GOLF DIGEST'S
PLACES *to* PLAY

FIFTH EDITION

Fodor's Travel Publications

New York • Toronto • London • Sydney • Auckland

Fodor's   **Golf Digest**

Fodor's is a registered trademark of Random House, Inc. All rights reserved under International and Pan-American Copyright Conventions. Published in the United States by Fodor's Travel Publications, a unit of Fodors LLC, a subsidiary of Random House, Inc., New York, and simultaneously in Canada by Random House of Canada Limited, Toronto. Distributed by Random House, Inc., New York.

*No portions of this book may be reproduced in
any form without written permission from the publishers.*

ISBN 0-676-90879-9
ISSN 1534-1356
FIFTH EDITION

SPECIAL SALES

Fodor's Travel Publications are available at special discounts for bulk purchases for sales promotions or premiums. Special editions, including personalized covers, excerpts of existing guides, and corporate imprints, can be created in large quantities for special needs. For more information, contact your local bookseller or write to Special Markets, Fodor's Travel Publications, 280 Park Avenue, New York, NY 10017. Inquiries from Canada should be directed to your local Canadian bookseller or sent to Random House of Canada, Ltd., Marketing Department, 2775 Matheson Boulevard East, Mississauga, Ontario L4W 4P7. Inquiries from the United Kingdom should be sent to Fodor's Travel Publications, 20 Vauxhall Bridge Road, London SW1V 2SA, England.

PRINTED IN THE UNITED STATES OF AMERICA
10 9 8 7 6 5 4 3 2 1

Contents

Welcome to Golf Digest's Places to Play

Every year, hundreds of new courses open up offering golfers new opportunities to challenge their games. With all the choices out there, how is the golfer to choose? Enter *Golf Digest's Places to Play*.

Places to Play began in 1963 as a magazine insert. With this 5th edition, some 20,000 GOLF DIGEST readers have filled out course ballots, sharing their opinions and experiences on more than 6,500 courses in the United States, Canada, Mexico and the Caribbean.

Places to Play provides you with the most comprehensive information on public-access golf courses in North America. Our readers reviewed thousands of courses they played over the previous year and rated them using a five-point scale for five separate criteria: the overall golf experience, the value for the money, the standard of service at the facility, the overall conditioning of the course, and the normal pace of play for an 18-hole round of golf. In addition, readers were invited to write comments on their experiences at each of the courses they rated—both the good and the bad.

A team of 8 editors reviewed every comment—great care was taken to use comments that were fair, accurate and representative of the sample. Another team contacted all 6,500-plus courses by mail, fax or phone to get their latest, up-to-date information, such as their name, address, green fee and walking policy.

Reader star ratings were averaged, then compiled on a bell curve to reflect a course's relative strength. The top 200 courses in the Value, Service, Conditioning, and Pace of Play categories have received special designations in this book for their outstanding achievement. The top 50 and ties received the highest awards of Great Value, Great Service, Great Conditioning and Great Pace of Play. The next 150 and ties received Good Value, Good Service, Good Conditioning and Good Pace of Play awards.

We think GOLF DIGEST's *Places to Play* is the only book you'll need to plan your next golf vacation or find that new course to play in your neck of the woods. Have fun—and let us know how it went at golfdigest.com.

Executive Editor: Bob Carney. **Project Manager:** Sue Sawyer. **Editors:** Mike Johnson, Ron Kaspriske, Mary Jane McGirr, Sue Sawyer, Topsy Siderowf, Kathy Stachura, Mike Stachura, Melissa Yow. **Editorial Assistants/Fact Checkers/Proofreaders:** Agnes Farkas, Mary Ann Hegedus, Jill Plonski, Ginnie Preuss, Kathy Stachura, Joan Sweet, Lisa Sweet, Melissa Yow, Danielle Zions. **IT/EPP:** Michael Astolfi, Nancy Boudreau, Byrute Johnson, Larry Kother, John Kulhawik, Kristofor Lefebvre, Charles Letezeio, Liz Quinones, Christian Sauer, Timothy Smith.

So You Wanna Take a Golf Trip

By Mike Stachura, *Golf Digest* Travel Editor

Years ago, before I knew what the Internet was (I still don't, but that's another story), before I had a cell phone (I have one now, but lose it more often than I use it) and before cars came with dashboard computers that can navigate you to any golf course on the planet, my idea of golf travel consisted of a hastily packed duffel bag, a trunk full of golf clubs, golf bag and shoes, a Waffle House pocket guide and a rolled up, nacho-chip-stained copy of Golf Digest's 1990 Places to Play guide.

This was a while ago, mind you. Well before Places to Play became the comprehensive golf tome you hold in your hands now. But even then, which according to the National Golf Foundation was approximately 3,000 new golf course openings ago, that little 16-page volume of course listings and phone numbers and eight-word course descriptions was my Rosetta Stone, my Book of Revelation, my treasure map. Anytime I turned a corner and noticed unusually green grass through a stand of trees, I slowed the car and found the listing for some soon-to-be-discovered pot of golf gold in my rumpled up Places to Play. In it, I would find my way to golf courses I might never have known or seen and, more often than not, never saw again. To me, they became legendary places, not because of their stature or rank, but solely for the good fortune of having found my way to them and then spending four hours or so building a lifetime of memories. There was that November afternoon playing Penn National's original 18 in a snow squall, that January side trip that led me and a buddy to a sporty Pete Dye municipal course in High Point, N.C. (Oak Hollow, green fee: eight bucks), that lonely Fourth of July when I stumbled upon the Lewisburg (W.Va.) Elks Country Club and that Christmas present trip my dad and I took to Sea Trail Plantation in Sunset Beach, N.C., where we sang country songs and alternately navigated by way of the Waffle House guide and Places to Play.

Though I still prefer to travel the old way, it is not the method I'd recommend. In fact, that's why I went to some golf travel planners, people whose job it is to figure out what works and what doesn't on a golf trip. Keep their thoughts in mind when that old golf wanderlust starts to kick in. Plan accordingly, certainly, but stick that copy of Places to Play in your glove compartment or carry-on luggage. You never know when some green grass might catch your eye and lead you to your own new promised land.

These are what I like to call the emergency nine of golf travel advice.

1. Information. We live in the information age. This book is testimony to that fact. It took the Internet, the reach of the world's largest golf publication, a squadron of editors and a team of computer programmers to get this information in your hands. Your job is to use it. There is more information available about golf courses and golf resorts than ever before thought humanly possible. If you want to know what kind of sand they use in the facial scrub mixture at the new spa at Pinehurst, you can check out their website for all the details. If you want to get your hands on a Whistling Straits yardage book before you actually arrive at The American Club, you can call the resort's toll-free number and have them send you the glossy picture book overnight. If you want to read up on the 10 best resorts in Northern California, you can go to your local bookstore and buy at least one volume on the subject, maybe two. The point is, don't simply acknowledge that this information is out there, consume it. It helps you decide whether Myrtle Beach fits your needs better than Palm Springs. It helps you find the best deals and the type of courses you're looking for. Most importantly, it gets every aspect of your trip straight in the collective mind of your group. And that's an often-overlooked essential, whether you're planning your own trip or going through a travel planner.

2. Timing/scheduling. There are only two crucial aspects involved in planning a golf trip: When and where. This sounds easy; it's not, especially when you're talking about a first-time trip. I know a group that goes on two trips a year, and they haven't had an excursion yet that didn't require at least four conference calls and 45 e-mails. And they all work in the same building. Here's the simple solution from John Yaker, vice president of sales and marketing at Pam's Golf Getaways: "Plan the trip before you call the planner, then call the planner to put together the package, then go. It doesn't have to be any harder than that." A good trip packager will provide you with everything you need from transportation to accommodations to driving directions and restaurant advice. The key is understanding what experience you're after. Mike Ryan of Golf Destinations says there are some basic questions that need to be settled before you make any calls: "Do you want a stay and play resort with golf on premises or a hotel and golf package that includes play at daily fee courses around the area? If it is a golf-around package, how close do you want the golf courses? What caliber of golf are you looking for?" Finally, remember what your budget is and factor that into the timing of your trip. Discount prices during the shoulder seasons at the popular destinations may give you an opportunity to play at some places outside your budget. Figure out when and where. The how—that's where it gets interesting.

3. Simpatico. Mark Twain once opined, "I have found out that there ain't no surer way to find out whether you like people or hate them than to travel with them." A golf trip involves a lot of time spent not playing golf. Perhaps you have learned to tolerate your pals on the golf course because you don't have to spend a lot of time talking to them. That's not an option on a golf trip, when you are surrounded by these same guys every waking—and sleeping—hour of every day. Snoring, which can make for some great grill room laughs during the day, can put some people in homicidal rage, especially when they're working on their third night in a row without some decent shuteye. To avoid old friends becoming new enemies make sure the size of your group is healthy (always equally divisible by four). Generally speaking, those who know suggest eight, but if that seems a bit ambitious, be comfortable with four. The joy of a larger number is that it allows for breakout groups that provide a natural release valve to potential tensions. The other thing to remember with your group dynamic is to make sure that it is dynamic. Hand out assignments, whether they be meal procurement, driving duties or social direction. The real benefit of having a specific duty for each member of the team is that while it splits up the workload, more importantly, it forces the group to depend on each member for some aspect of the experience. It's what the young kids call team spirit. And whatever you do, find someone who has people skills straight out of the Norman Vincent Peale playbook.

4. Trip content. Life's Little Instruction Book suggestion No. 399 reads, "Focus on making things better not bigger." Translation: mandatory 36-hole days are only a good idea when everybody in the group thinks so. Let's play two is a fine sentiment if you're dealing with a room full of young Ernie Banks clones. Some of us, however, aren't as young as we used to be. We like a leisurely breakfast, a chance to linger over the morning paper, perhaps, or maybe just to sleep in. We prefer to let others warm up the golf course for us, so that at a reasonable hour, we can approach the first tee in much the manner of one of those prime time U.S. Open pairings. So maybe we don't belong on your golf trip. The key is to set the ground rules early, probably even before you decide when and where you're going. Be prepared to be a little flexible in your schedule. Maybe leave a morning or afternoon open to see something like the Hockey Hall of Fame and the World's Largest Hockey Stick in Ely, Minn., before you tee it up a few miles down the road at Giants Ridge in Biwabik. State the mission clearly from the outset, and everyone will be satisfied

5. Gamesmanship. Donald Ross, whose American home, Pinehurst, became the foundation for the golf travel industry we know and love today, was not an especially jocular fellow. He once said, "I used to be apprenticed to Old Tom Morris at St. Andrews. Old Tom used to say, 'Why make a horse race out of a grand game like golf?' I've always felt that way, too. Golf is too good a game to go out for gambling purposes. You go out for the enjoyment of the game and the company, and not for the money which you may win at it." Well, old D.R. might have known a thing or two about elevated greens and cross bunkers, but he would have been about as much fun on a golf trip as castor oil is on pancakes. The key to any golf trip is playing games, whether you've got three guys playing eight rounds in four days, or 10 couples on a weekend getaway. And while the obvious contests are always good, it doesn't hurt to mix in team events, and oddball games like Wolf and blind partner games. Money isn't the issue here, either. Find a comfortable sum to play for and then have the winners buy the losers drinks afterward. I know a group that takes a trip every year with eight guys. They play for an old tin cup that looks like it might have been a used spitoon in its heyday. The Ryder Cup should have so much intensity. It also should have so much good feelings on both sides at the end of the day. It's the competition and the smack talking before and the laughs afterwards that should be as much a part of any decent golf trip as delayed flights and lost hotel keys.

6. Serendipity. Charles Kuralt, the late CBS newsman and storyteller was the model traveler, mainly because every day was an adventure for him. He welcomed the unexpected, even searched for it, and made a great point when he said, "Thanks to the interstate highway system, it is now possible to travel across the country from coast to coast without seeing anything." It is tempting and convenient to stick to the package deal, the famous courses that everybody knows about because of their big marketing budgets, the full-service, amenity-laden resorts. (Frankly, you should visit all of these places at least once because they are the best. Places like Pebble Beach, Pinehurst, the American Club, the Cloister at Sea Island, the Greenbrier and the Homestead didn't become famous because they have recognizable logos. They know what you want and generally they get it for you before you ask. We like that.) But, you have to allow room for the unexpected. That's why sometimes you have to turn left when the itinerary says go right. The quick nine at the end of the day at the nine-hole Great Dunes Course on Jekyll Island might end up being the highlight of your trip. Planning is crucial, but deviating from the plan just slightly is almost as important.

7. Golf trip anxiety. A travel writer I know once remarked, "Most travel is best of all in the anticipation or the remembering; the reality has more to do with losing your luggage." The reality of golf trips is that they are a lot like the game itself. You know that perfect drive that ends up in a divot? That perfect iron shot that hits the flagstick and bounds 25 feet away from the hole? That perfect putt that hits a spike mark six inches from the hole? Golf gives us these sorts of disruptions, just to remind us that we can never master this game. Well, golf trips can produce their own hiccups. Somebody's golf bag doesn't make the trip. Somebody gets bumped from his flight. It rains. Hard. The key is to be light on your feet. If you don't trust the airlines, try shipping your clubs via an overnight service dedicated to golfers like ShipGolf. Or revel in the opportunity to play a slick new set of rental clubs. Many of the top golf resorts have outstanding rental sets. Missed flights will happen. One solution is to avoid scheduling a tee time for the minute your plane touches down. Travel the afternoon before and get in an hour on the range, a good meal and a good night's sleep before the games begin. And, of course, bring a rainsuit. Always. Some of the latest golf travel packages include optional "rain insurance" that refunds money spent for a round that never happens. It's not as good as guaranteed sunshine, but it gives you peace of mind, if that's important to you. But again, be willing to adjust. Expect uncertainty. Don't go to Scotland and expect 70-degree windless days. Don't go to Palm Springs in July, and be all hot and bothered after skipping the sunblock and getting a third-degree burn on the back of your neck. As Dr. Bob Rotella, the famed sports psychologist, says, "thinking badly won't help you play better."

8. Transportation. Yogi Berra always knew what he was talking about. Nobody else did. Nevertheless, his understanding of the importance of good directions was pretty clear. "You got to be careful if you don't know where you're going," he said, "because you might not get there." A golf trip is all about getting there. It is also a good deal about getting there well ahead of time. That means calling the pro shop in advance to get directions, calling the resort in advance to get directions, calling the rental car company to make sure you've got the right size car. This last point is very big, and it's a big mistake a lot of golf trippers make. Efficiency outweighs style in this department every time. As travel expert John Yaker reminded me, "It may not be very macho to rent a minivan, but you get four golfers and eight bags together and all of a sudden that Lincoln or Cadillac can look pretty silly."

9. Details. More than 200 years ago, a storied traveler came up with the definitive advice for anyone going on any excursion. "When preparing to travel," this sage explained, "lay out all your clothes and all your money. Then take half the clothes and twice the money." The tendency for golfers is to overpack. This is why golf bag travel covers tend to be so bulky. Resist the temptation to pack three changes of clothes for each day of your trip. Nevertheless, it is important to be prepared. Always call the courses a few days before you leave and make sure they'll all be playable. For one, it's reassuring if they are. If they aren't and they tell you, you still have time to alter your itinerary. And if they aren't and they say they are, then you've got a legitimate gripe and grounds for a refund. Make tee times. Sounds easy, but it sometimes gets overlooked. Not only that, make sure you have documentation so you know that Tuesday is an 8:39 tee time, not a 9:38. Again, this can be one of the major benefits of going through a trip planner. They'll take care of the itinerary and the details. They'll often also get you better rates than you could on your own. Because they tend to do a lot of business with the courses and hotels in a resort area, they are less likely to be taken for granted. If you go on your own, you may not be operating from as strong a position as you'd like.

The benefit of preparation is that it eliminates future discomfort. In short, it saves you and your buddies from turning into whining existentialists. I think Wittgenstein was three hours into a golf trip to Phoenix when he famously remarked to his foursome, "I don't know why we are here, but I'm pretty sure that it is not in order to enjoy ourselves."

★★★★★
The *Five Star* Courses

These are the 12 sublime courses that received the highest *Places to Play* rating from GOLF DIGEST readers: the maximum five stars.

Belgrade Lakes Golf Club, Belgrade Lakes, ME

Blackwolf Run Golf Club (River Cse.), Kohler, WI

Bulle Rock (South Cse.), Havre de Grace, MD

The Broadmoor Golf Club (East Cse.), Colorado Springs, CO

Casa de Campo Resort & Country Club (Teeth of the Dog), Dominican Republic

The Challenge at Manele, Lanai City, HI

Grand View Lodge (The Pines), Breeze Point Township, MN

Kiawah Island Resort (Ocean Cse.), Kiawah Island, S.C.

Pebble Beach Golf Links, Pebble Beach, CA

Pinehurst Country Club (No. 2 Course), Pinehurst, N.C.

Timber Ridge Golf Club, East Lansing, MI

Whistling Straits Golf Club (Straits Cse.), Sheboygan, WI

The *Great Value* Courses

The top-50 golf courses in North America in terms of value for money, as rated by GOLF DIGEST readers.

UNITED STATES
Alabama
R.T. Jones Golf Trail at Grand National G.C. (Short Cse.)
R.T. Jones Golf Trail at Highland Oaks (Highlands/Magnolia)
R.T. Jones Golf Trail at Cambrian Ridge G.C. (Canyon/Loblolly)
Arkansas
Big Creek G.&C.C.
Colorado
Eisenhower G.C. (Silver Cse.)
Florida
PGA Golf Club (South Cse.)
Georgia
Southern Hills G.C.
Hawaii
Kaneohe Klipper G.C.
Wailua G.Cse.
Indiana
The Trophy Club
Iowa
Muscatine Municipal G.Cse.

Kansas
Buffalo Dunes G.Cse.
Louisiana
Gray Plantation G.C.
Massachusetts
Taconic G.C.
Westover G.Cse.
Michigan
Grand View G.Cse.
Heather Hills G.Cse.
Hidden Oaks G.Cse.
L.E. Kaufman G.C.
The Legacy G.C.
Pinecroft Plantation
Timber Ridge G.C.
TimberStone G.Cse.
Wild Bluff G.Cse.
Minnesota
Grand View Lodge Resort (The Pines)
Minnewaska G.C.
Mississippi
Quail Hollow G.Cse.
Nebraska
Wild Horse G.C.
Woodland Hills G.Cse.
New Mexico
Pinon Hills G.Cse.
New York
Bethpage State Park (Black Cse.)
Bethpage State Park (Red Cse.)
Seneca Lake C.C.
North Dakota
Hawktree G.C.
Pennsylvania
Stoughton Acres G.C.
South Carolina
Cheraw State Park G.Cse.
Texas
Painted Dunes Desert G.Cse. (East/West)
Squaw Valley G.Cse.
Utah
Wasatch State Park G.C. (Lake Cse.)
Wasatch State Park G.C. (Mountain)
Washington
Lake Padden G.Cse.
Wisconsin
Brown County G.Cse.
Washington County G.Cse.
CANADA
Alberta
Banff Springs G.Cse. (Stanley Thompson 18)
Kananaskis Country G.C. (Mt. Kidd Cse.)
Kananaskis Country G.C. (Mt. Lorette Cse.)
Ontario
Forest City National G.C.
Timberwolf G.C.
Prince Edward Island
The Links at Crowbush Cove
MEXICO
Jalisco
El Tamarindo G.Cse.

The *Good Value* Courses

The next 150 (and ties) Golf Courses in North America in terms of value as rated by GOLF DIGEST readers.

UNITED STATES

Alabama
Capitol Hill G.C. (Legislator Cse.)
Capitol Hill G.C. (Senator Cse.)
Goose Pond Colony G.Cse.
Limestone Springs G.C.
R.T. Jones Golf Trail at Grand National G.C. (Lake Cse.)
R.T. Jones Golf Trail at Grand National G.C. (Links Cse.)
R.T. Jones Golf Trail at Magnolia Grove (Crossings Cse.)

Arizona
Aguila G.Cse.
Apache Stronghold G.C.

California
Cimarron G. Resort (Long Cse.)
Graeagle Meadows G.Cse.
Madera Municipal G.Cse.
Pacific Grove Municipal G. Links
Poppy Hills G.Cse.
Rio Vista G.C.

Colorado
The Broadmoor G.C. (East Cse.)
Buffalo Run G.Cse.
Eisenhower G.C. (Blue Cse.)
Fairway Pines G.C.
Hyland Hills G.Cse. (Gold Cse.)
Riverdale G.C. (Dunes Cse.)
Ute Creek G.Cse.

Connecticut
Great River G.C.
Rockledge C.C.
Timberlin G.C.
Twin Hills C.C.

Florida
The Club at Eaglebrooke
El Diablo G.&C.C.
Palisades G.Cse.
PGA G.C. (North Cse.)
Sherman Hills G.C.
World Woods G.C. (Pine Barrens Cse.)
World Woods G.C. (Rolling Oaks Cse.)

Georgia
Cateechee G.C.
Fields Ferry G.C.
Nob North G.Cse.
Osprey Cove G.C.

Hawaii
The Dunes at Maui Lani G.Cse.
Hickam G.Cse. (Mamala Bay Championship G.C.)
Kiahuna G.C.
Leilehua G.Cse.

Iowa
Glynns Creek G.Cse.

Idaho
BanBury G.C.

Illinois
Bon Vivant C.C. (Championship Cse.)
Bonnie Brook G.C.
Heritage Bluffs G.C.
Lick Creek G.Cse.
Orchard Valley G.C.
Piper Glen G.C.
Prairie Bluff G.C.
Prairie Vista G.Cse.
Rend Lake G.Cse. (East/South)

Indiana
Birck Boilermaker G. Complex (Kampen Cse.)
Cobblestone G.Cse.
The Cse. at Aberdeen
The Fort G.Cse.
Rock Hollow G.C.

Kentucky
Drake Creek on the Ohio
Lafayette G.C. at Green Farm Resort

Maine
Bangor Municipal G.Cse.
Belgrade Lakes G.C.
Biddeford Saco C.C.
Natanis G.Cse. (Arrowhead)

Massachusetts
Braintree Municipal G.Cse.
Kettle Brook G.C.

Michigan
Black Forest & Wilderness Valley G. Resort (Valley Cse.)
Black Lake G.C.
Cascades G.Cse.
Fox Run C.C.
Gaylord C.C.
Groesbeck Municipal G.Cse.
Milham Park Municipal G.C.
Pierce Lake G.Cse.
Pilgrim's Run G.C.
Stony Creek G.Cse.

Minnesota
Albion Ridges G.Cse.
Baker National G.Cse.
Bellwood Oaks G.Cse.
Grand View Lodge Resort (Preserve G.Cse.)
Hidden Greens G.C.

Mississippi
Timberton G.C. (Lakeview)

Missouri
Eagle Lake G.C.

Montana
Old Works G.Cse.

Nebraska
Grand Island Municipal G.Cse.
Heritage Hills G.Cse.

New Jersey
Hominy Hill G.Cse.
Howell Park G. Cse.

New York
Bethpage State Park G.Cse. (Green Cse.)
Bethpage State Park G.Cse. (Yellow Cse.)
Colgate University Seven Oaks G.C.
Conklin Players Club
Eisenhower Park Golf (Red Cse.)
Inlet G.C.
The Links at Hiawatha Landing

McCann Memorial G.C.
McConnellsville G.C.
Montauk Downs State Park G.Cse.
Saratoga Spa G.Cse.
Thendara G.C.
Town of Colonie G.Cse. (Blue/Red Cse.)
North Carolina
Keith Hills C.C.
Legacy G. Links
Lockwood Folly C.C.
Mount Mitchell G.C.
The Neuse G.C.
North Shore C.C.
Pine Needles Lodge & G.C.
Thistle G.C. (North/West)
North Dakota
The Links of North Dakota at Red Mike
   Resort
Ohio
Cassel Hills G.Cse.
Mill Creek Park G.Cse. (South Cse.)
Mohican Hills G.C.
Red Hawk Run G.C.
Weatherwax G.Cse.
   (Woodside/Meadows)
Oklahoma
Chickasaw Point G.Cse.
Oregon
Bandon Dunes G. Resort (Bandon Dunes
   Cse.)
Eagle Point G.Cse.
Elkhorn Valley G.Cse.
Running Y Ranch Resort
Tokatee G.C.
Pennsylvania
Armitage G.Cse.
Bethlehem Municipal G.C. (Bethlehem G.C.)
Sugarloaf G.C.
South Carolina
Crowfield G.& C.C.
Daufuskie Island Club & Resort (Melrose
   Cse.)
Fripp Island Resort (Ocean Creek)
Wild Wing Plantation (Hummingbird Cse.)
South Dakota
The Bluffs
Texas
Bay Forest G.Cse.
The Falls G.C. & Resort
Sugartree G.C.
Utah
Moab G.C.
Sky Mountain G.Cse.
Valley View G.Cse.
Wingpointe G.Cse.
Virginia
Kingsmill Resort & C. (Woods Cse.)
Riverfront G.C.
Shenandoah Valley G.C.
Washington
Canyon Lakes G.Cse.
Gold Mountain G. Complex (Cascade Cse.)
Gold Mountain G. Complex (Olympic Cse.)
Hangman Valley G.Cse.
Indian Canyon G.Cse.

MeadowWood G.Cse.
Wisconsin
Brighton Dale G.C. (Blue Spruce Cse.)
Clifton Highlands G.Cse.
Hawthorne Hills G.C.
Kikarney Hills G.C.
Lake Arrowhead G.Cse. (Pines Cse.)
Naga-Waukee G.Cse.
NorthBrook C.C.
Northwood G.Cse.
Rolling Meadows G.Cse. (Blue/Red)
Whispering Springs G.C.
CANADA
Alberta
Jasper Park Lodge G.Cse.
British Columbia
Fairview Mountain G.C.
Golden G. & C.C.
Manitoba
Hecla G.Cse. at Gull Harbor Resort
Nova Scotia
Highlands Links G.Cse.
Northumberland Links
Ontario
Silver Lakes G. & C.C.
Upper Canada G.Cse.
Prince Edward Island
Brudenell River Resort (Brudenell River
   G.Cse.)
Brudenell River Resort (Dundarave G.Cse.)
ISLANDS
Dominican Republic
Casa de Campo Resort & C.C. (Links Cse.)
Campo de Golf Playa Grande

The *Great Service* Facilities

The top-50 golf facilities in North America in terms of service, as rated by Golf Digest readers.

UNITED STATES
Alabama
Limestone Springs G.C.
R.T. Jones Golf Trail at Grand National
   G.C.
R.T. Jones Golf Trail at Highland Oaks
Arizona
The Boulders Club
Grayhawk G.C.
The Raven G.C. at Sabino Springs
The Raven G.C. at South Mountain
Troon North G.C.
Arkansas
Big Creek G. & C.C.
California
La Costa Resort & Spa
La Quinta Resort & Club
Colorado
The Broadmoor G.C.
The Ridge at Castle Pines North
Florida
Grand Cypress G.C.

Lely Resort G. & C.C.
Naples Grande G.C.
PGA G.C.
Tiburon G.C.
Walt Disney World Resort
Georgia
Southern Hills G.C.
Hawaii
The Challenge at Manele
Hualalai G.C.
Wailea G.C.
Idaho
Coeur d'Alene Resort G.Cse.
Kentucky
Lafayette G.C. at Green Farm Resort
Maine
Belgrade Lakes G.C.
Maryland
Bulle Rock
Michigan
Black Lake G.C.
The Legacy G.C.
Timber Ridge G.C.
Minnesota
Grand View Lodge Resort
Nevada
Primm Valley G.C.
Royal Links G.C.
New York
Seneca Lake C.C.
North Carolina
Pine Needles Lodge & G.C.
Pinehurst Resort & C.C.
Oregon
Bandon Dunes G. Resort
Pennsylvania
Skytop Lodge
South Carolina
Daufuskie Island C. & Resort
Palmetto Dunes Resort
Texas
The Houstonian G.C.
Virginia
Ford's Colony C.C.
Kingsmill Resort & Club
West Virginia
The Greenbrier
Wisconsin
Blackwolf Run G.C.
Whistling Straits G.C.
CANADA
British Columbia
Westwood Plateau G. & C.C.
Nova Scotia
Glen Arbour G.C.
ISLANDS
Dominican Republic
Casa de Campo Resort & C.C.Resort

The *Good Service* Facilities

The next 150 (and ties) golf facilities in North America in terms of service, as

rated by GOLF DIGEST readers.
UNITED STATES
Alabama
Capitol Hill G.C.
Rock Creek G.C.
R.T. Jones Golf Trail at Cambrian Ridge G.C.
R.T. Jones Golf Trail at Hampton Cove G.C.
R.T. Jones Golf Trail at Silver Lakes G.C.
Arizona
Las Sendas G.C.
The Phoenician G.C.
Talking Stick G.C.
Ventana Canyon G. & Racquet Club
California
Cimarron G. Resort
Desert Willow G. Resort
Diablo Grande Resort
Four Seasons Resort Aviara
Eagle Glen G.C.
The Links at Spanish Bay
Marriott's Desert Springs Resort & Spa
Ojai Valley Inn & Spa
Pebble Beach G. Links
PGA West Resort
Spyglass Hill G.Cse.
Colorado
Beaver Creek G.C.
The Club at Cordillera
Eisenhower G.C.
Omni Interlocken Resort G.C.
Connecticut
Great River G.C.
Florida
Amelia Island Plantation
Arnold Palmer's Bay Hill Club & Lodge
Celebration G.C.
Falcon's Fire G.C.
Gateway G. & C.C.
Kelly Plantation G.C.
Orange County National G. Center & Lodge
Ponte Vedra Inn & Club
PGA National Golf Club
Saddlebrook Resort
Sandestin Resort
Tournament Players Club at Heron Bay
Tournament Players Club at Sawgrass
Tournament Players Club of Tampa Bay
The Westin Innisbrook Resort
World Golf Village
World Woods G.C.
Georgia
Barnsley Gardens
Reynolds Plantation
Sea Island G.C.
Hawaii
The Experience at Koele
Hapuna G.Cse.
Kapalua G.C.
Kauai Lagoons Resort
Mauna Lani Resort
Poipu Bay G.C.
Princeville Resort
Idaho

BanBury G.C.
Illinois
Cantigny Golf
Eagle Ridge Inn & Resort
Tournament Players Club at Deere Run
Indiana
The Course at Aberdeen
The Links at Heartland Crossing
Rock Hollow G.C.
Iowa
The Meadows G.C.
Louisiana
Gray Plantation G.C.
Maine
Sugarloaf G.C.
Maryland
The Links at Lighthouse Sound G.C.
Whiskey Creek G.C.
Massachusetts
Cyprian Keyes G.C.
Taconic G.C.
Michigan
Black Forest & Wilderness Valley G.
　Resort
Boyne Mountain Resort
Cherry Creek G.C.
Crystal Mountain Resort
Garland
George Young Recreational Complex
Grand Traverse Resort & Spa
Hidden Oaks G.Cse.
Hidden River G. & Casting Club
The Orchards G.C.
Pilgrim's Run G.C.
Red Hawk G.C.
St. Ives G.C.
Shanty Creek
Thousand Oaks G.C.
TimberStone G.Cse.
Treetops Sylvan Resort
Minnesota
Deacon's Lodge G.Cse.
Madden's on Gull Lake
Mississippi
Dancing Rabbit G.C.
Grand Bear G.Cse.
Missouri
Branson Creek G.C.
Nebraska
Woodland Hills G.Cse.
Nevada
Desert Inn G.C.
Edgewood Tahoe G.Cse.
Las Vegas Paiute Resort
New Hampshire
The Balsams Grand Resort Hotel
Mount Washington Hotel & Resort
New Jersey
Blue Heron Pines G.C.
Marriott's Seaview Resort
Pine Barrens G.C.
New York
The Links at Hiawatha Landing
North Carolina
Legacy G. Links

Mid Pines Inn & G.C.
The Neuse G.C.
North Shore C.C.
Pearl G. Links
Rivers Edge G.C.
North Dakota
Hawktree G.C.
Ohio
Longaberger G.C.
Mohican Hills G.C.
Quail Hollow Resort & C.C.
Yankee Run G.Cs.e
Oklahoma
Chickasaw Point G.Cse.
Karsten Creek
Oregon
Lost Tracks G.C.
Persimmon C.C.
The Reserve Vineyards & G.C.
Pennsylvania
Chestnut Ridge G.C.
Nemacolin Woodlands Resort & Spa
Penn National G.C. & Inn
South Carolina
Barefoot Resort & Golf
Caledonia Golf & Fish Club
Fripp Island Resort
Glen Dornoch Waterway G. Links
Harbour Town G. Links
Kiawah Island Resort
Litchfield Beach & G. Resort
The Long Bay Club
Myrtle Beach National G.C.
Pine Lakes International C.C.
Wild Wing Plantation
Tennessee
Graysburg Hills G.Cse.
Woodlake G.C.
Texas
Barton Creek Resort & C.C.
Four Seasons Resort & Club
The G.C. of Texas
La Cantera G.C.
Meadowbrook Farms G.C.
Utah
The G.C. at Thanksgiving Point
Vermont
Gleneagles G.Cse. at The Equinox
Vermont National C.C.
Virginia
The Homestead Resort
The Legends at Stonehouse
Tradition at Stonehouse
Wintergreen Resort
Washington
Port Ludlow G.Cse.
Trophy Lake G. & Casting Club
West Virginia
Oglebay Resort & Conf. Center
Snowshoe Mountain Resort
Wisconsin
Geneva National G.C.
CANADA
Alberta
Banff Springs G.Cse.

Jasper Park Lodge G.Cse.
Kananaskis Country G.C.
British Columbia
Chateau Whistler G.C.
Predator Ridge G. Resort
Ontario
Forest City National G.C.
Lionhead G. & C.C.
Quebec
Tremblant G. Resort

The *Great Condition* Courses

The top 50 Golf Courses in North America in terms of optimum course conditions, as rated by GOLF DIGEST readers.

UNITED STATES
Alabama
Limestone Springs G.C.
Arizona
Grayhawk G.C. (Talon Cse.)
Troon North G.C. (Monument Cse.)
Colorado
The Broadmoor G.C. (East Cse.)
Eisenhower G.C. (Silver Cse.)
Florida
Grand Cypress G.C. (New Cse.)
Tiburon G.C. (North/South)
Georgia
Southern Hills G.C.
Hawaii
The Challenge at Manele
Idaho
Coeur d'Alene Resort G.Cse.
Illinois
Harborside International G. Ctr. (Starboard Cse.)
Harborside International G. Ctr. (Port Cse.)
Indiana
Brickyard Crossing G.C.
Iowa
Spencer G. & C.C.
Kansas
Buffalo Dunes G.Cse.
Maine
Belgrade Lakes G.C.
Maryland
Bulle Rock (South Cse.)
Massachusetts
Taconic G.C.
Michigan
Black Lake G.C.
The Legacy G.C.
Timber Ridge G.C.
Treetops Sylvan Resort (R.T. Jones Masterpiece)
Minnesota
Grand View Lodge Resort (The Pines)
Missouri
The Club at Old Kinderhook
Nevada

Lake Las Vegas Resort (Reflection Bay G.C.)
Las Vegas Paiute Resort (ANu-Wav Kaiv Cse.)
New York
Bethpage State Park G.Cse. (Black Cse.)
Conklin Players Club
Shenendoah G.C.
North Carolina
Pinehurst Resort & C.C. (No. 2)
Pinehurst Resort & C.C. (No. 8)
North Dakota
Hawktree G.C.
Ohio
Longaberger G.C.
Oklahoma
Chickasaw Point G.Cse.
Karsten Creek (Karsten Creek)
Oregon
Bandon Dunes G. Resort (Bandon Dunes Cse.)
South Carolina
Daufuskie Island Club & Resort (Melrose Cse.)
Virginia
Riverfront G.C.
Tradition at Stonehouse
West Virginia
The Greenbrier (Greenbrier Cse.)
Snowshoe Mountain Resort (Raven G.C.)
Wisconsin
Blackwolf Run G.C. (Meadow Valleys Cse.)
Blackwolf Run G.C. (River Cse.)
Whistling Straits G.C. (Straits Cse.)
CANADA
Alberta
SilverTip G.Cse.
Nova Scotia
Glen Arbour G.C.
Prince Edward Island
The Links at Crowbush Cove
Quebec
Tremblant G. Resort (Le Diable)
MEXICO
Baja Sur
Cabo del Sol (Ocean Cse.)
Jalisco
El Tamindo Resort (El Tamarindo G.Cse.)

The *Good Condition* Courses

The next 150 Golf Courses in North America in terms of optimum course conditions, as rated by GOLF DIGEST readers.

UNITED STATES
Alabama
Kiva Dunes G.C.
R.T. Jones Golf Trail at Cambrian Ridge G.C. (Canyon/Loblolly)
Arizona
The Boulders Club (North Cse.)

The Boulders Club (South Cse.)
Estrella Mountain Ranch G.C.
The G.C. at Vistoso
Gold Canyon G. Resort (Dinosaur Mountain)
Grayhawk G.C. (Raptor Cse.)
La Paloma C.C. (Canyon/Hill)
Las Sendas G.C.
Legend Trail G.C.
The Raven G.C. at Sabino Springs
The Raven G.C. at South Mountain
SunRidge Canyon G.C.
Troon North G.C. (Pinnacle Cse.)
Ventana Canyon G. & Racquet Club
   (Canyon Cse.)

Arkansas
Big Creek G. & C.C.

California
Desert Willow G. Resort (Firecliff Cse.)
Diablo Grande Ranch (Legends West
   Cse.)
Diablo Grande Ranch (Ranch Cse.)
The G.C. at Whitehawk Ranch
Marriott's Desert Springs Resort & Spa
   (Valley Cse.)
Pebble Beach G. Links
Poppy Hills G.Cse.
PGA of Southern California G.C. at Oak
   Valley
PGA West Resort (Jack Nicklaus
   Tournament Cse.)
PGA West Resort (TPC Stadium Cse.)
Rancho San Marcos G.C.
Spyglass Hill G. Cse.
Twelve Bridges G.C.

Colorado
The Broadmoor G.C. (West Cse.)
The Club at Cordillera (Mountain Cse.)
Eisenhower G.C. (Blue Cse.)
Omni Interlocken Resort G.C.
   (Vista/Sunshine)
The Ridge at Castle Pines North

Connecticut
Great River G.C.

Florida
Arnold Palmer's Bay Hill Club & Lodge
   (Challenger/Champion)
The Club at Eaglebrooke
Emerald Dunes G.Cse.
Grand Haven G.C.
Kelly Plantation G.C.
LPGA International (Champions)
Orange County National G. Center &
   Lodge (Panther Lake Cse.)
PGA G.C. (South Cse.)
Tournament Players Club at Sawgrass
   (Stadium Cse.)
Walt Disney World Resort (Eagle Pines
   G. Cse.)
Walt Disney World Resort (Osprey Ridge
   G.Cse.)
The Westin Innisbrook Resort (Island Cse.)
World Golf Village (Slammer & Squire)
World Woods G.C. (Pine Barrens Cse.)
World Woods G.C. (Rolling Oaks Cse.)

Georgia

The Frog at The Georgian Resort
The G.C. at Cuscowilla
Reynolds Plantation (Great Waters Cse.)
Sea Island G.C. (Plantation Cse.)
Sea Island G.C. (Seaside Cse.)
White Columns G.C.

Hawaii
Hualalai G.C.
Mauna Lani Resort (North Cse.)
Poipu Bay G.C.
Wailea G.C. (Emerald Cse.)
Wailea G.C. (Gold Cse.)

Illinois
Cantigny Golf (Lakeside/Hillside)
Eagle Ridge Inn & Resort (The General
   Cse.)
Kemper Lakes G.Cse.
Pine Meadow G.C.

Indiana
Rock Hollow G.C.

Louisiana
Gray Plantation G.C.

Maine
Dunegrass G.C.

Maryland
Whiskey Creek G.C.

Massachusetts
Farm Neck G.C.
Waverly Oaks G.C.

Michigan
Garland (Swampfire Cse.)
Glacier Club
The Orchards G.C.
Pilgrim's Run G.C.
TimberStone G.Cse.
Treetops Sylvan Resort (Tom Fazio
   Premier)

Minnesota
Grand View Lodge Resort (The Preserve
   G.Cse.)
The Wilds G.C.
Willinger's G.C.

Mississippi
Canebrake G.C.
Dancing Rabbit G.C. (The Azaleas)
Grand Bear G.Cse.

Missouri
Tiffany Greens G.C.

Nebraska
Wild Horse G.C.

Nevada
Las Vegas Paiute Resort (Tav-ai Kaiv Cse.)
Primm Valley G.C. (Desert Cse.)
Primm Valley G.C. (Lakes Cse.)
Tournament Players Club at The
   Canyons

New Jersey
Crystal Springs G. & Spa Resort
   (Ballyowen G.C.)
Harbor Pines G.C.
Pine Barrens G.C.

New Mexico
Pinon Hills G.Cse.

New York
The Links at Hiawatha Landing

North Carolina
Grandover Resort & Conf. Center (East Cse.)
Magnolia Greens Golf Plantation
   (Magnolia/Camelia)
Mount Mitchell G.C.
The Neuse G.C.
Tobacco Road G.C.
Trillium Links & Lake Club (Trillium Links)
Ohio
EagleSticks G.C.
Elks Run G.C.
Quail Hollow Resort & C.C. (Devlin-Von
   Hagge Cse.)
Quail Hollow Resort & C.C. (Weiskopf-
   Morrish Cse.)
StoneWater G.C.
Oklahoma
Forest Ridge G.C.
Oregon
The Reserve Vineyards & G.C. (Cupp
   Cse.)
The Reserve Vineyards & G.C. (Fought
   Cse)
Running Y Ranch Resort
Sunriver Lodge & Resort (Crosswater
   Club)
Pennsylvania
Chestnut Ridge G.C. (Tom's Run Cse.)
Penn National G. C. & Inn (Iron Forge
   Cse.)
Skytop Lodge
South Carolina
Caledonia Golf & Fish Club
Kiawah Island Resort (The Ocean Cse.)
Palmetto Dunes Resort (Arthur Hills Cse.)
Wild Wing Plantation (Avocet Cse.)
Wild Wing Plantation (Hummingbird Cse.)
Wild Wing Plantation (Wood Stork Cse.)
Tennessee
Graysburg Hills G. Cse.
   (Fodderstack/Chimneytop)
Texas
Barton Creek Resort & C.C. (Fazio Cse.)
Horseshoe Bay Resort (Applerock Cse.)
Horseshoe Bay Resort (Slick Rock)
La Cantera G.C. (The Resort Cse.)
Painted Dunes Desert G. Cse.
   (East/West)
Squaw Valley G.Cse.
Tierra Santa G.C.
Vermont
Vermont National C.C.
Virginia
Ford's Colony C.C. (Marsh Hawk Cse.)
Golden Horseshoe G.C. (Gold Cse.)
Kingsmill Resort & Club (Woods Cse.)
Lansdowne G.C.
Royal New Kent G.C.
Washington
Desert Canyon Golf Resort
West Virginia
The Greenbrier (Old White Cse.)
Wisconsin
Bristlecone Pines G.C.
Geneva National G.C. (Trevino Cse.)

The House on The Rock Resort (North
   Nine)
University Ridge G. Cse.
Washington County G. Cse.
CANADA
Alberta
Kananaskis Country G.C. (Mt. Lorette
   Cse.)
British Columbia
Trickle Creek G. Resort
Nova Scotia
Bell Bay G.C.
Ontario
Angus Glen G.C.
Eagle Creek G.Cse.
Lionhead G. & C.C.
National Pines G.C.
Quebec
Tremblant G. Resort (Le Geant)
ISLANDS
Dominican Republic
Campo de Golf Playa Grande
Casa de Campo Resort & C.C. (Links
   Cse.)
MEXICO
Baja Sur
Eldorado G.Cse.

# Standard Abbreviations:
C. = Club
C.C. = Country Club
Cse. = Course
G. = Golf
G. & C.C. = Golf & Country Club
G. & Conf. Ctr. = Golf & Conference Center
G.C. = Golf Club
G.Cse. = Golf Course
G. Ctr. = Golf Center
G.L. = Golf Links
Plant. = Plantation

How to Use This Guide

Sample Entry

ANYWHERE GOLF RESORT

★★★ **ANYWHERE GOLF COURSE.** *Service+, Condition*

PU-100 Anywhere Drive, Centerville, 10001, Nice County, (212)000-9999, (888)123-4567, 25 miles from Nowhere. **E-mail:** good golf@xyz.com **Web:** www.anywheregolf-course.com

Facility Holes: 18. **Yards:** 6,500/5,500. **Par:** 70/71. **Course Rating:** 72.5/71.5. **Slope:** 145/135. **Green Fee:** $75/$125. **Cart Fee:** Included in Green Fee. **Walking Policy:** Walking at certain times. **Walkability:** 4. **Opened:** 1920. **Architect:** AW Tillinghast. **Season:** April-Oct. **High:** April-Oct. **To obtain tee times:** Call golf shop.

Miscellaneous: Reduced fees (seniors, juniors), metal spikes, range (grass), caddies, lodging (200 rooms), credit cards (MC, V, AE, DC), BF, FF.

Notes: Ranked 5th in 2001 Best in State.

Reader comments: I always play here while on vacation ... One of my favorites.

Special Notes: Also has a 9-hole par-3 course. Formerly Somewhere Golf Club.

Explanation

ANYWHERE GOLF RESORT—The name of the resort or facility.

★★★—The Star Rating; a rating of the golf experience according to GOLF DIGEST readers. See ratings chart below.

ANYWHERE GOLF COURSE—The name of the course at Anywhere Golf Resort (generally only appears when there is more than one course at the facility).

Service+, Condition—Indicators of major award winners. Award categories include: Great Value (Value+), Great Service (Service+), Great Conditioning (Condition+), Great Pace of Play (Pace+) to the top 50 (and ties) vote getters in each category; Good Value (Value), Good Service (Service), Good Conditioning (Condition), and Good Pace of Play (Pace) to the next 150 (and ties) winners.

PU—Public course, including Municipal or County owned courses. **R**: Resort course. **SP**: Semi-private course. **M**: Military course.

100 Anywhere Drive, Centerville, 10001, Nice County—The address, zip code and county.

(212)000-9999—The phone number of the facility. Please note that all phone numbers were current at the time of publication, but *numbers and area codes are subject to change.*

(888)123-4567—The toll free number for the course, if available.

25 miles from Nowhere—Approximate mileage to the nearest major city.

E-mail—The e-mail address for the course.

Web—The web site address for the course.

Facility Holes—The number of holes at the facility.

(18)—The number of holes for the individual course. 27-hole courses are shown in combinations (18-combo).

Yards—The yardage from the back/front tees.

Par—The figures shown represent the par from the back/front tees.

Course Rating—The USGA course rating from the back/front tees.

Slope—The USGA Slope rating from the back/front tees.

Green Fee—Fees listed represent the lowest/highest fee for an 18-hole rounds of golf. *Published fees are subject to change.*

Golf Carts—Price of renting golf carts at the course either per person or per cart as designated by the club. If the cart fee is included in the green fee, that information will be listed instead. Some facilities allow the player to walk even though the cart fee is included in the green fee. See Walking Policy for further information. *Published fees are subject to change.*

Walking policy—Unrestricted walking: Walking is allowed at any time. Walking at certain times: Carts may be mandatory at certain (usually busy) times. Mandatory cart: Walking is never an option.

Walkability—On a 1 to 5 scale, with 1 being flat and 5 extremely hilly, courses have rated the terrain of their course.

Opened—The year the course first opened.

Architect—The architect of the golf course.

Season—Months of the year when the course is open for play.

High—When the course is likely to be busiest and the rates typically higher.

To obtain tee times—The number of days prior to play that reservations can be made.

Miscellaneous—This category reflects amenities available and certain policies at the course including reduced fees, if metal spikes are allowed, golf range, if caddies are available, lodging and the number of rooms, credit cards, if the facility is beginner friendly or female friendly.

Notes—Relevant additional information, including GOLF DIGEST rankings and GOLF DIGEST school sites.

Reader comments—A representative sample of comments made by GOLF DIGEST readers in response to the February, 2001 survey. These comments come from readers' impressions of the course based on their playing experiences between January 1, 2000 and January 31, 2001 and may not be indicative of current conditions or changes in course ownership.

Special Notes—Additional information such as the former name of a club or if the club has a 9-hole or par-3 course affiliated with it.

Course conditions, prices and policies may vary from time to time, so plan on calling the course prior to playing.

Star Rating Explanation

★ Basic golf.

★★ Good, but not great.

★★★ Very good. Tell a friend it's worth getting off the highway to play.

★★★★ Outstanding. Plan your next vacation around it.

★★★★★ Golf at its absolute best. Pay any price to play at least once in your life.

½ The equivalent of one-half star.

Please note that a number of courses do not have a Star Rating. A course that did not receive a minimum of 10 ballots, either because it is very new or simply was not visited by a sufficient number of GOLF DIGEST subscribers, remains unrated.

America's 100 Greatest Golf Courses, 2001-2002

The following courses, both public and private, are the top 100 in the United States as ranked by GOLF DIGEST in its biennial ranking. Courses marked in red are public-access facilities and are featured in this book.

FIRST 10

1. **Pebble Beach G. Links,** Pebble Beach, Calif.
2. **Pine Valley G.C.,** Pine Valley, N.J.
3. **Augusta National G.C.,** Augusta, Ga.
4. **Cypress Point Club,** Pebble Beach, Calif.
5. **Oakmont C.C.,** Oakmont, Pa.
6. **Shinnecock Hills G.C.,** Southampton, N.Y.
7. **Merion G.C. (East),** Ardmore, Pa.
8. **Winged Foot G.C. (West),** Mamaroneck, N.Y
9. **Pinehurst Resort & C.C. (No. 2),** Pinehurst, N.C.
10. **Oakland Hills C.C. (South),** Bloomfield Hills, Mich.

SECOND 10

11. **The Olympic Club (Lake),** San Francisco
12. **Seminole G.C.,** North Palm Beach, Fla.
13. **The Country Club (Clyde/Squirrel),** Brookline, Mass.
14. **Medinah C.C. (No. 3),** Medinah, Ill.
15. **Southern Hills C.C.,** Tulsa, Okla.
16. **National Golf Links,** Southampton, N.Y.
17. **Muirfield Village G.C.,** Dublin, Ohio
18. **San Francisco G.C.,** San Francisco
19. **Crystal Downs C.C.,** Frankfort, Mich.
20. **Quaker Ridge G.C.,** Scarsdale, N.Y.

THIRD 10

21. **Riviera C.C.,** Pacific Palisades, Calif.
22. **Los Angeles C.C. (North),** Los Angeles
23. **Oak Hill C.C. (East),** Rochester, N.Y.
24. **Inverness Club,** Toledo, Ohio
25. **Cherry Hills C.C.,** Englewood, Colo.
26. **Prairie Dunes C.C.,** Hutchinson, Kan.
27. **Garden City G.C.,** Garden City, N.Y
28. **Baltusrol G.C. (Lower),** Springfield, N.J.
29. **Scioto C.C.,** Columbus, Ohio
30. **Olympia Fields C.C. (North),** Olympia Fields, Ill.

FOURTH 10

31. **Shadow Creek G.C.,** North Las Vegas, Nev.
32. **Winged Foot G.C. (East),** Mamaroneck, N.Y.
33. **Peachtree G.C.,** Atlanta, Ga.
34. **Spyglass Hill G. Cse.,** Pebble Beach, Calif.
35. **Wannamoisett C.C.,** Rumford, R.I.
36. **Sand Hills G.C.,** Mullen, Nebraska
37. **Wade Hampton G.C.,** Cashiers, N.C.
38. **Interlachen C.C.,** Edina, Minn.
39. **The Golf Club,** New Albany, Ohio
40. **Colonial C.C.,** Fort Worth

FIFTH 10

41. **Bandon Dunes,** Bandon, Ore.
42. **Maidstone Club,** East Hampton, N.Y.
43. **Chicago G.C.,** Wheaton, Ill.
44. **Fishers Island Club,** Fishers Island, N.Y.
45. **Somerset Hills C.C.,** Bernardsville, N.J.
46. **Bethpage G. Cse. (Black),** Farmingdale, N.Y.
47. **Plainfield C.C.,** Plainfield, N.J.
48. **Cascades G. Cse.,** Homestead Resort, Hot Springs, Va.

49. **Kittansett Club,** Marion, Mass.
50. **Milwaukee C.C.,** Milwaukee, Wis.

SIXTH 10
51. **Prince Course,** Princeville Resort, Kauai HI
52. **Victoria National G.C.,** Newburgh, Ind.
53. **The Honors Course,** Chattanooga, Tenn.
54. **Hazeltine National G.C.,** Chaska, Minn.
55. **Sand Ridge G.C.,** Chardon, Ohio
56. **Canterbury G.C.,** Beachwood, Ohio
57. **Baltimore C.C. (East),** Timonium, Md.
58. **Butler National G.C.,** Oak Brook, Ill.
59. **Valley C. of Montecito,** Santa Barbara, Calif.
60. **East Lake G.C.,** Atlanta, Ga.

SEVENTH 10
61. **Laurel Valley G.C.,** Ligonier, Pa.
62. **Whistling Straits (Straits),** Haven, Wis.
63. **TPC At Sawgrass (Stadium),** Ponte Vedra Beach, Fla.
64. **Cog Hill G. & C.C. (No. 4),** Lemont, Ill.
65. **Salem C.C.,** Peabody, Mass.
66. **Harbour Town G. Links,** Hilton Head Island, S.C.
67. **The Ocean Course,** Kiawah Island, S.C.
68. **Shoal Creek,** Shoal Creek, Ala.
69. **Desert Forest G.C.,** Carefree, Ariz.
70. **Blackwolf Run (River),** Kohler, Wis.

EIGHTH 10
71. **Congressional C.C.(Blue),** Bethesda, Md.
72. **Crooked Stick G.C.,** Carmel, Ind.
73. **Bellerive C.C.,** Creve Coeur, Mo.
74. **Castle Pines G.C.,** Castle Rock, Colo.
75. **Camargo Club,** Indian Hill, Ohio
76. **Mauna Kea G. Cse.,** Kamuela, Hi.
77. **Pasatiempo G.C.,** Santa Cruz, Calif.
78. **Valhalla G.C.,** Louisville, Ky.
79. **Grandfather G. & C.C.,** Linville, N.C.
80. **Point O'Woods G. & C.C.,** Benton Harbor, Mich.

NINTH 10
81. **The Estancia Club,** Scottsdale, Ariz.
82. **Sahalee C.C. (South/North),** Redmond, Wash.
83. **Black Diamond Ranch G & C.C. (Quarry),** Lecanto, Fla.
84. **Jupiter Hills Club (Hills),** Tequesta, Fla.
85. **NCR C.C. (South),** Kettering, Ohio
86. **Forest Highlands G.C. (Canyon),** Flagstaff, Ariz.
87. **Shoreacres,** Lake Bluff, Ill.
88. **Eugene C.C.,** Eugene, Ore.
89. **Sanctuary G.C.,** Sedalia, Co.
90. **Double Eagle Club,** Galena, Oh.

TENTH 10
91. **The Quarry at La Quinta,** La Quinta, Calif.
92. **Stanwich Club,** Greenwich, Conn.
93. **Long Cove Club,** Hilton Head Island, S.C.
94. **Sycamore Hills G.C.,** Fort Wayne, Ind.
95. **Greenville C.C. (Chanticleer),** Greenville, S.C.
96. **Crosswater,** Sunriver Lodge, Sunriver, Ore.
97. **World Woods G.C. (Pine Barrens),** Brooksville, Fla.
98. **Aronimink G.C.,** Newtown Square, Pa.
99. **Wilmington C.C.(South),** Greenville, Del.
100. **Atlantic G.C.,** Bridgehampton, N.Y.

America's Best New Courses—2001

The Golf Digest annual survey of America's Best New Courses.

BEST NEW UPSCALE COURSES:
Maximum green fee more than $50.
1. **Pacific Dunes G. Links**, Bandon, Ore.
2. **Arcadia Bluffs G.C.**, Arcadia, Mich.
3. **Wolf Creek at Paradise Canyon,** Mesquite, Nev.
4. **Great River G.C.**, Milford, Conn.
5. **Saratoga National G.C.**, Saratoga, N.Y.
6. **Shepherd's Hollow G.C. (2nd/3rd 9s)**, Clarkston, Mich.
7. **The G. Cse. at Glen Mills**, Glen Mills, Pa.
8. **Avalon Lakes G. Cse.**, Warren, Ohio
9. **Shenandoah G.C.**, Verona, N.Y.
10. **Ocean Hammock G.C.**, Palm Coast, Fla.

Best New Affordable Public Courses

Maximum green fee $50 or less.
1. **The G.C. at Redlands Mesa.**, Grand Junction, Colo.
2. **The Harvester G.C.**, Harvester, Iowa
3. **Dacotah Ridge G.C.**, Morton, Minn.
4. **Olympia Hills G. & Conf. Ctr.**, Universal City, Texas
5. **Ol' Colony G. Complex**, Tuscaloosa, Ala.
6. **Old Silo G.C.**, Mount Sterling, Ky.
7. **Coyote Crossing G. Cse.**, West Lafayette, Ind.
8. **Aspen Lakes G.C. (Faith/Hope 9s)**, Sisters, Ore.
9. **New Albany Links G.C.**, New Albany, Ohio
10. **Murphy Creek G. Cse.**, Aurora, Co.

Best New Canadian

1. **Fox Harb'r Resort**, Wallace, Nova Scotia
2. **Stewart Creek G.C.**, Canmore, Alberta
3. **St. Eugene Mission G. Resort**, Cranbrook, British Columbia

Part I

The United States

★★ ALPINE BAY GOLF & COUNTRY CLUB
R-9855 Renfore Rd., Alpine, 35014, Talladega County, (256)268-2920, 40 miles from Birmingham. **E-mail:** bobame76@aol.com. **Facility Holes:** 18. **Yards:** 6,518/5,392. **Par:** 72/72. **Course Rating:** 70.9/69.8. **Slope:** 129/120. **Green Fee:** $30/$39. **Cart Fee:** Included in green fee. **Walking Policy:** Walking at certain times. **Walkability:** 3. **Opened:** 1972. **Architect:** Robert Trent Jones. **Season:** Year-round. **High:** May-Sept. **To obtain tee times:** Call up to 30 days in advance. **Miscellaneous:** Reduced fees (twilight, seniors), range (grass), credit cards (MC, V, AE, D), BF, FF.

★★★½ AUBURN LINKS AT MILL CREEK
PU-826 Shell-Toomer Pkwy., Auburn, 36830, Lee County, (334)887-5151, 4 miles from Auburn-Opelika. **E-mail:** kbasz@mindspring. **Web:** auburnlinks.com. **Facility Holes:** 18. **Yards:** 7,145/5,320. **Par:** 72/72. **Course Rating:** 72.5/68.5. **Slope:** 129/118. **Green Fee:** $35/$42. **Cart Fee:** Included in green fee. **Walking Policy:** Walking at certain times. **Walkability:** 3. **Opened:** 1991. **Architect:** Ward Northrup. **Season:** Year-round. **To obtain tee times:** Call up to 7 days in advance. **Miscellaneous:** Reduced fees (weekdays, guests, twilight, seniors, juniors), metal spikes, range (grass), credit cards (MC, V, D), BF, FF.
Reader Comments: Large bent-grass greens, nice practice areas … Watch out for the woods … Tricky sloping greens, good par 3s … Good greens, fun course … Beautiful course, difficult but fair layout, good service … Good people.

★★★ AZALEA CITY GOLF COURSE
PU-1000 Gaillard Dr., Mobile, 36608, Mobile County, (334)342-4221, 10 miles from Mobile. **Facility Holes:** 18. **Yards:** 6,850/5,347. **Par:** 72/72. **Course Rating:** 72.1/70.3. **Slope:** 126/122. **Green Fee:** $10/$17. **Cart Fee:** $12/Person. **Walking Policy:** Unrestricted walking. **Walkability:** 2. **Opened:** 1957. **Architect:** R.B Harris. **Season:** Year-round. **To obtain tee times:** Call up to 14 days in advance. **Miscellaneous:** Reduced fees (weekdays, twilight), metal spikes, range (grass), credit cards (MC, V, AE), BF, FF.
Reader Comments: Player-friendly course made for amateurs … Very quiet and in good shape … New greens will be good when they soften … Good for long drives off the tee.

★½ BAY OAKS GOLF CLUB
SP-7960 Edgar Roberts Road, Irvington, 36544, Mobile County, (334)824-2429, (800)338-9826, 10 miles from Mobile. **E-mail:** bayoaks01@cs.com. **Facility Holes:** 18. **Yards:** 6,623/5,504. **Par:** 72/72. **Course Rating:** 69.3/70.3. **Slope:** 126/114. **Green Fee:** $12/$14. **Cart Fee:** $13/Person. **Walking Policy:** Unrestricted walking. **Walkability:** 2. **Opened:** 1963. **Season:** Year-round. **To obtain tee times:** Call golf shop. **Miscellaneous:** Reduced fees (weekdays, twilight), range (grass), credit cards (MC, V, AE, D), FF.

★★★½ BENT BROOK GOLF COURSE
PU-7900 Dickey Springs Rd., Bessemer, 35022, Jefferson County, (205)424-2368, 10 miles from Birmingham. **Facility Holes:** 27. **Green Fee:** $20/$40. **Cart Fee:** $30/Person. **Walking Policy:** Walking at certain times. **Opened:** 1988. **Architect:** Ward Northrup. **Season:** Year-round. **High:** April-July. **To obtain tee times:** Call up to 3 days in advance. **Miscellaneous:** Reduced fees (weekdays), range (grass), credit cards (MC, V, AE, D), BF, FF.
BROOK/GRAVEYARD (18 Combo)
Yards: 7,053/5,364. **Par:** 71/71. **Course Rating:** 71.7/70.9. **Slope:** 121/124. **Walkability:** 3.
WINDMILL/BROOK (18 Combo)
Yards: 6,934/5,333. **Par:** 71/71. **Course Rating:** 69.6/70.3. **Slope:** 117/120. **Walkability:** 3.
WINDMILL/GRAVEYARD (18 Combo)
Yards: 6,847/5,321. **Par:** 70/70. **Course Rating:** 69.2/70.6. **Slope:** 116/123. **Walkability:** 2.
Reader Comments: One of Alabama's best … Tee times are even easy to get on a moment's notice … Well-kept fairways and greens … Good shape, open fairways, good greens … Great condition, superb service.

★★ BLACKBERRY TRAIL GOLF COURSE
PU-112 Clubhouse Dr., Florence, 35630, Lauderdale County, (256)760-6428, 120 miles from Birmingham. **E-mail:** cparrish@floweb.com. **Facility Holes:** 18. **Yards:** 6,851/4,664. **Par:** 72/72. **Green Fee:** $10/$22. **Walking Policy:** Unrestricted walking. **Walkability:** 3. **Opened:** 2001. **Architect:** Steve Plumer. **Season:** Year-round. **To obtain tee times:** Call golf shop. **Miscellaneous:** Reduced fees (seniors, juniors), range (grass), credit cards (MC, V), BF, FF. **Special Notes:** Formerly McFarland Park Golf Course.
round. **To obtain tee times:** Call up to 7 days in advance. **Miscellaneous:** Range (grass), credit cards (MC, V, AE, D), BF, FF.

CAPITOL HILL GOLF CLUB
PU-2600 Constitution Ave., Prattville, 36066, Autauga County, (334)285-1114, (800)949-4444, 10 miles from Montgomery. **E-mail:** jcannon@rtjgolf.com. **Web:** www.rtjgolf.com. **Facility**

Holes: 54. **Cart Fee:** $15/Person. **Walking Policy:** Unrestricted walking. **Walkability:** 2. **Opened:** 1999. **Season:** Year-round. **High:** Feb.-May. **To obtain tee times:** Call up to 120 days in advance. **Miscellaneous:** Range (grass), lodging (90 rooms), credit cards (MC, V, AE, D), BF, FF.

JUDGE COURSE (18)
Yards: 7,794/4,955. **Par:** 72/72. **Course Rating:** 77.8/68.3. **Slope:** 144/121. **Green Fee:** $45/$65. **Architect:** Robert Trent Jones Jr.

★★★★ LEGISLATOR COURSE (18) *Value*
Yards: 7,323/5,414. **Par:** 72/72. **Course Rating:** 74.1/70.7. **Slope:** 126/121. **Green Fee:** $35/$55. **Architect:** Roger Rulewich.
Notes: Ranked 9th in 2000 Best New Affordable Courses.
Reader Comments: Awesome views … Good golf, cheap … Difficult for most … Pretty, fair, fun, a good time … Service is top-of-the-line … Some of the best public golf you can find, especially for the price … Very playable, huge greens … Hilly, some blind shots … Good traditional golf course.

★★★★½ SENATOR COURSE (18) *Value*
Yards: 7,697/5,122. **Par:** 72/72. **Course Rating:** 76.6/68.8. **Slope:** 131/112. **Green Fee:** $35/$55. **Architect:** Roger Rulewich.
Reader Comments: Great, great, what is there to say? … Looks like British Open … Hilly, some blind shots … Great place for foursome visit … Bring plenty of balls … Fun, no need to go to Scotland … Played with wind blowing 35 mph, thought I was in Scotland … Great challenge.

★★★½ CHESLEY OAKS GOLF COURSE *Pace*
PU-1035 Co. Rd. 1583, Cullman, 35058, Cullman County, (256)796-9808, 40 miles from Huntsville. **E-mail:** Chesleyl@mindspring.com. **Web:** chesleyoaksgolf.com. **Facility Holes:** 18. **Yards:** 6,738/4,981. **Par:** 71/71. **Course Rating:** 71.0. **Slope:** 113. **Green Fee:** $11/$24. **Cart Fee:** $11/Person. **Walking Policy:** Unrestricted walking. **Walkability:** 2. **Opened:** 1996. **Architect:** Steve Plumer. **Season:** Year-round. **High:** April-Nov. **To obtain tee times:** Call up to 5 days in advance. **Miscellaneous:** Reduced fees (weekdays, twilight, seniors, juniors), range (grass/mats), credit cards (MC, V, D), BF, FF.
Reader Comments: Great course, Scottish links flavor, staff makes you feel right at home, fees are an unbelievable value … Employees very friendly, outstanding course … Excellent rural course, excellent greens & fairways … Wide open, great for beginners.

★★ CITRONELLE MUNICIPAL GOLF COURSE
PU-18350 Lakeview Dr., Citronelle, 36522, Mobile County, (334)866-7881, 45 miles from Mobile. **Facility Holes:** 18. **Yards:** 5,916/5,201. **Par:** 71/71. **Course Rating:** 70.0/69.4. **Slope:** 126/116. **Green Fee:** $12. **Cart Fee:** $10/Person. **Walking Policy:** Walking at certain times. **Walkability:** 4. **Opened:** 1975. **Season:** Year-round. **High:** May-Aug. **To obtain tee times:** Call golf shop. **Miscellaneous:** Metal spikes, range (grass), credit cards (MC, V).

★★ COLONIAL GOLF CLUB
PU-400 Colonial Dr., Meridianville, 35759, Madison County, (256)828-0431. **Facility Holes:** 18. **Yards:** 6,571/6,153. **Par:** 72/72. **Course Rating:** 69.5/67.6. **Slope:** 114/110. **Green Fee:** $16/$18. **Cart Fee:** $9/Person. **Walking Policy:** Unrestricted walking. **Walkability:** 2. **Opened:** 1963. **Season:** Year-round. **High:** March-Nov. **To obtain tee times:** Call up to 7 days in advance. **Miscellaneous:** Reduced fees (weekdays), metal spikes, credit cards (MC, V, D), BF, FF.

CRAFT FARMS COASTAL GOLF RESORT
PU-104 Cotton Creek Dr., Gulf Shores, 36542, Baldwin County, (334)968-7766, (800)327-2657, 40 miles from Mobile. **Web:** www.craftfarms.com. **Facility Holes:** 54. **Cart Fee:** Included in green fee. **Walkability:** 2. **Season:** Year-round. **High:** Feb.-April. **To obtain tee times:** Call up to 60 days in advance. **Miscellaneous:** Reduced fees (twilight, juniors), lodging (114 rooms), credit cards (MC, V, AE).

★★★★ COTTON CREEK COURSE (18)
Yards: 7,028/5,175. **Par:** 72/72. **Course Rating:** 74.1/70.9. **Slope:** 136/122. **Green Fee:** $42/$70. **Walking Policy:** Mandatory carts. **Opened:** 1987. **Architect:** Arnold Palmer/Ed Seay. **Miscellaneous:** Range (grass/mats).
Reader Comments: I play this course every summer vacation … Excellent course, a real challenge … Pricey, beautiful course … Very slow … Pleasant round of golf … Nice staff … One of the finest Gulf Coast complexes … Fun course, friendly people.

★★★ CYPRESS BEND COURSE (18)
Yards: 6,848/5,045. **Par:** 72/72. **Course Rating:** 72.4/68.4. **Slope:** 127/112. **Green Fee:** $42/$70. **Walking Policy:** Mandatory carts. **Opened:** 1987. **Architect:** Arnold Palmer. **Miscellaneous:** Metal spikes, range (grass).
Reader Comments: Really fun & scoreable … Hole design is a little watered down compared to other Craft Farms designs, but a fun play … Wide open, but you must shape shots … Fair shape, over-played, nice staff.

★★★½ THE WOODLANDS COURSE (18)
Yards: 6,484/5,145. **Par:** 72/72. **Course Rating:** 70.8/67.9. **Slope:** 123/109. **Green Fee:**

$42/$65. **Walking Policy:** Walking at certain times. **Opened:** 1994. **Architect:** Larry Nelson. **Miscellaneous:** Metal spikes, range (grass).
Reader Comments: By far the best scenery, service & golf … Come here to avoid the crowds and still get a great round … Pricey, beautiful … Good ladies' course … Snake warnings … Great course, a little short, great staff.

★★½ CULLMAN GOLF COURSE
PU-2321 County Rd. 490, Hanceville, 35077, Cullman County, (256)739-2386, 50 miles from Birmingham. **E-mail:** golf@cullmanrecreation.org. **Facility Holes:** 18. **Yards:** 6,361/4,495. **Par:** 72/72. **Course Rating:** 70.6/67.7. **Slope:** 131/115. **Green Fee:** $17/$21. **Cart Fee:** $12/Person. **Walking Policy:** Unrestricted walking. **Walkability:** 3. **Opened:** 1950. **Architect:** Curtis Davis. **Season:** Year-round. **High:** April-Sept. **To obtain tee times:** Call golf shop. **Miscellaneous:** Reduced fees (weekdays, twilight, seniors, juniors), range (grass), credit cards (MC, V, D), BF, FF.

★★★ CYPRESS LAKES GOLF & COUNTRY CLUB
SP-1311 E. 6th St., Muscle Shoals, 35661, Colbert County, (256)381-1232, 50 miles from Huntsville. **Facility Holes:** 18. **Yards:** 6,562/5,100. **Par:** 71/71. **Course Rating:** 71.8/69.3. **Slope:** 126/128. **Green Fee:** $36/$48. **Cart Fee:** $13/Person. **Walking Policy:** Walking at certain times. **Walkability:** 3. **Opened:** 1991. **Architect:** Gary Roger Baird. **Season:** Year-round. **High:** March-Oct. **To obtain tee times:** Call golf shop. **Miscellaneous:** Reduced fees (weekdays, juniors), range (grass), credit cards (MC, V, AE), BF, FF.
Reader Comments: Lots of trees & narrow fairways … Challenging, lots of water … Short but demanding … Excellent greens, little sand.
Special Notes: Formerly The Oaks Golf Club.

★★★ DEER RUN GOLF COURSE
PU-1175 County Rd. 100, Moulton, 35650, Lawrence County, (256)974-7384, 24 miles from Decatur. **Facility Holes:** 18. **Yards:** 6,745/5,457. **Par:** 72/72. **Course Rating:** 70.9/70.9. **Slope:** 119/111. **Green Fee:** $16/$20. **Cart Fee:** $22/Cart. **Walking Policy:** Unrestricted walking. **Walkability:** 3. **Opened:** 1981. **Architect:** Earl Stone. **Season:** Year-round. **High:** April-Sept. **To obtain tee times:** Call golf shop. **Miscellaneous:** Range (grass), credit cards (MC, V), BF, FF.
Reader Comments: Good & challenging … Tight, quaint, enjoyable … Beautiful course, windy … Unbelievable bang for the buck! … Very challenging, lots of water, sand and value = the best course I have played.

DOTHAN NATIONAL GOLF CLUB & HOTEL
PU-7410 Hwy 231S, Dothan, 36301, Houston County, (334)677-3326, 4 miles from Dothan. **Facility Holes:** 18. **Yards:** 7,242/5,470. **Par:** 72/72. **Course Rating:** 74.5/71.1. **Slope:** 123/113. **Green Fee:** $12/$18. **Cart Fee:** $11/Person. **Walking Policy:** Walking at certain times. **Opened:** 1968. **Architect:** Bob Simmons. **Season:** Year-round. **High:** March-June. **To obtain tee times:** Call golf shop. **Miscellaneous:** Reduced fees (twilight), metal spikes, range (grass), credit cards (MC, V, AE, D, Diners Club).
Special Notes: Formerly Olympia Spa Golf Resort.

★★★½ EAGLE POINT GOLF CLUB
PU-4500 Eagle Point Dr., Birmingham, 35242, Shelby County, (205)991-9070, 18 miles from Birmingham. **Facility Holes:** 18. **Yards:** 6,470/4,691. **Par:** 71/70. **Course Rating:** 70.2/61.9. **Slope:** 127/108. **Green Fee:** $27/$37. **Cart Fee:** $12/Person. **Walking Policy:** Unrestricted walking. **Walkability:** 3. **Opened:** 1990. **Architect:** Earl Stone. **Season:** Year-round. **High:** April-Sept. **To obtain tee times:** Call golf shop. **Miscellaneous:** Reduced fees (seniors), range (grass), credit cards (MC, V, AE, D).
Reader Comments: Very nice, fun to play … Tight layout, still fun for high-handicapper, friendly folks … Very good course and staff for the money … Very nice greens … Another favorite … Pace enforced, need every club.

EMERALD MOUNTAIN GOLF CLUB
SP-245 Mountain View Dr., Wetumpka, 36093, Elmore County, (334)514-8082, 6 miles from Montgomery. **E-mail:** golfemgc@aol.com. **Facility Holes:** 18. **Yards:** 7,023/5,396. **Par:** 72/72. **Course Rating:** 73.5/70.8. **Slope:** 133/119. **Green Fee:** $11/$35. **Cart Fee:** $12/Cart. **Walking Policy:** Mandatory carts. **Walkability:** 3. **Opened:** 2000. **Architect:** Ward Northrup. **Season:** Year-round. **High:** March-Nov. **To obtain tee times:** Call up to 7 days in advance. **Miscellaneous:** Reduced fees (weekdays, twilight, seniors, juniors), range (grass), credit cards (MC, V, AE, D), BF, FF.

★★ FRANK HOUSE MUNICIPAL GOLF CLUB
PU-801 Golf Course Rd., Bessemer, 35022, Jefferson County, (205)424-9540, 15 miles from Birmingham. **Facility Holes:** 18. **Yards:** 6,320/5,034. **Par:** 72/75. **Course Rating:** 69.0/63.3.

Slope: 119/107. **Green Fee:** $12/$15. **Cart Fee:** $10/Person. **Walking Policy:** Walking at certain times. **Walkability:** 5. **Opened:** 1972. **Architect:** Earl Stone. **Season:** Year-round. **High:** May-Aug. **To obtain tee times:** Call golf shop. **Miscellaneous:** Reduced fees (weekdays, guests, twilight, seniors), metal spikes, credit cards (MC, V, AE, D).

★★★½ GLENLAKES GOLF CLUB
SP-9530 Clubhouse Dr., Foley, 36535, Baldwin County, (334)955-1220, 35 miles from Pensacola. **Web:** www.glenlakesgolf.com. **Facility Holes:** 27. **Yards:** 6,938/5,384. **Par:** 72/72. **Course Rating:** 72.9/70.2. **Slope:** 125/114. **Green Fee:** $23/$37. **Cart Fee:** $16/Person. **Walking Policy:** Mandatory carts. **Walkability:** 3. **Opened:** 1987. **Architect:** Robert von Hagge/Bruce Devlin. **Season:** Year-round. **High:** Feb.-April. **To obtain tee times:** Call up to 7 days in advance. **Miscellaneous:** Reduced fees (weekdays, guests, twilight, juniors), range (grass), credit cards (MC, V, AE, D), BF, FF.
Reader Comments: Short course. Very easy … Price good … Outstanding … Back nine is a 4 or 4 1/2, first nine is nice but ordinary … Playing condition good … Great value.
Special Notes: Also has 9-hole Lakes Course.

★★★½ GOOSE POND COLONY GOLF COURSE *Value*
PU-417 Ed Hembree Dr., Scottsboro, 35769, Jackson County, (256)574-5353, (800)268-2884, 40 miles from Huntsville. **Web:** WWW.GPC.ORG. **Facility Holes:** 18. **Yards:** 6,860/5,370. **Par:** 72/72. **Course Rating:** 71.7/70.0. **Slope:** 125/115. **Green Fee:** $18/$23. **Cart Fee:** $11/Person. **Walking Policy:** Walking at certain times. **Opened:** 1968. **Architect:** George Cobb. **Season:** Year-round. **High:** April-Aug. **To obtain tee times:** Call golf shop. **Miscellaneous:** Reduced fees (weekdays, guests, seniors, juniors), range (grass), credit cards (MC, V, D).
Reader Comments: One of the best in North Alabama … Outstanding greens … A vista from every hole, a great test of your golf skills … Beautiful layout … Challenging but reasonable … Nice course, can be crowded & slow on weekends, very challenging.

★★ GULF SHORES GOLF CLUB
SP-520 Clubhouse Dr., Gulf Shores, 36547, Baldwin County, (334)968-7366, 20 miles from Pensacola. **Facility Holes:** 18. **Yards:** 6,570/5,522. **Par:** 72/72. **Course Rating:** 70.2/70.9. **Slope:** 110/118. **Green Fee:** $32/$40. **Cart Fee:** Included in green fee. **Walkability:** 1. **Opened:** 1964. **Architect:** Earl Stone. **Season:** Year-round. **High:** Jan.-Aug. **To obtain tee times:** Call golf shop. **Miscellaneous:** Reduced fees (juniors), range (grass), credit cards (MC, V).

★★★ GULF STATE PARK GOLF COURSE
PU-20115 State Hwy. 135, Gulf Shores, 36542, Baldwin County, (334)948-4653, 50 miles from Mobile. **Facility Holes:** 18. **Yards:** 6,563/5,310. **Par:** 72/72. **Course Rating:** 72.5/70.4. **Green Fee:** $24/$27. **Cart Fee:** $13/Person. **Walking Policy:** Walking at certain times. **Walkability:** 1. **Opened:** 1974. **Architect:** Earl Stone. **Season:** Year-round. **High:** Year-round. **To obtain tee times:** Call golf shop. **Miscellaneous:** Reduced fees (guests, seniors), metal spikes, range (grass), lodging (144 rooms), credit cards (MC, V, AE), BF, FF.
Reader Comments: A fun municipal course … Friendliest staff I've ever encountered in 35 years of golf … Very scenic, some interesting gambling holes … One of the best values the area … Very good. Could be a bit faster in the pace of play.

★★★★ GUNTER'S LANDING GOLF COURSE
SP-1000 Gunter's Landing Rd., Guntersville, 35976, Marshall County, (256)582-3586, (800)833-6663, 35 miles from Huntsville. **E-mail:** gunterslanding@mindspring.com. **Web:** gunterslanding.com. **Facility Holes:** 18. **Yards:** 6,863/5,274. **Par:** 72/72. **Course Rating:** 73.0/70.0. **Slope:** 144/113. **Green Fee:** $35/$45. **Cart Fee:** Included in green fee. **Walking Policy:** Walking at certain times. **Walkability:** 5. **Opened:** 1992. **Architect:** Jim Kennamer. **Season:** Year-round. **High:** April-Sept. **To obtain tee times:** Call up to 14 days in advance. **Miscellaneous:** Reduced fees (weekdays, twilight, seniors, juniors), range (grass), lodging (4 rooms), credit cards (MC, V, AE, D), BF, FF.
Reader Comments: Better bring lots of balls … All new greens, great course … Tough course if you don't know it … Overpriced for area, beautiful course … Hard but fair course, good value.

HIGHLAND PARK GOLF CLUB
PU-3300 Highland Ave., Birmingham, 35205, Jefferson County, (205)322-1902. **Facility Holes:** 18. **Yards:** 5,801/4,793. **Par:** 70/70. **Course Rating:** 68.1/63.8. **Slope:** 128/114. **Green Fee:** $24/$31. **Cart Fee:** $11/Person. **Walking Policy:** Walking at certain times. **Walkability:** 3. **Opened:** 1998. **Architect:** Bob Cupp. **Season:** Year-round. **High:** April-Sept. **To obtain tee times:** Call up to 5 days in advance. **Miscellaneous:** Reduced fees (twilight, seniors, juniors), range (grass/mats), credit cards (MC, V, AE), BF, FF.

HORSE CREEK GOLF CLUB
PU-1745 Highway 78, Dora, 35062, Walker County, (205)648-1494, 23 miles from Birmingham. **Facility Holes:** 18. **Yards:** 6,883/4,805. **Par:** 72/72. **Course Rating:** 72.6. **Slope:**

128. **Green Fee:** $27/$32. **Cart Fee:** Included in green fee. **Walking Policy:** Mandatory carts. **Walkability:** 3. **Opened:** 2000. **Architect:** R. Kirk. **Season:** Year-round. **To obtain tee times:** Call golf shop. **Miscellaneous:** Reduced fees (weekdays, twilight, juniors), range (grass), credit cards (MC, V, AE), BF, FF.

★★ HUNTSVILLE MUNICIPAL GOLF COURSE
PU-2151 Airport Rd., Huntsville, 35801, Madison County, (256)880-1151. **Facility Holes:** 18. **Yards:** 6,719/4,782. **Par:** 72/72. **Course Rating:** 70.2/63.4. **Slope:** 122/109. **Green Fee:** $14/$15. **Cart Fee:** $8/Person. **Walking Policy:** Unrestricted walking. **Walkability:** 2. **Opened:** 1986. **Architect:** Ron Kirby/Denis Griffiths. **Season:** Year-round. **High:** April-Oct. **To obtain tee times:** Call golf shop. **Miscellaneous:** Reduced fees (weekdays, twilight, juniors), metal spikes, credit cards (MC, V, AE).

★★★ INDIAN PINES GOLF CLUB
PU-900 Country Club Lane, Auburn, 36830, Lee County, (334)821-0880, 50 miles from Montgomery. **Facility Holes:** 18. **Yards:** 6,213/4,751. **Par:** 71/71. **Course Rating:** 68.8/62.1. **Slope:** 119/105. **Green Fee:** $11/$16. **Cart Fee:** $10/Person. **Walking Policy:** Unrestricted walking. **Walkability:** 2. **Opened:** 1976. **Season:** Year-round. **High:** March-Oct. **To obtain tee times:** Call up to 7 days in advance. **Miscellaneous:** Reduced fees (juniors), metal spikes, range (grass/mats), credit cards (MC, V), BF, FF.
Reader Comments: Much improved, good value ... Beautiful course, but windy ... Can't beat the value. Lots of beginners, but still a solid municipal course ... A great course to walk.

★½ ISLE DAUPHINE GOLF CLUB
PU-100 Orleans Dr., P.O. Box 39, Dauphin Island, 36528, Mobile County, (334)861-2433, 30 miles from Mobile. **Facility Holes:** 18. **Yards:** 6,620/5,619. **Par:** 72/72. **Course Rating:** 70.8/72.6. **Slope:** 123/122. **Green Fee:** $13/$14. **Cart Fee:** $12/Person. **Walking Policy:** Unrestricted walking. **Walkability:** 2. **Opened:** 1958. **Architect:** Charles Maddox. **Season:** Year-round. **High:** Jan.-April. **To obtain tee times:** Call up to 7 days in advance. **Miscellaneous:** Reduced fees (weekdays, twilight, juniors), metal spikes, credit cards (MC, V), BF, FF.

★★★ JOE WHEELER STATE PARK GOLF COURSE
R-Rte. 4, Box 369A, Rogersville, 35652, Lauderdale County, (256)247-9308, (800)252-7275, 20 miles from Florence. **Facility Holes:** 18. **Yards:** 7,251/6,055. **Par:** 72/72. **Course Rating:** 73.1/67.7. **Slope:** 120/109. **Green Fee:** $15. **Cart Fee:** $18/Cart. **Walking Policy:** Unrestricted walking. **Walkability:** 4. **Opened:** 1974. **Architect:** Earl Stone. **Season:** Year-round. **High:** March-Oct. **To obtain tee times:** Call golf shop. **Miscellaneous:** Reduced fees (guests, seniors), metal spikes, range (grass), lodging (75 rooms), credit cards (MC, V, AE).
Reader Comments: Lots of hills, some fun holes, neat lodge ... Great layout ... Course is in good condition, worth the money, challenging ... Worth the trip, fair, beautiful ... Always a fun course, friendly people, good rates.

★★★★½ KIVA DUNES GOLF CLUB *Condition*
PU-815 Plantation Dr., Gulf Shores, 36542, Baldwin County, (334)540-7000, (888)833-5482, 45 miles from Pensacola. **E-mail:** kivadune@gulftel.com. **Web:** kivadunes-golf.com. **Facility Holes:** 18. **Yards:** 7,092/4,994. **Par:** 72/72. **Course Rating:** 73.9/68.5. **Slope:** 132/115. **Green Fee:** $65/$90. **Cart Fee:** Included in green fee. **Walking Policy:** Unrestricted walking. **Walkability:** 2. **Opened:** 1995. **Architect:** Jerry Pate. **Season:** Year-round. **High:** Feb.-Oct. **To obtain tee times:** Call up to 90 days in advance. **Miscellaneous:** Range (grass), lodging (23 rooms), credit cards (MC, V, AE, D).
Notes: Ranked 3rd in 2001 Best in State; 2nd in 1995 Best New Public Courses.
Reader Comments: Fairways like plush carpet. BIG greens ... Excellent course designed around wind ... In such great shape I didn't want to make a divot ... Wonderful links design on the Gulf of Mexico. Bring the camera ... Hell for average golfer ... Very tough, but fun ... Nice layout, windy, very challenging.

★★★ LAGOON PARK GOLF COURSE
PU-2855 Lagoon Park Dr., Montgomery, 36109, Montgomery County, (334)271-7000. **Facility Holes:** 18. **Yards:** 6,773/5,342. **Par:** 72/72. **Course Rating:** 71.1/69.6. **Slope:** 124/113. **Green Fee:** $15/$25. **Cart Fee:** $12/Person. **Walking Policy:** Unrestricted walking. **Walkability:** 1. **Opened:** 1978. **Architect:** Charles M. Graves. **Season:** Year-round. **High:** April-Oct. **To obtain tee times:** Call golf shop. **Miscellaneous:** Reduced fees (weekdays), range (grass/mats), credit cards (MC, V, D).
Reader Comments: Great driving course ... Lace up your shoes from the tips ... Good course ... Slow play ... Tight course, well maintained ... Narrow fairways, many doglegs ... Good municipal course ... Long, very good condition, felt rushed.

ALABAMA

★★★ LAKE GUNTERSVILLE GOLF CLUB
PU-7966 Alabama Hwy. 227, Guntersville, 35976, Marshall County, (205)582-0379, 40 miles from Huntsville. **Facility Holes:** 18. **Yards:** 6,785/5,776. **Par:** 72/72. **Course Rating:** 71.2/70.3. **Slope:** 128/124. **Green Fee:** $16. **Cart Fee:** $20/Cart. **Walking Policy:** Unrestricted walking. **Walkability:** 4. **Opened:** 1974. **Architect:** Earl Stone. **Season:** Year-round. **High:** March-Oct. **To obtain tee times:** Call up to 3 days in advance. **Miscellaneous:** Reduced fees (twilight, seniors), metal spikes, range (grass), lodging (100 rooms), credit cards (MC, V, AE), FF.
Reader Comments: Nicely bunkered. Very hilly … Great people who make up staff, need to speed up play … Hardest course in North Alabama … Beautiful golf course … Course in good shape, range not long enough.

★½ LAKEPOINT RESORT GOLF COURSE
R-Hwy. 431, Eufaula, 36027, Barbour County, (334)687-6677, (800)544-5253, 50 miles from Columbus. **Facility Holes:** 18. **Yards:** 6,752/5,363. **Par:** 72/72. **Course Rating:** 73.6/69.2. **Slope:** 123. **Green Fee:** $14. **Cart Fee:** $9/Person. **Walking Policy:** Unrestricted walking. **Walkability:** 3. **Opened:** 1971. **Architect:** Thomas Nicol. **Season:** Year-round. **High:** March-June. **To obtain tee times:** Call golf shop. **Miscellaneous:** Reduced fees (seniors), metal spikes, range (grass), lodging (250 rooms), credit cards (MC, V, AE).

LAKEWOOD GOLF COURSE
PU-2800 Lakewood Dr., Phenix City, 36867, Russell County, (334)291-4726, 3 miles from Columbus. **Facility Holes:** 18. **Yards:** 6,476/5,114. **Par:** 72/72. **Course Rating:** 70.1/69.0. **Slope:** 124/124. **Green Fee:** $24/$26. **Cart Fee:** Included in green fee. **Walking Policy:** Walking at certain times. **Walkability:** 3. **Opened:** 1997. **Architect:** John LaFoy. **Season:** Year-round. **High:** April-Sept. **To obtain tee times:** Call golf shop. **Miscellaneous:** Metal spikes, range (grass), credit cards (MC, V), BF, FF.

★★★★½ LIMESTONE SPRINGS G.C. *Service+, Value, Condition+, Pace+*
SP-3000 Colonial Dr., Oneonta, 35121, Blount County, (205)274-4653, 31 miles from Birmingham. **Web:** limestonesprings.com. **Facility Holes:** 18. **Yards:** 6,987/5,042. **Par:** 72/72. **Course Rating:** 74.2/69.6. **Slope:** 139/128. **Green Fee:** $50/$65. **Cart Fee:** $13/Person. **Walking Policy:** Unrestricted walking. **Walkability:** 2. **Opened:** 1999. **Architect:** Jerry Pate. **Season:** Year-round. **To obtain tee times:** Call up to 7 days in advance. **Miscellaneous:** Reduced fees (twilight, juniors), range (grass), lodging (4 rooms), credit cards (MC, V, AE, D), BF, FF.
Notes: Ranked 5th in 2001 Best in State; 8th in 1999 Best New Upscale Public.
Reader Comments: A hidden gem, good imaginative golf … Beautiful layout, very fair course … Good length, very demanding … Great views, natural layout, challenging … This course is a gem with super greens & scenic holes … Great design, excellent maintenance … Best in north Alabama.

★★ THE LINKSMAN GOLF CLUB
PU-3700 St. Andrews Dr., Mobile, 36693, Mobile County, (334)661-0018, 50 miles from Pensacola. **Facility Holes:** 18. **Yards:** 6,275/5,416. **Par:** 72/72. **Course Rating:** 70.1/71.0. **Slope:** 123/121. **Green Fee:** $18. **Cart Fee:** $11/Person. **Walking Policy:** Unrestricted walking. **Opened:** 1987. **Season:** Year-round. **High:** March-June. **To obtain tee times:** Call golf shop. **Miscellaneous:** Reduced fees (weekdays, guests, twilight, seniors, juniors), metal spikes, range (grass), credit cards (MC, V, AE, D).

MARRIOTT'S LAKEWOOD GOLF CLUB
R-Marriott's Grand Hotel, Scenic Hwy. 98, Point Clear, 36564, Baldwin County, (334)990-6312, (800)544-9933, 30 miles from Mobile. **E-mail:** dclark@rtjgolf.com. **Web:** www.marriottgrand.com. **Facility Holes:** 36. **Green Fee:** $44/$57. **Cart Fee:** Included in green fee. **Walking Policy:** Unrestricted walking. **Walkability:** 2. **Opened:** 1947. **Season:** Year-round. **To obtain tee times:** Call golf shop. **Miscellaneous:** Reduced fees (twilight, juniors), metal spikes, range (grass), lodging (300 rooms), credit cards (MC, V, AE, D), BF, FF.
★★★ AZALEA COURSE (18)
Yards: 6,770/5,307. **Par:** 72/72. **Course Rating:** 72.5/71.3. **Slope:** 128/118. **Architect:** Perry Maxwell/Ron Garl.
Reader Comments: Great old Southern course with live oaks and Spanish moss. Moderate difficulty but plenty of features to keep it interesting … Pricey.
★★½ DOGWOOD COURSE (18)
Yards: 6,676/5,532. **Par:** 71/72. **Course Rating:** 72.1/72.6. **Slope:** 124/122. **Architect:** Perry Maxwell/Joe Lee.

★★½ THE MEADOWS GOLF CLUB
PU-1 Plantation Dr., Harpersville, 35078, Shelby County, (205)672-7529, 20 miles from Birmingham. **Facility Holes:** 18. **Yards:** 6,823/5,275. **Par:** 72/72. **Course Rating:** 71.6/70.1.

Slope: 122/119. **Green Fee:** $32/$42. **Cart Fee:** Included in green fee. **Walking Policy:** Walking at certain times. **Walkability:** 2. **Opened:** 1995. **Architect:** Steve Plumer. **Season:** Year-round. **High:** April-Sept. **To obtain tee times:** Call golf shop. **Miscellaneous:** Reduced fees (twilight, seniors, juniors), range (grass), credit cards (MC, V, AE, D), BF, FF.

MOORE'S MILL GOLF CLUB
SP-2320 Moore's Mill Rd. #600, Auburn, 36830, Lee County, (334)826-8989, 1.5 miles from Auburn. **Facility Holes:** 18. **Yards:** 6,873/4,733. **Par:** 72/72. **Course Rating:** 73.0/67.3. **Slope:** 132/125. **Green Fee:** $12/$25. **Cart Fee:** $12/Person. **Walking Policy:** Unrestricted walking. **Walkability:** 3. **Opened:** 2001. **Architect:** Day-Blalock Golf. **Season:** Year-round. **High:** April-Oct. **To obtain tee times:** Call up to 7 days in advance. **Miscellaneous:** Reduced fees (twilight), range (grass), credit cards (MC, V, AE, D), BF, FF.

★★½ MOUNTAIN VIEW GOLF CLUB
PU-3200 Mountain View Dr., Graysville, 35073, Jefferson County, (205)674-8362, 17 miles from Birmingham. **Web:** golf.bizhosting.com. **Facility Holes:** 27. **Green Fee:** $25/$30. **Cart Fee:** Included in green fee. **Opened:** 1991. **Architect:** James Thursby. **Season:** Year-round. **High:** March-Oct. **To obtain tee times:** Call golf shop. **Miscellaneous:** Reduced fees (twilight, seniors), credit cards (MC, V, D).
RED/BLUE (18 Combo)
Yards: 6,070/4,816. **Par:** 71/71. **Course Rating:** 69.3/69.4. **Slope:** 114/120.
RED/WHITE (18 Combo)
Yards: 5,800/4,702. **Par:** 71/71. **Course Rating:** 67.5/67.5. **Slope:** 111/116.
WHITE/BLUE (18 Combo)
Yards: 5,890/4,718. **Par:** 70/70. **Course Rating:** 68.4/68.5. **Slope:** 114/123.

★★½ OAK MOUNTAIN STATE PARK GOLF COURSE
PU-Findley Dr., Pelham, 35124, Shelby County, (205)620-2522, 15 miles from Birmingham. **Web:** www.bham.net/oakmtn. **Facility Holes:** 18. **Yards:** 6,748/5,615. **Par:** 72/72. **Course Rating:** 71.5/66.5. **Slope:** 127/117. **Green Fee:** $12/$18. **Cart Fee:** $18/Person. **Walking Policy:** Unrestricted walking. **Walkability:** 2. **Opened:** 1974. **Architect:** Earl Stone. **Season:** Year-round. **High:** May-Sept. **To obtain tee times:** Call golf shop. **Miscellaneous:** Reduced fees (seniors), metal spikes, range (grass), credit cards (MC, V, AE).

OL' COLONY GOLF COMPLEX
PU-401 Old Colony Rd., Tuscaloosa, 35406, Tuscaloosa County, (205)562-3201, 40 miles from Birmingham. **Facility Holes:** 18. **Yards:** 7,041/4,975. **Par:** 72/72. **Course Rating:** 73.9. **Slope:** 135. **Green Fee:** $25/$31. **Cart Fee:** $9/Person. **Walking Policy:** Unrestricted walking. **Walkability:** 3. **Opened:** 2000. **Architect:** Jerry Pate. **Season:** Year-round. **High:** March-July. **To obtain tee times:** Call up to 7 days in advance. **Miscellaneous:** Reduced fees (juniors), range (grass), credit cards (MC, V), BF, FF.
Notes: Ranked 5th in 2001 Best New Affordable Courses.

★★★★ THE PENINSULA GOLF CLUB
SP-20 Peninsula Blvd., Gulf Shores, 36542, Baldwin County, (334)968-8009, 50 miles from Mobile. **Facility Holes:** 27. **Green Fee:** $45/$78. **Cart Fee:** Included in green fee. **Walking Policy:** Walking at certain times. **Walkability:** 2. **Opened:** 1995. **Architect:** Earl Stone. **Season:** Year-round. **To obtain tee times:** Call golf shop. **Miscellaneous:** Reduced fees (twilight, juniors), metal spikes, range (grass), credit cards (MC, V, AE, D), BF, FF.
CYPRESS/LAKES (18 combo)
Yards: 7,055/4,978. **Par:** 72/72. **Course Rating:** 74.0/69.6. **Slope:** 131/121.
MARSH/CYPRESS (18 combo)
Yards: 7,179/5,080. **Par:** 72/72. **Course Rating:** 74.7/70.1. **Slope:** 133/120.
MARSH/LAKES (18 combo)
Yards: 7,026/5,072. **Par:** 72/72. **Course Rating:** 73.8/68.7. **Slope:** 130/115.
Reader Comments: Scoreable, fun & well laid out ... Great track, heavy traffic ... All you want from the tips. Customer service is a top priority ... Flat ... Good course, well kept ... Excellent course for golfers of all skill levels.

★★★½ POINT MALLARD GOLF COURSE
PU-1800 Point Mallard Dr., Decatur, 35601, Morgan County, (256)351-7776, 20 miles from Huntsville. **Facility Holes:** 18. **Yards:** 7,113/5,437. **Par:** 72/73. **Course Rating:** 73.7/69.9. **Slope:** 125/115. **Green Fee:** $16/$20. **Cart Fee:** $12/Person. **Walking Policy:** Unrestricted walking. **Walkability:** 1. **Opened:** 1970. **Architect:** Charles M. Graves. **Season:** Year-round. **To obtain tee times:** Call up to 2 days in advance. **Miscellaneous:** Reduced fees (weekdays, seniors, juniors), range (grass/mats), credit cards (MC, V), BF, FF.
Reader Comments: Outstanding design ... Majestic setting, well-maintained ... Nice layout, need better maintenance ... Good variety of holes, mostly easy ... Short hitters beware. Lots of water. Staff is excellent.

★½ QUAIL CREEK GOLF COURSE
PU-19841 Quail Creek Dr., Fairhope, 36532, Baldwin County, (334)990-0240, (888)701-2202, 20 miles from Mobile. **Web:** cofairhope.com. **Facility Holes:** 18. **Yards:** 6,426/5,305. **Par:** 72/72. **Course Rating:** 70.6/70.2. **Slope:** 123/122. **Green Fee:** $24. **Cart Fee:** $12/Person. **Walking Policy:** Walking at certain times. **Walkability:** 1. **Opened:** 1988. **Season:** Year-round. **High:** Jan.-May. **To obtain tee times:** Call up to 3 days in advance. **Miscellaneous:** Reduced fees (twilight), metal spikes, range (grass), credit cards (MC, V, AE, D), BF, FF.

RIVER RUN GOLF COURSE
PU-1501 Dozier Rd., Montgomery, 36117, Montgomery County, (334)271-2811, 3 miles from Montgomery. **Facility Holes:** 36. **Green Fee:** $17/$25. **Cart Fee:** $14/Person. **Walking Policy:** Walking at certain times. **Walkability:** 2. **Season:** Year-round. **High:** March-Oct. **To obtain tee times:** Call up to 4 days in advance. **Miscellaneous:** Reduced fees (weekdays, twilight, juniors), range (grass), credit cards (MC, V, AE, D, Debit Card), BF, FF.
★★ ORANGE AND BLUE (18)
Yards: 6,585/5,079. **Par:** 72/72. **Course Rating:** 69.4/68.6. **Slope:** 114/109.
RED AND WHITE (18)
Yards: 6,535/5,093. **Par:** 72/72. **Course Rating:** 69.4. **Slope:** 116.

ROBERT TRENT JONES GOLF TRAIL AT CAMBRIAN RIDGE GOLF CLUB
PU-101 Sunbelt Pkwy., Greenville, 36037, Butler County, (334)382-9787, (800)949-4444, 40 miles from Montgomery. **Facility Holes:** 36. **Green Fee:** $35/$57. **Cart Fee:** $15/Person. **Walking Policy:** Unrestricted walking. **Opened:** 1993. **Architect:** Robert Trent Jones. **Season:** Year-round. **High:** Feb.-May. **To obtain tee times:** Call up to 7 days in advance. **Miscellaneous:** Reduced fees (juniors), metal spikes, range (grass), credit cards (MC, V, AE, D), BF, FF.
★★★★½ CANYON/LOBLOLLY/SHERLING (27) *Value+, Condition, Pace*
CANYON/LOBLOLLY (18 combo)
Yards: 7,297/4,772. **Par:** 71/71. **Course Rating:** 74.6/67.8. **Slope:** 140/126. **Walkability:** 5.
CANYON/SHERLING (18 combo)
Yards: 7,424/4,857. **Par:** 72/72. **Course Rating:** 75.4/68.1. **Slope:** 142/127. **Walkability:** 5.
Notes: Ranked 6th in 2001 Best in State; 13th in 1996 America's Top 75 Affordable Courses.
LOBLOLLY/SHERLING (18 combo)
Yards: 7,130/4,785. **Par:** 71/71. **Course Rating:** 73.9/67.0. **Slope:** 133/119. **Walkability:** 4.
Reader Comments: Amazing! Drove 9 hours each way to play it; worth it … Tough for average golfer. Very good staff. Every hole memorable and tough, don't sweat your score, enjoy the challenge … Visually majestic and fun … Best layout of the RTJ Trail … Great value.
Special Notes: Also has a 9-hole par-3 course.

ROBERT TRENT JONES GOLF TRAIL AT GRAND NATIONAL GOLF CLUB
PU-3000 Sunbelt Pkwy., Opelika, 36801, Lee County, (334)749-9042, (800)949-4444, 55 miles from Montgomery. **E-mail:** prouillard@rtjgolf.com. **Web:** rtjgolf.com. **Facility Holes:** 54. **Walking Policy:** Unrestricted walking. **Opened:** 1992. **Architect:** Robert Trent Jones. **Season:** Year-round. **To obtain tee times:** Call golf shop. **Miscellaneous:** Reduced fees (juniors), range (grass), credit cards (MC, V, AE, D), BF, FF.
★★★★ LAKE COURSE (18) *Value*
Yards: 7,149/4,910. **Par:** 72/72. **Course Rating:** 74.9/68.7. **Slope:** 138/117. **Green Fee:** $35/$55. **Cart Fee:** $15/Person. **Walkability:** 3. **High:** March-May.
Notes: Ranked 8th in 2001 Best in State; 7th in 1996 America's Top 75 Affordable Courses.
Reader Comments: Don't miss this one. Excellent course. Nice layout, great service … Playing 36 holes here was never … Tests all shots … Elegant, playable … Nice people, great bargain … Long & tight … Quality from beginning to end.
★★★★½ LINKS COURSE (18) *Value*
Yards: 7,311/4,843. **Par:** 72/72. **Course Rating:** 74.9/69.6. **Slope:** 141/113. **Green Fee:** $35/$55. **Cart Fee:** $15/Person. **Walkability:** 4. **High:** March-May.
Notes: Ranked 9th in 2001 Best in State; 9th in 1996 America's Top 75 Affordable Courses.
Reader Comments: Great course … Tough, enjoyable … Great par 3s, fantastic scenery … Too much target golf … Incredibly beautiful, amazingly difficult, trouble around every green … One of my all-time favorite rounds.
★★★★½ SHORT COURSE (18) *Value+, Pace+*
Yards: 3,328/1,715. **Par:** 54/54. **Green Fee:** $18. **Cart Fee:** $10/Person. **Walkability:** 4.
Miscellaneous: Metal spikes.
Reader Comments: Interesting, scenic, sporty! …If there's a better par-3 course in the world, I'd be surprised … Best 18-hole par 3 in country … Power par-3 course, use all clubs … First class … Hardest short course you'll ever play.

ROBERT TRENT JONES GOLF TRAIL AT HAMPTON COVE GOLF CLUB
PU-450 Old Hwy. 431 S., Huntsville, 35763, Madison County, (256)551-1818, (800)949-4444, 5 miles from Huntsville. **Facility Holes:** 54. **Walking Policy:** Unrestricted walking. **Architect:** Robert Trent Jones. **Season:** Year-round. **High:** March-Oct. **To obtain tee times:** Call golf shop.

Miscellaneous: Metal spikes, range (grass), credit cards (MC, V, AE, D).

★★★★ **HIGHLANDS COURSE** (18) *Pace*

Yards: 7,262/4,766. **Par:** 72/72. **Course Rating:** 74.1/66.0. **Slope:** 134/118. **Green Fee:** $34/$49. **Cart Fee:** $19/Person. **Walkability:** 3. **Opened:** 1992. **Miscellaneous:** Reduced fees (weekdays, twilight, seniors, juniors).

Reader Comments: Great experience, reasonable price … Target golf at its best … Used every club … Service great from the minute the clubs were dropped off … Little pricey, beautiful … Excellent design, good service, challenging.

★★★½ **RIVER COURSE** (18)

Yards: 7,507/5,283. **Par:** 72/72. **Course Rating:** 75.6/67.0. **Slope:** 135/118. **Green Fee:** $34/$49. **Cart Fee:** $19/Person. **Walkability:** 2. **Opened:** 1993. **Miscellaneous:** Reduced fees (weekdays, twilight, juniors).

Reader Comments: Better than the Highlands course … Lots of H2O. Take enough balls … Nice facilities and service, attractive course … Price slightly high, very challenging course … Only course on the trail without bunkers. Good test.

★★★½ **SHORT COURSE** (18)

Yards: 3,140/1,829. **Par:** 59/59. **Green Fee:** $15. **Cart Fee:** $12/Person. **Walkability:** 2. **Opened:** 1993. **Miscellaneous:** Reduced fees (juniors).

Reader Comments: A good par 3 … Nice par 3 course, many sets of tees ranging from wedge to driver … Great fun, good price, good place to work on iron play.

ROBERT TRENT JONES GOLF TRAIL AT HIGHLAND OAKS

PU-904 Royal Pkwy., Dothan, 36305, Houston County, (334)712-2820, (800)949-4444, 100 miles from Montgomery. **E-mail:** RTJDothan@cyber-south.com. **Web:** www.rtjgolf.com. **Facility Holes:** 36. **Green Fee:** $29/$45. **Cart Fee:** $15/Person. **Walking Policy:** Unrestricted walking. **Walkability:** 2. **Opened:** 1993. **Architect:** Robert Trent Jones. **Season:** Year-round. **To obtain tee times:** Call up to 7 days in advance. **Miscellaneous:** Reduced fees (twilight, seniors, juniors), metal spikes, range (grass), credit cards (MC, V, AE, D), BF, FF.

★★★★½ **HIGHLANDS/MAGNOLIA/MARSHWOOD** (27) *Value+, Pace+*

HIGHLANDS/MAGNOLIA (18 combo)

Yards: 7,591/6,025. **Par:** 72/72. **Course Rating:** 76.0/67.6. **Slope:** 135/118. **High:** Feb.-May.

HIGHLANDS/MARSHWOOD (18 combo)

Yards: 7,704/5,085. **Par:** 72/72. **Course Rating:** 76.9/68.3. **Slope:** 138/120.

MARSHWOOD/MAGNOLIA (18 combo)

Yards: 7,511/6,002. **Par:** 72/72. **Course Rating:** 75.7/67.3. **Slope:** 133/116.

Notes: Ranked 10th in 2001 Best in State; 31st in 1996 America's Top 75 Affordable Courses.

Reader Comments: Tremendous value, beautiful, challenging and fair layout. Staff treats you like a king … Fantastic golf course! Fantastic Value! Generous off the tee, punishing around the green … Course was fantastic … Great setup.

Special Notes: Also has a 9-hole par-3 course.

ROBERT TRENT JONES GOLF TRAIL AT MAGNOLIA GROVE

PU-7000 Lamplighter Dr., Semmes, 36575, Mobile County, (334)645-0075, (800)949-4444, 5 miles from Mobile. **E-mail:** jmorgan@rtjgolf.com. **Web:** www.rtjgolf.com. **Facility Holes:** 54. **Walking Policy:** Unrestricted walking. **Opened:** 1992. **Architect:** Robert Trent Jones. **Season:** Year-round. **High:** Feb.-May. **Miscellaneous:** Range (grass), credit cards (MC, V, AE, D), BF, FF.

★★★★½ **CROSSINGS COURSE** (18) *Value, Pace*

Yards: 7,151/5,184. **Par:** 72/72. **Course Rating:** 74.6/70.4. **Slope:** 134/131. **Green Fee:** $35/$55. **Cart Fee:** $15/Person. **Walkability:** 3. **To obtain tee times:** Call up to 120 days in advance. **Miscellaneous:** Reduced fees (weekdays, twilight, juniors), metal spikes.

Notes: Ranked 50th in 1996 America's Top 75 Affordable Courses.

Reader Comments: Excellent course. Excellent hospitality and value … Hard for average golfer … Tough, fun … Scenic and hilly … Southern Hospitality at its best … Great for all levels … Better hit it straight. Tough & tight.

★★★★ **FALLS COURSE** (18)

Yards: 7,239/5,253. **Par:** 72/72. **Course Rating:** 75.1/71.0. **Slope:** 137/126. **Green Fee:** $35/$55. **Cart Fee:** $15/Person. **Walkability:** 4. **To obtain tee times:** Call golf shop. **Miscellaneous:** Reduced fees (weekdays, twilight, juniors).

Notes: Ranked 10th in 1999 Best in State; 43rd in 1996 America's Top 75 Affordable Courses.

Reader Comments: Challenging course, but playable by all levels of golfers … World-class golf at a very affordable price … Always excellent test … 2 days of golf=2 months of enjoyment … Lots of sand … Very tough, fun.

★★★★½ **SHORT COURSE** (18)

Yards: 3,140/1,829. **Par:** 54/54. **Green Fee:** $18. **Cart Fee:** $10/Person. **Walkability:** 3. **To obtain tee times:** Call golf shop. **Miscellaneous:** Reduced fees (weekdays, juniors), metal spikes.

Reader Comments: Absolutely wonderful par-3 course … Short doesn't mean easy … Bring all your irons and leave your ego at the clubhouse … Par 3 is a great test.

ALABAMA

ROBERT TRENT JONES GOLF TRAIL AT OXMOOR VALLEY GOLF CLUB

PU-100 Sunbelt Pkwy., Birmingham, 35211, Jefferson County, (205)942-1177, (800)949-4444. **E-mail:** oxmoor@mindspring.com. **Web:** www.rtjgolf.com. **Facility Holes:** 54. **Walking Policy:** Unrestricted walking. **Opened:** 1992. **Architect:** Robert Trent Jones. **Season:** Year-round. **To obtain tee times:** Call up to 7 days in advance. **Miscellaneous:** Metal spikes, credit cards (MC, V, AE, D), BF, FF.

★★★★ **RIDGE COURSE** (18)
Yards: 7,055/4,974. **Par:** 72/72. **Course Rating:** 73.5/69.1. **Slope:** 140/122. **Green Fee:** $35/$55. **Cart Fee:** $15/Person. **Walkability:** 4. **High:** March-June. **Miscellaneous:** Reduced fees (weekdays, juniors), range (grass).
Reader Comments: Terrific layout. Miss the greens and you're in trouble ... Hilly, challenging, fun, scenic ... Tough for average golfer ... High quality course, great value ... Greens severe ... Lots of elevation changes, scenic.

★★★½ **SHORT COURSE** (18)
Yards: 3,154/1,990. **Par:** 54/54. **Green Fee:** $18. **Cart Fee:** $10/Person. **Walkability:** 4. **Miscellaneous:** Reduced fees (juniors), range (grass).
Reader Comments: Excellent ... Beautiful and challenging ... Fun course, lots of tees and lots of variety.

★★★½ **VALLEY COURSE** (18)
Yards: 7,292/4,866. **Par:** 72/72. **Course Rating:** 73.9/69.4. **Slope:** 135/122. **Green Fee:** $35/$55. **Cart Fee:** $15/Person. **Walkability:** 2. **Miscellaneous:** Reduced fees (weekdays, juniors), range (grass/mats).
Reader Comments: The last hole will eat your lunch if you play too aggressively ... Good layout and lots of fun ... Rolling terrain, challenging ... Lovely setting, good golf ... Very women friendly.

ROBERT TRENT JONES GOLF TRAIL AT SILVER LAKES GOLF CLUB

PU-1 Sunbelt Pkwy., Glencoe, 35905, Calhoun County, (256)892-3268, (800)949-4444, 15 miles from Anniston. **E-mail:** aland@rtjgolf.com. **Web:** www.rtjgolf.com. **Facility Holes:** 36. **Green Fee:** $35/$45. **Cart Fee:** $15/Person. **Walking Policy:** Unrestricted walking. **Walkability:** 3. **Opened:** 1993. **Architect:** Robert Trent Jones. **Season:** Year-round. **High:** March-May. **To obtain tee times:** Call golf shop. **Miscellaneous:** Reduced fees (weekdays, twilight, juniors), range (grass), credit cards (MC, V, AE, D), BF, FF.

★★★★½ **HEARTBREAKER/BACKBREAKER/MINDBREAKER** (27) *Pace*
HEARTBREAKER/BACKBREAKER (18 combo)
Yards: 7,674/4,907. **Par:** 72/72. **Course Rating:** 77.7/68.8. **Slope:** 152/120.
MINDBREAKER/BACKBREAKER (18 combo)
Yards: 7,425/4,681. **Par:** 72/72. **Course Rating:** 76.1/67.5. **Slope:** 148/119.
MINDBREAKER/HEARTBREAKER (18 combo)
Yards: 7,407/4,860. **Par:** 72/72. **Course Rating:** 76.4/68.3. **Slope:** 142/122.
Reader Comments: Very beautiful layout, tough ... A joyous death for your game on a heavenly course ... The most zigzaging fairways you'll see in one round ... Beautiful course, almost no flat ground ... Not real playable for average/less golfer ... They'll even clean your clubs when you're done.
Special Notes: Also has a 9-hole par-3 course.

★★★★½ **ROCK CREEK GOLF CLUB** *Service, Pace*
SP-140 Clubhouse Dr., Fairhope, 36532, Baldwin County, (334)928-4223, (800)458-8815, 10 miles from Mobile. **E-mail:** rockcreek@honoursgolf.com. **Web:** www.rockcreekgolf.com. **Facility Holes:** 18. **Yards:** 6,920/5,157. **Par:** 72/72. **Course Rating:** 72.2/69.2. **Slope:** 129/123. **Green Fee:** $50/$70. **Cart Fee:** Included in green fee. **Walking Policy:** Mandatory carts. **Walkability:** 3. **Opened:** 1993. **Architect:** Earl Stone. **Season:** Year-round. **High:** Feb.-May. **To obtain tee times:** Call up to 30 days in advance. **Miscellaneous:** Reduced fees (twilight, juniors), range (grass), credit cards (MC, V, AE, D), BF, FF.
Reader Comments: Nice place, service great ... Jewel, crowded because of great holes ... Good condition, friendly service ... Price OK, I like this course ... Some elevation changes, fun ... Well-maintained, beautiful ... Tough par 3s.

STILL WATERS RESORT

R-797 Moonbrook Dr., Dadeville, 36853, Tallapoosa County, (256)825-1353, (888)797-3767, 55 miles from Montgomery. **E-mail:** swrgolfshop@aol.com. **Web:** www.stillwaters.com. **Facility Holes:** 36. **Green Fee:** $20/$30. **Cart Fee:** $15/Person. **Walking Policy:** Unrestricted walking. **Season:** Year-round. **High:** April-Oct. **To obtain tee times:** Call up to 7 days in advance. **Miscellaneous:** Reduced fees (weekdays, twilight, juniors), metal spikes, range (grass), lodging (93 rooms), credit cards (MC, V, AE, D), BF, FF.

★★★½ **THE LEGEND COURSE** (18)
Yards: 6,407/5,287. **Par:** 72/72. **Course Rating:** 69.9/71.5. **Slope:** 124/125. **Walkability:** 3. **Opened:** 1972. **Architect:** George Cobb.
Reader Comments: Great test ... Well-kept and beautiful layout on Lake Martin ... Narrow and hilly ... Beautiful course, tight for the most part.

★★★ **THE TRADITION COURSE** (18)
Yards: 6,906/5,048. **Par:** 72/72. **Course Rating:** 73.5/69.5. **Slope:** 139/126. **Walkability:** 5.
Opened: 1997. **Architect:** Kurt Sandness.
Reader Comments: Great place to play golf … Good variety … Limited views of lake, course well groomed … Nice resort, quiet, good golf.

★★ **STONEY MOUNTAIN GOLF COURSE**
PU-5200 Georgia Mountain Rd., Guntersville, 35976, Marshall County, (256)582-2598, 25 miles from Huntsville. **Facility Holes:** 18. **Yards:** 5,931/4,711. **Par:** 72/72. **Course Rating:** 67.6/66.2. **Slope:** 118/117. **Green Fee:** $17/$23. **Cart Fee:** $15/Person. **Walking Policy:** Walking at certain times. **Walkability:** 3. **Opened:** 1977. **Season:** Year-round. **High:** April-Nov. **To obtain tee times:** Call golf shop. **Miscellaneous:** Reduced fees (weekdays, twilight, seniors), credit cards (MC, V), BF, FF.

★★★½ **TANNEHILL NATIONAL GOLF COURSE**
PU-12863 Tannehill Pkwy., McCalla, 35111, Tuscaloosa County, (205)477-4653, (888)218-7888, 15 miles from Birmingham. **Web:** www.tannehill.com. **Facility Holes:** 18. **Yards:** 6,630/5,440. **Par:** 72/72. **Course Rating:** 71.1/70.5. **Slope:** 121/119. **Green Fee:** $21/$31. **Cart Fee:** $14/Person. **Walking Policy:** Walking at certain times. **Walkability:** 2. **Opened:** 1996. **Architect:** Steve Plumer. **Season:** Year-round. **High:** April-Nov. **To obtain tee times:** Call up to 4 days in advance. **Miscellaneous:** Reduced fees (weekdays), range (grass), credit cards (MC, V, AE, D), BF, FF.
Reader Comments: Very good course for the money. Nice layout and in good condition … Crowded, but playable … An outstanding & enjoyable course … A well-maintained interesting course for all types of golfers. Good service.

TARTAN PINES GOLF CLUB
PU-423 Tartan Way, Enterprise, 36330, Coffee County, (334)393-800, 30 miles from Dothan. **Facility Holes:** 18. **Yards:** 6,787/4,619. **Par:** 72/72. **Course Rating:** 72.3. **Slope:** 129. **Green Fee:** $17/$24. **Cart Fee:** $11/Person. **Walking Policy:** Unrestricted walking. **Walkability:** 3. **Opened:** 2000. **Architect:** Glen Day/Alan Blalock. **Season:** Year-round. **High:** May-Sept. **To obtain tee times:** Call up to 14 days in advance. **Miscellaneous:** Reduced fees (twilight, seniors, juniors), range (grass), credit cards (MC, V, AE), BF, FF.

★★ **TIMBER RIDGE GOLF CLUB**
PU-101 Ironaton Rd., Talladega, 35160, Talladega County, (256)362-0346, 50 miles from Birmingham. **Facility Holes:** 18. **Yards:** 6,521/5,028. **Par:** 71/71. **Course Rating:** 71.2/70.9. **Slope:** 126/122. **Green Fee:** $14/$30. **Cart Fee:** Included in green fee. **Walking Policy:** Unrestricted walking. **Walkability:** 3. **Opened:** 1989. **Architect:** Charlie Carter. **Season:** Year-round. **High:** June-Aug. **To obtain tee times:** Call golf shop. **Miscellaneous:** Reduced fees (weekdays, twilight, seniors, juniors), range (grass), credit cards (MC, V, AE).

★★★½ **TIMBERCREEK GOLF CLUB**
PU-9650 TimberCreek Blvd., Daphne, 36527, Baldwin County, (334)621-9900, (877)621-9900, 10 miles from Mobile. **E-mail:** timberck@gulftel.com. **Web:** www.golftimbercreek.com. **Facility Holes:** 27. **Green Fee:** $29/$34. **Cart Fee:** $15/Person. **Walking Policy:** Walking at certain times. **Walkability:** 3. **Opened:** 1993. **Architect:** Earl Stone. **Season:** Year-round. **To obtain tee times:** Call golf shop. **Miscellaneous:** Reduced fees (weekdays, guests, twilight, juniors), range (grass), credit cards (MC, V, AE).
DOGWOOD/MAGNOLIA (18 Combo)
Yards: 7,062/4,885. **Par:** 72/72. **Course Rating:** 73.8/66.7. **Slope:** 144/106.
DOGWOOD/PINES (18 Combo)
Yards: 6,928/4,911. **Par:** 72/72. **Course Rating:** 72.9/66.7. **Slope:** 137/105.
MAGNOLIA/PINES (18 Combo)
Yards: 7,090/4,990. **Par:** 72/72. **Course Rating:** 74.3/67.8. **Slope:** 143/107.
Reader Comments: Great experience … Very challenging, nice clubhouse … With improved management, course has great potential … Lovely layout, nice outing … Enjoyable for amateur players … Good course, fun to play.

★½ **TWIN LAKES GOLF COURSE**
PU-211 Golfview Dr., Arab, 35016, Marshall County, (256)586-3269, (800)213-3938, 15 miles from Huntsville. **Facility Holes:** 18. **Yards:** 6,711/5,609. **Par:** 72/72. **Course Rating:** 70.9/67.4. **Slope:** 130/114. **Green Fee:** $15/$18. **Cart Fee:** $9/Person. **Walking Policy:** Unrestricted walking. **Walkability:** 2. **Opened:** 1963. **Season:** Feb.-Dec. **To obtain tee times:** Call golf shop. **Miscellaneous:** Reduced fees (weekdays, seniors), metal spikes, credit cards (MC, V, D), BF, FF.

ALABAMA

★★ UNIVERSITY OF ALABAMA HARRY PRITCHETT GOLF COURSE

PU-University of Alabama, Tuscaloosa, 35487, Tuscaloosa County, (205)348-7041. **Facility Holes:** 18. **Yards:** 6,180/5,047. **Par:** 71/71. **Course Rating:** 69.7/67.2. **Slope:** 126/121. **Green Fee:** $15/$17. **Cart Fee:** $12/Person. **Walking Policy:** Unrestricted walking. **Walkability:** 3. **Architect:** Harold Williams/Thomas H. Nicol. **Season:** Year-round. **High:** May-Sept. **To obtain tee times:** Call golf shop. **Miscellaneous:** Reduced fees (weekdays, seniors, juniors), range (grass), credit cards (MC, V, D), BF, FF.

★½ WILLOW OAKS GOLF CLUB

PU-330 Willow Oaks Dr., Ozark, 36360, Dale County, (334)774-7388. **Facility Holes:** 18. **Yards:** 6,001/6,001. **Par:** 72/72. **Course Rating:** 67.0/67.0. **Slope:** 110/110. **Green Fee:** $15/$21. **Cart Fee:** Included in green fee. **Walking Policy:** Unrestricted walking. **Walkability:** 4. **Season:** Year-round. **To obtain tee times:** Call golf shop. **Miscellaneous:** Metal spikes, range (grass).

★★½ ANCHORAGE GOLF COURSE
PU-3651 O'Malley Rd., Anchorage, 99516, Anchorage County, (907)522-3363. **E-mail:** golf@alyeskiresort.com. **Facility Holes:** 18. **Yards:** 6,616/4,848. **Par:** 72/72. **Course Rating:** 72.1/68.2. **Slope:** 130/119. **Green Fee:** $17/$45. **Cart Fee:** $13/Person. **Walking Policy:** Walking at certain times. **Walkability:** 4. **Opened:** 1987. **Architect:** William Newcomb. **Season:** May-Oct. **High:** June-Aug. **To obtain tee times:** Call up to 5 days in advance. **Miscellaneous:** Reduced fees (guests, seniors, juniors), range (grass), credit cards (MC, V, AE, D, DC), BF, FF.
Notes: Ranked 5th in 2001 Best in State.

BIRCH RIDGE GOLF COURSE
PU-P.O. Box 828, Soldotna, 99669, Kenai County, (907)262-5270, 2 miles from Soldotna. **E-mail:** birchridge@att.net. **Web:** www.birchridgegolf.com. **Facility Holes:** 9. **Yards:** 6,080/5,025. **Par:** 70/69. **Course Rating:** 68.8/67.8. **Slope:** 120/115. **Green Fee:** $14/$22. **Cart Fee:** $20/Cart. **Walking Policy:** Unrestricted walking. **Walkability:** 3. **Opened:** 1973. **Architect:** Thomas R. Smith. **Season:** May-Oct. **High:** June-Sept. **To obtain tee times:** Call golf shop. **Miscellaneous:** Reduced fees (weekdays, guests, seniors, juniors), range (grass/mats), lodging (8 rooms), credit cards (MC, V, AE, D), BF, FF.

CHENA BEND GOLF CLUB
PU-Bldg. 2092 Gaffney Rd., Fort Wainwright, 99703, Fairbanks County, (907)353-6223. **Facility Holes:** 18. **Yards:** 7,012/5,516. **Par:** 72/72. **Course Rating:** 73.6/71.6. **Slope:** 128/117. **Green Fee:** $11/$30. **Cart Fee:** $21/Cart. **Walking Policy:** Unrestricted walking. **Walkability:** 3. **Opened:** 1996. **Architect:** Jerry Matthews. **Season:** May-Sept. **High:** June-July. **To obtain tee times:** Call golf shop. **Miscellaneous:** Reduced fees (twilight, seniors, juniors), range (grass/mats), credit cards (MC, V).
Notes: Ranked 2nd in 2001 Best in State.

★★★ EAGLEGLEN GOLF COURSE
PU-4414 1st Street, Elmendorf AFB, 99506, Anchorage County, (907)552-3821, 2 miles from Anchorage. **Web:** elmendorfservices.com. **Facility Holes:** 18. **Yards:** 6,689/5,457. **Par:** 72/72. **Course Rating:** 71.6/70.4. **Slope:** 128/123. **Green Fee:** $25/$35. **Cart Fee:** $24/Cart. **Walking Policy:** Unrestricted walking. **Walkability:** 2. **Opened:** 1973. **Architect:** Robert Trent Jones Jr. **Season:** May-Sept. **To obtain tee times:** Call golf shop. **Miscellaneous:** Reduced fees (twilight, seniors, juniors), range (mats), credit cards (MC, V), BF, FF.
Notes: Ranked 1st in 2001 Best in State.
Reader Comments: Gorgeous setting on Ship Creek ... Military course, very well kept ... Great golf course.

FAIRBANKS GOLF & COUNTRY CLUB
PU-1735 Farmers Loop, Fairbanks, 99709, Fairbanks County, (907)479-6555. **Facility Holes:** 9. **Yards:** 6,264/5,186. **Par:** 72/72. **Course Rating:** 69.8/69.9. **Slope:** 120/115. **Green Fee:** $22/$30. **Cart Fee:** $20/Cart. **Walking Policy:** Unrestricted walking. **Walkability:** 3. **Opened:** 1946. **Season:** May-Oct. **High:** June-Sept. **To obtain tee times:** Call up to 7 days in advance. **Miscellaneous:** Reduced fees (seniors, juniors), range (grass), credit cards (MC, V, AE), BF, FF.

★★ KENAI GOLF COURSE
PU-1420 Lawton Dr., Kenai, 99611, Kenai County, (907)283-7500, 180 miles from Anchorage. **Facility Holes:** 18. **Yards:** 6,641/5,644. **Par:** 72/72. **Course Rating:** 73.2/74.4. **Slope:** 135/133. **Green Fee:** $18/$22. **Cart Fee:** $20/Cart. **Walking Policy:** Unrestricted walking. **Walkability:** 3. **Opened:** 1986. **Architect:** R. Morgan/R. Collins/M. Davis. **Season:** May-Sept. **High:** June-July. **To obtain tee times:** Call golf shop. **Miscellaneous:** Reduced fees (weekdays, seniors, juniors), range (mats), credit cards (MC, V), BF, FF.

MOOSE RUN GOLF COURSE
M-P.O. Box 5130, Fort Richardson, 99505, Anchorage County, (907)428-0056, 1 mile from Anchorage. **Facility Holes:** 36. **Green Fee:** $30/$35. **Cart Fee:** $20/Cart. **Walking Policy:** Unrestricted walking. **Walkability:** 2. **Architect:** U.S. Army. **Season:** May-Sept. **High:** May-Sept. **To obtain tee times:** Call up to 4 days in advance. **Miscellaneous:** Reduced fees (twilight, seniors, juniors), credit cards (MC, V, AE, D), BF, FF.
THE CREEK COURSE (18)
Yards: 7,324/5,783. **Par:** 72/72. **Course Rating:** 78.0/72.0. **Slope:** 142/134. **Opened:** 2000.
★★★ THE HILL COURSE (18)
Yards: 6,499/5,382. **Par:** 72/72. **Course Rating:** 69.8/70.0. **Slope:** 119/120. **Opened:** 1951.
Notes: Ranked 4th in 2001 Best in State.

ALASKA

NORTH STAR GOLF COURSE
SP-330 Golf Club Dr., Fairbanks, 99712, Fairbanks County, (907)457-4653, 4 miles from Fairbanks. **E-mail:** northstargolf@mosquitonet.com. **Web:** www.golf-alaska.com. **Facility Holes:** 18. **Yards:** 6,328/4,933. **Par:** 71/71. **Course Rating:** 70.4/68.4. **Slope:** 113/113. **Green Fee:** $25. **Cart Fee:** $20/Cart. **Walking Policy:** Unrestricted walking. **Walkability:** 1. **Opened:** 1993. **Architect:** Jack Stallings/Roger Evans. **Season:** May-Sept. **High:** June-July. **To obtain tee times:** Call golf shop. **Miscellaneous:** Reduced fees (weekdays, juniors), range (grass/mats), credit cards (MC, V, D), BF, FF.

★★★ PALMER GOLF COURSE
PU-1000 Lepak Ave., Palmer, 99645, Matanuska County, (907)745-4653, 42 miles from Anchorage. **E-mail:** Jeffgolf@mtAonline.net. **Facility Holes:** 18. **Yards:** 7,125/5,895. **Par:** 72/73. **Course Rating:** 74.5/74.6. **Slope:** 132/127. **Green Fee:** $20/$30. **Cart Fee:** $20/Person. **Walking Policy:** Unrestricted walking. **Walkability:** 1. **Opened:** 1990. **Architect:** Illiad Group. **Season:** May-Sept. **High:** May-July. **To obtain tee times:** Call golf shop. **Miscellaneous:** Reduced fees (seniors, juniors), range (grass), credit cards (MC, V), BF, FF.
Reader Comments: Lots of wind … Stunning mountain and glacier views, windy most of the time … Surrounded by majestic, snow-capped mountains … Bring your camera … Fastest greens in the west … Wonderful management … Long course, when wind blows.

★★½ SETTLERS BAY GOLF CLUB
PU-Mile 8 Knik Rd., Wasilla, 99687, Matanuska County, (907)376-5466, 50 miles from Anchorage. **Facility Holes:** 18. **Yards:** 6,596/5,461. **Par:** 72/72. **Course Rating:** 71.4/70.8. **Slope:** 129/123. **Green Fee:** $18/$30. **Cart Fee:** $22/Cart. **Walking Policy:** Unrestricted walking. **Walkability:** 3. **Opened:** 1977. **Season:** April-Sept. **High:** June-Aug. **To obtain tee times:** Call up to 7 days in advance. **Miscellaneous:** Reduced fees (twilight, seniors, juniors), range (grass/mats), credit cards (MC, V, D), BF, FF.
Notes: Ranked 3rd in 2001 Best in State.

SLEEPY HOLLOW GOLF CLUB
PU-Mile .5 Leeuen St., Wasilla, 99654, Matanuska County, (907)376-5948, 7 miles from Wasilla. **Facility Holes:** 9. **Yards:** 1,304/1,215. **Par:** 27/27. **Green Fee:** $20/$22. **Cart Fee:** $18/Person. **Walking Policy:** Unrestricted walking. **Walkability:** 1. **Opened:** 1989. **Architect:** Carney Bros. **Season:** May-Sept. **High:** May-July. **To obtain tee times:** Call golf shop. **Miscellaneous:** Reduced fees (weekdays, seniors, juniors), metal spikes, range (grass/mats), BF, FF.

ARIZONA

★★★½ THE 500 CLUB
PU-4707 W. Pinnacle Peak Rd., Glendale, 85310, Maricopa County, (623)492-9500, 20 miles from Downtown Phoenix. **E-mail:** the500club@aol.com. **Facility Holes:** 18. **Yards:** 6,867/5,601. **Par:** 72/73. **Course Rating:** 71.5/69.8. **Slope:** 121/112. **Green Fee:** $18/$55. **Cart Fee:** $10/Person. **Walking Policy:** Unrestricted walking. **Walkability:** 2. **Opened:** 1989. **Architect:** Brian Whitcomb. **Season:** Year-round. **High:** Jan.-March. **To obtain tee times:** Call golf shop. **Miscellaneous:** Reduced fees (weekdays, twilight, juniors), metal spikes, range (grass), credit cards (MC, V, AE, D, Diners Club).
Reader Comments: Staff congenial and personable ... Hole No. 11 cool par-3 straight up hill ... Course is in incredible shape ... Beautiful desert mountain course ... Good value ... Excellent fairways, tee boxes.

★★★ AGUILA GOLF COURSE *Value*
PU-8440 S. 35th Ave., Laveen, 85339, Maricopa County, (602)237-9601. **E-mail:** DESCOBEDO@61.PHOENIX.AZ.USNE. **Facility Holes:** 27. **Yards:** 6,962/5,491. **Par:** 72/72. **Course Rating:** 73.0/70.8. **Slope:** 125/117. **Green Fee:** $20/$35. **Cart Fee:** $20/Cart. **Walking Policy:** Unrestricted walking. **Walkability:** 3. **Opened:** 1999. **Architect:** Gary Panks. **Season:** Year-round. **To obtain tee times:** Call up to 2 days in advance. **Miscellaneous:** Reduced fees (weekdays, twilight, seniors, juniors), range (grass/mats), credit cards (MC, V, AE, D), BF, FF.
Reader Comments: Best new city course ... Great value, even in the winter ... Requires variety of shots ... Best course I played in Arizona — and the least expensive! Great design, good maintenance and quality amenities ... Could rival Papago as best muni in Phoenix.
Special Notes: Also has a 9-hole par-3 course.

ANTELOPE HILLS GOLF COURSES
PU-1 Perkins Dr., Prescott, 86301, Yavapai County, (520)776-7888, 1-(800)972-6818, 90 miles from Phoenix. **E-mail:** jim.noe@cityofprescott.net. **Web:** antelopehillsgolf.com. **Facility Holes:** 36. **Green Fee:** $25/$36. **Cart Fee:** $12/Person. **Walking Policy:** Unrestricted walking. **Walkability:** 2. **Season:** Year-round. **High:** May-Nov. **To obtain tee times:** Call up to 7 days in advance. **Miscellaneous:** Reduced fees (twilight, juniors), metal spikes, range (grass), credit cards (MC, V, AE, D), BF, FF.
★★★ NORTH COURSE (18)
Yards: 6,829/6,029. **Par:** 72/72. **Course Rating:** 72.1/72.7. **Slope:** 128/127. **Opened:** 1956. **Architect:** Lawrence Hughes.
Reader Comments: Fair challenge on typical mature course ... Overall in pretty good shape ... Good layout ... I love this place! ... Traditional and solid ... Mature trees, old-style course.
★★★ SOUTH COURSE (18)
Yards: 7,014/5,570. **Par:** 72/72. **Course Rating:** 71.3/69.9. **Slope:** 124/118. **Opened:** 1992. **Architect:** Gary Panks.
Reader Comments: Links style, a fair challenge ... Wide open, very forgiving ... My first time there, we were treated very well ... Course was in good shape for the middle of winter.

★★★ APACHE CREEK GOLF CLUB
PU-3401 S. Ironwood Dr., Apache Junction, 85220, Pinal County, (480)982-2677, 20 miles from Phoenix. **E-mail:** acgolf@usasn.com. **Web:** apachecreek.com. **Facility Holes:** 18. **Yards:** 6,591/5,516. **Par:** 72/72. **Course Rating:** 71.6/65.4. **Slope:** 128/110. **Green Fee:** $15/$49. **Cart Fee:** Included in green fee. **Walking Policy:** Unrestricted walking. **Walkability:** 1. **Opened:** 1994. **Season:** Year-round. **High:** Dec.-May. **To obtain tee times:** Call up to 3 days in advance. **Miscellaneous:** Reduced fees (weekdays, twilight, juniors), range (grass), credit cards (MC, V), BF, FF.
Reader Comments: Desert golf at a decent cost ... Sits just west of the base of Superstition Mountain ... Desert golf at its finest! ... Greens don't bite ... Short hitter's paradise, a little narrow at times.

★★★½ APACHE STRONGHOLD GOLF CLUB *Value*
R-Hwy. 70, San Carlos, 85550, Gila County, (928)425-7800, (800)272-2438. **E-mail:** apachestrongholdgc@ezlinksgolf.com. **Web:** apachegoldcasinoresort.com. **Facility Holes:** 18. **Yards:** 7,519/5,535. **Par:** 72/72. **Course Rating:** 74.9/70.5. **Slope:** 138/117. **Green Fee:** $45/$60. **Cart Fee:** $20/Person. **Walking Policy:** Walking at certain times. **Walkability:** 4. **Opened:** 1999. **Architect:** Tom Doak. **Season:** Year-round. **High:** Feb.-July. **To obtain tee times:** Call up to 14 days in advance. **Miscellaneous:** Reduced fees (juniors), range (grass), lodging (147 rooms), credit cards (MC, V, AE), BF, FF.
Reader Comments: Pristine high desert location ... Nice variety of elevation changes ... Great layout ... Not vicious ... Out of the way, but worth the trip ... Excellent hospitality ... Natural, rugged course.

ARIZONA BILTMORE COUNTRY CLUB
SP-2400 E. Missouri Ave., Phoenix, 85016, Maricopa County, (602)955-9655. **Facility Holes:** 36. **Green Fee:** $48/$165. **Cart Fee:** Included in green fee. **Walking Policy:** Mandatory carts.

ARIZONA

Season: Year-round. **High:** Jan.-April. **To obtain tee times:** Call up to 7 days in advance. **Miscellaneous:** Metal spikes, range (grass), credit cards (MC, V, AE), BF, FF.

★★½ **ADOBE COURSE** (18)
Yards: 6,449/5,796. **Par:** 72/73. **Course Rating:** 70.1/72.2. **Slope:** 119/118. **Walkability:** 1. **Opened:** 1929. **Architect:** William P. Bell.
Reader Comments: Old course… Holes blend together … This resort course is always in good condition … Grounds beautiful … Good service, nice staff … Ball sat up in fairway, rough was good—not too hard to get out of..

★★★½ **LINKS COURSE** (18)
Yards: 6,300/4,747. **Par:** 71/71. **Course Rating:** 69.7/66.5. **Slope:** 126/106. **Walkability:** 3. **Opened:** 1979. **Architect:** Bill Johnston.
Reader Comments: Each hole is unique … Played 18 holes in 3 hours and 30 minutes … Grounds beautiful … Not very challenging but well maintained and a lot of fun … Great service, great restaurant, course is beautiful.

★★½ **THE ARIZONA GOLF RESORT & CONFERENCE CENTER**
R-425 S. Power Rd., Mesa, 85206, Maricopa County, (480)832-1661, (800)458-8330, 25 miles from Phoenix. **E-mail:** azgolf@earthlink.net. **Web:** www.azgolfresort.com. **Facility Holes:** 18. **Yards:** 6,574/6,195. **Par:** 71/71. **Course Rating:** 71.2/68.6. **Slope:** 123/117. **Green Fee:** $29/$84. **Cart Fee:** Included in green fee. **Walking Policy:** Mandatory carts. **Walkability:** 2. **Opened:** 1961. **Architect:** Arthur Jack Snyder. **Season:** Year-round. **High:** Jan.-April. **To obtain tee times:** Call up to 7 days in advance. **Miscellaneous:** Reduced fees (twilight), metal spikes, range (grass), lodging (187 rooms), BF, FF.

★½ **ARTHUR PACK DESERT GOLF CLUB**
PU-9101 N. Thornydale Rd., Tucson, 85742, Pima County, (520)744-3322. **Facility Holes:** 18. **Yards:** 6,900/5,100. **Par:** 72/72. **Course Rating:** 71.8/68.2. **Slope:** 130/117. **Green Fee:** $15/$36. **Cart Fee:** $18/Cart. **Walking Policy:** Unrestricted walking. **Walkability:** 2. **Opened:** 1975. **Architect:** Dave Bennet/Lee Trevino. **Season:** Year-round. **High:** Nov.-May. **To obtain tee times:** Call up to 7 days in advance. **Miscellaneous:** Reduced fees (weekdays, seniors, juniors), metal spikes, range (grass/mats), credit cards (MC, V), BF, FF.

★★★★ **THE ASU KARSTEN GOLF COURSE**
R-1125 E. Rio Salado Pkwy., Tempe, 85281, Maricopa County, (480)921-8070, 5 miles from Phoenix. **E-mail:** info@asukarsten. **Web:** asukarsten.com. **Facility Holes:** 18. **Yards:** 7,057/4,765. **Par:** 72/72. **Course Rating:** 74.3/63.4. **Slope:** 133/110. **Green Fee:** $25/$93. **Cart Fee:** Included in green fee. **Walking Policy:** Mandatory carts. **Walkability:** 4. **Opened:** 1989. **Architect:** Pete Dye/Perry Dye. **Season:** Year-round. **To obtain tee times:** Call golf shop. **Miscellaneous:** Reduced fees (weekdays, juniors), range (grass/mats), credit cards (MC, V, AE), BF, FF.
Reader Comments: As busy as course is, made you feel at home … Lots of moguls and water … Wonderful experience … When done watch ASU golfers on range and DREAM! … A good value … Very challenging, well maintained, excellent greens.

BEAR CREEK GOLF COURSE
PU-500 E. Riggs Rd., Chandler, 85249, Maricopa County, (480)883-8200, 7 miles from Chandler. **E-mail:** dstrand@bearcreekaz.com. **Web:** www.bearcreekaz.com. **Facility Holes:** 36. **Yards:** 6,858/5,017. **Par:** 71/71. **Course Rating:** 71.7/67.4. **Slope:** 118/110. **Green Fee:** $22/$95. **Cart Fee:** $7/Person. **Walking Policy:** Unrestricted walking. **Walkability:** 2. **Opened:** 2000. **Architect:** Nicklaus Design/Bill O'Leary. **Season:** Year-round. **High:** Nov.-April. **To obtain tee times:** Call up to 7 days in advance. **Miscellaneous:** Reduced fees (weekdays, twilight, juniors), metal spikes, range (grass), credit cards (MC, AE, D), BF, FF.
Special Notes: Also has an 18-hole executive course.

BOUGANVILLEA GOLF CLUB
PU-5740 W Baseline, Laveen, 85339, Maricopa County, (602)237-4567, 5 miles from Phoenix. **Facility Holes:** 18. **Yards:** 6,740/5,793. **Par:** 71/71. **Course Rating:** 70.9/71.9. **Slope:** 118/114. **Green Fee:** $15/$50. **Cart Fee:** Included in green fee. **Walking Policy:** Unrestricted walking. **Walkability:** 2. **Opened:** 1993. **Architect:** Dan Pohl. **Season:** Year-round. **High:** Jan.-March. **To obtain tee times:** Call up to 14 days in advance. **Miscellaneous:** Reduced fees (weekdays, twilight, seniors, juniors), range (grass), credit cards (MC, V), BF, FF.

THE BOULDERS CLUB
R-34631 N. Tom Darlington Dr., Carefree, 85377, Maricopa County, (480)488-9028, 33 miles from Phoenix. **Facility Holes:** 36. **Cart Fee:** Included in green fee. **Walking Policy:** Walking at certain times. **Opened:** 1984. **Architect:** Jay Morrish. **Season:** Year-round. **High:** Feb.-May. **To obtain tee times:** Call golf shop. **Miscellaneous:** Range (grass), lodging (200 rooms), credit cards (MC, V, AE, Diners Club).

★★★★½ **NORTH COURSE** (18) *Condition, Pace+*
Yards: 6,811/4,900. **Par:** 72/72. **Course Rating:** 72.3/68.2. **Slope:** 135/111. **Green Fee:** $75/$200. **Walkability:** 3. **Miscellaneous:** Caddies ().
Notes: Ranked 23rd in 1999 Best in State.
Reader Comments: Wonderful golf course ... Course you can play everyday and always be challenged ... Great people ... Expensive but worth it ... South is better ... Beautiful ambience and service.

★★★★½ **SOUTH COURSE** (18) *Condition, Pace+*
Yards: 6,701/5,141. **Par:** 71/71. **Course Rating:** 72.0/71.8. **Slope:** 140/114. **Green Fee:** $72/$195. **Walkability:** 4.
Notes: Ranked 22nd in 1999 Best in State.
Reader Comments: Awesome scenery, beautiful ... Wonderful... Pricey, but not too bad for region ... Prettiest course I ever played ... Perfect golf, unbelievable scenery ... Cuisine and service outstanding.

★★½ **CANOA HILLS GOLF COURSE**
SP-1401 W. Calle Urbano, Green Valley, 85614, Pima County, (520)648-1880, 25 miles from Tucson. **Facility Holes:** 18. **Yards:** 6,610/5,158. **Par:** 72/72. **Course Rating:** 70.8/68.5. **Slope:** 126/116. **Green Fee:** $21/$70. **Cart Fee:** Included in green fee. **Walking Policy:** Mandatory carts. **Walkability:** 3. **Opened:** 1984. **Architect:** Dave Bennett. **Season:** Year-round. **High:** Jan.-March. **To obtain tee times:** Call up to 7 days in advance. **Miscellaneous:** Reduced fees (twilight, juniors), metal spikes, range (grass), credit cards (MC, V, AE, D), BF, FF.

★★ **CASA GRANDE MUNICIPAL GOLF COURSE**
PU-2121 N.Thornton Rd., Casa Grande, 85222, Pinal County, (520)836-9216, 35 miles from Phoenix. **Facility Holes:** 18. **Yards:** 6,396/5,400. **Par:** 72/72. **Course Rating:** 68.6/67.6. **Slope:** 114/110. **Green Fee:** $7/$17. **Cart Fee:** $9/Person. **Walking Policy:** Unrestricted walking. **Walkability:** 2. **Opened:** 1981. **Architect:** G. Panks/A. Snyder, F. Richardson. **Season:** Year-round. **High:** Nov.-April. **To obtain tee times:** Call golf shop. **Miscellaneous:** Reduced fees (weekdays, twilight, seniors, juniors), metal spikes, range (grass), credit cards (MC, V).

★★★½ **CAVE CREEK GOLF CLUB**
PU-15202 N. 19th Ave., Phoenix, 85023, Maricopa County, (602)866-8076. **Facility Holes:** 18. **Yards:** 6,876/5,614. **Par:** 72/72. **Course Rating:** 71.1/70.0. **Slope:** 122/112. **Green Fee:** $19/$28. **Cart Fee:** $15/Cart. **Walking Policy:** Unrestricted walking. **Walkability:** 3. **Opened:** 1984. **Architect:** Jack Snyder. **Season:** Year-round. **High:** Nov.-April. **To obtain tee times:** Call golf shop. **Miscellaneous:** Reduced fees (twilight, seniors, juniors), metal spikes, range (grass), credit cards (MC, V, AE, D).
Reader Comments: Some outstanding holes ... Good muni ... Fun layout ... Has a lot of potential ... Good muni course ... Fantastic back 9 ... Nice, good service.

★★★½ **CLUB WEST GOLF CLUB**
PU-16400 S. 14th Ave., Phoenix, 85045, Maricopa County, (480)460-4400, 10 miles from Phoenix. **E-mail:** shawn.mcgechie@suncorgolf.com. **Web:** clubwestgolf.com. **Facility Holes:** 18. **Yards:** 7,142/4,985. **Par:** 72/72. **Course Rating:** 73.1/67.0. **Slope:** 129/107. **Green Fee:** $35/$110. **Cart Fee:** Included in green fee. **Walking Policy:** Mandatory carts. **Walkability:** 4. **Opened:** 1993. **Architect:** Brian Whitcomb. **Season:** Year-round. **High:** Jan.-April. **To obtain tee times:** Call up to 7 days in advance. **Miscellaneous:** Reduced fees (seniors), range (grass), credit cards (MC, V, AE, Diners Club), BF, FF.
Reader Comments: Great clubhouse ... Professional staff... Interesting layout ... Great scenery ... Nice landscaped holes, variety in elevations on back 9 was refreshing ... Fine facility ... Good variety.

COLDWATER GOLF CLUB
PU-100 North Clubhouse Dr., Avondale, 85323, Maricopa County, (623)932-9000, 4 miles from Phoenix. **E-mail:** jkuhry@coldwatergolfclub.com. **Web:** www.coldwatergolfclub.com. **Facility Holes:** 18. **Yards:** 6,758/5,147. **Par:** 72/72. **Course Rating:** 71.3. **Slope:** 121. **Green Fee:** $25/$65. **Cart Fee:** Included in green fee. **Walking Policy:** Mandatory carts. **Walkability:** 4. **Opened:** 2000. **Architect:** Forrest Richardson. **Season:** Year-round. **High:** Jan.-April. **To obtain tee times:** Call up to 14 days in advance. **Miscellaneous:** Reduced fees (weekdays, twilight), range (grass), credit cards (MC, V, AE), BF, FF.

CONCHO VALLEY COUNTRY CLUB
SP-HC-30, Box 57, Concho, 85924, Apache County, (520)337-4644, (800)658-8071, 28 miles from Show Low. **Facility Holes:** 18. **Yards:** 6,656/5,559. **Par:** 72/72. **Course Rating:** 69.1/70.0. **Slope:** 119/128. **Green Fee:** $12/$23. **Cart Fee:** $10/Person. **Walking Policy:** Unrestricted walking. **Walkability:** 3. **Opened:** 1975. **Architect:** Arthur Jack Snyder. **Season:** Year-round. **High:** May-Sept. **To obtain tee times:** Call golf shop. **Miscellaneous:** Reduced fees (guests, twilight, seniors, juniors), metal spikes, range (grass/mats), lodging (9 rooms), credit cards (MC, V).

★★★ COYOTE LAKES GOLF CLUB
PU-18800 N. Coyote Lakes Pkwy., Surprise, 85374, Maricopa County, (602)566-2323, 12 miles from Phoenix. **Web:** www.americangolf.com. **Facility Holes:** 18. **Yards:** 6,159/4,708. **Par:** 71/71. **Course Rating:** 69.2/65.9. **Slope:** 117/103. **Green Fee:** $16/$69. **Cart Fee:** Included in green fee. **Walking Policy:** Mandatory carts. **Walkability:** 3. **Opened:** 1993. **Architect:** Arthur Jack Snyder/Forrest Richardson. **Season:** Year-round. **High:** Jan.-Oct. **To obtain tee times:** Call up to 7 days in advance. **Miscellaneous:** Reduced fees (weekdays, twilight), metal spikes, range (grass), credit cards (MC, V, AE, D), BF, FF.
Reader Comments: Excellent place to play, friendly people … The course, although relatively short, is a great challenge … A gem in the desert … Nice variety of holes … Fun to play.

DEL LAGO GOLF CLUB
PU-14155 E. Via Rancho del Lago, Vail, 85641, Pima County, (520)647-1100, 20 miles from Tucson. **E-mail:** craigbauley@dellagogolfclub.com. **Web:** www.dellagogolfclub.com. **Facility Holes:** 18. **Yards:** 7,206/5,044. **Par:** 72/72. **Course Rating:** 73.9/70.3. **Slope:** 135/118. **Green Fee:** $33/$79. **Cart Fee:** Included in green fee. **Walking Policy:** Walking at certain times. **Walkability:** 4. **Opened:** 2000. **Architect:** Nugent & Associates. **Season:** Year-round. **High:** Jan.-April. **To obtain tee times:** Call up to 14 days in advance. **Miscellaneous:** Reduced fees (weekdays), range (grass), credit cards (MC, V, AE, D, DC), BF, FF.

★★ DESERT CANYON GOLF CLUB
PU-10440 Indian Wells Dr., Fountain Hills, 85268, Maricopa County, (602)837-1173, 14 miles from Scottsdale. **E-mail:** fhgolf@primenet.com. **Web:** www.desertcanyon-golfclub.com. **Facility Holes:** 18. **Yards:** 6,415/5,352. **Par:** 71/71. **Course Rating:** 69.9/68.9. **Slope:** 123/114. **Green Fee:** $56/$125. **Cart Fee:** Included in green fee. **Walking Policy:** Unrestricted walking. **Walkability:** 4. **Opened:** 1971. **Architect:** John Allen. **Season:** Year-round. **High:** Jan.-April. **To obtain tee times:** Call up to 7 days in advance. **Miscellaneous:** Reduced fees (weekdays, twilight, juniors), range (grass), credit cards (MC, V, AE, D), BF, FF. **Special Notes:** Formerly Fountain Hills Golf Club.

★★★ DESERT HILLS GOLF COURSE
PU-1245 Desert Hills Dr., Yuma, 85364, Yuma County, (520)344-4653, 175 miles from Phoenix. **E-mail:** deserthills@excite.com. **Facility Holes:** 18. **Yards:** 6,800/5,726. **Par:** 72/74. **Course Rating:** 71.1/72.4. **Slope:** 117/122. **Green Fee:** $10/$32. **Cart Fee:** $10/Person. **Walking Policy:** Unrestricted walking. **Walkability:** 3. **Opened:** 1973. **Season:** Year-round. **High:** Dec. **To obtain tee times:** Call up to 7 days in advance. **Miscellaneous:** Reduced fees (juniors), range (grass), credit cards (MC, V, AE, D), BF, FF.
Reader Comments: Best municipal course in Arizona … Great course for very little money! … Great golf, greens very fast … Great value.

★★★½ DESERT SPRINGS GOLF CLUB
PU-19900 N Remington Dr, Surprise, 85374, Maricopa County, (623)546-7400, 18 miles from Phoenix. **E-mail:** laruej@delwebb.com. **Facility Holes:** 18. **Yards:** 7,006/5,250. **Par:** 72/72. **Course Rating:** 73.4/69.6. **Slope:** 131/119. **Green Fee:** $19/$65. **Cart Fee:** Included in green fee. **Walkability:** 3. **Opened:** 1996. **Architect:** Billy Casper/Greg Nash. **Season:** Year-round. **High:** Jan.-April. **To obtain tee times:** Call golf shop. **Miscellaneous:** Reduced fees (weekdays, twilight, seniors), range (grass), credit cards (MC, V, AE), BF, FF.
Reader Comments: Great views, good challenge from tips … Well laid out, well groomed … Nice but too slow … Great finishing hole … 3 hrs 45 minutes, great … Best of the Sun City Grand courses … Beautiful landscaping and course appearance.

★★½ DOBSON RANCH GOLF CLUB
PU-2155 S. Dobson Rd., Mesa, 85202, Maricopa County, (480)644-2270, 15 miles from Phoenix. **E-mail:** golfphd@netscape.net. **Facility Holes:** 18. **Yards:** 6,593/5,598. **Par:** 72/72. **Course Rating:** 71.0/71.3. **Slope:** 117/116. **Green Fee:** $13/$22. **Cart Fee:** $20/Cart. **Walking Policy:** Unrestricted walking. **Walkability:** 1. **Opened:** 1973. **Architect:** Red Lawrence. **Season:** Year-round. **High:** Nov.-April. **To obtain tee times:** Call up to 4 days in advance. **Miscellaneous:** Reduced fees (twilight, juniors), metal spikes, range (grass), credit cards (MC, V), BF, FF.

★★★ DOVE VALLEY RANCH GOLF CLUB
PU-33244 N. Black Mtn. Pkwy., Cave Creek, 85331, Maricopa County, (480)473-1444, 10 miles from Phoenix. **Web:** www.dovevalleyranch.com. **Facility Holes:** 18. **Yards:** 7,011/5,337. **Par:** 72/72. **Course Rating:** 72.7/70.5. **Slope:** 131/114. **Green Fee:** $55/$125. **Cart Fee:** Included in green fee. **Walking Policy:** Unrestricted walking. **Walkability:** 2. **Opened:** 1998. **Architect:** Robert Trent Jones Jr. **Season:** Year-round. **High:** Jan.-April. **To obtain tee times:** Call up to 30 days in advance. **Miscellaneous:** Range (grass), credit cards (MC, V, AE, D), BF, FF.

ARIZONA

Reader Comments: New course, great condition. I'd play it again and recommend it to my friend … Tight back 9, challenging course … Love the split fairway … Personal service begins when you park your car… Greens a little spotty, but rolled pretty true … Cheap for Scottsdale—nice desert layout.

★★★ EAGLE'S NEST COUNTRY CLUB AT PEBBLE CREEK
SP-3645 Clubhouse Dr., Goodyear, 85338, Maricopa County, (623)935-6750, (800)795-4663, 15 miles from Phoenix. **Facility Holes:** 18. **Yards:** 6,860/5,030. **Par:** 72/72. **Course Rating:** 72.6/68.1. **Slope:** 130/111. **Green Fee:** $21/$51. **Cart Fee:** $9/Person. **Walking Policy:** Unrestricted walking. **Walkability:** 2. **Opened:** 1991. **Architect:** Keith Foster. **Season:** Year-round. **High:** Jan.-March. **To obtain tee times:** Call golf shop. **Miscellaneous:** Reduced fees (twilight), metal spikes, range (grass), credit cards (MC, V, AE).
Reader Comments: Nice … A jewel in the middle of nowhere. Staff very nice. Great shape … Long, wide open … Some screwy holes but fun.

★★★ ELDEN HILLS GOLF CLUB
PU-2380 N. Oakmont Dr., Flagstaff, 86004, Coconino County, (520)527-7999. **E-mail:** info@golfflgstaff.com. **Web:** golfflagstaff.com. **Facility Holes:** 18. **Yards:** 6,029/5,380. **Par:** 72/73. **Course Rating:** 66.6/68.7. **Slope:** 115/126. **Green Fee:** $32/$43. **Cart Fee:** $13/Person. **Walking Policy:** Unrestricted walking. **Walkability:** 4. **Opened:** 1960. **Architect:** Bob Baldock. **Season:** April-Nov. **High:** June-Sept. **To obtain tee times:** Call up to 14 days in advance. **Miscellaneous:** Reduced fees (weekdays, twilight, juniors), range (grass), credit cards (MC, V, AE, D), BF, FF.
Reader Comments: The course is in very good shape, and even though it's usually crowded in the summer, the staff does a good job getting you on and keeps the pace of play moving.

★★★ ELEPHANT ROCKS GOLF CLUB
PU-2200 Country Club Rd., Williams, 86046, Coconino County, (520)635-4935, 30 miles from Flagstaff. **Facility Holes:** 18. **Yards:** 6,695/5,423. **Par:** 72/72. **Course Rating:** 70.8/69.2. **Slope:** 128/127. **Green Fee:** $24/$39. **Cart Fee:** $10/Person. **Walking Policy:** Walking at certain times. **Walkability:** 5. **Opened:** 1990. **Architect:** Gary Panks. **Season:** March-Nov. **High:** May-Sept. **To obtain tee times:** Call up to 7 days in advance. **Miscellaneous:** Reduced fees (weekdays, twilight, juniors), range (grass), credit cards (MC, V), BF, FF.
Reader Comments: A beautiful mountain course that has improved with the addition of a new 9 … Worth the drive, about 50 miles from the Grand Canyon and 32 miles from Flagstaff … Three great closing holes … Scenery is almost distracting … Wonderful greens.

★★★½ EMERALD CANYON GOLF COURSE
PU-7351 Riverside Dr., Parker, 85344, La Paz County, (520)667-3366, 150 miles from Phoenix. **Facility Holes:** 18. **Yards:** 6,657/4,769. **Par:** 72/71. **Course Rating:** 71.5/67.2. **Slope:** 131/117. **Green Fee:** $18/$45. **Cart Fee:** Included in green fee. **Walking Policy:** Mandatory carts. **Walkability:** 4. **Opened:** 1989. **Architect:** Bill Phillips. **Season:** Year-round. **High:** Dec.-March. **To obtain tee times:** Call golf shop. **Miscellaneous:** Reduced fees (weekdays, twilight, juniors), range (grass), credit cards (MC, V), BF, FF.
Reader Comments: A jewel! If heading from Vegas to Phoenix or anywhere near—allow the time to play this course… Staff is friendly and helpful … Fascinating, tight track built in the desert wastelands along the Colorado River … Elevation changes, great views of the river and coyotes to keep you company.

★★½ ENCANTO GOLF COURSE
PU-2775 N. 15th Ave., Phoenix, 85007, Maricopa County, (602)253-3963. **Facility Holes:** 27. **Yards:** 6,386/5,731. **Par:** 70/72. **Course Rating:** 69.0/70.5. **Slope:** 114/111. **Green Fee:** $8/$35. **Cart Fee:** $18/Cart. **Walking Policy:** Unrestricted walking. **Walkability:** 1. **Opened:** 1937. **Architect:** William P. Bell. **Season:** Year-round. **To obtain tee times:** Call up to 4 days in advance. **Miscellaneous:** Reduced fees (twilight, juniors), metal spikes, range (grass), credit cards (MC, V), BF, FF.
Special Notes: Also has a 9-hole par-3 course.

★★★½ ESTRELLA MOUNTAIN GOLF COURSE
PU-15205 West Vineyard Dr., Goodyear, 85338, Maricopa County, (602)932-3714, 15 miles from Phoenix. **E-mail:** estrellagolf@qwest.net. **Web:** www.estrella-golf.com. **Facility Holes:** 18. **Yards:** 6,868/5,297. **Par:** 71/72. **Course Rating:** 71.9/68.5. **Slope:** 117/113. **Green Fee:** $10/$30. **Cart Fee:** $10/Person. **Walking Policy:** Unrestricted walking. **Walkability:** 2. **Opened:** 1962. **Architect:** Red Lawrence. **Season:** Year-round. **To obtain tee times:** Call up to 30 days in advance. **Miscellaneous:** Reduced fees (twilight, seniors, juniors), range (grass), credit cards (MC, V, D), BF, FF.
Reader Comments: Equals the other Great Phoenix area courses in challenge and beauty… Great value … Can be tough on windy days … Course in great shape.

ARIZONA

★★★★½ **ESTRELLA MOUNTAIN RANCH GOLF CLUB** *Condition*
PU-11800 S. Golf Club Dr., Goodyear, 85338, Maricopa County, (623)386-2600, 20 miles from Phoenix. **Web:** www.estrellamtnranch/golf.com. **Facility Holes:** 18. **Yards:** 7,102/5,124. **Par:** 72/72. **Course Rating:** 73.8/68.2. **Slope:** 138/115. **Green Fee:** $40/$120. **Cart Fee:** Included in green fee. **Walking Policy:** Unrestricted walking. **Walkability:** 3. **Opened:** 1999. **Architect:** Jack Nicklaus II. **Season:** Year-round. **High:** Jan.-April. **To obtain tee times:** Call up to 60 days in advance. **Miscellaneous:** Reduced fees (weekdays, twilight, juniors), range (grass), credit cards (MC, V, AE, D, DC), BF, FF.
Reader Comments: Hidden jewel, nice variety of mountains and desert ... Tough ... Friendly, helpful personnel ... Excellent value for the Phoenix area ... Unbelievable desert views ... Best new course ... Make the trek, it's worth it—the silence is deafening ... Many carries over natural washes.

★★★½ **THE FOOTHILLS GOLF CLUB**
SP-2201 E. Clubhouse Dr., Phoenix, 85048, Maricopa County, (480)460-4653, 15 miles from Phoenix. **E-mail:** foothills732@hotmail.com. **Web:** americangolf.com. **Facility Holes:** 18. **Yards:** 6,968/5,441. **Par:** 72/72. **Course Rating:** 73.2/70.1. **Slope:** 132/114. **Green Fee:** $29/$125. **Cart Fee:** Included in green fee. **Walking Policy:** Mandatory carts. **Walkability:** 2. **Opened:** 1987. **Architect:** Tom Weiskopf/Jay Morrish. **Season:** Year-round. **High:** Jan.-April. **To obtain tee times:** Call golf shop. **Miscellaneous:** Reduced fees (weekdays, guests, twilight, juniors), range (grass), credit cards (MC, V, AE, D, DC, Diners), BF, FF.
Reader Comments: Great course ... Staff is wonderful... Desert golf at its best ... Fair prices ... Made friends with a rattler ... Not tough, but fair... Even on the weekends a great value ... Good layout, true greens ... Good conditions, a little crowded.

★★ **FRANCISCO GRANDE RESORT & GOLF CLUB**
R-26000 Gila Bend Hwy., Casa Grande, 85222, Pinal County, (520)836-6444, (800)237-4238, 45 miles from Phoenix. **E-mail:** sdes@franciscogrande. **Web:** www.franciscogrande.com. **Facility Holes:** 18. **Yards:** 7,594/5,554. **Par:** 72/72. **Course Rating:** 74.9/69.9. **Slope:** 126/112. **Green Fee:** $18/$65. **Cart Fee:** Included in green fee. **Walking Policy:** Unrestricted walking. **Walkability:** 2. **Opened:** 1961. **Architect:** Ralph Plummer. **Season:** Year-round. **High:** Jan.-March. **To obtain tee times:** Call up to 2 days in advance. **Miscellaneous:** Reduced fees (weekdays, guests, twilight), metal spikes, range (grass), lodging (112 rooms), credit cards (MC, V, AE, DC, Diners Club), BF, FF.

★★½ **FRED ENKE GOLF COURSE**
PU-8251 E. Irvington Rd., Tucson, 85730, Pima County, (520)791-2539. **Facility Holes:** 18. **Yards:** 6,567/5,003. **Par:** 72/72. **Course Rating:** 71.3/70.1. **Slope:** 135/121. **Green Fee:** $12/$32. **Cart Fee:** $18/Cart. **Walking Policy:** Unrestricted walking. **Walkability:** 4. **Opened:** 1982. **Architect:** Brad Benz/Michael Poellot. **Season:** Year-round. **To obtain tee times:** Call up to 6 days in advance. **Miscellaneous:** Reduced fees (weekdays, twilight, seniors, juniors), metal spikes, range (grass), credit cards (MC, V, D), BF, FF.

★★★½ **GAINEY RANCH GOLF CLUB**
R-7600 Gainey Club Dr., Scottsdale, 85258, Maricopa County, (480)483-2582. **Facility Holes:** 27. **Green Fee:** $70/$105. **Cart Fee:** Included in green fee. **Opened:** 1984. **Architect:** Bradford Benz/J. Michael Poellot. **Season:** Year-round. **High:** Jan.-April. **To obtain tee times:** Call golf shop. **Miscellaneous:** Metal spikes, range (grass), credit cards (Must charge to hotel room).
DUNES/ARROYO (18 Combo)
Yards: 6,662/5,151. **Par:** 72/72. **Course Rating:** 70.7/68.5. **Slope:** 124/113.
DUNES/LAKES (18 Combo)
Yards: 6,614/4,993. **Par:** 72/72. **Course Rating:** 71.1/67.9. **Slope:** 126/115.
LAKES/ARROYO (18 Combo)
Yards: 6,800/5,312. **Par:** 72/72. **Course Rating:** 71.9/70.4. **Slope:** 128/116.
Reader Comments: Great layout that's not desert style ... Short, interesting course ... Wonderful condition ... Fun experience ... Overall, a good short course ... A nice change.

GOLD CANYON GOLF RESORT
R-6100 S. Kings Ranch Rd., Gold Canyon, 85219, Pinal County, (480)982-9449, 35 miles from Phoenix. **E-mail:** scott@gcgr.com. **Web:** www.gcgr.com. **Facility Holes:** 36. **Cart Fee:** Included in green fee. **Walking Policy:** Mandatory carts. **Season:** Year-round. **High:** Jan.-March. **Miscellaneous:** Reduced fees (weekdays, guests, twilight, juniors), lodging (101 rooms), credit cards (MC, V, AE, D, DC, Diners Club), BF, FF.
★★★★ **DINOSAUR MOUNTAIN** (18) *Condition*
Yards: 6,584/4,883. **Par:** 70/72. **Course Rating:** 71.1/67.4. **Slope:** 140/115. **Green Fee:** $50/$165. **Walkability:** 5. **Opened:** 1997. **Architect:** Ken Kavanaugh. **To obtain tee times:** Call up to 10 days in advance. **Miscellaneous:** Range (grass).
Reader Comments: What a great layout! ... Bring your camera ... Beautiful design in a beautiful setting ... Elevation changes make for memorable golf holes ... Beautiful course ... Super 3 pars.

★★★½ **SIDEWINDER** (18)
Yards: 6,530/4,529. **Par:** 71/72. **Course Rating:** 71.8/66.5. **Slope:** 133/119. **Green Fee:** $35/$85. **Walkability:** 2. **Opened:** 1998. **Architect:** G. Nash/K. Kavanaugh/S. Penge. **To obtain tee times:** Call golf shop. **Miscellaneous:** Range (grass/mats).
Reader Comments: Fun course ... Well-maintained, interesting ... Great course ... Lots of wildlife, good pace, great staff ... Breathtaking ... Good value in summer ... Outstanding golf day.

★★★★ **THE GOLF CLUB AT EAGLE MOUNTAIN**
PU-14915 E. Eagle Mtn. Pkwy., Fountain Hills, 85268, Maricopa County, (602)816-1234, 5 miles from Scottsdale. **E-mail:** therbst@eaglemtn.com. **Web:** www.eaglemtn.com. **Facility Holes:** 18. **Yards:** 6,755/5,065. **Par:** 71/71. **Course Rating:** 71.7/67.9. **Slope:** 139/118. **Green Fee:** $50/$175. **Cart Fee:** Included in green fee. **Walking Policy:** Mandatory carts. **Walkability:** 5. **Opened:** 1996. **Architect:** Scott Miller. **Season:** Year-round. **High:** Jan.-July. **To obtain tee times:** Call up to 30 days in advance. **Miscellaneous:** Reduced fees (weekdays, twilight, juniors), range (grass), lodging (42 rooms), credit cards (MC, V, AE), BF, FF.
Reader Comments: Good variety of holes, very playable, nice greens ... Beautiful piece of real estate ... Liked it better than Troon North ... A great desert layout with spectacular elevation changes ... A pleasant surprise—one of the best in a golfer's paradise.

★★★★½ **THE GOLF CLUB AT VISTOSO** *Condition*
PU-955 W. Vistoso Highlands Dr., Tucson, 85737, Pima County, (520)797-9900, 12 miles from Tucson. **E-mail:** gcatv@aol.com. **Web:** www.vistosogolf.net. **Facility Holes:** 18. **Yards:** 6,905/5,165. **Par:** 72/72. **Course Rating:** 72.1/65.4. **Slope:** 145/111. **Green Fee:** $39/$140. **Cart Fee:** Included in green fee. **Walking Policy:** Walking at certain times. **Walkability:** 2. **Opened:** 1995. **Architect:** Tom Weiskopf. **Season:** Year-round. **To obtain tee times:** Call up to 30 days in advance. **Miscellaneous:** Reduced fees (weekdays, twilight), range (grass), credit cards (MC, V, AE, D), BF, FF.
Notes: Ranked 19th in 2001 Best in State.
Reader Comments: One of Tucson's top 5 ... In true Weiskopf fashion most holes offer multiple options ... Target golf, terrific course ... Friendly staff ... A great course but harder than it looks ... Gets better each time you play ... Amazing view.

★★★ **GRANDE VALLE GOLF CLUB**
PU-1505 S. Toltec Rd., Eloy, 85231, Pinal County, (520)466-7734, 47 miles from Phoenix. **Facility Holes:** 18. **Yards:** 7,100/5,363. **Par:** 72/72. **Course Rating:** 72.3/69.8. **Slope:** 117/112. **Green Fee:** $11/$25. **Cart Fee:** $10/Person. **Walking Policy:** Unrestricted walking. **Opened:** 1992. **Architect:** Forrest Richardson. **Season:** Year-round. **High:** Oct.-April. **To obtain tee times:** Call golf shop. **Miscellaneous:** Reduced fees (weekdays, twilight, juniors), metal spikes, range (grass), credit cards (MC, V, AE).
Reader Comments: Greens are better under new ownership ... Fun track, can be windy in p.m. ... This could turn into a great course ... Nice course in the desert.
Special Notes: Formerly Eloy Tohono Municipal Golf Course.

★★★★ **GRANITE FALLS GOLF CLUB**
SP-15949 W. Clearview Blvd, Surprise, 85374, Maricopa County, (623)546-7575, 18 miles from Phoenix. **Facility Holes:** 18. **Yards:** 6,840/5,214. **Par:** 72/72. **Course Rating:** 72.1/68.8. **Slope:** 127/114. **Green Fee:** $21/$79. **Cart Fee:** Included in green fee. **Opened:** 1996. **Architect:** Billy Casper/Greg Nash. **Season:** Year-round. **High:** Nov.-April. **To obtain tee times:** Call golf shop. **Miscellaneous:** Reduced fees (weekdays, twilight), range (grass), credit cards (MC, V, AE).
Reader Comments: Great test of golf with beauty ... Out of the way, but go play; worth it ... Great to play in summer when snowbirds have left ... Great views, good challenge, good food ... No complaints.

GRAYHAWK GOLF CLUB
PU-8620 E Thompson Peak Pkwy., Scottsdale, 85255, Maricopa County, (480)502-1800, (800)472-9429. **E-mail:** golf@grayhawk.com. **Web:** www.grayhawk.com. **Facility Holes:** 36. **Green Fee:** $50/$225. **Cart Fee:** Included in green fee. **Walking Policy:** Unrestricted walking. **Season:** Year-round. **High:** Jan.-March. **To obtain tee times:** Call up to 90 days in advance. **Miscellaneous:** Metal spikes, range (grass), credit cards (MC, V, AE), BF, FF.
★★★★½ **RAPTOR COURSE** (18) *Condition*
Yards: 7,135/5,309. **Par:** 72/72. **Course Rating:** 74.1/71.3. **Slope:** 143/127. **Walkability:** 3. **Opened:** 1995. **Architect:** Tom Fazio. **Miscellaneous:** Reduced fees (weekdays, guests, juniors).
Notes: Ranked 21st in 2001 Best in State.
Reader Comments: Unsurpassed service ... First-class all the way ... Excellent layout, well maintained ... Wonderful Fazio courses in the desert ... It doesn't get any better than this ... Worth the money and the balls.

ARIZONA

★★★★½ **TALON COURSE** (18) *Condition+*
Yards: 6,973/5,143. **Par:** 72/72. **Course Rating:** 74.3/70.0. **Slope:** 141/121. **Walkability:** 2. **Opened:** 1994. **Architect:** David Graham/Gary Panks. **Miscellaneous:** Reduced fees (weekdays, twilight, juniors).
Notes: Ranked 18th in 2001 Best in State; 56th in 1996 America's Top 75 Upscale Courses.
Reader Comments: Outstanding service ... Like a country club ... Immaculate conditions ... A fantastic bargain in the summer—and they'll bring you iced towels to keep cool ... Beautiful course, target golf ... Treat you like royalty, good shots rewarded.

★★★ **HAPPY TRAILS RESORT**
SP-17200 W. Bell Rd., Surprise, 85374, Maricopa County, (623)584-6000, 20 miles from Phoenix. **Facility Holes:** 18. **Yards:** 6,646/5,146. **Par:** 72/72. **Course Rating:** 72.1/68.7. **Slope:** 124/113. **Green Fee:** $19/$51. **Cart Fee:** Included in green fee. **Walkability:** 3. **Opened:** 1983. **Architect:** Greg Nash/Ken Cavanaugh. **Season:** Year-round. **High:** Nov.-April. **To obtain tee times:** Call golf shop. **Miscellaneous:** Reduced fees (weekdays, guests, twilight, juniors), range (grass), credit cards (MC, V, AE, D).
Reader Comments: Tougher than it looks ... Wow, excellent course and priced right ... Excellent greens ... Great off-season course, good layout ... Fun course for everyone.

★★½ **HAVEN GOLF CLUB**
PU-110 N. Abrego, Green Valley, 85614, Pima County, (520)625-4281, 25 miles from Tucson. **Facility Holes:** 18. **Yards:** 6,867/5,588. **Par:** 72/72. **Course Rating:** 72.0/70.6. **Slope:** 123/120. **Green Fee:** $15/$30. **Cart Fee:** $16/Cart. **Walking Policy:** Unrestricted walking. **Walkability:** 1. **Opened:** 1966. **Architect:** Arthur Jack Snyder. **Season:** Year-round. **High:** Nov.-March. **To obtain tee times:** Call up to 7 days in advance. **Miscellaneous:** Metal spikes, range (grass), credit cards (MC, V, D), FF.

★★★ **HERITAGE HIGHLANDS GOLF & COUNTRY CLUB**
SP-4949 W. Heritage Club Blvd., Marana, 85653, Pima County, (520)579-7000, 10 miles from Tucson. **E-mail:** golf@heritagehighlands.com. **Web:** www.heritagehighlands.com. **Facility Holes:** 18. **Yards:** 6,904/4,843. **Par:** 72/72. **Course Rating:** 72.5/67.1. **Slope:** 136/115. **Green Fee:** $45/$125. **Cart Fee:** Included in green fee. **Walking Policy:** Mandatory carts. **Walkability:** 3. **Opened:** 1997. **Architect:** Arthur Hills. **Season:** Year-round. **High:** Jan.-April. **To obtain tee times:** Call up to 7 days in advance. **Miscellaneous:** Reduced fees (twilight), range (grass), credit cards (MC, V, D), BF, FF.
Reader Comments: Desert course ... A little overpriced but worth a try ... A couple of gimmicky holes ... Very well maintained ... Beautiful clubhouse ... Beautiful course—wonderful shape.

★★★½ **HILLCREST GOLF CLUB**
PU-20002 N. Star Ridge Dr., Sun City West, 85375, Maricopa County, (623)584-1500, 19 miles from Phoenix. **E-mail:** Hillcrestaz@westmail.net. **Web:** www.teematic.com/hillcrestaz. **Facility Holes:** 18. **Yards:** 7,002/5,489. **Par:** 72/72. **Course Rating:** 72.7/70.7. **Slope:** 126/120. **Green Fee:** $29/$65. **Cart Fee:** Included in green fee. **Walkability:** 2. **Opened:** 1979. **Architect:** Jeff Hardin/Greg Nash. **Season:** Year-round. **High:** Nov.-April. **To obtain tee times:** Call golf shop. **Misc:** Reduced fees (weekdays, twilight), range (grass), credit cards (MC, V, AE, D).
Reader Comments: Good challenge, plays well ... More typical of a Midwest course than an AZ course ... The finishing 3 holes are a great challenge ... Excellent, open design with a nice feel and flow.

★★★ **KEN MCDONALD GOLF COURSE**
PU-800 Divot Dr., Tempe, 85283, Maricopa County, (480)350-5256, 4 miles from Phoenix. **E-mail:** kennymocgolf@qwest.net. **Facility Holes:** 18. **Yards:** 6,743/5,872. **Par:** 72/73. **Course Rating:** 70.8/70.8. **Slope:** 115/112. **Green Fee:** $15/$29. **Cart Fee:** $10/Person. **Walking Policy:** Unrestricted walking. **Walkability:** 2. **Opened:** 1974. **Architect:** Jack Snyder. **Season:** Year-round. **To obtain tee times:** Call golf shop. **Miscellaneous:** Reduced fees (twilight, seniors, juniors), range (grass), credit cards (MC, V), BF, FF.
Reader Comments: Well-kept secret ... City course, busy excellent value ... 18 holes of great golf! ... From the first tee to the final green, you will truely enjoy your golf.

★★★★ **KIERLAND GOLF CLUB**
PU-15636 N. Clubgate Dr., Scottsdale, 85254, Maricopa County, (480)922-9283, 20 miles from Phoenix. **Facility Holes:** 27. **Green Fee:** $40/$140. **Cart Fee:** Included in green fee. **Walking Policy:** Unrestricted walking. **Walkability:** 3. **Opened:** 1996. **Architect:** Scott Miller. **Season:** Year-round. **To obtain tee times:** Call golf shop. **Miscellaneous:** Reduced fees (weekdays, twilight, juniors), metal spikes, range (grass), credit cards (MC, V, AE, D), BF, FF.
IRONWOOD/ACACIA (18 Combo)
Yards: 6,974/4,985. **Par:** 72/72. **Course Rating:** 72.9/69.2. **Slope:** 130/116.
IRONWOOD/MESQUITE (18 Combo)
Yards: 7,017/5,017. **Par:** 72/72. **Course Rating:** 73.3/69.4. **Slope:** 133/120.

MESQUITE/ACACIA (18 Combo)
Yards: 6,913/4,898. **Par:** 72/72. **Course Rating:** 72.6/69.0. **Slope:** 133/115.
Notes: Golf Digest School site.
Reader Comments: User-friendly course, wide open fairways … Pleasant staff, good location … Much less "target golf" than most desert courses … Charles Barkley played in group right behind us … An exquisite 27-hole course in the heart of Scottsdale.

★★★ KOKOPELLI GOLF RESORT
PU-1800 W. Guadalupe, Gilbert, 85233, Maricopa County, (480)926-3589, (800)468-7918, 10 miles from Phoenix. **Facility Holes:** 18. **Yards:** 6,716/4,992. **Par:** 72/72. **Course Rating:** 72.2/68.8. **Slope:** 132/120. **Green Fee:** $40/$100. **Cart Fee:** Included in green fee. **Walking Policy:** Mandatory carts. **Walkability:** 4. **Opened:** 1993. **Architect:** Bill Phillips. **Season:** Year-round. **To obtain tee times:** Call up to 7 days in advance. **Miscellaneous:** Reduced fees (weekdays, guests, twilight), metal spikes, range (grass), credit cards (MC, V, AE), BF, FF.
Reader Comments: Great rate, long course, great holes … Tough course, nothing's flat, like playing on a rollercoaster … Pace of play is good, well laid out greens … A great time.

★★★★ LA PALOMA COUNTRY CLUB *Condition*
R-3660 E. Sunrise Dr., Tucson, 85718, Pima County, (520)299-1500, (800)222-1249. **Facility Holes:** 27. **Green Fee:** $85/$185. **Cart Fee:** Included in green fee. **Walking Policy:** Mandatory carts. **Opened:** 1984. **Architect:** Jack Nicklaus. **Season:** Year-round. **To obtain tee times:** Call golf shop. **Miscellaneous:** Reduced fees (guests, juniors), metal spikes, range (grass), credit cards (MC, V, AE, D, DC), BF, FF.
CANYON/HILL (18 Combo)
Yards: 6,997/5,057. **Par:** 72/72. **Course Rating:** 74.8/67.4. **Slope:** 155/114. **Walkability:** 5.
Miscellaneous: Lodging (487 rooms).
RIDGE/CANYON (18 Combo)
Yards: 7,088/5,075. **Par:** 72/72. **Course Rating:** 75.2/67.9. **Slope:** 155/121.
Notes: Ranked 25th in 1999 Best in State.
RIDGE/HILL (18 Combo)
Yards: 7,017/4,878. **Par:** 72/72. **Course Rating:** 74.2/66.9. **Slope:** 155/110.
Reader Comments: Nice weekend golf getaway, very scenic … Good grass … Challenging, very expensive … Spectacular desert/mountain views and a challenging but playable course … This is heaven … Good service … Tough holes but beautiful … Stay-and-play packages are excellent .

LAKE POWELL NATIONAL GOLF CLUB
PU-Bitter Springs Rd., Page, 86040, Coconino County, (520)645-2715, 270 miles from Phoenix. **Web:** www.lakepowellgolf.com. **Facility Holes:** 27. **Season:** Year-round. **High:** March-Oct. **To obtain tee times:** Call up to 7 days in advance. **Miscellaneous:** Range (grass), lodging (150 rooms), credit cards (MC, V, AE, D), BF, FF.
GLEN CANYON COURSE (9)
Yards: 6,493/5,645. **Par:** 72/72. **Course Rating:** 68.3/71.2. **Slope:** 110/113. **Green Fee:** $23.
Cart Fee: $10/Cart. **Walking Policy:** Unrestricted walking. **Walkability:** 2. **Opened:** 1959.
Miscellaneous: Reduced fees (juniors).
★★★★ MESA COURSE (18)
Yards: 7,064/5,097. **Par:** 72/72. **Course Rating:** 73.4/68.0. **Slope:** 139/122. **Green Fee:** $35/$60. **Cart Fee:** Included in green fee. **Walking Policy:** Mandatory carts. **Walkability:** 4. **Opened:** 1995. **Architect:** Bill Phillips. **Miscellaneous:** Reduced fees (guests, twilight, juniors).
Reader Comments: Next to the Grand Canyon, Arizona's greatest natural wonder! … Fun and forgiving … Magnificent setting, challenging holes … The golf course is set in a beautiful location above Lake Powell and the Glen Canyon Dam … Good course.

★★★★½ LAS SENDAS GOLF CLUB *Service, Condition*
PU-7555 E. Eagle Crest Dr., Mesa, 85207, Maricopa County, (480)396-4000, 14 miles from Phoenix. **Web:** www.lassendas.com. **Facility Holes:** 18. **Yards:** 6,836/5,100. **Par:** 71/71. **Course Rating:** 73.8/69.9. **Slope:** 149/126. **Green Fee:** $45/$160. **Cart Fee:** Included in green fee. **Walking Policy:** Unrestricted walking. **Walkability:** 4. **Opened:** 1995. **Architect:** Robert Trent Jones Jr. **Season:** Year-round. **High:** Jan.-April. **To obtain tee times:** Call golf shop. **Miscellaneous:** Reduced fees (twilight), range (grass), credit cards (MC, V, AE), BF, FF.
Notes: Ranked 22nd in 2001 Best in State.
Reader Comments: Great course! … A beautiful course carved out of the rugged foothills east of Mesa … A true desert experience, bring plenty of reloads … You will need your A+ short game to successfully get up down from around these greens … Golf Heaven! … Lightning fast greens.

★★★½ THE LEGACY GOLF RESORT
PU-6808 S. 32nd, Phoenix, 85040, Maricopa County, (602)305-3550, (888)828-3673. **Web:** www.legacygolfresort.com. **Facility Holes:** 18. **Yards:** 6,802/5,471. **Par:** 71/71. **Course Rating:** 71.8/70.4. **Slope:** 125/117. **Green Fee:** $65/$140. **Cart Fee:** Included in green fee. **Walking Policy:** Walking at certain times. **Walkability:** 2. **Opened:** 1999. **Architect:** Gary Panks.

Season: Year-round. **To obtain tee times:** Call up to 60 days in advance. **Misc:** Reduced fees (weekdays, guests, twilight), range (grass), credit cards (MC, V, AE, D, CB), BF, FF.
Reader Comments: Great views ... One to play ... Excellent value ... Fabulous condition ... Plenty of room off tee ... Wonderful mix of par 3s ... Good variety of holes, fairways and bunkers.

★★★ THE LEGEND AT ARROWHEAD GOLF CLUB

R-21027 N. 67th Ave., Glendale, 85308, Maricopa County, (623)561-1902, (800)468-7918, 15 miles from Phoenix. **Facility Holes:** 18. **Yards:** 7,005/5,233. **Par:** 72/72. **Course Rating:** 73.0/71.2. **Slope:** 129/119. **Green Fee:** $29/$80. **Cart Fee:** Included in green fee. **Walkability:** 4. **Opened:** 1989. **Architect:** Arnold Palmer/Ed Seay. **Season:** Year-round. **High:** Jan.-April. **To obtain tee times:** Call golf shop. **Miscellaneous:** Reduced fees (weekdays, twilight, juniors), metal spikes, range (grass), credit cards (MC, V, AE).
Reader Comments: Good price ... Very nice course, one of my favorite places to play ... Great views, generous fairways ... Beautiful ... Interesting holes.

★★★★ LEGEND TRAIL GOLF CLUB *Condition*

PU-9462 E. Legendary Lane, Scottsdale, 85262, Maricopa County, (480)488-7434. **Web:** www.troongolf.com. **Facility Holes:** 18. **Yards:** 6,845/5,000. **Par:** 72/72. **Course Rating:** 72.3/68.2. **Slope:** 135/122. **Green Fee:** $45/$190. **Cart Fee:** Included in green fee. **Walking Policy:** Unrestricted walking. **Walkability:** 2. **Opened:** 1995. **Architect:** Rees Jones. **Season:** Year-round. **To obtain tee times:** Call up to 60 days in advance. **Misc:** Reduced fees (weekdays, twilight, juniors), metal spikes, range (grass), caddies, credit cards (MC, V, AE), BF, FF.
Notes: Ranked 19th in 1999 Best in State.
Reader Comments: This is a great course ... No two holes alike ... Most enjoyable in Arizona for me ... Best maintained course in Scottsdale ... One of most playable desert courses ... Troon golf at its best.

★★★ THE LINKS AT CONTINENTAL RANCH

PU-8480 N. Continental Links Dr., Tucson, 85743, Pima County, (520)744-7443. **E-mail:** dpgolfguy@yahoo.com. **Web:** www.linksatcrgolf.com. **Facility Holes:** 18. **Yards:** 6,854/5,182. **Par:** 72/72. **Course Rating:** 71.8/69.3. **Slope:** 122/115. **Green Fee:** $20/$79. **Cart Fee:** $15/Person. **Walking Policy:** Unrestricted walking. **Walkability:** 2. **Opened:** 1997. **Architect:** Brian Huntley. **Season:** Year-round. **High:** Jan.-March. **To obtain tee times:** Call up to 7 days in advance. **Miscellaneous:** Reduced fees (weekdays, twilight, juniors), metal spikes, range (grass), credit cards (MC, V, AE, D), BF, FF.
Reader Comments: Narrow fairways with very heavy grass rough ... Great value ... Great staff and driving range ... Links style expensive ... Nice links style course—good value.

★★½ THE LINKS AT QUEEN CREEK

PU-445 E. Ocotillo Rd., Queen Creek, 85242, Maricopa County, (480)987-1910, 12 miles from Mesa. **Facility Holes:** 18. **Yards:** 6,100/5,000. **Par:** 70/71. **Slope:** 100/92. **Green Fee:** $18/$30. **Cart Fee:** Included in green fee. **Walking Policy:** Unrestricted walking. **Walkability:** 2. **Opened:** 1993. **Architect:** Sam West. **Season:** Nov.-May. **High:** Dec.-March. **To obtain tee times:** Call golf shop. **Miscellaneous:** Reduced fees (twilight), range (grass/mats), credit cards (MC, V), FF.

LONDON BRIDGE GOLF CLUB

SP-2400 Clubhouse Dr., Lake Havasu City, 86406, Mohave County, (520)855-2719, 150 miles from Las Vegas, NV. **E-mail:** americangolf.com. **Web:** www.americangolf.com. **Facility Holes:** 36. **Season:** Year-round. **High:** Oct.-April. **Miscellaneous:** Metal spikes, range (grass/mats), credit cards (MC, V, AE, D), BF, FF.
★½ **EAST COURSE** (18)
Yards: 6,140/5,045. **Par:** 71/71. **Course Rating:** 68.9/68.2. **Slope:** 118/111. **Green Fee:** $30/$45. **Cart Fee:** $15/Person. **Walking Policy:** Unrestricted walking. **Walkability:** 4. **Opened:** 1979. **Architect:** Arthur Jack Snyder. **To obtain tee times:** Call up to 60 days in advance. **Miscellaneous:** Reduced fees (weekdays, guests, twilight, seniors, juniors).
★★ **WEST COURSE** (18)
Yards: 6,678/5,756. **Par:** 71/72. **Course Rating:** 71.7/72.7. **Slope:** 128/123. **Green Fee:** $35/$79. **Walking Policy:** Mandatory carts. **Walkability:** 3. **Opened:** 1969. **Architect:** Jack Snyder. **To obtain tee times:** Call golf shop. **Miscellaneous:** Reduced fees (twilight, seniors).

★★★½ LONGBOW GOLF CLUB

PU-5400 E. McDowell Rd., Mesa, 85215, Maricopa County, (480)807-5400, 15 miles from Phoenix. **Web:** www.longbowgolf.com. **Facility Holes:** 18. **Yards:** 6,750/4,890. **Par:** 70/70. **Course Rating:** 71.8/67.0. **Slope:** 128/111. **Green Fee:** $35/$85. **Cart Fee:** Included in green fee. **Walking Policy:** Unrestricted walking. **Walkability:** 2. **Opened:** 1997. **Architect:** Ken Kavanaugh. **Season:** Year-round. **To obtain tee times:** Call up to 7 days in advance. **Miscellaneous:** Reduced fees (weekdays, twilight, juniors), range (grass), credit cards

ARIZONA

(MC, V, AE), BF, FF.
Reader Comments: Pleasureable experience ... Nice value for desert golf... Very playable for all skill levels ... Friendly staff ... Long, long, long ... Immaculate condition ... An undiscovered jewel.

★★★★½ **LOS CABALLEROS GOLF CLUB** *Pace+*
R-1551 S. Vulture Mine Rd., Wickenburg, 85390, Maricopa County, (520)684-2704, 50 miles from Phoenix. **Facility Holes:** 18. **Yards:** 6,962/5,264. **Par:** 72/72. **Course Rating:** 73.5/71.2. **Slope:** 138/124. **Green Fee:** $49/$120. **Cart Fee:** Included in green fee. **Walking Policy:** Mandatory carts. **Walkability:** 4. **Opened:** 1979. **Architect:** Greg Nash/Jeff Hardin. **Season:** Year-round. **High:** Dec.-April. **To obtain tee times:** Call up to 30 days in advance. **Miscellaneous:** Reduced fees (guests), range (grass), credit cards (MC, V), BF, FF.
Reader Comments: Mellow pace, windy ... Lots of good holes ... Best challenge in Arizona ... Excellent layout ... Well worth a trip to play ... Great course in middle of nowhere.

MARRIOTT'S CAMELBACK GOLF CLUB
R-7847 N. Mockingbird Lane, Scottsdale, 85253, Maricopa County, (602)596-7050, (800)242-2635, 5 miles from Phoenix. **E-mail:** lgrundyecamelbackgolf.com. **Web:** camelbackinn.com. **Facility Holes:** 36. **Cart Fee:** Included in green fee. **Walking Policy:** Mandatory carts. **Season:** Year-round. **High:** Jan.-April. **To obtain tee times:** Call up to 30 days in advance. **Miscellaneous:** Reduced fees (weekdays, guests, twilight, juniors), metal spikes, range (grass), credit cards (MC, V, AE, D, DC), BF, FF.
★★½ **CLUB COURSE** (18)
Yards: 7,014/5,917. **Par:** 72/72. **Course Rating:** 72.6/72.0. **Slope:** 122/118. **Green Fee:** $30/$105. **Walkability:** 2. **Opened:** 1980. **Architect:** Jack Snyder.
★★ **RESORT COURSE** (18)
Yards: 6,559/5,626. **Par:** 72/72. **Course Rating:** 71.0/72.0. **Slope:** 125/124. **Green Fee:** $40/$155. **Walkability:** 3. **Opened:** 2000. **Architect:** Arthur Hills.

★★★½ **MARYVALE GOLF CLUB**
PU-5902 W. Indian School Rd., Phoenix, 85033, Maricopa County, (623)846-4022. **Facility Holes:** 18. **Yards:** 6,539/5,656. **Par:** 72/72. **Course Rating:** 69.8/70.2. **Slope:** 115/113. **Green Fee:** $8/$28. **Cart Fee:** $18/Person. **Walking Policy:** Unrestricted walking. **Walkability:** 1. **Opened:** 1961. **Architect:** William F. Bell. **Season:** Year-round. **High:** Nov.-April. **To obtain tee times:** Call golf shop. **Miscellaneous:** Reduced fees (weekdays, twilight, seniors, juniors), metal spikes, range (grass), credit cards (MC, V, AE, D).
Reader Comments: Old, flat, well maintained, lots of trees, fun ... Nice muni in Phoenix ... Very mature with tall eucalyptus trees ... Good layout and tough.

MCCORMICK RANCH GOLF CLUB
PU-7505 E. McCormick Pkwy., Scottsdale, 85258, Maricopa County, (480)948-0260. **Facility Holes:** 36. **Green Fee:** $40/$110. **Cart Fee:** Included in green fee. **Walkability:** 1. **Opened:** 1972. **Architect:** Desmond Muirhead. **Season:** Year-round. **High:** Jan.-April. **To obtain tee times:** Call golf shop. **Miscellaneous:** Reduced fees (twilight, juniors), metal spikes, range (grass/mats), credit cards (MC, V, AE).
★★★ **PALM COURSE** (18)
Yards: 7,044/5,057. **Par:** 72/72. **Course Rating:** 74.4/69.9. **Slope:** 137/117.
Reader Comments: Very enjoyable—pleasant experience ... Expected more ... Palm trees, water-holes ... Whites too short, blues too long ... Difficult course unless you stay on fairways ... Lots of water, trees and bunkers ... Landscape is beautiful.
★★★½ **PINE COURSE** (18)
Yards: 7,187/5,333. **Par:** 72/72. **Course Rating:** 74.4/69.9. **Slope:** 135/117.
Reader Comments: Great service and a fun course to play ... Old style course with little to get excited about ... Difficult course unless you stay on fairways ... Lots of water, trees and bunkers.

MESA DEL SOL GOLF COURSE
PU-12213 Calle Del Cid, Yuma, 85367, Yuma County, (520)342-1283, 10 miles from Yuma. **E-mail:** c-medrow@hotmail.com. **Web:** mesadelsolgolf.com. **Facility Holes:** 18. **Yards:** 6,767/5,367. **Par:** 72/72. **Course Rating:** 71.8/69.4. **Slope:** 124/112. **Green Fee:** $18/$30. **Cart Fee:** $11/Person. **Walking Policy:** Unrestricted walking. **Walkability:** 2. **Architect:** Arnold Palmer. **Season:** Year-round. **High:** Jan.-March. **To obtain tee times:** Call up to 7 days in advance. **Misc:** Reduced fees (twilight, juniors), range (grass), credit cards (MC, V), BF, FF.

MOUNT GRAHAM MUNICIPAL GOLF COURSE
PU-Golf Course Rd., Safford, 85546, Graham County, (602)348-3140, 120 miles from Tucson. **Facility Holes:** 18. **Yards:** 6,354/5,691. **Par:** 72/73. **Course Rating:** 69.5/70.6. **Slope:** 116/117. **Green Fee:** $15/$16. **Cart Fee:** $16/Cart. **Walking Policy:** Unrestricted walking. **Walkability:** 1. **Season:** Year-round. **To obtain tee times:** Call golf shop. **Miscellaneous:** Reduced fees (twilight, juniors), metal spikes, range (grass/mats), BF, FF.

ARIZONA

MOUNTAIN BROOK GOLF CLUB
PU-5783 S. Mountain Brook Dr., Gold Canyon, 85219, Pinal County, (480)671-1000.
Facility Holes: 18. **Yards:** 6,710/5,277. **Par:** 71/71. **Course Rating:** 69.9/66.2. **Slope:** 124/103.
Green Fee: $20/$65. **Cart Fee:** Included in green fee. **Walking Policy:** Walking at certain
times. **Walkability:** 2. **Opened:** 1996. **Architect:** Brian Whitcomb. **Season:** Year-round. **High:**
Nov.-April. **To obtain tee times:** Call up to 6 days in advance. **Miscellaneous:** Reduced fees
(twilight, juniors), range (grass), credit cards (MC, V), BF, FF.

★★★ **MOUNTAIN SHADOWS**
PU-5641 E. Lincoln Dr, Scottsdale, 85253, Maricopa County, (480)951-5427. **E-mail:**
mtnshadowgolf@aol.com. **Web:** mountainshadowsgolf.com. **Facility Holes:** 18. **Yards:**
3,083/2,650. **Par:** 56/56. **Course Rating:** 56.9/55.4. **Slope:** 92/89. **Green Fee:** $30/$75.
Walking Policy: Mandatory carts. **Opened:** 1959. **Architect:** Jack Snyder. **Season:** Year-round.
To obtain tee times: Call up to 7 days in advance. **Miscellaneous:** Reduced fees (weekdays,
twilight), range (grass), lodging (337 rooms), credit cards (MC, V, AE, D), BF, FF.
Reader Comments: Excellent executive course … Keep straight or hit a condo … Challenging your
irons, OB problems, pretty course … Sharpen short game here … Must be one of best executive
courses in world … Great test also.

★★★★ **OAKCREEK COUNTRY CLUB**
SP-690 Bell Rock Blvd., Sedona, 86351, Yavapai County, (520)284-1660, (888)703-9489,
100 miles from Phoenix. **E-mail:** OCCC@Sedona.net. **Facility Holes:** 18. **Yards:** 6,824/5,579.
Par: 72/72. **Course Rating:** 72.2/71.0. **Slope:** 132/128. **Green Fee:** $70/$80. **Cart Fee:** Included
in green fee. **Walking Policy:** Walking at certain times. **Walkability:** 2. **Opened:** 1968.
Architect: Robert Trent Jones. **Season:** Year-round. **To obtain tee times:** Call up to 30 days in
advance. **Miscellaneous:** Reduced fees (twilight, juniors), range (grass/mats), caddies, credit
cards (MC, V, AE, D), BF, FF.
Reader Comments: Old original, still great … Treelined course in Arizona; tough, fair, fun …
Beautiful location … Friendly, scenic … Breathtaking views … Good test of golf … Red rocks
beautiful … Great staff.

★★★★ **OCOTILLO GOLF CLUB**
R-3751 S. Clubhouse Dr., Chandler, 85248, Maricopa County, (480)917-6660,
(888)624-8899, 15 miles from Phoenix. **E-mail:** dbogue@ocotillogolf.com. **Web:** www.ocotillo-
golf.com. **Facility Holes:** 27. **Cart Fee:** Included in green fee. **Walking Policy:** Walking at cer-
tain times. **Walkability:** 2. **Opened:** 1986. **Architect:** Ted Robinson. **Season:** Year-round. **High:**
Dec.-March. **To obtain tee times:** Call up to 30 days in advance. **Miscellaneous:** Reduced fees
(twilight, juniors), range (grass), Credit cards (MC, V, AE, D), BF, FF.
BLUE/GOLD (18 Combo)
Yards: 6,729/5,128. **Par:** 72/72. **Course Rating:** 71.3/71.3. **Slope:** 131/128. **Fee:** $45/$155.
BLUE/WHITE (18 Combo)
Yards: 6,533/5,134. **Par:** 71/71. **Course Rating:** 70.8/71.0. **Slope:** 128/127. **Fee:** $35/$155.
WHITE/GOLD (18 Combo)
Yards: 6,612/5,124. **Par:** 71/71. **Course Rating:** 71.4/68.4. **Slope:** 128/122. **Fee:** $45/$155.
Reader Comments: Beautiful course and clubhouse … No.1 course in Arizona, hands down
Wonderful course with water galore … Ocotillo is a great value in the winter … A beautiful course,
but tight!! Just plain beautiful … Taste of Florida … Miles of lake shoreline.

★★★★ **OMNI TUCSON NATIONAL GOLF RESORT & SPA**
R-2727 W. Club Dr., Tucson, 85741, Pima County, (520)575-7540, (800)528-4856, 20 miles
from Tucson. **Facility Holes:** 27. **Green Fee:** $55/$135. **Cart Fee:** Included in green fee.
Walking Policy: Mandatory carts. **Opened:** 1962. **Architect:** R.B. Harris/R. von Hagge/B.
Devlin. **Season:** Year-round. **High:** Jan.-April. **To obtain tee times:** Call up to 30 days in
advance. **Miscellaneous:** Reduced fees (twilight, juniors), range (grass/mats), lodging (169
rooms), credit cards (MC, V, AE, D, DC, Diners Club), BF, FF.
GOLD/GREEN (18 Combo)
Yards: 6,782/5,440. **Par:** 72/72. **Course Rating:** 72.6/71.2. **Slope:** 140/127. **Walkability:** 3.
GREEN/ORANGE (18 Combo)
Yards: 6,609/5,375. **Par:** 71/71. **Course Rating:** 72.0/71.2. **Slope:** 135/122. **Walkability:** 2.
ORANGE/GOLD (18 Combo)
Yards: 7,103/5,679. **Par:** 73/73. **Course Rating:** 74.6/73.0. **Slope:** 136/127. **Walkability:** 2.
Reader Comments: Fast greens … The PGA plays there for a reason … A fine traditional course
… Great ambience … Price is high but great course, great service … Operates like a private club.

★★½ **ORANGE TREE GOLF RESORT**
R-10601 N. 56th St., Scottsdale, 85254, Maricopa County, (480)948-3730, (800)228-0386.
E-mail: randyw@orangetree.com. **Web:** www.orangetree.com. **Facility Holes:** 18. **Yards:**
6,775/5,704. **Par:** 72/72. **Course Rating:** 71.3/71.8. **Slope:** 122/116. **Green Fee:** $32/$109.
Cart Fee: Included in green fee. **Walking Policy:** Mandatory carts. **Walkability:** 2. **Opened:**

1957. **Architect:** Johnny Bulla/Lawrence Hughes. **Season:** Year-round. **High:** Dec.-April. **To obtain tee times:** Call up to 30 days in advance. **Miscellaneous:** Reduced fees (twilight), metal spikes, range (grass), lodging (160 rooms), credit cards (MC, V, AE, D, DC), BF, FF.

★★★ PAINTED MOUNTAIN GOLF CLUB
PU-6210 E. McKellips Rd., Mesa, 85215, Maricopa County, (480)832-0156, 20 miles from Phoenix. **Facility Holes:** 18. **Yards:** 6,021/4,651. **Par:** 70/70. **Course Rating:** 67.2/64.3. **Slope:** 104/97. **Green Fee:** $17/$44. **Cart Fee:** $9/Person. **Walking Policy:** Unrestricted walking. **Walkability:** 1. **Architect:** Milt Coggins. **Season:** Year-round. **To obtain tee times:** Call up to 7 days in advance. **Misc:** Reduced fees (weekdays, twilight, juniors), range, cards (MC, V). **Reader Comments:** Absolutely outstanding—great course, value for dollar ... A nice course in the middle of a typical desert neighborhood ... Need more courses like this ... Fun golf, good food, great prices ... Easy layout, great greens. **Special Notes:** Formerly Camelot Golf Club.

PALM VALLEY GOLF CLUB
SP-2211 N. Litchfield Rd., Goodyear, 85338, Maricopa County, (623)935-2500, (800)475-2978, 15 miles from Phoenix. **Web:** www.suncgolf.com. **Facility Holes:** 36. **Walking Policy:** Unrestricted walking. **Season:** Year-round. **To obtain tee times:** Call up to 7 days in advance. **Miscellaneous:** Reduced fees (weekdays, twilight, juniors), range (grass), lodging (109 rooms), credit cards (MC, V, AE), BF, FF.
★★★★ ARTHUR HILLS CHAMPIONSHIP COURSE (18)
Yards: 7,015/5,300. **Par:** 72/72. **Course Rating:** 72.8/68.7. **Slope:** 130/109. **Green Fee:** $19/$82. **Cart Fee:** $14/Person. **Walkability:** 4. **Opened:** 1993. **Architect:** Arthur Hills. **T Reader Comments:** Playable ... Need every club in your bag ... The best course for the price ... Fine course always in good condition with a very nice feel and flow ... Excellent practice area ... Probably the most underrated course in Phoenix area.
★★★½ HALE IRWIN MID-LENGTH COURSE (18)
Yards: 4,700/3,200. **Par:** 62/62. **Green Fee:** $6/$50. **Cart Fee:** Included in green fee. **Walkability:** 3. **Opened:** 1999. **Architect:** Hale Irwin. **High:** Nov.-March.
Reader Comments: Good track at a fair price ... Best deal in Arizona ... Always first on our list of courses to play in Phoenix area ... Great condition, nice golf shop and staff ... Beautiful clubhouse ... Great bunkers, good long course ... Must be straight hitter... Fun course, constantly improving, great practice area.

★★★ PAPAGO GOLF COURSE
PU-5595 E. Moreland St., Phoenix, 85008, Maricopa County, (602)275-8428. **Facility Holes:** 18. **Yards:** 7,068/5,937. **Par:** 72/72. **Course Rating:** 73.3/72.4. **Slope:** 132/119. **Green Fee:** $8/$35. **Cart Fee:** $21/Cart. **Walking Policy:** Unrestricted walking. **Walkability:** 3. **Opened:** 1963. **Architect:** William F. Bell. **Season:** Year-round. **To obtain tee times:** Call up to 2 days in advance. **Miscellaneous:** Reduced fees (twilight, seniors, juniors), range (grass/mats), credit cards (MC, V), FF.
Notes: Ranked 51st in 1996 America's Top 75 Affordable Courses.
Reader Comments: Great municipal course ... Can carry your own bag ... Walking is great ... Excellent layout, good test, good value ... A great desert course, lots of variety and challenge ... Price is great but hard to get tee times.

★½ PAVILION LAKES GOLF CLUB
PU-8870 E. Indian Bend Rd., Scottsdale, 85250, Maricopa County, (480)948-3370. **Web:** www.pavilolakes.com. **Facility Holes:** 18. **Yards:** 6,515/5,135. **Par:** 71/71. **Course Rating:** 70.1/68.2. **Slope:** 120/110. **Green Fee:** $18/$59. **Cart Fee:** Included in green fee. **Walking Policy:** Walking at certain times. **Walkability:** 1. **Opened:** 1992. **Season:** Year-round. **High:** Jan.-April. **To obtain tee times:** Call golf shop. **Miscellaneous:** Reduced fees (weekdays, twilight, juniors), metal spikes, range (grass), credit cards (MC, V, AE, DC).

★★ PAYSON GOLF COURSE
PU-1504 W. Country Club Dr., Payson, 85541, Gila County, (520)474-2273, 85 miles from Phoenix. **Facility Holes:** 18. **Yards:** 5,894/5,094. **Par:** 71/71. **Course Rating:** 66.9/66.7. **Slope:** 114/113. **Green Fee:** $24/$29. **Cart Fee:** $22/Cart. **Walking Policy:** Unrestricted walking. **Walkability:** 1. **Opened:** 1959. **Architect:** Frank Hughes/Russ Zakarisen. **Season:** Year-round. **High:** May-Sept. **To obtain tee times:** Call golf shop. **Miscellaneous:** Reduced fees (weekdays, juniors), metal spikes, range (grass/mats), credit cards (MC, V, AE), FF.

★★★½ THE PHOENICIAN GOLF CLUB
R-6000 E. Camelback Rd., Scottsdale, 85251, Maricopa County, (480)423-2449, (800)888-8234. **E-mail:** johnjackson@starwoodhotels.com. **Web:** www.thephoenician.com. **Facility Holes:** 27. **Green Fee:** $90/$170. **Cart Fee:** Included in green fee. **Walking Policy:** Mandatory carts. **Walkability:** 3. **Opened:** 1988. **Architect:** Homer Flint/Ted Robinson. **Season:** Year-round. **High:** Oct.-May. **To obtain tee times:** Call up to 60 days in advance.

Miscellaneous: Reduced fees (twilight, juniors), metal spikes, range (grass), lodging (654 rooms), credit cards (MC, V, AE, D, DC, CB, TCB), BF, FF.
DESERT/CANYON (18 Combo)
Yards: 6,068/4,777. **Par:** 70/70. **Course Rating:** 69.4/67.7. **Slope:** 131/114.
OASIS/CANYON (18 Combo)
Yards: 6,258/4,871. **Par:** 70/70. **Course Rating:** 70.1/69.1. **Slope:** 130/111.
OASIS/DESERT (18 Combo)
Yards: 6,310/5,024. **Par:** 70/70. **Course Rating:** 70.3/69.7. **Slope:** 130/113.
Reader Comments: Immaculate, it's a major emergency if a leaf is on the course … Above average resort course … Uncrowded … Very hilly, must stay on fairways … Excellent shape … Short course … Beautiful landscape-great to just ride it … Lovely views … Top quality pro shop.

★★★★ THE POINTE HILTON RESORT AT TAPATIO CLIFFS

R-11111 N. 7th St., Phoenix, 85020, Maricopa County, (602)866-6356. **Web:** www.pointe-hilton.com. **Facility Holes:** 18. **Yards:** 6,700/5,000. **Par:** 72/72. **Course Rating:** 71.2/68.4. **Slope:** 135/128. **Green Fee:** $45/$145. **Cart Fee:** Included in green fee. **Walking Policy:** Mandatory carts. **Walkability:** 4. **Opened:** 1989. **Architect:** Bill Johnston. **Season:** Year-round. **To obtain tee times:** Call up to 30 days in advance. **Miscellaneous:** Reduced fees (weekdays, guests, twilight), metal spikes, range (grass), caddies, lodging (585 rooms), credit cards (MC, V, AE, D, DC), BF, FF.
Reader Comments: Great staff … No. 10 teeing off from top of mountain a thrill … Good resort course … Fantastic practice facility and a real test … A desert favorite resort … Greens putt true … Great course! … Nice desert setting … Great location … Good desert course in town.

★★★½ POINTE SOUTH MOUNTAIN RESORT

R-7777 S. Pointe Pkwy., Phoenix, 85044, Maricopa County, (602)431-6480, (800)876-4683. **E-mail:** vdemis@destinationhotels.com. **Web:** www.pointesouthmtn.com. **Facility Holes:** 18. **Yards:** 6,211/4,550. **Par:** 70/70. **Course Rating:** 69.1/66.2. **Slope:** 124/107. **Green Fee:** $30/$125. **Cart Fee:** Included in green fee. **Walking Policy:** Mandatory carts. **Walkability:** 3. **Opened:** 1988. **Architect:** Forrest Richardson. **Season:** Year-round. **High:** Dec.-April. **To obtain tee times:** Call up to 7 days in advance. **Miscellaneous:** Reduced fees (weekdays, guests, twilight, juniors), range (grass), caddies, lodging (648 rooms), credit cards (MC, V, AE, D, Diners Club), BF, FF.
Reader Comments: Great airport course, nice golf and great condition … Great views and challenging array of par 3s … Beautiful course and great service … Challenging golf course … Target golf, short course … Best greens I've ever played.

★★★ PRESCOTT GOLF & COUNTRY CLUB

SP-1030 Prescott C.C. Blvd., Dewey, 86327, Yavapai County, (520)772-8984, (800)717-7274. **E-mail:** timpgcc@cableone.lnet. **Web:** prescottcc.com. **Facility Holes:** 18. **Yards:** 6,783/5,771. **Par:** 72/72. **Course Rating:** 71.2/71.1. **Slope:** 124/124. **Green Fee:** $19/$49. **Cart Fee:** Included in green fee. **Walking Policy:** Unrestricted walking. **Walkability:** 3. **Opened:** 1971. **Architect:** Milt Coggins. **Season:** Year-round. **To obtain tee times:** Call up to 7 days in advance. **Miscellaneous:** Reduced fees (weekdays, twilight, juniors), range (grass), credit cards (MC, V, AE, D), BF, FF.
Reader Comments: Put this one on your list of courses to play … Best in Prescott area … Great summer getaway …Very cool, not expensive and some challenging play. I did not expect red carpet treatment … A fine traditional course … Rolling hills and vistas … Up north, beautiful and cool.

PRESCOTT LAKES GOLF CLUB

SP-315 E. Smoke Tree Lane, Prescott, 86301, Yavapai County, (928)443-3500, (877)643-3501, 45 miles from Phoenix. **E-mail:** kkrause@m3comp.com. **Web:** www.prescott-lakes.com. **Facility Holes:** 18. **Yards:** 7,216/4,724. **Par:** 72/72. **Course Rating:** 72.7/65.8. **Slope:** 132/117. **Green Fee:** $65/$95. **Cart Fee:** Included in green fee. **Walking Policy:** Unrestricted walking. **Walkability:** 4. **Opened:** 2000. **Architect:** Hale Irwin. **Season:** Year-round. **High:** May-Nov. **To obtain tee times:** Call up to 7 days in advance. **Miscellaneous:** Reduced fees (guests, juniors), range (grass), credit cards (MC, V, AE, D), BF, FF.

★★½ PUEBLO DEL SOL COUNTRY CLUB

SP-2770 St. Andrews Dr., Sierra Vista, 85650, Cochise County, (520)378-6444, 70 miles from Tucson. **E-mail:** pkelly@castle-cooke.com. **Web:** pdscountryclub.com. **Facility Holes:** 18. **Yards:** 7,074/5,896. **Par:** 72/74. **Course Rating:** 73.1/73.1. **Slope:** 128/126. **Green Fee:** $15/$40. **Cart Fee:** $20/Cart. **Walking Policy:** Unrestricted walking. **Walkability:** 1. **Opened:** 1975. **Architect:** Tenneco Engineers. **Season:** Year-round. **High:** Jan.-April. **To obtain tee times:** Call up to 7 days in advance. **Miscellaneous:** Reduced fees (weekdays, twilight, seniors, juniors), metal spikes, range (grass/mats), credit cards (MC, V, D), BF, FF.

★½ PUEBLO EL MIRAGE RESORT

R-11201 N. El Mirage Rd., El Mirage, 85335, Maricopa County, (623)583-0425, 10 miles from Phoenix. **Facility Holes:** 18. **Yards:** 6,596/5,826. **Par:** 72/72. **Course Rating:** 71.1/71.0. **Slope:** 125/117. **Green Fee:** $12/$39. **Cart Fee:** Included in green fee. **Walking Policy:** Walking at certain times. **Walkability:** 2. **Opened:** 1985. **Architect:** Ken Killian/Fuzzy Zoeller. **Season:** Year-round. **High:** Nov.-March. **To obtain tee times:** Call golf shop. **Miscellaneous:** Reduced fees (weekdays, guests, twilight, juniors), metal spikes, range (grass), credit cards (MC, V).

★★★★ RANCHO MANANA GOLF CLUB

R-5734 E. Rancho Manana Blvd., Cave Creek, 85331, Maricopa County, (480)488-0398, 10 miles from Phoenix. **Web:** www.ranchomanana.com. **Facility Holes:** 18. **Yards:** 6,378/5,910. **Par:** 71/71. **Course Rating:** 67.8/68.8. **Slope:** 125/114. **Green Fee:** $45/$145. **Cart Fee:** Included in green fee. **Walking Policy:** Mandatory carts. **Walkability:** 5. **Opened:** 1988. **Architect:** Bill Johnston/Mike Allred. **Season:** Year-round. **High:** Jan.-April. **To obtain tee times:** Call up to 7 days in advance. **Miscellaneous:** Reduced fees (weekdays, twilight, juniors), metal spikes, range (grass), credit cards (MC, V, AE, D), BF, FF.
Reader Comments: I am a dedicated junior golfer and the pros here are the most helpful and friendly you will ever find ... Target golf—narrow fairways—excellent always ... Great Bloody Marys ... Great views ... High desert is better than low ... Course has all types of challenges ... Awesome elevation changes for Phoenix.

RANDOLPH PARK GOLF COURSE

PU-600 S. Alvernon Way, Tucson, 85711, Pima County, (520)791-4161. **Web:** tucsoncitygolf.com. **Facility Holes:** 36. **Green Fee:** $10/$37. **Cart Fee:** $9/Person. **Walking Policy:** Unrestricted walking. **Season:** Year-round. **High:** Oct.-March. **To obtain tee times:** Call up to 6 days in advance. **Miscellaneous:** Reduced fees (weekdays, twilight, seniors, juniors), metal spikes, range (grass/mats), credit cards (MC, V, D), BF, FF.

★★★ DELL ULRICH MUNICIPAL GOLF COURSE (18)

Yards: 6,633/5,270. **Par:** 70/70. **Course Rating:** 70.3/68.8. **Slope:** 119/113. **Walkability:** 3. **Opened:** 1996. **Architect:** Ken Kavanaugh.
Reader Comments: Good muni, nice layout ...Tough course for my legs ... Move the LPGA here, more character and better condition than North ... OK ... Best of Tuscon city courses.

★★★ NORTH COURSE (18)

Yards: 6,863/5,972. **Par:** 72/73. **Course Rating:** 72.5/73.7. **Slope:** 125/124. **Walkability:** 1. **Opened:** 1925. **Architect:** William P. Bell.
Reader Comments: The water hazards eat my golf balls ....The same beautiful Tucson setting for a fraction of the $ ... Great old course ... LPGA plays here ... Best public course I've played ... Still a favorite of mine ... Condition fading a bit.

★★★★½ THE RAVEN G.C. AT SABINO SPRINGS *Service+, Condition, Pace*

PU-9777 E. Sabino Greens Dr., Tucson, 85749, Pima County, (520)749-3636. **E-mail:** ehoffman@intrawest.com. **Web:** www.ravengolf.com. **Facility Holes:** 18. **Yards:** 6,776/4,733. **Par:** 71/71. **Course Rating:** 73.2/66.6. **Slope:** 144/112. **Green Fee:** $55/$175. **Cart Fee:** Included in green fee. **Walking Policy:** Unrestricted walking. **Walkability:** 5. **Opened:** 1996. **Architect:** Robert Trent Jones Jr. **Season:** Year-round. **High:** Jan.-April. **To obtain tee times:** Call up to 30 days in advance. **Miscellaneous:** Reduced fees (twilight, juniors), metal spikes, range (grass), credit cards (MC, V, AE, D, DC), BF, FF.
Notes: Ranked 20th in 2001 Best in State; 7th in 1996 Best New Upscale Courses.
Reader Comments: Best value among "elite" courses in Phoenix-Tucson area during winter season ... Elevation changes make for great vistas and excellent golf holes ... Unbelievable views and some tough, tough holes ... Course was in great shape and tested all aspects of your game ... 18th is a great finish to a great course.

★★★★½ THE RAVEN G.C. AT SOUTH MOUNTAIN *Service+, Condition*

PU-3636 E. Baseline Rd., Phoenix, 85040, Maricopa County, (602)243-3636. **E-mail:** jgunby@intrawest.com. **Web:** ravengolf.com. **Facility Holes:** 18. **Yards:** 7,078/5,759. **Par:** 72/72. **Course Rating:** 73.9/72.9. **Slope:** 133/124. **Green Fee:** $50/$170. **Cart Fee:** Included in green fee. **Walking Policy:** Unrestricted walking. **Walkability:** 2. **Opened:** 1995. **Architect:** David Graham/Gary Panks. **Season:** Year-round. **High:** Jan.-March. **To obtain tee times:** Call up to 30 days in advance. **Miscellaneous:** Reduced fees (weekdays, twilight, juniors), metal spikes, range (grass), credit cards (MC, V, AE, D, DC), BF, FF.
Notes: Ranked 24th in 2001 Best in State.
Reader Comments: Thinking man's course ... Great course ... A good change from the 'usual' desert courses ... Outstanding service, better than at private club ... Greens, fairways immaculate—definitely one of the very best courses in the state ... Close to the airport, great place to play on a day of travel.

ARIZONA

★★★½ RIO RICO RESORT & COUNTRY CLUB
R-1069 Camino Caralampi, Rio Rico, 85648, Santa Cruz County, (520)281-8567, (800)288-4746, 50 miles from Tucson. **Web:** www.rioricoresort.com. **Facility Holes:** 18. **Yards:** 7,119/5,649. **Par:** 72/72. **Course Rating:** 72.9/70.4. **Slope:** 128/126. **Green Fee:** $25/$75. **Cart Fee:** Included in green fee. **Walking Policy:** Mandatory carts. **Walkability:** 2. **Opened:** 1972. **Architect:** Robert Trent Jones. **Season:** Year-round. **High:** Jan.-April. **To obtain tee times:** Call up to 5 days in advance. **Miscellaneous:** Reduced fees (weekdays, guests), range (grass), lodging (189 rooms), credit cards (MC, V, AE, D, DC), BF, FF.
Reader Comments: Best course in southern Arizona, great layout … Well maintained, wide open, with water… Nice place if you stay overnight … 3-hour rounds, good greens … Fast greens, some tight holes, great fun … Good resort course … Hidden treasure.

★★★★ SAN IGNACIO GOLF CLUB
SP-4201 S. Camino Del Sol, Green Valley, 85614, Pima County, (520)648-3468, 25 miles from Tucson. **Web:** www.irigolfgroup.com. **Facility Holes:** 18. **Yards:** 6,704/5,200. **Par:** 72/70.5. **Course Rating:** 71.4/68.7. **Slope:** 135/125. **Green Fee:** $25/$69. **Cart Fee:** Included in green fee. **Walking Policy:** Mandatory carts. **Walkability:** 4. **Opened:** 1989. **Architect:** Arthur Hills. **Season:** Year-round. **High:** Jan.-May. **To obtain tee times:** Call up to 6 days in advance. **Miscellaneous:** Reduced fees (weekdays, guests, twilight, seniors, juniors), range (grass), credit cards (MC, V, AE, D, DC), BF, FF.
Reader Comments: Good course and good facilities … Good grass, well marked … Nicely laid out, par-5 13th is unbelievable! Jacobs Golf School is excellent … Well worth the drive and green fee … Tight course, great value in summer … Green Valley bargain … New staff has great attitude.

★★★ THE SANCTUARY GOLF COURSE AT WESTWORLD
PU-10690 E. Sheena Dr., Scottsdale, 85259, Maricopa County, (480)502-8200, 10 miles from Phoenix. **E-mail:** jay.haffner@suncorgolf.com. **Web:** www.sanctuarygolf.com. **Facility Holes:** 18. **Yards:** 6,696/5,924. **Par:** 71/71. **Course Rating:** 71.7/68.1. **Slope:** 135/118. **Green Fee:** $35/$115. **Cart Fee:** Included in green fee. **Walking Policy:** Unrestricted walking. **Walkability:** 2. **Opened:** 1999. **Architect:** Randy Heckenkemper. **Season:** Year-round. **High:** Feb.-April. **To obtain tee times:** Call up to 30 days in advance. **Miscellaneous:** Reduced fees (weekdays, twilight, juniors), range (grass), caddies, credit cards (MC, V, AE), BF, FF.
Reader Comments: Environmentally sensitive area … Good course, may be overpriced … Power lines nearby … Bad piece of property turns into a good course.

★★½ SANTA RITA GOLF CLUB
SP-16461 Houghton Rd., Corona, 85641, Pima County, (520)762-5620, 6 miles from Tucson. **E-mail:** santaritagolf@aol.com. **Facility Holes:** 18. **Yards:** 6,523/5,400. **Par:** 72/73. **Course Rating:** 70.9/70.9. **Slope:** 125/123. **Green Fee:** $18/$40. **Cart Fee:** $8/Person. **Walking Policy:** Unrestricted walking. **Walkability:** 3. **Opened:** 1962. **Architect:** Red Lawrence. **Season:** Year-round. **High:** Jan.-April. **To obtain tee times:** Call up to 7 days in advance. **Miscellaneous:** Reduced fees (weekdays, twilight, seniors, juniors), metal spikes, range (grass/mats), credit cards (MC, V, AE, D), BF, FF.

SCOTTSDALE SILVERADO GOLF CLUB
R-7605 E. Indian Bend Rd., Scottsdale, 85250, Maricopa County, (480)778-0100, 15 miles from Phoenix. **Facility Holes:** 18. **Yards:** 6,354/5,794. **Par:** 70/70. **Course Rating:** 66.3/65.7. **Slope:** 109/106. **Green Fee:** $22/$59. **Cart Fee:** Included in green fee. **Walking Policy:** Mandatory carts. **Walkability:** 2. **Opened:** 2000. **Architect:** Gilmore Graves. **Season:** Year-round. **To obtain tee times:** Call up to 7 days in advance. **Miscellaneous:** Reduced fees (weekdays, twilight, juniors), metal spikes, credit cards (MC, V, AE), FF.

★★★★ SEDONA GOLF RESORT *Pace*
R-35 Ridge Trail Dr., Sedona, 86351, Yavapai County, (928)284-9355, (877)733-9888, 100 miles from Phoenix. **E-mail:** mikemadore@suncorgolf.com. **Web:** www.suncorgolf.com. **Facility Holes:** 18. **Yards:** 6,646/5,059. **Par:** 71/71. **Course Rating:** 70.3/67.0. **Slope:** 129/114. **Green Fee:** $82/$99. **Cart Fee:** Included in green fee. **Walking Policy:** Unrestricted walking. **Walkability:** 4. **Opened:** 1988. **Architect:** Gary Panks. **Season:** Year-round. **To obtain tee times:** Call up to 60 days in advance. **Miscellaneous:** Reduced fees (twilight, juniors), range (grass), lodging (225 rooms), credit cards (MC, V, AE), BF, FF.
Notes: Ranked 23rd in 2001 Best in State.
Reader Comments: Worth the trip cost … Solid course, AWESOME views … Beautiful setting, with green fairways against red mountains … Range balls included, helpful course rangers … Great clubhouse and staff … Treated like kings … Difficult to keep focused it was so beautiful.

SHADOW MOUNTAIN GOLF CLUB
SP-1105 Irene St., Pearce, 85625, Cochise County, (520)826-3412, 70 miles from Tucson. **Facility Holes:** 18. **Yards:** 6,632/5,876. **Par:** 72/72. **Course Rating:** 71.1/72.3. **Slope:** 126/125.

Green Fee: $10/$17. **Cart Fee:** $17/Cart. **Walking Policy:** Unrestricted walking. **Walkability:** 1. **Opened:** 1960. **Season:** Year-round. **High:** Jan.-May. **To obtain tee times:** Call golf shop. **Miscellaneous:** Reduced fees (twilight, juniors), credit cards (MC, V, AE).

SHERATON EL CONQUISTADOR COUNTRY CLUB
R-10555 N. La Canada, Tucson, 85737, Pima County, (520)544-1800. **Facility Holes:** 36. **Green Fee:** $25/$125. **Cart Fee:** Included in green fee. **Walking Policy:** Mandatory carts. **Opened:** 1984. **Architect:** Greg Nash/Jeff Hardin. **Season:** Year-round. **High:** Dec.-April. **To obtain tee times:** Call up to 60 days in advance. **Miscellaneous:** Reduced fees (guests, twilight, juniors), range (grass), lodging (460 rooms), credit cards (MC, V, AE, D).
★★½ **CANADA COURSE** (18)
Yards: 6,819/5,255. **Par:** 72/72. **Course Rating:** 71.7/69.4. **Slope:** 123/116. **Walkability:** 4.
★★½ **CONQUISTADOR COURSE** (18)
Yards: 6,763/5,323. **Par:** 71/71. **Course Rating:** 71.2/69.5. **Slope:** 123/114. **Walkability:** 3.

★★½ SHERATON SAN MARCOS GOLF CLUB
SP-100 N. Dakota St., Chandler, 85224, Maricopa County, (480)963-3358, 15 miles from Phoenix. **Facility Holes:** 18. **Yards:** 6,551/5,431. **Par:** 72/73. **Course Rating:** 70.0/69.4. **Slope:** 117/112. **Green Fee:** $30/$79. **Cart Fee:** Included in green fee. **Walking Policy:** Walking at certain times. **Walkability:** 4. **Opened:** 1923. **Architect:** Watson. **Season:** Year-round. **High:** Jan.-April. **To obtain tee times:** Call golf shop. **Miscellaneous:** Reduced fees (weekdays, twilight, juniors), range (grass), credit cards (MC, V, AE, D).

★★★½ SILVER CREEK GOLF CLUB
PU-2051 Silver Lake Blvd., Show Low, 85901, Navajo County, (520)537-2744, (800)909-5981, 12 miles from Show Low. **E-mail:** scgc@whitemtns.com. **Web:** www.silvercreekgolfclub.com. **Facility Holes:** 18. **Yards:** 6,813/5,193. **Par:** 71/71. **Course Rating:** 71.7/68.6. **Slope:** 135/127. **Green Fee:** $18/$42. **Cart Fee:** $28/Cart. **Walking Policy:** Unrestricted walking. **Walkability:** 3. **Opened:** 1985. **Architect:** Gary Panks. **Season:** Year-round. **To obtain tee times:** Call up to 3 days in advance. **Miscellaneous:** Reduced fees (weekdays, twilight, seniors, juniors), range (grass), credit cards (MC, V, AE, D), BF, FF.
Reader Comments: Great course, great price ... Probably best value in the state. Greens great condition, lightning fast! ... Out of the way, but worth it ... All you want from tips—even at 6,000 foot elevation ... Par 3s were a challenge.

★★★ SILVERBELL GOLF COURSE
PU-3600 N. Silverbell, Tucson, 85745, Pima County, (520)791-5235. **Facility Holes:** 18. **Yards:** 6,824/5,800. **Par:** 72/73. **Course Rating:** 71.2/72.2. **Slope:** 123/125. **Green Fee:** $17/$32. **Cart Fee:** $9/Person. **Walking Policy:** Unrestricted walking. **Walkability:** 2. **Opened:** 1978. **Architect:** Jack Snyder. **Season:** Year-round. **To obtain tee times:** Call golf shop. **Miscellaneous:** Reduced fees (weekdays, twilight, seniors, juniors), metal spikes, range (grass), credit cards (MC, V, D), BF, FF.
Reader Comments: Flat, friendly course; pumps the ego ... Mediocre, flat, forgiving ... Not a bad course, the price is more than right ... Good muni.

★★½ STARFIRE GOLF CLUB AT SCOTTSDALE COUNTRY CLUB
SP-11500 N. Hayden Rd., Scottsdale, 85260, Maricopa County, (480)948-6000. **E-mail:** golfshop@starfiregolf club.com. **Web:** www.starfiregolfclub.com. **Facility Holes:** 27. **Green Fee:** $29/$89. **Cart Fee:** Included in green fee. **Walking Policy:** Walking at certain times. **Walkability:** 2. **Opened:** 1954. **Architect:** Arnold Palmer/Ed Seay. **Season:** Year-round. **High:** Jan.-April. **To obtain tee times:** Call up to 7 days in advance. **Miscellaneous:** Reduced fees (weekdays, twilight), range (grass). credit cards (MC, V, AE), BF, FF.
NORTH/EAST (18 Combo)
Yards: 6,011/5,096. **Par:** 70/70. **Course Rating:** 68.8/68.9. **Slope:** 120/119.
NORTH/SOUTH (18 Combo)
Yards: 5,598/4,734. **Par:** 68/68. **Course Rating:** 67.6/67.5. **Slope:** 123/115.
SOUTH/EAST (18 Combo)
Yards: 6,093/5,084. **Par:** 70/70. **Course Rating:** 68.9/68.4. **Slope:** 123/118.

★★★★ STARR PASS GOLF CLUB
SP-3645 W. Starr Pass Blvd., Tucson, 85745, Pima County, (520)670-0400, (800)503-2898, 4 miles from Tucson. **Web:** www.starrpasstucson.com. **Facility Holes:** 18. **Yards:** 6,910/5,071. **Par:** 71/71. **Course Rating:** 74.6/70.7. **Slope:** 139/121. **Green Fee:** $48/$125. **Cart Fee:** Included in green fee. **Opened:** 1986. **Architect:** Bob Cupp. **Season:** Year-round. **High:** Jan.-May. **To obtain tee times:** Call golf shop. **Miscellaneous:** Reduced fees (guests, twilight), range (grass), credit cards (MC, V, AE, D).
Reader Comments: A class place with a great driving range ... Tough greens! ... Immaculately groomed ... Worth playing even at the current rate ... Great course, but tight and long ... Have to play well ... True desert course, great pro shop ... No. 15 is awesome! ... Excellent desert course.

★★★★ STONECREEK GOLF CLUB
SP-4435 E. Paradise Village Pkwy. S., Phoenix, 85032, Maricopa County, (602)953-9111.
Facility Holes: 18. **Yards:** 6,839/5,098. **Par:** 71/71. **Course Rating:** 72.6/68.4. **Slope:** 134/118.
Green Fee: $20/$125. **Cart Fee:** Included in green fee. **Walking Policy:** Mandatory carts.
Walkability: 3. **Opened:** 1989. **Architect:** Arthur Hills. **Season:** Year-round. **High:** Jan.-April.
To obtain tee times: Call up to 7 days in advance. **Miscellaneous:** Reduced fees (weekdays,
guests, twilight, juniors), range (grass), credit cards (MC, V, AE, D, DC), BF, FF.
Reader Comments: Liked the creek in play so often … Well-maintained, Stonecreek requires a full
bag of skills … Big, undulating greens, some narrow fairways on an exciting layout … A bargain
even in the more expensive winter season.

★★★★ SUNRIDGE CANYON GOLF CLUB *Condition*
PU-13100 N. SunRidge Dr., Fountain Hills, 85268, Maricopa County, (480)837-5100,
(800)562-5178, 1 mile from Scottsdale. **E-mail:** joel.schafer@suncorgolf.com. **Web:** www.sun-
ridgecanyongolf.com. **Facility Holes:** 18. **Yards:** 6,823/5,141. **Par:** 71/71. **Course Rating:**
73.4/70.1. **Slope:** 140/125. **Green Fee:** $65/$175. **Cart Fee:** Included in green fee. **Walking
Policy:** Mandatory carts. **Walkability:** 4. **Opened:** 1995. **Architect:** Keith Foster. **Season:** Year-
round. **High:** Jan.-April. **To obtain tee times:** Call up to 30 days in advance. **Miscellaneous:**
Reduced fees (juniors), range (grass), credit cards (MC, V, AE), BF, FF.
Reader Comments: Best course we played by far … Canyon golf, and incredible journey … Nice
layout for a residential course … Desert golf, hilly fun … One of the top 3 in Scottsdale … Nice
layout, lots of elevation change … Good in-season value.

★★★½ SUPERSTITION SPRINGS GOLF CLUB
R-6542 E. Baseline Rd., Mesa, 85206, Maricopa County, (480)985-5622, (800)468-7918,
20 miles from Phoenix. **Web:** www.americangolf.com. **Facility Holes:** 18. **Yards:** 7,005/5,328.
Par: 72/72. **Course Rating:** 74.1/70.9. **Slope:** 135/120. **Green Fee:** $30/$125. **Cart Fee:**
Included in green fee. **Walking Policy:** Mandatory carts. **Walkability:** 3. **Opened:** 1986.
Architect: Greg Nash. **Season:** Year-round. **High:** Nov.-March. **To obtain tee times:** Call up to
7 days in advance. **Miscellaneous:** Reduced fees (weekdays, guests, twilight, juniors), metal
spikes, range (grass/mats), credit cards (MC, V, AE, D, DC), BF, FF.
Reader Comments: Tough finishing holes … Super layout, attentive staff … A great course that
would challenge any pro from the tips … The last two holes are world class … First class.

TALKING STICK GOLF CLUB
PU-9998 East Indian Bend Rd., Scottsdale, 85256, Maricopa County, (602)860-2221, 2 miles
from Scottsdale. **Web:** www.troongolf.com. **Facility Holes:** 36. **Green Fee:** $45/$140. **Cart Fee:**
Included in green fee. **Walking Policy:** Unrestricted walking. **Walkability:** 2. **Opened:** 1998.
Architect: Ben Crenshaw/Bill Coore. **Season:** Year-round. **High:** Jan.-May. **To obtain tee times:**
Call up to 60 days in advance. **Miscellaneous:** Reduced fees (weekdays, juniors), metal
spikes, range (grass), credit cards (MC, V, AE), BF, FF.
★★★ NORTH COURSE (18)
Yards: 7,133/5,532. **Par:** 70/70. **Course Rating:** 73.8/70.0. **Slope:** 125/116.
Notes: Golf Digest School site. Ranked 21st in 1999 Best in State.
Reader Comments: Excellent service … Wonderful experience … Wide open fairways … Links
golf, long and challenging … Tremendous service everywhere! Met Charles Barkley hanging out at
the driving range … Another great course from Troon Golf.
★★★★ SOUTH COURSE (18)
Yards: 6,833/5,428. **Par:** 71/71. **Course Rating:** 72.7/69.1. **Slope:** 129/118.
Notes: Golf Digest school site.
Reader Comments: Easier than North Course … Excellent test of golf, fair, well-conditioned …
Traditional course … Will get better as trees grow … More traditional than North, but liked it better.

★★★½ TATUM RANCH GOLF CLUB
SP-29888 N. Tatum Ranch Dr., Cave Creek, 85331, Maricopa County, (480)585-2399,
25 miles from Phoenix. **Web:** tatumranchgc.com. **Facility Holes:** 18. **Yards:** 6,856/5,081.
Par: 72/72. **Course Rating:** 71.8/69.3. **Slope:** 127/115. **Green Fee:** $45/$150. **Cart Fee:**
Included in green fee. **Walking Policy:** Mandatory carts. **Walkability:** 2. **Opened:** 1987.
Architect: Bob Cupp. **Season:** Year-round. **High:** Jan.-April. **To obtain tee times:** Call up to
7 days in advance. **Miscellaneous:** Reduced fees (weekdays, guests, twilight, juniors),
metal spikes, range (grass), credit cards (MC, V, AE, D, DC), BF, FF.
Reader Comments: Great test … Excellent course … Extra friendly staff … Don't want to drive it
bad here.

TONTO VERDE GOLF CLUB
SP-18401 El Circulo Dr., Rio Verde, 85263, Maricopa County, (480)471-2710, 20 miles from
Scottsdale. **E-mail:** dogtontoverde@hotmail.com. **Web:** tontoverdegolfaz.com. **Facility Holes:**
36. **Green Fee:** $50/$140. **Cart Fee:** Included in green fee. **Season:** Year-round. **High:** Dec.-
April. **To obtain tee times:** Call up to 7 days in advance. **Miscellaneous:** Reduced fees

(guests), range (grass), credit cards (MC, V, AE, D), BF, FF.

★★★½ **PEAKS COURSE** (18)
Yards: 6,736/5,376. **Par:** 72/72. **Course Rating:** 71.1/70.8. **Slope:** 132/124. **Walking Policy:** Mandatory carts. **Walkability:** 2. **Opened:** 1994. **Architect:** David Graham/Gary Panks.
Reader Comments: Tight fairways … Firm course … Very playable, fun … Long way from Scottsdale … Great fairways; ordinary layout … Excellent service … Great desert layout and enjoyable holes … Nice staff … Pretty desert course. Too narrow, with fairways sloped toward desert edges. Great place to eat … Great views.

★★★★ **RANCH COURSE** (18)
Yards: 6,988/5,788. **Par:** 72/72. **Course Rating:** 73.1/72.2. **Slope:** 133/127. **Walking Policy:** Walking at certain times. **Opened:** 1998. **Architect:** Gary Panks.
Reader Comments: Good traditional golf course with very good clubhouse facilities … Scenic, short and easy to score well … Great views, easy to get on, great 18-hole putting course.

★★★ **TORRES BLANCAS GOLF CLUB**
PU-3233 S. Abrego, Green Valley, 85614, Pima County, (520)625-5200, 20 miles from Tucson. **Facility Holes:** 18. **Yards:** 6,894/5,077. **Par:** 72/72. **Course Rating:** 71.6/67.8. **Slope:** 125/119. **Green Fee:** $19/$60. **Cart Fee:** Included in green fee. **Walking Policy:** Mandatory carts. **Walkability:** 2. **Opened:** 1996. **Architect:** O'Campo,Fernandez,Trevino. **Season:** Year-round. **High:** Jan.-March. **To obtain tee times:** Call up to 7 days in advance. **Miscellaneous:** Reduced fees (seniors), range (grass), credit cards (MC, V, AE), BF, FF.
Reader Comments: Pleasant design. Fast greens. Good kitchen … A good place to work out the rust … Getting better every year … Heavy play, easy course, good personnel … A nice course, tough on a windy day.

TOURNAMENT PLAYERS CLUB OF SCOTTSDALE
R-17020 N. Hayden Rd., Scottsdale, 85255, Maricopa County, (480)585-3939. **Web:** www.pgatour.com. **Facility Holes:** 36. **Walkability:** 2. **Architect:** Tom Weiskopf/Jay Morrish. **Season:** Year-round. **To obtain tee times:** Call golf shop. **Miscellaneous:** Metal spikes, range (grass/mats), credit cards (MC, V, AE).

★★★ **DESERT COURSE** (18)
Yards: 6,552/4,715. **Par:** 71/71. **Course Rating:** 71.4/66.3. **Slope:** 112/109. **Green Fee:** $31/$41. **Walking Policy:** Unrestricted walking. **Opened:** 1987. **High:** Oct.-April. **Miscellaneous:** Reduced fees (twilight, seniors, juniors).
Reader Comments: Short, but challenging enough to test course management skills and short irons … Overshadowed by the Stadium Course, but this is almost as great, and much easier on the wallet … Best value in Scottsdale.

★★★½ **STADIUM COURSE** (18)
Yards: 7,509/5,567. **Par:** 71/71. **Course Rating:** 73.9/71.6. **Slope:** 131/122. **Green Fee:** $62/$149. **Cart Fee:** $16/Person. **Opened:** 1986. **High:** Jan.-April. **Miscellaneous:** Reduced fees (twilight).
Reader Comments: The course is worth playing … Greens are great and while some complain about slow play we played it in four hours … A little pricey but hey this is where the pros play … Great finishing holes … Great staff, from director of golf down … Play in the summer, not worth winter rate.

★★½ **TRINI ALVAREZ EL RIO MUNICIPAL GOLF COURSE**
PU-1400 W. Speedway Blvd., Tucson, 85745, Pima County, (520)791-4229, (520)791-4336. **Facility Holes:** 18. **Yards:** 6,316/5,645. **Par:** 70/73. **Course Rating:** 69.7/72.3. **Slope:** 121/123. **Green Fee:** $11/$27. **Cart Fee:** $16/Cart. **Walking Policy:** Unrestricted walking. **Walkability:** 1. **Opened:** 1936. **Architect:** William P. Bell. **Season:** Year-round. **High:** Nov.-April. **To obtain tee times:** Call golf shop. **Miscellaneous:** Reduced fees (weekdays, twilight, seniors, juniors), metal spikes, range (grass), credit cards (MC, V, D).
Special Notes: Formerly El Rio Golf Course.

TROON NORTH GOLF CLUB
SP-10320 E. Dynamite Blvd., Scottsdale, 85255, Maricopa County, (602)585-5300. **Web:** www.troonnorthgolf.com. **Facility Holes:** 36. **Green Fee:** $75/$240. **Cart Fee:** Included in green fee. **Walking Policy:** Unrestricted walking. **Season:** Year-round. **High:** Jan.-May. **To obtain tee times:** Call up to 30 days in advance. **Miscellaneous:** Reduced fees (juniors), metal spikes, range (grass), credit cards (MC, V, AE), FF.

★★★★½ **MONUMENT COURSE** (18) *Condition+*
Yards: 7,008/5,050. **Par:** 72/72. **Course Rating:** 73.3/68.5. **Slope:** 147/117. **Walkability:** 4. **Opened:** 1990. **Architect:** Tom Weiskopf/Jay Morrish.
Notes: Golf Digest School site. Ranked 91st in 1997-98 America's 100 Greatest; 5th in 2001 Best in State; 10th in 1996 America's Top 75 Upscale Courses.
Reader Comments: Every hole a postcard, tight, tough course … Excellent track, but overpriced … Pinnacle Course has better views … Target course that is not forgiving to slicers or hookers … Up there with the best … Great holes, easy walk … Excellent service, friendly staff … The ultimate in upscale public golf.

ARIZONA

★★★★½ **PINNACLE COURSE** (18) *Condition*
Yards: 7,044/4,980. **Par:** 72/72. **Course Rating:** 73.4/68.6. **Slope:** 147/120. **Walkability:** 5.
Opened: 1996. **Architect:** Tom Weiskopf.
Notes: Golf Digest School site. Ranked 16th in 2001 Best in State; 2nd in 1996 Best New
Upscale Courses.
Reader Comments: Outstanding condition and superb views ... The prettiest course I have ever
played ... About as good as it gets for golf ... The better of the two Troon courses ... Super hard
target course, excellent ... Great greens ... Great target course ... Expensive, but like golf heaven!
... Best desert course in the U.S.

★★★½ **TUBAC GOLF RESORT**
R-One Otero Rd., Tubac, 85646, Santa Cruz County, (520)398-2021, (800)848-7893,
35 miles from Tucson. **E-mail:** tgr@theriver.com. **Web:** www.tubacgolfresort.com. **Facility
Holes:** 18. **Yards:** 6,776/5,384. **Par:** 71/71. **Course Rating:** 72.4/70.5. **Slope:** 128/120. **Green
Fee:** $29/$70. **Cart Fee:** Included in green fee. **Walking Policy:** Walking at certain times.
Walkability: 3. **Opened:** 1960. **Architect:** Red Lawrence. **Season:** Year-round. **High:** Jan.-April.
To obtain tee times: Call golf shop. **Miscellaneous:** Reduced fees (guests, twilight), range
(grass), lodging (46 rooms), credit cards (MC, V, AE, D), BF, FF.
Reader Comments: Fun course to play ... Easy layout ... Short, but very tough greens ... If you
want a quiet getaway, this is it, easy to walk to play golf, eat and sleep ... Monster par 3s.

★★★ **VALLE VISTA COUNTRY CLUB**
SP-9686 Concho Dr, Kingman, 86401, Mohave County, (520)757-8744. **Facility Holes:** 18.
Yards: 6,266/5,585. **Par:** 72/72. **Course Rating:** 68.3/68.2. **Slope:** 112/115. **Green Fee:**
$15/$17. **Opened:** 1972. **Architect:** Fred Bolton. **Season:** Year-round. **To obtain tee times:**
Call golf shop. **Miscellaneous:** Metal spikes.
Reader Comments: Enjoyable ... Wonderful atmosphere ... Pretty desert setting ... Nondescript,
short, windy ... Very good layout ... Beautiful desert views ... Greens nicely contoured.

VENTANA CANYON GOLF & RACQUET CLUB
R-6200 N. Clubhouse Lane, Tucson, 85750, Pima County, (520)577-4061, (800)828-5701.
Facility Holes: 36. **Green Fee:** $99/$199. **Cart Fee:** Included in green fee. **Walking Policy:**
Mandatory carts. **Walkability:** 3. **Architect:** Tom Fazio. **Season:** Year-round. **High:** Jan.-April.
To obtain tee times: Call golf shop. **Miscellaneous:** Reduced fees (guests, twilight), range
(grass), lodging (50 rooms), credit cards (MC, V, AE, D, DC), BF, FF.
★★★★ **CANYON COURSE** (18) *Condition, Pace*
Yards: 6,819/4,919. **Par:** 72/72. **Course Rating:** 72.6/70.2. **Slope:** 140/119. **Opened:** 1987.
Reader Comments: Not a true desert course ... More grass than cacti and desert ... Good layout,
challenging ... If I could only play one course, this would be it ... Golf at its very best ... Views and
condition great ... Get your driver out ... Fantastic layout.
★★★★½ **MOUNTAIN COURSE** (18)
Yards: 6,907/4,709. **Par:** 72/72. **Course Rating:** 73.0/70.2. **Slope:** 147/114. **Opened:** 1984.
Notes: Ranked 20th in 1999 Best in State.
Reader Comments: A good resort course ... Excellent, difficult but well maintained ... Tight ...
Excellent layout, worth the cost ... One of Arizona's must-plays ... Don't be fooled—everything
breaks away from the mountains ... Spectacular par-3 across a canyon.

WESTBROOK VILLAGE GOLF CLUB
SP-19260 N. Westbrook Pkwy., Peoria, 85382, Maricopa County, (623)566-3439. **Facility
Holes:** 36. **Green Fee:** $35/$74. **Cart Fee:** Included in green fee. **Walking Policy:** Unrestricted
walking. **Walkability:** 2. **Season:** Year-round. **High:** Dec.-April. **To obtain tee times:** Call golf
shop. **Miscellaneous:** Range (grass), credit cards (MC, V).
★★★ **LAKES COURSE** (18)
Yards: 6,412/5,370. **Par:** 71/71. **Course Rating:** 69.9/69.5. **Slope:** 120/111. **Opened:** 1980.
Architect: Ted Robinson.
Reader Comments: Several great holes ... A nice course always in great shape ... The last two
holes (the par-3 along Union Hills and the par-5 18th) are memorable—perhaps the best two
finishing holes in Arizona.
★★★ **VISTAS COURSE** (18)
Yards: 6,544/5,225. **Par:** 72/73. **Course Rating:** 70.3/68.2. **Slope:** 121/109. **Opened:** 1990.
Reader Comments: Links-style course ... Some short holes ... The 14th hole is a beautiful
signature hole ... Well kept—lots of play ... Several great holes.
Special Notes: Formerly The Vistas Club.

★★½ **WESTERN SKIES GOLF CLUB**
PU-1245 E. Warner Rd., Gilbert, 85234, Maricopa County, (480)545-8542, 20 miles from
Phoenix. **Facility Holes:** 18. **Yards:** 6,673/5,639. **Par:** 72/72. **Course Rating:** 70.0/68.6. **Slope:**
120/116. **Green Fee:** $20/$50. **Cart Fee:** Included in green fee. **Walking Policy:** Unrestricted
walking. **Walkability:** 3. **Opened:** 1992. **Architect:** Brian Whitcomb. **Season:** Year-round.

High: Jan.-March. **To obtain tee times:** Call golf shop. **Miscellaneous:** Reduced fees (twilight), metal spikes, range (grass), credit cards (MC, V, AE).

WHIRLWIND GOLF CLUB

R-5692 W. North Loop Rd., Chandler, 85226, Maricopa County, (480)940-1500, 12 miles from Phoenix. **Web:** www.whirlwindgolf.com. **Facility Holes:** 18. **Yards:** 7,017/5,523. **Par:** 72/72. **Course Rating:** 72.8/71.4. **Slope:** 131/121. **Green Fee:** $45/$145. **Cart Fee:** Included in green fee. **Walking Policy:** Unrestricted walking. **Walkability:** 2. **Opened:** 2000. **Architect:** Gary Panks. **Season:** Year-round. **High:** Nov.-April. **To obtain tee times:** Call up to 7 days in advance. **Miscellaneous:** Reduced fees (weekdays, twilight, seniors, juniors), metal spikes, range (grass), credit cards (MC, V, AE), BF, FF.

THE WIGWAM GOLF & COUNTRY CLUB

R-451 N. Litchfield Rd., Litchfield Park, 85340, Maricopa County, (602)272-4653, (800)909-4224, 20 miles from Phoenix. **Facility Holes:** 54. **Green Fee:** $37/$120. **Cart Fee:** Included in green fee. **Walking Policy:** Mandatory carts. **Walkability:** 1. **Season:** Year-round. **To obtain tee times:** Call up to 5 days in advance. **Miscellaneous:** Reduced fees (guests), range (grass/mats), lodging (351 rooms), credit cards (MC, V, AE), FF.

★★★ **BLUE COURSE** (18)
Yards: 6,130/5,235. **Par:** 70/70. **Course Rating:** 67.9/69.3. **Slope:** 122/115. **Opened:** 1961. **Architect:** Robert Trent Jones.
Reader Comments: Short but challenging … Great courses on beautiful resort property … Old course—reminds me of a city park … Played all three Wigwam courses … A great golf experience with very good accommodations and food.

★★★ **GOLD COURSE** (18)
Yards: 7,021/5,737. **Par:** 72/72. **Course Rating:** 74.1/72.8. **Slope:** 133/126. **Opened:** 1961. **Architect:** Robert Trent Jones.
Reader Comments: Tough course in 30-mile wind … Very challenging—lots of sand—bring your shovel … Great course … One of the best ever.

★★★ **RED COURSE** (18)
Yards: 6,867/5,821. **Par:** 72/72. **Course Rating:** 72.4/72.4. **Slope:** 126/118. **Opened:** 1974. **Architect:** Red Lawrence.
Reader Comments: Good resort … Great finishing hole … Neat little course for the average player … My favorite of the three at Wigwam … Tough greens … Really fun, forgiving course. Pretty … Traditional layout … Most interesting of three at Wigwam.

★★★★ WILDFIRE AT DESERT RIDGE GOLF CLUB

PU-5225 E. Pathfinder Dr, Phoenix, 85054, Maricopa County, (480)473-0205, (888)705-7775, 10 miles from Phoenix. **E-mail:** kevinstockford@marriott.com. **Web:** www.wildfiregolf.com. **Facility Holes:** 18. **Yards:** 7,170/5,505. **Par:** 72/72. **Course Rating:** 73.3/70.1. **Slope:** 135/116. **Green Fee:** $50/$135. **Cart Fee:** Included in green fee. **Walking Policy:** Unrestricted walking. **Walkability:** 3. **Opened:** 1997. **Architect:** Arnold Palmer. **Season:** Year-round. **High:** Jan.-March. **To obtain tee times:** Call up to 30 days in advance. **Miscellaneous:** Reduced fees (weekdays, twilight), metal spikes, range (grass), credit cards (MC, V, AE, D), BF, FF.
Reader Comments: Good course, I liked it … Target golf but forgiving fairways … Awesome greens, wonderful variety of golf holes … Arizona's laws on irrigation have made designers think … Worth the trip to Phoenix just to play … Extremely quick greens.

★★★½ BELVEDERE COUNTRY CLUB
SP-385 Belvedere Dr., Hot Springs, 71901, Garland County, (501)623-2305. **Facility Holes:** 18. **Yards:** 6,800/5,400. **Par:** 72/72. **Course Rating:** 72.8/72.8. **Slope:** 134/132. **Green Fee:** $55/$65. **Walking Policy:** Unrestricted walking. **Walkability:** 4. **Opened:** 1963. **Architect:** Tom Clark. **Season:** Year-round. **High:** April-Sept. **To obtain tee times:** Call golf shop. **Miscellaneous:** Range (grass), lodging (20 rooms), credit cards (MC, V), BF, FF.
Reader Comments: Best in Hot Springs. You can't go wrong here ... Everything is first class ... Tough.

★★½ BEN GEREN REGIONAL PARK GOLF COURSE
PU-7200 S. Zero, Fort Smith, 72903, Sebastian County, (501)646-5301. **Facility Holes:** 27. **Green Fee:** $13/$17. **Cart Fee:** $24/Cart. **Walking Policy:** Unrestricted walking. **Walkability:** 2. **Opened:** 1972. **Architect:** Marvin Ferguson/Jeff Brauer. **Season:** Year-round. **To obtain tee times:** Call golf shop. **Miscellaneous:** Reduced fees (weekdays, twilight, seniors, juniors), range (grass/mats), credit cards (MC, V), BF, FF.
MAGNOLIA/WILLOW (18 Combo)
Yards: 6,782/5,023. **Par:** 72/73. **Course Rating:** 71.7/67.7. **Slope:** 120/109.
SILO HILL/MAGNOLIA (18 Combo)
Yards: 6,840/5,347. **Par:** 72/74. **Course Rating:** 69.3/68.5. **Slope:** 114/112.
SILO HILL/WILLOW (18 Combo)
Yards: 6,812/5,126. **Par:** 72/73. **Course Rating:** 69.3/68.5. **Slope:** 114/112.

★★★★½ BIG CREEK G. & C.C. *Service+, Value+, Condition, Pace+*
SP-452 Country Club Dr., Mountain Home, 72653, Baxter County, (870)425-8815, 120 miles from Little Rock. **E-mail:** langz@mtnhome.com. **Web:** www.membership@bigcreekgolf.com. **Facility Holes:** 18. **Yards:** 7,320/5,068. **Par:** 72/72. **Course Rating:** 75.1/69.7. **Slope:** 133/120. **Green Fee:** $45/$55. **Cart Fee:** Included in green fee. **Walking Policy:** Walking at certain times. **Walkability:** 3. **Opened:** 2000. **Architect:** Tom Clark. **Season:** Year-round. **High:** March-Nov. **To obtain tee times:** Call up to 180 days in advance. **Miscellaneous:** Reduced fees (weekdays), range (grass), credit cards (MC, V, AE, D), BF, FF.
Reader Comments: Outstanding ... This is a most pleasurable course to play, from the time your bag is picked up until the time they take it back to your car... You can see the entire course from almost any location ... Difficult, beautiful, elegant, professional, great service.

BURNS PARK GOLF COURSE
PU-30 Championship Dr., North Little Rock, 72115, Pulaski County, (501)758-5800, 10 miles from Little Rock. **Facility Holes:** 36. **Green Fee:** $9/$14. **Cart Fee:** $24/Cart. **Walking Policy:** Unrestricted walking. **Walkability:** 5. **Season:** Year-round. **High:** March-Nov. **To obtain tee times:** Call up to 4 days in advance. **Miscellaneous:** Reduced fees (twilight, seniors, juniors), range (grass), BF, FF.
★★ **CHAMPIONSHIP COURSE** (18)
Yards: 6,450/4,900. **Par:** 71/71. **Course Rating:** 69.7/67.7. **Slope:** 116/114. **Opened:** 1964. **Architect:** Joe Finger/Steve Ralston. **Miscellaneous:** Credit cards (MC, V, AE).
★★ **TOURNAMENT COURSE** (18)
Yards: 5,710/5,400. **Par:** 70/70. **Course Rating:** 65.1/70.8. **Slope:** 102/117. **Opened:** 1991. **Architect:** Joe Finger. **Miscellaneous:** Credit cards (MC, V, AE, D).

★★★½ CHEROKEE VILLAGE GOLF CLUB
R-5 Laguna Dr., Cherokee Village, 72529, Fulton County, (870)257-2555, 120 miles from Little Rock. **E-mail:** dwebb@poKynet.com. **Facility Holes:** 36. **Yards:** 7,058/5,270. **Par:** 72/72. **Course Rating:** 73.5/70.4. **Slope:** 128/116. **Green Fee:** $16/$27. **Cart Fee:** $11/Person. **Walking Policy:** Walking at certain times. **Walkability:** 4. **Opened:** 1972. **Architect:** Edmund Ault. **Season:** Year-round. **High:** May-Oct. **To obtain tee times:** Call golf shop. **Miscellaneous:** Reduced fees (juniors), range (grass), credit cards (MC, V), BF, FF.
Reader Comments: By far the finest course in immediate area ... Pro shop very economical, greens great, poor sand traps ... Not bad for a rural retirement community ... A very nice course. The facilities are very good. I will go back.
Special Notes: Also has a private North Course.

★½ THE CREEKS GOLF COURSE
PU-1499 S. Main, Cave Springs, 72718, Benton County, (501)248-1000, 1 mile from Fayetteville. **Web:** www.realark.com/creeks. **Facility Holes:** 18. **Yards:** 6,009/5,031. **Par:** 71/71. **Course Rating:** 67.5/64.2. **Slope:** 111/104. **Green Fee:** $18/$25. **Cart Fee:** $20/Cart. **Walking Policy:** Unrestricted walking. **Walkability:** 2. **Opened:** 1990. **Architect:** Reed & Hughes. **Season:** Year-round. **To obtain tee times:** Call up to 1 day in advance. **Miscellaneous:** Reduced fees (weekdays, twilight, seniors, juniors), range (grass), credit cards (MC, V, AE), BF, FF.

ARKANSAS

★★½ DAWN HILL GOLF & RACQUET CLUB
R-R-R. No.1 Dawn Hill Rd., Siloam Springs, 72761, Benton County, (501)524-4838, (800)423-3786, 35 miles from Fayetteville. **Facility Holes:** 18. **Yards:** 6,852/5,330. **Par:** 72/73. **Course Rating:** 71.3/69.1. **Slope:** 114/110. **Green Fee:** $20/$22. **Cart Fee:** $10/Person. **Walking Policy:** Walking at certain times. **Walkability:** 2. **Opened:** 1966. **Architect:** Ralph Jones. **Season:** Year-round. **High:** May-Oct. **To obtain tee times:** Call golf shop. **Miscellaneous:** Reduced fees (twilight), range (grass), credit cards (MC, V, AE, D).

★★½ DEGRAY LAKE RESORT STATE PARK GOLF COURSE
PU-2027 State Park Entrance Rd., Bismarck, 71929, Hot Spring County, (501)865-2807, (800)737-8355, 25 miles from Hot Springs. **Facility Holes:** 18. **Yards:** 6,930/5,731. **Par:** 72/72. **Course Rating:** 72.4/71.8. **Slope:** 134/123. **Green Fee:** $13/$15. **Cart Fee:** $18/Cart. **Walking Policy:** Unrestricted walking. **Walkability:** 3. **Opened:** 1977. **Season:** Year-round. **High:** May-Sept. **To obtain tee times:** Call up to 365 days in advance. **Miscellaneous:** Reduced fees (weekdays, twilight, seniors), range (grass/mats), credit cards (MC, V, AE, D), FF.

★★ DIAMOND HILLS COUNTRY CLUB
SP-Rte. 7 N. Diamond Blvd., Diamond City, 72630, Boone County, (870)422-7613, 35 miles from Branson. **Facility Holes:** 18. **Yards:** 6,311/5,491. **Par:** 69/72. **Course Rating:** 69.7/71.1. **Slope:** 125/115. **Green Fee:** $20. **Cart Fee:** $20/Cart. **Walking Policy:** Unrestricted walking. **Walkability:** 2. **Opened:** 1971. **Architect:** Maury Bell. **Season:** Year-round. **High:** July-Aug. **To obtain tee times:** Call golf shop. **Miscellaneous:** Metal spikes, range (grass), credit cards (MC, V), FF.

EAGLE CREST GOLF COURSE
PU-3926 Golf Course Dr., Alma, 72921, Crawford County, (501)632-8857, (888)966-4653, 15 miles from Fort Smith. **E-mail:** eaglecrest@alltel.net. **Web:** www.golfeaglecrest.com. **Facility Holes:** 18. **Yards:** 6,869/5,254. **Par:** 71/71. **Course Rating:** 73.3/70.4. **Slope:** 132/117. **Green Fee:** $27/$37. **Cart Fee:** Included in green fee. **Walking Policy:** Unrestricted walking. **Walkability:** 4. **Opened:** 1997. **Architect:** Mark Hayes. **Season:** Year-round. **To obtain tee times:** Call up to 4 days in advance. **Miscellaneous:** Reduced fees (weekdays, twilight, seniors, juniors), range (grass), credit cards (MC, V, AE, D, DC, CB), BF, FF.

★★ FOXWOOD COUNTRY CLUB
SP-701 Foxwood Dr., Jacksonville, 72076, Pulaski County, (501)982-1254, 15 miles from North Little Rock. **Facility Holes:** 18. **Yards:** 6,413/5,225. **Par:** 72/72. **Course Rating:** 69.8/69.2. **Slope:** 110/111. **Green Fee:** $10/$17. **Cart Fee:** $16/Cart. **Walking Policy:** Walking at certain times. **Walkability:** 1. **Opened:** 1975. **Season:** Year-round. **High:** April-Oct. **To obtain tee times:** Call golf shop. **Miscellaneous:** Reduced fees (seniors, juniors), range (grass), credit cards (MC, V, AE, D).

★★★★½ GLENWOOD COUNTRY CLUB
PU-584 Hwy. 70 East, Glenwood, 71943, Pike County, (870)356-4422, (800)833-3110, 32 miles from Hot Springs. **E-mail:** gcc@ipa.net. **Web:** www.glenwoodcountryclub.com. **Facility Holes:** 18. **Yards:** 6,550/5,076. **Par:** 72/72. **Course Rating:** 70.8/64.1. **Slope:** 128/114. **Green Fee:** $19/$29. **Cart Fee:** $20/Cart. **Walking Policy:** Unrestricted walking. **Walkability:** 4. **Opened:** 1994. **Architect:** Bobby McGee. **Season:** Year-round. **To obtain tee times:** Call golf shop. **Miscellaneous:** Reduced fees (weekdays, guests, twilight, seniors), range (grass), lodging (12 rooms), credit cards (MC, V, AE, D), FF.
Reader Comments: Excellent value. Fun to play … Great course … Tucked in the wilderness … A must-play course. The par 3s were beautiful with water surrounding 2 of them. The price was incredible … Best bargain, great course, beautiful setting.

THE GOLF CLUB AT VALLEY VIEW
PU-11520 Clubhouse Pkwy., Farmington, 72730, Washington County, (501)267-1096, 10 miles from Fayetteville. **E-mail:** golfvalleyview@aol.com. **Facility Holes:** 18. **Yards:** 7,046/4,757. **Par:** 72/72. **Course Rating:** 73.3/66.6. **Slope:** 137/113. **Green Fee:** $15/$35. **Cart Fee:** $10/Person. **Walking Policy:** Unrestricted walking. **Walkability:** 3. **Opened:** 2000. **Architect:** Hurdzan/Fry. **Season:** Year-round. **High:** April-June. **To obtain tee times:** Call up to 5 days in advance. **Miscellaneous:** Reduced fees (twilight), range (grass), credit cards (MC, V, AE, D), BF, FF.

★★ HARRISON COUNTRY CLUB
SP-Hwy 62-65 N., Harrison, 72601, Boone County, (870)741-4947. **Facility Holes:** 18. **Yards:** 6,066/5,049. **Par:** 70/72. **Course Rating:** 69.3/69.7. **Slope:** 121/122. **Green Fee:** $23/$27. **Cart Fee:** $19/Cart. **Walking Policy:** Unrestricted walking. **Walkability:** 4. **Opened:** 1920. **Season:** Year-round. **High:** March-Oct. **To obtain tee times:** Call golf shop. **Miscellaneous:** Reduced fees (twilight), range (grass/mats), credit cards (MC, V).

★★ HINDMAN PARK GOLF COURSE
PU-60 Brookview Dr., Little Rock, 72209, Pulaski County, (501)565-6450. **Facility Holes:** 36.
Yards: 6,393/4,349. **Par:** 72/72. **Course Rating:** 68.9/68.6. **Slope:** 109/121. **Green Fee:** $8/$10.
Cart Fee: $18/Cart. **Walking Policy:** Unrestricted walking. **Walkability:** 3. **Opened:** 1969.
Architect: Dave Bennett/Leon Howard. **Season:** Year-round. **High:** April-Sept. **To obtain tee
times:** Call golf shop. **Miscellaneous:** Reduced fees (twilight, seniors, juniors), metal spikes,
range (grass), credit cards (MC, V, D), BF, FF.
Special Notes: Also has an 18-hole War Memorial Golf Course.

HOT SPRINGS COUNTRY CLUB
R-101 Country Club Dr., Hot Springs, 71901, Garland County, (501)624-2661, 60 miles from
Little Rock. **Facility Holes:** 45. **Green Fee:** $95. **Cart Fee:** Included in green fee. **Walking
Policy:** Unrestricted walking. **Season:** Year-round. **High:** March-Nov. **To obtain tee times:** Call
golf shop. **Miscellaneous:** Reduced fees (guests), range (grass/mats), credit cards (MC, V,
AE), FF.
★★★★ ARLINGTON COURSE (18)
Yards: 6,646/6,206. **Par:** 72/74. **Course Rating:** 73.9/75.6. **Slope:** 127/137. **Walkability:** 4.
Opened: 1932. **Architect:** William H. Diddel.
Notes: Ranked 7th in 2001 Best in State.
Reader Comments: Recent Ben Crenshaw renovation, lots of play … A nice surprise … Varied
shotmaking needed … Deep bunkers and fast greens … Pleasing to the eye … Very nice …
Beautiful layout, long.
★★★ MAJESTIC COURSE (18)
Yards: 6,715/5,541. **Par:** 72/72. **Course Rating:** 72.7/70.9. **Slope:** 131/121. **Walkability:** 2.
Opened: 1908. **Architect:** Willie Park Jr.
Reader Comments: Greens were fantastic. Very playable course for golfers who are not long
hitters … Traditional old 1908 course, a classic.
Special Notes: Also has a 9-hole Pineview Course.

★★ LONGHILLS GOLF CLUB
SP-327 Hwy. 5 N., Benton, 72018, Saline County, (501)316-3000, 9 miles from Little Rock.
E-mail: LHPRO@aol.com. **Facility Holes:** 18. **Yards:** 6,539/5,350. **Par:** 72/73. **Course Rating:**
70.2/70.5. **Slope:** 116/114. **Green Fee:** $16/$20. **Cart Fee:** $18/Cart. **Walking Policy:**
Unrestricted walking. **Walkability:** 3. **Opened:** 1955. **Architect:** William T. Martin. **Season:**
Year-round. **High:** April-Oct. **To obtain tee times:** Call golf shop. **Miscellaneous:** Reduced fees
(juniors), range (grass), credit cards (MC, V), FF.

★★★★½ MOUNTAIN RANCH GOLF CLUB
R-820 Lost Creek Pkwy., Fairfield Bay, 72088, Van Buren County, (501)884-3400, 84 miles
from Little Rock. **E-mail:** markbrouwer@linkscorp.com. **Web:** www.mountainranchgolf.com.
Facility Holes: 18. **Yards:** 6,780/5,325. **Par:** 72/72. **Course Rating:** 71.8/69.8. **Slope:** 129/121.
Green Fee: $30/$50. **Cart Fee:** $12/Person. **Walking Policy:** Walking at certain times.
Walkability: 4. **Opened:** 1983. **Architect:** Edmund B. Ault. **Season:** Year-round. **High:** April-Oct.
To obtain tee times: Call golf shop. **Miscellaneous:** Reduced fees (weekdays, guests, twilight),
metal spikes, range (grass/mats), credit cards (MC, V, AE, D), BF, FF.
Reader Comments: In the Ozarks … Great track … Great Edmond Ault mountain course, tough …
Tough layout, spectacular design … Very nice course and staff. Challenging, playable and
affordable. Friendly marshals helped on blind tee shots … In the top-10 courses in Arkansas.
Outstanding.

★★★½ PRAIRIE CREEK COUNTRY CLUB
M-Hwy. 12 E.,1585 Rountree Dr., Rogers, 72757, Benton County, (501)925-2414, 100 miles
from Tulsa, OK. **Facility Holes:** 18. **Yards:** 6,707/5,599. **Par:** 72/77. **Course Rating:** 73.1/72.6.
Slope: 135/120. **Green Fee:** $15/$17. **Cart Fee:** $20/Person. **Walking Policy:** Unrestricted
walking. **Walkability:** 2. **Opened:** 1968. **Architect:** Joe Sanders. **Season:** Year-round. **High:**
June-Aug. **To obtain tee times:** Call golf shop. **Miscellaneous:** Reduced fees (weekdays,
guests, twilight), range (grass), BF, FF.
Reader Comments: Tough, but fair. Course has two separate nines. Front is on top of hill. Bottom
nine is in valley with nice creek … If you score well here, you can play anywhere and do well …
Small but excellent bent-grass greens … Very enjoyable. I'm ready to go back.

★ RAZORBACK PARK GOLF COURSE
PU-2514 W. Lori Dr., Fayetteville, 72704, Washington County, (501)443-5862. **Facility Holes:**
18. **Yards:** 6,622/5,620. **Par:** 72/72. **Course Rating:** 66.9/71.5. **Slope:** 108/110. **Green Fee:** $11.
Cart Fee: $17/Cart. **Walking Policy:** Unrestricted walking. **Walkability:** 2. **Opened:** 1959.
Architect: E.H. Sonneman/David Taylor. **Season:** Year-round. **High:** May-Sept. **To obtain tee
times:** Call golf shop. **Miscellaneous:** Credit cards (MC, V, D).

★★★ REBSAMEN PARK GOLF COURSE
PU-3400 Rebsamen Park Rd., Little Rock, 72202, Pulaski County, (501)666-7965. **Facility Holes:** 27. **Yards:** 6,271/5,651. **Par:** 71/71. **Course Rating:** 67.9/68.8. **Slope:** 100/106. **Green Fee:** $9/$11. **Cart Fee:** $17/Cart. **Walking Policy:** Unrestricted walking. **Walkability:** 2. **Opened:** 1999. **Architect:** Tom Clark. **Season:** Year-round. **High:** May-Aug. **To obtain tee times:** Call golf shop. **Miscellaneous:** Metal spikes.
Reader Comments: Great renovation ... Very good golf course ... Very well priced course ... Fairways and greens are in excellent shape ... Course is long but a mid-handicapper can score well. Good winter course to play.
Special Notes: Also has a 9-hole executive course.

★★ THE RED APPLE INN & COUNTRY CLUB
R-325 Club Rd., Heber Springs, 72543, Cleburne County, (501)362-3131, (800)733-2775, 65 miles from Little Rock. **E-mail:** appleinn&suebell.net. **Web:** www.redappleinn.com. **Facility Holes:** 18. **Yards:** 6,402/5,137. **Par:** 71/71. **Course Rating:** 71.5/65.5. **Slope:** 128/117. **Green Fee:** $35. **Cart Fee:** $22/Cart. **Walking Policy:** Unrestricted walking. **Walkability:** 3. **Opened:** 1984. **Architect:** Gary Panks. **Season:** Year-round. **High:** April-Nov. **To obtain tee times:** Call up to 1 day in advance. **Miscellaneous:** Reduced fees (juniors), range (grass), lodging (59 rooms), credit cards (MC, V, AE, D), BF, FF.

SAGE MEADOWS GOLF CLUB
PU-4406 Clubhouse Drive, Jonesboro, 72401, Craighead County, (870)932-4420. **E-mail:** Driddle@sagemeadows.com. **Web:** www.sagemeadows.com. **Facility Holes:** 18. **Yards:** 6,901/4,947. **Par:** 72/72. **Course Rating:** 72.5/69.2. **Slope:** 129/119. **Green Fee:** $14/$24. **Cart Fee:** $11/Person. **Walking Policy:** Unrestricted walking. **Walkability:** 4. **Opened:** 1998. **Architect:** Kevin Tucker. **Season:** Year-round. **High:** April-Oct. **To obtain tee times:** Call golf shop. **Miscellaneous:** Reduced fees (seniors, juniors), range (grass), credit cards (MC, V, AE, D).

★★ SOUTH HAVEN GOLF CLUB
PU-Route 10, Box 201, Texarkana, 71854, Miller County, (870)774-5771. **Facility Holes:** 18. **Yards:** 6,227/4,951. **Par:** 71/71. **Course Rating:** 69.3/69.8. **Slope:** 123/117. **Green Fee:** $10/$12. **Cart Fee:** $16/Cart. **Walking Policy:** Unrestricted walking. **Walkability:** 2. **Opened:** 1931. **Architect:** Jeff Miers. **Season:** Year-round. **High:** April-Sept. **To obtain tee times:** Call golf shop. **Miscellaneous:** Reduced fees (seniors, juniors), metal spikes, range (grass/mats).

STONEBRIDGE MEADOWS GOLF CLUB
PU-3495 E. Goff Farms Rd., Fayetteville, 72701, Washington County, (501)571-3673, 3 miles from Fayetteville. **Web:** www.stonebridgemeadows.com. **Facility Holes:** 18. **Yards:** 7,150/5,225. **Par:** 72/72. **Course Rating:** 74.8/70.7. **Slope:** 138/128. **Green Fee:** $25/$42. **Cart Fee:** Included in green fee. **Walking Policy:** Unrestricted walking. **Walkability:** 4. **Opened:** 1997. **Architect:** Randy Heckenkemper. **Season:** Year-round. **High:** April-Oct. **To obtain tee times:** Call up to 3 days in advance. **Miscellaneous:** Reduced fees (weekdays, twilight), range (grass), credit cards (MC, V, AE, D), BF, FF.
Notes: Ranked 10th in 2001 Best in State.

★★½ STONELINKS
PU-110 St. Hwy. 391 N., North Little Rock, 72117, Pulaski County, (501)945-0945. **Web:** www.stonelinks.com. **Facility Holes:** 18. **Yards:** 7,050/5,118. **Par:** 72/72. **Course Rating:** 72.8/70.3. **Slope:** 125/120. **Green Fee:** $15/$30. **Cart Fee:** Included in green fee. **Walking Policy:** Unrestricted walking. **Walkability:** 3. **Opened:** 1993. **Architect:** Tommy Thomason/Tim Deibel/Steve Holden. **Season:** Year-round. **High:** March-Oct. **To obtain tee times:** Call golf shop. **Miscellaneous:** Reduced fees (weekdays, twilight, seniors, juniors), range (grass/mats), credit cards (MC, V).
Special Notes: Formerly Quapaw Golf Links.

★★★ TURKEY MOUNTAIN GOLF CLUB
SP-3 Club Rd., Horseshoe Bend, 72512, Izard County, (870)670-5252. **Facility Holes:** 18. **Yards:** 6,477/5,455. **Par:** 73/73. **Course Rating:** 10.0/65.0. **Slope:** 112/102. **Green Fee:** $20. **Walking Policy:** Unrestricted walking. **Walkability:** 4. **Season:** Year-round. **High:** March-Nov. **To obtain tee times:** Call up to 2 days in advance. **Miscellaneous:** Range (grass), credit cards (MC, V, D), BF, FF.
Reader Comments: Scenic mountain course ... Short course, great to work on wedge play ... Great views.

★½ TWIN LAKES GOLF CLUB
SP-70 Elkway, Mountain Home, 72653, Baxter County, (870)425-9265, 120 miles from Springfield. **Facility Holes:** 18. **Yards:** 5,910/5,018. **Par:** 70/70. **Course Rating:** 67.2/69.1.

Slope: 110/106. **Green Fee:** $17/$22. **Cart Fee:** $20/Cart. **Walking Policy:** Unrestricted walking. **Walkability:** 2. **Opened:** 1959. **Architect:** Cecil B. Hollingsworth. **Season:** Year-round. **To obtain tee times:** Call up to 7 days in advance. **Miscellaneous:** Reduced fees (juniors), credit cards (V), BF, FF.

★½ VACHE GRASSE COUNTRY CLUB
SP-Country Club Rd., Greenwood, 72936, Sebastian County, (501)996-4191, 15 miles from Ft. Smith. **Facility Holes:** 18. **Yards:** 6,502/4,966. **Par:** 72/72. **Course Rating:** 70.5/67.4. **Slope:** 114/113. **Green Fee:** $12/$15. **Cart Fee:** $18/Cart. **Walking Policy:** Unrestricted walking. **Walkability:** 3. **Opened:** 1968. **Architect:** William T. Martin. **Season:** Year-round. **High:** May-Sept. **To obtain tee times:** Call golf shop. **Miscellaneous:** Reduced fees (twilight), range (grass).

★★ WAR MEMORIAL GOLF COURSE
PU-5511 W. Markham, Little Rock, 72205, Pulaski County, (501)663-0854. **Facility Holes:** 18. **Yards:** 4,432/4,260. **Par:** 65/65. **Course Rating:** 60.8. **Slope:** 92. **Green Fee:** $11/$14. **Cart Fee:** $15/Cart. **Walking Policy:** Unrestricted walking. **Walkability:** 4. **Season:** Year-round. **High:** April-Sept. **To obtain tee times:** Call up to 7 days in advance. **Miscellaneous:** Reduced fees (weekdays, twilight, seniors, juniors), credit cards (MC, V), BF, FF.

CALIFORNIA

★★½ ADOBE CREEK GOLF CLUB
PU-1901 Frates Rd., Petaluma, 94954, Sonoma County, (707)765-3000, 35 miles from San Francisco. **E-mail:** nsmith@adobecreek.com. **Facility Holes:** 18. **Yards:** 6,886/5,085. **Par:** 72/72. **Course Rating:** 73.8/69.4. **Slope:** 131/120. **Green Fee:** $10/$47. **Cart Fee:** $13/Person. **Walking Policy:** Unrestricted walking. **Walkability:** 2. **Opened:** 1990. **Architect:** Robert Trent Jones Jr. **Season:** Year-round. **To obtain tee times:** Call up to 7 days in advance. **Miscellaneous:** Reduced fees (weekdays, twilight, seniors, juniors), range (grass/mats), credit cards (MC, V, AE, D), BF, FF.

★★ ALHAMBRA MUNICIPAL GOLF COURSE
PU-630 S. Almansor St., Alhambra, 91801, Los Angeles County, (626)570-5059, 8 miles from Los Angeles. **E-mail:** info@alhambragolf.com. **Web:** www.alhambragolf.com. **Facility Holes:** 18. **Yards:** 5,214/4,501. **Par:** 70/71. **Course Rating:** 64.5/64.7. **Slope:** 107/105. **Green Fee:** $20/$24. **Cart Fee:** $11/Person. **Walking Policy:** Unrestricted walking. **Walkability:** 3. **Opened:** 1956. **Architect:** William F. Bell. **Season:** Year-round. **To obtain tee times:** Call up to 7 days in advance. **Miscellaneous:** Reduced fees (weekdays, twilight, seniors, juniors), range (mats), credit cards (MC, V), BF, FF.

★★★½ THE ALISAL RANCH GOLF COURSE
R-1054 Alisal Rd., Solvang, 93463, Santa Barbara County, (805)688-4215, 40 miles from Santa Barbara. **Web:** www.alisal.com. **Facility Holes:** 18. **Yards:** 6,551/5,752. **Par:** 72/73. **Course Rating:** 72.0/74.5. **Slope:** 133/133. **Green Fee:** $75. **Cart Fee:** $26/Cart. **Walking Policy:** Unrestricted walking. **Walkability:** 1. **Opened:** 1955. **Architect:** William F. Bell. **Season:** Year-round. **To obtain tee times:** Call golf shop. **Miscellaneous:** Reduced fees (juniors), range (grass), lodging (75 rooms), credit cards (MC, V), BF, FF.
Reader Comments: Great condition. Tight, tough ... Aesthetics abound, water hazards in all the right places ... Perfect weather, great layout, will play here again ... Great trees and setting, longer than yards suggest ... Beautiful layout.

★★★★ ALISO VIEJO GOLF CLUB
PU-25002 Golf Dr., Aliso Viejo, 92656, Orange County, (949)598-9200, 40 miles from Los Angeles. **E-mail:** meri.merrigan@ourclub.com. **Web:** alisogolf.com. **Facility Holes:** 27. **Green Fee:** $45/$125. **Cart Fee:** Included in green fee. **Walking Policy:** Mandatory carts. **Walkability:** 4. **Opened:** 1999. **Architect:** Jack Nicklaus/Jack Nicklaus II. **Season:** Year-round. **To obtain tee times:** Call up to 14 days in advance. **Miscellaneous:** Reduced fees (weekdays, twilight, seniors, juniors), range (mats), credit cards (MC, V, AE), BF, FF.
CREEK/VALLEY (18 combo)
Yards: 6,435/4,878. **Par:** 71/71. **Course Rating:** 71.3/68.6. **Slope:** 131/122.
RIDGE/CREEK (18 combo)
Yards: 6,277/4,736. **Par:** 70/70. **Course Rating:** 70.5/68.6. **Slope:** 129/121.
VALLEY/RIDGE (18 combo)
Yards: 6,268/4,740. **Par:** 71/71. **Course Rating:** 70.0/67.5. **Slope:** 128/117.
Reader Comments: Great course with 27 holes. Ridge course is the best nine. Needs a clubhouse to make it great ... Outstanding but killer greens, many 3-putts ... Another fine work of art and challenge from Jack Nicklaus ... Friendly staff, course in great shape ... Absolutely a gorgeous golf course.

★½ ALONDRA PARK GOLF COURSE
PU-16400 S. Prairie Ave., Lawndale, 90260, Los Angeles County, (310)217-9915, 10 miles from Los Angeles. **Facility Holes:** 18. **Yards:** 6,450/5,976. **Par:** 72/73. **Course Rating:** 70.6/74.4. **Slope:** 120/117. **Green Fee:** $20/$25. **Cart Fee:** $22/Cart. **Walking Policy:** Unrestricted walking. **Walkability:** 1. **Season:** Year-round. **To obtain tee times:** Call up to 7 days in advance. **Miscellaneous:** Reduced fees (twilight, seniors, juniors), range (mats), credit cards (MC, V), BF, FF.

★★★ ALTA SIERRA COUNTRY CLUB
SP-11897 Tammy Way, Grass Valley, 95949, Nevada County, (530)273-2010, 50 miles from Sacramento. **E-mail:** teeoff@altasierragolf.com. **Web:** www.altasierragolf.com. **Facility Holes:** 18. **Yards:** 6,537/5,984. **Par:** 72/73. **Course Rating:** 70.9/74.8. **Slope:** 127/136. **Green Fee:** $45/$50. **Cart Fee:** $22/Cart. **Walking Policy:** Unrestricted walking. **Walkability:** 3. **Opened:** 1964. **Architect:** Bob Baldock. **Season:** Year-round. **To obtain tee times:** Call golf shop. **Misc:** Reduced fees (weekdays, juniors), range (grass/mats), credit cards (MC, V), BF, FF.
Reader Comments: Great design, no adjacent fairways ... Mountain course, lots of trees ... Hill course, challenging, hidden trouble ... Relaxed, friendly.

★★★ ANAHEIM HILLS GOLF COURSE
PU-6501 Nohl Ranch Rd., Anaheim, 92807, Orange County, (714)998-3041, 25 miles from Los Angeles. **Facility Holes:** 18. **Yards:** 6,245/5,361. **Par:** 71/72. **Course Rating:** 69.6/70.0.

42

Slope: 117/115. **Green Fee:** $30/$36. **Cart Fee:** Included in green fee. **Walkability:** 5. **Opened:** 1972. **Architect:** Richard Bigler. **Season:** Year-round. **To obtain tee times:** Call golf shop. **Miscellaneous:** Reduced fees (twilight, seniors, juniors), range (mats), credit cards (MC, V).
Reader Comments: Great views ... Good greens, lots of blind shots, my home course keep it a secret ... What a view! ... Real good muni ... Senior rate good price ... Course layout is nice, view from every tee.

★★★ ANCIL HOFFMAN GOLF COURSE
PU-6700 Tarshes Dr., Carmichael, 95608, Sacramento County, (916)575-4653, 12 miles from Sacramento. **E-mail:** ahgc@calweb.com. **Facility Holes:** 18. **Yards:** 6,794/5,954. **Par:** 72/73. **Course Rating:** 72.5/73.4. **Slope:** 123/123. **Green Fee:** $21/$26. **Cart Fee:** $24/Cart. **Walking Policy:** Unrestricted walking. **Walkability:** 2. **Opened:** 1965. **Architect:** William F. Bell. **Season:** Year-round. **High:** April-Oct. **To obtain tee times:** Call up to 7 days in advance. **Miscellaneous:** Reduced fees (weekdays, twilight, seniors, juniors), metal spikes, range (grass/mats), credit cards (MC, V), BF, FF.
Reader Comments: Great, classic course. Great value ... Very friendly environment ... Good course, always fun to play ... Great course, all you could want from the back tees ... One of the better low cost muni courses.

THE AULD COURSE
PU-525 Hunte Pkwy., Chula Vista, 91915, San Diego County, (619)480-4666, 10 miles from San Diego. **E-mail:** aulddog@theauldcourse.com. **Web:** www.theauldcourse.com. **Facility Holes:** 18. **Yards:** 6,855/4,814. **Par:** 72/72. **Course Rating:** 73.4/68.9. **Slope:** 135/116. **Green Fee:** $25/$78. **Cart Fee:** Included in green fee. **Walking Policy:** Mandatory carts. **Walkability:** 4. **Opened:** 2001. **Architect:** John Cook/Cary Bickler. **Season:** Year-round. **To obtain tee times:** Call up to 60 days in advance. **Miscellaneous:** Reduced fees (weekdays, twilight, juniors), range (grass/mats), credit cards (MC, V, AE, D), BF, FF.

★★½ AVILA BEACH GOLF RESORT
PU-P.O. Box 2140, Avila Beach, 93424, San Luis Obispo County, (805)595-4000, 8 miles from San Luis Obispo. **E-mail:** info@avilabeachresort.com. **Web:** www.avilabeachresort.com. **Facility Holes:** 18. **Yards:** 6,443/5,116. **Par:** 71/71. **Course Rating:** 70.9/69.9. **Slope:** 122/126. **Green Fee:** $42/$52. **Cart Fee:** $14/Person. **Walking Policy:** Unrestricted walking. **Walkability:** 3. **Opened:** 1969. **Architect:** Desmond Muirhead. **Season:** Year-round. **High:** May-Oct. **To obtain tee times:** Call up to 7 days in advance. **Miscellaneous:** Reduced fees (twilight, juniors), metal spikes, range (grass), credit cards (MC, V, AE), BF, FF.

★½ AZUSA GREENS GOLF COURSE
PU-919 W. Sierra Madre Blvd., Azusa, 91702, Los Angeles County, (626)969-1727, 12 miles from Pasadena. **Facility Holes:** 18. **Yards:** 6,220/5,601. **Par:** 70/72. **Course Rating:** 69.1/70.9. **Slope:** 112/115. **Green Fee:** $22/$36. **Cart Fee:** Included in green fee. **Walking Policy:** Mandatory carts. **Walkability:** 1. **Opened:** 1963. **Architect:** Bob Baldock. **Season:** Year-round. **To obtain tee times:** Call up to 7 days in advance. **Miscellaneous:** Reduced fees (weekdays, twilight, seniors, juniors), range (grass/mats), credit cards (MC, V, AE), BF, FF.

★★½ BALBOA PARK GOLF CLUB
PU-2600 Golf Course Dr., San Diego, 92102, San Diego County, (619)239-1632. **Facility Holes:** 18. **Yards:** 6,267/5,369. **Par:** 72/72. **Course Rating:** 69.8/71.4. **Slope:** 119/119. **Green Fee:** $17/$34. **Cart Fee:** $22/Cart. **Walking Policy:** Unrestricted walking. **Walkability:** 4. **Opened:** 1915. **Architect:** William P. Bell. **Season:** Year-round. **High:** June-Aug. **To obtain tee times:** Call golf shop. **Miscellaneous:** Reduced fees (twilight), metal spikes, range (mats), credit cards (MC, V).

BARONA CREEK GOLF CLUB
R-1932 Wildcat Canyon Rd., Lakeside, 92040, San Diego County, (619)387-7018, (888)722-7662. **E-mail:** dking@barona.com. **Web:** www.barona.com. **Facility Holes:** 18. **Yards:** 7,018/5,296. **Par:** 72/72. **Course Rating:** 74.5/70.6. **Slope:** 139/126. **Green Fee:** $75. **Cart Fee:** Included in green fee. **Walking Policy:** Unrestricted walking. **Opened:** 2001. **Architect:** Gary Roger Baird. **Season:** Year-round. **To obtain tee times:** Call up to 7 days in advance. **Miscellaneous:** Range (grass), credit cards (MC, V, AE), BF, FF.

★★½ BARTLEY W. CAVANAUGH GOLF COURSE
PU-8301 Freeport Blvd., Sacramento, 95832, Sacramento County, (916)665-2020. **Web:** www.capitolcity.com. **Facility Holes:** 18. **Yards:** 6,265/4,723. **Par:** 71/71. **Course Rating:** 69.0/66.3. **Slope:** 114/107. **Green Fee:** $13/$26. **Cart Fee:** $24/Cart. **Walking Policy:** Unrestricted walking. **Walkability:** 1. **Opened:** 1995. **Architect:** Perry Dye. **Season:** Year-round. **High:** April-Aug. **To obtain tee times:** Call up to 7 days in advance. **Miscellaneous:** Reduced fees (weekdays, twilight, seniors, juniors), credit cards (MC, V), BF, FF.

CALIFORNIA

BAYONET/BLACK HORSE GOLF COURSES
PU-1 McClure Way, Seaside, 93955, Monterey County, (831)899-7271, 8 miles from Pebble Beach. **Facility Holes:** 36. **Green Fee:** $70/$95. **Cart Fee:** $16/Person. **Walking Policy:** Walking at certain times. **Season:** Year-round. **High:** May-Oct. **To obtain tee times:** Call golf shop. **Miscellaneous:** Reduced fees (weekdays, twilight, seniors, juniors), metal spikes, range (grass/mats), credit cards (MC, V, AE), BF, FF.

★★★★ **BAYONET COURSE** (18)
Yards: 7,094/5,763. **Par:** 72/74. **Course Rating:** 75.1/73.7. **Slope:** 139/134. **Walkability:** 3. **Opened:** 1954. **Architect:** General Bob McClure.
Notes: Ranked 71st in 1996 America's Top 75 Affordable Courses.
Reader Comments: Superb test, good value … Subtle, deceptive design makes course difficult. A challenge, bring your 'A' game … A lot of work has gone into this course in last 2-3 years … Don't miss it … One of the greatest, very underrated … Another Monterey toughie, rough can be nightmarish … In the forest by the ocean with the best greens around.

★★★★½ **BLACK HORSE COURSE** (18)
Yards: 7,009/5,648. **Par:** 72/72. **Course Rating:** 74.4/72.5. **Slope:** 135/129. **Walkability:** 4. **Opened:** 1963. **Architect:** General Karnes/General McClure.
Reader Comments: Nicely maintained. Well managed and good service … Redone a few years ago, this course is now as tough and beautiful as its more notable companion, the Bayonet Course. Wonderful job in remaking this track … Outstanding, play and service … It's PGA quality, the courses are excellent … Awesome.
Special Notes: Formerly Fort Ord Golf Course.

★★ BEAU PRE GOLF CLUB
SP-1777 Norton Rd., McKinleyville, 95519, Humboldt County, (707)839-2342, (800)931-6690, 10 miles from Eureka. **E-mail:** golf@beaupregc.com. **Web:** beaupregc.com. **Facility Holes:** 18. **Yards:** 5,910/4,976. **Par:** 71/72. **Course Rating:** 68.1/67.6. **Slope:** 118/112. **Green Fee:** $21/$30. **Cart Fee:** $20/Cart. **Walking Policy:** Unrestricted walking. **Walkability:** 4. **Opened:** 1967. **Architect:** Don Harling. **Season:** Year-round. **High:** May-Oct. **To obtain tee times:** Call golf shop. **Miscellaneous:** Reduced fees (weekdays, twilight, juniors), metal spikes, range (grass/mats), credit cards (MC, V, D), BF, FF.

★★★ BENNETT VALLEY GOLF COURSE
PU-3330 Yulupa Ave., Santa Rosa, 95405, Sonoma County, (707)528-3673, 50 miles from San Francisco. **Facility Holes:** 18. **Yards:** 6,600/5,958. **Par:** 72/75. **Course Rating:** 70.6/72.5. **Slope:** 112/123. **Green Fee:** $10/$25. **Cart Fee:** $22/Cart. **Walking Policy:** Unrestricted walking. **Walkability:** 2. **Opened:** 1969. **Architect:** Ben Harmon. **Season:** Year-round. **To obtain tee times:** Call up to 7 days in advance. **Miscellaneous:** Reduced fees (weekdays, twilight, seniors, juniors), metal spikes, range (grass/mats), credit cards (MC, V), BF, FF.
Reader Comments: For the price, this is a great course. Very good condition considering the amount of play. Friendly and knowledgeable pros. This is a muni course at its best … Best course in northern CA for the money.

★★½ BETHEL ISLAND GOLF COURSE
PU-3303 Gateway Rd., Bethel Island, 94511, Contra Costa County, (925)684-2654, 25 miles from Stockton. **Facility Holes:** 18. **Yards:** 6,632/5,813. **Par:** 72/74. **Course Rating:** 70.8/72.2. **Slope:** 118/117. **Green Fee:** $13/$23. **Cart Fee:** $22/Cart. **Walking Policy:** Unrestricted walking. **Opened:** 1960. **Architect:** Ted Robinson. **Season:** Year-round. **High:** April-Oct. **To obtain tee times:** Call golf shop. **Miscellaneous:** Reduced fees (weekdays, twilight, seniors), metal spikes, range (grass), credit cards (MC, V, AE, D).

★★½ BIDWELL PARK GOLF COURSE
PU-3199 Golf Course Road, Chico, 95973, Butte County, (530)891-8417, 90 miles from Sacramento. **Facility Holes:** 18. **Yards:** 6,363/5,855. **Par:** 72/71. **Course Rating:** 70.2/73.1. **Slope:** 123/123. **Green Fee:** $14/$22. **Cart Fee:** $19/Cart. **Walking Policy:** Unrestricted walking. **Walkability:** 2. **Opened:** 1930. **Architect:** City of Chico. **Season:** Year-round. **To obtain tee times:** Call golf shop. **Miscellaneous:** Reduced fees (twilight, seniors, juniors), metal spikes, credit cards (MC, V, AE, D, DC), BF, FF.

★★ BING MALONEY GOLF COURSE
PU-6801 Freeport Blvd., Sacramento, 95822, Sacramento County, (916)433-2283. **Facility Holes:** 27. **Yards:** 6,558/5,972. **Par:** 72/73. **Course Rating:** 70.3/72.6. **Slope:** 113/119. **Green Fee:** $18/$26. **Cart Fee:** $23/Cart. **Walking Policy:** Unrestricted walking. **Walkability:** 1. **Opened:** 1952. **Architect:** Mike McDonagh. **Season:** Year-round. **To obtain tee times:** Call up to 7 days in advance. **Miscellaneous:** Reduced fees (weekdays, twilight, seniors, juniors), range (mats), credit cards (MC, V), BF, FF.
Special Notes: Also has a 9-hole executive course.

★★½ BIRCH HILLS GOLF COURSE
PU-2250 E. Birch St., Brea, 92821, Orange County, (714)990-0201. **Facility Holes:** 18. **Yards:** 3,481/3,003. **Par:** 59/59. **Course Rating:** 57.7/55.9. **Slope:** 91/85. **Green Fee:** $18/$26. **Walking Policy:** Unrestricted walking. **To obtain tee times:** Call golf shop.

★★★ BLACK LAKE GOLF RESORT
R-1490 Golf Course Lane, Nipomo, 93444, San Luis Obispo County, (805)343-1214, 10 miles from Santa Maria. **Web:** www.blacklake.com. **Facility Holes:** 27. **Green Fee:** $20/$54. **Cart Fee:** $19/Person. **Walking Policy:** Unrestricted walking. **Walkability:** 3. **Opened:** 1964. **Architect:** Ted Robinson. **Season:** Year-round. **To obtain tee times:** Call up to 7 days in advance. **Miscellaneous:** Reduced fees (weekdays, guests, twilight, seniors, juniors), metal spikes, range (grass/mats), credit cards (MC, V, AE, D, DC), BF, FF.
CANYON/OAKS (18 Combo)
Yards: 6,034/5,047. **Par:** 71/71. **Course Rating:** 69.3/70.5. **Slope:** 121/120.
LAKES/CANYON (18 Combo)
Yards: 6,401/5,628. **Par:** 72/72. **Course Rating:** 70.9/72.9. **Slope:** 123/126.
LAKES/OAKS (18 Combo)
Yards: 6,185/5,161. **Par:** 71/71. **Course Rating:** 69.7/70.8. **Slope:** 121/124.
Reader Comments: The 3 nines they have are nice and challenging. It's target golf … A fun place to play … Fine resort course, challenging … Very comfortable experience.

★★★½ BODEGA HARBOUR GOLF LINKS
R-21301 Heron Dr., Bodega Bay, 94923, Sonoma County, (707)875-3538, 20 miles from Santa Rosa. **Web:** www.bedegaharbourgolf.com. **Facility Holes:** 18. **Yards:** 6,265/4,749. **Par:** 70/69. **Course Rating:** 72.4/69.7. **Slope:** 134/120. **Green Fee:** $40/$90. **Cart Fee:** Included in green fee. **Walking Policy:** Walking at certain times. **Walkability:** 4. **Opened:** 1976. **Architect:** Robert Trent Jones Jr. **Season:** Year-round. **High:** June-Oct. **To obtain tee times:** Call up to 90 days in advance. **Miscellaneous:** Reduced fees (weekdays, guests, twilight, seniors, juniors), metal spikes, range (mats), caddies, credit cards (MC, V, AE), BF, FF.
Reader Comments: Great ocean views, tough golf … Great ambience and superb customer service! … You can't get any closer to the ocean than this. Beautiful views at a good price.

★★½ BONITA GOLF CLUB
PU-5540 Sweetwater Rd., Bonita, 91902, San Diego County, (619)267-1103, 20 miles from San Diego. **E-mail:** rscribner@bonitagolfclub.com. **Web:** www.bonitagolfclub.com. **Facility Holes:** 18. **Yards:** 6,287/5,442. **Par:** 71/71. **Course Rating:** 68.8/71.0. **Slope:** 117/119. **Green Fee:** $22/$34. **Cart Fee:** $22/Cart. **Walking Policy:** Unrestricted walking. **Walkability:** 2. **Opened:** 1978. **Architect:** William F. Bell. **Season:** Year-round. **To obtain tee times:** Call up to 7 days in advance. **Miscellaneous:** Range (grass/mats), credit cards (MC, V, AE), BF, FF.

BORREGO SPRINGS COUNTRY CLUB
PU-1112 Tilting T Dr., Borrego Springs, 92004, San Diego County, (760)767-3330, 45 miles from San Diego. **Facility Holes:** 18. **Yards:** 6,569/4,754. **Par:** 71/71. **Course Rating:** 70.4/66.7. **Slope:** 117/104. **Green Fee:** $54/$64. **Walkability:** 1. **Opened:** 1998. **Architect:** Cary Bickler. **Season:** Year-round. **High:** Nov.-April. **To obtain tee times:** Call golf shop. **Miscellaneous:** Range (grass), lodging (100 rooms).

★★½ BOULDER CREEK GOLF & COUNTRY CLUB
R-16901 Big Basin Hwy., Boulder Creek, 95006, Santa Cruz County, (408)338-2121, 15 miles from Santa Cruz. **Web:** www.webfairway.com. **Facility Holes:** 18. **Yards:** 4,396/4,027. **Par:** 65/67. **Course Rating:** 61.5/63.3. **Slope:** 104/104. **Green Fee:** $14/$40. **Cart Fee:** $19/Cart. **Walking Policy:** Unrestricted walking. **Walkability:** 2. **Opened:** 1961. **Architect:** Jack Fleming. **Season:** Year-round. **High:** April-Oct. **To obtain tee times:** Call up to 7 days in advance. **Miscellaneous:** Reduced fees (weekdays, guests, twilight, seniors, juniors), lodging (21 rooms), credit cards (MC, V, AE, D), BF, FF.

★★★ BOUNDARY OAK COUNTRY CLUB
PU-3800 Valley Vista Rd., Walnut Creek, 94596, Contra Costa County, (925)934-6212, 1 mile from Oakland. **Web:** www.boundaryoak.com. **Facility Holes:** 18. **Yards:** 7,063/5,699. **Par:** 72/72. **Course Rating:** 73.9/72.0. **Slope:** 130/120. **Green Fee:** $12/$25. **Cart Fee:** $25/Cart. **Walking Policy:** Unrestricted walking. **Walkability:** 4. **Opened:** 1969. **Architect:** Bob Boldt. **Season:** Year-round. **High:** Year-round. **To obtain tee times:** Call up to 7 days in advance. **Miscellaneous:** Reduced fees (weekdays, twilight, seniors, juniors), range (grass/mats), credit cards (MC, V), BF, FF.
Reader Comments: Best value golf, anywhere! … Exceptional service … For a public course it's great, with very good variety … Best public course in northern California for the dollar.

★★★ THE BRIDGES GOLF CLUB
PU-9000 S. Gale Ridge Rd., San Ramon, 94583, Contra Costa County, (925)735-4253, 25 miles from Oakland. **E-mail:** sgates@thebridgesgolf.com. **Web:** www.thebridgesgolf.com. **Facility Holes:** 18. **Yards:** 7,081/5,274. **Par:** 73/73. **Course Rating:** 74.5/71.4. **Slope:** 134/123. **Green Fee:** $55/$95. **Cart Fee:** Included in green fee. **Walking Policy:** Unrestricted walking. **Walkability:** 3. **Opened:** 1999. **Architect:** Damian Pascuzzo & Robert Muir Graves. **Season:** Year-round. **High:** March-Sept. **To obtain tee times:** Call up to 30 days in advance. **Miscellaneous:** Reduced fees (weekdays, twilight, seniors, juniors), range (grass/mats), caddies, credit cards (MC, V, AE), BF, FF.
Reader Comments: Very nice course and very challenging. As with many tough courses, you will need to play it a few times to zero in the right club … Outstanding course! Great service … Just a great day … Very penal, many canyons.

BROOKSIDE GOLF CLUB
PU-1133 N. Rosemont Ave., Pasadena, 91103, Los Angeles County, (626)796-0177, 7 miles from Los Angeles. **Facility Holes:** 36. **Green Fee:** $30/$40. **Cart Fee:** $24/Cart. **Walking Policy:** Unrestricted walking. **Walkability:** 1. **Architect:** William P. Bell. **Season:** Year-round. **High:** April-Oct. **To obtain tee times:** Call golf shop. **Miscellaneous:** Reduced fees (weekdays, twilight, seniors, juniors), range (mats), credit cards (MC, V, AE, D).
★★★ C.W. KOINER COURSE (18)
Yards: 7,037/6,104. **Par:** 72/75. **Course Rating:** 73.6/74.7. **Slope:** 128/128. **Opened:** 1928.
Reader Comments: Both courses have great layouts criss-crossing the river … Flat terrain … Fine traditional layout … Very scenic but tough … People are helpful. Course is fun to play … A wonderful great old public course.
★★★ E.O. NAY COURSE (18)
Yards: 6,046/5,377. **Par:** 70/71. **Course Rating:** 68.4/70.5. **Slope:** 115/117. **Opened:** 1952.
Reader Comments: Good course … A good golf course—old fashioned.

★★★ BUENAVENTURA GOLF COURSE
PU-5882 Olivas Park Dr., Ventura, 93003, Ventura County, (805)642-2231. **Facility Holes:** 18. **Yards:** 6,376/5,443. **Par:** 72/72. **Course Rating:** 70.7/71.8. **Slope:** 126/123. **Green Fee:** $11/$26. **Cart Fee:** $12/Person. **Walking Policy:** Unrestricted walking. **Season:** Year-round. **To obtain tee times:** Call up to 7 days in advance. **Miscellaneous:** Reduced fees (weekdays, twilight, seniors, juniors), credit cards (MC, V, AE), BF, FF.
Reader Comments: Inexpensive, good condition, well managed … Great seaside course. Tight tree-lined. Nice clubhouse and people … Consistently good course.

★★ CALIMESA COUNTRY CLUB
PU-1300 S3rd St, Calimesa, 92320, Riverside County, (909)795-2488, 8 miles from Redlands. **Facility Holes:** 18. **Yards:** 5,970/5,293. **Par:** 70/72. **Course Rating:** 67.3/69.6. **Slope:** 114/112. **Green Fee:** $9/$22. **Cart Fee:** $10/Person. **Walking Policy:** Unrestricted walking. **Walkability:** 1. **Opened:** 1965. **Season:** Year-round. **To obtain tee times:** Call golf shop. **Miscellaneous:** Reduced fees (weekdays, twilight), metal spikes, credit cards (MC, V, AE).

★★½ CAMARILLO SPRINGS GOLF COURSE
PU-791 Camarillo Springs Rd., Camarillo, 93012, Ventura County, (805)484-1075, 54 miles from Los Angeles. **Facility Holes:** 18. **Yards:** 6,375/5,297. **Par:** 72/72. **Course Rating:** 70.2/70.2. **Slope:** 115/116. **Green Fee:** $22/$46. **Cart Fee:** $12/Person. **Walking Policy:** Walking at certain times. **Walkability:** 3. **Opened:** 1972. **Architect:** Ted Robinson. **Season:** Year-round. **High:** March-Aug. **To obtain tee times:** Call up to 7 days in advance. **Miscellaneous:** Reduced fees (weekdays, guests, twilight, seniors, juniors), metal spikes, range (mats), credit cards (MC, V, AE, D, DC), BF, FF.

★★½ CANYON LAKES COUNTRY CLUB
PU-640 Bollinger Canyon Way, San Ramon, 94583, Contra Costa County, (925)735-6511, 30 miles from San Francisco. **Facility Holes:** 18. **Yards:** 6,373/5,191. **Par:** 71/71. **Course Rating:** 71.4/69.9. **Slope:** 129/121. **Green Fee:** $65/$80. **Cart Fee:** Included in green fee. **Walking Policy:** Mandatory carts. **Walkability:** 4. **Opened:** 1987. **Architect:** Ted Robinson. **Season:** Year-round. **To obtain tee times:** Call up to 7 days in advance. **Miscellaneous:** Metal spikes, credit cards (MC, V), FF.

★★★ CANYON SOUTH GOLF COURSE
PU-1097 Murray Canyon Dr., Palm Springs, 92264, Riverside County, (760)327-2019, 100 miles from Los Angeles. **E-mail:** canyonsouthgolf@earthlink.net. **Facility Holes:** 18. **Yards:** 6,536/5,685. **Par:** 71/71. **Course Rating:** 70.8/72.0. **Slope:** 119/116. **Green Fee:** $25/$70. **Cart Fee:** Included in green fee. **Walking Policy:** Mandatory carts. **Walkability:** 1. **Opened:** 1963. **Architect:** William F. Bell. **Season:** Year-round. **High:** Jan.-March. **To obtain tee times:** Call up to 7 days in advance. **Miscellaneous:** Reduced fees (weekdays, twilight),

metal spikes, range (grass), credit cards (MC, V, AE), BF, FF.
Reader Comments: Easy to play & pay. Back tees a must. Course on which to relax and enjoy … Good value for Palm Springs. Good basic course for intermediate and beginners … A gem in outskirts of Palm Springs. Challenging, located outside and away from roads. Quiet. I love this course.

★★★ CARLTON OAKS COUNTRY CLUB
PU-9200 Inwood Dr., Santee, 92071, San Diego County, (619)448-8500, (800)831-6757, 20 miles from San Diego. **Facility Holes:** 18. **Yards:** 7,088/4,548. **Par:** 72/72. **Course Rating:** 74.6/62.1. **Slope:** 137/114. **Green Fee:** $55/$80. **Cart Fee:** Included in green fee. **Walking Policy:** Unrestricted walking. **Walkability:** 3. **Opened:** 1990. **Architect:** Perry Dye. **Season:** Year-round. **High:** Feb.-April. **To obtain tee times:** Call golf shop. **Miscellaneous:** Reduced fees (weekdays, guests, twilight, seniors), range (grass/mats), lodging (58 rooms), credit cards (MC, V, AE), BF, FF.
Reader Comments: Great facilities, good course, good room accommodations, good restaurant and bar … Always a challenge … Excellent course, great restaurant … Tough 18 … Flat course … Rough is mostly sandy with rocks … Best course in San Diego … Great weekend getaway.

★★★½ CARMEL MOUNTAIN RANCH COUNTRY CLUB
PU-14050 Carmel Ridge Rd., San Diego, 92128, San Diego County, (858)487-9224, 15 miles from San Diego. **Facility Holes:** 18. **Yards:** 6,728/5,372. **Par:** 72/72. **Course Rating:** 71.9/71.0. **Slope:** 131/122. **Green Fee:** $50/$85. **Cart Fee:** Included in green fee. **Walkability:** 4. **Opened:** 1986. **Architect:** Ron Fream. **Season:** Year-round. **To obtain tee times:** Call golf shop. **Miscellaneous:** Reduced fees (twilight, seniors, juniors), metal spikes, range (mats), credit cards (MC, V, AE).
Reader Comments: Hilly course, some really nice holes … Narrow and challenging. Outstanding weekday rates. Plays like a private club … Not very forgiving but interesting … A tight but fun course … Very nice course … Nice, play often.

★★★½ CARMEL VALLEY RANCH GOLF CLUB
R-1 Old Ranch Rd., Carmel, 93923, Monterey County, (831)626-2510, (800)422-7635, 6 miles from Carmel by the Sea. **E-mail:** tsprister@toongolf.com. **Web:** www.cvrgolf.com. **Facility Holes:** 18. **Yards:** 6,515/5,088. **Par:** 70/70. **Course Rating:** 70.1/69.6. **Slope:** 124/135. **Green Fee:** $90/$180. **Cart Fee:** Included in green fee. **Walking Policy:** Walking at certain times. **Walkability:** 3. **Opened:** 1981. **Architect:** Pete Dye. **Season:** Year-round. **High:** May-Oct. **To obtain tee times:** Call up to 30 days in advance. **Miscellaneous:** Reduced fees (guests, twilight, juniors), range (grass), lodging (144 rooms), credit cards (MC, V, AE, D, DC, CB), BF, FF.
Reader Comments: A very, very, enjoyable resort course … Very service oriented … Very good resort course … Weekender value & light play … Good food, good golf, good lodging … Expensive but worth it, had course to ourselves … Nice, well run course … Great location.

★★½ THE CASCADES GOLF CLUB
PU-16325 Silver Oaks Dr., Sylmar, 91342, Los Angeles County, (818)833-8900, 30 miles from Los Angeles. **Facility Holes:** 18. **Yards:** 6,610/5,080. **Par:** 71/71. **Course Rating:** 72.6/69.4. **Slope:** 139/124. **Green Fee:** $30/$85. **Cart Fee:** Included in green fee. **Walking Policy:** Mandatory carts. **Walkability:** 5. **Opened:** 1999. **Architect:** Steve Timm. **Season:** Year-round. **To obtain tee times:** Call up to 7 days in advance. **Miscellaneous:** Reduced fees (weekdays, twilight, seniors), range (grass), credit cards (MC, V, AE, D, DC), BF, FF.

★★½ CASTLE CREEK COUNTRY CLUB
SP-8797 Circle R Dr., Escondido, 92026, San Diego County, (760)749-2422, (800)619-2465, 30 miles from San Diego. **Facility Holes:** 18. **Yards:** 6,396/4,800. **Par:** 72/72. **Course Rating:** 70.8/67.4. **Slope:** 124/108. **Green Fee:** $22/$40. **Cart Fee:** $10/Person. **Walking Policy:** Unrestricted walking. **Walkability:** 5. **Opened:** 1956. **Architect:** Jack Daray Sr. **Season:** Year-round. **High:** Jan.-April. **To obtain tee times:** Call golf shop. **Miscellaneous:** Reduced fees (weekdays, twilight), credit cards (MC, V, AE).

★★★★ CASTLE OAKS GOLF CLUB
PU-1000 Castle Oaks Dr., Ione, 95640, Amador County, (209)274-0167, 30 miles from Sacramento. **Facility Holes:** 18. **Yards:** 6,739/4,953. **Par:** 71/71. **Course Rating:** 72.7/67.3. **Slope:** 131/114. **Green Fee:** $18/$48. **Cart Fee:** Included in green fee. **Walking Policy:** Walking at certain times. **Walkability:** 3. **Opened:** 1994. **Architect:** Bradford Benz. **Season:** Year-round. **To obtain tee times:** Call up to 7 days in advance. **Miscellaneous:** Reduced fees (weekdays, twilight, seniors, juniors), range (grass), credit cards (MC, V), BF, FF.
Reader Comments: Best value near Sacramento. Great Track! No two holes alike … Greens in great condition. Hard to get to golf course (out in nowhere), but worth it … Rolling fairways. Fast, firm, undulating greens. Nice layout. Very good conditioning. A good test … Best hidden jewel in northern California, fast greens.

★★★ **CATHEDRAL CANYON COUNTRY CLUB**
SP-68311 Paseo Real, Cathedral City, 92234, Riverside County, (760)328-6571, 10 miles from Palm Springs. **E-mail:** terry.ferraro@ourclub.com. **Facility Holes:** 27. **Green Fee:** $25/$85. **Cart Fee:** Included in green fee. **Walking Policy:** Mandatory carts. **Walkability:** 3. **Opened:** 1975. **Architect:** David Rainville. **Season:** Year-round. **To obtain tee times:** Call golf shop. **Miscellaneous:** Reduced fees (weekdays, twilight), metal spikes, range (grass), credit cards (MC, V, AE, D), BF, FF.
LAKE VIEW/ARROYO (18 Combo)
Yards: 6,366/5,183. **Par:** 72/72. **Course Rating:** 70.3/70.1. **Slope:** 125/124.
LAKE VIEW/MOUNTAIN VIEW (18 Combo)
Yards: 6,505/5,423. **Par:** 72/72. **Course Rating:** 71.1/71.6. **Slope:** 130/127.
MOUNTAIN VIEW/ARROYO (18 Combo)
Yards: 6,477/5,182. **Par:** 72/72. **Course Rating:** 70.9/70.8. **Slope:** 126/124.
Reader Comments: Lots of fun, great greens and wide fairways ... 27 adventurous holes.

★★½ **CHALK MOUNTAIN GOLF CLUB**
PU-10000 El Bordo Ave., Atascadero, 93422, San Luis Obispo County, (805)466-8848, 10 miles from San Luis Obispo. **Facility Holes:** 18. **Yards:** 6,299/5,330. **Par:** 72/72. **Course Rating:** 69.2/71.1. **Slope:** 126/125. **Green Fee:** $10/$29. **Architect:** Robert Muir Graves. **Season:** Year-round. **To obtain tee times:** Call golf shop. **Miscellaneous:** Metal spikes, credit cards (MC, V, AE).

THE CHARDONNAY GOLF CLUB
SP-2555 Jameson Canyon Rd. Hwy. 12, Napa, 94558, Napa County, (707)257-1900, (800)788-0136, 38 miles from San Francisco. **Web:** www.chardonnaygolfclub.com. **Facility Holes:** 36. **Cart Fee:** Included in green fee. **Walking Policy:** Mandatory carts. **Walkability:** 3. **Architect:** Johnny Miller/Jack Barry. **Season:** Year-round. **High:** April-Oct. **To obtain tee times:** Call up to 30 days in advance. **Miscellaneous:** Metal spikes, range (grass), credit cards (MC, V, AE, D, DC, JCB), BF, FF.
★★★½ **CLUB SHAKESPEARE** (18)
Yards: 7,001/5,448. **Par:** 72/72. **Course Rating:** 74.5/70.9. **Slope:** 137/125. **Green Fee:** $110/$130. **Opened:** 1992. **Miscellaneous:** Reduced fees (twilight).
Reader Comments: A great golf test ... Good value, tough greens ... Excellent facilities, underrated California course ... A jewel in the wine country, gorgeous.
★★★½ **VINEYARDS COURSE** (18)
Yards: 6,811/5,200. **Par:** 71/71. **Course Rating:** 73.7/70.1. **Slope:** 133/126. **Green Fee:** $55/$95. **Opened:** 1987. **Miscellaneous:** Reduced fees (weekdays, twilight).
Reader Comments: Beautiful course. Challenging but fair ... Fall special with cart ... Relaxing picturesque course ... Better than most, bring your A game ... Vineyards make for interesting visual aesthetics ... Classy place ... Tough public course, great practice areas ... Real sleeper, tough challenge from back tees.

★★★ **CHERRY ISLAND GOLF COURSE**
PU-2360 Elverta Rd., Elverta, 95626, Sacramento County, (916)991-7293, 10 miles from Sacramento. **Facility Holes:** 18. **Yards:** 6,562/5,163. **Par:** 72/72. **Course Rating:** 71.1/70.0. **Slope:** 124/117. **Green Fee:** $17/$23. **Cart Fee:** $22/Cart. **Walking Policy:** Unrestricted walking. **Walkability:** 2. **Opened:** 1990. **Architect:** Robert Muir Graves. **Season:** Year-round. **High:** April-Nov. **To obtain tee times:** Call golf shop. **Miscellaneous:** Reduced fees (weekdays, twilight, seniors, juniors), metal spikes, range (grass/mats).
Reader Comments: Nice layout, friendly management.

★½ **CHESTER WASHINGTON GOLF COURSE**
PU-1930 W. 120th St., Los Angeles, 90047, Los Angeles County, (323)756-6975, 20 miles from Los Angeles. **Facility Holes:** 18. **Yards:** 6,348/5,646. **Par:** 70/70. **Course Rating:** 69.6/71.8. **Slope:** 107/115. **Green Fee:** $20/$25. **Walking Policy:** Unrestricted walking. **Walkability:** 2. **Season:** Year-round. **High:** June-Aug. **To obtain tee times:** Call golf shop. **Miscellaneous:** Reduced fees (weekdays, twilight, seniors, juniors), metal spikes, credit cards (MC, V, AE).

★★ **CHINA LAKE GOLF CLUB**
M-411 Midway, China Lake, 93555, Kern County, (760)939-2990, 65 miles from Bakersfield. **Facility Holes:** 18. **Yards:** 6,850/5,925. **Par:** 72/72. **Course Rating:** 72.5/73.8. **Slope:** 119/123. **Green Fee:** $16/$18. **Cart Fee:** $16/Cart. **Walking Policy:** Unrestricted walking. **Walkability:** 1. **Opened:** 1952. **Architect:** William F. Bell. **Season:** Year-round. **To obtain tee times:** Call golf shop. **Miscellaneous:** Reduced fees (twilight, juniors), range (grass/mats), credit cards (MC, V, AE), BF, FF.

CHUCK CORICA GOLF COMPLEX
PU-No.1 Clubhouse Memorial Rd., Alameda, 94501, Alameda County, (510)522-4321,
5 miles from Oakland. **Facility Holes:** 36. **Green Fee:** $16/$29. **Cart Fee:** $26/Cart. **Walking Policy:** Unrestricted walking. **Walkability:** 1. **Season:** Year-round. **High:** April-Oct. **To obtain tee times:** Call up to 7 days in advance. **Miscellaneous:** Reduced fees (weekdays, twilight, seniors, juniors), range (mats), credit cards (MC, V), BF, FF.
★★½ **EARL FRY COURSE** (18)
Yards: 6,310/5,202. **Par:** 71/72. **Course Rating:** 70.9/69.9. **Slope:** 123/113. **Opened:** 1927. **Architect:** William P. Bell/Desmond Muirhead.
★★ **JACK CLARK SOUTH COURSE** (18)
Yards: 6,560/5,284. **Par:** 71/71. **Course Rating:** 71.8/69.3. **Slope:** 119/109. **Opened:** 1952. **Architect:** William P. Bell/Robert Muir Graves.

★★½ **CHULA VISTA MUNICIPAL GOLF COURSE**
PU-4475 Bonita Rd., Bonita, 91902, San Diego County, (619)479-4141, (800)833-8463, 10 miles from San Diego. **Facility Holes:** 18. **Yards:** 6,759/5,776. **Par:** 73/74. **Course Rating:** 72.3/72.7. **Slope:** 128/124. **Green Fee:** $21/$28. **Cart Fee:** $12/Person. **Walking Policy:** Unrestricted walking. **Walkability:** 1. **Opened:** 1963. **Architect:** Harry Rainville. **Season:** Year-round. **High:** July-Sept. **To obtain tee times:** Call golf shop. **Miscellaneous:** Reduced fees (weekdays, twilight, seniors, juniors), metal spikes, range (grass/mats), credit cards (MC, V, AE).

★★★★ **CIMARRON GOLF RESORT** *Service, Value*
PU-67-603 30th Ave., Cathedral City, 92234, Riverside County, (760)770-6060, (877)955-6233, 1 mile from Palm Springs. **E-mail:** info@cimarrongolf.com. **Web:** cimarrongolf.com. **Facility Holes:** 27. **Yards:** 6,858/5,127. **Par:** 71/71. **Course Rating:** 72.4/69.7. **Slope:** 123/117. **Green Fee:** $55/$115. **Cart Fee:** Included in green fee. **Walking Policy:** Unrestricted walking. **Walkability:** 2. **Opened:** 2000. **Architect:** John Fought. **Season:** Year-round. **High:** Jan.-April. **To obtain tee times:** Call up to 60 days in advance. **Miscellaneous:** Reduced fees (weekdays, guests, twilight, juniors), range (grass), lodging (80 rooms), credit cards (MC, V, AE, D), BF, FF.
Reader Comments: Superb layout ... Nice course. Great deals ... Great bang for my buck. An interesting track to play and the service is great. The restaurant was excellent ... Great staff. Golf course was in perfect shape. The best in the desert!! ... Both courses were great!! ... Great value. A must play for avid golfers. Their Short Course was equally good.
Special Notes: Also has a 9-hole executive course.

★★★½ **CINNABAR HILLS GOLF CLUB**
PU-23600 McKean Rd., San Jose, 95141, Santa Clara County, (408)323-7812. **Facility Holes:** 27. **Green Fee:** $80/$120. **Cart Fee:** Included in green fee. **Opened:** 1998. **Architect:** John Harbottle. **Season:** Year-round. **To obtain tee times:** Call golf shop.
CANYON/MOUNTAIN (18)
Yards: 6,641/4,859. **Par:** 72/72. **Course Rating:** 72.5/68.1. **Slope:** 137/118.
LAKE/CANYON (18)
Yards: 6,688/4,959. **Par:** 72/72. **Course Rating:** 72.9/68.4. **Slope:** 138/121.
LAKE/MOUNTAIN (18)
Yards: 6,853/5,010. **Par:** 72/72. **Course Rating:** 73.6/68.1. **Slope:** 142/120.
Reader Comments: Tremendous course close to the city. Twilight is great value ... Great course ... One of the nicest courses in the San Jose area, including private country clubs ... A new, well-conditioned, public test of unbelievably tough golf holes. Great vistas and some hellacious places to lose your ball.

★½ **COLTON GOLF CLUB**
PU-1901 W. Valley Blvd., Colton, 92324, San Bernardino County, (909)877-1712, 10 miles from Riverside. **Facility Holes:** 18. **Yards:** 310/2,626. **Par:** 57/57. **Course Rating:** 54.2/54.2. **Slope:** 82/82. **Green Fee:** $13/$20. **Cart Fee:** $17/Person. **Walking Policy:** Unrestricted walking. **Walkability:** 2. **Opened:** 1961. **Architect:** Robert Trent Jones. **Season:** Year-round. **High:** April-Nov. **To obtain tee times:** Call golf shop. **Miscellaneous:** Reduced fees (weekdays, twilight, seniors, juniors), range (grass/mats), credit cards (MC, V), BF, FF.

★½ **CORDOVA GOLF COURSE**
PU-9425 Jackson Rd, Sacramento, 95826, Sacramento County, (916)362-1196, 9 miles from Sacramento. **Facility Holes:** 18. **Yards:** 4,755/4,728. **Par:** 63/66. **Course Rating:** 61.2/64.9. **Slope:** 90/96. **Green Fee:** $8/$12. **Cart Fee:** $18/Cart. **Walking Policy:** Unrestricted walking. **Walkability:** 1. **Opened:** 1960. **Season:** Year-round. **To obtain tee times:** Call up to 7 days in advance. **Miscellaneous:** Reduced fees (weekdays, seniors, juniors), range (grass/mats), credit cards (MC, V, ATM), BF, FF.

CALIFORNIA

★★★★ **CORONADO GOLF COURSE**
PU-2000 Visalia Row, Coronado, 92118, San Diego County, (619)435-3121, 2 miles from San Diego. **E-mail:** ronthepro@net.com. **Facility Holes:** 18. **Yards:** 6,590/5,742. **Par:** 72/72. **Course Rating:** 71.5/73.7. **Slope:** 124/126. **Green Fee:** $20. **Cart Fee:** $12/Person. **Walking Policy:** Walking at certain times. **Walkability:** 1. **Opened:** 1957. **Architect:** Jack Daray Sr. **Season:** Year-round. **High:** Year-round. **To obtain tee times:** Call up to 2 days in advance. **Misc:** Reduced fees (twilight, juniors), range (grass/mats), credit cards (MC, V), BF, FF.
Reader Comments: Beauty rivaled by no course in California, including Pebble! Great bargain! ... Not hard to walk ... Beautiful view of bay ... Good maintenance, great facilities, nice layout ... Excellent back 9 ... 20 bucks all year round. Beautiful scenery ... A great price. Convenient.

COSTA MESA COUNTRY CLUB
PU-1701 Golf Course Dr., Costa Mesa, 92626, Orange County, (714)540-7500, 25 miles from Los Angeles. **Facility Holes:** 36. **Cart Fee:** $22/Cart. **Walking Policy:** Unrestricted walking. **Walkability:** 2. **Architect:** William F. Bell. **Season:** Year-round. **To obtain tee times:** Call golf shop. **Miscellaneous:** Reduced fees (twilight, seniors, juniors), range (grass/mats), BF, FF.
★★★ **LOS LAGOS COURSE** (18)
Yards: 6,542/5,925. **Par:** 72/72. **Course Rating:** 70.7/73.3. **Slope:** 116/118. **Green Fee:** $27/$39.
Reader Comments: Course improved greatly in 2 years ... Good value, excellent shape, good test ... Best So. Cal city course, greens A1 ... Fantastic greens for the price ... City-owned muni, great greens, lots of play ... Tight ... Best greens in the area for a muni.
★★★ **MESA LINDA COURSE** (18)
Yards: 5,486/4,591. **Par:** 70/70. **Course Rating:** 66.0/65.6. **Slope:** 104/103. **Green Fee:** $20/$30.
Reader Comments: Local secret value with great greens ... Shorter than Los Lagos course, good greens ... Tight lots of trees ... Steady improvement ... Heavily played, but fun design ... Good bargain.

COTTONWOOD AT RANCHO SAN DIEGO GOLF CLUB
PU-3121 Willow Glen Dr., El Cajon, 92019, San Diego County, (619)442-9891, (800)455-1902, 20 miles from San Diego. **E-mail:** cottonwoodgolf@aol.com. **Web:** cottonwoodgolf.com. **Facility Holes:** 36. **Cart Fee:** $11/Person. **Walking Policy:** Unrestricted walking. **Walkability:** 1. **Architect:** O.W. Moorman/A.C. Sears. **Season:** Year-round. **To obtain tee times:** Call up to 14 days in advance. **Misc:** Range (grass/mats), credit cards (MC, V, D), BF, FF.
★★★ **IVANHOE COURSE** (18)
Yards: 6,837/5,686. **Par:** 72/73. **Course Rating:** 72.6/72.4. **Slope:** 126/121. **Green Fee:** $20/$42. **Opened:** 1962. **Miscellaneous:** Reduced fees (weekdays, twilight, seniors).
Reader Comments: Best value in San Diego County. Clean, neat, well kept ...Fast greens, lot of trees ... Well worth playing. Super value ... Best greens around, outstanding staff ... Good for beginners ... Good, standard course.
★★½ **MONTE VISTA COURSE** (18)
Yards: 6,302/5,531. **Par:** 71/72. **Course Rating:** 69.5/75.7. **Slope:** 117/134. **Green Fee:** $18/$39. **Opened:** 1963. **Miscellaneous:** Reduced fees (weekdays, twilight, seniors, juniors).

★★★½ **THE COURSE AT WENTE VINEYARDS**
PU-5050 Arroyo Rd., Livermore, 94550, Alameda County, (925)456-2475, 35 miles from Oakland. **Web:** www.wentegolf.com. **Facility Holes:** 18. **Yards:** 6,949/4,975. **Par:** 72/72. **Course Rating:** 74.5/69.4. **Slope:** 142/122. **Green Fee:** $85/$115. **Walking Policy:** Unrestricted walking. **Walkability:** 4. **Opened:** 1998. **Architect:** Greg Norman. **Season:** Year-round. **To obtain tee times:** Call up to 30 days in advance. **Miscellaneous:** Reduced fees (weekdays, juniors), range (grass), credit cards (MC, V, AE, D, DC), FF.
Reader Comments: Great condition, nice track ... Spectacular layout. Norman did himself proud. A little pricey but worth it once a year ... Very pretty. Premium is on the elevated tee shots ... Great course for a treat.

★★★ **COYOTE CREEK GOLF CLUB**
PU-One Coyote Creek Golf Dr., San Jose, 95037, Santa Clara County, (408)463-1400, 10 miles from San Jose. **Web:** www.coyotecreekgolf.com. **Facility Holes:** 36. **Yards:** 7,027/5,184. **Par:** 72/72. **Course Rating:** 75.5/70.4. **Slope:** 141/124. **Green Fee:** $25/$125. **Cart Fee:** $15/Person. **Walking Policy:** Mandatory carts. **Walkability:** 3. **Opened:** 1999. **Architect:** Jack Nicklaus. **Season:** Year-round. **High:** March-Oct. **To obtain tee times:** Call up to 21 days in advance. **Miscellaneous:** Reduced fees (weekdays, twilight, seniors, juniors), range (grass), credit cards (MC, V), BF, FF.
Reader Comments: Interesting layout carved out of mountain ... Like playing two courses, great clubhouse ... Great course now, needs 20 years for trees to mature ... Strong, interesting finishing holes ... High-end Jack Nicklaus course ... Great finishing holes.
Special Notes: Also has Valley Course.

★★★★ COYOTE HILLS GOLF COURSE
PU-1440 E. Bastachury Rd., Fullerton, 92835, Orange County, (714)672-6800, 5 miles from Anaheim. **E-mail:** campuscoyote@msn.com. **Facility Holes:** 18. **Yards:** 6,510/4,437. **Par:** 70/70. **Course Rating:** 71.1/64.2. **Slope:** 128/108. **Green Fee:** $29/$105. **Cart Fee:** Included in green fee. **Walking Policy:** Mandatory carts. **Walkability:** 4. **Opened:** 1996. **Architect:** Cal Olson/Payne Stewart. **Season:** Year-round. **To obtain tee times:** Call golf shop. **Miscellaneous:** Reduced fees (weekdays, twilight, seniors, juniors), range (grass/mats), credit cards (MC, V, AE, D, DC), BF, FF.
Reader Comments: Excellent challenge … Treated like a king, year after year … A little pricey, but a fun course … Hidden valley very nice touch … Very nice Payne Stewart design … Great tract, great friendly service … Payne's legacy, great practice area … Good layout.

COYOTE MOON
PU-10685 Northwoods Blvd., Truckee, 96161, Nevada County, (530)587-0886. **E-mail:** tahoe-tracy@mindspring.com. **Facility Holes:** 18. **Yards:** 7,177/5,022. **Par:** 72/72. **Course Rating:** 74.1/68.4. **Slope:** 138/127. **Green Fee:** $135. **Cart Fee:** Included in green fee. **Walking Policy:** Unrestricted walking. **Walkability:** 3. **Opened:** 2000. **Architect:** Brad Bell. **Season:** May-Oct. **To obtain tee times:** Call up to 30 days in advance. **Miscellaneous:** Reduced fees (twilight), credit cards (MC, V, AE), BF, FF.

★★ CREEKSIDE GOLF COURSE
PU-701 Lincoln Ave., Modesto, 95354, Stanislaus County, (209)571-5123, 25 miles from Stockton. **Facility Holes:** 18. **Yards:** 6,610/5,496. **Par:** 72/72. **Course Rating:** 70.3/69.5. **Slope:** 115/108. **Green Fee:** $14/$26. **Cart Fee:** $20/Cart. **Walking Policy:** Unrestricted walking. **Walkability:** 2. **Opened:** 1992. **Architect:** Halsey/Durey. **Season:** Year-round. **To obtain tee times:** Call up to 7 days in advance. **Miscellaneous:** Reduced fees (weekdays, twilight, seniors, juniors), metal spikes, range (grass), credit cards (MC, V), BF, FF.

CROSSCREEK GOLF CLUB
PU-43860 Glen Meadows Rd., Temecula, 92590, Riverside County, (909)506-3402, 50 miles from San Diego. **Web:** crosscreekgolfclub.com. **Facility Holes:** 18. **Yards:** 6,831/4,606. **Par:** 71/71. **Course Rating:** 74.1/67.4. **Slope:** 142/118. **Green Fee:** $60/$85. **Cart Fee:** Included in green fee. **Walking Policy:** Unrestricted walking. **Walkability:** 3. **Opened:** 2001. **Architect:** Arthur Hills. **Season:** Year-round. **To obtain tee times:** Call up to 7 days in advance. **Misc:** Reduced fees (weekdays, juniors), range (grass), credit cards (MC, V, AE), BF, FF.

★★ CRYSTAL SPRINGS GOLF CLUB
SP-6650 Golf Course Dr., Burlingame, 94010, San Mateo County, (650)342-0603, 20 miles from San Francisco. **E-mail:** csgcpro@pacbell.net. **Web:** www.playcrystalsprings.com. **Facility Holes:** 18. **Yards:** 6,683/5,420. **Par:** 72/72. **Course Rating:** 72.1/74.0. **Slope:** 125/130. **Green Fee:** $42/$80. **Cart Fee:** $14/Person. **Walking Policy:** Walking at certain times. **Walkability:** 3. **Opened:** 1920. **Architect:** Herbert Fowler. **Season:** Year-round. **To obtain tee times:** Call golf shop. **Miscellaneous:** Reduced fees (weekdays, twilight, seniors, juniors), range (mats), credit cards (MC, V, AE), BF, FF.

★★★ CYPRESS GOLF CLUB
PU-4921 Katella Ave., Los Alamitos, 90720, Orange County, (714)527-1800, 22 miles from Los Angeles. **E-mail:** shimanosan@aol.com. **Web:** www.cypressgolfclub.com. **Facility Holes:** 18. **Yards:** 6,476/5,188. **Par:** 71/71. **Course Rating:** 71.4/69.0. **Slope:** 129/122. **Green Fee:** $45/$75. **Cart Fee:** Included in green fee. **Walking Policy:** Unrestricted walking. **Walkability:** 5. **Opened:** 1992. **Architect:** Perry Dye. **Season:** Year-round. **To obtain tee times:** Call up to 14 days in advance. **Miscellaneous:** Reduced fees (weekdays, twilight, juniors), range (grass/mats), credit cards (MC, V, AE, D, JCB - Diners), BF, FF.
Reader Comments: Wonderful value as a walk-on … Late fall/early winter are perfect tee-to-green conditions, better than many private clubs. Newly renovated, very short course, can't use driver or long irons. Excellent practice facilities … Newer configuration, much impressed … Tough course, but fair! Bring your A game.

★★★½ CYPRESS RIDGE GOLF CLUB
PU-780 Cypress Ridge Pkwy., Arroyo Grande, 93420, San Luis Obispo County, (805)474-7979, 15 miles from San Luis Obispo. **E-mail:** crproshop@charter.net. **Web:** www.cypressridge.com. **Facility Holes:** 18. **Yards:** 6,803/5,087. **Par:** 72/72. **Course Rating:** 73.0/70.3. **Slope:** 133/120. **Green Fee:** $30/$55. **Cart Fee:** $12/Person. **Walking Policy:** Walking at certain times. **Walkability:** 3. **Opened:** 1999. **Architect:** Peter Jacobsen & Jim Hardy. **Season:** Year-round. **High:** May-Nov. **To obtain tee times:** Call up to 10 days in advance. **Miscellaneous:** Reduced fees (weekdays, twilight, juniors), range (grass), credit cards (MC, V, AE, D), BF, FF.

CALIFORNIA

Reader Comments: Stunning … Well-balanced design … A very good course that will get better with age … Nice clubhouse. Course is manicured very well. Bring all of your clubs, you will need them. Outstanding finishing par 5 … Beautiful new course … Beautiful course and facilities, excellent staff.

★★½ DAD MILLER GOLF COURSE
PU-430 N. Gilbert St., Anaheim, 92801, Orange County, (714)765-3481, 20 miles from Los Angeles. **Facility Holes:** 18. **Yards:** 6,025/5,362. **Par:** 71/71. **Course Rating:** 68.0/70.2. **Slope:** 108/116. **Green Fee:** $20/$32. **Cart Fee:** $24/Cart. **Walking Policy:** Unrestricted walking. **Walkability:** 1. **Opened:** 1961. **Architect:** Dick Miller/Wayne Friday. **Season:** Year-round. **To obtain tee times:** Call up to 7 days in advance. **Miscellaneous:** Reduced fees (weekdays, seniors), range (grass/mats), credit cards (MC, V, D), BF, FF.

★★½ DAIRY CREEK GOLF COURSE
PU-2990 Dairy Creek Rd., San Luis Obispo, 93405, San Luis Obispo County, (805)782-8060. **Facility Holes:** 18. **Yards:** 6,548/4,965. **Par:** 71/71. **Course Rating:** 71.9/69.0. **Slope:** 127/121. **Green Fee:** $25/$35. **Cart Fee:** $20/Cart. **Walking Policy:** Unrestricted walking. **Opened:** 1996. **Architect:** John Harbottle. **To obtain tee times:** Call golf shop.

★★½ DAVIS GOLF COURSE
PU-24439 Fairway Dr.; Davis, 95616, Yolo County, (530)756-4010, 12 miles from Sacramento. **Facility Holes:** 18. **Yards:** 4,953/4,428. **Par:** 67/67. **Course Rating:** 62.9/63.9. **Slope:** 102/95. **Green Fee:** $8/$16. **Cart Fee:** $9/Person. **Walking Policy:** Unrestricted walking. **Walkability:** 1. **Opened:** 1964. **Architect:** Bob Baldock. **Season:** Year-round. **To obtain tee times:** Call up to 7 days in advance. **Miscellaneous:** Reduced fees (weekdays, twilight, seniors, juniors), metal spikes, range (mats), credit cards (MC, V), BF, FF.

★★½ DEBELL GOLF CLUB
PU-1500 Walnut Ave., Burbank, 91504, Los Angeles County, (818)845-0022, 3 miles from Los Angeles. **Facility Holes:** 18. **Yards:** 5,610/5,412. **Par:** 71/73. **Course Rating:** 67.4/72.9. **Slope:** 108/126. **Green Fee:** $15/$19. **Cart Fee:** $20/Cart. **Walking Policy:** Unrestricted walking. **Walkability:** 4. **Opened:** 1958. **Architect:** William F. Bell/William H. Johnson. **Season:** Year-round. **To obtain tee times:** Call golf shop. **Miscellaneous:** Reduced fees (weekdays, twilight, seniors, juniors), metal spikes, range (mats), credit cards (MC, V).

★★★½ DELAVEAGA GOLF CLUB
PU-401 Upper Park Rd., Santa Cruz, 95065, Santa Cruz County, (831)423-7214, 25 miles from San Jose. **E-mail:** davel@delaveagagolf.com. **Web:** www.Delaveagagolf.com. **Facility Holes:** 18. **Yards:** 6,010/5,331. **Par:** 72/72. **Course Rating:** 70.4/70.6. **Slope:** 133/125. **Green Fee:** $35/$45. **Cart Fee:** $17/Person. **Walking Policy:** Unrestricted walking. **Walkability:** 3. **Opened:** 1970. **Architect:** Bert Stamps. **Season:** Year-round. **To obtain tee times:** Call up to 7 days in advance. **Miscellaneous:** Reduced fees (weekdays, twilight), range (mats), credit cards (MC, V, AE, D), BF, FF.
Reader Comments: A real test. Beautiful scenery … This is a very fun course to play. It is pretty narrow with canyons, hillsides, and trees lining almost every fairway … What a course! Bring your A game, and lots of balls … Excellent value, sporty, fun layout.

★★★★ DESERT DUNES GOLF CLUB
PU-19300 Palm Dr., Desert Hot Springs, 92240, Riverside County, (760)251-5367, (888)423-8637, 5 miles from Palm Springs. **Web:** www.desertdunes.com. **Facility Holes:** 18. **Yards:** 6,876/5,359. **Par:** 72/72. **Course Rating:** 73.8/70.7. **Slope:** 142/122. **Green Fee:** $30/$120. **Cart Fee:** Included in green fee. **Walking Policy:** Mandatory carts. **Walkability:** 2. **Opened:** 1989. **Architect:** Robert Trent Jones Jr. **Season:** Year-round. **High:** Jan.-April. **To obtain tee times:** Call up to 7 days in advance. **Miscellaneous:** Reduced fees (weekdays, guests, twilight), range (grass/mats), credit cards (MC, V, AE), FF.
Reader Comments: I've played this course during the summer for $20! It's a links course and sometimes it can be very windy!!! … One of the best in the desert, tough, windy, beautiful … Good condition … Good variety and fun … Very good links course.

★★★★ DESERT FALLS COUNTRY CLUB
SP-1111 Desert Falls Pkwy., Palm Desert, 92211, Riverside County, (760)340-4653. **Web:** www.desertfalls.com. **Facility Holes:** 18. **Yards:** 7,017/5,313. **Par:** 72/72. **Course Rating:** 75.0/71,7. **Slope:** 145/124. **Green Fee:** $30/$180. **Cart Fee:** Included in green fee. **Walkability:** 4. **Opened:** 1984. **Architect:** Ron Fream. **Season:** Year-round. **High:** Nov.-April. **To obtain tee times:** Call golf shop. **Misc:** Reduced fees (twilight), range (grass), credit cards (MC, V).
Reader Comments: Good layout, challenging greens … Good desert course … Nice design, good use of desert plants … From the back tees one of the best in the desert … Meticulously kept … This is a must-play when in the Palm Springs area.

CALIFORNIA

★★★★ DESERT PRINCESS COUNTRY CLUB & RESORT
R-28-555 Landau Blvd., Cathedral City, 92234, Riverside County, (760)322-2280, (800)637-0577, 2 miles from Palm Springs. **Facility Holes:** 27. **Green Fee:** $45/$120. **Cart Fee:** Included in green fee. **Walking Policy:** Mandatory carts. **Walkability:** 4. **Opened:** 1984. **Architect:** David Rainville. **Season:** Nov.-Sept. **High:** Nov.-April. **To obtain tee times:** Call up to 2 days in advance. **Miscellaneous:** Reduced fees (weekdays, guests, twilight), range (grass), credit cards (MC, V, AE), FF.
CIELO/VISTA (18 Combo)
Yards: 6,764/5,273. **Par:** 72/72. **Course Rating:** 72.5/70.3. **Slope:** 126/118.
LAGOS/CIELO (18 Combo)
Yards: 6,587/5,217. **Par:** 72/72. **Course Rating:** 71.2/69.8. **Slope:** 121/119.
VISTA/LAGOS (18 Combo)
Yards: 6,667/5,298. **Par:** 72/72. **Course Rating:** 71.8/69.9. **Slope:** 123/117.
Reader Comments: Took lessons, excellent beautiful course … Target golf, requires accuracy off tee. … Friendly staff.

DESERT WILLOW GOLF RESORT
PU-38-995 Desert Willow Drive, Palm Desert, 92260, Riverside County, (760)346-7060, (800)320-3323, 130 miles from Los Angeles. **E-mail:** ggoodsell@desertwillow.com. **Web:** www.desertwillow.com. **Facility Holes:** 36. **Green Fee:** $65/$165. **Cart Fee:** Included in green fee. **Walking Policy:** Mandatory carts. **Walkability:** 3. **Architect:** Michael Hurdzan/Dana Fry/John Cook. **Season:** Year-round. **High:** Jan.-April. **To obtain tee times:** Call up to 30 days in advance. **Miscellaneous:** Reduced fees (weekdays, guests, twilight, seniors, juniors), range (grass), lodging (300 rooms), credit cards (MC, V, AE, D), BF, FF.
★★★★½ FIRECLIFF COURSE (18) *Condition*
Yards: 7,056/5,079. **Par:** 72/72. **Course Rating:** 74.1/69.0. **Slope:** 138/120. **Opened:** 1997.
Reader Comments: Great scenery, wonderful staff … This is one of the best courses in an area full of great golf courses … Great views. Lots of sand. Bring your straight game or lots of trouble in the sand. Terrific deal for locals … Always in great condition … The Pride of Palm Desert.
MOUNTAIN VIEW COURSE (18)
Yards: 6,913/4,997. **Par:** 72/72. **Course Rating:** 73.4/69.0. **Slope:** 129/119. **Opened:** 1998.

★★½ DIABLO CREEK GOLF COURSE
PU-4050 Port Chicago Hwy., Concord, 94520, Contra Costa County, (925)686-6262, 40 miles from San Francisco. **E-mail:** sandy@ci.concord.ca.us. **Facility Holes:** 18. **Yards:** 6,876/5,891. **Par:** 71/72. **Course Rating:** 72.4/73.1. **Slope:** 123/122. **Green Fee:** $20/$28. **Cart Fee:** $12/Person. **Walking Policy:** Unrestricted walking. **Walkability:** 1. **Opened:** 1962. **Architect:** Robert Muir Graves. **Season:** Year-round. **High:** Year-round. **To obtain tee times:** Call up to 7 days in advance. **Miscellaneous:** Reduced fees (weekdays, twilight, seniors, juniors), metal spikes, range (mats), credit cards (MC, V, AE, D), BF, FF.

DIABLO GRANDE RESORT
R-10001 Oak Flat Rd., Patterson, 95363, Stanislaus County, (209)892-4653, 75 miles from Sacramento. **Facility Holes:** 36. **Cart Fee:** Included in green fee. **Walking Policy:** Unrestricted walking. **Walkability:** 4. **Season:** Year-round. **To obtain tee times:** Call up to 7 days in advance. **Miscellaneous:** Range (grass/mats), credit cards (MC, V, AE, D), BF, FF.
★★★★½ LEGENDS WEST COURSE AT DIABLO GRANDE (18) *Condition, Pace*
Yards: 7,112/4,905. **Par:** 72/72. **Course Rating:** 74.3/68.1. **Slope:** 143/120. **Fee:** $80/$100. **Opened:** 1998. **Architect:** Jack Nicklaus/Gene Sarazen. **Misc:** Reduced fees (guests).
Reader Comments: Awesome course. Great experience. Can't wait to get out there again … Remote location, worth the drive … Very nice course. Women friendly … Strong par 3s … A course that plays easier than the scorecard … Great course, challenging. Treat people right … Staff is excellent, hilly with tricky greens … Excellent course, very challenging, hilly fairways. An all weather course, playable even after heavy rains.
★★★★½ RANCH COURSE AT DIABLO GRANDE (18) *Condition, Pace*
Yards: 7,243/5,026. **Par:** 72/71. **Course Rating:** 75.1/69.0. **Slope:** 139/116. **Green Fee:** $40/$85. **Opened:** 1996. **Architect:** Denis Griffiths. **Miscellaneous:** Reduced fees (weekdays).
Reader Comments: A tough long course from the tips with a few holes that are just monsters. Would pay to see the pros play this yardage monster … One of the finest resorts I have ever been to. Great time … This is one of the most challenging courses I have played … You'll need all 14 clubs here … Staff is excellent … A truly awesome facility.

★★ DIAMOND BAR GOLF CLUB
PU-22751 E. Golden Springs Dr., Diamond Bar, 91765, Los Angeles County, (909)861-8282, 25 miles from Los Angeles. **Facility Holes:** 18. **Yards:** 6,810/6,009. **Par:** 72/73. **Course Rating:** 72.8/73.9. **Slope:** 125/122. **Green Fee:** $20/$25. **Cart Fee:** $11/Person. **Walking Policy:** Unrestricted walking. **Walkability:** 2. **Opened:** 1964. **Architect:** William F. Bell. **Season:** Year-round. **To obtain tee times:** Call up to 7 days in advance. **Misc:** Reduced fees (weekdays, twilight, seniors, juniors), range (mats), credit cards (MC, V, AE, D), BF, FF.

CALIFORNIA

★★★★ DIAMOND VALLEY GOLF CLUB
PU-31220 Sage Rd., Hemet, 92543, Riverside County, (909)767-0828, 25 miles from Riverside. **E-mail:** diamondvalleygolf.com. **Web:** www.diamondvalleygolf.com. **Facility Holes:** 18. **Yards:** 6,720/5,634. **Par:** 72/72. **Course Rating:** 73.0/72.3. **Slope:** 135/128. **Green Fee:** $25/$60. **Cart Fee:** $11/Person. **Walking Policy:** Unrestricted walking. **Walkability:** 3. **Opened:** 1999. **Architect:** Art Magnuson. **Season:** Year-round. **To obtain tee times:** Call up to 7 days in advance. **Miscellaneous:** Reduced fees (twilight, seniors, juniors), range (grass), credit cards (MC, V, AE, D), BF, FF.
Reader Comments: For $, it is excellent. Target golf at its best! It's a long drive to get to but worth it!! ... For pure golf, great value coming out of the Los Angeles/Orange County area with not too far a drive. Course is off the beaten path, conditions were good ... Fast undulating greens, excellent value ... Fun tract, great value.

★★★ DOUBLETREE CARMEL HIGHLAND RESORT
R-14455 Penasquitos Dr., San Diego, 92129, San Diego County, (619)672-9100, (866)912-4653, 20 miles from San Diego. **E-mail:** irishpro@pga.com. **Web:** www.highlanddoubletreehotels.com. **Facility Holes:** 18. **Yards:** 6,428/5,361. **Par:** 72/72. **Course Rating:** 70.7/71.9. **Slope:** 123/125. **Green Fee:** $50/$75. **Cart Fee:** Included in green fee. **Walking Policy:** Walking at certain times. **Walkability:** 4. **Opened:** 1967. **Architect:** Jack Daray. **Season:** Year-round. **High:** Jan.-April. **To obtain tee times:** Call golf shop. **Miscellaneous:** Reduced fees (weekdays, guests, twilight, seniors, juniors), range (grass/mats), credit cards (MC, V, AE, D), BF, FF.
Reader Comments: Enjoyable golf ... Challenging course, fun to play ... Greens are tough to read. For the most part, everything breaks down the hill toward the freeway ... Great conditions, great food, bar and service ... Tight layout ... Good scoring course ... Hilly, fairly short resort course.

DRAGON AT GOLD MOUNTAIN
R-3887 County Rd. A15, Clio, 96106, Plumas County, (530)832-4887, (800)368-7786, 55 miles from Reno, NV. **E-mail:** dragongf@psln.com. **Web:** www.dragongolf.com. **Facility Holes:** 18. **Yards:** 7,077/4,611. **Par:** 72/72. **Course Rating:** 74.2/66.6. **Slope:** 147/128. **Green Fee:** $65/$120. **Cart Fee:** Included in green fee. **Walking Policy:** Unrestricted walking. **Walkability:** 3. **Opened:** 2000. **Architect:** Robin Nelson. **Season:** May-Oct. **High:** June-Sept. **To obtain tee times:** Call up to 365 days in advance. **Miscellaneous:** Reduced fees (twilight, juniors), range (grass/mats), lodging (30 rooms), credit cards (MC, V, AE, D), BF, FF.

★★★½ DRY CREEK RANCH GOLF COURSE
PU-809 Crystal Way, Galt, 95632, Sacramento County, (209)745-4653, 20 miles from Sacramento. **E-mail:** drycreek@softcom.net. **Web:** www.drycreekranch.play18.com. **Facility Holes:** 18. **Yards:** 6,773/5,952. **Par:** 72/74. **Course Rating:** 72.7/73.9. **Slope:** 129/134. **Green Fee:** $18/$30. **Cart Fee:** $20/Cart. **Walking Policy:** Unrestricted walking. **Walkability:** 3. **Opened:** 1962. **Architect:** Jim Fleming. **Season:** Year-round. **High:** April-Oct. **To obtain tee times:** Call up to 14 days in advance. **Miscellaneous:** Reduced fees (weekdays, twilight, seniors, juniors), metal spikes, range (grass), credit cards (MC, V), BF, FF.
Reader Comments: One of our area's best; underrated ... Outstanding course at a great price ... Challenging course that nobody knows about, extremely cheap, great greens and fairways ... A very good course.

★½ DRYDEN PARK GOLF COURSE
PU-920 Sunset Ave., Modesto, 95351, Stanislaus County, (209)577-5359, 40 miles from Stockton. **Facility Holes:** 18. **Yards:** 6,574/6,048. **Par:** 72/74. **Course Rating:** 69.8/72.5. **Slope:** 119/115. **Green Fee:** $13/$23. **Cart Fee:** $22/Cart. **Walking Policy:** Unrestricted walking. **Walkability:** 2. **Opened:** 1953. **Architect:** William F. Bell/William P. Bell. **Season:** Year-round. **To obtain tee times:** Call up to 7 days in advance. **Miscellaneous:** Reduced fees (weekdays, twilight, seniors, juniors), metal spikes, range (grass), credit cards (MC, V), BF, FF.

★★★½ EAGLE CREST GOLF CLUB
PU-2492 Old Ranch Road, Escondido, 92027, San Diego County, (760)737-9762, 20 miles from San Diego. **Facility Holes:** 18. **Yards:** 6,417/4,941. **Par:** 72/72. **Course Rating:** 71.6/69.9. **Slope:** 136/123. **Green Fee:** $43/$65. **Cart Fee:** Included in green fee. **Walkability:** 4. **Opened:** 1993. **Architect:** David Rainville. **Season:** Year-round. **High:** Jan.-May. **To obtain tee times:** Call up to 7 days in advance. **Miscellaneous:** Reduced fees (guests, twilight, seniors, juniors), range (grass/mats), credit cards (MC, V, AE, D, DC), BF, FF.
Reader Comments: Beautiful setting! I have seen ostrich, coyotes, hawks, rattlesnakes ... Good layout, challenging, good variety of holes ... Beautiful setting, peaceful. Keep it straight ... Good risk/reward course ... Tough but fun ... Long and challenging, need to think your way around this course ... Very quiet and relaxing course.

CALIFORNIA

★★★★ **EAGLE GLEN GOLF CLUB** *Service*
PU-1800 Eagle Glen Pkwy., Corona, 92883-0620, Riverside County, (909)272-4653, 50 miles from Los Angeles. **E-mail:** jfairchild@troongolf.com. **Web:** www.troongolf.com. **Facility Holes:** 18. **Yards:** 6,930/4,998. **Par:** 72/72. **Course Rating:** 73.0/67.7. **Slope:** 129/113. **Green Fee:** $75/$100. **Cart Fee:** Included in green fee. **Walking Policy:** Unrestricted walking. **Walkability:** 4. **Opened:** 1999. **Architect:** Gary Roger Baird. **Season:** Year-round. **High:** Year-round. **To obtain tee times:** Call up to 60 days in advance. **Miscellaneous:** Reduced fees (weekdays, twilight, seniors, juniors), range (grass), credit cards (MC, V, AE, D), BF, FF.
Reader Comments: Great experience! … A first-class golf course with great service. Their goal is to make you feel like a country club member and they succeed … Very nice, worth the money … Excellent … One of the best new public access courses I played in Los Angeles area … Spectacular …

★★★½ **EAGLE RIDGE GOLF CLUB**
PU-2951 Club Dr., Gilroy, 95020, Santa Clara County, (408)846-4531, 30 miles from San Jose. **E-mail:** tmejia@eagleridgegc.com. **Web:** www.eagleridgegc.com. **Facility Holes:** 18. **Yards:** 7,005/5,102. **Par:** 72/72. **Course Rating:** 74.0/69.6. **Slope:** 138/119. **Green Fee:** $25/$80. **Cart Fee:** $15/Person. **Walking Policy:** Unrestricted walking. **Opened:** 1999. **Architect:** R Fream/D Dale/J Miller. **Season:** Year-round. **To obtain tee times:** Call up to 30 days in advance. **Miscellaneous:** Reduced fees (weekdays, twilight, seniors, juniors), range (grass/mats), credit cards (MC, V, AE).
Reader Comments: Great variety … One of the better courses in Santa Clara Valley. Great service in pro shop, starters, and restaurant … Perfectly maintained, challenging course, great clubhouse.

★★★½ **EASTLAKE COUNTRY CLUB**
PU-2375 Clubhouse Dr., Chula Vista, 91915, San Diego County, (619)482-5757, 15 miles from San Diego. **Facility Holes:** 18. **Yards:** 6,606/5,118. **Par:** 72/72. **Course Rating:** 70.7/68.8. **Slope:** 116/114. **Green Fee:** $35/$61. **Cart Fee:** Included in green fee. **Walking Policy:** Walking at certain times. **Walkability:** 3. **Opened:** 1991. **Architect:** Ted Robinson. **Season:** Year-round. **High:** Jan.-June. **To obtain tee times:** Call golf shop. **Miscellaneous:** Reduced fees (weekdays, twilight, seniors, juniors), range (grass), credit cards (MC, V, AE).
Reader Comments: Great confidence building course, open wide … Very quiet. Nice layout … Wide open, grip it and rip it.

★★★ **EL DORADO PARK GOLF CLUB**
PU-2400 Studebaker Rd., Long Beach, 90815, Los Angeles County, (562)430-5411, 15 miles from Anaheim. **Facility Holes:** 18. **Yards:** 6,401/5,918. **Par:** 72/73. **Course Rating:** 70.6/74.3. **Slope:** 121/126. **Green Fee:** $15/$23. **Cart Fee:** $21/Cart. **Walking Policy:** Unrestricted walking. **Walkability:** 1. **Opened:** 1960. **Architect:** Ted Robinson. **Season:** Year-round. **To obtain tee times:** Call golf shop. **Miscellaneous:** Metal spikes, range (grass/mats), credit cards (MC, V, AE).
Reader Comments: Old course with character, nice improvements … New pro shop, good course overall … Since they upgraded, it's very good, but not for high-handicapper … Good greens, remodel job great improvement … Public municipal course, very good condition, lots of trees.

EL PRADO GOLF COURSE
PU-6555 Pine Ave., Chino, 91710, San Bernardino County, (909)597-1751, 30 miles from Los Angeles. **Facility Holes:** 36. **Green Fee:** $10/$34. **Cart Fee:** $24/Cart. **Walking Policy:** Unrestricted walking. **Walkability:** 2. **Opened:** 1976. **Architect:** Harry Rainville/David Rainville. **Season:** Year-round. **To obtain tee times:** Call golf shop. **Miscellaneous:** Reduced fees (weekdays, twilight, seniors, juniors), range (grass), credit cards (MC, V), BF, FF.
★★½ **BUTTERFIELD STAGE COURSE** (18)
Yards: 6,508/5,503. **Par:** 72/73. **Course Rating:** 70.6/72.0. **Slope:** 116/118.
★★½ **CHINO CREEK** (18)
Yards: 6,671/5,596. **Par:** 72/73. **Course Rating:** 71.5/72.1. **Slope:** 119/121.

★★ **EL RANCHO VERDE ROYAL VISTA GOLF COURSE**
PU-355 E Country Club Drive, Rialto, 92377, San Bernardino County, (909)875-5346, 5 miles from San Bernardino. **E-mail:** tmagtotoerv@cs.com. **Facility Holes:** 18. **Yards:** 6,822/5,563. **Par:** 72/72. **Course Rating:** 72.8/71.9. **Slope:** 126/118. **Green Fee:** $16/$30. **Cart Fee:** $12/Person. **Walking Policy:** Unrestricted walking. **Walkability:** 1. **Opened:** 1955. **Architect:** Harry Rainville/David Rainville. **Season:** Year-round. **To obtain tee times:** Call up to 7 days in advance. **Miscellaneous:** Reduced fees (weekdays, twilight, seniors, juniors), metal spikes, range (grass/mats), credit cards (MC, V, D), BF, FF.

CALIFORNIA

★★★ EL RIVINO COUNTRY CLUB
PU-5530 El Rivino Rd, Riverside, 92519, Riverside County, (909)684-8905, 3 miles from San Bernardino. **Facility Holes:** 18. **Yards:** 6,466/5,863. **Par:** 73/73. **Slope:** 111/116. **Green Fee:** $13/$31. **Cart Fee:** $24/Cart. **Walkability:** 3. **Opened:** 1956. **Architect:** Joseph Calwell. **Season:** Year-round. **To obtain tee times:** Call golf shop. **Miscellaneous:** Reduced fees (weekdays, twilight), credit cards (MC, V).
Reader Comments: First hole par 6, wide course … A good value, very nice layout … Reachable par 4s for seniors … Fun, wide open course … Worth going out of way for, very challenging … Lots of fun, inexpensive.

★★★ ELKINS RANCH GOLF COURSE
SP-1386 Chambersburg Rd., Fillmore, 93015, Ventura County, (805)524-1440, 20 miles from Valencia. **Facility Holes:** 18. **Yards:** 6,303/5,700. **Par:** 71/72. **Course Rating:** 69.9/72.7. **Slope:** 117/123. **Green Fee:** $24/$30. **Cart Fee:** $24/Person. **Walking Policy:** Unrestricted walking. **Walkability:** 3. **Opened:** 1959. **Architect:** William H. Tucker Jr./Bob Schipper. **Season:** Year-round. **To obtain tee times:** Call up to 10 days in advance. **Miscellaneous:** Reduced fees (weekdays, twilight, seniors, juniors), range (grass/mats), credit cards (MC, V), BF, FF.
Reader Comments: Old parklands course in hills among citrus … It is a gem, nice to play … Beautiful location, good value … A favorite place to play … A little gem.

★★★½ EMPIRE LAKES GOLF COURSE
PU-11015 Sixth St., Rancho Cucamonga, 91730, San Bernardino County, (909)481-6663, 1 mile from Ontario. **E-mail:** info@empirelakes.com. **Web:** www.empirelakes.com. **Facility Holes:** 18. **Yards:** 6,923/5,200. **Par:** 72/72. **Course Rating:** 73.4/70.5. **Slope:** 133/125. **Green Fee:** $55/$80. **Cart Fee:** Included in green fee. **Walking Policy:** Unrestricted walking. **Walkability:** 2. **Opened:** 1996. **Architect:** Arnold Palmer/Ed Seay. **Season:** Year-round. **To obtain tee times:** Call up to 7 days in advance. **Miscellaneous:** Reduced fees (weekdays, twilight, seniors, juniors), range (grass/mats), credit cards (MC, V, AE, D, DC), BF, FF.
Reader Comments: You may want to walk it … Palmer design keeps you working for a good score … Very challenging and very good … Beautiful … Good senior rate … Very nicely maintained. Nice design … In very good shape. Nice layout … Great course and service.

★★★ ENCINITAS RANCH GOLF CLUB
PU-1275 Quail Gardens Dr., Encinitas, 92024, San Diego County, (760)944-1936, 22 miles from San Diego. **E-mail:** rlinville@jcresorts.com. **Facility Holes:** 18. **Yards:** 6,523/5,235. **Par:** 72/72. **Course Rating:** 71.2/70.3. **Slope:** 127/118. **Green Fee:** $35/$73. **Cart Fee:** $12/Person. **Walking Policy:** Unrestricted walking. **Walkability:** 3. **Opened:** 1998. **Architect:** Cary Bickler. **Season:** Year-round. **To obtain tee times:** Call up to 7 days in advance. **Miscellaneous:** Reduced fees (twilight, juniors), range (grass/mats), credit cards (MC, V, AE, D), BF, FF.
Reader Comments: Great ocean views, unique layout … Somewhat easy new course, small trees … Every hole different, great views and interesting. Potentially great … Nice course, well managed, excellent condition … Ocean view on 12 holes.

★★★★½ FALL RIVER VALLEY GOLF & COUNTRY CLUB
PU-42889 State Hwy., 299 E., Fall River Mills, 96028, Shasta County, (530)336-5555, 70 miles from Redding. **Facility Holes:** 18. **Yards:** 7,365/6,020. **Par:** 72/72. **Course Rating:** 74.9/73.2. **Slope:** 131/128. **Green Fee:** $16/$29. **Cart Fee:** $24/Cart. **Walking Policy:** Unrestricted walking. **Walkability:** 2. **Opened:** 1978. **Architect:** Clark Glasson. **Season:** April-Nov. **High:** June-Oct. **To obtain tee times:** Call up to 14 days in advance. **Miscellaneous:** Reduced fees (weekdays, twilight, seniors, juniors), metal spikes, range (grass/mats), credit cards (MC, V), BF, FF.
Reader Comments: A very nice course that not a lot of people know about and that makes it kind of nice … Great golfing experience … The combination of challenge, fairness, scenic beauty and affordability make this course one of the best in all California … Big, powerful, surprisingly memorable.

★★½ FALLBROOK GOLF CLUB
PU-2757 Gird Rd., Fallbrook, 92028, San Diego County, (760)728-8334, 40 miles from San Diego. **E-mail:** flbkgolf@adnc.com. **Facility Holes:** 18. **Yards:** 6,223/5,597. **Par:** 72/72. **Course Rating:** 69.9/73.8. **Slope:** 119/130. **Green Fee:** $13/$35. **Cart Fee:** $24/Cart. **Walking Policy:** Unrestricted walking. **Walkability:** 2. **Opened:** 1961. **Architect:** Harry Rainville. **Season:** Year-round. **High:** March-May. **To obtain tee times:** Call up to 10 days in advance. **Miscellaneous:** Reduced fees (weekdays, twilight, juniors), range (grass/mats), credit cards (MC, V, D), BF, FF.

★★★½ FIG GARDEN GOLF CLUB
SP-7700 N. Van Ness Blvd., Fresno, 93711, Fresno County, (559)439-2928. **E-mail:** Affordablegolf@juno.com. **Facility Holes:** 18. **Yards:** 6,700/5,510. **Par:** 72/72. **Course Rating:**

69.6/71.6. **Slope:** 119/124. **Green Fee:** $15/$50. **Cart Fee:** $25/Cart. **Walking Policy:** Unrestricted walking. **Walkability:** 2. **Opened:** 1958. **Architect:** Nick Lombardo. **Season:** Year-round. **To obtain tee times:** Call golf shop. **Miscellaneous:** Reduced fees (weekdays, twilight, juniors), metal spikes, range (mats), credit cards (MC, V, AE, D), BF, FF.
Reader Comments: A very nice course, although a little on the short side. Tests your accuracy, short game, and putting … Short but challenging … Loved this course.

★★★★ **THE FOUNTAINGROVE CLUB**
SP-1525 Fountaingrove Pkwy., Santa Rosa, 95403, Sonoma County, (707)579-4653, 50 miles from San Francisco. **Web:** www.fountaingrovegolf.com. **Facility Holes:** 18. **Yards:** 6,990/5,424. **Par:** 72/72. **Course Rating:** 73.3/71.0. **Slope:** 135/125. **Green Fee:** $75/$95. **Cart Fee:** Included in green fee. **Walking Policy:** Mandatory carts. **Walkability:** 3. **Opened:** 1985. **Architect:** Ted Robinson. **Season:** Year-round. **To obtain tee times:** Call up to 2 days in advance. **Miscellaneous:** Reduced fees (weekdays, twilight), range (grass), credit cards (MC, V, AE), BF, FF.
Reader Comments: Course has matured well in its 15 years … Nice course … Very nice course for the $ … Play it while it is still public … What a layout! Worth every dime. Best in area … Beautiful atmosphere, good course.
Special Notes: Formerly Fountaingrove Resort & Country Club.

★★★★½ **FOUR SEASONS RESORT AVIARA** *Service, Pace*
R-7447 Batiquitos Dr., Carlsbad, 92009, San Diego County, (760)603-6900, 30 miles from San Diego. **Facility Holes:** 18. **Yards:** 7,007/5,007. **Par:** 72/72. **Course Rating:** 74.2/69.1. **Slope:** 137/119. **Green Fee:** $175/$195. **Cart Fee:** Included in green fee. **Walking Policy:** Mandatory carts. **Walkability:** 3. **Opened:** 1991. **Architect:** Arnold Palmer/Ed Seay. **Season:** Year-round. **To obtain tee times:** Call up to 6 days in advance. **Miscellaneous:** Reduced fees (guests, juniors), range (grass/mats), lodging (329 rooms), credit cards (MC, V, AE, DC, Diners Club, JCB), BF, FF.
Reader Comments: With California being the most expensive place to play golf and all the choices in the $100 bracket, this is worth the week's grocery money … A truly beautiful course, with a great staff … Worth the price … Great track, well maintained … Beautiful … Just a paradise to play.

★★½ **FRANKLIN CANYON GOLF COURSE**
PU-Highway 4, Hercules, 94547, Contra Costa County, (510)799-6191, 22 miles from San Francisco. **Web:** mgow43@aol.com. **Facility Holes:** 18. **Yards:** 6,776/5,516. **Par:** 72/72. **Course Rating:** 70.9/71.2. **Slope:** 118/123. **Green Fee:** $26/$48. **Cart Fee:** $13/Person. **Walking Policy:** Unrestricted walking. **Walkability:** 3. **Opened:** 1968. **Architect:** Robert Muir Graves. **Season:** Year-round. **To obtain tee times:** Call up to 7 days in advance. **Miscellaneous:** Reduced fees (weekdays, twilight, seniors, juniors), metal spikes, range (mats), credit cards (MC, V, AE, D, DC), BF, FF.

★½ **FURNACE CREEK GOLF COURSE**
R-Hwy. 190, Death Valley, 92328, Inyo County, (760)786-2301, 140 miles from Las Vegas. **Web:** www.furnacecreekresort.com. **Facility Holes:** 18. **Yards:** 6,215/4,724. **Par:** 70/70. **Course Rating:** 69.6/66.0. **Slope:** 114/109. **Green Fee:** $30/$50. **Cart Fee:** $13/Person. **Walking Policy:** Unrestricted walking. **Walkability:** 2. **Opened:** 1937. **Architect:** William P. Bell/Perry Dye. **Season:** Year-round. **High:** Oct.-May. **To obtain tee times:** Call up to 365 days in advance. **Miscellaneous:** Reduced fees (guests, twilight, juniors), range (grass), lodging (224 rooms), credit cards (MC, V, AE, D, DC, CB), BF, FF.

★★½ **GENERAL OLD GOLF COURSE**
PU-6104 Village West Dr., Riverside, 92518, Riverside County, (909)697-6690, 10 miles from Riverside. **Facility Holes:** 18. **Yards:** 6,783/5,923. **Par:** 72/72. **Course Rating:** 71.9/73.1. **Slope:** 118/120. **Green Fee:** $13/$29. **Cart Fee:** $11/Person. **Walking Policy:** Unrestricted walking. **Walkability:** 2. **Opened:** 1955. **Season:** Year-round. **To obtain tee times:** Call up to 7 days in advance. **Miscellaneous:** Reduced fees (weekdays, twilight, seniors, juniors), metal spikes, range (grass), credit cards (MC, V, AE, D), BF, FF.

★★★½ **GLEN ANNIE GOLF COURSE**
PU-405 Glen Annie Rd., Goleta, 93117, Santa Barbara County, (805)968-6400, 5 miles from Santa Barbara. **E-mail:** glenannie@aol.com. **Web:** www.glenannie-golf.com. **Facility Holes:** 18. **Yards:** 6,420/5,036. **Par:** 71/71. **Course Rating:** 71.1/69.5. **Slope:** 122/118. **Green Fee:** $60/$75. **Cart Fee:** Included in green fee. **Walking Policy:** Unrestricted walking. **Walkability:** 5. **Opened:** 1997. **Architect:** R.M. Graves/D. Pascuzzo/N. Meagher. **Season:** Year-round. **To obtain tee times:** Call up to 7 days in advance. **Miscellaneous:** Reduced fees (weekdays, twilight, seniors, juniors), range (grass), credit cards (MC, V, AE, D, DC, Diners Club), BF, FF.
Reader Comments: Fun layout with elevation changes … Beautiful course … Very thick rough … Beautiful ocean views from most holes. Newer course, need to have all the shots … Nice new course, rewards good shots. Requires smart play … Challenging, tough but fair.

CALIFORNIA

★★ GOLD HILLS GOLF CLUB

PU-1950 Gold Hill Dr, Redding, 96003, Shasta County, (530)246-7867, 3 miles from Redding. **Facility Holes:** 18. **Yards:** 6,562/4,836. **Par:** 72/72. **Course Rating:** 72.2/68.8. **Slope:** 135/120. **Green Fee:** $30/$40. **Cart Fee:** $10/Person. **Walking Policy:** Unrestricted walking. **Walkability:** 4. **Opened:** 1978. **Season:** Year-round. **To obtain tee times:** Call up to 7 days in advance. **Miscellaneous:** Reduced fees (seniors, juniors), range (grass/mats), credit cards (MC, V, D), BF, FF.

★★★★ THE GOLF CLUB AT RODDY RANCH

PU-1 Tour Way, Antioch, 94509, Contra Costa County, (925)978-4653, 30 miles from Oakland. **E-mail:** Fitz@PGA.com. **Web:** www.roddyranch.com. **Facility Holes:** 18. **Yards:** 6,945/5,390. **Par:** 72/72. **Course Rating:** 74.3/71.7. **Slope:** 131/120. **Green Fee:** $55/$75. **Cart Fee:** Included in green fee. **Walking Policy:** Walking at certain times. **Walkability:** 3. **Opened:** 2000. **Architect:** J. Michael Poellet. **Season:** Year-round. **To obtain tee times:** Call up to 30 days in advance. **Miscellaneous:** Reduced fees (twilight, seniors, juniors), range (grass), credit cards (MC, V, AE, D, DC), BF, FF.
Reader Comments: Great new course, with nary a house in sight … Magnificent setting and views. No clubhouse yet but staff was nice and the owner was around! Interesting holes, nice variety … A hidden jewel with only two quirky holes. A must-play for the price … Superb new course design and condition.

★★★★ THE GOLF CLUB AT WHITEHAWK RANCH *Condition*

R-1137 Hwy. 89, Clio, 96106, Plumas County, (530)836-0394, (800)332-4295, 60 miles from Reno, NV. **E-mail:** golfshop@golfwhitehawk.com. **Web:** www.golfwhitehawk.com. **Facility Holes:** 18. **Yards:** 6,928/4,816. **Par:** 71/71. **Course Rating:** 72.4/64.2. **Slope:** 130/115. **Green Fee:** $75/$115. **Cart Fee:** Included in green fee. **Walking Policy:** Unrestricted walking. **Walkability:** 2. **Opened:** 1996. **Architect:** Dick Bailey. **Season:** May-Nov. **High:** June-Oct. **To obtain tee times:** Call up to 180 days in advance. **Miscellaneous:** Reduced fees (guests, twilight, juniors), range (grass), lodging (12 rooms), credit cards (MC, V, AE), BF, FF.
Reader Comments: Best conditioned course in the Sierra … One of the best golf experiences ever … Tops: beauty, condition, service, best practice facility I know … One of my favorite courses. Great layout and views. Worth the drive.

GOLF RESORT AT INDIAN WELLS

R-44-500 Indian Wells Lane, Indian Wells, 92210, Riverside County, (760)346-4653, 19 miles from Palm Springs. **Facility Holes:** 36. **Green Fee:** $40/$120. **Cart Fee:** Included in green fee. **Walking Policy:** Mandatory carts. **Walkability:** 2. **Opened:** 1986. **Architect:** Ted Robinson. **Season:** Year-round. **To obtain tee times:** Call up to 14 days in advance. **Miscellaneous:** Reduced fees (weekdays, guests, twilight), metal spikes, range (grass/mats), credit cards (MC, V, AE, Diners Club), FF.
★★★★ EAST COURSE (18)
Yards: 6,631/5,516. **Par:** 72/72. **Course Rating:** 71.7/71.5. **Slope:** 122/113.
Reader Comments: Beautiful course, pro shop and starter are all great. Course is challenging … Beautiful resort course, fair play, excellent facilities … Nice resort course, joy to play … Pricey but fun.
★★★½ WEST COURSE (18)
Yards: 6,500/5,408. **Par:** 72/72. **Course Rating:** 70.7/71.0. **Slope:** 120/127.
Reader Comments: Elevated tees and mountainside make tee shots challenging … Beautiful views. Friendly staff … Really a fun golf course, fairly easy, but very good.

★★★½ GOOSE CREEK GOLF CLUB

PU-11418 68th St., Mira Loma, 91752, Riverside County, (909)735-3982, 10 miles from Ontario. **Facility Holes:** 18. **Yards:** 6,520/5,052. **Par:** 70/70. **Course Rating:** 71.1/69.4. **Slope:** 127/115. **Green Fee:** $32/$52. **Cart Fee:** $8/Person. **Walking Policy:** Unrestricted walking. **Walkability:** 1. **Opened:** 1999. **Architect:** Brian Curley and Lee Schmidt. **Season:** Year-round. **To obtain tee times:** Call up to 7 days in advance. **Miscellaneous:** Reduced fees (twilight, seniors, juniors), range (grass), credit cards (MC, V, AE), BF, FF.
Reader Comments: Great course for the price. Easy to walk … A nice little course, friendly with good service … Rolling greens are challenge. Front nine narrow. Tough in the wind. Outstanding new course … It's one of the best bargains around and the course is in excellent condition … Prices great for this course.

★★★½ GRAEAGLE MEADOWS GOLF COURSE *Value*

R-Highway 89, Graeagle, 96103, Plumas County, (530)836-2323, 58 miles from Reno. **E-mail:** teetimes@playgraeagle.com. **Web:** www.playgraeagle.com. **Facility Holes:** 18. **Yards:** 6,725/5,589. **Par:** 72/72. **Course Rating:** 72.1/71.0. **Slope:** 129/127. **Green Fee:** $25/$45. **Cart Fee:** $30/Cart. **Walking Policy:** Unrestricted walking. **Walkability:** 3. **Opened:** 1967. **Architect:** Ellis Van Gorder. **Season:** April-Nov. **High:** June-Sept. **To obtain tee times:** Call up to 180 days in advance. **Miscellaneous:** Reduced fees (weekdays, twilight), metal spikes, range (grass),

credit cards (MC, V, D), BF, FF.
Reader Comments: You have to use every club in the bag ... Best kept secret in the mountains ... Wide open, let'er rip, excellent mountain resort ... Great layout, a river runs through it.

GREEN RIVER GOLF COURSE
PU-5215 Green River Rd., Corona, 91720, Riverside County, (909)737-7393, 25 miles from San Bernardino. **Facility Holes:** 36. **Green Fee:** $15/$30. **Cart Fee:** $11/Person. **Walking Policy:** Unrestricted walking. **Walkability:** 1. **Opened:** 1965. **Season:** Year-round. **High:** May-Oct. **To obtain tee times:** Call golf shop. **Miscellaneous:** Reduced fees (weekdays, twilight, seniors, juniors), range (grass), credit cards (MC, V, AE, D).
★★½ **ORANGE COURSE** (18)
Yards: 6,470/5,725. **Par:** 71/72. **Course Rating:** 71.1/72.8. **Slope:** 126/125. **Architect:** Harry Rainville.
★★½ **RIVERSIDE COURSE** (18)
Yards: 6,275/5,467. **Par:** 72/71. **Course Rating:** 70.6/71.0. **Slope:** 122/115. **Architect:** Harry Rainville/Cary Bickler.

GREEN TREE GOLF CLUB
PU-999 Leisure Town Rd., Vacaville, 95687, Solano County, (707)448-1420, 30 miles from Sacramento. **Facility Holes:** 27. **Walking Policy:** Unrestricted walking. **Walkability:** 1. **Opened:** 1962. **Season:** Year-round. **High:** March-Nov. **To obtain tee times:** Call golf shop. **Miscellaneous:** Range (mats), credit cards (MC, V).
EXECUTIVE COURSE (9)
Yards: 3,104. **Par:** 29. **Course Rating:** 28.2. **Slope:** 80. **Green Fee:** $9/$12. **Cart Fee:** $0/Person. **Miscellaneous:** Reduced fees (seniors, juniors).
★★½ **GREEN TREE COURSE** (18)
Yards: 6,301/5,261. **Par:** 71/71. **Course Rating:** 70.2/69.9. **Slope:** 119/118. **Green Fee:** $12/$25. **Cart Fee:** $11/Person. **Miscellaneous:** Reduced fees (twilight, seniors, juniors).

★★½ **GREEN TREE GOLF COURSE**
SP-14144 Green Tree Blvd., Victorville, 92392, San Bernardino County, (760)245-4860, 25 miles from San Bernardio. **E-mail:** jlynch@ci.victorville.ca.us. **Facility Holes:** 18. **Yards:** 6,643/5,874. **Par:** 72/72. **Course Rating:** 71.3/72.5. **Slope:** 123/124. **Green Fee:** $19/$23. **Cart Fee:** $11/Person. **Walking Policy:** Walking at certain times. **Walkability:** 3. **Opened:** 1965. **Architect:** William F. Bell. **Season:** Year-round. **To obtain tee times:** Call up to 14 days in advance. **Miscellaneous:** Reduced fees (weekdays, guests, twilight, seniors, juniors), credit cards (MC, V), BF, FF.

★★★½ **GREENHORN CREEK GOLF CLUB**
R-676 McCauley Ranch Rd., Angels Camp, 95222, Calaveras County, (209)736-8111, 50 miles from Stockton. **E-mail:** request@greenhorncreek.com. **Web:** www.greenhorncreek.com. **Facility Holes:** 18. **Yards:** 6,870/5,214. **Par:** 72/72. **Course Rating:** 72.7/70.1. **Slope:** 130/119. **Green Fee:** $30/$53. **Cart Fee:** $18/Person. **Walking Policy:** Unrestricted walking. **Walkability:** 3. **Opened:** 1996. **Architect:** Donald Boos/Patty Sheehan/Dick Lotz. **Season:** Year-round. **High:** March-Oct. **To obtain tee times:** Call golf shop. **Miscellaneous:** Reduced fees (weekdays, guests, twilight, juniors), range (grass/mats), lodging (60 rooms), credit cards (MC, V, AE).
Reader Comments: Redone, big improvement ... Scenic, beautiful country ... Challenging ... Mountain course, great setting, some interesting and fun holes to play ... Lots of variety ... Great views. Good greens. Good wine ... Foothill gem. Underrated ... Staff is outstanding, as are some holes.

GRIFFITH PARK
PU-4730 Crystal Springs Dr., Los Angeles, 90027, Los Angeles County, (323)664-2255. **Facility Holes:** 36. **Green Fee:** $10/$21. **Cart Fee:** $21/Cart. **Walking Policy:** Unrestricted walking. **Walkability:** 4. **Season:** Year-round. **High:** March-Sept. **To obtain tee times:** Call golf shop. **Miscellaneous:** Reduced fees (weekdays, twilight, seniors, juniors), metal spikes, range (mats).
★★½ **HARDING COURSE** (18)
Yards: 6,536/6,028. **Par:** 72/73. **Course Rating:** 70.4/72.5. **Slope:** 115/121. **Opened:** 1924. **Architect:** George C. Thomas, Jr.
★★★ **WILSON COURSE** (18)
Yards: 6,942/6,330. **Par:** 72/73. **Course Rating:** 72.7/74.6. **Slope:** 117/128. **Opened:** 1923. **Architect:** Carl Worthing.
Reader Comments: Great muni track, slow pace of play but worth the wait. Beautiful par-5 1st hole and solid par- 4, uphill finishing hole make it more challenging of the 2 Griffith Park courses ... Aesthetically better than most resorts, condition outstanding considering volume of play ... Good course, hilly in Los Angeles, CA ... Top municipal course in Los Angeles.

HAGGIN OAKS GOLF COURSE
PU-3645 Fulton Ave., Sacramento, 95821, Sacramento County, (916)575-2526. **Facility Holes:** 36. **Cart Fee:** $12/Person. **Walking Policy:** Unrestricted walking. **Walkability:** 1. **Season:** Year-round. **High:** April-Sept. **To obtain tee times:** Call up to 7 days in advance. **Miscellaneous:** Reduced fees (weekdays, twilight, seniors, juniors), range (mats), credit cards (MC, V, AE, D), BF, FF.
★★½ **ALISTER MACKENZIE COURSE** (18)
Yards: 6,683/5,747. **Par:** 72/72. **Course Rating:** 70.6/72.5. **Slope:** 112/124. **Green Fee:** $9/$25. **Opened:** 1932. **Architect:** Alister Mackenzie.
★★ **ARCADE CREEK COURSE** (18)
Yards: 6,903/5,832. **Par:** 72/72. **Course Rating:** 71.4/71.7. **Slope:** 115/111. **Green Fee:** $10/$24. **Opened:** 1962. **Architect:** Michael J. McDonagh.

HALF MOON BAY GOLF CLUB
PU-2000 Fairway Dr., Half Moon Bay, 94019, San Mateo County, (650)726-4438, 20 miles from San Francisco. **Facility Holes:** 36. **Cart Fee:** Included in green fee. **Season:** Year-round. **High:** April-Sept. **To obtain tee times:** Call golf shop. **Miscellaneous:** Lodging (80 rooms), credit cards (MC, V, AE), reduced fees (weekdays, guests, twilight).
★★★½ **LINKS COURSE** (18)
Yards: 7,131/5,769. **Par:** 72/72. **Course Rating:** 75.0/73.3. **Slope:** 135/128. **Green Fee:** $95/$115. **Opened:** 1973. **Architect:** Francis Duane/Arnold Palmer.
Reader Comments: An Arnold Palmer course that is one of his best designs. If you don't mind paying the high price tag, then you'll enjoy this beautiful tree-lined course with the links-style finish … Beautiful ocean views, very forgiving for a links course … Scotland in N. California.
★★★★ **OCEAN COURSE** (18)
Yards: 6,732/5,109. **Par:** 72/72. **Course Rating:** 71.8/71.6. **Slope:** 125/119. **Green Fee:** $115/$135. **Walking Policy:** Unrestricted walking. **Walkability:** 3. **Opened:** 1997. **Architect:** Arthur Hills.
Notes: Ranked 16th in 1999 Best in State.
Reader Comments: Who needs Pebble Beach, this course gives you the ocean views at half the price. Great challenge and incredible scenery. Will play it whenever in the area … Beautiful course demanding from the tips … A beautiful seaside course with ocean views on almost every hole. Wide open links style, no trees. Easy to score when the wind is calm. When the wind blows, it's tough as nails.

★★ HANSEN DAM GOLF COURSE
PU-10400 Glen Oaks Blvd., Pacoima, 91331, Los Angeles County, (818)896-0050, 15 miles from Los Angeles. **Facility Holes:** 18. **Yards:** 6,715/6,090. **Par:** 72/75. **Course Rating:** 70.8/73.8. **Slope:** 115/123. **Green Fee:** $17/$23. **Cart Fee:** $21/Cart. **Walking Policy:** Unrestricted walking. **Walkability:** 3. **Opened:** 1977. **Architect:** Ray Goates. **Season:** Year-round. **High:** April-Sept. **To obtain tee times:** Call golf shop. **Miscellaneous:** Reduced fees (weekdays, twilight, seniors, juniors), metal spikes, range (mats).

★★½ HARDING PARK GOLF CLUB
PU-Harding Park Rd. at Skyline Blvd., San Francisco, 94132, San Francisco County, (415)661-1865. **Facility Holes:** 27. **Yards:** 6,743/6,205. **Par:** 72/73. **Course Rating:** 72.1/74.1. **Slope:** 124/120. **Green Fee:** $26/$31. **Cart Fee:** $22/Person. **Walking Policy:** Unrestricted walking. **Walkability:** 3. **Opened:** 1925. **Architect:** Willie Watson. **Season:** Year-round. **High:** April-Oct. **To obtain tee times:** Call up to 6 days in advance. **Miscellaneous:** Reduced fees (weekdays, twilight, seniors, juniors), metal spikes, range (mats), credit cards (MC, V, ATM), BF, FF.
Special Notes: Also has a 9-hole executive course.

★★★★ HERITAGE PALMS GOLF CLUB
SP-44291 Heritage Palms Dr. S., Indio, 92201, Riverside County, (760)772-7334, 15 miles from Palm Springs. **Facility Holes:** 18. **Yards:** 6,727/4,885. **Par:** 72/72. **Course Rating:** 71.9/66.6. **Slope:** 124/107. **Green Fee:** $40/$115. **Cart Fee:** Included in green fee. **Walking Policy:** Mandatory carts. **Walkability:** 2. **Opened:** 1996. **Architect:** Arthur Hills. **Season:** Year-round. **To obtain tee times:** Call up to 10 days in advance. **Miscellaneous:** Reduced fees (twilight), range (grass), credit cards (MC, V, AE, D), BF, FF.
Reader Comments: Great golf course for a new course … Fastest, truest greens I have ever played … Outstanding … This course is very rewarding.

★★★ HESPERIA GOLF & COUNTRY CLUB
SP-17970 Bangor Ave., Hesperia, 92345, San Bernardino County, (760)244-9301, 30 miles from San Bernardino. **E-mail:** hesperiacc@aol.co. **Web:** www.hesperiagolf.com. **Facility Holes:** 18. **Yards:** 6,996/6,136. **Par:** 72/72. **Course Rating:** 73.5/73.9. **Slope:** 131/128. **Green Fee:** $20/$25. **Cart Fee:** $20/Cart. **Walking Policy:** Unrestricted walking. **Walkability:** 2. **Opened:** 1955. **Architect:** William F. Bell. **Season:** Year-round. **To obtain tee times:** Call golf shop.

Miscellaneous: Reduced fees (weekdays, twilight, seniors, juniors), range (mats), credit cards (MC, V), BF, FF.
Reader Comments: Old course still a challenge … A little oasis in a desert valley. Neat traditional layout with fine greens.

★★★★ HIDDEN VALLEY GOLF CLUB
PU-10 Clubhouse Dr., Norco, 91760, Riverside County, (909)737-1010, 10 miles from Riverside. **E-mail:** sales@hiddenvalleygolf.com. **Web:** www.hiddenvalleygolf.com. **Facility Holes:** 18. **Yards:** 6,721/4,649. **Par:** 72/71. **Course Rating:** 73.3/66.6. **Slope:** 140/116. **Green Fee:** $45/$90. **Walkability:** 4. **Opened:** 1997. **Architect:** Casey O'Callaghan. **Season:** Year-round. **High:** Oct.-May. **To obtain tee times:** Call golf shop. **Miscellaneous:** Reduced fees (twilight, seniors, juniors), range (grass), credit cards (MC, V).
Reader Comments: Great course in the hills. Hard to walk. Very challenging … If you like changes in elevation, this is a must course. A real jewel … Nice people, fun course … For a new course it is excellent … Breathtaking vistas. A fun and challenging course … A slice of heaven in the desert … Never saw anyone in front or behind all day.

★★½ HIDDEN VALLEY LAKE GOLF & COUNTRY CLUB
SP-19210 Hartman Rd., Middletown, 95461, Lake County, (707)987-3035, 40 miles from Santa Rosa. **Web:** www.hiddenvalleylake.org. **Facility Holes:** 18. **Yards:** 6,667/5,546. **Par:** 72/74. **Course Rating:** 72.5/71.5. **Slope:** 124/124. **Green Fee:** $20/$30. **Cart Fee:** $15/Person. **Walking Policy:** Walking at certain times. **Walkability:** 5. **Opened:** 1970. **Architect:** William F. Bell. **Season:** Year-round. **To obtain tee times:** Call golf shop. **Miscellaneous:** Reduced fees (twilight, seniors, juniors), range (grass), credit cards (MC, V, AE, D).

★★★★ HIDDENBROOKE GOLF CLUB
PU-1095 Hiddenbrooke Parkway, Vallejo, 94591, Solano County, (707)558-1140, (888)773-0330, 35 miles from San Francisco. **E-mail:** info@hiddenbrookgolf.com. **Web:** www.hidden-brookegolf.com. **Facility Holes:** 18. **Yards:** 6,678/4,648. **Par:** 72/72. **Course Rating:** 72.8/66.4. **Slope:** 142/117. **Green Fee:** $75/$100. **Cart Fee:** Included in green fee. **Walking Policy:** Walking at certain times. **Walkability:** 4. **Opened:** 1995. **Architect:** Arnold Palmer/Ed Seay. **Season:** Year-round. **High:** April-Nov. **To obtain tee times:** Call up to 14 days in advance. **Miscellaneous:** Reduced fees (weekdays, seniors, juniors), range (grass/mats), credit cards (MC, V, AE, D), BF, FF.
Reader Comments: Outstanding new course. Approach shots are key … Wonderful experience, difficult track … A bit expensive, but an amazing layout … LPGA tournament course, hilly layout … Great course, nice staff … Difficult but fun course.

★★★★½ HORSE THIEF COUNTRY CLUB
R-28930 Horse Thief Dr., Stallion Spring, Tehachapi, 93561, Kern County, (661)822-5581, 50 miles from Bakersfield. **Web:** www.stallionsprings.com. **Facility Holes:** 18. **Yards:** 6,719/5,677. **Par:** 72/72. **Course Rating:** 72.0/73.1. **Slope:** 131/129. **Green Fee:** $28/$48. **Cart Fee:** $24/Person. **Walking Policy:** Unrestricted walking. **Walkability:** 4. **Opened:** 1972. **Architect:** Bob Baldock. **Season:** Year-round. **High:** March-Oct. **To obtain tee times:** Call up to 10 days in advance. **Miscellaneous:** Reduced fees (weekdays, twilight, seniors, juniors), range (grass/mats), lodging (75 rooms), credit cards (MC, V, AE, D), FF.
Reader Comments: Excellent mountain course with fresh air and scenery that would be hard to beat. If you are ever in the area play it … Great small-town course in excellent mountain setting. Good value for golf dollar … Secluded and restful … Challenging and pretty … One of my favorites.

★★★★ HUNTER RANCH GOLF COURSE
PU-4041 Hwy. 46 E., Paso Robles, 93446, San Luis Obispo County, (805)237-7444, 25 miles from San Luis Obispo. **E-mail:** mbremer@hunterranchgolf.com. **Web:** www.hunterranchgolf.com. **Facility Holes:** 18. **Yards:** 6,741/5,639. **Par:** 72/72. **Course Rating:** 72.2/72.8. **Slope:** 136/132. **Green Fee:** $25/$55. **Cart Fee:** $24/Cart. **Walking Policy:** Unrestricted walking. **Walkability:** 3. **Opened:** 1994. **Architect:** Ken Hunter Jr./Mike McGinnis. **Season:** Year-round. **To obtain tee times:** Call golf shop. **Miscellaneous:** Reduced fees (twilight, juniors), range (grass), credit cards (MC, V), BF, FF.
Reader Comments: Beautiful clubhouse, very pleasant … Fantastic slick and true greens. Great elevation changes and scenery. Could use some yardage markers on the course … This is a gorgeous course without the crowds. It's out there a bit, but well worth the trip. I can't think of a better way to spend 25 dollars … All around good experience/great value.

★★ INDIAN HILLS GOLF CLUB
PU-5700 Clubhouse Dr., Riverside, 92509, Riverside County, (909)360-2090, (800)600-2090. **E-mail:** info@indianhillsgolf.com. **Web:** www.indianhillsgolf.com. **Facility Holes:** 18. **Yards:** 6,104/5,562. **Par:** 70/72. **Course Rating:** 70.0/72.5. **Slope:** 126/120. **Green Fee:** $29/$47. **Cart Fee:** Included in green fee. **Walking Policy:** Mandatory carts. **Walkability:** 4. **Opened:** 1965. **Architect:** Harold Heers. **Season:** Year-round. **To obtain tee times:** Call up to 7 days in

advance. **Miscellaneous:** Reduced fees (weekdays, twilight, seniors, juniors), metal spikes, credit cards (MC, V), FF.

★★ INDIAN PALMS COUNTRY CLUB & RESORT

R-48-630 Monroe St., Indio, 92201, Riverside County, (760)347-2326, (800)778-5288, 20 miles from Palm Springs. **Web:** www.indianpalms.com. **Facility Holes:** 27. **Green Fee:** $25/$70. **Cart Fee:** Included in green fee. **Walking Policy:** Mandatory carts. **Walkability:** 1. **Opened:** 1948. **Architect:** Jackie Cochran/Helen Detweiler. **Season:** Year-round. **High:** Jan.-March. **To obtain tee times:** Call up to 7 days in advance. **Miscellaneous:** Reduced fees (weekdays, guests, twilight), range (grass), lodging (59 rooms), credit cards (MC, V, AE), BF, FF.
INDIAN/MOUNTAIN (18 combo)
Yards: 6,708/5,849. **Par:** 72/73. **Course Rating:** 72.7/72.1. **Slope:** 131/120.
MOUNTAIN/ROYAL (18combo)
Yards: 6,713/5,622. **Par:** 72/72. **Course Rating:** 72.9/70.0. **Slope:** 129/116.
ROYAL/INDIAN (18combo)
Yards: 6,700/5,547. **Par:** 72/72. **Course Rating:** 72.7/70.0. **Slope:** 127/116.

★★★ INDIAN SPRINGS COUNTRY CLUB

SP-46-080 Jefferson St., La Quinta, 92253, Riverside County, (760)775-3360, 6 miles from Palm Desert. **Facility Holes:** 18. **Yards:** 6,661/5,297. **Par:** 72/72. **Course Rating:** 71.3/70.2. **Slope:** 123/120. **Cart Fee:** Included in green fee. **Walking Policy:** Mandatory carts. **Walkability:** 2. **Opened:** 2000. **Architect:** Dave Ginkel. **Season:** Year-round. **To obtain tee times:** Call up to 7 days in advance. **Miscellaneous:** Reduced fees (weekdays, guests, twilight), range (grass), credit cards (MC, V, AE, D), FF.
Reader Comments: Great course and people ... Best value in Palm Springs area ... Long distances between holes ... Easy design, in good shape, good value.

★★★ INDIAN VALLEY GOLF CLUB

PU-3035 Novato Blvd., Novato, 94948, Marin County, (415)897-1118, 22 miles from San Francisco. **E-mail:** golf@ivgc.com. **Web:** www.ivgc.com. **Facility Holes:** 18. **Yards:** 6,253/5,238. **Par:** 72/72. **Course Rating:** 69.2/70.9. **Slope:** 119/128. **Green Fee:** $15/$49. **Cart Fee:** $24/Cart. **Walking Policy:** Walking at certain times. **Walkability:** 4. **Opened:** 1958. **Architect:** Robert Nyberg. **Season:** Year-round. **To obtain tee times:** Call up to 7 days in advance. **Miscellaneous:** Reduced fees (weekdays, twilight, seniors, juniors), metal spikes, range (mats), credit cards (MC, V, AE), BF, FF.
Reader Comments: Friendly place ... Steep hills on back side ... Unusual setting, hills, good challenge ... Course is beautiful.

INDUSTRY HILLS SHERATON RESORT & CONFERENCE CENTER

R-One Industry Hills Pkwy., City of Industry, 91744, Los Angeles County, (626)810-4653, 25 miles from Los Angeles. **Facility Holes:** 36. **Green Fee:** $39/$85. **Cart Fee:** Included in green fee. **Walking Policy:** Mandatory carts. **Architect:** William F. Bell. **Season:** Year-round. **To obtain tee times:** Call up to 7 days in advance. **Miscellaneous:** Range (mats), lodging (294 rooms), BF, FF.
★★★ BABE DIDRIKSON ZAHARIAS COURSE (18)
Yards: 6,600/5,363. **Par:** 71/71. **Course Rating:** 72.5/72.4. **Slope:** 134/133. **Walkability:** 5. **Opened:** 1980. **Miscellaneous:** Reduced fees (weekdays, twilight, seniors), credit cards (MC, V, AE, D, DC).
Reader Comments: Tight but fair, challenging ... Good difficult course ... Good value for your money ... Hard, hard, hard ... Great golf course, good test ... If you conquer this course, you've made it.
★★★★ EISENHOWER COURSE (18)
Yards: 6,735/5,589. **Par:** 72/73. **Course Rating:** 72.9/73.1. **Slope:** 136/135. **Opened:** 1979. **Miscellaneous:** Reduced fees (weekdays, twilight, seniors, juniors), credit cards (MC, V, AE, D, DC).
Reader Comments: Spectacular course, difficult, but worth every stroke!! Very customer friendly ... Tough course, great design ... Challenging, great variety ... Course has matured well, remains long and challenging ... Good track for corporate outings.

JACK TONE GOLF

PU-1500 Ruess Rd., Ripon, 95366, San Joaquin County, (209)599-2973, 5 miles from Modesto. **E-mail:** tbuzzini@aol.com. **Web:** www.jacktonegolf.com. **Facility Holes:** 18. **Yards:** 3,693/3,292. **Par:** 62/62. **Course Rating:** 58.2/57.4. **Slope:** 82/85. **Green Fee:** $13/$19. **Cart Fee:** $18/Cart. **Walking Policy:** Unrestricted walking. **Walkability:** 2. **Opened:** 1997. **Architect:** George Buzzini. **Season:** Year-round. **To obtain tee times:** Call up to 7 days in advance. **Miscellaneous:** Reduced fees (weekdays, twilight, seniors, juniors), range (grass), credit cards (MC, V, AE), BF, FF.

CALIFORNIA

★½ **JAVIER'S FRESNO WEST GOLF & COUNTRY CLUB**
PU-23986 W. Whitesbridge Rd., Kerman, 93630, Fresno County, (559)846-8655, 23 miles from Fresno. **E-mail:** progolf606@aol.com. **Facility Holes:** 18. **Yards:** 6,959/6,000. **Par:** 72/73. **Course Rating:** 72.6/74.1. **Slope:** 118/118. **Green Fee:** $10/$13. **Cart Fee:** $20/Cart. **Walking Policy:** Walking at certain times. **Walkability:** 1. **Opened:** 1966. **Architect:** Bob Baldock. **Season:** Year-round. **To obtain tee times:** Call golf shop. **Miscellaneous:** Reduced fees (weekdays, twilight, seniors, juniors), range (grass), credit cards (MC, V), BF, FF.

★★½ **JURUPA HILLS COUNTRY CLUB**
PU-6161 Moraga Ave., Riverside, 92509, Riverside County, (909)685-7214, 5 miles from Riverside. **E-mail:** rrwedge@aol.com. **Facility Holes:** 18. **Yards:** 6,022/5,773. **Par:** 70/71. **Course Rating:** 69.5/73.4. **Slope:** 122/123. **Green Fee:** $24/$40. **Cart Fee:** Included in green fee. **Walking Policy:** Walking at certain times. **Walkability:** 3. **Opened:** 1960. **Architect:** William F. Bell. **Season:** Year-round. **To obtain tee times:** Call up to 7 days in advance. **Miscellaneous:** Reduced fees (weekdays, twilight, seniors, juniors), range (grass), credit cards (MC, V), BF, FF.

★★ **KERN RIVER GOLF COURSE**
PU-Rudal Rd., Bakersfield, 93386, Kern County, (805)872-5128. **Facility Holes:** 18. **Yards:** 6,458/5,971. **Par:** 70/73. **Course Rating:** 70.5/72.3. **Slope:** 120/123. **Green Fee:** $12/$15. **Cart Fee:** $10/Cart. **Walking Policy:** Unrestricted walking. **Walkability:** 3. **Opened:** 1952. **Architect:** William P. Bell. **Season:** Year-round. **To obtain tee times:** Call up to 7 days in advance. **Miscellaneous:** Reduced fees (weekdays, twilight, seniors, juniors), metal spikes, range (grass/mats), credit cards (MC, V, AE, D), BF, FF.

★★½ **KNOLLWOOD COUNTRY CLUB**
PU-12040 Balboa Blvd., Granada Hills, 91344, Los Angeles County, (818)363-1810. **Facility Holes:** 18. **Yards:** 6,379/5,802. **Par:** 72/72. **Course Rating:** 70.5/72.6. **Slope:** 125/118. **Green Fee:** $20/$25. **Cart Fee:** $22/Cart. **Walking Policy:** Unrestricted walking. **Opened:** 1957. **Architect:** William F. Bell. **To obtain tee times:** Call golf shop.

★★★ **LA CONTENTA GOLF CLUB**
SP-1653 Hwy. 26, Valley Springs, 95252, Calaveras County, (209)772-1081, (800)446-5321, 30 miles from Stockton. **E-mail:** lcgc@caltel.com. **Facility Holes:** 18. **Yards:** 6,425/5,120. **Par:** 71/72. **Course Rating:** 70.1/70.8. **Slope:** 133/120. **Green Fee:** $21/$35. **Cart Fee:** $12/Person. **Walking Policy:** Unrestricted walking. **Walkability:** 3. **Opened:** 1972. **Architect:** Richard Bigler. **Season:** Year-round. **To obtain tee times:** Call up to 14 days in advance. **Miscellaneous:** Reduced fees (weekdays, guests, twilight, seniors, juniors), metal spikes, credit cards (MC, V, D), BF, FF.
Reader Comments: If you keep in play you can score … Course layout great. No two holes alike … Fun, hilly, blind shots, short … Best value in the area … Fun course, always treat you well.

LA COSTA RESORT & SPA
R-Costa Del Mar Rd., Carlsbad, 92009, San Diego County, (760)438-9111, 30 miles from San Diego. **E-mail:** info@lacosta.com. **Web:** www.lacosta.com. **Facility Holes:** 36. **Green Fee:** $140/$195. **Cart Fee:** Included in green fee. **Opened:** 1964. **Season:** Year-round. **To obtain tee times:** Call golf shop. **Miscellaneous:** Reduced fees (twilight), metal spikes, range (grass), caddies, lodging (497 rooms), credit cards (MC, V, AE, D, Diners Club, JCB).
★★★★½ **NORTH COURSE** (18)
Yards: 7,021/5,939. **Par:** 72/73. **Course Rating:** 74.8/76.3. **Slope:** 137/137. **Walkability:** 2. **Architect:** Dick Wilson/Joe Lee.
Reader Comments: Nice to play a course the pros have played … Great shape, crowded, colorful … A great course but very expensive … Testing and surprisingly tight … Great resort, great courses … Breathtaking … Wish I could afford to play more often.
★★★★½ **SOUTH COURSE** (18) *Pace*
Yards: 7,004/5,612. **Par:** 72/74. **Course Rating:** 74.4/74.2. **Slope:** 138/134. **Walkability:** 3. **Architect:** Dick Wilson.
Reader Comments: First-class operation … Enjoy the pampered life … Excellent resort course … Courses are well maintained and long because one gets absolutely no roll. Tough greens to hit.

★★½ **LA MIRADA GOLF COURSE**
PU-15501 E. Alicante Rd., La Mirada, 90638, Los Angeles County, (562)943-7123, 20 miles from Los Angeles. **Facility Holes:** 18. **Yards:** 6,056/5,652. **Par:** 70/71. **Course Rating:** 68.6/71.6. **Slope:** 114/117. **Green Fee:** $19/$23. **Cart Fee:** $22/Cart. **Walking Policy:** Unrestricted walking. **Walkability:** 4. **Opened:** 1962. **Season:** Year-round. **To obtain tee times:** Call golf shop. **Miscellaneous:** Reduced fees (weekdays, twilight, seniors, juniors), metal spikes, range (grass/mats), credit cards (MC, V, AE).

★★★★½ **LA PURISIMA GOLF COURSE**
PU-3455 State Hwy. 246, Lompoc, 93436, Santa Barbara County, (805)735-8395, 40 miles from Santa Barbara. **E-mail:** lapurisimagolf@yahoo.com. **Web:** www.lapurisimagolf.com. **Facility Holes:** 18. **Yards:** 7,105/5,762. **Par:** 72/72. **Course Rating:** 74.9/74.3. **Slope:** 143/131. **Green Fee:** $50/$60. **Cart Fee:** $30/Cart. **Walking Policy:** Unrestricted walking. **Walkability:** 3. **Opened:** 1986. **Architect:** Robert Muir Graves. **Season:** Year-round. **To obtain tee times:** Call up to 30 days in advance. **Miscellaneous:** Reduced fees (weekdays, twilight, juniors), range (grass), credit cards (MC, V), BF, FF.
Notes: Ranked 61st in 1996 America's Top 75 Affordable Courses.
Reader Comments: An outstanding test, bring your 'A' game. A wonderful mix of beauty and sport … Best of the best. My #1 … Outstanding layout … Very challenging when the wind is up … Central California's hidden gem, that may be the best course in the state … The best! … Favorite course to play. Great layout. Excellent bargain.

LA QUINTA RESORT & CLUB
R-50-200 Vista Bonita, La Quinta, 92253, Riverside County, (760)564-7686, (800)598-3828, 15 miles from Palm Springs. **E-mail:** sgustavson@kslmail.com. **Web:** www.laquintaresort.com. **Facility Holes:** 36. **Cart Fee:** Included in green fee. **Walking Policy:** Mandatory carts. **Architect:** Pete Dye. **Season:** Year-round. **High:** Dec.-May. **To obtain tee times:** Call golf shop. **Miscellaneous:** Reduced fees (weekdays, guests, twilight), range (grass), lodging (920 rooms), Credit cards (MC, V, AE, DC, JCB), FF.
★★★★ **DUNES COURSE** (18)
Yards: 6,747/4,997. **Par:** 72/72. **Course Rating:** 73.1/69.1. **Slope:** 137/125. **Green Fee:** $50/$145. **Walkability:** 3. **Opened:** 1981.
Reader Comments: Great … Great course, difficult … Love this golf course … Boasts one of the hardest holes in golf. Fabulous golf. … Great course … Great summer bargain.
★★★★½ **MOUNTAIN COURSE** (18) *Pace+*
Yards: 6,756/5,005. **Par:** 72/72. **Course Rating:** 74.1/71.0. **Slope:** 140/123. **Green Fee:** $75/$235. **Walkability:** 4. **Opened:** 1980.
Reader Comments: Great layout. Great views. A classic. A must play sometime in your life … The holes keep getting better and better. Back nine is awesome. Would play there every week if it weren't for the drive … Best kept secret in desert. Now I know why … Hole #16 one of the prettiest I've ever played. Beautiful course built around mountains. The entire staff made us feel as if we were longtime members.

★★★½ **LAGUNA SECA GOLF CLUB**
PU-10520 York Rd., Monterey, 93940, Monterey County, (831)373-3701, (888)524-8629, 7 miles from Monterey. **E-mail:** laguna@golf-monterey.com. **Web:** www.golf-monterey.com. **Facility Holes:** 18. **Yards:** 6,157/5,204. **Par:** 71/72. **Course Rating:** 70.7/70.8. **Slope:** 127/121. **Green Fee:** $65. **Cart Fee:** $34/Cart. **Walking Policy:** Unrestricted walking. **Walkability:** 4. **Opened:** 1970. **Architect:** Robert Trent Jones. **Season:** Year-round. **To obtain tee times:** Call golf shop. **Miscellaneous:** Reduced fees (twilight), credit cards (MC, V, AE), BF, FF.
Reader Comments: Great landscape … Great 15th hole … My home course, I love it! … Sporty track … Gets a lot of play, nice area … Native oaks give "Old California" setting … The 15th hole goes over the water twice, beautiful scenery … Nice course, interesting, hilly layout, good value.

★★ **LAKE CHABOT GOLF COURSE**
PU-11450 Golf Links Rd., Oakland, 94605, Alameda County, (510)351-5812, 10 miles from Oakland. **Facility Holes:** 18. **Yards:** 5,982/5,268. **Par:** 72/71. **Course Rating:** 68.6/68.5. **Slope:** 115/116. **Green Fee:** $10/$23. **Cart Fee:** $22/Cart. **Walking Policy:** Unrestricted walking. **Walkability:** 5. **Opened:** 1927. **Architect:** William Lock. **Season:** Year-round. **High:** April-Sept. **To obtain tee times:** Call golf shop. **Miscellaneous:** Reduced fees (weekdays, twilight, seniors, juniors), metal spikes, range (mats), credit cards (MC, V).

★★★½ **LAKE SHASTINA GOLF RESORT**
R-5925 Country Club Dr., Weed, 96094, Siskiyou County, (530)938-3205, (800)358-4653, 90 miles from Eureka. **E-mail:** info@lakeshastinagolfresort.net. **Web:** www.lakeshastinagolfresort.net. **Facility Holes:** 27. **Yards:** 6,969/5,530. **Par:** 72/72. **Course Rating:** 72.6/70.0. **Slope:** 132/121. **Green Fee:** $22/$45. **Cart Fee:** $15/Person. **Walking Policy:** Unrestricted walking. **Walkability:** 2. **Opened:** 1973. **Architect:** Robert Trent Jones. **Season:** Year-round. **To obtain tee times:** Call up to 30 days in advance. **Miscellaneous:** Reduced fees (guests, twilight, juniors), range (mats), credit cards (MC, V, AE, D), BF, FF.
Reader Comments: Pretty setting, very easy … Interesting layout … Scottish feel.

★★★½ **LAKE TAHOE GOLF COURSE**
PU-2500 Emerald Bay Rd. Hwy. 50, South Lake Tahoe, 96150, El Dorado County, (530)577-0788, 60 miles from Reno. **Facility Holes:** 18. **Yards:** 6,741/5,654. **Par:** 71/72. **Course Rating:** 70.8/70.1. **Slope:** 126/115. **Green Fee:** $47/$67. **Cart Fee:** Included in green fee. **Walking Policy:** Walking at certain times. **Walkability:** 2. **Opened:** 1960. **Architect:** William

F. Bell. **Season:** April-Oct. **High:** June-Sept. **To obtain tee times:** Call up to 60 days in advance. **Miscellaneous:** Reduced fees (twilight, juniors), metal spikes, range (grass), credit cards (MC, V, AE), BF, FF.

Reader Comments: Good value ... A mountain jewel, views to die for! ... Too bad only open for short season ... Pretty setting, high altitude ... Could use more H2O, pretty in mountains... A perfect mix of Sierra sun, beautiful greens, and blue skies ... Fun course. A good walk in the woods.

★★½ LAKEWOOD COUNTRY CLUB

PU-3101 E. Carson St., Lakewood, 90712, Los Angeles County, (562)421-3741. **Facility Holes:** 18. **Yards:** 7,045/5,920. **Par:** 72/73. **Course Rating:** 72.9/74.1. **Slope:** 113/121. **Green Fee:** $20/$25. **Cart Fee:** $22/Cart. **Walking Policy:** Unrestricted walking. **Walkability:** 1. **Opened:** 1935. **Architect:** William P. Bell. **Season:** Year-round. **High:** April-Oct. **To obtain tee times:** Call golf shop. **Miscellaneous:** Reduced fees (weekdays, twilight, seniors, juniors), metal spikes, range (mats), credit cards (MC, V, AE).

LANDMARK GOLF CLUB

PU-88-000 Landmark Pkwy., Indio, 92203, Riverside County, (760)775-2000, 25 miles from Palm Springs. **E-mail:** lmgc@earthlink.net. **Web:** www.landmarkgc.com. **Facility Holes:** 36. **Green Fee:** $45/$145. **Cart Fee:** Included in green fee. **Walking Policy:** Mandatory carts. **Walkability:** 3. **Opened:** 1999. **Architect:** Lee Schmidt/Brian Curley. **Season:** Year-round. **To obtain tee times:** Call up to 60 days in advance. **Miscellaneous:** Reduced fees (weekdays, twilight), range (grass), credit cards (MC, V, AE, D, DC), BF, FF.

★★★★ SKINS NORTH COURSE (18) *Pace*

Yards: 7,123/5,015. **Par:** 72/72. **Course Rating:** 74.3/69.7. **Slope:** 135/124. **High:** Jan.-May.

Reader Comments: Great service, great challenge ... Great staff ... May be best in desert. Strong all around ... Scenic and challenging ... Loved the holes up in the rocks! ... Best public course in the desert! Wonderful layout, perfect conditions, service was great at all times, playing times averaged 4 hrs 15 min! Pricey but worth every penny.

★★★★ SKINS SOUTH COURSE (18)

Yards: 7,229/5,094. **Par:** 72/72. **Course Rating:** 75.1/70.9. **Slope:** 136/128. **High:** Jan.-June.

Reader Comments: Great service, challenging ... Outstanding staff ... Go again ... Terrific desert courses ... Treated juniors very well ... Loved the water hole ... They are first-class in all aspects, great practice facility.

LANDMARK GOLF CLUB AT OAK QUARRY

PU-7151 Sierra Ave., Riverside, 92509, Riverside County, (909)685-1440, 5 miles from Riverside. **E-mail:** oakquarrygolfclub@msn. **Web:** oakquarry.com. **Facility Holes:** 18. **Yards:** 7,002/5,408. **Par:** 72/72. **Course Rating:** 73.9/75.4. **Slope:** 137/131. **Green Fee:** $65/$95. **Cart Fee:** Included in green fee. **Walking Policy:** Mandatory carts. **Walkability:** 2. **Opened:** 2000. **Architect:** Dr. Gil Morgan/Schmidt-Curley. **Season:** Year-round. **High:** Nov.-June. **To obtain tee times:** Call up to 14 days in advance. **Miscellaneous:** Reduced fees (weekdays, twilight, seniors, juniors), range (grass), credit cards (MC, V, AE, D), BF, FF.

★★★½ LAS POSITAS GOLF COURSE

PU-917 Clubhouse Dr., Livermore, 94550, Alameda County, (925)455-7820, 1 mile from Livermore. **Web:** laspositasgolf.com. **Facility Holes:** 27. **Yards:** 6,725/5,270. **Par:** 72/72. **Course Rating:** 72.1/70.1. **Slope:** 127/120. **Green Fee:** $25/$36. **Cart Fee:** $12/Person. **Walking Policy:** Unrestricted walking. **Walkability:** 1. **Opened:** 1966. **Architect:** Robert Muir Graves. **Season:** Year-round. **To obtain tee times:** Call up to 7 days in advance. **Miscellaneous:** Reduced fees (weekdays, twilight, seniors, juniors), range (grass/mats), credit cards (MC, V), BF, FF.

Reader Comments: Fun, challenging muni ... No. 9 is very difficult! ... A good solid muni ... Overall, very good municipal course ... Watch out for the wind and airplanes.

Special Notes: Also has a 9-hole executive course.

★★ LEMOORE GOLF COURSE

PU-350 Iona Ave., Lemoore, 93245, Kings County, (559)924-9658, 30 miles from Fresno. **Facility Holes:** 18. **Yards:** 6,431/5,126. **Par:** 72/72. **Course Rating:** 70.8/68.8. **Slope:** 121/115. **Green Fee:** $16/$20. **Cart Fee:** $20/Cart. **Walking Policy:** Unrestricted walking. **Walkability:** 1. **Opened:** 1930. **Architect:** Bob Baldock/Bill Phillips. **Season:** Year-round. **To obtain tee times:** Call up to 5 days in advance. **Miscellaneous:** Reduced fees (weekdays, twilight, seniors), range (grass/mats), credit cards (MC, V), BF, FF.

★★½ LINCOLN PARK GOLF COURSE

PU-34th Ave. and Clement St., San Francisco, 94121, San Francisco County, (415)221-9911. **Facility Holes:** 18. **Yards:** 5,149/4,984. **Par:** 68/70. **Course Rating:** 64.4/67.4. **Slope:** 106/108. **Green Fee:** $23/$27. **Cart Fee:** $22/Cart. **Walking Policy:** Unrestricted walking. **Walkability:** 4. **Opened:** 1916. **Architect:** Jack Fleming. **Season:** Year-round. **High:** April-Nov. **To obtain tee times:** Call golf shop. **Miscellaneous:** Reduced fees (weekdays, twilight, juniors), metal spikes, credit cards (MC, V).

CALIFORNIA

THE LINKS AT RIVERLAKES RANCH
PU-5201 Riverlakes Dr., Bakersfield, 93312, Kern County, (661)587-5465. **Web:** www.river-lakes.com. **Facility Holes:** 18. **Yards:** 6,800/5,180. **Par:** 72/72. **Course Rating:** 72.6/70.4. **Slope:** 133/120. **Green Fee:** $18/$46. **Cart Fee:** $12/Person. **Walking Policy:** Walking at certain times. **Walkability:** 4. **Opened:** 1999. **Architect:** R Fream/D Dale/R Elliot. **Season:** Year-round. **High:** March-Dec. **To obtain tee times:** Call up to 7 days in advance. **Miscellaneous:** Reduced fees (twilight, seniors, juniors), range (grass), credit cards (MC, V, AE, D), BF, FF.

★★★★½ THE LINKS AT SPANISH BAY *Service*
R-2700 17 Mile Dr., Pebble Beach, 93953, Monterey County, (408)647-7495, (800)654-9300, 2 miles from Monterey. **E-mail:** ramseyv@pebblebeach.com. **Web:** www.pebblebeach.com. **Facility Holes:** 18. **Yards:** 6,820/5,309. **Par:** 72/72. **Course Rating:** 74.8/70.6. **Slope:** 146/129. **Green Fee:** $105/$210. **Cart Fee:** $25/Cart. **Walking Policy:** Unrestricted walking. **Walkability:** 2. **Opened:** 1987. **Architect:** R.T. Jones Jr./T. Watson/S. Tatum. **Season:** Year-round. **To obtain tee times:** Call up to 60 days in advance. **Miscellaneous:** Reduced fees (guests, twilight), caddies, lodging (270 rooms), credit cards (MC, V, AE, D, JCB), BF, FF.
Notes: Ranked 99th in 1997-98 America's 100 Greatest; 23rd in 2001 Best in State; 48th in 1996 America's Top 75 Upscale Courses.
Reader Comments: Wow!! ... A true links course. Played it in the wind and the rain and loved every minute of it ... It's a 'must' play on the Monterey Pennisula ... Spectacular layout, very unforgiving, great hotel ... Worth every cent. Make sure you see the Scotsman walk up the 2nd fairway at about 6 pm with full bagpipes.

★½ THE LINKS AT VICTORIA GOLF CLUB
PU-340 E 192nd St., Carson, 90746, Los Angeles County, (310)323-6981, 10 miles from Los Angeles. **E-mail:** landerson@palmergolf.com. **Facility Holes:** 18. **Yards:** 6,804/5,855. **Par:** 72/72. **Course Rating:** 71.3/73.0. **Slope:** 119/134. **Green Fee:** $20/$25. **Cart Fee:** $11/Person. **Walking Policy:** Unrestricted walking. **Walkability:** 2. **Opened:** 1966. **Architect:** Casey O'Callaghan. **Season:** Year-round. **To obtain tee times:** Call up to 7 days in advance. **Miscellaneous:** Reduced fees (weekdays, twilight, seniors, juniors), metal spikes, range (grass/mats), credit cards (MC, V, AE), BF, FF.

★★★ LOCKEFORD SPRINGS GOLF COURSE
PU-16360 N. Hwy. 88, Lodi, 95240, San Joaquin County, (209)333-6275, 35 miles from Sacramento. **E-mail:** sara@lockefordsprings.com. **Web:** www.lockefordsprings.com. **Facility Holes:** 18. **Yards:** 6,861/5,951. **Par:** 72/72. **Course Rating:** 73.2/74.0. **Slope:** 130/123. **Green Fee:** $22/$33. **Cart Fee:** $14/Person. **Walking Policy:** Unrestricted walking. **Walkability:** 1. **Opened:** 1995. **Architect:** Jim Summers/Sandy Tatum. **Season:** Year-round. **To obtain tee times:** Call up to 7 days in advance. **Miscellaneous:** Reduced fees (weekdays, twilight, seniors, juniors), range (grass), credit cards (MC, V), BF, FF.
Reader Comments: Par 5s true 3-shot holes, great greens ... Underrated course, very enjoyable ... Nice layout, few trees, flat ... Small town, big heart, must play ... Meandering the vineyards of Lodi ... Worth the drive from Bay Area ... Nice clubhouse.

★★½ LOS ANGELES ROYAL VISTA GOLF COURSE
SP-20055 E. Colima Rd., Walnut, 91789, Los Angeles County, (909)595-7441, 22 miles from Los Angeles. **E-mail:** dcrooke1@ix.netcom.com. **Web:** www.larv.com. **Facility Holes:** 27. **Green Fee:** $24/$35. **Cart Fee:** $12/Person. **Walking Policy:** Walking at certain times. **Walkability:** 4. **Opened:** 1963. **Architect:** William F. Bell. **Season:** Year-round. **To obtain tee times:** Call up to 7 days in advance. **Miscellaneous:** Reduced fees (weekdays, guests, twilight, seniors, juniors), metal spikes, range (mats), credit cards (MC, V, D), BF, FF.
EAST/NORTH (18 Combo)
Yards: 6,537/5,545. **Par:** 71/71. **Course Rating:** 70.6/71.3. **Slope:** 121/118.
NORTH/SOUTH (18 Combo)
Yards: 6,243/5,316. **Par:** 71/71. **Course Rating:** 69.3/69.8. **Slope:** 119/117.
SOUTH/EAST (18 Combo)
Yards: 6,182/5,595. **Par:** 72/72. **Course Rating:** 68.5/71.1. **Slope:** 112/117.

★★½ LOS ROBLES GOLF COURSE
PU-299 S. Moorpark Rd., Thousand Oaks, 91360, Ventura County, (805)495-6421, 30 miles from Los Angeles. **Facility Holes:** 18. **Yards:** 6,134/5,184. **Par:** 69/69. **Course Rating:** 68.7/69.0. **Slope:** 116/115. **Green Fee:** $16/$27. **Cart Fee:** $22/Cart. **Walking Policy:** Unrestricted walking. **Walkability:** 2. **Opened:** 1965. **Architect:** William F. Bell. **Season:** Year-round. **To obtain tee times:** Call golf shop. **Miscellaneous:** Reduced fees (weekdays, twilight, seniors, juniors), metal spikes, range (grass/mats), credit cards (MC, V).

LOS SERRANOS GOLF & COUNTRY CLUB
PU-15656 Yorba Ave., Chino Hills, 91709, San Bernardino County, (909)597-1711, 40 miles from Los Angeles. **E-mail:** golflscc@gte.net. **Web:** www.losserranoscountryclub.com. **Facility Holes:** 36. **Green Fee:** $17/$48. **Cart Fee:** $12/Person. **Walking Policy:** Walking at certain times. **Opened:** 1925. **Season:** Year-round. **To obtain tee times:** Call up to 7 days in advance. **Miscellaneous:** Reduced fees (weekdays, twilight, seniors, juniors), metal spikes, range (grass/mats), credit cards (MC, V, AE, D),.BF, FF.

★★★½ **NORTH COURSE** (18)
Yards: 6,440/5,949. **Par:** 72/74. **Course Rating:** 71.3/73.9. **Slope:** 129/125. **Walkability:** 3.
Architect: Harry Rainville/John Dunne.
Reader Comments: Locals' favorite. Greens good … Well-run course in great shape for the amount of play, senior rates make it a bargain … Take the time to play, scenic … My favorite course to play.

★★★½ **SOUTH COURSE** (18)
Yards: 7,470/5,957. **Par:** 74/74. **Course Rating:** 76.1/73.9. **Slope:** 135/128. **Walkability:** 4.
Architect: Zell Eaton.
Reader Comments: Great greens, well laid out … Older course. Good rates … Have enjoyed playing there for years … A long course and a true test of golf. Excellent course, service and price … Good value for the money … Site of numerous qualifying events. Long, difficult, but fair. Excellent staff.
Special Notes: Formerly Los Serranos Lakes Golf & Country Club.

★★½ LOS VERDES GOLF COURSE
PU-7000 W. Los Verdes Dr., Rancho Palos Verdes, 90275, Los Angeles County, (310)377-7888, 25 miles from Los Angeles. **Web:** www.americangolf.com. **Facility Holes:** 18. **Yards:** 6,651/5,738. **Par:** 71/72. **Course Rating:** 71.7/71.8. **Slope:** 122/118. **Green Fee:** $21/$27. **Cart Fee:** $10/Person. **Walking Policy:** Unrestricted walking. **Walkability:** 3. **Opened:** 1964. **Architect:** William F. Bell. **Season:** Year-round. **High:** June-Aug. **To obtain tee times:** Call up to 7 days in advance. **Miscellaneous:** Reduced fees (weekdays, twilight, seniors, juniors), range (mats), credit cards (MC, V, AE, D, DC), BF, FF.

LOST CANYONS GOLF CLUB
PU-3301 Lost Canyons Dr., Simi Valley, 93063, Ventura County, (805)522-4653, 35 miles from Los Angeles. **Web:** lostcanyons.com. **Facility Holes:** 36. **Green Fee:** $80/$145. **Cart Fee:** Included in green fee. **Walking Policy:** Mandatory carts. **Walkability:** 3. **Opened:** 2000. **Architect:** Pete Dye. **Season:** Year-round. **High:** March-Oct. **To obtain tee times:** Call golf shop. **Miscellaneous:** Reduced fees (twilight, seniors, juniors), range (grass), included in fee), credit cards (MC, V, AE, D, DC, JCB), BF, FF.
SHADOW COURSE (18)
Yards: 7,005/4,795. **Par:** 72/72. **Course Rating:** 75.0/64.1. **Slope:** 149/125.
SKY COURSE (18)
Yards: 7,250/4,885. **Par:** 72/72. **Course Rating:** 76.1/70.0. **Slope:** 149/120.

★★½ MACE MEADOW GOLF & COUNTRY CLUB
SP-26570 Fairway Dr., Pioneer, 95666, Amador County, (209)295-7020, 19 miles from Jackson. **E-mail:** flashraider@yahoo.com. **Web:** www.macemeadow.com. **Facility Holes:** 18. **Yards:** 6,285/5,387. **Par:** 72/72. **Course Rating:** 70.0/70.0. **Slope:** 125/118. **Green Fee:** $14/$29. **Cart Fee:** $11/Person. **Walking Policy:** Unrestricted walking. **Walkability:** 2. **Opened:** 1973. **Architect:** Jack Fleming. **Season:** Year-round. **To obtain tee times:** Call up to 14 days in advance. **Miscellaneous:** Reduced fees (twilight, juniors), metal spikes, range (grass/mats), credit cards (MC, V), BF, FF.

★★★ MADERA MUNICIPAL GOLF COURSE *Value*
PU-23200 Ave. 17, Madera, 93637, Madera County, (209)675-3504, 25 miles from Fresno. **Facility Holes:** 18. **Yards:** 6,831/5,519. **Par:** 72/72. **Course Rating:** 71.7/70.6. **Slope:** 121/112. **Green Fee:** $12/$17. **Cart Fee:** $19/Cart. **Walking Policy:** Unrestricted walking. **Walkability:** 2. **Opened:** 1991. **Architect:** Bob Putman. **Season:** Year-round. **High:** April-Sept. **To obtain tee times:** Call golf shop. **Miscellaneous:** Metal spikes, range (grass), credit cards (MC, V, D).
Reader Comments: Excellent greens and fairways … Nice links-type with water everywhere. Best greens, anywhere! … Fairly long course, open and forgiving. Greens are very undulating and are outstanding … The best greens around … Great greens, head pro is great … Best buy in the area.

★★★★ MADERAS COUNTRY CLUB
SP-17750 Old Coach Rd., Poway, 92064, San Diego County, (858)451-8100, 30 miles from San Diego. **Web:** www.maderasgolf.com. **Facility Holes:** 18. **Yards:** 7,115/5,100. **Par:** 72/72. **Course Rating:** 75.2/70.0. **Slope:** 143/128. **Green Fee:** $50/$135. **Cart Fee:** Included in green fee. **Walking Policy:** Mandatory carts. **Opened:** 1999. **Architect:** D. Pascuzzo/R.M. Graves/J. Miller. **Season:** Year-round. **To obtain tee times:** Call up to 60 days in advance. **Misc:** Reduced fees (twilight, seniors, juniors), range (grass), credit cards (MC, V, AE), BF, FF.

CALIFORNIA

Notes: Golf Digest School site.
Reader Comments: Great test of golf … Pretty San Diego area course … First class … One of my favorites in San Diego County … Outstanding design … Super course … Challenging course, especially when windy. Looks more mature than it really is … A great layout, great value for the $.

★★★½ MALIBU COUNTRY CLUB
PU-901 Encinal Canyon Rd., Malibu, 90265, Los Angeles County, (818)889-6680, 30 miles from Los Angeles. **E-mail:** dmeherin@malibucountryclub.net. **Web:** www.malibucountryclub.net. **Facility Holes:** 18. **Yards:** 6,740/5,627. **Par:** 72/72. **Course Rating:** 72.3/71.4. **Slope:** 132/120. **Green Fee:** $55/$80. **Cart Fee:** Included in green fee. **Walking Policy:** Mandatory carts. **Walkability:** 4. **Opened:** 1976. **Architect:** William F. Bell. **Season:** Year-round. **To obtain tee times:** Call up to 10 days in advance. **Miscellaneous:** Reduced fees (seniors, juniors), metal spikes, credit cards (MC, V, AE, DC, JCB).
Reader Comments: Beautiful mountain course … Tough greens. Lots of fun holes with beautiful surroundings … Tough course … Beautiful course that is in mint condition, challenging … Good layout, provides some picturesque locations.

MARRIOTT'S DESERT SPRINGS RESORT & SPA
R-74-855 Country Club Dr., Palm Desert, 92260, Riverside County, (760)341-1756, (800)331-3112, 85 miles from Los Angeles. **E-mail:** tim.skogen@marriott.com. **Facility Holes:** 36. **Cart Fee:** Included in green fee. **Walking Policy:** Mandatory carts. **Walkability:** 3. **Opened:** 1987. **Architect:** Ted Robinson. **Season:** Year-round. **High:** Jan.-April. **To obtain tee times:** Call up to 21 days in advance. **Miscellaneous:** Metal spikes, range (grass), lodging (800 rooms), credit cards (MC, V, AE, D, DC, Diners Club), BF, FF.
★★★★½ PALM COURSE (18)
Yards: 6,761/5,492. **Par:** 72/72. **Course Rating:** 72.1/70.8. **Slope:** 130/116. **Green Fee:** $55/$165. **Miscellaneous:** Reduced fees (weekdays, guests, twilight, juniors).
Reader Comments: As good as resort golf gets … Great resort courses … Parkland type courses in desert, water in play on both courses, ranger gives you fruit! … Beautiful desert course. Great layout, a bit expensive, … Expensive, but beautiful, great conditions … Great service, fast greens.
★★★★½ VALLEY COURSE (18) *Condition*
Yards: 6,627/5,262. **Par:** 72/72. **Course Rating:** 71.5/69.6. **Slope:** 127/110. **Green Fee:** $50/$150. **Miscellaneous:** Reduced fees (weekdays, guests, twilight).
Reader Comments: Desert and mountain views. Thousands of hummingbirds and other wildlife. A well-designed playable course and off season rates were less then $50 per round. Is this heaven or what?! … Great resort courses … Beautiful.

★★½ MARRIOTT'S RANCHO LAS PALMAS RESORT & COUNTRY CLUB
R-42000 Bob Hope Dr., Rancho Mirage, 92270, Riverside County, (760)862-4551, 5 miles from Palm Springs. **E-mail:** Bshollenberger@cclinksgolf.com. **Facility Holes:** 27. **Green Fee:** $59/$129. **Cart Fee:** Included in green fee. **Walking Policy:** Mandatory carts. **Opened:** 1978. **Architect:** Ted Robinson. **Season:** Year-round. **To obtain tee times:** Call up to 7 days in advance. **Miscellaneous:** Reduced fees (weekdays, guests, twilight), metal spikes, range (grass/mats), lodging (450 rooms), credit cards (MC, V, AE, D), BF, FF.
NORTH/SOUTH (18 Combo)
Yards: 6,019/5,421. **Par:** 71/71. **Course Rating:** 67.1/69.7. **Slope:** 115/113.
NORTH/WEST (18 Combo)
Yards: 6,113/5,308. **Par:** 71/71. **Course Rating:** 67.8/66.9. **Slope:** 116/105.
SOUTH/WEST (18 Combo)
Yards: 6,128/5,271. **Par:** 70/70. **Course Rating:** 67.8/66.8. **Slope:** 115/110.

MARRIOTT'S SHADOW RIDGE RESORT
R-9002 Shadow Ridge Rd., Palm Desert, 92211, Riverside County, (760)674-2700, 110 miles from Los Angeles. **E-mail:** martyhoeffken@marriottgolf.com. **Web:** golfshadowridge.com. **Facility Holes:** 18. **Yards:** 6,923/6,114. **Par:** 71/71. **Course Rating:** 73.2/69.2. **Slope:** 132/122. **Green Fee:** $50/$145. **Cart Fee:** Included in green fee. **Walking Policy:** Mandatory carts. **Walkability:** 2. **Opened:** 2000. **Architect:** Nick Faldo. **Season:** Year-round. **High:** Jan.-April. **To obtain tee times:** Call up to 90 days in advance. **Miscellaneous:** Reduced fees (guests), metal spikes, range (grass), credit cards (MC, V, AE, D, DC), BF, FF.

★★★ MATHER GOLF COURSE
PU-4103 Eagles Nest Rd., Mather, 95655, Sacramento County, (916)364-4354, 7 miles from Sacramento. **E-mail:** mathergc@pacbell.net. **Web:** www.courseco.com. **Facility Holes:** 18. **Yards:** 6,721/5,976. **Par:** 72/74. **Course Rating:** 71.3/72.4. **Slope:** 121/119. **Green Fee:** $21/$26. **Cart:** $12/Cart. **Walking Policy:** Unrestricted walking. **Walkability:** 2. **Opened:** 1963. **Architect:** Jack Fleming. **Season:** Year-round. **To obtain tee times:** Call up to 7 days ahead. **Misc:** Reduced fees (weekdays, twilight, seniors, juniors), range, cards (MC, V), BF, FF.
Reader Comments: Nice greens and wide fairways … Has potential, could be upgraded … Former military course, but it is wide open course.

CALIFORNIA

★★★ MEADOW LAKE GOLF COURSE
SP-10333 Meadow Glen Way, Escondido, 92026, San Diego County, (760)749-1620, (800)523-2655, 30 miles from San Diego. **Facility Holes:** 18. **Yards:** 6,419/5,610. **Par:** 71/73. **Course Rating:** 71.0/73.3. **Slope:** 128/133. **Green Fee:** $26/$38. **Cart Fee:** $13/Person. **Walking Policy:** Walking at certain times. **Walkability:** 3. **Opened:** 1965. **Architect:** Tom Sanderson. **Season:** Year-round. **To obtain tee times:** Call golf shop. **Miscellaneous:** Reduced fees (weekdays, guests, twilight, seniors, juniors), range (grass/mats), credit cards (MC, V, AE, DC), BF, FF.
Reader Comments: A fun course ... Fun golf, need some local knowledge, small greens, nice setting ... Interesting variety of holes, think about the club you use off the tee ... Beautiful setting, great personnel and challenging ... #10 is the toughest hole in San Diego.

★★½ MEADOWLARK GOLF CLUB
PU-16782 Graham St., Huntington Beach, 92649, Orange County, (714)846-1364, 22 miles from Los Angeles. **Facility Holes:** 18. **Yards:** 5,609/5,251. **Par:** 70/71. **Course Rating:** 66.8/69.9. **Slope:** 113/117. **Green Fee:** $25/$35. **Cart Fee:** $12/Cart. **Walking Policy:** Unrestricted walking. **Walkability:** 2. **Opened:** 1929. **Architect:** William F. Bell. **Season:** Year-round. **To obtain tee times:** Call up to 21 days in advance. **Miscellaneous:** Reduced fees (weekdays, twilight, seniors, juniors), range (grass/mats), credit cards (MC, V, AE, D, DC), BF, FF.

★★★★ THE MEADOWS DEL MAR GOLF CLUB
R-5300 Meadows Del Mar, San Diego, 92130, San Diego County, (858)792-6200, (877)530-0636. **E-mail:** hmoore@meadowsdelmar.com. **Web:** www.meadowsdelmar.com. **Facility Holes:** 18. **Yards:** 6,885/4,929. **Par:** 71/71. **Course Rating:** 73.7/68.3. **Slope:** 138/116. **Green Fee:** $70/$160. **Cart Fee:** Included in green fee. **Walking Policy:** Mandatory carts. **Walkability:** 4. **Opened:** 1999. **Architect:** Tom Fazio. **Season:** Year-round. **High:** May-Oct. **To obtain tee times:** Call up to 60 days in advance. **Miscellaneous:** Reduced fees (weekdays, twilight, juniors), range (grass/mats), credit cards (MC, V, AE, D, DC), BF, FF.
Reader Comments: It's great, fun, tough ... Very solid ... Great design, use every club ... Well maintained, nice personnel, a bit pricey ... Great new Southern CA course ... Fun course, good holes ... Outstanding course and service, the best we have seen in the San Diego area ... Great holes.

★★★ MENIFEE LAKES COUNTRY CLUB
SP-29875 Menifee Lakes Dr., Menifee, 92584, Riverside County, (909)672-3090, 20 miles from Riverside. **Facility Holes:** 27. **Green Fee:** $24/$58. **Cart Fee:** Included in green fee. **Walking Policy:** Unrestricted walking. **Walkability:** 2. **Opened:** 1989. **Architect:** Ted Robinson. **Season:** Year-round. **To obtain tee times:** Call up to 7 days in advance. **Miscellaneous:** Reduced fees (weekdays, twilight, juniors), metal spikes, range (grass), credit cards (MC, V), BF, FF.
FALLS/LAKES COURSE (18 Combo)
Yards: 6,500/5,500. **Par:** 72/72. **Course Rating:** 70.7/72.4. **Slope:** 121/122.
LAKES/PALMS COURSE (18 Combo)
Yards: 6,500/5,500. **Par:** 72/72. **Course Rating:** 70.5/71.5. **Slope:** 120/120.
PALMS/FALLS COURSE (18 Combo)
Yards: 6,500/5,500. **Par:** 72/72. **Course Rating:** 71.1/72.2. **Slope:** 122/121.
Reader Comments: Fun course, semi-private but well managed. Course conditions were great, service was good. Well worth a little drive from LA/Orange County ... Service is great, tough rough ... Fun, short course ... Very nice course. Multiple tiered greens.

★★ MERCED HILLS GOLF CLUB
PU-5320 North Lake Rd., Merced, 95340, Merced County, (209)383-4943, 40 miles from Modesto. **E-mail:** mercedhills.com. **Web:** www.mercedhill.com. **Facility Holes:** 18. **Yards:** 6,831/5,397. **Par:** 72/72. **Course Rating:** 72.8/70.6. **Slope:** 128/115. **Green Fee:** $17/$24. **Cart Fee:** $10/Person. **Walking Policy:** Unrestricted walking. **Walkability:** 3. **Opened:** 1995. **Season:** Year-round. **High:** April-Oct. **To obtain tee times:** Call golf shop. **Misc:** Reduced fees (weekdays, twilight, seniors, juniors), range (grass), credit cards (MC, V, D), BF, FF.

★★★ MESQUITE GOLF CLUB
PU-2700 E. Mesquite Ave., Palm Springs, 92262, Riverside County, (760)323-1502, 120 miles from Los Angeles. **Facility Holes:** 18. **Yards:** 6,328/5,281. **Par:** 72/72. **Course Rating:** 69.5/70.8. **Slope:** 122/120. **Green Fee:** $30/$85. **Cart Fee:** Included in green fee. **Walking Policy:** Walking at certain times. **Walkability:** 1. **Opened:** 1984. **Architect:** Bert Stamps. **Season:** Year-round. **High:** Nov.-April. **To obtain tee times:** Call up to 14 days in advance. **Miscellaneous:** Reduced fees (weekdays, guests, twilight, juniors), metal spikes, range (grass/mats), credit cards (MC, V, AE, D, DC), BF, FF.
Reader Comments: Great practice area ... Has 6 par 5s, 6 par 4s, 6 par 3s ... Not too tough but beautiful ... Nice people, nice course.

★★★½ MICKE GROVE GOLF LINKS
PU-11401 N. Micke Grove Rd., Lodi, 95240, San Joaquin County, (209)369-4410, 5 miles from Stockton. **Facility Holes:** 18. **Yards:** 6,565/5,286. **Par:** 72/72. **Course Rating:** 71.1/69.7. **Slope:** 118/111. **Green Fee:** $17/$27. **Cart Fee:** $11/Person. **Walking Policy:** Unrestricted walking. **Walkability:** 1. **Opened:** 1989. **Architect:** Garrett Gill/George B. Williams. **Season:** Year-round. **High:** March-Nov. **To obtain tee times:** Call golf shop. **Misc:** Reduced fees (weekdays, twilight, seniors, juniors), metal spikes, range (grass/mats), credit cards (MC, V).
Reader Comments: Well manicured public course, friendly and helpful staff … Great course to play for local area … … Nice course, well maintained.

MILE SQUARE GOLF COURSE
PU-10401 Warner Ave., Fountain Valley, 92708, Orange County, (714)968-4556, 30 miles from Los Angeles. **Web:** www.milesquaregolf.com. **Facility Holes:** 36. **Walking Policy:** Unrestricted walking. **Walkability:** 2. **Architect:** David Rainville. **Season:** Year-round. **To obtain tee times:** Call up to 7 days in advance. **Miscellaneous:** Reduced fees (weekdays, twilight), range (mats), credit cards (MC, V), BF, FF.
★★½ CLASSIC COURSE (18)
Yards: 6,629/5,545. **Par:** 72/72. **Course Rating:** 71.0/70.5. **Slope:** 119/109. **Green Fee:** $26/$35. **Cart Fee:** $22/Cart. **Opened:** 1969.
PLAYERS COURSE (18)
Yards: 6,759/5,747. **Par:** 72/72. **Course Rating:** 72.3. **Slope:** 125/125. **Green Fee:** $40/$60. **Cart Fee:** $12/Person. **Opened:** 2001.

★★★ MISSION LAKES COUNTRY CLUB
SP-8484 Clubhouse Blvd., Desert Hot Springs, 92240, Riverside County, (760)329-8061, 10 miles from Palm Springs. **Facility Holes:** 18. **Yards:** 6,737/5,390. **Par:** 71/72. **Course Rating:** 72.8/71.2. **Slope:** 131/122. **Green Fee:** $30/$75. **Cart Fee:** Included in green fee. **Opened:** 1973. **Architect:** Ted Robinson. **Season:** Year-round. **High:** Jan.-May. **To obtain tee times:** Call golf shop. **Miscellaneous:** Reduced fees (weekdays, guests, twilight, juniors), metal spikes, range (grass), credit cards (MC, V).
Reader Comments: Beautiful golf course. Good challenge for all levels of golfers because of its multiple tees … Good golf course, fun to play … One of my favorites.

★★ MONARCH BAY GOLF CLUB
PU-13800 Neptune Dr., San Leandro, 94577, Alameda County, (510)895-2162, 5 miles from Oakland. **E-mail:** info@americangolf.com. **Facility Holes:** 27. **Yards:** 7,015/5,140. **Par:** 71/71. **Course Rating:** 73.5/69.8. **Slope:** 121/117. **Green Fee:** $15/$70. **Cart Fee:** $13/Person. **Walking Policy:** Unrestricted walking. **Walkability:** 4. **Opened:** 1973. **Architect:** John Harbottle III. **Season:** Year-round. **To obtain tee times:** Call up to 30 days in advance. **Miscellaneous:** Reduced fees (twilight, seniors, juniors), range (grass/mats), credit cards (MC, V, AE, D, DC), BF, FF.
Special Notes: Formerly Tony Lema Golf Course. Also has a 9-hole executive course.

★★★ MONARCH BEACH GOLF LINKS
R-33033 Niguel Rd., Dana Point, 92629, Orange County, (949)240-8247, 60 miles from Los Angeles. **E-mail:** adeck@troongolf.com. **Facility Holes:** 18. **Yards:** 6,344/5,046. **Par:** 70/70. **Course Rating:** 71.4/70.4. **Slope:** 134/125. **Green Fee:** $135/$175. **Cart Fee:** Included in green fee. **Walking Policy:** Unrestricted walking. **Walkability:** 3. **Opened:** 1984. **Architect:** Robert Trent Jones Jr. **Season:** Year-round. **To obtain tee times:** Call up to 30 days in advance. **Miscellaneous:** Reduced fees (twilight, juniors), range (mats), credit cards (MC, V, AE, DC), FF.
Reader Comments: A nice layout, dolphins a nice touch … Ocean views are great … Lowest priced high-end course, great staff … Coastal setting, good views, must play once.

★★ MONTEBELLO COUNTRY CLUB
PU-901 Via San Clemente, Montebello, 90640, Los Angeles County, (323)725-0892, 9 miles from Los Angeles. **Facility Holes:** 18. **Yards:** 6,671/5,979. **Par:** 71/72. **Course Rating:** 70.4/72.4. **Slope:** 114/117. **Green Fee:** $28/$38. **Cart Fee:** $24/Cart. **Walking Policy:** Unrestricted walking. **Walkability:** 3. **Opened:** 1928. **Architect:** William P. Bell. **Season:** Year-round. **High:** April-Oct. **To obtain tee times:** Call golf shop. **Miscellaneous:** Reduced fees (twilight, seniors, juniors), metal spikes, range (mats), credit cards (MC, V).

★★★½ MORENO VALLEY RANCH GOLF CLUB
PU-28095 John F. Kennedy Dr., Moreno Valley, 92555, Riverside County, (909)924-4444, 15 miles from Riverside. **Web:** www.mvrgolf.com. **Facility Holes:** 27. **Green Fee:** $31/$65. **Cart Fee:** Included in green fee. **Walking Policy:** Mandatory carts. **Opened:** 1988. **Architect:** Pete Dye. **Season:** Year-round. **To obtain tee times:** Call up to 7 days in advance. **Miscellaneous:**

Reduced fees (weekdays, twilight, seniors, juniors), metal spikes, range (grass/mats), credit cards (MC, V, AE, D), BF, FF.
LAKE/VALLEY (18 Combo)
Yards: 6,898/5,196. **Par:** 72/72. **Course Rating:** 74.1/70.1. **Slope:** 138/122. **Walkability:** 3.
MOUNTAIN/LAKE (18 Combo)
Yards: 6,684/5,108. **Par:** 72/72. **Course Rating:** 73.1/69.6. **Slope:** 139/121. **Walkability:** 4.
MOUNTAIN/VALLEY (18 Combo)
Yards: 6,880/5,196. **Par:** 72/72. **Course Rating:** 74.2/70.1. **Slope:** 140/122. **Walkability:** 3.
Reader Comments: Great course. Great people ... Wonderful scenery, great variety of holes. Quite challenging ... Excellent!!! ... Good value, lots of hills ... 3 nines all different, all great layouts ... Fun Pete Dye design, bargain ... Great greens, wind a factor.

★★★ **MORGAN RUN RESORT & CLUB**
R-5690 Cancha de Golf, Rancho Santa Fe, 92067, San Diego County, (858)756-3255, 20 miles from San Diego. **Facility Holes:** 27. **Green Fee:** $50/$90. **Cart Fee:** $20/Person. **Architect:** H. Rainville. **Season:** Year-round. **To obtain tee times:** Call golf shop. **Miscellaneous:** Reduced fees (twilight), credit cards (MC, V, AE).
EAST/NORTH (18 Combo)
Yards: 6,141/5,860. **Par:** 71/71. **Course Rating:** 68.8/70.2. **Slope:** 110/113. **Walkability:** 2.
Miscellaneous: Lodging (89 rooms).
EAST/SOUTH (18 Combo)
Yards: 6,443/6,136. **Par:** 72/72. **Course Rating:** 70.2/71.3. **Slope:** 112/117. **Walkability:** 1.
Miscellaneous: Lodging (89 rooms).
SOUTH/NORTH (18 Combo)
Yards: 6,346/6,344. **Par:** 71/71. **Course Rating:** 69.7/70.7. **Slope:** 112/115. **Walkability:** 1.
Reader Comments: Great course, worth the travel time from Indian Wells ... East and South nines best ... Very simple, a beginners' course ... Good framing on each hole ... Four-star accommodations. Challenging course.

★★★ **MORRO BAY GOLF COURSE**
PU-201 State Park Rd., Morro Bay, 93442, San Luis Obispo County, (805)772-8751, 15 miles from San Luis Obispo. **E-mail:** jasonhayes@pga.com. **Facility Holes:** 18. **Yards:** 6,360/5,055. **Par:** 71/72. **Course Rating:** 70.7/69.5. **Slope:** 115/117. **Green Fee:** $29/$36. **Cart Fee:** $20/Cart. **Walking Policy:** Unrestricted walking. **Walkability:** 4. **Opened:** 1929. **Architect:** Russell Noyes. **Season:** Year-round. **To obtain tee times:** Call up to 7 days in advance. **Miscellaneous:** Reduced fees (twilight, seniors, juniors), metal spikes, range (grass/mats), credit cards (MC, V, D), BF, FF.
Reader Comments: Nifty old-fashioned style design and greens ... Fun course, great views ... This course is quite a bargain considering the amazing views you have of the harbor. Your putts always break towards the ocean even if goes uphill. Overall, well worth the money ... Great public course ... Superb views, challenging layout.

★★★★ **MOUNT WOODSON GOLF CLUB**
SP-16422 N. Woodson Dr., Ramona, 92065, San Diego County, (760)788-3555, 25 miles from San Diego. **Web:** www.mtwoodson.com. **Facility Holes:** 18. **Yards:** 6,180/4,441. **Par:** 70/70. **Course Rating:** 68.8/64.7. **Slope:** 130/108. **Green Fee:** $55/$80. **Cart Fee:** Included in green fee. **Walking Policy:** Mandatory carts. **Walkability:** 5. **Opened:** 1991. **Architect:** Lee Scmidt/Brian Curley. **Season:** Year-round. **To obtain tee times:** Call up to 7 days in advance. **Miscellaneous:** Reduced fees (weekdays, twilight, juniors), credit cards (MC, V, AE), BF, FF.
Reader Comments: Great par 3, outstanding views ... Gorgeous setting in mountains of San Diego ... Great views. Good service and fees ... Most fun course in county. Short but challenging ... Short course but can best you up if you are not playing well ... People great, course very challenging ... Great wooden bridge for carts.

★★½ **MOUNTAIN MEADOWS GOLF CLUB**
PU-1875 N. Fairplex Dr., Pomona, 91768, Los Angeles County, (909)623-3704, 20 miles from Los Angeles. **Web:** www.americangolf.com. **Facility Holes:** 18. **Yards:** 6,509/5,637. **Par:** 72/72. **Course Rating:** 71.5/71.5. **Slope:** 125/117. **Green Fee:** $20/$25. **Cart Fee:** $11/Person. **Walking Policy:** Unrestricted walking. **Walkability:** 4. **Opened:** 1977. **Architect:** Ted Robinson. **Season:** Year-round. **To obtain tee times:** Call up to 7 days in advance. **Miscellaneous:** Reduced fees (weekdays, twilight, seniors, juniors), metal spikes, range (grass), credit cards (MC, V, AE, D, DC), BF, FF.

MOUNTAIN SHADOWS GOLF COURSE
PU-100 Golf Course Dr., Rohnert Park, 94928, Sonoma County, (707)584-7766, 7 miles from Santa Rosa. **Facility Holes:** 36. **Cart Fee:** $13/Person. **Season:** Year-round. **High:** April-Oct. **To obtain tee times:** Call golf shop. **Miscellaneous:** Reduced fees (weekdays, twilight, seniors, juniors), metal spikes, range (mats), lodging (500 rooms), credit cards (MC, V, AE).

★★ **NORTH COURSE** (18)
Yards: 7,035/5,503. **Par:** 72/72. **Course Rating:** 72.1/70.5. **Slope:** 0/117. **Green Fee:** $20/$55. **Walking Policy:** Walking at certain times. **Walkability:** 3. **Opened:** 1974. **Architect:** Gary Roger Baird.
★★ **SOUTH COURSE** (18)
Yards: 6,720/5,805. **Par:** 72/72. **Course Rating:** 70.1/71.4. **Slope:** 115/122. **Green Fee:** $15/$40. **Walking Policy:** Unrestricted walking. **Walkability:** 2. **Opened:** 1963. **Architect:** Bob Baldock.

★★★ MOUNTAIN SPRINGS GOLF CLUB
PU-17566 Lime Kiln Road, Sonora, 95370, Tuolumne County, (209)532-1000, 45 miles from Stockton. **Web:** www.mountainspringsgolf.com. **Facility Holes:** 18. **Yards:** 6,665/5,195. **Par:** 72/72. **Course Rating:** 72.1/70.2. **Slope:** 131/120. **Green Fee:** $25/$36. **Cart Fee:** $13/Person. **Walking Policy:** Unrestricted walking. **Walkability:** 4. **Opened:** 1990. **Architect:** Robert Muir Graves. **Season:** Year-round. **To obtain tee times:** Call up to 14 days in advance. **Miscellaneous:** Reduced fees (twilight, seniors, juniors), metal spikes, range (mats), credit cards (MC, V), BF, FF.
Reader Comments: Best value in the Mother Lode ... Unusual, hilly course, but fun ... Slow but nice, challenging course.

★★ MOUNTAIN VIEW COUNTRY CLUB
PU-2121 Mountain View Dr., Corona, 92882, Riverside County, (909)737-9798, 10 miles from Riverside. **Facility Holes:** 18. **Yards:** 6,456/5,432. **Par:** 72/73. **Course Rating:** 70.9/71.7. **Slope:** 129/120. **Green Fee:** $24/$45. **Cart Fee:** Included in green fee. **Walking Policy:** Walking at certain times. **Walkability:** 3. **Opened:** 1963. **Season:** Year-round. **High:** Oct.-July. **To obtain tee times:** Call up to 7 days in advance. **Miscellaneous:** Reduced fees (weekdays, twilight, seniors, juniors), range (grass), credit cards (MC, V), BF, FF.

MOUNTAIN VISTA GOLF CLUB
SP-38-180 Del Webb Blvd., Palm Desert, 92211, Riverside County, (760)200-2200, 10 miles from Palm Springs. **E-mail:** hochmanj@delwebb.com. **Web:** www.delwebb.com. **Facility Holes:** 36. **Green Fee:** $33/$89. **Cart Fee:** Included in green fee. **Walking Policy:** Mandatory carts. **Walkability:** 3. **Architect:** Billy Casper/Greg Nash. **Season:** Year-round. **High:** Nov.-April. **To obtain tee times:** Call up to 30 days in advance. **Miscellaneous:** Reduced fees (twilight), range (grass), credit cards (MC, V), BF, FF.
SAN GORGONIO (18)
Yards: 6,700/5,000. **Par:** 72/72. **Opened:** 2001.
★★★½ **SANTA ROSA** (18)
Yards: 6,720/5,305. **Par:** 72/72. **Course Rating:** 72.3/71.5. **Slope:** 125/116. **Opened:** 1992.
Reader Comments: Nice, player friendly ... Hot in summer, good course ... Beautiful scenery, very playable ... One of the best in Palm Springs area.
Special Notes: Formerly Sun City Palm Desert Golf Club.

★★★ NAPA GOLF COURSE AT KENNEDY PARK
PU-2295 Streblow Dr., Napa, 94558, Napa County, (707)255-4333, 45 miles from San Francisco. **Web:** www.playnapa.com. **Facility Holes:** 18. **Yards:** 6,704/5,690. **Par:** 72/73. **Course Rating:** 72.3/71.9. **Slope:** 123/123. **Green Fee:** $17/$40. **Cart Fee:** $12/Person. **Walking Policy:** Unrestricted walking. **Walkability:** 2. **Opened:** 1968. **Architect:** Jack Fleming/Bob Baldock. **Season:** Year-round. **To obtain tee times:** Call up to 14 days in advance. **Miscellaneous:** Reduced fees (weekdays, twilight, seniors, juniors), metal spikes, range (mats), credit cards (MC, V), BF, FF.
Reader Comments: A steal for this true test of golf. The greens are tour fast and the layout is narrow. You need to hit all your clubs for this course and you better be hitting them well ... Best value in the North Bay! Better than all for value.
Special Notes: Formerly Napa Municipal Golf Club.

★★½ NEEDLES MUNICIPAL GOLF COURSE
PU-144 Marina Dr., Needles, 92363, San Bernardino County, (760)326-3931, 100 miles from Las Vegas. **E-mail:** ndlsgolf@ctaz.com. **Web:** www.needlesgolf.com. **Facility Holes:** 18. **Yards:** 6,550/5,850. **Par:** 70/70. **Course Rating:** 71.4/71.1. **Slope:** 117/114. **Green Fee:** $25/$35. **Cart Fee:** $10/Person. **Walking Policy:** Unrestricted walking. **Walkability:** 2. **Opened:** 1962. **Season:** Year-round. **High:** Dec.-April. **To obtain tee times:** Call up to 7 days in advance. **Misc:** Reduced fees (seniors, juniors), range (grass/mats), credit cards (MC, V, AE), BF, FF.

★★★½ NORTHSTAR-AT-TAHOE RESORT GOLF COURSE
R-Hwy. 267 and Northstar Dr., Truckee, 96160, Nevada County, (530)562-2490, (800)466-6784, 40 miles from Reno. **E-mail:** northstar@boothcreek.com. **Web:** www.skinorthstar.com. **Facility Holes:** 18. **Yards:** 6,897/5,470. **Par:** 72/72. **Course Rating:** 72.4/71.2. **Slope:** 137/134. **Green Fee:** $65/$95. **Cart Fee:** Included in green fee. **Walking Policy:** Unrestricted

walking. **Walkability:** 3. **Opened:** 1975. **Architect:** Robert Muir Graves. **Season:** May-Nov. **High:** June-Oct. **To obtain tee times:** Call up to 45 days in advance. **Miscellaneous:** Reduced fees (guests, twilight, seniors, juniors), range (mats), lodging (257 rooms), credit cards (MC, V, AE, D), BF, FF.

Reader Comments: Fun playing in the mountains … Front/back like two different courses. Need length and accuracy … Great mountain course, must be able to work the ball, must play for sure … Back 9 through tall timber is spectacular … Mountain 9 extremely tight. Meadow 9 wide open. Interesting change of pace.

★★★½ OAK CREEK GOLF CLUB
PU-1 Golf Club Dr., Irvine, 92618, Orange County, (949)653-5300, 60 miles from Los Angeles. **Facility Holes:** 18. **Yards:** 6,834/5,605. **Par:** 71/71. **Course Rating:** 72.7/71.2. **Slope:** 132/121. **Green Fee:** $95/$135. **Cart Fee:** Included in green fee. **Walking Policy:** Mandatory carts. **Walkability:** 1. **Opened:** 1996. **Architect:** Tom Fazio. **Season:** Year-round. **To obtain tee times:** Call golf shop. **Miscellaneous:** Reduced fees (twilight, seniors, juniors), range (grass), credit cards (MC, V, AE, D, DC, JCB), BF, FF.

Reader Comments: Outstanding value for the money … A well maintained course, a pleasure to play … User friendly. Enjoyed the layout. Fazio did a good job here as well as Pelican sister courses and the same quality golf and staff … Fair course for all levels.

★★★★ OAK VALLEY GOLF CLUB
PU-1888 Golf Club Dr., Beaumont, 92223, Riverside County, (909)769-7200, (877)625-2582, 20 miles from San Bernadino. **E-mail:** oakgc@aol.com. **Web:** www.oakvalleygolf.com. **Facility Holes:** 18. **Yards:** 7,003/5,494. **Par:** 72/72. **Course Rating:** 73.9/71.1. **Slope:** 136/122. **Green Fee:** $32/$75. **Cart Fee:** Included in green fee. **Walking Policy:** Mandatory carts. **Walkability:** 4. **Opened:** 1991. **Architect:** Lee Schmidt/Brian Curley. **Season:** Year-round. **High:** Oct.-May. **To obtain tee times:** Call up to 7 days in advance. **Miscellaneous:** Reduced fees (weekdays, twilight, seniors, juniors), range (grass), credit cards (MC, V, AE, D), BF, FF.

Reader Comments: Nobody in front of me all day and the green fees make it worth the drive to the middle of nowhere … Top-notch. Play early to avoid wind … Lots of water, hilly, very scenic … Run a good ship. Professional staff … A special course now in great condition. Bring your 'A' game.

★★½ OAKHURST COUNTRY CLUB
SP-1001 Peacock Creek Dr., Clayton, 94517, Contra Costa County, (925)672-9737, (888)455-0300, 2 miles from Concord. **Facility Holes:** 18. **Yards:** 6,739/5,285. **Par:** 72/72. **Course Rating:** 73.1/70.3. **Slope:** 132/123. **Green Fee:** $80. **Cart Fee:** Included in green fee. **Walking Policy:** Mandatory carts. **Walkability:** 3. **Opened:** 1990. **Architect:** Ron Fream. **Season:** Year-round. **To obtain tee times:** Call up to 7 days in advance. **Miscellaneous:** Range (grass/mats), credit cards (MC, V, AE, D), BF, FF.

OAKMONT GOLF CLUB
SP-7025 Oakmont Dr., Santa Rosa, 95409, Sonoma County, (707)538-2454, 55 miles from Santa Rosa. **Facility Holes:** 36. **Cart Fee:** $24/Person. **Walking Policy:** Unrestricted walking. **Walkability:** 1. **Architect:** Ted Robinson. **Season:** Year-round. **High:** June-Oct. **To obtain tee times:** Call golf shop. **Miscellaneous:** Reduced fees (twilight), metal spikes, range (grass/mats), credit cards (MC, V).
EAST COURSE (18)
Yards: 4,293/4,067. **Par:** 63/63. **Course Rating:** 59.8/62.8. **Slope:** 94/102. **Green Fee:** $22/$28. **Opened:** 1976.
★★★ **WEST COURSE** (18)
Yards: 6,379/5,573. **Par:** 72/72. **Course Rating:** 70.5/71.9. **Slope:** 121/128. **Green Fee:** $27/$35. **Opened:** 1963.

Reader Comments: Very friendly staff, good price … One of best values in all of northern California … Nothing great but solid golf course … Wide open, a walk in the park.

★★½ OCEANSIDE MUNICIPAL GOLF COURSE
PU-825 Douglas Dr., Oceanside, 92054, San Diego County, (760)433-1360, 30 miles from San Diego. **Facility Holes:** 18. **Yards:** 6,450/5,398. **Par:** 72/72. **Course Rating:** 70.8/71.6. **Slope:** 118/123. **Green Fee:** $18/$24. **Cart Fee:** $20/Cart. **Walking Policy:** Unrestricted walking. **Walkability:** 2. **Opened:** 1974. **Architect:** Richard Bigler. **Season:** Year-round. **To obtain tee times:** Call golf shop. **Miscellaneous:** Reduced fees (weekdays, twilight, seniors, juniors), metal spikes, range (grass), credit cards (MC, V, AE), BF, FF.

★★★★½ OJAI VALLEY INN & SPA *Service*
R-Country Club Rd., Ojai, 93023, Ventura County, (805)646-2420, (800)422-6524, 60 miles from Los Angeles. **E-mail:** mark_creenslit@golfojai.com. **Web:** www.golfojai.com. **Facility Holes:** 18. **Yards:** 6,235/5,225. **Par:** 70/71. **Course Rating:** 70.2/70.2. **Slope:** 122/123. **Green Fee:** $103/$118. **Cart Fee:** $17/Person. **Walking Policy:** Unrestricted walking. **Walkability:** 4. **Opened:** 1923. **Architect:** George Thomas/Jay Morrish. **Season:** Year-round. **High:** April-Nov.

To obtain tee times: Call golf shop. **Miscellaneous:** Reduced fees (guests, twilight, juniors), range (grass), lodging (208 rooms), credit cards (MC, V, AE, D), BF, FF.

Reader Comments: Great course. I've played here several times and always return ... A great course ... All you can play deals (can't beat it). Played 54 holes one day and 36 the next. Beautiful course that's challenging ... Nothing second rate. You arrive and leave smiling ... Loved everything, go there often.

★★★★ OLD DEL MONTE GOLF COURSE
PU-1300 Sylvan Rd., Monterey, 93940, Monterey County, (831)373-2700, 60 miles from San Jose. **Facility Holes:** 18. **Yards:** 6,339/5,526. **Par:** 72/74. **Course Rating:** 71.3/71.1. **Slope:** 122/118. **Green Fee:** $80. **Cart Fee:** $18/Person. **Walking Policy:** Unrestricted walking. **Walkability:** 2. **Opened:** 1897. **Architect:** C. Maud. **Season:** Year-round. **High:** April-Oct. **To obtain tee times:** Call golf shop. **Miscellaneous:** Reduced fees (guests, twilight, juniors), metal spikes, caddies, credit cards (MC, V, AE, D, JCB).

Reader Comments: Super, love to play ... Good challenge for everyone ... A pleasure ... Superior, elegant course ... Great old course, cheap for Monterey ... Lush fairways, tough greens ... Very good value, good service ... Small fast greens, course usually wins ... A good secret in Monterey.

★★★ OLIVAS PARK GOLF COURSE
PU-3750 Olivas Park Dr., Ventura, 93001, Ventura County, (805)642-4303, 60 miles from Los Angeles. **E-mail:** djones@eaglgolf.com. **Facility Holes:** 18. **Yards:** 6,760/5,501. **Par:** 72/72. **Course Rating:** 72.6/72.4. **Slope:** 124/119. **Green Fee:** $20/$29. **Cart Fee:** $24/Cart. **Walking Policy:** Unrestricted walking. **Walkability:** 1. **Opened:** 1964. **Architect:** William F. Bell. **Season:** Year-round. **To obtain tee times:** Call up to 7 days in advance. **Miscellaneous:** Reduced fees (weekdays, twilight, seniors, juniors), metal spikes, range (grass/mats), caddies, credit cards (MC, V, AE), BF, FF.

Reader Comments: Good Ventura County course. Fast fun muni ... Good little course, flat ... Windy ... Open course. Good variety of holes ... Fun. Great course to play with wife ... Good muni course, usually busy.

★★★★ PACIFIC GROVE MUNICIPAL GOLF LINKS *Value*
PU-77 Asilomar Blvd., Pacific Grove, 93950, Monterey County, (831)648-5775, 2 miles from Monterey. **Web:** www.ci.pacific-grove.ca.us. **Facility Holes:** 18. **Yards:** 5,732/5,305. **Par:** 70/72. **Course Rating:** 67.5/70.5. **Slope:** 117/114. **Green Fee:** $32/$38. **Cart Fee:** $18/Cart. **Walking Policy:** Unrestricted walking. **Walkability:** 2. **Opened:** 1932. **Architect:** Jack Neville/Chandler Egan. **Season:** Year-round. **To obtain tee times:** Call golf shop. **Miscellaneous:** Reduced fees (twilight, juniors), range (grass/mats), credit cards (MC, V), FF.

Reader Comments: Tremendous value. Great course to walk. Funky layout (starts with back to back par 3s) ... Everyone should play ... Best public course in USA. Great views, great courses, great value ... Poor man's Pebble Beach ... Best kept secret in Northern Calif. A must play for the price.

★★★ PAJARO VALLEY GOLF CLUB
SP-967 Salinas Rd., Watsonville, 95076, Santa Cruz County, (831)724-3851, 20 miles from Santa Cruz. **Facility Holes:** 18. **Yards:** 6,218/5,696. **Par:** 72/72. **Course Rating:** 70.0/72.3. **Slope:** 122/123. **Green Fee:** $27/$55. **Cart Fee:** $28/Cart. **Walking Policy:** Unrestricted walking. **Walkability:** 4. **Opened:** 1927. **Architect:** Robert Muir Graves. **Season:** Year-round. **High:** April-Oct. **To obtain tee times:** Call golf shop. **Miscellaneous:** Reduced fees (weekdays, twilight), metal spikes, range (grass/mats), credit cards (MC, V, AE).

Reader Comments: Tight old golf course, fair test ... Challenging, nice variety of holes ... Some holes of this course were very scenic, and I had a lot of fun here. There were just places here and there that could have been in better condition.

★★★★ PALA MESA RESORT
R-2001 S. Hwy. 395, Fallbrook, 92028, San Diego County, (760)731-6803, (800)722-4700, 40 miles from San Diego. **Facility Holes:** 18. **Yards:** 6,502/5,632. **Par:** 72/72. **Course Rating:** 72.0/74.0. **Slope:** 131/134. **Green Fee:** $39/$80. **Cart Fee:** Included in green fee. **Walkability:** 2. **Opened:** 1964. **Architect:** Dick Rossen. **Season:** Year-round. **High:** Jan.-May. **To obtain tee times:** Call golf shop. **Miscellaneous:** Reduced fees (weekdays, guests, twilight), range (grass/mats), credit cards (MC, V, AE).

Reader Comments: Classy, fun course ... Great routing. No parallel fairways ... Good short tight resort course ... Best golf course I have ever played ... A course I play a lot in the summer, a good value midweek twilight ... Great course, great restaurant, great setting ... One of the better courses.

★★★½ PALM DESERT RESORT COUNTRY CLUB
SP-77-333 Country Club Dr., Palm Desert, 92211, Riverside County, (760)345-2791. **Facility Holes:** 18. **Yards:** 6,585/5,670. **Par:** 72/72. **Course Rating:** 70.8/71.8. **Slope:** 117/123. **Green Fee:** $25/$70. **Cart Fee:** Included in green fee. **Walkability:** 3. **Opened:** 1980. **Architect:** Joe Mulleneaux. **Season:** Nov.-Sept. **High:** Nov.-April. **To obtain tee times:** Call golf shop.

Miscellaneous: Reduced fees (weekdays, twilight), metal spikes, range (grass), credit cards (MC, V, D).
Reader Comments: Nice course, some holes a challenge … Wide open fairways cut 5-6 strokes off your game … Another relaxing easy-to-play course from back tees … Good course for the money

---

★★½ PALM SPRINGS COUNTRY CLUB

PU-2500 Whitewater Club Dr., Palm Springs, 92262, Riverside County, (760)323-2626, 110 miles from Los Angeles. **Facility Holes:** 18. **Yards:** 6,396/4,991. **Par:** 72/72. **Course Rating:** 68.9/71.4. **Slope:** 115/113. **Green Fee:** $15/$50. **Cart Fee:** Included in green fee. **Walking Policy:** Mandatory carts. **Walkability:** 1. **Opened:** 1960. **Season:** Oct.-May. **High:** Dec.-March. **To obtain tee times:** Call up to 7 days in advance. **Misc:** Reduced fees (weekdays, guests, twilight, juniors), metal spikes, range (grass), credit cards (MC, V, AE, D, DC).

★★½ PALO ALTO MUNICIPAL GOLF COURSE

PU-1875 Embarcadero Rd., Palo Alto, 94303, Santa Clara County, (650)856-0881, 15 miles from San Jose. **E-mail:** bradloz@aol.com. **Facility Holes:** 18. **Yards:** 6,820/5,679. **Par:** 72/72. **Course Rating:** 72.4/71.8. **Slope:** 118/118. **Green Fee:** $20/$39. **Cart Fee:** $22/Cart. **Walking Policy:** Walking at certain times. **Walkability:** 1. **Opened:** 1956. **Architect:** William F. Bell/William P. Bell. **Season:** Year-round. **High:** May-Oct. **To obtain tee times:** Call up to 7 days in advance. **Miscellaneous:** Reduced fees (twilight, juniors), range (mats), credit cards (MC, V, AE), BF, FF.

★★★★ PALOS VERDES GOLF CLUB

SP-3301 Via Campesina, Palos Verdes Estates, 90274, Los Angeles County, (310)375-2759, 20 miles from Los Angeles. **Facility Holes:** 18. **Yards:** 6,116/5,506. **Par:** 71/70. **Course Rating:** 70.4/68.9. **Slope:** 131/126. **Green Fee:** $205. **Cart Fee:** Included in green fee. **Walking Policy:** Mandatory carts. **Walkability:** 5. **Opened:** 1924. **Architect:** George C. Thomas, Jr. **Season:** Year-round. **High:** June-Aug. **To obtain tee times:** Call golf shop. **Miscellaneous:** Credit cards (MC, V, AE).
Reader Comments: Great views!! Good challenge … Difficult and challenging … Good view of the ocean … Great value, beautiful views, toward ocean … Toughest course for its length in state … Good layout.

★★★ PARADISE VALLEY GOLF COURSE

PU-3950 Paradise Valley Dr., Fairfield, 94533, Solano County, (707)426-1600, 45 miles from San Francisco. **E-mail:** pv0492@aol.com. **Facility Holes:** 18. **Yards:** 6,993/5,413. **Par:** 72/72. **Course Rating:** 74.1/71.1. **Slope:** 135/119. **Green Fee:** $18/$36. **Cart Fee:** $15/Person. **Walking Policy:** Unrestricted walking. **Walkability:** 1. **Opened:** 1993. **Architect:** Robert Muir Graves. **Season:** Year-round. **To obtain tee times:** Call up to 7 days in advance. **Miscellaneous:** Reduced fees (weekdays, twilight, seniors, juniors), range (grass/mats), credit cards (MC, V, AE, D), BF, FF.
Reader Comments: They make every effort to get you to play if you don't have a tee time. Very nice … Fun course, easy to score … Beautiful and good staff and program … Excellent overall facility … Great wet weather course … Outstanding golf for the money.

★★★★½ PASATIEMPO GOLF CLUB *Pace*

SP-18 Clubhouse Rd., Santa Cruz, 95060, Santa Cruz County, (831)459-9155, 30 miles from San Jose. **E-mail:** jmonroe@pasatiempo.com. **Web:** www.pasatiempo.com. **Facility Holes:** 18. **Yards:** 6,445/5,629. **Par:** 70/72. **Course Rating:** 72.7/73.6. **Slope:** 141/135. **Green Fee:** $135/$150. **Cart Fee:** $20/Person. **Walking Policy:** Unrestricted walking. **Walkability:** 4. **Opened:** 1929. **Architect:** Alister Mackenzie. **Season:** Year-round. **High:** May-Oct. **To obtain tee times:** Call up to 7 days in advance. **Miscellaneous:** Range (grass/mats), caddies, credit cards (MC, V, AE), BF, FF.
Notes: Ranked 77th in 2001-2002 America's 100 Greatest; 9th in 2001 Best in State.
Reader Comments: Tremendous Alister Mackenzie course, very challenging … One of my top-10 courses in the world … Tough back 9 … Great par 3s, very tough to score … Every hole was a treat! Great for shotmaking … 18 different holes, very challenging from tips … Awesome … As good as advertised. Could play this course 100 times and not get bored.

★★½ PEACOCK GAP GOLF & COUNTRY CLUB

SP-333 Biscayne Dr., San Rafael, 94901, Marin County, (415)453-4940, 12 miles from San Francisco. **E-mail:** peacockgap@worldnet.att.net. **Facility Holes:** 18. **Yards:** 6,354/5,629. **Par:** 71/73. **Course Rating:** 70.0/71.9. **Slope:** 118/126. **Green Fee:** $33/$47. **Cart Fee:** $13/Cart. **Walking Policy:** Walking at certain times. **Walkability:** 2. **Opened:** 1960. **Architect:** William F. Bell. **Season:** Year-round. **To obtain tee times:** Call up to 7 days in advance. **Miscellaneous:** Reduced fees (weekdays, twilight), range (grass/mats), credit cards (MC, V, AE), BF, FF.

CALIFORNIA

★★★★★ **PEBBLE BEACH GOLF LINKS** *Service, Condition*
R-1700 17-Mile Dr., Pebble Beach, 93953, Monterey County, (831)624-3811, (800)654-9300, 115 miles from San Francisco. **E-mail:** ramseyv@pebblebeach.com. **Web:** www.pebble-beach.com. **Facility Holes:** 18. **Yards:** 6,719/5,198. **Par:** 72/72. **Course Rating:** 73.8/71.9. **Slope:** 142/130. **Green Fee:** $350. **Cart Fee:** $25/Person. **Walking Policy:** Unrestricted walking. **Walkability:** 3. **Opened:** 1919. **Architect:** Jack Neville and Douglas Grant. **Season:** Year-round. **To obtain tee times:** Call golf shop. **Miscellaneous:** Range (grass/mats), caddies, credit cards (MC, V, AE, D, DC), BF, FF.
Notes: Ranked 1st in 2001-2002 America's 100 Greatest; 1st in 2001 Best in State.
Reader Comments: A place every avid golfer should experience at least once ... America's St. Andrews. A must play, even at outrageous prices. Variety of golf holes is what makes this course great. A little history also helps ... Worth every penny for an experience of a lifetime ... Historic, 1st class everything ... Nothing better, a must no matter $. ... Heaven on earth.

PELICAN HILL GOLF CLUB
R-22651 Pelican Hill Rd. South, Newport Coast, 92657, Orange County, (949)760-0707, 40 miles from Los Angeles. **Web:** www.pelicanhill.com. **Facility Holes:** 36. **Green Fee:** $175/$270. **Cart Fee:** Included in green fee. **Walking Policy:** Mandatory carts. **Architect:** Tom Fazio. **Season:** Year-round. **To obtain tee times:** Call up to 60 days in advance. **Miscellaneous:** Reduced fees (guests, twilight, seniors, juniors), range (grass), credit cards (MC, V, AE, D, DC), BF, FF.
★★★★½ **OCEAN NORTH COURSE** (18)
Yards: 6,856/5,800. **Par:** 71/71. **Course Rating:** 73.6/73.0. **Slope:** 133/125. **Walkability:** 3. **Opened:** 1993.
Notes: Ranked 24th in 2001 Best in State; 51st in 1996 America's Top 75 Upscale Courses.
Reader Comments: Five Star all the way. Course is in great shape. Staff is wonderful. You can find the reduced price fit for you if you ask what they have. Great day ... Some of the best views of any course I have ever played. Challenging finishing hole ... Prime course on prime coastal land ... A real treat to play here, beautiful course, well maintained. Fairly expensive but with reason.
★★★★½ **OCEAN SOUTH COURSE** (18)
Yards: 6,634/5,366. **Par:** 70/70. **Course Rating:** 72.1/72.5. **Slope:** 130/124. **Walkability:** 4. **Opened:** 1991.
Notes: Ranked 21st in 1997 Best in State; 59th in 1996 America's Top 75 Upscale Courses.
Reader Comments: A great design and well manicured ... I think this course is as beautiful as it is fair to play. As a woman golfer I enjoy being welcomed on to a course as I was at Pelican Hill. The apres golf is wonderful too ... As good as golf gets. I've been to Augusta several times. It's not Augusta, but it's close. Incredible views Manicured to a tee. Expensive but worth every penny. Great staff.

PGA OF SOUTH CALIFORNIA GOLF CLUB AT OAK VALLEY
PU-36211 Champions Dr., Calimesa, 92320, Riverside County, (909)845-8996, (877)742-2500, 16 miles from San Bernardino. **E-mail:** SCPGAgolfclub@aol.com. **Web:** www.scpgagolf.com. **Facility Holes:** 36. **Green Fee:** $32/$75. **Cart Fee:** Included in green fee. **Walking Policy:** Unrestricted walking. **Walkability:** 4. **Opened:** 2000. **Architect:** Lee Schmidt/Brian Curley. **Season:** Year-round. **To obtain tee times:** Call up to 7 days in advance. **Miscellaneous:** Reduced fees (twilight, seniors, juniors), range (grass), credit cards (MC, V, AE), BF, FF.
★★★★½ **CHAMPIONS COURSE** (18) *Condition*
Yards: 7,377/5,274. **Par:** 72/72. **Course Rating:** 76.5/72.4. **Slope:** 141/128.
Reader Comments: New course in great shape. Challenging ... 36 holes, new course, must play ... One of Southern California's best. Wait till you see the bunkers! ... Beautiful course, great view and shape ... Great new course, totally isolated.
LEGENDS COURSE (18)
Yards: 7,442/5,169. **Par:** 72/72. **Course Rating:** 76.6/70.9. **Slope:** 144/130.

PGA WEST RESORT
R-81405 Kingston Heath, La Quinta, 92253, Riverside County, (760)564-3900, (800)742-9378, 30 miles from Palm Springs. **E-mail:** sgustavson@kslmail.com. **Web:** www.pgawest.com. **Facility Holes:** 54. **Green Fee:** $75/$235. **Cart Fee:** Included in green fee. **Season:** Year-round. **High:** Dec.-May. **To obtain tee times:** Call golf shop. **Miscellaneous:** Reduced fees (weekdays, guests, twilight), range (grass), lodging (920 rooms), credit cards (MC, V, AE, DC, JCB), FF.
★★★ **GREG NORMAN COURSE** (18)
Yards: 7,156/5,281. **Par:** 72/72. **Course Rating:** 74.0/70.5. **Slope:** 134/115. **Walking Policy:** Walking with Caddie. **Walkability:** 3. **Opened:** 1999. **Architect:** Greg Norman.
Reader Comments: Very unique and challenging course with beautiful landscaping and wonderful views ... Good layout, young course ... Interesting design ... Really good fairways ... Wonderful golf experience ... Very attractive course ... Nice variety of holes. Pretty bunkering. Will improve with age.

CALIFORNIA

★★★★½ **JACK NICKLAUS TOURNAMENT COURSE** (18) *Condition*
Yards: 7,204/5,023. **Par:** 72/72. **Course Rating:** 74.7/69.0. **Slope:** 139/116. **Walking Policy:**
Mandatory carts. **Walkability:** 3. **Opened:** 1987. **Architect:** Jack Nicklaus.
Reader Comments: All the courses, both public and private are A-1. I rate the entire resort as 5-star! … Met Arnie at the clubhouse. Wonderful staff … Awesome … Toughest course I've ever played, lots of hidden problems. Site of PGA qualifying school … Great stuff.

★★★★½ **TPC STADIUM COURSE** (18) *Condition*
Yards: 7,266/5,092. **Par:** 72/72. **Course Rating:** 75.9/69.0. **Slope:** 150/124. **Walking Policy:**
Mandatory carts. **Walkability:** 4. **Opened:** 1986. **Architect:** Pete Dye.
Notes: Ranked 25th in 2001 Best in State.
Reader Comments: Longest, toughest course I ever played … Great clubhouse … A premier course. Toughest … The one must-play in the area. Defintely worth the money … Very tough and challenging … Must play at least once … Special, don't mind a high score.

★★★★½ **PINE MOUNTAIN LAKE COUNTRY CLUB**
SP-12765 Mueller Dr., Groveland, 95321, Tuolumne County, (209)962-8620, 90 miles from
Sacramento. **E-mail:** cborrego@pinemtlake.com. **Web:** www.pinemountainlake.com. **Facility
Holes:** 18. **Yards:** 6,363/5,726. **Par:** 70/72. **Course Rating:** 70.1/73.3. **Slope:** 125/128. **Green
Fee:** $20/$42. **Cart Fee:** $26/Cart. **Walking Policy:** Walking at certain times. **Walkability:** 3.
Opened: 1969. **Architect:** William F. Bell. **Season:** Year-round. **High:** June-Sept. **To obtain tee
times:** Call up to 10 days in advance. **Miscellaneous:** Reduced fees (twilight), range
(grass/mats), credit cards (MC, V, AE, D), BF, FF.
Reader Comments: Scenic mountain views from every hole. The 6th hole is the best. Par this hole
and you will not forget it! … Great course, great experience.

★★★ **PITTSBURG DELTA VIEW GOLF COURSE**
PU-2242 Golf Club Rd., Pittsburg, 94565, Contra Costa County, (925)439-4040, 40 miles
from San Francisco. **Facility Holes:** 18. **Yards:** 6,359/5,405. **Par:** 71/72. **Course Rating:**
71.4/70.0. **Slope:** 130/124. **Green Fee:** $13/$24. **Cart Fee:** $20/Cart. **Walking Policy:**
Unrestricted walking. **Walkability:** 5. **Opened:** 1947. **Architect:** Robert Muir Graves/Alistair
Mackenzie. **Season:** Year-round. **To obtain tee times:** Call golf shop. **Miscellaneous:** Reduced
fees (twilight, seniors, juniors), metal spikes, range (grass/mats), credit cards (MC, V).
Reader Comments: Great muni … Short course, but good value … The front 9 is somewhat quirky
going through the hills, but the back 9 is a masterpiece created by Alistair Mackenzie … Much
improved and well maintained course, combination of hilly and flat fairways, very affordable rate,
friendly personnel.

★★½ **PLUMAS LAKE GOLF & COUNTRY CLUB**
SP-1551 Country Club Rd., Marysville, 95901, Yuba County, (530)742-3201, 40 miles from
Sacramento. **E-mail:** office@plumaslake.com. **Web:** www.plumaslake.com. **Facility Holes:** 18.
Yards: 6,437/5,753. **Par:** 71/72. **Course Rating:** 70.5/73.4. **Slope:** 122/127. **Green Fee:**
$21/$26. **Cart Fee:** $10/Person. **Walking Policy:** Unrestricted walking. **Walkability:** 1. **Opened:**
1926. **Architect:** Jack Bosley/Bob Baldock. **Season:** Year-round. **High:** March-Oct. **To obtain
tee times:** Call up to 7 days in advance. **Miscellaneous:** Reduced fees (weekdays, twilight,
seniors, juniors), range (grass/mats), credit cards (MC, V), BF, FF.

★★★ **PLUMAS PINES COUNTRY CLUB**
PU-402 Poplar Valley Rd., Blairsden, 96103, Plumas County, (530)836-1420, (888)236-8725,
63 miles from Reno, NV. **E-mail:** pprgolf@psln.com. **Web:** www.plumaspinesgolf.com. **Facility
Holes:** 18. **Yards:** 6,504/5,240. **Par:** 72/72. **Course Rating:** 71.3/69.9. **Slope:** 132/126. **Green
Fee:** $50/$70. **Cart Fee:** Included in green fee. **Walking Policy:** Unrestricted walking.
Walkability: 5. **Opened:** 1980. **Architect:** Homer Flint. **Season:** May-Nov. **High:** June-Sept.
To obtain tee times: Call golf shop. **Miscellaneous:** Reduced fees (weekdays, twilight), range
(grass/mats), credit cards (MC, V, AE, D, DC, CB), BF, FF.
Reader Comments: Beautiful setting, tight holes, challenging … A must play mountain course …
Nice mountain course … Beautiful! Great play deals.

★½ **POPLAR CREEK GOLF COURSE - SAN MATEO**
PU-1700 Coyote Point Dr., San Mateo, 94401, San Mateo County, (650)522-4653, 18 miles
from San Francisco. **E-mail:** heck@ci.sanmateo.ca.us. **Web:** www.poplarcreekgolf.com.
Facility Holes: 18. **Yards:** 6,042/5,642. **Par:** 70/71. **Course Rating:** 69.0/72.8. **Slope:** 113/122.
Green Fee: $20/$38. **Cart Fee:** $24/Cart. **Walking Policy:** Unrestricted walking. **Walkability:** 1.
Opened: 1933. **Architect:** WPA. **Season:** Year-round. **To obtain tee times:** Call up to 7 days in
advance. **Misc:** Reduced fees (weekdays, twilight, seniors, juniors), cards (MC, V), BF, FF.
Special Notes: Formerly City of San Mateo Golf Course.

★★★★½ **POPPY HILLS GOLF COURSE** *Value, Condition*
PU-3200 Lopez Rd., Pebble Beach, 93953, Monterey County, (831)625-2154, 60 miles from
San Jose. **E-mail:** tjones@ncga.org. **Web:** www.ncga.org. **Facility Holes:** 18. **Yards:**

6,835/5,403. **Par:** 72/72. **Course Rating:** 74.6/72.1. **Slope:** 144/131. **Green Fee:** $45/$150. **Cart Fee:** $30/Cart. **Walking Policy:** Unrestricted walking. **Walkability:** 3. **Opened:** 1986. **Architect:** Robert Trent Jones Jr. **Season:** Year-round. **High:** April-Nov. **To obtain tee times:** Call up to 30 days in advance. **Miscellaneous:** Reduced fees (juniors), range (grass), caddies, credit cards (MC, V, AE), BF, FF.
Reader Comments: One of the best in California … Beautiful course, best deal for the money … Very nice course that was a lot of fun to play. Not as rushed as the other more famous courses in the area. Fun design. Beautiful forest setting … Best deal on 17-Mile Drive. An outstanding course in pristine condition year-round.

★★★★ **POPPY RIDGE GOLF COURSE**
PU-4280 Greenville Rd., Livermore, 94550, Alameda County, (925)456-8202, 10 miles from Pleasanton. **E-mail:** prgolfops@poppyridgegolf.com. **Web:** www.ncga.org. **Facility Holes:** 27. **Green Fee:** $35/$70. **Cart Fee:** $24/Cart. **Walking Policy:** Unrestricted walking. **Opened:** 1996. **Architect:** Rees Jones. **Season:** Year-round. **To obtain tee times:** Call up to 30 days in advance. **Miscellaneous:** Reduced fees (weekdays, twilight), range (grass), credit cards (MC, V, AE), BF, FF.
CHARDONNAY/ZINFANDEL (18 Combo)
Yards: 7,048/5,267. **Par:** 72/72. **Course Rating:** 74.6/70.2. **Slope:** 139/120. **Walkability:** 4.
MERLOT/CHARDONNAY (18 Combo)
Yards: 7,106/5,212. **Par:** 72/72. **Course Rating:** 74.6/70.2. **Slope:** 139/120. **Walkability:** 5.
ZINFANDEL/MERLOT (18 Combo)
Yards: 7,128/5,265. **Par:** 72/72. **Course Rating:** 74.6/70.2. **Slope:** 139/120. **Walkability:** 5.
Reader Comments: Outstanding course! Good service, super value … The place to test your wind game … Great course and model organization! … A challenge, add the wind, real fun … Beautiful … Great value for NCGA members, course is always in excellent condition … Best value around Bay area … Excellent course, even in the winter.

★★★½ **PRESIDIO GOLF COURSE**
PU-300 Finley Rd at Arguello Gate, San Francisco, 94129, San Francisco County, (415)561-4661. **E-mail:** cdaly@palmergolf.com. **Web:** www.presidiogolf.com. **Facility Holes:** 18. **Yards:** 6,477/5,785. **Par:** 72/73. **Course Rating:** 72.2/74.2. **Slope:** 136/131. **Green Fee:** $42/$72. **Cart Fee:** $15/Person. **Walking Policy:** Unrestricted walking. **Walkability:** 4. **Opened:** 1895. **Architect:** Robert Johnstone. **Season:** Year-round. **To obtain tee times:** Call up to 30 days in advance. **Miscellaneous:** Reduced fees (weekdays, twilight), range (grass/mats), credit cards (MC, V, AE), BF, FF.
Reader Comments: All fours here but very close to being fives. I played here in the early morning and it was great … Great golf in a gorgeous setting. I've been told that flat lies exist, but I have yet to find one! No. 12 is a gem.

★★★ **QUAIL RANCH GOLF CLUB**
PU-15960 Gilman Springs Rd., Moreno Valley, 92555, Riverside County, (909)654-2727, 20 miles from Riverside. **Facility Holes:** 18. **Yards:** 6,690/5,320. **Par:** 72/72. **Course Rating:** 72.9/71.9. **Slope:** 134/122. **Green Fee:** $29/$45. **Cart Fee:** Included in green fee. **Walking Policy:** Unrestricted walking. **Walkability:** 5. **Opened:** 1968. **Architect:** Desmond Muirhead. **Season:** Year-round. **High:** Nov.-June. **To obtain tee times:** Call golf shop. **Miscellaneous:** Reduced fees (weekdays, twilight, seniors, juniors), range (grass), credit cards (MC, V, AE), FF.
Reader Comments: Super resort course … Outstanding staff … River holes very challenging, fun round … Good value for the money … Tricky greens, excellent summer specials … Best value.

★★★½ **RAMS HILL COUNTRY CLUB**
R-1881 Rams Hill Rd., Borrego Springs, 92004, San Diego County, (760)767-5124, (800)292-2944, 87 miles from San Diego. **E-mail:** ramshill@nia.net. **Web:** www.ramshill.com. **Facility Holes:** 18. **Yards:** 6,866/5,694. **Par:** 72/72. **Course Rating:** 72.9/73.4. **Slope:** 130/128. **Green Fee:** $40/$105. **Cart Fee:** Included in green fee. **Walking Policy:** Mandatory carts. **Walkability:** 3. **Opened:** 1983. **Architect:** Ted Robinson. **Season:** Year-round. **High:** Nov.-May. **To obtain tee times:** Call golf shop. **Miscellaneous:** Reduced fees (guests, twilight), range (grass/mats), lodging (15 rooms), credit cards (MC, V, AE), FF.
Reader Comments: Great golf course in a great setting … A jewel away from Palm Springs, worth the trip … Has to be one of the best! Expensive … Watch out of the road runners… Lovely course … Gem in the desert … Beautiful desert course and resort, good food.

★★★½ **RANCHO BERNARDO INN RESORT**
R-17550 Bernardo Oaks Dr., San Diego, 92128, San Diego County, (858)675-8470, (800)662-6439. **Facility Holes:** 18. **Yards:** 6,458/5,448. **Par:** 72/72. **Course Rating:** 70.6/71.2. **Slope:** 122/119. **Green Fee:** $85/$110. **Cart Fee:** Included in green fee. **Walking Policy:** Walking at certain times. **Walkability:** 2. **Opened:** 1962. **Architect:** William F. Bell. **Season:** Year-round. **High:** Dec.-May. **To obtain tee times:** Call golf shop. **Miscellaneous:** Reduced fees

CALIFORNIA

(weekdays, guests, twilight, juniors), metal spikes, range (grass/mats), lodging (288 rooms), credit cards (MC, V, AE, D).

Reader Comments: Beautiful place and course … Outstanding course, good customer service … Fine layout, US Open rough, magnificent resort … Was the best course we played on vacation … Very good resort course. Four sets of tee boxes for each hole which accommodates several levels of play.

RANCHO CANADA GOLF CLUB
PU-4860 Carmel Valley Rd., Carmel, 93923, Monterey County, (831)624-0111, (800)536-9459, 8 miles from Monterey. **E-mail:** rnchoglf@carmel-golf.com. **Web:** www.ranchocanada.com. **Facility Holes:** 36. **Cart Fee:** $34/Cart. **Walking Policy:** Unrestricted walking. **Walkability:** 2. **Opened:** 1970. **Architect:** Robert Dean Putman. **Season:** Year-round. **To obtain tee times:** Call golf shop. **Miscellaneous:** Reduced fees (twilight, juniors), range (grass/mats), credit cards (MC, V, AE, DC), BF, FF.

★★★ **EAST COURSE** (18)
Yards: 6,109/5,267. **Par:** 71/72. **Course Rating:** 68.7/69.4. **Slope:** 120/114. **Green Fee:** $30/$65.
Reader Comments: Played in the rain but still a fun time … Ample practice facilities. Challenging … Rebuilt after El NiOo, great. No. 12 a winner.

★★★ **WEST COURSE** (18)
Yards: 6,349/5,568. **Par:** 71/72. **Course Rating:** 70.4/71.9. **Slope:** 125/118. **Green Fee:** $40/$80.
Reader Comments: The first of many good courses in Carmel Valley … Cozy clubhouse, relaxing layout … They go out of their way to make your day … East Course easier … In good shape for all the play it gets.

★★ RANCHO DEL RAY GOLF CLUB
PU-5250 Green Sands Ave., Atwater, 95301, Merced County, (209)358-7131, 30 miles from Modesto. **Facility Holes:** 18. **Yards:** 6,703/5,987. **Par:** 72/75. **Course Rating:** 72.5/73.6. **Slope:** 124/125. **Green Fee:** $15/$25. **Cart Fee:** $20/Cart. **Walking Policy:** Unrestricted walking. **Walkability:** 1. **Season:** Year-round. **To obtain tee times:** Call golf shop. **Miscellaneous:** Reduced fees (weekdays, twilight), range (grass/mats), credit cards (MC, V, AE, D), FF.

★★ RANCHO MARIA GOLF CLUB
PU-1950 Casmalia Rd., Santa Maria, 93455, Santa Barbara County, (805)937-2019, 5 miles from Santa Maria. **Web:** www.ranchomariagolf.com. **Facility Holes:** 18. **Yards:** 6,390/5,504. **Par:** 72/73. **Course Rating:** 70.2/71.3. **Slope:** 119/123. **Green Fee:** $17/$28. **Cart Fee:** $18/Cart. **Walking Policy:** Unrestricted walking. **Walkability:** 2. **Opened:** 1965. **Architect:** Bob Baldock. **Season:** Year-round. **To obtain tee times:** Call up to 7 days in advance. **Miscellaneous:** Reduced fees (weekdays, twilight, seniors, juniors), metal spikes, range (grass), credit cards (MC, V), BF, FF.

★★★ RANCHO PARK GOLF COURSE
PU-10460 W. Pico Blvd., Los Angeles, 90064, Los Angeles County, (310)839-4374. **Facility Holes:** 18. **Yards:** 6,585/5,928. **Par:** 71/71. **Slope:** 124/122. **Green Fee:** $17/$23. **Cart Fee:** $20/Cart. **Walking Policy:** Unrestricted walking. **Walkability:** 2. **Opened:** 1949. **Architect:** William P. Bell/William H. Johnson. **Season:** Year-round. **High:** April-Oct. **To obtain tee times:** Call golf shop. **Miscellaneous:** Reduced fees (weekdays, twilight), metal spikes.
Reader Comments: Design and track still hold up to make a challenge in this, one of the most played courses in the U.S. … Great value when you can get on. Always busy … For the money it is hard to beat … Where old Los Angeles Open used to be played, great diversity of challenging terrain … Rebuilt greens improve playability.

★★ RANCHO SAN JOAQUIN GOLF CLUB
PU-1 Sandburg Way, Irvine, 92612, Orange County, (949)451-0840, 18 miles from Los Angeles. **Facility Holes:** 18. **Yards:** 6,453/5,794. **Par:** 72/72. **Course Rating:** 70.6/73.1. **Slope:** 118/121. **Green Fee:** $13/$60. **Cart Fee:** Included in green fee. **Walking Policy:** Unrestricted walking. **Walkability:** 3. **Opened:** 1971. **Architect:** William F. Bell. **Season:** Year-round. **To obtain tee times:** Call golf shop. **Miscellaneous:** Reduced fees (weekdays, twilight, seniors, juniors), metal spikes, range (mats), credit cards (MC, V, AE).

★★★★ RANCHO SAN MARCOS GOLF CLUB *Condition*
PU-4600 Hwy. 154, Santa Barbara, 93105, Santa Barbara County, (805)683-6334, (877)776-1804, 12 miles from Santa Barbara. **E-mail:** cpaulson@rms1804.com. **Web:** www.rsm1804.com. **Facility Holes:** 18. **Yards:** 6,801/5,018. **Par:** 71/71. **Course Rating:** 73.1/69.2. **Slope:** 135/117. **Green Fee:** $79/$139. **Cart Fee:** Included in green fee. **Walking Policy:** Unrestricted walking. **Walkability:** 4. **Opened:** 1998. **Architect:** Robert Trent Jones Jr. **Season:** Year-round. **High:** March-Oct. **To obtain tee times:** Call golf shop. **Miscellaneous:**

Reduced fees (weekdays, guests, twilight, juniors), range (grass), caddies, credit cards (MC, V, AE), BF, FF.
Notes: Ranked 28th in 1999 Best in State.
Reader Comments: One of my favorite courses. Fun, beautiful and challenging. Tough Greens … Terrific course. Wonderful views. Good variety of hole designs. Great shape … Frequent MJ and Jimmy Connors sightings … Great course, staff, and atmosphere!! … The best course I played all year. Beautiful. Challenging.

★★★½ RANCHO SOLANO GOLF COURSE
PU-3250 Rancho Solano Pkwy., Fairfield, 94533, Solano County, (707)429-4653, 40 miles from San Francisco. **Web:** www.ranchosolanoclub.com. **Facility Holes:** 18. **Yards:** 6,705/5,206. **Par:** 72/72. **Course Rating:** 72.1/69.6. **Slope:** 128/117. **Green Fee:** $20/$43. **Cart Fee:** $15/Person. **Walking Policy:** Unrestricted walking. **Walkability:** 3. **Opened:** 1990. **Architect:** Gary Roger Baird. **Season:** Year-round. **To obtain tee times:** Call up to 7 days in advance. **Miscellaneous:** Reduced fees (weekdays, twilight, seniors, juniors), metal spikes, range (mats), credit cards (MC, V, AE, D), BF, FF.
Reader Comments: Great value for a very dynamic golf course … Altogether great experience … Course in great shape. Huge greens! Love the computer screens on carts that give yardages to green … Well designed and well maintained golf course, friendly personnel, affordable rates with seasonal discount offers.

★★★ RECREATION PARK GOLF COURSE
PU-5001 Deukmejian Dr., Long Beach, 90804, Los Angeles County, (562)494-5000, 15 miles from Los Angeles. **Facility Holes:** 18. **Yards:** 6,405/5,930. **Par:** 72/74. **Course Rating:** 69.9/72.4. **Slope:** 111/119. **Green Fee:** $19/$23. **Cart Fee:** $21/Cart. **Walking Policy:** Unrestricted walking. **Walkability:** 2. **Opened:** 1924. **Architect:** William P. Bell. **Season:** Year-round. **To obtain tee times:** Call golf shop. **Miscellaneous:** Reduced fees (weekdays, twilight, seniors, juniors), metal spikes, range (mats), credit cards (MC, V, AE).
Reader Comments: Great muni course … Challenging, good condition, enjoyed playing it … Home court, good layout … Order the Birdie for breakfast in the coffee shop. Municipal course, a few sand traps, no water, a good walk.

★★★★ REDHAWK GOLF CLUB
PU-45100 Redhawk Pkwy., Temecula, 92592, Riverside County, (909)602-3850, (800)451-4295, 30 miles from Riverside. **E-mail:** redhawkgc@earthlink.net. **Web:** www.red-hawkgolfcourse.com. **Facility Holes:** 18. **Yards:** 7,139/5,510. **Par:** 72/72. **Course Rating:** 75.7/72.0. **Slope:** 149/124. **Green Fee:** $49/$69. **Cart Fee:** Included in green fee. **Walking Policy:** Mandatory carts. **Walkability:** 4. **Opened:** 1991. **Architect:** Ron Fream. **Season:** Feb.-Dec. **To obtain tee times:** Call up to 7 days in advance. **Miscellaneous:** Reduced fees (twilight, seniors, juniors), range (grass/mats), credit cards (MC, V, AE, D), FF.
Reader Comments: Many great holes Definitely a challenge … Beautiful, great condition will repeat … Great twilight rates, super conditions … Very good course. Good layout and greens are nice … Magnificent target course … Great course. Price high but a must. Bring a weed whacker if you don't hit straight.

★★★½ THE RESERVE AT SPANOS PARK
SP-6301 West Eight Mile Rd., Stockton, 95219, San Joaquin County, (209)477-4653, 2 miles from Stockton. **Facility Holes:** 18. **Yards:** 7,000/5,490. **Par:** 72/72. **Course Rating:** 74.2/69.9. **Slope:** 133/118. **Green Fee:** $22/$70. **Cart Fee:** $13/Person. **Walking Policy:** Walking at certain times. **Walkability:** 1. **Opened:** 1999. **Architect:** Andy Raugust. **Season:** Year-round. **High:** April-Sept. **To obtain tee times:** Call up to 7 days in advance. **Miscellaneous:** Reduced fees (twilight, seniors, juniors), range (grass), credit cards (MC, V, AE, D), BF, FF.
Reader Comments: This course is a fun links-style course. There were very few trees, but lots of thick rough, wind, and water. And the greens are lightning fast, making it a very difficult course … Outstanding greens!!! … Good layout, wide open, forgiving … Hasn't caught on in Bay area yet, but this hidden gem will.

★★★½ RESORT AT SQUAW CREEK
R-400 Squaw Creek Rd., Olympic Valley, 96146, Placer County, (530)581-6637, (800)327-3353, 45 miles from Reno, Nevada. **E-mail:** dflynn@benchmarkmanagement.com. **Web:** www.squawcreek.com. **Facility Holes:** 18. **Yards:** 6,931/5,097. **Par:** 71/71. **Course Rating:** 72.9/68.9. **Slope:** 143/127. **Green Fee:** $85/$115. **Cart Fee:** Included in green fee. **Walking Policy:** Unrestricted walking. **Walkability:** 2. **Opened:** 1992. **Architect:** Robert Trent Jones Jr. **Season:** May-Oct. **High:** July-Aug. **To obtain tee times:** Call up to 30 days in advance. **Miscellaneous:** Reduced fees (weekdays, twilight, juniors), range (mats), caddies, lodging (403 rooms), credit cards (MC, V, AE, D, DC), BF, FF.
Reader Comments: Outstanding course! … Target golf at its best … Great shotmaking course, great test mentally … What a pleasant surprise, this was a great course.

★★★★ **THE RIDGE GOLF COURSE**
PU-2020 Golf Course Rd., Auburn, 95602, Placer County, (530)888-7888, 25 miles from Sacramento. **E-mail:** KBickel@RidgeGC.com. **Web:** www.RidgeGC.com. **Facility Holes:** 18. **Yards:** 6,734/5,855. **Par:** 71/71. **Course Rating:** 72.3/70.7. **Slope:** 137/128. **Green Fee:** $35/$55. **Cart Fee:** $14/Person. **Walking Policy:** Unrestricted walking. **Walkability:** 3. **Opened:** 1999. **Architect:** Robert Trent Jones Jr. **Season:** Year-round. **High:** March-Oct. **To obtain tee times:** Call up to 7 days in advance. **Miscellaneous:** Reduced fees (twilight), range (grass/mats), credit cards (MC, V, AE), BF, FF.
Reader Comments: This is a great course that challenges even the best of golfers with narrow fairways and some long holes … Fun course on rugged terrain … Nice course with good vistas… A must play. Some super holes … An excellent track melding a rugged environment with the beauty of a well maintained golf course.

RIDGEMARK GOLF & COUNTRY CLUB
R-3800 Airline Hwy., Hollister, 95023, San Benito County, (408)634-2222, (800)637-8151, 40 miles from San Jose. **E-mail:** golf@ridgemark.com. **Web:** www.ridgemark.com. **Facility Holes:** 36. **Green Fee:** $58/$70. **Cart Fee:** Included in green fee. **Walking Policy:** Walking at certain times. **Opened:** 1972. **Architect:** Richard Bigler. **Season:** Year-round. **To obtain tee times:** Call up to 30 days in advance. **Miscellaneous:** Reduced fees (twilight), metal spikes, range (grass/mats), lodging (32 rooms), credit cards (MC, V, AE, D, DC), BF, FF.
★★★½ **DIABLO COURSE** (18)
Yards: 6,603/5,475. **Par:** 72/72. **Course Rating:** 72.5/71.7. **Slope:** 128/118. **Walkability:** 4.
Reader Comments: Excellent value and good condition. It is a secret place where weekday tee times can be made the day before … Best course for value in Bay area! … Play with the coupon.
★★★ **GABILAN COURSE** (18)
Yards: 6,781/5,683. **Par:** 72/72. **Course Rating:** 72.9/71.6. **Slope:** 129/118. **Walkability:** 2.
Reader Comments: It will challenge you … Excellent value and good condition. Pace of play during the week is exceptional. Little known secret and is a must play … Nice views. Greens break towards ocean.

★★½ **RIO HONDO GOLF CLUB**
PU-10627 Old River School Rd., Downey, 90241, Los Angeles County, (562)927-2329, 15 miles from Los Angeles. **Facility Holes:** 18. **Yards:** 6,360/5,103. **Par:** 71/71. **Course Rating:** 70.5/69.4. **Slope:** 122/117. **Green Fee:** $30/$40. **Walking Policy:** Unrestricted walking. **Walkability:** 2. **Opened:** 1994. **Architect:** John Duncan Dunn/Jerry Pierkel. **Season:** Year-round. **High:** March-Oct. **To obtain tee times:** Call up to 7 days in advance. **Miscellaneous:** Reduced fees (twilight, seniors, juniors), range (mats), credit cards (MC, V), BF, FF.

RIO LA PAZ GOLF CLUB
SP-201 Lee Rd., Nicolaus, 95659, Sutter County, (530)656-2182, 25 miles from Sacramento. **Web:** www.riolapazgolf.com. **Facility Holes:** 18. **Yards:** 6,504/4,774. **Par:** 71/71. **Course Rating:** 71.3/67.5. **Slope:** 126/117. **Green Fee:** $18/$29. **Cart Fee:** $10/Person. **Walking Policy:** Unrestricted walking. **Walkability:** 2. **Opened:** 2000. **Season:** Year-round. **High:** April-Oct. **To obtain tee times:** Call up to 7 days in advance. **Miscellaneous:** Reduced fees (weekdays, twilight, seniors, juniors), range (grass), credit cards (MC, V), FF.

★★★★ **RIO VISTA GOLF CLUB** *Value, Pace*
PU-1000 Summerset Dr., Rio Vista, 94571, Solano County, (707)374-2900, 35 miles from Berkeley. **Web:** www.riovistagolf.com. **Facility Holes:** 18. **Yards:** 6,800/5,330. **Par:** 72/72. **Course Rating:** 73.9/72.4. **Slope:** 131/124. **Green Fee:** $34/$49. **Cart Fee:** $16/Person. **Walking Policy:** Unrestricted walking. **Walkability:** 2. **Opened:** 1998. **Architect:** Ted Robinson/Ted Robinson Jr. **Season:** Year-round. **To obtain tee times:** Call up to 7 days in advance. **Miscellaneous:** Reduced fees (twilight, seniors, juniors), range (grass/mats), credit cards (MC, V, AE), BF, FF.
Reader Comments: Good value, pretty, fair course … Course plays dry in wet season … Good new course but windy … Great holes! Water always in play! Don't miss it, it's a memorable course … Beautiful 9th and 18th holes … Maturing well.

★★★½ **RIVER COURSE AT THE ALISAL**
PU-150 Alisal Rd., Solvang, 93463, Santa Barbara County, (805)688-6042, 35 miles from Santa Barbara. **E-mail:** rivercourse@alisal.com. **Web:** www.rivercourse.com. **Facility Holes:** 18. **Yards:** 6,830/5,815. **Par:** 72/72. **Course Rating:** 73.1/73.4. **Slope:** 126/127. **Green Fee:** $45/$55. **Cart Fee:** $26/Cart. **Walking Policy:** Unrestricted walking. **Walkability:** 2. **Opened:** 1992. **Architect:** Halsey/Daray. **Season:** Year-round. **To obtain tee times:** Call up to 7 days in advance. **Miscellaneous:** Reduced fees (weekdays, guests, twilight, seniors, juniors), range (grass/mats), credit cards (MC, V, AE), BF, FF.
Reader Comments: Several tight holes but beautiful setting … Very challenging layout. Great variety of holes … One of my favorites to play … Nice facilities, nice people and nice course.

★★★ RIVER RIDGE GOLF CLUB

PU-2401 W. Vineyard Ave., Oxnard, 93030, Ventura County, (805)983-4653, 50 miles from Los Angeles. **Facility Holes:** 18. **Yards:** 6,718/5,351. **Par:** 72/72. **Course Rating:** 72.3/71.3. **Slope:** 121/124. **Green Fee:** $20/$35. **Cart Fee:** $24/Cart. **Walking Policy:** Unrestricted walking. **Walkability:** 4. **Opened:** 1986. **Architect:** William F. Bell. **Season:** Year-round. **To obtain tee times:** Call up to 7 days in advance. **Miscellaneous:** Reduced fees (weekdays, twilight, seniors, juniors), range (grass), lodging (251 rooms), credit cards (MC, V, D), BF, FF.
Reader Comments: Good municipal course … Nice layout and challenging … Nice course, good practice facility. Friendly staff. Course tends to play slow at times … Fun course, not too difficult … Great price.

★½ RIVER VIEW GOLF COURSE

PU-1800 West Santa Clara, Santa Ana, 92706, Orange County, (714)543-1115. **Web:** www.riverviewgolf.com. **Facility Holes:** 18. **Yards:** 6,100/5,800. **Par:** 70/70. **Course Rating:** 69.0/66.1. **Slope:** 106/103. **Green Fee:** $15/$26. **Cart Fee:** $22/Cart. **Walking Policy:** Walking at certain times. **Walkability:** 4. **Opened:** 1964. **Architect:** Novel James. **Season:** Year-round. **To obtain tee times:** Call up to 10 days in advance. **Miscellaneous:** Reduced fees (weekdays, guests, twilight, seniors, juniors), metal spikes, range (mats), credit cards (MC, V), BF, FF.

★★½ RIVERSIDE GOLF COURSE

PU-9770 Monterey Rd., Morgan Hill, 95037, Santa Clara County, (408)463-0622, 8 miles from San Jose. **Facility Holes:** 18. **Yards:** 6,579/5,639. **Par:** 71/72. **Course Rating:** 70.5/71.1. **Slope:** 122/115. **Green Fee:** $26/$36. **Cart Fee:** $24/Cart. **Walking Policy:** Unrestricted walking. **Walkability:** 1. **Opened:** 1957. **Architect:** Pike Ross. **Season:** Year-round. **High:** April-Oct. **To obtain tee times:** Call golf shop. **Miscellaneous:** Reduced fees (weekdays, twilight, seniors, juniors), metal spikes, range (grass), credit cards (MC, V).

★★★ RIVERSIDE GOLF COURSE

PU-7672 N. Josephine, Fresno, 93722, Fresno County, (559)275-5900. **E-mail:** rivere@pac-bell.net. **Web:** www.playriverside.com. **Facility Holes:** 18. **Yards:** 6,592/5,979. **Par:** 72/75. **Course Rating:** 71.0/73.8. **Slope:** 122/125. **Green Fee:** $15/$18. **Cart Fee:** $22/Cart. **Walking Policy:** Unrestricted walking. **Walkability:** 2. **Opened:** 1939. **Architect:** William P. Bell. **Season:** Year-round. **High:** April-Sept. **To obtain tee times:** Call up to 7 days in advance. **Miscellaneous:** Reduced fees (weekdays, twilight, seniors, juniors), metal spikes, range (grass), credit cards (MC, V), BF, FF.
Reader Comments: Good track with some very interesting holes, especially Nos. 10 and 11 … Golf course was in great shape, practice facility is the best in the area. New golf carts, lighted driving range, and exceptional service made for an enjoyable day. A great value for such a challenging course.

★★★½ RIVERWALK GOLF CLUB

PU-1150 Fashion Valley Rd., San Diego, 92108, San Diego County, (619)296-4653, 7 miles from San Diego. **Facility Holes:** 27. **Green Fee:** $35/$95. **Cart Fee:** Included in green fee. **Walking Policy:** Unrestricted walking. **Opened:** 1998. **Architect:** Ted Robinson/Ted Robinson Jr. **Season:** Year-round. **High:** Nov.-April. **To obtain tee times:** Call golf shop. **Miscellaneous:** Reduced fees (weekdays, twilight, juniors), range (grass/mats), lodging (40 rooms), credit cards (MC, V, AE).
MISSION/FRYERS (18 Combo)
Yards: 6,483/5,215. **Par:** 72/72. **Course Rating:** 70.5/69.5. **Slope:** 120/114. **Walkability:** 2.
PRESIDIO/FRYERS (18 Combo)
Yards: 6,627/5,532. **Par:** 72/72. **Course Rating:** 71.6/70.9. **Slope:** 123/115. **Walkability:** 2.
PRESIDIO/MISSIONS (18 Combo)
Yards: 6,550/5,427. **Par:** 72/72. **Course Rating:** 71.5/74.3. **Slope:** 120/115. **Walkability:** 4.
Reader Comments: Nice remodel of Stardust … I've only played here once. Nice layout, and greens were in good shape … Great course, good prices … Tough with afternoon wind … Pricey, good instruction … Played in the rain and still enjoyed the course.
Special Notes: Formerly Stardust Country Club.

ROBINSON RANCH GOLF CLUB

PU-27734 Sand Canyon Rd., Santa Clarita, 91351, Los Angeles County, (661)252-7666, 25 miles from Los Angeles. **E-mail:** rsmith@robinsonranchgolf.com. **Web:** www.robinson-ranchgolf.com. **Facility Holes:** 36. **Cart Fee:** Included in green fee. **Walking Policy:** Unrestricted walking. **Opened:** 2000. **Architect:** T Robinson/T Robinson, Jr. **Season:** Year-round. **To obtain tee times:** Call up to 8 days in advance. **Miscellaneous:** Range (grass/mats), credit cards (MC, V, AE), BF, FF.
★★★★ MOUNTAIN COURSE (18) *Pace*
Yards: 6,508/5,076. **Par:** 71/71. **Course Rating:** 72.1/69.5. **Slope:** 133/121. **Green Fee:** $85/$105. **Miscellaneous:** Reduced fees (weekdays, twilight).
Reader Comments: Very tough course. Don't miss the fairways. Excellent greens. Good layout …

CALIFORNIA

Plenty of variety, you'll use every club in the bag! Not overly long, the course is a bit tight, but in no way does it make you feel claustrophobic. The green are some of the best in the state. It's in a beautiful setting … What a great place.
VALLEY COURSE (18)
Yards: 6,903/5,408. **Par:** 72/72. **Course Rating:** 74.5/72.2. **Slope:** 140/126. **Green Fee:** $85/$125. **Walkability:** 3. **Miscellaneous:** Reduced fees (weekdays, twilight, juniors).

★★★ ROOSTER RUN GOLF CLUB
PU-2301 East Washington St., Petaluma, 94954, Sonoma County, (707)778-1211, 30 miles from San Francisco. **Facility Holes:** 18. **Yards:** 7,001/5,139. **Par:** 72/72. **Course Rating:** 73.9/69.1. **Slope:** 128/117. **Green Fee:** $32/$49. **Cart Fee:** $24/Cart. **Walking Policy:** Unrestricted walking. **Walkability:** 2. **Opened:** 1998. **Architect:** Fred Bliss. **Season:** Year-round. **To obtain tee times:** Call up to 7 days in advance. **Miscellaneous:** Reduced fees (twilight, seniors, juniors), range (grass), credit cards (MC, V), BF, FF.
Reader Comments: Nice staff, great winter condition, good $ … Great course … This is a new course that plays older, nice layout, you can hold the green … The teeth of the course is all in the greens … Best wet weather course north of San Francisco.

★★ ROSEVILLE DIAMOND OAKS MUNICIPAL GOLF COURSE
PU-349 Diamond Oaks Rd., Roseville, 95678, Placer County, (916)783-4947, 15 miles from Sacramento. **Web:** www.golfroseville.com. **Facility Holes:** 18. **Yards:** 6,283/5,608. **Par:** 72/73. **Course Rating:** 69.5/70.5. **Slope:** 115/112. **Green Fee:** $13/$23. **Cart Fee:** $12/Cart. **Walking Policy:** Unrestricted walking. **Walkability:** 2. **Opened:** 1963. **Architect:** Ted Robinson. **Season:** Year-round. **High:** April-Sept. **To obtain tee times:** Call up to 7 days in advance. **Miscellaneous:** Reduced fees (weekdays, twilight, seniors, juniors), metal spikes, range (mats), credit cards (MC, V, AE, D), BF, FF.

★★★★½ SADDLE CREEK GOLF CLUB
SP-1001 Saddle Creek Dr., Copperopolis, 95228, Calaveras County, (209)785-3700, (800)852-5787, 35 miles from Stockton. **E-mail:** proshop@caltel.com. **Web:** www.saddle-creek.com. **Facility Holes:** 18. **Yards:** 6,829/4,488. **Par:** 72/72. **Course Rating:** 73.0/65.4. **Slope:** 134/111. **Green Fee:** $35/$62. **Cart Fee:** $13/Person. **Walking Policy:** Unrestricted walking. **Walkability:** 3. **Opened:** 1996. **Architect:** Carter Morrish & Associates. **Season:** Year-round. **High:** May-Sept. **To obtain tee times:** Call golf shop. **Miscellaneous:** Reduced fees (weekdays, twilight, seniors, juniors), range (grass), credit cards (MC, V, AE).
Reader Comments: Beautiful area. A little high in the price, but it is worth every penny … That says it all. Great track … Every hole is a postcard. This is as close to Augusta as you can get … Best new course in some time … Sierra foothills, top flight golf.

★★½ SALINAS FAIRWAYS GOLF COURSE
PU-45 Skyway Blvd., Salinas, 93905, Monterey County, (831)758-7300. **Web:** www.golfsali-nas.com. **Facility Holes:** 18. **Yards:** 6,479/5,121. **Par:** 72/72. **Course Rating:** 69.8/67.9. **Slope:** 115/105. **Green Fee:** $20/$28. **Cart Fee:** $22/Cart. **Walking Policy:** Unrestricted walking. **Walkability:** 1. **Opened:** 1965. **Architect:** Robert Muir Graves/Steve Halsey. **Season:** Year-round. **High:** May-Aug. **To obtain tee times:** Call up to 7 days in advance. **Miscellaneous:** Reduced fees (weekdays, juniors), range (grass/mats), credit cards (MC, V, AE), BF, FF.

★★½ SAN BERNARDINO GOLF CLUB
PU-1494 S. Waterman, San Bernardino, 92408, San Bernardino County, (909)885-2414, 45 miles from Palm Springs. **Facility Holes:** 18. **Yards:** 5,779/5,218. **Par:** 70/73. **Course Rating:** 67.5/69.9. **Slope:** 111/114. **Green Fee:** $10/$28. **Cart Fee:** $9/Person. **Walking Policy:** Unrestricted walking. **Walkability:** 1. **Opened:** 1967. **Architect:** Dan Brown. **Season:** Year-round. **To obtain tee times:** Call up to 7 days in advance. **Miscellaneous:** Reduced fees (weekdays, twilight, seniors, juniors), metal spikes, range (grass/mats), credit cards (MC, V, AE, D), FF.

★★★½ SAN CLEMENTE MUNICIPAL GOLF CLUB
PU-150 E. Magdalena, San Clemente, 92672, Orange County, (949)361-8380, 60 miles from San Diego. **Facility Holes:** 18. **Yards:** 6,447/5,722. **Par:** 72/73. **Course Rating:** 70.6/73.0. **Slope:** 121/120. **Green Fee:** $27/$33. **Cart Fee:** $24/Cart. **Walking Policy:** Unrestricted walking. **Walkability:** 2. **Opened:** 1929. **Architect:** William P. Bell. **Season:** Year-round. **To obtain tee times:** Call golf shop. **Misc:** Reduced fees (weekdays, twilight), range (mats), BF, FF.
Reader Comments: Pleasant layout in city, well kept, good use of hillside and valley … Low key, low pressure course, with some good challenges … Best value in Orange County, very friendly people … Great last 4 holes … One of the best values in So Cal.

★★½ SAN DIMAS CANYON GOLF CLUB
PU-2100 Terrebonne Ave., San Dimas, 91773, Los Angeles County, (909)599-2313, 25 miles from Los Angeles. **Facility Holes:** 18. **Yards:** 6,309/5,539. **Par:** 72/74. **Course Rating:**

70.3/73.9. **Slope:** 118/123. **Green Fee:** $20/$39. **Cart Fee:** $12/Person. **Walking Policy:** Walking at certain times. **Walkability:** 3. **Opened:** 1962. **Architect:** Jeff Brauer. **Season:** Year-round. **High:** April-Sept. **To obtain tee times:** Call golf shop. **Miscellaneous:** Reduced fees (weekdays, twilight, seniors, juniors), metal spikes, range (mats), credit cards (MC, V, AE, D).

★★★ **SAN GERONIMO GOLF COURSE**
PU-5800 Sir Francis Drake Blvd., San Geronimo, 94963, Marin County, (415)488-4030, (888)526-4653, 20 miles from San Francisco. **Facility Holes:** 18. **Yards:** 6,801/5,140. **Par:** 72/72. **Course Rating:** 73.3/69.9. **Slope:** 130/125. **Green Fee:** $25/$60. **Cart Fee:** $12/Person. **Walking Policy:** Unrestricted walking. **Walkability:** 3. **Opened:** 1963. **Architect:** A. Vernon Macan. **Season:** Year-round. **High:** April-Nov. **To obtain tee times:** Call up to 10 days in advance. **Miscellaneous:** Reduced fees (weekdays, twilight, seniors, juniors), credit cards (MC, V, AE, D, DC), BF, FF.
Reader Comments: My course, can't get enough, very challenging ... A well maintained friendly golf course with scenic views, affordable rates and good seasonal discounts ... Challenging layout ... Completely satisfying golf, super layout.

★★½ **SAN JOSE MUNICIPAL GOLF COURSE**
PU-1560 Oakland Rd., San Jose, 95131, Santa Clara County, (408)441-4653. **Facility Holes:** 18. **Yards:** 6,602/5,594. **Par:** 72/72. **Course Rating:** 70.1/69.7. **Slope:** 108/112. **Green Fee:** $14/$38. **Walking Policy:** Unrestricted walking. **Walkability:** 1. **Opened:** 1968. **Architect:** Robert Muir Graves. **Season:** Year-round. **To obtain tee times:** Call golf shop. **Miscellaneous:** Reduced fees (weekdays, twilight, seniors, juniors), metal spikes, range (mats), credit cards (MC, V, AE, D).

★★½ **SAN JUAN HILLS COUNTRY CLUB**
PU-32120 San Juan Creek Rd., San Juan Capistrano, 92675, Orange County, (949)493-1167, 60 miles from Los Angeles. **E-mail:** sanjuanhills@aol.com. **Facility Holes:** 18. **Yards:** 6,295/5,402. **Par:** 71/71. **Course Rating:** 69.5/71.4. **Slope:** 116/122. **Green Fee:** $22/$35. **Cart Fee:** $10/Person. **Walking Policy:** Walking at certain times. **Walkability:** 3. **Opened:** 1966. **Architect:** Harry Rainville. **Season:** Year-round. **High:** April-Oct. **To obtain tee times:** Call up to 10 days in advance. **Miscellaneous:** Reduced fees (weekdays, twilight, seniors, juniors), metal spikes, range (mats), credit cards (MC, V), BF, FF.

★★★★½ **SAN JUAN OAKS GOLF CLUB**
PU-3825 Union Rd., Hollister, 95023, San Benito County, (831)636-6113, (800)453-8337, 45 miles from San Jose. **E-mail:** sfuller@sanjuanoaks.com. **Web:** www.sanjuanoaks.com. **Facility Holes:** 18. **Yards:** 7,133/4,770. **Par:** 72/72. **Course Rating:** 75.6/67.1. **Slope:** 145/116. **Green Fee:** $55/$80. **Cart Fee:** $15/Person. **Walking Policy:** Unrestricted walking. **Walkability:** 3. **Opened:** 1996. **Architect:** Fred Couples/Gene Bates. **Season:** Year-round. **To obtain tee times:** Call up to 30 days in advance. **Miscellaneous:** Reduced fees (weekdays, twilight, seniors, juniors), range (grass), credit cards (MC, V, AE), BF, FF.
Reader Comments: Five-star experience from top to bottom, great layout, great condition, great service ... The best Northern California public access course not on the Monterey Peninsula ... Excellent variety in beautiful setting ... Great course, a lot like Fred Couples, relaxed and classy!!! Super design, impeccable conditioning, great staff. A perfect 10.

★★★ **SAN LUIS REY DOWNS GOLF RESORT**
R-31474 Golf Club Dr., Bonsall, 92003, San Diego County, (760)758-9699, (800)783-6967, 40 miles from San Diego. **E-mail:** slrd@earthlink.net. **Web:** www.slrd.com. **Facility Holes:** 18. **Yards:** 6,750/5,493. **Par:** 72/72. **Course Rating:** 73.0/72.1. **Slope:** 136/124. **Green Fee:** $25/$62. **Cart Fee:** Included in green fee. **Walking Policy:** Walking at certain times. **Walkability:** 1. **Opened:** 1963. **Architect:** William F. Bell. **Season:** Year-round. **High:** Year-round. **To obtain tee times:** Call up to 7 days in advance. **Miscellaneous:** Reduced fees (twilight, juniors), range (grass), lodging (28 rooms), credit cards (MC, V, AE, D), BF, FF.
Reader Comments: Straightforward. Good golf ... Great shot values ... Golf passbook rates. Long water holes from tee! ... Narrow, good course ... Pretty course.

★★ **SAN RAMON ROYAL VISTA GOLF CLUB**
PU-9430 Fircrest Lane, San Ramon, 94583, Contra Costa County, (925)828-6100, 15 miles from Walnut Creek. **E-mail:** mreedsrrv@aol.com. **Facility Holes:** 18. **Yards:** 6,460/5,770. **Par:** 72/73. **Course Rating:** 71.1/72.7. **Slope:** 121/119. **Green Fee:** $22/$39. **Cart Fee:** $26/Cart. **Walking Policy:** Walking at certain times. **Walkability:** 2. **Opened:** 1961. **Architect:** Clark Glasson. **Season:** Year-round. **To obtain tee times:** Call up to 7 days in advance. **Miscellaneous:** Reduced fees (twilight, seniors, juniors), range (mats), credit cards (MC, V), BF, FF.

CALIFORNIA

★★★ SAN VICENTE INN & GOLF CLUB
R-24157 San Vicente Rd., Ramona, 92065, San Diego County, (760)789-3477, 25 miles from San Diego. **Web:** www.sanvicenteresort.com. **Facility Holes:** 18. **Yards:** 6,633/5,543. **Par:** 72/72. **Course Rating:** 71.5/72.8. **Slope:** 123/128. **Green Fee:** $49/$59. **Cart Fee:** Included in green fee. **Walking Policy:** Walking at certain times. **Walkability:** 2. **Opened:** 1972. **Architect:** Ted Robinson. **Season:** Year-round. **To obtain tee times:** Call up to 5 days in advance. **Miscellaneous:** Reduced fees (weekdays, guests, twilight), range (grass/mats), lodging (28 rooms), credit cards (MC, V, AE), BF, FF.
Reader Comments: My favorite, mature course, best conditions, challenge for amateurs ... Very playable, varied hole layout ... Good resort course, easy when dry ... Play twilight! Great old course! Great trees! ... Good greens and fairways, nice setting ... Good golf package. Course plays long.

★★★★ SANDPIPER GOLF COURSE
PU-7925 Hollister Ave., Santa Barbara, 93117, Santa Barbara County, (805)968-1541, 100 miles from Los Angeles. **Facility Holes:** 18. **Yards:** 7,068/5,725. **Par:** 72/73. **Course Rating:** 74.5/73.3. **Slope:** 134/125. **Green Fee:** $118. **Cart Fee:** $24/Cart. **Walking Policy:** Unrestricted walking. **Walkability:** 3. **Opened:** 1972. **Architect:** William F. Bell. **Season:** Year-round. **To obtain tee times:** Call golf shop. **Miscellaneous:** Reduced fees (weekdays, twilight, juniors), range (grass), caddies, credit cards (MC, V, AE), BF, FF.
Notes: Ranked 28th in 1997 Best in State; 70th in 1996 America's Top 75 Upscale Courses.
Reader Comments: Wonderful views and a good test ... Best on the West Coast ... The ocean views are great and the golf course is equally very good ... Extremely challenging course ... This course is simply beautiful. Great seaside course! Great walk ... Classic ... Great views, solid golf, costly.

★★½ SANTA ANITA GOLF COURSE
PU-405 S. Santa Anita Ave., Arcadia, 91006, Los Angeles County, (626)447-7156, 6 miles from Pasadena. **Facility Holes:** 18. **Yards:** 6,368/5,908. **Par:** 71/74. **Course Rating:** 70.4/73.1. **Slope:** 122/121. **Green Fee:** $20/$25. **Cart Fee:** $22/Cart. **Walking Policy:** Unrestricted walking. **Walkability:** 3. **Opened:** 1936. **Architect:** L.A. County. **Season:** Year-round. **To obtain tee times:** Call golf shop. **Miscellaneous:** Reduced fees (twilight, seniors, juniors), range (grass/mats), credit cards (MC, V), BF, FF.

★★★ SANTA BARBARA GOLF CLUB
PU-3500 McCaw Ave., Santa Barbara, 93105, Santa Barbara County, (805)687-7087, 90 miles from Los Angeles. **Facility Holes:** 18. **Yards:** 6,014/5,541. **Par:** 70/72. **Course Rating:** 67.6/71.9. **Slope:** 113/121. **Green Fee:** $18/$35. **Cart Fee:** $24/Cart. **Walking Policy:** Unrestricted walking. **Walkability:** 4. **Opened:** 1958. **Architect:** Lawrence Hughes. **Season:** Year-round. **To obtain tee times:** Call golf shop. **Miscellaneous:** Reduced fees (weekdays, twilight, seniors, juniors), range (mats), credit cards (MC, V), BF, FF.
Reader Comments: Great value for a muni ... A good collection of easy and tough holes ... Best muni in California! ... Well kept ... Best value in Santa Barbara. Well maintained ... Great twilight rates ... Short, but challenging.

★★½ SANTA CLARA GOLF & TENNIS CLUB
PU-5155 Stars and Stripes Dr., Santa Clara, 95054, Santa Clara County, (408)980-9515, 12 miles from San Jose. **Facility Holes:** 18. **Yards:** 6,822/5,639. **Par:** 72/72. **Course Rating:** 73.0/71.5. **Slope:** 126/115. **Green Fee:** $15/$34. **Cart Fee:** $22/Cart. **Walking Policy:** Unrestricted walking. **Walkability:** 2. **Opened:** 1987. **Architect:** Robert Muir Graves. **Season:** Year-round. **High:** April-Sept. **To obtain tee times:** Call golf shop. **Miscellaneous:** Reduced fees (weekdays, guests, twilight, seniors, juniors), metal spikes, range (mats), credit cards (MC, V, AE).

★★½ SANTA TERESA GOLF CLUB
PU-260 Bernal Rd., San Jose, 95119, Santa Clara County, (408)225-2650. **Facility Holes:** 27. **Yards:** 6,742/6,032. **Par:** 71/73. **Course Rating:** 71.1/73.5. **Slope:** 121/125. **Green Fee:** $30/$44. **Cart Fee:** $24/Cart. **Walking Policy:** Unrestricted walking. **Walkability:** 2. **Opened:** 1962. **Architect:** George Santana. **Season:** Year-round. **High:** April-Sept. **To obtain tee times:** Call golf shop. **Miscellaneous:** Reduced fees (weekdays, twilight, seniors, juniors), metal spikes, range (mats), credit cards (MC, V, D).
Special Notes: Also has a 9-hole course.

★★★★ THE SCGA MEMBERS' CLUB AT RANCHO CALIFORNIA
PU-38275 Murrieta Hot Springs Rd., Murrieta, 92563, Riverside County, (909)677-7446, (800)752-9724, 45 miles from San Diego. **Facility Holes:** 18. **Yards:** 7,059/5,355. **Par:** 72/72. **Course Rating:** 73.9/70.5. **Slope:** 132/116. **Green Fee:** $40/$70. **Cart Fee:** Included in green fee. **Walking Policy:** Unrestricted walking. **Walkability:** 3. **Opened:** 1972. **Architect:**

Robert Trent Jones. **Season:** Year-round. **To obtain tee times:** Call up to 7 days in advance. **Miscellaneous:** Reduced fees (weekdays, twilight, juniors), range (grass), credit cards (MC, V, AE), BF, FF.

Reader Comments: Great diverse layout … Well managed and maintained … Good greens, well placed bunkers … Figure-8 layout, challenging … Good and easy to get a tee time … A gem! My favorite course! … Good value for the money … Third hole a classic.

★★ SCHOLL CANYON GOLF COURSE

PU-3800 E Glen Oaks Blvd, Glendale, 91206, Los Angeles County, (818)243-4100, 8 miles from Los Angeles. **Facility Holes:** 18. **Yards:** 3,039/2,400. **Par:** 60/60. **Course Rating:** 56.8. **Slope:** 81. **Green Fee:** $12/$16. **Cart Fee:** $18/Cart. **Walking Policy:** Unrestricted walking. **Walkability:** 3. **Opened:** 1994. **Architect:** George Williams. **Season:** Year-round. **High:** June-Sept. **To obtain tee times:** Call golf shop. **Miscellaneous:** Reduced fees (weekdays, twilight, seniors, juniors), metal spikes, range (grass/mats), credit cards (MC, V, AE).

★★★ THE SEA RANCH GOLF LINKS

R-4200 Highway 1, The Sea Ranch, 95497, Sonoma County, (707)785-2468, (800)842-3270, 37 miles from Santa Rosa. **E-mail:** srgi@mcn.com. **Web:** www.searanchvillage.com. **Facility Holes:** 18. **Yards:** 6,598/5,105. **Par:** 72/72. **Course Rating:** 73.2/71.5. **Slope:** 136/123. **Green Fee:** $45/$65. **Cart Fee:** $13/Person. **Walking Policy:** Unrestricted walking. **Walkability:** 3. **Opened:** 1996. **Architect:** Robert Muir Graves. **Season:** Year-round. **High:** July-Nov. **To obtain tee times:** Call golf shop. **Miscellaneous:** Reduced fees (weekdays, twilight, juniors), metal spikes, range (grass), credit cards (MC, V, AE).

Reader Comments: Great seaside course! Hard to get to … Best kept secret in Northern California. Tough but rewarding. Beautiful ocean views … Links golf on the lost coast. Great fun.

★★★ SEASCAPE GOLF CLUB

SP-610 Clubhouse Dr., Aptos, 95003, Santa Cruz County, (831)688-3213, 20 miles from San Jose. **Facility Holes:** 18. **Yards:** 6,034/5,514. **Par:** 71/72. **Course Rating:** 70.2/72.6. **Slope:** 129/127. **Green Fee:** $45/$70. **Cart Fee:** $32/Cart. **Walking Policy:** Unrestricted walking. **Walkability:** 3. **Opened:** 1926. **Season:** Year-round. **High:** June-Aug. **To obtain tee times:** Call golf shop. **Miscellaneous:** Reduced fees (weekdays, guests, twilight, juniors), metal spikes, range (mats), credit cards (MC, V, AE, D, DC), BF, FF.

Reader Comments: Good playability, short but testing … Hills, huge mature trees. Favors accuracy over length … Beautiful Pacific Coast views. Good risk/reward tester … Beautiful place.

Special Notes: Formerly Aptos Seascape Golf Course.

★½ SELMA VALLEY GOLF COURSE

PU-12389 E. Rose Ave., Selma, 93662, Fresno County, (559)896-2424, 15 miles from Fresno. **Facility Holes:** 18. **Yards:** 5,332/5,038. **Par:** 69/70. **Course Rating:** 65.3/69.6. **Slope:** 112/118. **Green Fee:** $14/$18. **Cart Fee:** $22/Cart. **Walking Policy:** Unrestricted walking. **Walkability:** 2. **Opened:** 1963. **Architect:** Bob Baldock. **Season:** Year-round. **To obtain tee times:** Call up to 7 days in advance. **Miscellaneous:** Metal spikes, range (grass/mats).

SEPULVEDA GOLF COURSE

PU-16821 Burbank Blvd., Encino, 91436, Los Angeles County, (818)986-4560, 15 miles from Los Angeles. **Facility Holes:** 36. **Green Fee:** $20/$25. **Cart Fee:** $21/Cart. **Walking Policy:** Unrestricted walking. **Walkability:** 1. **Season:** Year-round. **High:** Year-round. **To obtain tee times:** Call up to 7 days in advance. **Miscellaneous:** Reduced fees (weekdays, twilight, seniors, juniors), metal spikes, range (mats), credit cards (MC, V, AE, D), BF, FF.

★★ BALBOA COURSE (18)

Yards: 6,359/5,912. **Par:** 70/72. **Course Rating:** 68.8/70.9. **Slope:** 107/115. **Opened:** 1954. **Architect:** W.F. Bell/W.H. Johnson.

★★★ ENCINO COURSE (18)

Yards: 6,863/6,133. **Par:** 72/75. **Course Rating:** 71.5/73.4. **Slope:** 116/118. **Opened:** 1957. **Architect:** W.F. Bell/W.P. Bell/W.H. Johnson.

Reader Comments: Pretty municipal course, heavily used but good condition. Challenging … Longer than Balboa. Flat, tree-lined, good greens. Hit it long and straight, you'll go low.

★★★ SEVEN HILLS GOLF CLUB

PU-1537 S. Lyon St., Hemet, 92545, Riverside County, (909)925-4815, 100 miles from Los Angeles. **Facility Holes:** 18. **Yards:** 6,557/5,771. **Par:** 72/72. **Course Rating:** 70.2/70.0. **Slope:** 116/109. **Green Fee:** $14/$25. **Cart Fee:** $10/Person. **Walking Policy:** Unrestricted walking. **Walkability:** 1. **Opened:** 1970. **Architect:** Harry Rainville/David Rainville. **Season:** Year-round. **High:** Nov.-March. **To obtain tee times:** Call golf shop. **Miscellaneous:** Reduced fees (weekdays, twilight, seniors, juniors), range (grass/mats), credit cards (MC, V, AE, D).

Reader Comments: Good walkers' course, flat with mature trees and tricky greens … Good mature course … Good challenge.

CALIFORNIA

★★★ SHANDIN HILLS GOLF CLUB
PU-3380 Little Mountain Dr., San Bernardino, 92407, San Bernardino County, (909)886-0669, 60 miles from Los Angeles. **Facility Holes:** 18. **Yards:** 6,517/5,592. **Par:** 72/72. **Course Rating:** 70.3/71.6. **Slope:** 120/122. **Green Fee:** $9/$28. **Cart Fee:** $10/Person. **Walking Policy:** Unrestricted walking. **Walkability:** 3. **Opened:** 1980. **Architect:** Cary Bickler. **Season:** Year-round. **To obtain tee times:** Call golf shop. **Miscellaneous:** Reduced fees (weekdays, twilight, seniors, juniors), metal spikes, range (grass/mats), credit cards (MC, V, AE, D).
Reader Comments: Very friendly, good shape, accommodating ... Best course I've played.

★★★ SHARP PARK GOLF COURSE
PU-Highway 1, Pacifica, 94044, San Mateo County, (650)359-3380, 15 miles from San Francisco. **Facility Holes:** 18. **Yards:** 6,273/6,095. **Par:** 72/74. **Course Rating:** 70.6/73.0. **Slope:** 119/120. **Green Fee:** $23/$27. **Cart Fee:** $22/Cart. **Walking Policy:** Unrestricted walking. **Walkability:** 2. **Opened:** 1929. **Architect:** Alister Mackenzie. **Season:** Year-round. **High:** April-Nov. **To obtain tee times:** Call up to 6 days in advance. **Miscellaneous:** Reduced fees (weekdays, twilight, juniors), metal spikes, BF, FF.
Reader Comments: Worth the every dollar paid ... An affordable public golf course with scenic views of Pacific Ocean and mountains. Gets muddy on rainy days. Courteous personnel ... Good deal ... Mackenzie design, good setting, bargain.

★★★ SHERWOOD FOREST GOLF CLUB
PU-79 N. Frankwood Ave., Sanger, 93657, Fresno County, (559)787-2611, 18 miles from Fresno. **Facility Holes:** 18. **Yards:** 6,345/5,597. **Par:** 71/72. **Course Rating:** 69.2/71.4. **Slope:** 118/118. **Green Fee:** $19/$23. **Cart Fee:** $22/Cart. **Walking Policy:** Unrestricted walking. **Walkability:** 1. **Opened:** 1968. **Architect:** Bob Baldock. **Season:** Year-round. **To obtain tee times:** Call up to 7 days in advance. **Miscellaneous:** Reduced fees (twilight, juniors), metal spikes, range (grass), credit cards (MC, V, D), BF, FF.
Reader Comments: This is a fun course to play. It is not so difficult that a beginner is discouraged, but not an easy course for the above average golfer ... Good layout, excellent service/food ... All the holes are named after Robin Hood characters ... New greenkeeper, greens are fast, firm, and smooth. Don't let the short yardage fool you.

★★ SHORECLIFFS GOLF CLUB
PU-501 Avenida Vaquero, San Clemente, 92762, Orange County, (949)492-1177. **Web:** www.Suntessa.com. **Facility Holes:** 18. **Yards:** 6,228/5,223. **Par:** 72/72. **Course Rating:** 71.3/71.1. **Slope:** 130/123. **Green Fee:** $30/$60. **Cart Fee:** Included in green fee. **Walkability:** 5. **Opened:** 1965. **Architect:** Joe Williams. **Season:** Year-round. **High:** May-Oct. **To obtain tee times:** Call golf shop. **Miscellaneous:** Reduced fees (weekdays, twilight, seniors), metal spikes, range (mats), credit cards (MC, V, AE, D).

★★½ SHORELINE GOLF LINKS AT MOUNTAIN VIEW
PU-2940 N. Shoreline Blvd., Mountain View, 94043-1347, Santa Clara County, (650)969-2041, 8 miles from San Jose. **Facility Holes:** 18. **Yards:** 6,578/5,399. **Par:** 72/72. **Course Rating:** 71.9/66.4. **Slope:** 124/111. **Green Fee:** $30/$42. **Cart Fee:** $22/Cart. **Walking Policy:** Unrestricted walking. **Walkability:** 2. **Opened:** 1982. **Architect:** Robert Trent Jones Jr. **Season:** Year-round. **High:** March-Oct. **To obtain tee times:** Call up to 7 days in advance. **Miscellaneous:** Reduced fees (weekdays, twilight, seniors, juniors), range (grass/mats), credit cards (MC, V, AE), BF, FF.

SIERRA LAKES GOLF CLUB
PU-16600 Clubhouse Dr., Fonatana, 92336, San Bernardino County, (909)350-2500, 15 miles from Ontario. **E-mail:** rdanruther@earthlink.net. **Web:** www.sierralakes.com. **Facility Holes:** 18. **Yards:** 6,805/5,324. **Par:** 72/72. **Course Rating:** 73.0/70.7. **Slope:** 125/118. **Green Fee:** $39/$70. **Cart Fee:** Included in green fee. **Walking Policy:** Unrestricted walking. **Walkability:** 2. **Opened:** 2000. **Architect:** Ted Robinson. **Season:** Year-round. **To obtain tee times:** Call up to 8 days in advance. **Miscellaneous:** Reduced fees (weekdays, twilight, seniors, juniors), range (grass), credit cards (MC, V, AE), BF, FF.

SIERRA STAR GOLF CLUB
PU-2001 Sierra Star Pkwy., Mammoth Lakes, 93546, Mono County, (760)924-2200, 160 miles from Reno. **E-mail:** dschacht@sierrastargolf.com. **Web:** www.mammoth-golf.com. **Facility Holes:** 18. **Yards:** 6,708/4,912. **Par:** 70/70. **Course Rating:** 71.0/68.7. **Slope:** 133/128. **Green Fee:** $85/$115. **Cart Fee:** Included in green fee. **Walking Policy:** Walking at certain times. **Opened:** 1999. **Architect:** Cal Olson. **Season:** June-Oct. **High:** June-Oct. **To obtain tee times:** Call golf shop. **Miscellaneous:** Reduced fees (weekdays, guests, twilight), credit cards (MC, V, AE), FF.

SILVERADO COUNTRY CLUB & RESORT
R-1600 Atlas Peak Rd., Napa, 94558, Napa County, (707)257-5460, (800)532-0500, 50 miles from San Francisco. **Facility Holes:** 36. **Green Fee:** $70/$150. **Cart Fee:** Included in green fee. **Walking Policy:** Mandatory carts. **Opened:** 1955. **Season:** Year-round. **To obtain tee times:** Call up to 2 days in advance. **Miscellaneous:** Reduced fees (guests, twilight), metal spikes, range (grass/mats), lodging (275 rooms), credit cards (MC, V, AE, D), BF, FF.
★★★½ **NORTH COURSE** (18)
Yards: 6,900/5,857. **Par:** 72/72. **Course Rating:** 73.1/73.1. **Slope:** 134/128. **Walkability:** 2.
Architect: Robert Trent Jones.
Reader Comments: Great resort course with plenty of challenge ... Expensive, but beautiful ... Excellent country club atmosphere, tough track ... Challenging greens ... Wonderful accommodations ... Beautiful valley layout.
★★★½ **SOUTH COURSE** (18)
Yards: 6,685/5,672. **Par:** 72/72. **Course Rating:** 72.1/72.7. **Slope:** 131/127. **Walkability:** 3.
Architect: Robert Trent Jones Jr.
Reader Comments: Treat you like a king ... Cannot say enough, good stuff ... Great resort course ... Oh yes, you must enjoy this course! ... Beautiful course, tough greens ... Beautiful course layout. Helpful staff ... Good layout, challenge with forgiveness.

★★★ **SIMI HILLS GOLF CLUB**
PU-5031 Alamo, Simi Valley, 93063, Ventura County, (805)522-0803, 10 miles from Thousand Oaks. **Facility Holes:** 18. **Yards:** 6,509/5,505. **Par:** 71/71. **Course Rating:** 70.6/65.9. **Slope:** 125/112. **Green Fee:** $25/$35. **Cart Fee:** $13/Person. **Walking Policy:** Unrestricted walking. **Walkability:** 2. **Opened:** 1981. **Architect:** Ted Robinson. **Season:** Year-round. **To obtain tee times:** Call up to 7 days in advance. **Miscellaneous:** Reduced fees (weekdays, twilight, seniors, juniors), range (grass/mats), credit cards (MC, V, AE, D, DC), BF, FF.
Reader Comments: Very good layout ... Best kept secret in Ventura County ... Challenging course with many undulations and uphill fairways. Lots of doglegs, good greens ... Interesting layout. Good value ... Very crowded but good public course.

SINGING HILLS RESORT AT SYCUAN
R-3007 Dehesa Rd., El Cajon, 92019, San Diego County, (619)442-3425, (800)457-5568, 17 miles from San Diego. **E-mail:** golfshop@singinghills.com. **Web:** www.singinghills.com. **Facility Holes:** 54. **Green Fee:** $37/$45. **Cart Fee:** $22/Cart. **Walking Policy:** Unrestricted walking. **Walkability:** 2. **Opened:** 1956. **Architect:** Ted Robinson/Dave Fleming. **Season:** Year-round. **To obtain tee times:** Call up to 7 days in advance. **Miscellaneous:** Reduced fees (weekdays, twilight, juniors), range (grass/mats), lodging (102 rooms), credit cards (MC, V, AE, D).BF, FF.
★★★★ **OAK GLEN COURSE** (18)
Yards: 6,597/5,549. **Par:** 72/72. **Course Rating:** 71.3/71.4. **Slope:** 122/124. **Reader Comments:** Great track just outside San Diego ... Lots of trees, very green ... Good facilities, excellent golf ... Great family service ... Nice money. Easy play.
★★★½ **WILLOW GLEN COURSE** (18)
Yards: 6,605/5,585. **Par:** 72/72. **Course Rating:** 72.0/72.8. **Slope:** 124/122.
Reader Comments: Excellent atmosphere ... Feel very comfortable at this course ... A beautiful course with challenging holes and it is beautifully laid out. The greens are challenging but true and the course will demand a variety of shots to play it well. Very enjoyable.
Special Notes: Also has an 18-hole executive Pine Glen Course.

★★½ **SKYLINKS GOLF COURSE**
PU-4800 E. Wardlow Rd., Long Beach, 90808, Los Angeles County, (562)429-0030, 15 miles from Los Angeles. **Facility Holes:** 18. **Yards:** 6,372/5,933. **Par:** 72/74. **Course Rating:** 70.3/74.0. **Slope:** 118/121. **Green Fee:** $17/$27. **Cart Fee:** $22/Cart. **Walking Policy:** Unrestricted walking. **Walkability:** 1. **Opened:** 1956. **Architect:** William F. Bell. **Season:** Year-round. **To obtain tee times:** Call golf shop. **Miscellaneous:** Reduced fees (twilight, seniors, juniors), metal spikes, range (grass/mats), credit cards (MC, V, AE, D), BF, FF.

★★ **SKYWEST GOLF COURSE**
PU-1401 Golf Course Rd., Hayward, 94541, Alameda County, (510)317-2300, 22 miles from San Francisco. **E-mail:** suhd@haywandrec.org. **Facility Holes:** 18. **Yards:** 6,930/6,171. **Par:** 72/73. **Course Rating:** 72.9/74.3. **Slope:** 121/123. **Green Fee:** $15/$31. **Cart Fee:** $12/Person. **Walking Policy:** Unrestricted walking. **Walkability:** 1. **Opened:** 1965. **Architect:** Bob Baldock. **Season:** Year-round. **To obtain tee times:** Call golf shop. **Miscellaneous:** Reduced fees (seniors, juniors), range (mats), credit cards (MC, V), BF, FF.

★★★ **SOBOBA SPRINGS ROYAL VISTA GOLF COURSE**
SP-1020 Soboba Rd., San Jacinto, 92583, Riverside County, (909)654-9354, 25 miles from Palm Springs. **E-mail:** ssrvgreg@lagercom.net. **Web:** www.sobobasprings.com. **Facility Holes:** 18. **Yards:** 6,846/5,777. **Par:** 73/74. **Course Rating:** 72.7/73.1. **Slope:** 130/126. **Green Fee:**

$29/$55. **Cart Fee:** Included in green fee. **Walking Policy:** Unrestricted walking. **Walkability:** 1. **Opened:** 1967. **Architect:** Desmond Muirhead. **Season:** Year-round. **To obtain tee times:** Call up to 7 days in advance. **Miscellaneous:** Reduced fees (weekdays, guests, twilight, juniors), range (grass), credit cards (MC, V), BF, FF.
Reader Comments: Old course. Great play … Forgiving fairways. Hot in summer… Great old design, all the shots required … Good challenge course, requires all skills of the game … Surprisingly good.

★★★½ SONOMA MISSION INN GOLF & COUNTRY CLUB
R-17700 Arnold Dr., Sonoma, 95476, Sonoma County, (707)996-0300, 45 miles from San Francisco. **Web:** www.SonomaMissionInn.com. **Facility Holes:** 18. **Yards:** 7,087/5,511. **Par:** 72/72. **Course Rating:** 74.1/71.8. **Slope:** 132/125. **Green Fee:** $40/$125. **Cart Fee:** $15/Person. **Walking Policy:** Unrestricted walking. **Walkability:** 2. **Opened:** 1926. **Architect:** Robert Muir Graves. **Season:** Year-round. **High:** March-Oct. **To obtain tee times:** Call up to 14 days in advance. **Miscellaneous:** Reduced fees (weekdays, twilight), range (grass/mats), caddies, lodging (250 rooms), credit cards (MC, V, AE), BF, FF.
Reader Comments: Has been a PGA and US Open qualifying course. A must-play to see how you stack up to the pros … Staff great, posh course … You gotta play this one … Old classic course, fun to play … Beautifully positioned at the foot of the mountains … Best course in wine country.

★★★½ SOULE PARK GOLF COURSE
PU-1033 E. Ojai Ave., Ojai, 93024, Ventura County, (805)646-5633, 16 miles from Ventura. **Facility Holes:** 18. **Yards:** 6,475/5,639. **Par:** 72/72. **Course Rating:** 70.5/71.8. **Slope:** 121/121. **Green Fee:** $23/$34. **Cart Fee:** $24/Cart. **Walking Policy:** Unrestricted walking. **Walkability:** 3. **Opened:** 1962. **Architect:** William F. Bell. **Season:** Year-round. **To obtain tee times:** Call up to 7 days in advance. **Miscellaneous:** Reduced fees (weekdays, twilight, seniors, juniors), range (grass), credit cards (MC, V, D), BF, FF.
Reader Comments: Very good municipal course … Nice public course … A gem for the value. Not fancy. Some holes are a real challenge … Beautiful setting, great value for golf dollar … Another favorite course … Well used but great.

★★★ SOUTHRIDGE GOLF CLUB
SP-9413 S. Butte Rd., Sutter, 95982, Sutter County, (530)755-0457, 8 miles from Yuba City. **Web:** www.southridge.com. **Facility Holes:** 18. **Yards:** 7,047/5,541. **Par:** 72/72. **Course Rating:** 72.7/71.3. **Slope:** 130/122. **Green Fee:** $19/$29. **Cart Fee:** $10/Person. **Walking Policy:** Walking at certain times. **Walkability:** 5. **Opened:** 1992. **Architect:** Cal Olson. **Season:** Year-round. **High:** March-Dec. **To obtain tee times:** Call golf shop. **Miscellaneous:** Reduced fees (weekdays, twilight, seniors, juniors), range (grass), credit cards (MC, V, AE), BF, FF.
Reader Comments: Challenging back 9, nice layout … Fun course … Most improved course in Sacramento Valley … Nice layout … Very challenging. Used all the clubs … Nice clubhouse.

★★½ SPRING VALLEY GOLF CLUB
PU-3441 E. Calaveras Blvd., Milpitas, 95035, Santa Clara County, (408)262-1722, 8 miles from San Jose. **Facility Holes:** 18. **Yards:** 6,100/5,613. **Par:** 70/73. **Course Rating:** 67.7/71.2. **Slope:** 110/120. **Green Fee:** $19/$42. **Cart Fee:** $24/Cart. **Walking Policy:** Unrestricted walking. **Walkability:** 2. **Opened:** 1956. **Architect:** Ray Anderson. **Season:** Year-round. **High:** May-Aug. **To obtain tee times:** Call golf shop. **Miscellaneous:** Metal spikes, range (mats), credit cards (MC, V), FF.

★★★★½ SPYGLASS HILL GOLF COURSE *Service, Condition*
R-Spyglass Hill Rd. & Stevenson Dr., Pebble Beach, 93953, Monterey County, (831)625-8563, (800)654-9300. **Facility Holes:** 18. **Yards:** 6,855/5,642. **Par:** 72/74. **Course Rating:** 75.3/73.7. **Slope:** 148/133. **Green Fee:** $195/$225. **Cart Fee:** $25/Person. **Walking Policy:** Unrestricted walking. **Walkability:** 5. **Opened:** 1966. **Architect:** Robert Trent Jones. **Season:** Year-round. **High:** Aug.-Nov. **To obtain tee times:** Call golf shop. **Miscellaneous:** Reduced fees (guests, twilight), metal spikes, range (grass/mats), caddies, credit cards (MC, V, AE, D, Diners Club, JCB).
Notes: Ranked 34th in 2001-2002 America's 100 Greatest; 7th in 2001 Best in State; 3rd in 1996 America's Top 75 Upscale Courses.
Reader Comments: Beautiful!! … A must to play … It doesn't get any better … Don't miss it … Best combo of ocean and forest … Good value if you play with a member, the best in Monterey … Early tee time equals a 4 hr 15 min round walking. Unbelievable mix of holes and terrain … Superb condition. Excellent service staff. A beautiful walk in the woods … One of the all time greatest.

★★★★ STEELE CANYON GOLF CLUB - SAN DIEGO
SP-3199 Stonefield Dr., San Diego, 91935, San Diego County, (619)441-6900, 20 miles from San Diego. **E-mail:** marketing@steelecanyon.com. **Web:** www.steelecanyon.com. **Facility Holes:** 27. **Green Fee:** $75/$95. **Cart Fee:** Included in green fee. **Walking Policy:** Mandatory

carts. **Walkability:** 3. **Opened:** 1991. **Architect:** Gary Player. **Season:** Year-round. **To obtain tee times:** Call up to 7 days in advance. **Miscellaneous:** Reduced fees (twilight, seniors, juniors), range (grass/mats), credit cards (MC, V, AE, D), BF, FF.
CANYON/MEADOW (18 Combo)
Yards: 6,672/4,813. **Par:** 71/71. **Course Rating:** 72.2/67.9. **Slope:** 134/118.
CANYON/RANCH (18 Combo)
Yards: 6,741/4,655. **Par:** 71/71. **Course Rating:** 72.7/66.6. **Slope:** 135/112.
RANCH/MEADOW (18 Combo)
Yards: 7,001/5,026. **Par:** 72/72. **Course Rating:** 74.0/69.5. **Slope:** 137/124.
Reader Comments: An outstanding day of golf. Challenging, but fair course. Several holes call for plenty of carry … Easy to get on in the middle of the week … Very nice day, just short of 5 stars. A must play if you're in the area … Fabulous, unbelievable 3 9s all different, great views and elevation changes, best 27 I ever played.

★★★ **STERLING HILLS GOLF CLUB**
PU-901 Sterling Hills Dr., Camarillo, 93010, Ventura County, (805)987-3446, 45 miles from Los Angeles. **E-mail:** mdziabo@env.com. **Web:** www.sterlinghills-golf.com. **Facility Holes:** 18.
Yards: 6,813/5,445. **Par:** 71/71. **Course Rating:** 72.7/72.0. **Slope:** 131/120. **Green Fee:** $39/$58. **Cart Fee:** $11/Person. **Walking Policy:** Walking at certain times. **Walkability:** 3.
Opened: 1999. **Architect:** D. Pascuzzo/R.M. Graves. **Season:** Year-round. **To obtain tee times:** Call up to 7 days in advance. **Miscellaneous:** Reduced fees (weekdays, twilight, seniors, juniors), range (grass/mats), credit cards (MC, V, AE), BF, FF.
Reader Comments: Excellent, challenging design but still immature turf conditions. This course has a good future … You will use every club in your bag … Good value for the money. Course is in good shape. Nice variety of holes … Challenging, fair, enjoyable … Overall, one of the best values near LA I have found.

★★★★ **STEVINSON RANCH GOLF CLUB**
PU-2700 N. Van Clief Rd., Stevinson, 95374, Merced County, (209)668-8200, (877)752-9276, 9 miles from Turlock. **E-mail:** info@stevinsonranch.com. **Web:** www.stevinsonranch.com.
Facility Holes: 18. **Yards:** 7,205/5,461. **Par:** 72/72. **Course Rating:** 74.3/71.9. **Slope:** 140/124.
Green Fee: $35/$85. **Cart Fee:** Included in green fee. **Walking Policy:** Unrestricted walking.
Walkability: 2. **Opened:** 1995. **Architect:** John Harbottle/George Kelley. **Season:** Year-round.
High: March-Oct. **To obtain tee times:** Call up to 30 days in advance. **Miscellaneous:** Reduced fees (weekdays, twilight, juniors), range (grass), caddies, lodging (20 rooms), credit cards (MC, V, AE), BF, FF.
Notes: Ranked 25th in 1997 Best in State; 8th in 1996 Best New Upscale Courses.
Reader Comments: A true test of golf from the two back tees. You better bring your A game, otherwise you might as well enjoy the scenery … A real jewel in the middle of the Great San Joaquin Valley … Scottish golf in Calif., excellent condition … Great stay and play package. A must do.

STONETREE GOLF CLUB
PU-9 Stone Tree Lane, Novato, 94945, Marin County, (415)209-6090. **E-mail:** sl@stonetree-golf.com. **Web:** www.stonetreegolf.com. **Facility Holes:** 18. **Yards:** 6,810/5,237. **Par:** 72/72.
Course Rating: 72.7/71.2. **Slope:** 137/127. **Green Fee:** $85/$115. **Cart Fee:** Included in green fee. **Walking Policy:** Unrestricted walking. **Walkability:** 4. **Opened:** 2000. **Architect:** S. Tatum/J. Summers/J. Miller/F. Bliss. **Season:** Year-round. **High:** April-Oct. **To obtain tee times:** Call up to 60 days in advance. **Miscellaneous:** Reduced fees (weekdays), credit cards (MC, V, AE, D), BF, FF.

★★★ **STRAWBERRY FARMS GOLF CLUB**
PU-11 Strawberry Farms Rd., Irvine, 92612, Orange County, (949)551-1811, 25 miles from Los Angeles. **Facility Holes:** 18. **Yards:** 6,700/4,832. **Par:** 71/72. **Course Rating:** 72.7/68.7.
Slope: 134/114. **Green Fee:** $85/$135. **Cart Fee:** Included in green fee. **Walking Policy:** Unrestricted walking. **Walkability:** 2. **Opened:** 1997. **Architect:** Jim Lipe. **Season:** Year-round.
To obtain tee times: Call up to 30 days in advance. **Miscellaneous:** Reduced fees (weekdays, twilight, seniors, juniors), range (grass/mats), credit cards (MC, V, AE), BF, FF.
Reader Comments: Very tough layout from the back tees … Tough layout, no room for errors, high $ … Nice track … Very well maintained for young course, interesting holes make for a fun outing … Good layout. Good greens. GPS carts.

★★★ **SUMMIT POINTE GOLF CLUB**
PU-1500 Country Club Dr., Milpitas, 95035, Santa Clara County, (408)262-8813, (800)422-4653, 5 miles from San Jose. **Web:** www.americangolf.com. **Facility Holes:** 18.
Yards: 6,331/5,496. **Par:** 72/72. **Course Rating:** 70.9/70.6. **Slope:** 125/121. **Green Fee:** $12/$80. **Cart Fee:** $16/Person. **Walking Policy:** Walking at certain times. **Walkability:** 5.
Opened: 1968. **Architect:** Marvin Orgill. **Season:** Year-round. **High:** April-Sept. **To obtain tee times:** Call up to 7 days in advance. **Miscellaneous:** Reduced fees (weekdays, twilight,

seniors, juniors), range (mats), credit cards (MC, V, AE, D, DC), FF.

Reader Comments: Challenging layout with each hole having its own characteristics. Practice your uneven-lie shots and get used to the fast greens before playing. Spectacular view of the Silicon Valley … Very good senior rates.

★★ SUNNYVALE GOLF COURSE
PU-605 Macara Lane, Sunnyvale, 94086, Santa Clara County, (408)738-3666, 5 miles from San Jose. **Facility Holes:** 18. **Yards:** 6,249/5,305. **Par:** 70/71. **Course Rating:** 69.7/70.2. **Slope:** 119/120. **Green Fee:** $18/$32. **Cart Fee:** $23/Cart. **Walking Policy:** Unrestricted walking. **Walkability:** 1. **Opened:** 1968. **Architect:** David W. Kent. **Season:** Year-round. **High:** March-Sept. **To obtain tee times:** Call golf shop. **Miscellaneous:** Reduced fees (weekdays, twilight, seniors, juniors), metal spikes, credit cards (MC, V).

SUNOL VALLEY GOLF COURSE
PU-6900 Mission Rd., Sunol, 94586, Alameda County, (925)862-0414, 5 miles from Fremont. **Web:** www.sunolvalley.com. **Facility Holes:** 36. **Green Fee:** $20/$55. **Cart Fee:** Included in green fee. **Walking Policy:** Walking at certain times. **Opened:** 1968. **Architect:** Clark Glasson. **Season:** Year-round. **To obtain tee times:** Call up to 7 days in advance. **Miscellaneous:** Reduced fees (twilight, juniors), range (grass/mats), credit cards (MC, V), BF, FF.
★★½ **CYPRESS COURSE** (18)
Yards: 6,195/5,458. **Par:** 72/72. **Course Rating:** 69.8/71.5. **Slope:** 120/120. **Walkability:** 2.
★★½ **PALM COURSE** (18)
Yards: 6,843/5,997. **Par:** 72/74. **Course Rating:** 72.4/74.8. **Slope:** 126/126. **Walkability:** 3.

★★ SWENSON PARK GOLF CLUB
PU-6803 Alexandria Place, Stockton, 95207, San Joaquin County, (209)937-7360, 6 miles from Stockton. **Facility Holes:** 27. **Yards:** 6,485/6,266. **Par:** 72/74. **Course Rating:** 70.0/73.8. **Slope:** 110/117. **Green Fee:** $9/$17. **Cart Fee:** $20/Cart. **Walking Policy:** Unrestricted walking. **Walkability:** 1. **Opened:** 1952. **Architect:** William P. Bell. **Season:** Year-round. **High:** May-Sept. **To obtain tee times:** Call up to 7 days in advance. **Miscellaneous:** Reduced fees (weekdays, twilight, seniors, juniors), metal spikes, range (grass), BF, FF.
Special Notes: Also has a 9-hole par-3 course.

★★ SYCAMORE CANYON GOLF CLUB
PU-500 Kenmar Lane, Arvin, 93203, Kern County, (661)854-3163, 25 miles from Bakersfield. **Facility Holes:** 18. **Yards:** 7,100/5,744. **Par:** 72/73. **Course Rating:** 72.8/71.6. **Slope:** 125/120. **Green Fee:** $10/$13. **Walking Policy:** Unrestricted walking. **Opened:** 1989. **Architect:** Bob Putman. **Season:** Year-round. **High:** Feb.-Oct. **To obtain tee times:** Call golf shop. **Miscellaneous:** Reduced fees (weekdays, twilight, seniors, juniors), metal spikes, range (grass), credit cards (MC, V).

★★½ TABLE MOUNTAIN GOLF COURSE
PU-2700 Oro Dam Blvd. W., Oroville, 95965, Butte County, (916)533-3922, 70 miles from Sacramento. **Facility Holes:** 18. **Yards:** 6,500/5,000. **Par:** 72/68. **Course Rating:** 69.8/66.5. **Slope:** 116/104. **Green Fee:** $17/$21. **Cart Fee:** $19/Cart. **Walking Policy:** Unrestricted walking. **Walkability:** 2. **Opened:** 1956. **Architect:** Louis Bertolone. **Season:** Year-round. **To obtain tee times:** Call up to 7 days in advance. **Miscellaneous:** Reduced fees (weekdays, twilight, seniors, juniors), metal spikes, range (grass/mats), credit cards (MC, V, AE), BF, FF.

★★★½ TAHOE DONNER GOLF CLUB
SP-11509 Northwoods Blvd., Truckee, 96161, Nevada County, (530)587-9440, 40 miles from Reno. **Facility Holes:** 18. **Yards:** 6,917/6,032. **Par:** 72/74. **Course Rating:** 72.4/73.1. **Slope:** 133/138. **Green Fee:** $32/$100. **Cart Fee:** $15/Person. **Walking Policy:** Unrestricted walking. **Walkability:** 3. **Opened:** 1975. **Architect:** Joseph B. Williams. **Season:** June-Oct. **High:** July-Sept. **To obtain tee times:** Call up to 10 days in advance. **Miscellaneous:** Reduced fees (twilight), metal spikes, range (grass/mats), credit cards (MC, V), BF, FF.
Reader Comments: Love those mountains and trees … Views of lake are everywhere. Beautiful course. Tough and over-priced … Nice design, tree-lined with views … Best course in Tahoe area (sorry Edgewood) … Gorgeous! … A course that you could play every day! … Mountain course, tough, good test.

TAHQUITZ CREEK GOLF RESORT
PU-1885 Golf Club Dr., Palm Springs, 92264, Riverside County, (760)328-1005, (800)743-2211, 40 miles from Riverside. **E-mail:** rmcdonald@palmergolf.com. **Web:** www.palmergolf.com. **Facility Holes:** 36. **Cart Fee:** Included in green fee. **Season:** Year-round. **To obtain tee times:** Call up to 5 days in advance. **Miscellaneous:** Reduced fees (weekdays, guests, twilight, juniors), metal spikes, range (grass), credit cards (MC, V, AE), BF, FF.
★★★½ **LEGEND COURSE** (18)
Yards: 6,775/5,861. **Par:** 71/74. **Course Rating:** 71.0/72.2. **Slope:** 118/116. **Green Fee:**

$20/$70. **Walking Policy:** Walking at certain times. **Walkability:** 2. **Opened:** 1960. **Architect:** William F. Bell.

Reader Comments: This public course has been upgraded and looks great, some holes still need more care, but overall it is good … Good value, nice course … Golf passbook and summer rate … Nothing better than a Palmer-managed course.

★★★★ **RESORT COURSE** (18)
Yards: 6,705/5,206. **Par:** 72/72. **Course Rating:** 71.8/70.0. **Slope:** 125/119. **Green Fee:** $25/$95. **Walking Policy:** Mandatory carts. **Walkability:** 3. **Opened:** 1995. **Architect:** Ted Robinson.

Reader Comments: Great par 3s … Fun course, could play every day … Well laid-out, fairly easy though … Great course, great rates … They are very well organized … Very challenging, scenic holes … Tough course … Great summer rates, fun course … Great value, interesting.

TALEGA GOLF CLUB

PU-990 Avenida Talega, San Clemente, 92673, Orange County, (949)369-6226, 45 miles from San Diego. **Web:** talegagolfclub.com. **Facility Holes:** 18. **Yards:** 6,951/5,245. **Par:** 72/72. **Course Rating:** 73.6/71.1. **Slope:** 137/121. **Green Fee:** $70/$115. **Cart Fee:** Included in green fee. **Walking Policy:** Mandatory carts. **Walkability:** 3. **Opened:** 2001. **Architect:** Lee Schmidt/Brian Curley/Fred Couples. **Season:** Year-round. **To obtain tee times:** Call up to 10 days in advance. **Miscellaneous:** Reduced fees (weekdays, twilight, seniors, juniors), credit cards (MC, V, AE, D), BF, FF.

★★★★ **TEMECULA CREEK INN**
R-44501 Rainbow Canyon Rd., Temecula, 92592, Riverside County, (909)676-2405, (800)962-7335, 50 miles from San Diego. **E-mail:** gbotti@jcresorts.com. **Web:** www.temeculacreekinn.com. **Facility Holes:** 27. **Green Fee:** $50/$80. **Cart Fee:** Included in green fee. **Walking Policy:** Walking at certain times. **Opened:** 1970. **Architect:** Dick Rossen/Ted Robinson. **Season:** Year-round. **To obtain tee times:** Call up to 7 days in advance. **Miscellaneous:** Reduced fees (weekdays, guests, twilight, juniors), range (grass/mats), lodging (80 rooms), credit cards (MC, V, AE, D), BF, FF.
CREEK/OAKS (18 Combo)
Yards: 6,784/5,737. **Par:** 72/72. **Course Rating:** 72.6/72.8. **Slope:** 126/123. **Walkability:** 2.
CREEK/STONEHOUSE (18 Combo)
Yards: 6,605/5,686. **Par:** 72/72. **Course Rating:** 71.4/71.9. **Slope:** 129/120. **Walkability:** 3.
OAKS/STONEHOUSE (18 Combo)
Yards: 6,693/5,683. **Par:** 72/72. **Course Rating:** 72.2/72.4. **Slope:** 128/125. **Walkability:** 5.
Reader Comments: All three 9s are great layouts … Good overnite value package … Excellent value … Mature. Immaculate care, excellent accommodations … Best greens in So Cal. Play the Stonehouse 9 for an experience … Outstanding course, all three 9s are fun and challenging. Stay at the Inn for a couple of days and get treated like royalty.

★★★½ **TEMEKU HILLS GOLF & COUNTRY CLUB**
PU-41687 Temeku Dr., Temecula, 92591, Riverside County, (909)694-9998, (800)839-9949, 65 miles from San Diego. **Web:** www.temecula.com. **Facility Holes:** 18. **Yards:** 6,636/5,013. **Par:** 72/72. **Course Rating:** 72.4/70.5. **Slope:** 131/123. **Green Fee:** $28/$58. **Cart Fee:** Included in green fee. **Walking Policy:** Mandatory carts. **Walkability:** 4. **Opened:** 1995. **Architect:** Ted Robinson/Pete Dye. **Season:** Year-round. **To obtain tee times:** Call up to 7 days in advance. **Miscellaneous:** Reduced fees (twilight, seniors, juniors), range (grass/mats), credit cards (MC, V, AE, D), BF, FF.
Reader Comments: Lots of fun, just tough enough … Really nice place … Doing a lot of improvements lately … Nice layout, fun to play … Excellent greens and fairways, nice clubhouse, challenging course, affordable.

★★ **TIERRA DEL SOL GOLF CLUB**
PU-10300 N. Loop Dr., California City, 93505, Kern County, (619)373-2384, (888)465-3837, 45 miles from Bakersfield. **Facility Holes:** 18. **Yards:** 6,908/5,225. **Par:** 72/72. **Course Rating:** 74.1/68.6. **Slope:** 130/122. **Green Fee:** $14/$18. **Cart Fee:** $20/Cart. **Walking Policy:** Unrestricted walking. **Walkability:** 1. **Opened:** 1977. **Architect:** Robert von Hagge/Bruce Devlin. **Season:** Year-round. **To obtain tee times:** Call golf shop. **Miscellaneous:** Metal spikes, range (grass), credit cards (MC, V), FF.

★★½ **TIERRA REJADA GOLF CLUB**
PU-15187 Tierra Rejada Rd., Moorpark, 93021, Ventura County, (805)531-9300. **Facility Holes:** 18. **Yards:** 7,015/5,148. **Par:** 72/72. **Course Rating:** 73.3/69.4. **Slope:** 132/123. **Green Fee:** $40/$75. **Cart Fee:** Included in green fee. **Walking Policy:** Unrestricted walking. **Walkability:** 4. **Opened:** 1999. **Architect:** Brad Bell/Steve Timm. **Season:** Year-round. **High:** Year-round. **To obtain tee times:** Call up to 7 days in advance. **Miscellaneous:** Range (grass), credit cards (MC, V, AE).

CALIFORNIA

★★★½ TIJERAS CREEK GOLF CLUB
PU-29082 Tijeras Creek Rd., Rancho Santa Margarita, 92688, Orange County, (949)589-9793, 50 miles from Los Angeles. **Web:** www.tijerascreek.com. **Facility Holes:** 18. **Yards:** 6,613/5,130. **Par:** 72/72. **Course Rating:** 71.7/69.8. **Slope:** 126/120. **Green Fee:** $80/$115. **Cart Fee:** Included in green fee. **Walking Policy:** Unrestricted walking. **Walkability:** 5. **Opened:** 1990. **Architect:** Ted Robinson. **Season:** Year-round. **To obtain tee times:** Call up to 14 days in advance. **Miscellaneous:** Reduced fees (twilight, seniors, juniors), range (grass/mats), credit cards (MC, V, AE, DC), BF, FF.
Reader Comments: Front longer and flatter, back shorter, hillier and more fun … Challenging course, well worth the money … The 2 nines are totally different … Great place to take customers … Great course, one of best in So Cal.

★★★ TILDEN PARK GOLF COURSE
PU-Grizzly Peak and Shasta Rd., Berkeley, 94708, Alameda County, (510)848-7373, 10 miles from San Francisco. **Facility Holes:** 18. **Yards:** 6,300/5,400. **Par:** 70/71. **Course Rating:** 69.9/69.2. **Slope:** 120/116. **Green Fee:** $18/$35. **Cart Fee:** $12/Person. **Walking Policy:** Unrestricted walking. **Walkability:** 4. **Opened:** 1936. **Architect:** William P. Bell. **Season:** Year-round. **High:** April-Oct. **To obtain tee times:** Call golf shop. **Miscellaneous:** Reduced fees (weekdays, twilight, seniors, juniors), metal spikes, range (mats), credit cards (MC, V, AE).
Reader Comments: A good place to play for the price … Good course … Very picturesque setting … Good condition, nice blend of space and hills … Good local course. A bit busy … Played it 4 times over Thanksgiving, had a ball.

TORREY PINES GOLF COURSE
PU-11480 N. Torrey Pines Rd., La Jolla, 92037, San Diego County, (858)452-3226, (800)985-4653, 3 miles from La Jolla. **Facility Holes:** 36. **Green Fee:** $95/$150. **Cart Fee:** $30/Cart. **Walking Policy:** Unrestricted walking. **Walkability:** 2. **Opened:** 1957. **Architect:** William F. Bell. **Season:** Year-round. **To obtain tee times:** Call golf shop. **Miscellaneous:** Reduced fees (twilight), range (grass/mats), credit cards (MC, V, AE), BF, FF.
★★★★ **NORTH COURSE** (18)
Yards: 6,874/6,122. **Par:** 72/74. **Course Rating:** 72.1/75.4. **Slope:** 129/134.
Reader Comments: Don't look at the views you will hold up the course, putts really do break toward the ocean … Little buddy to South, just as good, fun golf … Very beautiful course. Well worth it … Good experience, value … Thank you Buick! Course upgrades are good … Good ocean view.
★★★★ **SOUTH COURSE** (18)
Yards: 7,055/6,457. **Par:** 72/76. **Course Rating:** 74.6/77.3. **Slope:** 136/139.
Notes: Ranked 28th in 2001 Best in State; 58th in 1996 America's Top 75 Upscale Courses.
Reader Comments: Exciting course to play for the first time. Will come back again and again when in Southern California … Still no better deal in the county when you are a resident … Vacationing there recently, I did a 'walk-on' and got right on the course and my wife went along to ride in the cart. No problem … Still the best golf overall in San Diego. A must play.

★★★★ TURKEY CREEK GOLF CLUB
PU-1525 Hwy. 193, Lincoln, 95648, Placer County, (916)434-9100, (888)236-8715. **Web:** www.turkeycreekgc.com. **Facility Holes:** 18. **Yards:** 7,021/4,887. **Par:** 72/72. **Course Rating:** 73.4/67.3. **Slope:** 136/121. **Green Fee:** $45/$65. **Opened:** 1999. **Architect:** Brad Bell. **Season:** Year-round. **To obtain tee times:** Call golf shop.
Reader Comments: Excellent customer service … Challenge, yet great course … Very women friendly … Great course with exciting holes … Beautiful course, outstanding layout … Excellent layout and scenery. No houses yet … Very good course.

★★★½ TUSTIN RANCH GOLF CLUB
PU-12442 Tustin Ranch Rd., Tustin, 92780, Orange County, (714)730-1611, 10 miles from Anaheim. **E-mail:** tustinranch@crowngolf.com. **Web:** www.tustinranchgolf.com. **Facility Holes:** 18. **Yards:** 6,803/5,263. **Par:** 72/72. **Course Rating:** 72.4/70.3. **Slope:** 129/118. **Green Fee:** $85/$125. **Cart Fee:** Included in green fee. **Walking Policy:** Walking with Caddie. **Walkability:** 2. **Opened:** 1989. **Architect:** Ted Robinson. **Season:** Year-round. **High:** April-Oct. **To obtain tee times:** Call up to 7 days in advance. **Miscellaneous:** Reduced fees (twilight, seniors, juniors), range (grass/mats), caddies, credit cards (MC, V, AE, DC), BF, FF.
Reader Comments: Not very difficult, but a must play … Definitely a hidden jewel … The perfect place to take a client … Excellent signature par 3 on No. 11.

★★★★ TWELVE BRIDGES GOLF CLUB *Condition*
PU-3070 Twelve Bridges Dr., Lincoln, 95648, Placer County, (916)645-7200, (888)893-5832, 25 miles from Sacramento. **Web:** www.twelvebridges.com. **Facility Holes:** 18. **Yards:** 7,150/5,310. **Par:** 72/72. **Course Rating:** 74.6/71.0. **Slope:** 139/123. **Green Fee:** $30/$60. **Cart Fee:** $15/Person. **Walking Policy:** Unrestricted walking. **Walkability:** 4. **Opened:** 1996. **Architect:** Dick Phelps. **Season:** Year-round. **To obtain tee times:** Call up to 30 days in advance. **Misc:** Reduced fees (twilight, juniors), range, credit cards (MC, V, AE), BF, FF.

CALIFORNIA

Notes: Ranked 10th in 1996 Best New Upscale Courses.
Reader Comments: This is one of my favorites. The course is always in excellent condition, and it is out away from the city, and is a very peaceful and enjoyable round of golf … The best public-access course I have ever played … Best in Sacramento, LPGA stop … My favorite course, very secluded … Challenging course in excellent condition.

★★★★ **TWIN OAKS GOLF COURSE**
PU-1425 N. Twin Oaks Valley Rd., San Marcos, 92069, San Diego County, (760)591-4653, 3 miles from Escondido. **E-mail:** aschutak@jcresorts.com. **Web:** www.twinoaksgolf.com. **Facility Holes:** 18. **Yards:** 6,535/5,423. **Par:** 72/72. **Course Rating:** 71.2/71.6. **Slope:** 124/120. **Green Fee:** $29/$67. **Cart Fee:** Included in green fee. **Walking Policy:** Mandatory carts. **Walkability:** 3. **Opened:** 1993. **Architect:** Ted Robinson. **Season:** Year-round. **High:** Dec.-March. **To obtain tee times:** Call up to 7 days in advance. **Misc:** Reduced fees (weekdays, twilight, seniors, juniors), range (grass/mats), credit cards (MC, V, AE, D, DC), BF, FF.
Reader Comments: A well-kept course and great value … Fine condition, challenging greens, friendly service, good variety in holes … Helpful service, beautiful course.

★★½ **UPLAND HILLS COUNTRY CLUB**
SP-1231 E. 16th St., Upland, 91786, San Bernardino County, (909)946-4711, 20 miles from Los Angeles. **Facility Holes:** 18. **Yards:** 5,827/4,813. **Par:** 70/70. **Course Rating:** 67.1/66.5. **Slope:** 111/106. **Green Fee:** $17/$31. **Cart Fee:** $11/Person. **Walking Policy:** Walking at certain times. **Opened:** 1983. **Architect:** H. Rainville. **Season:** Year-round. **To obtain tee times:** Call golf shop. **Miscellaneous:** Metal spikes, credit cards (MC, V, AE, D).

★ **VALLE GRANDE GOLF COURSE**
PU-1119 Watts Dr., Bakersfield, 93307, Kern County, (661)832-2259. **Facility Holes:** 18. **Yards:** 6,331/5,318. **Par:** 72/72. **Course Rating:** 68.7/68.4. **Slope:** 112/109. **Green Fee:** $13/$16. **Cart Fee:** $22/Cart. **Walking Policy:** Unrestricted walking. **Walkability:** 1. **Opened:** 1952. **Architect:** William P. Bell. **Season:** Year-round. **To obtain tee times:** Call up to 7 days in advance. **Miscellaneous:** Reduced fees (twilight, seniors, juniors), range (grass/mats), credit cards (MC, V), BF, FF.

VAN BUREN GOLF CENTER
PU-6720 Van Buren Blvd., Riverside, 92503, Riverside County, (909)688-2563. **E-mail:** vbsales@earthlink.net. **Web:** www.vanburengolf.com. **Facility Holes:** 18. **Yards:** 2,700/2,109. **Par:** 57/57. **Green Fee:** $12/$15. **Cart Fee:** $8/Person. **Walking Policy:** Unrestricted walking. **Walkability:** 3. **Opened:** 1997. **Architect:** Murray Nonhoff. **Season:** Year-round. **To obtain tee times:** Call up to 14 days in advance. **Miscellaneous:** Reduced fees (weekdays, twilight, seniors, juniors), metal spikes, range (grass/mats), credit cards (MC, V, AE, D), BF, FF.

★★ **VAN BUSKIRK PARK GOLF COURSE**
PU-1740 Houston Ave., Stockton, 95206, San Joaquin County, (209)937-7357, 3 miles from Stockton. **Facility Holes:** 18. **Yards:** 6,928/5,927. **Par:** 72/74. **Course Rating:** 72.2/72.2. **Slope:** 118/113. **Green Fee:** $18/$23. **Cart Fee:** $20/Cart. **Walking Policy:** Unrestricted walking. **Walkability:** 1. **Opened:** 1961. **Architect:** Larry Norstrom. **Season:** Year-round. **High:** April-Sept. **To obtain tee times:** Call up to 7 days in advance. **Miscellaneous:** Reduced fees (twilight, seniors, juniors), metal spikes, range (grass/mats), BF, FF.

★★★★ **THE VINEYARD AT ESCONDIDO**
PU-925 San Pasqual Rd., Escondido, 92025, San Diego County, (760)735-9545, 15 miles from San Diego. **Facility Holes:** 18. **Yards:** 6,531/5,073. **Par:** 70/70. **Course Rating:** 70.3/70.3. **Slope:** 125/117. **Green Fee:** $30/$61. **Cart Fee:** Included in green fee. **Walking Policy:** Walking at certain times. **Walkability:** 3. **Opened:** 1993. **Architect:** David Rainville. **Season:** Year-round. **To obtain tee times:** Call up to 7 days in advance. **Miscellaneous:** Reduced fees (weekdays, twilight, seniors, juniors), range (grass/mats), credit cards (MC, V, AE, D, DC), BF, FF.
Reader Comments: Good golf, a little of everything. Fun play … Interesting holes, some room for errors. Great service … Golf and wine a perfect match … Target golf. Good condition. Love the back 9 … Exclusive course. Beautiful greens.

★★★ **WASCO VALLEY ROSE GOLF COURSE**
PU-301 N. Leonard Ave., Wasco, 93280, Kern County, (661)758-8301, 19 miles from Bakersfield. **E-mail:** wvr@aol.com. **Facility Holes:** 18. **Yards:** 6,862/5,356. **Par:** 72/72. **Course Rating:** 73.1/70.5. **Slope:** 117/120. **Green Fee:** $8/$14. **Cart Fee:** $18/Cart. **Walking Policy:** Unrestricted walking. **Walkability:** 1. **Opened:** 1991. **Architect:** Bob Putman. **Season:** Year-round. **High:** March-Sept. **To obtain tee times:** Call up to 7 days in advance. **Miscellaneous:** Reduced fees (weekdays, twilight, seniors, juniors), range (grass), credit cards (MC, V, AE), BF, FF.
Reader Comments: Exceptional value … Great greens … Good challenging course … Big and open, mostly easy, variety nice … Great value, best muni course.

★★★½ **WELK RESORT CENTER**
R-8860 Lawrence Welk Dr., Escondido, 92026, San Diego County, (760)749-3225, (800)932-9355, 35 miles from San Diego. **E-mail:** t.roberts@welkgroup.com. **Web:** www.welkresort.com. **Facility Holes:** 36. **Yards:** 4,041/3,099. **Par:** 62/62. **Course Rating:** 59.1/57.7. **Slope:** 99/90. **Green Fee:** $11/$42. **Cart Fee:** Included in green fee. **Walking Policy:** Walking at certain times. **Walkability:** 4. **Opened:** 1964. **Architect:** David Rainville. **Season:** Year-round. **High:** Jan.-May. **To obtain tee times:** Call up to 7 days in advance. **Misc:** Reduced fees (guests, twilight, juniors), lodging (186 rooms), credit cards (MC, V, AE, D), BF, FF.
Reader Comments: If you like executive-style courses this is a good one … Fun to play … Executive course that you'll play all day and every day … Best executive course I've seen. Bring every club! … First class … A small gem in the foothills, panoramic, a good couples course.
Special Notes: Also has an 18-hole par-3 Oaks Course.

THE WESTIN MISSION HILLS RESORT
R-70-705 Ramon Rd., Rancho Mirage, 92270, Riverside County, (760)770-2908, (800)358-2211, 5 miles from Palm Springs. **Web:** www.troongolf.com. **Facility Holes:** 36. **Cart Fee:** Included in green fee. **Walking Policy:** Mandatory carts. **Season:** Year-round. **High:** Jan.-April. **Misc:** Range (grass), lodging (500 rooms), credit cards (MC, V, AE, D, DC), BF, FF.
★★★★½ **MISSION HILLS NORTH (18)**
Yards: 7,062/4,907. **Par:** 72/72. **Course Rating:** 73.4/68.0. **Slope:** 131/118. **Green Fee:** $55/$145. **Walkability:** 2. **Opened:** 1991. **Architect:** Gary Player. **To obtain tee times:** Call up to 30 days in advance. **Miscellaneous:** Reduced fees (weekdays, guests, twilight).
Notes: Golf Digest School site.
Reader Comments: Very nice desert course. Play it off season for a real bargain … First-class experience at great rates. Loved the layout … One of the few courses in Palm Springs that didn't have houses built all around it, which made the experience more pleasurable … Great summer stay & play rates.
★★★★½ **PETE DYE GOLF COURSE (18)**
Yards: 6,706/4,841. **Par:** 70/70. **Course Rating:** 73.5/67.4. **Slope:** 137/107. **Green Fee:** $55/$175. **Walkability:** 3. **Opened:** 1987. **Architect:** Pete Dye. **To obtain tee times:** Call golf shop. **Miscellaneous:** Reduced fees (guests, twilight).
Notes: Golf Digest School site.
Reader Comments: Fantastic desert course. Challenging … A very good experience … Beautiful courses … Course is extremely well maintained. Fast greens with complex undulations. Fairways are somewhat generous off the tee and views of the mountains are incredible … Player friendly.

★★½ **WESTRIDGE GOLF CLUB**
PU-1400 La Habra Hills Dr., La Habra, 90631, Orange County, (562)690-4200, 20 miles from Los Angeles. **Facility Holes:** 18. **Yards:** 6,342/5,081. **Par:** 72/72. **Course Rating:** 71.1/75.3. **Slope:** 134/139. **Green Fee:** $40/$80. **Cart Fee:** Included in green fee. **Walkability:** 5. **Opened:** 1999. **Architect:** D. Pascuzzo/R.M. Graves. **Season:** Year-round. **High:** April-July. **To obtain tee times:** Call up to 30 days in advance. **Miscellaneous:** Reduced fees (weekdays, twilight, seniors, juniors), range (mats), credit cards (MC, V, AE), BF, FF.

★½ **WHISPERING LAKES GOLF COURSE**
PU-2525 Riverside Dr., Ontario, 91761, San Bernardino County, (909)923-3673, 15 miles from San Bernardino. **Facility Holes:** 18. **Yards:** 6,700/6,000. **Par:** 72/74. **Course Rating:** 71.4/72.8. **Slope:** 122/117. **Green Fee:** $19/$23. **Cart Fee:** $22/Cart. **Walking Policy:** Unrestricted walking. **Walkability:** 2. **Opened:** 1960. **Season:** Year-round. **To obtain tee times:** Call golf shop. **Miscellaneous:** Reduced fees (twilight, seniors, juniors), metal spikes, range (grass), credit cards (MC, V).

★★★½ **WHITNEY OAKS GOLF CLUB**
PU-2305 Clubhouse Dr., Rocklin, 95765, Placer County, (916)632-8333, 30 miles from Sacramento. **E-mail:** info@whitneyoaks.com. **Web:** www.whitneyoaks.com. **Facility Holes:** 18. **Yards:** 6,793/4,983. **Par:** 71/71. **Course Rating:** 74.2/70.9. **Slope:** 138/127. **Green Fee:** $30/$70. **Cart Fee:** Included in green fee. **Walking Policy:** Unrestricted walking. **Walkability:** 3. **Opened:** 1997. **Architect:** Johnny Miller. **Season:** Year-round. **To obtain tee times:** Call up to 7 days in advance. **Miscellaneous:** Reduced fees (weekdays, twilight, seniors, juniors), range (grass), credit cards (MC, V, AE), BF, FF.
Reader Comments: Bring your mental A-game … Tough course for high handicap, slow … Staff are great! … Sensitively built in wetlands and oak woodlands … Well established for new course … Bring lots of balls. Target golf. Narrow. Penalizing … Each shot is a unique challenge.

★★ **WHITTIER NARROWS GOLF COURSE**
PU-8640 E. Rush St., Rosemead, 91770, Los Angeles County, (626)288-1044, 6 miles from Los Angeles. **E-mail:** jvelasco@palmergolf.com. **Facility Holes:** 27. **Yards:** 6,864/5,965. **Par:** 72/74. **Course Rating:** 72.3/73.6. **Slope:** 121/117. **Green Fee:** $20/$25. **Cart Fee:** $22/Cart. **Walking Policy:** Unrestricted walking. **Walkability:** 3. **Opened:** 1954. **Architect:** William F. Bell.

Season: Year-round. **High:** May-Oct. **To obtain tee times:** Call golf shop. **Misc:** Reduced fees (twilight, seniors, juniors), metal spikes, range (grass/mats), credit cards (MC, V, AE), BF, FF. **Special Notes:** Also have a 9-hole executive course.

★★★½ WILDHAWK GOLF CLUB
PU-7713 Vineyard Rd., Sacramento, 95829, Sacramento County, (916)688-4653. **Web:** www.wildhawkgolf.com. **Facility Holes:** 18. **Yards:** 6,695/4,847. **Par:** 72/72. **Course Rating:** 71.2/67.2. **Slope:** 124/109. **Green Fee:** $30/$43. **Cart Fee:** $6/Person. **Walking Policy:** Unrestricted walking. **Walkability:** 3. **Opened:** 1997. **Architect:** J. Michael Poellot with Mark Hollinger. **Season:** Year-round. **High:** March-Nov. **To obtain tee times:** Call golf shop. **Miscellaneous:** Range (grass/mats), credit cards (MC, V, AE, Diners).
Reader Comments: Nice course, a little pricey, would play again … Fun course to play … Friendly helpful staff, course will improve as it matures … Good value for the Sacramento area … Most reasonable for this quality.

★★★ WILDHORSE GOLF CLUB
PU-2323 Rockwell Dr., Davis, 95616, Yolo County, (530)753-4900, (800)467-6132, 12 miles from Sacramento. **Facility Holes:** 18. **Yards:** 6,786/5,386. **Par:** 72/73. **Course Rating:** 72.9/68.0. **Slope:** 134/122. **Green Fee:** $35/$50. **Cart Fee:** Included in green fee. **Walking Policy:** Unrestricted walking. **Walkability:** 3. **Opened:** 1998. **Architect:** Jeff Brauer. **Season:** Year-round. **High:** March-Oct. **To obtain tee times:** Call up to 7 days in advance. **Miscellaneous:** Reduced fees (twilight, seniors, juniors), range (grass), credit cards (MC, V, AE, DC), BF, FF.
Reader Comments: With maturity will be a great course … Good course … Good new course, winds nicely through walnut grove…. Excellent greens … Great value and design in new course … Tough test, forced carries, good variety.

★★½ WILLOW PARK GOLF CLUB
PU-17007 Redwood Rd., Castro Valley, 94546, Alameda County, (510)537-8989, 20 miles from Oakland. **Facility Holes:** 18. **Yards:** 5,700/5,193. **Par:** 71/71. **Course Rating:** 67.4/69.2. **Slope:** 110/117. **Green Fee:** $22/$31. **Cart Fee:** $24/Cart. **Walking Policy:** Unrestricted walking. **Walkability:** 2. **Opened:** 1967. **Architect:** Bob Baldock. **Season:** Year-round. **High:** June-Nov. **To obtain tee times:** Call golf shop. **Misc:** Range (mats), credit cards (MC, V), FF.

★★½ WILLOWICK GOLF CLUB
PU-3017 W. Fifth St., Santa Ana, 92703, Orange County, (714)554-0672. **Facility Holes:** 18. **Yards:** 6,063/5,742. **Par:** 71/71. **Course Rating:** 67.7/72.3. **Slope:** 110/118. **Green Fee:** $16/$33. **Cart Fee:** $12/Person. **Walking Policy:** Unrestricted walking. **Walkability:** 1. **Season:** Year-round. **To obtain tee times:** Call up to 7 days in advance. **Miscellaneous:** Reduced fees (weekdays, twilight), metal spikes, range (grass), credit cards (MC, V), FF.

★★★½ WINDSOR GOLF CLUB
PU-1340 19th Hole Dr., Windsor, 95492, Sonoma County, (707)838-7888, 6 miles from Santa Rosa. **Facility Holes:** 18. **Yards:** 6,650/5,116. **Par:** 72/72. **Course Rating:** 71.7/69.3. **Slope:** 127/125. **Green Fee:** $24/$42. **Cart Fee:** $22/Cart. **Walking Policy:** Unrestricted walking. **Walkability:** 2. **Opened:** 1989. **Architect:** Fred Bliss. **Season:** Year-round. **To obtain tee times:** Call golf shop. **Miscellaneous:** Reduced fees (weekdays, twilight, seniors, juniors), range (grass), credit cards (MC, V), BF, FF.
Reader Comments: Very nice course for the money … Nicer, now that they built clubhouse … A fun course. Very good for seniors.

★★★★ WOODCREEK GOLF CLUB
PU-5880 Woodcreek Oaks Blvd., Roseville, 95747, Placer County, (916)771-4653, 15 miles from Sacramento. **Web:** www.golfroseville.com. **Facility Holes:** 18. **Yards:** 6,518/4,739. **Par:** 72/70. **Course Rating:** 72.4/66.2. **Slope:** 128/112. **Green Fee:** $25/$40. **Cart Fee:** $14/Person. **Walking Policy:** Mandatory carts. **Walkability:** 2. **Opened:** 1995. **Architect:** Robert Muir Graves. **Season:** Year-round. **High:** March-Sept. **To obtain tee times:** Call up to 7 days in advance. **Miscellaneous:** Reduced fees (weekdays, twilight, seniors, juniors), metal spikes, range (grass/mats), credit cards (MC, V, AE, D), BF, FF.
Reader Comments: Very fun course with variety of holes … Some dynamic holes for a muni … Outstanding staff … Difficult & beautiful grounds … Distance between some holes, excellent greens.

★★½ WOODLEY LAKES GOLF COURSE
PU-6331 Woodley Ave., Van Nuys, 91406, Los Angeles County, (818)787-8163, 15 miles from Los Angeles. **Facility Holes:** 18. **Yards:** 6,782/6,242. **Par:** 72/72. **Course Rating:** 70.9/74.3. **Slope:** 111/112. **Green Fee:** $18/$23. **Cart Fee:** $21/Cart. **Walking Policy:** Unrestricted walking. **Walkability:** 1. **Opened:** 1965. **Architect:** City of Los Angeles/Ray Goates. **Season:** Year-round. **To obtain tee times:** Call golf shop. **Misc:** Reduced fees (twilight, seniors, juniors), metal spikes, range (grass), credit cards (MC, V, AE, D), BF, FF.

YUCAIPA VALLEY GOLF CLUB
PU-33725 Chapman Heights Rd., Yucaipa, 92399, San Bernardino County, (909)790-6522, 50 miles from Los Angeles. **Web:** www.yvgc.com. **Facility Holes:** 18. **Yards:** 6,803/5,273. **Par:** 72/72. **Course Rating:** 72.8/70.9. **Slope:** 128/119. **Green Fee:** $17/$36. **Cart Fee:** $11/Person. **Walking Policy:** Unrestricted walking. **Walkability:** 2. **Opened:** 2000. **Architect:** David Rainville/Gary Bye. **Season:** Year-round. **High:** Oct.-May. **To obtain tee times:** Call up to 7 days in advance. **Miscellaneous:** Reduced fees (twilight, juniors), range (grass/mats), credit cards (MC, V, D), BF, FF.

★★½ ADOBE CREEK NATIONAL GOLF COURSE
PU-876 18 1/2 Rd., Fruita, 81521, Mesa County, (970)858-0521, 9 miles from Grand Junction. **E-mail:** adobecrk@acsol.net. **Facility Holes:** 27. **Yards:** 6,997/4,980. **Par:** 72/72. **Course Rating:** 71.2/55.1. **Slope:** 119/97. **Green Fee:** $15/$24. **Walking Policy:** Unrestricted walking. **Walkability:** 1. **Opened:** 1992. **Architect:** Ned Wilson. **Season:** Year-round. **To obtain tee times:** Call up to 3 days in advance. **Miscellaneous:** Reduced fees (weekdays, twilight, seniors, juniors), range (grass), credit cards (MC, V), BF, FF.
Special Notes: Also has a 9-hole course.

★★★ APPLETREE GOLF COURSE
PU-10150 Rolling Ridge Rd., Colorado Springs, 80925, El Paso County, (719)382-3649, (800)844-6531, 8 miles from Denver. **Web:** www.apple-tree.com. **Facility Holes:** 18. **Yards:** 6,407/5,003. **Par:** 72/72. **Course Rating:** 68.6/66.9. **Slope:** 122/113. **Green Fee:** $10/$20. **Cart Fee:** $20/Cart. **Walking Policy:** Unrestricted walking. **Walkability:** 1. **Opened:** 1972. **Architect:** Lee Trevino/Dave Bennett. **Season:** Year-round. **High:** May-Sept. **To obtain tee times:** Call golf shop. **Miscellaneous:** Reduced fees (weekdays, twilight, seniors, juniors), range (grass), credit cards (MC, V, AE).
Reader Comments: Lots of sand and water… Good mixture of easy playing holes … Low price goes with pace of play … Variety of difficulty from easy to hard.

★½ APPLEWOOD GOLF COURSE
PU-14001 W. 32nd Ave., Golden, 80401, Jefferson County, (303)279-3003, 13 miles from Golden. **Facility Holes:** 18. **Yards:** 5,992/5,374. **Par:** 71/72. **Course Rating:** 68.2/69.0. **Slope:** 112/118. **Green Fee:** $20/$23. **Cart Fee:** $10/Person. **Walking Policy:** Unrestricted walking. **Walkability:** 3. **Opened:** 1954. **Architect:** Press Maxwell. **Season:** Year-round. **High:** April-Oct. **To obtain tee times:** Call golf shop. **Miscellaneous:** Reduced fees (weekdays, twilight, seniors, juniors), range (grass/mats), credit cards (MC, V, AE).

★★★½ ARROWHEAD GOLF CLUB
R-10850 W. Sundown Trail, Littleton, 80125, Douglas County, (303)973-9614, 25 miles from Denver. **Facility Holes:** 18. **Yards:** 6,682/5,465. **Par:** 70/72. **Course Rating:** 70.9/71.1. **Slope:** 134/127. **Green Fee:** $45/$110. **Cart Fee:** Included in green fee. **Walking Policy:** Mandatory carts. **Walkability:** 4. **Opened:** 1972. **Architect:** Robert Trent Jones Jr. **Season:** Feb.-Nov. **High:** May-Sept. **To obtain tee times:** Call golf shop. **Miscellaneous:** Reduced fees (weekdays, twilight, seniors), range (grass/mats), credit cards (MC, V, AE, D), BF, FF.
Reader Comments: Incredible views and very demanding shots … Watch for snakes … A delight … Price tag is a bit much for what you get … Deer abundant … Course built into the Red Rocks west of Denver … A lot of tournaments.

★★★ ASPEN GOLF COURSE
R-39551 Hwy. 82, Aspen, 81612, Pitkin County, (970)925-2145, 2 miles from Aspen. **E-mail:** lhkpga@hotmail.com. **Facility Holes:** 18. **Yards:** 7,165/5,591. **Par:** 71/72. **Course Rating:** 72.2/69.9. **Slope:** 125/116. **Green Fee:** $45/$80. **Walking Policy:** Unrestricted walking. **Walkability:** 2. **Opened:** 1962. **Architect:** Frank Hummel/Dick Phelps. **Season:** April-Oct. **High:** June-Sept. **To obtain tee times:** Call golf shop. **Miscellaneous:** Reduced fees (twilight, seniors, juniors), range (grass), credit cards (MC, V, AE, D), BF, FF.
Reader Comments: Affordable golf in Aspen … Wonderful condition, great views, a real test, challenging greens, super town … Majestic view of Maroon Bell … Nice course, tough greens, thin air.

★★½ AURORA HILLS GOLF COURSE
PU-50 S. Peoria St., Aurora, 80012, Arapahoe County, (303)364-6111, 2 miles from Denver. **Web:** www.golfaurora.com. **Facility Holes:** 18. **Yards:** 6,735/5,919. **Par:** 72/73. **Course Rating:** 70.1/71.5. **Slope:** 115/120. **Green Fee:** $13/$20. **Cart Fee:** $20/Cart. **Walking Policy:** Unrestricted walking. **Walkability:** 2. **Opened:** 1968. **Architect:** Henry Hughes. **Season:** Year-round. **High:** April-Sept. **To obtain tee times:** Call golf shop. **Miscellaneous:** Reduced fees (twilight, seniors, juniors), range (grass/mats), credit cards (MC, V, D), BF, FF.

★★★★ BATTLEMENT MESA GOLF CLUB
PU-3930 N. Battlement Pkwy., Battlement Mesa, 81635, Garfield County, (970)285-7274, (888)285-7274, 42 miles from Glenwood Springs. **E-mail:** jgbmgc@aol.com. **Facility Holes:** 18. **Yards:** 7,309/5,386. **Par:** 72/72. **Course Rating:** 73.7/68.7. **Slope:** 135/116. **Green Fee:** $22/$35. **Cart Fee:** $14/Person. **Walking Policy:** Unrestricted walking. **Walkability:** 4. **Opened:** 1987. **Architect:** Finger/Dye/Spann. **Season:** Feb.-Nov. **High:** May-Sept. **To obtain tee times:** Call up to 3 days in advance. **Miscellaneous:** Reduced fees (guests, juniors), range (grass), lodging (16 rooms), credit cards (MC, V, AE, D), BF, FF.
Reader Comments: Fun on the Mesa … Talking bird in the clubhouse … Have to play more than

once … Wind a factor, many blind tee shots … Great view of Colorado River on back 9 … Lot of elevation changes … No. 7 is worth the trip.

★★★★ BEAVER CREEK GOLF CLUB *Service*
R-103 Offerson Rd., Avon, 81620, Eagle County, (970)845-5775, 8 miles from Vail. **Facility Holes:** 18. **Yards:** 6,752/5,200. **Par:** 70/70. **Course Rating:** 69.6/70.3. **Slope:** 140/124. **Green Fee:** $75/$135. **Cart Fee:** Included in green fee. **Walking Policy:** Mandatory carts. **Walkability:** 5. **Opened:** 1982. **Architect:** Robert Trent Jones Jr. **Season:** May-Oct. **High:** June-Sept. **To obtain tee times:** Call golf shop. **Miscellaneous:** Reduced fees (guests), range (grass/mats), credit cards (MC, V, AE, D, DC, Diners), BF, FF.
Reader Comments: Tough course, local info is key … This course makes you feel like royalty … Excellent service … Takes your breath away.

★★★½ BOOMERANG LINKS
PU-7309 W. 4th St., Greeley, 80634, Weld County, (970)351-8934, (970)351-8934, 40 miles from Denver. **Web:** www.ci.greeley.co.us. **Facility Holes:** 18. **Yards:** 7,214/5,285. **Par:** 72/72. **Course Rating:** 72.6/68.5. **Slope:** 131/113. **Green Fee:** $17/$27. **Cart Fee:** $26/Cart. **Walking Policy:** Unrestricted walking. **Walkability:** 2. **Opened:** 1991. **Architect:** William H. Neff. **Season:** Year-round. **High:** May-Sept. **To obtain tee times:** Call up to 7 days in advance. **Miscellaneous:** Reduced fees (weekdays, twilight, seniors, juniors), range (grass), credit cards (MC, V, D), BF, FF.
Reader Comments: Putting and chipping area very good, pace needs to improve … 18th very dangerous, driving range on other side … You've got to be straight off the tee … Good test from the tips … Getting better.

★★★★ BRECKENRIDGE GOLF CLUB
PU-200 Clubhouse Dr., Breckenridge, 80424, Summit County, (970)453-9104, 80 miles from Denver. **Web:** www.golfcolorado.com/breckenridge. **Facility Holes:** 18. **Yards:** 7,276/5,063. **Par:** 72/72. **Course Rating:** 73.3/67.6. **Slope:** 149/129. **Green Fee:** $55/$90. **Cart Fee:** $15/Person. **Walking Policy:** Walking at certain times. **Walkability:** 3. **Opened:** 1985. **Architect:** Jack Nicklaus. **Season:** May-Oct. **High:** June-Sept. **To obtain tee times:** Call up to 4 days in advance. **Miscellaneous:** Reduced fees (twilight), range (grass), credit cards (MC, V, AE), BF, FF.
Notes: Ranked 13th in 2001 Best in State.
Reader Comments: Tight layout … Very good condition for such heavy play … Local knowledge a plus … Fantastic mountain course, real tough from back … Beautiful, well laid out.

★★★ THE BROADLANDS GOLF COURSE
PU-4380 W. 144th Ave., Broomfield, 80020, Boulder County, (303)466-8285, 5 miles from Denver. **E-mail:** broadland@eaglgolf.com. **Web:** www.eaglgolf.com. **Facility Holes:** 18. **Yards:** 7,263/5,348. **Par:** 72/72. **Course Rating:** 72.9/72.4. **Slope:** 125/124. **Green Fee:** $24/$35. **Cart Fee:** $11/Person. **Walking Policy:** Unrestricted walking. **Opened:** 1999. **Architect:** Rick Phelps. **Season:** Year-round. **High:** March-Nov. **To obtain tee times:** Call up to 3 days in advance. **Miscellaneous:** Reduced fees (weekdays, twilight, seniors, juniors), range (grass), credit cards (MC, V, AE), BF, FF.
Reader Comments: New course, needs maturing … Greens were in great shape … Challenging … Very crowded.

THE BROADMOOR GOLF CLUB
R-1 Pourtales Rd., Colorado Springs, 80906, El Paso County, (719)577-5790, (800)634-7711, 60 miles from Denver. **Web:** www.broadmoor.com. **Facility Holes:** 54. **Cart Fee:** Included in green fee. **Walking Policy:** Walking at certain times. **To obtain tee times:** Call up to 60 days in advance. **Miscellaneous:** Range (grass), caddies, lodging (700 rooms), credit cards (MC, V, AE, D, DC), BF, FF.
★★★★★ EAST COURSE (18) *Value, Condition+, Pace+*
Yards: 7,091/5,847. **Par:** 72/72. **Course Rating:** 73.0/72.7. **Slope:** 129/139. **Green Fee:** $90/$155. **Walkability:** 3. **Opened:** 1918. **Architect:** Donald Ross/Robert Trent Jones. **Season:** Year-round. **High:** April-Nov. **Miscellaneous:** Reduced fees (twilight).
Notes: Ranked 12th in 2001 Best in State.
Reader Comments: Simply fantastic … Wow … Bring your best putting touch with you or expect more than just a three putt … Always keep the Mountain in mind when putting … The views are magnificent … The service is first class.
★★★★ MOUNTAIN COURSE (18) *Pace*
Yards: 6,781/5,609. **Par:** 72/71. **Course Rating:** 72.1/71.5. **Slope:** 135/126. **Walkability:** 5. **Opened:** 1976. **Architect:** Arnold Palmer/Ed Seay. **Season:** May-Oct. **High:** May-Oct. **Miscellaneous:** Reduced fees (twilight, juniors).
Reader Comments: The view from the Broadmoor Mountain is breathtaking … Challenging layout is tough even for the seasoned competitor … Target-style course … Tough.
★★★★½ WEST COURSE (18) *Condition, Pace*

Yards: 6,937/5,375. **Par:** 72/73. **Course Rating:** 73.0/70.5. **Slope:** 133/127. **Green Fee:** $90/$155. **Walkability:** 4. **Opened:** 1918. **Architect:** Donald Ross/Robert Trent Jones. **Season:** Year-round. **High:** April-Nov. **Miscellaneous:** Reduced fees (twilight, juniors).
Reader Comments: The 11th hole is definitely a favorite … Beautiful … Good change in elevation … Fun to play … Pamper yourself.

★★★★ BUFFALO RUN GOLF COURSE *Value*
PU-15700 E. 112th Ave., Commerce City, 80022, Adams County, (303)289-1500, 15 miles from Denver. **Facility Holes:** 18. **Yards:** 7,411/5,227. **Par:** 72/71. **Course Rating:** 73.5/68.1. **Slope:** 121/119. **Green Fee:** $18/$38. **Cart Fee:** $11/Person. **Walking Policy:** Unrestricted walking. **Walkability:** 3. **Opened:** 1996. **Architect:** Keith Foster. **Season:** Year-round. **High:** April-Oct. **To obtain tee times:** Call golf shop. **Miscellaneous:** Reduced fees (seniors, juniors), range (grass), caddies, credit cards (MC, V, AE, D), BF, FF.
Notes: Ranked 6th in 1997 Best New Affordable Public Courses.
Reader Comments: True links course, you won't a tree on the course … Quite a walk from cart path, slows play … Play early and avoid wind … Worth the drive, will challenge you from the tips … Tranquil setting but hard to locate.

★★½ CANTERBERRY GOLF COURSE
PU-11400 Canterberry Pkwy., Parker, 80134, Douglas County, (303)840-3100, 20 miles from Denver. **Facility Holes:** 18. **Yards:** 7,180/5,600. **Par:** 72/72. **Course Rating:** 73.0/63.9. **Slope:** 138/104. **Green Fee:** $14/$30. **Cart Fee:** $10/Person. **Walking Policy:** Walking at certain times. **Walkability:** 3. **Opened:** 1996. **Architect:** Jeff Brauer. **Season:** Year-round. **High:** March-Oct. **To obtain tee times:** Call golf shop. **Miscellaneous:** Reduced fees (weekdays, twilight, seniors, juniors), metal spikes, range (grass), credit cards (MC, V, AE).

★★ CATTAILS GOLF CLUB
PU-6615 N. River Rd., Alamosa, 81101, Alamosa County, (719)589-9515. **Web:** www.alamosagolf.com. **Facility Holes:** 18. **Yards:** 6,527/5,107. **Par:** 71/72. **Course Rating:** 69.1/69.0. **Slope:** 123/116. **Green Fee:** $16/$30. **Cart Fee:** $18/Cart. **Walking Policy:** Unrestricted walking. **Walkability:** 1. **Architect:** Dick Phelps. **Season:** April-Nov. **High:** May-Sept. **To obtain tee times:** Call golf shop. **Miscellaneous:** Reduced fees (twilight, seniors, juniors), range (grass/mats), credit cards (MC, V, AE, D), BF, FF.

★★½ CITY PARK GOLF CLUB
PU-2500 York, Denver, 80218, Denver County, (303)295-4420. **Facility Holes:** 18. **Yards:** 6,318/6,181. **Par:** 72/74. **Course Rating:** 68.0/74.1. **Slope:** 111/116. **Green Fee:** $19/$20. **Cart Fee:** $20/Cart. **Walking Policy:** Unrestricted walking. **Walkability:** 3. **Opened:** 1913. **Architect:** Tom Bendelow. **Season:** Year-round. **High:** April-Sept. **To obtain tee times:** Call golf shop. **Miscellaneous:** Range (mats), credit cards (MC, V).

THE CLUB AT CORDILLERA
SP-650 Clubhouse Dr., Edwards, 81632, Eagle County, (970)926-5100, (800)877-3529, 100 miles from Denver. **E-mail:** ptofferi@cordillera-vail.com. **Web:** www.cordillera-vail.com. **Facility Holes:** 63. **Cart Fee:** Included in green fee. **Walking Policy:** Mandatory carts. **To obtain tee times:** Call golf shop. **Miscellaneous:** Reduced fees (guests), caddies (included in fee), range (grass/mats), lodging (56 rooms), credit cards (MC, V, AE, D), BF, FF.
★★★★ MOUNTAIN COURSE (18) *Condition, Pace*
Yards: 7,416/5,226. **Par:** 72/72. **Course Rating:** 74.7/68.6. **Slope:** 145/128. **Green Fee:** $97/$237. **Walkability:** 5. **Opened:** 1994. **Architect:** Hale Irwin/Dick Phelps. **Season:** March-Oct. **High:** July-Sept.
Notes: Ranked 20th in 1999 Best in State.
Reader Comments: Beautiful course … Best greens ever … Mandatory forecaddie … Gorgeous but very pricey … What's not to like? … By far the best Colorado-style course in state … Luxury personified.
SUMMIT COURSE (18)
Yards: 7,441/5,425. **Par:** 72/72. **Course Rating:** 74.0/69.5. **Slope:** 135/130. **Green Fee:** $95/$235. **Walkability:** 4. **Opened:** 2001. **Architect:** Jack Nicklaus. **Season:** June-Oct. **High:** June-Sept.
VALLEY COURSE (18)
Yards: 7,005/5,087. **Par:** 71/71. **Course Rating:** 71.9/68.1. **Slope:** 125/121. **Green Fee:** $97/$192. **Walkability:** 4. **Opened:** 1997. **Architect:** Tom Fazio/Dennis Wise. **Season:** April-Nov. **High:** June-Sept.
Notes: Ranked 14th in 2001 Best in State.

★★★★ THE CLUB AT CRESTED BUTTE
SP-385 Country Club Dr., Crested Butte, 81224, Gunnison County, (970)349-6131, (800)628-5496, 28 miles from Gunnison. **E-mail:** cbcc@crestedbutte.net. **Web:** www.golfcolorado.net. **Facility Holes:** 18. **Yards:** 7,208/5,702. **Par:** 72/72. **Course Rating:** 73.0/72.3.

COLORADO

Slope: 133/128. **Green Fee:** $65/$120. **Cart Fee:** Included in green fee. **Walking Policy:** Mandatory carts. **Walkability:** 5. **Opened:** 1983. **Architect:** Robert Trent Jones Jr. **Season:** May-Oct. **High:** June-Sept. **To obtain tee times:** Call up to 14 days in advance. **Miscellaneous:** Reduced fees (guests, twilight), range (grass), credit cards (MC, V, AE, D), BF, FF.
Reader Comments: Small creek runs through course and in blind spots … The course grows on you … Like Scotland up to 9,000 feet … Bring your gold card, things here are not cheap … Nice course.

★★★½ COAL CREEK GOLF COURSE
PU-585 W. Dillon Rd., Louisville, 80027, Boulder County, (303)666-7888, 10 miles from Boulder. **E-mail:** coalcreekgolf@earthlink.net. **Web:** www.coalcreekgolf.com. **Facility Holes:** 18. **Yards:** 7/5,185. **Par:** 72/72. **Course Rating:** 72.4/67.3. **Slope:** 136/118. **Green Fee:** $27/$40. **Cart Fee:** $15/Person. **Walking Policy:** Unrestricted walking. **Walkability:** 3. **Opened:** 1990. **Architect:** Dick Phelps. **Season:** Year-round. **High:** May-Sept. **To obtain tee times:** Call up to 3 days in advance. **Miscellaneous:** Reduced fees (weekdays, twilight, seniors, juniors), range (grass/mats), credit cards (MC, V, DC), BF, FF.
Reader Comments: Use the GPS cart if it is your first time … Challenges for the better golfer but rookies will still fare okay … Weekend play slow … Water, bunkers and elevation changes make for nice track … Masterful design, lots of trouble … Never boring.

★★★ COLLINDALE GOLF CLUB
PU-1441 E. Horsetooth Rd., Fort Collins, 80525, Larimer County, (970)221-6651, 60 miles from Denver. **Facility Holes:** 18. **Yards:** 7,011/5,472. **Par:** 71/73. **Course Rating:** 71.5/69.9. **Slope:** 126/113. **Green Fee:** $19/$21. **Cart Fee:** $21/Cart. **Walking Policy:** Unrestricted walking. **Walkability:** 1. **Opened:** 1972. **Architect:** Frank Hummel. **Season:** Year-round. **High:** April-Sept. **To obtain tee times:** Call up to 3 days in advance. **Miscellaneous:** Reduced fees (weekdays, twilight, seniors, juniors), range (grass/mats), credit cards (MC, V), BF, FF.
Reader Comments: A terrific test … Don't be above the hole … Good muni, tough greens … Trees have matured and are now a factor … Park style … No room for error on approaches … Forgiving yet challenging … I would play there every day … Best greens in the area.

★★★ CONQUISTADOR GOLF COURSE
PU-2018 N. Delores Rd., Cortez, 81321, Montezuma County, (970)565-9208, 45 miles from Durango. **E-mail:** mrudosky@hotmail.com. **Facility Holes:** 18. **Yards:** 6,852/5,576. **Par:** 72/72. **Course Rating:** 69.5/70.2. **Slope:** 113/121. **Green Fee:** $18. **Cart Fee:** $21/Cart. **Walking Policy:** Unrestricted walking. **Walkability:** 2. **Opened:** 1963. **Season:** March-Nov. **High:** May-Sept. **To obtain tee times:** Call up to 3 days in advance. **Miscellaneous:** Reduced fees (juniors), range (grass/mats), credit cards (MC, V), BF, FF.
Reader Comments: A great course at a reasonable price … Wide open but balanced by small fast greens … It was a very fair and challenging course.

★★★ COPPER MOUNTAIN RESORT
R-104 Wheeler Circle, Copper Mountain, 80443, Summit County, (970)968-3333, (800)458-8386, 75 miles from Denver. **E-mail:** twohigd@ski-copper.com. **Web:** www.ski-copper.com. **Facility Holes:** 18. **Yards:** 6,053/4,445. **Par:** 70/70. **Course Rating:** 68.2/63.2. **Slope:** 115/111. **Green Fee:** $60/$79. **Cart Fee:** Included in green fee. **Walking Policy:** Mandatory carts. **Walkability:** 4. **Opened:** 1976. **Architect:** Pete Dye/Perry Dye. **Season:** June-Oct. **High:** July-Sept. **To obtain tee times:** Call up to 7 days in advance. **Miscellaneous:** Reduced fees (guests, twilight, juniors), range (mats), lodging (800 rooms), credit cards (MC, V, AE, D, DC), BF, FF.
Reader Comments: Back nine especially scenic … A good overall test of golf … A fun course but tricked up some … Mountain golf with a lot of straightaway holes … High altitude so you get great distance … Great views … Course seems forced into small area.

★★★★ COTTON RANCH CLUB
SP-530 Cotton Ranch Dr., Gypsum, 81637, Eagle County, (970)524-6200, (800)404-3542, 35 miles from Vail. **Web:** www.cottonranch.com. **Facility Holes:** 18. **Yards:** 7,052/5,197. **Par:** 72/72. **Course Rating:** 73.6/70.4. **Slope:** 136/121. **Green Fee:** $55/$100. **Cart Fee:** Included in green fee. **Walking Policy:** Walking at certain times. **Walkability:** 4. **Opened:** 1997. **Architect:** Pete Dye. **Season:** March-Nov. **High:** July-Sept. **To obtain tee times:** Call golf shop. **Miscellaneous:** Reduced fees (twilight, juniors), range (grass), credit cards (MC, V, AE, D), BF, FF.
Reader Comments: This Pete Dye design won't let you down … Course has two personalities … They treat you like a member … Some good holes … Accuracy counts … Need local knowledge.

★★★½ COUNTRY CLUB OF COLORADO
R-125 E. Clubhouse Dr., Colorado Springs, 80906, El Paso County, (719)538-4095. **Facility Holes:** 18. **Yards:** 7,028/5,357. **Par:** 71/71. **Course Rating:** 72.4/69.3. **Slope:** 138/124. **Green Fee:** $120. **Walking Policy:** Unrestricted walking. **Walkability:** 3. **Opened:** 1973. **Architect:**

Pete Dye. **Season:** Year-round. **High:** May-Sept. **To obtain tee times:** Call up to 3 days in advance. **Miscellaneous:** Range (grass/mats), lodging (300 rooms), credit cards (MC, V, AE, D), BF, FF.

Reader Comments: One of Pete Dye's better designs ... Great layout ... Beautiful course with excellent service ... A challenging layout ... Stay out of the rough.

★★½ COYOTE CREEK GOLF COURSE

PU-2 Clubhouse Dr., Fort Lupton, 80621, Weld County, (303)857-6152, 22 miles from Denver. **Facility Holes:** 18. **Yards:** 6,412/5,166. **Par:** 71/71. **Course Rating:** 69.3/67.8. **Slope:** 116/115. **Green Fee:** $15/$26. **Walkability:** 2. **Opened:** 1999. **Architect:** Matt Eccles. **Season:** Year-round. **To obtain tee times:** Call up to 7 days in advance. **Miscellaneous:** Reduced fees (weekdays, twilight, seniors, juniors), range (grass/mats), credit cards (MC, V), BF, FF.

★★★★ DALTON RANCH GOLF CLUB

SP-589 C.R. 252, Durango, 81301, La Plata County, (970)247-8774, 210 miles from Albuquerque. **E-mail:** dalton@frontier.net. **Web:** www.daltonranch.com. **Facility Holes:** 18. **Yards:** 6,934/5,539. **Par:** 72/72. **Course Rating:** 72.4/71.7. **Slope:** 135/127. **Green Fee:** $30/$59. **Cart Fee:** $10/Person. **Walking Policy:** Unrestricted walking. **Walkability:** 3. **Opened:** 1993. **Architect:** Ken Dye. **Season:** March-Nov. **High:** June-Sept. **To obtain tee times:** Call up to 7 days in advance. **Miscellaneous:** Reduced fees (guests, twilight, juniors), range (grass), credit cards (MC, V, AE), BF, FF.

Reader Comments: Plenty of water and sand ... Great track, terrific setting on river ... Challenging from back ... Service makes up for the price ... Great views ... Thoroughly enjoyable.

★★½ DEER CREEK GOLF CLUB AT MEADOW RANCH

SP-8135 Shaffer Pkwy., Littleton, 80127, Jefferson County, (303)978-1800, 15 miles from Denver. **Web:** www.golfexperience.com/deercreek. **Facility Holes:** 18. **Yards:** 7,003/5,004. **Par:** 72/72. **Course Rating:** 73.2/63.2. **Slope:** 135/108. **Walkability:** 4. **Opened:** 2000. **Architect:** Scott Miller. **Season:** Year-round. **To obtain tee times:** Call up to 7 days in advance. **Miscellaneous:** Range (grass), BF, FF.

★★★½ DEER CREEK VILLAGE GOLF CLUB

PU-500 S.E. Jay Ave., Cedaredge, 81413, Delta County, (970)856-7781, 30 miles from Grand Junction. **E-mail:** deergolf@gvii.net. **Web:** www.golfcolorado.com/deercreek. **Facility Holes:** 18. **Yards:** 6,418/5,077. **Par:** 72/72. **Course Rating:** 69.8/68.4. **Slope:** 128/122. **Green Fee:** $21/$23. **Cart Fee:** $22/Cart. **Walking Policy:** Unrestricted walking. **Walkability:** 4. **Opened:** 1992. **Architect:** Byron Coker. **Season:** Feb.-Dec. **High:** May-Oct. **To obtain tee times:** Call up to 7 days in advance. **Miscellaneous:** Reduced fees (juniors), range (grass), credit cards (MC, V, D), BF, FF.

Reader Comments: Great course, outstanding service ... Back 9 narrow and rocky ... I shot even on the front and 17 over on the back ... Back 9 is the hardest I have ever played ... Very difficult, great course ... Goofy back 9.

★★ DESERT HAWK GOLF COURSE AT PUEBLO WEST

PU-251 S. McCulloch, Pueblo West, 81007, Pueblo County, (719)547-2280, 8 miles from Pueblo. **E-mail:** heathermf19@hotmail.com. **Facility Holes:** 18. **Yards:** 7,368/5,688. **Par:** 72/72. **Course Rating:** 73.3/71.4. **Slope:** 125/117. **Green Fee:** $19/$25. **Cart Fee:** $9/Person. **Walking Policy:** Unrestricted walking. **Walkability:** 2. **Opened:** 1972. **Architect:** Clyde B. Young. **Season:** Year-round. **High:** May-Oct. **To obtain tee times:** Call up to 10 days in advance. **Miscellaneous:** Reduced fees (weekdays, twilight, seniors, juniors), range (grass), credit cards (MC, V), BF, FF.

★★★½ THE DIVIDE AT KING'S DEER

PU-19255 Royal Troon Dr., Monument, 80132, El Paso County, (719)481-1518, 20 miles from Colorado Springs. **E-mail:** thedivide@earthlink.net. **Web:** www.thedivide.net. **Facility Holes:** 18. **Yards:** 6,945/5,138. **Par:** 71/71. **Course Rating:** 72.0/68.7. **Slope:** 136/124. **Green Fee:** $45/$55. **Cart Fee:** Included in green fee. **Walking Policy:** Mandatory carts. **Walkability:** 3. **Opened:** 1999. **Architect:** Redstone Golf. **Season:** Year-round. **High:** June-Oct. **To obtain tee times:** Call up to 7 days in advance. **Miscellaneous:** Reduced fees (juniors), range (grass), credit cards (MC, V), BF, FF.

Reader Comments: No. 10 is one hard hole ... Beautiful setting ... Interesting design ... A little rough still, but has potential to be great ... Tough but fair ... The wind was up a little and I felt like I was in Scotland ... Course really tests your driving.

★★★ DOS RIOS GOLF CLUB

SP-501 Camino Del Rio Drive, Gunnison, 81230, Gunnison County, (970)641-1482. **Facility Holes:** 18. **Yards:** 6,566/5,453. **Par:** 71/71. **Course Rating:** 69.4/69.4. **Slope:** 127/125. **Green Fee:** $45/$65. **Cart Fee:** Included in green fee. **Walking Policy:** Unrestricted walking. **Walkability:** 2. **Opened:** 1966. **Architect:** John Cochran. **Season:** April-Oct. **High:** June-Sept.

COLORADO

To obtain tee times: Call up to 10 days in advance. **Miscellaneous:** Reduced fees (twilight, juniors), range (grass), credit cards (MC, V), BF, FF.
Reader Comments: Not a very hard course ... Some holes unfair ... Gotten a little pricey over the years ... Nice place to enjoy life ... Lots of water, deep rough.

★★½ EAGLE TRACE GOLF CLUB
PU-1200 Clubhouse Dr., Broomfield, 80020, Boulder County, (303)466-3322, 15 miles from Denver. **Facility Holes:** 18. **Yards:** 6,609/5,745. **Par:** 71/71. **Course Rating:** 70.1/65.8. **Slope:** 121/111. **Green Fee:** $19/$28. **Cart Fee:** $10/Person. **Walking Policy:** Unrestricted walking. **Walkability:** 2. **Opened:** 1968. **Architect:** Dick Phelps. **Season:** Year-round. **To obtain tee times:** Call up to 7 days in advance. **Miscellaneous:** Reduced fees (weekdays, twilight, seniors, juniors), range (mats), credit cards (MC, V), BF, FF.

★★★★ EAGLE VAIL GOLF CLUB
PU-0431 Eagle Dr., Avon, 81620, Eagle County, (970)949-5267, (800)341-8051, 107 miles from Denver. **Facility Holes:** 18. **Yards:** 6,819/4,856. **Par:** 72/72. **Course Rating:** 71.3/67.4. **Slope:** 131/123. **Green Fee:** $55/$105. **Cart Fee:** Included in green fee. **Walking Policy:** Mandatory carts. **Walkability:** 5. **Opened:** 1975. **Architect:** Bruce Devlin/Bob von Hagge. **Season:** May-Oct. **High:** June-Sept. **To obtain tee times:** Call golf shop. **Miscellaneous:** Reduced fees (twilight), range (grass/mats), credit cards (MC, V, AE), BF, FF.
Reader Comments: Funky layout ... Excellent condition, difficult elevation changes, great service ... This course has some excellent holes ... Fun to play ... Adventure golf at its best ... Can see eagles over the course.

EISENHOWER GOLF CLUB
M-USAF Academy, Bldg. 3170, Colorado Springs, 80840, El Paso County, (719)333-4735, 1 mile from Colorado Springs. **E-mail:** edward.ainsworth@usafa.af.mil. **Facility Holes:** 36. **Green Fee:** $10/$50. **Cart Fee:** $20/Person. **Walkability:** 4. **Season:** Year-round. **High:** May-Oct. **To obtain tee times:** Call golf shop. **Miscellaneous:** Reduced fees (twilight, juniors), range (grass/mats), credit cards (MC, V), BF, FF.
★★★★½ BLUE COURSE (18) *Value, Condition, Pace*
Yards: 7,301/5,559. **Par:** 72/72. **Course Rating:** 74.2/65.3. **Slope:** 137/130. **Opened:** 1963. **Architect:** Robert Trent Jones.
Reader Comments: Played this course as a youngster and went back this past year, felt like I was in heaven. It just feels golf ... Beautiful mountain setting ... Scatter my ashes here ... You use all of your shots ... Beautiful scenery ... Best military course I've played.
★★★★½ SILVER COURSE (18) *Value+, Condition+, Pace*
Yards: 6,519/5,215. **Par:** 72/72. **Course Rating:** 70.5/69.0. **Slope:** 121/119. **Opened:** 1976. **Architect:** Frank Hummell.
Reader Comments: Shorter than Blue but a good test ... 6 or 7 really nice holes ... A treat to play, super setting ... Target golf at its best ... Tough for high-handicappers.

★★★ ENGLEWOOD GOLF COURSE
PU-2101 W. Oxford Ave., Englewood, 80110, Arapahoe County, (303)762-2670, 5 miles from Denver. **E-mail:** bspada@ci.englewood.co.us. **Facility Holes:** 27. **Yards:** 6,836/5,967. **Par:** 72/72. **Course Rating:** 71.0/72.2. **Slope:** 125/128. **Green Fee:** $15/$24. **Cart Fee:** $22/Cart. **Walking Policy:** Unrestricted walking. **Walkability:** 3. **Opened:** 1977. **Architect:** Dick Phelps. **Season:** Year-round. **To obtain tee times:** Call up to 4 days in advance. **Miscellaneous:** Reduced fees (weekdays, twilight, seniors, juniors), range (grass/mats), credit cards (MC, V), BF, FF.
Reader Comments: Solid course, lots of water ... Each 9 totally different, fun course ... For the price this is a good play ... Very good practice facilities ... Some nice holes and some odd holes ... A great course that concentrates on service.
Special Notes: Also has a 9-hole course.

★★★ ESTES PARK GOLF COURSE
PU-1080 S. Saint Vrain Ave., Estes Park, 80517, Larimer County, (970)586-8146, 60 miles from Denver. **E-mail:** epgolf@charter.net. **Web:** www.estesvalleyrecreation.com. **Facility Holes:** 27. **Yards:** 6,326/5,250. **Par:** 71/72. **Course Rating:** 69.0/68.3. **Slope:** 121/125. **Green Fee:** $25/$36. **Cart Fee:** $12/Person. **Walking Policy:** Unrestricted walking. **Walkability:** 3. **Opened:** 1917. **Architect:** Henry Hughes/Dick Phelps. **Season:** April-Nov. **High:** June-Oct. **To obtain tee times:** Call up to 7 days in advance. **Miscellaneous:** Reduced fees (twilight), range (grass/mats), credit cards (MC, V), BF, FF.
Reader Comments: Beautiful course in the midst of the Rocky Mountains ... Fun to play ... Low-key resort course ... Watch out for the elk ... Worth the money ... Has to be a favorite ... Ball sails a long way ... Very good vacation course.
Special Notes: Also has a 9-hole course.

★★½ EVERGREEN GOLF COURSE

PU-29614 Upper Bear Creek Rd., Evergreen, 80439, Jefferson County, (303)674-6351, 18 miles from Denver. **Facility Holes:** 18. **Yards:** 4,877/4,494. **Par:** 69/69. **Course Rating:** 62.4/66.7. **Slope:** 111/115. **Green Fee:** $17/$19. **Cart Fee:** $12/Person. **Walking Policy:** Unrestricted walking. **Walkability:** 5. **Opened:** 1924. **Architect:** Babe Lind. **Season:** March-Nov. **To obtain tee times:** Call golf shop. **Miscellaneous:** Reduced fees (seniors, juniors), credit cards (MC, V), BF, FF.

★★★★½ FAIRWAY PINES GOLF CLUB *Value, Pace*

SP-117 Ponderosa Dr., Ridgway, 81432, Ouray County, (970)626-5284, 25 miles from Montrose. **E-mail:** golf@ouraycolorado.net. **Web:** www.fairwaypines.com. **Facility Holes:** 18. **Yards:** 6,841/5,291. **Par:** 72/72. **Course Rating:** 71.6/72.2. **Slope:** 130/123. **Green Fee:** $42/$60. **Cart Fee:** $13/Person. **Walking Policy:** Unrestricted walking. **Walkability:** 3. **Opened:** 1993. **Architect:** Byron Coker. **Season:** April-Nov. **High:** July-Aug. **To obtain tee times:** Call up to 7 days in advance. **Miscellaneous:** Reduced fees (twilight, juniors), metal spikes, range (grass/mats), credit cards (MC, V), BF, FF.
Reader Comments: The most beautiful course I have ever seen … A very pleasant surprise—after finding it … Try to find a local if 1st time … Don't miss this one … Slow play, but everyone is looking at the views.

★★½ FITZSIMONS GOLF COURSE

PU-2323 Scranton St., Aurora, 80010, Arapahoe County, (303)364-8125, 5 miles from Denver. **Web:** www.golfaurora.com. **Facility Holes:** 18. **Yards:** 6,530/5,914. **Par:** 72/72. **Course Rating:** 69.5/73.3. **Slope:** 119/128. **Green Fee:** $13/$20. **Cart Fee:** $22/Cart. **Walking Policy:** Unrestricted walking. **Walkability:** 2. **Opened:** 1941. **Season:** Year-round. **To obtain tee times:** Call golf shop. **Miscellaneous:** Reduced fees (twilight, seniors, juniors), range (grass), credit cards (MC, V, AE, D), BF, FF.

★★★ FLATIRONS GOLF COURSE

PU-5706 Arapahoe Rd., Boulder, 80303, Boulder County, (303)442-7851, 15 miles from Denver. **Facility Holes:** 18. **Yards:** 6,782/5,226. **Par:** 70/70. **Course Rating:** 71.7/68.3. **Slope:** 126/119. **Green Fee:** $19/$26. **Cart Fee:** $20/Cart. **Walking Policy:** Unrestricted walking. **Walkability:** 1. **Opened:** 1933. **Architect:** Robert Bruce Harris. **Season:** Year-round. **High:** March-Sept. **To obtain tee times:** Call golf shop. **Miscellaneous:** Range (grass/mats), credit cards (MC, V).
Reader Comments: Public course—many beginners … Tough muni … Easiest walking course in Colorado … Old course and lots of trees, plays fair … Good greens-fairways too close together.

★★★½ FOOTHILLS GOLF COURSE

PU-3901 S. Carr St., Denver, 80235, Denver County, (303)989-3901, 1 mile from Denver. **Web:** www.ifoothills.com. **Facility Holes:** 27. **Yards:** 6,908/6,028. **Par:** 72/74. **Course Rating:** 71.1/72.9. **Slope:** 122/130. **Green Fee:** $13/$24. **Cart Fee:** $12/Person. **Walking Policy:** Unrestricted walking. **Walkability:** 3. **Opened:** 1971. **Architect:** Dick Phelps. **Season:** Year-round. **To obtain tee times:** Call golf shop. **Miscellaneous:** Reduced fees (weekdays, seniors, juniors), range (grass/mats), credit cards (MC, V), BF, FF.
Reader Comments: Good muni course … Heavily played … Test from the back tees … Fine tuning would make foothills outstanding … Good price for a fair course … A few too many parallel holes … Lots of variety.
Special Notes: Also has 9-hole executive course and a par-3 course.

★★★ FORT CARSON GOLF CLUB

M-Bldg. 7800 Titus Blvd., Fort Carson, 80913, El Paso County, (719)526-4122. **Facility Holes:** 18. **Yards:** 6,919/6,599. **Par:** 72/72. **Course Rating:** 71.6/70.2. **Slope:** 126/123. **Green Fee:** $8/$22. **Cart Fee:** $8/Person. **Walkability:** 4. **Opened:** 1972. **Season:** Year-round. **High:** May-Oct. **To obtain tee times:** Call golf shop. **Miscellaneous:** Reduced fees (weekdays, twilight, seniors, juniors), range (grass/mats), credit cards (MC, V, AE).
Reader Comments: Excellent course to practice your shots … Military course open to the public … Excellent greens … Expensive for civilians … What a great time … Hilly, walking 18 is strenuous.
Special Notes: Formerly Cheyenne Shadow Golf Course.

★½ FORT MORGAN GOLF COURSE

PU-17586 County Rd. T.5, Fort Morgan, 80701, Morgan County, (970)867-5990, 70 miles from Denver. **E-mail:** fmgcpro@twol.com. **Web:** www.fortmorgangolfclub.com. **Facility Holes:** 18. **Yards:** 6,575/5,457. **Par:** 72/74. **Course Rating:** 71.0/70.2. **Slope:** 128/118. **Green Fee:** $17/$22. **Cart Fee:** $22/Cart. **Walking Policy:** Unrestricted walking. **Walkability:** 4. **Opened:** 1927. **Architect:** Henry B. Hughes. **Season:** Year-round. **To obtain tee times:** Call golf shop. **Miscellaneous:** Range (grass/mats), credit cards (MC, V), BF, FF.

COLORADO

★★★★ **FOX HOLLOW AT LAKEWOOD GOLF COURSE**
PU-13410 W. Morrison Rd., Lakewood, 80228, Jefferson County, (303)986-7888, 15 miles from Denver. **E-mail:** judyb@lakewood.org. **Web:** www.golffoxhollow.com. **Facility Holes:** 27. **Green Fee:** $38. **Cart Fee:** $12/Person. **Walking Policy:** Unrestricted walking. **Opened:** 1993. **Architect:** Denis Griffiths. **Season:** Year-round. **To obtain tee times:** Call up to 6 days in advance. **Miscellaneous:** Reduced fees (seniors, juniors), range (grass/mats), credit cards (MC, V), BF, FF.
CANYON/LINKS (18 Combo)
Yards: 7,030/4,802. **Par:** 71/71. **Course Rating:** 72.3/67.5. **Slope:** 134/112. **Walkability:** 5.
CANYON/MEADOW (18 Combo)
Yards: 6,808/4,439. **Par:** 71/71. **Course Rating:** 71.2/65.3. **Slope:** 138/107. **Walkability:** 2.
Notes: Ranked 24th in 1996 America's Top 75 Affordable Courses.
MEADOW/LINKS (18 Combo)
Yards: 6,888/4,801. **Par:** 72/72. **Course Rating:** 71.1/66.6. **Slope:** 132/107. **Walkability:** 2.
Reader Comments: Three 9's with different character … Speed of play is monitored and kept up … Best combination is Canyon and Meadows … Great use of terrain … Every hole kept me interested … Bring all your shots! … Don't overlook this gem … Tough to get on … Play this course from tips, if you dare.

★★½ **GLENEAGLE GOLF CLUB**
SP-345 Mission Hills Way, Colorado Springs, 80908, El Paso County, (719)488-0900, 5 miles from Colorado Springs. **Facility Holes:** 18. **Yards:** 7,276/5,655. **Par:** 72/72. **Course Rating:** 73.9/73.2. **Slope:** 128/120. **Green Fee:** $14/$29. **Cart Fee:** $22/Person. **Walking Policy:** Unrestricted walking. **Walkability:** 4. **Opened:** 1972. **Architect:** Frank Hummel. **Season:** Year-round. **High:** March-Oct. **To obtain tee times:** Call golf shop. **Miscellaneous:** Reduced fees (weekdays, twilight), range (grass), credit cards (MC, V, AE, D).

THE GOLF CLUB AT REDLANDS MESA
PU-2325 W. Ridges Blvd., Grand Junction, 81503, Mesa County, (970)263-9270, 240 miles from Denver. **E-mail:** redlandsgolf@cs.com. **Web:** www.redlandsgolf.com. **Facility Holes:** 18. **Yards:** 7,007/4,916. **Par:** 72/72. **Course Rating:** 71.7/68.6. **Slope:** 135/113. **Green Fee:** $39/$50. **Cart Fee:** $12/Person. **Walking Policy:** Unrestricted walking. **Walkability:** 4. **Opened:** 2001. **Architect:** Jim Engh. **Season:** Year-round. **High:** March-Oct. **To obtain tee times:** Call up to 5 days in advance. **Miscellaneous:** Reduced fees (weekdays, juniors), range (grass), credit cards (MC, V, AE, D), BF, FF.
Notes: Ranked 1st in 2001 Best New Affordable Courses.

★★★★ **GRAND LAKE GOLF COURSE**
PU-1415 County Rd. 48, Grand Lake, 80447, Grand County, (970)627-8008, 100 miles from Denver. **Facility Holes:** 18. **Yards:** 6,542/5,685. **Par:** 72/74. **Course Rating:** 70.5/70.9. **Slope:** 131/123. **Green Fee:** $55. **Cart Fee:** $25/Cart. **Walking Policy:** Unrestricted walking. **Walkability:** 3. **Opened:** 1964. **Architect:** Dick Phelps. **Season:** May-Nov. **High:** July-Aug. **To obtain tee times:** Call up to 2 days in advance. **Miscellaneous:** Metal spikes, range (grass/mats), credit cards (MC, V, D), BF, FF.
Reader Comments: Feels like you are alone … Better be straight or you're with the bears! … Likely to see deer or fox … Nice course in deep woods … Excellent views … Tricky track, interesting.

★★★½ **GRANDOTE PEAKS GOLF CLUB**
PU-5540 Hwy. 12, La Veta, 81055, Huerfano County, (719)742-3391, (800)457-9986, 60 miles from Pueblo. **E-mail:** granpeak@rmi.net. **Web:** www.grandotepeaks.com. **Facility Holes:** 18. **Yards:** 7,085/5,608. **Par:** 72/73. **Course Rating:** 72.9/70.6. **Slope:** 133/130. **Green Fee:** $24/$65. **Cart Fee:** $11/Person. **Walking Policy:** Unrestricted walking. **Walkability:** 3. **Opened:** 1986. **Architect:** Tom Weiskopf/Jay Morrish. **Season:** April-Oct. **High:** June-Sept. **To obtain tee times:** Call golf shop. **Miscellaneous:** Reduced fees (weekdays, twilight, seniors, juniors), range (grass), credit cards (MC, V, AE, D), BF, FF.
Reader Comments: Out of the way, but a must play … A couple of unfair holes … Mountain 9 and links 9 … Enjoyable to play … An under-appreciated gem … Not crowded, good value … Beautiful surroundings … Take an extra sleeve of balls … High altitude makes for long drives.

★★★ **HAYMAKER GOLF COURSE**
PU-34855 U.S. Hwy. 40 E., Steamboat Springs, 80477, Routt County, (970)870-1846, (888)282-2969, 80 miles from Boulder. **Facility Holes:** 18. **Yards:** 7,308/5,059. **Par:** 72/72. **Course Rating:** 73.3/66.9. **Slope:** 131/117. **Green Fee:** $54/$79. **Cart Fee:** $16/Person. **Walking Policy:** Unrestricted walking. **Walkability:** 2. **Opened:** 1997. **Architect:** Keith Foster. **Season:** May-Oct. **High:** June-Sept. **To obtain tee times:** Call golf shop. **Miscellaneous:** Reduced fees (weekdays, guests, twilight), range (grass/mats), credit cards (MC, V, AE, D), BF, FF.
Reader Comments: Great design … Playing the course and seeing the rolling dunes is much

different than the expectation driving by on the highway :.. Very difficult greens to putt ... Links in the mountains ... Great course ... Fair course with OB trouble on every hole.

HERITAGE EAGLE BEND GOLF CLUB
SP-23155 E. Heritage Pkwy., Aurora, 80016, Arapahoe County, (303)400-6700, 20 miles from Denver. **E-mail:** eaglebendgc@cs.com. **Web:** www.heritageeaglebend.com. **Facility Holes:** 18. **Green Fee:** $20/$70. **Cart Fee:** Included in green fee. **Walking Policy:** Mandatory carts. **Walkability:** 5. **Opened:** 2000. **Architect:** Arthur Hills. **Season:** Year-round. **High:** April-Oct. **To obtain tee times:** Call up to 7 days in advance. **Miscellaneous:** Reduced fees (twilight, juniors), credit cards (MC, V, AE), FF.

★★★½ THE HERITAGE GOLF COURSE AT WESTMOOR
PU-10555 Westmoor Dr., Westminster, 80021, Adams County, (303)469-2974, 8 miles from Denver. **E-mail:** bcarlson@ci.westminster.co.us. **Web:** www.ci.westminster.co.us. **Facility Holes:** 18. **Yards:** 7,345/5,200. **Par:** 72/72. **Course Rating:** 74.0/68.0. **Slope:** 131/116. **Green Fee:** $26/$41. **Cart Fee:** $13/Person. **Walking Policy:** Unrestricted walking. **Walkability:** 4. **Opened:** 1999. **Architect:** M. Hurdzan/D. Fry. **Season:** Year-round. **High:** April-Oct. **To obtain tee times:** Call up to 7 days in advance. **Miscellaneous:** Reduced fees (weekdays, seniors, juniors), range (grass/mats), credit cards (MC, V, AE, D), BF, FF.
Reader Comments: Don't try to walk ... No. 13 is a great par 5 ... A fun course with a lot of different holes ... Friendly people, good marshals ... Incredible shape for new track ... Hit it straight.

★★★½ HIGHLAND HILLS GOLF COURSE
PU-2200 Clubhouse Dr., Greeley, 80634, Weld County, (970)330-7327, 50 miles from Denver. **Facility Holes:** 18. **Yards:** 6,723/6,002. **Par:** 71/75. **Course Rating:** 73.1/73.4. **Slope:** 129/129. **Green Fee:** $17/$27. **Cart Fee:** $26/Cart. **Walking Policy:** Unrestricted walking. **Walkability:** 3. **Opened:** 1961. **Architect:** Frank Hummel. **Season:** Feb.-Nov. **High:** May-Oct. **To obtain tee times:** Call up to 7 days in advance. **Miscellaneous:** Reduced fees (twilight, seniors), credit cards (MC, V, D), BF, FF.
Reader Comments: Very challenging, a lot of trees, pace needs to improve ... Good value ... It's laid out for all class of players ... Front 9 is long and straight while back side is short and crooked ... Lots of trees.

★★★★ HIGHLANDS RANCH GOLF CLUB
SP-9000 Creekside Way, Highlands Ranch, 80129, Douglas County, (303)471-0000, 15 miles from Denver. **Facility Holes:** 18. **Yards:** 7,192/5,405. **Par:** 72/72. **Course Rating:** 71.6/69.9. **Slope:** 123/120. **Green Fee:** $45/$70. **Cart Fee:** Included in green fee. **Walking Policy:** Unrestricted walking. **Walkability:** 4. **Opened:** 1998. **Architect:** Hale Irwin. **Season:** Year-round. **High:** June-Oct. **To obtain tee times:** Call up to 5 days in advance. **Miscellaneous:** Reduced fees (weekdays, seniors, juniors), range (grass), credit cards (MC, V, AE, D), BF, FF.
Reader Comments: Wish this was a muni ... Great service ... Very playable ... Nice variety of holes ... Pace of play is fast ... Nice course, new clubhouse ... Plays like a private country club ... The higher cost limits play.

★★★ HILLCREST GOLF CLUB
PU-2300 Rim Dr., Durango, 81301, La Plata County, (970)247-1499, 1 mile from Durango. **Facility Holes:** 18. **Yards:** 6,838/5,252. **Par:** 71/71. **Course Rating:** 71.2/68.1. **Slope:** 125/111. **Green Fee:** $20. **Cart Fee:** $18/Cart. **Walking Policy:** Unrestricted walking. **Walkability:** 3. **Opened:** 1969. **Architect:** Frank Hummel. **Season:** March-Dec. **High:** May-Sept. **To obtain tee times:** Call golf shop. **Miscellaneous:** Reduced fees (twilight), metal spikes, range (grass/mats), credit cards (MC, V, D), BF, FF.
Reader Comments: The course is basic by design but is maintained excellently ... Fast greens ... For the price it's quite a deal ... Very nice public course ... Pace of play was a little slow.

THE HOMESTEAD AT MURPHY CREEK
PU-1700 S. Old Tom Morris Rd., Aurora, 80018, Arapahoe County, (303)361-7300, 20 miles from Denver. **E-mail:** mcreekgolf@aol.com. **Web:** www.golfaurora.com. **Facility Holes:** 18. **Yards:** 7,456/5,335. **Par:** 72/72. **Course Rating:** 74.6/68.7. **Slope:** 131/120. **Green Fee:** $28/$38. **Cart Fee:** $12/Person. **Walking Policy:** Unrestricted walking. **Walkability:** 2. **Opened:** 2000. **Architect:** Ken Kavanaugh. **Season:** Year-round. **High:** April-Oct. **To obtain tee times:** Call up to 4 days in advance. **Miscellaneous:** Reduced fees (twilight, seniors, juniors), range (grass), credit cards (MC, V, AE, D), BF, FF.

★★★ HYLAND HILLS GOLF COURSE *Value*
PU-9650 N. Sheridan Blvd., Westminster, 80030, Adams County, (303)428-6526, 10 miles from Denver. **Facility Holes:** 43. **Yards:** 7,021/5,654. **Par:** 72/73. **Course Rating:** 71.9/71.9. **Slope:** 132/120. **Green Fee:** $16/$21. **Cart Fee:** $20/Cart. **Walking Policy:** Unrestricted walking. **Walkability:** 2. **Opened:** 1964. **Architect:** Henry Hughes. **Season:** Year-round. **High:** June-Aug. **To obtain tee times:** Call golf shop. **Miscellaneous:** Reduced fees (twilight), range

(grass/mats), caddies, credit cards (MC, V, AE).
Notes: Ranked 18th in 2001 Best in State.
Reader Comments: A nice course, but impossible to get times … Pace of play on weekends is 5-6 hours … Greens are always excellent condition … Good course, fun to play … A fair test for mid-high handicappers … Front tight, many trees, back open and fair.
Special Notes: Also has a 9-hole regulation Blue Course, 9-hole South Course and 7-hole North Course.

★★★★ INDIAN PEAKS GOLF CLUB
PU-2300 Indian Peaks Trail, Lafayette, 80026, Boulder County, (303)666-4706, 10 miles from Boulder. **Facility Holes:** 18. **Yards:** 7,083/5,468. **Par:** 72/72. **Course Rating:** 72.5/69.9. **Slope:** 134/116. **Green Fee:** $34/$38. **Cart Fee:** $24/Cart. **Walking Policy:** Unrestricted walking. **Opened:** 1993. **Architect:** Hale Irwin/Dick Phelps. **Season:** Year-round. **High:** May-Sept. **To obtain tee times:** Call up to 7 days in advance. **Miscellaneous:** Reduced fees (weekdays), range (grass/mats), credit cards (MC, V, D), BF, FF.
Reader Comments: The price is a little steep if you aren't a resident … All a municipal course should be—wide fairways, but real rough if you miss them, large greens in great shape, not a lot of out-of-bounds … True greens … Good test … Great practice facilities and service.

★★½ INDIAN TREE GOLF CLUB
PU-7555 Wadsworth Blvd., Arvada, 80003, Jefferson County, (303)403-2541, 10 miles from Denver. **E-mail:** proabrams@yahoo.com. **Facility Holes:** 27. **Yards:** 6,742/5,850. **Par:** 70/75. **Course Rating:** 69.6/71.4. **Slope:** 114/116. **Green Fee:** $25. **Cart Fee:** $22/Cart. **Walking Policy:** Unrestricted walking. **Walkability:** 3. **Opened:** 1970. **Architect:** Dick Phelps. **Season:** Year-round. **To obtain tee times:** Call up to 2 days in advance. **Miscellaneous:** Reduced fees (juniors), range (grass/mats), credit cards (MC, V, AE), BF, FF.
Special Notes: Also has a 9-hole course.

★★★★ INVERNESS HOTEL & GOLF CLUB
SP-200 Inverness Dr. W., Englewood, 80112, Arapahoe County, (303)397-7878, (800)346-4891, 3 miles from Denver. **Facility Holes:** 18. **Yards:** 6,889/5,681. **Par:** 70/71. **Course Rating:** 71.8/71.7. **Slope:** 131/133. **Green Fee:** $65/$115. **Cart Fee:** Included in green fee. **Walking Policy:** Unrestricted walking. **Walkability:** 3. **Opened:** 1974. **Architect:** Press Maxwell. **Season:** Year-round. **To obtain tee times:** Call golf shop. **Miscellaneous:** Reduced fees (twilight), range (grass), lodging (200 rooms), credit cards (MC, V, AE, D, DC), BF, FF.
Reader Comments: Very fast greens and well kept … Will test any golfer … Well worth the money … Great par 3 from back tees … Need to stay at hotel to play … Nice track, good service.

★★½ JOHN F. KENNEDY GOLF CLUB
PU-10500 E. Hampden Ave., Aurora, 80014, Arapahoe County, (303)755-0105, (800)661-1419, 8 miles from Denver. **Facility Holes:** 36. **Green Fee:** $17/$21. **Cart Fee:** $24/Cart. **Walking Policy:** Unrestricted walking. **Walkability:** 4. **Opened:** 1963. **Architect:** Henry Hughes/Dick Phelps. **Season:** Year-round. **High:** April-Sept. **To obtain tee times:** Call golf shop. **Miscellaneous:** Reduced fees (seniors, juniors), range (grass/mats), credit cards (MC, V).
EAST/CREEK (18 combo)
Yards: 6,886/5,769. **Par:** 71/71. **Course Rating:** 71.6. **Slope:** 131.
WEST/CREEK (18 combo)
Yards: 6,751/5,729. **Par:** 74/71. **Course Rating:** 70.9. **Slope:** 124.
WEST/EAST (18 combo)
Yards: 7,035/6,456. **Par:** 75/73. **Course Rating:** 71.7. **Slope:** 119.
Special Notes: Also has a 9-hole course.

KEYSTONE RANCH
R-1239 Keystone Ranch Rd., Keystone, 80435, Summit County, (970)496-4250, (800)354-4386, 70 miles from Denver. **E-mail:** skeiser@vailresorts.com. **Facility Holes:** 36. **Cart Fee:** Included in green fee. **Walking Policy:** Walking at certain times. **Season:** May-Oct. **High:** July-Sept. **To obtain tee times:** Call up to 7 days in advance. **Miscellaneous:** Reduced fees (guests, twilight, juniors), range (grass/mats), lodging (2500 rooms), credit cards (MC, V, AE, D, DC), BF, FF.
★★★★ KEYSTONE RANCH GOLF COURSE (18)
Yards: 7,090/5,596. **Par:** 72/72. **Course Rating:** 71.4/70.7. **Slope:** 130/129. **Green Fee:** $125/$140. **Walkability:** 3. **Opened:** 1980. **Architect:** Robert T. Jones Jr.
Notes: Ranked 17th in 1999 Best in State.
Reader Comments: Great mountain course … Incredible views … Favors long hitters … Scenic, well managed … Big, long bruiser even for high altitude.
RIVER COURSE AT KEYSTONE (18)
Yards: 6,886/4,762. **Par:** 72/70. **Course Rating:** 70.3/64.5. **Slope:** 131/113. **Green Fee:** $90/$140. **Walkability:** 5. **Opened:** 2000. **Architect:** Hurdzan/Fry.

★★½ LAKE ARBOR GOLF COURSE
PU-8600 Wadsworth Blvd., Arvada, 80003, Jefferson County, (303)423-1650, 15 miles from Denver. **E-mail:** lkauffman@ci.arvada.co.us. **Web:** www.lakearborgolf.com. **Facility Holes:** 18. **Yards:** 5,865/4,965. **Par:** 70/69. **Course Rating:** 66.7/71.1. **Slope:** 108/113. **Green Fee:** $19/$23. **Cart Fee:** $23/Cart. **Walking Policy:** Unrestricted walking. **Walkability:** 1. **Opened:** 1971. **Architect:** Clark Glasson. **Season:** Year-round. **High:** April-Sept. **To obtain tee times:** Call golf shop. **Miscellaneous:** Range (mats), credit cards (MC, V), BF, FF.

★★★★ LEGACY RIDGE GOLF COURSE
PU-10801 Legacy Ridge Pkwy., Westminster, 80030, Adams County, (303)438-8997, 15 miles from Denver. **E-mail:** rfielder@cl.westminster.co.us. **Facility Holes:** 18. **Yards:** 7,212/5,383. **Par:** 72/72. **Course Rating:** 74.0/70.6. **Slope:** 144/122. **Green Fee:** $26/$41. **Cart Fee:** $26/Cart. **Walking Policy:** Unrestricted walking. **Walkability:** 3. **Opened:** 1994. **Architect:** Arthur Hills. **Season:** Year-round. **High:** April-Oct. **To obtain tee times:** Call up to 7 days in advance. **Miscellaneous:** Reduced fees (weekdays, twilight, seniors, juniors), range (grass/mats), credit cards (MC, V, AE, D), BF, FF.
Reader Comments: Keep it on the fairway ... Bring extra balls ... Narrow fairways, fast greens ... Homes everywhere ... A must play ... Long rough penalizes errant shots ... Arthur Hills grace and excellence ... Great practice area ... Hard to believe its not a country club ... Extra tough when wind blows.

★★★½ LONE TREE GOLF CLUB & HOTEL
PU-9808 Sunningdale Blvd., Littleton, 80124, Arapahoe County, (303)799-9940, 15 miles from Denver. **Facility Holes:** 18. **Yards:** 7,012/5,340. **Par:** 72/72. **Course Rating:** 72.1/70.6. **Slope:** 127/120. **Green Fee:** $34/$53. **Cart Fee:** $11/Person. **Walking Policy:** Unrestricted walking. **Walkability:** 3. **Opened:** 1983. **Architect:** Arnold Palmer/Ed Seay. **Season:** Year-round. **High:** March-Oct. **To obtain tee times:** Call golf shop. **Miscellaneous:** Reduced fees (guests, twilight, seniors), range (grass), lodging (15 rooms), credit cards (MC, V, AE, D), BF, FF.
Reader Comments: Pricey but worth it ... Pace of play is slow ... Great views, lots of elevation changes and challenging ... Very challenging track, each hole different.

★★½ MAD RUSSIAN GOLF COURSE
PU-2100 Country Club Pkwy., Milliken, 80543, Weld County, (970)587-5157, 40 miles from Denver. **Facility Holes:** 18. **Yards:** 5,665/4,375. **Par:** 70/70. **Course Rating:** 65.2/64.1. **Slope:** 117/103. **Green Fee:** $16/$27. **Cart Fee:** $24/Cart. **Walking Policy:** Unrestricted walking. **Walkability:** 4. **Opened:** 1987. **Architect:** Robert Ehrlich. **Season:** Year-round. **To obtain tee times:** Call up to 7 days in advance. **Miscellaneous:** Reduced fees (weekdays, twilight, seniors, juniors), range (grass), credit cards (MC, V), BF, FF.

★★★★ MARIANA BUTTE GOLF COURSE
PU-701 Clubhouse Dr., Loveland, 80537, Larimer County, (970)667-8308, 45 miles from Denver. **Facility Holes:** 18. **Yards:** 6,572/5,420. **Par:** 72/72. **Course Rating:** 71.5/70.2. **Slope:** 132/121. **Green Fee:** $26/$33. **Cart Fee:** $24/Cart. **Walking Policy:** Unrestricted walking. **Walkability:** 4. **Opened:** 1992. **Architect:** Dick Phelps. **Season:** Year-round. **To obtain tee times:** Call up to 5 days in advance. **Miscellaneous:** Reduced fees (twilight), range (grass/mats), credit cards (MC, V, D).
Reader Comments: Good variety including a few fun elevation changes ... Extremely nice for a public course ... Remains one of my favorites ... Must play when in Colorado ... It's a blast ... Fun course, water, greens good ... Hard to get to, but very nice ... Picture perfect—wish I had a camera ... Gorgeous views.

★★★½ MEADOW HILLS GOLF COURSE
PU-3609 S. Dawson St., Aurora, 80014, Arapahoe County, (303)690-2500, 6 miles from Denver. **Facility Holes:** 18. **Yards:** 6,492/5,417. **Par:** 70/72. **Course Rating:** 70.5/70.2. **Slope:** 133/120. **Green Fee:** $22/$26. **Cart Fee:** $11/Person. **Walking Policy:** Unrestricted walking. **Walkability:** 2. **Opened:** 1957. **Architect:** Henry Hughes. **Season:** Year-round. **High:** April-Oct. **To obtain tee times:** Call up to 4 days in advance. **Miscellaneous:** Reduced fees (weekdays, twilight, seniors, juniors), range (grass/mats), caddies, credit cards (MC, V, AE, D), BF, FF.
Reader Comments: Lots of trees, must keep it in the fairway to score ... Sneaky long ... Easy to walk ... Tight course, fun layout, small greens ... For a city-run course, always busy and hard to get on ... Good test ... Love this course! ... Nice relaxing round of golf—woman friendly.

★★★½ THE MEADOWS GOLF CLUB
PU-6937 S. Simms, Littleton, 80127, Jefferson County, (303)972-8831, 15 miles from Denver. **Facility Holes:** 18. **Yards:** 7,011/5,437. **Par:** 72/72. **Course Rating:** 72.2/71.1. **Slope:** 135/124. **Green Fee:** $14/$31. **Cart Fee:** $12/Person. **Walking Policy:** Unrestricted walking. **Walkability:** 4. **Opened:** 1984. **Architect:** Dick Phelps. **Season:** Year-round. **High:** May-Sept. **To obtain tee times:** Call up to 5 days in advance. **Miscellaneous:** Reduced fees (seniors, juniors), range

(grass), credit cards (MC, V), BF, FF.

Reader Comments: Food is good, nice layout ... A good test with variety ... Play is slow ... Can't beat this for the money.

★★½ MIRA VISTA GOLF COURSE
PU-10110 E. Golfer's Way, Aurora, 80010, Arapahoe County, (303)340-1520, 5 miles from Denver. **E-mail:** mvgolf@gte.net. **Facility Holes:** 18. **Yards:** 6,870/5,919. **Par:** 72/73. **Course Rating:** 71.7/70.5. **Slope:** 130/124. **Green Fee:** $14/$27. **Cart Fee:** $11/Cart. **Walking Policy:** Unrestricted walking. **Walkability:** 2. **Opened:** 1972. **Architect:** Bob Baldock. **Season:** Year-round. **To obtain tee times:** Call up to 5 days in advance. **Miscellaneous:** Reduced fees (weekdays, twilight, seniors, juniors), range (grass), credit cards (MC, V), BF, FF.

MURPHY CREEK GOLF COURSE
PU-1700 S. Old Tom Morris Rd., Aurora, 80018, Arapahoe County, (303)361-7300, 20 miles from Denver. **Web:** www.golfaurora.com. **Facility Holes:** 18. **Yards:** 7,456/5,335. **Par:** 72/72. **Course Rating:** 74.6/68.7. **Slope:** 131/120. **Green Fee:** $30/$38. **Cart Fee:** $12/Person. **Walking Policy:** Unrestricted walking. **Walkability:** 5. **Opened:** 2000. **Architect:** Ken Kavanaugh. **Season:** Year-round. **High:** June-Aug. **To obtain tee times:** Call up to 4 days in advance. **Miscellaneous:** Reduced fees (weekdays, twilight, seniors, juniors), range (grass), credit cards (MC, V, AE, D), BF, FF.
Notes: Ranked 10th in 2001 Best New Affordable Courses.

★★★★ THE OLDE COURSE AT LOVELAND
PU-2115 W. 29th St., Loveland, 80538, Larimer County, (970)667-5256, 45 miles from Denver. **Facility Holes:** 18. **Yards:** 6,870/5,498. **Par:** 72/72. **Course Rating:** 70.9/70.6. **Slope:** 125/124. **Green Fee:** $16/$25. **Cart Fee:** $24/Cart. **Walking Policy:** Unrestricted walking. **Walkability:** 2. **Opened:** 1959. **Architect:** Dick Phelps/Henry Hughes. **Season:** Year-round. **To obtain tee times:** Call up to 5 days in advance. **Miscellaneous:** Reduced fees (twilight, juniors), range (grass/mats), credit cards (MC, V), BF, FF.

Reader Comments: Love to play this one, especially back 9 ... Nice elevation changes ... Solid old course ... Greens in very good shape ... Getting better with age ... All time favorite, hard from the back ... Lots of big 'old' trees.

★★★★½ OMNI INTERLOCKEN RESORT GOLF CLUB *Condition*
R-800 Eldorado Blvd., Broomfield, 80021, Boulder County, (303)464-9000, 20 miles from Denver. **E-mail:** lcollins@omnihotels.com. **Web:** www.omnihotels.com. **Facility Holes:** 27. **Green Fee:** $55/$85. **Cart Fee:** Included in green fee. **Walking Policy:** Unrestricted walking. **Walkability:** 4. **Opened:** 1999. **Architect:** D. Graham/G. Panks/G. Stephenson. **Season:** Year-round. **High:** April-Sept. **To obtain tee times:** Call up to 14 days in advance. **Miscellaneous:** Reduced fees (twilight), range (grass), lodging (390 rooms), credit cards (MC, V, AE, D, DC), BF, FF.
ELDORADO /VISTA (18 combo)
Yards: 6,957/5,161. **Par:** 72/72. **Course Rating:** 72.3/68.2. **Slope:** 136/130.
SUNSHINE/ELDORADO (18 combo)
Yards: 6,955/5,200. **Par:** 72/72. **Course Rating:** 72.2/69.4. **Slope:** 133/132.
VISTA/SUNSHINE COURSE (18 combo)
Yards: 7,040/5,655. **Par:** 72/72. **Course Rating:** 72.5/71.8. **Slope:** 136/142.
Notes: Ranked 5th in 2001 Best in State.

Reader Comments: A quality, classy golf facility. Outstanding use of terrain. Great view ... Excellent course, somewhat short. Very upscale, classy, luxurious. Staff especially thoughtful. Great links, great service.

★★½ OVERLAND PARK GOLF COURSE
PU-1801 S. Huron St., Denver, 80223, Denver County, (303)777-7331, 2 miles from Denver. **Facility Holes:** 18. **Yards:** 6,312/6,126. **Par:** 72/74. **Course Rating:** 69.2/72.7. **Slope:** 114/115. **Green Fee:** $17/$21. **Cart Fee:** $22/Cart. **Walking Policy:** Unrestricted walking. **Walkability:** 1. **Opened:** 1895. **Season:** Year-round. **High:** April-Nov. **To obtain tee times:** Call golf shop. **Miscellaneous:** Reduced fees (weekdays, seniors, juniors), range (grass/mats), credit cards (MC, V).

★★★★ PAGOSA SPRINGS GOLF CLUB
R-One Pines Club Place, Pagosa Springs, 81147, Archuleta County, (970)731-4755, 55 miles from Durango. **Web:** www.pagosagolf@pagosa.net. **Facility Holes:** 27. **Green Fee:** $20/$38. **Cart Fee:** $12/Person. **Walking Policy:** Unrestricted walking. **Walkability:** 4. **Opened:** 1972. **Architect:** Johnny Bulla. **Season:** April-Oct. **High:** July-Aug. **To obtain tee times:** Call golf shop. **Miscellaneous:** Reduced fees (twilight, juniors), range (grass/mats), credit cards (MC, V, AE, D).
PINON/MEADOWS COURSE (18 Combo)
Yards: 7,221/5,400. **Par:** 72/72. **Course Rating:** 72.9/68.0. **Slope:** 125/110.

COLORADO

PINON/PONDEROSA COURSE (18 Combo)
Yards: 6,670/5,320. **Par:** 71/71. **Course Rating:** 69.4/67.4. **Slope:** 119/107.
PONDEROSA/MEADOWS COURSE (18 Combo)
Yards: 6,913/5,074. **Par:** 71/71. **Course Rating:** 70.9/66.2. **Slope:** 123/108.
Reader Comments: If you are in the area, stop and play this one ... Beautiful scenery to go along with a beautiful course ... Excellent greens and fairways ... Three very different 9s ... Typical resort course ... Good holes with nice elevation charges.

★★½ **PARK HILL GOLF CLUB**
PU-4141 E. 35th Ave., Denver, 80207, Arapahoe County, (303)333-5411, 1 mile from Denver.
Facility Holes: 18. **Yards:** 6,585/5,811. **Par:** 71/72. **Course Rating:** 69.4/73.4. **Slope:** 120/124.
Green Fee: $19/$22. **Walking Policy:** Unrestricted walking. **Opened:** 1931. **Season:** Year-round. **High:** May-Aug. **To obtain tee times:** Call golf shop. **Miscellaneous:** Metal spikes, credit cards (MC, V).

★★★ **PATTY JEWETT GOLF COURSE**
PU-900 E. Espanola, Colorado Springs, 80907, El Paso County, (719)385-6938. **E-mail:** gimmiegolf1@msd.com. **Facility Holes:** 27. **Yards:** 6,928/5,758. **Par:** 72/75. **Course Rating:** 71.5/73.0. **Slope:** 124/124. **Green Fee:** $20/$27. **Cart Fee:** $22/Cart. **Walking Policy:** Unrestricted walking. **Walkability:** 2. **Opened:** 1898. **Architect:** Willy Campbell/Mark Mahanna. **Season:** Year-round. **High:** April-Oct. **To obtain tee times:** Call up to 7 days in advance. **Miscellaneous:** Range (mats), BF, FF.
Reader Comments: Great breakfast ... Friendly, helpful personnel ... Nice old course ... Layout and scenery are terrific, I have played this course for 30 years, enjoy more than Pebble Beach ... Very busy, well groomed, great greens.
Special Notes: Also has a 9-hole course.

★★★★ **PELICAN LAKES GOLF & COUNTRY CLUB**
SP-1600 Pelican Lakes Point, Windsor, 80550, Weld County, (970)674-0930, (877)837-4653. **E-mail:** pelicanlakescc@aol.com. **Web:** www.pelicanlakesgolf.com. **Facility Holes:** 18. **Yards:** 7,214/6,039. **Par:** 72/72. **Course Rating:** 72.6/68.8. **Slope:** 127/120. **Green Fee:** $36/$46. **Cart Fee:** $12/Person. **Walking Policy:** Unrestricted walking. **Walkability:** 2. **Opened:** 1999. **Architect:** Ted Robinson. **Season:** Year-round. **High:** May-Sept. **To obtain tee times:** Call up to 7 days in advance. **Miscellaneous:** Reduced fees (weekdays, seniors, juniors), range (grass), credit cards (MC, V, AE, D), BF, FF.
Reader Comments: Great layout along the lakes ... Takes solid shots.... Neat log clubhouse ... Friendly, small town hominess ... Water, rivers, lakes everywhere ... Not as difficult as may seem, however very intimidating ... See how many you keep on land.

★★★★ **PINE CREEK GOLF CLUB**
PU-9850 Divot Trail, Colorado Springs, 80920, El Paso County, (719)594-9999, 2 miles from Colorado Springs. **E-mail:** pinecreek@codenet.net. **Web:** www.pinecreek.com. **Facility Holes:** 18. **Yards:** 7,194/5,314. **Par:** 72/72. **Course Rating:** 72.6/70.2. **Slope:** 139/122. **Green Fee:** $35. **Cart Fee:** $12/Person. **Walking Policy:** Walking at certain times. **Walkability:** 3. **Opened:** 1988. **Architect:** Dick Phelps. **Season:** Year-round. **High:** April-Oct. **To obtain tee times:** Call up to 7 days in advance. **Miscellaneous:** Reduced fees (weekdays), range (grass), credit cards (MC, V, AE, D), BF, FF.
Reader Comments: Good layout, several good holes ... Great course and usually not crowded ... A golf course that makes you think, from the first tee to the last green ... Very tough ... Subtle contours in greens. Uses the natural ravines and dunes.

POLE CREEK GOLF CLUB
PU-P.O. Box 3348, Winter Park, 80482, Grand County, (970)726-8847, (800)511-5076, 67 miles from Denver. **E-mail:** info@polecreekgolf.com. **Web:** www.polecreekgolf.com. **Facility Holes:** 27. **Green Fee:** $55/$80. **Cart Fee:** $13/Person. **Walking Policy:** Unrestricted walking. **Opened:** 1984. **Architect:** Denis Griffiths. **Season:** May-Oct. **High:** June-Sept. **To obtain tee times:** Call golf shop. **Miscellaneous:** Reduced fees (twilight, juniors), range (grass), credit cards (MC, V, AE, D), BF, FF.
★★★★ **MEADOW/RANCH** (18)
Yards: 7,106/5,008. **Par:** 72/72. **Course Rating:** 73.7/68.5. **Slope:** 145/130. **Walkability:** 2.
Notes: Ranked 19th in 2001 Best in State.
Reader Comments: Spectacular ... My favorite mountain course ... Great layout, beautiful views ... Elevated tee—about as heavenly as you can get ... Challenging for high-handicaps, very enjoyable experience.
RANCH/RIDGE (18)
Yards: 7,112/5,157. **Par:** 72/72. **Course Rating:** 73.8/69.0. **Slope:** 142/132. **Walkability:** 3.
RIDGE/MEADOW (18)
Yards: 7,100/5,101. **Par:** 72/72. **Course Rating:** 73.3/69.7. **Slope:** 139/132. **Walkability:** 3.

COLORADO

★★ PUEBLO CITY PARK GOLF COURSE
PU-3900 Thatcher Ave., Pueblo, 81005, Pueblo County, (719)561-4946, 40 miles from Colorado Springs. **Facility Holes:** 27. **Yards:** 6,500/5,974. **Par:** 70/73. **Course Rating:** 68.9/72.5. **Slope:** 111/114. **Green Fee:** $24/$26. **Cart Fee:** $18/Cart. **Walking Policy:** Unrestricted walking. **Walkability:** 1. **Opened:** 1908. **Architect:** WPS Project. **Season:** Year-round. **High:** April-Sept. **To obtain tee times:** Call golf shop. **Miscellaneous:** Reduced fees (weekdays, seniors, juniors), range (grass/mats), credit cards (MC, V), BF, FF. **Special Notes:** Also has a 9-hole executive course.

★★★ RACCOON CREEK GOLF COURSE
PU-7301 W. Bowles Ave., Littleton, 80123, Arapahoe County, (303)973-4653, 3 miles from Littleton. **Facility Holes:** 18. **Yards:** 7,045/5,130. **Par:** 72/72. **Course Rating:** 72.6/68.2. **Slope:** 128/125. **Green Fee:** $32/$40. **Cart Fee:** $12/Person. **Walking Policy:** Unrestricted walking. **Walkability:** 4. **Opened:** 1983. **Architect:** Dick Phelps/Brad Benz. **Season:** Year-round. **High:** May-Sept. **To obtain tee times:** Call golf shop. **Miscellaneous:** Reduced fees (weekdays, twilight, seniors, juniors), range (grass), credit cards (MC, V, D).
Reader Comments: Too much play on the course ... Pretty in the fall ... Flat course, good range, good food ... Fairways too narrow and lots of water ... Course begs to be played again ... Challenging greens ... Challenging par 3 over water.

THE RAVEN GOLF CLUB AT THREE PEAKS
SP-2929 Golden Eagle Rd., Silverthorne, 80498, Summit County, (970)262-3636, 65 miles from Denver. **E-mail:** kishr@ski-copper.com. **Web:** www.ravengolf.com. **Facility Holes:** 18. **Yards:** 7,413/5,235. **Par:** 72/72. **Course Rating:** 73.8/69.0. **Slope:** 129/117. **Green Fee:** $65/$140. **Cart Fee:** Included in green fee. **Walking Policy:** Mandatory carts. **Walkability:** 5. **Opened:** 2000. **Architect:** Lehman/Hurdzan/Fry. **Season:** May-Oct. **High:** July-Sept. **To obtain tee times:** Call up to 7 days in advance. **Miscellaneous:** Reduced fees (guests, twilight, juniors), range (grass), credit cards (MC, V, AE, D), BF, FF.

★★★★½ RED HAWK RIDGE GOLF CLUB
PU-2156 Red Hawk Ridge Dr., Castle Rock, 80104, Douglas County, (303)663-7150, 800-663-7150, 20 miles from Denver. **Web:** www.redhawkridge.com. **Facility Holes:** 18. **Yards:** 6,942/4,636. **Par:** 72/72. **Course Rating:** 71.6/67.5. **Slope:** 129/107. **Green Fee:** $40/$50. **Cart Fee:** $12/Person. **Walking Policy:** Unrestricted walking. **Walkability:** 4. **Opened:** 1999. **Architect:** Jim Engh. **Season:** Year-round. **High:** June-Sept. **To obtain tee times:** Call up to 7 days in advance. **Miscellaneous:** Reduced fees (weekdays, twilight, seniors, juniors), range (grass), credit cards (MC, V, AE), BF, FF.
Notes: Ranked 7th in 1999 Best New Affordable Public.
Reader Comments: The layout is outstanding ... Great views ... Very enjoyable, fair course ... Lots of elevation changes ... Wide fairways ... Hit it in the fairway and scoring on this course can boost the ego ... A shotmakers course ... Par 5s too short ... Great finishing hole.

★★★★½ THE RIDGE AT CASTLE PINES NORTH *Service+, Condition, Pace*
PU-1414 Castle Pines Pkwy., Castle Rock, 80104, Douglas County, (303)688-0100, 16 miles from Denver. **E-mail:** jsmall@troongolf.com. **Web:** www.troongolf.com. **Facility Holes:** 18. **Yards:** 7,013/5,001. **Par:** 71/71. **Course Rating:** 71.8/67.6. **Slope:** 143/123. **Green Fee:** $75/$120. **Cart Fee:** Included in green fee. **Walking Policy:** Walking at certain times. **Walkability:** 4. **Opened:** 1997. **Architect:** Tom Weiskopf. **Season:** March-Dec. **High:** May-Sept. **To obtain tee times:** Call up to 7 days in advance. **Miscellaneous:** Reduced fees (twilight), range (grass), credit cards (MC, V, AE), BF, FF.
Notes: Ranked 16th in 1999 Best in State.
Reader Comments: A country club for a day ... Everyone's favorite ... Each hole a new challenge ... Beauty is unsurpassed ... Great par 5s ... A 'must play' ... Front is open and rolling hills—back has majestic views of the rockies with many elevated tee boxes overlooking expansive fairways ... Love this course.

★★★ RIFLE CREEK GOLF COURSE
SP-3004 State Hwy.325, Rifle, 81650, Garfield County, (970)625-1093, (888)247-0370, 60 miles from Grand Junction. **Facility Holes:** 18. **Yards:** 6,241/5,131. **Par:** 72/72. **Course Rating:** 69.3/68.1. **Slope:** 123/120. **Green Fee:** $18/$34. **Cart Fee:** $12/Person. **Walking Policy:** Unrestricted walking. **Walkability:** 4. **Opened:** 1960. **Architect:** Dick Phelps. **Season:** Feb.-Nov. **High:** June-Sept. **To obtain tee times:** Call up to 4 days in advance. **Miscellaneous:** Reduced fees (twilight, juniors), range (grass/mats), credit cards (MC, V, D), BF, FF.
Reader Comments: Front 9 is old course, back 9 breathtaking views ... Some very unique holes on the mountain ... The back 9 will blow your mind.

★★★★ RIVER VALLEY RANCH GOLF CLUB
PU-303 River Valley Ranch Dr., Carbondale, 81623, Garfield County, (970)963-3625, 15 miles from Glenwood Springs. **Web:** www.rvrgolf.com. **Facility Holes:** 18. **Yards:** 7,348/5,168. **Par:** 72/72. **Course Rating:** 73.2/68.8. **Slope:** 125/114. **Green Fee:** $50/$65. **Cart Fee:** Included in green fee. **Walking Policy:** Unrestricted walking. **Walkability:** 2. **Opened:** 1998. **Architect:** Jay Morrish/Carter Morrish. **Season:** March-Nov. **High:** June-Sept. **To obtain tee times:** Call up to 90 days in advance. **Miscellaneous:** Reduced fees (twilight, seniors), range (grass), credit cards (MC, V, AE), BF, FF.
Reader Comments: Lovely course … Great scenery, challenging course … Great design … Holes 12-15 are a slice of heaven with long views in every direction … Very playable but challenging.

RIVERDALE GOLF CLUB
PU-13300 Riverdale Rd., Brighton, 80601, Adams County, (303)659-6700, 10 miles from Denver. **E-mail:** Riverdalegolf.com. **Web:** www.riverdalegolf.com. **Facility Holes:** 36. **Cart Fee:** $23/Cart. **Walking Policy:** Unrestricted walking. **Walkability:** 2. **Season:** Year-round. **High:** May-Oct. **To obtain tee times:** Call up to 7 days in advance. **Miscellaneous:** Range (grass/mats), credit cards (MC, V, AE), BF, FF.
★★★★½ **DUNES COURSE** (18) *Value*
Yards: 7,067/4,903. **Par:** 72/72. **Course Rating:** 72.1/67.5. **Slope:** 129/109. **Green Fee:** $25/$33. **Opened:** 1985. **Architect:** Pete Dye.
Notes: Ranked 17th in 2001 Best in State; 22nd in 1996 America's Top 75 Affordable Courses.
Reader Comments: For the money you can't do better … Excellent use of tall, native grass to define holes … Hit straight … Shotmaker's paradise! Gets jammed on weekends … Starter worked me in as a single without problem … Great practice facilities … Greens are outstanding.
★★★½ **KNOLLS COURSE** (18)
Yards: 6,784/5,876. **Par:** 71/73. **Course Rating:** 70.2/72.2. **Slope:** 118/117. **Green Fee:** $18/$23. **Opened:** 1963. **Architect:** Henry B. Hughes.
Reader Comments: Tough track from the tips … A very nice course … Great greens, nice walk … Don't like placement of canals … Couple holes need reworking.

★★★ RIVERVIEW GOLF COURSE
PU-13064 County Rd. 370, Sterling, 80751, Logan County, (970)522-3035, 120 miles from Denver. **E-mail:** peplspro@kci.com. **Web:** www.kci.net/~rivervw. **Facility Holes:** 18. **Yards:** 6,466/5,032. **Par:** 71/71. **Course Rating:** 69.6/67.7. **Slope:** 126/110. **Green Fee:** $18. **Walking Policy:** Unrestricted walking. **Walkability:** 3. **Opened:** 1980. **Architect:** Val Heim. **Season:** Year-round. **To obtain tee times:** Call up to 7 days in advance. **Miscellaneous:** Reduced fees (juniors), range (grass), credit cards (MC, AE, DC, CB), BF, FF.
Reader Comments: A lot of fun, especially the back-9.

★★★★ SADDLE ROCK GOLF COURSE
PU-21705 E. Arapahoe Rd., Aurora, 80016, Arapahoe County, (303)699-3939, 7 miles from Denver. **E-mail:** saddlerockgc@aol.com. **Facility Holes:** 18. **Yards:** 7,351/5,407. **Par:** 72/72. **Course Rating:** 73.7/70.9. **Slope:** 136/126. **Green Fee:** $32/$40. **Cart Fee:** $24/Cart. **Walking Policy:** Unrestricted walking. **Walkability:** 3. **Opened:** 1997. **Architect:** Dick Phelps. **Season:** Year-round. **High:** June-Aug. **To obtain tee times:** Call up to 4 days in advance. **Miscellaneous:** Reduced fees (weekdays, twilight, seniors, juniors), range (grass), caddies, credit cards (MC, V, AE, D), BF, FF.
Reader Comments: I love it … Great test of golf … Elevation changes, fast & fun greens … Tough course from the back tees … 10th hole is tough … Thinking man's course, tough when wind blows … Toughest pin placements in city—don't expect to score 1st time out.

SADDLEBACK GOLF CLUB
PU-8631 Frontier St., Firestone, 80520, Weld County, (303)833-5000, 15 miles from Denver. **E-mail:** rfielder@saddlebackgolf.com. **Web:** www.saddlebackgolf.com. **Facility Holes:** 18. **Green Fee:** $26/$36. **Cart Fee:** $20/Cart. **Walking Policy:** Unrestricted walking. **Walkability:** 2. **Opened:** 2001. **Architect:** Andy Johnson. **Season:** Year-round. **To obtain tee times:** Call up to 7 days in advance. **Miscellaneous:** Reduced fees (weekdays, twilight, seniors, juniors), range (grass), credit cards (MC, V), BF, FF.

★★★★½ SHERATON STEAMBOAT RESORT & GOLF CLUB
R-2000 Clubhouse Dr., Steamboat Springs, 80477, Routt County, (970)879-1391, (800)848-8878, 157 miles from Denver. **Web:** www.steamboat-sheraton.com. **Facility Holes:** 18. **Yards:** 6,902/5,536. **Par:** 72/72. **Course Rating:** 72.0/71.5. **Slope:** 138/127. **Green Fee:** $62/$110. **Cart Fee:** $20/Person. **Walking Policy:** Walking at certain times. **Walkability:** 4. **Opened:** 1974. **Architect:** Robert Trent Jones Jr. **Season:** May-Nov. **High:** June-Sept. **To obtain tee times:** Call golf shop. **Miscellaneous:** Reduced fees (guests, twilight, seniors, juniors), range (grass/mats), lodging (317 rooms), credit cards (MC, V, AE, D, All major), BF, FF.
Reader Comments: Wildlife galore … What views … Fun mountain course.

COLORADO

★★★★½ SHERATON TAMARRON RESORT
R-40292 Hwy. 550 N, Durango, 81301, La Plata County, (970)382-6700, (800)678-1000, 280 miles from Denver. **Facility Holes:** 18. **Yards:** 6,885/5,330. **Par:** 72/72. **Course Rating:** 73.0/70.6. **Slope:** 142/124. **Green Fee:** $69/$129. **Cart Fee:** Included in green fee. **Walking Policy:** Mandatory carts. **Walkability:** 5. **Opened:** 1974. **Architect:** Arthur Hills. **Season:** May-Oct. **High:** July-Sept. **To obtain tee times:** Call pro shop. **Miscellaneous:** Reduced fees (guests, juniors), range (mats), lodging (325 rooms), credit cards (MC, V, AE, D, DC, All major cards), BF, FF.
Notes: Ranked 14th in 1999 Best in State.
Reader Comments: Tough to get to but worth it ... Very nice resort course ... Wonderful track in wonderful setting, fantastic greens ... Who couldn't fall in love with this setting?.

★★★ SHINING MOUNTAIN GOLF CLUB
SP-100 Lucky Lady Dr., Woodland Park, 80863, Teller County, (719)687-7587, 18 miles from Colorado Springs. **Facility Holes:** 18. **Yards:** 6,617/5,092. **Par:** 72/71. **Course Rating:** 71.5/69.6. **Slope:** 133/126. **Green Fee:** $28/$38. **Cart Fee:** $12/Person. **Walking Policy:** Unrestricted walking. **Walkability:** 4. **Opened:** 1995. **Architect:** John Harbottle. **Season:** Year-round. **High:** July-Sept. **To obtain tee times:** Call up to 7 days in advance. **Miscellaneous:** Reduced fees (weekdays, seniors, juniors), range (grass/mats), credit cards (MC, V, AE, D), BF, FF.
Reader Comments: Good tough course ... Narrow fairways, serious rough ... Very challenging ... Beautiful mountain course ... Doesn't appear to be that tough, until you add it up ... Fun.
Special Notes: Formerly Woodland Park Fujiki Golf & Country Club.

★★★½ SNOWMASS CLUB GOLF COURSE
R-P.O. Box G-2, Snowmass Village, 81615, Pitkin County, (970)923-3148, (800)525-6200, 7 miles from Aspen. **Facility Holes:** 18. **Yards:** 6,662/5,056. **Par:** 71/71. **Course Rating:** 70.1/67.5. **Slope:** 134/127. **Green Fee:** $60/$98. **Cart Fee:** Included in green fee. **Walking Policy:** Unrestricted walking. **Walkability:** 4. **Opened:** 1970. **Architect:** Arnold Palmer/Ed Seay. **Season:** May-Oct. **High:** July-Sept. **To obtain tee times:** Call golf shop. **Miscellaneous:** Reduced fees (guests, twilight, juniors), range (grass), lodging (74 rooms), credit cards (MC, V, AE, D).
Reader Comments: Tough in the wind ... Mountain views are fantastic.

★★★★½ SONNENALP GOLF CLUB *Pace+*
R-1265 Berry Creek Rd., Edwards, 81632, Eagle County, (970)477-5370, (800)-654-8312, 110 miles from Denver. **E-mail:** golf@sonnenalp.com. **Web:** www.sonnenalp.com. **Facility Holes:** 18. **Yards:** 7,059/5,293. **Par:** 71/71. **Course Rating:** 73.1/69.4. **Slope:** 139/125. **Green Fee:** $52/$160. **Cart Fee:** Included in green fee. **Walking Policy:** Unrestricted walking. **Walkability:** 3. **Opened:** 1981. **Architect:** Bob Cupp/Jay Morrish. **Season:** April-Nov. **High:** June-Sept. **To obtain tee times:** Call up to 7 days in advance. **Miscellaneous:** Reduced fees (weekdays, guests, twilight, juniors), metal spikes, range (grass), credit cards (MC, V, AE, D), BF, FF.
Reader Comments: Shh! Don't let too many people know ... Lots of condos, houses ... Best greens in the mountains ... Nice variety of holes ... Overall, very nice but a little pricey.

★★½ SOUTH SUBURBAN GOLF COURSE
PU-7900 S. Colorado Blvd., Centennial, 80122, Arapahoe County, (303)770-5508, 9 miles from Denver. **Web:** www.sspr.org. **Facility Holes:** 27. **Yards:** 6,790/5,274. **Par:** 72/72. **Course Rating:** 70.1/69.3. **Slope:** 122/119. **Green Fee:** $20/$36. **Cart Fee:** $11/Person. **Walking Policy:** Unrestricted walking. **Walkability:** 3. **Opened:** 1973. **Architect:** Dick Phelps. **Season:** Year-round. **High:** May-Oct. **To obtain tee times:** Call golf shop. **Miscellaneous:** Reduced fees (seniors), range (grass/mats), credit cards (MC, V, D), BF, FF.
Special Notes: Also has a 9-hole course.

★★★ SOUTHRIDGE GOLF CLUB
PU-5750 S. Lemay Ave., Fort Collins, 80525, Larimer County, (970)226-2828, 60 miles from Denver. **Facility Holes:** 18. **Yards:** 6,363/5,508. **Par:** 71/71. **Course Rating:** 69.1/69.3. **Slope:** 122/118. **Green Fee:** $19/$22. **Cart Fee:** $21/Cart. **Walking Policy:** Unrestricted walking. **Walkability:** 3. **Opened:** 1984. **Architect:** Frank Hummel. **Season:** Year-round. **High:** April-Sept. **To obtain tee times:** Call up to 3 days in advance. **Miscellaneous:** Reduced fees (weekdays, twilight, seniors, juniors), range (grass/mats), credit cards (MC, V), BF, FF.
Reader Comments: Course gets lots of play ... Good value ... Too many houses along fairways ... Short but tight ... Easy when hitting straight ... Fun to walk, great workout.

★★★ SPRINGS RANCH GOLF CLUB
PU-3525 Tutt Blvd., Colorado Springs, 80922, El Paso County, (719)573-4863, (800)485-9771. **Facility Holes:** 18. **Yards:** 7,107/5,004. **Par:** 72/72. **Course Rating:** 72.3/67.2.

Slope: 127/112. **Green Fee:** $18/$22. **Cart Fee:** $28/Person. **Walking Policy:** Unrestricted walking. **Walkability:** 3. **Opened:** 1997. **Architect:** Dick Phelps/Rick Phelps. **Season:** Year-round. **High:** May-Sept. **To obtain tee times:** Call golf shop. **Miscellaneous:** Range (grass), credit cards (MC, V).
Reader Comments: Great course but expect to finish in 5 hours on weekends ... The course is still growing up ... A winding target course with a view ... Challenging, will improve with age.

★★½ THORNCREEK GOLF CLUB
PU-13555 N. Washington St., Thornton, 80241, Adams County, (303)450-7055, 18 miles from Denver. **Facility Holes:** 18. **Yards:** 7,268/5,547. **Par:** 72/72. **Course Rating:** 73.7/70.5. **Slope:** 136/120. **Green Fee:** $30/$35. **Cart Fee:** $12/Person. **Walking Policy:** Unrestricted walking. **Walkability:** 4. **Opened:** 1992. **Architect:** Baxter Spann. **Season:** Year-round. **To obtain tee times:** Call up to 7 days in advance. **Miscellaneous:** Reduced fees (weekdays, twilight, seniors, juniors), range (grass), credit cards (MC, V, AE, D, DC), BF, FF.

★★½ TIARA RADO GOLF COURSE
PU-2063 S. Broadway, Grand Junction, 81503, Mesa County, (970)254-3830, 4 miles from Grand Junction. **Facility Holes:** 18. **Yards:** 6,289/4,967. **Par:** 71/71. **Course Rating:** 69.0/66.9. **Slope:** 120/113. **Green Fee:** $18/$21. **Cart Fee:** $20/Cart. **Walking Policy:** Unrestricted walking. **Walkability:** 3. **Opened:** 1972. **Season:** Year-round. **High:** April-Oct. **To obtain tee times:** Call up to 2 days in advance. **Miscellaneous:** Reduced fees (weekdays, juniors), range (grass), credit cards (MC, V, D), BF, FF.

★★½ TWIN PEAKS GOLF COURSE
PU-1200 Cornell Dr., Longmont, 80503, Boulder County, (303)772-1722, 35 miles from Denver. **Facility Holes:** 18. **Yards:** 6,810/5,398. **Par:** 70/71. **Course Rating:** 71.7/68.8. **Slope:** 123/117. **Green Fee:** $23. **Cart Fee:** $20/Cart. **Walking Policy:** Unrestricted walking. **Opened:** 1977. **Architect:** Frank Hummel. **Season:** Year-round. **High:** May-Sept. **To obtain tee times:** Call golf shop. **Miscellaneous:** Reduced fees (weekdays, seniors, juniors), range (grass), credit cards (MC, V).

★★★★ UTE CREEK GOLF COURSE *Value*
PU-2000 Ute Creek Dr., Longmont, 80501, Boulder County, (303)776-7662. **Facility Holes:** 18. **Yards:** 7,167/5,509. **Par:** 72/72. **Course Rating:** 73.1/69.2. **Slope:** 131/124. **Green Fee:** $15/$30. **Cart Fee:** $22/Cart. **Walking Policy:** Unrestricted walking. **Walkability:** 4. **Opened:** 1997. **Architect:** Robert Trent Jones Jr./Gary Linn. **Season:** Year-round. **High:** May-Oct. **To obtain tee times:** Call golf shop. **Miscellaneous:** Reduced fees (twilight, seniors, juniors), range (grass/mats), caddies, credit cards (MC, V).
Reader Comments: Each hole is a unique challenge ... Nice open tract ... Relatively new course that has an excellent layout and is fun to play ... Great value ... Fast greens, excellent par 5s ... Lots of sand.

★★★ VAIL GOLF CLUB
PU-1778 Vail Valley Dr., Vail, 81657, Eagle County, (970)479-2260, 100 miles from Denver. **Facility Holes:** 18. **Yards:** 7,100/5,291. **Par:** 77/72. **Course Rating:** 70.8/69.5. **Slope:** 121/114. **Green Fee:** $50/$100. **Cart Fee:** $15/Person. **Walking Policy:** Walking at certain times. **Walkability:** 3. **Opened:** 1966. **Architect:** Press Maxwell. **Season:** May-Oct. **High:** June-Sept. **To obtain tee times:** Call up to 2 days in advance. **Miscellaneous:** Range (grass), credit cards (MC, V, AE, D), BF, FF.
Reader Comments: My wife loves this course ... Mountain course ... Good value in the land of rip-offs ... Nicer than it looks from the highway ... Beautiful scenery ... Tight fairways, out of bounds on many holes ... Winter takes its toll on this course.

★★½ VALLEY HI GOLF COURSE
PU-610 S. Chelton Rd., Colorado Springs, 80910, El Paso County, (719)385-6911. **Facility Holes:** 18. **Yards:** 6,818/5,388. **Par:** 72/73. **Course Rating:** 70.8/69.3. **Slope:** 114/120. **Green Fee:** $20/$27. **Cart Fee:** $22/Cart. **Walking Policy:** Unrestricted walking. **Walkability:** 2. **Opened:** 1954. **Architect:** Henry B. Hughes. **Season:** Year-round. **High:** May-Sept. **To obtain tee times:** Call up to 7 days in advance. **Miscellaneous:** Reduced fees (seniors, juniors), range (grass/mats), credit cards (MC, V), BF, FF.

★★★★ WALKING STICK GOLF COURSE
PU-4301 Walking Stick Blvd., Pueblo, 81001, Pueblo County, (719)584-3400, 40 miles from Colorado Springs. **Facility Holes:** 18. **Yards:** 7,147/5,181. **Par:** 72/72. **Course Rating:** 72.6/69.0. **Slope:** 130/114. **Green Fee:** $26/$28. **Cart Fee:** $18/Cart. **Walking Policy:** Unrestricted walking. **Walkability:** 4. **Opened:** 1991. **Architect:** Arthur Hills. **Season:** Year-round. **High:** March-Oct. **To obtain tee times:** Call golf shop. **Miscellaneous:** Reduced fees (weekdays, twilight, seniors, juniors), range (grass/mats), credit cards (MC, V, D), BF, FF.

COLORADO

★★½ WELLSHIRE GOLF COURSE
PU-3333 S. Colorado Blvd., Denver, 80222, Denver County, (303)757-1352. **Facility Holes:** 18. **Yards:** 6,608/5,890. **Par:** 71/73. **Course Rating:** 70.1/69.3. **Slope:** 124/121. **Green Fee:** $19/$22. **Cart Fee:** $22/Cart. **Walking Policy:** Unrestricted walking. **Walkability:** 3. **Opened:** 1926. **Architect:** Donald Ross. **Season:** Year-round. **High:** April-Oct. **To obtain tee times:** Call golf shop. **Miscellaneous:** Reduced fees (weekdays, seniors, juniors), range (mats), credit cards (MC, V), BF, FF.

★★★ WEST WOODS GOLF CLUB
PU-6655 Quaker St., Arvada, 80403, Jefferson County, (303)424-3334, 14 miles from Denver. **Facility Holes:** 27. **Green Fee:** $25/$30. **Cart Fee:** $23/Cart. **Walking Policy:** Unrestricted walking. **Walkability:** 3. **Opened:** 1994. **Architect:** Dick Phelps. **Season:** Year-round. **High:** May-Aug. **To obtain tee times:** Call up to 5 days in advance. **Miscellaneous:** Reduced fees (seniors, juniors), range (grass/mats), credit cards (MC, V), BF, FF.
COTTONWOOD/SILO (18 combo)
Yards: 6,761/5,107. **Par:** 72/72. **Course Rating:** 72.7/69.9. **Slope:** 138/119.
SLEEPING INDIAN/COTTONWOOD (18 combo)
Yards: 7,035/5,197. **Par:** 72/72. **Course Rating:** 73.0/69.3. **Slope:** 136/119.
SLEEPING INDIAN/SILO (18 combo)
Yards: 6,722/5,074. **Par:** 72/72. **Course Rating:** 72.3/69.2. **Slope:** 138/121.

★★★ WILLIS CASE GOLF COURSE
PU-4999 Vrain St., Denver, 80212, Denver County, (303)455-9801. **Facility Holes:** 18. **Yards:** 6,306/6,122. **Par:** 72/75. **Course Rating:** 68.6/72.0. **Slope:** 119/115. **Green Fee:** $18/$20. **Cart Fee:** $20/Cart. **Walking Policy:** Unrestricted walking. **Walkability:** 4. **Opened:** 1929. **Season:** Year-round. **High:** May-Sept. **To obtain tee times:** Call golf shop. **Miscellaneous:** Reduced fees (weekdays, seniors, juniors), credit cards (MC, V), BF, FF.

★★★ YAMPA VALLEY GOLF CLUB
PU-2194 Hwy. 394, Craig, 81625, Moffat County, (970)824-3673, 200 miles from Denver. **E-mail:** yvgc@cmn.net. **Facility Holes:** 18. **Yards:** 6,514/5,242. **Par:** 72/72. **Course Rating:** 69.9/67.9. **Slope:** 126/120. **Green Fee:** $27. **Cart Fee:** $9/Person. **Walking Policy:** Unrestricted walking. **Walkability:** 1. **Opened:** 1968. **Architect:** William H. Neff. **Season:** Year-round. **High:** May-Sept. **To obtain tee times:** Call up to 3 days in advance. **Miscellaneous:** Reduced fees (seniors, juniors), range (grass), credit cards (MC, V, AE), BF, FF.

CONNECTICUT

★★ AIRWAYS GOLF CLUB
PU-1070 S. Grand St., West Suffield, 06093, Hartford County, (860)668-4973, 18 miles from Hartford. **E-mail:** bobkemp1@msn.com. **Web:** airwaygolf.com. **Facility Holes:** 18. **Yards:** 6,000/5,400. **Par:** 71/72. **Course Rating:** 67.2/65.0. **Slope:** 108/103. **Green Fee:** $20/$22. **Cart Fee:** $20/Cart. **Walking Policy:** Unrestricted walking. **Walkability:** 1. **Opened:** 1976. **Season:** Year-round. **To obtain tee times:** Call up to 7 days in advance. **Miscellaneous:** Reduced fees (weekdays, seniors), credit cards (MC, V), FF.

★½ ALLING MEMORIAL GOLF COURSE
PU-35 Eastern St., New Haven, 06513, New Haven County, (203)946-8014. **Facility Holes:** 18. **Yards:** 6,283/5,071. **Par:** 72/72. **Course Rating:** 71.9/71.0. **Slope:** 127/129. **Green Fee:** $16/$25. **Cart Fee:** $20/Cart. **Walking Policy:** Unrestricted walking. **Walkability:** 4. **Opened:** 1930. **Architect:** Robert Pryde/Al Zikorus. **Season:** April-Dec. **High:** June-Sept. **To obtain tee times:** Call up to 7 days in advance. **Miscellaneous:** Reduced fees (twilight, seniors, juniors), BF, FF.

★★ BANNER RESORT & COUNTRY CLUB
PU-10 Banner Rd., Moodus, 06469, Middlesex County, (860)873-9075, 18 miles from Hartford. **Facility Holes:** 18. **Yards:** 6,100/5,600. **Par:** 72/74. **Course Rating:** 68.9. **Slope:** 118. **Green Fee:** $25/$27. **Cart Fee:** $24/Cart. **Walking Policy:** Unrestricted walking. **Walkability:** 3. **Opened:** 1958. **Architect:** Frank Gamberdella. **Season:** April-Nov. **High:** June-Aug. **To obtain tee times:** Call golf shop. **Miscellaneous:** Reduced fees (weekdays, seniors, juniors), metal spikes, range (grass).

BLACKLEDGE COUNTRY CLUB
PU-180 W. St., Hebron, 06248, Tolland County, (860)228-0250, 15 miles from Hartford. **E-mail:** blackledge@msn.com. **Web:** www.ctgolfer.com/blackledge. **Facility Holes:** 36. **Green Fee:** $31/$35. **Cart Fee:** $24/Cart. **Walking Policy:** Unrestricted walking. **Season:** March-Dec. **High:** June-Aug. **To obtain tee times:** Call golf shop. **Miscellaneous:** Reduced fees (weekdays, twilight, seniors, juniors), credit cards (MC, V), BF, FF.
★★★ ANDERSON'S GLEN (18)
Yards: 6,787/5,458. **Par:** 72/72. **Course Rating:** 72.0/71.7. **Slope:** 128/123. **Walkability:** 2. **Opened:** 1964. **Architect:** Geoffrey Cornish.
Reader Comments: Two 18-hole courses with plenty of diversity ... Very good layout ... I used all my clubs ... Old 18 excellent ... Used for many outings ... Went up as a single and the staff made every effort to get me on the course ... Great test of golf.
GILEAD HIGHLANDS (18)
Yards: 6,537/4,951. **Par:** 72/72. **Course Rating:** 71.6/69.5. **Slope:** 131/122. **Walkability:** 3. **Opened:** 1994. **Architect:** Cornish/Silva/Mungeam.

★★★½ BLUE FOX RUN GOLF CLUB
PU-65 Nod Rd., Avon, 06001, Hartford County, (860)678-1679, 10 miles from Hartford. **Facility Holes:** 18. **Yards:** 6,779/5,171. **Par:** 71/72. **Course Rating:** 71.9/69.5. **Slope:** 125/123. **Green Fee:** $24/$34. **Cart Fee:** $15/Person. **Walking Policy:** Unrestricted walking. **Walkability:** 1. **Opened:** 1974. **Architect:** Joe Brunoli. **Season:** March-Dec. **High:** May-Sept. **To obtain tee times:** Call golf shop. **Miscellaneous:** Reduced fees (weekdays, twilight, seniors, juniors), range (mats), credit cards (MC, V, AE), BF, FF.

★★★ CANDLEWOOD VALLEY COUNTRY CLUB
PU-401 Danbury Rd., New Milford, 06776, Litchfield County, (860)354-9359, (860)354-9359, 8 miles from Danbury. **Facility Holes:** 18. **Yards:** 6,404/5,362. **Par:** 72/72. **Course Rating:** 72.0/72.5. **Slope:** 129/123. **Green Fee:** $28/$35. **Cart Fee:** $25/Cart. **Walking Policy:** Unrestricted walking. **Walkability:** 2. **Opened:** 1961. **Architect:** Geoffry Cornish/Stephen Kay. **Season:** April-Dec. **High:** June-Oct. **To obtain tee times:** Call up to 4 days in advance. **Misc:** Reduced fees (weekdays, twilight, seniors), range (mats), credit cards (MC, V, D), BF, FF.

★★ CANTON PUBLIC GOLF COURSE
PU-110 Rte. 44, Canton, 06019-0305, Hartford County, (860)693-8305, 12 miles from Hartford. **Facility Holes:** 9. **Yards:** 3,068/2,569. **Par:** 36/36. **Course Rating:** 68.2/67.0. **Slope:** 117/123. **Green Fee:** $24/$30. **Cart Fee:** $28/Cart. **Walking Policy:** Unrestricted walking. **Walkability:** 3. **Opened:** 1932. **Architect:** Jack Ross. **Season:** March-Jan. **High:** June-Sept. **To obtain tee times:** Call up to 7 days in advance. **Miscellaneous:** Reduced fees (seniors, juniors), metal spikes, credit cards (MC, V, AE), BF, FF.

★★★ CEDAR KNOB GOLF CLUB
PU-Billings Rd., Somers, 06071, Tolland County, (860)749-3550, 11 miles from Springfield. **Facility Holes:** 18. **Yards:** 6,734/5,784. **Par:** 72/74. **Course Rating:** 72.3/73.9. **Slope:** 126/129. **Green Fee:** $21/$26. **Cart Fee:** $24/Cart. **Walking Policy:** Unrestricted walking. **Walkability:** 3.

Opened: 1963. Architect: Geoffrey Cornish. Season: Year-round. High: April-Oct. To obtain tee times: Call golf shop. Miscellaneous: Reduced fees (weekdays, seniors, juniors), metal spikes, BF, FF.
Reader Comments: Best drainage of any course I've ever seen ... If no snow on the ground the course is always open and with surprisingly good conditions ... Slow greens ... A little rustic ... Some blind holes—need to know course ... Very scenic ... 18 a great finishing hole ... Steamed dogs in clubhouse ... Tough 3 pars.

★★ CEDAR RIDGE GOLF CLUB
PU-34 Drabik Rd., East Lyme, 06333, New London County, (860)691-4568, 1 mile from East Lyme. E-mail: alrustici@home.com. Web: www.cedarridgegolf.com. Facility Holes: 18. Yards: 3,025. Par: 54. Green Fee: $16/$23. Cart Fee: $20/Cart. Walking Policy: Unrestricted walking. Walkability: 2. Opened: 1964. Season: March-Dec. To obtain tee times: Call up to 7 days in advance. Miscellaneous: Reduced fees (weekdays, seniors, juniors), metal spikes, credit cards (MC, V, D), BF, FF.

★★★ CRESTBROOK PARK GOLF CLUB
PU-834 Northfield Rd., Watertown, 06795, Litchfield County, (860)945-5249, 5 miles from Waterbury. Facility Holes: 18. Yards: 6,915/5,696. Par: 71/75. Course Rating: 73.6/73.8. Slope: 128/128. Green Fee: $12/$22. Cart Fee: $24/Cart. Walking Policy: Unrestricted walking. Walkability: 4. Opened: 1970. Architect: Cornish/Zikoras. Season: April-Dec. High: June-Aug. To obtain tee times: Call golf shop. Miscellaneous: Reduced fees (weekdays, seniors, juniors), range (grass).
Reader Comments: Some very oddly contrived holes ... Fast greens ... Extremely slow, but nice layout and condition ... Always enjoyable, but 18th hole is absurd ... Two different 9s ... Front 9 greens faster than fast.

D. FAIRCHILD-WHEELER GOLF COURSE
PU-2390 Easton Tpke., Fairfield, 06432, Fairfield County, (203)373-5911. Web: www.fairchild-wheeler.com. Facility Holes: 36. Green Fee: $16/$36. Walking Policy: Unrestricted walking. Opened: 1931. Architect: Robert White. Season: Year-round. High: April-Oct. To obtain tee times: Call up to 7 days in advance. Miscellaneous: Reduced fees (weekdays, twilight, seniors, juniors), range (mats), credit cards (MC, V), BF, FF.
★★ BLACK COURSE (18)
Yards: 6,402/5,764. Par: 71/73. Course Rating: 70.0/71.9. Slope: 124/114. Walkability: 3.
★½ RED COURSE (18)
Yards: 6,775/6,382. Par: 72/79. Course Rating: 71.0/78.0. Slope: 124/122.

★★ E. GAYNOR BRENNAN MUNICIPAL GOLF COURSE
PU-451 Stillwater Rd., Stamford, 06902, Fairfield County, (203)356-0046, 1 mile from Stamford. Facility Holes: 18. Yards: 6,107/5,736. Par: 71/71. Course Rating: 69.8. Slope: 122. Green Fee: $13/$38. Cart Fee: $23/Cart. Walking Policy: Unrestricted walking. Walkability: 5. Opened: 1931. Architect: Maurice McCarthy. Season: Year-round. To obtain tee times: Call golf shop. Miscellaneous: Reduced fees (twilight, seniors, juniors), BF, FF.
Special Notes: Also known as Hubbard Heights Golf Course.

★★ EAST HARTFORD GOLF COURSE
PU-130 Long Hill St., East Hartford, 06108, Hartford County, (860)528-5082, 3 miles from Hartford. Facility Holes: 18. Yards: 6,186/5,072. Par: 71/72. Course Rating: 69.1/68.9. Slope: 124/113. Green Fee: $21/$23. Cart Fee: $10/Person. Walking Policy: Unrestricted walking. Walkability: 2. Opened: 1930. Architect: Orrin Smith. Season: April-Dec. To obtain tee times: Call up to 7 days in advance. Miscellaneous: Reduced fees (seniors, juniors), BF, FF.

★★ EAST MOUNTAIN GOLF CLUB
PU-171 E. Mountain Rd., Waterbury, 06706, New Haven County, (203)756-1676. Facility Holes: 18. Yards: 5,817/5,211. Par: 67/67. Course Rating: 68.0/67.0. Slope: 118/113. Green Fee: $13/$21. Cart Fee: $20/Cart. Walking Policy: Unrestricted walking. Walkability: 1. Opened: 1933. Architect: Wayne Stiles. Season: April-Dec. High: June-Sept. To obtain tee times: Call up to 3 days in advance. Miscellaneous: Reduced fees (weekdays, seniors, juniors), BF, FF.

★★★ ELMRIDGE GOLF COURSE
SP-Elmridge Rd., Pawcatuck, 06379, New London County, (860)599-2248, 14 miles from New London. Facility Holes: 27. Green Fee: $31/$35. Cart Fee: $25/Cart. Walking Policy: Unrestricted walking. Walkability: 2. Opened: 1968. Architect: Joe Rustici/Charlie Rustici. Season: March-Dec. High: July-Oct. To obtain tee times: Call golf shop. Miscellaneous: Reduced fees (twilight), range (grass), credit cards (MC, V, AE), BF, FF.

BLUE/WHITE (18 combo)
Yards: 6,683/5,648. **Par:** 72/72. **Course Rating:** 72.3/70.1. **Slope:** 124/117.
RED/BLUE (18 combo)
Yards: 6,404/5,376. **Par:** 71/71. **Course Rating:** 70.5/69.5. **Slope:** 117/110.
RED/WHITE (18 combo)
Yards: 6,347/5,430. **Par:** 71/71. **Course Rating:** 70.8/69.0. **Slope:** 115/109.
Reader Comments: Course has potential to be better … Three beautiful 9-hole courses … Very picturesque … 27 holes for a variety of 18 combos.

FAIRVIEW FARM GOLF COURSE
PU-300 Hill Rd., Harwinton, 06791, Litchfield County, (860)689-1000, 15 miles from Waterbury. **E-mail:** bsparks@aol.com. **Web:** www.fairviewfarmgolfcourse.com. **Facility Holes:** 18. **Yards:** 6,660/4,780. **Par:** 72/72. **Course Rating:** 71.7/67.6. **Slope:** 125/118. **Green Fee:** $32/$38. **Cart Fee:** $14/Person. **Walking Policy:** Walking at certain times. **Walkability:** 3. **Opened:** 2000. **Architect:** Dick Christian. **Season:** April-Nov. **To obtain tee times:** Call up to 7 days in advance. **Miscellaneous:** Range (mats), credit cards (MC, V, AE), BF, FF.

★★★ GOODWIN PARK GOLF COURSE
PU-1130 Maple Ave., Hartford, 06114, Hartford County, (860)956-3601. **Facility Holes:** 27. **Yards:** 5,929/5,343. **Par:** 70/70. **Course Rating:** 67.8/69.6. **Slope:** 110/109. **Green Fee:** $20/$23. **Walkability:** 1. **Architect:** Everett Pyle. **Season:** April-Nov. **To obtain tee times:** Call golf shop. **Miscellaneous:** Metal spikes.
Special Notes: Also 9 hole executive course.

GRASSMERE COUNTRY CLUB
PU-130 Town Farm Rd., Enfield, 06082, Hartford County, (860)749-7740, 14 miles from Hartford. **E-mail:** margot10@aol.com. **Facility Holes:** 9. **Yards:** 6,430/5,346. **Par:** 70/70. **Course Rating:** 69.1/71.0. **Slope:** 111/113. **Green Fee:** $23/$28. **Walkability:** 2. **Opened:** 1965. **Season:** March-Dec. **High:** March-Dec. **To obtain tee times:** Call up to 14 days in advance. **Misc:** Reduced fees (weekdays, seniors, juniors), credit cards (MC, V), BF, FF.

★★½ GRASSY HILL COUNTRY CLUB
PU-441 Clark Lane, Orange, 06477, New Haven County, (203)795-1422, 8 miles from New Haven. **Facility Holes:** 18. **Yards:** 6,208/5,209. **Par:** 70/71. **Course Rating:** 70.5/71.1. **Slope:** 122/118. **Green Fee:** $20/$42. **Cart Fee:** Included in green fee. **Walking Policy:** Walking at certain times. **Walkability:** 2. **Opened:** 1927. **Season:** April-Nov. **High:** April-Oct. **To obtain tee times:** Call golf shop. **Miscellaneous:** Reduced fees (weekdays, seniors), metal spikes, range (grass/mats), credit cards (MC, V, AE).

★★★★½ GREAT RIVER GOLF CLUB *Service, Value, Condition, Pace+*
PU-130 Coram Lane, Milford, 06460, New Haven County, (203)876-8051, 15 miles from New Haven. **Web:** www.greatrivergolfclub.com. **Facility Holes:** 18. **Yards:** 7,209/4,975. **Par:** 72/72. **Course Rating:** 75.5/70.7. **Slope:** 152/125. **Green Fee:** $100/$125. **Cart Fee:** Included in green fee. **Walking Policy:** Unrestricted walking. **Walkability:** 2. **Opened:** 2001. **Architect:** Tommy Fazio. **Season:** Year-round. **High:** June-Sept. **To obtain tee times:** Call up to 5 days in advance. **Miscellaneous:** Reduced fees (twilight), range (grass), credit cards (MC, V, AE, D), BF, FF.
Notes: Ranked 4th in 2001 Best New Upscale Courses.
Reader Comments: Decide on a tee box, then move up one … Bring an extra sleeve … Impressive … Course condition was better than the private courses in the Met area … I want to play there every day … The services are incredible … You can tell a lot of hard work went into it … The architect and superintendent should be commended.

★★½ GRIFFITH E. HARRIS GOLF CLUB
SP-1300 King St., Greenwich, 06831, Fairfield County, (203)531-7261, 20 miles from New York City. **Facility Holes:** 18. **Yards:** 6,512/5,710. **Par:** 71/73. **Course Rating:** 70.5/73.6. **Slope:** 120/128. **Green Fee:** $11/$16. **Cart Fee:** $23/Cart. **Walking Policy:** Unrestricted walking. **Walkability:** 3. **Opened:** 1963. **Architect:** Robert Trent Jones. **Season:** March-Dec. **To obtain tee times:** Call golf shop. **Misc:** Reduced fees (weekdays, seniors, juniors), range, BF, FF.

★★★ H. SMITH RICHARDSON GOLF COURSE
PU-2425 Morehouse Hwy., Fairfield, 06430, Fairfield County, (203)255-7300, (203)255-7300, 50 miles from New York. **Facility Holes:** 18. **Yards:** 6,700/5,764. **Par:** 72/72. **Course Rating:** 71.0/72.8. **Slope:** 127/129. **Green Fee:** $13/$40. **Cart Fee:** $24/Person. **Walking Policy:** Unrestricted walking. **Walkability:** 5. **Opened:** 1972. **Architect:** Hal Purdy. **Season:** April-Dec. **High:** May-Sept. **To obtain tee times:** Call golf shop. **Miscellaneous:** Reduced fees (weekdays, seniors, juniors), range (grass/mats), BF, FF.
Reader Comments: Loved it … Some of back-9 greens very difficult to two putt … One of the best laid out and prettiest public courses I've ever played … Great course, but just try to get on it!

CONNECTICUT

★★★ HUNTER GOLF CLUB
PU-685 Westfield Rd., Meriden, 06450, New Haven County, (203)634-3366, 12 miles from Hartford. **Facility Holes:** 18. **Yards:** 6,604/5,569. **Par:** 71/72. **Course Rating:** 71.9/72.7. **Slope:** 124/131. **Green Fee:** $20/$29. **Cart Fee:** $23/Cart. **Walking Policy:** Unrestricted walking. **Walkability:** 3. **Opened:** 1929. **Architect:** Robert Pryde/Al Zikorus. **Season:** March-Dec. **High:** June-Aug. **To obtain tee times:** Call up to 14 days in advance. **Miscellaneous:** Reduced fees (weekdays, seniors, juniors), range (grass), credit cards (MC, V), BF, FF.
Reader Comments: Very popular, very crowded, fairly slow ... New grounds keeper has made many improvements ... A fun, playable challenge for my level of play ... Good muni course ... Good hot dogs ... Fun.

★★★ KENEY GOLF COURSE
PU-280 Tower Ave., Hartford, 06120, Hartford County, (860)525-3656. **Facility Holes:** 18. **Yards:** 5,969/5,005. **Par:** 70/70. **Course Rating:** 68.2/67.2. **Slope:** 118/107. **Green Fee:** $11/$18. **Walking Policy:** Unrestricted walking. **Opened:** 1927. **Architect:** D. Emmet/G.S. Cornish/W.G Robinson. **Season:** April-Nov. **High:** May-Sept. **To obtain tee times:** Call golf shop. **Miscellaneous:** Reduced fees (weekdays, twilight, seniors, juniors), metal spikes, credit cards (MC, V).
Reader Comments: Great old layout ... Done a lot of work on course, still needs more ... Old, natural golf course—if you're not a golf snob, you'll love it ... Overlooked ... For a public course in the city, the play was good.

★★½ LAUREL VIEW GOLF COURSE
PU-310 W. Shepard Ave., Hamden, 06514, New Haven County, (203)287-2656, 15 miles from New Haven. **Facility Holes:** 18. **Yards:** 6,899/5,558. **Par:** 72/72. **Course Rating:** 72.7/71.8. **Slope:** 130/130. **Green Fee:** $9/$25. **Cart Fee:** $20/Cart. **Walking Policy:** Unrestricted walking. **Walkability:** 3. **Opened:** 1969. **Architect:** Geoffrey S. Cornish/William G. Robinson. **Season:** March-Dec. **High:** May-Aug. **To obtain tee times:** Call golf shop. **Miscellaneous:** Metal spikes.

★★½ LONGSHORE CLUB PARK
SP-260 Compo Rd. S., Westport, 06880, Fairfield County, (203)222-7535, 13 miles from Bridgeport. **Facility Holes:** 18. **Yards:** 5,845/5,227. **Par:** 69/73. **Course Rating:** 69.3/69.9. **Slope:** 115/113. **Green Fee:** $11/$13. **Cart Fee:** $25/Cart. **Walkability:** 1. **Opened:** 1925. **Architect:** Orrin Smith. **Season:** March-Dec. **High:** May-Sept. **To obtain tee times:** Call up to 3 days in advance. **Miscellaneous:** Reduced fees (weekdays, seniors, juniors), range (mats), BF, FF.

LYMAN ORCHARDS GOLF CLUB
SP-Rte. 157, Middlefield, 06455, Middlesex County, (888)995-9626, (888)995-9626, 15 miles from New Haven. **Web:** www.lymanorchards.com. **Facility Holes:** 36. **Green Fee:** $31/$48. **Cart Fee:** $12/Person. **Season:** March-Dec. **To obtain tee times:** Call up to 7 days in advance. **Miscellaneous:** Reduced fees (weekdays, twilight, seniors, juniors), range (grass/mats), credit cards (MC, V, AE), BF, FF.
★★★ GARY PLAYER COURSE (18)
Yards: 6,725/4,900. **Par:** 71/71. **Course Rating:** 73.1/68.7. **Slope:** 134/119. **Walking Policy:** Mandatory carts. **Walkability:** 4. **Opened:** 1994. **Architect:** Gary Player.
Reader Comments: Need to know where to hit it ... Leave driver at home ... Short but challenging ... Great views ... Love finishing with 2 par 5s ... Target golf ... The course drains poorly after hard rains ... Nice clubhouse.
★★★½ ROBERT TRENT JONES COURSE (18)
Yards: 7,011/5,812. **Par:** 72/72. **Course Rating:** 73.2/72.0. **Slope:** 129/124. **Walking Policy:** Unrestricted walking. **Walkability:** 3. **Opened:** 1969. **Architect:** Robert Trent Jones.
Reader Comments: Outstanding course, price is high ... The Titanic had better drainage ... Usually in good shape ... Use all your clubs, high-handicapper's nightmare ... Front 9 good layout—too much like Florida on back ... Deceptively hard ... Great day playing 36 very interesting holes ... Good test of golf.

★★★ MANCHESTER COUNTRY CLUB
SP-305 South Main St., Manchester, 06040, Hartford County, (860)646-0226, 12 miles from Hartford. **E-mail:** mancc@prodigy.net. **Web:** www.mancc.com. **Facility Holes:** 18. **Yards:** 6,285/5,610. **Par:** 72/72. **Course Rating:** 70.8/72.0. **Slope:** 125/120. **Green Fee:** $31/$36. **Cart Fee:** $12/Person. **Walking Policy:** Unrestricted walking. **Walkability:** 3. **Opened:** 1917. **Architect:** Tom Bendelow/D. Emmitt. **Season:** April-Nov. **High:** May-July. **To obtain tee times:** Call golf shop. **Miscellaneous:** Reduced fees (seniors, juniors), range (grass/mats), credit cards (MC, V, AE, D).
Reader Comments: Very, very fast greens ... 14th a super hole ... Great old-style course ... Great food and atmosphere ... 4-hour rounds, all the time! ... Improved most greens and bunkers.

★★★ NORWICH GOLF COURSE

PU-685 New London Tpke., Norwich, 06360, New London County, (860)889-6973. **E-mail:** norwich.golf@snet.net. **Facility Holes:** 18. **Yards:** 6,183/5,104. **Par:** 71/71. **Course Rating:** 69.5/70.2. **Slope:** 129/118. **Green Fee:** $22/$31. **Cart Fee:** $10/Person. **Walking Policy:** Unrestricted walking. **Walkability:** 4. **Opened:** 1926. **Architect:** Donald Ross. **Season:** March-Dec. **High:** April-Oct. **To obtain tee times:** Call up to 3 days in advance. **Miscellaneous:** Reduced fees (twilight), range (grass/mats), lodging (100 rooms), credit cards (MC, V), BF, FF.

Reader Comments: Good layout, positioning gives reward ... Great beginners course ... Very hard to get a tee time ... Nice old course ... Variety of holes, no flat lies ... Beautiful in autumn.

★★ OAK HILLS GOLF CLUB

PU-165 Fillow St., Norwalk, 06850, Fairfield County, (203)853-8400, 53 miles from New York. **E-mail:** oakhills1969@aol.com. **Facility Holes:** 18. **Yards:** 6,407/5,221. **Par:** 71/72. **Course Rating:** 70.5/69.2. **Slope:** 125/119. **Green Fee:** $23/$40. **Cart Fee:** $24/Cart. **Walking Policy:** Unrestricted walking. **Walkability:** 3. **Opened:** 1969. **Architect:** Alfred H. Tull. **Season:** Year-round. **High:** April-Nov. **To obtain tee times:** Call golf shop. **Miscellaneous:** Reduced fees (twilight), BF, FF.

★★★½ ORANGE HILLS COUNTRY CLUB

PU-389 Racebrook Rd., Orange, 06477, New Haven County, (203)795-4161, 7 miles from New Haven. **E-mail:** mlvkin4@hotmail.com. **Facility Holes:** 18. **Yards:** 6,499/5,729. **Par:** 71/74. **Course Rating:** 72.3/71.5. **Slope:** 126/120. **Green Fee:** $32/$42. **Cart Fee:** $27/Cart. **Walking Policy:** Unrestricted walking. **Walkability:** 2. **Opened:** 1940. **Architect:** Geoffrey Cornish. **Season:** March-Dec. **High:** June-Aug. **To obtain tee times:** Call up to 7 days in advance. **Miscellaneous:** Credit cards (MC, V), BF, FF.

Reader Comments: Front open, back wooded ... In the country while you're next to the city ... Family run, great course, good food ... Nice mix of holes ... Like new 9th hole ... Pro shop almost nonexistent.

★★ PATTONBROOK COUNTRY CLUB

SP-201 Pattonwood Dr., Southington, 06489, Hartford County, (860)793-6000. **Facility Holes:** 18. **Yards:** 4,433/3,640. **Par:** 61/61. **Course Rating:** 60.6/59.1. **Slope:** 97/92. **Green Fee:** $16/$22. **Cart Fee:** $22/Cart. **Walking Policy:** Unrestricted walking. **Walkability:** 3. **Opened:** 1967. **Architect:** Geoffrey S. Cornish. **Season:** March-Nov. **High:** May-Aug. **To obtain tee times:** Call golf shop. **Miscellaneous:** Reduced fees (weekdays, seniors), credit cards (MC, V).

★★★ PEQUABUCK GOLF CLUB

SP-School St., Pequabuck, 06781, Litchfield County, (860)583-7307, 12 miles from Waterbury. **E-mail:** office@pequabuckgolf.com. **Web:** www.pequabuckgolf.com. **Facility Holes:** 18. **Yards:** 6,015/5,388. **Par:** 69/72. **Course Rating:** 69.1/71.0. **Slope:** 122/117. **Green Fee:** $40. **Cart Fee:** $14/Person. **Walking Policy:** Unrestricted walking. **Walkability:** 4. **Opened:** 1902. **Architect:** Geoffrey S. Cornish/William G. Robinson. **Season:** April-Dec. **High:** April-Oct. **To obtain tee times:** Call up to 14 days in advance. **Miscellaneous:** Range (grass/mats), BF, FF.

Reader Comments: Short but tricky ... 10th hole tricky par 3 ... Outstanding back nine. Front nine easier to score ... 11th hole a classic ... Great greens ... Need accurate iron play ... Unusual layout but a fun course to play.

★★ PEQUOT GOLF CLUB

PU-127 Wheeler Rd., Stonington, 06378, New London County, (860)535-1898, 15 miles from New London. **Facility Holes:** 18. **Yards:** 5,903/5,246. **Par:** 70/70. **Course Rating:** 68.7/69.4. **Slope:** 108/112. **Green Fee:** $23/$28. **Cart Fee:** $24/Cart. **Walking Policy:** Unrestricted walking. **Walkability:** 3. **Opened:** 1959. **Architect:** Wendal Ross. **Season:** Feb.-Dec. **High:** June-Sept. **To obtain tee times:** Call golf shop. **Miscellaneous:** Reduced fees (seniors, juniors), credit cards (MC, V).

★★★½ PINE VALLEY GOLF COURSE

PU-300 Welch Rd., Southington, 06489, Hartford County, (860)628-0879, 15 miles from Hartford. **Facility Holes:** 18. **Yards:** 6,325/5,482. **Par:** 71/73. **Course Rating:** 70.6/72.0. **Slope:** 123/122. **Green Fee:** $29/$34. **Cart Fee:** $27/Cart. **Walking Policy:** Unrestricted walking. **Walkability:** 2. **Opened:** 1960. **Architect:** Orrin Smith. **Season:** March-Dec. **To obtain tee times:** Call golf shop. **Miscellaneous:** Range (grass), BF, FF.

Reader Comments: Beautiful, challenging course ... Leave the driver in the bag ... Lets keep this place a secret, so it stays 4 hrs ... Challenging but forgiving, plays longer than it is ... Tight fairways ... Requires precise irons ... My favorite place in CT.

★★★½ **PORTLAND GOLF COURSE**
SP-169 Bartlett St., Portland, 06480, Middlesex County, (860)342-6107, 20 miles from Hartford. **Facility Holes:** 18. **Yards:** 6,213/5,039. **Par:** 71/71. **Course Rating:** 70.8/68.6. **Slope:** 124/118. **Green Fee:** $29/$37. **Cart Fee:** $12/Person. **Walking Policy:** Unrestricted walking. **Walkability:** 3. **Opened:** 1974. **Architect:** Geoffrey Cornish/William Robinson. **Season:** March-Dec. **High:** April-Oct. **To obtain tee times:** Call golf shop. **Miscellaneous:** Reduced fees (weekdays, seniors, juniors), range (grass/mats), BF, FF.
Reader Comments: Too crowded in summer … Small fast greens … Some blind tee shots, club selection important … Easy play, not too difficult, friendly staff always willing to fit you in when able … Rolling hills, nice layout.

★★★½ **QUARRY RIDGE GOLF COURSE**
PU-9A Rose Hill Rd., Portland, 06480, Middlesex County, (860)342-6113, 20 miles from Hartford. **E-mail:** qrpro@aol.com. **Web:** www.quarryridge.com. **Facility Holes:** 18. **Yards:** 6,369/4,948. **Par:** 72/72. **Course Rating:** 70.8. **Slope:** 129. **Green Fee:** $35/$44. **Cart Fee:** Included in green fee. **Walking Policy:** Mandatory carts. **Walkability:** 5. **Opened:** 1993. **Architect:** Joe Kelly/Al Zikorus. **Season:** March-Dec. **High:** April-Oct. **To obtain tee times:** Call golf shop. **Miscellaneous:** Reduced fees (seniors, juniors), credit cards (MC, V), FF.
Reader Comments: Ho-hum target golf … Narrow hilly fairways … Do not expect a lot of level lies … I will definitly play it again … Only the young or young at heart can walk this course … Built on an old stone quarry, tee to green elevations can be 50 feet … Tight fairways, leave your driver in the car.

★½ **RACEWAY GOLF CLUB**
SP-205 E. Thompson Rd., Thompson, 06277, Windham County, (860)923-9591, 60 miles from Hartford. **E-mail:** raceway@neca.com. **Web:** www.racewaygolf@neca.com. **Facility Holes:** 18. **Yards:** 6,412/5,437. **Par:** 71/71. **Course Rating:** 70.0/71.3. **Slope:** 111/117. **Green Fee:** $21/$36. **Cart Fee:** $24/Cart. **Walking Policy:** Walking at certain times. **Walkability:** 2. **Opened:** 1940. **Architect:** Donald Hoenig. **Season:** April-Nov. **High:** April-Oct. **To obtain tee times:** Call golf shop. **Miscellaneous:** Reduced fees (weekdays, twilight, juniors), range (grass/mats), credit cards (MC, V, AE, D), BF, FF.

★★★★½ **RICHTER PARK GOLF CLUB**
PU-100 Aunt Hack Rd., Danbury, 06811, Fairfield County, (203)792-2552, 60 miles from New York City. **E-mail:** richterpro@aol.com. **Web:** www.ctgolfer.com. **Facility Holes:** 18. **Yards:** 6,740/5,627. **Par:** 72/72. **Course Rating:** 73.0/72.8. **Slope:** 130/122. **Green Fee:** $17/$48. **Cart Fee:** $23/Cart. **Walking Policy:** Unrestricted walking. **Walkability:** 4. **Opened:** 1971. **Architect:** Edward Ryder. **Season:** April-Nov. **High:** June-Aug. **To obtain tee times:** Call golf shop. **Miscellaneous:** Reduced fees (twilight), credit cards (MC, V), BF, FF.
Notes: Ranked 8th in 2001 Best in State.
Reader Comments: Beautiful layout and very well maintained … Challenging, especially for women … Nonresidents don't always seem welcome … Hard to get tee times … Every hole has risk/reward … Tricky greens … Tough walk … Mirrors in trees on blind tee shots … Best in Connecticut … Lots of water.

★★★ **RIDGEFIELD GOLF COURSE**
PU-545 Ridgebury Rd., Ridgefield, 06877, Fairfield County, (203)748-7008, 1 mile from Danbury. **Facility Holes:** 18. **Yards:** 6,444/5,295. **Par:** 71/74. **Course Rating:** 70.9/70.6. **Slope:** 123/119. **Green Fee:** $10/$40. **Cart Fee:** $24/Cart. **Walking Policy:** Unrestricted walking. **Walkability:** 3. **Opened:** 1974. **Architect:** George Fazio/Tom Fazio. **Season:** April-Dec. **High:** June-Aug. **To obtain tee times:** Call golf shop. **Miscellaneous:** Reduced fees (twilight, seniors, juniors), range (grass), credit cards (MC, V).
Reader Comments: Keep the ball below the hole, fast tricky greens … Very wet, flat track … New 6th hole terrific … Back nine is most challenging.

RIVER RIDGE GOLF COURSE
PU-Rte. 164, Griswold, 06351, Middlesex County, (860)376-3268. **Facility Holes:** 18. **Yards:** 6,548/5,340. **Par:** 72/72. **Course Rating:** 70.7/70.4. **Slope:** 122/119. **Green Fee:** $31/$35. **Cart Fee:** $13/Person. **Walking Policy:** Unrestricted walking. **Opened:** 1999. **Architect:** Joe Rustici/Charles Rustici. **To obtain tee times:** Call golf shop. **Miscellaneous:** Reduced fees (weekdays).

★★★★ **ROCKLEDGE COUNTRY CLUB** *Value*
PU-289 S. Main St., West Hartford, 06107, Hartford County, (860)521-3156, 7 miles from Hartford. **Facility Holes:** 18. **Yards:** 6,366/5,608. **Par:** 72/74. **Course Rating:** 71.3/71.5. **Slope:** 121/118. **Green Fee:** $16/$27. **Cart Fee:** $20/Cart. **Walking Policy:** Unrestricted walking. **Walkability:** 3. **Opened:** 1949. **Architect:** Orrin Smith. **Season:** April-Dec. **High:** June-July. **To obtain tee times:** Call golf shop. **Miscellaneous:** Reduced fees (seniors), range (grass/mats),

CONNECTICUT

credit cards (MC, V).

Reader Comments: Nice layout, very good condition ... Excellent service, good pace of play ... Conditions have improved over the last few years ... Great course to walk ... Very pretty & relaxing.

★★★ SHENNECOSSETT MUNICIPAL GOLF COURSE
PU-93 Plant St., Groton, 06340, New London County, (860)445-0262, 2 miles from New London. **Facility Holes:** 18. **Yards:** 6,491/5,796. **Par:** 71/75. **Course Rating:** 71.5/73.2. **Slope:** 122/122. **Green Fee:** $20/$35. **Cart Fee:** $13/Person. **Walking Policy:** Unrestricted walking. **Walkability:** 2. **Opened:** 1898. **Architect:** Donald Ross. **Season:** Year-round. **High:** April-Oct. **To obtain tee times:** Call up to 3 days in advance. **Miscellaneous:** Reduced fees (weekdays, juniors), credit cards (MC, V), BF, FF.
Reader Comments: View at 15 is worth the price—wow! ... 15-16-17 nice layout ... Wonderful old course with a Scottish essence ... Turtle-back greens ... Nice shore view ... 16th is prettiest hole in CT.

★★★★ SIMSBURY FARMS GOLF CLUB
PU-100 Old Farms Rd., West Simsbury, 06092, Hartford County, (860)658-6246, 15 miles from Hartford. **Facility Holes:** 18. **Yards:** 6,421/5,439. **Par:** 72/72. **Course Rating:** 71.1/70.1. **Slope:** 124/117. **Green Fee:** $14/$26. **Cart Fee:** $22/Cart. **Walking Policy:** Unrestricted walking. **Walkability:** 3. **Opened:** 1972. **Architect:** Geoffrey Cornish/William Robinson. **Season:** April-Nov. **High:** May-Sept. **To obtain tee times:** Call golf shop. **Miscellaneous:** Metal spikes, range (mats), credit cards (MC, V).
Reader Comments: Very good muni course ... Great greens ... Difficult for beginners ... A scenic course ... Just needs a 19th hole.

★★ SKUNGAMAUG RIVER GOLF CLUB
PU-104 Folly Lane, Coventry, 06238, Tolland County, (860)742-9348, 20 miles from Hartford. **Facility Holes:** 18. **Yards:** 5,785/4,838. **Par:** 70/71. **Course Rating:** 69.4/69.3. **Slope:** 120/123. **Green Fee:** $28/$31. **Walking Policy:** Unrestricted walking. **Walkability:** 3. **Opened:** 1963. **Architect:** Chet Jenkins/John Motycka. **Season:** April-Jan. **To obtain tee times:** Call up to 5 days in advance. **Miscellaneous:** Reduced fees (twilight, seniors, juniors), range (grass), credit cards (MC, V, AE), BF, FF.

★★½ SOUTHINGTON COUNTRY CLUB
SP-Savage St., Southington, 06489, Hartford County, (860)628-7032, 22 miles from Hartford. **Facility Holes:** 18. **Yards:** 5,675/5,103. **Par:** 71/73. **Course Rating:** 67.0/69.8. **Slope:** 123/119. **Green Fee:** $26/$30. **Cart Fee:** $27/Cart. **Walking Policy:** Unrestricted walking. **Walkability:** 3. **Opened:** 1922. **Season:** April-Nov. **To obtain tee times:** Call up to 4 days in advance. **Miscellaneous:** Reduced fees (seniors, juniors), FF.

★★★½ STANLEY GOLF CLUB
PU-245 Hartford Rd., New Britain, 06053, Hartford County, (860)827-8144, 8 miles from Hartford. **Facility Holes:** 27. **Green Fee:** $24/$28. **Cart Fee:** $26/Cart. **Walking Policy:** Unrestricted walking. **Walkability:** 2. **Opened:** 1930. **Architect:** R.J. Ross/O. Smith/G.S. Cornish. **Season:** April-Dec. **To obtain tee times:** Call golf shop. **Miscellaneous:** Reduced fees (weekdays, seniors), BF, FF.
BLUE/RED (18 Combo)
Yards: 6,453/5,681. **Par:** 72/73. **Course Rating:** 71.1/71.6. **Slope:** 115/118. **High:** May-Oct.
RED/WHITE (18 Combo)
Yards: 6,156/5,359. **Par:** 72/72. **Course Rating:** 69.0/69.5. **Slope:** 108/112. **High:** May-Oct.
WHITE/BLUE COURSE (18 Combo)
Yards: 6,329/5,557. **Par:** 72/73. **Course Rating:** 69.8/70.3. **Slope:** 112/118. **High:** June-Oct.
Reader Comments: Very impressed with this public course ... A fun, playable challenge for my level of play ... Good value, slow round ... 3 nines—two flat one hilly—all good.

★★★ STERLING FARMS GOLF CLUB
PU-1349 Newfield Ave., Stamford, 06905, Fairfield County, (203)329-7888. **Facility Holes:** 18. **Yards:** 6,410/5,600. **Par:** 72/73. **Course Rating:** 71.7/72.6. **Slope:** 127/121. **Green Fee:** $14/$45. **Cart Fee:** $24/Cart. **Walking Policy:** Unrestricted walking. **Walkability:** 4. **Opened:** 1969. **Architect:** Geoffrey Cornish/William Robinson. **Season:** Year-round. **To obtain tee times:** Call golf shop. **Miscellaneous:** Reduced fees (weekdays, twilight, seniors, juniors), range (mats), BF, FF.
Reader Comments: Excellent municipal course ... Nice variety of holes ... Bring a pillow for the nap between shots ... Short course, greens a little shaggy ... If a resident, best value anywhere ... Greens are too slow ... Course always in great condition.

★★★½ TALLWOOD COUNTRY CLUB
PU-91 North St., Rte. 85, Hebron, 06248, Tolland County, (860)646-3437, 15 miles from Glastonbury. **Web:** www.ctgolfer/tallwood.com. **Facility Holes:** 18. **Yards:** 6,353/5,424.

CONNECTICUT

Par: 72/72. **Course Rating:** 70.4/70.6. **Slope:** 123/121. **Green Fee:** $30/$32. **Cart Fee:** $24/Cart. **Walking Policy:** Unrestricted walking. **Walkability:** 3. **Opened:** 1970. **Architect:** Mike Ovian. **Season:** March-Dec. **High:** June-Sept. **To obtain tee times:** Call up to 7 days in advance. **Miscellaneous:** Reduced fees (twilight, seniors, juniors), metal spikes, range (grass), credit cards (MC, V), BF, FF.

Reader Comments: Nice layout, good conditions ... Limited food ... Very challenging course ... Scenic front 9 a warmup for much tougher back 9 ... Plenty of water ... Rural setting.

★★★ TASHUA KNOLLS GOLF COURSE
PU-40 Tashua Knolls Lane, Trumbull, 06611, Fairfield County, (203)261-5989, 7 miles from Bridgeport. **Facility Holes:** 18. **Yards:** 6,534/5,454. **Par:** 72/72. **Course Rating:** 71.9/71.7. **Slope:** 125/124. **Green Fee:** $15/$30. **Cart Fee:** $23/Cart. **Walking Policy:** Unrestricted walking. **Walkability:** 3. **Opened:** 1976. **Architect:** Al Zikorus. **Season:** March-Dec. **High:** May-Sept. **To obtain tee times:** Call golf shop. **Miscellaneous:** Reduced fees (seniors, juniors), range (grass/mats).

Reader Comments: Very enjoyable ... Fun to play ... The play is slow, but fun.

★★★★ TIMBERLIN GOLF CLUB *Value*
PU-Don Bates Dr., Kensington, 06037, Hartford County, (860)828-3228, 18 miles from Hartford. **Facility Holes:** 18. **Yards:** 6,733/5,477. **Par:** 72/72. **Course Rating:** 72.2/72.0. **Slope:** 129/125. **Green Fee:** $26/$28. **Cart Fee:** $26/Cart. **Walking Policy:** Unrestricted walking. **Walkability:** 2. **Opened:** 1970. **Architect:** Al Zikorus. **Season:** April-Dec. **High:** May-Oct. **To obtain tee times:** Call up to 2 days in advance. **Miscellaneous:** Range (grass/mats), credit cards (MC, V, D), BF, FF.

Reader Comments: Easy walk, good greens ... Very peaceful, good variety of holes ... Busy course ... One of my favorites ... Excellent grillroom ... Great golf course but too overcrowded ... Slick, true greens.

★★★ TOPSTONE GOLF CLUB
PU-516 Griffin Rd., South Windsor, 06074, Hartford County, (860)648-4653, 10 miles from Hartford. **Facility Holes:** 18. **Yards:** 6,649/5,000. **Par:** 72/72. **Course Rating:** 70.9/68.4. **Slope:** 124/113. **Green Fee:** $33/$36. **Cart Fee:** $12/Person. **Walking Policy:** Unrestricted walking. **Opened:** 1987. **Season:** March-Dec. **To obtain tee times:** Call up to 7 days in advance. **Miscellaneous:** Credit cards (MC, V), BF, FF.

Reader Comments: Great staff, good condition, mediocre design ... Top shelf ... All the traps are in front of the greens ... Will be back ... Growing in beautifully ... 6-hour rounds ... Too many bunkers ... Pace of play needs improvement ... Nice smooth greens ... Ultra challenging 14th hole.

★★½ THE TRADITION GOLF CLUB AT WALLINGFORD
PU-37 Harrison Rd., Wallingford, 06492, New Haven County, (203)269-6023, (888)560-8476, 12 miles from New Haven. **Facility Holes:** 18. **Yards:** 6,200/4,900. **Par:** 70/70. **Course Rating:** 70.0/68.0. **Slope:** 125/117. **Green Fee:** $28/$55. **Cart Fee:** $13/Person. **Walking Policy:** Walking at certain times. **Walkability:** 5. **Season:** March-Nov. **High:** May-Oct. **To obtain tee times:** Call up to 7 days in advance. **Miscellaneous:** Reduced fees (weekdays, twilight, seniors, juniors), range (grass/mats), credit cards (MC, V, AE, D), BF, FF. **Special Notes:** Formerly Harbour Ridge Golf Club.

★★★ THE TRADITION GOLF CLUB AT WINDSOR
PU-147 Pigeon Hill Rd., Windsor, 06095, Hartford County, (860)688-2575, (888)399-8484, 10 miles from Hartford. **E-mail:** mbgolf@tiac.net. **Facility Holes:** 18. **Yards:** 6,068/4,877. **Par:** 71/71. **Course Rating:** 69.8/68.9. **Slope:** 119/117. **Green Fee:** $23/$41. **Cart Fee:** $13/Person. **Walking Policy:** Unrestricted walking. **Walkability:** 4. **Architect:** Geoffrey S. Cornish. **Season:** March-Dec. **To obtain tee times:** Call up to 7 days in advance. **Miscellaneous:** Reduced fees (weekdays, twilight, seniors, juniors), credit cards (MC, V, AE), BF, FF.

Reader Comments: New ownership ... Compact layout ... Parallel fairways dangerous ... Overpriced, but nice course ... Too hilly ... One of my favorites ... Unusual layout but a fun course to play.

TUNXIS PLANTATION COUNTRY CLUB
PU-87 Town Farm Rd., Farmington, 06032, Hartford County, (860)677-1367, 10 miles from Hartford. **Facility Holes:** 45. **Green Fee:** $29/$35. **Cart Fee:** $27/Cart. **Walking Policy:** Unrestricted walking. **Walkability:** 1. **Opened:** 1962. **Architect:** Al Zikorus. **Season:** April-Nov. **High:** May-Aug. **To obtain tee times:** Call golf shop. **Miscellaneous:** Reduced fees (weekdays, seniors, juniors), range (grass/mats), credit cards (MC, V, AE, D), BF, FF.
★★★½ **GREEN COURSE** (18)
Yards: 6,354/4,883. **Par:** 70/70. **Course Rating:** 70.0/71.0. **Slope:** 120/117.

Reader Comments: This course has the new 9 combined with an older 9 ... Wide open, easy walk ... Too easy. White course more challenging ... Two different 9s ... Good for high-handicapper.

CONNECTICUT

★★★½ **WHITE COURSE** (18)
Yards: 6,638/5,744. **Par:** 72/72. **Course Rating:** 72.2/71.5. **Slope:** 121/116.
Reader Comments: Always a great place to play ... When you go there you get treated well, and have a good time ... Enough water holes to keep your attention ... Nice variety of holes ... Relaxing, wide open, love everything ... A nice course for a new golfer ... Slow greens, flat, but enjoyable.
Special Notes: Also has a 9-hole Red Course.

★★★½ **TWIN HILLS COUNTRY CLUB** *Value*
PU-Rte. 31, Coventry, 06238, Tolland County, (860)742-9705, 10 miles from Hartford. **Facility Holes:** 18. **Yards:** 6,257/5,249. **Par:** 71/71. **Course Rating:** 68.7/69.5. **Slope:** 118/116. **Green Fee:** $30/$32. **Cart Fee:** $24/Cart. **Walking Policy:** Unrestricted walking. **Walkability:** 3. **Opened:** 1971. **Architect:** Mike McDermott/George McDermott. **Season:** Year-round. **High:** May-Sept. **To obtain tee times:** Call up to 7 days in advance. **Miscellaneous:** Reduced fees (seniors, juniors), metal spikes, credit cards (MC, V), BF, FF.
Reader Comments: Constant improvement, underrated ... Needs work ... Neat little course ... Owners who make you feel relaxed ... Friendly staff ... Short, scenic, fast greens ... Doglegs and water hazards.

★½ **WESTERN HILLS GOLF CLUB**
PU-Park Rd., Waterbury, 06708, New Haven County, (203)755-6828, 60 miles from New York. **Facility Holes:** 18. **Yards:** 6,427/5,393. **Par:** 72/72. **Course Rating:** 69.6/69.6. **Slope:** 125/122. **Green Fee:** $17/$24. **Cart Fee:** $24/Cart. **Walking Policy:** Unrestricted walking. **Walkability:** 3. **Opened:** 1961. **Architect:** Al Zikorus. **Season:** April-Dec. **High:** April-Aug. **To obtain tee times:** Call up to 3 days in advance. **Miscellaneous:** Reduced fees (weekdays, seniors, juniors),BF, FF.

★★★ **WHITNEY FARMS GOLF COURSE**
PU-175 Shelton Rd., Monroe, 06468, Fairfield County, (203)268-0707, 20 miles from Bridgeport. **Facility Holes:** 18. **Yards:** 6,628/5,832. **Par:** 72/73. **Course Rating:** 72.4/72.9. **Slope:** 130/124. **Green Fee:** $50/$60. **Cart Fee:** Included in green fee. **Walking Policy:** Mandatory carts. **Walkability:** 1. **Opened:** 1981. **Architect:** Hal Purdy. **Season:** March-Dec. **High:** June-Aug. **To obtain tee times:** Call up to 7 days in advance. **Miscellaneous:** Reduced fees (seniors), range (mats), credit cards (MC, V, AE), BF, FF.
Reader Comments: Difficult course, excellent condition ... Driving range is an eyesore and cuts into 18th ... Go on a weekday ... Be straight or else!

★★★½ **WILLIMANTIC COUNTRY CLUB**
SP-184 Club Rd., Windham, 06280, Windham County, (860)456-1971, 28 miles from Hartford. **E-mail:** webmaster@wiligolf.com. **Web:** www.wiligolf.com. **Facility Holes:** 18. **Yards:** 6,278/5,106. **Par:** 71/71. **Course Rating:** 70.5/68.5. **Slope:** 123/113. **Green Fee:** $45. **Cart Fee:** $11/Person. **Walking Policy:** Walking at certain times. **Walkability:** 3. **Opened:** 1922. **Architect:** Designed by members. **Season:** April-Dec. **High:** May-Sept. **To obtain tee times:** Call golf shop. **Miscellaneous:** Credit cards (MC, V, AE).
Reader Comments: Expensive if you go up as a daily fee player ... Not an especially long course, but challenging ... Fun to play ... Old style course ... Nice greens ... Excellent condition.

★★½ **WOODHAVEN COUNTRY CLUB**
PU-275 Miller Rd., Bethany, 06524, New Haven County, (203)393-3230, 5 miles from New Haven. **E-mail:** woodhaven@snet.net. **Facility Holes:** 9. **Yards:** 3,387/2,859. **Par:** 36/37. **Course Rating:** 72.7/73.0. **Slope:** 128/125. **Green Fee:** $27/$37. **Cart Fee:** $26/Cart. **Walking Policy:** Unrestricted walking. **Walkability:** 2. **Opened:** 1968. **Architect:** Al Zikorus. **Season:** Year-round. **High:** May-Sept. **To obtain tee times:** Call golf shop. **Miscellaneous:** Reduced fees (weekdays, seniors), range (mats), credit cards (MC, V), FF.

★★★★ **YALE GOLF COURSE**
SP-200 Conrad Dr., New Haven, 06515, New Haven County, (203)432-0895. **E-mail:** peterpulaski@yale.edu. **Facility Holes:** 18. **Yards:** 6,750/5,209. **Par:** 70/70. **Course Rating:** 72.9/70.2. **Slope:** 132/123. **Green Fee:** $100. **Cart Fee:** $34/Cart. **Walking Policy:** Unrestricted walking. **Walkability:** 5. **Opened:** 1926. **Architect:** C.B. Macdonald. **Season:** April-Dec. **To obtain tee times:** Call golf shop. **Miscellaneous:** Metal spikes, range (grass), credit cards (MC, V),BF, FF.
Notes: Ranked 4th in 2001 Best in State.
Reader Comments: My favorite place in CT to play! ... A classic test of shotmaking ... Charges like a country club for a course which is really like an above average public course ... Very difficult ... There aren't many courses like this one ... Memorable 9th hole ... Bunkers are deep.

DELAWARE

★★★½ BACK CREEK GOLF CLUB
PU-101 Back Creek Dr., Middletown, 19709, New Castle County, (302)378-6499, 20 miles from Wilmington. **E-mail:** backcreekgc@dol.net. **Web:** www.backcreekgc.com. **Facility Holes:** 18. **Yards:** 7,003/5,014. **Par:** 71/71. **Course Rating:** 74.2/69.3. **Slope:** 134/115. **Green Fee:** $22/$46. **Cart Fee:** $16/Person. **Walking Policy:** Unrestricted walking. **Walkability:** 2. **Opened:** 1997. **Architect:** David Horn/Allen Liddicoat. **Season:** Year-round. **High:** April-Oct. **To obtain tee times:** Call up to 7 days in advance. **Miscellaneous:** Reduced fees (weekdays, twilight, seniors, juniors), range (grass/mats), credit cards (MC, V, D), BF, FF.
Reader Comments: 13th plays narrow but is visually open—plays with your mind ... Great new course ... Worth the time it took to get from Jersey ... Not too long but errant shots will cost you in the high grass ... Great deals during the week ... Greens were awesome! ... Wind is super tough ... Good short par 4s.

BAYWOOD GREENS
PU-Long Neck Rd. off Rte. 24, Long Neck, 19966, Sussex County, (302)947-9800, (888)844-2254, 8 miles from Rehoboth Beach. **E-mail:** info@baywoodgreens.com. **Web:** www.baywoodgreens.com. **Facility Holes:** 18. **Yards:** 6,983/5,136. **Par:** 72/72. **Course Rating:** 73.2/70.9. **Slope:** 129/124. **Green Fee:** $48/$78. **Cart Fee:** Included in green fee. **Walking Policy:** Unrestricted walking. **Walkability:** 2. **Opened:** 1998. **Season:** Year-round. **High:** April-Oct. **To obtain tee times:** Call up to 180 days in advance. **Miscellaneous:** Reduced fees (weekdays, twilight, juniors), range (grass/mats), credit cards (MC, V), BF, FF.

★★★★ BEAR TRAP DUNES GOLF CLUB
PU-Central Ave., Ocean View, 19970, New Castle County, (302)537-5600, (877)232-7872, 125 miles from Philadelphia. **E-mail:** bmarshall@seacolony.com. **Web:** www.beartrapdunes.com. **Facility Holes:** 18. **Yards:** 6,834/5,208. **Par:** 72/72. **Course Rating:** 72.1/69.8. **Slope:** 125/120. **Cart Fee:** Included in green fee. **Opened:** 1999. **Architect:** Rick Jacobson. **Season:** Year-round. **High:** April-Oct. **To obtain tee times:** Call up to 270 days in advance. **Miscellaneous:** Reduced fees (weekdays, twilight, juniors), range (grass/mats), credit cards (MC, V, AE), BF, FF.
Reader Comments: You would think you were playing right on the ocean ... Very enjoyable despite the wind ... A must play ... Possibly the best golf in Delaware ... Good course for tourist and novice golfers ... Strong contouring of greens ... Fun course, does not beat you up.

★★½ DEL CASTLE GOLF CLUB
PU-801 McKennans Church Rd., Wilmington, 19808, New Castle County, (302)995-1990, 20 miles from Philadelphia. **Facility Holes:** 18. **Yards:** 6,625/6,326. **Par:** 72/72. **Course Rating:** 71.0/69.7. **Slope:** 123/120. **Green Fee:** $16/$22. **Cart Fee:** $14/Person. **Walking Policy:** Unrestricted walking. **Walkability:** 3. **Opened:** 1972. **Architect:** Edmund B. Ault. **Season:** Year-round. **High:** May-Sept. **To obtain tee times:** Call up to 14 days in advance. **Miscellaneous:** Reduced fees (twilight, seniors, juniors), metal spikes, range (grass/mats), credit cards (MC, V, AE, D), BF, FF.

EAGLE CREEK GOLF CLUB
M-Building 827, Dover, 19902, Kent County, (302)677-6039. **Facility Holes:** 18. **Yards:** 5,904/4,791. **Par:** 69/69. **Course Rating:** 67.8/62.5. **Slope:** 121/103. **Green Fee:** $9/$16. **Cart Fee:** $11/Person. **Walking Policy:** Unrestricted walking. **Walkability:** 1. **Season:** Year-round. **High:** April-Sept. **To obtain tee times:** Call golf shop. **Miscellaneous:** Reduced fees (twilight, juniors), range (grass), credit cards (MC, V).

★★ ED 'PORKY' OLIVER GOLF CLUB
PU-800 N. DuPont Rd., Wilmington, 19807, New Castle County, (302)571-9041, 25 miles from Philadelphia. **E-mail:** jsurrette@mggi.com. **Facility Holes:** 18. **Yards:** 6,115/5,674. **Par:** 69/71. **Course Rating:** 69.8/71.8. **Slope:** 118/121. **Green Fee:** $15/$31. **Cart Fee:** $27/Cart. **Walking Policy:** Unrestricted walking. **Walkability:** 1. **Opened:** 1901. **Architect:** Wilfrid Reid/Ed Ault. **Season:** Year-round. **To obtain tee times:** Call golf shop. **Miscellaneous:** Reduced fees (weekdays, twilight, seniors, juniors), metal spikes, range (grass/mats), credit cards (MC, V), BF, FF.

FROG HOLLOW GOLF CLUB
SP-1 E. Whittington Way, Middletown, 19709, New Castle County, (302)376-6500, 25 miles from Wilmington. **Web:** www.froghollowgolf.com. **Facility Holes:** 18. **Yards:** 6,608/4,750. **Par:** 71/71. **Course Rating:** 72.1/63.4. **Slope:** 128/114. **Green Fee:** $48/$65. **Cart Fee:** Included in green fee. **Walking Policy:** Unrestricted walking. **Walkability:** 2. **Opened:** 2000. **Architect:** Daneil Horn/AllenLiddicoat. **Season:** Year-round. **High:** April-Oct. **To obtain tee times:** Call up to 7 days in advance. **Miscellaneous:** Reduced fees (weekdays, twilight, seniors, juniors), range (grass), credit cards (MC, V), FF.

★★½   GARRISONS LAKE COUNTRY CLUB
PU-101 Fairways Circle, Smyrna, 19977, Kent County, (302)653-6349, (800)546-5745,
5 miles from Dover. **E-mail:** rjgarslake.com. **Web:** www.garrisonslake.com. **Facility Holes:** 18.
Yards: 7,028/5,460. **Par:** 72/72. **Course Rating:** 73.1/71.6. **Slope:** 125/126. **Green Fee:**
$24/$43. **Walking Policy:** Walking at certain times. **Walkability:** 1. **Opened:** 1963. **Architect:**
Edmund B. Ault. **Season:** Year-round. **High:** April-Sept. **To obtain tee times:** Call golf shop.
Miscellaneous: Reduced fees (weekdays, twilight, seniors), range (grass/mats), credit cards
(MC, V, AE, D), BF, FF.

★½   OLD LANDING GOLF CLUB
PU-300 Old Landing Road, Rehoboth Beach, 19971, Sussex County, (302)227-3131, 40
miles from Dover. **Facility Holes:** 18. **Yards:** 6,097/5,383. **Par:** 71/71. **Course Rating:** 68.2.
Slope: 108. **Green Fee:** $30. **Opened:** 1965. **Season:** Year-round. **To obtain tee times:** Call
golf shop. **Miscellaneous:** Metal spikes.

★★   ROCK MANOR GOLF COURSE
PU-1319 Caruthers Lane, Wilmington, 19803, New Castle County, (302)652-4083. **Facility
Holes:** 18. **Yards:** 5,779/5,201. **Par:** 69/69. **Course Rating:** 66.3/67.8. **Slope:** 111/107. **Green
Fee:** $18/$21. **Opened:** 1938. **Season:** Year-round. **To obtain tee times:** Call golf shop.

THE ROOKERY GOLF CLUB
PU-27052 Broadkill Rd., Milton, 19968, Sussex County, (302)684-3000, (866)313-4653,
9 miles from Rehoboth Beach. **E-mail:** butch@rookerygolf.com. **Web:** www.rookerygolf.com.
Facility Holes: 18. **Yards:** 6,461/4,785. **Par:** 71/71. **Course Rating:** 70.5. **Slope:** 117. **Green
Fee:** $29/$54. **Cart Fee:** Included in green fee. **Walking Policy:** Unrestricted walking.
Walkability: 1. **Opened:** 2000. **Architect:** Chris Adkins. **Season:** Year-round. **To obtain tee
times:** Call up to 30 days in advance. **Miscellaneous:** Reduced fees (weekdays, twilight,
seniors, juniors), range (grass/mats), credit cards (MC, V), BF, FF.

★★★½   THREE LITTLE BAKERS COUNTRY CLUB
SP-3542 Foxcroft Dr., Wilmington, 19808, New Castle County, (302)737-1877, 65 miles from
Philadelphia. **Facility Holes:** 18. **Yards:** 6,609/5,209. **Par:** 71/72. **Course Rating:** 71.9/70.3.
Slope: 130/120. **Green Fee:** $47/$52. **Cart Fee:** Included in green fee. **Walking Policy:** Walking
at certain times. **Walkability:** 5. **Opened:** 1973. **Architect:** Edmund B. Ault. **Season:** Year-
round. **High:** April-Oct. **To obtain tee times:** Call golf shop. **Miscellaneous:** Reduced fees
(weekdays, twilight, seniors, juniors), credit cards (MC, V, AE, D), BF, FF.
Reader Comments: Worth the bucks, go back again … Keep it in play … Greens are very true …
Hilly, interesting par 3s, country club character … Try and get a tee time in morning … Very challenging … Not a flat spot on the course … Exceptional service … Can play long with unkind rough.

DISTRICT OF COLUMBIA

★½ EAST POTOMAC PARK GOLF COURSE
PU-Ohio Dr., Washington D.C., 20024, District of Columbia County, (202)554-7660. **E-mail:** mbyrd@capitalcitygolf.net. **Web:** www.golfde.com. **Facility Holes:** 36. **Yards:** 6,303/5,761. **Par:** 72/72. **Course Rating:** 68.5. **Slope:** 109. **Green Fee:** $12/$24. **Cart Fee:** $20/Cart. **Walking Policy:** Unrestricted walking. **Walkability:** 1. **Opened:** 1920. **Architect:** Robert White/Walter Travis. **Season:** Year-round. **High:** May-Sept. **To obtain tee times:** Call golf shop. **Miscellaneous:** Reduced fees (weekdays, seniors), metal spikes, range (mats), credit cards (MC, V), BF, FF.
Special Notes: Also has an 18-hole executive course.

★★ LANGSTON GOLF COURSE
PU-2600 Benning Rd. N.E., Washington D.C., 20001, District of Columbia County, (202)397-8638, 33 miles from Baltimore. **Facility Holes:** 18. **Yards:** 6,340. **Par:** 72. **Course Rating:** 69.6. **Slope:** 112. **Green Fee:** $11/$17. **Cart Fee:** $19/Cart. **Walking Policy:** Unrestricted walking. **Opened:** 1939. **Architect:** William Gordon. **Season:** Year-round. **High:** March-Oct. **To obtain tee times:** Call golf shop. **Miscellaneous:** Reduced fees (weekdays), metal spikes, range (grass).

★½ ROCK CREEK PARK GOLF COURSE
PU-16th & Rittenhouse N.W., Washington D.C., 20011, District of Columbia County, (202)882-7332. **Facility Holes:** 18. **Yards:** 4,715/4,715. **Par:** 65/65. **Course Rating:** 62.5/65.5. **Slope:** 112/102. **Green Fee:** $11/$19. **Cart Fee:** $18/Cart. **Walking Policy:** Unrestricted walking. **Walkability:** 3. **Opened:** 1923. **Architect:** William S. Flynn. **Season:** Year-round. **High:** June-Aug. **To obtain tee times:** Call golf shop. **Miscellaneous:** Reduced fees (weekdays, seniors), metal spikes, credit cards (MC, V).

★★★ ABACOA GOLF CLUB
PU-105 Barbados Dr., Jupiter, 33458, Palm Beach County, (561)622-0036, 15 miles from West Palm Beach. **E-mail:** abacoa@bellsouth.net. **Web:** www.abacoagolfclub.com. **Facility Holes:** 18. **Yards:** 7,200/5,391. **Par:** 72/72. **Course Rating:** 74.6/71.7. **Slope:** 137/128. **Green Fee:** $29/$79. **Cart Fee:** Included in green fee. **Walking Policy:** Mandatory carts. **Opened:** 1999. **Architect:** Joe Lee. **Season:** Year-round. **High:** June-April. **To obtain tee times:** Call up to 30 days in advance. **Miscellaneous:** Reduced fees (twilight, juniors), range (grass), credit cards (MC, V, AE), BF, FF.
Reader Comments: Great new course challenging & fun … Wide open, nice … Lots of wind … Hard course, slow pace, good value … Great fun, sporty excellent course. Friendly staff … Housing overpowers course.

ADMIRAL LEHIGH GOLF RESORT
R-225 East Joel Blvd., Lehigh, 33972, Lee County, (941)369-2121, 13 miles from Fort Myers. **Facility Holes:** 36. **Cart Fee:** Included in green fee. **Walking Policy:** Walking at certain times. **Season:** Year-round. **To obtain tee times:** Call up to 4 days in advance. **Miscellaneous:** Reduced fees (guests, twilight), range (grass/mats), lodging (131 rooms), credit cards (MC, V, AE, D), BF, FF.
★★ **NORTH COURSE** (18)
Yards: 6,085/4,703. **Par:** 70/70. **Course Rating:** 70.0/67.3. **Slope:** 119/116. **Green Fee:** $17/$62. **Walkability:** 2. **Opened:** 1958. **Architect:** Mark Mahannah.
★★½ **SOUTH COURSE AT MIRROR LAKES** (18)
Yards: 7,058/5,697. **Par:** 73/73. **Course Rating:** 74.0/72.9. **Slope:** 123/125. **Green Fee:** $17/$60. **Walkability:** 3. **Opened:** 1973. **Architect:** Mark Mahannah.

AMELIA ISLAND PLANTATION
R-6800 1st Coast Hwy., Amelia Island, 32035, Nassau County, (904)277-5907, (800)874-6878, 35 miles from Jacksonville. **Web:** www.aipfl.com. **Facility Holes:** 54. **Cart Fee:** Included in green fee. **Opened:** 1987. **Architect:** Tom Fazio. **Season:** Year-round. **To obtain tee times:** Call golf shop. **Miscellaneous:** Reduced fees (guests, twilight, juniors), range (grass), lodging (400 rooms), credit cards (MC, V, AE, D, Resort Charge Card).
★★★★½ **LONG POINT GOLF CLUB** (18)
Yards: 6,775/4,927. **Par:** 72/72. **Course Rating:** 72.9/69.1. **Slope:** 129/121. **Green Fee:** $125/$155. **Walkability:** 2. **High:** Oct.-Nov.
Reader Comments: Great views, layout sequence weird … Tight, windy, small greens, bring 'A' game … Easy to get tee time … Very pricey, great holes, speedy greens … Nice course but expensive … A great golf challenge.
★★★★ **OAK MARSH** (18) *Pace*
Yards: 6,108/4,341. **Par:** 70/70. **Course Rating:** 70.3/66.4. **Slope:** 134/115. **Green Fee:** $115/$145. **High:** March-May.
Reader Comments: Great resort links course, beautiful ocean holes … Target golf, fun to play … Layout interesting … Great all-around experience … Ocean-front holes … First-class course.
★★★★ **OCEAN LINKS** (18)
Yards: 6,592/4,983. **Par:** 72/72. **Course Rating:** 71.7/66.4. **Slope:** 130/115. **Green Fee:** $95/$115. **Walkability:** 1. **High:** Oct.-Nov.
Reader Comments: Amazing views … Tight, windy, small greens, bring "A" game … Will be better when it matures … Ocean holes are beautiful & challenging … A few good holes, but overall not great … Wind makes it challenging.

★★ APOLLO BEACH GOLF & SEA CLUB
PU-801 Golf and Sea Blvd., Apollo Beach, 33572, Hillsborough County, (813)645-6212, 15 miles from Tampa. **Facility Holes:** 18. **Yards:** 7,070/4,831. **Par:** 72/72. **Course Rating:** 73.9/69.1. **Slope:** 130/115. **Green Fee:** $22/$40. **Cart Fee:** Included in green fee. **Walking Policy:** Mandatory carts. **Walkability:** 1. **Opened:** 1972. **Architect:** Robert Trent Jones. **Season:** Year-round. **High:** Nov.-April. **To obtain tee times:** Call up to 7 days in advance. **Miscellaneous:** Reduced fees (twilight, juniors), range (grass), credit cards (MC, V, AE, D), BF, FF.

ARNOLD PALMER'S BAY HILL CLUB & LODGE
R-9000 Bay Hill Blvd., Orlando, 32819, Orange County, (407)876-2429x630, 15 miles from Orlando. **Web:** www.bayhill.com. **Facility Holes:** 18. **Cart Fee:** Included in green fee. **Walkability:** 2. **Architect:** Dick Wilson/Arnold Palmer/Ed Seay. **Season:** Year-round. **To obtain tee times:** Call golf shop. **Miscellaneous:** Reduced fees (guests, juniors), range (grass), caddies, lodging (68 rooms), credit cards (MC, V, AE).
★★★★½ **CHALLENGER/CHAMPION** (18) *Condition*
Yards: 7,207/5,235. **Par:** 72/72. **Course Rating:** 75.1/72.7. **Slope:** 139/130. **Walking Policy:** Walking with Caddie. **Opened:** 1961. **Miscellaneous:** BF, FF.
Notes: Ranked 97th in 1997-98 America's 100 Greatest; 8th in 2001 Best in State; 25th in 1996 America's Top 75 Upscale Courses.

FLORIDA

Reader Comments: Multiple tees for varying abilities … Terrific golf environment … Arnie played just ahead of us … Well-trained staff, friendly people … Outstanding course … Arnold talked to us on the putting green … Great caddies.
CHARGER (9)
Yards: 3,409/2,635. **Par:** 36/36. **Walking Policy:** Unrestricted walking. **Opened:** 1965.

★★ ARROWHEAD GOLF COURSE
PU-8201 S.W. 24th St., Ft. Lauderdale, 33324, Broward County, (954)475-8200, 5 miles from Ft. Lauderdale. **Facility Holes:** 18. **Yards:** 6,311/4,838. **Par:** 70/70. **Course Rating:** 70.8/68.7. **Slope:** 115/109. **Green Fee:** $24/$47. **Cart Fee:** Included in green fee. **Walking Policy:** Mandatory carts. **Walkability:** 2. **Opened:** 1976. **Architect:** Bill Watts. **Season:** Year-round. **High:** Dec.-April. **To obtain tee times:** Call up to 14 days in advance. **Miscellaneous:** Reduced fees (weekdays, twilight, juniors), metal spikes, range (grass/mats), credit cards (MC, V, AE, D), BF, FF.

★★★ ATLANTIS COUNTRY CLUB & INN
R-190 Atlantis Blvd., Atlantis, 33462, Palm Beach County, (561)968-1300, (800)393-2224, 7 miles from West Palm Beach. **E-mail:** atlkin@aol.com. **Facility Holes:** 18. **Yards:** 6,610/5,242. **Par:** 72/72. **Course Rating:** 71.5/70.9. **Slope:** 129/123. **Green Fee:** $20/$60. **Cart Fee:** $17/Person. **Walking Policy:** Mandatory carts. **Walkability:** 1. **Opened:** 1972. **Architect:** Bob Simmons. **Season:** Year-round. **High:** Jan.-March. **To obtain tee times:** Call up to 5 days in advance. **Miscellaneous:** Reduced fees (weekdays, guests, twilight), range (grass), lodging (24 rooms), credit cards (MC, V, D), BF, FF.
Reader Comments: Narrow fairways, not a long course … Country club amenities, small greens, putt from rear of greens best … Friendly, efficient staff … Accuracy on approach rewarded with good scores.

★★ BABE ZAHARIAS GOLF COURSE
PU-11412 Forest Hills Dr., Tampa, 33612, Hillsborough County, (813)631-4374, 20 miles from St. Petersburg. **E-mail:** bzbillhp@prodisy.net. **Facility Holes:** 18. **Yards:** 6,039/4,989. **Par:** 70/72. **Course Rating:** 68.4/68.8. **Slope:** 117/119. **Green Fee:** $17/$36. **Cart Fee:** Included in green fee. **Walking Policy:** Unrestricted walking. **Walkability:** 1. **Opened:** 1974. **Architect:** Ron Garl. **Season:** Year-round. **High:** Dec.-April. **To obtain tee times:** Call golf shop. **Miscellaneous:** Reduced fees (weekdays, twilight, seniors, juniors), metal spikes, credit cards (MC, V, D), BF, FF.

★★★ BARDMOOR GOLF & TENNIS CLUB
SP-8001 Cumberland Rd., Largo, 33777, Pinellas County, (727)392-1234, 15 miles from Tampa. **E-mail:** bardmoor@crown-golf.com. **Web:** www.bardmoor.com. **Facility Holes:** 18. **Yards:** 7,000/4,990. **Par:** 72/72. **Course Rating:** 74.4/69.4. **Slope:** 131/120. **Green Fee:** $35/$100. **Cart Fee:** Included in green fee. **Walking Policy:** Mandatory carts. **Walkability:** 2. **Opened:** 1970. **Architect:** William Diddel. **Season:** Year-round. **To obtain tee times:** Call up to 30 days in advance. **Miscellaneous:** Reduced fees (weekdays, twilight, juniors), range (grass), credit cards (MC, V, AE, D), BF, FF.
Reader Comments: Average to above public course … Very challenging … OK old FL course … many water hazards … Average throughout … Responsive staff.

★★ BAYMEADOWS GOLF CLUB
SP-7981 Baymeadows Circle W., Jacksonville, 32256, Duval County, (904)731-5701. **Facility Holes:** 18. **Yards:** 6,939/5,309. **Par:** 72/72. **Course Rating:** 73.7/72.2. **Slope:** 130/130. **Green Fee:** $20/$45. **Cart Fee:** Included in green fee. **Walking Policy:** Mandatory carts. **Walkability:** 2. **Opened:** 1969. **Architect:** Desmond Muirhead/Gene Sarazen. **Season:** Year-round. **To obtain tee times:** Call up to 7 days in advance. **Miscellaneous:** Reduced fees (weekdays, guests, twilight, seniors, juniors), range (grass/mats), lodging (200 rooms), credit cards (MC, V, AE, D, DC), BF, FF.

★★ BAYSHORE GOLF COURSE
PU-2301 Alton Rd., Miami Beach, 33140, Dade County, (305)532-3350. **Facility Holes:** 18. **Yards:** 6,903/5,538. **Par:** 72/73. **Course Rating:** 73.0/71.6. **Slope:** 127/120. **Green Fee:** $30/$55. **Cart Fee:** Included in green fee. **Walking Policy:** Mandatory carts. **Walkability:** 1. **Opened:** 1927. **Architect:** Robert von Hagge/Bruce Devlin. **Season:** Year-round. **High:** Nov.-April. **To obtain tee times:** Call up to 7 days in advance. **Miscellaneous:** Reduced fees (weekdays, twilight, juniors), metal spikes, range (mats), credit cards (MC, V, AE), BF, FF.

★★★★ BAYTREE NATIONAL GOLF LINKS
SP-8207 National Dr., Melbourne, 32940, Brevard County, (321)259-9060, (888)955-1234, 50 miles from Orlando. **E-mail:** bnglmgr@metrolink.net. **Web:** www.golfbaytree.com. **Facility Holes:** 18. **Yards:** 7,043/4,803. **Par:** 72/72. **Course Rating:** 74.4/67.5. **Slope:** 138/118. **Green Fee:** $34/$85. **Cart Fee:** Included in green fee. **Walking Policy:** Mandatory carts.

Walkability: 2. **Opened:** 1994. **Architect:** Gary Player. **Season:** Year-round. **High:** Jan.-April. **To obtain tee times:** Call golf shop. **Miscellaneous:** Reduced fees (guests, twilight), range (grass), credit cards (MC, V, AE), BF, FF.

Reader Comments: Fair challenge ... Convex fairways are hard to hold ... Fine course ... Layout good, course in great shape ... Nice people, loved the waste areas! ... This was a fun course.

★★ BELLA VISTA GOLF & YACHT CLUB

SP-P.O. Box 66, Hwy. 48, Howey in the Hills, 34737, Lake County, (352)324-3233, (800)955-7001, 25 miles from Orlando. **Facility Holes:** 18. **Yards:** 6,321/5,386. **Par:** 71/71. **Course Rating:** 68.4/71.9. **Slope:** 119/123. **Green Fee:** $16/$38. **Cart Fee:** Included in green fee. **Walking Policy:** Mandatory carts. **Walkability:** 2. **Opened:** 1990. **Architect:** Lloyd Clifton. **Season:** Year-round. **High:** Jan.-April. **To obtain tee times:** Call golf shop. **Miscellaneous:** Reduced fees (weekdays, guests, twilight, seniors, juniors), range (grass), credit cards (MC, V, AE, D), FF.

★★ BELLEVIEW BILTMORE RESORT & GOLF CLUB

R-1501 Indian Rocks Rd., Belleair, 33756, Pinellas County, (727)581-5498, 1 mile from Clearwater. **E-mail:** ssarb@mindspring.com. **Web:** www.belleviewbiltmore.com. **Facility Holes:** 18. **Yards:** 6,695/5,703. **Par:** 72/74. **Course Rating:** 70.7/72.1. **Slope:** 118/119. **Green Fee:** $35/$75. **Cart Fee:** Included in green fee. **Walking Policy:** Mandatory carts. **Walkability:** 2. **Opened:** 1926. **Architect:** Donald Ross. **Season:** Year-round. **High:** Jan.-April. **To obtain tee times:** Call up to 4 days in advance. **Miscellaneous:** Reduced fees (weekdays, guests, twilight), range (grass), lodging (250 rooms), credit cards (MC, V, AE, D), BF, FF.

★★½ THE BILTMORE GOLF COURSE

PU-1210 Anastasia Ave., Coral Gables, 33134, Dade County, (305)460-5364, 3 miles from Miami. **E-mail:** biltcggolf@aol.com. **Facility Holes:** 18. **Yards:** 6,642/5,237. **Par:** 71/73. **Course Rating:** 71.5/70.1. **Slope:** 119/115. **Green Fee:** $13/$53. **Cart Fee:** $17/Person. **Walking Policy:** Walking at certain times. **Walkability:** 1. **Opened:** 1925. **Architect:** Donald Ross. **Season:** Year-round. **High:** Dec.-April. **To obtain tee times:** Call up to 2 days in advance. **Miscellaneous:** Reduced fees (guests, twilight, juniors), range (grass/mats), credit cards (MC, V, AE), BF, FF.

★★★½ BINKS FOREST GOLF COURSE

SP-400 Binks Forest Dr., Wellington, 33414, Palm Beach County, (561)795-0595, 15 miles from West Palm Beach. **Facility Holes:** 18. **Yards:** 7,065/5,599. **Par:** 72/72. **Course Rating:** 75.0/71.9. **Slope:** 138/127. **Green Fee:** $20/$55. **Cart Fee:** Included in green fee. **Walkability:** 1. **Opened:** 1990. **Architect:** Johnny Miller. **Season:** Year-round. **High:** Nov.-April. **To obtain tee times:** Call golf shop. **Miscellaneous:** Reduced fees (weekdays, guests, twilight), metal spikes, range (grass), credit cards (MC, V, AE, D).

Reader Comments: Good test ... Plays long, very challenging but great rewards when hitting solidly ... Liked it so well played it twice ... Overbooked! Back up on every hole ... North Carolina course in Florida.

★★★ BLACK BEAR GOLF CLUB

PU-24505 Calusa Blvd., Eustis, 32736, Lake County, (352)357-4732, (800)423-2718, 40 miles from Orlando. **Facility Holes:** 18. **Yards:** 7,002/5,044. **Par:** 72/72. **Course Rating:** 74.7/70.5. **Slope:** 134/121. **Green Fee:** $35/$65. **Cart Fee:** Included in green fee. **Walking Policy:** Unrestricted walking. **Walkability:** 3. **Opened:** 1995. **Architect:** P.B. Dye. **Season:** Year-round. **High:** Jan.-March. **To obtain tee times:** Call golf shop. **Miscellaneous:** Reduced fees (weekdays, twilight, juniors), metal spikes, range (grass), credit cards (MC, V, AE, D).

Reader Comments: Elevations make it a challenge, beautiful ... Great, dry, hilly, tough greens ... PGA Tour caliber from back tees. Huge practice green ... Some neat holes, love those mounds ... Mound greens require skill & patience.

★★★ BLOOMINGDALE GOLFERS CLUB

PU-4113 Great Golfers Place, Valrico, 33594, Hillsborough County, (813)685-4105, 15 miles from Tampa. **E-mail:** tkrebs@eaglgolf.com. **Web:** www.bgcgolf.com. **Facility Holes:** 18. **Yards:** 7,165/5,506. **Par:** 72/73. **Course Rating:** 74.4/72.1. **Slope:** 131/132. **Green Fee:** $30/$66. **Cart Fee:** Included in green fee. **Walking Policy:** Mandatory carts. **Walkability:** 1. **Opened:** 1983. **Architect:** Ron Garl. **Season:** Year-round. **High:** Dec.-April. **To obtain tee times:** Call golf shop. **Miscellaneous:** Reduced fees (weekdays, twilight, seniors, juniors), range (grass/mats), credit cards (MC, V, AE), BF, FF.

Reader Comments: On the way back to being great ... Fast greens, excellent service ... Great value for area ... Condition has upped, very good driving holes (must work the ball) ... Thinker's course, quick greens. Be straight or you pay.

BLUEWATER BAY RESORT

R-1950 Bluewater Blvd., Niceville, 32578, Okaloosa County, (850)897-3241, (800)274-2128, 60 miles from Pensacola. **E-mail:** golf@bwbresort.com. **Web:** bwbresort.com. **Facility Holes:**

36. **Green Fee:** $35/$50. **Cart Fee:** $15/Person. **Walking Policy:** Walking at certain times. **Walkability:** 1. **Opened:** 1981. **Architect:** Tom Fazio/Jerry Pate. **Season:** Year-round. **To obtain tee times:** Call golf shop. **Miscellaneous:** Reduced fees (guests, juniors), range (grass), lodging (90 rooms), credit cards (MC, V, AE, D), BF, FF.

★★★ **BAY/LAKE COURSE** (18)
Yards: 6,803/5,378. **Par:** 72/72. **Course Rating:** 73.0/70.6. **Slope:** 140/124.
Reader Comments: Excellent course, value price … Friendly staff. Scenic and challenging holes … Best service anywhere … Good facilities, moderate green fee, course condition average.

★★★ **MAGNOLIA/MARSH COURSE** (18)
Yards: 6,669/5,048. **Par:** 72/72. **Course Rating:** 72.2/68.4. **Slope:** 132/117.
Reader Comments: Friendly … Layout a mixed bag … Outstanding! … Quiet and very nice place … Out of the way, but worth it … Very good condition, enjoyable … Terrific value.

BOBBY JONES GOLF COMPLEX
PU-1000 Circus Blvd., Sarasota, 34232, Sarasota County, (941)955-8097, 60 miles from Tampa. **E-mail:** gjgc@gte.net. **Facility Holes:** 45. **Green Fee:** $9/$24. **Cart Fee:** $12/Person. **Walking Policy:** Walking at certain times. **Season:** Year-round. **High:** Dec.-March. **To obtain tee times:** Call up to 3 days in advance. **Miscellaneous:** Reduced fees (twilight, juniors), range (mats), credit cards (MC, V), BF, FF.

★★½ **AMERICAN COURSE** (18)
Yards: 6,039/4,326. **Par:** 71/71. **Course Rating:** 69.8/70.4. **Slope:** 120/117. **Walkability:** 2.
Opened: 1957. **Architect:** Ron Garl.

★★½ **BRITISH COURSE** (18)
Yards: 6,537/5,268. **Par:** 72/72. **Course Rating:** 71.3/70.4. **Slope:** 120/117. **Walkability:** 1.
Opened: 1927. **Architect:** Donald Ross.
Special Notes: Also has a 9-hole executive course.

★★★★½ BOBCAT TRAIL GOLF & COUNTRY CLUB
PU-1350 Bobcat Trail, North Port, 34286, Sarasota County, (941)429-0500, 35 miles from Sarasota. **E-mail:** fdawson@bobcattrail.com. **Web:** bobcattrail.com. **Facility Holes:** 18. **Yards:** 6,748/4,741. **Par:** 71/71. **Course Rating:** 72.9/68.7. **Slope:** 129/115. **Green Fee:** $24/$60. **Cart Fee:** $15/Person. **Walking Policy:** Mandatory carts. **Walkability:** 3. **Opened:** 1998. **Architect:** Lee Singletary, Bob Tway. **Season:** Year-round. **High:** Oct.-April. **To obtain tee times:** Call up to 7 days in advance. **Miscellaneous:** Reduced fees (twilight), range (grass), credit cards (MC, V, AE, D), BF, FF.
Reader Comments: Water every hole but one … Excellent course, scenic, challenging … Nice layout … Deep bunkers, fine facilities … GPS on carts is nice. Good layout, good condition … Pace of play little slow.

BOCA RATON RESORT & CLUB
R-17751 Boca Club Blvd., Boca Raton, 33487, Palm Beach County, (561)997-8205, (800)327-0101, 17 miles from West Palm Beach. **E-mail:** rsc@bocaresort.com. **Web:** www.bocaresort.com. **Facility Holes:** 36. **Cart Fee:** $25/Person. **Season:** Year-round. **High:** Oct.-May. **To obtain tee times:** Call golf shop. **Miscellaneous:** Reduced fees (twilight), range (grass), lodging (965 rooms), credit cards (MC, V, AE, D, DC).

★★★★ **COUNTRY CLUB COURSE** (18)
Yards: 6,513/5,365. **Par:** 72/72. **Course Rating:** 71.8/72.1. **Slope:** 131/128. **Green Fee:** $50/$100. **Walkability:** 2. **Opened:** 1984. **Architect:** Joe Lee.
Reader Comments: Very nice course. Staff pleasant and efficient. Rental clubs are excellent … Marshals everywhere, smoked course in less than 4 hours … Excellent service/clear course … Well maintained, fair, challenging.

★★★½ **RESORT COURSE** (18)
Yards: 6,253/5,160. **Par:** 71/71. **Course Rating:** 69.3/68.7. **Slope:** 128/122. **Green Fee:** $65/$125. **Walkability:** 3. **Opened:** 1926. **Architect:** William Flynn. **Miscellaneous:**
Reader Comments: Old, traditional course, medium test … Good course, greens too sandy … Nice resort course for tourists … Beautiful course. Great flowers … Redesign is a significant improvement.

BONAVENTURE COUNTRY CLUB
R-200 Bonaventure Blvd., Weston, 33326, Broward County, (954)389-2100, 10 miles from Ft. Lauderdale. **E-mail:** edunes@aol.com. **Facility Holes:** 36. **Cart Fee:** Included in green fee. **Walking Policy:** Mandatory carts. **Season:** Year-round. **High:** Jan.-April. **To obtain tee times:** Call up to 365 days in advance. **Miscellaneous:** Reduced fees (guests, twilight), metal spikes, range (grass/mats), credit cards (MC, V, AE, D, DC, CB), FF.

★★★ **EAST** (18)
Yards: 7,011/5,345. **Par:** 72/72. **Course Rating:** 74.2/71.6. **Slope:** 132/122. **Green Fee:** $45/$95. **Walkability:** 2. **Opened:** 1968. **Architect:** Joe Lee.
Reader Comments: Nicely maintained, somewhat overcrowded during season … Great condition … Not most interesting course … Course we like to play as many times as possible … Ho-hum with an indifferent staff … Average.

★★½ **WEST** (18)
Yards: 6,189/4,993. **Par:** 70/70. **Course Rating:** 70.0/69.0. **Slope:** 118/114. **Green Fee:** $40/$70. **Walkability:** 1. **Opened:** 1974. **Architect:** Charles Mahannah.

★★½ **BONITA SPRINGS GOLF CLUB**
SP-10200 Maddox Lane, Bonita Springs, 34135, Lee County, (941)992-2800, 10 miles from Naples. **Facility Holes:** 18. **Yards:** 6,761/5,306. **Par:** 72/72. **Course Rating:** 71.2/70.1. **Slope:** 129/121. **Green Fee:** $15/$60. **Cart Fee:** Included in green fee. **Walking Policy:** Walking at certain times. **Walkability:** 1. **Opened:** 1977. **Architect:** William Maddox. **Season:** Year-round. **To obtain tee times:** Call up to 2 days in advance. **Miscellaneous:** Reduced fees (twilight), metal spikes, credit cards (MC, V, D), BF, FF.

BRAMBLE RIDGE GOLF COURSE
PU-2505 Bramble Ridge Dr., Lakeland, 33813, Polk County, (863)667-1988, 2 miles from Lakeland. **E-mail:** proshop@brgolf.com. **Web:** www.brgolf.com. **Facility Holes:** 18. **Yards:** 6,000/4,263. **Par:** 72/72. **Course Rating:** 68.1/63.8. **Slope:** 117/101. **Green Fee:** $10/$14. **Cart Fee:** $10/Person. **Walking Policy:** Unrestricted walking. **Walkability:** 2. **Opened:** 1991. **Architect:** Ed Holloway. **Season:** Year-round. **High:** Jan.-March. **To obtain tee times:** Call up to 7 days in advance. **Miscellaneous:** Reduced fees (guests, twilight, juniors), metal spikes, range (grass), credit cards (MC, V, D), BF, FF.

THE BREAKERS
R-1550 Flagler Pkwy., West Palm Beach, 33411, Palm Beach County, (561)653-6320, 15 miles from West Palm Beach. **Web:** www.thebreakers.com. **Facility Holes:** 36. **Cart Fee:** Included in green fee. **Walking Policy:** Walking at certain times. **Walkability:** 1. **Season:** Year-round. **Miscellaneous:** Lodging (500 rooms), BF, FF.
BREAKERS WEST (18)
Yards: 6,905/5,420. **Par:** 71/72. **Course Rating:** 73.7/72.1. **Slope:** 135/131. **Green Fee:** $85/$155. **Opened:** 1969. **Architect:** Wylard Byrd. **High:** Nov.-April. **To obtain tee times:** Call up to 7 days in advance. **Miscellaneous:** Reduced fees (twilight), range (grass), credit cards (MC, V, AE, D, DC).
★★½ **OCEAN COURSE** (18)
Yards: 6,167/5,254. **Par:** 70/72. **Course Rating:** 69.3/72.6. **Slope:** 121/122. **Fee:** $60/$145. **Opened:** 2000. **Architect:** Brian Silva. **High:** Dec.-April. **To obtain tee times:** Call up to 30 days in advance. **Misc:** Reduced fees (juniors), range, caddies, credit cards (MC, V, AE, D, DC).

★★★½ **BUFFALO CREEK**
PU-8100 Erie Rd., Palmetto, 34221, Manatee County, (941)776-2611, 20 miles from Tampa. **Facility Holes:** 18. **Yards:** 7,005/5,261. **Par:** 72/72. **Course Rating:** 73.1/69.7. **Slope:** 125/114. **Green Fee:** $37. **Walking Policy:** Unrestricted walking. **Walkability:** 2. **Opened:** 1989. **Architect:** Ron Garl. **Season:** Year-round. **To obtain tee times:** Call up to 2 days in advance. **Miscellaneous:** Range (grass), credit cards (MC, V, D), BF, FF.
Reader Comments: A pleasure to play, for all abilities ... Very good municipal course. If wind blows, this links course can bite back ... Long holes, alligators & deep rough ... Could use ranger ... Good for long hitters, need a good drive.

★★½ **CALIFORNIA CLUB**
SP-20898 San Simeon Way, North Miami, 33179, Dade County, (305)651-3590, 5 miles from Miami. **Facility Holes:** 18. **Yards:** 6,670/5,675. **Par:** 72/72. **Course Rating:** 70.9/69.7. **Slope:** 125/117. **Green Fee:** $22/$45. **Cart Fee:** Included in green fee. **Walkability:** 2. **Season:** Year-round. **High:** Dec.-April. **To obtain tee times:** Call golf shop. **Miscellaneous:** Reduced fees (weekdays, twilight), metal spikes, range (grass/mats), credit cards (MC, V, AE).

★★½ **CALUSA COUNTRY CLUB**
SP-9400 S.W. 130th Ave., Miami, 33186, Dade County, (305)386-5533, 5 miles from Miami. **Facility Holes:** 18. **Yards:** 7,172/5,476. **Par:** 72/72. **Course Rating:** 74.3/70.9. **Slope:** 123/118. **Green Fee:** $23/$55. **Cart Fee:** Included in green fee. **Walkability:** 1. **Opened:** 1968. **Architect:** Mark Mahannah. **Season:** Year-round. **High:** Nov.-April. **To obtain tee times:** Call golf shop. **Miscellaneous:** Reduced fees (weekdays, guests, twilight), range (grass/mats), lodging (300 rooms), credit cards (MC, V, AE).

★★½ **CALUSA LAKES GOLF COURSE**
SP-1995 Calusa Lakes Blvd., Nokomis, 34275, Sarasota County, (941)484-8995, 5 miles from Sarasota. **Facility Holes:** 18. **Yards:** 6,760/5,197. **Par:** 72/72. **Course Rating:** 72.4/70.0. **Slope:** 124/118. **Green Fee:** $30/$55. **Cart Fee:** Included in green fee. **Walking Policy:** Walking at certain times. **Walkability:** 2. **Opened:** 1991. **Architect:** Ted McAnlis. **Season:** Year-round. **High:** Jan.-April. **To obtain tee times:** Call up to 2 days in advance. **Misc:** Reduced fees (twilight), range (grass), credit cards (MC, V), BF, FF.

FLORIDA

★★★ CAPE CORAL GOLF & TENNIS RESORT
R-4003 Palm Tree Blvd., Cape Coral, 33904, Lee County, (941)542-7879, (800)648-1475, 10 miles from Fort Myers. **E-mail:** info@capecoralgolfresort.com. **Web:** www.capecoralgolfresort. **Facility Holes:** 18. **Yards:** 6,707/5,152. **Par:** 72/72. **Course Rating:** 72.0/71.2. **Slope:** 127/119. **Green Fee:** $18/$65. **Cart Fee:** Included in green fee. **Walkability:** 2. **Opened:** 1963. **Architect:** Dick Wilson. **Season:** Year-round. **High:** Jan.-March. **To obtain tee times:** Call golf shop. **Miscellaneous:** Reduced fees (guests, twilight, juniors), range (grass/mats), credit cards (MC, V, AE, D).
Reader Comments: Kind of a so-so golf course … Too many rounds played but a good price … OK … An impeccable course, great condition, all-around fun.

★★½ CAPRI ISLES GOLF CLUB
SP-849 Capri Isles Blvd., Venice, 34292, Sarasota County, (941)485-3371, 60 miles from Tampa. **E-mail:** caprigolf@aol.com. **Facility Holes:** 18. **Yards:** 6,472/5,480. **Par:** 72/72. **Course Rating:** 70.6/70.9. **Slope:** 122/116. **Green Fee:** $29/$48. **Cart Fee:** Included in green fee. **Walking Policy:** Walking at certain times. **Walkability:** 2. **Opened:** 1972. **Architect:** Andy Anderson. **Season:** Year-round. **High:** Jan.-April. **To obtain tee times:** Call up to 3 days in advance. **Miscellaneous:** Reduced fees (twilight), metal spikes, range (grass), credit cards (MC, V), BF, FF.

★★½ CAROLINA CLUB
SP-3011 Rock Island Rd., Margate, 33063, Broward County, (954)753-4000, 10 miles from Fort Lauderdale. **Web:** www.carolinagolfclub.com. **Facility Holes:** 18. **Yards:** 6,584/4,978. **Par:** 71/71. **Course Rating:** 72.1/69.8. **Slope:** 135/124. **Green Fee:** $29/$69. **Cart Fee:** Included in green fee. **Walking Policy:** Mandatory carts. **Walkability:** 1. **Opened:** 1990. **Architect:** Karl Litton. **Season:** Year-round. **High:** Nov.-May. **To obtain tee times:** Call up to 7 days in advance. **Miscellaneous:** Reduced fees (weekdays, twilight, juniors), metal spikes, range (grass), credit cards (MC, V), BF, FF.

★★★★ CELEBRATION GOLF CLUB *Service*
PU-701 Golf Park Dr., Celebration, 34747, Osceola County, (407)566-4653, (888)275-2918, 15 miles from Orlando. **E-mail:** andrew.walls@celebration.fl.us.com. **Web:** www.celebrationgolf.com. **Facility Holes:** 18. **Yards:** 6,786/5,724. **Par:** 72/72. **Course Rating:** 73.0/68.1. **Slope:** 135/122. **Green Fee:** $75/$130. **Cart Fee:** Included in green fee. **Walking Policy:** Walking at certain times. **Walkability:** 3. **Opened:** 1996. **Architect:** Robert Trent Jones/Robert Trent Jones Jr. **Season:** Year-round. **High:** Jan.-April. **To obtain tee times:** Call up to 30 days in advance. **Miscellaneous:** Reduced fees (twilight, juniors), range (grass), credit cards (MC, V, AE, D, DC), BF, FF.
Reader Comments: Imaginative layout, tough at times … Superb condition, excellent service … Tight layout, bring lots of balls … Has children's tees … A looker, tough, target play, fun … Too pricey … Very fair, lot of danger.

★★★ CHAMPIONS CLUB AT JULINGTON CREEK
SP-1111 Durbin Creek Blvd., Jacksonville, 32259, Duval County, (904)287-4653, 15 miles from Jacksonville. **Web:** www.championsclubgolf.com. **Facility Holes:** 18. **Yards:** 6,872/4,994. **Par:** 72/72. **Course Rating:** 72.8/68.6. **Slope:** 126/114. **Green Fee:** $45/$65. **Cart Fee:** Included in green fee. **Walking Policy:** Mandatory carts. **Walkability:** 1. **Opened:** 1992. **Architect:** Bob Walker/Steve Melynk. **Season:** Year-round. **High:** Feb.-May. **To obtain tee times:** Call up to 14 days in advance. **Miscellaneous:** Reduced fees (weekdays, twilight, seniors, juniors), range (grass), credit cards (MC, V, AE, D), BF, FF.
Reader Comments: Good condition, nice people, fair layout … Felt somewhat pushed when clock didn't warrant it … Slow play at times … Too many holes the same length & layout.

★★★ THE CHAMPIONS CLUB AT SUMMERFIELD
PU-3400 S.E. Summerfield Way, Stuart, 34997, Martin County, (561)283-1500, 25 miles from West Palm Beach. **E-mail:** champllb@gate.net. **Web:** www.thechampionsclub.com. **Facility Holes:** 18. **Yards:** 6,809/4,941. **Par:** 72/72. **Course Rating:** 72.8/71.0. **Slope:** 131/120. **Green Fee:** $20/$65. **Cart Fee:** Included in green fee. **Walking Policy:** Walking at certain times. **Walkability:** 2. **Opened:** 1994. **Architect:** Tom Fazio. **Season:** Year-round. **High:** Jan.-April. **To obtain tee times:** Call up to 5 days in advance. **Miscellaneous:** Reduced fees (weekdays, guests, twilight, juniors), range (grass), credit cards (MC, V, AE, D), BF, FF.
Reader Comments: Beautiful course …Better hit it straight … Never see a condo or adjacent fairway. All the challenge you want. The greens are not the smoothest … Gorgeous vistas throughout marshes … A real value, a sleeper.

CHAMPIONSGATE GOLF RESORT
R-1400 Masters Blvd., ChampionsGate, 33896, Osceola County, (407)787-4653, (888)558-9301, 5 miles from Orlando. **E-mail:** sbertrand@mggi.com. **Web:** championsgate-

golf.com. **Facility Holes:** 36. **Green Fee:** $40/$150. **Cart Fee:** Included in green fee. **Walking Policy:** Mandatory carts. **Walkability:** 3. **Opened:** 2000. **Architect:** Greg Norman. **Season:** Year-round. **High:** Jan.-April. **To obtain tee times:** Call up to 60 days in advance. **Miscellaneous:** Reduced fees (weekdays, twilight), range (grass), credit cards (MC, V, AE, D), FF.
INTERNATIONAL COURSE (18)
Yards: 7,363/5,618. **Par:** 72/72. **Course Rating:** 76.3/72.3. **Slope:** 143/123.
NATIONAL COURSE (18)
Yards: 7,128/5,150. **Par:** 72/72. **Course Rating:** 75.1/69.8. **Slope:** 133/122.

★★★ CHI CHI RODRIGUEZ GOLF CLUB
PU-3030 McMullen Booth Rd., Clearwater, 33761, Pinellas County, (727)726-4673, 15 miles from Tampa. **Web:** www.chichi.org. **Facility Holes:** 18. **Yards:** 5,454/3,929. **Par:** 69/71. **Course Rating:** 67.6/64.0. **Slope:** 118/110. **Green Fee:** $25/$45. **Cart Fee:** Included in green fee. **Walking Policy:** Walking at certain times. **Walkability:** 3. **Opened:** 1989. **Architect:** Denis Griffiths. **Season:** Year-round. **High:** Nov.-May. **To obtain tee times:** Call up to 4 days in advance. **Miscellaneous:** Reduced fees (weekdays), credit cards (MC, V, AE, D), BF, FF.
Reader Comments: Nice course, good condition ... Tight, nice course, somewhat tough at times. Short but fun, fast play. You can walk it comfortably ... A routing nightmare ... Lots of room to get in trouble.

★★★½ CIMARRONE GOLF & COUNTRY CLUB
SP-2690 Cimarrone Blvd., Jacksonville, 32259, Duval County, (904)287-2000, 22 miles from Jacksonville. **Web:** www.cimarronegolf.com. **Facility Holes:** 18. **Yards:** 6,891/4,707. **Par:** 72/72. **Course Rating:** 72.7/67.8. **Slope:** 132/119. **Green Fee:** $25/$44. **Cart Fee:** Included in green fee. **Walking Policy:** Mandatory carts. **Walkability:** 4. **Opened:** 1989. **Architect:** David Postlethwait. **Season:** Year-round. **To obtain tee times:** Call up to 7 days in advance. **Miscellaneous:** Reduced fees (weekdays, twilight, juniors), range (grass), credit cards (MC, V, AE, D).
Reader Comments: Tight, tough in the wind ... Lots of teeing options. Lots of water beside fairways. Requires shot placement rather than length ... Decent challenge, enjoyable ... Good layout ... Water always in play.

CITRUS HILLS GOLF & COUNTRY CLUB
SP-509 E. Hartford St., Hernando, 34442, Citrus County, (352)746-4425, 90 miles from Tampa. **E-mail:** hhurley@citrushills.com. **Facility Holes:** 36. **Green Fee:** $14/$38. **Cart Fee:** Included in green fee. **Architect:** Phil Friel. **Season:** Year-round. **High:** Jan.-April. **To obtain tee times:** Call up to 5 days in advance. **Miscellaneous:** Reduced fees (twilight), range (grass/mats), credit cards (MC, V, AE, D), BF, FF.
★★★ MEADOWS COURSE (18)
Yards: 5,885/4,585. **Par:** 70/70. **Course Rating:** 68.5/66.9. **Slope:** 114/112. **Walking Policy:** Walking at certain times. **Walkability:** 2. **Opened:** 1983.
Reader Comments: Nothing spectacular, wide-open fairways, mostly straight, fairly easy, good course for beginning golfers, excellent pro shop & 19th hole ... Great design, fair and playable ... Nice place to play.
★★★ OAKS COURSE (18)
Yards: 6,323/4,647. **Par:** 70/70. **Course Rating:** 71.0/67.0. **Slope:** 121/114. **Walkability:** 4. **Opened:** 1985.
Reader Comments: Narrow fairways, trees along the sides ... Hard, hills, narrow ... Challenging course.

★★★ CITRUS SPRINGS GOLF & COUNTRY CLUB
SP-8690 N. Golfview Dr., Citrus Springs, 34434, Citrus County, (352)489-5045, (877)405-4653, 4 miles from Dunellon. **Web:** brassboys.com. **Facility Holes:** 18. **Yards:** 6,600/6,242. **Par:** 72/72. **Course Rating:** 72.0/71.0. **Slope:** 126/118. **Green Fee:** $15/$32. **Cart Fee:** Included in green fee. **Walking Policy:** Mandatory carts. **Walkability:** 5. **Opened:** 1972. **Architect:** Deltona Corporation. **Season:** Year-round. **To obtain tee times:** Call golf shop. **Miscellaneous:** Range (grass), credit cards (MC, V), FF.
Reader Comments: Easy course to play ... Good shape, friendly staff.

★½ CLEARWATER COUNTRY CLUB
SP-525 N. Betty Lane, Clearwater, 33755-4709, Pinellas County, (727)443-5078, 2 miles from Clearwater. **E-mail:** eal4ccc@juno.com. **Facility Holes:** 18. **Yards:** 6,231/5,202. **Par:** 72/72. **Course Rating:** 69.4/69.7. **Slope:** 123/118. **Green Fee:** $20/$55. **Cart Fee:** Included in green fee. **Walking Policy:** Walking at certain times. **Walkability:** 2. **Opened:** 1922. **Season:** Year-round. **High:** Jan.-March. **To obtain tee times:** Call golf shop. **Miscellaneous:** Reduced fees (weekdays, twilight), range (grass), credit cards (MC, V).

★★½ CLEVELAND HEIGHTS GOLF COURSE

PU-2900 Buckingham Ave., Lakeland, 33803, Polk County, (863)682-3277, 45 miles from Tampa. **E-mail:** rmccl@city.lakeland.net. **Web:** www.city.lakeland.net. **Facility Holes:** 27. **Green Fee:** $18/$29. **Cart Fee:** $10/Person. **Walking Policy:** Walking at certain times. **Walkability:** 2. **Opened:** 1925. **Season:** Year-round. **High:** Dec.-March. **To obtain tee times:** Call golf shop. **Miscellaneous:** Reduced fees (twilight, juniors), range (grass), credit cards (MC, V).
A/B (18 Combo)
Yards: 6,378/5,389. **Par:** 72/72. **Course Rating:** 70.3/70.1. **Slope:** 118/116.
A/C (18 Combo)
Yards: 6,517/5,546. **Par:** 72/72. **Course Rating:** 71.0/71.5. **Slope:** 120/115.
B/C (18 Combo)
Yards: 6,459/5,455. **Par:** 72/72. **Course Rating:** 70.3/70.8. **Slope:** 119/116.

★★★★½ THE CLUB AT EAGLEBROOKE *Value, Condition, Pace+*

SP-1300 Eaglebrooke Blvd., Lakeland, 33813, Polk County, (863)701-0101, 30 miles from Tampa. **Web:** www.eaglebrooke.com. **Facility Holes:** 18. **Yards:** 7,005/4,981. **Par:** 72/72. **Course Rating:** 74.0/69.0. **Slope:** 136/115. **Green Fee:** $20/$51. **Cart Fee:** $14/Person. **Walking Policy:** Mandatory carts. **Walkability:** 3. **Opened:** 1997. **Architect:** Ron Garl. **Season:** Year-round. **High:** Jan.-May. **To obtain tee times:** Call golf shop. **Miscellaneous:** Reduced fees (weekdays, twilight, juniors), range (grass), credit cards (MC, V, AE, D), BF, FF.
Reader Comments: Challenging and carefully groomed. Greens are fast and true ... Excellent for new course, will only get better ... Will use all your clubs ... Long and difficult ... H2O, H2O, everywhere ... Long carries over water.

★★★½ THE CLUB AT EMERALD HILLS

SP-4100 N. Hills Dr., Hollywood, 33021, Broward County, (954)961-4000, 5 miles from Fort Lauderdale. **E-mail:** skjeldgard@aol.com. **Web:** www.theclubatemeraldhills.com. **Facility Holes:** 18. **Yards:** 7,117/5,032. **Par:** 72/72. **Course Rating:** 74.6/70.1. **Slope:** 142/116. **Green Fee:** $25/$125. **Cart Fee:** $25/Person. **Walking Policy:** Mandatory carts. **Walkability:** 3. **Opened:** 1969. **Architect:** B. Devlin/R. von Hagge/C. Ankrom. **Season:** Year-round. **High:** Dec.-April. **To obtain tee times:** Call up to 5 days in advance. **Miscellaneous:** Reduced fees (weekdays, twilight), range (grass/mats), credit cards (MC, V, AE, D), BF, FF.
Reader Comments: Most difficult course in Broward County, tips are for 0- to 4-handicap. Excellent condition ... Tough course ... Lots of variety ... Enjoyable, good pace, good condition.

★★★★½ THE CLUB AT HIDDEN CREEK

SP-3070 PGA Blvd., Navarre, 32566, Santa Rosa County, (850)939-4604, 20 miles from Pensacola. **E-mail:** bross@kslf.com. **Web:** www.kslfairways.com. **Facility Holes:** 18. **Yards:** 6,862/5,213. **Par:** 72/72. **Course Rating:** 73.2/70.1. **Slope:** 139/124. **Green Fee:** $25/$55. **Cart Fee:** Included in green fee. **Walking Policy:** Mandatory carts. **Walkability:** 2. **Opened:** 1988. **Architect:** Ron Garl. **Season:** Year-round. **To obtain tee times:** Call up to 7 days in advance. **Miscellaneous:** Reduced fees (weekdays, twilight, juniors), range (grass), credit cards (MC, V), BF, FF.
Reader Comments: Lots of sand ... Many tough approaches ... A little overated, but attractive layout ... Fine shape as usual ... Good greens, accurate tee shots a must.

★★★½ THE CLUB AT WINSTON TRAILS

SP-6101 Winston Trails Blvd., Lake Worth, 33463, Palm Beach County, (561)439-3700, 15 miles from West Palm Beach. **Web:** www.winstontrails.com. **Facility Holes:** 18. **Yards:** 6,835/5,405. **Par:** 72/72. **Course Rating:** 73.0/70.0. **Slope:** 130/119. **Green Fee:** $30/$75. **Cart Fee:** Included in green fee. **Walking Policy:** Walking at certain times. **Walkability:** 2. **Opened:** 1993. **Architect:** Joe Lee. **Season:** Year-round. **To obtain tee times:** Call golf shop. **Miscellaneous:** Reduced fees (weekdays, twilight), range (grass), credit cards (MC, V, AE), BF, FF.
Reader Comments: Nice people, nice course ... Can be put under pressure to play fast ... Excellent practice facilities ... Typical course within a development, plays harder than it looks ... Lots of water, good conditions.

CLUB MED SANDPIPER

R-3500 S.E. Morningside Blvd., Port St. Lucie, 34952, St. Lucie County, (561)398-5007, 35 miles from West Palm Beach. **Facility Holes:** 36. **Cart Fee:** Included in green fee. **Walking Policy:** Mandatory carts. **Walkability:** 2. **Opened:** 1961. **Architect:** Mark Mahannah. **Season:** Year-round. **To obtain tee times:** Call up to 3 days in advance. **Miscellaneous:** Reduced fees (juniors), metal spikes, range (grass), . credit cards (MC, V, AE), BF, FF.
★½ **SAINTS COURSE** (18)
Yards: 6,478/5,379. **Par:** 72/72. **Course Rating:** 70.7/71.3. **Slope:** 120/119. **Green Fee:** $18/$45.

★½ **SINNERS COURSE** (18)
Yards: 6,888/5,384. **Par:** 72/72. **Course Rating:** 72.3/71.1. **Slope:** 123/116. **Green Fee:** $25/$45.

★★½ **COCOA BEACH GOLF COURSE**
PU-5000 Tom Warriner Blvd., Cocoa Beach, 32931, Brevard County, (321)868-3351, 40 miles from Orlando. **E-mail:** jtucker@cityofcocoabeach.com. **Web:** www.cityofcocoabeach.com. **Facility Holes:** 27. **Green Fee:** $18/$28. **Cart Fee:** $9/Person. **Walking Policy:** Walking at certain times. **Walkability:** 1. **Opened:** 1992. **Architect:** Charles Ankrom. **Season:** Year-round. **To obtain tee times:** Call up to 28 days in advance. **Miscellaneous:** Reduced fees (twilight, juniors), metal spikes, range (grass), credit cards (MC, V, AE), BF, FF.
DOLPHIN/LAKES (18 Combo)
Yards: 6,393/4,985. **Par:** 71/71. **Course Rating:** 70.1/68.0. **Slope:** 115/109.
RIVER/DOLPHIN (18 Combo)
Yards: 6,363/4,903. **Par:** 71/71. **Course Rating:** 69.9/67.5. **Slope:** 116/108.
RIVER/LAKES (18 Combo)
Yards: 6,714/5,294. **Par:** 72/72. **Course Rating:** 71.7/69.3. **Slope:** 119/113.

COLONY WEST COUNTRY CLUB
PU-6800 N.W. 88th Ave., Tamarac, 33321, Broward County, (954)726-8430, 10 miles from Fort Lauderdale. **E-mail:** colrle@pop.prodigy. **Facility Holes:** 36. **Cart Fee:** Included in green fee. **Walkability:** 1. **Opened:** 1970. **Architect:** Bruce Devlin/Robert von Hagge. **Season:** Year-round. **High:** Dec.-April. **To obtain tee times:** Call golf shop. **Miscellaneous:** Reduced fees (weekdays, twilight), credit cards (MC, V, AE).
★★★★ **CHAMPIONSHIP COURSE** (18)
Yards: 7,312/4,415. **Par:** 71/71. **Course Rating:** 75.5. **Slope:** 146. **Green Fee:** $45/$90. **Walking Policy:** Mandatory carts.
Reader Comments: Long course, great challenge ... Good condition, value ... Slow play, course conditions not great ... Lots of trees, not too much water, very long ... Buy the course guide ... Excellent for all levels, overcrowded ... Fair value.
★★★ **GLADES COURSE** (18)
Yards: 4,207/3,331. **Par:** 65/65. **Course Rating:** 59.3/59.1. **Slope:** 89/85. **Green Fee:** $25/$30. **Walking Policy:** Walking at certain times.
Reader Comments: Walkable, executive length ... Tough course, overpriced ... Good course to learn and practice on.

★★ **CONTINENTAL COUNTRY CLUB**
SP-50 Continental Blvd., Wildwood, 34785, Sumter County, (352)748-3293, 5 miles from Leesburg. **Facility Holes:** 18. **Yards:** 6,461/5,438. **Par:** 72/73. **Course Rating:** 70.1/71.1. **Slope:** 123/122. **Green Fee:** $20/$35. **Cart Fee:** Included in green fee. **Walking Policy:** Mandatory carts. **Walkability:** 1. **Opened:** 1972. **Architect:** Ron Garl. **Season:** Year-round. **High:** Nov.-May. **To obtain tee times:** Call up to 2 days in advance. **Miscellaneous:** Reduced fees (twilight), range (grass), credit cards (MC, V, D), BF, FF.

★★★ **CORAL OAKS GOLF COURSE**
PU-1800 N.W. 28th Ave., Cape Coral, 33993, Lee County, (941)573-3100, 12 miles from Fort Myers. **E-mail:** robo_pro@yahoo.com. **Web:** www.coraloaks.com. **Facility Holes:** 18. **Yards:** 6,623/4,803. **Par:** 72/72. **Course Rating:** 73.3/68.3. **Slope:** 139/115. **Green Fee:** $23/$27. **Cart Fee:** $15/Person. **Walking Policy:** Walking at certain times. **Walkability:** 2. **Opened:** 1988. **Architect:** Arthur Hills. **Season:** Year-round. **To obtain tee times:** Call up to 4 days in advance. **Miscellaneous:** Reduced fees (juniors), range (grass), credit cards (MC, V, AE, D), BF, FF.
Reader Comments: Slow play, otherwise a fun course to play ... Excellent condition at all times ... Good course. Out of the way ... Very nice.

COUNTRY CLUB OF MIAMI
PU-6801 Miami Gardens Dr., Miami, 33015, Dade County, (305)829-4700, 20 miles from Miami. **E-mail:** ccofmiami@mindspring.com. **Web:** www.countryclubofmiami.com. **Facility Holes:** 36. **Green Fee:** $25/$65. **Cart Fee:** Included in green fee. **Walking Policy:** Mandatory carts. **Walkability:** 3. **Season:** Year-round. **High:** Dec.-April. **To obtain tee times:** Call golf shop. **Miscellaneous:** Reduced fees (weekdays, twilight), range (grass/mats), credit cards (MC, V, AE, D), BF, FF.
★★½ **EAST COURSE** (18)
Yards: 6,553/5,025. **Par:** 70/70. **Course Rating:** 70.3/68.8. **Slope:** 124/117. **Opened:** 1959. **Architect:** Robert Trent Jones.
★★★ **WEST COURSE** (18)
Yards: 7,017/5,298. **Par:** 72/72. **Course Rating:** 73.5/70.1. **Slope:** 130/123. **Opened:** 1960. **Architect:** Robert Trent Jones/Bobby Weed.

Reader Comments: Greens need some work because of so much play ... Dollar for dollar, one of the best ... Consistently good all year-round ... Nice clubhouse.

★★★ COUNTRY CLUB OF MOUNT DORA
SP-1900 Country Club Blvd., Mount Dora, 32757, Lake County, (352)735-2263, 30 miles from Orlando. **Facility Holes:** 18. **Yards:** 6,571/5,002. **Par:** 72/72. **Course Rating:** 72.1/71.0. **Slope:** 125/120. **Green Fee:** $18/$55. **Cart Fee:** Included in green fee. **Walking Policy:** Walking at certain times. **Walkability:** 3. **Opened:** 1991. **Architect:** Lloyd Clifton. **Season:** Year-round. **High:** Jan.-April. **To obtain tee times:** Call up to 7 days in advance. **Miscellaneous:** Reduced fees (weekdays, guests, twilight, seniors, juniors), range (grass), caddies, credit cards (MC, V), BF, FF.
Reader Comments: Lots of water ... Very good for this low price ... Short ... Lots of water, good test, excellent value.

★★★½ COUNTRY CLUB OF SEBRING
SP-4800 Haw Branch Rd., Sebring, 33875, Highlands County, (863)382-3500, 70 miles from Orlando. **E-mail:** ccsgc@tnni.net. **Web:** www.countryclubofsebring.com. **Facility Holes:** 18. **Yards:** 6,722/4,938. **Par:** 71/71. **Course Rating:** 72.0/67.7. **Slope:** 124/112. **Green Fee:** $20/$50. **Cart Fee:** Included in green fee. **Walking Policy:** Mandatory carts. **Walkability:** 2. **Opened:** 1984. **Architect:** Ron Garl. **Season:** Year-round. **High:** Dec.-March. **To obtain tee times:** Call up to 30 days in advance. **Miscellaneous:** Reduced fees (twilight, juniors), range (grass), credit cards (MC, V, AE, D), BF, FF.
Reader Comments: Back 9 through a nature preserve, well done ... Tight course, fun to play 2nd time ... Good pro shop ... Great course with good people ... Lots of sand ... A great little woodland course ... Good contrast between 2 9s.

★★ THE COURSE AT WESTLAND
PU-7502 Plantation Bay Dr., Jacksonville, 32244, Duval County, (904)778-4653. **E-mail:** mark.brunt@mccumbergolf.com. **Web:** www.mccumbergolf.com. **Facility Holes:** 18. **Yards:** 6,347/5,380. **Par:** 71/71. **Course Rating:** 70.3/71.2. **Slope:** 121/118. **Green Fee:** $18/$33. **Cart Fee:** Included in green fee. **Walking Policy:** Walking at certain times. **Walkability:** 1. **Opened:** 1974. **Architect:** Lloyd Clifton. **Season:** Year-round. **To obtain tee times:** Call up to 7 days in advance. **Miscellaneous:** Reduced fees (weekdays, twilight, seniors, juniors), metal spikes, range (grass), credit cards (MC, V, AE, D, ATM Debit Cards), BF, FF.

★★★½ CRANDON GOLF AT KEY BISCAYNE
PU-6700 Crandon Blvd., Key Biscayne, 33149, Dade County, (305)361-9120, 7 miles from Miami. **Facility Holes:** 18. **Yards:** 7,180/5,380. **Par:** 72/73. **Course Rating:** 75.4/71.8. **Slope:** 129/125. **Green Fee:** $52/$131. **Cart Fee:** Included in green fee. **Walking Policy:** Walking at certain times. **Walkability:** 2. **Opened:** 1972. **Architect:** Robert von Hagge/Bruce Devlin. **Season:** Year-round. **High:** Dec.-May. **To obtain tee times:** Call golf shop. **Miscellaneous:** Reduced fees (weekdays, twilight), range (grass), credit cards (MC, V, AE), BF, FF. **Notes:** Ranked 22nd in 2001 Best in State.
Reader Comments: Unmatched scenery ... Long ... Next to the ocean ... Beautiful views of bay, lots of wildlife, be considerate of resident iguanas ... Challenging, fun, good greens, nice fairways, expensive, but worth the price ... Nice and flat.

CRYSTAL LAKE COUNTRY CLUB
SP-3800 Crystal Lake Dr., Pompano Beach, 33064, Broward County, (954)942-1900, 5 miles from Fort Lauderdale. **Facility Holes:** 36. **Cart Fee:** Included in green fee. **Walking Policy:** Mandatory carts. **Architect:** Rees Jones. **Season:** Year-round. **High:** Nov.-April. **Miscellaneous:** Reduced fees (twilight), range (mats), credit cards (MC, V, AE), BF, FF.
★★½ **SOUTH COURSE** (18)
Yards: 6,873/5,458. **Par:** 72/72. **Course Rating:** 73.5/71.5. **Slope:** 135/121. **Green Fee:** $28/$55. **Walkability:** 3. **Opened:** 1963. **To obtain tee times:** Call up to 2 days in advance.
★★½ **TAM O'SHANTER NORTH COURSE** (18)
Yards: 6,390/5,205. **Par:** 70/72. **Course Rating:** 71.0/70.0. **Slope:** 122/118. **Green Fee:** $28/$48. **Walkability:** 2. **Opened:** 1967. **To obtain tee times:** Call golf shop.

★★★ CYPRESS CREEK GOLF COURSE
SP-9400 N. Military Trail, Boynton Beach, 33436, Palm Beach County, (561)732-4202, 10 miles from West Palm Beach. **Facility Holes:** 18. **Yards:** 6,808/5,425. **Par:** 72/72. **Course Rating:** 72.0/67.1. **Slope:** 129/109. **Green Fee:** $30/$65. **Cart Fee:** Included in green fee. **Walking Policy:** Walking at certain times. **Walkability:** 2. **Opened:** 1964. **Architect:** Robert von Hagge. **Season:** Year-round. **High:** Nov.-April. **To obtain tee times:** Call golf shop. **Miscellaneous:** Reduced fees (weekdays, twilight), metal spikes, range (grass), credit cards (MC, V, AE, D).
Reader Comments: Lots of water, hit it straight ... Undulating greens very challenging ... OK ... Very good ... Water on half of the holes ...Great course and a great value.

DAYTONA BEACH GOLF COURSE

PU-600 Wilder Blvd., Daytona Beach, 32114, Volusia County, (386)671-3500. **E-mail:** cameronjohn@ci.daytona-beach.fl.us. **Web:** www.ci.daytona-beach.fl.us. **Facility Holes:** 36. **Green Fee:** $8/$17. **Cart Fee:** $10/Cart. **Walkability:** 1. **Season:** Year-round. **High:** Dec.-April. **Miscellaneous:** Reduced fees (twilight, juniors), range (mats), credit cards (MC, V), BF, FF.

★★ **NORTH COURSE (18)**
Yards: 6,338/4,938. **Par:** 72/72. **Course Rating:** 70.0/68.3. **Slope:** 120/119. **Walking Policy:** Walking at certain times. **Opened:** 1997. **Architect:** Lloyd Clifton/Slim Deathridge. **To obtain tee times:** Call up to 3 days in advance.

★★ **SOUTH COURSE (18)**
Yards: 6,229/5,346. **Par:** 71/71. **Course Rating:** 69.8/70.2. **Slope:** 118/118. **Walking Policy:** Unrestricted walking. **Opened:** 1921. **Architect:** Donald Ross. **To obtain tee times:** Call golf shop. **Miscellaneous:** Metal spikes.

★★★★ DEBARY GOLF & COUNTRY CLUB

SP-300 Plantation Dr., DeBary, 32713, Volusia County, (407)668-2061, 15 miles from Orlando. **Facility Holes:** 18. **Yards:** 6,776/5,060. **Par:** 72/72. **Course Rating:** 72.3/68.8. **Slope:** 128/122. **Green Fee:** $19/$60. **Cart Fee:** Included in green fee. **Walking Policy:** Mandatory carts. **Walkability:** 3. **Opened:** 1990. **Architect:** Lloyd Clifton. **Season:** Year-round. **To obtain tee times:** Call golf shop. **Miscellaneous:** Reduced fees (twilight, juniors), range (grass), credit cards (MC, V, AE), BF, FF.
Reader Comments: Very nice course, in good condition ... Beautiful & nice to play ... Not to be missed ... A challenging course, enjoyable ... A surprise, elevations, trees, almost no water ... Wooded, hilly course.

★★½ DEEP CREEK GOLF CLUB

SP-1260 San Cristobal Ave., Port Charlotte, 33983, Charlotte County, (941)625-6911, 25 miles from Fort Myers. **E-mail:** pab@deepcreekgc.com. **Web:** www.deepcreekgc.com. **Facility Holes:** 18. **Yards:** 6,005/4,860. **Par:** 70/70. **Course Rating:** 67.5/68.0. **Slope:** 112/110. **Green Fee:** $16/$32. **Cart Fee:** $12/Person. **Walking Policy:** Walking at certain times. **Walkability:** 1. **Opened:** 1985. **Architect:** Mark McCumber. **Season:** Year-round. **To obtain tee times:** Call up to 7 days in advance. **Miscellaneous:** Reduced fees (weekdays, twilight, seniors, juniors), range (grass), credit cards (MC, V, D), BF, FF.

★★★½ DEER CREEK GOLF CLUB

SP-2801 Country Club Blvd., Deerfield Beach, 33442, Broward County, (954)421-5550, 6 miles from Fort Lauderdale. **E-mail:** dcreek95@aol.com. **Web:** www.deercreekflorida.com. **Facility Holes:** 18. **Yards:** 7,038/5,319. **Par:** 72/72. **Course Rating:** 74.8/71.6. **Slope:** 133/120. **Green Fee:** $45/$135. **Cart Fee:** Included in green fee. **Walking Policy:** Unrestricted walking. **Walkability:** 3. **Opened:** 1971. **Architect:** Bill Watts/Arthur Hills. **Season:** Year-round. **To obtain tee times:** Call up to 3 days in advance. **Miscellaneous:** Reduced fees (weekdays, guests, twilight, seniors, juniors), range (grass), credit cards (MC, V, AE), BF, FF.
Reader Comments: Orange trees, greens are challenging ... Mucho dinero, slow pace ... Great condition but you pay too much ... Average layout, overrated ... Good course, first-class public.

★★★★ DEER ISLAND GOLF & LAKE CLUB

SP-18000 Eagles Way, Tavares, 32778, Lake County, (352)343-7550, (800)269-0006, 30 miles from Orlando. **Web:** www.deerislandgolf.com. **Facility Holes:** 18. **Yards:** 6,676/5,139. **Par:** 72/72. **Course Rating:** 73.1/70.4. **Slope:** 137/118. **Green Fee:** $25/$59. **Cart Fee:** Included in green fee. **Walking Policy:** Mandatory carts. **Walkability:** 2. **Opened:** 1994. **Architect:** Joe Lee. **Season:** Year-round. **High:** Jan.-April. **To obtain tee times:** Call up to 7 days in advance. **Miscellaneous:** Reduced fees (weekdays, twilight, seniors), range (grass), credit cards (MC, V, AE, D), BF, FF.
Reader Comments: Very good course, pleasure to play ... Difficult, fun ... Don't let anybody know about this ... Lots & lots of water ... Tight layout with lots of water, yet playable ... They put everything together, my favorite in Florida.

★½ DEERFIELD LAKES GOLF COURSE

PU-3825 Deerfield Country Club Rd., Callahan, 32011, Nassau County, (904)879-1210, 7 miles from Jacksonville. **E-mail:** candm@ilnk.com. **Facility Holes:** 18. **Yards:** 6,700/5,266. **Par:** 72/74. **Course Rating:** 70.2/69.0. **Slope:** 114/102. **Green Fee:** $18/$30. **Cart Fee:** Included in green fee. **Walking Policy:** Walking at certain times. **Walkability:** 1. **Opened:** 1970. **Season:** Year-round. **To obtain tee times:** Call golf shop. **Miscellaneous:** Reduced fees (weekdays, seniors), metal spikes, range (grass/mats), credit cards (MC, V, D), BF, FF.

★★½ DELRAY BEACH GOLF CLUB

PU-2200 Highland Ave., Delray Beach, 33445, Palm Beach County, (561)243-7380, 18 miles from West Palm Beach. **E-mail:** delraygc@aol.com. **Web:** affordablegolf.com. **Facility Holes:**

FLORIDA

18. **Yards:** 6,907/5,189. **Par:** 72/72. **Course Rating:** 73.0/69.8. **Slope:** 126/117. **Green Fee:** $22/$53. **Cart Fee:** Included in green fee. **Walking Policy:** Walking at certain times. **Walkability:** 1. **Opened:** 1923. **Architect:** Donald Ross. **Season:** Year-round. **High:** Jan.-April. **To obtain tee times:** Call up to 3 days in advance. **Miscellaneous:** Reduced fees (juniors), range (mats), credit cards (MC, V), BF, FF.

★★★½ DIAMOND PLAYERS CLUB
PU-200 Hunt Club Blvd., Longwood, 32779, Seminole County, (407)862-5113, (877)372-4653, 10 miles from Downtown Orlando. **Web:** www.dpcgolf.com. **Facility Holes:** 18. **Yards:** 6,640/5,745. **Par:** 72/73. **Course Rating:** 71.9/73.2. **Slope:** 123/126. **Green Fee:** $20/$49. **Cart Fee:** $15/Person. **Walking Policy:** Mandatory carts. **Walkability:** 2. **Opened:** 1970. **Architect:** Ward Northrup. **Season:** Year-round. **To obtain tee times:** Call up to 14 days in advance. **Miscellaneous:** Reduced fees (weekdays, twilight, seniors, juniors), range (grass), credit cards (MC, V, AE, D), BF, FF.
Reader Comments: Beautiful, fun challenging greens … Very hilly for Florida. Good layout … Lots of hills for a Florida course … A bit tight.

DIAMOND PLAYERS CLUB
PU-2601 Diamond Club Dr., Clermont, 34711, Lake County, (352)243-0411, 15 miles from Downtown Orlando. **E-mail:** Thomason@ibm.net. **Web:** www.dpcgolf.com. **Facility Holes:** 18. **Yards:** 7,000/5,200. **Par:** 71/71. **Green Fee:** $35/$65. **Cart Fee:** $15/Person. **Walking Policy:** Mandatory carts. **Walkability:** 4. **Opened:** 1999. **Architect:** Terrell Legree. **Season:** Year-round. **High:** Sept.-March. **To obtain tee times:** Call golf shop. **Miscellaneous:** Reduced fees (weekdays, seniors, juniors), range (grass).

★★★★ DIAMONDBACK GOLF CLUB
SP-6501 S.R. 544 E., Haines City, 33844, Polk County, (863)421-0437, (800)222-5629, 25 miles from Orlando. **E-mail:** dmdbackgc@aol.com. **Web:** www.Diamondbackgc.com. **Facility Holes:** 18. **Yards:** 6,805/5,061. **Par:** 72/72. **Course Rating:** 73.3/70.3. **Slope:** 138/122. **Green Fee:** $30/$75. **Cart Fee:** Included in green fee. **Walking Policy:** Mandatory carts. **Walkability:** 5. **Opened:** 1995. **Architect:** Joe Lee. **Season:** Year-round. **High:** Jan.-April. **To obtain tee times:** Call up to 7 days in advance. **Miscellaneous:** Reduced fees (weekdays, twilight, juniors), range (grass), credit cards (MC, V, AE), BF, FF.
Reader Comments: Not recommended for casual golfer. Tight fairways, good greens … Good, tight and exciting … Tight fairways, accommodating staff … Beautiful layout, hilly & wooded … Top to bottom everything is perfect.

THE DIPLOMAT COUNTRY CLUB & SPA
R-501 Diplomat Pkwy., Hallandale Beach, 33009, Broward County, (954)883-4444, (800)327-1212, 10 miles from Miami. **E-mail:** dtinling@diplomatresort.com. **Web:** www.diplomatresort.com. **Facility Holes:** 18. **Yards:** 6,728/5,354. **Par:** 72/72. **Course Rating:** 72.9/71.4. **Slope:** 136/119. **Green Fee:** $80/$165. **Cart Fee:** Included in green fee. **Walking Policy:** Walking with Caddie. **Walkability:** 2. **Opened:** 2000. **Architect:** Joe Lee. **Season:** Year-round. **High:** Jan.-May. **To obtain tee times:** Call golf shop. **Miscellaneous:** Reduced fees (guests), range (grass), caddies, credit cards (MC, V, AE, D, DC), BF, FF.

★★ DODGER PINES COUNTRY CLUB
SP-4600 26th St., Vero Beach, 32966, Indian River County, (561)569-4400, 60 miles from West Palm Beach. **Facility Holes:** 18. **Yards:** 6,692/5,615. **Par:** 73/74. **Course Rating:** 72.3/73.0. **Slope:** 129/123. **Green Fee:** $25/$45. **Cart Fee:** Included in green fee. **Walking Policy:** Walking at certain times. **Walkability:** 1. **Opened:** 1971. **Architect:** Marion Luke. **Season:** Year-round. **High:** Jan.-April. **To obtain tee times:** Call golf shop. **Miscellaneous:** Reduced fees (guests, twilight), range (grass), credit cards (MC, V, AE), BF, FF.

★★★½ DON SHULA'S GOLF CLUB *Pace*
R-7601 Miami Lakes Dr., Miami Lakes, 33014, Dade County, (305)820-8106, 5 miles from Miami. **Web:** www.donshula.com. **Facility Holes:** 36. **Yards:** 7,055/5,287. **Par:** 72/72. **Course Rating:** 72.3/70.1. **Slope:** 121/117. **Green Fee:** $40/$125. **Cart Fee:** Included in green fee. **Walking Policy:** Mandatory carts. **Walkability:** 2. **Opened:** 1963. **Architect:** Bill Watts. **Season:** Year-round. **High:** Nov.-May. **To obtain tee times:** Call up to 3 days in advance. **Miscellaneous:** Reduced fees (weekdays, guests, twilight), range (grass/mats), lodging (200 rooms), credit cards (MC, V, AE, D), BF, FF.
Reader Comments: Nice layout, a good test of golf, with atmosphere … Beautiful trees frame many holes … Nice length, good service … Decent track, great greens … Expensive & you get what you pay for… Several nice holes with water.
Special Notes: Also has an 18-hole par-3 course.

★★★½ DON VELLER SEMINOLE GOLF COURSE
PU-2550 Pottsdamer St., Tallahassee, 32310, Leon County, (850)644-2582. **E-mail:**

tmellot@mggi.com. **Web:** www.seminolegolfcourse.com. **Facility Holes:** 18. **Yards:** 7,033/5,930. **Par:** 72/72. **Course Rating:** 73.4/73.0. **Slope:** 121/111. **Green Fee:** $13/$19. **Cart Fee:** $12/Person. **Walking Policy:** Walking at certain times. **Walkability:** 2. **Opened:** 1962. **Architect:** Bill Amick. **Season:** Year-round. **High:** April-June. **To obtain tee times:** Call up to 7 days in advance. **Miscellaneous:** Reduced fees (weekdays, twilight, juniors), range (grass/mats), credit cards (MC, V, D), BF, FF.

Reader Comments: Wide open, great for those who are not straight off the tee. A high-quality clubhouse and related facilities … Best ever played … Best course I play, excellent service … Top 10 … Packed … Nice course.

DORAL GOLF RESORT & SPA
R-4400 N.W. 87th Ave., Miami, 33178, Dade County, (305)592-2000x2105, (800)713-6725. **E-mail:** golfinfo@doralresort.com. **Web:** www.doralresort.com. **Facility Holes:** 90. **Walkability:** 1. **Season:** Year-round. **Misc:** Lodging (693 rooms), credit cards (MC, V, AE, D, DC), BF, FF.

★★★★ **BLUE COURSE** (18)
Yards: 7,125/5,392. **Par:** 72/72. **Course Rating:** 74.5/73.0. **Slope:** 130/124. **Green Fee:** $175/$250. **Cart Fee:** Included in green fee. **Walking Policy:** Walking at certain times. **Opened:** 1961. **Architect:** Dick Wilson. **High:** Dec.-April. **To obtain tee times:** Call golf shop. **Miscellaneous:** Reduced fees (weekdays, guests, twilight), range (grass/mats), caddies, . **Notes:** Ranked 20th in 2001 Best in State; 42nd in 1996 America's Top 75 Upscale Courses.

Reader Comments: Tough & long … Expensive … Better with less sand, great Bermuda greens … Too much sand in the wrong places for average golfer … Pricey but service is incredible … A mustplay course.

★★★½ **GOLD COURSE** (18) *Pace*
Yards: 6,602/5,179. **Par:** 70/70. **Course Rating:** 73.3/71.4. **Slope:** 129/123. **Green Fee:** $100/$225. **Cart Fee:** Included in green fee. **Walking Policy:** Walking at certain times. **Opened:** 1961. **Architect:** Robert von Hagge. **High:** Dec.-April. **To obtain tee times:** Call golf shop. **Miscellaneous:** Reduced fees (weekdays, guests, twilight), range (grass/mats), caddies.

Reader Comments: Decent course … Hectic clubhouse … Almost like the Blue only cheaper … Better value than Blue … Very nice for average player … Doral has the best maintained courses in Miami with excellent facilities & services.

★★★ **GREAT WHITE COURSE** (18)
Yards: 6,208/5,286. **Par:** 72/72. **Course Rating:** 69.7/70.1. **Slope:** 117/116. **Green Fee:** $175/$250. **Cart Fee:** Included in green fee. **Walking Policy:** Walking at certain times. **Opened:** 2000. **Architect:** Greg Norman. **High:** Dec.-April. **To obtain tee times:** Call golf shop. **Miscellaneous:** Reduced fees (weekdays, guests, twilight, seniors, juniors), range (grass), caddies.

Reader Comments: Nice course, not too scenic, Doral thinks it's Pebble, $$$ … Good shape, very difficult … Fine course, a very fair test & challenging … Pricey … Very challenging, some very special holes.

★★½ **RED COURSE** (18)
Yards: 6,214/5,216. **Par:** 70/70. **Course Rating:** 69.9/70.6. **Slope:** 118/118. **Green Fee:** $85/$200. **Cart Fee:** Included in green fee. **Walking Policy:** Walking at certain times. **Opened:** 1961. **Architect:** Robert von Hagge. **High:** Dec.-April. **To obtain tee times:** Call golf shop. **Miscellaneous:** Reduced fees (weekdays, guests, twilight), range (grass/mats), caddies.

★★★ **SILVER COURSE** (18)
Yards: 6,567/5,589. **Par:** 71/71. **Course Rating:** 72.5/68.7. **Slope:** 131/123. **Green Fee:** $100/$250. **Cart Fee:** $35/Cart. **Walking Policy:** Mandatory carts. **Opened:** 1984. **Architect:** B. Devlin/R. von Hagge/J. Pate. **High:** Jan.-April. **To obtain tee times:** Call up to 30 days in advance. **Miscellaneous:** Reduced fees (weekdays, guests, twilight), range (grass/mats).

Reader Comments: Too many lateral hazards off each hole … Lots & lots of water … Good test, good clubhouse.

★½ DOUG FORD'S LACUNA GOLF CLUB
SP-6400 Grand Lacuna Blvd., Lake Worth, 33467, Palm Beach County, (561)433-3006, 5 miles from West Palm Beach. **Facility Holes:** 18. **Yards:** 6,700/5,119. **Par:** 71/71. **Slope:** 121/111. **Green Fee:** $20/$40. **Cart Fee:** Included in green fee. **Walking Policy:** Mandatory carts. **Walkability:** 1. **Opened:** 1985. **Architect:** Joe Lee. **Season:** Year-round. **High:** Dec.-May. **To obtain tee times:** Call up to 4 days in advance. **Miscellaneous:** Reduced fees (juniors), metal spikes, range (grass), credit cards (MC, V), FF.

★★★ DUNEDIN COUNTRY CLUB
SP-1050 Palm Blvd., Dunedin, 34698, Pinellas County, (727)733-7836, 20 miles from Tampa. **Facility Holes:** 18. **Yards:** 6,565/5,726. **Par:** 72/73. **Course Rating:** 71.5/73.1. **Slope:** 125/120. **Green Fee:** $37/$45. **Cart Fee:** Included in green fee. **Walking Policy:** Walking at certain times. **Walkability:** 1. **Opened:** 1928. **Architect:** Donald Ross. **Season:** Year-round. **High:** Dec.-April. **To obtain tee times:** Call golf shop. **Miscellaneous:** Reduced fees (twilight), range (grass), credit cards (MC, V).

Reader Comments: Former PGA course … Nice course … Mounded greens make it challenging … Lets you see what a pro course is like, excellent condition.

FLORIDA

★★½ THE DUNES GOLF & TENNIS CLUB
R-949 Sandcastle Rd., Sanibel Island, 33957, Lee County, (941)472-2535, 15 miles from Fort Myers. **E-mail:** kevin.mccune@merista.com. **Web:** www.dunesgolfsanibel.com. **Facility Holes:** 18. **Yards:** 5,578/4,002. **Par:** 70/70. **Course Rating:** 68.0/64.5. **Slope:** 123/111. **Green Fee:** $26/$92. **Cart Fee:** $22/Person. **Walking Policy:** Mandatory carts. **Walkability:** 2. **Opened:** 1973. **Architect:** Mark McCumber. **Season:** Year-round. **High:** Jan.-March. **To obtain tee times:** Call up to 4 days in advance. **Miscellaneous:** Reduced fees (guests, twilight, juniors), range (grass), lodging (400 rooms), credit cards (MC, V, AE, D, DC), BF, FF.

★★★ THE DUNES GOLF CLUB AT SEVILLE
PU-18200 Seville Clubhouse Dr., Brooksville, 34614, Hernando County, (352)596-7888, (800)232-1363, 70 miles from Tampa. **Facility Holes:** 18. **Yards:** 7,140/5,236. **Par:** 72/72. **Course Rating:** 74.9/70.8. **Slope:** 138/126. **Green Fee:** $25/$45. **Cart Fee:** Included in green fee. **Walkability:** 4. **Opened:** 1988. **Architect:** Arthur Hills. **Season:** Year-round. **High:** Jan.-April. **To obtain tee times:** Call golf shop. **Miscellaneous:** Reduced fees (weekdays, twilight), metal spikes, range (grass), credit cards (MC, V).
Reader Comments: Nice surroundings … Huge bunkers, hilly, good layout … OK condition … Hilly … A favorite … Great value … Poor man's World Woods … Hard to get to.
Special Notes: Formerly Seville Golf & Country Club.

★★★½ EAGLE HARBOR GOLF CLUB *Pace*
SP-2217 Eagle Harbor Pkwy., Orange Park, 32003, Clay County, (904)269-9300, 15 miles from Jacksonville. **E-mail:** aaronm@eagle-harbor.com. **Web:** www.eagleharborfl.com. **Facility Holes:** 18. **Yards:** 6,840/4,980. **Par:** 72/72. **Course Rating:** 72.6/68.2. **Slope:** 133/121. **Green Fee:** $47/$56. **Cart Fee:** Included in green fee. **Walking Policy:** Walking at certain times. **Walkability:** 1. **Opened:** 1993. **Architect:** Clyde Johnston. **Season:** Year-round. **High:** March-May. **To obtain tee times:** Call up to 4 days in advance. **Miscellaneous:** Reduced fees (weekdays, twilight, juniors), range (grass), credit cards (MC, V), BF, FF.
Reader Comments: Great layout, great amenities, can't go wrong … Always in great shape … Price is right … Always in good condition … Beautiful course.

★★★½ EAGLE MARSH GOLF CLUB
SP-3869 N.W. Royal Oak Drive, Jensen Beach, 34957, Martin County, (561)692-3322, 45 miles from West Palm Beach. **E-mail:** golf@eaglemarsh.com. **Web:** www.eaglemarsh.com. **Facility Holes:** 18. **Yards:** 6,904/4,765. **Par:** 72/72. **Course Rating:** 74.0/69.1. **Slope:** 144/113. **Green Fee:** $25/$70. **Cart Fee:** Included in green fee. **Walkability:** 4. **Opened:** 1998. **Architect:** Tommy Fazio. **Season:** Year-round. **High:** Jan.-April. **To obtain tee times:** Call golf shop. **Miscellaneous:** Reduced fees (juniors), range (grass), credit cards (MC, V, AE, D).
Reader Comments: Narrow … Lots of water, need to be accurate … Excellent target course if you use right tees, fun, good value … Semi-tough course … Good condition. Play from tees relative to handicap.

THE EAGLES GOLF CLUB
SP-16101 Nine Eagles Dr., Odessa, 33556, Hillsborough County, (813)920-6681, 10 miles from Tampa. **E-mail:** freynolds@eaglesgolf.com. **Web:** www.eaglesgolf.com. **Facility Holes:** 36. **Green Fee:** $32/$65. **Cart Fee:** Included in green fee. **Walking Policy:** Mandatory carts. **Walkability:** 2. **Architect:** Rick Robbins/Gary Koch/Ron Garl. **Season:** Year-round. **High:** Jan.-May. **To obtain tee times:** Call up to 7 days in advance. **Miscellaneous:** Reduced fees (weekdays, twilight), range (grass), credit cards (MC, V, AE, D), BF, FF.
FOREST (18)
Yards: 6,712/4,911. **Par:** 72/72. **Course Rating:** 72.1/70.0. **Slope:** 122/114. **Opened:** 1973.
★★½ LAKES (18)
Yards: 7,134/5,453. **Par:** 72/72. **Course Rating:** 74.7/71.3. **Slope:** 132/123. **Opened:** 1970.

★★★½ EASTWOOD GOLF CLUB
SP-13950 Golfway Blvd., Orlando, 32828, Orange County, (407)281-4653, 10 miles from Orlando. **Facility Holes:** 18. **Yards:** 7,176/5,393. **Par:** 72/72. **Course Rating:** 73.9/70.5. **Slope:** 124/117. **Green Fee:** $22/$70. **Cart Fee:** Included in green fee. **Walkability:** 3. **Opened:** 1989. **Architect:** Lloyd Clifton. **Season:** Year-round. **High:** Jan.-April. **To obtain tee times:** Call golf shop. **Miscellaneous:** Reduced fees (weekdays, twilight, seniors, juniors), range (grass), credit cards (MC, V, AE, D).
Reader Comments: Overall a good value … Fair but challenging … Always in great shape, good play … Great public course, fun, easy layout, one of the best … Water, water everywhere.

★★★½ EASTWOOD GOLF COURSE
PU-4600 Bruce Herd Lane, Fort Myers, 33994, Lee County, (941)275-4848, 130 miles from Tampa. **Facility Holes:** 18. **Yards:** 6,772/5,116. **Par:** 72/72. **Course Rating:** 73.3/68.9. **Slope:** 130/120. **Green Fee:** $28/$55. **Cart Fee:** Included in green fee. **Walking Policy:** Walking at certain times. **Walkability:** 1. **Opened:** 1977. **Architect:** Robert von Hagge/Bruce Devlin. **Season:** Year-round. **High:** Nov.-April. **To obtain tee times:** Call up to 1 day in advance.

Miscellaneous: Reduced fees (twilight, juniors), range (grass), credit cards (MC, V, D), BF, FF.
Reader Comments: Beautiful ... Unusual to play in Florida and not be surrounded by housing ... One of the best places you can play ... I played it once and bought a lot by the 3rd green.

★★★★½ EL DIABLO GOLF & COUNTRY CLUB *Value, Pace*
PU-10405 N. Sherman Dr., Citrus Springs, 34434, Citrus County, (352)465-0986, (877)353-4225, 20 miles from Ocala. **E-mail:** robpyle@aol.com. **Web:** www.eldiablo.cc.
Facility Holes: 18. **Yards:** 7,045/5,144. **Par:** 72/72. **Course Rating:** 75.3/69.8. **Slope:** 147/117.
Green Fee: $25/$49. **Walking Policy:** Unrestricted walking. **Walkability:** 4. **Opened:** 1998.
Architect: Jim Fazio. **Season:** Year-round. **To obtain tee times:** Call golf shop.
Miscellaneous: Reduced fees (twilight), range (grass), credit cards (MC, V, AE), BF, FF.
Notes: Ranked 12th in 2001 Best in State; 1st in 1999 Best New Affordable Public.
Reader Comments: Very exciting and beautiful course. Challenging, worth every penny ... In the middle on nowhere, well worth the drive ... A ball buster, tight and tough ... Reminded me of Royal Dornoch, gently rolling fairways, large bunkers, a fair and interesting test.

★★★½ EMERALD BAY GOLF COURSE
SP-40001 Emerald Coast Pkwy., Destin, 32541, Okaloosa County, (850)837-5197, (888)465-3229, 15 miles from Fort Walton Beach. **Facility Holes:** 18. **Yards:** 6,802/5,184. **Par:** 72/72. **Course Rating:** 73.1/70.1. **Slope:** 135/122. **Green Fee:** $40/$75. **Walking Policy:** Mandatory carts. **Walkability:** 1. **Opened:** 1991. **Architect:** Bob Cupp. **Season:** Year-round. **High:** March-Nov. **To obtain tee times:** Call golf shop. **Miscellaneous:** Reduced fees (weekdays, guests, juniors), range (grass), lodging (8 rooms), credit cards (MC, V, AE, D, DC), BF, FF.
Reader Comments: Very pricey ... Great course, excellent staff & service ... Sporty course. Water on most holes. Course in very good shape, slightly costly ... Some very long and tight, some short and wide.

★★★★½ EMERALD DUNES GOLF COURSE *Condition*
PU-2100 Emerald Dunes Dr., West Palm Beach, 33411, Palm Beach County, (561)684-4653, (888)650-4653, 3 miles from West Palm Beach. **E-mail:** edunes@aol.com. **Web:** www.emeralddunes.com. **Facility Holes:** 18. **Yards:** 7,006/4,676. **Par:** 72/72. **Course Rating:** 73.8/67.1.
Slope: 133/115. **Green Fee:** $80/$175. **Cart Fee:** Included in green fee. **Walking Policy:** Unrestricted walking. **Walkability:** 3. **Opened:** 1990. **Architect:** Tom Fazio. **Season:** Year-round. **High:** Dec.-April. **To obtain tee times:** Call up to 60 days in advance. **Miscellaneous:** Reduced fees (weekdays, twilight), range (grass), credit cards (MC, V, AE, D, DC, Diners Club), BF, FF.
Reader Comments: Player friendly, perfect shape ... Service is great, the GPS system a nice addition ... Beautiful, slow and pricey ... One of the best, getting expensive ... Terrific & fun ... Pricey, but first class ... Best course in Fla.

★★★ FAIRWINDS GOLF COURSE
PU-4400 Fairwinds Dr., Fort Pierce, 34946, St. Lucie County, (561)462-2722, (800)894-1781, 40 miles from West Palm Beach. **Facility Holes:** 18. **Yards:** 6,783/5,392. **Par:** 72/72. **Course Rating:** 71.1/68.5. **Slope:** 119/112. **Green Fee:** $20/$40. **Cart Fee:** Included in green fee. **Walking Policy:** Walking at certain times. **Walkability:** 1. **Opened:** 1991. **Architect:** Jim Fazio. **Season:** Year-round. **To obtain tee times:** Call up to 3 days in advance. **Miscellaneous:** Reduced fees (twilight, juniors), range (grass), credit cards (MC, V, AE, D), BF, FF.
Reader Comments: Fair ... Pro shop stuff very good, slow play ... Inexpensive good golf ... Convenient, priced right, challenging ... Nice vacation course ... Nice shape, real good value.

★★★★ FALCON'S FIRE GOLF CLUB *Service*
PU-3200 Seralago Blvd., Kissimmee, 34746, Osceola County, (407)239-5445, 3 miles from Orlando. **E-mail:** proshop@falconsfire.com. **Web:** www.falconsfire.com. **Facility Holes:** 18.
Yards: 6,901/5,417. **Par:** 72/72. **Course Rating:** 72.5/70.4. **Slope:** 125/118. **Green Fee:** $56/$117. **Cart Fee:** Included in green fee. **Walking Policy:** Mandatory carts. **Walkability:** 1.
Opened: 1993. **Architect:** Rees Jones. **Season:** Year-round. **High:** Jan.-March. **To obtain tee times:** Call golf shop. **Miscellaneous:** Reduced fees (twilight, juniors), metal spikes, range (grass), credit cards (MC, V, AE, D), BF, FF.
Reader Comments: Back 9 will get ya. Wonderful risk-reward course ... Blast away, wide open and fun ... Great staff, good condition ... Solid, but not exciting ... Not the most demanding course ... Greens are quick and true, fairways are lush.

★★★ FERNANDINA BEACH MUNICIPAL GOLF COURSE
PU-2800 Bill Melton Rd., Fernandina Beach, 32034, Nassau County, (904)277-7370, (800)646-5997, 35 miles from Jacksonville. **Facility Holes:** 27. **Green Fee:** $24/$40. **Cart Fee:** $13/Person. **Walking Policy:** Walking at certain times. **Walkability:** 1. **Opened:** 1954. **Architect:** Ed Mattson/Tommy Birdsong. **Season:** Year-round. **To obtain tee times:** Call up to 5 days in advance. **Miscellaneous:** Reduced fees (weekdays, twilight, juniors), range (grass), credit

cards (MC, V), BF, FF.
NORTH/WEST (18 Combo)
Yards: 6,803/5,720. **Par:** 72/72. **Course Rating:** 71.5/71.7. **Slope:** 124/118.
SOUTH/NORTH (18 Combo)
Yards: 6,400/5,156. **Par:** 71/72. **Course Rating:** 69.7/68.7. **Slope:** 124/116.
WEST/SOUTH (18 Combo)
Yards: 7,027/5,308. **Par:** 73/73. **Course Rating:** 72.6/69.4. **Slope:** 128/115.
Reader Comments: Very nice muni course … Fun course which you can walk … Pretty good public track … Many holes formed by large trees, nice … A little scruffy, but a great 27 holes.

FONTAINEBLEAU GOLF COURSE
PU-9603 Fontainebleau Blvd., Miami, 33172, Dade County, (305)221-5181, 5 miles from Miami. **Facility Holes:** 36. **Green Fee:** $15/$32. **Cart Fee:** Included in green fee. **Walking Policy:** Mandatory carts. **Walkability:** 1. **Architect:** Mark Mahannah. **Season:** Year-round. **High:** Nov.-March. **To obtain tee times:** Call up to 60 days in advance. **Miscellaneous:** Reduced fees (weekdays, guests, twilight), metal spikes, range (grass/mats), credit cards (MC, V, AE, DC), FF.
★★ **EAST COURSE** (18)
Yards: 7,035/5,586. **Par:** 72/72. **Course Rating:** 73.3/71.5. **Slope:** 122/119. **Opened:** 1969.
★ **WEST COURSE** (18)
Yards: 6,944/5,565. **Par:** 72/72. **Course Rating:** 72.5/71.0. **Slope:** 120/118. **Opened:** 1976.

★★★½ FOREST LAKE GOLF CLUB OF OCOEE
PU-10521 Clarcona-Ocoee Rd., Ocoee, 34761, Orange County, (407)654-4653, 5 miles from Orlando. **E-mail:** kaddy99@aol.com. **Web:** www.forestlake.com. **Facility Holes:** 18. **Yards:** 7,113/5,103. **Par:** 72/72. **Course Rating:** 74.4/69.2. **Slope:** 127/113. **Green Fee:** $29/$68. **Cart Fee:** Included in green fee. **Walking Policy:** Mandatory carts. **Walkability:** 2. **Opened:** 1994. **Architect:** Clifton/Ezell/Clifton. **Season:** Year-round. **High:** Dec.-March. **To obtain tee times:** Call up to 5 days in advance. **Miscellaneous:** Reduced fees (weekdays, twilight, juniors), range (grass), credit cards (MC, V), BF, FF.
Reader Comments: Beautiful surroundings, most enjoyable … Great par 5s and 3s. Play through the woods, no houses … Flat scenic course, wide fairways & fast, challenging greens … 18 challenging holes, bring all your clubs.

★★★ FOREST LAKES GOLF CLUB
SP-2401 Beneva Rd., Sarasota, 34232, Sarasota County, (941)922-1312, 40 miles from Tampa. **Facility Holes:** 18. **Yards:** 6,500/5,500. **Par:** 71/71. **Course Rating:** 70.8/71.3. **Slope:** 124/117. **Green Fee:** $16/$42. **Cart Fee:** Included in green fee. **Walking Policy:** Walking at certain times. **Walkability:** 1. **Opened:** 1964. **Architect:** Andy Anderson. **Season:** Year-round. **High:** Jan.-March. **To obtain tee times:** Call up to 4 days in advance. **Miscellaneous:** Reduced fees (weekdays, guests, twilight, juniors), metal spikes, range (grass/mats), credit cards (MC, V, AE, D), FF.
Reader Comments: Nice course, long course, great greens … Each hole a different nightmare.

★★★ FORT MYERS COUNTRY CLUB
PU-3591 McGregor Blvd., Fort Myers, 33901, Lee County, (941)936-3126, 120 miles from Tampa. **Facility Holes:** 18. **Yards:** 6,414/5,135. **Par:** 71/71. **Course Rating:** 70.5/70.6. **Slope:** 118/117. **Green Fee:** $13/$32. **Cart Fee:** $15/Person. **Walking Policy:** Unrestricted walking. **Walkability:** 1. **Opened:** 1917. **Architect:** Donald Ross. **Season:** Year-round. **High:** Nov.-April. **To obtain tee times:** Call up to 1 day in advance. **Miscellaneous:** Reduced fees (weekdays, twilight), credit cards (MC, V), BF, FF.
Reader Comments: Harder than it looks, very nice … Love Donald Ross course, but it needs touching up … Different 9s, really enjoyable day.

FORT WALTON BEACH GOLF CLUB
PU-1909 Lewis Turner Blvd., Fort Walton Beach, 32547, Okaloosa County, (850)833-9530, 50 miles from Pensacola. **Facility Holes:** 36. **Cart Fee:** $9/Person. **Walking Policy:** Unrestricted walking. **Walkability:** 1. **Season:** Year-round. **To obtain tee times:** Call golf shop. **Miscellaneous:** Reduced fees (twilight), range (grass/mats), credit cards (MC, V).
★★★ **OAKS COURSE** (18)
Yards: 6,416/5,059. **Par:** 72/72. **Course Rating:** 70.7/69.1. **Slope:** 123/121. **Green Fee:** $15/$19. **Opened:** 1993. **Architect:** David Smith.
Reader Comments: Plain, basic, but easy … Flat, nice … Nice course and good value.
★★½ **PINES COURSE** (18)
Yards: 6,761/5,263. **Par:** 72/72. **Course Rating:** 72.5/70.0. **Slope:** 123/118. **Green Fee:** $19. **Opened:** 1961. **Architect:** Bill Amick. **Miscellaneous:** BF, FF.

★★★½ FOX HOLLOW GOLF CLUB
PU-10050 Robert Trent Jones Pkwy., New Port Richey, 34655, Pasco County, (813)376-6333,

(800)943-1902, 25 miles from Tampa. **Web:** www.sandri.com. **Facility Holes:** 18. **Yards:** 7,138/5,203. **Par:** 71/71. **Course Rating:** 75.1/70.6. **Slope:** 137/127. **Green Fee:** $33/$85. **Cart Fee:** Included in green fee. **Walking Policy:** Unrestricted walking. **Walkability:** 2. **Opened:** 1994. **Architect:** Robert Trent Jones/Roger Rulewich. **Season:** Year-round. **High:** Jan.-April. **To obtain tee times:** Call up to 4 days in advance. **Miscellaneous:** Reduced fees (weekdays, twilight, juniors), metal spikes, range (grass), credit cards (MC, V, AE, D, DC), BF, FF.
Reader Comments: Super people ... Nice layout. A pleasure to play ... Long course, many water hazards, beautiful track ... Long ... Excellent design & conditions ... Tee boxes are long, good options ... Huge greens, a variety of tees.

★★★ FOXFIRE GOLF CLUB
PU-7200 Proctor Rd., Sarasota, 34241, Sarasota County, (941)921-7757, 50 miles from Tampa. **Facility Holes:** 27. **Green Fee:** $16/$49. **Cart Fee:** Included in green fee. **Walking Policy:** Unrestricted walking. **Walkability:** 2. **Opened:** 1975. **Architect:** Andy Anderson. **Season:** Year-round. **High:** Dec.-March. **To obtain tee times:** Call up to 7 days in advance. **Miscellaneous:** Reduced fees (weekdays, guests, twilight, juniors), metal spikes, range (grass), credit cards (MC, V, D), BF, FF.
PALM/OAK (18 Combo)
Yards: 6,280/5,024. **Par:** 72/72. **Course Rating:** 70.0/67.7. **Slope:** 123/129.
PINE/OAK (18 Combo)
Yards: 6,101/4,941. **Par:** 72/72. **Course Rating:** 69.8/67.6. **Slope:** 121/127.
PINE/PALM (18 Combo)
Yards: 6,213/4,983. **Par:** 72/72. **Course Rating:** 69.8/67.5. **Slope:** 119/115.
Reader Comments: Great course ... We were treated well and were able to play quickly ... OK shape, open fairways, not long course ... I was welcomed quite royally ... Hit the ball straight, great 27 holes ... Fun course, tees for all games.

★★ FOXWOOD COUNTRY CLUB
SP-4927 Antioch Rd., Crestview, 32536, Okaloosa County, (850)682-2012, 40 miles from Pensacola. **Facility Holes:** 18. **Yards:** 6,282/5,016. **Par:** 72/72. **Course Rating:** 69.6/69.7. **Slope:** 127/118. **Green Fee:** $12/$16. **Cart Fee:** $18/Person. **Walking Policy:** Walking at certain times. **Walkability:** 2. **Opened:** 1962. **Architect:** Bill Amick/Earl Stone. **Season:** Year-round. **To obtain tee times:** Call up to 7 days in advance. **Miscellaneous:** Reduced fees (weekdays, twilight, seniors), range (grass), included in fee), credit cards (MC, V, AE, D), BF, FF.

★★★★ GATEWAY GOLF & COUNTRY CLUB *Service*
SP-11360 Championship Dr., Fort Myers, 33913, Lee County, (941)561-2621. **Facility Holes:** 18. **Yards:** 6,974/5,323. **Par:** 72/72. **Course Rating:** 74.1/70.1. **Slope:** 129/121. **Green Fee:** $35/$115. **Cart Fee:** Included in green fee. **Walkability:** 1. **Opened:** 1989. **Architect:** Tom Fazio. **Season:** Year-round. **High:** Jan.-March. **To obtain tee times:** Call golf shop. **Miscellaneous:** Reduced fees (twilight), range (grass), credit cards (MC, V, AE).
Reader Comments: Great course, very well kept ... Fine course ... Amazing design, a great course and great service ... You can reach 2 of the par 5s in two, but small greens.

★★½ GATOR TRACE GOLF & COUNTRY CLUB
SP-4302 Gator Trace Dr., Fort Pierce, 34982, St. Lucie County, (561)464-7442, 40 miles from West Palm Beach. **Facility Holes:** 18. **Yards:** 6,092/4,573. **Par:** 70/70. **Course Rating:** 68.9/67.1. **Slope:** 123/123. **Green Fee:** $18/$40. **Cart Fee:** $15/Person. **Walking Policy:** Walking at certain times. **Walkability:** 3. **Opened:** 1986. **Architect:** Arthur Hills. **Season:** Year-round. **High:** Dec.-May. **To obtain tee times:** Call golf shop. **Miscellaneous:** Reduced fees (weekdays, twilight), metal spikes, credit cards (MC, V, D).

★★★★ THE GOLDEN BEAR CLUB AT KEENE'S POINTE
SP-6300 Jack Nicklaus Pkwy., Windermere, 34786, Orange County, (408)876-5775, 10 miles from Orlando. **Facility Holes:** 18. **Yards:** 7,173/5,071. **Par:** 72/72. **Course Rating:** 74.8/69.1. **Slope:** 136/118. **Cart Fee:** Included in green fee. **Walking Policy:** Mandatory carts. **Walkability:** 2. **Opened:** 1999. **Architect:** Jack Nicklaus/Bruce Borland. **Season:** Year-round. **High:** Jan.-April. **To obtain tee times:** Call up to 7 days in advance. **Miscellaneous:** Reduced fees (twilight, juniors), range (grass), credit cards (MC, V), BF, FF.
Reader Comments: Very solid course, very enjoyable to play ... Great potential ... Very nice facility, slow play ... Good course, flat, expensive ... Typical Florida, not typical Nicklaus ... Very playable for a Nicklaus design ... Long and hard.

★★★½ GOLDEN BEAR GOLF CLUB AT HAMMOCK CREEK
SP-2400 Golden Bear Way, Palm City, 34990, Martin County, (561)220-2599, (888)841-5225, 35 miles from West Beach. **E-mail:** steve.harrop@ourclub.com. **Web:** www.gbgc-hammock-creek.com. **Facility Holes:** 18. **Yards:** 7,119/5,045. **Par:** 72/72. **Course Rating:** 73.6/68.9. **Slope:** 132/111. **Green Fee:** $20/$70. **Cart Fee:** Included in green fee. **Walking Policy:** Walking at certain times. **Walkability:** 1. **Opened:** 1996. **Architect:** Jack Nicklaus/Jack Nicklaus Jr.

Season: Year-round. **High:** Dec.-April. **To obtain tee times:** Call up to 7 days in advance. **Miscellaneous:** Reduced fees (weekdays, guests, twilight, seniors, juniors), range (grass), credit cards (MC, V, AE, D, DC), BF, FF.
Reader Comments: Great for the average golfer ... Long & wide ... Juniors are treated respectfully ... Nice layout, good test ... Fast, firm greens, good variety of holes ... Offers everything an amateur could want ... Wide but challenging.

★★★ GOLDEN OCALA GOLF & COUNTRY CLUB
SP-7340 US Hwy. 27 N.W., Ocala, 34482, Marion County, (352)629-6229, 85 miles from Orlando. **E-mail:** jdonnelly@goldenocala.com. **Web:** www.goldenocala.com. **Facility Holes:** 18. **Yards:** 6,735/5,595. **Par:** 72/72. **Course Rating:** 72.2/72.2. **Slope:** 132/124. **Green Fee:** $35/$75. **Cart Fee:** Included in green fee. **Walking Policy:** Mandatory carts. **Walkability:** 3. **Opened:** 1986. **Architect:** Ron Garl. **Season:** Year-round. **High:** Dec.-April. **To obtain tee times:** Call golf shop. **Miscellaneous:** Range (grass), credit cards (MC, V, AE), BF, FF.
Reader Comments: Wonderful replica holes ... New clubhouse being built ... Challenging but fair. Replica holes are fun but the other holes are more interesting tests of golf. If you are looking for golf rather than amenities, play this.

★★★½ THE GOLF CLUB AT AMELIA ISLAND
R-4700 Amelia Island Pkwy., Amelia Island, 32034, Nassau County, (904)277-0012, (800)245-4224, 26 miles from Jacksonville. **Facility Holes:** 18. **Yards:** 6,692/5,039. **Par:** 72/72. **Course Rating:** 72.9/70.4. **Slope:** 136/124. **Green Fee:** $130/$140. **Cart Fee:** Included in green fee. **Walking Policy:** Mandatory carts. **Walkability:** 3. **Opened:** 1987. **Architect:** Mark McCumber. **Season:** Year-round. **To obtain tee times:** Call golf shop. **Miscellaneous:** Reduced fees (twilight, juniors), range (grass), credit cards (MC, V, AE, D), BF, FF.
Reader Comments: Looks harder than it plays ... Good condition, enjoyable to play ... Nice layout, but overpriced.

★★★ THE GOLF CLUB AT CYPRESS HEAD
PU-6231 Palm Vista St., Port Orange, 32124, Volusia County, (904)756-5449, 5 miles from Daytona Beach. **Facility Holes:** 18. **Yards:** 6,814/4,909. **Par:** 72/72. **Course Rating:** 72.4/68.3. **Slope:** 133/116. **Green Fee:** $30/$48. **Cart Fee:** Included in green fee. **Walking Policy:** Walking at certain times. **Walkability:** 3. **Opened:** 1992. **Architect:** Arthur Hills. **Season:** Year-round. **High:** Jan.-April. **To obtain tee times:** Call golf shop. **Miscellaneous:** Reduced fees (weekdays, guests, twilight, juniors), metal spikes, range (grass), credit cards (MC, V).
Reader Comments: Fine course and staff... Good greens ... Very playable ... Best golf for the money ... Great place to raise handicap ... Some weird holes.

THE GOLF CLUB AT FLEMING ISLAND PLANTATION
SP-2260 Town Center Blvd., Orange Park, 32003, Clay County, (904)269-1440. **Facility Holes:** 18. **Yards:** 6,801/4,881. **Par:** 71/71. **Course Rating:** 72.7/68.0. **Slope:** 136/116. **Green Fee:** $30/$50. **Cart Fee:** Included in green fee. **Walking Policy:** Mandatory carts. **Opened:** 2000. **Architect:** Bobby Weed. **Season:** Year-round. **To obtain tee times:** Call up to 7 days in advance. **Miscellaneous:** Reduced fees (weekdays, twilight, seniors, juniors), range (grass), credit cards (MC, V, AE), BF, FF.

★★★½ THE GOLF CLUB AT MARCO
R-3433 Marriott Club Dr., Naples, 34114, Collier County, (941)793-6060, 35 miles from Fort Myers. **E-mail:** cvliet@earthlink.net. **Web:** www.marriottgolf.com. **Facility Holes:** 18. **Yards:** 6,898/5,416. **Par:** 72/72. **Course Rating:** 73.1/70.9. **Slope:** 137/122. **Green Fee:** $35/$125. **Cart Fee:** Included in green fee. **Walking Policy:** Mandatory carts. **Walkability:** 1. **Opened:** 1991. **Architect:** Joe Lee. **Season:** Year-round. **High:** Jan.-May. **To obtain tee times:** Call up to 30 days in advance. **Miscellaneous:** Reduced fees (twilight, juniors), metal spikes, range (grass), lodging (400 rooms), credit cards (MC, V, AE, D, DC), BF, FF.
Reader Comments: I want to play No. 18 over and over ... Beautiful, beware of gators ... Staff is friendly ... Excellent facilities and restaurant ... Good course, bugs were bad ... Wonderful staff ... Good test in high winds, a bit pricey.

★★★½ GOLF CLUB OF JACKSONVILLE
PU-10440 Tournament Lane, Jacksonville, 32222, Duval County, (904)779-0800, 15 miles from Downtown Jacksonville. **Web:** www.golfclubofjacksonville.com. **Facility Holes:** 18. **Yards:** 6,620/5,021. **Par:** 71/71. **Course Rating:** 71.7/68.3. **Slope:** 129/119. **Green Fee:** $26/$55. **Cart Fee:** Included in green fee. **Walking Policy:** Walking at certain times. **Walkability:** 2. **Opened:** 1989. **Architect:** Bobby Weed/Mark McCumber. **Season:** Year-round. **To obtain tee times:** Call up to 14 days in advance. **Miscellaneous:** Reduced fees (weekdays, twilight, seniors, juniors), metal spikes, range (grass), credit cards (MC, V, AE), BF, FF.
Reader Comments: Great track ... A secret gem in the Jacksonville area ... Nice people ... Very challenging. Excellent condition ... Slow play, well-run golf shop.

FLORIDA

★★ THE GOLF CLUB OF JUPITER
PU-1800 Central Blvd., Jupiter, 33458, Palm Beach County, (561)747-6262. **Facility Holes:** 18. **Yards:** 6,265/5,150. **Par:** 70/71. **Course Rating:** 69.9/69.5. **Slope:** 117/118. **Green Fee:** $26/$55. **Cart Fee:** Included in green fee. **Walking Policy:** Mandatory carts. **Walkability:** 1. **Opened:** 1982. **Architect:** Lamar Smith. **Season:** Year-round. **High:** Jan.-March. **To obtain tee times:** Call up to 21 days in advance. **Miscellaneous:** Reduced fees (weekdays, twilight), range (grass), credit cards (MC, V), BF, FF.

★★½ GOLF HAMMOCK COUNTRY CLUB
SP-2222 Golf Hammock Dr., Sebring, 33872, Highlands County, (863)382-2151, 90 miles from Orlando. **Facility Holes:** 18. **Yards:** 6,431/5,352. **Par:** 72/72. **Course Rating:** 71.0/70.2. **Slope:** 127/118. **Green Fee:** $14/$40. **Cart Fee:** Included in green fee. **Walking Policy:** Mandatory carts. **Walkability:** 1. **Opened:** 1976. **Architect:** Ron Garl. **Season:** Year-round. **High:** Jan.-March. **To obtain tee times:** Call up to 2 days in advance. **Miscellaneous:** Reduced fees (guests, twilight, juniors), range (grass), credit cards (MC, V), BF, FF.

GRAND CYPRESS GOLF CLUB
R-One N. Jacaranda, Orlando, 32836, Orange County, (407)239-1904, (800)835-7377. **E-mail:** keshle9257@aol.com. **Web:** www.grandcypress.com. **Facility Holes:** 45. **Green Fee:** $115/$170. **Cart Fee:** Included in green fee. **Walkability:** 2. **Architect:** Jack Nicklaus. **Season:** Year-round. **To obtain tee times:** Call golf shop. **Miscellaneous:** Reduced fees (twilight, juniors), range (grass), caddies, lodging (896 rooms), credit cards (MC, V, AE, D, DC, CB), BF, FF.
★★★★½ NEW COURSE (18) *Condition+, Pace*
Yards: 6,773/5,314. **Par:** 72/72. **Course Rating:** 72.2/69.8. **Slope:** 122/115. **Walking Policy:** Unrestricted walking. **Opened:** 1988.
Reader Comments: Not Scotland, but it sure is close! Love the double greens ... Open course ... Expensive, but worth it ... Wonderful facilities, fair course, great service ... St. Andrews lookalike.
★★★★½ NORTH/EAST (18 combo)
Yards: 6,955/5,056. **Par:** 72/72. **Course Rating:** 75.0/69.5. **Slope:** 139/118. **Walking Policy:** Mandatory carts. **Opened:** 1984.
NORTH/SOUTH (18 combo)
Yards: 6,993/5,328. **Par:** 72/72. **Course Rating:** 75.1/71.6. **Slope:** 137/121.
SOUTH/EAST (18 combo)
Yards: 6,906/5,126. **Par:** 72/72. **Course Rating:** 74.7/70.3. **Slope:** 138/121.
Reader Comments: Very nice facility ... Best course I have ever played (including Bay Hill & Isleworth)... A pleasure and a challenge ... Very nice overall facility ... Save up your lunch money to afford this one.

★★★★ GRAND HAVEN GOLF CLUB *Condition*
SP-2001 Waterside Pkwy., Palm Coast, 32137, Flagler County, (904)445-2327, (888)522-5642, 30 miles from Daytona Beach. **Web:** www.palmcoastresort.com. **Facility Holes:** 18. **Yards:** 7,069/4,985. **Par:** 72/72. **Course Rating:** 74.9/70.4. **Slope:** 135/123. **Green Fee:** $53/$73. **Cart Fee:** Included in green fee. **Walkability:** 3. **Opened:** 1998. **Architect:** Jack Nicklaus. **Season:** Year-round. **High:** Jan.-April. **To obtain tee times:** Call golf shop. **Miscellaneous:** Reduced fees (guests, juniors), range (grass), lodging (150 rooms), credit cards (MC, V, AE). **Notes:** 1999 U.S. Open Qualifier; 1999 U.S. Junior Amateur Qualifier.
Reader Comments: Great experience ... Fantastic course to play ... Great design ... A fun course to play ... Fantastic layout, super conditioning ... New course, but in great shape.

★★★ GRAND PALMS GOLF & COUNTRY CLUB RESORT
R-110 Grand Palms Dr., Pembroke Pines, 33027, Broward County, (954)437-3334, (800)327-9246, 15 miles from Fort Lauderdale. **E-mail:** zachary@pga.com. **Facility Holes:** 27. **Green Fee:** $35/$75. **Cart Fee:** Included in green fee. **Walking Policy:** Mandatory carts. **Walkability:** 1. **Opened:** 1987. **Architect:** Ward Northrup. **Season:** Year-round. **To obtain tee times:** Call up to 3 days in advance. **Miscellaneous:** Reduced fees (weekdays, twilight), range (grass/mats), lodging (140 rooms), credit cards (MC, V, AE), BF, FF.
GRAND/ROYAL (18 Combo)
Yards: 6,816/5,245. **Par:** 72/72. **Course Rating:** 71.6/70.8. **Slope:** 127/126.
ROYAL/SABAL (18 Combo)
Yards: 6,736/5,391. **Par:** 73/73. **Course Rating:** 71.9/71.5. **Slope:** 128/122.
SABAL/GRAND (18 Combo)
Yards: 6,653/5,198. **Par:** 71/71. **Course Rating:** 71.5/70.7. **Slope:** 124/123.
Reader Comments: Great 9 hole courses ... Lots of water... Not bad, not great ... Satisfactory, enjoyable ... Comfortable, relaxing, good service, practice areas ... Not very long but demanding ... Great greens.

GRENELEFE GOLF & TENNIS RESORT

R-3200 State Rd. 546, Haines City, 33844, Polk County, (863)422-7511, (800)237-9549, 5 miles from Haines City. **Facility Holes:** 54. **Cart Fee:** Included in green fee. **Walking Policy:** Mandatory carts. **Walkability:** 3. **Season:** Year-round. **To obtain tee times:** Call golf shop. **Miscellaneous:** Reduced fees (weekdays, guests, twilight), metal spikes, range (grass), lodging (750 rooms), credit cards (MC, V, AE, DC).

★★★ **EAST COURSE** (18)

Yards: 6,802/5,114. **Par:** 72/72. **Course Rating:** 72.7/69.5. **Slope:** 131/118. **Green Fee:** $25/$110. **Opened:** 1978. **Architect:** Arnold Palmer/Ed Seay.

Reader Comments: Narrow course ... Good challenge ... Long course, nice greens... A great place to spend multiple days playing golf, excellent facilities ... Great golf at a fair price ... Tight course, bunkers need work.

★★★½ **SOUTH COURSE** (18)

Yards: 6,869/5,174. **Par:** 71/71. **Course Rating:** 72.6/69.5. **Slope:** 132/120. **Green Fee:** $25/$110. **Opened:** 1983. **Architect:** Ron Garl.

Reader Comments: A lot of fun ... Great resort! Reasonable prices ... It lost a bit of its perfection but still is a good course ... Great course ... Great holes ... Great golf at a fair price.

★★★ **WEST COURSE** (18)

Yards: 7,325/5,398. **Par:** 72/72. **Course Rating:** 75.0/71.3. **Slope:** 133/124. **Green Fee:** $25/$120. **Opened:** 1971. **Architect:** Robert Trent Jones/David Wallace.

Reader Comments: Lot's of fun to play. Should play all 3 during stay ... Incredibly challenging, lots of bunkers, facilities above average ... Could be great ... Too much money.

★★★½ GULF HARBOUR GOLF & COUNTRY CLUB

SP-14700 Portsmouth Blvd. S.W., Fort Myers, 33908, Lee County, (941)433-4211. **Facility Holes:** 18. **Yards:** 6,708/5,248. **Par:** 72/72. **Course Rating:** 72.5/70.1. **Slope:** 130/121. **Green Fee:** $28/$115. **Cart Fee:** Included in green fee. **Walkability:** 1. **Opened:** 1984. **Architect:** Ron Garl/Chip Powell. **Season:** Year-round. **High:** Jan.-May. **To obtain tee times:** Call golf shop. **Miscellaneous:** Reduced fees (twilight), metal spikes, range (grass), credit cards (MC, V, AE, D).

Reader Comments: Lots of water, fast greens ... Good course, great amenities ... Has potential.

★★★ HABITAT GOLF COURSE

PU-3591 Fairgreen St., Valkaria, 32905, Brevard County, (321)952-6312, 16 miles from Melbourne. **E-mail:** habitat@digital.net. **Web:** www.golfspacecoast.com. **Facility Holes:** 18. **Yards:** 6,836/4,969. **Par:** 72/72. **Course Rating:** 73.7/70.0. **Slope:** 141/119. **Green Fee:** $13/$30. **Cart Fee:** $11/Person. **Walking Policy:** Walking at certain times. **Walkability:** 4. **Opened:** 1991. **Architect:** Charles Ankrom. **Season:** Year-round. **High:** Dec.-April. **To obtain tee times:** Call up to 3 days in advance. **Miscellaneous:** Reduced fees (weekdays, guests, juniors), range (grass), credit cards (MC, V), BF, FF.

Reader Comments: Average ... Greatest golf deal in the area. Beautiful layout with challenging holes ... Great layout in a nature preserve. Small airplanes always flying over because of municipal airport located next to course.

★★★½ HALIFAX PLANTATION GOLF CLUB

SP-3400 Halifax Clubhouse Dr., Ormond Beach, 32174, Volusia County, (386)676-9600, (800)839-4044, 6 miles from Ormond Beach. **E-mail:** manager@halifax plantation.com. **Web:** www.halifaxplantation.com. **Facility Holes:** 18. **Yards:** 7,128/4,971. **Par:** 72/72. **Course Rating:** 74.1/68.3. **Slope:** 128/118. **Green Fee:** $10/$40. **Cart Fee:** $15/Person. **Walking Policy:** Walking at certain times. **Walkability:** 1. **Opened:** 1993. **Architect:** Bill Amick. **Season:** Year-round. **To obtain tee times:** Call up to 4 days in advance. **Miscellaneous:** Reduced fees (weekdays, guests, twilight), range (grass), credit cards (MC, V, AE), BF, FF.

Reader Comments: Nice range, greens are inconsistent ... Staff friendly, nice layout ... Enjoyable place to play golf ... Beautiful surroundings ... Friendly staff, easy location ...Traditional layout ... Very reasonable, a challenge.

★★★★ HARBOR HILLS COUNTRY CLUB

SP-6538 Lake Griffin Rd., Lady Lake, 32159, Lake County, (352)753-7711. **Facility Holes:** 18. **Yards:** 6,910/5,363. **Par:** 72/72. **Course Rating:** 72.8/70.3. **Slope:** 128/115. **Green Fee:** $28/$49. **Cart Fee:** Included in green fee. **To obtain tee times:** Call golf shop.

Reader Comments: Remote location, but worth the trip ... Good value worth your time ... Great fairways, tough good greens, fine facility, nice people ... Hilly Pinehurst in Florida.

★½ HARDER HALL COUNTRY CLUB

PU-3600 Golfview Dr., Sebring, 33872, Highlands County, (941)382-0500, 80 miles from Orlando. **Facility Holes:** 18. **Yards:** 6,300/5,003. **Par:** 72/72. **Course Rating:** 70.5/69.0. **Slope:** 125/108. **Green Fee:** $13/$34. **Walking Policy:** Mandatory carts. **Opened:** 1956. **Architect:** Dick Wilson. **Season:** Year-round. **High:** Jan.-April. **To obtain tee times:** Call golf shop. **Miscellaneous:** Reduced fees (guests, twilight), range (grass), credit cards (MC, V, D), BF, FF.

★★★★ HERON CREEK GOLF & COUNTRY CLUB
PU-5303 Heron Creek Blvd., North Port, 34287, Sarasota County, (941)423-6955, (800)877-1433, 15 miles from Sarasota. **E-mail:** paul@heron-ceek.com. **Web:** www.heron-creek.com. **Facility Holes:** 18. **Yards:** 6,869/4,787. **Par:** 72/72. **Course Rating:** 73.1/69.9. **Slope:** 140/124. **Green Fee:** $30/$65. **Cart Fee:** Included in green fee. **Walking Policy:** Walking at certain times. **Walkability:** 2. **Opened:** 2000. **Architect:** Arthur Hills/Brian Yoder. **Season:** Year-round. **High:** Jan.-April. **To obtain tee times:** Call up to 4 days in advance. **Miscellaneous:** Reduced fees (twilight), range (grass), credit cards (MC, V, AE), BF, FF. **Reader Comments:** Attractive, good elevation changes … A hills & yodel course, beautiful, graceful & fun … Will get better with age … Lots of doglegs, plenty of water… One of the best in area & getting better … Good, typical Florida.

★★★½ HIGHLANDS RESERVE GOLF CLUB
PU-500 Highlands Reserve Blvd., Davenport, 33837, Polk County, (863)420-1724, (877)508-4653, 5 miles from Orlando. **Web:** www.highlandsreserve.com. **Facility Holes:** 18. **Yards:** 6,673/4,875. **Par:** 72/72. **Course Rating:** 72.1/67.4. **Slope:** 118/107. **Green Fee:** $28/$65. **Cart Fee:** Included in green fee. **Walking Policy:** Unrestricted walking. **Walkability:** 2. **Opened:** 1998. **Architect:** Mike Dasher. **Season:** Year-round. **To obtain tee times:** Call up to 90 days in advance. **Miscellaneous:** Reduced fees (weekdays, guests, twilight, seniors, juniors), range (grass), credit cards (MC, V, AE, D, DC, CB), BF, FF. **Reader Comments:** Staff was friendly, course was open but fair … Very windy, lots of sand … Very enjoyable round … Good putter is essential … Hilly & wide open, challenging greens, friendly staff

★½ HILAMAN PARK MUNICIPAL GOLF COURSE
PU-2737 Blairstone Rd., Tallahassee, 32301, Leon County, (850)891-3935. **E-mail:** zimmerb@talgov.com. **Web:** www.talgov.com. **Facility Holes:** 18. **Yards:** 6,333/5,365. **Par:** 72/72. **Course Rating:** 70.1/70.8. **Slope:** 121/116. **Green Fee:** $11/$15. **Cart Fee:** $11/Person. **Walking Policy:** Walking at certain times. **Walkability:** 3. **Opened:** 1972. **Architect:** Edward Lawrence Packard. **Season:** Year-round. **High:** March-June. **To obtain tee times:** Call up to 7 days in advance. **Miscellaneous:** Reduced fees (weekdays, twilight, seniors, juniors), range (grass), credit cards (MC, V, AE, D), BF, FF.

★★★½ HOMBRE GOLF CLUB
SP-120 Coyote Pass, Panama City Beach, 32407, Bay County, (850)234-3673, 100 miles from Pensacola. **E-mail:** hombre@knology.net. **Web:** www.hombregolfclub.com. **Facility Holes:** 27. **Green Fee:** $65/$75. **Cart Fee:** Included in green fee. **Walking Policy:** Mandatory carts. **Walkability:** 1. **Opened:** 1990. **Architect:** Wes Burnham. **Season:** Year-round. **To obtain tee times:** Call up to 7 days in advance. **Miscellaneous:** Reduced fees (weekdays, guests, twilight, juniors), range (grass), lodging (26 rooms), credit cards (MC, V, D), BF, FF.
BAD/UGLY (18 combo)
Yards: 6,820/4,793. **Par:** 72/74. **Course Rating:** 73.8/68.9. **Slope:** 137/132.
GOOD/BAD (18 combo)
Yards: 6,563/4,949. **Course Rating:** 72.4/69.5. **Slope:** 137/131.
UGLY/GOOD (18 combo)
Yards: 6,596/4,910. **Course Rating:** 72.6/69.6. **Slope:** 133/127.
Reader Comments: A good value. Wide fairways with plenty of trouble for the wayward shot. A great place for high- and low-handicappers alike … Typical Florida, very flat and lots of water. Nice course, but overpriced … Not a pushover.

★★★ HUNTER'S CREEK GOLF CLUB
R-14401 Sports Club Way, Orlando, 32837, Orange County, (407)240-4653, 50 miles from Tampa. **Web:** www.golfhunterscreek.com. **Facility Holes:** 18. **Yards:** 7,432/5,755. **Par:** 72/72. **Course Rating:** 76.1/72.5. **Slope:** 137/120. **Green Fee:** $35/$80. **Cart Fee:** Included in green fee. **Walking Policy:** Mandatory carts. **Walkability:** 1. **Opened:** 1986. **Architect:** Lloyd Clifton. **Season:** Year-round. **High:** Jan.-March. **To obtain tee times:** Call golf shop. **Miscellaneous:** Reduced fees (weekdays, twilight, juniors), range (grass), credit cards (MC, V, D), FF. **Reader Comments:** Its greatest feature is its length—huge if played from the tips … Overrated, bland … Got to be the greenest course ever … Good mix of holes … Nice & open … Better bring your big stick … Nice greens.

★★★½ HUNTINGTON HILLS GOLF & COUNTRY CLUB
SP-2626 Duff Rd., Lakeland, 33809, Polk County, (863)859-3689, 33 miles from Tampa. **Facility Holes:** 18. **Yards:** 6,631/5,011. **Par:** 72/72. **Course Rating:** 72.5/68.7. **Slope:** 122/115. **Green Fee:** $25/$45. **Cart Fee:** Included in green fee. **Opened:** 1992. **Architect:** Ron Garl. **Season:** Year-round. **High:** Dec.-March. **To obtain tee times:** Call golf shop. **Miscellaneous:** Reduced fees (weekdays, twilight), range (grass), credit cards (MC, V, AE, D, Diners Club). **Reader Comments:** Fair course, challenging, nice greens … One of the nicer mid-level courses, can get slow at times, but usually it plays around 4 hours … Solid golf, no frills … Short but fun … Solid course at fair price.

★★ HYDE PARK GOLF CLUB
PU-6439 Hyde Grove Ave., Jacksonville, 32210, Duval County, (904)786-5410, 5 miles from Jacksonville. **Facility Holes:** 18. **Yards:** 6,500/5,500. **Par:** 72/73. **Course Rating:** 70.3/71.0. **Slope:** 120/122. **Green Fee:** $15/$18. **Cart Fee:** $14/Person. **Walking Policy:** Walking at certain times. **Walkability:** 2. **Opened:** 1925. **Architect:** Donald Ross. **Season:** Year-round. **High:** Year-round. **To obtain tee times:** Call up to 14 days in advance. **Miscellaneous:** Reduced fees (weekdays, twilight, seniors, juniors), range (grass), credit cards (MC, V, AE), BF, FF.

★★★ IMPERIAL LAKEWOODS GOLF CLUB
SP-6807 Buffalo Rd., Palmetto, 34221, Manatee County, (941)747-4653, (800)642-2193, 20 miles from Tampa. **E-mail:** imperiallakewoods,com. **Web:** www.imperiallakewoods.com. **Facility Holes:** 18. **Yards:** 7,019/5,270. **Par:** 72/72. **Course Rating:** 73.9/69.9. **Slope:** 136/117. **Green Fee:** $32/$55. **Cart Fee:** Included in green fee. **Walking Policy:** Walking at certain times. **Walkability:** 3. **Opened:** 1987. **Architect:** Ted McAnlis. **Season:** Year-round. **To obtain tee times:** Call up to 2 days in advance. **Miscellaneous:** Reduced fees (weekdays, twilight, juniors), metal spikes, range (grass), credit cards (MC, V, D), BF, FF.
Reader Comments: The 18th hole is the best, most demanding, fair finishing hole I have ever played … Fast, good value … Customer service great, makes you want to come back.
Special Notes: New 18-hole course planned for 2002.

★★½ INDIAN BAYOU GOLF & COUNTRY CLUB
SP-1 Country Club Dr. E., Destin, 32541, Okaloosa County, (850)837-6191, 30 miles from Pensacola. **Facility Holes:** 27. **Green Fee:** $50/$85. **Cart Fee:** Included in green fee. **Walking Policy:** Walking at certain times. **Walkability:** 1. **Opened:** 1978. **Architect:** Earl Stone. **Season:** Year-round. **To obtain tee times:** Call up to 14 days in advance. **Miscellaneous:** Reduced fees (twilight, juniors), range (grass), credit cards (MC, V, AE, D), BF, FF.
CHOCTAW/CREEK (18 Combo)
Yards: 6,939/4,928. **Par:** 72/71. **Course Rating:** 74.1/69.0. **Slope:** 139/122.
SEMINOLE/CHOCTAW (18 Combo)
Yards: 7,078/5,226. **Par:** 72/72. **Course Rating:** 74.6/70.7. **Slope:** 132/121.
SEMINOLE/CREEK (18 Combo)
Yards: 7,089/5,002. **Par:** 72/71. **Course Rating:** 74.7/69.1. **Slope:** 142/124.

★★★½ INDIGO LAKES GOLF CLUB *Pace*
SP-312 Indigo Dr., Daytona Beach, 32114, Volusia County, (386)254-3607,.1 mile from Daytona Beach. **Facility Holes:** 18. **Yards:** 7,168/5,159. **Par:** 72/72. **Course Rating:** 73.5/69.1. **Slope:** 128/123. **Green Fee:** $30/$55. **Cart Fee:** Included in green fee. **Walkability:** 1. **Opened:** 1977. **Architect:** Lloyd Clifton. **Season:** Year-round. **High:** Jan.-May. **To obtain tee times:** Call golf shop. **Miscellaneous:** Reduced fees (weekdays, twilight), metal spikes, range (grass/mats), credit cards (MC, V, AE).
Reader Comments: Nice course, busy … Enjoyable city course … Wet at times but good course … Good course for all skill levels … Great place to play. Kept in great shape … An interesting layout with a good value … Friendly staff.
Special Notes: Formerly Holiday Inn Crowne Plaza Resort.

★★½ INTERNATIONAL GOLF CLUB
PU-6351 International Golf Club Rd., Orlando, 32821, Orange County, (407)239-6909, (800)371-1165. **E-mail:** todd.howard@vacationclub.com. **Web:** www.internationalgolfclub.com. **Facility Holes:** 18. **Yards:** 6,776/5,077. **Par:** 72/72. **Course Rating:** 73.0/69.2. **Slope:** 134/117. **Green Fee:** $60/$105. **Cart Fee:** Included in green fee. **Walking Policy:** Mandatory carts. **Walkability:** 1. **Opened:** 1986. **Architect:** Joe Lee. **Season:** Year-round. **High:** Jan.-April. **To obtain tee times:** Call up to 60 days in advance. **Miscellaneous:** Reduced fees (guests, twilight, juniors), range (grass/mats), credit cards (MC, V, AE, D), BF, FF.

★★½ INTERNATIONAL LINKS OF MIAMI AT MELREESE GOLF COURSE
PU-1802 N.W. 37th Ave., Miami, 33125, Dade County, (305)633-4583. **Facility Holes:** 18. **Yards:** 7,173/5,534. **Par:** 71/71. **Course Rating:** 73.5/71.2. **Slope:** 132/118. **Green Fee:** $45/$90. **Cart Fee:** Included in green fee. **Walking Policy:** Walking at certain times. **Walkability:** 2. **Opened:** 1997. **Architect:** Charles Mahannah. **Season:** Year-round. **High:** Dec.-April. **To obtain tee times:** Call golf shop. **Miscellaneous:** Reduced fees (weekdays, twilight, juniors), range (grass/mats), credit cards (MC, V, AE, D).

★★ IRONWOOD GOLF COURSE
PU-2100 N.E. 39th Ave., Gainesville, 32609, Alachua County, (352)334-3120. **Facility Holes:** 18. **Yards:** 6,465/5,234. **Par:** 72/72. **Course Rating:** 71.3/70.2. **Slope:** 122/117. **Green Fee:** $11/$14. **Cart Fee:** $8/Person. **Walking Policy:** Unrestricted walking. **Walkability:** 1. **Opened:** 1964. **Architect:** David Wallace. **Season:** Year-round. **High:** Feb.-June. **To obtain tee times:**

FLORIDA

Call golf shop. **Miscellaneous:** Reduced fees (weekdays, twilight, seniors, juniors), range (grass), caddies, credit cards (MC, V, D).

JACARANDA GOLF CLUB
SP-9200 W. Broward Blvd., Plantation, 33324, Broward County, (954)472-5836, (888)955-1234, 12 miles from Fort Lauderdale. **E-mail:** jacarand@paradise.net. **Web:** www.scratch-golf.com. **Facility Holes:** 36. **Green Fee:** $35/$99. **Walking Policy:** Walking at certain times. **Walkability:** 2. **Season:** Year-round. **High:** Nov.-May. **To obtain tee times:** Call golf shop. **Miscellaneous:** Reduced fees (weekdays, twilight), range (grass/mats), credit cards (MC, V, AE), BF, FF.
★★★½ **EAST COURSE** (18)
Yards: 7,195/5,638. **Par:** 72/72. **Course Rating:** 74.0/72.3. **Slope:** 130/124. **Cart Fee:** Included in green fee. **Opened:** 1971. **Architect:** Mark Mahannah.
Reader Comments: Great value, underrated … Long course, good test … Nice track not worth the full ticket price … Standard South Florida facility … I play here as often as I can.
★★★½ **WEST COURSE** (18)
Yards: 6,729/5,314. **Par:** 72/72. **Course Rating:** 72.5/71.1. **Slope:** 132/118. **Opened:** 1972. **Architect:** Mark Mahannah/Charles Mahannah.
Reader Comments: Shotmaker's course … Good treatment by staff, reasonably priced, nice challenge … Always well prepared, condition is outstanding, even during the dog days of summer… Satisfactory, enjoyable … Good course.

★½ **JACKSONVILLE BEACH GOLF CLUB**
PU-605 South Penman Rd., Jacksonville, 32250, Duval County, (904)247-6184, 10 miles from Jacksonville. **Facility Holes:** 18. **Yards:** 6,510/5,245. **Par:** 72/72. **Course Rating:** 70.5/69.2. **Slope:** 119/114. **Green Fee:** $17/$19. **Walking Policy:** Walking at certain times. **Walkability:** 1. **Opened:** 1959. **Architect:** Robert Walker. **Season:** Year-round. **High:** Sept.-June. **To obtain tee times:** Call golf shop. **Miscellaneous:** Reduced fees (weekdays, twilight, juniors), metal spikes, range (grass/mats), credit cards (MC, V), BF, FF.

★★★★½ **KELLY PLANTATION GOLF CLUB** *Service, Condition*
SP-307 Kelly Plantation Dr., Destin, 32541, Okaloosa County, (850)650-7600, (800)811-6757, 3 miles from Destin. **E-mail:** swright@kellyplantation.com. **Web:** www.kellyplantation.com. **Facility Holes:** 18. **Yards:** 7,099/5,170. **Par:** 72/72. **Course Rating:** 74.2/70.9. **Slope:** 146/124. **Green Fee:** $75/$120. **Cart Fee:** Included in green fee. **Walking Policy:** Unrestricted walking. **Walkability:** 2. **Opened:** 1998. **Architect:** Fred Couples/Gene Bates. **Season:** Year-round. **To obtain tee times:** Call up to 30 days in advance. **Miscellaneous:** Reduced fees (twilight, juniors), range (grass), lodging (100 rooms), credit cards (MC, V, AE, D), BF, FF.
Reader Comments: Scenic bay view from some holes … Really interesting, challenging tract … Beautiful course, expensive … Service is exceptional & the course is wonderful.

★★★ **KEY WEST GOLF CLUB**
PU-6450 E. College Rd., Key West, 33040, Monroe County, (305)294-5232. **E-mail:** kwgolf@aol.com. **Web:** keywestgolf.com. **Facility Holes:** 18. **Yards:** 6,526/5,183. **Par:** 70/70. **Course Rating:** 71.2/70.1. **Slope:** 124/118. **Green Fee:** $75/$140. **Cart Fee:** Included in green fee. **Walking Policy:** Walking at certain times. **Walkability:** 1. **Architect:** Rees Jones. **Season:** Year-round. **High:** Oct.-May. **To obtain tee times:** Call up to 7 days in advance. **Miscellaneous:** Reduced fees (twilight, juniors), range (mats), credit cards (MC, V, AE), BF, FF.
Reader Comments: Course was fun and challenging … Price is steep, but considering it's the only game it town, put up or shut up … Southernmost course in the U.S., no other public course within miles, and they act like it.

★★½ **KISSIMMEE BAY COUNTRY CLUB**
SP-2801 Kissimmee Bay Blvd., Kissimmee, 34744, Osceola County, (407)348-4653, 10 miles from Orlando. **Facility Holes:** 18. **Yards:** 6,846/5,171. **Par:** 71/71. **Course Rating:** 70.1/71.0. **Slope:** 125/122. **Green Fee:** $42/$79. **Cart Fee:** Included in green fee. **Walking Policy:** Mandatory carts. **Walkability:** 1. **Opened:** 1990. **Architect:** Lloyd Clifton. **Season:** Year-round. **To obtain tee times:** Call up to 7 days in advance. **Miscellaneous:** Reduced fees (weekdays, twilight), range (grass), credit cards (MC, V, D), BF, FF.

★★★ **KISSIMMEE GOLF CLUB**
SP-3103 Florida Coach Dr., Kissimmee, 34741, Osceola County, (407)847-2816, 15 miles from Orlando. **Web:** golfkiss@aol.com. **Web:** www.kissgolfclub.com. **Facility Holes:** 18. **Yards:** 6,537/5,083. **Par:** 72/72. **Course Rating:** 73.0/68.6. **Slope:** 126/116. **Green Fee:** $30/$52. **Cart Fee:** Included in green fee. **Walking Policy:** Walking at certain times. **Walkability:** 1. **Opened:** 1970. **Architect:** Bill Bulmer/Gordon Lewis. **Season:** Year-round. **To obtain tee times:** Call up to 4 days in advance. **Miscellaneous:** Reduced fees (guests, twilight, juniors), metal spikes, range (grass), credit cards (MC, V), BF, FF.

FLORIDA

★★★★½ LAKE JOVITA GOLF & COUNTRY CLUB
SP-12900 Lake Jovita Blvd., Dade City, 33525, Pasco County, (352)588-9200, (877)481-2652, 20 miles from Tampa. **Web:** www.lakejovita.com. **Facility Holes:** 18. **Yards:** 7,151/5,091. **Par:** 72/72. **Course Rating:** 74.4/68.4. **Slope:** 140/136. **Green Fee:** $65/$95. **Cart Fee:** Included in green fee. **Walking Policy:** Unrestricted walking. **Walkability:** 3. **Opened:** 1999. **Architect:** Kurt Sandness/Tom Lehman. **Season:** Year-round. **High:** Jan.-May. **To obtain tee times:** Call golf shop. **Miscellaneous:** Range (grass), credit cards (MC, V, AE), BF, FF. **Notes:** Ranked 11th in 2001 Best in State; 9th in 2000 Best New Upscale Courses.
Reader Comments: Challenging and a real bargain ... Nice change over other Florida courses ... Play here if you can ... Excellent, a few strange holes ... Nice, fun & fair course ... Beautiful course, rolling terrain.

★½ LAKE ORLANDO GOLF CLUB
PU-4224 Clubhouse Rd., Orlando, 32808, Orange County, (407)298-4144, 3 miles from Orlando. **E-mail:** lakeorlandogolf@yahoo.com. **Web:** www.golflakeorlando.com. **Facility Holes:** 18. **Yards:** 6,803/5,488. **Par:** 72/72. **Course Rating:** 72.3/70.3. **Slope:** 130/114. **Green Fee:** $27/$55. **Cart Fee:** Included in green fee. **Walking Policy:** Mandatory carts. **Walkability:** 1. **Opened:** 1970. **Architect:** Lloyd Clifton. **Season:** Year-round. **High:** Jan.-May. **To obtain tee times:** Call up to 7 days in advance. **Miscellaneous:** Reduced fees (weekdays, twilight, juniors), metal spikes, range (grass/mats), credit cards (MC, V, AE, D), BF, FF.

★½ LAKE WORTH GOLF CLUB
PU-1-7th Ave. N., Lake Worth, 33460, Palm Beach County, (561)582-9713, 7 miles from Palm Beach. **Web:** lakeworthgc@flinet.com. **Facility Holes:** 18. **Yards:** 6,113/5,413. **Par:** 70/70. **Course Rating:** 68.6/69.6. **Slope:** 116/113. **Green Fee:** $16/$42. **Cart Fee:** Included in green fee. **Walking Policy:** Unrestricted walking. **Walkability:** 1. **Opened:** 1926. **Architect:** Ward Northrup/Dick Wilson. **Season:** Year-round. **High:** Jan.-April. **To obtain tee times:** Call up to 2 days in advance. **Miscellaneous:** Reduced fees (twilight, juniors), metal spikes, credit cards (MC, V, Debit), BF, FF.

★★★ LANSBROOK GOLF COURSE
SP-4605 Village Center Dr., Palm Harbor, 34685, Pinellas County, (727)784-7333, 20 miles from Tampa. **E-mail:** lansgolf@aol.com. **Web:** www.lansbrookgolf.com. **Facility Holes:** 18. **Yards:** 6,862/5,333. **Par:** 72/72. **Course Rating:** 73.2/70.2. **Slope:** 131/124. **Green Fee:** $27/$65. **Cart Fee:** Included in green fee. **Walking Policy:** Mandatory carts. **Walkability:** 1. **Opened:** 1975. **Architect:** Lane Marshall. **Season:** Year-round. **To obtain tee times:** Call up to 7 days in advance. **Miscellaneous:** Reduced fees (weekdays, twilight, seniors), range (grass/mats), credit cards (MC, V, AE, D), BF, FF.
Reader Comments: Course maintained very well ... Layout is just OK ... Narrow fairways, good greens ... Great for short hitters ... Tight through trees ... Many risk-reward shots.

★★★★½ THE LEGACY CLUB AT ALAQUA LAKES
SP-1700 Alaqua Lakes Blvd., Longwood, 32779, Seminole County, (407)444-9995, 10 miles from Orlando. **E-mail:** rparris@taylorwoodrowhomer.com. **Web:** www.legacyclubgolf.com. **Facility Holes:** 18. **Yards:** 7,160/5,383. **Par:** 72/72. **Course Rating:** 74.5/70.7. **Slope:** 132/119. **Green Fee:** $59/$109. **Cart Fee:** Included in green fee. **Walking Policy:** Walking at certain times. **Walkability:** 3. **Opened:** 1998. **Architect:** Tom Fazio. **Season:** Year-round. **High:** Jan.-May. **To obtain tee times:** Call up to 3 days in advance. **Miscellaneous:** Reduced fees (weekdays, guests, twilight), range (grass), credit cards (MC, V), BF, FF.
Reader Comments: Rolling hills, not typical Florida course ... Terrific course, pricey ... Staff treats people well and keeps things moving. Keep it straight and long or pay the price... Great layout, fantastic condition.

★★★★ THE LEGACY GOLF COURSE AT LAKEWOOD RANCH
PU-8255 Legacy Blvd., Bradenton, 34202, Manatee County, (941)907-7067, 30 miles from Tampa. **Facility Holes:** 18. **Yards:** 7,067/4,886. **Par:** 72/72. **Course Rating:** 73.7/68.2. **Slope:** 143/125. **Green Fee:** $45/$95. **Cart Fee:** Included in green fee. **Walkability:** 3. **Opened:** 1997. **Architect:** Arnold Palmer/Ed Seay/Vici Martz. **Season:** Year-round. **High:** Jan.-April. **To obtain tee times:** Call golf shop. **Miscellaneous:** Reduced fees (weekdays, twilight), metal spikes, range (grass), credit cards (MC, V, AE).
Reader Comments: Every hole into the wind ... Average ... Great course and well maintained ... Tough when the wind is up. Absolutely beautiful ... Challenge off the back ... Good value, long way between tees.

FLORIDA

★★★½ **THE LEGENDS GOLF & COUNTRY CLUB**
PU-8600 Legends Blvd., Fort Myers, 33912, Lee County, (941)561-7757, (941)561-7767.
Facility Holes: 18. **Yards:** 6,652/5,212. **Par:** 72/72. **Course Rating:** 72.5/70.6. **Slope:** 133/121.
Green Fee: $20/$68. **Walking Policy:** Mandatory carts. **Walkability:** 1. **Opened:** 1999.
Architect: Joe Lee. **Season:** Year-round. **High:** Nov.-March. **To obtain tee times:** Call up to 3
days in advance. **Miscellaneous:** Reduced fees (twilight), range (grass), credit cards (MC, V,
AE, D), BF, FF.
Reader Comments: Lovely, graceful, fair & very enjoyable course for all … A most enjoyable
course to play … Very nice layout in fine condition … Excellent service & facilities … Great course.

LELY RESORT GOLF & COUNTRY CLUB
R-8004 Lely Resort Blvd., Naples, 34113, Collier County, (941)793-2223, (800)388-4653,
30 miles from Fort Myers. **Facility Holes:** 36. **Green Fee:** $35/$125. **Cart Fee:** Included in
green fee. **Walking Policy:** Mandatory carts. **Season:** Year-round. **High:** Nov.-April. **To obtain
tee times:** Call up to 3 days in advance. **Miscellaneous:** Reduced fees (twilight), range
(grass), credit cards (MC, V, AE, D, DC).
★★★★ **LELY FLAMINGO ISLAND CLUB** (18) *Pace*
Yards: 7,171/5,377. **Par:** 72/72. **Course Rating:** 73.9/70.6. **Slope:** 135/126. **Opened:** 1990.
Architect: Robert Trent Jones. **Miscellaneous:** BF, FF.
Reader Comments: Superb in every respect, but price … Great water holes, nice people … Great
layout, every hole a challenge, tough but fair, lots of water and sand.
★★★★½ **LELY MUSTANG GOLF CLUB** (18) *Pace+*
Yards: 7,217/5,197. **Par:** 72/72. **Course Rating:** 75.2/70.5. **Slope:** 141/120. **Opened:** 1996.
Architect: Lee Trevino.
Reader Comments: Great service, beautiful course, lot of sand … Great variety of par 3s … Really
wonderful course … Outstanding service, facilities, and course … Challenging but not overly difficult, roomy fairways, long from back tees.

THE LINKS AT BOYNTON BEACH
PU-8020 Jog Rd., Boynton Beach, 33437, Palm Beach County, (561)742-6501, 10 miles from
West Palm Beach. **E-mail:** defessef@ci.boynton-beach.fl.us. **Web:** www.thelinksatboynton-
beach.com. **Facility Holes:** 27. **Walkability:** 1. **Opened:** 1984. **Architect:** von
Hagge/Devlin/Ankrom. **Season:** Year-round. **High:** Jan.-March. **To obtain tee times:** Call up to
2 days in advance. **Miscellaneous:** Range (grass), credit cards (MC, V), BF, FF.
★★★ **CHAMPIONSHIP COURSE** (18)
Yards: 6,231/4,913. **Par:** 71/71. **Course Rating:** 70.4/68.9. **Slope:** 132/113. **Green Fee:**
$12/$19. **Cart Fee:** $13/Person. **Walking Policy:** Walking at certain times.
Reader Comments: Great value with outstanding pace of play and customer service programs.
Particularly liked being chosen "VIP of the day" … Good experience … Nice little course … Playable
for all levels.
EXECUTIVE COURSE (9)
Yards: 1,981/1,626. **Par:** 30/30. **Green Fee:** $9/$16. **Cart Fee:** $11/Person. **Walking Policy:**
Unrestricted walking.

THE LINKS AT MADISON GREEN
PU-2001 Crestwood Blvd. N., Royal Palm Beach, 33411, Palm Beach County,
(561)784-5225, 12 miles from West Palm Beach. **Web:** empiregolfusa.com. **Facility Holes:** 18.
Yards: 7,051/4,863. **Par:** 72/72. **Green Fee:** $35/$75. **Cart Fee:** Included in green fee. **Walking
Policy:** Walking at certain times. **Walkability:** 1. **Opened:** 2001. **Architect:** John Sandford.
Season: Year-round. **High:** Nov.-April. **To obtain tee times:** Call up to 6 days in advance.
Miscellaneous: Reduced fees (weekdays), range (grass), credit cards (MC, V, AE, D), BF, FF.

THE LINKS AT POINTE WEST
SP-7510 14th Lane, Vero Beach, 32968, Indian River County, (561)794-2904, 45 miles from
Orlando. **E-mail:** linksatpw@cs.com. **Web:** pointewestflorida.com. **Facility Holes:** 18. **Yards:**
6,951/5,166. **Par:** 72/72. **Course Rating:** 73.0/70.6. **Slope:** 129/119. **Green Fee:** $30/$60. **Cart
Fee:** Included in green fee. **Walking Policy:** Unrestricted walking. **Walkability:** 2. **Opened:**
2000. **Architect:** John Sanford. **Season:** Year-round. **To obtain tee times:** Call up to 5 days in
advance. **Miscellaneous:** Reduced fees (juniors), range (grass), credit cards (MC, V, AE),
BF, FF.

★★½ THE LINKS OF LAKE BERNADETTE
SP-5430 Links Lane, Zephyrhills, 33541, Pasco County, (813)788-4653, 20 miles from
Tampa. **Facility Holes:** 18. **Yards:** 6,392/5,031. **Par:** 71/71. **Course Rating:** 70.0/68.0. **Slope:**
119/118. **Green Fee:** $20/$35. **Cart Fee:** Included in green fee. **Walkability:** 1. **Opened:** 1985.
Architect: Dean Refram. **Season:** Year-round. **High:** Jan.-April. **To obtain tee times:** Call
golf shop. **Miscellaneous:** Reduced fees (weekdays, twilight), metal spikes, credit cards
(MC, V, AE).

FLORIDA

★★★ LOCHMOOR COUNTRY CLUB
SP-3911 Orange Grove Blvd., North Fort Myers, 33903, Lee County, (941)995-0501, 5 miles from Fort Myers. **Facility Holes:** 18. **Yards:** 6,908/5,152. **Par:** 72/72. **Course Rating:** 73.1/69.1. **Slope:** 128/116. **Green Fee:** $14/$50. **Cart Fee:** Included in green fee. **Walking Policy:** Walking at certain times. **Walkability:** 1. **Opened:** 1972. **Architect:** William F. Mitchell. **Season:** Year-round. **High:** Jan.-April. **To obtain tee times:** Call golf shop. **Miscellaneous:** Reduced fees (twilight, juniors), range (grass), credit cards (MC, V, AE).
Reader Comments: Course OK, needs work … Good course, lots of water, some narrow fairways … Nice layout.

LONG MARSH GOLF CLUB
SP-20 White Marsh Rd., Rotonda, 33947, Charlotte County, (941)698-0918, 30 miles from Sarasota. **E-mail:** longmarshgolf@eusl.com. **Web:** www.longmarsh.com. **Facility Holes:** 18. **Yards:** 7,120/5,257. **Par:** 72/72. **Course Rating:** 74.2/69.3. **Slope:** 127/112. **Green Fee:** $25/$56. **Cart Fee:** Included in green fee. **Walking Policy:** Mandatory carts. **Walkability:** 1. **Opened:** 1999. **Architect:** Ted McAnlis. **Season:** Year-round. **High:** Feb.-March. **To obtain tee times:** Call up to 365 days in advance. **Miscellaneous:** Reduced fees (juniors), range (grass), credit cards (MC, V), BF, FF.

LONGBOAT KEY CLUB
R-3200 Harbourside Dr., Longboat Key, 34228, Sarasota County, (941)387-1632, (800)237-8821, 3 miles from Sarasota. **E-mail:** golf@longboatkeyclub.com. **Web:** www.longboatkeyclub.com. **Facility Holes:** 45. **Green Fee:** $84/$150. **Cart Fee:** Included in green fee. **Walking Policy:** Mandatory carts. **Walkability:** 1. **Season:** Year-round. **High:** Dec.-April. **To obtain tee times:** Call up to 2 days in advance. **Miscellaneous:** Reduced fees (twilight, juniors), lodging (230 rooms), credit cards (MC, V, AE), BF, FF.
HARBOURSIDE COURSE
Opened: 1982. **Architect:** William Byrd. **Miscellaneous:** Range (grass).
(BLUE/RED) (18 combo)
Yards: 6,709/5,198. **Par:** 72/72. **Course Rating:** 72.6/69.5. **Slope:** 130/123.
(RED/WHITE) (18 combo)
Yards: 6,749/5,469. **Par:** 72/72. **Course Rating:** 72.7/71.3. **Slope:** 131/125.
(WHITE/BLUE) (18 combo)
Yards: 6,812/5,135. **Par:** 72/72. **Course Rating:** 73.1/70.3. **Slope:** 132/126.
★★½ **ISLANDSIDE COURSE** (18)
Yards: 6,792/5,198. **Par:** 72/72. **Course Rating:** 73.8/68.6. **Slope:** 138/121. **Opened:** 1960. **Architect:** William F. Mitchell. **Miscellaneous:** Range (mats).

★★★½ LOST KEY PLANTATION
PU-625 Lost Key Dr., Perdido Key, 32507, Escambia County, (850)492-1300, (888)256-7853, 5 miles from Pensacola. **E-mail:** proshop@lostkey.com. **Web:** www.lostkey.com. **Facility Holes:** 18. **Yards:** 6,810/4,825. **Par:** 72/72. **Course Rating:** 74.3/69.6. **Slope:** 144/121. **Green Fee:** $50/$70. **Cart Fee:** Included in green fee. **Walking Policy:** Mandatory carts. **Walkability:** 2. **Opened:** 1997. **Architect:** A. Palmer/E. Seay/H. Minchew/E. Wiltse. **Season:** Year-round. **High:** Feb.-May. **To obtain tee times:** Call up to 30 days in advance. **Miscellaneous:** Reduced fees (twilight, juniors), metal spikes, range (grass), credit cards (MC, V, AE), BF, FF.
Reader Comments: Target golf, not for average players … Shotmaking is at a premium here. If you grip it and rip it, this is not the course for you. A lot of fun … Tight, but fair … Very beautiful, very hard without any gimmicks.

★★★½ LOST LAKE GOLF CLUB
SP-8300 S.E. Fazio Dr., Hobe Sound, 33455, Martin County, (561)220-6666, 25 miles from West Plam Beach. **Facility Holes:** 18. **Yards:** 6,850/5,106. **Par:** 72/72. **Course Rating:** 73.4/69.5. **Slope:** 135/123. **Green Fee:** $22/$60. **Cart Fee:** Included in green fee. **Walking Policy:** Mandatory carts. **Walkability:** 3. **Opened:** 1992. **Architect:** Jim Fazio. **Season:** Year-round. **High:** Jan.-April. **To obtain tee times:** Call golf shop. **Miscellaneous:** Range (grass), credit cards (MC, V, D), BF, FF.
Reader Comments: Nice conditions, excellent greens … Average … A really fun course, good shape … Excellent layout, challenge, friendly staff.

★★★ LOST OAKS GOLF CLUB
PU-1100 Tarpon Woods Blvd., Palm Harbor, 34685, Pinellas County, (727)784-7606, 20 miles from Tampa. **E-mail:** lostaoaks@e2linksgolf.com. **Facility Holes:** 18. **Yards:** 6,515/5,245. **Par:** 72/72. **Course Rating:** 72.1/69.5. **Slope:** 128/115. **Green Fee:** $28/$55. **Cart Fee:** Included in green fee. **Walking Policy:** Mandatory carts. **Walkability:** 2. **Opened:** 1970. **Architect:** Lane Marshall. **Season:** Year-round. **High:** Jan.-April. **To obtain tee times:** Call up to 7 days in advance. **Miscellaneous:** Reduced fees (weekdays, guests, twilight, seniors, juniors), metal spikes, range (grass), credit cards (MC, V, AE, D), BF, FF.
Reader Comments: Good & challenging course … Best value in Bay Area, challenging.

LPGA INTERNATIONAL

PU-1000 Champions Dr., Daytona Beach, 32124, Volusia County, (386)523-2001, 50 miles from Orlando. **E-mail:** nacey.henderson@bvhg.com. **Web:** www.lpgainternational.com. **Facility Holes:** 36. **Green Fee:** $30/$85. **Cart Fee:** Included in green fee. **Walking Policy:** Mandatory carts. **Season:** Year-round. **High:** Jan.-April. **To obtain tee times:** Call up to 7 days in advance. **Miscellaneous:** Reduced fees (twilight, juniors), range (grass), credit cards (MC, V, AE), BF, FF.

★★★★ **CHAMPIONS** (18) *Condition*
Yards: 7,088/5,131. **Par:** 72/72. **Course Rating:** 74.0/68.9. **Slope:** 134/122. **Walkability:** 2. **Opened:** 1994. **Architect:** Rees Jones.
Reader Comments: Excellent condition ... Tough layout, lots of sand, great GPS ... Beautiful course ... Good test ... Great course, best value in the world ... Beautiful course, scenic, great condition ... Great course, great staff.

★★★★ **LEGENDS** (18)
Yards: 6,984/5,131. **Par:** 72/72. **Course Rating:** 74.5/70.2. **Slope:** 138/123. **Walkability:** 3. **Opened:** 1998. **Architect:** Arthur Hills.
Reader Comments: Back 9 is awesome ... Fun ... Terrific layout, options and decisions on every shot! Great par 4s that demand precise shotmaking ... Staff extremely friendly ... Wide open course, windy ... Good course, fine staff.

MAGNOLIA PLANTATION GOLF CLUB

SP-600 Shadowmoss Circle, Lake Mary, 32746, Seminole County, (407)833-0818, (866)511-4653, 10 miles from Orlando. **Facility Holes:** 18. **Yards:** 7,175/5,240. **Par:** 72/72. **Course Rating:** 75.2/71.8. **Slope:** 137/134. **Green Fee:** $45/$90. **Cart Fee:** Included in green fee. **Walking Policy:** Walking at certain times. **Walkability:** 3. **Opened:** 2000. **Architect:** David Harmon. **Season:** Year-round. **High:** Jan.-March. **To obtain tee times:** Call up to 7 days in advance. **Miscellaneous:** Reduced fees (weekdays, twilight, juniors), range (grass), credit cards (MC, V, AE), BF, FF.

★★½ **MAGNOLIA VALLEY GOLF CLUB**
SP-7223 Massachusetts Ave., New Port Richey, 34653, Pasco County, (727)847-2342, 20 miles from Tampa. **Facility Holes:** 27. **Yards:** 6,106/4,869. **Par:** 71/72. **Course Rating:** 69.1/67.2. **Slope:** 121/112. **Green Fee:** $15/$20. **Cart Fee:** Included in green fee. **Walking Policy:** Walking at certain times. **Walkability:** 1. **Opened:** 1965. **Architect:** Phil Leckey. **Season:** Year-round. **High:** Nov.-April. **To obtain tee times:** Call up to 5 days in advance. **Miscellaneous:** Reduced fees (twilight), metal spikes, range (grass), credit cards (MC, V, D), FF.
Special Notes: Also has a 9-hole executive course.

★★★ **MANATEE COUNTY GOLF CLUB**
PU-6415 53rd Ave. W., Bradenton, 34210, Manatee County, (941)792-6773, 40 miles from Tampa. **Facility Holes:** 18. **Yards:** 6,703/5,587. **Par:** 72/72. **Course Rating:** 72.3/71.9. **Slope:** 126/121. **Green Fee:** $16/$27. **Cart Fee:** $10/Person. **Walking Policy:** Unrestricted walking. **Walkability:** 2. **Opened:** 1977. **Architect:** Lane Marshall. **Season:** Year-round. **High:** Dec.-April. **To obtain tee times:** Call up to 2 days in advance. **Miscellaneous:** Reduced fees (weekdays, twilight), range (grass), credit cards (MC, V, D), BF, FF.

★★★ **MANGROVE BAY GOLF COURSE**
PU-875 62nd Ave. N.E., St. Petersburg, 33702, Pinellas County, (727)893-7800, 15 miles from Tampa. **E-mail:** jghollis@stpete.org. **Web:** www.stpete.org. **Facility Holes:** 18. **Yards:** 6,656/5,176. **Par:** 72/72. **Course Rating:** 71.5/68.5. **Slope:** 120/112. **Green Fee:** $18/$24. **Cart Fee:** $12/Person. **Walking Policy:** Unrestricted walking. **Walkability:** 2. **Opened:** 1978. **Architect:** Bill Amick. **Season:** Year-round. **To obtain tee times:** Call up to 7 days in advance. **Miscellaneous:** Reduced fees (twilight), range (grass), credit cards (MC, V, AE, D, Debit), BF, FF.
Reader Comments: Busy city course ... Outstanding value, good condition ... Good condition for a city course ... Played 2 times while vacationing, treated with courtesy and respect, very good value ... Great public course, excellent value.

★★ **MARCO SHORES COUNTRY CLUB**
PU-1450 Mainsail Dr., Naples, 34114, Collier County, (941)394-2581, 30 miles from Fort Myers. **E-mail:** info@marco-shores-golf.com. **Web:** www.marco-shores-golf.com. **Facility Holes:** 18. **Yards:** 6,879/5,634. **Par:** 72/72. **Course Rating:** 73.0/72.3. **Slope:** 125/121. **Green Fee:** $26/$79. **Cart Fee:** Included in green fee. **Walking Policy:** Mandatory carts. **Walkability:** 1. **Opened:** 1974. **Architect:** Bruce Devlin/Robert von Hagge. **Season:** Year-round. **High:** Jan.-April. **To obtain tee times:** Call up to 5 days in advance. **Miscellaneous:** Reduced fees (twilight, juniors), metal spikes, range (grass), credit cards (MC, V, D), BF, FF.

★★★½ MARCUS POINTE GOLF CLUB
PU-2500 Oak Pointe Dr., Pensacola, 32505, Escambia County, (850)484-9770, (800)362-7287. **Facility Holes:** 18. **Yards:** 6,737/5,185. **Par:** 72/72. **Course Rating:** 72.3/69.5. **Slope:** 129/119. **Green Fee:** $27/$36. **Cart Fee:** $13/Person. **Walking Policy:** Walking at certain times. **Walkability:** 3. **Opened:** 1990. **Architect:** Earl Stone. **Season:** Year-round. **High:** Feb.-May. **To obtain tee times:** Call golf shop. **Miscellaneous:** Reduced fees (weekdays, twilight, juniors), metal spikes, range (grass), credit cards (MC, V).
Reader Comments: In great shape and quite remarkable terrain for a Florida golf course. I liked it … User-friendly design … Friendly staff … First-class operation … Only played twice in winter, great job … Good public course.

MARRIOTT'S BAY POINT RESORT
R-P.O. Box 27880, Panama City Beach, 32411, Bay County, (850)235-6950, 90 miles from Pensacola. **E-mail:** baypoint@panamacity.com. **Web:** www.baypointgolf.com. **Facility Holes:** 36. **Cart Fee:** Included in green fee. **Walking Policy:** Mandatory carts. **Season:** Year-round. **To obtain tee times:** Call up to 60 days in advance. **Miscellaneous:** Reduced fees (guests, twilight, juniors), range (grass), lodging (500 rooms), credit cards (MC, V, AE, D), BF, FF.
★★★ CLUB MEADOWS COURSE (18)
Yards: 6,913/4,999. **Par:** 72/72. **Course Rating:** 73.3/68.0. **Slope:** 126/118. **Green Fee:** $50/$75. **Walkability:** 1. **Opened:** 1973. **Architect:** Willard Byrd.
Reader Comments: People are great, reasonable fees, nice conditions … My favorite overall course … Good for husband-wife golf.
★★★★ LAGOON LEGEND (18)
Yards: 6,921/4,942. **Par:** 72/72. **Course Rating:** 75.3/69.8. **Slope:** 152/127. **Green Fee:** $60/$90. **Walkability:** 2. **Opened:** 1986. **Architect:** Bruce Devlin/Robert von Hagge. **High:** Feb.-May.
Reader Comments: Not nearly as difficult as they say … Hard for average golfer. Water everywhere. In 3 rounds, my foursome lost 72 balls in the water … I give it high marks, but it's only for scratch golfers … Target golf in the extreme.

★★★★ MARSH LANDING COUNTRY CLUB
R-25655 Marsh Landing Pkwy., Ponte Vedra Beach, 32082, St. Johns County, (904)285-6459, (800)457-4653, 15 miles from Jacksonville. **Facility Holes:** 18. **Yards:** 6,821/5,097. **Par:** 72/72. **Slope:** 135/124. **Green Fee:** $100/$175. **Cart Fee:** $26/Person. **Walking Policy:** Walking at certain times. **Opened:** 1986. **Architect:** Ed Seay. **Season:** Year-round. **To obtain tee times:** Call golf shop. **Miscellaneous:** Range (grass), credit cards (MC, V), BF, FF.
Reader Comments: Greens slick & tricky, 2 9s very different … Best condition of any course I ever played … Good holes, a lot of marsh & water … Worth the money … Gets better each time I play … Great layout, very friendly staff.
Special Notes: Limited access available to guests staying at Marriott at Sawgrass.

MARTIN COUNTY GOLF & COUNTRY CLUB
PU-2000 S.E. Saint Lucie Blvd., Stuart, 34996, Martin County, (561)287-3747, 40 miles from West Palm Beach. **Facility Holes:** 36. **Green Fee:** $10/$22. **Walking Policy:** Walking at certain times. **Opened:** 1925. **Architect:** Ron Garl. **Season:** Year-round. **High:** Dec.-April. **To obtain tee times:** Call golf shop. **Miscellaneous:** Reduced fees (juniors), metal spikes, range (grass).
★★★ BLUE/GOLD COURSE (18)
Yards: 5,900/5,236. **Par:** 72/72. **Course Rating:** 67.5/69.1. **Slope:** 120/120.
Reader Comments: Great shape for amount of play … Blue & gold are different courses, one open and one narrow … Flat, fairly easy, economical.
★★ RED/WHITE COURSE (18)
Yards: 6,200/5,400. **Par:** 72/73. **Course Rating:** 69.1/70.4. **Slope:** 116/120.

★★ MAYFAIR COUNTRY CLUB
PU-3536 Country Club Rd., Sanford, 32771, Seminole County, (407)322-2531, (800)279-5098, 15 miles from Orlando. **Facility Holes:** 18. **Yards:** 6,403/5,051. **Par:** 72/74. **Course Rating:** 69.7/69.3. **Slope:** 119/115. **Green Fee:** $25/$40. **Cart Fee:** Included in green fee. **Walking Policy:** Mandatory carts. **Walkability:** 2. **Opened:** 1920. **Architect:** Donald Ross. **Season:** Year-round. **High:** Dec.-April. **To obtain tee times:** Call up to 7 days in advance. **Miscellaneous:** Reduced fees (weekdays), metal spikes, range (grass), credit cards (MC, V, AE, D), BF, FF.

★½ MEADOWBROOK GOLF CLUB
SP-3200 N.W. 98th St., Gainesville, 32606, Alachua County, (352)332-0577, 60 miles from Jacksonville. **E-mail:** w_smith@pga.com. **Web:** www.gainesvillesbestgolf.com. **Facility Holes:** 18. **Yards:** 6,289/4,720. **Par:** 72/72. **Course Rating:** 69.9/66.7. **Slope:** 119/117. **Green Fee:** $7/$24. **Walking Policy:** Walking at certain times. **Walkability:** 3. **Opened:** 1987. **Architect:** Steve Smyers. **Season:** Year-round. **To obtain tee times:** Call up to 5 days in advance.

Miscellaneous: Reduced fees (weekdays, twilight, juniors), range (grass), credit cards (MC, V, D), BF, FF.

★★★★ **METROWEST COUNTRY CLUB** *Pace*
SP-2100 S. Hiawassee Rd., Orlando, 32835, Orange County, (407)299-1099, 5 miles from Orlando. **E-mail:** dscott@metrowestorlando.com. **Web:** www.metrowestorlando.com. **Facility Holes:** 18. **Yards:** 7,051/5,325. **Par:** 72/72. **Course Rating:** 74.1/70.3. **Slope:** 132/122. **Green Fee:** $49/$115. **Cart Fee:** Included in green fee. **Walking Policy:** Mandatory carts. **Walkability:** 4. **Opened:** 1987. **Architect:** Robert Trent Jones. **Season:** Year-round. **High:** Dec.-April. **To obtain tee times:** Call golf shop. **Miscellaneous:** Reduced fees (twilight, juniors), metal spikes, range (grass), credit cards (MC, V, AE), BF, FF.
Reader Comments: Challenging but beautiful … Easy par 5s, harder par 4 … They treat you well … Beautiful, open, expensive … Excellent condition and a beautiful layout … Gently rolling, excellent layout, fast greens.

★★★ **MIAMI NATIONAL GOLF CLUB**
SP-6401 Kendale Lakes Dr., Miami, 33183, Dade County, (305)382-3930. **E-mail:** cwggp@aol.com. **Facility Holes:** 27. **Green Fee:** $25/$45. **Cart Fee:** Included in green fee. **Walking Policy:** Mandatory carts. **Walkability:** 3. **Opened:** 1970. **Architect:** Mark Mahannah. **Season:** Year-round. **To obtain tee times:** Call up to 7 days in advance. **Miscellaneous:** Reduced fees (weekdays, twilight, juniors), range (grass/mats), credit cards (MC, V, AE), BF, FF.
BARRACUDA/MARLIN COURSE (18 Combo)
Yards: 6,719/5,445. **Par:** 72/74. **Course Rating:** 73.6/70.1. **Slope:** 132/118.
DOLPHIN/BARRACUDA COURSE (18 Combo)
Yards: 6,679/5,281. **Par:** 72/73. **Course Rating:** 73.1/69.3. **Slope:** 130/119.
Reader Comments: Journeyman course, good practice … Inexpensive, several interesting holes … Greens poor, pace slow … Short but a challenge.

★★★ **MIAMI SHORES COUNTRY CLUB**
SP-10000 Biscayne Blvd., Miami Shores, 33138, Dade County, (305)795-2366, 15 miles from Miami. **Web:** www.pcmgolf.com. **Facility Holes:** 18. **Yards:** 6,400/5,400. **Par:** 71/72. **Course Rating:** 70.0/72.8. **Slope:** 122/122. **Green Fee:** $35/$75. **Cart Fee:** Included in green fee. **Walking Policy:** Mandatory carts. **Walkability:** 3. **Opened:** 1938. **Architect:** Red Lawrence. **Season:** Year-round. **High:** Jan.-April. **To obtain tee times:** Call up to 3 days in advance. **Miscellaneous:** Reduced fees (weekdays, twilight), range (grass/mats), credit cards (MC, V, AE, DC), BF, FF.
Reader Comments: Some good holes. Slow on weekends … Old course, user friendly … Good layout! Course needs a little work.

★★ **MILL COVE GOLF CLUB**
PU-1700 Monument Rd., Jacksonville, 32225, Duval County, (904)646-4653. **E-mail:** xtc-new@aol.com. **Web:** www.millcovegolf.com. **Facility Holes:** 18. **Yards:** 6,671/4,719. **Par:** 71/71. **Course Rating:** 71.7/66.3. **Slope:** 129/112. **Green Fee:** $14/$27. **Cart Fee:** $16/Person. **Walking Policy:** Walking at certain times. **Walkability:** 1. **Opened:** 1990. **Architect:** Arnold Palmer/Ed Seay. **Season:** Year-round. **To obtain tee times:** Call up to 7 days in advance. **Miscellaneous:** Reduced fees (weekdays, twilight, seniors, juniors), range (grass/mats), credit cards (MC, V, AE), BF, FF.

MISSION INN GOLF & TENNIS RESORT
R-10400 County Rd. 48, Howey in the Hills, 34737, Lake County, (352)324-3885, (800)874-9053, 30 miles from Orlando. **E-mail:** golf@missioninnresort.com. **Web:** www.missioninnresort.com. **Facility Holes:** 36. **Cart Fee:** Included in green fee. **Walking Policy:** Mandatory carts. **Season:** Year-round. **High:** Nov.-April. **To obtain tee times:** Call up to 7 days in advance. **Miscellaneous:** Range (grass), lodging (187 rooms), BF, FF.
★★★★ **EL CAMPEON COURSE** (18)
Yards: 6,923/4,811. **Par:** 72/73. **Course Rating:** 73.6/67.3. **Slope:** 133/118. **Green Fee:** $60/$125. **Walkability:** 3. **Opened:** 1926. **Architect:** Charles Clark. **Miscellaneous:** Credit cards (MC, V, AE, D).
Reader Comments: A real bargain … Slow play but it's a resort … Tough uphill holes … Old park course, excellent facilities, great people … Hills in Florida, gators … Outstanding layout … A classic, lots of elevation changes.
★★★½ **LAS COLINAS COURSE** (18)
Yards: 6,879/4,651. **Par:** 72/72. **Course Rating:** 73.2/64.3. **Slope:** 128/103. **Green Fee:** $50/$105. **Walkability:** 2. **Opened:** 1992. **Architect:** Gary Koch. **Miscellaneous:** Credit cards (MC, V, AE).
Reader Comments: Absolutely beautiful, loved it … Nice layout … Played in off-season, excellent condition … Newer layout is also a good one … A shotmaker's course, challenging.

FLORIDA

MONARCH GOLF COURSE
SP-5325 St. Andrews Arc, Leesburg, 34748, Lake County, (352)314-9000, 35 miles from Orlando. **E-mail:** monarchrh@aol.com. **Web:** www.monarchgolf.com. **Facility Holes:** 18. **Yards:** 6,084/5,149. **Par:** 72/72. **Course Rating:** 68.8/68.2. **Slope:** 113/106. **Green Fee:** $22/$38. **Cart Fee:** Included in green fee. **Walking Policy:** Walking at certain times. **Walkability:** 4. **Opened:** 1997. **Architect:** Len DeBoer. **Season:** Year-round. **High:** Nov.-May. **To obtain tee times:** Call up to 4 days in advance. **Miscellaneous:** Reduced fees (weekdays, twilight, seniors), range (grass), credit cards (MC, V, AE, D), BF, FF.

★★★★½ THE MOORS GOLF CLUB
PU-3220 Avalon Blvd., Milton, 32583, Santa Rosa County, (850)995-4653, (800)727-1010, 6 miles from Pensacola. **E-mail:** themoors@pensacola.com. **Web:** www.moors.com. **Facility Holes:** 18. **Yards:** 6,828/5,259. **Par:** 70/70. **Course Rating:** 72.9/70.3. **Slope:** 126/117. **Green Fee:** $33/$47. **Cart Fee:** $12/Person. **Walking Policy:** Walking at certain times. **Walkability:** 2. **Opened:** 1993. **Architect:** John B. LaFoy. **Season:** Year-round. **High:** Feb.-May. **To obtain tee times:** Call up to 7 days in advance. **Miscellaneous:** Reduced fees (weekdays, guests), range (grass/mats), lodging (8 rooms), credit cards (MC, V, AE, D), BF, FF.
Reader Comments: Great fun. Felt like we were in England.... Best play & stay deal I've ever seen ... Beautifully manicured! Heaven on earth ... Great links-style course, reasonable rates.

★★★ MOUNT DORA GOLF CLUB
SP-1100 S. Highland, Mount Dora, 32757, Lake County, (352)383-3954, 20 miles from Orlando. **E-mail:** r55001@cs.com. **Facility Holes:** 18. **Yards:** 5,719/5,238. **Par:** 70/72. **Course Rating:** 67.3/70.6. **Slope:** 118/118. **Green Fee:** $18/$33. **Cart Fee:** Included in green fee. **Walking Policy:** Unrestricted walking. **Walkability:** 3. **Opened:** 1945. **Season:** Year-round. **High:** Jan.-April. **To obtain tee times:** Call up to 7 days in advance. **Miscellaneous:** Reduced fees (twilight), metal spikes, credit cards (MC, V, D), BF, FF.
Reader Comments: Classic, walking course, let's keep it a secret ... Hilly & fair to all golfers. Staff very good ... Excellent layout. Pleasure to play ... Short, tight, walking course, small greens ... Can always walk.

★★½ MYAKKA PINES GOLF CLUB
SP-2550 S. River Rd., Englewood, 34223, Sarasota County, (941)474-1745, 11 miles from Venice. **Facility Holes:** 27. **Green Fee:** $15/$30. **Cart Fee:** $28/Cart. **Walking Policy:** Walking at certain times. **Walkability:** 1. **Opened:** 1977. **Architect:** Lane Marshall. **Season:** Year-round. **High:** Jan.-April. **To obtain tee times:** Call up to 2 days in advance. **Miscellaneous:** Reduced fees (twilight), range (grass), credit cards (MC, V), BF, FF.
BLUE/RED (18 Combo)
Yards: 6,500/5,208. **Par:** 72/72. **Course Rating:** 71.1/69.7. **Slope:** 118/118.
RED/WHITE (18 Combo)
Yards: 6,137/5,085. **Par:** 72/72. **Course Rating:** 69.2/68.8. **Slope:** 114/116.
WHITE/BLUE (18 Combo)
Yards: 6,046/5,121. **Par:** 72/72. **Course Rating:** 69.0/68.9. **Slope:** 115/115.

★★★½ THE NAPLES BEACH HOTEL & GOLF CLUB
R-851 Gulf Shore Blvd. N., Naples, 34102, Collier County, (941)435-2475, (800)237-7600, 25 miles from Fort Myers. **E-mail:** j_gantzer@naplesbeachhotel.com. **Web:** www.naplesbeach-hotel.com. **Facility Holes:** 18. **Yards:** 6,488/5,142. **Par:** 72/72. **Course Rating:** 71.7/70.0. **Slope:** 134/121. **Green Fee:** $40/$120. **Cart Fee:** Included in green fee. **Walking Policy:** Mandatory carts. **Walkability:** 1. **Opened:** 1930. **Architect:** Ron Garl. **Season:** Year-round. **To obtain tee times:** Call golf shop. **Miscellaneous:** Reduced fees (guests, twilight, juniors), range (grass/mats), lodging (315 rooms), credit cards (MC, V, AE, D), BF, FF.
Reader Comments: Beautiful trees & flowers, good condition ... A little overpriced, but great golf ... Flat and short with ordinary holes, not much of a challenge, expensive ... Staff very accommodating ... Nice course, great service.

★★★★½ NAPLES GRANDE GOLF CLUB *Service+, Pace*
R-7760 Golden Gate Pkwy., Naples, 34105, Collier County, (941)659-3710. **E-mail:** mbrooks@naplesgrande.com. **Web:** www.naplesgrande.com. **Facility Holes:** 18. **Yards:** 7,078/5,209. **Par:** 72/72. **Course Rating:** 75.1/70.5. **Slope:** 143/119. **Green Fee:** $70/$170. **Cart Fee:** Included in green fee. **Walking Policy:** Unrestricted walking. **Walkability:** 3. **Opened:** 2000. **Architect:** Rees Jones. **Season:** Year-round. **High:** Jan.-April. **To obtain tee times:** Call golf shop. **Miscellaneous:** Reduced fees (twilight), range (grass), credit cards (MC, V, AE, D), BF, FF.
Reader Comments: Beautiful, graceful & great fun to play ... Beautiful, expensive ... User friendly ... Good course ... May be the best course in southwest Florida ... Terrific practice facility.

★★★ NAPLES LAKES COUNTRY CLUB
PU-4788 Inverness Club Dr., Naples, 34112, Collier County, (941)732-1011, 75 miles from Miami. **Web:** www.napleslakes.com. **Facility Holes:** 18. **Yards:** 6,804/5,073. **Par:** 72/72. **Course Rating:** 74.3/70.3. **Slope:** 142/121. **Green Fee:** $39/$98. **Cart Fee:** Included in green fee. **Walking Policy:** Mandatory carts. **Walkability:** 3. **Opened:** 2000. **Architect:** Arnold Palmer/Ed Seay/Greg Stang. **Season:** Year-round. **High:** Jan.-March. **To obtain tee times:** Call up to 3 days in advance. **Miscellaneous:** Range (grass), credit cards (MC, V, AE), BF, FF.
Reader Comments: Good layout ... A top-notch course ... Flat, long distance between holes ... Needs some time, but very promising ... New course, will only get better ... Excellent course ... Tricked up, not my favorite.

★½ NORMANDY SHORES GOLF COURSE
PU-2401 Biarritz Dr., Miami Beach, 33141, Dade County, (305)868-6502. **Facility Holes:** 18. **Yards:** 6,402/5,527. **Par:** 71/73. **Course Rating:** 70.5/71.0. **Slope:** 120/119. **Green Fee:** $30/$45. **Cart Fee:** Included in green fee. **Walking Policy:** Walking at certain times. **Walkability:** 2. **Opened:** 1938. **Architect:** William S. Flynn/Howard Toomey. **Season:** Year-round. **To obtain tee times:** Call golf shop. **Miscellaneous:** Reduced fees (weekdays, twilight, juniors), range (grass/mats), credit cards (MC, V, AE), BF, FF.

★★ NORTH PALM BEACH COUNTRY CLUB
PU-951 U.S. Hwy. 1, North Palm Beach, 33408, Palm Beach County, (561)691-3433, 5 miles from West Palm Beach. **Facility Holes:** 18. **Yards:** 6,281/5,033. **Par:** 72/72. **Course Rating:** 69.9/68.9. **Slope:** 120/114. **Green Fee:** $26/$62. **Cart Fee:** Included in green fee. **Walking Policy:** Walking at certain times. **Walkability:** 2. **Opened:** 1963. **Architect:** Mark McCumber. **Season:** Year-round. **High:** Nov.-May. **To obtain tee times:** Call up to 1 day in advance. **Miscellaneous:** Reduced fees (guests, juniors), range (grass/mats), credit cards (MC, V), BF, FF.

★★ NORTHDALE GOLF & TENNIS CLUB
SP-4417 Northdale Blvd., Tampa, 33624, Hillsborough County, (813)962-0428. **E-mail:** rstunley@crown-golf.com. **Web:** www.northdalegc.com. **Facility Holes:** 18. **Yards:** 6,824/5,404. **Par:** 72/72. **Course Rating:** 72.8/71.0. **Slope:** 129/120. **Green Fee:** $25/$55. **Cart Fee:** Included in green fee. **Walking Policy:** Walking at certain times. **Walkability:** 2. **Opened:** 1978. **Architect:** Ron Garl. **Season:** Year-round. **To obtain tee times:** Call up to 5 days in advance. **Miscellaneous:** Reduced fees (weekdays, twilight, juniors), credit cards (MC, V, AE, D), FF.

★★½ OAK BRIDGE CLUB AT SAWGRASS
SP-254 Alta Mar Dr., Ponte Vedra Beach, 32082, St. Johns County, (904)285-0204, 12 miles from Jacksonville. **Facility Holes:** 18. **Yards:** 6,368/4,869. **Par:** 70/70. **Course Rating:** 70.5/67.6. **Slope:** 129/119. **Green Fee:** $100/$125. **Cart Fee:** Included in green fee. **Walking Policy:** Walking at certain times. **Walkability:** 1. **Opened:** 1972. **Architect:** Arnold Palmer. **Season:** Year-round. **High:** Feb.-May. **To obtain tee times:** Call golf shop. **Miscellaneous:** Range (grass), credit cards (MC, V).

★★★½ OAK FORD GOLF CLUB
SP-1552 Palm View Rd., Sarasota, 34240, Sarasota County, (941)371-3680, (888)881-3673, 60 miles from Tampa. **Web:** www.oakfordgolfclub.com. **Facility Holes:** 27. **Green Fee:** $15/$60. **Cart Fee:** Included in green fee. **Walking Policy:** Mandatory carts. **Walkability:** 2. **Opened:** 1989. **Architect:** Ron Garl. **Season:** Year-round. **High:** Jan.-April. **To obtain tee times:** Call up to 7 days in advance. **Miscellaneous:** Reduced fees (twilight), range (grass), credit cards (MC, V), FF.
MYRTLE/LIVE OAK (18 Combo)
Yards: 6,750/5,085. **Par:** 72/72. **Course Rating:** 72.7/69.0. **Slope:** 131/118.
MYRTLE/PALMS (18 Combo)
Yards: 6,750/5,085. **Par:** 72/72. **Course Rating:** 72.7/69.0. **Slope:** 131/118.
PALMS/LIVE OAK (18 Combo)
Yards: 6,750/5,085. **Par:** 72/72. **Course Rating:** 72.7/69.0. **Slope:** 131/118.
Reader Comments: Wow. Nice blending of golf course and swamplands ... Good value, interesting course ... Has been better ... Great service, out of way, challenging ... Feels primeval in live oaks... Play through woods & jungle, tight fairways.

★★ OAK HILLS GOLF CLUB
PU-10059 Northcliff Blvd., Spring Hill, 34608, Hernando County, (352)683-6830, 37 miles from Tampa. **Facility Holes:** 18. **Yards:** 6,774/5,468. **Par:** 72/72. **Course Rating:** 72.2/71.1. **Slope:** 123/119. **Green Fee:** $18/$27. **Cart Fee:** Included in green fee. **Walking Policy:** Walking at certain times. **Walkability:** 3. **Opened:** 1982. **Architect:** Chuck Almony. **Season:** Year-round. **High:** Dec.-March. **To obtain tee times:** Call golf shop. **Miscellaneous:** Reduced fees (weekdays, twilight, seniors, juniors), metal spikes, range (grass), credit cards (MC, V, D).

FLORIDA

★★★½ **OKEEHEELEE GOLF COURSE**
PU-1200 Country Club Way, West Palm Beach, 33413, Palm Beach County, (561)964-4653,
1 mile from West Palm Beach. **Facility Holes:** 27. **Green Fee:** $22/$49. **Cart Fee:** Included in
green fee. **Walking Policy:** Walking at certain times. **Walkability:** 1. **Opened:** 1995. **Architect:**
Roy Case. **Season:** Year-round. **High:** Dec.-April. **To obtain tee times:** Call golf shop.
Miscellaneous: Range (grass), credit cards (MC, V, AE), BF, FF.
EAGLE/OSPREY (BLUE/WHITE) (18 Combo)
Yards: 6,648/4,591. **Par:** 72/72. **Course Rating:** 71.7/62.7. **Slope:** 130/103.
HERON/EAGLE (RED/BLUE) (18 Combo)
Yards: 6,916/4,842. **Par:** 72/72. **Course Rating:** 72.9/63.4. **Slope:** 128/103.
OSPREY/HERON (WHITE/RED) (18 Combo)
Yards: 6,826/4,731. **Par:** 72/72. **Course Rating:** 72.6/62.9. **Slope:** 130/102.
Reader Comments: Challenging, inexpensive course … Great staff, they treat you like they want
you there … Good layout … Service is outstanding from start to finish, excellent value, nice variety
… Best value for the buck.

ORANGE COUNTY NATIONAL GOLF CENTER & LODGE
PU-16301 Phil Ritson Way, Winter Garden, 34787, Orange County, (407)656-2626,
(888)727-3672, 5 miles from Orlando. **E-mail:** Info@ocngolf.com. **Web:** www.ocngolf.com.
Facility Holes: 36. **Cart Fee:** Included in green fee. **Walking Policy:** Mandatory carts.
Walkability: 5. **Architect:** Phil Ritson/David Harman/Isao Aoki. **Season:** Year-round. **To obtain
tee times:** Call golf shop. **Miscellaneous:** Reduced fees (weekdays, guests, twilight, juniors),
range (grass), lodging (50 rooms), credit cards (MC, V, AE, DC), BF, FF.
★★★★½ **CROOKED CAT COURSE** (18)
Yards: 7,277/5,262. **Par:** 72/72. **Course Rating:** 75.4/70.3. **Slope:** 140/120. **Green Fee:**
$19/$65. **Opened:** 1999.
Reader Comments: Great practice area, very expenseive … Large fairways, visually beautiful …
You will not be disappointed … Back 9 turns tough … Best course in Orlando … Great course & set
up … Best course I have ever played.
★★★★½ **PANTHER LAKE COURSE** (18) *Condition, Pace*
Yards: 7,295/5,073. **Par:** 72/72. **Course Rating:** 75.7/71.5. **Slope:** 137/125. **Green Fee:**
$19/$75. **Opened:** 1997.
Reader Comments: Excellent course. Great design and very well maintained, challenging … Great
variety of holes … New, remote, beautiful, pricey … Definitely go back again … Open but definitely
not easy … Good escape from the glitz of Disney World … World-class public facility … Golf
Nirvana.

ORANGE LAKE COUNTRY CLUB
R-8505 W. Irlo Bronson Mem. Hwy., Kissimmee, 34747, Osceola County, (407)239-1050,
15 miles from Orlando. **Facility Holes:** 54. **Cart Fee:** Included in green fee. **Season:** Year-
round. **High:** Jan.-April. **To obtain tee times:** Call golf shop. **Miscellaneous:** Reduced fees
(weekdays, guests, twilight, juniors), range (grass/mats), credit cards (MC, V, AE).
★★★★ **THE LEGENDS AT ORANGE LAKE** (18)
Yards: 7,072/5,188. **Par:** 72/72. **Course Rating:** 74.3/69.6. **Slope:** 132/120. **Green Fee:**
$40/$125. **Opened:** 1982. **Architect:** Arnold Palmer.
Reader Comments: Open fairways … Course was fun to play … Great course architecture, club-
house, driving range … Typical Arnold Palmer course … Great place to stay and play … Good time
… Best-kept secret in central Florida.
★★★½ **THE RESORT COURSE AT ORANGE LAKE**
Green Fee: $30/$85. **Opened:** 1998. **Architect:** Joe Lee.
(CYPRESS/LAKE) (18 combo)
Yards: 6,571/5,456. **Par:** 72/72. **Course Rating:** 72.3/72.1. **Slope:** 131/128.
(LAKE/ORANGE) (18 combo)
Yards: 6,531/5,289. **Par:** 72/72. **Course Rating:** 72.2/71.1. **Slope:** 132/126.
(ORANGE/CYPRESS) (18 combo)
Yards: 6,670/5,467. **Par:** 72/72. **Course Rating:** 72.6/70.5. **Slope:** 131/128.
Reader Comments: Too great to be true … Plenty of variety … Forced carries over water … Too
short … Well-placed bunkers … Saw an eagle with fish in talons.
Special Notes: Also has a 9-hole course.

★★ **ORIOLE GOLF & TENNIS CLUB OF MARGATE**
PU-8000 W. Margate Blvd., Margate, 33063, Broward County, (954)972-8140, 5 miles from
Fort Lauderdale. **Facility Holes:** 18. **Yards:** 6,418/4,875. **Par:** 72/72. **Course Rating:** 70.9/67.7.
Slope: 120/112. **Green Fee:** $6/$30. **Cart Fee:** $15/Person. **Walkability:** 2. **Opened:** 1972.
Architect: Bill Dietsch Jr. **Season:** Year-round. **High:** Jan.-April. **To obtain tee times:** Call golf
shop. **Miscellaneous:** Reduced fees (twilight), metal spikes, range (grass/mats), credit cards
(MC, V).

FLORIDA

★★★½ **ORLANDO WORLD CENTER - MARRIOTT**
R-8701 World Center Dr., Orlando, 32821, Orange County, (407)238-8660, (800)567-2623, 10 miles from Orlando. **E-mail:** tony.austin@marriott.com. **Web:** www.golfhawkslanding.com. **Facility Holes:** 18. **Yards:** 6,810/4,890. **Par:** 72/72. **Course Rating:** 73.2/68.4. **Slope:** 134/117. **Green Fee:** $65/$165. **Cart Fee:** Included in green fee. **Walking Policy:** Unrestricted walking. **Walkability:** 2. **Opened:** 1999. **Architect:** Bob Cup. **Season:** Year-round. **High:** Jan.-April. **To obtain tee times:** Call up to 30 days in advance. **Miscellaneous:** Reduced fees (guests, twilight, juniors), range (grass), lodging (2000 rooms), credit cards (MC, V, AE, D, DC), BF, FF.
Reader Comments: Nice course, great facilities … Outstanding, in perfect shape and very challenging … Apparently the course had just been redone, and it was a quality experience in all aspects … Immaculate … Too close, need more land.

OYSTER CREEK GOLF & COUNTRY CLUB
SP-6651 Orivle Blvd., Englewood, 34224, Charlotte County, (941)475-0334, 10 miles from Venice. **Facility Holes:** 18. **Yards:** 4,000/2,600. **Par:** 60/60. **Course Rating:** 59.7/57.3. **Slope:** 100/85. **Green Fee:** $16/$30. **Cart Fee:** Included in green fee. **Walkability:** 1. **Opened:** 1993. **Architect:** Ted McAnlis. **Season:** Year-round. **High:** Nov.-April. **To obtain tee times:** Call golf shop. **Miscellaneous:** Reduced fees (twilight), metal spikes, credit cards (MC, V), BF, FF.

★★★★ **PALISADES GOLF COURSE** *Value*
SP-16510 Palisades Blvd., Clermont, 34711, Lake County, (352)394-0085, 20 miles from Orlando. **E-mail:** tgolf18@hotmail.com. **Web:** www.golfpalisades.com. **Facility Holes:** 18. **Yards:** 7,004/5,528. **Par:** 72/72. **Course Rating:** 73.8/72.1. **Slope:** 127/122. **Green Fee:** $30/$55. **Cart Fee:** Included in green fee. **Walking Policy:** Walking at certain times. **Walkability:** 5. **Opened:** 1991. **Architect:** Joe Lee. **Season:** Year-round. **High:** Jan.-March. **To obtain tee times:** Call golf shop. **Miscellaneous:** Reduced fees (weekdays, twilight, seniors), range (grass), credit cards (MC, V, AE, D), BF, FF.
Reader Comments: Rolling hills, beautifully manicured, a pleasure to play … Remote, hilly good course … A very nice layout … Excellent hilly design, could play everyday … Lack of water has hurt, but still a great layout.

★★½ **PALM BEACH GARDENS GOLF COURSE**
PU-11401 Northlake Blvd., Palm Beach Gardens, 33418, Palm Beach County, (561)626-7888, 8 miles from West Palm Beach. **E-mail:** sgrfla@aol.com. **Web:** www.gardens-golf.com. **Facility Holes:** 18. **Yards:** 6,375/4,663. **Par:** 72/72. **Course Rating:** 70.2/66.5. **Slope:** 128/110. **Green Fee:** $44. **Cart Fee:** Included in green fee. **Walking Policy:** Walking at certain times. **Walkability:** 3. **Opened:** 1991. **Architect:** Roy Case. **Season:** Year-round. **High:** Dec.-April. **To obtain tee times:** Call up to 7 days in advance. **Misc:** Reduced fees (weekdays, twilight, juniors), metal spikes, range (grass), credit cards (MC, V), BF, FF.

PALM COAST GOLF RESORT
R-53 Easthampton Blvd., Palm Coast, 32164, Flagler County, (386)437-5807, (800)654-6538, 25 miles from Daytona Beach. **E-mail:** kkoshko@destinationhotels.com. **Web:** www.palm-coastgolfresort.com. **Facility Holes:** 90. **Cart Fee:** Included in green fee. **Walkability:** 2. **Season:** Year-round. **High:** Jan.-April. **To obtain tee times:** Call up to 6 days in advance. **Misc:** Reduced fees (guests, juniors), range (grass), credit cards (MC, V, AE, D), BF, FF.
★★★ CYPRESS KNOLL GOLF CLUB (18)
Yards: 6,591/5,386. **Par:** 72/72. **Course Rating:** 71.6/70.5. **Slope:** 130/121. **Green Fee:** $55/$80. **Walking Policy:** Mandatory carts. **Opened:** 1991. **Architect:** Gary Player.
Reader Comments: Extremely tight, water everywhere, watch for gators … Very tight … Staff very helpful … Tough but fair.
★★★★ MATANZAS WOODS GOLF CLUB (18)
Yards: 6,929/5,236. **Par:** 72/72. **Course Rating:** 74.9/71.0. **Slope:** 141/121. **Green Fee:** $55/$80. **Walking Policy:** Mandatory carts. **Opened:** 1986. **Architect:** Arnold Palmer/Ed Seay.
Reader Comments: Very good condition … Tougher than it looks … Tough course … Excellent course … Sand traps need work.
OCEAN HAMMOCK GOLF CLUB (18)
Yards: 7,201/5,115. **Par:** 72/72. **Course Rating:** 77.0/71.5. **Slope:** 147/131. **Green Fee:** $95/$175. **Walking Policy:** Unrestricted walking. **Opened:** 2000. **Architect:** Jack Nicklaus. **Notes:** Ranked 10th in 2001 Best New Upscale Courses.
★★½ PALM HARBOR GOLF CLUB (18)
Yards: 6,572/5,346. **Par:** 72/72. **Course Rating:** 71.8/71.2. **Slope:** 127/128. **Green Fee:** $55/$80. **Walking Policy:** Mandatory carts. **Opened:** 1971. **Architect:** Bill Amick.
★★★★ PINE LAKES COUNTRY CLUB (18)
Yards: 7,074/5,166. **Par:** 72/72. **Course Rating:** 73.5/71.4. **Slope:** 126/124. **Green Fee:** $55/$80. **Walking Policy:** Mandatory carts. **Opened:** 1981. **Architect:** Arnold Palmer/Ed Seay.
Reader Comments: Felt like top private C.C. … Excellent value … Sand, water, undulating greens. Wide open.

FLORIDA

PALM-AIRE COUNTRY CLUB
SP-3701 Oaks Clubhouse Dr., Pompano Beach, 33069, Broward County, (954)978-1737, 12 miles from Fort Lauderdale. **E-mail:** info@palmairegolf.com. **Web:** www.palmairecountryclub.com. **Facility Holes:** 94. **Cart Fee:** Included in green fee. **Season:** Year-round. **To obtain tee times:** Call up to 4 days in advance. **Miscellaneous:** Reduced fees (twilight), range (grass), lodging (300 rooms), credit cards (MC, V, AE), BF, FF.
★★★ **CYPRESS COURSE** (18)
Yards: 6,826/5,307. **Par:** 72/72. **Course Rating:** 74.1/71.8. **Slope:** 143/127. **Green Fee:** $49/$85. **Walking Policy:** Mandatory carts. **Walkability:** 2. **Opened:** 1972. **Architect:** George Fazio/Tom Fazio.
Reader Comments: Needs work ... Great tracks ... Enjoyable, easy access ... Very good course ... Great course, a little pricey.
★★★½ **OAKS COURSE** (18)
Yards: 6,910/4,860. **Par:** 71/71. **Course Rating:** 73.3/62.9. **Slope:** 131/103. **Green Fee:** $59/$99. **Walking Policy:** Mandatory carts. **Walkability:** 2. **Opened:** 1959. **Architect:** George Fazio/Tom Fazio.
Reader Comments: Crowded, crowded, crowded ... Excellent Florida golf ... Short, thick rough, harder than it looks ... Great value ... Nice course & layout, condition varies.
Special Notes: Also has a 4-hole practice loop.
★★★ **PALMS COURSE** (18)
Yards: 6,931/5,431. **Par:** 72/72. **Course Rating:** 73.3/71.1. **Slope:** 128/118. **Green Fee:** $49/$85. **Walking Policy:** Mandatory carts. **Walkability:** 1. **Opened:** 1959. **Architect:** William F. Mitchell.
Reader Comments: Very nice.
★★ **PINES COURSE** (18)
Yards: 6,610/5,232. **Par:** 72/72. **Course Rating:** 72.5/70.0. **Slope:** 133/116. **Green Fee:** $39/$65. **Walking Policy:** Mandatory carts. **Walkability:** 1. **Opened:** 1959. **Architect:** Robert von Hagge.
SABALS COURSE (18)
Yards: 3,401/3,069. **Par:** 60/60. **Green Fee:** $25/$34. **Walking Policy:** Unrestricted walking. **Walkability:** 1. **Opened:** 1969. **Architect:** William F. Mitchell.

★★ PALMETTO GOLF COURSE
PU-9300 S.W. 152nd St., Miami, 33157, Dade County, (305)238-2922. **Facility Holes:** 18. **Yards:** 6,648/5,710. **Par:** 70/73. **Course Rating:** 72.2/73.4. **Slope:** 128/125. **Green Fee:** $12/$25. **Walking Policy:** Unrestricted walking. **Walkability:** 1. **Opened:** 1959. **Architect:** Dick Wilson. **Season:** Year-round. **To obtain tee times:** Call up to 7 days in advance. **Miscellaneous:** Reduced fees (weekdays, twilight, juniors), range (mats), credit cards (MC, V, AE), BF, FF.

★★★ PELICAN BAY COUNTRY CLUB
SP-350 Pelican Bay Dr., Daytona Beach, 32119, Volusia County, (904)788-6496, 5 miles from Daytona Beach. **E-mail:** echick@mggi.com. **Facility Holes:** 18. **Yards:** 6,630/5,278. **Par:** 72/72. **Course Rating:** 71.9/70.8. **Slope:** 123/127. **Green Fee:** $25/$45. **Cart Fee:** Included in green fee. **Walking Policy:** Mandatory carts. **Walkability:** 2. **Opened:** 1985. **Architect:** Lloyd Clifton. **Season:** Year-round. **High:** Jan.-April. **To obtain tee times:** Call up to 6 days in advance. **Miscellaneous:** Reduced fees (weekdays, twilight), credit cards (MC, V, D), BF, FF.
Reader Comments: Friendly staff. Lots of water on both sides ... Greens very receptive to good shots, good irrigation, well-managed course ... Nice layout ... Good value course, pace too slow ... Average course.

★★★ PELICAN POINTE GOLF & COUNTRY CLUB
SP-575 Center Rd., Venice, 34292, Sarasota County, (941)496-4653, 15 miles from Sarasota. **Facility Holes:** 18. **Yards:** 7,192/4,939. **Par:** 72/72. **Course Rating:** 75.1/68.9. **Slope:** 138/113. **Green Fee:** $35/$60. **Cart Fee:** Included in green fee. **Walking Policy:** Mandatory carts. **Walkability:** 1. **Opened:** 1995. **Architect:** Ted McAnlis. **Season:** Year-round. **High:** Jan.-May. **To obtain tee times:** Call up to 3 days in advance. **Miscellaneous:** Reduced fees (twilight), range (grass), credit cards (MC, V, AE, D), FF.
Reader Comments: Interesting holes, good use of water ... Will improve when housing construction ends ... Very challenging course ... Easy, wide open, not worth it.

PELICAN SOUND GOLF & RIVER CLUB
SP-4561 Pelican Sound Blvd., Estero, 33928, Lee County, (941)948-4333, 2 miles from Ft. Myers. **Web:** wci.com. **Facility Holes:** 27. **Green Fee:** $40/$110. **Cart Fee:** Included in green fee. **Walking Policy:** Mandatory carts. **Opened:** 1999. **Architect:** Chip Powell/Mike Hill. **Season:** Year-round. **To obtain tee times:** Call up to 3 days in advance. **Miscellaneous:** Reduced fees (twilight, juniors), range (grass), credit cards (MC, V, AE), BF, FF.
LAKE/SOUND (18 combo)
Yards: 7,062/5,386. **Par:** 72/72. **Course Rating:** 74.0/71.4. **Slope:** 143/130. **Walkability:** 3.

RIVER/LAKES (18 combo)
Yards: 6,781/5,237. **Par:** 71/71. **Course Rating:** 73.0/70.8. **Slope:** 142/123. **Walkability:** 2.
RIVER/SOUND (18 combo)
Yards: 6,842/5,317. **Par:** 72/72. **Course Rating:** 74.4/72.1. **Slope:** 141/128. **Walkability:** 3.

PGA GOLF CLUB
PU-1916 Perfect Dr., Port St. Lucie, 34986, St. Lucie County, (800)800-4653, (800)800-4653, 45 miles from West Palm Beach. **E-mail:** btaylor@pgahq.com. **Web:** www.pgavillage.com. **Facility Holes:** 54. **Green Fee:** $15/$75. **Cart Fee:** Included in green fee. **Walking Policy:** Unrestricted walking. **Walkability:** 2. **Season:** Year-round. **High:** Jan.-March. **To obtain tee times:** Call up to 9 days in advance. **Miscellaneous:** Reduced fees (twilight, juniors), range (grass), lodging (300 rooms), credit cards (MC, V, AE, D), BF, FF.
★★★★½ **NORTH COURSE** (18) *Value, Pace*
Yards: 7,026/4,993. **Par:** 72/72. **Course Rating:** 73.8/68.8. **Slope:** 133/114. **Opened:** 1996.
Architect: Tom Fazio.
Notes: Ranked 7th in 1996 Best New Affordable Courses.
Reader Comments: Friendly & beautiful course … Good design, great practice areas, challenging … Nice complex … Excellent, great golf, great food, great service … Fairly priced and well managed … Outstanding value, a must … Great experience and value … Can't ask for more.
★★★★ **PETE DYE COURSE** (18)
Yards: 7,150/5,015. **Par:** 72/72. **Course Rating:** 74.7/67.8. **Slope:** 133/109. **Opened:** 1999.
Architect: Pete Dye.
Reader Comments: Design is uniquely fun … Needs to mature a bit … Good design, great practice areas, challenging … Everybody friendly … The moguls and sand were daunting, but manageable … Best course I've played this year.
★★★★½ **SOUTH COURSE** (18) *Value+, Condition*
Yards: 7,076/4,933. **Par:** 72/72. **Course Rating:** 74.5/68.7. **Slope:** 141/119. **Opened:** 1996.
Architect: Tom Fazio.
Notes: Ranked 21st in 2001 Best in State; 1st in 1996 Best New Affordable Courses.
Reader Comments: Simply fantastic and inexpensive, too … Nice layout, nice pro shop & clubhouse … Very challenging but manageable for the average golfer … Can't beat prices … Florida's Pinehurst … Life doesn't get much better than this.

PGA NATIONAL GOLF CLUB
R-1000 Ave.of the Champions, Palm Beach Gardens, 33418, Palm Beach County, (561)627-1800, (800)633-9150, 15 miles from West Palm Beach. **Facility Holes:** 90. **Cart Fee:** $30/Person. **Walking Policy:** Mandatory carts. **Walkability:** 1. **Season:** Year-round. **High:** Nov.-April. **To obtain tee times:** Call golf shop. **Miscellaneous:** Metal spikes, range (grass/mats), lodging (300 rooms), credit cards (MC, V, AE, D), BF, FF.
★★★★ **CHAMPION COURSE** (18)
Yards: 7,022/5,377. **Par:** 72/72. **Course Rating:** 74.7/71.1. **Slope:** 142/123. **Green Fee:** $109/$225. **Opened:** 1981. **Architect:** Tom Fazio/Jack Nicklaus.
Reader Comments: Great shape, good greens and challenging … Great course, challenging … Beautiful, good test … Great golf course. Very expensive to play … Great layout that seems never to be in good shape.
★★★½ **ESTATE COURSE** (18)
Yards: 6,784/4,903. **Par:** 72/72. **Course Rating:** 73.4/68.4. **Slope:** 131/118. **Green Fee:** $65/$130. **Opened:** 1984. **Architect:** Karl Litten.
Reader Comments: Needs some work done. Interesting … Fairly long, nice course … Awesome place, courses were great … First hole a bear. Lots of water … Super course, fast pace of play.
★★★★ **GENERAL COURSE** (18)
Yards: 6,768/5,324. **Par:** 72/72. **Course Rating:** 73.0/71.0. **Slope:** 130/122. **Green Fee:** $68/$130. **Opened:** 1984. **Architect:** Arnold Palmer.
Reader Comments: Service was excellent … Nice course and underrated … Fun resort course … Grounds and courses are beautiful, courses are difficult, expensive, but worth it … Play slow and expensive, good condition, nice facilities.
★★★½ **HAIG COURSE** (18)
Yards: 6,806/5,645. **Par:** 72/72. **Course Rating:** 73.0/72.5. **Slope:** 130/121. **Green Fee:** $68/$130. **Opened:** 1980. **Architect:** Tom Fazio.
Reader Comments: May be the best at PGA National … Grounds and courses are beautiful … Open fairways, large greens, overpriced … Valid test of skills … A great Florida layout … Flat, boring course.
★★★★ **SQUIRE COURSE** (18)
Yards: 6,478/4,982. **Par:** 72/72. **Course Rating:** 71.3/69.8. **Slope:** 127/123. **Green Fee:** $68/$130. **Opened:** 1981. **Architect:** Tom Fazio.
Reader Comments: A place to go back to … Middle of the road, OK … Lots of water … Perfection … Tight course, a good test.

★★ PINE LAKES GOLF CLUB
PU-153 Northside Dr. S., Jacksonville, 32218, Duval County, (904)757-0318. **Facility Holes:**

18. Yards: 6,631/5,192. **Par:** 72/72. **Course Rating:** 71.1/69.8. **Slope:** 127/118. **Green Fee:** $18/$35. **Cart Fee:** Included in green fee. **Walking Policy:** Walking at certain times. **Walkability:** 2. **Opened:** 1965. **Season:** Year-round. **To obtain tee times:** Call up to 14 days in advance. **Miscellaneous:** Reduced fees (weekdays, twilight, seniors, juniors), metal spikes, range (grass), credit cards (MC, V, AE, D), FF.

★★★ PLANTATION INN & GOLF RESORT

R-9301 W. Fort Island Trail, Crystal River, 34429, Citrus County, (352)795-7211, (800)632-6262, 80 miles from Orlando. **Facility Holes:** 27. **Yards:** 6,531/5,203. **Par:** 72/72. **Course Rating:** 72.0/70.7. **Slope:** 128/118. **Green Fee:** $21/$48. **Cart Fee:** Included in green fee. **Walking Policy:** Walking at certain times. **Walkability:** 1. **Opened:** 1956. **Architect:** Mark Mahannah. **Season:** Year-round. **To obtain tee times:** Call up to 3 days in advance. **Miscellaneous:** Reduced fees (weekdays, guests, twilight, juniors), metal spikes, range (grass), lodging (150 rooms), credit cards (MC, V, AE, D), BF, FF.
Reader Comments: Old, flat, easy … Front 9 open and easy, 2nd 9 a bit more difficult … Have more play than they can handle with the schools … Always in great shape.
Special Notes: Also has a 9-hole course.

★★½ POINCIANA GOLF & RACQUET RESORT

R-500 E. Cypress Pkwy., Kissimmee, 34759, Osceola County, (407)933-5300, (800)331-7743, 14 miles from Orlando. **E-mail:** golfing@poincianaresort.com. **Web:** www.poincianaresort.com. **Facility Holes:** 18. **Yards:** 6,700/4,938. **Par:** 72/72. **Course Rating:** 72.2/68.4. **Slope:** 125/118. **Green Fee:** $35/$65. **Cart Fee:** Included in green fee. **Walkability:** 1. **Opened:** 1973. **Architect:** Bruce Devlin/Robert von Hagge. **Season:** Year-round. **High:** Jan.-April. **To obtain tee times:** Call golf shop. **Miscellaneous:** Reduced fees (guests, twilight, juniors), metal spikes, range (grass), credit cards (MC, V, AE).

★★★½ POLO TRACE GOLF COURSE

SP-13481 Polo Trace Dr., Delray Beach, 33446, Palm Beach County, (561)495-5300, (888)650-4653, 30 miles from West Palm Beach. **E-mail:** emeralddunes@aol.com. **Web:** www.emeralddunes.com. **Facility Holes:** 18. **Yards:** 7,096/5,314. **Par:** 72/72. **Course Rating:** 73.4/71.0. **Slope:** 134/124. **Green Fee:** $35/$130. **Cart Fee:** Included in green fee. **Walking Policy:** Mandatory carts. **Walkability:** 3. **Opened:** 1989. **Architect:** Karl Litten/Joey Sindelar. **Season:** Year-round. **High:** Dec.-May. **To obtain tee times:** Call up to 30 days in advance. **Miscellaneous:** Reduced fees (weekdays, guests, twilight, seniors, juniors), metal spikes, range (grass/mats), credit cards (MC, V, AE, D, DC), BF, FF.
Reader Comments: Tough & pricey … Good par 3s, very expensive … Unique links-type layout that I would absolutely recommend … No trees, OK … Fun to play, scenic … Excellent layout & challenge.

POMPANO BEACH GOLF COURSE

PU-1101 N. Federal Hwy., Pompano Beach, 33062, Broward County, (954)781-0426, 7 miles from Fort Lauderdale. **Facility Holes:** 36. **Green Fee:** $22/$45. **Cart Fee:** Included in green fee. **Walking Policy:** Unrestricted walking. **Walkability:** 1. **Opened:** 1954. **Architect:** Robert von Hagge/Bruce Devlin. **Season:** Year-round. **To obtain tee times:** Call golf shop. **Miscellaneous:** Reduced fees (twilight, juniors), range (grass), BF, FF.
★★★ PALMS COURSE (18)
Yards: 6,345/5,133. **Par:** 71/72. **Course Rating:** 69.8/69.5. **Slope:** 113/122.
Reader Comments: For a public course had a professional air about it … Great new holes, nice mounding … Course has been revamped, they did a good job … Nice course, needs more sand traps … Good playable course, good value.
★★★ PINES COURSE (18)
Yards: 6,995/5,530. **Par:** 72/72. **Course Rating:** 72.7/71.5. **Slope:** 120/123.
Reader Comments: Excellent … Good test.

PONTE VEDRA INN & CLUB

R-200 Ponte Vedra Blvd., Ponte Vedra Beach, 32082, St. Johns County, (904)285-1111, (800)234-7842, 20 miles from Jacksonville. **Facility Holes:** 36. **Cart Fee:** Included in green fee. **Walking Policy:** Walking at certain times. **Season:** Year-round. **High:** March-Nov. **To obtain tee times:** Call golf shop. **Miscellaneous:** Range (grass), lodging (221 rooms), credit cards (MC, V, AE, D, DC), BF, FF.
★★½ LAGOON COURSE (18)
Yards: 5,574/4,571. **Par:** 70/70. **Course Rating:** 67.3/66.6. **Slope:** 116/113. **Green Fee:** $100. **Walkability:** 1. **Opened:** 1962. **Architect:** Robert Trent Jones.
★★★½ OCEAN COURSE (18)
Yards: 6,811/4,967. **Par:** 72/73. **Course Rating:** 73.2/69.5. **Slope:** 138/117. **Green Fee:** $160. **Walkability:** 2. **Opened:** 1928. **Architect:** Herbert Strong.
Reader Comments: Windy, terrain mostly flat, greens tough … Severely undulating greens … Elevated greens keep your approach shots honest … Great practice course, great for short hitters.

THE PRESERVE GOLF CLUB AT TARA
SP-7310 Tara Preserve Lane, Bradenton, 34203, Manatee County, (941)756-2944, 50 miles from Tampa. **Facility Holes:** 18. **Yards:** 7,000/5,300. **Par:** 72/72. **Course Rating:** 74.0/68.9. **Slope:** 141/114. **Walking Policy:** Walking at certain times. **Walkability:** 2. **Opened:** 2001. **Architect:** Ted McAnlis. **Season:** Year-round. **High:** Oct.-April. **To obtain tee times:** Call up to 3 days in advance. **Miscellaneous:** Range (grass), credit cards (MC, V), BF, FF.

★★½ PRESIDENTIAL COUNTRY CLUB
SP-19600 Presidential Way, North Miami Beach, 33179, Dade County, 305-935-7500, 3 miles from Fort Lauderdale. **E-mail:** a.mandatta@ourclub.com. **Web:** www.presidential.com. **Facility Holes:** 18. **Yards:** 6,576/4,980. **Par:** 71/71. **Course Rating:** 71.8/70.0. **Slope:** 126/117. **Green Fee:** $32/$90. **Cart Fee:** Included in green fee. **Walking Policy:** Mandatory carts. **Walkability:** 3. **Opened:** 1999. **Architect:** Tommy Fazio. **Season:** Year-round. **To obtain tee times:** Call up to 3 days in advance. **Miscellaneous:** Reduced fees (twilight), range (mats), credit cards (MC, V, AE), BF, FF.

★★ QUALITY INN & SUITES GOLF RESORT
R-4100 Golden Gate Pkwy., Naples, 34116, Collier County, (941)455-9498, (800)277-0017, 6 miles from Naples. **E-mail:** info@naplesgolfresort.com. **Web:** www.naplesgolfresort.com. **Facility Holes:** 18. **Yards:** 6,570/5,374. **Par:** 72/72. **Course Rating:** 70.8/70.3. **Slope:** 125/123. **Green Fee:** $20/$65. **Cart Fee:** Included in green fee. **Walking Policy:** Walking at certain times. **Walkability:** 1. **Opened:** 1964. **Architect:** Dick Wilson/Joe Lee. **Season:** Year-round. **High:** Jan.-April. **To obtain tee times:** Call up to 7 days in advance. **Miscellaneous:** Reduced fees (guests, twilight, juniors), range (grass), lodging (181 rooms), credit cards (MC, V, AE, D, DC), BF, FF.

★★★ RADISSON PONCE DE LEON GOLF & CONFERENCE RESORT
R-4000 U.S. Hwy. 1 N., St. Augustine, 32095, St. Johns County, (904)829-5314, (888)829-5314, 25 miles from Jacksonville. **E-mail:** mhafe@aol.com. **Facility Holes:** 18. **Yards:** 6,823/5,308. **Par:** 72/72. **Course Rating:** 72.9/70.7. **Slope:** 131/125. **Green Fee:** $25/$55. **Cart Fee:** Included in green fee. **Walking Policy:** Mandatory carts. **Walkability:** 1. **Opened:** 1916. **Architect:** Donald Ross. **Season:** Year-round. **To obtain tee times:** Call up to 4 days in advance. **Miscellaneous:** Reduced fees (weekdays, guests, twilight, juniors), range (grass), lodging (200 rooms), credit cards (MC, V, AE, D, DC), BF, FF.
Reader Comments: Interesting holes, can be very windy ... Well-maintained track, well-managed course ... One of my favorite Ross gems.

★★★ RAINTREE GOLF RESORT
R-1600 S. Hiatus Rd., Pembroke Pines, 33025, Broward County, (954)432-4400, (800)346-5332, 8 miles from Fort Lauderdale. **E-mail:** info@raintreegolf.com. **Web:** www.raintreegolf.com. **Facility Holes:** 18. **Green Fee:** $30/$75. **Cart Fee:** Included in green fee. **Walking Policy:** Mandatory carts. **Walkability:** 1. **Opened:** 1985. **Architect:** Charles M. Mahannah. **Season:** Year-round. **To obtain tee times:** Call golf shop. **Miscellaneous:** Reduced fees (weekdays, guests, twilight), range (mats), lodging (24 rooms), credit cards (MC, V, AE, D), BF, FF.

★★★ RAVINES GOLF & COUNTRY CLUB
SP-2932 Ravines Rd., Middleburg, 32068, Clay County, (904)282-7888, 3 miles from Jacksonville. **Web:** www.theravines.com. **Facility Holes:** 18. **Yards:** 6,733/4,817. **Par:** 72/70. **Course Rating:** 72.4/67.4. **Slope:** 133/120. **Green Fee:** $35/$75. **Cart Fee:** Included in green fee. **Walking Policy:** Mandatory carts. **Walkability:** 4. **Opened:** 1979. **Architect:** Mark McCumber/Ron Garl. **Season:** Year-round. **To obtain tee times:** Call golf shop. **Miscellaneous:** Reduced fees (twilight, seniors, juniors), range (grass), lodging (30 rooms), credit cards (MC, V, AE, D), BF, FF.
Reader Comments: Extremely hilly for Florida. Very dramatic holes. Watch for snakes when looking for lost ball ... Hilly, tough as nails ... Very scenic & challenging ... True elevation changes in Florida.

★★★★ REGATTA BAY GOLF & COUNTRY CLUB
SP-465 Regatta Bay Blvd., Destin, 32541, Okaloosa County, (850)650-7800, (800)648-0123. **Web:** www.regattabay.com. **Facility Holes:** 18. **Yards:** 6,864/5,092. **Par:** 72/72. **Course Rating:** 73.8/70.8. **Slope:** 148/119. **Green Fee:** $44/$94. **Cart Fee:** $15/Person. **Walking Policy:** Mandatory carts. **Walkability:** 3. **Opened:** 1998. **Architect:** Bob Walker. **Season:** Year-round. **To obtain tee times:** Call golf shop. **Miscellaneous:** Reduced fees (twilight, juniors), range (grass), credit cards (MC, V, AE), BF, FF.
Reader Comments: Excellent layout, pricey ... Really enjoyable course ... Beautiful, challenging, top condition, great staff ... Too expensive, great layout ... Good shape, awesome service ... Good course, good conditions, overpriced.

FLORIDA

★★★ REMINGTON GOLF CLUB
PU-2995 Remington Blvd., Kissimmee, 34741, Osceola County, (407)344-4004, 12 miles from Orlando. **Web:** www.remington-gc.com. **Facility Holes:** 18. **Yards:** 7,111/5,178. **Par:** 72/72. **Course Rating:** 73.9/69.8. **Slope:** 134/118. **Green Fee:** $24/$75. **Cart Fee:** Included in green fee. **Walking Policy:** Mandatory carts. **Walkability:** 2. **Opened:** 1996. **Architect:** Lloyd Clifton/George Clifton/Ken Ezell. **Season:** Year-round. **High:** Jan.-April. **To obtain tee times:** Call golf shop. **Miscellaneous:** Reduced fees (weekdays, guests, twilight, seniors, juniors), range (grass), credit cards (MC, V, AE), BF, FF.
Reader Comments: Sporty ... Bring plenty of balls, water everywhere ... Lots of water, fairly short ... OK, nothing fancy ... Friendly staff, nice course, hidden trouble ... Nice course definitely worth playing ... Great price, too slow.

★★★ RIDGEWOOD LAKES GOLF CLUB
SP-200 Eagle Ridge Dr., Davenport, 33837, Polk County, (941)424-8688, (800)684-8800, 35 miles from Orlando. **E-mail:** bboeling@pga.com. **Web:** www.ridgewoodlakes.cc. **Facility Holes:** 18. **Yards:** 7,016/5,217. **Par:** 72/72. **Course Rating:** 73.7/64.5. **Slope:** 140/114. **Green Fee:** $40/$99. **Cart Fee:** Included in green fee. **Walking Policy:** Mandatory carts. **Walkability:** 1. **Opened:** 1994. **Architect:** Ted McAnlis. **Season:** Year-round. **To obtain tee times:** Call golf shop. **Miscellaneous:** Reduced fees (guests, twilight, seniors, juniors), range (grass), credit cards (MC, V), BF, FF.
Reader Comments: Great layout, typical Florida course, great for the price ... Challenging course, nice greens. Good layout ... Tough, tight course, water in play on every hole, fun ... Average Florida course.

★★½ RIVER BEND GOLF CLUB
SP-730 Airport Rd., Ormond Beach, 32174, Volusia County, (386)673-6000, 3 miles from Daytona Beach. **E-mail:** rbmanatee@aol.com. **Facility Holes:** 18. **Yards:** 6,821/5,112. **Par:** 72/72. **Course Rating:** 72.3/69.6. **Slope:** 126/120. **Green Fee:** $28/$45. **Cart Fee:** Included in green fee. **Walking Policy:** Mandatory carts. **Walkability:** 2. **Opened:** 1990. **Architect:** Lloyd Clifton. **Season:** Year-round. **High:** Jan.-April. **To obtain tee times:** Call up to 4 days in advance. **Miscellaneous:** Reduced fees (twilight, juniors), range (grass), credit cards (MC, V, AE), BF, FF.

★★★½ THE RIVER CLUB
SP-6600 River Club Blvd., Bradenton, 34202, Manatee County, (941)751-4211, 45 miles from Tampa. **Web:** www.bradentonriverclub.com. **Facility Holes:** 18. **Yards:** 7,026/5,252. **Par:** 72/72. **Course Rating:** 74.5/70.4. **Slope:** 135/121. **Green Fee:** $30/$60. **Cart Fee:** Included in green fee. **Walking Policy:** Walking at certain times. **Walkability:** 3. **Opened:** 1988. **Architect:** Ron Garl. **Season:** Year-round. **High:** Nov.-April. **To obtain tee times:** Call golf shop. **Miscellaneous:** Reduced fees (weekdays, guests, twilight), range (grass), credit cards (MC, V, AE, D), BF, FF.
Reader Comments: Great design, condition of the course has slipped ... A nice test and a good value, staff is friendly, and you may see an alligator or 2 ... Very nice, a pleasant afternoon ... Great course ... Good course. Friendly people.

★★★½ RIVER HILLS COUNTRY CLUB
SP-3943 New River Hills Pkwy., Valrico, 33594, Hillsborough County, (813)653-3323, 20 miles from Tampa. **Facility Holes:** 18. **Yards:** 7,004/5,236. **Par:** 72/72. **Course Rating:** 74.0/70.4. **Slope:** 132/124. **Green Fee:** $50/$85. **Cart Fee:** Included in green fee. **Walking Policy:** Mandatory carts. **Walkability:** 2. **Opened:** 1989. **Architect:** Joe Lee. **Season:** Year-round. **To obtain tee times:** Call up to 4 days in advance. **Miscellaneous:** Reduced fees (twilight), range (grass), credit cards (MC, V, AE, DC), BF, FF.
Reader Comments: Slow, uneventful ... Nice layout, challenging ... Good layout 18 great holes.

★★★ RIVER RUN GOLF LINKS
PU-1801 27th St. E., Bradenton, 34208, Manatee County, (941)747-6331, 30 miles from St. Petersburg. **E-mail:** riverrun44@aol.com. **Facility Holes:** 18. **Yards:** 5,825/4,579. **Par:** 70/70. **Course Rating:** 68.0/67.8. **Slope:** 113/113. **Green Fee:** $9/$18. **Cart Fee:** $10/Person. **Walking Policy:** Unrestricted walking. **Opened:** 1987. **Architect:** Ward Northrup. **Season:** Year-round. **High:** Jan.-April. **To obtain tee times:** Call golf shop. **Miscellaneous:** Reduced fees (weekdays, twilight), BF, FF.
Reader Comments: Very good course to play ... Short and tight ... Great public course ... About average city course ... Very good city course.

★★★★½ RIVERWOOD GOLF CLUB
SP-4100 Riverwood Dr., Port Charlotte, 33953, Charlotte County, (941)764-6661, 45 miles from Sarasota. **E-mail:** mburtz3@home.com. **Facility Holes:** 18. **Yards:** 6,938/4,695. **Par:** 72/72. **Course Rating:** 73.8/68.0. **Slope:** 133/114. **Green Fee:** $50/$90. **Cart Fee:** Included in

green fee. **Walking Policy:** Mandatory carts. **Walkability:** 2. **Opened:** 1993. **Architect:** Gene Bates. **Season:** Year-round. **To obtain tee times:** Call golf shop. **Miscellaneous:** Reduced fees (guests, twilight, juniors), range (grass), credit cards (MC, V), BF, FF.
Reader Comments: Great test, always in good condition, great practice facility ... Great value ... Difficult from back tees, challenging ... Top course around, somewhat overpriced ... Good test, hard greens, shotmaker course.

★★ RIVIERA COUNTRY CLUB
SP-500 Calle Grande, Ormond Beach, 32174, Volusia County, (904)677-2464, 4 miles from Daytona Beach. **Facility Holes:** 18. **Yards:** 6,302/5,207. **Par:** 71/72. **Course Rating:** 68.0/69.9. **Slope:** 113/122. **Green Fee:** $18/$35. **Cart Fee:** Included in green fee. **Walking Policy:** Mandatory carts. **Walkability:** 1. **Opened:** 1935. **Architect:** David Wallace. **Season:** Year-round. **High:** Jan.-April. **Miscellaneous:** Reduced fees (guests, twilight, juniors), metal spikes, range (grass), credit cards (MC, V), BF, FF.

★½ ROCKY POINT GOLF COURSE
PU-4151 Dana Shores Dr., Tampa, 33634, Hillsborough County, (813)673-4316. **Facility Holes:** 18. **Yards:** 6,301/4,925. **Par:** 71/71. **Course Rating:** 70.5/67.9. **Slope:** 119/118. **Green Fee:** $21/$36. **Cart Fee:** Included in green fee. **Walking Policy:** Unrestricted walking. **Walkability:** 1. **Opened:** 1900. **Architect:** Ron Garl. **Season:** Year-round. **To obtain tee times:** Call golf shop. **Miscellaneous:** Reduced fees (twilight, juniors), metal spikes, credit cards (MC, V, D), BF, FF.

★★ ROGERS PARK GOLF COURSE
PU-7910 N. 30th St., Tampa, 33610, Hillsborough County, (813)673-4396. **Facility Holes:** 18. **Yards:** 6,593/5,922. **Par:** 72/72. **Course Rating:** 71.0/67.3. **Slope:** 120/110. **Green Fee:** $35. **Cart Fee:** Included in green fee. **Walking Policy:** Unrestricted walking. **Walkability:** 1. **Opened:** 1950. **Architect:** Ron Garl. **Season:** Year-round. **High:** Jan.-April. **To obtain tee times:** Call golf shop. **Miscellaneous:** Reduced fees (twilight, juniors), metal spikes, range (grass), credit cards (MC, V, D).

★★½ ROLLING GREEN GOLF CLUB
SP-4501 N. Tuttle Ave., Sarasota, 34234, Sarasota County, (941)355-7621. **Facility Holes:** 18. **Yards:** 6,343/5,010. **Par:** 72/72. **Course Rating:** 69.7/67.9. **Slope:** 119/110. **Green Fee:** $10/$28. **Cart Fee:** $16/Person. **Walking Policy:** Walking at certain times. **Walkability:** 1. **Opened:** 1968. **Architect:** R. Albert Anderson. **Season:** Year-round. **High:** Dec.-April. **To obtain tee times:** Call golf shop. **Miscellaneous:** Range (grass), credit cards (MC, V, AE, D), FF.

★★½ ROSEDALE GOLF & COUNTRY CLUB
SP-5100 87th St. E., Bradenton, 34202, Manatee County, (941)756-0004, 30 miles from Tampa. **E-mail:** rosedalememb@acun.com. **Facility Holes:** 18. **Yards:** 6,779/5,169. **Par:** 72/72. **Course Rating:** 72.9/70.4. **Slope:** 134/114. **Green Fee:** $20/$70. **Cart Fee:** Included in green fee. **Walking Policy:** Walking at certain times. **Walkability:** 2. **Opened:** 1993. **Architect:** Ted McAnlis. **Season:** Year-round. **High:** Jan.-May. **To obtain tee times:** Call up to 3 days in advance. **Miscellaneous:** Reduced fees (weekdays, guests, twilight), range (grass), credit cards (MC, V), BF, FF.

★★★½ ROYAL OAK GOLF CLUB
SP-2150 Country Club Dr., Titusville, 32780, Brevard County, (321)268-1550, (800)884-2150, 45 miles from Orlando. **Facility Holes:** 18. **Yards:** 6,709/5,471. **Par:** 71/72. **Course Rating:** 72.3/71.5. **Slope:** 126/128. **Green Fee:** $16/$45. **Cart Fee:** Included in green fee. **Walking Policy:** Unrestricted walking. **Walkability:** 3. **Opened:** 1964. **Architect:** Dick Wilson. **Season:** Year-round. **High:** Jan.-April. **To obtain tee times:** Call golf shop. **Miscellaneous:** Reduced fees (weekdays, guests, twilight, juniors), metal spikes, range (grass), credit cards (MC, V, AE).
Reader Comments: Fun, friendly, won't burn-out your wallet ... Excellent greens, fairways OK ... Good design, great value ... Good conditions and facilities, poor irrigation, pace of play fair, management good ... Busy, championship layout.

★★★½ ROYAL TEE COUNTRY CLUB
SP-11460 Royal Tee Circle, Cape Coral, 33991, Lee County, (941)283-5522, 15 miles from Fort Myers. **Facility Holes:** 27. **Green Fee:** $15/$49. **Cart Fee:** Included in green fee. **Walking Policy:** Walking at certain times. **Walkability:** 1. **Opened:** 1985. **Architect:** Gordon Lewis. **Season:** Year-round. **High:** Jan.-April. **To obtain tee times:** Call golf shop. **Miscellaneous:** Reduced fees (twilight, seniors), metal spikes, range (grass), credit cards (MC, V, D), FF.
PRINCE/KING COURSE (18 Combo)
Yards: 6,736/4,685. **Par:** 72/72. **Course Rating:** 71.5/67.0. **Slope:** 126/114.
PRINCE/QUEEN COURSE (18 Combo)
Yards: 6,606/4,670. **Par:** 72/72. **Course Rating:** 71.3/66.4. **Slope:** 126/114.

QUEEN/KING COURSE (18 Combo)
Yards: 6,574/4,631. **Par:** 72/72. **Course Rating:** 71.4/66.2. **Slope:** 128/110.
Reader Comments: Just a day in the sun … A good course to play while on vacation … Interesting layout with lots of water, fine value, lateral water hazards often pinch into fairways making seemingly easy holes more difficult. Marshy areas make for target golf on a few holes.

★★★ SABAL POINT COUNTRY CLUB
SP-2662 Sabal Club Way, Longwood, 32779, Seminole County, (407)869-4622, 5 miles from Orlando. **E-mail:** tkoch@mggi.com. **Web:** www.sabalpointcountryclub.com. **Facility Holes:** 18.
Yards: 6,603/5,278. **Par:** 72/72. **Course Rating:** 71.6/70.0. **Slope:** 129/120. **Green Fee:** $25/$55. **Cart Fee:** Included in green fee. **Walking Policy:** Mandatory carts. **Walkability:** 2.
Opened: 1981. **Architect:** Wade Northrup. **Season:** Year-round. **High:** Dec.-April. **To obtain tee times:** Call golf shop. **Miscellaneous:** Reduced fees (weekdays, twilight, juniors), range (mats), credit cards (MC, V, AE), BF, FF.
Reader Comments: Unknown gem in Orlando … New management has started improvements.

SADDLEBROOK RESORT
R-5700 Saddlebrook Way, Wesley Chapel, 33543, Pasco County, (813)973-1111, (800)729-8383, 20 miles from Tampa. **Web:** www.saddlebrookresort.com. **Facility Holes:** 36.
Green Fee: $45/$120. **Cart Fee:** $25/Person. **Walking Policy:** Mandatory carts. **Season:** Year-round. **To obtain tee times:** Call golf shop. **Miscellaneous:** Reduced fees (guests), range (grass), credit cards (MC, V, AE, D), BF, FF.
★★★★ PALMER COURSE (18)
Yards: 6,469/5,187. **Par:** 71/71. **Course Rating:** 71.9/71.0. **Slope:** 134/127. **Opened:** 1986.
Architect: Arnold Palmer/Ed Seay.
Reader Comments: Expensive Florida golf … Great instructional staff for beginners … Overpriced … Great course, interesting, easy and hard … Great and beautiful. Facilities and service outrank the course.
★★★★ SADDLEBROOK COURSE (18)
Yards: 6,564/4,941. **Par:** 70/70. **Course Rating:** 72.0/70.6. **Slope:** 127/126. **Opened:** 1976.
Architect: Dean Refram.
Reader Comments: Terrific picturebook, demanding .·. Not a spectacular course, but fast pace, a few gators, and amazing food made it worth the trip … Tight, interesting.

SANDESTIN RESORT
R-9300 Hwy. 98 W., Destin, 32541, Walton County, (850)267-8155, (800)277-0800, 20 miles from Fort Walton Beach. **E-mail:** j.osenkowski@ sandestin.com. **Web:** www.sandestin.com.
Facility Holes: 73. **Cart Fee:** Included in green fee. **Walkability:** 2. **Season:** Year-round.
Miscellaneous: Range (grass), lodging (740 rooms), credit cards (MC, V, AE, D, DC), BF, FF.
★★★★½ BAYTOWNE GOLF CLUB AT SANDESTIN (18)
Yards: 6,890/4,862. **Par:** 72/72. **Course Rating:** 73.4/68.5. **Slope:** 127/114. **Green Fee:** $68/$86. **Walking Policy:** Mandatory carts. **Opened:** 1985. **Architect:** Tom Jackson. **High:** Feb.-May. **To obtain tee times:** Call up to 14 days in advance. **Miscellaneous:** Reduced fees (guests, twilight, juniors).
Reader Comments: Easiest of the Sandestin courses, but plenty of challenging, fun holes. Great course to start your Destin golf adventure.
★★★★ BURNT PINES COURSE (18) *Pace*
Yards: 7,046/5,950. **Par:** 72/72. **Course Rating:** 74.1/68.7. **Slope:** 135/124. **Green Fee:** $88/$145. **Walking Policy:** Unrestricted walking. **Opened:** 1994. **Architect:** Rees Jones. **To obtain tee times:** Call up to 14 days in advance. **Miscellaneous:** Reduced fees (guests, juniors).
Notes: Ranked 29th in 1999 Best in State; 64th in 1996 America's Top 75 Upscale Courses; 3rd in 1995 Best New Resort Courses.
Reader Comments: First-class from start to finish … Great condition … Big course, big price. Play at least once … Overrated course … Nice experience, but not exceptional … Very good layout, cold towels … Best course in the area.
★★★★ LINKS COURSE (18)
Yards: 6,710/4,969. **Par:** 72/72. **Course Rating:** 72.8/69.2. **Slope:** 124/115. **Green Fee:** $68/$105. **Walking Policy:** Unrestricted walking. **Opened:** 1977. **Architect:** Tom Jackson. **To obtain tee times:** Call golf shop. **Miscellaneous:** Reduced fees (guests, twilight, juniors).
Reader Comments: Wet and wild target golf. Water and wind on every hole … Fun layout for all levels, awesome shape … Very scenic bayside holes. Tight driving holes … Beautiful, fun to play, hit it straight or bring a lot of balls.
★★★★ THE RAVEN GOLF CLUB (19)
Yards: 6,910/5,065. **Par:** 71/71. **Course Rating:** 73.8/70.6. **Slope:** 138/126. **Green Fee:** $65/$145. **Walking Policy:** Unrestricted walking. **Opened:** 2000. **Architect:** Robert Trent Jones, Jr. **High:** Feb.-Aug. **To obtain tee times:** Call up to 14 days in advance. **Miscellaneous:** Reduced fees (guests, twilight, juniors).
Reader Comments: Awesome in every way … Perfect Florida golf … Outstanding service, staff really made us feel welcome. Challenging but fair, lots of fun … Good design but too congested …

Unbelievable service at a fantastic course.
Special Notes: 16th hole has twin par 3s played on alternate days.

★★½ SANDPIPER GOLF CLUB
SP-6001 Sandpipers Dr., Lakeland, 33809, Polk County, (863)859-5461, 30 miles from Tampa. **Web:** www.golfmatrix.com. **Facility Holes:** 18. **Yards:** 6,442/5,024. **Par:** 70/70. **Course Rating:** 70.1/65.9. **Slope:** 123/114. **Green Fee:** $18/$30. **Cart Fee:** Included in green fee. **Walking Policy:** Mandatory carts. **Walkability:** 1. **Opened:** 1987. **Architect:** Steve Smyers. **Season:** Year-round. **High:** Oct.-May. **To obtain tee times:** Call up to 4 days in advance. **Miscellaneous:** Reduced fees (weekdays, twilight), credit cards (MC, V), FF.

SANDRIDGE GOLF CLUB
PU-5300 73rd St., Vero Beach, 32967, Indian River County, (561)770-5000, 70 miles from West Palm Beach. **E-mail:** bgnern@msn.com. **Facility Holes:** 36. **Green Fee:** $16/$38. **Cart Fee:** Included in green fee. **Walking Policy:** Walking at certain times. **Architect:** Ron Garl. **Season:** Year-round. **High:** Jan.-April. **To obtain tee times:** Call up to 2 days in advance. **Miscellaneous:** Reduced fees (weekdays, twilight, juniors), range (grass), credit cards (MC, V, D), BF, FF.

★★★½ DUNES COURSE (18)
Yards: 6,900/4,922. **Par:** 72/72. **Course Rating:** 74.0/69.3. **Slope:** 131/120. **Walkability:** 4. **Opened:** 1987.
Reader Comments: Good county-owned course ... Will not break you finacially but will make for a great day of golf. Not long but target golf ... Average, good layout ... Great course, great value, wish I lived closer ... Excellent county course.

★★★★ LAKES COURSE (18)
Yards: 6,200/4,625. **Par:** 72/72. **Course Rating:** 70.1/67.1. **Slope:** 128/112. **Walkability:** 2. **Opened:** 1992.
Reader Comments: A hidden jewel. Very surprised by the quality of the course at such a reasonable price ... Bring a lot of balls ... As nice as any private course ... Good value ... A bargain, difficult to get on, nice course.

★★ SANTA ROSA GOLF & BEACH CLUB
SP-334 Golf Club Dr., Santa Rosa Beach, 32459, Walton County, (904)267-2229, 15 miles from Destin. **E-mail:** srgruss@gnt.net. **Web:** www.santarosaclub.com. **Facility Holes:** 18. **Yards:** 6,474/4,988. **Par:** 72/72. **Course Rating:** 72.0/73.1. **Slope:** 139/128. **Green Fee:** $40/$60. **Cart Fee:** $15/Person. **Walking Policy:** Walking at certain times. **Walkability:** 2. **Opened:** 1969. **Architect:** Tom Jackson. **Season:** Year-round. **To obtain tee times:** Call golf shop. **Miscellaneous:** Reduced fees (twilight, juniors), range (grass), credit cards (MC, V, AE, DC), FF.

★★½ SARASOTA GOLF CLUB
SP-7280 N. Leewynn Dr., Sarasota, 34240, Sarasota County, (941)371-2431. **E-mail:** ceston99@an.com. **Web:** www.kollstar.com. **Facility Holes:** 18. **Yards:** 7,066/5,004. **Par:** 72/72. **Course Rating:** 71.2/67.4. **Slope:** 122/108. **Green Fee:** $22/$40. **Cart Fee:** Included in green fee. **Walking Policy:** Walking at certain times. **Walkability:** 1. **Opened:** 1950. **Architect:** Wayne Tredway. **Season:** Year-round. **High:** Jan.-April. **To obtain tee times:** Call golf shop. **Miscellaneous:** Reduced fees (guests, twilight, seniors, juniors), metal spikes, range (grass), credit cards (MC, V, AE, D).

★★★ SAVANNAHS AT SYKES CREEK GOLF CLUB
PU-3915 Savannahs Trail, Merritt Island, 32953, Brevard County, (321)455-1375, 40 miles from Orlando. **E-mail:** savannah@digital.net. **Web:** www.golfspacecoast.com. **Facility Holes:** 18. **Yards:** 6,636/4,795. **Par:** 72/72. **Course Rating:** 72.2/68.6. **Slope:** 135/121. **Green Fee:** $14/$28. **Cart Fee:** $11/Person. **Walking Policy:** Walking at certain times. **Opened:** 1990. **Architect:** Gordon Lewis. **Season:** Year-round. **High:** Dec.-April. **To obtain tee times:** Call up to 2 days in advance. **Miscellaneous:** Reduced fees (guests, twilight, juniors), range (grass), credit cards (MC, V), BF, FF.
Reader Comments: Much improved, some very tough holes ... Nice challenging course, winding through development.

★★½ SCENIC HILLS COUNTRY CLUB
SP-8891 Burning Tree Rd., Pensacola, 32514, Escambia County, (904)476-0611. **Facility Holes:** 18. **Yards:** 6,689/5,187. **Par:** 71/71. **Course Rating:** 71.3/70.0. **Slope:** 131/116. **Green Fee:** $25/$45. **Walking Policy:** Mandatory carts. **Walkability:** 3. **Opened:** 1956. **Architect:** Chic Adams/Jerry Pate. **Season:** Year-round. **High:** Feb.-May. **To obtain tee times:** Call up to 60 days in advance. **Miscellaneous:** Reduced fees (weekdays, guests, twilight), range (grass/mats), credit cards (MC, V), BF, FF.

FLORIDA

★★½ SCHALAMAR CREEK GOLF & COUNTRY CLUB
SP-4500 U.S. Hwy. 92 E., Lakeland, 33801, Polk County, (941)666-1623, 30 miles from Tampa. **Facility Holes:** 18. **Yards:** 6,399/4,363. **Par:** 72/72. **Course Rating:** 70.9/64.8. **Slope:** 124/106. **Green Fee:** $8/$21. **Walking Policy:** Walking at certain times. **Walkability:** 1. **Opened:** 1987. **Architect:** Ron Garl. **Season:** Year-round. **High:** Jan.-April. **To obtain tee times:** Call golf shop. **Misc:** Reduced fees (weekdays, twilight), range (grass), credit cards (MC, V).

★★ SEASCAPE RESORT
R-100 Seascape Dr., Destin, 32550, Walton County, (850)654-7888, (800)874-9106, 6 miles from Destin. **Facility Holes:** 18. **Yards:** 6,480/5,014. **Par:** 70/70. **Course Rating:** 72.7/70.9. **Slope:** 123/116. **Green Fee:** $55/$75. **Cart Fee:** Included in green fee. **Walking Policy:** Walking at certain times. **Walkability:** 1. **Opened:** 1973. **Architect:** Joe Lee. **Season:** Year-round. **High:** March-Oct. **To obtain tee times:** Call up to 7 days in advance. **Miscellaneous:** Reduced fees (guests, juniors), range (grass), credit cards (MC, V, AE, D), BF, FF.

★★ SEBASTIAN MUNICIPAL GOLF COURSE
PU-101 E. Airport Dr., Sebastian, 32958, Indian River County, (561)589-6801, 75 miles from Orlando. **Web:** www.cityofsebastian.org. **Facility Holes:** 18. **Yards:** 6,717/5,414. **Par:** 72/72. **Course Rating:** 71.0/71.1. **Slope:** 112/121. **Green Fee:** $14/$31. **Walking Policy:** Walking at certain times. **Walkability:** 1. **Opened:** 1981. **Architect:** Charles Ankrom. **Season:** Year-round. **To obtain tee times:** Call up to 4 days in advance. **Miscellaneous:** Reduced fees (twilight, juniors), range (grass), credit cards (MC, V), BF, FF.

★★½ SEVEN HILLS GOLFERS CLUB
SP-10599 Fairchild Rd., Spring Hill, 34608, Hernando County, (352)688-8888, 35 miles from Tampa. **E-mail:** 7hillsgolf@msn.com. **Facility Holes:** 18. **Yards:** 6,715/4,902. **Par:** 72/72. **Course Rating:** 70.5/66.5. **Slope:** 126/109. **Green Fee:** $24/$40. **Cart Fee:** Included in green fee. **Walking Policy:** Mandatory carts. **Walkability:** 3. **Opened:** 1989. **Architect:** Denis Griffiths. **Season:** Year-round. **To obtain tee times:** Call up to 7 days in advance. **Miscellaneous:** Reduced fees (weekdays, twilight), range (grass), credit cards (MC, V), BF, FF.

SEVEN SPRINGS GOLF & COUNTRY CLUB
SP-3535 Trophy Blvd., New Port Richey, 34655, Pasco County, (813)376-0035, 12 miles from Tampa. **Facility Holes:** 36. **Walking Policy:** Mandatory carts. **Season:** Year-round. **To obtain tee times:** Call up to 2 days in advance. **Miscellaneous:** Reduced fees (twilight), range (grass), credit cards (MC, V), BF, FF.
★★★½ **CHAMPIONSHIP COURSE** (18)
Yards: 6,566/5,250. **Par:** 72/72. **Slope:** 128/125. **Green Fee:** $31/$45. **Walkability:** 3. **Architect:** Ron Garl. **High:** Oct.-May.
Reader Comments: Bring a lot of balls … Reasonable even in season, pro shop bargains … Well taken care of, friendly atmosphere.
EXECUTIVE COURSE (18)
Yards: 4,310/4,030. **Par:** 64/64. **Slope:** 112/113. **Green Fee:** $18/$25. **Cart Fee:** Included in green fee. **Walkability:** 1.

★★★½ SHALIMAR POINTE GOLF & COUNTRY CLUB
SP-302 Country Club Rd., Shalimar, 32579, Okaloosa County, (850)651-1416, (800)964-2833, 45 miles from Pensacola. **Facility Holes:** 18. **Yards:** 6,765/5,427. **Par:** 72/72. **Course Rating:** 72.9/70.7. **Slope:** 125/115. **Green Fee:** $21/$49. **Cart Fee:** $18/Person. **Walking Policy:** Mandatory carts. **Walkability:** 2. **Opened:** 1968. **Architect:** Joe Finger/Ken Dye. **Season:** Year-round. **To obtain tee times:** Call up to 30 days in advance. **Misc:** Reduced fees (weekdays, guests, twilight, juniors), range , credit cards (MC, V), BF, FF.
Reader Comments: Nicest staff, a great course, fun to play … Best value in bunch.

★★★ SHERMAN HILLS GOLF CLUB *Value*
PU-31200 Eagle Falls Dr., Brooksville, 34602, Hernando County, (352)544-0990, (866)743-7445, 30 miles from Tampa. **E-mail:** shgc@innet.com. **Web:** www.shermanhills.com. **Facility Holes:** 18. **Yards:** 6,778/4,959. **Par:** 72/72. **Course Rating:** 71.4/68.1. **Slope:** 130/117. **Green Fee:** $15/$30. **Cart Fee:** Included in green fee. **Walking Policy:** Mandatory carts. **Walkability:** 3. **Opened:** 1993. **Architect:** Ted McAnlis. **Season:** Year-round. **High:** Jan.-March. **To obtain tee times:** Call up to 7 days in advance. **Miscellaneous:** Reduced fees (weekdays, twilight, juniors), range (grass), credit cards (MC, V), BF, FF.
Reader Comments: Well-maintained, greens in excellent condition. Good layout … Good value … Very good, nice layout … Fast greens, wide-open front 9 … Half links, half woodlands, great value … Good test when windy, great prices.

★★½ SHOAL RIVER COUNTRY CLUB
SP-1100 Shoal River Dr., Crestview, 32539, Okaloosa County, (850)689-1010, 25 miles from

Fort Walton Beach. **Facility Holes:** 18. **Yards:** 6,782/5,183. **Par:** 72/72. **Course Rating:** 73.5/70.3. **Slope:** 136/124. **Green Fee:** $18. **Cart Fee:** $20/Person. **Walking Policy:** Walking at certain times. **Walkability:** 3. **Opened:** 1986. **Architect:** Dave Bennett. **Season:** Year-round. **High:** Jan.-March. **To obtain tee times:** Call golf shop. **Miscellaneous:** Reduced fees (weekdays, twilight, juniors), range (grass), credit cards (MC, V, AE, D), BF, FF.

★★½ SIGNAL HILL GOLF COURSE

PU-9615 N. Thomas Dr., Panama City Beach, 32407, Bay County, (850)234-5051, 10 miles from Panama City. **E-mail:** signal@signalhillgolfcourse.com. **Facility Holes:** 18. **Yards:** 5,617/4,790. **Par:** 71/71. **Course Rating:** 66.5/67.4. **Slope:** 118/107. **Green Fee:** $25/$40. **Cart Fee:** Included in green fee. **Walking Policy:** Unrestricted walking. **Walkability:** 2. **Opened:** 1962. **Architect:** John Henry Sherman. **Season:** Year-round. **To obtain tee times:** Call golf shop. **Miscellaneous:** Reduced fees (twilight), credit cards (MC, V), BF, FF.

★★ SILVER OAKS GOLF & COUNTRY CLUB

SP-36841 Clubhouse Dr., Zephyrhills, 33541, Pasco County, (813)788-1225, (800)853-4653, 20 miles from Tampa. **Web:** silveroaksgolf.com. **Facility Holes:** 27. **Yards:** 6,702/5,147. **Par:** 72/72. **Course Rating:** 72.5/68.8. **Slope:** 126/109. **Green Fee:** $10/$35. **Cart Fee:** Included in green fee. **Walking Policy:** Mandatory carts. **Walkability:** 2. **Opened:** 1988. **Architect:** Bob Simmons. **Season:** Year-round. **High:** Dec.-April. **To obtain tee times:** Call up to 7 days in advance. **Miscellaneous:** Reduced fees (weekdays, guests, twilight, seniors, juniors), range (grass), credit cards (MC, V), BF, FF.
Special Notes: Also has a 9-hole Replica Course.

★★★½ SILVERTHORN COUNTRY CLUB

SP-4550 Golf Club Lane, Brooksville, 34609, Hernando County, (352)799-2600, 65 miles from Tampa. **E-mail:** silverthorn@atlantic.net. **Facility Holes:** 18. **Yards:** 6,827/5,259. **Par:** 72/72. **Course Rating:** 72.3/70.4. **Slope:** 131/120. **Green Fee:** $32/$65. **Cart Fee:** Included in green fee. **Walking Policy:** Mandatory carts. **Walkability:** 3. **Opened:** 1995. **Architect:** Joe Lee. **Season:** Year-round. **High:** Nov.-May. **To obtain tee times:** Call up to 7 days in advance. **Miscellaneous:** Reduced fees (weekdays, twilight, juniors), range (grass), credit cards (MC, V, AE, D), BF, FF.
Reader Comments: Fantastic golf, beautiful ... Worth the drive. Excellent greens ... Good challenge, great staff & facility ... Worth playing ... Worth the money ... Nice track ... Excellent.

★★★★½ SOUTHERN DUNES GOLF & COUNTRY CLUB

PU-2888 Southern Dunes Blvd., Haines City, 33844, Polk County, (863)421-4653, (800)632-6400, 20 miles from Orlando. **E-mail:** shane@southerndunes.com. **Web:** www.southerndunes.com. **Facility Holes:** 18. **Yards:** 7,727/5,200. **Par:** 72/72. **Course Rating:** 74.7/72.4. **Slope:** 135/126. **Green Fee:** $35/$100. **Cart Fee:** Included in green fee. **Walking Policy:** Mandatory carts. **Walkability:** 3. **Opened:** 1993. **Architect:** Steve Smyers. **Season:** Year-round. **High:** Jan.-April. **To obtain tee times:** Call up to 30 days in advance. **Miscellaneous:** Reduced fees (weekdays, guests, twilight, juniors), range (grass/mats), credit cards (MC, V, AE, D), BF, FF.
Reader Comments: If you like sand, this is one for you ... Great challenge. Nothing like it in Florida. Love it ... Long and different ... A real find, don't tell anyone about this bargain ... Feel of links with hills, many bunkers ... Open, fair, fun.

★★ SOUTHWINDS GOLF COURSE

PU-19557 Lyons Rd., Boca Raton, 33434, Palm Beach County, (561)483-1305, 5 miles from Boca Raton. **Web:** www.affordablegolf.com. **Facility Holes:** 18. **Yards:** 6,029/4,453. **Par:** 70/70. **Course Rating:** 69.2/66.4. **Slope:** 129/118. **Green Fee:** $20/$47. **Cart Fee:** Included in green fee. **Walking Policy:** Walking at certain times. **Walkability:** 1. **Opened:** 1955. **Season:** Year-round. **To obtain tee times:** Call up to 4 days in advance. **Miscellaneous:** Reduced fees (twilight, juniors), range (mats), credit cards (MC, V), BF, FF.

★★ THE SPORTSMAN OF PERDIDO GOLF RESORT

R-One Doug Ford Dr., Pensacola, 32507, Escambia County, (850)492-1223, (866)319-2471. **Web:** www.sportsmanresort.com. **Facility Holes:** 18. **Yards:** 7,154/5,478. **Par:** 72/72. **Course Rating:** 74.2/69.4. **Slope:** 133/119. **Green Fee:** $25/$50. **Cart Fee:** $15/Person. **Walking Policy:** Walking at certain times. **Walkability:** 1. **Opened:** 1963. **Architect:** Bill Amick. **Season:** Year-round. **High:** Feb.-Aug. **To obtain tee times:** Call up to 7 days in advance. **Miscellaneous:** Reduced fees (twilight, juniors), range (grass), credit cards (MC, V, AE, D), BF, FF.

★★ SPRING HILL GOLF CLUB

SP-12079 Coronado Dr., Spring Hill, 34609, Hernando County, (352)683-2261, 35 miles from Tampa. **Facility Holes:** 18. **Yards:** 6,917/5,588. **Par:** 72/73. **Course Rating:** 73.0/71.8. **Slope:** 133/127. **Green Fee:** $11/$28. **Cart Fee:** Included in green fee. **Walking Policy:** Walking at certain times. **Walkability:** 3. **Opened:** 1969. **Architect:** David Wallace. **Season:** Year-round. **High:**

Sept.-March. **To obtain tee times:** Call up to 7 days in advance. **Miscellaneous:** Reduced fees (twilight), metal spikes, range (grass), credit cards (MC, V), FF.

★★½ SPRING LAKE GOLF & TENNIS RESORT
R-100 Clubhouse Lane, Sebring, 33876, Highlands County, (863)655-1276, (800)635-7277, 65 miles from Orlando. **E-mail:** slc@strato.net. **Web:** www.springlakegolf.com. **Facility Holes:** 36. **Green Fee:** $17/$36. **Cart Fee:** Included in green fee. **Walking Policy:** Walking at certain times. **Walkability:** 1. **Opened:** 1980. **Architect:** Michael Tellshow. **Season:** Year-round. **High:** Jan.-March. **To obtain tee times:** Call golf shop. **Miscellaneous:** Reduced fees (guests, twilight), metal spikes, range (grass/mats), lodging (120 rooms), credit cards (MC, V, AE, D), BF, FF.
EAGLE/HAWK (18)
Yards: 6,578/5,000. **Par:** 72/72. **Course Rating:** 71.8/68.8. **Slope:** 126/116.
HAWK/OSPREY (18)
Yards: 6,496/4,939. **Par:** 71/71. **Course Rating:** 71.3/68.4. **Slope:** 122/113.
OSPREY/EAGLE (18)
Yards: 6,272/4,973. **Par:** 71/71. **Course Rating:** 70.1/68.2. **Slope:** 121/113.
Special Notes: Also has a 9-hole executive course.

★★★½ SPRUCE CREEK COUNTRY CLUB
SP-1900 Country Club Dr., Daytona Beach, 32124, Volusia County, (386)756-6114, 45 miles from Orlando. **E-mail:** sccc24@bellsouth.net. **Web:** golfdaytonabeach.com. **Facility Holes:** 18. **Yards:** 6,894/5,176. **Par:** 72/72. **Course Rating:** 73.1/70.7. **Slope:** 128/123. **Green Fee:** $16/$50. **Cart Fee:** Included in green fee. **Walking Policy:** Mandatory carts. **Walkability:** 1. **Opened:** 1971. **Architect:** Bill Amick. **Season:** Year-round. **High:** Jan.-April. **To obtain tee times:** Call up to 4 days in advance. **Miscellaneous:** Reduced fees (weekdays, guests, twilight, juniors), range (grass), credit cards (MC, V), BF, FF.
Reader Comments: Very good condition, wide open, very forgiving. Tight, expansive medium fast greens ... Excellent, well-kept course ... Fun to play. Beautiful homes & scenery ... Fun to play, cost low ... Very good greens, fast pace of play.

★½ ST. AUGUSTINE SHORES GOLF CLUB
PU-707 Shores Blvd., St. Augustine, 32086, St. Johns County, (904)794-4653, 50 miles from Jacksonville. **Facility Holes:** 18. **Yards:** 5,719/4,151. **Par:** 71/71. **Course Rating:** 67.5/64.8. **Slope:** 112/106. **Green Fee:** $27/$29. **Cart Fee:** Included in green fee. **Walking Policy:** Walking at certain times. **Walkability:** 1. **Opened:** 1974. **Architect:** Chuck Almony. **Season:** Year-round. **To obtain tee times:** Call up to 5 days in advance. **Miscellaneous:** Reduced fees (twilight, juniors), range (grass/mats), credit cards (MC, V), BF, FF.

★★★ ST. JOHNS COUNTY GOLF CLUB
PU-4900 Cypress Links Blvd., Elkton, 32033, St. Johns County, (904)825-4900, 7 miles from St Augustine. **Facility Holes:** 18. **Yards:** 6,926/5,173. **Par:** 72/72. **Course Rating:** 72.9/68.8. **Slope:** 130/117. **Green Fee:** $17/$20. **Cart Fee:** $10/Person. **Walking Policy:** Walking at certain times. **Walkability:** 3. **Opened:** 1989. **Architect:** Robert Walker. **Season:** Year-round. **High:** Jan.-April. **To obtain tee times:** Call golf shop. **Miscellaneous:** Reduced fees (twilight), range (grass), credit cards (MC, V).
Reader Comments: Very nice course, well-maintained, nice clubhouse ... Very scenic, friendly staff ... Probably the best bargain in Fla., but play sometimes slow ... Great course ... Nice course, reasonable cost.

ST. JOHNS GOLF & COUNTRY CLUB
SP-205 St. Johns Golf Dr., St. Augustine, 32092, St. Johns County, (904)940-3200, (866)467-5422, 15 miles from Jacksonville. **E-mail:** emory-pater@aruida.com. **Web:** www.aruida.com. **Facility Holes:** 18. **Yards:** 7,236/5,286. **Par:** 72/72. **Course Rating:** 75.3/70.8. **Slope:** 142/123. **Green Fee:** $45/$80. **Cart Fee:** Included in green fee. **Walking Policy:** Walking at certain times. **Walkability:** 2. **Opened:** 2001. **Architect:** Clyde Johnston. **Season:** Year-round. **High:** March-May. **To obtain tee times:** Call up to 7 days in advance. **Miscellaneous:** Reduced fees (weekdays, twilight), range (grass/mats), credit cards (MC, V, AE, D), BF, FF.

STONEGATE GOLF CLUB AT SOLIVITA
SP-404 Village Dr., Poinciana, 34759, Polk County, (863)427-7150, 10 miles from Orlando. **Web:** solivita.com. **Facility Holes:** 18. **Yards:** 7,011/5,285. **Par:** 72/72. **Course Rating:** 73.3/70.2. **Slope:** 131/113. **Green Fee:** $29/$85. **Cart Fee:** Included in green fee. **Walking Policy:** Mandatory carts. **Walkability:** 2. **Opened:** 2000. **Architect:** Ron Garl. **Season:** Year-round. **To obtain tee times:** Call up to 14 days in advance. **Miscellaneous:** Reduced fees (twilight, seniors, juniors), range (grass), credit cards (MC, V, AE, D), BF, FF.

STONEY BROOK WEST GOLF CLUB
PU-15501 Towne Commons Blvd., Winter Garden, 34787, Orange County, (407)877-7533,

13 miles from Orlando. **E-mail:** info@stoneybrookgolf.com. **Web:** www.stoneybrookgolf.com. **Facility Holes:** 18. **Yards:** 7,101/5,173. **Par:** 72/72. **Course Rating:** 74.8/70.1. **Slope:** 135/117. **Green Fee:** $27/$80. **Cart Fee:** Included in green fee. **Walking Policy:** Mandatory carts. **Walkability:** 2. **Opened:** 2000. **Architect:** Arthur Hills. **Season:** Year-round. **High:** Jan.-Aug. **To obtain tee times:** Call up to 7 days in advance. **Miscellaneous:** Reduced fees (weekdays, twilight, seniors, juniors), range (grass), credit cards (MC, V, AE), BF, FF.

★★★ STONEYBROOK GOLF & COUNTRY CLUB
SP-8801 Stoneybrook Blvd., Sarasota, 34238, Sarasota County, (941)966-1800, 50 miles from Tampa. **Facility Holes:** 18. **Yards:** 6,561/4,984. **Par:** 72/72. **Course Rating:** 72.0/69.4. **Slope:** 133/119. **Green Fee:** $35/$70. **Cart Fee:** Included in green fee. **Walking Policy:** Mandatory carts. **Walkability:** 2. **Opened:** 1994. **Architect:** Arthur Hills. **Season:** Year-round. **High:** Nov.-April. **To obtain tee times:** Call golf shop. **Miscellaneous:** Range (grass), credit cards (MC, V), BF, FF.
Reader Comments: Outstanding! Best course in Florida ... Too many houses on course ... Overall good experience ... Mostly for residents, tough tee time ... Average layout & design ... A solid course.

STONEYBROOK GOLF CLUB
PU-21251 Stoneybrook Golf Blvd., Estero, 33928, Lee County, (941)948-3933, 6 miles from Fort Myers. **Facility Holes:** 18. **Yards:** 7,353/4,672. **Par:** 72/72. **Course Rating:** 75.8/67.0. **Slope:** 141/115. **Green Fee:** $5/$45. **Cart Fee:** $15/Person. **Walking Policy:** Mandatory carts. **Walkability:** 2. **Opened:** 1999. **Architect:** Gordon Lewis/Jed Azinger. **Season:** Year-round. **High:** Jan.-May. **To obtain tee times:** Call up to 7 days in advance. **Miscellaneous:** Reduced fees (twilight, juniors), range (grass), credit cards (MC, V), BF, FF.

★★★ SUMMERFIELD GOLF CLUB
PU-13050 Summerfield Blvd., Riverview, 33569, Hillsborough County, (813)671-3311, 15 miles from Tampa. **Facility Holes:** 18. **Yards:** 6,903/5,139. **Par:** 71/71. **Course Rating:** 73.0/69.6. **Slope:** 125/114. **Green Fee:** $10/$43. **Cart Fee:** $16/Person. **Walking Policy:** Mandatory carts. **Walkability:** 2. **Opened:** 1986. **Architect:** Ron Garl. **Season:** Year-round. **High:** Jan.-April. **To obtain tee times:** Call up to 7 days in advance. **Miscellaneous:** Reduced fees (twilight), range (grass), credit cards (MC, V, AE, D, DC), BF, FF.
Reader Comments: Lots of waiting ... Good staff makes it fun. Needs maintenance ... Reasonable rates in the summertime ... Links-style course, very windy.

★½ SUNRISE COUNTRY CLUB
SP-7400 N.W. 24th Place, Sunrise, 33313, Broward County, (954)742-4333, 7 miles from Fort Lauderdale. **Facility Holes:** 18. **Yards:** 6,624/5,317. **Par:** 72/72. **Course Rating:** 71.8/69.8. **Slope:** 126/119. **Green Fee:** $25/$45. **Cart Fee:** Included in green fee. **Walking Policy:** Mandatory carts. **Walkability:** 1. **Opened:** 1959. **Architect:** Bill Watts. **Season:** Year-round. **To obtain tee times:** Call up to 7 days in advance. **Miscellaneous:** Reduced fees (twilight), range (grass), credit cards (MC, V, AE), BF, FF.

★★★ SUNRISE GOLF CLUB
SP-5710 Draw Lane, Sarasota, 34238, Sarasota County, (941)924-1402. **Facility Holes:** 18. **Yards:** 6,455/5,271. **Par:** 72/72. **Course Rating:** 70.6/69.3. **Slope:** 122/117. **Green Fee:** $19/$47. **Cart Fee:** Included in green fee. **Walking Policy:** Walking at certain times. **Walkability:** 2. **Opened:** 1970. **Architect:** Andy Anderson. **Season:** Year-round. **High:** Jan.-April. **To obtain tee times:** Call golf shop. **Miscellaneous:** Reduced fees (twilight, juniors), metal spikes, range (grass), credit cards (MC, V, AE, D).
Reader Comments: Very nice ... Some of the best greens around ... Nice layout ... Fair, but not very interesting ... Flat.

★★ TANGLEWOOD GOLF & COUNTRY CLUB
PU-5916 Tanglewood Dr., Milton, 32570, Santa Rosa County, (904)623-6176, 10 miles from Pensacola. **E-mail:** tanglewoodgolf@aol.com. **Web:** www.tanglewoodgolf.com. **Facility Holes:** 18. **Yards:** 6,455/5,295. **Par:** 72/72. **Course Rating:** 70.0/69.9. **Slope:** 115/118. **Green Fee:** $20/$23. **Walking Policy:** Unrestricted walking. **Walkability:** 1. **Opened:** 1964. **Season:** Year-round. **To obtain tee times:** Call up to 4 days in advance. **Miscellaneous:** Reduced fees (seniors), range (grass), credit cards (MC, V, AE, D), FF.

★★ TARPON SPRINGS GOLF CLUB
PU-1310 Pinellas Ave., S. (Alt. 19), Tarpon Springs, 34689, Pinellas County, (727)937-6906, 25 miles from Tampa. **Facility Holes:** 18. **Yards:** 6,156/5,338. **Par:** 72/72. **Course Rating:** 68.9/71.5. **Slope:** 112/110. **Green Fee:** $20/$25. **Walking Policy:** Walking at certain times. **Walkability:** 2. **Opened:** 1927. **Architect:** John Van Kleek/Wayne Stiles. **Season:** Year-round. **High:** Dec.-May. **To obtain tee times:** Call up to 3 days in advance. **Miscellaneous:** Reduced fees (twilight), metal spikes, range (grass), credit cards (MC, V), BF, FF.

FLORIDA

★★½ TATUM RIDGE GOLF LINKS
SP-421 N. Tatum Rd., Sarasota, 34240, Sarasota County, (941)378-4211, 55 miles from Tampa. **E-mail:** tatumridgegolf@aol.com. **Facility Holes:** 18. **Yards:** 6,757/5,149. **Par:** 72/72. **Course Rating:** 71.9/68.9. **Slope:** 124/114. **Green Fee:** $17/$52. **Cart Fee:** Included in green fee. **Walking Policy:** Mandatory carts. **Walkability:** 1. **Opened:** 1989. **Architect:** Ted McAnlis. **Season:** Year-round. **High:** Nov.-April. **To obtain tee times:** Call golf shop. **Miscellaneous:** Reduced fees (seniors), range (grass), credit cards (MC, V), BF, FF.

★★★★½ TIBURON GOLF CLUB *Condition+, Pace*
R-2620 Tiburon Dr., Naples, 34109, Collier County, (941)594-2040, (888)387-8417, 12 miles from Fort Myers. **E-mail:** bobradunz@wcicommunities.com. **Web:** www.wcigolf.com. **Facility Holes:** 27. **Green Fee:** $55/$215. **Cart Fee:** Included in green fee. **Walking Policy:** Mandatory carts. **Walkability:** 2. **Opened:** 1998. **Architect:** Greg Norman. **Season:** Year-round. **High:** Jan.-April. **To obtain tee times:** Call up to 60 days in advance. **Misc:** Reduced fees (guests, twilight, juniors), range (grass), lodging (463 rooms), credit cards (MC, V, AE), BF, FF.
NORTH/SOUTH (18 combo)
Yards: 7,170/5,140. **Par:** 72/72. **Course Rating:** 74.5/70.6. **Slope:** 137/124.
NORTH/WEST (18 combo)
Yards: 7,193/5,148. **Par:** 72/72. **Course Rating:** 74.5/69.6. **Slope:** 135/122.
WEST/SOUTH (18 combo)
Yards: 6,977/4,988. **Par:** 72/72. **Course Rating:** 73.4/70.4. **Slope:** 131/123.
Reader Comments: Great services, excellent condition, and unique layout. No rough, but marshes abound ... Excellent conditions, beautifully manicured ... Tight and narrow ... You either love it, hate it ... Very good but very expensive.

TIGER POINT GOLF & COUNTRY CLUB
SP-1255 Country Club Rd., Gulf Breeze, 32561, Santa Rosa County, (850)932-1333, (888)218-8463, 15 miles from Pensacola. **Web:** www.mggi.com. **Facility Holes:** 36. **Cart Fee:** Included in green fee. **Walking Policy:** Mandatory carts. **Season:** Year-round. **High:** Jan.-April. **To obtain tee times:** Call up to 7 days in advance. **Miscellaneous:** Reduced fees (weekdays, twilight), range (grass), credit cards (MC, V, AE, Lung Card & Golf Card), BF, FF.
★★★ EAST COURSE (18)
Yards: 7,033/5,217. **Par:** 72/72. **Course Rating:** 74.2/70.8. **Slope:** 141/125. **Green Fee:** $38/$70. **Walkability:** 2. **Opened:** 1979. **Architect:** B. Amick/R. Garl/J. Pate.
Reader Comments: Many holes where you could risk as much as you dared off tee. Very reasonable ... Older resort. Price is high.
★★★ WEST COURSE (18)
Yards: 6,737/5,314. **Par:** 71/72. **Course Rating:** 72.9/71.3. **Slope:** 138/123. **Green Fee:** $30/$49. **Walkability:** 3. **Opened:** 1965. **Architect:** Bill Amick.
Reader Comments: Slightly easier than East Course. Very reasonable ... Nice along the bay ... Save your $ ... Long and challenging. Good course.

★★★½ TIMACUAN GOLF & COUNTRY CLUB
SP-550 Timacuan Blvd., Lake Mary, 32746, Seminole County, (407)321-0010, (888)955-1234, 15 miles from Orlando. **Facility Holes:** 18. **Yards:** 6,915/4,576. **Par:** 71/71. **Course Rating:** 73.2/66.8. **Slope:** 133/118. **Green Fee:** $40/$94. **Cart Fee:** Included in green fee. **Walking Policy:** Mandatory carts. **Walkability:** 3. **Opened:** 1987. **Architect:** Ron Garl/Bobby Weed. **Season:** Year-round. **High:** Jan.-April. **To obtain tee times:** Call up to 5 days in advance. **Miscellaneous:** Reduced fees (weekdays, guests, twilight), range (grass), credit cards (MC, V, AE), BF, FF.
Reader Comments: Excellent, but busy. Variety of holes, strategic thinking called for ... Good course, condition & layout good ... Great driving course, water can be managed ...A course with character ... Hilly, tough test, playable.

★★★ TOMOKA OAKS GOLF & COUNTRY CLUB
SP-20 Tomoka Oaks Blvd., Ormond Beach, 32174, Volusia County, (904)677-7117, 5 miles from Daytona Beach. **E-mail:** sryals8572@aol.com. **Facility Holes:** 18. **Yards:** 6,745/5,385. **Par:** 72/72. **Course Rating:** 72.0/71.4. **Slope:** 131/124. **Green Fee:** $25/$32. **Cart Fee:** Included in green fee. **Walking Policy:** Walking at certain times. **Walkability:** 2. **Opened:** 1962. **Architect:** J. Porter Gibson. **Season:** Year-round. **High:** Jan.-April. **To obtain tee times:** Call golf shop. **Miscellaneous:** Reduced fees (twilight, juniors), range (grass), credit cards (MC, V, AE, D), BF, FF.
Reader Comments: Available, some good holes ... Doglegs galore. Fun course, lots of trees ... Extremely heavy play, lots of trees ... Good course, good condition, good staff.

★★★★ TOURNAMENT PLAYERS CLUB AT HERON BAY *Service, Pace*
PU-11801 Heron Bay Blvd., Coral Springs, 33076, Broward County, (954)796-2000, (800)511-6616, 20 miles from Fort Lauderdale. **E-mail:** tpchb@aol.com. **Web:** www.pgatour.com. **Facility Holes:** 18. **Yards:** 7,268/4,961. **Par:** 72/72. **Course Rating:**

74.9/68.7. **Slope:** 133/113. **Green Fee:** $59/$110. **Cart Fee:** Included in green fee. **Walking Policy:** Unrestricted walking. **Walkability:** 3. **Opened:** 1996. **Architect:** Mark McCumber/Mike Beebe. **Season:** Year-round. **High:** Dec.-April. **To obtain tee times:** Call golf shop. **Miscellaneous:** Reduced fees (weekdays, twilight, juniors), metal spikes, range (grass), lodging (224 rooms), credit cards (MC, V, AE, Diners Club).
Reader Comments: Wide open, long, lots of sand ... No wind = no challenge, sand play a must, needs to mature ... Expensive, but worth it ... Needs time to grow in.

TOURNAMENT PLAYERS CLUB AT SAWGRASS
R-110 TPC Blvd., Ponte Vedra Beach, 32082, St. Johns County, (904)273-3235, 15 miles from Jacksonville. **E-mail:** 4/20/2001. **Web:** www.pgatour.com. **Facility Holes:** 36. **Cart Fee:** $28/Person. **Walking Policy:** Walking with Caddie. **Season:** Year-round. **High:** Feb.-May. **To obtain tee times:** Call golf shop. **Miscellaneous:** Reduced fees (juniors), range (grass), lodging (515 rooms), credit cards (MC, V, AE, DC, Resort Charge).
★★★★½ **STADIUM COURSE** (18) *Condition, Pace*
Yards: 6,937/5,000. **Par:** 72/72. **Course Rating:** 73.3/64.9. **Slope:** 138/120. **Green Fee:** $110/$265. **Walkability:** 3. **Opened:** 1980. **Architect:** Pete Dye.
Notes: Ranked 63rd in 2001-2002 America's 100 Greatest; 2nd in 2001 Best in State.
Reader Comments: Women's tees are extraordinarily well-placed ... Keep it in the middle or else ... Golf heaven. Perfect ... Playable if you select the correct tees ... Pricey, when greens are slick, forget it ... Best greens, very expensive.
★★★★ **VALLEY COURSE** (18) *Pace*
Yards: 6,864/5,126. **Par:** 72/72. **Course Rating:** 72.8/68.7. **Slope:** 130/120. **Green Fee:** $80/$135. **Walkability:** 4. **Opened:** 1987. **Architect:** Pete Dye/Bobby Weed.
Reader Comments: Tough from the tips ... Nice course, but not what you'd expect at TPC ... Pricey, as tricky as Stadium ... Fun to play ... Felt like I was playing the same hole over and over ... Lots of water.

★★★★ **TOURNAMENT PLAYERS CLUB OF TAMPA BAY** *Service, Pace*
PU-5300 W. Lutz Lake Fern Rd., Lutz, 33549, Hillsborough County, (813)949-0090, 15 miles from Tampa. **E-mail:** lapp@pgatourtpc.com. **Web:** www.playatpc.com. **Facility Holes:** 18.
Yards: 6,898/5,036. **Par:** 71/71. **Course Rating:** 73.4/69.1. **Slope:** 130/119. **Green Fee:** $71/$136. **Cart Fee:** Included in green fee. **Walking Policy:** Mandatory carts. **Walkability:** 3. **Opened:** 1991. **Architect:** Bobby Weed/Chi Chi Rodriguez. **Season:** Year-round. **High:** Jan.-March. **To obtain tee times:** Call golf shop. **Miscellaneous:** Reduced fees (weekdays, twilight, juniors), range (grass), credit cards (MC, V, AE, DC), BF, FF.
Reader Comments: Greens were fun & real fast ... Great design ... Beautiful course ... Not worth it ... Great design, fast greens, good challenge ... Nice layout, very classy ... Lots of water off the tee ... This is ultimate golf.

TURNBERRY ISLE RESORT & CLUB
R-19999 W. Country Club Dr., Aventura, 33180, Dade County, (305)933-6929, (800)327-7208, 10 miles from Fort Lauderdale. **Web:** www.turnberryisle.com. **Facility Holes:** 36. **Green Fee:** $65/$105. **Cart Fee:** $21/Person. **Walking Policy:** Mandatory carts. **Walkability:** 2. **Opened:** 1971. **Architect:** Robert Trent Jones. **Season:** Year-round. **To obtain tee times:** Call up to 60 days in advance. **Miscellaneous:** Reduced fees (twilight), range (grass/mats), lodging (395 rooms), credit cards (MC, V, AE), BF, FF.
★★★★ **NORTH COURSE** (18)
Yards: 6,348/4,991. **Par:** 70/70. **Course Rating:** 70.3/67.9. **Slope:** 127/107.
Reader Comments: Course in good shape, pace of play slow ... Great course, overpriced ... Great resort course, excellent service ... Great layout.
★★★★½ **SOUTH COURSE** (18)
Yards: 7,003/5,581. **Par:** 72/72. **Course Rating:** 73.7/71.3. **Slope:** 136/116.
Reader Comments: Great place to play golf, great rates ... Great resort course, excellent service.

★★★ TURNBULL BAY GOLF COURSE
SP-2600 Turnbull Estates Dr., New Smyrna Beach, 32168, Volusia County, (386)427-8727, 2 miles from New Smyrna Beach. **Web:** www.turnbullbaygolfcourse.com. **Facility Holes:** 18.
Yards: 6,400/4,836. **Par:** 72/72. **Course Rating:** 71.6/68.6. **Slope:** 129/119. **Green Fee:** $28/$45. **Cart Fee:** Included in green fee. **Walking Policy:** Mandatory carts. **Walkability:** 2. **Opened:** 1995. **Architect:** Gary Wintz. **Season:** Year-round. **High:** Jan.-April. **To obtain tee times:** Call up to 4 days in advance. **Miscellaneous:** Reduced fees (twilight), range (grass), credit cards (MC, V).
Reader Comments: Excellent condition, well-managed, great service, greens not receptive to good shots ... Tight, real tight ... Good layout, poor condition.

★★★ TURTLE CREEK GOLF CLUB
PU-1278 Admiralty Blvd., Rockledge, 32955, Brevard County, (321)638-0603, 35 miles from Orlando. **E-mail:** turtlecreekgc@yahoo.com. **Web:** www.turtlecreekgolfclub.com. **Facility**

Holes: 18. **Yards:** 6,709/4,880. **Par:** 72/72. **Course Rating:** 70.1/68.8. **Slope:** 129/113. **Green Fee:** $20/$54. **Cart Fee:** Included in green fee. **Walking Policy:** Mandatory carts. **Walkability:** 1. **Opened:** 1970. **Architect:** Robert Renaud. **Season:** Year-round. **High:** Jan.-March. **To obtain tee times:** Call up to 7 days in advance. **Miscellaneous:** Reduced fees (weekdays, twilight, juniors), range (grass/mats), credit cards (MC, V, AE), BF, FF.
Reader Comments: Only downside is that it is surrounded by housing, but the course is in great shape, with excellent greens, perhaps a bit fast. Water on many holes, and very sporty ... Great narrow course with water on almost every hole.

★★★ TWIN RIVERS GOLF CLUB
SP-2100 Ekana Dr., Oviedo, 32765, Seminole County, (407)366-1211, 10 miles from Orlando. **E-mail:** dmoore@mggi.com. **Facility Holes:** 18. **Yards:** 6,683/5,544. **Par:** 72/72. **Course Rating:** 72.0/72.1. **Slope:** 130/128. **Green Fee:** $22/$60. **Walking Policy:** Mandatory carts. **Walkability:** 3. **Opened:** 1989. **Architect:** Joe Lee. **Season:** Year-round. **High:** Dec.-March. **To obtain tee times:** Call golf shop. **Miscellaneous:** Reduced fees (weekdays, twilight), range (grass), credit cards (MC, V), BF, FF.
Reader Comments: Fun public course, great layout, gets crowded ... Needs a facelift ... Worth playing ... Some areas could use some work.

★★★ TWISTED OAKS GOLF CLUB
PU-4545 Forest Ridge Blvd., Beverly Hills, 34465, Citrus County, (352)746-6257, 60 miles from Tampa. **Facility Holes:** 18. **Yards:** 6,876/4,641. **Par:** 72/72. **Course Rating:** 72.9/66.5. **Slope:** 126/114. **Green Fee:** $18/$40. **Cart Fee:** Included in green fee. **Walking Policy:** Mandatory carts. **Walkability:** 2. **Opened:** 1990. **Architect:** Karl Litten. **Season:** Year-round. **High:** Nov.-May. **To obtain tee times:** Call up to 7 days in advance. **Miscellaneous:** Reduced fees (twilight), range (grass), credit cards (MC, V, D), BF, FF.
Reader Comments: Good value ... Good, hilly course ... Course isn't bad but pace of play is ridiculous ... Great value with layout & condition ... Great value ... Nice layout, elevation changes, greens OK, good $$ ... Great shape.

★★½ UNIVERSITY OF SOUTH FLORIDA GOLF COURSE
PU-13801 N. 46th Street, Tampa, 33612, Hillsborough County, (813)632-6893, 8 miles from Tampa. **E-mail:** cbruno@admin.usf.edu. **Web:** www.usfgolf.com. **Facility Holes:** 18. **Yards:** 6,876/5,353. **Par:** 71/71. **Course Rating:** 74.2/70.9. **Slope:** 132/115. **Green Fee:** $16/$40. **Cart Fee:** $13/Person. **Walking Policy:** Unrestricted walking. **Walkability:** 1. **Opened:** 1967. **Architect:** William F. Mitchell. **Season:** Year-round. **High:** Nov.-April. **To obtain tee times:** Call golf shop. **Miscellaneous:** Reduced fees (weekdays, twilight, seniors, juniors), metal spikes, range (grass/mats), credit cards (MC, V), BF, FF.

★★★★ UNIVERSITY PARK COUNTRY CLUB
SP-7671 Park Blvd., University Park, 34201, Manatee County, (941)359-9999, 1 mile from Sarasota. **E-mail:** mclayton@universitypark-fl.com. **Facility Holes:** 27. **Green Fee:** $50/$100. **Cart Fee:** Included in green fee. **Walking Policy:** Walking at certain times. **Walkability:** 1. **Opened:** 1991. **Architect:** Ron Garl. **Season:** Year-round. **High:** Nov.-April. **To obtain tee times:** Call up to 3 days in advance. **Miscellaneous:** Reduced fees (weekdays, twilight), range (grass/mats), credit cards (MC, V, D), BF, FF.
COURSE 1 & 19 (18 Combo)
Yards: 7,247/5,576. **Par:** 72/72. **Course Rating:** 74.4/71.8. **Slope:** 132/122.
COURSE 10 & 1 (18 Combo)
Yards: 7,001/5,511. **Par:** 72/72. **Course Rating:** 73.6/71.6. **Slope:** 138/126.
COURSE 19 & 10 (18 Combo)
Yards: 7,152/5,695. **Par:** 72/72. **Course Rating:** 74.0/72.4. **Slope:** 134/124.
Reader Comments: A bit expensive, but worth it ... Truly one of the top courses in the state ... Beautiful ... Good golf course, overrated ... Play original 18, skip new 9 ... Superb organization ... Excellent course but pricey.

★★★½ VALENCIA GOLF COURSE AT ORANGETREE
PU-1725 Double Eagle Trail, Naples, 34120, Collier County, (941)352-0777, 10 miles from Naples. **Facility Holes:** 18. **Yards:** 7,145/4,786. **Par:** 72/72. **Course Rating:** 74.3/67.4. **Slope:** 130/113. **Green Fee:** $20/$55. **Cart Fee:** $15/Person. **Walking Policy:** Walking at certain times. **Walkability:** 1. **Opened:** 1997. **Architect:** Gordon Lewis. **Season:** Year-round. **High:** Dec.-May. **To obtain tee times:** Call golf shop. **Miscellaneous:** Reduced fees (juniors), range (grass), credit cards (MC, V, D).
Reader Comments: Too much money ... High-handicappers will love this one ... Gulf Coast gem, residential development has not ruined layout.

★★★★ VIERA EAST GOLF CLUB
PU-2300 Clubhouse Dr., Viera, 32955, Brevard County, (407)639-6500, (888)843-7232, 5 miles from Melbourne. **E-mail:** golf@vieragolf.com. **Web:** www.vieragolf.com. **Facility Holes:**

18. Yards: 6,720/5,428. **Par:** 72/72. **Course Rating:** 72.1/71.0. **Slope:** 129/122. **Green Fee:** $24/$59. **Cart Fee:** Included in green fee. **Walking Policy:** Walking at certain times. **Walkability:** 1. **Opened:** 1994. **Architect:** Joe Lee. **Season:** Year-round. **High:** Jan.-April. **To obtain tee times:** Call up to 7 days in advance. **Miscellaneous:** Reduced fees (guests, twilight, juniors), range (grass), credit cards (MC, V, AE, D), BF, FF.
Reader Comments: Long course … Great condition, good price … Great value, great shape, lots of challenging holes … Greens usually good, though fast. Fairways rather generous. Pace of play usually good.

★★½ **THE VILLAGE GOLF CLUB**
PU-122 Country Club Dr., Royal Palm Beach, 33411, Palm Beach County, (561)793-1400, 1 mile from Royal Palm Beach. **E-mail:** villagegolf@aol.com. **Facility Holes:** 18. **Yards:** 6,883/5,455. **Par:** 72/72. **Course Rating:** 73.3/71.7. **Slope:** 134/126. **Green Fee:** $24/$50. **Cart Fee:** Included in green fee. **Opened:** 1971. **Season:** Year-round. **High:** Nov.-April. **To obtain tee times:** Call golf shop. **Miscellaneous:** Metal spikes, range (grass), credit cards (MC, V, AE, D).

THE VILLAGES HACIENDA HILLS GOLF & COUNTRY CLUB
SP-1200 Morse Blvd., The Villages, 32159, Sumter County, (352)753-5155, 50 miles from Orlando. **E-mail:** greenb@villages.com. **Facility Holes:** 27. **Green Fee:** $17/$42. **Cart Fee:** Included in green fee. **Walking Policy:** Unrestricted walking. **Walkability:** 3. **Opened:** 1990. **Architect:** Clifton/Ezell/Clifton. **Season:** Year-round. **High:** Nov.-April. **To obtain tee times:** Call golf shop. **Miscellaneous:** Reduced fees (guests, twilight), metal spikes, range (grass/mats), credit cards (MC, V, AE).
LAKES/OAKS (18 Combo)
Yards: 6,417/5,224. **Par:** 72/72. **Course Rating:** 70.4/65.1. **Slope:** 115/112.
OAKS/PALMS (18 Combo)
Yards: 6,365/5,230. **Par:** 72/72. **Course Rating:** 69.7/65.2. **Slope:** 122/109.
PALMS/LAKES (18 Combo)
Yards: 6,446/5,220. **Par:** 72/72. **Course Rating:** 69.9/64.9. **Slope:** 121/107.

WALDEN LAKES GOLF & COUNTRY CLUB
SP-2001 Clubhouse Dr., Plant City, 33567, Hillsborough County, (813)754-8575, (888)218-8463, 20 miles from Tampa. **E-mail:** chendrick@mggi.com. **Web:** www.walden-lakecc.com. **Facility Holes:** 36. **Green Fee:** $25/$50. **Cart Fee:** Included in green fee. **Walking Policy:** Mandatory carts. **Walkability:** 2. **Opened:** 1977. **Architect:** Garl/Cupp/Morrish/Nicklaus. **Season:** Year-round. **High:** Nov.-May. **To obtain tee times:** Call up to 7 days in advance. **Misc:** Reduced fees (weekdays, twilight), range (grass), credit cards (MC, V, AE), BF, FF.
★★★ **HILLS COURSE** (18)
Yards: 6,610/4,800. **Par:** 72/72. **Course Rating:** 71.5/68.6. **Slope:** 131/120.
Reader Comments: Factors vary with season … Fast greens! Lots of hills.
LAKES COURSE (18)
Yards: 6,561/4,953. **Par:** 72/72. **Course Rating:** 72.0/70.5. **Slope:** 132/124.

WALT DISNEY WORLD RESORT
R-3451 Golf View Dr., Lake Buena Vista, 32830, Orange County, (407)939-4653, 20 miles from Orlando Airport. **Web:** www.disney.go.com/disneyworld. **Facility Holes:** 99. **Season:** Year-round. **High:** Jan.-April. **To obtain tee times:** Call golf shop. **Miscellaneous:** Reduced fees (guests, twilight), metal spikes, range (grass/mats), credit cards (MC, V, AE, D, DC, The Disney Card).
★★★★½ **EAGLE PINES GOLF COURSE** (18) *Condition*
Yards: 6,772/4,838. **Par:** 72/72. **Course Rating:** 72.3/68.0. **Slope:** 131/111. **Green Fee:** $100/$140. **Cart Fee:** Included in green fee. **Opened:** 1992. **Architect:** Pete Dye.
Reader Comments: Very playable … Difficult for average golfer, many long carries … Enjoyable in all areas … Challenging but fair … Excellent, great condition, best of Disney courses … Friendly, well-maintained. Great for family.
★★★★ **LAKE BUENA VISTA GOLF COURSE** (18)
Yards: 6,819/5,194. **Par:** 72/73. **Course Rating:** 72.7/69.4. **Slope:** 128/120. **Green Fee:** $90/$120. **Cart Fee:** Included in green fee. **Walking Policy:** Walking at certain times. **Walkability:** 1. **Opened:** 1972. **Architect:** Joe Lee.
Reader Comments: Fun to play … Paid more, but worth it … Typical Disney—great service, a little pricey … Long & tough … No character … A great course … Like all Disney courses, great shape, great staff, always fun.
★★★★ **MAGNOLIA GOLF COURSE** (18)
Yards: 7,190/5,232. **Par:** 72/72. **Course Rating:** 73.9/70.5. **Slope:** 133/123. **Green Fee:** $90/$120. **Cart Fee:** Included in green fee. **Walkability:** 1. **Opened:** 1971. **Architect:** Joe Lee.
Reader Comments: Typical Disney, good condition … I expected standard resort golf. This is first-class … Leave kids at the park and have a great time … Expected more from Disney … Good value, friendly staff … Great for family vacations.
★★★½ **OAK TRAIL GOLF COURSE** (9)
Yards: 2,913/2,532. **Par:** 36/36. **Walking Policy:** Unrestricted walking. **Walkability:** 2. **Opened:**

1971. **Architect:** Ron Garl/Larry Kanphaus.
Reader Comments: Always in good condition … Great walk approaching sunset.

★★★★½ **OSPREY RIDGE GOLF COURSE** (18) *Condition*
Yards: 7,101/5,402. **Par:** 72/72. **Course Rating:** 73.9/70.5. **Slope:** 135/122. **Green Fee:** $100/$140. **Cart Fee:** Included in green fee. **Walkability:** 4. **Opened:** 1992. **Architect:** Tom Fazio.
Reader Comments: Disney knows how to treat guests and it shows … Best of Disney courses … Everything was outstanding … Excellent resort course … Not my first choice … My long-standing favorite Disney course … Last 3 holes are tough.

★★★★ **PALM GOLF COURSE** (18)
Yards: 6,957/5,311. **Par:** 72/72. **Course Rating:** 73.0/70.4. **Slope:** 133/124. **Green Fee:** $90/$120. **Cart Fee:** Included in green fee. **Opened:** 1971. **Architect:** Joe Lee.
Reader Comments: Excellent resort course … Able to use military discount, great experience … Nice flat course, rough could be higher … Traditional with well-placed traps … Unable to finish, took more than 5 hours.

★★★ **WATERFORD GOLF CLUB**
SP-1454 Gleneagles Dr., Venice, 34292, Sarasota County, (941)484-6621, 11 miles from Sarasota. **Facility Holes:** 27. **Green Fee:** $25/$55. **Cart Fee:** Included in green fee. **Walking Policy:** Walking at certain times. **Opened:** 1989. **Architect:** Ted McAnlis. **Season:** Year-round. **To obtain tee times:** Call up to 2 days in advance. **Miscellaneous:** Reduced fees (twilight), range (grass/mats), credit cards (MC, V), FF.
GLENEAGLES/SAWGRASS COURSE (18 Combo)
Yards: 6,498/4,998. **Par:** 72/72. **Course Rating:** 71.4/68.6. **Slope:** 124/115. **Walkability:** 2.
GLENEAGLES/TURNBERRY COURSE (18 Combo)
Yards: 6,504/5,168. **Par:** 72/72. **Course Rating:** 71.5/69.4. **Slope:** 126/115. **Walkability:** 2.
TURNBERRY/SAWGRASS COURSE (18 Combo)
Yards: 6,670/5,124. **Par:** 72/72. **Course Rating:** 72.3/69.2. **Slope:** 128/115. **Walkability:** 1.
Reader Comments: Very friendly, fun holes, lots of water … Nice surprise … Very good value.

★★★★ **WATERLEFE GOLF & RIVER CLUB**
PU-1022 Fish Hook Cove, Bradenton, 34202, Manatee County, 941-744-9771, 40 miles from Tampa. **E-mail:** waterlefegolfclub@wcicommunities.com. **Web:** www.wcigolf.com. **Facility Holes:** 18. **Yards:** 6,908/4,770. **Par:** 72/72. **Course Rating:** 73.8/68.0. **Slope:** 141/119. **Green Fee:** $30/$85. **Cart Fee:** Included in green fee. **Walking Policy:** Walking at certain times. **Walkability:** 2. **Opened:** 2000. **Architect:** Ted McAnlis. **Season:** Year-round. **High:** Jan.-May. **To obtain tee times:** Call up to 7 days in advance. **Miscellaneous:** Reduced fees (weekdays), range (grass), credit cards (MC, V, AE), BF, FF.
Reader Comments: Best in Florida … Fun! Last holes terrific … Very attractive, fair course you can walk … Outstanding, has more character and beauty than any course I've played on Florida.

★½ **WEDGEWOOD GOLF & COUNTRY CLUB**
SP-401 Carpenter's Way, Lakeland, 33809, Polk County, (863)858-4451, 25 miles from Tampa. **Facility Holes:** 18. **Yards:** 6,402/4,885. **Par:** 70/70. **Course Rating:** 69.1/68.1. **Slope:** 115/113. **Green Fee:** $18/$25. **Cart Fee:** Included in green fee. **Walking Policy:** Mandatory carts. **Walkability:** 3. **Opened:** 1984. **Architect:** Ron Garl. **Season:** Year-round. **High:** Dec.-April. **To obtain tee times:** Call golf shop. **Miscellaneous:** Reduced fees (weekdays, twilight), range (grass), credit cards (MC, V, AE), BF, FF.

★★★ **WEST PALM BEACH MUNICIPAL COUNTRY CLUB**
PU-7001 Parker Ave., West Palm Beach, 33405, Palm Beach County, (561)582-2019. **E-mail:** wpbcc@mindspring.com. **Web:** www.wpalmbeachcountryclub.com. **Facility Holes:** 18. **Yards:** 6,759/6,223. **Par:** 72/72. **Course Rating:** 71.8/75.2. **Slope:** 122/131. **Green Fee:** $14/$36. **Cart Fee:** $12/Person. **Walking Policy:** Walking at certain times. **Walkability:** 2. **Opened:** 1947. **Architect:** Dick Wilson. **Season:** Year-round. **High:** Dec.-April. **To obtain tee times:** Call golf shop. **Misc:** Reduced fees (twilight, juniors), range (grass), credit cards (MC, V, D), BF, FF.
Reader Comments: No water, but not an easy course … Long, good track … This is the most fun course (of 25) I've played in Florida. From the back tees I use every club in the bag … Dick Wilson gem not given attention it deserves.

★★★½ **WESTCHASE GOLF CLUB**
PU-11602 Westchase Dr., Tampa, 33626, Hillsborough County, (813)854-2331. **Facility Holes:** 18. **Yards:** 6,710/5,205. **Par:** 72/72. **Course Rating:** 71.8/69.1. **Slope:** 130/121. **Green Fee:** $29/$69. **Cart Fee:** Included in green fee. **Walking Policy:** Mandatory carts. **Walkability:** 2. **Opened:** 1992. **Architect:** Clifton/Ezell/Clifton. **Season:** Year-round. **High:** Jan.-April. **To obtain tee times:** Call golf shop. **Miscellaneous:** Reduced fees (weekdays, twilight, juniors), range (grass/mats), credit cards (MC, V, AE), BF, FF.
Reader Comments: Lots of water, good course … Good value … Nice course, too many homes … Convenient, fun, affordable … Above-average course, conditions & value.

FLORIDA

★★★ **WESTCHESTER GOLF & COUNTRY CLUB**
SP-12250 Westchester Club Dr., Boynton Beach, 33437, Palm Beach County,
(561)734-6300, 12 miles from West Palm Beach. **Facility Holes:** 27. **Green Fee:** $19/$65. **Cart
Fee:** Included in green fee. **Walkability:** 1. **Opened:** 1988. **Architect:** Karl Litten, Inc. **Season:**
Year-round. **High:** Nov.-April. **To obtain tee times:** Call golf shop. **Miscellaneous:** Reduced
fees (weekdays, guests), range (grass), credit cards (MC, V, AE).
BLUE/GOLD COURSE (18 Combo)
Yards: 6,735/4,728. **Par:** 72/72. **Course Rating:** 72.8/69.7. **Slope:** 137/121.
GOLD/RED COURSE (18 Combo)
Yards: 6,657/4,808. **Par:** 72/72. **Course Rating:** 72.3/70.0. **Slope:** 134/120.
RED/BLUE COURSE (18 Combo)
Yards: 6,772/4,758. **Par:** 72/72. **Course Rating:** 72.9/70.3. **Slope:** 136/119.
Reader Comments: Friendly local course … Easy to get a tee time … Good value in the winter …
Women-friendly tees … Lots of water… Good value … Water, water, alligators, nice course.

THE WESTIN INNISBROOK RESORT
R-36750 Hwy. 19 N., Palm Harbor, 34684, Pinellas County, (727)942-2000, 25 miles from
Tampa. **Web:** www.westin-innisbrook.com. **Facility Holes:** 72. **Cart Fee:** Included in green fee.
Walking Policy: Mandatory carts. **Walkability:** 3. **Season:** Year-round. **High:** Nov.-March. **To
obtain tee times:** Call golf shop. **Miscellaneous:** Reduced fees (guests, juniors), range
(grass/mats), lodging (1000 rooms), credit cards (MC, V, AE, D), BF, FF.
★★★★ **COPPERHEAD COURSE** (18)
Yards: 7,291/5,537. **Par:** 71/71. **Course Rating:** 74.4/72.0. **Slope:** 140/128. **Green Fee:**
$120/$210. **Opened:** 1972. **Architect:** Lawrence Packard/Roger Packard.
Notes: Ranked 25th in 2001 Best in State.
Reader Comments: Very challenging holes throughout … Long and narrow … Fantastic layout, lots
of hills … Condition of course varies, but a great layout … Nice staff … Good rolling terrain …
Excellent course, large alligators.
★★★ **HIGHLANDS NORTH COURSE** (18)
Yards: 6,405/4,955. **Par:** 71/71. **Course Rating:** 70.5/68.4. **Slope:** 125/118. **Green Fee:**
$60/$130. **Opened:** 1971. **Architect:** Lawrence Packard.
Reader Comments: Fun & challenging … Great place to play … Fair … Lots of challenge … Nice
design … Shorter course, some good holes.
★★★½ **HIGHLANDS SOUTH COURSE** (18)
Yards: 6,635/4,975. **Par:** 71/71. **Course Rating:** 72.0/68.4. **Slope:** 127/121. **Green Fee:**
$60/$130. **Opened:** 1997. **Architect:** Lawrence Packard.
Reader Comments: Great challenge, wonderful, swift greens … Fair … Great front 9 … Very nice,
definitely play it … Outstanding, pricey but worth it.
★★★★½ **ISLAND COURSE** (18) *Condition*
Yards: 6,999/5,578. **Par:** 72/72. **Course Rating:** 74.1/73.0. **Slope:** 132/129. **Green Fee:**
$70/$185. **Opened:** 1970. **Architect:** Lawrence Packard.
Reader Comments: Lots of fun for the finesse player … 2nd only to Copperhead … Pleasant front
9, uneven back 9 … My favorite at Innisbrook.

★★★★ **WINDSOR PARKE GOLF CLUB**
SP-13823 Sutton Park Dr. N., Jacksonville, 32224, Duval County, (904)223-4653, 12 miles
from Jacksonville. **E-mail:** jackie@windsorparke.com. **Web:** www.windsorparke.com. **Facility
Holes:** 18. **Yards:** 6,740/5,206. **Par:** 72/72. **Course Rating:** 71.9/69.4. **Slope:** 133/123. **Green
Fee:** $50/$70. **Cart Fee:** Included in green fee. **Walking Policy:** Walking at certain times.
Walkability: 1. **Opened:** 1991. **Architect:** Arthur Hills. **Season:** Year-round. **High:** Feb.-April. **To
obtain tee times:** Call up to 14 days in advance. **Miscellaneous:** Reduced fees (weekdays,
twilight, seniors, juniors), range (grass), credit cards (MC, V, AE, D), BF, FF.
Reader Comments: Great par 5s … Excellent potential … Lots of sand & water. Probably not much
fun for high-handicappers … Best value in the area, don't miss it.

WORLD GOLF VILLAGE
R-1 King and Bear Dr., St. Augustine, 32092, St. Johns County, (904)940-6200, 5 miles from
St. Augustine. **E-mail:** dianag@aug.com. **Web:** www.kingandbeargolf.com. **Facility Holes:** 36.
Cart Fee: Included in green fee. **Walking Policy:** Unrestricted walking. **Walkability:** 2. **Season:**
Year-round. **High:** March-April. **To obtain tee times:** Call up to 30 days in advance.
Miscellaneous: Reduced fees (guests, twilight, juniors), metal spikes, range (grass), lodging
(600 rooms), credit cards (MC, V, AE, D), BF, FF.
KING & BEAR (18)
Yards: 7,279/5,119. **Par:** 72/72. **Course Rating:** 75.2/70.1. **Slope:** 141/123. **Green Fee:**
$125/$200. **Opened:** 2000. **Architect:** Arnold Palmer/Jack Nicklaus.
★★★★ **SLAMMER & SQUIRE** (18) *Condition, Pace*
Yards: 6,940/5,001. **Par:** 72/72. **Course Rating:** 73.8/69.1. **Slope:** 135/116. **Green Fee:**
$95/$170. **Opened:** 1998. **Architect:** Bobby Weed.

FLORIDA

WORLD WOODS GOLF CLUB
R-17590 Ponce De Leon Blvd., Brooksville, 34614, Hernando County, (352)796-5500, 60 miles from Tampa. **E-mail:** worldwoods@hitter.net. **Web:** www.worldwoods.com. **Facility Holes:** 45. **Green Fee:** $50/$85. **Cart Fee:** Included in green fee. **Walking Policy:** Unrestricted walking. **Walkability:** 4. **Opened:** 1993. **Architect:** Tom Fazio. **Season:** Year-round. **To obtain tee times:** Call golf shop. **Miscellaneous:** Reduced fees (weekdays, twilight), range (grass), credit cards (MC, V, AE, D, DC), BF, FF.

★★★★½ **PINE BARRENS COURSE** (18) *Value, Condition, Pace*
Yards: 6,902/5,301. **Par:** 71/71. **Course Rating:** 73.7/70.9. **Slope:** 140/132.
Notes: Ranked 97th in 2000-2001 America's 100 Greatest; 5th in 2001 Best in State; 9th in 1996 America's Top 75 Upscale Courses.
Reader Comments: Unbelievable, nothing else like it in Florida ... What an awesome place ... Can't wait to go back ... Pure joy to play ... Great course, very challenging, long drive but worth the trip ... As good as it gets.

★★★★½ **ROLLING OAKS COURSE** (18) *Value, Condition, Pace*
Yards: 6,985/5,245. **Par:** 72/72. **Course Rating:** 73.5/70.7. **Slope:** 136/128.
Notes: Ranked 24th in 2001 Best in State; 73rd in 1996 America's Top 75 Upscale Courses.
Reader Comments: Practice facility must be best on earth ... I could play it every day, best complex in America ... Suprised to find a couple of mediocre holes ... What a bargain ... Superb architecture ... Easier and more pleasant of the 2 ... Nice, scenic, fun course and good specials ... Fun and fair.
Special Notes: Also has 9-hole executive course.

★★½ ZELLWOOD STATION COUNTRY CLUB
SP-2126 Spillman Dr., Zellwood, 32798, Orange County, (407)886-3303, 20 miles from Orlando. **Facility Holes:** 18. **Yards:** 6,400/5,377. **Par:** 72/74. **Course Rating:** 70.5/71.1. **Slope:** 122/122. **Green Fee:** $22/$30. **Cart Fee:** Included in green fee. **Walking Policy:** Mandatory carts. **Opened:** 1977. **Architect:** William Maddox. **Season:** Year-round. **High:** Nov.-April. **To obtain tee times:** Call golf shop. **Miscellaneous:** Reduced fees (twilight), FF.

★★ BACON PARK GOLF COURSE
PU-Shorty Cooper Dr., Savannah, 31406, Chatham County, (912)354-2625, 2 miles from Savannah. **Web:** www.cityofsavannah.com. **Facility Holes:** 27. **Green Fee:** $15/$17. **Cart Fee:** $12/Person. **Walking Policy:** Walking at certain times. **Walkability:** 2. **Opened:** 1926. **Architect:** Donald Ross/Ron Kirby/Denis Griffiths. **Season:** Year-round. **To obtain tee times:** Call golf shop. **Miscellaneous:** Reduced fees (weekdays, twilight, seniors, juniors), range (grass/mats), credit cards (MC, V, AE), BF, FF.
CYPRESS/LIVE OAK (18 Combo)
Yards: 6,679/5,160. **Par:** 72/72. **Course Rating:** 70.5/68.3. **Slope:** 119/116.
CYPRESS/MAGNOLIA (18 Combo)
Yards: 6,573/4,943. **Par:** 72/72. **Course Rating:** 69.9/66.9. **Slope:** 118/114.
MAGNOLIA/LIVE OAK (18 Combo)
Yards: 6,740/5,309. **Par:** 72/72. **Course Rating:** 70.7/69.4. **Slope:** 120/118.

★★★★½ BARNSLEY GARDENS *Service, Pace*
R-597 Barnsley Garden Rd., Adairsville, 30103, Bartow County, (770)773-7480, (877)773-2447, 60 miles from Atlanta. **E-mail:** smahr@barnsleyinn.com. **Web:** www.barnsleyinn.com. **Facility Holes:** 18. **Yards:** 7,200/6,200. **Par:** 72/72. **Course Rating:** 74.5/76.2. **Slope:** 141/138. **Green Fee:** $75/$100. **Cart Fee:** Included in green fee. **Walking Policy:** Unrestricted walking. **Walkability:** 4. **Opened:** 1999. **Architect:** Jim Fazio. **Season:** Year-round. **To obtain tee times:** Call up to 7 days in advance. **Miscellaneous:** Reduced fees (juniors), range (grass), lodging (70 rooms), credit cards (MC, V, AE, D, DC, CB), BF, FF. **Notes:** Ranked 13th in 2001 Best in State.
Reader Comments: Beautiful scenery, excellent resort-level service. Best group of par 3s ever seen … One of Georgia's best-kept secrets. Great series of extraordinary holes that flow naturally through the land. Surprising elevation changes require care in club selection … High end, but well worth it.

★★★ BARRINGTON HALL GOLF CLUB
SP-104 Stoney Creek Dr., Macon, 31220, Bibb County, (478)757-8358, 65 miles from Atlanta. **Facility Holes:** 18. **Yards:** 7,062/5,012. **Par:** 72/72. **Course Rating:** 73.8/69.3. **Slope:** 138/118. **Green Fee:** $19/$29. **Cart Fee:** $10/Person. **Walking Policy:** Mandatory carts. **Walkability:** 3. **Opened:** 1992. **Architect:** Tom Clark. **Season:** Year-round. **High:** March-Sept. **To obtain tee times:** Call up to 3 days in advance. **Miscellaneous:** Reduced fees (weekdays, twilight, juniors), range (grass/mats), credit cards (MC, V), BF, FF.
Reader Comments: Super layout except for No. 2 and No. 11 where development won out over design. Super bent-grass greens … Nice course and pretty well taken care of. Not a bargain for the condition it is kept in … Good course, member friendly.

BEAR CREEK GOLF & COUNTRY CLUB
SP-5450 Country Manor Dr., Douglasville, 30135, Douglas County, (770)949-4653, 35 miles from Atlanta. **E-mail:** bstubbs@pga.com. **Web:** bearcreekatlanta.com. **Facility Holes:** 18. **Yards:** 6,562/5,861. **Par:** 71/72. **Course Rating:** 72.6/75.4. **Slope:** 139/142. **Green Fee:** $25/$49. **Cart Fee:** Included in green fee. **Walking Policy:** Walking at certain times. **Walkability:** 5. **Opened:** 2000. **Architect:** Jim Ganley. **Season:** Year-round. **High:** March-Oct. **To obtain tee times:** Call up to 14 days in advance. **Miscellaneous:** Reduced fees (weekdays, twilight, seniors, juniors), range (grass), credit cards (MC, V, AE), BF, FF.

★★ BELLE MEADE COUNTRY CLUB
SP-2660 Twin Pine Rd. N.W., Thomson, 30824, McDuffie County, (706)595-4511, 35 miles from Augusta. **Facility Holes:** 18. **Yards:** 6,403/5,362. **Par:** 72/73. **Course Rating:** 69.9/68.6. **Slope:** 120/113. **Green Fee:** $13/$23. **Cart Fee:** $10/Person. **Walking Policy:** Unrestricted walking. **Walkability:** 3. **Opened:** 1968. **Architect:** Boone A. Knox, Pete Knox. **Season:** Year-round. **High:** April-Aug. **To obtain tee times:** Call golf shop. **Miscellaneous:** Reduced fees (weekdays), metal spikes, range (grass), credit cards (MC, V).

BENTWATER GOLF CLUB
SP-100 Golf Links Dr., Acworth, 30101, Paulding County, (770)529-9554, 20 miles from Atlanta. **Facility Holes:** 18. **Yards:** 6,833/4,646. **Par:** 72/72. **Course Rating:** 73.0/67.5. **Slope:** 139/116. **Green Fee:** $35/$59. **Cart Fee:** Included in green fee. **Walking Policy:** Unrestricted walking. **Walkability:** 3. **Opened:** 2000. **Architect:** Mike Dasher. **Season:** Year-round. **To obtain tee times:** Call up to 7 days in advance. **Miscellaneous:** Reduced fees (weekdays, twilight, seniors, juniors), range (grass), credit cards (MC, V, AE, D), BF, FF.

★★★ BLACK CREEK GOLF CLUB
SP-Bill Futch Rd., Ellabell, 31308, Bryan County, (912)858-4653, 30 miles from Savannah. **Web:** www.blackcreek.com. **Facility Holes:** 18. **Yards:** 6,287/4,551. **Par:** 72/72. **Course Rating:** 70.4/66.0. **Slope:** 130/109. **Green Fee:** $27/$34. **Cart Fee:** Included in green fee. **Walking**

Policy: Walking at certain times. **Walkability:** 1. **Opened:** 1994. **Architect:** Jim Bevins. **Season:** Year-round. **High:** April-Sept. **To obtain tee times:** Call golf shop. **Miscellaneous:** Reduced fees (weekdays, twilight, seniors, juniors), range (grass), credit cards (MC, V, D).
Reader Comments: The greens were great. The fairway facilities were good … Interesting back 9 with bridges crossing marsh swamps … Short but tight track … Keep driver in the bag.

★★ BOBBY JONES GOLF CLUB
PU-384 Woodward Way, Atlanta, 30305, Fulton County, (404)355-1009. **Facility Holes:** 18.
Yards: 6,155/4,661. **Par:** 71/71. **Course Rating:** 69.0/67.6. **Slope:** 119/114. **Green Fee:** $19/$33. **Walkability:** 3. **Opened:** 1932. **Architect:** J. Van Kleek/G. Gill/G. B. Williams. **Season:** Year-round. **High:** May-Sept. **To obtain tee times:** Call golf shop. **Miscellaneous:** Reduced fees (weekdays, twilight, seniors, juniors), metal spikes, credit cards (MC, V, AE).

★½ BOWDEN GOLF COURSE
PU-3111 Millerfield Rd., Macon, 31201, Bibb County, (912)742-1610. **Facility Holes:** 18.
Yards: 6,570/4,955. **Par:** 72/73. **Course Rating:** 70.7/68.0. **Slope:** 119/106. **Green Fee:** $22/$24. **Cart Fee:** Included in green fee. **Walking Policy:** Unrestricted walking. **Walkability:** 3.
Opened: 1940. **Architect:** Dick Cotton. **Season:** Year-round. **High:** May-Aug. **To obtain tee times:** Call golf shop. **Miscellaneous:** Reduced fees (weekdays, twilight, seniors, juniors), metal spikes, range (grass).

★★★½ BRASSTOWN VALLEY RESORT
R-6321 U.S. Hwy. 76, Young Harris, 30582, Towns County, (706)379-4613, (800)201-3205, 90 miles from Atlanta. **E-mail:** jjohnson@brasstownvalley.com. **Web:** www.brasstownvalley.com. **Facility Holes:** 18. **Yards:** 7,000/5,028. **Par:** 72/72. **Course Rating:** 73.9/69.2. **Slope:** 139/116. **Green Fee:** $65/$75. **Cart Fee:** Included in green fee. **Walking Policy:** Mandatory carts. **Walkability:** 3. **Opened:** 1995. **Architect:** Denis Griffiths. **Season:** Year-round. **High:** Aug.-Nov. **To obtain tee times:** Call golf shop. **Miscellaneous:** Reduced fees (weekdays, twilight, seniors, juniors), metal spikes, range (grass/mats), lodging (134 rooms), credit cards (MC, V, AE, D, DC), BF, FF.
Notes: Ranked 16th in 1997 Best in State.
Reader Comments: A fantastic weekend getaway … Awesome mountain course, greens are in great shape … Expected more elevation changes … Fee's too high—should do 90 degrees to pick up pace … Great course, friendly staff.

★★½ BRICKYARD PLANTATION GOLF CLUB
SP-1619 U.S. 280 E., Americus, 31709, Sumter County, (912)874-1234, 7 miles from Americus. **E-mail:** bpgcdeb@sowega.net. **Web:** www.brickyardgolfclub.com. **Facility Holes:** 27.
Green Fee: $16. **Cart Fee:** $12/Person. **Walking Policy:** Unrestricted walking. **Walkability:** 1.
Opened: 1979. **Architect:** W.N. Clark. **Season:** Year-round. **High:** May-Aug. **To obtain tee times:** Call golf shop. **Miscellaneous:** Range (grass), credit cards (MC, V, AE, D).
DITCHES/MOUNDS (18 Combo)
Yards: 6,700/5,300. **Par:** 72/72. **Course Rating:** 70.5/69.9. **Slope:** 129/114.
DITCHES/WATERS (18 Combo)
Yards: 6,300/5,100. **Par:** 72/72. **Course Rating:** 70.0/70.6. **Slope:** 128/120.
WATERS/MOUNDS (18 Combo)
Yards: 6,400/5,100. **Par:** 72/72. **Course Rating:** 67.7/69.8. **Slope:** 124/116.

★★★½ BRIDGEMILL ATHLETIC CLUB
SP-1190 BridgeMill Ave., Canton, 30114, Cherokee County, (770)345-5500, 32 miles from Atlanta. **Facility Holes:** 18. **Yards:** 7,085/4,828. **Par:** 72/72. **Course Rating:** 74.0/69.0. **Slope:** 140/119. **Green Fee:** $59/$79. **Cart Fee:** Included in green fee. **Walking Policy:** Unrestricted walking. **Walkability:** 3. **Opened:** 1998. **Architect:** Desmond Muirhead/Larry Mize. **Season:** Year-round. **To obtain tee times:** Call up to 7 days in advance. **Miscellaneous:** Reduced fees (twilight), range (grass), credit cards (MC, V, AE, D), BF, FF.
Reader Comments: Interesting layout, conditions very windy … Great course for weekend play … Tight driving areas on most holes require accuracy and better than average length … Nice layout, expensive, but good quality.

★★½ BROWNS MILL GOLF COURSE
PU-480 Cleveland Ave., Atlanta, 30354, Fulton County, (404)366-3573. **Facility Holes:** 18.
Yards: 6,539/5,545. **Par:** 72/72. **Course Rating:** 71.0/71.4. **Slope:** 123/118. **Green Fee:** $17/$22. **Cart Fee:** $10/Person. **Walking Policy:** Unrestricted walking. **Walkability:** 2. **Opened:** 1969. **Architect:** George W. Cobb. **Season:** Year-round. **High:** March-Oct. **To obtain tee times:** Call golf shop. **Miscellaneous:** Reduced fees (weekdays, twilight, seniors, juniors), metal spikes, range (grass), credit cards (MC, V, AE).

BULL CREEK GOLF COURSE
PU-7333 Lynch Rd., Midland, 31820, Muscogee County, (706)561-1614, 10 miles from

181

Columbus. **Facility Holes:** 36. **Green Fee:** $16/$18. **Cart Fee:** $13/Person. **Walking Policy:** Unrestricted walking. **Opened:** 1972. **Architect:** Joe Lee/Ward Northrup. **Season:** Year-round. **To obtain tee times:** Call up to 3 days in advance. **Miscellaneous:** Reduced fees (weekdays, seniors, juniors), range (grass), credit cards (MC, V), BF, FF.

★★★½ **EAST COURSE** (18)
Yards: 6,705/5,430. **Par:** 72/74. **Course Rating:** 71.2/69.8. **Slope:** 124/114. **Walkability:** 3.
Reader Comments: Fairways narrow in places … Excellent conditions, value and service.

★★★½ **WEST COURSE** (18)
Yards: 6,921/5,385. **Par:** 72/74. **Course Rating:** 72.5/69.9. **Slope:** 130/121. **Walkability:** 5.
Reader Comments: Hard layout, lots of challenges … Long and tough with hard greens and up-and-down fairways … Excellent conditions, value and service.

CALLAWAY GARDENS RESORT
R-U.S. Highway 27, Pine Mountain, 31822, Harris County, (706)663-2281, (800)225-5292, 30 miles from Columbus. **E-mail:** info@callawaygardens.com. **Web:** www.callawaygardens.com. **Facility Holes:** 63. **Cart Fee:** Included in green fee. **Season:** Year-round. **To obtain tee times:** Call up to 3 days in advance. **Miscellaneous:** Reduced fees (twilight), metal spikes, range (grass), credit cards (MC, V, AE, D), BF, FF.

★★★★ **GARDENS VIEW COURSE** (18)
Yards: 6,392/5,848. **Par:** 72/72. **Course Rating:** 70.9/73.4. **Slope:** 119/125. **Green Fee:** $55/$75. **Walking Policy:** Walking at certain times. **Walkability:** 2. **Opened:** 1964. **Architect:** Joe Lee.
Reader Comments: The experience at Callaway is awesome. One of America's most beautiful resorts with the finest of Southern hospitality … Great conditioned course with fairly basic design, great service at a PGA quality course.

★★★½ **LAKE VIEW COURSE** (18) *Pace*
Yards: 6,051/5,347. **Par:** 70/71. **Course Rating:** 68.6/71.1. **Slope:** 123/121. **Green Fee:** $55/$75. **Walking Policy:** Walking at certain times. **Walkability:** 3. **Opened:** 1952. **Architect:** J.B. McGovern.
Reader Comments: Nice course, not too difficult … Pricey but a good location … Excellent course—pricey … Target golf with a twist … Beautiful in spring & summer … Great area, great course.

★★★★ **MOUNTAIN VIEW COURSE** (18)
Yards: 7,057/5,848. **Par:** 72/74. **Course Rating:** 73.9/74.3. **Slope:** 136/131. **Green Fee:** $70/$110. **Walking Policy:** Mandatory carts. **Opened:** 1965. **Architect:** Dick Wilson/Joe Lee.
Reader Comments: Good chance to play a PGA Tour venue. Fall is great time of year to go there … Long for the average hitter. Fairways are plush … Good condition, challenging greens … Beautiful scenery … Great course, very challenging.
Special Notes: Also has a 9-hole Sky View Course.

★★★★ CATEECHEE GOLF CLUB *Value, Pace*
SP-140 Cateechee Trail, Hartwell, 30643, Hart County, (706)856-4653, 20 miles from Anderson, S.C.. **E-mail:** cateechee@hartcom.net. **Web:** www.cateechee.com. **Facility Holes:** 18. **Yards:** 6,611/5,102. **Par:** 71/71. **Course Rating:** 70.8/67.9. **Slope:** 130/118. **Green Fee:** $40/$50. **Cart Fee:** Included in green fee. **Walking Policy:** Unrestricted walking. **Walkability:** 3. **Opened:** 1998. **Architect:** Mike Young. **Season:** Year-round. **To obtain tee times:** Call up to 7 days in advance. **Miscellaneous:** Reduced fees (twilight, seniors, juniors), range (grass), credit cards (MC, V, AE), BF, FF.
Notes: Ranked 6th in 1999 Best New Affordable Public.
Reader Comments: Very good layout, good shot values, challenging but fair, great value … Great golf course that not many know about … Off the beaten path, superb value … Some holes & greens quirky, has potential.

★★½ CENTENNIAL GOLF CLUB
PU-5225 Woodstock Rd., Acworth, 30102, Cherokee County, (770)975-1000, 15 miles from Atlanta. **E-mail:** centgc@yahoo.com. **Web:** centennialatlanta.com. **Facility Holes:** 18. **Yards:** 6,850/5,095. **Par:** 72/72. **Course Rating:** 73.1/69.5. **Slope:** 134/122. **Green Fee:** $45/$55. **Cart Fee:** Included in green fee. **Walking Policy:** Walking at certain times. **Walkability:** 3. **Opened:** 1990. **Architect:** Larry Nelson. **Season:** Year-round. **High:** March-Oct. **To obtain tee times:** Call up to 7 days in advance. **Miscellaneous:** Reduced fees (twilight, seniors), range (grass), credit cards (MC, V, AE, D), BF, FF.

CHATEAU ELAN RESORT
R-6060 Golf Club Dr., Braselton, 30517, Barrow County, (678)425-6050, (800)233-9463, 45 miles from Atlanta. **E-mail:** gsarazen@chateuelan.com. **Web:** wwwchateauelan.com. **Facility Holes:** 54. **Green Fee:** $32/$77. **Cart Fee:** Included in green fee. **Walking Policy:** Walking at certain times. **Architect:** Denis Griffiths. **Season:** Year-round. **High:** March-Nov. **To obtain tee times:** Call golf shop. **Miscellaneous:** Reduced fees (weekdays, guests, twilight), range (grass), lodging (300 rooms), credit cards (MC, V, AE, D, DC), BF, FF.

GEORGIA

★★★½ **CHATEAU ELAN COURSE** (18)
Yards: 7,030/5,092. **Par:** 71/71. **Course Rating:** 73.5/70.8. **Slope:** 136/124. **Walkability:** 4.
Opened: 1989.
Reader Comments: Very well maintained. Greens were in excellent shape … Tough course if you don't get off the tee well … Best bunkers in GA … Fun course with some truly challenging holes, course makes you play every club in the bag.

★★★★ **WOODLANDS COURSE** (18)
Yards: 6,738/4,850. **Par:** 72/72. **Course Rating:** 72.6/68.5. **Slope:** 131/123. **Walkability:** 5.
Opened: 1996.
Reader Comments: Tight course with fast, undulating greens … Bring your A+ game, great elevation changes … A lot of the holes are on a rolling terrain with some blind shots that can be fun … Well-maintained course.
Special Notes: Also has a private 18-hole Legends Course.

★★★ **CHATTAHOOCHEE GOLF CLUB**
PU-301 Tommy Aaron Dr., Gainesville, 30506, Hall County, (770)532-0066, 50 miles from Atlanta. **Facility Holes:** 18. **Yards:** 6,700/5,000. **Par:** 72/72. **Course Rating:** 72.6/67.4. **Slope:** 127/113. **Green Fee:** $14/$39. **Cart Fee:** $10/Person. **Walking Policy:** Walking at certain times. **Walkability:** 2. **Opened:** 1955. **Architect:** Robert Trent Jones. **Season:** Year-round. **High:** April-Sept. **To obtain tee times:** Call golf shop. **Miscellaneous:** Reduced fees (twilight, juniors), range (grass), credit cards (MC, V, AE).
Reader Comments: Good course, crowded, slow play … Home course, I love it! … Good for all levels.

★★★½ **CHEROKEE RUN GOLF CLUB**
SP-1595 Centennial Olympic Pkwy., Conyers, 30013, Rockdale County, (770)785-7904, 20 miles from Atlanta. **E-mail:** info@cherokeerun.com. **Web:** www.cherokeerun.com. **Facility Holes:** 18. **Yards:** 7,016/4,948. **Par:** 72/72. **Course Rating:** 74.9/70.0. **Slope:** 142/123. **Green Fee:** $30/$65. **Cart Fee:** Included in green fee. **Walking Policy:** Walking at certain times. **Walkability:** 5. **Opened:** 1995. **Architect:** Arnold Palmer/Ed Seay. **Season:** Year-round. **High:** April-Sept. **To obtain tee times:** Call up to 7 days in advance. **Miscellaneous:** Reduced fees (weekdays, twilight, seniors, juniors), range (grass), lodging (80 rooms), credit cards (MC, V, AE, D), BF, FF.
Notes: Ranked 19th in 1999 Best in State.
Reader Comments: No wait during the week. Great course, very different … Tough, but very good … New superintendent has made a difference … Up and down hills, rolling, bending through Georgia Pines … Interesting layout, good variety.

★★★½ **CHESTATEE GOLF CLUB**
SP-777 Dogwood Way, Dawsonville, 30534, Dawson County, (706)216-7336, (800)520-8675, 35 miles from Atlanta. **Web:** www.chestategolf.net. **Facility Holes:** 18. **Yards:** 6,877/4,947. **Par:** 71/71. **Course Rating:** 72.5/68.4. **Slope:** 135/121. **Green Fee:** $39/$79. **Cart Fee:** Included in green fee. **Walking Policy:** Walking at certain times. **Walkability:** 3. **Opened:** 1999. **Architect:** Denis Griffiths. **Season:** Year-round. **To obtain tee times:** Call up to 7 days in advance. **Miscellaneous:** Reduced fees (twilight, seniors), range (grass), credit cards (MC, V, AE), BF, FF.
Reader Comments: Very difficult, but fair … Hilly, beautiful course, challenging & fun … This is a very scenic and well cared for course. The housing is mostly well back from the fairways. The price is high.

★★★ **CHICOPEE WOODS GOLF COURSE**
PU-2515 Atlanta Hwy., Gainesville, 30504, Hall County, (770)534-7322, 30 miles from Atlanta. **E-mail:** arendtgolf@hotmail.com. **Facility Holes:** 27. **Yards:** 7,040/5,001. **Par:** 72/72. **Course Rating:** 74.0/69.0. **Slope:** 135/117. **Green Fee:** $33/$38. **Cart Fee:** $12/Person. **Walking Policy:** Unrestricted walking. **Walkability:** 4. **Opened:** 1991. **Architect:** Denis Griffiths. **Season:** Year-round. **To obtain tee times:** Call up to 6 days in advance. **Miscellaneous:** Reduced fees (twilight, seniors, juniors), range (grass), credit cards (MC, V, AE), BF, FF.
Reader Comments: Many elevation changes. Well-maintained, diverse layout … Great public course, very affordable … Narrow fairways, lots of blind shots … Nice hilly course—good value.
Special Notes: Also has a 9-hole course.

★★ **CITY CLUB MARIETTA**
PU-510 Powder Spring St., Marietta, 30064, Cobb County, (770)528-4653, 15 miles from Atlanta. **E-mail:** proshop@city.marietta.ga.us. **Facility Holes:** 18. **Yards:** 5,721/4,715. **Par:** 71/71. **Course Rating:** 67.3/67.5. **Slope:** 118/115. **Green Fee:** $39/$49. **Cart Fee:** Included in green fee. **Walking Policy:** Unrestricted walking. **Walkability:** 3. **Opened:** 1991. **Architect:** Mike Young. **Season:** Year-round. **High:** April-Sept. **To obtain tee times:** Call up to 7 days in advance. **Miscellaneous:** Reduced fees (weekdays, twilight, seniors, juniors), range (grass/mats), lodging (200 rooms), credit cards (MC, V, AE), BF, FF.

GEORGIA

★★★★ **THE CLUB AT JONES CREEK**
SP-4101 Hammond's Ferry Rd., Evans, 30809, Columbia County, (706)860-4228, 5 miles from Augusta. **Facility Holes:** 18. **Yards:** 7,008/5,430. **Par:** 72/72. **Course Rating:** 73.8/72.4. **Slope:** 137/130. **Green Fee:** $22/$37. **Cart Fee:** $11/Person. **Walking Policy:** Walking at certain times. **Walkability:** 3. **Opened:** 1986. **Architect:** Rees Jones. **Season:** Year-round. **High:** April-Aug. **To obtain tee times:** Call golf shop. **Miscellaneous:** Reduced fees (seniors, juniors), metal spikes, range (grass), credit cards (MC, V, AE).
Reader Comments: Bring all your shots and putts … Very penal course … Very nice, interesting layout … Little expensive, but good course … Accuracy required, good target course.

★★★★ **THE CLUB AT SAVANNAH HARBOR**
R-Two Resort Drive, Savannah, 31421, Chatham County, (912)201-2007, 1 mile from Savannah. **E-mail:** Rcarter@premierweb/net. **Facility Holes:** 18. **Yards:** 7,288/5,261. **Par:** 72/72. **Course Rating:** 74.6/70.4. **Slope:** 134/117. **Green Fee:** $85/$115. **Cart Fee:** Included in green fee. **Walking Policy:** Walking at certain times. **Walkability:** 1. **Opened:** 2000. **Architect:** Bob Cupp/Sam Snead. **Season:** Year-round. **High:** Sept.-Nov. **To obtain tee times:** Call up to 5 days in advance. **Miscellaneous:** Reduced fees (twilight), range (grass), lodging (400 rooms), credit cards (MC, V, AE, D, DC, CB), BF, FF.
Reader Comments: A memorable golf experience … Hot, humid, bright, bring sunblock! … Much better than expected! … Nice pro shop—great food … Good links-style layout.

★★★★ **COBBLESTONE GOLF COURSE**
PU-4200 Nance Rd., Acworth, 30101, Cobb County, (770)917-5151, 20 miles from Atlanta. **Web:** cobblestonegolf.com. **Facility Holes:** 18. **Yards:** 6,759/5,400. **Par:** 71/71. **Course Rating:** 73.1/71.5. **Slope:** 140/129. **Green Fee:** $34/$49. **Cart Fee:** $10/Person. **Walking Policy:** Walking at certain times. **Walkability:** 3. **Opened:** 1993. **Architect:** Ken Dye. **Season:** Year-round. **To obtain tee times:** Call up to 4 days in advance. **Miscellaneous:** Reduced fees (weekdays, twilight, seniors, juniors), metal spikes, range (grass), credit cards (MC, V), BF, FF.
Notes: Ranked 15th in 1999 Best in State.
Reader Comments: Very hard muni. Wonderful design demands you hit straight and long … Awesome, great layout … Can't beat it for the money, but everyone knows it, heavy traffic … Great layout, tough to get tee times.

★½ **COLLINS HILL GOLF CLUB**
PU-585 Camp Perrin Rd., Lawrenceville, 30043, Gwinnett County, (770)822-5400, 35 miles from Atlanta. **E-mail:** info@colllinshillgolf.com. **Web:** collinshillgolf.com. **Facility Holes:** 18. **Yards:** 6,000/4,738. **Par:** 71/72. **Course Rating:** 68.0/67.1. **Slope:** 120/113. **Green Fee:** $30/$40. **Cart Fee:** Included in green fee. **Walking Policy:** Walking at certain times. **Walkability:** 3. **Opened:** 1963. **Architect:** Perrin Walker. **Season:** Year-round. **To obtain tee times:** Call up to 3 days in advance. **Miscellaneous:** Reduced fees (weekdays, twilight, seniors, juniors), range (grass), credit cards (MC, V, AE, D), BF, FF.

★★★ **COVINGTON PLANTATION GOLF CLUB**
SP-10400 Covington Bypass SE, Covington, 30014, Newton County, (770)385-0064, 30 miles from Atlanta. **Facility Holes:** 18. **Yards:** 6,906/4,803. **Par:** 72/72. **Green Fee:** $39/$49. **Cart Fee:** Included in green fee. **Walking Policy:** Walking at certain times. **Walkability:** 3. **Opened:** 1996. **Architect:** Desmond Muirhead. **Season:** Year-round. **High:** March-May. **To obtain tee times:** Call golf shop. **Miscellaneous:** Reduced fees (twilight, seniors), range (grass/mats), credit cards (MC, V, AE).
Reader Comments: Course in good shape, greens need attention … No yardage markers, long distance hole-to-hole … Bring your A game … Good course—needs some work, has one of the toughest par 4s I've seen.

★★ **CREEKSIDE GOLF & COUNTRY CLUB**
PU-591 Westchester Club Dr., Hiram, 30141, Paulding County, (770)445-7655, 20 miles from Atlanta. **Web:** jjc2374@aol.com. **Facility Holes:** 18. **Yards:** 6,700/5,352. **Par:** 72/72. **Course Rating:** 71.7/70.7. **Slope:** 131/128. **Green Fee:** $26/$36. **Cart Fee:** $12/Person. **Walking Policy:** Walking at certain times. **Walkability:** 3. **Opened:** 1999. **Architect:** Rich Mandell. **Season:** Year-round. **To obtain tee times:** Call golf shop. **Miscellaneous:** Reduced fees (weekdays, twilight, seniors), range (grass/mats), credit cards (MC, V, AE), BF, FF.

★★★★ **CROOKED CREEK GOLF CLUB**
SP-3430 Highway 9, Alpharetta, 30004, Fulton County, (770)475-2300, 20 miles from Atlanta. **Facility Holes:** 18. **Yards:** 6,917/4,985. **Par:** 72/72. **Course Rating:** 73.4/70.0. **Slope:** 141/120. **Green Fee:** $48/$89. **Cart Fee:** Included in green fee. **Walking Policy:** Mandatory carts. **Walkability:** 3. **Opened:** 1996. **Architect:** Michael Riley. **Season:** Year-round. **To obtain tee times:** Call golf shop. **Miscellaneous:** Reduced fees (weekdays, twilight, juniors), range

(grass), credit cards (MC, V, AE), BF, FF.

Reader Comments: Great design, beautifully maintained. No boring series of driver, short iron, wedge here. You will need an accurate driver on every hole ... Tremendous clubhouse & traditional-style course ... Great finishing par 5.

CROSSWINDS GOLF CLUB

SP-232 James B. Blackburn Dr., Savannah, 31408, Chatham County, (912)966-1909, 5 miles from Savannah. **Facility Holes:** 27. **Yards:** 6,600/4,700. **Par:** 72/72. **Course Rating:** 71.7/67.7. **Slope:** 132/110. **Green Fee:** $29/$46. **Cart Fee:** Included in green fee. **Walking Policy:** Mandatory carts. **Walkability:** 2. **Opened:** 2000. **Architect:** Rusty Simmons. **Season:** Year-round. **High:** Nov.-March. **To obtain tee times:** Call up to 7 days in advance. **Miscellaneous:** Reduced fees (weekdays, guests, twilight, seniors, juniors), range (grass), credit cards (MC, V, AE), BF, FF.
Special Notes: Also has a 9-hole par-3 course.

EAGLE CREEK GOLF CLUB

SP-7436 Georgia Hwy. 46, Statesboro, 30458, Bulloch County, (912)839-3933, 6 miles from Statesboro. **Facility Holes:** 18. **Yards:** 6,700/5,200. **Par:** 72/72. **Course Rating:** 71.6/68.5. **Slope:** 124/114. **Green Fee:** $15/$18. **Cart Fee:** $12/Person. **Walking Policy:** Walking at certain times. **Walkability:** 2. **Opened:** 1997. **Architect:** Paul Massey. **Season:** Year-round. **To obtain tee times:** Call up to 7 days in advance. **Miscellaneous:** Reduced fees (weekdays, twilight, seniors, juniors), range (grass), credit cards (MC, V, D), BF, FF.

★★★½ EAGLE WATCH GOLF CLUB

SP-3055 Eagle Watch Dr., Woodstock, 30189, Cherokee County, (770)591-1000, 25 miles from Atlanta. **Facility Holes:** 18. **Yards:** 6,900/5,243. **Par:** 72/72. **Course Rating:** 72.6/68.9. **Slope:** 136/126. **Green Fee:** $50/$70. **Cart Fee:** Included in green fee. **Opened:** 1989. **Architect:** Arnold Palmer/Ed Seay. **Season:** Year-round. **High:** June-Aug. **To obtain tee times:** Call golf shop. **Miscellaneous:** Reduced fees (weekdays, twilight, seniors, juniors), range (grass), credit cards (MC, V, AE).
Reader Comments: The course is heavily played by a mix of members and the public ... The course is in excellent condition and can be enjoyed by all gofers ... Nice course, good value ... Nice layout, beautiful fairways & greens.

★★★ EMERALD POINTE GOLF RESORT & CONFERENCE CENTER

R-7000 Holiday Rd., Buford, 30518, Hall County, (770)945-8789, (800)768-5253, 35 miles from Atlanta. **E-mail:** rnash@lumac.com. **Web:** www.lakelanierislands.com. **Facility Holes:** 18. **Yards:** 6,341/4,935. **Par:** 72/72. **Course Rating:** 70.1/68.3. **Slope:** 124/117. **Green Fee:** $27/$56. **Cart Fee:** $19/Person. **Walking Policy:** Mandatory carts. **Walkability:** 4. **Opened:** 1989. **Architect:** Joe Lee. **Season:** Year-round. **High:** April-Nov. **To obtain tee times:** Call up to 14 days in advance. **Miscellaneous:** Reduced fees (weekdays, twilight, seniors, juniors), range (grass), lodging (250 rooms), credit cards (MC, V, AE, D, Diners Club), FF.
Reader Comments: Tough in the wind ... Lots of water & hills, inexpensive ... Up and down hills, rolling, bending through Georgia Pines. It doesn't get any better.

★★★★ FIELDS FERRY GOLF CLUB *Value*

PU-581 Fields Ferry Dr., Calhoun, 30701, Gordon County, (706)625-5666, 50 miles from Atlanta. **Facility Holes:** 18. **Yards:** 6,824/5,355. **Par:** 72/72. **Course Rating:** 71.8/70.5. **Slope:** 123/120. **Green Fee:** $13/$33. **Cart Fee:** $12/Person. **Walking Policy:** Unrestricted walking. **Walkability:** 2. **Opened:** 1992. **Architect:** Arthur Davis. **Season:** Year-round. **To obtain tee times:** Call up to 3 days in advance. **Miscellaneous:** Reduced fees (weekdays, twilight, seniors, juniors), range (grass/mats), credit cards (MC, V), BF, FF.
Reader Comments: Beautiful location, great layout, course is in great shape ... Great closing holes ... Super muni course, challenging but still fun ... 16 is an amazing hole ... Front side long, wind always blows ... Good value.

★★★½ THE FIELDS GOLF CLUB

SP-257 S. Smith Rd., LaGrange, 30241, Troup County, (706)845-7425, 30 miles from Columbus. **E-mail:** fgilliii@aol.com. **Web:** www.teaweb.com/fields. **Facility Holes:** 18. **Yards:** 6,800/5,200. **Par:** 72/72. **Course Rating:** 71.4/67.4. **Slope:** 128/113. **Green Fee:** $21/$27. **Cart Fee:** $11/Person. **Walking Policy:** Walking at certain times. **Walkability:** 4. **Opened:** 1990. **Architect:** Butch Gill. **Season:** Year-round. **To obtain tee times:** Call up to 7 days in advance. **Miscellaneous:** Reduced fees (weekdays, twilight, seniors, juniors), range (grass/mats), credit cards (MC, V, AE), BF, FF.
Reader Comments: Outstanding course, excellent greens & fairways ... Good variety ... Long and tough, great bent-grass greens ... Good course, play a little too slow.

★★ FIELDSTONE COUNTRY CLUB

SP-2720 Salem Rd. SE, Conyers, 30013, Rockdale County, (770)483-4372, 35 miles from

Atlanta. **Facility Holes:** 18. **Yards:** 6,562/5,268. **Par:** 72/72. **Course Rating:** 68.8/70.4. **Slope:** 120/114. **Green Fee:** $20/$35. **Cart Fee:** Included in green fee. **Walking Policy:** Walking at certain times. **Walkability:** 2. **Opened:** 1969. **Architect:** Harold Zink. **Season:** Year-round. **High:** March-June. **To obtain tee times:** Call golf shop. **Miscellaneous:** Reduced fees (twilight), range (grass), credit cards (MC, V), FF.

★★★ **FOREST HILLS GOLF CLUB**
PU-1500 Comfort Rd., Augusta, 30909, Richmond County, (706)733-0001, 140 miles from Atlanta. **Facility Holes:** 18. **Yards:** 6,875/4,875. **Par:** 72/72. **Course Rating:** 72.2/68.3. **Slope:** 126/116. **Green Fee:** $15/$22. **Cart Fee:** $12/Person. **Walking Policy:** Unrestricted walking. **Walkability:** 2. **Opened:** 1926. **Architect:** Donald Ross. **Season:** Year-round. **High:** March-Nov. **To obtain tee times:** Call golf shop. **Miscellaneous:** Reduced fees (juniors), metal spikes, range (grass), credit cards (MC, V, AE, D), FF.
Reader Comments: A great course for anyone looking to enjoy a challenging round for under $20 … Nice layout. Very affordable … Friendly staff … Fun, traditional layout.

★½ **FOX CREEK GOLF CLUB**
PU-1501 Windy Hill Rd., Smyrna, 30080, Cobb County, (770)435-1000, 10 miles from Atlanta. **E-mail:** boliver@legacygolfmgmt.com. **Facility Holes:** 18. **Yards:** 3,879/2,973. **Par:** 61/61. **Course Rating:** 60.0/57.5. **Slope:** 102/92. **Green Fee:** $26/$36. **Cart Fee:** Included in green fee. **Walking Policy:** Unrestricted walking. **Walkability:** 3. **Opened:** 1985. **Architect:** John LaFoy. **Season:** Year-round. **High:** March-Nov. **To obtain tee times:** Call golf shop. **Miscellaneous:** Reduced fees (twilight, seniors, juniors), range (grass/mats), credit cards (MC, V, AE, Diners Club).

★★ **FRANCIS LAKE GOLF CLUB**
SP-5366 Golf Dr., Lake Park, 31636, Lowndes County, (912)559-7961, 12 miles from Valdosta. **E-mail:** leonard@datasys.net. **Facility Holes:** 18. **Yards:** 6,653/5,709. **Par:** 72/72. **Course Rating:** 71.4/70.1. **Slope:** 124/117. **Green Fee:** $22/$30. **Cart Fee:** Included in green fee. **Walking Policy:** Walking at certain times. **Walkability:** 1. **Opened:** 1973. **Architect:** Williard C. Byrd. **Season:** Year-round. **High:** Jan.-March. **To obtain tee times:** Call golf shop. **Miscellaneous:** Reduced fees (weekdays, guests, twilight, seniors, juniors), range (mats), credit cards (MC, V, AE).

★★★★½ **THE FROG AT THE GEORGIAN RESORT** *Condition, Pace*
PU-1900 Georgian Pkwy., Villa Rica, 30180, Paulding County, (770)459-4400, 35 miles from Atlanta. **Facility Holes:** 18. **Yards:** 7,018/5,336. **Par:** 72/72. **Course Rating:** 73.7/68.2. **Slope:** 137/118. **Green Fee:** $65/$79. **Cart Fee:** Included in green fee. **Walking Policy:** Unrestricted walking. **Walkability:** 2. **Opened:** 1998. **Architect:** Tom Fazio. **Season:** Year-round. **High:** April-Nov. **To obtain tee times:** Call up to 14 days in advance. **Miscellaneous:** Reduced fees (twilight), range (grass), credit cards (MC, V, AE, D, DC), BF, FF.
Notes: Ranked 14th in 2001 Best in State.
Reader Comments: Every type hole possible. Long and tough … Nice layout, needs time to mature … True, true, true greens … Peaceful, fantastic layout, use every club … Professional staff who pay attention to detail.

★★★★ **GEORGIA NATIONAL GOLF CLUB** *Pace*
SP-1715 Lake Dow Rd., McDonough, 30252, Henry County, (770)914-9994, 30 miles from Atlanta. **Facility Holes:** 18. **Yards:** 6,874/5,005. **Par:** 71/71. **Course Rating:** 74.1/70.5. **Slope:** 140/128. **Green Fee:** $40/$65. **Cart Fee:** Included in green fee. **Walking Policy:** Walking at certain times. **Walkability:** 5. **Opened:** 1994. **Architect:** Denis Griffiths. **Season:** Year-round. **High:** April-July. **To obtain tee times:** Call up to 7 days in advance. **Miscellaneous:** Reduced fees (weekdays, twilight, seniors, juniors), range (grass), credit cards (MC, V, AE, D), BF, FF.
Reader Comments: Course has tees for seniors to the scratch player. The hospitality of the employees was great … Course is always in great shape … Nice layout and condition was great for winter … Long, but wide. Well-kept even in drought.

★★★★ **GEORGIA VETERANS MEMORIAL GOLF COURSE**
PU-2315 Hwy. 280 W., Cordele, 31015, Crisp County, (229)276-2377, 45 miles from Macon. **Facility Holes:** 18. **Yards:** 7,088/5,171. **Par:** 72/72. **Course Rating:** 72.1/73.5. **Slope:** 130/124. **Green Fee:** $17/$21. **Cart Fee:** $10/Cart. **Walking Policy:** Unrestricted walking. **Walkability:** 1. **Opened:** 1990. **Architect:** Denis Griffiths. **Season:** Year-round. **High:** April-Sept. **To obtain tee times:** Call golf shop. **Miscellaneous:** Reduced fees (weekdays, twilight, seniors, juniors), range (grass), credit cards (MC, V, AE, D), BF, FF.
Reader Comments: Nice scenery, alligators in lakes … Great course, nice service and tournament-like course conditions … Clean, pretty, hills … Well-kept greens … Fine state-owned course.

GEORGIA

★ ★ ★ GOLD CREEK RESORT
R-1 Gold Creek Dr./P. O. Box 1357, Dawsonville, 30534, Dawson County, (770)844-1327, 45 miles from Atlanta. **Web:** www.goldcreek.com. **Facility Holes:** 27. **Yards:** 6,924/4,760. **Par:** 72/72. **Course Rating:** 73.3/67.2. **Slope:** 130/106. **Green Fee:** $52/$68. **Cart Fee:** Included in green fee. **Walking Policy:** Walking at certain times. **Walkability:** 3. **Opened:** 1995. **Architect:** Mike Young/David DeVictor. **Season:** Year-round. **High:** March-Nov. **To obtain tee times:** Call golf shop. **Miscellaneous:** Reduced fees (twilight, seniors, juniors), range (grass), lodging (74 rooms), credit cards (MC, V, AE).
Reader Comments: 27 holes, good condition … Steep, rolling mountains, lots of lost balls … Nice, fast greens, new 9 pretty rough, has promise … Very good course—very good service … Very attractive scenery.

★ ★ ½ THE GOLF CLUB AT BRADSHAW FARM
SP-3030 Bradshaw Club Dr., Woodstock, 30188, Cherokee County, (770)592-2222, 20 miles from Atlanta. **Facility Holes:** 18. **Yards:** 6,838/4,972. **Par:** 72/72. **Course Rating:** 73.5/68.6. **Slope:** 138/117. **Green Fee:** $35/$73. **Cart Fee:** Included in green fee. **Walking Policy:** Mandatory carts. **Walkability:** 5. **Opened:** 1995. **Architect:** Michael O'Shea. **Season:** Year-round. **To obtain tee times:** Call up to 8 days in advance. **Miscellaneous:** Reduced fees (weekdays, twilight, seniors, juniors), range (grass), credit cards (MC, V, AE, D, DC), BF, FF.

★ ★ ★ ★ ½ THE GOLF CLUB AT CUSCOWILLA *Condition, Pace+*
SP-354 Cuscowilla Dr., Eatonton, 31024, Putnam County, (706)485-0094, (800)458-5351, 90 miles from Atlanta. **Facility Holes:** 18. **Yards:** 6,847/5,348. **Par:** 70/72. **Course Rating:** 72.2/69.9. **Slope:** 132/123. **Green Fee:** $75/$90. **Cart Fee:** $15/Person. **Walking Policy:** Unrestricted walking. **Walkability:** 1. **Opened:** 1998. **Architect:** Bill Coore/Ben Crenshaw. **Season:** Year-round. **To obtain tee times:** Call up to 14 days in advance. **Miscellaneous:** Reduced fees (guests, juniors), range (grass), caddies, lodging (30 rooms), credit cards (MC, V, AE, D), BF, FF.
Notes: Ranked 9th in 2001 Best in State; 7th in 1999 Best New Upscale Public.
Reader Comments: One of the best courses I've played, 5 stars … Coore and Crenshaw are the best … Caddies, great greens, fun … An all-time classic … A bit pricey, but with it's a walker's delight! … Testing layout, nearly great.

★ ★ ½ GOSHEN PLANTATION COUNTRY CLUB
SP-1601 Goshen Clubhouse Dr., Augusta, 30906, Richmond County, (706)793-1168. **Facility Holes:** 18. **Yards:** 6,722/5,269. **Par:** 72/72. **Course Rating:** 72.5/70.3. **Slope:** 131/125. **Green Fee:** $24/$37. **Cart Fee:** Included in green fee. **Walking Policy:** Walking at certain times. **Opened:** 1970. **Architect:** Ellis Maples. **Season:** Year-round. **High:** March-Oct. **To obtain tee times:** Call golf shop. **Miscellaneous:** Reduced fees (weekdays, twilight, seniors, juniors), range (grass), credit cards (MC, V).

★ ★ ★ ½ HAMILTON MILL GOLF COURSE
PU-1995 Hamilton Mill Pkwy., Dacula, 30211, Gwinnett County, (770)945-4653, 10 miles from Buford. **E-mail:** golfshop@hamiltonmillgolf.com. **Web:** www.hamiltonmillgolf.com. **Facility Holes:** 18. **Yards:** 6,810/4,744. **Par:** 72/72. **Course Rating:** 73.7/68.4. **Slope:** 137/116. **Green Fee:** $49/$79. **Cart Fee:** Included in green fee. **Walking Policy:** Unrestricted walking. **Walkability:** 5. **Opened:** 1995. **Architect:** Gene Bates/Fred Couples. **Season:** Year-round. **To obtain tee times:** Call up to 10 days in advance. **Miscellaneous:** Reduced fees (weekdays, twilight, seniors, juniors), range (grass), credit cards (MC, V, AE, D), BF, FF.
Reader Comments: Nice track, slow play … Rates are a bit pricey … Quality course, excellent service … Tough hilly course … Fun, challenging, can score … Long course, good condition.

★ ★ ★ ½ HAMPTON CLUB *Pace*
R-100 Tabbystone, St. Simons Island, 31522, Glynn County, (912)634-0255, 70 miles from Jacksonville, FL. **E-mail:** hampton@hamptonclub.com. **Web:** www.hamptonclub.com. **Facility Holes:** 18. **Yards:** 6,400/5,233. **Par:** 72/72. **Course Rating:** 71.4/71.0. **Slope:** 130/123. **Green Fee:** $68. **Cart Fee:** $19/Person. **Walking Policy:** Mandatory carts. **Walkability:** 2. **Opened:** 1989. **Architect:** Joe Lee. **Season:** Year-round. **High:** Feb.-April. **To obtain tee times:** Call golf shop. **Miscellaneous:** Reduced fees (guests, juniors), range (grass), credit cards (MC, V, AE, D), BF, FF.
Reader Comments: Good design, lot of hills … New superintendent, tough par 3s … Outstanding back 9, beautiful holes … Nice marsh holes … What a wonderful experience.

HAMPTON GOLF VILLAGE
PU-6310 Hampton Golf Club Dr., Cumming, 30041, Forsyth County, (770)205-7070, 30 miles from Atlanta. **E-mail:** keithmelvin@mindspring.com. **Web:** www.hamptongolfvillage.net. **Facility Holes:** 18. **Yards:** 6,903/4,929. **Par:** 71/71. **Course Rating:** 72.9/68.3. **Slope:** 140/118. **Green Fee:** $25/$65. **Cart Fee:** Included in green fee. **Walking Policy:** Mandatory carts. **Walkability:**

3. **Opened:** 2000. **Architect:** Clyde Johnston. **Season:** Year-round. **To obtain tee times:** Call up to 7 days in advance. **Miscellaneous:** Reduced fees (weekdays, twilight, seniors), range (grass), credit cards (MC, V, AE), BF, FF.

★★★½ **HARBOR CLUB**
SP-One Club Dr., Greensboro, 30642, Greene County, (706)453-4414, (800)505-4653, 70 miles from Atlanta. **E-mail:** harborclub@plantation.net. **Web:** www.harborclub.com. **Facility Holes:** 18. **Yards:** 7,014/5,207. **Par:** 72/72. **Course Rating:** 73.7/70.2. **Slope:** 135/123. **Green Fee:** $59/$89. **Cart Fee:** Included in green fee. **Walking Policy:** Walking at certain times. **Walkability:** 3. **Opened:** 1991. **Architect:** Tom Weiskopf/Jay Morrish. **Season:** Year-round. **High:** March-Nov. **To obtain tee times:** Call up to 7 days in advance. **Miscellaneous:** Reduced fees (weekdays, guests, seniors, juniors), range (grass), credit cards (MC, V, AE), BF, FF.
Reader Comments: Great layout, a bit expensive … Very nice course. Friendly staff … Elevation changes over water are exciting.

★★★½ **HARD LABOR CREEK STATE PARK GOLF COURSE** *Pace*
PU-1400 Knox Chapel Rd., Rutledge, 30663, Morgan County, (706)557-3006, 45 miles from Atlanta. **Facility Holes:** 18. **Yards:** 6,444/4,854. **Par:** 72/75. **Course Rating:** 71.5/68.6. **Slope:** 129/123. **Green Fee:** $23/$28. **Cart Fee:** $12/Person. **Walking Policy:** Unrestricted walking. **Walkability:** 4. **Opened:** 1967. **Architect:** James B. McCloud. **Season:** Year-round. **To obtain tee times:** Call up to 14 days in advance. **Miscellaneous:** Reduced fees (seniors, juniors), range (grass), lodging (20 rooms), credit cards (MC, V, AE, D), BF, FF.
Reader Comments: Hilly and tight … Nice place to play 36 on a weekday … Clean, well-groomed course … Best Scenery & Value. Great on weekends, fast play … Keep it in the fairway … Good layout, wildlife abundant, several challenges.

★★½ **HENDERSON GOLF CLUB**
PU-1 A1 Henderson Dr., Savannah, 31419, Chatham County, (912)920-4653, 16 miles from Savannah. **Facility Holes:** 18. **Yards:** 6,650/4,788. **Par:** 71/71. **Course Rating:** 72.4/67.7. **Slope:** 136/115. **Green Fee:** $30/$44. **Cart Fee:** Included in green fee. **Walking Policy:** Walking at certain times. **Walkability:** 2. **Opened:** 1995. **Architect:** Mike Young. **Season:** Year-round. **To obtain tee times:** Call golf shop. **Miscellaneous:** Reduced fees (seniors, juniors), range (grass), credit cards (MC, V, AE), BF, FF.

★★½ **THE HERITAGE GOLF CLUB**
SP-4445 Britt Rd., Tucker, 30084, Gwinnett County, (770)493-4653, 12 miles from Downtown Atlanta. **Web:** www.heritagegolfclub.com. **Facility Holes:** 27. **Yards:** 6,903/5,153. **Par:** 72/72. **Course Rating:** 73.6/68.8. **Slope:** 145/120. **Green Fee:** $90. **Cart Fee:** Included in green fee. **Walking Policy:** Mandatory carts. **Walkability:** 4. **Opened:** 1996. **Architect:** Mike Young. **Season:** Year-round. **High:** March-Nov. **To obtain tee times:** Call golf shop. **Miscellaneous:** Range (grass), credit cards (MC, V, AE, D), BF, FF.
Notes: Ranked 20th in 1999 Best in State.
Special Notes: Also has a 9-hole executive course.

★★★½ **HIGHLAND GOLF CLUB**
SP-2271 Flat Shoals Rd., Conyers, 30013, Rockdale County, (770)483-4235, 30 miles from Atlanta. **Facility Holes:** 18. **Yards:** 6,817/5,383. **Par:** 72/72. **Course Rating:** 72.7/71.0. **Slope:** 128/118. **Green Fee:** $31/$47. **Cart Fee:** Included in green fee. **Walking Policy:** Mandatory carts. **Walkability:** 2. **Opened:** 1961. **Architect:** Neil Edwards. **Season:** Year-round. **High:** April-Oct. **To obtain tee times:** Call up to 5 days in advance. **Miscellaneous:** Reduced fees (weekdays, twilight, seniors, juniors), range (grass/mats), credit cards (MC, V), BF, FF.
Reader Comments: Fun, not long course, good greens … Always welcome, friendly … Good greens, pro shop. Picturesque with lots of wildlife … Wide open, hard to lose a ball.

HINSON HILLS GOLF COURSE
PU-3179 Hwy. 32 E, Douglas, 31533, Coffee County, (912)384-8984, 2 miles from Douglas. **Web:** www.hinsonhillsgolf.com. **Facility Holes:** 18. **Yards:** 3,020/1,736. **Par:** 54/54. **Course Rating:** 54.8/56.7. **Slope:** 85/87. **Green Fee:** $19/$22. **Cart Fee:** Included in green fee. **Walking Policy:** Unrestricted walking. **Walkability:** 2. **Opened:** 1992. **Architect:** L. Hinson. **Season:** Year-round. **High:** March-Oct. **To obtain tee times:** Call golf shop. **Miscellaneous:** Reduced fees (seniors), range (grass/mats), lodging (4 rooms), credit cards (MC, V, D), BF, FF.

★★★½ **HOUSTON LAKE COUNTRY CLUB**
SP-2323 Highway 127, Perry, 31069, Houston County, (478)218-5252, 20 miles from Macon. **Facility Holes:** 18. **Yards:** 6,800/5,100. **Par:** 72/72. **Course Rating:** 71.8/70.0. **Slope:** 132/122. **Green Fee:** $30/$37. **Cart Fee:** Included in green fee. **Walking Policy:** Unrestricted walking. **Walkability:** 1. **Opened:** 1966. **Architect:** O.C. Jones. **Season:** Year-round. **To obtain tee times:** Call golf shop. **Miscellaneous:** Reduced fees (juniors), range (grass/mats), credit cards (MC, V, AE), BF, FF.

GEORGIA

Reader Comments: Interesting, fun course … Beautiful lake views, in great condition … Lots of water … Great value, nice clubhouse facility … Super layout, friendly environment … Excellent course, fine personnel … Real challenge.

★★★ INNSBRUCK RESORT & GOLF CLUB
PU-Bahn Innsbruck, Helen, 30545, White County, (706)878-2100, (800)642-2709, 65 miles from Atlanta. **Facility Holes:** 18. **Yards:** 6,748/5,174. **Par:** 72/72. **Course Rating:** 72.4. **Slope:** 136/118. **Green Fee:** $30/$40. **Cart Fee:** Included in green fee. **Walkability:** 5. **Opened:** 1987. **Architect:** Bill Watts. **Season:** Year-round. **High:** April-Oct. **To obtain tee times:** Call golf shop. **Miscellaneous:** Reduced fees (guests, twilight, seniors, juniors), range (grass), credit cards (MC, V, AE).
Reader Comments: Friendly folks … Outstanding mountain course, nice greens … Exquisite setting, interesting holes, wildlife … A really difficult course … Short, but challenging … Hilly, nice facilities, should be cheaper.

★½ INTERNATIONAL CITY MUNICIPAL GOLF COURSE
PU-100 Sandy Run Lane, Warner Robins, 31088, Houston County, (912)922-3892, 15 miles from Macon. **Facility Holes:** 18. **Yards:** 6,071/4,425. **Par:** 71/71. **Course Rating:** 66.4/66.7. **Slope:** 109/110. **Green Fee:** $10/$14. **Cart Fee:** $10/Person. **Walking Policy:** Unrestricted walking. **Walkability:** 2. **Opened:** 1957. **Architect:** Lew Burnette/Arnie Smith. **Season:** Year-round. **High:** Aug.-Dec. **To obtain tee times:** Call golf shop. **Miscellaneous:** Reduced fees (seniors, juniors), metal spikes, range (grass), credit cards (MC, V).

JEKYLL ISLAND GOLF RESORT
R-Beachview Dr., Jekyll Island, 31527, Glynn County, (912)635-2170, (877)453-5955, 60 miles from Jacksonville, FL. **E-mail:** jigolf@hotmail.com. **Web:** www.jekyllisland.com. **Facility Holes:** 63. **Walkability:** 1. **Season:** Year-round. **To obtain tee times:** Call golf shop. **Miscellaneous:** Reduced fees (guests, twilight, juniors), metal spikes, range (grass), credit cards (MC, V, AE, D), FF.

★★★ GREAT DUNES COURSE (9)
Yards: 3,023/2,570. **Par:** 36/36. **Course Rating:** 70.9/70.3. **Slope:** 126/123. **Green Fee:** $21. **Walking Policy:** Unrestricted walking. **Opened:** 1898. **Architect:** Walter Travis.
Reader Comments: Awesome course, not in good shape, disappointing … 9-hole course, windy, small greens … Great price for an aesthetically beautiful course … Daily fee, all day play … Old course seaside.

★★★½ INDIAN MOUND COURSE (18)
Yards: 6,469/4,964. **Par:** 72/72. **Course Rating:** 71.3/68.8. **Slope:** 130/118. **Green Fee:** $35. **Cart Fee:** $15/Person. **Walking Policy:** Unrestricted walking. **Opened:** 1975. **Architect:** Joe Lee.
Reader Comments: Outstanding value & service … What a surprise. Great course in great shape for very reasonable price … A fun course … These people really treat you right … Enjoyable facilities, not well kept … Good design, rather narrow.

★★★ OLEANDER COURSE (18)
Yards: 6,521/4,913. **Par:** 72/72. **Course Rating:** 71.7/64.5. **Slope:** 126/110. **Green Fee:** $35. **Cart Fee:** $15/Person. **Walking Policy:** Unrestricted walking. **Opened:** 1964. **Architect:** Dick Wilson.
Reader Comments: Great grass, good lies consistently, good use of traps … Tough when the wind blows … Best of 3 … Friendly service … Great course to walk.

★★★ PINE LAKES COURSE (18)
Yards: 6,620/5,079. **Par:** 72/72. **Course Rating:** 71.3/64.2. **Slope:** 130/112. **Green Fee:** $35. **Cart Fee:** $15/Person. **Walking Policy:** Walking at certain times. **Opened:** 1968. **Architect:** Dick Wilson/Joe Lee.
Reader Comments: Outstanding value & service … Great layout … Good design, real challenge … Interesting wooded course … Longest and tightest of Jekyll courses … Small island, lots of motels! Some challenging holes. Good off season.

★★ LAKE ARROWHEAD COUNTRY CLUB
SP-L.A. Station 20, 598 Country Club Dr., Waleska, 30183, Cherokee County, (770)479-5500, 55 miles from Atlanta. **Facility Holes:** 18. **Yards:** 6,400/4,468. **Par:** 72/71. **Course Rating:** 72.4/67.2. **Slope:** 140/124. **Green Fee:** $32/$49. **Cart Fee:** Included in green fee. **Walkability:** 5. **Opened:** 1975. **Season:** Year-round. **High:** May-Aug. **To obtain tee times:** Call golf shop. **Miscellaneous:** Reduced fees (weekdays, guests, juniors), metal spikes, range (grass), credit cards (MC, V, AE, D).

★★★ LAKE BLACKSHEAR GOLF CLUB
PU-2078 Antioch Church Rd., Cordele, 31015, Crisp County, (912)535-4653, 24 miles from Albany. **Facility Holes:** 18. **Yards:** 6,930/5,372. **Par:** 72/72. **Course Rating:** 71.6/70.0. **Slope:** 129/120. **Green Fee:** $14/$19. **Cart Fee:** $9/Person. **Walking Policy:** Walking at certain times. **Walkability:** 3. **Opened:** 1995. **Architect:** Don McMillan/Ray Jensen/Don Marbury. **Season:**

Year-round. **High:** March-Nov. **To obtain tee times:** Call golf shop. **Miscellaneous:** Metal spikes, range (grass), credit cards (MC, V, AE).

Reader Comments: Good local course. Cheap green fees ... Enjoyable for average golfer ... Nice links-style layout ... Worth playing again ... Long course. Fun and challenging to play. Will visit often.

★★½ LAKESIDE COUNTRY CLUB

PU-3600 Old Fairburn Rd., Atlanta, 30331, Fulton County, (404)344-3629, 10 miles from Atlanta. **Facility Holes:** 18. **Yards:** 6,522/5,279. **Par:** 71/71. **Course Rating:** 71.4/70.7. **Slope:** 127/121. **Green Fee:** Included in green fee. **Opened:** 1962. **Architect:** George Cobb. **Season:** Year-round. **High:** March-May. **To obtain tee times:** Call golf shop. **Miscellaneous:** Reduced fees (weekdays, twilight, seniors), range (grass), credit cards (MC, V, AE).

★★★ LANDINGS GOLF CLUB

SP-309 Statham's Way, Warner Robins, 31088, Houston County, (912)923-5222, 15 miles from Macon. **E-mail:** pgagolfprolgc@aol.com. **Web:** www.landingsgolfclub.com. **Facility Holes:** 27. **Green Fee:** $30/$40. **Cart Fee:** Included in green fee. **Walking Policy:** Unrestricted walking. **Walkability:** 2. **Opened:** 1987. **Architect:** Tom Clark. **Season:** Year-round. **To obtain tee times:** Call up to 7 days in advance. **Miscellaneous:** Reduced fees (weekdays), range (grass), credit cards (MC, V, AE), BF, FF.
BLUFF/CREEK (18 Combo)
Yards: 6,671/5,157. **Par:** 72/73. **Course Rating:** 71.9/70.6. **Slope:** 130/118.
TRESTLE/BLUFF (18 Combo)
Yards: 6,998/5,481. **Par:** 72/74. **Course Rating:** 73.1/72.0. **Slope:** 133/119.
TRESTLE/CREEK (18 Combo)
Yards: 6,819/5,174. **Par:** 72/73. **Course Rating:** 72.6/71.8. **Slope:** 131/121.

Reader Comments: Good restaurant. Golf design not friendly ... Challenging, fun course ... Nice golf course set around many large homes ... 27-hole facility, good challenge ... Good course for residential area ... Very nice, favorite course to play.

★★★ LANE CREEK GOLF CLUB

PU-1201 Club Dr., Bishop, 30621, Oconee County, (706)769-6699, (800)842-6699, 8 miles from Athens. **Facility Holes:** 18. **Yards:** 6,752/5,293. **Par:** 72/72. **Course Rating:** 71.9/68.4. **Slope:** 130/115. **Green Fee:** $23/$43. **Cart Fee:** Included in green fee. **Walking Policy:** Walking at certain times. **Walkability:** 3. **Opened:** 1992. **Architect:** Mike Young. **Season:** Year-round. **High:** April-June. **To obtain tee times:** Call golf shop. **Miscellaneous:** Reduced fees (weekdays, twilight, seniors, juniors), range (grass/mats), credit cards (MC, V, D).

Reader Comments: Hidden gem in the rolling pine woods. Good shots rewarded, poor shots penalized fairly ... Best kept secret, fun, can rip it ... Good senior rate, unique holes (4 of them) ... Good course, reasonably good condition, nice price.

★★★ LAURA WALKER GOLF COURSE

PU-5500 Laura Walker Rd., Waycross, 31503, Ware County, (912)285-6154, 68 miles from Jacksonville. **E-mail:** lwgc@acmatel.net. **Web:** www.golfgeorge.org. **Facility Holes:** 18. **Yards:** 6,719/5,536. **Par:** 72/72. **Course Rating:** 71.9/66.6. **Slope:** 122/106. **Green Fee:** $10/$26. **Cart Fee:** $12/Person. **Walking Policy:** Walking at certain times. **Walkability:** 1. **Opened:** 1996. **Architect:** Steve Burns. **Season:** Year-round. **To obtain tee times:** Call golf shop. **Miscellaneous:** Reduced fees (weekdays, twilight, seniors, juniors), range (grass), credit cards (MC, V, AE, D), BF, FF.

Reader Comments: The best $35 you can spend on golf. Course is as good as a $90 course in Hilton Head. Requires good short game ... Very good for a state course.

LAUREL SPRINGS GOLF CLUB

SP-6400 Golf Club Dr., Suwanee, 30174, Gwinnett County, (770)884-0064, 30 miles from Atlanta. **E-mail:** todd.beiers@ovrclub.com. **Facility Holes:** 18. **Yards:** 6,804/5,119. **Par:** 71/71. **Course Rating:** 72.3/69.3. **Slope:** 137/125. **Green Fee:** $72/$90. **Cart Fee:** Included in green fee. **Walkability:** 4. **Opened:** 1998. **Architect:** Jack Nicklaus. **Season:** Year-round. **To obtain tee times:** Call up to 5 days in advance. **Miscellaneous:** Reduced fees (twilight, juniors), range (grass), credit cards (MC, V, AE), BF, FF.

★★½ THE LINKS AT LOST PLANTATION

SP-1 Clubhouse Dr., Rincon, 31326, Effingham County, (912)826-2092, 20 miles from Savannah. **Facility Holes:** 18. **Yards:** 6,800/5,250. **Par:** 72/72. **Course Rating:** 72.4/69.1. **Slope:** 127/123. **Green Fee:** $18/$32. **Cart Fee:** Included in green fee. **Walking Policy:** Walking at certain times. **Walkability:** 3. **Opened:** 1988. **Architect:** Ward Northrup. **Season:** Year-round. **To obtain tee times:** Call up to 7 days in advance. **Miscellaneous:** Reduced fees (weekdays, seniors, juniors), range (grass), credit cards (MC, V, AE, D), BF, FF.

★★ THE LINKS GOLF CLUB

PU-340 Hewell Rd., Jonesboro, 30238, Fayette County, (770)461-5100, 3 miles from Jonesboro. **E-mail:** linksglf@aol.com. **Web:** www.linksgolfclub.com. **Facility Holes:** 18. **Yards:** 6,376/4,398. **Par:** 70/70. **Course Rating:** 69.4/64.7. **Slope:** 118/111. **Green Fee:** $17/$25. **Cart Fee:** $15/Person. **Walking Policy:** Walking at certain times. **Walkability:** 2. **Opened:** 1991. **Season:** Year-round. **High:** April-Oct. **To obtain tee times:** Call up to 7 days in advance. **Misc:** Reduced fees (twilight, seniors, juniors), range (grass), credit cards (MC, V, AE, D), BF, FF. **Special Notes:** Also has a 9-hole par-3 course.

★★ LITTLE FISHING CREEK GOLF CLUB

PU-Highway 22 W., Milledgeville, 31061, Baldwin County, (912)445-0796, 35 miles from Macon. **Facility Holes:** 18. **Yards:** 6,718/5,509. **Par:** 72/73. **Course Rating:** 72.4/73.6. **Slope:** 121/121. **Green Fee:** $7/$12. **Cart Fee:** $9/Person. **Walking Policy:** Unrestricted walking. **Walkability:** 5. **Opened:** 1981. **Season:** Year-round. **High:** March-June. **To obtain tee times:** Call golf shop. **Miscellaneous:** Reduced fees (twilight, seniors, juniors), metal spikes, range (grass), credit cards (MC, V, AE, D).

★★ LITTLE MOUNTAIN GOLF COURSE

PU-1850 Little Mountain Rd., Ellenwood, 30294, Henry County, (770)981-7921, 15 miles from Atlanta. **Facility Holes:** 27. **Yards:** 5,737/4,647. **Par:** 72/72. **Course Rating:** 68.1/66.8. **Slope:** 117/114. **Green Fee:** $14/$23. **Cart Fee:** $24/Cart. **Walking Policy:** Unrestricted walking. **Walkability:** 3. **Opened:** 1969. **Season:** Year-round. **To obtain tee times:** Call up to 5 days in advance. **Misc:** Reduced fees (twilight, seniors), range, credit cards (MC, V), FF. **Special Notes:** Also has a 9-hole course.

★★½ METROPOLITAN GOLF CLUB

SP-300 Fairington Pkwy., Lithonia, 30038, De Kalb County, (770)981-7696, 10 miles from Atlanta. **Facility Holes:** 18. **Yards:** 6,030/5,966. **Par:** 72/72. **Course Rating:** 74.2/74.8. **Slope:** 138/131. **Green Fee:** $32/$43. **Cart Fee:** Included in green fee. **Walking Policy:** Walking at certain times. **Opened:** 1967. **Architect:** Robert Trent Jones. **Season:** Year-round. **High:** April-Sept. **To obtain tee times:** Call golf shop. **Miscellaneous:** Reduced fees (weekdays, twilight), metal spikes, range (grass), credit cards (MC, V, AE).

★★½ MYSTERY VALLEY GOLF COURSE

PU-6094 Shadowrock Dr., Lithonia, 30058, De Kalb County, (770)469-6913, 5 miles from Stone Mountain. **Facility Holes:** 18. **Yards:** 6,705/5,815. **Par:** 72/75. **Course Rating:** 71.7/73.1. **Slope:** 125/124. **Green Fee:** $15/$25. **Cart Fee:** $11/Person. **Walking Policy:** Unrestricted walking. **Walkability:** 3. **Opened:** 1965. **Architect:** Dick Wilson. **Season:** Year-round. **To obtain tee times:** Call up to 7 days in advance. **Miscellaneous:** Reduced fees (weekdays, seniors, juniors), range (grass), credit cards (MC, V, AE), BF, FF.

NICKLAUS GOLF CLUB AT BIRCH RIVER

SP-639 Birch River Dr., Dahlonega, 30533, Lumpkin County, (866)271-5700, (866)271-5700, 50 miles from Atlanta. **E-mail:** jonkitchen@ourclub.com. **Web:** nicklausgolfbirchriver.com. **Facility Holes:** 18. **Yards:** 6,937/4,992. **Par:** 72/72. **Course Rating:** 72.8/67.9. **Slope:** 134/118. **Green Fee:** $65/$85. **Cart Fee:** Included in green fee. **Walking Policy:** Mandatory carts. **Walkability:** 1. **Opened:** 2000. **Architect:** Jack Nicklaus. **Season:** Year-round. **To obtain tee times:** Call up to 7 days in advance. **Miscellaneous:** Reduced fees (weekdays, twilight, juniors), range (grass), credit cards (MC, V), BF, FF.

★★★★ NOB NORTH GOLF COURSE *Value*

PU-298 Nob N. Dr., Cohutta, 30710, Whitfield County, (706)694-8505, 25 miles from Chattanooga, TN. **E-mail:** afnobnorth@alltel.net. **Facility Holes:** 18. **Yards:** 6,573/5,448. **Par:** 72/72. **Course Rating:** 71.7/71.7. **Slope:** 128/126. **Green Fee:** $21/$25. **Cart Fee:** $12/Person. **Walking Policy:** Unrestricted walking. **Walkability:** 3. **Opened:** 1978. **Architect:** Ron Kirby/Gary Player. **Season:** Year-round. **To obtain tee times:** Call up to 5 days in advance. **Miscellaneous:** Reduced fees (seniors, juniors), range (grass), credit cards (MC, V), BF, FF.
Reader Comments: 1st is a great par-5 starting hole you can score on, if you hit good shots ... Great public course ... Wide open, beautiful greens and fairways ... Always fun and in good shape ... Well maintained, they constantly make improvements.

★★½ NORTH FULTON GOLF COURSE

PU-216 W. Wieuca Rd., Atlanta, 30342, Fulton County, (404)255-0723. **Facility Holes:** 18. **Yards:** 6,570/5,120. **Par:** 71/71. **Course Rating:** 71.8/69.5. **Slope:** 126/118. **Green Fee:** $14/$16. **Cart Fee:** $10/Person. **Walking Policy:** Unrestricted walking. **Walkability:** 2. **Opened:** 1935. **Architect:** H. Chandler Egan. **Season:** Year-round. **High:** June-July. **To obtain tee times:** Call golf shop. **Miscellaneous:** Reduced fees (weekdays, twilight, seniors, juniors), metal spikes, credit cards (MC, V, AE).

★★★ OAK GROVE ISLAND GOLF CLUB
SP-100 Clipper Bay, Brunswick, 31523, Glynn County, (912)280-9525, 45 miles from Savannah. **Facility Holes:** 18. **Yards:** 6,910/4,855. **Par:** 72/72. **Course Rating:** 73.2/67.6. **Slope:** 132/116. **Green Fee:** $6/$22. **Cart Fee:** $15/Person. **Walking Policy:** Mandatory carts. **Walkability:** 3. **Opened:** 1993. **Architect:** Mike Young. **Season:** Year-round. **High:** Feb.-May. **To obtain tee times:** Call up to 7 days in advance. **Miscellaneous:** Reduced fees (weekdays, guests, twilight, seniors, juniors), range (grass), credit cards (MC, V, AE, D), BF, FF.
Reader Comments: Cheap & good ... What a deal ... Poor condition, boring layout ... Love the layout, never crowded, senior blitz activity.

OAK MOUNTAIN CHAMPIONSHIP GOLF CLUB
SP-409 Birkdale Blvd., Carrollton, 30116, Carroll County, (770)834-7065, 35 miles from Atlanta. **Facility Holes:** 18. **Yards:** 7,056/5,187. **Par:** 72/72. **Course Rating:** 72.8/69.4. **Slope:** 134/127. **Green Fee:** $25/$52. **Cart Fee:** Included in green fee. **Walking Policy:** Unrestricted walking. **Walkability:** 4. **Opened:** 1997. **Architect:** Ward Northrup. **Season:** Year-round. **To obtain tee times:** Call golf shop. **Miscellaneous:** Reduced fees (weekdays, twilight, seniors, juniors), range (grass/mats), credit cards (MC, V, AE, D), BF, FF.

★★★½ THE OAKS GOLF COURSE
SP-11240 Brown Bridge Rd., Covington, 30014, Newton County, (770)786-3801, 30 miles from Atlanta. **E-mail:** golf@golfoaks. **Web:** www.golfoaks.com. **Facility Holes:** 18. **Yards:** 6,437/4,600. **Par:** 70/70. **Course Rating:** 70.2/64.5. **Slope:** 121/107. **Green Fee:** $28/$45. **Cart Fee:** Included in green fee. **Walking Policy:** Walking at certain times. **Walkability:** 3. **Opened:** 1990. **Architect:** Richard M. Schulz. **Season:** Year-round. **High:** March-Nov. **To obtain tee times:** Call up to 7 days in advance. **Miscellaneous:** Reduced fees (weekdays, guests, twilight, seniors, juniors), range (grass), credit cards (MC, V, AE, D), BF, FF.
Reader Comments: Outstanding course for your money! ... Good for seniors ... Always good place to play ... One of the best values around ... Fun course with chance to score ... Super staff.

★★★ OAKVIEW GOLF & COUNTRY CLUB
PU-129 Oakview Club Dr., Macon, 31216, Bibb County, (478)784-8700, 65 miles from Atlanta. **E-mail:** glcoxe@oakviewgolf.com. **Web:** www.oakviewgolf.com. **Facility Holes:** 18. **Yards:** 6,722/4,894. **Par:** 72/72. **Course Rating:** 72.7/68.7. **Slope:** 135/121. **Green Fee:** $12/$24. **Cart Fee:** $12/Person. **Walking Policy:** Walking at certain times. **Walkability:** 4. **Opened:** 1999. **Architect:** Barry Edgar. **Season:** Year-round. **High:** April-Oct. **To obtain tee times:** Call golf shop. **Miscellaneous:** Reduced fees (weekdays, juniors), range (grass), credit cards (MC, V, AE, D).
Reader Comments: Very new course with good potential. Time will tell ... Good new course, but grass hasn't fully developed, nice service though ... Scenic new course, hilly, fun.

★★★ OLDE ATLANTA GOLF CLUB
SP-5750 Olde Atlanta Pkwy., Suwanee, 30024, Gwinnett County, (770)497-0097, 15 miles from Atlanta. **E-mail:** oldeatlanta@mindspring.com. **Web:** www.oldeatlanta.com. **Facility Holes:** 18. **Yards:** 6,800/5,147. **Par:** 71/71. **Course Rating:** 73.5/69.3. **Slope:** 136/120. **Green Fee:** $61/$78. **Walking Policy:** Walking at certain times. **Walkability:** 3. **Opened:** 1993. **Architect:** Arthur Hills. **Season:** Year-round. **High:** April-Sept. **To obtain tee times:** Call up to 7 days in advance. **Miscellaneous:** Reduced fees (twilight, seniors, juniors), range (grass/mats), credit cards (MC, V, AE), BF, FF.
Reader Comments: Lots of hills! Another North Atlanta gem ... Good conditions, considering the volume of play ... Quirky, good greens, Hills deserved more land ... Marshals were very helpful with pace of play.

★★★½ ORCHARD HILLS GOLF CLUB
PU-600 E. Hwy. 16, Newnan, 30263, Coweta County, (770)251-5683, 33 miles from Atlanta. **Facility Holes:** 27. **Green Fee:** $44/$55. **Cart Fee:** Included in green fee. **Walking Policy:** Walking at certain times. **Walkability:** 3. **Opened:** 1990. **Architect:** Don Cottle Jr. **Season:** Year-round. **High:** April-May. **To obtain tee times:** Call golf shop. **Miscellaneous:** Reduced fees (weekdays, twilight, seniors, juniors), range (grass), credit cards (MC, V, AE, D).
LOGO/ROCK GARDEN (18 Combo)
Yards: 7,002/5,052. **Par:** 72/72. **Course Rating:** 73.4/68.4. **Slope:** 134/118.
ORCHARD/LOGO (18 Combo)
Yards: 7,012/5,153. **Par:** 72/72. **Course Rating:** 73.4/68.9. **Slope:** 131/116.
ROCK GARDEN/ORCHARD (18 Combo)
Yards: 7,014/5,245. **Par:** 72/72. **Course Rating:** 72.8/68.4. **Slope:** 132/118.
Reader Comments: Excellent course for the cost ... Very nice course, friendly personnel, the clubhouse could be bigger and in better condition for this course ... Some of the best greens anywhere ... Variety of holes, something for everyone.

GEORGIA

★★★★ **OSPREY COVE GOLF CLUB** *Value, Pace+*
SP-123 Osprey Dr., St. Marys, 31558, Camden County, (912)882-5575, (800)352-5575, 35
miles from Jacksonville, FL. **Facility Holes:** 18. **Yards:** 6,791/5,145. **Par:** 72/72. **Course Rating:**
72.9/69.7. **Slope:** 132/120. **Green Fee:** $25/$85. **Cart Fee:** Included in green fee. **Walking
Policy:** Mandatory carts. **Walkability:** 3. **Opened:** 1990. **Architect:** Mark McCumber. **Season:**
Year-round. **High:** Feb.-April. **To obtain tee times:** Call up to 7 days in advance. **Misc:**
Reduced fees (twilight, juniors), range (grass), credit cards (MC, V, AE), BF, FF.
Reader Comments: You've got to be able to hit every club in your bag, but it's a good test of golf ...
Great value, neat course ... Marsh-links, double green (9 & 18) ... Scenic, wide fairways ... Well laid
out and fun to play.

★★★½ **PINE BLUFF GOLF & COUNTRY CLUB**
PU-Hwy. 341 S., Eastman, 31023, Dodge County, (912)374-0991, 50 miles from Macon.
E-mail: mooret@public.ub.ga.us. **Web:** www.pinebluffcc.com. **Facility Holes:** 18. **Yards:**
6,499/5,065. **Par:** 72/72. **Course Rating:** 70.6/69.1. **Slope:** 125/119. **Green Fee:** $8/$12. **Cart
Fee:** $8/Person. **Walking Policy:** Walking at certain times. **Opened:** 1994. **Architect:** Tim
Moore. **Season:** Year-round. **High:** March-May. **To obtain tee times:** Call golf shop. **Misc:**
Reduced fees (twilight, seniors, juniors), metal spikes, range (grass), credit cards (MC, V, D).
Reader Comments: Outstanding course, great layout, for such a small town ... Great course for
small green fee ... Open front, tight back ... Super friendly staff.

★★★½ **PORT ARMOR RESORT & COUNTRY CLUB**
R-One Port Armor Pkwy., Greensboro, 30642, Greene County, (706)453-4564,
(800)804-7678, 50 miles from Atlanta. **Facility Holes:** 18. **Yards:** 6,926/5,177. **Par:** 72/72.
Course Rating: 74.0/72.8. **Slope:** 140/131. **Green Fee:** $30/$69. **Cart Fee:** Included in green
fee. **Walkability:** 4. **Opened:** 1986. **Architect:** Bob Cupp. **Season:** Year-round. **High:** April-Oct.
To obtain tee times: Call golf shop. **Miscellaneous:** Reduced fees (guests), metal spikes,
range (grass), credit cards (MC, V, AE), FF.
Reader Comments: Superb, great, play black tees ... Super layout, beautiful views ... Beautiful
championship course ... New, great greens.

RAINTREE GOLF CLUB
PU-1495 Hwy. 19 S., Thomaston, 30286, Upson County, (706)647-7358. **Facility Holes:** 18.
Yards: 6,463/4,873. **Par:** 72/72. **Course Rating:** 70.1/66.3. **Slope:** 127/118. **Green Fee:**
$20/$38. **Cart Fee:** Included in green fee. **Opened:** 2000. **Architect:** Mark Bennett/
Don McMillan. **Season:** Year-round. **To obtain tee times:** Call golf shop. **Misc:** Reduced fees
(weekdays, seniors).

★★★½ **RENAISSANCE PINEISLE RESORT**
R-9000 Holiday Rd., Lake Lanier Islands, 30518, Hall County, (770)945-8921, 45 miles from
Atlanta. **Facility Holes:** 18. **Yards:** 6,527/5,297. **Par:** 72/72. **Course Rating:** 71.6/70.6. **Slope:**
132/127. **Green Fee:** $39/$69. **Cart Fee:** Included in green fee. **Walking Policy:** Walking at certain times. **Walkability:** 4. **Opened:** 1973. **Architect:** Gary Player/Ron Kirby. **Season:** Year-
round. **High:** April-Nov. **To obtain tee times:** Call up to 14 days in advance. **Miscellaneous:**
Reduced fees (weekdays, twilight, seniors, juniors), range (grass), lodging (254 rooms), credit
cards (MC, V, AE, D, DC), BF, FF.
Reader Comments: Tricky course if you don't play smart ... A short, target-oriented course. Do not
try to overpower and you can score on this beautiful track. Plenty of water.

REYNOLDS PLANTATION
R-100 Plantation Drive, Eatonton, 31024, Putnam County, (706)485-0235, (800)852-5885, 70
miles from Macon. **Facility Holes:** 54. **Cart Fee:** $20/Person. **Walking Policy:** Walking at cer-
tain times. **Season:** Year-round. **To obtain tee times:** Call golf shop. **Miscellaneous:** Lodging
(99 rooms), credit cards (MC, V, AE, D).
★★★★½ **GREAT WATERS COURSE** (18) *Condition*
Yards: 7,058/5,057. **Par:** 72/72. **Course Rating:** 73.8/69.2. **Slope:** 135/114. **Green Fee:** $110.
Walkability: 3. **Opened:** 1992. **Architect:** Jack Nicklaus. **High:** April-Oct. **Miscellaneous:**
Reduced fees (weekdays), range (grass).
Notes: Ranked 8th in 2001 Best in State.
Reader Comments: Quiet start and noisy finish, beautiful ... Great 2nd & 18th holes ... Pricey, but
terrific track, beautiful holes around lake ... Tough, tight course especially in windy conditions ...
Worth it. A must-play course ... Great course, greens excellent.
★★★★ **NATIONAL COURSE** (18)
Yards: 7,015/5,292. **Par:** 72/72. **Course Rating:** 72.7/69.5. **Slope:** 127/116. **Green Fee:** $110.
Walkability: 4. **Opened:** 1997. **Architect:** Tom Fazio. **High:** April-Aug. **Miscellaneous:** Reduced
fees (weekdays), range (grass/mats).
Notes: Ranked 18th in 2001 Best in State.
Reader Comments: Good companion to Great Waters. Challenging layout, nice greens ... Very
enjoyable, challenging course ... Pricey, great layout, fun to play.

★★★★½ **PLANTATION COURSE** (18)
Yards: 6,698/5,121. **Par:** 72/72. **Course Rating:** 71.7/68.9. **Slope:** 128/115. **Green Fee:** $85/$95. **Walkability:** 3. **Opened:** 1987. **Architect:** Bob Cupp/Fuzzy Zoeller/Hubert Green. **High:** April-Aug. **Miscellaneous:** Reduced fees (weekdays, juniors), range (mats).
Reader Comments: The oldest and shortest of the Reynolds Plantation courses, but fun layout and nice facilities … As tough as it gets from the blues … Beautiful course.

★★½ **RIVER'S EDGE GOLF COURSE**
SP-40 Southern Golf Court, Fayetteville, 30214, Fayette County, (770)460-1098, 19 miles from Atlanta. **Facility Holes:** 18. **Yards:** 6,810/5,641. **Par:** 71/71. **Course Rating:** 72.9/69.9. **Slope:** 135/121. **Green Fee:** $35/$49. **Cart Fee:** Included in green fee. **Walkability:** 4. **Opened:** 1990. **Architect:** Bobby Weed. **Season:** Year-round. **High:** March-Oct. **To obtain tee times:** Call golf shop. **Miscellaneous:** Reduced fees (weekdays, twilight, seniors, juniors), range (grass), credit cards (MC, V, AE).

★★★½ **RIVERPINES GOLF CLUB**
PU-4775 Old Alabama Rd., Alpharetta, 30022, Fulton County, (770)442-5960, 20 miles from Atlanta. **E-mail:** rpgolfpro@mindspring.com. **Web:** www.riverpinesgolf.com. **Facility Holes:** 18. **Yards:** 6,511/4,279. **Par:** 70/70. **Course Rating:** 71.4/65.1. **Slope:** 128/106. **Green Fee:** $60/$70. **Cart Fee:** Included in green fee. **Walking Policy:** Walking at certain times. **Walkability:** 3. **Opened:** 1992. **Architect:** Denis Griffiths. **Season:** Year-round. **High:** April-Sept. **To obtain tee times:** Call golf shop. **Miscellaneous:** Reduced fees (twilight, juniors), range (grass/mats), credit cards (MC, V, AE), BF, FF.
Reader Comments: Good pace, I like that they speed up hackers … Good layout with greens in good shape … Course is always kept up … Great practice facilities … Good course maintenance, good service … Tougher than it looks.

★★★½ **ROYAL LAKES GOLF & COUNTRY CLUB**
SP-4700 Royal Lakes Dr., Flowery Branch, 30542, Hall County, (770)535-8800, 35 miles from Atlanta. **Web:** www.royallakes.com. **Facility Holes:** 18. **Yards:** 6,871/5,325. **Par:** 72/72. **Course Rating:** 72.0/70.4. **Slope:** 135/118. **Green Fee:** $27/$59. **Cart Fee:** Included in green fee. **Walking Policy:** Walking at certain times. **Walkability:** 3. **Opened:** 1989. **Architect:** Arthur Davis. **Season:** Year-round. **To obtain tee times:** Call up to 4 days in advance. **Miscellaneous:** Reduced fees (weekdays, twilight, seniors, juniors), range (grass), credit cards (MC, V, AE), FF.
Reader Comments: Very good course maintenance, good service … Hilly, some challenging shots, tough par 3s. Excellent fast greens … Nice course, not worth price.

★½ **ROYAL OAKS GOLF CLUB**
SP-256 Summit Ridge Dr., Cartersville, 30120, Bartow County, (770)382-3999, 40 miles from Atlanta. **E-mail:** royaloaks@mindsrpring.com. **Web:** www.royaloaksgolf.com. **Facility Holes:** 18. **Yards:** 6,409/4,890. **Par:** 71/75. **Course Rating:** 70.0/71.0. **Slope:** 124/121. **Green Fee:** $20/$30. **Cart Fee:** $12/Person. **Walking Policy:** Walking at certain times. **Walkability:** 3. **Opened:** 1978. **Architect:** Kirby/Davis/Bingaman. **Season:** Year-round. **High:** April-Oct. **To obtain tee times:** Call golf shop. **Miscellaneous:** Reduced fees (weekdays, twilight, seniors, juniors), range (grass/mats), credit cards (MC, V).

SCALES CREEK GOLF CLUB
PU-474 Samples-Scales Rd., Homer, 30547, Banks County, (706)677-3333, 65 miles from Atlanta. **E-mail:** scalescreek@alltel.net. **Web:** www.scalescreek.com. **Facility Holes:** 18. **Yards:** 6,985/4,778. **Par:** 72/72. **Course Rating:** 73.4/66.5. **Slope:** 132/116. **Green Fee:** $29/$55. **Cart Fee:** Included in green fee. **Walking Policy:** Mandatory carts. **Walkability:** 3. **Opened:** 1998. **Architect:** Mark McCumber. **Season:** Year-round. **To obtain tee times:** Call golf shop. **Miscellaneous:** Reduced fees (weekdays, twilight, seniors, juniors), range (grass), credit cards (MC, V, D), FF.

SEA ISLAND GOLF CLUB
R-100 Retreat Ave., St. Simons Island, 31522, Glynn County, (912)638-5118, (800)732-4752, 50 miles from Jacksonville. **E-mail:** branenveal@seaisland.com. **Facility Holes:** 54. **Cart Fee:** Included in green fee. **Season:** Year-round. **To obtain tee times:** Call golf shop. **Miscellaneous:** Reduced fees (juniors), range (grass/mats), credit cards (MC, V, AE, D, Sea Island Card), BF, FF.
★★★★½ **PLANTATION COURSE** (18) *Condition, Pace*
Yards: 7,043/5,223. **Par:** 72/74. **Course Rating:** 73.9/69.8. **Slope:** 135/124. **Green Fee:** $145/$175. **Walking Policy:** Walking with Caddie. **Walkability:** 2. **Opened:** 1998. **Architect:** Rees Jones. **Miscellaneous:** Lodging (300 rooms).
Reader Comments: Greens like Pinehurst #2 … Everything was as nice as possible … Expensive, caddies available, good course … Typical seaside course … Loved the entire experience … Better than average resort course.

GEORGIA

★★★★½ **SEASIDE COURSE** (18) *Condition, Pace*
Yards: 6,945/5,048. **Par:** 70/70. **Course Rating:** 73.1/69.3. **Slope:** 131/119. **Green Fee:** $185/$215. **Walking Policy:** Walking at certain times. **Walkability:** 1. **Opened:** 1999. **Architect:** Tom Fazio. **Miscellaneous:** Lodging (40 rooms).
Notes: Ranked 4th in 2000 Best New Upscale Courses.
Reader Comments: Unbelievably gorgeous layout. Don't pass up a chance to play here … Great golf course! Fun to play … Beautiful and challenging … Sand & water everywhere … Outstanding in all areas … A great caddie program, a course with no homes.
Special Notes: Also has 18-hole private course.

★★★ **SEA PALMS RESORT**
R-5445 Frederica Rd., St. Simons Island, 31522, Glynn County, (912)638-9041, (800)841-6268, 65 miles from Jacksonville. **Facility Holes:** 27. **Walking Policy:** Mandatory carts. **Walkability:** 2. **Opened:** 1966. **Season:** Year-round. **High:** Feb.-May. **To obtain tee times:** Call up to 7 days in advance. **Miscellaneous:** Reduced fees (weekdays, guests, twilight, juniors), range (grass/mats), credit cards (MC, V, AE), BF, FF.
GREAT OAKS/SEA PALMS (18 Combo)
Yards: 6,350/5,200. **Par:** 72/72. **Course Rating:** 71.8/69.3. **Slope:** 128/124. **Green Fee:** $35/$52. **Cart Fee:** $18/Person. **Architect:** George Cobb/Tom Jackson.
TALL PINES/GREAT OAKS (18 Combo)
Yards: 6,658/5,350. **Par:** 72/72. **Course Rating:** 72.1/70.9. **Slope:** 131/120. **Green Fee:** $35/$50. **Cart Fee:** $17/Person. **Architect:** George Cobb.
TALL PINES/SEA PALMS (18 Combo)
Yards: 6,198/5,249. **Par:** 72/72. **Course Rating:** 70.6/70.8. **Slope:** 129/127. **Green Fee:** $35/$50. **Cart Fee:** $17/Person. **Architect:** George Cobb.

★★★ **SKY VALLEY GOLF & SKI RESORT**
R-696 Sky Valley Way #1, Sky Valley, 30537, Rabun County, (706)746-5303, (800)437-2416, 100 miles from Atlanta. **E-mail:** info@skyvalley.com. **Web:** www.skyvalley.com. **Facility Holes:** 18. **Yards:** 6,452/5,017. **Par:** 72/72. **Course Rating:** 7.0/68.3. **Slope:** 133/119. **Green Fee:** $30/$50. **Cart Fee:** Included in green fee. **Walking Policy:** Walking at certain times. **Walkability:** 3. **Opened:** 1971. **Architect:** Bill Watts. **Season:** Year-round. **High:** April-Oct. **To obtain tee times:** Call up to 20 days in advance. **Miscellaneous:** Reduced fees (weekdays, guests, twilight, juniors), range (grass), credit cards (MC, V, AE, D), BF, FF.
Reader Comments: This course is still fun after lots of play over several years. Good tee designs make it enjoyable for both high-and-low-handicappers. Very pretty course without being over the top … New irrigation system really helps fairways … A really fun mountain course.

★★½ **SOUTHBRIDGE GOLF CLUB**
SP-415 Southbridge Blvd., Savannah, 31405, Chatham County, (912)651-5455. **E-mail:** southbridge@hmsgolf.com. **Web:** www.southbridgegolf.com. **Facility Holes:** 18. **Yards:** 6,990/5,181. **Par:** 72/72. **Course Rating:** 73.4/69.2. **Slope:** 136/118. **Green Fee:** $38/$44. **Cart Fee:** Included in green fee. **Walking Policy:** Mandatory carts. **Walkability:** 1. **Opened:** 1988. **Architect:** Rees Jones. **Season:** Year-round. **To obtain tee times:** Call up to 7 days in advance. **Miscellaneous:** Reduced fees (weekdays, twilight, seniors, juniors), range (grass), credit cards (MC, V, AE, D), BF, FF.

★★★★½ **SOUTHERN HILLS G. C.** *Service+, Value+, Condition+, Pace+*
SP-Hwy. 247, Hawkinsville, 31036, Pulaski County, (478)783-0600, 40 miles from Macon. **E-mail:** southernhill@cstel.net. **Web:** www.southernhillsgolf.com. **Facility Holes:** 18. **Yards:** 6,741/5,290. **Par:** 72/72. **Course Rating:** 72.7/70.6. **Slope:** 134/122. **Green Fee:** $21/$32. **Cart Fee:** Included in green fee. **Walking Policy:** Unrestricted walking. **Walkability:** 1. **Opened:** 1997. **Architect:** Mike Young/Ernest Jones. **Season:** Year-round. **High:** March-Oct. **To obtain tee times:** Call golf shop. **Miscellaneous:** Reduced fees (weekdays, twilight, seniors, juniors), range (grass), credit cards (MC, V, AE), BF, FF.
Reader Comments: Great new course. Staff is friendly and take good care of you. The layout is good and the course is in extremely good shape … Tough front 9 but easier back, quick hard greens … One of the best courses I've played.

★★★ **SOUTHERNESS GOLF CLUB**
SP-4871 Flat Bridge Rd., Stockbridge, 30281, Rockdale County, (770)808-6000, 20 miles from Atlanta. **Facility Holes:** 18. **Yards:** 6,756/4,916. **Par:** 72/72. **Course Rating:** 73.6/69.0. **Slope:** 136/119. **Green Fee:** $14/$36. **Cart Fee:** $14/Person. **Walking Policy:** Mandatory carts. **Walkability:** 3. **Opened:** 1991. **Architect:** Clyde Johnston. **Season:** Year-round. **To obtain tee times:** Call up to 5 days in advance. **Miscellaneous:** Reduced fees (twilight, seniors, juniors), range (grass/mats), credit cards (MC, V, AE).
Reader Comments: Nice layout, but drainage is a problem, wonderful practice areas … New owners, will be excellent … Great course for women.

★★★ ST. MARLO COUNTRY CLUB

PU-7755 St. Marlo Country Club Pkwy., Duluth, 30097, Forsyth County, (770)495-7725, 25 miles from Atlanta. **E-mail:** amy.donahue@mindspring. **Web:** www.stmarlo.com. **Facility Holes:** 18. **Yards:** 6,923/5,085. **Par:** 72/72. **Course Rating:** 73.5/70.3. **Slope:** 138/119. **Green Fee:** $66/$84. **Cart Fee:** Included in green fee. **Walking Policy:** Unrestricted walking. **Walkability:** 4. **Opened:** 1995. **Architect:** Denis Griffiths. **Season:** Year-round. **To obtain tee times:** Call up to 7 days in advance. **Miscellaneous:** Reduced fees (weekdays, twilight, seniors, juniors), range (grass/mats), credit cards (MC, V, AE, D, DC), BF, FF.
Notes: Ranked 10th in 1995 Best New Public Courses.
Reader Comments: You need 14 clubs here, strategic layout ... Not very long, but in great shape. Some of the fastest greens you will ever play ... Some holes are difficult ... Some holes needed work ... Beautiful course, great service & price.

★★★ STONE CREEK GOLF CLUB

SP-4300 Coleman Rd., Valdosta, 31602, Lowndes County, (229)247-2527. **E-mail:** Stnck@datasys.net. **Facility Holes:** 18. **Yards:** 6,850/4,750. **Par:** 72/72. **Course Rating:** 71.7/67.5. **Slope:** 121/114. **Green Fee:** $31/$40. **Cart Fee:** Included in green fee. **Walking Policy:** Mandatory carts. **Walkability:** 2. **Opened:** 1992. **Architect:** Franzman-Davis. **Season:** Year-round. **To obtain tee times:** Call golf shop. **Miscellaneous:** Reduced fees (weekdays), range (grass/mats), credit cards (MC, V, AE, D, DC), BF, FF.
Reader Comments: Interesting layout, good value.

STONE MOUNTAIN GOLF CLUB

PU-1145 Stonewall Jackson Drive, Stone Mountain, 30083, De Kalb County, (770)465-3278, 16 miles from Atlanta. **E-mail:** steve/hupe@marriott.com. **Web:** www.stonemountaingolf.com. **Facility Holes:** 36. **Green Fee:** $34/$57. **Cart Fee:** Included in green fee. **Walking Policy:** Walking at certain times. **Walkability:** 4. **Season:** Year-round. **High:** April-Nov. **To obtain tee times:** Call up to 7 days in advance. **Miscellaneous:** Reduced fees (weekdays, twilight, juniors), metal spikes, range (grass/mats), lodging (450 rooms), credit cards (MC, V, AE, D, DC, CB), BF, FF.

★★★ LAKEMONT COURSE (18)

Yards: 6,444/4,762. **Par:** 71/71. **Course Rating:** 71.6/68.1. **Slope:** 133/132. **Opened:** 1987. **Architect:** John LaFoy.
Reader Comments: Excellent layout ... Nice views ... Much better since managed by Marriott ... Very busy ... Remarkable service.

★★★★ STONEMONT COURSE (18)

Yards: 6,769/5,522. **Par:** 70/71. **Course Rating:** 73.4/73.6. **Slope:** 133/132. **Opened:** 1969. **Architect:** Robert Trent Jones.
Reader Comments: Excellent layout ... Nice views, well manicured, great service ... This very challenging course is in super condition. This is an outstanding value with excellent service.

★★★½ STONEBRIDGE GOLF CLUB

PU-585 Stonebridge Dr., Rome, 30165, Floyd County, (706)236-5046, (800)336-5046, 50 miles from Atlanta. **Facility Holes:** 18. **Yards:** 6,816/5,130. **Par:** 72/72. **Course Rating:** 72.8/64.6. **Slope:** 123/109. **Green Fee:** $10/$30. **Cart Fee:** $12/Person. **Walking Policy:** Walking at certain times. **Walkability:** 2. **Opened:** 1994. **Architect:** Arthur Davis. **Season:** Year-round. **High:** March-Sept. **To obtain tee times:** Call golf shop. **Miscellaneous:** Reduced fees (weekdays, twilight, seniors, juniors), range (grass/mats), credit cards (MC, V, AE).
Notes: Ranked 20th in 2001 Best in State.
Reader Comments: Play smart on #9, so you don't sink too many balls in the water trying to go for the green in 2. In excellent condition ... Facilities, very clean & nice ... Needs work on course, good layout that could be outstanding.

★★ SUGAR HILL GOLF CLUB

PU-6094 Suwanee Dam Rd., Sugar Hill, 30518, Gwinnett County, (770)271-0519, 35 miles from Atlanta. **E-mail:** Shgclub@bellsouth.net. **Web:** www.sugarhillgolfclub.com. **Facility Holes:** 18. **Yards:** 6,423/4,207. **Par:** 72/72. **Course Rating:** 70.7/65.3. **Slope:** 127/112. **Green Fee:** $35/$48. **Cart Fee:** Included in green fee. **Walking Policy:** Walking at certain times. **Walkability:** 5. **Opened:** 1992. **Architect:** Willard Byrd. **Season:** Year-round. **High:** April-Oct. **To obtain tee times:** Call up to 2 days in advance. **Miscellaneous:** Reduced fees (twilight, seniors, juniors), range (grass/mats), credit cards (MC, V), BF, FF.

★★★½ SUMMERGROVE GOLF CLUB

PU-335 SummerGrove Pkwy., Newnan, 30265, Coweta County, (770)251-1800, 35 miles from Atlanta. **Facility Holes:** 18. **Yards:** 6,953/5,128. **Par:** 72/72. **Course Rating:** 73.3/70.1. **Slope:** 127/117. **Green Fee:** $35. **Cart Fee:** $10/Person. **Walking Policy:** Unrestricted walking. **Walkability:** 3. **Opened:** 1999. **Architect:** Jeff Burton/Joe T. Jemsek. **Season:** Year-round. **To obtain tee times:** Call up to 6 days in advance. **Miscellaneous:** Reduced fees (twilight, seniors, juniors), range (grass/mats), credit cards (MC, V, D), BF, FF.

GEORGIA

Notes: Ranked 10th in 2000 Best New Affordable Courses.
Reader Comments: Fairways are lush, thick zoysia grass. Clubhouse gives an old fashioned country club atmosphere ... Great greens, rest of course needs time to grow in ... Playable and fun, but crowded ... Greens too hard & fast for average player.

★★★ TOWNE LAKE HILLS GOLF CLUB
PU-1003 Towne Lake Hills E., Woodstock, 30189, Cherokee County, (770)592-9969, 25 miles from Atlanta. **E-mail:** townelake@hmsgolf.com. **Web:** www.townelakehills.com. **Facility Holes:** 18. **Yards:** 6,757/4,984. **Par:** 72/72. **Course Rating:** 72.3/69.0. **Slope:** 133/116. **Green Fee:** $55/$70. **Cart Fee:** Included in green fee. **Walking Policy:** Unrestricted walking. **Walkability:** 4. **Opened:** 1994. **Architect:** Arthur Hills. **Season:** Year-round. **To obtain tee times:** Call up to 7 days in advance. **Miscellaneous:** Reduced fees (weekdays, twilight, seniors), metal spikes, range (grass), credit cards (MC, V, AE, D), BF, FF.
Reader Comments: Great greens ... Nothing fancy, too expensive ... Beautiful course, good greens.

★★★ THE TROPHY CLUB OF APALACHEE
SP-1008 Dacula Rd., Dacula, 30211, Gwinnett County, (770)822-9220, 30 miles from Atlanta. **Facility Holes:** 18. **Yards:** 6,620/5,685. **Par:** 72/72. **Course Rating:** 72.5/68.0. **Slope:** 137/116. **Green Fee:** $35/$65. **Cart Fee:** included in green fee. **Walking Policy:** Mandatory carts. **Walkability:** 4. **Opened:** 1994. **Architect:** D.J. DeVictor/Steve Melnyk. **Season:** Year-round. **High:** May-Oct. **To obtain tee times:** Call golf shop. **Miscellaneous:** Reduced fees (weekdays, twilight, seniors, juniors), range (grass), credit cards (MC, V, AE).
Reader Comments: Good course, friendly staff, 2 bad holes ... Several interesting holes.

★★★ THE TROPHY CLUB OF ATLANTA
SP-15135 Hopewell Rd., Alpharetta, 30004, Fulton County, (770)343-9700, 20 miles from Atlanta. **Facility Holes:** 18. **Yards:** 6,725/4,470. **Par:** 72/72. **Course Rating:** 72.9/65.2. **Slope:** 131/108. **Green Fee:** $49/$85. **Cart Fee:** Included in green fee. **Walking Policy:** Mandatory carts. **Walkability:** 3. **Opened:** 1991. **Architect:** D.J. DeVictor/Steve Melnyk. **Season:** Year-round. **To obtain tee times:** Call up to 7 days in advance. **Miscellaneous:** Reduced fees (twilight, seniors, juniors), range (grass), credit cards (MC, V, AE), BF, FF.
Reader Comments: Scenic, excellent layout ... Pro shop wonderful. Good off-season twilight fees.

★★★ TROPHY CLUB OF GWINNETT
SP-3254 Clubside View Court, Snellville, 30039, Gwinnett County, (770)978-7755, 25 miles from Atlanta. **Facility Holes:** 18. **Yards:** 6,305/4,861. **Par:** 72/72. **Course Rating:** 70.6/68.8. **Slope:** 132/119. **Green Fee:** $35/$67. **Cart Fee:** Included in green fee. **Walking Policy:** Mandatory carts. **Walkability:** 3. **Opened:** 1993. **Architect:** Steve Melnyk. **Season:** Year-round. **To obtain tee times:** Call up to 7 days in advance. **Miscellaneous:** Reduced fees (twilight, seniors, juniors), range (grass/mats), credit cards (MC, V, AE), BF, FF.
Reader Comments: Most difficult 18th, great greens ... Blind approach shots ... Nice course north of Atlanta ... Good layout, very good greens ... Short but a good test.

★★½ UNIVERSITY OF GEORGIA GOLF CLUB
PU-2600 Riverbend Rd., Athens, 30605, Clarke County, (706)369-5739, (800)936-4833, 60 miles from Atlanta. **Facility Holes:** 18. **Yards:** 6,890/5,713. **Par:** 72/73. **Course Rating:** 73.4/74.0. **Slope:** 133/128. **Green Fee:** $15/$24. **Cart Fee:** $11/Person. **Walking Policy:** Unrestricted walking. **Opened:** 1968. **Architect:** Robert Trent Jones/John LaFoy. **Season:** Year-round. **High:** March-June. **To obtain tee times:** Call golf shop. **Miscellaneous:** Reduced fees (weekdays, twilight), metal spikes, range (grass), credit cards (MC, V).

★★★★ WHITE COLUMNS GOLF CLUB *Condition*
SP-300 White Columns Dr., Alpharetta, 30004, Fulton County, (770)343-9025, 25 miles from Atlanta. **E-mail:** whitecol@mildspring.com. **Web:** www.whitecolumns.com. **Facility Holes:** 18. **Yards:** 7,053/6,015. **Par:** 72/72. **Course Rating:** 73.6/69.0. **Slope:** 137/116. **Green Fee:** $85/$120. **Cart Fee:** Included in green fee. **Walking Policy:** Unrestricted walking. **Walkability:** 3. **Opened:** 1994. **Architect:** Tom Fazio. **Season:** Year-round. **To obtain tee times:** Call up to 10 days in advance. **Miscellaneous:** Reduced fees (twilight), range (grass), credit cards (MC, V, AE), BF, FF.
Notes: Ranked 16th in 2001 Best in State; 6th in 1995 Best New Public Course.
Reader Comments: Great course, too pricey ... Course well kept ... Great Fazio layout always in good shape ... Wonderful course set in the pine trees ... Good, challenging course, but a bit overrated ... Excellent undulating fairways.

★★½ WHITEPATH GOLF CLUB
PU-1156 Shenendoah Dr., Ellijay, 30540, Gilmer County, (706)276-3080, 40 miles from Chattanooga. **Facility Holes:** 18. **Yards:** 6,511/4,900. **Par:** 72/72. **Course Rating:** 70.0/72.1.

Slope: 131/128. **Green Fee:** $34/$39. **Cart Fee:** Included in green fee. **Walking Policy:** Mandatory carts. **Walkability:** 5. **Opened:** 1984. **Season:** Year-round. **High:** May-Sept. **To obtain tee times:** Call golf shop. **Miscellaneous:** Reduced fees (weekdays, guests, twilight, seniors, juniors), range (grass), credit cards (MC, V, AE, D), BF, FF.

★★★½ WHITEWATER COUNTRY CLUB

SP-175 Birkdale Dr., Fayetteville, 30214, Fayette County, (770)461-6545, 30 miles from Atlanta. **Facility Holes:** 18. **Yards:** 6,739/4,909. **Par:** 72/72. **Course Rating:** 72.3/68.2. **Slope:** 133/123. **Green Fee:** $15/$38. **Cart Fee:** $15/Person. **Walkability:** 3. **Opened:** 1988. **Architect:** Arnold Palmer/Ed Seay. **Season:** Year-round. **High:** March-Oct. **To obtain tee times:** Call golf shop. **Miscellaneous:** Reduced fees (weekdays, twilight, seniors, juniors), range (grass), credit cards (MC, V, AE).

Reader Comments: Very good all-around course, will come back many times ... Nice layout.

WINDERMERE GOLF CLUB

PU-5000 Davis Love Dr., Cumming, 30041, Forsyth County, (678)513-1000, 35 miles from Atlanta. **E-mail:** mnoles@eaglgolf.com. **Web:** windermeregolfclub.com. **Facility Holes:** 18. **Yards:** 6,902/4,763. **Par:** 71/71. **Course Rating:** 73.6/68.8. **Slope:** 140/120. **Green Fee:** $60/$80. **Cart Fee:** Included in green fee. **Walking Policy:** Mandatory carts. **Walkability:** 5. **Opened:** 2000. **Architect:** Davis Love III. **Season:** Year-round. **High:** April-Oct. **To obtain tee times:** Call up to 30 days in advance. **Miscellaneous:** Reduced fees (weekdays, twilight, seniors, juniors), credit cards (MC, V, AE, DC), BF, FF.

★★★½ WINDSTONE GOLF CLUB

SP-9230 Windstone Dr., Ringgold, 30736, Catoosa County, (423)894-1231, 6 miles from Chattanooga. **E-mail:** windstonegolf@aol.com. **Web:** www.windstone.com. **Facility Holes:** 18. **Yards:** 6,626/4,956. **Par:** 72/72. **Course Rating:** 71.7/66.8. **Slope:** 127/108. **Green Fee:** $17/$26. **Cart Fee:** $13/Person. **Walking Policy:** Unrestricted walking. **Walkability:** 3. **Opened:** 1990. **Architect:** Jeff Brauer. **Season:** Year-round. **High:** April-Oct. **To obtain tee times:** Call up to 7 days in advance. **Miscellaneous:** Reduced fees (twilight, seniors), range (grass), credit cards (MC, V, AE, D), BF, FF.

Reader Comments: Flat front, mountain back, fast greens ... Interesting layout, narrow fairways ... Good course ... Short, but tight and demanding ... Nice course, less than what I expected.

WOODLAND HILLS GOLF CLUB

PU-592 Day Lake Dr., Midland, 31820, Harris County, (706)563-5511. **Facility Holes:** 18. **Yards:** 7,004/5,185. **Par:** 72/72. **Course Rating:** 74.0/71.0. **Slope:** 140/124. **Green Fee:** $28/$30. **Cart Fee:** Included in green fee. **Opened:** 1999. **Architect:** Lisa Maki. **Season:** Year-round. **To obtain tee times:** Call golf shop. **Miscellaneous:** Reduced fees (weekdays).

★★★★ WOODMONT GOLF CLUB

SP-3105 Gaddis Rd., Canton, 30115, Cherokee County, (770)345-9260, 30 miles from Atlanta. **E-mail:** matt.risse@jwhome.com. **Web:** www.woodmontgolfclub.com. **Facility Holes:** 18. **Yards:** 6,830/5,198. **Par:** 72/72. **Course Rating:** 72.8/70.6. **Slope:** 138/126. **Green Fee:** $38/$75. **Cart Fee:** Included in green fee. **Walking Policy:** Unrestricted walking. **Walkability:** 3. **Opened:** 1999. **Architect:** Robert Trent Jones, Jr. **Season:** Year-round. **High:** April-Oct. **To obtain tee times:** Call up to 7 days in advance. **Miscellaneous:** Reduced fees (weekdays, twilight, seniors, juniors), range (grass), credit cards (MC, V, AE, D), BF, FF.

Reader Comments: The architect's design philosophy was always hard par, easy bogey. That's what you get from any set of tees ... Great design and terrain ... Very slow play, a bit pricey for quality ... Great experience.

★★ ALA WAI GOLF COURSE
PU-404 Kapahulu Ave., Honolulu, 96815, Oahu County, (808)735-6534. **Facility Holes:** 18. **Yards:** 6,208/5,095. **Par:** 70/70. **Course Rating:** 67.2/67.2. **Slope:** 116/109. **Green Fee:** $7/$42. **Cart Fee:** $16/Cart. **Walking Policy:** Unrestricted walking. **Walkability:** 1. **Opened:** 1931. **Architect:** Donald MacKay/B. Baldock/R. Nelson. **Season:** Year-round. **High:** May-Aug. **To obtain tee times:** Call up to 3 days in advance. **Miscellaneous:** Reduced fees (weekdays, seniors, juniors), range (mats), credit cards (MC, V), BF, FF.

★★½ BARBERS POINT GOLF COURSE
M-NAS, Barbers Point, 96862, Oahu County, (808)682-1911. **Facility Holes:** 18. **Yards:** 6,400/5,522. **Par:** 72/72. **Course Rating:** 69.5. **Slope:** 120/114. **Green Fee:** $10/$38. **Walking Policy:** Unrestricted walking. **Walkability:** 1. **Opened:** 1968. **Architect:** William P. Bell. **Season:** Year-round. **High:** June-Aug. **To obtain tee times:** Call golf shop. **Miscellaneous:** Reduced fees (twilight, juniors), range (grass/mats), credit cards (MC, V, AE, D).

★★★★★ THE CHALLENGE AT MANELE *Service+, Condition+, Pace+*
R-P.O. Box 630310, Lanai City, 96763, Lanai County, (808)565-2222, 13 miles from Airport. **Web:** www.lanairesorts.com. **Facility Holes:** 18. **Yards:** 7,039/5,024. **Par:** 72/72. **Course Rating:** 73.3/68.8. **Slope:** 132/119. **Green Fee:** $100/$205. **Cart Fee:** Included in green fee. **Walking Policy:** Mandatory carts. **Walkability:** 5. **Opened:** 1993. **Architect:** Jack Nicklaus. **Season:** Year-round. **High:** Jan.-April. **To obtain tee times:** Call up to 90 days in advance. **Miscellaneous:** Reduced fees (guests), range (grass), lodging (250 rooms), credit cards (MC, V, AE, DC), BF, FF.
Notes: Ranked 4th in 2001 Best in State; 55th in 1996 America's Top 75 Upscale Courses.
Reader Comments: Spectacular views … Great setting … A good course but somewhat overrated … Beautiful ocean views, staff wonderful … Wow! … Must play, outstanding layout … Finest resort course played … Heaven! Must play … Experience it before course-side houses are built.

★★★★ CORAL CREEK GOLF COURSE
PU-91-1111 Geiger Rd., Ewa Beach, 96706, Oahu County, (808)441-4653, 15 miles from Honolulu. **E-mail:** ccgc@aloha.net. **Web:** www.coralcreekgolf.com. **Facility Holes:** 18. **Yards:** 6,808/4,935. **Par:** 72/72. **Course Rating:** 72.2/68.3. **Slope:** 135/111. **Green Fee:** $45/$125. **Cart Fee:** Included in green fee. **Walking Policy:** Unrestricted walking. **Walkability:** 2. **Opened:** 1999. **Architect:** Robin Nelson. **Season:** Year-round. **High:** June-Sept. **To obtain tee times:** Call golf shop. **Miscellaneous:** Reduced fees (weekdays, twilight), range (grass/mats), credit cards (MC, V, AE).

★★★★ THE DUNES AT MAUI LANI GOLF COURSE *Value*
PU-1333 Maui Lani Parkway, Kahului, 96732, Maui County, (808)873-0422, 2 miles from Kahului. **E-mail:** dgleason@mauilani.com. **Web:** www.mauilani.com. **Facility Holes:** 18. **Yards:** 6,841/4,768. **Par:** 72/72. **Course Rating:** 73.5/67.9. **Slope:** 136/114. **Green Fee:** $44/$85. **Cart Fee:** Included in green fee. **Walking Policy:** Walking at certain times. **Walkability:** 3. **Opened:** 1999. **Architect:** Robin Nelson. **Season:** Year-round. **To obtain tee times:** Call up to 30 days in advance. **Miscellaneous:** Reduced fees (twilight, juniors), range (grass), credit cards (MC, V, AE), FF.
Reader Comments: After third hole, they all get harder to play … Links style … Very inexpensive … Service was great, course was in excellent condition … Play it in the morning before the gale force winds rip through … Best new course in Maui.

★★★½ ELLEAIR MAUI GOLF CLUB
PU-1345 Piilani Hwy., Kihei, 96753, Maui County, (808)874-0777, 12 miles from Kahului. **Facility Holes:** 18. **Yards:** 6,801/5,265. **Par:** 71/71. **Course Rating:** 72.0/70.0. **Slope:** 124/118. **Green Fee:** $75. **Cart Fee:** Included in green fee. **Walking Policy:** Mandatory carts. **Walkability:** 3. **Opened:** 1987. **Architect:** William J. Newis. **Season:** Year-round. **To obtain tee times:** Call up to 30 days in advance. **Miscellaneous:** Reduced fees (twilight), metal spikes, range (grass/mats), credit cards (MC, V), BF, FF.
Reader Comments: Nice course, great value … A must-play when in Maui … Wonderful public course, great price, very nice layout … Beautiful scenery, course could use an overhaul.
Special Notes: Formerly Silversword Golf Club.

★★★ EWA VILLAGE GOLF COURSE
PU-91-1760 Park Row St., Ewa Beach, 96706, Oahu County, (808)681-0220. **Facility Holes:** 18. **Yards:** 6,959/5,595. **Par:** 73/73. **Course Rating:** 73.3/73.6. **Slope:** 127/124. **Green Fee:** $12/$42. **Cart Fee:** $16/Cart. **To obtain tee times:** Call golf shop.
Reader Comments: Par 73, tough when windy (almost always) … Bring a good book, pace slow … Pace of play better since allowing carts/fairways … Nice course, good facilities … Good course for average golfer … Wind blows every afternoon.

★★★★ THE EXPERIENCE AT KOELE *Service, Pace*
R-730 Lanai Ave., Lanai City, 96763, Lanai County, (808)565-4653. **Web:** www.lanai-resorts.com. **Facility Holes:** 18. **Yards:** 7,014/5,425. **Par:** 72/72. **Course Rating:** 73.3/66.0. **Slope:** 141/123. **Green Fee:** $100/$200. **Cart Fee:** Included in green fee. **Walking Policy:** Mandatory carts. **Walkability:** 3. **Opened:** 1991. **Architect:** Ted Robinson/Greg Norman. **Season:** Year-round. **High:** Jan.-March. **To obtain tee times:** Call up to 30 days in advance. **Miscellaneous:** Reduced fees (guests, twilight, juniors), range (grass), credit cards (MC, V, AE, D, DC, JCB), BF, FF.
Notes: Ranked 15th in 1997 Best in State.
Reader Comments: First 9 open links and the back 9 in the trees ... 18-hole putting course, great time ... Great resort course ... Good value, great service, good staff ... Drought has hurt conditions.

★★★★½ HAPUNA GOLF COURSE *Service, Pace+*
R-62-100 Kauna'oa Dr., Kamuela, 96743, Hawaii County, (808)880-3000, 34 miles from Kailua-Kona. **Web:** www.maunakearesort.com. **Facility Holes:** 18. **Yards:** 6,875/5,067. **Par:** 72/72. **Course Rating:** 72.1/63.9. **Slope:** 134/117. **Green Fee:** $85/$135. **Cart Fee:** $20/Person. **Walking Policy:** Walking at certain times. **Walkability:** 3. **Opened:** 1992. **Architect:** Arnold Palmer/Ed Seay. **Season:** Year-round. **To obtain tee times:** Call golf shop. **Miscellaneous:** Reduced fees (guests, juniors), range (grass), lodging (350 rooms), credit cards (MC, V, AE, CB, JCB).
Notes: Ranked 11th in 1997 Best in State.
Reader Comments: A truly superb links course nestled in paradise ... Kind of tricky, but it kept you interested and there were spectacular views ... Leave the driver in your hotel room ... Can see volcanoes and the ocean from most holes.

HAWAII KAI GOLF COURSE
PU-8902 Kalanianaole Hwy., Honolulu, 96825, Oahu County, (808)395-2358, 10 miles from Waikiki. **Web:** www.hawaiikaigolf.com. **Facility Holes:** 36. **Season:** Year-round. **To obtain tee times:** Call golf shop. **Miscellaneous:** Metal spikes, range (grass/mats), credit cards (MC, V, AE, DC, JCB), BF, FF.
★★½ **CHAMPIONSHIP COURSE** (18)
Yards: 6,614/5,591. **Par:** 72/72. **Course Rating:** 71.4/72.7. **Slope:** 127/124. **Green Fee:** $80/$100. **Cart Fee:** Included in green fee. **Walking Policy:** Mandatory carts. **Walkability:** 3. **Opened:** 1973. **Architect:** William F. Bell. **High:** Nov.-Feb. **Miscellaneous:** Reduced fees (weekdays, twilight).
EXECUTIVE COURSE (18)
Yards: 2,386/2,094. **Par:** 55/55. **Green Fee:** $29/$34. **Cart Fee:** $9/Cart. **Walking Policy:** Unrestricted walking. **Walkability:** 4. **Opened:** 1950. **Architect:** Robert Trent Jones. **Miscellaneous:** Reduced fees (weekdays, twilight, juniors).

★★★ HAWAII PRINCE GOLF CLUB
R-91-1200 Fort Weaver Rd., Ewa Beach, 96706, Oahu County, (808)944-4567, 20 miles from Honolulu. **E-mail:** giwamuro@hiprince.com. **Facility Holes:** 27. **Green Fee:** $50/$135. **Cart Fee:** Included in green fee. **Walking Policy:** Mandatory carts. **Walkability:** 3. **Opened:** 1992. **Architect:** Arnold Palmer/Ed Seay. **Season:** Year-round. **To obtain tee times:** Call golf shop. **Miscellaneous:** Reduced fees (weekdays, guests, twilight, seniors, juniors), range (grass), credit cards (MC, V, AE, DC, JCB), BF, FF.
A/B (18 Combo)
Yards: 7,117/5,275. **Par:** 72/72. **Course Rating:** 74.2/70.4. **Slope:** 131/120.
A/C (18 Combo)
Yards: 7,166/5,300. **Par:** 72/72. **Course Rating:** 74.4/69.9. **Slope:** 134/118.
B/C (18 Combo)
Yards: 7,255/5,205. **Par:** 72/72. **Course Rating:** 75.0/69.5. **Slope:** 132/117.
Reader Comments: Breezy with plenty of water hazards on A and C courses ... Very good greens, holes look alike ... Very challenging with water, wind and brush ... Twilight is an excellent deal.

★★★★ HICKAM GOLF COURSE *Value*
M-Bldg. 3572, Hickam AFB, Hickam AFB, 96853, Oahu County, (808)449-6490. **E-mail:** thomas.stanfill@hickam.at.mil.org. **Web:** www.hickam.services/golf.com. **Facility Holes:** 27. **Yards:** 6,868/5,675. **Par:** 72/73. **Course Rating:** 71.9/72.9. **Slope:** 129/120. **Green Fee:** $9/$32. **Cart Fee:** $8/Person. **Walking Policy:** Unrestricted walking. **Walkability:** 1. **Opened:** 1965. **Season:** Year-round. **High:** March-July. **To obtain tee times:** Call up to 4 days in advance. **Misc:** Reduced fees (twilight, juniors), range (grass/mats), credit cards (MC, V), BF, FF.
Reader Comments: Outstanding, don't miss this one ... Next to Honolulu International Airport and Hickam Air Field ... Great condition, best military course ... Great views ... Can't beat the military price ... Good greens, noisy from aircraft.
Special Notes: Also has a 9-hole par-3 course.

★★★★½ **HUALALAI GOLF CLUB** *Service+, Condition, Pace+*
SP-Mile Marker 87, Queen Kaahumanu Hwy., Kailua Kona, 96745, Hawaii County, (808)325-8480, 15 miles from Kona. **E-mail:** jfreitas@hualalairesort.com. **Facility Holes:** 18. **Yards:** 7,117/5,374. **Par:** 72/72. **Course Rating:** 75.7/70.4. **Slope:** 131/118. **Green Fee:** $160. **Cart Fee:** Included in green fee. **Walking Policy:** Unrestricted walking. **Walkability:** 2. **Opened:** 1996. **Architect:** Jack Nicklaus. **Season:** Year-round. **To obtain tee times:** Call golf shop. **Miscellaneous:** Reduced fees (juniors), range (grass), caddies, credit cards (MC, V, AE, D, DC, JCB), BF, FF.
Notes: Ranked 12th in 1999 Best in State.
Reader Comments: Most enjoyable round of the year! ... Beautiful views and wide fairways make this course a dream ... Resort golf at its best ... Fantastic experience playing along the acres of black punishing lava ... A relatively generous course for the average player ... Easy course, expensive because you have to stay there to play.

KAANAPALI GOLF COURSES
R-Kaanapali Resort, Lahaina, 96761, Maui County, (808)661-3691, 5 miles from Historic Lahaina Town. **E-mail:** kgcgolf@maui.net. **Web:** www.kaanapali-golf.com. **Facility Holes:** 36. **Cart Fee:** Included in green fee. **Walking Policy:** Mandatory carts. **Season:** Year-round. **To obtain tee times:** Call up to 30 days in advance. **Miscellaneous:** Reduced fees (guests, twilight), range (grass/mats), credit cards (MC, V, AE, JCB), FF.
★★★½ **NORTH COURSE (18)**
Yards: 6,994/5,417. **Par:** 71/72. **Course Rating:** 72.8/71.1. **Slope:** 134/123. **Green Fee:** $130/$150. **Walkability:** 4. **Opened:** 1963. **Architect:** Robert Trent Jones.
Reader Comments: Lush lava ... Burnt out, boring layout, nice on the eyes though ... Beautiful views & good golf ... The winds were murder ... Good golfing experience.
★★★½ **SOUTH COURSE (18)**
Yards: 6,555/5,485. **Par:** 71/71. **Course Rating:** 70.7/69.8. **Slope:** 127/120. **Green Fee:** $117/$142. **Walkability:** 3. **Opened:** 1976. **Architect:** Jack Snyder.
Reader Comments: Excellent golf, great experience ... Good resort course, accommodating to guests ... Fun course, wide open ... Crossing over the freeway ... Nice greens, good mix of tough and easy holes.

★★★½ **KALAKAUA GOLF COURSE**
M-Building 1283 Schofield Barracks, Wahiawa, 96857, Oahu County, (808)655-9833, 25 miles from Honolulu. **Facility Holes:** 18. **Yards:** 6,186/5,818. **Par:** 72/73. **Course Rating:** 69.0/75.1. **Slope:** 119/133. **Green Fee:** $9/$55. **Cart Fee:** $8/Person. **Walking Policy:** Unrestricted walking. **Walkability:** 1. **Season:** Year-round. **High:** April-Aug. **To obtain tee times:** Call golf shop. **Miscellaneous:** Range (grass/mats).
Reader Comments: One of the finest of the US Army golf system! ... Good value, easy course ... Great, cheap golf on Oahu ... Short, flat, good for ego ... Needs work ... Nice inland military course.

★★★ **KALUAKOI HOTEL & GOLF CLUB**
R-P.O. Box 26, Maunaloa, 96770, Molokai County, (808)552-2555, 20 miles from Kaunakakai. **E-mail:** Kaluakoi@juno.com. **Facility Holes:** 18. **Yards:** 6,600/5,461. **Par:** 72/72. **Course Rating:** 72.3/71.4. **Slope:** 129/119. **Green Fee:** $60/$80. **Cart Fee:** Included in green fee. **Walkability:** 2. **Opened:** 1977. **Architect:** Ted Robinson. **Season:** Year-round. **High:** Nov.-Feb. **To obtain tee times:** Call golf shop. **Miscellaneous:** Reduced fees (guests, twilight, juniors), metal spikes, range (grass), credit cards (MC, V, AE, D, DC, JCB).
Reader Comments: Many holes on ocean-front ... Course could be excellent if weather cooperates ... Lack of water, still challenging ... Felt like we owned the place. Quiet.

★★★½ **KANEOHE KLIPPER GOLF CLUB** *Value+*
M-Kaneohe Marine Corps Air Station, Kanehoe Bay, 96863, Oahu County, (808)254-1745, 15 miles from Waikiki. **Facility Holes:** 18. **Yards:** 6,739/5,575. **Par:** 72/71. **Course Rating:** 71.0/76.3. **Slope:** 130/133. **Green Fee:** $8/$37. **Cart Fee:** $16/Cart. **Walking Policy:** Unrestricted walking. **Walkability:** 3. **Opened:** 1948. **Architect:** William P. Bell. **Season:** Year-round. **To obtain tee times:** Call golf shop. **Miscellaneous:** Range (grass/mats), credit cards (MC, V, AE, D), BF, FF.
Reader Comments: A new irrigation system has this course in top shape ... The holes along the ocean are breathtaking ... The most scenic golf ... Super value on the ocean ... Usually in bad shape, great back 9 ... Good military layout.
Special Notes: Open to military personnel and their guests.

KAPALUA GOLF CLUB
R-300 Kapalua Dr., Kapalua, 96761, Maui County, (808)669-8820, (877)527-2582, 8 miles from Lahaina. **E-mail:** teetimes@kapaluamaui.com. **Web:** www.kapaluamaui.com. **Facility Holes:** 54. **Cart Fee:** Included in green fee. **Season:** Year-round. **To obtain tee times:** Call up to 4 days in advance. **Miscellaneous:** Reduced fees (guests, twilight, juniors), metal spikes,

range (grass), caddies, credit cards (MC, V, AE, D, DC, JCB), BF, FF.

★★★★½ **THE BAY COURSE** (18)

Yards: 6,600/5,124. **Par:** 72/72. **Course Rating:** 71.7/69.6. **Slope:** 138/121. **Green Fee:** $115/$160. **Walking Policy:** Walking with Caddie. **Walkability:** 2. **Opened:** 1975. **Architect:** Francis Duane/Arnold Palmer.

Notes: Ranked 13th in 2001 Best in State.

Reader Comments: Expensive and a once-in-a-lifetime treat ... Sites, views, service ... The most playable of the Kapalua courses ... Beautiful, manicured holes ... Crowded but good experience ... Scenery is amazing ... Staff treats you like royalty.

★★★★½ **THE PLANTATION COURSE** (18)

Yards: 7,263/5,627. **Par:** 73/73. **Course Rating:** 75.2/73.2. **Slope:** 142/129. **Green Fee:** $125/$200. **Walking Policy:** Walking with Caddie. **Walkability:** 4. **Opened:** 1991. **Architect:** Bill Coore/Ben Crenshaw.

Notes: Ranked 5th in 2001 Best in State; 63rd in 1996 America's Top 75 Upscale Courses.

Reader Comments: Most beautiful scenery ... Worth every cent you pay ... Windy and rainy at times ... Keep the ball low and hit more club than you think ... Fantastic views ... Slow going ... Great fun to play a course and then watch the pros on TV, especially 18.

★★★★ **THE VILLAGE COURSE** (18) *Pace*

Yards: 6,632/5,134. **Par:** 71/71. **Course Rating:** 73.3/70.9. **Slope:** 139/122. **Green Fee:** $115/$160. **Walking Policy:** Mandatory carts. **Opened:** 1980. **Architect:** Arnold Palmer/Ed Seay.

Reader Comments: The least memorable of our Maui courses ... Facilities were top notch ... Beautiful course.

★★★★½ **KAPOLEI GOLF COURSE**

PU-91-701 Farrington Hwy., Kapolei, 96707, Oahu County, (808)674-2227, (877)674-2225, 25 miles from Waikiki. **E-mail:** kapgc@gte.net. **Facility Holes:** 18. **Yards:** 7,001/5,490. **Par:** 72/72. **Course Rating:** 72.7/71.9. **Slope:** 134/124. **Green Fee:** $130/$150. **Cart Fee:** Included in green fee. **Walking Policy:** Mandatory carts. **Walkability:** 3. **Opened:** 1995. **Architect:** Ted Robinson. **Season:** Year-round. **To obtain tee times:** Call up to 30 days in advance.

Miscellaneous: Reduced fees (twilight), metal spikes, range (mats), credit cards (MC, V, AE, DC, JCB), FF.

Reader Comments: Really enjoy playing here ... Well protected greens, very good test ... From No. 9 on, lots of water ... Tricky greens in great shape ... Straightforward Hawaiian golf, tropical, windy, pretty ... Excellent in every aspect.

KAUAI LAGOONS RESORT

R-3351 Hoolaulea Way, Lihue, 96766, Kauai County, (808)241-6000, (800)634-6400, 2 miles from Lihue. **E-mail:** kennethk@kauailagoonsgolf.com. **Web:** www.kauailagoonsgolf.com. **Facility Holes:** 36. **Cart Fee:** Included in green fee. **Architect:** Jack Nicklaus. **Season:** Year-round. **To obtain tee times:** Call up to 30 days in advance. **Miscellaneous:** Reduced fees (guests, twilight, juniors), metal spikes, range (grass), credit cards (MC, V, AE, DC), BF, FF.

★★★★½ **KIELE COURSE** (18) *Pace*

Yards: 7,070/5,417. **Par:** 72/72. **Course Rating:** 73.7/70.5. **Slope:** 137/123. **Green Fee:** $120/$170. **Walking Policy:** Mandatory carts. **Walkability:** 3. **Opened:** 1988.

Notes: Ranked 6th in 2001 Best in State; 60th in 1996 America's Top 75 Upscale Courses.

Reader Comments: The scenery helps you forget about the bad shots! ... A real treat to play ... Excellent resort course ... Worth the $ to play it once ... Two great par 3s ... Expensive but a must play! ... Nine great holes, nine plain holes. ... Putts in paradise! ... Don't miss this course if there.

★★★★ **MOKIHANA COURSE** (18)

Yards: 6,960/5,607. **Par:** 72/72. **Course Rating:** 73.1/71.8. **Slope:** 127/116. **Green Fee:** $75/$120. **Walking Policy:** Walking at certain times. **Walkability:** 1. **Opened:** 1989.

Reader Comments: Price low enough for retirees to play ... Flat course, holes look the same ... Busy on weekends, good for beginners ... Airport noise is a distraction.

★★★½ **KIAHUNA GOLF CLUB** *Value, Pace*

R-2545 Kiahuna Plantation Dr., Poipu, 96756, Kauai County, (808)742-9595, 15 miles from Lihue. **E-mail:** aloha@aloha.net. **Web:** www.kiahunagolf.com. **Facility Holes:** 18. **Yards:** 6,366/5,521. **Par:** 70/70. **Course Rating:** 70.0/66.7. **Slope:** 127/115. **Green Fee:** $45/$75. **Cart Fee:** Included in green fee. **Walking Policy:** Mandatory carts. **Walkability:** 3. **Opened:** 1984. **Architect:** Robert Trent Jones Jr. **Season:** Year-round. **High:** Dec.-March. **To obtain tee times:** Call up to 30 days in advance. **Miscellaneous:** Reduced fees (weekdays, guests, twilight, juniors), range (grass), credit cards (MC, V, AE, D, JCB), BF, FF.

Reader Comments: Short, fun, friendly, scenic ... Plays among Hawaii ruins ... One of the best values on the islands ... Challenging, shorter course with historical lava walls ... Well planned, has ocean views from a distance.

★★★★ **KO OLINA GOLF CLUB**

R-92-1220 Aliinui Dr., Kapolei, 96707, Oahu County, (808)676-5300, 20 miles from Honolulu. **E-mail:** koolina@aloha.net. **Web:** www.koolinagolf.com. **Facility Holes:** 18. **Yards:** 6,867/5,392.

Par: 72/72. **Course Rating:** 72.3/71.3. **Slope:** 135/126. **Green Fee:** $98/$145. **Walking Policy:** Walking at certain times. **Walkability:** 3. **Opened:** 1990. **Architect:** Ted Robinson. **Season:** Year-round. **High:** Nov.-Feb. **To obtain tee times:** Call golf shop. **Miscellaneous:** Reduced fees (guests, twilight), range (grass/mats), credit cards (MC, V, AE, D, DC, JCB), BF, FF.
Reader Comments: Excellent resort course … Always windy … Not as difficult as it appears … A bit pricey, but if you have the cash, you will not be disappointed … Fairways & greens in excellent condition.

KONA COUNTRY CLUB
R-78-7000 Alii Dr., Kailua Kona, 96740, Hawaii County, (808)322-2595. **E-mail:** gmolina@lava.net. **Web:** www.konagolf.com. **Facility Holes:** 36. **Green Fee:** $95/$150. **Cart Fee:** Included in green fee. **Walking Policy:** Mandatory carts. **Season:** Year-round. **To obtain tee times:** Call up to 7 days in advance. **Miscellaneous:** Metal spikes, range (grass/mats), lodging (500 rooms), credit cards (MC, V, AE, DC, JCB), BF, FF.
★★★★½ **ALII MOUNTAIN COURSE** (18)
Yards: 6,471/4,906. **Par:** 72/72. **Course Rating:** 71.5/69.2. **Slope:** 133/125. **Walkability:** 3. **Opened:** 1985. **Architect:** W. F. Bell/R. Nelson/R. Wright. **Miscellaneous:** Reduced fees (guests, twilight, juniors).
Reader Comments: Mountain course to the max … Popular, gets heavy play … Just a super place to be! … Some of the best views of Pacific in Hawaii … Spectacular view … Hilly, uneven lies, great condition … Great place for golf.
★★★★ **OCEAN COURSE** (18)
Yards: 6,579/5,499. **Par:** 72/73. **Course Rating:** 71.6/71.9. **Slope:** 129/127. **Walkability:** 2. **Opened:** 1968. **Architect:** William F. Bell. **Miscellaneous:** Reduced fees (guests, twilight).
Reader Comments: Great facility, very fair, worth the money … Wonderful, lots of lava … Best grass conditions in Hawaii … The greens were tough to putt.

★★★★ KOOLAU GOLF CLUB *Pace*
PU-45-550 Kionaole, Kaneohe, 96744, Oahu County, (808)236-4653, 13 miles from Honolulu. **Web:** www.americangolf.koolau.com. **Facility Holes:** 18. **Yards:** 7,310/5,119. **Par:** 72/72. **Course Rating:** 76.4/72.9. **Slope:** 162/134. **Green Fee:** $54/$125. **Cart Fee:** Included in green fee. **Walking Policy:** Walking at certain times. **Walkability:** 4. **Opened:** 1992. **Architect:** Dick Nugent. **Season:** Year-round. **High:** Nov.-Feb. **To obtain tee times:** Call up to 30 days in advance. **Miscellaneous:** Reduced fees (weekdays, twilight), metal spikes, range (grass), caddies, credit cards (MC, V, AE, D, DC), BF, FF.
Notes: Ranked 3rd in 2001 Best in State.
Reader Comments: You can't beat the scenery, was waiting for King Kong to come out of the mountains … All bunkers need better drainage … Plays a little slow, so darned tough.

★★★★ LEILEHUA GOLF COURSE *Value*
M-USAG Hawaii Golf, Schofield Barracks, 96857, Oahu County, (808)655-4653. **Facility Holes:** 18. **Yards:** 6,916/6,174. **Par:** 72/75. **Course Rating:** 72.2/75.5. **Slope:** 131/133. **Green Fee:** $10/$32. **Cart Fee:** $8/Person. **Walking Policy:** Unrestricted walking. **Walkability:** 1. **Season:** Year-round. **High:** June-Aug. **To obtain tee times:** Call golf shop. **Miscellaneous:** Credit cards (MC, V, AE).
Reader Comments: Best military course on Oahu … Good test of golf skills … Greens need work, old-style layout … Quality inland military course.

★★★★ MAHAKA RESORT GOLF CLUB
R-84-626 Makaha Valley Rd., Waianae, 96792, Oahu County, (808)695-9544, (800)757-8060, 40 miles from Honolulu. **Facility Holes:** 18. **Yards:** 7,077/5,856. **Par:** 72/72. **Course Rating:** 73.2/73.9. **Slope:** 139/129. **Green Fee:** $90/$125. **Cart Fee:** Included in green fee. **Walking Policy:** Mandatory carts. **Walkability:** 4. **Opened:** 1969. **Architect:** William F. Bell. **Season:** Year-round. **To obtain tee times:** Call golf shop. **Miscellaneous:** Reduced fees (weekdays, guests, twilight, seniors, juniors), range (mats), credit cards (MC, V, AE, D, DC, JCB), BF, FF.
Reader Comments: Best course for money on Oahu's Leeward coast … Great ocean and mountain views … We make a point of playing this course every year … Absolutely breathtaking … Much improved.

★★★★ MAKAHA VALLEY COUNTRY CLUB
PU-84-627 Makaha Valley Rd., Waianea, 96792, Oahu County, (808)695-7111, 40 miles from Honolulu. **Facility Holes:** 18. **Yards:** 6,369/5,720. **Par:** 71/71. **Course Rating:** 69.2/72.7. **Slope:** 133/120. **Green Fee:** $55/$100. **Cart Fee:** Included in green fee. **Walkability:** 5. **Opened:** 1969. **Architect:** William F. Bell. **Season:** Year-round. **High:** Dec.-March. **To obtain tee times:** Call golf shop. **Miscellaneous:** Metal spikes, range (grass), credit cards (MC, V, AE, D, DC).
Reader Comments: It's easy to lose your golf ball as it flies in front of the gorgeous vistas … Course and service are superb … A nice valley course.

★★★ MAKALEI HAWAII COUNTRY CLUB
PU-72-3890 Hawaii Belt Rd., Kailua-Kona, 96740, Hawaii County, (808)325-6625, (800)606-9606, 5 miles from Kailua-Kona. **Web:** www.makaleihawaiigolf.com. **Facility Holes:** 18. **Yards:** 7,091/5,242. **Par:** 72/72. **Course Rating:** 73.5/64.9. **Slope:** 143/125. **Green Fee:** $110. **Cart Fee:** Included in green fee. **Walking Policy:** Mandatory carts. **Walkability:** 4. **Opened:** 1992. **Architect:** Dick Nugent. **Season:** Year-round. **High:** Dec.-March. **To obtain tee times:** Call up to 7 days in advance. **Miscellaneous:** Reduced fees (weekdays, guests, twilight, seniors, juniors), metal spikes, range (grass), credit cards (MC, V, AE, DC, JCB), BF, FF.
Reader Comments: Target golf on hillside … Bent greens, fairways in bad shape, hilly course … What a contrast! … Uphill, downhill, wildlife appealing … Great landscape, wildlife.

MAKENA RESORT GOLF COURSE
R-5415 Makena Alanui, Kihei, 96753, Maui County, (808)879-3344, (800)321-6284, 6 miles from Kihei. **Facility Holes:** 36. **Green Fee:** $90/$155. **Cart Fee:** Included in green fee. **Walking Policy:** Walking at certain times. **Opened:** 1993. **Architect:** Robert Trent Jones Jr. **Season:** Year-round. **High:** Nov.-April. **To obtain tee times:** Call up to 30 days in advance. **Miscellaneous:** Reduced fees (guests, twilight, juniors), range (grass/mats), caddies, lodging (310 rooms), credit cards (MC, V, AE, DC, CB), BF, FF.
★★★★ NORTH COURSE (18)
Yards: 6,914/5,303. **Par:** 72/72. **Course Rating:** 72.1/70.9. **Slope:** 139/128. **Walkability:** 5. **Notes:** Ranked 14th in 2001 Best in State.
Reader Comments: The greens are hard to read … Expensive but good pace of play … Scenic … Some of the most gorgeous holes.
★★★★½ SOUTH COURSE (18)
Yards: 7,017/5,529. **Par:** 72/72. **Course Rating:** 72.6/71.1. **Slope:** 138/130. **Walkability:** 3. **Notes:** Ranked 10th in 2001 Best in State.
Reader Comments: Hitting up to mountain and down to ocean … Very scenic … Hard course, but the ocean views are great … Wonderful track … Every hole a winner … Not as visually striking as the North Course but more of a players' track.

★★★★½ MAUNA KEA BEACH GOLF COURSE *Pace*
R-62-100 Mauna Kea Beach Dr., Kamuela, 96743, Hawaii County, (808)882-5400, 34 miles from Kailua-Kona. **E-mail:** maunakeabeachhotel.com. **Web:** www.maunakeabeachhotel.com. **Facility Holes:** 18. **Yards:** 7,114/5,277. **Par:** 72/72. **Course Rating:** 73.6/70.2. **Slope:** 143/124. **Green Fee:** $110/$195. **Cart Fee:** Included in green fee. **Walking Policy:** Walking at certain times. **Walkability:** 5. **Opened:** 1965. **Architect:** Robert Trent Jones. **Season:** Year-round. **High:** Dec.-April. **To obtain tee times:** Call golf shop. **Miscellaneous:** Reduced fees (guests, twilight, juniors), range (grass), lodging (315 rooms), credit cards (MC, V, AE, CB, JCB), BF, FF. **Notes:** Ranked 76th in 2001-2002 America's 100 Greatest; 2nd in 2001 Best in State.
Reader Comments: A golfer could not want more … The best … One hole on the ocean does not make a great course … When I die I want my ashes spread on the third hole … Great ocean par 3.

MAUNA LANI RESORT
R-68-1310 Mauna Lani Dr., Suite 103, Kohala Coast, 96743, Hawaii County, (808)885-6655, 30 miles from Kailua-Kona. **Facility Holes:** 36. **Green Fee:** $95/$185. **Cart Fee:** Included in green fee. **Walking Policy:** Mandatory carts. **Walkability:** 1. **Opened:** 1981. **Architect:** Nelson/Wright/Haworth. **Season:** Year-round. **To obtain tee times:** Call golf shop. **Miscellaneous:** Reduced fees (guests, twilight, juniors), metal spikes, range (grass), credit cards (MC, V, AE, D, DC), BF, FF.
★★★★½ NORTH COURSE (18) *Condition*
Yards: 6,993/5,474. **Par:** 72/72. **Course Rating:** 73.2/71.4. **Slope:** 136/124. **Notes:** Ranked 15th in 2001 Best in State.
Reader Comments: For my money, it's the best in Hawaii … Excellent condition, playable for all levels of player … Very windy! Hit it low … Awesome! … Excellent pro shop … Challenging, enjoyable, scenic … Good golf course, lots of lava.
★★★★½ SOUTH COURSE (18)
Yards: 7,029/5,331. **Par:** 72/72. **Course Rating:** 72.8/69.6. **Slope:** 133/122. **Notes:** Ranked 12th in 1997 Best in State.
Reader Comments: Prettiest course on the planet, awesome par-3 holes along the ocean … Beautiful views … Like playing on the moon … Having junior rates made it even better by bringing my son along … My all-time favorite … Great course with great views.

★★½ MILILANI GOLF CLUB
SP-95-176 Kuahelani Ave., Mililani, 96789, Oahu County, (808)623-2222, 12 miles from Honolulu. **Facility Holes:** 18. **Yards:** 6,455/5,985. **Par:** 72/72. **Course Rating:** 69.3/73.6. **Slope:** 121/127. **Green Fee:** $89/$95. **Cart Fee:** Included in green fee. **Walkability:** 1. **Opened:** 1967. **Architect:** Bob Baldock. **Season:** Year-round. **High:** Jan.-June. **To obtain tee times:** Call golf shop. **Miscellaneous:** Reduced fees (weekdays, twilight), metal spikes, range (mats), credit cards (MC, V, AE, DC).

★★★★ **NAVY MARINE GOLF COURSE**
M-943 Valkenburgh St., Honolulu, 96818, Oahu County, (808)471-0142. **Facility Holes:** 18.
Yards: 6,771/5,740. **Par:** 72/72. **Course Rating:** 72.2/75.8. **Slope:** 127/125. **Green Fee:** $40.
Opened: 1948. **Architect:** William P. Bell. **Season:** Year-round. **To obtain tee times:** Call golf
shop.
Reader Comments: Challenging and good value … Best military course in Hawaii … Fast greens,
good layout, good condition … Pace of play slow … Best greens in Oahu … Flat, windy … Holding
its own.

★★★ **NEW EWA BEACH GOLF CLUB**
SP-91-050 Fort Weaver Rd., Ewa Beach, 96706, Oahu County, (808)689-8351, 18 miles from
Honolulu. **Facility Holes:** 18. **Yards:** 6,541/5,230. **Par:** 72/72. **Course Rating:** 71.3/70.5. **Slope:**
125/121. **Green Fee:** $55/$135. **Cart Fee:** Included in green fee. **Walkability:** 2. **Opened:** 1992.
Architect: Robin Nelson/Rodney Wright. **Season:** Year-round. **High:** Aug.-March. **To obtain tee
times:** Call golf shop. **Miscellaneous:** Reduced fees (twilight, seniors, juniors), metal spikes,
credit cards (MC, V, AE).
Reader Comments: Tough and interesting, especially with the wind … Unusual layout … A nice
shorter playing course in good condition.

★★½ **OLOMANA GOLF LINKS**
SP-41-1801 Kalanianaole Hwy., Waimanalo, 96795, Oahu County, (808)259-7926, 9 miles
from Honolulu. **Facility Holes:** 18. **Yards:** 6,304/5,465. **Par:** 72/73. **Course Rating:** 69.8/72.4.
Slope: 126/128. **Green Fee:** $65/$90. **Cart Fee:** Included in green fee. **Walking Policy:** Walking
at certain times. **Walkability:** 2. **Opened:** 1967. **Architect:** Bob Baldock/Robert L. Baldock.
Season: Year-round. **To obtain tee times:** Call golf shop. **Miscellaneous:** Reduced fees (weekdays, twilight), metal spikes, range (mats), credit cards (MC, V, D, JCB), FF.

★★★ **PALI MUNICIPAL GOLF COURSE**
PU-45-050 Kamehameha Hwy., Kaneohe, 96744, Oahu County, (808)266-7612, 5 miles from
Honolulu. **Facility Holes:** 18. **Yards:** 6,500/6,050. **Par:** 72/74. **Course Rating:** 78.8/70.4. **Slope:**
126/127. **Green Fee:** $20/$40. **Cart Fee:** Included in green fee. **Walking Policy:** Unrestricted
walking. **Opened:** 1954. **Architect:** Willard Wilkinson. **Season:** Year-round. **High:** June-Aug. **To
obtain tee times:** Call golf shop. **Miscellaneous:** Reduced fees (twilight, seniors, juniors),
metal spikes, range (grass), credit cards (MC, V).
Reader Comments: City course, hilly mountain views, small greens … Public course, hilly, lots a
rain … Greens fast … Great views of Pali Mountains near Koolau … Local rates excellent. Tourist
rates best on island.

★★★ **PEARL COUNTRY CLUB**
PU-98-535 Kaonohi St., Aiea, 96701, Oahu County, (808)487-3802, 10 miles from Honolulu.
E-mail: pearlcc@hi.net. **Web:** www.pearlcc.com. **Facility Holes:** 18. **Yards:** 6,787/5,536. **Par:**
72/72. **Course Rating:** 72.0/72.1. **Slope:** 135/130. **Green Fee:** $39/$100. **Cart Fee:** Included in
green fee. **Walking Policy:** Mandatory carts. **Walkability:** 4. **Opened:** 1967. **Architect:** Akiro
Sato. **Season:** Year-round. **High:** Nov.-Feb. **To obtain tee times:** Call up to 30 days in advance.
Miscellaneous: Reduced fees (twilight), metal spikes, range (mats), credit cards (MC, V, AE,
D, DC, CB, JCB), FF.
Reader Comments: Very good greens, don't care for layout … Occasionally rainy and slow play
(cartpath only) … Great views of Pearl Harbor.

★★★★½ **POIPU BAY GOLF CLUB** *Service, Condition, Pace*
R-2250 Ainako St., Koloa, 96756, Kauai County, (808)742-8711, (800)858-6300, 16 miles
from Lihue. **E-mail:** mcastillo@alona.net. **Facility Holes:** 18. **Yards:** 6,959/5,241. **Par:** 72/72.
Course Rating: 73.4/70.9. **Slope:** 132/121. **Green Fee:** $120/$170. **Cart Fee:** Included in green
fee. **Walking Policy:** Mandatory carts. **Walkability:** 3. **Opened:** 1990. **Architect:** Robert Trent
Jones Jr. **Season:** Year-round. **To obtain tee times:** Call golf shop. **Miscellaneous:** Reduced
fees (guests, twilight, juniors), range (grass/mats), lodging (610 rooms), credit cards (MC, V,
AE, DC, JCB), FF.
Notes: Ranked 12th in 2001 Best in State.
Reader Comments: What a great course, very windy … Really a well operated and maintained
course … Concentration is a must … Great finishing holes … Ocean holes outstanding … Rough
was too penal … One of the best … Nice course, expensive.

PRINCEVILLE RESORT
R-1 Lei O Papa Rd., Princeville, 96722, Kauai County, (808)826-3580, (800)826-4400, 30
miles from Lihue. **Web:** www.princeville.com. **Facility Holes:** 45. **Cart Fee:** Included in green
fee. **Architect:** Robert Trent Jones Jr. **To obtain tee times:** Call up to 30 days in advance.
Misc: Metal spikes, range (grass/mats), credit cards (MC, V, AE, D, DC, JCB), BF, FF.

★★★★ **MAKAI GOLF CLUB**
Green Fee: $100/$120. **Walking Policy:** Unrestricted walking. **Walkability:** 2. **Opened:** 1973. **Season:** Year-round. **Misc:** Reduced fees (weekdays, guests, twilight, juniors).
(LAKES/WOODS) (18 combo)
Yards: 6,901/5,543. **Par:** 72/72. **Course Rating:** 72.5/69.6. **Slope:** 129/115.
(OCEAN/LAKES) (18 combo)
Yards: 6,886/5,516. **Par:** 72/72. **Course Rating:** 73.2/69.9. **Slope:** 132/116.
Notes: Ranked 8th in 2001 Best in State.
(OCEAN/WOODS) (18 combo)
Yards: 6,875/5,631. **Par:** 72/72. **Course Rating:** 72.9/70.4. **Slope:** 131/116.
Reader Comments: The Prince may be better known, but Makai is for those who want to enjoy the game … Less play than on the Ocean nine … Greens were in excellent condition.
★★★★½ **PRINCE COURSE** (18) *Pace+*
Yards: 7,309/5,338. **Par:** 72/72. **Course Rating:** 75.3/72.0. **Slope:** 145/127. **Green Fee:** $115/$155. **Walking Policy:** Walking at certain times. **Walkability:** 5. **Opened:** 1991.
Season: Year-round. **High:** April-Sept. **Miscellaneous:** Reduced fees (weekdays, guests, twilight, juniors).
Notes: Ranked 51st in 2001-2002 America's 100 Greatest; 1st in 2001 Best in State.
Reader Comments: This is the best, most beautiful and challenging course I've ever played … Expensive, but so worth it … Hilly, over canyons, difficult for higher handicapper … Hard to keep course up with all the rain, but still a great course … Bring plenty of ammo … Breathtaking, watch out for wild roosters.

★★½ **PUKALANI COUNTRY CLUB**
PU-360 Pukalani St., Pukalani, 96768, Maui County, (808)572-1314, 9 miles from Kahului.
E-mail: nishida@maui.net. **Web:** www.pukalanigolf.com. **Facility Holes:** 18. **Yards:** 6,945/5,612. **Par:** 72/74. **Course Rating:** 72.8/71.6. **Slope:** 128/133. **Green Fee:** $35/$55. **Cart Fee:** Included in green fee. **Walking Policy:** Mandatory carts. **Walkability:** 3. **Opened:** 1981.
Architect: Bob Baldock. **Season:** Year-round. **High:** Jan.-March. **To obtain tee times:** Call up to 30 days in advance. **Miscellaneous:** Reduced fees (twilight), range (grass), credit cards (MC, V, AE), FF.

★★★ **SANDALWOOD GOLF COURSE**
PU-2500 Honoapiilani Hwy., Wailuku, 96793, Maui County, (808)242-4653, 4 miles from Wailuku. **E-mail:** gwrgolf@maui.net. **Facility Holes:** 18. **Yards:** 6,469/6,011. **Par:** 72/72. **Course Rating:** 70.6/68.3. **Slope:** 129/125. **Green Fee:** $50/$75. **Cart Fee:** Included in green fee.
Walking Policy: Mandatory carts. **Walkability:** 3. **Opened:** 1991. **Architect:** Nelson & Wright.
Season: Year-round. **High:** Jan.-April. **To obtain tee times:** Call up to 365 days in advance.
Miscellaneous: Reduced fees (weekdays, guests, twilight), metal spikes, range (grass), credit cards (MC, V, AE, DC), BF, FF.
Reader Comments: Middle-of-road Hawaiian course … Great valley views, tough in wind … Great bang for the buck … Very windy, but enjoyable.

★★½ **SEAMOUNTAIN GOLF COURSE**
R-Off Hwy. 11, Punaluu, 96777, Hawaii County, (808)928-6222, 56 miles from Hilo. **Facility Holes:** 18. **Yards:** 6,416/5,590. **Par:** 72/72. **Course Rating:** 71.1/70.9. **Slope:** 129/116. **Green Fee:** $25/$45. **Cart Fee:** Included in green fee. **Walking Policy:** Mandatory carts. **Walkability:** 3. **Opened:** 1973. **Architect:** Arthur Jack Snyder. **Season:** Year-round. **High:** Dec.-March. **To obtain tee times:** Call golf shop. **Miscellaneous:** Reduced fees (guests, juniors), metal spikes, range (grass), credit cards (MC, V), BF, FF.

TURTLE BAY RESORT GOLF CLUB
R-57-049 Kuilima Dr., Kahuku, 96731, Oahu County, (808)293-8574, 35 miles from Honolulu.
E-mail: thelinks@kuilima.com. **Web:** www.kuilima.com. **Facility Holes:** 36. **Green Fee:** $95/$140. **Cart Fee:** Included in green fee. **Walking Policy:** Unrestricted walking. **Walkability:** 3. **Architect:** Arnold Palmer/Ed Seay. **High:** Jan.-April. **Misc:** Reduced fees (guests, twilight, juniors), range (grass), lodging (487 rooms), credit cards (MC, V, AE, D, DC, JCB), BF, FF.
★★★★ **THE ARNOLD PALMER COURSE** (18) *Pace*
Yards: 7,199/4,851. **Par:** 72/72. **Course Rating:** 75.0/64.3. **Slope:** 141/121. **Opened:** 1992.
Season: Feb.-Dec. **To obtain tee times:** Call up to 90 days in advance.
Notes: Ranked 9th in 2001 Best in State.
Reader Comments: Excellent variety to holes … Best tee-to-green course on Oahu … Beautiful, but greens are not well kept … Pricey, tough course conditions … Underrated … Best fairways in Hawaii … Approach to 17th green unforgetable.
★★★★ **THE GEORGE FAZIO COURSE** (18)
Yards: 6,822/5,518. **Par:** 72/72. **Opened:** 1972. **Season:** Year-round. **To obtain tee times:** Call golf shop.
Reader Comments: Nice course, great value, conditions … A challenging links-style course, much tougher when windy … Scenic and not very difficult.
Special Notes: 9 new holes opening in 2002.

★★½ VOLCANO GOLF & COUNTRY CLUB

PU-Pii Mauna Dr., Hawaii Volcanoes Nat'l Pk, Volcano National Park, 96718, Hawaii County, (808)967-7331, 32 miles from Hilo. **Facility Holes:** 18. **Yards:** 6,547/5,567. **Par:** 72/72. **Course Rating:** 70.8/70.7. **Slope:** 128/117. **Green Fee:** $63. **Cart Fee:** Included in green fee. **Walking Policy:** Mandatory carts. **Walkability:** 2. **Opened:** 1922. **Architect:** Arthur Jack Snyder. **Season:** Year-round. **To obtain tee times:** Call golf shop. **Miscellaneous:** Reduced fees (juniors), metal spikes, range (grass), credit cards (MC, V, AE, D), BF, FF.

★★½ WAIEHU GOLF COURSE

PU-P.O. Box 507, Wailuku, 96793, Maui County, (808)244-5934, 4 miles from Waliuku. **Facility Holes:** 18. **Yards:** 6,330/5,511. **Par:** 72/71. **Course Rating:** 69.8/70.6. **Slope:** 111/115. **Green Fee:** $25/$30. **Cart Fee:** $16/Cart. **Walking Policy:** Unrestricted walking. **Walkability:** 1. **Architect:** Arthur Jack Snyder. **Season:** Year-round. **To obtain tee times:** Call up to 2 days in advance. **Miscellaneous:** Range (grass/mats), credit cards (MC, V, AE), BF, FF.

★★★ WAIKELE GOLF CLUB

SP-94-200 Paioa Place, Waipahu, 96797, Oahu County, (808)676-9000, 15 miles from Honolulu. **E-mail:** wglgolf@ahoha.net. **Web:** www.golfwaikele.com. **Facility Holes:** 18. **Yards:** 6,663/5,226. **Par:** 72/72. **Course Rating:** 71.7/65.6. **Slope:** 126/113. **Green Fee:** $107/$112. **Cart Fee:** Included in green fee. **Walking Policy:** Mandatory carts. **Walkability:** 2. **Opened:** 1993. **Architect:** Ted Robinson. **Season:** Year-round. **To obtain tee times:** Call up to 90 days in advance. **Miscellaneous:** Reduced fees (weekdays, twilight), metal spikes, range (grass), credit cards (MC, V, AE, D, DC, JCB), BF, FF.

Reader Comments: Lots of water … Great driving range with nearby outlet stores … Nice challenge … Some of the holes have homes nearby … Nice shopping area near course … Needs tender love and care.

WAIKOLOA BEACH RESORT

R-1020 Keana Place, Waikoloa, 96738, Hawaii County, (808)886-6060, (877)924-5656, 23 miles from Kailua-Kona. **E-mail:** kstrauss@waikoloaland.com. **Web:** www.waikoloagolf.com. **Facility Holes:** 36. **Green Fee:** $105/$205. **Cart Fee:** Included in green fee. **Walking Policy:** Mandatory carts. **Walkability:** 2. **Season:** Year-round. **High:** Jan.-April. **To obtain tee times:** Call up to 365 days in advance. **Miscellaneous:** Reduced fees (guests, twilight, juniors), metal spikes, range (grass), lodging (2000 rooms), credit cards (MC, V, AE, D, JCB), BF, FF.

★★★★½ **BEACH GOLF COURSE** (18) *Pace+*
Yards: 6,566/5,094. **Par:** 70/70. **Course Rating:** 71.5/69.4. **Slope:** 133/119. **Opened:** 1981. **Architect:** Robert Trent Jones Jr.

Reader Comments: Many greens guarded by lava, fun to watch whales while trying to putt … Nice layout, only one hole (No. 12) plays out to the ocean … Beautiful course and fun to play in paradise … Rarely crowded … Lots of lava.

★★★★ **KINGS GOLF COURSE** (18) *Pace*
Yards: 7,074/5,459. **Par:** 72/72. **Course Rating:** 73.9/71.0. **Slope:** 133/121. **Opened:** 1990. **Architect:** Tom Weiskopf/Jay Morrish.

Reader Comments: Hawaii at its best … Tougher than Beach, but not as scenic … A lot of lava rock … A good Hawaii course, but there are better. I'm having a hard time remembering the holes.

★★★ WAIKOLOA VILLAGE GOLF CLUB

R-68-1792 Melia St., Waikoloa, 96738, Hawaii County, (808)883-9621, 18 miles from Kailua-Kona. **E-mail:** golfwaikoloa@aol.com. **Web:** www.waikoloa.org. **Facility Holes:** 18. **Yards:** 6,814/5,479. **Par:** 72/72. **Course Rating:** 71.8/72.1. **Slope:** 130/119. **Green Fee:** $45/$80. **Cart Fee:** $15/Cart. **Walking Policy:** Walking at certain times. **Walkability:** 2. **Opened:** 1972. **Architect:** Robert Trent Jones Jr. **Season:** Year-round. **To obtain tee times:** Call golf shop. **Miscellaneous:** Reduced fees (guests, twilight, juniors), range (grass/mats), credit cards (MC, V, AE, D, DC. JCB), BF, FF.

Reader Comments: Beautiful course, fun … Tropical, bring your wind game … Old course, price is right … Very dry conditions, too expensive … Friendly staff.

WAILEA GOLF CLUB

R-120 Kaukahi St., Wailea, 96753, Maui County, (808)875-5111, (800)332-1614, 17 miles from Kahului. **E-mail:** golf@waileagolf.com. **Web:** www.waileagolf.com. **Facility Holes:** 54. **Cart Fee:** Included in green fee. **Walking Policy:** Mandatory carts. **Season:** Year-round. **High:** Jan.-April. **To obtain tee times:** Call up to 30 days in advance. **Miscellaneous:** Range (grass/mats), credit cards (MC, V, AE, D, JCB), BF, FF.

★★★★ **BLUE COURSE** (18)
Yards: 6,758/5,291. **Par:** 72/72. **Course Rating:** 71.6/72.0. **Slope:** 130/117. **Green Fee:** $80/$140. **Opened:** 1972. **Architect:** Arthur Jack Snyder. **Miscellaneous:** Reduced fees (guests, twilight, juniors), lodging (2500 rooms).

Reader Comments: Great condition, a real challenge for the average golfer … Worth the money … Expensive, beautiful … Wide fairways.

★★★★½ **EMERALD COURSE** (18) *Condition, Pace*
Yards: 6,825/5,256. **Par:** 72/72. **Course Rating:** 71.7/69.6. **Slope:** 130/115. **Green Fee:** $125/$150. **Opened:** 1994. **Architect:** Robert Trent Jones Jr. **Miscellaneous:** Reduced fees (guests).
Notes: Ranked 11th in 2001 Best in State; 2nd in 1995 Best New Resort Courses.
Reader Comments: They have the whole deal here ... Fun, friendly, a beautifully manicured course with exquisite views ... Golf in heaven, what can you say? ... Too pricey ... My favorite golf course on the island ... Unbelievable customer relations ... Only the Gold was better .. A real challenge for the average golfer.

★★★★½ **GOLD COURSE** (18) *Condition, Pace*
Yards: 7,070/5,317. **Par:** 72/72. **Course Rating:** 73.0/70.3. **Slope:** 139/121. **Green Fee:** $135/$160. **Opened:** 1994. **Architect:** Robert Trent Jones Jr. **Miscellaneous:** Reduced fees (guests).
Reader Comments: Sparkling Pacific everywhere ... Fairly open, big greens and great ocean views ... Unbelivable for its condition and beauty ... Lots of volcanic outcroppings in play ... Not as good as the Emerald, but enjoyable.

★★★★ **WAILUA GOLF COURSE** *Value+*
PU-3-5350 Kuhio Hwy., Lihue, 96766, Kauai County, (808)246-2793, 3 miles from Lihue.
E-mail: pwgolf@kauaigov.com. **Facility Holes:** 18. **Yards:** 6,981/5,974. **Par:** 36/36. **Course Rating:** 73.0/73.1. **Slope:** 136/122. **Green Fee:** $25/$35. **Cart Fee:** $14/Cart. **Walking Policy:** Unrestricted walking. **Walkability:** 3. **Opened:** 1963. **Architect:** Toyo Shirai. **Season:** Year-round. **High:** Jan.-March. **To obtain tee times:** Call up to 7 days in advance. **Miscellaneous:** Reduced fees (twilight, seniors), range (grass/mats), FF.
Notes: Ranked 7th in 2001 Best in State.
Reader Comments: One of the country's great muni courses, the condition is more like a private course ... Tough course ... The best value in Hawaii.

★★★½ **WAIMEA COUNTRY CLUB**
SP-47-5220 Mamalohoa Hwy., Kamuela, 96743, Hawaii County, (808)885-8777, 51 miles from Hilo. **Facility Holes:** 18. **Yards:** 6,661/5,673. **Par:** 72/72. **Course Rating:** 71.7/71.3. **Slope:** 130/119. **Green Fee:** $50/$65. **Cart Fee:** Included in green fee. **Walking Policy:** Unrestricted walking. **Walkability:** 2. **Opened:** 1994. **Architect:** John Sanford. **Season:** Year-round. **High:** Dec.-March. **To obtain tee times:** Call up to 7 days in advance. **Misc:** Reduced fees (twilight, seniors, juniors), metal spikes, range (grass/mats), credit cards (MC, V, AE, D, DC, JCB), FF.
Reader Comments: When weather is good, best value ... A solid value and a different look from resorts ... Very interesting ... Hidden bargain, completely different from the resort courses ... Nice change of pace from the Kona area courses.

★★ **WEST LOCH GOLF COURSE**
PU-91-1126 Okupe St., Ewa Beach, 96706, Oahu County, (808)671-2292, 15 miles from Honolulu. **Facility Holes:** 18. **Yards:** 6,479/5,296. **Par:** 72/72. **Course Rating:** 70.3/68.6. **Slope:** 123/117. **Green Fee:** $17/$21. **Cart Fee:** Included in green fee. **Walkability:** 2. **Opened:** 1990. **Architect:** Robin Nelson/Rodney Wright. **Season:** Year-round. **High:** April-Sept. **To obtain tee times:** Call golf shop. **Miscellaneous:** Reduced fees (twilight, seniors, juniors), metal spikes, range (grass/mats), credit cards (MC, V).

ASPEN ACRES GOLF CLUB
PU-4179 E 1100 N, Ashton, 83420, Fremont County, (208)652-3524, (800)845-2374. **Facility Holes:** 18. **Yards:** 3,000/3,000. **Par:** 60/62. **Course Rating:** 50.5/52.4. **Slope:** 73/73. **Green Fee:** $11/$17. **Season:** May-Nov. **To obtain tee times:** Call golf shop. **Misc:** Reduced fees (juniors).

★★★½ AVONDALE GOLF CLUB
SP-10745 Avondale Loop Rd., Hayden Lake, 83835, Kootenai County, (208)772-5963, (877)286-6429, 35 miles from Spokane. **E-mail:** avondale@dmi.net. **Web:** www.avondalegolf-course.com. **Facility Holes:** 18. **Yards:** 6,773/5,180. **Par:** 72/74. **Course Rating:** 71.8/70.9. **Slope:** 124/123. **Green Fee:** $24/$38. **Cart Fee:** $24/Cart. **Walking Policy:** Walking at certain times. **Walkability:** 3. **Opened:** 1972. **Architect:** Mel (Curley) Hueston. **Season:** March-Oct. **High:** June-Aug. **To obtain tee times:** Call golf shop. **Miscellaneous:** Reduced fees (twilight, seniors, juniors), range (mats), credit cards (MC, V, D), BF, FF.
Reader Comments: There's a lot of hidden beauty, play it twice ... Nice course but kind of narrow ... Love the holes along the waterfall! ... One of the best courses I have played ... 11th hole beautiful par 3 ... Turned into a real good course.

★★★★½ BANBURY GOLF CLUB *Service, Value*
PU-2626 Mary Post Place, Eagle, 83616, Ada County, (208)939-3600, 8 miles from Boise. **E-mail:** becker@banburygolf.com. **Web:** www.banburygolf.com. **Facility Holes:** 18. **Yards:** 6,900/5,257. **Par:** 71/71. **Course Rating:** 71.7/69.8. **Slope:** 125/119. **Green Fee:** $29/$39. **Cart Fee:** $11/Person. **Walking Policy:** Unrestricted walking. **Walkability:** 2. **Opened:** 1999. **Architect:** John Harbottle III. **Season:** Feb.-Nov. **High:** April-Sept. **To obtain tee times:** Call up to 7 days in advance. **Miscellaneous:** Reduced fees (twilight, seniors, juniors), range (grass/mats), credit cards (MC, V, AE, D), BF, FF.
Notes: Ranked 2nd in 2001 Best in State.
Reader Comments: Fun golf ... Top 5 in Idaho, good price to play it ... A course to score on, if you can avoid the water on 17 holes ... Has everything, variety, water, bunkers, quality ... Friendly staff, all aspects of course excellent condition ... Back 9 is much more difficult.

BIGWOOD GOLF COURSE
R-Hwy. 75 North of Ketchum, Ketchum/Sun Valley, 83340, Blaine County, (208)726-4024, 1 mile from Sun Valley. **Facility Holes:** 9. **Yards:** 3,335/2,912. **Par:** 36/37. **Course Rating:** 36.0/37.0. **Slope:** 115/121. **Green Fee:** $45. **Cart Fee:** $16/Person. **Walking Policy:** Unrestricted walking. **Walkability:** 2. **Opened:** 1972. **Architect:** Robert Muir Graves. **Season:** May-Nov. **High:** July-Aug. **To obtain tee times:** Call up to 7 days in advance. **Miscellaneous:** Range (grass), credit cards (MC, V, AE, D), BF, FF.

★★★ BLACKFOOT MUNICIPAL GOLF COURSE
PU-3115 Teeples Dr., Blackfoot, 83221, Bingham County, (208)785-9960, 19 miles from Pocatello. **Facility Holes:** 18. **Yards:** 6,899/6,385. **Par:** 72/78. **Course Rating:** 71.0/75.0. **Slope:** 123/124. **Green Fee:** $17. **Cart Fee:** $16/Cart. **Walking Policy:** Unrestricted walking. **Walkability:** 1. **Opened:** 1959. **Architect:** George Von Elm. **Season:** March-Nov. **High:** June-Sept. **To obtain tee times:** Call up to 7 days in advance. **Miscellaneous:** Reduced fees (weekdays), range (grass), credit cards (MC, V, D), BF, FF.
Reader Comments: Tough front 9 ... Wonderful small-town course, greens and course always in excellent shape, pro and help are all friendly and accommodating ... Excellent greens ... One of the better courses in eastern Idaho.

★★½ BRYDEN CANYON PUBLIC GOLF COURSE
PU-445 O'Connor Rd., Lewiston, 83501, Nez Perce County, (208)746-0863, 100 miles from Spokane. **Facility Holes:** 18. **Yards:** 6,103/5,380. **Par:** 71/72. **Course Rating:** 67.4/69.9. **Slope:** 106/111. **Green Fee:** $16. **Cart Fee:** $21/Cart. **Walking Policy:** Unrestricted walking. **Walkability:** 4. **Opened:** 1975. **Season:** Year-round. **High:** Feb.-Sept. **To obtain tee times:** Call golf shop. **Miscellaneous:** Metal spikes, range (grass), credit cards (MC, V, D).

BURLEY GOLF COURSE
PU-131 E. Highway 81, Burley, 83318, Minnadka County, (208)878-9807, 35 miles from Twin Falls. **Facility Holes:** 18. **Yards:** 6,437/5,565. **Par:** 72/75. **Course Rating:** 69.5/69.7. **Slope:** 115/116. **Green Fee:** $18/$19. **Cart Fee:** $9/Person. **Walking Policy:** Unrestricted walking. **Walkability:** 1. **Opened:** 1928. **Season:** Year-round. **High:** April-Sept. **To obtain tee times:** Call up to 3 days in advance. **Miscellaneous:** Reduced fees (weekdays, seniors, juniors), range (grass), credit cards (MC, V, AE, D), BF, FF.

★★½ CANYON SPRINGS GOLF COURSE
PU-199 Canyon Springs Rd., Twin Falls, 83301, Twin Falls County, (208)734-7609, 110 miles from Boise. **E-mail:** info@canyonspringsgolf.com. **Web:** www.canyonspringsgolf.com. **Facility Holes:** 18. **Yards:** 6,452/5,190. **Par:** 72/74. **Course Rating:** 68.7/67.1. **Slope:** 116/112.

Green Fee: $15/$29. **Cart Fee:** $22/Cart. **Walking Policy:** Unrestricted walking. **Walkability:** 3. **Opened:** 1975. **Architect:** Max Mueller. **Season:** Year-round. **High:** May-Sept. **To obtain tee times:** Call up to 3 days in advance. **Miscellaneous:** Reduced fees (weekdays, twilight, juniors), range (grass), credit cards (MC, V), BF, FF.

★★½ CENTENNIAL GOLF CLUB
PU-2600 Centennial Dr., Nampa, 83651, Canyon County, (208)467-3011. **E-mail:** golfprol@micron.net. **Web:** www.golfcentennial.com. **Facility Holes:** 18. **Yards:** 6,499/5,505. **Par:** 72/72. **Course Rating:** 69.6/69.6. **Slope:** 113/112. **Green Fee:** $15/$18. **Cart Fee:** $17/Cart. **Walking Policy:** Unrestricted walking. **Walkability:** 2. **Opened:** 1987. **Architect:** Robert L. Baldock. **Season:** Year-round. **High:** April-Sept. **To obtain tee times:** Call up to 2 days in advance. **Miscellaneous:** Reduced fees (twilight), range (grass), credit cards (MC, V, D), BF, FF.

★★★ CLEAR LAKE COUNTRY CLUB
SP-403 Clear Lake Lane, Buhl, 83316, Twin Falls County, (208)543-4849, 90 miles from Boise. **Facility Holes:** 18. **Yards:** 5,905/5,378. **Par:** 72/73. **Course Rating:** 68.2/69.4. **Slope:** 112/113. **Green Fee:** $15/$22. **Walking Policy:** Unrestricted walking. **Walkability:** 5. **Opened:** 1987. **Architect:** Dutch Kuse. **Season:** Year-round. **To obtain tee times:** Call golf shop. **Miscellaneous:** Reduced fees (weekdays, juniors), range (grass), credit cards (MC, V), BF, FF.
Reader Comments: Everything slopes toward river... Lots of elevation changes ... Course always in good shape ... Right next to Snake River—beautiful! Great spring golf in Snake River Canyon ... Intriguing, high risk, high rewards. Fun!... Pleasant short course ... Bring your trout rod.

★★★★½ COEUR D'ALENE RESORT G. CSE. *Service+, Condition+, Pace*
R-900 Floating Green Dr., Coeur d'Alene, 83814, Kootenai County, (208)667-4653, (800)688-5253, 32 miles from Spokane. **E-mail:** mdelong@cdaresort.com. **Web:** www.cdaresort.com. **Facility Holes:** 18. **Yards:** 6,309/5,490. **Par:** 71/71. **Course Rating:** 69.9/70.3. **Slope:** 121/118. **Green Fee:** $75/$210. **Cart Fee:** Included in green fee. **Walking Policy:** Walking with Caddie. **Walkability:** 3. **Opened:** 1991. **Architect:** Scott Miller. **Season:** April-Oct. **High:** July-Sept. **To obtain tee times:** Call golf shop. **Miscellaneous:** Reduced fees (guests), range (grass), caddies (included in fee), lodging (338 rooms), credit cards (MC, V, AE, D), BF, FF. **Notes:** Ranked 2nd in 1999 Best in State.
Reader Comments: An unbelievable experience ... The Coeur d'Alene Resort Golf Course is the most beautiful course I've ever played ... Great service, the course is manicured in every detail ... Always exciting ... They treat you like a tour player ... King for a day ... Floating green a real treat.

★★½ EAGLE HILLS GOLF COURSE
PU-605 N. Edgewood Lane, Eagle, 83616, Ada County, (208)939-0402, 4 miles from Boise. **Facility Holes:** 18. **Yards:** 6,485/5,305. **Par:** 72/72. **Course Rating:** 70.5/70.2. **Slope:** 119/114. **Green Fee:** $20/$27. **Cart Fee:** $10/Person. **Walking Policy:** Unrestricted walking. **Walkability:** 3. **Opened:** 1968. **Architect:** C. Edward Trout. **Season:** Year-round. **High:** March-Oct. **To obtain tee times:** Call golf shop. **Miscellaneous:** Reduced fees (weekdays, twilight, seniors, juniors), metal spikes, range (grass/mats), credit cards (MC, V).

★★★½ ELKHORN RESORT & GOLF CLUB
SP-1 Elkhorn Rd., Sun Valley, 83354, Blaine County, (208)622-3300, (800)355-4676, 150 miles from Boise. **E-mail:** golf117@meristar.com. **Facility Holes:** 18. **Yards:** 7,034/5,414. **Par:** 72/72. **Course Rating:** 72.2/69.3. **Slope:** 127/114. **Green Fee:** $100. **Cart Fee:** Included in green fee. **Walking Policy:** Mandatory carts. **Walkability:** 5. **Opened:** 1974. **Architect:** R.T. Jones/R.T. Jones Jr. **Season:** May-Oct. **High:** July-Sept. **To obtain tee times:** Call golf shop. **Miscellaneous:** Reduced fees (weekdays, guests, twilight, juniors), range (grass/mats), credit cards (MC, V, AE, D), BF, FF. **Notes:** Ranked 5th in 1999 Best in State.
Reader Comments: Great mountain resort ... Course great in summer and fall ... Big course from the tips... Very fair... Every hole has great views ... Fairways lined by condos ... We were treated like royal guests. Our bags were collected from the car and at the end our clubs were cleaned ... New clubhouse.

EMMETT CITY GOLF COURSE
PU-2102 W. Sales Yard Rd., Emmett, 83617, Gem County, (208)365-2675, 2 miles from Emmett. **Facility Holes:** 9. **Yards:** 2,910/2,737. **Par:** 36/36. **Course Rating:** 67.4/67.7. **Slope:** 111/115. **Green Fee:** $13. **Walking Policy:** Unrestricted walking. **Walkability:** 1. **Opened:** 1959. **Season:** Year-round. **High:** May-Oct. **To obtain tee times:** Call golf shop. **Miscellaneous:** Reduced fees (twilight), credit cards (V).

IDAHO

★★★★ HIDDEN LAKES GOLF RESORT
R-151 Clubhouse Way, Sandpoint, 83864, Bonner County, (208)263-1642, (888)806-6673, 86 miles from Spokane. **E-mail:** golfidkap@nidlink.com. **Web:** www.hiddenlakesgolf.com. **Facility Holes:** 18. **Yards:** 7,077/5,269. **Par:** 72/72. **Course Rating:** 73.5/70.3. **Slope:** 139/120. **Green Fee:** $38. **Cart Fee:** $13/Person. **Walking Policy:** Unrestricted walking. **Walkability:** 3. **Opened:** 1986. **Architect:** Jim Krause. **Season:** April-Nov. **To obtain tee times:** Call golf shop. **Miscellaneous:** Reduced fees (guests, twilight, seniors, juniors), range (grass/mats), credit cards (MC, V, AE, D, DC, CB), BF, FF.
Reader Comments: Excellent layout … A sleeper … Good test of golf … Moose! … Very nice people … Outstanding site … New clubhouse … Need golf balls, you need to hit straight … Very exciting, many lakes.

★★★ HIGHLAND GOLF COURSE
PU-201 Vonelm Rd., Pocatello, 83201, Bannock County, (208)237-9922. **Facility Holes:** 18. **Yards:** 6,512/6,100. **Par:** 72/76. **Course Rating:** 67.5/73.0. **Slope:** 114/117. **Green Fee:** $12/$13. **Walking Policy:** Unrestricted walking. **Opened:** 1963. **Architect:** Babe Hiskey. **Season:** March-Oct. **High:** May-Sept. **To obtain tee times:** Call golf shop. **Miscellaneous:** Reduced fees (seniors, juniors), metal spikes, range (grass).
Reader Comments: Rolling fairways provide challenge … A nice course overall … Good shots required … Tough greens to putt …. Hilly course … Getting better each year, a great golf test … Improvements being made, very good … An easy but immaculate course.

★★★ THE HIGHLANDS GOLF & COUNTRY CLUB
PU-5500 E. Mullan, Post Falls, 83854, Kootenai County, (208)773-3673, (800)797-7339, 30 miles from Spokane. **Web:** www.highlandsgcc.com. **Facility Holes:** 18. **Yards:** 6,036/5,125. **Par:** 72/73. **Course Rating:** 70.0/69.3. **Slope:** 125/125. **Green Fee:** $23/$27. **Cart Fee:** $23/Cart. **Walking Policy:** Unrestricted walking. **Walkability:** 4. **Opened:** 1990. **Architect:** Jim Kraus. **Season:** April-Oct. **High:** June-Aug. **To obtain tee times:** Call up to 7 days in advance. **Miscellaneous:** Reduced fees (weekdays, twilight, seniors, juniors), range (grass/mats), credit cards (MC, V, AE, D), BF, FF.
Reader Comments: Water holes, surprising layout … Requires well placed shots … Great course, nice people … Several blind shots … Highlands Golf and Country Club is one of those 'love it or hate it' courses … The practice range is arguably the best in North Idaho.

★★★ JEROME COUNTRY CLUB
SP-6 mi. S of Town, Jerome, 83338, Jerome County, (208)324-5281, 6 miles from Jerome. **Facility Holes:** 18. **Yards:** 6,429/5,644. **Par:** 72/73. **Course Rating:** 68.8/71.2. **Slope:** 106/114. **Green Fee:** $30. **Cart Fee:** $20/Cart. **Walking Policy:** Unrestricted walking. **Walkability:** 3. **Opened:** 1930. **Architect:** Ed Hunnicutt. **Season:** March-Dec. **High:** May-Sept. **To obtain tee times:** Call golf shop. **Miscellaneous:** Range (grass), credit cards (MC, V).
Reader Comments: Windy … Back 9 more interesting … Good track, many tournaments … Well manicured, relaxed atmosphere … Distinctly different front and back 9s … Flat front 9, challenging back 9, good layout … 'Deals' abound.

★★½ MCCALL MUNICIPAL GOLF COURSE
PU-1000 Reedy Lane, McCall, 83638, Valley County, (208)634-7200, 102 miles from Boise. **Facility Holes:** 27. **Green Fee:** $20/$30. **Cart Fee:** $22/Cart. **Walking Policy:** Unrestricted walking. **Walkability:** 2. **Season:** May-Nov. **High:** June-Sept. **To obtain tee times:** Call golf shop. **Misc:** Reduced fees (weekdays, twilight), range (grass/mats), credit cards (MC, V, D). BF, FF.
ASPEN/BIRCH COURSE (18 combo)
Yards: 6,295/5,552. **Par:** 71/71. **Course Rating:** 69.1/71.2. **Slope:** 124/119. **Opened:** 1926.
BIRCH/CEDAR COURSE (18 combo)
Yards: 6,221/5,298. **Par:** 71/71. **Course Rating:** 68.6/69.2. **Slope:** 116/118. **Opened:** 1991.
CEDAR/ASPEN COURSE (18 combo)
Yards: 6,222/5,232. **Par:** 70/70. **Course Rating:** 68.8/68.7. **Slope:** 117/118. **Opened:** 1991.

MONTPELIER GOLF COURSE
PU-210 Boise St., Montpelier, 83254, Bear Lake County, (208)847-1981, 150 miles from Salt Lake City. **Facility Holes:** 9. **Yards:** 6,400/6,000. **Par:** 72/72. **Course Rating:** 68.3/67.6. **Slope:** 111/116. **Green Fee:** $16. **Cart Fee:** $16/Cart. **Walking Policy:** Unrestricted walking. **Walkability:** 2. **Opened:** 1964. **Architect:** Ernie Schneiter. **Season:** April-Oct. **High:** June-July. **To obtain tee times:** Call golf shop. **Miscellaneous:** Reduced fees (juniors), metal spikes, range (grass), credit cards (MC, V), BF, FF.

OREGON TRAIL COUNTRY CLUB
SP-2525 Hwy. 30, Soda Springs, 83276, Caribou County, (208)547-2204. **Facility Holes:** 9. **Yards:** 3,066/2,700. **Par:** 36/36. **Course Rating:** 67.7/68.7. **Slope:** 108/104. **Green Fee:** $9. **Walkability:** 2. **Opened:** 1964. **Season:** March-Oct. **To obtain tee times:** Call golf shop.

★★★★ PINECREST MUNICIPAL GOLF COURSE

PU-701 E. Elva St., Idaho Falls, 83401, Bonneville County, (208)529-1485, 180 miles from Salt Lake City. **Facility Holes:** 18. **Yards:** 6,419/6,123. **Par:** 70/75. **Course Rating:** 69.4/72.5. **Slope:** 116/123. **Green Fee:** $17/$18. **Cart Fee:** $15/Cart. **Walking Policy:** Unrestricted walking. **Walkability:** 3. **Opened:** 1934. **Architect:** W. H. Tucker. **Season:** March-Nov. **High:** May-Sept. **To obtain tee times:** Call up to 2 days in advance. **Miscellaneous:** Credit cards (MC, V, D), BF, FF.

Reader Comments: A great course in a beautiful town ... Wonderful old course ... Relaxing, open and casual ... Classic old golf course, tall trees, beautiful ... Quality pro/quality staff ... One of the oldest and best courses in Idaho.

PRESTON GOLF & COUNTRY CLUB

SP-1215 N. 800 E., Preston, 83263, Franklin County, (208)852-2408. **E-mail:** pete13golf@aol.com. **Facility Holes:** 18. **Yards:** 6,254/5,813. **Par:** 71/71. **Course Rating:** 68.4/69.0. **Slope:** 104/110. **Green Fee:** $6. **Walking Policy:** Unrestricted walking. **Walkability:** 1. **Opened:** 1960. **Architect:** Ernie Schneider. **Season:** March-Nov. **To obtain tee times:** Call golf shop. **Miscellaneous:** Reduced fees (seniors, juniors), credit cards (MC, V), BF, FF.

PRIEST LAKE GOLF COURSE

PU-152 Fairway Dr., Priest Lake, 83856, Bonner County, (208)443-2525. **E-mail:** golfclub@povn.com. **Web:** www.priestlakegolfcourse.com. **Facility Holes:** 18. **Yards:** 6,344/6,166. **Par:** 72/72. **Course Rating:** 65.6/69.2. **Slope:** 110/115. **Green Fee:** $20/$26. **Cart Fee:** $25/Cart. **Walking Policy:** Unrestricted walking. **Walkability:** 2. **Opened:** 1965. **Season:** April-Nov. **High:** June-Sept. **To obtain tee times:** Call up to 30 days in advance. **Miscellaneous:** Reduced fees (twilight, juniors), range (grass), credit cards (MC, V, D), BF, FF.

★★½ PURPLE SAGE GOLF COURSE

PU-15192 Purple Sage Rd., Caldwell, 83607, Canyon County, (208)459-2223, 25 miles from Boise. **Facility Holes:** 18. **Yards:** 6,753/5,343. **Par:** 71/72. **Course Rating:** 70.8/69.2. **Slope:** 123/114. **Green Fee:** $15/$17. **Cart Fee:** $18/Person. **Walking Policy:** Unrestricted walking. **Walkability:** 1. **Opened:** 1963. **Architect:** A. Vernon Macan. **Season:** Year-round. **To obtain tee times:** Call golf shop. **Miscellaneous:** Reduced fees (weekdays), range (grass), credit cards (MC, V), BF, FF.

★★½ QUAIL HOLLOW GOLF CLUB

SP-4520 N. 36th St., Boise, 83703, Ada County, (208)344-7807. **Facility Holes:** 18. **Yards:** 6,444/4,530. **Par:** 70/70. **Course Rating:** 70.7/68.0. **Slope:** 128/129. **Green Fee:** $18/$27. **Cart Fee:** $9/Person. **Walking Policy:** Unrestricted walking. **Walkability:** 4. **Opened:** 1982. **Architect:** Robert von Hagge/Bruce Devlin. **Season:** Year-round. **High:** March-Oct. **To obtain tee times:** Call up to 5 days in advance. **Miscellaneous:** Reduced fees (weekdays, seniors, juniors), range (grass), credit cards (MC, V), BF, FF.

★★★½ · RIDGECREST GOLF CLUB

PU-3730 Ridgecrest Dr., Nampa, 83687, Canyon County, (208)468-9073, 15 miles from Boise. **Web:** www.ridgecrestgolf.com. **Facility Holes:** 27. **Yards:** 6,888/5,193. **Par:** 72/72. **Course Rating:** 72.0/68.8. **Slope:** 125/120. **Green Fee:** $16/$19. **Cart Fee:** $18/Cart. **Walking Policy:** Unrestricted walking. **Walkability:** 2. **Opened:** 1996. **Architect:** John Harbottle. **Season:** Year-round. **High:** April-Sept. **To obtain tee times:** Call golf shop. **Miscellaneous:** Reduced fees (weekdays, twilight, juniors), metal spikes, range (grass), credit cards (MC, V). **Notes:** Ranked 1st in 1999 Best in State.

Reader Comments: Best public course in Idaho! ... Some tough holes ... Great course, worth finding ... Outstanding ... Hard but fun to play ... Windy and dry... Design is good... Fairly new with promise to be one of the best public courses in Idaho ... A must play. Bring all clubs! .... Popular and crowded ... Well run ...New clubhouse ... Good course.

Special Notes: Also has a 9-hole par-3 course.

★★½ RIVERSIDE GOLF COURSE

PU-3500 S. Bannock Hwy., Pocatello, 83204, Bannock County, (208)232-9515. **Facility Holes:** 18. **Yards:** 6,397/5,710. **Par:** 72/75. **Course Rating:** 69.7/72.2. **Slope:** 114/119. **Green Fee:** $16/$17. **Cart Fee:** $19/Person. **Walking Policy:** Unrestricted walking. **Walkability:** 2. **Opened:** 1963. **Architect:** Babe Hiskey. **Season:** March-Oct. **High:** May-Aug. **To obtain tee times:** Call golf shop. **Miscellaneous:** Metal spikes, range (grass), credit cards (MC, V).

★★★ SAGE LAKES MUNICIPAL GOLF

PU-100 E. 65N, Idaho Falls, 83401, Bonneville County, (208)528-5535. **Facility Holes:** 18. **Yards:** 6,566/4,883. **Par:** 70/70. **Course Rating:** 70.4/66.4. **Slope:** 115/108. **Green Fee:** $14/$17. **Walking Policy:** Unrestricted walking. **Walkability:** 2. **Opened:** 1993. **Season:** March-Nov. **High:** May-Sept. **To obtain tee times:** Call up to 2 days in advance.

IDAHO

Miscellaneous: Range (grass), credit cards (MC, V, D), BF, FF.
Reader Comments: Developing into a very good course ... Courteous, friendly staff ... Open ... A really fun, quiet course ... Watch the water... Beautiful place, well maintained.

★★★ SAND CREEK GOLF CLUB
PU-5200 S.E. Hackman Rd., Idaho Falls, 83403, Bonneville County, (208)529-1115. **Facility Holes:** 18. **Yards:** 6,805/5,770. **Par:** 72/73. **Course Rating:** 70.5/72.2. **Slope:** 115/116. **Green Fee:** $11/$12. **Walking Policy:** Unrestricted walking. **Opened:** 1978. **Architect:** William F. Bell. **Season:** March-Nov. **High:** June-Aug. **To obtain tee times:** Call golf shop. **Miscellaneous:** Reduced fees (seniors, juniors), metal spikes, credit cards (MC, V).
Reader Comments: Easy walk ... Friendly, accommodating staff ... Excellent maintenance ... Scenic sand dunes located on course ... A confidence builder, makes me feel like a 6-handicap ... Flat course ... Fun course, well managed ... Play this in a 30 m.p.h. breeze, it is a hoot.

SAND POINT ELKS GOLF COURSE
PU-30196 Hwy. 200 East, Sandpoint, 83864, Bonner County, (208)263-4321, 1 mile from Sandpoint. **Facility Holes:** 9. **Yards:** 5,701/5,463. **Par:** 70/70. **Course Rating:** 65.9/71.1. **Slope:** 106/108. **Green Fee:** $20. **Cart Fee:** $20/Cart. **Walking Policy:** Unrestricted walking. **Walkability:** 1. **Opened:** 1925. **Season:** April-Oct. **High:** July-Aug. **To obtain tee times:** Call golf shop. **Miscellaneous:** Reduced fees (weekdays, twilight), credit cards (MC, V, AE), BF, FF.

★★★½ SCOTCH PINES GOLF COURSE
PU-10610 Scotch Pines Rd., Payette, 83661, Payette County, (208)642-1829, 58 miles from Boise. **E-mail:** ramz@fmtc.com. **Facility Holes:** 18. **Yards:** 6,605/5,512. **Par:** 72/72. **Course Rating:** 69.4/70.3. **Slope:** 111/116. **Green Fee:** $20. **Cart Fee:** $10/Person. **Walking Policy:** Unrestricted walking. **Walkability:** 3. **Opened:** 1960. **Architect:** Cliff Masingill/Scott Masingill. **Season:** Year-round. **High:** April-Oct. **To obtain tee times:** Call up to 7 days in advance. **Misc:** Reduced fees (weekdays, twilight), range (grass), credit cards (MC, V, AE), BF, FF.
Reader Comments: Best course in the Treasure Valley ... Front 9 narrow, back 9 open ... Rolling terrain ... Great course for such a small community ... Fast play, elevation changes, fun ... Homey, quaint, personable ... Best kept secret in the valley.

★★★½ SHADOW VALLEY GOLF CLUB
PU-15711 Hwy. 55, Boise, 83703, Ada County, (208)939-6699, (800)936-7035, 10 miles from Boise. **E-mail:** svgolf@micron.net. **Web:** www.shadowvalley.com. **Facility Holes:** 18. **Yards:** 6,433/5,394. **Par:** 72/72. **Course Rating:** 69.2/71.8. **Slope:** 117/117. **Green Fee:** $21/$30. **Cart Fee:** $20/Person. **Walking Policy:** Unrestricted walking. **Walkability:** 3. **Opened:** 1973. **Architect:** Ed Trout. **Season:** Year-round. **High:** April-Oct. **To obtain tee times:** Call up to 5 days in advance. **Miscellaneous:** Reduced fees (weekdays, seniors, juniors), range (grass), credit cards (MC, V, AE, D), BF, FF.
Reader Comments: Walkable, fun, elevation changes ... First time out course is hard to play ... Always improving, go to extreme on pace of play ... Challenging, lots of doglegs and streams with water hazards ... Marshals keep pace.

SHOSHONE GOLF & TENNIS CLUB
SP-Gold Run Mountain, Kellogg, 83873, Shoshone County, (208)784-0161, 10 miles from Wallace. **Facility Holes:** 9. **Yards:** 6,270/5,959. **Par:** 72/72. **Course Rating:** 69.3/75.1. **Slope:** 119/128. **Green Fee:** $12/$22. **Cart Fee:** $22/Cart. **Walking Policy:** Unrestricted walking. **Walkability:** 3. **Opened:** 1979. **Architect:** Keith Hellstrum. **Season:** April-Oct. **High:** June-Sept. **To obtain tee times:** Call golf shop. **Miscellaneous:** Reduced fees (weekdays), range (mats), credit cards (MC, V, AE), BF, FF.

★★ STONERIDGE COUNTRY CLUB
SP-1 Blanchard Rd., Blanchard, 83804, Bonner County, (208)437-4682, 35 miles from Spokane. **Web:** www.stoneridgeidaho.com. **Facility Holes:** 18. **Yards:** 6,612/5,678. **Par:** 72/72. **Course Rating:** 71.4/72.4. **Slope:** 127/126. **Green Fee:** $15/$20. **Cart Fee:** $23/Cart. **Walking Policy:** Unrestricted walking. **Walkability:** 4. **Opened:** 1971. **Architect:** Jim Krause. **Season:** April-Oct. **High:** May-Sept. **To obtain tee times:** Call golf shop. **Miscellaneous:** Reduced fees (guests, twilight, seniors, juniors), range (grass), credit cards (MC, V).

★★★★ SUN VALLEY RESORT GOLF COURSE
R-Sun Valley Rd., Sun Valley, 83353, Blaine County, (208)622-2251, (800)786-8259. **Facility Holes:** 18. **Yards:** 6,565/5,241. **Par:** 72/73. **Course Rating:** 71.1/70.4. **Slope:** 128/125. **Green Fee:** $49/$83. **Cart Fee:** Included in green fee. **Walking Policy:** Walking at certain times. **Opened:** 1938. **Architect:** William P. Bell/Robert Trent Jones Jr. **Season:** April-Oct. **High:** June-Sept. **To obtain tee times:** Call golf shop. **Miscellaneous:** Reduced fees (guests), metal spikes, range (grass), credit cards (MC, V, AE, D).
Notes: Golf Digest School site. Ranked 3rd in 1999 Best in State.

IDAHO

★★½ TETON LAKES GOLF COURSE

PU-2000 W. Hibbard Pkwy., Rexburg, 83440, Madison County, (208)359-3036. **Facility Holes:** 18. **Yards:** 6,397/5,116. **Par:** 71/73. **Course Rating:** 69.4/66.6. **Slope:** 119/112. **Green Fee:** $14. **Cart Fee:** $17/Cart. **Walking Policy:** Unrestricted walking. **Opened:** 1979. **Season:** March-Nov. **High:** June-Aug. **To obtain tee times:** Call golf shop. **Miscellaneous:** Credit cards (MC, V, AE, D).

★½ TWIN FALLS MUNICIPAL GOLF COURSE

PU-Grandview Dr., Twin Falls, 83301, Twin Falls County, (208)733-3326. **Facility Holes:** 18. **Yards:** 5,234/4,961. **Par:** 68/71. **Course Rating:** 64.8/68.0. **Slope:** 106/105. **Green Fee:** $14. **Cart Fee:** $20/Person. **Walking Policy:** Unrestricted walking. **Walkability:** 1. **Season:** Year-round. **High:** Feb.-Nov. **To obtain tee times:** Call golf shop. **Miscellaneous:** Reduced fees (weekdays, twilight, seniors, juniors), metal spikes, range (grass), credit cards (MC, V).

★★★ TWIN LAKES VILLAGE GOLF COURSE

SP-5416 W. Village Blvd., Rathdrum, 83858, Kootenai County, (208)687-1311, (888)836-7949, 15 miles from Coeur d'Alene. **E-mail:** info@golfnorthidaho.com. **Web:** www.golfnorthidaho.com. **Facility Holes:** 18. **Yards:** 6,277/5,363. **Par:** 72/72. **Course Rating:** 70.0/70.5. **Slope:** 121/118. **Green Fee:** $20/$25. **Cart Fee:** $20/Cart. **Walking Policy:** Unrestricted walking. **Walkability:** 2. **Opened:** 1975. **Architect:** William Robinson. **Season:** April-Oct. **High:** June-Aug. **To obtain tee times:** Call golf shop. **Miscellaneous:** Reduced fees (weekdays, twilight, seniors, juniors), range (grass), credit cards (MC, V, AE), BF, FF.

UNIVERSITY OF IDAHO GOLF COURSE

PU-1215 Nez Perce, Moscow, 83843, Latah County, (208)885-6171, 85 miles from Spokane. **E-mail:** dawesm@uidaho.edu. **Web:** www.its.uidaho.edu/golf. **Facility Holes:** 18. **Yards:** 6,639/5,770. **Par:** 72/72. **Course Rating:** 72.0/73.0. **Slope:** 130/130. **Green Fee:** $14/$22. **Cart Fee:** $20/Cart. **Walking Policy:** Unrestricted walking. **Walkability:** 3. **Opened:** 1933. **Architect:** Francis L. James. **Season:** March-Oct. **High:** May-Aug. **To obtain tee times:** Call up to 7 days in advance. **Miscellaneous:** Reduced fees (weekdays, twilight, seniors, juniors), range (grass), credit cards (MC, V, D), BF, FF.

★★ WARM SPRINGS GOLF COURSE

PU-2495 Warm Springs Ave., Boise, 83712, Ada County, (208)343-5661. **Facility Holes:** 18. **Yards:** 6,719/5,660. **Par:** 72/72. **Course Rating:** 70.9/73.4. **Slope:** 113/113. **Green Fee:** $18/$22. **Cart Fee:** $10/Person. **Walking Policy:** Unrestricted walking. **Walkability:** 2. **Season:** Year-round. **High:** May-Sept. **To obtain tee times:** Call golf shop. **Miscellaneous:** Reduced fees (weekdays, twilight, seniors, juniors), range (grass/mats), credit cards (MC, V, D), BF, FF.

★★★ THE ACORNS GOLF LINKS
PU-3933 Ahne Rd., Waterloo, 62298, Monroe County, (618)939-7800, (888)922-2676, 20 miles from St. Louis. **Facility Holes:** 18. **Yards:** 6,701/4,623. **Par:** 72/72. **Course Rating:** 72.3/67.0. **Slope:** 125/105. **Green Fee:** $11/$24. **Cart Fee:** Included in green fee. **Walking Policy:** Unrestricted walking. **Walkability:** 3. **Opened:** 1997. **Architect:** William Ebeler. **Season:** Year-round. **High:** April-Nov. **To obtain tee times:** Call up to 7 days in advance. **Misc:** Reduced fees (weekdays, twilight, seniors, juniors), range (grass), credit cards (MC, V, AE, D), BF, FF.
Reader Comments: Very pleasurable day … Very fair with great greens … Good course for the price, fairways inconsistent.

★★★★ ALDEEN GOLF CLUB
PU-1900 Reid Farm Rd., Rockford, 61107, Winnebago County, (815)282-4653, (888)425-3336, 90 miles from Chicago. **E-mail:** dgpgapro@aol.com. **Web:** www.aldeengolf-club.com. **Facility Holes:** 18. **Yards:** 7,058/5,038. **Par:** 72/72. **Course Rating:** 73.6/69.1. **Slope:** 126/115. **Green Fee:** $38/$44. **Cart Fee:** $24/Cart. **Walking Policy:** Unrestricted walking. **Walkability:** 2. **Opened:** 1991. **Architect:** Dick Nugent. **Season:** April-Nov. **High:** June-Sept. **To obtain tee times:** Call up to 7 days in advance. **Miscellaneous:** Reduced fees (weekdays, twilight), range (grass), credit cards (MC, V, D), BF, FF.
Reader Comments: Plenty of water. Scenic course elevated greens, island green, and plenty of strategic water and bunkers. Good clubhouse, too many geese!! … No. 18 is a great finishing hole … Well designed, good pace, great value.

★★★★½ ANNBRIAR GOLF COURSE *Pace*
PU-1524 Birdie Lane, Waterloo, 62298, Monroe County, (618)939-4653, (888)939-5191, 25 miles from St. Louis. **E-mail:** annbriar@htc.net. **Web:** www.annbriar.com. **Facility Holes:** 18. **Yards:** 6,841/4,792. **Par:** 72/72. **Course Rating:** 72.3/66.4. **Slope:** 141/110. **Green Fee:** $53/$63. **Cart Fee:** Included in green fee. **Walking Policy:** Mandatory carts. **Walkability:** 3. **Opened:** 1993. **Architect:** Michael Hurdzan. **Season:** Year-round. **High:** April-Nov. **To obtain tee times:** Call up to 7 days in advance. **Miscellaneous:** Reduced fees (twilight, seniors, juniors), range (grass), credit cards (MC, V, AE), BF, FF.
Reader Comments: Excellent layout … No. 11 is as good as it gets … Great layout. Beautiful course & people. Great restaurant … Enjoyable, 2 different 9s … Breathtaking back 9 … Outstanding, makes you want to walk, enjoy … Nice course, challenging with plenty of hills … Great course. I love the zoysia grass.

★★½ ANTIOCH GOLF CLUB
PU-40150 N. Rte. 59, Antioch, 60002, Lake County, (847)395-3004, 60 miles from Chicago. **Web:** www.antiochgolfclub.com. **Facility Holes:** 18. **Yards:** 6,172/5,703. **Par:** 71/72. **Course Rating:** 70.1/69.7. **Slope:** 126/122. **Green Fee:** $22/$42. **Cart Fee:** Included in green fee. **Walking Policy:** Unrestricted walking. **Walkability:** 3. **Opened:** 1925. **Architect:** Michael Hurdzan/Dave Esler. **Season:** Year-round. **To obtain tee times:** Call golf shop. **Miscellaneous:** Reduced fees (weekdays, twilight, juniors), range (mats), credit cards (MC, V, AE, D), BF, FF.

★★★ THE ARBORETUM CLUB
PU-401 Half Day Rd., Buffalo Grove, 60089, Lake County, (847)913-1112, 15 miles from Chicago. **E-mail:** jschwister@vbg.org. **Web:** www.arboretumgolf.com. **Facility Holes:** 18. **Yards:** 6,477/5,039. **Par:** 72/72. **Course Rating:** 71.1/68.7. **Slope:** 132/118. **Green Fee:** $28/$50. **Cart Fee:** $26/Cart. **Walking Policy:** Walking at certain times. **Walkability:** 2. **Opened:** 1990. **Architect:** Dick Nugent. **Season:** March-Dec. **High:** March-Dec. **To obtain tee times:** Call up to 7 days in advance. **Misc:** Reduced fees (weekdays, twilight), credit cards (MC, V, AE, D), FF.
Reader Comments: Water on most of the holes, tight and challenging … Front and back very different 9s. Nice condition. Trouble on most holes. Expensive for non-resident … Townhouses everywhere … Too many blind shots to enjoy the experience.

★★★½ ARROWHEAD GOLF CLUB
PU-26 W. 151 Butterfield Rd., Wheaton, 60187, Du Page County, (630)653-5800, 35 miles from Chicago. **E-mail:** wpdgolf@aol.com. **Web:** www.wheatonparkdistrict.com. **Facility Holes:** 27. **Green Fee:** $37/$44. **Cart Fee:** $25/Cart. **Walking Policy:** Unrestricted walking. **Walkability:** 3. **Opened:** 1924. **Architect:** Ralph Weimer/Ken Killian. **Season:** April-Nov. **High:** May-Sept. **To obtain tee times:** Call golf shop. **Miscellaneous:** Reduced fees (twilight, seniors, juniors), range (mats), credit cards (MC, V), BF, FF.
EAST/WEST (18 Combo)
Yards: 6,632/4,868. **Par:** 72/72. **Course Rating:** 71.9/68.1. **Slope:** 128/116.
SOUTH/EAST (18 Combo)
Yards: 6,734/5,033. **Par:** 72/72. **Course Rating:** 72.4/69.1. **Slope:** 131/118.
SOUTH/WEST (18 Combo)
Yards: 6,692/5,077. **Par:** 72/72. **Course Rating:** 72.1/69.2. **Slope:** 132/119.
Reader Comments: Very good condition, need to be a shotmaker, challenging … Outstanding redesign, blending old with new … Some interesting holes … Great value … Good course.

ATWOOD HOMESTEAD GOLF COURSE
PU-8890 Old River Rd., Rockford, 61103, Winnebago County, (815)623-2411, 5 miles from Rockford. **Web:** www.wcfpd.org. **Facility Holes:** 18. **Yards:** 7,420/5,818. **Par:** 72/72. **Course Rating:** 74.9/72.6. **Slope:** 120/116. **Green Fee:** $14/$25. **Cart Fee:** $24/Cart. **Walking Policy:** Unrestricted walking. **Walkability:** 2. **Opened:** 1971. **Architect:** Charles Maddox. **Season:** March-Nov. **To obtain tee times:** Call golf shop. **Miscellaneous:** Reduced fees (twilight, seniors, juniors), range (grass), credit cards (MC, V, D), BF, FF.

★★★½ BALMORAL WOODS COUNTRY CLUB
PU-26732 S. Balmoral Woods Dr., Crete, 60417, Will County, (708)672-7448, 40 miles from Chicago. **E-mail:** info@balmoralwoods.com. **Web:** www.balmoralwoods.com. **Facility Holes:** 18. **Yards:** 6,683/5,282. **Par:** 72/72. **Course Rating:** 72.6/71.8. **Slope:** 128/117. **Green Fee:** $38/$60. **Cart Fee:** Included in green fee. **Walking Policy:** Unrestricted walking. **Walkability:** 4. **Opened:** 1976. **Architect:** Don Mortell. **Season:** March-Nov. **High:** June-Sept. **To obtain tee times:** Call up to 7 days in advance. **Miscellaneous:** Reduced fees (weekdays, twilight, seniors, juniors), range (grass), credit cards (MC, V, AE, D), BF, FF.
Reader Comments: Shotmaker's course. Equal number of dogleg lefts and rights … Mature, lots of variation … Excellent track on rolling terrain … Challenging to a 16 handicap, but several easy holes keep the score down … 5 challenging par 5s.

★★★ BARTLETT HILLS GOLF COURSE
PU-800 W. Oneida, Bartlett, 60103, Cook County, (630)837-2741, 25 miles from Chicago. **E-mail:** plenz@vbartlett.org. **Facility Holes:** 18. **Yards:** 6,482/5,488. **Par:** 71/71. **Course Rating:** 71.2/71.8. **Slope:** 124/121. **Green Fee:** $21/$38. **Cart Fee:** $13/Person. **Walking Policy:** Unrestricted walking. **Walkability:** 4. **Opened:** 1923. **Architect:** Charles Maddox/Bob Lohmann. **Season:** Year-round. **High:** May-Sept. **To obtain tee times:** Call up to 7 days in advance. **Miscellaneous:** Reduced fees (weekdays, twilight, seniors, juniors), range (grass/mats), credit cards (MC, V), BF, FF.
Reader Comments: Well run, good people … Lots of variety … Rolling hills, large oak trees … Overpriced.

★★★½ BELK PARK GOLF COURSE
PU-880 Belk Park Rd., Wood River, 62095, Madison County, (618)251-3115, 10 miles from St. Louis. **Facility Holes:** 18. **Yards:** 6,872/5,003. **Par:** 72/72. **Course Rating:** 71.9/67.3. **Slope:** 121/105. **Green Fee:** $27/$33. **Cart Fee:** $11/Person. **Walking Policy:** Walking at certain times. **Walkability:** 2. **Opened:** 1970. **Architect:** E.L. Packard. **Season:** Year-round. **High:** May-Nov. **To obtain tee times:** Call up to 14 days in advance. **Miscellaneous:** Reduced fees (weekdays, twilight, seniors, juniors), range (grass), credit cards (MC, V), BF, FF.
Reader Comments: Basic fun with subtle tee ball demands … Great condition … A decent-kept course that is very affordable, nice staff, a walkable course … New zoysia fairways, hard greens … Beautiful tight back 9. Friendly and polite staff.

BENT TREE GOLF COURSE
PU-14618 E. CR 400 N, Charleston, 61920, Coles County, (217)348-1611. **Facility Holes:** 18. **Yards:** 6,300/5,645. **Par:** 70/70. **Green Fee:** $12/$16. **Cart Fee:** $10/Person. **Opened:** 1986. **Architect:** Pat Kaiser. **Season:** Year-round. **To obtain tee times:** Call golf shop. **Miscellaneous:** Credit cards (MC, V).

★★★½ BIG RUN GOLF CLUB
PU-17211 W. 135th St., Lockport, 60441, Will County, (815)838-1057, 35 miles from Chicago. **Web:** www.bigrungolf.com. **Facility Holes:** 18. **Yards:** 7,025/5,420. **Par:** 72/72. **Course Rating:** 74.4/71.9. **Slope:** 142/130. **Green Fee:** $34/$51. **Cart Fee:** $16/Person. **Walking Policy:** Walking at certain times. **Walkability:** 5. **Opened:** 1930. **Architect:** Muhlenford/Sneed/Didier/Killian/Nugent. **Season:** Year-round. **High:** April-Nov. **To obtain tee times:** Call up to 7 days in advance. **Miscellaneous:** Reduced fees (weekdays, twilight, juniors), metal spikes, credit cards (MC, V, D), BF, FF.
Reader Comments: Long and difficult … Great par 5s. Lots of uphill approaches … Very tough, greens are severe … Elevations make this course more enjoyable … Wide open but tough, No. 18 is a killer! … Superb layout, definitely not for beginners.

★★★ BITTERSWEET GOLF CLUB
PU-875 Almond St., Gurnee, 60031, Lake County, (847)855-9031, 40 miles from Chicago. **Facility Holes:** 18. **Yards:** 6,754/5,027. **Par:** 72/72. **Course Rating:** 72.8/69.6. **Slope:** 130/115. **Green Fee:** $45. **Cart Fee:** $14/Person. **Walking Policy:** Walking at certain times. **Walkability:** 2. **Opened:** 1996. **Architect:** Jack Porter/Harry Vignocchi. **Season:** April-Nov. **High:** May-Oct. **To obtain tee times:** Call golf shop. **Miscellaneous:** Reduced fees (twilight, seniors), metal spikes, range (grass/mats), credit cards (MC, V, AE, D).

ILLINOIS

Reader Comments: Tight target golf, good facilities, pricey … Very challenging with lots of water … Play smart, the greens are hard & fast … Thinking course, must play positions … Front 9 around housing, back 9 scenic & tough but fun.

★★★ BLACKBERRY OAKS GOLF COURSE
PU-2245 Kennedy Rd., Bristol, 60512, Kendall County, (630)553-7170, 40 miles from Chicago. **E-mail:** bboaksgc@aol.com. **Facility Holes:** 18. **Yards:** 6,332/5,218. **Par:** 72/72. **Course Rating:** 70.5/70.8. **Slope:** 125/123. **Green Fee:** $21/$39. **Cart Fee:** $14/Person. **Walking Policy:** Unrestricted walking. **Walkability:** 2. **Opened:** 1993. **Architect:** David Gill. **Season:** April-Nov. **High:** May-Sept. **To obtain tee times:** Call up to 7 days in advance. **Miscellaneous:** Reduced fees (twilight, seniors, juniors), range (grass/mats), credit cards (MC, V, AE, D), BF, FF.
Reader Comments: Course is in great shape, staff very customer service minded, good value … Short but challenging, lots of wate … Excellent finishing hole … Water on 14 of 18 holes, a real challenge , but a very enjoyable course.

★★★ BLACKHAWK GOLF CLUB
SP-5N748 Burr Rd., St. Charles, 60175, Kane County, (630)443-3500, 50 miles from Chicago. **E-mail:** golflll@meristar.com. **Web:** www.blackhawkgolfclub.com. **Facility Holes:** 18. **Yards:** 6,647/5,111. **Par:** 72/72. **Course Rating:** 72.5/70.9. **Slope:** 132/120. **Green Fee:** $26/$50. **Cart Fee:** $14/Person. **Walking Policy:** Walking at certain times. **Walkability:** 4. **Opened:** 1974. **Architect:** Charles Maddox. **Season:** Year-round. **To obtain tee times:** Call up to 7 days in advance. **Miscellaneous:** Reduced fees (twilight, seniors, juniors), range (grass), credit cards (MC, V, AE, D), BF, FF.
Reader Comments: Variety of hole designs with elevation changes … Crowned greens, tight fairways … getting new clubhouse … Excellent service. Nice facility … Tough in the wind.

★★½ BLOOMINGDALE GOLF CLUB
PU-181 Glen Ellyn Rd., Bloomingdale, 60108, Du Page County, (630)529-6232, 20 miles from Chicago. **Facility Holes:** 18. **Yards:** 5,992/5,313. **Par:** 72/72. **Course Rating:** 68.2/70.5. **Slope:** 108/111. **Green Fee:** $23/$34. **Cart Fee:** $14/Person. **Walking Policy:** Walking at certain times. **Walkability:** 2. **Opened:** 1934. **Architect:** Bob Lohmann. **Season:** April-Nov. **High:** May-Sept. **To obtain tee times:** Call up to 7 days in advance. **Miscellaneous:** Reduced fees (weekdays, twilight, seniors, juniors), credit cards (MC, V), FF.

BON VIVANT COUNTRY CLUB
PU-Career Center Rd., Bourbonnais, 60914, Kankakee County, (815)935-0400, (800)248-7775, 2 miles from Kankakee. **Facility Holes:** 36. **Cart Fee:** $10/Person. **Walking Policy:** Unrestricted walking. **Walkability:** 2. **Opened:** 1980. **Season:** March-Nov. **High:** May-Sept. **To obtain tee times:** Call up to 7 days in advance. **Misc:** Reduced fees (weekdays, twilight, seniors, juniors), metal spikes, range (grass), credit cards (MC, V, AE, D), BF, FF.
★★★½ CHAMPIONSHIP COURSE (18) *Value*
Yards: 7,498/5,631. **Par:** 72/75. **Course Rating:** 75.8/74.8. **Slope:** 130/122. **Fee:** $17/$27.
Reader Comments: Shortest par-5 is 570 yards … Friendly, accommodating, challenging course … Super value … Bon Vivant is an oasis in the cornfields … Beautiful flowers everywhere. Demanding and fair.
NORTH COURSE (18)
Yards: 6,723/5,240. **Par:** 72/72. **Course Rating:** 71.2/68.9. **Slope:** 118/113. **Fee:** $14/$24.

★★★★ BONNIE BROOK GOLF CLUB *Value*
PU-2800 N. Lewis Ave., Waukegan, 60087, Lake County, (847)360-4730, 25 miles from Chicago. **Web:** www.waukeganparks.org. **Facility Holes:** 18. **Yards:** 6,701/5,559. **Par:** 72/73. **Course Rating:** 72.4/72.2. **Slope:** 126/124. **Green Fee:** $21/$35. **Cart Fee:** $26/Cart. **Walking Policy:** Unrestricted walking. **Walkability:** 2. **Opened:** 1927. **Architect:** Jim Foulis. **Season:** April-Nov. **High:** May-Sept. **To obtain tee times:** Call golf shop. **Miscellaneous:** Reduced fees (twilight, seniors, juniors), range (grass/mats), credit cards (MC, V), BF, FF.
Reader Comments: Plenty of challenge & variety, however not too intimidating to an average player as myself … Friendly, accommodating, good open course … Good muni course, good value, not much trouble … Excellent for players of all abilities.

★★ BONNIE DUNDEE GOLF CLUB
PU-270 Kennedy Dr., Carpentersville, 60110, Kane County, (847)426-5511, 25 miles from Chicago. **Facility Holes:** 18. **Yards:** 6,021/5,464. **Par:** 69/75. **Course Rating:** 68.3/71.1. **Slope:** 112/114. **Green Fee:** $15/$26. **Cart Fee:** $13/Person. **Walking Policy:** Unrestricted walking. **Walkability:** 1. **Opened:** 1924. **Architect:** C. D. Wagstaff. **Season:** March-Dec. **To obtain tee times:** Call up to 7 days in advance. **Miscellaneous:** Reduced fees (weekdays, seniors, juniors), credit cards (MC, V, D), BF, FF.

BOONE CREEK GOLF CLUB
PU-6912 Mason Hill Rd., McHenry, 60050, McHenry County, (815)455-6900, 5 miles from Crystal Lake. **Facility Holes:** 27. **Yards:** 6,524/5,213. **Par:** 71/71. **Course Rating:** 69.5/68.6. **Slope:** 114/110. **Green Fee:** $19/$24. **Cart Fee:** $11/Person. **Walking Policy:** Unrestricted walking. **Walkability:** 2. **Opened:** 1997. **Architect:** Gordon Cunningham. **Season:** Feb.-Nov. **To obtain tee times:** Call up to 7 days in advance. **Miscellaneous:** Reduced fees (juniors), range (grass), credit cards (MC, V), BF, FF.
Special Notes: Also has a 9-hole executive course.

★★½ THE BOURNE GOLF CLUB
PU-2359 N. 35th Rd., Marseilles, 61341, La Salle County, (815)496-2301. **Facility Holes:** 9. **Yards:** 3,156/2,717. **Par:** 36/36. **Green Fee:** $32/$40. **Walking Policy:** Mandatory carts. **Walkability:** 4. **Opened:** 1990. **Season:** April-Nov. **High:** June-Sept. **To obtain tee times:** Call golf shop. **Miscellaneous:** Range (grass), FF.
Reader Comments: A different and difficult course ... Target golf, great setting, tee off cliffs on 3 holes ... Lots of hidden landing areas, tough to find ball.

★★ BRAE LOCH GOLF CLUB
PU-33600 N. Route 45, Grayslake, 60030, Lake County, (847)223-5542, 55 miles from Chicago. **Facility Holes:** 18. **Yards:** 5,979/5,299. **Par:** 70/70. **Course Rating:** 67.5/69.6. **Slope:** 114/115. **Green Fee:** $21/$25. **Cart Fee:** $25/Cart. **Walking Policy:** Unrestricted walking. **Walkability:** 1. **Opened:** 1931. **Season:** Year-round. **To obtain tee times:** Call golf shop. **Miscellaneous:** Reduced fees (twilight), credit cards (MC, V), FF.

★★★ BROKEN ARROW GOLF CLUB
PU-16325 W. Broken Arrow Dr., Lockport, 60441, Will County, (815)836-8858, 30 miles from Chicago. **E-mail:** info@brokenarrowgolfclub.com. **Web:** www.brokenarrowgolfclub.com. **Facility Holes:** 27. **Green Fee:** $27/$44. **Cart Fee:** $15/Person. **Walking Policy:** Unrestricted walking. **Walkability:** 2. **Opened:** 1996. **Architect:** Bob Lohmann. **Season:** Year-round. **High:** May-Oct. **To obtain tee times:** Call up to 14 days in advance. **Miscellaneous:** Reduced fees (weekdays, twilight, seniors, juniors), range (grass/mats), credit cards (MC, V), BF, FF.
EAST/NORTH COURSE (18 Combo)
Yards: 7,034/5,182. **Par:** 72/72. **Course Rating:** 74.1/70.3. **Slope:** 131/121.
NORTH/SOUTH COURSE (18 Combo)
Yards: 7,027/5,255. **Par:** 72/72. **Course Rating:** 73.9/70.5. **Slope:** 131/121.
SOUTH/EAST (18 Combo)
Yards: 6,945/5,211. **Par:** 72/72. **Course Rating:** 73.6/70.4. **Slope:** 129/121.
Reader Comments: Great value for seniors & interesting course ... Lots of water but not many forced carries. Nice variety of holes ... Difficult in the wind ... Good design, innovative features ... Don't like double greens on North Course.

★★ BUFFALO GROVE GOLF CLUB
PU-48 Raupp Blvd., Buffalo Grove, 60089, Lake County, (847)459-5520, 40 miles from Chicago. **Facility Holes:** 18. **Yards:** 6,892/6,003. **Par:** 72/75. **Course Rating:** 71.5/73.5. **Slope:** 120/122. **Green Fee:** $16/$34. **Cart Fee:** $26/Cart. **Walking Policy:** Unrestricted walking. **Walkability:** 1. **Opened:** 1965. **Architect:** Dick Nugent. **Season:** March-Dec. **To obtain tee times:** Call up to 5 days in advance. **Miscellaneous:** Reduced fees (twilight, seniors, juniors), range (grass), credit cards (MC, V, AE, D), BF, FF.

★★½ BUNKER LINKS MUNICIPAL GOLF COURSE
PU-3500 Lincoln Park Dr., Galesburg, 61401, Knox County, (309)344-1818, 42 miles from Peoria. **Facility Holes:** 18. **Yards:** 5,934/5,354. **Par:** 71/73. **Course Rating:** 67.4/69.4. **Slope:** 106/108. **Green Fee:** $8/$9. **Walking Policy:** Unrestricted walking. **Opened:** 1922. **Architect:** D.C. Bunker. **Season:** March-Nov. **High:** April-Sept. **To obtain tee times:** Call golf shop. **Miscellaneous:** Reduced fees (twilight), metal spikes, range (grass).

★½ BUNN GOLF COURSE
PU-2500 S. 11th, Springfield, 62703, Sangamon County, (217)522-2633. **Facility Holes:** 18. **Yards:** 6,104/5,355. **Par:** 72/73. **Course Rating:** 68.7/68.4. **Slope:** 118/119. **Green Fee:** $11/$15. **Cart Fee:** $10/Person. **Walking Policy:** Unrestricted walking. **Walkability:** 2. **Opened:** 1901. **Architect:** Edward Lawrence Packard. **Season:** March-Nov. **High:** June-July. **To obtain tee times:** Call golf shop. **Misc:** Reduced fees (seniors, juniors), credit cards (MC, V).

★★★½ BYRON HILLS GOLF COURSE
PU-23316 94th Ave. N., Port Byron, 61275, Rock Island County, (800)523-9306. **Facility Holes:** 18. **Yards:** 6,441/5,258. **Par:** 71/71. **Course Rating:** 70.5/69.6. **Slope:** 115/112. **Green Fee:** $14/$20. **Cart Fee:** $11/Person. **Walking Policy:** Unrestricted walking. **Walkability:** 3. **Opened:** 1967. **Season:** March-Nov. **High:** May-Sept. **To obtain tee times:** Call golf shop.

ILLINOIS

Miscellaneous: Reduced fees (seniors, juniors), credit cards (MC, V, D), FF.
Reader Comments: Excellent course at a great value ... Nice course ... Good, fast and easy to play course ... Great family-owned, always improving ... Great layout ... Good for weekend golfer.

★★★★½ **CANTIGNY GOLF** *Condition*
PU-27 W. 270 Mack Rd., Wheaton, 60187, Du Page County, (630)668-3323, 40 miles from Chicago. **E-mail:** mrjones@tribune.com. **Web:** www.rrmtf.org/cantigny/golf/. **Facility Holes:** 36.
Green Fee: $80. **Cart Fee:** $15/Person. **Opened:** 1989. **Architect:** Roger Packard. **Season:** April-Oct. **High:** May-Sept. **Walking Policy:** Unrestricted walking. **Walkability:** 3. **To obtain tee times:** Call up to 14 days in advance. **Miscellaneous:** Reduced fees (seniors, juniors), range (grass), caddies, credit cards (MC, V, AE, D), BF, FF.
LAKESIDE/HILLSIDE (18 combo)
Yards: 6,830/5,183. **Par:** 72/72. **Course Rating:** 72.6/70.1. **Slope:** 131/119.
WOODSIDE/HILLSIDE (18 combo)
Yards: 6,939/5,236. **Par:** 72/72. **Course Rating:** 73.4/70.3. **Slope:** 132/120.
WOODSIDE/LAKESIDE (18 combo)
Yards: 6,981/5,425. **Par:** 72/72. **Course Rating:** 73.8/71.9. **Slope:** 138/127.
Notes: Ranked 24th in 1999 Best in State; 57th in 1996 America's Top 75 Upscale Courses.
Reader Comments: it was nice to take a caddie and not have to take a cart ... Some wonderful holes ... Well groomed, good service ... Great balance. Not too tough, not too easy. Getting pricey ... The course is "friendly" to golfers of all skill levels ... Fun to play. Requires decisions ... Expensive but worth it.
YOUTH LINKS (9)
Yards: 939. **Par:** 27. **Opened:** 1997. **Architect:** Roger Packard/Andy North. **Season:** May-Oct.

★★★ **CARDINAL CREEK GOLF COURSE**
SP-615 Dixie Hwy., Beecher, 60401, Will County, (708)946-2800, 30 miles from Chicago.
Facility Holes: 27. **Green Fee:** $19/$26. **Cart Fee:** $24/Person. **Walking Policy:** Unrestricted walking. **Walkability:** 3. **Opened:** 1971. **Architect:** R. Albert Anderson. **Season:** Year-round. **To obtain tee times:** Call golf shop. **Miscellaneous:** Reduced fees (seniors), credit cards (MC, V).
NORTH/CENTER (18 combo)
Yards: 6,413/5,592. **Par:** 72/72. **Course Rating:** 69.2/67.8. **Slope:** 114/110.
NORTH/SOUTH (18 combo)
Yards: 6,558/5,734. **Par:** 72/72. **Course Rating:** 69.5/68.4. **Slope:** 115/112.
SOUTH/CENTER (18 combo)
Yards: 6,423/5,574. **Par:** 72/72. **Course Rating:** 69.1/68.9. **Slope:** 112/110.
Reader Comments: Very friendly staff, course is always in excellent shape. A definite bargain ... Wide-open course ... Major changes over the years, a nice challenge ... Tough course, but fair. Nice facilities.

★½ **CARDINAL GOLF COURSE**
PU-15737 N. Beach Rd., Effingham, 62401, Effingham County, (217)868-2860. **Facility Holes:** 18. **Yards:** 5,899/5,247. **Par:** 72/72. **Green Fee:** $16. **Cart Fee:** $16/Cart. **Walking Policy:** Unrestricted walking. **Walkability:** 1. **Opened:** 1963. **Season:** March-Oct. **To obtain tee times:** Call golf shop. **Miscellaneous:** Metal spikes.

★★★½ **CARILLON GOLF CLUB**
PU-21200 S. Carillon, Plainfield, 60544, Will County, (815)886-2132, 30 miles from Chicago.
E-mail: jlong@carillongolf.com. **Web:** www.carillongolf.com. **Facility Holes:** 27. **Yards:** 6,607/5,194. **Par:** 72/72. **Course Rating:** 72.5/70.2. **Slope:** 125/120. **Green Fee:** $40/$50. **Cart Fee:** $15/Person. **Walking Policy:** Unrestricted walking. **Walkability:** 3. **Opened:** 1990.
Architect: Greg Martin. **Season:** April-Dec. **High:** May-Sept. **To obtain tee times:** Call up to 7 days in advance. **Miscellaneous:** Reduced fees (weekdays, twilight, seniors, juniors), range (grass/mats), credit cards (MC, V, AE, D, DC, CB), BF, FF.
Reader Comments: Not overly crowded, tight fairways, nice greens ... Excellent conditions, great prices, good restaurant ... No trees, can be windy. GPS on carts is a nice feature ... 18th hole a memorable par 5! ... Tough to walk due to distance.
Special Notes: Also has a 9-hole executive course.

★★½ **CARRIAGE GREENS COUNTRY CLUB**
PU-8700 Carriage Greens Dr., Darien, 60561, Du Page County, (630)985-3730, 25 miles from Chicago. **Facility Holes:** 18. **Yards:** 6,451/6,009. **Par:** 70/72. **Course Rating:** 70.9/73.5. **Slope:** 121/123. **Green Fee:** $30/$51. **Cart Fee:** Included in green fee. **Walking Policy:** Walking at certain times. **Walkability:** 2. **Opened:** 1969. **Season:** Year-round. **To obtain tee times:** Call up to 14 days in advance. **Miscellaneous:** Reduced fees (weekdays, twilight, seniors), credit cards (MC, V, AE, D), FF.

★★★ CARY COUNTRY CLUB
SP-2400 Grove Lane, Cary, 60013, McHenry County, (847)639-3161, 40 miles from Chicago. **E-mail:** ilpgawork@aol.com. **Web:** www.carycountryclub.com. **Facility Holes:** 18. **Yards:** 6,135/5,595. **Par:** 72/77. **Course Rating:** 68.9/71.5. **Slope:** 117/119. **Green Fee:** $28/$35. **Cart Fee:** $30/Cart. **Walking Policy:** Unrestricted walking. **Walkability:** 4. **Opened:** 1923. **Season:** April-Oct. **High:** June-Sept. **To obtain tee times:** Call up to 7 days in advance. **Miscellaneous:** Reduced fees (weekdays, seniors), credit cards (MC, V, AE, D), FF.
Reader Comments: 78-year-old course with lots of rolling hills … Pretty course, great panoramic views of the Fox River Valley. It's obvious management works hard at continuous conditioning … Some interesting holes … Fun layout, great holes.

★★★★ CHALET HILLS GOLF CLUB
PU-943 Rawson Bridge Rd., Cary, 60013, McHenry County, (847)639-0666, 40 miles from Chicago. **E-mail:** Chaletgo@mc.net. **Web:** www.chaletgolf.com. **Facility Holes:** 18. **Yards:** 6,877/4,934. **Par:** 73/73. **Course Rating:** 73.4/68.1. **Slope:** 131/114. **Green Fee:** $43/$74. **Cart Fee:** $15/Person. **Walking Policy:** Walking at certain times. **Walkability:** 4. **Opened:** 1995. **Architect:** Ken Killian. **Season:** March-Dec. **High:** June-Sept. **To obtain tee times:** Call up to 7 days in advance. **Miscellaneous:** Reduced fees (weekdays, twilight, seniors, juniors), range (mats), credit cards (MC, V, AE, D), BF, FF.
Reader Comments: Beautiful course with a nice mix of holes from easy to difficult … Great new clubhouse … Use of contour and native vegetation, great … Bring your "A" game. This one is a challenge … Elevation changes force you to make shots.

★★ CHAPEL HILL COUNTRY CLUB
PU-2500 Chapel Hill Rd., McHenry, 60005, McHenry County, (815)385-3337. **Facility Holes:** 18. **Yards:** 6,021/5,359. **Par:** 70/72. **Course Rating:** 68.7/70.4. **Slope:** 117/117. **Green Fee:** $14/$29. **Cart Fee:** $12/Person. **Walking Policy:** Walking at certain times. **Walkability:** 3. **Opened:** 1928. **Season:** Year-round. **High:** April-Nov. **To obtain tee times:** Call up to 14 days in advance. **Miscellaneous:** Reduced fees (weekdays, twilight, seniors, juniors), range (grass), credit cards (MC, V, AE, D), BF, FF.

★½ CHERRY HILLS GOLF CLUB
PU-191 St . & Kedzie Ave., Flossmoor, 60422, Cook County, (708)799-5600. **Facility Holes:** 18. **Yards:** 6,151/5,801. **Par:** 72/74. **Course Rating:** 69.3/72.6. **Slope:** 115/120. **Green Fee:** $20/$28. **Cart Fee:** $23/Cart. **Walking Policy:** Unrestricted walking. **Walkability:** 1. **Opened:** 1932. **Architect:** Jack Daray/Harry Collis. **Season:** March-Nov. **High:** June-Sept. **To obtain tee times:** Call golf shop. **Miscellaneous:** Reduced fees (twilight, seniors), BF, FF.

★★ CHEVY CHASE GOLF CLUB
PU-1000 N. Milwaukee Ave., Wheeling, 60090, Cook County, (847)537-0082, 30 miles from Chicago. **Facility Holes:** 18. **Yards:** 6,608/5,215. **Par:** 72/72. **Course Rating:** 71.7/69.3. **Slope:** 126/119. **Green Fee:** $20/$32. **Cart Fee:** $28/Cart. **Walking Policy:** Unrestricted walking. **Walkability:** 2. **Opened:** 1923. **Architect:** Tom Bendelow. **Season:** Year-round. **High:** April-Oct. **To obtain tee times:** Call up to 7 days in advance. **Miscellaneous:** Reduced fees (twilight, seniors, juniors), credit cards (MC, V, D), BF, FF.
Special Notes: Closing all year 2002 for reconstruction. Re-opening spring 2003.

★½ CHICK EVANS GOLF COURSE
PU-6145 Golf Rd., Morton Grove, 60053, Cook County, (847)965-5353. **Facility Holes:** 18. **Yards:** 5,680/5,680. **Par:** 73/71. **Course Rating:** 64.7/69.7. **Slope:** 94/105. **Green Fee:** $16/$19. **Cart Fee:** $20/Cart. **Walking Policy:** Unrestricted walking. **Walkability:** 2. **Opened:** 1940. **Architect:** Dick Nugent. **Season:** March-Dec. **High:** May-Sept. **To obtain tee times:** Call up to 7 days in advance. **Miscellaneous:** Reduced fees (weekdays, twilight, seniors, juniors), metal spikes, range (grass), credit cards (MC, V, AE, D), BF, FF.

★★★ CINDER RIDGE GOLF LINKS
PU-24801 Lakepoint Dr., Wilmington, 60481, Will County, (815)476-4000, 55 miles from Chicago. **Facility Holes:** 18. **Yards:** 6,938/4,810. **Par:** 72/72. **Course Rating:** 74.1/72.9. **Slope:** 139/126. **Green Fee:** $40/$50. **Cart Fee:** Included in green fee. **Walking Policy:** Unrestricted walking. **Walkability:** 3. **Opened:** 1995. **Architect:** George Kappos. **Season:** Year-round. **To obtain tee times:** Call up to 7 days in advance. **Miscellaneous:** Reduced fees (weekdays, twilight, seniors, juniors), range (grass/mats), credit cards (MC, V, AE, D), BF, FF.
Reader Comments: Very interesting track built on an old strip mine site … Fun course, takes the driver out of your hand … Great service … Difficult, fun course to play … Forced carries everywhere, dynamite par 3s.

★★★½ CLINTON HILL GOLF COURSE

PU-3700 Old Collinsville Rd., Swansea, 62226, St. Clair County, (618)277-3700, 15 miles from St. Louis. **E-mail:** chccbob@aol.com. **Web:** www.clintonhillgc.com. **Facility Holes:** 18. **Yards:** 6,568/5,176. **Par:** 71/71. **Course Rating:** 70.6/68.4. **Slope:** 121/101. **Green Fee:** $14/$27. **Cart Fee:** $12/Person. **Walking Policy:** Walking at certain times. **Walkability:** 3. **Opened:** 1969. **Architect:** Clete Idoux. **Season:** Year-round. **To obtain tee times:** Call up to 7 days in advance. **Miscellaneous:** Reduced fees (twilight, seniors, juniors), range (grass/mats), credit cards (MC, V, D), BF, FF.

Reader Comments: Some blind shots ... Play 50 rounds a year here. Gets better every year ... Fun to play, huge greens ... You'll use every club in the bag ... Outstanding value ... Will test the best from the tips ... Staff and facilities outstanding.

★★½ CLOVERLEAF GOLF COURSE

PU-3555 Fosterburg Rd., Alton, 62002, Madison County, (618)462-3022, 25 miles from St. Louis. **Facility Holes:** 18. **Yards:** 5,671/4,867. **Par:** 70/70. **Course Rating:** 66.8/66.7. **Slope:** 113/103. **Green Fee:** $15/$17. **Cart Fee:** $9/Person. **Walking Policy:** Unrestricted walking. **Walkability:** 3. **Opened:** 1931. **Architect:** Paul E. Cabriel. **Season:** Year-round. **To obtain tee times:** Call up to 7 days in advance. **Miscellaneous:** Reduced fees (seniors, juniors), metal spikes, BF, FF.

COG HILL GOLF CLUB

PU-12294 Archer Ave., Lemont, 60439, Cook County, (630)257-5872, 32 miles from Chicago. **E-mail:** coghillgolfclub@worldnet.att.net. **Web:** www.coghillgolf.com. **Facility Holes:** 72. **Walking Policy:** Unrestricted walking. **Season:** Year-round. **High:** May-Oct. **Miscellaneous:** Reduced fees (weekdays, twilight, juniors), range (grass/mats), caddies, credit cards (MC, V, D, DC), BF, FF.

★★★ COURSE NO. 1 (18)

Yards: 6,267/5,328. **Par:** 71/72. **Course Rating:** 69.6/70.3. **Slope:** 118/117. **Green Fee:** $11/$38. **Cart Fee:** $31/Cart. **Walkability:** 2. **Opened:** 1927. **Architect:** David McIntosh/Bert Coghill.

Reader Comments: Great traditional course, old style club ... A great value. Very good, not as tough as No. 4 ... Facilities very good ... Nice for high handicappers. Old growth trees ... Tough front 9 ... Interesting holes, nice break from modern course.

★★★½ COURSE NO. 2 (RAVINES) (18)

Yards: 6,268/5,564. **Par:** 72/72. **Course Rating:** 69.8/70.5. **Slope:** 120/115. **Green Fee:** $25/$48. **Cart Fee:** $31/Cart. **Walkability:** 4. **Opened:** 1930. **Architect:** Bert Coghill.

Reader Comments: Poor man's "Dobsdread" ... For the amount of play it gets, this is a fine course. One of my favorites. Getting a little expensive ... Designed for average golfer.

★★★ COURSE NO. 3 (18)

Yards: 6,384/5,213. **Par:** 72/71. **Course Rating:** 69.7/69.0. **Slope:** 116/111. **Green Fee:** $11/$38. **Cart Fee:** $31/Cart. **Walkability:** 2. **Opened:** 1964. **Architect:** Dick Wilson.

Reader Comments: Beautiful shape on a sunny October day ... Shorter, but perhaps more interesting than No. 1... Nice course, some tough holes ... You better know how to work the ball ... Easy layout, fun to score well ... Tough back 9.

★★★★½ COURSE NO. 4 (DUBSDREAD) (18)

Yards: 6,940/5,889. **Par:** 72/72. **Course Rating:** 75.4/78.5. **Slope:** 142/140. **Green Fee:** $120. **Cart Fee:** Included in green fee. **Walkability:** 4. **Opened:** 1964. **Architect:** Dick Wilson. **Season:** March-Nov. **To obtain tee times:** Call golf shop.

Notes: Ranked 40th in 1999-2000 America's 100 Greatest; 3rd in 1999 Best in State; 5th in 1996 America's Top 75 Upscale Courses.

Reader Comments: Classic design, don't choose wrong tees (be humble or be humbled)... Great variety of holes, doglegs, long, short. Always a pleasure to play. Good pace of play ... A classic! Unfortunately very expensive ... Site of Western Open. Big old trees. Small firm greens.

★★ COLONIAL GOLF COURSE

PU-Old Route 51 S., Sandoval, 62882, Marion County, (618)247-3307. **Facility Holes:** 18. **Yards:** 5,657/4,739. **Par:** 70/70. **Course Rating:** 65.1/65.1. **Slope:** 102/102. **Green Fee:** $10/$11. **Walking Policy:** Unrestricted walking. **Walkability:** 2. **Opened:** 1964. **Season:** Year-round. **High:** June-Aug. **To obtain tee times:** Call golf shop.

★★ COLUMBIA GOLF CLUB

PU-125 AA Rd., Columbia, 62236, Monroe County, (618)286-4455, 15 miles from St. Louis, MO. **Facility Holes:** 18. **Yards:** 6,200/4,873. **Par:** 72/72. **Course Rating:** 69.4/66.3. **Slope:** 110/103. **Green Fee:** $14/$18. **Cart Fee:** $10/Person. **Walking Policy:** Unrestricted walking. **Walkability:** 3. **Opened:** 1969. **Architect:** Gary Kearns. **Season:** Year-round. **High:** April-Oct. **To obtain tee times:** Call golf shop. **Miscellaneous:** Reduced fees (weekdays, seniors), metal spikes, credit cards (MC, V).

★½ COUNTRY LAKES GOLF CLUB
PU-1601 Fairway Dr., Naperville, 60563, Du Page County, (630)420-1060, 18 miles from Chicago. **E-mail:** gcountry@aol.com. **Facility Holes:** 18. **Yards:** 6,875/5,340. **Par:** 73/75. **Course Rating:** 71.9/72.9. **Slope:** 121/124. **Green Fee:** $16/$32. **Cart Fee:** $16/Person. **Walking Policy:** Unrestricted walking. **Walkability:** 2. **Opened:** 1970. **Architect:** Rolf Campbell. **Season:** Year-round. **High:** April-Sept. **To obtain tee times:** Call up to 15 days in advance. **Miscellaneous:** Reduced fees (weekdays, twilight, seniors, juniors), range (grass), credit cards (MC, V, AE, D), BF, FF.

COUNTRYSIDE GOLF COURSE
PU-20800 W. Hawley St., Mundelein, 60060, Lake County, (847)566-5544, 30 miles from Chicago. **Facility Holes:** 36. **Green Fee:** $15/$31. **Cart Fee:** $25/Cart. **Walking Policy:** Unrestricted walking. **Walkability:** 3. **Architect:** Bob Lohmann. **High:** May-Sept. **To obtain tee times:** Call golf shop. **Miscellaneous:** Reduced fees (weekdays, twilight, seniors, juniors), range (grass/mats), credit cards (MC, V).
★★★ PRAIRIE COURSE (18)
Yards: 6,757/5,050. **Par:** 72/72. **Course Rating:** 71.5/68.3. **Slope:** 123/114. **Opened:** 1990. **Season:** March-Dec. .
Reader Comments: A good Sunday afternoon, a nice walk … Good layout, challenging, ok facilities … Excellent value … Nice muni … Wide fairways and natural habitat areas … Good beginners' course.
★★★ TRADITIONAL COURSE (18)
Yards: 6,178/5,111. **Par:** 72/72. **Course Rating:** 69.4/68.8. **Slope:** 114/112. **Opened:** 1927. **Season:** Year-round.
Reader Comments: Have been playing it for 33 years and still go back a couple times a summer … Can get crowded … No. 5 is 585 yards … Good value, nice terrain … Traditional more difficult but Prairie gets more play cause it's newer design.

★★ CRAB ORCHARD GOLF CLUB
SP-901 W. Grand Ave., Carterville, 62918, Williamson County, (618)985-2321, 100 miles from St. Louis. **Facility Holes:** 18. **Yards:** 6,448/5,058. **Par:** 70/71. **Course Rating:** 71.0/68.4. **Slope:** 129/114. **Green Fee:** $20. **Cart Fee:** $10/Person. **Walking Policy:** Unrestricted walking. **Walkability:** 3. **Opened:** 1959. **Architect:** Roy Glenn. **Season:** Year-round. **High:** May-Sept. **To obtain tee times:** Call golf shop. **Miscellaneous:** Reduced fees (twilight, seniors), range (grass), credit cards (MC, V, D), BF, FF.

★★½ CRYSTAL WOODS GOLF CLUB
SP-5915 S. Rte. 47, Woodstock, 60098, McHenry County, (815)338-3111, 3 miles from Woodstock. **E-mail:** cwoods@owc.net. **Facility Holes:** 18. **Yards:** 6,403/5,488. **Par:** 72/73. **Course Rating:** 70.3/70.5. **Slope:** 117/114. **Green Fee:** $26/$48. **Cart Fee:** Included in green fee. **Walking Policy:** Walking at certain times. **Walkability:** 3. **Opened:** 1957. **Architect:** William B. Langford. **Season:** March-Dec. **High:** May-Oct. **To obtain tee times:** Call golf shop. **Misc:** Reduced fees (twilight, seniors), range (grass), credit cards (MC, V, AE, D), FF.

★★★½ DEER CREEK GOLF CLUB
PU-25055 Western Ave., University Park, 60466, Will County, (708)672-6667, 30 miles from Chicago. **E-mail:** golf@deercreekgolfcourse.com. **Web:** www.deercreekgolfcourse.com. **Facility Holes:** 18. **Yards:** 6,905/5,835. **Par:** 72/72. **Course Rating:** 72.9/73.2. **Slope:** 124/120. **Green Fee:** $15/$32. **Cart Fee:** $12/Person. **Walking Policy:** Unrestricted walking. **Walkability:** 1. **Opened:** 1972. **Architect:** Edward Lawrence Packard. **Season:** Year-round. **To obtain tee times:** Call up to 7 days in advance. **Miscellaneous:** Reduced fees (weekdays, twilight, seniors, juniors), metal spikes, range (grass/mats), credit cards (MC, V, AE, D), BF, FF.
Reader Comments: Best greens at a public track in suburban Chicago. New owners and friendly staff … Well kept and a good pace of play … Just a bit overpriced … Good test, great price … Good shape, fast greens, great value.

★★½ DEERFIELD PARK DISTRICT GOLF CLUB
PU-1201 Saunders Rd., Riverwoods, 60015, Lake County, (847)945-8333, 6 miles from Highland Park. **Facility Holes:** 18. **Yards:** 6,756/5,635. **Par:** 72/74. **Course Rating:** 71.8/71.9. **Slope:** 125/121. **Green Fee:** $26/$32. **Cart Fee:** $24/Cart. **Walking Policy:** Unrestricted walking. **Architect:** Edward Lawrence Packard. **Season:** March-Dec. **High:** June-Sept. **To obtain tee times:** Call up to 6 days in advance. **Miscellaneous:** Reduced fees (weekdays, twilight), credit cards (MC, V, D), FF.

★★★ DEERPATH PARK GOLF COURSE
PU-500 W. Deerpath, Lake Forest, 60045, Lake County, (847)615-4290, 25 miles from Chicago. **Facility Holes:** 18. **Yards:** 6,105/5,542. **Par:** 70/72. **Course Rating:** 69.8/72.2. **Slope:** 128/125. **Green Fee:** $27/$30. **Cart Fee:** $20/Cart. **Walking Policy:** Unrestricted walking.

Walkability: 2. **Opened:** 1927. **Architect:** Alex Pirie. **Season:** April-Dec. **To obtain tee times:** Call golf shop. **Miscellaneous:** Reduced fees (seniors, juniors), range (grass/mats), credit cards (MC, V), BF, FF.

Reader Comments: Excellent condition, not difficult, fair value … Nice upkeep, not too tough … Ladies & students in summer … Very pleasant environment … Fun course … Extremely fast greens.

★★★★ THE DEN AT FOX CREEK GOLF CLUB
PU-3002 Fox Creek Rd., Bloomington, 61704, McLean County, (309)434-2300. **E-mail:** jkennedy@cityblm.org. **Web:** www.thedengc.com. **Facility Holes:** 18. **Yards:** 6,926/5,345. **Par:** 72/72. **Course Rating:** 72.9/70.1. **Slope:** 128/116. **Green Fee:** $28/$35. **Cart Fee:** $11/Person. **Walking Policy:** Unrestricted walking. **Walkability:** 3. **Opened:** 1997. **Architect:** Arnold Palmer/Ed Seay. **Season:** March-Nov. **High:** May-Sept. **To obtain tee times:** Call up to 7 days in advance. **Miscellaneous:** Reduced fees (twilight, seniors, juniors), range (grass/mats), credit cards (MC, V, AE, D), BF, FF.

Reader Comments: Great layout, multiple tees, fair for all golfers … Terrific track especially from the back. Always windy on this links layout … Fast greens, accurate tee shots required great variety, picturesque.

★★★ DOWNERS GROVE PARK DISTRICT GOLF COURSE
PU-2420 Haddow Ave., Downers Grove, 60515, Du Page County, (630)963-1306, 25 miles from Chicago. **Facility Holes:** 9. **Yards:** 3,230/2,629. **Par:** 38/35. **Course Rating:** 70.5/69.4. **Slope:** 122/115. **Green Fee:** $24/$35. **Cart Fee:** $24/Cart. **Walking Policy:** Unrestricted walking. **Walkability:** 4. **Opened:** 1892. **Architect:** C.B. Macdonald/D. Gill/S. Halberg. **Season:** March-Nov. **High:** May-Sept. **To obtain tee times:** Call golf shop. **Miscellaneous:** Reduced fees (weekdays, seniors, juniors), range (grass/mats), credit cards (MC, V), BF, FF.

Reader Comments: Small, undulating greens and plenty of elevation change … Good little 9 holer—tough … Oldest 9- holer around, long and fun to play … Good course for a park district … Take 3 to 4 hours to play.

★★ DWIGHT COUNTRY CLUB
SP-31577N 2400 E Road, Dwight, 60420, Livingston County, (815)584-1399, 80 miles from Chicago. **Facility Holes:** 18. **Yards:** 6,269/5,221. **Par:** 71/71. **Course Rating:** 69.6/68.3. **Slope:** 121/115. **Green Fee:** $13/$20. **Cart Fee:** $10/Person. **Walking Policy:** Unrestricted walking. **Walkability:** 1. **Opened:** 1913. **Season:** Year-round. **To obtain tee times:** Call golf shop. **Miscellaneous:** Range (grass), credit cards (MC, V), BF, FF.

★★★★ EAGLE CREEK RESORT
R-Eagle Creek State Park, Findlay, 62534, Shelby County, (217)756-3456, (800)876-3245, 35 miles from Decatur. **E-mail:** golf@eaglecreekresort.com. **Web:** www.eaglecreekresort.com. **Facility Holes:** 18. **Yards:** 6,908/4,978. **Par:** 72/72. **Course Rating:** 73.5/69.1. **Slope:** 132/115. **Green Fee:** $27/$65. **Cart Fee:** Included in green fee. **Walking Policy:** Mandatory carts. **Walkability:** 3. **Opened:** 1989. **Architect:** Ken Killian. **Season:** Year-round. **To obtain tee times:** Call golf shop. **Miscellaneous:** Reduced fees (weekdays, guests, twilight, seniors, juniors), range (grass), lodging (138 rooms), credit cards (MC, V, AE, D, DC), BF, FF.

Reader Comments: Tough, challenging course carved through the woods surrounding Lake Shelbyville … Improved since last year … Driver can get you into trouble on several holes … They have added outdoor pool, miniature golf for children.

EAGLE RIDGE INN & RESORT
R-10 Clubhouse Dr., Galena, 61036, Jo Daviess County, (815)777-4525, (800)892-2269, 20 miles from Dubuque. **Web:** www.eagleridge.com/golf/. **Facility Holes:** 63. **Cart Fee:** Included in green fee. **Season:** March-Nov. **High:** May-Sept. **To obtain tee times:** Call golf shop. **Miscellaneous:** Reduced fees (weekdays, guests, twilight, juniors), range (grass), credit cards (MC, V, AE, D, DC), BF, FF.

★★★★½ **THE GENERAL COURSE (18)** *Condition*
Yards: 6,820/5,335. **Par:** 72/72. **Course Rating:** 73.8/66.7. **Slope:** 137/119. **Green Fee:** $77/$120. **Walking Policy:** Mandatory carts. **Walkability:** 5. **Opened:** 1997. **Architect:** Roger Packard/Andy North.
Notes: Golf Digest School site. Ranked 18th in 1999 Best in State.

Reader Comments: No. 14 par 4, tee box 180' above fairway … Beautiful course, but don't miss the fairway … Scenic views from elevated tees … Very long and challenging, very scenic … Must use cart path most of the time, very hilly.

Special Notes: Also has a 9-hole East Course.
★★★★ **NORTH COURSE (18)**
Yards: 6,836/5,578. **Par:** 72/72. **Course Rating:** 73.4/72.3. **Slope:** 134/127. **Green Fee:** $55/$100. **Walking Policy:** Unrestricted walking. **Walkability:** 3. **Opened:** 1977. **Architect:** Larry Packard/Roger Packard.
Notes: Golf Digest School site.

Reader Comments: Most playable of Eagle Ridge's courses. Slower greens ... Great fun to play, awesome greens! ... Course kept in great shape. Challenging greens ... Great fall rates, outstanding golf! ... Great resort, views, steady course.

★★★★ **SOUTH COURSE** (18)
Yards: 6,762/5,609. **Par:** 72/72. **Course Rating:** 72.9/72.4. **Slope:** 133/128. **Green Fee:** $55/$100. **Walking Policy:** Unrestricted walking. **Walkability:** 3. **Opened:** 1984. **Architect:** Roger Packard.
Notes: Golf Digest School site. 75th in 1996 America's Top 75 Upscale Courses.
Reader Comments: Great weekend getaway ... Great setting with a varity of holes that are challenging and fun ... Excellent course, need to hit it straight ... Lots of blind shots, with so many hills tough to locate ball.
Special Notes: Also has a 9-hole East Course.

★★½ **EDGEBROOK COUNTRY CLUB**
SP-2100 Sudyam Rd., Sandwich, 60548, De Kalb County, (815)786-3058, 35 miles from Chicago. **Facility Holes:** 18. **Yards:** 6,500/5,134. **Par:** 72/73. **Course Rating:** 69.1/69.5. **Slope:** 123/114. **Green Fee:** $18/$32. **Cart Fee:** $14/Person. **Walking Policy:** Unrestricted walking. **Walkability:** 2. **Opened:** 1968. **Architect:** Ken Killian/Dick Nugent. **Season:** March-Dec. **High:** June-Aug. **To obtain tee times:** Call up to 7 days in advance. **Miscellaneous:** Reduced fees (weekdays, twilight, seniors, juniors), range (grass/mats), credit cards (MC, V, AE, D), BF, FF.

★½ **EDGEBROOK GOLF CLUB**
PU-6100 North Central Ave., Chicago, 60646, Cook County, (773)763-8320. **Facility Holes:** 18. **Yards:** 4,626/4,626. **Par:** 66/66. **Course Rating:** 61.2/64.8. **Slope:** 88/96. **Green Fee:** $16/$19. **Opened:** 1910. **Season:** March-Dec. **To obtain tee times:** Call golf shop. **Miscellaneous:** Reduced fees (weekdays, twilight, seniors, juniors), metal spikes, credit cards (MC, V, D).

★★½ **EDGEWOOD GOLF CLUB**
PU-16497 Kennedy Rd., Auburn, 62615, Sangamon County, (217)438-3221, 10 miles from Springfield. **E-mail:** golf@edgewoodgc.com. **Web:** www.edgewoodgc.com. **Facility Holes:** 18. **Yards:** 6,400/5,234. **Par:** 71/71. **Course Rating:** 70.5/70.1. **Slope:** 126/121. **Green Fee:** $14/$20. **Walking Policy:** Unrestricted walking. **Walkability:** 3. **Opened:** 1968. **Season:** Year-round. **High:** April-Oct. **To obtain tee times:** Call up to 8 days in advance. **Miscellaneous:** Reduced fees (weekdays, twilight, seniors, juniors), credit cards (MC, V, AE, D), BF, FF.
Special Notes: This is an 18 hole course listed under course code 13068.

EDGEWOOD PARK GOLF CLUB
PU-Box 104 Rte 89, McNabb, 61335, Putnam County, (815)882-2317, 2 miles from McNabb. **Facility Holes:** 18. **Yards:** 6,660/5,780. **Par:** 72/74. **Course Rating:** 70.9/72.0. **Slope:** 117/118. **Green Fee:** $16. **Cart Fee:** $20/Cart. **Walking Policy:** Unrestricted walking. **Walkability:** 2. **Opened:** 1968. **Architect:** Jim Spear. **Season:** Year-round. **To obtain tee times:** Call up to 3 days in advance. **Miscellaneous:** Reduced fees (seniors, juniors), range (grass), credit cards (MC, V), FF.

★★★½ **EL PASO GOLF CLUB**
SP-2860 County Rd., El Paso, 61738, Woodford County, (309)527-5225, 10 miles from Bloomington. **Facility Holes:** 18. **Yards:** 6,111/5,053. **Par:** 71/71. **Course Rating:** 70.1/69.9. **Slope:** 122/121. **Green Fee:** $20. **Cart Fee:** $20/Cart. **Walking Policy:** Unrestricted walking. **Walkability:** 4. **Opened:** 1924. **Architect:** James Spear. **Season:** March-Nov. **High:** May-Sept. **To obtain tee times:** Call up to 4 days in advance. **Misc:** Credit cards (MC, V), BF, FF.
Reader Comments: A wonderful setting for golf ... Challenging course ... Excellent, well-kept course very reasonable price ... Great value—another small-town gem.

★★½ **ELLIOT GOLF COURSE**
PU-888 South Lyford Rd., Cherry Valley, 61108, Winnebago County, (815)987-1687. **Web:** www.rockfordparks.org. **Facility Holes:** 18. **Yards:** 6,393/6,253. **Par:** 72/69. **Course Rating:** 69.4/70.7. **Slope:** 107/113. **Green Fee:** $16/$21. **Cart Fee:** $24/Cart. **Walking Policy:** Unrestricted walking. **Walkability:** 2. **Opened:** 1968. **Architect:** Edward Lawrence Packard. **Season:** March-Nov. **High:** June-Aug. **To obtain tee times:** Call up to 7 days in advance. **Miscellaneous:** Reduced fees (twilight), range (mats), credit cards (MC, V, D), BF, FF.

★★½ **EMERALD HILL GOLF & LEARNING CENTER**
PU-16802 Prairie Ville Rd., Sterling, 61081, Whiteside County, (815)622-6204. **Facility Holes:** 18. **Yards:** 6,244/4,869. **Par:** 71/71. **Course Rating:** 69.5/66.8. **Slope:** 113/108. **Green Fee:** $21. **Cart Fee:** $21/Cart. **Walking Policy:** Unrestricted walking. **Walkability:** 3. **Opened:** 1923. **Season:** March-Nov. **High:** June-Aug. **To obtain tee times:** Call golf shop. **Miscellaneous:** Reduced fees (weekdays, seniors, juniors), metal spikes, credit cards (MC, V).

★½ EVERGREEN GOLF & COUNTRY CLUB

PU-9140 South Western Ave., Evergreen Park, 60805, Cook County, (773)238-6680. **Facility Holes:** 18. **Yards:** 6,355/6,355. **Par:** 72/72. **Course Rating:** 71.2. **Slope:** 119. **Green Fee:** $23/$28. **Walkability:** 1. **Opened:** 1921. **Season:** Year-round. **To obtain tee times:** Call golf shop. **Miscellaneous:** Metal spikes.

★½ FAIRLAKES GOLF COURSE

PU-RR 1, Box 122, Secor, 61771, Woodford County, (309)744-2222, 10 miles from Bloomington. **Facility Holes:** 18. **Yards:** 5,400/4,274. **Par:** 67/69. **Course Rating:** 64.1/64.8. **Slope:** 102/103. **Green Fee:** $11/$14. **Cart Fee:** $18/Cart. **Walking Policy:** Unrestricted walking. **Walkability:** 4. **Opened:** 1989. **Architect:** Harold Sparks. **Season:** March-Oct. **High:** June-Aug. **To obtain tee times:** Call golf shop. **Miscellaneous:** Reduced fees (weekdays, seniors), metal spikes, range (grass/mats), credit cards (MC, V).

★★★★½ FAR OAKS GOLF CLUB

PU-419 Old Collinsville Rd., Caseyville, 62232, St. Clair County, (618)628-2900, (314)386-4653. **E-mail:** farnaks@apci.net. **Facility Holes:** 27. **Yards:** 7,016/4,897. **Par:** 72/72. **Course Rating:** 73.3/71.8. **Slope:** 141/114. **Cart Fee:** Included in green fee. **Walking Policy:** Unrestricted walking. **Walkability:** 4. **Opened:** 1997. **Architect:** Bob Goalby/Kye Goalby. **Season:** Year-round. **High:** April-Oct. **To obtain tee times:** Call up to 7 days in advance. **Miscellaneous:** Reduced fees (twilight), range (grass), credit cards (MC, V, AE), BF, FF.
Reader Comments: This course is first class, love the prairie grass ... Priced well, great greens, long-hitter's dream. Will play again ... Spectacular back 9 ... Variety, fair but tough.
Special Notes: Also has a 9-hole executive course.

★★★ FARIES PARK GOLF COURSE

PU-1 Faries Park, Decatur, 62521, Macon County, (217)422-2211. **Facility Holes:** 18. **Yards:** 6,708/5,763. **Par:** 72/75. **Course Rating:** 70.8/73.0. **Slope:** 117/113. **Green Fee:** $12/$17. **Cart Fee:** $16/Cart. **Walking Policy:** Unrestricted walking. **Walkability:** 2. **Opened:** 1961. **Architect:** Edward Lawrence Packard. **Season:** March-Nov. **To obtain tee times:** Call up to 7 days in advance. **Miscellaneous:** Metal spikes, range (grass/mats), credit cards (MC, V).
Reader Comments: Pretty scenery—good test ... Good layout.

★★½ FOSS PARK GOLF CLUB

PU-3124 Argonne Dr., North Chicago, 60064, Lake County, (847)689-7490, 1 mile from Waukegan. **E-mail:** fpgolf@aol.com. **Facility Holes:** 18. **Yards:** 6,914/5,888. **Par:** 72/74. **Course Rating:** 71.9/72.5. **Slope:** 113/117. **Green Fee:** $26/$32. **Walking Policy:** Unrestricted walking. **Walkability:** 1. **Opened:** 1974. **Season:** March-Nov. **High:** June-Aug. **To obtain tee times:** Call golf shop. **Miscellaneous:** Reduced fees (weekdays, twilight, seniors, juniors), range (grass), credit cards (MC, V, AE, D), BF, FF.

★★½ FOUR WINDS GOLF CLUB

PU-Rte. 176, Mundelein, 60060, Lake County, (847)566-8502, 40 miles from Chicago. **Facility Holes:** 18. **Yards:** 6,501/4,943. **Par:** 71/72. **Course Rating:** 71.5/68.5. **Slope:** 122/114. **Green Fee:** $34/$57. **Cart Fee:** Included in green fee. **Walking Policy:** Walking at certain times. **Walkability:** 3. **Opened:** 1963. **Architect:** Herman Schwinge. **Season:** March-Nov. **High:** June-Sept. **To obtain tee times:** Call up to 10 days in advance. **Miscellaneous:** Reduced fees (weekdays, twilight, seniors), range (grass/mats), credit cards (MC, V, AE, D), BF, FF.

★★★½ FOX BEND GOLF COURSE

PU-Rte. 34, Oswego, 60543, Kendall County, (630)554-3939, 9 miles from Aurora. **E-mail:** leon@foxbendgolfcourse.com. **Web:** www.foxbendgolfcourse.com. **Facility Holes:** 18. **Yards:** 6,800/5,400. **Par:** 72/72. **Course Rating:** 72.1/70.1. **Slope:** 124/116. **Green Fee:** $30/$41. **Cart Fee:** $15/Person. **Walking Policy:** Unrestricted walking. **Walkability:** 3. **Opened:** 1967. **Architect:** Brent Wadsworth/Paul Loague. **Season:** March-Dec. **High:** May-Sept. **To obtain tee times:** Call golf shop. **Miscellaneous:** Reduced fees (weekdays, twilight, seniors, juniors), range (grass/mats), credit cards (MC, V, AE), BF, FF.
Reader Comments: Love a par 4 that you can try and drive the green ... Enjoyable course, nice setting ... It gets better every year ... Great course, slow play ... A fun day, tough but average course ... Another great deal. First 9 is gorgeous.

★★★★ FOX CREEK GOLF CLUB

PU-6555 Fox Creek Dr., Edwardsville, 62025, Madison County, (618)692-9400, 20 miles from St. Louis, MO. **Facility Holes:** 18. **Yards:** 7,027/5,185. **Par:** 72/72. **Course Rating:** 74.9/72.1. **Slope:** 144/132. **Green Fee:** $25/$45. **Cart Fee:** Included in green fee. **Walking Policy:** Mandatory carts. **Walkability:** 5. **Opened:** 1992. **Architect:** Gary Kern. **Season:** Year-round. **High:** April-Oct. **To obtain tee times:** Call up to 7 days in advance. **Miscellaneous:** Reduced

fees (weekdays, twilight, seniors), metal spikes, range (grass), credit cards (MC, V), BF, FF.
Reader Comments: Great service, nice setting ... Narrow fairways, hilly ... Bring the set that hits the ball straight ... Some really interesting holes with teeth ... Good layout—demanding ... Excellent course, bent-grass fairways, reasonable price.

★★★ FOX LAKE COUNTRY CLUB

PU-7220 N. State Park Rd., Fox Lake, 60020, Lake County, (847)587-6411, 35 miles from Chicago. **Facility Holes:** 18. **Yards:** 6,347/5,852. **Par:** 72/73. **Course Rating:** 71.7/73.9. **Slope:** 128/125. **Green Fee:** $30/$57. **Cart Fee:** Included in green fee. **Walking Policy:** Mandatory carts. **Opened:** 1920. **Season:** March-Dec. **High:** March-Dec. **To obtain tee times:** Call golf shop. **Miscellaneous:** Range (grass), credit cards (MC, V), BF, FF.
Reader Comments: Very hilly & long but I feel over priced, course always in good shape ... A couple of weak opening holes, but very good overall ... An under-used beauty, a secret gem.

★★★ FOX RUN GOLF LINKS

PU-333 Plum Grove Rd., Elk Grove Village, 60007, Cook County, (847)228-3544, 20 miles from Chicago. **Facility Holes:** 18. **Yards:** 6,287/5,288. **Par:** 70/70. **Course Rating:** 70.5/70.2. **Slope:** 117/114. **Green Fee:** $12/$32. **Cart Fee:** $13/Person. **Walking Policy:** Unrestricted walking. **Walkability:** 2. **Opened:** 1984. **Architect:** William Newcomb. **Season:** April-Dec. **High:** May-Sept. **To obtain tee times:** Call golf shop. **Miscellaneous:** Reduced fees (weekdays, twilight, seniors, juniors), range (grass/mats), credit cards (MC, V, AE), BF, FF.
Reader Comments: Short, tricky course in super condition. Lots of challanges. A great value ... Links style ... Nice change of pace.

★★½ FOX VALLEY GOLF CLUB

PU-Rte. 25, North Aurora, 60542, Kane County, (630)879-1030, 3 miles from Aurora. **Facility Holes:** 18. **Yards:** 5,927/5,279. **Par:** 72/72. **Course Rating:** 68.2/70.4. **Slope:** 118/117. **Green Fee:** $22/$29. **Cart Fee:** $24/Cart. **Walking Policy:** Unrestricted walking. **Walkability:** 3. **Opened:** 1930. **Season:** March-Nov. **High:** May-Sept. **To obtain tee times:** Call up to 6 days in advance. **Miscellaneous:** Reduced fees (twilight), credit cards (MC, V), FF.

★★ FRESH MEADOWS GOLF COURSE

PU-2144 S. Wolf Rd., Hillside, 60162, Cook County, (708)449-3434, 12 miles from Chicago. **E-mail:** freshmeadowsgc@aol.com. **Facility Holes:** 18. **Yards:** 6,276/5,956. **Par:** 70. **Course Rating:** 69.6/68.2. **Slope:** 111/108. **Green Fee:** $29/$41. **Cart Fee:** $10/Person. **Walking Policy:** Walking at certain times. **Walkability:** 1. **Opened:** 1927. **Season:** Year-round. **High:** May-Sept. **To obtain tee times:** Call up to 7 days in advance. **Misc:** Reduced fees (weekdays, twilight, seniors, juniors), metal spikes, range (grass/mats), credit cards (MC, V, AE, D, DC), BF, FF.

GAMBIT GOLF CLUB

PU-1550 St. Rte. 146 E., Vienna, 62995, Johnson County, (618)658-6022, (800)942-6248, 27 miles from Paducah, KY. **Web:** www.cambitgolf.com. **Facility Holes:** 18. **Yards:** 6,546/4,725. **Par:** 71/72. **Course Rating:** 72.4/66.1. **Slope:** 137/102. **Green Fee:** $32/$38. **Cart Fee:** $12/Person. **Walking Policy:** Walking at certain times. **Walkability:** 3. **Opened:** 1996. **Architect:** Richard Osborne. **Season:** Year-round. **High:** April-Oct. **To obtain tee times:** Call up to 7 days in advance. **Miscellaneous:** Reduced fees (twilight, seniors, juniors), range (grass), credit cards (MC, V, AE), BF, FF.

★★★★ GATEWAY NATIONAL GOLF LINKS

PU-18 Golf Dr., Madison, 62060, Madison County, (618)482-4653, 4 miles from St. Louis. **E-mail:** sbarnesgn@msn.com. **Web:** www.gatewaynational.com. **Facility Holes:** 18. **Yards:** 7,178/5,187. **Par:** 71/71. **Course Rating:** 75.0/69.4. **Slope:** 138/114. **Green Fee:** $29/$55. **Cart Fee:** $8/Person. **Walking Policy:** Unrestricted walking. **Walkability:** 1. **Opened:** 1998. **Architect:** Keith Foster. **Season:** Year-round. **High:** April-Nov. **To obtain tee times:** Call golf shop. **Miscellaneous:** Reduced fees (weekdays, twilight, seniors, juniors), range (grass), credit cards (MC, V, AE), BF, FF.
Reader Comments: Many excellent holes ... Great facilities, links-style course, long from blues ... Long links-style course. Bent-grass fairways and challenging greens. Bring the driver.

★★★½ GEORGE W. DUNNE NATIONAL GOLF COURSE

PU-16310 S. Central, Oak Forest, 60452, Cook County, (708)614-2600, 25 miles from Chicago. **Facility Holes:** 18. **Yards:** 7,170/5,535. **Par:** 72/72. **Course Rating:** 75.1/71.4. **Slope:** 135/121. **Green Fee:** $30/$40. **Cart Fee:** Included in green fee. **Walking Policy:** Unrestricted walking. **Walkability:** 2. **Opened:** 1982. **Architect:** Killian & Nugent. **Season:** March-Dec. **High:** May-Aug. **To obtain tee times:** Call golf shop. **Miscellaneous:** Reduced fees (weekdays, twilight, seniors, juniors), metal spikes, range (mats), credit cards (MC, V, D).
Notes: Ranked 25th in 1996 America's Top 75 Affordable Courses.
Reader Comments: Nice fairways—lots of sand traps, long-ball hitter's paradise ... The layout is a gem, a little scruffy, but hard to score ... Big greens, long course.

★★★ GIBSON WOODS GOLF COURSE
PU-1321 N. 11th St., Monmouth, 61462, Warren County, (309)734-9968, 16 miles from Galesburg. **Facility Holes:** 18. **Yards:** 6,362/5,885. **Par:** 71/75. **Course Rating:** 70.9/73.9. **Slope:** 119/119. **Green Fee:** $12/$17. **Cart Fee:** $20/Cart. **Walking Policy:** Unrestricted walking. **Walkability:** 4. **Opened:** 1966. **Architect:** Homer Fieldhouse. **Season:** March-Nov. **High:** May-Sept. **To obtain tee times:** Call up to 7 days in advance. **Miscellaneous:** Reduced fees (weekdays, twilight, seniors), range (grass), credit cards (MC, V), BF, FF.
Reader Comments: Definitely woody … Very challenging course, always in good shape, great greens … Shorter than expected, but tight and challenging. Friendly staff. Good value … Very hilly and tight … Good layout— demanding.

★★ GLENCOE GOLF CLUB
PU-621 Westley Rd., Glencoe, 60022, Cook County, (847)835-0981. **E-mail:** smiller@earth-links.net. **Facility Holes:** 18. **Yards:** 6,517/5,713. **Par:** 72/73. **Course Rating:** 70.4/71.8. **Slope:** 121/117. **Green Fee:** $37/$43. **Cart Fee:** $30/Cart. **Walking Policy:** Unrestricted walking. **Walkability:** 2. **Opened:** 1921. **Season:** April-Dec. **High:** May-Aug. **To obtain tee times:** Call up to 6 days in advance. **Miscellaneous:** Reduced fees (twilight), range (grass), credit cards (MC, V, AE, D, DC), FF.

★★½ GLENDALE LAKES GOLF COURSE
PU-1550 President St., Glendale Heights, 60139, Du Page County, (630)260-0018, 30 miles from Chicago. **Facility Holes:** 18. **Yards:** 6,143/5,390. **Par:** 71/71. **Course Rating:** 62.1/71.1. **Slope:** 121/124. **Green Fee:** $16/$30. **Cart Fee:** $14/Person. **Walking Policy:** Walking at certain times. **Walkability:** 1. **Opened:** 1987. **Architect:** Dick Nugent. **Season:** March-Nov. **High:** June-Aug. **To obtain tee times:** Call golf shop. **Miscellaneous:** Reduced fees (weekdays, twilight, seniors, juniors), metal spikes, credit cards (MC, V, AE, D, Diners Club).

GLENEAGLES GOLF CLUB
PU-13070 McCarthy Rd., Lemont, 60439, Cook County, (630)257-5466, 25 miles from Chicago. **Facility Holes:** 36. **Green Fee:** $23/$30. **Cart Fee:** $13/Person. **Walking Policy:** Unrestricted walking. **Walkability:** 3. **Opened:** 1924. **Architect:** Charles Maddox/Frank P. Macdonald. **Season:** March-Dec. **High:** June-Aug. **To obtain tee times:** Call golf shop. **Miscellaneous:** Reduced fees (twilight, seniors), metal spikes, range (grass/mats).
★★★ **RED COURSE** (18)
Yards: 6,090/6,090. **Par:** 70/74. **Course Rating:** 67.6/71.3. **Slope:** 112/111.
Reader Comments: Old, but a goodie. Tight fairways and small greens … Beautiful conditioning … Fair test, good mix … Short, but tough … Well kept. Challenging but not too tough.
★★½ **WHITE COURSE** (18)
Yards: 6,250/6,080. **Par:** 70/75. **Course Rating:** 70.1/72.3. **Slope:** 120/114.

★★ GLENVIEW PARK DISTRICT GOLF CLUB
PU-800 Shermer Rd., Glenview, 60025, Cook County, (847)724-0250, 5 miles from Northbrook. **Facility Holes:** 18. **Yards:** 6,057/5,734. **Par:** 70/70. **Course Rating:** 68.6/72.5. **Slope:** 121/122. **Green Fee:** $38/$43. **Cart Fee:** $28/Cart. **Walking Policy:** Unrestricted walking. **Walkability:** 2. **Opened:** 1955. **Architect:** Joe Roseman. **Season:** March-Dec. **High:** May-Oct. **To obtain tee times:** Call up to 2 days in advance. **Miscellaneous:** Reduced fees (weekdays, twilight), credit cards (MC, V), FF.

★★½ GLENWOODIE GOLF COURSE
PU-193rd and State, Glenwood, 60425, Cook County, (708)758-1212, 25 miles from Downtown Chicago. **E-mail:** Glenwoodie@crown-golf.com. **Facility Holes:** 18. **Yards:** 6,715/5,176. **Par:** 72/72. **Course Rating:** 71.4/68.4. **Slope:** 120/108. **Green Fee:** $19/$33. **Cart Fee:** $12/Person. **Walking Policy:** Unrestricted walking. **Walkability:** 2. **Opened:** 1926. **Architect:** Harry Collis. **Season:** Year-round. **To obtain tee times:** Call golf shop. **Miscellaneous:** Reduced fees (weekdays, twilight, seniors, juniors), range (grass), credit cards (MC, V), BF, FF.

★★★ GOLF CLUB OF ILLINOIS
PU-1575 Edgewood Rd., Algonquin, 60102, McHenry County, (847)658-4400, 35 miles from Chicago. **Facility Holes:** 18. **Yards:** 7,011/4,896. **Par:** 71/71. **Course Rating:** 74.6/68.6. **Slope:** 133/115. **Green Fee:** $33/$43. **Cart Fee:** $13/Person. **Walking Policy:** Walking at certain times. **Opened:** 1987. **Architect:** Dick Nugent. **Season:** March-Nov. **High:** May-Sept. **To obtain tee times:** Call golf shop. **Miscellaneous:** Reduced fees (weekdays, twilight, seniors, juniors), metal spikes, range (grass/mats), credit cards (MC, V, AE, D).
Reader Comments: Must be straight off tee or you'll lose lots of golf balls … Links-style course with hidden trouble … Great late season deals … Course is fun, but too many houses … Challenging, windy.

★★½ GOLFMOHR GOLF COURSE
PU-16724 Hubbard Rd., East Moline, 61244, Rock Island County, (309)496-2434. **E-mail:** birdie@revealed.net. **Facility Holes:** 18. **Yards:** 6,659/5,402. **Par:** 72/72. **Course Rating:** 71.2/70.0. **Green Fee:** $16/$19. **Cart Fee:** $20/Cart. **Walking Policy:** Unrestricted walking. **Walkability:** 1. **Opened:** 1965. **Architect:** Ted Lockie. **Season:** March-Nov. **High:** May-Sept. **To obtain tee times:** Call up to 7 days in advance. **Miscellaneous:** Reduced fees (weekdays, twilight, seniors), range (mats), credit cards (MC, V), FF.

★★ GRAND MARAIS GOLF COURSE
PU-5802 Lake Dr., Centerville, 62205, St. Clair County, (618)398-9999, (888)398-9002, 7 miles from St. Louis, MO. **E-mail:** metbet@prodigy.net. **Facility Holes:** 18. **Yards:** 6,600/5,324. **Par:** 72/72. **Course Rating:** 71.7/68.1. **Slope:** 126/120. **Green Fee:** $16/$22. **Cart Fee:** $10/Person. **Walking Policy:** Unrestricted walking. **Walkability:** 1. **Opened:** 1936. **Architect:** Joseph A. Roseman. **Season:** Year-round. **High:** April-Nov. **To obtain tee times:** Call up to 7 days in advance. **Miscellaneous:** Reduced fees (weekdays, twilight, seniors, juniors), range (grass/mats), caddies, credit cards (MC, V, AE, D), BF, FF.

GREAT RIVER ROAD GOLF CLUB
PU-771 E. County Rd. 1850, Nauvoo, 62354, Hancock County, (217)453-2417. **Facility Holes:** 18. **Yards:** 4,904/3,972. **Par:** 65/65. **Course Rating:** 70.5/69.0. **Slope:** 123/112. **Green Fee:** $12/$14. **Cart Fee:** $10/Person. **Opened:** 1970. **Architect:** Steve Sanders. **To obtain tee times:** Call golf shop.

★½ GREEN ACRES GOLF COURSE
SP-Rte. 148 S., Energy, 62933, Williamson County, (618)942-6816, 10 miles from Carbondale. **Facility Holes:** 18. **Yards:** 5,889/4,372. **Par:** 72/72. **Course Rating:** 67.0/66.0. **Slope:** 107/105. **Green Fee:** $13/$15. **Walkability:** 2. **Opened:** 1969. **Architect:** Val Gene Could. **Season:** Year-round. **To obtain tee times:** Call golf shop. **Miscellaneous:** Reduced fees (weekdays, seniors), range (mats), FF.

GREEN GARDEN COUNTRY CLUB
PU-9511 W. Monee Manhattan Rd., Frankfort, 60423, Will County, (815)469-3350, 30 miles from Chicago. **Web:** www.greengardencc.com. **Facility Holes:** 36. **Green Fee:** $15/$36. **Cart Fee:** $14/Person. **Walkability:** 1. **Season:** Year-round. **To obtain tee times:** Call up to 7 days in advance. **Miscellaneous:** Reduced fees (weekdays, twilight, seniors, juniors), range (grass/mats), credit cards (MC, V, AE, D), BF, FF.
★★★ BLUE COURSE (18)
Yards: 6,665/5,652. **Par:** 72/73. **Course Rating:** 70.1/69.5. **Slope:** 112/110. **Walking Policy:** Walking at certain times. **Opened:** 1972. **Architect:** Tom Walsh. **Miscellaneous:** Metal spikes.
Reader Comments: Great value, great food, good courses … Flat … Rough is never too long … Average all the way … Both courses in very nice shape, design, service outstanding.
★★★½ GOLD COURSE (18)
Yards: 6,519/5,442. **Par:** 72/72. **Course Rating:** 70.2/70.2. **Slope:** 115/116. **Opened:** 1992. **Architect:** Buzz Didier.
Reader Comments: Maturing into great course for $ … All types of hole designs, no bad points.

★★★ GREENVIEW COUNTRY CLUB
PU-2801 Putter Lane, Centralia, 62801, Marion County, (618)532-7395, 50 miles from St. Louis, MO. **Facility Holes:** 18. **Yards:** 6,600/5,343. **Par:** 72/72. **Course Rating:** 69.2/73.2. **Slope:** 116/113. **Green Fee:** $22. **Cart Fee:** $22/Cart. **Walking Policy:** Unrestricted walking. **Walkability:** 3. **Opened:** 1966. **Architect:** Oral Telford. **Season:** March-Dec. **High:** April-Sept. **To obtain tee times:** Call golf shop. **Miscellaneous:** Metal spikes, credit cards (MC, V), BF, FF.
Reader Comments: A fun course to play … Worth the drive.

HARBORSIDE INTERNATIONAL GOLF CENTER
PU-11001 S. Doty Ave. E., Chicago, 60628, Cook County, (312)782-7837, 12 miles from Chicago. **E-mail:** km3480@aol.com. **Facility Holes:** 36. **Green Fee:** $70/$80. **Cart Fee:** Included in green fee. **Walking Policy:** Unrestricted walking. **Walkability:** 3. **Opened:** 1995. **Architect:** Dick Nugent. **Season:** April-Nov. **High:** June-Aug. **To obtain tee times:** Call up to 14 days in advance. **Miscellaneous:** Reduced fees (twilight), range (grass/mats), credit cards (MC, V, AE), FF.
★★★★ PORT COURSE (18) *Condition+*
Yards: 7,164/5,164. **Par:** 72/72. **Course Rating:** 75.1/70.8. **Slope:** 136/122.
Reader Comments: Different, but nice … Very tough when windy … Best practice facility and great skyline view … A great test every hole … One of Chicago's best and tough nicest design.
★★★★½ STARBOARD COURSE (18) *Condition+*
Yards: 7,152/5,106. **Par:** 72/72. **Course Rating:** 75.2/70.4. **Slope:** 137/122.
Notes: 1997 Golf Digest's Environmental Leaders in Golf Award.

ILLINOIS

Reader Comments: Cool sandtrap on 15. Great finish … Great views of city … Wonderful, good enough for major event … Very tough links style, greens in great shape … Great layout, wonderful practice facility … Best practice facility around! … A great links course, very hard when windy.

★★ HARRISON PARK GOLF COURSE
PU-1300 W. Voorhees, Danville, 61832, Vermillion County, (217)431-2266, 25 miles from Champaign. **Facility Holes:** 18. **Yards:** 6,330/5,015. **Par:** 71/71. **Course Rating:** 70.3/68.5. **Slope:** 119/110. **Green Fee:** $12/$14. **Walkability:** 2. **Opened:** 1900. **Season:** Year-round. **To obtain tee times:** Call golf shop. **Miscellaneous:** Reduced fees (weekdays, seniors), metal spikes.

★★★½ HAWTHORN RIDGE GOLF CLUB
PU-621 State Hwy. 94, Aledo, 61231, Mercer County, (309)582-5641. **E-mail:** birdie@revealed.net. **Facility Holes:** 18. **Yards:** 6,701/5,674. **Par:** 72/72. **Course Rating:** 71.4/71.6. **Green Fee:** $9/$18. **Cart Fee:** $19/Cart. **Walking Policy:** Unrestricted walking. **Walkability:** 3. **Opened:** 1977. **Architect:** William James Spear. **Season:** March-Nov. **High:** May-Sept. **To obtain tee times:** Call up to 7 days in advance. **Miscellaneous:** Reduced fees (weekdays, twilight, seniors), metal spikes, range (grass), credit cards (MC, V).
Reader Comments: Course has grown the past 5 years to be a very good shotmaker's course, very affordable & worth the trip … Challenging and the greens are always in good shape, large, rolling, difficult … Good layout, good condition, friendly.

★★★★ HAWTHORN SUITES AT MIDLANE GOLF RESORT
R-4555 W. Yorkhouse Rd., Wadsworth, 60083, Lake County, (847)623-4653, 39 miles from Chicago. **Facility Holes:** 27. **Green Fee:** $39/$65. **Cart Fee:** Included in green fee. **Walking Policy:** Unrestricted walking. **Walkability:** 3. **Opened:** 1964. **Architect:** Robert Bruce Harris. **Season:** March-Nov. **To obtain tee times:** Call up to 7 days in advance. **Miscellaneous:** Reduced fees (weekdays, guests, twilight, seniors, juniors), metal spikes, range (grass), credit cards (MC, V, AE, D), BF, FF.
BACK/FRONT (18 combo)
Yards: 7,015/5,367. **Par:** 72/72. **Course Rating:** 74.5/71.4. **Slope:** 135/125.
FRONT/MIDDLE (18 combo)
Yards: 7,073/5,635. **Par:** 72/73. **Course Rating:** 74.4/72.7. **Slope:** 132/124.
MIDDLE/BACK (18 combo)
Yards: 6,932/5,160. **Par:** 72/72. **Course Rating:** 73.8/70.5. **Slope:** 134/123.
Reader Comments: 3 excellent 9s … Unbelievable greens, very tough … Beautiful course and facility, a little high on price … Great value with early bird rates … Loads of outings, treat people very well … A big course in great condition.

★★★★ HERITAGE BLUFFS GOLF CLUB *Value*
PU-24355 W. Bluff Rd., Channahon, 60410, Will County, (815)467-7888, 45 miles from Chicago. **Facility Holes:** 18. **Yards:** 7,106/4,967. **Par:** 72/72. **Course Rating:** 73.9/68.6. **Slope:** 138/114. **Green Fee:** $31/$43. **Cart Fee:** $13/Person. **Walking Policy:** Unrestricted walking. **Walkability:** 4. **Opened:** 1993. **Architect:** Dick Nugent. **Season:** April-Dec. **High:** June-Sept. **To obtain tee times:** Call up to 7 days in advance. **Miscellaneous:** Reduced fees (weekdays, twilight, seniors, juniors), range (grass/mats), credit cards (MC, V, D), BF, FF.
Reader Comments: No. 18 is a great finishing hole … Traditional golf at its finest, worth the drive … Course was interesting and fair … Fun track. Wide open … Always a treat to play this course … Should be in "play again" file … Long & tough.

★★ HICKORY HILLS COUNTRY CLUB
PU-8201 West 95th St., Hickory Hills, 60457, Cook County, (708)598-6460, 20 miles from Chicago. **Facility Holes:** 18. **Yards:** 6,018/5,928. **Par:** 71/71. **Course Rating:** 67.9/67.9. **Slope:** 116/116. **Green Fee:** $25/$30. **Cart Fee:** $13/Person. **Walking Policy:** Walking at certain times. **Walkability:** 4. **Opened:** 1930. **Season:** Year-round. **High:** May-Sept. **To obtain tee times:** Call golf shop. **Miscellaneous:** Reduced fees (weekdays, twilight, seniors), metal spikes, range (mats), credit cards (MC, V, AE).
Special Notes: Also has 9-hole executive course.

★★★ HICKORY POINT GOLF COURSE
PU-727 Weaver Road, Forsyth, 62535, Macon County, (217)421-7444. **Facility Holes:** 18. **Yards:** 6,855/5,896. **Par:** 72/72. **Course Rating:** 71.4/73.0. **Slope:** 121. **Green Fee:** $17/$18. **Cart Fee:** $18/Cart. **Walking Policy:** Unrestricted walking. **Walkability:** 1. **Opened:** 1970. **Architect:** Larry Packard. **Season:** March-Nov. **High:** June-Aug. **To obtain tee times:** Call golf shop. **Miscellaneous:** Reduced fees (twilight, seniors, juniors), metal spikes, range (grass), credit cards (MC, V).
Reader Comments: This course hosts a Futures Tour event each year. Friendly staff, excellent value … Wide fairways, good greens … Fun to play, nice course … Good practice area … As much play as this course gets it's always in great shape.

★★★★ **HICKORY RIDGE GOLF CENTER**
PU-2727 W. Glenn Rd., Carbondale, 62902, Jackson County, (618)529-4386, 100 miles from St. Louis. **Facility Holes:** 18. **Yards:** 6,863/5,506. **Par:** 72/72. **Course Rating:** 73.3/71.6. **Slope:** 137/134. **Green Fee:** $18/$24. **Cart Fee:** $9/Person. **Walking Policy:** Unrestricted walking. **Walkability:** 4. **Opened:** 1993. **Architect:** William James Spear. **Season:** Year-round. **High:** April-Sept. **To obtain tee times:** Call golf shop. **Miscellaneous:** Reduced fees (twilight, seniors, juniors), range (grass), credit cards (MC, V), BF, FF.
Reader Comments: Fairways awesome … Tough back 9 … Good value.

★★★ **HIGHLAND PARK COUNTRY CLUB**
PU-1201 Park Ave. W., Highland Park, 60035, Lake County, (847)433-9015, 20 miles from Chicago. **Facility Holes:** 18. **Yards:** 6,522/5,353. **Par:** 70/70. **Course Rating:** 72.1/71.8. **Slope:** 130/122. **Green Fee:** $29/$52. **Cart Fee:** $15/Person. **Walking Policy:** Walking at certain times. **Walkability:** 1. **Opened:** 1966. **Architect:** Ted Lockie. **Season:** Year-round. **To obtain tee times:** Call up to 14 days in advance. **Miscellaneous:** Reduced fees (weekdays, twilight, juniors), range (grass), credit cards (MC, V, AE), BF, FF.
Reader Comments: Getting better, pace of play needs work … Very friendly and courteous people … Remodeled a few years ago, great conditions, a bit pricey … Short, tight, decent course … Manicured to a tee … Improving every year.

★★½ **HIGHLAND PARK GOLF COURSE**
PU-1613 S. Main, Bloomington, 61701, McLean County, (309)434-2200, 120 miles from Chicago. **Facility Holes:** 18. **Yards:** 5,725/5,530. **Par:** 70/70. **Course Rating:** 66.9/70.8. **Slope:** 111/115. **Green Fee:** $14. **Cart Fee:** $16/Cart. **Walking Policy:** Unrestricted walking. **Walkability:** 3. **Opened:** 1923. **Season:** Year-round. **To obtain tee times:** Call golf shop. **Miscellaneous:** Reduced fees (twilight), credit cards (MC, V).

★★★ **HIGHLAND SPRINGS GOLF CLUB**
PU-9500 35th. St. W., Rock Island, 61201, Rock Island County, (309)732-7265, 5 miles from Davenport. **E-mail:** wcdapro@pga.com. **Facility Holes:** 18. **Yards:** 6,800/5,875. **Par:** 72/72. **Course Rating:** 73.1/69.0. **Slope:** 125/122. **Green Fee:** $15/$17. **Cart Fee:** $20/Cart. **Walking Policy:** Unrestricted walking. **Walkability:** 3. **Opened:** 1968. **Architect:** William James Spear. **Season:** April-Nov. **High:** May-Aug. **To obtain tee times:** Call golf shop. **Miscellaneous:** Reduced fees (twilight, seniors, juniors), metal spikes, range (grass), credit cards (MC, V).
Reader Comments: Nice course … Outstanding course with flowers and wildlife. Good service … Good all-around course.

★★ **HIGHLAND WOODS GOLF COURSE**
PU-2775 N. Ela Rd., Hoffman Estates, 60172, Cook County, (847)358-3727, 20 miles from Chicago. **Facility Holes:** 18. **Yards:** 6,846/5,831. **Par:** 72/72. **Course Rating:** 72.1/72.6. **Slope:** 120/121. **Green Fee:** $21/$25. **Cart Fee:** $20/Cart. **Walking Policy:** Unrestricted walking. **Opened:** 1975. **Architect:** William James Spear. **Season:** March-Dec. **High:** May-Sept. **To obtain tee times:** Call golf shop. **Miscellaneous:** Reduced fees (weekdays, twilight), metal spikes, credit cards (MC, V).

★★★½ **HILLDALE GOLF CLUB**
PU-1625 Ardwick Dr., Hoffman Estates, 60195, Cook County, (847)310-1100, 40 miles from Chicago. **E-mail:** cheryl@hilldalegolf.com. **Web:** www.hilldalegolf.com. **Facility Holes:** 18. **Yards:** 6,432/5,409. **Par:** 71/72. **Course Rating:** 71.3/72.1. **Slope:** 130/125. **Green Fee:** $37/$43. **Cart Fee:** $13/Person. **Walking Policy:** Walking at certain times. **Walkability:** 3. **Opened:** 1971. **Architect:** Robert Trent Jones. **Season:** April-Nov. **High:** March-Dec. **To obtain tee times:** Call up to 7 days in advance. **Miscellaneous:** Reduced fees (weekdays, twilight), range (grass), credit cards (MC, V, AE, D), FF.
Reader Comments: Tough, challenging course in great shape. Nos. 10 and 11 are monsters … Best public course greens … Pricey, but excellent layout … Short but fun, great conditioned course.

HUBBARD TRAIL GOLF & COUNTRY CLUB
SP-13937 E.3680 N. Road, Hoopeston, 60942, Vermillion County, (217)748-6759, 20 miles from Danville. **E-mail:** grfix@ktb.net. **Facility Holes:** 9. **Yards:** 6,107/5,248. **Par:** 72/72. **Course Rating:** 66.6/70.8. **Slope:** 104/112. **Green Fee:** $18/$20. **Cart Fee:** $10/Person. **Walking Policy:** Unrestricted walking. **Walkability:** 1. **Opened:** 1925. **Season:** March-Nov. **High:** May-Sept. **To obtain tee times:** Call golf shop. **Miscellaneous:** Reduced fees (weekdays), credit cards (MC, V), FF.

★★★ **HUGHES CREEK GOLF CLUB**
PU-1749 Spring Valley Dr., Elburn, 60119, Kane County, (630)365-9200, 30 miles from Chicago. **Facility Holes:** 18. **Yards:** 6,506/5,561. **Par:** 72/72. **Course Rating:** 70.9/71.7. **Slope:** 117/115. **Green Fee:** $14/$22. **Walking Policy:** Unrestricted walking. **Opened:** 1993. **Architect:**

Gordon Cunningham. **Season:** April-Nov. **High:** June-Aug. **To obtain tee times:** Call golf shop. **Misc:** Reduced fees (weekdays, twilight, seniors, juniors), metal spikes, credit cards (MC, V). **Reader Comments:** Hilly, good condition, slow play on weekends, nice greens … In boondocks, needs to mature … Needs a new clubhouse … Way cool layout in great shape & fantastic views.

★½ HUNTER COUNTRY CLUB
PU-5419 Kenosha St., Richmond, 60071, McHenry County, (815)678-2631. **Facility Holes:** 18. **Yards:** 6,381/5,534. **Par:** 72/74. **Course Rating:** 69.2/70.2. **Slope:** 115/114. **Green Fee:** $14/$18. **Season:** April-Nov. **To obtain tee times:** Call golf shop. **Miscellaneous:** Metal spikes.

★★★ ILLINOIS STATE UNIVERSITY GOLF COURSE
PU-W. Gregory St., Normal, 61790, McLean County, (309)438-8065, 100 miles from Chicago. **E-mail:** ljprovo@ilstu.edu. **Web:** www.rec.ilstu.edu. **Facility Holes:** 18. **Yards:** 6,533/5,581. **Par:** 71/73. **Course Rating:** 71.1/71.8. **Slope:** 120/119. **Green Fee:** $25. **Cart Fee:** $11/Person. **Walking Policy:** Unrestricted walking. **Walkability:** 2. **Opened:** 2000. **Architect:** R.B. Harris/D.A. Weibring/G.R.I. **Season:** March-Dec. **High:** May-Oct. **To obtain tee times:** Call up to 7 days in advance. **Miscellaneous:** Reduced fees (weekdays, twilight, seniors, juniors), credit cards (MC, V, D), BF, FF. **Reader Comments:** Tough, lots of traps & water. Great personnel … Great price, good course.

★★★ INDIAN BLUFF GOLF COURSE
PU-6200 78th Ave., Milan, 61264, Rock Island County, (309)799-3868, 185 miles from Chicago. **Facility Holes:** 18. **Yards:** 5,516/4,510. **Par:** 70/71. **Course Rating:** 66.7/67.1. **Slope:** 111/108. **Green Fee:** $13/$14. **Cart Fee:** $10/Person. **Walking Policy:** Unrestricted walking. **Walkability:** 4. **Season:** April-Nov. **High:** May-Aug. **To obtain tee times:** Call golf shop. **Miscellaneous:** Reduced fees (twilight, seniors, juniors), metal spikes, credit cards (MC, V, D). **Reader Comments:** Lots of hills … Unusual layout—great food, service … Very nice greens, funny layout, fun … Short, some hills—interesting … Well maintained.

★½ INDIAN BOUNDARY GOLF COURSE
PU-8600 W. Forest Preserve Dr, Chicago, 60634, Cook County, (773)625-2013. **Facility Holes:** 18. **Yards:** 5,838/5,621. **Par:** 70/70. **Course Rating:** 66.3/70.2. **Slope:** 98/107. **Green Fee:** $19. **Cart Fee:** $20/Cart. **Walking Policy:** Unrestricted walking. **Walkability:** 1. **Season:** Year-round. **High:** April-Aug. **To obtain tee times:** Call golf shop. **Miscellaneous:** Reduced fees (weekdays, twilight, seniors, juniors), metal spikes, credit cards (MC, V).

★★½ INDIAN HILLS GOLF COURSE
PU-20 Indian Trail Dr., Mt. Vernon, 62864, Jefferson County, (618)244-9697. **Facility Holes:** 18. **Yards:** 6,263/4,816. **Par:** 72/71. **Course Rating:** 69.6/67.0. **Slope:** 119/99. **Green Fee:** $10/$11. **Cart Fee:** $10/Person. **Architect:** Tom Puckett. **Season:** Year-round. **To obtain tee times:** Call golf shop. **Miscellaneous:** Credit cards (MC, V).

INDIAN LAKES RESORT
R-250 W. Schick Rd., Bloomingdale, 60108, Du Page County, (630)529-6466, (800)334-3417, 30 miles from Chicago. **Web:** www.indianlakesresort.com. **Facility Holes:** 36. **Green Fee:** $30/$90. **Cart Fee:** Included in green fee. **Walking Policy:** Unrestricted walking. **Walkability:** 3. **Opened:** 1965. **Architect:** Robert Bruce Harris. **Season:** March-Nov. **To obtain tee times:** Call up to 7 days in advance. **Miscellaneous:** Reduced fees (weekdays, guests, twilight, seniors, juniors), range (mats), lodging (350 rooms), credit cards (MC, V, AE, D, DC), BF, FF.
★★½ EAST COURSE (18)
Yards: 6,890/5,031. **Par:** 72/72. **Course Rating:** 72.4/67.7. **Slope:** 120/106.
★★ WEST COURSE (18)
Yards: 6,901/5,088. **Par:** 72/72. **Course Rating:** 72.1/68.3. **Slope:** 123/110.

★½ INDIAN VALLEY COUNTRY CLUB
PU-25224 N. Hwy. 83, Mundelein, 60060, Lake County, (847)566-1313. **E-mail:** supfr-priesty@webt.net. **Facility Holes:** 27. **Yards:** 6,173/5,576. **Par:** 72/72. **Course Rating:** 68.9. **Slope:** 110. **Green Fee:** $18/$24. **Cart Fee:** $26/Cart. **Walking Policy:** Unrestricted walking. **Walkability:** 4. **Opened:** 1960. **Architect:** Tony Fillichio. **Season:** Year-round. **To obtain tee times:** Call golf shop. **Miscellaneous:** Reduced fees (seniors), metal spikes, credit cards (MC, V), BF, FF.

★★½ INGERSOLL GOLF COURSE
PU-101 Daisyfield Rd., Rockford, 61102, Winnebago County, (815)987-8887. **Facility Holes:** 18. **Yards:** 6,107/5,820. **Par:** 71/75. **Course Rating:** 68.9/72.6. **Slope:** 111/116. **Green Fee:** $16/$21. **Cart Fee:** $22/Cart. **Walking Policy:** Unrestricted walking. **Walkability:** 2. **Opened:** 1922. **Architect:** Tom Bendelow. **Season:** March-Oct. **High:** June-Aug. **To obtain tee times:** Call up to 7 days in advance. **Miscellaneous:** Reduced fees (twilight), range (mats), credit cards (MC, V, D), BF, FF.

★★ INWOOD GOLF COURSE
PU-3200 W. Jefferson, Joliet, 60435, Will County, (815)741-7265, 40 miles from Chicago.
Facility Holes: 18. **Yards:** 6,078/5,559. **Par:** 71/71. **Course Rating:** 69.4/71.4. **Slope:** 117/121.
Green Fee: $12/$24. **Walking Policy:** Unrestricted walking. **Opened:** 1931. **Architect:** Edward
Lawrence Packard. **Season:** April-Oct. **High:** June-Aug. **To obtain tee times:** Call golf shop.
Miscellaneous: Reduced fees (weekdays, twilight, seniors, juniors), metal spikes, range
(grass), credit cards (MC, V, D).

★★★★½ IRONHORSE GOLF COURSE
PU-200 Ironhorse Dr., Tuscola, 61953, Douglas County, (217)253-6644. **Facility Holes:** 18.
Yards: 7,046/6,093. **Par:** 72/72. **Course Rating:** 72.7/74.1. **Slope:** 120/118. **Green Fee:**
$15/$32. **Cart Fee:** $11/Person. **Walking Policy:** Unrestricted walking. **Walkability:** 4. **Opened:**
1997. **Architect:** Paul Loague. **Season:** Year-round. **To obtain tee times:** Call golf shop.
Miscellaneous: Reduced fees (weekdays, twilight, seniors), range (grass/mats), credit cards
(MC, V), BF, FF.
Reader Comments: Nice course, rural setting … This links-style course is a joy … Wind can make
a difference … Lots of water, no trees.

★★½ IRONWOOD GOLF COURSE
PU-1901 N. Towanda Ave., Normal, 61761, McLean County, (309)454-9620, 100 miles from
Chicago. **E-mail:** golfpro@normal.org. **Web:** www.normal.org. **Facility Holes:** 18. **Yards:**
6,960/5,385. **Par:** 72/72. **Course Rating:** 72.4/69.8. **Slope:** 126/113. **Green Fee:** $13/$19. **Cart
Fee:** $12/Person. **Walking Policy:** Unrestricted walking. **Walkability:** 2. **Opened:** 1990.
Architect: Roger Packard. **Season:** March-Nov. **High:** June-Aug. **To obtain tee times:** Call up
to 7 days in advance. **Miscellaneous:** Reduced fees (weekdays, twilight, seniors, juniors),
range (grass/mats), credit cards (MC, V, AE, D), BF, FF.

★½ JACKSON PARK GOLF CLUB
PU-6300 Hayes Dr., Chicago, 60637, Cook County, (312)747-2763. **Facility Holes:** 18. **Yards:**
5,508/5,307. **Par:** 70/72. **Green Fee:** $18/$19. **Cart Fee:** $4/Cart. **Opened:** 1899. **Season:** April-
Nov. **To obtain tee times:** Call golf shop. **Miscellaneous:** Reduced fees (twilight, seniors,
juniors), metal spikes, credit cards (MC, V).

JOE LOUIS GOLF CLUB
PU-13100 South Halstead, Riverdale, 60827, Cook County, (708)841-6340. **Facility Holes:**
18. **Yards:** 6,869/5,228. **Par:** 72/72. **Course Rating:** 71.7/70.5. **Slope:** 123/121. **Green Fee:**
$16/$19. **Opened:** 1918. **Architect:** Dick Nugent. **Season:** April-Nov. **To obtain tee times:** Call
golf shop. **Miscellaneous:** Metal spikes.

★★★½ KANKAKEE ELKS COUNTRY CLUB
SP-2283 Bittersweet Dr., St. Anne, 60964, Kankakee County, (815)937-9547. **Facility Holes:**
18. **Yards:** 6,329/5,509. **Par:** 71/74. **Course Rating:** 70.5/71.6. **Slope:** 118/119. **Green Fee:**
$18/$30. **Season:** March-Nov. **To obtain tee times:** Call golf shop.
Reader Comments: Old line and lovely layout, fun to play … A hilly course with a lot of trees …
Very few courses this good … Small elevated greens are fast, tough chips when you miss.

KELLOGG GOLF COURSE
PU-7716 N. Radnor Rd., Peoria, 61615, Peoria County, (309)691-0293. **Facility Holes:** 27.
Cart Fee: $18/Cart. **Walking Policy:** Unrestricted walking. **Walkability:** 2. **Season:** March-Dec.
High: May-Aug. **Miscellaneous:** Reduced fees (weekdays, twilight, juniors), range
(grass/mats), credit cards (MC, V, D, Check Card), BF, FF.
★★★½ EXECUTIVE COURSE (9)
Yards: 2,901/2,407. **Par:** 35/35. **Course Rating:** 33.5/33.2. **Green Fee:** $9. **To obtain tee times:**
Call golf shop.
Reader Comments: Always crowded … New learning center is a great addition … Wide open and
windy … Some challenging holes … Good test.
★★★½ KELLOGG COURSE (18)
Yards: 6,735/5,675. **Par:** 72/72. **Course Rating:** 70.9/71.5. **Slope:** 117/120. **Green Fee:**
$13/$17. **Opened:** 1974. **Architect:** Larry Packard/Roger Packard. **To obtain tee times:** Call up
to 6 days in advance.
Reader Comments: Excellent public course with wide fairways. Excellent value.

★★★★ KEMPER LAKES GOLF COURSE *Condition*
PU-Old McHenry Rd., Long Grove, 60049, Lake County, (847)320-3450, 25 miles from
Chicago. **Facility Holes:** 18. **Yards:** 7,217/5,638. **Par:** 72/72. **Course Rating:** 75.7/67.9. **Slope:**
140/125. **Green Fee:** $135. **Cart Fee:** Included in green fee. **Walking Policy:** Unrestricted walk-
ing. **Walkability:** 2. **Opened:** 1979. **Architect:** Dick Nugent/Ken Killian. **Season:** April-Nov. **High:**
June-Sept. **To obtain tee times:** Call up to 14 days in advance. **Miscellaneous:** Reduced fees

(twilight), range (grass), credit cards (MC, V, AE), BF, FF.
Notes: Golf Digest School site. Ranked 12th in 1999 Best in State; 1989 National PGA Championship; 1986, 1987, 1989 Grand Slam of Golf; 1998, 1998, 1999 Ameritech Senior Open.
Reader Comments: Real quality golf, a little pricey, but nice … Great layout, greens awesome, tough, windy … Long course, not for high handicappers … Fast greens … Must play from the tips, 17 & 18 are great finishing holes.

★★★ KLEIN CREEK GOLF CLUB
PU-1 N. 333 Pleasant Hill Rd., Winfield, 60190, Du Page County, (630)690-0101, 2 miles from Wheaton. **E-mail:** pgolden854@aol.com. **Web:** www.kleincreek.com. **Facility Holes:** 18. **Yards:** 6,701/4,509. **Par:** 72/72. **Course Rating:** 71.9/66.2. **Slope:** 127/110. **Green Fee:** $49/$80. **Cart Fee:** Included in green fee. **Walking Policy:** Unrestricted walking. **Walkability:** 2. **Opened:** 1994. **Architect:** Dick Nugent. **Season:** March-Dec. **High:** May-Sept. **To obtain tee times:** Call up to 14 days in advance. **Miscellaneous:** Reduced fees (weekdays, twilight), credit cards (MC, V, AE, DC), BF, FF.
Reader Comments: Sometimes tight to adjacent homes, but gets better every time you play it … Shotmaker's course, hard & fast … Very tough No. 5, par-4, 150 yard tunnel to fairway … Greens in great shape … Either love it or hate it.

KOKOPELLI GOLF CLUB
SP-1401 Champions Dr., Marion, 62959, Williamson County, (618)997-5656, 100 miles from St. Louis. **E-mail:** golfpro@kokopelligolf.com. **Web:** www.kokopelligolf.com. **Facility Holes:** 18. **Yards:** 7,150/5,375. **Par:** 72/72. **Course Rating:** 75.2/70.6. **Slope:** 139/122. **Green Fee:** $24/$30. **Cart Fee:** $12/Person. **Walking Policy:** Walking at certain times. **Walkability:** 3. **Opened:** 1997. **Architect:** Steve Smyers. **Season:** Year-round. **High:** May-Oct. **To obtain tee times:** Call up to 30 days in advance. **Miscellaneous:** Reduced fees (weekdays, seniors), range (grass), credit cards (MC, V, D), BF, FF.

LACOMA GOLF COURSE
PU-8080 Timmerman Rd., East Dubuque, 61025, Jo Daviess County, (815)747-3874, 1 mile from Dubuque. **E-mail:** golflacoma@aol.com. **Web:** www.lacomagolf.com. **Facility Holes:** 45. **Cart Fee:** $20/Cart. **Walking Policy:** Unrestricted walking. **Opened:** 1967. **Architect:** Gordon Cunningham. **Season:** Year-round. **High:** May-Sept. **To obtain tee times:** Call up to 7 days in advance. **Misc:** Reduced fees (twilight), range (grass/mats), credit cards (MC, V, D), BF, FF.
★★★ BLUE COURSE (18)
Yards: 6,705/5,784. **Par:** 71/71. **Course Rating:** 71.8/70.0. **Slope:** 123/117. **Green Fee:** $12/$16. **Walkability:** 4.
Reader Comments: Very good public course that offers some nice scenery and challenging … Price is right … Made new holes, challenging, always crowded … Great layout, tight fairways.
★★ RED/GOLD COURSE (18)
Yards: 5,552/4,895. **Par:** 69/69. **Course Rating:** 63.5/63.8. **Slope:** 105/102. **Green Fee:** $12/$15. **Walkability:** 2.
Special Notes: Also has a 9-hole par-3 course.

★★★ LAKE BLUFF GOLF CLUB
PU-Green Bay Rd. & Washington St., Lake Bluff, 60044, Lake County, (847)234-6771, 10 miles from Waukegan. **Facility Holes:** 18. **Yards:** 6,537/5,450. **Par:** 72/72. **Course Rating:** 71.6/69.7. **Slope:** 120/114. **Green Fee:** $23/$38. **Cart Fee:** $28/Cart. **Walking Policy:** Unrestricted walking. **Walkability:** 2. **Opened:** 1969. **Season:** April-Dec. **To obtain tee times:** Call up to 6 days in advance. **Miscellaneous:** Reduced fees (weekdays, twilight, seniors, juniors), range (grass/mats), credit cards (MC, V), BF, FF.
Reader Comments: Bent-grass fairways, No. 8 ranks with par 5s anywhere … Most holes look the same—straight, no challenge … Lots of uphill scored shots, greens are fast … Pace of play is consistently fast.

★★★ LAKE OF THE WOODS GOLF CLUB
PU-405 N. Lake of the Woods Rd., Mahomet, 61853, Champaign County, (217)586-2183, 8 miles from Champaign. **E-mail:** lakeshop@aol.com. **Web:** www.mah-online.com/lowgc/. **Facility Holes:** 27. **Yards:** 6,520/5,187. **Par:** 72/72. **Course Rating:** 70.6/68.9. **Slope:** 120/115. **Green Fee:** $18/$20. **Cart Fee:** $10/Person. **Walking Policy:** Unrestricted walking. **Walkability:** 2. **Opened:** 1954. **Architect:** Robert Bruce Harris. **Season:** March-Dec. **High:** May-Sept. **To obtain tee times:** Call up to 7 days in advance. **Miscellaneous:** Reduced fees (twilight, seniors, juniors), range (grass/mats), credit cards (MC, V), BF, FF.
Reader Comments: Has great potential … A fair, pretty course in central Illinois … Well-run course … Nice, mature tree-lined course. Can be hard to find … Good challenge from the tips.
Special Notes: Also has a 9-hole executive course.

★★★ LAKE SHORE GOLF COURSE
PU-1460 E. 1000 North Rd., Taylorville, 62568, Christian County, (217)824-5521, 26 miles from Springfield. **E-mail:** jjpga2000@aol.com. **Facility Holes:** 18. **Yards:** 6,778/5,581. **Par:** 72/74. **Course Rating:** 72.0/74.0. **Slope:** 117/114. **Green Fee:** $20. **Cart Fee:** $24/Cart. **Walking Policy:** Unrestricted walking. **Walkability:** 4. **Opened:** 1969. **Architect:** William James Spear. **Season:** March-Dec. **High:** May-Oct. **To obtain tee times:** Call up to 7 days in advance. **Miscellaneous:** Reduced fees (twilight, juniors), range (grass), credit cards (MC, V, D), BF, FF. **Reader Comments:** Gotta think your way around this one. A fair test if played from the proper tees, but danger can be found on most every hole … For the money can't beat it … Long & strong course … A nice course that gets a lot of play.

★½ LAKE VIEW COUNTRY CLUB
SP-23319 Hazel Rd., Sterling, 61081, Whiteside County, (815)626-2886. **Facility Holes:** 18. **Yards:** 6,171/5,612. **Par:** 70/75. **Course Rating:** 68.7. **Slope:** 116. **Green Fee:** $15/$17. **Opened:** 1970. **Season:** March-Nov. **To obtain tee times:** Call golf shop. **Misc:** Metal spikes.

★★ LAUREL GREENS PUBLIC GOLFERS CLUB
PU-1133 Hwy. 150 E., Knoxville, 61448, Knox County, (309)289-4146, 3 miles from Peoria. **Facility Holes:** 36. **Green Fee:** $12/$13. **Cart Fee:** $9/Person. **Walking Policy:** Unrestricted walking. **Walkability:** 3. **Architect:** Clyde Raible. **Season:** March-Dec. **High:** May-Oct. **To obtain tee times:** Call up to 7 days in advance. **Miscellaneous:** Metal spikes, FF.
1-9 EAST/1-9 SOUTH COURSE (18)
Yards: 6,397/4,935. **Par:** 72/72. **Opened:** 1994.
1-9 WEST/10-18 EAST COURSE (18)
Yards: 6,703/5,089. **Par:** 72/72. **Opened:** 1971.
Special Notes: Four 9-hole courses played as two 18-hole courses.

LAWRENCE COUNTY COUNTRY CLUB
SP-US No. 50, Lawrenceville, 62439, Lawrence County, (618)943-2011, 150 miles from St. Louis. **E-mail:** lccc72@midwest.net. **Facility Holes:** 9. **Yards:** 6,252/5,388. **Par:** 72. **Course Rating:** 68.9. **Slope:** 113. **Green Fee:** $17. **Cart Fee:** $20/Cart. **Walking Policy:** Unrestricted walking. **Walkability:** 3. **Opened:** 1915. **Architect:** Tom Bendelow. **Season:** March-Nov. **High:** April-Oct. **To obtain tee times:** Call golf shop. **Miscellaneous:** Range (grass), BF, FF.

★★★ THE LEDGES GOLF CLUB
PU-7111 McCurry Rd., Roscoe, 61073, Winnebago County, (815)389-0979, 10 miles from Rockford. **Web:** www.wcfpd.org. **Facility Holes:** 18. **Yards:** 6,417/5,881. **Par:** 72/72. **Course Rating:** 71.1/74.1. **Slope:** 124/129. **Green Fee:** $14/$25. **Cart Fee:** $24/Cart. **Walking Policy:** Unrestricted walking. **Walkability:** 3. **Opened:** 1965. **Architect:** Edward Lawrence Packard. **Season:** April-Nov. **High:** May-Aug. **To obtain tee times:** Call golf shop. **Miscellaneous:** Reduced fees (twilight, seniors, juniors), range (grass). **Reader Comments:** A very scenic course with a variety of challenging holes … Great price for great golf … Beautiful local course … A fun course … Needs work.

★★ LEGACY GOLF CLUB
PU-3500 Cargill Rd., Granite City, 62040, Madison County, (618)931-4653, 12 miles from St. Louis. **Facility Holes:** 18. **Yards:** 6,300/5,600. **Par:** 71/71. **Course Rating:** 70.4/69.4. **Slope:** 114/110. **Green Fee:** $14/$21. **Cart Fee:** $10/Person. **Walking Policy:** Unrestricted walking. **Walkability:** 0. **Opened:** 1990. **Architect:** Jerry Loomis. **Season:** Year-round. **High:** April-Oct. **To obtain tee times:** Call golf shop. **Miscellaneous:** Reduced fees (weekdays, twilight, seniors, juniors), metal spikes, range (grass), credit cards (MC, V, AE, D).

★★ LEO DONOVAN GOLF COURSE
PU-5805 Knoxville Ave., Peoria, 61614, Peoria County, (309)691-8361. **Facility Holes:** 18. **Yards:** 6,735/5,675. **Par:** 72/72. **Course Rating:** 70.9/71.5. **Slope:** 117/120. **Green Fee:** $11/$15. **Walking Policy:** Unrestricted walking. **Walkability:** 2. **Opened:** 1929. **Season:** March-Nov. **High:** April-Aug. **To obtain tee times:** Call golf shop. **Miscellaneous:** Reduced fees (weekdays, twilight, juniors), credit cards (MC, V).

★★★★ LICK CREEK GOLF COURSE *Value*
PU-2210 N. Pkwy. Dr., Pekin, 61554, Tazewell County, (309)346-0077, 12 miles from Peoria. **Facility Holes:** 18. **Yards:** 6,909/5,729. **Par:** 72/72. **Course Rating:** 72.8/72.9. **Slope:** 128/126. **Green Fee:** $7/$22. **Cart Fee:** $18/Cart. **Walking Policy:** Unrestricted walking. **Walkability:** 4. **Opened:** 1976. **Architect:** Edward Lawrence Packard. **Season:** March-Nov. **High:** May-Aug. **To obtain tee times:** Call up to 7 days in advance. **Miscellaneous:** Reduced fees (weekdays, twilight, seniors, juniors), range (grass), credit cards (MC, V), FF. **Reader Comments:** Challenging public course that is well maintained and an excellent value … Long, sporty course … Lots of hills and side-sloped fairways … Very tight & demanding course.

ILLINOIS

★★ LINCOLN GREENS GOLF COURSE
PU-700 E. Lake Dr., Springfield, 62707, Sangamon County, (217)786-4000, 90 miles from St. Louis. **Facility Holes:** 18. **Yards:** 6,582/5,625. **Par:** 72/72. **Course Rating:** 70.3/70.9. **Slope:** 112/114. **Green Fee:** $7/$22. **Cart Fee:** $18/Cart. **Walking Policy:** Unrestricted walking. **Walkability:** 1. **Opened:** 1957. **Architect:** Robert Bruce Harris. **Season:** March-Dec. **High:** June-Aug. **To obtain tee times:** Call golf shop. **Miscellaneous:** Reduced fees (weekdays, twilight, seniors, juniors), metal spikes, range (grass), credit cards (MC, V).

★★½ LINCOLN OAKS GOLF COURSE
PU-390 Richton Rd., Crete, 60417, Will County, (708)672-9401, 25 miles from Chicago. **Facility Holes:** 18. **Yards:** 6,087/4,699. **Par:** 71/73. **Course Rating:** 68.1/65.8. **Slope:** 112/105. **Green Fee:** $10/$25. **Cart Fee:** $12/Person. **Walking Policy:** Unrestricted walking. **Walkability:** 1. **Opened:** 1927. **Architect:** Tom Bendelow. **Season:** Year-round. **High:** June-Aug. **To obtain tee times:** Call golf shop. **Miscellaneous:** Reduced fees (weekdays, twilight, seniors, juniors), metal spikes, range (grass), credit cards (MC, V).

★★★½ THE LINKS GOLF COURSE
PU-Nichols Park, Jacksonville, 62650, Morgan County, (217)479-4663, 30 miles from Springfield. **Facility Holes:** 27. **Yards:** 6,836/5,310. **Par:** 72/72. **Course Rating:** 71.3/69.0. **Slope:** 116/108. **Green Fee:** $14/$18. **Cart Fee:** $11/Person. **Walking Policy:** Unrestricted walking. **Walkability:** 1. **Opened:** 1979. **Architect:** David Gill. **Season:** Year-round. **High:** April-Oct. **To obtain tee times:** Call up to 7 days in advance. **Miscellaneous:** Reduced fees (weekdays, seniors, juniors), range (grass), BF, FF.
Reader Comments: Good municipal course ... Long course, very large, very nice greens, challenging ... Greens always in good shape, wind comes into play.
Special Notes: Also has a 9-hole executive course.

★★½ LOCUST HILLS GOLF CLUB
PU-1015 Belleville St., Lebanon, 62254, St. Clair County, (618)537-4590, 22 miles from St. Louis, MO. **Web:** www.locusthillsgolf.com. **Facility Holes:** 18. **Yards:** 6,014/4,459. **Par:** 71/71. **Course Rating:** 68.2/71.0. **Slope:** 109/113. **Green Fee:** $13/$22. **Cart Fee:** $11/Cart. **Walking Policy:** Unrestricted walking. **Walkability:** 2. **Opened:** 1967. **Season:** Year-round. **High:** May-Oct. **To obtain tee times:** Call golf shop. **Miscellaneous:** Reduced fees (weekdays, twilight, seniors, juniors), credit cards (MC, V, AE, D, DC, CB), BF, FF.

★★ LONGWOOD COUNTRY CLUB
SP-3503 E. Steger Rd., Crete, 60417, Will County, (708)758-1811, 40 miles from Chicago. **E-mail:** lcountrycl@aol.com. **Facility Holes:** 18. **Yards:** 6,404/6,536. **Par:** 70/72. **Course Rating:** 70.5/72.1. **Slope:** 121/120. **Green Fee:** $16/$31. **Cart Fee:** $14/Person. **Walking Policy:** Unrestricted walking. **Walkability:** 4. **Opened:** 1957. **Season:** Year-round. **To obtain tee times:** Call golf shop. **Miscellaneous:** Reduced fees (weekdays, twilight, seniors, juniors), metal spikes, range (grass), credit cards (MC, V, AE, D).

★★★ LOST NATION GOLF CLUB
PU-6931 S. Lost Nation Rd., Dixon, 61021, Ogle County, (815)652-4212, 90 miles from Chicago. **Facility Holes:** 18. **Yards:** 6,275/5,626. **Par:** 71/72. **Course Rating:** 69.5/72.0. **Slope:** 114/114. **Green Fee:** $18/$22. **Cart Fee:** $24/Cart. **Walking Policy:** Unrestricted walking. **Walkability:** 3. **Opened:** 1965. **Season:** March-Dec. **High:** May-Sept. **To obtain tee times:** Call up to 14 days in advance. **Miscellaneous:** Reduced fees (twilight, seniors), credit cards (MC, V), FF.
Reader Comments: Lots of sand and pine trees, tight fairways, very scenic and natural. Some long, tough holes and greens ... Nice greens ... Good place to play during the week ... Good first impression, enjoyed, will return.

★★½ MACKTOWN GOLF COURSE
PU-2221 Freeport Rd., Rockton, 61072, Winnebago County, (815)624-7410. **Facility Holes:** 18. **Yards:** 5,770/5,403. **Par:** 71/71. **Course Rating:** 67.1/70.3. **Slope:** 109/111. **Green Fee:** $14/$25. **Cart Fee:** $24/Cart. **Walking Policy:** Unrestricted walking. **Walkability:** 3. **Opened:** 1931. **Architect:** R. Welsh. **Season:** April-Oct. **High:** May-Aug. **To obtain tee times:** Call golf shop. **Miscellaneous:** Reduced fees (weekdays, twilight, seniors, juniors).

★½ MADISON PARK GOLF COURSE
PU-2735 W. Martin Luther King Dr., Peoria, 61604, Peoria County, (309)673-7161. **Facility Holes:** 18. **Yards:** 5,476/5,120. **Par:** 69/69. **Course Rating:** 64.5/67.7. **Slope:** 96/100. **Green Fee:** $12/$13. **Cart Fee:** $18/Cart. **Walking Policy:** Unrestricted walking. **Walkability:** 1. **Opened:** 1909. **Season:** March-Dec. **High:** June-Sept. **To obtain tee times:** Call golf shop. **Miscellaneous:** Reduced fees (weekdays, twilight, juniors), range (grass), credit cards (MC, V, D), BF, FF.

MANTENO GOLF CLUB
PU-Village Hall 269 N. Main St., Manteno, 60950, Kankakee County, (815)468-8827. **Facility Holes:** 18. **Yards:** 6,435/5,145. **Par:** 72/72. **Course Rating:** 70.1/68.5. **Slope:** 118/112. **Green Fee:** $17/$20. **Walking Policy:** Unrestricted walking. **Walkability:** 2. **Opened:** 1974. **Architect:** John Krutilla. **Season:** Year-round. **High:** April-Oct. **To obtain tee times:** Call up to 2 days in advance. **Miscellaneous:** Reduced fees (twilight, seniors), range (grass), credit cards (MC, V), BF, FF.

★★★ **MAPLE MEADOWS GOLF COURSE**
PU-271 South Addison Rd., Wood Dale, 60191, Du Page County, (630)616-8424, 19 miles from Chicago. **Facility Holes:** 27. **Yards:** 6,438/6,057. **Par:** 70/70. **Course Rating:** 70.1/68.3. **Slope:** 122/118. **Green Fee:** $27/$45. **Cart Fee:** $14/Person. **Walking Policy:** Walking at certain times. **Walkability:** 5. **Opened:** 1998. **Season:** April-Dec. **High:** June-Sept. **To obtain tee times:** Call golf shop. **Miscellaneous:** Reduced fees (weekdays), credit cards (MC, V).
Reader Comments: New 9 an excellent addition, will get better ... Good all-round layout ... Open setting, not many trees ... Excellent value ... Very windy at most times ... Good course, fair test, wide open.
Special Notes: Also has a 9-hole executive course.

★★★★ **MARENGO RIDGE GOLF CLUB**
PU-9508 Harmony Hill Rd., Marengo, 60152, McHenry County, (815)923-2332, 35 miles from Chicago. **E-mail:** rwitek@mc.net. **Facility Holes:** 18. **Yards:** 6,636/5,659. **Par:** 72/73. **Course Rating:** 71.4/72.2. **Slope:** 122/120. **Green Fee:** $20/$40. **Walking Policy:** Unrestricted walking. **Walkability:** 3. **Opened:** 1965. **Architect:** William James Spear. **Season:** Year-round. **High:** March-Oct. **To obtain tee times:** Call up to 7 days in advance. **Miscellaneous:** Reduced fees (weekdays, twilight, seniors, juniors), range (grass), credit cards (MC, V, D), BF, FF.
Reader Comments: One of the few courses to space tee times 10 minutes apart ... Two totally different 9s, front new, open and upscale; back is older, more mature trees and overall look ... Greens make this course tough ... Excellent staff.

★★★ **MARRIOTT'S LINCOLNSHIRE RESORT**
R-Ten Marriott Dr., Lincolnshire, 60069, Lake County, (847)634-5935, 30 miles from Chicago. **Facility Holes:** 18. **Yards:** 6,313/4,892. **Par:** 70/69. **Course Rating:** 71.1/68.9. **Slope:** 129/117. **Green Fee:** $55/$69. **Cart Fee:** Included in green fee. **Walking Policy:** Walking at certain times. **Walkability:** 2. **Opened:** 1975. **Architect:** Tom Fazio/George Fazio. **Season:** April-Nov. **High:** June-Sept. **To obtain tee times:** Call up to 14 days in advance. **Miscellaneous:** Reduced fees (weekdays, twilight, juniors), range (mats), credit cards (MC, V, AE, D), BF, FF.
Reader Comments: Course is tougher than it looks ... Tight fairways ... Nice, sporty layout and overnight packages ... Short, but narrow course. Course in good condition.

MEADOWLARK GOLF COURSE
PU-11599 W. 31st Street, Hinsdale, 60523, Cook County, (708)562-2977, 16 miles from Chicago. **Facility Holes:** 9. **Yards:** 3,324/2,918. **Par:** 36/36. **Course Rating:** 70.8/67.4. **Slope:** 110/104. **Walking Policy:** Unrestricted walking. **Walkability:** 2. **Opened:** 1966. **Season:** March-Dec. **High:** June-Aug. **To obtain tee times:** Call golf shop. **Miscellaneous:** Reduced fees (twilight, seniors, juniors), metal spikes, credit cards (MC, V, AE, D, DC).

★½ **THE MEADOWS GOLF CLUB OF BLUE ISLAND**
PU-2802 W. 123rd St., Blue Island, 60406, Cook County, (708)385-1994. **Facility Holes:** 18. **Yards:** 6,549/5,040. **Par:** 71/71. **Course Rating:** 71.3/67.7. **Slope:** 121/107. **Green Fee:** $18/$30. **Cart Fee:** $12/Person. **Walking Policy:** Unrestricted walking. **Walkability:** 2. **Opened:** 1994. **Architect:** J. Porter Gibson. **Season:** Year-round. **High:** July-Aug. **To obtain tee times:** Call golf shop. **Miscellaneous:** Reduced fees (seniors, juniors), range (grass/mats), credit cards (MC, V).

★★½ **MEADOWVIEW GOLF COURSE**
PU-6489 Meadowview Lane, Mattoon, 61938, Coles County, (217)258-7888, 50 miles from Champaign. **Web:** www.meadowviewgolf.com. **Facility Holes:** 18. **Yards:** 6,907/5,559. **Par:** 72/72. **Course Rating:** 72.6/71.3. **Slope:** 121/117. **Green Fee:** $12/$21. **Cart Fee:** $11/Person. **Walking Policy:** Unrestricted walking. **Walkability:** 2. **Opened:** 1991. **Architect:** William James Spear. **Season:** Year-round. **High:** April-Oct. **To obtain tee times:** Call up to 21 days in advance. **Miscellaneous:** Reduced fees (weekdays, twilight, seniors, juniors), range (grass), credit cards (MC, V, D), BF, FF.

★★★ **MILL CREEK GOLF CLUB**
PU-39 W. 525 Herrington Dr., Geneva, 60134, Kane County, (630)208-7272, 5 miles from Geneva. **Facility Holes:** 27. **Yards:** 6,724/4,833. **Par:** 73/73. **Course Rating:** 72.1/67.5. **Slope:** 130/118. **Green Fee:** $55/$80. **Cart Fee:** Included in green fee. **Walking Policy:** Mandatory

carts. **Walkability:** 3. **Opened:** 1996. **Architect:** Roy Case. **Season:** March-Dec. **High:** May-Sept. **To obtain tee times:** Call up to 14 days in advance. **Miscellaneous:** Reduced fees (weekdays, twilight, seniors, juniors), range (grass), credit cards (MC, V, AE, D, DC), BF, FF.
Reader Comments: Need to play couple times to figure blind shots ... Design requires use of all clubs ... Great greens with a number of challenging holes ... Short course, back tees must be played ... Good practice facility.
Special Notes: Also has a 9-hole pitch & putt.

★★★ MINNE MONESSE GOLF CLUB
SP-15944 E. Six Mi Grove Rd., Grant Park, 60940, Kankakee County, (815)465-6653, (800)339-3126, 20 miles from Kankakee. **E-mail:** minnemonesse@aol.com. **Facility Holes:** 18. **Yards:** 6,500/5,100. **Par:** 72/72. **Course Rating:** 71.1. **Slope:** 121. **Green Fee:** $25/$37. **Cart Fee:** Included in green fee. **Walking Policy:** Unrestricted walking. **Walkability:** 4. **Opened:** 1926. **Architect:** Ted Lockie, Bob Lohmann. **Season:** Year-round. **High:** May-Oct. **To obtain tee times:** Call up to 7 days in advance. **Miscellaneous:** Reduced fees (weekdays, twilight, seniors, juniors), range (grass), credit cards (MC, V, AE, D), BF, FF.
Reader Comments: Good for iron control, some long par 5s, narrow fairways.

★★★½ MISTWOOD GOLF COURSE
PU-1700 W. Renwick Rd., Romeoville, 60446, Joliet County, (815)254-3333, 25 miles from Chicago. **Facility Holes:** 18. **Yards:** 6,727/5,231. **Par:** 72/72. **Course Rating:** 72.1. **Slope:** 132. **Green Fee:** $20/$55. **Cart Fee:** $13/Person. **Walking Policy:** Unrestricted walking. **Walkability:** 3. **Opened:** 1998. **Architect:** Ray Hearn. **Season:** March-Nov. **High:** May-Oct. **To obtain tee times:** Call up to 10 days in advance. **Miscellaneous:** Reduced fees (seniors, juniors), range (grass/mats), credit cards (MC, V, AE, D), BF, FF.
Notes: Illinois Womens Open.
Reader Comments: Requires use of every club in the bag ... Last 5 holes around quarry very tough. 5 sets of tees ... Great back 9, getting a little pricey ... Best set of par 5s around. Tough on a windy day ... Great use of hills, moguls, and water.

★★ MOUNT CARMEL MUNICIPAL GOLF CLUB
PU-700 Park Rd., Mt. Carmel, 62863, Wabash County, (618)262-5771. **Facility Holes:** 18. **Yards:** 6,233/5,417. **Par:** 71/72. **Course Rating:** 69.2/67.9. **Slope:** 123/119. **Green Fee:** $12/$16. **Cart Fee:** $22/Cart. **Walking Policy:** Unrestricted walking. **Walkability:** 3. **Opened:** 1928. **Season:** March-Nov. **High:** May-Sept. **To obtain tee times:** Call golf shop. **Miscellaneous:** BF, FF.

★★★ MOUNT PROSPECT GOLF CLUB
PU-600 See Gwum Ave., Mt. Prospect, 60056, Cook County, (847)632-9300, 6 miles from Chicago. **E-mail:** mpgcoo@aol.com. **Facility Holes:** 18. **Yards:** 6,200/5,355. **Par:** 71/73. **Course Rating:** 70.3/70.8. **Slope:** 128/123. **Green Fee:** $37/$47. **Cart Fee:** $28/Cart. **Walking Policy:** Unrestricted walking. **Walkability:** 2. **Opened:** 1927. **Architect:** Unknown. **Season:** March-Nov. **High:** May-Sept. **To obtain tee times:** Call up to 5 days in advance. **Miscellaneous:** Reduced fees (twilight), range (grass/mats), credit cards (MC, V, D), BF, FF.
Reader Comments: Bent-grass fairways are rare for area. Greens are challanging. Course rewards accuracy ... Long and hard ... Nice design ... Most unique course I have ever played ... A tough course, but overpriced and overplayed.

★★★ NAPERBROOK GOLF COURSE
PU-22204 111th St., Plainfield, 60544, Will County, (630)378-4215, 24 miles from Chicago. **Facility Holes:** 18. **Yards:** 6,755/5,381. **Par:** 72/72. **Course Rating:** 72.2/70.5. **Slope:** 125/118. **Green Fee:** $26/$48. **Cart Fee:** $14/Person. **Walking Policy:** Unrestricted walking. **Walkability:** 1. **Opened:** 1990. **Architect:** Roger Packard. **Season:** March-Dec. **High:** June-Aug. **To obtain tee times:** Call up to 7 days in advance. **Miscellaneous:** Reduced fees (weekdays, twilight, seniors, juniors), range (grass), credit cards (MC, V), BF, FF.
Reader Comments: Well-maintained public course ... Flat, but plenty of interest ... Long, tough course, good greens ... Nice muni. You get what you pay for ... Good condition—fun course ... Fair & wide open ... Challenging—many traps & water.

★½ NELSON PARK GOLF COURSE
PU-200 Nelson Blvd., Decatur, 62521, Macon County, (217)422-7241, 45 miles from Springfield. **Facility Holes:** 18. **Yards:** 4,793/4,378. **Par:** 65/65. **Course Rating:** 63.2/63.2. **Slope:** 101/101. **Green Fee:** $11/$20. **Cart Fee:** $22/Cart. **Walking Policy:** Unrestricted walking. **Walkability:** 5. **Opened:** 1916. **Season:** Year-round. **High:** June-Aug. **To obtain tee times:** Call up to 7 days in advance. **Miscellaneous:** Reduced fees (weekdays, twilight, seniors, juniors), metal spikes, credit cards (MC, V), BF, FF.

★★★ NETTLE CREEK COUNTRY CLUB

PU-5355 Saratoga Rd., Morris, 60450, Grundy County, (815)941-4300, 50 miles from Chicago. **Web:** www.nettlecreek.com. **Facility Holes:** 18. **Yards:** 6,489/5,059. **Par:** 71/71. **Course Rating:** 70.4/68.9. **Slope:** 117/114. **Green Fee:** $34/$44. **Cart Fee:** Included in green fee. **Walking Policy:** Walking at certain times. **Walkability:** 2. **Opened:** 1993. **Architect:** Buzz Didier. **Season:** March-Nov. **High:** June-Aug. **To obtain tee times:** Call golf shop. **Miscellaneous:** Reduced fees (twilight, seniors, juniors), metal spikes, credit cards (MC, V).

Reader Comments: Service for outings was excellent ... Good course and conditions, good bargain ... Very good yardage markers ... Excellent layout, fun to play, pace is great ... Well manicured, fast greens.

★★★★ NEWMAN GOLF COURSE

PU-2021 W. Nebraska, Peoria, 61604, Peoria County, (309)674-1663. **E-mail:** michellemorse5@yahoo.com. **Web:** www.peoriaparks.org. **Facility Holes:** 18. **Yards:** 6,838/5,933. **Par:** 71/74. **Course Rating:** 71.8/74.2. **Slope:** 119/120. **Green Fee:** $5/$17. **Cart Fee:** $18/Cart. **Walking Policy:** Unrestricted walking. **Walkability:** 3. **Opened:** 1934. **Season:** March-Jan. **High:** April-Nov. **To obtain tee times:** Call up to 6 days in advance. **Miscellaneous:** Reduced fees (weekdays, twilight, juniors), credit cards (MC, V, D), FF.

Reader Comments: Best public course in Peoria ... Tough from back tees ... Nice layout.

★★½ NORDIC HILLS RESORT

R-Nordic Rd., Itasca, 60143, Du Page County, (630)773-2750, 20 miles from Chicago. **Facility Holes:** 18. **Yards:** 5,732/4,747. **Par:** 70/72. **Course Rating:** 67.9/69.6. **Slope:** 115/118. **Green Fee:** $17/$35. **Cart Fee:** Included in green fee. **Walking Policy:** Walking at certain times. **Walkability:** 3. **Architect:** Charles Maddox/Frank P. MacDonald. **Season:** March-Nov. **High:** May-Sept. **To obtain tee times:** Call up to 14 days in advance. **Miscellaneous:** Reduced fees (weekdays, twilight), credit cards (MC, V, AE, D), FF.

★★★ OAK BROOK GOLF CLUB

PU-2606 York Rd., Oak Brook, 60523, Du Page County, (630)990-3032, 15 miles from Chicago. **Facility Holes:** 18. **Yards:** 6,541/5,341. **Par:** 72/72. **Course Rating:** 71.1/70.7. **Slope:** 126/120. **Green Fee:** $40/$44. **Cart Fee:** $14/Person. **Walking Policy:** Walking at certain times. **Walkability:** 2. **Opened:** 1980. **Architect:** Roger Packard. **Season:** April-Nov. **High:** May-Sept. **To obtain tee times:** Call up to 7 days in advance. **Miscellaneous:** Reduced fees (twilight), range (grass), credit cards (MC, V, AE), BF, FF.

Reader Comments: Nice—not great ... Two different 9s ... Really great value considering urban location. Challenging and long. Great greens. Nice layout with some water ... Nothing exceptional ... Management is super.

★★★ OAK BROOK GOLF COURSE

PU-9157 Fruit Rd., Edwardsville, 62025, Madison County, (618)656-5600, 30 miles from St. Louis. **Facility Holes:** 27. **Yards:** 6,641/5,176. **Par:** 71/71. **Course Rating:** 68.2/67.2. **Slope:** 113/103. **Green Fee:** $15/$17. **Cart Fee:** $10/Person. **Walking Policy:** Unrestricted walking. **Walkability:** 3. **Opened:** 1972. **Architect:** Larry Suhre. **Season:** Year-round. **To obtain tee times:** Call up to 7 days in advance. **Miscellaneous:** Reduced fees (seniors, juniors), metal spikes, range (grass), credit cards (MC, V), BF, FF.

Reader Comments: One of my favorite courses ... Course gets a lot of play ... Very affordable ... Nice course, not too difficult ... Fair with a lot of risk—reward ... Pace of play was slow. Improved back 9. Nice & tight front 9.

Special Notes: Also has a 9-hole executive course.

★★★ OAK BROOK HILLS HOTEL & RESORT

R-3500 Midwest Rd., Oak Brook, 60522, Du Page County, (630)850-5530, (800)445-3315, 20 miles from Chicago. **Facility Holes:** 18. **Yards:** 6,397/4,952. **Par:** 70/69. **Course Rating:** 70.4/69.2. **Slope:** 130/120. **Green Fee:** $38/$78. **Cart Fee:** Included in green fee. **Walking Policy:** Unrestricted walking. **Walkability:** 3. **Opened:** 1987. **Architect:** Dick Nugent. **Season:** April-Dec. **To obtain tee times:** Call up to 14 days in advance. **Misc:** Reduced fees (twilight, seniors, juniors), metal spikes, lodging (384 rooms), credit cards (MC, V, AE, D, DC), BF, FF.

Reader Comments: Hotel course—nice, not great ... Beautiful fairways ... Overpriced resort course ... Fun to play. Good condition, nice facility :.. Hit all 6 par 3s in regulation.

★★★ THE OAK CLUB OF GENOA

PU-11770 Ellwood Greens Rd., Genoa, 60135, De Kalb County, (815)784-5678, 60 miles from Chicago. **E-mail:** jmgila@tbc.net. **Web:** www.oakclubofgenoa.com. **Facility Holes:** 18. **Yards:** 6,990/5,556. **Par:** 72/72. **Course Rating:** 74.1/72.5. **Slope:** 135/127. **Green Fee:** $13/$33. **Cart Fee:** Included in green fee. **Walking Policy:** Walking at certain times. **Walkability:** 3. **Opened:** 1973. **Architect:** Charles Maddox. **Season:** March-Dec.

High: May-Aug. **To obtain tee times:** Call up to 7 days in advance. **Miscellaneous:** Reduced fees (weekdays, twilight, juniors), credit cards (MC, V, AE, D), BF, FF.
Reader Comments: Quite nice! ... Water, woods & hills ... Good service and great greens ... Hidden gem—ssshhh! ... Great test of golf ... An undiscovered gem.

OAK GLEN GOLF COURSE
PU-Stoy Rd., Robinson, 62454, Crawford County, (618)592-3030, 50 miles from Effingham.
Facility Holes: 18. **Yards:** 6,086/5,220. **Par:** 71/71. **Course Rating:** 67.7/67.8. **Slope:** 112/108.
Green Fee: $15. **Cart Fee:** $20/Cart. **Walking Policy:** Unrestricted walking. **Walkability:** 2.
Opened: 1963. **Season:** March-Nov. **High:** May-Aug. **To obtain tee times:** Call golf shop.
Miscellaneous: Reduced fees (twilight), range (grass/mats).

OAK GROVE GOLF COURSE
PU-16914 Oak Grove Rd., Harvard, 60033, McHenry County, (815)648-2550, (877)648-4653, 12 miles from Lake Geneva, WI. **E-mail:** rob@oakgrovegolfcourse.com. **Web:** www.oakgrove-olfcourse.com. **Facility Holes:** 18. **Yards:** 7,021/5,254. **Par:** 71/71. **Course Rating:** 74.6/70.1.
Slope: 135/120. **Green Fee:** $65/$80. **Cart Fee:** Included in green fee. **Walking Policy:**
Mandatory carts. **Walkability:** 5. **Opened:** 1998. **Architect:** Steven Halberg. **Season:** April-Nov.
High: June-Sept. **To obtain tee times:** Call up to 365 days in advance. **Miscellaneous:**
Reduced fees (seniors, juniors), range (grass/mats), credit cards (MC, V, D), BF, FF.
Notes: 1999 Illinois P.G.A. and Stroke Play Tournament.

★★½ OAK MEADOWS GOLF CLUB
PU-900 N. Wood Dale Rd., Addison, 60101, Du Page County, (630)595-0071, 20 miles from Chicago. **Facility Holes:** 18. **Yards:** 6,718/5,954. **Par:** 71/73. **Course Rating:** 72.1/73.8.
Slope: 126/128. **Green Fee:** $30/$35. **Cart Fee:** $16/Person. **Walking Policy:** Walking at certain times. **Walkability:** 2. **Opened:** 1925. **Season:** April-Nov. **To obtain tee times:** Call up to 7 days in advance. **Miscellaneous:** Reduced fees (twilight), range (grass), credit cards (MC, V, AE, D), BF, FF.

★★½ OAK SPRINGS GOLF COURSE
PU-6740 E.3500 South Rd., St. Anne, 60964, Kankakee County, (815)937-1648, 7 miles from Kankakee. **Facility Holes:** 18. **Yards:** 6,260/5,038. **Par:** 72/72. **Course Rating:** 68.6/68.1. **Slope:** 118/111. **Green Fee:** $17/$24. **Cart Fee:** $11/Person. **Walking Policy:** Unrestricted walking.
Walkability: 3. **Opened:** 1968. **Architect:** John Krutila. **Season:** March-Nov. **High:** June-Aug.
To obtain tee times: Call up to 8 days in advance. **Miscellaneous:** Reduced fees (weekdays, twilight, seniors), credit cards (MC, V), FF.

★★★½ OAK TERRACE GOLF COURSE
PU-100 Beyers Lake Rd, Pana, 62557, Shelby County, (217)539-4477, (800)-577-7598, 30 miles from Decatur. **Web:** www.oakterrace.com. **Facility Holes:** 18. **Yards:** 6,375/4,898. **Par:** 72/72. **Course Rating:** 70.1/67.8. **Slope:** 112/107. **Green Fee:** $30/$38. **Cart Fee:** Included in green fee. **Walking Policy:** Unrestricted walking. **Walkability:** 1. **Opened:** 1991. **Season:**
March-Nov. **High:** June-Aug. **To obtain tee times:** Call golf shop. **Miscellaneous:** Reduced fees (weekdays, guests, twilight, seniors, juniors), range (grass), lodging (37 rooms), credit cards (MC, V, AE, D).
Reader Comments: The back 9 is great. Hills, ponds and lush fairways make it seem like Augusta in Illinois ... The front 9 is easy but the back 9 is tough.

★★ THE OAKS GOLF COURSE
PU-851 Dave Stockton Dr., Springfield, 62707-3116, Sangamon County, (217)528-6600.
Web: www.theoaksgolfcourse.com. **Facility Holes:** 18. **Yards:** 6,054/4,587. **Par:** 70/70. **Course Rating:** 68.4/65.5. **Slope:** 112/112. **Green Fee:** $10/$19. **Cart Fee:** $10/Person. **Walking Policy:**
Unrestricted walking. **Walkability:** 4. **Opened:** 1926. **Season:** Year-round. **High:** June-Sept. **To obtain tee times:** Call up to 7 days in advance. **Miscellaneous:** Reduced fees (weekdays, seniors, juniors), metal spikes, credit cards (MC, V), BF, FF.

★★★½ ODYSSEY COUNTRY CLUB & GOLF ACADEMY
PU-19110 S. Ridgeland, Tinley Park, 60477, Cook County, (708)429-7400, 20 miles from Chicago. **Facility Holes:** 18. **Yards:** 7,095/5,564. **Par:** 72/72. **Course Rating:** 73.1/69.3. **Slope:** 131/116. **Green Fee:** $21/$57. **Cart Fee:** $15/Person. **Walking Policy:** Walking at certain times.
Walkability: 3. **Opened:** 1992. **Architect:** Harry Bowers/Curtis Strange. **Season:** March-Nov.
High: May-Oct. **To obtain tee times:** Call up to 14 days in advance. **Miscellaneous:** Reduced fees (weekdays, twilight), metal spikes, range (grass/mats), credit cards (MC, V, AE), BF, FF.
Reader Comments: Layout is challenging, but fair. Staff is nice ... Getting expensive ... Lots of water, plenty of sand, easy to walk ... Big slick greens ... 9s should be reversed ... A little too open to the wind. Too short from men's regular tees.

★★★½ OLD OAK COUNTRY CLUB

PU-14200 S. Parker Rd., Lockport, 60441, Will County, (708)301-3344, 19 miles from Chicago. **Facility Holes:** 18. **Yards:** 6,535/5,274. **Par:** 71/72. **Course Rating:** 70.1. **Slope:** 124. **Green Fee:** $29/$60. **Cart Fee:** $15/Person. **Walking Policy:** Walking at certain times. **Walkability:** 2. **Opened:** 1926. **Architect:** Kingman. **Season:** April-Nov. **High:** June-Aug. **To obtain tee times:** Call up to 7 days in advance. **Miscellaneous:** Reduced fees (weekdays, twilight, seniors, juniors), credit cards (MC, V, D), BF, FF.
Reader Comments: Much improved ... Beautiful course—nice fairways and greens, must be accurate on all clubs ... Fun to play old course ... Surprising tree-lined track with reasonable hills ... Average course, average priced, needs more sand.

★★★ OLD ORCHARD COUNTRY CLUB

PU-700 W. Rand Rd., Mt. Prospect, 60056, Cook County, (847)255-2025, 10 miles from Chicago. **E-mail:** mheidk123@aol.com. **Facility Holes:** 18. **Yards:** 6,119/5,731. **Par:** 70/70. **Course Rating:** 70.1/68.7. **Slope:** 131/127. **Green Fee:** $36/$55. **Cart Fee:** Included in green fee. **Walking Policy:** Walking at certain times. **Walkability:** 2. **Opened:** 1930. **Architect:** Al Wickersham. **Season:** March-Dec. **High:** May-Sept. **To obtain tee times:** Call up to 14 days in advance. **Miscellaneous:** Reduced fees (weekdays, twilight), metal spikes, credit cards (MC, V, AE, D, DC), BF, FF.
Reader Comments: Short, tight course in great condition. Pace of play can get pretty slow ... Playable, great doglegs ... No range, nice course.

★★ ORCHARD HILLS GOLF COURSE

PU-38342 N. Green Bay Rd., Waukegan, 60087, Lake County, (847)336-5118, 40 miles from Chicago. **Facility Holes:** 18. **Yards:** 6,458/5,448. **Par:** 71/71. **Course Rating:** 69.7/65.3. **Slope:** 107/96. **Green Fee:** $26/$28. **Cart Fee:** $13/Person. **Walking Policy:** Walking at certain times. **Walkability:** 2. **Opened:** 1930. **Architect:** Robert Bruce Harris. **Season:** Year-round. **To obtain tee times:** Call up to 7 days in advance. **Miscellaneous:** Reduced fees (weekdays, twilight), range (grass), credit cards (MC, V, D), FF.

★★★★½ ORCHARD VALLEY GOLF CLUB *Value*

PU-2411 W. Illinois Ave., Aurora, 60506, Kane County, (630)907-0500, 35 miles from Chicago. **Facility Holes:** 18. **Yards:** 6,745/5,162. **Par:** 72/72. **Course Rating:** 72.8/70.3. **Slope:** 134/123. **Green Fee:** $48/$55. **Cart Fee:** $14/Person. **Walking Policy:** Unrestricted walking. **Walkability:** 2. **Opened:** 1993. **Architect:** Ken Kavanaugh. **Season:** April-Nov. **To obtain tee times:** Call up to 10 days in advance. **Miscellaneous:** Reduced fees (twilight, seniors, juniors), range (grass/mats), credit cards (MC, V, AE, D), BF, FF.
Reader Comments: Several holes cut around lakes and wetlands ... Fairways & greens in perfect shape, a well-planned facility ... Great value, tough course from backs ... Best par 3s and great staff ... 10 minute intervals on tee times are a huge plus! Female-friendly layout ... Good variety of holes. Use every club.

★★★½ THE ORCHARDS GOLF CLUB

PU-1499 Golf Course Dr., Belleville, 62220, St. Clair County, (618)233-8921, (800)452-0358, 20 miles from St. Louis. **Facility Holes:** 18. **Yards:** 6,405/5,001. **Par:** 71/71. **Course Rating:** 69.0/70.1. **Slope:** 121/120. **Green Fee:** $24/$35. **Walking Policy:** Walking at certain times. **Walkability:** 3. **Opened:** 1991. **Architect:** Bob Goalby. **Season:** Year-round. **High:** April-Oct. **To obtain tee times:** Call golf shop. **Miscellaneous:** Reduced fees (weekdays, twilight, seniors, juniors), range (grass), credit cards (MC, V, AE).
Reader Comments: Great layout, a pleasure to play ... A quirk here an there but pretty ... Nicepriced course ... Good course to shoot well ... Long, tight, tough. Beautiful facilities and staff.

★★★ PALATINE HILLS GOLF COURSE

PU-512 W. Northwest Hwy., Palatine, 60067, Cook County, (847)359-4020, 25 miles from Chicago. **Facility Holes:** 18. **Yards:** 6,800/5,975. **Par:** 72/72. **Course Rating:** 72.5/73.9. **Slope:** 128/127. **Green Fee:** $32/$37. **Cart Fee:** $14/Person. **Walking Policy:** Unrestricted walking. **Walkability:** 3. **Opened:** 1965. **Architect:** Edward L. Packard. **Season:** April-Nov. **To obtain tee times:** Call golf shop. **Miscellaneous:** Reduced fees (weekdays, twilight), metal spikes, range (grass/mats), credit cards (MC, V), BF, FF.
Reader Comments: Good for municipal course ... Long even from the whites, deceptively tricky ... Well-kept greens and fairways. Good test of golf. You'll need every club in your bag ... Solid park district golf ... Fun course to play.

★★ PALOS COUNTRY CLUB

PU-13100 S.W. Hwy., Palos Park, 60464, Cook County, (708)448-6550, 30 miles from Chicago. **Web:** www.paloscountryclub.com. **Facility Holes:** 27. **Green Fee:** $29/$40. **Cart Fee:** $30/Cart. **Walking Policy:** Walking at certain times. **Walkability:** 3. **Opened:** 1917. **Architect:** Charles Maddox/Frank P. MacDonald. **Season:** Year-round. **High:** March-Oct. **To obtain tee**

times: Call golf shop. **Miscellaneous:** Reduced fees (weekdays, twilight, seniors), range (grass/mats), credit cards (MC, V), BF, FF.
BLUE/WHITE (18 Combo)
Yards: 6,701/5,873. **Par:** 72/72. **Course Rating:** 71.3/72.9. **Slope:** 127/124.
RED/BLUE (18 Combo)
Yards: 6,007/5,215. **Par:** 72/72. **Course Rating:** 68.7/69.7. **Slope:** 118/117.
RED/WHITE (18 Combo)
Yards: 6,076/5,280. **Par:** 70/70. **Course Rating:** 69.1/70.1. **Slope:** 120/119.

PARK HILLS GOLF CLUB
PU-3240 W. Stephenson Road, Freeport, 61032, Stephenson County, (815)235-3611, 100 miles from Chicago. **Facility Holes:** 36. **Green Fee:** $20/$24. **Cart Fee:** $11/Person. **Walking Policy:** Unrestricted walking. **Walkability:** 3. **Architect:** C.D. Wagstaff. **Season:** April-Nov. **High:** June-Aug. **To obtain tee times:** Call golf shop. **Miscellaneous:** Reduced fees (weekdays, juniors), metal spikes, range (grass), credit cards (MC, V), BF, FF.
★★★½ **EAST COURSE** (18)
Yards: 6,477/5,401. **Par:** 72/72. **Course Rating:** 69.9/69.8. **Slope:** 116/115. **Opened:** 1955.
Reader Comments: One of the best public courses in Illinois. Tremendous value, especially for a course of this caliber, design and condition. Exceptional pace of play … Well-run club … Holes 12-16 toughest set of holes you'll face on a muni.
★★★½ **WEST COURSE** (18)
Yards: 6,622/5,940. **Par:** 72/73. **Course Rating:** 71.3/76.2. **Slope:** 121/127. **Opened:** 1966.
Reader Comments: An outstanding course, very mature course and very well kept … Stunning scenery, challenging length and layout, top-level maintenance. Best public value in area. Pace is never a problem … Hard par 3s and long par 5s.

★★ **PARKVIEW GOLF COURSE**
PU-2300 Broadway, Pekin, 61554, Tazewell County, (309)346-8494, 12 miles from Peoria. **Facility Holes:** 18. **Yards:** 6,002/5,376. **Par:** 70/76. **Course Rating:** 65.4/63.6. **Slope:** 102/100. **Green Fee:** $7/$17. **Cart Fee:** $18/Cart. **Walking Policy:** Unrestricted walking. **Walkability:** 3. **Season:** Year-round. **High:** May-Aug. **To obtain tee times:** Call up to 7 days in advance. **Miscellaneous:** Reduced fees (weekdays, twilight, seniors, juniors), credit cards (MC, V), FF.

★★½ **PHEASANT RUN RESORT GOLF COURSE**
R-4051 East Main St., St. Charles, 60174, Kane County, (630)584-4914, 40 miles from Chicago. **E-mail:** djohnson@pheasantrun.com. **Web:** www.pheasantrun.com. **Facility Holes:** 18. **Yards:** 6,315/5,109. **Par:** 71/72. **Course Rating:** 70.4/71.1. **Slope:** 123/120. **Green Fee:** $22/$45. **Cart Fee:** Included in green fee. **Walking Policy:** Unrestricted walking. **Walkability:** 2. **Opened:** 1963. **Architect:** Bill Maddox. **Season:** March-Nov. **High:** June-Sept. **To obtain tee times:** Call up to 7 days in advance. **Miscellaneous:** Reduced fees (weekdays, twilight, juniors), metal spikes, lodging (473 rooms), credit cards (MC, V, AE, D, DC), FF.

★½ **PHILLIPS PARK GOLF COURSE**
PU-901 Moses Dr., Aurora, 60507, Kane County, (630)898-7352, 40 miles from Chicago. **Facility Holes:** 18. **Yards:** 5,634. **Par:** 71. **Course Rating:** 66.8. **Slope:** 109. **Green Fee:** $15/$20. **Cart Fee:** $21/Cart. **Walking Policy:** Unrestricted walking. **Walkability:** 4. **Opened:** 1930. **Season:** March-Nov. **High:** June-Sept. **To obtain tee times:** Call golf shop. **Miscellaneous:** Reduced fees (twilight), metal spikes, credit cards (MC, V).

★★½ **PINE LAKES GOLF CLUB**
PU-25130 Schuck Rd., Washington, 61571, Tazewell County, (309)745-9344. **Facility Holes:** 18. **Yards:** 6,385/5,187. **Par:** 71/72. **Course Rating:** 69.9/69.8. **Slope:** 119/117. **Green Fee:** $15/$20. **Cart Fee:** $18/Cart. **Walking Policy:** Unrestricted walking. **Walkability:** 3. **Opened:** 1963. **Architect:** Day Ault. **Season:** March-Nov. **High:** June-Sept. **To obtain tee times:** Call up to 6 days in advance. **Miscellaneous:** Credit cards (MC, V), BF, FF.

★★★★½ **PINE MEADOW GOLF CLUB** *Condition, Pace*
PU-1 Pine Meadow Lane, Mundelein, 60060, Lake County, (847)566-4653, 30 miles from Chicago. **E-mail:** pinemeadow@ameritech.net. **Web:** www.pinemeadowgc.com. **Facility Holes:** 18. **Yards:** 7,141/5,203. **Par:** 72/71. **Course Rating:** 74.6/70.9. **Slope:** 138/125. **Green Fee:** $75. **Cart Fee:** $31/Cart. **Walking Policy:** Unrestricted walking. **Walkability:** 2. **Opened:** 1985. **Architect:** Joe Lee/Rocky Roquemore. **Season:** March-Dec. **High:** May-Nov. **To obtain tee times:** Call up to 120 days in advance. **Miscellaneous:** Reduced fees (twilight, juniors), range (grass/mats), caddies, credit cards (MC, V, D, DC), BF, FF.
Notes: Ranked 11th in 1999 Best in State; 27th in 1996 America's Top 75 Upscale Courses.
Reader Comments: A bit pricey, but a must at least once a season … Difficult rough … Excellent course regardless of handicap … Excellent practice facilities … Basic holes with dramatic changes makes course very memorable … Beautiful, scenic … For the money, a great challenge, especially from the tips.

ILLINOIS

★★★ PINECREST GOLF & COUNTRY CLUB
PU-11220 Algonquin Rd., Huntley, 60142, McHenry County, (847)669-3111, 50 miles from Chicago. **Web:** www.pinecrestgc.com. **Facility Holes:** 18. **Yards:** 6,636/5,061. **Par:** 72/72. **Course Rating:** 71.4/68.9. **Slope:** 119/112. **Green Fee:** $28/$49. **Cart Fee:** $14/Person. **Walking Policy:** Walking at certain times. **Walkability:** 2. **Opened:** 1972. **Architect:** Ted Lockie/Bob Lohmann. **Season:** March-Dec. **High:** May-Oct. **To obtain tee times:** Call up to 14 days in advance. **Miscellaneous:** Reduced fees (twilight, seniors, juniors), metal spikes, range (grass), credit cards (MC, V, AE, D), BF, FF.
Reader Comments: With the housing boom, this course will get a lot of play … Fine greens, but fairway turn makes iron play difficult … Well maintained & managed … Good old course, fast greens, good par 3s … Nice people, nice course.

★★★★½ PIPER GLEN GOLF CLUB *Value*
PU-7112 Piper Glen Dr., Springfield, 62707, Sangamon County, (217)483-6537, 100 miles from St. Louis, MO. **E-mail:** proshop@piperglen.com. **Web:** www.piperglen.com. **Facility Holes:** 18. **Yards:** 6,985/5,138. **Par:** 72/72. **Course Rating:** 73.6/70.3. **Slope:** 133/123. **Green Fee:** $28/$33. **Cart Fee:** $12/Person. **Walking Policy:** Unrestricted walking. **Walkability:** 4. **Opened:** 1996. **Architect:** Bob Lohmann. **Season:** March-Dec. **High:** May-Sept. **To obtain tee times:** Call up to 7 days in advance. **Miscellaneous:** Reduced fees (weekdays, seniors, juniors), range (grass), credit cards (MC, V, D), BF, FF.
Reader Comments: Challenging, but fair. Good shots are rewarded poor shots make for a long day. Pin placements can be killers. Never be above the hole … Great course, great service. Two 9s that are quite a bit different but very challenging … Excellent fairways. Greens putt true, but are just average speed.

★★★½ PLUM TREE NATIONAL GOLF CLUB
PU-19511 Lembcke Rd., Harvard, 60033, McHenry County, (815)943-7474, (800)851-3578, 35 miles from Chicago. **Web:** www.plumtreegolf.com. **Facility Holes:** 18. **Yards:** 6,648/5,954. **Par:** 72/72. **Course Rating:** 71.8/74.9. **Slope:** 126/132. **Green Fee:** $44/$65. **Cart Fee:** Included in green fee. **Walking Policy:** Walking at certain times. **Walkability:** 3. **Opened:** 1969. **Architect:** Joe Lee. **Season:** March-Nov. **High:** June-Aug. **To obtain tee times:** Call golf shop. **Miscellaneous:** Reduced fees (weekdays, twilight, seniors, juniors), range (grass), credit cards (MC, V, AE, D), BF, FF.
Reader Comments: Hard to get to but one of the best, awesome greens … Worth the ride … Another hidden jewel! … Doglegs make course good test of driving … Not crowded, even on weekends … Great course, excellent conditions.

★★★½ PONTIAC ELKS COUNTRY CLUB
SP-Rte. 116 W., Pontiac, 61764, Livingston County, (815)842-1249, 100 miles from Chicago. **Facility Holes:** 18. **Yards:** 6,804/5,507. **Par:** 72/72. **Course Rating:** 72.2/70.6. **Slope:** 122/113. **Green Fee:** $18/$22. **Cart Fee:** $11/Person. **Walking Policy:** Unrestricted walking. **Walkability:** 2. **Opened:** 1975. **Season:** March-Nov. **High:** June-Sept. **To obtain tee times:** Call up to 7 days in advance. **Miscellaneous:** Range (grass), credit cards (MC, V), FF.
Reader Comments: Good layout, needs work … One of my top 2 to play … Hole No. 1—tough hole … Great food, tight front 9, excellent greens … Mix of old & modern, fast greens, challenging

★★½ POPLAR CREEK COUNTRY CLUB
PU-1400 Poplar Creek Dr., Hoffman Estates, 60194, Cook County, (847)781-3681, 30 miles from Chicago. **E-mail:** jamannina@yahoo.com. **Web:** www.heparks.org. **Facility Holes:** 18. **Yards:** 6,311/5,402. **Par:** 70/70. **Course Rating:** 70.2/69.8. **Slope:** 126/122. **Green Fee:** $15/$35. **Cart Fee:** $28/Cart. **Walking Policy:** Walking at certain times. **Walkability:** 2. **Opened:** 1971. **Architect:** Dick Nugent/Ken Killian. **Season:** March-Nov. **To obtain tee times:** Call up to 7 days in advance. **Miscellaneous:** Reduced fees (weekdays, twilight, seniors, juniors), range (grass/mats), credit cards (MC, V, AE, D), BF, FF.

★★★ POTTAWATOMIE GOLF COURSE
PU-845 N. 2nd Ave., St. Charles, 60174, Kane County, (630)584-8356, 50 miles from Chicago. **E-mail:** pgc.wheeler@juno.com. **Facility Holes:** 9. **Yards:** 3,005/2,546. **Par:** 35/37. **Course Rating:** 69.4/69.6. **Slope:** 118/115. **Green Fee:** $30. **Cart Fee:** $30/Cart. **Walking Policy:** Unrestricted walking. **Walkability:** 2. **Opened:** 1939. **Architect:** Robert Trent Jones. **Season:** March-Dec. **High:** May-Sept. **To obtain tee times:** Call golf shop. **Miscellaneous:** Credit cards (MC, V, D), BF, FF.
Reader Comments: A quite nice 9-holer adjacent to the Fox River … Good walking course … Easy fairways, tough greens, great island green.

★★★★ PRAIRIE BLUFF GOLF CLUB *Value*
PU-19433 Renwick Rd., Lockport, 60441, Will County, (815)836-4653, 30 miles from Chicago. **Facility Holes:** 18. **Yards:** 6,832/5,314. **Par:** 72/72. **Course Rating:** 72.1/70.1. **Slope:**

122/115. **Green Fee:** $29/$37. **Cart Fee:** $13/Person. **Walking Policy:** Unrestricted walking. **Walkability:** 3. **Opened:** 1998. **Architect:** Roger Packard/Andy North. **Season:** March-Dec. **High:** June-Sept. **To obtain tee times:** Call up to 7 days in advance. **Miscellaneous:** Reduced fees (weekdays, twilight, seniors, juniors), range (grass), credit cards (MC, V, AE, D), BF, FF. **Reader Comments:** Some interesting holes on the back 9 …Great use of the old Joliet Prison farm! … In top condition year-round and changing winds make it a new challenge every time you play it … Great clubhouse, great practice facility.

★★★½ PRAIRIE ISLE GOLF CLUB
SP-2216 Rte. 176, Prairie Grove, 60012, McHenry County, (815)356-0202, 50 miles from Chicago. **E-mail:** prairiepro@aol.com. **Facility Holes:** 18. **Yards:** 6,562/5,398. **Par:** 72/73. **Course Rating:** 70.8/71.3. **Slope:** 124/117. **Green Fee:** $26/$43. **Cart Fee:** $14/Person. **Walking Policy:** Walking at certain times. **Walkability:** 2. **Opened:** 1994. **Architect:** Gordon Cunningham. **Season:** March-Dec. **High:** May-Oct. **To obtain tee times:** Call up to 14 days in advance. **Miscellaneous:** Reduced fees (weekdays, twilight, seniors, juniors), credit cards (MC, V, AE, D), BF, FF. **Reader Comments:** A good variety of holes and elevations … Good course, good value … Very nice for the price … A great mix of holes, always in great shape, friendly staff … Good par 3s … A number of distinctive holes.

★★★★ PRAIRIE LANDING GOLF CLUB
PU-2325 Longest Dr., West Chicago, 60185, Du Page County, (630)208-7600, 30 miles from Chicago. **E-mail:** plshop@aol.com. **Web:** www.prairielanding.com. **Facility Holes:** 18. **Yards:** 6,862/4,859. **Par:** 72/72. **Course Rating:** 73.8/69.3. **Slope:** 131/119. **Green Fee:** $58/$90. **Cart Fee:** Included in green fee. **Walking Policy:** Unrestricted walking. **Walkability:** 3. **Opened:** 1994. **Architect:** Robert Trent Jones,Jr. **Season:** April-Nov. **High:** May-Oct. **To obtain tee times:** Call up to 14 days in advance. **Miscellaneous:** Reduced fees (twilight, juniors), metal spikes, range (grass), credit cards (MC, V, AE, D, DC), BF, FF. **Reader Comments:** Practice holes are a nice added bonus … Wide fairways and fast greens: Good practice facility … Usual windy conditions increase difficulty … Treeless but tough … Great service … Design holds interest for repeated play.

★★★★ PRAIRIE VISTA GOLF COURSE *Value*
PU-502 W. Hamilton Rd., Bloomington, 61704, McLean County, (309)434-2217, 140 miles from Chicago. **E-mail:** nsampson@cityblm.org. **Web:** www.prairievistagc.com. **Facility Holes:** 18. **Yards:** 6,748/5,224. **Par:** 72/71. **Course Rating:** 71.8/68.9. **Slope:** 128/114. **Green Fee:** $20/$25. **Cart Fee:** $11/Person. **Walking Policy:** Unrestricted walking. **Walkability:** 3. **Opened:** 1991. **Architect:** Roger B. Packard. **Season:** March-Nov. **High:** May-Sept. **To obtain tee times:** Call up to 7 days in advance. **Miscellaneous:** Reduced fees (twilight, seniors, juniors), range (grass/mats), credit cards (MC, V, AE, D), BF, FF. **Reader Comments:** Challenging, hilly conditions. Excellent greens … Very nice—complete experience … Open, windy, but well maintained with bent-grass fairways and a good variety of holes—fun to play and worth the green fee.

★★★★ PRAIRIEVIEW GOLF COURSE
PU-7993 N. River Rd., Byron, 61010, Ogle County, (815)234-4653, 12 miles from Rockford. **Web:** www.prairieview.com. **Facility Holes:** 18. **Yards:** 7,117/5,269. **Par:** 72/72. **Course Rating:** 72.3/71.6. **Slope:** 123/117. **Green Fee:** $24/$30. **Cart Fee:** $24/Cart. **Walking Policy:** Unrestricted walking. **Walkability:** 4. **Opened:** 1992. **Architect:** William James Spear. **Season:** March-Nov. **High:** June-Aug. **To obtain tee times:** Call up to 7 days in advance. **Misc:** Reduced fees (weekdays, twilight, seniors, juniors), range (grass/mats), credit cards (MC, V, D), BF, FF. **Reader Comments:** Great elevated tees … Commitment to continual course improvements. Some real signature holes where strategy becomes key . … Super layout using Mother Nature. Long and tough … Excellent place to play.

★½ PRESTBURY COUNTRY CLUB
PU-Golfview & Hankes, Sugar Grove, 60554, Kane County, (630)466-4177. **Facility Holes:** 18. **Yards:** 5,516/4,651. **Par:** 69/69. **Course Rating:** 65.1/64.9. **Slope:** 106/110. **Green Fee:** $16/$26. **Cart Fee:** $26/Cart. **Walking Policy:** Unrestricted walking. **Walkability:** 1. **Season:** March-Sept. **High:** May-Aug. **To obtain tee times:** Call golf shop. **Miscellaneous:** Reduced fees (weekdays, twilight, seniors, juniors), credit cards (MC, V).

★★½ QUAIL MEADOWS GOLF COURSE
PU-2215 Centennial Dr., Washington, 61571, Tazewell County, (309)694-3139, 3 miles from Peoria. **E-mail:** quailtom@worldnet.att.net. **Facility Holes:** 18. **Yards:** 6,647/5,492. **Par:** 72/72. **Course Rating:** 71.3/71.6. **Slope:** 121/117. **Green Fee:** $12/$17. **Cart Fee:** $18/Cart. **Walking Policy:** Unrestricted walking. **Walkability:** 2. **Opened:** 1972. **Season:** March-Dec. **High:** May-Sept. **To obtain tee times:** Call up to 7 days in advance. **Miscellaneous:** Reduced fees (twilight, seniors, juniors), metal spikes, range (grass), credit cards (MC, V), BF, FF.

★★★★ **THE RAIL GOLF CLUB**

PU-1400 S. Clubhouse Dr., Springfield, 62707, Sangamon County, (217)525-0365, 100 miles from St. Louis, MO. **Web:** www.therailgc.com. **Facility Holes:** 18. **Yards:** 6,583/5,406. **Par:** 72/72. **Course Rating:** 71.1/70.6. **Slope:** 120/116. **Green Fee:** $30/$38. **Cart Fee:** $12/Person. **Walking Policy:** Unrestricted walking. **Walkability:** 2. **Opened:** 1968. **Architect:** Robert Trent Jones. **Season:** March-Dec. **High:** May-Oct. **To obtain tee times:** Call up to 10 days in advance. **Miscellaneous:** Reduced fees (weekdays, seniors, juniors), range (grass), credit cards (MC, V, AE, D), BF, FF.
Notes: LPGA State Farm Rail Classic.
Reader Comments: Challenging golf with water hazards, greens fast, flat topography ... Good greens. LPGA Tour stop usually in good condition ... Always well maintained ... Lots of traps make this course tough.

★★★½ **RAILSIDE GOLF CLUB**

PU-120 W. 19th St., Gibson City, 60936, Ford County, (217)784-5000, 25 miles from Bloomington. **E-mail:** golf@railside.com. **Web:** www.railside.com. **Facility Holes:** 18. **Yards:** 6,801/5,320. **Par:** 72/72. **Course Rating:** 71.8/69.9. **Slope:** 122/114. **Green Fee:** $19/$22. **Cart Fee:** $13/Person. **Walking Policy:** Unrestricted walking. **Walkability:** 2. **Opened:** 1993. **Architect:** Paul Loague. **Season:** Feb.-Dec. **To obtain tee times:** Call golf shop. **Miscellaneous:** Reduced fees (weekdays, twilight, seniors, juniors), range (grass), credit cards (MC, V, AE, D), BF, FF.
Reader Comments: A great play-all-day deal ... good-conditioned course, uncrowded, good value with shorter holes protected by difficult greens ... Staff does a great job accommodating everyone from beginners to large outings ... Always windy.

★★★½ **RANDALL OAKS GOLF CLUB**

PU-37 W. 361 Binnie Rd., Dundee, 60118, Kane County, (847)428-5661, 35 miles from Chicago. **Facility Holes:** 18. **Yards:** 6,208/5,379. **Par:** 71/71. **Course Rating:** 70.4/71.3. **Slope:** 118/119. **Green Fee:** $18/$35. **Cart Fee:** $15/Person. **Walking Policy:** Unrestricted walking. **Walkability:** 3. **Opened:** 1966. **Architect:** William James Spear. **Season:** April-Dec. **High:** June-Sept. **To obtain tee times:** Call up to 7 days in advance. **Miscellaneous:** Reduced fees (weekdays, twilight, seniors, juniors), range (grass), credit cards (MC, V, D), BF, FF.
Reader Comments: Tough undulating greens, well maintained park district course ... Great course for price ... Tricky greens and fairways are kept in great condition ... Fun course—dogleg heaven ... Hit them straight.

★★ **RED HAWK COUNTRY CLUB**

SP-Rte. 154, Tamaroa, 62888, Perry County, (618)357-9704. **Facility Holes:** 18. **Yards:** 6,111/4,343. **Par:** 70/71. **Course Rating:** 69.5/68.0. **Slope:** 111/97. **Green Fee:** $15/$20. **Cart Fee:** $10/Person. **Walking Policy:** Unrestricted walking. **Walkability:** 3. **Opened:** 1921. **Season:** Year-round. **To obtain tee times:** Call golf shop. **Miscellaneous:** Range (grass), credit cards (MC, V), BF, FF.

★★★½ **REDTAIL GOLF CLUB**

PU-7900 Redtail Dr., Lakewood, 60014, McHenry County, (815)477-0055, 30 miles from Chicago. **Web:** www.redtailgolf.com. **Facility Holes:** 18. **Yards:** 6,902/5,455. **Par:** 72/72. **Course Rating:** 72.8/71.3. **Slope:** 130/122. **Green Fee:** $42/$59. **Cart Fee:** Included in green fee. **Walking Policy:** Walking at certain times. **Walkability:** 3. **Opened:** 1991. **Architect:** Roger Packard. **Season:** March-Nov. **High:** May-Sept. **To obtain tee times:** Call up to 14 days in advance. **Miscellaneous:** Reduced fees (weekdays, twilight, seniors, juniors), range (grass), credit cards (MC, V, AE, D), BF, FF.
Reader Comments: Good elevation changes, good mix of holes ... Great value ... Tough challenging course ... Much improved ... Fun par 3s, par 5s within reach ... Requires variety of shots.

★★★★½ **REND LAKE GOLF COURSE** *Value*

PU-12476 Golf Course Dr., Whittington, 62897, Franklin County, (618)629-2353, (800)999-0977, 90 miles from St. Louis, MO. **E-mail:** golf@rendlake.org. **Web:** www.rendlake.org. **Facility Holes:** 27. **Green Fee:** $25/$29. **Cart Fee:** $10/Person. **Walking Policy:** Walking at certain times. **Walkability:** 3. **Opened:** 1976. **Architect:** Edward Lawrence Packard. **Season:** March-Nov. **High:** May-Oct. **To obtain tee times:** Call golf shop. **Miscellaneous:** Reduced fees (weekdays, twilight, seniors), lodging (62 rooms), credit cards (MC, V, AE), BF, FF.
EAST/SOUTH (18 Combo)
Yards: 6,861/5,830. **Par:** 72/72. **Course Rating:** 72.2/72.5. **Slope:** 130/116.
EAST/WEST (18 Combo)
Yards: 6,812/5,849. **Par:** 72/72. **Course Rating:** 71.8/72.6. **Slope:** 131/116.
WEST/SOUTH (18 Combo)
Yards: 6,835/5,861. **Par:** 72/72. **Course Rating:** 73.0/72.6. **Slope:** 133/116.

Reader Comments: 27 holes of pure pleasure … Best & cheapest course to play, Great greens. Excellent value … Beautiful course, but challenging … Beautifully manicured fairways … Zoysia fairways takes getting use to … A nice layout.

★★★ RENWOOD GOLF COURSE
PU-701 E. Shorewood Rd., Round Lake Beach, 60073, Lake County, (847)231-4711, 50 miles from Chicago. **Facility Holes:** 18. **Yards:** 6,062/5,445. **Par:** 72/72. **Course Rating:** 69.1/71.1. **Slope:** 123/122. **Green Fee:** $16/$32. **Cart Fee:** $13/Person. **Walking Policy:** Unrestricted walking. **Walkability:** 1. **Opened:** 1920. **Season:** April-Nov. **High:** June-Sept. **To obtain tee times:** Call up to 7 days in advance. **Misc:** Reduced fees (weekdays, twilight, seniors, juniors), range (mats), credit cards (MC, V, AE, D), BF, FF.
Reader Comments: Nice short course. Well worth the very inexpensive cost … Easy course but very short par 4s really slow down pace … Will improve with addition of clubhouse, more parking.

★★½ RIVER OAKS GOLF COURSE
PU-1 Park Ave., Calumet City, 60409, Cook County, (708)366-9466, 3 miles from Chicago. **Facility Holes:** 18. **Yards:** 5,863/5,457. **Par:** 72/72. **Course Rating:** 68.6/73.6. **Slope:** 115/123. **Green Fee:** $6/$21. **Cart Fee:** $21/Cart. **Walking Policy:** Unrestricted walking. **Walkability:** 2. **Opened:** 1976. **Architect:** Dick Nugent. **Season:** April-Dec. **High:** May-Nov. **To obtain tee times:** Call up to 7 days in advance. **Miscellaneous:** Reduced fees (weekdays, twilight, seniors, juniors), metal spikes, credit cards (MC, V, AE, D), BF, FF.

★★★ ROLLING HILLS GOLF COURSE
PU-5801 Pierce Lane, Godfrey, 62035, Madison County, (618)466-8363, 15 miles from St. Louis. **E-mail:** rollinhills@piasrnet.com. **Facility Holes:** 18. **Yards:** 5,687/4,814. **Par:** 71/71. **Course Rating:** 66.1/66.5. **Slope:** 100/101. **Green Fee:** $16/$18. **Cart Fee:** $11/Person. **Walking Policy:** Unrestricted walking. **Walkability:** 3. **Opened:** 1964. **Season:** Year-round. **High:** April-Sept. **To obtain tee times:** Call golf shop. **Miscellaneous:** Reduced fees (twilight, seniors, juniors), range (grass), credit cards (MC, V, AE, D, Diners Club).
Reader Comments: Fun course, friendly staff … Short & fun course … Good practice course.

★★★½ RUFFLED FEATHERS GOLF CLUB
SP-1 Pete Dye Dr., Lemont, 60439, Cook County, (630)257-1000, 20 miles from Chicago. **E-mail:** gluvsj@aol.com. **Facility Holes:** 18. **Yards:** 6,878/5,273. **Par:** 72/72. **Course Rating:** 73.1/65.7. **Slope:** 134/110. **Green Fee:** $55/$125. **Cart Fee:** Included in green fee. **Walking Policy:** Unrestricted walking. **Walkability:** 2. **Opened:** 1992. **Architect:** Pete Dye/P. B. Dye. **Season:** April-Nov. **High:** May-Sept. **To obtain tee times:** Call up to 14 days in advance. **Miscellaneous:** Reduced fees (weekdays, twilight), range (grass/mats), credit cards (MC, V, AE, D, DC), BF, FF.
Notes: Ranked 23rd in 1999 Best in State.
Reader Comments: A great layout with water on most holes. Difficult to judge distances playing for the first time … Good course, too pricey … Bring all facets for your game. Tough … Slightly overrated—greens were great.

SALINE GOLF & COUNTRY CLUB
SP-355 Golf Course Rd., Eldorado, 62930, Saline County, (618)273-9002. **Facility Holes:** 18. **Yards:** 5,973/5,603. **Par:** 70/70. **Course Rating:** 66.9/66.9. **Slope:** 108/103. **Green Fee:** $14/$16. **Opened:** 1962. **Season:** Year-round. **To obtain tee times:** Call golf shop. **Miscellaneous:** Metal spikes.

★★★½ THE SANCTUARY GOLF COURSE
PU-485 N. Marley Rd., New Lenox, 60451, Will County, (815)462-4653, 35 miles from Chicago. **E-mail:** servis@adsnet.com. **Facility Holes:** 18. **Yards:** 6,701/5,120. **Par:** 72/72. **Course Rating:** 72.1/69.1. **Slope:** 122/114. **Green Fee:** $21/$37. **Cart Fee:** $13/Person. **Walking Policy:** Unrestricted walking. **Walkability:** 2. **Opened:** 1996. **Architect:** Steven Halberg. **Season:** March-Dec. **High:** May-Sept. **To obtain tee times:** Call golf shop. **Miscellaneous:** Reduced fees (weekdays, twilight, seniors, juniors), range (grass/mats), credit cards (MC, V, AE, D), BF, FF.
Reader Comments: Great value for the money … Challenging course with excellent value … Hard to get to but worth it. Back 9 is pretty and tough … Tough & tight. Good layout … Several holes tricky 1st time through.

★★★ SANDY HOLLOW GOLF COURSE
PU-2500 Sandy Hollow Rd., Rockford, 61109, Winnebago County, (815)987-8836, 70 miles from Chicago. **Facility Holes:** 18. **Yards:** 6,228/5,883. **Par:** 71/76. **Course Rating:** 69.4/72.8. **Slope:** 115/120. **Green Fee:** $16/$21. **Walking Policy:** Unrestricted walking. **Walkability:** 3. **Opened:** 1930. **Architect:** Charles Dudley Wagstaff. **Season:** April-Oct. **High:** June-Aug. **To obtain tee times:** Call golf shop. **Miscellaneous:** Reduced fees (twilight), credit cards (MC, V, D).

ILLINOIS

Reader Comments: An older established course with a variety of holes that challenge your shot-making. Play can be slow, especially on weekends ... Inexpensive, fun, average course.

★★ SAUKIE GOLF CLUB
PU-3101 38th St., Rock Island, 61201, Rock Island County, (309)732-2278, 2 miles from Rock Island. **E-mail:** wcdapro@pga.com. **Facility Holes:** 18. **Yards:** 5,186/4,496. **Par:** 66/66. **Green Fee:** $14/$16. **Cart Fee:** $20/Cart. **Walking Policy:** Unrestricted walking. **Walkability:** 4. **Opened:** 1926. **Season:** Year-round. **High:** May-Aug. **To obtain tee times:** Call golf shop. **Miscellaneous:** Reduced fees (twilight, seniors, juniors), metal spikes, credit cards (MC, V).

SCHAUMBURG GOLF CLUB
PU-401 N. Roselle Rd., Schaumburg, 60194, Cook County, (847)885-9000, 30 miles from Chicago. **Facility Holes:** 27. **Walking Policy:** Unrestricted walking. **Walkability:** 3. **Opened:** 1926. **Architect:** Robert Lohmann. **Season:** April-Nov. **High:** June-Aug. **To obtain tee times:** Call up to 7 days in advance. **Miscellaneous:** Reduced fees (weekdays, twilight, seniors, juniors), range (grass/mats), credit cards (MC, V, AE, D), BF, FF.
PLAYER COURSE (9)
Yards: 3,091/2,372. **Par:** 35/35. **Course Rating:** 69.6/66.8. **Slope:** 117/114.
★★★½ **TOURNAMENT COURSE (18)**
Yards: 6,542/4,885. **Par:** 72/72. **Course Rating:** 70.7/67.5. **Slope:** 121/114. **Green Fee:** $36/$42. **Cart Fee:** $15/Person.
Reader Comments: Very good municipal course. 10-minute intervals on tee times helps pace a lot ... Bent-grass fairways and tees, elevated tees and greens give it that upscale look, yet it's still easy to shoot low scores.

★★★ SCOVILL GOLF CLUB
PU-3909 West Main St., Decatur, 62522, Macon County, (217)429-6243, 120 miles from St. Louis. **E-mail:** rick@decparks.com. **Web:** www.decatur-parks.org. **Facility Holes:** 18. **Yards:** 5,900/4,303. **Par:** 71/71. **Course Rating:** 67.8/64.8. **Slope:** 119/108. **Green Fee:** $14/$22. **Cart Fee:** $22/Cart. **Walking Policy:** Unrestricted walking. **Walkability:** 5. **Opened:** 1925. **Architect:** Dick Nugent. **Season:** March-Dec. **High:** April-Sept. **To obtain tee times:** Call up to 7 days in advance. **Miscellaneous:** Reduced fees (guests, twilight, seniors, juniors), metal spikes, range (grass/mats), credit cards (MC, V), BF, FF.
Reader Comments: Pretty course ... Moderate length, but hilly and tight. Carts are voluntary, but almost a must, due to the terrain. Good value for a muni course ... it's affordable for all.

★★★ SENICA OAK RIDGE GOLF CLUB
SP-658 E. Rte. 6, La Salle, 61301, La Salle County, (815)223-7273, 90 miles from Chicago. **E-mail:** sherrysenica@hotmail.com. **Web:** www.senicasoakridge.com. **Facility Holes:** 18. **Yards:** 6,900/5,397. **Par:** 72/72. **Course Rating:** 72.6/70.3. **Slope:** 131/120. **Green Fee:** $22/$26. **Cart Fee:** $14/Person. **Walking Policy:** Walking at certain times. **Walkability:** 4. **Opened:** 1994. **Architect:** William James Spear. **Season:** March-Nov. **High:** April-Aug. **To obtain tee times:** Call golf shop. **Miscellaneous:** Reduced fees (weekdays, seniors), range (grass/mats), credit cards (MC, V, D), BF, FF.
Reader Comments: Very nice and pleasant personnel ... Course has everything—sand, water, hills ... Very nice course. Front 9 easier than back 9.

★★★ SETTLER'S HILL GOLF COURSE
PU-919 E. Fabyan Pkwy., Batavia, 60510, Kane County, (630)232-1636, 40 miles from Chicago. **Facility Holes:** 18. **Yards:** 6,630/4,945. **Par:** 72/72. **Course Rating:** 72.1/68.9. **Slope:** 130/120. **Green Fee:** $20/$36. **Cart Fee:** $14/Person. **Walking Policy:** Unrestricted walking. **Walkability:** 4. **Opened:** 1988. **Architect:** Bob Lohmann. **Season:** March-Dec. **To obtain tee times:** Call up to 7 days in advance. **Miscellaneous:** Reduced fees (twilight, seniors, juniors), credit cards (MC, V, AE, D, DC).
Reader Comments: Great elevation changes. Great value, but pace of play on weekends is brutal ... Tough course to play in wind, 17 & 18 are great finishing holes ... Good par 5s ... Built on land-fill. Every hole an adventure ... Not a course to walk.

★★★ SEVEN BRIDGES GOLF CLUB
PU-One Mulligan Dr., Woodridge, 60517, Du Page County, (630)964-7777, 25 miles from Chicago. **Web:** www.sevenbridges.com. **Facility Holes:** 18. **Yards:** 7,118/5,277. **Par:** 72/72. **Course Rating:** 74.6/70.4. **Slope:** 135/121. **Green Fee:** $49/$99. **Cart Fee:** Included in green fee. **Walking Policy:** Unrestricted walking. **Walkability:** 3. **Opened:** 1991. **Architect:** Dick Nugent. **Season:** April-Nov. **High:** May-Oct. **To obtain tee times:** Call golf shop. **Miscellaneous:** Reduced fees (weekdays, twilight, seniors, juniors), range (grass/mats), caddies, credit cards (MC, V, AE, DC), BF, FF.
Reader Comments: You'd better like water to play here ... Fantastic layout, greens are the best ... Good, but expensive ... Good mix of old- and new-style course ... No driving range ... Great holes.

SHADY OAKS COUNTRY CLUB
PU-Rte. 52 S. Amboy, Amboy, 61310, Lee County, (815)849-5424, 110 miles from Chicago. **Facility Holes:** 18. **Yards:** 6,212/4,542. **Par:** 71/72. **Course Rating:** 69.6/66.1. **Slope:** 123/114. **Green Fee:** $14/$23. **Walking Policy:** Unrestricted walking. **Walkability:** 3. **Opened:** 1963. **Season:** March-Nov. **High:** May-Oct. **To obtain tee times:** Call up to 7 days in advance. **Misc:** Reduced fees (weekdays, twilight, seniors, juniors), credit cards (MC, V), BF, FF.

★★★ SHEPHERD'S CROOK GOLF COURSE
PU-43125 Green Bay Rd., Zion, 60099, Lake County, (847)872-2080. **Facility Holes:** 18. **Yards:** 6,769/6,002. **Par:** 71/71. **Course Rating:** 71.9/73.2. **Slope:** 126/126. **Green Fee:** $25/$35. **Cart Fee:** $26/Cart. **Walking Policy:** Unrestricted walking. **Walkability:** 3. **Opened:** 1999. **Architect:** Keith Foster. **Season:** April-Dec. **To obtain tee times:** Call up to 10 days in advance. **Miscellaneous:** Reduced fees (weekdays, twilight, seniors, juniors), credit cards (MC, V).
Reader Comments: A nice variety of par 3s, the 5s are very tough and most all the par 4s are birdie opportunities ... Will be a top course in time ... Great course, great value, needs some maturing ... New clubhouse ... Friendly staff.

SILVER LAKE COUNTRY CLUB
PU-147th St. and 82nd Ave., Orland Park, 60462, Cook County, (708)349-6940, (800)525-3465, 22 miles from Chicago. **Web:** www.silverlakecc.com. **Facility Holes:** 45. **Green Fee:** $29/$35. **Cart Fee:** $14/Person. **Walking Policy:** Unrestricted walking. **Walkability:** 2. **Season:** March-Dec. **To obtain tee times:** Call up to 14 days in advance. **Miscellaneous:** Reduced fees (weekdays, twilight, seniors, juniors), credit cards (MC, V, AE, D), BF, FF.
★★★½ **NORTH COURSE** (18)
Yards: 6,826/5,659. **Par:** 72/77. **Course Rating:** 71.9/71.5. **Slope:** 116/116. **Opened:** 1927. **Architect:** Lenoard Macomber.
Reader Comments: Challenging, fun course ... Nice course, tough from tips ... Great staff ... Long and narrow ... Lots of traffic but kept up well.
★★★½ **SOUTH COURSE** (18)
Yards: 5,948/5,138. **Par:** 70/72. **Course Rating:** 67.9/69.3. **Slope:** 108/109. **Opened:** 1929. **Architect:** Raymond Didier.
Reader Comments: Much more sporty than North Course ... More difficult than its slope rating! ... Would recommend to play ... Enough water and length for most ... 2 good courses.
Special Notes: Also has a 9-hole executive course.

★★★½ SILVER RIDGE GOLF COURSE
SP-3069 N. Hill Rd., Oregon, 61061, Ogle County, (815)734-4440, (800)762-6301, 2 miles from Oregon. **E-mail:** steven.fridley@worldnet.com. **Facility Holes:** 18. **Yards:** 6,614/5,181. **Par:** 72/72. **Course Rating:** 71.2/72.0. **Slope:** 116/106. **Green Fee:** $21/$25. **Cart Fee:** $12/Person. **Walking Policy:** Walking at certain times. **Walkability:** 5. **Opened:** 1983. **Architect:** Lowell Beggs. **Season:** Year-round. **High:** June-Aug. **To obtain tee times:** Call golf shop. **Miscellaneous:** Reduced fees (twilight, seniors, juniors), range (grass), credit cards (MC, V, D), BF, FF.
Reader Comments: Scenic, with trees and hills, and a variety of holes that challenge your shot-making ... Good use of Mother Nature. Many blind approach shots and length ... Great par 3s, accurate tee shot required, good variety of par 4s .

SINNISSIPPI GOLF COURSE
PU-1401 N. Second Street, Rockford, 61107, Winnebago County, (815)987-8889, 70 miles from Chicago. **Facility Holes:** 9. **Yards:** 3,230/2,903. **Par:** 37/38. **Walking Policy:** Unrestricted walking. **Walkability:** 4. **Opened:** 1912. **Architect:** Tom Bendelow. **Season:** April-Oct. **High:** June-Aug. **To obtain tee times:** Call golf shop. **Miscellaneous:** Credit cards (MC, V, D), BF, FF.

★★½ SNAG CREEK GOLF COURSE
PU-RR 1, Washburn, 61570, Woodford County, (309)248-7300, (309)248-7300, 25 miles from Peoria. **E-mail:** golfsnag@mtco.com. **Facility Holes:** 18. **Yards:** 6,300/5,635. **Par:** 72/73. **Course Rating:** 70.1/70.9. **Slope:** 115/116. **Green Fee:** $11/$15. **Cart Fee:** $10/Person. **Walking Policy:** Unrestricted walking. **Walkability:** 2. **Opened:** 1965. **Season:** April-Oct. **High:** June-Aug. **To obtain tee times:** Call up to 7 days in advance. **Miscellaneous:** Metal spikes, credit cards (MC, V), BF, FF.

★★ SOUTH SHORE GOLF COURSE
PU-1727 N. River South Rd., Momence, 60954, Kankakee County, (815)472-4407, 7 miles from Kankakee. **Facility Holes:** 18. **Yards:** 6,174/5,439. **Par:** 72/72. **Course Rating:** 68.9/70.2. **Slope:** 122/115. **Green Fee:** $10/$20. **Cart Fee:** $22/Person. **Walking Policy:** Unrestricted walking. **Walkability:** 2. **Opened:** 1927. **Season:** Year-round. **To obtain tee times:** Call golf shop. **Misc:** Reduced fees (weekdays, twilight, seniors), range (grass), credit cards (MC, V, D), FF.

★★★ SPARTAN MEADOWS GOLF CLUB
PU-1969 Spartan, Elgin, 60123, Kane County, (847)931-5950, 40 miles from Chicago.
Facility Holes: 18. **Yards:** 6,853/5,353. **Par:** 72/72. **Course Rating:** 72.7/70.3. **Slope:** 123/116. **Green Fee:** $19/$31. **Cart Fee:** $27/Cart. **Walking Policy:** Unrestricted walking. **Walkability:** 1. **Opened:** 1971. **Architect:** Edward Lawrence Packard/Greg Bayor. **Season:** Year-round. **High:** May-Oct. **To obtain tee times:** Call up to 7 days in advance. **Misc:** Reduced fees (weekdays, twilight, seniors, juniors), range (mats), credit cards (MC, V, D), BF, FF. **Reader Comments:** Fun and affordable ... Your first impression of a flat course will dissipate after each extremely different hole ... Low price course needing a facelift ... Great muni value ... Excellent course, flat but tough.

SPENCER T. OLIN COMMUNITY GOLF COURSE
PU-4701 College Ave., Alton, 62002, Madison County, (618)465-3111, 25 miles from St. Louis. **E-mail:** sspansick@palmergolf.com. **Web:** www.spencertolingolf.com. **Facility Holes:** 27. **Walkability:** 3. **Season:** Year-round. **Miscellaneous:** Range (grass), credit cards (MC, V, AE), BF, FF.
★★★★ SPENCER T. OLIN COURSE (18)
Yards: 6,941/5,049. **Par:** 72/72. **Course Rating:** 73.8/68.5. **Slope:** 135/117. **Green Fee:** $20/$60. **Cart Fee:** Included in green fee. **Walking Policy:** Walking at certain times. **Opened:** 1989. **Architect:** Arnold Palmer/Ed Seay. **High:** April-Oct. **To obtain tee times:** Call up to 14 days in advance. **Miscellaneous:** Reduced fees (weekdays, guests, twilight, seniors, juniors). **Reader Comments:** Challenging, best for the money ... Many excellent holes ... User friendly, fun, classy like Arnie ... Magnificent ... Requires all the shots ... All around good deal—can score well here.
SPENCER T. OLIN LEARNING CENTER COURSE (9)
Yards: 1,795/1,300. **Par:** 30/30. **Walking Policy:** Unrestricted walking. **Opened:** 2000. **Architect:** Arnold Palmer. **High:** April-Sept. **To obtain tee times:** Call golf shop. **Miscellaneous:** Reduced fees (seniors, juniors).

SPORTSMAN'S COUNTRY CLUB
PU-3535 Dundee Rd., Northbrook, 60062, Cook County, (847)291-2351, 2 miles from Deerfield. **Facility Holes:** 27. **Green Fee:** $34/$41. **Cart Fee:** $26/Cart. **Walking Policy:** Unrestricted walking. **Walkability:** 3. **Season:** March-Dec. **Miscellaneous:** Reduced fees (twilight), range (mats), credit cards (MC, V, AE), BF, FF.
★★½ 18-HOLE COURSE (18)
Yards: 6,354/5,470. **Par:** 70/72. **Course Rating:** 70.7/71.9. **Slope:** 124/122. **Opened:** 1931. **Architect:** Edward B. Dearie Jr. **To obtain tee times:** Call up to 2 days in advance.
9-HOLE COURSE (9)
Yards: 3,016/2,667. **Par:** 35/35. **Course Rating:** 34.6/35.2. **Slope:** 122/120. **Opened:** 1990. **High:** June-Sept. **To obtain tee times:** Call up to 3 days in advance.

★★ SPRING CREEK GOLF COURSE
PU-286 Golf Course Rd., Spring Valley, 61362, Bureau County, (815)894-2137, 60 miles from Peoria. **E-mail:** springcreek@thegolfcourse.com. **Facility Holes:** 18. **Yards:** 6,465/5,196. **Par:** 72/73. **Course Rating:** 71.6/70.9. **Slope:** 128/120. **Green Fee:** $16/$19. **Cart Fee:** $22/Cart. **Walking Policy:** Unrestricted walking. **Walkability:** 4. **Opened:** 1964. **Architect:** Ken Killian/Dick Nugent. **Season:** March-Nov. **High:** April-Oct. **To obtain tee times:** Call golf shop. **Miscellaneous:** Reduced fees (weekdays), range (grass), BF, FF.

★★★ SPRINGBROOK GOLF COURSE
PU-2220 83rd St., Naperville, 60564, Du Page County, (630)848-5060, 28 miles from Chicago. **Facility Holes:** 18. **Yards:** 6,896/5,850. **Par:** 72/73. **Course Rating:** 72.6/72.7. **Slope:** 124/125. **Green Fee:** $26/$48. **Cart Fee:** $14/Person. **Walking Policy:** Unrestricted walking. **Walkability:** 3. **Opened:** 1974. **Architect:** Edward Lawrence Packard. **Season:** April-Nov. **High:** May-Aug. **To obtain tee times:** Call up to 7 days in advance. **Miscellaneous:** Reduced fees (weekdays, twilight, seniors, juniors), range (grass/mats), credit cards (MC, V), BF, FF. **Reader Comments:** Resident rates great, holes 14 thru 18 are super tough! ... Traditional midwestern layout with some trees and water ... Beautiful trees—greens fast with many breaks ... Good all-around course.

ST. ANDREWS GOLF & COUNTRY CLUB
PU-3N 441 Rte. 59, West Chicago, 60185, Du Page County, (630)231-3100, 30 miles from Chicago. **Facility Holes:** 36. **Green Fee:** $30/$35. **Cart Fee:** $29/Person. **Walking Policy:** Unrestricted walking. **Walkability:** 1. **Opened:** 1926. **Season:** Year-round. **To obtain tee times:** Call golf shop. **Miscellaneous:** Reduced fees (weekdays, twilight, juniors), range (grass/mats), credit cards (MC, V, D, DC), BF, FF.
★★★ LAKEWOOD COURSE (18)
Yards: 6,666/5,353. **Par:** 72/72. **Course Rating:** 70.9/69.4. **Slope:** 115/112. **Architect:** E. B. Dearie Jr.

Reader Comments: Good place for winter golf … Old course and affordable … Great traditional course with fast play … Service excellent … Well taken care of, challenging, pace is good.

★★★½ **ST. ANDREWS COURSE** (18)
Yards: 6,759/5,138. **Par:** 71/71. **Course Rating:** 71.1/67.9. **Slope:** 116/108. **Architect:** John McGregor.
Reader Comments: Expensive, in great shape, challenging layout … A course you will always come back to … Older course, lot of trouble, fast greens … Course is always in good shape, rangers control pace.

★★★★ **STEEPLE CHASE GOLF CLUB**
PU-200 N. La Vista Dr., Mundelein, 60060, Lake County, (847)949-8900, 35 miles from Chicago. **Facility Holes:** 18. **Yards:** 6,827/4,831. **Par:** 72/72. **Course Rating:** 73.1/68.1. **Slope:** 129/113. **Green Fee:** $25/$52. **Cart Fee:** $14/Person. **Walking Policy:** Walking at certain times. **Walkability:** 3. **Opened:** 1993. **Architect:** Ken Killian. **Season:** March-Nov. **High:** June-Sept. **To obtain tee times:** Call up to 7 days in advance. **Miscellaneous:** Reduced fees (weekdays, twilight, seniors, juniors), credit cards (MC, V, AE, D), BF, FF.
Reader Comments: Enjoyable from all tee boxes … Gets better every year, awesome greens … Great finishing hole, nice clubhouse … Always in good shape. Challenging but fun. Good clubhouse … Fun layout, needs a range.

★★★½ **STONE CREEK GOLF CLUB**
PU-2600 S. Stone Creek Blvd., Urbana, 61802, Champaign County, (217)367-3000. **E-mail:** perryg@stonecreekgolfclub.com. **Web:** www.stonecreekgolfclub.com. **Facility Holes:** 18. **Yards:** 7,118/5,048. **Par:** 72/72. **Course Rating:** 73.9/68.9. **Slope:** 124/111. **Green Fee:** $32/$65. **Cart Fee:** Included in green fee. **Walking Policy:** Mandatory carts. **Walkability:** 2. **Opened:** 1999. **Architect:** Dick Nugent/Tim Nugent. **Season:** March-Dec. **High:** May-Sept. **To obtain tee times:** Call up to 14 days in advance. **Miscellaneous:** Reduced fees (weekdays, twilight, seniors, juniors), range (grass/mats), credit cards (MC, V, AE, D), BF, FF.
Reader Comments: Terrific course. Difficult from back tees. Windy conditions make this very hard. Great practice facility … Strong design with great facilities, well-conditioned … A lot of variety … A bit pricey, but very professional.

STONE CREEK GOLF CLUB
PU-503 Stone Creek Dr., Makanda, 62958, Jackson County, (618)457-5455, 100 miles from St. Louis. **Facility Holes:** 18. **Yards:** 6,875/5,402. **Par:** 72/72. **Course Rating:** 74.0/67.0. **Slope:** 140/120. **Green Fee:** $12/$27. **Cart Fee:** $12/Person. **Walking Policy:** Unrestricted walking. **Walkability:** 3. **Opened:** 2000. **Architect:** Jerry Lemons. **Season:** Year-round. **High:** April-Oct. **To obtain tee times:** Call golf shop. **Miscellaneous:** Reduced fees (weekdays, guests, twilight, seniors, juniors), range (grass), BF, FF.

★★★★ **STONEWALL ORCHARD GOLF CLUB**
PU-25675 W. Hwy. 60, Grayslake, 60030, Lake County, (847)740-4890, 45 miles from Chicago. **Web:** www.stonewallorchard.com. **Facility Holes:** 18. **Yards:** 7,074. **Par:** 72. **Course Rating:** 74.1. **Slope:** 140. **Walking Policy:** Unrestricted walking. **Walkability:** 2. **Opened:** 1999. **Architect:** Arthur Hills/Steve Forrest. **Season:** March-Dec. **High:** May-Oct. **To obtain tee times:** Call up to 7 days in advance. **Miscellaneous:** Reduced fees (weekdays, twilight, seniors, juniors), range (grass), credit cards (MC, V, AE, D, DC), BF, FF.
Notes: Ranked 23rd in 2001 Best in State.
Reader Comments: Very tough course. Brutal 18th hole … Juniors play free with parent after 4:30 p.m. … What a treat in conditioning and natural beauty … Will become a good one … Nice course but a bit overpriced … Difficult but fair.

★★★★ **STONEWOLF GOLF CLUB**
PU-1195 Stonewolf Trail, Fairview Heights, 62208, St. Clair County, (618)624-4653, (877)721-4653, 12 miles from St. Louis. **Web:** www.stonewolfgolf.com. **Facility Holes:** 18. **Yards:** 6,943/4,849. **Par:** 71/72. **Course Rating:** 74.0/67.2. **Slope:** 141/126. **Green Fee:** $55/$65. **Cart Fee:** Included in green fee. **Walking Policy:** Unrestricted walking. **Walkability:** 5. **Opened:** 1996. **Architect:** Jack Nicklaus. **Season:** Year-round. **To obtain tee times:** Call up to 10 days in advance. **Miscellaneous:** Reduced fees (weekdays, twilight, seniors), range (grass), credit cards (MC, V, D), BF, FF.
Notes: Ranked 14th in 1999 Best in State.
Reader Comments: Course management is a must, you'll need every club in the bag … Many excellent holes … Too expensive … Fantastic layout. Always in excellent condition. Nice pro shop … Stay out of bunkers … Tough from back tees.

★★ **STORYBROOK COUNTRY CLUB**
SP-2124 W Storybrook Rd., Hanover, 61041, Jo Daviess County, (815)591-2210, 40 miles from Dubuque, IA. **Facility Holes:** 18. **Yards:** 6,194/5,501. **Par:** 72/75. **Course Rating:** 69.6. **Slope:** 118. **Green Fee:** $14/$16. **Cart Fee:** $18/Cart. **Walking Policy:** Unrestricted walking.

Walkability: 5. **Opened:** 1965. **Season:** March-Nov. **High:** June-Sept. **To obtain tee times:** Call golf shop. **Miscellaneous:** Range (grass), credit cards (MC, V), BF, FF.

★★★½ SUNSET VALLEY GOLF CLUB

PU-1390 Sunset Rd., Highland Park, 60035, Lake County, (847)432-7140, 20 miles from Chicago. **E-mail:** pdhpsunset.com. **Facility Holes:** 18. **Yards:** 6,458/5,465. **Par:** 72/72. **Course Rating:** 70.5/71.6. **Slope:** 121/119. **Walking Policy:** Unrestricted walking. **Opened:** 1922. **Architect:** Bob Lohman. **Season:** March-Nov. **High:** March-Aug. **To obtain tee times:** Call golf shop. **Miscellaneous:** Reduced fees (weekdays, twilight, seniors, juniors), metal spikes, credit cards (MC, V).

Reader Comments: Older municipal course in much better shape with irrigation improvement … Really nice public course, some real nice holes … Must hit drives straight … Expensive, but exciting … Tough old course, very narrow, nice staff.

SYCAMORE GOLF CLUB

PU-940 E. State Street, Sycamore, 60178, De Kalb County, (815)895-3884, 50 miles from Chicago. **Facility Holes:** 18. **Yards:** 6,213/5,364. **Par:** 71/72. **Course Rating:** 67.7/69.9. **Slope:** 116/118. **Green Fee:** $25/$29. **Cart Fee:** $12/Person. **Walking Policy:** Unrestricted walking. **Walkability:** 1. **Opened:** 1923. **Season:** April-Dec. **High:** June-Aug. **To obtain tee times:** Call up to 7 days in advance. **Miscellaneous:** Reduced fees (twilight), credit cards (MC, V, D), BF, FF.

★★ SYCAMORE HILLS GOLF CLUB

SP-928 Clinton Rd., Paris, 61944, Edgar County, (217)465-4031, 120 miles from Indianapolis, IN. **E-mail:** boiler@tigerpaw.com. **Web:** wwwl.tigerpaw/sycamore. **Facility Holes:** 18. **Yards:** 6,589/5,222. **Par:** 72/72. **Course Rating:** 72.2/70.6. **Slope:** 124/117. **Green Fee:** $15/$20. **Cart Fee:** $10/Person. **Walking Policy:** Unrestricted walking. **Walkability:** 4. **Opened:** 1927. **Season:** Year-round. **High:** May-Aug. **To obtain tee times:** Call golf shop. **Miscellaneous:** Reduced fees (weekdays), range (grass), credit cards (MC, V, D).

★★★ TAMARACK COUNTRY CLUB

PU-800 Tamarack Lane, O'Fallon, 62269, St. Clair County, (618)632-6666, 20 miles from St. Louis, MO. **E-mail:** tamarackgc@yahoo.com. **Facility Holes:** 18. **Yards:** 6,300/5,120. **Par:** 71/74. **Course Rating:** 68.2/67.7. **Slope:** 106/104. **Green Fee:** $18/$25. **Cart Fee:** $10/Person. **Walking Policy:** Unrestricted walking. **Walkability:** 1. **Opened:** 1965. **Architect:** Pete Dye. **Season:** Year-round. **High:** March-Nov. **To obtain tee times:** Call golf shop. **Miscellaneous:** Reduced fees (seniors), metal spikes, range (grass), credit cards (MC, V), BF, FF.

Reader Comments: Great value … Good links course … Short course, difficult greens … Facilities need work. Very good layout, but not too tough.

★★★ TAMARACK GOLF CLUB

SP-24032 Royal Worlington Dr., Naperville, 60564, Will County, (630)904-4000, 20 miles from Chicago. **Facility Holes:** 18. **Yards:** 6,901/5,016. **Par:** 70/70. **Course Rating:** 74.2/68.8. **Slope:** 131/114. **Green Fee:** $25/$69. **Cart Fee:** Included in green fee. **Walking Policy:** Mandatory carts. **Walkability:** 2. **Opened:** 1989. **Architect:** David Gill. **Season:** Year-round. **High:** May-Sept. **To obtain tee times:** Call up to 7 days in advance. **Miscellaneous:** Reduced fees (weekdays, twilight), credit cards (MC, V, AE, D), BF, FF.

Reader Comments: Water on 16 of 18 holes, often in important places, wonderful service and food in the clubhouse … Large greens … Some tight holes.

★★½ THUNDERBIRD COUNTRY CLUB

SP-1010 East NW Hwy., Barrington, 60010, Cook County, (847)381-6500, 30 miles from Chicago. **Facility Holes:** 18. **Yards:** 6,274/5,472. **Par:** 71/72. **Course Rating:** 69.5/70.9. **Slope:** 121/118. **Green Fee:** $20/$39. **Walking Policy:** Unrestricted walking. **Walkability:** 3. **Opened:** 1958. **Season:** Year-round. **To obtain tee times:** Call up to 7 days in advance. **Miscellaneous:** Reduced fees (weekdays, seniors, juniors), range (grass), credit cards (MC, V, D), BF, FF.

★★★★½ THUNDERHAWK GOLF CLUB

PU-39700 N. Lewis Ave., Beach Park, 60099, Lake County, (847)872-4295, 50 miles from Chicago. **E-mail:** forestpreserve@co.lake.il.us. **Web:** www.co.lake.il.us/forest. **Facility Holes:** 18. **Yards:** 7,031/5,046. **Par:** 72/72. **Course Rating:** 73.8/69.2. **Slope:** 136/122. **Green Fee:** $56/$84. **Cart Fee:** $28/Cart. **Walking Policy:** Walking at certain times. **Walkability:** 3. **Opened:** 1999. **Architect:** Robert Trent Jones Jr./Bruce Charlton. **Season:** March-Nov. **High:** May-Sept. **To obtain tee times:** Call up to 14 days in advance. **Miscellaneous:** Reduced fees (weekdays, twilight, seniors, juniors), range (grass/mats), credit cards (MC, V, AE), BF, FF.

Notes: Ranked 24th in 2001 Best in State.

Reader Comments: Great new course. Facing a wall of boulders bordering the 18th green, it's an intriguing approach shot … Great service, friendly staff … Nice, expensive though … Some hidden water hazards … Very well-maintained course … Wide landing areas … Long very tough with wind … Variety of challenges.

ILLINOIS

★★★½ TIMBER TRAILS COUNTRY CLUB
PU-11350 Plainfield Rd., La Grange, 60525, Cook County, (708)246-0275, 20 miles from Chicago. **Facility Holes:** 18. **Yards:** 6,197/5,581. **Par:** 71/73. **Course Rating:** 68.7/71.1. **Slope:** 113/116. **Green Fee:** $40/$50. **Cart Fee:** $30/Person. **Walking Policy:** Unrestricted walking. **Walkability:** 3. **Opened:** 1931. **Architect:** Robert Bruce Harris. **Season:** March-Nov. **High:** May-Oct. **To obtain tee times:** Call up to 7 days in advance. **Miscellaneous:** Reduced fees (twilight, seniors), metal spikes, credit cards (MC, V), BF, FF.
Reader Comments: Trees, trees, trees. Audubon sanctuary … Interesting wooded course … Oak trees occasionally keep you in bounds! … Old course, tight fairways with large oaks … Needs a driving range.

★★★★ TOURNAMENT PLAYERS CLUB AT DEERE RUN *Service*
PU-3100 Heather Knoll, Silvis, 61282, Rock Island County, (309)796-6000. **E-mail:** bde-john@pgatour.com. **Web:** www.pgatour.com. **Facility Holes:** 18. **Yards:** 7,183/5,179. **Par:** 71/71. **Course Rating:** 75.1/70.1. **Slope:** 130/119. **Green Fee:** $81/$88. **Cart Fee:** $18/Person. **Walking Policy:** Mandatory carts. **Opened:** 2000. **Architect:** D.A. Weibring/Chris Gray. **Season:** March-Nov. **To obtain tee times:** Call up to 45 days in advance. **Miscellaneous:** Reduced fees (juniors), range (grass), credit cards (MC, V, AE), BF, FF.
Notes: Ranked 17th in 2001 Best in State; 8th in 2000 Best New Upscale Courses.
Reader Comments: A little pricey, but it is super … Exceptional land & layout … Greens need to mature. Great value … A bit pricy for the location … Great holes that are challenging and fun to play … Very nice track, great test & views.

★½ TRIPLE LAKES GOLF COURSE
PU-6942 Triple Lakes Rd., Millstadt, 62260, St. Clair County, (618)476-9985, 10 miles from St. Louis, MO. **Facility Holes:** 18. **Yards:** 6,227/4,857. **Par:** 72/71. **Course Rating:** 69.1. **Slope:** 112. **Green Fee:** $14/$28. **Cart Fee:** $11/Person. **Walking Policy:** Unrestricted walking. **Walkability:** 3. **Opened:** 1962. **Architect:** EB Jones. **Season:** Year-round. **High:** April-Dec. **To obtain tee times:** Call up to 7 days in advance. **Miscellaneous:** Reduced fees (weekdays, twilight, seniors), credit cards (MC, V, AE), FF.

★★½ TUCKAWAY GOLF COURSE
SP-27641 Stony Island, Crete, 60417, Will County, (708)946-2259, 25 miles from Chicago. **Facility Holes:** 18. **Yards:** 6,245/5,581. **Par:** 72/74. **Course Rating:** 68.7/72.2. **Slope:** 110/116. **Green Fee:** $32/$40. **Cart Fee:** Included in green fee. **Walking Policy:** Unrestricted walking. **Walkability:** 3. **Opened:** 1961. **Architect:** John Ellis. **Season:** March-Dec. **High:** June-Sept. **To obtain tee times:** Call golf shop. **Miscellaneous:** Reduced fees (twilight, seniors, juniors), range (grass), credit cards (MC, V).

UNIVERSITY OF ILLINOIS GOLF COURSE
PU-800 Hartwell Dr., Savoy, 61874, Champaign County, (217)359-5613, 120 miles from Chicago. **Facility Holes:** 36. **Walking Policy:** Unrestricted walking. **Architect:** C.W. Wagstaff. **Season:** Year-round. **To obtain tee times:** Call up to 7 days in advance. **Miscellaneous:** Reduced fees (twilight, seniors), range (grass), credit cards (MC, V, D), BF, FF.
★★★½ BLUE COURSE (18)
Yards: 6,579/6,129. **Par:** 73/74. **Course Rating:** 70.4/74.1. **Slope:** 114/118. **Green Fee:** $12/$17. **Cart Fee:** $22/Cart. **Walkability:** 1. **Opened:** 1966.
Reader Comments: A great course for longer hitters … Easier than its sister course (Orange) … New management improved … Good value.
★★★½ ORANGE COURSE (18)
Yards: 6,817/5,721. **Par:** 72/76. **Course Rating:** 72.1/72.2. **Slope:** 120/121. **Green Fee:** $14/$20. **Opened:** 1950.
Reader Comments: A great course for shotmaking … Very well-maintained. Clean facilities … The greens are the challenge here … Good course. Fun to play … Good value … Needs up-grading.

★★½ URBAN HILLS COUNTRY CLUB
PU-23520 Crawford Ave., Richton Park, 60471, Will County, (708)747-0306, 20 miles from Chicago. **Facility Holes:** 18. **Yards:** 6,650/5,266. **Par:** 71/71. **Course Rating:** 71.1/69.1. **Slope:** 114/110. **Green Fee:** $22/$30. **Cart Fee:** $23/Cart. **Walking Policy:** Unrestricted walking. **Walkability:** 2. **Opened:** 1967. **Architect:** Larry Packard. **Season:** Year-round. **High:** April-Oct. **To obtain tee times:** Call up to 7 days in advance. **Miscellaneous:** Reduced fees (weekdays, twilight, seniors, juniors), credit cards (MC, V), BF, FF.

★★ VILLA OLIVIA COUNTRY CLUB
PU-Rte. 20 and Naperville Rd., Bartlett, 60103, Cook County, (630)289-1000, 45 miles from Chicago. **E-mail:** info@villaolivia.com. **Web:** www.villaolivia.com. **Facility Holes:** 18. **Yards:** 6,510/5,546. **Par:** 73/72. **Course Rating:** 71.3/72.5. **Slope:** 124/122. **Green Fee:** $20/$40. **Cart Fee:** $15/Person. **Walking Policy:** Walking at certain times. **Walkability:** 2. **Architect:**

Dick Nugent. **Season:** March-Nov. **High:** May-Oct. **To obtain tee times:** Call up to 7 days in advance. **Miscellaneous:** Reduced fees (weekdays, twilight, seniors), credit cards (MC, V, AE, D, DC), BF, FF.

★★ VILLAGE GREEN COUNTRY CLUB

PU-2501 N. Midlothian Rd., Mundelein, 60060, Lake County, (847)566-7373, 25 miles from Chicago. **Facility Holes:** 18. **Yards:** 6,235/5,600. **Par:** 70/70. **Course Rating:** 69.2/69.2. **Slope:** 115/118. **Green Fee:** $21/$28. **Cart Fee:** $28/Cart. **Walking Policy:** Walking at certain times. **Walkability:** 2. **Opened:** 1963. **Architect:** William B. Langford. **Season:** April-Oct. **High:** June-Aug. **To obtain tee times:** Call golf shop. **Miscellaneous:** Reduced fees (weekdays, twilight, seniors, juniors), credit cards (MC, V).

★★½ VILLAGE GREENS OF WOODRIDGE

PU-1575 W. 75th St., Woodridge, 60517, Du Page County, (630)985-3610, 25 miles from Chicago. **Facility Holes:** 18. **Yards:** 6,650/5,847. **Par:** 72/72. **Course Rating:** 71.2/72.2. **Slope:** 121/119. **Green Fee:** $22/$38. **Cart Fee:** $13/Person. **Walking Policy:** Unrestricted walking. **Walkability:** 2. **Opened:** 1959. **Architect:** Robert Bruce Harris. **Season:** Year-round. **High:** May-Sept. **To obtain tee times:** Call up to 7 days in advance. **Miscellaneous:** Reduced fees (weekdays, twilight, seniors, juniors), range (grass), credit cards (MC, V), BF, FF.

★★★½ VILLAGE LINKS OF GLEN ELLYN

PU-485 Winchell Way, Glen Ellyn, 60137, Du Page County, (630)469-8180, 20 miles from Chicago. **E-mail:** jeffv.@pga.com. **Web:** www.villagelinks.com. **Facility Holes:** 27. **Yards:** 6,933/5,753. **Par:** 71/73. **Course Rating:** 73.6/73.3. **Slope:** 128/127. **Green Fee:** $47/$50. **Cart Fee:** $15/Cart. **Walking Policy:** Unrestricted walking. **Walkability:** 2. **Opened:** 1967. **Architect:** David Gill. **Season:** March-Nov. **High:** May-Aug. **To obtain tee times:** Call up to 7 days in advance. **Miscellaneous:** Reduced fees (weekdays), range (grass/mats), caddies, credit cards (MC, V, AE, D), BF, FF.
Reader Comments: Nice 27-hole layout is a bargain for residents, but too expensive for others … Great layout, enjoyable challenge … Plenty of hazards … Good condition—long par 4s … Excellent test, great value, good pro shop.
Special Notes: Also has a 9-hole executive course.

★★½ WATER'S EDGE GOLF CLUB

PU-7205 W. 115th St., Worth, 60482-1732, Cook County, (708)671-1032, 20 miles from Chicago. **E-mail:** watersedgec@aol.com. **Web:** www.watersedgegolf.com. **Facility Holes:** 18. **Yards:** 6,904/5,332. **Par:** 72/72. **Course Rating:** 72.9/70.4. **Slope:** 131/122. **Green Fee:** $20/$48. **Cart Fee:** $12/Person. **Walking Policy:** Walking at certain times. **Walkability:** 3. **Opened:** 1999. **Architect:** Gary Koch/Rick Robbins. **Season:** March-Dec. **High:** May-Sept. **To obtain tee times:** Call up to 7 days in advance. **Miscellaneous:** Reduced fees (weekdays, twilight, seniors, juniors), range (grass/mats), credit cards (MC, V), BF, FF.

★★★★½ WEAVERRIDGE GOLF CLUB

PU-5100 WeaverRidge Blvd., Peoria, 61615, Peoria County, (309)691-3344. **Web:** www.weaverridge.com. **Facility Holes:** 18. **Yards:** 7,030/5,046. **Par:** 72/72. **Course Rating:** 73.1/68.9. **Slope:** 136/115. **Green Fee:** $30/$73. **Cart Fee:** $15/Person. **Walking Policy:** Unrestricted walking. **Walkability:** 4. **Opened:** 1997. **Architect:** Michael Hurdzan/Dana Fry. **Season:** April-Nov. **High:** April-Dec. **To obtain tee times:** Call up to 14 days in advance. **Miscellaneous:** Reduced fees (weekdays, twilight, juniors), range (grass/mats), credit cards (MC, V), BF, FF.
Notes: Ranked 6th in 1999 Best in State.
Reader Comments: Awesome course, awesome setting! Elevation changes and course layout are outstanding, GPS on carts extremely helpful… Exciting hole after hole … Fun to play, but overpriced … A little too pricey, but gorgeous.

★★★½ WEDGEWOOD GOLF COURSE

PU-Rte.59 and Caton Farm Rd., Joliet, 60435, Will County, (815)741-7270, 40 miles from Chicago. **Facility Holes:** 18. **Yards:** 6,836/5,792. **Par:** 72/72. **Course Rating:** 72.0/72.4. **Slope:** 119/123. **Green Fee:** $13/$32. **Cart Fee:** $26/Cart. **Walking Policy:** Unrestricted walking. **Walkability:** 3. **Opened:** 1970. **Architect:** Edward Lawrence Packard. **Season:** March-Nov. **High:** May-Oct. **To obtain tee times:** Call golf shop. **Miscellaneous:** Reduced fees (weekdays, twilight, seniors, juniors), range (grass/mats), credit cards (MC, V, D), BF, FF.
Reader Comments: Good layout and fun to play … Not a great course, but its very well maintained … Long course from back tees, real bitch in the wind … Elevation changes … Superior course condition.

★★★ WESTVIEW GOLF COURSE

PU-2150 S. 36th St., Quincy, 62301, Adams County, (217)223-7499, 100 miles from St. Louis, MO. **E-mail:** mcqpd@adams.net. **Web:** www.westviewgolf.com. **Facility Holes:** 27.

Yards: 6,441/4,946. **Par:** 71/71. **Course Rating:** 69.1/67.0. **Slope:** 117/105. **Green Fee:** $17/$21. **Cart Fee:** $12/Person. **Walking Policy:** Unrestricted walking. **Walkability:** 3. **Opened:** 1999. **Architect:** D.A. Weibring. **Season:** March-Dec. **High:** April-Oct. **To obtain tee times:** Call up to 7 days in advance. **Misc:** Reduced fees (twilight), credit cards (MC, V, D), BF, FF.
Reader Comments: Very nice course, great clubhouse & pro shop. Large, very fast greens, always improving course ... Tees & traps redone. A-1 course for value & challenge ... Pace of play slow.
Special Notes: Also has a 9-hole executive course.

WHISPER CREEK GOLF CLUB
PU-12840 Del Webb Blvd., Huntley, 60142, McHenry County, (847)515-7682, (877)246-4653, 40 miles from Chicago. **E-mail:** karrasj@delwebb.com. **Facility Holes:** 18. **Yards:** 7,103/5,550. **Par:** 72/72. **Course Rating:** 73.9/71.6. **Slope:** 131/124. **Green Fee:** $50/$105. **Cart Fee:** $17/Person. **Walking Policy:** Walking at certain times. **Walkability:** 2. **Opened:** 2000. **Architect:** Billy Casper/Greg Nash. **Season:** April-Oct. **High:** May-Sept. **To obtain tee times:** Call up to 7 days in advance. **Miscellaneous:** Reduced fees (weekdays, twilight, seniors, juniors), range (grass/mats), credit cards (MC, V, AE), BF, FF.

★★★½ WHITE DEER RUN GOLF CLUB
PU-250 W. Gregg's Pkwy., Vernon Hills, 60061, Lake County, (847)680-6100, 25 miles from Chicago. **E-mail:** mwilliams@whitedeergolf.com. **Web:** www.whitedeergolf.com. **Facility Holes:** 18. **Yards:** 7,101/4,916. **Par:** 72/72. **Course Rating:** 74.6/68.4. **Slope:** 137/116. **Green Fee:** $45/$82. **Cart Fee:** Included in green fee. **Walking Policy:** Unrestricted walking. **Walkability:** 3. **Opened:** 1998. **Architect:** Dick Nugent/Tim Nugent. **Season:** April-Nov. **High:** May-Aug. **To obtain tee times:** Call up to 14 days in advance. **Miscellaneous:** Reduced fees (twilight), range (grass/mats), credit cards (MC, V, AE, D, DC, CB), BF, FF.
Reader Comments: Great greens & fairways ... Good value for a great new track ... Many tee box options, very nice for a young course.

WHITE PINES GOLF CLUB
PU-500 W. Jefferson St., Bensenville, 60106, Du Page County, (630)766-0304x1, 10 miles from Chicago. **Web:** www.whitepinesgolf.com. **Facility Holes:** 36. **Walking Policy:** Unrestricted walking. **Walkability:** 2. **Opened:** 1930. **Architect:** Jack Daray. **Miscellaneous:** Reduced fees (weekdays, twilight), range (grass/mats), credit cards (MC, V, AE, D, Debit Cards), BF, FF.
★★★ **EAST COURSE** (18)
Yards: 6,371/5,331. **Par:** 70/73. **Course Rating:** 70.2/70.3. **Slope:** 122/117. **Green Fee:** $29/$34. **Cart Fee:** $27/Cart. **Season:** March-Dec. **To obtain tee times:** Call golf shop.
Reader Comments: Well-kept course ... Nice layout, fair greens ... Price is right ... Smallest greens around, no need for driver ... Very fun course to play, short with hard greens ... Too many trees. It slows play.
★★★ **WEST COURSE** (18)
Yards: 6,601/5,998. **Par:** 72/72. **Course Rating:** 71.1/73.2. **Slope:** 118/120. **Green Fee:** $33/$34. **Cart Fee:** $27/Person. **Season:** April-Dec. **High:** June-Aug. **To obtain tee times:** Call up to 6 days in advance.
Reader Comments: Good test on water & other hazards ... Well run, great day, good condition ... Tough course. Accuracy needed ... Price is right ... Good layout only getting better with age ... A good challenge, in decent condition.

★★ WILLOW POND GOLF COURSE
PU-1126 Country Club Lane, Rantoul, 61868, Champaign County, (217)893-9000, 15 miles from Champaign. **Facility Holes:** 18. **Yards:** 6,799/6,550. **Par:** 72/72. **Course Rating:** 71.8/71.9. **Slope:** 115/114. **Green Fee:** $14/$18. **Cart Fee:** $18/Cart. **Walking Policy:** Unrestricted walking. **Walkability:** 1. **Opened:** 1956. **Architect:** Edward Lawrence Packard. **Season:** March-Nov. **High:** June-Aug. **To obtain tee times:** Call golf shop. **Miscellaneous:** Reduced fees (twilight, seniors, juniors), range (grass/mats), credit cards (MC, V, D).

★★½ WILMETTE GOLF COURSE
PU-3900 Fairway Dr., Wilmette, 60091, Cook County, (847)256-9646, 10 miles from Chicago. **E-mail:** jamc0@aol.com. **Web:** www.wilmettepark.org. **Facility Holes:** 18. **Yards:** 6,375/4,855. **Par:** 70/70. **Course Rating:** 70.7/63.5. **Slope:** 127/115. **Green Fee:** $40/$45. **Cart Fee:** $28/Cart. **Walking Policy:** Unrestricted walking. **Walkability:** 3. **Opened:** 1922. **Architect:** Joseph A. Roseman. **Season:** March-Nov. **High:** June-Sept. **To obtain tee times:** Call up to 6 days in advance. **Miscellaneous:** Reduced fees (weekdays, twilight, juniors), range (mats), credit cards (MC, V, D), BF, FF.

★★★ WINNETKA GOLF CLUB
PU-1300 Oak St., Winnetka, 60093, Cook County, (847)501-2050, 12 miles from Chicago. **Facility Holes:** 27. **Yards:** 6,485/5,857. **Par:** 71/72. **Course Rating:** 70.9/73.3. **Slope:** 125/124. **Green Fee:** $24/$46. **Cart Fee:** $28/Cart. **Walking Policy:** Unrestricted walking. **Walkability:** 1. **Opened:** 1917. **Architect:** W.H. Langford. **Season:** April-Nov. **High:** May-Sept. **To obtain tee

times: Call up to 6 days in advance. **Miscellaneous:** Reduced fees (weekdays, twilight), range (mats), credit cards (MC, V), BF, FF.

Reader Comments: Excellent municipal course ... Too many hazards ... Short and sporty. Tough layout, water on half of the holes ... A decent public course, very good greens.

Special Notes: Also has a 9-hole executive course.

★★½ WOLF CREEK GOLF CLUB

PU-Old #66, Pontiac, 61764, Livingston County, (815)842-9008, 35 miles from Bloomington.
Facility Holes: 18. **Yards:** 6,674/5,470. **Par:** 72/72. **Course Rating:** 70.1/72.8. **Slope:** 119/121.
Green Fee: $16. **Cart Fee:** $16/Person. **Walking Policy:** Unrestricted walking. **Walkability:** 2.
Opened: 1973. **Season:** March-Nov. **High:** June-Aug. **To obtain tee times:** Call golf shop.
Miscellaneous: Metal spikes, range (grass).

WOLVES CROSSING GOLF COURSE

PU-1374 Centennial Rd., Jerseyville, 62052, Jersey County, (618)498-7715. **Facility Holes:** 18. **Yards:** 5,986/4,564. **Par:** 70/70. **Course Rating:** 67.3/65.2. **Slope:** 107/101. **Green Fee:** $12/$13. **Cart Fee:** $12/Person. **Walking Policy:** Unrestricted walking. **Walkability:** 2. **Season:** Year-round. **To obtain tee times:** Call golf shop. **Miscellaneous:** Reduced fees (seniors), range (grass), credit cards (MC, V).

★★★ WOODBINE GOLF COURSE

PU-14240 W. 151st St., Lockport, 60441, Will County, (708)301-1252, 30 miles from Chicago.
E-mail: woodbinegc@aol.com. **Facility Holes:** 18. **Yards:** 6,020/5,618. **Par:** 70/70. **Course Rating:** 68.3/71.7. **Slope:** 115/119. **Green Fee:** $28/$37. **Cart Fee:** $14/Person. **Walking Policy:** Unrestricted walking. **Walkability:** 2. **Opened:** 1988. **Architect:** Gordon Cunningham. **Season:** March-Nov. **High:** May-Aug. **To obtain tee times:** Call golf shop. **Miscellaneous:** Reduced fees (weekdays, twilight, seniors, juniors), credit cards (MC, V, AE), BF, FF.

Reader Comments: A good value ... Good conditions, pace not so hot ... Great place for couples. Course not long but equal for all handicaps ... No Marshal.

THE WOODLANDS GOLF CLUB

PU-2839 Harris Lane, Alton, 62002, Madison County, (618)462-1456, (800)745-4306, 25 miles from St. Louis, MO. **E-mail:** toddmcress@aol.com. **Web:** www.woodlandsgolfclub.com. **Facility Holes:** 18. **Yards:** 6,401/4,775. **Par:** 71/71. **Course Rating:** 69.8/68.4. **Slope:** 123/109. **Green Fee:** $30/$38. **Cart Fee:** Included in green fee. **Walking Policy:** Walking at certain times. **Walkability:** 2. **Opened:** 1994. **Architect:** Hansen. **Season:** Year-round. **High:** April-Oct. **To obtain tee times:** Call up to 7 days in advance. **Miscellaneous:** Reduced fees (twilight, seniors, juniors), credit cards (MC, V, AE, D), BF, FF.

★★ WOODRUFF GOLF COURSE

PU-621 N. Gouger Rd., Joliet, 60432, Will County, (815)741-7272, 40 miles from Chicago.
Facility Holes: 18. **Yards:** 5,424/5,059. **Par:** 68/68. **Course Rating:** 64.9/67.8. **Slope:** 99/105.
Green Fee: $14/$32. **Cart Fee:** $26/Cart. **Walking Policy:** Unrestricted walking. **Walkability:** 4.
Opened: 1921. **Architect:** Edward Lawrence Packard. **Season:** March-Nov. **High:** May-Sept.
To obtain tee times: Call golf shop. **Miscellaneous:** Reduced fees (weekdays, twilight, seniors, juniors), credit cards (MC, V, D), BF, FF.

INDIANA

★★ ARBOR TRACE GOLF CLUB
PU-2500 E. 550 N., Marion, 46952, Grant County, (765)662-8236, 4 miles from Marion.
E-mail: jack@arbortracegc.com. **Web:** www.arbortracegc.com. **Facility Holes:** 18. **Yards:** 6,535/5,060. **Par:** 72/72. **Course Rating:** 69.5/67.6. **Slope:** 108/106. **Green Fee:** $16/$18. **Cart Fee:** $10/Person. **Walking Policy:** Unrestricted walking. **Walkability:** 1. **Opened:** 1966. **Architect:** H. Lamboley. **Season:** Feb.-Dec. **To obtain tee times:** Call golf shop. **Miscellaneous:** Reduced fees (seniors, juniors), credit cards (MC, V, D), BF, FF.
Special Notes: Formerly Hart Golf Course.

★★★ AUTUMN RIDGE GOLF CLUB
SP-11420 Old Auburn Rd., Fort Wayne, 46845, Allen County, (219)637-8727, 2 miles from Fort Wayne. **E-mail:** autumnridgegc@aol.com. **Web:** www.golfus.com/autumnridge. **Facility Holes:** 18. **Yards:** 7,103/5,273. **Par:** 72/72. **Course Rating:** 73.9/70.1. **Slope:** 134/122. **Green Fee:** $35/$45. **Cart Fee:** Included in green fee. **Walking Policy:** Mandatory carts. **Walkability:** 3. **Opened:** 1993. **Architect:** Ernie Schrock. **Season:** March-Dec. **High:** May-Oct. **To obtain tee times:** Call golf shop. **Miscellaneous:** Reduced fees (weekdays, twilight, seniors, juniors), range (grass), credit cards (MC, V, AE), BF, FF.
Reader Comments: The greens are country club caliber. Clubhouse facilities were excellent … Course plays firm and fast. Suits a right-to-left big hitter best … Average course … Every hole is an adventure, bring all your clubs.

★★★★ BEAR SLIDE GOLF CLUB
PU-6770 E. 231st St., Cicero, 46034, Hamilton County, (317)984-3837, (800)252-8337, 20 miles from Indianapolis. **E-mail:** bslidem@aol.com. **Web:** bearslide.com. **Facility Holes:** 18. **Yards:** 7,041/4,831. **Par:** 71/71. **Course Rating:** 74.6/69.5. **Slope:** 136/117. **Green Fee:** $35/$45. **Cart Fee:** $13/Person. **Walking Policy:** Unrestricted walking. **Walkability:** 4. **Opened:** 1993. **Architect:** Dean Refram. **Season:** Year-round. **To obtain tee times:** Call golf shop. **Miscellaneous:** Range (grass), credit cards (MC, V, AE, D), BF, FF.
Notes: Ranked 10th in 1999 Best in State.
Reader Comments: Couple of quirky holes, but a nice experience overall … Great price … Totally different 9s. Links front, trees back … Fun course, except on windy days … Fast greens.

BIRCK BOILERMAKER GOLF COMPLEX
PU-1202 Cherry Lane, West Lafayette, 47907, Tippecanoe County, (765)494-3216, 50 miles from Indianapolis. **E-mail:** drhill@purdue.edu. **Web:** www.purdue.edu/athletics/golf. **Facility Holes:** 36. **Season:** Year-round. **To obtain tee times:** Call up to 7 days in advance. **Miscellaneous:** Range (grass/mats), credit cards (MC, V, D), FF.
ACKERMAN COURSE (18)
Yards: 6,436/5,918. **Par:** 71/71. **Course Rating:** 70.3/68.7. **Slope:** 124/112. **Green Fee:** $21/$27. **Cart Fee:** $13/Person. **Walking Policy:** Unrestricted walking. **Walkability:** 4. **Miscellaneous:** Reduced fees (twilight, seniors, juniors).
★★★★½ KAMPEN COURSE (18) *Value*
Yards: 7,272/5,216. **Par:** 72/72. **Course Rating:** 76.5/65.5. **Slope:** 145/115. **Green Fee:** $48/$55. **Cart Fee:** Included in green fee. **Walking Policy:** Mandatory carts. **Walkability:** 3. **Opened:** 1998. **Architect:** Pete Dye. **Miscellaneous:** Reduced fees (weekdays, twilight, juniors).
Reader Comments: Good design with a lot of waste bunkers … Very tough around the greens. Need to play more than once. Excellent experience … Beautiful layout, a little pricey … 4 or 5 tee boxes, suit anyone's game … The course and practice facility is great. Great for the price.

★★½ BLACK SQUIRREL GOLF CLUB
PU-Hwy. 119 S., Goshen, 46526, Elkhart County, (219)533-1828, 19 miles from South Bend. **E-mail:** blacksquirrelgc@juno.com. **Web:** www.blacksquirrelgc.com. **Facility Holes:** 18. **Yards:** 6,483/5,018. **Par:** 72/72. **Course Rating:** 69.8/67.8. **Slope:** 115/110. **Green Fee:** $15/$25. **Cart Fee:** $12/Person. **Walking Policy:** Unrestricted walking. **Walkability:** 2. **Opened:** 1989. **Architect:** Larimer Development. **Season:** March-Dec. **High:** April-Oct. **To obtain tee times:** Call up to 14 days in advance. **Miscellaneous:** Reduced fees (weekdays, juniors), credit cards (MC, V, AE, D), BF, FF.

★★★★½ BLACKTHORN GOLF CLUB
PU-6100 Nimtz Pkwy., South Bend, 46628, St. Joseph County, (219)232-4653, 90 miles from Chicago. **Web:** www.blackthorngolf.com. **Facility Holes:** 18. **Yards:** 7,106/5,036. **Par:** 72/72. **Course Rating:** 75.2/71.0. **Slope:** 135/120. **Green Fee:** $30/$48. **Cart Fee:** $14/Person. **Walking Policy:** Unrestricted walking. **Walkability:** 3. **Opened:** 1994. **Architect:** Michael Hurdzan. **Season:** March-Dec. **High:** May-Sept. **To obtain tee times:** Call up to 14 days in advance. **Miscellaneous:** Reduced fees (weekdays, twilight, juniors), metal spikes, range (grass), credit cards (MC, V, AE), BF, FF.
Notes: Ranked 9th in 1999 Best in State; 4th in 1995 Best New Public Courses.
Reader Comments: Play the different tees for an interesting variety … From tee to green, this

course is always in excellent condition. Very nice practice facility. Great food ... You need every club in the bag ... Outstanding service people ... Incredibly fun layout ... Every hole is unique. **Special Notes:** Also has a 19th practice hole.

★★½ BRASSIE GOLF CLUB

PU-1110 Pearson Rd., Chesterton, 46304, Porter County, (219)921-1192, (219)921-1192, 45 miles from Chicago. **Web:** www.thebrassie.com. **Facility Holes:** 18. **Yards:** 7,008/5,493. **Par:** 72/72. **Course Rating:** 73.2/70.9. **Slope:** 129/116. **Green Fee:** $30/$50. **Cart Fee:** Included in green fee. **Walking Policy:** Unrestricted walking. **Walkability:** 1. **Opened:** 1999. **Architect:** Jim Fazio. **Season:** March-Dec. **High:** May-Oct. **To obtain tee times:** Call up to 7 days in advance. **Miscellaneous:** Reduced fees (weekdays, twilight), range,cards (MC, V, AE, D), BF, FF.

★½ BRIAR LEAF GOLF CLUB

PU-3233 N. State Rd. 39, La Porte, 46350, La Porte County, (219)326-1992, (877)274-2753, 60 miles from Chicago. **Web:** www.briarleaf.com. **Facility Holes:** 18. **Yards:** 6,850/5,391. **Par:** 72/72. **Course Rating:** 72.1/70.7. **Slope:** 130/121. **Green Fee:** $23/$33. **Cart Fee:** $13/Person. **Walking Policy:** Walking at certain times. **Walkability:** 3. **Opened:** 1973. **Season:** Year-round. **High:** April-Oct. **To obtain tee times:** Call up to 21 days in advance. **Miscellaneous:** Reduced fees (weekdays, twilight, seniors, juniors), range (grass), credit cards (MC, V, AE, D), BF, FF.

★★★★½ BRICKYARD CROSSING GOLF CLUB *Condition+*

R-4400 W. 16th St., Indianapolis, 46222, Marion County, (317)484-6572. **Facility Holes:** 18. **Yards:** 6,994/5,038. **Par:** 72/72. **Course Rating:** 74.5/68.3. **Slope:** 137/116. **Green Fee:** $90. **Cart Fee:** Included in green fee. **Walking Policy:** Walking at certain times. **Walkability:** 3. **Opened:** 1993. **Architect:** Pete Dye. **Season:** March-Nov. **To obtain tee times:** Call golf shop. **Miscellaneous:** Reduced fees (guests), range (grass), credit cards (MC, V, AE, D). **Notes:** Ranked 6th in 1999 Best in State. Senior PGA Tour Comfort Classic. Reader Comments: Awesome feeling hearing the race cars circling the track beside you as you try to hit a shot ... Costly but worth it, excellent layout with great greens ... Holes inside the track are the weakest. Once you come out of the track, the course goes from good to great. Finishing 5 holes make the course.

★★★½ BRIDGEWATER GOLF CLUB

PU-1818 Morningstar Rd., Auburn, 46706, DeKalb County, (219)925-8184, (800)377-1012, 15 miles from Fort Wayne. **Web:** www.bridgewatergolf.com. **Facility Holes:** 18. **Yards:** 7,239/5,128. **Par:** 72/72. **Course Rating:** 75.1/70.2. **Slope:** 137/117. **Green Fee:** $40. **Cart Fee:** Included in green fee. **Walking Policy:** Mandatory carts. **Walkability:** 3. **Opened:** 1999. **Architect:** Ernie Schrock. **Season:** Year-round. **To obtain tee times:** Call up to 7 days in advance. **Misc:** Reduced fees (twilight, seniors, juniors), credit cards (MC, V, AE, D), BF, FF. Reader Comments: Fairly open, too many irons off the tee, 9th might be the best hole in Indiana ... Better than you expect in farm country ... Very long, nice ... Fairly expensive ... Great practice area. Tough opening par 5 ... Very difficult.

★½ BROADMOOR COUNTRY CLUB

PU-4300 W. 81st St., Merrillville, 46410, Lake County, (219)769-5444, 10 miles from Gary. **Facility Holes:** 18. **Yards:** 6,021/5,181. **Par:** 71/71. **Course Rating:** 69.8/71.4. **Slope:** 117/110. **Green Fee:** $15/$23. **Cart Fee:** Included in green fee. **Walking Policy:** Unrestricted walking. **Walkability:** 3. **Opened:** 1973. **Architect:** R. Albert Anderson. **Season:** Year-round. **High:** March-Oct. **To obtain tee times:** Call golf shop. **Miscellaneous:** Reduced fees (weekdays, twilight, seniors, juniors), range (grass/mats), credit cards (MC, V, AE, D), BF, FF.

★★★ BROOK HILL GOLF CLUB

SP-11175 Fairway Lane, Brookville, 47012, Franklin County, (765)647-4522, (800)708-4522, 35 miles from Cincinnati. **Web:** brookhillgc.com. **Facility Holes:** 18. **Yards:** 6,361/4,776. **Par:** 71/71. **Course Rating:** 70.2/67.9. **Slope:** 125/125. **Green Fee:** $15/$19. **Cart Fee:** $13/Person. **Walking Policy:** Unrestricted walking. **Walkability:** 3. **Opened:** 1975. **Season:** Year-round. **High:** May-Sept. **To obtain tee times:** Call up to 7 days in advance. **Miscellaneous:** Reduced fees (weekdays, twilight, seniors), range (grass), credit cards (MC, V, AE, D), BF, FF. Reader Comments: Very courteous staff ... Great for seniors. Good layout, challenging & fun ... Nice, but small.

★★ BROOKSHIRE GOLF CLUB

SP-12120 Brookshire Pkwy., Carmel, 46033, Hamilton County, (317)846-7431, 15 miles from Indianapolis. **E-mail:** alaneoff@pga.com. **Web:** brookshiregolf.com. **Facility Holes:** 18. **Yards:** 6,651/5,635. **Par:** 72/75. **Course Rating:** 71.8/74.4. **Slope:** 123/129. **Green Fee:** $30/$44. **Cart Fee:** Included in green fee. **Walking Policy:** Walking at certain times. **Walkability:** 2. **Opened:** 1970. **Architect:** William H. Diddel. **Season:** March-Nov. **High:** June-Aug. **To obtain tee times:** Call up to 10 days in advance. **Miscellaneous:** Reduced fees (weekdays, twilight, juniors), range (grass), credit cards (MC, V, AE), BF, FF.

INDIANA

★★★½ BROOKWOOD GOLF CLUB
PU-10304 Bluffton Rd., Fort Wayne, 46809, Allen County, (219)747-3136. **Web:** brookwood-golf.com. **Facility Holes:** 18. **Yards:** 6,700/6,250. **Par:** 72/73. **Course Rating:** 70.3/67.9. **Slope:** 123/111. **Green Fee:** $18/$20. **Cart Fee:** $20/Cart. **Walking Policy:** Unrestricted walking. **Walkability:** 3. **Opened:** 1925. **Season:** March-Dec. **High:** April-Sept. **To obtain tee times:** Call golf shop. **Miscellaneous:** Range (grass), credit cards (MC, V, AE, D), BF, FF.
Reader Comments: Seemed to be always busy ... Greens need some repair ... 4 tough par 3s. A treat to play ... Nice, short, fun course ... Challenging, but not unfair ... Great old-style course.

CAMBRIDGE GOLF CLUB
SP-1120 Cambridge Village Square, Evansville, 47725, Vanderburen County, (812)868-4653, 7 miles from Evansville. **E-mail:** pgapro@villageofcambridge.com. **Web:** villageofcambridge.com. **Facility Holes:** 18. **Yards:** 7,047/5,064. **Par:** 72/72. **Course Rating:** 74.6/69.5. **Slope:** 137/119. **Green Fee:** $27/$35. **Cart Fee:** $14/Person. **Walkability:** 2. **Opened:** 2000. **Architect:** Tim Liddy. **Season:** Feb.-Dec. **High:** April-Oct. **To obtain tee times:** Call up to 14 days in advance. **Miscellaneous:** Reduced fees (twilight, juniors), range (grass), credit cards (MC, V, AE), BF, FF.

★★★★ CHERRY HILL GOLF CLUB
PU-6615 Wheelock Rd., Fort Wayne, 46845, Allen County, (219)485-8727. **Facility Holes:** 18. **Yards:** 6,818/5,248. **Par:** 72/72. **Slope:** 129. **Green Fee:** $35/$44. **Cart Fee:** Included in green fee. **Walking Policy:** Mandatory carts. **Walkability:** 3. **Opened:** 1999. **Architect:** Max Robertson/Mark Slater. **Season:** March-Dec. **High:** May-Sept. **To obtain tee times:** Call up to 7 days in advance. **Miscellaneous:** Reduced fees (weekdays, twilight), range (grass), credit cards (MC, V, AE), FF.
Reader Comments: Very playable course ... Surprisingly well-designed ... Greens are hard as a rock, but course is beautiful ... Country-club setting, great layout, housing doesn't get in the way of the course, #6 still kills me.

★★★½ CHESTNUT HILL GOLF CLUB
PU-11502 Illinois Rd., Fort Wayne, 46804, Allen County, (219)625-4146. **Facility Holes:** 18. **Yards:** 6,996/5,206. **Par:** 72/72. **Course Rating:** 72.9/68.8. **Slope:** 132/117. **Green Fee:** $30. **Cart Fee:** $12/Person. **Walking Policy:** Unrestricted walking. **Walkability:** 3. **Opened:** 1995. **Architect:** Clyde Johnston/Fuzzy Zoeller. **Season:** Year-round. **To obtain tee times:** Call up to 7 days in advance. **Miscellaneous:** Range (grass), credit cards (MC, V, AE, D), BF, FF.
Reader Comments: Very nice course. Lots of variety ... Good golf course ... This course has come a long way in 4-5 years, much improved condition. Price continues to get higher ... Tough layout—great holes with views.

★★★ CHRISTMAS LAKE GOLF COURSE
PU-1 Country Club Dr., Santa Claus, 47579, Spencer County, (812)544-2271, (877)962-7463, 45 miles from Evansville. **E-mail:** tnelson@christmaslake.com. **Web:** www.christmaslake.com. **Facility Holes:** 18. **Yards:** 7,191/5,135. **Par:** 72/72. **Course Rating:** 74.4/69.2. **Slope:** 134/117. **Green Fee:** $24/$39. **Cart Fee:** Included in green fee. **Walking Policy:** Walking at certain times. **Walkability:** 3. **Opened:** 1968. **Architect:** Edmund Ault. **Season:** Year-round. **High:** April-Oct. **To obtain tee times:** Call up to 14 days in advance. **Miscellaneous:** Reduced fees (weekdays, twilight), range (grass/mats), credit cards (MC, V, D), BF, FF.
Reader Comments: Beautiful, challenging layout ... Fair front 9 but difficult back 9.

★★★★½ COBBLESTONE GOLF COURSE *Value, Pace*
PU-2702 Cobblestone Lane, Kendallville, 46755, Noble County, (219)349-1550, 25 miles from Ft. Wayne. **Web:** www.golfus.com/cobblestone. **Facility Holes:** 18. **Yards:** 6,863/4,779. **Par:** 72/72. **Course Rating:** 72.9/67.6. **Slope:** 129/112. **Green Fee:** $25/$30. **Cart Fee:** $11/Person. **Walking Policy:** Unrestricted walking. **Walkability:** 3. **Opened:** 1998. **Architect:** Steve Burns. **Season:** April-Nov. **High:** May-Sept. **To obtain tee times:** Call up to 7 days in advance. **Miscellaneous:** Reduced fees (twilight, seniors, juniors), range (grass), credit cards (MC, V, AE, D), BF, FF.
Notes: Ranked 8th in 1999 Best New Affordable Public.
Reader Comments: Good walking course, only a couple of long treks. Nice setting. Friendly driving course ... Nice course for a hacker like me ... Very enjoyable—lots of challenge ... Course test all parts of your game and is fair ... Simply a wonderful golf experience.

★★★ COFFIN GOLF CLUB
PU-2401 Cold Springs Rd., Indianapolis, 46222, Marion County, (317)327-7845, 2 miles from Indianapolis. **Facility Holes:** 18. **Yards:** 6,789/5,135. **Par:** 72/72. **Course Rating:** 73.7/70.3. **Slope:** 129/114. **Green Fee:** $20/$22. **Cart Fee:** $15/Person. **Walking Policy:** Unrestricted walking. **Walkability:** 3. **Opened:** 1995. **Architect:** Tim Liddy. **Season:** Year-round. **To obtain tee**

times: Call up to 7 days in advance. **Miscellaneous:** Reduced fees (weekdays, twilight, seniors, juniors), credit cards (MC, V, D), BF, FF.
Reader Comments: A great value ... Gem for the money, better upkeep needed ... One of the best city courses ... Tight fairways ... A well-groomed city course that can be slow at times.

★★½ COOL LAKE GOLF CLUB

PU-520 E. 750 N., Lebanon, 46052, Boone County, (765)325-9271, 35 miles from Indianapolis. **Web:** coollakegolf.com. **Facility Holes:** 18. **Yards:** 6,000/4,827. **Par:** 70/72. **Course Rating:** 67.4/67.1. **Slope:** 108/105. **Green Fee:** $14/$18. **Cart Fee:** $12/Person. **Walking Policy:** Walking at certain times. **Walkability:** 2. **Opened:** 1962. **Architect:** G&J Design Inc. **Season:** Year-round. **High:** April-Oct. **To obtain tee times:** Call golf shop. **Miscellaneous:** Range (grass), credit cards (MC, V, D), BF, FF.

★★★★ THE COURSE AT ABERDEEN *Service, Value*

SP-245 Tower Rd., Valparaiso, 46385, Porter County, (219)462-5050, 40 miles from Chicago. **E-mail:** aberdeen18@aol.com. **Web:** www.golfataberdeen.com. **Facility Holes:** 18. **Yards:** 6,917/4,949. **Par:** 72/72. **Course Rating:** 73.0/68.3. **Slope:** 134/120. **Green Fee:** $55/$65. **Cart Fee:** Included in green fee. **Walking Policy:** Unrestricted walking. **Walkability:** 3. **Opened:** 1997. **Architect:** Michael Hurdzan/Dana Fry/Bill Kerman. **Season:** March-Nov. **High:** May-Oct. **To obtain tee times:** Call up to 14 days in advance. **Miscellaneous:** Reduced fees (weekdays, twilight, seniors, juniors), range (grass), lodging (11 rooms), credit cards (MC, V, AE), BF, FF.
Reader Comments: Very scenic, beautiful layout, could be in better shape ... Gets better every year ... Great variety of holes. Fast greens. Wonderful value ... Some very thought provoking holes. Great 10th hole ... Good par 5s, fun, short par 4 .

★★★★ COVERED BRIDGE GOLF CLUB

SP-12510 Covered Bridge Rd., Sellersburg, 47172, Clark County, (812)246-8880, 12 miles from Louisville, KY. **Facility Holes:** 18. **Yards:** 6,832/5,943. **Par:** 72/72. **Course Rating:** 73.0/74.7. **Slope:** 128/126. **Green Fee:** $50/$60. **Cart Fee:** Included in green fee. **Walkability:** 1. **Opened:** 1994. **Architect:** Clyde Johnston/Fuzzy Zoeller. **Season:** Year-round. **High:** April-Oct. **To obtain tee times:** Call golf shop. **Miscellaneous:** Reduced fees (weekdays), metal spikes, range (grass), credit cards (MC, V, AE, D).
Reader Comments: Zoysia fairways great—greens improving ... Wonderful course, pricey ... A scenic course fun to play for all handicap levels ... Tough par 3s. Excellent layout ... Slow greens ... A must play! Friendly staff and a nice pro shop.

COYOTE CROSSING GOLF CLUB

PU-28 E. 500 North, West Lafayette, 47906, Tippecanoe County, (765)497-1061, 50 miles from Indianapolis. **Web:** coyotecrossinggolf.com. **Facility Holes:** 18. **Yards:** 6,839/4,881. **Par:** 72/72. **Course Rating:** 72.2/67.5. **Slope:** 136/121. **Green Fee:** $20/$38. **Cart Fee:** $12/Person. **Walking Policy:** Unrestricted walking. **Walkability:** 4. **Architect:** Hale Irwin. **Season:** March-Dec. **High:** May-Sept. **To obtain tee times:** Call golf shop. **Miscellaneous:** Reduced fees (twilight, juniors), range (grass), credit cards (MC, V, AE, D, DC, CB), BF, FF.
Notes: Ranked 7th in 2001 Best New Affordable Courses.

CREEKSIDE GOLF COURSE & TRAINING CENTER

PU-2355 Clifford Rd., Valparaiso, 46385, Porter County, (219)531-7888, 40 miles from Chicago. **Web:** www.valparaisogolf.com. **Facility Holes:** 12. **Yards:** 3,270. **Par:** 36. **Green Fee:** $18/$23. **Cart Fee:** $22/Cart. **Walking Policy:** Unrestricted walking. **Walkability:** 3. **Opened:** 2000. **Architect:** Don Childs. **Season:** March-Dec. **High:** June-Sept. **To obtain tee times:** Call up to 7 days in advance. **Miscellaneous:** Range (grass/mats), credit cards (MC, V), BF, FF.

CRESSMOOR COUNTRY CLUB

SP-601 N. Wisconsin St., Hobart, 46342, Lake County, (219)942-9300. **Facility Holes:** 18. **Yards:** 6,060/4,914. **Par:** 72/72. **Course Rating:** 68.0/68.0. **Slope:** 108/108. **Green Fee:** $20/$25. **Cart Fee:** Included in green fee. **Walking Policy:** Unrestricted walking. **Walkability:** 1. **Opened:** 1922. **Season:** Year-round. **High:** April-Oct. **To obtain tee times:** Call golf shop. **Miscellaneous:** Reduced fees (weekdays, twilight, seniors, juniors), BF, FF.

★★★ DEER CREEK GOLF CLUB

PU-7143 South SR #39, Clayton, 46118, Hendricks County, (317)539-2013, 18 miles from Indianapolis. **Web:** deercreekgolfclub.com. **Facility Holes:** 18. **Yards:** 6,510/5,033. **Par:** 71/72. **Course Rating:** 71.2/68.8. **Slope:** 128/120. **Green Fee:** $18/$25. **Cart Fee:** $12/Person. **Walking Policy:** Walking at certain times. **Walkability:** 3. **Opened:** 1991. **Season:** March-Dec. **High:** May-Sept. **To obtain tee times:** Call up to 14 days in advance. **Miscellaneous:** Reduced fees (weekdays, twilight), range (grass/mats), credit cards (MC, V), BF, FF.
Reader Comments: Really hilly, will use all the clubs, really nice staff ... Has 3 weird holes.

★★½ DYKEMAN PARK GOLF COURSE

PU-63 Eberts Rd., Logansport, 46947, Cass County, (219)753-0222. **E-mail:** bobrothgeb@lneti.com. **Facility Holes:** 18. **Yards:** 6,185/5,347. **Par:** 70/73. **Course Rating:** 69.4/69.8. **Slope:** 118/102. **Green Fee:** $18. **Cart Fee:** $20/Person. **Walking Policy:** Unrestricted walking. **Walkability:** 3. **Opened:** 1920. **Architect:** William B. Langford/Theodore J. Moreau. **Season:** March-Nov. **High:** May-Sept. **To obtain tee times:** Call golf shop. **Miscellaneous:** Reduced fees (twilight, seniors, juniors), range (grass), BF, FF.

EAGLE CREEK GOLF CLUB

PU-8802 W. 56th St., Indianapolis, 46234, Marion County, (317)297-3366, 12 miles from Indianapolis. **E-mail:** eaglecreek1@aol.com. **Web:** www.eaglecreekgolfclub.com. **Facility Holes:** 36. **Cart Fee:** $17/Person. **Walking Policy:** Unrestricted walking. **Season:** Year-round. **High:** May-Sept. **To obtain tee times:** Call up to 7 days in advance. **Miscellaneous:** Metal spikes, range (grass/mats), credit cards (MC, V), BF, FF.

★★★½ **PINES COURSE** (18)
Yards: 6,976/5,002. **Par:** 72/72. **Green Fee:** $21/$23. **Walkability:** 3. **Opened:** 1974. **Architect:** Pete Dye. **Miscellaneous:** Reduced fees (weekdays, twilight, seniors, juniors).
Reader Comments: A super-challenging course and a great value. Well-managed operation … Slow greens, lots of play, picturesque … Very walkable … Interesting—fun to play.

SYCAMORE COURSE (18)
Yards: 6,856/4,726. **Par:** 70/70. **Green Fee:** $23/$25. **Opened:** 2001. **Architect:** Pete Dye/Tim Liddy. **Miscellaneous:** Reduced fees (weekdays, twilight, seniors).

EAGLE PINES GOLF CLUB

SP-9373 N. Country Club Rd., Mooresville, 46158, Morgan County, (317)831-4774, 1 mile from Mooresville. **Facility Holes:** 18. **Yards:** 6,055/5,032. **Par:** 70/70. **Course Rating:** 67.7/67.3. **Slope:** 113/110. **Green Fee:** $17/$18. **Cart Fee:** $12/Person. **Walking Policy:** Unrestricted walking. **Walkability:** 2. **Opened:** 1968. **Architect:** Ron Kern. **Season:** Year-round. **High:** May-Sept. **To obtain tee times:** Call up to 7 days in advance. **Miscellaneous:** Reduced fees (weekdays, twilight, seniors), credit cards (MC, V, AE, D), BF, FF.
Special Notes: Formerly Mooresville Golf Club.

★★★½ EAGLE POINTE GOLF & TENNIS RESORT

R-2250 E. Pointe Rd., Bloomington, 47401, Monroe County, (812)824-4040, (800)860-8604, 65 miles from Indianapolis. **Facility Holes:** 18. **Yards:** 6,604/5,186. **Par:** 71/71. **Course Rating:** 73.0/71.2. **Slope:** 140/126. **Green Fee:** $31/$50. **Cart Fee:** Included in green fee. **Walking Policy:** Mandatory carts. **Walkability:** 3. **Opened:** 1973. **Architect:** Bob Simmons. **Season:** Year-round. **High:** May-Sept. **To obtain tee times:** Call golf shop. **Miscellaneous:** Reduced fees (weekdays, twilight), metal spikes, range (grass/mats), credit cards (MC, V, AE, D), BF, FF.
Reader Comments: Very underrated course, excellent condition, some really testing holes from back tees, premium on accuracy, most shots require a good amount of thought … Good course, good management … Fun course tied to a condo association.

EAGLE VALLEY GOLF CLUB

PU-10350 Petersburg Rd., Evansville, 47725, Vanderburgh County, (812)867-7888, 3 miles from Evansville. **Facility Holes:** 18. **Yards:** 6,692/4,955. **Par:** 70/70. **Course Rating:** 72.5/68.7. **Slope:** 131/118. **Green Fee:** $21. **Cart Fee:** $10/Person. **Walking Policy:** Unrestricted walking. **Walkability:** 3. **Opened:** 1999. **Architect:** Bob Lohmann/Mike Benkusky. **Season:** Year-round. **High:** May-Sept. **To obtain tee times:** Call golf shop. **Miscellaneous:** Range (grass), credit cards (MC, V, AE, D), BF, FF.

★★★½ ELBEL PARK GOLF COURSE

PU-26595 Auten Rd., South Bend, 46628, St. Joseph County, (219)271-9180. **Facility Holes:** 18. **Yards:** 6,700/5,750. **Par:** 72/73. **Course Rating:** 70.7/71.4. **Slope:** 113/114. **Green Fee:** $13/$21. **Cart Fee:** $12/Person. **Walking Policy:** Unrestricted walking. **Walkability:** 4. **Opened:** 1963. **Architect:** William James Spear. **Season:** March-Dec. **High:** May-Sept. **To obtain tee times:** Call up to 7 days in advance. **Miscellaneous:** Reduced fees (weekdays, twilight, seniors, juniors), range (grass), credit cards (MC, V), BF, FF.
Reader Comments: Narrow fairways, some water, and well-placed bunkers … Rolling terrain, making distance control a premium … 9 doglegs on this wide-open course give long hitters a tremendous advantage … Gets too much play.

★★★ ERSKINE PARK GOLF CLUB

PU-4200 Miami St., South Bend, 46614, St. Joseph County, (219)291-3216. **Facility Holes:** 18. **Yards:** 6,104/5,536. **Par:** 70/74. **Course Rating:** 68.5/70.9. **Slope:** 120/120. **Green Fee:** $10/$21. **Cart Fee:** $12/Person. **Walking Policy:** Unrestricted walking. **Walkability:** 3. **Opened:** 1925. **Architect:** William H. Diddel. **Season:** March-Dec. **High:** May-Sept. **Tee times:** Call golf shop. **Miscellaneous:** Reduced fees (twilight, seniors, juniors), credit cards (MC, V), BF, FF.

INDIANA

Reader Comments: Best value course I have played. Always in immaculate condition. This very hilly course plays up and down a lot so club selection is of great importance. The par 5s are great—a 625-yard 10th (from the back tees).

★★ ETNA ACRES GOLF COURSE
SP-9803 W. 600 S., Andrews, 46702, Huntington County, (219)468-2906, 11 miles from Marion. **Web:** www.golfus.com/etnaacres. **Facility Holes:** 18. **Yards:** 6,096/5,142. **Par:** 72/72. **Course Rating:** 68.6/68.9. **Slope:** 109/108. **Green Fee:** $13/$15. **Cart Fee:** $10/Person. **Walking Policy:** Unrestricted walking. **Walkability:** 3. **Opened:** 1960. **Architect:** Gene Kaufman. **Season:** March-Nov. **To obtain tee times:** Call golf shop. **Miscellaneous:** Reduced fees (weekdays, seniors, juniors), metal spikes, range (grass), BF, FF.

★★★ FAIRVIEW GOLF COURSE
PU-7102 S. Calhoun St., Fort Wayne, 46807, Allen County, (219)745-7093. **Facility Holes:** 18. **Yards:** 6,620/5,125. **Par:** 72/72. **Course Rating:** 70.8/71.1. **Slope:** 119/108. **Green Fee:** $10. **Walking Policy:** Unrestricted walking. **Opened:** 1927. **Architect:** Donald Ross. **Season:** March-Oct. **High:** May-Sept. **To obtain tee times:** Call golf shop. **Miscellaneous:** Metal spikes, range (grass), credit cards (MC, V).
Reader Comments: Good course for the beginner or weekender ... Needs updating ... Best value around. Weekend pace is slow.

★★ FENDRICH GOLF COURSE
PU-1900 Diamond Ave., Evansville, 47711, Vanderburgh County, (812)435-6070. **Facility Holes:** 18. **Yards:** 5,791/5,232. **Par:** 70/70. **Course Rating:** 67.1/69.2. **Slope:** 106/109. **Green Fee:** $10. **Walking Policy:** Unrestricted walking. **Opened:** 1945. **Architect:** William H. Diddel. **Season:** Year-round. **High:** April-Sept. **To obtain tee times:** Call golf shop. **Miscellaneous:** Metal spikes, range (grass).

★★ FOREST PARK GOLF COURSE
PU-P.O. Box 42, 1018 S. John Stelle Dr., Brazil, 47834, Clay County, (812)442-5681, 15 miles from Terre Haute. **Facility Holes:** 18. **Yards:** 6,012/5,647. **Par:** 71/73. **Course Rating:** 68.0/69.8. **Slope:** 110/112. **Green Fee:** $12/$14. **Cart Fee:** $12/Cart. **Walking Policy:** Unrestricted walking. **Walkability:** 1. **Opened:** 1963. **Architect:** Pete Dye. **Season:** Year-round. **High:** May-Sept. **To obtain tee times:** Call golf shop. **Miscellaneous:** Reduced fees (weekdays, twilight), range (grass), credit cards (MC, V), BF, FF.

★★ FOREST PARK GOLF COURSE
PU-1155 Sheffield Dr., Valparaiso, 46385, Porter County, (219)531-7888, 40 miles from Chicago. **Web:** www.valparaisogolf.com. **Facility Holes:** 18. **Yards:** 5,731/5,339. **Par:** 70/72. **Course Rating:** 67.4/70.7. **Slope:** 114/111. **Green Fee:** $18/$23. **Cart Fee:** $22/Cart. **Walking Policy:** Unrestricted walking. **Walkability:** 3. **Opened:** 1973. **Architect:** William James Spear. **Season:** March-Dec. **High:** June-Sept. **To obtain tee times:** Call up to 7 days in advance. **Miscellaneous:** Reduced fees (juniors), credit cards (MC, V), FF.

★★★★½ THE FORT GOLF COURSE *Value*
PU-6002 N. Post Rd., Indianapolis, 46216, Marion County, (317)543-9597. **E-mail:** fortgolfpro@dnr.state.in.us. **Web:** www.thefortgolf.com. **Facility Holes:** 18. **Yards:** 7,148/5,045. **Par:** 72/71. **Course Rating:** 74.5/69.2. **Slope:** 139/123. **Green Fee:** $33/$46. **Cart Fee:** $13/Person. **Walking Policy:** Unrestricted walking. **Walkability:** 3. **Opened:** 1997. **Architect:** Pete Dye/Tim Liddy. **Season:** March-Nov. **High:** May-Sept. **To obtain tee times:** Call golf shop. **Miscellaneous:** Reduced fees (twilight, juniors), range (grass), lodging (25 rooms), credit cards (MC, V, AE, D), BF, FF.
Notes: Ranked 7th in 1999 Best in State.
Reader Comments: Perfect conditions ... Don't try to walk it! Lots of memorable holes—especially # 11 ... Lots of elevation changes. Big old trees everywhere. Play the right tees and you will have fun ... New upscale look to a traditional layout, but still scoreable ... Excellent variety of holes.

★★★½ FOX PRAIRIE GOLF CLUB
PU-8465 E. 196th St., Noblesville, 46060, Hamilton County, (317)776-6357, 15 miles from Indianapolis. **Facility Holes:** 18. **Yards:** 6,946/5,533. **Par:** 72/75. **Course Rating:** 72.1/71.4. **Slope:** 119/114. **Green Fee:** $20/$26. **Cart Fee:** $13/Person. **Walking Policy:** Unrestricted walking. **Walkability:** 3. **Opened:** 1970. **Architect:** William Newcomb. **Season:** March-Dec. **To obtain tee times:** Call up to 7 days in advance. **Miscellaneous:** Range (grass), credit cards (MC, V), BF, FF.
Reader Comments: A fun course but gets a lot of play ... Great shape ... Adding 9 holes ... Very long from back tees—big greens.
Special Notes: 9 new holes scheduled to open in summer 2002.

INDIANA

★★ FOX RIDGE COUNTRY CLUB
PU-1364 N. Hillcrest Road, Vincennes, 47591, Knox County, (812)886-5929, 50 miles from Terre Haute. **Facility Holes:** 18. **Yards:** 6,578/5,412. **Par:** 72/72. **Course Rating:** 72.0/71.0. **Slope:** 131/124. **Green Fee:** $25/$30. **Cart Fee:** Included in green fee. **Walking Policy:** Walking at certain times. **Walkability:** 5. **Opened:** 1987. **Architect:** G. S. Ridgway. **Season:** Year-round. **High:** April-Oct. **To obtain tee times:** Call golf shop. **Miscellaneous:** Reduced fees (weekdays), range (grass/mats), credit cards (MC, V, D).

FRENCH LICK SPRINGS RESORT
R-Hwy. 56., French Lick, 47432, Orange County, (812)936-9300, (800)457-4042, 60 miles from Louisville. **Web:** www.frenchlick.com. **Facility Holes:** 36. **Cart Fee:** Included in green fee. **High:** May-Sept. **To obtain tee times:** Call up to 90 days in advance. **Miscellaneous:** Reduced fees (guests, twilight), metal spikes, range (grass/mats), credit cards (MC, V, AE, D, Hotel Chg.), BF, FF.
★★★★ **HILL COURSE (18)**
Yards: 6,650/5,927. **Par:** 70/71. **Course Rating:** 71.6/70.3. **Slope:** 119/116. **Green Fee:** $55/$66. **Walkability:** 5. **Opened:** 1920. **Architect:** Donald Ross. **Season:** March-Nov.
Reader Comments: Very challenging—tough greens to read … A fun challenging course to play. Hilly with interesting greens. Depending on the pin placement, very easy to 4-putt the 8th green … Nice, long, demanding pro-type course.
★★ **VALLEY COURSE (18)**
Yards: 6,001/5,627. **Par:** 70/71. **Course Rating:** 67.6/66.0. **Slope:** 110/106. **Green Fee:** $35/$39. **Walking Policy:** Walking at certain times. **Walkability:** 2. **Opened:** 1905. **Architect:** Tom Bendelow. **Season:** Year-round.

GARRETT COUNTRY CLUB
PU-401 N. Walsh St., Garrett, 46738, DeKalb County, (219)357-5586. **Facility Holes:** 18. **Yards:** 6,552/4,840. **Par:** 72/72. **Course Rating:** 70.8/67.6. **Slope:** 123/108. **Green Fee:** $17/$20. **Cart Fee:** $10/Person. **Walking Policy:** Unrestricted walking. **Walkability:** 2. **Opened:** 1918. **Architect:** Tom Bendelow. **Season:** March-Nov. **To obtain tee times:** Call golf shop. **Miscellaneous:** Reduced fees (weekdays), range (grass), credit cards (MC, V), BF, FF.

★★½ GENEVA HILLS GOLF CLUB
PU-13446 S. Geneva Rd., Clinton, 47842, Vermillion County, (765)832-8384, 15 miles from Terre Haute. **E-mail:** south@abcs.com. **Web:** www.golfus.com/genevahills. **Facility Holes:** 18. **Yards:** 6,768/4,785. **Par:** 72/72. **Course Rating:** 70.2/67.3. **Slope:** 118/115. **Green Fee:** $17/$20. **Cart Fee:** $12/Person. **Walking Policy:** Unrestricted walking. **Walkability:** 3. **Opened:** 1970. **Architect:** R. D. Shaw. **Season:** Year-round. **High:** April-Oct. **Tee times:** Call golf shop. **Misc:** Reduced fees (weekdays, twilight, seniors, juniors), range (grass), credit cards (MC, V).

★★★½ GOLF CLUB OF INDIANA
PU-I 65 at Zionsville Exit 130, Zionsville, 46077, Boone County, (317)769-6388, 16 miles from Indianapolis. **E-mail:** jrubenst@pop.iquest.net. **Web:** www.golfindiana.com. **Facility Holes:** 18. **Yards:** 7,151/5,156. **Par:** 72/72. **Course Rating:** 73.6/68.9. **Slope:** 132/119. **Green Fee:** $35/$44. **Cart Fee:** $10/Person. **Walking Policy:** Unrestricted walking. **Walkability:** 2. **Opened:** 1974. **Architect:** Charles Maddox. **Season:** Year-round. **High:** April-Nov. **Ttee times:** Call up to 7 ahead. **Misc:** Reduced fees (twilight), range, credit cards (MC, V), BF, FF.
Reader Comments: Always in good shape, slow play most times … A great value for the money … Very open, fun course … Classic design & challenging … Overpriced for what you get.

★★★½ GRAND OAK GOLF CLUB
SP-370 Grand Oak Dr., West Harrison, 47060, Dearborn County, (812)637-3943, 25 miles from Cincinnati. **E-mail:** golfgogc@aol.com. **Web:** www.grandoakgolfclub.com. **Facility Holes:** 18. **Yards:** 6,528/5,113. **Par:** 72/72. **Course Rating:** 71.0/70.1. **Slope:** 128/121. **Green Fee:** $21/$33. **Cart Fee:** $12/Person. **Walking Policy:** Unrestricted walking. **Walkability:** 4. **Opened:** 1989. **Architect:** Michael Hurdzan. **Season:** Feb.-Dec. **High:** June-Aug. **To obtain tee times:** Call up to 14 days in advance. **Miscellaneous:** Reduced fees (weekdays, twilight, seniors, juniors), range (grass/mats), credit cards (MC, V), BF, FF.
Reader Comments: Hard course for seniors. A lot of walking even with cart … Very nice country course … Some nice holes, some design features I didn't get.

★★ GREEN ACRES GOLF CLUB
PU-1300 Green Acres Dr., Kokomo, 46901-9546, Howard County, (765)883-5771, 9 miles from Kokomo. **Facility Holes:** 18. **Yards:** 6,811/5,257. **Par:** 72/72. **Course Rating:** 72.8/72.7. **Slope:** 129/118. **Green Fee:** $19/$24. **Cart Fee:** $11/Person. **Walking Policy:** Unrestricted walking. **Walkability:** 3. **Opened:** 1968. **Architect:** Bob Simmons. **Season:** Year-round. **To obtain tee times:** Call golf shop. **Miscellaneous:** Reduced fees (seniors, juniors), range (grass), credit cards (MC, V, AE, D), BF, FF.

★★★ GREENFIELD COUNTRY CLUB

SP-145 S. Morristown Pike, Greenfield, 46140, Hancock County, (317)462-2706, 15 miles from Indianapolis. **Facility Holes:** 18. **Yards:** 6,773/5,501. **Par:** 72/73. **Course Rating:** 71.2/73.5. **Slope:** 119/120. **Green Fee:** $18/$23. **Cart Fee:** $12/Person. **Walking Policy:** Unrestricted walking. **Opened:** 1927. **Architect:** Gary Kern. **Season:** March-Nov. **High:** May-Sept. **To obtain tee times:** Call golf shop. **Miscellaneous:** Reduced fees (weekdays), metal spikes, range (grass), credit cards (MC, V).
Reader Comments: Great place to play. Outstanding golf professional. Best teacher in state of Indiana … An old winner, some of the best greens.

★★★ HANGING TREE GOLF CLUB

SP-2302 W. 161st St., Westfield, 46074, Hamilton County, (317)896-2474, 20 miles from Indianapolis. **Web:** www.golfus.com/hangingtree. **Facility Holes:** 18. **Yards:** 6,519/5,151. **Par:** 71/71. **Course Rating:** 72.6/70.6. **Slope:** 130/122. **Green Fee:** $33/$44. **Cart Fee:** Included in green fee. **Walking Policy:** Mandatory carts. **Walkability:** 3. **Opened:** 1990. **Architect:** Gary Kern. **Season:** Year-round. **High:** April-Nov. **To obtain tee times:** Call up to 14 days in advance. **Miscellaneous:** Reduced fees (weekdays, twilight), range (grass), credit cards (MC, V, AE, D), BF, FF.
Reader Comments: A tough course. A creek crossing the fairway comes into play on many holes. A good value … Good layout, tough on a windy day … Well conditioned, has some quirky holes.

HARRISON HILLS GOLF & COUNTRY CLUB

PU-413 E. New St., Attica, 47918, Fountain County, (765)762-1135, 25 miles from Lafayette. **E-mail:** hhills@tctc.com. **Web:** www.harrisonhills.com. **Facility Holes:** 18. **Yards:** 6,820/5,223. **Par:** 72/72. **Course Rating:** 72.6/69.7. **Slope:** 130/120. **Green Fee:** $21/$26. **Cart Fee:** $12/Person. **Walking Policy:** Walking at certain times. **Walkability:** 3. **Opened:** 1924. **Architect:** William B. Langford/Tim Liddy. **Season:** March-Dec. **High:** May-Sept. **To obtain tee times:** Call golf shop. **Miscellaneous:** Reduced fees (weekdays), range (grass), cards (MC, V, D), BF, FF.

★½ HELFRICH GOLF COURSE

PU-1550 Mesker Park Dr., Evansville, 47720, Vanderburgh County, (812)435-6075. **E-mail:** dmcatee@pga.com. **Facility Holes:** 18. **Yards:** 6,306/5,506. **Par:** 71/74. **Course Rating:** 69.8/71.4. **Slope:** 124/117. **Green Fee:** $14. **Cart Fee:** $21/Person. **Walking Policy:** Unrestricted walking. **Walkability:** 5. **Opened:** 1923. **Architect:** Tom Bendelow. **Season:** Year-round. **To obtain tee times:** Call up to 7 days in advance. **Miscellaneous:** Credit cards (MC, V).

HICKORY STICK GOLF CLUB

SP-4422 Hickory Stick Blvd., Greenwood, 46143, Johnson County, (317)422-8300, 12 miles from Indianapolis. **Web:** hickorystickgolf.com. **Facility Holes:** 18. **Yards:** 6,832/4,944. **Par:** 71/71. **Course Rating:** 72.7/68.1. **Slope:** 135/114. **Green Fee:** $45/$55. **Cart Fee:** Included in green fee. **Walking Policy:** Walking at certain times. **Walkability:** 4. **Opened:** 2001. **Architect:** Tim Liddy. **Season:** April-Nov. **To obtain tee times:** Call up to 7 days in advance. **Miscellaneous:** Range (grass), credit cards (MC, V, AE), FF.

★★½ HIDDEN CREEK GOLF CLUB

PU-4975 Utica Sellersburg Rd., Sellersburg, 47172, Clark County, (812)246-2556, (800)822-2556, 10 miles from Louisville, KY. **E-mail:** info@kentucky-golfer.com. **Web:** www.kentucky-golfer.com. **Facility Holes:** 27. **Yards:** 6,785/5,100. **Par:** 71/71. **Course Rating:** 73.0/70.6. **Slope:** 133/123. **Green Fee:** $10/$31. **Cart Fee:** $10/Person. **Walking Policy:** Unrestricted walking. **Walkability:** 2. **Opened:** 1992. **Architect:** David Pfaff. **Season:** Year-round. **High:** April-Sept. **To obtain tee times:** Call golf shop. **Miscellaneous:** Reduced fees (weekdays, twilight, seniors, juniors), range (grass/mats), credit cards (MC, V, AE, D), BF, FF. **Special Notes:** Also has a 9-hole mid-size course.

★★★ HONEYWELL GOLF COURSE

PU-3360 W. Division Rd., Wabash, 46992, Wabash County, (219)563-8663, 45 miles from Fort Wayne. **E-mail:** rlundy@ctlnet.com. **Web:** www.honeywellgolf.com. **Facility Holes:** 18. **Yards:** 6,430/5,650. **Par:** 71/71. **Course Rating:** 69.4/70.4. **Slope:** 121/118. **Green Fee:** $20. **Cart Fee:** $10/Person. **Walking Policy:** Unrestricted walking. **Walkability:** 2. **Opened:** 1980. **Architect:** Arthur Hills. **Season:** March-Dec. **High:** June-Aug. **To obtain tee times:** Call golf shop. **Miscellaneous:** Reduced fees (weekdays, juniors), range (grass), credit cards (MC, V), BF, FF.
Reader Comments: Some real tricky holes … This is an excellent low-cost public course … Tight course, but a good course to walk … Condition varies with weather … Nice course layout—very accommodating.

★★★½ HULMAN LINKS GOLF COURSE
PU-990 N. Chamberlain St., Terre Haute, 47803, Vigo County, (812)877-2096, 75 miles from Indianapolis. **Facility Holes:** 18. **Yards:** 7,225/5,775. **Par:** 72/72. **Course Rating:** 74.9/68.7. **Slope:** 144/127. **Green Fee:** $26. **Cart Fee:** $13/Person. **Walking Policy:** Unrestricted walking. **Walkability:** 4. **Opened:** 1978. **Architect:** David Gill. **Season:** March-Dec. **High:** May-Nov. **To obtain tee times:** Call golf shop. **Miscellaneous:** Reduced fees (juniors), range (grass), credit cards (MC, V), BF, FF.
Reader Comments: Really tough course, could be taken care of much better, #18 great finishing hole ... Great public course, every hole different, good test.

★★★ INDIANA UNIVERSITY GOLF CLUB
PU-State Rd. 46 Bypass, Bloomington, 47401, Monroe County, (812)855-7543, 45 miles from Indianapolis. **E-mail:** mkemper@indiana.edu. **Facility Holes:** 27. **Yards:** 6,942/5,661. **Par:** 71/72. **Course Rating:** 72.4/73.1. **Slope:** 129/123. **Green Fee:** $19/$21. **Cart Fee:** $12/Person. **Walking Policy:** Walking at certain times. **Walkability:** 4. **Opened:** 1959. **Architect:** Jim Soutar. **Season:** March-Dec. **To obtain tee times:** Call golf shop. **Miscellaneous:** Range (grass/mats), credit cards (MC, V, D), BF, FF.
Reader Comments: Very tough course. A lot of slope changes, downhill and sidehill lies. Trees to the left & right on just about every hole. Long par 3s ... The course has little water or sand, but is an enjoyable challenge.
Special Notes: Also has 9-hole par-3 course.

IRONWOOD GOLF CLUB
SP-10955 Fall Rd., Fishers, 46038, Hamilton County, (317)842-0551, 15 miles from Indianapolis. **Web:** www.ironwoodgc.com. **Facility Holes:** 27. **Green Fee:** $25/$30. **Cart Fee:** $12/Person. **Walking Policy:** Walking at certain times. **Walkability:** 3. **Architect:** R. N. Thompson/Art Kaser. **Season:** Year-round. **High:** April-Oct. **To obtain tee times:** Call golf shop. **Miscellaneous:** Range (grass), credit cards (MC, V, D).
LAKES/RIDGE (18 combo)
Yards: 6,713/4,935. **Par:** 72/72. **Course Rating:** 73.6/69.5. **Slope:** 140/121.
RIDGE/VALLEY (18 combo)
Yards: 6,901/5,104. **Par:** 72/72. **Course Rating:** 74.5/70.4. **Slope:** 142/126.
VALLEY/LAKES (18 combo)
Yards: 6,901/5,104. **Par:** 72/72. **Course Rating:** 74.5/70.4. **Slope:** 142/126.

★★★ JASPER MUNICIPAL GOLF COURSE
PU-17th and Jackson, Jasper, 47546, Dubois County, (812)482-4600, 50 miles from Evansville. **Facility Holes:** 18. **Yards:** 5,985/5,055. **Par:** 71/71. **Course Rating:** 68.0/68.0. **Slope:** 105/105. **Green Fee:** $14. **Cart Fee:** $9/Person. **Walking Policy:** Unrestricted walking. **Walkability:** 4. **Opened:** 1971. **Architect:** William Newcomb. **Season:** Year-round. **High:** June-Aug. **To obtain tee times:** Call golf shop. **Miscellaneous:** Reduced fees (seniors), credit cards (MC, V).
Reader Comments: A challenging course with a great finishing hole. The 18th green is in a beautiful setting ... The beauty and toughness of this course.

★★★★ JUDAY CREEK GOLF COURSE
SP-14770 Lindy Dr., Granger, 46530, St. Joseph County, (219)277-4653, 5 miles from South Bend. **E-mail:** info@judaycreek.com. **Web:** www.judaycreek.com. **Facility Holes:** 18. **Yards:** 6,940/5,000. **Par:** 72/72. **Course Rating:** 73.3/67.1. **Slope:** 133/116. **Green Fee:** $25/$30. **Cart Fee:** $13/Person. **Walking Policy:** Walking at certain times. **Walkability:** 3. **Opened:** 1989. **Architect:** Ken Killian. **Season:** March-Oct. **High:** June-Aug. **To obtain tee times:** Call golf shop. **Miscellaneous:** Reduced fees (twilight, seniors, juniors), range (grass/mats), credit cards (MC, V, AE), BF, FF.
Reader Comments: Water, water everywhere ... The staff is some of the best I have ever encountered and the course is always in great shape ... Good layout, will go back again ... Very overrated, price is right.

★★ KI-ANN GOLF COURSE
PU-2436 E. SR 26, Hartford City, 47348, Blackford County, (765)348-4876, 2 miles from Hartford City. **Facility Holes:** 18. **Yards:** 5,962/4,868. **Par:** 70/71. **Course Rating:** 67.8/70.1. **Slope:** 111/115. **Green Fee:** $14/$17. **Cart Fee:** $12/Person. **Walking Policy:** Unrestricted walking. **Walkability:** 2. **Opened:** 1971. **Architect:** Mr. Hodges. **Season:** March-Dec. **High:** May-Oct. **To obtain tee times:** Call golf shop. **Miscellaneous:** Reduced fees (weekdays, seniors, juniors), credit cards (MC, V), BF, FF.

★★½ LAFAYETTE GOLF CLUB
PU-800 Golf View Dr., Lafayette, 47904, Tippecanoe County, (765)476-4588, 68 miles from Indianapolis. **Facility Holes:** 18. **Yards:** 7,018/5,241. **Par:** 72/75. **Course Rating:** 73.0/71.7.

Slope: 129/115. Green Fee: $15/$17. Cart Fee: $10/Person. Walking Policy: Unrestricted walking. Walkability: 2. Opened: 1972. Architect: Bob Simmons. Season: Year-round. To obtain tee times: Call up to 14 days in advance. Miscellaneous: Reduced fees (twilight), range (grass), credit cards (MC, V), BF, FF. Special Notes: Formerly Lafayette Municipal Golf Club.

LAKE HILLS GOLF CLUB
PU-10001 W. 85th Ave., St. John, 46373, Lake County, (219)365-8601, (888)274-4557, 35 miles from Chicago. Facility Holes: 54. Green Fee: $18/$40. Cart Fee: Included in green fee. Walking Policy: Unrestricted walking. Walkability: 5. Opened: 1925. Architect: Charles Maddox/Frank P. MacDonald. Season: April-Nov. High: June-Sept. To obtain tee times: Call golf shop. Miscellaneous: Credit cards (MC, V, AE, D).
★★ CLUB COURSE (18)
Yards: 5,888/4,648. Par: 71/72. Course Rating: 68.1/66.1. Slope: 110/105.
★★ COUNTRY COURSE (18)
Yards: 5,889/4,471. Par: 71/72. Course Rating: 68.0/65.4. Slope: 109/102. Miscellaneous: Reduced fees (weekdays, twilight, seniors, juniors).
★★ PLAYERS COURSE (18)
Yards: 6,194/4,504. Par: 70/70. Course Rating: 70.1/65.8. Slope: 124/111.

★★ LAKE JAMES GOLF CLUB
SP-1445 W. 275 N., Angola, 46703, Steuben County, (219)833-3967, 45 miles from Fort Wayne. Facility Holes: 18. Yards: 6,651/5,311. Par: 72/73. Course Rating: 72.6/69.3. Slope: 134/124. Green Fee: $20/$25. Cart Fee: $12/Person. Walking Policy: Unrestricted walking. Walkability: 4. Opened: 1926. Architect: Robert Beard. Season: March-Oct. High: June-Aug. To obtain tee times: Call up to 14 days in advance. Miscellaneous: Reduced fees (weekdays, seniors, juniors), credit cards (MC, V, D), BF, FF.

★★★ THE LEGENDS OF INDIANA GOLF COURSE
PU-2555 N. Hurricane Rd., Franklin, 46131, Johnson County, (317)736-8186, 22 miles from Indianapolis. E-mail: thelegends@aol.com. Web: www.legendsofindiana.com. Facility Holes: 27. Green Fee: $32/$45. Cart Fee: $10/Person. Walking Policy: Walking at certain times. Walkability: 2. Opened: 1991. Architect: Jim Fazio. Season: Year-round. High: May-Oct. To obtain tee times: Call up to 7 days in advance. Miscellaneous: Reduced fees (twilight, seniors), range (grass), credit cards (MC, V, AE, D), BF, FF.
CREEK/MIDDLE (18 Combo)
Yards: 7,029/5,287. Par: 72/72. Course Rating: 74.0/70.3. Slope: 132/120.
CREEK/ROAD (18 Combo)
Yards: 7,177/5,399. Par: 72/72. Course Rating: 74.8/71.0. Slope: 134/120.
MIDDLE/ROAD (18 Combo)
Yards: 7,044/5,244. Par: 72/72. Course Rating: 74.0/70.1. Slope: 133/120.
Reader Comments: Beautifully conditioned golf course, very playable, very flat but not boring. Some ordinary holes ... Excellent condition & practice facility, slightly overpriced ... Average layout with decent condition course.

★★½ LIBERTY COUNTRY CLUB
SP-1391 U.S. 27 N., Liberty, 47353, Union County, (765)458-5664, 35 miles from Cincinnati. Web: libertycountryclub.com. Facility Holes: 18. Yards: 6,375/4,544. Par: 70/71. Course Rating: 70.5/69.3. Slope: 128/115. Green Fee: $20/$25. Cart Fee: $12/Person. Walking Policy: Unrestricted walking. Walkability: 3. Opened: 1927. Architect: Nipper Campbell/Bob Simmons. Season: Year-round. High: April-Oct. To obtain tee times: Call up to 7 days in advance. Misc: Reduced fees (weekdays, twilight), range (grass), cards (MC, V), BF, FF.

LIMBERLOST GOLF CLUB
SP-3204 E. Rd 900 N, Rome City, 46784, Noble County, (219)854-4878, 32 miles from Fort Wayne. Facility Holes: 18. Yards: 5,770/4,973. Par: 70/70. Course Rating: 64.9/69.3. Slope: 101/109. Green Fee: $13/$15. Cart Fee: $17/Cart. Walking Policy: Unrestricted walking. Walkability: 3. Opened: 1927. Season: March-Nov. High: May-Sept. To obtain tee times: Call golf shop. Miscellaneous: Metal spikes, credit cards (MC, V, AE).

★★★ THE LINKS AT GRAND VICTORIA
PU-600 Grand Victoria Dr., Rising Sun, 47040, Ohio County, (812)438-5148, 35 miles from Cincinnati. E-mail: davidh@seidata.com. Facility Holes: 18. Yards: 6,406/5,006. Par: 71/71. Course Rating: 70.3/67.8. Slope: 125/112. Green Fee: $45/$55. Cart Fee: Included in green fee. Walking Policy: Mandatory carts. Walkability: 2. Opened: 2000. Architect: Tim Liddy. Season: April-Nov. To obtain tee times: Call up to 30 days in advance. Miscellaneous: Reduced fees (weekdays, twilight, seniors, juniors), credit cards (MC, V, AE, D, DC, CB), FF.
Reader Comments: No trees, but plenty of sand ... Very good ... Excellent facility ... It's better than I thought as I played it ... True links experience ... Good challenge.

★★★★ **THE LINKS AT HEARTLAND CROSSING** *Service*
PU-6701 S. Heartland Blvd., Camby, 46113, Morgan County, (317)630-1785, 5 miles from Indianapolis. **E-mail:** heartlandgolf@iquest.net. **Web:** heartlandcrossinggolf.com. **Facility Holes:** 18. **Yards:** 7,267/5,536. **Par:** 72/72. **Course Rating:** 75.4/69.0. **Slope:** 134/121. **Green Fee:** $23/$49. **Cart Fee:** $10/Person. **Walking Policy:** Unrestricted walking. **Walkability:** 1. **Opened:** 1998. **Architect:** Steve Smyers/Nick Price. **Season:** Year-round. **High:** May-Nov. **To obtain tee times:** Call up to 14 days in advance. **Miscellaneous:** Reduced fees (weekdays, twilight, juniors), range (grass), credit cards (MC, V, AE, D), BF, FF.
Reader Comments: Excellent layout, good service & practice facility ... Links style, huge bunkers, deep rough ... Great contrasting 9s ... Unique, championship style layout ... Too long & hard for most golfers ... For a challenge, play the back tees.

THE LINKS GOLF CLUB
PU-11425 N. Shelby 700 W., New Palestine, 46163, Shelby County, (317)861-4466, 15 miles from Indianapolis. **Facility Holes:** 18. **Yards:** 7,054/5,018. **Par:** 72/72. **Course Rating:** 73.3/68.4. **Slope:** 122/100. **Green Fee:** $32/$43. **Cart Fee:** $5/Person. **Walking Policy:** Walking at certain times. **Walkability:** 1. **Opened:** 1972. **Architect:** Charles Maddox. **Season:** Year-round. **To obtain tee times:** Call golf shop. **Miscellaneous:** Reduced fees (weekdays, twilight, seniors), range (grass), credit cards (MC, V, D, Novus), BF, FF.

★★ **LOGANSPORT GOLF CLUB**
PU-20 Cedar Island, Logansport, 46947, Cass County, (219)722-1110, 5 miles from Logansport. **Web:** www.usgolf.com. **Facility Holes:** 18. **Yards:** 6,100/5,400. **Par:** 71/72. **Course Rating:** 67.8/64.8. **Slope:** 109/103. **Green Fee:** $11/$14. **Cart Fee:** $13/Person. **Walking Policy:** Unrestricted walking. **Walkability:** 2. **Opened:** 1904. **Architect:** Bob A. Simmons. **Season:** Year-round. **High:** May-Oct. **To obtain tee times:** Call golf shop. **Miscellaneous:** Reduced fees (weekdays), range (grass), credit cards (MC, V), BF, FF.
Special Notes: Formerly Ironhorse Golf Club.

★½ **MAPLEWOOD GOLF CLUB**
SP-4261 E. County Rd. 700 S., Muncie, 47302, Delaware County, (765)284-8007, 7 miles from Muncie. **Facility Holes:** 18. **Yards:** 6,571/5,759. **Par:** 71/76. **Course Rating:** 70.0/68.5. **Slope:** 121/115. **Green Fee:** $15/$19. **Cart Fee:** $11/Person. **Walking Policy:** Unrestricted walking. **Walkability:** 2. **Opened:** 1961. **Season:** April-Oct. **High:** June-Sept. **To obtain tee times:** Call golf shop. **Miscellaneous:** Reduced fees (weekdays), range (grass), credit cards (MC, V, D).

★★ **MAXWELTON GOLF CLUB**
SP-5721 E. Elkhart County Line Rd., Syracuse, 46567, Kosciusko County, (219)457-3504, 45 miles from South Bend. **Web:** maxweltongolf.com. **Facility Holes:** 18. **Yards:** 6,490/5,992. **Par:** 72/72. **Course Rating:** 70.1/73.4. **Slope:** 124/128. **Green Fee:** $21/$25. **Cart Fee:** $12/Person. **Walking Policy:** Unrestricted walking. **Walkability:** 3. **Opened:** 1930. **Architect:** William B. Langford. **Season:** March-Nov. **High:** May-Sept. **To obtain tee times:** Call up to 7 days in advance. **Miscellaneous:** Credit cards (MC, V, AE, D), BF, FF.

MICHIGAN CITY MUNICIPAL COURSE
PU-4000 E. Michigan Blvd., Michigan City, 46360, La Porte County, (219)873-1516, 55 miles from Chicago. **Facility Holes:** 36. **Walking Policy:** Unrestricted walking. **Walkability:** 2. **Architect:** Ted Netz. **Season:** March-Nov. **High:** June-Aug. **To obtain tee times:** Call golf shop. **Miscellaneous:** Reduced fees (twilight, seniors, juniors).
★½ **NORTH COURSE** (18)
Yards: 3,531/3,223. **Par:** 60/60. **Green Fee:** $8/$11.
★½ **SOUTH COURSE** (18)
Yards: 6,169/5,363. **Par:** 72/74. **Course Rating:** 67.6/68.6. **Slope:** 113/113. **Green Fee:** $13/$17. **Cart Fee:** $20/Cart. **Opened:** 1930.

★★★½ **MYSTIC HILLS GOLF CLUB** *Pace*
PU-16788 20 B Rd., Culver, 46511, Marshall County, (219)842-2687, 35 miles from South Bend. **Web:** www.mystichills.com. **Facility Holes:** 18. **Yards:** 6,780/4,958. **Par:** 71/71. **Course Rating:** 72.0/67.5. **Slope:** 132/117. **Green Fee:** $15/$21. **Cart Fee:** $14/Person. **Walking Policy:** Walking at certain times. **Walkability:** 4. **Architect:** Pete Dye/Alice Dye/P.B. Dye. **Season:** March-Oct. **High:** July-Aug. **To obtain tee times:** Call golf shop. **Miscellaneous:** Reduced fees (weekdays, guests, twilight), range (grass), credit cards (MC, V, AE, D).
Notes: Ranked 9th in 1999 Best New Affordable Public.
Reader Comments: Links-style front 9 and wooded back 9 ... Wide fairways ... Shotmakers course, nice rolling course, good layout ... Incredibly inexpensive—very good par 4s ... In time, will grow up to be top-notch course.

OAK GROVE COUNTRY CLUB
SP-State Road 55 S., Oxford, 47971, Benton County, (765)385-2713, 15 miles from Lafayette. **Facility Holes:** 18. **Yards:** 6,050/5,410. **Par:** 71/73. **Course Rating:** 69.2/68.4. **Slope:** 113/113. **Green Fee:** $13/$15. **Cart Fee:** $10/Person. **Walking Policy:** Unrestricted walking. **Walkability:** 1. **Opened:** 1928. **Architect:** William H. Diddel. **Season:** Year-round. **High:** June-Sept. **To obtain tee times:** Call golf shop. **Miscellaneous:** Reduced fees (weekdays, juniors), credit cards (MC, V), BF, FF.

★½ OAK KNOLL GOLF COURSE
PU-11200 Whitcomb St., Crown Point, 46307, Lake County, (219)663-3349, 12 miles from Gary. **Facility Holes:** 18. **Yards:** 5,703/5,369. **Par:** 70/70. **Course Rating:** 67.3/72.3. **Slope:** 107/113. **Green Fee:** $13/$17. **Opened:** 1935. **Season:** Year-round. **To obtain tee times:** Call golf shop.

★★ OTIS PARK GOLF CLUB
PU-607 Tunnelton Rd., Bedford, 47421, Lawrence County, (812)279-9092, 75 miles from Indianapolis. **Facility Holes:** 18. **Yards:** 6,308/5,184. **Par:** 72/72. **Course Rating:** 70.0/68.1. **Slope:** 128/124. **Green Fee:** $14/$17. **Cart Fee:** $22/Cart. **Walking Policy:** Unrestricted walking. **Walkability:** 4. **Opened:** 1920. **Architect:** Harry S. Scoop. **Season:** Year-round. **High:** May-Oct. **To obtain tee times:** Call golf shop. **Miscellaneous:** Range (grass/mats), BF, FF.

OTTER CREEK GOLF COURSE
PU-11522 E. 50 N., Columbus, 47203, Bartholomew County, (812)579-5227, 35 miles from Indianapolis. **E-mail:** chad@hsonline.net. **Web:** www.ocgc.com. **Facility Holes:** 27. **Green Fee:** $45/$70. **Cart Fee:** Included in green fee. **Walking Policy:** Unrestricted walking. **Walkability:** 3. **Opened:** 1964. **Architect:** Robert Trent Jones/Rees Jones. **Season:** Year-round. **To obtain tee times:** Call golf shop. **Miscellaneous:** Reduced fees (weekdays, twilight), range (grass/mats), credit cards (MC, V, D), BF, FF.
★★★★ NORTH/EAST (18)
Yards: 7,224/5,581. **Par:** 72/72. **Course Rating:** 75.6/73.0. **Slope:** 137/125.
Reader Comments: Fun to play if you select the right tees ... Flat, but challenging ... Slightly expensive, but great traditional golf ... Nice variety of holes ... Good practice facility ... Long tough par 4s, great older course.
NORTH/WEST (18)
Yards: 7,258/5,690. **Par:** 72/72. **Course Rating:** 75.6/73.5. **Slope:** 138/128.
Notes: Ranked 3rd in 1999 Best in State; 45th in 1996 America's Top 75 Upscale Courses.
WEST/EAST (18)
Yards: 7,126/5,403. **Par:** 72/72. **Course Rating:** 75.0/71.9. **Slope:** 137/123.
Special Notes: Also has a 9-hole course.

★★★ PALMIRA GOLF & COUNTRY CLUB
SP-12111 W. 109th St., St. John, 46373, Lake County, (219)365-4331, 40 miles from Chicago. **E-mail:** nicpon@palmiragolf.com. **Web:** www.palmiragolf.com. **Facility Holes:** 18. **Yards:** 6,922/5,725. **Par:** 71/73. **Course Rating:** 72.7/74.6. **Slope:** 128/117. **Green Fee:** $16/$30. **Cart Fee:** $26/Cart. **Walking Policy:** Unrestricted walking. **Walkability:** 4. **Opened:** 1972. **Architect:** Bob Lohmann/Rich Nicpon. **Season:** Year-round. **To obtain tee times:** Call up to 7 days in advance. **Miscellaneous:** Reduced fees (weekdays, twilight, seniors, juniors), range (grass), credit cards (MC, V), BF, FF.
Reader Comments: Most-improved course in area ... Nice course, perfect for a 90s shooter ... Outstanding course, but pace was very slow ... Great course, a true challenge. A little expensive but worth the drive.

PEBBLE BROOK GOLF & COUNTRY CLUB
PU-3110 Westfield Rd., Noblesville, 46060, Hamilton County, (317)896-5596, 30 miles from Indianapolis. **Facility Holes:** 36. **Green Fee:** $27/$31. **Walking Policy:** Walking at certain times. **Walkability:** 1. **Season:** March-Dec. **To obtain tee times:** Call up to 7 days in advance. **Miscellaneous:** Reduced fees (weekdays, twilight), range (grass), credit cards (MC, V), BF, FF.
★★★ NORTH COURSE (18)
Yards: 6,392/5,806. **Par:** 70/70. **Course Rating:** 70.5/74.1. **Slope:** 118/115. **Cart Fee:** $14/Person. **Opened:** 1989. **Architect:** Gary Kern/Ron Kern.
Reader Comments: Newer 9, more open, modern design ... Golf factory & fun ... Always in great shape.
★★★ SOUTH COURSE (18)
Yards: 6,557/5,261. **Par:** 72/72. **Course Rating:** 70.5/71.9. **Slope:** 121/115. **Cart Fee:** $13/Person. **Opened:** 1974. **Architect:** James Dugan.
Reader Comments: Older 9 traditional layout. Good test ... Always in great shape ... Fun course ... Very upscale, deluxe accommodations.

INDIANA

★★★½ PHEASANT VALLEY COUNTRY CLUB
PU-3838 W. 141st Ave., Crown Point, 46307, Lake County, (219)663-5000, 30 miles from Chicago. **Web:** www.pheasantvalley.com. **Facility Holes:** 18. **Yards:** 6,869/6,166. **Par:** 72/73. **Course Rating:** 72.3/72.6. **Slope:** 126/120. **Green Fee:** $20/$25. **Cart Fee:** $10/Person. **Walking Policy:** Unrestricted walking. **Walkability:** 4. **Opened:** 1967. **Architect:** R. Albert Anderson. **Season:** Year-round. **High:** May-Oct. **To obtain tee times:** Call golf shop. **Miscellaneous:** Reduced fees (weekdays, twilight, seniors, juniors), credit cards (MC, V, AE, D), BF, FF.
Reader Comments: Toughest course to walk in Lake County … Best pro shop in the entire Midwest … Elevated tees make for an interesting time picking the right club. A long course that is well worth anyone's time … Good course, hard par 4s.

★★★ THE PLAYERS CLUB AT WOODLAND TRAILS
PU-6610 W. River Rd., Yorktown, 47396, Delaware County, (765)759-8536, 40 miles from Indianapolis. **Web:** www.theplayersclubgolf.com. **Facility Holes:** 18. **Yards:** 6,911/5,482. **Par:** 72/72. **Course Rating:** 72.7/71.0. **Slope:** 127/120. **Green Fee:** $16/$25. **Cart Fee:** $14/Person. **Walking Policy:** Walking at certain times. **Walkability:** 3. **Opened:** 1991. **Architect:** Gene Bates. **Season:** Year-round. **High:** May-Sept. **To obtain tee times:** Call golf shop. **Miscellaneous:** Reduced fees (weekdays, twilight, seniors, juniors), range (grass), credit cards (MC, V), BF, FF.
Reader Comments: Very good course, great green fees … Pace occasionally slow, a few long walks to the next tee … OK course, greens are very true … 18 excellent holes, fair price … A good place to play for condition and value.

★★★½ PLUM CREEK COUNTRY CLUB
SP-12401 Lynnwood Blvd., Carmel, 46033, Hamilton County, (317)573-9900, 4 miles from Indianapolis. **Web:** www.plumcreekcc.com. **Facility Holes:** 18. **Yards:** 6,766/5,209. **Par:** 72/72. **Course Rating:** 72.5/69.6. **Slope:** 127/117. **Green Fee:** $42/$49. **Cart Fee:** $15/Person. **Walking Policy:** Walking at certain times. **Walkability:** 2. **Opened:** 1997. **Architect:** Pete Dye. **Season:** March-Dec. **High:** May-Oct. **To obtain tee times:** Call up to 7 days in advance. **Misc:** Reduced fees (weekdays, twilight), range (grass), credit cards (MC, V), BF, FF.
Reader Comments: Fast greens. Shorter, tricky layout even though there are not a lot of trees in play … Lots of trouble … Good service and a nice layout … Very playable course for all handicaps.

PLYMOUTH ROCK GOLF COURSE
PU-12641 7B Rd., Plymouth, 46563, Marshall County, (219)936-4405, 20 miles from South Bend. **Facility Holes:** 18. **Yards:** 6,533/5,068. **Par:** 72/74. **Course Rating:** 70.0/68.2. **Slope:** 115/108. **Green Fee:** $12/$18. **Cart Fee:** $12/Person. **Walking Policy:** Unrestricted walking. **Walkability:** 2. **Opened:** 1960. **Architect:** Russel Rush. **Season:** Year-round. **To obtain tee times:** Call golf shop. **Miscellaneous:** Reduced fees (weekdays, twilight, seniors, juniors), range (grass), credit cards (MC, V), BF, FF.

★★ POND VIEW GOLF COURSE
PU-850 South 300 E., Star City, 46985, Pulaski County, (219)595-7431, (800)972-9636, 75 miles from Indianapolis. **E-mail:** Donnell@pwrtc.com. **Web:** www.indianagolfacademy.com. **Facility Holes:** 18. **Yards:** 6,270/5,115. **Par:** 70/72. **Course Rating:** 69.7/69.9. **Slope:** 121/121. **Green Fee:** $11/$14. **Cart Fee:** $12/Person. **Walking Policy:** Unrestricted walking. **Walkability:** 3. **Architect:** Steve Bonnell. **Season:** March-Nov. **High:** July-Aug. **To obtain tee times:** Call golf shop. **Miscellaneous:** Metal spikes, range (grass), credit cards (MC, V, D).

★★½ POND-A-RIVER GOLF CLUB
PU-26025 River Rd., Woodburn, 46797, Allen County, (219)632-5481, 20 miles from Fort Wayne. **Facility Holes:** 18. **Yards:** 4,701/3,612. **Par:** 69/67. **Course Rating:** 62.0/62.1. **Slope:** 99/98. **Green Fee:** $16. **Cart Fee:** $9/Person. **Walking Policy:** Unrestricted walking. **Walkability:** 3. **Opened:** 1968. **Season:** April-Nov. **High:** May-Sept. **To obtain tee times:** Call up to 14 days in advance. **Miscellaneous:** Reduced fees (seniors, juniors), metal spikes, BF, FF.

★★½ PORTLAND COUNTRY CLUB
SP-124 W. 200 S., Portland, 47371, Jay County, (219)726-4646, 45 miles from Ft. Wayne. **Facility Holes:** 18. **Yards:** 6,505/4,917. **Par:** 70/70. **Course Rating:** 70.7/69.2. **Slope:** 118/89. **Green Fee:** $15/$18. **Cart Fee:** $11/Person. **Walking Policy:** Unrestricted walking. **Walkability:** 2. **Opened:** 1922. **Season:** March-Dec. **High:** June-Sept. **To obtain tee times:** Call golf shop. **Miscellaneous:** Reduced fees (weekdays), range (grass), credit cards (MC, V, D), BF, FF.

★★★★ PRAIRIE VIEW GOLF CLUB
PU-7000 Longest Dr., Carmel, 46033, Hamilton County, (317)816-3100, (888)646-4653, 10 miles from Indianapolis. **Web:** www.prairieviewgc.com. **Facility Holes:** 18. **Yards:** 7,073/5,203. **Par:** 72/72. **Course Rating:** 74.3/70.5. **Slope:** 138/122. **Green Fee:** $50/$80. **Cart Fee:** Included

in green fee. **Walking Policy:** Unrestricted walking. **Walkability:** 3. **Opened:** 1997. **Architect:** Robert Trent Jones, Jr. **Season:** March-Dec. **High:** May-Oct. **To obtain tee times:** Call up to 14 days in advance. **Miscellaneous:** Reduced fees (weekdays, twilight, juniors), range (grass), credit cards (MC, V, AE, D), BF, FF.
Notes: Ranked 4th in 1999 Best in State.
Reader Comments: Very fast greens. Very long from the back tees ... Flat, but a solid tract ... Great diversity of holes, very scenic, nice clubhouse and pro shop ... Premier course but pricey ... Excellent links-type course.

PURGATORY GOLF CLUB
PU-12160 E. 216th St., Noblesville, 46060, Hamilton County, (317)776-4653, 12 miles from Indianapolis. **Web:** www.purgatorygolf.com. **Facility Holes:** 18. **Yards:** 7,754/4,562. **Par:** 72/72. **Course Rating:** 78.1/68.5. **Slope:** 142/121. **Green Fee:** $65. **Cart Fee:** Included in green fee. **Walking Policy:** Unrestricted walking. **Walkability:** 3. **Opened:** 2000. **Architect:** Ron Kern. **Season:** April-Oct. **To obtain tee times:** Call up to 30 days in advance. **Miscellaneous:** Range (grass), credit cards (MC, V, AE), BF, FF.

QUAIL CROSSING GOLF CLUB
PU-5 Quail Crossing Drive, Boonville, 47601, Warrick County, (812)897-1247, 12 miles from Evansville. **Facility Holes:** 18. **Yards:** 6,758/5,081. **Par:** 71/71. **Course Rating:** 72.3/68.8. **Slope:** 126/113. **Green Fee:** $22/$30. **Cart Fee:** $13/Person. **Walking Policy:** Unrestricted walking. **Walkability:** 3. **Opened:** 1997. **Architect:** Tom Doak/Bruce Hepner. **Season:** Year-round. **High:** June-Sept. **To obtain tee times:** Call golf shop. **Miscellaneous:** Reduced fees (weekdays, twilight, seniors, juniors), range (grass/mats), credit cards (MC, V, AE).

RABER GOLF COURSE
PU-19396 State Rd. 120, Bristol, 46507, Elkhart County, (219)848-4020, 20 miles from South Bend. **Facility Holes:** 27. **Green Fee:** $11/$15. **Opened:** 1960. **Architect:** William Daniel. **Season:** March-Nov. **To obtain tee times:** Call golf shop. **Miscellaneous:** Reduced fees (weekdays), metal spikes.
★½ **BLUE/RED** (18 Combo)
Yards: 6,642/5,771. **Par:** 72/74. **Course Rating:** 70.7. **Slope:** 115.
BLUE/WHITE (18 Combo)
Yards: 6,310/5,733. **Par:** 72/73. **Course Rating:** 70.3. **Slope:** 115.
WHITE/RED (18 Combo)
Yards: 6,616/6,292. **Par:** 72/75. **Course Rating:** 71.8. **Slope:** 119.

★★★ RIVERBEND GOLF COURSE
PU-7207 St. Joe Rd., Fort Wayne, 46835, Allen County, (219)485-2732, 1 mile from Fort Wayne. **Facility Holes:** 18. **Yards:** 6,702/5,633. **Par:** 72/72. **Course Rating:** 72.5/72.5. **Slope:** 127/124. **Green Fee:** $15/$21. **Cart Fee:** $10/Person. **Walking Policy:** Unrestricted walking. **Walkability:** 4. **Opened:** 1974. **Architect:** Ernie Schrock. **Season:** March-Nov. **High:** May-Sept. **To obtain tee times:** Call golf shop. **Miscellaneous:** Reduced fees (weekdays, twilight, seniors, juniors), credit cards (MC, V).
Reader Comments: Old home course keeps getting better.

★★½ RIVERSIDE GOLF COURSE
PU-3502 White River Pkwy., Indianapolis, 46222, Marion County, (317)327-7300, 3 miles from Indianapolis. **Facility Holes:** 18. **Yards:** 6,260/5,385. **Par:** 70/71. **Course Rating:** 67.9/69.7. **Slope:** 110/104. **Green Fee:** $9/$15. **Cart Fee:** $13/Person. **Walking Policy:** Unrestricted walking. **Walkability:** 2. **Opened:** 1901. **Architect:** William H. Diddel. **Season:** Year-round. **High:** May-Sept. **To obtain tee times:** Call golf shop. **Miscellaneous:** Reduced fees (weekdays, twilight, seniors, juniors), metal spikes, range, credit cards (MC, V, D).

★★★★½ ROCK HOLLOW GOLF CLUB *Service, Value, Condition, Pace*
PU-County Rd. 250 W., Peru, 46970, Miami County, (765)473-6100, 70 miles from Indianapolis. **E-mail:** rockgolf@hotmail.com. **Web:** www.rockhollowgolf.com. **Facility Holes:** 18. **Yards:** 6,944/4,967. **Par:** 72/72. **Course Rating:** 74.0/69.1. **Slope:** 136/118. **Green Fee:** $35/$45. **Cart Fee:** $10/Person. **Walking Policy:** Unrestricted walking. **Walkability:** 4. **Opened:** 1994. **Architect:** Tim Liddy. **Season:** April-Oct. **High:** June-Aug. **To obtain tee times:** Call golf shop. **Miscellaneous:** Reduced fees (weekdays), range (grass/mats), credit cards (MC, V), BF, FF.
Notes: Ranked 8th in 1999 Best in State; 8th in 1995 Best New Public Courses.
Reader Comments: A great course for the money ... Hard to beat, great conditioned all the time. Very challenging holes, built on an abandoned rock quarry. Beautiful & tough ... A tough course if you don't hit a straight ball. Fairways are tight with little rough before the lateral hazzards ... Several unique holes.

★★★ ROYAL HYLANDS GOLF CLUB

PU-7629 S. Greensboro Pike, Knightstown, 46148, Henry County, (765)345-2123, 23 miles from Indianapolis. **Web:** www.royalhylands.com. **Facility Holes:** 18. **Yards:** 6,500/5,000. **Par:** 71/71. **Course Rating:** 71.9/68.8. **Slope:** 130/122. **Green Fee:** $25/$28. **Cart Fee:** $12/Person. **Walking Policy:** Unrestricted walking. **Walkability:** 3. **Opened:** 1982. **Architect:** Ron Kern/Gary Kern. **Season:** March-Dec. **High:** June-Sept. **To obtain tee times:** Call up to 7 days in advance. **Miscellaneous:** Reduced fees (weekdays, twilight, seniors, juniors), range (grass), lodging (5 rooms), credit cards (MC, V), BF, FF.

Reader Comments: An excellent golf experience. The owners have really brought this course a long way. It is a great public course ... They treat you well and always welcome you back ... Another well-kept secret.

SADDLEBROOK GOLF CLUB

SP-RR 3, Box 51-A1, Orleans, 47452, Lawrence County, (812)849-4653, 50 miles from Louisville. **Facility Holes:** 18. **Yards:** 6,313/4,560. **Par:** 72/72. **Course Rating:** 70.2/66.5. **Slope:** 121/112. **Green Fee:** $9/$14. **Cart Fee:** $11/Person. **To obtain tee times:** Call golf shop. **Miscellaneous:** Reduced fees (weekdays), metal spikes. **Special Notes:** Formerly The Links Golf Course.

★★★ SADDLEBROOK GOLF CLUB

PU-5516 Arabian Rd., Indianapolis, 46228, Marion County, (317)290-0539, 7 miles from Indianapolis. **Web:** www.golfus.com/saddlebrook. **Facility Holes:** 18. **Yards:** 6,038/4,586. **Par:** 71/71. **Course Rating:** 70.0/68.1. **Slope:** 124/116. **Green Fee:** $20/$24. **Cart Fee:** $12/Person. **Walking Policy:** Walking at certain times. **Walkability:** 2. **Opened:** 1994. **Architect:** R.N. Thompson. **Season:** Year-round. **High:** May-Sept. **To obtain tee times:** Call golf shop. **Miscellaneous:** Reduced fees (weekdays, twilight, seniors), range (grass), credit cards (MC, V).

Reader Comments: Great shape, fun to play, scenic ... Not enough room, too short ... Fun course, short but challenging ... Very helpful in putting singles in a foursome.

★★★½ SALT CREEK GOLF CLUB

PU-2359 State Road 46 East, Nashville, 47448, Brown County, (812)988-7888, 45 miles from Indianapolis. **Web:** www.saltcreek.com. **Facility Holes:** 18. **Yards:** 6,407/5,001. **Par:** 72/72. **Course Rating:** 71.2/68.8. **Slope:** 132/122. **Green Fee:** $33/$39. **Cart Fee:** Included in green fee. **Walkability:** 5. **Opened:** 1992. **Architect:** Duane Dammeyer. **Season:** March-Nov. **High:** May-Oct. **To obtain tee times:** Call golf shop. **Miscellaneous:** Reduced fees (weekdays, twilight, juniors), metal spikes, range (grass), credit cards (MC, V, D).

Reader Comments: Good value & beautiful layout, needs conditioning ... Not long, but tricky, fun to play ... Another good course in Indiana.

★★★ SANDY PINES GOLF COURSE

SP-10527 Bunker Dr., De Motte, 46310, Jasper County, (219)987-6211, (877)987-3611, 60 miles from Chicago. **Facility Holes:** 18. **Yards:** 6,500/4,935. **Par:** 72/72. **Course Rating:** 69.9/67.3. **Slope:** 119/112. **Green Fee:** $25/$35. **Cart Fee:** Included in green fee. **Walking Policy:** Unrestricted walking. **Walkability:** 3. **Opened:** 1974. **Architect:** William James Spear. **Season:** April-Nov. **High:** April-Nov. **To obtain tee times:** Call up to 7 days in advance. **Miscellaneous:** Reduced fees (twilight, seniors, juniors), credit cards (MC, V), BF, FF.

Reader Comments: Nice improvement ... Many doglegs. Lots of trees. Excellent value ... New ownership, trying hard, "feel good" course.

★½ SARAH SHANK GOLF COURSE

PU-2901 S. Keystone, Indianapolis, 46203, Marion County, (317)784-0631. **Facility Holes:** 18. **Yards:** 6,491/5,352. **Par:** 72/72. **Course Rating:** 68.9/70.8. **Slope:** 106/115. **Green Fee:** $12/$13. **Walking Policy:** Unrestricted walking. **Opened:** 1940. **Architect:** City of Indianapolis. **Season:** Year-round. **High:** March-Sept. **To obtain tee times:** Call golf shop. **Miscellaneous:** Reduced fees (weekdays, twilight, seniors, juniors), metal spikes, credit cards (MC, V).

★★ SCHERWOOD GOLF COURSE

PU-600 E. Joliet St., Schererville, 46375-0567, Lake County, (219)865-2554, 25 miles from Chicago. **E-mail:** scherwoodmrh@worldnet.att.net. **Web:** www.scherwoodgolf.com. **Facility Holes:** 36. **Yards:** 6,900/5,053. **Par:** 71/72. **Course Rating:** 72.0/67.3. **Slope:** 127/108. **Green Fee:** $18/$27. **Cart Fee:** $23/Cart. **Walking Policy:** Unrestricted walking. **Walkability:** 1. **Opened:** 1967. **Architect:** Ted Locke. **Season:** March-Dec. **High:** May-Sept. **To obtain tee times:** Call up to 14 days in advance. **Miscellaneous:** Reduced fees (weekdays, twilight, seniors, juniors), range (grass), credit cards (MC, V, AE), BF, FF. **Special Notes:** Also has an 18-hole executive course.

★★★ SHADOWOOD GOLF COURSE
PU-333 N. Sandy Creek Dr, Seymour, 47274, Jackson County, (812)522-8164, 62 miles from Indianapolis. **Facility Holes:** 18. **Yards:** 6,713/5,416. **Par:** 72/73. **Course Rating:** 71.8/70.8. **Slope:** 127/118. **Green Fee:** $25/$30. **Cart Fee:** $11/Person. **Walking Policy:** Unrestricted walking. **Walkability:** 2. **Opened:** 1994. **Season:** Year-round. **High:** April-Oct. **To obtain tee times:** Call golf shop. **Miscellaneous:** Reduced fees (weekdays), metal spikes, range (grass/mats), credit cards (MC, V).
Reader Comments: Excellent value; great walkable old-style course.

SHADY HILLS GOLF COURSE
PU-1520 W. Chapel Pike, Marion, 46952, Grant County, (765)668-8256, 50 miles from Indianapolis. **Facility Holes:** 18. **Yards:** 6,513/5,595. **Par:** 71/72. **Course Rating:** 71.6/71.6. **Slope:** 123/110. **Green Fee:** $19/$21. **Cart Fee:** $12/Person. **Walking Policy:** Unrestricted walking. **Walkability:** 3. **Opened:** 1957. **Architect:** William H. Diddel. **Season:** March-Nov. **High:** May-July. **To obtain tee times:** Call golf shop. **Miscellaneous:** Reduced fees (weekdays, seniors, juniors), range (grass/mats), credit cards (MC, V).

★★ SMOCK GOLF COURSE
PU-3910 E. County Line Rd., Indianapolis, 46237, Marion County, (317)888-0036, 10 miles from Indianapolis. **E-mail:** jtellstrom@smockgolf.com. **Web:** www.smockgolf.com. **Facility Holes:** 18. **Yards:** 7,055/5,331. **Par:** 72/72. **Course Rating:** 73.7/69.7. **Slope:** 125/115. **Green Fee:** $16/$18. **Cart Fee:** $13/Person. **Walking Policy:** Unrestricted walking. **Walkability:** 2. **Opened:** 1976. **Architect:** Bob Simmons. **Season:** March-Nov. **High:** May-Oct. **To obtain tee times:** Call up to 7 days in advance. **Miscellaneous:** Reduced fees (twilight, seniors, juniors), range (grass), credit cards (MC, V), BF, FF.

★★½ SOUTH GROVE GOLF COURSE
PU-1800 W. 18th St., Indianapolis, 46202, Marion County, (317)327-7350. **Facility Holes:** 18. **Yards:** 6,259/5,126. **Par:** 70/74. **Course Rating:** 69.3/74.5. **Slope:** 108/108. **Green Fee:** $9/$18. **Cart Fee:** $13/Person. **Walking Policy:** Unrestricted walking. **Walkability:** 1. **Opened:** 1902. **Season:** Year-round. **High:** April-Oct. **To obtain tee times:** Call up to 7 days in advance. **Miscellaneous:** Reduced fees (weekdays, twilight, seniors, juniors), metal spikes, credit cards (MC, V), BF, FF.

★★ SOUTH SHORE GOLF CLUB
PU-10601 State Rd. 13, Syracuse, 46567, Kosciusko County, (219)457-2832, 2 miles from Syracuse. **Facility Holes:** 18. **Yards:** 6,258/5,245. **Par:** 71/71. **Course Rating:** 68.7/71.1. **Slope:** 120/110. **Green Fee:** $19/$23. **Cart Fee:** $12/Person. **Walking Policy:** Walking at certain times. **Walkability:** 2. **Opened:** 1929. **Architect:** William H. Diddel. **Season:** April-Nov. **High:** June-Aug. **To obtain tee times:** Call golf shop. **Miscellaneous:** Reduced fees (seniors), range (grass), credit cards (MC, V, D).

★★★ SUGAR RIDGE GOLF COURSE
PU-21010 Stateline Rd., Lawrenceburg, 47025, Dearborn County, (812)537-9300, 15 miles from Cincinnati. **Web:** www.pebblecreek-sugarridge.com. **Facility Holes:** 18. **Yards:** 7,000/4,812. **Par:** 72/72. **Course Rating:** 72.7/66.9. **Slope:** 127/109. **Green Fee:** $25/$40. **Cart Fee:** Included in green fee. **Walking Policy:** Mandatory carts. **Walkability:** 3. **Opened:** 1994. **Architect:** Brian Huntley/Mike Macke. **Season:** Year-round. **To obtain tee times:** Call up to 7 days in advance. **Miscellaneous:** Reduced fees (weekdays, twilight, seniors, juniors), credit cards (MC, V, AE, D), FF.
Reader Comments: Great prices, always available tee times … Difficult back 9 … I like it 3 or 4 times a year … High priced on weekends. Beautiful scenery. Needs to mature … I really enjoyed the layout. There are quick greens.

★★★★ SULTAN'S RUN GOLF COURSE
PU-1490 N. Meridian Rd., Jasper, 47546, Dubois County, (812)482-1009, (888)684-3287, 60 miles from Louisville. **E-mail:** sultan@psci.net. **Web:** www.sultansrun.com. **Facility Holes:** 18. **Yards:** 6,859/4,911. **Par:** 72/72. **Course Rating:** 72.9/68.0. **Slope:** 132/118. **Green Fee:** $31/$46. **Cart Fee:** $11/Person. **Walking Policy:** Walking at certain times. **Walkability:** 5. **Opened:** 1992. **Architect:** Tom Jones/Allen Sternberg/Tim Liddy. **Season:** Year-round. **High:** May-Oct. **To obtain tee times:** Call up to 14 days in advance. **Miscellaneous:** Reduced fees (weekdays, twilight, juniors), range (grass), credit cards (MC, V, AE, D), BF, FF.
Reader Comments: The par 3s are among the best in the area … Beautiful trees, elevation changes galore … What a fun course, every hole is unique.

★★ SUMMERTREE GOLF CLUB
PU-2323 E. 101st St., Crown Point, 46307, Lake County, (219)663-0800, 35 miles from Chicago. **Facility Holes:** 18. **Yards:** 6,586/5,654. **Par:** 71/72. **Course Rating:** 71.9/72.3. **Slope:**

124/117. **Green Fee:** $15/$21. **Walking Policy:** Unrestricted walking. **Opened:** 1975. **Architect:** Bruce Matthews/Jerry Matthews. **Season:** Year-round. **High:** April-Oct. **To obtain tee times:** Call golf shop. **Miscellaneous:** Reduced fees (seniors), metal spikes, range (grass), credit cards (MC, V).

SWAN LAKE GOLF CLUB
R-5203 Plymouth LaPorte Trail, Plymouth, 46563, Marshall County, (219)936-9798, (800)582-7539, 30 miles from South Bend. **Web:** www.usgolfacademy.com. **Facility Holes:** 36. **Green Fee:** $13/$20. **Cart Fee:** $12/Person. **Walking Policy:** Unrestricted walking. **Walkability:** 4. **Opened:** 1967. **Architect:** Al Humphrey. **Season:** March-Oct. **High:** April-June. **To obtain tee times:** Call golf shop. **Miscellaneous:** Reduced fees (weekdays, twilight, seniors), range (grass/mats), lodging (93 rooms), credit cards (MC, V, AE, D).

★★★½ **EAST COURSE** (18)
Yards: 6,854/5,289. **Par:** 72/72. **Course Rating:** 72.1/69.4. **Slope:** 121/109.
Reader Comments: Play them both for a great day of golf ... The East is chock full of water holes and is much more interesting. A fine driving range and down home service make this an enjoyable day ... Friendly management ... Challenging water.

★★★½ **WEST COURSE** (18)
Yards: 6,507/5,545. **Par:** 72/72. **Course Rating:** 70.5/71.7. **Slope:** 121/106.
Reader Comments: Play them both for a great day of golf ... Need good tee shots for usable approach.

★½ TAMEKA WOODS GOLF CLUB
PU-State Rd. 135 and County Rd. 450W, Trafalgar, 46181, Johnson County, (317)878-4331, 22 miles from Indianpolis. **Web:** www.golfus.com/tamekawoods. **Facility Holes:** 18. **Yards:** 6,526/5,341. **Par:** 72/72. **Course Rating:** 70.8/70.0. **Slope:** 123/119. **Green Fee:** $16/$18. **Cart Fee:** $12/Person. **Walking Policy:** Unrestricted walking. **Walkability:** 3. **Opened:** 1991. **Architect:** James A. Hague III. **Season:** Year-round. **High:** April-Sept. **To obtain tee times:** Call golf shop. **Miscellaneous:** Reduced fees (weekdays, twilight, seniors), metal spikes, credit cards (MC, V).

★★★ TIMBERGATE GOLF CLUB
PU-151 St. Andrews Ave., Edinburgh, 46124, Johnson County, (812)526-3523, 20 miles from Indianapolis. **E-mail:** golf@timbergate.com. **Web:** www.timbergate.com. **Facility Holes:** 18. **Yards:** 6,965/5,047. **Par:** 72/72. **Course Rating:** 73.7/69.1. **Slope:** 137/117. **Green Fee:** $27/$48. **Cart Fee:** Included in green fee. **Walking Policy:** Unrestricted walking. **Opened:** 1999. **Architect:** Clyde Johnston/Fuzzy Zoeller. **Season:** Year-round. **High:** April-Sept. **To obtain tee times:** Call up to 14 days in advance. **Miscellaneous:** Reduced fees (twilight), range (grass), credit cards (MC, V, AE), BF, FF.
Reader Comments: Wind really comes into play, open links-style course ... Pretty good value, playable track, well-conditioned, very good greens ... Player friendly ... Good practice range.

★★ TIPTON MUNICIPAL GOLF COURSE
PU-Golf Course Rd., Tipton, 46072, Tipton County, (765)675-6627, 35 miles from Indianapolis. **Facility Holes:** 18. **Yards:** 6,607/5,671. **Par:** 71/72. **Course Rating:** 70.5/66.3. **Slope:** 119/111. **Green Fee:** $15/$17. **Opened:** 1934. **Architect:** William H. Diddel. **Season:** March-Oct. **To obtain tee times:** Call golf shop.

★½ TRI COUNTY GOLF CLUB
PU-8170 N. CR 400 W., Middletown, 47356, Henry County, (765)533-4107, 40 miles from Indianapolis. **Facility Holes:** 18. **Yards:** 6,706/5,456. **Par:** 72/73. **Course Rating:** 76.1/70.3. **Slope:** 110/97. **Green Fee:** $15/$17. **Cart Fee:** $12/Person. **Walking Policy:** Unrestricted walking. **Walkability:** 2. **Opened:** 1964. **Architect:** Robert Solomon. **Season:** Year-round. **To obtain tee times:** Call golf shop. **Miscellaneous:** Reduced fees (seniors), range (grass), FF.

★½ TRI-WAY GOLF CLUB
PU-12939-4A Rd., Plymouth, 46563, Marshall County, (219)936-9517, 16 miles from South Bend. **Web:** www.triwaygolf.com. **Facility Holes:** 18. **Yards:** 6,175/5,386. **Par:** 71/71. **Course Rating:** 69.9/68.6. **Slope:** 110/110. **Green Fee:** $10/$15. **Cart Fee:** $16/Cart. **Walking Policy:** Unrestricted walking. **Walkability:** 3. **Opened:** 1966. **Architect:** Al Humphrey/Don Kinney/Dana Kinney. **Season:** March-Dec. **To obtain tee times:** Call golf shop. **Miscellaneous:** Reduced fees (weekdays), range (grass), credit cards (MC, V), BF, FF.

★★★★½ THE TROPHY CLUB *Value+, Pace*
PU-3887 N. US Hwy. 52, Lebanon, 46052, Boone County, (765)482-7272, (888)-730-7272, 15 miles from Indianapolis. **E-mail:** trophy@qserve.net. **Web:** www.thetrophyclubgolf.com. **Facility Holes:** 18. **Yards:** 7,208/5,050. **Par:** 72/72. **Course Rating:** 74.0/68.5. **Slope:** 131/117. **Green Fee:** $30/$60. **Cart Fee:** Included in green fee. **Walking Policy:** Unrestricted walking. **Walkability:** 3. **Opened:** 1998. **Architect:** Tim Liddy. **Season:** March-Dec. **High:** May-Aug.

INDIANA

To obtain tee times: Call up to 14 days in advance. **Miscellaneous:** Reduced fees (weekdays, twilight, seniors, juniors), range (grass), credit cards (MC, V), FF.
Notes: Ranked 4th in 1999 Best New Upscale Public.
Reader Comments: Excellent condition. Spray the ball on this links course and you probably can't find it in the heather … Lot of mounds and bump-and-run shots around the greens … Outstanding elevation changes … Good practice facility—very nice clubhouse.

★★ TURKEY CREEK COUNTRY CLUB
SP-6400 Harrison St., Merrillville, 46410, Lake County, (219)980-5170, 7 miles from Gary.
Facility Holes: 18. **Yards:** 6,200/5,787. **Par:** 70/70. **Course Rating:** 72.0/72.0. **Slope:** 116/116.
Green Fee: $15/$20. **Architect:** Charles Maddox/Frank P. MacDonald. **Season:** March-Nov. **To obtain tee times:** Call golf shop.

★★★ TURKEY RUN GOLF COURSE
PU-R.R. 1, Waveland, 47989, Montgomery County, (765)435-2048, 40 miles from Indianapolis. **Facility Holes:** 18. **Yards:** 6,607/4,834. **Par:** 72/72. **Course Rating:** 71.1/65.1. **Slope:** 120/85. **Green Fee:** $12/$14. **Cart Fee:** $10/Person. **Walking Policy:** Walking at certain times. **Walkability:** 5. **Opened:** 1971. **Architect:** Gary Kern. **Season:** Year-round. **High:** April-Sept. **To obtain tee times:** Call golf shop. **Miscellaneous:** Reduced fees (weekdays, twilight, juniors), credit cards (MC, V, D).
Reader Comments: Nothing really outstanding here … Very inexpensive, easy family-type course.

★★★½ TWIN BRIDGES GOLF CLUB
PU-1001 Cartersburg Rd., Danville, 46122, Hendricks County, (317)745-9098, 15 miles from Indianapolis. **E-mail:** jfewell@twinbridgesgolfclub.com. **Web:** www.twinbridgesgolfclub.com.
Facility Holes: 18. **Yards:** 7,058/5,470. **Par:** 72/72. **Course Rating:** 74.0/71.6. **Slope:** 130/120.
Green Fee: $25/$36. **Cart Fee:** $12/Person. **Walking Policy:** Unrestricted walking. **Walkability:** 4. **Opened:** 1997. **Architect:** Bob Lohmann/Michael Benkusky. **Season:** March-Oct. **High:** May-Oct. **To obtain tee times:** Call golf shop. **Miscellaneous:** Range (grass), credit cards (MC, V, D), BF, FF.
Reader Comments: Have to play more than once to know where to hit your tee shot. Has many interesting holes … Scenic, nice greens … Nice variety of holes, easy par 5s … Very hard greens.

★★½ VALLE VISTA GOLF CLUB & CONFERENCE CENTER.
PU-755 E. Main St., Greenwood, 46143, Johnson County, (317)888-5313, 10 miles from Indianapolis. **E-mail:** lew.sharp@vallevista.com. **Web:** www.vallevista.com. **Facility Holes:** 18. **Yards:** 6,306/5,680. **Par:** 70/74. **Course Rating:** 70.3/72.4. **Slope:** 127/124. **Green Fee:** $17/$23. **Cart Fee:** $10/Person. **Walking Policy:** Unrestricted walking. **Walkability:** 2. **Opened:** 1971. **Architect:** Bob Simmons. **Season:** Year-round. **High:** April-Sept. **To obtain tee times:** Call up to 7 days in advance. **Miscellaneous:** Reduced fees (weekdays, twilight, seniors, juniors), range (mats), credit cards (MC, V, AE, D), BF, FF.

★★½ VALLEY VIEW GOLF CLUB
PU-3748 Lawrence Banet Rd., Floyd Knobs, 47119, Floyd County, (812)923-7291, 5 miles from Louisville. **Facility Holes:** 18. **Yards:** 6,514/5,329. **Par:** 71/75. **Course Rating:** 71.0/71.0. **Slope:** 125/122. **Green Fee:** $21/$24. **Cart Fee:** $10/Person. **Walking Policy:** Unrestricted walking. **Walkability:** 3. **Opened:** 1962. **Season:** Year-round. **High:** April-Sept. **To obtain tee times:** Call golf shop. **Miscellaneous:** Reduced fees (weekdays, twilight, seniors, juniors), credit cards (MC, V).

★★★ VALLEY VIEW GOLF COURSE
SP-6950 W. County Rd. 850 N., Middletown, 47356, Henry County, (765)354-2698, 30 miles from Indianapolis. **E-mail:** valleyview@iquest.net. **Web:** www.valleyviewgc.com. **Facility Holes:** 18. **Yards:** 6,421/5,281. **Par:** 72/72. **Course Rating:** 70.3/69.9. **Slope:** 114/109. **Green Fee:** $16/$19. **Cart Fee:** $12/Person. **Walking Policy:** Unrestricted walking. **Walkability:** 4. **Opened:** 1964. **Architect:** E.V. Ratliff. **Season:** March-Nov. **High:** May-Sept. **To obtain tee times:** Call golf shop. **Misc:** Reduced fees (seniors), credit cards (MC, V, D), FF.
Reader Comments: The perfect golfing experience.

WABASH VALLEY GOLF CLUB
PU-207 North Dr., Geneva, 46740, Adams County, (219)368-7388, 32 miles from Fort Wayne. **E-mail:** wvgc@adamswells.com. **Web:** www.wabashvalleygc.com. **Facility Holes:** 18. **Yards:** 6,454/5,079. **Par:** 71/71. **Course Rating:** 70.5/68.4. **Slope:** 120/114. **Green Fee:** $13/$18. **Cart Fee:** $12/Person. **Walking Policy:** Unrestricted walking. **Walkability:** 1. **Opened:** 1963. **Architect:** Henry Culp/Gary Kern. **Season:** March-Nov. **To obtain tee times:** Call golf shop. **Miscellaneous:** Reduced fees (weekdays), credit cards (MC, V), BF, FF.

WALNUT CREEK GOLF COURSE

PU-7453 E. 400 S., Marion, 46953, Grant County, (765)998-7651, (800)998-7651, 35 miles from Fort Wayne. **E-mail:** randy@walnutcreekgolf.com. **Web:** www.walnutcreekgolf.com. **Facility Holes:** 36. **Green Fee:** $18/$22. **Cart Fee:** $12/Person. **Walking Policy:** Unrestricted walking. **Walkability:** 4. **Architect:** Randy Ballinger. **Season:** March-Dec. **To obtain tee times:** Call golf shop. **Miscellaneous:** Reduced fees (weekdays, guests), range (grass/mats), credit cards (MC, V), BF, FF.

CLUB RUN COURSE (18)
Yards: 6,226/4,230. **Par:** 72/72. **Course Rating:** 69.1/68.5. **Slope:** 122/118. **Opened:** 1995.
★★★ **WALNUT CREEK GOLF COURSE** (18)
Yards: 6,880/5,154. **Par:** 72/72. **Course Rating:** 72.1/68.5. **Slope:** 121/109. **Opened:** 1970.
Reader Comments: Great design. Fun to play.

★★★★ THE WARREN GOLF COURSE AT NOTRE DAME

PU-110 Warren Golf Course Dr., Notre Dame, 46556, St. Joseph County, (219)631-4653, 2 miles from South Bend. **E-mail:** Brian.D.Godfrey.7@nd.edu. **Web:** www.nd.edu. **Facility Holes:** 18. **Yards:** 6,744/5,302. **Course Rating:** 72.4/70.1. **Slope:** 129/119. **Green Fee:** $39/$49. **Cart Fee:** $16/Person. **Walking Policy:** Unrestricted walking. **Walkability:** 2. **Opened:** 2000. **Architect:** Bill Coore/Ben Crenshaw. **Season:** March-Nov. **High:** May-Oct. **To obtain tee times:** Call up to 7 days in advance. **Miscellaneous:** Reduced fees (twilight, juniors), range (grass), caddies, credit cards (MC, V, AE), BF, FF.
Notes: Ranked 5th in 2000 Best New Affordable Courses.
Reader Comments: Great facilities. Lack of par is a little gimmicky … Bring all of your wedges … When the wind is up this course is a test from the tips. Bring your putter and bump and run, the fun really starts within 40 yards of the green.

★★★ WESTCHASE GOLF CLUB

SP-4 Hollaway Blvd., Brownsburg, 46112, Hendricks County, (317)892-7888, 10 miles from Indianapolis. **Web:** www.westchasegolf.com. **Facility Holes:** 18. **Yards:** 6,700/4,869. **Par:** 71/71. **Course Rating:** 70.8/68.2. **Slope:** 129/112. **Green Fee:** $32/$37. **Cart Fee:** $12/Person. **Walking Policy:** Unrestricted walking. **Walkability:** 3. **Opened:** 1996. **Architect:** Ron Kern. **Season:** Year-round. **To obtain tee times:** Call golf shop. **Miscellaneous:** Reduced fees (weekdays, twilight, juniors), range (grass), credit cards (MC, V, AE), BF, FF.
Reader Comments: Back 9 is shorter, but has much more trouble. Fun to play … Boring front, original back 9 … Nice mix of holes, tough when the wind blows.

WHITE HAWK COUNTRY CLUB

SP-1001 White Hawk Dr., Crown Point, 46307, Lake County, (219)661-2323, 40 miles from Chicago. **E-mail:** managers@whitehawkcc.com. **Web:** www.whitehawkcc.com. **Facility Holes:** 27. **Green Fee:** $39/$59. **Cart Fee:** Included in green fee. **Walking Policy:** Walking at certain times. **Walkability:** 2. **Opened:** 1998. **Architect:** Dick Nugent. **Season:** March-Nov. **High:** May-Oct. **To obtain tee times:** Call up to 14 days in advance. **Miscellaneous:** Reduced fees (weekdays, twilight, juniors), range (grass), credit cards (MC, V, AE, D), BF, FF.

GREY HAWK/BLACK HAWK (18)
Yards: 7,004/5,159. **Par:** 72/72. **Course Rating:** 73.9/69.5. **Slope:** 141/122.
RED HAWK/BLACK HAWK (18)
Yards: 6,984/5,144. **Par:** 72/72. **Course Rating:** 73.5/69.5. **Slope:** 136/122.
RED HAWK/GREY HAWK (18)
Yards: 7,050/5,255. **Par:** 72/72. **Course Rating:** 74.0/70.4. **Slope:** 135/118.

★½ WICKER MEMORIAL PARK GOLF COURSE

PU-Indianapolis Blvd. and Ridge Rd., Highland, 46322, Lake County, (219)838-9809, 1 mile from Hammond. **Facility Holes:** 18. **Yards:** 6,515/5,301. **Par:** 72/73. **Course Rating:** 70.8/69.3. **Slope:** 106/107. **Green Fee:** $12/$16. **Walking Policy:** Unrestricted walking. **Walkability:** 1. **Opened:** 1930. **Architect:** Tom Bendelow. **Season:** Year-round. **To obtain tee times:** Call golf shop. **Misc:** Reduced fees (weekdays, twilight, seniors, juniors), range (grass), BF, FF.

WILDCAT CREEK GOLF COURSE

PU-3200 Timber Valley Dr., Kokomo, 46902, Howard County, (765)455-3673, 65 miles from Indianapolis. **E-mail:** wccgc@netusa7.net. **Web:** www.wildcatcreek.com. **Facility Holes:** 18. **Yards:** 6,882/5,219. **Par:** 72/72. **Course Rating:** 72.2/69.2. **Slope:** 125/117. **Green Fee:** $25/$33. **Cart Fee:** $11/Person. **Walking Policy:** Walking at certain times. **Walkability:** 2. **Opened:** 1994. **Architect:** Jim Fazio. **Season:** March-Nov. **High:** May-Oct. **To obtain tee times:** Call up to 7 days in advance. **Miscellaneous:** Reduced fees (weekdays, twilight, seniors, juniors), range (grass/mats), credit cards (MC, V, AE, D), BF, FF.

★½ WILLIAM S. REA GOLF COURSE

PU-3500 S. 7th St., Terre Haute, 47802, Vigo County, (812)232-0709, 70 miles from Indianapolis. **E-mail:** Bogeys6263@aol.com. **Web:** www.thcitygolf.com. **Facility Holes:** 18. **Yards:** 6,482/5,353. **Par:** 72/72. **Course Rating:** 70.2/71.7. **Slope:** 110/110. **Green Fee:** $9/$18. **Cart Fee:** $14/Person. **Walking Policy:** Unrestricted walking. **Walkability:** 1. **Opened:** 1900. **Architect:** Rea Family. **Season:** March-Dec. **High:** May-Aug. **To obtain tee times:** Call up to 6 days in advance. **Miscellaneous:** Reduced fees (juniors), range (grass), credit cards (MC, V), BF, FF.

★★½ WILLIAM SAHM GOLF COURSE

PU-6800 East 91st. St., Indianapolis, 46250, Marion County, (317)849-0036, 5 miles from Indianapolis. **Facility Holes:** 18. **Yards:** 6,347/5,459. **Par:** 70/70. **Course Rating:** 69.2/69.2. **Slope:** 105/104. **Green Fee:** $16/$18. **Cart Fee:** $12/Person. **Walking Policy:** Unrestricted walking. **Walkability:** 2. **Opened:** 1963. **Architect:** Pete Dye. **Season:** Year-round. **High:** April-Sept. **To obtain tee times:** Call up to 7 days in advance. **Miscellaneous:** Reduced fees (twilight, seniors), range (grass/mats), credit cards (MC, V), BF, FF.

WINCHESTER GOLF CLUB

PU-100 Simpson Dr., Winchester, 47394, Randolph County, (765)584-5151, 20 miles from Muncie. **Web:** www.winchestergc.com. **Facility Holes:** 27. **Green Fee:** $16/$20. **Cart Fee:** $14/Person. **Walking Policy:** Unrestricted walking. **Walkability:** 1. **Season:** Feb.-Dec. **High:** May-Sept. **To obtain tee times:** Call up to 14 days in advance. **Miscellaneous:** Reduced fees (weekdays), range (grass), credit cards (MC, V), BF, FF.
PONY 9 (9)
Yards: 3,250. **Par:** 36. **Opened:** 2001. **Architect:** Tim Liddy.
★★★ **WINCHESTER GOLF CLUB** (18)
Yards: 6,540/5,023. **Par:** 72/74. **Course Rating:** 70.4/67.6. **Slope:** 115/106. **Opened:** 1937. **Architect:** William H. Diddel/Tim Liddy.
Reader Comments: Very good public golf ... Love this course ... Most par 5s very short ... Consistent greens ... Looking good for future.

★★ WOODED VIEW GOLF CLUB

PU-2404 Greentree North, Clarksville, 47129, Clark County, (812)283-9274, 5 miles from Louisville. **Facility Holes:** 18. **Yards:** 6,514/5,006. **Par:** 71/73. **Course Rating:** 71.0/67.2. **Slope:** 126/114. **Green Fee:** $14/$19. **Cart Fee:** $11/Person. **Walking Policy:** Unrestricted walking. **Walkability:** 2. **Opened:** 1978. **Architect:** Jacobi/Tombs/Lanz. **Season:** Year-round. **To obtain tee times:** Call up to 3 days in advance. **Miscellaneous:** Reduced fees (weekdays, seniors, juniors), range (grass), credit cards (MC, V, D), BF, FF.

★★½ ZOLLNER GOLF COURSE AT TRI-STATE UNIVERSITY

PU-300 W. Park St., Angola, 46703, Steuben County, (219)665-4269, 30 miles from Fort Wayne. **E-mail:** alexanders@tristate.edu. **Web:** www.zollnergolfcourse.com. **Facility Holes:** 18. **Yards:** 6,628/5,204. **Par:** 72/73. **Course Rating:** 71.8/70.2. **Slope:** 129/122. **Green Fee:** $20/$23. **Cart Fee:** $12/Person. **Walking Policy:** Unrestricted walking. **Walkability:** 4. **Opened:** 1971. **Architect:** Robert Beard. **Season:** May-Nov. **High:** May-Sept. **To obtain tee times:** Call up to 7 days in advance. **Miscellaneous:** Reduced fees (weekdays, twilight, seniors, juniors), range (grass), credit cards (MC, V), BF, FF.

★★★ A.H. BLANK GOLF COURSE

PU-808 County Line Rd., Des Moines, 50315, Polk County, (515)285-0864, 1 mile from downtown Des Moines. **Facility Holes:** 18. **Yards:** 6,815/5,617. **Par:** 72/72. **Course Rating:** 72.0/70.4. **Slope:** 119/115. **Green Fee:** $16/$20. **Cart Fee:** $22/Cart. **Walking Policy:** Unrestricted walking. **Walkability:** 3. **Opened:** 1971. **Architect:** Edward Lawrence Packard. **Season:** March-Oct. **High:** May-Aug. **To obtain tee times:** Call golf shop. **Miscellaneous:** Reduced fees (twilight, seniors, juniors), range (grass/mats), cards (MC, V). **Reader Comments:** Best city course in DesMoines … Gets better every time I play … Good greens, hard fairways … OK test from back tees, hard grass … First rate muni … Last three holes very challenging.

★★ AIRPORT NATIONAL PUBLIC GOLF COMPLEX

PU-3001 Wright Bros Blvd. E., Cedar Rapids, 52404, Linn County, (319)848-4500, 3 miles from Cedar Rapids. **Web:** www.airportnationalpublicgolf.com. **Facility Holes:** 18. **Yards:** 4,500/3,826. **Par:** 63/64. **Course Rating:** 58.5. **Slope:** 80. **Green Fee:** $5/$15. **Cart Fee:** $22/Cart. **Walking Policy:** Unrestricted walking. **Walkability:** 4. **Opened:** 1994. **Architect:** T. Lockie/C. Pribble/M. Lemon/G. Mason. **Season:** March-Dec. **High:** June-Aug. **To obtain tee times:** Call golf shop. **Miscellaneous:** Reduced fees (weekdays, seniors, juniors), metal spikes, range (grass/mats), credit cards (MC, V, D), BF, FF.

★★★★ AMANA COLONIES GOLF COURSE

PU-451 27th Ave., Amana, 52203, Iowa County, (319)622-6222, (800)383-3636, 20 miles from Cedar Rapids. **E-mail:** golfacgc@netins.net. **Web:** www.amanagolfcourse.com. **Facility Holes:** 18. **Yards:** 6,824/5,228. **Par:** 72/72. **Course Rating:** 73.3/69.7. **Slope:** 136/115. **Green Fee:** $30/$60. **Cart Fee:** Included in green fee. **Walking Policy:** Mandatory carts. **Walkability:** 4. **Opened:** 1989. **Architect:** Jim Spear. **Season:** March-Nov. **High:** May-Sept. **To obtain tee times:** Call up to 30 days in advance. **Miscellaneous:** Reduced fees (weekdays, twilight), range (grass), credit cards (MC, V, AE, DC), BF, FF. **Notes:** Ranked 10th in 2001 Best in State. **Reader Comments:** Not a flat point on the course … Beautiful course in America's heartland … Play here if given an opportunity … Can't believe you're in Iowa! … Very good service and views … Best public course in Iowa … Superb blend of challenge and fairness.

AMERICAN LEGION COUNTRY CLUB

SP-1800 S. Elm St., Shenandoah, 51601, Page County, (712)246-3308, 60 miles from Omaha. **Facility Holes:** 18. **Yards:** 5,803/5,261. **Par:** 70/72. **Course Rating:** 67.4/69.1. **Slope:** 116/113. **Green Fee:** $17/$20. **Cart Fee:** $20/Cart. **Walking Policy:** Unrestricted walking. **Walkability:** 3. **Opened:** 1956. **Architect:** Chic Adams. **Season:** April-Oct. **High:** June-Aug. **To obtain tee times:** Call golf shop. **Miscellaneous:** Credit cards (MC, V), BF, FF.

AMERICAN LEGION GOLF & COUNTRY CLUB

SP-Rte. 3, Fort Dodge, 50501, Webster County, (515)576-5711, 3 miles from Fort Dodge. **Facility Holes:** 9. **Yards:** 3,161/2,821. **Par:** 37/37. **Green Fee:** $10/$12. **Cart Fee:** $14/Cart. **Walking Policy:** Unrestricted walking. **Walkability:** 3. **Opened:** 1920. **Season:** April-Nov. **High:** May-Aug. **Tee times:** Call golf shop. **Misc:** Reduced fees (twilight),cards (MC, V), BF, FF.

AMERICAN LEGION MEMORIAL GOLF COURSE

PU-1301 S. 6th St., Marshalltown, 50158, Marshall County, (641)752-1834. **Facility Holes:** 18. **Yards:** 6,123/5,409. **Par:** 70/71. **Course Rating:** .0/69.1. **Slope:** 0/109. **Green Fee:** $12/$15. **Opened:** 1956. **Season:** April-Nov. **To obtain tee times:** Call golf shop.

★★★★ BEAVER CREEK GOLF CLUB

PU-11200 N.W. Towner Dr., Grimes, 50111, Polk County, (515)986-3221, 5 miles from Des Moines. **Facility Holes:** 18. **Yards:** 6,779/5,245. **Par:** 72/72. **Course Rating:** 72.0/70.4. **Slope:** 128/122. **Green Fee:** $24/$26. **Cart Fee:** $12/Person. **Walking Policy:** Walking at certain times. **Walkability:** 2. **Opened:** 1991. **Architect:** Jerry Raible. **Season:** March-Nov. **High:** May-Oct. **To obtain tee times:** Call golf shop. **Miscellaneous:** Reduced fees (weekdays, seniors, juniors), range (grass), credit cards (MC, V, AE), BF, FF. **Reader Comments:** Good public course … Good condition, especially the greens … Staff is very accommodating … Well-run operation … Not long, enjoyable, new 9 unique addition.

BENT TREE GOLF CLUB

PU-23579 Hwy. 6, Council Bluffs, 51503, Pottawattamie County, (712)566-9441, 5 miles from Omaha. **Facility Holes:** 18. **Yards:** 7,022/5,152. **Par:** 72/72. **Course Rating:** 74.1/65.6. **Slope:** 126/109. **Green Fee:** $35/$40. **Cart Fee:** Included in green fee. **Walking Policy:** Walking at certain times. **Walkability:** 5. **Opened:** 2000. **Architect:** Jeffrey Brauer. **Season:** March-Nov. **High:** May-Aug. **To obtain tee times:** Call up to 7 days in advance. **Miscellaneous:** Reduced fees (seniors, juniors), range (grass), credit cards (MC, V, AE, D), BF, FF.

★★★★ BOS LANDEN GOLF RESORT
R-2411 Bos Landen Dr., Pella, 50219, Marion County, (641)628-4625, (800)916-7888, 35 miles from Des Moines. **E-mail:** information@boslanden.com. **Web:** www.boslanden.com. **Facility Holes:** 18. **Yards:** 6,932/5,132. **Par:** 72/72. **Course Rating:** 73.5/71.0. **Slope:** 131/125. **Green Fee:** $29/$50. **Cart Fee:** Included in green fee. **Walking Policy:** Walking at certain times. **Walkability:** 5. **Opened:** 1994. **Architect:** Dick Phelps. **Season:** March-Oct. **High:** May-Sept. **To obtain tee times:** Call up to 30 days in advance. **Miscellaneous:** Reduced fees (weekdays, guests, twilight, seniors, juniors), range (grass), lodging (87 rooms), credit cards (MC, V, AE), BF, FF.
Notes: Ranked 8th in 2001 Best in State.
Reader Comments: Great course for money … Nice variety of holes … Best public course in Iowa! … Tough test of golf … Tight layout through woods and hills … Great course in the middle of nowhere … Tough for high handicappers.

★★★★ BRIARWOOD GOLF COURSE
PU-3405 N.E. Trilein Dr., Ankeny, 50021, Polk County, (515)964-4653, 15 miles from Des Moines. **E-mail:** mmathias@newmancompanies.com. **Facility Holes:** 18. **Yards:** 7,019/5,250. **Par:** 72/72. **Course Rating:** 74.2/70.4. **Slope:** 128/119. **Green Fee:** $21/$27. **Cart Fee:** $12/Person. **Walking Policy:** Walking at certain times. **Walkability:** 3. **Opened:** 1995. **Architect:** Gordon Cunningham. **Season:** March-Nov. **High:** May-Oct. **To obtain tee times:** Call golf shop. **Miscellaneous:** Reduced fees (weekdays, twilight), range (grass), credit cards (MC, V), BF, FF.
Reader Comments: Great golf course … Good value … This is the best public course in Iowa … It gives you a resort course feel … Wide open and wind effects every shot.

★★½ BRIGGS WOODS GOLF COURSE
PU-2501 Briggs Woods Trail, Webster City, 50595, Hamilton County, (515)832-9572, 20 miles from Fort Dodge. **E-mail:** briggsw@netins.net. **Web:** www.briggswoods.com. **Facility Holes:** 18. **Yards:** 6,502/5,167. **Par:** 72/71. **Course Rating:** 72.0/70.0. **Slope:** 128/118. **Green Fee:** $13/$21. **Cart Fee:** $20/Cart. **Walking Policy:** Unrestricted walking. **Walkability:** 5. **Opened:** 1971. **Season:** April-Nov. **High:** May-Sept. **To obtain tee times:** Call up to 7 days in advance. **Miscellaneous:** Reduced fees (weekdays, twilight, juniors), range (grass), credit cards (MC, V, AE), BF, FF.

★★★ BROOKS GOLF CLUB
R-1201 Brooks Park Lane, Okoboji, 51355, Dickinson County, (712)332-5011, (800)204-0507, 90 miles from Sioux Falls, SD. **E-mail:** brooksgolfclub@iowaone.net. **Web:** www.brooksgolfclub.com. **Facility Holes:** 27. **Green Fee:** $40/$55. **Cart Fee:** Included in green fee. **Walking Policy:** Unrestricted walking. **Walkability:** 2. **Opened:** 2000. **Architect:** Joel Goldstrand. **Season:** April-Nov. **High:** June-Aug. **To obtain tee times:** Call golf shop. **Miscellaneous:** Reduced fees (twilight, seniors, juniors), range (grass), lodging (210 rooms), credit cards (MC, V, AE, D), BF, FF.
SCOTS' LINKS/THE MOUNDS (18)
Yards: 6,798/5,313. **Par:** 72/73. **Course Rating:** 71.9/69.6. **Slope:** 126/120.
VAL/SCOTS' LINKS (18)
Yards: 6,566/5,123. **Par:** 71/72. **Course Rating:** 71.0/68.6. **Slope:** 124/118.
VAL/THE MOUNDS (18)
Yards: 6,636/5,074. **Par:** 71/71. **Course Rating:** 71.1/68.3. **Slope:** 125/117.
Reader Comments: Nice course … Fun course to play, good service … Nice bent-grass fairways … New 9 … New holes that need to mature.

★★ BROWN DEER GOLF CLUB
PU-1900 Country Club Dr., Coralville, 52241, Johnson County, (319)337-8508, 111 miles from Des Moines. **Facility Holes:** 9. **Yards:** 3,192/2,694. **Par:** 35/36. **Course Rating:** 36.7/35.6. **Slope:** 132/118. **Green Fee:** $18/$22. **Cart Fee:** $12/Person. **Walking Policy:** Unrestricted walking. **Walkability:** 5. **Opened:** 1992. **Architect:** Jim Spears. **Season:** March-Nov. **High:** May-Aug. **To obtain tee times:** Call up to 7 days in advance. **Miscellaneous:** Reduced fees (weekdays, guests, twilight, seniors, juniors), range (grass), credit cards (MC, V), BF, FF.

★★★ BUNKER HILL GOLF COURSE
PU-2200 Bunker Hill Rd., Dubuque, 52001, Dubuque County, (319)589-4261. **Facility Holes:** 18. **Yards:** 5,316/4,318. **Par:** 69/69. **Course Rating:** 65.7/64.1. **Slope:** 111/113. **Green Fee:** $12/$14. **Cart Fee:** $9/Person. **Walking Policy:** Unrestricted walking. **Walkability:** 5. **Architect:** Gordon Cunningham. **Season:** March-Nov. **High:** May-Sept. **To obtain tee times:** Call golf shop. **Miscellaneous:** Reduced fees (weekdays, twilight, seniors, juniors), metal spikes, credit cards (MC, V), BF, FF.
Reader Comments: Hilly, short course … Big old trees … Laid-back atmosphere … Lots of hills, good price … Tough course from back tees … Above average muni, great in fall … Great golf pro … Very good condition. Not too difficult … Lots of practice with ball above or below your feet.

CARROLL MUNICIPAL GOLF COURSE
PU-2266 North West St., Carroll, 51401, Carroll County, (712)792-9190. **Facility Holes:** 18. **Yards:** 6,160/4,994. **Par:** 71/72. **Course Rating:** 66.0/67.0. **Slope:** 102/102. **Green Fee:** $16. **Cart Fee:** $18/Cart. **Walking Policy:** Unrestricted walking. **Walkability:** 2. **Opened:** 1968. **Architect:** Charles Calhoun. **Season:** April-Nov. **To obtain tee times:** Call up to 7 days in advance. **Miscellaneous:** Credit cards (MC, V).

CEDAR BEND GOLF
PU-2147 Underwood Ave., Charles City, 50616, Floyd County, (641)228-6465, 1 mile from Charles City. **Facility Holes:** 18. **Yards:** 6,765/5,337. **Par:** 72/72. **Course Rating:** 71.8/69.7. **Slope:** 118/113. **Green Fee:** $15/$18. **Cart Fee:** $22/Cart. **Walking Policy:** Unrestricted walking. **Walkability:** 2. **Opened:** 1964. **Season:** April-Nov. **High:** May-Sept. **To obtain tee times:** Call golf shop. **Miscellaneous:** Reduced fees (twilight), range (grass), FF.

★★ DODGE PARK GOLF COMPLEX
PU-4041 W. Broadway, Council Bluffs, 51501, Pottawattamie County, (712)322-9970, 4 miles from downtown Council Bluffs. **Facility Holes:** 18. **Yards:** 6,339/5,232. **Par:** 72/72. **Course Rating:** 70.0/69.2. **Slope:** 120/113. **Green Fee:** $18/$19. **Cart Fee:** $10/Person. **Walking Policy:** Unrestricted walking. **Walkability:** 1. **Opened:** 1927. **Architect:** Wyss Associates. **Season:** March-Dec. **To obtain tee times:** Call up to 7 days in advance. **Miscellaneous:** Reduced fees (weekdays), credit cards (MC, V, AE, D), BF, FF.

★★★ DON GARDNER MEMORIAL GOLF COURSE
PU-5101 Golf Course Rd., Marion, 52302, Linn County, (319)286-5586, (800)373-8433, 2 miles from Cedar Rapids. **Facility Holes:** 18. **Yards:** 6,629/5,574. **Par:** 72/72. **Slope:** 111/109. **Green Fee:** $14/$15. **Cart Fee:** $22/Cart. **Walking Policy:** Unrestricted walking. **Walkability:** 3. **Opened:** 1968. **Architect:** Herman Thompson. **Season:** March-Dec. **High:** April-Nov. **To obtain tee times:** Call up to 10 days in advance. **Miscellaneous:** Reduced fees (twilight, seniors, juniors), range (grass), credit cards (MC, V).
Reader Comments: What a shop, has everything … Facility is great … Course good shape … Easy to play, easy to get around … Great staff … Good length and quality greens … A good municipal course.

★★½ DUCK CREEK GOLF CLUB
PU-Locust and Marlow, Davenport, 52803, Scott County, (319)326-7824. **Facility Holes:** 18. **Yards:** 5,900/5,500. **Par:** 70/74. **Course Rating:** 67.9/72.0. **Slope:** 115/120. **Green Fee:** $9/$13. **Cart Fee:** $16/Person. **Walking Policy:** Unrestricted walking. **Opened:** 1930. **Architect:** William B. Langford. **Season:** April-Nov. **High:** April-Sept. **To obtain tee times:** Call golf shop. **Miscellaneous:** Reduced fees (seniors, juniors), range (grass).

★★ EDMUNDSON GOLF COURSE
PU-1608 Edmundson Dr., Oskaloosa, 52577, Mahaska County, (641)673-5120, 60 miles from Des Moines. **E-mail:** joemadsen@pga.com. **Facility Holes:** 18. **Yards:** 6,031/4,701. **Par:** 70/70. **Course Rating:** 68.6/66.9. **Slope:** 116/112. **Green Fee:** $15/$16. **Cart Fee:** $18/Cart. **Walking Policy:** Unrestricted walking. **Walkability:** 4. **Opened:** 1940. **Architect:** C.C. (Nick) Carter. **Season:** March-Dec. **High:** June-Sept. **To obtain tee times:** Call up to 2 days in advance. **Miscellaneous:** Reduced fees (twilight, seniors, juniors), range (grass), credit cards (MC, V, D), BF, FF.

★★★ ELLIS PARK MUNICIPAL GOLF COURSE
PU-1401 Zika Ave. N.W., Cedar Rapids, 52405, Linn County, (319)286-5589. **E-mail:** toml@cedar-rapids.org. **Facility Holes:** 18. **Yards:** 6,648/5,210. **Par:** 72/72. **Course Rating:** 72.1/68.0. **Slope:** 124/103. **Green Fee:** $14/$14. **Cart Fee:** $22/Cart. **Walking Policy:** Unrestricted walking. **Walkability:** 5. **Opened:** 1920. **Architect:** William B. Langford. **Season:** March-Nov. **High:** June-Aug. **To obtain tee times:** Call up to 10 days in advance. **Miscellaneous:** Reduced fees (weekdays, twilight, seniors, juniors), range (grass/mats), credit cards (MC, V, D), BF, FF.
Reader Comments: Scenic back 9 holes, pretty in the fall …Tight back 9 … One hard 9, one easy … Lots of play … Older course scheduled for makeover in 2002 … Hilly! … No. 15 is a bear … Good challenge … Variety.

★★★½ EMEIS GOLF CLUB
PU-4500 W. Central Park, Davenport, 52804, Scott County, (319)326-7825. **Facility Holes:** 18. **Yards:** 6,500/5,549. **Par:** 72/74. **Course Rating:** 71.9/74.0. **Slope:** 120/115. **Green Fee:** $16/$17. **Cart Fee:** $18/Person. **Walking Policy:** Unrestricted walking. **Walkability:** 3. **Opened:** 1961. **Architect:** C.D. Wagstaff. **Season:** April-Dec. **High:** May-Aug. **To obtain tee times:** Call up to 3 days in advance. **Miscellaneous:** Reduced fees (seniors, juniors), range (grass/mats), credit cards (MC, V), BF, FF.

IOWA

Reader Comments: Great par 4s ... New practice range ... Not much for a clubhouse, but the course more than makes up for it ... Long and challenging ... Good price for what you get.

★★★ EMERALD HILLS GOLF CLUB
SP-808 S. Hwy. 71, Arnolds Park, 51331, Dickinson County, (712)332-7100, 103 miles from Sioux City. **Facility Holes:** 18. **Yards:** 6,651/5,493. **Par:** 72/72. **Course Rating:** 72.6/72.2. **Slope:** 125/121. **Green Fee:** $25/$42. **Cart Fee:** $12/Person. **Walking Policy:** Unrestricted walking. **Walkability:** 3. **Opened:** 1972. **Architect:** Leo Johnson. **Season:** April-Nov. **High:** May-Sept. **To obtain tee times:** Call golf shop. **Miscellaneous:** Reduced fees (weekdays, twilight, juniors), range (grass/mats), credit cards (MC, V, D), BF, FF.
Reader Comments: Fun course ... Good challenge ... Nice vacation golf setting ... Mature course ... Friendly staff... Good condition ... Great atmosphere ... Long and rolling with interesting variety, very enjoyable ... Roller-coaster greens.

★★★★ FINKBINE GOLF COURSE
PU-1362 W. Melrose Ave., Iowa City, 52246, Johnson County, (319)335-9246, 110 miles from Des Moines. **Web:** www.finkbine.com. **Facility Holes:** 18. **Yards:** 7,030/5,645. **Par:** 72/72. **Course Rating:** 74.1/69.5. **Slope:** 134/118. **Green Fee:** $20/$37. **Cart Fee:** $22/Cart. **Walking Policy:** Unrestricted walking. **Walkability:** 3. **Opened:** 1955. **Architect:** Robert Bruce Harris. **Season:** April-Nov. **High:** June-Aug. **To obtain tee times:** Call up to 7 days in advance. **Miscellaneous:** Reduced fees (twilight), range (grass), credit cards (MC, V), BF, FF. **Notes:** Ranked 9th in 2001 Best in State.
Reader Comments: Great college course/clubhouse ... Beautiful course ... Head pro is a real people person ... Fun and tough layout ... Former home of the Amana VIP ... Lots of sand ... Island hole memorable ... Gets better every year... Good test of golf.

★★ FLINT HILLS MUNICIPAL GOLF CLUB
PU-12842 102 Ave. Hwy 61, Burlington, 52601, Des Moines County, (319)752-2018. **Facility Holes:** 18. **Yards:** 5,648/4,952. **Par:** 71/71. **Course Rating:** 66.7. **Slope:** 110. **Green Fee:** $10/$12. **Cart Fee:** $18/Cart. **Walking Policy:** Unrestricted walking. **Walkability:** 2. **Opened:** 1943. **Season:** April-Nov. **High:** July-Sept. **To obtain tee times:** Call golf shop. **Miscellaneous:** Reduced fees (weekdays, twilight, seniors, juniors), credit cards (MC, V).

FOX RUN GOLF COURSE
PU-3001 MacIneery Dr., Council Bluffs, 51501, Pottawattamie County, (712)366-4653, 1 mile from Omaha. **Web:** www.golfllc.com. **Facility Holes:** 18. **Yards:** 6,500/4,968. **Par:** 71/71. **Course Rating:** 70.3/69.2. **Slope:** 117/115. **Green Fee:** $13/$24. **Cart Fee:** $11/Person. **Walking Policy:** Unrestricted walking. **Walkability:** 1. **Opened:** 1985. **Season:** Year-round. **High:** March-Oct. **To obtain tee times:** Call up to 7 days in advance. **Miscellaneous:** Reduced fees (weekdays, twilight, seniors, juniors), range (grass/mats), credit cards (MC, V, AE, D), BF, FF.

GARDNER GOLF COURSE
PU-Hwy. 13, Marion, 52302, Linn County, (319)286-5586. **E-mail:** toml@cedar-rapids.org. **Facility Holes:** 18. **Course Rating:** 70.5/69.7. **Slope:** 111/109. **Green Fee:** $14/$14. **Cart Fee:** $22/Cart. **Walking Policy:** Unrestricted walking. **Walkability:** 3. **Season:** March-Nov. **High:** June-Aug. **To obtain tee times:** Call up to 10 days in advance. **Miscellaneous:** Reduced fees (weekdays, twilight, seniors, juniors), range (grass/mats), credit cards (MC, V, D), BF, FF.

★★★ GATES PARK GOLF COURSE
PU-820 E. Donald St., Waterloo, 50701, Black Hawk County, (319)291-4485, 115 miles from Des Moines. **Facility Holes:** 18. **Yards:** 6,839/5,568. **Par:** 72/72. **Course Rating:** 71.5/69.5. **Slope:** 118/113. **Green Fee:** $14. **Cart Fee:** $22/Cart. **Walking Policy:** Unrestricted walking. **Walkability:** 3. **Opened:** 1954. **Architect:** Robert Bruce Harris. **Season:** March-Nov. **Tee times:** Call golf shop. **Miscellaneous:** Reduced fees (seniors, juniors), cards (MC, V), BF, FF.
Reader Comments: Excellent old course for little money ... The staff was very helpful and convenient ... This track is a championship-caliber layout with a little work ... If you have a game play the back tees.

★★★★½ GLYNNS CREEK GOLF COURSE *Value*
PU-19251 290th St., Long Grove, 52756, Scott County, (563)285-6444, 10 miles from Davenport. **E-mail:** jvalliere@scottcountyiowa.com. **Facility Holes:** 18. **Yards:** 7,036/5,097. **Par:** 72/72. **Course Rating:** 73.5/68.3. **Slope:** 131/104. **Green Fee:** $17/$25. **Cart Fee:** $11/Person. **Walking Policy:** Walking at certain times. **Walkability:** 3. **Opened:** 1992. **Architect:** Dick Watson. **Season:** April-Nov. **High:** May-Sept. **To obtain tee times:** Call up to 30 days in advance. **Miscellaneous:** Reduced fees (weekdays, twilight, seniors, juniors), range (grass), credit cards (MC, V, D), BF, FF.
Reader Comments: Old-style course ... Excellent value, with good service ... Outstanding course and wildlife ... Seems to always be in great shape ... Fun place to play ... Great public course! ... Best value and course in the Quad Cities ... Challenging, but fun.

★★ GRANDVIEW GOLF COURSE
PU-2401 East 29th. St., Des Moines, 50317, Polk County, (515)262-8414. **Facility Holes:** 18. **Yards:** 5,422/5,147. **Par:** 70/71. **Course Rating:** 65.7. **Slope:** 108. **Green Fee:** $16/$20. **Cart Fee:** $11/Person. **Walking Policy:** Unrestricted walking. **Walkability:** 2. **Opened:** 1902. **Season:** March-Dec. **High:** May-Sept. **To obtain tee times:** Call golf shop. **Miscellaneous:** Reduced fees (twilight, seniors, juniors), credit cards (MC, V, D), BF, FF.

★★½ GREEN VALLEY MUNICIPAL GOLF CLUB
PU-4300 Donner Ave., Sioux City, 51106, Woodbury County, (712)252-2025. **Facility Holes:** 18. **Yards:** 7,085/5,349. **Par:** 72/72. **Course Rating:** 74.0/70.8. **Slope:** 124/116. **Green Fee:** $15. **Cart Fee:** $9/Person. **Walking Policy:** Unrestricted walking. **Walkability:** 3. **Opened:** 1963. **Architect:** David Gill. **Season:** April-Nov. **High:** May-Sept. **To obtain tee times:** Call up to 7 days in advance. **Miscellaneous:** Range (grass/mats), BF, FF.

THE HARVESTER GOLF CLUB
PU-1102 330th St., Rhodes, 50234, Marshall County, (877)963-4653, 25 miles from Des Moines. **Web:** www.harvestergolf.com. **Facility Holes:** 18. **Yards:** 7,340/5,115. **Par:** 72/72. **Course Rating:** 75.3/69.4. **Slope:** 133/120. **Green Fee:** $48/$60. **Cart Fee:** Included in green fee. **Walking Policy:** Unrestricted walking. **Walkability:** 4. **Opened:** 2000. **Architect:** Keith Foster. **Season:** March-Nov. **High:** May-Sept. **To obtain tee times:** Call up to 30 days in advance. **Miscellaneous:** Range (grass), credit cards (MC, V, AE, D), FF. **Notes:** Ranked 2nd in 2001 Best New Affordable Courses.

★½ HIDDEN HILLS GOLF COURSE
PU-4335 Indiana Ave., Bettendorf, 52722, Scott County, (319)332-5616. **Facility Holes:** 22. **Yards:** 7,105/5,220. **Par:** 70/74. **Green Fee:** $17. **Cart Fee:** $20/Cart. **Walkability:** 4. **Opened:** 1980. **Season:** Year-round. **To obtain tee times:** Call golf shop. **Miscellaneous:** Metal spikes. **Special Notes:** Course also has 4 bonus holes.

★★½ HIGHLAND PARK GOLF COURSE
PU-944 17th St., N.E., Mason City, 50401, Cerro Gordo County, (641)423-9693, 110 miles from Des Moines. **Facility Holes:** 18. **Yards:** 6,022/5,633. **Par:** 72/74. **Course Rating:** 70.9/70.9. **Slope:** 110/110. **Green Fee:** $10/$17. **Cart Fee:** $18/Cart. **Walking Policy:** Unrestricted walking. **Walkability:** 2. **Opened:** 1920. **Architect:** David Gill. **Season:** April-Oct. **To obtain tee times:** Call golf shop. **Miscellaneous:** Reduced fees (twilight), range (grass).

★★★★ HUNTER'S RIDGE GOLF CLUB
PU-2901 Hunter's Ridge Rd., Marion, 52302, Linn County, (319)377-3500, 1 mile from Cedar Rapids. **E-mail:** huntersridgegc@hotmail.com. **Web:** www.huntersridgegolfcourse.com. **Facility Holes:** 18. **Yards:** 7,007/5,090. **Par:** 72/72. **Course Rating:** 74.0/71.0. **Slope:** 132/118. **Green Fee:** $26/$35. **Cart Fee:** $13/Person. **Walking Policy:** Unrestricted walking. **Walkability:** 3. **Opened:** 1997. **Architect:** Bob Lohmann/Gordon G. Lewis. **Season:** March-Dec. **High:** May-Oct. **To obtain tee times:** Call up to 14 days in advance. **Miscellaneous:** Reduced fees (weekdays, twilight, seniors, juniors), range (grass), credit cards (MC, V). **Reader Comments:** Excellent design ... Back 9 like Florida course ... Bring extra balls ... For a young course, it is great!!! ... Great time, great track, it can be war! ... Wind always a problem ... Fast greens, great fairways.

★★½ IRV WARREN MEMORIAL GOLF COURSE
PU-1000 Fletcher Ave., Waterloo, 50701, Black Hawk County, (319)234-9271, 50 miles from Cedar Rapids. **Facility Holes:** 18. **Yards:** 6,268/5,325. **Par:** 72/72. **Course Rating:** 68.2/68.6. **Slope:** 113/102. **Green Fee:** $12. **Cart Fee:** $23/Cart. **Walking Policy:** Unrestricted walking. **Walkability:** 1. **Opened:** 1908. **Season:** March-Dec. **High:** May-Oct. **To obtain tee times:** Call golf shop. **Miscellaneous:** Reduced fees (seniors, juniors), metal spikes, range (grass), credit cards (MC, V), BF, FF.

★★★★ JESTER PARK GOLF COURSE
PU-R.R. No.1, Granger, 50109, Polk County, (515)999-2903, 10 miles from Des Moines. **E-mail:** pgadlane@aol.com. **Web:** www.conservationboard.org. **Facility Holes:** 27. **Yards:** 6,801/6,062. **Par:** 72/73. **Course Rating:** 72.7. **Slope:** 125. **Green Fee:** $18/$22. **Cart Fee:** $24/Cart. **Walking Policy:** Unrestricted walking. **Walkability:** 3. **Opened:** 1970. **Architect:** Dick Phelps. **Season:** March-Nov. **High:** April-Sept. **To obtain tee times:** Call up to 7 days in advance. **Miscellaneous:** Reduced fees (twilight, seniors, juniors), range (grass/mats), credit cards (MC, V, D), BF, FF. **Reader Comments:** Jester Park is a great value ... Well run ... Good mix of holes ... Nice range, par-3 course ... Long and tough when wind blows, big greens ... Need all my clubs. **Special Notes:** Also has a 9-hole par-3 course.

JONES GOLF COURSE
PU-2901 Fruitland Blvd. S.W., Cedar Rapids, 52404, Linn County, (319)286-5581. **E-mail:** toml@cedar-rapids.org. **Facility Holes:** 18. **Yards:** 6,009/4,785. **Par:** 72/72. **Course Rating:** 69.7/66.1. **Slope:** 121/100. **Green Fee:** $13/$14. **Cart Fee:** $22/Cart. **Walking Policy:** Unrestricted walking. **Walkability:** 2. **Season:** March-Nov. **High:** June-Aug. **To obtain tee times:** Call up to 10 days in advance. **Miscellaneous:** Reduced fees (weekdays, twilight, seniors, juniors), range (grass/mats), credit cards (MC, V, D), BF, FF.

★★★★ LAKE PANORAMA NATIONAL GOLF COURSE
R-5071 Clover Ridge Rd., Panora, 50216, Guthrie County, (641)755-2024, (800)879-1917, 45 miles from Des Moines. **Facility Holes:** 18. **Yards:** 7,015/5,765. **Par:** 72/72. **Course Rating:** 73.2/73.2. **Slope:** 131/121. **Green Fee:** $25/$40. **Cart Fee:** Included in green fee. **Walking Policy:** Walking at certain times. **Walkability:** 4. **Opened:** 1970. **Architect:** Richard Watson. **Season:** April-Nov. **High:** June-Aug. **To obtain tee times:** Call golf shop. **Miscellaneous:** Reduced fees (weekdays), range (grass/mats), lodging (39 rooms), credit cards (MC, V, AE, D).
Reader Comments: Enjoyable course, usually windy ... Surprisingly scenic, good variety of holes, difficult ... Long par- 3 holes ... Nice clubhouse.

★★½ LAKESIDE MUNICIPAL GOLF COURSE
PU-1417 Nelson Ave., Fort Dodge, 50501, Webster County, (515)576-6741. **Facility Holes:** 18. **Yards:** 6,436/5,540. **Par:** 72/72. **Course Rating:** 70.1/69.8. **Slope:** 114/109. **Green Fee:** $10/$11. **Cart Fee:** $14/Cart. **Walking Policy:** Unrestricted walking. **Opened:** 1976. **Architect:** City Engineers. **Season:** April-Nov. **High:** May-Aug. **To obtain tee times:** Call golf shop. **Miscellaneous:** Range (grass), credit cards (MC, V), BF, FF.

LAKEVIEW COUNTRY CLUB
SP-3724 Lakeview Lane, Winterset, 50273, Madison County, (515)462-9962, 40 miles from Des Moines. **Facility Holes:** 9. **Yards:** 2,880/2,575. **Par:** 35/35. **Course Rating:** 67.0/67.4. **Slope:** 0/110. **Green Fee:** $15/$20. **Cart Fee:** $20/Cart. **Walking Policy:** Unrestricted walking. **Walkability:** 3. **Season:** April-Oct. **High:** May-Aug. **To obtain tee times:** Call golf shop. **Miscellaneous:** Range (grass), BF, FF.

LANDSMEER GOLF CLUB
PU-902 7th St. N.E., Orange City, 51041, Sioux County, (712)737-3429, (866)510-4653, 40 miles from Sioux City. **Facility Holes:** 18. **Yards:** 6,370/5,252. **Par:** 71/71. **Course Rating:** 71.1/68.9. **Slope:** 122/107. **Green Fee:** $20/$22. **Cart Fee:** $11/Person. **Walking Policy:** Unrestricted walking. **Walkability:** 2. **Opened:** 1995. **Architect:** Don Sechrest. **Season:** April-Oct. **To obtain tee times:** Call up to 5 days in advance. **Miscellaneous:** Reduced fees (weekdays), range (grass/mats), credit cards (MC, V), BF, FF.

★★½ LE MARS MUNICIPAL GOLF COURSE
PU-935 Park Lane NE, Le Mars, 51031, Plymouth County, (712)546-6849, 25 miles from Sioux City. **E-mail:** schultz5@frontiernet.net. **Facility Holes:** 18. **Yards:** 6,762/5,300. **Par:** 72/71. **Course Rating:** 71.8/70.3. **Slope:** 126/120. **Green Fee:** $18/$20. **Cart Fee:** $17/Cart. **Walking Policy:** Unrestricted walking. **Walkability:** 2. **Season:** April-Oct. **To obtain tee times:** Call up to 7 days in advance. **Miscellaneous:** Reduced fees (juniors), range (grass), BF, FF.

LINCOLN VALLEY GOLF CLUB
SP-1538 235th St., State Center, 50247, Marshall County, (641)483-2054. **Facility Holes:** 18. **Yards:** 6,432/6,009. **Par:** 72/72. **Course Rating:** 69.7/67.1. **Slope:** 112/110. **Green Fee:** $16/$20. **Cart Fee:** $20/Cart. **Walking Policy:** Unrestricted walking. **Walkability:** 4. **Opened:** 1978. **Architect:** Larry W. Flatt/Gordy Cunningham. **Season:** April-Nov. **High:** May-Aug. **To obtain tee times:** Call golf shop. **Miscellaneous:** Reduced fees (weekdays), range (grass), credit cards (MC, V), BF, FF.

★★★★ THE MEADOWS GOLF CLUB *Service*
PU-15766 Clover Lane, Dubuque, 52001, Dubuque County, (563)583-7385, 190 miles from Chicago. **E-mail:** DWV3370@aol.com. **Web:** www.meadowgolf.com. **Facility Holes:** 18. **Yards:** 6,667/5,199. **Par:** 72/72. **Course Rating:** 72.6/68.7. **Slope:** 132/114. **Green Fee:** $23/$29. **Cart Fee:** $11/Person. **Walking Policy:** Unrestricted walking. **Walkability:** 3. **Opened:** 1996. **Architect:** Bob Lohmann. **Season:** March-Nov. **High:** June-Sept. **To obtain tee times:** Call up to 7 days in advance. **Miscellaneous:** Reduced fees (weekdays, seniors, juniors), credit cards (MC, V, AE, D), BF, FF.
Reader Comments: Rolling course ... Fun layout ... Firm greens ... Friendly staff ... Great new course, needs trees, love the bent-grass fairways ... Fun course, not long, lots of hills, and tight ... Knowledgeable golf pro.

★★★★ MUSCATINE MUNICIPAL GOLF COURSE *Value+*
PU-1820 Hwy. 38 N., Muscatine, 52761, Muscatine County, (319)263-4735, 1 mile from
Muscatine. **Facility Holes:** 18. **Yards:** 6,471/5,471. **Par:** 72/72. **Course Rating:** 69.7/72.5.
Slope: 117/108. **Green Fee:** $8/$10. **Cart Fee:** $10/Person. **Walking Policy:** Unrestricted walk-
ing. **Walkability:** 2. **Opened:** 1969. **Season:** March-Nov. **High:** May-June. **To obtain tee times:**
Call golf shop. **Miscellaneous:** Reduced fees (seniors, juniors), metal spikes, range (grass).
Reader Comments: Great muni, love to walk it ... Good shots required ... Well worth the trip if you
can get on ... The best value in Iowa! ... Nice course, super price, nice people ... Best muni course
played ... Hard to believe the quality of golf for such a low cost.

★½ OAKLAND ACRES GOLF CLUB
PU-13476 Hwy. 6, Grinnell, 50112, Poweshiek County, (641)236-7111, 60 miles from Des
Moines. **Facility Holes:** 18. **Yards:** 5,878/5,410. **Par:** 69/71. **Course Rating:** 69.0. **Slope:** 114.
Green Fee: $13/$14. **Cart Fee:** $16/Cart. **Walking Policy:** Unrestricted walking. **Season:** April-
Oct. **High:** June-Aug. **To obtain tee times:** Call golf shop. **Miscellaneous:** Reduced fees (week-
days, seniors, juniors), range (grass), credit cards (MC, V, D).

★★★ OKOBOJI VIEW GOLF COURSE
PU-1665 Hwy. 86, Spirit Lake, 51360, Dickinson County, (712)337-3372, 4 miles from Spirit
Lake. **E-mail:** Puttov@rconnect.com. **Web:** www.okoboj.view.play18.com. **Facility Holes:** 18.
Yards: 6,051/5,441. **Par:** 70/73. **Course Rating:** 68.5/70.1. **Slope:** 113/113. **Green Fee:**
$31/$37. **Cart Fee:** $12/Person. **Walking Policy:** Unrestricted walking. **Walkability:** 2. **Opened:**
1962. **Architect:** E.G. McCoy. **Season:** April-Nov. **High:** June-Sept. **To obtain tee times:** Call up
to 7 days in advance. **Miscellaneous:** Reduced fees (twilight), range (grass), credit cards
(MC, V, AE, D), BF, FF.
Reader Comments: Nice course for big hitters ... Good service and a nice course ... Good twilight
rates for a resort area ... Has developed into a dandy ... Great condition ... Several interesting
doglegs ... Nicest people ever, good course.

OLATHEA GOLF COURSE
PU-23200 Great River Rd., Le Claire, 52753, Scott County, (563)289-4653, 15 miles from
Davenport. **Facility Holes:** 9. **Yards:** 2,918/2,513. **Par:** 36/36. **Course Rating:** 33.9/33.5. **Slope:**
110/108. **Green Fee:** $8/$15. **Cart Fee:** $10/Person. **Walking Policy:** Unrestricted walking.
Walkability: 3. **Opened:** 1984. **Architect:** Randy Leander. **Season:** April-Nov. **To obtain tee
times:** Call golf shop. **Miscellaneous:** Reduced fees (seniors, juniors), range (grass/mats),
credit cards (MC, V), FF.

ONEOTA GOLF & COUNTRY CLUB
SP-1714 Golf Rd., Decorah, 52101, Winneshiek County, (319)382-9347, 70 miles from
Rochester, Minnesota. **Facility Holes:** 18. **Yards:** 6,472/5,656. **Par:** 72/72. **Course Rating:**
70.6/70.4. **Slope:** 122/110. **Green Fee:** $24/$30. **Cart Fee:** $22/Cart. **Walking Policy:**
Unrestricted walking. **Walkability:** 2. **Opened:** 1921. **Season:** April-Oct. **High:** May-Aug. **To
obtain tee times:** Call up to 7 days in advance. **Miscellaneous:** Range (grass).

★★★ OTTER CREEK GOLF COURSE
PU-1410 N.E. 36th, Ankeny, 50021, Polk County, (515)965-6464, 10 miles from Des Moines.
E-mail: kbeard@ci.ankeny.ia.us. **Facility Holes:** 18. **Yards:** 6,458/5,331. **Par:** 71/74. **Course
Rating:** 70.3. **Slope:** 115. **Green Fee:** $18/$21. **Cart Fee:** $12/Person. **Walking Policy:**
Unrestricted walking. **Walkability:** 3. **Opened:** 1981. **Architect:** Don Rippel. **Season:** April-Nov.
To obtain tee times: Call up to 7 days in advance. **Miscellaneous:** Reduced fees (weekdays),
range (grass), credit cards (MC, V, D), BF, FF.
Reader Comments: A real sleeper, looks easy, but will bite you ... Pretty open ... Good for hacker
like me ... Good buy and good golf ... Much improved, but a lot of play ... Best muni in world.

★★½ OTTUMWA MUNICIPAL GOLF COURSE
PU-13120 Angle Rd., Ottumwa, 52501, Wapello County, (641)683-0646, 90 miles from Des
Moines. **Facility Holes:** 18. **Yards:** 6,335/4,954. **Par:** 70/70. **Course Rating:** 70.4/66.7. **Slope:**
118/102. **Green Fee:** $15. **Cart Fee:** $20/Cart. **Walking Policy:** Unrestricted walking.
Walkability: 2. **Opened:** 1931. **Architect:** Tom Bendelow/Chic Adams. **Season:** April-Oct. **To
obtain tee times:** Call up to 7 days in advance. **Miscellaneous:** Range (grass), credit cards
(MC, V, D), BF, FF.

★★★★ PALMER HILLS MUNICIPAL GOLF COURSE
PU-2999 Middle Rd., Bettendorf, 52722, Scott County, (319)332-8296, 3 miles from
Davenport. **Facility Holes:** 18. **Yards:** 6,535/5,923. **Par:** 71/71. **Course Rating:** 71.5/74.0.
Slope: 124/130. **Green Fee:** $16/$17. **Cart Fee:** $22/Cart. **Walking Policy:** Unrestricted walk-
ing. **Walkability:** 4. **Opened:** 1975. **Architect:** William James Spear. **Season:** April-Nov. **High:**
May-Aug. **To obtain tee times:** Call up to 7 days in advance. **Miscellaneous:** Reduced fees

(weekdays, twilight, seniors, juniors), range (mats), credit cards (MC, V, D), BF, FF.

Reader Comments: Hilly, narrow, challenging course at a great value ...Tough, fair layout, fun, big greens ... Thinking man's course ... Hilly, lakes, streams uphill and down ... Wide open ... There is water in Iowa ... Great shape.

★★★½ PHEASANT RIDGE MUNICIPAL GOLF COURSE

PU-3205 W. 12th St., Cedar Falls, 50613, Black Hawk County, (319)266-8266, 5 miles from Waterloo. **Facility Holes:** 27. **Yards:** 6,730/5,179. **Par:** 72/70. **Course Rating:** 72.5/68.4. **Slope:** 122/101. **Green Fee:** $12. **Cart Fee:** $21/Person. **Walking Policy:** Unrestricted walking. **Walkability:** 1. **Opened:** 1972. **Architect:** Donald Brauer. **Season:** April-Nov. **High:** April-Sept. **To obtain tee times:** Call golf shop. **Miscellaneous:** Reduced fees (seniors, juniors), range (grass), credit cards (MC, V).

Reader Comments: Good facilities ... Long ... The wind makes this course a challenge ... Fair but tough test, lots of landing area ... Small greens ... Course is easy to walk ... When the winds are up it can be a killer.

Special Notes: Also has a 9-hole par-3 course.

★★★★ PLEASANT VALLEY GOLF COURSE

PU-4390 S.E. Sand Rd., Iowa City, 52240, Johnson County, (319)337-7209, 100 miles from Des Moines. **E-mail:** pvinc@inav.net. **Web:** www.pleasantvalley-ic.com. **Facility Holes:** 18. **Yards:** 6,472/5,067. **Par:** 72/72. **Course Rating:** 71.6/68.4. **Slope:** 127/111. **Green Fee:** $15/$25. **Cart Fee:** $20/Cart. **Walking Policy:** Unrestricted walking. **Walkability:** 1. **Opened:** 1987. **Architect:** William James Spear. **Season:** April-Nov. **To obtain tee times:** Call up to 7 days in advance. **Miscellaneous:** Reduced fees (weekdays, twilight, seniors, juniors), range (grass/mats), credit cards (MC, V, AE, D), BF, FF.

Reader Comments: Wonderfully maintained course ... This course makes you work and feel good about your day ... Out of the public eye ... Beautiful fairways ... Great service and value for the price ... An enjoyable venue ... Lots of water and plenty of trees keep you on your toes.

★★★½ QUAIL CREEK GOLF COURSE

PU-700 Clubhouse Rd. NE, North Liberty, 52317, Johnson County, (319)626-2281, 5 miles from Iowa City. **Facility Holes:** 9. **Yards:** 7,046/5,492. **Par:** 72/72. **Course Rating:** 73.6/74.5. **Slope:** 124/118. **Green Fee:** $19/$24. **Cart Fee:** $22/Cart. **Walking Policy:** Unrestricted walking. **Walkability:** 2. **Opened:** 1969. **Architect:** Johnson. **Season:** April-Dec. **To obtain tee times:** Call up to 7 days in advance. **Miscellaneous:** Reduced fees (weekdays), range (grass), BF, FF.

Reader Comments: The best 9-hole course ... Water comes into play on some holes, but don't let them scare you. There are easier holes also, and even a high handicapper will enjoy this course ... Greens in the best condition of any course.

★★ RED CARPET GOLF CLUB

PU-1409 Newell St., Waterloo, 50703, Black Hawk County, (319)235-1242. **Facility Holes:** 18. **Yards:** 6,557/5,754. **Par:** 72/73. **Course Rating:** 70.8/72.1. **Slope:** 119. **Green Fee:** $14. **Cart Fee:** $22/Cart. **Walking Policy:** Unrestricted walking. **Walkability:** 2. **Opened:** 1920. **Season:** March-Dec. **High:** May-Oct. **To obtain tee times:** Call golf shop. **Miscellaneous:** Range, BF, FF.

RICE LAKE GOLF & COUNTRY CLUB

SP-43080 Golf Av., Lake Mills, 50450, Winnebago County, (641)592-8022. **Facility Holes:** 18. **Yards:** 6,238/5,271. **Par:** 71/71. **Course Rating:** 69.6/69.4. **Slope:** 118/111. **Green Fee:** $12/$17. **Opened:** 1925. **Season:** April-Nov. **To obtain tee times:** Call golf shop.

★★★ RIVER VALLEY GOLF COURSE

PU-2267 Valley View Trail, Adel, 50003, Dallas County, (515)993-4029, 15 miles from Des Moines. **E-mail:** rivervalleygolf@aol.com. **Web:** www.rivervalleygolf.com. **Facility Holes:** 18. **Yards:** 6,635/5,482. **Par:** 72/72. **Course Rating:** 71.1/67.4. **Slope:** 121/114. **Green Fee:** $16/$39. **Cart Fee:** Included in green fee. **Walking Policy:** Walking at certain times. **Walkability:** 4. **Opened:** 1995. **Season:** Year-round. **High:** May-Oct. **To obtain tee times:** Call up to 30 days in advance. **Miscellaneous:** Reduced fees (weekdays, twilight, juniors), range (grass), credit cards (MC, V, AE), BF, FF.

Reader Comments: Log clubhouse ... A new course that will get better with time ... Three finishing holes are a real challenge ... Wide open ... Good value ... Playable and well kept ... New management has really improved course ... Challenging, fun and beautiful all in one.

SANBORN GOLF & COUNTRY CLUB

PU-Miller Park Dr., Sanborn, 51248, O'Brien County, (712)729-5600. **Facility Holes:** 18. **Yards:** 6,212/5,498. **Par:** 71/71. **Course Rating:** 70.4/71.5. **Slope:** 112/114. **Green Fee:** $9/$12. **Walkability:** 2. **Opened:** 1982. **Season:** April-Nov. **Tee times:** Call golf shop. **Miscellaneous:** Range (grass), FF.

SHADY OAKS GOLF COURSE
PU-1811 Hwy. 92, Ackworth, 50001, Warren County, (515)961-0262, 5 miles from Indianola. **Facility Holes:** 18. **Yards:** 3,101/2,976. **Par:** 35/37. **Course Rating:** 70.0. **Slope:** 116. **Green Fee:** $17/$18. **Cart Fee:** $17/Cart. **Walking Policy:** Unrestricted walking. **Walkability:** 4. **Opened:** 1972. **Season:** April-Nov. **High:** June-Aug. **To obtain tee times:** Call golf shop. **Miscellaneous:** Reduced fees (weekdays), credit cards (V).

★★★ SHEAFFER MEMORIAL GOLF PARK
PU-1760 308th Ave., Fort Madison, 52627, Lee County, (319)528-6214, 15 miles from Burlington. **Facility Holes:** 18. **Yards:** 6,303/5,441. **Par:** 72/73. **Course Rating:** 69.9/69.9. **Slope:** 118/113. **Green Fee:** $12/$15. **Cart Fee:** $20/Cart. **Walking Policy:** Unrestricted walking. **Walkability:** 1. **Opened:** 1962. **Architect:** C.D. Wagstaff. **Season:** March-Nov. **High:** June-Aug. **To obtain tee times:** Call golf shop. **Miscellaneous:** Reduced fees (weekdays, twilight, seniors, juniors), range (grass/mats), credit cards (MC, V, D), BF, FF.
Reader Comments: The best kept secret in Iowa ... A new clubhouse, super service and value, speedy play ... Short tight front 9, long open back 9 ... New very nice clubhouse, greens are large, fast and smooth.

SHORELINE GOLF COURSE
PU-210 Locust St., Carter Lake, 51510, Pottawattamie County, (712)347-5173, 1 mile from Omaha, NE. **E-mail:** theshore@radiks.net. **Web:** www.golfshoreline.com. **Facility Holes:** 18. **Yards:** 6,690/5,439. **Par:** 72/72. **Course Rating:** 72.2/72.0. **Slope:** 127/118. **Green Fee:** $16/$20. **Cart Fee:** $20/Cart. **Walking Policy:** Unrestricted walking. **Walkability:** 1. **Opened:** 1990. **Architect:** Pat Wyss. **Season:** Year-round. **High:** April-Oct. **To obtain tee times:** Call up to 7 days in advance. **Miscellaneous:** Reduced fees (weekdays, seniors, juniors), range (grass), credit cards (MC, V), BF, FF.

★★★★½ SPENCER GOLF & COUNTRY CLUB *Condition+*
SP-2200 W. 18th St., Spencer, 51301, Clay County, (712)262-2028, 100 miles from Sioux City. **E-mail:** tomsgolf@pionet.net. **Facility Holes:** 18. **Yards:** 6,888/5,412. **Par:** 72/72. **Course Rating:** 73.0/70.1. **Slope:** 127/112. **Green Fee:** $34/$43. **Cart Fee:** $12/Person. **Walking Policy:** Unrestricted walking. **Walkability:** 2. **Opened:** 1966. **Architect:** David Gill. **Season:** April-Nov. **High:** June-Sept. **To obtain tee times:** Call golf shop. **Miscellaneous:** Range (grass), credit cards (MC, V), BF, FF.
Reader Comments: Excellent mature set up ... For my money this is the best course in Iowa ... Imaculate facility that left me satisfied from the first tee to the 18th green ... Country club quality, open to the public.

SPIRIT HOLLOW GOLF COURSE
PU-5592 Clubhouse Dr., Burlington, 52601, Des Moines County, (319)752-0004, 80 miles from Iowa City. **Web:** www.spirithollowgolfcourse.com. **Facility Holes:** 18. **Yards:** 7,021/5,053. **Par:** 72/72. **Course Rating:** 73.6/70.3. **Slope:** 129/116. **Green Fee:** $55. **Cart Fee:** Included in green fee. **Walking Policy:** Unrestricted walking. **Walkability:** 5. **Opened:** 2000. **Architect:** Rick Jacobson. **Season:** April-Nov. **High:** June-Aug. **To obtain tee times:** Call up to 14 days in advance. **Miscellaneous:** Reduced fees (seniors, juniors), range (grass), credit cards (MC, V, AE), BF, FF.

SPRING VALLEY GOLF COURSE
PU-1107 140th Ave., Livermore, 50558, Kossuth County, (515)379-1259, (515)379-1259, 17 miles from Humboldt. **Facility Holes:** 18. **Yards:** 6,421/5,467. **Par:** 72/72. **Course Rating:** 70.2/69.2. **Slope:** 117/108. **Green Fee:** $16. **Cart Fee:** $16/Cart. **Walking Policy:** Unrestricted walking. **Walkability:** 3. **Opened:** 1979. **Season:** March-Oct. **High:** April-Sept. **To obtain tee times:** Call golf shop. **Miscellaneous:** Credit cards (MC, V), BF, FF.

★★½ ST. ANDREWS GOLF CLUB
SP-1866 Blairs Ferry Rd. N.E., Cedar Rapids, 52402, Linn County, (319)393-9915. **E-mail:** jeanpgirl@aol.com. **Facility Holes:** 18. **Yards:** 6,354/5,019. **Par:** 70/71. **Course Rating:** 69.8/67.3. **Slope:** 118/108. **Green Fee:** $13/$15. **Walking Policy:** Walking at certain times. **Walkability:** 2. **Opened:** 1988. **Architect:** Mike Hall. **Season:** Year-round. **To obtain tee times:** Call golf shop. **Miscellaneous:** Metal spikes, credit cards (MC, V), FF.

SUNNY BRAE COUNTRY CLUB
SP-3419 Golf Course Rd., Osage, 50461, Mitchell County, (641)732-3435, 2 miles from Osage. **Facility Holes:** 9. **Yards:** 2,638/2,474. **Par:** 35/36. **Course Rating:** 65.4/68.6. **Slope:** 115/115. **Green Fee:** $13. **Cart Fee:** $18/Cart. **Walking Policy:** Unrestricted walking. **Walkability:** 4. **Opened:** 1915. **Season:** April-Oct. **To obtain tee times:** Call golf shop. **Miscellaneous:** Reduced fees (weekdays), range (grass), BF, FF.

★★½ **TERRACE HILLS GOLF COURSE**
PU-8700 NE 46th. Ave., Altoona, 50009, Polk County, (515)967-2932. **Facility Holes:** 18.
Yards: 6,300/5,347. **Par:** 71/71. **Course Rating:** 68.8/70.0. **Slope:** 116/110. **Green Fee:**
$17/$19. **Walking Policy:** Unrestricted walking. **Walkability:** 3. **Opened:** 1964. **Season:** Year-round. **To obtain tee times:** Call golf shop. **Miscellaneous:** Metal spikes, range (grass).

★★★½ **TIMBERLINE GOLF COURSE**
PU-19804 E. Pleasant Grove Rd., Peosta, 52068, Dubuque County, (563)876-3422, 20 miles
from Dubuque. **Facility Holes:** 18. **Yards:** 6,545/5,318. **Par:** 72/73. **Course Rating:** 71.4/73.5.
Slope: 119/113. **Green Fee:** $14/$17. **Cart Fee:** $11/Person. **Walking Policy:** Unrestricted walking. **Walkability:** 5. **Opened:** 1979. **Season:** April-Nov. **To obtain tee times:** Call up to 7 days in
advance. **Miscellaneous:** Reduced fees (seniors, juniors), credit cards (MC, V, D), BF, FF.
Reader Comments: Greens better and better ... Vastly improved in the last year ... Good value ...
Out in the country but worth the trip! ... One of the most beautiful courses I've played ... Good
scenery ... Take a cart.

★★½ **TOAD VALLEY PUBLIC GOLF COURSE & DRIVING RANGE**
PU-237 NE 80th St., Runnells, 50237-2028, Polk County, (515)967-9575, 5 miles from Des
Moines. **Facility Holes:** 18. **Yards:** 6,170/5,295. **Par:** 71/71. **Course Rating:** 69.1/71.2. **Slope:**
114/114. **Green Fee:** $16/$21. **Cart Fee:** $22/Cart. **Walking Policy:** Unrestricted walking.
Walkability: 4. **Opened:** 1973. **Architect:** Tom Brady. **Season:** Year-round. **High:** April-Sept. **To
obtain tee times:** Call up to 7 days in advance. **Miscellaneous:** Reduced fees (seniors), range
(grass), credit cards (MC, V, D), FF.

★★½ **TWIN PINES GOLF COURSE**
PU-3800 42nd St. NE, Cedar Rapids, 52402, Linn County, (319)286-5583. **E-mail:**
toml@cedar-rapids.org. **Facility Holes:** 18. **Yards:** 5,932/5,655. **Par:** 72/73. **Course Rating:**
67.8/70.9. **Slope:** 107/107. **Green Fee:** $14/$14. **Cart Fee:** $22/Cart. **Walking Policy:**
Unrestricted walking. **Walkability:** 1. **Opened:** 1961. **Season:** March-Nov. **High:** June-Aug. **To
obtain tee times:** Call up to 10 days in advance. **Miscellaneous:** Reduced fees (weekdays,
twilight, seniors, juniors), range (grass/mats), credit cards (MC, V, D), BF, FF.

★★★★ **VALLEY OAKS GOLF CLUB**
SP-3330 Harts Mill Rd., Clinton, 52732, Clinton County, (563)242-7221, (800)796-6187, 40
miles from Davenport. **E-mail:** huestis@sanasys.com. **Facility Holes:** 27. **Yards:** 6,803/5,337.
Par: 72/73. **Course Rating:** 73.0/70.3. **Slope:** 127/121. **Green Fee:** $17/$20. **Cart Fee:**
$10/Person. **Walking Policy:** Unrestricted walking. **Walkability:** 3. **Opened:** 1966. **Architect:**
Robert Bruce Harris. **Season:** March-Nov. **To obtain tee times:** Call up to 7 days in advance.
Miscellaneous: Reduced fees (weekdays, juniors), range (grass/mats), credit cards (MC, V),
BF, FF.
Reader Comments: Some very tough holes ... Great course ... Fast greens ... Nice setting, good
greens ... A real hidden gem ... Lots of blind shots.
Special Notes: Also has a 9-hole par-3 course.

★★★★ **VEENKER MEMORIAL GOLF COURSE-IOWA STATE UNIVERSITY**
PU-Stange Rd., Ames, 50011, Story County, (515)294-6727, 30 miles from Des Moines.
E-mail: tbalsley@iastate.edu. **Web:** www.veenkergolf.com. **Facility Holes:** 18. **Yards:**
6,543/5,357. **Par:** 72/73. **Course Rating:** 71.3/70.6. **Slope:** 124/120. **Green Fee:** $19/$25. **Cart
Fee:** $11/Person. **Walking Policy:** Unrestricted walking. **Walkability:** 5. **Opened:** 1938.
Architect: Perry Maxwell. **Season:** March-Nov. **High:** June-Sept. **To obtain tee times:** Call up
to 7 days in advance. **Miscellaneous:** Reduced fees (weekdays, seniors, juniors), range
(grass), credit cards (MC, V, D), BF, FF.
Reader Comments: One of my favorite courses ... Tough course ... Good layout ... A tough test of
golf over a short, but demanding layout that puts a premium on accuracy and putting.

★★★½ **WAVELAND GOLF COURSE**
PU-4908 University Ave., Des Moines, 50311, Polk County, (515)271-8725. **E-mail:**
bvpro@aol.com. **Facility Holes:** 18. **Yards:** 6,419/5,295. **Par:** 72/71. **Course Rating:** 71.4/69.4.
Slope: 126/116. **Green Fee:** $16/$20. **Cart Fee:** $22/Cart. **Walking Policy:** Unrestricted walking. **Walkability:** 4. **Opened:** 1901. **Architect:** Warren Dickinson. **Season:** March-Dec. **High:**
June-Sept. **To obtain tee times:** Call golf shop. **Miscellaneous:** Reduced fees (twilight, seniors,
juniors), credit cards (MC, V, D), BF, FF.
Reader Comments: Short course, but lot of character, hilly ... Neat clubhouse ... Great old heavily
wooded course, you'll use all 14 clubs ... Mature muni ... Hilly and scenic ... No. 12 is a monster.

★★★ **WAVERLY GOLF COURSE**
PU-Hwy 218S Fairgrounds, Waverly, 50677, Bremer County, (319)352-1530, 15 miles from
Waterloo. **Web:** www.greenie@wl.p.net. **Facility Holes:** 18. **Yards:** 5,881/5,440. **Par:** 70/72.

IOWA

Course Rating: 69.2/69.5. Slope: 115/105. Green Fee: $13/$15. Cart Fee: $20/Cart. Walking Policy: Unrestricted walking. Walkability: 3. Opened: 1923. Season: March-Nov. High: June-Aug. To obtain tee times: Call up to 7 days in advance. Miscellaneous: Reduced fees (juniors), credit cards (MC, V, D), BF, FF.
Reader Comments: Nice small-town course ... Not too long ... Short but enjoyable ... Elevation changes ... Small, fast greens ... O.B. everywhere.

★★½ WESTWOOD GOLF CLUB
PU-3387 Hwy. F 48 W., Newton, 50208, Jasper County, (641)792-3087, 25 miles from Des Moines. Web: www.westwoodgolfcourse.com. Facility Holes: 18. Yards: 6,321/5,645. Par: 71/71. Course Rating: 70.5/74.5. Slope: 120. Green Fee: $17. Cart Fee: $18/Cart. Walking Policy: Unrestricted walking. Opened: 1927. Architect: David Gill. Season: April-Oct. High: June-Aug. To obtain tee times: Call up to 7 days in advance. Miscellaneous: Reduced fees (juniors), range (grass), credit cards (MC, V), BF, FF.

WILLOW CREEK GOLF COURSE
PU-140 Army Post Rd., West Des Moines, 50265, Polk County, (515)285-4558, 6 miles from Des Moines. Facility Holes: 36. Green Fee: $20/$24. Cart Fee: $12/Person. Walking Policy: Unrestricted walking. Opened: 1961. Season: April-Oct. High: June-Sept. To obtain tee times: Call up to 6 days in advance. Miscellaneous: Range (grass/mats), credit cards (MC, V, AE, D), BF, FF.
★★★ BLUE/WHITE COURSE (18)
Yards: 5,385/4,625. Par: 68/69. Course Rating: 65.5/67.0. Slope: 109/110. Walkability: 2.
Reader Comments: Short, but fun in a pinch ... New holes helped quality ... Good not too challenging course ... Back 9 overshadows front 9.
★★½ RED COURSE (18)
Yards: 6,473/5,572. Par: 72/73. Course Rating: 71.8/71.1. Slope: 121/113. Walkability: 3. Architect: Dick Phelps.

WOODLAND HILLS GOLF COURSE
PU-620 NE 66th Ave., Des Moines, 50313, Polk County, (515)289-1326, 3 miles from Des Moines. Facility Holes: 27. Green Fee: $12/$22. Cart Fee: $12/Person. Walking Policy: Unrestricted walking. Walkability: 3. Opened: 1928. Season: March-Oct. High: May-July. To obtain tee times: Call golf shop. Miscellaneous: Reduced fees (weekdays, seniors), credit cards (MC, V, AE, D), FF.
NORTH COURSE (18)
Yards: 5,568/4,903. Par: 70/70. Course Rating: 67.2/67.8. Slope: 116/114.
SOUTH COURSE (9)
Yards: 2,489/2,158. Par: 34/34. Course Rating: 31.5/32.0. Slope: 102/101.

★★★½ ALVAMAR GOLF CLUB
SP-1800 Crossgate Dr., Lawrence, 66047, Douglas County, (785)842-1907, 25 miles from Kansas City. **Web:** www.alvamar.com. **Facility Holes:** 18. **Yards:** 7,096/4,892. **Par:** 72/72. **Course Rating:** 75.5/68.1. **Slope:** 141/112. **Green Fee:** $25/$42. **Cart Fee:** $14/Person. **Walking Policy:** Unrestricted walking. **Walkability:** 4. **Opened:** 1968. **Architect:** Bob Dunning. **Season:** Year-round. **High:** April-Oct. **To obtain tee times:** Call golf shop. **Miscellaneous:** Reduced fees (weekdays, guests, twilight, seniors, juniors), range (grass/mats), credit cards (MC, V, AE, D).
Notes: Ranked 75th in 1996 America's Top 75 Affordable Courses.
Reader Comments: Magnificent greens, good strokes rewarded … Slightly overpriced, but a solid parkland course … Back 9 much stronger than front side … Country club style golf … Very crowded … Fast, sloping greens … Good test, heavy summer play.

★★★ ARTHUR B. SIM PARK GOLF COURSE
PU-2020 W. Murdock, Wichita, 67203, Sedgwick County, (316)337-9100. **E-mail:** gmfsim@swbelle.net. **Web:** www.simparkgolf.com. **Facility Holes:** 18. **Yards:** 6,330/5,026. **Par:** 71/71. **Course Rating:** 70.2/67.9. **Slope:** 113/110. **Green Fee:** $15/$16. **Cart Fee:** $19/Cart. **Walking Policy:** Unrestricted walking. **Walkability:** 1. **Opened:** 1922. **Season:** Year-round. **High:** March-Oct. **To obtain tee times:** Call golf shop. **Miscellaneous:** Reduced fees (twilight), credit cards (MC, V), BF, FF.
Reader Comments: Excellent pace of play … Relaxing course to play … Easy … Driveable par 4s.

AUBURN HILLS MUNICIPAL GOLF CLUB
PU-443 S. 135th St. W., Wichita, 67235, Sedgwick County, (316)721-7477, 6 miles from Wichita. **E-mail:** hendricks-t@ci.wichita.ks.us. **Web:** www.ci.wichita.ks.us. **Facility Holes:** 18. **Yards:** 7,169/4,923. **Par:** 72/72. **Course Rating:** 76.0/70.2. **Slope:** 142/124. **Green Fee:** $20/$25. **Cart Fee:** $20/Cart. **Walking Policy:** Unrestricted walking. **Walkability:** 3. **Opened:** 2001. **Architect:** Perry Dye. **Season:** Year-round. **High:** May-Sept. **Tee times:** Call up to 5 days ahead. **Miscellaneous:** Reduced fees (twilight), range (grass), credit cards (MC, V), BF, FF.

BERKSHIRE GOLF CLUB
SP-3720 SW 45th, Topeka, 66610, Shawnee County, (785)267-7888. **Facility Holes:** 18. **Yards:** 6,700/5,600. **Par:** 70/70. **Course Rating:** 70.6/69.6. **Slope:** 125/123. **Green Fee:** $12/$15. **Cart Fee:** $10/Person. **Walking Policy:** Unrestricted walking. **Walkability:** 2. **Opened:** 1990. **Season:** Year-round. **To obtain tee times:** Call golf shop. **Miscellaneous:** Reduced fees (juniors), range (grass), credit cards (MC, V), BF, FF.

★★½ BRAEBURN GOLF COURSE AT WICHITA STATE UNIVERSITY
PU-4201 E. 21st, Wichita, 67208, Sedgwick County, (316)978-4653. **Facility Holes:** 18. **Yards:** 6,451/5,257. **Par:** 70/71. **Course Rating:** 71.7/70.5. **Slope:** 128/117. **Green Fee:** $15/$18. **Cart Fee:** $18/Cart. **Walking Policy:** Unrestricted walking. **Walkability:** 2. **Opened:** 1924. **Season:** Year-round. **High:** April-Oct. **To obtain tee times:** Call up to 7 days in advance. **Miscellaneous:** Reduced fees (twilight, seniors, juniors), range (grass), credit cards (MC, V), BF, FF.

★★★★½ BUFFALO DUNES GOLF COURSE *Value+, Condition+, Pace*
PU-5675 S. Highway 83, Garden City, 67846, Finney County, (620)276-1210, 180 miles from Wichita. **E-mail:** buffalodunes@gcnet.com. **Web:** www.garden-city.org. **Facility Holes:** 18. **Yards:** 6,767/5,598. **Par:** 72/72. **Course Rating:** 72.5/72.0. **Slope:** 124/114. **Green Fee:** $12/$15. **Cart Fee:** $21/Cart. **Walking Policy:** Unrestricted walking. **Walkability:** 3. **Opened:** 1976. **Architect:** Frank Hummel. **Season:** Year-round. **High:** April-Oct. **To obtain tee times:** Call up to 7 days in advance. **Miscellaneous:** Reduced fees (twilight, juniors), range (grass/mats), credit cards (MC, V, D), BF, FF.
Reader Comments: Don't pass it up ..: Great course … Not glitzy and immaculate but by far the most precious course that I've ever played … Always in good shape, but gosh the wind blows! … Fantastic greens, very challenging, long course.

★★ CAREY PARK GOLF CLUB
PU-15 Emerson Lane, Hutchinson, 67501, Reno County, (620)694-2698, 40 miles from Wichita. **Facility Holes:** 18. **Yards:** 6,410/5,101. **Par:** 71/71. **Course Rating:** 70.4/69.3. **Slope:** 116/114. **Green Fee:** $10/$15. **Cart Fee:** $18/Cart. **Walking Policy:** Unrestricted walking. **Walkability:** 1. **Opened:** 1932. **Architect:** Ralph McCarroll. **Season:** Year-round. **To obtain tee times:** Call up to 7 days in advance. **Miscellaneous:** Reduced fees (weekdays), range (grass), credit cards (MC, V, D), BF, FF.

CEDARBROOK GOLF COURSE
PU-2700 N. Cottonwood St., Iola, 66749, Allen County, (620)365-2176, 80 miles from Kansas City. **Facility Holes:** 18. **Yards:** 6,363/4,935. **Par:** 72/72. **Course Rating:** 71.2/71.7. **Slope:** 122/114. **Green Fee:** $17/$18. **Cart Fee:** $11/Person. **Walking Policy:** Unrestricted walking.

Walkability: 2. **Architect:** Kevin Pargman. **Season:** Year-round. **To obtain tee times:** Call golf shop. **Miscellaneous:** Reduced fees (weekdays, twilight, seniors, juniors), range (grass), credit cards (MC, V), BF, FF.

CHISHOLM TRAIL GOLF COURSE

PU-645 2400 Ave., Abilene, 67410, Dickinson County, (785)263-3377, 2 miles from Abiline. **Facility Holes:** 18. **Yards:** 6,568/4,746. **Par:** 71/72. **Course Rating:** 72.4/71.0. **Slope:** 125/113. **Green Fee:** $12/$15. **Cart Fee:** $9/Person. **Walking Policy:** Unrestricted walking. **Walkability:** 3. **Opened:** 1999. **Architect:** JonThayer Sr./Bruce Dixon. **Season:** Year-round. **High:** June-Sept. **To obtain tee times:** Call golf shop. **Miscellaneous:** Reduced fees (weekdays, twilight, juniors), range (grass), credit cards (MC, V), BF, FF.

★★★★ COLBERT HILLS GOLF COURSE

PU-5200 Colbert Hills Dr., Manhattan, 66503, Riley County, (785)776-6475, (877)916-4653, 120 miles from Kansas City. **E-mail:** davidgourlay@excite.com. **Web:** www.colberthills.com. **Facility Holes:** 27. **Yards:** 7,525/4,947. **Par:** 72/72. **Course Rating:** 77.5/65.1. **Slope:** 152/119. **Green Fee:** $40/$79. **Cart Fee:** Included in green fee. **Walking Policy:** Unrestricted walking. **Walkability:** 4. **Opened:** 2000. **Architect:** Jeff Brauer/Jim Colbert. **Season:** Year-round. **High:** May-Oct. **To obtain tee times:** Call up to 21 days in advance. **Miscellaneous:** Reduced fees (weekdays, twilight), range (grass), credit cards (MC, V, AE, D), BF, FF.
Reader Comments: Spectacular, difficult from back ... Very long ... Long distances between tees, hidden trouble ... Expensive for golf in Kansas ... Outstanding view from #7 ... You must always contend with the wind here ... Will be even better once the grass matures.
Special Notes: Also has a 9-hole executive course.

★★½ CUSTER HILL GOLF CLUB

PU-5202 Normandy Dr., Fort Riley, 66442, Geary County, (785)784-6000, 4 miles from Junction City. **E-mail:** osbornk@riley.army.mil. **Facility Holes:** 18. **Yards:** 7,072/5,323. **Par:** 72/72. **Course Rating:** 74.2. **Slope:** 127. **Green Fee:** $13/$16. **Cart Fee:** $18/Cart. **Walking Policy:** Unrestricted walking. **Walkability:** 4. **Opened:** 1957. **Architect:** Robert Trent Jones. **Season:** Year-round. **High:** April-June. **To obtain tee times:** Call golf shop. **Miscellaneous:** Reduced fees (twilight), range (grass), credit cards (MC, V, AE, D), BF, FF.

★★★★ DEER CREEK GOLF CLUB

SP-7000 W. 133rd St., Overland Park, 66209, Johnson County, (913)681-3100, 15 miles from Kansas City. **Web:** www.americangolf.com. **Facility Holes:** 18. **Yards:** 6,811/5,120. **Par:** 72/72. **Course Rating:** 74.5/68.5. **Slope:** 137/113. **Green Fee:** $35/$80. **Cart Fee:** Included in green fee. **Walking Policy:** Unrestricted walking. **Walkability:** 4. **Opened:** 1989. **Architect:** Robert Trent Jones Jr. **Season:** Year-round. **High:** April-Oct. **To obtain tee times:** Call up to 3 days in advance. **Miscellaneous:** Reduced fees (weekdays, twilight), credit cards (MC, V, AE, D), FF.
Reader Comments: Tough but fair ... Great track ... Too bad there isn't a driving range ... Pro shop and staff are outstanding ... This was a treat. Every shot is a challenge ... Lots of bunkers, narrow fairways ... Some great holes ... Greens too slow ... Best beer cart service ... Use all your clubs.

★★½ DUB'S DREAD GOLF CLUB

PU-12601 Hollingsworth Rd., Kansas City, 66109, Wyandotte County, (913)721-1333. **Facility Holes:** 18. **Yards:** 6,987/5,454. **Par:** 72/72. **Course Rating:** 73.6/70.4. **Slope:** 131/121. **Green Fee:** $29/$52. **Cart Fee:** $12/Person. **Walking Policy:** Unrestricted walking. **Walkability:** 2. **Opened:** 1964. **Architect:** Harold McSpaden. **Season:** Year-round. **High:** April-Nov. **To obtain tee times:** Call up to 3 days in advance. **Miscellaneous:** Reduced fees (weekdays, twilight, seniors, juniors), range (grass/mats), credit cards (MC, V, AE, D), BF, FF.

★★★½ EAGLE BEND GOLF COURSE

PU-1250 E. 902 Rd., Lawrence, 66047, Douglas County, (785)748-0600, (877)861-4653, 30 miles from Kansas City. **E-mail:** jkane@ci.lawrence.ks.us. **Facility Holes:** 18. **Yards:** 6,850/6,004. **Par:** 72/72. **Course Rating:** 72.8/70.0. **Slope:** 124/113. **Green Fee:** $15/$18. **Cart Fee:** $11/Person. **Walking Policy:** Unrestricted walking. **Walkability:** 2. **Opened:** 1998. **Architect:** Jeff Brauer. **Season:** Year-round. **High:** April-Oct. **To obtain tee times:** Call up to 7 days in advance. **Miscellaneous:** Reduced fees (twilight, juniors), range (grass), credit cards (MC, V), BF, FF.
Notes: 1999 Lawrence City Amateur.
Reader Comments: Where else can you walk 18 for $20 ... The natural setting makes for an enjoyable round of golf ... Needs another year to mature ... Front and back totally different—fun ... Finishing 4 holes are fantastic ... Too many golfers going off the 10th in front of you.

★★ ECHO HILLS GOLF COURSE

PU-800 East 53rd North, Wichita, 67219, Sedgwick County, (316)838-0143, 2 miles from Wichita. **E-mail:** echohillsgolf@aol.com. **Web:** www.echohills.com. **Facility Holes:** 18. **Yards:**

5,785/5,381. **Par:** 70/71. **Course Rating:** 68.8/70.6. **Slope:** 116/115. **Green Fee:** $10/$17. **Cart Fee:** $20/Cart. **Walking Policy:** Unrestricted walking. **Walkability:** 3. **Opened:** 1930. **Architect:** Bert Henderson. **Season:** Year-round. **To obtain tee times:** Call up to 14 days in advance. **Miscellaneous:** Reduced fees (weekdays, twilight, seniors, juniors), credit cards (MC, V, D), BF, FF.

ELK'S COUNTRY CLUB
SP-1800 S. Marymount, Salina, 67401, Saline County, (785)827-8585, 90 miles from Wichita. **Facility Holes:** 18. **Yards:** 6,031/4,979. **Par:** 71/71. **Course Rating:** 69.2/66.8. **Slope:** 120/106. **Green Fee:** $22. **Cart Fee:** $11/Person. **Walking Policy:** Unrestricted walking. **Walkability:** 4. **Opened:** 1952. **Architect:** James Dagelish. **Season:** Year-round. **High:** April-Aug. **To obtain tee times:** Call golf shop. **Miscellaneous:** Range (grass), BF, FF.

★★ EMPORIA MUNICIPAL GOLF CLUB
PU-1133 S. Hwy. 99, Emporia, 66801, Lyon County, (316)342-7666, 6 miles from Emporia. **Facility Holes:** 18. **Yards:** 6,500/5,900. **Par:** 71/71. **Course Rating:** 71.4/71.0. **Slope:** 118/114. **Green Fee:** $14/$16. **Cart Fee:** $20/Cart. **Walking Policy:** Unrestricted walking. **Walkability:** 3. **Opened:** 1971. **Architect:** Bob Dunning. **Season:** Year-round. **High:** May-Oct. **To obtain tee times:** Call golf shop. **Miscellaneous:** Reduced fees (twilight, seniors, juniors), range (grass), credit cards (MC, V), BF, FF.

★★★★ FALCON RIDGE GOLF CLUB
PU-20200 Prairie Star Pkwy., Lenexa, 66220, Johnson County, (913)393-4653, 15 miles from Kansas City. **E-mail:** dralston@falconridgegolf.com. **Web:** www.falconridgegolf.com. **Facility Holes:** 18. **Yards:** 6,820/5,160. **Par:** 72/72. **Course Rating:** 72.3/69.6. **Slope:** 127/119. **Green Fee:** $40/$73. **Cart Fee:** Included in green fee. **Walking Policy:** Unrestricted walking. **Walkability:** 4. **Opened:** 1997. **Architect:** Craig Schreiner. **Season:** Year-round. **To obtain tee times:** Call up to 30 days in advance. **Miscellaneous:** Reduced fees (weekdays, seniors, juniors), range (grass/mats), credit cards (MC, V, AE, D), BF, FF. **Notes:** Ranked 9th in 1999 Best in State.
Reader Comments: Big fairways, tough shots everywhere … Firm, fast greens with sometimes ridiculous pins … Pricey, but best maintained in KC area … I love this course! … GPS on cart … Needs better marshaling … Excellent practice facilities … Resort-like atmosphere.

★½ GARDNER GOLF COURSE
PU-15810 S. Gardner, Gardner, 66030, Johnson County, (913)856-8858, 5 miles from Olathe. **Facility Holes:** 18. **Yards:** 6,165/5,222. **Par:** 71/71. **Course Rating:** 67.9/68.2. **Slope:** 116/108. **Green Fee:** $14/$15. **Cart Fee:** $10/Person. **Walking Policy:** Unrestricted walking. **Walkability:** 3. **Opened:** 1987. **Architect:** Kevin Pargman. **Season:** Year-round. **High:** June-Aug. **To obtain tee times:** Call golf shop. **Miscellaneous:** Reduced fees (weekdays, seniors, juniors), range (grass), credit cards (MC, V, D).

GIRARD GOLF COURSE
PU-East Hwy. 57, Girard, 66743, Crawford County, (620)724-8855, 45 miles from Joplin. **Facility Holes:** 9. **Yards:** 6,055/5,452. **Par:** 72/72. **Course Rating:** 68.9/67.1. **Slope:** 112/110. **Green Fee:** $7/$9. **Cart Fee:** $17/Cart. **Walking Policy:** Unrestricted walking. **Walkability:** 2. **Opened:** 1950. **Architect:** Vern Grassi. **Season:** Year-round. **To obtain tee times:** Call golf shop. **Miscellaneous:** Reduced fees (weekdays, twilight, juniors), FF.

GOLDEN BELT COUNTRY CLUB
SP-24th & Frye, Great Bend, 67530, Barton County, (316)792-4306, 80 miles from Wichita. **E-mail:** gm@goldenbeltcc.com. **Web:** www.goldenbelt.com. **Facility Holes:** 18. **Yards:** 6,383/5,029. **Par:** 71/72. **Course Rating:** 71.6/68.6. **Slope:** 125/112. **Green Fee:** $18/$25. **Cart Fee:** $20/Person. **Walking Policy:** Unrestricted walking. **Walkability:** 1. **Season:** Year-round. **High:** April-Oct. **To obtain tee times:** Call golf shop. **Miscellaneous:** Reduced fees (weekdays, twilight), credit cards (MC, V, AE).

★★½ HERITAGE PARK GOLF COURSE
PU-16445 Lackman Rd., Olathe, 66062, Johnson County, (913)829-4653, 12 miles from Kansas City. **Facility Holes:** 18. **Yards:** 6,876/5,797. **Par:** 71/71. **Course Rating:** 72.6/72.3. **Slope:** 131/121. **Green Fee:** $20/$26. **Cart Fee:** $24/Cart. **Walking Policy:** Unrestricted walking. **Walkability:** 3. **Opened:** 1990. **Architect:** Don Sechrest. **Season:** Year-round. **To obtain tee times:** Call up to 3 days in advance. **Miscellaneous:** Reduced fees (weekdays, twilight, seniors, juniors), range (grass), credit cards (MC, V), BF, FF.

★★★½ HESSTON GOLF PARK
PU-520 Golf Course Dr., Hesston, 67062, Harvey County, (620)327-2331, 35 miles from Wichita. **E-mail:** swsports@southwind.net. **Facility Holes:** 18. **Yards:** 6,526/5,475. **Par:** 71/71. **Course Rating:** 71.4/66.7. **Slope:** 125/118. **Green Fee:** $13/$16. **Cart Fee:** $9/Person. **Walking**

Policy: Unrestricted walking. **Walkability:** 2. **Opened:** 1976. **Architect:** Frank Hummel. **Season:** Year-round. **High:** April-Sept. **Tee times:** Call up to 7 days in advance. **Miscellaneous:** Reduced fees (seniors, juniors), range (grass/mats), credit cards (MC, V, D), BF, FF.

Reader Comments: Nice course, bargain price, seem to score well here … One of my favorite public courses … Fairly long with some challenging holes … Small town course that brings people in … Like that this course allows no alcohol … A good course to play if you want to play fast … Several long par 4s.

★★★½ HIDDEN LAKES GOLF COURSE
PU-6020 S. Greenwich Rd., Derby, 67037, Sedgwick County, (316)788-2855, 6 miles from Wichita. **E-mail:** hlgc18@netzero.net. **Web:** www.hiddenlakesgolfcourse.com. **Facility Holes:** 18. **Yards:** 6,584/5,381. **Par:** 72/71. **Course Rating:** 72.0/71.1. **Slope:** 128/117. **Green Fee:** $17/$23. **Cart Fee:** $19/Cart. **Walking Policy:** Unrestricted walking. **Walkability:** 2. **Opened:** 1960. **Architect:** Floyd Farley. **Season:** Year-round. **High:** April-Oct. **To obtain tee times:** Call up to 7 days in advance. **Miscellaneous:** Reduced fees (weekdays, twilight, seniors, juniors), range (grass), credit cards (MC, V), BF, FF.

Reader Comments: Has been upgraded considerably over the last several years … Due to it's location, this course plays fast and it's not crowded … Conditions are great during the summer time—country club like quality … Plenty of water … More enjoyable the 3rd or 4th time around.

★★★★ IRONHORSE GOLF CLUB
PU-15400 Mission Rd., Leawood, 66224, Johnson County, (913)685-4653, 15 miles from Kansas City. **E-mail:** ironhorse@leawood.org. **Web:** www.ironhorsegolf.com. **Facility Holes:** 18. **Yards:** 6,889/4,745. **Par:** 72/72. **Course Rating:** 73.8/67.5. **Slope:** 140/119. **Green Fee:** $37/$51. **Cart Fee:** $15/Person. **Walking Policy:** Unrestricted walking. **Walkability:** 5. **Opened:** 1995. **Architect:** Michael Hurdzan. **Season:** Year-round. **High:** April-Nov. **To obtain tee times:** Call up to 3 days in advance. **Miscellaneous:** Reduced fees (twilight, seniors, juniors), range (grass/mats), credit cards (MC, V, AE, D), BF, FF.
Notes: Ranked 3rd in 1996 Best New Affordable Courses.

Reader Comments: A great layout, some fun holes, difficult to walk … Awesome … Great practice area … Need to work on pace of play … I had to think on every shot … Dress code enforced … Great course except for sand traps … Friendly atmosphere.

★★½ L.W. CLAPP GOLF COURSE
PU-4611 E. Harry, Wichita, 67218, Sedgwick County, (316)688-9341. **Facility Holes:** 18. **Yards:** 6,087/4,965. **Par:** 70/70. **Course Rating:** 70.0/69.7. **Slope:** 120/110. **Green Fee:** $15/$16. **Cart Fee:** $18/Person. **Walking Policy:** Unrestricted walking. **Walkability:** 2. **Opened:** 1923. **Season:** Year-round. **To obtain tee times:** Call golf shop. **Miscellaneous:** Reduced fees (weekdays, twilight, seniors, juniors), credit cards (MC, V, AE, D), BF, FF.

★★ LAKESIDE HILLS GOLF COURSE
PU-2300 Golf Course Rd., Olathe, 66061, Johnson County, (913)782-4192, 2 miles from Olathe. **Facility Holes:** 18. **Yards:** 5,975/5,292. **Par:** 70/71. **Course Rating:** 67.3/69.5. **Slope:** 107/107. **Green Fee:** $16/$18. **Cart Fee:** $22/Person. **Walking Policy:** Unrestricted walking. **Walkability:** 3. **Opened:** 1963. **Season:** Year-round. **High:** May-Sept. **To obtain tee times:** Call golf shop. **Miscellaneous:** Reduced fees (twilight, seniors, juniors), range (grass), credit cards (MC, V, AE), BF, FF.

LAKIN MUNICIPAL GOLF COURSE
PU-West Hwy. 50, Lakin, 67860, Kearny County, (316)355-6946, 25 miles from Garden City. **E-mail:** lakiac@tld.com. **Facility Holes:** 9. **Yards:** 5,930/5,056. **Par:** 70/72. **Course Rating:** 70.4/69.1. **Slope:** 119/124. **Green Fee:** $10/$13. **Cart Fee:** $15/Cart. **Walking Policy:** Unrestricted walking. **Walkability:** 2. **Opened:** 1952. **Season:** Year-round. **High:** May-Aug. **To obtain tee times:** Call golf shop. **Miscellaneous:** Reduced fees (weekdays, twilight), FF.

★★★½ MACDONALD GOLF COURSE
PU-840 N. Yale, Wichita, 67208, Sedgwick County, (316)688-9391. **Facility Holes:** 18. **Yards:** 6,911/5,311. **Par:** 71/72. **Course Rating:** 73.9/70.3. **Slope:** 131/116. **Green Fee:** $15/$16. **Cart Fee:** $18/Cart. **Walking Policy:** Unrestricted walking. **Walkability:** 3. **Opened:** 1996. **Architect:** Mark Hayes. **Season:** Year-round. **To obtain tee times:** Call golf shop. **Miscellaneous:** Reduced fees (twilight), credit cards (MC, V), BF, FF.

Reader Comments: Takes a litttle while to start due to a 458-yard par 4 … Challenging and easy holes, great pace and a marshal who does his job well … Old course, well kept … Some nice doglegs, long par 3s … Even better after recent improvements.

★★★ MARIAH HILLS GOLF COURSE
PU-1800 Mattdown Lane, Dodge City, 67801, Ford County, (316)225-8182, 50 miles from Garden City. **Facility Holes:** 18. **Yards:** 6,868/5,458. **Par:** 71/73. **Course Rating:** 72.5/75.3. **Slope:** 112/124. **Green Fee:** $13/$15. **Cart Fee:** $19/Cart. **Walking Policy:** Unrestricted walk-

ing. **Walkability:** 3. **Opened:** 1975. **Architect:** Frank Hummel. **Season:** Year-round. **High:** April-Sept. **To obtain tee times:** Call golf shop. **Miscellaneous:** Reduced fees (twilight, juniors), range (grass), credit cards (MC, V, AE, D, Diners', Carte Blanche).
Reader Comments: Few trees ... Really nice for the area, course condition can vary throughout season ... Hot high winds sometimes take their toll ... Walkable small town course, nice clubhouse, fair condition.

NEWTON PUBLIC GOLF COURSE
PU-329 N.E. 36th Street, Newton, 67114, Harvey County, (316)283-4168, 18 miles from Wichita. **E-mail:** browngrens@aol.com. **Web:** www.golfnewton.com. **Facility Holes:** 9. **Yards:** 5,744/5,160. **Par:** 70/72. **Course Rating:** 67.2/68.2. **Slope:** 108/113. **Green Fee:** $10/$12. **Cart Fee:** $10/Person. **Walking Policy:** Unrestricted walking. **Walkability:** 2. **Opened:** 1960. **Architect:** Ray Schmidt. **Season:** Year-round. **High:** April-Oct. **To obtain tee times:** Call golf shop. **Miscellaneous:** Reduced fees (weekdays, seniors, juniors), metal spikes, range (grass/mats), BF, FF.

OAK COUNTRY GOLF COURSE
PU-8800 Scott Dr., Desoto, 66018, Johnson County, (913)583-3503, 40 miles from Kansas City. **E-mail:** ocountryclub@kcpro.com. **Facility Holes:** 18. **Yards:** 3,927/3,333. **Par:** 66/66. **Course Rating:** 59.7/68.0. **Slope:** 101/119. **Green Fee:** $20/$23. **Cart Fee:** Included in green fee. **Walking Policy:** Unrestricted walking. **Walkability:** 3. **Opened:** 1989. **Architect:** James Carpenter. **Season:** Year-round. **High:** May-Sept. **Tee times:** Call up to 7 days in advance. **Miscellaneous:** Reduced fees (weekdays, seniors, juniors), credit cards (MC, V, D), BF, FF.

OVERLAND PARK GOLF CLUB
PU-12501 Quivira Rd., Overland Park, 66213, Johnson County, (913)897-3809, 20 miles from Kansas City. **Facility Holes:** 36. **Green Fee:** $23. **Cart Fee:** $11/Person. **Walking Policy:** Walking at certain times. **Walkability:** 3. **Opened:** 1970. **Architect:** Floyd Farley/Craig Schreiner. **Season:** Year-round. **High:** April-Sept. **To obtain tee times:** Call golf shop. **Miscellaneous:** Reduced fees (weekdays, twilight, seniors, juniors), range (grass/mats), credit cards (MC, V, D, CB), BF, FF.
★★½ **NORTH/WEST** (18)
Yards: 6,455/5,038. **Par:** 70/70. **Course Rating:** 69.7/67.7. **Slope:** 119/108.
SOUTH/NORTH (18)
Yards: 6,446/5,143. **Par:** 70/71. **Course Rating:** 69.9/68.2. **Slope:** 113/105.
SOUTH/WEST (18)
Yards: 6,367/5,067. **Par:** 70/71. **Course Rating:** 69.9/67.9. **Slope:** 115/111.
Special Notes: Also has a 9-hole executive course.

★★½ PAINTED HILLS GOLF COURSE
PU-7101 Parallel Pkwy., Kansas City, 66112, Wyandotte County, (913)334-1111, 6 miles from Kansas City, MO. **Facility Holes:** 18. **Yards:** 5,914/4,698. **Par:** 70/70. **Course Rating:** 67.7/63.5. **Slope:** 119/107. **Green Fee:** $17/$20. **Cart Fee:** $12/Cart. **Walking Policy:** Unrestricted walking. **Opened:** 1927. **Architect:** James Dalgleish/Jeff Brauer. **Season:** Year-round. **High:** April-Sept. **To obtain tee times:** Call golf shop. **Miscellaneous:** Reduced fees (weekdays, twilight, seniors, juniors), metal spikes, credit cards (MC, V, AE).

★★★★ QUAIL RIDGE GOLF COURSE
PU-3805 Quail Ridge Dr., Winfield, 67156, Cowley County, (620)221-5645, 35 miles from Wichita. **E-mail:** mike-hammond@hit.net. **Web:** www.winfieldks.org/quail_ridge.htm. **Facility Holes:** 18. **Yards:** 6,826/5,328. **Par:** 72/72. **Course Rating:** 73.0/71.5. **Slope:** 125/119. **Green Fee:** $15/$16. **Cart Fee:** $10/Person. **Walking Policy:** Unrestricted walking. **Walkability:** 2. **Opened:** 1992. **Architect:** Jerry Slack. **Season:** Year-round. **High:** April-Oct. **To obtain tee times:** Call golf shop. **Miscellaneous:** Reduced fees (weekdays, seniors, juniors), range (grass), lodging (100 rooms), credit cards (MC, V, AE, D), BF, FF.
Reader Comments: Excellent golf course since the day it opened ... Great fairways, not crowded ... With normal Kansas winds this can be a monster with its Open class rough.

★★★½ ROLLING MEADOWS GOLF COURSE
PU-7550 Old Milford Rd., Milford, 66514, Geary County, (785)238-4303, 60 miles from Topeka. **E-mail:** bob@flinthills.com. **Web:** www.rollingmeadowsgc.com. **Facility Holes:** 18. **Yards:** 6,879/5,515. **Par:** 72/72. **Course Rating:** 74.0/70.7. **Slope:** 134/116. **Green Fee:** $10/$15. **Cart Fee:** $9/Person. **Walking Policy:** Unrestricted walking. **Walkability:** 1. **Opened:** 1981. **Architect:** Richard Watson. **Season:** Year-round. **High:** April-Sept. **To obtain tee times:** Call up to 3 days in advance. **Miscellaneous:** Reduced fees (weekdays, twilight), range (grass/mats), credit cards (MC, V, AE, D), BF, FF.
Reader Comments: Nice established course that offers it all—trees, water, sand, OB and a good time ... Some neat holes ... Very slow play, but course is worth return visit ... Good service, very pleasant ... Greens are challenging ... Great par 5s ... Good surprise—worth the trip.

KANSAS

RUSSELL COUNTRY CLUB
PU-2nd & Copeland, Russell, 67665, Russell County, (785)483-2852, 60 miles from Salina.
E-mail: ithompson@russellks.net. **Facility Holes:** 18. **Yards:** 6,282/5,516. **Par:** 72/72. **Course
Rating:** 71.0/72.9. **Slope:** 120/120. **Green Fee:** $13/$15. **Cart Fee:** $16/Cart. **Walking Policy:**
Unrestricted walking. **Walkability:** 1. **Season:** Year-round. **High:** April-Nov. **To obtain tee times:**
Call golf shop. **Miscellaneous:** Range (grass), credit cards (MC, V, AE, D).

★★★ **SALINA MUNICIPAL GOLF CLUB**
PU-2500 E. Crawford St., Salina, 67401, Saline County, (785)826-7450. **E-mail:** shard@infor-
matics.net. **Facility Holes:** 18. **Yards:** 6,500/4,800. **Par:** 70/70. **Course Rating:** 72.1/68.0.
Slope: 117/110. **Green Fee:** $13/$15. **Cart Fee:** $10/Person. **Walking Policy:** Unrestricted walk-
ing. **Walkability:** 3. **Opened:** 1969. **Architect:** Floyd Farley. **Season:** Year-round. **To obtain tee
times:** Call up to 5 days in advance. **Miscellaneous:** Reduced fees (twilight, juniors), range
(grass), credit cards (MC, V), BF, FF.
Reader Comments: Watch out for the wind … Always in excellent shape despite the volume of
golfers … Long for a par 70 … Greens were great … New par 3 will add to the value … Can you
spell W-I-N-D-Y? You know you're in the Plains.

SENECA GOLF CLUB
PU-1400 Elk Street, Seneca, 66538, Nemaha County, (785)336-3568, 80 miles from Topeka.
Facility Holes: 9. **Yards:** 5,897/5,557. **Par:** 72/72. **Course Rating:** 66.9/66.9. **Slope:** 103/103.
Green Fee: $13. **Cart Fee:** $15/Cart. **Walking Policy:** Unrestricted walking. **Walkability:** 2.
Season: Year-round. **To obtain tee times:** Call golf shop. **Miscellaneous:** BF, FF.

SIM PARK GOLF COURSE
PU-2020 W. Murdock, Wichita, 67203, Sedgwick County, (316)337-9100. **Facility Holes:** 18.
Yards: 6,330/5,026. **Par:** 71/71. **Course Rating:** 70.2/67.9. **Slope:** 113/103. **Green Fee:**
$15/$16. **Cart Fee:** $19/Cart. **To obtain tee times:** Call golf shop.

★★½ **ST. ANDREW'S GOLF COURSE**
PU-11099 W. 135th St., Overland Park, 66221, Johnson County, (913)897-3804, 10 miles
from Kansas City. **E-mail:** pgamp165@aol.com. **Facility Holes:** 18. **Yards:** 6,205/4,713. **Par:**
70/70. **Course Rating:** 69.5/67.7. **Slope:** 109/108. **Green Fee:** $13/$18. **Cart Fee:** $11/Person.
Walking Policy: Unrestricted walking. **Walkability:** 2. **Opened:** 1962. **Architect:** Jess
Nash/John Nash. **Season:** Year-round. **High:** March-Oct. **To obtain tee times:** Call golf shop.
Miscellaneous: Reduced fees (twilight, seniors, juniors), range (grass), cards (MC, V), BF, FF.

★★½ **STAGG HILL GOLF CLUB**
SP-4441 Fort Riley Blvd., Manhattan, 66502, Riley County, (785)539-1041, 60 miles from
Topeka. **Facility Holes:** 18. **Yards:** 6,697/5,524. **Par:** 72/72. **Course Rating:** 73.1/72.8. **Slope:**
131/117. **Green Fee:** $17/$19. **Cart Fee:** $21/Cart. **Walking Policy:** Unrestricted walking.
Walkability: 1. **Opened:** 1968. **Architect:** Richard Morse/Ray Weisenberger. **Season:** Year-
round. **To obtain tee times:** Call up to 7 days in advance. **Miscellaneous:** Reduced fees (twilight, juniors), range (mats), credit cards (MC, V, AE, D), BF, FF.

★★★ **SUNFLOWER HILLS GOLF CLUB**
PU-122 Riverview, Bonner Springs, 66012, Wyandotte County, (913)721-2727, 15 miles from
Kansas City. **Facility Holes:** 18. **Yards:** 7,001/5,850. **Par:** 72/73. **Course Rating:** 73.3/72.6.
Slope: 124/124. **Green Fee:** $13/$25. **Cart Fee:** $24/Cart. **Walking Policy:** Unrestricted walk-
ing. **Walkability:** 4. **Opened:** 1977. **Architect:** Roger Packard. **Season:** Year-round. **High:** April-
Sept. **To obtain tee times:** Call golf shop. **Miscellaneous:** Reduced fees (weekdays, twilight,
seniors, juniors), range (grass/mats), credit cards (MC, V), BF, FF.
Reader Comments: Long and fair … Hard to score, always tough … Nice layout needs TLC …
Slow rounds on weekends … Quite a hike for walkers.

SYCAMORE RIDGE GOLF COURSE
PU-21731 Clubhouse Dr., Spring Hill, 66083, Johnson County, (913)592-5292, 5 miles from
Olathe. **Facility Holes:** 18. **Yards:** 7,055/4,877. **Par:** 72/72. **Course Rating:** 76.2/65.4. **Slope:**
150/118. **Green Fee:** $37/$44. **Cart Fee:** $15/Person. **Walking Policy:** Unrestricted walking.
Walkability: 5. **Opened:** 2000. **Architect:** Jim Colbert/Baxter Spann. **Season:** Year-round. **High:**
May-Oct. **To obtain tee times:** Call golf shop. **Miscellaneous:** Reduced fees (twilight, seniors),
range (grass), credit cards (MC, V), BF, FF.

★★★★ **TERRADYNE RESORT HOTEL & COUNTRY CLUB** *Pace*
R-1400 Terradyne, Andover, 67002, Butler County, (316)733-5851, (800)892-4613, 10 miles
from Wichita. **Web:** www.terradyne-resort.com. **Facility Holes:** 18. **Yards:** 6,843/5,048. **Par:**
71/71. **Course Rating:** 75.3/70.2. **Slope:** 138/121. **Green Fee:** $35/$70. **Cart Fee:** $12/Person.
Walking Policy: Unrestricted walking. **Walkability:** 2. **Opened:** 1987. **Architect:** Don Sechrest.

Season: Year-round. **High:** May-Nov. **To obtain tee times:** Call golf shop. **Miscellaneous:** Reduced fees (guests, juniors), range (grass), lodging (42 rooms), credit cards (MC, V, AE, D), BF, FF.

Reader Comments: A great links course … Relies heavily on extreme rough … Tough but fair … Hardly any trees on the entire course … Front 9 layout was excellent … I thought I was in Scotland … Play it in the wind and brace yourself for a real test.

★★½ TEX CONSOLVER GOLF COURSE
PU-1931 S. Tyler Rd., Wichita, 67209, Sedgwick County, (316)721-7474, 1 mile from Wichita. **E-mail:** ghart38487@aol.com. **Facility Holes:** 18. **Yards:** 7,361/5,928. **Par:** 72/72. **Course Rating:** 74.8/73.3. **Slope:** 123/119. **Green Fee:** $15/$16. **Cart Fee:** $18/Cart. **Walking Policy:** Unrestricted walking. **Walkability:** 3. **Opened:** 1970. **Architect:** Bob Dunning. **Season:** Year-round. **High:** April-Sept. **To obtain tee times:** Call golf shop. **Miscellaneous:** Reduced fees (twilight, seniors, juniors), range (grass), credit cards (MC, V), BF, FF. **Special Notes:** Formerly Pawnee Prairie Golf Course.

★★ TOMAHAWK HILLS GOLF CLUB
PU-17501 Midland Dr., Shawnee, 66218, Johnson County, (913)631-8000, 5 miles from Kansas City. **E-mail:** jay.lispi@toloks.com. **Facility Holes:** 18. **Yards:** 6,003/5,643. **Par:** 70/71. **Course Rating:** 69.1/71.1. **Slope:** 118/117. **Green Fee:** $17/$22. **Cart Fee:** $24/Person. **Walking Policy:** Unrestricted walking. **Walkability:** 5. **Opened:** 1911. **Architect:** Bill Leonard. **Season:** Year-round. **To obtain tee times:** Call golf shop. **Miscellaneous:** Reduced fees (weekdays, twilight, seniors, juniors), range (grass/mats), credit cards (MC, V), BF, FF.

★★½ TOPEKA PUBLIC GOLF CLUB
PU-2533 S.W. Urish Rd., Topeka, 66614, Shawnee County, (785)272-0511. **Web:** www.topeka.org. **Facility Holes:** 18. **Yards:** 6,313/5,445. **Par:** 71/71. **Course Rating:** 70.4/72.6. **Slope:** 117/121. **Green Fee:** $13/$14. **Cart Fee:** $11/Person. **Walking Policy:** Unrestricted walking. **Walkability:** 3. **Opened:** 1954. **Architect:** William Leonard/L.J. (Dutch) McLellan. **Season:** Year-round. **High:** April-Sept. **To obtain tee times:** Call up to 30 days in advance. **Miscellaneous:** Reduced fees (seniors, juniors), range (grass), credit cards (MC, V), BF, FF.

★★★★ TURKEY CREEK GOLF COURSE & DEVELOPMENT
PU-1000 Fox Run, McPherson, 67460, McPherson County, (620)241-8530, 50 miles from Wichita. **E-mail:** turkeycreek@mpks.net. **Facility Holes:** 18. **Yards:** 6,241/5,327. **Par:** 70/70. **Course Rating:** 70.6/69.6. **Slope:** 126/116. **Green Fee:** $14/$16. **Cart Fee:** $20/Cart. **Walking Policy:** Unrestricted walking. **Walkability:** 3. **Opened:** 1991. **Architect:** Phillip Smith. **Season:** Year-round. **To obtain tee times:** Call golf shop. **Miscellaneous:** Reduced fees (twilight), range (grass), credit cards (MC, V, AE, D), BF, FF.

Reader Comments: A terrific layout that gives a variety of golfers a challenge … Well maintained … Friendly staff, lots of hazards, lots of fun … Very flat, wide open … Greens nice … Lots of trouble—rewards good shots … Will not need the driver here … Water can come into play on over half of the holes.

TWIN LAKES GOLF COURSE
M-53469 Mulvane Rd., Bldg 1336, McConnell AFB, 67221, Sedgwick County, (316)759-4038, 5 miles from Wichita. **Web:** www.mcconnell.af.mil. **Facility Holes:** 18. **Yards:** 6,904/5,151. **Par:** 72/72. **Course Rating:** 73.1/71.0. **Slope:** 120/120. **Green Fee:** $8/$16. **Cart Fee:** $16/Cart. **Walking Policy:** Unrestricted walking. **Walkability:** 1. **Season:** Year-round. **High:** June-Aug. **To obtain tee times:** Call golf shop. **Miscellaneous:** Reduced fees (twilight, juniors), range (grass), credit cards (MC, V), BF, FF.

★★★ VILLAGE GREENS GOLF CLUB
PU-5815 Highway 92, Meriden, 66512, Jefferson County, (785)876-2255, 20 miles from Topeka. **Facility Holes:** 18. **Yards:** 6,392/5,588. **Par:** 72/72. **Course Rating:** 70.2. **Slope:** 114. **Green Fee:** $12/$13. **Cart Fee:** $18/Cart. **Walking Policy:** Unrestricted walking. **Walkability:** 2. **Opened:** 1970. **Architect:** Buck Blankenship/L.J. McClellan. **Season:** Year-round. **High:** May-Sept. **To obtain tee times:** Call golf shop. **Miscellaneous:** Reduced fees (weekdays, juniors), metal spikes, range (grass/mats).

Reader Comments: Play all day one price … This course is the best public course in Kansas … A hidden gem … Mom & Pop course, but one of the most fun courses anywhere … Nice place to lower your handicap … Fun to play.

★★½ WELLINGTON GOLF CLUB
PU-1500 W. Harvey, Wellington, 67152, Sumner County, (620)326-7904, 28 miles from Wichita. **E-mail:** wellingtongolfclub@hotmail.com. **Web:** www.wellingtongolfclub.com. **Facility Holes:** 18. **Yards:** 6,201/5,384. **Par:** 70/70. **Course Rating:** 68.8/67.1. **Slope:** 114/111. **Green Fee:** $12/$15. **Cart Fee:** $17/Cart. **Walking Policy:** Unrestricted walking. **Walkability:** 2. **Opened:** 1919. **Architect:** Built by members. **Season:** Year-round. **To obtain tee times:** Call up

to 7 days in advance. **Miscellaneous:** Reduced fees (weekdays, twilight, juniors), range (grass/mats), credit cards (MC, V, AE), BF, FF.

★★½ **WESTERN HILLS GOLF CLUB**
SP-8533 S.W. 21st. St., Topeka, 66615, Shawnee County, (785)478-4000. **Facility Holes:** 18. **Yards:** 6,089/4,728. **Par:** 70/70. **Course Rating:** 69.2/66.1. **Slope:** 121/110. **Green Fee:** $13/$15. **Cart Fee:** $10/Person. **Walking Policy:** Unrestricted walking. **Walkability:** 2. **Opened:** 1967. **Architect:** Maury Bell. **Season:** Year-round. **High:** April-Sept. **To obtain tee times:** Call golf shop. **Miscellaneous:** Reduced fees (weekdays), credit cards (MC, V, AE, D).

WICHITA COUNTY MUNICIPAL GOLF COURSE
PU-East Hwy. 96, Leoti, 67861, Wichita County, (620)375-2263. **Facility Holes:** 18. **Yards:** 6,514/5,854. **Par:** 72/72. **Course Rating:** 73.6. **Slope:** 127/121. **Green Fee:** $12/$15. **Walking Policy:** Unrestricted walking. **Walkability:** 1. **Season:** April-Oct. **To obtain tee times:** Call golf shop. **Miscellaneous:** Reduced fees (weekdays, twilight, juniors), range (grass), BF, FF. **Special Notes:** Formerly Leoti Country Club.

WILLOW TREE GOLF COURSE
PU-1800 W. 15th St., Liberal, 67901, Seward County, (316)626-0175, 160 miles from Amarillo. **E-mail:** willowtree@swko.net. **Facility Holes:** 18. **Yards:** 5,900/5,052. **Par:** 72/72. **Course Rating:** 70.2. **Slope:** 121. **Green Fee:** $10/$13. **Cart Fee:** $18/Cart. **Walking Policy:** Unrestricted walking. **Walkability:** 1. **Season:** Year-round. **High:** May-Sept. **To obtain tee times:** Call golf shop. **Miscellaneous:** Reduced fees (weekdays, seniors, juniors), range (grass), caddies, credit cards (MC, V), BF, FF.

★★★ A.J. JOLLY GOLF COURSE
PU-5350 South U.S. 27, Alexandria, 41001, Campbell County, (859)635-2106, 15 miles from Cincinnati. **E-mail:** tjpro63@yahoo.com. **Web:** www.netcaddy.com. **Facility Holes:** 18. **Yards:** 6,219/5,418. **Par:** 71/75. **Course Rating:** 69.3/70.3. **Slope:** 118/115. **Green Fee:** $18/$20. **Cart Fee:** $12/Person. **Walking Policy:** Unrestricted walking. **Walkability:** 2. **Opened:** 1962. **Season:** Feb.-Dec. **High:** May-Aug. **To obtain tee times:** Call golf shop. **Miscellaneous:** Reduced fees (seniors, juniors), credit cards (MC, V), BF, FF.
Reader Comments: One of the best 19th-hole settings overlooking 10th & 18th holes situated between 2 lakes, and the beer is cold! … This is a good, fairly long course … Pretty course, way too slow … Long and open, good variety of holes.

★★½ BARREN RIVER STATE PARK GOLF COURSE
PU-1149 State Park Rd., Lucas, 42156, Barren County, (270)646-4653, (800)295-1876, 30 miles from Bowling Green. **E-mail:** golfpro@csip.net. **Facility Holes:** 18. **Yards:** 6,440/4,919. **Par:** 72/72. **Course Rating:** 69.1/66.6. **Slope:** 118/106. **Green Fee:** $18/$20. **Cart Fee:** $10/Person. **Walking Policy:** Unrestricted walking. **Walkability:** 5. **Opened:** 1967. **Architect:** Fred Rux. **Season:** Year-round. **High:** April-Sept. **To obtain tee times:** Call golf shop. **Miscellaneous:** Reduced fees (weekdays, twilight), range (grass), credit cards (MC, V, AE, D).

BEN HAWES STATE PARK GOLF
PU-400 Boothfield Rd., Owensboro, 42301, Daviess County, (270)684-9808. **Facility Holes:** 18. **Yards:** 6,632/5,371. **Par:** 71/71. **Course Rating:** 71.0/70.0. **Slope:** 118/115. **Green Fee:** $10/$15. **Cart Fee:** $10/Person. **Walking Policy:** Unrestricted walking. **Walkability:** 4. **Opened:** 1975. **Season:** Year-round. **High:** June-Aug. **To obtain tee times:** Call up to 5 days in advance. **Miscellaneous:** Range (grass), credit cards (MC, V, AE, D).

BIG HICKORY GOLF COURSE & COUNTRY CLUB
PU-Rte. 5, Manchester, 40962, Clay County, (606)598-8053. **Facility Holes:** 9. **Yards:** 5,844/4,910. **Par:** 72/72. **Slope:** 119/117. **Green Fee:** $12/$14. **Cart Fee:** $10/Person. **Walking Policy:** Unrestricted walking. **Architect:** Zenas Campbell Sr./Zenas Campbell Jr. **Season:** Year-round. **To obtain tee times:** Call golf shop. **Miscellaneous:** Credit cards (MC, V, AE, D).

★½ BOB-O-LINK GOLF ENTERPRISES
PU-1450 Fox Creek Rd, Lawrenceburg, 40342, Anderson County, (502)839-4029, 2 miles from Lawrenceburg. **Facility Holes:** 18. **Yards:** 6,650/4,889. **Par:** 71/71. **Course Rating:** 69.7/67.5. **Slope:** 109/105. **Green Fee:** $15/$17. **Cart Fee:** $10/Person. **Walking Policy:** Walking at certain times. **Walkability:** 2. **Opened:** 1968. **Architect:** Harold England/Jack Ridge. **Season:** Year-round. **High:** March-Nov. **Tee times:** Call golf shop. **Miscellaneous:** Reduced fees (weekdays, seniors, juniors), range (grass), credit cards (MC, V), BF, FF.

BOGIE BUSTERS GOLF CLUB
PU-346 Leesburg Rd., Georgetown, 40324, Scott County, (502)863-0754, 10 miles from Lexington. **Facility Holes:** 18. **Yards:** 6,300/5,240. **Par:** 72/72. **Green Fee:** $18/$20. **Cart Fee:** Included in green fee. **Walking Policy:** Unrestricted walking. **Walkability:** 3. **Opened:** 1993. **Architect:** Andy Adams. **Season:** Year-round. **High:** July-Sept. **Tee times:** Call golf shop. **Miscellaneous:** Reduced fees (seniors), range (grass/mats), credit cards (MC, V, AE, D).

★★★ BOONE LINKS
PU-19 Clubhouse Dr., Florence, 41042, Boone County, (859)371-7550, 10 miles from Cincinnati. **Web:** www.boonelinks.com. **Facility Holes:** 27. **Green Fee:** $23. **Cart Fee:** $12/Person. **Walking Policy:** Unrestricted walking. **Walkability:** 4. **Opened:** 1980. **Architect:** Robert von Hagge/Michael Hurdzan. **Season:** Year-round. **High:** May-Sept. **To obtain tee times:** Call golf shop. **Miscellaneous:** Reduced fees (weekdays, seniors, juniors), credit cards (MC, V), BF, FF.
BROOKVIEW/LAKEVIEW COURSE (18 Combo)
Yards: 6,634/5,648. **Par:** 72/72. **Course Rating:** 72.1/71.1. **Slope:** 128/123.
BROOKVIEW/RIDGEVIEW CSE (18 Combo)
Yards: 5,950/4,725. **Par:** 70/70. **Course Rating:** 68.4/69.2. **Slope:** 118/122.
RIDGEVIEW/LAKEVIEW COURSE (18 Combo)
Yards: 6,110/4,749. **Par:** 70/70. **Course Rating:** 69.2/66.8. **Slope:** 122/113.
Reader Comments: Good shape year round … Tough layout, good greens … Hilly, good greens … Very nice must have course management on shots … Very clean and well groomed.

BRECKENRIDGE COUNTY COMMUNITY CENTER
SP-Rte 3, Hardinsburg, 40143, Breckenridge County, (270)756-2841, 40 miles from Louisville. **Facility Holes:** 9. **Yards:** 3,362/2,614. **Par:** 36/36. **Course Rating:** 35.7/34.4. **Slope:** 123/116. **Green Fee:** $15/$25. **Walking Policy:** Unrestricted walking. **Walkability:** 3. **Opened:** 1969. **Season:** March-Nov. **High:** May-Aug. **To obtain tee times:** Call golf shop.

★★½ BRIGHT LEAF GOLF RESORT
R-1742 Danville Rd., Harrodsburg, 40330, Mercer County, (859)734-4231, (800)469-6038, 29 miles from Lexington. **E-mail:** blgr@kycom.net. **Web:** www.brightleafgolfresort.com. **Facility Holes:** 36. **Yards:** 6,474/5,800. **Par:** 72/77. **Course Rating:** 69.8/66.1. **Slope:** 118/109. **Green Fee:** $19/$25. **Cart Fee:** $20/Cart. **Walking Policy:** Unrestricted walking. **Walkability:** 3. **Opened:** 1964. **Architect:** Buck Blankenship. **Season:** Year-round. **High:** April-Oct. **To obtain tee times:** Call up to 7 days in advance. **Miscellaneous:** Reduced fees (weekdays, twilight), lodging (105 rooms), credit cards (MC, V, D), BF, FF.
Special Notes: Also has a 9-hole regulation and a 9-hole par-3 course.

★★★½ THE BULL AT BOONE'S TRACE GOLF CLUB
PU-175 Glen Eagle Blvd., Richmond, 40475, Madison County, (859)623-4653, 15 miles from Lexington. **Facility Holes:** 18. **Yards:** 6,659/4,879. **Par:** 72/72. **Course Rating:** 71.6/63.3. **Slope:** 136/119. **Green Fee:** $26/$31. **Cart Fee:** $10/Cart. **Walking Policy:** Walking at certain times. **Walkability:** 4. **Opened:** 1999. **Architect:** David Pfaff. **Season:** Year-round. **To obtain tee times:** Call up to 7 days in advance. **Miscellaneous:** Reduced fees (weekdays, twilight, juniors), range (grass), credit cards (MC, V, AE, D), FF.
Reader Comments: I like this course. It's a great challenge. A great course course for a low-handicapper ... Nice young course ... Too hilly ... Back 9 much better than front ... Very nice new course ... One of the best in this area.

★½ CABIN BROOK GOLF CLUB
PU-2260 Lexington Rd., Versailles, 40383, Woodford County, (859)873-8404, 7 miles from Lexington. **Facility Holes:** 18. **Yards:** 7,017/5,233. **Par:** 72/72. **Course Rating:** 72.4/68.3. **Slope:** 117/108. **Green Fee:** $13/$20. **Cart Fee:** $10/Person. **Walking Policy:** Unrestricted walking. **Walkability:** 1. **Opened:** 1965. **Architect:** Danny McQueen. **Season:** Year-round. **High:** May-Sept. **To obtain tee times:** Call up to 7 days in advance. **Miscellaneous:** Reduced fees (weekdays, twilight), range (grass), credit cards (MC, V), FF.

CALVERT CITY GOLF & COUNTRY CLUB
SP-199 Country Club Lane, Calvert City, 42029, Marshall County, (270)395-5831, 20 miles from Paducah. **Facility Holes:** 18. **Yards:** 6,405/5,005. **Par:** 72/72. **Course Rating:** 69.1/67.0. **Slope:** 107/103. **Green Fee:** $20/$25. **Cart Fee:** $20/Cart. **Walking Policy:** Unrestricted walking. **Walkability:** 2. **Opened:** 1970. **Season:** Year-round. **High:** May-Sept. **Tee times:** Call golf shop. **Miscellaneous:** Reduced fees (twilight), range (grass), credit cards (MC, V), FF.

CARDINAL HILLS GOLF COURSE
PU-335 Stark Lane, Bedford, 40006, Trimble County, (502)255-7770, 35 miles from Louisville. **Facility Holes:** 18. **Yards:** 5,700/4,800. **Par:** 70/70. **Green Fee:** $16/$22. **Cart Fee:** Included in green fee. **Walking Policy:** Walking at certain times. **Walkability:** 3. **Opened:** 1968. **Architect:** Stephen Stark. **Season:** Year-round. **High:** June-Aug. **To obtain tee times:** Call golf shop. **Miscellaneous:** Credit cards (MC, V).

CEDAR-FIL GOLF COURSE
PU-2330 New Shepardsville Rd., Bardstown, 40004, Nelson County, (502)348-8981, 30 miles from Louisville. **Facility Holes:** 18. **Yards:** 5,938/5,233. **Par:** 72/72. **Green Fee:** $10/$12. **Cart Fee:** $10/Person. **Walking Policy:** Unrestricted walking. **Walkability:** 1. **Opened:** 1967. **Architect:** Harold Filiatreau. **Season:** Year-round. **To obtain tee times:** Call golf shop. **Miscellaneous:** BF, FF.

★★ CHARLIE VETTINER GOLF COURSE
PU-10207 Mary Dell Lane, Jeffersontown, 40299, Jefferson County, (502)267-9958, 25 miles from Louisville. **Facility Holes:** 18. **Yards:** 6,914/5,388. **Par:** 72/73. **Course Rating:** 72.3/70.0. **Slope:** 123/116. **Green Fee:** $12. **Cart Fee:** $24/Cart. **Walking Policy:** Unrestricted walking. **Walkability:** 4. **Opened:** 1967. **Architect:** Jack Kidwell/Michael Hurdzan. **Season:** Year-round. **High:** April-Nov. **To obtain tee times:** Call golf shop. **Miscellaneous:** Reduced fees (twilight, seniors, juniors).

★★½ CONNEMARA GOLF LINKS
PU-2327 Lexington Rd., Nicholasville, 40356, Jessamine County, (859)885-4331, 5 miles from Lexington. **E-mail:** connemaragl@aol.com. **Web:** www.connemaragolf.com. **Facility Holes:** 18. **Yards:** 6,533/4,956. **Par:** 71/71. **Course Rating:** 71.1/69.5. **Slope:** 115/111. **Green Fee:** $8/$18. **Cart Fee:** $12/Person. **Walking Policy:** Walking at certain times. **Walkability:** 4. **Opened:** 1992. **Architect:** Jack Ridge. **Season:** Year-round. **To obtain tee times:** Call up to 7 days in advance. **Miscellaneous:** Reduced fees (weekdays, twilight, seniors, juniors), range (grass/mats), credit cards (MC, V, AE, D), BF, FF.

COUNTRY CREEK GOLF COURSE

PU-1075 Kenny Perry Dr., Franklin, 42134, Simpson County, (270)586-9373, 40 miles from Nashville, TN. **E-mail:** kpccgc@apex.net. **Web:** www.kpcountrycreek.com. **Facility Holes:** 18. **Yards:** 6,545/5,416. **Par:** 72/72. **Course Rating:** 69.5/64.0. **Slope:** 105/93. **Green Fee:** $15/$18. **Cart Fee:** $10/Person. **Walking Policy:** Unrestricted walking. **Walkability:** 3. **Opened:** 1995. **Architect:** Kenny Perry. **Season:** Year-round. **High:** March-Oct. **To obtain tee times:** Call golf shop. **Miscellaneous:** Reduced fees (seniors, juniors), metal spikes, range (grass), credit cards (MC, V, AE, D), FF.

CROOKED CREEK GOLF CLUB

SP-781 Crooked Creek Dr., London, 40744, Laurel County, (606)877-1993, 66 miles from Lexington. **E-mail:** crookedcreek@kih.net. **Web:** www.crookedcreekgolfclub.net. **Facility Holes:** 18. **Yards:** 7,007/5,087. **Par:** 72/72. **Course Rating:** 73.4/71.3. **Slope:** 134/122. **Green Fee:** $35/$40. **Cart Fee:** Included in green fee. **Walking Policy:** Unrestricted walking. **Walkability:** 4. **Opened:** 1993. **Architect:** Brian Silva. **Season:** Year-round. **To obtain tee times:** Call golf shop. **Miscellaneous:** Reduced fees (juniors), range (grass), credit cards (MC, V, AE, D), BF, FF.

★½ DEVOU PARK GOLF COURSE

PU-1344 Audubon Rd., Covington, 41011, Kenton County, (859)431-8030, 2 miles from Cincinnati, OH. **E-mail:** landrumgolf@landrumgolf.com. **Web:** www.landrumgolf.com. **Facility Holes:** 18. **Yards:** 6,103/5,052. **Par:** 70/70. **Course Rating:** 66.2/60.7. **Slope:** 114/103. **Green Fee:** $11/$21. **Cart Fee:** $12/Person. **Walking Policy:** Unrestricted walking. **Walkability:** 4. **Opened:** 1928. **Architect:** Gene Bates. **Season:** Year-round. **To obtain tee times:** Call up to 7 days in advance. **Miscellaneous:** Reduced fees (weekdays, seniors), metal spikes, credit cards (MC, V), BF, FF.

DIAMOND LINKS

PU-200 Fairway Dr., Cannonsburg, 41129, Boyd County, (606)928-5335, 6 miles from Ashland. **Facility Holes:** 18. **Yards:** 5,703/4,640. **Par:** 71/71. **Course Rating:** 67.7/63.2. **Slope:** 104/94. **Green Fee:** $19/$27. **Cart Fee:** Included in green fee. **Walking Policy:** Walking at certain times. **Walkability:** 5. **Opened:** 1989. **Season:** Year-round. **High:** June-Aug. **To obtain tee times:** Call golf shop. **Miscellaneous:** Reduced fees (weekdays, twilight, seniors, juniors), metal spikes, range (grass), credit cards (MC, V, AE, D). **Special Notes:** Formerly Bear Creek Country Club.

★★★ DOE VALLEY GOLF CLUB

SP-1 Doe Valley Pkwy., Brandenburg, 40108, Meade County, (270)422-3397, 30 miles from Louisville. **Facility Holes:** 18. **Yards:** 6,471/5,409. **Par:** 71/72. **Course Rating:** 69.8/70.3. **Slope:** 119/118. **Green Fee:** $11/$17. **Cart Fee:** $11/Person. **Walking Policy:** Walking at certain times. **Walkability:** 4. **Opened:** 1972. **Architect:** Dick Watson. **Season:** Year-round. **High:** April-Sept. **To obtain tee times:** Call golf shop. **Miscellaneous:** Reduced fees (weekdays, twilight), credit cards (MC, V).

Reader Comments: Excellent price ... Good layout, scenic ... Nice layout ... Wide open front 9, hilly difficult back 9 ... Nice course, quiet environment ... Very scenic and well-kept.

★★★½ DRAKE CREEK ON THE OHIO *Value, Pace*

PU-P. O. Box 306, Ledbetter, 42058, Livingston County, (270)898-4653, 150 miles from Nashville, TN. **E-mail:** golf@DrakeCreek.com. **Web:** www.DrakeCreek.com. **Facility Holes:** 18. **Yards:** 6,714/5,146. **Par:** 72/72. **Course Rating:** 71.6/68.8. **Slope:** 132/121. **Green Fee:** $20/$25. **Cart Fee:** $10/Person. **Walking Policy:** Unrestricted walking. **Walkability:** 3. **Opened:** 1999. **Architect:** Richard Osborne. **Season:** Year-round. **To obtain tee times:** Call up to 14 days in advance. **Miscellaneous:** Reduced fees (juniors), range (grass), credit cards (MC, V, AE), BF, FF.

Reader Comments: Excellent course. A bit tough ... Several good holes ... Will be a nice course ... Excellent course ... Still new, but real good course ... A good course and condition, people are accommodating, and a good price.

★★★★ EAGLE TRACE GOLF COURSE

SP-1275 Eagle Dr., Morehead, 40351, Rowan County, (606)783-9973, 60 miles from Lexington. **E-mail:** info@eagletrace.com. **Web:** www.eagletrace.com. **Facility Holes:** 18. **Yards:** 6,902/5,247. **Par:** 72/72. **Course Rating:** 73.8/70.8. **Slope:** 139/127. **Green Fee:** $12/$23. **Cart Fee:** $10/Person. **Walking Policy:** Unrestricted walking. **Walkability:** 3. **Opened:** 1995. **Architect:** David Pfaff. **Season:** Year-round. **To obtain tee times:** Call up to 14 days in advance. **Miscellaneous:** Reduced fees (twilight, seniors, juniors), range (grass/mats), credit cards (MC, V, AE, D), BF, FF.

Reader Comments: Excellent course cut out of huge pines ... Good variety of holes, some wooded, some open ... Very enjoyable course ... Very good ... Really nice for price ... Lots of tree-lined fairways ... Pretty.

KENTUCKY

★★★ **EAGLE'S NEST COUNTRY CLUB**
SP-Hwy. 39 N., Somerset, 42501, Pulaski County, (606)679-7754, 70 miles from Lexington. **Facility Holes:** 18. **Yards:** 6,404/5,010. **Par:** 71/72. **Course Rating:** 69.8/67.9. **Slope:** 123/117. **Green Fee:** $36/$45. **Cart Fee:** Included in green fee. **Walking Policy:** Unrestricted walking. **Walkability:** 5. **Opened:** 1979. **Architect:** Benjamin Wihry. **Season:** Feb.-Dec. **High:** May-Oct. **To obtain tee times:** Call golf shop. **Miscellaneous:** Range (grass), credit cards (MC, V).
Reader Comments: Everything good, a must ... Best-kept secret—a must play ... Quite beautiful & good hole variety ... Good design, well maintained, excellent staff.

FAIRWAY GOLF COURSE
PU-4940 Hwy. 227 N, Wheatley, 40359, Owen County, (502)463-2338, (888)463-1121, 50 miles from Louisville. **E-mail:** gilbyrd@aol.com. **Facility Holes:** 18. **Yards:** 5,900/5,400. **Par:** 70/70. **Course Rating:** 66.0/68.6. **Slope:** 100/101. **Green Fee:** $24/$28. **Cart Fee:** Included in green fee. **Walking Policy:** Walking at certain times. **Walkability:** 3. **Opened:** 1960. **Architect:** Harold England. **Season:** Year-round. **High:** April-Nov. **To obtain tee times:** Call golf shop. **Miscellaneous:** Reduced fees (juniors), range (grass), credit cards (MC, V, AE), BF, FF.

★★ **FLAGG SPRINGS GOLF CLUB**
PU-46 Smith Rd., California, 41007, Campbell County, (859)635-2170, 20 miles from Cincinnati. **Facility Holes:** 18. **Yards:** 6,137/4,634. **Par:** 71/71. **Course Rating:** 68.3/66.0. **Slope:** 111/104. **Green Fee:** $19. **Cart Fee:** $10/Person. **Walking Policy:** Unrestricted walking. **Walkability:** 3. **Opened:** 1997. **Season:** Year-round. **To obtain tee times:** Call golf shop. **Miscellaneous:** Reduced fees (twilight, seniors, juniors), metal spikes, range (grass/mats), credit cards (MC, V), BF, FF.

FORT KNOX
M-7955 Wilson Rd., Fort Knox, 40121, Hardin County, (502)943-9929, (888)548-5728, 20 miles from Louisville. **Facility Holes:** 36. **Green Fee:** $16/$18. **Cart Fee:** $10/Person. **Walking Policy:** Unrestricted walking. **Season:** Year-round. **High:** April-Oct. **To obtain tee times:** Call golf shop. **Miscellaneous:** Reduced fees (twilight), range (grass/mats), credit cards (MC, V, AE).
ANDERSON GOLF COURSE (18)
Yards: 6,509/5,135. **Par:** 72/72. **Course Rating:** 70.2/68.3. **Slope:** 120/114. **Walkability:** 4.
LINDSEY GOLF COURSE (18)
Yards: 6,668/5,314. **Par:** 72/72. **Course Rating:** 71.4/69.8. **Slope:** 122/116. **Walkability:** 3.

★★★ **FRANCES E. MILLER GOLF COURSE**
PU-2814 Pottertown Rd., Murray, 42071, Calloway County, (270)762-2238, (888)313-9862, 3 miles from Murray. **E-mail:** millergc@altavista.com. **Web:** www.murraystate.edu/millergolf. **Facility Holes:** 18. **Yards:** 6,592/5,058. **Par:** 71/71. **Course Rating:** 71.6/68.9. **Slope:** 125/117. **Green Fee:** $9/$17. **Cart Fee:** $10/Person. **Walking Policy:** Walking at certain times. **Walkability:** 3. **Opened:** 1983. **Architect:** Jack Kidwell/Michael Hurdzan. **Season:** Year-round. **High:** June-Aug. **To obtain tee times:** Call golf shop. **Miscellaneous:** Reduced fees (twilight, seniors, juniors), range (grass), credit cards (MC, V, AE), FF.
Reader Comments: Great public course, exceptional value ... You know before you go, always good ... Not plush, but a good fun course ... Nice hilly layout, some tight holes ... Challenging course, varied 9s.

★½ **GENERAL BURNSIDE STATE PARK GOLF COURSE**
PU-8801 S. Highway 27, Burnside, 42519, Pulaski County, (606)561-4104, 71 miles from Lexington. **Facility Holes:** 18. **Yards:** 5,905/5,905. **Par:** 71/71. **Course Rating:** 67.5/71.6. **Green Fee:** $18. **Cart Fee:** $10/Cart. **Walking Policy:** Unrestricted walking. **Walkability:** 4. **Opened:** 1958. **Season:** Year-round. **High:** June-Sept. **To obtain tee times:** Call golf shop. **Miscellaneous:** Reduced fees (weekdays, twilight, juniors), credit cards (MC, V, AE, D).

★★★★ **GIBSON BAY GOLF COURSE**
PU-2000 Gibson Bay Dr., Richmond, 40475, Madison County, (859)623-0225, 20 miles from Lexington. **E-mail:** eberlegolf@aol.com. **Web:** www.gibsonbay.com. **Facility Holes:** 18. **Yards:** 7,113/5,069. **Par:** 72/72. **Course Rating:** 74.1/69.1. **Slope:** 128/115. **Green Fee:** $4/$18. **Cart Fee:** $9/Person. **Walking Policy:** Walking at certain times. **Walkability:** 4. **Opened:** 1993. **Architect:** Michael Hurdzan. **Season:** Year-round. **High:** March-Oct. **To obtain tee times:** Call golf shop. **Miscellaneous:** Reduced fees (weekdays, twilight, seniors, juniors), range (grass/mats), credit cards (MC, V), BF, FF.
Reader Comments: Great course, excellent staff ... Best value I've ever seen ... Super nice & value ... Needs maturing ... Practice before you come, your clubs will thank you for it ... Average course ... Would play there everyday if I could.

THE GOLF COURSES AT KENTON COUNTY
PU-3908 Richardson Rd., Independence, 41051, Kenton County, (606)371-3200, 15 miles from Cincinnati. **E-mail:** jason@kentoncounty.org. **Web:** www.kentoncounty.org. **Facility Holes:** 54. **High:** May-Aug. **To obtain tee times:** Call golf shop. **Miscellaneous:** Reduced fees (weekdays, seniors, juniors), range (grass/mats), credit cards (MC, V), BF, FF.

★★★½ **FOX RUN COURSE** (18)
Yards: 7,055/4,707. **Par:** 72/72. **Course Rating:** 74.8/68.1. **Slope:** 143/123. **Green Fee:** $38/$44. **Cart Fee:** Included in green fee. **Walking Policy:** Mandatory carts. **Walkability:** 4. **Opened:** 1992. **Architect:** Arthur Hills. **Season:** March-Nov.
Notes: Ranked 9th in 1997 Best in State.
Reader Comments: Excellent but pricey … Hilly, long, a real workout for your driver and long irons … Good variety of holes … Tough course from back tees … Great test, fun to play … Hardest group of par 3s, great layout.

★★½ **PIONEER COURSE** (18)
Yards: 6,059/5,336. **Par:** 70/71. **Course Rating:** 67.9/69.5. **Slope:** 114/115. **Green Fee:** $9/$20. **Cart Fee:** $12/Person. **Walking Policy:** Unrestricted walking. **Walkability:** 3. **Opened:** 1968. **Architect:** Taylor Boyd. **Season:** Year-round.

★★★½ **WILLOWS COURSE** (18)
Yards: 6,791/5,669. **Par:** 72/72. **Course Rating:** 72.5/74.0. **Slope:** 130/129. **Green Fee:** $19/$22. **Cart Fee:** $12/Person. **Walking Policy:** Unrestricted walking. **Walkability:** 3. **Opened:** 1976. **Architect:** Jack Kidwell/Michael Hurzdan. **Season:** March-Nov.
Reader Comments: Great weekday course. Weekends make for very slow play … A fairly long course with a couple of tight holes.

★★½ HARTLAND MUNICIPAL GOLF COURSE
PU-1031 Wilkinson Trace, Bowling Green, 42103, Warren County, (270)393-3559, (800)786-7263, 45 miles from Nashville, TN. **Facility Holes:** 18. **Yards:** 6,523/5,016. **Par:** 71/72. **Course Rating:** 70.9/68.3. **Slope:** 123/114. **Green Fee:** $14/$17. **Cart Fee:** $10/Person. **Walking Policy:** Walking at certain times. **Walkability:** 3. **Opened:** 1989. **Architect:** Kevin Tucker. **Season:** Year-round. **High:** July-Aug. **To obtain tee times:** Call golf shop. **Miscellaneous:** Reduced fees (weekdays, twilight, seniors, juniors), credit cards (MC, V, AE).

HENRY COUNTY COUNTRY CLUB
SP-Hwy. 421, New Castle, 40050, Henry County, (502)845-2375, 30 miles from Louisville. **Facility Holes:** 18. **Yards:** 6,570/4,759. **Par:** 72/70. **Course Rating:** 70.7/67.4. **Slope:** 124/114. **Green Fee:** $11/$16. **Cart Fee:** $9/Person. **Walking Policy:** Walking at certain times. **Walkability:** 3. **Architect:** Buck Blankenship. **Season:** Year-round. **High:** May-Oct. **To obtain tee times:** Call golf shop. **Miscellaneous:** Reduced fees (seniors), range (grass).

HIDDEN VALLEY GOLF COURSE
PU-530 Hidden Valley Rd., Morgantown, 42261, Butler County, (270)526-4643, 20 miles from Bowling Green. **Facility Holes:** 18. **Yards:** 6,215/5,640. **Par:** 72/72. **Green Fee:** $12. **Cart Fee:** $8/Person. **Walking Policy:** Unrestricted walking. **Walkability:** 4. **Opened:** 1984. **Architect:** Gary Robbins. **Season:** Year-round. **High:** May-Oct. **To obtain tee times:** Call up to 14 days in advance. **Miscellaneous:** Metal spikes, BF, FF.

HIGH POINT GOLF CLUB
PU-1215 High Point Dr., Nicholasville, 40356, Jessamine County, (859)887-4614, 12 miles from Lexington. **Web:** www.highpointgolfclub.com. **Facility Holes:** 18. **Yards:** 6,114/5,431. **Par:** 72/72. **Course Rating:** 69.6. **Slope:** 121. **Green Fee:** $20/$26. **Cart Fee:** Included in green fee. **Walking Policy:** Unrestricted walking. **Walkability:** 3. **Opened:** 1992. **Architect:** Danny McQueen. **Season:** Year-round. **Tee times:** Call up to 7 days in advance. **Miscellaneous:** Reduced fees (weekdays, seniors, juniors), range (grass), credit cards (MC, V, AE), BF, FF.

★★★½ HOUSTON OAKS GOLF COURSE
SP-555 Houston Oaks Drive, Paris, 40361, Bourbon County, (606)987-5600, 12 miles from Lexington. **Facility Holes:** 18. **Yards:** 6,842/5,079. **Par:** 72/73. **Course Rating:** 73.9/69.3. **Slope:** 127/114. **Green Fee:** $20/$25. **Cart Fee:** $10/Person. **Walking Policy:** Unrestricted walking. **Walkability:** 3. **Opened:** 1996. **Architect:** Jack Ridge. **Season:** Year-round. **High:** May-Aug. **To obtain tee times:** Call up to 7 days in advance. **Miscellaneous:** Reduced fees (weekdays, twilight, seniors, juniors), range (grass), credit cards (MC, V, AE, D), FF.
Notes: Ranked 8th in 2001 Best in State.
Reader Comments: Good layout, long and longer when wet. Solid course, could be a real gem … Young, challenging course, will improve with time … Course in great shape.

★★½ INDIAN SPRINGS GOLF CLUB
SP-3408 Indian Lake Dr., Louisville, 40241, Jefferson County, (502)426-7111, 8 miles from Downtown Louisville. **E-mail:** blarson@isgolfclub.com. **Web:** www.isgolfclub.com. **Facility**

Holes: 18. **Yards:** 6,799/5,253. **Par:** 72/72. **Course Rating:** 71.4/68.4. **Slope:** 133/122. **Green Fee:** $25/$30. **Cart Fee:** $10/Person. **Walking Policy:** Walking at certain times. **Walkability:** 3. **Opened:** 1994. **Architect:** Kingsley Stratton. **Season:** Year-round. **To obtain tee times:** Call up to 5 days in advance. **Miscellaneous:** Reduced fees (juniors), range (grass), credit cards (MC, V, AE, D), FF.

★★ IROQUOIS GOLF COURSE

PU-1501 Rundill Rd., Louisville, 40214, Jefferson County, (502)363-9520. **Facility Holes:** 18. **Yards:** 6,151/4,636. **Par:** 71/73. **Course Rating:** 68.6/65.6. **Slope:** 119/110. **Green Fee:** $7/$12. **Cart Fee:** $11/Person. **Walking Policy:** Unrestricted walking. **Walkability:** 4. **Opened:** 1947. **Architect:** Robert Bruce Harris. **Season:** Year-round. **To obtain tee times:** Call golf shop. **Miscellaneous:** Reduced fees (twilight, seniors, juniors), BF, FF.

★★ JUNIPER HILLS GOLF COURSE

PU-800 Louisville Rd., Frankfort, 40601, Franklin County, (502)875-8559, 25 miles from Lexington. **Facility Holes:** 18. **Yards:** 6,200/5,904. **Par:** 70/74. **Course Rating:** 68.7/67.7. **Slope:** 111/106. **Green Fee:** $12/$15. **Cart Fee:** $10/Person. **Walking Policy:** Mandatory carts. **Walkability:** 3. **Opened:** 1956. **Architect:** Buck Blankenship. **Season:** Year-round. **To obtain tee times:** Call up to 7 days in advance. **Miscellaneous:** BF, FF.

★★★★ KEARNEY HILL GOLF LINKS

PU-3403 Kearney Rd., Lexington, 40511, Fayette County, (859)253-1981, 5 miles from Lexington. **Facility Holes:** 18. **Yards:** 6,987/5,362. **Par:** 72/72. **Course Rating:** 73.5/70.1. **Slope:** 128/118. **Green Fee:** $22. **Cart Fee:** $10/Person. **Walking Policy:** Unrestricted walking. **Walkability:** 2. **Opened:** 1989. **Architect:** P.B. Dye/Pete Dye. **Season:** Year-round. **To obtain tee times:** Call up to 7 days in advance. **Miscellaneous:** Reduced fees (twilight, seniors, juniors), range (grass), credit cards (MC, V, D). **Notes:** Ranked 9th in 2001 Best in State.
Reader Comments: Great condition, impeccable service, great layout … Challenging course … Very inexpensive, a little short, nice layout … Quality golf, good price, good service … Linksy.

★★★½ KENTUCKY DAM VILLAGE STATE RESORT PARK GOLF COURSE

R-Highway 641South, Gilbertsville, 42044, Marshall County, (270)362-8658, (800)295-1877, 20 miles from Paducah. **Web:** www.kystateparks.com. **Facility Holes:** 18. **Yards:** 6,704/5,094. **Par:** 72/72. **Course Rating:** 73.0/70.0. **Slope:** 135/124. **Green Fee:** $18/$25. **Cart Fee:** $10/Person. **Walking Policy:** Unrestricted walking. **Walkability:** 3. **Opened:** 1952. **Architect:** Perry Maxwell/Press Maxwell. **Season:** Year-round. **High:** March-Nov. **To obtain tee times:** Call up to 180 days in advance. **Miscellaneous:** Reduced fees (weekdays, twilight, juniors), range (grass), lodging (74 rooms), credit cards (MC, V, AE, D), FF.
Reader Comments: Challenging, fast. Very good shape … Good course, too crowded … Slow on weekends, beautiful course … 3 or 4 real nice holes.

★★★ KERRY LANDING GOLF COURSE *Pace*

PU-805 Valhalla Ln., Benton, 42025, Marshall County, (270)354-5050, (877)874-5050. **Web:** www.kerrylanding.com. **Facility Holes:** 18. **Opened:** 1999. **Architect:** Gary Roger Baird. **To obtain tee times:** Call golf shop.
Reader Comments: Beautiful course. Extremely well cared for. Excellence is rewarded. Can escape mis-hits … Will be a nice course … Good layout, will be a good course … Tight fairways, tall rough.

★★½ LA GRANGE WOODS COUNTRY CLUB

SP-2820 S. Hwy. 53, La Grange, 40031, Oldham County, (502)222-7927, 25 miles from Louisville. **E-mail:** birdcrawford1025@netscape.net. **Facility Holes:** 18. **Yards:** 6,104/4,577. **Par:** 71/71. **Course Rating:** 68.9/65.8. **Slope:** 115/106. **Green Fee:** $14/$19. **Cart Fee:** $9/Person. **Walking Policy:** Walking at certain times. **Walkability:** 3. **Opened:** 1970. **Architect:** Buck Blankenship/Rick Crawford. **Season:** Year-round. **High:** March-Oct. **To obtain tee times:** Call golf shop. **Miscellaneous:** Reduced fees (weekdays, seniors), credit cards (MC, V).

★★★★½ LAFAYETTE G. C. AT GREEN FARM RESORT *Service+, Value*

R-57 Jennie Green Rd., Falls of Rough, 40119, Grayson County, (270)257-2105, (888)257-2105, 45 miles from Owensboro. **E-mail:** info@lafayettegolfclub.com. **Web:** www.lafayettegolfclub.com. **Facility Holes:** 18. **Yards:** 6,888/5,286. **Par:** 72/72. **Course Rating:** 73.9/71.7. **Slope:** 133/124. **Green Fee:** $38/$42. **Cart Fee:** Included in green fee. **Walking Policy:** Walking at certain times. **Walkability:** 3. **Opened:** 1997. **Architect:** Jodie Kinney. **Season:** Year-round. **High:** April-Oct. **To obtain tee times:** Call golf shop. **Miscellaneous:** Reduced fees (weekdays, twilight, seniors), range (grass), lodging (9 rooms), credit cards (MC, V, AE, D), FF.
Reader Comments: Challenging course in beautiful country … Excellent service … Excellent new course, too expensive for area … Great experience … Best course in Central Kentucky, well worth a visit … Beautiful, scenic, demanding.

KENTUCKY

★★½ LAKE BARKLEY STATE PARK
PU-Hwy. 68 W., Cadiz, 42211, Trigg County, (270)924-9076, (800)295-1878, 65 miles from Bowling Green. **Web:** www.kystateparks.com. **Facility Holes:** 18. **Yards:** 6,751/5,191. **Par:** 72/72. **Course Rating:** 72.7/70.2. **Slope:** 131/121. **Green Fee:** $20/$25. **Cart Fee:** $10/Person. **Walking Policy:** Unrestricted walking. **Walkability:** 1. **Opened:** 1972. **Architect:** Edward Lawrence Packard. **Season:** Year-round. **To obtain tee times:** Call golf shop. **Miscellaneous:** Reduced fees (weekdays, twilight), range (grass/mats), lodging (150 rooms), credit cards (MC, V, AE, D), BF, FF.

★★★ LAKESIDE GOLF CLUB
PU-3725 Richmond Rd., Lexington, 40509, Fayette County, (859)263-5315. **Facility Holes:** 18. **Yards:** 6,844/5,269. **Par:** 72/72. **Course Rating:** 72.2/69.6. **Slope:** 123/116. **Green Fee:** $12. **Cart Fee:** $9/Person. **Walking Policy:** Unrestricted walking. **Walkability:** 2. **Opened:** 1970. **Architect:** Bob Carr. **Season:** Year-round. **To obtain tee times:** Call up to 7 days in advance. **Miscellaneous:** Reduced fees (twilight, seniors, juniors), range (grass), credit cards (MC, V, D), BF, FF.
Reader Comments: Green fees are reasonable. Decent layout ... Wide open, heavily played ... Average ... Good municipal course ... Nice.

LARUE COUNTY COUNTRY CLUB
SP-1175 Greensburg Rd., Hodgenville, 42748, Larue County, (270)358-9727, 45 miles from Louisville. **Facility Holes:** 18. **Yards:** 6,094/4,691. **Par:** 71/71. **Green Fee:** $12/$20. **Cart Fee:** $10/Person. **Walking Policy:** Unrestricted walking. **Walkability:** 3. **Season:** Year-round. **High:** April-July. **To obtain tee times:** Call golf shop. **Miscellaneous:** FF.

★★★★ LASSING POINTE GOLF COURSE
PU-2266 Double Eagle Dr., Union, 41091, Boone County, (859)384-2266, 12 miles from Cincinnati. **E-mail:** jkruempelman@boonecounty.org. **Web:** www.lassingpoint.com. **Facility Holes:** 18. **Yards:** 6,724/5,153. **Par:** 71/71. **Course Rating:** 72.2/69.5. **Slope:** 132/122. **Green Fee:** $34. **Cart Fee:** $12/Person. **Walking Policy:** Unrestricted walking. **Walkability:** 3. **Opened:** 1994. **Architect:** Michael Hurdzan. **Season:** April-Dec. **High:** May-Sept. **To obtain tee times:** Call up to 10 days in advance. **Miscellaneous:** Reduced fees (weekdays, seniors, juniors), range (grass), credit cards (MC, V), BF, FF.
Notes: Ranked 5th in 2001 Best in State: 29th in 1996 America's Top 75 Affordable Courses.
Reader Comments: Course is very plush ... One of my favorites, great layout ... Elevation changes. A real challenge ... Great course, really hard to get on ... A real gem—country club atomosphere at a bargain price.

★★★ LINCOLN HOMESTEAD STATE PARK
PU-5079 Lincoln Park Rd., Springfield, 40069, Washington County, (606)336-7461, 50 miles from Louisville. **E-mail:** gary.feldman@mail.state.ky.us. **Web:** http://www.state.ky.us/agencies/parks/linchome.htm **Facility Holes:** 18. **Yards:** 6,359/5,472. **Par:** 71/73. **Course Rating:** 70.0/71.0. **Slope:** 119/118. **Green Fee:** $15/$20. **Cart Fee:** $10/Person. **Walking Policy:** Walking at certain times. **Walkability:** 4. **Opened:** 1958. **Architect:** Buck Blankenship. **Season:** Year-round. **To obtain tee times:** Call golf shop. **Miscellaneous:** Reduced fees (weekdays, twilight, juniors), credit cards (MC, V, AE, D), BF, FF.
Reader Comments: Great value, good country golf course, 9th is one of my favorite holes anywhere ... Nice seniors' tees ... Beautiful course in the country, quiet.

★★★ LINCOLN TRAIL COUNTRY CLUB
SP-Country Club Road, Vine Grove, 40175, Hardin County, (270)877-2181, 40 miles from Louisville. **Facility Holes:** 18. **Yards:** 6,529/5,276. **Par:** 72/72. **Course Rating:** 70.6/69.9. **Slope:** 122/117. **Green Fee:** $15/$20. **Cart Fee:** $10/Person. **Walking Policy:** Walking at certain times. **Walkability:** 2. **Opened:** 1969. **Season:** Year-round. **High:** April-Oct. **To obtain tee times:** Call up to 7 days in advance. **Miscellaneous:** Range (grass/mats), credit cards (MC, V), FF.
Reader Comments: Great layout, needs more maintenance ... Good course when weather cooperates ... Nice course, quiet.

LINKS AT LILLY CREEK RESORT
PU-500 Lilly Creek Resort Rd., Jamestown, 42629, Russell County, (270)343-4653, 70 miles from Bowling Green. **E-mail:** thelinks@Duo-county.com. **Facility Holes:** 18. **Yards:** 6,105/4,730. **Par:** 72/72. **Course Rating:** 68.7/67.0. **Slope:** 112/106. **Green Fee:** $15. **Cart Fee:** $10/Person. **Walking Policy:** Unrestricted walking. **Opened:** 1996. **Architect:** Joe David Polston. **Season:** Year-round. **High:** April-Oct. **To obtain tee times:** Call golf shop. **Miscellaneous:** Reduced fees (guests, twilight, seniors, juniors), metal spikes, range (grass), credit cards (MC, V).

★★ **LONG RUN GOLF CLUB**
PU-1605 Flatrock Rd., Anchorage, 40245, Jefferson County, (502)245-9015, 10 miles from Louisville. **Facility Holes:** 18. **Yards:** 6,839/5,562. **Par:** 72/73. **Course Rating:** 71.5/71.4. **Slope:** 111/111. **Green Fee:** $9/$18. **Cart Fee:** $20/Cart. **Walking Policy:** Unrestricted walking. **Walkability:** 2. **Opened:** 1965. **Architect:** Benjamin Wihry. **Season:** Year-round. **High:** May-Aug. **To obtain tee times:** Call golf shop. **Miscellaneous:** Reduced fees (weekdays, twilight, seniors, juniors), range (grass).

LONGVIEW GOLF COURSE
PU-3243 Frankfort Pike, Georgetown, 40324, Scott County, (502)863-2165, (800)572-0210, 10 miles from Frankfort. **Facility Holes:** 18. **Yards:** 6,600/5,300. **Par:** 72/73. **Course Rating:** 70.7/67.0. **Slope:** 120/114. **Green Fee:** $25/$30. **Cart Fee:** Included in green fee. **Walking Policy:** Walking at certain times. **Walkability:** 3. **Opened:** 1967. **Architect:** Buck Blankenship. **Season:** Year-round. **High:** April-Sept. **To obtain tee times:** Call golf shop. **Miscellaneous:** Range (grass/mats), credit cards (MC, V, AE).

MAPLEHURST GOLF COURSE
PU-700 Bells Mill Rd., Shepherdsville, 40165, Bullitt County, (502)957-3370, 20 miles from Louisville. **E-mail:** miniaturemickey1@aol.com. **Facility Holes:** 18. **Yards:** 6,065/5,165. **Par:** 70/70. **Course Rating:** 67.0/66.0. **Slope:** 104/102. **Green Fee:** $10/$11. **Cart Fee:** $19/Cart. **Walking Policy:** Unrestricted walking. **Walkability:** 3. **Opened:** 1970. **Architect:** Sammy Tilford. **Season:** Year-round. **To obtain tee times:** Call golf shop. **Miscellaneous:** Reduced fees (weekdays, seniors), credit cards (MC, V, AE, D), FF.

★★★½ **MARRIOTT'S GRIFFIN GATE GOLF CLUB**
R-1720 Newtown Pike, Lexington, 40511, Fayette County, (859)231-5100. **E-mail:** kypgapro@aol.com. **Facility Holes:** 18. **Yards:** 6,830/4,994. **Par:** 72/72. **Course Rating:** 73.3/69.3. **Slope:** 132/119. **Green Fee:** $42/$52. **Cart Fee:** Included in green fee. **Walkability:** 1. **Opened:** 1981. **Architect:** Rees Jones. **Season:** Year-round. **High:** March-Oct. **To obtain tee times:** Call golf shop. **Miscellaneous:** Reduced fees (twilight, seniors), lodging (400 rooms), credit cards (MC, V, AE, D, Diners' Club).
Reader Comments: Houses close to fairways ... A typical resort course, not very exciting ,.. A little pricey, pace of play slow ... Well-run resort hotel course.

★★★★ **MAYWOOD GOLF CLUB**
PU-130 Maywood Ave., Bardstown, 40004, Nelson County, (502)348-6600, (800)791-8633, 34 miles from Louisville. **E-mail:** kevin@maywoodgolf.com. **Web:** www.kentucky-golfer.com. **Facility Holes:** 18. **Yards:** 6,965/4,711. **Par:** 72/72. **Course Rating:** 72.2/66.5. **Slope:** 121/107. **Green Fee:** $19/$22. **Cart Fee:** $10/Person. **Walking Policy:** Unrestricted walking. **Walkability:** 4. **Opened:** 1995. **Architect:** David Pfaff. **Season:** Year-round. **To obtain tee times:** Call up to 7 days in advance. **Miscellaneous:** Reduced fees (weekdays, twilight), range (grass), credit cards (MC, V, AE, D), BF, FF.
Reader Comments: Beautiful layout, very nice driving range, very well kept, easily worth the green fees ... Great condition, best value in area ... A good place to shoot a good score.

MEADOWOOD GOLF CLUB
PU-1911 Golf Club Dr, Burlington, 41005, Boone County, (859)586-0422. **Facility Holes:** 18. **Yards:** 5,083/4,212. **Par:** 69/69. **Course Rating:** 62.3/63.4. **Slope:** 100/100. **Green Fee:** $17. **Cart Fee:** $11/Person. **Walking Policy:** Unrestricted walking. **Walkability:** 2. **Opened:** 1954. **Architect:** Ted Williams. **Season:** Year-round. **High:** May-Aug. **To obtain tee times:** Call golf shop. **Miscellaneous:** Reduced fees (seniors, juniors), credit cards (MC, V, D).

★★½ **MY OLD KENTUCKY HOME STATE PARK GOLF CLUB**
PU-668 Loretto Road, Bardstown, 40004, Nelson County, (502)349-6542, (800)323-7803, 30 miles from Louisville. **Facility Holes:** 18. **Yards:** 6,065/5,239. **Par:** 70/71. **Course Rating:** 69.5/70.2. **Slope:** 119/118. **Green Fee:** $18/$20. **Cart Fee:** $10/Person. **Walking Policy:** Unrestricted walking. **Walkability:** 3. **Opened:** 1938. **Architect:** H.H. Rudy/David Pfaff. **Season:** Year-round. **To obtain tee times:** Call up to 7 days in advance. **Miscellaneous:** Reduced fees (weekdays, twilight, juniors), range (grass), credit cards (MC, V, AE, D), BF, FF.

★★★½ **NEVEL MEADE GOLF COURSE**
SP-3123 Nevel Meade Dr., Prospect, 40059, Oldham County, (502)228-9522, (502)228-2091, 10 miles from Louisville. **E-mail:** nevelmeade@aol.com. **Facility Holes:** 18. **Yards:** 6,956/5,616. **Par:** 72/72. **Course Rating:** 72.2/70.4. **Slope:** 122/117. **Green Fee:** $20/$27. **Cart Fee:** $12/Person. **Walking Policy:** Unrestricted walking. **Walkability:** 3. **Opened:** 1991. **Architect:** Steve Smyers. **Season:** Year-round. **High:** May-Sept. **To obtain tee times:** Call up to 3 days in advance. **Miscellaneous:** Reduced fees (weekdays, twilight, juniors), range (grass), credit cards (MC, V, AE), BF, FF.

KENTUCKY

★★ OLD BRIDGE GOLF CLUB

SP-1 Old Bridge Rd., Danville, 40422, Boyle County, (859)236-6051, (800)783-7153, 25 miles from Lexington. **E-mail:** oldbridgegc@hotmail.com. **Facility Holes:** 18. **Yards:** 6,400/4,600. **Par:** 72/72. **Course Rating:** 68.0/64.9. **Slope:** 117/104. **Green Fee:** $23/$28. **Cart Fee:** Included in green fee. **Walking Policy:** Walking at certain times. **Walkability:** 3. **Opened:** 1990. **Architect:** Benjamin Wihry. **Season:** Year-round. **To obtain tee times:** Call golf shop. **Miscellaneous:** Reduced fees (seniors, juniors), range (grass/mats), credit cards (MC, V), BF, FF.

OLD SILO GOLF CLUB

PU-350 Silver Lake Dr., Mt. Sterling, 40353, Montgomery County, (859)498-4697, (877)653-7456, 30 miles from Lexington. **E-mail:** oldsilo@mindspring.com. **Web:** www.oldsilo.com. **Facility Holes:** 18. **Yards:** 6,977/5,509. **Par:** 72/72. **Course Rating:** 74.5/67.8. **Slope:** 139/125. **Green Fee:** $42. **Cart Fee:** Included in green fee. **Walking Policy:** Unrestricted walking. **Walkability:** 4. **Opened:** 2001. **Architect:** Graham Marsh. **Season:** Year-round. **High:** April-Oct. **To obtain tee times:** Call up to 7 days in advance. **Miscellaneous:** Reduced fees (weekdays, twilight, seniors, juniors), range (grass), credit cards (MC, V, AE), BF, FF. **Notes:** Ranked 6th in 2001 Best New Affordable Courses.

OLDHAM COUNTY COUNTRY CLUB

SP-2300 N. Hwy. 393, La Grange, 40031, Oldham County, (502)222-9133, 25 miles from Louisville. **Facility Holes:** 18. **Yards:** 6,230/5,790. **Par:** 71/74. **Course Rating:** 69.2/71.8. **Slope:** 115/118. **Green Fee:** $17/$22. **Opened:** 1956. **Architect:** Buck Blankenship. **Season:** Year-round. **To obtain tee times:** Call golf shop. **Miscellaneous:** Reduced fees (weekdays).

PARK MAMMOTH RESORT

R-Hwy. U.S. 31W., Park City, 42160, Edmonson County, (270)749-4101, 19 miles from Bowling Green. **Facility Holes:** 36. **Green Fee:** $10. **Cart Fee:** $10/Person. **Walking Policy:** Unrestricted walking. **Walkability:** 4. **Opened:** 1964. **Season:** Year-round. **To obtain tee times:** Call golf shop. **Miscellaneous:** Lodging (92 rooms), credit cards (MC, V, AE, D), FF.

★½ NO. 1 COURSE (18)
Yards: 6,073/5,299. **Par:** 70/70. **Course Rating:** 68.0/69.0. **Slope:** 114/114. **Architect:** Buck Blankenship.

NO. 2 COURSE (18)
Yards: 6,306/6,047. **Par:** 72/72. **Course Rating:** 69.3/71.5. **Slope:** 109/113. **Architect:** Gary Robbins.

★★ PAXTON PARK GOLF COURSE

PU-841 Berger Rd., Paducah, 42002, McCracken County, (270)444-9514, 140 miles from Nashville, TN. **Web:** www.paxtonpark.com. **Facility Holes:** 18. **Yards:** 6,464/5,376. **Par:** 71/76. **Course Rating:** 70.1/65.4. **Slope:** 126/117. **Green Fee:** $14/$20. **Cart Fee:** $18/Cart. **Walking Policy:** Unrestricted walking. **Walkability:** 3. **Opened:** 1940. **Season:** Year-round. **To obtain tee times:** Call up to 5 days in advance. **Miscellaneous:** Reduced fees (weekdays, twilight, juniors), range (grass), credit cards (MC, V, AE, D), BF, FF.

★★★★½ THE PENINSULA GOLF RESORT

R-200 Club House Dr., Lancaster, 40444, Garrard County, (859)548-5055, (877)249-4747, 20 miles from Lexington. **E-mail:** peninsulagolf@aol.com. **Web:** www.peninsulagolf.com. **Facility Holes:** 18. **Yards:** 6,700/5,000. **Par:** 72/72. **Course Rating:** 71.5/68.5. **Slope:** 124/115. **Green Fee:** $25/$40. **Cart Fee:** Included in green fee. **Walking Policy:** Walking at certain times. **Walkability:** 3. **Opened:** 1997. **Architect:** Pete Dye/Tim Liddy. **Season:** Year-round. **High:** April-Oct. **To obtain tee times:** Call golf shop. **Miscellaneous:** Reduced fees (guests, twilight, seniors, juniors), range (grass), lodging (24 rooms), credit cards (MC, V, AE), BF, FF. **Notes:** Ranked 7th in 2001 Best in State.

PENN RUN GOLF COURSE

PU-12900 Christman Rd., Louisville, 40229, Jefferson County, (502)957-5940, 12 miles from Louisville. **Facility Holes:** 18. **Yards:** 6,217/5,511. **Par:** 71/73. **Course Rating:** 68.6/70.2. **Slope:** 111/113. **Green Fee:** $10/$12. **Cart Fee:** $18/Person. **Walking Policy:** Unrestricted walking. **Walkability:** 3. **Opened:** 1970. **Architect:** McCawley & Emberson. **Season:** Year-round. **High:** April-Aug. **To obtain tee times:** Call golf shop. **Miscellaneous:** Reduced fees (twilight, seniors, juniors), metal spikes.

PERRY PARK COUNTRY CLUB

PU-Rte. 355, Perry Park, 40363, Owen County, (502)484-5776, 50 miles from Cincinnati. **Facility Holes:** 18. **Yards:** 7,240/5,900. **Par:** 72/72. **Course Rating:** 73.4/72.3. **Slope:** 119/116. **Green Fee:** $21/$24. **Cart Fee:** $12/Person. **Walking Policy:** Unrestricted walking. **Walkability:** 2. **Opened:** 1968. **Season:** Feb.-Dec. **High:** June-Sept. **To obtain tee times:** Call golf shop. **Miscellaneous:** Reduced fees (seniors, juniors), range (grass), credit cards (MC, V).

PICADOME GOLF COURSE

PU-469 Parkway Dr., Lexington, 40504, Fayette County, (859)455-8454. **Facility Holes:** 18. **Yards:** 6,455/5,095. **Par:** 72/72. **Course Rating:** 71.0/69.1. **Slope:** 125/118. **Green Fee:** $12/$17. **Cart Fee:** $10/Person. **Walking Policy:** Unrestricted walking. **Walkability:** 1. **Opened:** 1927. **Architect:** Bob Lee. **Season:** Year-round. **High:** March-Oct. **To obtain tee times:** Call up to 7 days in advance. **Miscellaneous:** Reduced fees (twilight, seniors, juniors), lodging (500 rooms), credit cards (MC, V), BF, FF.
Special Notes: Formerly Campbell House Country Club.

★★ PINE VALLEY COUNTRY CLUB & RESORT

R-805 Pine Valley Dr., Elizabethtown, 42701, Hardin County, (270)737-8300, (800)844-1904, 35 miles from Louisville. **Facility Holes:** 18. **Yards:** 6,648/5,357. **Par:** 72/73. **Course Rating:** 71.3/69.6. **Slope:** 119/114. **Green Fee:** $20. **Cart Fee:** $10/Person. **Walking Policy:** Walking at certain times. **Walkability:** 3. **Opened:** 1968. **Architect:** Bill Amick/Jack Ridge. **Season:** Year-round. **High:** April-Oct. **To obtain tee times:** Call golf shop. **Miscellaneous:** Reduced fees (weekdays, guests, twilight, seniors, juniors), metal spikes, range (grass/mats), lodging (56 rooms), credit cards (MC, V, D).

★★★★ QUAIL CHASE GOLF CLUB

PU-7000 Cooper Chapel Rd., Louisville, 40229, Jefferson County, (502)239-2110, (877)239-2110. **E-mail:** quail@quailchase.com. **Web:** www.quailchase.com. **Facility Holes:** 27. **Green Fee:** $23/$30. **Cart Fee:** $10/Person. **Walking Policy:** Unrestricted walking. **Walkability:** 3. **Opened:** 1988. **Architect:** David Pfaff. **Season:** Year-round. **High:** March-Nov. **To obtain tee times:** Call up to 5 days in advance. **Miscellaneous:** Reduced fees (weekdays, twilight, seniors, juniors), range (grass/mats), credit cards (MC, V, AE), BF, FF.
EAST/SOUTH (18 Combo)
Yards: 6,769/5,320. **Par:** 72/72. **Course Rating:** 71.7/77.6. **Slope:** 127/136.
SOUTH/WEST (18 Combo)
Yards: 6,569/5,070. **Par:** 72/72. **Course Rating:** 70.5/76.3. **Slope:** 124/133.
WEST/EAST (18 Combo)
Yards: 6,790/5,053. **Par:** 72/72. **Course Rating:** 72.0/77.9. **Slope:** 133/141.
Reader Comments: Always busy, usually slow, nice course … Setting is breathtaking, staff extremely nice, very women friendly and encouraging to beginners and juniors … One of the best in the area … Exceptional value.

ROLLING HILLS GOLF COURSE

PU-1600 Pine Dr., Russellville, 42276, Logan County, (270)726-8700, 20 miles from Bowling Green. **Facility Holes:** 18. **Yards:** 6,379/4,877. **Par:** 71/71. **Course Rating:** 69.4/67.2. **Slope:** 111/106. **Green Fee:** $9/$15. **Cart Fee:** $8/Person. **Walking Policy:** Unrestricted walking. **Walkability:** 4. **Season:** Year-round. **To obtain tee times:** Call golf shop. **Miscellaneous:** Reduced fees (seniors), range (grass/mats), credit cards (MC, V, AE, D), FF.

★★★ SENECA GOLF COURSE

PU-2300 Seneca Park Rd., Louisville, 40206, Jefferson County, (502)458-9298. **E-mail:** LMD6@aol.com. **Facility Holes:** 18. **Yards:** 7,034/5,469. **Par:** 72/73. **Course Rating:** 73.7/71.5. **Slope:** 130/122. **Green Fee:** $7/$12. **Cart Fee:** $22/Cart. **Walking Policy:** Unrestricted walking. **Walkability:** 3. **Opened:** 1935. **Architect:** Michael Hurdzan/Alex McKay. **Season:** Year-round. **To obtain tee times:** Call up to 2 days in advance. **Miscellaneous:** Reduced fees (weekdays, twilight, seniors, juniors), range (grass), BF, FF.
Reader Comments: Rolling hills with grass mounds around greens, water comes into play … Good course to walk, a challenge to play water holes … Much improved … Great price … Best city course.

★★★ SHAWNEE GOLF COURSE

PU-460 Northwestern Pkwy., Louisville, 40212, Jefferson County, (502)776-9389. **Facility Holes:** 18. **Yards:** 6,402/5,476. **Par:** 70/70. **Course Rating:** 66.7/68.9. **Slope:** 100/105. **Green Fee:** $7/$12. **Walking Policy:** Unrestricted walking. **Walkability:** 2. **Opened:** 1933. **Architect:** Alex McKay. **Season:** Year-round. **High:** May-Oct. **To obtain tee times:** Call golf shop. **Miscellaneous:** Reduced fees (twilight, seniors, juniors), metal spikes, range (grass).
Reader Comments: Well-kept muni, popular course … My best round ever, plays left to right … Nice layout.

SHELBYVILLE COUNTRY CLUB
SP-Smithfield Rd., Shelbyville, 40066, Shelby County, (502)633-0542, 20 miles from Frankfort. **E-mail:** diceman@shelbyvillecc.com. **Web:** www.shelbyvillecc.com. **Facility Holes:** 18. **Yards:** 6,331/5,231. **Par:** 72/73. **Course Rating:** 70.2/69.7. **Slope:** 122/118. **Green Fee:** $35. **Cart Fee:** Included in green fee. **Walking Policy:** Mandatory carts. **Walkability:** 3. **Opened:** 1934. **Season:** Year-round. **To obtain tee times:** Call golf shop. **Miscellaneous:** Range (grass), credit cards (MC, V, D), BF, FF.

THE SILOS GOLF CLUB
SP-270 N. Country Club Lane KY 286, Paducah, 42002, McCracken County, (270)488-2182. **Facility Holes:** 18. **Yards:** 6,780/5,876. **Par:** 72/72. **Course Rating:** 73.3/69.9. **Slope:** 128/117. **Green Fee:** $22/$28. **Cart Fee:** $18/Cart. **Walking Policy:** Unrestricted walking. **Walkability:** 3. **Opened:** 1997. **Architect:** Jerry Lemons. **Season:** Year-round. **High:** July-Aug. **To obtain tee times:** Call golf shop. **Miscellaneous:** Range (grass).
Special Notes: Formerly The Golf Club.

★★ SOUTHWIND GOLF COURSE
SP-2480 New Boonesboro Rd., Winchester, 40391, Clark County, (859)744-0375, 15 miles from Lexington. **Facility Holes:** 18. **Yards:** 6,265/4,700. **Par:** 71/71. **Course Rating:** 67.1/70.0. **Slope:** 113/102. **Green Fee:** $11/$13. **Cart Fee:** $8/Person. **Walking Policy:** Walking at certain times. **Walkability:** 3. **Opened:** 1992. **Architect:** Dan McQueen/Ken Arnold. **Season:** Feb.-Dec. **High:** May-Sept. **To obtain tee times:** Call golf shop. **Miscellaneous:** Reduced fees (weekdays, seniors), range (grass/mats).

SPORTLAND GOLF COURSE
PU-4199 Lexington Rd., Winchester, 40391, Clark County, (859)744-9959, (800)273-5001, 18 miles from Lexington. **Facility Holes:** 18. **Yards:** 6,714/4,717. **Par:** 72/72. **Course Rating:** 70.0/64.6. **Slope:** 116/104. **Green Fee:** $16/$31. **Cart Fee:** Included in green fee. **Walking Policy:** Unrestricted walking. **Walkability:** 5. **Opened:** 1967. **Season:** March-Dec. **High:** May-Sept. **To obtain tee times:** Call up to 7 days in advance. **Miscellaneous:** Reduced fees (seniors), FF.

SUGAR BAY GOLF COURSE
SP-RR #1, Warsaw, 41095, Gallatin County, (859)567-2601, 25 miles from Cincinnati. **E-mail:** tbruceold@aol.com. **Facility Holes:** 18. **Yards:** 6,103/4,907. **Par:** 71/71. **Course Rating:** 68.7/67.4. **Slope:** 121/114. **Green Fee:** $23/$28. **Cart Fee:** $10/Person. **Walking Policy:** Unrestricted walking. **Walkability:** 2. **Opened:** 1989. **Season:** Year-round. **High:** May-Sept. **To obtain tee times:** Call golf shop. **Miscellaneous:** Reduced fees (weekdays), credit cards (MC, V), BF, FF.

★★★½ THE SUMMIT
SP-6501 Summit Dr., Owensboro, 42303, Daviess County, (502)281-4653, 6 miles from Owensboro. **E-mail:** summit@milesnmore.com. **Web:** www.summitky.com. **Facility Holes:** 18. **Yards:** 6,600/4,890. **Par:** 72/72. **Course Rating:** 71.3/67.6. **Slope:** 128/117. **Green Fee:** $29/$55. **Cart Fee:** Included in green fee. **Walking Policy:** Walking at certain times. **Walkability:** 4. **Opened:** 1993. **Architect:** Don Charles. **Season:** Year-round. **High:** April-Oct. **To obtain tee times:** Call golf shop. **Miscellaneous:** Reduced fees (weekdays, twilight), range (grass), credit cards (MC, V, AE), BF, FF.
Reader Comments: Good place to play, a little expensive … Great layout, tough greens especially No. 9 … Won't disappoint you … A long water hole, fun to drive … It plays a little long from the back tees.

SWEET HOLLOW GOLF COURSE
PU-424 Sweet Hollow Road, Corbin, 40701, Laurel County, (606)523-1241, 80 miles from Lexington. **Facility Holes:** 9. **Yards:** 3,022/2,649. **Par:** 36/36. **Course Rating:** 69.6/69.6. **Slope:** 125/119. **Green Fee:** $21/$23. **Cart Fee:** $10/Person. **Walkability:** 3. **Season:** Year-round. **To obtain tee times:** Call golf shop. **Miscellaneous:** Range (grass), credit cards (MC, V).

★★★½ TANGLEWOOD GOLF COURSE
SP-245 Tanglewood Ct., Taylorsville, 40071, Spencer County, (502)477-2468, 25 miles from Louisville. **Facility Holes:** 18. **Yards:** 6,626/5,275. **Par:** 72/72. **Course Rating:** 70.2/68.8. **Slope:** 121/115. **Green Fee:** $16/$23. **Cart Fee:** $12/Person. **Walking Policy:** Walking at certain times. **Walkability:** 4. **Opened:** 1984. **Architect:** Buck Blankenship. **Season:** Year-round. **High:** May-Aug. **To obtain tee times:** Call golf shop. **Miscellaneous:** Reduced fees (weekdays, twilight, seniors, juniors), metal spikes, range (grass), credit cards (MC, V), BF, FF.
Reader Comments: Good country golf course, nice greens … Decent, demanding country course … Sidehill lies lead to alibis.

KENTUCKY

★★½ **TATES CREEK GOLF COURSE**
PU-1400 Gainesway Dr., Lexington, 40502, Fayette County, (859)272-3428. **Facility Holes:** 18. **Yards:** 6,310/5,260. **Par:** 72/73. **Course Rating:** 69.5/69.3. **Slope:** 120/117. **Green Fee:** $12/$18. **Cart Fee:** $16/Person. **Walking Policy:** Unrestricted walking. **Walkability:** 3. **Opened:** 1957. **Architect:** Buck Blankenship. **Season:** Year-round. **To obtain tee times:** Call golf shop. **Miscellaneous:** Reduced fees (twilight, seniors, juniors), credit cards (MC, V, D), BF, FF.

★★★½ **TWIN OAKS GOLF & PLANTATION CLUB**
PU-43rd & Michigan Ave., Covington, 41015, Kenton County, (859)581-2410, 5 miles from Cincinnati, OH. **E-mail:** roswingos@aol.com. **Web:** www.golfatwinoaks.com. **Facility Holes:** 18. **Yards:** 6,400/5,078. **Par:** 70/70. **Course Rating:** 70.6/68.5. **Slope:** 121/114. **Green Fee:** $22. **Cart Fee:** $14/Person. **Walking Policy:** Unrestricted walking. **Walkability:** 1. **Opened:** 1928. **Season:** Feb.-Dec. **High:** April-Oct. **To obtain tee times:** Call up to 14 days in advance. **Miscellaneous:** Reduced fees (seniors, juniors), credit cards (MC, V, D), BF, FF.
Reader Comments: Open but has small greens … Very laid back, best value in Kentucky … Easy front 9, tough back 9.

WASIOTO WINDS GOLF COURSE
R-1050 State Park Rd., Pineville, 40977, Bell County, (606)377-1066, (800)814-8002, 60 miles from Knoxville. **Web:** www.kystateparks.com. **Facility Holes:** 18. **Yards:** 7,037/4,058. **Par:** 72/72. **Course Rating:** 73.9/61.6. **Slope:** 137/112. **Green Fee:** $25/$30. **Cart Fee:** $11/Person. **Walking Policy:** Walking at certain times. **Walkability:** 2. **Opened:** 2001. **Architect:** Michael Hurdzan. **Season:** Year-round. **High:** May-July. **To obtain tee times:** Call golf shop. **Miscellaneous:** Range (grass), credit cards (MC, V, AE, D), BF, FF.

★★★ **WEISSINGER HILLS GOLF COURSE**
PU-2240 Mt. Eden Rd., Shelbyville, 40065, Shelby County, (502)633-7332, (888)834-9442, 15 miles from Louisville. **E-mail:** whgc@skyl.net. **Facility Holes:** 18. **Yards:** 6,534/5,165. **Par:** 72/73. **Course Rating:** 70.8/69.0. **Slope:** 125/112. **Green Fee:** $13/$20. **Cart Fee:** $10/Person. **Walking Policy:** Walking at certain times. **Walkability:** 3. **Opened:** 1990. **Architect:** Jack Ridge. **Season:** Year-round. **High:** April-Oct. **To obtain tee times:** Call up to 7 days in advance. **Miscellaneous:** Reduced fees (weekdays, twilight, seniors, juniors), range (grass), credit cards (MC, V, AE), BF, FF.
Reader Comments: Windy every time I play it … OK … Wide open course … Reasonable rates … Very accessible, lots of local history, well maintained, good layout, staff, facilities … Easy to score, small greens.

★★★½ **WESTERN HILLS GOLF COURSE**
PU-2160 Russellville Rd., Hopkinsville, 42240, Christian County, (270)885-6023, 60 miles from Nashville, TN. **Facility Holes:** 18. **Yards:** 6,907/3,921. **Par:** 72/72. **Course Rating:** 73.8/64.0. **Slope:** 134/109. **Green Fee:** $14/$17. **Cart Fee:** $17/Cart. **Walking Policy:** Walking at certain times. **Walkability:** 4. **Opened:** 1985. **Architect:** Earl Stone. **Season:** Year-round. **To obtain tee times:** Call golf shop. **Miscellaneous:** Reduced fees (weekdays, seniors), range (grass/mats), credit cards (MC, V), BF, FF.
Reader Comments: My favorite course, very nice … Great staff and value for your money … Greens very fast, like putting on highway … Wide open, good course … Nice fairways.

★★★ **WIDOW'S WATCH GOLF COURSE**
SP-6000 Harrodsburg Rd., Nicholasville, 40356, Jessamine County, (859)223-4516, 5 miles from Lexington. **E-mail:** widowswatch@aol.com. **Web:** www.widowswatch.com. **Facility Holes:** 18. **Yards:** 6,949/4,951. **Par:** 72/72. **Course Rating:** 74.3/65.2. **Slope:** 135/116. **Green Fee:** $34/$39. **Cart Fee:** Included in green fee. **Walking Policy:** Walking at certain times. **Walkability:** 4. **Opened:** 1999. **Architect:** Barry Serafin. **Season:** Year-round. **High:** March-Oct. **To obtain tee times:** Call up to 10 days in advance. **Miscellaneous:** Reduced fees (weekdays, twilight, seniors), range (grass), credit cards (MC, V), BF, FF.
Reader Comments: Layout is very solid. Would like to see the course in 5 years, and if it matures, could be a top-10 course … Great design, I'll definitely be back … New course, needs more time … Pretty good, attractive.

WOODFORD HILLS COUNTRY CLUB
SP-3495 McCowans Ferry Rd., Versailles, 40383, Woodford County, (859)873-8122, 12 miles from Lexington. **Facility Holes:** 18. **Yards:** 6,142/5,214. **Par:** 70/73. **Course Rating:** 69.0. **Slope:** 115. **Green Fee:** $20/$23. **Cart Fee:** $10/Person. **Walking Policy:** Unrestricted walking. **Walkability:** 4. **Opened:** 1968. **Architect:** Buck Blankenship. **Season:** Year-round. **High:** May-Sept. **To obtain tee times:** Call golf shop. **Miscellaneous:** Reduced fees (juniors), range (grass), credit cards (MC, V, AE).

WOODLAWN SPRINGS GOLF CLUB
SP-103 Woodhill Rd., Bardstown, 40004, Nelson County, (502)348-2200, (877)748-2200.
Facility Holes: 18. **Yards:** 6,530/5,050. **Par:** 72/72. **Course Rating:** 71.5/69.0. **Slope:** 125/117.
Green Fee: $13/$18. **Cart Fee:** $11/Person. **Walking Policy:** Unrestricted walking. **Walkability:**
4. **Opened:** 1995. **Architect:** George Young. **Season:** Year-round. **To obtain tee times:** Call golf
shop. **Miscellaneous:** Reduced fees (seniors), range (grass), credit cards (MC, V, AE), BF, FF.

★★★ **WOODSON BEND RESORT**
R-14 Woodson Bend, Bronston, 42518, Wayne County, (606)561-5316, 75 miles from
Lexington. **E-mail:** dudleygolfpro@aol.com. **Facility Holes:** 18. **Yards:** 6,189/5,155. **Par:** 72/75.
Course Rating: 69.2/72.0. **Slope:** 117/113. **Green Fee:** $18/$23. **Cart Fee:** $12/Person.
Walking Policy: Mandatory carts. **Opened:** 1973. **Architect:** Dave Bennett/Lee Trevino.
Season: March-Dec. **High:** June-Oct. **To obtain tee times:** Call golf shop. **Miscellaneous:**
Reduced fees (juniors), credit cards (MC, V), BF, FF.
Reader Comments: A good track, typical resort course, a couple of tricked up holes, one a very
short par 3, overall a nice day, saw a family of red foxes.

LOUISIANA

★½ ABITA SPRINGS GOLF & COUNTRY CLUB
SP-73433 Oliver St., Abita Springs, 70420, St. Tammany County, (504)893-2463, 5 miles from Abita Springs. **Web:** www.Abitagolf.com. **Facility Holes:** 18. **Yards:** 6,384/4,756. **Par:** 72/72. **Course Rating:** 69.9. **Green Fee:** $15/$20. **Cart Fee:** $11/Person. **Walking Policy:** Unrestricted walking. **Walkability:** 2. **Season:** Year-round. **High:** March-Dec. **To obtain tee times:** Call golf shop. **Miscellaneous:** Reduced fees (twilight, seniors, juniors), range (grass), credit cards (MC, V, AE, D, DC).
Special Notes: Formerly Hillcrest Lake Resort & Club.

ALPINE GOLF & COUNTRY CLUB
PU-8311 Shreveport Hwy., Pineville, 71360, Alexandria County, (318)640-4030. **Facility Holes:** 9. **Yards:** 6,054/5,087. **Par:** 72/72. **Course Rating:** 71.2/72.1. **Slope:** 127/122. **Green Fee:** $10/$12. **Cart Fee:** $16/Cart. **Walking Policy:** Walking at certain times. **Walkability:** 5. **Season:** Year-round. **High:** April-Aug. **To obtain tee times:** Call golf shop. **Miscellaneous:** Reduced fees (seniors), credit cards (MC, V, AE, D).

★½ AUDUBON GOLF CLUB
PU-473 Walnut St., New Orleans, 70118, Orleans County, (504)865-8260. **Facility Holes:** 18. **Yards:** 5,739/5,181. **Par:** 68/69. **Course Rating:** 64.4/70.0. **Slope:** 96/115. **Green Fee:** $8/$12. **Cart Fee:** $18/Cart. **Walkability:** 1. **Opened:** 1898. **Season:** Year-round. **High:** April-Oct. **To obtain tee times:** Call golf shop. **Miscellaneous:** Reduced fees (twilight), metal spikes, credit cards (MC, V, AE, D).

BARKSDALE GOLF CLUB
M-185 Bossier Rd., Barksdale AFB, 71110, Bossier County, (318)456-2263, 5 miles from Bossier City/Shreveport. **E-mail:** Larry.busch@barksdale.af.mil. **Facility Holes:** 18. **Yards:** 5,904/5,075. **Par:** 70/71. **Course Rating:** 68.3/68.9. **Slope:** 118/113. **Green Fee:** $6/$18. **Cart Fee:** $13/Cart. **Walking Policy:** Unrestricted walking. **Walkability:** 1. **Opened:** 1999. **Architect:** Newgent. **Season:** Year-round. **High:** April-Oct. **To obtain tee times:** Call golf shop. **Miscellaneous:** Reduced fees (twilight), range (grass), credit cards (MC, V), BF, FF.

BAYOU OAKS GOLF COURSES
PU-1040 Filmore, New Orleans, 70124, Orleans County, (504)483-9396. **Facility Holes:** 54. **Cart Fee:** $18/Cart. **Walking Policy:** Unrestricted walking. **Walkability:** 1. **Opened:** 1936. **Season:** Year-round. **High:** April-Oct. **To obtain tee times:** Call golf shop. **Miscellaneous:** Reduced fees (twilight, seniors, juniors), metal spikes, range (grass/mats).
★★½ **CHAMPIONSHIP COURSE** (18)
Yards: 7,061/6,013. **Par:** 72/72. **Rating:** 71.5/73.3. **Slope:** 116/118. **Green Fee:** $12/$20.
★★ **LAKESIDE COURSE** (18)
Yards: 6,054/5,872. **Par:** 70/70. **Rating:** 68.5/70.5. **Slope:** 110/103. **Green Fee:** $9/$14.
★½ **WISNER COURSE** (18)
Yards: 6,465/5,707. **Par:** 72/72. **Rating:** 70.5/71.8. **Slope:** 111/116. **Green Fee:** $9/$14.

★★★ BELLE TERRE COUNTRY CLUB
SP-111 Fairway Dr., La Place, 70068, St. John the Baptist County, (504)652-5000, 20 miles from New Orleans. **Facility Holes:** 18. **Yards:** 6,840/5,510. **Par:** 72/72. **Course Rating:** 72.2/71.6. **Slope:** 130/113. **Green Fee:** $35/$54. **Cart Fee:** Included in green fee. **Walking Policy:** Mandatory carts. **Walkability:** 1. **Opened:** 1977. **Architect:** Pete Dye. **Season:** Year-round. **To obtain tee times:** Call golf shop. **Miscellaneous:** Reduced fees (weekdays, twilight, juniors), range (grass), credit cards (MC, V, AE, D), BF, FF.
Reader Comments: A very pleasurable round of golf ... Lot of water and the occasional gator too! ... Fun course, nice people ... Average track without much competition.

★½ BRECHTEL GOLF COURSE
PU-3700 Behrman Place, New Orleans, 70114, Orleans County, (504)362-4761. **E-mail:** fred83golf@aol.com. **Facility Holes:** 18. **Yards:** 6,065/5,556. **Par:** 70/70. **Course Rating:** 66.0. **Slope:** 97. **Green Fee:** $8/$10. **Cart Fee:** $16/Cart. **Walking Policy:** Unrestricted walking. **Walkability:** 1. **Opened:** 1965. **Architect:** R.W. LaConte/T. McAnlis. **Season:** Year-round. **To obtain tee times:** Call golf shop. **Miscellaneous:** Reduced fees (twilight, seniors, juniors), metal spikes, range (mats), BF, FF.

BRIARWOOD GOLF CLUB
PU-13209 Airline Hwy., Baton Rouge, 70817, East Baton Rouge County, (225)753-1989. **Facility Holes:** 18. **Yards:** 6,879/5,493. **Par:** 72/72. **Course Rating:** 71.2/70.0. **Slope:** 121/119. **Green Fee:** $19/$32. **Cart Fee:** Included in green fee. **Walking Policy:** Unrestricted walking. **Walkability:** 1. **Season:** Year-round. **High:** March-June. **To obtain tee times:** Call up to 7 days in advance. **Miscellaneous:** Reduced fees (seniors, juniors), metal spikes, credit cards (MC, V, AE, D).

CALVERT CROSSING GOLF CLUB
SP-515 Hodge-Watson Rd., Calhoun, 71225, Washouita County, (318)397-0064, 12 miles from West Monroe. **Facility Holes:** 18. **Yards:** 6,822/5,031. **Par:** 72/72. **Course Rating:** 73.6/70.6. **Slope:** 144/118. **Green Fee:** $37/$44. **Cart Fee:** Included in green fee. **Walking Policy:** Unrestricted walking. **Walkability:** 4. **Opened:** 1999. **Architect:** John Floyd. **Season:** Year-round. **High:** April-Sept. **To obtain tee times:** Call golf shop. **Miscellaneous:** Range (grass), credit cards (MC, V, AE).

★★ CHENNAULT PARK GOLF COURSE
PU-8475 Millhaven Rd., Monroe, 71203, Ouachita County, (318)329-2454. **Facility Holes:** 18. **Yards:** 7,044/5,783. **Par:** 72/72. **Course Rating:** 72.6/71.5. **Slope:** 115/113. **Green Fee:** $15/$16. **Cart Fee:** $16/Cart. **Walking Policy:** Unrestricted walking. **Walkability:** 1. **Opened:** 1975. **Architect:** Winnie Cole. **Season:** Year-round. **High:** May-Sept. **To obtain tee times:** Call golf shop. **Miscellaneous:** Reduced fees (seniors, juniors), metal spikes, range (grass), credit cards (MC, V).

CITY PARK GOLF COURSE
PU-1121 Mudd Ave., Lafayette, 70501, Lafayette County, (337)291-5557. **E-mail:** mikeguidry@worldnet.att.net. **Facility Holes:** 18. **Yards:** 6,426/5,447. **Par:** 72/72. **Course Rating:** 70.1/72.0. **Slope:** 117. **Green Fee:** $11. **Cart Fee:** $17/Cart. **Walking Policy:** Unrestricted walking. **Walkability:** 1. **Opened:** 1926. **Season:** Year-round. **High:** April-Dec. **To obtain tee times:** Call golf shop. **Miscellaneous:** Credit cards (MC, V, AE).

★★★★ THE CLUB & LODGE AT THE BLUFFS ON THOMPSON CREEK
R-Hwy. 965/Freeland Rd., St. Francisville, 70775, West Feliciana County, (225)634-5551, (888)634-3410, 25 miles from Baton Rouge. **E-mail:** info@the bluffs.com. **Web:** www.the-bluffs.com. **Facility Holes:** 18. **Yards:** 7,154/4,781. **Par:** 72/72. **Course Rating:** 75.3/68.6. **Slope:** 150/117. **Green Fee:** $40/$70. **Cart Fee:** $12/Person. **Walking Policy:** Walking at certain times. **Walkability:** 4. **Opened:** 1989. **Architect:** Arnold Palmer/Ed Seay. **Season:** Year-round. **To obtain tee times:** Call golf shop. **Miscellaneous:** Reduced fees (weekdays, guests), range (grass), lodging (39 rooms), credit cards (MC, V, AE, D), BF, FF.
Notes: Ranked 2nd in 1999 Best in State.
Reader Comments: Absolutely beautiful course, challenging, particularly the greens which are very quick … Beautiful course. Not easily playable by 20-handicapped players … Wonderful views … Played it in a morning fog, awesome.

★★ EMERALD HILLS GOLF RESORT
R-Hwy. 171 S., Florien, 71429, Sabine County, (318)586-4661, (800)533-5031, 22 miles from Leesville. **Facility Holes:** 18. **Yards:** 6,548/5,432. **Par:** 72/72. **Course Rating:** 71.0/69.4. **Slope:** 125/114. **Green Fee:** $20/$37. **Cart Fee:** Included in green fee. **Walking Policy:** Walking at certain times. **Walkability:** 5. **Season:** Year-round. **High:** April-Sept. **To obtain tee times:** Call golf shop. **Miscellaneous:** Reduced fees (guests, twilight), range (grass), lodging (50 rooms), credit cards (MC, V, AE, D), BF, FF.

GEMSTONE PLANTATION GOLF & COUNTRY CLUB
SP-101 Gemstone Dr., Franklinton, 70438, Washington County, (985)795-8900. **Facility Holes:** 18. **Yards:** 6,657/5,004. **Par:** 72/72. **Course Rating:** 72.5/69.3. **Slope:** 128/120. **Green Fee:** $28. **Cart Fee:** $9/Person. **Walking Policy:** Unrestricted walking. **Walkability:** 3. **Opened:** 1997. **Architect:** James Ray Carpenter. **Season:** Year-round. **To obtain tee times:** Call up to 7 days in advance. **Miscellaneous:** Reduced fees (weekdays, twilight, seniors, juniors), credit cards (MC, V, AE, D), BF, FF.

THE GOLF CLUB AT STONEBRIDGE
SP-301 StoneBridge Blvd., Bossier City, 71111, Bossier County, (318)747-2004, 200 miles from Dallas. **E-mail:** mbarnard@stonebridgegolf.org. **Web:** www.stonebridgegolf.org. **Facility Holes:** 18. **Yards:** 6,954/4,926. **Par:** 72/72. **Course Rating:** 74.0/65.3. **Slope:** 148/108. **Green Fee:** $35/$55. **Cart Fee:** Included in green fee. **Walking Policy:** Unrestricted walking. **Walkability:** 3. **Opened:** 1999. **Architect:** Gene Bates/Fred Couples. **Season:** Year-round. **To obtain tee times:** Call up to 7 days in advance. **Miscellaneous:** Reduced fees (guests, seniors, juniors), range (grass), credit cards (MC, V, AE, D), BF, FF.

THE GOLF CLUB OF NEW ORLEANS AT EASTOVER
SP-5889 Eastover Dr., New Orleans, 70128, Orleans County, (504)245-7347, 12 miles from Downtown New Orleans. **E-mail:** golfinfo@eastovercc.com. **Web:** www.eastovercc.com. **Facility Holes:** 36. **Green Fee:** $70/$105. **Cart Fee:** $13/Person. **Walking Policy:** Unrestricted walking. **Walkability:** 2. **Opened:** 2000. **Architect:** Joe Lee/Rocky Roquemore. **Season:** Year-round. **High:** March-June. **To obtain tee times:** Call golf shop. **Miscellaneous:** Range (grass), credit cards (MC, V, AE, D, DC), BF, FF.

LOUISIANA

★★★ **RABBIT'S FOOT** (18)
Yards: 6,825/5,470. **Par:** 72/72. **Course Rating:** 72.5/72.2. **Slope:** 129/123.
Reader Comments: Good for LA ... Great people well maintained, good challenge ... Very fair, great greens ... Playable, good value.

★★★½ **TEETH OF THE GATOR** (18)
Yards: 7,025/5,560. **Par:** 72/72. **Course Rating:** 72.7/72.3. **Slope:** 131/124.
Reader Comments: This course had to be named after hole No. 8 ... Wind blows hard here. Tight layout ... Great people, well maintained, good challenge ... A tough course, lots of water. A great layout.

★★★★½ **GRAY PLANTATION G. C.** *Service, Value+, Condition, Pace+*
SP-6150 Graywood Pkwy., Lake Charles, 70706, Calcasieu County, (337)562-1663, 125 miles from Houston. **Facility Holes:** 18. **Yards:** 6,946/5,392. **Par:** 72/72. **Course Rating:** 73.6/71.9. **Slope:** 138/128. **Green Fee:** $24/$28. **Cart Fee:** $11/Person. **Walking Policy:** Unrestricted walking. **Walkability:** 1. **Opened:** 1999. **Architect:** Rocky Roquemore. **Season:** Year-round. **To obtain tee times:** Call up to 2 days in advance. **Miscellaneous:** Reduced fees (twilight, seniors, juniors), range (grass), credit cards (MC, V, AE, D), BF, FF.
Notes: Ranked 2nd in 2001 Best in State; 3rd in 2000 Best New Affordable Courses.
Reader Comments: Awesome, great course, lots of water, sand, nice lush fairways, and great green ... Great new course, in good shape, treated well, great value, have traveled back three times ... Possibly the best course for the price.

HIDDEN OAKS GOLF COURSE
PU-200 Oak Dr., Braithwaite, 70040, Plaquemines County, (504)682-2685, 15 miles from New Orleans. **Web:** www.hiddenoaksgolfcourse.com. **Facility Holes:** 18. **Yards:** 6,775/5,424. **Par:** 72/72. **Course Rating:** 70.0/71.1. **Slope:** 117/109. **Green Fee:** $20/$25. **Cart Fee:** Included in green fee. **Walking Policy:** Walking at certain times. **Walkability:** 1. **Opened:** 1963. **Architect:** John Cottage. **Season:** Year-round. **To obtain tee times:** Call golf shop. **Miscellaneous:** Reduced fees (twilight), credit cards (MC, V, AE, D), FF.

★½ **HOWELL PARK GOLF COURSE**
PU-5511 Winbourne Ave., Baton Rouge, 70805, East Baton Rouge County, (225)357-9292. **Web:** www.brec.org. **Facility Holes:** 18. **Yards:** 5,662/4,442. **Par:** 70/70. **Course Rating:** 66.0/63.5. **Slope:** 118/114. **Green Fee:** $7. **Cart Fee:** $14/Cart. **Walking Policy:** Unrestricted walking. **Walkability:** 1. **Opened:** 1956. **Season:** Year-round. **High:** March-Nov. **To obtain tee times:** Call up to 48 days in advance. **Miscellaneous:** Reduced fees (twilight, seniors, juniors), credit cards (MC, V), BF, FF.

★★½ **HUNTINGTON PARK GOLF COURSE**
PU-8300 Pines Rd., Shreveport, 71129, Caddo County, (318)673-7765. **E-mail:** bic1979@aol.com. **Facility Holes:** 18. **Yards:** 7,294/6,171. **Par:** 72/74. **Course Rating:** 73.3/74.7. **Slope:** 119/124. **Green Fee:** $10/$13. **Cart Fee:** $8/Person. **Walking Policy:** Unrestricted walking. **Walkability:** 5. **Opened:** 1969. **Architect:** Tommy Moore. **Season:** Year-round. **High:** April-Oct. **To obtain tee times:** Call up to 2 days in advance. **Miscellaneous:** Reduced fees (weekdays, twilight, seniors, juniors), metal spikes, range (grass), credit cards (MC, V), FF.

THE ISLAND COUNTRY CLUB
SP-23560 Myrtle Grove Rd., Plaquemine, 70765, Iberville County, (225)685-0808, 20 miles from Baton Rouge. **Web:** www.theislandgolf.com. **Facility Holes:** 18. **Yards:** 7,010/5,408. **Par:** 72/72. **Course Rating:** 75.1/72.7. **Slope:** 143/128. **Green Fee:** $27/$37. **Cart Fee:** $12/Person. **Walking Policy:** Unrestricted walking. **Walkability:** 2. **Opened:** 1999. **Architect:** Mike Young. **Season:** Year-round. **High:** March-Oct. **To obtain tee times:** Call up to 3 days in advance. **Miscellaneous:** Range (grass), credit cards (MC, V, AE), BF, FF.

JOE BARTHOLOMEW GOLF COURSE
PU-6514 Congress Dr., New Orleans, 70126, Orleans County, (504)288-0928. **Facility Holes:** 18. **Yards:** 7,265/5,971. **Par:** 72/72. **Course Rating:** 70.4. **Slope:** 101. **Green Fee:** $8/$11. **Cart Fee:** $18/Cart. **Walking Policy:** Unrestricted walking. **Walkability:** 2. **Architect:** Joe Bartholomew. **Season:** Year-round. **High:** March-Dec. **To obtain tee times:** Call golf shop. **Miscellaneous:** Range (grass).

★★½ **LES VIEUX CHENES GOLF CLUB**
PU-340 Rue Des Vieux Chenes, Youngsville, 70592, Lafayette County, (337)837-1159, 9 miles from Lafayette. **Facility Holes:** 18. **Yards:** 6,900/5,600. **Par:** 72/74. **Course Rating:** 70.1/69.1. **Slope:** 119/113. **Green Fee:** $8/$10. **Cart Fee:** $8/Person. **Walking Policy:** Unrestricted walking. **Walkability:** 1. **Opened:** 1977. **Architect:** Dr. Marvin Ferguson. **Season:** Year-round. **To obtain tee times:** Call golf shop. **Miscellaneous:** Reduced fees (twilight, seniors, juniors), range (grass), credit cards (MC, V, AE), BF, FF.

LOUISIANA

LSU GOLF COURSE
PU-Nicholson Dr. & Burbank, Baton Rouge, 70803, East Baton Rouge County, (225)578-3394. **E-mail:** jthom16@lsu.edu. **Web:** www.LSU.edu/golf. **Facility Holes:** 27. **Yards:** 6,727/5,086. **Par:** 72/72. **Course Rating:** 72.3/69.3. **Slope:** 131/119. **Green Fee:** $15/$27. **Cart Fee:** $9/Person. **Walking Policy:** Unrestricted walking. **Walkability:** 3. **Opened:** 1958. **Architect:** Phil Thompson. **Season:** Year-round. **High:** Sept.-June. **To obtain tee times:** Call golf shop. **Miscellaneous:** Reduced fees (weekdays, twilight, seniors, juniors), range (grass), credit cards (MC, V), BF, FF.
Special Notes: Also has a 9-hole par-3 pitch & putt course.

★★★ **MALLARD COVE GOLF COURSE**
PU-Chennault Air Base, Lake Charles, 70601, Calcasieu County, (318)491-1204, 125 miles from Baton Rouge. **E-mail:** sreeves@mail.city-lakecharles.org. **Facility Holes:** 18. **Yards:** 6,903/5,294. **Par:** 72/72. **Course Rating:** 72.4/70.1. **Slope:** 125/117. **Green Fee:** $10/$17. **Cart Fee:** $11/Person. **Walking Policy:** Unrestricted walking. **Walkability:** 2. **Opened:** 2001. **Architect:** Kevin Tucker. **Season:** Year-round. **High:** April-Oct. **To obtain tee times:** Call up to 2 days in advance. **Miscellaneous:** Reduced fees (weekdays, twilight, seniors, juniors), range (grass/mats), credit cards (MC, V, D), BF, FF.
Reader Comments: Good value.

MEADOW LAKE GOLF & COUNTRY CLUB
SP-152 Golf Course Rd., Bernice, 71222, Union County, (318)285-7425, 25 miles from Ruston. **Facility Holes:** 9. **Yards:** 6,342/5,501. **Par:** 72/72. **Green Fee:** $5/$15. **Cart Fee:** $21/Cart. **Walking Policy:** Walking at certain times. **Walkability:** 2. **Opened:** 1985. **Season:** Year-round. **High:** March-July. **To obtain tee times:** Call golf shop. **Miscellaneous:** Reduced fees (weekdays, seniors), range (grass), credit cards (MC, V), FF.

★½ **MEADOWLAKE GOLF CLUB**
PU-5730 Meadowlake, Keithville, 71047, Caddo County, (318)925-9547, 5 miles from Shreveport. **Facility Holes:** 18. **Yards:** 6,473/5,345. **Par:** 72/72. **Course Rating:** 70.5/69.1. **Slope:** 113/108. **Green Fee:** $10/$12. **Cart Fee:** $16/Cart. **Walking Policy:** Unrestricted walking. **Walkability:** 1. **Opened:** 1962. **Season:** Year-round. **To obtain tee times:** Call golf shop. **Miscellaneous:** Reduced fees (twilight, seniors, juniors), credit cards (MC, V, AE, D), BF, FF.
Special Notes: Formerly Alpine Meadows Golf Club.

NAS GOLF COURSE
M-Morale Welfare & Rec. Bldg. 49 Code 100, New Orleans, 70143, Orleans County, (504)678-3453, 2 miles from New Orleans. **Facility Holes:** 18. **Yards:** 6,464/5,362. **Par:** 72/72. **Course Rating:** 69.1/69.8. **Slope:** 115/110. **Green Fee:** $14/$19. **Cart Fee:** $8/Person. **Walking Policy:** Unrestricted walking. **Walkability:** 1. **Opened:** 1964. **Season:** Year-round. **High:** May-Oct. **To obtain tee times:** Call golf shop. **Miscellaneous:** Reduced fees (twilight), credit cards (MC, V, AE, D), BF, FF.

NORTHWOOD GOLF & COUNTRY CLUB
SP-5000 Northwood Hills Dr., Shreveport, 71107, Caddo County, (318)929-2380. **Facility Holes:** 18. **Yards:** 6,550/5,165. **Par:** 72/73. **Course Rating:** 69.6/69.4. **Slope:** 116/110. **Green Fee:** $27/$40. **Cart Fee:** $11/Person. **Walking Policy:** Walking at certain times. **Walkability:** 4. **Architect:** Golf Scapes. **Season:** Year-round. **High:** Feb.-Dec. **Tee times:** Call golf shop. **Miscellaneous:** Reduced fees (twilight), range (grass), credit cards (MC, V, AE, D), BF, FF.

★★★½ **OAK HARBOR GOLF CLUB**
SP-201 Oak Harbor Blvd., Slidell, 70458, St. Tammany County, (504)646-0110, 25 miles from New Orleans. **Web:** www.oakharborgolf.com. **Facility Holes:** 18. **Yards:** 6,896/5,305. **Par:** 72/72. **Course Rating:** 72.7/70.0. **Slope:** 132/118. **Green Fee:** $32/$69. **Cart Fee:** Included in green fee. **Walkability:** 3. **Opened:** 1991. **Architect:** Lee Schmidt. **Season:** Year-round. **High:** April-Nov. **To obtain tee times:** Call golf shop. **Miscellaneous:** Reduced fees (twilight), metal spikes, range (grass), credit cards (MC, V, AE, D).
Reader Comments: Very good course, very challenging ... Nicest staff I've ever met ... Great golf experience ... A great layout, a fun place with lots of wind and good people ... Nice layout, pace of play slow at times.

OLDE OAKS GOLF CLUB
PU-60 Golf Club Dr., Haughton, 71037, Bossier County, (318)742-0333, 3 miles from Bossier City. **E-mail:** jguin@softdisk.com. **Web:** www.oldeoaksgolf.com. **Facility Holes:** 27. **Green Fee:** $25/$30. **Cart Fee:** $11/Person. **Walking Policy:** Walking at certain times. **Walkability:** 3. **Opened:** 1999. **Architect:** Kevin Tucker/Hal Sutton. **Season:** Year-round. **To obtain tee times:** Call up to 7 days in advance. **Miscellaneous:** Reduced fees (twilight), range (grass), credit cards (MC, V, AE, D), BF, FF.

CYPRESS/MEADOW COURSE (18)
Yards: 7,200/5,100. **Par:** 72/72. **Course Rating:** 74.8/69.2. **Slope:** 130/107.
OAK /MEADOW COURSE (18)
Yards: 7,200/5,100. **Par:** 72/72. **Course Rating:** 74.3/69.3. **Slope:** 134/111.
OAK/CYPRESS COURSE (18)
Yards: 7,100/5,000. **Par:** 72/72. **Course Rating:** 74.8/69.2. **Slope:** 130/107.

★★　**PINE SHADOWS GOLF CENTER**
PU-750 Goodman Rd., Lake Charles, 70615, Calcasieu County, (337)433-8681. **Facility Holes:** 18. **Yards:** 6,292/5,873. **Par:** 72/72. **Course Rating:** 69.5/70.0. **Slope:** 108/106. **Green Fee:** $12/$15. **Cart Fee:** $9/Person. **Walking Policy:** Unrestricted walking. **Walkability:** 1. **Opened:** 1985. **Season:** Year-round. **High:** May-July. **Tee times:** Call golf shop. **Miscellaneous:** Reduced fees (seniors), metal spikes, range (grass), credit cards (MC, V, AE, D).

★½　**PINEWOOD COUNTRY CLUB**
SP-405 Country Club Blvd., Slidell, 70458, St. Tammany County, (504)643-6893, 20 miles from New Orleans. **Facility Holes:** 18. **Yards:** 6,366/5,077. **Par:** 72/72. **Course Rating:** 68.5/70.2. **Slope:** 121/117. **Green Fee:** $29/$34. **Cart Fee:** Included in green fee. **Walking Policy:** Mandatory carts. **Walkability:** 2. **Opened:** 1963. **Architect:** Bill Bergin. **Season:** Year-round. **To obtain tee times:** Call golf shop. **Miscellaneous:** Reduced fees (juniors), range (grass), credit cards (MC, V, AE, D).

★½　**QUERBES PARK GOLF COURSE**
PU-3500 Beverly Place, Shreveport, 71104, Caddo County, (318)673-7773, 180 miles from Dallas. **Facility Holes:** 18. **Yards:** 6,207/5,360. **Par:** 71/71. **Course Rating:** 69.0/70.0. **Slope:** 118/110. **Green Fee:** $6/$13. **Cart Fee:** $16/Cart. **Walking Policy:** Unrestricted walking. **Walkability:** 1. **Opened:** 1922. **Season:** Year-round. **Tee times:** Call golf shop. **Misc:** Reduced fees (weekdays, twilight, seniors, juniors), range (grass/mats), credit cards (MC, V), BF, FF.

★★½　**ROYAL GOLF CLUB**
PU-201 Royal Dr., Slidell, 70460, St. Tammany County, (985)643-3000, 20 miles from New Orleans. **Facility Holes:** 18. **Yards:** 6,655/5,544. **Par:** 72/72. **Course Rating:** 73.1/68.0. **Slope:** 111/101. **Green Fee:** $11/$15. **Cart Fee:** $10/Person. **Walking Policy:** Unrestricted walking. **Walkability:** 1. **Opened:** 1969. **Architect:** Gerald Gatlin. **Season:** Year-round. **High:** April-Sept. **To obtain tee times:** Call golf shop. **Miscellaneous:** Reduced fees (weekdays, juniors), range (grass), credit cards (MC, V, D).

★★★　**SANTA MARIA GOLF CLUB**
PU-18460 Santa Maria Pkwy., Baton Rouge, 70810, East Baton Rouge County, (225)752-9667. **E-mail:** santamariagolf@brec.org. **Web:** www.brec.org. **Facility Holes:** 18. **Yards:** 6,826/5,202. **Par:** 72/72. **Course Rating:** 74.1/70.7. **Slope:** 136/120. **Green Fee:** $23/$27. **Cart Fee:** $10/Person. **Walking Policy:** Unrestricted walking. **Walkability:** 3. **Opened:** 1986. **Architect:** Robert Trent Jones. **Season:** Year-round. **High:** March-Nov. **To obtain tee times:** Call up to 6 days in advance. **Miscellaneous:** Reduced fees (twilight, seniors, juniors), range (grass), credit cards (MC, V), BF, FF.
Reader Comments: Best layout in Baton Rouge … Great value! Big fairways! … Good layout, bargain, 18 signature holes.

SOUTHERN OAKS GOLF CLUB
SP-1000 Bayou Black Dr., Houma, 70360, Terrebonne County, (985)851-6804, 60 miles from New Orleans. **Facility Holes:** 9. **Yards:** 6,245/5,518. **Par:** 71/74. **Course Rating:** 68.4/71.0. **Slope:** 116/116. **Green Fee:** $15/$20. **Cart Fee:** $9/Person. **Walking Policy:** Unrestricted walking. **Walkability:** 1. **Opened:** 1928. **Season:** Year-round. **High:** March-Dec. **To obtain tee times:** Call golf shop. **Miscellaneous:** Reduced fees (weekdays), credit cards (MC, V, AE, D).

SPANISH TRAIL GOLF CLUB
SP-1655 Old Spanish Trail, Cade, 70519, St. Martin County, (337)364-2263, 12 miles from Lafayette. **Facility Holes:** 18. **Yards:** 6,042/5,120. **Par:** 71/71. **Course Rating:** 69.9/69.1. **Slope:** 118/113. **Green Fee:** $19/$25. **Cart Fee:** $9/Person. **Walking Policy:** Unrestricted walking. **Walkability:** 3. **Opened:** 1955. **Season:** Year-round. **Tee times:** Call golf shop. **Miscellaneous:** Reduced fees (weekdays), range (grass), credit cards (MC, V, AE), BF, FF.

SUGAR OAKS GOLF & COUNTRY CLUB
SP-4002 Sugar Oaks Rd., New Iberia, 70560, Iberia County, (318)364-7611, (318)364-7611, 20 miles from Lafayette. **Facility Holes:** 18. **Yards:** 7,002/5,600. **Par:** 72/72. **Course Rating:** 70.0/70.0. **Slope:** 116/116. **Green Fee:** $15/$20. **Cart Fee:** $11/Person. **Walking Policy:** Unrestricted walking. **Walkability:** 1. **Opened:** 1959. **Architect:** Luca Barbato. **Season:** Year-round. **High:** April-Oct. **To obtain tee times:** Call up to 2 days in advance. **Miscellaneous:** Reduced fees (weekdays, juniors), metal spikes, range (grass), credit cards (MC, V), BF, FF.

TAMAHKA TRAILS GOLF CLUB
R-222 Slim Lemoine Rd., Marksville, 71351, Avoyelles County, (318)240-3600, (800)946-1946, 30 miles from Alexandria. **E-mail:** avorlw2@paragoncasinoresort.com. **Facility Holes:** 18. **Yards:** 7,019/5,087. **Par:** 71/70. **Course Rating:** 74.4/69.5. **Slope:** 133/121. **Green Fee:** $25/$50. **Cart Fee:** Included in green fee. **Walking Policy:** Walking at certain times. **Walkability:** 2. **Opened:** 2000. **Architect:** Steve Smyers. **Season:** Year-round. **High:** March-Oct. **To obtain tee times:** Call up to 5 days in advance. **Miscellaneous:** Reduced fees (guests, twilight), range (grass), credit cards (MC, V, AE), BF, FF.

WARRIOR HILLS GOLF COURSE
M-323 Patterson Dr., Fort Polk, 71459, Vernon County, (337)531-4661, 45 miles from Alexandria. **Web:** www.fortpolkmwr.com. **Facility Holes:** 18. **Yards:** 6,555/5,141. **Par:** 72/72. **Course Rating:** 71.0/68.4. **Slope:** 121/119. **Green Fee:** $11/$15. **Cart Fee:** $9/Person. **Walking Policy:** Unrestricted walking. **Walkability:** 5. **Opened:** 1957. **Season:** Year-round. **To obtain tee times:** Call up to 5 days in advance. **Miscellaneous:** Reduced fees (weekdays, twilight, juniors), range (grass/mats), credit cards (MC, V, AE), BF, FF.

★½ WEBB MEMORIAL GOLF COURSE
PU-1352 Country Club Dr., Baton Rouge, 70806, East Baton Rouge County, (225)383-4919. **Facility Holes:** 18. **Yards:** 6,412/5,442. **Par:** 72/72. **Course Rating:** 70.1/70.3. **Slope:** 120. **Green Fee:** $6. **Cart Fee:** $14/Cart. **Walking Policy:** Unrestricted walking. **Walkability:** 1. **Opened:** 1932. **Architect:** E.E. Evans/Al Michael. **Season:** Year-round. **High:** Feb.-Aug. **To obtain tee times:** Call golf shop. **Miscellaneous:** Reduced fees (twilight, juniors), credit cards (MC, V), BF, FF.

WESTSIDE GOLF CLUB
SP-Choctaw Rd., Brusly, 70719, West Baton Rouge County, (225)749-8832, 10 miles from Baton Rouge. **Facility Holes:** 18. **Yards:** 6,280/5,065. **Par:** 72/72. **Slope:** 112/112. **Green Fee:** $14/$18. **Walking Policy:** Walking at certain times. **Walkability:** 2. **Opened:** 1963. **Season:** Year-round. **High:** April-July. **Tee times:** Call golf shop. **Miscellaneous:** Reduced fees (twilight).

WILLOWDALE GOLF CLUB
SP-500 Willowdale Blvd., Luling, 70070, St. Charles County, (985)785-2478. **Facility Holes:** 18. **Yards:** 6,656/5,528. **Par:** 72/72. **Course Rating:** 70.5/71.0. **Slope:** 118/118. **Green Fee:** $13/$25. **Cart Fee:** $11/Person. **Walking Policy:** Unrestricted walking. **Walkability:** 2. **Opened:** 1968. **Season:** Year-round. **To obtain tee times:** Call up to 7 days in advance. **Miscellaneous:** Range (grass), credit cards (MC, V, AE), BF, FF.

WOODROW W. DUMAS GOLF COURSE
PU-3400 Lavey Lane, Baker, 70714, East Baton Rouge County, (225)775-9166, 9 miles from Baton Rouge. **Facility Holes:** 18. **Yards:** 6,700/5,208. **Par:** 72/72. **Course Rating:** 71.3. **Slope:** 119. **Green Fee:** $8. **Cart Fee:** $14/Cart. **Walking Policy:** Unrestricted walking. **Walkability:** 2. **Opened:** 1961. **Season:** Year-round. **High:** March-July. **To obtain tee times:** Call golf shop. **Miscellaneous:** Reduced fees (twilight, seniors, juniors), range (grass), credit cards (MC, V). **Special Notes:** Formerly Greenwood Park Golf Course.

MAINE

★★★½ **AROOSTOOK VALLEY COUNTRY CLUB**
SP-Russell Rd., Fort Fairfield, 04742, Aroostook County, (207)476-8083, 15 miles from Presque Isle. **Web:** www.intellis.net/avcc. **Facility Holes:** 18. **Yards:** 6,304/5,393. **Par:** 72/72. **Course Rating:** 69.8/70.0. **Slope:** 117/108. **Green Fee:** $25. **Cart Fee:** $22/Cart. **Walking Policy:** Unrestricted walking. **Walkability:** 4. **Opened:** 1927. **Architect:** Howard Watson. **Season:** May-Oct. **High:** July-Aug. **To obtain tee times:** Call up to 3 days in advance. **Miscellaneous:** Reduced fees (juniors), range (grass), credit cards (MC, V), BF, FF.
Reader Comments: Great views, fast greens … Each hole separate and distinct … Well worth the 4 hour drive from Bangor … A lot of fun … Fantastic risk/reward course.

★★★ **BANGOR MUNICIPAL GOLF COURSE** *Value*
PU-278 Webster Ave., Bangor, 04401, Penobscot County, (207)941-0232. **Facility Holes:** 27. **Yards:** 6,345/5,173. **Par:** 71/71. **Course Rating:** 67.9/69.1. **Slope:** 112/111. **Green Fee:** $21/$25. **Cart Fee:** $20/Cart. **Walking Policy:** Unrestricted walking. **Walkability:** 2. **Opened:** 1964. **Architect:** Geoffrey Cornish. **Season:** April-Nov. **High:** June-Sept. **To obtain tee times:** Call up to 5 days in advance. **Miscellaneous:** Reduced fees (weekdays, twilight), range (grass), credit cards (MC, V), BF, FF.
Reader Comments: Layout and length good for low scores … New 9 is totally different from the old 18 … Too busy for my blood most days.
Special Notes: Also has a 9-hole executive course.

★★½ **BAR HARBOR GOLF COURSE**
PU-51 Jordan River Rd., Trenton, 04605, Hancock County, (207)667-7505, 3 miles from Ellsworth. **Facility Holes:** 18. **Yards:** 6,680/5,542. **Par:** 71/73. **Course Rating:** 71.1/70.4. **Slope:** 122/119. **Green Fee:** $25/$35. **Cart Fee:** $28/Cart. **Walking Policy:** Unrestricted walking. **Walkability:** 2. **Opened:** 1968. **Architect:** Phil Wogan. **Season:** April-Nov. **To obtain tee times:** Call golf shop. **Miscellaneous:** Metal spikes, range (grass), credit cards (MC, V), BF, FF.

★★ **BATH COUNTRY CLUB**
SP-387 Wiskeag Road, Bath, 04530, Sagadahoc County, (207)442-8411, 30 miles from Portland. **Web:** bathcountryclub.com. **Facility Holes:** 18. **Yards:** 6,216/4,708. **Par:** 70/70. **Course Rating:** 70.2/67.0. **Slope:** 128/115. **Green Fee:** $18/$25. **Cart Fee:** $12/Person. **Walking Policy:** Unrestricted walking. **Walkability:** 3. **Opened:** 1932. **Season:** April-Nov. **High:** June-Aug. **To obtain tee times:** Call golf shop. **Miscellaneous:** Reduced fees (twilight), credit cards (MC, V, AE, D).

★★★★★ **BELGRADE LAKES G. C.** *Service+, Value, Condition+, Pace+*
PU-West Rd., Belgrade Lakes, 04918, Kennebec County, (207)495-4653, 13 miles from Augusta. **E-mail:** blgolfclub@aol.com. **Web:** www.belgradelakesgolf.com. **Facility Holes:** 18. **Yards:** 6,653/4,881. **Par:** 71/71. **Course Rating:** 71.6/67.1. **Slope:** 142/117. **Green Fee:** $50/$75. **Cart Fee:** $20/Person. **Walking Policy:** Unrestricted walking. **Walkability:** 3. **Opened:** 1998. **Architect:** Clive Clark. **Season:** May-Nov. **Tee times:** Call up to 7 days in advance. **Miscellaneous:** Reduced fees (twilight, juniors), caddies, credit cards (MC, V, AE), BF, FF.
Notes: Ranked 2nd in 2001 Best in State; 5th in 1999 Best New Upscale Public.
Reader Comments: Amazing layout and great views … Beautiful sights and a friendly staff … Wildlife along the course, including fox and beavers … Great food at the turn! If you order before you start you can ask them to bring up a lobster roll from their restaurant down the street.

★★½ **THE BETHEL INN & COUNTRY CLUB**
R-Broad St., Bethel, 04217, Oxford County, (207)824-6276, (800)654-0125, 70 miles from Portland. **Web:** www.bethelinn.com. **Facility Holes:** 18. **Yards:** 6,663/5,280. **Par:** 72/72. **Course Rating:** 72.3/71.4. **Slope:** 133/129. **Green Fee:** $30/$50. **Cart Fee:** $28/Cart. **Walking Policy:** Unrestricted walking. **Walkability:** 3. **Opened:** 1913. **Architect:** Geoffrey Cornish. **Season:** May-Oct. **High:** Aug.-Sept. **To obtain tee times:** Call golf shop. **Miscellaneous:** Reduced fees (weekdays, guests, twilight), range (grass/mats), lodging (116 rooms), credit cards (MC, V, AE, D), BF, FF.

★★★½ **BIDDEFORD SACO COUNTRY CLUB** *Value*
SP-101 Old Orchard Rd., Saco, 04072, York County, (207)282-5883, 13 miles from Portland. **Facility Holes:** 18. **Yards:** 6,192/5,053. **Par:** 71/72. **Course Rating:** 69.6/69.2. **Slope:** 123/110. **Green Fee:** $25/$40. **Cart Fee:** $25/Cart. **Walking Policy:** Unrestricted walking. **Walkability:** 2. **Opened:** 1921. **Architect:** Donald Ross. **Season:** April-Nov. **High:** June-Sept. **To obtain tee times:** Call golf shop. **Miscellaneous:** Reduced fees (twilight), range (grass/mats), credit cards (MC, V, AE, D), BF, FF.
Reader Comments: Excellent Donald Ross course … Great pro shop … Back 9 A OK … Classic front 9, back is tough … A pleasant experience in late afternoon.

MAINE

BOOTHBAY COUNTRY CLUB
R-Country Club Rd., Boothbay, 04537, Lincoln County, (207)633-6085. **Web:** www.boothbay-countryclub.com. **Facility Holes:** 18. **Yards:** 6,306/4,641. **Par:** 71/71. **Course Rating:** 68.3/67.2. **Slope:** 133/120. **Green Fee:** $30/$50. **Cart Fee:** $15/Person. **Walking Policy:** Mandatory carts. **Walkability:** 4. **Opened:** 1921. **Architect:** Wayne Stiles/John Van Kleek. **Season:** April-Nov. **High:** June-Sept. **To obtain tee times:** Call up to 5 days in advance. **Miscellaneous:** Range (mats), credit cards (MC, V, AE, D), BF, FF.

BRIDGTON HIGHLANDS COUNTRY CLUB
PU-RR 3 Box 1065 Highland Ridge, Bridgton, 04009, Cumberland County, (207)647-3491, 35 miles from Portland. **Web:** www.bridgtonhighlands.com. **Facility Holes:** 18. **Yards:** 6,059/2,527. **Par:** 72/74. **Course Rating:** 70.2/70.0. **Slope:** 126/119. **Green Fee:** $24/$32. **Cart Fee:** $12/Person. **Walking Policy:** Unrestricted walking. **Walkability:** 3. **Opened:** 1926. **Architect:** Ralph Martin Barton/Fred Ryan. **Season:** May-Nov. **High:** July-Sept. **To obtain tee times:** Call golf shop. **Miscellaneous:** Reduced fees (weekdays, guests, juniors), credit cards (MC, V, D), BF, FF.

★★★½ BRUNSWICK GOLF CLUB
SP-165 River Rd., Brunswick, 04011, Cumberland County, (207)725-8224, 30 miles from Portland. **E-mail:** brungolf@gwi.net. **Web:** www.brunswickgolfclub.com. **Facility Holes:** 18. **Yards:** 6,609/5,772. **Par:** 72/74. **Course Rating:** 69.5/72.9. **Slope:** 123/128. **Green Fee:** $30/$40. **Cart Fee:** $24/Cart. **Walking Policy:** Unrestricted walking. **Walkability:** 1. **Opened:** 1918. **Architect:** Stiles/Van Kleek/Cornish/Robinson. **Season:** April-Nov. **To obtain tee times:** Call up to 3 days in advance. **Miscellaneous:** Range (mats), credit cards (MC, V), FF.
Reader Comments: Local town course … Wonderful Maine layout … Mildly difficult. Good greens … Fun to play … Nice spot for lunch, fine pro shop, very friendly staff … A little slow at times.

★★★½ CAPE ARUNDEL GOLF CLUB
SP-19 River Rd., Kennebunkport, 04046, York County, (207)967-3494, 20 miles from Portland. **E-mail:** cagolf@cybertours.com. **Facility Holes:** 18. **Yards:** 5,869/5,134. **Par:** 69/70. **Course Rating:** 67.0/68.6. **Slope:** 117/106. **Green Fee:** $45. **Cart Fee:** $24/Cart. **Walking Policy:** Unrestricted walking. **Walkability:** 2. **Opened:** 1897. **Architect:** Walter Travis. **Season:** April-Nov. **High:** June-Sept. **To obtain tee times:** Call golf shop. **Miscellaneous:** Caddies, credit cards (MC, V, AE), BF, FF.
Reader Comments: Good for Bush, good for me! … Always have a good time … Fun links, nice people … Old-fashioned New England golf—small targets yield big rewards … Devilish greens … Somewhat short by today's standards but the long par 3s won't disappoint big hitters.

CARIBOU COUNTRY CLUB
PU-Sweeden Rd., Caribou, 04736, Aroostook County, (207)493-3933. **Facility Holes:** 9. **Yards:** 6,433/5,631. **Par:** 72/72. **Course Rating:** 69.6. **Slope:** 116. **Green Fee:** $18. **Cart Fee:** $15/Cart. **Walking Policy:** Unrestricted walking. **Walkability:** 4. **Opened:** 1971. **Architect:** Geoffrey Cornish. **Season:** May-Oct. **High:** May-Oct. **To obtain tee times:** Call golf shop. **Miscellaneous:** Range (grass), credit cards (MC, V).

CASTINE GOLF CLUB
SP-Battle Ave., Castine, 04421, Hancock County, (207)326-8844, 30 miles from Bangor. **E-mail:** twes649775@aol.com. **Facility Holes:** 9. **Yards:** 5,954/5,228. **Par:** 70/70. **Course Rating:** 68.1/71.4. **Slope:** 116/122. **Green Fee:** $22. **Opened:** 1887. **Architect:** Willie Park Jr. **Season:** May-Oct. **High:** July-Aug. **To obtain tee times:** Call golf shop. **Miscellaneous:** Range (grass/mats), BF, FF.

★★★★ DUNEGRASS GOLF CLUB *Condition*
PU-200 Wild Dunes Way, Old Orchard Beach, 04064, York County, (207)934-4513, (800)521-1029, 12 miles from Portland. **Web:** www.dunegrass.com. **Facility Holes:** 18. **Yards:** 6,644/4,920. **Par:** 71/71. **Course Rating:** 71.6/68.0. **Slope:** 134/113. **Cart Fee:** Included in green fee. **Walking Policy:** Walking at certain times. **Walkability:** 2. **Opened:** 1998. **Architect:** Dan Maples. **Season:** April-Nov. **High:** July-Aug. **To obtain tee times:** Call golf shop. **Miscellaneous:** Range (grass), credit cards (MC, V, AE), BF, FF.
Reader Comments: Fabulous public course with resort-like conditions … Some holes are tight … 5 sets of tees make this course enjoyable for all … On the expensive side, but worth every penny … If you are looking for a challenge, this is it … Not enough rangers … Interesting design.

★½ DUTCH ELM GOLF CLUB
PU-5 Brimstone Rd., Arundel, 04046, York County, (207)282-9850, 20 miles from Portland. **E-mail:** dutchelm@cybertours.com. **Web:** www.dutchelmgolf.com. **Facility Holes:** 18. **Yards:** 6,230/5,384. **Par:** 72/72. **Course Rating:** 71.0/70.1. **Slope:** 125/115. **Green Fee:** $20/$35. **Cart Fee:** $26/Cart. **Walking Policy:** Unrestricted walking. **Walkability:** 3. **Opened:** 1965. **Architect:**

MAINE

Lucian Bourque. **Season:** April-Nov. **High:** July-Oct. **To obtain tee times:** Call up to 7 days in advance. **Miscellaneous:** Reduced fees (weekdays, guests, twilight, seniors), range (grass/mats), credit cards (MC, V, D), BF, FF.

★★ **FAIRLAWN GOLF & COUNTRY CLUB**
SP-434 Empire Rd., Poland, 04274, Androscoggin County, (207)998-4277, 25 miles from Portland. **Facility Holes:** 18. **Yards:** 6,300/5,379. **Par:** 72/72. **Course Rating:** 69.4/69.9. **Slope:** 118/112. **Green Fee:** $18/$20. **Cart Fee:** $12/Cart. **Walking Policy:** Unrestricted walking. **Walkability:** 2. **Opened:** 1963. **Architect:** Chic Adams. **Season:** May-Oct. **High:** July-Aug. **To obtain tee times:** Call golf shop. **Miscellaneous:** Reduced fees (weekdays, twilight), metal spikes, range (grass), credit cards (MC, V), BF, FF.

FORT KENT GOLF CLUB
PU-St. John Rd., Fort Kent, 04743, Aroostook County, (207)834-3149, 3 miles from Presque Isle. **Facility Holes:** 18. **Yards:** 6,367/5,361. **Par:** 71/72. **Course Rating:** 69.0/69.0. **Slope:** 112/112. **Green Fee:** $15. **Cart Fee:** $16/Cart. **Walking Policy:** Unrestricted walking. **Walkability:** 3. **Opened:** 1968. **Architect:** Ben Gray. **Season:** April-Oct. **High:** June-Aug. **To obtain tee times:** Call golf shop. **Miscellaneous:** Range (grass), credit cards (MC, V).

FOXCROFT GOLF CLUB
PU-36 Foxcroft Center Rd., Dover-Foxcroft, 04426, Piscataquis County, (207)564-8887, 38 miles from Bangor. **Web:** wwwdover.foxcroft.org. **Facility Holes:** 9. **Yards:** 3,136/2,763. **Par:** 36/38. **Course Rating:** 67.7/67.1. **Slope:** 110/101. **Green Fee:** $18. **Cart Fee:** $18/Cart. **Walking Policy:** Unrestricted walking. **Walkability:** 3. **Opened:** 1964. **Architect:** Renaldo Reynolds. **Season:** May-Oct. **To obtain tee times:** Call golf shop. **Miscellaneous:** FF.

★½ **GORHAM COUNTRY CLUB**
PU-134 McClellan Rd., Gorham, 04038, Cumberland County, (207)839-3490, 10 miles from Portland. **Web:** www.megolf.com. **Facility Holes:** 18. **Yards:** 6,552/5,426. **Par:** 71/72. **Course Rating:** 70.1/70.5. **Slope:** 120/117. **Green Fee:** $24/$26. **Cart Fee:** $24/Person. **Walking Policy:** Unrestricted walking. **Walkability:** 3. **Opened:** 1960. **Architect:** Jim McDonald Sr. **Season:** April-Nov. **To obtain tee times:** Call golf shop. **Miscellaneous:** Reduced fees (twilight), metal spikes, range (grass/mats), credit cards (MC, V, AE), BF, FF.

★½ **HERMON MEADOW GOLF CLUB**
PU-281 Billings Rd., Harmon, 04401, Penobscot County, (207)848-3741, 3 miles from Bangor. **Facility Holes:** 18. **Yards:** 6,329/5,395. **Par:** 72/73. **Course Rating:** 69.4/70.9. **Slope:** 117/120. **Green Fee:** $15/$22. **Cart Fee:** $22/Person. **Walking Policy:** Unrestricted walking. **Walkability:** 3. **Opened:** 1964. **Architect:** Winn Pike. **Season:** April-Dec. **High:** July-Sept. **To obtain tee times:** Call golf shop. **Miscellaneous:** Reduced fees (weekdays, twilight), range (grass/mats), credit cards (MC, V, AE), BF, FF.

★★★★ **KEBO VALLEY GOLF COURSE**
PU-Eagle Lake Rd., Bar Harbor, 04609, Hancock County, (207)288-3000, 42 miles from Bangor. **E-mail:** bake@pga.com. **Web:** www.kebovalley.com. **Facility Holes:** 18. **Yards:** 6,131/5,440. **Par:** 70/72. **Course Rating:** 69.0/68.0. **Slope:** 124/121. **Green Fee:** $30/$69. **Cart Fee:** $34/Cart. **Walking Policy:** Unrestricted walking. **Walkability:** 3. **Opened:** 1888. **Architect:** H. Leeds/A.E. Liscombe- D Ross rev. 1926. **Season:** May-Oct. **High:** July-Sept. **To obtain tee times:** Call golf shop. **Miscellaneous:** Credit cards (MC, V, AE).
Notes: Ranked 5th in 2001 Best in State.
Reader Comments: A real challenge ... The greens border on sadistic, yet few courses are more enjoyable to play ... Located in one of the most beautiful spots in the country ... Toughest short course I ever played ... Traditional Ross design, classic ... Put it on your list when going to Maine.

★★★ **KENNEBEC HEIGHTS COUNTRY CLUB**
PU-1 Fairway Lane, Farmingdale, 04344, Kennebec County, (207)582-2000, 3 miles from Augusta. **Facility Holes:** 18. **Yards:** 6,003/4,820. **Par:** 70/70. **Course Rating:** 69.0/67.7. **Slope:** 129/119. **Green Fee:** $20/$25. **Cart Fee:** $22/Person. **Walking Policy:** Unrestricted walking. **Walkability:** 2. **Opened:** 1964. **Architect:** Brian Silva. **Season:** April-Oct. **High:** June-Aug. **To obtain tee times:** Call golf shop. **Miscellaneous:** Range (mats), credit cards (MC, V).
Reader Comments: Course is challenging and well maintained ... Clubhouse has little to offer but staff was friendly and helpful ... Enjoyed the experience ... The two 9s are very different: the back is open and short, the front is narrow, in the woods.

MAINE

LAKEWOOD GOLF COURSE
PU-Rte. 201 Lakewood Center, Madison, 04950, Somerset County, (207)474-5955, 5 miles from Madison. **Facility Holes:** 18. **Yards:** 6,300/5,500. **Par:** 72/72. **Course Rating:** 68.4/70.1. **Slope:** 122/121. **Green Fee:** $20/$23. **Cart Fee:** $24/Person. **Walking Policy:** Unrestricted walking. **Walkability:** 4. **Opened:** 1927. **Architect:** C.F. Humphrey/P. Wogan. **Season:** April-Dec. **High:** April-Dec. **To obtain tee times:** Call golf shop. **Miscellaneous:** Reduced fees (twilight, juniors), range (grass), lodging (9 rooms), BF, FF.

★★★★½ THE LEDGES GOLF CLUB
SP-1 Ledges Dr., York, 03909, York County, (207)351-3000, 15 miles from Portsmouth. **E-mail:** jacksullivan@ledgesgolf.com. **Web:** www.ledgesgolf.com. **Facility Holes:** 18. **Yards:** 6,981/4,988. **Par:** 72/72. **Course Rating:** 74.3/65.6. **Slope:** 144/129. **Green Fee:** $50/$65. **Cart Fee:** $15/Person. **Walking Policy:** Unrestricted walking. **Walkability:** 4. **Opened:** 1998. **Architect:** William Bradley Booth. **Season:** April-Dec. **High:** May-Oct. **To obtain tee times:** Call up to 4 days in advance. **Miscellaneous:** Reduced fees (twilight), range (grass), credit cards (MC, V), BF, FF.
Reader Comments: A beautiful course in the middle of nowhere … Great views of seacoast … Dollar for dollar, best deal around … Worth the ride … Continues to mature.

★★ MINGO SPRINGS GOLF COURSE
PU-Proctor Rd. and Rte. 4, Rangeley, 04970, Franklin County, (207)864-5021, 120 miles from Portland. **Facility Holes:** 18. **Yards:** 6,014/5,158. **Par:** 70/70. **Course Rating:** 66.3/67.4. **Slope:** 109/110. **Green Fee:** $28/$32. **Cart Fee:** $14/Person. **Walking Policy:** Unrestricted walking. **Walkability:** 4. **Opened:** 1925. **Architect:** Phil Wogan. **Season:** May-Oct. **To obtain tee times:** Call golf shop. **Miscellaneous:** Range (grass), credit cards (MC, V), BF, FF.

NAS BRUNSWICK GOLF COURSE
M-NASB Bldg. 78, Brunswick, 04011, Cumberland County, (207)921-2155, 2 miles from Brunswick. **E-mail:** verhey@nasb.navy.mil. **Web:** www.nfmwr.com/mwrbrunswick. **Facility Holes:** 9. **Yards:** 6,284/5,594. **Par:** 72/74. **Course Rating:** 68.9/71.4. **Slope:** 119/119. **Green Fee:** $17/$23. **Cart Fee:** $20/Cart. **Walking Policy:** Unrestricted walking. **Walkability:** 3. **Opened:** 1958. **Season:** May-Nov. **High:** July-Aug. **To obtain tee times:** Call golf shop. **Miscellaneous:** Range (grass/mats), credit cards (MC, V, AE), BF, FF.

NATANIS GOLF COURSE
PU-RR No. 1, Box 6820-J, Vassalboro, 04989, Kennebec County, (207)622-3561, 7 miles from Augusta. **E-mail:** rbrowne@powerlink.net. **Web:** www.mainebusiness.org/natanis. **Facility Holes:** 36. **Green Fee:** $30. **Cart Fee:** $24/Cart. **Walking Policy:** Unrestricted walking. **Walkability:** 3. **Opened:** 1965. **Season:** April-Nov. **High:** July-Sept. **To obtain tee times:** Call golf shop. **Miscellaneous:** Range (grass), credit cards (MC, V), BF, FF.
★★★½ ARROWHEAD (18) *Value*
Yards: 6,338/5,019. **Par:** 72/73. **Course Rating:** 67.8/68.7. **Slope:** 116/117. **Architect:** Phil Wogan.
Reader Comments: Great in every way … Best 36 holes in state … Love it … Something for everybody … Challenging course … Was three separate 9s with 9 more just completed.
TOMAHAWK (18)
Yards: 6,650. **Par:** 72. **Course Rating:** .0. **Slope:** 0. **Architect:** Dan Maples.

NORTHEAST HARBOR GOLF CLUB
SP-Sargent Dr., Northeast Harbor, 04662, Hancock County, (207)276-5335, 9 miles from Bar Harbor. **E-mail:** nehgc@yahoo.com. **Facility Holes:** 18. **Yards:** 5,492/4,562. **Par:** 69/71. **Course Rating:** 67.8/66.7. **Slope:** 120/118. **Green Fee:** $25/$80. **Cart Fee:** $36/Cart. **Walking Policy:** Unrestricted walking. **Walkability:** 3. **Opened:** 1895. **Architect:** Herbert Strong/Donald Ross. **Season:** May-Oct. **High:** July-Aug. **To obtain tee times:** Call golf shop. **Miscellaneous:** Credit cards (MC, V), BF, FF.

PALMYRA OUTDOOR RESORT
R-147 Lang Hill Rd., Palmyra, 04965, Somerset County, (207)938-4947, 3 miles from Newport. **E-mail:** palmyra@www.palmyra-me.com. **Web:** www.palmyra-me.com. **Facility Holes:** 18. **Yards:** 6,617/5,464. **Par:** 72/72. **Course Rating:** 70.1/69.9. **Slope:** 120/118. **Green Fee:** $20. **Cart Fee:** $20/Cart. **Walking Policy:** Unrestricted walking. **Walkability:** 3. **Opened:** 1965. **Architect:** Dick Cayer. **Season:** April-Oct. **High:** June-Sept. **To obtain tee times:** Call up to 7 days in advance. **Miscellaneous:** Reduced fees (guests), range (grass/mats), lodging (50 rooms), credit cards (MC, V, D), FF.

MAINE

★★★★ PENOBSCOT VALLEY COUNTRY CLUB
SP-366 Main St., Orono, 04473, Penobscot County, (207)866-2423, 5 miles from Bangor. E-mail: gilliesch2@cs.com. **Facility Holes:** 18. **Yards:** 6,450/5,856. **Par:** 72/74. **Course Rating:** 70.3/73.2. **Slope:** 123/126. **Green Fee:** $50. **Cart Fee:** $11/Person. **Walking Policy:** Unrestricted walking. **Walkability:** 4. **Opened:** 1924. **Architect:** Donald Ross. **Season:** April-Nov. **To obtain tee times:** Call up to 7 days in advance. **Miscellaneous:** Range (grass), credit cards (MC, V, D), BF, FF.
Notes: Ranked 4th in 1997 Best in State.
Reader Comments: Short and sweet, greens will either make you or break you ... Great old course, nice layout ... Always in good shape ... Tiny, well protected greens ... Wonderful Donald Ross design ... Diabolical greens, very challenging ... Tough par 3s and tougher par 4s.

★★★½ POINT SEBAGO GOLF & BEACH RESORT
R-261 Point Sebago Rd., Casco, 04015, Cumberland County, (207)655-2747, (800)655-1232, 20 miles from Portland. **E-mail:** info@pointsebago.com. **Web:** pointsebago.com. **Facility Holes:** 18. **Yards:** 7,002/4,866. **Par:** 72/72. **Course Rating:** 73.7/68.4. **Slope:** 135/117. **Green Fee:** $38/$55. **Cart Fee:** Included in green fee. **Walking Policy:** Walking at certain times. **Walkability:** 3. **Opened:** 1996. **Architect:** Phil Wogan/George Sargent. **Season:** May-Nov. **High:** July-Sept. **Tee times:** Call golf shop. **Miscellaneous:** Reduced fees (weekdays, guests, twilight, juniors), range (grass/mats), lodging (350 rooms), credit cards (MC, V, D), BF, FF.
Notes: Ranked 5th in 1997 Best in State; 4th in 1996 Best New Affordable Courses.
Reader Comments: Incredible scenery and views ... Terrific variety of holes ... A must play ... If you don't mind riding, this is a very good golf experience ... Nice range and practice greens ... Fair but not easy.

★★★½ POLAND SPRING COUNTRY CLUB
R-41 Ricker Rd., Poland Spring, 04274, Androscoggin County, (207)998-6002, 25 miles from Portland. **E-mail:** polandsprg@aol.com. **Web:** www.polandspringinns.com. **Facility Holes:** 18. **Yards:** 6,200/5,097. **Par:** 71/74. **Course Rating:** 68.2/68.6. **Slope:** 119/110. **Green Fee:** $22. **Cart Fee:** $21/Cart. **Walking Policy:** Unrestricted walking. **Walkability:** 4. **Opened:** 1896. **Architect:** A.H. Fenn/Donald Ross. **Season:** May-Oct. **To obtain tee times:** Call golf shop. **Miscellaneous:** Reduced fees (guests, twilight), lodging (210 rooms), credit cards (MC, V, AE, D), FF.
Reader Comments: Nice improvements ... Fun old course, 4th hole spectacular ... Donald Ross jewel, even today ... Nice course I would play again ... Wonderful views and layout.

★★½ PRESQUE ISLE COUNTRY CLUB
SP-35 Parkhurst Siding Rd. (Rte. 205), Presque Isle, 04769, Aroostook County, (207)764-0430, 4 miles from Presque Isle. **Facility Holes:** 18. **Yards:** 6,730/5,600. **Par:** 72/72. **Course Rating:** 71.4/72.5. **Slope:** 122/119. **Green Fee:** $20. **Cart Fee:** $20/Cart. **Walking Policy:** Unrestricted walking. **Walkability:** 3. **Opened:** 1958. **Architect:** Ben Gray/Geoffrey S. Cornish. **Season:** May-Nov. **To obtain tee times:** Call golf shop. **Miscellaneous:** Range (grass), credit cards (MC, V, AE), BF, FF.

★½ PROSPECT HILL GOLF COURSE
SP-694 S. Main St., Auburn, 04210, Androscoggin County, (207)782-9220, 5 miles from Lewiston. **Facility Holes:** 18. **Yards:** 5,846/5,227. **Par:** 71/73. **Course Rating:** 66.9/68.7. **Slope:** 111/119. **Green Fee:** $22. **Cart Fee:** $20/Cart. **Walking Policy:** Unrestricted walking. **Walkability:** 3. **Opened:** 1957. **Architect:** Arthur David Chapman. **Season:** April-Nov. **High:** June-Aug. **To obtain tee times:** Call golf shop. **Miscellaneous:** Reduced fees (twilight), credit cards (MC, V, D), BF, FF.

PROVINCE LAKE GOLF
PU-Rte. 153, Parsonsfield, 04047, York County, (207)793-4040, (800)325-4434, 24 miles from Conway, NH. **E-mail:** gpl@golfatprovlake.com. **Web:** www.provincelakegolf.com. **Facility Holes:** 18. **Yards:** 6,270/4,168. **Par:** 71/71. **Course Rating:** 70.1/63.8. **Slope:** 127/109. **Green Fee:** $20/$38. **Cart Fee:** $12/Person. **Walking Policy:** Walking at certain times. **Walkability:** 3. **Opened:** 1918. **Architect:** Brian Silva/Lawrence Van Etten. **Season:** April-Nov. **High:** June-Sept. **To obtain tee times:** Call up to 7 days in advance. **Miscellaneous:** Reduced fees (weekdays, twilight, juniors), range (grass/mats), credit cards (MC, V, D), BF, FF.

RIVER MEADOW GOLF CLUB
PU-216 Lincoln St., Westbook, 04092, Cumberland County, (207)854-1625, 2 miles from Portland. **Facility Holes:** 9. **Yards:** 2,915/2,610. **Par:** 35/36. **Course Rating:** 67.5/69.4. **Slope:** 112/117. **Green Fee:** $17/$20. **Cart Fee:** $16/Cart. **Walking Policy:** Unrestricted walking. **Walkability:** 1. **Opened:** 1963. **Architect:** Rufus Jordan. **Season:** April-Nov. **High:** June-Aug. **To obtain tee times:** Call golf shop. **Miscellaneous:** Reduced fees (weekdays, twilight, seniors).

★★ RIVERSIDE MUNICIPAL GOLF COURSE
PU-1158 Riverside St., Portland, 04103, Cumberland County, (207)797-3524. **Facility Holes:** 18. **Yards:** 6,450/5,640. **Par:** 72/72. **Course Rating:** 69.5/70.7. **Slope:** 115/112. **Green Fee:** $15/$18. **Cart Fee:** $22/Cart. **Walking Policy:** Unrestricted walking. **Walkability:** 4. **Opened:** 1935. **Architect:** Wayne Stiles. **Season:** April-Nov. **High:** July-Aug. **Tee times:** Call golf shop. **Miscellaneous:** Reduced fees (seniors, juniors), range (grass), credit cards (MC, V).

★★★ ROCKLAND GOLF CLUB
SP-606 Old County Rd., Rockland, 04841, Knox County, (207)594-9322, 45 miles from Augusta. **E-mail:** rgc@midcoast.com. **Facility Holes:** 18. **Yards:** 6,121/5,583. **Par:** 70/73. **Course Rating:** 67.8/71.8. **Slope:** 115/119. **Green Fee:** $20/$45. **Cart Fee:** $25/Cart. **Walking Policy:** Unrestricted walking. **Walkability:** 2. **Opened:** 1932. **Architect:** Wayne Stiles/Roger Sorrent. **Season:** April-Oct. **High:** June-Sept. **To obtain tee times:** Call up to 2 days in advance. **Miscellaneous:** Reduced fees (twilight, juniors), credit cards (MC, V, AE, D), BF, FF. **Reader Comments:** Greens hard and fast ... Slicer's delight ... Very friendly ... Good place to lower your handicap.

★★★★ SABLE OAKS GOLF CLUB
PU-505 Country Club Dr., South Portland, 04106, Cumberland County, (207)775-6257, 3 miles from Portland. **Facility Holes:** 18. **Yards:** 6,359/4,786. **Par:** 70/70. **Course Rating:** 71.9/68.0. **Slope:** 134/118. **Green Fee:** $25/$32. **Cart Fee:** $22/Cart. **Walking Policy:** Unrestricted walking. **Walkability:** 3. **Opened:** 1989. **Architect:** Geoffrey Cornish/Brian Silva. **Season:** April-Dec. **High:** April-Sept. **To obtain tee times:** Call golf shop. **Miscellaneous:** Reduced fees (weekdays, twilight), metal spikes, caddies, credit cards (MC, V). **Reader Comments:** Punishes mistakes, rewards great shots ... Toughest course in Maine after Sugarloaf ... Many interesting holes ... Very walkable if you have young legs ... Rather tight for 15+ handicappers ... Fall is the time to play.

SALMON FALLS COUNTRY CLUB
R-52 Golf Course Lane, Hollis, 04042, York County, (207)929-5233, (800)734-1616, 10 miles from Biddeford. **E-mail:** info@salmonfalls-resort.com. **Web:** www.salmonfalls-resort.com. **Facility Holes:** 18. **Yards:** 5,948/5,298. **Par:** 72/70. **Course Rating:** 67.6/69.5. **Slope:** 121/112. **Green Fee:** $15/$20. **Cart Fee:** $20/Cart. **Walking Policy:** Unrestricted walking. **Walkability:** 4. **Opened:** 1974. **Architect:** Jim Jones. **Season:** April-Nov. **High:** Jan.-Sept. **To obtain tee times:** Call up to 7 days in advance. **Miscellaneous:** Reduced fees (twilight), range (grass), lodging (7 rooms), credit cards (MC, V, AE, D), BF, FF.

★★★★ SAMOSET RESORT GOLF CLUB
R-220 Warrenton St., Rockport, 04856, Knox County, (207)594-1431, (800)341-1650, 80 miles from Portland. **E-mail:** christie@samoset.com. **Web:** www.samoset.com. **Facility Holes:** 18. **Yards:** 6,591/5,034. **Par:** 70/72. **Course Rating:** 70.7/71.2. **Slope:** 130/125. **Green Fee:** $55/$100. **Cart Fee:** Included in green fee. **Walking Policy:** Unrestricted walking. **Walkability:** 2. **Opened:** 1978. **Architect:** Robert Elder. **Season:** April-Nov. **High:** July-Sept. **To obtain tee times:** Call golf shop. **Miscellaneous:** Reduced fees (guests, twilight), range (grass/mats), lodging (222 rooms), credit cards (MC, V, AE, D, DC, CB), BF, FF. **Notes:** Ranked 4th in 2001 Best in State. **Reader Comments:** Absolutely beautiful ... Wonderful views ... Very challenging and great fun for all levels of proficiency ... Pebble Beach of Maine ... Tough in the wind.

SPRINGBROOK GOLF CLUB
PU-Route 202, Leeds, 04263, Androscoggin County, (207)946-5900, 15 miles from Augusta. **Facility Holes:** 18. **Yards:** 6,383/4,752. **Par:** 71/73. **Course Rating:** 68.1/66.0. **Slope:** 119/113. **Green Fee:** $20/$25. **Cart Fee:** $22/Cart. **Walking Policy:** Unrestricted walking. **Walkability:** 4. **Season:** April-Nov. **High:** June-Aug. **To obtain tee times:** Call golf shop. **Miscellaneous:** Reduced fees (twilight, seniors, juniors), range (grass), credit cards (MC, V).

ST. CROIX COUNTRY CLUB
SP-River Rd., Calais, 04619, Washington County, (207)454-8875. **Facility Holes:** 9. **Yards:** 2,767/2,567. **Par:** 35/36. **Course Rating:** 64.8/68.6. **Slope:** 102/111. **Green Fee:** $20. **Cart Fee:** $17/Cart. **Walking Policy:** Unrestricted walking. **Walkability:** 2. **Opened:** 1930. **Architect:** Earl T. Gray. **Season:** May-Oct. **High:** July-Sept. **To obtain tee times:** Call golf shop. **Miscellaneous:** Credit cards (MC, V), BF, FF.

★★★★½ SUGARLOAF GOLF CLUB *Service*
R-RR No.1, P.O. Box 5000, Carrabassett Valley, 04947, Franklin County, (207)237-2000, (800)843-5623, 100 miles from Portland. **E-mail:** shoisington@sugarloaf.com. **Web:** www.sugarloaf.com. **Facility Holes:** 18. **Yards:** 6,910/5,376. **Par:** 72/72. **Course Rating:** 74.3/73.7. **Slope:** 151/136. **Green Fee:** $53/$105. **Cart Fee:** $18/Person. **Walking Policy:** Unrestricted

walking. **Walkability:** 4. **Opened:** 1986. **Architect:** Robert Trent Jones Jr. **Season:** May-Oct. **High:** Aug.-Sept. **Tee times:** Call golf shop. **Misc:** Reduced fees (guests, twilight, juniors), metal spikes, range (grass/mats), lodging (1000 rooms), credit cards (MC, V, AE, D), BF, FF. **Notes:** Ranked 1st in 2001 Best in State.

Reader Comments: Everyone should get to play this course at least once … Thank goodness there are 4 sets of men's tees, even single digit players will struggle from the back … Stunningly beautiful mountain course … You won't believe the views from the tees on 10 and 11 … A magestical golf course surrounded by beauty.

★★★ VA JO WA GOLF COURSE

R-142A Walker Rd., Island Falls, 04747, Aroostook County, (207)463-2128, 85 miles from Bangor. **E-mail:** vajowa@webtv.net. **Web:** www.vajowa.com. **Facility Holes:** 18. **Yards:** 6,223/5,065. **Par:** 72/72. **Course Rating:** 70.4/69.6. **Slope:** 125/119. **Green Fee:** $25. **Cart Fee:** $24/Cart. **Walking Policy:** Unrestricted walking. **Walkability:** 5. **Opened:** 1964. **Architect:** Vaughan Walker/Warren Walker. **Season:** May-Oct. **High:** June-Sept. **To obtain tee times:** Call golf shop. **Miscellaneous:** Reduced fees (weekdays, guests, twilight, juniors), range (grass), lodging (35 rooms), credit cards (MC, V, D), BF, FF.

Reader Comments: Good variety of holes … Front 9 in a valley, bordering a lake—back 9 in mountains … Scenic … A good test … Friendly atmosphere.

★★★ VAL HALLA GOLF & RECREATION CENTER

PU-1 Val Halla Rd., Cumberland, 04021, Cumberland County, (207)829-2225, 10 miles from Portland. **Facility Holes:** 18. **Yards:** 6,574/5,437. **Par:** 72/72. **Course Rating:** 71.1/70.4. **Slope:** 126/116. **Green Fee:** $25/$30. **Cart Fee:** $30/Cart. **Walking Policy:** Unrestricted walking. **Walkability:** 3. **Opened:** 1965. **Architect:** Phil Wogan. **Season:** April-Nov. **High:** June-Sept. **To obtain tee times:** Call up to 7 days in advance. **Miscellaneous:** Reduced fees (weekdays, seniors, juniors), range (grass/mats), credit cards (MC, V, AE), BF, FF.

Reader Comments: Some long holes … Good local club atmosphere … Greens were good.

★★★½ WATERVILLE COUNTRY CLUB

SP-Country Club Rd., Oakland, 04963, Kennebec County, (207)465-9861, 5 miles from Waterville. **Facility Holes:** 18. **Yards:** 6,427/5,466. **Par:** 70/73. **Course Rating:** 69.6/71.3. **Slope:** 124/119. **Green Fee:** $48. **Cart Fee:** $28/Cart. **Walking Policy:** Unrestricted walking. **Walkability:** 3. **Opened:** 1916. **Architect:** Orrin Smith/Geoffrey S. Cornish. **Season:** April-Nov. **Tee times:** Call up to 2 days in advance. **Miscellaneous:** Range (grass/mats), BF, FF.

Reader Comments: Great northern Maine layout … Winds through pine forest … A great course, great service, nice people … Excellent old style of golf course … Hard to get tee time … Still the 'best kept secret' in New England.

★★½ WILLOWDALE GOLF CLUB

PU-52 Willowdale Rd., Scarborough, 04074, Cumberland County, (207)883-9351, 9 miles from Portland. **Facility Holes:** 18. **Yards:** 5,881/5,049. **Par:** 70/70. **Course Rating:** 67.7/68.9. **Slope:** 115/116. **Green Fee:** $27/$29. **Cart Fee:** $22/Cart. **Walking Policy:** Unrestricted walking. **Walkability:** 2. **Opened:** 1924. **Architect:** Eugene Wogan. **Season:** April-Nov. **To obtain tee times:** Call golf shop. **Miscellaneous:** Reduced fees (twilight), credit cards (MC, V, AE, D), FF.

MARYLAND

ANDREWS AFB GOLF COURSE
M-4442 Perimeter Rd., Andrews AFB, 20762, Prince George's County, (301)981-5010, 10 miles from Washington, DC. **E-mail:** aafbgc@aol.com. **Web:** www.aafbgc.com. **Facility Holes:** 54. **Green Fee:** $19/$30. **Cart Fee:** $18/Cart. **Walkability:** 3. **Architect:** Ault/Clark. **Season:** Year-round. **High:** April-Oct. **To obtain tee times:** Call golf shop. **Miscellaneous:** Reduced fees (twilight), metal spikes, range (grass/mats), credit cards (MC, V), BF, FF.
★★½ **EAST COURSE** (18)
Yards: 6,780/5,493. **Par:** 72/72. **Course Rating:** 72.0/72.1. **Slope:** 121/119. **Walking Policy:** Unrestricted walking. **Opened:** 1956.
SOUTH COURSE (18)
Yards: 6,748/5,371. **Par:** 72/72. **Course Rating:** 72.1/71.1. **Slope:** 128/115. **Walking Policy:** Mandatory carts. **Opened:** 1997.
★★★ **WEST COURSE** (18)
Yards: 6,346/5,436. **Par:** 70/73. **Course Rating:** 70.5/70.9. **Slope:** 120/124. **Walking Policy:** Unrestricted walking. **Opened:** 1961.
Reader Comments: Wonderful course; excellent whether you walk or use a cart ... Sunday mornings in the fall: Too many Redskins fans trying to get in 18 holes before the game ... Nice tournament outing, well kept up.

ANNAPOLIS GOLF CLUB
SP-2638 Carrollton Rd., Annapolis, 21403, Anne Arundel County, (410)263-6771, 30 miles from Baltimore. **E-mail:** annapolisgc@aol. **Facility Holes:** 9. **Yards:** 6,405/5,373. **Par:** 72/74. **Course Rating:** 70.1/75.9. **Slope:** 121/128. **Green Fee:** $18. **Cart Fee:** $12/Cart. **Walking Policy:** Unrestricted walking. **Walkability:** 3. **Opened:** 1928. **Architect:** Charles Banks. **Season:** Year-round. **High:** April-Oct. **To obtain tee times:** Call golf shop. **Miscellaneous:** BF, FF.

★★½ ATLANTIC GOLF AT POTOMAC RIDGE
PU-15800 Sharperville Rd., Accokeek, 20601, Prince George's County, (301)372-1305, (800)791-9078, 15 miles from Washington, DC. **E-mail:** jmichael@mdgolf.com. **Web:** mdgolf.com. **Facility Holes:** 18. **Yards:** 6,505/5,075. **Par:** 72/72. **Course Rating:** 71.6/69.5. **Slope:** 126/122. **Green Fee:** $25/$54. **Cart Fee:** Included in green fee. **Walking Policy:** Unrestricted walking. **Walkability:** 3. **Opened:** 1995. **Architect:** Tom Clark. **Season:** Year-round. **High:** May-Oct. **To obtain tee times:** Call up to 365 days in advance. **Miscellaneous:** Reduced fees (weekdays, twilight, seniors, juniors), metal spikes, range (grass/mats), credit cards (MC, V, AE, D), BF, FF.
Special Notes: Formerly Potomac Ridge Golf Links.

THE BAY CLUB
R-9122 Libertytown Rd., Berlin, 21811, Worcester County, (800)229-2582, (800)229-2582, 7 miles from Ocean City. **E-mail:** Bogey@shore.intercom.net. **Web:** www.thebayclub.com. **Facility Holes:** 36. **Green Fee:** $25/$69. **Cart Fee:** Included in green fee. **Walking Policy:** Unrestricted walking. **Walkability:** 1. **Season:** Year-round. **To obtain tee times:** Call up to 365 days in advance. **Miscellaneous:** Reduced fees (weekdays, guests, twilight, seniors, juniors), range (grass), credit cards (MC, V, AE), BF, FF.
★★★ **EAST COURSE** (18)
Yards: 7,004/5,231. **Par:** 72/72. **Course Rating:** 74.6/67.4. **Slope:** 134/115. **Opened:** 1999. **Architect:** Charles Priestley.
Reader Comments: Favorite eastern shore course all round ... Zoysia grass is a great change, your ball just sits up like you wouldn't believe ... Staff were very helpful.
★★★½ **WEST COURSE** (18)
Yards: 6,958/5,609. **Par:** 72/72. **Course Rating:** 73.1/71.3. **Slope:** 126/118. **Opened:** 1989. **Architect:** Russell Roberts.
Reader Comments: Good old-style course ... A joy to play ... Hard for average golfer ... A great classic. Very straightforward and very affordable ... Nice layout, very much a Myrtle Beach-type course, good staff & facilities, a sleeper.

★★½ BAY HILLS GOLF CLUB
SP-545 Bay Hills Dr., Arnold, 21012, Anne Arundel County, (410)974-0669, 10 miles from Annapolis. **Facility Holes:** 18. **Yards:** 6,423/5,029. **Par:** 70/70. **Course Rating:** 70.8/69.2. **Slope:** 118/121. **Green Fee:** $36/$50. **Cart Fee:** Included in green fee. **Walking Policy:** Mandatory carts. **Walkability:** 3. **Opened:** 1969. **Architect:** Ed Ault. **Season:** Year-round. **To obtain tee times:** Call up to 5 days in advance. **Miscellaneous:** Reduced fees (twilight), credit cards (MC, V, AE), BF, FF.

THE BEACH CLUB GOLF LINKS
SP-9715 Deer Park Dr., Berlin, 21811, Worcester County, (410)641-4653, (800)435-9223, 7 miles from Ocean City. **E-mail:** bchclb@dmv.com. **Web:** www.ocean-city.com/beahpsg.htm. **Facility Holes:** 36. **Green Fee:** $35/$72. **Cart Fee:** Included in green fee. **Walking Policy:** Walking at certain times. **Walkability:** 2. **Architect:** Brian Ault. **Season:** Year-round. **To obtain

tee times: Call golf shop. **Miscellaneous:** Reduced fees (twilight, juniors), range (mats), credit cards (MC, V, AE, D), BF, FF.
★★½ **INNER LINKS COURSE** (18)
Yards: 7,020/5,167. **Par:** 72/72. **Course Rating:** 73.0/69.0. **Slope:** 128/117. **Opened:** 1991.
★★★½ **OUTER LINKS COURSE** (18)
Yards: 6,548/5,022. **Par:** 72/72. **Course Rating:** 71.7/68.6. **Slope:** 134/119. **Opened:** 1996.
Reader Comments: Very tough course, narrow fairways, fast greens … Nice experience … Very good value … Must play.

★★½ **BEAR CREEK GOLF CLUB**
SP-2158 Littlestown Rd., Westminster, 21158, Carroll County, (410)876-4653, 30 miles from Baltimore. **E-mail:** beggp@aol.com. **Web:** www.gothamgolf.com. **Facility Holes:** 18. **Yards:** 6,319/5,397. **Par:** 71/72. **Course Rating:** 70.6/70.2. **Slope:** 124/123. **Green Fee:** $20/$43. **Cart Fee:** Included in green fee. **Walking Policy:** Walking at certain times. **Walkability:** 4. **Opened:** 1989. **Architect:** Paul HIcks. **Season:** Year-round. **High:** April-Sept. **To obtain tee times:** Call up to 7 days in advance. **Miscellaneous:** Reduced fees (twilight, seniors, juniors), range (grass/mats), credit cards (MC, V, AE), BF, FF.

★★★ **BEAVER CREEK COUNTRY CLUB**
SP-9535 Mapleville Rd., Hagerstown, 21740, Washington County, (301)733-5152, 60 miles from Baltimore. **E-mail:** plsteine@intrepid.net. **Facility Holes:** 18. **Yards:** 6,878/5,636. **Par:** 72/73. **Course Rating:** 71.6/71.4. **Slope:** 117/124. **Green Fee:** $24/$30. **Cart Fee:** $14/Person. **Walking Policy:** Walking at certain times. **Walkability:** 3. **Opened:** 1959. **Architect:** Reuben Hine/Jack Young. **Season:** Year-round. **High:** April-Oct. **To obtain tee times:** Call up to 3 days in advance. **Miscellaneous:** Reduced fees (weekdays, twilight, juniors), range (grass/mats), credit cards (MC, V), BF, FF.
Reader Comments: Tough course, target golf … Back nine very good … Challenging, many raised tee boxes … Nice course in a surprising location … Easy … Very fast shiny greens.

★★★★½ **BEECHTREE GOLF CLUB**
PU-811 South Stepney Rd., Aberdeen, 21001, Harford County, (410)297-9700, (877)233-2487. **Web:** www.beechtreegolf.com. **Facility Holes:** 18. **Yards:** 7,023/5,363. **Par:** 71/72. **Course Rating:** 74.9/70.4. **Slope:** 142/121. **Green Fee:** $70/$85. **Cart Fee:** Included in green fee. **Walking Policy:** Unrestricted walking. **Walkability:** 3. **Opened:** 1998. **Architect:** Tom Doak. **Season:** April-Dec. **High:** May-Oct. **To obtain tee times:** Call up to 30 days in advance. **Miscellaneous:** Range (grass), credit cards (MC, V, AE, D), FF.
Notes: Ranked 14th in 2001 Best in State.
Reader Comments: Simply great golf conditions … Outstanding service … Challenging holes, especially those where you can not see the landing area from the tee box. Staff was very friendly, helped guide us around the course … Anywhere else would cost $100+ … Challenging course with a lot of variety.

★★★★ **BLACK ROCK GOLF COURSE**
PU-20025 Mt. Aetna Rd., Hagerstown, 21742, Washington County, (301)791-3040, 70 miles from Baltimore. **E-mail:** dw1954@aol.com. **Web:** www.blackrockgolfcourse.com. **Facility Holes:** 18. **Yards:** 6,646/5,179. **Par:** 72/74. **Course Rating:** 70.7/64.7. **Slope:** 124/112. **Green Fee:** $16/$27. **Cart Fee:** $14/Person. **Walking Policy:** Walking at certain times. **Walkability:** 3. **Opened:** 1989. **Architect:** Bob Elder. **Season:** Year-round. **To obtain tee times:** Call up to 7 days in advance. **Miscellaneous:** Reduced fees (twilight, seniors, juniors), range (grass), credit cards (MC, V), BF, FF.
Reader Comments: Well designed muni … One of the best public courses in Maryland, a great value … Beautiful mountain views, long drive for most of state … Nice greens … Played by President Clinton … Player friendly course.

BOWIE GOLF & COUNTRY CLUB
SP-7420 Laurel-Bowie Road, Bowie, 20715, Prince George's County, (301)262-8141. **Facility Holes:** 18. **Yards:** 6,142/5,106. **Par:** 70/73. **Course Rating:** 69.8/69.6. **Slope:** 114/113. **Green Fee:** $25/$30. **Cart Fee:** $12/Person. **Walking Policy:** Walking at certain times. **Walkability:** 3. **Opened:** 1959. **Season:** Year-round. **High:** May-Oct. **To obtain tee times:** Call golf shop. **Miscellaneous:** Range (mats), credit cards (MC, V, AE).

★★½ **BRANTWOOD GOLF CLUB**
SP-1190 Augustine Herman Hwy., Elkton, 21921, Cecil County, (410)398-8848, 15 miles from Wilmington. **E-mail:** brantwoodgc@aol.com. **Facility Holes:** 18. **Yards:** 6,101/5,237. **Par:** 70/72. **Course Rating:** 67.6/70.5. **Slope:** 118/114. **Green Fee:** $17/$30. **Cart Fee:** $10/Person. **Walking Policy:** Walking at certain times. **Walkability:** 2. **Opened:** 1962. **Architect:** Wallace William. **Season:** Year-round. **To obtain tee times:** Call golf shop. **Miscellaneous:** Reduced fees (twilight, seniors, juniors), range (grass/mats), credit cards (MC, V), BF, FF.

★★★ BRETON BAY GOLF & COUNTRY CLUB
SP-21935 Society Hill Rd., Leonardtown, 20650, St. Mary's County, (301)475-2300, 7 miles from Leonardtown. **E-mail:** barnold@PGA.com. **Facility Holes:** 18. **Yards:** 6,933/5,457. **Par:** 72/73. **Course Rating:** 73.0/70.0. **Slope:** 126/117. **Green Fee:** $25. **Cart Fee:** $13/Person. **Walking Policy:** Walking at certain times. **Walkability:** 2. **Opened:** 1974. **Architect:** J. Porter Gibson. **Season:** Year-round. **To obtain tee times:** Call up to 5 days in advance. **Miscellaneous:** Reduced fees (twilight, seniors, juniors), range (grass/mats), credit cards (MC, V), BF, FF.
Reader Comments: Nice track, lots of hills, usually in excellent condition ... A good challenge, a long course, very scenic ... Fair on scoring.

★★★★★ BULLE ROCK *Service+, Condition+, Pace*
PU-320 Blenheim Lane, Havre de Grace, 21078, Harford County, (410)939-8887, . **E-mail:** BulleRock@iximd.com. **Web:** www.bullerock.com. **Facility Holes:** 18. **Yards:** 7,375/5,426. **Par:** 72/72. **Course Rating:** 76.4/71.1. **Slope:** 147/127. **Green Fee:** $105/$145. **Cart Fee:** Included in green fee. **Walking Policy:** Unrestricted walking. **Walkability:** 3. **Opened:** 1998. **Architect:** Pete Dye. **Season:** March-Nov. **High:** May-Oct. **To obtain tee times:** Call up to 30 days in advance. **Miscellaneous:** Reduced fees (weekdays), range (grass), caddies, credit cards (MC, V, AE, D), BF, FF.
Notes: Ranked 3rd in 2001 Best in State.
Reader Comments: Bring your wallet, but it is outstanding ... Pete Dye created a great course and the staff created a day to be remembered ... A caddie is a must ... Dramatic views, very challenging ... The rough is absolutely a penalty shot ... Great condition, one of Dye's best ... Only pros from the tips ... New 225 room hotel to be completed in 2003.

★½ CAMBRIDGE COUNTRY CLUB
SP-Horns Point Rd., Cambridge, 21613, Dorchester County, (410)228-4808, 40 miles from Salisbury. **Facility Holes:** 18. **Yards:** 6,387/5,416. **Par:** 72/73. **Course Rating:** 69.3/71.0. **Slope:** 113/118. **Green Fee:** $35. **Walking Policy:** Unrestricted walking. **Opened:** 1925. **Architect:** Russell Roberts. **Season:** Year-round. **High:** May-Oct. **To obtain tee times:** Call golf shop. **Miscellaneous:** Reduced fees (guests), metal spikes, range (grass), credit cards (MC, V).

★½ CARROLL PARK GOLF COURSE
PU-2100 Washington Blvd., Baltimore, 21230, Baltimore County, (410)685-8344, 3 miles from Baltimore. **Facility Holes:** 12. **Yards:** 3,214/2,862. **Par:** 44/43. **Course Rating:** 31.4/30.0. **Slope:** 109/101. **Green Fee:** $8. **Walking Policy:** Unrestricted walking. **Walkability:** 1. **Opened:** 1924. **Architect:** Gus Hook. **Season:** Year-round. **High:** April-Sept. **To obtain tee times:** Call up to 14 days in advance. **Miscellaneous:** Reduced fees (weekdays, twilight, seniors, juniors), metal spikes, credit cards (MC, V), BF, FF.

CEDAR POINT GOLF CLUB
M-Bldg. 663 - NAWC, Patuxent River, 20670, St. Mary's County, (301)342-3597, 45 miles from Washington, DC. **Facility Holes:** 18. **Yards:** 6,714/5,021. **Par:** 72/72. **Course Rating:** 71.6/68.3. **Slope:** 124/110. **Green Fee:** $12/$24. **Cart Fee:** $11/Person. **Walking Policy:** Unrestricted walking. **Walkability:** 3. **Opened:** 1964. **Season:** Year-round. **High:** April-Oct. **Tee times:** Call golf shop. **Miscellaneous:** Range (grass), credit cards (MC, V, AE, D).

CHESAPEAKE BAY GOLF CLUB
PU-1500 Chesapeake Club Dr., North East, 21901, Cecil County, (410)287-0200, 25 miles from Baltimore. **E-mail:** cbgc@chesapeakegolf.com. **Web:** www.chesapeakegolf.com. **Facility Holes:** 36. **Green Fee:** $20/$49. **Cart Fee:** Included in green fee. **Season:** Year-round. **To obtain tee times:** Call up to 7 days in advance. **Miscellaneous:** Reduced fees (weekdays, twilight, seniors, juniors), credit cards (MC, V, AE, D), BF, FF.
★★★ NORTH EAST COURSE (18)
Yards: 6,434/4,811. **Par:** 70/70. **Slope:** 138. **Walking Policy:** Unrestricted walking. **Walkability:** 3. **Opened:** 1994. **Architect:** Andrew Barbin. **Miscellaneous:** Range (grass/mats).
Reader Comments: The course winds through native wetlands and forests. Leadbetter practice facility/school ... Tough on high handicapper, shot maker course ... Very challenging, hilly, narrow fairways ... Love the greens.
★★★½ RISING SUN COURSE (18)
Yards: 6,636/5,233. **Par:** 71/71. **Course Rating:** 72.3/70.4. **Slope:** 130/119. **Walking Policy:** Walking at certain times. **Walkability:** 2. **Opened:** 1967. **Architect:** Russell Roberts. **High:** May-Oct. **Miscellaneous:** Range (grass).
Reader Comments: Best greens in the area ... '60s style East course ... These guys treat you right. Always a good experience ... Don't try to cut corner on 9th ... Price is right, great greens.
Special Notes: Formerly Chantilly Manor Country Club.

MARYLAND

CHESAPEAKE HILLS GOLF CLUB
SP-Rte. 765, Lusby, 20657, Calvert County, (410)326-4653, 50 miles from Washington, DC. **Facility Holes:** 18. **Yards:** 6,545/5,489. **Par:** 72/72. **Course Rating:** 72.3/71.8. **Slope:** 126/119. **Green Fee:** $20/$23. **Cart Fee:** $12/Person. **Walking Policy:** Walking at certain times. **Walkability:** 4. **Opened:** 1967. **Architect:** Dick Thompson. **Season:** Year-round. **High:** April-Nov. **To obtain tee times:** Call up to 6 days in advance. **Miscellaneous:** Reduced fees (juniors), range (grass), credit cards (MC, V), BF, FF.

CLIFTON PARK GOLF COURSE
PU-2701 St. Lo Dr., Baltimore, 21213, Baltimore County, (410)243-3500. **E-mail:** markp-gapro@prodigy.net. **Web:** bmgcgolf.com. **Facility Holes:** 18. **Yards:** 5,954/5,469. **Par:** 71/73. **Course Rating:** 68.0/66.6. **Slope:** 116/104. **Cart Fee:** Included in green fee. **Walking Policy:** Unrestricted walking. **Walkability:** 3. **Opened:** 1915. **Season:** Year-round. **To obtain tee times:** Call up to 14 days in advance. **Miscellaneous:** Reduced fees (weekdays, twilight, juniors), metal spikes, credit cards (MC, V), BF, FF.

★★★ CLUSTERED SPIRES GOLF COURSE
PU-8415 Gas House Pike, Frederick, 21701, Frederick County, (301)624-1295, 45 miles from Baltimore. **Facility Holes:** 18. **Yards:** 6,769/5,230. **Par:** 72/72. **Course Rating:** 70.5/70.0. **Slope:** 115/124. **Green Fee:** $18/$35. **Cart Fee:** $12/Person. **Walking Policy:** Unrestricted walking. **Walkability:** 1. **Opened:** 1991. **Architect:** Brian Ault. **Season:** Year-round. **To obtain tee times:** Call up to 5 days in advance. **Miscellaneous:** Reduced fees (weekdays, twilight, seniors, juniors), range (grass), credit cards (MC, V, AE), BF, FF.
Reader Comments: One of the best public courses in area, well kept, challenging, fun course to play ... Staff is glad you came to play ... Solid muni ... A good test at a decent price.

THE COURSES FORT MEADE
M-Bldg. 6800 Taylor Ave., Fort Meade, 20755, Anne Arundel County, (301)677-5326, 12 miles from Baltimore. **Web:** www.ftmeadegolf.com. **Facility Holes:** 36. **Green Fee:** $14/$26. **Cart Fee:** $17/Cart. **Walking Policy:** Unrestricted walking. **Walkability:** 2. **Season:** Year-round. **High:** April-Oct. **To obtain tee times:** Call golf shop. **Miscellaneous:** Reduced fees (twilight), range (grass/mats), credit cards (MC, V, AE, D).
APPLEWOOD COURSE (18)
Yards: 6,494/5,436. **Par:** 72/74. **Course Rating:** 70.8/70.2. **Slope:** 116/113. **Opened:** 1944.
★★★ **PARKS COURSE** (18)
Yards: 6,811/5,333. **Par:** 72/73. **Course Rating:** 71.6/69.0. **Slope:** 117/110. **Opened:** 1955.
Reader Comments: Wide open course, 3rd hole dogleg to right is fun hole over creek ... Well kept, especially for amount of play ... Back 9 particularly interesting. No. 12 in the spring is as pretty as any hole ever.

DEER RUN GOLF CLUB
PU-8804 Logtown Rd., Berlin, 21811, Worcester County, (410)629-0060, (888)790-4465, 6 miles from Ocean City. **E-mail:** golfpro@golfdeerrun.com. **Web:** www.golfdeerrun.com. **Facility Holes:** 18. **Yards:** 6,105/4,072. **Par:** 70/70. **Course Rating:** 69.4/68.8. **Slope:** 115/110. **Green Fee:** $30/$55. **Cart Fee:** Included in green fee. **Walking Policy:** Unrestricted walking. **Walkability:** 1. **Opened:** 1997. **Architect:** Lindsay Ervin. **Season:** Year-round. **High:** April-Oct. **To obtain tee times:** Call up to 14 days in advance. **Miscellaneous:** Reduced fees (twilight, seniors, juniors), range (grass/mats), credit cards (MC, V, AE, D), BF, FF.

DIAMOND RIDGE
PU-2309 Ridge Rd., Woodlawn, 21244, Baltimore County, (410)887-1349, 10 miles from Baltimore. **E-mail:** diamond1@baltimoregolfing.com. **Web:** www.baltimoregolfing.com. **Facility Holes:** 36. **Green Fee:** $17/$20. **Cart Fee:** $22/Cart. **Walking Policy:** Unrestricted walking. **Walkability:** 3. **Season:** Year-round. **To obtain tee times:** Call up to 7 days in advance. **Miscellaneous:** Reduced fees (twilight, seniors, juniors), range (mats), credit cards (MC, V, AE, D), BF, FF.
★★★ **DIAMOND RIDGE GOLF COURSE** (18)
Yards: 6,550/5,833. **Par:** 70/72. **Rating:** 71.0/73.2. **Slope:** 120/123. **Opened:** 1968. **Architect:** Ed Ault.
Reader Comments: Nice design ... As fun as it was 22 1/2 years ago ... Great scenery ... Use all in your bag ... Friendly staff ... Long ... Good value ... Always enjoy playing here.
WOODLAND GOLF COURSE (18)
Yards: 6,613/5,431. **Par:** 71/73. **Rating:** 71.6/72.7. **Slope:** 127/122. **Architect:** Linsay Irvin.

★★★★ EAGLE'S LANDING GOLF COURSE
PU-12367 Eagle's Nest Rd., Berlin, 21811, Worcester County, (410)213-7277, (800)283-3846, 3 miles from Ocean City. **E-mail:** broberts@ococean.com. **Web:** ocean-city.com/eagles-landing.htm. **Facility Holes:** 18. **Yards:** 7,003/4,896. **Par:** 72/72. **Course Rating:** 73.6/67.9.

Slope: 126/112. **Green Fee:** $20/$36. **Cart Fee:** $23/Person. **Walking Policy:** Unrestricted walking. **Walkability:** 1. **Opened:** 1991. **Architect:** Michael Hurdzan. **Season:** Year-round. **High:** April-Oct. **To obtain tee times:** Call up to 365 days in advance. **Miscellaneous:** Reduced fees (weekdays, twilight, juniors), range (grass), credit cards (MC, V, AE, D), BF, FF.
Notes: Ranked 13th in 1999 Best in State; 45th in 1996 America's Top 75 Affordable Courses.
Reader Comments: One tough course, a lot of carries over marshland ... Unbelievable muni ... Will kill you on windy days ... Best value in Ocean City ... Very organized, excellent scenic areas ... Best bang for your buck ... Every hole a different challenge ... The views are spectacular... Tough holes over water.

★★½ THE EASTON CLUB GOLF COURSE
PU-28449 Clubhouse Dr., Easton, 21601, Talbot County, (410)820-9800, (800)277-9800, 60 miles from Baltimore. **E-mail:** info@eastonclub.com. **Web:** www.eastonclub.com. **Facility Holes:** 18. **Yards:** 6,703/5,230. **Par:** 72/72. **Course Rating:** 72.3/70.2. **Slope:** 129/119. **Green Fee:** $34/$51. **Cart Fee:** $14/Person. **Walking Policy:** Walking at certain times. **Walkability:** 2. **Opened:** 1995. **Architect:** Robert Rauch. **Season:** Year-round. **High:** April-Oct. **To obtain tee times:** Call up to 14 days in advance. **Miscellaneous:** Reduced fees (twilight, juniors), range (grass/mats), credit cards (MC, V, D), BF, FF.

★★½ EISENHOWER GOLF COURSE
PU-1576 General Hwy., Crownsville, 21032, Anne Arundel County, (410)571-0973, 4 miles from Annapolis. **E-mail:** kleddy@eisenhowergolf.com. **Web:** www.eisenhowergolf.com. **Facility Holes:** 18. **Yards:** 6,659/4,884. **Par:** 71/70. **Course Rating:** 70.8/68.7. **Slope:** 122/115. **Green Fee:** $25/$30. **Cart Fee:** $13/Person. **Walking Policy:** Unrestricted walking. **Walkability:** 4. **Opened:** 1970. **Architect:** Edmund B. Ault. **Season:** Year-round. **High:** April-Oct. **To obtain tee times:** Call up to 7 days in advance. **Miscellaneous:** Reduced fees (twilight, seniors, juniors), range (mats), credit cards (MC, V, AE), BF, FF.

★★★½ ENTERPRISE GOLF COURSE
PU-2802 Enterprise Rd., Mitchellville, 20721, Prince George's County, (301)249-2040, 2 miles from Washington, DC. **Facility Holes:** 18. **Yards:** 6,586/5,157. **Par:** 72/72. **Course Rating:** 71.7/69.6. **Slope:** 128/114. **Green Fee:** $14/$30. **Cart Fee:** $24/Cart. **Walking Policy:** Walking at certain times. **Walkability:** 3. **Opened:** 1976. **Architect:** Dunovan & Assoc. **Season:** Year-round. **High:** March-Oct. **To obtain tee times:** Call golf shop. **Miscellaneous:** Reduced fees (weekdays, twilight, seniors, juniors), metal spikes, range (mats), credit cards (MC, V).
Reader Comments: One of the best conditioned public courses ... Lots of rounds, but management deals with crowds well. Fun test ... Would play again ... Fun course with good local feel.

★★½ FALLS ROAD GOLF CLUB
PU-10800 Falls Rd., Potomac, 20854, Montgomery County, (301)299-5156, 15 miles from Washington, DC. **E-mail:** jonlesage@pga.com. **Facility Holes:** 18. **Yards:** 6,257/5,476. **Par:** 71/75. **Course Rating:** 67.7/59.3. **Slope:** 120/111. **Green Fee:** $24/$29. **Cart Fee:** $27/Cart. **Walking Policy:** Unrestricted walking. **Walkability:** 2. **Opened:** 1955. **Architect:** Edward Ault. **Season:** Year-round. **To obtain tee times:** Call golf shop. **Miscellaneous:** Reduced fees (seniors, juniors), range (grass/mats), credit cards (MC, V, AE), BF, FF.

★★ FOREST PARK GOLF CLUB
PU-2900 Hillsdale Rd., Baltimore, 21207, Baltimore County, (410)448-4653. **Facility Holes:** 18. **Yards:** 6,127/4,824. **Par:** 71/71. **Course Rating:** 68.2/66.0. **Slope:** 116/100. **Green Fee:** $10. **Walking Policy:** Unrestricted walking. **Architect:** Alex (Nipper) Campbell. **Season:** Year-round. **High:** April-Oct. **To obtain tee times:** Call golf shop. **Miscellaneous:** Reduced fees (weekdays, twilight, seniors, juniors), metal spikes, credit cards (MC, V).

FREDERICK GOLF CLUB
PU-5519 South Renn Rd., Frederick, 21703, Frederick County, (301)846-0694, 45 miles from Baltimore. **Facility Holes:** 18. **Yards:** 5,160/3,985. **Par:** 69/69. **Course Rating:** 61.8/55.9. **Slope:** 100/98. **Green Fee:** $8/$12. **Cart Fee:** $19/Cart. **Walking Policy:** Unrestricted walking. **Walkability:** 2. **Opened:** 1997. **Architect:** R. Carels Milligan. **Season:** Year-round. **High:** April-Nov. **To obtain tee times:** Call golf shop. **Miscellaneous:** Reduced fees (weekdays, twilight, seniors), credit cards (MC, V), BF, FF.

★★½ GENEVA FARM GOLF CLUB
PU-217 Davis Rd., Street, 21154, Harford County, (410)452-8800, 30 miles from Baltimore. **Facility Holes:** 18. **Yards:** 6,450/5,394. **Par:** 72/73. **Course Rating:** 69.5/71.4. **Slope:** 120/116. **Green Fee:** $30/$35. **Cart Fee:** Included in green fee. **Walking Policy:** Unrestricted walking. **Walkability:** 3. **Opened:** 1990. **Architect:** Bob Elder. **Season:** Year-round. **High:** April-Sept. **To obtain tee times:** Call golf shop. **Miscellaneous:** Range (grass), credit cards (MC, V).

★★★½ GLADE VALLEY GOLF CLUB
PU-10502 Glade Rd., Walkersville, 21793, Frederick County, (301)898-5555, 4 miles from Frederick. **Facility Holes:** 18. **Yards:** 6,787/4,953. **Par:** 72/72. **Course Rating:** 72.5/67.4. **Slope:** 123/110. **Green Fee:** $20/$43. **Cart Fee:** Included in green fee. **Walking Policy:** Walking at certain times. **Walkability:** 2. **Opened:** 1991. **Architect:** Bob Elder. **Season:** Year-round. **High:** April-Nov. **To obtain tee times:** Call golf shop. **Miscellaneous:** Reduced fees (twilight, seniors, juniors), range (grass/mats), credit cards (MC, V).
Reader Comments: Friendly staff, good condition … Excellent value, unique holes … Upscale conditions without the high price … Good value mix of long and short, tight and open … Fast greens.

★★★ GLENN DALE GOLF CLUB
PU-11501 Old Prospect Hill Rd., Glenn Dale, 20769, Prince George's County, (301)262-1166, 15 miles from Washington, DC. **E-mail:** gdgc@erols.com. **Facility Holes:** 18. **Yards:** 6,282/4,809. **Par:** 70/70. **Course Rating:** 70.0/67.2. **Slope:** 115/107. **Green Fee:** $25/$34. **Cart Fee:** $13/Cart. **Walking Policy:** Walking at certain times. **Walkability:** 3. **Opened:** 1955. **Architect:** George W. Cobb. **Season:** Year-round. **High:** April-Oct. **To obtain tee times:** Call up to 7 days in advance. **Miscellaneous:** Reduced fees (twilight, seniors, juniors), range (mats), credit cards (MC, V), BF, FF.
Reader Comments: Good course, very hilly … Short, tight, iron play should be sharp here … Out of the way, but a good deal … Tough greens, they slope back to front.

GOBBLERS KNOB GOLF COURSE
PU-16302 Conda Way, Rawlings, 21557, Allegany County, (301)729-4000. **Facility Holes:** 18. **Yards:** 6,337/5,004. **Par:** 70/70. **Green Fee:** $19/$23. **Opened:** 1991. **Architect:** Bill Ward. **Season:** April-Oct. **To obtain tee times:** Call golf shop.

★★★½ THE GOLF CLUB AT WISP
R-296 Marsh Hill Rd., P.O. Box 629, McHenry, 21541, Garrett County, (301)387-4911, 90 miles from Pittsburgh, PA. **E-mail:** wispinfo@gcnet. **Web:** www.gcnet.net/wisp. **Facility Holes:** 18. **Yards:** 6,911/5,166. **Par:** 72/72. **Course Rating:** 73.7/75.8. **Slope:** 141/131. **Green Fee:** $48/$65. **Cart Fee:** Included in green fee. **Walking Policy:** Walking at certain times. **Walkability:** 4. **Opened:** 1979. **Architect:** Dominic Palombo. **Season:** April-Nov. **High:** June-Sept. **To obtain tee times:** Call golf shop. **Miscellaneous:** Reduced fees (guests, twilight), range (grass/mats), lodging (167 rooms), credit cards (MC, V, AE, D), BF, FF.
Reader Comments: Unknown gem, always in great shape … Excellent, tight mountain course … Vistas, views from mountainside tees … Very tough, hilly, long, tight, long water carries.

★★½ GREAT HOPE GOLF COURSE
PU-8380 Crisfield Hwy., Westover, 21871, Somerset County, (410)651-5900, (800)537-8009, 20 miles from Salisbury. **E-mail:** reroute18@hotmail.com. **Web:** www.greathopegolf.com. **Facility Holes:** 18. **Yards:** 7,047/5,204. **Par:** 72/72. **Course Rating:** 72.8/68.5. **Slope:** 125/112. **Green Fee:** $15/$29. **Cart Fee:** $12/Person. **Walking Policy:** Unrestricted walking. **Walkability:** 1. **Opened:** 1995. **Architect:** Michael Hurdzan. **Season:** Year-round. **High:** March-Nov. **To obtain tee times:** Call up to 365 days in advance. **Miscellaneous:** Reduced fees (weekdays, guests, twilight, seniors, juniors), range (grass), credit cards (MC, V), BF, FF.

★★½ GREEN HILL YACHT & COUNTRY CLUB
SP-5473 Whitehaven Rd., Quantico, 21856, Wicomico County, (410)749-1605, (888)465-3855, 30 miles from Ocean City. **Web:** greenhillgolf.com. **Facility Holes:** 18. **Yards:** 6,800/5,600. **Par:** 72/72. **Course Rating:** 72.2/72.0. **Slope:** 126/126. **Green Fee:** $30/$69. **Cart Fee:** Included in green fee. **Walkability:** 2. **Opened:** 1927. **Architect:** Alfred H. Tull. **Season:** Year-round. **High:** June-Aug. **To obtain tee times:** Call golf shop. **Miscellaneous:** Reduced fees (weekdays), range (grass), credit cards (MC, V, AE).

★★★★ GREYSTONE GOLF COURSE
PU-2115 White Hall Rd., White Hall, 21161, Baltimore County, (410)887-1945, 25 miles from Baltimore. **E-mail:** greystone1@baltimoregolfing.com. **Web:** Baltimoregolfing.com. **Facility Holes:** 18. **Yards:** 6,925/4,800. **Par:** 72/72. **Course Rating:** 73.5/67.5. **Slope:** 139/112. **Green Fee:** $39/$64. **Cart Fee:** Included in green fee. **Walking Policy:** Unrestricted walking. **Walkability:** 5. **Opened:** 1997. **Architect:** Joe Lee. **Season:** Year-round. **To obtain tee times:** Call up to 7 days in advance. **Miscellaneous:** Reduced fees (weekdays, twilight, seniors, juniors), range (grass), credit cards (MC, V, AE, D), BF, FF.
Notes: Ranked 15th in 1999 Best in State.
Reader Comments: Fairways are amazing … An impressive, challenging layout, requires you to bring your "A" game … Overlooks a beautiful environment, very challenging course … Excellent service, fun to play … Awesome, beautiful, tough, fast greens.

GUNPOWDER GOLF CLUB
PU-14300 Gunpowder Rd., Laurel, 20707, Prince George's County, (301)725-4532, 15 miles from Washington, DC. **Facility Holes:** 18. **Yards:** 6,061/4,710. **Par:** 70/70. **Course Rating:** 67.3/64.8. **Slope:** 98/105. **Green Fee:** $9/$14. **Cart Fee:** $19/Cart. **Walking Policy:** Unrestricted walking. **Walkability:** 5. **Opened:** 1956. **Architect:** R. Carels Milligan. **Season:** Year-round. **High:** July-Aug. **To obtain tee times:** Call golf shop. **Miscellaneous:** Reduced fees (weekdays, twilight, seniors), credit cards (MC, V), FF.

HAGERSTOWN MUNICIPAL
PU-2 S. Cleveland Ave., Hagerstown, 21740, Washington County, (301)733-8630. **Facility Holes:** 18. **Yards:** 2,554/2,554. **Par:** 34/37. **Green Fee:** $8/$9. **Opened:** 1957. **Architect:** Frank Murray & Russell Roberts. **Season:** Year-round. **To obtain tee times:** Call golf shop. **Miscellaneous:** Metal spikes.

★★½ HAMPSHIRE GREENS GOLF CLUB
PU-616 Firestone Dr., Silver Spring, 20905, Montgomery County, (301)476-7999, 15 miles from Washington, DC. **Facility Holes:** 18. **Yards:** 6,815/5,048. **Par:** 72/72. **Course Rating:** 72.4/68.5. **Slope:** 129/114. **Green Fee:** $38/$59. **Cart Fee:** Included in green fee. **Walking Policy:** Mandatory carts. **Walkability:** 3. **Opened:** 1999. **Architect:** Lisa Maki. **Season:** Year-round. **High:** April-Oct. **To obtain tee times:** Call up to 14 days in advance. **Miscellaneous:** Range (grass/mats), credit cards (MC, V, AE), BF, FF.

★★½ HARBOURTOWNE GOLF RESORT & COUNTRY CLUB
R-Rt. 33 at Martingham Dr., St. Michaels, 21663, Talbot County, (410)745-5183, (800)446-9066, 75 miles from Baltimore. **Facility Holes:** 18. **Yards:** 6,320/5,036. **Par:** 70/71. **Course Rating:** 69.5/68.5. **Slope:** 120/113. **Green Fee:** $49. **Cart Fee:** $16/Person. **Walking Policy:** Mandatory carts. **Walkability:** 3. **Opened:** 1971. **Architect:** Pete Dye/Roy Dye. **Season:** Year-round. **To obtain tee times:** Call golf shop. **Miscellaneous:** Reduced fees (guests), metal spikes, range (grass), lodging (111 rooms), credit cards (MC, V, AE, D), BF, FF.

★★★★ HOG NECK GOLF COURSE
PU-10142 Old Cordova Rd., Easton, 21601, Talbot County, (410)822-6079, (800)200-1790, 50 miles from Baltimore. **Facility Holes:** 18. **Yards:** 7,000/5,500. **Par:** 72/72. **Course Rating:** 73.8/71.3. **Slope:** 131/125. **Green Fee:** $36/$46. **Cart Fee:** $14/Person. **Walking Policy:** Unrestricted walking. **Walkability:** 2. **Opened:** 1976. **Architect:** Lindsay Ervin. **Season:** Feb.-Dec. **High:** April-Oct. **To obtain tee times:** Call golf shop. **Miscellaneous:** Reduced fees (weekdays, twilight, juniors), range (mats), credit cards (MC, V), BF, FF. **Notes:** Ranked 10th in 1999 Best in State. **Reader Comments:** Day in, day out, a great track … Best course on eastern shore! Don't tell anyone … Generous greens … Front 9, short, back 9, long, tight, 2 different courses … The windswept front, combined with the tight trees on the back, along with water everywhere will empty your bag, and your head.

★★½ LAKE ARBOR COUNTRY CLUB
SP-1401 Golf Course Dr., Mitchellville, 20721, Prince George's County, (301)336-7771, 10 miles from Washington, DC. **Facility Holes:** 18. **Yards:** 6,359/5,976. **Par:** 71/71. **Course Rating:** 73.1/71.2. **Slope:** 127/123. **Green Fee:** $25/$45. **Cart Fee:** Included in green fee. **Walking Policy:** Walking at certain times. **Walkability:** 3. **Opened:** 1968. **Season:** Year-round. **High:** March-Oct. **To obtain tee times:** Call up to 7 days in advance. **Miscellaneous:** Reduced fees (seniors, juniors), credit cards (MC, V, AE).

★★★ LAYTONSVILLE GOLF COURSE
PU-7130 Dorsey Rd., Laytonsville, 20882, Montgomery County, (301)948-5288, 18 miles from Washington, DC. **Web:** www.montgomerycountygolf.com. **Facility Holes:** 18. **Yards:** 6,311/5,439. **Par:** 70/73. **Course Rating:** 69.8/71.4. **Slope:** 117/113. **Green Fee:** $21/$28. **Cart Fee:** $24/Cart. **Walking Policy:** Unrestricted walking. **Walkability:** 2. **Opened:** 1973. **Architect:** Roger Peacock. **Season:** Year-round. **High:** April-Sept. **To obtain tee times:** Call golf shop. **Miscellaneous:** Reduced fees (seniors, juniors), range (grass/mats), credit cards (MC, V). **Reader Comments:** Old, much improved course. New clubhouse is nice … Respectable muni … Good for practice … Short, mostly open, good course to learn game … Friendly people, forgiving course … Flat, wide open, short.

★★★ THE LINKS AT CHALLEDON
PU-6166 Challedon Circle, Mount Airy, 21771, Carroll County, (301)829-3000, 18 miles from Baltimore. **Facility Holes:** 18. **Yards:** 6,730/5,355. **Par:** 72/72. **Course Rating:** 71.3/70.7. **Slope:** 124/122. **Green Fee:** $45/$60. **Cart Fee:** Included in green fee. **Walking Policy:** Walking at certain times. **Walkability:** 3. **Opened:** 1996. **Architect:** Brian Ault. **Season:** Year-round. **To obtain tee times:** Call up to 7 days in advance. **Miscellaneous:** Reduced fees (weekdays, twilight,

seniors, juniors), range (grass/mats), credit cards (MC, V, AE), BF, FF.
Reader Comments: Will improve as it matures … Great service and amenities … Watch for OB stakes on half of the holes … Scenic, links-style layout … Greens and fairways are well-groomed … The 4th hole is a terrific par 4.

★★★★½ THE LINKS AT LIGHTHOUSE SOUND GOLF CLUB *Service*
PU-12723 St. Martin's Neck Rd., Bishopville, 21813, Worcester County, (410)352-5767, (888)554-4557, 2 miles from Ocean City. **E-mail:** ruarkgolf@aol.com. **Web:** www.lighthous-esound.com. **Facility Holes:** 18. **Yards:** 7,031/4,553. **Par:** 72/72. **Course Rating:** 73.3/67.1. **Slope:** 144/107. **Green Fee:** $85/$135. **Cart Fee:** Included in green fee. **Walking Policy:** Unrestricted walking. **Walkability:** 3. **Opened:** 2000. **Architect:** Arthur Hills. **Season:** Year-round. **High:** April-Oct. **To obtain tee times:** Call up to 365 days in advance. **Miscellaneous:** Reduced fees (twilight), range (grass), credit cards (MC, V, AE, D), BF, FF.
Notes: Ranked 5th in 2001 Best in State.
Reader Comments: Great views of Ocean City from the course … Greens are huge & hard … Tough track in windy conditions … All four of the par 3s are tough … Dramatic holes and use of wetlands environment.

★★★★ LITTLE BENNETT GOLF COURSE
PU-25900 Prescott Rd., Clarksburg, 20871, Montgomery County, (301)253-1515, (800)366-2012, 15 miles from Frederick. **E-mail:** lcarroll@mncppc.state.md.us. **Facility Holes:** 18. **Yards:** 6,706/4,921. **Par:** 72/72. **Course Rating:** 72.9/68.2. **Slope:** 133/115. **Green Fee:** $32/$40. **Cart Fee:** $12/Person. **Walking Policy:** Unrestricted walking. **Walkability:** 5. **Opened:** 1994. **Architect:** Hurdzan Design Group. **Season:** Year-round. **High:** May-Oct. **To obtain tee times:** Call golf shop. **Miscellaneous:** Reduced fees (seniors, juniors), range (grass), credit cards (MC, V), BF, FF.
Reader Comments: Major elevation change … Beautiful views, but hilly … Two of the 'deepest' par 3s in the state, and count your hang-time.

LONGVIEW GOLF CLUB
PU-1 Cardigan Rd., Timonium, 21093, Baltimore County, (410)628-6362, 12 miles from Baltimore. **Web:** www.baltimoregolfing.com. **Facility Holes:** 18. **Yards:** 6,038/5,394. **Par:** 70/71. **Course Rating:** 68.2/66.6. **Slope:** 110/105. **Green Fee:** $16/$18. **Cart Fee:** $11/Person. **Walking Policy:** Unrestricted walking. **Walkability:** 1. **Opened:** 1964. **Architect:** Ed Ault. **Season:** Year-round. **High:** March-Oct. **To obtain tee times:** Call up to 7 days in advance. **Miscellaneous:** Reduced fees (weekdays, twilight, seniors, juniors), range (grass/mats), credit cards (MC, V, AE, D), BF, FF.

★★ MAPLE RUN GOLF COURSE
PU-13610-A Moser Rd., Thurmont, 21788, Frederick County, (301)271-7870, 15 miles from Frederick. **Facility Holes:** 18. **Yards:** 6,553/4,822. **Par:** 72/72. **Course Rating:** 71.2/66.1. **Slope:** 128/114. **Green Fee:** $16/$25. **Cart Fee:** $10/Person. **Walking Policy:** Unrestricted walking. **Walkability:** 2. **Opened:** 1992. **Architect:** Russell Moser/Joe Moser. **Season:** Year-round. **High:** April-Oct. **To obtain tee times:** Call up to 10 days in advance. **Miscellaneous:** Reduced fees (weekdays, twilight, seniors, juniors), range (mats), credit cards (MC, V, D), FF.

MAPLEHURST COUNTRY CLUB
SP-Grant Ave., Frostburg, 21532, Allegany County, (301)689-6602, 60 miles from Hagerston. **E-mail:** flowersr@prodigy.net. **Facility Holes:** 18. **Yards:** 6,677/5,506. **Par:** 72/74. **Course Rating:** 70.8/72.4. **Slope:** 126/129. **Green Fee:** $30. **Cart Fee:** $11/Person. **Walking Policy:** Unrestricted walking. **Walkability:** 4. **Opened:** 1955. **Season:** April-Nov. **High:** June-Sept. **To obtain tee times:** Call up to 7 days in advance. **Miscellaneous:** Reduced fees (weekdays), range (grass), credit cards (MC, V, D), BF, FF.

★★ MARLBOROUGH GOLF CLUB
SP-4750 John Rodgers Blvd., Upper Marlboro, 20772, Prince George's County, (301)952-1350, (888)218-8463, 20 miles from Washington, DC. **Facility Holes:** 18. **Yards:** 6,057/5,052. **Par:** 71/71. **Course Rating:** 69.0/69.5. **Slope:** 124/120. **Green Fee:** $20/$30. **Cart Fee:** $15/Person. **Walking Policy:** Walking at certain times. **Walkability:** 1. **Opened:** 1976. **Architect:** Algie Pulley. **Season:** Year-round. **High:** March-Nov. **To obtain tee times:** Call up to 7 days in advance. **Miscellaneous:** Reduced fees (weekdays, twilight), range (mats), credit cards (MC, V), BF, FF.

★★★½ MOUNT PLEASANT GOLF CLUB
PU-6001 Hillen Rd., Baltimore, 21239, Baltimore County, (410)254-5100. **Web:** www.bmgc-golf.com. **Facility Holes:** 18. **Yards:** 6,728/5,294. **Par:** 71/73. **Course Rating:** 71.8/69.4. **Slope:** 119/118. **Green Fee:** $16/$19. **Cart Fee:** Included in green fee. **Walking Policy:** Unrestricted walking. **Walkability:** 4. **Opened:** 1933. **Architect:** Gus Hook. **Season:** Year-round. **To obtain tee times:** Call golf shop. **Miscellaneous:** Reduced fees (weekdays, twilight, seniors, juniors),

metal spikes, credit cards (MC, V), BF, FF.
Reader Comments: Great value, old PGA stop in early '60s ... Incredible design, another hidden gem, like Bethpage, it too is awaiting it's long overdue rebirth, recognition ... Hilly, challenging, great greens ... Classic old style; still tough.

MOUNTAIN BRANCH GOLF COURSE
SP-1827 Mountain Rd., Joppa, 21085, Harford County, (410)836-9600, (877)588-1492, 12 miles from Baltimore. **Web:** mountainbranch.com. **Facility Holes:** 18. **Yards:** 6,969/5,279. **Par:** 72/72. **Course Rating:** 74.6. **Slope:** 138. **Green Fee:** $60/$92. **Cart Fee:** Included in green fee. **Walking Policy:** Unrestricted walking. **Walkability:** 3. **Opened:** 2001. **Architect:** Jeff Matthai/Davis Sezna. **Season:** Year-round. **High:** April-Oct. **To obtain tee times:** Call up to 14 days in advance. **Miscellaneous:** Reduced fees (twilight), range (grass/mats), credit cards (MC, V, AE, D), BF, FF.

★★ NASSAWANGO COUNTRY CLUB
SP-3940 Nassawango Rd., Snow Hill, 21863, Worcester County, (410)632-3114, 18 miles from Salisbury. **Facility Holes:** 18. **Yards:** 6,644/5,760. **Par:** 72/73. **Course Rating:** 70.2/72.1. **Slope:** 125/125. **Green Fee:** $27. **Cart Fee:** $12/Person. **Walkability:** 3. **Opened:** 1970. **Architect:** Russell Roberts. **Season:** Year-round. **High:** May-Oct. **To obtain tee times:** Call golf shop. **Miscellaneous:** Metal spikes, credit cards (MC, V).

★★★ NEEDWOOD GOLF COURSE
PU-6724 Needwood Rd., Derwood, 20855, Montgomery County, (301)948-1075, 22 miles from Washington, DC. **Facility Holes:** 27. **Yards:** 6,254/5,112. **Par:** 70/72. **Course Rating:** 69.1/69.2. **Slope:** 113/105. **Green Fee:** $26/$31. **Cart Fee:** $24/Cart. **Walking Policy:** Unrestricted walking. **Walkability:** 3. **Opened:** 1969. **Architect:** Lindsay Ervin. **Season:** Year-round. **To obtain tee times:** Call golf shop. **Miscellaneous:** Reduced fees (weekdays, seniors, juniors), range (mats), credit cards (MC, V), BF, FF.
Reader Comments: Excellent 18th hole ... Beautiful course ... Nice short public course ... Wide open, regular course.
Special Notes: Also has a 9-hole executive course.

NORTHWEST PARK GOLF COURSE
PU-15701 Layhill Rd., Wheaton, 20906, Montgomery County, (301)598-6100, 15 miles from Washington, DC. **E-mail:** www.insite.mncppc-mc.org. **Facility Holes:** 27. **Cart Fee:** $12/Person. **Walking Policy:** Unrestricted walking. **Walkability:** 3. **Opened:** 1964. **Architect:** Edmund B. Ault/Russell Roberts. **Season:** Year-round. **Miscellaneous:** Reduced fees (weekdays, seniors, juniors), range (mats), credit cards (MC, V).
★★★½ **18-HOLE COURSE** (18)
Yards: 7,376/6,184. **Par:** 72/74. **Course Rating:** 74.0/74.5. **Slope:** 122/126. **Green Fee:** $22/$31. **High:** April-Oct. **Tee times:** Call up to 6 days in advance. **Miscellaneous:** BF, FF.
Reader Comments: Long course ... Long, many par 4s to reach, new sprinkling system should help condition ... Great 18th hole ... Hit it hard ... Hit your long clubs.
INSIDE NINE (9)
Yards: 2,687/2,480. **Par:** 34/34. **Course Rating:** 31.2/32.8. **Slope:** 51/53. **Green Fee:** $22/$27. **High:** June-Aug. **To obtain tee times:** Call golf shop.

★★½ NUTTERS CROSSING GOLF CLUB
SP-30287 S. Hampton Bridge Rd., Salisbury, 21804, Wicomico County, (410)860-4653. **Web:** www.nutterscrossing.com. **Facility Holes:** 18. **Yards:** 6,033/4,800. **Par:** 70/70. **Course Rating:** 67.1/66.5. **Slope:** 115/110. **Green Fee:** $18/$42. **Cart Fee:** $12/Person. **Walking Policy:** Walking at certain times. **Walkability:** 3. **Opened:** 1991. **Architect:** Ault/Clark. **Season:** Year-round. **High:** April-Oct. **To obtain tee times:** Call golf shop. **Miscellaneous:** Reduced fees (twilight), range (grass), credit cards (MC, V).

OAKLAND GOLF CLUB
SP-433 N. Bradley Lane, Oakland, 21550, Garrett County, (301)334-3883. **Facility Holes:** 18. **Yards:** 6,417/5,226. **Par:** 71/71. **Course Rating:** 70.1/73.0. **Slope:** 117/118. **Green Fee:** $22/$34. **Cart Fee:** $15/Person. **Walking Policy:** Walking at certain times. **Walkability:** 4. **Architect:** Ault/Clark. **High:** March-Nov. **To obtain tee times:** Call golf shop. **Miscellaneous:** Reduced fees (weekdays), credit cards (MC, V), BF, FF.

★★½ OAKMONT GREEN GOLF COURSE
SP-2290 Golf View Lane, Hampstead, 21074, Carroll County, (410)374-1500, 25 miles from Baltimore. **Facility Holes:** 18. **Yards:** 6,600/5,139. **Par:** 72/72. **Course Rating:** 71.4/69.3. **Slope:** 122/116. **Green Fee:** $16/$26. **Cart Fee:** $10/Person. **Walking Policy:** Unrestricted walking. **Walkability:** 3. **Opened:** 1991. **Architect:** Leeland Snyder. **Season:** March-Dec. **High:** May-Sept. **To obtain tee times:** Call golf shop. **Miscellaneous:** Reduced fees (weekdays, twilight, seniors, juniors), metal spikes, range (grass/mats), credit cards (MC, V).

MARYLAND

OCEAN CITY GOLF & YACHT CLUB
R-11401 Country Club Dr., Berlin, 21811, Worcester County, (410)641-1779, (800)442-3570, 5 miles from Ocean City. **Facility Holes:** 36. **Cart Fee:** $21/Person. **Walking Policy:** Walking at certain times. **Walkability:** 1. **Season:** Year-round. **High:** April-Oct. **To obtain tee times:** Call golf shop. **Miscellaneous:** Reduced fees (weekdays, twilight, juniors), range (grass/mats), credit cards (MC, V), BF, FF.

★★★★ **NEWPORT BAY COURSE** (18)
Yards: 6,526/5,396. **Par:** 72/72. **Course Rating:** 71.7/71.3. **Slope:** 121/119. **Green Fee:** $13/$65. **Opened:** 1998. **Architect:** Russell Roberts/Lester George.
Reader Comments: Beautiful views … If they hung Spanish moss in the trees, you'd swear you were playing a low-country course in Myrtle Beach. The marsh holes are every bit as good as any in Myrtle … Great finishing hole … Scenic bay views & marshland, tough if windy … Great par 3s.

★★★ **SEASIDE COURSE** (18)
Yards: 6,520/5,848. **Par:** 73/75. **Course Rating:** 70.9/73.1. **Slope:** 115/119. **Green Fee:** $13/$49. **Opened:** 1959. **Architect:** William Gordon/David Gordon/Russell Robe.
Reader Comments: Private feel, very quiet, holes were isolated from each other … Best fairways & greens in the area … Great view of ocean.

★★★½ **P.B. DYE GOLF CLUB**
PU-9526 Dr. Perry Rd., Ijamsville, 21754, Frederick County, (301)607-4653, 10 miles from Frederick. **Web:** www.pbdyegolf.com. **Facility Holes:** 18. **Yards:** 7,036/5,391. **Par:** 72/73. **Course Rating:** 74.6/71.5. **Slope:** 141/129. **Green Fee:** $49/$89. **Cart Fee:** Included in green fee. **Walking Policy:** Unrestricted walking. **Walkability:** 3. **Opened:** 1999. **Architect:** P.B. Dye. **Season:** Year-round. **High:** April-Oct. **To obtain tee times:** Call up to 14 days in advance. **Miscellaneous:** Reduced fees (weekdays, twilight, juniors), range (grass/mats), credit cards (MC, V, AE), BF, FF.
Notes: Ranked 15th in 2001 Best in State.
Reader Comments: Great layout, challenging approach shots, tough greens, fun course to play if you like shaping your shots … Greens difficult … Fun slopes on greens … Keeps you thinking.

★★½ **PATUXENT GREENS COUNTRY CLUB**
SP-14415 Greenview Dr., Laurel, 20708, Prince George's County, (301)776-5533, 15 miles from Baltimore. **E-mail:** aczajka@mggi.com. **Facility Holes:** 18. **Yards:** 6,294/5,279. **Par:** 71/71. **Course Rating:** 71.1/70.1. **Slope:** 131/117. **Green Fee:** $28/$54. **Cart Fee:** Included in green fee. **Walking Policy:** Mandatory carts. **Walkability:** 1. **Opened:** 1970. **Architect:** George Cobb/Buddy Loving. **Season:** Year-round. **To obtain tee times:** Call up to 7 days in advance. **Miscellaneous:** Reduced fees (weekdays, twilight), credit cards (MC, V), BF, FF.

★★★½ **PINE RIDGE GOLF COURSE**
PU-2101 Dulaney Valley Rd., Lutherville, 21093, Baltimore County, (410)252-1408, 15 miles from Baltimore. **Facility Holes:** 18. **Yards:** 6,820/5,460. **Par:** 72/72. **Course Rating:** 71.9/71.3. **Slope:** 123/119. **Green Fee:** $21/$22. **Cart Fee:** Included in green fee. **Walking Policy:** Unrestricted walking. **Walkability:** 3. **Opened:** 1958. **Architect:** Gus Hook. **Season:** Year-round. **To obtain tee times:** Call up to 14 days in advance. **Miscellaneous:** Reduced fees (weekdays, twilight, seniors, juniors), metal spikes, range (mats), credit cards (MC, V), BF, FF.
Reader Comments: Great views of local river reservoir … Unbelievable views, every hole totally private from the others … Scenic and challenging … Lot of dogleg lefts, fun … Leave your driver home, target golf.

★★½ **POOLESVILLE GOLF COURSE**
PU-16601 W. Willard Rd, Poolesville, 20837, Montgomery County, (301)428-8143, 25 miles from Washington, DC. **Facility Holes:** 18. **Yards:** 6,811/5,521. **Par:** 71/73. **Course Rating:** 72.3/71.4. **Slope:** 123/118. **Green Fee:** $24/$28. **Cart Fee:** $28/Cart. **Walking Policy:** Unrestricted walking. **Walkability:** 2. **Opened:** 1959. **Architect:** Edmund B. Ault/Al Jamison. **Season:** Year-round. **To obtain tee times:** Call up to 7 days in advance. **Miscellaneous:** Reduced fees (seniors, juniors), range (grass/mats), credit cards (MC, V, AE), BF, FF.

QUEENSTOWN HARBOR GOLF LINKS
PU-310 Links Lane, Queenstown, 21658, Queen Anne's County, (410)827-6611, (800)827-5257, 45 miles from Baltimore. **Web:** www.mdgolf.com. **Facility Holes:** 36. **Cart Fee:** Included in green fee. **Walking Policy:** Unrestricted walking. **Walkability:** 2. **Opened:** 1991. **Architect:** Lindsay Ervin. **Season:** Year-round. **High:** April-Oct. **To obtain tee times:** Call up to 10 days in advance. **Miscellaneous:** Reduced fees (weekdays, twilight, seniors, juniors), metal spikes, range (grass/mats), credit cards (MC, V, AE, D), BF, FF.

★★★★ **LAKES COURSE** (18)
Yards: 6,537/4,576. **Par:** 71/71. **Course Rating:** 71.0/66.6. **Slope:** 124/111. **Green Fee:** $25/$68.
Notes: Ranked 11th in 1999 Best in State.

MARYLAND

Reader Comments: Great greens … Great hazards … Challenging holes … Great course, good service … Very scenic & well kept … Well run, some nice sights and wildlife … Both courses are nice, but tough if you don't keep it in play …Very scenic.

★★★★ RIVER COURSE (18)
Yards: 7,110/5,026. Par: 72/72. Course Rating: 74.2/69.0. Slope: 138/123. Green Fee: $35/$89.
Notes: Ranked 11th in 2001 Best in State.
Reader Comments: Scenic, good golf, enjoyable day, good service … Incredible water views & birds & deer! Great staff … In excellent condition … Greens always in great condition … Tough if you don't keep it in play … One of the best in state.

★★★½ REDGATE MUNICIPAL GOLF COURSE
PU-14500 Avery Rd., Rockville, 20853, Montgomery County, (301)309-3055, 10 miles from Washington, DC. Facility Holes: 18. Yards: 6,432/5,271. Par: 71/71. Course Rating: 71.7/70.2. Slope: 131/121. Green Fee: $26/$31. Cart Fee: $25/Cart. Walking Policy: Unrestricted walking. Walkability: 4. Opened: 1974. Architect: Thurman Donovan. Season: Year-round. High: April-Nov. To obtain tee times: Call up to 7 days in advance. Miscellaneous: Reduced fees (weekdays, seniors, juniors), range (grass/mats), credit cards (MC, V), BF, FF.
Reader Comments: Hilly, tight, but fun to play … Better known as 'Red-Badge' to the locals who know this course can test the best … A real sleeper… One of the best par 5s I've played … Beautiful city course, used every club.

★★★ RIVER DOWNS GOLFERS' CLUB
SP-1900 River Downs Dr., Finksburg, 21048, Carroll County, (410)526-2000, (800)518-7337, 30 miles from Baltimore. Facility Holes: 18. Yards: 6,873/5,003. Par: 72/72. Course Rating: 74.2/70.4. Slope: 135/122. Green Fee: $35/$65. Cart Fee: Included in green fee. Walking Policy: Mandatory carts. Walkability: 4. Opened: 1995. Architect: Arthur Hills. Season: Year-round. High: March-Oct. To obtain tee times: Call up to 7 days in advance. Miscellaneous: Reduced fees (weekdays, twilight), range (grass), credit cards (MC, V, AE), BF, FF.
Reader Comments: Good value for the $ … High handicappers beware, mistakes are punished … Very hilly, some holes wide open, wetlands and water come into play in several holes … Target golf, good use of elevation.

★★★½ RIVER RUN GOLF CLUB
R-11605 Masters Lane, Berlin, 21811, Worcester County, (410)641-7200, (800)733-7786, 110 miles from Washington, DC. E-mail: bpovr@aol. Web: riverrungolf.com. Facility Holes: 18. Yards: 6,705/5,002. Par: 71/71. Course Rating: 70.4/73.1. Slope: 128/117. Green Fee: $25/$89. Cart Fee: Included in green fee. Walking Policy: Walking at certain times. Walkability: 2. Opened: 1991. Architect: Gary Player. Season: Year-round. High: April-Oct. To obtain tee times: Call up to 180 days in advance. Miscellaneous: Reduced fees (weekdays, guests, twilight, seniors, juniors), range (grass), credit cards (MC, V, AE, D), BF, FF.
Reader Comments: Great challenging course … Front 9 is fairly open and the back 9 is tight through woods and a good amount of water … Excellent condition, great facility … A fair test & good for the ego … Have to play when going to Ocean City …Very playable … Nice greens.

★½ ROBIN DALE GOLF CLUB
PU-15851 McKendree Rd., Brandywine, 20613, Prince George's County, (301)372-8855, 22 miles from Washington, DC. E-mail: rdggp@aol.com. Facility Holes: 18. Yards: 6,667/5,888. Par: 72/73. Course Rating: 71.3/72.3. Slope: 123/117. Green Fee: $20/$39. Cart Fee: Included in green fee. Walking Policy: Walking at certain times. Walkability: 1. Opened: 1966. Season: Year-round. To obtain tee times: Call golf shop. Miscellaneous: Reduced fees (weekdays, twilight, seniors, juniors), range (mats), credit cards (MC, V, AE), BF, FF.

★★★ ROCKY GAP LODGE & GOLF RESORT
R-16710 Lakeview Dr. NE, Flintstone, 21530, Cumberland County, (391)784-8500, (800)724-0828. Web: www.rockygapresort.com. Facility Holes: 18. Yards: 7,006/5,212. Par: 72/72. Course Rating: 74.3/69.4. Slope: 141/123. Green Fee: $50/$65. Cart Fee: Included in green fee. Walking Policy: Mandatory carts. Walkability: 5. Opened: 1999. Architect: Jack Nicklaus. Season: Year-round. High: May-Oct. To obtain tee times: Call up to 14 days in advance. Miscellaneous: Reduced fees (guests, twilight, seniors, juniors), range (grass/mats), lodging (220 rooms), credit cards (MC, V, AE, D), BF, FF.
Reader Comments: The front 9 was a treat, very challenging … Outstanding course, spectacular scenery … Great elevation changes … Used every club in my bag.

★★★½ ROCKY POINT GOLF COURSE
PU-1935 Back River Neck Rd., Essex, 21221, Baltimore County, (410)391-2906, (888)246-5384, 9 miles from Baltimore. E-mail: rocky1@baltimoregolfing.com. Web: www.baltimore-county.com. Facility Holes: 18. Yards: 6,753/5,750. Par: 72/74. Course Rating: 72.3/73.1. Slope: 122/121. Green Fee: $15/$20. Cart Fee: $22/Cart. Walking Policy: Unrestricted walk-

ing. **Walkability:** 2. **Opened:** 1971. **Architect:** Russell Roberts. **Season:** Year-round. **High:** May-Aug. **To obtain tee times:** Call up to 10 days in advance. **Miscellaneous:** Reduced fees (weekdays, twilight, seniors, juniors), range (grass/mats), credit cards (MC, V, AE, D), BF, FF.
Reader Comments: Great greens … Overlooks a beautiful lake, very peaceful and comforting, very challenging.

RUGGLES GOLF COURSE
M-Bldg. 5600 Tank Rd., Aberdeen, 21005, Harford County, (410)671-2213, 25 miles from Baltimore. **Facility Holes:** 36. **Season:** Year-round. **To obtain tee times:** Call golf shop.
EDGEWOOD COURSE (9)
Yards: 2,940/2,750. **Par:** 35/35. **Course Rating:** 66.6/66.6. **Slope:** 112/112. **Green Fee:** $12/$13. **Opened:** 1921.
PLUMB POINT COURSE (9)
Yards: 2,557/2,557. **Par:** 34/36. **Green Fee:** $12/$13. **Walkability:** 1.
RUGGLES COURSE (18)
Yards: 7,044/5,546. **Par:** 72/72. **Course Rating:** 73.2/71.2. **Slope:** 0/125. **Green Fee:** $24/$28. **Opened:** 1965. **Architect:** Ed Ault.

★★★★½ RUM POINTE SEASIDE GOLF LINKS
R-7000 Rum Pointe Lane, Berlin, 21811, Worcester County, (410)629-1414, (888)809-4653, 7 miles from Ocean City. **E-mail:** Ruarkgolf@aol.com. **Web:** www.rumpointe.com. **Facility Holes:** 18. **Yards:** 7,001/5,276. **Par:** 72/72. **Course Rating:** 72.6/70.3. **Slope:** 122/120. **Green Fee:** $30/$99. **Cart Fee:** $12/Person. **Walking Policy:** Unrestricted walking. **Walkability:** 3. **Opened:** 1997. **Architect:** Pete Dye/P.B. Dye. **Season:** Year-round. **High:** April-Oct. **To obtain tee times:** Call up to 365 days in advance. **Miscellaneous:** Reduced fees (weekdays, guests, twilight, juniors), range (grass), lodging (1 rooms), credit cards (MC, V, AE, D), BF, FF.
Reader Comments: Try reaching any of the par 4s near the bay in regulation if the wind is even just puffing a little … Links style… A great finishing hole … Numerous holes played beside the bay …Water holes at 9, 18 are spectacular … No. 16 impossible in the wind.

★★★★ SOUTH RIVER GOLF LINKS
PU-3451 Solomon's Island Rd., Edgewater, 21037, Anne Arundel County, (410)798-5865, (800)767-4837, 4 miles from Annapolis. **E-mail:** bedwards@mdgolf.com. **Web:** www.mdgolf.com. **Facility Holes:** 18. **Yards:** 6,723/4,935. **Par:** 72/72. **Course Rating:** 71.8/66.9. **Slope:** 133/115. **Green Fee:** $30/$65. **Cart Fee:** Included in green fee. **Walking Policy:** Unrestricted walking. **Walkability:** 4. **Opened:** 1996. **Architect:** Brian Ault. **Season:** Year-round. **High:** May-Sept. **To obtain tee times:** Call golf shop. **Miscellaneous:** Reduced fees (twilight, seniors, juniors), metal spikes, range (mats), credit cards (MC, V, AE).
Notes: Ranked 10th in 2001 Best in State.
Reader Comments: Very good, tough … Homes are as pretty as the course … Tough, manicured course, bring balls … Use all clubs in bag.

★★★★ SWAN POINT GOLF YACHT & COUNTRY CLUB
SP-11550 Swan Point Blvd., Issue, 20645, Charles County, (301)259-0047, 50 miles from Washington, DC. **E-mail:** joey.spyccgolfpro@verison.net. **Facility Holes:** 18. **Yards:** 6,761/5,009. **Par:** 72/72. **Course Rating:** 72.5/69.3. **Slope:** 126/116. **Green Fee:** $37/$60. **Cart Fee:** $15/Cart. **Walking Policy:** Walking at certain times. **Walkability:** 2. **Opened:** 1990. **Architect:** Arthur Davis/Bob Cupp. **Season:** Year-round. **High:** April-Sept. **To obtain tee times:** Call up to 7 days in advance. **Miscellaneous:** Reduced fees (weekdays, twilight, seniors, juniors), range (grass/mats), credit cards (MC, V, BF, FF.
Reader Comments: An interesting blend of low-country and Pinehurst holes … Beautiful layout, best kept secret in Maryland … Punishing hazards & rough … A great little island green … Carries over scenic marshland and views of Potomac River … Playable for most skill levels.

★★★½ THE TIMBERS OF TROY
PU-6100 Marshalee Dr., Elkridge, 21075, Howard County, (410)313-4653, 10 miles from Baltimore. **Facility Holes:** 18. **Yards:** 6,652/4,926. **Par:** 72/72. **Course Rating:** 72.1/68.5. **Slope:** 134/115. **Green Fee:** $23/$37. **Cart Fee:** $13/Person. **Walking Policy:** Unrestricted walking. **Walkability:** 3. **Opened:** 1996. **Architect:** Brian Ault/Ken Killian. **Season:** Feb.-Dec. **High:** May-Sept. **To obtain tee times:** Call golf shop. **Miscellaneous:** Reduced fees (twilight), range (grass/mats), credit cards (MC, V, AE).
Reader Comments: Some forced carries, but very enjoyable … Not long but the greens will test the best of putters; position is key on this course … Narrow fairways surrounded by environmental area … Nice mix of holes, good short par 4s.

★★ TROTTERS GLEN GOLF COURSE
PU-16501 Batchellors Forest Rd., Olney, 20832, Montgomery County, (301)570-4951, 15 miles from Washington, DC. **Facility Holes:** 18. **Yards:** 6,220/4,983. **Par:** 72/72. **Course Rating:** 69.3/68.2. **Slope:** 113/111. **Green Fee:** $17/$29. **Cart Fee:** $13/Person. **Walking**

Policy: Unrestricted walking. **Walkability:** 1. **Opened:** 1993. **Architect:** Ault/Clark & Assoc. **Season:** Year-round. **High:** June-Aug. **To obtain tee times:** Call golf shop. **Miscellaneous:** Reduced fees (weekdays, twilight, seniors, juniors), range (grass/mats), credit cards (MC, V, AE).

TURF VALLEY RESORT

R-2700 Turf Valley Rd., Ellicott City, 21042, Howard County, (410)465-1504, (800)666-8873, 20 miles from Baltimore. **Web:** www.turfvalley.com. **Facility Holes:** 54. **Green Fee:** $37/$52. **Cart Fee:** $13/Person. **Walking Policy:** Walking at certain times. **Walkability:** 3. **Season:** Year-round. **High:** April-Oct. **To obtain tee times:** Call golf shop. **Miscellaneous:** Reduced fees (weekdays, guests, twilight), range (grass/mats), lodging (220 rooms), credit cards (MC, V, AE, D), BF, FF.

★★½ **EAST COURSE** (18)
Yards: 6,554/5,389. **Par:** 71/71. **Course Rating:** 71.1/71.6. **Slope:** 132/131. **Opened:** 1959. **Architect:** Edmund B. Ault/Al Jamison.

★★½ **NORTH COURSE** (18)
Yards: 6,586/5,466. **Par:** 71/71. **Course Rating:** 71.4/71.8. **Slope:** 126/124. **Opened:** 1959. **Architect:** Edmund B. Ault/Al Jamison.

★★ **SOUTH COURSE** (18)
Yards: 6,271/5,469. **Par:** 70/71. **Course Rating:** 70.3/72.3. **Slope:** 131/126. **Opened:** 1963. **Architect:** Edmund B. Ault.

★★★ TWIN SHIELDS GOLF CLUB

PU-2425 Roarty Rd., Dunkirk, 20754, Calvert County, (410)257-7800, 15 miles from Washington, DC. **Facility Holes:** 18. **Yards:** 6,527/5,318. **Par:** 70/71. **Course Rating:** 69.4/67.6. **Slope:** 119/113. **Green Fee:** $15/$32. **Cart Fee:** $26/Cart. **Walking Policy:** Walking at certain times. **Walkability:** 4. **Opened:** 1969. **Architect:** Roy Shields/Ray Shields. **Season:** Year-round. **High:** April-Sept. **To obtain tee times:** Call up to 7 days in advance. **Miscellaneous:** Reduced fees (twilight, seniors, juniors), range (grass/mats), BF, FF.
Reader Comments: Great beginner's course, very short ... Short, hilly; front 9 easy, back 9 more difficult ... Overall nice course ... Good, workman's course.

★★★½ UNIVERSITY OF MARYLAND GOLF COURSE

SP-Bldg. 166 University Blvd., College Park, 20740, Prince George's County, (301)403-4299, 5 miles from Washington, DC. **E-mail:** jmaynor@union.umd.edu. **Web:** www.terpgolf.umd.edu. **Facility Holes:** 18. **Yards:** 6,654/5,563. **Par:** 71/72. **Course Rating:** 71.6/71.7. **Slope:** 125/120. **Green Fee:** $17/$38. **Cart Fee:** $12/Person. **Walking Policy:** Walking at certain times. **Walkability:** 3. **Opened:** 1956. **Architect:** George W. Cobb. **Season:** Year-round. **High:** May-Sept. **To obtain tee times:** Call up to 5 days in advance. **Miscellaneous:** Reduced fees (weekdays, twilight, seniors, juniors), range (grass/mats), credit cards (MC, V, D), BF, FF.
Reader Comments: Great layout inside the beltway for DC. Only about 10 miles from Capitol Hill ... Tough course, old fashioned, trees, long ... Beautiful design, large greens ... Wide fairways ... Good shotmaker's course ... Demanding.

★★★★ WAKEFIELD VALLEY GOLF CLUB

SP-1000 Fenby Farm Rd., Westminster, 21158, Carroll County, (410)876-6662, 30 miles from Baltimore. **Web:** www.wakefieldvalley.com. **Facility Holes:** 27. **Green Fee:** $35/$42. **Cart Fee:** Included in green fee. **Walking Policy:** Walking at certain times. **Walkability:** 4. **Opened:** 1978. **Architect:** Wayne Weller/Russell Roberts. **Season:** Year-round. **High:** May-Oct. **To obtain tee times:** Call golf shop. **Miscellaneous:** Reduced fees (twilight, juniors), range (grass/mats), credit cards (MC, V, D).
GOLD/GREEN COURSE (18 combo)
Yards: 6,933/5,549. **Par:** 72/73. **Course Rating:** 74.4/73.3. **Slope:** 139/132.
GREEN/WHITE COURSE (18 combo)
Yards: 7,038/5,560. **Par:** 72/72. **Course Rating:** 74.1/72.5. **Slope:** 138/130.
WHITE/GOLD COURSE (18 combo)
Yards: 6,823/5,411. **Par:** 72/72. **Course Rating:** 73.6/71.8. **Slope:** 139/126.
Reader Comments: Our favorite, three interesting nines ... Greens very playable & fast, good accommodations ... Course is excellent with fantastic greens ... A tough course for mid-handicappers. Fast greens are a cornerstone ... 27 holes look easy but score high.

★★★★ WAVERLY WOODS GOLF CLUB

PU-2100 Warwick Way, Marriottsville, 21104, Howard County, (410)313-9182, 7 miles from Baltimore. **E-mail:** dkim@waverlywoods.com. **Web:** www.waverlywoods.com. **Facility Holes:** 18. **Yards:** 7,024/4,808. **Par:** 72/72. **Course Rating:** 73.1/67.8. **Slope:** 132/115. **Green Fee:** $38/$64. **Cart Fee:** $8/Person. **Walking Policy:** Unrestricted walking. **Walkability:** 3. **Opened:** 1998. **Architect:** Arthur Hills. **Season:** Year-round. **To obtain tee times:** Call up to 10 days in advance. **Miscellaneous:** Reduced fees (weekdays, twilight, seniors, juniors), range (grass), credit cards (MC, V, AE), BF, FF.

MARYLAND

Reader Comments: Combination of a thinking man's target course and a straight-up, brutal, beat-you-to-death-with-distance course ... Lightning fast greens and a layout that makes you use every club ... Not a bad hole to be found ... Challenging course fast greens ... Blind shots ... Good finishing holes.

★★★★½ **WHISKEY CREEK GOLF CLUB** *Service, Condition*
PU-4804 Whiskey Court, Ijamsville, 21754, Frederick County, (888)883-1174, 35 miles from Washington, DC. **E-mail:** whiskeycreek@crols. **Web:** whiskeycreekgolf.com. **Facility Holes:** 18. **Yards:** 7,001/5,296. **Par:** 72/72. **Course Rating:** 74.5/70.5. **Slope:** 137/121. **Green Fee:** $75/$90. **Cart Fee:** Included in green fee. **Walking Policy:** Unrestricted walking. **Walkability:** 5. **Opened:** 2000. **Architect:** JMP/Ernie Els. **Season:** March-Dec. **High:** May-Oct. **To obtain tee times:** Call up to 14 days in advance. **Miscellaneous:** Reduced fees (twilight), range (grass/mats), credit cards (MC, V, AE), BF, FF.
Reader Comments: A ruin in the middle of the fairway on the 18th hole ... Lots of variety ... Not a bad hole in bunch ... Spectacular views ... Very much a mountain-type course on the front side ... Great mix of interesting holes, no bad holes ... Felt like a VIP from the start.

★★½ **WHITE PLAINS REGIONAL PARK GOLF CLUB**
PU-1015 St. Charles Pkwy., White Plains, 20695, Charles County, (301)645-1300, 20 miles from Washington, DC. **Facility Holes:** 18. **Yards:** 6,277/5,365. **Par:** 70/70. **Course Rating:** 70.0/69.0. **Slope:** 125/122. **Green Fee:** $18/$23. **Cart Fee:** $24/Cart. **Walking Policy:** Unrestricted walking. **Walkability:** 3. **Opened:** 1974. **Architect:** J. Porter Gibson. **Season:** Year-round. **High:** April-Nov. **To obtain tee times:** Call up to 7 days in advance. **Miscellaneous:** Reduced fees (twilight, seniors, juniors), range (grass), credit cards (MC, V), BF, FF.

★★ **WICOMICO SHORES MUNICIPAL GOLF COURSE**
PU-Rt. 234, 20621 Aviation Yacht & CC Rd., Chaptico, 20621, St. Mary's County, (301)934-8191, 45 miles from Washington, DC. **Facility Holes:** 18. **Yards:** 6,482/5,460. **Par:** 72/72. **Course Rating:** 70.7/68.3. **Slope:** 120/120. **Green Fee:** $16/$20. **Cart Fee:** $12/Person. **Walking Policy:** Unrestricted walking. **Walkability:** 1. **Opened:** 1962. **Architect:** Edmund B. Ault. **Season:** Year-round. **High:** May-Sept. **To obtain tee times:** Call golf shop. **Miscellaneous:** Reduced fees (weekdays, twilight, seniors, juniors), metal spikes, range (grass/mats), credit cards (MC, V, AE).

★★★★ **THE WOODLANDS GOLF COURSE**
PU-2309 Ridge Rd., Woodlawn, 21244, Baltimore County, (410)887-1349, (888)246-5384, 18 miles from Baltimore. **Web:** www.baltimoregolfing.com. **Facility Holes:** 18. **Yards:** 7,014/5,452. **Par:** 72/72. **Course Rating:** 74.4/66.8. **Slope:** 143/122. **Green Fee:** $25/$59. **Cart Fee:** Included in green fee. **Walking Policy:** Unrestricted walking. **Walkability:** 4. **Opened:** 1998. **Architect:** Lindsay Ervin. **Season:** Year-round. **To obtain tee times:** Call up to 7 days in advance. **Miscellaneous:** Reduced fees (weekdays, twilight, seniors, juniors), range (mats), credit cards (MC, V, AE, D), BF, FF.
Reader Comments: Blind shots, small landing areas ... Beautiful, every hole separated by woods ... Undulations on greens.

★★★★ **WORTHINGTON MANOR GOLF CLUB**
PU-8329 Fingerboard Rd., Urbana, 21704, Frederick County, (301)874-5400, (888)987-2582, 30 miles from Washington, DC. **E-mail:** comments@worthingtonmanor.com. **Web:** www.worthingtonmanor.com. **Facility Holes:** 18. **Yards:** 7,014/5,206. **Par:** 72/72. **Course Rating:** 74.0/70.1. **Slope:** 143/116. **Green Fee:** $29/$64. **Cart Fee:** $11/Person. **Walking Policy:** Walking at certain times. **Walkability:** 4. **Opened:** 1998. **Architect:** Brian Ault/Eric Ault. **Season:** Year-round. **High:** March-Oct. **To obtain tee times:** Call golf shop. **Miscellaneous:** Reduced fees (weekdays, twilight, seniors, juniors), range (grass/mats), credit cards (MC, V, AE).
Reader Comments: Similar to links ... Beautiful & entertaining course, tough when windy ... Short, rolling terrain, greens severe ... Gorgeous greens that give you a great roll!! Great views ... The 18th split fairway makes for a wonderful close ... Toughest greens I've ever played.

★★½ **WORTHINGTON VALLEY COUNTRY CLUB**
SP-12425 Greenspring Ave., Owings Mills, 21117, Baltimore County, (410)356-8355, 12 miles from Baltimore. **Facility Holes:** 18. **Yards:** 6,346/5,760. **Par:** 70/75. **Course Rating:** 70.0/73.3. **Slope:** 119/110. **Green Fee:** $17/$24. **Cart Fee:** $10/Cart. **Walking Policy:** Unrestricted walking. **Walkability:** 3. **Opened:** 1954. **Architect:** James Duke. **Season:** Year-round. **High:** April-Oct. **To obtain tee times:** Call up to 7 days in advance. **Miscellaneous:** Reduced fees (twilight, seniors, juniors), range (grass), credit cards (MC, V), BF, FF.

YINGLING'S GOLF
PU-20220 Jefferson Blvd., Hagerstown, 21742, Washington County, (301)790-2494, 60 miles from Washington, DC. **Facility Holes:** 18. **Yards:** 1,729. **Par:** 54. **Green Fee:** $6/$7. **Walkability:** 2. **Opened:** 1973. **Season:** Year-round. **High:** March-Sept. **To obtain tee times:** Call golf shop. **Miscellaneous:** Reduced fees (seniors, juniors), range (grass/mats), BF, FF.

MASSACHUSETTS

★★★ ACUSHNET RIVER VALLEY GOLF COURSE
PU-685 Main St., Acushnet, 02743, Bristol County, (508)998-7777, 4 miles from New Bedford. **Web:** www.golfinmassachusetts.com. **Facility Holes:** 18. **Yards:** 6,807/5,099. **Par:** 72/72. **Course Rating:** 72.5/68.4. **Slope:** 124/115. **Green Fee:** $28/$35. **Cart Fee:** $14/Person. **Walking Policy:** Unrestricted walking. **Walkability:** 2. **Opened:** 1998. **Architect:** Brian Silva. **Season:** April-Nov. **High:** June-Sept. **To obtain tee times:** Call golf shop. **Miscellaneous:** Reduced fees (weekdays, twilight, juniors), range, credit cards (MC, V, AE, D), BF, FF. **Reader Comments:** Great value not far from the Cape … Tough if wind is up … Some holes on back 9 don't fit overall design … Excellent variety of holes … Unique topography—wooded hills, wetlands & links … Out of the way, very playable for average golfers.

★★★ AGAWAM MUNICIPAL GOLF COURSE
PU-128 Southwick, Feeding Hills, 01030, Hampden County, (413)786-2194, 7 miles from Springfield. **Facility Holes:** 18. **Yards:** 6,119/5,370. **Par:** 71/71. **Course Rating:** 67.0/70.2. **Slope:** 110/110. **Green Fee:** $14/$18. **Cart Fee:** $11/Person. **Walking Policy:** Unrestricted walking. **Walkability:** 4. **Opened:** 1927. **Season:** March-Dec. **High:** May-Oct. **To obtain tee times:** Call up to 3 days in advance. **Miscellaneous:** Reduced fees (weekdays, twilight, seniors, juniors), BF, FF. **Reader Comments:** Unusual layout … Confidence builder, fun course … Great deal for the price.

AMESBURY GOLF & COUNTRY CLUB
SP-50 Monroe St., Amesbury, 01913, Essex County, (978)388-5153. **Facility Holes:** 9. **Yards:** 6,312/5,381. **Par:** 70/70. **Course Rating:** 70.5/71.9. **Slope:** 125/126. **Green Fee:** $25/$27. **Cart Fee:** $12/Person. **Walking Policy:** Unrestricted walking. **Walkability:** 3. **Opened:** 1923. **Architect:** Wayne Stiles. **Season:** April-Nov. **High:** June-Sept. **To obtain tee times:** Call up to 5 days in advance. **Miscellaneous:** BF, FF.

★★ AMHERST GOLF CLUB
SP-365 S. Pleasant St., Amherst, 01002, Hampshire County, (413)256-6894, 25 miles from Springfield. **Facility Holes:** 9. **Yards:** 6,083/5,608. **Par:** 70/72. **Course Rating:** 68.6/71.6. **Slope:** 117/122. **Green Fee:** $25. **Cart Fee:** $20/Cart. **Walking Policy:** Unrestricted walking. **Walkability:** 3. **Opened:** 1900. **Architect:** Walter Hatch. **Season:** April-Nov. **High:** May-Sept. **To obtain tee times:** Call golf shop. **Miscellaneous:** Credit cards (MC, V), BF, FF.

★★★ ATLANTIC COUNTRY CLUB
PU-450 Little Sandy Pond Rd., Plymouth, 02360, Plymouth County, (508)759-6644, 50 miles from Boston. **E-mail:** acclspr@aol.com. **Facility Holes:** 18. **Yards:** 6,728/4,918. **Par:** 72/72. **Course Rating:** 71.5/67.4. **Slope:** 130/113. **Green Fee:** $37/$52. **Cart Fee:** $14/Person. **Walking Policy:** Unrestricted walking. **Walkability:** 3. **Opened:** 1994. **Architect:** G. Cornish/B. Silva/M. Mungeam. **Season:** March-Dec. **High:** June-Sept. **To obtain tee times:** Call up to 2 days in advance. **Miscellaneous:** Reduced fees (weekdays, twilight), range (grass/mats), credit cards (MC, V). **Reader Comments:** A good layout … Can be very windy at times … Excellent course design with elevated greens and prevailing winds … Unlike your traditional flat Cape Cod courses … Hit it straight and you'll score … I love it, seldom a flat lie … Always challenging.

★★★★ BALLYMEADE COUNTRY CLUB
SP-125 Falmouth Woods Rd., North Falmouth, 02556, Barnstable County, (508)540-4005, 58 miles from Boston. **E-mail:** jbshaw@aol.com. **Web:** www.ballymeade.com. **Facility Holes:** 18. **Yards:** 6,928/5,001. **Par:** 72/72. **Course Rating:** 74.3/68.9. **Slope:** 139/119. **Green Fee:** $40/$75. **Cart Fee:** Included in green fee. **Walkability:** 5. **Opened:** 1988. **Architect:** Jim Fazio. **Season:** Year-round. **High:** June-Aug. **To obtain tee times:** Call golf shop. **Miscellaneous:** Reduced fees (weekdays, twilight), range (grass), credit cards (MC, V, AE, D). **Reader Comments:** Very expensive, but that is the Cape … The service was excellent … Scenic, narrow, need variety of shots … On par 3 on the front side you can see bridge … Tough when wind is up … Challenging from back tees.

★★½ BASS RIVER GOLF COURSE
PU-Highbank Rd., South Yarmouth, 02664, Barnstable County, (508)398-9079, 90 miles from Boston. **Facility Holes:** 18. **Yards:** 6,129/5,343. **Par:** 72/72. **Course Rating:** 68.5/69.9. **Slope:** 115/115. **Green Fee:** $30/$45. **Cart Fee:** $25/Cart. **Walking Policy:** Unrestricted walking. **Walkability:** 1. **Opened:** 1900. **Architect:** P. Sheppard/Donald Ross. **Season:** Year-round. **High:** May-Sept. **To obtain tee times:** Call golf shop. **Miscellaneous:** Reduced fees (twilight), credit cards (MC, V).

★★½ BAY POINTE COUNTRY CLUB
SP-Onset Ave., Onset Beach, 02558, Plymouth County, (508)759-8802, 30 miles from Boston. **Facility Holes:** 18. **Yards:** 6,301. **Par:** 70. **Course Rating:** 69.1. **Slope:** 118. **Green Fee:**

$19/$40. **Cart Fee:** $15/Person. **Walking Policy:** Unrestricted walking. **Walkability:** 3. **Architect:** Geoff Cornish. **Season:** Year-round. **To obtain tee times:** Call golf shop. **Miscellaneous:** Credit cards (MC, V, AE, D).

★★★ **BAYBERRY HILLS GOLF COURSE**
PU-635 W. Yarmouth Rd., West Yarmouth, 02673, Barnstable County, (508)394-5597, 75 miles from Boston. **Facility Holes:** 18. **Yards:** 7,172/5,323. **Par:** 72/72. **Course Rating:** 74.3/69.7. **Slope:** 127/119. **Green Fee:** $25/$45. **Cart Fee:** $14/Person. **Walking Policy:** Mandatory carts. **Walkability:** 2. **Opened:** 1987. **Architect:** Brian Silva/Geoffrey S. Cornish. **Season:** Year-round. **High:** June-Oct. **To obtain tee times:** Call golf shop. **Miscellaneous:** Reduced fees (twilight, juniors), range (grass), credit cards (MC, V, D), BF, FF.
Reader Comments: Very playable course ... Very easy course to walk ... Several visually appealing holes ... Plays very long from gold tees.

BEVERLY GOLF & TENNIS CLUB
SP-134 McKay St., Beverly, 01915, Essex County, (978)922-9072, 18 miles from Boston. **E-mail:** frielgolf@aol.com. **Web:** www.northofboston.com. **Facility Holes:** 18. **Yards:** 6,237/5,429. **Par:** 70/73. **Course Rating:** 70.6/70.3. **Slope:** 123/113. **Green Fee:** $34/$40. **Cart Fee:** $26/Cart. **Walking Policy:** Unrestricted walking. **Walkability:** 3. **Opened:** 1910. **Season:** April-Nov. **To obtain tee times:** Call up to 7 days in advance. **Miscellaneous:** Reduced fees (twilight), range (grass), BF, FF.

BLACKSTONE NATIONAL GOLF CLUB
PU-227 Putnam Hill Rd., Sutton, 01590, Worcester County, (508)865-2111, 10 miles from Worcester. **E-mail:** cstella@bngc.net. **Web:** www.bngc.net. **Facility Holes:** 18. **Yards:** 6,909/5,203. **Par:** 72/72. **Course Rating:** 73.5/70.0. **Slope:** 132/122. **Green Fee:** $34/$59. **Cart Fee:** $15/Person. **Walking Policy:** Unrestricted walking. **Walkability:** 4. **Opened:** 2000. **Architect:** Rees Jones. **Season:** April-Nov. **High:** June-Sept. **To obtain tee times:** Call up to 5 days in advance. **Miscellaneous:** Reduced fees (weekdays, twilight, juniors), range (grass), credit cards (MC, V, AE, D), BF, FF.

★★★★ **BLISSFUL MEADOWS GOLF CLUB**
SP-801 Chockalog Rd., Uxbridge, 01569, Worcester County, (508)278-6113, 20 miles from Worcester. **E-mail:** jkane@blissfulmeadows.com. **Web:** www.blissfulmeadows.com. **Facility Holes:** 18. **Yards:** 6,656/5,072. **Par:** 72/72. **Course Rating:** 71.3/69.1. **Slope:** 128/122. **Green Fee:** $28/$38. **Cart Fee:** $14/Person. **Walking Policy:** Unrestricted walking. **Walkability:** 3. **Opened:** 1992. **Architect:** Geoffrey Cornish/Brian Silva. **Season:** Year-round. **To obtain tee times:** Call up to 4 days in advance. **Miscellaneous:** Reduced fees (weekdays, twilight, seniors), range (grass), credit cards (MC, V, AE), BF, FF.
Reader Comments: Great pace of play ... Some great holes on the back 9 ... Every hole different ... Narrow, back 9 real challenge ... Lots of fun to play ... Spectacular par 3s ... Super in fall.

★★★★ **BLUE ROCK GOLF COURSE**
PU-48 Todd Rd., South Yarmouth, 02664, Barnstable County, (508)398-9295, (800)237-8887, 70 miles from Boston. **Facility Holes:** 18. **Yards:** 3,000/2,200. **Par:** 54/54. **Course Rating:** 56.4/55.8. **Slope:** 83/80. **Green Fee:** $29/$33. **Cart Fee:** $4/Cart. **Walking Policy:** Unrestricted walking. **Walkability:** 2. **Opened:** 1962. **Architect:** Geoffrey Cornish. **Season:** Year-round. **To obtain tee times:** Call golf shop. **Miscellaneous:** Reduced fees (twilight), range (grass), lodging (40 rooms), credit cards (MC, V), BF, FF.
Reader Comments: Great par-3 course ... Best of its kind ... Very nice, demanding short course ... The course is too short even for a par 3 ... Can still use a wood on 3 holes ... Always fun to play.

★★½ **BRADFORD COUNTRY CLUB**
PU-201 Chadwick Rd., Bradford, 01835, Essex County, (978)372-8587, 25 miles from Boston. **Web:** www.bradfordcc.com. **Facility Holes:** 18. **Yards:** 6,311/4,614. **Par:** 70/70. **Course Rating:** 72.4/67.2. **Slope:** 132/123. **Green Fee:** $32/$40. **Cart Fee:** $13/Person. **Walking Policy:** Unrestricted walking. **Walkability:** 3. **Opened:** 1990. **Architect:** Geoffrey Cornish/Brian Silva. **Season:** March-Nov. **High:** May-Sept. **To obtain tee times:** Call up to 5 days in advance. **Miscellaneous:** Reduced fees (weekdays, twilight, seniors, juniors), metal spikes, credit cards (MC, V, AE), BF, FF.

★★★★ **BRAINTREE MUNICIPAL GOLF COURSE** *Value*
PU-101 Jefferson St., Braintree, 02184, Norfolk County, (781)843-6513, 15 miles from Boston. **E-mail:** golfshop@braintreegolf.com. **Web:** www.braintreegolf.com. **Facility Holes:** 18. **Yards:** 6,423/5,751. **Par:** 72/72. **Course Rating:** 71.2/72.1. **Slope:** 127/118. **Green Fee:** $29/$35. **Cart Fee:** $26/Cart. **Walking Policy:** Unrestricted walking. **Walkability:** 1. **Opened:** 1945. **Season:** March-Dec. **High:** June-Sept. **To obtain tee times:** Call up to 3 days in advance. **Miscellaneous:** Reduced fees (twilight, seniors, juniors), cards (MC, V), BF, FF.
Reader Comments: Nice layout ... Back much tougher ... Tight course, greens good.

BROOKLINE GOLF CLUB
PU-1281 W. Roxbury Pkwy., Brookline, 02467, Norfolk County, (617)730-2078, 5 miles from Boston. **Facility Holes:** 18. **Yards:** 6,307/5,680. **Par:** 71/72. **Course Rating:** 70.2/72.1. **Slope:** 123/121. **Green Fee:** $25/$35. **Cart Fee:** $28/Cart. **Walking Policy:** Unrestricted walking. **Walkability:** 3. **Opened:** 1931. **Architect:** Wayne Stiles/John Van Kleek. **Season:** Year-round. **High:** April-Nov. **To obtain tee times:** Call up to 4 days in advance. **Miscellaneous:** Reduced fees (twilight, seniors, juniors), credit cards (MC, V, AE), BF, FF.

★★★ **BROOKMEADOW COUNTRY CLUB**
PU-100 Everendon Rd., Canton, 02021, Norfolk County, (781)828-4444, 20 miles from Boston. **Facility Holes:** 18. **Yards:** 6,660/5,690. **Par:** 72/72. **Course Rating:** 71.6/71.2. **Slope:** 123/114. **Green Fee:** $30/$35. **Cart Fee:** $28/Cart. **Walking Policy:** Unrestricted walking. **Walkability:** 1. **Opened:** 1967. **Architect:** Samuel Mitchell. **Season:** Year-round. **High:** April-Oct. **To obtain tee times:** Call golf shop. **Miscellaneous:** Reduced fees (twilight, seniors, juniors), range (grass/mats), credit cards (MC, V, D), BF, FF.
Reader Comments: Electric water coolers on a few fairways … Very beautiful course, no caddies or beverage service … Great layout … Greens are fast & true … Getting better all the time.

★★★ **BROOKSIDE GOLF CLUB**
PU-1 Brigadoon Rd., Bourne, 02532, Barnstable County, (508)743-4653, 60 miles from Boston. **Web:** www.thebrooksideclub.com. **Facility Holes:** 18. **Yards:** 6,300/5,130. **Par:** 70/70. **Course Rating:** 71.1/69.6. **Slope:** 126/118. **Green Fee:** $40/$60. **Cart Fee:** Included in green fee. **Walking Policy:** Walking at certain times. **Walkability:** 4. **Opened:** 1997. **Architect:** John Sanford. **Season:** Year-round. **High:** April-Nov. **To obtain tee times:** Call up to 7 days in advance. **Miscellaneous:** Reduced fees (weekdays, twilight, seniors, juniors), range (grass/mats), credit cards (MC, V, AE, D), BF, FF.
Reader Comments: Good course, nice layout, many different types of holes … Parking lot and trailer clubhouse kind of cheesy, I think improvements are planned … Unfair tee shot landing areas … New layout better, but slow pace.

★★★½ **BUTTERNUT FARM GOLF CLUB**
PU-115 Wheeler Rd., Stow, 01775, Middlesex County, (978)897-3400, 22 miles from Boston. **E-mail:** bfgcgolf@aol.com. **Web:** www.butternutfarm.com. **Facility Holes:** 18. **Yards:** 6,205/4,778. **Par:** 70/70. **Course Rating:** 69.9/67.7. **Slope:** 125/117. **Green Fee:** $29/$38. **Cart Fee:** $24/Cart. **Walking Policy:** Unrestricted walking. **Walkability:** 1. **Opened:** 1993. **Architect:** Robert Page III. **Season:** April-Nov. **High:** May-Oct. **To obtain tee times:** Call golf shop. **Miscellaneous:** Reduced fees (seniors).
Reader Comments: Good value, some tough holes … A tight course with narrow fairways and hard greens … Nothing special but comfortable like an old pair of shoes … Nice neighborhood golf course … Tight, need long irons.

★★★ **CAPE COD COUNTRY CLUB**
PU-Theater Rd., North Falmouth, 02556, Barnstable County, (508)563-9842, 50 miles from Boston. **E-mail:** capecodccgolf@aol.com. **Facility Holes:** 18. **Yards:** 6,404/5,348. **Par:** 71/72. **Course Rating:** 71.0/70.6. **Slope:** 122/119. **Green Fee:** $39/$52. **Cart Fee:** $26/Cart. **Walking Policy:** Unrestricted walking. **Walkability:** 4. **Opened:** 1929. **Architect:** Devereux Emmett/Alfred H. Tull. **Season:** Year-round. **High:** May-Oct. **To obtain tee times:** Call up to 7 days in advance. **Miscellaneous:** Reduced fees (weekdays, twilight, juniors), metal spikes, credit cards (MC, V, AE, D), FF.
Reader Comments: Always want to return … Good value, some excellent, some weak holes … Not difficult, but a great place to swing the club … Flat, not many hazards … Greens were very fast, great service & beverage cart … Very busy on weekends … Couple of tough 4s … Nice elevation changes.

CAPTAINS GOLF COURSE
PU-1000 Freeman's Way, Brewster, 02631, Barnstable County, (508)896-1716, 100 miles from Boston. **E-mail:** proshop@captainsgolfcourse.com. **Web:** www.captainsgolfcourse.com. **Facility Holes:** 36. **Green Fee:** $35/$60. **Cart Fee:** $26/Cart. **Walking Policy:** Unrestricted walking. **Walkability:** 3. **Architect:** Geoffrey Cornish/Brian Silva. **Season:** Year-round. **High:** April-Oct. **To obtain tee times:** Call up to 2 days in advance. **Miscellaneous:** Reduced fees (twilight, juniors), range (grass), credit cards (MC, V), BF, FF.
★★★ **PORT COURSE** (18)
Yards: 6,724/5,345. **Par:** 72/72. **Course Rating:** 70.6/70.4. **Slope:** 121/120. **Opened:** 1999.
Reader Comments: It's a great tract … More hills than normal … Love the 3s … Difficult walking, not for seniors … The new 18 holes integrated into the original 18 elevates Captains from so-so to very good.
★★★½ **STARBOARD COURSE** (18)
Yards: 6,776/5,359. **Par:** 72/72. **Course Rating:** 70.9/70.4. **Slope:** 122/120. **Opened:** 1985.
Notes: Ranked 70th in 1996 America's Top 75 Affordable Courses.

MASSACHUSETTS

★★½ CHEQUESSETT YACHT & COUNTRY CLUB
SP-680 Chequessett Neck Rd., Wellfleet, 02667, Barnstable County, (508)349-3704, 45 miles from Hyannis. **E-mail:** cycc1@aol.com. **Web:** www.cycc.net. **Facility Holes:** 9. **Yards:** 2,581/2,304. **Par:** 35/37. **Course Rating:** 65.1/66.2. **Slope:** 110/113. **Green Fee:** $36/$42. **Cart Fee:** $21/Cart. **Walking Policy:** Unrestricted walking. **Walkability:** 3. **Opened:** 1929. **Season:** Year-round. **High:** May-Oct. **To obtain tee times:** Call golf shop. **Miscellaneous:** Reduced fees (twilight), credit cards (MC, V), BF, FF.

★★★½ CHICOPEE GOLF CLUB
PU-1290 Burnett Rd., Chicopee, 01020, Hampden County, (413)594-9295, 5 miles from Springfield. **Facility Holes:** 18. **Yards:** 6,742/5,123. **Par:** 71/71. **Course Rating:** 73.0/72.5. **Slope:** 126/115. **Green Fee:** $17/$21. **Cart Fee:** $22/Cart. **Walking Policy:** Unrestricted walking. **Walkability:** 1. **Opened:** 1964. **Architect:** Geoffrey S. Cornish. **Season:** April-Nov. **High:** June-Sept. **To obtain tee times:** Call up to 5 days in advance. **Miscellaneous:** Range (grass/mats), credit cards (MC, V, AE), BF, FF.

COLONIAL GOLF CLUB
R-427 Walnut St., Lynnfield, 01940, Essex County, (781)876-6031, 12 miles from Boston. **E-mail:** bjacobs@starlodge.com. **Facility Holes:** 18. **Yards:** 6,565/5,280. **Par:** 70/70. **Course Rating:** 72.8/70.5. **Slope:** 130/119. **Green Fee:** $50/$60. **Cart Fee:** Included in green fee. **Walking Policy:** Mandatory carts. **Walkability:** 3. **Opened:** 1961. **Season:** March-Nov. **High:** May-Sept. **To obtain tee times:** Call up to 3 days in advance. **Miscellaneous:** Reduced fees (twilight), range (grass), lodging (260 rooms), credit cards (MC, V, AE, DC), BF, FF.

COUNTRY CLUB OF BILLERICA
PU-51 Baldwin Rd., Billerica, 01821, Middlesex County, (978)667-8061, 15 miles from Boston. **Facility Holes:** 18. **Yards:** 5,368/4,185. **Par:** 66/66. **Course Rating:** 65.9/63.0. **Slope:** 112/99. **Green Fee:** $26/$28. **Cart Fee:** $24/Cart. **Walking Policy:** Unrestricted walking. **Walkability:** 2. **Opened:** 1972. **Architect:** Phil Wogan. **Season:** April-Nov. **High:** June-Aug. **To obtain tee times:** Call up to 2 days in advance. **Miscellaneous:** Reduced fees (weekdays, twilight), range (mats), credit cards (MC, V, AE, D), BF, FF.

COUNTRY CLUB OF GREENFIELD
SP-244 Country Club Rd., Greenfield, 01301, Franklin County, (413)773-7530. **Facility Holes:** 18. **Yards:** 6,453/5,444. **Par:** 72/73. **Course Rating:** 69.2/70.6. **Slope:** 117/119. **Green Fee:** $25/$40. **Cart Fee:** $21/Cart. **Walking Policy:** Unrestricted walking. **Walkability:** 3. **Opened:** 1896. **Architect:** George Barton. **Season:** April-Nov. **High:** June-Aug. **Tee times:** Call golf shop. **Miscellaneous:** Reduced fees (weekdays), range (grass), credit cards (MC, V), BF, FF.

★★★½ CRANBERRY VALLEY GOLF COURSE
PU-183 Oak St., Harwich, 02645, Barnstable County, (508)430-5234, 85 miles from Boston. **Facility Holes:** 18. **Yards:** 6,745/5,518. **Par:** 72/72. **Course Rating:** 71.9/71.3. **Slope:** 129/115. **Green Fee:** $55. **Cart Fee:** $26/Cart. **Walking Policy:** Unrestricted walking. **Walkability:** 2. **Opened:** 1974. **Architect:** Cornish/Robinson. **Season:** Year-round. **High:** July-Oct. **To obtain tee times:** Call golf shop. **Miscellaneous:** Reduced fees (weekdays, twilight), range (grass/mats), credit cards (MC, V), BF, FF.

★★★ CRANWELL RESORT & GOLF CLUB
R-55 Lee Rd, Lenox, 01240, Berkshire County, (413)637-1364, (800)272-6935, 8 miles from Pittsfield. **Web:** www.cranwell.com. **Facility Holes:** 18. **Yards:** 6,204/5,104. **Par:** 70/71. **Course Rating:** 70.0/72.4. **Slope:** 125/129. **Green Fee:** $50/$95. **Cart Fee:** Included in green fee. **Walking Policy:** Walking at certain times. **Walkability:** 4. **Opened:** 1926. **Architect:** Stiles/Van Kleek. **Season:** April-Nov. **High:** June-Sept. **To obtain tee times:** Call up to 5 days in advance. **Miscellaneous:** Reduced fees (weekdays, guests, twilight), range (grass/mats), lodging (105 rooms), credit cards (MC, V, AE, D, DC), BF, FF.
Notes: Golf Digest school site.

MASSACHUSETTS

★★★★½ CRUMPIN-FOX CLUB
SP-Parmenter Rd., Bernardston, 01337, Franklin County, (413)648-9101, 30 miles from Springfield. **E-mail:** crumpinfox@sandri.com. **Web:** www.sandri.com. **Facility Holes:** 18. **Yards:** 7,007/5,432. **Par:** 72/72. **Course Rating:** 73.8/71.5. **Slope:** 141/131. **Green Fee:** $64/$69. **Cart Fee:** $16/Person. **Walking Policy:** Unrestricted walking. **Walkability:** 4. **Opened:** 1978. **Architect:** Roger Rulewich. **Season:** April-Nov. **High:** May-Sept. **To obtain tee times:** Call golf shop. **Miscellaneous:** Reduced fees (guests, juniors), range (grass), caddies, lodging (28 rooms), credit cards (MC, V, AE, D), BF, FF.
Notes: Ranked 12th in 1999 Best in State.
Reader Comments: Great New England layout … Best course for the money … A great woodland course that challenges your best game … A true gem … Sharpen your game to score here … Elevation changes make this a track tough! … Bring all your clubs … Picturesque … Good test from back tees … Top notch in every way.

★★★ CRYSTAL SPRINGS GOLF CLUB
PU-940 N. Broadway, Haverhill, 01830, Essex County, (978)374-9621, 35 miles from Boston. **E-mail:** csbigpro@aol.com. **Facility Holes:** 18. **Yards:** 6,706/5,596. **Par:** 72/73. **Course Rating:** 72.0/71.1. **Slope:** 116/112. **Green Fee:** $20/$25. **Cart Fee:** $20/Cart. **Walking Policy:** Unrestricted walking. **Walkability:** 3. **Opened:** 1961. **Architect:** Geoffrey S. Cornish. **Season:** April-Dec. **To obtain tee times:** Call golf shop. **Miscellaneous:** Metal spikes, range (grass/mats).
Reader Comments: Front 9 is wet in spring … Strong par 4s … Working man's golf course … Confidence builder … Old flat course—some very challenging holes.

★★★★ CYPRIAN KEYES GOLF CLUB *Service*
PU-284 E. Temple St., Boylston, 01505, Worcester County, (508)869-9900, 5 miles from Worcester. **E-mail:** info@cypriankeyesgolfclub.com. **Facility Holes:** 27. **Yards:** 6,871/5,029. **Par:** 72/72. **Course Rating:** 72.7/69.2. **Slope:** 132/119. **Green Fee:** $44/$54. **Cart Fee:** $14/Person. **Walking Policy:** Unrestricted walking. **Walkability:** 4. **Opened:** 1997. **Architect:** Mark Mungeam. **Season:** May-Dec. **High:** April-Nov. **To obtain tee times:** Call up to 3 days in advance. **Miscellaneous:** Reduced fees (weekdays, twilight, juniors), range (grass/mats), credit cards (MC, V, AE, D, DC), BF, FF.
Notes: Ranked 10th in 1999 Best in State.
Reader Comments: If you walk, be prepared for a lot of hills … Nice mix of 3s, 4s and 5s … Narrow fairways and lots of doglegs … Country club atmosphere … Little pricey but anything over $50 is pricey for me. I would definitely play it again … I'm hooked on this place.
Special Notes: Also has a 9-hole par-3 course.

★★ D.W. FIELD GOLF CLUB
PU-331 Oak St., Brockton, 02401, Plymouth County, (508)580-7855. **Facility Holes:** 18. **Yards:** 5,972/5,415. **Par:** 70/70. **Course Rating:** 68.4/70.1. **Slope:** 127/111. **Green Fee:** $17/$21. **Cart Fee:** $22/Cart. **Walking Policy:** Unrestricted walking. **Opened:** 1926. **Architect:** Wayne Stiles/John Van Kleek. **Season:** Year-round. **High:** June-Aug. **To obtain tee times:** Call golf shop. **Miscellaneous:** Reduced fees (twilight, juniors), metal spikes.

★★★½ DENNIS HIGHLANDS GOLF COURSE
PU-825 Old Bass River Rd., Dennis, 02638, Barnstable County, (508)385-9826, 80 miles from Boston. **Facility Holes:** 18. **Yards:** 6,464/4,927. **Par:** 71/71. **Course Rating:** 70.9/67.8. **Slope:** 120/112. **Green Fee:** $35/$50. **Cart Fee:** $25/Cart. **Walking Policy:** Unrestricted walking. **Walkability:** 4. **Opened:** 1984. **Architect:** Jack Kidwell/Michael Hurdzan. **Season:** March-Dec. **High:** April-Nov. **To obtain tee times:** Call up to 4 days in advance. **Miscellaneous:** Reduced fees (weekdays, twilight), range (grass), credit cards (MC, V), BF, FF.
Reader Comments: Fun, sporty … Open off the tee, challenging greens … Awesome … Often crowded and tough to get tee time … Links style … Good layout, great greens … Treacherous green on #7.

★★★ DENNIS PINES GOLF COURSE
PU-Golf Course Rd., East Dennis, 02641, Barnstable County, (508)385-9826, 80 miles from Boston. **Facility Holes:** 18. **Yards:** 7,029/5,798. **Par:** 72/73. **Course Rating:** 74.2/73.6. **Slope:** 133/126. **Green Fee:** $35/$50. **Cart Fee:** $25/Cart. **Walking Policy:** Unrestricted walking. **Walkability:** 2. **Opened:** 1964. **Architect:** Henry Mitchell. **Season:** March-Dec. **High:** April-Nov. **To obtain tee times:** Call up to 4 days in advance. **Miscellaneous:** Reduced fees (weekdays, twilight), range (mats), credit cards (MC, V).
Reader Comments: Excellent food … Great layout, very challenging … Front and back sides differ a lot … Some very tight holes.

MASSACHUSETTS

★★½ **EAST MOUNTAIN COUNTRY CLUB**
PU-1458 E. Mountain Rd., Westfield, 01085, Hampden County, (413)568-1539, 7 miles from Springfield. **E-mail:** emcc@the-spa.com. **Web:** www.eastmountaincc.com. **Facility Holes:** 18. **Yards:** 6,118/4,564. **Par:** 71/71. **Course Rating:** 67.5/65.3. **Slope:** 107/101. **Green Fee:** $20/$23. **Cart Fee:** $22/Cart. **Walking Policy:** Unrestricted walking. **Walkability:** 1. **Opened:** 1963. **Architect:** Ted Perez Sr. **Season:** Year-round. **To obtain tee times:** Call up to 7 days in advance. **Miscellaneous:** Reduced fees (weekdays, twilight, seniors, juniors), range (grass/mats), credit cards (MC, V, AE), BF, FF.

★★★ **EASTON COUNTRY CLUB**
SP-265 Purchase St., South Easton, 02375, Bristol County, (508)238-2500, 25 miles from Boston. **Facility Holes:** 18. **Yards:** 6,328/5,271. **Par:** 71/72. **Course Rating:** 68.8/70.2. **Slope:** 119/112. **Green Fee:** $23/$35. **Cart Fee:** $22/Person. **Walking Policy:** Unrestricted walking. **Walkability:** 1. **Opened:** 1961. **Architect:** Sam Mitchell. **Season:** Year-round. **High:** May-Sept. **To obtain tee times:** Call golf shop. **Miscellaneous:** Reduced fees (weekdays, twilight, juniors), range (grass), credit cards (MC, V, D).
Reader Comments: Good course, forgivable fairways, redone clubhouse … Easy layout overall … A comfortable course with enough variety … Excellent value, excellent people.

★★½ **EDGEWOOD GOLF COURSE OF SOUTHWICK**
SP-161 Sheep Pasture Rd., Southwick, 01077, Hampden County, (413)569-6826, 15 miles from Springfield. **Facility Holes:** 18. **Yards:** 6,510/5,580. **Par:** 71/71. **Course Rating:** 69.1/71.8. **Slope:** 115/109. **Green Fee:** $16/$20. **Cart Fee:** $22/Person. **Walking Policy:** Unrestricted walking. **Walkability:** 3. **Opened:** 1963. **Architect:** Geoffrey Cornish. **Season:** March-Nov. **High:** June-Aug. **To obtain tee times:** Call golf shop. **Miscellaneous:** Reduced fees (seniors, juniors), metal spikes, range (grass), credit cards (MC, V, AE, D).

EGREMONT COUNTRY CLUB
SP-Rte. 23, Great Barrington, 01230, Berkshire County, (413)528-4222. **Facility Holes:** 18. **Yards:** 6,100/5,000. **Par:** 71/71. **Course Rating:** 68.7/68.1. **Slope:** 122/113. **Green Fee:** $35/$49. **Cart Fee:** Included in green fee. **Season:** April-Nov. **To obtain tee times:** Call golf shop. **Miscellaneous:** Reduced fees (weekdays, twilight, seniors).

ELLINWOOD COUNTRY CLUB
SP-1928 Pleasant St., Athol, 01331, Worcester County, (978)249-7460, 37 miles from Worcester. **Facility Holes:** 18. **Yards:** 6,207/5,737. **Par:** 71/71. **Course Rating:** 70.1/68.8. **Slope:** 123/117. **Green Fee:** $23/$28. **Cart Fee:** $25/Cart. **Walking Policy:** Unrestricted walking. **Walkability:** 4. **Opened:** 1929. **Architect:** Donald Ross. **Season:** April-Dec. **High:** June-Sept. **To obtain tee times:** Call up to 1 day in advance. **Miscellaneous:** Reduced fees (weekdays), credit cards (MC, V), BF, FF.

★★★½ **FALMOUTH COUNTRY CLUB**
PU-630 Carriage Shop Rd., East Falmouth, 02536, Barnstable County, (508)548-3211, 70 miles from Boston. **Facility Holes:** 27. **Yards:** 6,665/5,551. **Par:** 72/72. **Course Rating:** 72.9/72.7. **Slope:** 127/126. **Green Fee:** $28/$50. **Cart Fee:** $28/Cart. **Walking Policy:** Unrestricted walking. **Walkability:** 2. **Opened:** 1969. **Architect:** Vinnie Bartlet. **Season:** Year-round. **To obtain tee times:** Call golf shop. **Miscellaneous:** Reduced fees (twilight), range (grass/mats), credit cards (MC, V, AE), BF, FF.
Reader Comments: A laid-back, simple course and a good value … Hard to get on … New holes are great, wide open old holes … We were pleasantly surprised … Refreshing … Flat, uninspiring, but well kept.
Special Notes: Also has a 9-hole flat course for beginners and seniors.

★★½ **FAR CORNER GOLF CLUB**
PU-Main St. and Barker Rd., West Boxford, 01885, Essex County, (978)352-8300, 25 miles from Boston. **Facility Holes:** 27. **Green Fee:** $29/$32. **Opened:** 1971. **Architect:** Geoffrey S. Cornish/William G. Robinson. **Season:** April-Nov. **To obtain tee times:** Call golf shop. **Miscellaneous:** Reduced fees (weekdays).
BLUE/RED (18 combo)
Yards: 6,658/5,556. **Par:** 72/75. **Course Rating:** 71.6/74.2. **Slope:** 134/136.
RED/WHITE (18 combo)
Yards: 6,232/5,896. **Par:** 72/75.
WHITE/BLUE (18 combo)
Yards: 6,241/5,586. **Par:** 72/75.

★★★★½ **FARM NECK GOLF CLUB** *Condition*
SP-Farm Neck Way, Oak Bluffs, 02557, Dukes County, (508)693-3057, 10 miles from Falmouth. **Facility Holes:** 18. **Yards:** 6,807/5,004. **Par:** 72/72. **Course Rating:** 72.6/64.3. **Slope:**

133/121. **Green Fee:** $45/$125. **Cart Fee:** $13/Person. **Walking Policy:** Walking at certain times. **Walkability:** 2. **Opened:** 1979. **Architect:** Geoffrey S. Cornish/William G. Robinson. **Season:** April-Dec. **High:** June-Sept. **To obtain tee times:** Call up to 2 days in advance. **Miscellaneous:** Reduced fees (twilight), range (grass/mats), credit cards (MC, V, AE), BF, FF. **Reader Comments:** One of the most picturesque and interesting courses I've ever played ... The perfect vacation course, and one that you will never forget ... Beautiful course, fun to play, crowded in summer ... Incredible views of the ocean ... Love this old-style course.

★★★½ **FERNCROFT COUNTRY CLUB**
R-50 Ferncroft Rd., Danvers, 01923, Essex County, (978)777-5614, 15 miles from Boston. **E-mail:** tahern@starlodge.com. **Facility Holes:** 27. **Yards:** 6,601/5,543. **Par:** 72/73. **Course Rating:** 73.2/72.5. **Slope:** 132/128. **Green Fee:** $80/$110. **Cart Fee:** Included in green fee. **Walking Policy:** Mandatory carts. **Walkability:** 3. **Opened:** 1969. **Architect:** Robert Trent Jones. **Season:** April-Nov. **High:** May-Oct. **To obtain tee times:** Call up to 3 days in advance. **Miscellaneous:** Range (grass/mats), lodging (365 rooms), credit cards (MC, V, AE, D), FF. **Reader Comments:** Super outings package ... Tough to get on if you're not a member ... You will cry less if you play from the white tees ... Lovely lounge area to relax after ... Always a favorite for local players ... Challenging, shotmaker's delight ... Par-4 2nd memorable. **Special Notes:** Also has a 9-hole par-3 course.

FIREFLY GOLF COURSE
PU-320 Fall River Ave., Seekonk, 02771, Bristol County, (508)336-6622, 2 miles from Providence. **Facility Holes:** 18. **Yards:** 3,644/2,786. **Par:** 60/60. **Course Rating:** 58.0. **Slope:** 87. **Green Fee:** $22/$25. **Cart Fee:** $24/Cart. **Walking Policy:** Unrestricted walking. **Walkability:** 3. **Opened:** 1963. **Architect:** Joanne Carner. **Season:** Year-round. **High:** April-Sept. **Tee times:** Call golf shop. **Misc:** Reduced fees (seniors, juniors), range, cards (MC, V, AE), BF, FF.

★★★½ **FOXBOROUGH COUNTRY CLUB**
SP-33 Walnut St., Foxboro, 02035, Norfolk County, (508)543-4661, 12 miles from Providence. **Facility Holes:** 18. **Yards:** 6,850/5,627. **Par:** 72/73. **Course Rating:** 72.4/73.4. **Slope:** 130/122. **Green Fee:** $40/$50. **Cart Fee:** $23/Cart. **Walking Policy:** Unrestricted walking. **Walkability:** 3. **Opened:** 1955. **Architect:** Geoffrey Cornish. **Season:** April-Dec. **High:** May-Sept. **To obtain tee times:** Call golf shop. **Miscellaneous:** Reduced fees (weekdays), range (grass), credit cards (MC, V, AE, D), BF, FF. **Reader Comments:** Tough course, great greens, tree-lined fairways, rolling terrain ... Outstanding place ... Worth a weekday off, fine course with devilish greens ... Fair layout, killer greens.

★★ **FRANCONIA GOLF COURSE**
PU-619 Dwight Rd., Springfield, 01108, Hampden County, (413)734-9334, 3 miles from Springfield. **Facility Holes:** 18. **Yards:** 6,250/5,250. **Par:** 71/71. **Course Rating:** 68.5/68.5. **Slope:** 117/117. **Green Fee:** $16/$18. **Cart Fee:** $22/Cart. **Walking Policy:** Unrestricted walking. **Walkability:** 3. **Opened:** 1929. **Architect:** Wayne Stiles/John Van Kleek. **Season:** April-Nov. **High:** July-Sept. **To obtain tee times:** Call golf shop. **Miscellaneous:** Reduced fees (weekdays, twilight, seniors, juniors), credit cards (MC, V, AE), BF, FF.

FRANKLIN PARK GOLF COURSE
PU-1 Circuit Dr., Boston, 02121, Suffolk County, (617)265-4084. **E-mail:** fpgc18@aol.com. **Web:** www.sterlinggolf.com. **Facility Holes:** 18. **Yards:** 6,009/5,040. **Par:** 70/72. **Course Rating:** 69.8/69.3. **Slope:** 120/109. **Green Fee:** $21/$27. **Cart Fee:** $24/Cart. **Walking Policy:** Unrestricted walking. **Walkability:** 3. **Opened:** 1896. **Architect:** Donald Ross. **Season:** Year-round. **High:** May-Sept. **To obtain tee times:** Call up to 2 days in advance. **Miscellaneous:** Reduced fees (weekdays, seniors, juniors), range (grass), credit cards (MC, V, AE, D), BF, FF.

★★½ **GARDNER MUNICIPAL GOLF COURSE**
PU-152 Eaton St., Gardner, 01440, Worcester County, (978)632-9703, 20 miles from Worcester. **Facility Holes:** 18. **Yards:** 6,106/5,653. **Par:** 71/75. **Course Rating:** 68.9/72.2. **Slope:** 124/123. **Green Fee:** $17/$30. **Cart Fee:** $22/Cart. **Walking Policy:** Unrestricted walking. **Walkability:** 3. **Opened:** 1936. **Architect:** Samuel Mitchell. **Season:** April-Nov. **High:** June-Sept. **To obtain tee times:** Call up to 2 days in advance. **Miscellaneous:** Reduced fees (weekdays, twilight, juniors), range (grass/mats), BF, FF.

★★★ **GEORGE WRIGHT GOLF COURSE**
PU-420 West St., Hyde Park, 02136, Suffolk County, (617)361-8313, 5 miles from Boston. **Facility Holes:** 18. **Yards:** 6,400/5,500. **Par:** 70/70. **Course Rating:** 69.5/70.3. **Slope:** 126/115. **Green Fee:** $25/$28. **Cart Fee:** $26/Cart. **Walking Policy:** Unrestricted walking. **Walkability:** 3. **Opened:** 1938. **Architect:** Donald Ross. **Season:** Year-round. **To obtain tee times:** Call golf shop. **Miscellaneous:** Reduced fees (juniors), credit cards (MC, V, AE). **Reader Comments:** A fantastic old Donald Ross course, a bit rough around the edges, but great anyway. It makes you think ... Challenging holes ... Visually spooky course.

★★½ GLEN ELLEN COUNTRY CLUB
PU-84 Orchard St., Millis, 02054, Norfolk County, (508)376-2775, 25 miles from Boston. **Web:** www.glenellencc.com. **Facility Holes:** 18. **Yards:** 6,633/5,148. **Par:** 72/72. **Course Rating:** 72.0/69.4. **Slope:** 125/122. **Green Fee:** $31/$42. **Cart Fee:** $28/Cart. **Walking Policy:** Walking at certain times. **Walkability:** 2. **Opened:** 1963. **Architect:** Don Reynolds. **Season:** Year-round. **High:** May-Sept. **To obtain tee times:** Call up to 7 days in advance. **Miscellaneous:** Reduced fees (twilight, seniors), range (grass), credit cards (MC, V, AE), BF, FF.

GRANDVIEW COUNTRY CLUB
SP-454 Wachusett St., Leominster, 01453, Worcester County, (978)537-0614. **Facility Holes:** 18. **Yards:** 6,746/6,264. **Par:** 72/74. **Course Rating:** 68.8/68.8. **Slope:** 113/113. **Green Fee:** $22/$25. **Cart Fee:** $25/Cart. **Walking Policy:** Unrestricted walking. **Walkability:** 3. **Opened:** 1961. **Architect:** Eddie Vachon. **Season:** April-Nov. **To obtain tee times:** Call golf shop. **Miscellaneous:** Reduced fees (twilight), FF.

★★½ GREEN HARBOR GOLF CLUB
PU-624 Webster St., Marshfield, 02050, Plymouth County, (781)834-7303, 30 miles from Boston. **E-mail:** twtoll@aol.com. **Facility Holes:** 18. **Yards:** 6,251/4,972. **Par:** 71/71. **Course Rating:** 69.1/69.3. **Slope:** 115/107. **Green Fee:** $30/$35. **Walking Policy:** Unrestricted walking. **Walkability:** 1. **Opened:** 1971. **Architect:** Manuel Francis. **Season:** March-Dec. **High:** June-Aug. **To obtain tee times:** Call up to 2 days in advance. **Miscellaneous:** Reduced fees (twilight), metal spikes, BF, FF.

GREEN HILL MUNICIPAL GOLF COURSE
PU-1 Marsh Ave., Worcester, 01605, Worcester County, (508)799-1359. **Facility Holes:** 18. **Yards:** 6,487/5,547. **Par:** 72/71. **Course Rating:** 70.4/69.9. **Slope:** 122/116. **Green Fee:** $20/$25. **Cart Fee:** $24/Cart. **Walking Policy:** Unrestricted walking. **Walkability:** 4. **Opened:** 1929. **Season:** April-Dec. **High:** April-Dec. **To obtain tee times:** Call golf shop. **Miscellaneous:** Reduced fees (twilight, juniors), credit cards (MC, V).

★★★★ HAMPDEN COUNTRY CLUB
PU-128 Wilbraham Rd., Hampden, 01036, Hampden County, (413)566-8010, 10 miles from Springfield. **Facility Holes:** 18. **Yards:** 6,833/5,283. **Par:** 72/72. **Course Rating:** 72.5/72.3. **Slope:** 129/113. **Green Fee:** $25/$34. **Cart Fee:** $12/Person. **Walking Policy:** Unrestricted walking. **Walkability:** 5. **Opened:** 1975. **Season:** March-Dec. **High:** June-Sept. **To obtain tee times:** Call up to 7 days in advance. **Miscellaneous:** Reduced fees (weekdays, twilight), range (grass), credit cards (MC, V, AE), BF, FF.
Reader Comments: Very pretty and challenging course ... Fast, breaking greens ... Bring oxygen-pack for ascent to 9th tee ... Not easy to walk ... The hidden gem of New England. Perfect ... Hilly, fast greens, good service.

HEATHER HILL COUNTRY CLUB
PU-149 W. Bacon St., Plainville, 02762, Norfolk County, (508)695-0309, 12 miles from Providence. **Facility Holes:** 27. **Architect:** Elmo Finocchi. **To obtain tee times:** Call golf shop. **Miscellaneous:** Metal spikes.
★½ NORTH COURSE (9)
Yards: 3,368/2,681. **Par:** 36/36. **Course Rating:** .0/69.9. **Slope:** 127/112. **Green Fee:** $12. **Walkability:** 1. **Opened:** 1950. **Season:** Year-round.
SOUTH COURSE (18)
Yards: 6,005/4,736. **Par:** 70/70. **Course Rating:** 67.8/66.4. **Slope:** 117/103. **Green Fee:** $15/$22. **Walkability:** 3. **Opened:** 1955. **Miscellaneous:** Reduced fees (weekdays).

★★★ HERITAGE COUNTRY CLUB
SP-Sampson Rd., Charlton, 01507, Worcester County, (508)248-3591, 30 miles from Springfield. **Facility Holes:** 18. **Yards:** 6,335/5,415. **Par:** 71/71. **Course Rating:** 69.3/70.3. **Slope:** 118/114. **Green Fee:** $19/$25. **Opened:** 1964. **Architect:** Don Hoenig. **Season:** April-Nov. **To obtain tee times:** Call golf shop.
Reader Comments: The best par 3 around ... Very challenging greens, lots of hazards & water.

★★★½ HICKORY HILLS GOLF CLUB
PU-200 N. Lowell St., Methuen, 01844, Essex County, (978)686-0822, 4 miles from Lawrence. **Facility Holes:** 18. **Yards:** 6,276/5,397. **Par:** 71/73. **Course Rating:** 69.2/73.2. **Slope:** 122/127. **Green Fee:** $38/$42. **Cart Fee:** $26/Cart. **Walking Policy:** Unrestricted walking. **Walkability:** 3. **Opened:** 1968. **Architect:** Manuel Francis. **Season:** April-Dec. **High:** May-Sept. **To obtain tee times:** Call golf shop. **Miscellaneous:** Reduced fees (weekdays, twilight), range (grass), credit cards (MC, V), BF, FF.
Reader Comments: Excellent ... Fair test for average play, good track ... Play is a little slow but they try ... Nice greens and friendly staff ... Keeps you in condition walking.

MASSACHUSETTS

★★★½ HICKORY RIDGE COUNTRY CLUB
SP-191 W. Pomeroy Lane, Amherst, 01002, Hampshire County, (413)253-9320, 20 miles from Springfield. **E-mail:** hickorygolfshop@aol.com. **Web:** www.hickoryridgecc.com. **Facility Holes:** 18. **Yards:** 6,794/5,340. **Par:** 72/74. **Course Rating:** 72.8/71.1. **Slope:** 130/122. **Green Fee:** $45/$55. **Cart Fee:** $25/Cart. **Walking Policy:** Unrestricted walking. **Walkability:** 2. **Opened:** 1970. **Architect:** Geoffrey Cornish/William Robinson. **Season:** April-Nov. **High:** May-Aug. **To obtain tee times:** Call up to 1 day in advance. **Miscellaneous:** Reduced fees (weekdays, juniors), range (grass/mats), credit cards (MC, V, AE), BF, FF.
Reader Comments: A pleasant course to walk ... 9 & 18 are good holes; pace is very slow ... Tests your length from back tees.

★★★½ HIGHLAND GOLF LINKS
PU-Lighthouse Rd., P.O. Box 162, North Truro, 02652, Barnstable County, (508)487-9201, 45 miles from Hyannis. **Facility Holes:** 9. **Yards:** 5,299/4,782. **Par:** 70/74. **Course Rating:** 65.0/67.4. **Slope:** 103/107. **Green Fee:** $32/$40. **Cart Fee:** $21/Cart. **Walking Policy:** Unrestricted walking. **Walkability:** 3. **Opened:** 1892. **Architect:** Isiah Small. **Season:** April-Oct. **High:** June-Sept. **Tee times:** Call golf shop. **Misc:** Credit cards (MC, V), BF, FF.
Reader Comments: Great test in windy conditions ... Crowded in season ... Great views; I call it the poor man's Pebble Beach ... British golf on Cape ... Beautiful ocean views ... A lot of fun in wind and fog.

HILLCREST COUNTRY CLUB
PU-325 Pleasant St. Rte. 56, Leicester, 01524, Worcester County, (508)892-0963, 4 miles from Worcester. **Facility Holes:** 9. **Yards:** 2,920/2,310. **Par:** 36/37. **Course Rating:** 67.1/67.2. **Slope:** 103/113. **Green Fee:** $16/$20. **Cart Fee:** $16/Cart. **Walking Policy:** Unrestricted walking. **Walkability:** 2. **Opened:** 1940. **Architect:** J. Dolan. **Season:** March-Oct. **High:** July-April. **To obtain tee times:** Call golf shop. **Miscellaneous:** BF, FF.

HILLSIDE COUNTRY CLUB
SP-82 Hillside Ave., Rehoboth, 02769, Bristol County, (508)252-9761, 8 miles from Providence. **Facility Holes:** 18. **Yards:** 5,820/4,860. **Par:** 71/72. **Course Rating:** 69.5/72.8. **Slope:** 126/124. **Green Fee:** $20/$25. **Cart Fee:** $11/Person. **Walking Policy:** Unrestricted walking. **Walkability:** 4. **Opened:** 1999. **Architect:** George Cardono. **Season:** Year-round. **High:** April-Oct. **To obtain tee times:** Call golf shop. **Miscellaneous:** Reduced fees (weekdays, seniors, juniors), metal spikes, credit cards (MC, V, D).

HILLVIEW GOLF COURSE
PU-149 North St., North Reading, 01864, Middlesex County, (978)664-4435. **Facility Holes:** 18. **Yards:** 5,800/5,251. **Par:** 69/69. **Course Rating:** 67.4/66.0. **Slope:** 120/110. **Green Fee:** $29/$31. **Cart Fee:** $24/Cart. **Season:** April-Dec. **To obtain tee times:** Call golf shop. **Miscellaneous:** Reduced fees (weekdays, seniors).

HOLDEN HILLS COUNTRY CLUB
PU-1800 Main St., Jefferson, 01522, Worcester County, (508)829-3129, 10 miles from Worcester. **Web:** www.holdenhillsgolf.com. **Facility Holes:** 18. **Yards:** 6,088/5,878. **Par:** 71/74. **Course Rating:** 71.9/70.0. **Slope:** 125/115. **Green Fee:** $20/$32. **Cart Fee:** $15/Person. **Walking Policy:** Unrestricted walking. **Walkability:** 4. **Opened:** 1957. **Season:** March-Nov. **To obtain tee times:** Call golf shop. **Miscellaneous:** Reduced fees (weekdays, twilight, seniors, juniors), credit cards (MC, V), BF, FF.

★★★ HOLLY RIDGE GOLF CLUB
PU-121 Country Club Rd., South Sandwich, 02563, Barnstable County, (508)428-5577, 10 miles from Hyannis. **Web:** www.hollyridgegolf.com. **Facility Holes:** 36. **Yards:** 2,952/2,194. **Par:** 54/54. **Green Fee:** $17/$29. **Cart Fee:** $10/Person. **Walking Policy:** Unrestricted walking. **Walkability:** 2. **Opened:** 1966. **Architect:** Geoffrey Cornish. **Season:** Year-round. **To obtain tee times:** Call up to 7 days in advance. **Miscellaneous:** Reduced fees (weekdays, twilight, seniors, juniors), range (mats), credit cards (MC, V, AE), BF, FF.
Reader Comments: A fun par-3, always worth the visit ... Good warm up, nice setting, relatively easy ... Lots of children, seniors and women ... Very slow play.
Special Notes: Also has an 18-hole executive course.

HOLYOKE COUNTRY CLUB
SP-Smiths Ferry Rd., Holyoke, 01040, Hampden County, (413)534-1933. **Facility Holes:** 9. **Yards:** 6,309/5,411. **Par:** 72/74. **Course Rating:** 69.0/69.6. **Slope:** 118/120. **Green Fee:** $20. **Cart Fee:** $12/Person. **Walking Policy:** Unrestricted walking. **Walkability:** 4. **Opened:** 1906. **Season:** April-Nov. **High:** June-Aug. **To obtain tee times:** Call golf shop. **Miscellaneous:** Credit cards (MC, V, D).

343

HOPE DALE COUNTRY CLUB
SP-Mill St., Hopedale, 01747, Worcester County, (508)473-9876, 15 miles from Worcester. **Facility Holes:** 9. **Yards:** 6,008/5,836. **Par:** 70/70. **Course Rating:** 68.6/68.0. **Slope:** 122/122. **Green Fee:** $25/$30. **Cart Fee:** $20/Cart. **Walking Policy:** Unrestricted walking. **Walkability:** 2. **Opened:** 1953. **Season:** March-Nov. **To obtain tee times:** Call golf shop. **Miscellaneous:** Reduced fees (weekdays), credit cards (MC, V), FF.

★★★ HYANNIS GOLF CLUB AT IYANOUGH HILLS
PU-Rte. 132, Hyannis, 02601, Barnstable County, (508)362-2606, 1 mile from Hyannis. **Web:** www.golfcapecod.com. **Facility Holes:** 18. **Yards:** 6,711/5,149. **Par:** 71/72. **Course Rating:** 69.4/69.0. **Slope:** 121/125. **Green Fee:** $35/$55. **Cart Fee:** $15/Person. **Walking Policy:** Unrestricted walking. **Walkability:** 3. **Opened:** 1976. **Architect:** Geoffrey Cornish/William Robinson. **Season:** Year-round. **High:** May-Sept. **To obtain tee times:** Call golf shop. **Miscellaneous:** Reduced fees (weekdays, twilight, seniors), range (grass/mats), credit cards (MC, V, AE, D).
Reader Comments: Typical Cape Cod course. Elevated tees and greens … Par-5 5th is really tough, with blind 2nd shot … Cheap for Cape Cod … Course is beautiful … A great winter course … Good practice range.

JUNIPER HILL GOLF COURSE
PU-202 Brigham St., Northborough, 01532, Worcester County, (508)393-2444, 15 miles from Worcester. **E-mail:** ddarling@juniperhillgc.com. **Web:** www.juniperhillgc.com. **Facility Holes:** 36. **Green Fee:** $32/$37. **Cart Fee:** $24/Cart. **Walking Policy:** Walking at certain times. **Walkability:** 3. **Season:** April-Dec. **High:** May-Sept. **Tee times:** Call up to 7 days in advance. **Miscellaneous:** Reduced fees (seniors, juniors), range (grass), credit cards (MC, V), BF, FF.
★★★ LAKESIDE COURSE (18)
Yards: 6,140/4,707. **Par:** 71/71. **Course Rating:** 69.9/65.3. **Slope:** 127/102. **Opened:** 1991. **Architect:** Homer Darling/Philip Wogan.
Reader Comments: Must be accurate off the tee … New clubhouse adds a lot to the whole experience … Tight fairways … Target course … Steadily improving.
★★★ RIVERSIDE COURSE (18)
Yards: 6,266/5,373. **Par:** 71/71. **Course Rating:** 70.4/70.2. **Slope:** 123/117. **Opened:** 1931. **Architect:** Homer Darling/Geoff Cornish.
Reader Comments: Front and back are like two different courses … Front is hilly with one pond, back is flat with lots of water … Tight fairways … The Riverside course is a bit easier than Lakeside.

★★★★ KETTLE BROOK GOLF CLUB *Value*
PU-136 Marshall St., Paxton, 01612, Worcester County, (508)799-4653, 5 miles from Worcester. **Web:** www.kettlebrookgolfclub.com. **Facility Holes:** 18. **Yards:** 6,912/5,105. **Par:** 72/72. **Course Rating:** 73.1/70.2. **Slope:** 125/118. **Green Fee:** $29/$34. **Cart Fee:** $12/Person. **Walking Policy:** Walking at certain times. **Walkability:** 3. **Opened:** 1999. **Architect:** Brian Silva. **Season:** April-Nov. **High:** June-Sept. **To obtain tee times:** Call up to 7 days in advance. **Miscellaneous:** Reduced fees (twilight, seniors, juniors), credit cards (MC, V, AE), BF, FF.
Reader Comments: Very enjoyable and affordable … Generous landing areas … A new course that gets better every day … Links feel … A fun course to play.

★★★½ KINGS WAY GOLF CLUB
SP-Old Kings Hwy., Rte. 6A, Yarmouth Port, 02675, Barnstable County, (508)362-8870. **Facility Holes:** 18. **Yards:** 3,953/2,937. **Par:** 59/59. **Course Rating:** 60.5/55.8. **Slope:** 95/85. **Green Fee:** $40/$50. **Cart Fee:** Included in green fee. **Walking Policy:** Mandatory carts. **Walkability:** 3. **Opened:** 1988. **Architect:** Brian Silva. **Season:** April-Nov. **To obtain tee times:** Call golf shop. **Miscellaneous:** Reduced fees (twilight), credit cards (MC, V), BF, FF.
Reader Comments: One of best executive-style courses … Very picturesque … Great layout with several challenging holes.

★★★ LAKEVILLE COUNTRY CLUB
PU-44 Clear Pond Rd., Lakeville, 02347, Plymouth County, (508)947-6630, 50 miles from Boston. **Facility Holes:** 18. **Yards:** 6,335/4,863. **Par:** 72/72. **Course Rating:** 70.6/67.4. **Slope:** 125/111. **Green Fee:** $32/$37. **Cart Fee:** $14/Person. **Walking Policy:** Unrestricted walking. **Walkability:** 2. **Opened:** 1970. **Season:** Year-round. **To obtain tee times:** Call up to 7 days in advance. **Miscellaneous:** Credit cards (MC, V), FF.
Reader Comments: Open most of winter … Very nice … Short course, lots of tournament play … Water on 7 holes … Lots of H2O as the name implies … Greens are usually in good shape, but fairways suffer a little … Nice course, good condition … Easy to score on.

MASSACHUSETTS

★★★½ **LARRY GANNON GOLF CLUB**
PU-60 Great Woods Rd., Lynn, 01904, Essex County, (781)592-8238, 15 miles from Boston. **Web:** www.gannongolfclub.com. **Facility Holes:** 18. **Yards:** 6,106/5,215. **Par:** 70/71. **Course Rating:** 69.9/68.8. **Slope:** 118/115. **Green Fee:** $24/$32. **Cart Fee:** $24/Cart. **Walking Policy:** Unrestricted walking. **Walkability:** 5. **Opened:** 1932. **Architect:** Wayne Stiles. **Season:** March-Dec. **To obtain tee times:** Call golf shop. **Miscellaneous:** Reduced fees (seniors), BF, FF.
Reader Comments: Excellent test of golf ... Great vistas. Hard to believe severity of slope on many greens! ... Many blind shots and some pin positions are almost unfair ... Small fast greens.

LEICESTER COUNTRY CLUB
PU-1430 Main St., Leicester, 01524, Worcester County, (508)892-1390. **Web:** www.leicester-cc.com. **Facility Holes:** 18. **Yards:** 6,026/4,559. **Par:** 70/70. **Course Rating:** 69.8/67.4. **Slope:** 126/121. **Green Fee:** $20/$25. **Cart Fee:** $12/Person. **Opened:** 1884. **Season:** April-Nov. **To obtain tee times:** Call golf shop. **Miscellaneous:** Reduced fees (weekdays, twilight, seniors, juniors).

★½ **LEO J. MARTIN MEMORIAL MUNICIPAL GOLF COURSE**
PU-85 Park Rd., Weston, 02193, Middlesex County, (781)894-4903, 18 miles from Boston. **Facility Holes:** 18. **Yards:** 6,256/5,896. **Par:** 72/72. **Course Rating:** 72.0/69.7. **Slope:** 120/115. **Green Fee:** $17/$20. **Cart Fee:** $23/Cart. **Walking Policy:** Unrestricted walking. **Walkability:** 1. **Opened:** 1934. **Architect:** Donald Ross. **Season:** April-Dec. **To obtain tee times:** Call up to 2 days in advance. **Miscellaneous:** Range (mats), credit cards (MC, V, D), BF, FF.

★★½ **LITTLE HARBOR COUNTRY CLUB**
PU-Little Harbor Rd., Wareham, 02571, Plymouth County, (508)295-2617, (800)649-2617, 15 miles from New Bedford. **E-mail:** jjoneslhcc@aol.com. **Facility Holes:** 18. **Yards:** 3,038/2,692. **Par:** 56/56. **Course Rating:** 54.4/51.9. **Slope:** 79/72. **Green Fee:** $18/$23. **Cart Fee:** $20/Cart. **Walking Policy:** Unrestricted walking. **Walkability:** 2. **Opened:** 1963. **Season:** Year-round. **High:** July-Sept. **To obtain tee times:** Call golf shop. **Miscellaneous:** Reduced fees (weekdays, twilight, seniors, juniors), credit cards (MC, V), BF, FF.

★★★ **MAPLEGATE COUNTRY CLUB**
PU-160 Maple St., Bellingham, 02019, Norfolk County, (508)966-4040, 25 miles from Boston. **E-mail:** maplegate@ncounty.net. **Web:** www.maplegate.com. **Facility Holes:** 18. **Yards:** 6,815/4,852. **Par:** 72/72. **Course Rating:** 74.2/70.2. **Slope:** 133/124. **Green Fee:** $26/$46. **Cart Fee:** $14/Person. **Walking Policy:** Walking at certain times. **Walkability:** 2. **Opened:** 1990. **Architect:** Phil Wogan. **Season:** March-Dec. **High:** June-Aug. **To obtain tee times:** Call golf shop. **Miscellaneous:** Reduced fees (weekdays, twilight, juniors), range (grass/mats), credit cards (MC, V).
Reader Comments: A tough course from the back tees ... Many long carries over marshy areas ... Greens have great contours ... Nice target golf layout ... Outstanding in the fall.

★½ **MERRIMACK GOLF CLUB**
SP-210 Howe St., Methuen, 01844, Essex County, (978)685-9717, 25 miles from Boston. **Facility Holes:** 18. **Yards:** 6,220/5,151. **Par:** 71/72. **Course Rating:** 69.3/72.3. **Slope:** 120/116. **Green Fee:** $18/$28. **Cart Fee:** $24/Cart. **Walking Policy:** Unrestricted walking. **Walkability:** 3. **Opened:** 1910. **Architect:** Donald Ross. **Season:** Year-round. **High:** April-Oct. **To obtain tee times:** Call golf shop. **Miscellaneous:** Reduced fees (seniors, juniors).

★½ **MIACOMET GOLF CLUB**
PU-12 Miacomet Rd., Nantucket, 02554, Nantucket County, (508)325-0333, 25 miles from Hyannis. **E-mail:** miacomet@nantucket.net. **Web:** www.miacometgolf.com. **Facility Holes:** 9. **Yards:** 3,385/3,002. **Par:** 37/38. **Course Rating:** 72.4/76.2. **Slope:** 116/118. **Green Fee:** $50/$61. **Cart Fee:** $38/Cart. **Walking Policy:** Unrestricted walking. **Walkability:** 2. **Opened:** 1988. **Architect:** Ralph Marble. **Season:** Year-round. **To obtain tee times:** Call up to 4 days in advance. **Miscellaneous:** Reduced fees (seniors), range (mats), credit cards (MC, V, AE, D), BF, FF.

★★ **MINK MEADOWS GOLF CLUB**
SP-320 Golf Club Rd., Vineyard Haven, 02658, Dukes County, (508)693-0600, 10 miles from Falmouth. **E-mail:** minkmdws@gis.net. **Web:** www.minkmeadows.com. **Facility Holes:** 9. **Yards:** 6,091/5,569. **Par:** 71/71. **Course Rating:** 69.6/71.7. **Slope:** 125/123. **Green Fee:** $35/$63. **Cart Fee:** $28/Cart. **Walking Policy:** Unrestricted walking. **Walkability:** 2. **Opened:** 1936. **Architect:** Wayne Stiles/Ron Prichard. **Season:** Year-round. **To obtain tee times:** Call up to 2 days in advance. **Miscellaneous:** Range (grass), credit cards (MC, V), BF, FF.

MASSACHUSETTS

MONOOSNOCK COUNTRY CLUB
SP-25 Monoosnock Ave., Leominster, 01453, Worcester County, (978)534-9738, 15 miles from Worcester. **E-mail:** mcc@bicnet.net. **Facility Holes:** 9. **Yards:** 3,051/2,800. **Par:** 35/36. **Course Rating:** 69.8/71.9. **Slope:** 120/122. **Green Fee:** $26. **Cart Fee:** $12/Person. **Walking Policy:** Unrestricted walking. **Walkability:** 2. **Opened:** 1949. **Season:** March-Nov. **High:** May-Aug. **To obtain tee times:** Call golf shop. **Miscellaneous:** Range (grass).

MOUNT HOOD GOLF COURSE
PU-100 Slayton Rd., Melrose, 02176, Middlesex County, (781)665-8139. **Facility Holes:** 18. **Yards:** 5,553/5,318. **Par:** 69/74. **Course Rating:** 65.7/65.7. **Slope:** 107/107. **Green Fee:** $25/$28. **Cart Fee:** $21/Cart. **To obtain tee times:** Call golf shop. **Miscellaneous:** Reduced fees (seniors).

★★★★ NEW ENGLAND COUNTRY CLUB
PU-180 Paine St., Bellingham, 02019, Norfolk County, (508)883-2300, 35 miles from Boston. **Facility Holes:** 18. **Yards:** 6,430/4,908. **Par:** 71/71. **Course Rating:** 70.8/68.7. **Slope:** 130/121. **Green Fee:** $42/$63. **Cart Fee:** Included in green fee. **Walking Policy:** Walking at certain times. **Walkability:** 4. **Opened:** 1990. **Architect:** Hale Irwin. **Season:** April-Nov. **High:** June-Sept. **To obtain tee times:** Call golf shop. **Miscellaneous:** Reduced fees (weekdays, twilight), range (grass), credit cards (MC, V).
Reader Comments: 18th hole is great … Expensive for the area … Very challenging layout … Computerized yardage system in use on carts … Blind landing areas … Not an easy course for average player … Always in great shape.

NEW SEABURY COUNTRY CLUB
SP-Shore Drive West, Mashpee, 02649, Barnstable County, (508)477-9110, 15 miles from Hyannis. **Web:** www.newseabury.com. **Facility Holes:** 36. **Cart Fee:** Included in green fee. **Opened:** 1962. **Architect:** William F. Mitchell. **Season:** Year-round. **High:** June-Sept. **To obtain tee times:** Call golf shop. **Miscellaneous:** Range (grass/mats), lodging (100 rooms), credit cards (MC, V, AE).
★★★★½ **BLUE COURSE** (18)
Yards: 7,200/5,764. **Par:** 72/72. **Course Rating:** 75.3/73.8. **Slope:** 130/128. **Green Fee:** $56/$150. **Walkability:** 4.
Notes: Ranked 7th in 2001 Best in State.
Reader Comments: Always great, Pebble Beach of the East, big, fast greens … Tough front on ocean—tame back 9 … Scenery is wonderful, try this course on a windy day, good luck … One of the toughest courses I have ever played … Worth the $ …. #4 is the prettiest hole … Top shelf.
★★★★ **GREEN COURSE** (18) *Pace*
Yards: 6,035/4,827. **Par:** 70/70. **Course Rating:** 69.0/67.6. **Slope:** 120/112. **Green Fee:** $46/$90. **Walking Policy:** Mandatory cart. **Walkability:** 3.
Reader Comments: Sporty, short track is a great starter round early in the year … Short, target golf, still in great condition … Expensive, but worth it … Nice mix of resort guests and members.

★★ NEWTON COMMONWEALTH GOLF COURSE
PU-212 Kenrick St, Newton, 02458, Middlesex County, (617)630-1971, 5 miles from Boston. **Web:** www.sterlinggolf.com. **Facility Holes:** 18. **Yards:** 5,313/4,466. **Par:** 70/70. **Course Rating:** 67.0/69.4. **Slope:** 125/118. **Green Fee:** $25/$30. **Cart Fee:** $24/Cart. **Walking Policy:** Unrestricted walking. **Walkability:** 4. **Opened:** 1897. **Architect:** Donald Ross. **Season:** Year-round. **High:** May-Sept. **To obtain tee times:** Call up to 4 days in advance. **Miscellaneous:** Reduced fees (weekdays, twilight, seniors, juniors), credit cards (MC, V, AE, D), BF, FF.

NORTH HILL COUNTRY CLUB
PU-Merry Ave., Duxbury, 02332, Plymouth County, (781)934-3249, 30 miles from Boston. **Facility Holes:** 9. **Yards:** 3,501/2,492. **Par:** 37/37. **Course Rating:** 35.8. **Slope:** 121. **Green Fee:** $27/$30. **Cart Fee:** $26/Cart. **Walking Policy:** Unrestricted walking. **Walkability:** 4. **Opened:** 1960. **Season:** Year-round. **High:** July-Sept. **To obtain tee times:** Call up to 7 days in advance. **Miscellaneous:** Credit cards (MC, V, D), BF, FF.

★★★ NORTON COUNTRY CLUB
SP-188 Oak St., Norton, 02766, Bristol County, (508)285-2400, 15 miles from Providence. **E-mail:** pgadel@aol.com. **Facility Holes:** 18. **Yards:** 6,546/5,040. **Par:** 71/71. **Course Rating:** 72.2/70.0. **Slope:** 137/124. **Green Fee:** $35/$57. **Cart Fee:** $13/Person. **Walking Policy:** Walking at certain times. **Walkability:** 2. **Opened:** 1955. **Architect:** Brian Silva. **Season:** April-Dec. **High:** May-Sept. **To obtain tee times:** Call up to 3 days in advance. **Miscellaneous:** Reduced fees (twilight), credit cards (V), BF, FF.
Reader Comments: A subtle but true test … Course is fine but short.

MASSACHUSETTS

★½ NORWOOD COUNTRY CLUB
PU-400 Providence Hwy., Norwood, 02062, Norfolk County, (781)769-5880, 15 miles from Boston. **E-mail:** info@norwoodgolf.com. **Web:** www.norwoodgolf.com. **Facility Holes:** 18. **Yards:** 6,009/4,997. **Par:** 71/71. **Course Rating:** 67.1/68.7. **Slope:** 112/108. **Green Fee:** $20/$25. **Cart Fee:** $24/Cart. **Walking Policy:** Unrestricted walking. **Walkability:** 1. **Opened:** 1974. **Architect:** Samuel Mitchell. **Season:** Year-round. **High:** April-Oct. **Tee times:** Call golf shop. **Miscellaneous:** Reduced fees (weekdays, twilight, seniors),range, cards (MC, V, AE, D).

★★★½ OAK RIDGE GOLF CLUB
PU-850 S. Westfield St., Feeding Hills, 01030, Hampden County, (413)789-7307, 10 miles from Springfield. **E-mail:** jpmodz@aol.com. **Web:** www.oakridgegc.com. **Facility Holes:** 18. **Yards:** 6,819/5,307. **Par:** 70/70. **Course Rating:** 71.2/70.0. **Slope:** 124/124. **Green Fee:** $20/$35. **Cart Fee:** $14/Person. **Walking Policy:** Unrestricted walking. **Walkability:** 2. **Opened:** 1974. **Architect:** George Fazio/Tom Fazio. **Season:** March-Nov. **High:** May-Oct. **To obtain tee times:** Call golf shop. **Miscellaneous:** Reduced fees (weekdays, seniors, juniors), BF, FF.
Reader Comments: Little place, nice drive in the country ... Every hole has a good look ... Nice place that is well kept.

★★★ OCEAN EDGE GOLF CLUB
R-832 Villages Dr., Brewster, 02631, Barnstable County, (508)896-5911, (800)343-6074, 90 miles from Boston. **E-mail:** oceanedge@oceanedge. **Facility Holes:** 18. **Yards:** 6,665/5,098. **Par:** 72/72. **Course Rating:** 71.9/70.6. **Slope:** 129/123. **Green Fee:** $44/$64. **Cart Fee:** $15/Person. **Walking Policy:** Walking at certain times. **Walkability:** 5. **Opened:** 1986. **Architect:** Geoffrey S. Cornish/Brian M. Silva. **Season:** Year-round. **High:** June-Sept. **To obtain tee times:** Call golf shop. **Miscellaneous:** Reduced fees (weekdays, guests, juniors), range (grass), lodging (320 rooms), credit cards (MC, V, AE).
Reader Comments: Treated like you mean something ... Great staff ... Expensive, well maintained, but not fantastic ... Great design ... No ocean ... Must make shots ... Great challenge, has everything ... I used only a handful of the clubs in my bag ... Large resort crowd tends to slow play.

★★★ OLDE BARNSTABLE FAIRGROUNDS GOLF COURSE
PU-Rte. 149, Marstons Mills, 02648, Barnstable County, (508)420-1141, 5 miles from Hyannis. **Facility Holes:** 18. **Yards:** 6,503/5,162. **Par:** 71/71. **Course Rating:** 70.7/69.2. **Slope:** 123/118. **Green Fee:** $25/$55. **Cart Fee:** $26/Cart. **Walking Policy:** Unrestricted walking. **Walkability:** 2. **Opened:** 1992. **Architect:** Geoffrey Cornish/Brian Silva/Mark Mungea. **Season:** Year-round. **High:** April-Nov. **To obtain tee times:** Call golf shop. **Miscellaneous:** Reduced fees (weekdays, twilight), range (mats), credit cards (MC, V).
Reader Comments: Good test ... Lots of trouble on the swamps of Cape Cod ... Could be great except for price & pace ... Great year-round ... Friendly members, reasonable walk

OLDE SALEM GREENS GOLF COURSE
PU-Willson St., Salem, 01970, Essex County, (978)744-2149, 15 miles from Boston. **Facility Holes:** 9. **Yards:** 3,046/2,483. **Par:** 35/35. **Course Rating:** 68.4/70.7. **Slope:** 116/112. **Green Fee:** $22/$28. **Walking Policy:** Unrestricted walking. **Walkability:** 4. **Opened:** 1933. **Season:** April-Nov. **High:** May-Aug. **To obtain tee times:** Call golf shop. **Miscellaneous:** Reduced fees (weekdays, twilight, seniors, juniors).

★★★★ OLDE SCOTLAND LINKS AT BRIDGEWATER
PU-690 Pine St., Bridgewater, 02324, Plymouth County, (508)279-3344, 25 miles from Boston. **Facility Holes:** 18. **Yards:** 6,790/4,949. **Par:** 72/72. **Course Rating:** 72.6/68.4. **Slope:** 126/111. **Green Fee:** $34/$39. **Cart Fee:** $13/Person. **Walking Policy:** Unrestricted walking. **Walkability:** 1. **Opened:** 1997. **Architect:** Brian Silva/Mark Mungeam. **Season:** March-Dec. **High:** June-Oct. **To obtain tee times:** Call golf shop. **Miscellaneous:** Reduced fees (weekdays, seniors, juniors), range (grass/mats), credit cards (MC, V, AE), BF, FF.
Reader Comments: Two distinct 9s ... New England layout ... Links design, fun to play ... Wide open ... Charming and innovative ... Once was enough ... 5 sets of tees, only 4 holes are tree lined ... Nice putting practice area as well as grass tees for driving range ... Good for all players.

OULD NEWBURY GOLF CLUB
SP-Rte. 1, Newburyport, 01950, Essex County, (978)465-9888, 35 miles from Boston. **Facility Holes:** 9. **Yards:** 3,092/2,767. **Par:** 35/38. **Course Rating:** 69.6/71.5. **Slope:** 120/115. **Green Fee:** $30. **Cart Fee:** $24/Cart. **Walking Policy:** Unrestricted walking. **Walkability:** 4. **Opened:** 1916. **Architect:** Jim Lowe. **Season:** April-Nov. **To obtain tee times:** Call golf shop. **Miscellaneous:** Metal spikes, credit cards (MC, V, D), FF.

MASSACHUSETTS

★★½ **PAUL HARNEY GOLF COURSE**
PU-74 Club Valley Dr., East Falmouth, 02536, Barnstable County, (508)563-3454, 70 miles from Boston. **E-mail:** mharvey850@aol.com. **Facility Holes:** 18. **Yards:** 3,500/3,330. **Par:** 59/59. **Course Rating:** 58.9/56.7. **Slope:** 91/89. **Green Fee:** $30/$35. **Cart Fee:** $24/Cart. **Walking Policy:** Unrestricted walking. **Walkability:** 3. **Opened:** 1967. **Architect:** Paul Harney. **Season:** Year-round. **High:** June-Sept. **To obtain tee times:** Call golf shop. **Miscellaneous:** Reduced fees (twilight), credit cards (MC, V), BF, FF.

★★½ **PEMBROKE COUNTRY CLUB**
PU-W. Elm St., Pembroke, 02359, Plymouth County, (781)826-5191, 25 miles from Boston. **Web:** www.pembrokecc.com. **Facility Holes:** 18. **Yards:** 6,532/5,887. **Par:** 71/75. **Course Rating:** 71.1/73.4. **Slope:** 124/120. **Green Fee:** $15/$40. **Cart Fee:** $12/Person. **Walking Policy:** Unrestricted walking. **Walkability:** 2. **Opened:** 1972. **Architect:** Phil Wogan. **Season:** Year-round. **High:** June-Sept. **To obtain tee times:** Call golf shop. **Miscellaneous:** Reduced fees (weekdays, twilight), metal spikes, range (grass/mats), credit cards (MC, V).

PETERSHAM COUNTRY CLUB
PU-240 N. Main St., Petersham, 01366, Worcester County, (978)724-3388, 28 miles from Worcester. **Facility Holes:** 9. **Yards:** 6,007/5,053. **Par:** 70/72. **Course Rating:** 68.4/64.4. **Slope:** 118/112. **Green Fee:** $20/$22. **Cart Fee:** $12/Person. **Walking Policy:** Unrestricted walking. **Walkability:** 3. **Opened:** 1924. **Architect:** Donald Ross. **Season:** April-Nov. **High:** May-Sept. **To obtain tee times:** Call golf shop. **Miscellaneous:** Reduced fees (weekdays, twilight, juniors), BF, FF.

PINE GROVE GOLF COURSE
PU-254 Wilson Rd., Northampton, 01062, Hampshire County, (413)584-4570, 15 miles from Springfield. **Facility Holes:** 18. **Yards:** 6,115/4,890. **Par:** 72/72. **Course Rating:** 68.8/67.3. **Slope:** 121/114. **Green Fee:** $14/$20. **Cart Fee:** $20/Cart. **Walking Policy:** Unrestricted walking. **Walkability:** 3. **Architect:** Gill Verillo. **Season:** May-Oct. **High:** June-Sept. **To obtain tee times:** Call up to 1 day in advance. **Miscellaneous:** Reduced fees (weekdays, seniors), metal spikes, FF.

PINE RIDGE COUNTRY CLUB
SP-28 Pleasant St., North Oxford, 01537, Worcester County, (508)892-9188. **Facility Holes:** 18. **Yards:** 6,002/5,333. **Par:** 71/72. **Course Rating:** 69.7/69.6. **Slope:** 120/117. **Green Fee:** $38/$47. **Cart Fee:** Included in green fee. **Season:** April-Nov. **To obtain tee times:** Call golf shop. **Miscellaneous:** Reduced fees (weekdays, twilight, seniors).

PINECREST GOLF CLUB
PU-212 Prentice St., Holliston, 01746, Middlesex County, (508)429-9871, 25 miles from Boston. **Facility Holes:** 18. **Yards:** 4,696/4,050. **Par:** 65/65. **Course Rating:** 63.2. **Slope:** 103. **Green Fee:** $20/$27. **Cart Fee:** $24/Cart. **Walking Policy:** Unrestricted walking. **Walkability:** 2. **Opened:** 1958. **Season:** April-Nov. **To obtain tee times:** Call up to 7 days in advance. **Miscellaneous:** Reduced fees (weekdays, seniors, juniors), range (grass), BF, FF.

PINEHILLS GOLF CLUB
PU-54 Clubhouse Dr., Plymouth, 02360, Plymouth County, (508)209-3000, (866)855-4653, 45 miles from Boston. **Web:** www.pinehillsgolf.com. **Facility Holes:** 36. **Green Fee:** $75/$95. **Cart Fee:** Included in green fee. **Walking Policy:** Unrestricted walking. **Walkability:** 3. **Season:** April-Dec. **To obtain tee times:** Call up to 7 days in advance. **Miscellaneous:** Reduced fees (twilight), range (grass), credit cards (MC, V, AE), BF, FF.
JONES COURSE (18)
Yards: 7,175/5,380. **Par:** 72/72. **Course Rating:** 73.8/71.2. **Slope:** 135/125. **Opened:** 2001. **Architect:** Rees Jones.
NICKLAUS COURSE (18)
Yards: 7,243/5,185. **Par:** 72/72. **Opened:** 2002. **Architect:** Jack Nicklaus.

PLYMOUTH COUNTRY CLUB
SP-Warren Ave., Plymouth, 02361, Plymouth County, (508)746-0476, 40 miles from Boston. **Facility Holes:** 18. **Yards:** 6,164/5,524. **Par:** 69/69. **Course Rating:** 70.0/68.6. **Slope:** 125/121. **Green Fee:** $65. **Walkability:** 2. **Opened:** 1901. **Architect:** Donald Ross. **To obtain tee times:** Call golf shop.

PONKAPOAG GOLF CLUB
PU-2167 Washington St., Canton, 02021, Norfolk County, (781)575-1001, 10 miles from Boston. **Facility Holes:** 36. **Green Fee:** $12/$20. **Cart Fee:** $19/Cart. **Walking Policy:** Unrestricted walking. **Walkability:** 2. **Opened:** 1933. **Architect:** Donald Ross. **Season:** April-Dec. **High:** May-Aug. **To obtain tee times:** Call golf shop. **Miscellaneous:** Reduced fees (week-

days, seniors, juniors), range (grass/mats), credit cards (MC, V).
★★½ **COURSE 1 (18)**
Yards: 6,728/5,523. **Par:** 72/74. **Course Rating:** 72.0/70.8. **Slope:** 126/115.
Special Notes: Also has another 18-hole course.

PONTOOSUC LAKE COUNTRY CLUB
PU-Kirkwood Dr., Pittsfield, 01201, Berkshire County, (413)445-4217, 45 miles from
Springfield. **Facility Holes:** 18. **Yards:** 6,207/5,240. **Par:** 70/70. **Course Rating:** 68.1/68.2.
Slope: 114/115. **Green Fee:** $8/$20. **Cart Fee:** $20/Cart. **Walking Policy:** Unrestricted walking.
Walkability: 3. **Opened:** 1920. **Architect:** Wayne Stiles. **Season:** April-Nov. **To
obtain tee times:** Call golf shop. **Miscellaneous:** Reduced fees (weekdays, seniors), FF.

★★★★ POQUOY BROOK GOLF CLUB
PU-20 Leonard St., Lakeville, 02347, Plymouth County, (508)947-5261, 45 miles from
Boston. **E-mail:** shdickow@yahoo.com. **Web:** www.poquoybrook.com. **Facility Holes:** 18.
Yards: 6,762/5,415. **Par:** 72/73. **Course Rating:** 72.4/71.0. **Slope:** 128/114. **Green Fee:**
$35/$42. **Cart Fee:** $14/Person. **Walking Policy:** Unrestricted walking. **Walkability:** 2. **Opened:**
1962. **Architect:** Geoffrey S. Cornish. **Season:** Year-round. **High:** April-Nov. **To obtain tee
times:** Call up to 7 days in advance. **Miscellaneous:** Reduced fees (weekdays, twilight,
juniors), range (grass), credit cards (MC, V, AE, D), BF, FF.
Reader Comments: Very nice tree-lined layout … Fairways and tee boxes in terrific condition year
round … A course that good players love to play … A hidden beauty.

PRESIDENTS GOLF COURSE
PU-357 W. Squantum St., Quincy, 02171, Norfolk County, (617)328-3444. **Facility Holes:** 18.
Yards: 5,665/4,425. **Par:** 70/70. **Course Rating:** 67.0/65.8. **Slope:** 115/110. **Green Fee:**
$16/$30. **Cart Fee:** $12/Person. **Season:** March-Dec. **To obtain tee times:** Call golf shop.
Miscellaneous: Reduced fees (weekdays, twilight, seniors, juniors).

★★★★ QUASHNET VALLEY COUNTRY CLUB
PU-309 Old Barnstable Rd., Mashpee, 02649, Barnstable County, (508)477-4412,
(800)433-8633, 55 miles from Boston. **Web:** www.quashnetvalley.com. **Facility Holes:** 18.
Yards: 6,602/5,094. **Par:** 72/72. **Course Rating:** 71.7/70.3. **Slope:** 132/119. **Green Fee:**
$25/$56. **Cart Fee:** $14/Person. **Walking Policy:** Walking at certain times. **Walkability:** 3.
Opened: 1974. **Architect:** Geoffrey Cornish/William Robinson. **Season:** Year-round. **High:**
April-Nov. **To obtain tee times:** Call up to 7 days in advance. **Miscellaneous:** Reduced fees
(weekdays, twilight), metal spikes, range (grass), credit cards (MC, V), BF, FF.
Reader Comments: Friendly staff, shotmaker's course … A Cape Cod beauty … Good value for
the Cape … Very friendly and helpful … Nice layout … Have to have cart on weekend. UGH!! …
Target golf … Front 9 much better than back … Lovely scenery, quiet and well known.

THE RANCH GOLF CLUB
PU-100 Ranch Club Rd., Southwick, 01077, Hampshire County, (413)569-9333. **E-mail:**
info@theranchgolfclub.com. **Web:** www.theranchgolfclub.com. **Facility Holes:** 18. **Yards:**
7,174/4,983. **Par:** 72/72. **Course Rating:** 74.1/69.7. **Slope:** 140/122. **Green Fee:** $85/$100. **Cart
Fee:** Included in green fee. **Opened:** 2001. **Architect:** Damian Pascuzzo. **Season:** April-Nov. **To
obtain tee times:** Call golf shop. **Miscellaneous:** Reduced fees (twilight, juniors), credit cards
(MC, V, AE).

★★½ REHOBOTH COUNTRY CLUB
PU-155 Perryville Rd., Rehoboth, 02769, Bristol County, (508)252-6259, 15 miles from
Providence. **Facility Holes:** 18. **Yards:** 6,950/5,450. **Par:** 72/75. **Course Rating:** 72.5/70.4.
Slope: 125/115. **Green Fee:** $25/$30. **Cart Fee:** $24/Cart. **Walking Policy:** Unrestricted walk-
ing. **Walkability:** 1. **Opened:** 1966. **Architect:** Geoffrey Cornish/William Robinson. **Season:**
March-Dec. **High:** June-Sept. **To obtain tee times:** Call up to 7 days in advance.
Miscellaneous: Reduced fees (twilight, seniors, juniors), credit cards (MC, V, AE), BF, FF.

★★ RIDDER GOLF CLUB
PU-300 Oak St., Rte. 14, Whitman, 02382, Plymouth County, (781)447-9003, 25 miles from
Boston. **Facility Holes:** 18. **Yards:** 5,909/4,862. **Par:** 70/70. **Course Rating:** 68.1/67.1. **Slope:**
113/107. **Green Fee:** $29/$32. **Cart Fee:** $13/Person. **Walking Policy:** Unrestricted walking.
Walkability: 2. **Opened:** 1961. **Architect:** Henry Hohman/Geoffrey S. Cornish. **Season:** Year-
round. **High:** May-Nov. **To obtain tee times:** Call golf shop. **Miscellaneous:** Reduced fees
(weekdays, juniors), range (grass).

★★★½ RIVER BEND COUNTRY CLUB
PU-250 E. Center St., West Bridgewater, 02379, Plymouth County, (508)580-3673, 25 miles
from Boston. **E-mail:** doaneii@aol.com. **Web:** www.riverbendgc.com. **Facility Holes:** 18. **Yards:**
6,659/4,915. **Par:** 71/71. **Course Rating:** 70.9/67.7. **Slope:** 127/120. **Green Fee:** $37/$47. **Cart**

Fee: $13/Person. **Walking Policy:** Walking at certain times. **Opened:** 1999. **Architect:** Phil Wogan. **Season:** March-Dec. **High:** April-Oct. **To obtain tee times:** Call up to 5 days in advance. **Miscellaneous:** Reduced fees (seniors, juniors), credit cards (MC, V, AE, D), BF, FF. **Reader Comments:** Very good public course, greens in good shape … 2 very different 9s—much improved! … Well designed & delightful … The par 5s on the back 9 are awesome … Practice those bump and run shots.

ROCHESTER GOLF CLUB
PU-323 Roundsville Rd., Rochester, 02770, Plymouth County, (508)763-5155. **Facility Holes:** 18. **Yards:** 5,280/4,032. **Par:** 69/69. **Course Rating:** 66.0/58.0. **Slope:** 115/100. **Green Fee:** $24. **Cart Fee:** $20/Cart. **Walkability:** 1. **Season:** April-Nov. **To obtain tee times:** Call golf shop.

ROWLEY COUNTRY CLUB
PU-235 Dodge Rd., Rowley, 01969, Essex County, (978)948-2731, 33 miles from Boston. **Web:** www.rowleygolf.com. **Facility Holes:** 9. **Yards:** 3,325/2,470. **Par:** 36/35. **Course Rating:** 70.7/67.5. **Slope:** 127/109. **Green Fee:** $28/$36. **Cart Fee:** $24/Cart. **Walking Policy:** Unrestricted walking. **Walkability:** 3. **Opened:** 1971. **Season:** March-Dec. **High:** June-Sept. **To obtain tee times:** Call up to 7 days in advance. **Miscellaneous:** Reduced fees (twilight, seniors), range (grass/mats), credit cards (MC, V), BF, FF.

★★½ SADDLE HILL COUNTRY CLUB
PU-204 Saddle Hill Rd., Hopkinton, 01748, Middlesex County, (508)435-4630, 26 miles from Boston. **Facility Holes:** 18. **Yards:** 6,900/5,619. **Par:** 72/72. **Course Rating:** 72.8/70.3. **Slope:** 124/108. **Green Fee:** $27/$32. **Cart Fee:** $13/Person. **Walking Policy:** Walking at certain times. **Walkability:** 4. **Opened:** 1963. **Architect:** William F. Mitchell. **Season:** March-Dec. **High:** May-Sept. **To obtain tee times:** Call up to 7 days in advance. **Miscellaneous:** Reduced fees (twilight, seniors, juniors), metal spikes, range (mats), credit cards (MC, V), BF, FF.

★★★ SAGAMORE SPRING GOLF CLUB
PU-1287 Main St., Lynnfield, 01940, Essex County, (781)334-3151, 15 miles from Boston. **E-mail:** bkfellows@sagamorespring.com. **Web:** www.sagamorespring.com. **Facility Holes:** 18. **Yards:** 5,936/4,784. **Par:** 70/70. **Course Rating:** 68.6/66.5. **Slope:** 119/112. **Green Fee:** $33/$42. **Cart Fee:** $24/Cart. **Walking Policy:** Unrestricted walking. **Walkability:** 2. **Opened:** 1929. **Architect:** Richard Luff. **Season:** March-Jan. **High:** May-Sept. **To obtain tee times:** Call up to 4 days in advance. **Miscellaneous:** Reduced fees (weekdays, seniors), metal spikes, range (mats), credit cards (MC, V, D), BF, FF. **Reader Comments:** Challenging par 3s, check out #9 & 18 … A couple of forgiving par 5s … Usually have a ranger roaming to speed up play … Average round 5 hours, good driving range, food, proshop … A nice course for ladies … Both 9s finish with a tough par 3 … Short but fun.

★★★ SANDWICH HOLLOWS GOLF CLUB
PU-Round Hill Rd., East Sandwich, 02537, Barnstable County, (508)888-3384, 60 miles from Boston. **E-mail:** gmartzolf@sandwichhollows.com. **Web:** www.sandwichhollows.com. **Facility Holes:** 18. **Yards:** 6,220/4,894. **Par:** 71/70. **Course Rating:** 70.4/68.1. **Slope:** 124/115. **Green Fee:** $35/$47. **Cart Fee:** $24/Cart. **Walking Policy:** Walking at certain times. **Walkability:** 3. **Opened:** 1972. **Architect:** Richard Cross. **Season:** Year-round. **To obtain tee times:** Call golf shop. **Miscellaneous:** Reduced fees (weekdays, twilight), metal spikes, range (grass), credit cards (MC, V), BF, FF. **Reader Comments:** Very hilly … Fairly easy, great condition … New ownership improving a good course … Just OK … Hilly course … Fast greens. **Special Notes:** Formerly Round Hill Country Club.

★★★ SANDY BURR COUNTRY CLUB
SP-103 Cochituate Rd., Wayland, 01778, Middlesex County, (508)358-7211, 16 miles from Boston. **E-mail:** kmkee@aol.com. **Web:** www.sandyburr.com. **Facility Holes:** 18. **Yards:** 6,412/4,561. **Par:** 72/69. **Course Rating:** 70.8/66.2. **Slope:** 125/110. **Green Fee:** $35/$45. **Cart Fee:** $30/Cart. **Walking Policy:** Unrestricted walking. **Walkability:** 3. **Opened:** 1922. **Architect:** Donald Ross. **Season:** April-Dec. **High:** May-Sept. **To obtain tee times:** Call golf shop. **Miscellaneous:** Reduced fees (twilight, seniors, juniors), credit cards (MC, V, AE, D), FF. **Reader Comments:** A good Donald Ross layout … Play early … Some blind shots … Slow on weekends … Some greens crowned and tricky.

SCITUATE COUNTRY CLUB
SP-91 Old Driftway, Scituate, 02066, Plymouth County, (781)545-9768, 15 miles from Boston. **Facility Holes:** 18. **Yards:** 6,051/5,407. **Par:** 70/72. **Course Rating:** 69.9/72.2. **Slope:** 125/124. **Green Fee:** $30. **Cart Fee:** $12/Person. **Walking Policy:** Unrestricted walking. **Walkability:** 3. **Opened:** 1920. **Season:** March-Nov. **High:** June-Sept. **To obtain tee times:** Call up to 3 days in advance. **Miscellaneous:** BF, FF.

SHAKER FARMS COUNTRY CLUB

SP-866 Shaker Rd., Westfield, 01086, Hampden County, (413)562-2770. **Facility Holes:** 18. **Yards:** 6,485/5,954. **Par:** 72/72. **Course Rating:** 68.7/69.3. **Slope:** 118/116. **Green Fee:** $15/$29. **Cart Fee:** $12/Cart. **Season:** March-Nov. **To obtain tee times:** Call golf shop. **Miscellaneous:** Reduced fees (weekdays, twilight, juniors).

★★★★ SHAKER HILLS GOLF CLUB

PU-146 Shaker Rd., Harvard, 01451, Middlesex County, (978)772-2227, 35 miles from Boston. **Web:** www.shakerhills.com. **Facility Holes:** 18. **Yards:** 6,850/5,001. **Par:** 71/71. **Course Rating:** 72.3/67.9. **Slope:** 135/116. **Green Fee:** $60/$65. **Cart Fee:** Included in green fee. **Walking Policy:** Unrestricted walking. **Walkability:** 4. **Opened:** 1991. **Architect:** Brian Silva. **Season:** April-Nov. **High:** June-Sept. **To obtain tee times:** Call up to 4 days in advance. **Miscellaneous:** Reduced fees (twilight), range (grass/mats), credit cards (MC, V), BF, FF. **Notes:** Ranked 44th in 1996 America's Top 75 Affordable Courses.

Reader Comments: Outstanding course with a great layout but a little pricey ... Need all your clubs for this course ... Narrow and rocky ... Greens are fast and tricky ... Only 4 par-3 holes ... I would play this course more often if it were more affordable ... Picturesque ... Great wildlife—foxes & deer.

★★½ SHERATON COLONIAL GOLF CLUB

R-427 Walnut St., Lynnfield, 01940, Essex County, (781)876-6031, 12 miles from Boston. **Facility Holes:** 18. **Yards:** 6,565/5,280. **Par:** 70/72. **Course Rating:** 72.8/69.5. **Slope:** 130/109. **Green Fee:** $50/$60. **Cart Fee:** Included in green fee. **Walking Policy:** Mandatory carts. **Walkability:** 2. **Opened:** 1929. **Architect:** William F. Mitchell. **Season:** April-Nov. **High:** May-Oct. **To obtain tee times:** Call up to 3 days in advance. **Miscellaneous:** Reduced fees (twilight), range (grass/mats), lodging (280 rooms), credit cards (MC, V, AE, D, DC), BF, FF.

SHERATON TWIN BROOKS GOLF COURSE

R-35 Scudder Ave., Hyannis, 02601, Barnstable County, (508)862-6980, 75 miles from Boston. **E-mail:** twinbrooks@hotmail.com. **Web:** www.twinbrooksgolf.com. **Facility Holes:** 18. **Yards:** 2,621/2,239. **Par:** 54/54. **Green Fee:** $17/$33. **Cart Fee:** $22/Cart. **Walking Policy:** Unrestricted walking. **Walkability:** 2. **Opened:** 1965. **Architect:** Geoffrey Cornish/William Robinson. **Season:** Year-round. **To obtain tee times:** Call golf shop. **Miscellaneous:** Reduced fees (weekdays, twilight, seniors, juniors), lodging (243 rooms), credit cards (MC, V, AE, D, DC), BF, FF.

SIASCONSET GOLF CLUB

PU-250 Milestone Rd., Siasconset, 02564, Nantucket County, (508)257-6596, 90 miles from Boston. **Facility Holes:** 9. **Yards:** 2,472/2,472. **Par:** 34/34. **Course Rating:** 68.1/68.1. **Slope:** 113/113. **Green Fee:** $48. **Walking Policy:** Unrestricted walking. **Walkability:** 1. **Opened:** 1894. **Architect:** John Grout. **Season:** June-Oct. **High:** July-Aug. **To obtain tee times:** Call golf shop. **Miscellaneous:** BF, FF.

SKYLINE COUNTRY CLUB

PU-405 S. Main St., Lanesboro, 01237, Berkshire County, (413)445-5584. **Facility Holes:** 18. **Yards:** 6,197/4,814. **Par:** 72/72. **Course Rating:** 72.3/68.1. **Slope:** 128/110. **Green Fee:** $18/$23. **Cart Fee:** $11/Person. **Walkability:** 3. **Opened:** 1962. **Season:** April-Nov. **High:** May-Sept. **To obtain tee times:** Call up to 5 days in advance. **Miscellaneous:** Reduced fees (weekdays, twilight), range (grass), credit cards (MC, V), BF, FF.

★★★½ SOUTH HAMPTON COUNTRY CLUB

PU-329 College Hwy., Southampton, 01073, Hampshire County, (413)527-9815, 12 miles from Springfield. **Facility Holes:** 18. **Yards:** 6,520/5,370. **Par:** 72/71. **Course Rating:** 69.0/67.0. **Slope:** 114/113. **Green Fee:** $15/$24. **Cart Fee:** $18/Cart. **Walking Policy:** Unrestricted walking. **Walkability:** 3. **Opened:** 1951. **Architect:** John Strycharz. **Season:** Year-round. **High:** May-Sept. **To obtain tee times:** Call golf shop. **Miscellaneous:** FF.

Reader Comments: Nice little course ... Very well maintained ... Varied terrain, pace can be slow depending on day ... Keeps improving every year.

★★½ SOUTH SHORE COUNTRY CLUB

SP-274 South St., Hingham, 02043, Plymouth County, (781)749-8479, 19 miles from Boston. **E-mail:** jkgolfpro@aol.com. **Web:** www.jkgolfpro.com. **Facility Holes:** 18. **Yards:** 6,444/5,064. **Par:** 72/72. **Course Rating:** 71.0/69.3. **Slope:** 128/116. **Green Fee:** $25/$36. **Cart Fee:** $25/Cart. **Walking Policy:** Unrestricted walking. **Walkability:** 4. **Opened:** 1925. **Architect:** Wayne Stiles. **Season:** April-Dec. **High:** June-Sept. **To obtain tee times:** Call golf shop. **Miscellaneous:** Reduced fees (twilight, seniors, juniors), range (mats), credit cards (MC, V).

MASSACHUSETTS

SOUTHWICK COUNTRY CLUB
PU-739 College Hwy., Southwick, 01077, Hampden County, (413)569-0136, 8 miles from Springfield. **Facility Holes:** 18. **Yards:** 6,100/5,900. **Par:** 71/71. **Course Rating:** 64.8/64.7. **Slope:** 106/103. **Green Fee:** $17/$22. **Cart Fee:** $23/Cart. **Walking Policy:** Unrestricted walking. **Walkability:** 1. **Opened:** 1928. **Season:** Year-round. **High:** March-Nov. **To obtain tee times:** Call up to 1 day in advance. **Miscellaneous:** Reduced fees (weekdays, twilight, seniors), credit cards (MC, V), BF, FF.

★★★ SQUIRREL RUN GOLF & COUNTRY CLUB
PU-Rte. 44, Carver Rd., Plymouth, 02360, Plymouth County, (508)746-5001, 40 miles from Boston. **E-mail:** davidsquirrel1@aol.com. **Facility Holes:** 18. **Yards:** 2,859/1,990. **Par:** 57/57. **Course Rating:** 85.0/82.0. **Slope:** 55.4/53.7. **Green Fee:** $15/$25. **Cart Fee:** $10/Person. **Walking Policy:** Unrestricted walking. **Walkability:** 1. **Opened:** 1991. **Architect:** Ray Richard. **Season:** Year-round. **High:** July-Aug. **To obtain tee times:** Call golf shop. **Miscellaneous:** Reduced fees (twilight, seniors, juniors), range (grass/mats), credit cards (MC, V), BF, FF. Reader Comments: Fun par 3 … Slow pace … A good course to practice your irons … Great place to bring kids.

★★ ST. ANNE COUNTRY CLUB
PU-781 Shoemaker Lane, Feeding Hills, 01030, Hampden County, (413)786-2088, 6 miles from Springfield. **Facility Holes:** 18. **Yards:** 6,360/5,018. **Par:** 72/72. **Course Rating:** 70.8/70.0. **Slope:** 116/114. **Green Fee:** $16/$21. **Cart Fee:** $24/Cart. **Walking Policy:** Unrestricted walking. **Walkability:** 3. **Season:** March-Dec. **High:** June-Aug. **To obtain tee times:** Call up to 7 days in advance. **Miscellaneous:** Reduced fees (seniors), credit cards (MC, V, AE, D, DC), BF, FF.

STONE-E-LEA GOLF COURSE
PU-1411 County St., Attleboro, 02703, Bristol County, (508)222-9735, 30 miles from Boston. **Facility Holes:** 18. **Yards:** 6,042/5,150. **Par:** 70/70. **Course Rating:** 69.5/67.8. **Slope:** 116/112. **Green Fee:** $17/$24. **Cart Fee:** $20/Cart. **Walking Policy:** Unrestricted walking. **Walkability:** 2. **Opened:** 1958. **Architect:** Ed Lapierre Sr. **Season:** Year-round. **To obtain tee times:** Call golf shop. **Miscellaneous:** Reduced fees (seniors), FF.

STOW ACRES COUNTRY CLUB
PU-58 Randall Rd., Stow, 01775, Middlesex County, (978)568-1100, 25 miles from Boston. **E-mail:** mgiles@shore.net. **Web:** www.stowacres.com. **Facility Holes:** 36. **Green Fee:** $36/$45. **Cart Fee:** $27/Cart. **Walking Policy:** Unrestricted walking. **Architect:** Geoffrey S. Cornish. **Season:** March-Dec. **High:** April-Nov. **To obtain tee times:** Call golf shop. **Miscellaneous:** Reduced fees (weekdays, twilight, seniors, juniors), range (mats), credit cards (MC, V, AE).
★★★½ **NORTH COURSE** (18)
Yards: 6,950/6,011. **Par:** 72/72. **Course Rating:** 72.8/70.6. **Slope:** 130/120. **Walkability:** 2. **Opened:** 1965.
Notes: Ranked 12th in 2001 Best in State
Reader Comments: Best public course in New England … Great greens and layout … Well worth the trip … Beauty and challenge … Superior all around experience … They have a Top 100 golf shop for a reason … Great golf school… Stay in the game on the front nine, and score on the back.
★★★ **SOUTH COURSE** (18)
Yards: 6,520/5,642. **Par:** 72/72. **Course Rating:** 71.8/69.7. **Slope:** 120/116. **Walkability:** 4. **Opened:** 1922.
Reader Comments: Solid layout … Not as good as the North Course … Hilly, sporty layout.

SUN VALLEY GOLF COURSE
PU-329 Summer St., Rehoboth, 02769, Bristol County, (508)336-8686, 10 miles from Providence. **Facility Holes:** 18. **Yards:** 6,734/5,654. **Par:** 71/73. **Course Rating:** 71.4/68.0. **Slope:** 118/113. **Green Fee:** $23/$28. **Cart Fee:** $22/Cart. **Walking Policy:** Unrestricted walking. **Opened:** 1957. **Architect:** Geoffrey Cornish. **Season:** March-Nov. **High:** May-Sept. **To obtain tee times:** Call up to 7 days in advance. **Miscellaneous:** Reduced fees (seniors).

★★½ SWANSEA COUNTRY CLUB
PU-299 Market St., Swansea, 02777, Bristol County, (508)379-9886, 10 miles from Providence. **Facility Holes:** 27. **Yards:** 6,840/5,239. **Par:** 72/72. **Course Rating:** 72.7/69.9. **Slope:** 124/109. **Green Fee:** $25/$36. **Cart Fee:** $24/Cart. **Walking Policy:** Unrestricted walking. **Walkability:** 2. **Opened:** 1963. **Architect:** Geoffrey S. Cornish. **Season:** Year-round. **High:** May-Sept. **To obtain tee times:** Call golf shop. **Miscellaneous:** Reduced fees (weekdays, twilight, seniors, juniors), range (grass), credit cards (MC, V, AE, D), BF, FF.
Special Notes: Also has an executive 9-hole course.

★★★★½ **TACONIC GOLF CLUB** *Service, Value+, Condition+, Pace+*
SP-Meacham St., Williamstown, 01267, Berkshire County, (413)458-3997, 35 miles from Albany. **E-mail:** capohle@adelphia.net. **Facility Holes:** 18. **Yards:** 6,640/5,202. **Par:** 71/71. **Course Rating:** 71.7/69.9. **Slope:** 127/123. **Green Fee:** $140. **Cart Fee:** Included in green fee. **Walking Policy:** Mandatory carts. **Walkability:** 3. **Opened:** 1896. **Architect:** Wayne E. Stiles/John R. Van Kleek. **Season:** April-Nov. **To obtain tee times:** Call up to 7 days in advance. **Miscellaneous:** Range (grass/mats), credit cards (MC, V), BF, FF.
Reader Comments: A New England classic. Stiles is underrated … One of the finest golf courses in the country … Every blade of grass is perfect … Pace of play can be a problem but rangers do a good job … Walk this course to enjoy its beauty … Mountain setting … Calls for strategic play especially around greens.

★★★½ **TEKOA COUNTRY CLUB**
SP-459 Russell Rd., Westfield, 01085, Hampden County, (413)568-1064, 10 miles from Springfield. **Facility Holes:** 18. **Yards:** 6,002/5,115. **Par:** 70/74. **Course Rating:** 69.6/71.0. **Slope:** 118/116. **Green Fee:** $15/$27. **Cart Fee:** $24/Cart. **Walking Policy:** Unrestricted walking. **Walkability:** 1. **Opened:** 1929. **Architect:** Geoffrey Cornish/Donald Ross. **Season:** March-Dec. **High:** May-Sept. **To obtain tee times:** Call up to 5 days in advance. **Miscellaneous:** Reduced fees (twilight, seniors, juniors), BF, FF.
Reader Comments: 5 par 3s make for good skins game … Too tight … Easy walking course.

TOUISSET COUNTRY CLUB
PU-221 Pearse Rd., Swansea, 02777, Bristol County, (508)679-9577, 15 miles from Providence. **Facility Holes:** 9. **Yards:** 6,211/5,565. **Par:** 71/73. **Course Rating:** 69.1/71.0. **Slope:** 111/114. **Green Fee:** $15/$21. **Cart Fee:** $25/Cart. **Walking Policy:** Unrestricted walking. **Walkability:** 1. **Opened:** 1961. **Architect:** Ray Brigham. **Season:** Year-round. **To obtain tee times:** Call golf shop. **Miscellaneous:** Reduced fees (weekdays, twilight, seniors, juniors), credit cards (MC, V, D), BF, FF.

★★★½ **TRULL BROOK GOLF COURSE**
PU-170 River Rd., Tewksbury, 01876, Middlesex County, (978)851-6731, 28 miles from Boston. **Web:** www.trullbrookgolf.com. **Facility Holes:** 18. **Yards:** 6,350/5,193. **Par:** 72/72. **Course Rating:** 69.8/69.6. **Slope:** 123/118. **Green Fee:** $38/$40. **Cart Fee:** $29/Cart. **Walking Policy:** Unrestricted walking. **Walkability:** 4. **Opened:** 1963. **Architect:** Geoffrey S. Cornish. **Season:** March-Nov. **High:** June-Aug. **To obtain tee times:** Call up to 7 days in advance. **Miscellaneous:** Reduced fees (weekdays, twilight, seniors, juniors), cards (MC, V).
Reader Comments: Very interesting layout … Can be fast round of golf … Local favorite … On most fairways you are hitting downhill … Fun combination of doglegs, hills and views … Short course packs a punch.

VETERANS GOLF COURSE
PU-1059 S. Branch Pkwy., Springfield, 01118, Hampden County, (413)783-9611. **Facility Holes:** 18. **Yards:** 6,500/5,500. **Par:** 72/72. **Course Rating:** 70.1/69.9. **Slope:** 116/112. **Green Fee:** $10/$18. **Cart Fee:** $21/Cart. **Walking Policy:** Unrestricted walking. **Walkability:** 2. **Opened:** 1963. **Architect:** Geoffrey Cornish. **Season:** March-Dec. **To obtain tee times:** Call up to 3 days in advance. **Miscellaneous:** Reduced fees (seniors, juniors), BF, FF.

★★★★ **WACHUSETT COUNTRY CLUB**
SP-187 Prospect St., West Boylston, 01583, Worcester County, (508)835-2264, 7 miles from Worcester. **Web:** www.wachusettcountryclub.com. **Facility Holes:** 18. **Yards:** 6,608/6,216. **Par:** 72/72. **Course Rating:** 71.7/70.0. **Slope:** 124/120. **Green Fee:** $25/$45. **Cart Fee:** $28/Cart. **Walking Policy:** Unrestricted walking. **Walkability:** 2. **Opened:** 1928. **Architect:** Donald Ross. **Season:** April-Nov. **High:** May-Oct. **To obtain tee times:** Call up to 5 days in advance. **Miscellaneous:** Reduced fees (twilight), range (grass/mats), cards (MC, V, AE; D), BF, FF.
Reader Comments: A gem, but can be slow … Good Donald Ross design … Good condition, crowded but moved along … Need a cart—it's very hilly … For all levels of play … Score on the front, blind shots on back.

★★★½ **WAHCONAH COUNTRY CLUB**
SP-15 Orchard Rd., Dalton, 01226, Berkshire County, (413)684-1333, 4 miles from Pittsfield. **Facility Holes:** 18. **Yards:** 6,567/5,567. **Par:** 71/73. **Course Rating:** 71.9/72.5. **Slope:** 126/123. **Green Fee:** $50/$60. **Cart Fee:** $24/Cart. **Walking Policy:** Unrestricted walking. **Walkability:** 3. **Opened:** 1930. **Architect:** W. Stiles/G.S. Cornish/R. Armacost. **Season:** April-Nov. **High:** April-Nov. **To obtain tee times:** Call golf shop. **Miscellaneous:** Reduced fees (weekdays), metal spikes, range (grass), credit cards (MC, V).
Reader Comments: Nice little gem in the Berkshires … Used to play here as a kid—many upgrades since then … Great layout … Good service.

MASSACHUSETTS

★★★ WAUBEEKA GOLF LINKS
PU-137 New Ashford Rd., Williamstown, 01267, Berkshire County, (413)458-8355, 12 miles from Pittsfield. **Facility Holes:** 18. **Yards:** 6,394/5,023. **Par:** 72/72. **Course Rating:** 70.6/69.6. **Slope:** 126/119. **Green Fee:** $33/$42. **Cart Fee:** $25/Cart. **Walking Policy:** Unrestricted walking. **Walkability:** 3. **Opened:** 1966. **Architect:** Rowland Armacost. **Season:** April-Nov. **High:** June-Aug. **To obtain tee times:** Call up to 7 days in advance. **Miscellaneous:** Reduced fees (twilight, juniors), range (grass), credit cards (MC, V, AE, D), BF, FF.
Reader Comments: Very scenic … Delightful experience … Nice track in great mountain setting … Course tends to get soggy after it rains.

★★★★½ WAVERLY OAKS GOLF CLUB *Condition*
R-444 Long Pond Rd., Plymouth, 02360, Plymouth County, (508)224-6016, 40 miles from Boston. **E-mail:** waverlyoaks@adelphia.net. **Web:** www.waverlyoaksgolfclub.com. **Facility Holes:** 27. **Yards:** 7,114/5,587. **Par:** 72/72. **Course Rating:** 73.5/71.4. **Slope:** 130/127. **Green Fee:** $65/$85. **Cart Fee:** Included in green fee. **Walking Policy:** Mandatory carts. **Walkability:** 4. **Opened:** 1998. **Architect:** Brian Silva. **Season:** March-Dec. **High:** May-Oct. **To obtain tee times:** Call up to 7 days in advance. **Miscellaneous:** Reduced fees (weekdays, juniors), range (grass/mats), credit cards (MC, V, AE), BF, FF.
Reader Comments: A great design … High quality layout with breathtaking views … #17 is a blast from the tips - you better flush it … Pricey, but that is the Cape … Better bring your A game—big league course … Spectacular scenery of Plymouth.
Special Notes: Also has a 9-hole executive course.

WEBSTER DUDLEY GOLF CLUB
SP-80 Airport Rd., Dudley, 01571, Worcester County, (508)943-4538, 20 miles from Worcester. **E-mail:** maobell@aol.com. **Web:** www.dudleyhill.homestead.com. **Facility Holes:** 9. **Yards:** 3,241/2,848. **Par:** 36/36. **Course Rating:** 71.4/71.3. **Slope:** 123/115. **Green Fee:** $25. **Cart Fee:** $22/Cart. **Walking Policy:** Unrestricted walking. **Walkability:** 2. **Opened:** 1926. **Architect:** Devereaux Emmet. **Season:** April-Dec. **High:** May-Sept. **Tee times:** Call golf shop. **Miscellaneous:** Reduced fees (juniors), credit cards (MC, V), BF, FF.

★★ WESTMINSTER COUNTRY CLUB
SP-51 Ellis Rd., Westminster, 01473, Worcester County, (978)874-5938, 22 miles from Worcester. **E-mail:** westwcc@aol.com. **Web:** www.westminstercountryclub.com. **Facility Holes:** 18. **Yards:** 6,521/5,453. **Par:** 71/71. **Course Rating:** 71.2/71.3. **Slope:** 124/117. **Green Fee:** $25/$30. **Cart Fee:** $24/Cart. **Walking Policy:** Unrestricted walking. **Walkability:** 3. **Opened:** 1957. **Architect:** Manny Francis. **Season:** April-Nov. **High:** June-Aug. **To obtain tee times:** Call golf shop. **Miscellaneous:** Reduced fees (weekdays, twilight), credit cards (MC, V, AE, D), BF, FF.

★★★★ WESTOVER GOLF COURSE *Value+*
PU-South St., Granby, 01033, Hampshire County, (413)547-8610, 10 miles from Springfield. **Facility Holes:** 18. **Yards:** 7,025/5,980. **Par:** 72/72. **Course Rating:** 73.9/72.0. **Slope:** 131/118. **Green Fee:** $14/$19. **Cart Fee:** $20/Cart. **Walking Policy:** Unrestricted walking. **Walkability:** 2. **Opened:** 1950. **Architect:** Al Zikorus. **Season:** March-Dec. **To obtain tee times:** Call up to 3 days in advance. **Miscellaneous:** Reduced fees (twilight, seniors, juniors), range (grass), credit cards (MC, V, AE, D), BF, FF.
Reader Comments: All the golf you could ever want … Bring your 'A' game, fades and draws … Lots of long par 4s … Very enjoyable to walk … Can be busy at times … Excellent greens.

WHALING CITY GOLF COURSE
PU-561 Hathaway Rd., New Bedford, 02740, Bristol County, (508)996-9393, 22 miles from Providence. **Facility Holes:** 18. **Yards:** 6,544/5,908. **Par:** 72/74. **Course Rating:** 70.1/70.1. **Slope:** 120/111. **Green Fee:** $19/$29. **Cart Fee:** $24/Cart. **Walking Policy:** Unrestricted walking. **Walkability:** 3. **Season:** Year-round. **High:** June-Sept. **Tee times:** Call golf shop. **Miscellaneous:** Reduced fees (weekdays, twilight, juniors), range (grass/mats), credit cards (MC, V, AE).
Special Notes: Formerly New Bedford Municipal Golf Course.

★★½ WIDOW'S WALK GOLF COURSE
PU-250 The Driftway, Scituate, 02066, Plymouth County, (781)544-0032, 20 miles from Boston. **Facility Holes:** 18. **Yards:** 6,403/4,562. **Par:** 72/72. **Course Rating:** 71.2/66.2. **Slope:** 129/113. **Green Fee:** $25/$42. **Cart Fee:** $13/Person. **Walking Policy:** Unrestricted walking. **Walkability:** 4. **Opened:** 1997. **Architect:** Michael Hurdzan/Bill Kerman. **Season:** April-Dec. **High:** June-Aug. **To obtain tee times:** Call up to 4 days in advance. **Miscellaneous:** Reduced fees (weekdays, seniors, juniors), range (grass), credit cards (MC, V, AE), BF, FF.

WINCHENDON COUNTRY CLUB
PU-172 Ash St., Winchendon, 01475, Worcester County, (978)297-9897, 30 miles from Worcester. **Facility Holes:** 18. **Yards:** 5,427/5,030. **Par:** 70/72. **Course Rating:** 65.7/68.5. **Slope:** 114/116. **Green Fee:** $17/$21. **Cart Fee:** $11/Person. **Walking Policy:** Unrestricted walking. **Walkability:** 2. **Opened:** 1920. **Architect:** Donald Ross. **Season:** April-Nov. **High:** June-Aug. **To obtain tee times:** Call golf shop. **Miscellaneous:** Reduced fees (weekdays, twilight), credit cards (MC, V, D), BF, FF.

MICHIGAN

★★★½ A-GA-MING RESORT
R-627 A-Ga-Ming Dr., Kewadin, 49648, Antrim County, (231)264-5081, (800)678-0122, 9 miles from Elk Rapids. **E-mail:** agaminggc@aol.com. **Web:** www.a-ga-ming.com. **Facility Holes:** 18. **Yards:** 6,663/5,125. **Par:** 72/72. **Course Rating:** 73.2/69.2. **Slope:** 133/124. **Green Fee:** $30/$60. **Cart Fee:** Included in green fee. **Walking Policy:** Walking at certain times. **Walkability:** 5. **Opened:** 1986. **Architect:** Chick Harbert. **Season:** April-Nov. **High:** June-Sept. **To obtain tee times:** Call up to 120 days in advance. **Miscellaneous:** Reduced fees (weekdays, guests, twilight, juniors), range (grass), lodging credit cards (MC, V, AE, D), BF, FF.
Reader Comments: Great views of Torch Lake ... Nice course ... Greens were great, good food, service ... Lovely course ... Course built on 2 small pieces of land.

★★½ ALPENA GOLF CLUB
PU-1135 Golf Course Rd., Alpena, 49707, Alpena County, (517)354-5052. **E-mail:** agci@alpanagolf.com. **Web:** www.alpenagolf.com. **Facility Holes:** 18. **Yards:** 6,459/5,100. **Par:** 72/72. **Course Rating:** 70.0/68.8. **Slope:** 121/114. **Green Fee:** $23/$25. **Cart Fee:** $22/Cart. **Walking Policy:** Unrestricted walking. **Walkability:** 1. **Opened:** 1934. **Architect:** Warner Bowen. **Season:** April-Nov. **High:** June-Aug. **To obtain tee times:** Call golf shop. **Miscellaneous:** Reduced fees (seniors, juniors), range (grass), credit cards (MC, V, AE, D), BF, FF.

★★★★ ANTRIM DELLS GOLF CLUB
PU-12352 Antrim Dr., Atwood, 49729, Antrim County, (231)599-2679, (800)872-8561, 35 miles from Traverse City. **Web:** www.antrimdellsgolf.com. **Facility Holes:** 18. **Yards:** 6,606/5,493. **Par:** 72/72. **Course Rating:** 72.1/71.9. **Slope:** 125/121. **Green Fee:** $33/$52. **Cart Fee:** Included in green fee. **Walking Policy:** Walking at certain times. **Walkability:** 4. **Opened:** 1973. **Architect:** Bruce Matthews/Jerry Matthews. **Season:** April-Oct. **High:** July-Aug. **To obtain tee times:** Call up to 365 days in advance. **Miscellaneous:** Reduced fees (weekdays, twilight, juniors), range (grass), credit cards (MC, V), FF.
Reader Comments: This is one of my favorite courses when I go to Michigan ... Only its popularity hinders this course ... Greens and fairways were in great shape ... Play on a weekday when it's not as busy.

ARCADIA BLUFFS GOLF CLUB
PU-14710 Northwood Hwy., Arcadia, 49613, Manistee County, (231)889-3001, 40 miles from Traverse City. **E-mail:** PGA Golf Professional. **Web:** www.arcadiabluffs.com. **Facility Holes:** 18. **Yards:** 7,404/5,529. **Par:** 72/72. **Green Fee:** $130/$160. **Cart Fee:** Included in green fee. **Walking Policy:** Walking at certain times. **Walkability:** 2. **Opened:** 1999. **Architect:** Rick Smith. **Season:** May-Nov. **To obtain tee times:** Call golf shop. **Miscellaneous:** Reduced fees (twilight), range (grass), caddies, credit cards (MC, V, AE, D), FF.
Notes: Ranked 2nd in 2001 Best New Upscale Courses.

★★ BALD MOUNTAIN GOLF COURSE
PU-3350 Kern Rd., Lake Orion, 48360, Oakland County, (248)373-1110, 30 miles from Detroit. **Facility Holes:** 27. **Yards:** 6,624/5,775. **Par:** 71/72. **Course Rating:** 71.2/72.9. **Slope:** 120/120. **Green Fee:** $26/$31. **Cart Fee:** $24/Cart. **Walking Policy:** Unrestricted walking. **Walkability:** 4. **Opened:** 1929. **Architect:** Wilfrid Reid. **Season:** April-Nov. **High:** May-Sept. **To obtain tee times:** Call golf shop. **Miscellaneous:** Reduced fees (twilight), metal spikes, range (grass), credit cards (MC, V, AE, D).
Special Notes: Also has a 9-hole executive course.

★★★ BAY COUNTY GOLF COURSE
PU-584 Hampton Rd., Essexville, 48732, Bay County, (517)892-2161, 6 miles from Bay City. **E-mail:** bcgc@chartermi.net. **Facility Holes:** 18. **Yards:** 6,557/5,706. **Par:** 72/74. **Course Rating:** 71.3/72.4. **Slope:** 113/114. **Green Fee:** $14/$20. **Cart Fee:** $20/Cart. **Walking Policy:** Unrestricted walking. **Walkability:** 1. **Opened:** 1966. **Architect:** Moranci. **Season:** April-Oct. **High:** May-Aug. **To obtain tee times:** Call golf shop. **Miscellaneous:** Reduced fees (weekdays, seniors, juniors), range (grass), credit cards (MC, V), BF, FF.
Reader Comments: Nice, clean, well kept ... Very young course, will be nice ... Very open course ... Beautiful scenery ... Fun course, well managed ... Some of the best fairways in Saginaw valley ... Routing could be better ... Long but fair.

★★★★½ BAY HARBOR GOLF CLUB
SP-5800 Coastal Ridge Dr., Bay Harbor, 49770, Emmet County, (231)439-4028, (800)462-6963, 5 miles from Petoskey. **E-mail:** mbedells@boyne.com. **Web:** www.bayharbor.com. **Facility Holes:** 27. **Green Fee:** $68/$240. **Cart Fee:** Included in green fee. **Walking Policy:** Mandatory carts. **Walkability:** 4. **Opened:** 1997. **Architect:** Arthur Hills. **Season:** April-Oct. **High:** July-Aug. **To obtain tee times:** Call golf shop. **Miscellaneous:** Reduced fees (guests, twilight), range (grass), lodging (735 rooms), credit cards (MC, V, AE, D, DC), BF, FF.

LINKS/QUARRY (18 Combo)
Yards: 6,780/4,151. **Par:** 72/72. **Course Rating:** 72.2/69.3. **Slope:** 143/113.
Notes: Ranked 9th in 2001 Best in State; 3rd in 1999 Best New Upscale Public.
PRESERVE/LINKS (18 Combo)
Yards: 6,810/4,087. **Par:** 72/72. **Course Rating:** 72.7/69.4. **Slope:** 142/113.
QUARRY/PRESERVE (18 Combo)
Yards: 6,726/3,906. **Par:** 72/72. **Course Rating:** 72.5/69.1. **Slope:** 144/112.
Reader Comments: Best course in Michigan … Not overly difficult, very scenic … Best course I've ever played … Played at sunset, this course is as stunning as Pebble Beach … Beautiful golf course, tough … Spectacular 27 holes … Pricey but beautiful.

★★★½ BAY VALLEY GOLF CLUB
R-2470 Old Bridge Rd., Bay City, 48706, Bay County, (989)686-5400, (888)241-4653, 5 miles from Bay City. **Web:** www.bayvalley.com. **Facility Holes:** 18. **Yards:** 6,610/5,515. **Par:** 71/71. **Course Rating:** 71.9/68.5. **Slope:** 125/114. **Green Fee:** $45/$65. **Cart Fee:** Included in green fee. **Walking Policy:** Mandatory carts. **Walkability:** 1. **Opened:** 1973. **Architect:** Jack Nicklaus/Desmond Muirhead. **Season:** April-Nov. **High:** June-Aug. **To obtain tee times:** Call golf shop. **Miscellaneous:** Reduced fees (weekdays, guests, twilight), range, lodging, credit cards (MC, V, AE, D), FF.
Reader Comments: A few very interesting holes … Nice, but too expensive … Good mix of hole designs and layout … Easy access & fair layout … Play this one during the spring and fall.

★★★ BEAR LAKE COUNTY HIGHLANDS GOLF CLUB
SP-Hwy. 31S., Bear Lake, 49614, Manistee County, (231)864-3817, 40 miles from Traverse City. **Facility Holes:** 18. **Yards:** 6,527/5,188. **Par:** 72/72. **Course Rating:** 71.0/70.1. **Slope:** 121/121. **Green Fee:** $23/$27. **Cart Fee:** $12/Person. **Walking Policy:** Unrestricted walking. **Walkability:** 3. **Opened:** 1966. **Season:** April-Oct. **High:** July-Aug. **To obtain tee times:** Call golf shop. **Miscellaneous:** Reduced fees (twilight, juniors), credit cards (MC, V, D), FF.
Reader Comments: Tough course, must play … Very crowded, nice condition … Busy with tourists, needs a starter … A good value … A fair course for high handicappers … Needs some work.

★★ BEAVER CREEK GOLF LINKS
SP-850 Stoney Creek Rd., Oakland, 48363, Oakland County, (248)693-7170, 5 miles from Rochester. **Facility Holes:** 27. **Yards:** 6,306/4,847. **Par:** 71/71. **Course Rating:** 69.5/67.8. **Slope:** 129/116. **Green Fee:** $33/$43. **Cart Fee:** Included in green fee. **Walkability:** 5. **Opened:** 1991. **Architect:** Dave Calhoun. **Season:** Year-round. **High:** May-Oct. **To obtain tee times:** Call golf shop. **Miscellaneous:** Metal spikes, credit cards (MC, V, AE, D).
Special Notes: Also has 9-hole executive course.

★★ BEECH HOLLOW GOLF COURSE
PU-7494 Hospital Rd., Freeland, 48623, Freeland County, (989)695-5427, 5 miles from Saginaw. **Facility Holes:** 18. **Yards:** 5,700/4,929. **Par:** 72/72. **Course Rating:** 66.0/67.0. **Slope:** 112/110. **Green Fee:** $14/$21. **Cart Fee:** $22/Cart. **Walking Policy:** Unrestricted walking. **Walkability:** 1. **Opened:** 1969. **Season:** March-Nov. **High:** May-Sept. **To obtain tee times:** Call golf shop. **Miscellaneous:** Reduced fees (weekdays, seniors), credit cards (MC, V, D), BF, FF.

★★★ BELLE RIVER GOLF & COUNTRY CLUB
PU-12564 Belle River Rd., Memphis, 48041, St. Clair County, (810)392-2121, 20 miles from Port Huron. **Facility Holes:** 18. **Yards:** 6,556/5,159. **Par:** 72/72. **Course Rating:** 71.4/67.7. **Slope:** 118/111. **Green Fee:** $18/$22. **Cart Fee:** $20/Cart. **Walking Policy:** Unrestricted walking. **Walkability:** 4. **Opened:** 1981. **Season:** April-Nov. **High:** June-Sept. **To obtain tee times:** Call golf shop. **Miscellaneous:** Reduced fees (seniors, juniors), range (grass), credit cards (MC, V), BF, FF.
Reader Comments: Low green fee, very good value … Nice variety of holes … Long course overall, short par 3s … Rarely crowded … Course always playable … Great value, shotmaker's course … You will use all the clubs in your bag.

★★ BELLO WOODS GOLF CLUB
PU-23650-23 Mile Rd., Macomb, 48042, Macomb County, (810)949-1200, 36 miles from Detroit. **Facility Holes:** 27. **Green Fee:** $20/$25. **Cart Fee:** $22/Cart. **Walking Policy:** Unrestricted walking. **Walkability:** 3. **Opened:** 1969. **Season:** April-Nov. **High:** June-Sept. **To obtain tee times:** Call up to 7 days in advance. **Miscellaneous:** Reduced fees (weekdays, seniors, juniors), credit cards (MC, V), BF, FF.
RED/GOLD (18 Combo)
Yards: 6,093/5,242. **Par:** 72/72.
RED/WHITE (18 Combo)
Yards: 6,201/5,528. **Par:** 72/72.
WHITE/GOLD (18 Combo)
Yards: 6,020/5,062. **Par:** 72/72.

MICHIGAN

★★★½ **BELVEDERE GOLF CLUB** *Pace+*
SP-5731 Marion Center Rd., Charlevoix, 49720, Charlevoix County, (231)547-2611, 40 miles from Traverse City. **E-mail:** belgolf@freway.net. **Web:** www.belvederegolfclub.com. **Facility Holes:** 18. **Yards:** 6,715/5,489. **Par:** 72/72. **Course Rating:** 72.9/72.0. **Slope:** 129/123. **Green Fee:** $51/$84. **Cart Fee:** $16/Person. **Walking Policy:** Unrestricted walking. **Walkability:** 2. **Opened:** 1927. **Architect:** William Watson. **Season:** April-Oct. **High:** June-Sept. **To obtain tee times:** Call golf shop. **Miscellaneous:** Reduced fees (guests, twilight), range (grass), caddies, credit cards (MC, V), BF, FF.
Reader Comments: Old-time golf architecture, fun and interesting to play … My favorite in northern Michigan … A classic … Classic course, challenging but fair … Still one of Michigan's best … A true classic course … All about golf … Old course that stands up to the new ones.

★½ **BENT PINE GOLF CLUB**
PU-2480 Duck Lake Rd., Whitehall, 49461, Muskegon County, (231)766-2045, 8 miles from Muskegon. **E-mail:** bentpine@aol.com. **Web:** www.bentpine.com. **Facility Holes:** 18. **Yards:** 6,007/5,429. **Par:** 71/72. **Green Fee:** $12/$18. **Cart Fee:** $10/Person. **Walking Policy:** Unrestricted walking. **Walkability:** 1. **Opened:** 1969. **Architect:** Oiler Family. **Season:** April-Nov. **High:** May-Sept. **To obtain tee times:** Call up to 7 days in advance. **Miscellaneous:** Reduced fees (weekdays, seniors, juniors), range (grass), credit cards (MC, V, AE), BF, FF.

★★★ **BINDER PARK GOLF COURSE**
PU-7255 B Dr. S., Battle Creek, 49014, Calhoun County, (616)979-8250, 5 miles from Battle Creek. **Web:** www.bcparks.org/golf. **Facility Holes:** 27. **Green Fee:** $21/$22. **Cart Fee:** $12/Person. **Walking Policy:** Unrestricted walking. **Opened:** 1960. **Architect:** Charles Burke/Jerry Matthews. **Season:** April-Oct. **High:** June-Aug. **To obtain tee times:** Call up to 14 days in advance. **Miscellaneous:** Reduced fees (weekdays, twilight, seniors, juniors), range (grass/mats), credit cards (MC, V, D), BF, FF.
NATURAL/MARSH (18 Combo)
Yards: 6,696/5,044. **Par:** 71/71. **Course Rating:** 71.7/68.6. **Slope:** 130/109. **Walkability:** 4.
PRESERVE/MARSH (18 Combo)
Yards: 6,700/5,100. **Par:** 72/74. **Course Rating:** 71.9/69.2. **Slope:** 130/110. **Walkability:** 3.
PRESERVE/NATURAL (18 Combo)
Yards: 6,558/4,943. **Par:** 71/71. **Course Rating:** 71.4/67.8. **Slope:** 128/113. **Walkability:** 4.
Reader Comments: Great muni, new 9 nice, but greens are different … New 9 layout is beautiful, large new clubhouse … Great buy … Redone, one of the finest munis in Midwest … Fine conditioned course, crowded.

★★★½ **BLACK BEAR GOLF RESORT**
R-1500 W. Alexander Rd., Vanderbilt, 49795, Ostego County, (517)983-4505, (800)923-2711, 8 miles from Gaylord. **E-mail:** blackbeargts.@yahoo.com. **Web:** www.golfblackbear.net. **Facility Holes:** 18. **Yards:** 6,500/4,400. **Par:** 72/72. **Course Rating:** 136.0/124.0. **Slope:** 70.4/66.6. **Green Fee:** $25/$56. **Cart Fee:** Included in green fee. **Walking Policy:** Mandatory carts. **Walkability:** 4. **Opened:** 1996. **Architect:** Internal. **Season:** May-Oct. **High:** June-Sept. **To obtain tee times:** Call up to 365 days in advance. **Miscellaneous:** Reduced fees (weekdays, guests, twilight, seniors), range (grass), lodging (30 rooms), credit cards (MC, V, AE), BF, FF.
Reader Comments: No. 16 is underrated … Very nice layout, really liked the warm up hole … 2 holes were not playable … Needed water and manicuring … Very enjoyable.

BLACK FOREST & WILDERNESS VALLEY GOLF RESORT
R-7519 Mancelona Rd., Gaylord, 49735, Otsego County, (231)585-7090, 15 miles from Gaylord. **E-mail:** dsmith3319@aol.com. **Web:** www.blackforestgolf.com. **Facility Holes:** 36. **Cart Fee:** $18/Person. **Walking Policy:** Unrestricted walking. **Season:** April-Nov. **High:** June-Aug. **To obtain tee times:** Call golf shop. **Miscellaneous:** Reduced fees (weekdays, guests, twilight, seniors, juniors), range (grass/mats), credit cards (MC, V, AE, D), BF, FF.
★★★★ **BLACK FOREST COURSE** (18) *Pace*
Yards: 7,044/5,282. **Par:** 73/74. **Course Rating:** 75.3/71.8. **Slope:** 145/131. **Green Fee:** $20/$47. **Walkability:** 5. **Opened:** 1992. **Architect:** Tom Doak.
Notes: Ranked 23rd in 1999 Best in State.
Reader Comments: Course for all levels … Fun & good value, especially during week … 2nd best course I played in 2000 … Northern Michigan gem.
★★★★ **VALLEY COURSE** (18) *Value, Pace+*
Yards: 6,485/4,889. **Par:** 71/71. **Course Rating:** 70.6/67.8. **Slope:** 126/115. **Green Fee:** $15/$27. **Walkability:** 2. **Opened:** 1971. **Architect:** Al Watrous.
Reader Comments: Easy course … Dogleg central … Almost all holes left to right … Good staff … Best value in northern Michigan … Great walking course.

★★★★½ **BLACK LAKE GOLF CLUB** *Service+, Value, Condition+, Pace+*
PU-2000 Maxon Rd., Onaway, 49765, Presque Island County, (989)733-4653, (800)829-4653, 40 miles from Gaylord. **E-mail:** pphipps@uaw.net. **Web:** www.blacklakegolf.com. **Facility**

MICHIGAN

Holes: 18. Yards: 7,030/5,058. Par: 72/72. Course Rating: 74.3/69.9. Slope: 140/125. Green Fee: $14/$95. Cart Fee: Included in green fee. Walking Policy: Walking at certain times. Walkability: 3. Opened: 1999. Architect: Rees Jones. Season: April-Oct. High: June-Sept. To obtain tee times: Call up to 14 days in advance. Miscellaneous: Reduced fees (twilight, seniors, juniors), range (grass), credit cards (MC, V, AE), BF, FF.
Notes: Ranked 4th in 2001 Best in State; 2nd in 2000 Best New Upscale Courses.
Reader Comments: Outstanding venue ... Built for UAW union, public play ... Very friendly place ... Very nice golf course, excellent condition for a new course, took a little to get used to taking rake from the cart to the bunkers ... Absolutely phenomenal ... The best course in state with the exception of Arcadia.

BLACKBERRY PATCH GOLF CLUB
PU-608 One Straight Dr., Coldwater, 49036, Branch County, (517)238-8686, 6 miles from Coldwater. E-mail: blackberg@cbpo.com. Web: www.blackberrypatchgolf.com. Facility Holes: 18. Yards: 7,133/5,173. Par: 72/72. Course Rating: 73.8/70.8. Slope: 141/118. Green Fee: $30/$47. Cart Fee: Included in green fee. Walking Policy: Walking at certain times. Walkability: 4. Opened: 1998. Architect: Ernie Schrock. Season: March-Dec. High: May-Aug. To obtain tee times: Call up to 14 days in advance. Miscellaneous: Reduced fees (weekdays, twilight, seniors, juniors), range (grass), credit cards (MC, V, AE), BF, FF.

★★★ BLACKHEATH GOLF CLUB
PU-3311 N. Rochester Rd., Rochester Hills, 48309, Oakland County, (248)601-8000, 4 miles from Rochester. Facility Holes: 18. Yards: 6,768/5,354. Par: 71/71. Course Rating: 73.0/70.8. Slope: 137/124. Green Fee: $35/$60. Cart Fee: Included in green fee. Walking Policy: Walking at certain times. Walkability: 2. Opened: 1998. Architect: Kevin Aldridge. Season: March-Dec. High: May-Aug. To obtain tee times: Call golf shop. Miscellaneous: Reduced fees (twilight, seniors, juniors), range (grass), credit cards (MC, V, AE), BF, FF.
Reader Comments: Greens slightly deteriorated ... A bad attempt at a links course in a cow pasture ... Poor designed holes, east-to-west holes ... Follow-up to the Gailes course, same architect but no match ... Narrow.

★½ BLOSSOM TRAILS GOLF COURSE
PU-1565 E. Britain Ave., Benton Harbor, 49022, Berrien County, (616)925-4951, 90 miles from Chicago. Facility Holes: 27. Yards: 5,987/4,957. Par: 70/70. Course Rating: 68.3/68.3. Slope: 121/118. Green Fee: $17/$18. Cart Fee: $9/Person. Walking Policy: Unrestricted walking. Walkability: 1. Opened: 1959. Architect: Bruce Matthews. Season: March-Nov. High: May-Aug. To obtain tee times: Call golf shop. Miscellaneous: Reduced fees (weekdays), metal spikes, range (grass), credit cards (MC, V, D).
Special Notes: Also has a 9-hole par-3 course.

★★½ BOGIE LAKE GOLF CLUB
PU-11231 Bogie Lake Rd., White Lake, 48386, Oakland County, (248)363-4449, 10 miles from Pontiac. Facility Holes: 18. Yards: 6,020/5,031. Par: 71/71. Course Rating: 68.1/67.2. Slope: 120/115. Green Fee: $20/$24. Cart Fee: $22/Cart. Walking Policy: Unrestricted walking. Walkability: 5. Opened: 1963. Season: Year-round. High: June-Aug. To obtain tee times: Call golf shop. Miscellaneous: Reduced fees (weekdays, twilight, seniors, juniors), metal spikes, range (grass/mats).

★★★★ BOULDER CREEK GOLF CLUB
PU-5750 Brewer Ave., Belmont, 49306, Kent County, (616)363-1330, 6 miles from Grand Rapids. Facility Holes: 18. Yards: 6,975/4,996. Par: 72/72. Course Rating: 73.0/67.4. Slope: 122/109. Green Fee: $25/$49. Cart Fee: Included in green fee. Walking Policy: Walking at certain times. Walkability: 4. Opened: 1998. Architect: Mark DeVries. Season: March-Dec. High: April-Oct. To obtain tee times: Call up to 14 days in advance. Miscellaneous: Reduced fees (twilight, seniors, juniors), range, credit cards (MC, V, AE, D), BF, FF.
Reader Comments: New course, neat and clean ... Very nice condition, bland layout, 4-hour round ... good service ... Newer layout, needs maturity ... Great for women ... Fun course to play ... You can score on this beautiful gravel pit.

BOULDER POINTE GOLF CLUB
SP-One Champions Circle, Oxford, 48371, Oakland County, (248)969-1500, 15 miles from Pontiac. Facility Holes: 27. Green Fee: $55/$65. Cart Fee: Included in green fee. Walking Policy: Mandatory carts. Walkability: 4. Opened: 2000. Architect: Conroy-Dewling. Season: Year-round. High: March-Dec. To obtain tee times: Call up to 14 days in advance. Miscellaneous: Reduced fees (weekdays, twilight, seniors, juniors), range (mats), credit cards (MC, V, AE, D), BF, FF.
THE BLUFFS/THE PEAKS (18)
Yards: 7,034/5,297. Par: 72/72. Course Rating: 73.3/70.4. Slope: 139/124.

THE DUNES/THE BLUFFS (18)
Yards: 7,334/5,433. **Par:** 72/72. **Course Rating:** 73.9/71.1. **Slope:** 140/126.
THE PEAKS/THE DUNES (18)
Yards: 7,424/5,426. **Par:** 72/72. **Course Rating:** 74.7/71.3. **Slope:** 142/12.7.

BOYNE HIGHLANDS RESORT
R-600 Highland Dr., Harbor Springs, 49740, Emmet County, (231)526-3029, (800)462-6963, 6 miles from Petoskey. **E-mail:** info@boyne.com. **Web:** www.boynehighlands.com/summer/golf.html. **Facility Holes:** 72. **Cart Fee:** Included in green fee. **To obtain tee times:** Call golf shop. **Miscellaneous:** Reduced fees (guests, twilight), range (grass), lodging (500 rooms), credit cards (MC, V, AE, D, DC), BF, FF.
ARTHUR HILLS COURSE (18)
Yards: 7,312/4,811. **Par:** 73/73. **Green Fee:** $129. **Walking Policy:** Mandatory carts.
Walkability: 4. **Opened:** 2000. **Architect:** Arthur Hills. **Season:** May-Sept.
Special Notes: Course not rated or sloped.
★★★★ **DONALD ROSS MEMORIAL COURSE** (18)
Yards: 6,814/4,929. **Par:** 72/72. **Course Rating:** 73.4/68.5. **Slope:** 132/119. **Green Fee:** $66/$110. **Walking Policy:** Mandatory carts. **Walkability:** 3. **Opened:** 1985. **Architect:** Newcomb/E. Kircher/Flick/S. Kircher. **Season:** April-Nov. **High:** June-Aug.
Reader Comments: Too hard for average golfer .., Very nice layout, typical look of Ross holes … Nice redesign of Ross … Northern Michigan at its best … Great designer, great course.
★★★★½ **HEATHER COURSE** (18)
Yards: 6,870/5,245. **Par:** 72/72. **Course Rating:** 74.0/67.8. **Slope:** 131/111. **Green Fee:** $84/$140. **Walking Policy:** Walking at certain times. **Walkability:** 3. **Opened:** 1968. **Architect:** Robert Trent Jones. **Season:** April-Nov. **High:** June-Aug.
Notes: Ranked 15th in 2001 Best in State.
Reader Comments: Peaceful, beautiful, challenging … Nice resort experience … Must play at Boyne Highlands … Lots of H20, somewhat tight … An above average solid course … The best at Boyne, memorable holes, 18th is tough.
★★★★ **MOOR COURSE** (18)
Yards: 7,127/5,459. **Par:** 72/72. **Course Rating:** 74.0/70.0. **Slope:** 131/118. **Green Fee:** $57/$95. **Walking Policy:** Mandatory carts. **Walkability:** 3. **Opened:** 1972. **Architect:** William Newcomb. **Season:** May-Oct. **High:** June-Aug.
Reader Comments: Great layout … Scenic, tough, but fair … Boyne does well … Fine service, outstanding shape … Worth a try … Fantastic course … There are so many great courses in Michigan … My favorite Boyne … Pricey but beauty justifies cost … Lovely layout.

BOYNE MOUNTAIN RESORT
R-Deer Lake Rd., Boyne Falls, 49713, Charlevoix County, (231)549-6029, (800)462-6963, 18 miles from Petoskey. **E-mail:** dturcott@boyne.com. **Web:** www.boyne.com. **Facility Holes:** 36. **Green Fee:** $29/$79. **Cart Fee:** Included in green fee. **Walking Policy:** Mandatory carts. **Walkability:** 4. **Architect:** William Newcomb. **Season:** May-Nov. **High:** June-Sept. **To obtain tee times:** Call up to 150 days in advance. **Miscellaneous:** Reduced fees (guests, twilight), range (grass/mats), lodging (276 rooms), credit cards (MC, V, AE, D, DC), BF, FF.
★★★½ **ALPINE COURSE** (18)
Yards: 7,104/4,986. **Par:** 72/72. **Course Rating:** 73.4/68.4. **Slope:** 135/114. **Opened:** 1974.
Reader Comments: Played in fall, colors were beautiful … Long ride to the first tee … Enjoyed it.
★★★★½ **MONUMENT COURSE** (18) *Pace*
Yards: 7,086/4,909. **Par:** 72/72. **Course Rating:** 74.8/68.9. **Slope:** 141/122. **Opened:** 1986.
Reader Comments: Good shape, nice people … Challenging course, each hole separate from others … Beautiful course … Rare treat … Best for the money … Friendly staff … Long ride, too hilly & tight … Beautiful … Great design, memorable holes … Nice elevation change.

★★½ **BRAE BURN GOLF COURSE**
PU-10860 W. 5 Mile Rd., Plymouth, 48170, Wayne County, (734)453-1900, (800)714-6700, 20 miles from Detroit. **Facility Holes:** 18. **Yards:** 6,320/5,072. **Par:** 70/71. **Course Rating:** 70.0/70.6. **Slope:** 120/119. **Green Fee:** $20/$46. **Walking Policy:** Walking at certain times. **Walkability:** 4. **Opened:** 1923. **Architect:** Wilford Reed. **Season:** March-Dec. **To obtain tee times:** Call up to 7 days in advance. **Miscellaneous:** Reduced fees (weekdays, twilight, seniors, juniors), range (grass/mats), credit cards (MC, V, AE), BF, FF.

★★½ **BRAESIDE GOLF COURSE**
PU-5460 Eleven Mile Rd., Rockford, 49341, Kent County, (616)866-1402, 12 miles from Grand Rapids. **Facility Holes:** 18. **Yards:** 6,810/5,440. **Par:** 71/72. **Course Rating:** 72.8/71.5. **Slope:** 136/131. **Green Fee:** $22/$24. **Cart Fee:** $24/Cart. **Walking Policy:** Unrestricted walking. **Walkability:** 3. **Opened:** 1979. **Season:** April-Oct. **High:** June-Sept. **To obtain tee times:** Call golf shop. **Miscellaneous:** Reduced fees (weekdays, seniors, juniors), metal spikes, credit cards (MC, V).

MICHIGAN

★★ BRAMBLEWOOD GOLF COURSE
SP-2154 Bramblewood Rd., Holly, 48442, Oakland County, (248)634-3481, 20 miles from Pontiac. **Facility Holes:** 18. **Yards:** 6,005/5,052. **Par:** 70/72. **Course Rating:** 70.0/74.0. **Slope:** 113/113. **Green Fee:** $15/$21. **Cart Fee:** $10/Person. **Walking Policy:** Walking at certain times. **Walkability:** 4. **Opened:** 1985. **Season:** April-Oct. **High:** June-Aug. **To obtain tee times:** Call golf shop. **Miscellaneous:** Reduced fees (weekdays, seniors, juniors), metal spikes, credit cards (MC, V).

★★ BRANSON BAY GOLF COURSE
PU-215 Branson Bay Dr., Mason, 48854, Ingham County, (517)663-4144, 8 miles from Lansing. **Facility Holes:** 18. **Yards:** 6,497/5,145. **Par:** 72/73. **Course Rating:** 71.5/69.5. **Slope:** 124/116. **Green Fee:** $13/$23. **Cart Fee:** $22/Cart. **Walking Policy:** Unrestricted walking. **Walkability:** 3. **Opened:** 1968. **Season:** March-Nov. **To obtain tee times:** Call golf shop. **Miscellaneous:** Reduced fees (twilight, seniors, juniors), range (grass), credit cards (MC, V).

BRENTWOOD GOLF & COUNTRY CLUB
PU-2450 Havenwood, White Lake, 48383, Oakland County, (248)684-2662, 3 miles from Highland. **Facility Holes:** 18. **Yards:** 6,424/4,479. **Par:** 72/72. **Course Rating:** 69.4/66.6. **Slope:** 120/116. **Green Fee:** $25/$30. **Cart Fee:** Included in green fee. **Walking Policy:** Mandatory carts. **Walkability:** 3. **Opened:** 1993. **Architect:** Jim Ludwig. **Season:** Year-round. **High:** May-Sept. **To obtain tee times:** Call up to 14 days in advance. **Miscellaneous:** Reduced fees (weekdays), credit cards (MC, V, AE, D), BF, FF.

★★★ THE BRIAR AT MESICK
PU-5441 E. M-115, Mesick, 49668, Wexford County, (231)885-1220, (888)745-1220, 26 miles from Traverse City. **Facility Holes:** 18. **Yards:** 5,876/4,549. **Par:** 71/71. **Course Rating:** 69.4/67.3. **Slope:** 116/104. **Green Fee:** $28/$25. **Cart Fee:** $12/Person. **Walking Policy:** Walking at certain times. **Walkability:** 3. **Opened:** 1989. **Architect:** Orman Bishop. **Season:** April-Oct. **High:** June-Aug. **To obtain tee times:** Call golf shop. **Miscellaneous:** Reduced fees (weekdays, twilight, seniors, juniors), credit cards (MC, V), BF, FF.
Reader Comments: Great for the price … Average, but price is good … Very scenic … Nice course … Good iron course … Course was good, weather was bad … Nice greens, pretty in fall … Great value … Excellent value, pretty views.

★★½ BRIARWOOD
PU-2900 92nd St., Caledonia, 49316, Kent County, (616)698-8720, 10 miles from Grand Rapids. **Web:** www.golfbriairwood.com. **Facility Holes:** 27. **Green Fee:** $13/$24. **Cart Fee:** $24/Cart. **Walking Policy:** Unrestricted walking. **Walkability:** 2. **Opened:** 1963. **Season:** March-Nov. **High:** May-Aug. **To obtain tee times:** Call golf shop. **Miscellaneous:** Reduced fees (weekdays, seniors, juniors), range (grass), credit cards (MC, V, AE, D), BF, FF.
EAST/BACK (18 Combo)
Yards: 6,571/5,681. **Par:** 72/78. **Course Rating:** 69.8. **Slope:** 124.
FRONT/BACK (18 Combo)
Yards: 6,285/5,244. **Par:** 72/76. **Course Rating:** 68.6. **Slope:** 117.
FRONT/EAST (18 Combo)
Yards: 6,364/5,503. **Par:** 72/78. **Course Rating:** 68.6. **Slope:** 116.

BRIGADOON GOLF CLUB
PU-12559 Bagley Ave., Grant, 49327, Newaygo County, (231)834-8200, 30 miles from Grand Rapids. **E-mail:** info@brigadoongolf.com. **Web:** www.brigadoongolf.com. **Facility Holes:** 27. **Green Fee:** $25/$29. **Cart Fee:** Included in green fee. **Walking Policy:** Walking at certain times. **Walkability:** 5. **Architect:** Grant McKinley. **High:** May-Aug. **To obtain tee times:** Call golf shop. **Miscellaneous:** Reduced fees (weekdays, seniors), range (grass), credit cards (MC, V), BF, FF.
GOLD COURSE (9)
Yards: 2,720/2,105. **Par:** 36/36. **Opened:** 1995. **Season:** April-Oct.
★★½ **RED/BLUE** (18)
Yards: 6,195/4,821. **Par:** 72/72. **Course Rating:** 70.9/68.6. **Slope:** 135/124. **Opened:** 1989. **Season:** April-Nov.

★½ BROADMOOR COUNTRY CLUB
PU-7725 Kraft Ave. SE, Caledonia, 49316, Kent County, (616)891-8000, 8 miles from Grand Rapids. **Facility Holes:** 18. **Yards:** 6,400/5,800. **Par:** 72/74. **Course Rating:** 69.8/69.1. **Slope:** 119/118. **Green Fee:** $13/$23. **Cart Fee:** $23/Cart. **Walking Policy:** Unrestricted walking. **Walkability:** 3. **Opened:** 1964. **Season:** March-Nov. **High:** April-Sept. **To obtain tee times:** Call golf shop. **Miscellaneous:** Reduced fees (weekdays, seniors, juniors), range (grass), credit cards (MC, V, AE, D, DC), BF, FF.

★★★ BROOKWOOD GOLF COURSE
PU-6045 Davison Rd, Burton, 48509, Genesee County, (810)742-4930, 5 miles from Flint.
Facility Holes: 18. **Yards:** 6,972/5,977. **Par:** 72/72. **Course Rating:** 72.9/78.7. **Slope:** 123/122.
Green Fee: $16/$26. **Cart Fee:** $23/Cart. **Walking Policy:** Unrestricted walking. **Walkability:** 3.
Opened: 1938. **Season:** April-Nov. **High:** June-Aug. **To obtain tee times:** Call golf shop.
Miscellaneous: Metal spikes, range (grass), credit cards (MC, V).
Reader Comments: Great layout ... Lots of play ... Nice ... Even with all the rain, course was well kept ... Greens hard but smooth ... Woods, back-to-nature course ... Very nice.

BUCKS RUN GOLF CLUB
PU-1559 S. Chippewa Rd., Mt. Pleasant, 48858, Isabella County, (989)773-6830, 60 miles from Lansing. **Web:** www.bucksrun.com. **Facility Holes:** 18. **Yards:** 6,756/5,090. **Par:** 72/72.
Course Rating: 72.0/68.9. **Slope:** 130/116. **Green Fee:** $40/$65. **Cart Fee:** $15/Person.
Walking Policy: Walking at certain times. **Walkability:** 3. **Opened:** 2000. **Architect:** Jerry Matthews. **Season:** April-Nov. **High:** June-Sept. **To obtain tee times:** Call up to 30 days in advance. **Miscellaneous:** Reduced fees (twilight seniors, juniors), range, credit cards (MC, V, AE, D, DC), BF, FF.

★★ BURNING OAK COUNTRY CLUB
PU-4345 Redwood Dr., Roscommon, 48653, Roscommon County, (517)821-9821, 62 miles from Traverse City. **Facility Holes:** 18. **Yards:** 6,240/5,256. **Par:** 72/72. **Course Rating:** 69.7/70.0. **Slope:** 117/115. **Green Fee:** $20. **Cart Fee:** $9/Person. **Walking Policy:** Unrestricted walking. **Walkability:** 1. **Opened:** 1962. **Season:** April-Oct. **High:** June-Aug. **To obtain tee times:** Call golf shop. **Miscellaneous:** Reduced fees (juniors), range (grass/mats), credit cards (MC, V, D), BF, FF.

★★½ BURR OAK GOLF CLUB
PU-3491 N. Parma Rd., Parma, 49269, Jackson County, (517)531-4741, 5 miles from Jackson. **Facility Holes:** 18. **Yards:** 6,329/5,011. **Par:** 72/72. **Course Rating:** 69.2/65.4. **Green Fee:** $14/$16. **Cart Fee:** $9/Person. **Walking Policy:** Unrestricted walking. **Walkability:** 3. **Opened:** 1965. **Season:** April-Oct. **High:** May-Aug. **To obtain tee times:** Call golf shop. **Miscellaneous:** Reduced fees (twilight, seniors, juniors), metal spikes, range (grass).

★★★ BYRON HILLS GOLF CLUB
PU-7330 Burlingame Rd., Byron Center, 49315, Kent County, (616)878-1522, 10 miles from Grand Rapids. **Facility Holes:** 27. **Yards:** 5,622/5,041. **Par:** 71/75. **Course Rating:** 67.3/70.1. **Slope:** 110/112. **Green Fee:** $22/$24. **Cart Fee:** $25/Cart. **Walking Policy:** Unrestricted walking. **Walkability:** 2. **Opened:** 1963. **Architect:** Fred Ellis. **Season:** April-Nov. **High:** April-Oct. **To obtain tee times:** Call golf shop. **Miscellaneous:** Reduced fees (weekdays, seniors, juniors), credit cards (MC, V), BF, FF.
Reader Comments: Slow play, hard ground ... Excellent challenge for mid-handicapper ... Small track, nice change of pace, tough to score well, though ... Good local course, unimaginative layout, crowded ... Nice course.
Special Notes: Also has a 9-hole executive course.

★★½ CABERFAE PEAKS SKI & GOLF RESORT
R-Caberfae Rd., Cadillac, 49601, Wexford County, (231)862-3000, 12 miles from Cadillac.
E-mail: caberfae@michweb.net. **Web:** www.michiweb.com/cabpeaks. **Facility Holes:** 9. **Yards:** 3,341/2,186. **Par:** 36/36. **Green Fee:** $18/$24. **Cart Fee:** $14/Person. **Walking Policy:** Unrestricted walking. **Walkability:** 2. **Opened:** 1995. **Architect:** Harry Bowers. **Season:** May-Nov. **High:** June-Aug. **To obtain tee times:** Call golf shop. **Miscellaneous:** Reduced fees (weekdays, guests, twilight), metal spikes, range (grass), lodging (36 rooms), credit cards (MC, V), BF, FF.

★★★½ CANDLESTONE INN GOLF & RESORT
R-8100 N. Storey, Belding, 48809, Ionia County, (616)794-1541, 20 miles from Grand Rapids.
Facility Holes: 18. **Yards:** 6,692/5,547. **Par:** 72/74. **Course Rating:** 72.8/73.1. **Slope:** 129/126. **Green Fee:** $11/$30. **Cart Fee:** $14/Person. **Walking Policy:** Unrestricted walking. **Walkability:** 3. **Opened:** 1975. **Architect:** Bruce Matthews/Jerry Matthews. **Season:** March-Nov. **High:** May-Sept. **To obtain tee times:** Call golf shop. **Miscellaneous:** Reduced fees (weekdays, guests, twilight, seniors), range (grass), lodging (24 rooms), credit cards (MC, V, AE, D), BF, FF.
Reader Comments: Very nice course for a low rate ... Great putting course ... Not long, but tricky ... Fantastic, quick greens ... Not one complaint, if I lived in Mich., I'd play it every week.

★★ CARLETON GLEN GOLF CLUB
SP-13470 Grafton Rd., Carleton, 48117, Monroe County, (734)654-6201, 19 miles from Detroit. **Facility Holes:** 18. **Yards:** 6,496/5,602. **Par:** 71/71. **Course Rating:** 70.0/73.0. **Slope:** 114/112. **Green Fee:** $20/$27. **Cart Fee:** $12/Person. **Walking Policy:** Unrestricted walking.

MICHIGAN

Walkability: 3. **Opened:** 1960. **Architect:** Robert G. Milosch. **Season:** March-Dec. **High:** May-Sept. **To obtain tee times:** Call up to 7 days in advance. **Miscellaneous:** Reduced fees (weekdays, twilight, seniors, juniors), metal spikes, range (grass), credit cards (MC, V, AE, D), FF.

★★½ CARRINGTON GOLF CLUB
PU-911 St. James Park Ave., Monroe, 48161, Monroe County, (734)241-0707, (888)270-0707, 30 miles from Detroit. **E-mail:** carringolf@aol.com. **Web:** www.carringtongolfclub.com. **Facility Holes:** 18. **Yards:** 6,851/5,145. **Par:** 72/72. **Course Rating:** 73.4/68.7. **Slope:** 125/116. **Green Fee:** $29/$35. **Cart Fee:** $13/Person. **Walking Policy:** Unrestricted walking. **Walkability:** 1. **Opened:** 1999. **Architect:** Brian Huntley. **Season:** March-Dec. **High:** June-Sept. **To obtain tee times:** Call up to 7 days in advance. **Miscellaneous:** Reduced fees (weekdays, twilight, seniors, juniors), range (grass), credit cards (MC, V, AE, D), BF, FF.

★★★½ CASCADES GOLF COURSE *Value*
PU-1992 Warren Ave., Jackson, 49203, Jackson County, (517)788-4323, 37 miles from Ann Arbor. **Facility Holes:** 18. **Yards:** 6,614/5,282. **Par:** 72/73. **Course Rating:** 71.8/70.5. **Slope:** 126/117. **Green Fee:** $13/$17. **Cart Fee:** $10/Person. **Walking Policy:** Unrestricted walking. **Walkability:** 2. **Opened:** 1929. **Architect:** Tom Bendelow. **Season:** March-Oct. **High:** July-Sept. **To obtain tee times:** Call golf shop. **Miscellaneous:** Reduced fees (weekdays, twilight, seniors, juniors), range (grass), credit cards (MC, V), BF, FF.
Reader Comments: Enjoyable, very good value … Always a bargain … Best muni in state, great course at great price … Affordable, classic golf … Top notch, great price … Decent course, greens were not good … Nice clubhouse.

★★★½ CATTAILS GOLF CLUB
PU-57737 W. 9 Mile Rd., South Lyon, 48178, Oakland County, (248)486-8777, 25 miles from Detroit. **E-mail:** cattailsgc@aol.com. **Web:** www.cattailsgolfclub.com. **Facility Holes:** 18. **Yards:** 6,436/4,974. **Par:** 72/72. **Course Rating:** 72.1/70.2. **Slope:** 131/118. **Green Fee:** $29/$42. **Cart Fee:** $16/Person. **Walking Policy:** Walking at certain times. **Walkability:** 3. **Opened:** 1991. **Architect:** Doug Palm. **Season:** March-Nov. **High:** May-Sept. **To obtain tee times:** Call up to 7 days in advance. **Miscellaneous:** Reduced fees (weekdays, twilight, seniors, juniors), range (grass), credit cards (MC, V, AE), BF, FF.
Reader Comments: Could play in over and over again … Short, tricky course … Very reasonable and easy to get on for that area … Fast greens … Challenging holes, good value … Overpriced, challenging course … Tough course … Pretty.

★★★½ CEDAR CHASE GOLF CLUB
PU-7551 17 Mile Rd. NE, Cedar Springs, 49319, Kent County, (616)696-2308, 20 miles from Grand Rapids. **E-mail:** cedarchase@cmedic.net. **Facility Holes:** 18. **Yards:** 7,115/5,115. **Par:** 72/72. **Course Rating:** 74.6/69.7. **Slope:** 132/122. **Green Fee:** $25/$33. **Cart Fee:** $12/Person. **Walking Policy:** Unrestricted walking. **Walkability:** 3. **Opened:** 1993. **Architect:** Bruce Matthews III. **Season:** March-Nov. **High:** May-Sept. **To obtain tee times:** Call golf shop. **Miscellaneous:** Reduced fees (weekdays, seniors, juniors), range (grass), credit cards (MC, V, AE, D), BF, FF.
Reader Comments: Upper Michigan course in lower Michigan … Great layout, good service , quick round, good condition … Nice, tight driving areas.

★★½ CEDAR CREEK GOLF COURSE
PU-14000 Renton Rd., Battle Creek, 49015, Calhoun County, (616)965-6423, 10 miles from Kalamazoo. **Facility Holes:** 36. **Yards:** 6,422/4,914. **Par:** 72/72. **Course Rating:** 70.9/68.8. **Slope:** 124/115. **Green Fee:** $12/$19. **Cart Fee:** $10/Person. **Walking Policy:** Unrestricted walking. **Walkability:** 3. **Opened:** 1974. **Architect:** Robert Beard. **Season:** Year-round. **High:** May-Aug. **To obtain tee times:** Call golf shop. **Miscellaneous:** Reduced fees (seniors, juniors), range (grass), credit cards (MC, V), BF, FF.
Special Notes: Also has an 18-hole executive course.

★½ CEDAR GLEN GOLF CLUB
SP-36860 25 Mile Rd., New Baltimore, 48047, Macomb County, (810)725-8156, 16 miles from Mount Clemens. **Facility Holes:** 18. **Yards:** 6,140/5,052. **Par:** 71/71. **Course Rating:** 69.5/69.9. **Slope:** 118/119. **Green Fee:** $20/$26. **Cart Fee:** $20/Cart. **Walking Policy:** Unrestricted walking. **Walkability:** 1. **Opened:** 1968. **Architect:** Jerry Matthews. **Season:** April-Nov. **High:** May-Sept. **To obtain tee times:** Call golf shop. **Miscellaneous:** Reduced fees (weekdays, twilight, seniors, juniors), metal spikes, credit cards (MC, V).

★★ CENTENNIAL ACRES GOLF COURSE
PU-12485 Dow Rd., Sunfield, 48890, Eaton County, (517)566-8055, 20 miles from Lansing. **E-mail:** golfcentennial@voyager.net. **Web:** www.centennialacres.com. **Facility Holes:** 27. **Green Fee:** $21/$26. **Cart Fee:** $12/Person. **Walking Policy:** Unrestricted walking. **Opened:** 1979. **Architect:** Warner Bowen. **Season:** March-Dec. **High:** May-Sept. **To obtain tee times:**

Call up to 3 days in advance. **Miscellaneous:** Reduced fees (weekdays, twilight, seniors, juniors), range (grass), credit cards (MC, V, D), BF, FF.
MIDDAY/SUNSET COURSE (18 Combo)
Yards: 6,449/4,342. **Par:** 71/71. **Course Rating:** 72.5/68.3. **Slope:** 127/111. **Walkability:** 4.
SUNRISE/MIDDAY COURSE (18 Combo)
Yards: 6,689/4,965. **Par:** 72/72. **Course Rating:** 72.6/68.3. **Slope:** 127/111. **Walkability:** 3.
SUNRISE/SUNSET COURSE (18 Combo)
Yards: 6,554/4,455. **Par:** 71/71. **Course Rating:** 72.0/67.6. **Slope:** 126/109. **Walkability:** 4.

★½ CENTERVIEW GOLF COURSE
PU-5640 N. Adrian Hwy., Adrian, 49221, Lenawee County, (517)263-8081, 30 miles from Toledo. **Facility Holes:** 18. **Yards:** 6,668/5,226. **Par:** 71/72. **Green Fee:** $14/$18. **Cart Fee:** $18/Person. **Walking Policy:** Unrestricted walking. **Walkability:** 2. **Opened:** 1970. **Season:** March-Nov. **To obtain tee times:** Call golf shop. **Miscellaneous:** Reduced fees (weekdays, seniors, juniors), range (grass), FF.

CHAMPION HILL
PU-501 N. Marshall Rd., Beulah, 49617, Benzie County, (231)882-9200, 27 miles from Traverse City. **E-mail:** estone@coslink.net. **Web:** www.championhill.com. **Facility Holes:** 18. **Yards:** 6,884/5,125. **Par:** 72/72. **Course Rating:** 71.9/68.7. **Slope:** 121/116. **Green Fee:** $21/$35. **Cart Fee:** $10/Person. **Walking Policy:** Unrestricted walking. **Walkability:** 4. **Opened:** 2000. **Architect:** Stone/Cole. **Season:** April-Oct. **High:** June-Aug. **To obtain tee times:** Call golf shop. **Miscellaneous:** Reduced fees (twilight), range (grass), credit cards (MC, V), BF, FF.

★★★ CHARLEVOIX COUNTRY CLUB
SP-9600 Clubhouse Dr., Charlevoix, 49720, Charlevoix County, (231)547-1922, (800)618-9796, 40 miles from Traverse City. **Facility Holes:** 18. **Yards:** 6,520/5,084. **Par:** 72/72. **Course Rating:** 70.6/68.4. **Slope:** 127/115. **Green Fee:** $39/$60. **Cart Fee:** Included in green fee. **Walking Policy:** Mandatory cart. **Walkability:** 3. **Opened:** 1994. **Architect:** Jerry Matthews. **Season:** May-Oct. **High:** June-Aug. **Tee times:** Call golf shop. **Miscellaneous:** Reduced fees (weekdays, guests, twilight), metal spikes, range (grass), credit cards (MC, V, AE).
Reader Comments: Challenging but fair course ... The staff goes way out of their way to make everyone feel like a member ... Beautiful clubhouse and lounge for public use ... Fairly priced ... Very pretty, great pro ... Old & traditional.

★★★ CHASE HAMMOND GOLF COURSE
PU-2454 N. Putnam Rd., Muskegon, 49445, Muskegon County, (231)766-3035, 40 miles from Grand Rapids. **Facility Holes:** 18. **Yards:** 6,307/5,135. **Par:** 72/72. **Course Rating:** 71.2/71.1. **Slope:** 133/123. **Green Fee:** $13/$22. **Cart Fee:** $10/Person. **Walking Policy:** Unrestricted walking. **Walkability:** 2. **Opened:** 1970. **Architect:** Mark DeVries. **Season:** March-Nov. **High:** June-Aug. **To obtain tee times:** Call golf shop. **Miscellaneous:** Reduced fees (weekdays, twilight, seniors, juniors), range (grass), credit cards (MC, V, D).
Reader Comments: If you can play Chase, then you can play anywhere ... Very good, tough but fair ... Outstanding municipal course, narrow & tough ... New owners bringing it back to the greatness it once had ... 18th hole is awesome.

★★ CHEBOYGAN GOLF & COUNTRY CLUB
SP-1431 Old Mackinaw Rd., Cheboygan, 49721, Cheboygan County, (616)627-4264, 12 miles from Mackinaw City. **Facility Holes:** 18. **Yards:** 6,003/4,653. **Par:** 70/71. **Course Rating:** 67.4/67.7. **Slope:** 120/113. **Green Fee:** $19/$29. **Cart Fee:** $14/Person. **Walking Policy:** Unrestricted walking. **Walkability:** 3. **Opened:** 1922. **Architect:** William Newcomb. **Season:** April-Nov. **High:** June-Aug. **To obtain tee times:** Call golf shop. **Miscellaneous:** Reduced fees (twilight, seniors, juniors), range (grass/mats), credit cards (MC, V, AE, D), FF.

★★★★ CHERRY CREEK GOLF CLUB *Service*
PU-52000 Cherry Creek Dr., Shelby Township, 48316, Macomb County, (810)254-7700, 24 miles from Detroit. **E-mail:** leonhardmr@aol.com. **Web:** www.cherrycreekgolf.com. **Facility Holes:** 18. **Yards:** 6,784/5,012. **Par:** 72/72. **Course Rating:** 72.7/67.1. **Slope:** 139/114. **Green Fee:** $40/$65. **Cart Fee:** Included in green fee. **Walking Policy:** Walking at certain times. **Walkability:** 3. **Opened:** 1995. **Architect:** Lanny Wadkins/Mike Bylen. **Season:** Year-round. **High:** May-Sept. **Tee times:** Call up to 10 days in advance. **Miscellaneous:** Reduced fees (weekdays, twilight, seniors, juniors), range (grass/mats), credit cards (MC, V), BF, FF.
Reader Comments: Great early/late season discounts ... Good course condition and service was OK ... A little expensive.

★★½ CHESHIRE HILLS GOLF COURSE
PU-3829 - 102nd Ave., Allegan, 49010, Allegan County, (616)673-2882, 10 miles from Allegan. **Facility Holes:** 27. **Green Fee:** $19/$22. **Cart Fee:** $15/Person. **Walking Policy:** Unrestricted walking. **Walkability:** 3. **Opened:** 1972. **Architect:** Herb Johnson. **High:** April-Nov.

To obtain tee times: Call golf shop. **Miscellaneous:** Reduced fees (weekdays, juniors), range (grass/mats), credit cards (MC, V, D), BF, FF.
BLUE BIRD/RED FOX COURSE (18 Combo)
Yards: 6,112/4,564. **Par:** 70/70. **Course Rating:** 68.8/64.7. **Slope:** 114/103.
BLUE BIRD/WHITETAIL COURSE (18 Combo)
Yards: 5,904/4,482. **Par:** 70/70. **Course Rating:** 68.8/64.7. **Slope:** 114/103.
RED FOX/WHITETAIL COURSE (18 Combo)
Yards: 6,026/4,490. **Par:** 70/70. **Course Rating:** 68.8/64.7. **Slope:** 114/103.

★★★½ CHESTNUT VALLEY GOLF COURSE
SP-1875 Clubhouse Dr., Harbor Springs, 49740, Emmet County, (231)526-9100, (877)284-3688, 10 miles from Petoskey. **Facility Holes:** 18. **Yards:** 6,406/5,166. **Par:** 72/72. **Course Rating:** 71.8/72.1. **Slope:** 125/116. **Green Fee:** $40/$70. **Cart Fee:** Included in green fee. **Walking Policy:** Walking at certain times. **Walkability:** 4. **Opened:** 1994. **Architect:** Larry Mancour. **Season:** May-Nov. **High:** June-Sept. **To obtain tee times:** Call golf shop. **Miscellaneous:** Reduced fees (weekdays, guests, twilight), range (grass), credit cards (MC, V, D).
Reader Comments: Scorable, rolling course … Affordable … Not my 1st choice but I'd play it again … Challenging, inexpensive by northern Michigan standards … Deer and turkey on course.

★½ CHISHOLM HILLS COUNTRY CLUB
PU-2395 Washington Rd., Lansing, 48911, Ingham County, (517)694-0169. **Facility Holes:** 18. **Yards:** 6,134/5,285. **Par:** 72/72. **Course Rating:** 68.7/68.8. **Slope:** 119/118. **Green Fee:** $13/$23. **Cart Fee:** $11/Person. **Walking Policy:** Unrestricted walking. **Walkability:** 3. **Season:** March-Nov. **To obtain tee times:** Call up to 7 days in advance. **Miscellaneous:** Reduced fees (weekdays, guests, twilight, seniors, juniors), credit cards (MC, V), BF, FF.

★★ CHOCOLAY DOWNS GOLF COURSE
PU-125 Chocolay Downs Golf Dr., Marquette, 49855, Marquette County, (906)249-3111, 7 miles from Marquette. **Web:** www.marquettemi.com. **Facility Holes:** 18. **Yards:** 6,375/4,878. **Par:** 72/72. **Green Fee:** $20. **Cart Fee:** $18/Cart. **Walking Policy:** Unrestricted walking. **Walkability:** 2. **Opened:** 1992. **Architect:** Jerry Matthews. **Season:** May-Nov. **High:** June-Sept. **To obtain tee times:** Call golf shop. **Miscellaneous:** Reduced fees (seniors), range (grass/mats), credit cards (MC, V), BF, FF.

★★ CLARK LAKE GOLF CLUB
PU-5535 Wesch Rd., Brooklyn, 49230, Jackson County, (517)592-6259, 17 miles from Jackson. **Facility Holes:** 27. **Yards:** 6,632/5,511. **Par:** 73/73. **Green Fee:** $11/$15. **Cart Fee:** $24/Cart. **Walking Policy:** Unrestricted walking. **Walkability:** 2. **Opened:** 1919. **Season:** Year-round. **To obtain tee times:** Call golf shop. **Miscellaneous:** Reduced fees (weekdays, seniors), range (grass), credit cards (MC, V), BF, FF.
Special Notes: Also has a 9-hole executive course.

★½ CLARKSTON CREEK GOLF CLUB
SP-6060 Maybee Rd., Clarkston, 48346, Oakland County, (248)625-3731, 35 miles from Detroit. **E-mail:** ccgolf@clarkstoncreek.com. **Web:** www.clarkstoncreek.com. **Facility Holes:** 18. **Yards:** 6,316/5,300. **Par:** 71/74. **Course Rating:** 69.5/70.6. **Slope:** 126/120. **Green Fee:** $19/$30. **Cart Fee:** $22/Cart. **Walking Policy:** Unrestricted walking. **Walkability:** 3. **Opened:** 1969. **Architect:** William Newcomb. **Season:** March-Nov. **High:** May-Sept. **To obtain tee times:** Call golf shop. **Miscellaneous:** Reduced fees (weekdays, twilight, seniors, juniors), metal spikes, range (grass/mats), credit cards (MC, V, AE).
Special Notes: Formerly Spring Lake Country Club.

★★★ CLEARBROOK GOLF CLUB
PU-6494 Clearbrook Dr., Saugatuck, 49453, Allegan County, (616)857-2000, 25 miles from Grand Rapids. **Web:** www.clearbrookgolfclub.com. **Facility Holes:** 18. **Yards:** 6,516/5,153. **Par:** 72/74. **Course Rating:** 72.8/70.0. **Slope:** 132/127. **Green Fee:** $18/$39. **Cart Fee:** $12/Person. **Walking Policy:** Unrestricted walking. **Walkability:** 2. **Opened:** 1926. **Architect:** Charles Darl Scott. **Season:** March-Nov. **High:** June-Sept. **To obtain tee times:** Call golf shop. **Miscellaneous:** Reduced fees (weekdays, twilight, seniors, juniors), range (grass/mats), credit cards (MC, V, AE, D), BF, FF.
Reader Comments: Nice people and course … Too many blind shots … Nice but not great … Dandy … Need local knowledge … Great classic course at low price … Very difficult from front tees.

★★★ THE COLONIAL GOLF COURSE
PU-2763 N. 72nd Ave., Hart, 49420, Oceana County, (231)873-8333, 30 miles from Muskegon. **Web:** www.westmichgolf.com. **Facility Holes:** 18. **Yards:** 6,859/5,151. **Par:** 72/72. **Course Rating:** 73.6/68.4. **Slope:** 130/108. **Green Fee:** $13/$25. **Cart Fee:** $14/Person. **Walking Policy:** Unrestricted walking. **Walkability:** 3. **Opened:** 1999. **Architect:** Jeff Gorney.

Season: March-Dec. **High:** June-Aug. **To obtain tee times:** Call golf shop. **Miscellaneous:** Reduced fees (weekdays, twilight, seniors), range, credit cards (MC, V, AE, D), BF, FF.
Reader Comments: New course with nice layout ... Par 5s more like risk/reward par 4s ... Twilight special is great ... Strong course from back tees ... Better in time.

★★★½ CONCORD HILLS GOLF COURSE
PU-7331 Pulaski Rd., Concord, 49237, Jackson County, (517)524-8337, 12 miles from Jackson. **E-mail:** concordhills@concordhills.com. **Web:** www.concordhills.com. **Facility Holes:** 18. **Yards:** 6,422/5,104. **Par:** 72/72. **Course Rating:** 71.5/71.0. **Slope:** 125/125. **Green Fee:** $19/$22. **Cart Fee:** $13/Person. **Walking Policy:** Unrestricted walking. **Walkability:** 3. **Opened:** 1976. **Architect:** William Newcomb. **Season:** April-Oct. **High:** June-Aug. **To obtain tee times:** Call golf shop. **Miscellaneous:** Reduced fees (weekdays, guests, twilight, seniors, juniors), range (grass), credit cards (MC, V), BF, FF.
Reader Comments: Owners were very accommodating to a large group ... Hidden gem in central Michigan ... Some greens and tees are too close together ... Another hidden gem, in a resort area, would be double the price.

★★★ COPPER HILL GOLF & COUNTRY CLUB
SP-2125 Lakeville Rd., Oxford, 48370, Oakland County, (248)969-9808. **E-mail:** junglegolf@aol.com. **Web:** www.copperhills.com. **Facility Holes:** 27. **Green Fee:** $40/$60. **Cart Fee:** Included in green fee. **Walking Policy:** Unrestricted walking. **Walkability:** 5. **Opened:** 1997. **Architect:** Curtis Wright. **Season:** March-Dec. **High:** June-Sept. **To obtain tee times:** Call up to 14 days in advance. **Miscellaneous:** Reduced fees (weekdays, twilight, seniors, juniors), credit cards (MC, V, AE), BF, FF.
HILL/JUNGLE COURSE (18 Combo)
Yards: 6,539/4,673. **Par:** 72/72. **Course Rating:** 71.2/67.5. **Slope:** 141/123.
MARSH/HILL COURSE (18 Combo)
Yards: 6,734/4,754. **Par:** 72/72. **Course Rating:** 73.1/68.4. **Slope:** 145/127.
Notes: Ranked 16th in 1999 Best in State.
MARSH/JUNGLE COURSE (18 Combo)
Yards: 6,493/4,771. **Par:** 72/72. **Course Rating:** 72.1/68.7. **Slope:** 141/124.
Reader Comments: Target golf over wetlands ... Fantastic, very challenging ... Great design through wetlands & woods.

★★★½ COYOTE GOLF CLUB
PU-28700 Milford Rd., New Hudson, 48165, Oakland County, (248)486-1228, 30 miles from Detroit. **E-mail:** coyote@teemaster.com. **Web:** www.teemaster.com. **Facility Holes:** 18. **Yards:** 7,201/4,923. **Par:** 72/72. **Course Rating:** 73.8/68.4. **Slope:** 130/114. **Green Fee:** $19/$47. **Cart Fee:** $13/Person. **Walking Policy:** Walking at certain times. **Walkability:** 3. **Opened:** 1996. **Architect:** Scott Thacker. **Season:** March-Nov. **High:** June-Sept. **To obtain tee times:** Call up to 14 days in advance. **Miscellaneous:** Reduced fees (weekdays, twilight, seniors, juniors), range (grass/mats), credit cards (MC, V), BF, FF.
Reader Comments: Nice condition, fair and pretty course ... Food very good ... Course is nice.

★★★ CRACKLEWOOD GOLF CLUB
PU-18215 24 Mile Macomb Township, Macomb, 48042, Macomb County, (810)781-0808, 4 miles from Mt. Clemens. **Facility Holes:** 18. **Yards:** 6,538/4,764. **Par:** 72/72. **Course Rating:** 70.4/67.3. **Slope:** 122/112. **Green Fee:** $24/$28. **Cart Fee:** $12/Person. **Walking Policy:** Walking at certain times. **Walkability:** 2. **Opened:** 1989. **Architect:** Jerry Matthews. **Season:** April-Nov. **High:** May-Sept. **To obtain tee times:** Call up to 7 days in advance. **Miscellaneous:** Reduced fees (weekdays, twilight, seniors, juniors), metal spikes, range (grass), credit cards (MC, V, AE, D, DC), BF, FF.
Reader Comments: Several tree-lined fairways make accuracy a must ... Fivesomes allowed by pro shop ... The name says it all ... Front 9 tree lined, very narrow ... Good for average golfers.

★★ CRESTVIEW GOLF CLUB
PU-900 W D Ave., Kalamazoo, 49009, Kalamazoo County, (616)349-1111, 5 miles from Kalamazoo. **Facility Holes:** 18. **Yards:** 6,103/5,403. **Par:** 70/72. **Course Rating:** 68.1/69.8. **Slope:** 109/111. **Green Fee:** $12/$20. **Cart Fee:** $20/Cart. **Walking Policy:** Unrestricted walking. **Walkability:** 2. **Opened:** 1964. **Architect:** Dewayne Amsen. **Season:** March-Nov. **High:** May-Oct. **Tee times:** Call golf shop. **Miscellaneous:** Credit cards (MC, V), BF, FF.

★½ CROOKED CREEK GOLF CLUB
PU-9387 Gratiot Rd., Saginaw, 48609, Saginaw County, (517)781-0050. **Facility Holes:** 18. **Yards:** 5,600/4,883. **Par:** 72/78. **Course Rating:** 66.5/67.4. **Slope:** 110/114. **Green Fee:** $19/$20. **Cart Fee:** $22/Cart. **Walking Policy:** Unrestricted walking. **Walkability:** 2. **Opened:** 1959. **Season:** Year-round. **High:** June-Sept. **To obtain tee times:** Call golf shop. **Miscellaneous:** Reduced fees (seniors, juniors), range, credit cards (MC, V, D), BF, FF.

★★★½ CROOKED TREE GOLF CLUB
PU-600 Crooked Tree Dr., Petoskey, 49770, Emmet County, (616)439-4030, 65 miles from Traverse City. **Facility Holes:** 18. **Yards:** 6,671/4,631. **Par:** 71/71. **Course Rating:** 72.8/68.0. **Slope:** 140/121. **Green Fee:** $29/$79. **Cart Fee:** Included in green fee. **Walking Policy:** Walking at certain times. **Walkability:** 3. **Opened:** 1995. **Architect:** Harry Bowers. **Season:** May-Oct. **High:** June-Aug. **To obtain tee times:** Call golf shop. **Miscellaneous:** Reduced fees (weekdays, guests, twilight), range, credit cards (MC, V, AE, D), BF, FF.
Reader Comments: Good warm-up for Bay Harbor ... Difficult for average golfer ... Blind holes, windy ... A lot of elevation changes ... Natural beauty, but needs to cut fairways.

★★ CRYSTAL LAKE GOLF CLUB
R-Hwy. 31, Beulah, 49617, Benzie County, (231)882-4061, 30 miles from Traverse City. **Facility Holes:** 18. **Yards:** 6,535/5,325. **Par:** 70/72. **Course Rating:** 70.0/70.0. **Slope:** 120/115. **Green Fee:** $25. **Walking Policy:** Unrestricted walking. **Walkability:** 2. **Opened:** 1970. **Architect:** Matthews/Keillor/Keillor. **Season:** May-Nov. **High:** July-Aug. **To obtain tee times:** Call golf shop. **Miscellaneous:** Reduced fees (twilight, seniors, juniors), range, credit cards (MC, V), FF.

CRYSTAL MOUNTAIN RESORT
R-12500 Crystal Mountain Dr., Thompsonville, 49683, Benzie County, (231)378-2000, (800)968-7686, 30 miles from Traverse City. **E-mail:** info@crystalmountain.com. **Web:** www.crystalmountain.com. **Facility Holes:** 36. **Architect:** William Newcomb. **Season:** April-Nov. **High:** May-Aug. **To obtain tee times:** Call golf shop. **Miscellaneous:** Reduced fees (weekdays, guests, twilight, juniors), range, lodging (220 rooms), credit cards (MC, V, AE, D), BF, FF.

★★★ BETSIE VALLEY COURSE (18)
Yards: 6,357/4,902. **Par:** 71/71. **Course Rating:** 70.2/68.5. **Slope:** 127/121. **Green Fee:** $20/$42. **Cart Fee:** $13/Person. **Walking Policy:** Unrestricted walking. **Walkability:** 2. **Opened:** 1977.
Reader Comments: Good for high handicap golfers, excellent 1st hole ... Nice resort course, many trees, have to hit straight, narrow fairways ... Very challenging great staff ... Great golf packages ... Nice resort & course.

★★★★ MOUNTAIN RIDGE (18)
Yards: 7,007/4,956. **Par:** 72/72. **Course Rating:** 73.3/68.2. **Slope:** 132/119. **Green Fee:** $50/$82. **Cart Fee:** Included in green fee. **Walking Policy:** Mandatory carts. **Walkability:** 4. **Opened:** 1992.
Reader Comments: Beautiful view ... A unique setting, park like, in an urban area ... Good challenge, hospitality ... Views, wildlife (turkey & deer) ... An unknown gem ... Up and coming ... Excellent ... Beautiful views and wildlife.

★★½ CURRIE MUNICIPAL GOLF COURSE
PU-1006 Currie Pkwy., Midland, 48640, Midland County, (517)839-9600. **Facility Holes:** 27. **Yards:** 6,523/5,244. **Par:** 72/72. **Course Rating:** 71.0/69.2. **Slope:** 118/109. **Green Fee:** $17. **Cart Fee:** $12/Person. **Walking Policy:** Unrestricted walking. **Walkability:** 1. **Opened:** 1954. **Architect:** Gill Currie. **Season:** April-Nov. **High:** May-Sept. **To obtain tee times:** Call golf shop. **Miscellaneous:** Reduced fees (twilight, seniors, juniors), range (grass/mats). **Special Notes:** Also has a 9-hole West Course.

★★ DE MOR HILLS GOLF COURSE
PU-10275 Ranger Hwy., Morenci, 49256, Lenawee County, (517)458-6679, (800)871-5983, 15 miles from Adrian. **Facility Holes:** 18. **Yards:** 6,340/5,603. **Par:** 72/76. **Green Fee:** $18/$20. **Cart Fee:** $20/Cart. **Walking Policy:** Unrestricted walking. **Walkability:** 2. **Opened:** 1962. **Architect:** Robert Demeritt. **Season:** March-Nov. **High:** June-Sept. **To obtain tee times:** Call up to 14 days in advance. **Miscellaneous:** Reduced fees (seniors, juniors), metal spikes, credit cards (MC, V), BF, FF.

★★★ DEARBORN HILLS GOLF COURSE
PU-1300 S. Telegraph Rd., Dearborn, 48124, Wayne County, (313)563-4653. **Facility Holes:** 18. **Yards:** 4,495/3,217. **Par:** 60/60. **Course Rating:** 61.2/57.7. **Slope:** 100/92. **Green Fee:** $13/$25. **Cart Fee:** $23/Cart. **Walking Policy:** Unrestricted walking. **Walkability:** 3. **Opened:** 1992. **Architect:** Warner Bowen. **Season:** March-Dec. **To obtain tee times:** Call up to 2 days in advance. **Miscellaneous:** Reduced fees (twilight, seniors, juniors), credit cards (MC, V, AE), BF, FF.
Reader Comments: Great shorter course for beginners, good course for learning the game, a fun course to play over & over ... Nice executive-style course ... Fine executive course ... Staff friendly.

DEER RUN AT LAKES OF THE NORTH
SP-Pineview Dr., Mancelona, 49659, Antrim County, (231)585-6800, 45 miles from Traverse City. **Facility Holes:** 18. **Yards:** 6,996/5,465. **Par:** 72/72. **Course Rating:** 73.0/71.0. **Slope:** 130/123. **Green Fee:** $25. **Cart Fee:** $15/Person. **Walking Policy:** Walking at certain times.

Walkability: 2. **Architect:** William Newcomb. **Season:** April-Oct. **To obtain tee times:** Call golf shop. **Miscellaneous:** Reduced fees (twilight), credit cards (MC, V, D).

★★ DEER RUN GOLF CLUB

PU-13955 Cascade Rd., Lowell, 49331, Kent County, (616)897-8481, 15 miles from Grand Rapids. **Facility Holes:** 18. **Yards:** 6,964/5,327. **Par:** 72/72. **Course Rating:** 74.1/70.7. **Slope:** 134/118. **Green Fee:** $20/$25. **Cart Fee:** $20/Cart. **Walking Policy:** Walking at certain times. **Walkability:** 2. **Opened:** 1973. **Season:** March-Nov. **High:** May-Aug. **To obtain tee times:** Call up to 30 days in advance. **Miscellaneous:** Reduced fees (seniors), range (grass), credit cards (MC, V, D), BF, FF.

DEER RUN GOLF COURSE

PU-8151 Pineview Dr., Mancelona, 49659, Antrim County, (231)585-6800, (800)851-4653, 17 miles from Gaylord. **Facility Holes:** 18. **Yards:** 6,996/5,465. **Par:** 72/74. **Course Rating:** 73.3/71.3. **Slope:** 130/123. **Green Fee:** $27/$42. **Cart Fee:** Included in green fee. **Walking Policy:** Unrestricted walking. **Walkability:** 4. **Opened:** 1974. **Architect:** William Newcomb. **Season:** May-Oct. **High:** May-July. **To obtain tee times:** Call golf shop. **Miscellaneous:** Reduced fees (twilight, juniors), range (grass), credit cards (MC, V, D), BF, FF.

DEME ACRES GOLF COURSE

PU-17655 Albain Rd., Petersburg, 49270, Monroe County, (734)279-1151, 15 miles from Sylvania. **Facility Holes:** 18. **Yards:** 5,735/5,200. **Par:** 70/70. **Green Fee:** $14/$18. **Cart Fee:** $10/Person. **Walking Policy:** Unrestricted walking. **Walkability:** 1. **Opened:** 1962. **Season:** March-Nov. **High:** June-Aug. **To obtain tee times:** Call golf shop. **Miscellaneous:** Reduced fees (weekdays, seniors, juniors), BF, FF.

★★★½ DEVIL'S RIDGE GOLF CLUB

PU-3700 Metamora Rd., Oxford, 48371, Oakland County, (248)969-0100, 11 miles from Auburn Hills. **E-mail:** rick_f9@yahoo.com. **Web:** www.devilsridge.com. **Facility Holes:** 18. **Yards:** 6,722/4,130. **Par:** 72/72. **Course Rating:** 72.2/64.4. **Slope:** 123/100. **Green Fee:** $49/$60. **Cart Fee:** Included in green fee. **Walking Policy:** Mandatory carts. **Walkability:** 4. **Opened:** 1995. **Architect:** Pat Conroy. **Season:** March-Nov. **High:** May-Oct. **To obtain tee times:** Call up to 7 days in advance. **Miscellaneous:** Reduced fees (weekdays, twilight, seniors), range (grass/mats), credit cards (MC, V, AE, D), BF, FF.
Reader Comments: Well maintained and very challenging ... Course hilly, tight ... Too slow, people looking for lost balls ... Much better now that it is softened up ... Great course.

★★★★ THE DREAM

PU-5166 Old Hwy. 76, West Branch, 48661, Ogemaw County, (989)345-6300, (888)833-7326, 3 miles from West Branch. **Facility Holes:** 18. **Yards:** 7,000/5,118. **Par:** 72/72. **Course Rating:** 73.7/68.6. **Slope:** 135/117. **Green Fee:** $45/$68. **Cart Fee:** Included in green fee. **Walking Policy:** Mandatory carts. **Walkability:** 5. **Opened:** 1997. **Architect:** Jeff Gorney. **Season:** April-Nov. **High:** May-Sept. **To obtain tee times:** Call up to 30 days in advance. **Miscellaneous:** Reduced fees (weekdays, twilight), range, credit cards (MC, V, D), BF, FF.
Reader Comments: A family-owned course ... Great service ... There are several blind tee shots ... Long from the tips, beautiful course ... Very nice, but you pay dearly for it ... Best value in Mich., the customer is king.

★★ THE DUNES GOLF CLUB

PU-6489 W. Empire Hwy., Empire, 49630, Leelanau County, (616)326-5390, 18 miles from Traverse City. **E-mail:** cwall@centuryinter.net. **Web:** www.dunesgolf.com. **Facility Holes:** 18. **Yards:** 5,868/5,041. **Par:** 72/72. **Course Rating:** 67.3/68.1. **Slope:** 112/114. **Green Fee:** $16. **Cart Fee:** $18/Cart. **Walking Policy:** Walking at certain times. **Walkability:** 2. **Opened:** 1984. **Season:** April-Oct. **High:** July-Sept. **To obtain tee times:** Call golf shop. **Miscellaneous:** Reduced fees (twilight), credit cards (MC, V), BF, FF.

★★★ DUNHAM HILLS GOLF & COUNTRY CLUB

PU-13561 Dunham Rd., Hartland, 48353, Livingston County, (248)887-9170, 23 miles from Pontiac. **Facility Holes:** 18. **Yards:** 6,820/5,310. **Par:** 71/74. **Course Rating:** 72.5/71.1. **Slope:** 133/123. **Green Fee:** $48/$58. **Cart Fee:** Included in green fee. **Walking Policy:** Walking at certain times. **Walkability:** 5. **Opened:** 1968. **Architect:** Built by owners. **Season:** March-Nov. **High:** May-Sept. **To obtain tee times:** Call up to 7 days in advance. **Miscellaneous:** Reduced fees (weekdays, twilight, seniors, juniors), range (grass), credit cards (MC, V, AE), BF, FF.
Reader Comments: Used to be a great value, raised rates ... Many parallel fairways ... More difficult than scorecards show ... Very difficult ... A good test for a public golf course.

★★★½ DUNMAGLAS GOLF CLUB

PU-09031 Boyne City Rd., Charlevoix, 49720, Charlevoix County, (231)547-1022, (888)847-0909, 50 miles from Traverse City. **E-mail:** corporateservices@americangolf.com.

MICHIGAN

Web: www.americangolf.com. **Facility Holes:** 18. **Yards:** 6,897/5,259. **Par:** 72/73. **Course Rating:** 73.5/69.8. **Slope:** 139/123. **Green Fee:** $35/$70. **Cart Fee:** Included in green fee. **Walking Policy:** Mandatory carts. **Walkability:** 5. **Opened:** 1992. **Architect:** Larry Mancour. **Season:** April-Nov. **High:** June-Sept. **To obtain tee times:** Call golf shop. **Miscellaneous:** Reduced fees (twilight), range (grass), credit cards (MC, V, AE), BF, FF.
Notes: Ranked 22nd in 1999 Best in State.
Reader Comments: Challenging, quality layout with beautiful views … Spectacular, hilly course … Too many lay-up shots from tee box … Best par 3s in state … Very tough.

★½   DUTCH HOLLOW GOLF CLUB
PU-8500 E. Lansing Rd., Durand, 48429, Shiawassee County, (989)288-3960, 22 miles from Flint. **Facility Holes:** 18. **Yards:** 5,688/5,128. **Par:** 70/74. **Green Fee:** $13. **Cart Fee:** $15/Cart. **Walking Policy:** Unrestricted walking. **Opened:** 1948. **Architect:** Ellis Bowler. **Season:** April-Oct. **To obtain tee times:** Call golf shop. **Miscellaneous:** Reduced fees (juniors), FF.

★★★   EAGLE CREST RESORT
R-1275 Huron St., Ypsilanti, 48197, Washtenaw County, (734)487-2441, 30 miles from Detroit. **E-mail:** tom.pendlebury@emich.edu. **Web:** www.eaglecrestresort.com. **Facility Holes:** 18. **Yards:** 6,750/5,185. **Par:** 72/72. **Course Rating:** 73.6/69.7. **Slope:** 138/124. **Green Fee:** $45/$55. **Cart Fee:** Included in green fee. **Walking Policy:** Walking at certain times. **Walkability:** 2. **Opened:** 1989. **Architect:** Karl V. Litten. **Season:** March-Nov. **High:** June-Aug. **To obtain tee times:** Call up to 14 days in advance. **Miscellaneous:** Reduced fees (weekdays, twilight, seniors, juniors), range, lodging (240 rooms), credit cards (MC, V, AE), BF, FF.
Reader Comments: Good for couples … Beautiful setting, excellent greens … Slow play … Great view of tree tops from many holes … Great facility.

★★★   EAGLE GLEN GOLF COURSE
PU-1251 Club House Dr., Farwell, 48622, Clare County, (517)588-4653. **Facility Holes:** 18. **Yards:** 6,602/5,119. **Par:** 72/72. **Course Rating:** 71.1/69.2. **Slope:** 123/116. **Green Fee:** $21/$28. **Cart Fee:** $12/Person. **Walking Policy:** Walking at certain times. **Walkability:** 3. **Opened:** 1992. **Architect:** Jerry Matthews. **Season:** March-Nov. **To obtain tee times:** Call golf shop. **Miscellaneous:** Reduced fees (weekdays, guests, seniors, juniors), range (grass), credit cards (MC, V, D), BF, FF.
Reader Comments: Great value and great golf … My favorite in mid Michigan … Rough is tough.

★½   EAGLE VIEW GOLF CLUB
PU-2602 Tomlinson Rd., Mason, 48854, Eaton County, (517)676-5366, 10 miles from Lansing. **Facility Holes:** 18. **Yards:** 6,348/5,550. **Par:** 72/72. **Course Rating:** 69.7/70.5. **Green Fee:** $18/$20. **Cart Fee:** $10/Person. **Walking Policy:** Unrestricted walking. **Walkability:** 3. **Opened:** 1926. **Architect:** Henry Chisholm. **Season:** April-Nov. **To obtain tee times:** Call golf shop. **Miscellaneous:** Reduced fees (weekdays, twilight, seniors, juniors), range (grass), credit cards (MC, V).
Special Notes: Formerly Mason Hills Golf Course.

EASTERN HILLS GOLF CLUB
PU-6075 East G Ave., Kalamazoo, 49004, Kalamazoo County, (616)385-8175, 2 miles from Kalamazoo. **E-mail:** shecky4@aol.com. **Web:** www.kalamazoogolf.org. **Facility Holes:** 27. **Green Fee:** $18/$20. **Cart Fee:** $12/Person. **Walking Policy:** Unrestricted walking. **Walkability:** 2. **Opened:** 1957. **Season:** March-Nov. **High:** June-Aug. **To obtain tee times:** Call golf shop. **Miscellaneous:** Reduced fees (seniors, juniors), range (grass), credit cards (MC, V, AE, D).
BLUE/RED (18 Combo)
Yards: 6,023/4,844. **Par:** 72/72. **Course Rating:** 70.9/67.2. **Slope:** 119/107.
WHITE/BLUE (18 Combo)
Yards: 6,626/5,516. **Par:** 72/72. **Course Rating:** 70.5/70.4. **Slope:** 118/113.
WHITE/RED (18 Combo)
Yards: 5,999/5,015. **Par:** 72/72. **Course Rating:** 70.8/67.8. **Slope:** 120/106.

★★   EL DORADO COUNTRY CLUB
PU-2869 Pontiac Trail, Walled Lake, 48390, Oakland County, (248)624-1736, 40 miles from Detroit. **Facility Holes:** 18. **Yards:** 5,753/4,846. **Par:** 70/74. **Course Rating:** 68.3/68.0. **Slope:** 122/116. **Green Fee:** $25/$33. **Cart Fee:** $12/Person. **Walking Policy:** Walking at certain times. **Walkability:** 2. **Opened:** 1967. **Architect:** Walter R. Lorang Sr. **Season:** April-Oct. **High:** May-Aug. **To obtain tee times:** Call golf shop. **Miscellaneous:** Reduced fees (weekdays, twilight, seniors, juniors), range (grass), credit cards (MC, V, AE), BF, FF.

★★★½   ELDORADO   *Pace*
PU-1 Automotive Ave., Cadillac, 49601, Wexford County, (231)779-9977, (888)374-8318, 75 miles from Grand Rapids. **E-mail:** info@golfeldorado.com. **Web:** www.golfeldorado.com. **Facility Holes:** 18. **Yards:** 7,070/5,050. **Par:** 72/72. **Course Rating:** 73.0/68.2. **Slope:** 132/125.

Green Fee: $35/$50. Cart Fee: $15/Person. Walking Policy: Unrestricted walking. Walkability: 1. Opened: 1996. Architect: Bob Meyer. Season: April-Dec. High: May-Sept. To obtain tee times: Call up to 30 days in advance. Miscellaneous: Reduced fees (weekdays, twilight, juniors), metal spikes, range (grass), credit cards (MC, V), BF, FF.
Reader Comments: Greens are bigger than the fairways … Some greens are four-clubs deep … Score on the front and hold on during the back … Gets better every year … Long ball course.

★★ ELDORADO GOLF COURSE
PU-3750 Howell Rd., Mason, 48854, Ingham County, (517)676-2854, 7 miles from Lansing. Web: www.webgolfer.com/eldorado. Facility Holes: 27. Green Fee: $25/$29. Cart Fee: $12/Person. Walking Policy: Unrestricted walking. Walkability: 2. Opened: 1965. Architect: Jerry Matthews. Season: March-Nov. High: April-Oct. To obtain tee times: Call golf shop. Miscellaneous: Reduced fees (weekdays, twilight, seniors, juniors), range (grass), credit cards (MC, V, D), BF, FF.
BLUE/WHITE COURSE (18 Combo)
Yards: 6,536/5,488. Par: 71/71. Course Rating: 71.2/70.7. Slope: 117/118.
RED/BLUE COURSE (18 Combo)
Yards: 6,757/5,498. Par: 72/72. Course Rating: 71.0/70.2. Slope: 116/119.
RED/WHITE COURSE (18 Combo)
Yards: 6,445/5,405. Par: 71/71. Course Rating: 70.2/70.0. Slope: 112/116.

★★★★ ELK RIDGE GOLF CLUB
PU-9400 Rouse Rd., Atlanta, 49709, Montmorency County, (517)785-2275, (800)626-4355, 30 miles from Gaylord. E-mail: elkridgegc@aol.com. Web: www.elkridgegolf.com. Facility Holes: 18. Yards: 7,072/5,261. Par: 72/72. Course Rating: 74.7/72.3. Slope: 143/130. Green Fee: $50/$75. Cart Fee: Included in green fee. Walking Policy: Walking at certain times. Walkability: 4. Opened: 1991. Architect: Jerry Matthews. Season: May-Oct. High: June-Aug. To obtain tee times: Call golf shop. Miscellaneous: Reduced fees (weekdays, seniors, juniors), range (grass), credit cards (MC, V, AE, D), FF.
Notes: Ranked 17th in 2001 Best in State.
Reader Comments: The view from No. 10 is worth it … Beautiful setting … Fun 10th hole … Wildlife, views, great conditions, shotmaker's course … A walk in the wilderness.

★★★ ELLA SHARP PARK GOLF COURSE
PU-2800 4th St., Jackson, 49203, Jackson County, (517)788-4066, 35 miles from Lansing. Facility Holes: 18. Yards: 5,792/4,744. Par: 71/71. Course Rating: 67.4/69.1. Slope: 113/114. Green Fee: $15/$16. Cart Fee: $14/Cart. Walking Policy: Unrestricted walking. Walkability: 2. Opened: 1923. Architect: Tom Bendelow. Season: March-Dec. High: May-Sept. To obtain tee times: Call up to 14 days in advance. Miscellaneous: Reduced fees (weekdays, twilight, seniors, juniors), range (mats), BF, FF.
Reader Comments: Good muni … Tight, fairly cramped, but fantastic value … Great people and price … Short but cheap … Good place to start … Price, course, location, good … Old course … Newly renovated.

★★½ ELMBROOK GOLF COURSE
PU-1750 Townline Rd., Traverse City, 49684, Grand Traverse County, (231)946-9180. E-mail: elmbrookgolf@aol.com. Web: www.elmbrookgolf.com. Facility Holes: 18. Yards: 6,131/5,194. Par: 72/72. Course Rating: 68.4/68.5. Slope: 114/112. Green Fee: $22/$31. Cart Fee: $14/Person. Walking Policy: Unrestricted walking. Walkability: 3. Opened: 1964. Architect: Jerry Matthews. Season: April-Dec. High: June-Aug. To obtain tee times: Call golf shop. Miscellaneous: Reduced fees (guests), range (grass/mats), credit cards (MC, V, D).

★★ THE EMERALD AT MAPLE CREEK GOLF COURSE
PU-8103 N. U.S. 27, St. Johns, 48879, Clinton County, (517)224-6287, (800)924-5993, 25 miles from Lansing. Web: www.emeraldatmaplecreek.com. Facility Holes: 18. Yards: 6,644/5,166. Par: 72/72. Course Rating: 71.5/69.1. Slope: 128/114. Green Fee: $25/$40. Cart Fee: $28/Cart. Walking Policy: Unrestricted walking. Walkability: 3. Opened: 1996. Architect: Jerry Matthews. Season: April-Nov. High: June-Sept. Tee times: Call golf shop. Miscellaneous: Reduced fees (weekdays, twilight, juniors), range (grass), credit cards (MC, V, AE), BF, FF.

EMERALD VALE GOLF CLUB
PU-6867 E. Michigan Hwy. 42, Manton, 49663, Wexford County, (231)824-3631, (800)890-3407, 12 miles from Cadillac. E-mail: info@emeraldvale.com. Web: www.emeraldvale.com. Facility Holes: 18. Yards: 6,800/5,277. Par: 72/72. Course Rating: 72.6/70.0. Slope: 130/122. Green Fee: $30/$36. Cart Fee: $12/Person. Walking Policy: Unrestricted walking. Walkability: 4. Opened: 1998. Architect: Bruce Matthews III. Season: April-Nov. High: June-Aug. To obtain tee times: Call golf shop. Miscellaneous: Reduced fees (twilight, seniors), range (grass), credit cards (MC, V), BF, FF.

MICHIGAN

★★ ENGLISH HILLS GOLF COURSE
PU-1200 Four Mile Rd., Grand Rapids, 49504, Kent County, (616)784-3420, 3 miles from Grand Rapids. **Facility Holes:** 18. **Yards:** 5,575/4,915. **Par:** 69/69. **Course Rating:** 63.0. **Slope:** 117/117. **Green Fee:** $18/$20. **Cart Fee:** $20/Cart. **Walking Policy:** Unrestricted walking. **Walkability:** 3. **Opened:** 1955. **Architect:** Jerry Matthews. **Season:** March-Dec. **High:** May-Aug. **Tee times:** Call up to 1 day in advance. **Miscellaneous:** Reduced fees (weekdays, seniors, juniors), metal spikes, credit cards (MC, V, AE, D), BF, FF.

★★ FALCON HEAD GOLF CLUB
PU-13120 Northland Dr., Big Rapids, 49307, Mecosta County, (231)796-2613, (888)264-0407, 50 miles from Grand Rapids. **Facility Holes:** 18. **Yards:** 6,166/4,799. **Par:** 72/72. **Course Rating:** 71.8/68.8. **Slope:** 133/120. **Green Fee:** $13/$22. **Cart Fee:** $13/Person. **Walking Policy:** Walking at certain times. **Walkability:** 3. **Season:** Year-round. **High:** May-Sept. **To obtain tee times:** Call golf shop. **Miscellaneous:** Reduced fees (weekdays, guests, twilight, seniors, juniors), range (grass), credit cards (MC, V, AE, D).

★★★½ FAULKWOOD SHORES GOLF CLUB
PU-300 South Hughes Rd., Howell, 48843, Livingston County, (517)546-4180, 20 miles from Detroit. **Facility Holes:** 18. **Yards:** 6,828/5,341. **Par:** 72/72. **Course Rating:** 74.3/71.8. **Slope:** 140/128. **Green Fee:** $24/$37. **Cart Fee:** $12/Person. **Walking Policy:** Walking at certain times. **Walkability:** 2. **Opened:** 1967. **Architect:** Ralph Banfield. **Season:** April-Nov. **To obtain tee times:** Call golf shop. **Miscellaneous:** Reduced fees (weekdays, twilight, seniors, juniors), metal spikes, range (grass/mats), credit cards (MC, V), FF.
Reader Comments: A major league test of golf at minor league prices ... Toughest in area, very reasonable ... 140 slope, long, no tricks ... Good price.

★★★ FELLOWS CREEK GOLF CLUB
PU-2936 Lotz Rd., Canton, 48188, Washtenaw County, (734)728-1300, 20 miles from Detroit. **Facility Holes:** 27. **Green Fee:** $23/$26. **Cart Fee:** $11/Person. **Walking Policy:** Unrestricted walking. **Walkability:** 1. **Opened:** 1961. **Architect:** Bruce Matthews/Jerry Matthews. **Season:** April-Nov. **High:** June-Aug. **To obtain tee times:** Call golf shop. **Miscellaneous:** Reduced fees (weekdays, twilight, seniors, juniors), metal spikes, credit cards (MC, V).
EAST/SOUTH (18 Combo)
Yards: 6,489/5,276. **Par:** 72/72. **Course Rating:** 70.1/70.9. **Slope:** 118/123.
EAST/WEST (18 Combo)
Yards: 6,399/5,290. **Par:** 72/72. **Course Rating:** 70.9/70.3. **Slope:** 120/123.
SOUTH/WEST (18 Combo)
Yards: 6,430/5,346. **Par:** 72/72. **Course Rating:** 69.9/70.2. **Slope:** 118/119.
Reader Comments: Mixture of old and new holes, redesign has made this a tighter and more challenging course, fantastic greens, feel like soft carpet ... Nice local course, good value ... Nice muni ... Nice course, good value.

★★ FENTON FARMS GOLF CLUB
PU-12312 Torrey Rd., Fenton, 48430, Genesee County, (810)629-1212, 10 miles from Flint. **Facility Holes:** 18. **Yards:** 6,596/5,196. **Par:** 72/70. **Course Rating:** 71.7/69.8. **Slope:** 125/117. **Green Fee:** $18/$28. **Cart Fee:** $12/Person. **Walking Policy:** Walking at certain times. **Walkability:** 3. **Opened:** 1945. **Season:** March-Dec. **High:** May-Sept. **To obtain tee times:** Call up to 7 days in advance. **Miscellaneous:** Reduced fees (weekdays, twilight, seniors, juniors), range (grass), credit cards (MC, V), BF, FF.

★½ FERNHILL GOLF & COUNTRY CLUB
PU-17600 Clinton River Rd., Clinton Township, 48044, Macomb County, (810)286-4700, 20 miles from Detroit. **Facility Holes:** 18. **Yards:** 6,018/4,962. **Par:** 70/72. **Course Rating:** 67.6/65.7. **Slope:** 115/108. **Green Fee:** $18/$20. **Cart Fee:** $18/Cart. **Walking Policy:** Unrestricted walking. **Walkability:** 2. **Opened:** 1972. **Architect:** Fred Severini III. **Season:** April-Nov. **High:** June-Sept. **To obtain tee times:** Call golf shop. **Miscellaneous:** Reduced fees (twilight, seniors), credit cards (MC, V).

★★★ FERRIS STATE UNIVERSITY
PU-1003 Perry St., Big Rapids, 49307, Mecosta County, (231)591-3765, 50 miles from Grand Rapids. **E-mail:** tuccik@ferris.edu. **Web:** www.katkegolf.com. **Facility Holes:** 18. **Yards:** 6,729/5,344. **Par:** 72/72. **Course Rating:** 72.5/70.8. **Slope:** 124/119. **Green Fee:** $22/$24. **Cart Fee:** $13/Person. **Walking Policy:** Unrestricted walking. **Walkability:** 3. **Opened:** 1974. **Architect:** Robert Beard. **Season:** Year-round. **To obtain tee times:** Call up to 14 days in advance. **Miscellaneous:** Reduced fees (weekdays, seniors, juniors), range (grass/mats), lodging (118 rooms), credit cards (MC, V, D), BF, FF.
Reader Comments: I will drive 40 miles to play here, never busy ... Great warm up holes ... Nice inexpensive course ... Used to be in better condition.

★★★ FIELDSTONE GOLF CLUB OF AUBURN HILLS

PU-1984 Taylor Rd., Auburn Hills, 48326, Oakland County, (248)370-9354, 20 miles from Detroit. **E-mail:** gmarmion@fieldstonegolfclub.com. **Web:** www.fieldstonegolfclub.com. **Facility Holes:** 18. **Yards:** 6,978/4,941. **Par:** 72/72. **Course Rating:** 74.4/70.4. **Slope:** 142/123. **Green Fee:** $33/$58. **Cart Fee:** Included in green fee. **Walking Policy:** Unrestricted walking. **Walkability:** 4. **Opened:** 1998. **Architect:** Arthur Hills. **Season:** March-Dec. **High:** May-Oct. **Tee times:** Call up to 15 days in advance. **Miscellaneous:** Reduced fees (weekdays, seniors, juniors), range (grass), credit cards (MC, V, AE, D),BF, FF. **Reader Comments:** Difficult layout from back tees, especially during a windy day ... Small greens with long par 4s make distance and accuracy a must ... Very good par 3s ... Players have difficulty breaking par.

★★ FIREFLY GOLF LINKS

PU-7795 S. Clare Ave., Clare, 48617, Clare County, (517)386-3510, 45 miles from Saginaw. **Web:** www.fireflygolflinks.com. **Facility Holes:** 18. **Yards:** 5,929/4,515. **Par:** 72/72. **Course Rating:** 67.9/65.6. **Slope:** 124/113. **Green Fee:** $21/$27. **Cart Fee:** $12/Person. **Walking Policy:** Unrestricted walking. **Walkability:** 3. **Opened:** 1932. **Architect:** Darrell Loar/Fran Loar. **Season:** April-Nov. **High:** May-Sept. **To obtain tee times:** Call up to 60 days in advance. **Miscellaneous:** Reduced fees (weekdays, twilight, seniors), credit cards (MC, V, AE, D), FF.

FOREST AKERS GOLF COURSE AT MSU

PU-Mich. St. Univ. Harrison Rd., East Lansing, 48823, Ingham County, (517)355-1635, 3 miles from Lansing. **Web:** www.golfmsu.msu.edu. **Facility Holes:** 36. **Cart Fee:** $26/Cart. **Walking Policy:** Unrestricted walking. **To obtain tee times:** Call up to 7 days in advance. **Miscellaneous:** Range (grass/mats), lodging (128 rooms), credit cards (MC, V), BF, FF.
★★½ EAST COURSE (18)
Yards: 6,510/5,380. **Par:** 72/73. **Course Rating:** 71.4/70.4. **Slope:** 118/115. **Green Fee:** $13/$26. **Walkability:** 2. **Opened:** 1972. **Architect:** M.S.U. Campus Planning. **Season:** March-Nov.
★★½ WEST COURSE (18)
Yards: 7,003/5,251. **Par:** 72/72. **Course Rating:** 74.4/70.0. **Slope:** 139/119. **Green Fee:** $24/$41. **Walkability:** 4. **Opened:** 1958. **Architect:** Bruce Matthews/Arthur Hills. **Season:** April-Oct.

★★★★ THE FORTRESS

R-950 Flint St., Frankenmuth, 48734, Saginaw County, (989)652-0460, (800)863-7999, 15 miles from Saginaw. **E-mail:** nblack@zehnders.com. **Web:** www.zehnders.com. **Facility Holes:** 18. **Yards:** 6,813/4,837. **Par:** 72/72. **Course Rating:** 73.6/68.8. **Slope:** 138/124. **Green Fee:** $42/$69. **Cart Fee:** Included in green fee. **Walking Policy:** Walking at certain times. **Walkability:** 3. **Opened:** 1992. **Architect:** Dick Nugent. **Season:** April-Oct. **High:** June-Sept. **To obtain tee times:** Call golf shop. **Miscellaneous:** Reduced fees (weekdays, guests, twilight, seniors, juniors), range (grass), credit cards (MC, V, D), BF, FF.
Reader Comments: Wide open, always windy ... Fantastic condition, one unfair hole, very playable even 1st time ... Great condition ... Needs good 19th hole ... A pleasure ... Holes close together.

★★½ FOX CREEK GOLF COURSE

PU-36000 Seven Mile, Livonia, 48152, Wayne County, (248)471-3400, 15 miles from Detroit. **E-mail:** tomwelsh@pga.com. **Facility Holes:** 18. **Yards:** 6,612/5,231. **Par:** 71/71. **Course Rating:** 71.4/69.8. **Slope:** 123/117. **Green Fee:** $17/$25. **Cart Fee:** $24/Cart. **Walking Policy:** Unrestricted walking. **Walkability:** 3. **Opened:** 1988. **Architect:** Mark DeVries. **Season:** Year-round. **High:** April-Nov. **To obtain tee times:** Call golf shop. **Miscellaneous:** Reduced fees (twilight, seniors, juniors), credit cards (MC, V), BF, FF.

FOX HILLS GOLF & CONFERENCE CENTER

PU-8768 N. Territorial Rd., Plymouth, 48170, Washtenaw County, (734)453-7272, 25 miles from Detroit. **E-mail:** foxhillsinfo@foxhills.com. **Web:** www.foxhills.com. **Facility Holes:** 63. **Walkability:** 3. **Season:** March-Nov. **High:** May-Sept. **To obtain tee times:** Call up to 13 days in advance. **Miscellaneous:** Reduced fees (weekdays, twilight, seniors, juniors), credit cards (MC, V, AE, D), BF, FF.
★★★½ GOLDEN FOX COURSE (18)
Yards: 6,783/5,040. **Par:** 72/72. **Course Rating:** 73.0/69.7. **Slope:** 136/122. **Green Fee:** $59/$62. **Cart Fee:** Included in green fee. **Walking Policy:** Mandatory carts. **Opened:** 1989. **Architect:** Arthur Hills. **Miscellaneous:** Range (grass).
Reader Comments: Nice layout, sporty yet fair ... Well run ... 63 holes, good value ... Nice course and layout, too much $ ... A great course with tempting par 5s, Scottish style ... Great condition.
STRATEGIC FOX COURSE (18)
Yards: 2,554/1,738. **Par:** 54/54. **Green Fee:** $25/$29. **Cart Fee:** $20/Cart. **Opened:** 2001. **Architect:** Ray Hearn.

MICHIGAN

★★★ **HILLS/WOODLANDS/LAKES** (27)
Green Fee: $28/$31. **Cart Fee:** $28/Cart. **Walking Policy:** Unrestricted walking. **Opened:** 1921.
Architect: Jim Lipe. **Miscellaneous:** Range (grass).
(HILLS/WOODLANDS) (18 Combo)
Yards: 5,969/4,538. **Par:** 70/70. **Course Rating:** 67.5/66.5. **Slope:** 112/113.
(LAKES/HILLS) (18 Combo)
Yards: 6,207/5,399. **Par:** 70/70. **Course Rating:** 70.1/69.4. **Slope:** 121/119.
(WOODLANDS/LAKES) (18 Combo)
Yards: 6,120/4,649. **Par:** 70/70. **Course Rating:** 68.6/69.5. **Slope:** 121/123.
Reader Comments: Challenging and fun … Great fish fry … Some areas are congested with holes tightly packed … Great job with the two 9s that have been refurbished.

★★★★ **FOX RUN COUNTRY CLUB** *Value, Pace*
PU-5825 W. Four Mile Rd., Grayling, 49738, Crawford County, (989)348-4343,
(800)436-9786, 40 miles from Traverse City. **E-mail:** foxrun@i2k.com. **Web:**
www.foxruncc.com. **Facility Holes:** 18. **Yards:** 6,362/4,829. **Par:** 72/72. **Course Rating:**
71.0/69.7. **Slope:** 128/119. **Green Fee:** $29/$32. **Cart Fee:** $16/Person. **Walking Policy:**
Walking at certain times. **Walkability:** 3. **Opened:** 1990. **Architect:** J. John Gorney. **Season:**
April-Oct. **High:** June-Sept. **To obtain tee times:** Call golf shop. **Miscellaneous:** Reduced fees
(twilight, juniors), range (grass), credit cards (MC, V, AE), FF.
Reader Comments: Staff very helpful, a great value for the money … Great staff … Smooth
greens … About the best in service in the north … Short course, but nice layout with great people.

★½ **FRUITPORT COUNTRY CLUB**
PU-6334 S. Harvey, Muskegon, 49444, Muskegon County, (231)798-3355, 4 miles from
Grand Haven. **Facility Holes:** 18. **Yards:** 5,725/5,725. **Par:** 71/71. **Course Rating:** 68.9/68.9.
Green Fee: $17/$19. **Cart Fee:** $19/Cart. **Walking Policy:** Unrestricted walking. **Walkability:** 1.
Opened: 1971. **Architect:** Dennis Snider/Davis Snider. **Season:** April-Nov. **To obtain tee times:**
Call golf shop. **Miscellaneous:** Reduced fees (weekdays, seniors), range (grass).

GARLAND
R-4700 North Red Oak, Lewiston, 49756, Oscoda County, (989)786-2211, (800)968-0042, 30
miles from Gaylord. **E-mail:** andrew.braley@garlandusa.com. **Web:** www.garlandusa.com.
Facility Holes: 72. **Cart Fee:** Included in green fee. **Walking Policy:** Mandatory carts.
Walkability: 2. **Architect:** Ron Otto. **Season:** May-Oct. **High:** June-Sept. **To obtain tee times:**
Call golf shop. **Miscellaneous:** Reduced fees (weekdays, guests, twilight, juniors), range
(grass/mats), lodging (186 rooms), credit cards (MC, V, AE, D, DC), BF, FF.
★★★★ **FOUNTAINS COURSE** (18)
Yards: 6,760/4,617. **Par:** 72/72. **Course Rating:** 73.0/74.1. **Slope:** 130/128. **Green Fee:**
$95/$100. **Opened:** 1995.
Reader Comments: My favorite at Garland, a few gimmicks … Nice course, a little short, but fun,
yardage system in carts … Pricey but worth it … Picturesque … Great layout, overpriced … Nice
lodge, high price.
★★★★ **MONARCH COURSE** (18)
Yards: 7,188/4,904. **Par:** 72/72. **Course Rating:** 75.6/69.5. **Slope:** 140/123. **Green Fee:**
$80/$85. **Opened:** 1987.
Reader Comments: The best in the area … A championship course … Great everything … Nice
lodge, high price … Excellent service … All 4 courses are great.
★★★½ **REFLECTIONS COURSE** (18)
Yards: 6,407/4,778. **Par:** 72/72. **Course Rating:** 70.8/66.9. **Slope:** 127/110. **Green Fee:**
$60/$80. **Opened:** 1990.
Reader Comments: Good course & scenic … Fall colors on the fairways were outstanding … Free
driving range for players … Nice lodge, high price … Beautiful course & scenery.
★★★★ **SWAMPFIRE COURSE** (18) *Condition, Pace*
Yards: 6,854/4,791. **Par:** 72/72. **Course Rating:** 73.9/68.4. **Slope:** 138/121. **Green Fee:**
$80/$85. **Opened:** 1988.
Reader Comments: Water, water, water … Difficult for a high handicapper … Keep it straight,
beautiful … Nice lodge, high price … All of Garland courses are great layouts & great fun to play …
Bring lots of balls.

GATEWAY GOLF CLUB
PU-33290 Gateway Dr., Romulus, 48174, Wayne County, (734)721-4100. **Facility Holes:** 18.
Yards: 6,842/5,047. **Par:** 72/72. **Course Rating:** 71.4/67.4. **Slope:** 125/109. **Green Fee:**
$40/$50. **Cart Fee:** Included in green fee. **Walking Policy:** Unrestricted walking. **Walkability:** 3.
Opened: 2000. **Architect:** Jerry Mathews. **Season:** March-Dec. **High:** May-Sept. **To obtain tee
times:** Call up to 7 days in advance. **Miscellaneous:** Reduced fees (twilight, seniors, juniors),
range (grass/mats), credit cards (MC, V, AE, D), BF, FF.

MICHIGAN

★★★ GAUSS GREEN VALLEY
PU-5751 Brooklyn Rd., Jackson, 49201, Jackson County, (517)764-0270, 10 miles from Jackson. **Facility Holes:** 18. **Yards:** 6,035/5,000. **Par:** 70/70. **Course Rating:** 70.3. **Green Fee:** $14/$16. **Cart Fee:** $20/Cart. **Walking Policy:** Unrestricted walking. **Walkability:** 3. **Opened:** 1959. **Architect:** Lloyd Gauss. **Season:** March-Nov. **High:** June-Aug. **To obtain tee times:** Call golf shop. **Miscellaneous:** Reduced fees (seniors, juniors), range, credit cards (MC, V, D).
Reader Comments: Good value … Nice public course … Very well kept, play well here … Great course, great value, well kept.
Special Notes: Formerly Green Valley Golf Course.

★★★★ GAYLORD COUNTRY CLUB *Value*
SP-P.O. Box 207, Gaylord, 49735, Otsego County, (231)546-3376, 5 miles from Gaylord. **Facility Holes:** 18. **Yards:** 6,452/5,490. **Par:** 72/72. **Course Rating:** 70.9/71.4. **Slope:** 123/122. **Green Fee:** $30/$35. **Cart Fee:** $15/Person. **Walking Policy:** Unrestricted walking. **Walkability:** 3. **Opened:** 1924. **Architect:** Wilfried Reid. **Season:** April-Oct. **High:** June-Aug. **To obtain tee times:** Call golf shop. **Miscellaneous:** Reduced fees (twilight), range, credit cards (MC, V).
Reader Comments: Well managed, great greens, excellent condition, new clubhouse … An oldie but goodie … One of the best values in Michigan … Beautiful layout, scenery … Very nice … Don't be above the hole … Conditioning very good.

★★½ GENESEE VALLEY MEADOWS
PU-5499 Miller Rd., Swartz Creek, 48473, Genesee County, (810)732-1401, 5 miles from Flint. **Facility Holes:** 18. **Yards:** 6,867/5,057. **Par:** 72/72. **Course Rating:** 72.3/68.9. **Slope:** 133/122. **Green Fee:** $21/$24. **Cart Fee:** $24/Cart. **Walking Policy:** Walking at certain times. **Walkability:** 2. **Opened:** 1965. **Architect:** D. Sincerbaugh. **Season:** April-Nov. **High:** June-Aug. **To obtain tee times:** Call golf shop. **Miscellaneous:** Reduced fees (weekdays, twilight, seniors, juniors), metal spikes.

★★★★ GEORGE YOUNG RECREATIONAL COMPLEX *Service*
PU-Hwy. 424 159 Youngs Lane, Gaastra, 49927, Iron County, (906)265-3401, 125 miles from Green Bay. **E-mail:** georgeyoung@up.net. **Web:** www.georgeyoung.com. **Facility Holes:** 18. **Yards:** 6,076/5,338. **Par:** 72/72. **Course Rating:** 74.3/71.2. **Slope:** 130/120. **Green Fee:** $22. **Cart Fee:** $20/Cart. **Walking Policy:** Unrestricted walking. **Walkability:** 4. **Opened:** 1993. **Season:** May-Oct. **High:** July-Aug. **To obtain tee times:** Call up to 10 days ahead **Misc:neous:** Range (grass), FF.
Reader Comments: Long ride but worth the price and beautiful clubhouse … Fine clubhouse, relatively new, outstanding public facility … Very affordable, excellent layout, challenging … Take cart.

★★½ GIANT OAK GOLF CLUB
PU-1024 Valetta Dr., Temperance, 48182, Monroe County, (734)847-6733, 5 miles from Toledo. **Facility Holes:** 27. **Yards:** 6,415/4,994. **Par:** 72/72. **Course Rating:** 71.1/68.0. **Slope:** 124/111. **Green Fee:** $23/$26. **Cart Fee:** $13/Person. **Walking Policy:** Unrestricted walking. **Walkability:** 2. **Opened:** 1969. **Architect:** Arthur Hills. **Season:** March-Dec. **High:** June-Aug. **To obtain tee times:** Call up to 14 days in advance. **Miscellaneous:** Reduced fees (seniors), metal spikes, credit cards (MC, V).
Special Notes: Also has a 9-hole executive course.

★★★★ GLACIER CLUB *Condition*
SP-8000 Glacier Club Dr., Washington, 48094, Macomb County, (810)786-0800, 27 miles from Detroit. **Web:** www.glacierclub.com. **Facility Holes:** 18. **Yards:** 7,018/4,937. **Par:** 72/72. **Course Rating:** 74.3/69.7. **Slope:** 137/125. **Green Fee:** $35/$65. **Cart Fee:** Included in green fee. **Walking Policy:** Mandatory carts. **Walkability:** 3. **Opened:** 1994. **Architect:** William Newcomb. **Season:** March-Nov. **High:** May-Sept. **To obtain tee times:** Call up to 8 days in advance. **Miscellaneous:** Reduced fees (weekdays, twilight, seniors, juniors), range (grass/mats), credit cards (MC, V, AE), BF, FF.
Reader Comments: Great course, beautiful … This place has it all, I would take you there … Fastest greens in metro Detroit … In very nice shape … Very challenging, great condition.

★★★ GLADSTONE GOLF COURSE
PU-6514 Days River 24-1/2 Rd., Gladstone, 49837, Delta County, (906)428-9646, 10 miles from Escanaba. **Facility Holes:** 18. **Yards:** 6,504/5,427. **Par:** 72/74. **Green Fee:** $22. **Cart Fee:** $20/Cart. **Walking Policy:** Unrestricted walking. **Walkability:** 1. **Opened:** 1936. **Architect:** A. H. Jolly. **Season:** April-Oct. **High:** June-Aug. **To obtain tee times:** Call golf shop. **Miscellaneous:** Range (grass), credit cards (MC, V, AE, D), FF.
Reader Comments: Just neat layout … Some challenging holes … Lots of blind shots.

MICHIGAN

★★ GLADWIN HEIGHTS GOLF COURSE
PU-3551 W. M-61, Gladwin, 48624, Gladwin County, (517)426-9941, 30 miles from Midland.
Facility Holes: 18. **Yards:** 6,007/5,226. **Par:** 71/72. **Course Rating:** 68.7/69.7. **Slope:** 110/112.
Green Fee: $15/$16. **Cart Fee:** $18/Cart. **Walking Policy:** Unrestricted walking. **Walkability:** 2.
Opened: 1959. **Season:** April-Oct. **High:** July-Aug. **To obtain tee times:** Call golf shop.
Miscellaneous: Reduced fees (twilight, seniors), metal spikes, range (grass).

★★★ GLEN OAKS GOLF & COUNTRY CLUB
PU-30500 W-13 Mile Rd., Farmington Hills, 48334, Oakland County, (248)851-8356, 20 miles
from Detroit. **Web:** www.co.oakland.mi.us. **Facility Holes:** 18. **Yards:** 6,117/4,993. **Par:** 70/70.
Course Rating: 67.6/72.1. **Slope:** 114/120. **Green Fee:** $26/$37. **Cart Fee:** $12/Person.
Walking Policy: Unrestricted walking. **Walkability:** 2. **Season:** April-Nov. **High:** May-Aug. **To
obtain tee times:** Call golf shop. **Miscellaneous:** Reduced fees (weekdays, twilight, seniors,
juniors), credit cards (MC, V), FF.
Reader Comments: Gets better every year ... Value excellent ... Great course ... The course in in
great shape and it has a wonderful, newly-remodeled clubhouse ... Average quality course.

★★ GLENBRIER GOLF COURSE
PU-Box 500, 4178 W. Locke Rd., Perry, 48872, Shiawassee County, (517)625-3800, 15 miles
from Lansing. **E-mail:** gfink1955@yahoo.com. **Facility Holes:** 18. **Yards:** 6,310/5,245. **Par:**
72/72. **Course Rating:** 68.4/69.4. **Slope:** 120/115. **Green Fee:** $19/$23. **Cart Fee:** $20/Cart.
Walking Policy: Unrestricted walking. **Walkability:** 2. **Opened:** 1972. **Architect:** Bob Fink.
Season: April-Nov. **High:** March-Oct. **To obtain tee times:** Call golf shop. **Miscellaneous:**
Reduced fees (weekdays, twilight, seniors, juniors), range, credit cards (MC, V), BF, FF.

★★½ GLENEAGLE GOLF CLUB
SP-6150 14th Ave., Hudsonville, 49426, Ottawa County, (616)457-3680, (877)832-4537, 8
miles from Grand Rapids. **Facility Holes:** 18. **Yards:** 6,705/5,215. **Par:** 72/72. **Course Rating:**
73.1/70.8. **Slope:** 143/128. **Green Fee:** $15/$31. **Cart Fee:** $12/Person. **Walking Policy:**
Walking at certain times. **Walkability:** 4. **Opened:** 1960. **Architect:** Michael Shields. **Season:**
April-Nov. **High:** May-Aug. **To obtain tee times:** Call up to 7 days in advance. **Miscellaneous:**
Reduced fees (weekdays, twilight, seniors, juniors), range, credit cards (MC, V), BF, FF.

★★ GLENHURST GOLF COURSE
PU-25345 W. 6 Mile Rd., Redford, 48240, Wayne County, (313)592-8758, 18 miles from
Detroit. **Facility Holes:** 18. **Yards:** 5,502/4,962. **Par:** 70/72. **Course Rating:** 66.1/68.1. **Slope:**
112/111. **Green Fee:** $11/$23. **Cart Fee:** $22/Cart. **Walking Policy:** Unrestricted walking.
Walkability: 2. **Opened:** 1932. **Architect:** Mr. McClane. **Season:** Year-round. **High:** May-Sept.
To obtain tee times: Call up to 7 days in advance. **Miscellaneous:** Reduced fees (weekdays,
twilight, seniors, juniors), BF, FF.

GOGEBIC COUNTRY CLUB
PU-Country Club Rd., Ironwood, 49938, Gogebic County, (906)932-2515, 20 miles from
Wakefield. **Facility Holes:** 18. **Yards:** 5,752/5,132. **Par:** 71/71. **Course Rating:** 66.5/68.5. **Slope:**
109/111. **Green Fee:** $20. **Cart Fee:** $20/Cart. **Walking Policy:** Unrestricted walking.
Walkability: 3. **Opened:** 1922. **Season:** May-Nov. **To obtain tee times:** Call golf shop.
Miscellaneous: Reduced fees (twilight, juniors), credit cards (MC, V), BF, FF.

THE GOLF CLUB AT APPLE MOUNTAIN
R-4519 N. River Rd., Freeland, 48623, Saginaw County, (989)781-6789, (888)781-6789, 9
miles from Saginaw. **E-mail:** bredman@applemountain.com. **Web:** www.applemountain.com.
Facility Holes: 18. **Yards:** 6,962/4,978. **Par:** 72/72. **Course Rating:** 74.2/69.6. **Slope:** 145/127.
Green Fee: $45/$65. **Cart Fee:** Included in green fee. **Walking Policy:** Mandatory carts.
Opened: 1998. **Architect:** John Sanford. **Season:** April-Nov. **High:** May-Sept. **To obtain tee
times:** Call golf shop. **Miscellaneous:** Reduced fees (twilight, seniors, juniors), range (grass),
credit cards (MC, V, AE, D), BF, FF.

★★★½ THE GOLF CLUB AT THORNAPPLE POINTE
PU-4747 Champions Circle S.E., Grand Rapids, 49512, Kent County, (616)554-4747, 15
miles from Grand Rapids. **E-mail:** cmsob@prodigy.net. **Web:** www.thornapplepointe.com.
Facility Holes: 18. **Yards:** 6,821/4,878. **Par:** 72/72. **Course Rating:** 73.2/64.3. **Slope:** 133/107.
Green Fee: $55/$60. **Cart Fee:** Included in green fee. **Walking Policy:** Unrestricted walking.
Walkability: 4. **Opened:** 1997. **Architect:** William Newcomb. **Season:** March-Dec. **High:** May-
Sept. **To obtain tee times:** Call up to 14 days in advance. **Miscellaneous:** Reduced fees
(weekdays, twilight, seniors, juniors), range (grass/mats), credit cards (MC, V, AE, D), BF, FF.
Reader Comments: Well kept, great views ... Needs to mature ... Expensive, but outstanding lay-
out ... Planes, trains, automobiles ... New, grass in fairways needs maturity ... First class layout ...
Scenic river holes.

MICHIGAN

GOLF CLUB OF MICHIGAN
PU-9325 McClements Rd., Brighton, 48114, Livingston County, (810)225-4498, (888)649-0040, 50 miles from Detroit. **Facility Holes:** 18. **Yards:** 7,115/5,269. **Par:** 72/71. **Course Rating:** 74.8/71.3. **Slope:** 143/124. **Green Fee:** $50/$60. **Cart Fee:** Included in green fee. **Opened:** 2000. **Architect:** Patrick Grelac. **To obtain tee times:** Call up to 14 days in advance. **Miscellaneous:** Reduced fees (weekdays, twilight, seniors), credit cards (MC, V).

★★½ GOODRICH COUNTRY CLUB
SP-10080 Hegel Rd., Goodrich, 48438, Genesee County, (810)636-2493, 6 miles from Davison. **Facility Holes:** 18. **Yards:** 5,497/4,321. **Par:** 70/70. **Course Rating:** 66.4/65.0. **Slope:** 104/100. **Green Fee:** $22/$26. **Cart Fee:** $28/Cart. **Walking Policy:** Unrestricted walking. **Walkability:** 4. **Season:** April-Oct. **High:** June-Aug. **To obtain tee times:** Call golf shop. **Miscellaneous:** Reduced fees (weekdays, seniors, juniors), credit cards (MC, V), FF.

GRACEWIL COUNTRY CLUB
PU-2597 Four Mile Rd. N.W., Grand Rapids, 49504, Kent County, (616)784-2455. **Facility Holes:** 36. **Green Fee:** $20/$23. **Cart Fee:** $20/Cart. **Walking Policy:** Unrestricted walking. **Opened:** 1929. **Architect:** J. Morris Wilson. **Season:** March-Nov. **High:** March-Sept. **To obtain tee times:** Call golf shop. **Miscellaneous:** Reduced fees (weekdays, twilight, seniors, juniors), credit cards (MC, V, AE, D), BF, FF.
★½ EAST COURSE (18)
Yards: 6,155/4,995. **Par:** 72/72. **Course Rating:** 68.5/67.3. **Slope:** 108/101.
★½ WEST COURSE (18)
Yards: 6,055/4,817. **Par:** 72/72. **Course Rating:** 67.5/65.8. **Slope:** 106/101.

GRAND BLANC GOLF & COUNTRY CLUB
PU-5270 Perry Rd., Grand Blanc, 48439, Genesee County, (810)694-5960, 7 miles from Flint. **Facility Holes:** 36. **Green Fee:** $20/$26. **Cart Fee:** $22/Cart. **Walking Policy:** Walking at certain times. **Walkability:** 3. **Season:** Year-round. **High:** April-Sept. **To obtain tee times:** Call up to 7 days in advance. **Miscellaneous:** Reduced fees (twilight, seniors, juniors), range (grass), credit cards (MC, V), BF, FF.
★★★ NORTH COURSE (18)
Yards: 7,023/5,471. **Par:** 72/72. **Course Rating:** 73.5/71.0. **Slope:** 122/118. **Opened:** 1997. **Architect:** Ron Lenard/Joe Roeski.
Reader Comments: Greens in great shape and fast ... Wide open, much nicer than South course, confidence builder ... Ego boost ... Lots of leagues ... Good for ladies and beginers ... Very nice place for a new course.
★½ SOUTH COURSE (18)
Yards: 6,545/5,774. **Par:** 72/74. **Course Rating:** 71.0/72.8. **Slope:** 122/120. **Opened:** 1970. **Architect:** Bruce & Jerry Matthews.

★★★½ GRAND HAVEN GOLF CLUB
SP-17000 Lincoln St., Grand Haven, 49417, Ottawa County, (616)842-4040, 28 miles from Grand Rapids. **E-mail:** info@grandhavengolfclub.com. **Web:** www.grandhavengolfclub.com. **Facility Holes:** 18. **Yards:** 6,725/5,256. **Par:** 72/72. **Course Rating:** 73.3/70.6. **Slope:** 134/122. **Green Fee:** $27/$38. **Cart Fee:** $14/Person. **Walking Policy:** Walking at certain times. **Walkability:** 3. **Opened:** 1965. **Architect:** Bruce Matthews/Jerry Matthews. **Season:** March-Nov. **High:** May-Sept. **To obtain tee times:** Call up to 7 days in advance. **Miscellaneous:** Reduced fees (weekdays, twilight, seniors, juniors), range (grass), credit cards (MC, V, AE), BF, FF.
Reader Comments: Good course, continually improving the fairways, etc ... Pricey, nice layout, scenic ... Good greens, trees often seem unfair ... Gotta love trees.

★★ GRAND HOTEL GOLF CLUB
R-1 Grand Drive, Mackinac Island, 49757, Mackinac County, (906)847-3331, 250 miles from Detroit. **Facility Holes:** 18. **Yards:** 5,415/4,212. **Par:** 67/67. **Course Rating:** 65.7. **Slope:** 110/106. **Green Fee:** $75. **Cart Fee:** Included in green fee. **Walking Policy:** Unrestricted walking. **Walkability:** 2. **Opened:** 1911. **Architect:** Jerry Matthews. **Season:** May-Oct. **High:** June-Aug. **To obtain tee times:** Call golf shop. **Miscellaneous:** Metal spikes, lodging (340 rooms), credit cards (MC, V, AE).

★½ GRAND ISLAND GOLF RANCH
PU-6266 West River Dr., Belmont, 49306, Kent County, (616)363-1262, 8 miles from Grand Rapids. **Facility Holes:** 18. **Yards:** 6,266/5,522. **Par:** 72/73. **Course Rating:** 68.7/69.1. **Slope:** 109/110. **Green Fee:** $20. **Cart Fee:** $24/Cart. **Walking Policy:** Unrestricted walking. **Walkability:** 2. **Opened:** 1965. **Architect:** Jake Brunsink/Ade VanLiere. **Season:** March-Nov. **High:** May-Sept. **To obtain tee times:** Call up to 7 days in advance. **Miscellaneous:** Reduced fees (seniors, juniors), range (grass/mats), credit cards (MC, V), BF, FF.

MICHIGAN

★½ GRAND LEDGE COUNTRY CLUB
PU-5811 E St. Joseph Highway, Grand Ledge, 48837, Eaton County, (517)627-2495,
10 miles from Lansing. **Facility Holes:** 18. **Yards:** 6,347/4,714. **Par:** 72/72. **Course Rating:**
70.2/66.5. **Slope:** 116/111. **Green Fee:** $19/$21. **Cart Fee:** $20/Cart. **Walking Policy:**
Unrestricted walking. **Walkability:** 3. **Opened:** 1958. **Architect:** Steve Lipkowitz. **Season:** April-
Nov. **High:** June-Aug. **Tee times:** Call golf shop. **Miscellaneous:** Range, credit cards (MC, V).

GRAND PRAIRIE GOLF COURSE
PU-3620 Grand Prairie Rd., Kalamazoo, 49006, Kalamazoo County, (616)388-4447, 2 miles
from Kalamazoo. **E-mail:** shecky4@aol.com. **Web:** www.kalamazoogolf.org. **Facility Holes:** 9.
Yards: 1,710/1,589. **Par:** 30/30. **Green Fee:** $11. **Cart Fee:** $16/Cart. **Walking Policy:**
Unrestricted walking. **Walkability:** 2. **Opened:** 1961. **Architect:** William Spear. **Season:** April-
Nov. **To obtain tee times:** Call golf shop. **Miscellaneous:** Reduced fees (seniors, juniors),
credit cards (MC, V, AE, D), BF, FF.

★½ GRAND RAPIDS GOLF CLUB
PU-4300 Leonard N.E., Grand Rapids, 49525, Kent County, (616)949-2820, (800)709-1100,
5 miles from Grand Rapids. **Facility Holes:** 27. **Green Fee:** $22/$25. **Cart Fee:** $25/Cart.
Walking Policy: Unrestricted walking. **Walkability:** 4. **Opened:** 1969. **Architect:** Willie Park Jr.
Season: March-Dec. **High:** April-Oct. **To obtain tee times:** Call golf shop. **Miscellaneous:**
Reduced fees (weekdays, twilight, seniors, juniors), range (grass/mats), credit cards (MC, V),
BF, FF.
BLUE/RED (18 Combo)
Yards: 5,992/4,590. **Par:** 70/70. **Course Rating:** 68.5/66.2. **Slope:** 107/103.
RED/WHITE (18 Combo)
Yards: 6,140/4,818. **Par:** 72/71. **Course Rating:** 70.3/68.9. **Slope:** 116/113.
WHITE/BLUE (18 Combo)
Yards: 6,286/4,754. **Par:** 72/71. **Course Rating:** 69.8/67.9. **Slope:** 115/110.

GRAND TRAVERSE RESORT AND SPA
R-6300 U.S. 31 N., Acme, 49610, Grand Traverse County, (231)938-1620, (800)748-0303,
6 miles from Traverse City. **Web:** www.grandtraverseresort.com. **Facility Holes:** 54. **Cart Fee:**
Included in green fee. **Walking Policy:** Mandatory carts. **Season:** April-Nov. **High:** June-Sept.
To obtain tee times: Call golf shop. **Miscellaneous:** Reduced fees (weekdays, guests, twilight),
range (grass), credit cards (MC, V, AE, D, DC, JCB), BF, FF.
★★★★ THE BEAR (18)
Yards: 7,083/5,424. **Par:** 72/72. **Course Rating:** 76.8/73.1. **Slope:** 146/137. **Green Fee:**
$50/$130. **Walkability:** 4. **Opened:** 1985. **Architect:** Jack Nicklaus.
Notes: Ranked 20th in 1999 Best in State.
Reader Comments: Tests your skills & decision making ... Nice course ... Expensive ... Way over-
priced, nice course ... Maintenance always very good ... Great greens ... Fun course, somewhat
tricky, great layout ... Outstanding golf.
★★★★ SPRUCE RUN (18) *Pace*
Yards: 6,304/4,726. **Par:** 70/70. **Course Rating:** 70.8/68.2. **Slope:** 130/125. **Green Fee:**
$50/$90. **Walkability:** 2. **Opened:** 1979. **Architect:** William Newcomb.
Reader Comments: Liked better than the Bear ... You have to play all 3 courses ... Flat, nice, least
picturesque of the three ..: Fun & challenging for the average golfer ... Resort course, good enough
challenge ... A super course, but $$$.
★★★★½ THE WOLVERINE (18) *Pace*
Yards: 7,038/5,029. **Par:** 72/72. **Course Rating:** 73.9/68.1. **Slope:** 144/121. **Green Fee:**
$50/$130. **Walkability:** 2. **Opened:** 1999. **Architect:** Gary Player.
Reader Comments: Way too easy, way too pricey ... Great addition to this resort ... Not as difficult
as The Bear ... Well designed ... Play this instead of The Bear ... Very user friendly ... Variety of
shots, fast ... Nice pleasing views.

★★★★ GRAND VIEW GOLF COURSE *Value+*
PU-5464 S. 68th Ave., New Era, 49446, Oceana County, (231)861-6616, 20 miles from
Muskegon. **Facility Holes:** 18. **Yards:** 6,258/4,737. **Par:** 71/71. **Course Rating:** 69.5/66.7.
Slope: 120/113. **Green Fee:** $13/$22. **Cart Fee:** $10/Person. **Walking Policy:** Unrestricted walk-
ing. **Walkability:** 3. **Opened:** 1993. **Architect:** David Goerbig. **Season:** April-Nov. **High:** June-
Sept. **To obtain tee times:** Call golf shop. **Miscellaneous:** Reduced fees (weekdays, seniors),
range (grass), credit cards (MC, V, D), FF.
Reader Comments: Very nice view ... Wonderful course ... Excellent 'up north course' great value
... The name says it all ... Just a great value ... Great course, low rates ... This is the best golf in
the state ... 8th hole has island green.

★★★★ GRANDVIEW GOLF CLUB
PU-3003 Hagni Rd., Kalkaska, 49646, Kalkaska County, (231)258-3244, 30 miles from
Traverse City. **Facility Holes:** 18. **Yards:** 6,620/4,964. **Par:** 72/72. **Course Rating:** 72.2/68.4.

Slope: 133/122. **Green Fee:** $20/$32. **Cart Fee:** $14/Person. **Walking Policy:** Walking at certain times. **Walkability:** 5. **Opened:** 1993. **Season:** April-Oct. **High:** June-Aug. **Tee times:** Call golf shop. **Miscellaneous:** Reduced fees (weekdays), range (grass/mats), credit cards (MC, V). **Reader Comments:** Interesting variety of holes, greens hold ... Course is still growing in ... Play is very slow for first 5 holes ... Just great value ... One of the best values in Mich. ... Very nice ... Scenic, tough, overall nice.

★★ GRAYLING COUNTRY CLUB
SP-Business I-75 S., Grayling, 49738, Crawford County, (517)348-5618, 25 miles from Gaylord. **Facility Holes:** 18. **Yards:** 5,813/4,622. **Par:** 70/70. **Course Rating:** 68.9/66.8. **Slope:** 121/115. **Green Fee:** $23. **Cart Fee:** $14/Person. **Walking Policy:** Unrestricted walking. **Walkability:** 2. **Opened:** 1923. **Architect:** Jeff Gorney. **Season:** April-Oct. **High:** July-Aug. **To obtain tee times:** Call up to 2 days in advance. **Miscellaneous:** Reduced fees (seniors, juniors), range (grass), credit cards (MC, V, AE, D), BF, FF.

★★ GREEN ACRES GOLF COURSE
PU-7323 Dixie Hwy, Bridgeport, 48722, Saginaw County, (517)777-3510, 6 miles from Saginaw. **Facility Holes:** 18. **Yards:** 6,400/6,100. **Par:** 72/72. **Course Rating:** 72.0/69.1. **Slope:** 119/115. **Cart Fee:** $20/Cart. **Walking Policy:** Unrestricted walking. **Walkability:** 1. **Opened:** 1957. **Season:** April-Nov. **High:** June-Aug. **To obtain tee times:** Call golf shop. **Miscellaneous:** Reduced fees (twilight, seniors), metal spikes, range (grass), credit cards (MC, V).

★★ GREEN HILLS GOLF CLUB
PU-1699 N M-13, Pinconning, 48650, Bay County, (517)697-3011, 10 miles from Bay City. **Facility Holes:** 18. **Yards:** 6,000. **Par:** 71. **Course Rating:** 67.1. **Slope:** 112. **Green Fee:** $18/$20. **Cart Fee:** $20/Cart. **Walking Policy:** Unrestricted walking. **Walkability:** 1. **Opened:** 1971. **Architect:** William Newcomb. **Season:** March-Nov. **High:** June-Sept. **To obtain tee times:** Call golf shop. **Miscellaneous:** Reduced fees (seniors), metal spikes, credit cards (MC, V, D).

★★ GREEN MEADOWS GOLF COURSE
PU-1555 Strasburg Rd., Monroe, 48161, Monroe County, (734)242-5566, 35 miles from Detroit. **Facility Holes:** 18. **Yards:** 6,391/4,965. **Par:** 70/70. **Course Rating:** 68.6/67.6. **Slope:** 116/108. **Green Fee:** $20/$25. **Cart Fee:** $12/Person. **Walking Policy:** Unrestricted walking. **Walkability:** 1. **Opened:** 1973. **Season:** March-Nov. **High:** April-Oct. **To obtain tee times:** Call up to 7 days in advance. **Miscellaneous:** Reduced fees (weekdays, seniors, juniors), credit cards (MC, V, AE, D), BF, FF.

★★ GREEN OAKS GOLF COURSE
PU-1775 Clark Rd., Ypsilanti, 48198, Washtenaw County, (734)485-0881, 8 miles from Ann Arbor. **Facility Holes:** 18. **Yards:** 6,780/5,528. **Par:** 71/71. **Course Rating:** 72.4/71.4. **Slope:** 126/121. **Green Fee:** $18/$21. **Cart Fee:** $20/Cart. **Walking Policy:** Unrestricted walking. **Walkability:** 2. **Opened:** 1958. **Season:** March-Dec. **High:** July-Aug. **Tee times:** Call golf shop. **Miscellaneous:** Reduced fees (weekdays, guests), metal spikes, credit cards (MC, V).

★★ GREENBRIER BROOKLYN
PU-14820 Wellwood Rd., Brooklyn, 49230, Jackson County, (517)592-6952, 20 miles from Ann Arbor. **Facility Holes:** 18. **Yards:** 5,390/5,390. **Par:** 67/72. **Green Fee:** $11/$15. **Cart Fee:** $26/Cart. **Walking Policy:** Unrestricted walking. **Walkability:** 2. **Season:** April-Nov. **To obtain tee times:** Call golf shop. **Miscellaneous:** Reduced fees (weekdays, seniors).

★★ GREENBRIER GOLF CLUB
PU-9350 N. Lapeer Rd., Mayville, 48744, Tuscola County, (517)843-6575, 17 miles from Lapeer. **Facility Holes:** 18. **Yards:** 5,827/4,970. **Par:** 71/71. **Green Fee:** $20/$22. **Cart Fee:** $20/Person. **Walking Policy:** Unrestricted walking. **Walkability:** 2. **Opened:** 1971. **Architect:** Les Otto. **Season:** April-Oct. **To obtain tee times:** Call golf shop. **Miscellaneous:** Reduced fees (weekdays, twilight, seniors, juniors), FF.

★★★½ GREYSTONE GOLF CLUB & BANQUET CENTER
PU-67500 Mound Rd., Romeo, 48095, Macomb County, (810)752-7030, (888)418-3386, 15 miles from Detroit. **Web:** www.golfgreystone.com. **Facility Holes:** 18. **Yards:** 6,861/4,816. **Par:** 72/71. **Course Rating:** 73.6/68.5. **Slope:** 132/113. **Green Fee:** $45/$65. **Cart Fee:** Included in green fee. **Walking Policy:** Mandatory carts. **Walkability:** 3. **Opened:** 1992. **Architect:** Jerry Matthews. **Season:** March-Dec. **To obtain tee times:** Call up to 30 days in advance. **Miscellaneous:** Reduced fees (twilight, seniors, juniors), range (grass/mats), credit cards (MC, V, AE, D, DC, CB), BF, FF. **Reader Comments:** Great finishing holes ... Great layout, well maintained, pleasant experience ... OK course, expensive ... Great new course ... Play on weekend was a little slow ... Best finishing 3 holes ... Great finish ... Overpriced.

★★★ **GROESBECK MUNICIPAL GOLF COURSE** *Value*
PU-1600 Ormond Ave., Lansing, 48906, Ingham County, (517)483-4232. **E-mail:**
dballard@ci.lansing.mi.us. **Facility Holes:** 18. **Yards:** 6,166/4,814. **Par:** 71/73. **Course Rating:**
68.2/67.0. **Slope:** 126/116. **Green Fee:** $20/$24. **Cart Fee:** $12/Cart. **Walking Policy:**
Unrestricted walking. **Walkability:** 2. **Opened:** 1927. **Architect:** Jack Dara /Jerry Matthews.
Season: April-Nov. **High:** April-Sept. **To obtain tee times:** Call up to 7 days in advance.
Miscellaneous: Reduced fees (twilight, seniors, juniors), credit cards (MC, V, D), BF, FF.
Reader Comments: Nice muni that is fun to play ... Play from blue tees, good redesign of back 9.

GULL LAKE VIEW GOLF CLUB
R-23161 Waubascon Rd., Battle Creek, 49017, Calhoun County, (616)965-3384, (800)432-
7971, 10 miles from Battle Creek. **E-mail:** glvresorts@aol.com. **Web:** www.gulllakeview.com.
Facility Holes: 90. **Green Fee:** $34/$37. **Walking Policy:** Walking at certain times. **Season:**
March-Nov. **High:** May-Sept. **Tee times:** Call golf shop. **Miscellaneous:** Reduced fees (week-
days, guests, juniors), range (grass), lodging (128 rooms), credit cards (MC, V, D), BF, FF.
★★★½ **BEDFORD VALLEY COURSE** (18)
Yards: 6,915/5,104. **Par:** 71/72. **Course Rating:** 73.8/70.0. **Slope:** 135/119. **Cart Fee:** $26/Cart.
Walkability: 3. **Opened:** 1964. **Architect:** William F. Mitchell.
Reader Comments: Classic design, big sand traps ... Very good test of golf, but forgiving ...
Traditional style course ... Old world ... Nice course, played it 25 years ago, still good ...
Challenging track in decent condition.
★★★½ **EAST COURSE** (18)
Yards: 6,002/4,918. **Par:** 70/70. **Course Rating:** 69.4/68.5. **Slope:** 124/118. **Cart Fee:** $26/Cart.
Walkability: 4. **Opened:** 1963. **Architect:** Darl Scott.
Reader Comments: Excellent staff and accommodations ... An all-time favorite ... Great resort
courses ... Great place to play 36 holes ... Good place, choice of 5 courses, all in good shape ...
We played 4 of the courses, all nice.
★★★★ **NORTH COURSE AT STONEHEDGE** (18)
Yards: 6,673/5,785. **Par:** 72/72. **Course Rating:** 72.2/72.1. **Slope:** 127/114. **Cart Fee:**
$13/Person. **Walkability:** 5. **Opened:** 1988. **Architect:** Charles Scott.
Reader Comments: Beautiful course, terrible pace ... Great resort courses ... I like it because you
can let the shaft out on this one ... Well maintained ... Will go back.
★★★★ **SOUTH COURSE AT STONEHEDGE** (18)
Yards: 6,656/5,191. **Par:** 72/72. **Course Rating:** 72.4/70.3. **Slope:** 133/120. **Cart Fee:**
$13/Person. **Walkability:** 5. **Opened:** 1988. **Architect:** Charles Scott.
Reader Comments: Better than North Course, slow ... Great resort courses ... Hilly terrain &
wooded, loved it ... The challenge of hitting the ball straight ... Resort golf ... Needs pin locators.
★★★½ **WEST COURSE** (18)
Yards: 6,300/5,218. **Par:** 71/72. **Course Rating:** 70.6/69.0. **Slope:** 123/114. **Cart Fee:** $26/Cart.
Walkability: 3. **Opened:** 1963. **Architect:** Darl Scott.
Reader Comments: Original 18 of now 90 holes ... Back is as challenging ... Nice value but they
pack you in ... Play is slow ... The original 18 a fun round ... Great resort courses.

HAMPSHIRE COUNTRY CLUB
SP-29592 Pokagon Hwy., Dowagiac, 49047, Cass County, (616)782-7476, 18 miles from
South Bend, IN. **Facility Holes:** 36. **Green Fee:** $18/$20. **Cart Fee:** $22/Cart. **Walking Policy:**
Unrestricted walking. **Season:** March-Nov. **High:** June-Sept. **Tee times:** Call up to 6 days in
advance. **Miscellaneous:** Reduced fees (weekdays, twilight, juniors), credit cards (MC, V), FF.
DOGWOOD TRAIL (18)
Yards: 6,795/4,968. **Par:** 72/72. **Course Rating:** 71.8/66.7. **Slope:** 126/111. **Walkability:** 3.
Opened: 1995. **Architect:** Duane Dammeyer.
★★★ **HAMPSHIRE** (18)
Yards: 7,030/6,185. **Par:** 72/73. **Course Rating:** 72.6/73.0. **Slope:** 125/119. **Walkability:** 2.
Opened: 1962. **Architect:** Edward Packard.
Reader Comments: Blind shots, but very playable ... What they lack in design is made up in ser-
vice ... Very long, pro tour long ... Flat & open, not very interesting ... Good course for money.

★★★ **HARBOR POINT GOLF COURSE**
SP-8475 South Lake Shore Drive, Harbor Springs, 49740, Emmet County, (231)526-2951,
1 mile from Harbor Springs. **Facility Holes:** 18. **Yards:** 6,003/5,034. **Par:** 71/73. **Course Rating:**
68.7/68.8. **Slope:** 121/122. **Green Fee:** $14/$40. **Cart Fee:** $16/Person. **Walking Policy:**
Walking at certain times. **Walkability:** 2. **Opened:** 1896. **Architect:** David Gill. **Season:** April-
Oct. **Tee times:** Call shop. **Miscellaneous:** Range (grass), credit cards (MC, V), BF, FF.
Reader Comments: Views of Little Traverse Bay, 2 1/2 hours for 18 holes ... An old classic ...
Small, well trapped, mature trees, perfect greens ... Wonderful walker's course ... Short course.

HARTLAND GLEN GOLF & COUNTRY CLUB
PU-12400 Highland Rd., Hartland, 48353, Livingston County, (248)887-3777, 25 miles from
Ann Arbor. **Facility Holes:** 36. **Green Fee:** $20/$30. **Cart Fee:** $10/Person. **Walking Policy:**

Unrestricted walking. **Season:** April-Nov. **High:** July-Aug. **To obtain tee times:** Call up to 7 days in advance. **Miscellaneous:** Reduced fees (weekdays, twilight, seniors, juniors), range (grass/mats), credit cards (MC, V, AE), BF, FF.

★★ **NORTH COURSE** (18)
Yards: 6,280/5,109. **Par:** 72/72. **Course Rating:** 67.6/67.8. **Slope:** 107/105. **Walkability:** 2. **Opened:** 1972. **Architect:** K. Sustic/J. Neagles.

★★ **SOUTH COURSE** (18)
Yards: 6,175/4,661. **Par:** 71/71. **Course Rating:** 67.0/65.1. **Slope:** 112/107. **Walkability:** 1. **Opened:** 1992. **Architect:** G. Duke/K. Sustic/R. Boyt.

★★½ **HASTINGS COUNTRY CLUB**
SP-1550 N Broadway, Hastings, 49058, Barry County, (616)945-2756, 20 miles from Battle Creek. **Facility Holes:** 18. **Yards:** 6,331/6,201. **Par:** 72/73. **Course Rating:** 70.9/71.7. **Slope:** 126/119. **Green Fee:** $25. **Cart Fee:** $25/Cart. **Walking Policy:** Unrestricted walking. **Walkability:** 5. **Opened:** 1921. **Season:** April-Oct. **High:** May-Aug. **To obtain tee times:** Call golf shop. **Miscellaneous:** Range (grass), credit cards (MC, V).

HAWK HOLLOW GOLF COURSE
PU-15101 Chandler Rd., Bath, 48808, Clinton County, (517)641-4295, (888)411-4295, 2 miles from East Lansing. **E-mail:** kirksherman@aol.com. **Web:** www.hawkhollow.com. **Facility Holes:** 27. **Green Fee:** $40/$62. **Cart Fee:** Included in green fee. **Walking Policy:** Mandatory carts. **Opened:** 1996. **Architect:** Jerry Matthews. **Season:** March-Nov. **To obtain tee times:** Call up to 14 days in advance. **Miscellaneous:** Range (grass), credit cards (MC, V, AE), BF, FF.

★★★ **EAST/NORTH** (18 Combo)
Yards: 6,693/4,962. **Par:** 71/71. **Course Rating:** 72.8. **Slope:** 134.

EAST/WEST (18 Combo)
Yards: 6,974/5,078. **Par:** 72/72. **Course Rating:** 73.7/69.7. **Slope:** 136/120.

NORTH/WEST (18 Combo)
Yards: 6,487/4,934. **Par:** 71/71. **Course Rating:** 71.7. **Slope:** 129.

Reader Comments: Housing development has spoiled look ... Does not feel like a golf course.

★★½ **HAWK MEADOWS AT DAMA FARMS**
PU-410 E. Marr Rd., Howell, 48843, Livingston County, (517)546-4635, 45 miles from Detroit. **E-mail:** hawkmeadows@cac.net. **Web:** www.hawkmeadows.com. **Facility Holes:** 18. **Yards:** 6,377/4,820. **Par:** 72/72. **Course Rating:** 70.2/67.3. **Slope:** 122/114. **Green Fee:** $15/$25. **Cart Fee:** $12/Person. **Walking Policy:** Unrestricted walking. **Walkability:** 3. **Opened:** 1969. **Architect:** Bob Matheson. **Season:** March-Nov. **High:** May-Sept. **To obtain tee times:** Call up to 14 days in advance. **Miscellaneous:** Reduced fees (weekdays, twilight, seniors, juniors), range (grass), credit cards (MC, V), BF, FF.

★★★★ **HAWKSHEAD GOLF LINKS** *Pace*
PU-6959 105th Ave., South Haven, 49090, Allegan County, (616)639-2121, 25 miles from Holland. **Web:** www.hawksheadlinks.com. **Facility Holes:** 18. **Yards:** 6,984/4,960. **Par:** 72/72. **Course Rating:** 73.5/66.9. **Slope:** 131/109. **Green Fee:** $28/$48. **Cart Fee:** $12/Person. **Walking Policy:** Unrestricted walking. **Walkability:** 2. **Opened:** 1997. **Architect:** Arthur Hills. **Season:** March-Nov. **High:** June-Sept. **To obtain tee times:** Call golf shop. **Miscellaneous:** Reduced fees (weekdays, guests, twilight), range (grass), lodging (9 rooms), credit cards (MC, V, AE, D), BF, FF.

Notes: Ranked 24th in 1999 Best in State.

Reader Comments: Links course, lots of hole separation, I'd play it again ... Very fine challenge ... One of my favorites, old style course ... Nicely maintained, pricey ... Amazing conditions, many memorable holes ... Beautiful layout.

★★★½ **HEATHER HIGHLANDS GOLF CLUB**
PU-11450 East Holly Rd., Holly, 48442, Oakland County, (248)634-6800, 50 miles from Detroit. **Facility Holes:** 27. **Yards:** 6,879/5,752. **Par:** 72/72. **Course Rating:** 72.6/73.4. **Slope:** 124/122. **Green Fee:** $25/$33. **Cart Fee:** $24/Cart. **Walking Policy:** Walking at certain times. **Walkability:** 2. **Opened:** 1966. **Architect:** Robert Bruce Harris. **High:** April-Oct. **To obtain tee times:** Call up to 6 days in advance. **Miscellaneous:** Reduced fees (weekdays, twilight, seniors, juniors), range (grass), credit cards (MC, V, AE), BF, FF.

Reader Comments: Easy course if you can putt ... Good old-fashioned golf, thinking course ... Not as easy as it appears.... Also has 9-holer.

★★★★ **HEATHER HILLS GOLF COURSE** *Value+*
PU-3100 McKail Rd., Romeo, 48065, Macomb County, (810)798-3971, 17 miles from Rochester. **Facility Holes:** 18. **Yards:** 6,282/5,029. **Par:** 71/71. **Course Rating:** 69.7/68.5. **Slope:** 118/114. **Green Fee:** $22/$30. **Cart Fee:** $20/Cart. **Walking Policy:** Unrestricted walking. **Walkability:** 4. **Opened:** 1972. **Season:** April-Nov. **High:** May-Sept. **To obtain tee times:** Call up to 7 days in advance. **Miscellaneous:** Reduced fees (seniors, juniors), metal spikes,

range (grass), credit cards (MC, V, D), BF, FF.
Reader Comments: Severely sloped back-to-front greens are very fast ... Very inexpensive, relatively hidden golf course 15-20 minutes from town ... Challenging and sporty ... Great place to play.

THE HEATHLANDS
PU-6444 Farr Rd., Onekama, 49675, Manistee County, (231)889-5644, 50 miles from Traverse City. **E-mail:** jread@heathlands.com. **Web:** www.heathlands.com. **Facility Holes:** 18. **Yards:** 6,569/4,437. **Par:** 72/72. **Course Rating:** 72.3/66.4. **Slope:** 139/112. **Green Fee:** $25/$40. **Cart Fee:** $10/Person. **Walking Policy:** Walking at certain times. **Walkability:** 4. **Opened:** 1997. **Architect:** Jeff Gorney. **Season:** April-Oct. **Tee times:** Call shop. **Miscellaneous:** Reduced fees (weekdays, twilight, seniors), range, credit cards (MC, V, AE, D), BF, FF.

★★★★ HERITAGE GLEN GOLF CLUB
PU-29795 Heritage Lane, Paw Paw, 49079, Van Buren County, (616)657-2552, 10 miles from Kalamazoo. **Web:** www.heritageglengolf.com. **Facility Holes:** 18. **Yards:** 6,630/4,946. **Par:** 72/72. **Course Rating:** 72.1/68.4. **Slope:** 137/130. **Green Fee:** $32/$35. **Cart Fee:** $14/Person. **Walking Policy:** Unrestricted walking. **Walkability:** 3. **Opened:** 1994. **Architect:** Jerry Matthews. **Season:** March-Nov. **High:** May-Aug. **To obtain tee times:** Call up to 14 days in advance. **Miscellaneous:** Reduced fees (weekdays, twilight, seniors, juniors), range (grass), credit cards (MC, V, AE, D), BF, FF.
Reader Comments: Pro tees, fair for women ... A diamond in the rough ... Very nice layout and conditions, pricey ... Well designed, great course ... Good facilities, fair golf, well maintained ... Beautiful course but hard to find.

HESSEL RIDGE GOLF COURSE
PU-2061 N. Three Mile Rd., Hessel, 49745, Mackinac County, (906)484-3494, (888)660-9166, 35 miles from Sault Ste. Marie. **E-mail:** hrgolf@northernway.net. **Web:** www.hessel-ridge.com. **Facility Holes:** 18. **Yards:** 6,415/4,905. **Par:** 70/70. **Green Fee:** $23/$33. **Cart Fee:** $12/Person. **Walking Policy:** Unrestricted walking. **Walkability:** 2. **Opened:** 1997. **Architect:** Jeff Gorney. **Season:** May-Oct. **High:** June-Aug. **To obtain tee times:** Call golf shop. **Miscellaneous:** Reduced fees (weekdays, twilight, juniors), credit cards (MC, V, D), BF, FF.

HICKORY HILLS GOLF CLUB
PU-2540 Parview Dr., Jackson, 49201, Jackson County, (517)750-3636, 35 miles from Ann Arbor. **Facility Holes:** 36. **Green Fee:** $18/$20. **Walking Policy:** Unrestricted walking. **Walkability:** 4. **Season:** March-Nov. **To obtain tee times:** Call golf shop. **Miscellaneous:** Reduced fees (twilight, seniors, juniors), metal spikes, range (grass), FF.
★★★ **GREEN/WHITE** (18)
Yards: 6,723/5,377. **Par:** 72/72. **Course Rating:** 71.5/68.3. **Slope:** 126/116. **Cart Fee:** $20/Cart. **Opened:** 1969. **Architect:** Bruce Matthews.
Reader Comments: Lots of wildlife, secluded, nice layout ... Super nice ... Good value, challenging ... Great for the money ... Play this a lot before you can score well.
★★½ **MAIZE/BLUE** (18)
Yards: 6,715/5,445. **Par:** 72/72. **Course Rating:** 72.0/68.7. **Slope:** 128/118. **Cart Fee:** $18/Cart. **Opened:** 1974. **Architect:** William Newcomb.

★½ HICKORY HOLLOW GOLF COURSE
PU-49001 North Ave., Macomb, 48042, Macomb County, (810)949-9033, 4 miles from Mt. Clemens. **Web:** www.hickoryhollowgolf.com. **Facility Holes:** 18. **Yards:** 6,384/5,220. **Par:** 73/73. **Course Rating:** 70.1/68.9. **Slope:** 116/116. **Green Fee:** $16/$26. **Cart Fee:** $14/Person. **Walking Policy:** Unrestricted walking. **Walkability:** 3. **Opened:** 1963. **Season:** Year-round. **High:** April-Oct. **To obtain tee times:** Call up to 7 days in advance. **Miscellaneous:** Reduced fees (weekdays, twilight, seniors), credit cards (MC, V, AE, D), FF.

HICKORY KNOLL GOLF COURSE
PU-3065 West Alice Street, Whitehall, 49461, Muskegon County, (231)894-5535, 45 miles from Grand Rapids. **Facility Holes:** 36. **Green Fee:** $10. **Cart Fee:** $24/Cart. **Walking Policy:** Unrestricted walking. **Walkability:** 2. **Opened:** 1966. **Architect:** Malcolm Jackson. **Season:** April-Dec. **High:** June-Aug. **To obtain tee times:** Call golf shop. **Miscellaneous:** Reduced fees (seniors), metal spikes, BF, FF.
★½ **BLUE/WHITE COURSE** (18)
Yards: 6,155/6,155. **Par:** 72/72.
GOLD/RED COURSE (18)
Yards: 5,968/5,968. **Par:** 69/69.

★★★★ HIDDEN OAKS GOLF COURSE *Service, Value+, Pace+*
PU-1270 W. Monroe Rd., St. Louis, 48880, Gratiot County, (989)681-3404, 45 miles from Lansing. **Facility Holes:** 18. **Yards:** 6,555/4,970. **Par:** 72/72. **Course Rating:** 72.6/69.4. **Slope:** 129/121. **Green Fee:** $15/$30. **Cart Fee:** $24/Cart. **Walking Policy:** Unrestricted walking.

Walkability: 4. **Opened:** 1999. **Architect:** Jerry Matthews. **Season:** April-Nov. **High:** May-Sept. **To obtain tee times:** Call golf shop. **Miscellaneous:** Reduced fees (weekdays, guests, twilight, seniors), range (grass), credit cards (MC, V), BF, FF.
Reader Comments: Great time, I paid $40 for 18 holes with cart. It was better than courses twice the price. Great value.... One nice place to play golf ... Nice combination of challenge and beauty ... If you're in the neighborhood, you gotta stop.

★★★★ HIDDEN RIVER GOLF & CASTING CLUB *Service*
PU-7688 Maple River Rd., Brutus, 49716, Emmet County, (231)529-4653, (800)325-4653, 13 miles from Petoskey. **E-mail:** info@hiddenriver.com. **Web:** www.hiddenriver.com. **Facility Holes:** 18. **Yards:** 7,101/4,787. **Par:** 72/72. **Course Rating:** 74.3/67.4. **Slope:** 140/117. **Green Fee:** $45/$85. **Cart Fee:** $17/Person. **Walking Policy:** Walking at certain times. **Walkability:** 4. **Opened:** 1998. **Architect:** Bruce Matthews III. **Season:** May-Oct. **High:** June-Aug. **To obtain tee times:** Call up to 200 days in advance. **Miscellaneous:** Reduced fees (weekdays, twilight, juniors), range (grass), credit cards (MC, V), BF, FF.
Reader Comments: Excellent greens, 5 sets of tees ... Great value ... Best Matthews design, beautiful and great people ... Elevation changes ... Tests course management ... Beautiful clubhouse, wind can be a factor on several holes, long natural traps along several fairways ... Great golf, great food, great view.

★★★★ HIGH POINTE GOLF CLUB
PU-5555 Arnold Rd., Williamsburg, 49690, Grand Traverse County, (231)267-9900, (800)753-7888, 10 miles from Traverse City. **E-mail:** highpointegolf@coslink.net. **Web:** www.highpointegolf.com. **Facility Holes:** 18. **Yards:** 6,890/4,974. **Par:** 71/72. **Course Rating:** 73.3/68.7. **Slope:** 136/120. **Green Fee:** $30/$80. **Cart Fee:** Included in green fee. **Walking Policy:** Walking at certain times. **Walkability:** 4. **Opened:** 1989. **Architect:** Tom Doak. **Season:** April-Oct. **High:** June-Aug. **To obtain tee times:** Call up to 180 days in advance. **Miscellaneous:** Reduced fees (weekdays, twilight, juniors), range (grass/mats), credit cards (MC, V, AE, D), BF, FF.
Reader Comments: Very nice course for the money, great views ... Very pretty course, diverse style ... Front 9 links style, fairly long back 9, though forest is narrow and unforgiving ... Back 9 more exciting & challenging ... Overrated.

★★ HIGHLAND GOLF CLUB
SP-3011 U.S. 2-41, Escanaba, 49829, Delta County, (906)466-7457, 90 miles from Green Bay. **Facility Holes:** 18. **Yards:** 6,237/5,499. **Par:** 71/72. **Course Rating:** 69.3/71.0. **Slope:** 117/115. **Green Fee:** $24. **Cart Fee:** $22/Cart. **Walking Policy:** Unrestricted walking. **Walkability:** 1. **Opened:** 1930. **Architect:** Merrill Maissack/Reinhold Bittnor. **Season:** April-Oct. **High:** June-Aug. **To obtain tee times:** Call golf shop. **Miscellaneous:** Credit cards (MC, V).

★½ HIGHLAND HILLS GOLF COURSE
PU-1050 E Alward Rd., De Witt, 48820, Clinton County, (517)669-9873. **Facility Holes:** 18. **Yards:** 6,621/5,030, **Par:** 72/72. **Course Rating:** 70.2/67.3. **Slope:** 118/107. **Green Fee:** $10/$23. **Cart Fee:** $11/Cart. **Walking Policy:** Unrestricted walking. **Season:** May-Oct. **To obtain tee times:** Call golf shop. **Miscellaneous:** Credit cards (MC, V, D).

★★★ HILLS HEART OF THE LAKES GOLF COURSE
PU-500 Case Rd., Brooklyn, 49230, Jackson County, (517)592-2110, 20 miles from Jackson. **Facility Holes:** 18. **Yards:** 5,517/4,445. **Par:** 69/69. **Green Fee:** $15/$20. **Cart Fee:** $13/Person. **Walking Policy:** Unrestricted walking. **Walkability:** 4. **Opened:** 1965. **Architect:** Mike Hill. **Season:** April-Nov. **High:** June-Sept. **To obtain tee times:** Call golf shop. **Miscellaneous:** Reduced fees (seniors, juniors), FF.
Reader Comments: Always kept up beautifully ... Short course, but tough ... Nice relaxing course ... Hard to find but good course ... The owners seem to be proud of the course ... Good condition ... What a view on every hole ... Score well.

★★ HILLTOP GOLF COURSE
PU-47000 Powell Rd., Plymouth, 48170, Wayne County, (734)453-9800, 15 miles from Detroit. **E-mail:** hilltopgc@hotmail.com. **Web:** www.americangolf.com. **Facility Holes:** 18. **Yards:** 6,100/4,761. **Par:** 70/75. **Course Rating:** 69.7/73.0. **Slope:** 120/115. **Green Fee:** $29/$31. **Cart Fee:** $25/Cart. **Walking Policy:** Unrestricted walking. **Walkability:** 4. **Opened:** 1927. **Architect:** Jim Lipe. **Season:** Year-round. **High:** May-Oct. **To obtain tee times:** Call golf shop. **Miscellaneous:** Reduced fees (weekdays, twilight, seniors, juniors), metal spikes, credit cards (MC, V, AE, D, DC), BF, FF.

★★★ HUDSON MILLS METRO PARK GOLF COURSE
PU-4800 Dexter-Pickney Rd., Dexter, 48130, Washtenaw County, (734)426-0466, (800)477-3191, 12 miles from Ann Arbor. **E-mail:** jerry.cyr@metroparks.com. **Web:** www.metroparks.com. **Facility Holes:** 18. **Yards:** 6,560/5,411. **Par:** 71/71. **Course Rating:**

70.6/70.2. **Slope:** 118/115. **Green Fee:** $19/$23. **Cart Fee:** $22/Person. **Walking Policy:** Unrestricted walking. **Walkability:** 3. **Opened:** 1990. **Architect:** Sue Nyquist. **Season:** April-Nov. **High:** June-Sept. **To obtain tee times:** Call golf shop. **Miscellaneous:** Reduced fees (weekdays, seniors, juniors), credit cards (MC, V), FF.
Reader Comments: Consecutive par 5s on the back are worth a look, especially with the fall colors out … A very good test, excellent value … Good, as are all metro parks courses … Front 9 open.

★★★★ **HUNTER'S RIDGE GOLF COURSE**
PU-8101 Byron Rd., Howell, 48843, Livingston County, (517)545-4653, 35 miles from Lansing. **E-mail:** hrgolf@ismi.net. **Web:** www.ismi.net/huntersridge. **Facility Holes:** 18. **Yards:** 6,530/4,624. **Par:** 71/71. **Course Rating:** 71.9/66.6. **Slope:** 134/112. **Green Fee:** $25/$37. **Cart Fee:** $12/Person. **Walking Policy:** Walking at certain times. **Walkability:** 3. **Opened:** 1995. **Architect:** Jerry Matthews. **Season:** April-Nov. **High:** May-Oct. **To obtain tee times:** Call up to 7 days in advance. **Miscellaneous:** Reduced fees (weekdays, twilight, seniors, juniors), range (grass, included in fee), credit cards (MC, V, D), BF, FF.
Reader Comments: Expensive, good test of golf … Heather too high, slows play looking for a ball … Links style, not too long but very fun & challenging course … Don't tell too many people … Good value … Very nice course.

★★★★ **HURON BREEZE GOLF & COUNTRY CLUB**
PU-5200 Huron Breeze Dr., Au Gres, 48703, Arenac County, (517)876-6868, 50 miles from Bay City. **Facility Holes:** 18. **Yards:** 6,806/5,075. **Par:** 72/72. **Course Rating:** 73.1/69.4. **Slope:** 133/123. **Green Fee:** $20/$29. **Cart Fee:** $10/Person. **Walking Policy:** Unrestricted walking. **Walkability:** 2. **Opened:** 1988. **Architect:** William Newcomb. **Season:** April-Oct. **High:** June-Sept. **To obtain tee times:** Call up to 3 days in advance. **Miscellaneous:** Reduced fees (weekdays, twilight, seniors, juniors), range (grass), credit cards (MC, V, D), FF.
Reader Comments: Can't beat the price … Nice course, nice scenery … Flat & open, but fun when the wind blows … Best value I have ever seen … Great track for the price … Short and tight, leave the driver home … Narrow fairways.

★½ **HURON HILLS GOLF COURSE**
PU-3465 E. Huron River Dr., Ann Arbor, 48104, Washtenaw County, (734)971-6840. **Web:** www.ci.ann-arbor.mi.us. **Facility Holes:** 18. **Yards:** 5,071/4,237. **Par:** 67/67. **Course Rating:** 64.0/67.1. **Slope:** 107/108. **Green Fee:** $12/$19. **Walking Policy:** Unrestricted walking. **Walkability:** 3. **Opened:** 1922. **Architect:** Tom Bendelow. **Season:** March-Dec. **High:** April-Sept. **To obtain tee times:** Call up to 14 days in advance. **Miscellaneous:** Reduced fees (weekdays, twilight, seniors, juniors), credit cards (MC, V), BF, FF.

★★½ **HURON MEADOWS METRO PARK GOLF COURSE**
PU-8765 Hammel Rd., Brighton, 48116, Livingston County, (810)231-4084, (800)477-3193, 4 miles from Brighton. **E-mail:** jerry.cyr@metroparks.com. **Web:** www.metroparks.com. **Facility Holes:** 18. **Yards:** 6,663/5,344. **Par:** 72/71. **Course Rating:** 71.2/69.9. **Slope:** 122/116. **Green Fee:** $19. **Cart Fee:** $22/Cart. **Walking Policy:** Unrestricted walking. **Walkability:** 2. **Opened:** 1982. **Season:** April-Nov. **High:** June-Sept. **To obtain tee times:** Call up to 21 days in advance. **Miscellaneous:** Reduced fees (seniors, juniors), range (mats), credit cards (MC, V), BF, FF.

★½ **IDLE WYLD GOLF CLUB**
PU-35780 Five Mile Rd., Livonia, 48154, Wayne County, (734)464-6325, 10 miles from Detroit. **Facility Holes:** 18. **Yards:** 5,817/5,022. **Par:** 70/71. **Course Rating:** 67.3/66.3. **Slope:** 118/111. **Green Fee:** $17/$25. **Cart Fee:** $24/Cart. **Walking Policy:** Unrestricted walking. **Walkability:** 2. **Season:** March-Nov. **High:** March-Nov. **To obtain tee times:** Call golf shop. **Miscellaneous:** Reduced fees (weekdays, twilight), credit cards (MC, V), BF, FF.

★★★ **INDIAN LAKE HILLS GOLF COURSE**
PU-55321 Brush Lake Rd., Eau Claire, 49111, Cass County, (616)782-2540, (888)398-7897, 20 miles from South Bend. **Web:** www.indianlakehills.com. **Facility Holes:** 27. **Green Fee:** $16/$24. **Cart Fee:** $26/Cart. **Walking Policy:** Walking at certain times. **Walkability:** 3. **Opened:** 1924. **Season:** March-Nov. **High:** May-Sept. **To obtain tee times:** Call golf shop. **Miscellaneous:** Reduced fees (twilight, juniors), range, credit cards (MC, V), BF, FF.
EAST/NORTH (18 Combo)
Yards: 6,201/5,156. **Par:** 71/71. **Course Rating:** 67.5/69.8. **Slope:** 112/113.
WEST/EAST (18 Combo)
Yards: 6,043/5,170. **Par:** 71/73. **Course Rating:** 67.0/68.5. **Slope:** 111/111.
WEST/NORTH (18 Combo)
Yards: 6,532/5,450. **Par:** 72/73. **Course Rating:** 68.5/71.3. **Slope:** 113/114.
Reader Comments: Old 9 and new 9, a great combination … Friendly, treated well … Fun for the family … Reasonable rates … Great views … Fast Greens.

★★★½ INDIAN RIVER GOLF CLUB
SP-3301Chippewa Beach Rd., Indian River, 49749, Cheboygan County, 231)238-7011, (800)305-4742, 12 miles from Petoskey. **Facility Holes:** 18. **Yards:** 6,687/5,175. **Par:** 72/72. **Course Rating:** 73.4/70.8. **Slope:** 125/119. **Green Fee:** $27/$45. **Cart Fee:** $14/Person. **Walking Policy:** Unrestricted walking. **Walkability:** 3. **Opened:** 1921. **Architect:** Warner Bowen & Son. **Season:** April-Oct. **High:** July-Aug. **To obtain tee times:** Call golf shop. **Miscellaneous:** Reduced fees (weekdays, twilight, juniors), range (grass), credit cards (MC, V, D).
Reader Comments: Play during the week save a couple dollars …A little old and a little new … Two distinct 9s, hard greens … No complaints … Easy … Good condition, fair course.

★★½ INDIAN RUN GOLF CLUB
SP-6359 East RS Ave., Scotts, 49088, Kalamazoo County, (616)327-1327, 6 miles from Kalamazoo. **Facility Holes:** 18. **Yards:** 6,808/5,028. **Par:** 72/72. **Course Rating:** 72.6/69.9. **Slope:** 126/115. **Green Fee:** $17/$20. **Cart Fee:** $13/Person. **Walking Policy:** Unrestricted walking. **Walkability:** 3. **Opened:** 1966. **Architect:** Charles Darl Scott. **Season:** March-Nov. **High:** May-Sept. **To obtain tee times:** Call golf shop. **Miscellaneous:** Reduced fees (weekdays, twilight, seniors, juniors), metal spikes, range (grass), credit cards (MC, V, D), BF, FF.

★★½ INDIAN SPRINGS METRO PARK GOLF COURSE
PU-2776 Indian Trail, White Lake, 48386, Oakland County, (248)625-7870, (800)477-3192, 8 miles from Pontiac. **Web:** www.metroparks.com. **Facility Holes:** 18. **Yards:** 6,688/5,425. **Par:** 71/71. **Course Rating:** 71.0/70.1. **Slope:** 120/114. **Green Fee:** $19/$23. **Cart Fee:** $11/Person. **Walking Policy:** Unrestricted walking. **Walkability:** 2. **Opened:** 1989. **Architect:** Sue Nyquist. **Season:** April-Nov. **High:** May-Sept. **To obtain tee times:** Call up to 21 days in advance. **Miscellaneous:** Reduced fees (seniors, juniors), range (grass), credit cards (MC, V), FF.

INDIAN TRAILS GOLF COURSE
PU-2776 Kalamazoo Ave. S.E., Grand Rapids, 49507, Kent County, (616)245-2021. **Facility Holes:** 18. **Yards:** 5,100/4,785. **Par:** 68/72. **Course Rating:** 66.8/71.6. **Slope:** 118/123. **Green Fee:** $14/$15. **Cart Fee:** $12/Person. **Walking Policy:** Unrestricted walking. **Walkability:** 3. **Opened:** 1928. **Architect:** Jeffrey John Gorney. **Season:** March-Nov. **High:** July-Aug. **To obtain tee times:** Call up to 14 days in advance. **Miscellaneous:** Reduced fees (weekdays, juniors), metal spikes, credit cards (MC, V, AE), BF, FF.

★★★ INKSTER VALLEY GOLF COURSE
PU-2150 Middlebelt Rd., Inkster, 48141, Wayne County, (734)722-8020, 10 miles from Detroit. **Web:** www.waynecountyparks.com. **Facility Holes:** 18. **Yards:** 6,709/4,500. **Par:** 72/72. **Course Rating:** 72.0/66.3. **Slope:** 133/109. **Green Fee:** $26/$40. **Cart Fee:** Included in green fee. **Walking Policy:** Walking at certain times. **Walkability:** 2. **Opened:** 1998. **Architect:** Harry Bowers. **Season:** March-Nov. **To obtain tee times:** Call up to 7 days in advance. **Miscellaneous:** Reduced fees (twilight, seniors, juniors), credit cards (MC, V), BF, FF.
Reader Comments: Very nice design for a municipal … Easier the 2nd time around … New course, good layout … Nice layout, too new … A gem on the Rouge River, a pleasant surprise.

★★ INTERLOCHEN GOLF & COUNTRY CLUB
PU-10586 U.S. 31 S., Interlochen, 49643, Grand Traverse County, (231)275-7311, (877)480-7311, 13 miles from Traverse City. **E-mail:** interlochengolf@aol.com. **Web:** www.interlochengolf.com. **Facility Holes:** 18. **Yards:** 6,435/5,136. **Par:** 71/72. **Course Rating:** 70.2/69.2. **Slope:** 130/117. **Green Fee:** $15/$25. **Cart Fee:** $24/Cart. **Walking Policy:** Unrestricted walking. **Walkability:** 3. **Opened:** 1965. **Season:** April-Oct. **High:** June-Aug. **To obtain tee times:** Call up to 30 days in advance. **Miscellaneous:** Reduced fees (weekdays, twilight, seniors, juniors), range (grass), credit cards (MC, V), BF, FF.

★★ IRONWOOD GOLF CLUB
PU-6902 (M-59) Highland Rd., Howell, 48843, Livingston County, (517)546-3211, 31 miles from Lansing. **Facility Holes:** 18. **Yards:** 6,083/5,172. **Par:** 72/72. **Course Rating:** 68.3/67.7. **Slope:** 116/117. **Green Fee:** $15/$28. **Cart Fee:** $20/Cart. **Walking Policy:** Unrestricted walking. **Walkability:** 2. **Opened:** 1972. **Architect:** David Pardun. **Season:** March-Nov. **High:** June-Sept. **To obtain tee times:** Call golf shop. **Miscellaneous:** Reduced fees (weekdays, twilight, seniors, juniors), credit cards (MC, V, AE, D).

★½ IRONWOOD GOLF COURSE
PU-3750 64th St. S.W., Byron Center, 49315, Kent County, (616)538-4000, 10 miles from Grand Rapids. **Facility Holes:** 18. **Yards:** 5,405/4,870. **Par:** 71/71. **Green Fee:** $12/$21. **Cart Fee:** $21/Cart. **Walking Policy:** Unrestricted walking. **Walkability:** 1. **Opened:** 1976. **Architect:** George Wolfert. **Season:** March-Nov. **High:** May-Aug. **To obtain tee times:** Call golf shop. **Miscellaneous:** Reduced fees (seniors, juniors), credit cards (MC, V, AE, D), BF, FF.

★★★★ **ISLAND HILLS GOLF CLUB** *Pace*
PU-17510 Island Hills Dr., Centreville, 49032, St. Joseph County, (616)467-7261, 30 miles from Kalamazoo. **E-mail:** islandhills@islandhillsgolf.com. **Web:** www.islandhillsgolf.com. **Facility Holes:** 18. **Yards:** 7,055/4,954. **Par:** 72/72. **Course Rating:** 73.2/67.7. **Slope:** 130/113. **Green Fee:** $59/$69. **Cart Fee:** Included in green fee. **Walking Policy:** Unrestricted walking. **Walkability:** 4. **Opened:** 1999. **Architect:** Ray Hearn. **Season:** April-Nov. **High:** June-Aug. **To obtain tee times:** Call up to 21 days in advance. **Miscellaneous:** Reduced fees (guests, juniors), range (grass), credit cards (MC, V, AE, D, DC, CB), BF, FF.
Notes: Ranked 24th in 2001 Best in State.
Reader Comments: Great views ... Pricey, but a great design, last 5 holes are best 5 finishing holes I've seen ... Great course, layout, and design ... Too pricey ... Tough the 1st time around.

★★ **KEARSLEY LAKE GOLF COURSE**
PU-4266 E Pierson Rd., Flint, 48506, Genesee County, (810)736-0930. **Web:** www.ci.flint.mi.us/parks/golf.html. **Facility Holes:** 18. **Yards:** 6,594/5,766. **Par:** 72/72. **Course Rating:** 70.6/70.1. **Slope:** 113/112. **Green Fee:** $21/$23. **Cart Fee:** $24/Cart. **Walking Policy:** Unrestricted walking. **Walkability:** 2. **Opened:** 1932. **Architect:** City of Flint. **Season:** April-Nov. **High:** May-Aug. **To obtain tee times:** Call golf shop. **Miscellaneous:** Reduced fees (twilight, seniors, juniors), credit cards (MC, V), BF, FF.

★★★½ **KENSINGTON METRO PARK GOLF COURSE**
PU-2240 W. Buno Rd., Milford, 48380, Oakland County, (248)685-9332, (800)477-3178, 25 miles from Detroit. **Facility Holes:** 18. **Yards:** 6,556/5,206. **Par:** 71/71. **Course Rating:** 71.6/69.8. **Slope:** 116/112. **Green Fee:** $19/$23. **Cart Fee:** $11/Person. **Walking Policy:** Unrestricted walking. **Walkability:** 3. **Opened:** 1961. **Architect:** H.A. Lemley. **Season:** March-Nov. **High:** May-Sept. **To obtain tee times:** Call up to 21 days in advance. **Miscellaneous:** Reduced fees (weekdays, seniors, juniors), credit cards (MC, V), BF, FF.
Reader Comments: Better than average & great price ... Very good for Metro Park course ... Best course condition of all municipal courses played in area, has only a few bunkers ... A good public course, lots to look at ... Very few traps.

★★★½ **KIMBERLEY OAKS GOLF CLUB**
SP-1100 W Walnut St., St. Charles, 48655, Saginaw County, (517)865-8261, 10 miles from Saginaw. **Facility Holes:** 18. **Yards:** 6,663/5,156. **Par:** 72/74. **Course Rating:** 72.7/69.9. **Slope:** 134/117. **Green Fee:** $15/$26. **Cart Fee:** $22/Cart. **Walking Policy:** Unrestricted walking. **Walkability:** 4. **Opened:** 1967. **Season:** April-Nov. **High:** June-Sept. **To obtain tee times:** Call golf shop. **Miscellaneous:** Reduced fees (weekdays, twilight, seniors, juniors), range (grass), credit cards (MC, V), BF, FF.
Reader Comments: Keep forgetting how nice this course is, good value, especially with coupons ... Very tight, take a lot of golf balls ... Greens are too knobby, but overall a great value

★★★ **KINCHELOE MEMORIAL GOLF COURSE**
PU-50 Woodside Rd., Kincheloe, 49788, Chippewa County, (906)495-5706, 24 miles from Sault Ste. Marie. **Web:** www.kinross.net. **Facility Holes:** 18. **Yards:** 6,939/5,016. **Par:** 72/72. **Course Rating:** 73.6/69.2. **Slope:** 127/115. **Green Fee:** $26/$28. **Cart Fee:** $10/Person. **Walking Policy:** Unrestricted walking. **Walkability:** 3. **Opened:** 1966. **Architect:** Bob Baldock/Jack Specker. **Season:** April-Nov. **High:** June-Aug. **To obtain tee times:** Call up to 3 days in advance. **Miscellaneous:** Reduced fees (weekdays, twilight, juniors), range, credit cards (MC, V, D), BF, FF.
Reader Comments: Enjoyable challenging track, great value ... Wide fairways, lots of trees ... One of the nicest courses in area ... Will go back ... Good layout and the value can't be beat anywhere ... Need to spend some money on course.

★★½ **KING'S CHALLENGE GOLF CLUB**
SP-4600 S. Country Club Dr., Cedar, 49621, Leelanau County, (231)228-7400, (888)228-0121, 18 miles from Traverse City. **Web:** www.kingschallenge.com. **Facility Holes:** 18. **Yards:** 6,593/4,764. **Par:** 70/71. **Course Rating:** 73.3/68.6. **Slope:** 145/123. **Green Fee:** $35/$65. **Cart Fee:** Included in green fee. **Walking Policy:** Mandatory carts. **Walkability:** 5. **Opened:** 1997. **Architect:** Arnold Palmer. **Season:** April-Oct. **High:** June-Aug. **To obtain tee times:** Call up to 180 days in advance. **Miscellaneous:** Reduced fees (weekdays, twilight, juniors), range (grass/mats), credit cards (MC, V), BF, FF.

★★★★ **L.E. KAUFMAN GOLF CLUB** *Value+*
PU-4807 Clyde Park S.W., Wyoming, 49509, Kent County, (616)538-5050, 8 miles from Grand Rapids. **Facility Holes:** 18. **Yards:** 6,812/5,202. **Par:** 72/72. **Course Rating:** 72.0/69.7. **Slope:** 130/117. **Green Fee:** $23/$25. **Cart Fee:** $24/Cart. **Walking Policy:** Unrestricted walking. **Walkability:** 3. **Opened:** 1965. **Architect:** Bruce Matthews. **Season:** March-Nov. **High:** June-Aug. **To obtain tee times:** Call up to 7 days in advance. **Miscellaneous:** Reduced fees

(seniors, juniors), range (grass/mats), credit cards (MC, V), BF, FF.
Reader Comments: The nicest course for the money in Michigan ... Municipal, very tough ... Super greens ... Good test of your skills ... Best in western Michigan for the price ... Layout is strategic, well-groomed for public ... Nice course.

★★ LAKE CORA HILLS GOLF COURSE
PU-Red Arrow Hwy., Paw Paw, 49079, Van Buren County, (616)657-4074, 12 miles from Kalamazoo. **Facility Holes:** 18. **Yards:** 6,195/5,352. **Par:** 72/72. **Course Rating:** 68.5/70.2. **Slope:** 120/119. **Green Fee:** $14. **Cart Fee:** $20/Person. **Walking Policy:** Unrestricted walking. **Walkability:** 3. **Opened:** 1957. **Architect:** Al Humphrey. **To obtain tee times:** Call golf shop. **Miscellaneous:** Metal spikes, credit cards (MC, V).

★★★★ LAKE DOSTER GOLF CLUB
SP-116 Country Club Blvd., Plainwell, 49080, Allegan County, (616)685-5308, 10 miles from Kalamazoo. **E-mail:** parfiveinc@aol.com. **Facility Holes:** 18. **Yards:** 6,570/5,530. **Par:** 72/72. **Course Rating:** 72.7/72.8. **Slope:** 134/128. **Green Fee:** $24/$27. **Cart Fee:** $10/Person. **Walking Policy:** Walking at certain times. **Walkability:** 3. **Opened:** 1969. **Architect:** Charles Darl Scott. **Season:** April-Oct. **High:** June-Aug. **To obtain tee times:** Call golf shop. **Miscellaneous:** Metal spikes, range (grass), credit cards (MC, V, D).
Reader Comments: Fantastic layout with severely contoured greens, really makes you think ... Good variety of holes and a personal favorite in Kalamazoo area ... Best par 3s around ... A fun course with some good holes ... Always a challenge and fun ... Hidden gem.

LAKE FOREST GOLF CLUB
PU-3110 W. Ellsworth, Ann Arbor, 48103, Washtenaw County, (734)994-8580. **Web:** www.lakeforestgolfclub.com. **Facility Holes:** 18. **Yards:** 6,800/5,354. **Par:** 72/72. **Course Rating:** 71.4/70.2. **Slope:** 130/117. **Green Fee:** $25/$49. **Cart Fee:** $12/Person. **Walking Policy:** Walking at certain times. **Walkability:** 3. **Opened:** 1999. **Architect:** Golf Services Group. **Season:** March-Nov. **High:** June-Aug. **To obtain tee times:** Call up to 7 days in advance. **Miscellaneous:** Reduced fees (weekdays, guests, twilight, seniors, juniors), range (grass/mats), credit cards (MC, V, AE, D), BF, FF.

★★★½ LAKE MICHIGAN HILLS GOLF CLUB
SP-2520 Kerlikowske Rd., Benton Harbor, 49022, Berrien County, (616)849-2722, (800)247-3437, 90 miles from Chicago. **Web:** www.lmhgolf.com. **Facility Holes:** 18. **Yards:** 6,911/5,250. **Par:** 72/72. **Course Rating:** 73.9/70.8. **Slope:** 135/124. **Green Fee:** $28/$38. **Cart Fee:** $26/Cart. **Walking Policy:** Walking at certain times. **Walkability:** 4. **Opened:** 1969. **Architect:** Charles Maddox. **Season:** April-Oct. **High:** June-Aug. **To obtain tee times:** Call golf shop. **Miscellaneous:** Reduced fees (weekdays, twilight, seniors, juniors), range (grass), credit cards (MC, V, AE), BF, FF.
Reader Comments: Beautiful, challenging course ... Wish it were closer to my home ... A great hilly course, very affordable ... 2 hours from Chicago, cheap, superior hotel ... Tremendous.

★★ LAKELAND HILLS GOLF COURSE
PU-5119 Page Ave., Jackson, 49201, Jackson County, (517)764-5292, 50 miles from Detroit. **Web:** www.lakelandhills.com. **Facility Holes:** 18. **Yards:** 6,199/5,090. **Par:** 72/72. **Course Rating:** 68.9/68.4. **Slope:** 110/109. **Green Fee:** $13/$20. **Cart Fee:** $24/Cart. **Walking Policy:** Unrestricted walking. **Walkability:** 3. **Opened:** 1969. **Season:** Feb.-Dec. **High:** May-Sept. **To obtain tee times:** Call golf shop. **Miscellaneous:** Reduced fees (twilight, seniors, juniors), credit cards (MC, V, D), BF, FF.

★★★★ LAKES OF TAYLOR GOLF CLUB
PU-25505 Northline Rd., Taylor, 48180, Wayne County, (734)784-4653, 10 miles from Detroit. **Web:** www.taylorgolf.com. **Facility Holes:** 18. **Yards:** 7,028/5,119. **Par:** 72/72. **Course Rating:** 73.4/69.4. **Slope:** 136/121. **Green Fee:** $27/$40. **Cart Fee:** $26/Cart. **Walking Policy:** Walking at certain times. **Walkability:** 4. **Opened:** 1996. **Architect:** Arthur Hills/Steve Forrest. **Season:** March-Dec. **High:** April-Sept. **To obtain tee times:** Call up to 7 days in advance. **Miscellaneous:** Reduced fees (twilight, seniors, juniors), range (grass/mats), credit cards (MC, V, AE), BF, FF.
Reader Comments: Solid course ... Great layout, but overpriced muni ... Nice course, lots of rangers.

★★★ LAKES OF THE NORTH DEER RUN
PU-8151 Pineview, Mancelona, 49659, Antrim County, (231)585-6800, (800)851-4653, 15 miles from Gaylord. **Facility Holes:** 18. **Yards:** 6,996/5,465. **Par:** 72/74. **Course Rating:** 73.0. **Slope:** 130. **Green Fee:** $25. **Cart Fee:** $15/Person. **Walking Policy:** Unrestricted walking. **Walkability:** 3. **Opened:** 1989. **Architect:** Jerry Matthews/William Newcomb. **Season:** May-Oct. **High:** June-Aug. **To obtain tee times:** Call golf shop. **Miscellaneous:** Reduced fees (guests, twilight, juniors), metal spikes, range (grass), credit cards (MC, V).

MICHIGAN

Reader Comments: Have played a number of times over a decade—nice but never memorable ... Great price and pace ... No problem ... Good course.

★★½ LAKESIDE LINKS
PU-5369 W. Chauves Rd., Ludington, 49431, Mason County, (231)843-3660, 35 miles from Muskegon. **Facility Holes:** 27. **Green Fee:** $23. **Cart Fee:** $10/Person. **Walkability:** 2. **Season:** April-Oct. **High:** June-Sept. **To obtain tee times:** Call golf shop. **Miscellaneous:** Credit cards (MC, V, D).
EAST/SOUTH (18 Combo)
Yards: 6,468/5,041. **Par:** 72/72. **Course Rating:** 72.3/69.1. **Slope:** 122/113.
EAST/WEST (18 Combo)
Yards: 5,766/4,736. **Par:** 69/69. **Course Rating:** 68.2/66.2. **Slope:** 121/111.
WEST/SOUTH (18 Combo)
Yards: 6,466/4,853. **Par:** 71/71. **Course Rating:** 71.5/67.9. **Slope:** 126/112.

LAKEVIEW HILLS COUNTRY CLUB & RESORT
R-6560 Peck Rd. (M-90), Lexington, 48450, Sanilac County, (810)359-8901, 20 miles from Port Huron. **E-mail:** lakeview@greatlakes.net. **Web:** www.lakeviewhills.com. **Facility Holes:** 36. **Walkability:** 3. **Season:** April-Oct. **High:** July-Sept. **To obtain tee times:** Call golf shop. **Miscellaneous:** Reduced fees (weekdays, twilight, seniors, juniors), range (grass/mats), lodging (34 rooms), credit cards (MC, V, AE).
★★★ NORTH COURSE (18)
Yards: 6,852/4,995. **Par:** 72/74. **Course Rating:** 73.5/71.8. **Slope:** 139/131. **Green Fee:** $44/$50. **Cart Fee:** Included in green fee. **Opened:** 1991. **Architect:** Jeffery John Gorney.
Reader Comments: Fun and challenging course from the back tees ... Challenging ... Great course, but bring a saw ... North & South course are the best, treat yourself ... Most scenic in MI.
★★★ SOUTH COURSE (18)
Yards: 6,290/4,707. **Par:** 72/74. **Course Rating:** 70.1/67.6. **Slope:** 119/116. **Green Fee:** $27/$31. **Cart Fee:** $14/Person. **Walking Policy:** Unrestricted walking. **Opened:** 1928. **Architect:** Walter Hagen.
Reader Comments: Nice, challenging greens, worth the ride ... Traditional ... Open, rolling terrain ... Excellent changes in elevation ... Mountain hiking gear necessary ... Great challenge, provides traditional value ... Nice trip for golf.

LAKEWOOD SHORES RESORT
R-7751 Cedar Lake Rd., Oscoda, 48750, Iosco County, (989)739-2075, (800)882-2493, 80 miles from Saginaw. **E-mail:** lakewoodresort@voyager.net. **Web:** www.lakewoodshores.com. **Facility Holes:** 54. **Cart Fee:** $13/Person. **Walking Policy:** Unrestricted walking. **Season:** April-Nov. **High:** June-Sept. **To obtain tee times:** Call golf shop. **Miscellaneous:** Reduced fees (weekdays, guests, twilight, juniors), range, lodging (64 rooms), credit cards (MC, V), BF, FF.
BLACKSHIRE COURSE (18)
Yards: 6,898/4,936. **Par:** 72/72. **Course Rating:** 71.9/66.8. **Slope:** 125/105. **Green Fee:** $30/$62. **Walkability:** 2. **Opened:** 1992. **Architect:** Kevin Aldridge.
★★★★½ THE GAILES COURSE (18) *Pace*
Yards: 6,954/5,246. **Par:** 72/73. **Course Rating:** 75.0/72.2. **Slope:** 138/122. **Green Fee:** $30/$62. **Walkability:** 2. **Opened:** 1992. **Architect:** Kevin Aldridge.
Notes: Ranked 7th in 2001 Best in State.
Reader Comments: Beautiful!, Greens are fast, true & huge ... Huge greens, yardage guide a must for hazards ... A great place ... Links type course, a little expensive ... Watch out for Nos. 3, 4 and 5, play smart, it's not that tough ... Difficult but fair.
★★★½ SERRADELLA COURSE (18)
Yards: 6,806/5,295. **Par:** 72/74. **Course Rating:** 72.9/70.9. **Slope:** 124/116. **Green Fee:** $23/$35. **Walkability:** 1. **Opened:** 1969. **Architect:** Bruce Matthews/Jerry Matthews.
Reader Comments: Nice old course ... Best value in northeastern Michigan ... A great scenic resort course ... Long even from white tees ... Parkland course, good warm-up for tougher courses in area ... Always enjoyable to play the old course.
Special Notes: Also has an 18-hole pitch & putt course.

★★★ LAPEER COUNTRY CLUB
PU-3786 Hunt Rd., Lapeer, 48446, Lapeer County, (810)664-2442, 2 miles from Lapeer. **Facility Holes:** 18. **Yards:** 6,109/5,057. **Par:** 72/73. **Slope:** 122/120. **Green Fee:** $18/$20. **Cart Fee:** $23/Cart. **Walking Policy:** Unrestricted walking. **Walkability:** 4. **Opened:** 1927. **Season:** March-Nov. **High:** April-Sept. **To obtain tee times:** Call golf shop. **Miscellaneous:** Reduced fees (weekdays, seniors, juniors), credit cards (MC, V).
Reader Comments: Skills will be challenged at this course ... Well-kept greens and fairways, excellent deal, well worth the price ... User-friendly public course ... Not long, but not easy, use a cart.

MICHIGAN

★½ **LEDGE MEADOWS GOLF COURSE**
PU-1801 Grand Ledge Hwy, Grand Ledge, 48837, Eaton County, (517)627-7492,
(800) 727-8465, 7 miles from Lansing. **Web:** www.ia4u.net/~ledgegolf/. **Facility Holes:** 18.
Yards: 6,444/4,852. **Par:** 72/72. **Course Rating:** 70.6/67.2. **Slope:** 118/111. **Green Fee:**
$15/$19. **Cart Fee:** $11/Person. **Walking Policy:** Unrestricted walking. **Walkability:** 3. **Opened:**
1971. **Architect:** Scott Kelly/Harold Weeks. **Season:** March-Nov. **High:** May-Aug. **Tee times:**
Call golf shop. **Miscellaneous:** Reduced fees (twilight, seniors, juniors), cards (MC, V, D).

★★★★½ **THE LEGACY GOLF CLUB** *Service+, Value+, Condition+, Pace+*
PU-7677 U.S. Hwy. 223, Ottawa Lake, 49267, Monroe County, (734)854-1101, (877)854-
5100, 5 miles from Toledo. **E-mail:** mtdslim@hotmail.com. **Web:** www.thelegacygolfresort.com.
Facility Holes: 18. **Yards:** 6,840/4,961. **Par:** 72/72. **Course Rating:** 72.7/68.3. **Slope:** 134/115.
Green Fee: $50/$55. **Cart Fee:** Included in green fee. **Walking Policy:** Unrestricted walking.
Walkability: 3. **Opened:** 1997. **Architect:** Arthur Hills. **Season:** Year-round. **High:** May-Oct. **To
obtain tee times:** Call up to 20 days in advance. **Miscellaneous:** Reduced fees (weekdays,
twilight, seniors), range (grass), credit cards (MC, V, D), BF, FF.
Reader Comments: Super greens, great layout, one of Art Hills' best yet … GPS system is very
nice for pace of play … Island green was fun, greens were fast and true, friendly service, a must
stop every year … A golfing pleasure … Great layout, I loved the island green

★★★½ **LESLIE PARK GOLF COURSE**
PU-2120 Traver Rd., Ann Arbor, 48105, Washtenaw County, (734)994-1163. **E-mail:** mhorn-
ing@ci.ann-arbor.mi.us. **Web:** www.ci.ann-arbor.mi.us/framed/parks/index.html. **Facility Holes:**
18. **Yards:** 6,591/4,985. **Par:** 72/72. **Course Rating:** 71.9/68.6. **Slope:** 127/115. **Green Fee:**
$24/$31. **Cart Fee:** $24/Cart. **Walking Policy:** Unrestricted walking. **Walkability:** 4. **Opened:**
1968. **Architect:** Edward Lawrence Packard. **Season:** April-Nov. **High:** May-Sept. **To obtain tee
times:** Call golf shop. **Miscellaneous:** Reduced fees (weekdays, twilight, seniors, juniors),
credit cards (MC, V), BF, FF.
Reader Comments: Hilly, fast greens, challenging … A great challenge with tight fairways … Needs
a better clubhouse … Great municipal layout … Great course, but needs a little work.

★½ **LILAC GOLF CLUB**
PU-9090 Armstrong Rd., Newport, 48166, Monroe County, (734)586-7555, 20 miles from
Detroit. **Facility Holes:** 18. **Yards:** 7,050/5,900. **Par:** 72/72. **Course Rating:** 72.4/69.9. **Slope:**
125/118. **Green Fee:** $17/$20. **Cart Fee:** $12/Cart. **Walking Policy:** Unrestricted walking.
Walkability: 1. **Opened:** 1959. **Architect:** Al Lilac/Sam Lilac. **Season:** March-Nov. **High:** June-
Aug. **To obtain tee times:** Call up to 14 days in advance. **Miscellaneous:** Reduced fees (week-
days, twilight, seniors, juniors), range (grass), credit cards (MC, V, D), BF, FF.

★ **LINCOLN COUNTRY CLUB**
PU-3485 Lake Michigan Dr., Grand Rapids, 49544, Kent County, (616)453-6348. **Facility
Holes:** 18. **Yards:** 6,035/5,592. **Par:** 72/74. **Course Rating:** 67.7/71.3. **Slope:** 110/117. **Green
Fee:** $16/$17. **To obtain tee times:** Call golf shop. **Miscellaneous:** Reduced fees (weekdays).

★★½ **LINCOLN GOLF CLUB**
SP-4907 N Whitehall Rd., Muskegon, 49445, Muskegon County, (231)766-2226, 9 miles from
Muskegon. **Facility Holes:** 18. **Yards:** 6,083/5,209. **Par:** 72/76. **Course Rating:** 68.9/70.3.
Slope: 118/117. **Green Fee:** $22. **Cart Fee:** $20/Cart. **Walkability:** 3. **Opened:** 1927. **Architect:**
Jerry Matthews. **Season:** April-Nov. **High:** May-Sept. **To obtain tee times:** Call golf shop.
Miscellaneous: Range (grass), credit cards (MC, V), BF, FF.

LINCOLN HILLS GOLF CLUB
SP-1527 N. Lakeshore Dr., Ludington, 49431, Mason County, (231)843-4666, 100 miles from
Grand Rapids. **E-mail:** TABPGA@T-one.net. **Facility Holes:** 18. **Yards:** 6,570/5,070. **Par:**
72/72. **Course Rating:** 70.9/69.1. **Slope:** 130/117. **Green Fee:** $30/$40. **Cart Fee:** $16/Person.
Walking Policy: Unrestricted walking. **Walkability:** 3. **Opened:** 1921. **Architect:** Mark Mitchell.
Season: April-Nov. **High:** June-Aug. **To obtain tee times:** Call golf shop. **Miscellaneous:** Range
(grass), credit cards (MC, V), BF, FF.

★★★★ **THE LINKS AT BOWEN LAKE**
PU-12990 Bradshaw NE, Gowen, 49326, Kent County, (616)984-9916, (888)715-4657, 30
miles from Grand Rapids. **Web:** www.liinksatbowenlake.com. **Facility Holes:** 18. **Yards:**
6,828/5,379. **Par:** 71/72. **Green Fee:** $42/$49. **Cart Fee:** Included in green fee. **Walking Policy:**
Mandatory carts. **Walkability:** 4. **Opened:** 1999. **Architect:** William Newcomb. **Season:** April-
Oct. **High:** June-Aug. **To obtain tee times:** Call golf shop. **Miscellaneous:** Reduced fees (weekdays, twilight, seniors, juniors), range (grass/mats), credit cards (MC, V), FF.
Reader Comments: Very nice, has potential to be really good … Great for seniors … First time and
fell in love with course … Nicer course with reasonable rates and good people.

★★½ THE LINKS AT LAKE ERIE GOLF CLUB
PU-14727 La Plaisance Rd., Monroe, 48161, Monroe County, (734)384-1096, (888)643-6765, 40 miles from Detroit. **Web:** www.linksatlakeerie.com. **Facility Holes:** 18. **Yards:** 6,575/5,163. **Par:** 72/72. **Course Rating:** 70.0/67.0. **Slope:** 120/112. **Green Fee:** $25/$27. **Cart Fee:** $11/Person. **Walking Policy:** Unrestricted walking. **Opened:** 1999. **Architect:** Scott Thacker. **Season:** March-Nov. **To obtain tee times:** Call up to 7 days in advance. **Misc:** Reduced fees (weekdays, seniors, juniors), range , cards (MC, V), BF, FF.

★★★ THE LINKS AT PINEWOOD
PU-8600 P.G.A. Dr., Walled Lake, 48390, Oakland County, (248)669-9802, 30 miles from Detroit. **Facility Holes:** 18. **Yards:** 6,676/5,300. **Par:** 72/72. **Course Rating:** 71.9/70.8. **Slope:** 130/121. **Green Fee:** $40/$50. **Cart Fee:** Included in green fee. **Walking Policy:** Walking at certain times. **Walkability:** 2. **Opened:** 1985. **Architect:** Ernest Fuller. **Season:** March-Dec. **High:** May-Sept. **To obtain tee times:** Call up to 6 days in advance. **Miscellaneous:** Reduced fees (weekdays, twilight, seniors, juniors), range (grass/mats), credit cards (MC, V, AE), BF, FF. **Reader Comments:** Course gets a lot of outings and conditions reflect that ... Excellent course and staff ... Somewhat pricey ... Lost many balls in tight woods course.

★★★ THE LINKS OF NOVI
PU-50395 Ten Mile Rd., Novi, 48374, Oakland County, (248)380-9595, 15 miles from Detroit. **Facility Holes:** 27. **Green Fee:** $37/$43. **Cart Fee:** $12/Person. **Walking Policy:** Walking at certain times. **Walkability:** 3. **Opened:** 1991. **Architect:** Jerry Matthews. **Season:** March-Nov. **High:** May-Sept. **To obtain tee times:** Call up to 6 days in advance. **Miscellaneous:** Reduced fees (twilight, seniors, juniors), range (grass/mats), credit cards (MC, V), BF, FF.
EAST/SOUTH (18 Combo)
Yards: 6,072/4,646. **Par:** 69/72. **Course Rating:** 67.9/66.8. **Slope:** 118/115.
EAST/WEST (18 Combo)
Yards: 6,537/5,122. **Par:** 71/74. **Course Rating:** 71.2/70.4. **Slope:** 127/126.
SOUTH/WEST (18 Combo)
Yards: 6,093/4,862. **Par:** 70/74. **Course Rating:** 68.3/68.0. **Slope:** 119/121.
Reader Comments: Great public course, No. 4 East is one of the toughest holes I've seen yet.

★★★★½ LITTLE TRAVERSE BAY GOLF CLUB
PU-995 Hideaway Valley Rd., Harbor Springs, 49740, Emmet County, (616)526-6200, (888)995-6262, 80 miles from Traverse City. **Web:** www.ltbaygolf.com. **Facility Holes:** 18. **Yards:** 6,895/5,061. **Par:** 72/72. **Course Rating:** 73.9/69.3. **Slope:** 136/119. **Green Fee:** $55/$80. **Cart Fee:** Included in green fee. **Walking Policy:** Mandatory carts. **Walkability:** 5. **Opened:** 1992. **Architect:** Jeff Gorney. **Season:** May-Oct. **High:** June-Aug. **To obtain tee times:** Call up to 3 days in advance. **Misc:** Reduced fees (weekdays, juniors), range (grass/mats), credit cards (MC, V), BF, FF.
Reader Comments: My favorite course, Kodak moments at virtually every tee ... Driving range view a must ... Great views, well worth the price ... Outstanding views ... Great service ... We go back every year ... Beautiful, take camera ... Very nice, good food, 1st hole very scenic.

★½ LUM INTERNATIONAL GOLF CLUB
PU-5191 Lum Rd., Lum, 48412, Lapeer County, (810)724-0851, 30 miles from Flint. **Facility Holes:** 27. **Green Fee:** $17/$21. **Cart Fee:** $22/Cart. **Walking Policy:** Unrestricted walking. **Walkability:** 2. **Opened:** 1979. **Architect:** Joe Hawald/Rich Graves. **Season:** March-Nov. **To obtain tee times:** Call golf shop. **Miscellaneous:** Reduced fees (weekdays, twilight, seniors, juniors), range (grass), credit cards (MC, V, D), BF, FF.
RED/GOLD (18 Combo)
Yards: 6,695/5,239. **Par:** 71/71.
RED/WHITE (18 Combo)
Yards: 6,629/5,201. **Par:** 72/72.
WHITE/GOLD (18 Combo)
Yards: 6,274/5,082. **Par:** 71/71.

★★★ THE MAJESTIC AT LAKE WALDEN
PU-9600 Crouse Rd., Hartland, 48353, Livingston County, (810)632-5235, (800)762-3280, 45 miles from Detroit. **E-mail:** majestic @ismi.net. **Web:** www.majesticgolf.com. **Facility Holes:** 27. **Green Fee:** $40/$69. **Cart Fee:** Included in green fee. **Walking Policy:** Mandatory carts. **Walkability:** 5. **Opened:** 1994. **Architect:** Matthews and Associates. **Season:** Year-round. **To obtain tee times:** Call up to 14 days in advance. **Miscellaneous:** Reduced fees (weekdays, twilight, seniors, juniors), range (grass), credit cards (MC, V, AE, D), BF, FF.
FIRST/SECOND (18 Combo)
Yards: 7,035/5,045. **Par:** 72/72. **Course Rating:** 73.8/68.7. **Slope:** 136/111.
FIRST/THIRD (18 Combo)
Yards: 6,914/5,001. **Par:** 72/72. **Course Rating:** 71.4/67.9. **Slope:** 134/111.
SECOND/THIRD (18 Combo)

Yards: 6,930/4,916. **Par:** 72/72. **Course Rating:** 72.0/67.6. **Slope:** 137/111.
Reader Comments: Lots of trees, heather and water but they give you room to drive the ball … Several tough par 3 holes.

MANISTEE NATIONAL GOLF & RESORT
R-4797 U.S. 31 South, Manistee, 49660, Manistee County, (231)723-8874, (800)867-2604, 60 miles from Traverse City. **E-mail:** dbell@manisteenational.com. **Web:** www.manisteenational.com. **Facility Holes:** 36. **Green Fee:** $25/$48. **Cart Fee:** $12/Person. **Walkability:** 3. **Season:** April-Nov. **High:** June-Sept. **To obtain tee times:** Call up to 365 days in advance. **Miscellaneous:** Reduced fees (guests, twilight, seniors, juniors), metal spikes, range (grass/mats), lodging (42 rooms), credit cards (MC, V), BF, FF.
CANTHOOKE VALLEY (18)
Yards: 6,619/4,982. **Par:** 72/72. **Course Rating:** 72.1/69.6. **Slope:** 132/124. **Walking Policy:** Unrestricted walking. **Opened:** 1994. **Architect:** Gary Pulsipher.
CUTTERS RIDGE (18)
Yards: 6,707/5,037. **Par:** 72/72. **Course Rating:** 73.4/70.2. **Slope:** 148/114. **Walking Policy:** Mandatory carts. **Opened:** 2000. **Architect:** Jerry Mathews.

MAPLE GROVE GOLF COURSE
PU-6360 Secor Rd., Lambertville, 48144, Monroe County, (734)854-6777, 1 mile from Toledo. **Facility Holes:** 27. **Yards:** 5,403/4,849. **Par:** 69/71. **Green Fee:** $16. **Cart Fee:** $18/Cart. **Walking Policy:** Unrestricted walking. **Walkability:** 2. **Opened:** 1975. **Architect:** Richard Kimble. **Season:** Year-round. **High:** May-Sept. **To obtain tee times:** Call golf shop. **Miscellaneous:** Range (grass/mats), credit cards (MC, V, D), BF, FF.
Special Notes: Also has a 9-hole executive course.

★★ MAPLE HILL GOLF COURSE
PU-5555 Ivanrest Ave., Grandville, 49418, Kent County, (616)538-0290, (800)219-1113, 3 miles from Grand Rapids. **E-mail:** golf@maplehillgc.com. **Web:** www.maplehillgc.com. **Facility Holes:** 18. **Yards:** 4,724/3,760. **Par:** 68/70. **Green Fee:** $20/$21. **Cart Fee:** $20/Cart. **Walking Policy:** Unrestricted walking. **Walkability:** 2. **Opened:** 1967. **Architect:** Woolferd/Kitchen. **Season:** Year-round. **High:** May-Sept. **To obtain tee times:** Call golf shop. **Miscellaneous:** Reduced fees (weekdays, seniors, juniors), range (grass), credit cards (MC, V, D), BF, FF.

MAPLE LANE GOLF COURSE
PU-33203 Maple Lane Road, Sterling Heights, 48312, Macomb County, (810)795-4000, 15 miles from Detroit. **Facility Holes:** 54. **Green Fee:** $22/$25. **Opened:** 1926. **Architect:** Clarence Wolfrom. **To obtain tee times:** Call golf shop. **Miscellaneous:** Metal spikes.
★½ **EAST COURSE** (18)
Yards: 5,781/5,700. **Par:** 70/70. **Course Rating:** 65.7/65.7. **Slope:** 105/105.
★★ **NORTH COURSE** (18)
Yards: 5,926/5,800. **Par:** 71/71. **Course Rating:** 66.7/69.9. **Slope:** 108/114.
★½ **WEST COURSE** (18)
Yards: 6,154/6,087. **Par:** 71/71. **Course Rating:** 67.7/69.0. **Slope:** 111/109.

★★★½ MAPLE LEAF GOLF COURSE
PU-158 N. Mackinaw Rd., Linwood, 48634, Bay County, (989)697-3370, 10 miles from Bay City. **E-mail:** jezowski@toast.net. **Web:** www.golfmapleleaf.com. **Facility Holes:** 27. **Green Fee:** $19/$21. **Cart Fee:** $20/Cart. **Walking Policy:** Unrestricted walking. **Walkability:** 2. **Opened:** 1963. **Architect:** Robert W. Bills/Donald L. Childs. **Season:** April-Nov. **High:** May-Aug. **To obtain tee times:** Call up to 7 days in advance. **Miscellaneous:** Reduced fees (weekdays, seniors, juniors), range (grass/mats), credit cards (MC, V, D, DC), BF, FF.
EAST/NORTH (18 Combo)
Yards: 5,762/4,261. **Par:** 71/73. **Course Rating:** 67.6/66.2. **Slope:** 116/113.
EAST/WEST (18 Combo)
Yards: 5,983/4,588. **Par:** 71/74. **Course Rating:** 66.4/66.7. **Slope:** 109/109. BF.
NORTH/WEST (18 Combo)
Yards: 6,274/4,735. **Par:** 72/75. **Course Rating:** 68.3/67.5. **Slope:** 114/114.
Reader Comments: Friendly, challenging holes, always improving course … Busy… Great North 9, value good … 27 holes … Has island green, very fair layout … Good course, on the short side.

MAPLE RIDGE GOLF CLUB
PU-3459 US-31 North, Brutus, 49716, Emmet County, (231)529-6574, 12 miles from Petosky. **Facility Holes:** 36. **Cart Fee:** Included in green fee. **Walking Policy:** Unrestricted walking. **Walkability:** 3. **Season:** April-Oct. **High:** July-Aug. **To obtain tee times:** Call golf shop. **Miscellaneous:** Reduced fees (twilight, juniors), range (grass), credit cards (MC, V, AE), BF, FF.

MICHIGAN

EXECUTIVE COURSE (18)
Yards: 2,381/2,356. **Par:** 54/57. **Green Fee:** $15/$29.
★★★ **THE NARROWS** (18)
Yards: 6,181/4,576. **Par:** 71/72. **Course Rating:** 68.5/66.0. **Slope:** 123/110. **Green Fee:** $19/$33. **Opened:** 1991. **Architect:** ABK Inc.
Reader Comments: Got what I expected … Very nice public course … Was built in a Huckleberry swamp and lives up to its name.

★★½ **MARION OAKS GOLF CLUB**
PU-2255 Pinckney Rd., Howell, 48843, Livingston County, (517)548-0050, 30 miles from Lansing. **Facility Holes:** 18. **Yards:** 6,706/4,851. **Par:** 70/70. **Course Rating:** 72.6/67.7. **Slope:** 135/114. **Green Fee:** $18/$31. **Cart Fee:** $12/Person. **Walking Policy:** Unrestricted walking. **Walkability:** 3. **Opened:** 1990. **Architect:** Frank Godwin. **Season:** April-Nov. **High:** June-Sept. **To obtain tee times:** Call up to 7 days in advance. **Miscellaneous:** Reduced fees (weekdays, twilight, seniors, juniors), range (grass), credit cards (MC, V, AE), BF, FF.

★★★ **MARQUETTE GOLF & COUNTRY CLUB**
SP-1075 Grove St, Marquette, 49855, Marquette County, (906)225-0721. **Facility Holes:** 18. **Yards:** 6,260/5,161. **Par:** 71/73. **Course Rating:** 70.0/69.7. **Slope:** 124/118. **Green Fee:** $27/$42. **Cart Fee:** $22/Cart. **Walking Policy:** Unrestricted walking. **Walkability:** 3. **Opened:** 1926. **Architect:** David Gill. **Season:** April-Oct. **High:** June-Aug. **To obtain tee times:** Call golf shop. **Miscellaneous:** Range (grass), credit cards (MC, V).
Reader Comments: Hard to get on … Love the old-style layouts.

★★ **MARQUETTE TRAILS COUNTRY CLUB**
PU-6409 W. 76th St., Baldwin, 49304, Lake County, (231)898-2450, 8 miles from Baldwin. **E-mail:** cab1159@aol.com. **Web:** www.marquettetrailsgolf.com. **Facility Holes:** 18. **Yards:** 5,847/4,490. **Par:** 70/70. **Course Rating:** 68.0/67.0. **Slope:** 113/111. **Green Fee:** $18/$25. **Cart Fee:** $12/Person. **Walking Policy:** Unrestricted walking. **Walkability:** 3. **Opened:** 1964. **Season:** March-Nov. **High:** July-Sept. **To obtain tee times:** Call golf shop. **Miscellaneous:** Reduced fees (seniors, juniors), range (grass), credit cards (MC, V), BF, FF.

★★★★ **MARSH RIDGE RESORT**
R-4815 Old 27 S., Gaylord, 49735, Otsego County, (989)705-3912, (800)968-2633, 55 miles from Traverse City. **E-mail:** teetimes@marshridge.com. **Web:** www.marshridge.com. **Facility Holes:** 18. **Yards:** 6,141/4,488. **Par:** 71/71. **Course Rating:** 70.8/66.8. **Slope:** 130/119. **Green Fee:** $39/$59. **Cart Fee:** Included in green fee. **Walking Policy:** Mandatory carts. **Walkability:** 5. **Opened:** 1992. **Architect:** Mike Husby. **Season:** April-Nov. **High:** June-Aug. **To obtain tee times:** Call up to 240 days in advance. **Miscellaneous:** Reduced fees (weekdays, guests, twilight, seniors, juniors), range (grass), lodging (59 rooms), credit cards (MC, V, AE, D), BF, FF.
Reader Comments: Beautiful terrain, condition … Fun course, played in rain … Scenic views, some blind shots, short course … Nice course … Another great North course … Good test.

★★★½ **MARYSVILLE GOLF COURSE**
PU-2080 River Rd., Marysville, 48040, St. Clair County, (810)364-4653, 55 miles from Detroit. **E-mail:** mvgolf@tir.com. **Web:** www.cityofmarysvillemi.com. **Facility Holes:** 18. **Yards:** 6,542/5,311. **Par:** 72/72. **Course Rating:** 71.0/70.6. **Slope:** 120/117. **Green Fee:** $13/$22. **Cart Fee:** $11/Person. **Walking Policy:** Unrestricted walking. **Walkability:** 2. **Opened:** 1954. **Season:** March-Nov. **To obtain tee times:** Call golf shop. **Miscellaneous:** Reduced fees (weekdays, seniors, juniors), range (grass), credit cards (MC, V, AE, D), BF, FF.
Reader Comments: It's worth the drive … Great course for seniors … Challenging.

★★½ **MARYWOOD GOLF CLUB & BANQUET CENTER**
PU-21310 North Ave., Battle Creek, 49017, Calhoun County, (616)968-1168, (866)627-9966, 3 miles from Battle Creek. **Facility Holes:** 18. **Yards:** 6,631/5,233. **Par:** 72/72. **Course Rating:** 73.0/71.6. **Slope:** 132/126. **Green Fee:** $18/$33. **Cart Fee:** $12/Person. **Walking Policy:** Walking at certain times. **Walkability:** 4. **Opened:** 1926. **Architect:** Maurice McCarthy. **Season:** March-Sept. **High:** April-Aug. **Tee times:** Call golf shop. **Miscellaneous:** Reduced fees (weekdays, twilight, seniors, juniors), range (grass/mats), credit cards (MC, V, AE, D), BF, FF.

★★½ **MCGUIRE'S RESORT**
R-7880 Mackinaw Trail, Cadillac, 49601, Wexford County, (231)775-9947, (800)632-7302, 35 miles from Traverse City. **E-mail:** info@mcguiresresort.com. **Web:** www.mcguiresresort.com. **Facility Holes:** 27. **Yards:** 6,443/5,107. **Par:** 71/71. **Course Rating:** 71.3/69.6. **Slope:** 124/118. **Green Fee:** $40/$62. **Cart Fee:** Included in green fee. **Walking Policy:** Mandatory carts. **Walkability:** 3. **Opened:** 1959. **Architect:** Bruce Matthews. **Season:** April-Nov. **High:** June-Oct. **To obtain tee times:** Call golf shop. **Miscellaneous:** Reduced fees (weekdays, guests, twilight), range (grass), lodging (123 rooms), credit cards (MC, V, AE, D).
Special Notes: Also has a 9-hole course.

★★★★ **THE MEADOWS GOLF CLUB**
PU-4645 West Campus Dr., Allendale, 49401, Ottawa County, (616)895-1000, 15 miles from Grand Rapids. **E-mail:** sackt@gvsu.edu. **Web:** www.webgolfer.com/meadows. **Facility Holes:** 18. **Yards:** 7,034/4,777. **Par:** 71/72. **Course Rating:** 74.5/67.4. **Slope:** 133/117. **Green Fee:** $27/$41. **Cart Fee:** $13/Person. **Walking Policy:** Unrestricted walking. **Walkability:** 2. **Opened:** 1994. **Architect:** Michael Hurdzan. **Season:** March-Dec. **High:** May-Sept. **To obtain tee times:** Call up to 10 days in advance. **Miscellaneous:** Reduced fees (weekdays, juniors), range (grass/mats), credit cards (MC, V, AE, D), BF, FF.
Reader Comments: Target layout ... Tough layout, requires excellent control, irons ... The course & people were great ... Great pace on weekdays, 3 1/2 hrs ... Real nice course with reasonable rates ... Staff was very friendly.

MECEOLA COUNTRY CLUB
SP-14777 150th Ave., Big Rapids, 49307, Mecosta County, (231)796-9004, 50 miles from Grand Rapids. **Facility Holes:** 18. **Yards:** 6,504/5,890. **Par:** 72/74. **Course Rating:** 70.7/69.9. **Slope:** 117/121. **Green Fee:** $18/$23. **Cart Fee:** $24/Cart. **Walking Policy:** Unrestricted walking. **Walkability:** 3. **Opened:** 1919. **Architect:** Jeff Gorney. **Season:** April-Nov. **High:** May-Sept. **To obtain tee times:** Call up to 1 day in advance. **Miscellaneous:** Reduced fees (weekdays, seniors), range (grass), credit cards (MC, V), BF, FF.

THE MEDALIST GOLF CLUB
R-15701 N. Drive North, Marshall, 49068, Calhoun County, (616)789-4653, 10 miles from Battle Creek. **Web:** www.themedalist.com. **Facility Holes:** 18. **Yards:** 6,969/5,240. **Par:** 72/72. **Course Rating:** 71.7/70.7. **Slope:** 138/129. **Green Fee:** $24/$44. **Cart Fee:** $16/Person. **Walking Policy:** Walking at certain times. **Walkability:** 4. **Opened:** 1996. **Architect:** William Newcomb. **Season:** March-Dec. **High:** June-Sept. **To obtain tee times:** Call up to 14 days in advance. **Miscellaneous:** Reduced fees (weekdays, guests, twilight, seniors, juniors), range (grass), credit cards (MC, V, AE), FF.

MERIDIAN SUN GOLF COURSE
PU-1018 Haslett Rd., Haslett, 48840, Ingham County, (517)339-8281, 10 miles from Lansing. **E-mail:** billmory@pga.com. **Facility Holes:** 18. **Yards:** 6,155/4,677. **Par:** 71/71. **Course Rating:** 69.9/67.0. **Slope:** 122/113. **Green Fee:** $18/$20. **Cart Fee:** $12/Person. **Walking Policy:** Unrestricted walking. **Walkability:** 3. **Opened:** 1954. **Architect:** Bob Wilkens. **Season:** March-Nov. **High:** May-Oct. **Tee times:** Call up to 30 days in advance. **Miscellaneous:** Reduced fees (weekdays, twilight, seniors, juniors), range (grass), credit cards (MC, V), BF, FF.

★★★½ **MICHAYWE**
PU-1535 Opal Lake Rd., Gaylord, 49735, Otsego County, (989)939-8911, (888)746-3742, 5 miles from Traverse City. **E-mail:** admin@michaywe.org. **Web:** www.michaywe.com. **Facility Holes:** 18. **Yards:** 6,835/5,901. **Par:** 72/73. **Course Rating:** 73.5/75.0. **Slope:** 133/130. **Green Fee:** $30/$55. **Cart Fee:** Included in green fee. **Walking Policy:** Walking at certain times. **Walkability:** 2. **Opened:** 1972. **Architect:** Robert W. Bills/Donald L. Childs. **Season:** April-Nov. **High:** June-Sept. **To obtain tee times:** Call golf shop. **Miscellaneous:** Reduced fees (weekdays, guests, twilight, juniors), range (grass), credit cards (MC, V, AE, D), BF, FF.
Reader Comments: Classic course that challenges ... Great place to play... Fun to play ... Traditional northern course ... Beautiful, friendly ... Nice layout ... Very enjoyable.

★★★★ **MILHAM PARK MUNICIPAL GOLF CLUB** *Value*
PU-4200 Lovers Lane, Kalamazoo, 49001, Kalamazoo County, (616)344-7639. **E-mail:** shecky4@aol.com. **Web:** www.kalamazoogolf.org. **Facility Holes:** 18. **Yards:** 6,578/5,582. **Par:** 72/72. **Course Rating:** 71.6/71.6. **Slope:** 130/119. **Green Fee:** $22. **Cart Fee:** $12/Person. **Walking Policy:** Unrestricted walking. **Walkability:** 2. **Opened:** 1931. **Architect:** Robert Millar. **Season:** March-Dec. **High:** June-Aug. **To obtain tee times:** Call golf shop. **Miscellaneous:** Reduced fees (seniors, juniors), range (grass/mats), credit cards (MC, V, AE, D), FF.
Reader Comments: Best muni around ... Fabulous facility, too crowded ... Outstanding municipal course ... One of the best-kept secrets in Kalamazoo, excellent course, courteous service, great place ... Lots of play year round.

★★½ **MISSAUKEE GOLF CLUB**
SP-5300 S Morey Rd, Lake City, 49651, Missaukee County, (231)825-2756, 11 miles from Cadillac. **E-mail:** goldclub18@hotmail.com. **Web:** www.golfmichigan.net/missaukeegolf. **Facility Holes:** 18. **Yards:** 6,045/4,905. **Par:** 71/71. **Course Rating:** 67.0/68.0. **Slope:** 110/110. **Green Fee:** $20/$25. **Cart Fee:** $8/Person. **Walking Policy:** Unrestricted walking. **Walkability:** 2. **Opened:** 1970. **Season:** March-Nov. **High:** June-Aug. **To obtain tee times:** Call golf shop. **Miscellaneous:** Reduced fees (twilight), range (grass/mats), credit cards (MC, V, AE), BF, FF.

MICHIGAN

★★★★ MISTWOOD GOLF COURSE
PU-7568 Ole White Dr., Lake Ann, 49650, Benzie County, (231)275-5500, 18 miles from Traverse City. **E-mail:** mistwood@coslink.net. **Web:** www.mistwoodgolf.com. **Facility Holes:** 27. **Green Fee:** $26/$43. **Cart Fee:** $12/Person. **Walking Policy:** Unrestricted walking. **Walkability:** 3. **Opened:** 1993. **Architect:** Jerry Matthews/Ray Hearn. **Season:** April-Nov. **High:** June-Aug. **To obtain tee times:** Call golf shop. **Miscellaneous:** Reduced fees (weekdays, guests, twilight, seniors, juniors), range (grass), credit cards (MC, V, AE, D), BF, FF.
RED/BLUE (18 Combo)
Yards: 6,669/5,032. **Par:** 71/71. **Course Rating:** 72.9/70.2. **Slope:** 143/120.
RED/WHITE (18 Combo)
Yards: 6,460/4,874. **Par:** 70/70. **Course Rating:** 71.6/69.2. **Slope:** 140/117.
WHITE/BLUE (18 Combo)
Yards: 6,695/5,070. **Par:** 71/71. **Course Rating:** 72.9/70.2. **Slope:** 142/123.
Reader Comments: A good value in northern Michigan … Fastest greens I've ever played … Good deal for golf & 19th hole … Good variety of holes, another good Matthews design … 3 9s, great course, fast greens.

★★ MORRISON LAKE COUNTRY CLUB
PU-6425 West Portland Rd., Saranac, 48881, Ionia County, (616)642-9528, 28 miles from Grand Rapids. **Facility Holes:** 18. **Yards:** 5,368/5,368. **Par:** 70/72. **Course Rating:** 65.7/66.4. **Slope:** 102/108. **Green Fee:** $14/$15. **Cart Fee:** $18/Cart. **Walking Policy:** Unrestricted walking. **Walkability:** 3. **Opened:** 1927. **Season:** April-Nov. **High:** April-Sept. **To obtain tee times:** Call golf shop. **Miscellaneous:** Reduced fees (weekdays, twilight, seniors, juniors).

★★ MULBERRY FORE GOLF COURSE
PU-955 N Main St. (M-66), Nashville, 49073, Barry County, (517)852-0760, (800)450-0760, 20 miles from Battle Creek. **Facility Holes:** 18. **Yards:** 5,869/5,121. **Par:** 72/75. **Green Fee:** $15. **Cart Fee:** $11/Person. **Walking Policy:** Unrestricted walking. **Walkability:** 4. **Opened:** 1979. **Season:** March-Nov. **High:** May-Sept. **To obtain tee times:** Call golf shop. **Miscellaneous:** Reduced fees (weekdays, twilight, seniors, juniors), range (grass), credit cards (MC, V), FF.

★ MULBERRY HILLS GOLF CLUB
PU-3530 Noble Rd., Oxford, 48370, Oakland County, (248)628-2808, 40 miles from Detroit. **Web:** www.golf@mulberryhills.com. **Facility Holes:** 18. **Yards:** 6,508/4,713. **Par:** 71/71. **Course Rating:** 70.2/67.1. **Slope:** 118/109. **Green Fee:** $17/$22. **Cart Fee:** $22/Cart. **Walking Policy:** Unrestricted walking. **Walkability:** 3. **Opened:** 1962. **Architect:** Franklin D. Clayton. **Season:** April-Nov. **To obtain tee times:** Call up to 7 days in advance. **Miscellaneous:** Reduced fees (weekdays, twilight, seniors, juniors), range (grass/mats), credit cards (MC, V, AE, D), BF, FF.

★★ MULLENHURST GOLF COURSE
PU-9810 Mullen Rd., Delton, 49046, Barry County, (616)623-8383, 20 miles from Kalamazoo. **Facility Holes:** 18. **Yards:** 5,220/4,545. **Par:** 71/71. **Course Rating:** 64.9/65.4. **Slope:** 112/109. **Green Fee:** $15. **Cart Fee:** $18/Cart. **Walking Policy:** Unrestricted walking. **Walkability:** 2. **Opened:** 1974. **Architect:** Dick Enyard. **Season:** April-Nov. **To obtain tee times:** Call up to 7 days in advance. **Miscellaneous:** Reduced fees (seniors, juniors), range (grass), credit cards (MC, V, D), BF, FF.

★★★ MYSTIC CREEK GOLF CLUB
PU-1 Champions Circle, Milford, 48380, Oakland County, (248)684-3333, 45 miles from Detroit. **E-mail:** rayreypga@aol.com. **Web:** www.mystic-creek.com. **Facility Holes:** 27. **Green Fee:** $48/$58. **Cart Fee:** Included in green fee. **Walking Policy:** Walking at certain times. **Walkability:** 4. **Opened:** 1996. **Architect:** Pat Conroy/Jim Dewling. **Season:** April-Nov. **High:** June-Aug. **To obtain tee times:** Call up to 14 days in advance. **Miscellaneous:** Reduced fees (twilight, seniors, juniors), range (mats), credit cards (MC, V, AE, D), BF, FF.
LAKES/WOODS (18 Combo)
Yards: 6,802/5,800. **Par:** 72/72. **Course Rating:** 72.2/66.7. **Slope:** 130/114.
MEADOWS/LAKES (18 Combo)
Yards: 6,900/5,800. **Par:** 72/72. **Course Rating:** 71.1/65.4. **Slope:** 131/109.
MEADOWS/WOODS (18 Combo)
Yards: 6,900/5,800. **Par:** 72/72. **Course Rating:** 71.5/66.3. **Slope:** 130/116.
Reader Comments: Very scenic, but not very affordable … 3 separate 9s, Lakes course a gem … Better place for weddings than golf … Greens are too hard and need to be manicured

★★★★ THE NATURAL AT BEAVER CREEK RESORT
PU-5004 W. Otsego Lake Dr., Gaylord, 49735, Otsego County, (989)732-1785, (877)646-7529, 75 miles from Traverse City. **E-mail:** bcr@voyager.net. **Web:** www.thenatural.org. **Facility Holes:** 18. **Yards:** 6,350/4,830. **Par:** 71/71. **Course Rating:**

69.3/67.8. **Slope:** 129/118. **Green Fee:** $47/$57. **Cart Fee:** Included in green fee. **Walking Policy:** Walking at certain times. **Walkability:** 4. **Opened:** 1993. **Architect:** Jerry Matthews. **Season:** May-Oct. **High:** June-Aug. **To obtain tee times:** Call golf shop. **Miscellaneous:** Reduced fees (weekdays, guests, twilight), range (grass), lodging (31 rooms), credit cards (MC, V, D), FF.
Reader Comments: Fairways a little rough, nice course for the price ... Best of Gaylord courses, a must play ... Slow play but exciting holes ... One of my favorites in northern Michigan ... Variety.

★★★ NORTH KENT GOLF COURSE
PU-11029 Stout Ave. N.E., Rockford, 49341, Kent County, (616)866-2659, 10 miles from Grand Rapids. **Facility Holes:** 18. **Yards:** 6,326/5,002. **Par:** 70/70. **Course Rating:** 71.1/68.1. **Slope:** 127/117. **Green Fee:** $22/$24. **Cart Fee:** $21/Cart. **Walking Policy:** Unrestricted walking. **Walkability:** 3. **Opened:** 1980. **Architect:** Warner Bowen & Son. **Season:** April-Nov. **High:** June-Sept. **To obtain tee times:** Call up to 7 days in advance. **Miscellaneous:** Reduced fees (weekdays, twilight, seniors, juniors), range (grass), credit cards (MC, V), BF, FF.
Reader Comments: Simple course, great condition ... Really nice greens, close to home for me ... Gets busy ... Good greens, some areas need better watering ... Fun, busy.

NORTH SHORE GOLF CLUB
SP-N 2315 Hwy. M-35, Menominee, 49858, Menominee County, (906)863-8421, 6 miles from Menominee. **E-mail:** nrthshoregolfpro@aol.com. **Facility Holes:** 18. **Yards:** 6,436/5,318. **Par:** 72/71. **Course Rating:** 70.4/70.9. **Slope:** 119/116. **Green Fee:** $25/$30. **Cart Fee:** $25/Cart. **Walking Policy:** Unrestricted walking. **Walkability:** 1. **Opened:** 1926. **Season:** April-Nov. **High:** May-Aug. **To obtain tee times:** Call up to 7 days in advance. **Miscellaneous:** Reduced fees (juniors), range (grass), caddies, credit cards (MC, V, D), BF, FF.

★★ NORTHBROOK GOLF CLUB
PU-21690 27 Mile Rd., Ray Township, 48096, Macomb County, (810)749-3415, (800)477-7756, 6 miles from Shelby Township. **Facility Holes:** 18. **Yards:** 6,352/4,949. **Par:** 72/72. **Course Rating:** 70.3/68.5. **Slope:** 121/114. **Green Fee:** $13/$23. **Cart Fee:** $24/Cart. **Walking Policy:** Unrestricted walking. **Walkability:** 2. **Opened:** 1965. **Season:** March-Nov. **High:** May-Sept. **To obtain tee times:** Call up to 21 days in advance. **Miscellaneous:** Reduced fees (seniors, juniors), credit cards (MC, V), BF, FF.

NORTHVILLE HILLS GOLF CLUB
PU-15565 Bay Hill Dr., Northville, 48167, Wayne County, (734)667-4653, 25 miles from Detroit. **Web:** northvillehills.com. **Facility Holes:** 18. **Yards:** 7,003/4,956. **Par:** 72/72. **Course Rating:** 72.0/69.4. **Slope:** 132/120. **Green Fee:** $50/$75. **Cart Fee:** Included in green fee. **Walking Policy:** Unrestricted walking. **Walkability:** 3. **Opened:** 2000. **Architect:** Arnold Palmer. **Season:** April-Nov. **To obtain tee times:** Call up to 7 days in advance. **Miscellaneous:** Reduced fees (twilight, seniors, juniors), range (grass), credit cards (MC, V, AE), BF, FF.

★★ NORTHWOOD GOLF COURSE
PU-2888 Comstock Ave., Fremont, 49412, Newaygo County, (231)924-3380, 40 miles from Grand Rapids. **Facility Holes:** 18. **Yards:** 6,313/5,608. **Par:** 71/71. **Course Rating:** 69.7/66.1. **Slope:** 115/111. **Green Fee:** $17/$19. **Cart Fee:** $18/Cart. **Walking Policy:** Unrestricted walking. **Walkability:** 2. **Opened:** 1968. **Season:** April-Oct. **High:** July-Aug. **To obtain tee times:** Call golf shop. **Miscellaneous:** Reduced fees (seniors), range (mats), credit cards (MC, V).

★★★½ OAK CREST GOLF COURSE
PU-Highway US 8, Norway, 49870, Dickinson County, (906)563-5891. **Facility Holes:** 18. **Yards:** 6,158/5,430. **Par:** 72/74. **Course Rating:** 69.2/71.0. **Slope:** 120/121. **Green Fee:** $26. **Cart Fee:** $22/Cart. **Walking Policy:** Unrestricted walking. **Walkability:** 2. **Opened:** 1929. **Season:** April-Nov. **To obtain tee times:** Call up to 7 days in advance. **Miscellaneous:** Range (grass), credit cards (MC, V), FF.
Reader Comments: Tight fairways, small greens, lots of oaks ... Pretty ... Tree-lined fairways, requires good shotmaking ... A hidden gem of the far north ... Easy walking, challenging, excellent layout, very enjoyable.

★½ OAK LANE GOLF COURSE
PU-800 North Main St., Webberville, 48892, Ingham County, (517)521-3900, 20 miles from Lansing. **Facility Holes:** 18. **Yards:** 5,714/5,115. **Par:** 70/71. **Course Rating:** 67.3/69.1. **Slope:** 107/115. **Green Fee:** $17/$23. **Cart Fee:** $10/Person. **Walking Policy:** Unrestricted walking. **Walkability:** 3. **Opened:** 1967. **Architect:** Harley Hodges. **Season:** April-Nov. **High:** June-Sept. **To obtain tee times:** Call up to 14 days in advance. **Miscellaneous:** Reduced fees (twilight, seniors, juniors), credit cards (MC, V, D), FF.

MICHIGAN

OAK POINTE
SP-5341 Brighton Rd., Brighton, 48116, Livingston County, (810)227-4541, 25 miles from Detroit. **Facility Holes:** 36. **Cart Fee:** $15/Person. **Walkability:** 3. **Opened:** 1918. **Architect:** A. Aames. **To obtain tee times:** Call golf shop. **Miscellaneous:** Reduced fees (twilight), credit cards (MC, V).
★★★½ **CHAMPIONSHIP COURSE** (18)
Yards: 6,157/5,367. **Par:** 71/71. **Course Rating:** 68.5/69.4. **Slope:** 108/110. **Green Fee:** $27/$32. **Season:** April-Oct. **High:** June-Sept.
Reader Comments: Beautiful layout … Greens were picture-perfect as well were the fairways and tee boxes … Layout remarkable, service great … Good tournament course … Great course.
HONORS COURSE (18)
Yards: 6,540/4,521. **Par:** 71/71. **Course Rating:** 72.5/68.9. **Slope:** 145/126. **Green Fee:** $87. **Season:** April-Nov.

OAK RIDGE GOLF CLUB
PU-35035 26 Mile Rd., New Haven, 48048, Macomb County, (810)749-5151, 20 miles from Detroit. **E-mail:** clubhouse@oakridgegolf.com. **Web:** www.oakridgegolf.com. **Facility Holes:** 36. **Opened:** 1966 **Architect:** Bruce Matthews. **Season:** April-Nov. **High:** April-Sept. **To obtain tee times:** Call up to 7 days in advance. **Miscellaneous:** Reduced fees (weekdays, twilight, seniors, juniors), range (grass), credit cards (MC, V, AE, D).
MARSH OAKS AT OAK RIDGE (18)
Yards: 6,706/4,916. **Par:** 72/72. **Course Rating:** 72.4/68.7. **Slope:** 131/112. **Green Fee:** $50/$60. **Cart Fee:** Included in green fee. **Walking Policy:** Mandatory carts. **Walkability:** 3.
★★½ **OLD OAKS AT OAK RIDGE** (18)
Yards: 6,563/5,427. **Par:** 71/71. **Course Rating:** 71.0/72.6. **Slope:** 119/119. **Green Fee:** $26/$31. **Cart Fee:** $13/Person. **Walking Policy:** Unrestricted walking. **Walkability:** 1.

★★ OAK RIDGE GOLF CLUB
PU-513 W. Pontaluna Rd., Muskegon, 49444, Muskegon County, (231)798-3660, 4 miles from Muskegon. **Facility Holes:** 18. **Yards:** 6,010/5,166. **Par:** 72/73. **Course Rating:** 68.6/71.4. **Slope:** 126/120. **Green Fee:** $23/$24. **Cart Fee:** $22/Cart. **Walking Policy:** Unrestricted walking. **Walkability:** 3. **Opened:** 1930. **Season:** Year-round. **High:** April-Oct. **To obtain tee times:** Call golf shop. **Miscellaneous:** Reduced fees (juniors), range (grass), credit cards (MC, V, AE, D), BF, FF.

★★½ OAKLAND HILLS GOLF CLUB
PU-11619 H Dr. North, Battle Creek, 49014, Calhoun County, (616)965-0809, 6 miles from Battle Creek. **Facility Holes:** 18. **Yards:** 6,327/5,517. **Par:** 72/72. **Course Rating:** 71.5/73.3. **Green Fee:** $18/$19. **Cart Fee:** $20/Cart. **Walking Policy:** Unrestricted walking. **Walkability:** 3. **Opened:** 1973. **Architect:** George V. Nickolaou. **Season:** March-Nov. **High:** May-Aug. **To obtain tee times:** Call up to 1 day in advance. **Miscellaneous:** Reduced fees (weekdays, seniors), credit cards (MC, V, AE).

OAKLAND UNIVERSITY GOLF & LEARNING CENTER
SP-Oakland Univ Golf & Learning Center, Rochester, 48309, Oakland County, (218)370-4150, 20 miles from Detroit. **Web:** ongolf.com. **Facility Holes:** 36. **Green Fee:** $60/$65. **Cart Fee:** Included in green fee. **Walking Policy:** Mandatory carts. **Walkability:** 4. **Season:** April-Nov. **High:** May-Sept. **To obtain tee times:** Call up to 7 days in advance. **Miscellaneous:** Reduced fees (weekdays), range (grass/mats), credit cards (MC, V), BF, FF.
KATKE-COUSINS COURSE (18)
Yards: 7,109/5,047. **Par:** 72/72. **Course Rating:** 75.0/68.5. **Slope:** 138/122. **Opened:** 1977. **Architect:** Bob Beard/Bill Newcomb.
R & S SHARF COURSE (18)
Yards: 7,103/5,155. **Par:** 72/72. **Course Rating:** 73.8/64.5. **Slope:** 130/105. **Opened:** 2000. **Architect:** Rick Smith/Warren Henderson.

★★½ THE OAKS GOLF CLUB
PU-3711 Niles Rd., St. Joseph, 49085, Berrien County, (616)429-8411, 5 miles from St. Joseph. **Facility Holes:** 18. **Yards:** 6,776/5,860. **Par:** 72/74. **Course Rating:** 71.0/74.4. **Slope:** 126/130. **Green Fee:** $21/$29. **Cart Fee:** $13/Person. **Walking Policy:** Walking at certain times. **Walkability:** 2. **Opened:** 1986. **Season:** April-Nov. **High:** June-Aug. **To obtain tee times:** Call golf shop. **Miscellaneous:** Reduced fees (weekdays, twilight, seniors, juniors), range (grass), credit cards (MC, V, AE), BF, FF.

★★★ OCEANA GOLF CLUB
PU-3333 W. Weaver Rd., Shelby, 49455, Oceana County, (231)861-4211, 25 miles from Muskegon. **E-mail:** mringlis@voyager.net. **Web:** www.westmichgolf.com/courses/oceana.htm.

Facility Holes: 18. **Yards:** 6,288/5,103. **Par:** 73/73. **Course Rating:** 71.0/71.8. **Slope:** 121/123. **Green Fee:** $19. **Cart Fee:** $13/Person. **Walking Policy:** Unrestricted walking. **Walkability:** 3. **Opened:** 1962. **Architect:** Designed by members. **Season:** April-Oct. **High:** June-Sept. **To obtain tee times:** Call golf shop. **Miscellaneous:** Reduced fees (weekdays, juniors), range (grass/mats), credit cards (MC, V), BF, FF.

Reader Comments: Short course with a back-and-forth layout on most of the back 9 … Fast, sloping greens give the course its teeth … Some greens with extreme angles … Nice old layout, fast greens, nice views … Par 73.

★★★ OLD CHANNEL TRAIL GOLF CLUB
PU-8325 N. Old Channel Trail, Montague, 49437, Muskegon County, (231)894-5076, 20 miles from Muskegon. **E-mail:** pro@octgolf.com. **Web:** www.octgolf.com. **Facility Holes:** 30. **Green Fee:** $18/$24. **Cart Fee:** $13/Person. **Walking Policy:** Unrestricted walking. **Opened:** 1927. **Architect:** R.B. Harris/B. Matthews/J. Matthews. **Season:** April-Nov. **High:** July-Aug. **To obtain tee times:** Call up to 7 days in advance. **Miscellaneous:** Reduced fees (weekdays, twilight, seniors, juniors), range (grass), credit cards (MC, V), BF, FF.

VALLEY/MEADOWS COURSE (18 Combo)
Yards: 6,703/4,901. **Par:** 72/72. **Course Rating:** 70.1/68.7. **Slope:** 121/115. **Walkability:** 3.
WOODS/MEADOWS COURSE (18 Combo)
Yards: 6,542/5,045. **Par:** 71/71. **Course Rating:** 70.1/68.9. **Slope:** 120/120. **Walkability:** 3.
WOODS/VALLEY COURSE (18 Combo)
Yards: 6,605/5,004. **Par:** 71/71. **Course Rating:** 70.4/69.6. **Slope:** 125/116. **Walkability:** 4.

Reader Comments: Original 9 a classic … Very short, but kept up well, pricey … Nice mix of old & new style holes.
Special Notes: Also has a 3-hole practice facility.

★★ OLDE MILL GOLF CLUB
SP-6101 West XY Ave., Schoolcraft, 49087, Kalamazoo County, (616)679-5625, 13 miles from Kalamazoo. **Facility Holes:** 18. **Yards:** 6,195/5,139. **Par:** 72/72. **Course Rating:** 69.2/68.4. **Slope:** 117/114. **Green Fee:** $18/$30. **Cart Fee:** $20/Cart. **Walking Policy:** Unrestricted walking. **Walkability:** 3. **Opened:** 1968. **Season:** March-Nov. **High:** June-Sept. **To obtain tee times:** Call golf shop. **Miscellaneous:** Reduced fees (weekdays, twilight, seniors, juniors), range (grass), credit cards (MC, V, D).

★★½ ORCHARD HILLS GOLF COURSE
PU-714 125th Ave., Shelbyville, 49344, Allegan County, (616)672-7096, (866)672-7096, 20 miles from Grand Rapids. **Facility Holes:** 27. **Yards:** 6,000/5,200. **Par:** 72/74. **Course Rating:** 68.6/68.3. **Slope:** 116/116. **Green Fee:** $16/$23. **Cart Fee:** $12/Person. **Walking Policy:** Unrestricted walking. **Walkability:** 3. **Opened:** 1955. **Architect:** Art Young. **Season:** April-Oct. **High:** May-Aug. **To obtain tee times:** Call up to 14 days in advance. **Miscellaneous:** Reduced fees (weekdays, seniors, juniors), range (grass), credit cards (MC, V, AE, D), BF, FF.
Special Notes: Also has a 9-hole East course.

★★★★½ THE ORCHARDS GOLF CLUB *Service, Condition*
PU-62900 Campground Rd., Washington, 48094, Macomb County, (810)786-7200, 30 miles from Detroit. **E-mail:** jdstalcup@orchards.com. **Facility Holes:** 18. **Yards:** 7,036/5,158. **Par:** 72/72. **Course Rating:** 74.5/70.3. **Slope:** 136/123. **Green Fee:** $35/$75. **Cart Fee:** Included in green fee. **Walking Policy:** Unrestricted walking. **Walkability:** 3. **Opened:** 1993. **Architect:** Robert Trent Jones Jr. **Season:** March-Nov. **High:** May-Sept. **To obtain tee times:** Call up to 30 days in advance. **Miscellaneous:** Reduced fees (weekdays, twilight), metal spikes, range (grass), credit cards (MC, V, AE, D), BF, FF.

Reader Comments: Very well run, always in great condition … Best course in Detroit area … New course, greens in excellent shape … Beautiful, just beautiful … One of the best in lower Michigan … A favorite … Excellent layout … Public course as close to private as it gets … Too expensive, but fine.

OTSEGO CLUB
R-696 M-32 East Gaylord, Gaylord, 49735, Otsego County, (989)732-5181, (800)752-5510, 60 miles from Traverse City. **Web:** www.otsegoclub.com. **Facility Holes:** 72. **Cart Fee:** Included in green fee. **Season:** May-Nov. **High:** July-Aug. **To obtain tee times:** Call up to 120 days in advance. **Miscellaneous:** Reduced fees (weekdays, guests, twilight), range (grass), lodging (100 rooms), credit cards (MC, V, AE, D), BF, FF.

★★★ THE CLASSIC (18)
Yards: 6,305/5,591. **Par:** 72/71. **Course Rating:** 69.8/71.5. **Slope:** 121/113. **Green Fee:** $32/$64. **Walking Policy:** Walking at certain times. **Walkability:** 2. **Opened:** 1958. **Architect:** William H. Diddel.

Reader Comments: We enjoyed a 3-day, 54-hole blowout … Resort course, no trouble … Rolling hills, nice greens, views … Totally different front to back … Old, wide open layout … Good value.

MICHIGAN

★★★½ **THE LAKE** (18)
Yards: 6,310/4,952. **Par:** 71/71. **Course Rating:** 71.0/68.5. **Slope:** 136/122. **Green Fee:** $32/$64. **Walking Policy:** Walking at certain times. **Walkability:** 3. **Opened:** 1988. **Architect:** Jerry Matthews.
Reader Comments: Good value … Tough course … Great courses, northern Michigan at its best … Very pretty … Great value, great challenge … Plenty of trees and water.
★★★★ **THE LOON** (18)
Yards: 6,701/5,123. **Par:** 71/71. **Course Rating:** 72.7/71.1. **Slope:** 128/121. **Green Fee:** $37/$84. **Walking Policy:** Walking at certain times. **Walkability:** 2. **Opened:** 1994. **Architect:** Mike Husby.
Reader Comments: Good layout … A couple of gimmick holes … Good value … Beautiful clubhouse, challenging course … Greens inconsistent … Great course, northern Michigan at its best.
THE TRIBUTE (18)
Yards: 7,347/5,085. **Par:** 72/72. **Green Fee:** $105. **Walking Policy:** Mandatory carts. **Walkability:** 4. **Opened:** 2001. **Architect:** Gary Koch.

★★ **OXFORD HILLS GOLF CLUB**
PU-300 E. Drahner Rd., Oxford, 48371, Oakland County, (248)628-2518, 8 miles from Pontiac. **Facility Holes:** 18. **Yards:** 6,528/5,315. **Par:** 72/72. **Course Rating:** 71.5/70.4. **Slope:** 125/114. **Green Fee:** $15/$28. **Cart Fee:** $12/Person. **Walking Policy:** Unrestricted walking. **Walkability:** 2. **Opened:** 1964. **Architect:** John Hubbard. **Season:** April-Nov. **To obtain tee times:** Call up to 30 days in advance. **Miscellaneous:** Reduced fees (weekdays, seniors), metal spikes, credit cards (MC, V, AE), BF, FF.

★★ **PALMER PARK GOLF COURSE**
PU-19013 Woodward Avenue, Detroit, 48203, Wayne County, (313)883-2525. **Facility Holes:** 18. **Yards:** 6,081/5,351. **Par:** 71/71. **Course Rating:** 67.8. **Slope:** 104. **Green Fee:** $18/$20. **Cart Fee:** $24/Cart. **To obtain tee times:** Call golf shop. **Miscellaneous:** Metal spikes.

PARK SHORE GOLF COURSE
PU-610 Park Shore Dr., Cassopolis, 49031, Cass County, (616)445-2834, 25 miles from South Bend. **Facility Holes:** 18. **Yards:** 4,981/4,981. **Par:** 68/70. **Course Rating:** 62.8/63.4. **Slope:** 97/90. **Green Fee:** $12/$18. **Cart Fee:** $20/Cart. **Walking Policy:** Unrestricted walking. **Walkability:** 2. **Opened:** 1928. **Architect:** C. D. Wagstaff. **Season:** April-Oct. **High:** June-Sept. **To obtain tee times:** Call golf shop. **Miscellaneous:** Reduced fees (Twilight, seniors), BF, FF.

PARTRIDGE CREEK GOLF COURSE
PU-43843 Romeo Plank Rd., Clinton Township, 48038, Macomb County, (810)228-3030, 29 miles from Detroit. **Web:** www.partridgecreek.com. **Facility Holes:** 45. **Season:** March-Nov. **High:** May-Aug. **To obtain tee times:** Call golf shop. **Miscellaneous:** Reduced fees (twilight, seniors, juniors), range (grass), credit cards (MC, V, AE), BF, FF.
★★★ **THE HAWK** (18)
Yards: 7,024/5,366. **Par:** 72/72. **Course Rating:** 73.6/70.6. **Slope:** 132/123. **Green Fee:** $40/$60. **Cart Fee:** Included in green fee. **Walking Policy:** Mandatory carts. **Walkability:** 3. **Opened:** 1996. **Architect:** Jerry Matthews.
Reader Comments: Built in a low flood plain, some holes are unplayable after a wet spell … Greens are good, some excellent holes … Course was redone, very nice … Good layout, a little tricky the first time … A good solid course.
★★½ **NORTH/SOUTH/WEST COURSE** (27)
Green Fee: $21/$23. **Cart Fee:** $13/Person. **Walking Policy:** Unrestricted walking. **Walkability:** 2. **Opened:** 1960. **Architect:** Kenny Nieman.
(NORTH/SOUTH) (18 Combo) **Yards:** 6,455/5,165. **Par:** 72/72. **Course Rating:** 70.0/69.0. **Slope:** 114/114.
(NORTH/WEST) (18 Combo)
Yards: 6,439/5,220. **Par:** 72/72. **Course Rating:** 70.0/69.0. **Slope:** 114/114.
(SOUTH/WEST) (18 Combo)
Yards: 6,706/5,225. **Par:** 72/72. **Course Rating:** 70.0/69.0. **Slope:** 114/114.

★★ **PAW PAW LAKE GOLF COURSE**
PU-4548 Forest Beach Rd., Watervliet, 49098, Berrien County, (616)463-3831, 10 miles from Benton Harbor. **Facility Holes:** 18. **Yards:** 6,055/4,382. **Par:** 70/75. **Course Rating:** 68.9/67.4. **Green Fee:** $20/$25. **Cart Fee:** $11/Person. **Walking Policy:** Unrestricted walking. **Walkability:** 3. **Opened:** 1928. **Season:** April-Nov. **High:** June-Aug. **To obtain tee times:** Call up to 7 days in advance. **Miscellaneous:** Reduced fees (weekdays, twilight), credit cards (MC, V), BF, FF.

★★ **PEBBLE CREEK GOLF COURSE**
PU-20495 Currie Rd., South Lyon, 48178, Oakland County, (248)437-5411, 35 miles from Detroit. **Facility Holes:** 18. **Yards:** 6,110/4,781. **Par:** 72/72. **Course Rating:** 68.7. **Slope:** 107. **Green Fee:** $23/$27. **Cart Fee:** $12/Person. **Walking Policy:** Unrestricted walking. **Walkability:**

3. **Opened:** 1978. **Architect:** Don Geake. **Season:** April-Nov. **High:** May-Aug. **To obtain tee times:** Call up to 7 days in advance. **Miscellaneous:** Reduced fees (weekdays, seniors, juniors), credit cards (MC, V, AE, D), FF.

★★ **PEBBLEWOOD COUNTRY CLUB**
PU-9794 Jericho Rd., Bridgman, 49106, Berrien County, (616)465-5611, 35 miles from South Bend. **Facility Holes:** 18. **Yards:** 5,421/4,636. **Par:** 68/70. **Course Rating:** 65.6/65.6. **Slope:** 106/106. **Green Fee:** $18/$20. **Cart Fee:** $18/Cart. **Walking Policy:** Unrestricted walking. **Walkability:** 1. **Opened:** 1923. **Season:** March-Nov. **High:** May-Aug. **To obtain tee times:** Call golf shop. **Miscellaneous:** Credit cards (MC, V, AE, D), BF, FF.

★★★½ **PHEASANT RUN GOLF CLUB**
PU-46500 Summit Pkwy., Canton, 48188, Wayne County, 734)397-6460, 15 miles from Detroit. **Facility Holes:** 18. **Yards:** 7,001/5,143. **Par:** 72/72. **Course Rating:** 73.3/69.1. **Slope:** 142/117. **Green Fee:** $40/$60. **Cart Fee:** Included in green fee. **Walking Policy:** Mandatory carts. **Walkability:** 3. **Opened:** 1995. **Architect:** Arthur Hills/Steve Forrest. **Season:** April-Nov. **High:** May-Sept. **To obtain tee times:** Call up to 14 days in advance. **Miscellaneous:** Reduced fees (twilight), range (grass/mats), credit cards (MC, V, AE), BF, FF.
Reader Comments: Beautiful surroundings but new homes ... Very nice layout, bad location ... A user-friendly course within a housing community.

★★★★ **PIERCE LAKE GOLF COURSE** *Value*
PU-1175 South Main St., Chelsea, 48118, Washtenaw County, (734)475-5858, 15 miles from Ann Arbor. **Facility Holes:** 18. **Yards:** 6,874/4,772. **Par:** 72/72. **Course Rating:** 72.5/67.4. **Slope:** 135/109. **Green Fee:** $21/$27. **Cart Fee:** $11/Person. **Walking Policy:** Unrestricted walking. **Walkability:** 4. **Opened:** 1996. **Architect:** Harry Bowers. **Season:** March-Nov. **High:** April-Sept. **To obtain tee times:** Call up to 7 days in advance. **Miscellaneous:** Reduced fees (weekdays, twilight, seniors, juniors), credit cards (MC, V).
Reader Comments: Best muni in the state ... Beautiful ... Great country course, great condition ... Nice county-owned course ... Wish it were closer to home ... Lots of deer, tough back 9 ... Excellent fairways, well kept.

★½ **PIERCE PARK GOLF COURSE**
PU-2302 Brookside, Flint, 48503, Genesee County, (810)766-7297. **Facility Holes:** 18. **Yards:** 2,354/1,202. **Par:** 54/54. **Green Fee:** $14. **Cart Fee:** $15/Cart. **Walking Policy:** Unrestricted walking. **Opened:** 1964. **Architect:** Arnold Trusdale. **Season:** April-Nov. **To obtain tee times:** Call golf shop. **Miscellaneous:** Reduced fees (seniors, juniors), metal spikes.

★★★★½ **PILGRIM'S RUN GOLF CLUB** *Service, Value, Condition, Pace*
PU-11401 Newcosta Ave., Pierson, 49339, Newaygo County, (888)533-7742, (888)533-7742, 22 miles from Grand Rapids. **E-mail:** JOMalley@pilgrimsrun.com. **Web:** www.pilgrimsrun.com. **Facility Holes:** 18. **Yards:** 7,078/4,863. **Par:** 73/73. **Course Rating:** 74.1/67.7. **Slope:** 137/116. **Green Fee:** $39/$49. **Cart Fee:** $10/Person. **Walking Policy:** Unrestricted walking. **Walkability:** 4. **Opened:** 1998. **Architect:** Kris Shumaker/Mike DeVries. **Season:** April-Dec. **High:** June-Sept. **To obtain tee times:** Call up to 7 days in advance. **Miscellaneous:** Reduced fees (weekdays, twilight, seniors, juniors), metal spikes, range (grass/mats), credit cards (MC, V, AE, D, DC), BF, FF.
Notes: Ranked 4th in 1999 Best New Affordable Public.
Reader Comments: Worth the trip to get there ... Good course reasonably priced ... Very nice condition, especially like front-9 layout ... Great design, memorable holes ... Excellent course carved through rolling terrain and woods, good value ... Wooded course, challenging ... Exceptional ... Great course.

★★★ **PINE HOLLOW GOLF CLUB**
PU-5400 Trailer Park Dr., Jackson, 49201, Jackson County, (517)764-4200, 20 miles from Lansing & Ann Arbor. **Facility Holes:** 18. **Yards:** 6,170/4,405. **Par:** 72/72. **Course Rating:** 69.7. **Green Fee:** $15/$18. **Cart Fee:** $18/Cart. **Walking Policy:** Unrestricted walking. **Walkability:** 3. **Opened:** 1984. **Architect:** Morris Wilson. **Season:** March-Nov. **High:** June-Sept. **To obtain tee times:** Call golf shop. **Miscellaneous:** Reduced fees (weekdays, twilight, seniors, juniors), metal spikes, credit cards (MC, V, AE), BF, FF.
Reader Comments: Narrow, tree-lined fairways ... Nice people, surprising quality for the price ... Pretty little course, can score well ... Tight ... Leave your driver at home ... Scenic and low priced.
Special Notes: Formerly Gracewil Pines Golf Club.

★★★½ **PINE KNOB GOLF CLUB**
PU-5580 Waldon Rd., Clarkston, 48348, Oakland County, (248)625-4430, 9 miles from Pontiac. **Facility Holes:** 27. **Green Fee:** $45/$58. **Cart Fee:** Included in green fee. **Walkability:** 5. **Opened:** 1972. **Architect:** Leo Bishop/Lori Viola. **Season:** April-Oct. **High:** June-Sept. **To obtain tee times:** Call golf shop. **Miscellaneous:** Reduced fees (seniors), range (grass/mats),

credit cards (MC, V, AE, D).
FALCON/EAGLE (18 Combo)
Yards: 6,471/4,941. **Par:** 70/69. **Course Rating:** 71.3/67.8. **Slope:** 130/114.
HAWK/EAGLE (18 Combo)
Yards: 6,421/4,798. **Par:** 71/70. **Course Rating:** 70.9/69.3. **Slope:** 131/116. **Walking Policy:**
Mandatory cart.
HAWK/FALCON (18 Combo)
Yards: 6,662/4,969. **Par:** 71/71. **Course Rating:** 72.2/69.1. **Slope:** 126/115.
Reader Comments: Big greens, if you miss them, you are having a bad day … Very enjoyable
course, something for everyone … Very nice layout, No. 10 is a pretty hole.

★★★ PINE RIVER GOLF CLUB
PU-2244 Pine River Rd., Standish, 48658, Arenac County, (517)846-6819, (877)474-6374,
30 miles from Bay City. **Facility Holes:** 18. **Yards:** 6,250/5,156. **Par:** 71/74. **Course Rating:**
70.8/70.7. **Slope:** 126/126. **Green Fee:** $18/$22. **Cart Fee:** $11/Person. **Walking Policy:**
Unrestricted walking. **Walkability:** 3. **Opened:** 1966. **Architect:** Bruce Matthews/Jerry
Matthews. **Season:** April-Oct. **High:** June-Aug. **To obtain tee times:** Call golf shop.
Miscellaneous: Reduced fees (weekdays, seniors, juniors), range, credit cards (MC, V).
Reader Comments: Tough, tight back 9 … Great for average golfer … Still a great value …
Challenging … 2 totally different 9s … Holes nicely kept, great value for metro area, staff was excel-
lent … Reasonably priced.

★★★½ PINE TRACE GOLF CLUB
PU-3600 Pine Trace Blvd., Rochester Hills, 48309, Oakland County, (248)852-7100,
30 miles from Detroit. **Web:** www.pinetracegolf.com. **Facility Holes:** 18. **Yards:** 6,610/4,974.
Par: 72/72. **Course Rating:** 72.8/69.9. **Slope:** 139/125. **Green Fee:** $50/$65. **Cart Fee:**
Included in green fee. **Walking Policy:** Walking at certain times. **Walkability:** 3. **Opened:**
1989. **Architect:** Arthur Hills. **Season:** March-Dec. **To obtain tee times:** Call up to 7 days in
advance. **Miscellaneous:** Reduced fees (seniors, juniors), range (mats), credit cards (MC, V),
BF, FF.
Reader Comments: Lot of blind shots, course tough & unforgiving … Great public course for the
area, great pace of play, holes are spaced far apart … Very fast play … They keep play moving.

★★★½ PINE VALLEY GOLF CLUB
PU-16801 31 Mile Rd., Ray, 48096, Macomb County, (810)752-9633, 12 miles from Mt.
Clemens. **Facility Holes:** 27. **Green Fee:** $30/$40. **Cart Fee:** $20/Cart. **Walking Policy:** Walking
at certain times. **Walkability:** 2. **Opened:** 1968. **Architect:** Otis McKinley. **Season:** April-Nov.
High: May-Sept. **To obtain tee times:** Call golf shop. **Miscellaneous:** Reduced fees (weekdays,
twilight, seniors), metal spikes, range (grass/mats), credit cards (MC, V).
BLUE/GOLD (18 Combo)
Yards: 6,021/4,971. **Par:** 72/70. **Course Rating:** 68.3/64.5. **Slope:** 114/100.
RED/BLUE (18 Combo)
Yards: 6,209/5,102. **Par:** 72/72. **Course Rating:** 69.0/65.6. **Slope:** 118/106.
RED/GOLD (18 Combo)
Yards: 6,490/5,208. **Par:** 72/70. **Course Rating:** 69.0/64.7. **Slope:** 110/103.
Reader Comments: Good open valley setting … Nice shape, always fun to play … Good condi-
tions, fun to play … Nice layout … Best public course in the area.

★★½ PINE VIEW GOLF CLUB
PU-5820 Stoney Creek Rd., Ypsilanti, 48197, Washtenaw County, (734)481-0500,
(800)214-5963, 3 miles from Ypsilanti. **E-mail:** info@pineviewgc.com. **Web:**
www.pineviewgc.com. **Facility Holes:** 27. **Yards:** 6,533/5,267. **Par:** 72/72. **Course Rating:**
71.3/70.7. **Slope:** 124/119. **Green Fee:** $15/$33. **Cart Fee:** $14/Person. **Walking Policy:**
Unrestricted walking. **Walkability:** 3. **Opened:** 1990. **Architect:** Harley Hodges/Greg Hodges.
Season: March-Dec. **High:** May-Sept. **To obtain tee times:** Call golf shop. **Miscellaneous:**
Reduced fees (weekdays, twilight, seniors, juniors), range, credit cards (MC, V, AE), BF, FF.
Special Notes: Also has a 9-hole executive course.

★★★★ PINECROFT PLANTATION *Value+, Pace*
PU-8260 Henry Rd., Benzonia, 49617, Benzie County, (231)882-9100, 30 miles from
Traverse City. **E-mail:** estone@coslink.net. **Web:** www.pinecroftgolf.com. **Facility Holes:** 18.
Yards: 6,447/4,975. **Par:** 72/72. **Course Rating:** 70.9/68.5. **Slope:** 124/118. **Green Fee:**
$18/$32. **Cart Fee:** $10/Person. **Walking Policy:** Unrestricted walking. **Walkability:** 4. **Opened:**
1992. **Architect:** L. Stone/A. Normal/J. Cole/C. Carlson. **Season:** April-Oct. **High:** June-Aug. **To
obtain tee times:** Call golf shop. **Miscellaneous:** Reduced fees (twilight), range (grass), credit
cards (MC, V), BF, FF.
Reader Comments: Old-time layout … Great views … Nice people … Great value, a must play for
the money … Views of Crystal Lake … Great views, fun for all levels.

★★★ THE PINES GOLF COURSE
PU-7231 Clubhouse Dr., Weidman, 48893, Isabella County, (989)644-2300, (800)741-3435, 15 miles from Mt. Pleasant. **Web:** www.thepinesgolfcourse.com. **Facility Holes:** 18. **Yards:** 6,856/5,092. **Par:** 72/72. **Course Rating:** 72.9/69.6. **Slope:** 132/123. **Green Fee:** $26/$31. **Cart Fee:** $14/Person. **Walking Policy:** Unrestricted walking. **Walkability:** 2. **Opened:** 1969. **Architect:** Bruce Matthews. **Season:** April-Oct. **Tee times:** Call up to 365 days in advance. **Miscellaneous:** Reduced fees (weekdays), range (grass), credit cards (MC, V, D), BF, FF. **Reader Comments:** Nice course, some holes not made for left handers on front 9 ... Deceiving difficulty ... Plays tough in the wind ... One of the first places to open.

★½ THE PINES GOLF COURSE
PU-5050 Byron Center Ave., Wyoming, 49509, Kent County, (616)538-8380, 12 miles from Grand Rapids. **E-mail:** info@pinesgolfcourse.com. **Facility Holes:** 18. **Yards:** 5,542/5,124. **Par:** 70/72. **Course Rating:** 67.3. **Slope:** 110. **Green Fee:** $12/$23. **Cart Fee:** $24/Cart. **Walking Policy:** Unrestricted walking. **Walkability:** 2. **Opened:** 1967. **Architect:** Bill Austhof. **Season:** March-Dec. **To obtain tee times:** Call golf shop. **Miscellaneous:** Reduced fees (weekdays, seniors, juniors), metal spikes, range (grass), credit cards (MC, V, D), BF, FF.

★½ PIPESTONE CREEK GOLF COURSE
PU-6768 Naomi Rd., Eau Claire, 49111, Berrien County, (616)944-1611, 10 miles from Benton Harbor. **Facility Holes:** 18. **Yards:** 4,402/4,188. **Par:** 67/68. **Green Fee:** $17/$20. **Cart Fee:** $22/Cart. **Walking Policy:** Unrestricted walking. **Walkability:** 2. **Opened:** 1957. **Architect:** Bruce Dustin. **Season:** March-Nov. **High:** May-Sept. **To obtain tee times:** Call golf shop. **Miscellaneous:** Credit cards (MC, V), FF.

★★ PLEASANT HILLS GOLF CLUB
PU-4452 E. Millbrook Rd., Mt. Pleasant, 48858, Isabella County, (989)772-0487, 50 miles from Saginaw. **Facility Holes:** 18. **Yards:** 6,012/4,607. **Par:** 72/72. **Course Rating:** 68.2/65.9. **Slope:** 110/107. **Green Fee:** $18/$20. **Cart Fee:** $20/Cart. **Walking Policy:** Unrestricted walking. **Walkability:** 2. **Opened:** 1964. **Architect:** Richard Krauss Sr. **Season:** March-Nov. **High:** May-Sept. **To obtain tee times:** Call golf shop. **Miscellaneous:** Reduced fees (weekdays, twilight, seniors, juniors), credit cards (MC, V, D), BF, FF.

★★½ PLUM BROOK GOLF CLUB
PU-13390 Plum Brook Dr., Sterling Heights, 48312, Macomb County, (810)264-9411, 10 miles from Detroit. **Facility Holes:** 18. **Yards:** 6,300/5,500. **Par:** 71/71. **Course Rating:** 68.5/68.5. **Slope:** 115/117. **Green Fee:** $22/$26. **Cart Fee:** $22/Cart. **Walking Policy:** Unrestricted walking. **Walkability:** 2. **Opened:** 1927. **Architect:** William Beaupre. **Season:** March-Dec. **To obtain tee times:** Call golf shop. **Miscellaneous:** Reduced fees (weekdays, twilight, juniors), credit cards (MC, V), BF, FF.

★★★½ POHLCAT GOLF COURSE
R-6595 E. Airport Rd., Mt. Pleasant, 48858, Isabella County, (517)773-4221, (800)292-8891, 60 miles from Lansing. **E-mail:** pohlcat82@hotmail.com. **Web:** www.pohlcat.net. **Facility Holes:** 18. **Yards:** 6,810/5,140. **Par:** 72/72. **Course Rating:** 74.2/70.8. **Slope:** 139/124. **Green Fee:** $29/$69. **Cart Fee:** Included in green fee. **Walking Policy:** Walking at certain times. **Walkability:** 3. **Opened:** 1991. **Architect:** Dan Pohl. **Season:** April-Nov. **High:** June-Oct. **To obtain tee times:** Call up to 30 days in advance. **Miscellaneous:** Reduced fees (weekdays, guests, twilight, seniors, juniors), range (grass/mats), credit cards (MC, V, AE, D), BF, FF. **Reader Comments:** Very secluded & peaceful ... Not too tough, not too easy ... Overpriced ... Excellent course, will go back ... Pricey but very nice.

★★ PONTIAC COUNTRY CLUB
SP-4335 Elizabeth Lake Rd, Waterford, 48328, Oakland County, (248)682-6333, 3 miles from Pontiac. **Facility Holes:** 18. **Yards:** 6,366/5,552. **Par:** 72/74. **Course Rating:** 70.4/71.6. **Slope:** 125. **Green Fee:** $25/$34. **Cart Fee:** $24/Cart. **Walking Policy:** Unrestricted walking. **Walkability:** 2. **Opened:** 1914. **Season:** Year-round. **High:** April-Nov. **To obtain tee times:** Call up to 7 days in advance. **Miscellaneous:** Range (grass), credit cards (MC, V, AE, F), FF.

★★½ PONTIAC MUNICIPAL GOLF COURSE
PU-800 Golf Dr., Pontiac, 48341, Oakland County, (248)858-8990, 30 miles from Detroit. **Facility Holes:** 18. **Yards:** 5,571/4,320. **Par:** 70/70. **Course Rating:** 65.1/63.5. **Slope:** 107/103. **Green Fee:** $19/$24. **Cart Fee:** $24/Cart. **Walking Policy:** Walking at certain times. **Walkability:** 3. **Opened:** 1995. **Architect:** Michael Hurdzan. **Season:** April-Nov. **High:** May-Aug. **To obtain tee times:** Call up to 3 days in advance. **Miscellaneous:** Reduced fees (weekdays, twilight, seniors, juniors), credit cards (MC, V), BF, FF.

★★½ PORTAGE LAKE GOLF COURSE
PU-Michigan Tech. Univ., US 41, Houghton, 49931, Houghton County, (906)487-2641, 200 miles from Green Bay, WI. **Facility Holes:** 18. **Yards:** 6,266/5,297. **Par:** 72/72. **Course Rating:** 69.2/69.8. **Slope:** 115/113. **Green Fee:** $26. **Cart Fee:** $20/Cart. **Walking Policy:** Unrestricted walking. **Walkability:** 3. **Opened:** 1902. **Season:** May-Oct. **High:** July-Aug. **To obtain tee times:** Call golf shop. **Miscellaneous:** Range (/), credit cards (MC, V, D).

★★ PRAIRIE CREEK GOLF COURSE
PU-800 E. Webb Dr., De Witt, 48820, Clinton County, (517)669-1958, 8 miles from Lansing. **Facility Holes:** 18. **Yards:** 6,165/5,171. **Par:** 72/72. **Green Fee:** $10/$18. **Cart Fee:** $10/Person. **Walking Policy:** Unrestricted walking. **Walkability:** 3. **Opened:** 1979. **Season:** April-Nov. **To obtain tee times:** Call golf shop. **Miscellaneous:** Reduced fees (weekdays, twilight, seniors, juniors), BF, FF.

★★ PRAIRIEWOOD GOLF COURSE
PU-315 Prairiewood Dr., Otsego, 49078, Allegan County, (616)694-6633, 14 miles from Kalamazoo. **Facility Holes:** 18. **Yards:** 6,519/4,705. **Par:** 72/72. **Course Rating:** 70.4/66.2. **Slope:** 114/106. **Green Fee:** $16/$20. **Cart Fee:** $10/Person. **Walking Policy:** Unrestricted walking. **Walkability:** 1. **Opened:** 1990. **Architect:** Warner Bowen. **Season:** April-Nov. **High:** June-Aug. **To obtain tee times:** Call golf shop. **Miscellaneous:** Reduced fees (weekdays, seniors, juniors), range (grass/mats), credit cards (MC, V, D).

QUAIL RIDGE GOLF CLUB
PU-8375 36th St. S.E., Ada, 49301, Kent County, (616)676-2000, 15 miles from Grand Rapids. **Facility Holes:** 18. **Yards:** 6,883/4,709. **Par:** 72/72. **Course Rating:** 72.5/66.5. **Slope:** 127/109. **Green Fee:** $35/$55. **Cart Fee:** Included in green fee. **Walking Policy:** Mandatory carts. **Walkability:** 3. **Opened:** 1999. **Architect:** Ray Hearn. **Season:** March-Nov. **High:** June-Oct. **To obtain tee times:** Call up to 14 days in advance. **Miscellaneous:** Reduced fees (weekdays, twilight, seniors, juniors), range (grass), credit cards (MC, V, AE), BF, FF.

★★★½ THE QUEST GOLF CLUB
R-116 Questview Dr., Houghton Lake, 48629, Roscommon County, (517)422-4516, 115 miles from Lansing. **Facility Holes:** 18. **Yards:** 6,773/5,027. **Par:** 72/72. **Course Rating:** 72.0/69.4. **Slope:** 130/117. **Green Fee:** $48/$52. **Cart Fee:** Included in green fee. **Walking Policy:** Walking at certain times. **Walkability:** 2. **Opened:** 1994. **Architect:** Ken Green/John Sanford. **Season:** Feb.-Nov. **To obtain tee times:** Call golf shop. **Miscellaneous:** Reduced fees (weekdays, twilight, seniors, juniors), range (grass), credit cards (MC, V), BF, FF.
Reader Comments: Accomodating staff, good mix of dogleg and straight holes … Fairly good course including condition … Excellent value… Great course for as little play as it gets … Better than I had heard, I'll go back.

★★½ RACKHAM GOLF CLUB
PU-10100 W. Ten Mile Rd., Huntington Woods, 48070, Oakland County, (248)543-4040, 15 miles from Detroit. **E-mail:** rackhamgc@yahoo.com. **Facility Holes:** 18. **Yards:** 6,501/5,413. **Par:** 71/72. **Course Rating:** 71.1/70.7. **Slope:** 118/115. **Green Fee:** $24/$30. **Cart Fee:** $14/Person. **Walking Policy:** Unrestricted walking. **Walkability:** 2. **Opened:** 1924. **Architect:** Donald Ross. **Season:** Year-round. **High:** April-Oct. **To obtain tee times:** Call up to 7 days in advance. **Miscellaneous:** Reduced fees (weekdays, twilight, seniors, juniors), credit cards (MC, V, AE, D, DC), BF, FF.

RAISIN RIVER COUNTRY CLUB
PU-1500 N. Dixie Hwy., Monroe, 48162, Monroe County, (734)289-3700, (800)321-9564, 25 miles from Detroit. **Facility Holes:** 36. **Green Fee:** $19/$25. **Cart Fee:** $11/Person. **Walking Policy:** Unrestricted walking. **Season:** March-Dec. **High:** June-Aug. **To obtain tee times:** Call up to 10 days in advance. **Miscellaneous:** Reduced fees (weekdays, guests, twilight, seniors, juniors), range, credit cards (MC, V), BF, FF.
★★½ **EAST COURSE** (18)
Yards: 6,930/5,606. **Par:** 71/71. **Course Rating:** 72.9/70.1. **Slope:** 122/111. **Walkability:** 2. **Opened:** 1974. **Architect:** Charles Maddox.
★★ **WEST COURSE** (18)
Yards: 6,106/5,749. **Par:** 70/74. **Course Rating:** 66.9/70.6. **Slope:** 114/120. **Walkability:** 1. **Opened:** 1964.

★★ RAISIN VALLEY GOLF CLUB
PU-4057 Comfort Rd., Tecumseh, 49286, Lenawee County, (517)423-2050, 35 miles from Toledo, OH. **Facility Holes:** 18. **Yards:** 5,650/4,630. **Par:** 71/71. **Course Rating:** 67.5/69.0. **Slope:** 115. **Green Fee:** $15/$20. **Cart Fee:** $22/Cart. **Walking Policy:** Unrestricted walking. **Walkability:** 4. **Opened:** 1969. **Architect:** William Porter. **Season:** March-Dec. **High:** May-Oct.

MICHIGAN

To obtain tee times: Call up to 7 days in advance. Miscellaneous: Reduced fees (weekdays, seniors, juniors), credit cards (MC, V), BF, FF.

★★ **RAMMLER GOLF CLUB**
PU-38180 Utica Rd., Sterling Heights, 48312, Macomb County, (810)978-1411, 8 miles from Detroit. **Facility Holes:** 27. **Yards:** 6,305/4,951. **Par:** 71/71. **Course Rating:** 69.5/73.1. **Slope:** 113/119. **Green Fee:** $21/$24. **Cart Fee:** $22/Cart. **Walking Policy:** Unrestricted walking. **Walkability:** 1. **Opened:** 1922. **Season:** April-Nov. **High:** June-Aug. **To obtain tee times:** Call golf shop. **Miscellaneous:** Reduced fees (seniors), metal spikes, credit cards (MC, V). **Special Notes:** Also has a 9-hole par-3 course.

★★★½ **RATTLE RUN GOLF COURSE**
PU-7163 St. Clair Hwy., St. Clair, 48079, St. Clair County, (810)329-2070, 23 miles from Detroit. **E-mail:** info@rattlerun.com. **Web:** www.rattlerun.com. **Facility Holes:** 18. **Yards:** 6,891/5,085. **Par:** 72/75. **Course Rating:** 73.6/70.4. **Slope:** 140/124. **Green Fee:** $35/$49. **Cart Fee:** Included in green fee. **Walking Policy:** Walking at certain times. **Walkability:** 3. **Opened:** 1977. **Architect:** Lou Powers. **Season:** April-Nov. **High:** May-Sept. **To obtain tee times:** Call up to 14 days in advance. **Miscellaneous:** Reduced fees (twilight, seniors, juniors), range (grass), credit cards (MC, V, AE, D).
Reader Comments: Target golf … The course is a challenge … The sand traps need work but overall the course is beautiful and wonderful to play … Challenging.

★★★★ **THE RAVINES GOLF CLUB**
PU-3520 Palmer Dr., Saugatuck, 49453, Allegan County, (616)857-1616, 10 miles from Holland. **Web:** ravinesgolfclub.com. **Facility Holes:** 18. **Yards:** 7,132/5,081. **Par:** 72/72. **Course Rating:** 73.9/68.6. **Slope:** 142/115. **Green Fee:** $58/$89. **Cart Fee:** Included in green fee. **Walking Policy:** Mandatory carts. **Walkability:** 3. **Opened:** 1999. **Architect:** Arnold Palmer/Ed Seay/R Wiltse. **Season:** April-Nov. **High:** June-Sept. **To obtain tee times:** Call up to 90 days in advance. **Miscellaneous:** Reduced fees (weekdays, twilight, seniors, juniors), range (grass), credit cards (MC, V, AE, D), BF, FF.
Reader Comments: A great championship course … Like the way it's manicured … Very challenging … Palmer course … Beautiful… 600-yard par 5 with 200-yard carry.

RED FOX RUN GOLF COURSE
PU-217 Fifth St., Gwinn, 49841, Marquette County, (906)346-7010, 19 miles from Marquette. **E-mail:** rgmgt@aol.com. **Web:** www.redfoxrun.com. **Facility Holes:** 18. **Yards:** 6,075/4,650. **Par:** 70/70. **Course Rating:** 69.3/67.1. **Slope:** 116/114. **Green Fee:** $15/$25. **Cart Fee:** $11/Person. **Walking Policy:** Unrestricted walking. **Walkability:** 3. **Season:** April-Oct. **High:** June-Sept. **To obtain tee times:** Call up to 7 days in advance. **Miscellaneous:** Range (grass), credit cards (MC, V), BF, FF.

★★★★½ **RED HAWK GOLF CLUB** *Service, Pace*
PU-350 W. Davison Rd., East Tawas, 48730, Iosco County, (517)362-0800, (877)733-4259, 65 miles from Bay City. **E-mail:** redhawk@redhawkgolf.net. **Web:** redhawkgolf.net. **Facility Holes:** 18. **Yards:** 6,589/4,933. **Par:** 71/71. **Course Rating:** 71.0/67.4. **Slope:** 130/117. **Green Fee:** $39/$75. **Cart Fee:** Included in green fee. **Walking Policy:** Unrestricted walking. **Walkability:** 4. **Opened:** 1999. **Architect:** Arthur Hills/Chris Wilzynski. **Season:** April-Nov. **High:** May-Sept. **To obtain tee times:** Call up to 365 days in advance. **Miscellaneous:** Reduced fees (weekdays, twilight), range (grass), credit cards (MC, V, D), BF, FF.
Notes: Ranked 11th in 2001 Best in State.
Reader Comments: Very pretty course … Best set of par 5s I have seen … Arthur Hills created a beauty … Love the elevation change … Real value in comparison to high dollar Michigan courses … Beautiful course, a little expensive for everyday … New, needs time to grow.

★★½ **REDDEMAN FARMS GOLF CLUB**
PU-555 S. Dancer Rd., Chelsea, 48118, Washtenaw County, (734)475-3020, 8 miles from Ann Arbor. **E-mail:** reddemangc@aol.com. **Web:** www.annarbor.org. **Facility Holes:** 18. **Yards:** 6,525/5,034. **Par:** 72/72. **Course Rating:** 71.6/68.9. **Slope:** 122/120. **Green Fee:** $24/$29. **Cart Fee:** $10/Person. **Walking Policy:** Unrestricted walking. **Walkability:** 2. **Opened:** 1991. **Architect:** Bob Louhouse/Howard Smith. **Season:** April-Nov. **High:** June-Sept. **To obtain tee times:** Call golf shop. **Miscellaneous:** Reduced fees (weekdays, twilight, seniors, juniors), range (grass), credit cards (MC, V, D).

★★★ **RICHMOND FOREST GOLF CLUB**
PU-33300 32 Mile Rd., Lenox, 48050, Macomb County, (810)727-4742, 30 miles from Detroit. **Facility Holes:** 18. **Yards:** 6,682/4,849. **Par:** 72/72. **Course Rating:** 72.3/70.8. **Slope:** 124/117. **Green Fee:** $24/$31. **Cart Fee:** $12/Person. **Walking Policy:** Unrestricted walking. **Walkability:** 1. **Opened:** 1994. **Architect:** W. Bruce Matthews III. **Season:** March-Nov. **High:** June-Aug. **To obtain tee times:** Call up to 7 days in advance.

MICHIGAN

Miscellaneous: Reduced fees (weekdays, twilight, seniors, juniors), range (grass), credit cards (MC, V), BF, FF.
Reader Comments: Very enjoyable course … Great course, great price … Very friendly … Hidden jewel… Nice course, well kept bunkers … Needs a new clubhouse, nice practice area … Inexpensive, good value.

★½ RIDGEVIEW GOLF COURSE
PU-10360 W. Main, Kalamazoo, 49009, Kalamazoo County, (616)375-8821, 5 miles from Kalamazo. **Facility Holes:** 18. **Yards:** 6,980/5,800. **Par:** 71/72. **Green Fee:** $16/$20. **Cart Fee:** $12/Person. **Walking Policy:** Unrestricted walking. **Walkability:** 2. **Opened:** 1964. **Season:** March-Nov. **High:** June-Aug. **To obtain tee times:** Call golf shop. **Miscellaneous:** Reduced fees (weekdays, seniors, juniors), credit cards (MC, V, D), BF, FF.

RIVER BEND GOLF COURSE
PU-1370 W. State Rd., Hastings, 49058, Barry County, (616)945-3238, 18 miles from Grand Rapids. **Facility Holes:** 27. **Green Fee:** $16. **Cart Fee:** $26/Cart. **Walking Policy:** Unrestricted walking. **Walkability:** 2. **Opened:** 1962. **Architect:** Don Haywood Sr. **Season:** April-Oct. **High:** June-Sept. **Tee times:** Call golf shop. **Miscellaneous:** Metal spikes, range (grass), BF, FF.
RED/BLUE (18 Combo)
Yards: 5,912/5,457. **Par:** 72/72.
RED/WHITE (18 Combo)
Yards: 6,075/5,755. **Par:** 72/72.
WHITE/BLUE (18 Combo)
Yards: 5,947/5,472. **Par:** 72/72.

★★½ RIVERVIEW HIGHLANDS GOLF CLUB
PU-15015 Sibley Rd., Riverview, 48192, Wayne County, (734)479-2266, 20 miles from Detroit. **Facility Holes:** 27. **Green Fee:** $18/$23. **Cart Fee:** $22/Cart. **Walking Policy:** Unrestricted walking. **Opened:** 1973. **Architect:** William Newcomb/Arthur Hills. **Season:** Year-round. **High:** May-Oct. **To obtain tee times:** Call up to 7 days in advance. **Miscellaneous:** Reduced fees (weekdays, twilight, seniors, juniors), range (grass), credit cards (MC, V, AE, D), BF, FF.
BLUE/GOLD (18 Combo)
Yards: 6,667/5,293. **Par:** 72/72. **Course Rating:** 71.4/70.1. **Slope:** 119/118. **Walkability:** 3.
GOLD/RED (18 Combo)
Yards: 6,732/5,173. **Par:** 72/70. **Course Rating:** 69.2/69.0. **Slope:** 115/112. **Walkability:** 2.
RED/BLUE (18 Combo)
Yards: 6,485/5,224. **Par:** 72/72. **Course Rating:** 70.8/70.1. **Slope:** 119/118. **Walkability:** 3.

★★½ RIVERWOOD RESORT
R-1313 E. Broomfield Rd., Mt. Pleasant, 48858, Isabella County, (989)772-5726, (800)882-5211, 45 miles from Lansing. **E-mail:** riverwood@teemaster.com. **Web:** www.riverwoodresort.com. **Facility Holes:** 27. **Green Fee:** $23/$31. **Cart Fee:** $14/Person. **Walking Policy:** Walking at certain times. **Walkability:** 2. **Opened:** 1932. **Architect:** Jerry Matthews/Richard Figg. **Season:** April-Oct. **High:** June-Sept. **To obtain tee times:** Call golf shop. **Miscellaneous:** Reduced fees (weekdays, guests, twilight, seniors, juniors), range (grass), lodging (8 rooms), credit cards (MC, V, D), BF, FF.
RED/BLUE (18 Combo)
Yards: 6,182/4,462. **Par:** 72/72. **Course Rating:** 70.3/66.6. **Slope:** 121/106.
RED/WHITE (18 Combo)
Yards: 6,600/4,952. **Par:** 72/72. **Course Rating:** 72.0/69.4. **Slope:** 125/116.
WHITE/BLUE (18 Combo)
Yards: 6,100/4,667. **Par:** 72/72. **Course Rating:** 70.3/66.4. **Slope:** 116/109.

★★½ ROCHESTER HILLS GOLF & COUNTRY CLUB
PU-655 Michelson Rd., Rochester, 48073, Oakland County, (248)852-4800, 30 miles from Detroit. **Facility Holes:** 18. **Yards:** 6,800/5,747. **Par:** 72/72. **Course Rating:** 70.8/72.5. **Slope:** 121/123. **Green Fee:** $27/$38. **Cart Fee:** $13/Person. **Walking Policy:** Walking at certain times. **Walkability:** 3. **Opened:** 1920. **Architect:** Tom Bendelow. **High:** March-Dec. **To obtain tee times:** Call up to 7 days in advance. **Miscellaneous:** Reduced fees (weekdays, twilight), metal spikes, credit cards (MC, V, AE, D), FF.

★★★★ THE ROCK AT DRUMMOND ISLAND *Pace+*
R-33494 Maxton Rd., Drummond Island, 49726, Chippewa County, (906)493-1006, (800)999-6343, 60 miles from Sault Ste. Marie. **Web:** www.drummondisland.com. **Facility Holes:** 18. **Yards:** 6,837/4,992. **Par:** 71/71. **Course Rating:** 74.9/70.9. **Slope:** 142/130. **Green Fee:** $30/$69. **Cart Fee:** Included in green fee. **Walking Policy:** Mandatory carts. **Walkability:** 3. **Opened:** 1989. **Architect:** Harry Bowers. **Season:** April-Nov. **To obtain tee times:** Call golf shop. **Miscellaneous:** Reduced fees (weekdays, guests, twilight, juniors), range (grass), lodg-

ing (40 rooms), credit cards (MC, V, AE, D), BF, FF.

Reader Comments: Upper Michigan course, woods, water … A must play in the Upper Peninsula … Have played it three times and was impressed every time … Hard to get to … Great scenery, wildlife abounds … Great fun … Pretty course.

★★ ROGELL GOLF COURSE

PU-18601 Berg Rd., Detroit, 48219, Wayne County, (313)578-8007. **E-mail:** ctowne@rec.ci.detroit.mi.us. **Facility Holes:** 18. **Yards:** 6,075/4,985. **Par:** 70/70. **Course Rating:** 70.2/68.3. **Slope:** 129/117. **Green Fee:** $23. **Cart Fee:** $24/Cart. **Walking Policy:** Unrestricted walking. **Walkability:** 5. **Opened:** 1905. **Architect:** Donald Ross. **Season:** March-Dec. **High:** May-Oct. **To obtain tee times:** Call golf shop. **Miscellaneous:** Reduced fees (weekdays, seniors, juniors), metal spikes, BF, FF.

★★ ROGUE RIVER GOLF COURSE

PU-12994 Paine Ave. N.W., Sparta, 49345, Kent County, (616)887-7182, (888)779-4653, 15 miles from Grand Rapids. **Web:** www.westmichgolf.com\courses\rogueriver.htm. **Facility Holes:** 18. **Yards:** 5,344/4,300. **Par:** 70/70. **Course Rating:** 66.1. **Green Fee:** $15/$22. **Cart Fee:** $10/Person. **Walking Policy:** Unrestricted walking. **Walkability:** 2. **Opened:** 1962. **Architect:** Warner Bowen. **High:** April-Oct. **To obtain tee times:** Call golf shop. **Miscellaneous:** Reduced fees (weekdays, seniors, juniors), credit cards (MC, V, D), BF, FF.

★★½ ROLLING HILLS GOLF CLUB

PU-3274 Davison Rd., Lapeer, 48446, Lapeer County, (810)664-2281, 20 miles from Flint. **Facility Holes:** 18. **Yards:** 6,060/5,184. **Par:** 71/72. **Course Rating:** 69.3/69.8. **Slope:** 113/112. **Green Fee:** $18/$20. **Cart Fee:** $26/Cart. **Walking Policy:** Unrestricted walking. **Walkability:** 2. **Opened:** 1968. **Architect:** Reitz & Turdales. **Season:** March-Nov. **To obtain tee times:** Call golf shop. **Miscellaneous:** Reduced fees (weekdays, twilight, seniors, juniors), range (grass/mats), credit cards (MC, V, AE, D), BF, FF.

★½ ROLLING HILLS GOLF COURSE

PU-3100 Baldwin Dr., Hudsonville, 49426, Ottawa County, (616)669-9768, 15 miles from Grand Rapids. **Facility Holes:** 18. **Yards:** 5,832/4,693. **Par:** 70/71. **Course Rating:** 67.0/65.7. **Slope:** 106/102. **Green Fee:** $17/$18. **Cart Fee:** $20/Cart. **Walking Policy:** Unrestricted walking. **Walkability:** 3. **Season:** April-Nov. **High:** June-Aug. **To obtain tee times:** Call golf shop. **Miscellaneous:** Metal spikes, range (grass), credit cards (MC, V).

★★ ROLLING MEADOWS GOLF COURSE

PU-6484 Sutton Rd., Whitmore Lake, 48189, Washtenaw County, (734)662-5144, 5 miles from Ann Arbor. **Facility Holes:** 18. **Yards:** 6,474/4,908. **Par:** 70/72. **Course Rating:** 69.9/67.0. **Slope:** 119/110. **Green Fee:** $14/$24. **Cart Fee:** $24/Cart. **Walking Policy:** Unrestricted walking. **Walkability:** 2. **Opened:** 1978. **Season:** April-Oct. **To obtain tee times:** Call up to 1 day in advance. **Miscellaneous:** Reduced fees (weekdays, seniors, juniors), range (grass), credit cards (MC, V), FF.

ROMEO GOLF COURSE & COUNTRY CLUB

PU-14600 - E. 32 Mile Rd., Washington, 48095, Macomb County, (810)752-9673, 20 miles from Flint. **E-mail:** romeogolf@prodigy.net. **Facility Holes:** 36. **Green Fee:** $17/$28. **Cart Fee:** $12/Cart. **Walking Policy:** Unrestricted walking. **Walkability:** 1. **Architect:** Cotton Strickland. **Season:** March-Dec. **High:** June-Sept. **To obtain tee times:** Call up to 7 days in advance. **Miscellaneous:** Reduced fees (weekdays, twilight, seniors, juniors), range (grass), credit cards (MC, V, AE, D), BF, FF.

★★★ NORTH COURSE (18)

Yards: 6,439/4,706. **Par:** 72/72. **Course Rating:** 70.6/66.4. **Slope:** 121/113. **Opened:** 1958.

Reader Comments: A good course for locals, South Course is very nice … Caters to seniors … My personal Juliet … Making great strides.

SOUTH COURSE (18)

Yards: 6,248/4,826. **Par:** 72/72. **Course Rating:** 70.4/68.5. **Slope:** 125/115. **Opened:** 1994.

★★★ ROUGE PARK GOLF CLUB

PU-11701 Burt Rd., Detroit, 48228, Wayne County, (313)837-5900. **Facility Holes:** 18. **Yards:** 6,262/4,868. **Par:** 72/72. **Course Rating:** 70.1/69.2. **Slope:** 121/108. **Green Fee:** $10/$29. **Cart Fee:** $13/Person. **Walking Policy:** Unrestricted walking. **Walkability:** 3. **Opened:** 1923. **Season:** March-Nov. **High:** May-Aug. **To obtain tee times:** Call golf shop. **Miscellaneous:** Reduced fees (weekdays, twilight, seniors, juniors), metal spikes, range (grass/mats), credit cards (MC, V, AE).

Reader Comments: Tough but fair, improvements made … Improved a lot … Some unique holes … Overpriced … Great value … A classic, rejuvenated city course … Small greens, great golf, old-style design.

MICHIGAN

★★½ **ROYAL SCOT GOLF COURSE**
PU-4722 W. Grand River, Lansing, 48906, Clinton County, (517)321-4653. **Facility Holes:** 36.
Yards: 6,568/4,700. **Par:** 71/71. **Course Rating:** 71.7/66.8. **Slope:** 123/117. **Green Fee:**
$23/$42. **Cart Fee:** $24/Cart. **Walking Policy:** Unrestricted walking. **Walkability:** 3. **Opened:**
2001. **Architect:** Ray Hearn. **Season:** Year-round. **High:** April-Oct. **To obtain tee times:** Call up
to 14 days in advance. **Miscellaneous:** Reduced fees (weekdays, guests, twilight, seniors,
juniors), range (grass/mats), credit cards (MC, V, AE, D), BF, FF.
Special Notes: Also has new 18-hole course.

★★ **RUSH LAKE HILLS GOLF CLUB**
PU-3199 Rush Lake Rd., Pinckney, 48169, Livingston County, 734)878-9790, 20 miles from
Ann Arbor. **Facility Holes:** 18. **Yards:** 6,237/4,964. **Par:** 73/73. **Course Rating:** 69.9/67.3.
Slope: 120/114. **Green Fee:** $10/$21. **Cart Fee:** $22/Cart. **Walking Policy:** Unrestricted walk-
ing. **Walkability:** 3. **Opened:** 1960. **Season:** April-Oct. **High:** May-Aug. **Tee times:** Call golf
shop. **Miscellaneous:** Reduced fees (twilight, seniors, juniors), credit cards (MC, V, D).

★★½ **SAINT JOE VALLEY GOLF CLUB**
PU-24953 M 86, Sturgis, 49091, St. Joseph County, (616)467-6275, 10 miles from Sturgis.
E-mail: cpers90723@aol.com. **Facility Holes:** 18. **Yards:** 5,225/4,616. **Par:** 68/71. **Course
Rating:** 64.6/65.7. **Slope:** 109/108. **Green Fee:** $15/$19. **Cart Fee:** $11/Person. **Walking Policy:**
Unrestricted walking. **Walkability:** 2. **Opened:** 1962. **Season:** April-Nov. **High:** June-Aug. **To
obtain tee times:** Call golf shop. **Miscellaneous:** Reduced fees (seniors, juniors), credit cards
(MC, V), BF, FF.

★★★½ **SALEM HILLS GOLF CLUB**
PU-8810 W. Six Mile Rd., Northville, 48167, Washentaw County, (248)437-2152, 25 miles
from Detroit. **Facility Holes:** 18. **Yards:** 6,982/5,823. **Par:** 72/76. **Course Rating:** 72.4/72.8.
Slope: 120/120. **Green Fee:** $29/$36. **Cart Fee:** $11/Person. **Walking Policy:** Walking at certain
times. **Walkability:** 3. **Opened:** 1963. **Architect:** Bruce Matthews/Jerry Matthews. **Season:**
March-Dec. **To obtain tee times:** Call golf shop. **Miscellaneous:** Reduced fees (weekdays, twi-
light, seniors, juniors), range (grass), credit cards (MC, V, AE), BF, FF.
Reader Comments: Good course, good value … Long course, difficult, hilly & some water …
Salem Hills, played long, several long par 4s, appeared to be against prevailing winds … Wide open
… Very busy.

★★ **SALT RIVER COUNTRY CLUB**
PU-33633 23 Mile Rd., Chesterfield, 48047, Macomb County, (810)725-0311. **Facility Holes:**
18. **Yards:** 6,052/5,176. **Par:** 70/72. **Course Rating:** 69.0/69.6. **Slope:** 115/113. **Green Fee:**
$16/$30. **Cart Fee:** $11/Person. **Walking Policy:** Unrestricted walking. **Walkability:** 2. **High:**
May-Sept. **To obtain tee times:** Call up to 7 days in advance. **Miscellaneous:** Reduced fees
(twilight, seniors, juniors), metal spikes, credit cards (MC, V, AE, D), FF.

★★ **SANDY RIDGE GOLF COURSE**
PU-2750 W. Lauria Rd., Midland, 48642, Bay County, (517)631-6010, 100 miles from Detroit.
Facility Holes: 18. **Yards:** 6,409/5,304. **Par:** 72/72. **Course Rating:** 70.9/70.5. **Slope:** 132/124.
Green Fee: $20/$24. **Cart Fee:** $12/Person. **Walking Policy:** Unrestricted walking. **Walkability:**
1. **Opened:** 1966. **Architect:** Bruce Matthews. **High:** April-Oct. **To obtain tee times:** Call up to 7
days in advance. **Misc:** Reduced fees (seniors, juniors), range, credit cards (MC, V), BF, FF.

SASKATOON GOLF CLUB
PU-9038 92nd St., Alto, 49302, Kent County, (616)891-9229, 12 miles from Grand Rapids.
E-mail: golf@saskatoongolf.com. **Web:** www.saskatoongolf.com. **Facility Holes:** 36. **Green
Fee:** $22/$24. **Cart Fee:** $11/Person. **Walking Policy:** Unrestricted walking. **Walkability:** 2.
Architect: Mark DeVries. **Season:** March-Dec. **High:** May-July. **To obtain tee times:** Call golf
shop. **Misc:** Reduced fees (seniors, juniors), range, cards (MC, V, AE, D, DC, CB), BF, FF.
★★½ **BLUE/WHITE** (18)
Yards: 6,750/6,125. **Par:** 73/73. **Course Rating:** 70.7/71.7. **Slope:** 123/122. **Opened:** 1963.
★★★ **RED/GOLD** (18)
Yards: 6,254/5,300. **Par:** 71/70. **Course Rating:** 69.1/68.0. **Slope:** 123/114. **Opened:** 1970.
Reader Comments: If you can only play 9, go with the Gold … Great layout, OK conditions, great
price … Long round, poor greens … Nice course and practice facility with nice people working.

★★ **SAULT STE. MARIE COUNTRY CLUB**
SP-1520 Riverside Dr., Sault Ste. Marie, 49783, Chippewa County, (906)632-7812. **Facility
Holes:** 18. **Yards:** 6,295/5,100. **Par:** 71/72. **Course Rating:** 70.6/70.0. **Slope:** 125/119. **Green
Fee:** $18/$22. **Walking Policy:** Unrestricted walking. **Walkability:** 1. **Opened:** 1903. **Architect:**
Jerry Matthews. **Season:** April-Oct. **High:** June-Aug. **To obtain tee times:** Call golf shop.
Miscellaneous: Metal spikes, range (grass), credit cards (MC, V).

THE SAWMILL GOLF CLUB

PU-19 Sawmill Blvd., Saginaw, 48603, Saginaw County, (517)793-2692. **E-mail:** andy@the-sawmill.com. **Web:** www.thesawmill.com. **Facility Holes:** 18. **Yards:** 6,757/5,140. **Par:** 72/82. **Course Rating:** 72.7/70.4. **Slope:** 139/125. **Green Fee:** $28/$34. **Cart Fee:** $14/Person. **Walking Policy:** Walking at certain times. **Walkability:** 1. **Opened:** 1997. **Architect:** John Sanford. **Season:** April-Nov. **To obtain tee times:** Call golf shop. **Miscellaneous:** Reduced fees (twilight, seniors), range (grass), credit cards (MC, V, D), BF, FF.

★★★ SCENIC GOLF & COUNTRY CLUB

SP-8364 Fillion Rd., Pigeon, 48755, Huron County, (517)453-3350, 45 miles from Bay City. **Facility Holes:** 18. **Yards:** 6,166/4,577. **Par:** 71/71. **Course Rating:** 69.5/67.0. **Slope:** 121/113. **Green Fee:** $10/$25. **Cart Fee:** $12/Person. **Walking Policy:** Unrestricted walking. **Walkability:** 1. **Opened:** 1950. **Architect:** Tim Furnace/Ron Ferris. **Season:** March-Nov. **High:** June-Aug. **To obtain tee times:** Call up to 7 days in advance. **Miscellaneous:** Reduced fees (weekdays, twilight, seniors, juniors), range (grass), credit cards (MC, V, D), BF, FF.

★★½ SCOTT LAKE COUNTRY CLUB

PU-911 Hayes Rd. N.E., Comstock Park, 49321, Kent County, (616)784-1355, 10 miles from Grand Rapids. **E-mail:** Jeffmho@aol.com. **Web:** scottlake.com. **Facility Holes:** 27. **Green Fee:** $18/$24. **Cart Fee:** $11/Person. **Walking Policy:** Unrestricted walking. **Walkability:** 4. **Opened:** 1962. **Architect:** Bruce Matthews/Jeff Gorney. **Season:** April-Nov. **High:** May-Sept. **To obtain tee times:** Call golf shop. **Miscellaneous:** Reduced fees (weekdays, seniors, juniors), range (grass/mats), credit cards (MC, V, AE, D), BF, FF.
EAST/SOUTH COURSE (18 Combo)
Yards: 6,333/4,794. **Par:** 72/72. **Course Rating:** 70.8/67.6. **Slope:** 122/110.
SOUTH/WEST COURSE (18 Combo)
Yards: 6,313/4,644. **Par:** 70/70. **Course Rating:** 70.6/67.6. **Slope:** 122/110.
WEST/EAST COURSE (18 Combo)
Yards: 6,352/4,799. **Par:** 72/72. **Course Rating:** 70.8/67.6. **Slope:** 122/110.

★★★ SHADOW RIDGE GOLF CLUB

PU-1191 Kelsey Hwy., Ionia, 48846, Ionia County, (616)527-1180, 1 mile from Ionia. **Facility Holes:** 9. **Yards:** 2,989/2,350. **Par:** 35/35. **Course Rating:** 70.3/70.8. **Slope:** 123/122. **Green Fee:** $13/$15. **Cart Fee:** $22/Cart. **Walking Policy:** Unrestricted walking. **Walkability:** 4. **Opened:** 1916. **Architect:** Donald Ross. **Season:** April-Oct. **High:** June-Aug. **To obtain tee times:** Call golf shop. **Miscellaneous:** Reduced fees (twilight, seniors, juniors), credit cards (MC, V), BF, FF.
Reader Comments: Built on top of a hill, beautiful … Great par 3s … A true Donald Ross gem.

SHADY HOLLOW GOLF COURSE

PU-34777 Smith Rd. At Wayne, Romulus, 48174, Wayne County, (734)721-0430, 15 miles from Detroit. **Facility Holes:** 18. **Yards:** 5,884/5,171. **Par:** 71/72. **Green Fee:** $30/$33. **Cart Fee:** Included in green fee. **Walking Policy:** Unrestricted walking. **Walkability:** 1. **Opened:** 1972. **Season:** March-Dec. **High:** May-Sept. **To obtain tee times:** Call up to 3 days in advance. **Miscellaneous:** Reduced fees (weekdays, twilight, seniors, juniors), credit cards (MC, V), FF.

★★½ SHAGBARK GOLF CLUB

PU-80 106th Ave., Plainwell, 49080, Allegan County, (616)664-4653, 16 miles from Kalamazoo. **Facility Holes:** 18. **Yards:** 6,364/4,454. **Par:** 72/72. **Course Rating:** 69.9/67.6. **Slope:** 134/117. **Green Fee:** $30/$35. **Cart Fee:** $10/Person. **Walking Policy:** Unrestricted walking. **Walkability:** 5. **Opened:** 1997. **Architect:** Steve DeLoof. **Season:** April-Oct. **High:** June-Aug. **To obtain tee times:** Call golf shop. **Miscellaneous:** Reduced fees (weekdays, twilight, seniors, juniors), range (grass), credit cards (MC, V, AE).

SHAMROCK HILLS GOLF COURSE

PU-31071 CR 390, Gobles, 49055, Van Buren County, (616)628-2070, 14 miles from Kalamazoo. **Facility Holes:** 18. **Yards:** 5,972/4,985. **Par:** 71/71. **Green Fee:** $8/$16. **Cart Fee:** $18/Cart. **Walking Policy:** Unrestricted walking. **Season:** March-Oct. **High:** June-Aug. **To obtain tee times:** Call golf shop. **Miscellaneous:** Reduced fees (weekdays, seniors, juniors), range (grass), credit cards (MC, V), FF.

SHANTY CREEK

R-One Shanty Creek Rd., Bellaire, 49615, Antrim County, (231)533-8621, (800)678-4111, 35 miles from Traverse City. **E-mail:** info@shantycreek.com. **Web:** www.shantycreek.com. **Facility Holes:** 72. **Cart Fee:** Included in green fee. **Walking Policy:** Unrestricted walking. **High:** June-Sept. **To obtain tee times:** Call golf shop. **Miscellaneous:** Reduced fees (weekdays, guests, twilight, seniors), range (grass/mats), lodging (600 rooms), credit cards (MC, V, AE, D), FF.

MICHIGAN

★★★★ **CEDAR RIVER GOLF CLUB** (18)
Yards: 6,989/5,315. **Par:** 72/72. **Course Rating:** 73.6/70.5. **Slope:** 144/128. **Green Fee:** $65/$140. **Walkability:** 5. **Opened:** 1999. **Architect:** Tom Weiskopf. **Season:** May-Oct.
Reader Comments: Outstanding, tough but playable … Course was picture perfect … Service was great … A bit pricey … Great layout.

★★★★½ **THE LEGEND GOLF CLUB** (18)
Yards: 6,764/4,953. **Par:** 72/72. **Course Rating:** 73.6/69.6. **Slope:** 137/124. **Green Fee:** $75/$140. **Walkability:** 5. **Opened:** 1985. **Architect:** Arnold Palmer/Ed Seay. **Season:** May-Oct.
Notes: Ranked 25th in 2001 Best in State.
Reader Comments: Awesome views … Many elevated tees … Palmer did a nice job … Very nice, very fair, too expensive … A must if in the area … Picture perfect, great views.

★★★½ **SCHUSS MOUNTAIN GOLF CLUB** (18)
Yards: 6,922/5,383. **Par:** 72/72. **Course Rating:** 73.4/71.2. **Slope:** 127/126. **Green Fee:** $45/$85. **Walkability:** 3. **Opened:** 1972. **Architect:** Warner Bowen/Bill Newcomb. **Season:** May-Oct.
Reader Comments: A very good old course … Awesome views … Many elevated tees … Premium on accuracy … Favorite at Shanty … A great course that has gotten pricey.

★★½ **SUMMIT GOLF CLUB** (18)
Yards: 6,260/4,679. **Par:** 72/72. **Course Rating:** 71.7/70.7. **Slope:** 120/113. **Green Fee:** $35/$60. **Walkability:** 2. **Opened:** 1965. **Architect:** William H. Diddel. **Season:** April-Oct.

★★½ **SHENANDOAH GOLF & COUNTRY CLUB**
PU-5600 Walnut Lake Rd., West Bloomfield, 48323, Oakland County, (248)682-4300, 15 miles from Detroit. **Facility Holes:** 18. **Yards:** 6,620/6,409. **Par:** 72/72. **Course Rating:** 72.9/70.8. **Slope:** 131/129. **Green Fee:** $50/$60. **Cart Fee:** Included in green fee. **Walking Policy:** Mandatory carts. **Walkability:** 4. **Opened:** 1963. **Architect:** Bruce Matthews/Jerry Matthews. **Season:** March-Dec. **High:** April-Oct. **To obtain tee times:** Call up to 10 days in advance. **Miscellaneous:** Reduced fees (twilight, seniors, juniors), range (grass/mats), credit cards (MC, V), BF, FF.

SHEPHERD'S HOLLOW GOLF CLUB
PU-9085 Big Lake Rd., Clarkston, 48348, Oakland County, (248)922-0300, 15 miles from Pontiac. **Web:** shepherdshollow.com. **Facility Holes:** 27. **Green Fee:** $60/$85. **Cart Fee:** Included in green fee. **Walkability:** 5. **Opened:** 2000. **Architect:** Arthur Hills. **Season:** March-Nov. **High:** May-Sept. **To obtain tee times:** Call up to 7 days in advance. **Miscellaneous:** Reduced fees (weekdays, twilight), range (grass), credit cards (MC, V), BF, FF.
1-9/10-18 (18 Combo)
Yards: 7,236/4,906. **Par:** 72/72. **Course Rating:** 76.0/69.7. **Slope:** 152/120.
10-18/19-27 (18 Combo)
Yards: 7,235/4,982. **Par:** 72/72. **Course Rating:** 76.1/70.0. **Slope:** 148/120.
Notes: Ranked 6th in 2001 Best New Upscale Courses.
19-27/1-9 (18 Combo)
Yards: 7,169/4,960. **Par:** 72/72. **Course Rating:** 75.4/69.7. **Slope:** 146/120.

SINGING BRIDGE GOLF
PU-1920 Noble Rd., Tawas City, 48763, Iosco County, (989)362-0022, 10 miles from Tawas City. **Facility Holes:** 18. **Yards:** 5,986/4,788. **Par:** 71/71. **Course Rating:** 67.8/66.6. **Slope:** 113/106. **Green Fee:** $12/$20. **Cart Fee:** $10/Person. **Walking Policy:** Unrestricted walking. **Walkability:** 2. **Opened:** 1992. **Architect:** William Brown/Ken Brown. **Season:** April-Nov. **High:** June-Oct. **To obtain tee times:** Call golf shop. **Miscellaneous:** Reduced fees (weekdays, seniors), range (grass), credit cards (MC, V, D), BF, FF.

★★ **SLEEPING BEAR GOLF CLUB**
PU-4512 S. Townline Rd., Cedar, 49621, Leelanau County, (231)228-7400, (888)228-0121, 18 miles from Traverse City. **Web:** www.kingschallenge.com. **Facility Holes:** 18. **Yards:** 6,813/5,134. **Par:** 72/74. **Course Rating:** 73.3/70.5. **Slope:** 125/117. **Green Fee:** $25/$45. **Cart Fee:** Included in green fee. **Walking Policy:** Walking at certain times. **Walkability:** 4. **Opened:** 1966. **Architect:** C.D. Wagstaff. **Season:** April-Oct. **High:** June-Aug. **To obtain tee times:** Call up to 180 days in advance. **Miscellaneous:** Reduced fees (weekdays, twilight, juniors), range, credit cards (MC, V), BF, FF.
Special Notes: Formerly King's Challenge North Resort Course.

★★★ **SNOW SNAKE SKI & GOLF**
PU-3407 E. Mannsiding Rd., Harrison, 48625, Clare County, (989)539-6583, 25 miles from Mt. Pleasant. **E-mail:** snosnake@glecomputers.com. **Web:** www.snowsnake.net. **Facility Holes:** 18. **Yards:** 6,135/4,547. **Par:** 71/71. **Course Rating:** 69.8/66.3. **Slope:** 133/117. **Green Fee:** $25/$43. **Cart Fee:** Included in green fee. **Walking Policy:** Unrestricted walking. **Walkability:** 5. **Opened:** 1994. **Architect:** Jeff Gorney. **Season:** April-Dec. **High:** June-Aug. **To obtain tee times:** Call golf shop. **Miscellaneous:** Reduced fees (twilight, seniors), range (grass/mats), credit cards (MC, V, D), FF.

Reader Comments: Short but challenging … Requires creative shotmaking … Beautiful layout, great flowers … Great course to play … Fun course, bring balls.

★½ SOUTH HAVEN COUNTRY CLUB
PU-397 Adams Rd., South Haven, 49090, Allegan County, (616)637-3896, 40 miles from Grand Rapids. **Facility Holes:** 18. **Yards:** 6,735/5,550. **Par:** 72/73. **Course Rating:** 71.5. **Slope:** 123. **Green Fee:** $16/$20. **Walkability:** 3. **Opened:** 1920. **Architect:** Tom Bendelow. **To obtain tee times:** Call golf shop. **Miscellaneous:** Reduced fees (weekdays), metal spikes.

★½ SOUTHMOOR COUNTRY CLUB
PU-G-4312 S. Dort Highway, Burton, 48529, Genesee County, (810)743-4080, 5 miles from Flint. **Facility Holes:** 18. **Yards:** 5,205/4,810. **Par:** 69/69. **Course Rating:** 67.0/67.0. **Slope:** 109/109. **Green Fee:** $18/$20. **Cart Fee:** $21/Cart. **Walking Policy:** Unrestricted walking. **Walkability:** 2. **Opened:** 1963. **Architect:** Bruce Matthews. **Season:** March-Nov. **High:** May-Sept. **To obtain tee times:** Call golf shop. **Miscellaneous:** Reduced fees (weekdays, twilight, seniors, juniors), range (grass/mats), credit cards (MC, V), FF.

★★ SPRING VALLEY GOLF COURSE
PU-18396 W. U.S. 10, Hersey, 49639, Osceola County, (231)832-5041, 70 miles from Grand Rapids. **Facility Holes:** 18. **Yards:** 6,439/5,273. **Par:** 72/74. **Course Rating:** 71.5/73.3. **Slope:** 120/120. **Green Fee:** $12/$26. **Cart Fee:** $14/Person. **Walking Policy:** Unrestricted walking. **Walkability:** 3. **Opened:** 1962. **Architect:** Donald Semeyn. **Season:** April-Nov. **High:** June-Sept. **To obtain tee times:** Call golf shop. **Miscellaneous:** Reduced fees (weekdays, twilight, seniors), range (grass), credit cards (MC, V), BF, FF.

★★★ SPRINGFIELD OAKS GOLF COURSE
PU-12450 Andersonville Rd., Davisburg, 48350, Oakland County, (248)625-2540, 15 miles from Pontiac. **Facility Holes:** 18. **Yards:** 6,033/4,911. **Par:** 71/71. **Course Rating:** 68.4/68.1. **Slope:** 118/114. **Green Fee:** $14/$23. **Cart Fee:** $10/Person. **Walking Policy:** Unrestricted walking. **Walkability:** 4. **Architect:** Mark DeVries. **Season:** March-Nov. **High:** June-Aug. **To obtain tee times:** Call golf shop. **Miscellaneous:** Reduced fees (weekdays, twilight, seniors, juniors), metal spikes, credit cards (MC, V).
Reader Comments: Great greens, outstanding value … Nice muni course, great price … Oakland County's finest course … One of the best public county courses … Just as good as a resort but a county course … Great layout.

★★★ ST. CLAIR SHORES COUNTRY CLUB
PU-22185 Masonic Blvd., St. Clair Shores, 48082, Macomb County, (810)294-2000, 20 miles from Detroit. **Facility Holes:** 18. **Yards:** 6,040/4,820. **Par:** 70/70. **Course Rating:** 68.3/67.6. **Slope:** 123/116. **Green Fee:** $14/$22. **Cart Fee:** $20/Cart. **Walking Policy:** Unrestricted walking. **Walkability:** 2. **Opened:** 1976. **Architect:** Bruce Matthews/Jerry Matthews. **Season:** Year-round. **To obtain tee times:** Call golf shop. **Miscellaneous:** Reduced fees (twilight, seniors, juniors), credit cards (MC, V, AE, D).
Reader Comments: Many seniors … Very well kept up … Very busy … Great course for the price … Recent redesign adds challenge … You could use an entire roll of film on every hole … Clean, well maintained, well managed.

★★★★½ ST. IVES GOLF CLUB *Service*
PU-9900 St. Ives Dr., Stanwood, 49346, Mecosta County, (231)972-8410, (800)972-4837, 60 miles from Grand Rapids. **Web:** www.stivesgolf.com. **Facility Holes:** 18. **Yards:** 6,702/4,821. **Par:** 72/72. **Course Rating:** 73.3/68.7. **Slope:** 140/120. **Green Fee:** $35/$76. **Cart Fee:** $14/Person. **Walking Policy:** Unrestricted walking. **Walkability:** 5. **Opened:** 1996. **Architect:** Jerry Matthews. **Season:** April-Nov. **High:** June-Sept. **To obtain tee times:** Call golf shop. **Miscellaneous:** Reduced fees (weekdays, twilight, juniors), range (grass), credit cards (MC, V, AE, D), BF, FF.
Notes: Ranked 19th in 2001 Best in State.
Reader Comments: Great conditions, amazing course … Outstanding, everything about it … I was so sorry to have to leave after finishing my round … Class act, worth the money … Beautiful … Very nice course, scenic & fair test.

★★★ ST. JOHN'S GOLF & CONFERENCE CENTER
PU-44115 Five Mile Rd., Plymouth, 48170, Wayne County, (734)453-1047, 10 miles from Detroit. **E-mail:** www.stjohnsgolfcenter.com. **Web:** www.stjohnsgolfconference.com. **Facility Holes:** 27. **Green Fee:** $22/$50. **Cart Fee:** Included in green fee. **Walking Policy:** Walking at certain times. **Walkability:** 4. **Opened:** 1996. **Architect:** Pat Grelac. **Season:** April-Nov. **High:** May-Aug. **To obtain tee times:** Call golf shop. **Miscellaneous:** Reduced fees (weekdays, guests, twilight, seniors, juniors), range (grass/mats), credit cards (MC, V, AE, D), BF, FF.
LUKE/MATTHEW (18)
Yards: 6,184/4,871. **Par:** 72/71. **Course Rating:** 68.0/65.3. **Slope:** 120/108.

MARK/LUKE (18)
Yards: 6,193/4,835. **Par:** 72/71. **Course Rating:** 67.7/65.6. **Slope:** 121/108.
MATTHEW/MARK (18)
Yards: 5,955/4,686. **Par:** 70/70. **Course Rating:** 66.9/64.3. **Slope:** 119/106.
Reader Comments: Awesome clubhouse ... 27 holes with a confusing layout ... Outstanding conference and practice facility ... Crowded course.

★★★ **STATES GOLF COURSE**
PU-20 E. West Ave., Vicksburg, 49097, Kalamazoo County, (616)649-1931, 15 miles from Kalamazoo. **Facility Holes:** 18. **Yards:** 6,248/5,605. **Par:** 72/74. **Course Rating:** 69.7/73.2.
Green Fee: $14/$14. **Cart Fee:** $14/Cart. **Walking Policy:** Unrestricted walking. **Walkability:** 1.
Opened: 1925. **Season:** April-Nov. **High:** June-Sept. **To obtain tee times:** Call golf shop.
Miscellaneous: Reduced fees (weekdays, seniors), credit cards (MC, V, AE, D), BF, FF.
Reader Comments: Excellent, large greens ... Very enjoyable experience ... Very flat, walk ... Favorite, crowd pleaser.

★★★½ **STONEBRIDGE GOLF CLUB**
PU-5315 Stonebridge Dr. South, Ann Arbor, 48108, Washtenaw County, (734)429-8383, (888)473-2818, 30 miles from Detroit. **E-mail:** aasbridge@aol.com. **Web:** www.stonebridge-annarbor.com. **Facility Holes:** 18. **Yards:** 6,932/5,075. **Par:** 72/72. **Course Rating:** 73.6/68.6.
Slope: 136/122. **Green Fee:** $35/$45. **Cart Fee:** $14/Person. **Walking Policy:** Walking at certain times. **Walkability:** 4. **Opened:** 1991. **Architect:** Arthur Hills. **Season:** March-Nov. **High:** May-Sept. **To obtain tee times:** Call up to 5 days in advance. **Miscellaneous:** Reduced fees (twilight, seniors, juniors), range (grass), credit cards (MC, V, AE, D), BF, FF.
Reader Comments: Good test of skill with both long and short holes requiring most of the clubs in your bag ... New clubhouse just opened ... Fun to play.

★★★½ **STONY CREEK GOLF COURSE** *Value*
PU-5140 Main Pkwy., Shelby Township, 48316, Macomb County, (810)781-9166, 5 miles from Rochester. **Facility Holes:** 18. **Yards:** 6,900/5,023. **Par:** 72/72. **Course Rating:** 73.1/74.1.
Slope: 124/124. **Green Fee:** $22/$29. **Cart Fee:** $24/Cart. **Walking Policy:** Walking at certain times. **Walkability:** 3. **Opened:** 1979. **Architect:** William Newcomb. **Season:** April-Nov. **To obtain tee times:** Call up to 3 days in advance. **Miscellaneous:** Reduced fees (weekdays, seniors, juniors), range (grass), credit cards (MC, V, D), BF, FF.
Reader Comments: Conditioning greatly improved the last few years ... A great layout, no weak holes ... Good course, will play it more in 2001 ... Very scenic ... Very good greens, entire course in very good condition.

★★★ **SUGAR SPRINGS COUNTRY CLUB**
SP-1930 W. Sugar River Rd., Gladwin, 48624, Gladwin County, (989)426-4391, 11 miles from Gladwin. **Facility Holes:** 18. **Yards:** 6,737/5,636. **Par:** 72/72. **Course Rating:** 72.6/72.5. **Slope:** 124/121. **Green Fee:** $32. **Cart Fee:** $14/Person. **Walking Policy:** Unrestricted walking.
Walkability: 2. **Opened:** 1972. **Architect:** Jerry Matthews. **Season:** April-Oct. **High:** June-Aug.
To obtain tee times: Call up to 7 days in advance. **Miscellaneous:** Range (grass), credit cards (MC, V), BF, FF.
Reader Comments: Private on weekends, out-of-the-way location ... Excellent course and value ... Most holes have distinct personality ... A nice par 3 over the water ... Needs more trees ... A hidden gem in Michigan.

★★★★ **SUGARBUSH GOLF CLUB**
PU-1 Sugarbush Dr., Davison, 48423, Genesee County, (810)653-3326, 8 miles from Flint.
Facility Holes: 18. **Yards:** 7,285/5,035. **Par:** 72/72. **Course Rating:** 75.6/70.3. **Slope:** 146/127.
Green Fee: $39/$49. **Cart Fee:** Included in green fee. **Walking Policy:** Walking at certain times.
Walkability: 2. **Opened:** 1995. **Architect:** Larry Mancour. **Season:** April-Nov. **To obtain tee times:** Call golf shop. **Miscellaneous:** Reduced fees (weekdays, twilight, seniors, juniors), range (grass/mats), credit cards (MC, V, AE).
Reader Comments: Greens always fast ... Car dealer must have owed retired sheriff a favor, he's director of golf ... The best bargain in Michigan ... Extremely challenging, excellent value ... Very long, play from proper tees to enjoy.

SUNNYBROOK GOLF CLUB
PU-7191 - 17 Mile Rd., Sterling Heights, 48078, Macomb County, (810)264-2700, 150 miles from Detroit. **Facility Holes:** 27. **Green Fee:** $21/$24. **Cart Fee:** $20/Cart. **Walking Policy:** Unrestricted walking. **Walkability:** 2. **Season:** March-Nov. **High:** April-Sept. **To obtain tee times:** Call golf shop. **Miscellaneous:** Reduced fees (weekdays, twilight, seniors, juniors), range (grass), lodging (90 rooms).
★ **GREEN/RED COURSE** (18)
Yards: 6,310/5,730. **Par:** 70/70. **Course Rating:** 69.0. **Slope:** 121. **Opened:** 1951. **Architect:** Donald Ross.

ORANGE COURSE (9)
Yards: 2,903/2,593. **Par:** 36/36. **Opened:** 1962. **Architect:** Al Lopez.

★★ SWAN VALLEY GOLF COURSE
PU-9521 Highland Green Dr., Saginaw, 48609, Saginaw County, (517)781-4945, 4 miles from Saginaw. **Facility Holes:** 18. **Yards:** 5,985/4,693. **Par:** 70/72. **Course Rating:** 68.9/66.9. **Slope:** 119/112. **Green Fee:** $22/$23. **Cart Fee:** $22/Cart. **Walking Policy:** Unrestricted walking. **Walkability:** 4. **Opened:** 1960. **Architect:** Jerry Matthews. **Season:** March-Dec. **High:** July-Sept. **To obtain tee times:** Call up to 7 days in advance. **Miscellaneous:** Reduced fees (seniors, juniors), range (grass/mats), credit cards (MC, V, D), BF, FF.

★★½ SWARTZ CREEK GOLF COURSE
PU-1902 Hammerberg Rd., Flint, 48503, Genesee County, (810)766-7043, 45 miles from Detroit. **Facility Holes:** 27. **Yards:** 6,662/5,798. **Par:** 72/72. **Course Rating:** 72.1/73.0. **Slope:** 121/123. **Green Fee:** $19/$23. **Cart Fee:** $22/Cart. **Walking Policy:** Unrestricted walking. **Walkability:** 3. **Opened:** 1926. **Architect:** Frederick A. Ellis. **Season:** Year-round. **High:** April-Oct. **To obtain tee times:** Call golf shop. **Miscellaneous:** Reduced fees (twilight, seniors, juniors), credit cards (MC, V).
Special Notes: Also has a 9-hole executive course.

★★½ SYCAMORE HILLS GOLF CLUB
PU-48787 North Ave., Macomb, 48042, Macomb County, (810)598-9500, 20 miles from Detroit. **E-mail:** webmaster@sycamorehills. com. **Web:** www.sycamorehills.com. **Facility Holes:** 27. **Green Fee:** $24/$42. **Cart Fee:** $12/Person. **Walking Policy:** Walking at certain times. **Walkability:** 2. **Opened:** 1990. **Architect:** Jerry Matthews. **Season:** March-Dec. **High:** May-Sept. **To obtain tee times:** Call up to 30 days in advance. **Miscellaneous:** Reduced fees (weekdays, twilight, seniors, juniors), range (grass/mats), credit cards (MC, V, AE, D), BF, FF.
NORTH/WEST (18 Combo)
Yards: 6,305/5,070. **Par:** 72/72. **Course Rating:** 70.3/68.3. **Slope:** 123/119.
SOUTH/NORTH (18 Combo)
Yards: 6,267/4,934. **Par:** 72/72. **Course Rating:** 70.2/67.2. **Slope:** 132/121.
SOUTH/WEST (18 Combo)
Yards: 6,336/5,119. **Par:** 72/72. **Course Rating:** 70.7/68.5. **Slope:** 130/120.

★★ SYLVAN GLEN GOLF COURSE
PU-5725 Rochester Rd., Troy, 48098, Oakland County, (248)879-0040, 7 miles from Detroit. **Facility Holes:** 18. **Yards:** 6,566/5,295. **Par:** 70/70. **Course Rating:** 71.3/70.0. **Slope:** 115/113. **Green Fee:** $17/$29. **Cart Fee:** $28/Cart. **Walking Policy:** Unrestricted walking. **Walkability:** 3. **Season:** April-Nov. **High:** July-Aug. **To obtain tee times:** Call golf shop. **Miscellaneous:** Reduced fees (seniors, juniors), credit cards (MC, V).

★★★ THE TAMARACKS GOLF COURSE
PU-8900 N. Clare Ave., Harrison, 48625, Clare County, (989)539-5441, (888)838-1162, 30 miles from Mt. Pleasant. **Facility Holes:** 18. **Yards:** 5,760/4,370. **Par:** 70/70. **Green Fee:** $17/$25. **Cart Fee:** $26/Cart. **Walking Policy:** Unrestricted walking. **Walkability:** 3. **Opened:** 1984. **Architect:** Stephen Hawkins. **Season:** April-Nov. **High:** June-Aug. **To obtain tee times:** Call golf shop. **Miscellaneous:** Reduced fees (weekdays, guests, twilight, seniors, juniors), metal spikes, range (grass), credit cards (MC, V, AE, D), FF.
Reader Comments: Lots of blind shots ... Fun course with good variety ... Front 9 lots of water—challenging and fun, short ... Best-kept secret in middle of state ... Bargain, never crowded ... Could be good course ... Short but enjoyable.
Special Notes: Also has a 9-hole par-3 course.

★★★½ TANGLEWOOD GOLF CLUB
PU-53503 W. Ten Mile Rd., South Lyon, 48178, Oakland County, (248)486-3355, 25 miles from Detroit. **E-mail:** twoodproshop@aol. **Facility Holes:** 27. **Green Fee:** $45/$50. **Cart Fee:** $10/Person. **Walking Policy:** Walking at certain times. **Walkability:** 2. **Opened:** 1991. **Architect:** William Newcomb. **Season:** March-Dec. **To obtain tee times:** Call up to 7 days in advance. **Miscellaneous:** Reduced fees (twilight, seniors, juniors), range (grass/mats), credit cards (MC, V, AE), BF, FF.
NORTH/SOUTH (18 Combo)
Yards: 7,077/5,011. **Par:** 72/72. **Course Rating:** 73.6/72.9. **Slope:** 129/119.
NORTH/WEST (18 Combo)
Yards: 6,922/4,896. **Par:** 72/72. **Course Rating:** 73.0/72.1. **Slope:** 128/118.
SOUTH/WEST (18 Combo)
Yards: 7,117/5,031. **Par:** 72/72. **Course Rating:** 76.4/75.6. **Slope:** 138/128.
Reader Comments: A bit overpriced ... Very wide open ... Nice layout & value ... Very good overall course ... Very good golf course ... Money well spent ... Michigan hole is neat ... Very good local course ... Good course, pricey ... OK.

MICHIGAN

TANGLEWOOD MARSH GOLF COURSE
PU-2300 12th Ave., Sault Ste. Marie, 49783, Chippewa County, (906)635-0617, 45 miles from Mackinaw City. **Facility Holes:** 18. **Yards:** 6,000/5,100. **Par:** 72/72. **Green Fee:** $20. **Cart Fee:** $20/Cart. **Walking Policy:** Unrestricted walking. **Walkability:** 3. **Opened:** 1995. **Architect:** Jack Specker. **Season:** April-Nov. **To obtain tee times:** Call golf shop. **Miscellaneous:** Range (grass/mats), credit cards (MC, V).

★★ TAWAS CREEK GOLF CLUB
PU-1022 Monument Rd., Tawas City, 48763, Iosco County, (517)362-6262, (888)829-2727, 80 miles from Saginaw. **Facility Holes:** 18. **Yards:** 6,527/5,006. **Par:** 72/73. **Course Rating:** 71.9/69.3. **Slope:** 126/123. **Green Fee:** $15/$22. **Cart Fee:** $10/Person. **Walking Policy:** Unrestricted walking. **Walkability:** 2. **Season:** April-Oct. **High:** July-Aug. **To obtain tee times:** Call golf shop. **Miscellaneous:** Reduced fees (twilight), metal spikes, credit cards (MC, V).

★★★ TAYLOR MEADOWS GOLF CLUB
PU-25360 Ecorse Rd., Taylor, 48180, Wayne County, (313)295-0506, 15 miles from Detroit. **E-mail:** jsovitch@citaylor.mi.us. **Web:** www.taylorgolf.com. **Facility Holes:** 18. **Yards:** 6,049/5,160. **Par:** 71/71. **Course Rating:** 67.7/70.0. **Slope:** 115/115. **Green Fee:** $22/$29. **Cart Fee:** $24/Cart. **Walking Policy:** Unrestricted walking. **Walkability:** 3. **Opened:** 1989. **Architect:** Arthur Hills. **Season:** March-Dec. **High:** June-Sept. **To obtain tee times:** Call golf shop. **Miscellaneous:** Reduced fees (weekdays, twilight, seniors, juniors), range (mats), credit cards (MC, V), BF, FF.
Reader Comments: Too short, bad shape, too much money for a little course ... Wonder how much they'll raise prices this year? ... Short, but fairly challenging ... Some difficulty with green maintenance ... Fun to play.

★½ TERRA VERDE GOLF COURSE
PU-11741 W. Leonard Rd., Nunica, 49448, Ottawa County, (616)837-8249, 12 miles from Grand Rapids. **Facility Holes:** 18. **Yards:** 5,831/5,342. **Par:** 70/71. **Green Fee:** $15/$20. **Cart Fee:** $20/Cart. **Walking Policy:** Unrestricted walking. **Walkability:** 3. **Opened:** 1965. **Architect:** Jerry Matthews. **Season:** April-Oct. **High:** June-Sept. **Tee times:** Call up to 7 days ahead. **Misc** Reduced fees (weekdays, seniors, juniors), credit cards (MC, V, AE, D), BF, FF.

★★★ TERRACE BLUFF GOLF COURSE
SP-7527 Lake Bluff 19.4 Rd., Gladstone, 49837, Delta County, (906)428-2343, 4 miles from Escanaba. **Facility Holes:** 18. **Yards:** 7,001/5,900. **Par:** 72/72. **Course Rating:** 69.5/71.5. **Slope:** 124/115. **Green Fee:** $26/$28. **Cart Fee:** $22/Cart. **Walking Policy:** Unrestricted walking. **Walkability:** 1. **Opened:** 1972. **Architect:** Ted Locke. **Season:** April-Oct. **High:** June-Aug. **To obtain tee times:** Call up to 14 days in advance. **Miscellaneous:** Range (grass), lodging (71 rooms), credit cards (MC, V), BF, FF.
Reader Comments: Scenic ... A nice layout ... Overrated ... A good bargain ... Target golf, short and easy to score.

★★★½ THORNAPPLE CREEK GOLF CLUB
PU-6415 W. F Ave., Kalamazoo, 49009, Kalamazoo County, (616)344-0040, 5 miles from Kalamazoo. **Web:** www.thornapplecreek.com. **Facility Holes:** 18. **Yards:** 6,579/4,915. **Par:** 72/72. **Course Rating:** 71.2/68.1. **Slope:** 130/113. **Green Fee:** $28/$34. **Cart Fee:** $14/Person. **Walking Policy:** Walking at certain times. **Walkability:** 4. **Opened:** 1979. **Architect:** Mike Shields. **Season:** April-Nov. **High:** June-Sept. **Tee times:** Call golf shop. **Miscellaneous:** Reduced fees (weekdays, seniors), range (grass), credit cards (MC, V, AE, D), FF.
Reader Comments: Nice course, good value, tough greens ... Great layout, 3 unfair greens, pricey ... Beautiful, challenging course ... Beautiful layout ... Excellent course and most complete facilities in the area. Great restaurant.

★ THORNE HILLS GOLF COURSE
PU-12915 Sumpter Rd., Carleton, 48117, Monroe County, (734)587-2332, 9 miles from Belleville. **Web:** www.thornehills.com. **Facility Holes:** 18. **Yards:** 5,827/4,524. **Par:** 72/72. **Green Fee:** $14/$16. **Cart Fee:** $7/Person. **Walking Policy:** Unrestricted walking. **Walkability:** 2. **Opened:** 1981. **Architect:** Daniel G. Thorne. **Season:** April-Nov. **High:** May-Sept. **To obtain tee times:** Call up to 7 days in advance. **Miscellaneous:** Reduced fees (weekdays, seniors), FF.

★★★★ THOROUGHBRED GOLF CLUB AT DOUBLE JJ RESORT
R-6886 Water Rd., Rothbury, 49452, Oceana County, (231)893-4653, (800)368-2535, 20 miles from Muskegon. **E-mail:** inro@doublejj.com. **Web:** www.doublejj.com. **Facility Holes:** 18. **Yards:** 6,900/4,851. **Par:** 72/72. **Course Rating:** 74.4/69.5. **Slope:** 147/126. **Green Fee:** $49/$75. **Cart Fee:** Included in green fee. **Walking Policy:** Unrestricted walking. **Walkability:** 5. **Opened:** 1993. **Architect:** Arthur Hills. **Season:** April-Nov. **High:** June-Oct. **To obtain tee times:** Call golf shop. **Miscellaneous:** Reduced fees (weekdays, guests, twilight), metal spikes, range

(grass), lodging (200 rooms), credit cards (MC, V, AE, D), BF, FF.
Notes: Ranked 16th in 2001 Best in State.
Reader Comments: Played my best round, very good shape … Toughest course in Michigan … Beautiful layout … Tough layout, good facility & service … Great golf and service … A must play.

★★★★½ **THOUSAND OAKS GOLF CLUB** *Service, Pace*
PU-4100 Thousand Oaks Dr. N.E., Grand Rapids, 49525, Kent County, (616)447-7750, 12 miles from Grand Rapids. **E-mail:** smithsongolf72@aol.com. **Web:** www.thousandoaksgolf.com. **Facility Holes:** 18. **Yards:** 7,128/5,328. **Par:** 72/72. **Course Rating:** 74.1/69.7. **Slope:** 139/120. **Green Fee:** $60. **Cart Fee:** $15/Person. **Walking Policy:** Unrestricted walking. **Walkability:** 5. **Opened:** 1999. **Architect:** Rees Jones. **Season:** Year-round. **High:** May-Sept. **To obtain tee times:** Call up to 14 days in advance. **Miscellaneous:** Reduced fees (twilight, seniors, juniors), range (grass), credit cards (MC, V, AE, D), BF, FF.
Notes: Ranked 20th in 2001 Best in State; 4th in 2000 Best New Affordable Courses.
Reader Comments: Wonderful course, must play again … Ist class in every respect … Hills, just beautiful … Facilities great, I liked the wooded fairways … One of the best in every way … The trees … Ist class all the way.

★★★ **THUNDER BAY GOLF RESORT**
R-27800 M-32 E., Hillman, 49746, Montmorency County, (517)742-4875, (800)729-9375, 22 miles from Alpena. **Web:** thunderbaygolf.com. **Facility Holes:** 18. **Yards:** 6,677/5,004. **Par:** 73/73. **Course Rating:** 73.2/69.9. **Slope:** 131/121. **Green Fee:** $20/$30. **Cart Fee:** $15/Person. **Walking Policy:** Walking at certain times. **Walkability:** 3. **Opened:** 1971. **Architect:** Jack Matthias. **Season:** April-Nov. **High:** May-Oct. **To obtain tee times:** Call golf shop. **Miscellaneous:** Reduced fees (weekdays, guests, twilight, seniors, juniors), range (grass), lodging (40 rooms), credit cards (MC, V, AE, D), BF, FF.
Reader Comments: A solid, playable course at a good price … The course is kept up well … Three back-nine holes very similar … On the good side, the 17th hole is a real treat, to see and play.

★★★★★ **TIMBER RIDGE GOLF CLUB** *Service+, Value+, Condition+, Pace+*
PU-16339 Park Lake Rd., East Lansing, 48823, Ingham County, (517)339-8000, (800)874-3432, 5 miles from Lansing. **E-mail:** judy@golftimberridge.com. **Web:** www.golftim-berridge.com. **Facility Holes:** 18. **Yards:** 6,497/5,048. **Par:** 72/72. **Course Rating:** 72.4/70.9. **Slope:** 140/129. **Green Fee:** $25/$50. **Cart Fee:** $15/Person. **Walking Policy:** Unrestricted walking. **Walkability:** 4. **Opened:** 1989. **Architect:** Jerry Matthews. **Season:** March-Nov. **High:** May-Sept. **To obtain tee times:** Call up to 7 days in advance. **Miscellaneous:** Reduced fees (weekdays, twilight), range (grass/mats), credit cards (MC, V, AE), BF, FF.
Reader Comments: New course, improvements have made this a modern classic … World class … Prettiest course I have ever played … Incredible value, well worth the trip from Chicago.

★★★★ **TIMBER TRACE GOLF CLUB**
PU-1 Champions Circle, Pinckney, 48169, Livingston County, (734)878-1800, 2.5 miles from Downtown Pinckney. **E-mail:** tjttpga@hotmail.com. **Web:** migrandgolftrail.com. **Facility Holes:** 18. **Yards:** 7,020/5,100. **Par:** 72/72. **Course Rating:** 72.5/68.9. **Slope:** 129/120. **Green Fee:** $45/$55. **Cart Fee:** Included in green fee. **Walking Policy:** Mandatory carts. **Walkability:** 5. **Opened:** 1998. **Architect:** Pat Conroy/Jim Dewling. **Season:** April-Nov. **High:** June-Sept. **To obtain tee times:** Call up to 14 days in advance. **Miscellaneous:** Reduced fees (weekdays, twilight, seniors, juniors), range (grass/mats), credit cards (MC, V, AE, D), BF, FF.
Reader Comments: Great combination of trees & heather … Nice little track, expensive … 2nd best value around … Nice course to play … A new course …The food and management were very good … New, very interesting.

★★★½ **THE TIMBERS GOLF CLUB**
PU-7300 Bray Rd., Tuscola, 48769, Tuscola County, (989)871-4884, 4 miles from Frankenmuth. **Facility Holes:** 18. **Yards:** 6,674/4,886. **Par:** 18/18. **Course Rating:** 72.7/69.1. **Slope:** 133/113. **Green Fee:** $39/$49. **Cart Fee:** Included in green fee. **Walking Policy:** Walking at certain times. **Walkability:** 2. **Opened:** 1996. **Architect:** Lorrie Viola. **Season:** April-Nov. **High:** May-Sept. **To obtain tee times:** Call golf shop. **Miscellaneous:** Reduced fees (weekdays, twilight, seniors), range (grass/mats), credit cards (MC, V), BF, FF.
Reader Comments: Lots of wooded holes, management course, very good condition, good price … Fantastic scenery (mountain) … New owner, switched 9s, front 5 strokes easier than back, target golf … Could play this 5 days a week … Keep this one a secret … Worth your time!

★★★★½ **TIMBERSTONE GOLF COURSE** *Service, Value+, Condition, Pace*
PU-1 TimberStone Dr., Iron Mountain, 49801, Dickinson County, (906)776-0111, 55 miles from Marquette. **E-mail:** tsgolf@up.net. **Web:** www.timberstonegolf.com. **Facility Holes:** 18. **Yards:** 6,937/5,060. **Par:** 72/72. **Course Rating:** 75.2/72.0. **Slope:** 144/131. **Green Fee:** $35/$65. **Cart Fee:** Included in green fee. **Walking Policy:** Unrestricted walking. **Walkability:** 4. **Opened:** 1997. **Architect:** Jerry Matthews/Paul Albanese. **Season:** April-Oct. **High:** June-Aug.

MICHIGAN

To obtain tee times: Call up to 12 days in advance. **Miscellaneous:** Reduced fees (weekdays, twilight, juniors), range (grass), lodging (60 rooms), credit cards (MC, V, AE, D), BF, FF.
Reader Comments: Built on the backside of a ski hill with spectacular elevation drops … Very tricky greens … Wow, a marvel of golf course design … Better than Pinehurst … Top quality … Beautiful views, outstanding value … Exceptional conditions, great layout … The best … Fun course to play.

★★★ TOMAC WOODS GOLF COURSE
PU-14827 26 1/2 Mile Rd., Albion, 49224, Calhoun County, (517)629-8241, (800)835-9185, 15 miles from Jackson. **E-mail:** quailrun@internet1.net. **Facility Holes:** 18. **Yards:** 6,290/5,800. **Par:** 72/72. **Course Rating:** 69.8/72.2. **Green Fee:** $16/$19. **Cart Fee:** $11/Person. **Walking Policy:** Unrestricted walking. **Walkability:** 2. **Opened:** 1964. **Architect:** Robert Beard. **Season:** March-Nov. **High:** May-Sept. **To obtain tee times:** Call golf shop. **Miscellaneous:** Reduced fees (weekdays, seniors, juniors), range (grass/mats), credit cards (MC, V, D), BF, FF.
Reader Comments: Course has improved a lot … Excellent, challenging greens … I like this course, it's good to your game … Fun, little course, well maintained, small greens but tricky open front, woodsy back … Pretty nice.

TREETOPS SYLVAN RESORT
R-3962 Wilkinson Rd., Gaylord, 49735, Otsego County, (517)732-6711, (888)873-3867, 50 miles from Traverse City. **E-mail:** info@treetops.com. **Web:** www.treetops.com. **Facility Holes:** 72. **Cart Fee:** Included in green fee. **Season:** April-Oct. **High:** June-Sept. **Tee times:** Call golf shop. **Miscellaneous:** Reduced fees (guests, twilight, juniors), range, lodging (250 rooms), FF.

★★★★½ **RICK SMITH SIGNATURE** (18)
Yards: 6,653/4,604. **Par:** 70/70. **Course Rating:** 72.8/67.0. **Slope:** 140/123. **Green Fee:** $59/$98. **Walking Policy:** Mandatory carts. **Walkability:** 5. **Opened:** 1993. **Architect:** Rick Smith. **Miscellaneous:** Credit cards (MC, V, AE, DC).
Reader Comments: Wonderful golf course, should get more attention than it does … Great elevation changes … Fun course, not too many tough holes but just enough to keep you on your toes … Some terrific views … From the first tee, you know you're in for a treat. … Greens are deceptive.

★★★★½ **ROBERT TRENT JONES MASTERPIECE** (18) *Condition+, Pace*
Yards: 7,060/4,972. **Par:** 71/71. **Course Rating:** 75.8/70.2. **Slope:** 144/123. **Green Fee:** $59/$98. **Walking Policy:** Mandatory carts. **Walkability:** 5. **Opened:** 1987. **Architect:** Robert Trent Jones/Roger Rulewich. **Miscellaneous:** Credit cards (MC, V, AE, DC).
Notes: Ranked 22nd in 2001 Best in State; 46th in 1996 America's Top 75 Upscale Courses.
Reader Comments: Tough if you're not hitting straight … Worth every penny spent … Great design … Great Jones course, great views … Golf heaven … Super greens … Great design … Excellent fall value … Great course, outstanding … Very nice course, scenic, but overpriced.

★★★★½ **TOM FAZIO PREMIER** (18) *Condition*
Yards: 6,832/5,039. **Par:** 72/72. **Course Rating:** 73.2/70.1. **Slope:** 135/123. **Green Fee:** $59/$98. **Walking Policy:** Mandatory carts. **Walkability:** 5. **Opened:** 1992. **Architect:** Tom Fazio. **Miscellaneous:** Credit cards (MC, V, AE, DC).
Notes: Ranked 25nd in 1999 Best in State.
Reader Comments: Awesome views, awesome course … Fun, challenge … Great opening hole … Tough finish … All around fun … I'd like to live here, Fazio at its best … Must play … Every hole is a postcard … Challenging, nice people.

★★★★ **TRADITION COURSE** (18) *Pace*
Yards: 6,467/4,907. **Par:** 71/70. **Course Rating:** 70.3/67.3. **Slope:** 122/109. **Green Fee:** $33/$75. **Walking Policy:** Unrestricted walking. **Walkability:** 3. **Opened:** 1997. **Architect:** Rick Smith. **Miscellaneous:** Credit cards (MC, V, AE, D).
Reader Comments: Great track, love to play it … Scenery is the best … User-friendly course, a pleasure… Awesome views … Awesome course … Best we played last year … Short & simple.

TURTLE CREEK GOLF CLUB
PU-9044 R Dr. South, Burlington, 49029, Calhoun County, (517)765-2232, 10 miles from Battle Creek. **Facility Holes:** 27. **Yards:** 5,905/4,972. **Par:** 72/72. **Course Rating:** 66.5/65.6. **Slope:** 107/103. **Green Fee:** $15/$17. **Cart Fee:** $18/Cart. **Walking Policy:** Unrestricted walking. **Walkability:** 2. **Opened:** 1970. **Architect:** Rex Spoor. **Season:** March-Nov. **High:** June-Aug. **To obtain tee times:** Call golf shop. **Miscellaneous:** Reduced fees (weekdays, twilight, seniors), credit cards (MC, V), FF.
Special Notes: Also has a 9-hole executive course.

★★★ TWIN BIRCH GOLF COURSE
PU-1030 Highway 612 N.E., Kalkaska, 49646, Kalkaska County, (231)258-9691, (800)968-9699, 17 miles from Traverse City. **Facility Holes:** 18. **Yards:** 6,133/4,969. **Par:** 72/70. **Course Rating:** 69.9/67.8. **Slope:** 119/118. **Green Fee:** $27. **Cart Fee:** $16/Cart. **Walking Policy:** Unrestricted walking. **Walkability:** 2. **Season:** April-Oct. **To obtain tee times:** Call golf shop. **Miscellaneous:** Reduced fees (twilight, seniors, juniors), range (grass), credit cards (MC, V), BF, FF.
Reader Comments: Fun course … Nice country course … Pretty, great greens, friendly staff … Narrow course with smallish greens … Forget driver … Great course … Nice greens …Well-kept.

TWIN BROOK GOLF COURSE

PU-2200 Island Hwy., Charlotte, 48813, Eaton County, (517)543-0570, 12 miles from Lansing. **E-mail:** tbgc1@ia4u.net. **Facility Holes:** 18. **Yards:** 6,668/4,768. **Par:** 72/72. **Course Rating:** 73.1/68.3. **Slope:** 127/113. **Green Fee:** $15/$17. **Cart Fee:** $20/Cart. **Walking Policy:** Unrestricted walking. **Walkability:** 2. **Opened:** 1970. **Architect:** Delbert Palmer. **Season:** April-Oct. **High:** May-Aug. **To obtain tee times:** Call golf shop. **Miscellaneous:** Reduced fees (weekdays, twilight, seniors, juniors), range (grass), credit cards (MC, V, AE).
Special Notes: Formerly Butternut Brook Golf Club.

★★ TWIN BROOKS GOLF CLUB

PU-1005 McKeighan Rd., Chesaning, 48616, Saginaw County, (989)845-6403, 20 miles from Saginaw. **Facility Holes:** 18. **Yards:** 6,406/5,361. **Par:** 72/72. **Course Rating:** 71.1/71.4. **Slope:** 121/120. **Green Fee:** $18. **Cart Fee:** $20/Cart. **Walking Policy:** Unrestricted walking. **Walkability:** 2. **Opened:** 1960. **Season:** April-Oct. **High:** June-Sept. **To obtain tee times:** Call golf shop. **Miscellaneous:** Reduced fees, range, credit cards (MC, V), BF, FF.

★★★★ TWIN LAKES GOLF CLUB

SP-455 Twin Lakes Dr., Oakland, 48363, Oakland County, (248)650-4960, 35 miles from Detroit. **Web:** twinlakesgc.com. **Facility Holes:** 18. **Yards:** 6,745/4,701. **Par:** 71/71. **Course Rating:** 71.0/65.9. **Slope:** 122/109. **Green Fee:** $60/$70. **Cart Fee:** Included in green fee. **Walking Policy:** Unrestricted walking. **Walkability:** 3. **Opened:** 1996. **Architect:** Roy Hearn/Jerry Matthews. **Season:** March-Dec. **Tee times:** Call up to 14 days in advance. **Miscellaneous:** Reduced fees (twilight, seniors, juniors), range (grass), credit cards (MC, V, AE, D), BF, FF.
Reader Comments: Many well-designed holes … Keep tee times at 10 minutes … Outstanding in every respect … Expensive, but worth it … Pricey but nice … Just OK design, but excellent service.

★½ TWIN OAKS GOLF COURSE

PU-6710 W. Freeland, Freeland, 48623, Bay County, (989)695-9746, 4 miles from Saginaw. **Facility Holes:** 27. **Yards:** 5,608/4,362. **Par:** 70/71. **Green Fee:** $19/$21. **Cart Fee:** $22/Cart. **Walking Policy:** Unrestricted walking. **Walkability:** 1. **Opened:** 1965. **Season:** March-Nov. **High:** April-Sept. **To obtain tee times:** Call up to 7 days in advance. **Miscellaneous:** Reduced fees (weekdays, seniors), credit cards (MC, V), FF.
Special Notes: Also has a 9-hole East Course.

★★ TYLER CREEK RECREATION AREA

PU-13495 92nd St., Alto, 49302, Kent County, (616)868-6751, 25 miles from Grand Rapids. **Facility Holes:** 18. **Yards:** 6,200. **Par:** 70. **Course Rating:** 69.5. **Slope:** 117. **Green Fee:** $10/$18. **Cart Fee:** $10/Person. **Walking Policy:** Unrestricted walking. **Walkability:** 4. **Season:** March-Nov. **High:** June-Aug. **To obtain tee times:** Call golf shop. **Miscellaneous:** Reduced fees (weekdays, guests, seniors, juniors), metal spikes, credit cards (MC, V).

★★½ TYRONE HILLS GOLF COURSE

PU-8449 US Highway 23, Fenton, 48430, Livingston County, (810)629-5011, 20 miles from Flint. **Facility Holes:** 18. **Yards:** 6,400/5,200. **Par:** 72/72. **Course Rating:** 70.3/69.1. **Slope:** 123/118. **Green Fee:** $19/$25. **Cart Fee:** $12/Person. **Walking Policy:** Unrestricted walking. **Walkability:** 3. **Opened:** 1960. **Architect:** Bruce Matthews. **Season:** April-Dec. **Tee times:** Call golf shop. **Misc:** Reduced fees (twilight, seniors, juniors), credit cards (MC, V), BF, FF.

★★★★½ UNIVERSITY OF MICHIGAN GOLF COURSE

SP-500 E. Stadium Blvd., Ann Arbor, 48104, Washtenaw County, (734)615-4653. **E-mail:** cegreen@umich.edu. **Web:** www.mgoblue.com. **Facility Holes:** 18. **Yards:** 6,687/5,331. **Par:** 71/75. **Course Rating:** 72.5/71.0. **Slope:** 135/125. **Green Fee:** $42/$50. **Cart Fee:** $24/Cart. **Walking Policy:** Unrestricted walking. **Walkability:** 5. **Opened:** 1931. **Architect:** Alister Mackenzie. **Season:** April-Nov. **High:** May-Sept. **To obtain tee times:** Call up to 7 days in advance. **Miscellaneous:** Reduced fees (twilight), range (grass), credit cards (MC, V, AE), FF.
Notes: Ranked 10th in 2001 Best in State. Open to U of M students.
Reader Comments: Value which is unmatched in the Ann Arbor area.

★★½ VALLEY VIEW FARM GOLF COURSE

PU-1435 S. Thomas Rd., Saginaw, 48609, Saginaw County, (517)781-1248, 4 miles from Saginaw. **Facility Holes:** 18. **Yards:** 6,228/4,547. **Par:** 71/72. **Course Rating:** 70.1/65.8. **Slope:** 119/111. **Green Fee:** $14/$19. **Cart Fee:** $24/Cart. **Walking Policy:** Unrestricted walking. **Walkability:** 1. **Opened:** 1975. **Season:** April-Nov. **To obtain tee times:** Call golf shop. **Miscellaneous:** Reduced fees (seniors), credit cards (MC, V), FF.

★★½ VASSAR GOLF & COUNTRY CLUB
SP-3509 Kirk Rd., Vassar, 48768, Tuscola County, (517)823-7221, 17 miles from Saginaw. **Facility Holes:** 18. **Yards:** 6,439/5,482. **Par:** 72/72. **Course Rating:** 71.1/72.1. **Slope:** 126/125. **Green Fee:** $18/$29. **Cart Fee:** $11/Person. **Walking Policy:** Unrestricted walking. **Walkability:** 2. **Opened:** 1963. **Architect:** William Newcomb. **Season:** April-Oct. **High:** June-Sept. **To obtain tee times:** Call golf shop. **Miscellaneous:** Range (grass), credit cards (MC, V).

★★★ VERONA HILLS GOLF CLUB
SP-3175 Sand Beach Rd., Bad Axe, 48413, Huron County, (517)269-8132, 7 miles from Bad Axe. **Facility Holes:** 18. **Yards:** 6,497/5,144. **Par:** 71/72. **Course Rating:** 72.6/72.6. **Slope:** 127/127. **Green Fee:** $35. **Cart Fee:** $15/Person. **Walking Policy:** Unrestricted walking. **Walkability:** 4. **Opened:** 1924. **Season:** April-Oct. **High:** June-Aug. **To obtain tee times:** Call golf shop. **Miscellaneous:** Range (grass), credit cards (MC, V, D).
Reader Comments: Michigan thumb area's finest … Old layout, lots of doglegs … Old course, has aged very well, beautiful clubhouse … Some elevation changes, interesting layout. Enjoyable day.

★★ VIENNA GREENS GOLF COURSE
PU-1184 E. Tobias, Clio, 48420, Genesee County, (810)686-1443, 5 miles from Clio. **Facility Holes:** 18. **Yards:** 6,245/4,908. **Par:** 70/70. **Course Rating:** 69.8/67.4. **Slope:** 112/106. **Green Fee:** $16. **Cart Fee:** $17/Cart. **Walking Policy:** Unrestricted walking. **Walkability:** 1. **Opened:** 1969. **To obtain tee times:** Call golf shop. **Miscellaneous:** Reduced fees (seniors).

★★★½ WALLINWOOD SPRINGS GOLF CLUB
SP-8152 Weatherwax, Jenison, 49428, Ottawa County, (616)457-9920, 15 miles from Grand Rapids. **Facility Holes:** 18. **Yards:** 6,751/5,067. **Par:** 72/72. **Course Rating:** 72.4/69.1. **Slope:** 128/115. **Green Fee:** $20/$45. **Cart Fee:** $11/Person. **Walking Policy:** Walking at certain times. **Walkability:** 3. **Opened:** 1992. **Architect:** Jerry Matthews. **Season:** Year-round. **High:** May-Sept. **To obtain tee times:** Call up to 14 days in advance. **Miscellaneous:** Reduced fees (weekdays, twilight, seniors, juniors), range (grass), credit cards (MC, V, D), BF, FF.
Reader Comments: Easy front, difficult back … Great course, super facilities, great staff … Fun course, perfect if you could mix up holes … Tough, need good variety of shots … Back is tight.

WARREN VALLEY GOLF COURSE
PU-26116 W. Warren, Dearborn Heights, 48127, Wayne County, (313)561-1040, 10 miles from Detroit. **Facility Holes:** 36. **Green Fee:** $15/$24. **Cart Fee:** $22/Cart. **Walking Policy:** Unrestricted walking. **Walkability:** 4. **Opened:** 1927. **Architect:** Donald Ross. **Season:** March-Nov. **High:** May-Oct. **To obtain tee times:** Call golf shop. **Miscellaneous:** Reduced fees (weekdays, twilight, seniors, juniors), credit cards (MC, V).
★½ **EAST COURSE** (18)
Yards: 6,189/5,328. **Par:** 72/72. **Course Rating:** 69.1/70.0. **Slope:** 114/113.
★½ **WEST COURSE** (18)
Yards: 6,066/5,150. **Par:** 71/71. **Course Rating:** 68.5/69.2. **Slope:** 115/114.

★★★ WASHAKIE GOLF & RV RESORT
PU-3461 Burnside Rd., North Branch, 48461, Lapeer County, (810)688-3235, 30 miles from Flint. **Facility Holes:** 18. **Yards:** 5,805/5,152. **Par:** 72/72. **Green Fee:** $18/$20. **Cart Fee:** $21/Cart. **Walking Policy:** Unrestricted walking. **Walkability:** 3. **Opened:** 1986. **Architect:** Lyle Ferrier. **Season:** April-Dec. **To obtain tee times:** Call golf shop. **Miscellaneous:** Reduced fees (seniors, juniors), lodging (100 rooms), BF, FF.
Reader Comments: Excellent course for the beginner, not that long, most holes pretty wide open … For the experienced golfer, does have some challenging holes … Well-kept and beautiful.

★★★½ WAWASHKAMO GOLF CLUB
SP-British Landing Rd., Mackinac Island, 49757, Mackinac County, (906)847-3871. **E-mail:** lewisdc@hotmail.com. **Web:** www.wawashkamo.com. **Facility Holes:** 9. **Yards:** 2,999/2,380. **Par:** 36/36. **Course Rating:** 68.0. **Slope:** 117. **Green Fee:** $50. **Cart Fee:** $30/Cart. **Walking Policy:** Unrestricted walking. **Walkability:** 2. **Opened:** 1898. **Architect:** Al Smith. **Season:** May-Oct. **High:** June-Aug. **To obtain tee times:** Call golf shop. **Miscellaneous:** Reduced fees (twilight), credit cards (MC, V, D), BF, FF.
Reader Comments: It's the oldest continually played course in Michigan … Golf as it should be, many turn-of-the-century design features … Ancient course, modern attitude.

★★★ WAWONOWIN COUNTRY CLUB
SP-3432 County Rd. #478, Champion, 49814, Marquette County, (906)485-1435, 18 miles from Marquette. **Facility Holes:** 18. **Yards:** 6,487/5,379. **Par:** 72/72. **Course Rating:** 71.1/70.8. **Slope:** 124/119. **Green Fee:** $17/$33. **Cart Fee:** $12/Person. **Walking Policy:** Unrestricted walking. **Walkability:** 3. **Season:** April-Oct. **High:** June-Aug. **To obtain tee times:** Call golf shop. **Miscellaneous:** Range (grass), credit cards (MC, V).

MICHIGAN

WESBURN GOLF COURSE
PU-5617 S. Huron River Dr., South Rockwood, 48179, Monroe County, (734)379-3555, (888)427-3555. **Facility Holes:** 18. **Yards:** 5,981/4,816. **Par:** 72/71. **Green Fee:** $15/$22. **Cart Fee:** $11/Person. **Walking Policy:** Unrestricted walking. **Walkability:** 2. **Opened:** 1910. **Architect:** Dodge Family. **Season:** Year-round. **High:** April-Oct. **To obtain tee times:** Call golf shop. **Miscellaneous:** Reduced fees (weekdays, twilight, seniors, juniors), range (grass), credit cards (MC, V), BF, FF.

★★★★ WEST BRANCH COUNTRY CLUB
SP-198 Fairview, West Branch, 48661, Ogemaw County, (989)345-2501, 60 miles from Saginaw. **E-mail:** jst@ejourney.com. **Facility Holes:** 18. **Yards:** 6,402/5,436. **Par:** 72/73. **Course Rating:** 70.5/71.4. **Slope:** 122/119. **Green Fee:** $19/$35. **Cart Fee:** $15/Person. **Walking Policy:** Unrestricted walking. **Walkability:** 2. **Opened:** 1928. **Architect:** William Newcomb. **Season:** April-Nov. **High:** June-Sept. **To obtain tee times:** Call up to 14 days in advance. **Miscellaneous:** Reduced fees (twilight, seniors), range, credit cards (MC, V, D), BF, FF.

WEST OTTAWA GOLF CLUB
PU-6045 136th Ave., Holland, 49424, Ottawa County, (616)399-1678, 7 miles from Holland. **Facility Holes:** 27. **Green Fee:** $22/$24. **Cart Fee:** $20/Cart. **Walking Policy:** Unrestricted walking. **Walkability:** 1. **Opened:** 1962. **Architect:** Bruce Matthews. **Season:** March-Nov. **High:** July-Aug. **To obtain tee times:** Call golf shop. **Miscellaneous:** Reduced fees (weekdays, seniors, juniors), range (grass/mats), credit cards (MC, V), BF, FF.
BLUE/RED COURSE (18)
Yards: 6,030/5,175. **Par:** 70/73. **Course Rating:** 68.5/66.0. **Slope:** 110/105.
RED/WHITE COURSE (18)
Yards: 5,830/5,075. **Par:** 70/71. **Course Rating:** 68.5/66.0. **Slope:** 110/105.
WHITE/BLUE COURSE (18)
Yards: 6,250/5,700. **Par:** 70/67. **Course Rating:** 68.5/66.0. **Slope:** 110/105.

★½ WESTBROOKE GOLF COURSE
PU-26817 Beck Rd., Novi, 48734, Oakland County, (248)349-2723. **Facility Holes:** 18. **Yards:** 5,582/4,943. **Par:** 70/70. **Course Rating:** 68.5/64.9. **Slope:** 107/106. **Green Fee:** $24/$26. **Cart Fee:** $20/Cart. **Walking Policy:** Unrestricted walking. **Walkability:** 1. **Season:** April-Oct. **High:** June-Sept. **Tee times:** Call golf shop. **Miscellaneous:** Reduced fees (twilight, seniors).

★★ WESTERN GREENS GOLF COURSE
PU-2475 Johnson Rd., Marne, 49435, Ottawa County, (616)677-3677, 12 miles from Grand Rapids. **Facility Holes:** 18. **Yards:** 6,460/5,552. **Par:** 71/73. **Green Fee:** $22/$24. **Cart Fee:** $20/Cart. **Walking Policy:** Unrestricted walking. **Walkability:** 3. **Opened:** 1966. **Architect:** Mark DeVries. **Season:** April-Nov. **High:** June-Aug. **Tee times:** Call golf shop. **Miscellaneous:** Reduced fees (weekdays, twilight, seniors, juniors), range (grass), cards (MC, V), BF, FF.

★★½ WHIFFLE TREE HILL GOLF COURSE
PU-15730 Homer Rd., Concord, 49237, Jackson County, (517)524-6655, 15 miles from Jackson. **Facility Holes:** 18. **Yards:** 6,370/4,990. **Par:** 72/72. **Course Rating:** 69.8/68.9. **Slope:** 116/112. **Green Fee:** $8/$17. **Cart Fee:** $10/Person. **Walking Policy:** Unrestricted walking. **Walkability:** 3. **Opened:** 1969. **Architect:** Arthur Young. **Season:** Feb.-Nov. **High:** June-Sept. **To obtain tee times:** Call golf shop. **Miscellaneous:** Reduced fees (weekdays, twilight, seniors, juniors), range (grass), credit cards (MC, V).

★★★½ WHISPERING PINES GOLF CLUB
PU-2500 Whispering Pines Dr., Pinckney, 48169, Livingston County, (734)878-0009, 10 miles from Ann Arbor. **Web:** www.whisperingpinesgc.com. **Facility Holes:** 18. **Yards:** 6,440/4,813. **Par:** 71/73. **Course Rating:** 69.8/67.3. **Slope:** 126/117. **Green Fee:** $25/$49. **Cart Fee:** Included in green fee. **Walking Policy:** Walking at certain times. **Walkability:** 4. **Opened:** 1992. **Architect:** Donald Moon. **Season:** March-Nov. **To obtain tee times:** Call up to 7 days in advance. **Miscellaneous:** Reduced fees (weekdays, twilight, seniors, juniors), credit cards (MC, V, AE), BF, FF.

MICHIGAN

★★ WHISPERING WILLOWS GOLF COURSE
PU-20500 Newburg Rd., Livonia, 48152, Wayne County, (248)476-4493, 24 miles from Detroit. **Facility Holes:** 18. **Yards:** 6,056/5,424. **Par:** 70/72. **Course Rating:** 69.3/71.1. **Slope:** 114/117. **Green Fee:** $18/$27. **Cart Fee:** $12/Person. **Walking Policy:** Unrestricted walking. **Walkability:** 2. **Opened:** 1968. **Architect:** Mark DeVries. **Season:** April-Dec. **To obtain tee times:** Call up to 5 days in advance. **Miscellaneous:** Reduced fees (weekdays, twilight, seniors, juniors), range (grass), credit cards (MC, V), BF, FF.

★½ WHITE BIRCH HILLS GOLF COURSE
PU-360 Ott Rd., Bay City, 48706, Bay County, (989)662-6523, 15 miles from Saginaw. **Facility Holes:** 18. **Yards:** 5,625/5,300. **Par:** 71/74. **Green Fee:** $17. **Cart Fee:** $20/Cart. **Walking Policy:** Unrestricted walking. **Walkability:** 1. **Opened:** 1949. **Season:** March-Nov. **High:** June-Aug. **To obtain tee times:** Call golf shop. **Miscellaneous:** Reduced fees (seniors, juniors), range (grass), caddies, credit cards (MC, V, D).

★★ WHITE DEER COUNTRY CLUB
PU-1309 Bright Angel Dr., Prudenville, 48651, Roscommon County, (517)366-5812, 70 miles from Saginaw. **E-mail:** whitedeercc@hotmail.com. **Facility Holes:** 18. **Yards:** 6,311/5,290. **Par:** 72/72. **Course Rating:** 68.8/69.9. **Slope:** 115/116. **Green Fee:** $17/$18. **Cart Fee:** $9/Person. **Walking Policy:** Unrestricted walking. **Walkability:** 1. **Opened:** 1965. **Architect:** Glenn Gulder. **Season:** April-Nov. **High:** July-Aug. **To obtain tee times:** Call golf shop. **Miscellaneous:** Reduced fees (twilight, juniors), credit cards (MC, V, D), BF, FF.

★★ WHITE LAKE OAKS GOLF COURSE
PU-991 Williams Lake Rd., White Lake, 48386, Oakland County, (248)698-2700, 5 miles from Pontiac. **Facility Holes:** 18. **Yards:** 5,738/4,900. **Par:** 70/71. **Course Rating:** 67.1/67.9. **Slope:** 111/114. **Green Fee:** $15/$23. **Cart Fee:** $20/Cart. **Walking Policy:** Unrestricted walking. **Walkability:** 2. **Opened:** 1940. **Architect:** Van Tine Family. **Season:** April-Nov. **High:** May-Aug. **To obtain tee times:** Call golf shop. **Miscellaneous:** Reduced fees (weekdays, twilight, seniors, juniors), credit cards (MC, V), BF, FF.

★★★½ WHITE PINE NATIONAL GOLF COURSE
PU-3450 N. Hubbard Lake Rd., Spruce, 48762, Alcona County, (989)736-3279, 30 miles from Alpena. **E-mail:** wpn@northland.hb.mi.us. **Facility Holes:** 18. **Yards:** 6,883/5,268. **Par:** 72/72. **Course Rating:** 72.7/70.5. **Slope:** 127/124. **Green Fee:** $38/$48. **Cart Fee:** Included in green fee. **Walking Policy:** Walking at certain times. **Walkability:** 4. **Opened:** 1992. **Architect:** Bruce Wolfrom/Clem Wolfrom. **Season:** April-Nov. **High:** May-Sept. **To obtain tee times:** Call golf shop. **Miscellaneous:** Reduced fees (weekdays, twilight, seniors, juniors), range (grass), credit cards (MC, V, D), BF, FF.
Reader Comments: Best value in Michigan, don't tell anyone about this course ... Best & priciest course in Mich. ... Great course.

WHITEFISH LAKE GOLF CLUB
PU-2241 Bass Lake Rd., Pierson, 49339, Montcalm County, (616)636-5260, (888)368-5666, 25 miles from Grand Rapids. **E-mail:** wlgc@triton.net. **Facility Holes:** 18. **Yards:** 6,122/5,062. **Par:** 72/72. **Course Rating:** 70.0/69.1. **Slope:** 128/121. **Green Fee:** $17/$22. **Cart Fee:** $20/Cart. **Walking Policy:** Unrestricted walking. **Walkability:** 3. **Opened:** 1997. **Architect:** Jerry Matthews. **Season:** April-Oct. **High:** June-Sept. **To obtain tee times:** Call golf shop. **Miscellaneous:** Reduced fees (seniors, juniors), range, credit cards (MC, V), BF, FF.

WHITEFORD VALLEY GOLF CLUB
PU-7980 Beck Rd., Ottawa Lake, 49267, Monroe County, (734)856-4545, (888)395-9041, 3 miles from Toledo. **E-mail:** golfpros@whitefordgolf.com. **Web:** www.whitefordgolf.com. **Facility Holes:** 72. **Green Fee:** $13/$24. **Cart Fee:** $24/Cart. **Walking Policy:** Unrestricted walking. **Walkability:** 2. **Opened:** 1995. **Architect:** Harley Hodges. **Season:** Year-round. **High:** May-Sept. **To obtain tee times:** Call up to 7 days in advance. **Miscellaneous:** Reduced fees (twilight, seniors, juniors), metal spikes, range (grass), credit cards (MC, V, D), BF, FF.
★ EAST COURSE (18)
Yards: 6,631/5,176. **Par:** 72/71. **Course Rating:** 70.8/68.2. **Slope:** 116/108.
★½ NORTH COURSE (18)
Yards: 6,808/5,677. **Par:** 72/73. **Course Rating:** 71.8/71.4. **Slope:** 123/119.
★½ SOUTH COURSE (18)
Yards: 6,659/5,195. **Par:** 72/72. **Course Rating:** 70.4/68.7. **Slope:** 116/109.
WEST COURSE (18)
Yards: 6,719/5,098. **Par:** 72/72. **Course Rating:** 70.8/68.3. **Slope:** 120/108.

★★★½ **WHITTAKER WOODS GOLF COMMUNITY**
PU-12578 Wilson Rd., New Buffalo, 49117, Berrien County, (616)469-3400, 70 miles from Chicago. **E-mail:** juliewwgc@aol.com. **Web:** www.golfwhittaker.com. **Facility Holes:** 18. **Yards:** 7,071/4,912. **Par:** 72/72. **Course Rating:** 74.3/68.6. **Slope:** 144/121. **Green Fee:** $55/$75. **Cart Fee:** Included in green fee. **Walking Policy:** Mandatory carts. **Walkability:** 5. **Opened:** 1996. **Architect:** Ken Killian. **Season:** Year-round. **High:** May-Aug. **To obtain tee times:** Call golf shop. **Miscellaneous:** Reduced fees (weekdays, twilight), range, credit cards (MC, V, AE, D), FF.
Reader Comments: Bring lots of balls, a very good test ... Very deceiving, but fair, tight landing areas if you hit it long ... Nicest course I played ... Nothing monotonous here.

★★★★½ **WILD BLUFF GOLF COURSE** *Value+*
PU-11335 W. Lakeshore Dr., Brimley, 49715, Sault County, (906)248-5861, (888)422-9645, 12 miles from Sault Ste. Marie. **Web:** www.wildbluff.com. **Facility Holes:** 18. **Yards:** 7,022/5,299. **Par:** 72/72. **Course Rating:** 74.4/71.5. **Slope:** 136/125. **Green Fee:** $40/$60. **Cart Fee:** Included in green fee. **Walking Policy:** Mandatory carts. **Walkability:** 3. **Opened:** 1999. **Architect:** Mike Husby. **Season:** April-Nov. **To obtain tee times:** Call up to 240 days in advance. **Miscellaneous:** Reduced fees (guests, twilight), range (grass), lodging (155 rooms), credit cards (MC, V, AE, D), BF, FF.
Reader Comments: We had a package deal with the casino that included lodging, two meals and golf, it was great ... Best in the UP ... A solid course ... Casino next door ... Scenic, too tough ... This may well be the best course in Upper Penninsula ... Great vistas from the bluffs overlooking Lake Superior.

★★½ **WILLOW BROOK PUBLIC GOLF CLUB**
PU-311 W. Maple, Byron, 48418, Shiawassee County, (810)266-4660, 22 miles from Lansing. **Facility Holes:** 18. **Yards:** 6,077/4,578. **Par:** 72/72. **Course Rating:** 70.6/67.3. **Slope:** 122/111. **Green Fee:** $15/$20. **Walking Policy:** Unrestricted walking. **Opened:** 1967. **Architect:** Jerry Clark. **Season:** April-Oct. **High:** June-Sept. **To obtain tee times:** Call golf shop. **Miscellaneous:** Reduced fees (weekdays).

★★★ **WILLOW METROPARK GOLF COURSE**
PU-22900 Huron River Dr., New Boston, 48164, Wayne County, (734)753-4040, (800)234-6534, 4 miles from Romulus. **Facility Holes:** 18. **Yards:** 6,378/5,278. **Par:** 71/72. **Course Rating:** 71.0/70.9. **Slope:** 126/122. **Green Fee:** $19/$23. **Cart Fee:** $11/Person. **Walking Policy:** Unrestricted walking. **Walkability:** 3. **Opened:** 1979. **Architect:** William Newcomb. **Season:** April-Nov. **High:** May-Aug. **To obtain tee times:** Call golf shop. **Miscellaneous:** Reduced fees (weekdays, seniors, juniors), range (grass), credit cards (MC, V).
Reader Comments: Near Detroit airport, noisy ... Good value, several pretty holes ... Staff friendly.

★★½ **WINDING BROOK GOLF CLUB**
PU-8240 S. Genuine, Shepherd, 48883, Isabella County, (517)828-5688, 6 miles from Mt. Pleasant. **Facility Holes:** 18. **Yards:** 6,614/5,015. **Par:** 72/72. **Course Rating:** 72.6/69.2. **Slope:** 127/115. **Green Fee:** $21/$25. **Cart Fee:** $12/Person. **Walking Policy:** Unrestricted walking. **Walkability:** 3. **Opened:** 1970. **Season:** Year-round. **To obtain tee times:** Call golf shop. **Miscellaneous:** Reduced fees (weekdays, twilight, seniors, juniors), range (grass), credit cards (MC, V, D), BF, FF.
Special Notes: Formerly Valley View Golf Course.

WINDING CREEK GOLF COURSE
PU-4514 Ottogan St., Holland, 49423, Allegan County, (616)396-4516, 20 miles from Grand Rapids. **Facility Holes:** 27. **Green Fee:** $24. **Cart Fee:** $11/Person. **Walking Policy:** Unrestricted walking. **Season:** April-Oct. **High:** May-Aug. **To obtain tee times:** Call golf shop. **Miscellaneous:** Reduced fees (twilight, seniors, juniors), range, credit cards (MC, V).
GOLD COURSE (9)
Yards: 2,600/1,865. **Par:** 34/34. **Course Rating:** 64.4/61.8. **Slope:** 119/112. **Walkability:** 2. **Opened:** 1993. **Architect:** D. Wiersema.
★★½ **WHITE/BLUE COURSE (18)**
Yards: 6,665/5,027. **Par:** 72/72. **Course Rating:** 71.5/68.6. **Slope:** 128/112. **Walkability:** 1. **Opened:** 1968. **Architect:** Bruce Matthews/Jerry Matthews.

WOLVERINE GOLF CLUB
PU-17201 25 Mile Rd., Macomb, 48042, Macomb County, (810)781-5544, (800)783-4653, 30 miles from Detroit. **Facility Holes:** 45. **Cart Fee:** $14/Person. **Opened:** 1965. **Walking Policy:** Mandatory carts. **Walkability:** 2. **Architect:** Jerry Matthews. **Season:** Year-round. **High:** May-Sept. **To obtain tee times:** Call golf shop. **Miscellaneous:** Reduced fees (weekdays, twilight, seniors, juniors), range (grass/mats), credit cards (MC, V, AE, D).
★★½ **BLUE/GREEN (18)**
Yards: 6,455/4,967. **Par:** 72/72. **Course Rating:** 70.3/69.6. **Slope:** 120/116.

MICHIGAN

★★ **RED/GOLD** (18)
Yards: 6,443/4,825. **Par:** 72/72. **Course Rating:** 70.7/69.5. **Slope:** 122/119.
★½ **WHITE** (9)
Yards: 3,281/2,539. **Par:** 36/36. **Course Rating:** 35.5/34.5. **Slope:** 117/114.

★★½ **WOODFIELD GOLF & COUNTRY CLUB**

PU-1 Golfside Dr., Grand Blanc, 48439, Genesee County, (810)695-4653, 30 miles from Detroit. **Facility Holes:** 18. **Yards:** 6,780/5,047. **Par:** 72/72. **Course Rating:** 73.3/70.3. **Slope:** 133/123. **Green Fee:** $40/$55. **Cart Fee:** Included in green fee. **Walking Policy:** Unrestricted walking. **Walkability:** 1. **Opened:** 1994. **Architect:** Raymond Floyd/Harry F. Bowers. **Season:** April-Oct. **High:** June-Aug. **To obtain tee times:** Call golf shop. **Miscellaneous:** Reduced fees (weekdays, twilight, seniors, juniors), metal spikes, range (grass/mats), credit cards (MC, V, AE).

★★★ **WOODLAWN GOLF CLUB**

PU-4634 Treat Hwy., Adrian, 49221, Lenawee County, (517)263-3288, 25 miles from Toledo. **Facility Holes:** 18. **Yards:** 6,080/4,686. **Par:** 71/71. **Course Rating:** 69.0/66.0. **Slope:** 116/112. **Green Fee:** $14/$23. **Cart Fee:** $12/Person. **Walking Policy:** Unrestricted walking. **Walkability:** 1. **Opened:** 1954. **Season:** March-Nov. **To obtain tee times:** Call golf shop. **Miscellaneous:** Reduced fees (twilight, seniors, juniors), credit cards (MC, V, D).
Reader Comments: Just great, should get more play, best-kept secret in area … Fun to play … Great for all types of players … My favorite.

★½ AFTON ALPS GOLF COURSE
PU-6600 Peller Ave. S., Hastings, 55033, Washington County, (651)436-1320, (800)328-1328, 20 miles from St. Paul. **Facility Holes:** 18. **Yards:** 5,528/4,866. **Par:** 72/72. **Course Rating:** 67.0/68.4. **Slope:** 108/114. **Green Fee:** $16/$20. **Cart Fee:** $18/Cart. **Walking Policy:** Unrestricted walking. **Walkability:** 3. **Opened:** 1989. **Architect:** Paul Augustine. **Season:** April-Oct. **High:** June-Aug. **To obtain tee times:** Call golf shop. **Miscellaneous:** Reduced fees (weekdays, seniors), metal spikes, credit cards (MC, V).

★★ ALBANY GOLF COURSE
PU-500 Church Ave., Albany, 56307, Stearns County, (320)845-2505, 15 miles from St. Cloud. **Facility Holes:** 18. **Yards:** 6,415/5,268. **Par:** 72/74. **Course Rating:** 70.7/69.0. **Slope:** 122/113. **Green Fee:** $20/$23. **Cart Fee:** $22/Cart. **Walking Policy:** Unrestricted walking. **Walkability:** 2. **Opened:** 1960. **Architect:** Willie Kidd. **Season:** April-Oct. **High:** May-Aug. **To obtain tee times:** Call golf shop. **Miscellaneous:** Reduced fees (seniors, juniors), metal spikes, range (grass/mats), credit cards (MC, V).

★★★½ ALBION RIDGES GOLF COURSE *Value*
PU-7771 20th St. NW, Annandale, 55302, Wright County, (320)963-5500, (800)430-7888, 40 miles from Minneapolis. **E-mail:** albion@teemaster.com. **Web:** www.teemaster.com. **Facility Holes:** 18. **Yards:** 6,555/4,728. **Par:** 72/72. **Course Rating:** 71.1/67.7. **Slope:** 129/115. **Green Fee:** $20/$28. **Cart Fee:** $20/Cart. **Walking Policy:** Unrestricted walking. **Walkability:** 3. **Opened:** 1991. **Architect:** Todd Severud. **Season:** April-Nov. **High:** May-Sept. **To obtain tee times:** Call golf shop. **Miscellaneous:** Reduced fees (weekdays, seniors, juniors), range (grass), credit cards (MC, V, D), BF, FF.
Reader Comments: Open links-style, fast greens, good value … Windy and hilly, but fun … Good for intermediate players … Everything is excellent, love it … Outstanding greens … Wide variety of holes … Great service.

★★★★ BAKER NATIONAL GOLF COURSE *Value*
PU-2935 Parkview Dr., Medina, 55340, Hennepin County, (952)473-0800, 20 miles from Minneapolis. **E-mail:** jmay@hennepinparks.org. **Web:** www.bakernational.com. **Facility Holes:** 27. **Yards:** 6,762/5,395. **Par:** 72/72. **Course Rating:** 73.9/72.7. **Slope:** 135/128. **Green Fee:** $26/$32. **Cart Fee:** $25/Cart. **Walking Policy:** Unrestricted walking. **Walkability:** 4. **Opened:** 1990. **Architect:** Michael Hurdzan. **Season:** April-Nov. **High:** May-Sept. **To obtain tee times:** Call up to 3 days in advance. **Miscellaneous:** Reduced fees (seniors, juniors), range (grass), credit cards (MC, V, D), BF, FF.
Reader Comments: Good challenge … Top 5 track, you'll love it! … Excellent course … A gem—and it's a county course! … Beautiful course start to finish … Every hole is different and fun to play.
Special Notes: Also has a 9-hole executive course.

★★½ BALMORAL GOLF COURSE
PU-28294 State Hwy. 78, Battle Lake, 56515, Otter Tail County, (218)864-5414, (800)943-2077, 9 miles from Battle Lake. **E-mail:** balmoral@prtel.com. **Web:** www.golfbalmoral.com. **Facility Holes:** 18. **Yards:** 6,144/5,397. **Par:** 72/72. **Course Rating:** 69.3/71.2. **Slope:** 120/120. **Green Fee:** $25/$30. **Cart Fee:** $24/Cart. **Walking Policy:** Unrestricted walking. **Walkability:** 3. **Opened:** 1961. **Architect:** Arnold Hemquist. **Season:** April-Oct. **High:** June-Aug. **To obtain tee times:** Call up to 7 days in advance. **Miscellaneous:** Reduced fees (weekdays, twilight), credit cards (MC, V, D), BF, FF.

★★★½ BELLWOOD OAKS GOLF COURSE *Value*
PU-13239 210th St., Hastings, 55033, Dakota County, (651)437-4141, 25 miles from St. Paul. **Facility Holes:** 18. **Yards:** 6,775/5,707. **Par:** 73/74. **Course Rating:** 72.5/72.3. **Slope:** 123/126. **Green Fee:** $21/$24. **Cart Fee:** $24/Cart. **Walking Policy:** Unrestricted walking. **Walkability:** 3. **Opened:** 1972. **Architect:** Don Raskob. **Season:** April-Nov. **High:** May-Sept. **To obtain tee times:** Call up to 5 days in advance. **Miscellaneous:** Reduced fees (weekdays, seniors), range (grass), credit cards (MC, V), BF, FF.
Reader Comments: A great course, always in good condition … Long challenging, must play position to score … Great value … Beautiful, challenging greens … Easy getting on … Tough finish

★★★★ BEMIDJI TOWN & COUNTRY CLUB
R-Birchmont Beach Rd., Bemidji, 56601, Beltrami County, (218)751-9215, 220 miles from Minneapolis/St. Paul. **Web:** www.bemidjigolf.com. **Facility Holes:** 18. **Yards:** 6,535/5,058. **Par:** 72/72. **Course Rating:** 71.8/69.1. **Slope:** 127/120. **Green Fee:** $30/$45. **Cart Fee:** $27/Cart. **Walking Policy:** Unrestricted walking. **Walkability:** 3. **Opened:** 1920. **Architect:** Joel Goldstrand. **Season:** April-Oct. **High:** June-Aug. **To obtain tee times:** Call golf shop. **Miscellaneous:** Reduced fees (guests, twilight), range, credit cards (MC, V, AE, D), BF, FF.
Reader Comments: Classy, old, treelined, deer watch you play … Friendly, challenging, excellent condition … Fun, scenic, a sleeper in the North country … Great woodsy course with views of lake.

MINNESOTA

★★★★ **BLUEBERRY PINES GOLF CLUB** *Pace*
PU-39161 U.S. Hwy. 71, Menahga, 56464, Wadena County, (218)564-4653, (800)652-4940, 115 miles from Fargo. **E-mail:** bbpgolf@wcta.net. **Web:** www.blueberrypinesgolf.com. **Facility Holes:** 18. **Yards:** 6,693/5,024. **Par:** 72/72. **Course Rating:** 72.6/69.3. **Slope:** 135/123. **Green Fee:** $30/$32. **Cart Fee:** $12/Person. **Walking Policy:** Walking at certain times. **Walkability:** 3. **Opened:** 1991. **Architect:** Joel Goldstrand. **Season:** April-Oct. **High:** June-Aug. **To obtain tee times:** Call golf shop. **Miscellaneous:** Reduced fees (twilight, seniors, juniors), range (grass), credit cards (MC, V, D), BF, FF.
Reader Comments: Nice layout, has some beautiful holes ... Only 9 years old and becoming one of Minnesota's best and most challenging ... Nice northwoods course ... The flowers around the course are great ... Beautiful layout in the pines.

★★ **BLUFF CREEK GOLF COURSE**
PU-1025 Creekwood, Chaska, 55318, Carver County, (952)445-5685, 20 miles from Minneapolis. **Facility Holes:** 18. **Yards:** 6,398/5,398. **Par:** 72/72. **Course Rating:** 70.2/70.7. **Slope:** 118/118. **Green Fee:** $20/$33. **Cart Fee:** $28/Cart. **Walking Policy:** Unrestricted walking. **Walkability:** 4. **Opened:** 1972. **Architect:** Gerry Pirkl/Donald G. Brauer. **Season:** April-Nov. **High:** May-Sept. **To obtain tee times:** Call up to 7 days in advance. **Miscellaneous:** Reduced fees (weekdays, twilight, seniors, juniors), range (mats), credit cards (MC, V), BF, FF.

★★★½ **BRAEMAR GOLF COURSE**
PU-6364 John Harris Dr., Edina, 55439, Hennepin County, (952)826-6799, 8 miles from Minneapolis. **Facility Holes:** 36. **Green Fee:** $30. **Cart Fee:** $24/Cart. **Walking Policy:** Unrestricted walking. **Walkability:** 3. **Opened:** 1964. **Architect:** Don Brauer. **Season:** April-Oct. **To obtain tee times:** Call up to 1 day in advance. **Miscellaneous:** Reduced fees (juniors), range (grass/mats), credit cards (MC, V, AE, D), BF, FF.
CASTLE/HAYS (18 Combo)
Yards: 6,739/5,702. **Par:** 71/73. **Course Rating:** 71.9/72.7. **Slope:** 125/126.
CLUNIE/CASTLE (18 Combo)
Yards: 6,660/5,579. **Par:** 72/73. **Course Rating:** 72.2/72.5. **Slope:** 129/125.
HAYS/CLUNIE (18 Combo)
Yards: 6,330/5,361. **Par:** 71/72. **Course Rating:** 70.5/71.0. **Slope:** 126/120.
Reader Comments: Great golf complex—challenging but fair ... Best city course ever ... Great 27 holes ... Good traditional course, 3rd 9 is tight.
Special Notes: Also has a 9-hole executive course.

BREEZY POINT RESORT
R-9252 Breezy Point Dr., Breezy Point, 56472, Crow Wing County, (218)562-7166, (800)950-4960, 20 miles from Brainerd. **E-mail:** mjohnson@breezypointresort.com. **Web:** www.breezypointresort.com. **Facility Holes:** 36. **Walking Policy:** Unrestricted walking. **Season:** April-Oct. **High:** July-Aug. **To obtain tee times:** Call golf shop. **Miscellaneous:** Reduced fees (weekdays, guests, twilight), lodging (275 rooms), credit cards (MC, V, AE, D, DC), BF, FF.
★★ **TRADITIONAL COURSE** (18)
Yards: 5,192/5,127. **Par:** 68/72. **Course Rating:** 62.9/65.5. **Slope:** 114/111. **Green Fee:** $27/$34. **Cart Fee:** $15/Person. **Walkability:** 3. **Opened:** 1930. **Architect:** Bill Fawcett.
★★★ **WHITEBIRCH GOLF COURSE** (18)
Yards: 6,704/4,711. **Par:** 72/72. **Course Rating:** 71.8/72.8. **Slope:** 124/123. **Green Fee:** $32/$69. **Cart Fee:** $16/Person. **Walkability:** 5. **Opened:** 1981. **Architect:** Landecker/Hubbard. **Miscellaneous:** Range (grass).
Reader Comments: Some really pretty holes ... Needs to grow and mature ... It's always breezy at Breezy Point ... Typical resort course.

★★★ **BROOKTREE MUNICIPAL GOLF COURSE**
PU-1369 Cherry St., Owatonna, 55060, Steele County, (507)444-2467, 40 miles from Minneapolis/St. Paul. **Facility Holes:** 18. **Yards:** 6,648/5,534. **Par:** 71/72. **Course Rating:** 71.9/71.3. **Slope:** 121/121. **Green Fee:** $14/$16. **Walking Policy:** Unrestricted walking. **Opened:** 1957. **Architect:** Gerry Pirkl/Donald G. Brauer. **Season:** April-Oct. **High:** June-Aug. **To obtain tee times:** Call golf shop. **Miscellaneous:** Reduced fees (weekdays), metal spikes.
Reader Comments: Always in good shape, ... Nice city course ... Good muni ... 2 different 9s.

★★★ **BROOKVIEW GOLF COURSE**
PU-200 Brookview Pkwy., Golden Valley, 55426, Hennepin County, (763)512-2300, 5 miles from Minneapolis. **E-mail:** ktovson@ci.golden-valley.mn.us. **Facility Holes:** 27. **Yards:** 6,369/5,463. **Par:** 72/72. **Course Rating:** 70.3/71.4. **Slope:** 127/124. **Green Fee:** $20/$28. **Cart Fee:** $25/Cart. **Walking Policy:** Unrestricted walking. **Walkability:** 3. **Opened:** 1969. **Architect:** Garrett Gill. **Season:** April-Nov. **High:** June-Sept. **To obtain tee times:** Call up to 7 days in advance. **Miscellaneous:** Reduced fees (twilight), range, credit cards (MC, V), BF, FF.
Reader Comments: Good city course ... Great for seniors ... Gets a lot of play ... A lot of water.
Special Notes: Also has a 9-hole par-3 course.

★★★★ **BUNKER HILLS GOLF COURSE**
PU-Highway 242 and Foley Blvd., Coon Rapids, 55448, Anoka County, (763)755-4141, 15 miles from Minneapolis. **Facility Holes:** 36. **Green Fee:** $28/$34. **Cart Fee:** $24/Cart. **Walking Policy:** Unrestricted walking. **Walkability:** 2. **Opened:** 1968. **Architect:** David Gill. **Season:** March-Nov. **High:** June-Sept. **To obtain tee times:** Call up to 4 days in advance. **Miscellaneous:** Reduced fees (seniors, juniors), range, credit cards (MC, V, AE, D), BF, FF.
EAST/WEST (18 Combo)
Yards: 6,901/5,809. **Par:** 72/73. **Course Rating:** 73.4/74.2. **Slope:** 133/128.
Notes: Ranked 35th in 1996 America's Top 75 Affordable Courses.
NORTH/EAST (18 Combo)
Yards: 6,799/5,618. **Par:** 72/72. **Course Rating:** 72.7/72.6. **Slope:** 130/126.
NORTH/WEST (18 Combo)
Yards: 6,938/5,779. **Par:** 72/73. **Course Rating:** 73.1/73.6. **Slope:** 135/130.
Special Notes: Also has a 9-hole executive course.
Reader Comments: Great course for twice the price ... Tough to get on, but in great shape ... Will test your entire game, especially your putting ... Best course for price in MN ... Great muni ... Lots of pine trees, greens, fairways outstanding.

★★★½ **CANNON GOLF CLUB**
SP-8606 295th St. E., Cannon Falls, 55009, Dakota County, (507)263-3126, 25 miles from St. Paul. **E-mail:** cannon@rconnect.com. **Web:** www.cannongolfclub.com. **Facility Holes:** 18. **Yards:** 6,157/4,988. **Par:** 71/71. **Course Rating:** 69.5/70.1. **Slope:** 127/125. **Green Fee:** $26/$32. **Cart Fee:** $28/Cart. **Walking Policy:** Unrestricted walking. **Walkability:** 3. **Opened:** 1927. **Architect:** Joel Goldstrand. **Season:** April-Nov. **High:** May-Oct. **To obtain tee times:** Call up to 7 days in advance. **Miscellaneous:** Reduced fees (weekdays, twilight, seniors, juniors), range (grass), credit cards (MC, V, AE, D), BF, FF.
Reader Comments: This course is a sleeper—great value for the money ... Short but challenging and fun to play ... In very good shape with some unique holes ... Pace of play was great ... Great variety of challenging holes ... Need every club ... Very scenic.

★½ **CARRIAGE HILLS COUNTRY CLUB**
PU-3535 Wescott Woodlands Dr., Eagan, 55123, Dakota County, (651)452-7211. **Facility Holes:** 18. **Yards:** 5,800/4,920. **Par:** 71/72. **Course Rating:** 67.5/68.4. **Slope:** 119/111. **Green Fee:** $14/$27. **Cart Fee:** $22/Cart. **Walking Policy:** Unrestricted walking. **Walkability:** 4. **Opened:** 1965. **Season:** April-Oct. **High:** June-Aug. **Tee times:** Call golf shop. **Miscellaneous:** Reduced fees (weekdays, twilight, seniors, juniors), credit cards (MC, V), BF, FF.

★★ **CASTLE HIGHLANDS GOLF COURSE**
SP-City Road 23, Highway 71, Bemidji, 56601, Beltrami County, (218)586-2681, 230 miles from Minneapolis. **Facility Holes:** 18. **Yards:** 5,246/4,448. **Par:** 70/70. **Course Rating:** 65.8/65.5. **Slope:** 111/112. **Green Fee:** $26. **Cart Fee:** $20/Cart. **Walking Policy:** Unrestricted walking. **Walkability:** 3. **Opened:** 1970. **Architect:** Ray Castle. **Season:** April-Oct. **High:** May-Sept. **To obtain tee times:** Call golf shop. **Miscellaneous:** Range, credit cards (MC, V, D).

★★★ **CEDAR RIVER COUNTRY CLUB**
SP-14927 State Hwy. 56, Adams, 55909, Mower County, (507)582-3595, 16 miles from Austin. **Facility Holes:** 18. **Yards:** 6,298/5,553. **Par:** 72/74. **Course Rating:** 69.3/71.3. **Slope:** 117/119. **Green Fee:** $22/$23. **Cart Fee:** $25/Cart. **Walking Policy:** Unrestricted walking. **Walkability:** 2. **Opened:** 1969. **Architect:** Bob Carlson. **Season:** March-Nov. **High:** June-Aug. **To obtain tee times:** Call up to 7 days in advance. **Miscellaneous:** Range (grass), credit cards (MC, V, D), BF, FF.
Reader Comments: Lots of pines ... Rewarding ... Rural setting ... You wouldn't expect to find a course like this here ... Nice fairways, challenging.

★★★ **CEDAR VALLEY GOLF COURSE**
SP-County Rd. 9, Winona, 55987, Winona County, (507)457-3129, 100 miles from Minneapolis. **Facility Holes:** 27. **Yards:** 6,218/5,560. **Par:** 72/72. **Course Rating:** 69.5/71.7. **Slope:** 119/122. **Green Fee:** $24/$26. **Cart Fee:** $20/Cart. **Walking Policy:** Unrestricted walking. **Walkability:** 3. **Opened:** 1992. **Season:** April-Nov. **High:** June-Aug. **To obtain tee times:** Call golf shop. **Miscellaneous:** Range (grass), credit cards (MC, V).
Reader Comments: Friendly little place. Hate to share this hidden gem! ... Beautiful setting. Very good greens ... Valley golf, well-routed ... Will become more challenging as it matures ... Open front 9; back 9 difficult but interesting.
Special Notes: Also has a 9-hole executive course.

★★★★ **CHASKA TOWN COURSE**
PU-3000 Town Course Dr., Chaska, 55318, Carver County, (952)443-3748, 25 miles from Minneapolis. **E-mail:** dcahill@chaska.net. **Web:** www.chaskatowncourse.com. **Facility Holes:**

18. **Yards:** 6,817/4,853. **Par:** 72/72. **Course Rating:** 73.8/69.8. **Slope:** 142/116. **Green Fee:** $28/$49. **Cart Fee:** $26/Cart. **Walking Policy:** Unrestricted walking. **Walkability:** 3. **Opened:** 1997. **Architect:** Arthur Hills/Brian Yoder. **Season:** April-Oct. **High:** May-Oct. **To obtain tee times:** Call up to 4 days in advance. **Miscellaneous:** Reduced fees (weekdays, twilight), range (grass), credit cards (MC, V), BF, FF.
Notes: Ranked 15th in 2001 Best in State.
Reader Comments: Nice track! ... Some extremely tough par 4s ... A great experience! ... New yardage book and markers help immensely... Great clubhouse building and staff ... A real find! Most player walk and it's a treat. #18 is Minnesota's version of Pebble Beach's #18 ... Pace of play is a priority—thank you! ... 18 great golf holes.

★★★ CHISAGO LAKES GOLF COURSE
SP-12975 292nd St., Lindstrom, 55045, Chisago County, (651)257-1484, 35 miles from St. Paul. **E-mail:** chisagolakesgolf@yahoo.com. **Web:** www.chisagolakesgolf.com. **Facility Holes:** 18. **Yards:** 6,529/5,714. **Par:** 72/72. **Course Rating:** 71.2/72.7. **Slope:** 119/124. **Green Fee:** $22/$26. **Cart Fee:** $24/Cart. **Walking Policy:** Unrestricted walking. **Walkability:** 3. **Opened:** 1972. **Architect:** Donald Brauer/Joel Goldstrand. **Season:** April-Oct. **High:** June-Aug. **To obtain tee times:** Call up to 6 days in advance. **Miscellaneous:** Reduced fees (weekdays, twilight, seniors, juniors), range (grass), credit cards (MC, V, D), BF, FF.
Reader Comments: Tough starting holes ... Good practice facility ... Nice course, not too busy ... Easy to get on ... Beautiful course to walk. Front 9 good warmup for tougher back 9 ... Great small-town track ... Fun.

★★½ CHOMONIX GOLF COURSE
PU-646 Sandpiper Dr., Lino Lakes, 55014, Anoka County, (651)482-8484, 22 miles from Minneapolis. **E-mail:** chomonix1@juno.com. **Web:** www.chomonixgolf.com. **Facility Holes:** 18. **Yards:** 6,596/5,455. **Par:** 72/72. **Course Rating:** 72.2/72.3. **Slope:** 128/125. **Green Fee:** $21/$27. **Cart Fee:** $24/Cart. **Walking Policy:** Unrestricted walking. **Walkability:** 2. **Opened:** 1970. **Architect:** Don Herfort/Gerry Pirkl. **Season:** April-Nov. **High:** June-Aug. **To obtain tee times:** Call up to 4 days in advance. **Miscellaneous:** Reduced fees (seniors, juniors), range (grass), credit cards (MC, V, D), BF, FF.

★★½ COLUMBIA GOLF COURSE
PU-3300 Central Ave., Minneapolis, 55418, Hennepin County, (612)789-2627, 3 miles from Minneapolis (downtown). **E-mail:** timothy.a.kuebelbeck@ci.minneapolis.mn.us. **Facility Holes:** 18. **Yards:** 6,371/5,191. **Par:** 71/71. **Course Rating:** 70.0/69.3. **Slope:** 122/117. **Green Fee:** $22/$23. **Cart Fee:** $24/Cart. **Walking Policy:** Unrestricted walking. **Walkability:** 3. **Opened:** 1919. **Architect:** Edward Lawrence Packard. **Season:** April-Dec. **High:** May-Sept. **To obtain tee times:** Call up to 4 days in advance. **Miscellaneous:** Reduced fees (weekdays, twilight, seniors, juniors), range (grass/mats), credit cards (MC, V, AE, D), BF, FF.

★★½ COMO GOLF COURSE
PU-1431 N. Lexington Pkwy., St. Paul, 55103, Ramsey County, (651)488-9673. **E-mail:** john.shimpach@ci.stpaul.mn.us. **Web:** www.stpaul.gov/parks. **Facility Holes:** 18. **Yards:** 5,814/5,068. **Par:** 70/70. **Course Rating:** 67.6/69.0. **Slope:** 117/115. **Green Fee:** $25. **Cart Fee:** $23/Cart. **Walking Policy:** Unrestricted walking. **Walkability:** 3. **Opened:** 1988. **Architect:** Don Herfort. **Season:** April-Nov. **High:** May-Oct. **To obtain tee times:** Call up to 7 days in advance. **Miscellaneous:** Reduced fees (twilight, seniors, juniors), credit cards (MC, V), BF, FF.

CROSSWOODS GOLF COURSE
PU-35878 County Road #3, Crosslake, 56442, Crow Wing County, (218)692-4653, 23 miles from Brainerd. **E-mail:** crosswoods@crosslake.net. **Web:** www.angelfire.com/mn2/crosswoods. **Facility Holes:** 18. **Yards:** 5,236/4,445. **Par:** 68/68. **Course Rating:** 66.5/67.0. **Slope:** 116/118. **Green Fee:** $18/$24. **Cart Fee:** $20/Cart. **Walking Policy:** Unrestricted walking. **Walkability:** 3. **Opened:** 1997. **Architect:** Michael Stone. **Season:** April-Oct. **High:** June-Aug. **To obtain tee times:** Call golf shop. **Miscellaneous:** Reduced fees (weekdays, twilight, seniors, juniors), range (grass/mats), credit cards (MC, V, D), BF, FF.

★★★ CUYUNA COUNTRY CLUB
SP-20 Golf Country Club Road, Box 40, Deerwood, 56444, Crow Wing County, (218)534-3489, 90 miles from Minneapolis. **Facility Holes:** 18. **Yards:** 6,407/5,749. **Par:** 72/74. **Course Rating:** 71.9/74.2. **Slope:** 132/138. **Green Fee:** $28/$39. **Cart Fee:** $26/Cart. **Walking Policy:** Unrestricted walking. **Walkability:** 3. **Opened:** 1923. **Architect:** Don Herfort. **Season:** April-Oct. **High:** July-Aug. **To obtain tee times:** Call golf shop. **Miscellaneous:** Reduced fees (weekdays, guests, seniors, juniors), range (grass), credit cards (MC, V, D).
Reader Comments: Hidden gem ... Could play back 9 every day ... Front side has small greens; back side bigger, a lot of woods. A sleeper ... A great golfer's course ... The back 9 gets more scenic every year.

MINNESOTA

DACOTAH RIDGE GOLF CLUB
R-31042 County Hwy. 2, Morton, 56270, Redwood County, (507)644-5050, (800)946-2274, 100 miles from Minneapolis. **Web:** www.dacotahridge.com. **Facility Holes:** 18. **Yards:** 7,109/5,055. **Par:** 72/72. **Course Rating:** 73.9/68.9. **Slope:** 134/121. **Green Fee:** $24/$49. **Cart Fee:** $15/Person. **Walking Policy:** Unrestricted walking. **Walkability:** 4. **Opened:** 2000. **Architect:** Rees Jones. **Season:** April-Nov. **High:** May-Oct. **To obtain tee times:** Call up to 90 days in advance. **Miscellaneous:** Reduced fees (guests, twilight, juniors), range (grass), credit cards (MC, V, AE, D), BF, FF.
Notes: Ranked 3rd in 2001 Best New Affordable Courses.

★★★ DAHLGREEN GOLF CLUB
SP-6940 Dahlgreen Rd., Chaska, 55318, Carver County, (952)448-7463, 20 miles from Minneapolis. **E-mail:** tocsn714@aol.com. **Web:** www.dahlgreengolfclub.com. **Facility Holes:** 18. **Yards:** 6,761/5,113. **Par:** 72/72. **Course Rating:** 72.5/69.3. **Slope:** 130/120. **Green Fee:** $28/$35. **Cart Fee:** $25/Cart. **Walking Policy:** Unrestricted walking. **Walkability:** 2. **Opened:** 1969. **Architect:** Gerry Pirkl/Donald Brauer. **Season:** April-Nov. **High:** June-Aug. **To obtain tee times:** Call up to 5 days in advance. **Miscellaneous:** Reduced fees (weekdays, seniors, juniors), range (grass), credit cards (MC, V, AE, D), BF, FF.
Reader Comments: Nice setting ... Short facility ... Long, you'll need a long drive to reach par 4s ... Old course, many trees ... Needs better maintenance ... A hidden gem on the outskirts of town.

★★½ DAYTONA COUNTRY CLUB
PU-14730 Lawndale Lane, Dayton, 55327, Hennepin County, (763)427-6110, 20 miles from Minneapolis. **Web:** www.daytonacc.com. **Facility Holes:** 18. **Yards:** 6,352/5,365. **Par:** 72/73. **Course Rating:** 69.8/71.0. **Slope:** 121/117. **Green Fee:** $25/$30. **Cart Fee:** $25/Cart. **Walking Policy:** Unrestricted walking. **Walkability:** 3. **Opened:** 1964. **Architect:** Jerry McCann. **Season:** April-Dec. **High:** June-Sept. **To obtain tee times:** Call up to 7 days in advance. **Miscellaneous:** Reduced fees (weekdays, seniors, juniors), range (grass), credit cards (MC, V, AE, D), BF, FF.

★★★★½ DEACON'S LODGE GOLF COURSE *Service, Pace*
R-9348 Arnold Palmer Dr., Breezy Point, 56472, Crow Wing County, (218)562-6262, (888)549-5444, 20 miles from Brainerd. **Web:** www.deaconslodge.com. **Facility Holes:** 18. **Yards:** 6,964/4,766. **Par:** 72/72. **Course Rating:** 73.8/67.6. **Slope:** 128/114. **Green Fee:** $90/$98. **Cart Fee:** Included in green fee. **Walking Policy:** Unrestricted walking. **Walkability:** 3. **Opened:** 1999. **Architect:** Arnold Palmer/Ed Seay/Erik Larsen. **Season:** May-Oct. **To obtain tee times:** Call up to 60 days in advance. **Miscellaneous:** Reduced fees (weekdays, guests, twilight), range (grass), lodging (10 rooms), credit cards (MC, V, AE, D), BF, FF.
Notes: Ranked 13th in 2001 Best in State.
Reader Comments: Beautiful and tough ... Very natural layout ... Expensive, but worth it ... Make sure you get on the right tees ... This is a great place to enjoy nature at its best ... Gorgeous course with great carries.

★★★ DEER RUN GOLF CLUB
PU-8661 Deer Run Dr., Victoria, 55386, Carver County, (952)443-2351, 20 miles from Minneapolis. **E-mail:** tabts@deerrungolf.com. **Web:** www.deerrungolf.com. **Facility Holes:** 18. **Yards:** 6,265/5,541. **Par:** 71/71. **Course Rating:** 70.5/72.1. **Slope:** 122/121. **Green Fee:** $29/$35. **Cart Fee:** $26/Cart. **Walking Policy:** Unrestricted walking. **Walkability:** 4. **Opened:** 1989. **Season:** April-Nov. **High:** May-Sept. **To obtain tee times:** Call up to 5 days in advance. **Miscellaneous:** Reduced fees (twilight, seniors, juniors), range, credit cards (MC, V, AE), FF.
Reader Comments: Nice rural course ... Nice layout—always in good condition ... Loved it ... Easy course—good pace and value ... Pleasant staff ... Good maintenance.

★★★ DETROIT COUNTRY CLUB
R-24591 County Hwy. 22, Detroit Lakes, 56501, Becker County, (218)847-5790, 47 miles from Fargo. **Web:** www.detroitlakes.com/golf/index.html. **Facility Holes:** 36. **Yards:** 6,071/5,013. **Par:** 71/71. **Course Rating:** 69.2/68.7. **Slope:** 119/117. **Green Fee:** $32. **Cart Fee:** $23/Cart. **Walking Policy:** Unrestricted walking. **Walkability:** 4. **Opened:** 1916. **Architect:** Tom Bendelow/Don Herfort. **Season:** April-Sept. **High:** June-Aug. **To obtain tee times:** Call up to 7 days in advance. **Miscellaneous:** Range (grass), caddies, credit cards (MC, V), BF, FF.
Reader Comments: Short, but tight ... Super condition ... Fun course for all types of golfer ... Very challenging ... Excellent resort course, beautiful surroundings.
Special Notes: Also has an 18-hole executive course.

DOUBLE EAGLE GOLF CLUB
PU-R.R.1 County Box 117 Road #3, Eagle Bend, 56446, Todd County, (218)738-5155, 30 miles from Alexandria. **Facility Holes:** 18. **Green Fee:** $22/$24. **Cart Fee:** $20/Cart. **Walking Policy:** Unrestricted walking. **Walkability:** 2. **Opened:** 1982. **Architect:** Joel Goldstrand. **Season:** April-Oct. **High:** June-Sept. **To obtain tee times:** Call golf shop. **Miscellaneous:**

Reduced fees (weekdays), range (grass/mats), credit cards (MC, V), FF.
★★½ **GOLD COURSE** (9)
Yards: 3,556/2,920. **Par:** 37/37. **Course Rating:** 37.4/36.8. **Slope:** 134/128.
Special Notes: Reversible course; play Gold Course in one direction, play Green Course in reverse direction to make 18 holes.
★★★ **GREEN COURSE** (9)
Yards: 3,337/2,790. **Par:** 36/36. **Course Rating:** 36.0/36.0. **Slope:** 127/124.
Reader Comments: Well-maintained …. Reversible 9-hole course … Enjoyable course, some very hard holes.
Special Notes: Reversible course; play Green Course in one direction, then play Gold Course in reverse direction to make 18 holes.

★★½ **EAGLE CREEK**
SP-1000 26th. Ave. N.E., Willmar, 56201, Kandiyohi County, (320)235-1166, 80 miles from Minneapolis. **E-mail:** golfshop@eaglecreekgc.com. **Facility Holes:** 18. **Yards:** 6,342/5,271. **Par:** 72/73. **Course Rating:** 70.8/70.9. **Slope:** 129/127. **Green Fee:** $27/$30. **Cart Fee:** $23/Cart. **Walking Policy:** Unrestricted walking. **Walkability:** 2. **Opened:** 1930. **Architect:** Albert Anderson. **Season:** April-Oct. **High:** May-Aug. **To obtain tee times:** Call up to 4 days in advance. **Miscellaneous:** Reduced fees (weekdays), range, credit cards (MC, V), BF, FF.

★★★½ **EAGLE RIDGE GOLF COURSE**
PU-1 Green Way, Coleraine, 55722, Itasca County, (218)245-2217, (888)307-3245, 5 miles from Grand Rapids. **E-mail:** ergc@uslink.com. **Web:** www.golfeagleridge.com. **Facility Holes:** 18. **Yards:** 6,772/5,220. **Par:** 72/72. **Course Rating:** 72.2/70.0. **Slope:** 127/117. **Green Fee:** $26/$32. **Cart Fee:** $20/Cart. **Walking Policy:** Unrestricted walking. **Walkability:** 4. **Opened:** 1996. **Architect:** Garrett Gill. **Season:** April-Oct. **High:** June-Aug. **To obtain tee times:** Call up to 90 days in advance. **Miscellaneous:** Reduced fees (weekdays, guests, juniors), range (grass/mats), credit cards (MC, V, D), BF, FF.
Reader Comments: Great views … Carved through woods … Challenging … Excellent course, very pretty, very woodsy … Very picturesque … Front 9 wide open, back 9 better.

★★½ **EASTWOOD GOLF CLUB**
PU-3505 Eastwood Rd. S.E., Rochester, 55904, Olmsted County, (507)281-6173. **Facility Holes:** 18. **Yards:** 6,178/5,289. **Par:** 70/70. **Course Rating:** 69.4/70.3. **Slope:** 119/116. **Green Fee:** $22. **Cart Fee:** $20/Cart. **Walking Policy:** Unrestricted walking. **Walkability:** 4. **Opened:** 1968. **Architect:** Ray Keller. **Season:** April-Nov. **High:** May-Sept. **To obtain tee times:** Call up to 2 days in advance. **Miscellaneous:** Range (grass), credit cards (MC, V), BF, FF.

★★★★ **EDINBURGH USA GOLF CLUB**
PU-8700 Edinbrook Crossing, Brooklyn Park, 55443, Hennepin County, (763)315-8550, 12 miles from Minneapolis. **Web:** www.edinburghusa.org. **Facility Holes:** 18. **Yards:** 6,729/5,255. **Par:** 72/72. **Course Rating:** 73.1/71.4. **Slope:** 131/128. **Green Fee:** $43/$45. **Cart Fee:** $30/Cart. **Walking Policy:** Unrestricted walking. **Walkability:** 2. **Opened:** 1987. **Architect:** Robert Trent Jones Jr. **Season:** April-Oct. **High:** May-Sept. **To obtain tee times:** Call up to 4 days in advance. **Miscellaneous:** Reduced fees (weekdays, twilight, seniors, juniors), metal spikes, range (grass), caddies, credit cards (MC, V, AE), BF, FF.
Notes: Ranked 18th in 2001 Best in State; 23rd in 1996 America's Top 75 Affordable Courses.
Reader Comments: I wanted to play the course again as soon as I putted out on 18 … Target golf … Fun course, bunkers everywhere … Always a treat to play … Lots of rounds … Great design … Like the Island hole … Best public course in metro area.

★★★ **ELK RIVER COUNTRY CLUB**
SP-20015 Elk Lake Rd., Elk River, 55330, Sherburne County, (763)441-4111, 45 miles from Minneapolis. **Facility Holes:** 18. **Yards:** 6,480/5,590. **Par:** 72/75. **Course Rating:** 71.1/72.3. **Slope:** 121/122. **Green Fee:** $31/$34. **Cart Fee:** $26/Cart. **Walking Policy:** Unrestricted walking. **Walkability:** 3. **Opened:** 1960. **Architect:** Willie Kidd. **Season:** March-Nov. **High:** June-Aug. **To obtain tee times:** Call up to 7 days in advance. **Miscellaneous:** Reduced fees (seniors, juniors), range (grass), credit cards (MC, V, AE, D), BF, FF.
Reader Comments: Nice old course, small crowned greens … Some interesting holes, too many blind shots, nice clubhouse … Better than average course.

★★ **ELM CREEK GOLF LINKS OF PLYMOUTH**
PU-18940 Highway 55, Plymouth, 55446, Hennepin County, (612)478-6716, 10 miles from Minneapolis. **Web:** www.teemaster.com. **Facility Holes:** 18. **Yards:** 6,235/4,874. **Par:** 70/71. **Course Rating:** 70.4/68.0. **Slope:** 132/117. **Green Fee:** $23/$27. **Cart Fee:** $24/Cart. **Walking Policy:** Unrestricted walking. **Walkability:** 4. **Opened:** 1960. **Architect:** Michael Klatte/Mark Klatte. **Season:** April-Oct. **High:** June-Aug. **To obtain tee times:** Call golf shop. **Miscellaneous:** Reduced fees (weekdays, twilight, seniors, juniors), credit cards (MC, V, AE), BF, FF.

★★★½ ENGER PARK GOLF CLUB

PU-1801 W. Skyline Blvd., Duluth, 55806, St. Louis County, (218)723-3451, 149 miles from Minneapolis. **Facility Holes:** 27. **Green Fee:** $23. **Cart Fee:** $23/Cart. **Walking Policy:** Unrestricted walking. **Walkability:** 3. **Opened:** 1927. **Architect:** Dick Phelps. **Season:** April-Nov. **To obtain tee times:** Call up to 7 days in advance. **Miscellaneous:** Reduced fees (twilight, seniors, juniors), range (grass), credit cards (MC, V), BF, FF.
BACK NINE/FRONT NINE (18 Combo)
Yards: 6,499/5,617. **Par:** 72/72. **Course Rating:** 71.0/67.0. **Slope:** 120/117.
FRONT NINE/MIDDLE NINE (18 Combo)
Yards: 6,434/5,247. **Par:** 72/72. **Course Rating:** 70.9/65.3. **Slope:** 126/115.
MIDDLE NINE/BACK NINE (18 Combo)
Yards: 6,325/5,404. **Par:** 72/72. **Course Rating:** 70.3/66.6. **Slope:** 121/110.
Reader Comments: Great view of Lake Superior and Duluth … Decent place to play … Rolling hills; very challenging in wind … Nice city course … Old course, needs some greens work … Still best value in the world.

★★ FALCON RIDGE GOLF COURSE

PU-33942 Falcon Ave., Stacy, 55079, Chisago County, (651)462-5797, (877)535-9335, 3 miles from Stacy. **E-mail:** falconridge@teemaster.com. **Facility Holes:** 27. **Yards:** 5,787/5,070. **Par:** 72/72. **Course Rating:** 68.0/70.3. **Slope:** 115/120. **Green Fee:** $20/$25. **Cart Fee:** $24/Cart. **Walking Policy:** Unrestricted walking. **Walkability:** 1. **Opened:** 1993. **Architect:** Lyle Kleven/Martin Johnson/Doug Lien. **Season:** April-Oct. **To obtain tee times:** Call up to 7 days in advance. **Miscellaneous:** Reduced fees (weekdays, seniors, juniors), range (grass/mats), credit cards (MC, V, D), BF, FF.
Special Notes: Also has a 9-hole executive course.

★★ FOUNTAIN VALLEY GOLF CLUB

PU-2830 220th St. W., Farmington, 55024, Dakota County, (651)463-2121, 30 miles from Minneapolis. **E-mail:** fvgc@netzero.net. **Facility Holes:** 18. **Yards:** 6,540/5,980. **Par:** 72/72. **Course Rating:** 71.5/73.4. **Slope:** 119/122. **Green Fee:** $20/$25. **Cart Fee:** $13/Person. **Walking Policy:** Unrestricted walking. **Walkability:** 2. **Opened:** 1977. **Architect:** Ray Rahn. **Season:** April-Oct. **High:** June-Aug. **To obtain tee times:** Call up to 7 days in advance. **Miscellaneous:** Reduced fees (weekdays, seniors), range, credit cards (MC, V), BF, FF.

★★★ FOX HOLLOW GOLF CLUB

SP-4780 Palmgren Lane N.E., Rogers, 55374, Wright County, (763)428-4468, 30 miles from Minneapolis. **E-mail:** foxhollow@teemaster.com. **Web:** www.teemaster.com. **Facility Holes:** 27. **Green Fee:** $32/$42. **Cart Fee:** $13/Person. **Walking Policy:** Unrestricted walking. **Walkability:** 3. **Opened:** 1989. **Architect:** Joel Goldstrand. **Season:** April-Nov. **High:** May-Sept. **To obtain tee times:** Call up to 3 days in advance. **Miscellaneous:** Reduced fees (weekdays, seniors, juniors), range (grass), credit cards (MC, V, AE, D), BF, FF.
Reader Comments: Challenging but good course … Need every club in your bag—keep it in play … Very good layout, great island green … Great holes along Crow River … Pleasant staff … Fast/firm greens and fairways.

★★★ FRANCIS A. GROSS GOLF COURSE

PU-2201 St. Anthony Blvd., Minneapolis, 55418, Hennepin County, (612)789-2542. **E-mail:** gross@teemaster.com. **Web:** www.teemaster.com. **Facility Holes:** 18. **Yards:** 6,575/5,400. **Par:** 71/71. **Course Rating:** 70.8/73.2. **Slope:** 120/121. **Green Fee:** $24/$26. **Cart Fee:** $24/Cart. **Walking Policy:** Unrestricted walking. **Walkability:** 2. **Opened:** 1925. **Architect:** W. D. Clark. **Season:** April-Nov. **High:** May-Sept. **To obtain tee times:** Call up to 4 days in advance. **Miscellaneous:** Reduced fees (weekdays, twilight, seniors, juniors), metal spikes, range (grass), credit cards (MC, V, AE, D, DC), BF, FF.
Reader Comments: Classic old public course … As good a muni as you'll find in area … Great city course, but very busy … Short but not easy … Pace has improved.

★★★★½ GIANTS RIDGE GOLF & SKI RESORT

R-P.O. Box 190, Biwabik, 55708, St. Louis County, (218)865-4143, (800)688-7669, 4 miles from Biwabik. **E-mail:** jkendall@giantsridge.com. **Web:** www.giantsridge.com. **Facility Holes:** 18. **Yards:** 6,930/5,084. **Par:** 72/72. **Course Rating:** 74.3/70.3. **Slope:** 138/124. **Green Fee:** $45/$77. **Cart Fee:** Included in green fee. **Walking Policy:** Mandatory carts. **Walkability:** 3. **Opened:** 1997. **Architect:** Jeffrey Brauer/Lanny Wadkins. **Season:** May-Oct. **High:** June-Sept. **To obtain tee times:** Call up to 180 days in advance. **Miscellaneous:** Reduced fees (twilight, juniors), range (grass), lodging (93 rooms), credit cards (MC, V, AE), BF, FF.
Notes: Ranked 10th in 2001 Best in State.
Reader Comments: Wow!! Doesn't get much better than this … Beautiful course design! Great condition, and great bargain … Best 9 (back) I've ever played! … Don't miss it! … Best in northern Minnesota … What a view … Great course for the money.

★★★ GLENCOE COUNTRY CLUB
SP-1325 E. 1st. St., Glencoe, 55336, McLeod County, (320)864-3023, 54 miles from Minneapolis. **Facility Holes:** 18. **Yards:** 6,074/4,940. **Par:** 71/71. **Course Rating:** 69.7/69.7. **Slope:** 117/117. **Green Fee:** $22/$27. **Cart Fee:** $22/Cart. **Walking Policy:** Unrestricted walking. **Walkability:** 2. **Opened:** 1958. **Season:** April-Nov. **High:** April-Sept. **To obtain tee times:** Call up to 3 days in advance. **Miscellaneous:** Reduced fees (seniors, juniors), range (grass), credit cards (MC, V, AE, D), BF, FF.
Reader Comments: Long walks between holes … Fast, hard, pro-style greens … Bring your short game … Great place for the money.

GOLF AT THE LEGACY
PU-1515 Shumway Ave., Faribault, 55021, Rice County, (507)332-7177, 40 miles from Minneapolis. **Web:** www.legacygolfandhomes.com. **Facility Holes:** 18. **Yards:** 6,416/5,031. **Par:** 72/72. **Course Rating:** 71.1/69.2. **Slope:** 127/118. **Green Fee:** $25/$31. **Cart Fee:** $24/Cart. **Walking Policy:** Unrestricted walking. **Walkability:** 3. **Opened:** 1998. **Architect:** Garrett Gill/George Williams. **Season:** March-Nov. **High:** May-Sept. **To obtain tee times:** Call up to 5 days in advance. **Miscellaneous:** Reduced fees (weekdays, twilight, seniors, juniors), range (grass/mats), credit cards (MC, V), BF, FF.

★★★ GOODRICH GOLF COURSE
PU-1820 N. Van Dyke, Maplewood, 55109, Ramsey County, (651)777-7355, 3 miles from St. Paul. **Facility Holes:** 18. **Yards:** 6,228/5,124. **Par:** 70/70. **Course Rating:** 68.6/69.3. **Slope:** 110/113. **Green Fee:** $20/$24. **Cart Fee:** $23/Cart. **Walking Policy:** Unrestricted walking. **Walkability:** 2. **Opened:** 1959. **Architect:** Paul Coates. **Season:** April-Nov. **High:** June-Sept. **To obtain tee times:** Call golf shop. **Miscellaneous:** Reduced fees (weekdays, twilight, seniors, juniors), range (mats), credit cards (MC, V), BF, FF.
Reader Comments: Moves pretty quickly … Wide open … Heavy play … Easy walking … Good condition … Great price—typical muni course … Great improvements with changes.

★★★ GRAND NATIONAL GOLF CLUB
PU-300 Lady Luck Dr., Hinckley, 55037, Pine County, (320)384-7427, 60 miles from Minneapolis/St. Paul. **Facility Holes:** 18. **Yards:** 6,894/5,100. **Par:** 72/72. **Course Rating:** 73.6/69.6. **Slope:** 137/122. **Green Fee:** $27/$30. **Cart Fee:** $26/Cart. **Walking Policy:** Unrestricted walking. **Walkability:** 3. **Opened:** 1995. **Architect:** Joel Goldstrand. **Season:** April-Oct. **High:** May-Aug. **To obtain tee times:** Call golf shop. **Miscellaneous:** Reduced fees (guests, twilight, seniors), metal spikes, range, lodging (500 rooms), credit cards (MC, V).
Reader Comments: Flat, but testy … Challenging … Nice course … Good layout … Plush fairways, links style … Good value, some great holes … A lot of variety for the value.

GRAND VIEW LODGE RESORT
R-Weaver Point Rd., Breeze Point Township, 56472, Crow Wing County, (218)562-6262, (888)437-4637, 30 miles from Brainerd. **E-mail:** golf@grandviewlodge.com. **Web:** www.grand-viewlodge.com. **Facility Holes:** 72. **Cart Fee:** Included in green fee. **Walking Policy:** Unrestricted walking. **Season:** April-Oct. **High:** May-Sept. **To obtain tee times:** Call up to 90 days in advance. **Miscellaneous:** Reduced fees (weekdays, guests, twilight), range (grass), lodging (300 rooms), credit cards (MC, V, AE, D), BF, FF.
★★★★½ **DEACON'S LODGE** (18) *Pace*
Yards: 6,964/4,766. **Par:** 72/72. **Course Rating:** 73.8/67.6. **Slope:** 128/114. **Green Fee:** $90/$98. **Walkability:** 4. **Opened:** 1999. **Architect:** Arnold Palmer.
Reader Comments: Great shape and excellent service … Wonderful course—a very unique feel to it … Views are awesome … Beautiful course with a number of odd holes.
★★★★★ **THE PINES** (27) *Value+, Condition+, Pace+*
Green Fee: $75/$85. **Walkability:** 2. **Opened:** 1990. **Architect:** Joel Goldstrand.
(LAKES/WOODS) (18 Combo)
Yards: 6,874/5,134. **Par:** 72/72. **Course Rating:** 74.1/70.7. **Slope:** 143/128.
Notes: Ranked 68th in 1996 America's Top 75 Upscale Courses.
(MARSH/LAKES) (18 Combo)
Yards: 6,837/5,112. **Par:** 72/72. **Course Rating:** 74.2/71.0. **Slope:** 145/131.
(WOODS/MARSH) (18 Combo)
Yards: 6,883/5,210. **Par:** 72/72. **Course Rating:** 74.3/71.5. **Slope:** 145/128.
Reader Comments: Excellent restaurant and attentive beverage cart drivers … A classic 'up-north' course … Could hold a major event from the back tees … Best part is the people … Never boring.
★★★★½ **THE PRESERVE GOLF COURSE** (18) *Value, Condition, Pace+*
Yards: 6,601/4,816. **Par:** 72/72. **Course Rating:** 71.9/69.1. **Slope:** 139/119. **Green Fee:** $75/$85. **Walkability:** 4. **Opened:** 1996. **Architect:** Dan Helbling/Mike Morley.
Reader Comments: Don't miss this terrific course … By far my favorite course in Minnesota … Big fast greens! … A great track, beautiful and challenging … Service and amenities are well above average … Lots of course for the money … Great panorama from clubhouse.
Special Notes: Also has a 9-hole executive course.

★★ GREEN LEA GOLF COURSE
PU-101 Richway Dr., Albert Lea, 56007, Freeborn County, (507)373-1061, 90 miles from Minneapolis/St. Paul. **E-mail:** greenlea@smig.net. **Facility Holes:** 18. **Yards:** 6,166/5,404. **Par:** 72/72. **Course Rating:** 70.2/71.4. **Slope:** 122/126. **Green Fee:** $22/$25. **Cart Fee:** $10/Person. **Walking Policy:** Unrestricted walking. **Walkability:** 3. **Opened:** 1947. **Architect:** B.L. Greengo. **Season:** April-Nov. **To obtain tee times:** Call up to 3 days in advance. **Miscellaneous:** Reduced fees (weekdays, twilight, seniors, juniors), credit cards (MC, V, AE, D), BF, FF.

★★★ GREENHAVEN COUNTRY CLUB
PU-2800 Greenhaven Rd., Anoka, 55303, Anoka County, (763)427-3180, 25 miles from Minneapolis. **Facility Holes:** 18. **Yards:** 6,287/5,418. **Par:** 71/73. **Course Rating:** 69.1/71.5. **Slope:** 121/110. **Green Fee:** $27/$30. **Cart Fee:** $25/Cart. **Walking Policy:** Unrestricted walking. **Walkability:** 3. **Season:** April-Nov. **High:** June-Aug. **To obtain tee times:** Call golf shop. **Miscellaneous:** Reduced fees (seniors, juniors), credit cards (MC, V, AE, D), BF, FF.
Reader Comments: Easy course, wide fairways and slow play ... Always enjoyable, good value, easy to walk ... Old course, good front 9, short back 9 ... Another honest and diverse test.

GREENWOOD GOLF COURSE
PU-4520 E. Viking Blvd., Wyoming, 55092, Chisago County, (651)462-4653, 30 miles from Minneapolis. **Facility Holes:** 18. **Yards:** 5,518/4,791. **Par:** 72/72. **Course Rating:** 67.2/67.3. **Slope:** 105/112. **Green Fee:** $19/$23. **Cart Fee:** $24/Cart. **Walking Policy:** Unrestricted walking. **Walkability:** 2. **Opened:** 1986. **Architect:** C. M. Johnson. **Season:** April-Nov. **High:** July-Sept. **To obtain tee times:** Call golf shop. **Miscellaneous:** Reduced fees (seniors, juniors).

GREYSTONE GOLF CLUB
SP-St. Andrews Dr., Sauk Centre, 56378, Todd County, (320)351-4653, (877)350-8849, 43 miles from St. Cloud. **E-mail:** davidjr@greystonegolf.com. **Web:** greystonegolf.com. **Facility Holes:** 18. **Yards:** 7,059/5,395. **Par:** 72/72. **Course Rating:** 74.5/71.8. **Slope:** 137/127. **Green Fee:** $38/$48. **Cart Fee:** $15/Person. **Walking Policy:** Unrestricted walking. **Walkability:** 2. **Opened:** 2000. **Architect:** Tom Lehman/Dan Hempt/Kevin Norby. **Season:** April-Oct. **High:** June-Aug. **To obtain tee times:** Call up to 30 days in advance. **Miscellaneous:** Reduced fees (weekdays, twilight, seniors, juniors), range (grass), credit cards (MC, V, AE), BF, FF.

★½ HAMPTON HILLS GOLF COURSE
PU-5313 Juneau Lane, Plymouth, 55446, Hennepin County, (763)559-9800, 12 miles from Minneapolis. **Web:** www.tc.umn.edu/~hampt007. **Facility Holes:** 18. **Yards:** 6,135/5,321. **Par:** 73/73. **Course Rating:** 69.9/70.2. **Slope:** 111/122. **Green Fee:** $19/$22. **Cart Fee:** $20/Cart. **Walking Policy:** Unrestricted walking. **Walkability:** 3. **Opened:** 1966. **Season:** April-Oct. **High:** April-Sept. **To obtain tee times:** Call golf shop. **Miscellaneous:** Reduced fees (twilight, seniors, juniors), metal spikes, range (grass).

★★ HAWLEY GOLF & COUNTRY CLUB
PU-Highway 10, Hawley, 56549, Clay County, (218)483-4808, 22 miles from Fargo. **Facility Holes:** 18. **Yards:** 6,106/5,082. **Par:** 71/72. **Course Rating:** 68.6/68.6. **Slope:** 119/113. **Green Fee:** $18/$20. **Cart Fee:** $20/Cart. **Walking Policy:** Unrestricted walking. **Walkability:** 3. **Opened:** 1923. **Season:** April-Oct. **To obtain tee times:** Call up to 7 days in advance. **Miscellaneous:** Reduced fees (weekdays), range (grass), credit cards (MC, V), FF.

★★★ HEADWATERS COUNTRY CLUB
SP-P.O. Box 9, Park Rapids, 56470, Hubbard County, (218)732-4832, 112 miles from St. Cloud. **E-mail:** hcc@unitelc.com. **Facility Holes:** 18. **Yards:** 6,506/5,382. **Par:** 72/72. **Course Rating:** 70.7/71.7. **Slope:** 130/123. **Green Fee:** $20/$32. **Cart Fee:** $25/Cart. **Walking Policy:** Unrestricted walking. **Walkability:** 3. **Opened:** 1969. **Season:** April-Oct. **High:** June-Aug. **To obtain tee times:** Call golf shop. **Miscellaneous:** Reduced fees (twilight, juniors), range (grass), credit cards (MC, V), BF, FF.
Reader Comments: Beautiful layout, great day ... Terrific front 9; back 9 is too back and forth ... Very challenging ... Take the family ... Above expectations ... Lake country ... Loons fly over.

★★ HIAWATHA GOLF COURSE
PU-4553 Longfellow Ave. S., Minneapolis, 55407, Hennepin County, (612)724-7715. **Facility Holes:** 18. **Yards:** 6,613/5,122. **Par:** 73/72. **Course Rating:** 71.2/69.2. **Slope:** 122/118. **Green Fee:** $24/$26. **Cart Fee:** $24/Cart. **Walking Policy:** Unrestricted walking. **Walkability:** 1. **Opened:** 1934. **Season:** April-Nov. **To obtain tee times:** Call up to 4 days in advance. **Miscellaneous:** Reduced fees (weekdays, twilight, seniors, juniors), metal spikes, range (grass/mats), credit cards (MC, V, D), BF, FF.

★★★ HIDDEN GREENS GOLF CLUB *Value*
PU-12977 200th St. E., Hastings, 55033, Dakota County, (651)437-3085, 24 miles from

Minneapolis. **Facility Holes:** 18. **Yards:** 5,954/5,559. **Par:** 72/72. **Course Rating:** 68.8/72.2. **Slope:** 118/127. **Green Fee:** $19/$23. **Cart Fee:** $24/Cart. **Walking Policy:** Unrestricted walking. **Walkability:** 2. **Opened:** 1976. **Architect:** Joel Goldstrand. **Season:** April-Nov. **High:** July-Aug. **To obtain tee times:** Call golf shop. **Miscellaneous:** Reduced fees (weekdays, seniors), range (grass), credit cards (MC, V).

Reader Comments: Not just a clever name! ... Tight fairways ... Lots of pine trees ... Best to play in early fall ... A real honey of a course ... This course has gotten better every year.

HIDDEN HAVEN GOLF CLUB

PU-20520 NE Polk St., Cedar, 55011, Anoka County, (763)434-6867, 30 miles from Minneapolis. **E-mail:** mhetland@pga.com. **Web:** www.hiddenhavengolfclub.com. **Facility Holes:** 18. **Yards:** 5,806/4,996. **Par:** 71/71. **Course Rating:** 67.7/64.3. **Slope:** 119/111. **Green Fee:** $22/$26. **Cart Fee:** $24/Cart. **Walking Policy:** Unrestricted walking. **Walkability:** 3. **Opened:** 1988. **Season:** March-Nov. **High:** May-Sept. **To obtain tee times:** Call up to 3 days in advance. **Miscellaneous:** Reduced fees (weekdays, twilight, seniors, juniors), credit cards (MC, V, D), BF, FF.

★★½ HIGHLAND PARK GOLF COURSE

PU-1403 Montreal Ave., St. Paul, 55116, Ramsey County, (651)699-5825. **Facility Holes:** 18. **Yards:** 6,265/5,600. **Par:** 72/73. **Course Rating:** 69.0/71.1. **Slope:** 111/118. **Green Fee:** $19/$21. **Cart Fee:** $20/Cart. **Walking Policy:** Unrestricted walking. **Walkability:** 1. **Opened:** 1929. **Architect:** G. Pirkl/D. Brauer/E. Perret. **Season:** April-Nov. **High:** May-Sept. **To obtain tee times:** Call golf shop. **Miscellaneous:** Reduced fees (twilight, seniors, juniors), metal spikes, range (grass), credit cards (MC, V).

★★½ HOLLYDALE GOLF COURSE

PU-4710 Holly Lane N., Plymouth, 55446, Hennepin County, (763)559-9847, 10 miles from Minneapolis. **Facility Holes:** 18. **Yards:** 6,160/5,128. **Par:** 71/73. **Course Rating:** 70.1/69.9. **Slope:** 121/120. **Green Fee:** $24/$27. **Cart Fee:** $24/Cart. **Walking Policy:** Unrestricted walking. **Walkability:** 2. **Opened:** 1965. **Architect:** William Deziel. **Season:** April-Nov. **High:** May-Aug. **To obtain tee times:** Call up to 7 days in advance. **Miscellaneous:** Reduced fees (seniors, juniors), range (grass), FF.

★★★½ INVER WOOD GOLF COURSE

PU-1850 70th St. E., Inver Grove Heights, 55077, Dakota County, (651)457-3667, 8 miles from St. Paul. **Facility Holes:** 27. **Yards:** 6,724/5,175. **Par:** 72/72. **Course Rating:** 72.6/70.7. **Slope:** 140/128. **Green Fee:** $28. **Cart Fee:** $26/Cart. **Walking Policy:** Unrestricted walking. **Walkability:** 5. **Opened:** 1992. **Architect:** Garrett Gill/George B. Williams. **Season:** April-Oct. **High:** June-Aug. **To obtain tee times:** Call up to 3 days in advance. **Miscellaneous:** Reduced fees (juniors), range (grass/mats), credit cards (MC, V), BF, FF.

Reader Comments: Excellent course, good value ... Challenging ... One of my favorite courses in the metro area ... Tough track ... The true Minnesota golf feel ... Tough course in the wind ... Good practice facility.

Special Notes: Also has a 9-hole executive course.

IRONMAN GOLF COURSE

PU-20664 County Rd. 21, Detroit Lakes, 56501, Becker County, (218)847-5592. **E-mail:** ironman@tekstar.com. **Web:** www.ironmangolf.com. **Facility Holes:** 18. **Yards:** 2,824/2,456. **Par:** 54/54. **Course Rating:** 53.4/53.5. **Slope:** 79/74. **Green Fee:** $16/$17. **Cart Fee:** $15/Cart. **Walking Policy:** Unrestricted walking. **Walkability:** 2. **Opened:** 1960. **Season:** April-Oct. **High:** June-Aug. **To obtain tee times:** Call up to 30 days in advance. **Miscellaneous:** Reduced fees (twilight, seniors, juniors), range (grass), credit cards (MC, V), BF, FF.

★★★ ISLAND VIEW GOLF COURSE

SP-9150 Island View Rd., Waconia, 55387, Carver County, (952)442-6116, 20 miles from Minneapolis. **E-mail:** ivgc@black.hole.com. **Facility Holes:** 18. **Yards:** 6,552/5,382. **Par:** 72/72. **Course Rating:** 70.5/70.0. **Slope:** 129/124. **Green Fee:** $41/$46. **Cart Fee:** $28/Cart. **Walking Policy:** Unrestricted walking. **Walkability:** 3. **Opened:** 1957. **Architect:** Willie Kidd. **Season:** April-Oct. **High:** June-Aug. **To obtain tee times:** Call up to 2 days in advance. **Miscellaneous:** Reduced fees (twilight), range (grass), credit cards (MC, V, D), BF, FF.

Reader Comments: Great value—wonderful staff! ... Good layout for walkers ... Semi-private, many members ... Lake views ... Difficult to get tee time ... Good bargain.

IZATYS GOLF & YACHT CLUB

R-40005 85th Ave., Onamia, 56359, Mille Lacs County, (320)532-3101, (800)533-1728, 90 miles from Minneapolis. **E-mail:** izatys@teemaster.com. **Web:** www.izatys.com. **Facility Holes:** 36. **Cart Fee:** Included in green fee. **Walking Policy:** Unrestricted walking. **Walkability:** 3. **Architect:** John Harbottle III. **Season:** April-Nov. **High:** June-Sept. **To obtain tee times:** Call golf shop. **Miscellaneous:** Reduced fees (guests, twilight), range (grass/mats), lodging (100 rooms), credit cards (MC, V, AE, D, DC), BF, FF.

★★★½ **BLACK BROOK COURSE** (18)
Yards: 6,867/5,119. **Par:** 72/72. **Course Rating:** 74.2/71.1. **Slope:** 140/122. **Green Fee:**
$45/$90. **Opened:** 1999.
Reader Comments: Tough but fun to play ... Better of the two courses ... Some tight fairways, so
bring your 'A' game or lots of balls ... Outstanding Fall value I'm going back... ... Challenging.

★★★½ **THE SANCTUARY** (18)
Yards: 6,646/5,075. **Par:** 72/72. **Course Rating:** 72.6/70.3. **Slope:** 134/125. **Green Fee:**
$40/$80. **Opened:** 1998.
Reader Comments: 5-Star course ... Great lodging and food ... Very nice course in pretty woods
... New holes are fun and good design.

★★★ **KELLER GOLF COURSE**
PU-2166 Maplewood Dr., St. Paul, 55109-2599, Ramsey County, (651)764-170, 10 miles
from Minneapolis/St. Paul. **E-mail:** paul.diegnau@co.ramsey.mn.us. **Web:**
www.co.ramsey.mn.us/parks/golf_courses. **Facility Holes:** 18. **Yards:** 6,566/5,373. **Par:** 72/73.
Course Rating: 71.7/71.3. **Slope:** 128/125. **Green Fee:** $27. **Cart Fee:** $23/Cart. **Walking
Policy:** Unrestricted walking. **Walkability:** 3. **Opened:** 1929. **Architect:** Paul Coates. **Season:**
April-Nov. **High:** May-Sept. **To obtain tee times:** Call up to 4 days in advance. **Miscellaneous:**
Reduced fees (twilight, seniors, juniors), range (grass), credit cards (MC, V), BF, FF.
Reader Comments: A classic old course that was a 60s tour stop ... Nostalgic photos in clubhouse
... Fast greens and fun to play ... In better shape than in the past ... Love original layout, neat old
course ... Best course in St. Paul ... Greatly improved in the 90s ... Great history ... Friendly staff.

★★½ **LAKESIDE GOLF CLUB**
SP-37160 Clear Lake Drive, Waseca, 56093, Waseca County, (507)835-2574. **Facility Holes:**
18. **Yards:** 6,025. **Par:** 71/71. **Course Rating:** 68.6/70.3. **Slope:** 116/115. **Green Fee:** $13/$24.
Opened: 1969. **To obtain tee times:** Call golf shop. **Miscellaneous:** Metal spikes.

★½ **LAKEVIEW GOLF OF ORONO**
PU-710 North Shore Drive, W., Mound, 55364, Hennepin County, (952)472-3459, 25 miles
from Minneapolis. **Web:** www.teemaster.com. **Facility Holes:** 18. **Yards:** 5,424/4,894. **Par:**
70/70. **Course Rating:** 65.8/67.1. **Slope:** 108/109. **Green Fee:** $16/$24. **Cart Fee:** $24/Cart.
Walking Policy: Unrestricted walking. **Walkability:** 3. **Opened:** 1956. **Architect:** Russ
Wenkstern. **Season:** April-Oct. **High:** June-Aug. **To obtain tee times:** Call golf shop.
Miscellaneous: Reduced fees (twilight, seniors, juniors), credit cards (MC, V, AE).

LAKEVIEW NATIONAL GOLF COURSE
PU-1349 Highway 61, Two Harbors, 55616, Lake County, (218)834-2664, 20 miles from
Duluth. **Facility Holes:** 18. **Yards:** 6,773/5,364. **Par:** 72/72. **Course Rating:** 72.2/70.7. **Slope:**
126/123. **Green Fee:** $16/$22. **Cart Fee:** $24/Cart. **Walking Policy:** Unrestricted walking.
Walkability: 5. **Opened:** 1997. **Architect:** Garrett Gill/William Fitzpatrick. **Season:** April-Oct.
High: June-Aug. **To obtain tee times:** Call golf shop. **Miscellaneous:** Reduced fees (weekdays,
twilight, juniors), range (grass), credit cards (MC, V, AE).

THE LEGACY COURSES AT CRAGUN'S
PU-11000 Craguns Dr., Brainerd, 56401, Cass County, (218)825-2800, (800)272-4867,
8 miles from Brainerd. **E-mail:** golf@craguns.com. **Web:** www.craguns.com. **Facility Holes:** 45.
Green Fee: $35/$99. **Cart Fee:** Included in green fee. **Walking Policy:** Unrestricted walking.
Walkability: 2. **Opened:** 1999. **Architect:** Robert Trent Jones Jr. **Season:** April-Oct. **High:** June-
Sept. **Miscellaneous:** Reduced fees (guests, twilight), range (grass), lodging (300 rooms),
credit cards (MC, V, AE, D), BF, FF.
NORTH COURSE (18)
Yards: 6,928/5,300. **Par:** 72/72. **Course Rating:** 73.8/71.1. **Slope:** 145/132.
★★★½ **SOUTH COURSE** (18)
Yards: 6,897/5,250. **Par:** 72/72. **Course Rating:** 73.7/71.2. **Slope:** 145/131.
Reader Comments: The way a course should be designed ... Great staff, outstanding service...
New adventure ... Beautiful design, tough, expensive ... Robert Trent Jones Jr. did a super job.
Special Notes: Also has a 9-hole par-3 course.

★★★½ **LES BOLSTAD UNIV. OF MINNESOTA GOLF CLUB**
SP-2275 W. Larpenteur Ave., St. Paul, 55113, Ramsey County, (612)627-4000, 5 miles from
Minneapolis/St. Paul. **Facility Holes:** 18. **Yards:** 6,123/5,684. **Par:** 71/75. **Course Rating:**
69.2/75.2. **Slope:** 117/132. **Green Fee:** $15/$25. **Cart Fee:** $18/Cart. **Walking Policy:**
Unrestricted walking. **Walkability:** 3. **Opened:** 1922. **Architect:** Seth Raynor. **Season:** April-Oct.
High: June-Aug. **To obtain tee times:** Call golf shop. **Miscellaneous:** Reduced fees (weekdays,
twilight), range (grass), credit cards (MC, V, D).
Reader Comments: Course is a real gem for the price ... Interesting layout ... Beautiful old university course ... Busy, but fun to play ... Tight course, small greens, tough of high handicappers.

MINNESOTA

LESTER PARK GOLF CLUB
PU-1860 Lester River Rd., Duluth, 55804, St. Louis County, (218)525-0828, 3 miles from Duluth. **E-mail:** paulschintz@aol.com. **Web:** www.lesterpark.com. **Facility Holes:** 27. **Green Fee:** $23. **Cart Fee:** $23/Cart. **Walking Policy:** Unrestricted walking. **Opened:** 1931. **Architect:** Dick Phelps. **Season:** May-Nov. **High:** June-Aug. **To obtain tee times:** Call up to 7 days in advance. **Miscellaneous:** Reduced fees (twilight, seniors, juniors), range (grass), credit cards (MC, V), BF, FF.
LAKE COURSE (9)
Yards: 3,417/2,693. **Par:** 36/36. **Course Rating:** 72.6/66.8. **Slope:** 113/119. **Walkability:** 2.
★★½ **LESTER PARK COURSE** (18)
Yards: 6,371/5,582. **Par:** 72/74. **Course Rating:** 70.8/67.7. **Slope:** 117/111. **Walkability:** 3.

★★★★ **THE LINKS AT NORTHFORK**
PU-9333 153rd Ave., Ramsey, 55303, Anoka County, (763)241-0506, 20 miles from Minneapolis. **E-mail:** linksatnorthfork@prodigy.net. **Facility Holes:** 18. **Yards:** 6,989/5,242. **Par:** 72/72. **Course Rating:** 73.7/70.5. **Slope:** 127/117. **Green Fee:** $33/$42. **Cart Fee:** $24/Cart. **Walking Policy:** Unrestricted walking. **Walkability:** 3. **Opened:** 1992. **Architect:** Joel Goldstrand. **Season:** April-Oct. **High:** June-Aug. **To obtain tee times:** Call golf shop. **Miscellaneous:** Reduced fees (weekdays, twilight, seniors, juniors), metal spikes, range (grass), credit cards (MC, V, AE, D).
Reader Comments: Unique practice holes ...Tough, no trees ... Challenging ... Nice, good value.

★★ **LITCHFIELD GOLF COURSE**
PU-405 W. Pleasure Dr., Litchfield, 55355, Meeker County, (320)693-6059, 70 miles from Minneapolis. **Facility Holes:** 18. **Yards:** 6,350/5,011. **Par:** 70/70. **Course Rating:** 69.8/69.4. **Slope:** 123/121. **Green Fee:** $18/$24. **Cart Fee:** $18/Cart. **Walking Policy:** Unrestricted walking. **Walkability:** 2. **Opened:** 1974. **Season:** April-Oct. **High:** June-Aug. **To obtain tee times:** Call up to 3 days in advance. **Miscellaneous:** Credit cards (MC, V, D), BF, FF.

★★★ **LITTLE CROW COUNTRY CLUB**
SP-Highway 23, Spicer, 56288, Kandiyohi County, (320)354-2296, 47 miles from St. Cloud. **E-mail:** lccc@wecnet.com. **Web:** www.littlecrowgolf.com. **Facility Holes:** 27. **Yards:** 6,765/5,757. **Par:** 72/72. **Course Rating:** 72.3/73.1. **Slope:** 123/125. **Cart Fee:** $24/Cart. **Walking Policy:** Unrestricted walking. **Walkability:** 2. **Opened:** 1969. **Architect:** Don Herfort. **Season:** April-Nov. **High:** June-Aug. **To obtain tee times:** Call golf shop. **Miscellaneous:** Range (grass), credit cards (MC, V).
Reader Comments: Good layout ... Excellent value ... Short but challenging ... Hidden gem in central MN ... Busy new 9 great fun to play ... Short, playable, fun ... Love the original 18 holes.

★★ **LITTLE FALLS COUNTRY CLUB**
PU-1 Edgewater Dr., Little Falls, 56345, Morrison County, (320)632-3584, 30 miles from St. Cloud. **Facility Holes:** 18. **Yards:** 6,051/5,713. **Par:** 72/72. **Course Rating:** 69.0/72.0. **Slope:** 121/125. **Green Fee:** $18/$20. **Cart Fee:** $18/Cart. **Walking Policy:** Unrestricted walking. **Walkability:** 1. **Opened:** 1982. **Season:** April-Oct. **High:** June-Aug. **To obtain tee times:** Call golf shop. **Miscellaneous:** Reduced fees (weekdays, juniors), range, credit cards (MC, V, AE).

★★ **LONE PINE COUNTRY CLUB**
PU-15451 Howard Lake Rd., Shakopee, 55379, Scott County, (952)445-3575. **Facility Holes:** 18. **Yards:** 5,965/5,020. **Par:** 71/71. **Course Rating:** 69.2/69.3. **Slope:** 128/118. **Green Fee:** $19/$22. **To obtain tee times:** Call golf shop. **Miscellaneous:** Metal spikes.

LYNX NATIONAL GOLF CLUB
PU-40204 Primrose Lane, Sauk Centre, 56378, Stearns County, (320)352-0243, (888)637-0243, 38 miles from St. Cloud. **E-mail:** lynxnationalgolf@hotmail.com. **Web:** www.lynxnationalgolf.com. **Facility Holes:** 18. **Yards:** 6,700/5,244. **Par:** 72/72. **Course Rating:** 71.1/69.1. **Slope:** 124/113. **Green Fee:** $17/$24. **Cart Fee:** $22/Cart. **Walking Policy:** Unrestricted walking. **Walkability:** 2. **Opened:** 1999. **Architect:** Mike Morley. **Season:** April-Nov. **High:** June-Aug. **To obtain tee times:** Call up to 7 days in advance. **Miscellaneous:** Reduced fees (weekdays), range (grass), credit cards (MC, V), BF, FF.

MADDEN'S ON GULL LAKE
R-11266 Pine Beach Peninsula, Brainerd, 56401, Crow Wing County, (218)829-2811, (800)642-5363, 120 miles from Minneapolis. **E-mail:** golf@maddens.com. **Web:** www.maddens.com. **Facility Holes:** 63. **Walking Policy:** Unrestricted walking. **Walkability:** 3. **Season:** April-Oct. **To obtain tee times:** Call up to 30 days in advance. **Miscellaneous:** Reduced fees (weekdays, guests, twilight), range, lodging (400 rooms), credit cards (MC, V, AE), BF, FF.
★★★★½ **THE CLASSIC AT MADDEN'S RESORT** (18) *Pace*
Yards: 7,102/4,859. **Par:** 72/72. **Course Rating:** 75.0/69.4. **Slope:** 143/124. **Green Fee:**

$65/$105. **Cart Fee:** Included in green fee. **Opened:** 1997. **Architect:** Scott Hoffman.
Notes: Ranked 9th in 2001 Best in State; 7th in 1999 Best New Upscale Public Courses.
Reader Comments: The course is always in phenomenal shape, every other corner involves spectacular scenery, fast firm greens, pearl white bunkers, outside service staff is the best I have witnessed ... Best course in the nation ... Close to Giants Ridge ... Tough test of golf ... One of nicest courses I've played .

★★★½ **PINE BEACH EAST COURSE** (18)
Yards: 5,956/5,352. **Par:** 72/72. **Course Rating:** 67.9/69.7. **Slope:** 113/114. **Green Fee:**
$18/$40. **Cart Fee:** $32/Cart. **Opened:** 1926. **Architect:** James Delgleish.
Reader Comments: Coure was in excellent shape, outside service staff very friendly ... Resort course, mature trees ... Traditional resort course, high land.
Special Notes: Also has a 9-hole par-3 course.

★★★ **PINE BEACH WEST COURSE** (18)
Yards: 5,049/4,662. **Par:** 67/67. **Course Rating:** 62.7/65.2. **Slope:** 104/103. **Green Fee:**
$18/$40. **Cart Fee:** $32/Cart. **Opened:** 1950. **Architect:** Paul Coates/Jim Madden.
Reader Comments: Short course etched in the woods. Challenging par 3s ... Very beautiful course, course in unbelievable shape.
Special Notes: Also has a 9-hole par-3 course.

MAJESTIC OAKS GOLF CLUB
PU-701 Bunker Lake Blvd., Ham Lake, 55304, Anoka County, (763)755-2142, 20 miles from Minneapolis. **Facility Holes:** 45. **Cart Fee:** $25/Cart. **Walking Policy:** Unrestricted walking.
Walkability: 3. **Season:** April-Oct. **High:** June-Aug. **To obtain tee times:** Call up to 4 days in advance. **Miscellaneous:** Reduced fees (weekdays, twilight, seniors, juniors), metal spikes, range (grass), credit cards (MC, V, AE, D), BF, FF.

★★★ **GOLD COURSE** (18)
Yards: 6,396/4,848. **Par:** 72/72. **Course Rating:** 71.2/68.4. **Slope:** 123/120. **Green Fee:**
$22/$33. **Opened:** 1991. **Architect:** Garrett Gill.
Reader Comments: Not long. Pretty easy if you hit short irons close ... Small greens and big trees ... Getting better.

★★★ **PLATINUM COURSE** (18)
Yards: 7,013/5,268. **Par:** 72/72. **Course Rating:** 73.9/71.6. **Slope:** 129/126. **Green Fee:**
$24/$33. **Opened:** 1972. **Architect:** Charles Maddox.
Reader Comments: Demanding approach shots over bunkers ... Lot of doglegs ... Good course for seniors ... Crowded ... Big league.
Special Notes: Also has a 9-hole executive course.

★★★ MANITOU RIDGE GOLF COURSE
PU-3200 N. McKnight Rd., White Bear Lake, 55110, Ramsey County, (651)777-2987, 10 miles from St. Paul. **Facility Holes:** 18. **Yards:** 6,401/5,468. **Par:** 71/71. **Course Rating:**
70.4/71.6. **Slope:** 116/119. **Green Fee:** $25. **Cart Fee:** $23/Cart. **Walking Policy:** Unrestricted walking. **Walkability:** 4. **Opened:** 1930. **Architect:** Don Herfort. **Season:** April-Nov. **High:** May-Sept. **To obtain tee times:** Call up to 4 days in advance. **Miscellaneous:** Reduced fees (twilight, seniors, juniors), range (grass), credit cards (MC, V, D), BF, FF.
Reader Comments: For a public course that gets a lot of play, kept in great shape ... Most improved course in Minnesota, priced right ... Basic golf ... Tricky greens.

★★★ MAPLE VALLEY GOLF & COUNTRY CLUB
SP-8600 Maple Valley Rd. S.E., Rochester, 55904, Olmsted County, (507)285-9100, 8 miles from Rochester. **Facility Holes:** 18. **Yards:** 6,270/5,330. **Par:** 71/71. **Course Rating:** 68.9/68.5.
Slope: 108/108. **Green Fee:** $24. **Cart Fee:** $24/Cart. **Walking Policy:** Unrestricted walking.
Walkability: 4. **Opened:** 1964. **Architect:** Wayne Idso. **Season:** April-Dec. **High:** June-Oct. **To obtain tee times:** Call up to 5 days in advance. **Miscellaneous:** Credit cards (MC, V), BF, FF.
Reader Comments: Some nice holes ... Scenic bluffs, lush valley ... Fun ... Tough par 4s, good greens ... Challenging layout could be outstanding with a little work ... In the fall the scenery is breathtaking ... Water, trees, hills, sand.

★★★½ MARSHALL GOLF CLUB
SP-800 Country Club Dr., Marshall, 56258, Lyon County, (507)537-1622, 90 miles from Sioux Falls. **E-mail:** mgcatstar.dotnet. **Facility Holes:** 18. **Yards:** 6,601/5,136. **Par:** 71/72. **Course Rating:** 71.6/70.2. **Slope:** 130/124. **Green Fee:** $35. **Cart Fee:** $25/Cart. **Walking Policy:** Unrestricted walking. **Walkability:** 2. **Opened:** 1942. **Architect:** J.W. Whitney. **Season:** April-Oct.
High: May-Aug. **To obtain tee times:** Call up to 7 days in advance. **Miscellaneous:** Reduced fees (twilight), range (grass), credit cards (MC, V), BF, FF.
Reader Comments: Really improved over last 5 years ... Tough pin placements ... A great layout, new condition ... Great course in smaller town out of metro area.

★★½ MEADOWBROOK GOLF COURSE
PU-201 Meadowbrook Rd., Hopkins, 55343, Hennepin County, (952)929-2077, 3 miles from

Minneapolis. **E-mail:** scott.d.nelson@ci.minneapolis.mn.us. **Web:** www.teemaster.com. **Facility Holes:** 18. **Yards:** 6,529/5,640. **Par:** 72/72. **Course Rating:** 72.0/72.7. **Slope:** 132/127. **Green Fee:** $21/$26. **Cart Fee:** $23/Cart. **Walking Policy:** Unrestricted walking. **Walkability:** 3. **Opened:** 1926. **Architect:** J. Foulis/K. Killian/D.Nugent/D Kirscht. **Season:** April-Nov. **High:** June-Aug. **To obtain tee times:** Call up to 4 days in advance. **Miscellaneous:** Reduced fees (twilight, seniors, juniors), credit cards (MC, V, AE, D, DC, CB), BF, FF.

★★★½ THE MEADOWS GOLF COURSE
PU-401 34th St. S., Moorhead, 56560, Clay County, (218)299-7888, 2 miles from Fargo. **Web:** www.moorheadgolf.com. **Facility Holes:** 18. **Yards:** 6,862/5,150. **Par:** 72/72. **Course Rating:** 72.2/69.3. **Slope:** 125/114. **Green Fee:** $20/$23. **Cart Fee:** $22/Cart. **Walking Policy:** Unrestricted walking. **Walkability:** 2. **Opened:** 1994. **Architect:** Joel Goldstrand. **Season:** April-Nov. **High:** June-Aug. **To obtain tee times:** Call up to 3 days in advance. **Miscellaneous:** Reduced fees (seniors, juniors), range (grass), credit cards (MC, V, AE, D), BF, FF.
Reader Comments: Nice course for price you pay … Links course not 1 tree on it … The Meadows will surprise you with water on seven holes … Treeless links style, great design, condition and value … Can be difficult when windy.

★★★ MESABA COUNTRY CLUB
SP-415 E. 51st St., Hibbing, 55746, St. Louis County, (218)263-4826, 70 miles from Duluth. **Facility Holes:** 18. **Yards:** 6,792/5,747. **Par:** 72/74. **Course Rating:** 71.7/73.0. **Slope:** 131/129. **Green Fee:** $45. **Cart Fee:** $21/Cart. **Walking Policy:** Unrestricted walking. **Opened:** 1923. **Architect:** Charles Erickson. **Season:** April-Oct. **High:** June-Aug. **To obtain tee times:** Call golf shop. **Miscellaneous:** Range (grass/mats), credit cards (MC, V), BF, FF.
Reader Comments: Reasonable value … Nos. 2 and 3 are beautiful, challenging holes.

★★½ MILLE LACS GOLF RESORT
R-18517 Captive Lake Rd., Garrison, 56450, Mille Lacs County, (320)692-4325, (800)435-8720, 95 miles from Twin Cities. **E-mail:** mlgr@millelacsgolf.com. **Web:** www.millelacsgolf.com. **Facility Holes:** 18. **Yards:** 6,309/5,106. **Par:** 71/72. **Course Rating:** 69.7/68.7. **Slope:** 119/113. **Green Fee:** $23/$35. **Cart Fee:** $13/Person. **Walking Policy:** Unrestricted walking. **Walkability:** 4. **Opened:** 1964. **Architect:** Robert Murphy. **Season:** April-Nov. **High:** June-Sept. **To obtain tee times:** Call up to 60 days in advance. **Miscellaneous:** Reduced fees (weekdays, guests, twilight, juniors), range, lodging (16 rooms), credit cards (MC, V, D), FF.

★★★★½ MINNEWASKA GOLF CLUB *Value+, Pace*
SP-23518 Dero Drive, Glenwood, 56334, Pope County, (320)634-3680, 120 miles from Minneapolis. **Facility Holes:** 18. **Yards:** 6,457/5,398. **Par:** 72/73. **Course Rating:** 70.7/71.7. **Slope:** 122/123. **Green Fee:** $19/$25. **Cart Fee:** $23/Cart. **Walking Policy:** Unrestricted walking. **Walkability:** 3. **Opened:** 1923. **Architect:** Joel Goldstrand. **Season:** April-Oct. **High:** June-Aug. **To obtain tee times:** Call up to 7 days in advance. **Miscellaneous:** Reduced fees (weekdays, twilight), range (grass/mats), credit cards (MC, V), BF, FF.
Reader Comments: Good golf at a good price at a good pace … Hills and hills but in great shape … Nice older course … Hidden gem … If you haven't played it, try it.

★★½ MISSISSIPPI DUNES GOLF LINKS
SP-10351 Grey Cloud Trail, Cottage Grove, 55016, Washington County, (651)768-7611, 15 miles from Minneapolis/St. Paul. **Web:** www.mississippidunes.com. **Facility Holes:** 18. **Yards:** 6,694/4,954. **Par:** 72/72. **Course Rating:** 73.1/69.4. **Slope:** 135/115. **Green Fee:** $36/$42. **Cart Fee:** $14/Person. **Walking Policy:** Unrestricted walking. **Walkability:** 3. **Opened:** 1995. **Season:** April-Nov. **High:** May-Sept. **To obtain tee times:** Call golf shop. **Miscellaneous:** Reduced fees (weekdays, twilight, seniors, juniors), range (grass), credit cards (MC, V, AE, D), FF.

MISSISSIPPI NATIONAL GOLF LINKS
PU-409 Golf Links Dr., Red Wing, 55066, Goodhue County, (651)388-1874, 50 miles from Minneapolis/St. Paul. **E-mail:** mn@wpgolf.com. **Web:** www.wpgolf.com. **Facility Holes:** 36. **Green Fee:** $28/$30. **Cart Fee:** $29/Cart. **Opened:** 1987. **Architect:** Gordon Cunningham. **Season:** April-Nov. **High:** May-Sept. **To obtain tee times:** Call up to 7 days in advance. **Miscellaneous:** Reduced fees (weekdays), range (grass), credit cards (MC, V, D), BF, FF.
★★★½ **HIGHLANDS** (18)
Yards: 6,282/5,002. **Par:** 71/71. **Course Rating:** 70.5/69.3. **Slope:** 121/115. **Walking Policy:** Mandatory carts. **Walkability:** 5.
Reader Comments: Worth playing for scenery … Awesome views of the river valley … Long distances from greens to tees … Beer cart was great.
★★★½ **LOWLANDS** (18)
Yards: 6,484/5,450. **Par:** 71/72. **Course Rating:** 71.0/71.0. **Slope:** 126/121. **Walking Policy:** Unrestricted walking. **Walkability:** 3.
Reader Comments: Good potential! … Good clubhouse … Worth playing for scenery.

★★★½ MONTICELLO COUNTRY CLUB
SP-1201 Golf Course Rd., Monticello, 55362, Wright County, (763)295-4653, 30 miles from Minneapolis. **Web:** www.montigolf.com. **Facility Holes:** 18. **Yards:** 6,485/5,085. **Par:** 71/72. **Course Rating:** 71.7/69.8. **Slope:** 125/118. **Green Fee:** $25/$35. **Cart Fee:** $27/Cart. **Walking Policy:** Unrestricted walking. **Walkability:** 3. **Opened:** 1969. **Architect:** Tim Murphy/Joel Goldstrand. **Season:** April-Oct. **High:** April-Aug. **To obtain tee times:** Call golf shop. **Miscellaneous:** Reduced fees (weekdays, seniors), range, credit cards (MC, V, D), BF, FF.
Reader Comments: Good little course ... Great value ... Best greens in the state ... Pretty course.

★★★ MOUNT FRONTENAC GOLF COURSE
PU-Hwy. 61, Frontenac, 55026, Goodhue County, (651)388-5826, (800)488-5826, 9 miles from Red Wing. **Web:** www.ski-frontenac.com. **Facility Holes:** 18. **Yards:** 6,050/4,832. **Par:** 70/70. **Course Rating:** 69.2/67.7. **Slope:** 119/117. **Green Fee:** $16/$22. **Cart Fee:** $20/Cart. **Walking Policy:** Unrestricted walking. **Walkability:** 3. **Opened:** 1985. **Architect:** Gordon Emerson. **Season:** April-Oct. **High:** June-Aug. **To obtain tee times:** Call up to 10 days in advance. **Miscellaneous:** Reduced fees (weekdays, twilight, seniors), range (mats), credit cards (MC, V, AE, D), BF, FF.
Reader Comments: Great views for autumn golf ... Beautiful views of Lake Pepin ... Some really scenic holes ... Needs a ranger ... Beautiful views of Mississippi River ... A hidden gem.

★★★ NEW PRAGUE GOLF CLUB
PU-400 Lexington Ave.S., New Prague, 56071, Le Sueur County, (612)758-3126, 40 miles from Minneapolis. **E-mail:** scott@newpraguegolf.com. **Web:** www.newpraguegolf.com. **Facility Holes:** 18. **Yards:** 6,362/5,032. **Par:** 71/72. **Course Rating:** 69.9/68.6. **Slope:** 126/118. **Green Fee:** $22/$32. **Cart Fee:** $14/Person. **Walking Policy:** Unrestricted walking. **Walkability:** 3. **Opened:** 1929. **Architect:** Don Herfort/Bob Pomije. **Season:** April-Oct. **High:** May-Sept. **To obtain tee times:** Call up to 7 days in advance. **Miscellaneous:** Reduced fees (weekdays, twilight, seniors, juniors), range (grass/mats), credit cards (MC, V), BF, FF.
Reader Comments: Good, simple golf ... Very well kept ... Old, traditional course ... A great short course ... Too many driver, wedge shots ... Lots of trees in New Prague ... Hilly ... Grand old lady

★★★ NORTH LINKS GOLF COURSE
PU-Nicollet County Rd. 66, North Mankato, 56003, Nicollet County, (507)947-3355, 80 miles from Minneapolis. **Facility Holes:** 18. **Yards:** 6,073/4,659. **Par:** 72/72. **Course Rating:** 69.5/66.9. **Slope:** 117/114. **Green Fee:** $18/$20. **Cart Fee:** $18/Cart. **Walking Policy:** Unrestricted walking. **Walkability:** 2. **Opened:** 1993. **Architect:** Pat Wyss. **Season:** April-Nov. **High:** June-Aug. **To obtain tee times:** Call golf shop. **Miscellaneous:** Reduced fees (twilight, seniors, juniors), metal spikes, range (grass/mats), credit cards (MC, V).
Reader Comments: Great design ... Some tough holes ... Enjoy the links layout ... Nice links course ... Short course—can get in a quick 18 almost anytime.

★★½ NORTHERN HILLS GOLF COURSE
PU-4805 41st Ave. N.W., Rochester, 59901, Olmsted County, (507)281-6170, 65 miles from Minneapolis. **Facility Holes:** 18. **Yards:** 6,315/5,456. **Par:** 72/72. **Course Rating:** 70.4/71.6. **Slope:** 123/123. **Green Fee:** $22. **Cart Fee:** $20/Cart. **Walking Policy:** Unrestricted walking. **Walkability:** 2. **Opened:** 1976. **Architect:** Clayton Westrum. **Season:** April-Nov. **High:** May-Sept. **To obtain tee times:** Call up to 2 days in advance. **Miscellaneous:** Range (grass), credit cards (MC, V), BF, FF.

★★★½ NORTHFIELD GOLF CLUB
SP-707 Prairie St., Northfield, 55057, Rice County, (507)645-4026, 25 miles from Minneapolis. **Facility Holes:** 18. **Yards:** 6,389/5,103. **Par:** 71/71. **Course Rating:** 71.6/70.4. **Slope:** 134/126. **Green Fee:** $32/$44. **Cart Fee:** $14/Person. **Walking Policy:** Unrestricted walking. **Walkability:** 2. **Opened:** 1926. **Architect:** Craig Schreiner. **Season:** April-Nov. **To obtain tee times:** Call up to 2 days in advance. **Miscellaneous:** Reduced fees (weekdays), credit cards (MC, V, D), BF, FF.
Reader Comments: Course is usually in good shape ... A real challenge on some holes ... New holes have added length to course ... Very good course, fast undulating greens, tight fairways ... Always excellent, hidden jewel ... Short and hilly.

★★★½ OAK GLEN GOLF CLUB
PU-1599 McKusick Rd., Stillwater, 55082, Washington County, (651)439-6963, 20 miles from St. Paul. **Facility Holes:** 27. **Yards:** 6,550/5,626. **Par:** 72/72. **Course Rating:** 72.4/73.4. **Slope:** 131/130. **Green Fee:** $25/$30. **Cart Fee:** $12/Person. **Walking Policy:** Unrestricted walking. **Walkability:** 2. **Opened:** 1982. **Architect:** Don Herfort. **Season:** April-Nov. **To obtain tee times:** Call up to 3 days in advance. **Miscellaneous:** Reduced fees (weekdays, twilight, seniors), range (grass), credit cards (MC, V), FF.

MINNESOTA

Reader Comments: Friendly staff, steal at $26 a round, always in great shape, fast greens, 3 1/2 hour rounds ... Enjoyed the course, surroundings and people.
Special Notes: Also has a 9-hole executive course.

★★ OAK SUMMIT GOLF COURSE
PU-2751 County Rd. 16 S.W., Rochester, 55902, Olmsted County, (507)252-1808. Facility Holes: 18. Yards: 6,523/5,159. Par: 71/71. Course Rating: 71.3/69.1. Slope: 121/115. Green Fee: $15/$20. Cart Fee: $20/Cart. Walking Policy: Unrestricted walking. Walkability: 3. Opened: 1992. Architect: Leon DeCook. Season: March-Nov. To obtain tee times: Call up to 7 days in advance. Miscellaneous: Reduced fees (weekdays, twilight, seniors), metal spikes, range (grass/mats), credit cards (MC, V), BF, FF.

★★★ OAKS COUNTRY CLUB
SP-Country Club Rd., Hayfield, 55940, Dodge County, (507)477-3233, 20 miles from Rochester. Facility Holes: 18. Yards: 6,404/5,663. Par: 72/72. Course Rating: 69.7/71.7. Slope: 114/118. Green Fee: $16/$17. Cart Fee: $22/Person. Walking Policy: Unrestricted walking. Walkability: 1. Opened: 1977. Architect: John Queenland. Season: April-Oct. High: May-Aug. To obtain tee times: Call up to 5 days in advance. Miscellaneous: Range (grass), credit cards (MC, V), BF, FF.
Reader Comments: Wide open; could use more hazards ... Heck of a jewel hidden in the corn ... Fun course-some hills, some water, greens hard to read ... Good mix of hills and flat ... Nice layout.

★★½ ONEKA RIDGE GOLF COURSE
PU-5610 120th St. N., White Bear Lake, 55110, Ramsey County, (651)429-2390, 15 miles from St. Paul. Facility Holes: 18. Yards: 6,351/5,166. Par: 72/72. Course Rating: 70.8/69.7. Slope: 118/115. Green Fee: $26/$28. Cart Fee: $26/Cart. Walking Policy: Unrestricted walking. Walkability: 3. Opened: 1996. Season: March-Oct. To obtain tee times: Call up to 4 days in advance. Miscellaneous: Reduced fees (twilight, seniors, juniors), range (grass), credit cards (MC, V), BF, FF.

★★★½ ORTONVILLE MUNICIPAL GOLF COURSE
PU-RR 1, Ortonville, 56278, Big Stone County, (320)839-3606, 150 miles from Minneapolis. E-mail: rizz.zz@hotmail.com. Facility Holes: 18. Yards: 6,001/5,419. Par: 72/72. Course Rating: 68.1/70.6. Slope: 111/115. Green Fee: $18/$22. Cart Fee: $22/Cart. Walking Policy: Unrestricted walking. Walkability: 1. Architect: Joel Goldstrand. Season: March-Oct. High: June-Aug. To obtain tee times: Call up to 7 days in advance. Miscellaneous: Reduced fees (weekdays), range (grass), credit cards (MC, V), BF, FF.
Reader Comments: Nice, affordable course ... Hidden treasure ... Needs more trees ... 1st time I played it, I would play it again.

★★★★ PEBBLE CREEK GOLF CLUB
PU-14000 Club House Lane, Becker, 55308, Sherburne County, (763)261-4653, 17 miles from St. Cloud. E-mail: pebblecreek@sherbtel.net. Web: www.pebblecreekgolf.com. Facility Holes: 27. Green Fee: $28/$34. Cart Fee: $12/Person. Walking Policy: Unrestricted walking. Walkability: 1. Opened: 1987. Architect: Don Herfort/Garrett Gill. Season: April-Oct. To obtain tee times: Call up to 7 days in advance. Miscellaneous: Reduced fees (twilight, seniors, juniors), range (grass), credit cards (MC, V, AE, D), BF, FF.
BLUE/RED (18 Combo)
Yards: 6,757/5,374. Par: 72/72. Course Rating: 72.4/71.1. Slope: 129/125.
RED/WHITE (18 Combo)
Yards: 6,820/5,633. Par: 72/72. Course Rating: 73.2/72.9. Slope: 129/127.
WHITE/BLUE (18 Combo)
Yards: 6,657/5,304. Par: 72/72. Course Rating: 72.2/70.6. Slope: 126/126.
Reader Comments: Fantastic staff, best value ... Some holes outstanding ... Superb restaurant in clubhouse ... Well worth the extra travel time ... A touch of country not far from Twin Cities ... Quality operation and course ... Original 18 better then new 9 ... Love my home course, always in good shape.

★★★ PEBBLE LAKE GOLF CLUB
PU-County 82 S., Fergus Falls, 56537, Otter Tail County, (218)736-7404, 175 miles from Minneapolis. Facility Holes: 18. Yards: 6,711/5,531. Par: 72/74. Course Rating: 72.3/72.1. Slope: 128/126. Green Fee: $23/$28. Cart Fee: $22/Cart. Walking Policy: Unrestricted walking. Walkability: 3. Opened: 1941. Architect: Paul Coates. Season: April-Oct. To obtain tee times: Call up to 7 days in advance. Miscellaneous: Reduced fees (twilight, juniors), range (grass), credit cards (MC, V), BF, FF.
Reader Comments: Can be a test on occasion ... Good walk ... Great find ... Fun lower course, great greens ... Great grounds crew ... Good but nothing stands out.

★★★½ PERHAM LAKESIDE COUNTRY CLUB
PU-2727 450th St., Perham, 56573, Otter Tail County, (218)346-6070, 20 miles from Detroit Lakes. **E-mail:** lakeside@djam.com. **Facility Holes:** 18 **Yards:** 6,575/5,312. **Par:** 72/72. **Course Rating:** 72.5/71.1. **Slope:** 128/122. **Green Fee:** $30/$32. **Cart Fee:** $23/Cart. **Walking Policy:** Unrestricted walking. **Walkability:** 3. **Opened:** 1938. **Architect:** Joel Goldstrand. **Season:** April-Nov. **High:** June-Sept. **To obtain tee times:** Call up to 30 days in advance. **Miscellaneous:** Reduced fees (weekdays, twilight), range (grass), credit cards (MC, V, D), BF, FF.
Reader Comments: Very nice course and people ... Good shape for late-season play ... #11 is an outstanding par 3 over water; say your prayers ... Tough little track.

★★½ PEZHEKEE GOLF CLUB
R-2000 South Lakeshore Dr., Glenwood, 56334, Pope County, (320)634-4501, (800)356-8654, 120 miles from Minneapolis/St. Paul. **E-mail:** jim@petersresort.com. **Web:** www.petersresort.com. **Facility Holes:** 18. **Yards:** 6,454/5,465. **Par:** 72/75. **Course Rating:** 70.8/71.5. **Slope:** 119/122. **Green Fee:** $27/$32. **Cart Fee:** $25/Cart. **Walking Policy:** Unrestricted walking. **Walkability:** 4. **Opened:** 1967. **Architect:** Tim Murphy/Bill Peters. **Season:** May-Oct. **High:** June-Sept. **To obtain tee times:** Call golf shop. **Miscellaneous:** Reduced fees (weekdays, guests, twilight, juniors), metal spikes, lodging (52 rooms), credit cards (MC, V).

★★½ PHALEN PARK GOLF COURSE
PU-1615 Phalen Dr., St. Paul, 55106, Ramsey County, (651)778-0413. **Facility Holes:** 18. **Yards:** 6,101/5,439. **Par:** 70/71. **Course Rating:** 68.7/70.7. **Slope:** 121/121. **Green Fee:** $25. **Cart Fee:** $23/Cart. **Walking Policy:** Unrestricted walking. **Walkability:** 2. **Opened:** 1920. **Architect:** Don Herfort. **Season:** March-Nov. **High:** May-Sept. **To obtain tee times:** Call up to 7 days in advance. **Miscellaneous:** Reduced fees (twilight, seniors, juniors), range (grass), credit cards (MC, V), BF, FF.

★★★ PHEASANT ACRES GOLF CLUB
PU-10705 County Rd. 116, Rogers, 55374, Hennepin County, (763)428-8244, 20 miles from Minneapolis. **Facility Holes:** 18. **Yards:** 6,400/5,200. **Par:** 71/72. **Course Rating:** 69.9/68.7. **Slope:** 117/115. **Green Fee:** $14/$25. **Cart Fee:** $20/Cart. **Walking Policy:** Unrestricted walking. **Walkability:** 1. **Opened:** 1988. **Architect:** Lyle Johansen. **Season:** April-Dec. **To obtain tee times:** Call golf shop. **Miscellaneous:** Reduced fees (weekdays, twilight, seniors, juniors), range (grass/mats), credit cards (MC, V), BF, FF.
Reader Comments: Good condition, clubhouse with food ... Average golf course ... Super people running course, always fun ... Great head pro ... Wide open, not many hazards ... Best for the money, play over and over ... Young course getting better each year.

★★ PINE MEADOWS AT BRAINERD
SP-500 Golf Course Dr., Baxter, 56425, Crow Wing County, (218)829-5733, (800)368-2048, 120 miles from Minneapolis/St. Paul. **E-mail:** pinemeadows@teemaster.com. **Web:** www.brainerdgolf.com. **Facility Holes:** 18. **Yards:** 6,372/5,145. **Par:** 72/72. **Course Rating:** 71.5/68.2. **Slope:** 133/118. **Green Fee:** $32/$37. **Cart Fee:** $25/Cart. **Walking Policy:** Unrestricted walking. **Walkability:** 2. **Season:** April-Oct. **High:** June-Sept. **To obtain tee times:** Call up to 30 days in advance. **Miscellaneous:** Reduced fees (weekdays, guests, twilight, seniors, juniors), range (grass), credit cards (MC, V, AE, D), BF, FF.

PIONEER CREEK GOLF COURSE
PU-705 Copeland Rd., Maple Plain, 55359, Hennepin County, (952)955-3982, 20 miles from Minneapolis. **Web:** www.goldenlinksgolf.com. **Facility Holes:** 18. **Yards:** 6,953/5,147. **Par:** 72/72. **Course Rating:** 72.7/68.9. **Slope:** 134/118. **Green Fee:** $28/$35. **Cart Fee:** $12/Person. **Walking Policy:** Unrestricted walking. **Walkability:** 2. **Opened:** 1999. **Architect:** Joel Goldstrand. **Season:** April-Nov. **High:** May-Aug. **To obtain tee times:** Call up to 7 days in advance. **Miscellaneous:** Reduced fees (twilight, seniors, juniors), range, credit cards (MC, V)

★★★½ POKEGAMA GOLF CLUB
PU-3910 Golf Course Rd., Grand Rapids, 55744, Itasca County, (218)326-3444, (888)307-3444, 4 miles from Grand Rapids. **Facility Holes:** 18. **Yards:** 6,481/5,046. **Par:** 71/72. **Course Rating:** 70.3/67.7. **Slope:** 121/116. **Green Fee:** $28/$33. **Cart Fee:** $26/Cart. **Walking Policy:** Unrestricted walking. **Walkability:** 2. **Opened:** 1926. **Architect:** Donald Brauer. **Season:** April-Oct. **To obtain tee times:** Call up to 7 days in advance. **Miscellaneous:** Reduced fees (weekdays, guests, twilight), range (grass), credit cards (MC, V), BF, FF.
Reader Comments: For a course that gets used alot, it is kept in good shape ... Fun to play and close to home ... Front 9 mirrors back 9 ... Beautiful setting ... Tight layout ... Easy walk.

★★½ PRAIRIE VIEW GOLF LINKS
PU-Hwy. 266 N., Worthington, 56187, Nobles County, (507)372-8670, 50 miles from Sioux Falls. **Facility Holes:** 18. **Yards:** 6,366/5,103. **Par:** 71/71. **Course Rating:** 69.9/68.3. **Slope:**

112/113. **Green Fee:** $21/$23. **Cart Fee:** $21/Cart. **Walking Policy:** Unrestricted walking. **Opened:** 1983. **Architect:** Joel Goldstrand. **Season:** April-Oct. **High:** June-Aug. **To obtain tee times:** Call golf shop. **Miscellaneous:** Reduced fees (twilight), range, credit cards (MC, V).

★★★½ **PRESTWICK GOLF CLUB AT WEDGEWOOD**
SP-9555 Wedgewood Dr., Woodbury, 55125, Washington County, (651)731-4779, 10 miles from St. Paul. **E-mail:** plambert@pga.com. **Web:** www.prestwick.com. **Facility Holes:** 18. **Yards:** 6,699/5,252. **Par:** 72/72. **Course Rating:** 72.7/70.8. **Slope:** 128/120. **Green Fee:** $44/$49. **Cart Fee:** $15/Person. **Walking Policy:** Unrestricted walking. **Walkability:** 3. **Opened:** 1985. **Architect:** Norb Anderson. **Season:** April-Nov. **High:** June-Aug. **To obtain tee times:** Call up to 5 days in advance. **Miscellaneous:** Reduced fees (weekdays, twilight, juniors), range (grass/mats), credit cards (MC, V, AE, D, DC), BF, FF.
Reader Comments: Excellent layout and maintenance ... Nice course, overall ... Great venue, always in good condition, good people in pro shop ... Can drive No.1 ... Challenging but playable.

★★ **PRINCETON GOLF CLUB**
SP-Golf Club Rd., Princeton, 55371, Mille Lacs County, (763)389-5109, (800)882-0698, 45 miles from Minneapolis/St. Paul. **E-mail:** princeton@teemaster.com. **Web:** www.princetongc.com. **Facility Holes:** 18. **Yards:** 6,381/4,967. **Par:** 71/71. **Course Rating:** 71.6/70.6. **Slope:** 128/124. **Green Fee:** $24/$28. **Cart Fee:** $26/Cart. **Walking Policy:** Unrestricted walking. **Walkability:** 3. **Opened:** 1951. **Architect:** Joe Goldstrand. **Season:** April-Nov. **High:** May-Sept. **To obtain tee times:** Call up to 30 days in advance. **Miscellaneous:** Reduced fees (weekdays, twilight, seniors, juniors), range, credit cards (MC, V, D), BF, FF.

★★★½ **PURPLE HAWK COUNTRY CLUB**
SP-N. Hwy. 65, P. O. Box 528, Cambridge, 55008, Isanti County, (763)689-3800, 60 miles from Minneapolis/St. Paul. **E-mail:** phcc72@ecenet.com. **Web:** www.purplehawk.com. **Facility Holes:** 18. **Yards:** 6,679/5,748. **Par:** 72/74. **Course Rating:** 72.3/73.5. **Slope:** 132/131. **Green Fee:** $25/$31. **Cart Fee:** $26/Cart. **Walking Policy:** Unrestricted walking. **Walkability:** 2. **Opened:** 1970. **Architect:** Don Herfort. **Season:** April-Oct. **High:** May-Sept. **To obtain tee times:** Call up to 5 days in advance. **Miscellaneous:** Reduced fees (twilight, seniors, juniors), range (grass/mats), credit cards (MC, V, D), BF, FF.
Reader Comments: Good small-town course ... A few hole redesigns ... Interesting par 3s ... Excellent layout, quick, true greens.

★½ **RAMSEY GOLF CLUB**
PU-54384 244th St., Austin, 55912, Mower County, (507)433-9098, 95 miles from Minneapolis/St. Paul. **Facility Holes:** 18. **Yards:** 5,987/5,426. **Par:** 71/72. **Course Rating:** 67.6/70.1. **Slope:** 118/118. **Green Fee:** $22. **Cart Fee:** $20/Cart. **Walking Policy:** Unrestricted walking. **Walkability:** 2. **Opened:** 1940. **Architect:** Jim Vacura. **Season:** April-Nov. **High:** May-Sept. **Tee times:** Call up to 7 days ahead. **Misc:** Range, credit cards (MC, V, AE, D), BF, FF.

★★½ **RICH SPRING GOLF CLUB**
SP-17467 Fairway Circle, Cold Spring, 56320, Stearns County, (320)685-8810, 20 miles from St. Cloud. **Facility Holes:** 18. **Yards:** 6,517/5,336. **Par:** 72/72. **Course Rating:** 71.1/70.4. **Slope:** 129/118. **Green Fee:** $19/$26. **Cart Fee:** $24/Cart. **Walking Policy:** Unrestricted walking. **Walkability:** 3. **Opened:** 1962. **Season:** April-Nov. **To obtain tee times:** Call golf shop. **Miscellaneous:** Reduced fees (seniors, juniors), range, credit cards (MC, V, D), BF, FF.

RICH VALLEY GOLF CLUB
PU-3855 145th St. E., Rosemount, 55068, Dakota County, (651)437-4653, 4 miles from Rosemount. **Facility Holes:** 27. **Green Fee:** $14/$21. **Cart Fee:** $22/Cart. **Walking Policy:** Unrestricted walking. **Walkability:** 2. **Opened:** 1988. **Architect:** Ray Rahn. **Season:** April-Oct. **High:** June-Aug. **To obtain tee times:** Call up to 7 days in advance. **Miscellaneous:** Reduced fees (seniors, juniors), range (grass), credit cards (MC, V), BF, FF.
RED/BLUE (18 Combo)
Yards: 5,286/4,539. **Par:** 69/70. **Course Rating:** 64.1/64.4. **Slope:** 100/101.
RED/WHITE (18 Combo)
Yards: 5,289/4,680. **Par:** 67/69. **Course Rating:** 63.7/65.1. **Slope:** 95/99.
WHITE/BLUE (18 Combo)
Yards: 5,079/4,397. **Par:** 68/69. **Course Rating:** 63.0/63.7. **Slope:** 98/98.

RIDGES AT SAND CREEK
PU-21775 Ridges Dr., Jordan, 55352, Scott County, (952)492-2644. **Web:** www.ridgesatsandcreek.com. **Facility Holes:** 18. **Yards:** 6,936/5,136. **Par:** 72/72. **Course Rating:** 73.0/69.8. **Slope:** 133/119. **Green Fee:** $29/$34. **Cart Fee:** $13/Person. **Walking Policy:** Unrestricted walking. **Walkability:** 4. **Opened:** 2000. **Architect:** Joel Goldstrand. **Season:** April-Nov. **To obtain tee times:** Call up to 7 days in advance. **Miscellaneous:** Reduced fees (seniors, juniors), range (grass), credit cards (MC, V, AE, D), BF, FF.

MINNESOTA

RIDGEWOOD GOLF COURSE
PU-Highway 7, Longville, 56655, Cass County, (218)363-2444. **Web:** wwwridgewoodgolf.com.
Facility Holes: 27.
EXECUTIVE COURSE (9)
Yards: 1,023/1,023. **Par:** 29/29. **Green Fee:** $7. **Opened:** 1990. **To obtain tee times:** Call.
★★★ **RIDGEWOOD COURSE (18)**
Yards: 6,564/5,669. **Par:** 72/72. **Course Rating:** 72.0/72.9. **Slope:** 129/127. **Green Fee:**
$25/$30. **Cart Fee:** $20/Cart. **Walking Policy:** Unrestricted walking. **Walkability:** 3. **Opened:**
1986. **Season:** April-Oct. **High:** June-Sept. **To obtain tee times:** Call up to 2 days in advance.
Miscellaneous: Reduced fees (twilight), range (grass), credit cards (MC, V, AE, D), BF, FF.
Reader Comments: Front 9 more mature than back.

★★★★ **RIVER OAKS MUNICIPAL GOLF CLUB**
PU-11099 S. Highway 61, Cottage Grove, 55016, Washington County, (651)438-2121, 15
miles from St. Paul. **E-mail:** riveroaksmunigolf@earthlink.net. **Web:**
www.riveroaksmunigolf.com. **Facility Holes:** 18. **Yards:** 6,433/5,224. **Par:** 71/71. **Course
Rating:** 71.4/74.9. **Slope:** 131/137. **Green Fee:** $25/$28. **Cart Fee:** $27/Cart. **Walking Policy:**
Unrestricted walking. **Walkability:** 2. **Opened:** 1991. **Architect:** Don Herfort. **Season:** April-Nov.
High: May-Sept. **To obtain tee times:** Call golf shop. **Miscellaneous:** Reduced fees (twilight,
seniors, juniors), range (grass), credit cards (MC, V), BF, FF.
Reader Comments: Great course, good condition and many challenging holes ... Good staff ...
Easy walking muni course overlooking Mississippi River... The 10th and 18th holes are two you will
not forget ... Best value in town ... Women friendly/good pricing.

★★½ **ROSE LAKE GOLF COURSE**
SP-2456 104th St., Fairmont, 56031, Martin County, (507)235-5274, 3 miles from Fairmont.
E-mail: roselake@frontiernnet.net. **Facility Holes:** 18. **Yards:** 6,196/5,276. **Par:** 71/71. **Course
Rating:** 69.6/70.3. **Slope:** 121/120. **Green Fee:** $20/$25. **Cart Fee:** $20/Cart. **Walking Policy:**
Unrestricted walking. **Walkability:** 3. **Opened:** 1957. **Architect:** Joel Goldstrand. **Season:** April-
Oct. **To obtain tee times:** Call up to 7 days in advance. **Miscellaneous:** Range (grass), credit
cards (MC, V), BF, FF.

★★½ **RUM RIVER HILLS GOLF CLUB**
PU-16659 St. Francis Blvd., Anoka, 55303, Anoka County, (763)753-3339, 15 miles from
Minneapolis. **Web:** www.rumriverhills.com. **Facility Holes:** 18. **Yards:** 6,338/5,095. **Par:** 71/71.
Course Rating: 70.0/69.6. **Slope:** 117/120. **Green Fee:** $22/$29. **Cart Fee:** $24/Cart. **Walking
Policy:** Unrestricted walking. **Walkability:** 2. **Opened:** 1986. **Architect:** Joel Goldstrand.
Season: April-Nov. **High:** June-Aug. **To obtain tee times:** Call golf shop. **Miscellaneous:**
Reduced fees (twilight, seniors, juniors), range (grass), credit cards (MC, V, D, DC), BF, FF.

★★★½ **RUSH CREEK GOLF CLUB**
PU-7801 CR 101, Maple Grove, 55311, Hennepin County, (763)494-8844, 20 miles from
Minneapolis. **E-mail:** derek@rushcreek.com. **Web:** www.rushcreek.com. **Facility Holes:** 18.
Yards: 7,020/5,317. **Par:** 72/72. **Course Rating:** 74.2/71.1. **Slope:** 137/127. **Green Fee:**
$50/$100. **Cart Fee:** $10/Person. **Walking Policy:** Unrestricted walking. **Walkability:** 2. **Opened:**
1996. **Architect:** Bob Cupp/John Fought. **Season:** April-Oct. **To obtain tee times:** Call up to 14
days in advance. **Miscellaneous:** Reduced fees (twilight, juniors), range (grass/mats), caddies, credit cards (MC, V, AE, DC), BF, FF.
Notes: Ranked 19th in 1999 Best in State.
Reader Comments: Challenging but fair, very good condition, good pace of play, very tough finishing hole ... Great links course ... One of the best in the state ... Great experience ... A new course
with nice facilities ... Fun to play ... Very scenic, great finishing hole ... Much improved.

RUTTGER'S BAY LAKE LODGE
R-Rte. 2, Deerwood, 56401, Crow Wing County, (218)678-2885, (800)450-4545, 15 miles
from Brainerd. **Facility Holes:** 27. **Green Fee:** $34/$40. **Cart Fee:** $14/Cart. **Walking Policy:**
Unrestricted walking. **Walkability:** 4. **Architect:** Joel Goldstrand. **Season:** April-Oct. **High:** May-
Sept. **To obtain tee times:** Call golf shop. **Miscellaneous:** Reduced fees (guests, twilight),
metal spikes, range (grass), caddies, credit cards (MC, V, AE, D).
★★★½ **LAKES COURSE (18)**
Yards: 6,750/5,100. **Par:** 72/72. **Course Rating:** 72.5/69.3. **Slope:** 132/125. **Opened:** 1992.
Reader Comments: Just beautiful ... One of the best ... Some weird holes ... Good overall ...
What a small resort course should be like ... Fun layout ... Nice flowers.
LODGE NINE (9)
Yards: 2,285/2,176. **Par:** 34/34. **Course Rating:** 60.6/62.4. **Slope:** 95/95. **Opened:** 1920.

SARTELL GOLF CLUB
PU-801 Pinecone Rd. Box 363, Sartell, 56377, Stearns County, (320)259-0551, 5 miles from

St. Cloud. **Web:** www.sartellgolf.com. **Facility Holes:** 18. **Yards:** 6,363/5,321. **Par:** 72/72. **Course Rating:** 68.3/69.9. **Slope:** 113/115. **Green Fee:** $18/$21. **Cart Fee:** $20/Cart. **Walking Policy:** Unrestricted walking. **Walkability:** 1. **Opened:** 1983. **Season:** March-Nov. **High:** May-July. **To obtain tee times:** Call golf shop. **Miscellaneous:** Reduced fees (seniors, juniors), range (grass/mats), credit cards (MC, V), BF, FF.

★★★ SAWMILL GOLF CLUB
SP-11177 McKusick Rd., Grant, 55082, Washington County, (651)439-7862, 15 miles from St. Paul. **Facility Holes:** 18. **Yards:** 6,300/4,940. **Par:** 70/70. **Course Rating:** 71.1/69.5. **Slope:** 121/119. **Green Fee:** $22/$37. **Cart Fee:** $26/Cart. **Walking Policy:** Unrestricted walking. **Walkability:** 3. **Opened:** 1983. **Architect:** Dan Pohl/John McCarthy/Pat Rooney. **Season:** April-Nov. **High:** June-Aug. **To obtain tee times:** Call up to 4 days in advance. **Miscellaneous:** Reduced fees (twilight, seniors, juniors), range (grass), credit cards (MC, V, AE), BF, FF. **Reader Comments:** Beautiful, tough course … Good value … Not long, but a good test … Slow greens … Tucked nicely in the woods … Always changing and working it … Very tight, can't use driver on many holes.

★½ SHAMROCK GOLF COURSE
PU-19625 Larkin Rd., Corcoran, 55340, Hennepin County, (763)478-9977, 15 miles from Minneapolis. **E-mail:** keeper29@idt.net. **Facility Holes:** 18. **Yards:** 6,423/5,793. **Par:** 72/74. **Course Rating:** 69.8/72.1. **Slope:** 111/115. **Green Fee:** $24/$27. **Cart Fee:** $24/Cart. **Walking Policy:** Unrestricted walking. **Walkability:** 2. **Opened:** 1974. **Season:** April-Oct. **High:** May-Aug. **Tee times:** Call golf shop. **Miscellaneous:** Reduced fees (weekdays, seniors, juniors), BF, FF.

★½ SHORELAND COUNTRY CLUB
SP-Lake Emily/County 21, St. Peter, 56082, Nicollet County, (507)931-3470. **Facility Holes:** 18. **Yards:** 5,592/4,965. **Par:** 69/71. **Course Rating:** 66.6/68.9. **Slope:** 112/117. **Green Fee:** $25/$27. **Cart Fee:** $24/Cart. **Walking Policy:** Unrestricted walking. **Walkability:** 4. **Opened:** 1929. **Season:** April-Nov. **High:** May-Aug. **To obtain tee times:** Call up to 7 days in advance. **Miscellaneous:** Reduced fees (juniors), credit cards (MC, V), BF, FF.

SILVER SPRINGS GOLF COURSE
PU-CR 39 W., Monticello, 55362, Wright County, (763)295-2951, 30 miles from Minneapolis. **Web:** www.silverspringsgolf.com. **Facility Holes:** 36. **Green Fee:** $26/$32. **Cart Fee:** $27/Cart. **Walking Policy:** Unrestricted walking. **Walkability:** 1. **Architect:** Al Joyner. **Season:** April-Nov. **To obtain tee times:** Call up to 7 days in advance. **Miscellaneous:** Reduced fees (weekdays, twilight, seniors, juniors), range (grass), credit cards (MC, V, AE, D), BF, FF.
★★ GOLD COURSE (18)
Yards: 6,458/5,959. **Par:** 72/72. **Course Rating:** 69.8/72.6. **Slope:** 115/121. **Opened:** 1984.
★½ SILVER COURSE (18)
Yards: 6,622/6,176. **Par:** 72/74. **Course Rating:** 70.5/73.9. **Slope:** 115/126. **Opened:** 1974.

★★★ SOUTHERN HILLS GOLF CLUB
PU-18950 Chippendale Ave., Farmington, 55024, Dakota County, (612)463-4653, 20 miles from Minneapolis. **Facility Holes:** 18. **Yards:** 6,314/4,970. **Par:** 71/71. **Course Rating:** 70.4/68.3. **Slope:** 123/116. **Green Fee:** $18/$30. **Cart Fee:** $13/Person. **Walking Policy:** Unrestricted walking. **Walkability:** 2. **Opened:** 1989. **Architect:** Joel Goldstrand. **Season:** April-Oct. **High:** June-Aug. **To obtain tee times:** Call golf shop. **Miscellaneous:** Reduced fees (weekdays, twilight, seniors, juniors), metal spikes, range (grass), credit cards (MC, V). **Reader Comments:** A well-run course, a pleasure to play … Very tough on a windy day … The course will improve as it matures … Good overall, some blind and unforgiving spots … Outstanding layout.

★½ ST. CHARLES GOLF CLUB
SP-1920 Park Rd., St. Charles, 55972, Winona County, (507)932-5444, 20 miles from Rochester. **E-mail:** stcharlesgolfclub@worldnet.att.net. **Facility Holes:** 18. **Yards:** 6,439/5,330. **Par:** 72/72. **Course Rating:** 69.8/69.7. **Slope:** 118/111. **Green Fee:** $24. **Cart Fee:** $12/Person. **Walking Policy:** Unrestricted walking. **Walkability:** 3. **Opened:** 1991. **Architect:** Wayne Idso. **Season:** April-Oct. **High:** June-Aug. **To obtain tee times:** Call up to 7 days in advance. **Miscellaneous:** Range (grass), credit cards (MC, V), BF, FF.

★★★ STONEBROOKE GOLF CLUB
SP-2693 CR 79, Shakopee, 55379, Scott County, (612)496-3171, (800)263-3189, 20 miles from Minneapolis. **Web:** www.stonebrooke.com. **Facility Holes:** 27. **Yards:** 6,614/5,033. **Par:** 71/71. **Course Rating:** 72.3/69.7. **Slope:** 135/122. **Green Fee:** $39/$46. **Cart Fee:** $28/Cart. **Walking Policy:** Unrestricted walking. **Walkability:** 3. **Opened:** 1989. **Architect:** T.L. Haugen. **Season:** April-Nov. **High:** June-Sept. **To obtain tee times:** Call up to 3 days in advance. **Miscellaneous:** Reduced fees (twilight, seniors), metal spikes, range (grass), credit cards (MC, V, AE), BF, FF.

Reader Comments: Staff very friendly and helpful ... Par-4 8th requires a ferry ride across lake ... The 'boat' hole is blast ... Very good public course ... A hidden gem although a bit short.
Special Notes: Also has a 9-hole executive course.

★★★★ STONERIDGE GOLF CLUB

SP-13600 Hudson Blvd. N., Stillwater, 55082, Washington County, (651)436-4653, 10 miles from St. Paul. **Web:** www.stoneridgegc.com. **Facility Holes:** 18. **Yards:** 6,959/5,247. **Par:** 72/72. **Course Rating:** 73.3/68.6. **Slope:** 133/117. **Green Fee:** $50/$70. **Cart Fee:** $15/Person. **Walking Policy:** Unrestricted walking. **Opened:** 2000. **Architect:** Bobby Weed. **To obtain tee times:** Call up to 1 day in advance. **Miscellaneous:** Reduced fees (weekdays, twilight), range (grass), caddies, credit cards (MC, V, AE), BF, FF.
Reader Comments: In fantastic shape for a new course ... It's Ireland without the ocean ... Tough back 9 ... One of the best tracks in the state ... Some holes are not 'traditional' ... Very nice ... Good variety of holes.

★★½ SUGAR LAKE LODGE

R-37584 Otil Lane, Cohasset, 55721, Itasca County, (218)327-1462, (800)450-4555, 12 miles from Grand Rapids. **E-mail:** kelly@sugarlakelodge.com. **Web:** www.sugarlakelodge.com. **Facility Holes:** 18. **Yards:** 6,545/5,032. **Par:** 71/71. **Course Rating:** 71.6/69.3. **Slope:** 124/119. **Green Fee:** $30/$35. **Cart Fee:** $26/Cart. **Walking Policy:** Unrestricted walking. **Walkability:** 2. **Opened:** 1994. **Architect:** Joel Goldstrand. **Season:** April-Oct. **High:** July-Aug. **To obtain tee times:** Call up to 30 days in advance. **Miscellaneous:** Reduced fees (weekdays, guests, twilight), range (grass), lodging (120 rooms), credit cards (MC, V, AE, D), BF, FF.

★★½ SUNDANCE GOLF CLUB

PU-15240 113th Ave. N., Maple Grove, 55369, Hennepin County, (763)420-4700, (888)210-7052, 15 miles from Minneapolis. **Facility Holes:** 18. **Yards:** 6,446/5,548. **Par:** 72/72. **Course Rating:** 70.7/71.6. **Slope:** 127/126. **Green Fee:** $26/$30. **Cart Fee:** $25/Cart. **Walking Policy:** Unrestricted walking. **Walkability:** 3. **Opened:** 1970. **Architect:** Ade Simonsen. **Season:** March-Nov. **High:** May-Aug. **To obtain tee times:** Call golf shop. **Miscellaneous:** Reduced fees (weekdays, seniors, juniors), range (grass), credit cards (MC, V, AE, D), BF, FF.

SUPERIOR NATIONAL GOLF COURSE

R-P.O. Box 177, Lutsen, 55612, Cook County, (218)663-7195, (888)616-6784, 90 miles from Duluth. **Web:** www.superiornational.com. **Facility Holes:** 27. **Green Fee:** $50/$70. **Cart Fee:** Included in green fee. **Walking Policy:** Mandatory carts. **Walkability:** 4. **Opened:** 1991. **Architect:** Don Herfort/Joel Goldstrand. **Season:** May-Oct. **High:** June-Oct. **To obtain tee times:** Call golf shop. **Miscellaneous:** Reduced fees (weekdays, guests, twilight, juniors), range, credit cards (MC, V, AE), BF, FF.
MOUNTAIN/CANYON (18)
Yards: 6,768/5,166. **Par:** 72/72. **Course Rating:** 73.0/70.5. **Slope:** 133/119.
Special Notes: This combination played on Monday, Wednesday, Friday and Saturday. River played as 9-hole course.
RIVER/CANYON (18)
Yards: 6,369/4,969. **Par:** 72/72. **Course Rating:** 71.1/69.4. **Slope:** 127/119.
Special Notes: This combination played on Tuesday, Thursday and Sunday. Mountain played as 9-hole course.

★★½ THEODORE WIRTH GOLF COURSE

PU-1300 Theodore Wirth Pkwy., Golden Valley, 55422, Hennepin County, (763)522-4584, 3 miles from Minneapolis. **Facility Holes:** 27. **Yards:** 6,585/5,552. **Par:** 72/72. **Course Rating:** 72.7/72.6. **Slope:** 132/124. **Green Fee:** $20/$26. **Cart Fee:** $24/Cart. **Walking Policy:** Unrestricted walking. **Walkability:** 5. **Opened:** 1916. **Architect:** Garrett Gill. **Season:** April-Nov. **High:** May-Sept. **To obtain tee times:** Call up to 4 days in advance. **Miscellaneous:** Reduced fees (weekdays, twilight, seniors, juniors), credit cards (MC, V, AE, D), BF, FF.
Special Notes: Also has a 9-hole par-3 course.

★★★½ TIANNA COUNTRY CLUB

SP-7470 State 34 N.W., Walker, 56484, Cass County, (218)547-1712, 60 miles from Brainerd. **E-mail:** tianna@tianna.com. **Web:** www.tianna.com. **Facility Holes:** 18. **Yards:** 6,550/5,430. **Par:** 72/74. **Course Rating:** 71.7/71.6. **Slope:** 123/123. **Green Fee:** $32. **Cart Fee:** $24/Cart. **Walking Policy:** Unrestricted walking. **Walkability:** 5. **Opened:** 1925. **Architect:** Ernie Tardiff. **Season:** April-Oct. **To obtain tee times:** Call up to 90 days in advance. **Miscellaneous:** Reduced fees (twilight), range (grass), credit cards (MC, V, AE, D), BF, FF.
Reader Comments: Sporty, well-maintained, hilly course ... A very friendly lakes resort area course ... Rolling hills ... Bring your best game ... Play there every year ... Magnificent scenery.

★★½ TIMBER CREEK GOLF COURSE
SP-9750 CR #24, Watertown, 55388, Carver County, (612)955-3490, 20 miles from
Minneapolis. **Facility Holes:** 18. **Yards:** 6,625/5,425. **Par:** 72/72. **Course Rating:** 71.7/71.0.
Slope: 128/125. **Green Fee:** $20/$27. **Cart Fee:** $22/Cart. **Walking Policy:** Unrestricted walking. **Walkability:** 3. **Opened:** 1986. **Architect:** Tim O'Connor. **Season:** April-Nov. **High:** May-Sept. **To obtain tee times:** Call golf shop. **Miscellaneous:** Reduced fees (twilight, seniors), range (grass), credit cards (MC, V), BF, FF.

TIPSINAH MOUNDS GOLF COURSE
SP-CR #24 to 15185 Golf Course Rd., Elbow Lake, 56531, Grant County, (218)685-4271,
(800)660-8642, 75 miles from Fargo. **Facility Holes:** 18. **Yards:** 6,219/4,909. **Par:** 70/70.
Course Rating: 69.7/68.0. **Slope:** 116/109. **Green Fee:** $19/$22. **Cart Fee:** $20/Cart. **Walking Policy:** Unrestricted walking. **Walkability:** 2. **Opened:** 1982. **Architect:** Joel Goldstrand.
Season: April-Oct. **High:** June-Aug. **To obtain tee times:** Call golf shop. **Miscellaneous:**
Reduced fees (weekdays, twilight, juniors), range (grass), credit cards (MC, V), BF, FF.

★★ VALLEY GOLF ASSOCIATION
SP-1800 21st St. NW, East Grand Forks, 56721, Polk County, (218)773-1207, 5 miles from
Grand Forks. **Facility Holes:** 18. **Yards:** 6,210/5,261. **Par:** 72/72. **Course Rating:** 69.6/69.2.
Slope: 118/112. **Green Fee:** $17. **Cart Fee:** $18/Cart. **Walking Policy:** Unrestricted walking.
Walkability: 2. **Opened:** 1971. **Season:** April-Oct. **To obtain tee times:** Call up to 14 days in
advance. **Miscellaneous:** Reduced fees (twilight, juniors), credit cards (MC, V, D), BF, FF.

★★ VALLEY HIGH GOLF CLUB
PU-9203 Mound Prairie Dr., Houston, 55943, Houston County, (507)896-3239, 15 miles from
La Crosse. **Facility Holes:** 18. **Yards:** 6,168/5,319. **Par:** 71/75. **Course Rating:** 68.3/69.2.
Slope: 113/109. **Green Fee:** $15/$22. **Cart Fee:** $20/Cart. **Walking Policy:** Unrestricted walking. **Walkability:** 4. **Opened:** 1970. **Architect:** Homer Fieldhouse. **Season:** March-Oct. **High:**
June-Aug. **To obtain tee times:** Call up to 30 days in advance. **Miscellaneous:** Reduced fees
(weekdays, seniors, juniors), range (grass), credit cards (MC, V), BF, FF.

★★½ VALLEY VIEW GOLF CLUB
PU-23795 Laredo Ave., Belle Plaine, 56011, Scott County, (953)873-4653, 30 miles from
Minneapolis. **Facility Holes:** 18. **Yards:** 6,309/4,921. **Par:** 70/71. **Course Rating:** 70.1/68.4.
Slope: 121/113. **Green Fee:** $22/$25. **Cart Fee:** $22/Cart. **Walking Policy:** Unrestricted walking. **Walkability:** 4. **Opened:** 1992. **Architect:** S & H Golf, Inc. **Season:** April-Oct. **High:** June-Aug. **To obtain tee times:** Call golf shop. **Miscellaneous:** Reduced fees (weekdays, twilight,
seniors, juniors), metal spikes, range (grass/mats), credit cards (MC, V).

★★★½ VALLEYWOOD GOLF COURSE
PU-4851 West 125th St., Apple Valley, 55124, Dakota County, (612)953-2323, 10 miles from
Minneapolis. **Facility Holes:** 18. **Yards:** 6,421/5,144. **Par:** 71/72. **Course Rating:** 70.6/71.5.
Slope: 123/122. **Green Fee:** $27/$34. **Cart Fee:** $28/Cart. **Walking Policy:** Unrestricted walking. **Walkability:** 3. **Opened:** 1976. **Architect:** Don Ripple. **Season:** April-Nov. **High:** May-Sept.
To obtain tee times: Call up to 5 days in advance. **Miscellaneous:** Reduced fees (seniors,
juniors), range (mats), credit cards (MC, V, D), BF, FF.
Reader Comments: Good public venue ... Short but tight ... Challenging for all levels ... Nice setting ... Always in nice shape.

★½ VIKING MEADOWS GOLF COURSE
PU-1788 Viking Blvd., Cedar, 55011, Anoka County, (763)434-4205, 20 miles from
Minneapolis. **Web:** www.vikingmeadows.com. **Facility Holes:** 27. **Yards:** 6,364/5,534. **Par:**
72/73. **Course Rating:** 70.8/71.6. **Slope:** 124/122. **Green Fee:** $18/$26. **Cart Fee:** $21/Cart.
Walking Policy: Unrestricted walking. **Walkability:** 2. **Opened:** 1989. **Season:** April-Nov. **High:**
July-Aug. **To obtain tee times:** Call golf shop. **Miscellaneous:** Reduced fees (weekdays,
seniors, juniors), range (grass), credit cards (MC, V), BF, FF.
Special Notes: Also has a 9-hole executive course.

★★½ VIRGINIA GOLF COURSE
PU-1308 18th St. N., Virginia, 55792, St. Louis County, (218)748-7530, 59 miles from Duluth.
Facility Holes: 18. **Yards:** 6,226/5,460. **Par:** 71/74. **Course Rating:** 69.5/70.9. **Slope:** 118/129.
Green Fee: $21/$25. **Cart Fee:** $21/Cart. **Walking Policy:** Unrestricted walking. **Walkability:** 2.
Opened: 1932. **Architect:** Hugh Vincent Feehan. **Season:** May-Oct. **High:** June-Sept. **Tee
times:** Call golf shop. **Misc:** Reduced fees (twilight), range, credit cards (MC, V, D), BF, FF.

★★★ WAPICADA GOLF CLUB
SP-4498 15th St. NE, Sauk Rapids, 56379, Stearns County, (320)251-7804, 4 miles from
St. Cloud. **Facility Holes:** 18. **Yards:** 6,610/5,491. **Par:** 72/73. **Course Rating:** 70.1/71.5. **Slope:**

124/126. **Green Fee:** $23/$25. **Cart Fee:** $23/Cart. **Walking Policy:** Unrestricted walking. **Walkability:** 2. **Opened:** 1957. **Season:** April-Oct. **High:** June-Aug. **To obtain tee times:** Call golf shop. **Miscellaneous:** Reduced fees (twilight, seniors), range, credit cards (MC, V).
Reader Comments: Good challenge, fair price … Busy … Nice holes … After 30 years, it keeps getting better … Greens were fast.

★★★½ WENDIGO GOLF COURSE
PU-20108 Golf Crest Dr., Grand Rapids, 55744, Itasca County, (218)327-2211, 180 miles from Minneapolis. **Facility Holes:** 18. **Yards:** 6,756/5,151. **Par:** 72/72. **Course Rating:** 72.0/70.0. **Slope:** 132/127. **Green Fee:** $25/$30. **Cart Fee:** $24/Cart. **Walking Policy:** Unrestricted walking. **Walkability:** 4. **Opened:** 1995. **Architect:** Joel Goldstrand. **Season:** April-Oct. **High:** June-Aug. **To obtain tee times:** Call golf shop. **Miscellaneous:** Reduced fees (twilight), metal spikes, range (grass/mats), credit cards (MC, V).
Reader Comments: Good scenery … Has some great holes. Long par 3s over gorges or water … Lots of trees, hills … Wish I didn't have to drive an hour and a half to get there … A great golf course but needs TLC.

★★★½ WHITEFISH GOLF CLUB
SP-7883 CR 16, Pequot Lakes, 56472, Crow Wing County, (218)543-4900, 25 miles from Brainerd. **E-mail:** wfgolf@uslink.net. **Web:** www.whitefishgolf.com. **Facility Holes:** 18. **Yards:** 6,407/5,682. **Par:** 72/72. **Course Rating:** 70.7/72.6. **Slope:** 128/124. **Green Fee:** $29/$42. **Cart Fee:** $28/Cart. **Walking Policy:** Unrestricted walking. **Walkability:** 2. **Opened:** 1968. **Architect:** Don Herfort. **Season:** April-Nov. **High:** June-Sept. **To obtain tee times:** Call golf shop. **Miscellaneous:** Reduced fees (weekdays, guests, twilight), range (grass), credit cards (MC, V, AE), BF, FF.
Reader Comments: Last of new greens opened in 2000 … Very nice course in resort area … Some nice terrain changes … can be a good challenge for intermediate golfers … My favorite Minnesota course—great design.

★★★★ WILDFLOWER AT FAIR HILLS
PU-19790 County, Hwy 20, Detroit Lakes, 56501, Becker County, (218)439-3357, (888)752-9945, 45 miles from Fargo. **E-mail:** wildflower@teemaster.com. **Web:** www.fairhillsresort.com. **Facility Holes:** 18. **Yards:** 7,000/5,301. **Par:** 72/72. **Course Rating:** 74.2/71.6. **Slope:** 139/121. **Green Fee:** $25/$45. **Cart Fee:** $15/Person. **Walking Policy:** Unrestricted walking. **Walkability:** 4. **Opened:** 1993. **Architect:** Joel Goldstrand. **Season:** April-Oct. **High:** June-Aug. **To obtain tee times:** Call up to 28 days in advance. **Miscellaneous:** Reduced fees (weekdays, guests, twilight, seniors, juniors), range (grass), lodging (72 rooms), credit cards (MC, V, AE, D), BF, FF.
Reader Comments: Outstanding prairie links … Golf features like St. Andrews … Don't miss this. … Good links golf without ocean … Challenging course in great shape … You have to play here.

★★★★ THE WILDS GOLF CLUB *Condition*
PU-3151 Wilds Ridge, Prior Lake, 55372, Scott County, (952)445-3500, 30 miles from Minneapolis. **Web:** www.golfthewilds.com. **Facility Holes:** 18. **Yards:** 7,025/5,095. **Par:** 72/72. **Course Rating:** 74.7/70.2. **Slope:** 140/126. **Green Fee:** $50/$99. **Cart Fee:** Included in green fee. **Walking Policy:** Unrestricted walking. **Walkability:** 4. **Opened:** 1995. **Architect:** Tom Weiskopf/Jay Morrish. **Season:** April-Nov. **High:** May-Sept. **To obtain tee times:** Call up to 14 days in advance. **Miscellaneous:** Reduced fees (weekdays, guests, seniors, juniors), range (grass), credit cards (MC, V, D, DC), BF, FF.
Notes: Ranked 11th in 2001 Best in State; 4th in 1996 Best New Upscale Courses.
Reader Comments: Awesome condition … Great staff … I go here when someone else pays … Plenty of hills & trees keep things interesting, tough when the wind is blowing … Best in Twin Cities.

★★★★½ WILLINGER'S GOLF CLUB *Condition, Pace*
PU-6900 Canby Trail, Northfield, 55057, Rice County, (612)440-7000, 40 miles from Minneapolis. **Facility Holes:** 18. **Yards:** 6,711/5,166. **Par:** 72/72. **Course Rating:** 73.4/71.8. **Slope:** 148/136. **Green Fee:** $32/$42. **Cart Fee:** $14/Person. **Walking Policy:** Unrestricted walking. **Walkability:** 4. **Opened:** 1992. **Architect:** Garrett Gill. **Season:** April-Nov. **High:** April-Nov. **To obtain tee times:** Call golf shop. **Miscellaneous:** Reduced fees (twilight, seniors, juniors), range (grass), credit cards (MC, V), BF, FF.
Notes: Ranked 20th in 2001 Best in State.
Reader Comments: Condition of course is ALWAYS great, the contrast between front and back is an added value … Breathtaking scenery … Really tough course to test skill … 2 separate 9s … Great bargain …They know how to run a golf course … Excellent variety.

MISSISSIPPI

BAY BREEZE GOLF COURSE
M-81st St. SVS/SVBG, Keesler AFB, 39534, Harrison County, (228)377-3832, 5 miles from Biloxi. **Facility Holes:** 18. **Yards:** 6,047/5,110. **Par:** 70/70. **Course Rating:** 69.5/70.0. **Slope:** 121/117. **Green Fee:** $14/$16. **Walking Policy:** Unrestricted walking. **Walkability:** 1. **To obtain tee times:** Call golf shop.

★★½ BAY POINTE RESORT & GOLF CLUB
SP-800 Bay Pointe Dr., Brandon, 39047, Rankin County, (601)829-1862, 7 miles from Jackson. **Facility Holes:** 18. **Yards:** 6,600/4,668. **Par:** 72/72. **Course Rating:** 71.1/66.3. **Slope:** 123/112. **Green Fee:** $17/$22. **Cart Fee:** $12/Person. **Walking Policy:** Walking at certain times. **Walkability:** 3. **Opened:** 1987. **Architect:** Marvin Ferguson. **Season:** Year-round. **High:** April-Oct. **To obtain tee times:** Call up to 7 days in advance. **Miscellaneous:** Reduced fees (juniors), metal spikes, range (grass), credit cards (MC, V, AE, D), BF, FF.

BEAR CREEK GOLF CLUB
PU-Hwy. 84 West, Laurel, 39440, Jones County, (601)425-5670. **Facility Holes:** 18. **Yards:** 6,482/4,820. **Par:** 72/72. **Course Rating:** 70.3/67.9. **Slope:** 118/110. **Green Fee:** $10/$15. **Cart Fee:** $9/Person. **Walking Policy:** Unrestricted walking. **Walkability:** 3. **Opened:** 1985. **Season:** Year-round. **High:** April-Sept. **To obtain tee times:** Call golf shop. **Miscellaneous:** Reduced fees (twilight, seniors, juniors), range (grass), BF, FF.

BEAU PRE COUNTRY CLUB
PU-P. O. Box 18367, Natchez, 39122, Adams County, (601)442-8181, 90 miles from Baton Rouge. **E-mail:** Beauprecc@aol.com. **Facility Holes:** 18. **Yards:** 6,940/5,100. **Par:** 72/72. **Course Rating:** 73.3/69.1. **Slope:** 130/116. **Green Fee:** $50/$60. **Cart Fee:** Included in green fee. **Walking Policy:** Unrestricted walking. **Walkability:** 3. **Opened:** 1999. **Architect:** Mike Young. **Season:** Year-round. **High:** April-Sept. **Tee times:** Call up to 60 days in advance. **Miscellaneous:** Reduced fees (guests), range (grass), credit cards (MC, V, AE), BF, FF.

★★★ BIG OAKS GOLF CLUB
SP-3481 Big Oaks Blvd., Saltillo, 38866, Lee County, (662)844-8002, 1 mile from Tupelo. **E-mail:** bogc3481@aol.com. **Facility Holes:** 18. **Yards:** 6,784/5,098. **Par:** 72/72. **Course Rating:** 73.1/69.1. **Slope:** 124/114. **Green Fee:** $30/$36. **Cart Fee:** Included in green fee. **Walking Policy:** Unrestricted walking. **Walkability:** 1. **Opened:** 1996. **Architect:** Tracy May. **Season:** Year-round. **To obtain tee times:** Call golf shop. **Miscellaneous:** Reduced fees (twilight, juniors), range (grass), credit cards (MC, V), BF, FF.
Reader Comments: Great place to play, especially from April to July (greens absolutely perfect at this time). Not many links-style courses in this neck of the woods … Under new ownership … Changes already evident … Big, bent-grass greens.

★★★½ THE BRIDGES GOLF RESORT AT CASINO MAGIC
R-711 Casino Magic Dr., Bay St. Louis, 39520, Hancock County, (228)463-4047, (800)562-4425, 45 miles from New Orleans, LA. **Web:** http://www.casinomagic.com. **Facility Holes:** 18. **Yards:** 6,841/5,108. **Par:** 72/72. **Course Rating:** 73.5/70.1. **Slope:** 138/126. **Green Fee:** $50/$88. **Cart Fee:** Included in green fee. **Walking Policy:** Walking at certain times. **Walkability:** 3. **Opened:** 1997. **Architect:** Arnold Palmer/Ed Seay. **Season:** Year-round. **High:** Feb.-May. **To obtain tee times:** Call up to 180 days in advance. **Miscellaneous:** Reduced fees (guests, twilight), range (grass), lodging (203 rooms), credit cards (MC, V, AE), BF, FF. **Notes:** Ranked 8th in 1999 Best in State.
Reader Comments: Tight, scenic, every shot a challenge … A beautifully designed course … Helpful staff … Hotel accommodations … Good layout … Could be a great course.

BROOKWOOD COUNTRY CLUB
SP-5001 Forest Hill Rd., Jackson, 39212, Hines County, (601)373-1601. **E-mail:** bwcc19@bellsouth.net. **Web:** brookwoodcountryclub.com. **Facility Holes:** 18. **Yards:** 6,560/5,172. **Par:** 72/74. **Course Rating:** 71.0/69.2. **Slope:** 122/123. **Green Fee:** $23/$26. **Cart Fee:** $12/Person. **Walking Policy:** Unrestricted walking. **Walkability:** 4. **Opened:** 1954. **Season:** Year-round. **High:** April-Oct. **To obtain tee times:** Call up to 3 days in advance. **Miscellaneous:** Reduced fees (juniors), range (grass), credit cards (MC, V), BF, FF.

★★★★½ CANEBRAKE GOLF CLUB *Condition, Pace*
SP-1 Cane Dr., Hattiesburg, 39402, Lamar County, (601)271-2010, (888)875-5595, 7 miles from Hattiesburg. **E-mail:** jeffqsmith@aolcom. **Web:** canebrakegolf.com. **Facility Holes:** 18. **Yards:** 7,003/5,129. **Par:** 71/71. **Course Rating:** 73.3/69.5. **Slope:** 130/117. **Green Fee:** $38/$48. **Cart Fee:** $12/Person. **Walking Policy:** Unrestricted walking. **Walkability:** 3. **Opened:** 1998. **Architect:** Jerry Pate. **Season:** Year-round. **High:** March-June. **To obtain tee times:** Call golf shop. **Miscellaneous:** Reduced fees (weekdays, twilight), range (grass), lodging (8 rooms), credit cards (MC, V, AE, D), BF, FF.

MISSISSIPPI

Notes: Ranked 2nd in 1999 Best New Affordable Public.
Reader Comments: Fair test, use every club ... Rolling fairways, well kept ... Public golf in very upscale development ... Nice layout ... A real gem ... Difficult greens (slick) ... Course in excellent condition in spite of heat.

CAROLINE GOLF CLUB

SP-118 Caroline Club Circle, Madison, 39110, Madison County, (601)853-4554, 10 miles from Jackson. **E-mail:** cargolf@bellsouth.net. **Web:** www.carolinegolfclub.com. **Facility Holes:** 18. **Yards:** 6,845/5,127. **Par:** 72/72. **Course Rating:** 73.3/69.7. **Slope:** 125/119. **Green Fee:** $42/$54. **Cart Fee:** Included in green fee. **Walking Policy:** Unrestricted walking. **Walkability:** 2. **Opened:** 1997. **Architect:** Max Maxwell. **Season:** Year-round. **To obtain tee times:** Call up to 3 days in advance. **Miscellaneous:** Reduced fees (weekdays, twilight, seniors, juniors), range (grass), credit cards (MC, V), BF, FF.

★★★ CHEROKEE VALLEY GOLF CLUB

PU-6635 Crumpler Blvd., Olive Branch, 38654, De Soto County, (662)893-4444, 7 miles from Memphis, TN. **E-mail:** cv6635@aol.com. **Web:** www.olivebranchgolf.com. **Facility Holes:** 18. **Yards:** 6,751/4,422. **Par:** 72/72. **Course Rating:** 72.2/65.4. **Slope:** 128/116. **Green Fee:** $17/$33. **Cart Fee:** $12/Person. **Walking Policy:** Walking at certain times. **Walkability:** 3. **Opened:** 1996. **Architect:** Don Cottle, Jr. **Season:** Year-round. **High:** April-Oct. **To obtain tee times:** Call up to 5 days in advance. **Miscellaneous:** Reduced fees (weekdays, twilight, seniors, juniors), credit cards (MC, V, AE), BF, FF.
Reader Comments: Good course ... Enjoy the zoysia fairways ... Liked the back side better ... Great greens ... Fun course ... Beautiful clubhouse.

CLEAR CREEK GOLF CLUB

PU-1566 Tiffentown Rd., Vicksburg, 39180, Warren County, (601)638-9395, 7 miles from Vicksburg. **Facility Holes:** 18. **Yards:** 6,661/5,182. **Par:** 72/72. **Course Rating:** 71.8/68.7. **Slope:** 118/109. **Green Fee:** $13/$15. **Cart Fee:** $18/Cart. **Walking Policy:** Unrestricted walking. **Walkability:** 2. **Opened:** 1920. **Season:** Year-round. **To obtain tee times:** Call golf shop. **Miscellaneous:** Reduced fees (juniors), range (grass), credit cards (MC, V), BF, FF.

THE CLUB AT NORTH CREEK

SP-8770 North Creek Blvd., Southaven, 38671, Desoto County, (662)280-4653, (877)465-3647, 1 mile from Memphis. **E-mail:** mm2ncreek@aol.com. **Web:** www.golfmississippi.com. **Facility Holes:** 18. **Yards:** 6,433/4,418. **Par:** 72/72. **Course Rating:** 71.2/73.0. **Slope:** 125/113. **Green Fee:** $20/$35. **Cart Fee:** $15/Person. **Walking Policy:** Walking at certain times. **Walkability:** 4. **Opened:** 1999. **Architect:** Tracy May. **Season:** Year-round. **To obtain tee times:** Call up to 7 days in advance. **Miscellaneous:** Reduced fees (weekdays, guests, twilight), range (grass/mats), credit cards (MC, V, AE), BF, FF.

COAHOMA COUNTRY CLUB

SP-Davenport Rd., Clarksdale, 38614, Coahoma County, (662)624-9484, 1 mile from Clarksdale. **E-mail:** grmax@aol.com. **Facility Holes:** 9. **Yards:** 6,126/6,126. **Par:** 72/72. **Course Rating:** 68.0/67.5. **Slope:** 107/104. **Green Fee:** $20. **Walking Policy:** Walking at certain times. **Walkability:** 1. **Season:** Year-round. **High:** April-Oct. **To obtain tee times:** Call golf shop. **Miscellaneous:** BF, FF.

★★★★ COTTONWOODS AT GRAND CASINO TUNICA

R-13615 Old Hwy. 61 North, Robinsonville, 38664, Tunica County, (662)357-6079, (800)946-4946, 15 miles from Memphis, TN. **E-mail:** culver@grandcasinos.com. **Web:** www.grandcasinos.com. **Facility Holes:** 18. **Yards:** 7,000/5,250. **Par:** 72/72. **Course Rating:** 72.3/69.8. **Slope:** 119/116. **Green Fee:** $79. **Cart Fee:** Included in green fee. **Walking Policy:** Mandatory carts. **Walkability:** 2. **Opened:** 1998. **Architect:** Hale Irwin. **Season:** Year-round. **High:** March-Nov. **To obtain tee times:** Call golf shop. **Miscellaneous:** Reduced fees (guests), range (grass), lodging (1300 rooms), credit cards (MC, V, AE, D), FF.
Reader Comments: Very hilly ... Surroundings are excellent ... Great shape, complete test ... It is amazing what you can do with the flat land on the Mississippi Delta.

DANCING RABBIT GOLF CLUB

SP-One Choctaw Trail, Philadelphia, 39350, Neshoba County, (601)663-0011, (888)372-2248, 70 miles from Jackson. **E-mail:** drabbit@netalpha.net. **Web:** www.dancingrabbitgolf.com. **Facility Holes:** 36. **Green Fee:** $60/$96. **Cart Fee:** Included in green fee. **Walking Policy:** Unrestricted walking. **Walkability:** 5. **Architect:** Tom Fazio/Jerry Pate. **Season:** Year-round. **High:** March-Oct. **To obtain tee times:** Call up to 180 days in advance. **Miscellaneous:** Reduced fees (weekdays, guests, twilight, juniors), range (grass), lodging (500 rooms), credit cards (MC, V, AE, D), BF, FF.
★★★★½ **THE AZALEAS** (18) *Condition, Pace*
Yards: 7,128/4,909. **Par:** 72/72. **Course Rating:** 74.4/68.6. **Slope:** 135/115. **Opened:** 1997.

Notes: Ranked 2nd in 2001 Best in State.
Reader Comments: Staff treats you like you're Tiger… Tight, undulating, fair … Best in the state … One of the prettiest courses in the spring … Nice course, but not special … Immaculate condition. A bit pricey… Top course in state … Absolutely beautiful, a must-play course.
★★★★½   **THE OAKS** (18) *Pace*
Yards: 7,076/5,097. **Par:** 72/72. **Course Rating:** 74.6/69.0. **Slope:** 139/123. **Opened:** 1999.
Notes: Ranked 7th in 2001 Best in State.
Reader Comments: Complex is best in MS … Outstanding facility, championship course in the middle of nowhere … Charge way too much … Tremendous design balance with 18 unique holes … Not as good as Azalea … Fine facility … Good course, cost high … Excellent, almost as good as sister course.

DIAMONDHEAD COUNTRY CLUB
R-7600 Country Club Circle, Diamondhead, 39525, Hancock County, (228)255-3910, (800)346-8741, 20 miles from Gulfport. **Facility Holes:** 36. **Green Fee:** $45/$55. **Cart Fee:** $15/Person. **Walking Policy:** Mandatory carts. **Walkability:** 3. **Season:** Year-round. **High:** Feb.-May. **To obtain tee times:** Call golf shop. **Miscellaneous:** Reduced fees (guests, juniors), range (grass), credit cards (MC, V, AE, D), BF, FF.
★★★   **CARDINAL COURSE** (18)
Yards: 6,831/5,065. **Par:** 72/72. **Course Rating:** 72.7/68.9. **Slope:** 132/117. **Opened:** 1972.
Architect: Bill Atkins.
Reader Comments: Very fair … Busy, enjoyable, tough to putt … Showing its age. Nice community course, not really resort-style golf. Nothing real remarkable about layout. Starter was helpful and friendly … Great layout, slow play.
★★★   **PINE COURSE** (18)
Yards: 6,817/5,313. **Par:** 72/72. **Course Rating:** 73.6/71.1. **Slope:** 133/118. **Opened:** 1977.
Architect: Earl Stone.
Reader Comments: Always liked this course, rolling terrain … OK, just OK … A great layout.

★★½   **DOGWOOD HILLS GOLF CLUB**
SP-17476 Dogwood Hills Dr., Biloxi, 39532, Harrison County, (228)392-9805, 12 miles from Biloxi. **Web:** www.dogwoodhills.com. **Facility Holes:** 18. **Yards:** 6,076/4,687. **Par:** 72/72. **Course Rating:** 69.0/68.7. **Slope:** 118/115. **Green Fee:** $22/$33. **Cart Fee:** Included in green fee. **Walking Policy:** Walking at certain times. **Walkability:** 4. **Opened:** 1993. **Architect:** Brent Williams. **Season:** Year-round. **High:** Oct.-April. **To obtain tee times:** Call golf shop. **Miscellaneous:** Reduced fees (juniors), metal spikes, range (grass), credit cards (MC, V).

DUNCAN PARK GOLF COURSE
PU-57 Duncan Park Road, Natchez, 39120, Adams County, (601)442-5955. **E-mail:** graympro@bkbank.com. **Facility Holes:** 18. **Yards:** 6,017/4,766. **Par:** 71/71. **Course Rating:** 69.4/70.4. **Slope:** 117/119. **Green Fee:** $12/$15. **Cart Fee:** $9/Person. **Walking Policy:** Unrestricted walking. **Walkability:** 3. **Opened:** 1994. **Architect:** Brian Ault. **Season:** Year-round. **To obtain tee times:** Call golf shop. **Miscellaneous:** Reduced fees (twilight, seniors, juniors), range (grass/mats), credit cards (MC, V), BF, FF.

★★   **EAGLE RIDGE GOLF COURSE**
PU-Hwy. 18 S., Raymond, 39154, Hinds County, (601)857-5993, 10 miles from Jackson. **Facility Holes:** 18. **Yards:** 6,500/5,135. **Par:** 72/72. **Course Rating:** 68.5. **Slope:** 113. **Green Fee:** $10/$13. **Cart Fee:** $18/Cart. **Walking Policy:** Unrestricted walking. **Walkability:** 2. **Opened:** 1955. **Architect:** Hinds Community College. **Season:** Year-round. **High:** March-Aug. **To obtain tee times:** Call golf shop. **Miscellaneous:** Reduced fees (weekdays, twilight, seniors), metal spikes, range (grass), lodging (40 rooms), credit cards (MC, V).

★★   **EDGEWATER BAY GOLF COURSE**
SP-2674 Pass Rd., Biloxi, 39531, Harrison County, (228)388-9670, 75 miles from New Orleans. **Facility Holes:** 18. **Yards:** 6,200/5,114. **Par:** 71/71. **Course Rating:** 70.0/69.8. **Slope:** 125/121. **Green Fee:** $15/$25. **Cart Fee:** $12/Person. **Walking Policy:** Walking at certain times. **Walkability:** 2. **Opened:** 1927. **Season:** Year-round. **High:** Jan.-March. **To obtain tee times:** Call golf shop. **Miscellaneous:** Reduced fees (weekdays, twilight), credit cards (MC, V).

FOREST COUNTRY CLUB
SP-Hwy. 35 South, Forest, 39074, Scott County, (601)469-9137, 50 miles from Jackson. **Facility Holes:** 18. **Yards:** 6,500/5,128. **Par:** 72/72. **Course Rating:** 69.3. **Slope:** 122. **Green Fee:** $23/$26. **Cart Fee:** Included in green fee. **Walking Policy:** Unrestricted walking. **Walkability:** 3. **Opened:** 1952. **Season:** Year-round. **High:** April-Aug. **To obtain tee times:** Call golf shop. **Miscellaneous:** Reduced fees (weekdays, juniors).

MISSISSIPPI

★★★★½ **GRAND BEAR GOLF COURSE** *Service, Condition, Pace+*
R-12040 Grand Way Blvd., Saucier, 39574, Harrison County, (228)604-7100, (800)946-7777.
E-mail: redmanb@grandcasinos.com. **Facility Holes:** 18. **Yards:** 7,200/4,800. **Par:** 72/72.
Course Rating: 73.8/63.5. **Slope:** 126/98. **Green Fee:** $79/$125. **Cart Fee:** Included in green
fee. **Walking Policy:** Unrestricted walking. **Opened:** 1999. **Architect:** Jack Nicklaus. **Season:**
Year-round. **High:** Feb.-May. **To obtain tee times:** Call golf shop. **Miscellaneous:** Reduced fees
(guests), range (grass), credit cards (MC, V, AE, D, DC), BF, FF.
Notes: Ranked 4th in 2001 Best in State.
Reader Comments: Perfect. Expensive … New, when mature a great course … Great design …
Very fair … Fabulous but expensive … Beautiful, pure golf … Wow! Plays long and you can't hit the
approach shots over the green. Generous landing areas, and a lot of doglegs. No gimmicks. A hellu-
va test … Class act.
Special Notes: Only Grand Casino Resort guests may play this course.

★½ **GRAND OAKS RESORT GOLF COURSE**
PU-Corner of Lyles Dr. and Hwy. 7, Oxford, 38655, Lafayette County, (601)236-3008,
(800)541-3881, 60 miles from Memphis, TN. **Facility Holes:** 18. **Yards:** 6,355/5,090. **Par:**
70/70. **Course Rating:** 69.7/69.7. **Slope:** 121/121. **Green Fee:** $29/$35. **Cart Fee:** Included in
green fee. **Walking Policy:** Walking at certain times. **Walkability:** 4. **Opened:** 1994. **Architect:**
Greg Clark. **Season:** Year-round. **High:** March-Oct. **To obtain tee times:** Call golf shop.
Miscellaneous: Reduced fees (weekdays, twilight, seniors, juniors), metal spikes, range
(grass), credit cards (MC, V, AE, D).

★½ **THE GREAT SOUTHERN GOLF CLUB**
SP-2000 Beach Dr., Gulfport, 39507, Harrison County, (228)896-3536, 69 miles from New
Orleans. **E-mail:** gsgc1908@aol.com. **Web:** www.gsgc1908.com. **Facility Holes:** 18. **Yards:**
6,200/4,881. **Par:** 71/71. **Course Rating:** 69.7/67.5. **Slope:** 117/114. **Green Fee:** $30/$50. **Cart
Fee:** Included in green fee. **Walking Policy:** Walking at certain times. **Walkability:** 1. **Opened:**
1908. **Architect:** Donald Ross. **Season:** Year-round. **High:** Feb.-May. **To obtain tee times:** Call
golf shop. **Miscellaneous:** Reduced fees (twilight), credit cards (MC, V, AE, D), BF, FF.

GREENVILLE PUBLIC GOLF COURSE
PU-465 Base Golf Rd., Greenville, 38703, Washington County, (662)332-4079, 7 miles from
Greenville. **Facility Holes:** 18. **Yards:** 6,430/5,650. **Par:** 72/73. **Course Rating:** 70.8. **Slope:**
114. **Green Fee:** $3/$10. **Cart Fee:** $14/Cart. **Walking Policy:** Unrestricted walking. **Walkability:**
1. **Opened:** 1956. **Season:** Year-round. **To obtain tee times:** Call golf shop. **Miscellaneous:**
Reduced fees (weekdays, seniors, juniors), range (grass), credit cards (MC, V), BF, FF.

GULF HILLS GOLF CLUB
SP-13700 Paso Rd., Ocean Springs, 39564, Jackson County, (228)872-9663, 4 miles from
Biloxi. **E-mail:** info@gulfhillsgolf.com. **Web:** gulfhillsgolf.com. **Facility Holes:** 18. **Yards:**
6,266/5,210. **Par:** 71/71. **Course Rating:** 70.0/69.5. **Slope:** 119/114. **Green Fee:** $30/$45. **Cart
Fee:** Included in green fee. **Walking Policy:** Mandatory carts. **Walkability:** 4. **Opened:** 1927.
Architect: Jack Daray. **Season:** Year-round. **High:** Feb.-April. **To obtain tee times:** Call golf
shop. **Miscellaneous:** Reduced fees (weekdays, twilight), credit cards (MC, V, AE, D), FF.

HILLANDALE COUNTRY CLUB
SP-Oakland School Rd., Corinth, 38834, Alcorn County, (662)286-8020, 75 miles from
Memphis. **Facility Holes:** 18. **Yards:** 6,232/4,842. **Par:** 71/71. **Course Rating:** 70.1/67.5. **Slope:**
120/107. **Green Fee:** $15. **Walkability:** 4. **Opened:** 1930. **Season:** Year-round. **High:** May-Oct.
To obtain tee times: Call golf shop.

★★★½ **KIRKWOOD NATIONAL GOLF CLUB**
SP-785 Hwy. 4 West, Holly Springs, 38635, Marshall County, (662)252-4888, (800)461-4653,
40 miles from Memphis. **E-mail:** kirkwood@dixie-net.com. **Web:** www.kirkwoodgolf.com.
Facility Holes: 18. **Yards:** 7,129/4,898. **Par:** 72/72. **Course Rating:** 73.6/68.2. **Slope:** 135/116.
Green Fee: $35/$55. **Cart Fee:** Included in green fee. **Walking Policy:** Walking at certain times.
Walkability: 5. **Opened:** 1994. **Season:** Year-round. **Tee times:** Call up to 7 days in advance.
Miscellaneous: Reduced fees (weekdays), range (grass), credit cards (MC, V, AE), BF, FF.
Notes: Ranked 10th in 2001 Best in State; 42nd in 1996 America's Top 75 Affordable
Courses; 5th in 1995 Best New Public Courses.
Reader Comments: Good challenge, long & narrow … Beautiful, challenging. So wooded you feel
you're the only group. Great golf … Greens very good, fast … Wonderful course, beautiful wooded
setting. Wildlife in abundance.

★★ **LINKS OF WHISPERING WOODS**
SP-11300 Goodman Rd., Olive Branch, 38654, De Soto County, (901)525-2402, 2 miles from
Memphis, TN. **E-mail:** mfulton@bristolhotels.com. **Facility Holes:** 18. **Yards:** 6,905/5,200. **Par:**

72/72. **Course Rating:** 72.6/69.1. **Slope:** 128/117. **Green Fee:** $22/$28. **Cart Fee:** $10/Person. **Walking Policy:** Walking at certain times. **Walkability:** 3. **Opened:** 1975. **Architect:** D.A. Weibring. **Season:** Year-round. **High:** April-Sept. **To obtain tee times:** Call up to 7 days in advance. **Miscellaneous:** Reduced fees (twilight, seniors, juniors), range (grass), lodging (181 rooms), credit cards (MC, V, AE, D, DC), BF, FF.

LUCEDALE GOLF & RECREATION
SP-9177 Hwy 63 S., Lucedale, 39452, George County, (601)947-8347, 30 miles from Biloxi. **Facility Holes:** 9. **Yards:** 5,845/4,820. **Par:** 71/71. **Walking Policy:** Walking at certain times. **Walkability:** 3. **Opened:** 1979. **To obtain tee times:** Call golf shop. **Miscellaneous:** Metal spikes, range (grass).

★★★½ MALLARD POINTE GOLF COURSE
PU-John Kyle State Park, Sardis, 39236, Panola County, (662)487-2400, (888)833-6477, 6 miles from Sardis. **Facility Holes:** 18. **Yards:** 7,005/5,300. **Par:** 72/72. **Course Rating:** 73.8/71.5. **Slope:** 131/122. **Green Fee:** $36. **Cart Fee:** Included in green fee. **Walking Policy:** Unrestricted walking. **Walkability:** 5. **Opened:** 1997. **Architect:** Bob Cupp. **Season:** Year-round. **High:** April-Oct. **To obtain tee times:** Call golf shop. **Miscellaneous:** Range (grass), lodging (35 rooms), credit cards (MC, V, AE).
Reader Comments: Tough for medium- to high-handicapper... Nice course, demands accuracy to hit large, generous fairways! Bermuda greens are true ... Hilly course, very challenging.

MILLBROOK COUNTRY CLUB
SP-Highway 11 North, Picayune, 39466, Pearl River County, (601)798-8711. **Facility Holes:** 18. **Yards:** 6,477/4,917. **Par:** 72/72. **Course Rating:** 71.0/68.7. **Slope:** 130/115. **Green Fee:** $20/$25. **Cart Fee:** $11/Person. **Walking Policy:** Walking at certain times. **Walkability:** 3. **Opened:** 1953. **Season:** Year-round. **To obtain tee times:** Call golf shop. **Miscellaneous:** Reduced fees (twilight), range (grass), credit cards (MC, V), BF, FF.

★★★ MISSISSIPPI NATIONAL GOLF CLUB
SP-900 Hickory Hill Dr., Gautier, 39553, Jackson County, (228)497-2372, 15 miles from Biloxi. **E-mail:** bobstrohecker@linkscorp.com. **Web:** www.linkscorp.com. **Facility Holes:** 18. **Yards:** 6,983/5,229. **Par:** 72/72. **Course Rating:** 73.1/69.6. **Slope:** 128/113. **Green Fee:** $20/$60. **Cart Fee:** $12/Person. **Walking Policy:** Walking at certain times. **Walkability:** 1. **Opened:** 1965. **Architect:** Earl Stone. **Season:** Year-round. **To obtain tee times:** Call golf shop. **Miscellaneous:** Reduced fees (weekdays, guests, twilight), metal spikes, range (grass/mats), credit cards (MC, V), BF, FF.
Reader Comments: Great old-style layout. Quick trip from the casinos, but don't tell anybody ... Greens too slow ... An absolute great older golf course. I could play everyday and not tire ... Course good for amount of play.
Special Notes: Formerly Hickory Hills Country Club.

★★★ MISSISSIPPI STATE UNIVERSITY GOLF COURSE
PU-1520 Old Hwy. 82E., Starkville, 39759, Oktibbeha County, (662)325-3028, 120 miles from Jackson. **E-mail:** hbm@ra.msstate.edu. **Facility Holes:** 18. **Yards:** 6,926/5,443. **Par:** 72/72. **Course Rating:** 73.5/71.8. **Slope:** 130/121. **Green Fee:** $12/$17. **Cart Fee:** $10/Person. **Walking Policy:** Unrestricted walking. **Walkability:** 3. **Opened:** 1989. **Architect:** Brian Ault. **Season:** Year-round. **High:** March-Sept. **To obtain tee times:** Call golf shop. **Miscellaneous:** Reduced fees (weekdays, juniors), range (grass/mats), credit cards (MC, V, AE, D).
Reader Comments: Great practice facility, great value ... Can be slow & crowded ... Nice layout & challenge, but heavily played & slow ... Best university course in the state ... Best turf ever.

★★ THE NATCHEZ TRACE GOLF CLUB
SP-Beech Springs Rd., 978A CR 681, Saltillo, 38866, Lee County, (662)869-2166, 1 mile from Tupelo. **E-mail:** probill@pga.com. **Facility Holes:** 18. **Yards:** 6,669/4,731. **Par:** 72/72. **Course Rating:** 72.6/67.6. **Slope:** 128/107. **Green Fee:** $15/$24. **Cart Fee:** $18/Person. **Walking Policy:** Unrestricted walking. **Walkability:** 5. **Opened:** 1964. **Architect:** John Frazier. **Season:** Year-round. **To obtain tee times:** Call up to 1 day in advance. **Miscellaneous:** Reduced fees (twilight), range (grass), credit cards (MC, V, AE), BF, FF.

★★★½ THE OAKS GOLF CLUB
PU-24384 Clubhouse Dr., Pass Christian, 39571, Harrison County, (228)452-0909, 10 miles from Gulfport. **E-mail:** theoaksgc@msn.com. **Web:** www.gcww.com/theoaks. **Facility Holes:** 18. **Yards:** 6,900/4,700. **Par:** 72/72. **Course Rating:** 72.5/66.4. **Slope:** 131/107. **Green Fee:** $28/$71. **Cart Fee:** $13/Person. **Walking Policy:** Unrestricted walking. **Walkability:** 3. **Opened:** 1998. **Architect:** Chris Cole/Steve Caplinger. **Season:** Year-round. **High:** Feb.-May. **To obtain tee times:** Call up to 30 days in advance. **Miscellaneous:** Reduced fees (twilight, juniors), range (grass), credit cards (MC, V), BF, FF.
Notes: Ranked 8th in 2001 Best in State.

Reader Comments: Stay in fairway, underbrush & woods, otherwise fair. Friendly starter... Long enough, tough, great condition ... Great! Fast, fast greens ... Watery, marshy, well-kept ... Challenging ... Somebody get a Stimpmeter out here.

OKATOMA GOLF COURSE
SP-25 Oakhills Blvd., Collins, 39428, Covington County, (601)765-1841, 50 miles from Jackson. **E-mail:** okatomagolf@megagate.com. **Facility Holes:** 18. **Yards:** 6,440/4,645. **Par:** 72/72. **Course Rating:** 68.9/66.5. **Slope:** 114/111. **Green Fee:** $25/$30. **Cart Fee:** Included in green fee. **Walking Policy:** Unrestricted walking. **Walkability:** 3. **Opened:** 1994. **Architect:** Milton/Schell. **Season:** Year-round. **High:** March-Sept. **To obtain tee times:** Call golf shop. **Miscellaneous:** Reduced fees (seniors), range (grass), credit cards (MC, V, D), FF.

★★ OLE MISS GOLF CLUB
PU-U of MS, College Hill Rd. #147 CR 1056, Oxford, 38655, Lafayette County, (662)234-4816, 70 miles from Memphis, TN. **Facility Holes:** 18. **Yards:** 6,563/5,306. **Par:** 72/72. **Course Rating:** 72.8/70.9. **Slope:** 129/120. **Green Fee:** $12/$15. **Cart Fee:** $18/Cart. **Walking Policy:** Unrestricted walking. **Walkability:** 3. **Opened:** 1965. **Architect:** Sonny Guy. **Season:** Year-round. **High:** May-Aug. **To obtain tee times:** Call golf shop. **Miscellaneous:** Reduced fees (seniors, juniors), metal spikes, range (grass/mats), credit cards (MC, V).

★★ PASS CHRISTIAN ISLES GOLF CLUB
SP-150 Country Club Dr., Pass Christian, 39571, Harrison County, (228)452-3830, 16 miles from Gulfport. **E-mail:** mcbpga@pgalinks. **Facility Holes:** 18. **Yards:** 6,438/5,428. **Par:** 72/72. **Course Rating:** 69.7/71.6. **Slope:** 124/120. **Green Fee:** $24/$26. **Cart Fee:** $14/Person. **Walking Policy:** Walking at certain times. **Walkability:** 1. **Opened:** 1951. **Architect:** Tom Bendelow. **Season:** Year-round. **High:** Feb.-April. **To obtain tee times:** Call up to 90 days in advance. **Miscellaneous:** Credit cards (MC, V, AE, D), BF, FF.

PEARL MUNICIPAL GOLF COURSE
PU-1001 Center City Dr., Pearl, 39208, Rankin County, (601)932-3534, 10 miles from Jackson. **Facility Holes:** 18. **Yards:** 5,947/4,441. **Par:** 70/70. **Course Rating:** 68.9/63.9. **Slope:** 122/104. **Green Fee:** $10/$12. **Cart Fee:** $9/Person. **Walking Policy:** Unrestricted walking. **Walkability:** 3. **Opened:** 1996. **Architect:** Frank Maxwell. **Season:** Year-round. **High:** May-Aug. **To obtain tee times:** Call up to 3 days in advance. **Miscellaneous:** Reduced fees (weekdays), credit cards (MC, V), BF, FF.

PEARL RIVER GOLF CLUB
PU-33 South Valley Road, Poplarville, 39470, Pearl River County, (601)795-8887, 60 miles from New Orleans. **Facility Holes:** 18. **Yards:** 6,366/4,973. **Par:** 72/72. **Course Rating:** 68.5/68.7. **Slope:** 107/113. **Green Fee:** $6/$13. **Cart Fee:** $10/Person. **Walking Policy:** Unrestricted walking. **Walkability:** 2. **Season:** Year-round. **High:** May-July. **To obtain tee times:** Call golf shop. **Miscellaneous:** Reduced fees (weekdays, seniors, juniors), metal spikes, range (grass), credit cards (MC, V, AE, D).

★★★ PINE BURR COUNTRY CLUB
SP-800 Pine Burr Dr., Wiggins, 39577, Stone County, (601)928-4911, 32 miles from Gulfport. **Facility Holes:** 18. **Yards:** 6,501/4,854. **Par:** 72/72. **Course Rating:** 71.3/68.5. **Slope:** 131/114. **Green Fee:** $15. **Cart Fee:** $10/Person. **Walking Policy:** Unrestricted walking. **Walkability:** 5. **Opened:** 1972. **Architect:** Earl Stone. **Season:** Year-round. **To obtain tee times:** Call up to 30 days in advance. **Miscellaneous:** Reduced fees (twilight, seniors, juniors), range (grass), credit cards (MC, V, AE, D), BF, FF.
Reader Comments: Tricky layout. The greens are extremely undulated, and the hills are deceptive. Very challenging ... Nice challenge ... Outstanding, hilly and narrow.

PINE CREEK GOLF CLUB
SP-61 Clubhouse Dr., Purvis, 39475, Lamar County, (601)794-6427, (877)234-0385, 10 miles from Hattiesburg. **E-mail:** mlvivien@aol. **Web:** www.golfpinecreek.com. **Facility Holes:** 18. **Yards:** 6,152/4,661. **Par:** 71/72. **Course Rating:** 68.8/67.0. **Slope:** 112/110. **Green Fee:** $7/$11. **Cart Fee:** $10/Cart. **Walking Policy:** Unrestricted walking. **Walkability:** 5. **Opened:** 1965. **Architect:** Larry Adams. **Season:** Year-round. **To obtain tee times:** Call up to 7 days in advance. **Miscellaneous:** Reduced fees (weekdays, seniors, juniors), range (grass), BF, FF.

★★★ PLANTATION GOLF CLUB
PU-9425 Plantation Rd., Olive Branch, 38654, De Soto County, (601)895-3530, 5 miles from Memphis, TN. **E-mail:** cv6635@aol.com. **Facility Holes:** 18. **Yards:** 6,773/5,055. **Par:** 72/72. **Course Rating:** 72.0/64.4. **Slope:** 122/109. **Green Fee:** $35/$40. **Cart Fee:** Included in green fee. **Walking Policy:** Walking at certain times. **Walkability:** 2. **Opened:** 1990. **Architect:** William Leathers. **Season:** Year-round. **High:** April-Nov. **To obtain tee times:** Call up to 7 days in advance. **Miscellaneous:** Reduced fees (weekdays, twilight, seniors, juniors), range

(grass/mats), credit cards (MC, V, AE), BF, FF.
Reader Comments: Too many houses, good greens and fairways … Excellent condition … Pricey. Fun course, great finishing hole … zoysia fairways are great, good greens, great values.

PONTOTOC COUNTRY CLUB
SP-Hwy. 6 East, Pontotoc, 38863, Pontotoc County, (662)489-1962, 5 miles from Pontotoc. **Facility Holes:** 18. **Yards:** 6,377/4,683. **Par:** 72/72. **Course Rating:** 70.9/67.6. **Slope:** 130/128. **Green Fee:** $30/$40. **Cart Fee:** Included in green fee. **Walking Policy:** Mandatory carts. **Walkability:** 3. **Opened:** 1964. **Season:** Year-round. **High:** March-Sept. **Tee times:** Call golf shop. **Miscellaneous:** Reduced fees (juniors), range (grass), credit cards (MC, V, D), BF, FF.

★★ PRESIDENT BROADWATER GOLF COURSE
R-200 Beauvoir Rd., Biloxi, 39531, Harrison County, (228)385-4081, (800)843-7737, 3 miles from Gulfport. **E-mail:** presgolf@digiscape.com. **Web:** presidentbroadwater.com. **Facility Holes:** 18. **Yards:** 7,140/5,398. **Par:** 72/72. **Course Rating:** 74.1/70.4. **Slope:** 134/120. **Green Fee:** $55. **Cart Fee:** Included in green fee. **Walking Policy:** Mandatory carts. **Walkability:** 1. **Opened:** 1968. **Architect:** Earl Stone. **Season:** Year-round. **High:** Feb.-May. **To obtain tee times:** Call golf shop. **Miscellaneous:** Reduced fees (guests, twilight, juniors), range (grass), lodging (530 rooms), credit cards (MC, V, AE, D), BF, FF.

★★★★½ QUAIL HOLLOW GOLF COURSE *Value+, Pace*
PU-1102 Percy Quin Dr., McComb, 39648, Pike County, (601)684-2903, (888)465-3647, 90 miles from Baton Rouge, LA. **E-mail:** waughgolf@hotmail.com. **Facility Holes:** 27. **Yards:** 6,754/4,944. **Par:** 72/72. **Course Rating:** 71.9/68.5. **Slope:** 118/116. **Green Fee:** $18/$23. **Cart Fee:** $12/Person. **Walking Policy:** Unrestricted walking. **Opened:** 1997. **Architect:** Arthur Hills. **Season:** Year-round. **To obtain tee times:** Call up to 14 days in advance. **Miscellaneous:** Reduced fees (twilight), range (grass), lodging (30 rooms), credit cards (MC, V, AE), BF, FF.
Notes: Ranked 5th in 1999 Best New Affordable Public Courses.
Reader Comments: Everything a state park course should be … Excellent course, staff and price … It was more than I expected … Must play … Private course at public price! … Beautiful holes … Greens inconsistent on different trips.
Special Notes: Also has a 9-hole par-3 course.

SHELL LANDING GOLF CLUB
PU-3499 Shell Landing Blvd., Gautier, 39553, Jackson County, (228)497-5683, (866)851-0541, 14 miles from Biloxi. **Web:** www.shelllanding.com. **Facility Holes:** 18. **Yards:** 6,978/4,989. **Par:** 72/72. **Course Rating:** 73.2/68.6. **Slope:** 128/112. **Green Fee:** $43/$63. **Cart Fee:** $17/Person. **Walking Policy:** Mandatory carts. **Walkability:** 3. **Opened:** 2000. **Architect:** Davis Love III. **Season:** Year-round. **High:** Feb.-April. **To obtain tee times:** Call up to 30 days in advance. **Miscellaneous:** Range (grass), credit cards (MC, V, AE, D), BF, FF.

SHILOH RIDGE GOLF & RACQUET CLUB
PU-3303 Shiloh Ridge Rd., Corinth, 38834, Alcorn County, (662)286-8000, 85 miles from Memphis. **Facility Holes:** 18. **Yards:** 6,525/5,072. **Par:** 72/72. **Course Rating:** 73.3. **Slope:** 123. **Green Fee:** $10/$20. **Cart Fee:** $10/Person. **Walking Policy:** Walking at certain times. **Walkability:** 3. **Opened:** 1989. **Architect:** Archie Anderson. **Season:** Year-round. **High:** April-Oct. **Tee times:** Call golf shop. **Miscellaneous:** Reduced fees (seniors), cards (MC, V, AE, D).

★½ SONNY GUY MUNICIPAL GOLF COURSE
PU-3200 Woodrow Wilson Dr., Jackson, 39209, Hinds County, (601)960-1905. **Facility Holes:** 18. **Yards:** 7,200/5,200. **Par:** 72/72. **Course Rating:** 71.1/67.8. **Slope:** 117/110. **Green Fee:** $8. **Cart Fee:** $14/Cart. **Walking Policy:** Unrestricted walking. **Walkability:** 1. **Opened:** 1949. **Architect:** Sonny Guy. **Season:** Year-round. **High:** March-Nov. **To obtain tee times:** Call golf shop. **Miscellaneous:** Reduced fees (weekdays, seniors, juniors), metal spikes, caddies, credit cards (MC, V), BF, FF.

★★ ST. ANDREWS GOLF CLUB
SP-2 Golfing Green Dr., Ocean Springs, 39564, Jackson County, (228)875-7730, (888)875-7730, 10 miles from Biloxi. **E-mail:** sagc@bellsouth.net. **Web:** standrewsgolfcourse.com. **Facility Holes:** 18. **Yards:** 6,540/4,960. **Par:** 72/72. **Course Rating:** 69.7/67.8. **Slope:** 119/111. **Green Fee:** $23/$43. **Cart Fee:** $12/Person. **Walking Policy:** Walking at certain times. **Walkability:** 1. **Opened:** 1968. **Architect:** J. Thompson. **Season:** Year-round. **High:** Feb.-April. **To obtain tee times:** Call up to 7 days in advance. **Miscellaneous:** Reduced fees (weekdays, guests), range (grass), lodging (20 rooms), credit cards (MC, V, AE), BF, FF.

★★½ **SUNKIST COUNTRY CLUB**
SP-2381 Sunkist Country Club Rd., Biloxi, 39532, Harrison County, (228)388-3961. **E-mail:** sunkistgolf@msn.com. **Facility Holes:** 18. **Yards:** 6,350/5,300. **Par:** 72/72. **Course Rating:** 69.3/71.0. **Slope:** 121/117. **Green Fee:** $25/$49. **Cart Fee:** Included in green fee. **Walking Policy:** Mandatory carts. **Walkability:** 2. **Opened:** 1953. **Architect:** Roland (Robby) Robertson. **Season:** Year-round. **To obtain tee times:** Call golf shop. **Miscellaneous:** Range (grass/mats), credit cards (MC, V), BF, FF.

TIMBERTON GOLF CLUB
PU-22 Clubhouse Dr., Hattiesburg, 39401, Forest County, (601)584-4653, (800)848-3222, 90 miles from New Orleans, LA. **E-mail:** timberton@megate.com. **Web:** timberton-golf.com. **Facility Holes:** 27. **Green Fee:** $19/$40. **Cart Fee:** $20/Cart. **Walking Policy:** Unrestricted walking. **Opened:** 1991. **Architect:** Mark McCumber/J.R. Carpenter/Ron Hickman. **Season:** Year-round. **High:** March-April. **To obtain tee times:** Call golf shop. **Miscellaneous:** Reduced fees (twilight), lodging (15 rooms), credit cards (MC, V, AE, D), BF, FF.
★★★★½ **CREEKSIDE/VALLEY** (18)
Yards: 7,003/5,439. **Par:** 72/72. **Course Rating:** 73.4/69.7. **Slope:** 135/129. **Walkability:** 3. **Miscellaneous:** Range (grass).
Reader Comments: Holes memorable and varied. High marks for challenge, beauty and fun … Difficult, but fair … One of the prettiest in the South, great value … Play from back tees and let rip … Pro is terrific … Beautiful, each fairway isolated from others … Back 9 as good as any.
★★★★½ **LAKEVIEW** (9) *Value, Pace*
Yards: 3,245/2,739. **Par:** 36/36. **Walkability:** 5. **Miscellaneous:** Range (grass/mats).
Reader Comments: Outstanding! Best in every way … Excellent course out in middle of forest … A top course, worth the trip … Scenic, difficult, but still enjoyable to all … Great, straightforward golf … The tallest pines I've ever seen … Natural design, very friendly, priced right.

★★ **TRAMARK GOLF COURSE**
PU-Washington Avenue, Gulfport, 39503, Harrison County, (228)863-7808, 65 miles from New Orleans. **Facility Holes:** 18. **Yards:** 6,350/5,800. **Par:** 72/72. **Course Rating:** 68.5/69.5. **Slope:** 116/109. **Green Fee:** $14. **Cart Fee:** $20/Person. **Walking Policy:** Unrestricted walking. **Walkability:** 1. **Opened:** 1967. **Architect:** Floyd Trehern. **Season:** Year-round. **High:** Feb.-April. **To obtain tee times:** Call golf shop. **Miscellaneous:** Reduced fees (juniors), metal spikes, range (grass), credit cards (MC, V).

TWIN PINES COUNTRY CLUB
SP-1 Tee Time Dr., Petal, 39465, Forrest County, (601)544-8318, 10 miles from Hattiesburg. **Facility Holes:** 9. **Yards:** 6,690/4,772. **Par:** 72/72. **Course Rating:** 68.5/64.6. **Slope:** 117/106. **Green Fee:** $10/$16. **Cart Fee:** $9/Person. **Walking Policy:** Walking at certain times. **Walkability:** 4. **Opened:** 1986. **Season:** Year-round. **High:** April-July. **To obtain tee times:** Call golf shop. **Miscellaneous:** Credit cards (MC, V).

★★ **USM'S VAN HOOK GOLF COURSE**
PU-One Golf Course Rd., Hattiesburg, 39402, Forest County, (601)264-1872, 60 miles from Biloxi. **Facility Holes:** 18. **Yards:** 6,429/4,903. **Par:** 72/73. **Course Rating:** 72.2/67.8. **Slope:** 117/110. **Green Fee:** $10/$15. **Cart Fee:** $20/Cart. **Walking Policy:** Unrestricted walking. **Walkability:** 4. **Opened:** 1957. **Architect:** Sonny Guy. **Season:** Year-round. **High:** May-Dec. **Tee times:** Call shop. **Misc:** Reduced fees (weekdays, twilight, seniors, juniors), cards (MC, V).

★★½ **WEDGEWOOD GOLF COURSE**
SP-5206 Tournament Dr., Olive Branch, 38654, De Soto County, (901)521-8275, 5 miles from Memphis. **E-mail:** www.golfsolf.com. **Facility Holes:** 18. **Yards:** 6,863/5,627. **Par:** 72/72. **Course Rating:** 72.8/69.1. **Slope:** 127/118. **Green Fee:** $29/$45. **Cart Fee:** Included in green fee. **Walking Policy:** Walking at certain times. **Walkability:** 2. **Opened:** 1990. **Architect:** John Floyd. **Season:** Year-round. **High:** May-Sept. **Tee times:** Call golf shop. **Miscellaneous:** Reduced fees (weekdays, guests, twilight, seniors, juniors), range (grass), credit cards (MC, V).

WHISPERING PINES GOLF CLUB
PU-555 Simlar Blvd., Columbus, 39710, Lowndes County, (662)434-7932, 8 miles from Columbus. **Facility Holes:** 9. **Yards:** 5,195/4,650. **Par:** 70/72. **Course Rating:** 66.7/67.7. **Slope:** 128/120. **Green Fee:** $8/$15. **Cart Fee:** $12/Person. **Walking Policy:** Unrestricted walking. **Walkability:** 1. **Season:** Year-round. **High:** April-Oct. **To obtain tee times:** Call golf shop. **Miscellaneous:** Range (grass), credit cards (MC, V).

WILLOW CREEK GOLF CLUB
PU-1300 Willowcreek Lane, Brandon, 39042, Rankin County, (601)825-8343. **Facility Holes:** 18. **Yards:** 6,424/4,864. **Par:** 72/72. **Course Rating:** 70.1/73.1. **Slope:** 113/117. **Green Fee:** $12/$18. **To obtain tee times:** Call golf shop.

★★★½ **WINDANCE COUNTRY CLUB**
SP-19385 Champion Circle, Gulfport, 39503, Harrison County, (228)832-4871, 60 miles from
New Orleans. **Facility Holes:** 18. **Yards:** 6,678/5,179. **Par:** 72/72. **Course Rating:** 73.1/70.1.
Slope: 129/120. **Green Fee:** $60. **Cart Fee:** $15/Person. **Walking Policy:** Mandatory carts.
Walkability: 2. **Opened:** 1986. **Architect:** Mark McCumber. **Season:** Year-round. **High:** Feb.-
April. **To obtain tee times:** Call golf shop. **Miscellaneous:** Range (grass), credit cards (MC, V,
AE), BF, FF.
Reader Comments: Good test, needs work, can be real good … Small-town hospitality … One of
the best on the coast, great condition … Excellent course … Some good holes, several gimmicky …
Nice coastal layout, nice experience.

WINONA COUNTRY CLUB
SP-535 Highway 407, Winona, 38967, Montgomery County, (662)283-4211, 90 miles from
Jackson. **E-mail:** winonacc@duckwood.net. **Facility Holes:** 9. **Yards:** 6,045/5,146. **Par:** 72/74.
Green Fee: $15/$20. **Cart Fee:** $12/Cart. **Walking Policy:** Unrestricted walking. **Walkability:** 4.
Season: Year-round. **To obtain tee times:** Call golf shop. **Miscellaneous:** Credit cards
(MC, V, D).

★★★½ ADAMS POINTE GOLF CLUB
PU-1601 R.D. Mize Rd., Blue Springs, 64014, Jackson County, (816)220-3673, 15 miles from Kansas City. **E-mail:** apgolf@gte.net. **Web:** www.eaglgolf.com. **Facility Holes:** 18. **Yards:** 6,938/5,060. **Par:** 72/72. **Course Rating:** 73.8/68.1. **Slope:** 131/114. **Green Fee:** $17/$39. **Cart Fee:** $12/Person. **Walking Policy:** Unrestricted walking. **Walkability:** 3. **Opened:** 1998. **Architect:** Don Sechrest. **Season:** Year-round. **High:** June-Aug. **To obtain tee times:** Call up to 5 days in advance. **Miscellaneous:** Reduced fees (twilight, seniors, juniors), range (grass/mats), lodging (100 rooms), credit cards (MC, V, AE), BF, FF.
Reader Comments: Great finishing hole … Variety of holes … Very pretty, new course but great condition … Still developing, excellent service … Good course … A definite play when in Kansas City, top 5 list.

ARTHUR HILLS GOLF CLUB
PU-Highway 22 - 2 miles W., Mexico, 65265, Audrain County, (573)581-1330, 90 miles from St. Louis. **Facility Holes:** 18. **Yards:** 6,148/5,097. **Par:** 71/72. **Course Rating:** 68.8/64.0. **Slope:** 118/108. **Green Fee:** $18. **Cart Fee:** $9/Person. **To obtain tee times:** Call golf shop.

★★★★ BENT CREEK GOLF COURSE
PU-2200 Bent Creek Dr., Jackson, 63755, Cape Girardeau County, (573)243-6060, 90 miles from St. Louis. **Web:** www.bentcreek.net. **Facility Holes:** 18. **Yards:** 6,958/5,148. **Par:** 72/72. **Course Rating:** 72.5/69.8. **Slope:** 136/112. **Green Fee:** $33/$43. **Cart Fee:** Included in green fee. **Walking Policy:** Walking at certain times. **Walkability:** 3. **Opened:** 1990. **Architect:** Gary Kern. **Season:** Year-round. **To obtain tee times:** Call up to 7 days in advance. **Miscellaneous:** Reduced fees (weekdays, twilight, seniors, juniors), range (grass/mats), credit cards (MC, V, AE, D), BF, FF.
Reader Comments: One of the best values in the state … Very nice course, great for the money … A hidden gem … The fairways have been resodded … Tough course has many elevated greens … A beautiful layout.

★★★½ BENT OAK GOLF CLUB
PU-1300 S.E. 30th, Oak Grove, 64075, Jackson County, (816)690-3028, 20 miles from Kansas City. **Web:** www.bentoakgolfclub.com. **Facility Holes:** 18. **Yards:** 6,855/5,500. **Par:** 72/73. **Course Rating:** 73.1/71.0. **Slope:** 134/119. **Green Fee:** $13/$24. **Cart Fee:** $14/Person. **Walking Policy:** Unrestricted walking. **Walkability:** 3. **Opened:** 1980. **Architect:** Bob Simmons. **Season:** Year-round. **High:** March-Nov. **To obtain tee times:** Call up to 7 days in advance. **Miscellaneous:** Reduced fees (weekdays, twilight, seniors, juniors), metal spikes, range (grass), credit cards (MC, V, AE, D), BF, FF.
Reader Comments: Laid back, easy going, pleasant… Recent upgrades … Back 9 is tough.

★★ BILL & PAYNE STEWART GOLF COURSE
PU-1825 E. Norton, Springfield, 65803, Greene County, (417)833-9962. **Facility Holes:** 18. **Yards:** 6,162/5,360. **Par:** 70/71. **Course Rating:** 68.4/70.6. **Slope:** 113/113. **Green Fee:** $12/$17. **Cart Fee:** $20/Cart. **Walking Policy:** Unrestricted walking. **Walkability:** 2. **Opened:** 1947. **Architect:** Perry Maxwell. **Season:** Year-round. **High:** March-Oct. **To obtain tee times:** Call golf shop. **Miscellaneous:** Reduced fees (weekdays, seniors, juniors), range (grass), credit cards (MC, V).
Special Notes: Also has a 9-hole par-3 course.

BOOTHEEL GOLF CLUB
SP-1218 N. Ingram, Sikeston, 63801, Scott County, (573)472-6111, (888)472-6111, 150 miles from St. Louis. **Facility Holes:** 18. **Yards:** 6,880/5,825. **Par:** 72/72. **Course Rating:** 73.0/70.0. **Slope:** 123/113. **Green Fee:** $17/$20. **Cart Fee:** $11/Person. **Walking Policy:** Mandatory carts. **Walkability:** 1. **Opened:** 1996. **Architect:** David Pfaff. **Season:** Year-round. **To obtain tee times:** Call up to 7 days in advance. **Miscellaneous:** Reduced fees (weekdays, twilight, seniors, juniors), range (grass/mats), credit cards (MC, V, AE), BF, FF.

★★★★½ BRANSON CREEK GOLF CLUB *Service, Pace*
PU-Hwy. 65 & Branson Creek Dr., Branson, 65615, Taney County, (417)339-4653, (888)772-9990, 3 miles from Branson. **E-mail:** mschisler@troongolf.com. **Web:** www.branson-creekgolf.com. **Facility Holes:** 18. **Yards:** 7,036/5,845. **Par:** 71/71. **Course Rating:** 73.0/64.5. **Slope:** 133/116. **Green Fee:** $59/$85. **Cart Fee:** Included in green fee. **Walking Policy:** Unrestricted walking. **Walkability:** 3. **Opened:** 2000. **Architect:** Tom Fazio/Dennis Wise. **Season:** Year-round. **High:** March-Oct. **Tee times:** Call up to 30 days in advance. **Miscellaneous:** Reduced fees (twilight, juniors), range credit cards (MC, V, AE), BF, FF.
Notes: Ranked 5th in 2001 Best in State; 5th in 2000 Best New Upscale Courses.
Reader Comments: Challenging, but fair… Back 9 is simply superb … Great practice facilities … Excellent course, very challenging, beautiful scenery … Beautiful course and staff doesn't get any better … Best public course in MO … Great layout.

BRIARBROOK COUNTRY CLUB
SP-502 Briarbrook Dr., Carl Junction, 64834, Jasper County, (417)649-4653, 5 miles from Joplin. **E-mail:** brairbrook@aol.com. **Web:** www.briarbrookgolf.com. **Facility Holes:** 27. **Green Fee:** $16. **Cart Fee:** $9/Person. **Walking Policy:** Unrestricted walking. **Walkability:** 4. **Opened:** 1962. **Season:** Year-round. **High:** April-Oct. **To obtain tee times:** Call golf shop. **Miscellaneous:** Range (grass/mats), credit cards (MC, V, D), BF, FF.
HILLSIDE/LAKESIDE (18 Combo)
Yards: 6,799/5,805. **Par:** 72/72. **Course Rating:** 71.6/74.1. **Slope:** 128/133.
HILLSIDE/VALLEYSIDE (18 Combo)
Yards: 6,663/5,925. **Par:** 72/73. **Course Rating:** 71.2/74.0. **Slope:** 127/133.
LAKESIDE/VALLEYSIDE (18 Combo)
Yards: 6,756/5,666. **Par:** 72/73. **Course Rating:** 71.6/74.1. **Slope:** 128/133.

CAPE JAYCEE MUNICIPAL GOLF COURSE
PU-Perryville Rd., Cape Girardeau, 63701, Cape Girardeau County, (573)334-2031, 100 miles from St. Louis. **Facility Holes:** 18. **Yards:** 5,616/4,492. **Par:** 70/70. **Course Rating:** 65.2/64.7. **Slope:** 106/101. **Green Fee:** $9/$11. **Cart Fee:** $17/Cart. **Walking Policy:** Unrestricted walking. **Walkability:** 3. **Season:** Year-round. **High:** April-Oct. **To obtain tee times:** Call golf shop. **Miscellaneous:** Reduced fees (juniors), credit cards (MC, V). **Special Notes:** Formerly Cape Girardeau Municipal Golf Course.

★★½ CARTHAGE MUNICIPAL GOLF COURSE
PU-2000 Richard Webster Dr., Carthage, 64836, Jasper County, (417)237-7030, 10 miles from Joplin. **E-mail:** mpeter@ipa.net. **Facility Holes:** 18. **Yards:** 6,402/5,469. **Par:** 71/73. **Course Rating:** 69.4/70.5. **Slope:** 124/115. **Green Fee:** $10/$12. **Cart Fee:** $18/Cart. **Walking Policy:** Unrestricted walking. **Walkability:** 3. **Opened:** 1937. **Architect:** Tom Bendelow/Don Sechrest. **Season:** Year-round. **To obtain tee times:** Call golf shop. **Miscellaneous:** Reduced fees (weekdays, twilight), range (grass/mats), credit cards (MC, V), BF, FF.

★★½ CASSVILLE GOLF CLUB
SP-Hwy. 112 S., Cassville, 65625, Barry County, (417)847-2399, 55 miles from Springfield. **Facility Holes:** 18. **Yards:** 6,620/5,802. **Par:** 72/72. **Course Rating:** 71.3/79.9. **Slope:** 118/117. **Green Fee:** $17/$21. **Cart Fee:** $21/Cart. **Walking Policy:** Unrestricted walking. **Walkability:** 2. **Opened:** 1966. **Architect:** Ken Sisney. **Season:** Year-round. **High:** April-Oct. **To obtain tee times:** Call golf shop. **Miscellaneous:** Range (grass/mats), credit cards (MC, V), BF, FF.

CHAPEL RIDGE GOLF CLUB
PU-3750 N.E. Ralph Powell Rd., Lee's Summit, 64064, Jackson County, (816)347-8000, 15 miles from Kansas City. **E-mail:** tab605@smsu.edu. **Web:** www.chapelridgegc.com. **Facility Holes:** 18. **Yards:** 6,376/5,052. **Par:** 70/70. **Course Rating:** 70.1/68.7. **Slope:** 120/113. **Green Fee:** $29/$36. **Cart Fee:** $14/Person. **Walking Policy:** Unrestricted walking. **Walkability:** 3. **Opened:** 2000. **Architect:** Don Secrest. **Season:** Year-round. **High:** May-Nov. **To obtain tee times:** Call up to 5 days in advance. **Miscellaneous:** Reduced fees (weekdays, twilight, seniors, juniors), credit cards (MC, V, AE), BF, FF.

★★½ CHERRY HILLS GOLF CLUB
SP-16700 Manchester Rd., St. Louis, 63040, St. Louis County, (636)458-4113, 12 miles from St. Louis. **E-mail:** swyatt01@earthlink.net. **Web:** www.cherryhillsgc.com. **Facility Holes:** 18. **Yards:** 6,450/5,491. **Par:** 71/72. **Course Rating:** 71.1/72.6. **Slope:** 132/120. **Green Fee:** $30/$50. **Cart Fee:** $9/Person. **Walking Policy:** Unrestricted walking. **Walkability:** 3. **Opened:** 1964. **Architect:** Art Linkogel/Gary Kern. **Season:** Year-round. **High:** April-Sept. **To obtain tee times:** Call up to 7 days in advance. **Miscellaneous:** Reduced fees (twilight, seniors, juniors), range (grass/mats), credit cards (MC, V, AE), BF, FF.

★★½ CLAYCREST GOLF CLUB
SP-925 N. Lightburne, Liberty, 64068, Clay County, (816)781-6522, 15 miles from Kansas City. **Facility Holes:** 18. **Yards:** 6,457/5,375. **Par:** 72/72. **Course Rating:** 69.5/68.2. **Slope:** 115/109. **Green Fee:** $15/$17. **Cart Fee:** $24/Cart. **Walking Policy:** Unrestricted walking. **Walkability:** 3. **Opened:** 1967. **Architect:** Chet Mendenhall. **Season:** Year-round. **High:** April-Nov. **To obtain tee times:** Call golf shop. **Miscellaneous:** Reduced fees (seniors), metal spikes, range (/), credit cards (MC, V).

CLINTON COUNTRY CLUB
SP-225 NE 100, Clinton, 64735, Henry County, (816)885-2521, 60 miles from Kansas City. **Facility Holes:** 18. **Yards:** 6,507/5,022. **Par:** 72/72. **Course Rating:** 71.6/67.5. **Slope:** 116/108. **Green Fee:** $24/$26. **Cart Fee:** $20/Cart. **Walking Policy:** Walking at certain times. **Walkability:** 2. **Opened:** 1993. **Architect:** Kevin Pargman. **Season:** Year-round. **To obtain tee times:** Call golf shop. **Miscellaneous:** Range (grass), FF.

★★★★½ **THE CLUB AT OLD KINDERHOOK** *Condition+*
PU-Lake Rd. 54-80, Camdenton, 65020, Camden County, (573)346-4444, (888)346-4949, 140 miles from St. Louis. **E-mail:** kraft@oldkinderhook.com. **Web:** www.oldkinderhook.com. **Facility Holes:** 18. **Yards:** 6,855/4,962. **Par:** 71/71. **Course Rating:** 72.8/69.5. **Slope:** 137/123. **Green Fee:** $55/$95. **Cart Fee:** Included in green fee. **Walkability:** 3. **Opened:** 1999. **Architect:** Tom Weiskopf. **Season:** Year-round. **High:** April-Nov. **To obtain tee times:** Call up to 30 days in advance. **Miscellaneous:** Reduced fees (weekdays, twilight, juniors), range (grass), lodging (30 rooms), credit cards (MC, V, AE), BF, FF.
Reader Comments: Beautiful layout and scenery ... Challenging ... Nice big greens ... Course was immaculate in late May ... I'd save my money, and play here again ... Great layout ... Manicured, slick greens.

COUNTRY CREEK GOLF CLUB
PU-21601 E. State Route P, Pleasant Hill, 64080, Cass County, (816)540-5225, 25 miles from Kansas City. **Facility Holes:** 36. **Green Fee:** $12/$17. **Walking Policy:** Unrestricted walking. **Walkability:** 1. **Architect:** Jeff McKee. **Season:** Year-round. **High:** May-Sept. **To obtain tee times:** Call golf shop. **Miscellaneous:** Reduced fees (twilight, seniors, juniors), range (grass), credit cards (MC, V, AE, D), FF.
THE QUARRY (9)
Yards: 5,942/5,656. **Par:** 71/72. **Course Rating:** 67.2/65.9. **Slope:** 105/103. **Opened:** 1994.
★★★ **THE ROCK** (18)
Yards: 6,721/5,656. **Par:** 72/72. **Course Rating:** 71.6/71.1. **Slope:** 118/118. **Opened:** 1991.
Reader Comments: When the trees grow to supply some shelter from the prairie winds this course will be a real winner.. Very good value ... Course maturing nicely ... Will be adding another 18-hole championship ... Fun to play ... Good greens and good pace of play.

★★ **CRACKERNECK GOLF COURSE**
PU-18800 E. 40 Hwy., Independence, 64055, Jackson County, (816)795-7771, 13 miles from Kansas City. **Facility Holes:** 18. **Yards:** 6,246/5,175. **Par:** 72/74. **Course Rating:** 69.1/68.8. **Slope:** 115/108. **Green Fee:** $15/$18. **Cart Fee:** $22/Cart. **Walking Policy:** Unrestricted walking. **Walkability:** 2. **Opened:** 1964. **Architect:** Charles Maddox/William Maddox. **Season:** Year-round. **High:** June-Aug. **To obtain tee times:** Call golf shop. **Miscellaneous:** Reduced fees (weekdays, twilight, seniors), range (mats), credit cards (MC, V).

★★★ **CRYSTAL HIGHLANDS GOLF CLUB**
PU-3030 U.S. Highway 61, Crystal City, 63028, Jefferson County, (636)931-3880, 30 miles from St. Louis. **E-mail:** crystalgc@mindspring.com. **Web:** www.golfstl.com. **Facility Holes:** 18. **Yards:** 6,480/4,946. **Par:** 72/72. **Course Rating:** 71.6/68.0. **Slope:** 135/109. **Green Fee:** $20/$30. **Cart Fee:** $10/Person. **Walking Policy:** Walking at certain times. **Walkability:** 4. **Opened:** 1988. **Architect:** Michael Hurdzan. **Season:** Year-round. **High:** May-Oct. **To obtain tee times:** Call up to 7 days in advance. **Miscellaneous:** Reduced fees (weekdays, twilight, seniors, juniors), metal spikes, range (grass), credit cards (MC, V, D), BF, FF.
Reader Comments: Exciting layout with the toughest greens in the area ... Nice clubhouse ... An affordable course that struggles with their greens.

DAVID DAYNE GLASS MUNICIPAL GOLF COURSE
PU-P.O. Box 1090, Mountain View, 65548, Howell County, (417)934-6959, 99 miles from Springfield. **Facility Holes:** 18. **Yards:** 6,185/4,973. **Par:** 72/72. **Slope:** 98.5. **Green Fee:** $13/$15. **Cart Fee:** $15/Cart. **Walking Policy:** Unrestricted walking. **Architect:** Bob Stevens. **Season:** Year-round. **To obtain tee times:** Call golf shop.

★★½ **DOGWOOD HILLS GOLF CLUB & RESORT INN**
R-1252 State Hwy. KK, Osage Beach, 65065, Camden County, (573)348-3153, 160 miles from St. Louis. **E-mail:** info@dogwoodhillsresort.com. **Web:** www.dogwoodhillsresort.com. **Facility Holes:** 18. **Yards:** 6,157/4,641. **Par:** 70/71. **Course Rating:** 68.5/66.1. **Slope:** 116/106. **Green Fee:** $28/$47. **Cart Fee:** Included in green fee. **Walking Policy:** Walking at certain times. **Walkability:** 4. **Opened:** 1962. **Architect:** Herman Hackbarth. **Season:** Year-round. **High:** May-Sept. **To obtain tee times:** Call up to 14 days in advance. **Miscellaneous:** Reduced fees (weekdays, guests, twilight), range (grass/mats), lodging (57 rooms), credit cards (MC, V, AE, D), BF, FF.

EAGLE CREST GOLF & COUNTRY CLUB
SP-1545 S. Beal, Republic, 65738, Greene County, (417)732-8500, 15 miles from Springfield. **Facility Holes:** 18. **Yards:** 6,621/5,202. **Par:** 72/73. **Slope:** 123. **Green Fee:** $12/$15. **Cart Fee:** $9/Person. **Opened:** 1990. **Architect:** Tom Riddell. **To obtain tee times:** Call golf shop. **Miscellaneous:** Reduced fees (weekdays).

★★★★ EAGLE KNOLL GOLF CLUB *Pace*
PU-5757 E. Eagle Knoll Dr., Hartsburg, 65039, Boone County, (573)761-4653, (800)909-0564, 18 miles from Columbia. **E-mail:** info@eagleknoll.com. **Web:** www.eagleknoll.com. **Facility Holes:** 18. **Yards:** 6,920/5,323. **Par:** 72/72. **Course Rating:** 73.8/69.1. **Slope:** 141/113. **Green Fee:** $28/$44. **Cart Fee:** Included in green fee. **Walking Policy:** Unrestricted walking. **Walkability:** 5. **Opened:** 1996. **Architect:** Gary Kern. **Season:** Year-round. **High:** April-Oct. **To obtain tee times:** Call up to 30 days in advance. **Miscellaneous:** Reduced fees (twilight, seniors, juniors), range (grass/mats), credit cards (MC, V, AE, D), BF, FF.
Notes: Ranked tied for 8th in 1996 Best New Affordable Courses.
Reader Comments: Narrow fairways but very playable … Excellent conditions … All par 3s the same … Bring extra balls.

★★★★½ EAGLE LAKE GOLF CLUB *Value*
SP-4215 Hunt Rd., Farmington, 63640, St. Francois County, (573)756-6660, 55 miles from St. Louis. **Facility Holes:** 18. **Yards:** 7,093/5,648. **Par:** 72/72. **Course Rating:** 73.9/71.0. **Slope:** 130/113. **Green Fee:** $25/$40. **Cart Fee:** Included in green fee. **Walking Policy:** Walking at certain times. **Walkability:** 2. **Opened:** 1993. **Architect:** Gary Kern. **Season:** Year-round. **High:** April-Oct. **To obtain tee times:** Call up to 14 days in advance. **Miscellaneous:** Reduced fees (weekdays, twilight, seniors), range (grass/mats), credit cards (MC, V, AE, D), BF, FF.
Reader Comments: Outstanding value, very desirable … Excellent value and conditions … Great layout … Long par 4s … All-around good deal … Beautiful, good greens … Wide open and well groomed … Excellent course, wish it was closer.

★★★ EAGLE SPRINGS GOLF COURSE
PU-2575 Redman Rd., St. Louis, 63136, St. Louis County, (314)355-7277, 6 miles from St. Louis. **E-mail:** davport2@aol.com. **Web:** www.eaglesprings.com. **Facility Holes:** 27. **Yards:** 6,583/5,221. **Par:** 72/72. **Course Rating:** 71.4/72.3. **Slope:** 122/121. **Green Fee:** $18/$30. **Cart Fee:** $11/Person. **Walking Policy:** Unrestricted walking. **Walkability:** 3. **Opened:** 1989. **Architect:** David Gill. **Season:** Year-round. **High:** March-Nov. **To obtain tee times:** Call golf shop. **Miscellaneous:** Reduced fees (weekdays, seniors, juniors), range (grass), credit cards (MC, V, D), BF, FF.
Reader Comments: Quirky design, very hilly, great finishing holes … Nice course … Good value … It has a nice 9-hole par 3 course … Good course, easy to walk, fun to play.
Special Notes: Also has a 9-hole par-3 course.

★★½ EAGLE'S LANDING GOLF COURSE
PU-4200 Bong Ave., Belton, 64012, Cass County, (816)318-0004, 25 miles from Kansas City. **E-mail:** eglslndg@swbell.net. **Facility Holes:** 18. **Yards:** 6,888/4,909. **Par:** 72/72. **Course Rating:** 73.4/64.5. **Slope:** 135/117. **Green Fee:** $22/$28. **Cart Fee:** $13/Person. **Walking Policy:** Unrestricted walking. **Walkability:** 3. **Opened:** 1999. **Architect:** Jeff Klaiber. **Season:** Year-round. **High:** May-Sept. **To obtain tee times:** Call golf shop. **Miscellaneous:** Reduced fees (twilight, seniors, juniors), credit cards (MC, V).

ELDON GOLF CLUB
SP-35 Golf Club Rd., Eldon, 65026, Miller County, (573)392-4172, 20 miles from Jefferson City. **Facility Holes:** 18. **Yards:** 6,373/4,754. **Par:** 71/73. **Course Rating:** 70.0/66.6. **Slope:** 124/110. **Green Fee:** $35/$40. **Cart Fee:** $10/Person. **Walking Policy:** Mandatory cart. **Walkability:** 3. **Season:** Year-round. **High:** May-Oct. **To obtain tee times:** Call golf shop. **Miscellaneous:** Reduced fees (juniors), range (grass), credit cards (MC, V).

★★★ EXCELSIOR SPRINGS GOLF CLUB
PU-1201 E. Golf Hill Dr., Excelsior Springs, 64024, Ray County, (816)630-3731, 28 miles from Kansas City. **Facility Holes:** 18. **Yards:** 6,075/5,119. **Par:** 72/72. **Course Rating:** 72.0/65.8. **Slope:** 120/107. **Green Fee:** $18/$23. **Cart Fee:** $12/Person. **Walking Policy:** Unrestricted walking. **Walkability:** 4. **Opened:** 1915. **Architect:** Tom Bendelow. **Season:** Feb.-Dec. **High:** May-Sept. **To obtain tee times:** Call golf shop. **Miscellaneous:** Reduced fees (weekdays, twilight), metal spikes, range (grass), BF, FF.
Reader Comments: Classic public golf course consistently maintained … Small greens with a lot of slope … Quick greens, tight fairways … Old traditional layout.

★★½ FAIRVIEW GOLF COURSE
PU-33rd and Pacific Sts., St. Joseph, 64507, Buchanan County, (816)271-5350, 40 miles from Kansas City. **Facility Holes:** 18. **Yards:** 6,312/5,490. **Par:** 72/73. **Course Rating:** 69.5/72.0. **Slope:** 116/120. **Green Fee:** $16/$18. **Cart Fee:** $24/Cart. **Walking Policy:** Unrestricted walking. **Walkability:** 3. **Season:** Year-round. **High:** May-Sept. **To obtain tee times:** Call golf shop. **Miscellaneous:** Reduced fees (twilight, seniors, juniors), range (mats), credit cards (MC, V, D), BF, FF.

★★★ THE FALLS GOLF CLUB
PU-1170 Turtle Creek Dr., O'Fallon, 63366, St. Charles County, (314)240-4653, (800)653-2557, 17 miles from St. Louis. **E-mail:** fallgolfnothnbut.net. **Facility Holes:** 18. **Yards:** 6,520/4,933. **Par:** 71/71. **Course Rating:** 70.6/67.2. **Slope:** 126/107. **Green Fee:** $25/$34. **Cart Fee:** $11/Person. **Walking Policy:** Walking at certain times. **Walkability:** 2. **Opened:** 1995. **Architect:** John Allen. **Season:** Year-round. **High:** May-Oct. **To obtain tee times:** Call up to 7 days in advance. **Miscellaneous:** Reduced fees (twilight), range (grass/mats), credit cards (MC, V), BF, FF.
Reader Comments: Greens are in great shape! ...Houses too close to fairways ... Not as plush but an excellent value ... Great value, good condition and fairly easy ... Challenging plus value.

★★½ FOREST PARK GOLF COURSE
PU-5591 Grand Dr., St. Louis, 63112, St. Louis County, (314)367-1337. **Facility Holes:** 18. **Yards:** 6,024/5,528. **Par:** 71/74. **Course Rating:** 67.8/67.8. **Slope:** 113/113. **Green Fee:** $13/$31. **Cart Fee:** Included in green fee. **Walking Policy:** Unrestricted walking. **Walkability:** 4. **Opened:** 1912. **Architect:** Robert Foulis. **Season:** Year-round. **High:** May-Sept. **To obtain tee times:** Call golf shop. **Miscellaneous:** Reduced fees (twilight, seniors), metal spikes, credit cards (MC, V, AE).

★★★★ FOURCHE' VALLEY GOLF CLUB
PU-Rt. 4, Box 800, Potosi, 63664, Washington County, (573)438-7888, 75 miles from St. Louis. **E-mail:** fvgolf@centurytel.net. **Web:** www.fourchevalley.org. **Facility Holes:** 18. **Yards:** 6,829/5,833. **Par:** 72/72. **Green Fee:** $16/$24. **Cart Fee:** $13/Person. **Walking Policy:** Unrestricted walking. **Walkability:** 3. **Opened:** 2000. **Architect:** Gary Kern. **Season:** Year-round. **High:** May-Sept. **Tee times:** Call up to 5 days ahead. **Miscellaneous:** Reduced fees (weekdays, twilight, seniors, juniors), range (grass), credit cards (MC, V, AE, D, DC, CB), BF, FF.
Reader Comments: One of the most scenic courses that I have ever played ... Excellent layout in middle of nowhere ... Old front 9 majestic ... New back 9 needs work ... One of the prettiest courses in the state.

FRANK E. PETERS MUNICIPAL GOLF COURSE
PU-RR 4, Box 432, Nevada, 64772, Vernon County, (417)448-2750, 100 miles from Kansas City. **Facility Holes:** 18. **Yards:** 6,608/5,159. **Par:** 72/72. **Course Rating:** 69.5/68.2. **Slope:** 117/110. **Green Fee:** $8/$14. **Cart Fee:** $18/Cart. **Walking Policy:** Unrestricted walking. **Walkability:** 2. **Opened:** 1978. **Architect:** Jim Lewis. **Season:** Year-round. **High:** June-Sept. **To obtain tee times:** Call golf shop. **Miscellaneous:** Reduced fees (weekdays, twilight, seniors, juniors), range (grass/mats), credit cards (MC, V), BF, FF.

★★½ GUSTIN GOLF CLUB
PU-Stadium Blvd., Columbia, 65211, Boone County, (573)882-6016, 30 miles from Jefferson City. **E-mail:** golfsd@showme.missouri.edu. **Facility Holes:** 18. **Yards:** 6,400/5,565. **Par:** 70/70. **Course Rating:** 69.7/71.3. **Slope:** 123/116. **Green Fee:** $18/$21. **Cart Fee:** $22/Cart. **Walking Policy:** Unrestricted walking. **Walkability:** 5. **Architect:** Floyd Farley. **Season:** Year-round. **To obtain tee times:** Call up to 7 days in advance. **Miscellaneous:** Reduced fees (twilight, juniors), range (grass/mats), credit cards (MC, V, D), BF, FF.

HIDDEN TRAILS COUNTRY CLUB
SP-11601 Hidden Trails Dr., Dexter, 63841, Stoddard County, (573)624-3638, 120 miles from St. Louis. **Facility Holes:** 18. **Yards:** 6,688/5,506. **Par:** 72/72. **Course Rating:** 70.2/70.0. **Slope:** 122/115. **Green Fee:** $18/$24. **Cart Fee:** $9/Person. **Walking Policy:** Mandatory carts. **Walkability:** 3. **Opened:** 1975. **Season:** March-Oct. **High:** May-Sept. **To obtain tee times:** Call golf shop. **Miscellaneous:** Reduced fees (juniors), range (grass),

HIDDEN VALLEY GOLF COURSE
PU-800 W. 184th St., Lawson, 64062, Clay County, (816)580-3444, 15 miles from Kansas City. **Facility Holes:** 18. **Yards:** 6,707/5,489. **Par:** 72/72. **Course Rating:** 70.9. **Slope:** 115. **Green Fee:** $16/$18. **Cart Fee:** $10/Person. **Walking Policy:** Unrestricted walking. **Walkability:** 2. **Opened:** 1995. **Architect:** Leo Johnson. **Season:** Year-round. **High:** May-Oct. **To obtain tee times:** Call golf shop. **Miscellaneous:** Reduced fees (weekdays, seniors, juniors), range (grass), credit cards (MC, V).

★★ HIDDEN VALLEY GOLF LINKS
PU-4455 Hidden Valley Rd., Clever, 65631, Stone County, (417)743-2860, 18 miles from Springfield. **Facility Holes:** 18. **Yards:** 6,611/5,237. **Par:** 73/73. **Course Rating:** 71.9. **Slope:** 118. **Green Fee:** $15/$20. **Cart Fee:** $20/Cart. **Walking Policy:** Unrestricted walking. **Walkability:** 2. **Opened:** 1975. **Architect:** Mario Alfonzo. **Season:** Year-round. **To obtain tee times:** Call up to 6 days in advance. **Miscellaneous:** Reduced fees (seniors), credit cards (MC, V, D), BF, FF.

★★½ **HODGE PARK GOLF COURSE**
PU-7000 N.E. Barry Rd., Kansas City, 64156, Clay County, (816)781-4152, 10 miles from Kansas City. **E-mail:** mmattingly@kempersports.com. **Facility Holes:** 18. **Yards:** 6,223/5,293. **Par:** 71/71. **Course Rating:** 69.5/69.4. **Slope:** 117/115. **Green Fee:** $19/$22. **Cart Fee:** $12/Person. **Walking Policy:** Unrestricted walking. **Walkability:** 3. **Opened:** 1975. **Architect:** Larry Runyon/Michael H. Malyn. **Season:** Year-round. **High:** April-Oct. **To obtain tee times:** Call up to 7 days in advance. **Miscellaneous:** Reduced fees (twilight, seniors, juniors), range (mats), credit cards (MC, V, AE, D), BF, FF.

HOLIDAY HILLS RESORT & GOLF CLUB
R-630 East Rockford Dr., Branson, 65616, Taney County, (417)334-4838, 40 miles from Springfield. **E-mail:** proshop@holidayhillsgolf.com. **Web:** www.holidayhillsgolf.com. **Facility Holes:** 18. **Yards:** 5,800/4,414. **Par:** 68/68. **Course Rating:** 69.5/68.5. **Slope:** 118/112. **Green Fee:** $55/$65. **Cart Fee:** Included in green fee. **Walking Policy:** Walking at certain times. **Walkability:** 3. **Opened:** 1938. **Season:** Year-round. **High:** April-Sept. **To obtain tee times:** Call up to 30 days in advance. **Miscellaneous:** Reduced fees (twilight, juniors), lodging (100 rooms), credit cards (MC, V, AE, D), BF, FF.

★★½ **HONEY CREEK GOLF CLUB**
PU-R.R. 1, Aurora, 65605, Lawrence County, (417)678-3353, 28 miles from Springfield. **Facility Holes:** 18. **Yards:** 6,732/5,972. **Par:** 71/79. **Course Rating:** 71.9. **Slope:** 133. **Green Fee:** $14/$18. **Cart Fee:** $20/Cart. **Walking Policy:** Unrestricted walking. **Walkability:** 3. **Opened:** 1948. **Architect:** H. Smith/M. Welch/B. Welch/S. Welch. **Season:** Year-round. **High:** May-Oct. **To obtain tee times:** Call golf shop. **Miscellaneous:** Reduced fees (weekdays, twilight, seniors, juniors), range (grass), credit cards (MC, V, D), BF, FF.

★★½ **HORTON SMITH GOLF COURSE**
PU-2409 S. Scenic, Springfield, 65807, Greene County, (417)891-1639. **Facility Holes:** 18. **Yards:** 6,317/5,199. **Par:** 70/71. **Course Rating:** 69.5/68.5. **Slope:** 103/101. **Green Fee:** $8/$18. **Cart Fee:** $10/Person. **Walking Policy:** Unrestricted walking. **Walkability:** 1. **Opened:** 1962. **Architect:** Tom Talbot. **Season:** Year-round. **High:** March-Oct. **To obtain tee times:** Call up to 7 days in advance. **Miscellaneous:** Reduced fees (weekdays, seniors, juniors), range (grass), credit cards (MC, V, AE, D), BF, FF.

★★★★ **INNSBROOK RESORT & CONFERENCE CENTER**
R-1 Aspen Circle, Innsbrook, 63390, Warren County, (636)928-6886, 20 miles from St. Charles. **E-mail:** mark.waltman@innsbrook-resort.com. **Web:** www.innsbrook-resort.com. **Facility Holes:** 18. **Yards:** 6,465/5,035. **Par:** 70/70. **Course Rating:** 70.0/67.7. **Slope:** 130/120. **Green Fee:** $22/$36. **Cart Fee:** $15/Person. **Walking Policy:** Walking at certain times. **Walkability:** 3. **Opened:** 1982. **Architect:** Jay Randolph/Mark Waltman. **Season:** Year-round. **High:** April-Oct. **To obtain tee times:** Call golf shop. **Miscellaneous:** Reduced fees (weekdays, guests, twilight, seniors), range (grass), lodging (100 rooms), credit cards (MC, V), BF, FF. **Reader Comments:** Greens are the best, friendly, great restaurant … This resort was first class, great track, great greens … Very, very nice … Above average … Best kept secret in St. Louis … Very narrow and long.

KENNETT COUNTRY CLUB
SP-Hwy. 412 E., Kennett, 63857, Dunklin County, (573)888-9945, 100 miles from Memphis. **Facility Holes:** 18. **Yards:** 6,389/4,890. **Par:** 72/72. **Course Rating:** 70.5/67.6. **Slope:** 112/107. **Green Fee:** $20/$25. **Cart Fee:** $20/Cart. **Walking Policy:** Unrestricted walking. **Walkability:** 1. **Season:** Year-round. **High:** May-Sept. **Tee times:** Call shop. **Miscellaneous:** Range, BF, FF.

KETH MEMORIAL GOLF COURSE
PU-S. Holden St., Warrensburg, 64093, Johnson County, (660)543-4182, 50 miles from Kansas City. **Facility Holes:** 18. **Yards:** 6,068/4,913. **Par:** 71/71. **Course Rating:** 68.7/67.5. **Slope:** 113/113. **Green Fee:** $12/$14. **Walkability:** 4. **Opened:** 1972. **To obtain tee times:** Call golf shop. **Miscellaneous:** Reduced fees (weekdays).

★★½ **KIRKSVILLE COUNTRY CLUB**
SP-S. Hwy. 63, Kirksville, 63501, Adair County, (660)665-5335, 85 miles from Columbia. **Facility Holes:** 18. **Yards:** 6,418/5,802. **Par:** 71/71. **Course Rating:** 70.9/71.6. **Slope:** 118/114. **Green Fee:** $20/$25. **Cart Fee:** $20/Cart. **Walking Policy:** Unrestricted walking. **Walkability:** 3. **Opened:** 1921. **Season:** Year-round. **High:** April-Aug. **To obtain tee times:** Call golf shop. **Miscellaneous:** Reduced fees (twilight), range (grass/mats), credit cards (MC, V, D), BF, FF.

★★ **L.A. NICKELL GOLF COURSE**
PU-1800 Parkside Dr., Columbia, 65202, Boone County, (573)445-4213, 110 miles from Kansas City. **Web:** www.ci.columbia.mo.us. **Facility Holes:** 18. **Yards:** 6,007/4,869. **Par:** 70/70.

Course Rating: 65.1/67.7. **Slope:** 100/103. **Green Fee:** $14/$18. **Cart Fee:** $10/Person. **Walking Policy:** Unrestricted walking. **Walkability:** 1. **Opened:** 1952. **Season:** Year-round. **High:** April-Sept. **To obtain tee times:** Call golf shop. **Miscellaneous:** Reduced fees (twilight), metal spikes, range (mats), credit cards (MC, V, D), BF, FF.

LAKE OF THE WOODS GOLF COURSE
PU-6700 St. Charles Rd., Columbia, 65202, Boone County, (573)474-7011, 90 miles from St. Louis. **E-mail:** aab@ci.columbia.mo.us. **Web:** www.ci.columbia.mo.us. **Facility Holes:** 18. **Yards:** 6,149/4,901. **Par:** 71/71. **Course Rating:** 68.4/68.7. **Slope:** 119/120. **Green Fee:** $14/$18. **Cart Fee:** $10/Person. **Walking Policy:** Unrestricted walking. **Walkability:** 2. **Season:** Year-round. **To obtain tee times:** Call up to 4 days in advance. **Miscellaneous:** Reduced fees (weekdays, twilight), credit cards (MC, V, D), BF, FF.

★★★★ LAKE VALLEY GOLF & COUNTRY CLUB
SP-Lake Rd. 54-79, Camdenton, 65020, Camden County, (573)346-7218, 60 miles from Springfield. **E-mail:** lakevalleygolf.com. **Web:** www.lakevalleygolf.com. **Facility Holes:** 18. **Yards:** 6,430/5,320. **Par:** 72/74. **Course Rating:** 71.1/70.5. **Slope:** 121/118. **Green Fee:** $34/$60. **Cart Fee:** Included in green fee. **Walking Policy:** Walking at certain times. **Walkability:** 3. **Opened:** 1967. **Architect:** Floyd Farley. **Season:** Year-round. **High:** April-Oct. **To obtain tee times:** Call golf shop. **Miscellaneous:** Reduced fees (guests, twilight, juniors), range (grass/mats), credit cards (MC, V), BF, FF.
Reader Comments: Very enjoyable for price … Beautiful views, good greens … Player friendly, tricky greens … Country-club quality, a pleasure to play.

LEBANON COUNTRY CLUB
SP-W. Hwy. 64, Lebanon, 65536, Laclede County, (417)532-2901, 40 miles from Springfield. **Facility Holes:** 18. **Yards:** 6,435/5,174. **Par:** 72/72. **Course Rating:** 70.4/69.7. **Slope:** 119/111. **Green Fee:** $38/$40. **Cart Fee:** Included in green fee. **Walking Policy:** Mandatory carts. **Walkability:** 3. **Opened:** 1950. **Season:** Year-round. **To obtain tee times:** Call up to 90 days in advance. **Miscellaneous:** Reduced fees (weekdays), range (grass), credit cards (MC, V), FF.

THE LODGE OF FOUR SEASONS
R-State Rd. HH at HK's Restaurant, Lake Ozark, 65049, Camden County, (573)365-8532, (800)843-5253, 150 miles from St. Louis. **E-mail:** jcunningham@4seasonsresort.com. **Web:** www.4seasonsresort.com. **Facility Holes:** 36. **Cart Fee:** Included in green fee. **Walking Policy:** Mandatory carts. **Walkability:** 4. **To obtain tee times:** Call up to 14 days in advance. **Miscellaneous:** Reduced fees (weekdays, guests, twilight), range (grass/mats), lodging (302 rooms), credit cards (MC, V, AE, D), BF, FF.
★★★★ ROBERT TRENT JONES COURSE (18)
Yards: 6,557/5,238. **Par:** 71/71. **Course Rating:** 71.4/70.8. **Slope:** 136/124. **Green Fee:** $75/$85. **Opened:** 1971. **Architect:** Robert Trent Jones. **Season:** March-Nov. **High:** May-Oct.
Reader Comments: Two thumbs up … These greens are fast … Hilly, crowded, expensive … Rebuilt greens, excellent fairways, shotmaker's course … Nice but spicy … Very scenic.
★★★½ SEASONS RIDGE COURSE (18)
Yards: 6,447/4,617. **Par:** 72/72. **Course Rating:** 71.4/71.0. **Slope:** 130/118. **Green Fee:** $63/$79. **Opened:** 1991. **Architect:** Ken Kavanaugh. **Season:** Year-round. **High:** May-Sept.
Reader Comments: Beautifully done … Don't let the lack of length from the tips bother you … Par 3 over water was fun … Just enough trouble for the bogey golfer … Nice resort course … Target course with major elevation changes … Good value.

LOMA LINDA COUNTRY CLUB
R-2407 Douglas Fir Rd., Joplin, 64804, Newton County, (417)623-2901, (800)633-3542, 5 miles from Joplin. **E-mail:** lomalinda@4state.com. **Web:** www.lomalindagolf.com. **Facility Holes:** 36. **Walking Policy:** Unrestricted walking. **Season:** Year-round. **High:** April-Sept. **To obtain tee times:** Call golf shop. **Miscellaneous:** Reduced fees (weekdays, seniors), range (grass), lodging (115 rooms), credit cards (MC, V, AE, D, DC, CB), BF, FF.
★★★ NORTH COURSE (18)
Yards: 6,628/5,333. **Par:** 72/73. **Course Rating:** 71.8/70.8. **Slope:** 123/125. **Green Fee:** $27. **Cart Fee:** $11/Person. **Walkability:** 5. **Opened:** 1984. **Architect:** Don Sechrest.
Reader Comments: Fun course to play … Loved greens, some real good holes … Challenging holes, par-3 hole No. 12 depending on wind can go from 6-iron to driver.
★½ SOUTH COURSE (18)
Yards: 6,397/4,663. **Par:** 71/71. **Course Rating:** 69.2/68.2. **Slope:** 118/120. **Green Fee:** $9/$11. **Cart Fee:** $9/Person. **Walkability:** 4. **Architect:** Scott Brown.
Special Notes: Must be guest of resort.

★★★½ LONGVIEW LAKE GOLF COURSE
PU-11100 View High Dr., Kansas City, 64134, Jackson County, (816)761-9445. **Facility Holes:** 27. **Yards:** 6,835/5,534. **Par:** 72/72. **Course Rating:** 71.9/70.8. **Slope:** 121/113. **Green**

MISSOURI

Fee: $12/$16. **Cart Fee:** $22/Cart. **Walking Policy:** Unrestricted walking. **Opened:** 1986. **Architect:** Benz/Poellot. **Season:** Year-round. **High:** May-Aug. **To obtain tee times:** Call golf shop. **Miscellaneous:** Reduced fees (weekdays, seniors, juniors), metal spikes, range (grass), credit cards (MC, V).
Reader Comments: Good, solid course … Best muni in Kansas City area … Wide open layout, tough on a windy day … Made my top 5 list in Kansas City … A must play … A links-style by a lake.
Special Notes: Also has a 9-hole par-3 course.

MEADOW LAKE COUNTRY CLUB
SP-1000 Watson Pkwy., Clinton, 64735, Henry County, (660)885-5124, 90 miles from Kansas City. **Facility Holes:** 18. **Yards:** 6,172/5,915. **Par:** 71/71. **Course Rating:** 69.1/71.6. **Slope:** 113/113. **Green Fee:** $24/$25. **Cart Fee:** $14/Person. **Walking Policy:** Mandatory carts. **Walkability:** 1. **Opened:** 1963. **Architect:** Jim Lewis. **Season:** Year-round. **High:** April-Oct. **To obtain tee times:** Call golf shop. **Miscellaneous:** Reduced fees (twilight), range (grass), credit cards (MC, V).

MERAMEC LAKES GOLF CLUB
PU-321 Birdie Lane, St. Clair, 63077, Franklin County, (636)451-5183, 40 miles from St. Louis. **E-mail:** golfthelakes@earthlink.net. **Facility Holes:** 18. **Yards:** 6,171/5,029. **Par:** 71/71. **Green Fee:** $9/$18. **Cart Fee:** $12/Person. **Walking Policy:** Unrestricted walking. **Walkability:** 3. **Opened:** 1995. **Architect:** Jerry Raible. **Season:** Year-round. **To obtain tee times:** Call golf shop. **Miscellaneous:** Reduced fees (weekdays, seniors, juniors), range (grass/mats), credit cards (MC, V), BF, FF.

★★½ MID-RIVERS GOLF COURSE
PU-4100 Mid-Rivers Mall Dr., St. Peters, 63376, St. Charles County, (636)939-3663, 20 miles from St. Louis. **Facility Holes:** 18. **Yards:** 6,466/5,375. **Par:** 71/72. **Course Rating:** 70.9/67.6. **Slope:** 125/110. **Green Fee:** $22. **Cart Fee:** $7/Person. **Architect:** Ned Story. **To obtain tee times:** Call golf shop.

★★★★½ MILLWOOD GOLF & RACQUET CLUB *Pace*
SP-3700 E. Millwood Dr., Springfield, 65809, Greene County, (417)889-2889, 2 miles from Springfield. **Web:** www.millwoodgolf.com. **Facility Holes:** 18. **Yards:** 6,700/4,815. **Par:** 71/72. **Course Rating:** 72.4/68.6. **Slope:** 134/116. **Green Fee:** $50. **Cart Fee:** Included in green fee. **Walkability:** 4. **Opened:** 1996. **Architect:** Greg Martin. **Season:** Year-round. **High:** May-Oct. **To obtain tee times:** Call golf shop. **Miscellaneous:** Range (grass/mats), credit cards (MC, V, AE).
Reader Comments: Driving range is on a lake! … Worth the stop in Springfield and close to Branson, MO … Beautiful course, narrow fairways … Tough, but playable… Excellent service.

★½ MINOR PARK GOLF CLUB
PU-11215 Holmes Rd., Kansas City, 64131, Jackson County, (816)942-4033, 10 miles from Kansas City. **E-mail:** mpelzl@eaglgolf.com. **Facility Holes:** 18. **Yards:** 5,704/4,781. **Par:** 70/71. **Course Rating:** 66.9/66.2. **Slope:** 107/101. **Green Fee:** $15/$19. **Cart Fee:** $12/Person. **Walking Policy:** Unrestricted walking. **Walkability:** 2. **Opened:** 1952. **Architect:** Larry W. Flatt. **Season:** Year-round. **High:** May-Oct. **To obtain tee times:** Call up to 4 days in advance. **Miscellaneous:** Reduced fees (weekdays, twilight, seniors, juniors), range (grass/mats), credit cards (MC, V, AE), BF, FF.

★★★½ MISSOURI BLUFFS GOLF CLUB
PU-18 Research Park Circle, St. Charles, 63304, St. Charles County, (636)939-6494, 20 miles from St. Louis. **Facility Holes:** 18. **Yards:** 7,047/5,197. **Par:** 71/71. **Course Rating:** 74.4/69.2. **Slope:** 140/115. **Green Fee:** $35/$78. **Cart Fee:** Included in green fee. **Walking Policy:** Unrestricted walking. **Walkability:** 5. **Opened:** 1994. **Architect:** Tom Fazio. **Season:** Year-round. **High:** April-Oct. **To obtain tee times:** Call up to 7 days in advance. **Miscellaneous:** Reduced fees (twilight, seniors, juniors), range (grass), credit cards (MC, V, AE), BF, FF. **Notes:** Ranked 9th in 1999 Best in State; 43rd in 1996 America's Top 75 Upscale Courses; 3rd in 1995 Best New Public Courses.
Reader Comments: Best in Missouri … Unique design, spectacular holes … An excellent value … Country club for the day… All employees are extremely nice … Beautiful course … Excellent pro shop… Nice clubhouse.

★★★½ MOZINGO LAKE GOLF COURSE
PU-25055 Liberty Rd., Maryville, 64468, Nodaway County, (660)562-3864, (888)562-3864, 90 miles from Kansas City. **E-mail:** Mozingolf@msc.net. **Web:** www.mozingolf.com. **Facility Holes:** 18. **Yards:** 7,072/5,583. **Par:** 72/72. **Course Rating:** 73.5/71.3. **Slope:** 134/124. **Green Fee:** $17/$20. **Cart Fee:** $11/Person. **Walking Policy:** Unrestricted walking. **Walkability:** 3. **Opened:** 1996. **Architect:** Don Sechrest. **Season:** Year-round. **High:** May-Sept. **To obtain tee times:** Call up to 14 days in advance. **Miscellaneous:** Reduced fees (weekdays, juniors), range (grass), credit cards (MC, V, D), BF, FF.

MISSOURI

Reader Comments: Best secret in north Missouri ... Very affordable course ... Very good experience ... A great golf course for a green fee under $20... Good condition ... Beautiful course.

★★★ NEW MELLE LAKES GOLF CLUB
PU-404 Foristel Rd., New Melle, 63365, St. Charles County, (314)398-4653, 30 miles from St. Louis. **Facility Holes:** 18. **Yards:** 6,348/4,905. **Par:** 71/71. **Course Rating:** 69.8/68.6. **Slope:** 126/120. **Green Fee:** $30/$40. **Cart Fee:** Included in green fee. **Walking Policy:** Walking at certain times. **Walkability:** 4. **Opened:** 1993. **Architect:** Theodore Christener & Assoc. **Season:** Year-round. **High:** April-Oct. **To obtain tee times:** Call golf shop. **Miscellaneous:** Reduced fees (twilight, seniors, juniors), metal spikes, range (grass/mats), credit cards (MC, V, AE, D).
Reader Comments: Very good course love it ... Small, tight, fun, quirky ... Fun to play once in a while ... Some different holes ... Most beautiful course I've played.

★★½ NORMANDIE GOLF CLUB
PU-7605 St. Charles Rock Rd., St. Louis, 63133, St. Louis County, (314)862-4884. **Facility Holes:** 18. **Yards:** 6,534/5,943. **Par:** 71/77. **Course Rating:** 71.1/73.1. **Slope:** 120/133. **Green Fee:** $19/$25. **Cart Fee:** $10/Person. **Walking Policy:** Unrestricted walking. **Walkability:** 4. **Opened:** 1901. **Architect:** Robert Foulis. **Season:** Year-round. **To obtain tee times:** Call up to 7 days in advance. **Miscellaneous:** Reduced fees (weekdays, twilight, seniors, juniors), metal spikes, range (grass/mats), credit cards (MC, V, AE, D), BF, FF.

OAKWOOD GOLF COURSE
PU-7453 Country Club Lane, Houston, 65483, Texas County, (417)967-3968, 70 miles from Springfield. **Facility Holes:** 9. **Yards:** 6,195/4,448. **Par:** 72/72. **Course Rating:** 68.6/65.6. **Slope:** 112/105. **Green Fee:** $11. **Cart Fee:** $20/Cart. **Walking Policy:** Unrestricted walking. **Walkability:** 2. **Season:** Year-round. **High:** April-Oct. **To obtain tee times:** Call golf shop. **Miscellaneous:** Reduced fees (seniors), range (grass), BF, FF.

★★½ OLD FLEURISSANT GOLF CLUB
PU-50 Country Club Lane, Florissant, 63033, St. Louis County, (314)741-7444, 15 miles from St. Louis. **E-mail:** killergolf@aol.com. **Facility Holes:** 18. **Yards:** 6,585/4,994. **Par:** 72/71. **Course Rating:** 70.7/69.0. **Slope:** 127/115. **Green Fee:** $18/$28. **Cart Fee:** $12/Person. **Walking Policy:** Unrestricted walking. **Walkability:** 4. **Opened:** 1964. **Architect:** Homer Herpel. **Season:** Year-round. **High:** May-Sept. **To obtain tee times:** Call up to 7 days in advance. **Miscellaneous:** Reduced fees (weekdays, twilight, seniors, juniors), range (grass), credit cards (MC, V, D), BF, FF.

★★★ OSAGE NATIONAL GOLF CLUB
R-Osage Hills Rd., Lake Ozark, 65049, Miller County, (573)365-1950, 150 miles from St. Louis. **Facility Holes:** 27. **Green Fee:** $38/$85. **Cart Fee:** Included in green fee. **Walking Policy:** Mandatory carts. **Walkability:** 4. **Opened:** 1992. **Architect:** Arnold Palmer/Ed Seay. **Season:** Year-round. **High:** April-Oct. **To obtain tee times:** Call up to 30 days in advance. **Miscellaneous:** Reduced fees (weekdays, guests, twilight), range (grass), credit cards (MC, V, AE, D), BF, FF.
MOUNTAIN/LINKS (18 Combo)
Yards: 7,165/5,076. **Par:** 72/72. **Course Rating:** 74.7/69.9. **Slope:** 139/121.
MOUNTAIN/RIVER (18 Combo)
Yards: 7,150/5,252. **Par:** 72/72. **Course Rating:** 75.6/70.5. **Slope:** 145/122.
RIVER/LINKS (18 Combo)
Yards: 7,103/5,026. **Par:** 72/72. **Course Rating:** 74.6/69.1. **Slope:** 141/120.
Reader Comments: Good golf experience ... Great course set in river valley and hills ... Outstanding view ... One of the best courses at the Lake of the Ozarks.

PARADISE POINTE GOLF COMPLEX
PU-18212 Golf Course Rd., Smithville, 64089, Clay County, (816)532-4100, 25 miles from Kansas City. **Facility Holes:** 36. **Cart Fee:** $27/Cart. **Walking Policy:** Unrestricted walking. **Season:** Feb.-Dec. **High:** March-Oct. **To obtain tee times:** Call up to 4 days in advance. **Miscellaneous:** Reduced fees (weekdays, seniors, juniors), range (grass), credit cards (MC, V, AE, D), BF, FF.
★★★★ OUTLAW COURSE (18)
Yards: 7,003/5,322. **Par:** 72/72. **Course Rating:** 73.8/67.0. **Slope:** 138/118. **Green Fee:** $23/$24. **Walkability:** 3. **Opened:** 1994. **Architect:** Craig Schriener.
Reader Comments: Lake views all around, real honest golf ... Fairway bunkers are well placed ... Scenic ... Good course, too slow ... Short, narrow course, lots of doglegs and elevation changes.
★★★½ POSSE COURSE (18)
Yards: 6,663/5,600. **Par:** 72/73. **Course Rating:** 71.8/70.0. **Slope:** 125/115. **Green Fee:** $21/$22. **Walkability:** 2. **Opened:** 1982. **Architect:** Tom Clark/Brian Ault.
Reader Comments: This course has several great holes ... No. 6 is a real score buster ... Jammed on weekends ... Good challenge ... Great lakeside holes ... Relaxing ... Great views.

MISSOURI

★★ PARADISE VALLEY GOLF & COUNTRY CLUB
PU-Old Hillsboro Rd., Valley Park, 63088, St. Louis County, (636)225-5157, 19 miles from St. Louis. **E-mail:** parvalgolf@aol.com. **Web:** www.paradisevalleygolf.com. **Facility Holes:** 18. **Yards:** 6,097/4,769. **Par:** 70/72. **Course Rating:** 68.6/66.4. **Slope:** 116/109. **Green Fee:** $31/$35. **Cart Fee:** Included in green fee. **Walking Policy:** Walking at certain times. **Walkability:** 3. **Opened:** 1965. **Architect:** James Cochran. **Season:** Year-round. **High:** May-Sept. **To obtain tee times:** Call golf shop. **Miscellaneous:** Reduced fees (weekdays, juniors), range (grass/mats), credit cards (MC, V, AE).

★★★★ PEVELY FARMS GOLF CLUB
SP-400 Lewis Rd., St. Louis, 63025, St. Louis County, (636)938-7000, 25 miles from St. Louis. **E-mail:** fehrways@aol.com. **Web:** www.pevelygolf.com. **Facility Holes:** 18. **Yards:** 7,115/5,250. **Par:** 72/72. **Course Rating:** 74.6/70.7. **Slope:** 138/115. **Green Fee:** $59/$69. **Cart Fee:** Included in green fee. **Walking Policy:** Mandatory carts. **Walkability:** 5. **Opened:** 1998. **Architect:** Arthur Hills. **Season:** Year-round. **High:** Sept.-Nov. **To obtain tee times:** Call up to 7 days in advance. **Miscellaneous:** Reduced fees (weekdays, twilight, seniors, juniors), range (grass), credit cards (MC, V, AE), BF, FF.
Reader Comments: Best course with the least amount of hype ... Pleasantly surprised at the beauty and natural setting ... Amazing scenery and wonderful conditions ... They actually acted as though they wanted me there ... I'd visit for the food on the veranda ... My new St Louis favorite.

PINEY VALLEY GOLF COURSE
M-Bldg. 10221 Waterintake Rd., Fort Leonard Wood, 65473, Pulaski County, (573)329-4770, 88 miles from Springfield. **E-mail:** jamesj@wood.army.mil. **Facility Holes:** 18. **Yards:** 7,014/5,067. **Par:** 72/72. **Course Rating:** 72.8/68.2. **Slope:** 121/104. **Green Fee:** $18/$20. **Cart Fee:** $15/Cart. **Walking Policy:** Unrestricted walking. **Walkability:** 3. **Architect:** U. S. Army Engineers. **Season:** Year-round. **High:** June-Aug. **To obtain tee times:** Call golf shop. **Miscellaneous:** Reduced fees (weekdays, twilight, juniors), credit cards (MC, V, AE).

★★★½ POINTE ROYALE GOLF CLUB
R-1000 Pointe Royale Dr., Branson, 65616, Taney County, (417)334-4477, (866)334-4477, 40 miles from Springfield. **E-mail:** ptrogolf@aol.com. **Web:** www.pointeroyalegolf.com. **Facility Holes:** 18. **Yards:** 6,200/4,390. **Par:** 70/70. **Course Rating:** 70.3/64.4. **Slope:** 126/112. **Green Fee:** $40/$65. **Cart Fee:** Included in green fee. **Walking Policy:** Mandatory carts. **Walkability:** 4. **Opened:** 1987. **Architect:** Ault/Clark. **Season:** Year-round. **High:** June-Oct. **To obtain tee times:** Call up to 14 days in advance. **Miscellaneous:** Reduced fees (guests, juniors), lodging (200 rooms), credit cards (MC, V, AE, D), BF, FF.
Reader Comments: Good resort course ... Challenging course, winds through homes ... Some real challenges ... Tough par 3s.

★★★ QUAIL CREEK GOLF CLUB
PU-6022 Wells Rd., St. Louis, 63128, St. Louis County, (314)487-1988, 15 miles from St. Louis. **Facility Holes:** 18. **Yards:** 6,984/5,244. **Par:** 72/72. **Course Rating:** 73.6/70.0. **Slope:** 141/118. **Green Fee:** $34/$55. **Cart Fee:** $12/Person. **Walking Policy:** Walking at certain times. **Walkability:** 2. **Opened:** 1988. **Architect:** Gary Kern/Hale Irwin. **Season:** Year-round. **To obtain tee times:** Call up to 7 days in advance. **Miscellaneous:** Reduced fees (weekdays, twilight, seniors, juniors), range (grass/mats), credit cards (MC, V, AE, D), BF, FF.
Reader Comments: Great! ... Tough layout ... Some funky holes, not for beginners or short hitters ... Great experience ... My favorite muni! Always in great condition.

RAILWOOD GOLF CLUB
PU-12025 CR 4037, Holts Summit, 65043, Callaway County, (573)896-4653, 3 miles from Jefferson City. **Facility Holes:** 18. **Yards:** 6,664/4,855. **Par:** 72/72. **Course Rating:** 71.2/67.1. **Slope:** 126/110. **Green Fee:** $16. **Cart Fee:** $10/Person. **Walking Policy:** Unrestricted walking. **Walkability:** 4. **Opened:** 1999. **Architect:** Larry Flatt. **Season:** Year-round. **To obtain tee times:** Call up to 7 days in advance. **Miscellaneous:** Reduced fees (weekdays, twilight), range (grass), credit cards (MC, V, AE), BF, FF.

★★ RAINTREE COUNTRY CLUB
SP-5925 Plantation Dr., Hillsboro, 63050, Jefferson County, (636)797-4020, 45 miles from St. Louis. **Facility Holes:** 18. **Yards:** 6,125/4,959. **Par:** 72/71. **Course Rating:** 70.0/68.2. **Slope:** 124/112. **Green Fee:** $10/$18. **Cart Fee:** $10/Person. **Walking Policy:** Walking at certain times. **Walkability:** 4. **Opened:** 1980. **Season:** Year-round. **High:** May-Sept. **To obtain tee times:** Call golf shop. **Miscellaneous:** Reduced fees (weekdays, seniors, juniors), metal spikes, range (grass), credit cards (MC, V, D).

MISSOURI

★★ RIVER OAKS GOLF CLUB
PU-14204 St. Andrews Dr., Grandview, 64030, Jackson County, (816)966-8111, 20 miles from Kansas City. **Facility Holes:** 18. **Yards:** 6,354/5,036. **Par:** 71/73. **Course Rating:** 70.2/69.9. **Slope:** 119/114. **Green Fee:** $16/$19. **Cart Fee:** $24/Cart. **Walking Policy:** Unrestricted walking. **Walkability:** 3. **Opened:** 1973. **Architect:** Larry Runyon/Michael H. Malyn. **To obtain tee times:** Call golf shop. **Miscellaneous:** Reduced fees (weekdays, twilight, seniors, juniors), metal spikes, credit cards (MC, V, D).

RIVERCUT GOLF COURSE
PU-2850 W. Farm Rd. 190, Springfield, 65810, Greene County, (417)891-1645, 3 miles from Springfield. **E-mail:** kingsk@gateway.net. **Facility Holes:** 18. **Yards:** 7,066/5,483. **Par:** 72/72. **Course Rating:** 74.2/71.3. **Slope:** 134/118. **Green Fee:** $32/$38. **Cart Fee:** Included in green fee. **Walking Policy:** Mandatory carts. **Walkability:** 4. **Opened:** 1999. **Architect:** Ken Dye. **Season:** Year-round. **To obtain tee times:** Call golf shop. **Miscellaneous:** Range (grass), credit cards (MC, V, AE, D), BF, FF.

★★ RIVERSIDE GOLF COURSE
PU-1210 Larkin Williams Rd., Fenton, 63026, St. Louis County, (314)343-6333, 10 miles from St. Louis. **Facility Holes:** 27. **Yards:** 5,500/5,400. **Par:** 69/70. **Course Rating:** 67.5/67.5. **Slope:** 99/99. **Green Fee:** $20/$22. **Cart Fee:** $20/Cart. **Walking Policy:** Unrestricted walking. **Walkability:** 1. **Opened:** 1964. **Architect:** Walter Wolfner/Jack Wolfner. **Season:** Year-round. **High:** April-Oct. **To obtain tee times:** Call golf shop. **Miscellaneous:** Reduced fees (weekdays, twilight, seniors, juniors), credit cards (MC, V, AE), BF, FF. **Special Notes:** Also has a 9-hole par-3 course.

★★ ROCKWOOD GOLF CLUB
PU-2400 Maywood, Independence, 64052, Jackson County, (816)252-2002, 2 miles from Kansas City. **E-mail:** rockwood@kempersports.com. **Facility Holes:** 18. **Yards:** 6,009/5,465. **Par:** 70/71. **Course Rating:** 67.0/69.0. **Slope:** 113/105. **Green Fee:** $15/$20. **Cart Fee:** $11/Person. **Walking Policy:** Unrestricted walking. **Walkability:** 2. **Opened:** 1946. **Architect:** J. Davis. **Season:** Year-round. **To obtain tee times:** Call up to 7 days in advance. **Miscellaneous:** Reduced fees (weekdays, twilight, seniors, juniors), credit cards (MC, V, D), BF, FF.

ROLLING HILLS COUNTRY CLUB
SP-Hwy. 5 N., Versailles, 65084, Morgan County, (573)378-5109, 30 miles from Jefferson City. **Facility Holes:** 18. **Yards:** 6,429/4,998. **Par:** 71/71. **Course Rating:** 70.0. **Slope:** 121. **Green Fee:** $22. **Cart Fee:** $12/Person. **To obtain tee times:** Call golf shop.

★★ ROYAL MEADOWS GOLF COURSE
PU-10501 E. 47th, Kansas City, 64133, Jackson County, (816)353-1323, 10 miles from Kansas City. **Facility Holes:** 27. **Green Fee:** $17/$20. **Cart Fee:** $6/Person. **Walking Policy:** Unrestricted walking. **Walkability:** 3. **Opened:** 1930. **Architect:** Charles Stayton. **Season:** Year-round. **High:** March-Oct. **To obtain tee times:** Call golf shop. **Miscellaneous:** Reduced fees (weekdays, twilight, seniors, juniors), credit cards (MC, V, AE, D).
EAST/NORTH (18 Combo)
Yards: 5,991/4,860. **Par:** 71/71. **Course Rating:** 67.4/67.4. **Slope:** 109/109.
WEST/EAST (18 Combo)
Yards: 6,220/5,211. **Par:** 73/73. **Course Rating:** 68.3/68.8. **Slope:** 110/113.
WEST/NORTH (18 Combo)
Yards: 6,143/4,945. **Par:** 72/72. **Course Rating:** 68.0/68.0. **Slope:** 111/111.

★★★½ ROYAL OAKS GOLF CLUB
PU-533 N. Lincoln Dr., Troy, 63379, Lincoln County, (636)462-8633, 55 miles from St. Louis. **Web:** www.royaloaksgc@juno.com. **Facility Holes:** 18. **Yards:** 6,256/4,830. **Par:** 72/72. **Course Rating:** 68.7/66.3. **Slope:** 112/100. **Green Fee:** $16/$22. **Cart Fee:** $12/Person. **Walking Policy:** Unrestricted walking. **Walkability:** 3. **Opened:** 1993. **Architect:** Lee Redman. **Season:** Year-round. **High:** April-Oct. **To obtain tee times:** Call up to 7 days in advance. **Miscellaneous:** Reduced fees (weekdays, seniors), metal spikes, range (grass), credit cards (MC, V, AE, D, Debit cards), BF, FF.
Reader Comments: Outstanding value, staff is superb ... Very hilly ... Needs a few more years seasoning ... Short course, a few interesting holes, good for morale ... Great course for seniors.

ROYAL OAKS GOLF COURSE
M-Bldg 3076, Whiteman AFB, 65305, Johnson County, (660)687-5572. **Facility Holes:** 18. **Yards:** 6,880/5,150. **Par:** 72/72. **Course Rating:** 74.7/71.4. **Slope:** 134/127. **Green Fee:** $8/$16. **Cart Fee:** $16/Cart. **To obtain tee times:** Call golf shop.

★★★½ SCHIFFERDECKER GOLF COURSE
PU-506 Schifferdecker, Joplin, 64801, Jasper County, (417)624-3533. **E-mail:** jwhite@joplin-mo.org. **Facility Holes:** 18. **Yards:** 6,123/5,251. **Par:** 71/72. **Course Rating:** 68.7/69.7. **Slope:** 108/117. **Green Fee:** $9/$10. **Cart Fee:** $16/Cart. **Walking Policy:** Unrestricted walking. **Walkability:** 3. **Opened:** 1920. **Architect:** Perk Latimere. **Season:** Year-round. **High:** April-Sept. **To obtain tee times:** Call up to 7 days in advance. **Miscellaneous:** Reduced fees (twilight, seniors, juniors), credit cards (MC, V), BF, FF.
Reader Comments: Best value in Southwest MO, and fun to play ... Wide open ... Best greens I have ever played. Lots of play. True roll ... Straightforward layout with no water, greens in nice condition ... For a public course, it is in great shape ... No surprises ... Nice little course.

★★½ SHAMROCK HILLS GOLF COURSE
PU-3161 S. M. 291, Lees Summit, 64082, Jackson County, (816)537-6556, 20 miles from Kansas City. **Facility Holes:** 18. **Yards:** 6,332/5,188. **Par:** 71/73. **Course Rating:** 69.8/68.8. **Slope:** 108/106. **Green Fee:** $15/$17. **Cart Fee:** $11/Person. **Walking Policy:** Unrestricted walking. **Walkability:** 2. **Opened:** 1961. **Architect:** Jim Weaver. **Season:** Year-round. **High:** March-Oct. **To obtain tee times:** Call golf shop. **Miscellaneous:** Reduced fees (twilight, seniors, juniors), credit cards (MC, V, D).

★★½ SHILOH SPRINGS GOLF CLUB
SP-Bethel Rd., Platte City, 64079, Platte County, (816)270-4653, 25 miles from Kansas City. **E-mail:** psshilohsprings@aol.com. **Facility Holes:** 18. **Yards:** 6,470/5,178. **Par:** 71/71. **Course Rating:** 71.2/70.1. **Slope:** 125/113. **Green Fee:** $20/$25. **Cart Fee:** $13/Person. **Walking Policy:** Unrestricted walking. **Walkability:** 4. **Opened:** 1995. **Architect:** Gary Martin. **Season:** Year-round. **High:** March-Nov. **To obtain tee times:** Call up to 7 days in advance. **Miscellaneous:** Reduced fees (twilight, seniors, juniors), range (mats), credit cards (MC, V, AE, D), BF, FF.

★★★★ SHIRKEY GOLF CLUB
SP-901 Wollard Blvd., Richmond, 64085, Ray County, (816)470-2582, 32 miles from Kansas City. **E-mail:** nbnet@hotmail.com. **Web:** www.shirkeygolfclub.com. **Facility Holes:** 18. **Yards:** 6,907/5,516. **Par:** 71/74. **Course Rating:** 74.0/73.0. **Slope:** 139/129. **Green Fee:** $25/$30. **Cart Fee:** $13/Person. **Walking Policy:** Unrestricted walking. **Walkability:** 3. **Opened:** 1969. **Architect:** Chet Mendenhall. **Season:** Year-round. **To obtain tee times:** Call up to 3 days in advance. **Miscellaneous:** Range (grass/mats), credit cards (MC, V, AE), BF, FF.
Reader Comments: Classic old course ... One solid hole after another ... Worth the drive ... Best greens in the state, best value ... Do not miss this one.

SIKESTON COUNTRY CLUB
SP-Country Club Rd., Sikeston, 63801, Scott County, (573)472-4225, 120 miles from St. Louis. **Facility Holes:** 18. **Yards:** 6,385/5,090. **Par:** 71/72. **Course Rating:** 71.5/68.5. **Slope:** 109/112. **Green Fee:** $18/$28. **Cart Fee:** $16/Cart. **Walking Policy:** Unrestricted walking. **Walkability:** 1. **Season:** Year-round. **High:** May-Sept. **To obtain tee times:** Call golf shop. **Miscellaneous:** Range (grass), credit cards (MC, V), BF, FF.

SILO RIDGE GOLF & COUNTRY CLUB
SP-4551 Fairway Dr., Bolivar, 65613, Polk County, (417)326-7456, (800)743-5279. **E-mail:** kevins@ipa.net. **Facility Holes:** 18. **Yards:** 6,840/5,356. **Par:** 72/72. **Course Rating:** 72.6/70.4. **Slope:** 129/119. **Green Fee:** $39/$45. **Cart Fee:** Included in green fee. **Opened:** 1999. **Architect:** Don Sechrest. **To obtain tee times:** Call golf shop.

★★ SOUTHVIEW GOLF CLUB
PU-16001 S. 71 Hwy., Belton, 64012, Cass County, (816)331-4042, 5 miles from Kansas City. **Facility Holes:** 27. **Yards:** 6,594/5,805. **Par:** 72/73. **Course Rating:** 70.6/73.0. **Slope:** 115/113. **Green Fee:** $17/$22. **Cart Fee:** $24/Cart. **Walking Policy:** Unrestricted walking. **Walkability:** 1. **Opened:** 1955. **Architect:** Jess Nash. **Season:** Year-round. **To obtain tee times:** Call up to 5 days in advance. **Miscellaneous:** Reduced fees (weekdays, seniors, juniors), metal spikes, range (grass/mats), credit cards (MC, V).
Special Notes: Also has a 9-hole par-3 course.

★★★½ ST. ANDREWS GOLF COURSE
PU-2121 St. Andrews Lane, St. Charles, 63301, St. Charles County, (636)946-7777, 15 miles from St. Louis. **Web:** www.standrews-golf.com. **Facility Holes:** 18. **Yards:** 6,003/5,094. **Par:** 68/72. **Course Rating:** 68.3/68.7. **Slope:** 116/113. **Green Fee:** $22/$32. **Cart Fee:** $11/Person. **Walking Policy:** Unrestricted walking. **Walkability:** 3. **Opened:** 1967. **Architect:** Stewart Mertz. **Season:** Year-round. **High:** April-Oct. **To obtain tee times:** Call up to 5 days ahead **Misc:** Reduced fees (weekdays, twilight, seniors, juniors), credit cards (MC, V, D), BF, FF.
Reader Comments: Lots of trees ... Great value ... Fun course to play ... Great back 9 ... Easy playing course.

★★½ SUGAR CREEK GOLF CLUB

PU-5224 Country Club Dr., High Ridge, 63049, Jefferson County, (636)677-4070, 3 miles from Fenton. **Facility Holes:** 18. **Yards:** 6,316/4,713. **Par:** 70/70. **Course Rating:** 71.3/65.5. **Slope:** 127/112. **Green Fee:** $9/$30. **Cart Fee:** $15/Person. **Walking Policy:** Walking at certain times. **Walkability:** 4. **Opened:** 1989. **Architect:** Gary Kern. **Season:** Year-round. **High:** April-Oct. **To obtain tee times:** Call golf shop. **Miscellaneous:** Reduced fees (weekdays, guests, twilight, seniors, juniors), range (grass/mats), credit cards (MC, V), BF, FF.

★★★½ SUN VALLEY GOLF COURSE

PU-Rte. 2, Elsberry, 63343, Lincoln County, (573)898-2613, (800)737-4653, 55 miles from St. Louis. **Facility Holes:** 18. **Yards:** 6,395/5,036. **Par:** 70/70. **Course Rating:** 70.5/69.3. **Slope:** 134/109. **Green Fee:** $16/$21. **Cart Fee:** $9/Person. **Walking Policy:** Unrestricted walking. **Walkability:** 4. **Opened:** 1988. **Architect:** Gary Kern. **Season:** Year-round. **High:** June-Sept. **To obtain tee times:** Call golf shop. **Miscellaneous:** Reduced fees (weekdays, seniors, juniors), range (grass/mats), credit cards (MC, V), BF, FF.
Reader Comments: Nice staff and service … Good course out in the country, worth the drive … Needs work, but much has been done … Too long for seniors.

★★ SUNSET LAKES GOLF CLUB

PU-13366 W. Watson Rd., St. Louis, 63127, St. Louis County, (314)843-3000. **Facility Holes:** 18. **Yards:** 6,452/4,900. **Par:** 72/72. **Course Rating:** 70.5/67.1. **Slope:** 117/117. **Green Fee:** $20/$24. **Walkability:** 1. **Opened:** 1989. **Architect:** Bob Lohman. **To obtain tee times:** Call golf shop. **Miscellaneous:** Reduced fees (weekdays).

★★½ SWOPE MEMORIAL GOLF COURSE

PU-6900 Swope Memorial Dr., Kansas City, 64132, Jackson County, (816)513-8910. **Facility Holes:** 18. **Yards:** 6,274/4,517. **Par:** 72/72. **Course Rating:** 70.9/65.9. **Slope:** 128/107. **Green Fee:** $20/$23. **Cart Fee:** $12/Person. **Walking Policy:** Unrestricted walking. **Walkability:** 3. **Opened:** 1934. **Architect:** A.W. Tillinghast. **Season:** Year-round. **High:** May-Sept. **Tee times:** Call shop. **Misc:** Reduced fees (twilight, seniors, juniors), credit cards (MC, V, AE), BF, FF.

SYCAMORE CREEK GOLF CLUB

PU-1270 Nichols Rd, Osage Beach, 65065, Osage County, (573)348-9593, 90 miles from Springfield. **Facility Holes:** 18. **Yards:** 6,078/4,379. **Par:** 72/72. **Course Rating:** 68.6/66.3. **Slope:** 123/110. **Green Fee:** $29/$43. **Cart Fee:** Included in green fee. **Walking Policy:** Mandatory carts. **Walkability:** 4. **Opened:** 1995. **Architect:** Pete Kahrs. **Season:** Year-round. **To obtain tee times:** Call up to 30 days in advance. **Miscellaneous:** Reduced fees (weekdays), metal spikes, credit cards (MC, V, AE, D), FF.

★★★½ TAN-TAR-A RESORT GOLF CLUB & SPA

R-State Rd. KK, Osage Beach, 65065, Camden County, (573)348-8521, (800)826-8272, 45 miles from Jefferson City. **E-mail:** pd/captain@aol.com. **Web:** www.tan-tar-a.com. **Facility Holes:** 27. **Yards:** 6,442/3,943. **Par:** 71/70. **Course Rating:** 72.1/62.5. **Slope:** 134/103. **Green Fee:** $39/$79. **Cart Fee:** Included in green fee. **Walking Policy:** Mandatory carts. **Walkability:** 4. **Opened:** 1980. **Architect:** Bruce Devlin/Robert von Hagge. **Season:** Year-round. **High:** April-Nov. **To obtain tee times:** Call up to 14 days in advance. **Miscellaneous:** Reduced fees (twilight, juniors), range (grass/mats), lodging (900 rooms), credit cards (MC, V, AE, D, DC), BF, FF.
Reader Comments: Friendliest people anywhere … Heavily used weekend course … Great track, good test … Resort course makes for slow play … Beautiful, tough course.
Special Notes: Also has 9-hole Hidden Lakes Course.

★★★½ TAPAWINGO NATIONAL GOLF CLUB

PU-13001 Gary Player Dr., St. Louis, 63127, St. Louis County, (636)349-3100, 15 miles from St. Louis. **Facility Holes:** 27. **Green Fee:** $50/$60. **Cart Fee:** Included in green fee. **Walking Policy:** Walking at certain times. **Walkability:** 4. **Opened:** 1994. **Architect:** Gary Player. **Season:** Year-round. **High:** April-Sept. **To obtain tee times:** Call up to 7 days in advance. **Miscellaneous:** Reduced fees (weekdays, twilight, seniors, juniors), range (grass), credit cards (MC, V, AE), BF, FF.
PRAIRIE/MERAMEC (18 Combo)
Yards: 7,093/5,452. **Par:** 72/72. **Course Rating:** 74.3/71.0. **Slope:** 141/139.
WOODLANDS/MERAMEC (18 Combo)
Yards: 6,982/5,208. **Par:** 72/72. **Course Rating:** 73.7/69.3. **Slope:** 139/120.
WOODLANDS/PRAIRIE (18 Combo)
Yards: 7,151/5,530. **Par:** 72/72. **Course Rating:** 75.0/71.3. **Slope:** 141/120.
Reader Comments: A super course with good service … Great value , 27 holes; good location … Nice Layout … Needs better clubhouse … Some outstanding holes … Three different 9s, original 18 the best.

THAYER COUNTRY CLUB
SP-N. Hwy. 63, Thayer, 65791, Oregon County, (417)264-7854, 85 miles from Springfield.
Facility Holes: 9. **Yards:** 3,015/2,593. **Par:** 36/36. **Course Rating:** 34.4. **Slope:** 110. **Green Fee:** $15. **Cart Fee:** $15/Cart. **To obtain tee times:** Call golf shop.

★★★ **THOUSAND HILLS GOLF RESORT**
PU-245 S Wildwood Dr, Branson, 65616, Taney County, (417)334-4553, (800)864-4145.
E-mail: bstorie@thousandhills.com. **Web:** www.thousandhills.com. **Facility Holes:** 18. **Yards:** 5,111/3,616. **Par:** 64/64. **Course Rating:** 66.5/64.1. **Slope:** 125/113. **Green Fee:** $29/$62. **Cart Fee:** Included in green fee. **Walking Policy:** Mandatory carts. **Walkability:** 5. **Opened:** 1995. **Architect:** Mike Riley. **Season:** Year-round. **High:** May-Sept. **To obtain tee times:** Call up to 60 days in advance. **Miscellaneous:** Reduced fees (guests, twilight, juniors), lodging (82 rooms), credit cards (MC, V, AE, D), BF, FF.
Reader Comments: Fun short course, but needs bunker maintenance ... Short but challenging ... Mostly par 3s, good location.

★★★★ **TIFFANY GREENS GOLF CLUB** *Condition*
PU-6100 N.W. Tiffany Springs Pkwy., Kansas City, 64154, Platte County, (816)880-9600, 15 miles from Kansas City. **Web:** www.tiffanygreensgolf.com. **Facility Holes:** 18. **Yards:** 6,977/5,391. **Par:** 72/72. **Course Rating:** 73.5/70.6. **Slope:** 133/121. **Green Fee:** $79. **Cart Fee:** Included in green fee. **Walking Policy:** Unrestricted walking. **Walkability:** 3. **Opened:** 1999. **Architect:** Robert Trent Jones Jr. **Season:** Year-round. **High:** April-Nov. **To obtain tee times:** Call up to 7 days in advance. **Miscellaneous:** Reduced fees (twilight, juniors), range (grass), credit cards (MC, V, AE, D), BF, FF.
Notes: Ranked 8th in 2001 Best in State.
Reader Comments: Nice variety ... Fast greens ... Good variety ... New course, wide fairways ... I'd enjoy playing the course more often ... Beautiful, sculpted course, but expensive ... Generous fairways ... A golfer's delight.

TIMBER LAKE GOLF COURSE
PU-County Rd. 110B, Moberly, 65270, Randolph County, (660)263-8542, 100 miles from St. Louis. **E-mail:** timberlake@mcmsys.com. **Facility Holes:** 18. **Yards:** 6,029/5,226. **Par:** 70/70. **Course Rating:** 69.3/67.9. **Slope:** 118/103. **Green Fee:** $14/$15. **Cart Fee:** $16/Cart. **Walking Policy:** Unrestricted walking. **Walkability:** 3. **Opened:** 1994. **Architect:** John Allen. **Season:** Year-round. **High:** May-Sept. **To obtain tee times:** Call golf shop. **Miscellaneous:** Reduced fees (weekdays, seniors, juniors), credit cards (MC, V, D), FF.

★½ **VALLEY HILLS GOLF CLUB**
PU-1600 Mize Rd., Grain Valley, 64029, Jackson County, (816)229-3032, 18 miles from Kansas City. **Facility Holes:** 18. **Yards:** 6,333/5,152. **Par:** 71/71. **Green Fee:** $12/$15. **Cart Fee:** $18/Cart. **Walkability:** 2. **Opened:** 1975. **To obtain tee times:** Call golf shop.

VANDALIA COUNTRY CLUB
SP-Hwy. 54, Vandalia, 63382, Audrain County, (573)594-6666, 55 miles from St. Louis.
Facility Holes: 9. **Yards:** 6,269/5,813. **Par:** 72/76. **Green Fee:** $10/$13. **Cart Fee:** $17/Cart. **Walking Policy:** Unrestricted walking. **Walkability:** 3. **Opened:** 1959. **Architect:** Albert Linkogel, Sr. **Season:** April-Oct. **To obtain tee times:** Call golf shop. **Miscellaneous:** BF.

WEST PLAINS COUNTRY CLUB
SP-1402 Country Club Dr., West Plains, 65775, Howell County, (417)257-2726, 70 miles from Springfield. **Facility Holes:** 18. **Yards:** 6,048/4,807. **Par:** 70/70. **Course Rating:** 68.5/68.0. **Slope:** 113/114. **Green Fee:** $25. **Cart Fee:** $20/Cart. **Walking Policy:** Unrestricted walking. **Walkability:** 1. **Season:** Year-round. **High:** May-Aug. **To obtain tee times:** Call golf shop. **Miscellaneous:** Range (grass/mats).

★★★★ **WINGHAVEN COUNTRY CLUB**
SP-7777 Winghaven Blvd., O'Fallon, 63366, St. Charles County, (636)561-9464, 20 miles from St. Louis. **E-mail:** dashby@winghavencc.com. **Facility Holes:** 18. **Yards:** 7,230/5,342. **Par:** 72/72. **Course Rating:** 74.4/68.4. **Slope:** 134/113. **Green Fee:** $54/$69. **Cart Fee:** $13/Person. **Walking Policy:** Walking at certain times. **Walkability:** 3. **Opened:** 1999. **Architect:** Nicklaus Design. **Season:** Year-round. **To obtain tee times:** Call up to 14 days in advance. **Miscellaneous:** Reduced fees (twilight), range (grass), credit cards (MC, V, AE, D), BF, FF.
Reader Comments: Nice new course! .. Some good holes ... Wonderful ... The wind can whip you! ... When it matures, it will be great ... Real classy course.

★★★ **WOLF HOLLOW GOLF CLUB**
PU-4504 Hwy. 100, Labadie, 63055, Franklin County, (636)390-8100, 25 miles from St. Louis.
E-mail: doug@wolfhollowgolf.com. **Web:** www.wolfhollowgolf.com. **Facility Holes:** 18. **Yards:**

6,803/4,913. **Par:** 71/71. **Course Rating:** 72.3/68.4. **Slope:** 129/113. **Green Fee:** $23/$45. **Cart Fee:** Included in green fee. **Walking Policy:** Unrestricted walking. **Walkability:** 4. **Opened:** 1999. **Architect:** Gary Kern. **Season:** Year-round. **High:** April-Oct. **To obtain tee times:** Call up to 5 days in advance. **Miscellaneous:** Reduced fees (weekdays, twilight, seniors, juniors), range (grass), credit cards (MC, V, AE, D), BF, FF.
Reader Comments: Creative layout, requires creative shots … Tough layout … Nice pro shop … Much improved, will be excellent … Good condition.

★★★ WOODS FORT COUNTRY CLUB

SP-1 Country Club Dr., Troy, 63379, Lincoln County, (636)462-6600, 35 miles from St. Louis.
Facility Holes: 18. **Yards:** 6,404/4,889. **Par:** 72/72. **Course Rating:** 71.8/68.0. **Slope:** 131/106. **Green Fee:** $28/$35. **Cart Fee:** Included in green fee. **Walking Policy:** Unrestricted walking. **Walkability:** 3. **Opened:** 1994. **Architect:** Jerry Loomis. **Season:** Year-round. **To obtain tee times:** Call up to 7 days in advance. **Miscellaneous:** Reduced fees (seniors, juniors), range (grass), credit cards (MC, V, AE, D), FF.
Reader Comments: Lot of golf for the money … OK course … Getting better … Challenging, some interesting holes … Tremendous clubhouse.

MONTANA

AIRPORT GOLF CLUB
PU-Hwy. 25 East, Wolf Point, 59201, Roosevelt County, (406)653-2161, 50 miles from Glasgow. **Facility Holes:** 18. **Yards:** 6,499/5,360. **Par:** 72/72. **Course Rating:** 69.2/69.6. **Slope:** 108/109. **Green Fee:** $16/$22. **Walking Policy:** Unrestricted walking. **Season:** April-Oct. **High:** June-Aug. **To obtain tee times:** Call golf shop. **Miscellaneous:** BF, FF.

★★ **BIG SKY GOLF CLUB**
R-2160 Black Otter Rd., Meadow Village, Big Sky, 59716, Gallatin County, (406)995-5780, 45 miles from Bozeman. **Facility Holes:** 18. **Yards:** 6,748/5,374. **Par:** 72/72. **Course Rating:** 69.0/67.4. **Slope:** 111/104. **Green Fee:** $40/$52. **Cart Fee:** Included in green fee. **Walking Policy:** Mandatory cart. **Walkability:** 3. **Opened:** 1973. **Architect:** Arnold Palmer. **Season:** May-Oct. **High:** June-Sept. **To obtain tee times:** Call golf shop. **Miscellaneous:** Reduced fees (guests, twilight, juniors), range (grass), lodging (500 rooms), credit cards (MC, V, AE, D).

★★ **BILL ROBERTS MUNICIPAL GOLF COURSE**
PU-2200 N. Benton, Helena, 59601, Lewis and Clark County, (406)442-2191. **E-mail:** helenagolf@aol.com. **Web:** www.members.aol.com/helenagolf. **Facility Holes:** 18. **Yards:** 6,782/5,612. **Par:** 72/72. **Course Rating:** 71.2/71.2. **Slope:** 117/120. **Green Fee:** $18/$22. **Cart Fee:** $22/Cart. **Walking Policy:** Unrestricted walking. **Walkability:** 2. **Opened:** 1950. **Architect:** Robert Muir Graves. **Season:** March-Nov. **High:** April-Sept. **To obtain tee times:** Call up to 2 days in advance. **Miscellaneous:** Reduced fees (twilight, seniors, juniors), range (grass/mats), credit cards (MC, V, D), BF, FF.

★★★ **THE BRIARWOOD**
SP-3429 Briarwood Blvd., Billings, 59101, Yellowstone County, (406)248-2702. **Facility Holes:** 18. **Yards:** 7,010/5,454. **Par:** 72/75. **Course Rating:** 73.0/71.0. **Slope:** 132/120. **Green Fee:** $39. **Cart Fee:** $18/Cart. **Walking Policy:** Unrestricted walking. **Walkability:** 4. **Opened:** 1985. **Architect:** Benz/Poellot. **Season:** Year-round. **High:** April-Nov. **To obtain tee times:** Call golf shop. **Miscellaneous:** Range (grass), credit cards (MC, V, AE), BF, FF.
Reader Comments: Wonderful layout ... Difficult back 9 can slow play ... Resort course, overpriced ... Par-3 16th great hole, challenging course ... Layout crosses creek 14 times, bring lots of balls. **Special Notes:** Reciprocal agreement with other clubs.

★★ **BRIDGER CREEK GOLF COURSE**
PU-2710 McIlahattan Rd., Bozeman, 59715, Gallatin County, (406)586-2333. **Facility Holes:** 18. **Yards:** 6,511/4,902. **Par:** 71/71. **Course Rating:** 69.9/66.2. **Slope:** 119/112. **Green Fee:** $26/$28. **Cart Fee:** $24/Cart. **Walking Policy:** Unrestricted walking. **Walkability:** 3. **Opened:** 1996. **Architect:** Mac Hunter/Mark Holiday/Dane Gamble. **Season:** April-Nov. **High:** May-Sept. **To obtain tee times:** Call up to 7 days in advance. **Miscellaneous:** Reduced fees (weekdays, juniors), range (grass), credit cards (MC, V), BF, FF.

BUFFALO HILL GOLF COURSE
PU-1176 N. Main St., Kalispell, 59901, Flathead County, (406)756-4547, 200 miles from Spokane. **E-mail:** steve@golfbuffalohill.com. **Facility Holes:** 27. **Walking Policy:** Unrestricted walking. **Walkability:** 4. **Season:** April-Nov. **High:** June-Sept. **To obtain tee times:** Call golf shop. **Miscellaneous:** Reduced fees (twilight), range (mats), credit cards (MC, V, AE), BF, FF.
CAMERON COURSE (9)
Yards: 3,001/2,950. **Par:** 35/35. **Course Rating:** 68.0/73.7. **Slope:** 122/132. **Green Fee:** $20/$30. **Cart Fee:** $26/Cart. **Architect:** John Robinson/Bill Robinson.
★★★½ **CHAMPIONSHIP COURSE** (18)
Yards: 6,525/5,258. **Par:** 72/74. **Course Rating:** 71.4/70.3. **Slope:** 131/125. **Green Fee:** $25/$38. **Cart Fee:** $22/Cart. **Opened:** 1933. **Architect:** Robert Muir Graves.
Notes: Ranked 5th in 2001 Best in State.
Reader Comments: Layout of course is hard to follow for the first 4 holes ... Beautiful clubhouse, hilly course ... This is one tough course, better be a mountain goat ... Lots of sidehill lies ... Traditional layout, natural beauty ....

COTTONWOOD COUNTRY CLUB
PU-Sidney Hwy., Glendive, 59330, Dawson County, (406)377-8797, 190 miles from Billings. **E-mail:** ccgs@midrivers.com. **Facility Holes:** 9. **Yards:** 3,163/2,752. **Par:** 36/36. **Course Rating:** 69.0/70.0. **Slope:** 115/114. **Green Fee:** $19/$26. **Walking Policy:** Unrestricted walking. **Walkability:** 3. **Opened:** 1962. **Architect:** Leo Johnson. **Season:** April-Nov. **To obtain tee times:** Call up to 1 day in advance. **Miscellaneous:** Range (grass), credit cards (MC, V), BF, FF.

COTTONWOOD HILLS GOLF COURSE
PU-8955 River Rd., Bozeman, 59718, Gallatin County, (406)587-1118, 7 miles from Bozeman. **Web:** www.cottonwoodhillsgolf.com. **Facility Holes:** 27. **Yards:** 6,753/5,186. **Par:**

70/71. **Course Rating:** 70.8/67.9. **Slope:** 121/110. **Green Fee:** $35. **Cart Fee:** $20/Cart. **Walking Policy:** Unrestricted walking. **Walkability:** 2. **Opened:** 1986. **Architect:** Robert Quick. **Season:** Feb.-Nov. **High:** June-Aug. **To obtain tee times:** Call golf shop. **Miscellaneous:** Reduced fees (seniors, juniors), range (grass), credit cards (MC, V, D), BF, FF.
Special Notes: Also has a 9-hole executive course.

EAGLE BEND GOLF CLUB
SP-279 Eagle Bend Dr., Bigfork, 59911, Flathead County, (406)837-7310, (800)255-5641, 15 miles from Kalispell. **E-mail:** golfmt@digisys.net. **Web:** www.golfmt.com. **Facility Holes:** 27. **Green Fee:** $32/$55. **Cart Fee:** $14/Person. **Walkability:** 3. **Season:** March-Oct. **High:** June-Sept. **To obtain tee times:** Call golf shop. **Miscellaneous:** Reduced fees (twilight, juniors), range (grass/mats), credit cards (MC, V, AE, D), BF, FF.
★★★★ **CHAMPIONSHIP** (18)
Yards: 6,724/5,397. **Par:** 72/72. **Course Rating:** 71.2/70.1. **Slope:** 121/119. **Walking Policy:** Walking at certain times. **Opened:** 1988. **Architect:** William Hull/Jack Nicklaus Jr.
Notes: Ranked 4th in 2001 Best in State.
Reader Comments: Nice layout, easy to score, too pricey … Good course with good amenities & staff … Makes you work … One of best … Wildlife galore.
LAKE (9)
Yards: 3,497/2,574. **Par:** 36/36. **Course Rating:** 71.9/68.5. **Slope:** 124/120. **Walking Policy:** Unrestricted walking. **Opened:** 1995. **Architect:** William Hull.

★★ FAIRMONT HOT SPRINGS RESORT
R-1500 Fairmont Rd., Fairmont, 59711, Silver Bow County, (406)797-3241, (800)332-3272, 20 miles from Butte. **E-mail:** edmilehigh@aol.com. **Web:** www.fairmontmontana.com. **Facility Holes:** 18. **Yards:** 6,741/5,921. **Par:** 72/72. **Course Rating:** 68.5/70.7. **Slope:** 107/109. **Green Fee:** $26/$37. **Cart Fee:** $27/Cart. **Walking Policy:** Unrestricted walking. **Walkability:** 3. **Opened:** 1974. **Architect:** Lloyd Wilder. **Season:** April-Nov. **High:** June-Oct. **To obtain tee times:** Call up to 90 days in advance. **Miscellaneous:** Reduced fees (weekdays, guests), range (grass), lodging (152 rooms), credit cards (MC, V, AE, D), BF, FF.

★½ GLACIER VIEW GOLF COURSE
PU-River Bend Rd., West Glacier, 59936, Flathead County, (406)888-5471, 15 miles from Columbia Falls. **Facility Holes:** 18. **Yards:** 5,116/4,432. **Par:** 69/69. **Course Rating:** 62.3/63.0. **Slope:** 96/102. **Green Fee:** $20. **Cart Fee:** $18/Cart. **Walking Policy:** Unrestricted walking. **Walkability:** 1. **Opened:** 1969. **Architect:** Bob Baldock. **Season:** April-Oct. **High:** June-Aug. **To obtain tee times:** Call golf shop. **Miscellaneous:** Credit cards (MC, V).

★★½ HAMILTON GOLF CLUB
PU-1004 Golf Course Rd., Hamilton, 59840, Ravalli County, (406)363-4251, 3 miles from Hamilton. **Facility Holes:** 18. **Yards:** 6,847/5,924. **Par:** 72/73. **Course Rating:** 72.3/72.9. **Slope:** 120/126. **Green Fee:** $24. **Cart Fee:** $22/Cart. **Walking Policy:** Unrestricted walking. **Walkability:** 3. **Opened:** 1925. **Architect:** Gary Jacobson. **Season:** March-Nov. **High:** June-Aug. **Tee times:** Call up to 7 days in advance. **Miscellaneous:** Credit cards (MC, V, AE), BF, FF.

HIGHLANDS GOLF CLUB
PU-102 Ben Hogan Dr., Missoula, 59803, Missoula County, (406)728-7360. **Facility Holes:** 9. **Yards:** 6,100/5,500. **Par:** 69/72. **Course Rating:** 68.4/70.6. **Slope:** 116/114. **Green Fee:** $20/$25. **Cart Fee:** $12/Cart. **Walking Policy:** Unrestricted walking. **Walkability:** 4. **Season:** April-Oct. **High:** May-Sept. **To obtain tee times:** Call golf shop. **Miscellaneous:** Reduced fees (weekdays, juniors).

★½ LAKE HILLS GOLF COURSE
SP-1930 Clubhouse Way, Billings, 59105, Yellowstone County, (406)252-9244. **Facility Holes:** 18. **Yards:** 6,802/5,126. **Par:** 72/74. **Course Rating:** 70.1/67.0. **Slope:** 112/104. **Green Fee:** $21. **Cart Fee:** $20/Cart. **Walking Policy:** Unrestricted walking. **Walkability:** 3. **Opened:** 1956. **Architect:** George Schneiter Sr. **Season:** Year-round. **High:** May-Aug. **To obtain tee times:** Call up to 3 days in advance. **Miscellaneous:** Reduced fees (seniors), metal spikes, range (grass/mats), credit cards (MC, V, AE, D), BF, FF.

★★★½ LARCHMONT GOLF COURSE
PU-3200 Old Fort Rd., Missoula, 59801, Missoula County, (406)721-4416. **Facility Holes:** 18. **Yards:** 7,114/5,936. **Par:** 72/72. **Course Rating:** 72.7/72.9. **Slope:** 118/118. **Green Fee:** $16/$18. **Cart Fee:** $20/Cart. **Walking Policy:** Unrestricted walking. **Walkability:** 2. **Opened:** 1982. **Architect:** Randy Lilje. **Season:** March-Oct. **High:** May-Aug. **To obtain tee times:** Call golf shop. **Miscellaneous:** Reduced fees (weekdays, seniors, juniors), metal spikes, range (grass), credit cards (MC, V, AE, D).
Reader Comments: Enjoyable … Nice, fast greens … Good course, greens slow … Fairly simple course … Lots of play…Wide open, flat and long … Huge greens … Watch out for lightning.

MADISON MEADOWS GOLF CLUB

PU-Golf Course Rd., Ennis, 59729, Madison County, (406)682-7468, 40 miles from Bozeman. **Facility Holes:** 9. **Yards:** 6,490/4,966. **Par:** 72/72. **Course Rating:** 68.7/66.1. **Slope:** 111/101. **Green Fee:** $10. **Walkability:** 5. **Opened:** 1982. **Architect:** Frank Hummel. **To obtain tee times:** Call golf shop.

MARIAS VALLEY GOLF & COUNTRY CLUB

PU-P.O. Box 784, Shelby, 59474, Toole County, (406)434-5940, 5 miles from Shelby. **Web:** www.mvgcc.com. **Facility Holes:** 18. **Yards:** 6,779/5,042. **Par:** 72/72. **Course Rating:** 71.5/67.7. **Slope:** 122/115. **Green Fee:** $24. **Cart Fee:** $24/Cart. **Walking Policy:** Unrestricted walking. **Walkability:** 2. **Opened:** 1969. **Architect:** N. Woods/R.M. Graves/C. Thuesen. **Season:** March-Nov. **To obtain tee times:** Call up to 7 days in advance. **Miscellaneous:** Reduced fees (twilight), range (grass), credit cards (MC, V), BF, FF.

★★★½ MEADOW LAKE GOLF RESORT

R-490 St. Andrews Dr., Columbia Falls, 59912, Flathead County, (406)892-2111, (800)321-4653, 12 miles from Kalispell. **Facility Holes:** 18. **Yards:** 6,714/5,344. **Par:** 72/73. **Course Rating:** 70.9/69.8. **Slope:** 124/121. **Green Fee:** $25/$45. **Cart Fee:** $14/Person. **Walking Policy:** Unrestricted walking. **Walkability:** 2. **Opened:** 1984. **Architect:** Dick Phelps. **Season:** April-Nov. **High:** June-Sept. **To obtain tee times:** Call golf shop. **Miscellaneous:** Reduced fees (guests, twilight), range (grass/mats), credit cards (MC, V, AE, D).

Reader Comments: Very fun and challenging, well maintained ... Pretty good service ... Lots of trees ... Fantastic resort course ... Best in the Flathead ... Beautiful, laid out among the trees ... Walkable ... Nice course in average shape, pretty setting.

★★★½ MISSION MOUNTAIN COUNTRY CLUB

SP-640 Stagecoach Trail, Ronan, 59864, Lake County, (406)676-4653, 60 miles from Missoula. **E-mail:** mmcc@ronan.net. **Facility Holes:** 18. **Yards:** 6,479/5,125. **Par:** 72/73. **Course Rating:** 70.1/69.1. **Slope:** 115/115. **Green Fee:** $27. **Cart Fee:** $24/Cart. **Walking Policy:** Unrestricted walking. **Walkability:** 2. **Opened:** 1988. **Architect:** Gary Roger Baird. **Season:** March-Oct. **High:** June-Aug. **To obtain tee times:** Call up to 2 days in advance. **Miscellaneous:** Range (grass), credit cards (MC, V), BF, FF.

Reader Comments: Weird! A fun but strange set-up ... Somewhat easy, except for the 550-yard 15th ... Hole 7 was cool ... Beautiful mountain views... Love this course ... Visual stunner.

★★★½ NORTHERN PINES GOLF CLUB

PU-3230 Hwy. 93 North, Kalispell, 59901, Flathead County, (406)751-1950, (800)255-5641, 2 miles from Kalispell. **E-mail:** golfmt@digisys.net. **Web:** www.golfmt.com. **Facility Holes:** 18. **Yards:** 7,015/5,421. **Par:** 72/72. **Course Rating:** 72.5/69.9. **Slope:** 121/118. **Green Fee:** $30/$45. **Cart Fee:** $14/Person. **Walking Policy:** Walking at certain times. **Walkability:** 3. **Opened:** 1996. **Architect:** Andy North/Roger Packard. **Season:** April-Oct. **High:** June-Sept. **To obtain tee times:** Call golf shop. **Miscellaneous:** Reduced fees (twilight, juniors), range (grass), credit cards (MC, V, AE, D), BF, FF.

Notes: Ranked 3rd in 2001 Best in State.

Reader Comments: A challenging but fun course ... Interesting terrain ... Good service ... Enjoyed back 9 ... Very nice ... Easy to lose golf balls—tall rough and narrow fairways ... Links in the mountains ... Lots of challenges, but fair ... Young course but promising.

★★★★½ OLD WORKS GOLF COURSE *Value*

PU-1205 Pizzini Way, Anaconda, 59711, Deer Lodge County, (406)563-5989, (888)229-4833, 26 miles from Butte. **E-mail:** mngr-professional@oldworks.org. **Web:** www.oldworks.org. **Facility Holes:** 18. **Yards:** 7,705/5,348. **Par:** 72/72. **Course Rating:** 76.0/70.3. **Slope:** 133/124. **Green Fee:** $29/$38. **Cart Fee:** $12/Person. **Walking Policy:** Unrestricted walking. **Walkability:** 3. **Opened:** 1997. **Architect:** Jack Nicklaus. **Season:** May-Nov. **High:** June-Sept. **To obtain tee times:** Call up to 3 days in advance. **Miscellaneous:** Reduced fees (twilight), range (grass), credit cards (MC, V, AE, D), BF, FF.

Notes: Ranked 2nd in 2001 Best in State.

Reader Comments: An extemely interesting, immaculately conditioned course ... Very playable ... Wonderful and affordable ... Pace of play is too slow ... Unique black sand ... Built on the site of a historic copper smelter ... Too far from cart path to fairway ball on cart path only course—as a senior would not play here again.

★½ PETER YEGEN JR. GOLF CLUB

PU-3400 Grand Ave., Billings, 59102, Yellowstone County, (406)656-8099. **Facility Holes:** 18. **Yards:** 6,617/4,994. **Par:** 71/71. **Course Rating:** 69.7/67.0. **Slope:** 112/109. **Green Fee:** $15/$16. **Cart Fee:** $15/Cart. **Walking Policy:** Unrestricted walking. **Walkability:** 1. **Opened:** 1993. **Architect:** Carl Thuesen. **Season:** Year-round. **High:** May-Oct. **To obtain tee times:** Call golf shop. **Miscellaneous:** Range (grass/mats), credit cards (MC, V, AE), BF, FF.

PINE MEADOWS GOLF COURSE
PU-35 Country Club Rd., Lewistown, 59457, Fergus County, (406)538-7075, 110 miles from Great Falls. **Facility Holes:** 9. **Yards:** 6,605/5,853. **Par:** 72/74. **Course Rating:** 69.4/71.1. **Slope:** 109/111. **Green Fee:** $21/$23. **Cart Fee:** $17/Cart. **Walking Policy:** Unrestricted walking. **Walkability:** 3. **Opened:** 1947. **Season:** April-Nov. **High:** June-Sept. **To obtain tee times:** Call up to 7 days in advance. **Miscellaneous:** Reduced fees (weekdays), range (grass), credit cards (MC, V, D), BF, FF.

POLSON COUNTRY CLUB
PU-111 Bayview Dr., Polson, 59860, Lake County, (406)883-8230, 60 miles from Missoula. **E-mail:** polsoncc@digisys.net. **Web:** www.polsoncc.com. **Facility Holes:** 27. **Green Fee:** $26. **Cart Fee:** $23/Cart. **Walking Policy:** Unrestricted walking. **Walkability:** 3. **Architect:** John Steidel. **Season:** March-Dec. **High:** June-Sept. **To obtain tee times:** Call golf shop. **Miscellaneous:** Reduced fees (twilight), range (grass/mats), credit cards (MC, V), BF, FF.
★★★ **NEW 18** (18)
Yards: 6,964/5,431. **Par:** 72/72. **Course Rating:** 72.5/70.0. **Slope:** 123/124. **Opened:** 1989.
Reader Comments: Nice lake view ... Worth the stop ... Beautiful setting ... New 9 is great ... Good variety ... Country style, not crowded ... Beautiful scenery with mountain ranges to east and the Flathead Lake adjacent to course ... Great for seniors.
OLD 9 (9)
Yards: 3,219/2,593. **Par:** 36/36. **Course Rating:** 69.4/63.7. **Slope:** 119/110. **Opened:** 1936.

PONDEROSA BUTTE GOLF COURSE
PU-1 Long Dr., Colstrip, 59323, Rosebud County, (406)748-2700, 120 miles from Billings. **Facility Holes:** 9. **Yards:** 6,469/5,309. **Par:** 72/72. **Course Rating:** 69.8/68.3. **Slope:** 116/110. **Green Fee:** $16. **Cart Fee:** $16/Cart. **Walking Policy:** Unrestricted walking. **Walkability:** 4. **Opened:** 1992. **Architect:** Carl Thuesen. **Season:** March-Oct. **High:** April-June. **To obtain tee times:** Call golf shop. **Miscellaneous:** Reduced fees (seniors, juniors), range (grass), credit cards (MC, V, AE, D).

★½ R.O. SPECK MUNICIPAL GOLF COURSE
PU-29th and River Drive N., Great Falls, 59401, Cascade County, (406)761-1078, 60 miles from Helena. **Facility Holes:** 18. **Yards:** 6,830/5,817. **Par:** 72/73. **Course Rating:** 69.6/71.4. **Slope:** 111/115. **Green Fee:** $17. **Walking Policy:** Unrestricted walking. **Walkability:** 1. **Season:** March-Oct. **High:** April-Oct. **To obtain tee times:** Call golf shop. **Miscellaneous:** Reduced fees (twilight, juniors), metal spikes, range (grass).

★★★ RED LODGE MOUNTAIN RESORT GOLF COURSE
R-828 Upper Continental Dr., Red Lodge, 59068, Carbon County, (406)446-3344, (800)514-3088, 60 miles from Billings. **Facility Holes:** 18. **Yards:** 6,863/5,678. **Par:** 72/72. **Course Rating:** 69.3/70.4. **Slope:** 115/115. **Green Fee:** $25/$30. **Cart Fee:** $19/Cart. **Walking Policy:** Unrestricted walking. **Walkability:** 3. **Opened:** 1983. **Architect:** Bob Baldock. **Season:** April-Nov. **High:** June-Sept. **To obtain tee times:** Call up to 14 days in advance. **Miscellaneous:** Reduced fees (weekdays, twilight, juniors), range (grass), credit cards (MC, V, D), BF, FF.
Reader Comments: Very attractive, not forgiving ... Greens small and hard ... Nice course, could use some trees ... Lots of water, great view of mountains ... Fun course with lots of little streams ... Beautiful ... Lose balls easily ... Elevated boxes ... Nice course in mountains.

★★★ VILLAGE GREENS GOLF CLUB
PU-500 Palmer Dr., Kalispell, 59901, Flathead County, (406)752-4666, 230 miles from Spokane. **E-mail:** tee@montanagolf.com. **Web:** www.montanagolf.com. **Facility Holes:** 18. **Yards:** 6,401/5,208. **Par:** 70/70. **Course Rating:** 69.8/68.3. **Slope:** 114/114. **Green Fee:** $20/$29. **Cart Fee:** $20/Cart. **Walking Policy:** Unrestricted walking. **Walkability:** 1. **Opened:** 1992. **Architect:** William Robinson. **Season:** April-Nov. **High:** July-Aug. **To obtain tee times:** Call up to 3 days in advance. **Miscellaneous:** Reduced fees (weekdays, twilight, seniors, juniors), range (grass), credit cards (MC, V, D), BF, FF.
Reader Comments: It is fun and easy, relaxing course providing quick play ... Good greens ... Not too difficult ... Pleasant experience ... Nice, flat course ... An excellent senior course with very good grass ... Lush course conditions.

WHITEFISH LAKE GOLF CLUB
PU-Hwy. 93 N., Whitefish, 59937, Flathead County, (406)862-5960, 130 miles from Missoula. **E-mail:** wlgc@cyberport.net. **Web:** www.golfwhitefish.com. **Facility Holes:** 36. **Green Fee:** $32/$37. **Cart Fee:** $25/Cart. **Walking Policy:** Unrestricted walking. **Walkability:** 2. **Architect:** John Steidel. **Season:** April-Oct. **High:** June-Sept. **To obtain tee times:** Call golf shop. **Miscellaneous:** Reduced fees (twilight), range (grass/mats), credit cards (MC, V), BF, FF.

MONTANA

★★★ **NORTH COURSE** (18)
Yards: 6,556/5,556. **Par:** 72/72. **Course Rating:** 69.8/70.1. **Slope:** 118/115. **Opened:** 1936.
Notes: Ranked 2nd in 1997 Best in State.
Reader Comments: First class course and restaurant at tourist class cost … Ski a.m., golf p.m. … Really like to play this course … Wide fairways, grass a negative … Very average, nice setting … Very difficult to get tee-times.
★★★★ **SOUTH COURSE** (18)
Yards: 6,551/5,361. **Par:** 71/72. **Course Rating:** 70.5/70.3. **Slope:** 122/120. **Opened:** 1980.
Reader Comments: Tight, pretty … This course will take your breath away, great track … No one hole like another … Greens are fast and true … What can I say, I enjoy it … #1 in the valley … Better than North Course … Wonderful, old, treed course.

WILD HORSE PLAINS GOLF COURSE
PU-328 Hwy. 200 W., Plains, 59859, Sanders County, (406)826-4015. **Facility Holes:** 9.
Yards: 5,681/4,379. **Par:** 72/72. **Green Fee:** $12/$14. **Cart Fee:** $14/Cart. **Opened:** 1918.
Season: March-Oct. **To obtain tee times:** Call golf shop. **Miscellaneous:** Credit cards (MC, V).

★★½ **ASHLAND COUNTRY CLUB**
SP-16119 Hwy. 6, Ashland, 68003, Cass County, (402)944-3388, 25 miles from Omaha.
Facility Holes: 18. **Yards:** 6,337/5,606. **Par:** 71/74. **Course Rating:** 70.2/72.3. **Slope:** 121/115.
Green Fee: $20/$24. **Cart Fee:** $11/Person. **Walking Policy:** Unrestricted walking. **Walkability:**
1. **Opened:** 1967. **Architect:** Dick Watson. **Season:** Year-round. **High:** May-Sept. **To obtain tee
times:** Call up to 5 days in advance. **Miscellaneous:** BF, FF.

★½ **BAY HILLS GOLF COURSE**
SP-3200 Buccaneer Blvd., Plattsmouth, 68048, Cass County, (402)298-8191, 15 miles from
Omaha. **E-mail:** bayhills@mail.com. **Web:** www.bayhills.com. **Facility Holes:** 18. **Yards:**
6,348/4,923. **Par:** 72/74. **Course Rating:** 72.5/76.5. **Slope:** 135/137. **Green Fee:** $15/$21. **Cart
Fee:** $12/Person. **Walking Policy:** Unrestricted walking. **Walkability:** 5. **Opened:** 1994. **Season:**
March-Nov. **High:** April-Oct. **To obtain tee times:** Call golf shop. **Miscellaneous:** Reduced fees
(weekdays, twilight, seniors, juniors), range (grass/mats), credit cards (MC, V, AE, D), FF.

★★½ **BENSON PARK GOLF COURSE**
PU-5333 N. 72nd St., Omaha, 68134, Douglas County, (402)444-4626. **Facility Holes:** 18.
Yards: 6,814/6,085. **Par:** 72/78. **Course Rating:** 72.1/73.4. **Slope:** 120/121. **Green Fee:**
$12/$13. **Cart Fee:** $16/Cart. **Walking Policy:** Unrestricted walking. **Opened:** 1964. **Architect:**
Edward Lawrence Packard. **Season:** March-Dec. **High:** May-Sept. **To obtain tee times:** Call
golf shop. **Miscellaneous:** Reduced fees (seniors, juniors), metal spikes.

CEDAR VIEW COUNTRY CLUB
PU-Calcavecchia Dr., Laurel, 68745, Cedar County, (402)256-3184. **Facility Holes:** 9. **Yards:**
3,015/2,491. **Par:** 36/36. **Course Rating:** 34.0/34.0. **Slope:** 112/112. **Green Fee:** $16/$20. **Cart
Fee:** $14/Cart. **Walking Policy:** Unrestricted walking. **Walkability:** 4. **Opened:** 1965. **Season:**
April-Nov. **High:** May-Sept. **To obtain tee times:** Call golf shop. **Miscellaneous:** Reduced fees
(weekdays), BF, FF.

COVINGTON LINKS GOLF COURSE
PU-497 Golf Rd., South Sioux City, 68776, Dakota County, (402)494-9841, 1 mile from South
Sioux City. **Facility Holes:** 18. **Yards:** 5,977/5,263. **Par:** 71/71. **Course Rating:** 68.8/69.2.
Slope: 115/114. **Green Fee:** $16. **Cart Fee:** $16/Cart. **Walking Policy:** Unrestricted walking.
Walkability: 2. **Opened:** 1977. **Architect:** Marty Johnson. **Season:** March-Nov. **To obtain tee
times:** Call golf shop. **Miscellaneous:** Credit cards (MC, V), FF.

★★½ **CROOKED CREEK GOLF CLUB**
PU-134th & O St., Lincoln, 68520, Lancaster County, (402)489-7899, 3 miles from Lincoln.
Facility Holes: 18. **Yards:** 6,720/5,024. **Par:** 72/72. **Course Rating:** 70.8/68.2. **Slope:** 113/109.
Green Fee: $16/$20. **Cart Fee:** $11/Person. **Walking Policy:** Unrestricted walking. **Walkability:**
3. **Opened:** 1995. **Architect:** Pat Wyss. **Season:** Year-round. **High:** April-Oct. **To obtain tee
times:** Call golf shop. **Miscellaneous:** Reduced fees (seniors, juniors), range (grass/mats),
credit cards (MC, V).

EAGLE HILLS GOLF COURSE
PU-501 Eagle Hill Dr., Papillion, 68133, Sarpy County, (402)592-7788, 7 miles from Omaha.
Facility Holes: 18. **Yards:** 6,515/4,615. **Par:** 72/72. **Course Rating:** 71.4/70.0. **Slope:** 130/113.
Green Fee: $17/$22. **Cart Fee:** $10/Person. **Walking Policy:** Unrestricted walking. **Walkability:**
3. **Opened:** 2000. **Season:** Year-round. **To obtain tee times:** Call up to 6 days in advance.
Miscellaneous: Reduced fees (weekdays), range (grass), credit cards (MC, V), BF, FF.

ELDORADO HILLS GOLF CLUB
SP-1227 Eldorado Rd., Norfolk, 68701, Madison County, (402)371-1453, 45 miles from
Columbus. **E-mail:** eldorado@ncfcomn.com. **Facility Holes:** 18. **Yards:** 6,700/5,566. **Par:**
72/72. **Course Rating:** 71.8/72.6. **Slope:** 116/115. **Green Fee:** $18. **Cart Fee:** $10/Person.
Walking Policy: Unrestricted walking. **Walkability:** 4. **Opened:** 1987. **Architect:** Bob Hupp.
Season: March-Nov. **To obtain tee times:** Call golf shop. **Miscellaneous:** Reduced fees (week-
days), credit cards (MC, V), BF, FF.

ELK'S COUNTRY CLUB
SP-5113 63rd St., Columbus, 68601, Platte County, (402)564-4930, 65 miles from Omaha.
Facility Holes: 18. **Yards:** 6,565/5,369. **Par:** 72/72. **Course Rating:** 72.0/72.2. **Slope:** 122/121.
Green Fee: $40. **Cart Fee:** $12/Person. **Walking Policy:** Unrestricted walking. **Walkability:** 3.
Architect: Dick Phelps. **Season:** April-Nov. **High:** May-Aug. **To obtain tee times:** Call up to 7
days in advance. **Miscellaneous:** Range (grass/mats), credit cards (MC, V), BF, FF.

ELKHORN ACRES GOLF COURSE
PU-56611 Golf Course Rd., Stanton, 68779, Stanton County, (402)439-2191, 14 miles from Norfolk. **Facility Holes:** 9. **Yards:** 3,278/2,628. **Par:** 36/36. **Course Rating:** 68.7/74.4. **Slope:** 117/125. **Green Fee:** $14/$17. **Cart Fee:** $18/Cart. **Walking Policy:** Unrestricted walking. **Walkability:** 1. **Opened:** 1974. **Season:** March-Oct. **High:** July-Aug. **To obtain tee times:** Call up to 3 days in advance. **Miscellaneous:** Reduced fees (weekdays), range (grass), FF.

ELMWOOD PARK GOLF COURSE
PU-6232 Pacific St., Omaha, 68106, Douglas County, (402)444-4683. **Facility Holes:** 18. **Yards:** 5,000/4,300. **Par:** 68/68. **Course Rating:** 64.0/64.0. **Slope:** 101/101. **Green Fee:** $16/$20. **Cart Fee:** $11/Person. **Walking Policy:** Unrestricted walking. **Walkability:** 3. **Opened:** 1934. **Season:** March-Dec. **High:** May-Sept. **To obtain tee times:** Call up to 7 days in advance. **Miscellaneous:** Reduced fees (seniors, juniors).

FAIRPLAY GOLF CLUB
SP-55427 837 Road, Norfolk, 68701, Madison County, (402)371-9877. **Facility Holes:** 18. **Yards:** 6,444/2,717. **Par:** 72/72. **Course Rating:** 68.1/70.4. **Slope:** 107/108. **Green Fee:** $17. **Cart Fee:** $17/Cart. **Walking Policy:** Unrestricted walking. **Walkability:** 1. **Architect:** Martin Johnson. **Season:** March-Nov. **High:** May-July. **To obtain tee times:** Call golf shop. **Miscellaneous:** Range (grass).

FALLS CITY COUNTRY CLUB
SP-West Hwy. 8, Falls City, 68355, Richardson County, (402)245-3624, 100 miles from Kansas City. **Facility Holes:** 18. **Yards:** 5,986/5,615. **Par:** 70/77. **Course Rating:** 68.6/72.0. **Slope:** 113/118. **Green Fee:** $15/$18. **Cart Fee:** $15/Cart. **Walking Policy:** Unrestricted walking. **Walkability:** 3. **Season:** Year-round. **High:** May-Sept. **To obtain tee times:** Call golf shop. **Miscellaneous:** Range (grass), BF, FF.

GORDON GOLF & COUNTRY CLUB
SP-West 2nd St., Gordon, 69343, Sheridan County, (308)282-1146. **Facility Holes:** 9. **Yards:** 3,209/2,906. **Par:** 36/37. **Course Rating:** 71.8/75.8. **Slope:** 119/127. **Green Fee:** $12/$17. **Cart Fee:** $15/Cart. **Walking Policy:** Unrestricted walking. **Walkability:** 2. **Opened:** 1969. **Architect:** Jack Korita. **Season:** April-Oct. **High:** June-July. **To obtain tee times:** Call golf shop. **Miscellaneous:** Reduced fees (weekdays), range (grass), BF, FF.

★★★½ GRAND ISLAND MUNICIPAL GOLF COURSE *Value*
PU-2803 Shady Bend Rd., Grand Island, 68801, Hall County, (308)385-5340, 90 miles from Lincoln. **Facility Holes:** 18. **Yards:** 6,752/5,487. **Par:** 72/72. **Course Rating:** 71.1/70.5. **Slope:** 110/104. **Green Fee:** $12/$14. **Cart Fee:** $10/Person. **Walking Policy:** Unrestricted walking. **Walkability:** 1. **Opened:** 1977. **Architect:** Frank Hummel. **Season:** Year-round. **High:** April-Oct. **To obtain tee times:** Call golf shop. **Miscellaneous:** Reduced fees (seniors, juniors), range (grass), credit cards (MC, V), BF, FF.
Reader Comments: Very nice municipal course … Flat course, easy to walk.

★★★★ HERITAGE HILLS GOLF COURSE *Value*
PU-6000 Clubhouse Dr., McCook, 69001, Red Willow County, (308)345-5032, 240 miles from Lincoln. **E-mail:** golf@ocsmccook.com. **Web:** www.mccookgolf.com. **Facility Holes:** 18. **Yards:** 6,715/5,475. **Par:** 72/72. **Course Rating:** 72.7/74.8. **Slope:** 130/130. **Green Fee:** $27. **Cart Fee:** $22/Cart. **Walking Policy:** Unrestricted walking. **Walkability:** 5. **Opened:** 1981. **Architect:** Phelps/Benz. **Season:** Year-round. **To obtain tee times:** Call up to 100 days in advance. **Miscellaneous:** Reduced fees (juniors), range (grass), credit cards (MC, V), BF, FF.
Notes: Ranked 10th in 1999 Best in State.
Reader Comments: Friendliest staff … Many great holes … Awesome vistas … Kind of unusual … Really terrific golf course in the middle of nowhere … A lot of blind shots, both from the tee box and on approach to greens … Take a cart & watch out for snakes in the rough.

HIDDEN VALLEY GOLF COURSE
PU-10501 Pine Lake Rd., Lincoln, 68526, Lancaster County, (402)483-2532. **E-mail:** mandrhemminger@msn.com. **Facility Holes:** 27. **Green Fee:** $14/$19. **Cart Fee:** $13/Person. **Walking Policy:** Unrestricted walking. **Walkability:** 3. **Opened:** 1962. **Architect:** C.J. Dietrich. **Season:** Year-round. **To obtain tee times:** Call up to 7 days in advance. **Miscellaneous:** Reduced fees (weekdays, seniors, juniors), range (grass), credit cards (MC, V, D), BF, FF.
BLUE/RED (18)
Yards: 5,711/4,952. **Par:** 70/71. **Course Rating:** 67.4/66.5. **Slope:** 106/104.
GREEN/BLUE (18)
Yards: 5,850/5,063. **Par:** 70/72. **Course Rating:** 68.2/67.8. **Slope:** 113/107.
GREEN/RED (18)
Yards: 5,951/5,221. **Par:** 70/73. **Course Rating:** 68.6/69.1. **Slope:** 115/109.

NEBRASKA

★★★ HIGHLANDS GOLF COURSE
PU-5501 N.W. 12th St., Lincoln, 68521, Lancaster County, (402)441-6081. **E-mail:** hgcpro@aol.com. **Facility Holes:** 18. **Yards:** 7,021/5,280. **Par:** 72/72. **Course Rating:** 72.5/69.4. **Slope:** 119/111. **Green Fee:** $15/$20. **Cart Fee:** $12/Person. **Walking Policy:** Unrestricted walking. **Walkability:** 4. **Opened:** 1993. **Architect:** Jeff Brauer. **Season:** Year-round. **High:** April-Nov. **To obtain tee times:** Call up to 7 days in advance. **Miscellaneous:** Reduced fees (twilight, seniors, juniors), range (grass/mats), credit cards (MC, V, D), BF, FF.
Reader Comments: Nice Scottish set up for a muni course, pace was slow at times ... Nice if you like links ... Lots of challenging holes ... Not a flat spot on any green ... Beautifully maintained ... Windy and long for average golfer.

HILLSIDE GOLF COURSE
PU-2616 Hillside Dr., Sidney, 69162, Cheyenne County, (308)254-2311, 170 miles from Denver. **E-mail:** sidgolf@wheatbelt.com. **Facility Holes:** 18. **Yards:** 6,924/5,308. **Par:** 72/73. **Course Rating:** 72.5/70.0. **Slope:** 121/110. **Green Fee:** $15. **Cart Fee:** $16/Cart. **Walking Policy:** Unrestricted walking. **Walkability:** 4. **Season:** March-Dec. **High:** May-Aug. **To obtain tee times:** Call golf shop. **Miscellaneous:** Reduced fees (seniors, juniors), range (grass), credit cards (MC, V, AE, D).

★★ HIMARK GOLF COURSE
PU-90th and Augusta Dr., Lincoln, 68520, Lancaster County, (402)488-7888. **Facility Holes:** 27. **Yards:** 6,637/4,969. **Par:** 72/72. **Course Rating:** 71.8/69.3. **Slope:** 128/117. **Green Fee:** $11/$28. **Cart Fee:** $13/Person. **Walking Policy:** Unrestricted walking. **Walkability:** 3. **Opened:** 1993. **Architect:** Larry Glatt/Lammle Brothers. **Season:** Year-round. **High:** April-Sept. **To obtain tee times:** Call up to 8 days in advance. **Miscellaneous:** Reduced fees (twilight, seniors, juniors), range (grass/mats), credit cards (MC, V), BF, FF.
Special Notes: Also has a 9-hole Blue Course.

★★★ HOLMES PARK GOLF COURSE
PU-3701 S. 70th St., Lincoln, 68506, Lancaster County, (402)441-8960. **Facility Holes:** 18. **Yards:** 6,805/6,054. **Par:** 72/74. **Course Rating:** 72.2/73.8. **Slope:** 120/126. **Green Fee:** $11/$16. **Cart Fee:** $20/Cart. **Walking Policy:** Unrestricted walking. **Walkability:** 3. **Opened:** 1964. **Architect:** Floyd Farley. **Season:** Year-round. **High:** May-June. **To obtain tee times:** Call golf shop. **Miscellaneous:** Reduced fees (weekdays, seniors, juniors), range (grass/mats), credit cards (MC, V).
Reader Comments: Very playable ... The best in Lincoln, not for the beginner ... Nice course, good value ... High-traffic course ... Great pro shop ... Too many fivesomes ... Good course, over-used.

★★★½ INDIAN CREEK GOLF COURSE
PU-20100 W. Maple Rd., Elkhorn, 68022, Douglas County, (402)289-0900, 5 miles from Omaha. **E-mail:** pato@gottsch.net. **Web:** www.indcrk.com. **Facility Holes:** 27. **Green Fee:** $26/$32. **Cart Fee:** $12/Person. **Walking Policy:** Unrestricted walking. **Walkability:** 4. **Opened:** 1992. **Architect:** Frank Hummel/Mark Rathert. **Season:** Year-round. **High:** April-Oct. **To obtain tee times:** Call up to 10 days in advance. **Miscellaneous:** Reduced fees (weekdays, seniors, juniors), range (grass/mats), credit cards (MC, V), BF, FF.
BLACKBIRD/GRAYHAWK (18 Combo)
Yards: 7,154/5,282. **Par:** 72/72. **Course Rating:** 74.1/68.5. **Slope:** 128/113.
RED FEATHER/BLACKBIRD (18 Combo)
Yards: 7,157/5,040. **Par:** 72/72. **Course Rating:** 75.0/68.1. **Slope:** 131/112.
RED FEATHER/GRAYHAWK (18 Combo)
Yards: 7,041/5,120. **Par:** 72/72. **Course Rating:** 73.9/69.4. **Slope:** 131/115.
Reader Comments: Very beautiful vistas ... Holes are fair, pick the right tee ... Improving steadily ... Nice greens ... The new 9 needs a few years ... Indian Creek requires concentration the moment you leave the clubhouse ... Shotmaking a necessity at this must play ... Play the original 18.

INDIAN MEADOWS GOLF COURSE
PU-2746 W. Walker Rd., North Platte, 69101, Lincoln County, (308)532-6955. **Facility Holes:** 9. **Yards:** 3,250/2,784. **Par:** 36/36. **Course Rating:** 70.1/71.0. **Slope:** 111/117. **Green Fee:** $12/$13. **Cart Fee:** $18/Cart. **Walking Policy:** Unrestricted walking. **Walkability:** 1. **Opened:** 1970. **Season:** Year-round. **High:** May-Sept. **To obtain tee times:** Call golf shop. **Miscellaneous:** Range (grass/mats), credit cards (MC, V, AE), BF, FF.

★★★ INDIAN TRAILS COUNTRY CLUB
SP-Highway 275, Beemer, 68716, Cuming County, (402)528-3404, 30 miles from Norfolk. **Facility Holes:** 18. **Yards:** 6,302/5,692. **Par:** 71/73. **Course Rating:** 68.8/74.2. **Slope:** 115/120. **Green Fee:** $12/$16. **Cart Fee:** $14/Cart. **Walkability:** 3. **Opened:** 1960. **Season:** March-Nov. **High:** May-Aug. **To obtain tee times:** Call golf shop. **Miscellaneous:** Metal spikes, range (grass), credit cards (MC, V).

NEBRASKA

Reader Comments: Lose your concentration for one shot, par is no longer an option … Spread over very rough terrain calls on the golfer to have every shot in his bag that day … Elevated tees to raised greens, sidehill lies in the fairways and undulating greens will challenge every golfer.

INDIANHEAD GOLF CLUB
PU-4100 W. Husker Hwy., Grand Island, 68803, Hall County, (308)381-4653, 90 miles from Lincoln. **Facility Holes:** 18. **Yards:** 6,597/5,664. **Par:** 72/72. **Course Rating:** 70.9/71.9. **Slope:** 122/117. **Green Fee:** $10/$12. **Cart Fee:** $9/Person. **Walking Policy:** Unrestricted walking. **Walkability:** 1. **Opened:** 1990. **Season:** Year-round. **High:** May-Sept. **To obtain tee times:** Call golf shop. **Miscellaneous:** Metal spikes, range (grass/mats), credit cards (MC, V).

IRON EAGLE MUNICIPAL GOLF COURSE
PU-2401 Halligan Dr, North Platte, 69101, Lincoln County, (308)535-6730, 260 miles from Denver/Omaha. **E-mail:** kaibl@ci.northplatte.ne.us. **Facility Holes:** 18. **Yards:** 6,401/4,459. **Par:** 72/72. **Course Rating:** 71.5/66.3. **Slope:** 124/114. **Green Fee:** $14/$17. **Cart Fee:** $9/Person. **Walking Policy:** Unrestricted walking. **Walkability:** 1. **Opened:** 1994. **Architect:** Pat Wyss. **Season:** Year-round. **Tee times:** Call up to 7 days in advance. **Miscellaneous:** Reduced fees (seniors, juniors), range (grass/mats), credit cards (MC, V), BF, FF.

★★½ JOHNNY GOODMAN GOLF COURSE
PU-6111 S. 99th St., Omaha, 68127, Douglas County, (402)444-4656. **Facility Holes:** 18. **Yards:** 6,928/6,026. **Par:** 72/76. **Course Rating:** 73.7/75.3. **Slope:** 124/126. **Green Fee:** $17/$21. **Cart Fee:** $11/Person. **Walking Policy:** Unrestricted walking. **Walkability:** 3. **Opened:** 1971. **Architect:** Dave Bennett/Leon Howard. **Season:** Year-round. **High:** May-Sept. **To obtain tee times:** Call up to 7 days in advance. **Miscellaneous:** Reduced fees (weekdays, seniors, juniors), range (grass), BF, FF.

★★½ THE KNOLLS GOLF COURSE
PU-11630 Sahler St., Omaha, 68164, Douglas County, (402)493-1740. **Facility Holes:** 18. **Yards:** 6,300/5,111. **Par:** 71/71. **Course Rating:** 69.8/69.8. **Slope:** 123/115. **Green Fee:** $17/$24. **Cart Fee:** $10/Person. **Walking Policy:** Unrestricted walking. **Walkability:** 3. **Opened:** 1976. **Season:** Year-round. **High:** April-Oct. **To obtain tee times:** Call golf shop. **Miscellaneous:** Reduced fees (weekdays, twilight, seniors, juniors), credit cards (MC, V, AE).

LAKE MALONEY GOLF COURSE
SP-608 Birdie Lane, North Platte, 69101, Lincoln County, (308)532-9998. **Facility Holes:** 18. **Yards:** 6,550/5,050. **Par:** 72/72. **Course Rating:** 72.6/70.1. **Slope:** 124/115. **Green Fee:** $9/$14. **Cart Fee:** $15/Cart. **Walking Policy:** Unrestricted walking. **Walkability:** 3. **Opened:** 1990. **Architect:** Bill Burns. **Season:** March-Nov. **High:** May-Aug. **To obtain tee times:** Call golf shop. **Miscellaneous:** Reduced fees (weekdays), range (grass/mats).

LAKESIDE COUNTRY CLUB
PU-74839 Hwy. 283, Elwood, 68937, Gosper County, (308)785-2818, 40 miles from Kearney. **Facility Holes:** 18. **Yards:** 6,200/5,200. **Par:** 72/72. **Course Rating:** 70.0/67.2. **Slope:** 115/115. **Green Fee:** $15/$25. **Cart Fee:** $20/Cart. **Walking Policy:** Unrestricted walking. **Walkability:** 4. **Opened:** 1961. **Architect:** Marty Johnson. **Season:** Year-round. **High:** May-Oct. **To obtain tee times:** Call golf shop. **Miscellaneous:** Reduced fees (juniors), range (grass), credit cards (MC, V, D), BF, FF.

LEGENDS BUTTE GOLF CLUB
PU-W. Highway 20, Crawford, 69339, Dawes County, (308)665-2431. **Facility Holes:** 9. **Yards:** 3,178/2,461. **Par:** 36/36. **Course Rating:** 70.4/67.4. **Slope:** 125/110. **Green Fee:** $16/$17. **Cart Fee:** $15/Cart. **Walking Policy:** Unrestricted walking. **Walkability:** 3. **Opened:** 1992. **Season:** March-Nov. **High:** June-Aug. **To obtain tee times:** Call golf shop. **Miscellaneous:** Range (grass), credit cards (MC, V, D, Novus), BF, FF.

LOGAN VALLEY GOLF COURSE
SP-Rte. 1, Wakefield, 68784, Wayne County, (402)287-2343, 80 miles from Omaha. **Facility Holes:** 9. **Yards:** 5,973/5,496. **Par:** 72/76. **Course Rating:** 67.7/67.7. **Slope:** 105/105. **Green Fee:** $7. **Cart Fee:** $16/Cart. **Walking Policy:** Unrestricted walking. **Walkability:** 3. **Opened:** 1932. **Architect:** Wilbar Peterson. **Season:** March-Oct. **High:** June-Aug. **To obtain tee times:** Call golf shop. **Miscellaneous:** Range (grass/mats), BF, FF.

★★ MAHONEY GOLF COURSE
PU-7900 Adams St., Lincoln, 68507, Lancaster County, (402)441-8969, 40 miles from Omaha. **Facility Holes:** 18. **Yards:** 6,459/5,582. **Par:** 70/72. **Course Rating:** 69.9/72.6. **Slope:** 113/120. **Green Fee:** $14/$18. **Cart Fee:** $12/Person. **Walking Policy:** Unrestricted walking. **Walkability:** 3. **Opened:** 1975. **Architect:** Floyd Farley. **High:** June-Aug. **To obtain tee times:**

Call golf shop. **Miscellaneous:** Reduced fees (twilight, seniors, juniors), metal spikes, range (grass/mats), credit cards (MC, V, AE, D).

★★★½ MEADOWLARK HILLS GOLF COURSE
PU-3300 30th Ave., Kearney, 68845, Buffalo County, (308)233-3265, 120 miles from Lincoln. **E-mail:** mhills@nebi.com. **Web:** www.meadowlark.nebi.com. **Facility Holes:** 18. **Yards:** 6,485/4,967. **Par:** 71/72. **Course Rating:** 70.4/68.2. **Slope:** 119/112. **Green Fee:** $14/$20. **Cart Fee:** $12/Person. **Walking Policy:** Unrestricted walking. **Walkability:** 5. **Opened:** 1994. **Architect:** David Gill/Steven Halberg. **Season:** Year-round. **High:** May-Aug. **To obtain tee times:** Call golf shop. **Miscellaneous:** Reduced fees (weekdays, seniors, juniors), range (grass/mats), credit cards (MC, V), BF, FF.
Reader Comments: Imaginative hilly layout … Great muni course … Course is so well maintained, it's hard to believe its a municipal course … Excellent variety of holes … Long par 3s … Priced right … Nice view of Platte River Valley.

★★½ MIRACLE HILL GOLF & TENNIS CENTER
PU-1401 N. 120th St., Omaha, 68154, Douglas County, (402)498-0220. **Facility Holes:** 18. **Yards:** 6,412/5,069. **Par:** 70/70. **Course Rating:** 71.0/69.0. **Slope:** 129/117. **Green Fee:** $20/$29. **Cart Fee:** $22/Cart. **Walking Policy:** Unrestricted walking. **Walkability:** 3. **Opened:** 1960. **Architect:** Floyd Farley. **Season:** Year-round. **To obtain tee times:** Call up to 7 days in advance. **Miscellaneous:** Reduced fees (twilight, seniors), range (grass/mats), credit cards (MC, V), BF, FF.

OAKLAND GOLF CLUB
SP-100 Parsons St., Oakland, 68045, Burt County, (402)685-5339, 50 miles from Omaha. **Facility Holes:** 18. **Yards:** 6,446/5,262. **Par:** 72/72. **Course Rating:** 70.5/69.8. **Slope:** 119/117. **Green Fee:** $16/$20. **Walkability:** 1. **Opened:** 1959. **Architect:** Jim White. **To obtain tee times:** Call golf shop. **Miscellaneous:** Reduced fees (weekdays).

★★½ THE PINES COUNTRY CLUB
SP-7516 N. 286th St., Valley, 68064, Douglas County, (402)359-4311, 30 miles from Omaha. **Facility Holes:** 18. **Yards:** 6,629/5,190. **Par:** 72/72. **Course Rating:** 72.1/70.2. **Slope:** 121/116. **Green Fee:** $16/$28. **Cart Fee:** $11/Person. **Walking Policy:** Unrestricted walking. **Walkability:** 1. **Opened:** 1979. **Architect:** Bill Kubly. **Season:** March-Oct. **High:** May-Aug. **To obtain tee times:** Call golf shop. **Miscellaneous:** Reduced fees (weekdays, seniors, juniors), range (grass/mats), credit cards (MC, V), BF, FF.

★★★ PIONEERS GOLF COURSE
PU-3403 W. Van Dorn, Lincoln, 68522, Lancaster County, (402)441-8966, 2 miles from Lincoln. **Facility Holes:** 18. **Yards:** 6,478/5,771. **Par:** 71/74. **Course Rating:** 69.2/73.2. **Slope:** 110/114. **Green Fee:** $13/$16. **Cart Fee:** $20/Cart. **Walking Policy:** Unrestricted walking. **Walkability:** 3. **Opened:** 1930. **Architect:** W. H. Tucker. **Season:** Year-round. **To obtain tee times:** Call up to 7 days in advance. **Miscellaneous:** Reduced fees (weekdays, twilight, seniors, juniors), range (grass), credit cards (MC, V), BF, FF.
Reader Comments: Beautiful, mature course … Well maintained … Nice elevation changes … Greens & fairways nice, very slow, lots of golfers on the older course … Could be great … Great layout … Excellent muni, easy to get on.

PLAYER'S CLUB AT DEER CREEK
SP-12101 Deer Creek Dr., Omaha, 68142, Douglas County, (402)963-9950, 2 miles from Omaha. **Web:** www.playersclubomaha.com. **Facility Holes:** 18. **Yards:** 7,088/5,277. **Par:** 71/71. **Course Rating:** 74.1/65.1. **Slope:** 140/116. **Green Fee:** $27/$62. **Cart Fee:** Included in green fee. **Walking Policy:** Walking at certain times. **Walkability:** 3. **Opened:** 2000. **Architect:** Arnold Palmer. **Season:** Year-round. **High:** April-Aug. **Tee times:** Call up to 7 days ahead **Misc:** Reduced fees (weekdays, twilight, seniors, juniors), credit cards (MC, V, AE), FF.

★★★ QUAIL RUN GOLF COURSE
PU-327 S. 5th St., Columbus, 68601, Platte County, (402)564-1313, 80 miles from Omaha. **E-mail:** jdgolf@quailrungolf.com. **Web:** www.quailrungolf.com. **Facility Holes:** 18. **Yards:** 7,024/5,147. **Par:** 72/72. **Course Rating:** 73.4/70.1. **Slope:** 127/114. **Green Fee:** $15/$19. **Cart Fee:** $11/Person. **Walking Policy:** Unrestricted walking. **Walkability:** 1. **Opened:** 1991. **Architect:** Frank Hummel. **Season:** April-Oct. **High:** May-Aug. **To obtain tee times:** Call golf shop. **Miscellaneous:** Reduced fees (weekdays, twilight, seniors, juniors), range (grass/mats), credit cards (MC, V), BF, FF.
Reader Comments: Very challenging 18 holes for the average golfer … Very busy at times, but always an enjoyable experience … Nice scenic view by the river, big cotton woods … Great holes on back 9 … under new management in 2002.

★★★½ QUARRY OAKS GOLF CLUB

PU-16600 Quarry Oaks Dr., Ashland, 68003-3820, Cass County, (402)944-6000, (888)944-6001, 25 miles from Omaha. **Web:** www.quarryoaks.com. **Facility Holes:** 18. **Yards:** 7,077/5,378. **Par:** 72/72. **Course Rating:** 73.2/70.0. **Slope:** 135/131. **Green Fee:** $40/$50. **Cart Fee:** $12/Person. **Walking Policy:** Unrestricted walking. **Walkability:** 5. **Opened:** 1997. **Architect:** John LaFoy. **Season:** March-Nov. **To obtain tee times:** Call up to 7 days in advance. **Miscellaneous:** Reduced fees (weekdays, twilight, seniors, juniors), range (grass), credit cards (MC, V, AE, D), FF.
Notes: Ranked 7th in 2001 Best in State; 1st Best New Affordable Public Course of 1997.
Reader Comments: This is a beautiful golf course … Very nice, in an unexpected setting in Nebraska … Work a little bit on drainage and overall course condition, and this will be a keeper … Breathtaking views … Long and narrow fairways … 17th hole is best hole in midwest.

★★½ RIVERVIEW GOLF & COUNTRY CLUB

PU-100928 CR 19, Scottsbluff, 69361, Scotts Bluff County, (308)635-1555, 200 miles from Denver. **Facility Holes:** 18. **Yards:** 6,024/5,598. **Par:** 70/74. **Course Rating:** 68.1/70.7. **Slope:** 116/120. **Green Fee:** $13. **Cart Fee:** $14/Cart. **Walking Policy:** Unrestricted walking. **Walkability:** 1. **Opened:** 1941. **Season:** Year-round. **To obtain tee times:** Call golf shop. **Miscellaneous:** Range (grass), credit cards (MC, V, D), BF, FF.

ROLLING GREEN GOLF CLUB

PU-400 S. Walsh St., Morrill, 69358, Scotts Bluff County, (308)247-2817, 180 miles from Denver. **Facility Holes:** 9. **Yards:** 3,186/2,767. **Par:** 36/38. **Course Rating:** 69.0/68.7. **Slope:** 106/111. **Green Fee:** $10. **Cart Fee:** $14/Cart. **Walking Policy:** Unrestricted walking. **Walkability:** 3. **Season:** Year-round. **High:** June-Aug. **To obtain tee times:** Call golf shop. **Miscellaneous:** Range (grass), FF.

SKYVIEW GOLF COURSE

PU-2613 CR 57, Alliance, 69301, Box Butte County, (308)762-1446, 45 miles from Scottsbluff. **Facility Holes:** 18. **Yards:** 6,501/5,364. **Par:** 70/72. **Course Rating:** 70.0/70.6. **Slope:** 112/115. **Green Fee:** $15/$17. **Cart Fee:** $7/Person. **Walking Policy:** Unrestricted walking. **Walkability:** 2. **Opened:** 1953. **Architect:** Henry B. Hughes. **High:** April-Oct. **To obtain tee times:** Call golf shop. **Miscellaneous:** Reduced fees (juniors), range (grass), BF, FF.

SOUTHERN HILLS GOLF COURSE

SP-3005 S. Southern Hills Dr., Hastings, 68901, Adams County, (402)463-8006, 150 miles from Omaha. **Facility Holes:** 18. **Yards:** 6,351/5,195. **Par:** 72/72. **Course Rating:** 70.7/69.6. **Slope:** 127/116. **Green Fee:** $14. **Cart Fee:** $17/Person. **Walking Policy:** Unrestricted walking. **Walkability:** 4. **To obtain tee times:** Call golf shop. **Miscellaneous:** Range (grass).

STONE CREEK GOLF CLUB

PU-6220 N. 160th Ave., Omaha, 68116, Douglas County, (402)965-9000. **Facility Holes:** 27. **Green Fee:** $12/$26. **Cart Fee:** $13/Person. **Walking Policy:** Unrestricted walking. **Walkability:** 3. **Opened:** 2000. **Architect:** Grant Wentzel. **Season:** Year-round. **High:** April-Sept. **Tee times:** Call up to 7 days in advance. **Miscellaneous:** Range (grass), credit cards (MC, V, AE), BF, FF.
BLACKSTONE/SANDSTONE (18)
Yards: 6,320/4,623. **Par:** 72/72. **Course Rating:** 70.5. **Slope:** 127.
GREYSTONE/BLACKSTONE (18)
Yards: 6,273/4,590. **Par:** 72/72. **Course Rating:** 70.6/64.2. **Slope:** 127/110.
SANDSTONE/GREYSTONE (18)
Yards: 6,247/4,543. **Par:** 72/72. **Course Rating:** 70.1. **Slope:** 127.

TARA HILLS GOLF COURSE

PU-1410 Western Hills Dr., Papillion, 68046, Sarpy County, (402)592-7550, 2 miles from Omaha. **E-mail:** joeostrem@alwaysgolfing.com. **Facility Holes:** 18. **Yards:** 6,160/4,879. **Par:** 70/72. **Course Rating:** 69.0/68.8. **Slope:** 120/118. **Green Fee:** $17/$22. **Cart Fee:** $10/Person. **Walking Policy:** Unrestricted walking. **Walkability:** 1. **Opened:** 1981. **Architect:** Wyss Associates. **Season:** March-Oct. **High:** March-Oct. **Tee times:** Call up to 6 days in advance. **Miscellaneous:** Reduced fees (weekdays, seniors, juniors), credit cards (MC, V), BF, FF.

★★★½ TIBURON GOLF CLUB

SP-10302 S. 168th St., Omaha, 68136, Sarpy County, (402)895-2688. **E-mail:** info@tiburongolf.com. **Web:** www.tiburongolf.com. **Facility Holes:** 27. **Green Fee:** $22/$29. **Cart Fee:** $12/Person. **Walking Policy:** Walking at certain times. **Walkability:** 3. **Opened:** 1989. **Architect:** Dave Bennett/Larry Hagewood. **Season:** Year-round. **High:** April-Sept. **To obtain tee times:** Call up to 7 days in advance. **Miscellaneous:** Reduced fees (weekdays, twilight, seniors, juniors), range (grass/mats), credit cards (MC, V, AE, D), BF, FF.

GREAT WHITE/HAMMERHEAD (18)
Yards: 7,005/5,435. **Par:** 72/72. **Course Rating:** 74.1/72.0. **Slope:** 131/127.
MAKO/GREAT WHITE (18)
Yards: 6,932/5,410. **Par:** 72/72. **Course Rating:** 73.3/71.8. **Slope:** 130/126.
MAKO/HAMMERHEAD (18)
Yards: 6,887/5,335. **Par:** 72/72. **Course Rating:** 73.4/71.0. **Slope:** 131/126.
Reader Comments: Enjoyable from the time you drive through the gates until the second you leave … Red is my least favorite but the best for my scores—go figure! … Play the original 18 holes, the 'new nine' is too short … Longer players MUST play the back tees … Best greens in area.

★★★ **TREGARON GOLF COURSE**
PU-13909 Glen Garry Circle, Bellevue, 68123, Sarpy County, (402)292-9300, 3 miles from Omaha. **E-mail:** tregaron@radtics.net. **Web:** www.tregarongolf.com. **Facility Holes:** 18. **Yards:** 6,508/4,417. **Par:** 71/71. **Course Rating:** 70.9/65.1. **Slope:** 122/104. **Green Fee:** $15/$25. **Cart Fee:** $10/Person. **Walking Policy:** Unrestricted walking. **Walkability:** 4. **Opened:** 1997. **Architect:** Craig Schreiner. **Season:** Year-round. **High:** April-Nov. **To obtain tee times:** Call up to 7 days in advance. **Miscellaneous:** Reduced fees (weekdays, twilight, seniors, juniors), credit cards (MC, V, AE), BF, FF.
Reader Comments: A good course … Pace of play a problem … Very short, some nice holes … Open layout … Links style … Good food … New course, improving yearly … Avoid windy days.

VALLEY VIEW GOLF COURSE
PU-1126 CR X, Fremont, 68025, Saunders County, (402)721-7772. **Facility Holes:** 18. **Yards:** 5,295/4,982. **Par:** 71/71. **Course Rating:** 64.6/67.9. **Slope:** 108/116. **Green Fee:** $15/$17. **Cart Fee:** $18/Cart. **Walking Policy:** Unrestricted walking. **Walkability:** 4. **Opened:** 1960. **Season:** March-Nov. **To obtain tee times:** Call golf shop. **Miscellaneous:** Range (grass/mats).

VAN BERG GOLF COURSE
PU-Pawnee Park, Rt. 4, Columbus, 68601, Platte County, (402)564-0761, 75 miles from Omaha. **E-mail:** jdgolf@quailrungolf.com. **Facility Holes:** 9. **Yards:** 2,905/2,455. **Par:** 36/36. **Course Rating:** 64.0/64.0. **Slope:** 99/99. **Green Fee:** $11/$15. **Cart Fee:** $11/Person. **Walking Policy:** Unrestricted walking. **Walkability:** 1. **Opened:** 1923. **Season:** Year-round. **High:** May-Aug. **To obtain tee times:** Call up to 3 days in advance. **Miscellaneous:** Reduced fees (weekdays, twilight, seniors, juniors), FF.

WAYNE COUNTRY CLUB
PU-RR #2, Wayne, 68787, Wayne County, (402)375-1152, 100 miles from Omaha. **Facility Holes:** 18. **Yards:** 6,315/5,500. **Par:** 72/72. **Course Rating:** 70.1/71.7. **Slope:** 113/117. **Green Fee:** $18/$22. **Cart Fee:** $16/Cart. **Walking Policy:** Unrestricted walking. **Walkability:** 3. **Season:** April-Oct. **High:** June-July. **Tee times:** Call golf shop. **Miscellaneous:** Range, BF, FF.

★★★★½ **WILD HORSE GOLF CLUB** *Value+, Condition, Pace*
SP-41150 Rd. 768, Gothenburg, 69138, Dawson County, (308)537-7700, 45 miles from North Platte. **Facility Holes:** 18. **Yards:** 6,805/4,688. **Par:** 72/72. **Course Rating:** 73.0/71.7. **Slope:** 125/123. **Green Fee:** $30/$33. **Cart Fee:** $10/Person. **Walking Policy:** Unrestricted walking. **Walkability:** 3. **Opened:** 1999. **Architect:** Dan Proctor/Dave Axland. **Season:** March-Oct. **To obtain tee times:** Call golf shop. **Miscellaneous:** Reduced fees (juniors), range (grass), credit cards (MC, V, D), BF, FF.
Notes: Ranked 3rd in 2001 Best in State; 3rd in 1999 Best New Affordable Public.
Reader Comments: No trees, no water, but you better stay in the fairway … Fastest greens I played on all season … Greens take some getting used to, but they putt true … Tough course … What a treat! … The greens are like billiard tables … We loved every minute … Outstanding links.

WILDWOOD GOLF COURSE
PU-1101 Wildwood Lane, Nebraska City, 68410, Otoe County, (402)873-3661, 45 miles from Omaha. **Facility Holes:** 9. **Yards:** 6,100/5,254. **Par:** 72/72. **Course Rating:** 69.4/69.6. **Slope:** 119/118. **Green Fee:** $14/$18. **Cart Fee:** $10/Person. **Walking Policy:** Unrestricted walking. **Opened:** 1972. **Season:** March-Nov. **High:** June-Aug. **To obtain tee times:** Call golf shop. **Miscellaneous:** Reduced fees (juniors), range (grass), credit cards (MC, V).

WILLOW LAKES GOLF COURSE
PU-Bldg. 9950 Offutt AFB, 25th St., Bellevue, 68113, Sarpy County, (402)292-1680, 10 miles from Omaha. **Facility Holes:** 18. **Yards:** 6,850/5,504. **Par:** 72/72. **Course Rating:** 72.8/71.5. **Slope:** 128/125. **Green Fee:** $14/$22. **Cart Fee:** $8/Person. **Walking Policy:** Unrestricted walking. **Walkability:** 2. **Opened:** 1962. **Architect:** Robert Trent Jones. **Season:** March-Nov. **High:** May-Aug. **To obtain tee times:** Call golf shop. **Miscellaneous:** Reduced fees (twilight, seniors), metal spikes, range (mats), credit cards (MC, V).

NEBRASKA

★★★★½ **WOODLAND HILLS GOLF COURSE** *Service, Value+, Pace+*
PU-6000 Woodland Hills Dr., Eagle, 68347, Otoe County, (402)475-4653, 12 miles from Lincoln. **E-mail:** woodland@direcpc.com. **Web:** www.woodlandhillsgolf.com. **Facility Holes:** 18.
Yards: 6,592/4,945. **Par:** 71/71. **Course Rating:** 72.6/70.3. **Slope:** 132/122. **Green Fee:** $15/$35. **Cart Fee:** $13/Person. **Walking Policy:** Unrestricted walking. **Walkability:** 3. **Opened:** 1991. **Architect:** Jeffrey D. Brauer. **Season:** Year-round. **High:** June-Aug. **To obtain tee times:** Call up to 7 days in advance. **Miscellaneous:** Reduced fees (weekdays, twilight, seniors, juniors), range (grass), credit cards (MC, V, AE, D), BF, FF.
Reader Comments: We love playing on this course … Feels like you are in another part of country … Lots of pine trees and water … I have played many of the 5-star courses and this is as good if not better … This is one to remember … Fun and women friendly … Lots of pine trees and water.

YORK COUNTRY CLUB
SP-W. Elm St., York, 68467, York County, (402)362-3721. **Facility Holes:** 18. **Yards:** 5,975/5,100. **Par:** 70/70. **Course Rating:** 68.9/69.8. **Slope:** 125/118. **Green Fee:** $20/$35. **Cart Fee:** $10/Person. **Walking Policy:** Unrestricted walking. **Walkability:** 3. **Opened:** 1919. **Season:** Year-round. **High:** April-Sept. **To obtain tee times:** Call up to 7 days in advance.
Miscellaneous: Range (grass), credit cards (MC, V), BF, FF.

NEVADA

ANGEL PARK GOLF CLUB
PU-100 S. Rampart Blvd., Las Vegas, 89145, Clark County, (702)254-4653, (888)446-5358, 5 miles from Las Vegas. **Web:** www.angelpark.com. **Facility Holes:** 48. **Green Fee:** $65/$155. **Cart Fee:** Included in green fee. **Walking Policy:** Mandatory carts. **Walkability:** 3. **Opened:** 1989. **Architect:** Arnold Palmer/Ed Seay/Bob Cupp. **Season:** Year-round. **To obtain tee times:** Call up to 60 days in advance. **Miscellaneous:** Reduced fees (weekdays, twilight, juniors), range (grass/mats), credit cards (MC, V, AE, D, DC), BF, FF.
★★★ **MOUNTAIN COURSE** (18)
Yards: 6,722/5,164. **Par:** 71/72. **Course Rating:** 72.4/69.9. **Slope:** 128/119.
Reader Comments: Solid golf experience … Beautiful course, excellent greens … Greens break toward the Stratosphere … Scenic views … Rather golf than gamble.
★★★ **PALM COURSE** (18)
Yards: 6,530/4,570. **Par:** 70/70. **Course Rating:** 70.9/66.2. **Slope:** 129/111.
Reader Comments: A joy to play … A bit pricey … Clubhouse employees are always looking to help … Comfortable resort course … Fun for average golfer.
Special Notes: Also has a 12-hole short course.

★★★★½ **ARROWCREEK GOLF CLUB**
PU-2905 ArrowCreek Pkwy., Reno, 89511, Sparks County, (775)850-4653, 10 miles from Downtown Reno. **Web:** www.arrowhead.com. **Facility Holes:** 36. **Yards:** 7,115/5,007. **Par:** 72/72. **Course Rating:** 74.0/68.6. **Slope:** 135/126. **Green Fee:** $30/$90. **Cart Fee:** Included in green fee. **Walking Policy:** Mandatory carts. **Walkability:** 4. **Opened:** 1999. **Architect:** Arnold Palmer/Ed Seay. **Season:** Year-round. **High:** April-Sept. **To obtain tee times:** Call up to 60 days in advance. **Miscellaneous:** Reduced fees (weekdays, twilight), range (grass/mats), credit cards (MC, V, AE), BF, FF.
Reader Comments: Great view of Truckee Meadows … Very good greens … Fun course to play … Not easily walkable … True mountain course … Lots of blind shots … Very tough for high handicappers … Watch out for snakes.
Special Notes: Also has a members only Challenge Course.

★★★★ **THE BADLANDS GOLF CLUB**
R-9119 Alta Dr., Las Vegas, 89145, Clark County, (702)242-4653, 10 miles from Las Vegas. **Web:** www.americangolf.com. **Facility Holes:** 27. **Green Fee:** $60/$225. **Cart Fee:** Included in green fee. **Walking Policy:** Mandatory carts. **Walkability:** 5. **Opened:** 1995. **Architect:** Johnny Miller. **Season:** Year-round. **Tee times:** Call up to 60 days in advance. **Miscellaneous:** Reduced fees (weekdays, twilight), range (grass/mats), credit cards (MC, V, AE, D), BF, FF.
DESPERADO/DIABLO (18 Combo)
Yards: 6,926/5,221. **Par:** 72/72. **Course Rating:** 73.8/71.0. **Slope:** 134/132.
DESPERADO/OUTLAW (18 Combo)
Yards: 6,602/5,037. **Par:** 72/72.
DIABLO/OUTLAW (18 Combo)
Yards: 6,802/5,066. **Par:** 72/72. **Course Rating:** 72.7/70.1. **Slope:** 129/126.
Reader Comments: Be accurate, or pay the price … Beautiful definition between course & desert … A tough, tough course when the wind blows … Hard! hard! hard! … Too expensive, but worth it once… Lots of carries over canyons … Fantastic layout … Use your irons … Difficult layout.

BALI HAI GOLF CLUB
PU-5160 Las Vegas Blvd., Las Vegas, 89119, Clark County, (702)597-2400, (888)397-2499. **E-mail:** sahern@waltersgolf.com. **Web:** www.waltersgolf.com. **Facility Holes:** 18. **Yards:** 7,002/5,535. **Par:** 71/71. **Course Rating:** 73.0/71.5. **Slope:** 130/121. **Green Fee:** $169/$325. **Cart Fee:** Included in green fee. **Walking Policy:** Walking with Caddie. **Walkability:** 3. **Opened:** 2000. **Architect:** Schmit/Curly. **Season:** Year-round. **High:** Jan.-June. **To obtain tee times:** Call up to 180 days in advance. **Miscellaneous:** Reduced fees (weekdays, twilight), range (mats), caddies, credit cards (MC, V, AE, D, DC), BF, FF.

★★½ **BLACK MOUNTAIN GOLF & COUNTRY CLUB**
SP-500 Greenway Rd., Henderson, 89015, Clark County, (702)565-7933, 15 miles from Las Vegas. **E-mail:** golfbmtn@aol.com. **Web:** www.golfblackmountain.com. **Facility Holes:** 18. **Yards:** 6,541/5,478. **Par:** 72/72. **Course Rating:** 71.2/71.6. **Slope:** 123/120. **Green Fee:** $40/$100. **Cart Fee:** Included in green fee. **Walking Policy:** Mandatory carts. **Walkability:** 2. **Opened:** 1959. **Architect:** Bob Baldock. **Season:** Year-round. **To obtain tee times:** Call golf shop. **Miscellaneous:** Reduced fees (twilight, seniors, juniors), range (grass/mats), credit cards (MC, V, AE), BF, FF.

★★★ **BOULDER CITY GOLF CLUB**
PU-1 Clubhouse Dr., Boulder City, 89005, Clark County, (702)293-9236, 20 miles from Las Vegas. **Facility Holes:** 18. **Yards:** 6,561/5,566. **Par:** 72/72. **Course Rating:** 70.2/70.7. **Slope:** 110/113. **Green Fee:** $25/$35. **Cart Fee:** $10/Person. **Walking Policy:** Unrestricted walking. **Walkability:** 2. **Opened:** 1972. **Architect:** David Rainville/Billy Casper. **Season:** Year-round.

NEVADA

High: Sept.-May. **To obtain tee times:** Call golf shop. **Miscellaneous:** Reduced fees (twilight, juniors), range (grass/mats), credit cards (MC, V), BF, FF.

Reader Comments: Best value in Vegas area … Excellent municipal … Back 9 really nice … Tight, tough, short laid back trees … What a pleasant surprise, tough on a windy day … Cheap for Vegas.

CHIMNEY ROCK MUNICIPAL GOLF COURSE
PU-144 Ventosa Ave., Wells, 89835, Elko County, (775)752-3928. **E-mail:** golf@rabbitbrush.com. **Facility Holes:** 9. **Yards:** 6,118/5,510. **Par:** 70/74. **Course Rating:** 67.0/70.8. **Slope:** 109/115. **Green Fee:** $16. **Cart Fee:** $18/Cart. **Walking Policy:** Unrestricted walking. **Walkability:** 2. **Opened:** 1978. **Season:** April-Nov. **To obtain tee times:** Call golf shop. **Miscellaneous:** Reduced fees (juniors), range (grass), credit cards (MC, V), BF, FF.

★½   CRAIG RANCH GOLF COURSE
PU-628 W. Craig Rd., North Las Vegas, 89030, Clark County, (702)642-9700. **Facility Holes:** 18. **Yards:** 6,001/5,221. **Par:** 70/70. **Course Rating:** 66.8/67.4. **Slope:** 105/101. **Green Fee:** $17. **Cart Fee:** $8/Person. **Walking Policy:** Unrestricted walking. **Walkability:** 1. **Opened:** 1962. **Architect:** John F. Stimson/John C. Stimson. **Season:** Year-round. **High:** March-Nov. **To obtain tee times:** Call golf shop. **Miscellaneous:** Metal spikes, range (grass).

D'ANDREA GOLF AND COUNTRY CLUB
SP-2351 N. D'Andrea Pkwy., Sparks, 89434, Washoe County, (775)331-6363, 10 miles from Reno. **Facility Holes:** 18. **Yards:** 6,849/5,162. **Par:** 71/71. **Course Rating:** 71.8/69.2. **Slope:** 129/123. **Green Fee:** $25/$85. **Cart Fee:** Included in green fee. **Walking Policy:** Walking at certain times. **Walkability:** 5. **Opened:** 2000. **Architect:** Keith Foster. **Season:** Year-round. **High:** March-Oct. **To obtain tee times:** Call up to 7 days in advance. **Miscellaneous:** Reduced fees (weekdays, twilight, juniors), range (grass/mats), credit cards (MC, V, AE, D), BF, FF.

★★★★   DAYTON VALLEY GOLF CLUB *Pace*
SP-51 Palmer Dr., Dayton, 89403, Lyon County, (775)246-7888, (800)644-3822, 35 miles from Reno. **E-mail:** golfdvgc@aol.com. **Web:** www.daytonvalley.com. **Facility Holes:** 18. **Yards:** 7,218/5,161. **Par:** 72/72. **Course Rating:** 74.2/68.4. **Slope:** 143/121. **Green Fee:** $30/$85. **Cart Fee:** Included in green fee. **Walking Policy:** Unrestricted walking. **Walkability:** 2. **Opened:** 1991. **Architect:** Arnold Palmer/Ed Seay. **Season:** Year-round. **High:** May-Oct. **To obtain tee times:** Call up to 14 days in advance. **Miscellaneous:** Reduced fees (weekdays, twilight), range (grass), credit cards (MC, V), BF, FF.

Reader Comments: Good value … Getting better with age … Middle of nowhere, but well kept … Bring a shovel, lots of sand! … Nice views … Water on 13 holes.

★★★★   DESERT INN GOLF CLUB *Service*
R-3145 Las Vegas Blvd. S., Las Vegas, 89109, Clark County, (702)733-4290. **E-mail:** kgraves@wynnresort.com. **Web:** www.thedesertinn.com. **Facility Holes:** 18. **Yards:** 7,066/5,791. **Par:** 72/72. **Course Rating:** 73.9/72.7. **Slope:** 124/121. **Green Fee:** $160/$225. **Cart Fee:** Included in green fee. **Walking Policy:** Mandatory carts. **Walkability:** 1. **Opened:** 1952. **Architect:** Lawrence Hughes. **Season:** Year-round. **High:** Jan.-June. **To obtain tee times:** Call up to 180 days in advance. **Miscellaneous:** Reduced fees (twilight), metal spikes, range (grass), credit cards (MC, V, AE, D).

Reader Comments: Historic course, but expensive … Play it before its gone, this course is set to be completely rebuilt at the end of the 2002 season … Well worth the cost … Excellent course, facility & great staff! … A classic, timeless test.

★★   DESERT LAKES GOLF COURSE
PU-4000 Farm District Rd., Fernley, 89408, Lyon County, (775)575-4653, 35 miles from Reno. **Facility Holes:** 18. **Yards:** 6,507/5,197. **Par:** 71/71. **Course Rating:** 69.9/68.3. **Slope:** 124. **Green Fee:** $20/$35. **Cart Fee:** Included in green fee. **Walking Policy:** Unrestricted walking. **Walkability:** 2. **Opened:** 1996. **Architect:** Bob Bingham. **Season:** Year-round. **High:** March-Oct. **To obtain tee times:** Call golf shop. **Miscellaneous:** Reduced fees (weekdays, twilight, seniors, juniors), metal spikes, range (grass), credit cards (MC, V).

★★½   DESERT PINES GOLF CLUB
PU-3415 E. Bonanza Ave., Las Vegas, 89101, Clark County, (702)388-4400, (888)397-2499. **E-mail:** awright@waltersgolf.com. **Web:** www.waltersgolf.com. **Facility Holes:** 18. **Yards:** 6,810/5,873. **Par:** 71/71. **Course Rating:** 70.4/69.4. **Slope:** 122/116. **Green Fee:** $70/$129. **Cart Fee:** Included in green fee. **Walking Policy:** Mandatory carts. **Walkability:** 3. **Opened:** 1996. **Architect:** Perry Dye. **Season:** Year-round. **To obtain tee times:** Call golf shop. **Miscellaneous:** Reduced fees (weekdays, twilight), range (mats), credit cards (MC, V, AE, DC), BF, FF.

★½ DESERT ROSE GOLF COURSE
PU-5483 Clubhouse Dr., Las Vegas, 89142, Clark County, (702)431-4653, 6 miles from Las Vegas. **Facility Holes:** 18. **Yards:** 6,511/5,458. **Par:** 71/71. **Course Rating:** 70.7/69.6. **Slope:** 112/107. **Green Fee:** $51/$75. **Cart Fee:** Included in green fee. **Walking Policy:** Unrestricted walking. **Walkability:** 3. **Opened:** 1962. **Architect:** Dick Wilson/Jeff Brauer. **Season:** Year-round. **High:** Sept.-June. **To obtain tee times:** Call golf shop. **Miscellaneous:** Reduced fees (twilight, seniors, juniors), metal spikes, range (grass/mats), credit cards (MC, V, AE, D).

EAGLE VALLEY GOLF COURSE
PU-3999 Centennial Park Dr., Carson City, 89706, Carson County, (775)887-2380, 30 miles from Reno. **Facility Holes:** 36. **Architect:** Homer Flint. **Season:** Year-round. **High:** May-Sept. **To obtain tee times:** Call golf shop. **Miscellaneous:** Reduced fees (twilight), BF, FF.

★★ EAST COURSE (18)
Yards: 6,658/5,980. **Par:** 72/72. **Course Rating:** 68.7/72.8. **Slope:** 117/123. **Green Fee:** $18. **Walking Policy:** Walking at certain times. **Walkability:** 2. **Opened:** 1977. **Miscellaneous:** Range (grass), credit cards (MC, V).

★★★ WEST COURSE (18)
Yards: 6,851/5,293. **Par:** 72/72. **Course Rating:** 73.5/68.8. **Slope:** 131/117. **Green Fee:** $27/$38. **Cart Fee:** $18/Cart. **Walking Policy:** Mandatory carts. **Walkability:** 5. **Opened:** 1987. **Miscellaneous:** Range (grass/mats).
Reader Comments: Outstanding muni … Good value for the dollar … Yardage not marked well … Hard to tell where some greens were located.

★★★★ EDGEWOOD TAHOE GOLF COURSE *Service, Pace*
PU-180 Lake Pkwy., Stateline, 89449, Douglas County, (775)588-3566, 50 miles from Reno. **E-mail:** randy@edgewood-tahoe.com. **Web:** www.edgewood-tahoe.com. **Facility Holes:** 18. **Yards:** 7,470/5,547. **Par:** 72/72. **Course Rating:** 75.7/71.3. **Slope:** 139/136. **Green Fee:** $200. **Cart Fee:** Included in green fee. **Walking Policy:** Unrestricted walking. **Walkability:** 2. **Opened:** 1968. **Architect:** George Fazio/Tom Fazio. **Season:** May-Oct. **High:** July-Sept. **Tee times:** Call up to 90 days in advance. **Misc:** Range (grass/mats), credit cards (MC, V, AE), BF, FF.
Notes: Ranked 99th in 1999-2000 America's 100 Greatest; 4th in 2001 Best in State; 37th in 1996 America's Top 75 Upscale Courses.
Reader Comments: Incredible scenery … Love the large pine trees … Don't pass this one up! … Excellent experience … 16, 17 and 18 alone are worth the green fee … A course with caddies … Beautiful shoreline setting at Lake Tahoe … Pace of play could improve … Large, undulating greens with sweeping breaks make it an interesting course … Beautiful, excellent condition.

★★★ EMERALD RIVER GOLF COURSE
PU-1155 W. Casino Dr., Laughlin, 89029, Clark County, (702)298-0061, 90 miles from Las Vegas. **Facility Holes:** 18. **Yards:** 6,572/5,230. **Par:** 72/72. **Course Rating:** 73.6/71.3. **Slope:** 144/129. **Green Fee:** $40/$75. **Cart Fee:** Included in green fee. **Walking Policy:** Mandatory carts. **Walkability:** 4. **Opened:** 1990. **Architect:** Tom Clark. **Season:** Year-round. **To obtain tee times:** Call golf shop. **Miscellaneous:** Reduced fees (weekdays, guests, twilight, seniors), metal spikes, range (grass), credit cards (MC, V, AE, D), BF, FF.
Reader Comments: This is one to play, you won't forget it … Keep it on the fairway if you can … Great desert course, good condition … The wind always blows … Tough greens … A real challenge for middle handicaps.

★★★ EMPIRE RANCH GOLF COURSE
PU-1875 Fair Way, Carson City, 89701, Carson County, (775)885-2100, (888)227-1335, 3 miles from Carson City. **E-mail:** prosho@empireranchgolf.com. **Web:** www.empireranchgolf.com. **Facility Holes:** 27. **Green Fee:** $25/$40. **Cart Fee:** Included in green fee. **Walking Policy:** Walking at certain times. **Walkability:** 3. **Opened:** 1997. **Architect:** Cary Bickler. **Season:** Year-round. **Tee times:** Call golf shop. **Miscellaneous:** Reduced fees (weekdays, twilight, seniors, juniors), range (grass), credit cards (MC, V), BF, FF.

BLUE/RED (18 Combo)
Yards: 6,603/4,719. **Par:** 72/72. **Course Rating:** 70.5/67.4. **Slope:** 127/118.
BLUE/WHITE (18 Combo)
Yards: 6,763/4,883. **Par:** 72/72. **Course Rating:** 71.6/68.1. **Slope:** 129/119.
RED/WHITE (18 Combo)
Yards: 6,840/4,854. **Par:** 72/72. **Course Rating:** 71.3/68.3. **Slope:** 128/123.
Reader Comments: Tough greens … Very nice golf course … 27 holes with a good practice facility … Not difficult, but well conditioned and interesting … Lots of look-a-like holes.

FALLON GOLF COURSE
PU-2655 Country Club Dr., Fallon, 89406, Churchill County, (775)423-4616. **Facility Holes:** 9. **Yards:** 6,254/5,360. **Par:** 70/70. **Course Rating:** 68.9/69.0. **Slope:** 121/115. **Green Fee:** $12. **Opened:** 1958. **Season:** Year-round. **To obtain tee times:** Call golf shop.

★★★★ THE GOLF CLUB AT GENOA LAKES
PU-1 Genoa Lakes Dr., Genoa, 89411, Douglas County, (775)782-4653, 15 miles from So. Lake Tahoe. **E-mail:** info@genoalakes.com. **Web:** www.genoalakes.com. **Facility Holes:** 18. **Yards:** 7,263/5,008. **Par:** 72/72. **Course Rating:** 73.5/67.6. **Slope:** 134/117. **Green Fee:** $45/$105. **Cart Fee:** Included in green fee. **Walking Policy:** Unrestricted walking. **Walkability:** 2. **Opened:** 1993. **Architect:** John Harbottle/Peter Jacobsen. **Season:** Year-round. **High:** June-Oct. **To obtain tee times:** Call up to 30 days in advance. **Miscellaneous:** Reduced fees (weekdays, twilight, juniors), range (grass), credit cards (MC, V, AE, D), BF, FF.
Notes: Ranked 10th in 2001 Best in State; 54th in 1996 America's Top 75 Upscale Courses.
Reader Comments: Conditioning is consistently excellent ... Great course for the price ... Must be long to score ... A wonderful golf experience ... The best in Reno area ... Play early to beat the wind ... Abundance of wildlife ... Very helpful staff. Descriptive play book.

THE GOLF COURSES AT INCLINE VILLAGE
PU-955 Fairway Blvd., Incline Village, 89451, Washoe County, (775)832-1146, (888)236-8725, 30 miles from Reno. **Web:** www.golfincline.com. **Cart Fee:** Included in green fee. **Walking Policy:** Unrestricted walking. **Season:** May-Oct. **To obtain tee times:** Call up to 14 days in advance. **Miscellaneous:** Reduced fees (twilight), credit cards (MC, V, AE), FF.
★★★★ CHAMPIONSHIP COURSE (18)
Yards: 6,931/5,245. **Par:** 72/72. **Course Rating:** 72.2/69.2. **Slope:** 133/128. **Green Fee:** $35/$125. **Walkability:** 4. **Opened:** 1964. **Architect:** Robert Trent Jones. **Miscellaneous:** Range (mats), BF.
Notes: Ranked 8th in 1999 Best in State.
Reader Comments: Worth the money ... Setting takes off the edge ... Need to adjust club selection for the altitude ... Blind shots-narrow-beautiful scenery.
MOUNTAIN COURSE (18)
Yards: 3,513/3,002. **Par:** 58/58. **Course Rating:** 56.6/57.3. **Slope:** 94/85. **Green Fee:** $25/$50. **Walkability:** 5. **Opened:** 1969. **Architect:** Robert Trent Jones, Jr.

HUNEWILL'S MASON VALLEY COUNTRY CLUB
SP-111 Hwy. 208, Yerington, 89447, Lyon County, (775)463-3300. **Facility Holes:** 18. **Yards:** 6,638/5,854. **Par:** 72/72. **Course Rating:** 69.2/71.0. **Slope:** 118/115. **Green Fee:** $24/$26. **Opened:** 1964. **Season:** Year-round. **To obtain tee times:** Call golf shop.

★★½ JACKPOT GOLF CLUB
R-P.O. Box 370, Jackpot, 89825, Elko County, (775)755-2260, 165 miles from Boise. **Facility Holes:** 18. **Yards:** 6,934/5,590. **Par:** 72/72. **Course Rating:** 69.4/69.3. **Slope:** 111/108. **Green Fee:** $15/$18. **Cart Fee:** $10/Person. **Walking Policy:** Walking at certain times. **Walkability:** 4. **Opened:** 1970. **Architect:** Robert Muir Graves. **Season:** March-Nov. **High:** May-Sept. **To obtain tee times:** Call golf shop. **Miscellaneous:** Reduced fees (weekdays, juniors), range (grass), credit cards (MC, V).

★★★★½ LAKE LAS VEGAS RESORT *Condition+, Pace*
R-75 MonteLago Blvd., Henderson, 89011, Clark County, (702)740-4653, (877)698-4653, 17 miles from Las Vegas Strip. **Web:** www.lakelasvegas.com. **Facility Holes:** 18. **Yards:** 7,261/5,166. **Par:** 72/72. **Course Rating:** 74.8/70.0. **Slope:** 138/127. **Green Fee:** $200/$250. **Cart Fee:** Included in green fee. **Walking Policy:** Mandatory carts. **Walkability:** 5. **Opened:** 1998. **Architect:** Jack Nicklaus. **Season:** Year-round. **High:** Jan.-May. **To obtain tee times:** Call up to 30 days in advance. **Miscellaneous:** Reduced fees (twilight), range (grass), lodging (496 rooms), credit cards (MC, V, AE), BF, FF.
Notes: Ranked 5th in 2001 Best in State; 6th in 1999 Best New Upscale Public.
Reader Comments: A must play ... First-class resort track ... A great course, but get out your wallet ... Finishing holes are superb! ... Always in perfect condition.

★★★½ LAKE RIDGE GOLF COURSE
PU-1200 Razorback Rd., Reno, 89509, Washoe County, (775)825-2200, (800)815-6999. **E-mail:** lakeridge@golf.reno.nv.us. **Web:** www.lakeridgegolf.com. **Facility Holes:** 18. **Yards:** 6,703/5,159. **Par:** 71/71. **Course Rating:** 72.3/68.5. **Slope:** 137/117. **Green Fee:** $45/$88. **Cart Fee:** Included in green fee. **Walking Policy:** Walking at certain times. **Walkability:** 4. **Opened:** 1969. **Architect:** Robert Trent Jones. **Season:** March-Dec. **High:** April-Oct. **To obtain tee times:** Call up to 7 days in advance. **Miscellaneous:** Reduced fees (twilight), metal spikes, range (mats), credit cards (MC, V, AE), BF, FF.
Reader Comments: Very hilly, especially back 9 ... Stands the test of time as the best in Reno ... A treat to play ... Island 15th hole is worth the round ... Nice layout, fun course to play ... Good value, open but tricky ... Excellent greens.

★★½ LAS VEGAS GOLF CLUB

PU-4300 W. Washington, Las Vegas, 89107, Clark County, (702)646-3003. **E-mail:** lvgolfclub@visto.com. **Web:** www.americangolf.com. **Facility Holes:** 18. **Yards:** 6,631/5,715. **Par:** 72/72. **Course Rating:** 71.8/71.2. **Slope:** 117/113. **Green Fee:** $49/$109. **Cart Fee:** $18/Cart. **Walking Policy:** Unrestricted walking. **Walkability:** 2. **Opened:** 1947. **Architect:** William P. Bell. **Season:** Year-round. **High:** Sept.-May. **Tee times:** Call golf shop. **Miscellaneous:** Reduced fees (twilight, seniors, juniors), range (grass/mats), credit cards (MC, V, AE, D), BF, FF.

★★½ LAS VEGAS NATIONAL GOLF CLUB

R-1911 E. Desert Inn Rd., Las Vegas, 89109, Clark County, (702)734-1796, (800)468-7918. **Facility Holes:** 18. **Yards:** 6,815/5,741. **Par:** 71/71. **Course Rating:** 72.1/69.5. **Slope:** 130/103. **Green Fee:** $50/$225. **Cart Fee:** Included in green fee. **Walking Policy:** Mandatory carts. **Walkability:** 1. **Opened:** 1961. **Architect:** Bert Stamps. **Season:** Year-round. **High:** Jan.-April. **To obtain tee times:** Call golf shop. **Miscellaneous:** Reduced fees (weekdays, guests, twilight, juniors), range (grass/mats), credit cards (MC, V, AE, D, DC), BF, FF.

LAS VEGAS PAIUTE RESORT

PU-10325 Nu-Wav Kaiv Blvd., Las Vegas, 89124, Clark County, (702)658-1400, (800)711-2833. **E-mail:** teeup@lvpaiutegolf.com. **Web:** www.lvpaiutegolf.com. **Facility Holes:** 36. **Green Fee:** $60/$160. **Cart Fee:** Included in green fee. **Walking Policy:** Mandatory carts. **Walkability:** 3. **Architect:** Pete Dye. **Season:** Year-round. **To obtain tee times:** Call up to 60 days in advance. **Miscellaneous:** Reduced fees (weekdays, twilight), range (grass), credit cards (MC, V, AE, D), FF.

★★★★½ **NU-WAV KAIV COURSE (SNOW MOUNTAIN)** (18) *Condition+*
Yards: 7,158/5,341. **Par:** 72/72. **Course Rating:** 73.9/70.4. **Slope:** 125/117. **Opened:** 1995. **Notes:** Ranked 8th in 1997 Best in State.
Reader Comments: A great layout in superb condition … Tough water carries … You get your money's worth and then some … Much better than most Las Vegas courses that charge more … Clubhouse has a spectacular view of the two courses … Nice mountain views … Want to come back!!! … Out in the middle of nowhere.

★★★★ **TAV-AI KAIV COURSE (SUN MOUNTAIN)** (18) *Condition*
Yards: 7,112/5,465. **Par:** 72/72. **Course Rating:** 73.3/71.0. **Slope:** 130/123. **Opened:** 1997.
Reader Comments: Perhaps the best course value in Vegas … A very nice golf experience … A bit overrated … It's a hike from the Strip … Will use all your clubs … Tough desert track.

★★★ THE LEGACY GOLF CLUB

PU-130 Par Excellence Dr., Henderson, 89014, Clark County, (702)897-2187, (888)446-5358, 10 miles from Las Vegas. **E-mail:** info@thelegacygolf.com. **Web:** www.thelegacygc.com. **Facility Holes:** 18. **Yards:** 7,233/5,340. **Par:** 72/72. **Course Rating:** 74.9/71.0. **Slope:** 136/120. **Green Fee:** $135. **Cart Fee:** Included in green fee. **Walking Policy:** Mandatory carts. **Opened:** 1989. **Architect:** Arthur Hills. **Season:** Year-round. **High:** Sept.-June. **To obtain tee times:** Call golf shop. **Miscellaneous:** Reduced fees (weekdays, twilight, juniors), range (grass/mats), credit cards (MC, V, AE, DC), BF, FF.
Reader Comments: Solid course, try it … Good layout, but pace of play a little slow … Homes too tight to the course.

★★★★ MOJAVE RESORT GOLF CLUB

PU-9905 Aha Macav Pkwy., Laughlin, 89029, Clark County, (702)535-4653. **Web:** www.mojaveresort.com. **Facility Holes:** 18. **Yards:** 6,939/5,520. **Par:** 72/72. **Course Rating:** 73.2/72.3. **Slope:** 126/124. **Green Fee:** $45/$75. **Cart Fee:** Included in green fee. **Walking Policy:** Mandatory carts. **Walkability:** 2. **Opened:** 1997. **Architect:** Landmark Golf Company. **Season:** Year-round. **To obtain tee times:** Call up to 30 days in advance. **Miscellaneous:** Reduced fees (guests, twilight, seniors), range (grass), credit cards (MC, V, AE, D), BF, FF.
Reader Comments: Beautiful hotel course … Water holes are challenging and fun to play … Beautiful in winter … Great reason to get away from the tables in Laughlin.

★★½ NORTHGATE GOLF COURSE

PU-1111 Clubhouse Dr., Reno, 89523, Washoe County, (775)747-7577, 5 miles from Reno. **Facility Holes:** 18. **Yards:** 6,966/5,521. **Par:** 72/72. **Course Rating:** 72.3/70.2. **Slope:** 131/127. **Green Fee:** $33/$58. **Cart Fee:** Included in green fee. **Walking Policy:** Unrestricted walking. **Walkability:** 5. **Opened:** 1988. **Architect:** Benz/Poellot. **Season:** Year-round. **To obtain tee times:** Call golf shop. **Miscellaneous:** Reduced fees (weekdays, guests, twilight), range (grass/mats), credit cards (MC, V, AE), BF, FF.

THE OASIS GOLF CLUB

SP-100 Palmer Lane, Mesquite, 89027, Clark County, (702)346-7820, 85 miles from Las Vegas. **Web:** www.theoasisgolfclub.com. **Facility Holes:** 27. **Cart Fee:** Included in green fee. **Walking Policy:** Mandatory carts. **Season:** Year-round. **High:** Jan.-May. **Tee times:** Call up to

60 days in advance. **Miscellaneous:** Range (grass), credit cards (MC, V, AE, D), FF.
★★★★ **OASIS COURSE** (18)
Yards: 6,737/4,513. **Par:** 71/71. **Course Rating:** 73.2/65.7. **Slope:** 141/110. **Green Fee:** $55/$135. **Walkability:** 5. **Opened:** 1995. **Architect:** Arnold Palmer/Ed Seay. **Miscellaneous:** Reduced fees (twilight).
Notes: Ranked 9th in 2001 Best in State; 5th in 1995 Best New Resort Courses.
Reader Comments: Incredible views … Pricey, but worth it … The best overall golf experience I have had in Nevada … Mountain views and elevation changes on the back nine are spectacular … A must play … Some breathtaking holes.
VISTAS COURSE (9)
Yards: 3,524/3,636. **Par:** 37/37. **Course Rating:** 72.0/60.7. **Slope:** 131/110. **Walkability:** 3. **Opened:** 1997.

★★★ **PAINTED DESERT GOLF CLUB**
R-5555 Painted Mirage Way, Las Vegas, 89129, Clark County, (702)645-2570. **Facility Holes:** 18. **Yards:** 6,840/5,711. **Par:** 72/72. **Course Rating:** 73.7/72.7. **Slope:** 136/127. **Green Fee:** $45/$140. **Cart Fee:** Included in green fee. **Walking Policy:** Mandatory carts. **Opened:** 1987. **Architect:** Jay Morrish. **Season:** Year-round. **High:** Sept.-June. **To obtain tee times:** Call golf shop. **Miscellaneous:** Reduced fees (weekdays, guests, twilight, juniors), range (grass/mats), credit cards (MC, V, AE), BF, FF.
Reader Comments: Target golf at its finest … Mundane layout … Good value in this resort town … Nice desert track.

PALM VALLEY GOLF COURSE
SP-9201 Del Webb Blvd., Las Vegas, 89134, Clark County, (702)363-4373. **Facility Holes:** 18. **Yards:** 6,849/5,502. **Par:** 72/72. **Course Rating:** 72.3/70.7. **Slope:** 127/119. **Green Fee:** $42/$101. **Cart Fee:** Included in green fee. **Walkability:** 3. **Architect:** Greg Nash/Billy Casper. **Season:** Oct.-Sept. **High:** Oct.-May. **To obtain tee times:** Call golf shop. **Miscellaneous:** Range (grass/mats), credit cards (MC, V, AE, D).

PALMS GOLF COURSE
R-711 Palms Blvd., Mesquite, 89027, Clark County, (800)621-0187, (800)621-0187, 85 miles from Las Vegas. **E-mail:** kent@oasis-resort.com. **Facility Holes:** 18. **Yards:** 7,008/5,016. **Par:** 72/72. **Course Rating:** 74.9/70.4. **Slope:** 137/122. **Green Fee:** $55/$110. **Cart Fee:** Included in green fee. **Walking Policy:** Mandatory carts. **Walkability:** 4. **Opened:** 1990. **Architect:** William Hull. **Season:** Year-round. **High:** Oct.-May. **To obtain tee times:** Call up to 60 days in advance. **Miscellaneous:** Reduced fees (guests, twilight), range (grass), lodging (1000 rooms), credit cards (MC, V, AE, D, DC), FF.

PRIMM VALLEY GOLF CLUB
R-1 Yates Well Rd., Primm, 89019, Clark County, (702)679-5510, (800)386-7867, 40 miles from Las Vegas. **Facility Holes:** 36. **Green Fee:** $55/$195. **Cart Fee:** Included in green fee. **Walking Policy:** Unrestricted walking. **Walkability:** 3. **Architect:** Tom Fazio. **Season:** Year-round. **To obtain tee times:** Call up to 60 days in advance. **Miscellaneous:** Reduced fees (weekdays, guests), range (grass), credit cards (MC, V, AE, D, DC), BF, FF.
★★★★½ **DESERT COURSE** (18) *Condition, Pace*
Yards: 7,131/5,397. **Par:** 72/72. **Course Rating:** 74.6/72.1. **Slope:** 138/124. **Opened:** 1998.
Notes: Ranked 25th in 1999 Best in State.
Reader Comments: One of the best golf courses I ever played … I was treated like a king … We played in the offseason so it was pretty inexpensive. I played 36 holes in 115 degrees and was ready for more. Excellent course and very challenging … A must play … What a deal! Stay & play package … A jewel in a big desert.
★★★★½ **LAKES COURSE** (18) *Condition*
Yards: 6,945/5,019. **Par:** 71/71. **Course Rating:** 74.0/69.1. **Slope:** 134/118. **Opened:** 1997.
Notes: Ranked 24th in 1999 Best in State.
Reader Comments: Service outstanding! Taken care of the minute you arrive … Every amenity that you could imagine … Great Fazio course … Both courses provide great golf at great prices. One of the best values in America. You can frolic at one of the Primm resorts and drive to the Strip in Las Vegas in less than 45 minutes.

RED HAWK GOLF CLUB
R-6600 N. Wingfield Pkwy., Sparks, 89436, Washoe County, (775)626-6000, 12 miles from Reno. **E-mail:** lanef@wingfieldsprings.com. **Web:** www.wingfieldsprings.com. **Facility Holes:** 36. **Green Fee:** $55/$95. **Cart Fee:** Included in green fee. **Walking Policy:** Unrestricted walking. **Walkability:** 3. **Opened:** 1997. **Architect:** Robert Trent Jones Jr. **Season:** Year-round. **High:** April-Oct. **To obtain tee times:** Call up to 6 days in advance. **Miscellaneous:** Reduced fees (weekdays, twilight, juniors), range (grass), credit cards (MC, V, AE), BF, FF.
★★★½ **LAKES COURSE** (18)
Yards: 7,127/5,115. **Par:** 72/72. **Course Rating:** 72.9/69.2. **Slope:** 137/125.

NEVADA

Reader Comments: Long irons a must … Memorable guest service … Consistent green speed … Pro shop has excellent staff … Great practice facility … Interesting wind factor … Overpriced, but always in superb condition.
Special Notes: Also has 18-hole putting course.

★★★ THE REVERE AT ANTHEM
PU-2600 Evergreen Oaks, Henderson, 89052, Clark County, (702)259-4653, (877)273-8373, 15 miles from Las Vegas. E-mail: villanoj@delwebb.com. Web: www.revereatanthem.com. Facility Holes: 18. Yards: 7,143/5,305. Par: 72/72. Course Rating: 73.6/73.5. Slope: 139/122. Green Fee: $85/$185. Cart Fee: Included in green fee. Walking Policy: Walking at certain times. Walkability: 4. Opened: 1999. Architect: Billy Casper/Greg Nash. Season: Year-round. To obtain tee times: Call up to 60 days in advance. Miscellaneous: Reduced fees (twilight), range (grass), credit cards (MC, V, AE), BF, FF.
Reader Comments: Interesting canyons & arroyos … Great, tough layout in excellent condition … Challenges keep you pumped.

★★★½ RHODES RANCH COUNTRY CLUB
PU-20 Rhodes Ranch Pkwy., Las Vegas, 89113, Clark County, (702)740-4114, (888)311-8337. Web: www.rhodesranch.com. Facility Holes: 18. Yards: 6,909/5,238. Par: 72/72. Course Rating: 73.0/64.8. Slope: 122/110. Cart Fee: Included in green fee. Walking Policy: Unrestricted walking. Walkability: 2. Opened: 1997. Architect: Ted Robinson/Ted Robinson Jr. Season: Year-round. High: March-Nov. To obtain tee times: Call golf shop. Miscellaneous: Reduced fees (weekdays, twilight), range (grass/mats), credit cards (MC, V, D).
Reader Comments: Expensive, but flawless … Will surely play there again … Quick playing and friendly staff … Fairly easy track, nothing spectacular … Good par 3s.

RIO SECCO GOLF CLUB
R-2851 Grand Hills Dr., Henderson, 89052, Clark County, (702)889-2400, (888)867-3226. Web: www.playrio.com. Facility Holes: 18. Yards: 7,332/5,684. Par: 72/72. Course Rating: 75.7/70.0. Slope: 142/127. Green Fee: $125/$250. Cart Fee: Included in green fee. Walking Policy: Walking at certain times. Walkability: 5. Opened: 1997. Architect: Rees Jones. Season: Year-round. High: Feb.-May. Tee times: Call up to 90 days in advance. Misc: Reduced fees (guests), range (grass), caddies, credit cards (MC, V, AE, D), FF.
Notes: Ranked 6th in 2001 Best in State.

★★★ ROSEWOOD LAKES GOLF COURSE
PU-6800 Pembroke Dr., Reno, 89502, Washoe County, (775)857-2892, (888)236-8725. E-mail: rosewoodpro@aol.com. Web: www.rosewoodlakes.com. Facility Holes: 18. Yards: 6,693/5,073. Par: 72/72. Course Rating: 70.7/67.8. Slope: 125/118. Green Fee: $15/$36. Cart Fee: $22/Cart. Walking Policy: Unrestricted walking. Walkability: 2. Opened: 1991. Architect: Bradford Benz. Season: Year-round. To obtain tee times: Call up to 7 days in advance. Misc: Reduced fees (twilight, juniors), metal spikes, range (grass), credit cards (MC, V), BF, FF.
Reader Comments: One of Nevada's hidden gems … Lots of water parallels the fairways … Short course with decent greens … Great muni track.

★★★★ ROYAL LINKS GOLF CLUB *Service+, Pace*
PU-5995 E. Vegas Valley Rd., Las Vegas, 89142, Clark County, (702)450-8123, (888)427-6682, 5 miles from Las Vegas. E-mail: rrandall@waltersgolf.com. Web: www.walters-golf.com. Facility Holes: 18. Yards: 7,029/5,142. Par: 72/72. Course Rating: 73.7/69.8. Slope: 135/115. Green Fee: $195/$250. Cart Fee: Included in green fee. Walking Policy: Unrestricted walking. Walkability: 2. Opened: 1999. Architect: Perry Dye. Season: Year-round. To obtain tee times: Call golf shop. Miscellaneous: Reduced fees (weekdays, twilight), range (grass), caddies, credit cards (MC, V, AE, D), BF, FF.
Notes: Ranked 8th in 2001 Best in State.
Reader Comments: Resemblance to holes on famous courses in Scotland remarkable … Good layout and excellent service, but not deserving of the Pebble Beach type green fee … Lots of bunkers and they are deep! … A caddie is optional. Expensive … Fun alternative to a trip to Scotland.

★★★ RUBY VIEW GOLF COURSE
PU-2100 Ruby View Dr., Elko, 89801, Elko County, (775)777-7277. Web: golfelko.com. Facility Holes: 18. Yards: 6,945/5,332. Par: 71/72. Course Rating: 69.5/67.5. Slope: 118/117. Green Fee: $19/$22. Cart Fee: $22/Cart. Walking Policy: Unrestricted walking. Walkability: 2. Opened: 1967. Architect: Jack Snyder. Season: March-Nov. High: June-Aug. To obtain tee times: Call golf shop. Miscellaneous: Reduced fees (weekdays, seniors, juniors), range (grass), credit cards (MC, V).
Reader Comments: Good course, lush fairways … Outstanding for this country desert … Outstanding par 4s.

486

SHADOW CREEK GOLF CLUB
R-5400 Losee Rd., North Las Vegas, 89030, Clark County, (702)399-7111. **Facility Holes:** 18.
Yards: 7,100/5,985. **Par:** 72/72. **Course Rating:** 71.0/69.2. **Slope:** 115/114. **Opened:** 1990.
Architect: Tom Fazio/Andy Banfield. **Season:** Year-round. **To obtain tee times:** Call golf shop.
Notes: Ranked 31st in 2001-2002 America's 100 Greatest; 1st in 2001 Best in State.

SIENA GOLF CLUB
R-10575 Siena Monte Ave., Las Vegas, 89135, Clark County, (702)341-9200, (888)689-6469,
12 miles from Las Vegas. **Web:** www.sienagolfclub.com. **Facility Holes:** 18. **Yards:**
6,816/4,978. **Par:** 72/72. **Course Rating:** 71.5/68.0. **Slope:** 129/112. **Green Fee:** $90/$160. **Cart
Fee:** Included in green fee. **Walking Policy:** Mandatory carts. **Walkability:** 3. **Opened:** 2000.
Architect: Schmidt/Curley. **Season:** Year-round. **High:** Sept.-June. **To obtain tee times:** Call up
to 60 days in advance. **Miscellaneous:** Reduced fees (twilight, juniors), range (grass), credit
cards (MC, V, AE), BF, FF.

★★★★ SIERRA NEVADA GOLF RANCH *Pace*
PU-2901 Jacks Valley Rd., Genoa, 89411, Douglas County, (775)782-7700, (888)452-4653,
6 miles from Carson City. **Facility Holes:** 18. **Yards:** 7,358/5,129. **Par:** 72/72. **Course Rating:**
75.3/69.5. **Slope:** 137/119. **Green Fee:** $25/$100. **Cart Fee:** Included in green fee. **Walking
Policy:** Walking at certain times. **Walkability:** 5. **Opened:** 1998. **Architect:** Johnny Miller/John
Harbottle. **Season:** Year-round. **To obtain tee times:** Call golf shop. **Miscellaneous:** Reduced
fees (weekdays, twilight, juniors), range (grass), credit cards (MC, V, AE), BF, FF.
Reader Comments: A must play for Tahoe ... Holes literally cut out of the Sierras ... Great views of
Genoa Valley ... Excellent greens ... Bring your A game! ... Finishing holes superb ... Tremendous
service, good experience.

★★ SIERRA SAGE GOLF COURSE
PU-6355 Silverlake Rd., Reno, 89506, Washoe County, (775)972-1564, 12 miles from Reno.
Facility Holes: 19. **Yards:** 6,605/5,630. **Par:** 71/72. **Course Rating:** 70.4/70.3. **Slope:** 122/120.
Green Fee: $21/$27. **Cart Fee:** $11/Person. **Walking Policy:** Unrestricted walking. **Walkability:**
3. **Opened:** 1963. **Season:** Year-round. **High:** April-Oct. **To obtain tee times:** Call up to 3 days
in advance. **Miscellaneous:** Reduced fees (weekdays, twilight, seniors, juniors), range (grass),
credit cards (MC, V), BF, FF.
Special Notes: Has an additional par-3 hole after regulation 18.

★★½ SILVER OAK GOLF COURSE
PU-1251 Country Club Dr., Carson City, 89703, Carson County, (775)841-7000. **Facility
Holes:** 18. **Yards:** 6,564/4,725. **Par:** 71/72. **Course Rating:** 70.8/65.9. **Slope:** 130/116. **Green
Fee:** $30/$40. **Cart Fee:** Included in green fee. **Walking Policy:** Walking at certain times.
Walkability: 3. **Opened:** 1999. **Architect:** Tom Duncan/Sid Salomon. **Season:** Feb.-Nov. **High:**
April-Oct. **To obtain tee times:** Call up to 14 days in advance. **Miscellaneous:** Reduced fees
(twilight), range (grass), credit cards (MC, V), BF, FF.

SILVERSTONE GOLF CLUB
R-8317 Mt. Geneva Ct., Las Vegas, 89131, Clark County, (702)562-3770, (877)888-2127, 15
miles from Las Vegas Strip. **Web:** www.silverstonegolf.com. **Facility Holes:** 27. **Green Fee:**
$145/$180. **Cart Fee:** Included in green fee. **Walking Policy:** Mandatory carts. **Walkability:** 2.
Opened: 2001. **Architect:** Robert Cupp. **Season:** Year-round. **High:** Sept.-May. **To obtain tee
times:** Call up to 60 days in advance. **Miscellaneous:** Reduced fees (weekdays, twilight,
juniors), range (grass), credit cards (MC, V, AE, D), BF, FF.
DESERT/VALLEY (18 Combo)
Yards: 6,958/5,191. **Par:** 72/72. **Course Rating:** 72.4/69.0. **Slope:** 143/113.
MOUNTAIN/DESERT (18 Combo)
Yards: 7,159/5,282. **Par:** 72/72. **Course Rating:** 73.3/69.5. **Slope:** 145/114.
VALLEY/MOUNTAIN (18 Combo)
Yards: 6,997/5,241. **Par:** 72/72. **Course Rating:** 72.4/69.2. **Slope:** 140/114.

SPRING CREEK GOLF COURSE
PU-431 E. Spring Creek Pkwy., Elko, 89801, Elko County, (775)753-6331, 240 miles
from Salt Lake City. **Facility Holes:** 18. **Yards:** 6,258/5,658. **Par:** 71/71. **Course Rating:**
70.6/70.5. **Slope:** 125/119. **Green Fee:** $14/$16. **Walkability:** 5. **Season:** March-Nov. **High:**
June-Aug. **To obtain tee times:** Call golf shop. **Miscellaneous:** Range (grass/mats), credit
cards (MC, V).

SUN CITY LAS VEGAS GOLF CLUB
SP-10201 Sun City Blvd., Las Vegas, 89134, Clark County, (702)254-7010. **Web:** www.suncitygolf.com. **Facility Holes:** 36. **Green Fee:** $59/$101. **Cart Fee:** Included in green fee. **Walking
Policy:** Mandatory carts. **Architect:** Billy Casper/Greg Nash. **Season:** Year-round. **High:** Oct.-

May. **To obtain tee times:** Call golf shop. **Miscellaneous:** Reduced fees (twilight), range (grass/mats), credit cards (MC, V, AE, D).

HIGHLAND FALLS COURSE (18)
Yards: 6,512/5,099. **Par:** 72/72. **Course Rating:** 71.2/68.8. **Slope:** 126/110. **Walkability:** 3. **Opened:** 1993.

PALM VALLEY COURSE (18)
Yards: 6,849/5,502. **Par:** 72/72. **Course Rating:** 72.3/71.5. **Slope:** 127/124. **Walkability:** 2. **Opened:** 1989.

★★★ **SUNRISE VISTA GOLF CLUB**
M-2841 Kinley Dr., Nellis AFB, 89191, Clark County, (702)652-2602, 12 miles from Las Vegas. **Facility Holes:** 27. **Green Fee:** $35. **Cart Fee:** $9/Person. **Walking Policy:** Unrestricted walking. **Walkability:** 2. **Opened:** 1962. **Architect:** Ted Robinson. **Season:** Year-round. **High:** Sept.-April. **To obtain tee times:** Call golf shop. **Miscellaneous:** Range (grass/mats), credit cards (MC, V).

EAGLE/FALCON (18 Combo)
Yards: 7,200/5,380. **Par:** 72/72. **Course Rating:** 73.8. **Slope:** 127.

PHANTOM/EAGLE (18 Combo)
Yards: 7,102/5,460. **Par:** 72/72. **Course Rating:** 72.3/69.1. **Slope:** 119/109.

PHANTOM/FALCON (18 Combo)
Yards: 6,950/5,370. **Par:** 72/72. **Course Rating:** 71.8. **Slope:** 119.
Reader Comments: Limited access, good bargain ... Value golf in Vegas area ... Loud jet fighters.

★★★½ **TOANA VISTA GOLF COURSE**
PU-2319 Pueblo Blvd., P. O. Box 2290, Wendover, 89883, Elko County, (775)664-4300, (800)352-4330, 110 miles from Salt Lake City. **Facility Holes:** 18. **Yards:** 6,911/5,220. **Par:** 72/72. **Course Rating:** 72.6/71.0. **Slope:** 124/124. **Green Fee:** $40. **Cart Fee:** Included in green fee. **Walking Policy:** Mandatory carts. **Walkability:** 3. **Opened:** 1986. **Architect:** Homer Flint. **Season:** March-Nov. **High:** May-Sept. **To obtain tee times:** Call up to 14 days in advance. **Misc:** Reduced fees (guests, juniors), range (grass/mats), credit cards (MC, V), BF, FF.
Reader Comments: A jewel in the desert. Watch out for snakes and lizards! ... Narrow and tough putting ... Stop here! Play this one.

★★★★ **TOURNAMENT PLAYERS CLUB AT THE CANYONS** *Condition*
R-9851 Canyon Run Dr., Las Vegas, 89144, Clark County, (702)256-2000, 8.1 miles from Las Vegas. **E-mail:** jland@pgatourtpc.com. **Web:** www.pgatour.com. **Facility Holes:** 18. **Yards:** 7,063/5,039. **Par:** 71/71. **Course Rating:** 73.0/67.0. **Slope:** 131/109. **Green Fee:** $35/$235. **Cart Fee:** Included in green fee. **Walking Policy:** Walking at certain times. **Walkability:** 5. **Opened:** 1996. **Architect:** Bobby Weed/Raymond Floyd. **Season:** Year-round. **Tee times:** Call up to 180 days ahead. **Misc:** Reduced fees (juniors), range, credit cards (MC, V, AE, DC), BF, FF. **Notes:** Ranked 9th in 1999 Best in State.
Reader Comments: Great test of shotmaking ... This course is immaculate! ... Hilly, narrow fairways, good test for accuracy ... Not long enough for big hitters.

★★½ **WASHOE COUNTY GOLF CLUB**
PU-2601 S. Arlington, Reno, 89509, Washoe County, (775)828-6640, 3 miles from Reno (downtown). **Web:** www.washoegolf.com. **Facility Holes:** 18. **Yards:** 6,695/5,863. **Par:** 72/74. **Course Rating:** 70.0/72.9. **Slope:** 119/122. **Green Fee:** $21/$27. **Cart Fee:** $22/Cart. **Walking Policy:** Unrestricted walking. **Walkability:** 3. **Opened:** 1936. **Architect:** WPA. **Season:** Year-round. **High:** April-Sept. **To obtain tee times:** Call up to 10 days in advance. **Miscellaneous:** Reduced fees (twilight, seniors, juniors), range (mats), credit cards (MC, V), BF, FF.

★★ **WILD HORSE GOLF CLUB**
R-2100 Warm Springs Rd., Henderson, 89014, Clark County, (702)434-9000, (800)468-7918, 8 miles from Las Vegas. **E-mail:** lvwildhorse@yahoo.com. **Facility Holes:** 18. **Yards:** 7,053/5,372. **Par:** 72/72. **Course Rating:** 75.2/71.3. **Slope:** 135/125. **Green Fee:** $50/$140. **Cart Fee:** Included in green fee. **Walking Policy:** Mandatory carts. **Walkability:** 3. **Opened:** 1959. **Architect:** Bob Cupp/Hubert Green. **Season:** Year-round. **High:** Sept.-June. **To obtain tee times:** Call golf shop. **Miscellaneous:** Reduced fees (weekdays, guests, twilight, juniors), range (grass/mats), credit cards (MC, V, AE), BF, FF.

★★½ **WILDCREEK GOLF COURSE**
PU-3500 Sullivan Lane, Sparks, 89431, Washoe County, (775)673-3100, 1 mile from Reno. **E-mail:** wcnggolf@rscva.com. **Web:** www.wcnggolf@rscva.com. **Facility Holes:** 27. **Yards:** 6,932/5,472. **Par:** 72/72. **Course Rating:** 72.5/69.9. **Slope:** 133/127. **Green Fee:** $42/$60. **Cart Fee:** Included in green fee. **Walking Policy:** Mandatory carts. **Walkability:** 5. **Opened:** 1978. **Architect:** Benz/Phelps. **Season:** Year-round. **High:** April-Oct. **To obtain tee times:** Call golf shop. **Miscellaneous:** Reduced fees (twilight), range (grass), credit cards (MC, V), BF, FF. **Special Notes:** Also has a 9-hole par-3 course.

★★ WILLOW CREEK GOLF COURSE

PU-1500 Red Butte, Pahrump, 89048, Nye County, (775)727-4653, (877)779-4653, 60 miles from Las Vegas. **E-mail:** willowcreek@wizard.com. **Web:** www.wcgolf.com. **Facility Holes:** 18. **Yards:** 7,025/5,948. **Par:** 71/73. **Course Rating:** 73.2/74.3. **Slope:** 124/123. **Green Fee:** $25/$60. **Cart Fee:** Included in green fee. **Walking Policy:** Mandatory carts. **Walkability:** 2. **Opened:** 1978. **Architect:** William F. Bell. **Season:** Year-round. **High:** Oct.-April. **To obtain tee times:** Call up to 7 days in advance. **Miscellaneous:** Reduced fees (weekdays), range (grass/mats), credit cards (MC, V, AE), BF, FF.
Special Notes: Formerly Calvada Valley Golf & Country Club.

WOLF CREEK AT PARADISE CANYON

PU-401 Paradise Pkwy., Ste 20, Mesquite, 89027, Clark County, (702)346-9020, 80 miles from Las Vegas. **Facility Holes:** 18. **Yards:** 7,073/4,169. **Par:** 72/72. **Course Rating:** 75.4/61.0. **Slope:** 154/106. **Green Fee:** $150. **Cart Fee:** Included in green fee. **Walking Policy:** Mandatory carts. **Walkability:** 4. **Opened:** 2000. **Architect:** Dennis Rider. **Season:** Year-round. **High:** Jan.-June. **To obtain tee times:** Call up to 60 days in advance. **Miscellaneous:** Range (grass), credit cards (MC, V, AE, D), BF, FF.
Notes: Ranked 3rd in 2001 Best New Upscale Courses.

★★★½ WOLF RUN GOLF CLUB

SP-1400 Wolf Run Rd., Reno, 89511, Washoe County, (775)851-3301, 10 miles from Reno. **Facility Holes:** 18. **Yards:** 6,936/5,294. **Par:** 71/71. **Course Rating:** 72.1/69.7. **Slope:** 130/128. **Green Fee:** $20/$60. **Cart Fee:** $15/Person. **Walking Policy:** Unrestricted walking. **Walkability:** 3. **Opened:** 1998. **Architect:** John Fleming/Steve van Meter/Lou Eiguren. **Season:** Year-round. **High:** May-Sept. **Tee times:** Call up to 14 days in advance. **Miscellaneous:** Reduced fees (weekdays, twilight, seniors, juniors), range (grass/mats), credit cards (MC, V, AE), BF, FF.
Reader Comments: All clubs are used ... Great condition and a good variety of holes ... Hard course.

NEW HAMPSHIRE

★★★ AMHERST COUNTRY CLUB
PU-72 Ponemah Rd., Amherst, 03031, Hillsborough County, (603)673-9908, 10 miles from Nashua. **E-mail:** ddiskin@amherstcountryclub.com. **Web:** www.amherstcountryclub.com. **Facility Holes:** 18. **Yards:** 6,520/5,532. **Par:** 72/74. **Course Rating:** 71.0/74.2. **Slope:** 123/129. **Green Fee:** $32/$42. **Cart Fee:** $14/Person. **Walking Policy:** Unrestricted walking. **Walkability:** 2. **Opened:** 1965. **Architect:** William F. Mitchell. **Season:** March-Dec. **High:** June-Aug. **To obtain tee times:** Call up to 5 days in advance. **Miscellaneous:** Reduced fees (weekdays, twilight, seniors), range (grass/mats), credit cards (MC, V), BF, FF.
Reader Comments: Good layout, very accommodating ... Greens were in excellent condition ... Short but beautiful greens, friendly ... Improved over years.

ANDROSCOGGIN VALLEY COUNTRY CLUB
SP-2 Main Street, Gorham, 03581, Coos County, (603)466-9468, 22 miles from N. Conway. **Facility Holes:** 18. **Yards:** 5,764/4,808. **Par:** 70/70. **Course Rating:** 67.0/70.1. **Slope:** 114/118. **Green Fee:** $24/$28. **Cart Fee:** $25/Cart. **Walking Policy:** Unrestricted walking. **Walkability:** 1. **Opened:** 1922. **Season:** May-Oct. **To obtain tee times:** Call up to 2 days in advance. **Miscellaneous:** Reduced fees (weekdays, juniors), range (grass), lodging (150 rooms), credit cards (MC, V), BF, FF.

★★★★ THE BALSAMS GRAND RESORT HOTEL   *Service, Pace*
R-Rte. 26, Dixville Notch, 03576, Coos County, (603)255-4961, 110 miles from Manchester. **E-mail:** thebalsams@aol.com. **Web:** www.thebalsams.com. **Facility Holes:** 18. **Yards:** 6,804/5,069. **Par:** 72/72. **Course Rating:** 72.8/67.8. **Slope:** 130/115. **Green Fee:** $50/$60. **Cart Fee:** $18/Person. **Walking Policy:** Unrestricted walking. **Walkability:** 4. **Opened:** 1912. **Architect:** Donald Ross. **Season:** May-Oct. **High:** July-Sept. **To obtain tee times:** Call up to 3 days in advance. **Miscellaneous:** Reduced fees (guests, twilight), metal spikes, range (grass/mats), lodging (204 rooms), credit cards (MC, V, AE, D), BF, FF.
Notes: Ranked 3rd in 2001 Best in State.
Reader Comments: Resort is fantastic ... Spectacular views, great food ... Need a cart ... Favorite course in NH—360 degree view ... A Donald Ross mountain classic, great stay packages ... It's very hard to lose a ball ... Not long but greens are very hard to read.

★★★ BEAVER MEADOW GOLF CLUB
PU-1 Beaver Meadow Dr., Concord, 03301, Merrimack County, (603)228-8954. **E-mail:** deshaies@mediaone.net. **Facility Holes:** 18. **Yards:** 6,356/5,519. **Par:** 72/72. **Course Rating:** 70.0/71.8. **Slope:** 121/123. **Green Fee:** $28/$32. **Cart Fee:** $26/Cart. **Walking Policy:** Unrestricted walking. **Walkability:** 1. **Opened:** 1896. **Architect:** Geoffrey Cornish. **Season:** April-Nov. **High:** May-Sept. **To obtain tee times:** Call golf shop. **Miscellaneous:** Reduced fees (weekdays, twilight), range (grass/mats), credit cards (MC, V), BF, FF.
Reader Comments: The 'Beav' returns to its former position of a good, solid test at a bargain price ... Very friendly staff ... Always busy ... Good muni, nice greens ... No reserved tee times.

★★ BETHLEHEM COUNTRY CLUB
PU-1901 Main St., Rte. 302, Bethlehem, 03574, Grafton County, (603)869-5745, 80 miles from Concord. **Web:** www.bethlehemccnhgolf.com. **Facility Holes:** 18. **Yards:** 5,808/5,008. **Par:** 70/70. **Course Rating:** 68.2/67.8. **Slope:** 114/109. **Green Fee:** $25/$30. **Cart Fee:** $13/Person. **Walking Policy:** Unrestricted walking. **Walkability:** 1. **Opened:** 1898. **Architect:** Donald Ross. **Season:** May-Oct. **High:** July-Aug. **To obtain tee times:** Call golf shop. **Miscellaneous:** Reduced fees (weekdays, guests, twilight, juniors), range (grass), credit cards (MC, V), BF, FF.

BREAKFAST HILL GOLF CLUB
PU-339 Breakfast Hill Rd., Greenland, 03840, Rockingham County, (603)436-5001, 50 miles from Boston. **E-mail:** bhgc@ttlc.net. **Web:** www.breakfasthill.com. **Facility Holes:** 18. **Yards:** 6,469/4,983. **Par:** 71/71. **Course Rating:** 70.5/68.5. **Slope:** 133/120. **Green Fee:** $42/$50. **Cart Fee:** $12/Person. **Walking Policy:** Unrestricted walking. **Walkability:** 3. **Opened:** 2000. **Architect:** Brian Silva. **Season:** April-Dec. **High:** July-Aug. **To obtain tee times:** Call up to 5 days in advance. **Miscellaneous:** Reduced fees (weekdays, twilight), range (grass/mats), credit cards (MC, V, AE), BF, FF.

BRETWOOD GOLF COURSE
PU-East Surry Rd., Keene, 03431, Cheshire County, (603)352-7626. **Facility Holes:** 36. **Green Fee:** $29/$36. **Cart Fee:** $22/Cart. **Walking Policy:** Unrestricted walking. **Walkability:** 3. **Opened:** 1968. **Architect:** Geoffrey Cornish/Hugh Barrett. **Season:** April-Nov. **High:** May-Oct. **To obtain tee times:** Call golf shop. **Miscellaneous:** Metal spikes, range (grass), credit cards (MC, V, D), BF, FF.
   ★★★★ **NORTH COURSE** (18)
Yards: 6,974/5,140. **Par:** 72/72. **Course Rating:** 73.7/70.1. **Slope:** 136/120.

NEW HAMPSHIRE

Notes: Ranked 6th in 2001 Best in State.
Reader Comments: Great staff, good value, two good courses … Very pretty, nice scenery … Beautiful course! … Good warm up for South Course … Both courses are treasures … Great condition … Must be played when visiting New Hampshire.

★★★★ **SOUTH COURSE** (18)
Yards: 6,952/4,990. **Par:** 72/71. **Course Rating:** 73.3/70.0. **Slope:** 139/121.
Reader Comments: Tough par 3s, good value to play both … Longer than North, be ready for back 9! … 2 Great 18s—I wish it was closer.

★★★½ **CAMPBELL'S SCOTTISH HIGHLANDS GOLF COURSE**
PU-79 Brady Ave., Salem, 03079, Rockingham County, (603)894-4653, 30 miles from Boston. **Facility Holes:** 18. **Yards:** 6,249/5,056. **Par:** 71/71. **Course Rating:** 68.9/68.4. **Slope:** 124/114. **Green Fee:** $30/$38. **Cart Fee:** $12/Person. **Walking Policy:** Unrestricted walking. **Walkability:** 3. **Opened:** 1994. **Architect:** George F. Sargent & MHF Design. **Season:** March-Nov. **High:** June-Aug. **To obtain tee times:** Call up to 5 days in advance. **Miscellaneous:** Reduced fees (weekdays, twilight, seniors), range (grass/mats), credit cards (MC, V), BF, FF.
Reader Comments: Many interesting holes, hard to find … Short track … Rough too heavy for average player … Good links course … Slow pace of play … A fun course.

★★½ **CANDIA WOODS GOLF LINKS**
PU-313 S. Rd., Candia, 03034, Rockingham County, (603)483-2307, (800)564-4344, 10 miles from Manchester. **E-mail:** candiawds@aol.com. **Web:** www.candiawoods.com. **Facility Holes:** 18. **Yards:** 6,558/5,582. **Par:** 71/73. **Course Rating:** 70.9/71.7. **Slope:** 121/127. **Green Fee:** $35/$45. **Cart Fee:** $12/Person. **Walking Policy:** Unrestricted walking. **Walkability:** 3. **Opened:** 1964. **Architect:** Phil Wogan. **Season:** April-Nov. **High:** June-Sept. **To obtain tee times:** Call up to 5 days in advance. **Miscellaneous:** Reduced fees (weekdays, twilight, seniors, juniors), range (grass/mats), credit cards (MC, V, D), BF, FF.

★★★ **COUNTRY CLUB OF NEW HAMPSHIRE**
PU-Kearsarge Valley Rd., P.O. Box 142, North Sutton, 03260, Merrimack County, (603)927-4246, 30 miles from Concord. **E-mail:** ccnh@conknet.com. **Web:** www.playgolfnh.com. **Facility Holes:** 18. **Yards:** 6,743/5,416. **Par:** 72/72. **Course Rating:** 72.5/71.7. **Slope:** 134/127. **Green Fee:** $29/$36. **Cart Fee:** $13/Person. **Walking Policy:** Unrestricted walking. **Walkability:** 3. **Opened:** 1957. **Architect:** William F. Mitchell. **Season:** April-Nov. **High:** April-Aug. **To obtain tee times:** Call up to 7 days in advance. **Miscellaneous:** Reduced fees (weekdays, twilight), range (grass), lodging (28 rooms), credit cards (MC, V, AE, D), FF.
Notes: Ranked 10th in 2001 Best in State.
Reader Comments: For people who love a great course with varied holes that make you think … Scenery is great too … Excellent layout … Greens are good but slow … Course is very picturesque, needs better conditioning … Solid course that is overplayed.

DEN BRAE GOLF COURSE
PU-80 Prescott Rd., Sanborton, 03269, Belknap County, (603)934-9818, 18 miles from Concord. **Web:** www.denbrae.com. **Facility Holes:** 9. **Yards:** 6,040/5,326. **Par:** 72/72. **Course Rating:** 67.0/70.0. **Slope:** 112/123. **Green Fee:** $22/$24. **Cart Fee:** $20/Cart. **Walking Policy:** Unrestricted walking. **Walkability:** 3. **Opened:** 1958. **Season:** April-Nov. **To obtain tee times:** Call golf shop. **Miscellaneous:** Reduced fees (twilight, juniors), range (grass), credit cards (MC, V, AE), BF, FF.

★½ **DERRYFIELD COUNTRY CLUB**
PU-625 Mammoth Rd., Manchester, 03104, Hillsborough County, (603)669-0235. **E-mail:** ryangolf@juno.com. **Web:** www.derryfieldgolf.com. **Facility Holes:** 18. **Yards:** 6,100/5,535. **Par:** 70/74. **Course Rating:** 68.7/71.0. **Slope:** 113/125. **Green Fee:** $29. **Cart Fee:** $24/Cart. **Walking Policy:** Unrestricted walking. **Walkability:** 3. **Opened:** 1932. **Architect:** Wayne Stiles/John Van Kleek. **Season:** April-Nov. **High:** May-Sept. **To obtain tee times:** Call golf shop. **Miscellaneous:** Credit cards (MC, V).

★★★½ **EASTMAN GOLF LINKS**
SP-Clubhouse Lane, Grantham, 03753, Sullivan County, (603)863-4500, 43 miles from Concord. **Facility Holes:** 18. **Yards:** 6,731/5,499. **Par:** 71/73. **Course Rating:** 72.0/72.3. **Slope:** 131/120. **Green Fee:** $42. **Cart Fee:** $16/Person. **Walking Policy:** Walking at certain times. **Walkability:** 3. **Opened:** 1973. **Architect:** Geoffrey Cornish. **Season:** May-Nov. **High:** June-Sept. **To obtain tee times:** Call up to 2 days in advance. **Miscellaneous:** Reduced fees (juniors), range (grass/mats), credit cards (MC, V, AE), BF, FF.
Notes: Ranked 9th in 2001 Best in State.
Reader Comments: Fine layout in the hills of New Hampshire … Play was slow on the day we were there but enjoyed the golf course … Great golf course.

GREEN MEADOW GOLF CLUB
PU-59 Steele Rd., Hudson, 03051, Hillsborough County, (603)889-1555, 11 miles from Manchester. **Facility Holes:** 36. **Green Fee:** $30/$38. **Cart Fee:** $24/Cart. **Walking Policy:** Unrestricted walking. **Opened:** 1959. **Architect:** Philip Friel/David Friel. **Season:** March-Dec. **To obtain tee times:** Call golf shop. **Miscellaneous:** Reduced fees (weekdays, twilight, seniors, juniors), metal spikes, caddies, credit cards (MC, V, AE, D), BF, FF.
★★½ **THE JUNGLE** (18)
Yards: 6,940/5,352. **Par:** 72/72. **Course Rating:** 71.4/69.7. **Slope:** 122/114. **Walkability:** 3.
Miscellaneous: Range (grass/mats).
★★½ **THE PRAIRIE** (18)
Yards: 6,160/5,102. **Par:** 72/72. **Course Rating:** 68.2/66.6. **Slope:** 112/106. **Walkability:** 2.
Miscellaneous: Range (grass).

★★★ **HANOVER COUNTRY CLUB**
SP-Rope Ferry Rd., Hanover, 03755, Grafton County, (603)646-2000, 10 miles from Lebanon. **E-mail:** www.dartmouthedu~/hccweb/. **Facility Holes:** 18. **Yards:** 5,876/5,468. **Par:** 69/73. **Course Rating:** 68.7/72.7. **Slope:** 118/127. **Green Fee:** $31. **Cart Fee:** $14/Person. **Walking Policy:** Unrestricted walking. **Walkability:** 3. **Opened:** 1899. **Architect:** Barton/Smith/Cornish/Robinson. **Season:** April-Nov. **High:** June-Sept. **To obtain tee times:** Call golf shop. **Miscellaneous:** Reduced fees (twilight, juniors), range (grass), caddies, credit cards (MC, V, AE), BF, FF.
Reader Comments: Well maintained, play with a local ... Old time college course ready for renovation.

★★½ **HOOPER GOLF CLUB**
SP-Prospect Hill, Walpole, 03608, Cheshire County, (603)756-4080, 16 miles from Keene. **Facility Holes:** 9. **Yards:** 3,019/2,748. **Par:** 71/72. **Course Rating:** 69.3/73.5. **Slope:** 122/132. **Green Fee:** $25. **Cart Fee:** $25/Cart. **Walking Policy:** Unrestricted walking. **Walkability:** 3. **Opened:** 1927. **Architect:** Wayne Stiles/John Van Kleek. **Season:** April-Oct. **High:** July-Aug. **Miscellaneous:** Lodging (3 rooms), credit cards (MC, V), FF.

INDIAN MOUND GOLF CLUB
PU-Old Rte. 16, Center Ossipee, 03814, Carroll County, (603)539-7733. **Facility Holes:** 18. **Yards:** 5,675/4,713. **Par:** 70/70. **Course Rating:** 68.5/67.5. **Slope:** 118/117. **Green Fee:** $25/$36. **Cart Fee:** $22/Cart. **Walking Policy:** Unrestricted walking. **Walkability:** 3. **Opened:** 1972. **Architect:** Phil Wogan. **Season:** May-Nov. **High:** June-Sept. **To obtain tee times:** Call up to 7 days in advance. **Miscellaneous:** Reduced fees (twilight), credit cards (MC, V), BF, FF.

★★★½ **JACK O'LANTERN RESORT**
R-Rte. 3, Box A, Woodstock, 03292, Grafton County, (603)745-3636, 60 miles from Manchester. **Web:** www.jackolanternresort.com. **Facility Holes:** 18. **Yards:** 6,003/4,917. **Par:** 70/71. **Course Rating:** 68.6/67.5. **Slope:** 117/113. **Green Fee:** $38/$42. **Cart Fee:** $26/Cart. **Walking Policy:** Walking at certain times. **Walkability:** 1. **Opened:** 1947. **Architect:** Robert Keating. **Season:** May-Oct. **To obtain tee times:** Call golf shop. **Miscellaneous:** Reduced fees (weekdays, guests, twilight), lodging (96 rooms), credit cards (MC, V, AE, D).
Reader Comments: Some narrow fairways ... One of best in NH ... Staying in the condos and using this course daily is a benefit ... The course crosses train tracks and water comes into play at the oddest times.

★★★ **JOHN H. CAIN GOLF CLUB**
SP-Unity Rd., Newport, 03773, Sullivan County, (603)863-7787, 35 miles from Concord. **Web:** www.johncain.com. **Facility Holes:** 18. **Yards:** 6,415/4,738. **Par:** 71/71. **Course Rating:** 72.4/63.8. **Slope:** 134/112. **Green Fee:** $20/$34. **Cart Fee:** $24/Cart. **Walking Policy:** Unrestricted walking. **Walkability:** 2. **Opened:** 1920. **Architect:** Phil Wogan. **Season:** April-Nov. **High:** June-Oct. **To obtain tee times:** Call golf shop. **Miscellaneous:** Reduced fees (weekdays, twilight, seniors, juniors), range (grass/mats), credit cards (MC, V), BF, FF.
Reader Comments: Interesting layout ... Variety in hole design ... Enjoyable to play ... Good value—I would go back ... A little of everything, lots of water.

★★★½ **KEENE COUNTRY CLUB**
SP-755 W. Hill Rd., Keene, 03431, Cheshire County, (603)352-9722, 60 miles from Manchester. **Facility Holes:** 18. **Yards:** 6,200/5,900. **Par:** 72/75. **Course Rating:** 69.0/72.2. **Slope:** 124/130. **Green Fee:** $88. **Cart Fee:** Included in green fee. **Walking Policy:** Mandatory carts. **Walkability:** 3. **Opened:** 1900. **Architect:** Wayne Stiles. **Season:** May-Oct. **High:** June-Sept. **To obtain tee times:** Call golf shop. **Miscellaneous:** Range (grass), credit cards (MC, V, AE), BF, FF.
Reader Comments: Treated well by all, expensive ... Back 9 beautiful ... Very friendly pro and staff ... Excellent course, not too hilly for area.

KINGSTON FAIRWAYS GOLF CLUB
PU-65 Depot Road - Route 107, Kingston, 03848, Rockingham County, (603)642-7722, 8 miles from Exeter. **Facility Holes:** 18. **Yards:** 5,800/5,100. **Par:** 70/69. **Course Rating:** 71.1. **Slope:** 113. **Green Fee:** $25/$29. **Cart Fee:** $22/Person. **Walking Policy:** Unrestricted walking. **Walkability:** 2. **Opened:** 1994. **Architect:** Colanton. **Season:** April-Nov. **To obtain tee times:** Call golf shop. **Miscellaneous:** Reduced fees (weekdays, seniors, juniors), FF.

KINGSWOOD COUNTRY CLUB
SP-Rte. 28 South Main/24 Kingswood Road, Wolfeboro, 03894, Carroll County, (603)569-3569. **Facility Holes:** 18. **Yards:** 6,360/5,860. **Par:** 72/72. **Course Rating:** 70.9/68.6. **Slope:** 125/122. **Green Fee:** $20/$60. **Cart Fee:** Included in green fee. **Walking Policy:** Walking at certain times. **Walkability:** 3. **Opened:** 1926. **Architect:** Donald Ross. **Season:** April-Nov. **To obtain tee times:** Call golf shop. **Miscellaneous:** Reduced fees (twilight, juniors), range (grass), credit cards (MC, V, D), BF, FF.

★★★ LACONIA COUNTRY CLUB
SP-607 Elm St., Laconia, 03246, Belknap County, (603)524-1273, 7 miles from Lake Winnipesaukee. **Facility Holes:** 18. **Yards:** 6,483/5,552. **Par:** 72/72. **Course Rating:** 71.7/72.1. **Slope:** 128/125. **Green Fee:** $65. **Cart Fee:** Included in green fee. **Walking Policy:** Mandatory carts. **Walkability:** 3. **Opened:** 1926. **Architect:** Wayne Stiles. **Season:** May-Nov. **High:** June-Sept. **To obtain tee times:** Call golf shop. **Miscellaneous:** Reduced fees (guests, juniors), range (grass), caddies, credit cards (MC, V), BF, FF.
Reader Comments: Good layout … Course renovation project is completed.

★★★ LOCHMERE GOLF & COUNTRY CLUB
SP-Rte. 3, Tilton, 03276, Belknap County, (603)528-4653. **Web:** www.lochmeregolf.com. **Facility Holes:** 18. **Yards:** 6,697/5,267. **Par:** 72/72. **Course Rating:** 71.8/68.9. **Slope:** 127/120. **Green Fee:** $30/$38. **Cart Fee:** $24/Cart. **Opened:** 1999. **Architect:** Phil Wogan/George Sargent. **Season:** April-Oct. **To obtain tee times:** Call golf shop. **Miscellaneous:** Reduced fees (twilight), credit cards (MC, V).
Reader Comments: Interesting course, minimal food … Good course … Playable with sidehill shot-making … Great in the fall … Great vistas … New 9 will get better … Very hilly, narrow fairways, bring lots of balls … Rarely crowded … Superb conditioning … Some funky holes.

★★½ MAPLEWOOD COUNTRY CLUB
PU-Rte. 302, Bethlehem, 03574, Grafton County, (603)869-3335, (877)869-3335, 80 miles from Concord. **Facility Holes:** 18. **Yards:** 6,100/5,200. **Par:** 72/72. **Course Rating:** 67.5/68.4. **Slope:** 113/114. **Green Fee:** $27/$32. **Cart Fee:** $12/Person. **Walkability:** 3. **Opened:** 1907. **Architect:** Donald Ross. **Season:** May-Oct. **High:** May-Sept. **To obtain tee times:** Call golf shop. **Miscellaneous:** Reduced fees (weekdays, twilight), metal spikes, range (grass), credit cards (MC, V, AE, D).

MOUNT WASHINGTON HOTEL & RESORT
R-Rte. 302, Bretton Woods, 03575, Carroll County, (603)278-4653, (800)258-0330, 90 miles from Concord. **E-mail:** golf@mtwashington.com. **Web:** www.mtwashington.com. **Facility Holes:** 27. **Green Fee:** $60/$75. **Walking Policy:** Unrestricted walking. **Season:** May-Nov. **To obtain tee times:** Call up to 7 days in advance. **Miscellaneous:** Range (grass), lodging (284 rooms), credit cards (MC, V, AE, D), BF, FF.
MOUNT PLEASANT GOLF COURSE (9)
Yards: 3,215/2,475. **Par:** 35/35. **Course Rating:** 71.0. **Slope:** 122. **Cart Fee:** Included in green fee. **Walkability:** 2. **Opened:** 1895. **Architect:** Alex Findlay/G. Cornish/B. Silva. **High:** July-Aug. **Miscellaneous:** Reduced fees (weekdays, guests, twilight).
★★★★ MOUNT WASHINGTON GOLF COURSE (18)
Yards: 6,638/5,336. **Par:** 71/71. **Course Rating:** 70.1/70.1. **Slope:** 123/118. **Cart Fee:** $30/Cart. **Walkability:** 3. **Opened:** 1915. **Architect:** Donald Ross. **High:** June-Sept. **Miscellaneous:** Reduced fees (weekdays, guests, twilight, juniors).
Reader Comments: Course speaks for itself … Scenery is the best … Great location & views … Once in a lifetime experience … A great Donald Ross layout with spectacular views of Mt. Washington … A first class operation … Fun resort course … Time on the practice green is a must! … Sentimental favorite.

MOUNTAIN VIEW COUNTRY CLUB
PU-Mountain View Rd., Whitefield, 03598, Coos County, (603)837-2100, 20 miles from St. Johnsbury, VT. **Facility Holes:** 9. **Yards:** 3,120/2,870. **Par:** 35/35. **Course Rating:** 69.7/71.9. **Slope:** 112/103. **Green Fee:** $18/$28. **Cart Fee:** $12/Person. **Walking Policy:** Walking at certain times. **Walkability:** 4. **Opened:** 1908. **Architect:** Ralph Barton. **Season:** May-Oct. **To obtain tee times:** Call golf shop. **Miscellaneous:** Reduced fees (weekdays, guests, twilight, juniors), credit cards (MC, V, AE), BF, FF.

NEW HAMPSHIRE

★★★½ NORTH CONWAY COUNTRY CLUB
SP-Norcross Circle, North Conway, 03860, Carroll County, (603)356-9391. **Facility Holes:** 18. **Yards:** 6,522/5,394. **Par:** 71/71. **Course Rating:** 71.9/70.1. **Slope:** 126/118. **Green Fee:** $35/$55. **Cart Fee:** $24/Cart. **Walking Policy:** Walking at certain times. **Walkability:** 2. **Opened:** 1895. **Architect:** Alex Findlay/Phil Wogan. **Season:** May-Oct. **High:** June-Oct. **To obtain tee times:** Call golf shop. **Miscellaneous:** Reduced fees (twilight, seniors, juniors), range (grass), credit cards (MC, V, AE).
Reader Comments: Love the scenery, beautiful ... A nice mix of hard & not-so-hard holes ... If possible, the pace was too fast! ... Great vacation value ... Good time worth trip & time.

★★½ OVERLOOK COUNTRY CLUB
PU-5 Overlook Dr., Hollis, 03049, Hillsborough County, (603)465-2909, 10 miles from Nashua. **E-mail:** overlookgolf@aol.com. **Facility Holes:** 18. **Yards:** 6,290/5,230. **Par:** 71/72. **Course Rating:** 70.2/68.9. **Slope:** 127/117. **Green Fee:** $32/$44. **Cart Fee:** $26/Cart. **Walking Policy:** Unrestricted walking. **Walkability:** 4. **Opened:** 1989. **Architect:** David E. Friel. **Season:** March-Dec. **High:** May-Aug. **To obtain tee times:** Call golf shop. **Miscellaneous:** Reduced fees (weekdays, twilight, juniors), credit cards (MC, V, AE, D), BF, FF.

★★★★ OWL'S NEST GOLF CLUB
PU-1 Club House Lane, Campton, 03223, Grafton County, (603)726-3076, (888)695-6378, 60 miles from Concord. **E-mail:** golf@owlsnestgolf.com. **Web:** www.owlsnestgolf.com. **Facility Holes:** 18. **Yards:** 6,818/5,296. **Par:** 72/72. **Course Rating:** 74.0/69.8. **Slope:** 133/115. **Green Fee:** $39/$54. **Cart Fee:** $16/Person. **Walking Policy:** Walking at certain times. **Walkability:** 4. **Opened:** 1998. **Architect:** Cornish/Silva/Mungeam. **Season:** April-Nov. **High:** June-Oct. **To obtain tee times:** Call up to 7 days in advance. **Miscellaneous:** Reduced fees (weekdays, twilight, seniors, juniors), range (grass), credit cards (MC, V, AE, D), BF, FF.
Reader Comments: Beauty in the hills of New Hampshire ... Views of mountains outstanding ... A great design featuring a front 9 in the valley and a back 9 where you literally traverse the mountain ... First class ... A true gem ... A new adventure at each turn, but very playable.

★★★½ PASSACONAWAY COUNTRY CLUB
PU-12 Midway Ave., Litchfield, 03052, Hillsborough County, (603)424-4653, 5 miles from Manchester. **Facility Holes:** 18. **Yards:** 6,855/5,369. **Par:** 71/72. **Course Rating:** 72.2/70.3. **Slope:** 126/118. **Green Fee:** $22/$39. **Cart Fee:** $12/Person. **Walking Policy:** Unrestricted walking. **Walkability:** 2. **Opened:** 1989. **Architect:** Cornish/Silva. **Season:** April-Dec. **High:** May-Sept. **To obtain tee times:** Call golf shop. **Miscellaneous:** Reduced fees (weekdays, twilight, seniors, juniors), credit cards (MC, V).
Reader Comments: Numerous parallel fairways ... Need to be accurate ... Wetlands are in play on various holes ... Fairly long course ... Holes are beautiful, absolutely beautiful, my favorite in New Hampshire ... Very tough when windy ... Bring the Big Dog! ... Some great par 4s, good food.

★★★ PEASE GOLF COURSE
PU-200 Grafton Dr., Portsmouth, 03801, Rockingham County, (603)433-1331. **E-mail:** t.seavey@peasedev.org. **Web:** www.peasedev.org. **Facility Holes:** 27. **Yards:** 6,328/5,324. **Par:** 71/71. **Course Rating:** 70.8/69.9. **Slope:** 128/120. **Green Fee:** $34. **Cart Fee:** $12/Person. **Walking Policy:** Unrestricted walking. **Walkability:** 2. **Opened:** 1901. **Architect:** Alex Findlay. **Season:** April-Nov. **High:** July-Aug. **To obtain tee times:** Call up to 3 days in advance. **Miscellaneous:** Range (grass), credit cards (MC, V, AE), BF, FF.
Reader Comments: Small greens ... 2 very different 9s; front links, back tree-lined and tough ... Needs drainage improvements ... Adding additional 9 holes ... Very busy, difficult but playable.
Special Notes: Additional 9 holes opening in 2002.

★★½ PERRY HOLLOW GOLF & COUNTRY CLUB
PU-250 Perry Hollow Rd., Wolfeboro, 03894, Carroll County, (603)569-3055, 3 miles from Wolfeboro. **Facility Holes:** 18. **Yards:** 6,338/4,788. **Par:** 71/71. **Course Rating:** 71.0/67.0. **Slope:** 132/115. **Green Fee:** $28. **Cart Fee:** $24/Cart. **Walking Policy:** Unrestricted walking. **Walkability:** 4. **Architect:** Geoffrey S. Cornish/Brian Silva. **Season:** April-Nov. **High:** June-Oct. **To obtain tee times:** Call golf shop. **Miscellaneous:** Reduced fees (juniors), range (grass), credit cards (MC, V, AE, D).

★★½ PLAUSAWA VALLEY COUNTRY CLUB
SP-42 Whittemore Rd., Pembroke, 03275, Merrimack County, (603)224-6267, 3 miles from Concord. **Facility Holes:** 18. **Yards:** 6,545/5,391. **Par:** 72/73. **Course Rating:** 72.6/71.5. **Slope:** 131/128. **Green Fee:** $28/$37. **Cart Fee:** $28/Cart. **Walking Policy:** Unrestricted walking. **Walkability:** 3. **Opened:** 1963. **Architect:** Geoffrey Cornish/Brian Silva/W.Mitchell. **Season:** March-Nov. **High:** May-Oct. **To obtain tee times:** Call up to 5 days in advance. **Miscellaneous:** Reduced fees (weekdays, twilight, seniors, juniors), range (grass), credit cards (MC, V), BF, FF.

PONEMAH GREEN FAMILY GOLF CENTER

SP-55 Ponemah Road, Amherst, 03031, Hillsboro County, (603)672-4732, 8 miles from Nashua. **Web:** ponemahgreen.com. **Facility Holes:** 9. **Yards:** 4,420/3,608. **Par:** 68/68. **Course Rating:** 61.9/62.5. **Slope:** 114/109. **Green Fee:** $25/$27. **Cart Fee:** $24/Cart. **Walking Policy:** Unrestricted walking. **Walkability:** 2. **Opened:** 1989. **Architect:** Geoffrey Cornish. **Season:** March-Dec. **High:** June-Sept. **To obtain tee times:** Call golf shop. **Miscellaneous:** Reduced fees (weekdays, seniors, juniors), range (grass/mats), credit cards (MC, V).

★★★★ PORTSMOUTH COUNTRY CLUB

SP-80 Country Club Lane, Greenland, 03840, Rockingham County, (603)436-9719, 3 miles from Portsmouth. **Facility Holes:** 18. **Yards:** 7,050/5,511. **Par:** 72/76. **Course Rating:** 74.1/72.6. **Slope:** 127/126. **Green Fee:** $70. **Cart Fee:** $26/Cart. **Walking Policy:** Walking at certain times. **Walkability:** 2. **Opened:** 1957. **Architect:** Robert Trent Jones. **Season:** April-Nov. **High:** June-Oct. **To obtain tee times:** Call up to 3 days in advance. **Miscellaneous:** Reduced fees (twilight, juniors), range (grass), credit cards (MC, V, D), BF, FF. **Notes:** Ranked 4th in 2001 Best in State.

Reader Comments: Best track in NH ... Expensive but worth it at least once a year ... Wow—nice course ... Long course, lots of fairway woods needed, a bear in the wind ... Hidden gem ... Still a favorite especially in fall.

★★½ RAGGED MOUNTAIN GOLF CLUB

R-RR 1, Box 106E Ragged Mountain Rd., Danbury, 03230, Merrimack County, (603)768-3300, 28 miles from Concord. **Facility Holes:** 18. **Yards:** 7,059/4,963. **Par:** 72/72. **Course Rating:** 74.9/71.0. **Slope:** 149/125. **Green Fee:** $39/$59. **Cart Fee:** Included in green fee. **Walking Policy:** Walking at certain times. **Walkability:** 3. **Opened:** 1999. **Architect:** Jeff Julian. **Season:** April-Oct. **High:** June-Sept. **To obtain tee times:** Call up to 14 days in advance. **Miscellaneous:** Reduced fees (twilight), range (grass), credit cards (MC, V, AE, D), BF, FF.

RIDGEWOOD COUNTRY CLUB

SP-Rte. 109 S., Moultonborough, 03254, Carroll County, (603)476-5930. **E-mail:** ridgewood-cc@hotmail.com. **Web:** www.golfridgewood.com. **Facility Holes:** 9. **Yards:** 3,275/2,355. **Par:** 36/36. **Course Rating:** 35.9/34.0. **Slope:** 127/110. **Green Fee:** $28/$34. **Cart Fee:** $11/Person. **Walking Policy:** Unrestricted walking. **Walkability:** 3. **Opened:** 1998. **Architect:** Wogan and Sargeant. **Season:** April-Nov. **High:** July-Aug. **To obtain tee times:** Call up to 3 days in advance. **Miscellaneous:** Reduced fees (twilight, seniors, juniors), range (mats), credit cards (MC, V), BF, FF.

ROCKINGHAM COUNTRY CLUB

PU-Rte. 108 (200 Exeter Road), New Market, 03857, Rockingham County, (603)659-9956, 10 miles from Portsmouth. **Facility Holes:** 9. **Yards:** 2,875/2,622. **Par:** 35/37. **Course Rating:** 65.3/69.4. **Slope:** 104/114. **Green Fee:** $20/$23. **Cart Fee:** $22/Cart. **Walking Policy:** Unrestricted walking. **Walkability:** 2. **Opened:** 1933. **Season:** April-Nov. **High:** June-Sept. **To obtain tee times:** Call up to 5 days in advance. **Miscellaneous:** Reduced fees (weekdays, seniors, juniors), credit cards (MC, V, D), BF, FF.

★★★½ SAGAMORE-HAMPTON GOLF CLUB

PU-101 North Rd., North Hampton, 03862, Rockingham County, (603)964-5341, 50 miles from Boston. **E-mail:** info@sagamorehampton.com. **Web:** www.sagamorehampton.com. **Facility Holes:** 18. **Yards:** 6,014/5,647. **Par:** 71/71. **Course Rating:** 68.0/71.7. **Slope:** 116/121. **Green Fee:** $25/$29. **Cart Fee:** $22/Cart. **Walking Policy:** Unrestricted walking. **Walkability:** 3. **Opened:** 1962. **Architect:** C.S. Luff. **Season:** April-Dec. **High:** June-Sept. **To obtain tee times:** Call golf shop. **Miscellaneous:** Reduced fees (seniors, juniors), range (grass/mats), credit cards (MC, V, AE), BF, FF.

Reader Comments: Enjoyed ... Need lots of balls in spring, often wet ... Popular course.

★★★★ SHATTUCK GOLF COURSE

PU-28 Dublin Rd., Jaffrey, 03452, Cheshire County, (603)532-4521, 20 miles from Keene. **Facility Holes:** 18. **Yards:** 6,764/4,632. **Par:** 71/71. **Course Rating:** 74.1/73.1. **Slope:** 145/139. **Green Fee:** $35. **Cart Fee:** $12/Person. **Walking Policy:** Unrestricted walking. **Walkability:** 4. **Opened:** 1991. **Architect:** Brian Silva. **Season:** May-Oct. **High:** June-Sept. **To obtain tee times:** Call golf shop. **Miscellaneous:** Reduced fees (weekdays, twilight), metal spikes, range (grass/mats), credit cards (MC, V, D). **Notes:** Ranked 7th in 2001 Best in State.

Reader Comments: Technical course with no mercy for off-fairway shots ... Beautiful setting ... Bring lots of extra balls ... Fast greens ... Toughest course I've played ... Yikes! If not at the top of your game, stay home & paint the house ... Target golf at its best.

★★★ SOUHEGAN WOODS GOLF CLUB

PU-65 Thorton Ferry Rd., Amherst, 03031, Hillsborough County, (603)673-0200, 10 miles from Nashua. **Facility Holes:** 18. **Yards:** 6,497/5,423. **Par:** 72/71. **Course Rating:** 70.4/65.6. **Slope:** 122/111. **Green Fee:** $34/$44. **Cart Fee:** $26/Cart. **Walking Policy:** Unrestricted walking. **Walkability:** 1. **Opened:** 1992. **Architect:** Phil Friel. **Season:** April-Dec. **To obtain tee times:** Call up to 5 days in advance. **Miscellaneous:** Reduced fees (weekdays, twilight), range (grass), credit cards (MC, V, AE, D), BF, FF.

Reader Comments: My absolute favorite course! ... Tight, long course to walk, long distances between holes ... Great new find ... Too many traps—do not encourage fast play.

★★★★ STONEBRIDGE COUNTRY CLUB

PU-161 Gorham Pond Rd., Goffstown, 03045, Hillsboro County, (603)497-8633, 7 miles from Manchester. **E-mail:** info@golfstonebridge.com. **Web:** www.golfstonebridge.com. **Facility Holes:** 18. **Yards:** 6,808/4,747. **Par:** 72/72. **Course Rating:** 73.0/67.6. **Slope:** 138/116. **Green Fee:** $35/$45. **Cart Fee:** $15/Person. **Walking Policy:** Unrestricted walking. **Walkability:** 3. **Opened:** 1998. **Architect:** Phil Wogan/George Sargent. **Season:** April-Nov. **High:** June-Sept. **To obtain tee times:** Call up to 3 days in advance. **Miscellaneous:** Reduced fees (weekdays, twilight, juniors), range (grass), credit cards (MC, V, AE, D), BF, FF. **Notes:** Ranked 8th in 2001 Best in State.

Reader Comments: A little on the high side but well worth it ... Condition improving with age ... Nice surprise. I'd go back ... Good risk reward challenges ... Plenty of elevation changes on each hole ... Front 9 tough but back 9 was tougher ... Don't miss it.

★★★ TORY PINES GOLF CLUB

R-Rte. 47 740 2nd NH Tpke North, Francestown, 03043, Hillsborough County, (603)588-2923, (800)227-8679. **Facility Holes:** 18. **Yards:** 6,111/4,604. **Par:** 71/71. **Course Rating:** 70.7/68.4. **Slope:** 138/121. **Green Fee:** $28/$38. **Cart Fee:** $14/Person. **Walking Policy:** Unrestricted walking. **Walkability:** 5. **Architect:** Donald Ross. **Season:** May-Oct. **To obtain tee times:** Call up to 3 days in advance. **Miscellaneous:** Reduced fees (twilight), range (grass), lodging (36 rooms), credit cards (MC, V, AE, D).

Reader Comments: Undiscovered jewel, great staff, excellent food and fun course ... Out of the way but fun ... Hilly & challenging ... Very small, tough greens ... Is there a flat lie here? Didn't think so.

★★½ WAUKEWAN GOLF CLUB

PU-Waukewan Rd., Center Harbor, 03226, Belknap County, (603)279-6661, 50 miles from Concord. **Facility Holes:** 18. **Yards:** 5,828/5,020. **Par:** 72/72. **Course Rating:** 67.4/68.3. **Slope:** 117/112. **Green Fee:** $22/$30. **Cart Fee:** $24/Cart. **Walking Policy:** Unrestricted walking. **Walkability:** 3. **Opened:** 1961. **Architect:** Melvyn D. Hale. **Season:** May-Nov. **High:** June-Sept. **To obtain tee times:** Call up to 7 days in advance. **Miscellaneous:** Range (grass), credit cards (MC, V), BF, FF.

WAUMBEK GOLF CLUB

PU-Route 2, Jefferson, 03583, Coos County, (603)586-7777, 85 miles from Concord. **Facility Holes:** 18. **Yards:** 6,128/4,772. **Par:** 71/71. **Course Rating:** 69.9/69.9. **Slope:** 107/107. **Green Fee:** $20/$25. **Cart Fee:** $20/Cart. **Walking Policy:** Unrestricted walking. **Walkability:** 2. **Opened:** 1895. **Architect:** Willie Norton/Ralph Barton. **Season:** April-Nov. **High:** July-Sept. **To obtain tee times:** Call golf shop. **Miscellaneous:** Reduced fees (weekdays, guests, twilight, seniors, juniors), credit cards (MC, V, AE), BF, FF.

★★½ WENTWORTH GOLF CLUB

SP-Rt. 16A, Jackson, 03846, Carroll County, (603)383-9641, 10 miles from North Conway. **E-mail:** info@wentworthgolf.com. **Web:** www.wentworthgolf.com. **Facility Holes:** 18. **Yards:** 5,581/5,087. **Par:** 70/70. **Course Rating:** 66.0/66.7. **Slope:** 115/114. **Green Fee:** $15/$38. **Cart Fee:** $12/Person. **Walking Policy:** Walking at certain times. **Walkability:** 2. **Opened:** 1895. **Season:** May-Oct. **High:** July-Sept. **Tee times:** Call golf shop. **Miscellaneous:** Reduced fees (weekdays, twilight, juniors), credit cards (MC, V, AE, D), BF, FF.

★★★ WHITE MOUNTAIN COUNTRY CLUB

PU-North Ashland Road, Ashland, 03217, Grafton County, (603)536-2227, 25 miles from Concord. **Facility Holes:** 18. **Yards:** 6,464/5,963. **Par:** 71/72. **Course Rating:** 70.4/67.9. **Slope:** 122/119. **Green Fee:** $27/$34. **Cart Fee:** $24/Cart. **Walking Policy:** Unrestricted walking. **Walkability:** 1. **Opened:** 1974. **Architect:** Geoffrey S. Cornish. **Season:** May-Oct. **High:** July-Sept. **To obtain tee times:** Call golf shop. **Miscellaneous:** Reduced fees (weekdays, guests, twilight), metal spikes, range (grass), lodging (4 rooms), credit cards (MC, V, D).

Reader Comments: Nice views. Greens could be better ... Nice layout ... Big greens, driving accuracy needed, great finishing hole ... A fantastic golf weekend package ... Nice greens.

NEW HAMPSHIRE

★★★½ **WINDHAM GOLF & COUNTRY CLUB**
PU-One Country Club Rd., Windham, 03087, Rockingham County, (603)434-2093, 20 miles
from Boston, MA. **E-mail:** joanne@windhamcc.com. **Web:** www.windhamcc.com. **Facility
Holes:** 18. **Yards:** 6,442/5,127. **Par:** 72/72. **Course Rating:** 71.3/69.1. **Slope:** 137/123. **Green
Fee:** $35/$42. **Cart Fee:** $12/Person. **Walking Policy:** Unrestricted walking. **Walkability:** 3.
Opened: 1995. **Architect:** Dean Bowen. **Season:** Year-round. **To obtain tee times:** Call golf
shop. **Miscellaneous:** Reduced fees (juniors), metal spikes, range (grass), credit cards
(MC, V), BF, FF.
Notes: Ranked 10th in 1999 Best in State.
Reader Comments: Tight, hard greens, challenging … Green fees too high … Creative layout—
hole #12 will make you think … Awesome course, great 16th hole … Very hilly first 9 with blind
drives second 9 … Will go back … Every hole a challenge, be prepared.

★★½ **APPLE MOUNTAIN GOLF CLUB**
PU-369 Hazen Oxford Rd., Rte. 624, Belvidere, 07823, Warren County, (908)453-3023, (800)752-9465, 80 miles from New York City. **E-mail:** applemt@nac.net. **Facility Holes:** 18. **Yards:** 6,593/5,214. **Par:** 71/71. **Course Rating:** 71.8/69.8. **Slope:** 122/123. **Green Fee:** $22/$49. **Cart Fee:** Included in green fee. **Walking Policy:** Walking at certain times. **Walkability:** 4. **Opened:** 1973. **Architect:** Andrew Kiszonak. **Season:** Year-round. **High:** June-Aug. **To obtain tee times:** Call golf shop. **Miscellaneous:** Reduced fees (weekdays, twilight, seniors, juniors), metal spikes, credit cards (MC, V, AE).

THE ARCHITECTS CLUB
PU-700 Strykers Rd., Lopatcong, 08865, Warren County, (908)213-3080. **Web:** www.thearchitectsclub.com. **Facility Holes:** 18. **Yards:** 6,863/5,233. **Par:** 71/71. **Course Rating:** 73.3/71.0. **Slope:** 130/123. **Green Fee:** $35/$85. **Cart Fee:** Included in green fee. **Walking Policy:** Unrestricted walking. **Walkability:** 2. **Opened:** 2001. **Architect:** Stephen Kay/Ron Whitten. **Season:** March-Nov. **High:** April-Oct. **To obtain tee times:** Call up to 6 days in advance. **Miscellaneous:** Reduced fees (weekdays, twilight), range (mats), FF. **Special Notes:** Holes based on designs by architects from 1885 to 1955.

★★★ **ASH BROOK GOLF COURSE**
PU-1210 Raritan Rd., Scotch Plains, 07076, Union County, (908)668-8503, 15 miles from Newark. **Facility Holes:** 18. **Yards:** 6,962/5,661. **Par:** 72/72. **Course Rating:** 72.1/71.8. **Slope:** 117/119. **Green Fee:** $24/$50. **Cart Fee:** $22/Cart. **Walking Policy:** Unrestricted walking. **Walkability:** 2. **Opened:** 1958. **Architect:** Alfred H. Tull. **Season:** Year-round. **High:** March-Oct. **Tee times:** Call golf shop. **Miscellaneous:** Reduced fees (weekdays, seniors, juniors). **Reader Comments:** Great price ... Tough county course ... Long course, very flat ... It's length and water hazards make it a great course for tournament play. The long par-4 14th hole is a monster ... Remodeling wonderful, new green contours.

★★½ **AVALON GOLF CLUB**
SP-1510 Route 9 N., Cape May Court House, 08210, Cape May County, (609)465-4653, (800)643-4766, 30 miles from Atlantic City. **Web:** www.avalongolfclub.net. **Facility Holes:** 18. **Yards:** 6,325/4,924. **Par:** 71/72. **Course Rating:** 70.3/70.7. **Slope:** 122/122. **Green Fee:** $29/$87. **Cart Fee:** Included in green fee. **Walking Policy:** Walking at certain times. **Walkability:** 2. **Opened:** 1971. **Architect:** Bob Hendricks. **Season:** Year-round. **To obtain tee times:** Call up to 14 days in advance. **Miscellaneous:** Reduced fees (weekdays, twilight, juniors), range (mats), credit cards (MC, V, D), BF, FF.

★★½ **BEAVER BROOK COUNTRY CLUB**
SP-25 Country Club Dr., Annandale, 08801, Hunterdon County, (908)735-4022, (800)433-8567, 45 miles from New York City. **E-mail:** beaverbrook@americangolf.com. **Web:** www.americangolf.com. **Facility Holes:** 18. **Yards:** 6,601/5,343. **Par:** 72/72. **Course Rating:** 71.7/71.7. **Slope:** 125/122. **Green Fee:** $45/$85. **Cart Fee:** Included in green fee. **Walking Policy:** Walking at certain times. **Walkability:** 4. **Opened:** 1964. **Architect:** Alec Ternyei. **Season:** Year-round. **High:** April-Oct. **To obtain tee times:** Call up to 7 days in advance. **Miscellaneous:** Reduced fees (weekdays, twilight), credit cards (MC, V, AE), FF.

★★ **BECKETT GOLF CLUB**
PU-Old Kings Highway, Swedesboro, 08085, Gloucester County, (856)467-4700, 5 miles from Philadelphia. **Facility Holes:** 27. **Green Fee:** $15/$19. **Opened:** 1964. **Season:** Year-round. **To obtain tee times:** Call golf shop. **Miscellaneous:** Metal spikes.
BLUE/WHITE (18 Combo)
Yards: 6,415/5,895. **Par:** 72/72. **Course Rating:** 69.7/73.4. **Slope:** 115/119.
RED/BLUE (18 Combo)
Yards: 6,418/5,690. **Par:** 73/73. **Course Rating:** 69.9/72.3. **Slope:** 116/117.
WHITE/RED (18 Combo)
Yards: 6,321/5,655. **Par:** 72/72. **Course Rating:** 69.7/71.9. **Slope:** 115/113.

★★½ **BEY LEA GOLF CLUB**
PU-1536 N. Bay Ave., Toms River, 08753, Ocean County, (732)349-0566. **Facility Holes:** 18. **Yards:** 6,677/5,793. **Par:** 72/72. **Course Rating:** 71.3/72.2. **Slope:** 122/117. **Green Fee:** $7/$32. **Cart Fee:** $26/Cart. **Walking Policy:** Unrestricted walking. **Walkability:** 1. **Opened:** 1969. **Architect:** Hal Purdy. **Season:** Year-round. **To obtain tee times:** Call up to 5 days in advance. **Miscellaneous:** Reduced fees (twilight, seniors, juniors), credit cards (MC, V), FF.

BLUE HERON PINES GOLF CLUB
PU-550 W. Country Club Dr., Cologne, Galloway Twsp., 08213, Atlantic County, (609)965-4653, (888)478-2746, 16 miles from Atlantic City. **E-mail:** info@blueheronpines.com. **Web:** www.blueheronpines.com. **Facility Holes:** 36. **Cart Fee:** Included in green fee. **Walking Policy:**

Unrestricted walking. **Walkability:** 1. **Season:** Year-round. **High:** June-Sept. **To obtain tee times:** Call up to 10 days in advance. **Miscellaneous:** Reduced fees (weekdays, twilight, juniors), range (grass/mats), credit cards (MC, V, AE, D, DC), BF, FF.

★★★★ **EAST COURSE** (18)
Yards: 7,300/5,500. **Par:** 71/71. **Course Rating:** 74.8/69.0. **Slope:** 135/120. **Green Fee:** $51/$130. **Opened:** 2000. **Architect:** Steve Smyers.
Notes: Golf Digest School site.
Reader Comments: One of NJ's best … Very difficult greens with a lot of undulation and tough pin placements … Feels like a 'southern' resort course … Many bunkers, tough … Fairways wide open, excellent greens … Excellent test from back tees … Expensive, but enjoyable experience.

★★★★½ **WEST COURSE** (18)
Yards: 6,777/5,053. **Par:** 72/72. **Course Rating:** 72.9/69.2. **Slope:** 132/119. **Green Fee:** $51/$125. **Opened:** 1993. **Architect:** Stephen Kay.
Notes: Golf Digest School site.
Reader Comments: Well maintained. Good layout … Great service, great conditions, great course … Just great golf … Pricey but worth it … First three warm-up holes followed by 15 beauties.

★★★ **BOWLING GREEN GOLF CLUB**
SP-53 Schoolhouse Rd., Milton, 07438, Morris County, (973)697-8688, 45 miles from New York City. **Facility Holes:** 18. **Yards:** 6,689/4,966. **Par:** 72/72. **Course Rating:** 72.9/69.4. **Slope:** 131/122. **Green Fee:** $37/$57. **Cart Fee:** $19/Person. **Walking Policy:** Unrestricted walking. **Walkability:** 3. **Opened:** 1966. **Architect:** Geoffrey Cornish. **Season:** March-Dec. **To obtain tee times:** Call up to 7 days in advance. **Miscellaneous:** Reduced fees (weekdays, twilight), range (mats), credit cards (MC, V, AE), BF, FF.
Reader Comments: Solid test … Good walking course. Par-5 4th a little too tricked up … Course is tight … Nice variety of holes. Bring your best driver because fairways are narrow and tree-lined … A true test of golf. You'll need to be creative around the greens. Front nine is carved through the trees.

★★½ **BRIGANTINE GOLF LINKS**
PU-1075 North Shore Dr., Brigantine, 08203, Atlantic County, (609)266-1388, 5 miles from Atlantic City. **Web:** www.brigantinegolf.com. **Facility Holes:** 18. **Yards:** 6,570/5,460. **Par:** 72/72. **Course Rating:** 71.9/66.9. **Slope:** 123/113. **Green Fee:** $30/$60. **Cart Fee:** Included in green fee. **Walking Policy:** Walking at certain times. **Walkability:** 1. **Opened:** 1926. **Architect:** Stiles/Van Kleek/Gill/Williams. **Season:** Year-round. **High:** May-Oct. **To obtain tee times:** Call up to 5 days in advance. **Miscellaneous:** Reduced fees (weekdays, guests, twilight), credit cards (MC, V, AE, D, DC, CB), BF, FF.

★★★ **BUENA VISTA COUNTRY CLUB**
PU-Box 307, Rte. 40 & Country Club Lane, Buena, 08310, Atlantic County, (609)697-3733, 25 miles from Philadelphia. **E-mail:** info@allforeclub.com. **Web:** www.allforeclub.com. **Facility Holes:** 18. **Yards:** 6,869/5,651. **Par:** 72/72. **Course Rating:** 71.8/72.6. **Slope:** 127/124. **Green Fee:** $27/$35. **Cart Fee:** $28/Cart. **Walking Policy:** Walking at certain times. **Walkability:** 1. **Opened:** 1957. **Architect:** William Gordon & Son. **Season:** Year-round. **To obtain tee times:** Call golf shop. **Miscellaneous:** Reduced fees (weekdays, twilight), range (grass), credit cards (MC, V), BF, FF.
Reader Comments: Very nice course and conditions … Excellent design for play & walking, sufficiently challenging … One of the most challenging in South Jersey, pines remind you of Carolina, good character, No. 10 a bear … Nice course, good price.

★★½ **BUNKER HILL GOLF COURSE**
PU-220 Bunker Hill Rd, Princeton, 08540, Somerset County, (908)359-6335, 8 miles from New Brunswick. **E-mail:** dwasnick@aol.com. **Web:** www.distinctgolf.com. **Facility Holes:** 18. **Yards:** 6,200/5,766. **Par:** 72/72. **Course Rating:** 67.9/72.6. **Slope:** 111/113. **Green Fee:** $13/$22. **Cart Fee:** $28/Cart. **Walking Policy:** Walking at certain times. **Walkability:** 3. **Opened:** 1972. **Season:** Year-round. **High:** May-Oct. **Tee times:** Call up to 7 days in advance. **Misc:** Reduced fees (weekdays, twilight, seniors, juniors), credit cards (MC, V), BF, FF.

★★★ **CAPE MAY NATIONAL GOLF CLUB**
SP-Rte. 9 & Florence Ave., Cape May, 08204, Cape May County, (609)884-1563, (800)227-3874, 35 miles from Atlantic City. **E-mail:** cmngc@bellatlantic.net. **Web:** www.cmngc.com. **Facility Holes:** 18. **Yards:** 6,905/4,711. **Par:** 71/71. **Course Rating:** 72.9/68.8. **Slope:** 136/115. **Green Fee:** $35/$85. **Cart Fee:** Included in green fee. **Walking Policy:** Unrestricted walking. **Walkability:** 2. **Opened:** 1991. **Architect:** Karl Litten/Robert Mullock. **Season:** Year-round. **Tee times:** Call up to 30 days in advance. **Miscellaneous:** Reduced fees (weekdays, guests, twilight, juniors), range (grass/mats), credit cards (MC, V), BF, FF.
Reader Comments: Very natural, great conditions. Second hole, par 4 and the 18th two of the best anywhere … Great water holes and par 3s … Bird sanctuary in the heart of course, challenging rounds here … Great golf course, not enough recognition, but I like it that way … Another winter favorite.

★★ CEDAR CREEK GOLF COURSE
PU-Bill Zimmermann Way, Bayville, 08721, Ocean County, (732)269-4460, 50 miles from Atlantic City. **Facility Holes:** 18. **Yards:** 6,325/5,154. **Par:** 72/72. **Course Rating:** 70.5/69.5. **Slope:** 120/118. **Green Fee:** $8/$27. **Cart Fee:** $14/Person. **Walking Policy:** Unrestricted walking. **Walkability:** 3. **Opened:** 1981. **Architect:** Nicholas Psiahas. **Season:** Year-round. **High:** May-Oct. **To obtain tee times:** Call up to 7 days in advance. **Miscellaneous:** Reduced fees (weekdays, twilight, seniors, juniors), range (mats), credit cards (MC, V, AE), FF.

★★★ CENTERTON GOLF CLUB
PU-Rte. 540-Almond Rd., Elmer, 08318, Salem County, (856)358-2220, 10 miles from Vineland. **Facility Holes:** 18. **Yards:** 6,725/5,525. **Par:** 71/71. **Course Rating:** 69.2/71.5. **Slope:** 120/120. **Green Fee:** $15/$28. **Cart Fee:** $26/Cart. **Walking Policy:** Walking at certain times. **Walkability:** 2. **Opened:** 1962. **Architect:** Ed Carmen. **Season:** Year-round. **High:** May-Aug. **To obtain tee times:** Call golf shop. **Miscellaneous:** Reduced fees (weekdays, twilight), metal spikes, range (grass/mats), credit cards (MC, V).
Reader Comments: Almost don't want to talk about this hidden gem, but the course deserves kudos for providing good golf at prices that skip pretension and allow participation. Open nature allows for high handicappers to enjoy … Fun but easy, short par 5s, 18 a good finishing hole.

★★★½ CHARLESTON SPRINGS GOLF COURSE
PU-193 Sweetman's Lane, Millstone Township, 07726, Monmouth County, (732)409-7227, 7 miles from Freehold Borough. **Facility Holes:** 18. **Yards:** 7,018/5,143. **Par:** 72/72. **Course Rating:** 73.1/69.4. **Slope:** 125/119. **Green Fee:** $30/$60. **Cart Fee:** $30/Cart. **Walking Policy:** Unrestricted walking. **Walkability:** 2. **Opened:** 1998. **Architect:** Mark Mungeam. **Season:** March-Dec. **High:** May-Sept. **To obtain tee times:** Call golf shop. **Miscellaneous:** Reduced fees (twilight, seniors), credit cards (MC, V).
Reader Comments: Links style with lots of hidden surprises … Best muni I have ever seen … Great public course. Makes me want to move to Monmouth county … Lots of fairway space … Almost resort condition … Getting better all the time … Fast greens … A great bargain.

★½ COHANZICK COUNTRY CLUB
PU-Bridgeton-Fairton Rd., Fairton, 08320, Cumberland County, (856)455-2127. **Facility Holes:** 18. **Yards:** 6,285/5,470. **Par:** 71/71. **Course Rating:** 70.2/70.5. **Slope:** 123/120. **Green Fee:** $15/$32. **Cart Fee:** $14/Cart. **Walking Policy:** Walking at certain times. **Walkability:** 5. **Architect:** Alex Findlay. **Season:** Year-round. **To obtain tee times:** Call up to 7 days in advance. **Miscellaneous:** Reduced fees (weekdays, twilight, juniors), metal spikes, credit cards (MC, V), BF, FF.

★★★ CRANBURY GOLF CLUB
SP-49 Southfield Rd., West Windsor, 08550, Mercer County, (609)799-0341, 6 miles from Princeton. **E-mail:** mike@cranburygolf.com. **Web:** www.cranburygolf.com. **Facility Holes:** 18. **Yards:** 6,495/5,010. **Par:** 70/71. **Course Rating:** 69.5/69.1. **Slope:** 122/123. **Green Fee:** $22/$40. **Cart Fee:** $15/Person. **Walking Policy:** Walking at certain times. **Walkability:** 2. **Opened:** 1963. **Architect:** Garrett Renn. **Season:** Year-round. **High:** May-Sept. **To obtain tee times:** Call golf shop. **Miscellaneous:** Reduced fees (weekdays, twilight, seniors, juniors), range (grass/mats), credit cards (MC, V, AE), BF, FF.
Reader Comments: We call this course 'Cran-birdie.' Nice course that is normally in good condition … Staff is among the friendliest around; you always feel welcome. Good course for all levels of golfer … Traditional course with outstanding food. Fast greens … Tight with high rough.

★★★ CREAM RIDGE GOLF CLUB
SP-181 Rte. 539, Cream Ridge, 08514, Monmouth County, (609)259-2849, (800)345-4957, 12 miles from Trenton. **Facility Holes:** 18. **Yards:** 6,491/5,150. **Par:** 71/70. **Course Rating:** 71.8/69.6. **Slope:** 124/119. **Green Fee:** $18/$37. **Cart Fee:** $15/Person. **Walking Policy:** Walking at certain times. **Walkability:** 2. **Opened:** 1958. **Architect:** Frank Miscoski. **Season:** Year-round. **To obtain tee times:** Call up to 7 days in advance. **Miscellaneous:** Reduced fees (weekdays, twilight, seniors, juniors), range (mats), credit cards (MC, V, AE), BF, FF.
Reader Comments: Nice local people … Fair layout, good condition … Nice scenery, well maintained, No. 18 toughest hole, long with water in play … Well maintained facility … Tough course, lots of water, several blind shots.

CRUZ GOLF & COUNTRY CLUB
PU-55 Birdsall Rd., Farmingdale, 07727, Monmouth County, (732)938-3378. **Facility Holes:** 18. **Yards:** 5,062/4,270. **Par:** 70/70. **Course Rating:** 64.3/32.1. **Slope:** 114/115. **Green Fee:** $20/$28. **Cart Fee:** $28/Cart. **To obtain tee times:** Call golf shop.

CRYSTAL SPRINGS GOLF & SPA RESORT

R-105-137 Wheatsworth Rd., Hamburg, 07419, Sussex County, (973)827-5996, 56 miles from New York City. **E-mail:** cheuttig@crystalgolfresort.com. **Web:** www.crystalgolfresort.com. **Facility Holes:** 81. **Cart Fee:** Included in green fee. **High:** May-Sept. **To obtain tee times:** Call up to 10 days in advance. **Miscellaneous:** Reduced fees (weekdays, guests, twilight), range (grass), lodging (100 rooms), credit cards (MC, V, AE), BF, FF.

★★★★½ **BALLYOWEN GOLF CLUB** (18) *Condition*
Yards: 7,032/4,903. **Par:** 72/72. **Course Rating:** 73.1/67.7. **Slope:** 127/109. **Green Fee:** $65/$125. **Walking Policy:** Walking at certain times. **Walkability:** 3. **Opened:** 1998. **Architect:** Roger Rulewich. **Season:** March-Dec.
Reader Comments: Scotland West, nice links course … Tough to get out of fescue … Simply breathtaking. Course condition is near perfect and the greens are best I've seen … Challenging with a lot of elevation changes … A windy day can become a real test of nerves … No. 7 a great, brutal par 4 … Worth the ride.

★★★ **BLACK BEAR GOLF CLUB** (18)
Yards: 6,673/4,756. **Par:** 72/72. **Course Rating:** 72.2/67.7. **Slope:** 130/116. **Green Fee:** $35/$75. **Walking Policy:** Mandatory carts. **Walkability:** 3. **Opened:** 1996. **Architect:** Jack Kurlander/David Glenz. **Season:** Year-round.
Reader Comments: Excellent shape and very challenging … If you hit it straight, can really score … A challenging mountain setting course, good value … A few gimmicky holes … White tees too short … Greens hold true. Fairways are open enough for big handicap.

★★★½ **CRYSTAL SPRINGS GOLF CLUB** (18)
Yards: 6,816/5,091. **Par:** 72/72. **Course Rating:** 74.1/70.5. **Slope:** 137/123. **Green Fee:** $40/$90. **Walking Policy:** Mandatory carts. **Walkability:** 5. **Opened:** 1991. **Architect:** Robert von Hagge. **Season:** March-Dec.
Reader Comments: Great golf course in scenic and hilly Northwest N.J. … Wicked awesome 10th … Not very forgiving … A must play, you'll love it or hate it, a lot of uneven lies. The scenery alone makes it a great day … Too many great holes to list … Who Every hole an adventure.

THE SPA GOLF CLUB (9)
Yards: 2,305/1,726. **Par:** 31/31. **Course Rating:** 62.8/62.1. **Slope:** 104/97. **Green Fee:** $18/$39. **Walking Policy:** Unrestricted walking. **Walkability:** 3. **Opened:** 1987. **Architect:** Robert Trent Jones. **Season:** March-Dec.

WILD TURKEY GOLF CLUB (18)
Yards: 7,100/5,015. **Par:** 71/71. **Green Fee:** $40/$90. **Walking Policy:** Mandatory carts. **Walkability:** 4. **Opened:** 2001. **Architect:** Roger Rulewich. **Season:** March-Dec.

★★★ **DARLINGTON COUNTY GOLF COURSE**
PU-2777 Campgaw Rd., Mahwah, 07430, Bergen County, (201)327-8770, 8 miles from Paramus. **Facility Holes:** 18. **Yards:** 6,457/5,300. **Par:** 71/72. **Course Rating:** 70.6/69.9. **Slope:** 122/117. **Green Fee:** $13/$45. **Cart Fee:** $20/Cart. **Walking Policy:** Unrestricted walking. **Walkability:** 5. **Architect:** Nicholas Psiahas. **Season:** March-Dec. **High:** July-Sept. **To obtain tee times:** Call golf shop. **Miscellaneous:** Reduced fees (weekdays, twilight, seniors, juniors), range (mats), credit cards (MC, V).
Reader Comments: Best county course, condition is very good to excellent … Hard to get a tee time … Best public course in Bergen County … Tight driving holes.

★★★★ **DEERWOOD COUNTRY CLUB**
SP-845 Woodland Rd., Westampton, 08060, Burlington County, (609)265-1800, 15 miles from Cherry Hill. **E-mail:** golf@deerwoodcc.com. **Web:** www.deerwoodcc.com. **Facility Holes:** 18. **Yards:** 6,231/4,807. **Par:** 70/70. **Course Rating:** 69.6/67.2. **Slope:** 124/111. **Green Fee:** $70/$82. **Cart Fee:** Included in green fee. **Walking Policy:** Mandatory carts. **Walkability:** 2. **Opened:** 1996. **Architect:** Jim Blaukovitch/Dick Alaimo. **Season:** Year-round. **To obtain tee times:** Call up to 7 days in advance. **Miscellaneous:** Reduced fees (weekdays), range (grass), credit cards (MC, V, AE, D), BF, FF.
Reader Comments: This is the best course in Burlington County, play it from the very back tees. Tough on windy days. Greens are best in the area and are always fast and true … One of the East Coast's finest. Great staff and great clubhouse … Beautiful at twice the price.

★★★½ **EAGLE RIDGE GOLF COURSE**
SP-2 August Blvd., Lakewood, 08701, Ocean County, (732)901-4900, 60 miles from New York City. **E-mail:** erlabel@aol.com. **Web:** www.eagleridgegolf.com. **Facility Holes:** 18. **Yards:** 6,607/4,792. **Par:** 71/71. **Course Rating:** 72.4/68.3. **Slope:** 132/125. **Green Fee:** $37/$57. **Cart Fee:** $16/Person. **Walking Policy:** Walking at certain times. **Walkability:** 4. **Opened:** 1999. **Architect:** Brian Ault. **Season:** Year-round. **High:** June-Sept. **To obtain tee times:** Call golf shop. **Miscellaneous:** Reduced fees (weekdays, twilight, seniors, juniors), range (grass/mats), credit cards (MC, V, AE), BF, FF.
Reader Comments: Tight little track … Course for all players … Clubhouse, restaurant and service were great … Surprisingly straightforward to play. Good shots are rewarded and poor shots are penalized … Great addition to local area, rough, bunker sand, water add challenge, elevated tees.

★½ EAST ORANGE GOLF COURSE
SP-440 Parsonage Hill Rd., Short Hills, 07078, Essex County, (973)379-7190, 10 miles from Newark. **Facility Holes:** 18. **Yards:** 6,120/5,640. **Par:** 72/73. **Course Rating:** 67.6/69.8. **Slope:** 117/122. **Green Fee:** $30/$35. **Cart Fee:** $20/Cart. **Walking Policy:** Unrestricted walking. **Walkability:** 1. **Opened:** 1920. **Architect:** Tom Bendelow. **Season:** Year-round. **High:** April-Sept. **To obtain tee times:** Call golf shop. **Miscellaneous:** Reduced fees (weekdays, twilight, juniors), range (mats), FF.

★★½ EMERSON GOLF CLUB
PU-99 Palisade Ave., Emerson, 07630, Bergen County, (201)261-1100, 15 miles from New York City. **Web:** www.emersongolfclub.com. **Facility Holes:** 18. **Yards:** 6,737/5,554. **Par:** 71/71. **Course Rating:** 71.5/70.8. **Slope:** 121/117. **Green Fee:** $45/$80. **Cart Fee:** Included in green fee. **Walking Policy:** Walking at certain times. **Walkability:** 1. **Opened:** 1963. **Architect:** Alec Ternyei. **Season:** Year-round. **High:** April-Oct. **To obtain tee times:** Call up to 5 days in advance. **Miscellaneous:** Reduced fees (weekdays, twilight, juniors), range (grass), credit cards (MC, V, AE), BF, FF.

★★★½ FARMSTEAD GOLF & COUNTRY CLUB
PU-88 Lawrence Rd., Lafayette, 07848, Sussex County, (973)383-1666, 5 miles from Sparta. **Facility Holes:** 27. **Green Fee:** $25/$47. **Cart Fee:** $28/Cart. **Walking Policy:** Walking at certain times. **Walkability:** 3. **Opened:** 1963. **Architect:** Byron Phoebus. **Season:** March-Dec. **High:** May-Oct. **To obtain tee times:** Call up to 7 days in advance. **Miscellaneous:** Reduced fees (weekdays, twilight, seniors), credit cards (MC, V, AE), FF.
CLUBVIEW/LAKEVIEW (18 Combo)
Yards: 6,680/4,987. **Par:** 71/71. **Course Rating:** 71.1/68.1. **Slope:** 127/116.
CLUBVIEW/VALLEYVIEW (18 Combo)
Yards: 6,221/4,822. **Par:** 69/70. **Course Rating:** 68.4/68.1. **Slope:** 119/117.
LAKEVIEW/VALLEYVIEW (18 Combo)
Yards: 6,161/4,636. **Par:** 68/69. **Course Rating:** 69.3/67.1. **Slope:** 118/116.
Reader Comments: You get value for the money … Wildlife was spectacular this time of year. Easy course to get on when you need a last minute starting time … Fun, real variety of holes … Nice layout, long, well maintained, nice clubhouse and food … Tests all skills … Biggest hot dogs in N.J.

FLANDERS VALLEY GOLF COURSE
PU-Pleasant Hill Rd., Flanders, 07836, Morris County, (973)584-5382, 50 miles from New York City. **Facility Holes:** 36. **Green Fee:** $16/$60. **Cart Fee:** $26/Cart. **Walking Policy:** Unrestricted walking. **Opened:** 1963. **Architect:** Hal Purdy/Rees Jones. **Season:** April-Dec. **To obtain tee times:** Call golf shop. **Miscellaneous:** Reduced fees (weekdays, twilight, seniors), credit cards (MC, V).
★★★½ **RED/GOLD COURSE** (18)
Yards: 6,770/5,540. **Par:** 72/73. **Course Rating:** 72.6/72.0. **Slope:** 126/123. **Walkability:** 4.
Reader Comments: Challenging, very hilly; great course … For amount of play, Morris County courses are outstanding … Easy to see why it's continually rated as one of the best in the US. The 10th is quite an uphill hike.
★★★½ **WHITE/BLUE COURSE** (18)
Yards: 6,765/5,534. **Par:** 72/72. **Course Rating:** 72.7/71.6. **Slope:** 126/122. **Walkability:** 2.
Reader Comments: Tough tee time, great value … Long, hard, fair … A real challenge to your game. The course is the thing … Nice place for a day of fun golf.

★★½ FRANCIS A. BYRNE GOLF CLUB
PU-1100 Pleasant Valley Way, West Orange, 07052, Essex County, (973)736-2306, 25 miles from New York City. **Facility Holes:** 18. **Yards:** 6,653/5,384. **Par:** 70/72. **Course Rating:** 70.2/73.0. **Slope:** 128/125. **Green Fee:** $22/$75. **Cart Fee:** $12/Person. **Walking Policy:** Walking at certain times. **Walkability:** 3. **Opened:** 1920. **Architect:** Charles H. Banks. **Season:** April-Dec. **High:** June-Aug. **To obtain tee times:** Call golf shop. **Miscellaneous:** Reduced fees (seniors, juniors), metal spikes.

★½ FREEWAY GOLF COURSE
PU-1858 Sicklerville Rd., Sicklerville, 08081, Camden County, (856)227-1115, 16 miles from Philadelphia. **Facility Holes:** 18. **Yards:** 6,536/5,395. **Par:** 72/72. **Course Rating:** 71.0/70.3. **Slope:** 121/118. **Green Fee:** $13/$30. **Cart Fee:** $15/Person. **Walking Policy:** Walking at certain times. **Walkability:** 3. **Opened:** 1968. **Architect:** Horace Smith. **Season:** Year-round. **High:** May-Oct. **To obtain tee times:** Call up to 7 days in advance. **Miscellaneous:** Reduced fees (weekdays, twilight, seniors, juniors), range (grass/mats), credit cards (MC, V, AE), BF, FF.

★★★ GALLOPING HILL GOLF COURSE

PU-P.O. Box 898, Union, 07083, Union County, (908)686-1556, 4 miles from Newark. **Facility Holes:** 27. **Yards:** 6,690/5,514. **Par:** 73/76. **Course Rating:** 71.3. **Slope:** 133. **Green Fee:** $32/$36. **Cart Fee:** $24/Cart. **Walking Policy:** Unrestricted walking. **Walkability:** 4. **Opened:** 1920. **Architect:** Willard Wilkinson. **Season:** Year-round. **High:** June-Sept. **To obtain tee times:** Call golf shop. **Miscellaneous:** Reduced fees (weekdays, seniors, juniors), BF, FF.

Reader Comments: Not a bad muni but very short … Great layout, hilly … Changes are great, love the rolling terrain … Reconstruction makes course easier, layout interesting … Good time, flat, not too difficult.

Special Notes: Also has a 9-hole course.

★★ GAMBLER RIDGE GOLF CLUB

PU-121 Burlington Path, Cream Ridge, 08514, Monmouth County, (609)758-3588, (800)427-8463, 10 miles from Trenton. **E-mail:** gmblrrdg@aol.com. **Web:** gogolfnj.com/gambler. **Facility Holes:** 18. **Yards:** 6,370/5,140. **Par:** 71/71. **Course Rating:** 70.2/69.3. **Slope:** 119/115. **Green Fee:** $11/$38. **Cart Fee:** $12/Person. **Walking Policy:** Walking at certain times. **Walkability:** 2. **Opened:** 1983. **Architect:** Nickelsen/Rockhill. **Season:** Year-round. **High:** April-Oct. **To obtain tee times:** Call up to 7 days in advance. **Miscellaneous:** Reduced fees (weekdays, twilight, seniors), range (mats), credit cards (MC, V, AE), FF.

★★½ GOLDEN PHEASANT GOLF CLUB

SP-141 Country Club Dr. & Eayrestown Rd., Medford, 08055, Burlington County, (609)267-4276, 20 miles from Philadelphia. **E-mail:** goldenphez@aol.com. **Web:** www.golfgoldenpheasant.com. **Facility Holes:** 18. **Yards:** 6,273/5,105. **Par:** 72/72. **Course Rating:** 68.1/68.4. **Slope:** 119/114. **Green Fee:** $14/$32. **Cart Fee:** $12/Person. **Walking Policy:** Walking at certain times. **Walkability:** 3. **Opened:** 1963. **Architect:** Richard Kidder/Carmen N. Capri. **Season:** Year-round. **High:** April-Oct. **To obtain tee times:** Call golf shop. **Miscellaneous:** Reduced fees (weekdays, twilight, seniors), metal spikes, range (grass/mats), credit cards (MC, V).

★★★½ GREAT GORGE COUNTRY CLUB

PU-Rte. 517, McAfee, 07428, Sussex County, (973)827-5757, 50 miles from New York City. **Facility Holes:** 27. **Green Fee:** $59/$89. **Cart Fee:** Included in green fee. **Walking Policy:** Mandatory carts. **Opened:** 1971. **Architect:** George Fazio. **Season:** April-Nov. **High:** May-Oct. **To obtain tee times:** Call golf shop. **Miscellaneous:** Reduced fees (weekdays, guests, twilight, seniors), metal spikes, range (grass/mats), credit cards (MC, V, AE), BF, FF.

LAKE/QUARRY (18 Combo)
Yards: 6,819/5,390. **Par:** 71/71. **Course Rating:** 73.4/71.4. **Slope:** 132/126. **Walkability:** 4.

LAKE/RAIL (18 Combo)
Yards: 6,921/5,555. **Par:** 72/72. **Course Rating:** 73.5/71.9. **Slope:** 129/125. **Walkability:** 3.

QUARRY/RAIL (18 Combo)
Yards: 6,826/5,539. **Par:** 71/71. **Course Rating:** 72.8/71.7. **Slope:** 128/122. **Walkability:** 3.

Reader Comments: 27 holes, no two the same, great holes especially among the rock … Mountain course … Tough lake side, interesting holes … Good condition for heavily played course … Always well kept, nice variety of holes … Out of the way, expensive, but pretty, interesting and fair course.

★★★ GREEN KNOLL GOLF COURSE

PU-587 Garretson Rd., Bridgewater, 08807, Somerset County, (908)722-1301, 30 miles from New York City. **E-mail:** banderson@parks.co.somerset.nj.us. **Facility Holes:** 18. **Yards:** 6,443/5,324. **Par:** 71/72. **Course Rating:** 70.5/71.1. **Slope:** 120/124. **Cart Fee:** $26/Cart. **Walking Policy:** Unrestricted walking. **Walkability:** 3. **Opened:** 1960. **Architect:** William Gordon. **Season:** Year-round. **High:** May-Oct. **To obtain tee times:** Call up to 7 days in advance. **Miscellaneous:** Reduced fees (weekdays, twilight, seniors, juniors), credit cards (MC, V, AE), BF, FF.

Reader Comments: Hilly in places but a nice walk, lots of variety … Very forgiving driving course with some interesting holes … Good all around service and conditions … Nice county course, many hills … Great views of mountains.

Special Notes: Also has a 9-hole pitch & putt course.

GREEN TREE GOLF COURSE

PU-1030 Somers Pt. Mays Landing Rd., Egg Harbor Township, 08234, Atlantic County, (609)625-9131. **Facility Holes:** 18. **Yards:** 5,709/4,804. **Par:** 70/70. **Course Rating:** 661.0. **Slope:** 109. **Green Fee:** $24/$30. **Cart Fee:** $20/Cart. **To obtain tee times:** Call golf shop.

★★½ HANOVER COUNTRY CLUB
PU-133 Larrison Rd., Jacobstown, 08562, Burlington County, (609)758-8301. **Facility Holes:** 18. **Yards:** 6,730/5,550. **Par:** 70/70. **Green Fee:** $21/$54. **Walking Policy:** Unrestricted walking. **Walkability:** 3. **Season:** Year-round. **To obtain tee times:** Call up to 7 days in advance. **Miscellaneous:** Reduced fees (weekdays, twilight, seniors, juniors), range (grass/mats), credit cards (MC, V, AE), BF, FF.

★★★★ HARBOR PINES GOLF CLUB *Condition*
PU-500 St. Andrews Dr., Egg Harbor Township, 08234, Atlantic County, (609)927-0006, 1 mile from Somers Point. **E-mail:** harborpines@msn.com. **Web:** www.harborpines.com. **Facility Holes:** 18. **Yards:** 6,827/5,099. **Par:** 72/72. **Course Rating:** 72.3/68.8. **Slope:** 129/118. **Green Fee:** $54/$120. **Cart Fee:** Included in green fee. **Walking Policy:** Mandatory carts. **Walkability:** 1. **Opened:** 1996. **Architect:** Stephen Kay. **Season:** Year-round. **High:** July-Aug. **To obtain tee times:** Call up to 7 days in advance. **Miscellaneous:** Reduced fees (weekdays, twilight, juniors), range (grass/mats), credit cards (MC, V, AE, D), BF, FF.
Reader Comments: Very well done, scenic ... Must go when in Atlantic City ... Wide fairways ... Nice course with large greens ... Great experience. Fair and challenging, and a beauty ... Treacherous greens.

HAWK POINTE GOLF CLUB
SP-294 Rte. 31 S., Washington, 07882, Warren County, (908)689-1870, (877)322-4295, 50 miles from New York City. **Web:** hawkpointegolf.com. **Facility Holes:** 18. **Yards:** 6,970/4,789. **Par:** 72/72. **Course Rating:** 73.4/67.9. **Slope:** 137/117. **Green Fee:** $75/$100. **Cart Fee:** Included in green fee. **Walking Policy:** Walking at certain times. **Walkability:** 3. **Opened:** 2000. **Architect:** Kelly Blake Moran. **Season:** April-Dec. **High:** June-Oct. **To obtain tee times:** Call up to 7 days in advance. **Miscellaneous:** Reduced fees (twilight, seniors, juniors), range (grass), caddies, credit cards (MC, V, AE), BF, FF.

★½ HENDRICKS FIELD GOLF COURSE
PU-240 Franklin Ave., Belleville, 07109, Essex County, (973)751-0178. **Facility Holes:** 18. **Yards:** 6,223/5,160. **Par:** 70/69. **Course Rating:** 68.6. **Slope:** 116. **Green Fee:** $22/$26. **Opened:** 1897. **Architect:** Tom Bendelow. **Season:** Year-round. **To obtain tee times:** Call golf shop. **Miscellaneous:** Metal spikes.

★★★ HIGH BRIDGE HILLS GOLF CLUB
PU-203 Cregar Rd., High Bridge, 08829, Hunterdon County, (908)638-5055. **E-mail:** hbhills@earthlink.net. **Facility Holes:** 18. **Yards:** 6,650/4,928. **Par:** 71/71. **Course Rating:** 71.7/68.3. **Slope:** 125/114. **Green Fee:** $65. **Walking Policy:** Unrestricted walking. **Walkability:** 4. **Opened:** 1999. **Architect:** Mark Mungeam. **Season:** Year-round. **High:** May-Oct. **To obtain tee times:** Call up to 7 days in advance. **Miscellaneous:** Reduced fees (twilight, seniors, juniors), range (grass), credit cards (MC, V, AE, D), BF, FF.
Reader Comments: Very challenging, rolling; links-like, great views ... You pay the price for errant shots. Very tough when wind is blowing ... A lot of hills on this course ... Bring many balls ... Walkable for first eight holes then call a taxi ... No. 18 tough finishing hole.

★★ HIGH MOUNTAIN GOLF CLUB
SP-845 Ewing Ave., Franklin Lakes, 07417, Bergen County, (201)891-4653, 8 miles from Ridgewood. **E-mail:** pgapro310@aol.com. **Web:** www.highmountaingolf.com. **Facility Holes:** 18. **Yards:** 6,347/5,426. **Par:** 71/71. **Course Rating:** 69.5/70.0. **Slope:** 118/117. **Green Fee:** $61/$71. **Cart Fee:** Included in green fee. **Walking Policy:** Walking at certain times. **Walkability:** 1. **Opened:** 1967. **Architect:** Alec Ternyei. **Season:** March-Dec. **High:** May-July. **To obtain tee times:** Call golf shop. **Miscellaneous:** Reduced fees (weekdays, twilight), range (grass), credit cards (MC, V, AE), BF, FF.

★★★ HIGH POINT COUNTRY CLUB
SP-P.O. Box 1729, Montague, 07827, Sussex County, (973)293-3282, 2 miles from Milford. **Web:** www.hpccnj.com. **Facility Holes:** 18. **Yards:** 6,783/5,355. **Par:** 73/73. **Course Rating:** 73.3/70.0. **Slope:** 128/120. **Green Fee:** $37/$60. **Cart Fee:** Included in green fee. **Walking Policy:** Mandatory carts. **Walkability:** 5. **Opened:** 1964. **Architect:** Gerald Roby. **Season:** April-Nov. **High:** June-Aug. **To obtain tee times:** Call up to 14 days in advance. **Miscellaneous:** Reduced fees (weekdays, twilight, seniors), metal spikes, range (grass), credit cards (MC, V, AE), FF.
Reader Comments: This is a fun place. Bring lots of golf balls, bring all clubs, bring brain ... Good solid course, 13 water holes.... Long and lots of water... Excellent greens ... Very long, blind shots.

★★ **HILLSBOROUGH COUNTRY CLUB**
SP-146 Wertsville Rd., P.O. Box 365, Neshanic, 08853, Somerset County, (908)369-3322, 7 miles from Flemington. **E-mail:** hccgolf@eclipse.net. **Web:** www.hillsboroughgolf.com. **Facility Holes:** 18. **Yards:** 5,840/5,445. **Par:** 70/73. **Course Rating:** 68.2/74.1. **Slope:** 114/119. **Green Fee:** $15/$38. **Cart Fee:** $15/Person. **Walking Policy:** Walking at certain times. **Walkability:** 4. **Season:** Year-round. **To obtain tee times:** Call up to 7 days in advance. **Miscellaneous:** Reduced fees (weekdays, twilight, seniors, juniors), range (grass), credit cards (MC, V, AE, D), BF, FF.

★★½ **HOLLY HILLS GOLF CLUB**
PU-374 Freisburg Rd., Alloway, 08001, Salem County, (856)455-5115, 15 miles from Wilmington. **E-mail:** mikezack@yahoo.com. **Facility Holes:** 18. **Yards:** 6,376/5,056. **Par:** 72/72. **Course Rating:** 71.4/68.0. **Slope:** 124/114. **Green Fee:** $30/$40. **Cart Fee:** Included in green fee. **Walking Policy:** Walking at certain times. **Walkability:** 5. **Opened:** 1970. **Architect:** Horace Smith. **Season:** Year-round. **High:** April-Oct. **To obtain tee times:** Call golf shop. **Miscellaneous:** Reduced fees (twilight, juniors), metal spikes, range (grass/mats), credit cards (MC, V, AE), BF, FF.

★★★★½ **HOMINY HILL GOLF COURSE** *Value*
PU-92 Mercer Rd., Colts Neck, 07722, Monmouth County, (732)462-9222, 50 miles from New York City. **Facility Holes:** 18. **Yards:** 7,056/5,794. **Par:** 72/72. **Course Rating:** 74.4/73.9. **Slope:** 132/128. **Green Fee:** $23/$56. **Cart Fee:** $28/Cart. **Walking Policy:** Unrestricted walking. **Walkability:** 3. **Opened:** 1964. **Architect:** Robert Trent Jones. **Season:** March-Dec. **To obtain tee times:** Call up to 7 days in advance. **Miscellaneous:** Reduced fees (weekdays, twilight, seniors, juniors), range (grass/mats), credit cards (MC, V), FF.
Notes: Ranked 13th in 2001 Best in State; Ranked 3rd in 1996 America's Top 75 Affordable Courses.
Reader Comments: Old school golf, in a great little town. Try playing from the tips when they let the rough grow out … Par-5 9th a favorite with second shot choice of over water to an elevated and bunkered green … Beautiful, horse farms … U.S. Open-type layout … Challenging, great shape, elevated greens.

★★★★½ **HOWELL PARK GOLF COURSE** *Value*
PU-Yellow Brook and Preventorium Rd., Farmingdale, 07727, Monmouth County, (732)938-4771, 40 miles from Philadelphia. **Facility Holes:** 18. **Yards:** 6,916/5,725. **Par:** 72/72. **Course Rating:** 73.0/72.5. **Slope:** 126/125. **Green Fee:** $20/$41. **Cart Fee:** $30/Cart. **Walking Policy:** Unrestricted walking. **Walkability:** 3. **Opened:** 1972. **Architect:** Frank Duane. **Season:** March-Dec. **High:** April-Oct. **To obtain tee times:** Call golf shop. **Miscellaneous:** Reduced fees (weekdays, twilight, seniors, juniors), range (mats).
Notes: Ranked 62nd in 1996 America's Top 75 Affordable Courses.
Reader Comments: Great course, one of the best in N.J., greens and pin placements always very challenging … Friendly course … Wide open layout … I love the wooded setting, lots of unique holes … Tough, well kept … Fast greens.

INDIAN SPRING COUNTRY CLUB
PU-115 S. Elmwood Rd., Marlton, 08053, Burlington County, (856)983-0222. **E-mail:** matteo@twp.evesham.nj.us. **Facility Holes:** 18. **Yards:** 6,409/5,590. **Par:** 70/70. **Course Rating:** 68.9/70.8. **Slope:** 113/116. **Green Fee:** $28/$32. **Cart Fee:** $14/Person. **Walking Policy:** Unrestricted walking. **Architect:** Fonse Design. **Season:** Year-round. **To obtain tee times:** Call golf shop. **Miscellaneous:** Range (grass/mats), credit cards (MC, V, AE, D), BF, FF.

★★★ **KNOB HILL GOLF CLUB**
SP-360 Rte. 33 West, Manalapan, 07726, Monmouth County, (732)792-8118, 4 miles from Freehold. **Facility Holes:** 18. **Yards:** 6,513/4,917. **Par:** 70/70. **Course Rating:** 72.2/69.5. **Slope:** 130/125. **Green Fee:** $25/$60. **Cart Fee:** $18/Person. **Walking Policy:** Walking at certain times. **Walkability:** 3. **Opened:** 1998. **Architect:** Mark McCumber. **Season:** Feb.-Dec. **High:** May-Sept. **To obtain tee times:** Call up to 3 days in advance. **Miscellaneous:** Reduced fees (weekdays, twilight), credit cards (MC, V, AE, D), FF.
Reader Comments: Needs maturity … Well kept … Short, but fun to play.

KNOLL COUNTRY CLUB
SP-Knoll and Green Bank Rds., Parsippany, 07054, Morris County, (973)263-7110, 16 miles from Newark. **Facility Holes:** 36. **Season:** March-Dec. **To obtain tee times:** Call up to 1 day in advance. **Miscellaneous:** Reduced fees (weekdays, twilight), range (grass), FF.
★★½ **EAST COURSE** (18)
Yards: 5,884/5,309. **Par:** 70/71. **Course Rating:** 67.9. **Slope:** 112. **Green Fee:** $22/$31. **Cart Fee:** $14/Person. **Walking Policy:** Unrestricted walking. **Walkability:** 2. **Opened:** 1963. **Architect:** Hal Purdy.

★★★½ **WEST COURSE** (18)
Yards: 6,735/5,840. **Par:** 70/74. **Course Rating:** 72.2/74.4. **Slope:** 128/128. **Green Fee:** $38/$51. **Cart Fee:** $15/Person. **Walking Policy:** Walking at certain times. **Walkability:** 1. **Opened:** 1928. **Architect:** Charles Banks.
Reader Comments: Very demanding … No. 18 is tough par four, long course, old style … Good course with some beautiful holes, excellent greens … Par 4s long for average golfer … Great course, great shape … Getting better, great value.

★★★ **LAKEWOOD COUNTRY CLUB**
SP-145 Country Club Dr., Lakewood, 08701, Ocean County, (732)364-8899, 40 miles from New York City. **Web:** www.lakewoodcountryclub-nj.com. **Facility Holes:** 18. **Yards:** 6,566/5,135. **Par:** 72/72. **Course Rating:** 71.7/65.9. **Slope:** 133/116. **Green Fee:** $27/$32. **Cart Fee:** $30/Cart. **Walking Policy:** Unrestricted walking. **Walkability:** 2. **Opened:** 1902. **Architect:** Willie Dunn Jr. **Season:** Year-round. **High:** May-Oct. **To obtain tee times:** Call golf shop. **Miscellaneous:** Reduced fees (weekdays, twilight), metal spikes, range (grass/mats), credit cards (MC, V, AE), FF.
Reader Comments: Love the hole on the side of hill … Fun course to play, good walking course and an excellent value. Difficult when the wind kicks up … The course has come a long way … Old course, interesting layout, long and tough par 3s … Good value, new holes on front 9.

★★ **MAPLE RIDGE GOLF CLUB**
PU-Woodbury-Glassboro Rd., Sewell, 08080, Gloucester County, (856)468-3542, 12 miles from Camden. **Facility Holes:** 18. **Yards:** 6,380/5,177. **Par:** 71/71. **Course Rating:** 70.4/67.9. **Slope:** 123/111. **Green Fee:** $25/$47. **Cart Fee:** Included in green fee. **Walking Policy:** Walking at certain times. **Walkability:** 3. **Architect:** William Gordon/David Gordon. **Season:** Year-round. **High:** April-Oct. **To obtain tee times:** Call golf shop. **Miscellaneous:** Reduced fees (weekdays, twilight, seniors), metal spikes, credit cards (MC, V, AE).

MARRIOTT'S SEAVIEW RESORT
R-401 S. New York Rd., Absecon, 08201, Atlantic County, (609)748-7680, 10 miles from Atlantic City. **E-mail:** seaviewpro@aol.com. **Web:** www.marriott.com. **Facility Holes:** 36. **Green Fee:** $49/$135. **Cart Fee:** Included in green fee. **Walking Policy:** Walking at certain times. **Season:** Year-round. **High:** May-Oct. **To obtain tee times:** Call golf shop. **Miscellaneous:** Reduced fees (weekdays, twilight, juniors), range (grass), caddies, credit cards (MC, V, AE, D, DC), BF, FF.
★★★★ **BAY COURSE** (18)
Yards: 6,247/5,017. **Par:** 71/71. **Course Rating:** 70.7/68.4. **Slope:** 122/114. **Walkability:** 2. **Opened:** 1914. **Architect:** Donald Ross/A. W. Tillinghast.
Reader Comments: Excellent course, great staff, fun to play … Tough seaside course … Impeccably restored Ross gem, not too tough unless the wind is blowing, greens are small and tricky … Deceptively hard … A lot of wind … Great course, beautiful layout … Greens fast and hard to hold in the wind.
★★★★ **PINES COURSE** (18)
Yards: 6,371/5,276. **Par:** 71/71. **Course Rating:** 71.7/69.8. **Slope:** 128/119. **Walkability:** 3. **Opened:** 1929. **Architect:** Toomey/Flynn/Gordon.
Reader Comments: Winds through the woods … Good layout and good shape … Go with a caddie, challenging course … Wooded pine forest, lightning greens, great … Tough tree-lined holes … After the first tee, never see anyone else on the course … Narrow, hard.

★★★ **MATTAWANG GOLF CLUB**
SP-P.O. Box 577, Belle Mead, 08502, Somerset County, (908)281-0778, 8 miles from Princeton. **Facility Holes:** 18. **Yards:** 6,800/5,469. **Par:** 72/75. **Course Rating:** 73.1/71.8. **Slope:** 130/123. **Green Fee:** $17/$42. **Cart Fee:** $16/Person. **Walking Policy:** Walking at certain times. **Walkability:** 2. **Opened:** 1962. **Architect:** Mike Myles. **Season:** March-Jan. **High:** May-Sept. **To obtain tee times:** Call golf shop. **Miscellaneous:** Reduced fees (twilight, seniors, juniors), range (mats), credit cards (MC, V, AE, D).
Reader Comments: Plays longer than card … Fair layout and good shape … Very challenging with lots of parallel and tight fairways, a little hilly and approach shots into greens are tough to hold … Tough back 9, small greens … Short, sporty, nice greens, well run.

★★★ **MAYS LANDING COUNTRY CLUB**
PU-1855 Cates Rd., Mays Landing, 08330, Atlantic County, (609)641-4411, 10 miles from Atlantic City. **Web:** www.mayslandinggolf.com. **Facility Holes:** 18. **Yards:** 6,662/5,432. **Par:** 72/71. **Course Rating:** 71.8/69.7. **Slope:** 123/114. **Green Fee:** $20/$60. **Cart Fee:** $16/Person. **Walking Policy:** Walking at certain times. **Walkability:** 2. **Opened:** 1962. **Architect:** Hal Purdy. **Season:** Year-round. **High:** May-Sept. **To obtain tee times:** Call up to 7 days in advance. **Miscellaneous:** Reduced fees (weekdays, guests, twilight), range (grass), credit cards (MC, V, AE, D, DC), BF, FF.

NEW JERSEY

THE MEADOWS AT MIDDLESEX
PU-70 Hunters Glen Drive, Plainsboro, 08536, Middlesex County, (609)799-4000, 5 miles from Princeton. **Facility Holes:** 18. **Yards:** 6,277/4,762. **Par:** 70/70. **Course Rating:** 70.3/71.5. **Slope:** 121/122. **Green Fee:** $16/$60. **Cart Fee:** $26/Cart. **Walking Policy:** Unrestricted walking. **Walkability:** 1. **Opened:** 1972. **Architect:** Joe Finger/Tom Fazio. **Season:** Year-round. **Tee times:** Call golf shop. **Miscellaneous:** Reduced fees (weekdays, guests, seniors, juniors), FF.

★★ MEADOWS GOLF CLUB
SP-79 Two Bridges Rd., Lincoln Park, 07035, Morris County, (973)696-7212, 22 miles from New York City. **Facility Holes:** 18. **Yards:** 6,193/4,600. **Par:** 68/70. **Green Fee:** $27/$47. **Cart Fee:** $30/Cart. **Walking Policy:** Walking at certain times. **Walkability:** 2. **Opened:** 1963. **Season:** Year-round. **High:** April-Oct. **To obtain tee times:** Call golf shop. **Miscellaneous:** Reduced fees (weekdays, twilight, seniors).

★★★½ MERCER OAKS GOLF CLUB
PU-725 Village Rd., West Windsor, 08550, Mercer County, (609)936-1383, 5 miles from Princeton. **Facility Holes:** 18. **Yards:** 7,012/6,330. **Par:** 72/72. **Course Rating:** 73.5/70.3. **Slope:** 126/120. **Green Fee:** $17/$38. **Cart Fee:** $25/Cart. **Walking Policy:** Unrestricted walking. **Walkability:** 3. **Opened:** 1993. **Architect:** Bill Love/Brian Ault. **Season:** March-Jan. **High:** April-Oct. **To obtain tee times:** Call golf shop. **Miscellaneous:** Reduced fees (weekdays, twilight, seniors, juniors), range (grass), credit cards (MC, V), BF, FF.

★½ MINEBROOK GOLF CLUB
PU-500 Schooley's Mt. Rd., Hackettstown, 07840, Morris County, (908)979-0366, 45 miles from Newark. **Facility Holes:** 18. **Yards:** 6,349/5,505. **Par:** 70/72. **Course Rating:** 70.9/73.0. **Slope:** 128/122. **Green Fee:** $22/$41. **Cart Fee:** $14/Person. **Walking Policy:** Walking at certain times. **Walkability:** 4. **Opened:** 1919. **Architect:** M. Coopman/J. Rocco. **Season:** Year-round. **To obtain tee times:** Call up to 7 days in advance. **Miscellaneous:** Reduced fees (twilight, seniors, juniors), credit cards (MC, V, AE), BF, FF.

★★½ MIRY RUN COUNTRY CLUB
SP-106 B. Sharon Rd., Robbinsville, 08691, Mercer County, (609)259-1010, 8 miles from Trenton. **Web:** www.snjgolf.com. **Facility Holes:** 18. **Yards:** 6,893/5,562. **Par:** 72/72. **Course Rating:** 71.7/70.7. **Slope:** 119/113. **Green Fee:** $15/$25. **Cart Fee:** $15/Person. **Walking Policy:** Walking at certain times. **Walkability:** 2. **Opened:** 1961. **Architect:** Fred Lambert. **Season:** Year-round. **High:** May-Sept. **To obtain tee times:** Call golf shop. **Miscellaneous:** Reduced fees (twilight), metal spikes, range (grass).

★★★ MOUNTAIN VIEW GOLF COURSE
PU-Bear Tavern Rd., West Trenton, 08650, Mercer County, (609)882-4093. **Facility Holes:** 18. **Yards:** 6,775/5,500. **Par:** 72/73. **Course Rating:** 72.0/70.8. **Slope:** 124/118. **Green Fee:** $12/$28. **Cart Fee:** $25/Cart. **Walking Policy:** Unrestricted walking. **Walkability:** 4. **Opened:** 1958. **Season:** Year-round. **High:** April-Sept. **Tee times:** Call golf shop. **Miscellaneous:** Reduced fees (twilight, seniors, juniors), range (grass), credit cards (MC, V), BF, FF.

★★★ NEW JERSEY NATIONAL GOLF CLUB
SP-579 Allen Rd., Basking Ridge, 07920, Somerset County, (908)781-9400, 6 miles from Basking Ridge. **Web:** www.newjerseynational.com. **Facility Holes:** 18. **Yards:** 7,056/5,019. **Par:** 72/72. **Course Rating:** 73.7/68.8. **Slope:** 137/121. **Green Fee:** $95/$125. **Cart Fee:** Included in green fee. **Walking Policy:** Unrestricted walking. **Walkability:** 4. **Opened:** 1997. **Architect:** Roy Case. **Season:** Year-round. **To obtain tee times:** Call golf shop. **Miscellaneous:** Reduced fees (weekdays, twilight), range (grass/mats), credit cards (MC, V, AE), BF, FF.

★★½ OAK RIDGE GOLF COURSE
PU-136 Oak Ridge Rd., Clark, 07066, Union County, (732)574-0139, 15 miles from Newark. **Facility Holes:** 18. **Yards:** 6,388/5,275. **Par:** 70/72. **Course Rating:** 70.0/69.9. **Slope:** 110/112. **Green Fee:** $24/$28. **Cart Fee:** $22/Cart. **Walking Policy:** Unrestricted walking. **Walkability:** 1. **Opened:** 1975. **Season:** Year-round. **High:** April-Oct. **To obtain tee times:** Call golf shop. **Miscellaneous:** Reduced fees (twilight, seniors, juniors).

★★ OCEAN ACRES COUNTRY CLUB

SP-925 Buccaneer Lane, Manahawkin, 08050, Ocean County, (609)597-9393, 12 miles from Long Beach Island. **Facility Holes:** 18. **Yards:** 6,548/5,412. **Par:** 72/72. **Course Rating:** 70.5/70.7. **Slope:** 120/118. **Green Fee:** $24/$27. **Cart Fee:** $20/Cart. **Walking Policy:** Walking at certain times. **Opened:** 1967. **Architect:** Hal Purdy/John Davies. **Season:** Year-round. **High:** June-Aug. **To obtain tee times:** Call golf shop. **Miscellaneous:** Reduced fees (twilight), metal spikes, credit cards (MC, V, AE).

★★★½ OCEAN COUNTY GOLF COURSE AT ATLANTIS

PU-Country Club Blvd., Tuckerton, 08087, Ocean County, (609)296-2444, 30 miles from Atlantic City. **Facility Holes:** 18. **Yards:** 6,848/5,579. **Par:** 72/72. **Course Rating:** 73.6/71.8. **Slope:** 134/124. **Green Fee:** $15/$42. **Cart Fee:** $24/Person. **Walking Policy:** Walking at certain times. **Walkability:** 1. **Opened:** 1961. **Architect:** George Fazio. **Season:** Year-round. **To obtain tee times:** Call up to 8 days in advance. **Miscellaneous:** Reduced fees (twilight, seniors, juniors), range (mats), credit cards (MC, V), FF.
Reader Comments: Make part of your winter tour ... Tight track, good test of golf, George Fazio's first course ... Tough track. Some locals won't play it because their scores rise too much ... Older but enjoyable ... A real bang for your buck ... Nice combo of difficult and forgiving holes.

★★½ OLD ORCHARD COUNTRY CLUB

SP-54 Monmouth Rd., Eatontown, 07724, Monmouth County, (732)542-7666, 40 miles from New York City. **E-mail:** gjc.pro@worldnet.att.net. **Facility Holes:** 18. **Yards:** 6,588/5,575. **Par:** 72/72. **Course Rating:** 70.5/70.8. **Slope:** 116/115. **Green Fee:** $28/$45. **Cart Fee:** $36/Cart. **Walking Policy:** Unrestricted walking. **Walkability:** 2. **Opened:** 1929. **Season:** Year-round. **High:** May-Sept. **To obtain tee times:** Call golf shop. **Miscellaneous:** Reduced fees (weekdays, twilight, seniors), range (grass), credit cards (MC, V, AE), BF, FF.

★½ OVERPECK COUNTY GOLF COURSE

PU-E. Cedar Lane, Teaneck, 07666, Bergen County, (201)837-8395, 10 miles from New York City. **Facility Holes:** 18. **Yards:** 6,559/5,557. **Par:** 72/72. **Course Rating:** 72.6/73.7. **Slope:** 124/127. **Green Fee:** $45. **Cart Fee:** $20/Cart. **Walking Policy:** Unrestricted walking. **Opened:** 1968. **Architect:** Nicholas Psiahas. **Season:** March-Dec. **High:** June-Sept. **To obtain tee times:** Call golf shop. **Miscellaneous:** Reduced fees (weekdays, twilight, seniors, juniors), metal spikes, range (grass).

★★★ PARAMUS GOLF CLUB

PU-314 Paramus Rd., Paramus, 07652, Bergen County, (201)447-6067, 15 miles from New York City. **Facility Holes:** 18. **Yards:** 6,212/5,241. **Par:** 71/70. **Course Rating:** 69.1/72.0. **Slope:** 118/117. **Green Fee:** $20/$40. **Cart Fee:** $24/Cart. **Walking Policy:** Unrestricted walking. **Walkability:** 2. **Opened:** 1976. **Architect:** Stephen Kay. **Season:** Year-round. **To obtain tee times:** Call golf shop. **Miscellaneous:** Reduced fees (weekdays, seniors, juniors), range (mats), BF, FF.
Reader Comments: For a municipal course, it's a good small course ... Surprise course ... Great value, nice open course ... Renovations & conditions have really improved.

★★½ PASCACK BROOK GOLF & COUNTRY CLUB

PU-15 Rivervale Rd., River Vale, 07675, Bergen County, (201)664-5886, 15 miles from New York City. **Facility Holes:** 18. **Yards:** 5,991/5,117. **Par:** 71/71. **Course Rating:** 69.0/69.3. **Slope:** 119/117. **Green Fee:** $60. **Cart Fee:** Included in green fee. **Walking Policy:** Walking at certain times. **Walkability:** 2. **Opened:** 1962. **Architect:** John Handwerg Jr. **Season:** Year-round. **High:** May-Sept. **To obtain tee times:** Call golf shop. **Miscellaneous:** Reduced fees (weekdays, twilight, seniors, juniors), metal spikes, credit cards (MC, V, AE).

PASSAIC COUNTY GOLF COURSE

PU-209 Totowa Rd., Wayne, 07470, Passaic County, (973)881-4921. **Facility Holes:** 36. **Green Fee:** $45. **Cart Fee:** $22/Cart. **Walking Policy:** Unrestricted walking. **Walkability:** 3. **Architect:** Alfred H. Tull. **Season:** Year-round. **High:** April-Oct. **To obtain tee times:** Call golf shop. **Miscellaneous:** Reduced fees (twilight, seniors, juniors), BF, FF.
★½ **BLUE COURSE** (18)
Yards: 6,080/6,080. **Par:** 70/73. **Course Rating:** 69.5/74.0. **Slope:** 120/128. **Opened:** 1892.
★½ **RED COURSE** (18)
Yards: 6,457/6,080. **Par:** 69/73. **Course Rating:** 71.2/74.8. **Slope:** 122/128. **Opened:** 1925.

★★★★ PENNSAUKEN COUNTRY CLUB

PU-3800 Haddonfield Rd., Pennsauken, 08109, Camden County, (856)662-4961, 5 miles from Philadelphia. **Facility Holes:** 18. **Yards:** 5,990/4,926. **Par:** 70/70. **Course Rating:** 68.1/67.9. **Slope:** 119/111. **Green Fee:** $25/$32. **Cart Fee:** $16/Person. **Walking Policy:** Walking at certain times. **Walkability:** 2. **Opened:** 1930. **Season:** Year-round. **To obtain tee**

times: Call golf shop. **Miscellaneous:** Reduced fees (twilight), credit cards (MC, V), BF, FF.
Reader Comments: Always in excellent condition. Flat and short. Great food at the 19th hole …
Always in great shape for a busy muni … Improved 400% in past 6 years … Place gets a lot of play,
but always in great shape.

★★★½ PINCH BROOK GOLF COURSE
PU-234 Ridgedale Ave., Florham Park, 07932, Morris County, (973)377-2039, 25 miles from
Newark. **Facility Holes:** 18. **Yards:** 5,007/4,117. **Par:** 65/65. **Course Rating:** 64.2/63.3. **Slope:**
105/103. **Green Fee:** $16/$25. **Cart Fee:** $26/Cart. **Walking Policy:** Unrestricted walking.
Opened: 1965. **Season:** April-Nov. **High:** May-July. **Tee times:** Call up to 7 days in advance.
Miscellaneous: Reduced fees (twilight, seniors, juniors), credit cards (MC, V), BF, FF.
Reader Comments: Go relax enjoy … Busy course, short back 9 has lots of water, feels cramped
in some areas, higher handicappers could feel 'pushed' … Play here once a month to work on your
long iron and short game. This course will improve your ability to score.

★★★★½ PINE BARRENS GOLF CLUB *Service, Condition*
PU-540 S. Hope Chapel Rd., Jackson, 08527, Ocean County, (732)408-1151,
(877)746-3227, 65 miles from Newark. **Web:** www.pinebarrensgolf.com. **Facility Holes:** 18.
Yards: 7,118/5,209. **Par:** 72/72. **Course Rating:** 74.2/70.2. **Slope:** 132/120. **Green Fee:**
$60/$105. **Cart Fee:** Included in green fee. **Walking Policy:** Unrestricted walking. **Walkability:**
2. **Opened:** 1999. **Architect:** Eric Bergstol. **Season:** Year-round. **High:** April-Sept. **To obtain tee
times:** Call golf shop. **Miscellaneous:** Reduced fees (twilight), range (grass), credit cards
(MC, V, AE).
Notes: Ranked 15th in 2001 Best in State; tied for 10th in 1999 Best New Upscale Public.
Reader Comments: Very fun to play … Course requires numerous forced carries … Great work on
a great piece of land … Long par 3 on the back 9 demands tee shot over a waste area some 50
yards below … Stunning and difficult, but fair … Reminds me of a Pinehurst area course.

★★★½ PINE BROOK GOLF COURSE
PU-1 Covered Bridge Blvd., Englishtown, 07726, Monmouth County, (732)536-7272, 70 miles
from New York City. **Facility Holes:** 18. **Yards:** 4,168/3,441. **Par:** 61/61. **Course Rating:**
61.0/61.0. **Slope:** 90/90. **Green Fee:** $10/$32. **Cart Fee:** $23/Cart. **Walking Policy:** Unrestricted
walking. **Walkability:** 2. **Opened:** 1980. **Architect:** Hal Purdy. **Season:** March-Dec. **High:** June-
Aug. **To obtain tee times:** Call golf shop. **Miscellaneous:** Reduced fees (weekdays, twilight,
seniors, juniors), BF, FF.
Reader Comments: Fun, executive course.

PINE HILL GOLF CLUB
PU-500 W. Branch Ave., Pine Hill, 08021, Camden County, (865)435-3100, (877)450-8866,
15 miles from Philadelpha. **E-mail:** ghproman@aol.com. **Facility Holes:** 18. **Yards:**
6,969/4,922. **Par:** 70/70. **Course Rating:** 74.2/68.3. **Slope:** 140/121. **Green Fee:** $65/$130. **Cart
Fee:** Included in green fee. **Walking Policy:** Walking at certain times. **Walkability:** 4. **Opened:**
2001. **Architect:** Tom Fazio. **Season:** March-Dec. **High:** June-Sept. **To obtain tee times:** Call up
to 6 days in advance. **Miscellaneous:** Reduced fees (twilight), range (grass), credit cards
(MC, V, AE, D), BF, FF.

★★ PINELANDS GOLF CLUB
PU-887 S. Mays Landing Rd., Winslow, 08037, Camden County, (609)561-8900, 25 miles from
Altantic City. **Facility Holes:** 18. **Yards:** 6,224/5,375. **Par:** 71/71. **Course Rating:** 69.7/70.4.
Slope: 114/119. **Green Fee:** $18/$24. **Cart Fee:** $24/Cart. **Walking Policy:** Walking at certain
times. **Walkability:** 2. **Opened:** 1963. **Season:** Year-round. **High:** May-Nov. **To obtain tee times:**
Call golf shop. **Miscellaneous:** Reduced fees (weekdays, twilight), metal spikes, range
(grass/mats), credit cards (MC, V).

★★½ PITMAN GOLF COURSE
PU-501 Pitman Rd., Sewell, 08080, Gloucester County, (856)589-6688. **E-mail:**
owells@co.gloucester.nj.us.com. **Web:** www.co.gloucester.nj.us/golf. **Facility Holes:** 18.
Yards: 6,125/4,942. **Par:** 70/73. **Course Rating:** 68.4/67.9. **Slope:** 113/106. **Green Fee:**
$18/$33. **Cart Fee:** $14/Person. **Walking Policy:** Unrestricted walking. **Walkability:** 2. **Opened:**
1927. **Architect:** Alex Findlay. **Season:** Year-round. **High:** June-Sept. **Tee times:** Call golf shop.
Miscellaneous: Reduced fees (twilight, seniors, juniors), range (grass/mats), BF, FF.

PONDERLODGE
SP-7 Shawmont Ave., Villas, 08251, Cape May County, (609)886-8065. **Facility Holes:** 18.
Yards: 6,200/4,800. **Par:** 71/71. **Course Rating:** 69.6/68.6. **Slope:** 120/117. **Green Fee:**
$18/$53. **Cart Fee:** $12/Person. **To obtain tee times:** Call golf shop.

NEW JERSEY

★★ PRINCETON GOLF CLUB
PU-Wheeler Way, Princeton, 08540, Mercer County, (609)452-9382, 2 miles from Princeton. **Facility Holes:** 18. **Yards:** 6,038/5,005. **Par:** 70/71. **Course Rating:** 68.6/69.9. **Slope:** 113/113. **Green Fee:** $14/$28. **Cart Fee:** $25/Cart. **Walking Policy:** Unrestricted walking. **Walkability:** 2. **Opened:** 1959. **Architect:** William Gordon/David Gordon. **Season:** Year-round. **High:** April-Sept. **To obtain tee times:** Call golf shop. **Miscellaneous:** Reduced fees (twilight, seniors, juniors), range (grass), credit cards (MC, V), BF, FF.

★★½ QUAIL BROOK GOLF COURSE
PU-625 New Brunswick Rd., Somerset, 08873, Somerset County, (732)560-9199, 30 miles from New York City. **E-mail:** banderson@parks.co.somerset.nj.us. **Facility Holes:** 18. **Yards:** 6,614/5,385. **Par:** 71/72. **Course Rating:** 71.4/70.9. **Slope:** 123/119. **Green Fee:** $14/$32. **Cart Fee:** $26/Cart. **Walking Policy:** Unrestricted walking. **Walkability:** 4. **Opened:** 1982. **Architect:** Edmund Ault. **Season:** March-Nov. **High:** May-Sept. **To obtain tee times:** Call up to 7 days in advance. **Miscellaneous:** Reduced fees (weekdays, twilight, seniors, juniors), range (mats), credit cards (MC, V, AE), BF, FF.

★★½ RAMBLEWOOD COUNTRY CLUB
PU-200 Country Club Pkwy., Mt. Laurel, 08054, Burlington County, (856)235-2118, 8 miles from Philadelphia. **Facility Holes:** 27. **Green Fee:** $31/$43. **Cart Fee:** $16/Person. **Walking Policy:** Walking at certain times. **Walkability:** 1. **Opened:** 1962. **Architect:** Edmund Ault. **Season:** Year-round. **High:** April-Oct. **To obtain tee times:** Call golf shop. **Miscellaneous:** Reduced fees (weekdays, twilight, seniors), credit cards (MC, V).
RED/BLUE (18 Combo)
Yards: 6,723/5,499. **Par:** 72/73. **Course Rating:** 72.1/71.4. **Slope:** 130/126.
RED/WHITE (18 Combo)
Yards: 6,883/5,741. **Par:** 72/74. **Course Rating:** 72.9/72.7. **Slope:** 130/128.
WHITE/BLUE (18 Combo)
Yards: 6,624/5,308. **Par:** 72/73. **Course Rating:** 71.1/70.1. **Slope:** 129/123.

★★½ RANCOCAS GOLF CLUB
PU-12 Club Ridge Lane, Willingboro, 08046, Burlington County, (609)877-5344, 10 miles from Philadelphia. **Web:** agpa.com. **Facility Holes:** 18. **Yards:** 6,634/5,284. **Par:** 71/72. **Course Rating:** 73.0/70.0. **Slope:** 130/120. **Green Fee:** $42/$55. **Cart Fee:** Included in green fee. **Walking Policy:** Unrestricted walking. **Walkability:** 2. **Opened:** 1968. **Architect:** Robert Trent Jones. **Season:** Year-round. **High:** May-Oct. **To obtain tee times:** Call golf shop. **Miscellaneous:** Reduced fees (weekdays, twilight, seniors, juniors), range (mats), credit cards (MC, V, AE), BF, FF.

★★★ RIVER VALE COUNTRY CLUB
PU-660 Rivervale Rd., River Vale, 07675, Bergen County, (201)391-2300, 20 miles from New York City. **E-mail:** info@rivervalecc.com. **Web:** www.rivervalecc.com. **Facility Holes:** 18. **Yards:** 6,470/5,293. **Par:** 72/74. **Course Rating:** 71.4/70.7. **Slope:** 128/123. **Green Fee:** $66/$93. **Cart Fee:** Included in green fee. **Walking Policy:** Mandatory carts. **Walkability:** 3. **Opened:** 1928. **Architect:** Orrin Smith. **Season:** Year-round. **High:** March-Oct. **To obtain tee times:** Call up to 14 days in advance. **Miscellaneous:** Reduced fees (twilight), range (mats), credit cards (MC, V, AE, JCB), FF.
Reader Comments: Excellent course, challenging and manicured ... They have a nice restaurant, good course ... Radio waves cut off cart engine if cart strays off blacktop onto grass ... Varied hilly terrain.

ROCKLEIGH GOLF COURSE
PU-15 Paris Ave., Rockleigh, 07647, Bergen County, (201)768-6353. **Facility Holes:** 27. **Green Fee:** $24/$31. **Season:** March-Dec. **To obtain tee times:** Call golf shop.
BLUE COURSE (9)
Yards: 6,254/5,744. **Par:** 72/72. **Course Rating:** 68.5/68.5. **Slope:** 117/118. **Opened:** 1964. **Architect:** Alfred H. Tull.
★½ RED/WHITE COURSE (18)
Yards: 6,243/5,611. **Par:** 72/72. **Course Rating:** 69.5/69.5. **Slope:** 117/118. **Opened:** 1959. **Architect:** Robert Trent Jones.

★½ ROLLING GREENS GOLF CLUB
PU-214 Newton-Sparta Rd, Newton, 07860, Sussex County, (973)383-3082, 60 miles from New York City. **Web:** www.rollinggreensgolf.com. **Facility Holes:** 18. **Yards:** 5,189/4,679. **Par:** 65/67. **Course Rating:** 64.8/62.1. **Slope:** 116/98. **Green Fee:** $10/$28. **Cart Fee:** $12/Person. **Walking Policy:** Unrestricted walking. **Walkability:** 1. **Opened:** 1969. **Architect:** Nicholas Psiahas. **Season:** Year-round. **High:** April-Oct. **Tee times:** Call up to 7 days in advance. **Misc:** Reduced fees (weekdays, twilight, seniors), range (grass), credit cards (MC, V, AE), BF, FF.

★★★ RON JAWORSKI'S VALLEYBROOK GOLF CLUB
PU-200 Golfview, Blackwood, 08012, Camden County, (856)227-3171, 10 miles from Philadelphia. **E-mail:** valleybrookgc@aol.com. **Web:** www.valleybrookgolf.com. **Facility Holes:** 18. **Yards:** 6,123/5,319. **Par:** 72/72. **Course Rating:** 70.6/69.1. **Slope:** 125/120. **Green Fee:** $25/$49. **Cart Fee:** Included in green fee. **Walking Policy:** Walking at certain times. **Walkability:** 3. **Opened:** 1990. **Season:** Year-round. **High:** March-Oct. **To obtain tee times:** Call golf shop. **Miscellaneous:** Reduced fees (weekdays, twilight), range (grass/mats), credit cards (MC, V, AE, D), BF, FF.
Reader Comments: Very good … Small greens, player's course … Fun course, getting better … Good scenic holes.

ROYCE BROOK GOLF CLUB
SP-201 Hamilton Rd., Hillsborough, 08844, Somerset County, (888)434-3673, (888)434-3673, 10 miles from Princeton. **E-mail:** wtroyanoski@roycebrook.com. **Web:** www.roycebrook.com. **Facility Holes:** 36. **Green Fee:** $75/$95. **Cart Fee:** Included in green fee. **Walking Policy:** Walking at certain times. **Walkability:** 2. **Opened:** 1998. **Architect:** Steve Smyers. **High:** May-Oct. **To obtain tee times:** Call up to 7 days in advance. **Miscellaneous:** Reduced fees (weekdays), range (grass), credit cards (MC, V, AE, D), BF, FF.
★★★★ EAST COURSE (18)
Yards: 6,983/5,014. **Par:** 72/72. **Course Rating:** 73.6/69.4. **Slope:** 132/114. **Season:** Year-round.
Reader Comments: Part of a great facility. It is a total golf experience. Excellent course … Most challenging … Best service in NJ! Beautiful natural turf range and practice areas … Nice layout with quick play … Lots of bunkers.
★★★★ WEST COURSE (18)
Yards: 7,158/5,366. **Par:** 72/72. **Course Rating:** 74.2/70.6. **Slope:** 134/119. **Season:** March-Dec.
Reader Comments: Traditional look but user friendly … Feel like Peter O'Toole playing this one—sand, sand, sand … If you want good golf, play here. A real gem of a course … Bring your sand wedge and enjoy. Seems no two holes in same direction. Strong westerly winds … A special course.

★★★½ RUTGERS UNIVERSITY GOLF COURSE
PU-777 Hoes Lane, Piscataway, 08854, Middlesex County, (732)445-2631, 3 miles from New Brunswick. **Facility Holes:** 18. **Yards:** 6,337/5,359. **Par:** 71/72. **Course Rating:** 70.6/71.3. **Slope:** 123/121. **Green Fee:** $22/$31. **Cart Fee:** $28/Cart. **Walking Policy:** Unrestricted walking. **Walkability:** 2. **Opened:** 1963. **Architect:** Hal Purdy. **Season:** March-Dec. **High:** April-Oct. **To obtain tee times:** Call golf shop. **Miscellaneous:** Reduced fees (weekdays, twilight, seniors, juniors), credit cards (MC, V), BF, FF.
Reader Comments: Excellent course and very challenging, always in great shape … Fun course, plenty room for error, some challenging holes, easy walking … Quick greens make up for short layout … Best kept secret in Jersey … Excellent walking design, greens have subtle breaks and can be fast.

★★★★ SAND BARRENS GOLF CLUB
SP-1765 Rte. 9 North, Swainton, 08210, Cape May County, (609)465-3555, (800)465-3122, 60 miles from Philadelphia, PA. **E-mail:** jzaborowski@sandbarrens.com. **Web:** www.sandbarrens.com. **Facility Holes:** 27. **Green Fee:** $42/$125. **Cart Fee:** Included in green fee. **Walking Policy:** Unrestricted walking. **Walkability:** 2. **Opened:** 1997. **Architect:** Michael Hurdzan/Dana Fry. **Season:** Year-round. **High:** June-Sept. **To obtain tee times:** Call up to 7 days in advance. **Miscellaneous:** Reduced fees (weekdays, twilight), range (grass), credit cards (MC, V, D), BF, FF.
NORTH/WEST (18)
Yards: 7,092/4,951. **Par:** 72/72. **Course Rating:** 73.2/67.9. **Slope:** 135/119.
SOUTH/NORTH (18)
Yards: 6,969/4,946. **Par:** 72/72. **Course Rating:** 72.7/68.0. **Slope:** 133/120.
Notes: Ranked 14th in 1999 Best in State.
SOUTH/WEST (18)
Yards: 6,895/4,971. **Par:** 72/72. **Course Rating:** 71.7/68.3. **Slope:** 130/119.
Reader Comments: Great course, beautiful … Lots and lots of sand, large greens … Must-play list for South Jersey … Great layout with easy and difficult holes. Generous landing areas but wayward shots are penalized by waste areas … Intimidating, but it plays fairly and rewards good shots, always in top shape.

★★★★ SCOTLAND RUN GOLF CLUB
PU-2626 Fries Mill Rd., Williamstown, 08094, Gloucester County, (856)863-3737, 15 miles from Philadelphia. **E-mail:** golfshop@scotlandrun.com. **Web:** www.scotlandrun.com. **Facility Holes:** 18. **Yards:** 6,810/5,010. **Par:** 71/71. **Course Rating:** 71.9/69.1. **Slope:** 131/119. **Green Fee:** $55/$105. **Cart Fee:** Included in green fee. **Walking Policy:** Unrestricted walking. **Walkability:** 3. **Opened:** 1999. **Architect:** Stephen Kay. **Season:** Year-round. **High:** May-Oct.

To obtain tee times: Call up to 7 days in advance. **Miscellaneous:** Reduced fees (weekdays, twilight), range (grass/mats), credit cards (MC, V, AE, D), BF, FF.
Reader Comments: Serious golfers only, a real challenge, but fair, tough greens, need all the clubs and shot making is a must, never a boring hole … The last three holes alone, are worth the price … Every hole different and fun … Tough back 9, long and hard … Huge greens.

SEA OAKS GOLF CLUB
SP-99 Golf View Dr., Little Egg Harbor Twshp., 08087, Ocean County, (609)296-2656, 20 miles from Atlantic City. **E-mail:** seaoaksgolf@aol.com. **Web:** www.seaoaksgolf.com. **Facility Holes:** 18. **Yards:** 6,950/5,150. **Par:** 72/72. **Course Rating:** 72.4/73.8. **Slope:** 129/129. **Green Fee:** $90/$105. **Cart Fee:** Included in green fee. **Walking Policy:** Unrestricted walking. **Architect:** Ray Hearn. **Season:** Year-round. **To obtain tee times:** Call golf shop.

★★★ SHARK RIVER GOLF COURSE
PU-320 Old Corlies Ave., Neptune, 07753, Monmouth County, (732)922-4141, (888)435-3613, 50 miles from Newark. **Facility Holes:** 18. **Yards:** 6,176/5,532. **Par:** 71/71. **Course Rating:** 70.3/72.0. **Slope:** 130/130. **Green Fee:** $14/$46. **Cart Fee:** $29/Cart. **Walking Policy:** Unrestricted walking. **Walkability:** 2. **Opened:** 1921. **Architect:** Joseph "Scotty" Anson. **Season:** Year-round. **To obtain tee times:** Call golf shop. **Miscellaneous:** Reduced fees (weekdays, twilight, seniors, juniors), credit cards (MC, V), BF, FF.
Reader Comments: Very challenging layout with numerous opportunities to score, if accurate. Some short par 3s and 4s, but par 5s are long and tough … Lots of water.

★★★ SPOOKY BROOK GOLF COURSE
PU-582 Elizabeth Ave., Somerset, 08873, Somerset County, (732)873-2242, 30 miles from New York City. **Facility Holes:** 18. **Yards:** 6,634/5,085. **Par:** 71/71. **Course Rating:** 71.0/69.0. **Slope:** 121/116. **Green Fee:** $14/$32. **Cart Fee:** $26/Cart. **Walking Policy:** Unrestricted walking. **Walkability:** 1. **Opened:** 1970. **Architect:** Edmund Ault. **Season:** March-Nov. **High:** May-Sept. **Tee times:** Call up to 7 days in advance. **Miscellaneous:** Reduced fees (weekdays, twilight, seniors, juniors), range (grass/mats), credit cards (MC, V, AE), BF, FF.
Reader Comments: Nice wide fairways, not much water, not a lot of trees, manageable for the beginner … Very open, mature course … Hit balls before you start. No. 1 is 430 yards into wind.

★★★ SPRING MEADOW GOLF COURSE
PU-4181 Atlantic Ave., Farmingdale, 07727, Monmouth County, (732)449-0806, 40 miles from Trenton. **E-mail:** smgc@superlink.net. **Web:** www.smgc@superlink.net. **Facility Holes:** 18. **Yards:** 6,224/5,074. **Par:** 72/76. **Course Rating:** 70.4/70.6. **Slope:** 125/121. **Green Fee:** $19/$23. **Cart Fee:** $26/Cart. **Walking Policy:** Unrestricted walking. **Walkability:** 3. **Opened:** 1920. **Architect:** Ron Faulseit. **Season:** Year-round. **To obtain tee times:** Call golf shop. **Miscellaneous:** Reduced fees (weekdays, twilight, seniors), metal spikes, range (grass/mats), credit cards (MC, V, AE, D), FF.
Reader Comments: Not a bad course. You can play 18 in reasonable time and have an enjoyable time … State run, very nice … Course in great shape, challenging holes , difficult pin placements … Nos. 10 and 11 are excellent … Good value, lot of walkers.

SPRINGFIELD GOLF CENTER
PU-855 Jacksonville Rd., Mt. Holly, 08060, Burlington County, (609)267-8440, 4 miles from Burlington. **Facility Holes:** 18. **Yards:** 5,005. **Par:** 68. **Green Fee:** $30/$33. **Walking Policy:** Walking at certain times. **Walkability:** 2. **Opened:** 1972. **Season:** Year-round. **High:** April-Oct. **To obtain tee times:** Call up to 7 days in advance. **Miscellaneous:** Reduced fees (twilight), range (grass/mats), BF, FF.

STONY BROOK GOLF CLUB
SP-Stoney Brook Rd., Hopewell, 08525, Mercer County, (609)466-2215, 13 miles from Trenton. **Facility Holes:** 18. **Yards:** 3,603/3,435. **Par:** 62/62. **Course Rating:** 57.3. **Slope:** 91. **Green Fee:** $27. **Cart Fee:** $20/Cart. **To obtain tee times:** Call golf shop. **Special Notes:** Formerly Ron Jaworski's Stony Brook Country Club.

★★★½ SUNSET VALLEY GOLF COURSE
PU-W. Sunset Rd., Pompton Plains, 07444, Morris County, (973)835-1515, 18 miles from Morristown. **Facility Holes:** 18. **Yards:** 6,483/5,274. **Par:** 70/70. **Course Rating:** 71.4/70.2. **Slope:** 129/122. **Green Fee:** $13/$60. **Cart Fee:** $26/Cart. **Walking Policy:** Unrestricted walking. **Walkability:** 4. **Opened:** 1974. **Architect:** Hal Purdy. **Season:** April-Nov. **High:** June-Aug. **To obtain tee times:** Call golf shop. **Miscellaneous:** Reduced fees (twilight, seniors), BF, FF.
Reader Comments: The last 3 holes are the hardest I play … Fast greens … Can you say four putt? The 7th hole is thinner than Heidi Klum … Great course for the money … Nice layout, good condition, stay below the hole … A great place to play in the fall … Hilly, beautiful, tough.

TAMARACK GOLF COURSE
PU-97 Hardenburg Lane, East Brunswick, 08816, Middlesex County, (732)821-8881, 6 miles from New Brunswick. **Facility Holes:** 36. **Cart Fee:** $26/Cart. **Walking Policy:** Unrestricted walking. **Walkability:** 2. **Opened:** 1970. **Architect:** Hal Purdy. **Season:** Year-round. **High:** April-Sept. **To obtain tee times:** Call golf shop. **Miscellaneous:** Reduced fees (weekdays, seniors, juniors), range (mats), BF, FF.
★★ **EAST COURSE** (18)
Yards: 6,226/5,346. **Par:** 71/71. **Course Rating:** 68.7/69.7. **Slope:** 111/113. **Green Fee:** $10/$30.
★★ **WEST COURSE** (18)
Yards: 7,025/5,810. **Par:** 72/72. **Course Rating:** 72.9/72.5. **Slope:** 124/122. **Green Fee:** $9/$60.

★★★ TOWN AND COUNTRY GOLF LINKS
PU-197 East Ave., Woodstown, 08098, Salem County, (856)769-8333, (877)825-4657, 15 miles from Wilmington. **Web:** www.tcgolflinks.com. **Facility Holes:** 18. **Yards:** 6,509/4,768. **Par:** 72/71. **Course Rating:** 71.3/66.1. **Slope:** 124/114. **Green Fee:** $36/$48. **Cart Fee:** $14/Person. **Walking Policy:** Unrestricted walking. **Walkability:** 2. **Opened:** 1999. **Architect:** Carl Gaskill. **Season:** Year-round. **High:** April-Nov. **To obtain tee times:** Call up to 7 days in advance. **Miscellaneous:** Reduced fees (weekdays, twilight, seniors, juniors), range (grass/mats), caddies, credit cards (MC, V, AE, D, DC, CB, Debit Card), BF, FF.
Reader Comments: Very accessible gem … Inexpensive, low key … Fun to play … Playable, friendly staff … Great layout, fine clubhouse, good test … Tough layout, carts have GPS.

TWISTED DUNE
PU-2101 Ocean Heights Ave., Egg Harbor Township, 08234, Atlantic County, (609)653-8019. **Facility Holes:** 18. **Yards:** 7,283/5,617. **Par:** 72/72. **Green Fee:** $60/$125. **Cart Fee:** Included in green fee. **Walking Policy:** Unrestricted walking. **Walkability:** 3. **Opened:** 2001. **Architect:** Archie Struthers. **Season:** Year-round. **To obtain tee times:** Call golf shop. **Miscellaneous:** Range (grass), caddies, credit cards (MC, V, AE), BF, FF.

★★½ WARRENBROOK GOLF COURSE
PU-500 Warrenville Rd., Warren, 07059, Somerset County, (908)754-8402, 30 miles from New York City. **E-mail:** banderson@parks.co.somerset.nj.us. **Facility Holes:** 18. **Yards:** 6,372/5,095. **Par:** 71/71. **Course Rating:** 70.8/69.9. **Slope:** 124/119. **Green Fee:** $14/$32. **Cart Fee:** $26/Cart. **Walking Policy:** Unrestricted walking. **Walkability:** 5. **Opened:** 1978. **Architect:** Hal Purdy. **Season:** March-Nov. **High:** May-Sept. **To obtain tee times:** Call up to 7 days in advance. **Miscellaneous:** Reduced fees (weekdays, twilight, seniors, juniors), credit cards (MC, V, AE), BF, FF.

★★ WEDGEWOOD COUNTRY CLUB
PU-200 Hurffville Rd., Turnersville, 08012, Camden County, (856)227-5522, 10 miles from Philadelphia. **Facility Holes:** 18. **Yards:** 7,074/6,356. **Par:** 72/72. **Course Rating:** 73.7/70.6. **Slope:** 133/129. **Green Fee:** $40/$50. **Cart Fee:** $15/Person. **Walking Policy:** Walking at certain times. **Walkability:** 3. **Architect:** Gary Wrenn. **Season:** Year-round. **High:** May-Oct. **To obtain tee times:** Call golf shop. **Miscellaneous:** Reduced fees (twilight), credit cards (MC, V), FF.

★★½ WESTWOOD GOLF CLUB
PU-850 Kings Hwy., Woodbury, 08096, Gloucester County, (856)845-2000, 10 miles from Philadelphia. **Web:** www.westwoodgolfclub.com. **Facility Holes:** 18. **Yards:** 5,968/5,182. **Par:** 71/72. **Course Rating:** 68.2/69.2. **Slope:** 120/116. **Green Fee:** $22/$35. **Cart Fee:** $28/Cart. **Walking Policy:** Walking at certain times. **Walkability:** 3. **Opened:** 1961. **Architect:** Horace W. Smith. **Season:** Year-round. **High:** May-Oct. **To obtain tee times:** Call up to 7 days in advance. **Miscellaneous:** Reduced fees (twilight), credit cards (MC, V), BF, FF.

WHITE OAKS COUNTRY CLUB
SP-2951 Dutch Mill Rd., Newfield, 08344, Gloucester County, (856)697-8900, 30 miles from Philadelphia. **E-mail:** frankgriser@earthlink.net. **Web:** whiteoaksgolf.com. **Facility Holes:** 18. **Yards:** 6,532/5,195. **Par:** 71/71. **Course Rating:** 70.7/68.9. **Slope:** 118/118. **Green Fee:** $40/$75. **Cart Fee:** Included in green fee. **Walking Policy:** Walking at certain times. **Walkability:** 2. **Opened:** 1999. **Architect:** Steve Filipone. **Season:** Year-round. **High:** May-Oct. **To obtain tee times:** Call up to 10 days in advance. **Miscellaneous:** Reduced fees (weekdays, twilight, juniors), credit cards (MC, V), BF, FF.

★★★ WILD OAKS GOLF CLUB
PU-75 Wild Oaks Dr., Salem, 08079, Salem County, (856)935-0705, 45 miles from Philadelphia. **Facility Holes:** 27. **Green Fee:** $17/$34. **Cart Fee:** Included in green fee. **Walking Policy:** Walking at certain times. **Walkability:** 2. **Opened:** 1968. **Architect:** Joe Hassler. **Season:** Year-round. **High:** May-Sept. **To obtain tee times:** Call golf shop. **Miscellaneous:**

Reduced fees (weekdays, twilight, seniors, juniors), credit cards (MC, V), BF, FF.
PIN OAKS/WHITE CEDAR (18 Combo)
Yards: 6,505/5,336. **Par:** 72/72. **Course Rating:** 71.4/71.0. **Slope:** 125/119.
WHITE CEDAR/WILLOW OAKS (18 Combo)
Yards: 6,726/5,322. **Par:** 72/72. **Course Rating:** 72.1/71.4. **Slope:** 126/118.
WILLOW OAKS/PIN OAKS (18 Combo)
Yards: 6,633/5,360. **Par:** 72/72. **Course Rating:** 71.8/71.1. **Slope:** 122/119.
Reader Comments: Long course, tough to score … Great views and layout … Very well kept … They get a lot done with limited resources. Fairly easy targets.

★★½ **WILLOW BROOK COUNTRY CLUB**
SP-4310 Bridgeboro Rd., Moorestown, 08057, Burlington County, (856)461-0131, 10 miles from Cherry Hills. **E-mail:** bfeld131@aol.com. **Web:** www.willowbrookcountryclub.com. **Facility Holes:** 18. **Yards:** 6,487/5,027. **Par:** 72/72. **Course Rating:** 71.2/68.3. **Slope:** 125/110. **Green Fee:** $18/$38. **Cart Fee:** $30/Cart. **Walking Policy:** Walking at certain times. **Walkability:** 2. **Opened:** 1968. **Architect:** William Gordon. **Season:** Year-round. **To obtain tee times:** Call up to 7 days in advance. **Miscellaneous:** Reduced fees (weekdays, twilight, seniors, juniors), range (grass), credit cards (MC, V, AE, D), BF, FF.

NEW MEXICO

★★ ANGEL FIRE RESORT GOLF COURSE
PU-Country Club Dr. & Angel Fire, Angel Fire, 87710, Taos County, (505)377-3055, 150 miles from Albuquerque. **Facility Holes:** 18. **Yards:** 6,641/5,453. **Par:** 72/72. **Course Rating:** 71.1/69.2. **Slope:** 136/130. **Green Fee:** $25/$55. **Cart Fee:** $25/Cart. **Walking Policy:** Mandatory carts. **Walkability:** 2. **Opened:** 1961. **Architect:** Lebus Ortiz/Paul Ortiz. **Season:** May-Oct. **High:** July-Sept. **To obtain tee times:** Call golf shop. **Miscellaneous:** Reduced fees (guests, twilight), range (grass), lodging (139 rooms), credit cards (MC, V, AE, D), BF, FF.

★★★ ARROYO DEL OSO MUNICIPAL GOLF COURSE
PU-7001 Osuna Rd. N.E., Albuquerque, 87109, Bernalillo County, (505)884-7505. **Facility Holes:** 27. **Yards:** 6,892/5,998. **Par:** 72/73. **Course Rating:** 72.3/72.3. **Slope:** 125/120. **Green Fee:** $16/$20. **Cart Fee:** $10/Person. **Walking Policy:** Unrestricted walking. **Walkability:** 3. **Opened:** 1966. **Architect:** Arthur Jack Snyder. **Season:** Year-round. **To obtain tee times:** Call golf shop. **Miscellaneous:** Reduced fees (twilight, seniors, juniors), range (grass/mats), credit cards (MC, V, AE, D), BF, FF.
Reader Comments: Good variety of holes ... Slow play due to crowded conditions ... Very busy course ... Great practice facility ... Best to play during the week.
Special Notes: Also has a 9-hole Dam Course.

CANNON AFB GOLF COURSE (WHISPERING WINDS)
M-105 Forrest Dr., Clovis, 88103, Curry County, (505)784-2800, 90 miles from Lubbock. **Facility Holes:** 18. **Yards:** 6,032/4,954. **Par:** 70/70. **Course Rating:** 66.9/64.5. **Slope:** 112/97. **Green Fee:** $12. **Cart Fee:** $15/Cart. **Walking Policy:** Unrestricted walking. **Walkability:** 1. **Opened:** 1994. **Season:** Year-round. **High:** March-Sept. **To obtain tee times:** Call golf shop. **Miscellaneous:** Reduced fees (twilight, seniors, juniors), range (grass), credit cards (MC, V), BF, FF.

CLAYTON GOLF COURSE
PU-P.O. Box 4, Clayton, 88415, Union County, (505)374-9957. **Facility Holes:** 9. **Yards:** 6,536/5,422. **Par:** 72/72. **Course Rating:** 68.2/68.2. **Slope:** 105/104. **Green Fee:** $8/$10. **Walkability:** 1. **Opened:** 1953. **Season:** Year-round. **High:** April-Oct. **To obtain tee times:** Call golf shop. **Miscellaneous:** Reduced fees (weekdays), metal spikes, range (grass).

COLONIAL PARK COUNTRY CLUB
SP-1300 Colonial Pkwy., Clovis, 88101, Curry County, (505)762-4775. **Facility Holes:** 27. **Yards:** 6,532/6,064. **Par:** 72/75. **Course Rating:** 69.7/71.9. **Slope:** 111/116. **Green Fee:** $9/$14. **Cart Fee:** $9/Person. **Walking Policy:** Unrestricted walking. **Walkability:** 1. **Opened:** 1964. **Season:** Year-round. **To obtain tee times:** Call golf shop. **Miscellaneous:** Metal spikes, range (grass), BF, FF.
Special Notes: Also has a 9-hole par-3 course.

CONCHAS DAM GOLF COURSE
PU-Conchas Dam State Park, Conchas Dam, 88416, San Miguel County, (505)868-2988. **Facility Holes:** 9. **Yards:** 6,726/6,000. **Par:** 72/72. **Green Fee:** $7/$9. **Cart Fee:** $5/Cart. **To obtain tee times:** Call golf shop.

COYOTE DE MALPAIS
PU-2001 Golf Course Road, Grants, 87020, Cibola County, (505)285-5544, (800)748-2142, 79 miles from Albuquerque. **E-mail:** coyote@7cities.net. **Web:** www.coyotegolfcourse.com. **Facility Holes:** 18. **Yards:** 7,087/5,158. **Par:** 71/71. **Course Rating:** 71.8/67.2. **Slope:** 120/117. **Green Fee:** $14/$16. **Cart Fee:** $9/Person. **Walking Policy:** Unrestricted walking. **Walkability:** 2. **Opened:** 1994. **Architect:** William H. Neff. **Season:** Year-round. **High:** May-Oct. **To obtain tee times:** Call up to 7 days in advance. **Miscellaneous:** Reduced fees (weekdays, twilight, juniors), range (grass), credit cards (MC, V), BF, FF.

CREE MEADOWS COUNTRY CLUB
PU-301 Country Club Dr., Ruidoso, 88345, Lincoln County, (505)257-5815, 65 miles from Roswell. **Facility Holes:** 18. **Yards:** 5,952/4,775. **Par:** 71/71. **Course Rating:** 66.2/66.4. **Slope:** 113/104. **Green Fee:** $25/$30. **Walkability:** 2. **Opened:** 1945. **Season:** Year-round. **To obtain tee times:** Call golf shop. **Miscellaneous:** Reduced fees (weekdays).

DESERT LAKES GOLF COURSE
PU-2351 Hamilton Rd., Alamogordo, 88310, Otero County, (505)437-0290, 86 miles from El Paso. **E-mail:** glgolf@zianet.com. **Facility Holes:** 18. **Yards:** 6,524/5,124. **Par:** 72/72. **Course Rating:** 70.2/67.9. **Slope:** 120/114. **Green Fee:** $14/$19. **Cart Fee:** $18/Cart. **Walking Policy:** Unrestricted walking. **Walkability:** 2. **Opened:** 1950. **Architect:** Williams/Gill. **Season:** Year-round. **High:** April-Oct. **To obtain tee times:** Call up to 7 days in advance. **Miscellaneous:** Reduced fees (twilight, seniors, juniors), range (grass), credit cards (MC, V), BF, FF.

DOS LAGOS GOLF CLUB
PU-1150 Duffer Lane, Anthony, 88021, Dona Ana County, (505)882-2830, 20 miles from El Paso. **Facility Holes:** 18. **Yards:** 6,424/5,658. **Par:** 71/72. **Course Rating:** 69.4/70.6. **Slope:** 119/111. **Green Fee:** $7/$17. **Cart Fee:** $18/Person. **Walking Policy:** Unrestricted walking. **Walkability:** 1. **Opened:** 1963. **Season:** Year-round. **High:** April-Sept. **To obtain tee times:** Call golf shop. **Miscellaneous:** Reduced fees (twilight, juniors), metal spikes, range (grass), credit cards (MC, V), BF, FF.

EUNICE MUNICIPAL GOLF COURSE
PU-Carlsbad Hwy, Eunice, 88231, Lea County, (505)394-2881. **Facility Holes:** 9. **Yards:** 6,655/5,127. **Par:** 72/72. **Course Rating:** 68.7. **Slope:** 109. **Green Fee:** $6/$8. **Cart Fee:** $8/Person. **To obtain tee times:** Call golf shop.

GALLUP MUNICIPAL GOLF COURSE
PU-1109 Susan St., Gallup, 87301, McKinley County, (505)863-9224, 120 miles from Albuquerque. **Facility Holes:** 18. **Yards:** 6,379/4,854. **Par:** 72/72. **Course Rating:** 68.4/66.6. **Slope:** 114/112. **Green Fee:** $10/$14. **Opened:** 1965. **Architect:** Leon Howard. **Season:** Year-round. **Tee times:** Call golf shop. **Miscellaneous:** Reduced fees (weekdays).

HIDDEN VALLEY COUNTRY CLUB
PU-29 County Rd. 3025, Aztec, 87410, San Juan County, (505)334-3248, 2 miles from Aztec. **Facility Holes:** 18. **Yards:** 6,850/5,710. **Par:** 72/72. **Green Fee:** $15/$20. **Walkability:** 2. **Architect:** Ken Lacy. **Season:** Year-round. **High:** April-Sept. **To obtain tee times:** Call golf shop. **Miscellaneous:** Reduced fees (guests), range (grass), credit cards (MC, V, D).

★★★★ INN OF THE MOUNTAIN GODS GOLF COURSE
R-P.O. Box 269, Rte. 4, Mescalero, 88340, Otero County, (505)257-5141, (800)446-2963, 80 miles from Las Cruces. **Facility Holes:** 18. **Yards:** 6,834/5,478. **Par:** 72/72. **Course Rating:** 72.1/70.2. **Slope:** 132/128. **Green Fee:** $40/$60. **Cart Fee:** $20/Cart. **Walkability:** 5. **Opened:** 1975. **Architect:** Ted Robinson. **Season:** March-Dec. **High:** May-Oct. **Tee times:** Call golf shop. **Miscellaneous:** Range (grass/mats), lodging (250 rooms), credit cards (MC, V, AE, D). **Notes:** Ranked 8th in 2001 Best in State.
Reader Comments: Beautiful, quiet, love it … Lightning fast greens … Nice mountain course … Fun to play at high altitude, but can't walk … Course is beautifully nestled among tall pines … Wind can howl, extremely fast greens … Great views.

★★★½ ISLETA EAGLE GOLF COURSE
PU-4001 Hwy. 47 SE, Albuquerque, 87105, Bernalillo County, (505)869-0950, (888)293-9146, 5 miles from Albuquerque. **Facility Holes:** 27. **Green Fee:** $35/$42. **Cart Fee:** Included in green fee. **Walking Policy:** Unrestricted walking. **Walkability:** 4. **Opened:** 1996. **Architect:** Bill Phillips. **Season:** Year-round. **High:** April-Sept. **To obtain tee times:** Call up to 5 days in advance. **Miscellaneous:** Reduced fees (weekdays, twilight, seniors, juniors), range (grass), credit cards (MC, V, AE, D), BF, FF.
LAKES/ARROYO (18 Combo)
Yards: 7,136/5,307. **Par:** 72/72. **Course Rating:** 72.9/68.1. **Slope:** 128/119.
LAKES/MESA (18 Combo)
Yards: 7,572/5,620. **Par:** 72/72. **Course Rating:** 75.1/71.3. **Slope:** 131/125.
Notes: Ranked 9th in 2001 Best in State.
MESA/ARROYO (18 Combo)
Yards: 7,218/5,311. **Par:** 72/72. **Course Rating:** 73.2/68.9. **Slope:** 127/123.
Reader Comments: Very nice course, some tricky holes … Overall pleasant experience … Long and usually windy, very challenging … Stay in fairway or lose a ball.

★★ LADERA GOLF COURSE
PU-3401 Ladera Dr. N.W., Albuquerque, 87120, Bernalillo County, (505)836-4449. **Facility Holes:** 27. **Yards:** 7,307/5,966. **Par:** 72/72. **Course Rating:** 73.0/72.8. **Slope:** 130/116. **Green Fee:** $8/$16. **Cart Fee:** $21/Cart. **Walking Policy:** Unrestricted walking. **Walkability:** 2. **Opened:** 1980. **Architect:** Dick Phelps. **Season:** Year-round. **High:** April-Sept. **To obtain tee times:** Call golf shop. **Miscellaneous:** Reduced fees (twilight, seniors, juniors), range (grass/mats), credit cards (MC, V, AE, D), BF, FF.
Special Notes: Also has a 9-hole executive course.

LAKE CARLSBAD GOLF COURSE
PU-901 North Muscatel, Carlsbad, 88220, Eddy County, (505)885-5444, 110 miles from El Paso. **Facility Holes:** 27. **Yards:** 6,067/5,452. **Par:** 72/72. **Course Rating:** 66.5/71.3. **Slope:** 105/110. **Green Fee:** $8/$10. **Walkability:** 4. **Opened:** 1971. **Season:** Year-round. **To obtain tee times:** Call golf shop. **Miscellaneous:** Reduced fees (weekdays).
Special Notes: Also has a 9-hole executive course.

NEW MEXICO

LAS CRUCES COUNTRY CLUB
SP-P.O. Box 876, Las Cruces, 88004, Dona Ana County, (505)526-8731, 40 miles from El Paso. **Facility Holes:** 18. **Yards:** 6,324/5,406. **Par:** 72/72. **Course Rating:** 69.5/69.0. **Slope:** 119/119. **Green Fee:** $25/$30. **Cart Fee:** $9/Person. **Walkability:** 1. **Opened:** 1923. **Season:** Year-round. **High:** Year-round. **To obtain tee times:** Call golf shop. **Miscellaneous:** Reduced fees (weekdays), range (grass/mats), credit cards (MC, V, AE, D).

★★★★½ THE LINKS AT SIERRA BLANCA
R-105 Sierra Blanca Dr., Ruidoso, 88345, Lincoln County, (505)258-5330, (800)854-6571, 135 miles from El Paso. **E-mail:** links@ruidoso.org. **Web:** www.trekwest.com. **Facility Holes:** 18. **Yards:** 6,793/5,071. **Par:** 72/72. **Course Rating:** 71.9/62.7. **Slope:** 127/104. **Green Fee:** $26/$65. **Cart Fee:** $12/Person. **Walking Policy:** Walking at certain times. **Walkability:** 3. **Opened:** 1990. **Architect:** Jeff Brauer/Jim Colbert. **Season:** Year-round. **High:** June-Oct. **To obtain tee times:** Call up to 14 days in advance. **Miscellaneous:** Reduced fees (weekdays, guests, twilight, seniors, juniors), range (grass), lodging (120 rooms), credit cards (MC, V, AE, D), BF, FF.
Notes: Ranked 6th in 2001 Best in State.
Reader Comments: Challenging, staff very friendly … They let me play before the first tee time, pro & staff couldn't be friendlier … Nice views … Good practice area … 15 is a true golf hole … Links course—difficult.

THE LODGE GOLF CLUB
R-1 Corona Place, Cloudcroft, 88317, Otero County, (505)682-2098, (800)395-6343, 100 miles from El Paso. **Facility Holes:** 9. **Yards:** 2,471/2,036. **Par:** 34/34. **Course Rating:** 63.0/65.0. **Slope:** 97/103. **Green Fee:** $18/$26. **Cart Fee:** $10/Person. **Walking Policy:** Unrestricted walking. **Walkability:** 5. **Opened:** 1899. **Season:** April-Nov. **High:** June-Aug. **To obtain tee times:** Call golf shop. **Miscellaneous:** Reduced fees (weekdays, guests, twilight), metal spikes, range (grass/mats), credit cards (MC, V, AE, D).

★★★ LOS ALAMOS GOLF CLUB
PU-4250 Diamond Dr., Los Alamos, 87544, Los Alamos County, (505)662-8139, 35 miles from Santa Fe. **E-mail:** torresd@lac.losalamos.nm.us.. **Facility Holes:** 18. **Yards:** 6,496/5,301. **Par:** 72/72. **Course Rating:** 70.2/69.3. **Slope:** 124/120. **Green Fee:** $21/$26. **Cart Fee:** $20/Cart. **Walking Policy:** Unrestricted walking. **Walkability:** 4. **Opened:** 1947. **Architect:** Bill Keith/William H. Tucker. **Season:** March-Dec. **To obtain tee times:** Call golf shop. **Miscellaneous:** Reduced fees (weekdays), range (mats), credit cards (MC, V), BF, FF.
Reader Comments: Ample lightning shelters … Tiny greens … Back 9 is better … Because of surrounding mountains, greens very difficult to read.

★★½ LOS ALTOS GOLF COURSE
PU-9717 Copper N.E. St., Albuquerque, 87123, Bernalillo County, (505)298-1897. **E-mail:** cemoya@aol.com. **Web:** www.golfatlosaltos.com. **Facility Holes:** 27. **Yards:** 6,459/5,895. **Par:** 71/74. **Course Rating:** 69.9/71.9. **Slope:** 110/113. **Green Fee:** $15. **Cart Fee:** $13/Person. **Walking Policy:** Unrestricted walking. **Walkability:** 2. **Opened:** 1960. **Architect:** Bob Baldock. **Season:** Year-round. **To obtain tee times:** Call golf shop. **Miscellaneous:** Reduced fees (weekdays, twilight, seniors, juniors), range (grass/mats), credit cards (MC, V, D), BF, FF.
Special Notes: Also has a 9-hole executive course.

★★★½ MARTY SANCHEZ LINKS DE SANTA FE
PU-205 Caja del Rio, Santa Fe, 87501, Santa Fe County, (505)955-4400, 6 miles from Santa Fe. **E-mail:** rossnettles@hotmail.com. **Web:** www.golfnewmexico.com. **Facility Holes:** 27. **Yards:** 7,415/5,045. **Par:** 72/72. **Course Rating:** 72.7/67.8. **Slope:** 124/126. **Green Fee:** $29/$49. **Cart Fee:** $11/Person. **Walking Policy:** Unrestricted walking. **Walkability:** 3. **Opened:** 1998. **Architect:** Baxter Spann. **Season:** Year-round. **High:** May-Sept. **To obtain tee times:** Call up to 7 days in advance. **Miscellaneous:** Reduced fees (twilight, juniors), range (grass/mats), credit cards (MC, V, AE, D), BF, FF.
Reader Comments: Very good young course, great views … Challenging … Good rates for seniors … Very expensive for non Santa Fean's … Needs to mature to become a better course … Shots require imagination … Gem in the rough.
Special Notes: Also has a 9-hole par-3 course.

NEW MEXICO MILITARY INSTITUTE GOLF COURSE
PU-201 West Nineteenth St., Roswell, 88201, Chaves County, (505)622-6033, 200 miles from Albuquerque. **Facility Holes:** 18. **Yards:** 6,639/5,275. **Par:** 72/72. **Course Rating:** 70.1/68.2. **Slope:** 116/113. **Green Fee:** $15. **Cart Fee:** $9/Person. **Walking Policy:** Unrestricted walking. **Walkability:** 2. **Season:** Year-round. **High:** June-Aug. **To obtain tee times:** Call golf shop. **Miscellaneous:** Reduced fees (seniors, juniors), range (grass), lodging (80 rooms), credit cards (MC, V, AE, D).

★★★★ NEW MEXICO STATE UNIVERSITY GOLF COURSE

PU-P.O. Box 30001, Dept. 3595, Las Cruces, 88003, Dona Ana County, (505)646-3219, 45 miles from El Paso. **E-mail:** dankoest@nmsu.edu. **Facility Holes:** 18. **Yards:** 7,017/5,494. **Par:** 72/74. **Course Rating:** 72.5/70.7. **Slope:** 128/120. **Green Fee:** $20/$25. **Cart Fee:** $8/Person. **Walking Policy:** Unrestricted walking. **Walkability:** 3. **Opened:** 1962. **Architect:** Floyd Farley. **Season:** Year-round. **To obtain tee times:** Call golf shop. **Miscellaneous:** Reduced fees (weekdays, twilight), range (grass/mats), credit cards (MC, V, D), BF, FF.
Reader Comments: Challenging greens … Beautiful views … Can be very crowded … When you think you're playing your best, this course brings you back to reality … Lightning fast greens and killer sloping fairways … If you hook it you're in trouble.

★★★ NEW MEXICO TECH GOLF COURSE

PU-1 Canyon Rd., Socorro, 87801, Socorro County, (505)835-5335, 75 miles from Albuquerque. **E-mail:** eltigre@post.com. **Web:** www.nmt.edu/~nmtgolf. **Facility Holes:** 18. **Yards:** 6,688/5,887. **Par:** 72/73. **Course Rating:** 71.2/72.8. **Slope:** 126/122. **Green Fee:** $15/$20. **Cart Fee:** $20/Cart. **Walking Policy:** Unrestricted walking. **Walkability:** 4. **Opened:** 1953. **Architect:** James Voss. **Season:** Year-round. **High:** April-Sept. **To obtain tee times:** Call up to 7 days in advance. **Miscellaneous:** Reduced fees (twilight, seniors, juniors), range (grass/mats), credit cards (MC, V, AE, D), BF, FF.
Reader Comments: Fun course, few nice holes, well worth the price … Good value, good challenge, a sleeper … Lots of trees.
Special Notes: Formerly New Mexico Institute of Mining Golf Course.

★★ OCOTILLO PARK GOLF COURSE

PU-5001 Jack Gomez Blvd., Hobbs, 88240, Lea County, (505)397-9297, 130 miles from Lubbock. **E-mail:** ocotillo2@msn.com. **Facility Holes:** 18. **Yards:** 6,716/5,245. **Par:** 72/72. **Course Rating:** 70.5/69.0. **Slope:** 121/108. **Green Fee:** $8/$10. **Cart Fee:** $10/Person. **Walking Policy:** Unrestricted walking. **Walkability:** 1. **Opened:** 1955. **Architect:** Warren Cantrell/M. Ferguson. **Season:** Year-round. **To obtain tee times:** Call golf shop. **Miscellaneous:** Reduced fees (weekdays, twilight, seniors, juniors), range (grass), credit cards (MC, V, AE, D), BF, FF.

★★★★½ PAA-KO RIDGE GOLF CLUB

PU-1 Clubhouse Dr., Sandia Park, 87047, Bernalillo County, (505)281-6000, (866)898-5987, 17 miles from Albuquerque. **E-mail:** wlehr@paakoridge.com. **Web:** www.paakoridge.com. **Facility Holes:** 18. **Yards:** 7,562/5,702. **Par:** 72/72. **Course Rating:** 75.2/71.8. **Slope:** 138/134. **Green Fee:** $25/$45. **Cart Fee:** $17/Person. **Walking Policy:** Unrestricted walking. **Walkability:** 5. **Opened:** 2000. **Architect:** Ken Dye. **Season:** March-Dec. **High:** April-Sept. **To obtain tee times:** Call up to 5 days in advance. **Miscellaneous:** Reduced fees (weekdays, twilight, seniors, juniors), range (grass), credit cards (MC, V, AE, D), BF, FF.
Notes: Ranked 1st in 2001 Best in State; 1st in 2000 Best New Affordable Courses.
Reader Comments: Beautiful course, but it punishes every mediocre shot … This is a golfers' paradise! From the way you are treated to the condition of the course and the scenic vistas … Bring 2-3 sleeves of balls … Probably best in NM … Play very slow due to difficulty of course.

★★½ PARADISE HILLS GOLF CLUB

PU-10035 Country Club Lane, Albuquerque, 87114, Bernalillo County, (505)898-7001. **Facility Holes:** 18. **Yards:** 6,801/6,090. **Par:** 72/74. **Course Rating:** 71.7/73.5. **Slope:** 125/118. **Green Fee:** $22/$31. **Cart Fee:** $7/Person. **Walkability:** 2. **Opened:** 1963. **Architect:** Red Lawrence. **Season:** Year-round. **High:** March-Oct. **To obtain tee times:** Call golf shop. **Miscellaneous:** Reduced fees (weekdays, twilight, seniors, juniors), range (grass), credit cards (MC, V, AE, D).

PENDARIES VILLAGE GOLF CLUB

R-P.O. Box 847, Rociada, 87742, San Miguel County, (505)425-9890, (800)733-5267, 140 miles from Albuquerque. **E-mail:** pendaries@newmexico.com. **Web:** www.pendaries.net. **Facility Holes:** 18. **Yards:** 6,056/5,021. **Par:** 72/72. **Course Rating:** 67.4/67.1. **Slope:** 119/121. **Green Fee:** $32/$40. **Walking Policy:** Unrestricted walking. **Walkability:** 4. **Opened:** 1972. **Architect:** Don Burns. **Season:** May-Nov. **High:** June-Oct. **To obtain tee times:** Call golf shop. **Miscellaneous:** Reduced fees (guests, twilight), range (mats), lodging (18 rooms), credit cards (MC, V, AE, D), BF, FF.

PICACHO HILLS COUNTRY CLUB

SP-6861 Via Campestre, Las Cruces, 88005, Dona Ana County, (505)523-8641, 30 miles from El Paso. **E-mail:** bpushak@forestargolfinc.com. **Web:** www.picachohills.com. **Facility Holes:** 18. **Yards:** 6,880/5,214. **Par:** 72/72. **Course Rating:** 72.9/70.0. **Slope:** 136/123. **Green Fee:** $25/$40. **Cart Fee:** $11/Person. **Walking Policy:** Unrestricted walking. **Walkability:** 3. **Opened:** 1978. **Architect:** Joe Finger. **Season:** Year-round. **High:** Feb.-April. **To obtain tee times:** Call golf shop. **Miscellaneous:** Range (grass), credit cards (MC, V, AE, D), BF, FF.

NEW MEXICO

★★★★½ PINON HILLS GOLF COURSE *Value+, Condition*
PU-2101 Sunrise Pkwy., Farmington, 87402, San Juan County, (505)326-6066, 180 miles from Albuquerque. **Facility Holes:** 18. **Yards:** 7,249/5,522. **Par:** 72/72. **Course Rating:** 73.3/71.1. **Slope:** 130/126. **Green Fee:** $20/$25. **Cart Fee:** $16/Cart. **Walking Policy:** Unrestricted walking. **Walkability:** 5. **Opened:** 1989. **Architect:** Ken Dye. **Season:** Year-round. **High:** April-Oct. **To obtain tee times:** Call golf shop. **Miscellaneous:** Reduced fees (weekdays), range (grass/mats), credit cards (MC, V), BF, FF.
Notes: Ranked 3rd in 2001 Best in State; 1st in 1996 America's Top 75 Affordable Courses.
Reader Comments: Still a great value, super course … Cheap but excellent … Love coming back here … Best value in the West … Certainly lives up to its reputation … Best golf for the price … Golf as it should be … I would never have expected such a great course in Farmington … Spectacular scenery.

★★★ PUEBLO DE COCHITI GOLF COURSE
PU-5200 Cochiti Hwy., Cochiti Lake, 87083, Sandoval County, (505)465-2239, 35 miles from Santa Fe. **Facility Holes:** 18. **Yards:** 6,817/5,100. **Par:** 72/72. **Course Rating:** 71.0/68.3. **Slope:** 132/113. **Green Fee:** $20/$35. **Cart Fee:** $11/Person. **Walking Policy:** Unrestricted walking. **Walkability:** 5. **Opened:** 1981. **Architect:** Robert Trent Jones Jr. **Season:** Year-round. **High:** April-Oct. **To obtain tee times:** Call up to 7 days in advance. **Miscellaneous:** Reduced fees (weekdays, twilight, seniors, juniors), range (grass), credit cards (MC, V, AE, D), BF, FF.
Notes: Ranked 5th in 2001 Best in State; 47th in 1996 America's Top 75 Affordable Courses.
Reader Comments: Undergoing renovations, should be great … Wonderful course … Bring plenty of balls … Wonderful vistas of surrounding buttes … Improvements are removing challenges, a great walk in the mountains … Must think to play well here … Driver stays in bag most of round.

RIO MIMBRES COUNTRY CLUB
SP-2500 E. Pine St., Deming, 88030, Luna County, (505)546-9481, 100 miles from El Paso. **Facility Holes:** 18. **Yards:** 6,701/5,454. **Par:** 72/72. **Course Rating:** 72.0/69.0. **Slope:** 125/111. **Green Fee:** $14/$22. **Walking Policy:** Unrestricted walking. **Walkability:** 1. **Opened:** 1950. **Architect:** Keith Foster. **Season:** Year-round. **High:** June-Aug. **To obtain tee times:** Call up to 7 days in advance. **Miscellaneous:** Reduced fees (weekdays, juniors), range (grass), credit cards (MC, V), BF, FF.

RIVER VIEW GOLF COURSE
PU-4146 U. S. Hwy. 64, Farmington, 87417, San Juan County, (505)598-0140, 7 miles from Farmington. **E-mail:** yostt@sjc.cc.nm.us. **Facility Holes:** 18. **Yards:** 6,853/5,238. **Par:** 72/72. **Course Rating:** 70.5/70.4. **Slope:** 121/118. **Green Fee:** $13/$15. **Cart Fee:** $8/Person. **Walking Policy:** Unrestricted walking. **Walkability:** 3. **Opened:** 1998. **Architect:** Baxter Spann. **Season:** Year-round. **High:** March-Sept. **Tee times:** Call up to 7 days in advance. **Miscellaneous:** Reduced fees (weekdays), range (grass/mats), credit cards (MC, V, D), BF, FF.

★★★★ SANTA ANA GOLF CLUB
PU-288 Prairie Star Rd., Bernalillo, 87004, Sandoval County, (505)867-9464, 15 miles from Albuquerque. **Web:** www.santaanagolf.com. **Facility Holes:** 27. **Green Fee:** $29/$35. **Cart Fee:** $11/Person. **Walking Policy:** Unrestricted walking. **Walkability:** 3. **Opened:** 1991. **Architect:** Ken Killian. **Season:** Year-round. **High:** May-Sept. **To obtain tee times:** Call golf shop. **Miscellaneous:** Reduced fees (weekdays, twilight, seniors, juniors), range (grass), credit cards (MC, V, AE, D), BF, FF.
CHEENA/STAR (18 Combo)
Yards: 7,152/5,058. **Par:** 71/71. **Course Rating:** 72.9/67.3. **Slope:** 134/121.
TAMAYA/CHEENA (18 Combo)
Yards: 7,258/5,044. **Par:** 71/71. **Course Rating:** 74.1/68.2. **Slope:** 132/122.
Notes: Ranked 7th in 2001 Best in State.
TAMAYA/STAR (18 Combo)
Yards: 7,192/4,924. **Par:** 72/72. **Course Rating:** 73.1/68.3. **Slope:** 133/118.
Reader Comments: Nice layout, fun, different 9s, try and play them all … Wonderful scenic views … I liked the desert scene … Kind of pricey, but not too bad … Beautiful view of Sandia mountains … GPS in carts gives accurate range … A must course if you are in Albuquerque … Generally fair for seniors.

SANTA FE COUNTRY CLUB
SP-Airport Rd., Santa Fe, 87592, Santa Fe County, (505)471-0601, 50 miles from Albuquerque. **Facility Holes:** 18. **Yards:** 7,098/5,862. **Par:** 72/74. **Course Rating:** 71.7/72.1. **Slope:** 125/129. **Green Fee:** $55. **Cart Fee:** $22/Person. **Walking Policy:** Unrestricted walking. **Walkability:** 1. **Opened:** 1941. **Season:** Year-round. **High:** May-Oct. **To obtain tee times:** Call golf shop. **Miscellaneous:** Reduced fees (juniors), range (grass), credit cards (MC, V).

SILVER CITY GOLF COURSE AT SCOTT PARK

PU-720 Fairway Dr., Silver City, 88062, Grant County, (505)538-5041, 100 miles from Las Cruces. **Web:** www.scottpark.com. **Facility Holes:** 18. **Yards:** 6,367/5,240. **Par:** 72/72. **Course Rating:** 68.2/68.9. **Slope:** 115/119. **Green Fee:** $16/$21. **Cart Fee:** $20/Cart. **Walking Policy:** Unrestricted walking. **Walkability:** 4. **Opened:** 1962. **Season:** Year-round. **High:** May-Sept. **To obtain tee times:** Call golf shop. **Miscellaneous:** Reduced fees (weekdays, twilight, seniors, juniors), range (grass), credit cards (MC, V), BF, FF.

★★★½ SONOMA RANCH GOLF COURSE

PU-1274 Golf Club Rd., Las Cruces, 88011, Dona Ana County, (505)521-1818, 30 miles from El Paso. **E-mail:** rhinds@zianet.com. **Web:** www.sonomaranchgolf.com. **Facility Holes:** 18. **Yards:** 7,028/5,169. **Par:** 72/72. **Course Rating:** 71.1/67.1. **Slope:** 124/109. **Green Fee:** $20/$27. **Cart Fee:** $10/Person. **Walking Policy:** Walking at certain times. **Walkability:** 3. **Opened:** 2000. **Architect:** Cal Olson. **Season:** Year-round. **To obtain tee times:** Call up to 7 days in advance. **Miscellaneous:** Reduced fees (twilight, seniors), range (grass), credit cards (MC, V, AE).
Reader Comments: Some blind second shots ... Great clubhouse and 19th hole ... Incredible views ... Tough greens ... Every hole a challenge.

SPRING RIVER GOLF COURSE

PU-1612 W. 8th St., Roswell, 88201, Chaves County, (505)622-9506. **E-mail:** jfowler @dfn.com. **Facility Holes:** 18. **Yards:** 6,488/5,419. **Par:** 71/71. **Course Rating:** 68.8/70.0. **Slope:** 120/115. **Green Fee:** $15. **Cart Fee:** $10/Person. **Walking Policy:** Unrestricted walking. **Walkability:** 2. **Opened:** 1935. **Season:** Year-round. **To obtain tee times:** Call up to 7 days in advance. **Miscellaneous:** Range (grass), credit cards (MC, V, D), BF, FF.

★★★½ TAOS COUNTRY CLUB

SP-54 Golf Course Dr., Rancho de Taos, 87557, Taos County, (505)758-7300, (888)826-7465, 58 miles from Santa Fe. **Facility Holes:** 18. **Yards:** 7,302/5,343. **Par:** 72/72. **Course Rating:** 72.8/68.7. **Slope:** 124/121. **Green Fee:** $35/$63. **Cart Fee:** $12/Person. **Walking Policy:** Unrestricted walking. **Walkability:** 3. **Opened:** 1992. **Architect:** Jep Wille. **Season:** Year-round. **High:** May-Sept. **To obtain tee times:** Call up to 30 days in advance. **Miscellaneous:** Reduced fees (weekdays, twilight, juniors), range (grass/mats), caddies, credit cards (MC, V, AE, D, DC), BF, FF.
Notes: Ranked 10th in 2001 Best in State; 15th in 1996 America's Top 75 Affordable Courses.
Reader Comments: Beautiful views, uncrowded ... Mountain scenery ... Can be difficult, but very golfer friendly.

★★★ TIERRA DEL SOL GOLF COURSE

SP-1000 Golf Course Rd., Belen, 87002, Valencia County, (505)864-1000, 34 miles from Albuquerque. **Facility Holes:** 27. **Yards:** 6,703/5,512. **Par:** 72/72. **Course Rating:** 71.0/71.2. **Slope:** 117/114. **Green Fee:** $18/$20. **Cart Fee:** $9/Person. **Walking Policy:** Walking at certain times. **Opened:** 1971. **Architect:** Gary Panks. **Season:** Year-round. **High:** April-Oct. **To obtain tee times:** Call golf shop. **Miscellaneous:** Reduced fees (weekdays, twilight, juniors), metal spikes, range (grass), credit cards (MC, V).
Reader Comments: This was so much fun let's do it again ... Too many 90-degree doglegs ... OB on both sides of several holes ... Easy to get on.
Special Notes: Also has a 9-hole executive course.

TIJERAS ARROYO GOLF COURSE

M-Kirtland AFB, Albuquerque, 87117, Bernalillo County, (505)846-1169. **Facility Holes:** 18. **Yards:** 6,970/6,445. **Par:** 72/72. **Course Rating:** 71.9/69.8. **Slope:** 126/121. **Green Fee:** $12/$20. **Cart Fee:** $16/Cart. **Walking Policy:** Unrestricted walking. **Walkability:** 2. **Opened:** 1971. **Season:** Year-round. **High:** Feb.-Oct. **To obtain tee times:** Call up to 3 days in advance. **Miscellaneous:** Reduced fees (twilight, seniors, juniors), range (grass/mats), credit cards (MC, V), BF, FF.

TIMBERON GOLF CLUB

PU-Pleasant Valley Rd., Timberon, 88350, Otero County, (505)987-2260, (877)550-9714, 50 miles from Alamogordo. **Facility Holes:** 18. **Yards:** 6,772/4,648. **Par:** 72/72. **Course Rating:** 71.4/65.0. **Slope:** 126/114. **Green Fee:** $13/$16. **Cart Fee:** $17/Person. **Walking Policy:** Unrestricted walking. **Walkability:** 5. **Opened:** 1978. **Architect:** Basil Smith. **Season:** April-Oct. **High:** May-Aug. **To obtain tee times:** Call golf shop. **Miscellaneous:** Reduced fees (twilight, juniors), range (grass), credit cards (MC, V, D, DC), BF, FF.

NEW MEXICO

TRUTH OR CONSEQUENCES MUNICIPAL GOLF COURSE
PU-685 Marie St., Truth or Consequences, 87901, Sierra County, (505)894-2603, 100 miles from El Paso. **Facility Holes:** 9. **Yards:** 6,446/5,647. **Par:** 72/72. **Course Rating:** 68.4/73.4. **Slope:** 102/109. **Green Fee:** $11/$14. **Cart Fee:** $14/Cart. **Walking Policy:** Unrestricted walking. **Walkability:** 1. **Season:** Year-round. **To obtain tee times:** Call golf shop. **Miscellaneous:** Reduced fees (weekdays, twilight, juniors).

TUCUMCARI MUNICIPAL GOLF COURSE
PU-4465 C. Rte. 66, Tucumcari, 88401, Quay County, (505)461-1849, 5 miles from Tucumcari. **E-mail:** jcgolf@sr66.com. **Facility Holes:** 9. **Yards:** 6,643/5,702. **Par:** 72/74. **Course Rating:** 70.6/71.0. **Slope:** 113/118. **Green Fee:** $7/$11. **Cart Fee:** $18/Cart. **Walking Policy:** Unrestricted walking. **Walkability:** 3. **Opened:** 1946. **Season:** Year-round. **High:** May-Sept. **To obtain tee times:** Call golf shop. **Miscellaneous:** Reduced fees (juniors), range (grass), BF, FF.

TWIN WARRIORS GOLF CLUB
R-1301 Tuyuna Trail, Bernalillo, 87004, Sandoval County, (507)771-6155, 15 miles from Albuquerque. **Facility Holes:** 18. **Yards:** 7,736/5,843. **Par:** 72/73. **Course Rating:** 75.0/75.9. **Slope:** 130/134. **Green Fee:** $80/$125. **Cart Fee:** Included in green fee. **Walking Policy:** Unrestricted walking. **Walkability:** 4. **Opened:** 2001. **Architect:** Gary Panks. **Season:** Year-round. **High:** March-Oct. **To obtain tee times:** Call up to 7 days in advance. **Miscellaneous:** Reduced fees (twilight, juniors), range (grass), lodging (350 rooms), credit cards (MC, V, AE, D), BF, FF.

★★★½ UNIVERSITY OF NEW MEXICO GOLF COURSE
PU-3601 University Blvd., S.E., Albuquerque, 87106, Bernalillo County, (505)277-4546. **Web:** http://www.unm.edu/~golf. **Facility Holes:** 21. **Yards:** 7,248/6,031. **Par:** 72/73. **Course Rating:** 74.3/75.1. **Slope:** 134/131. **Green Fee:** $38/$67. **Cart Fee:** Included in green fee. **Walking Policy:** Unrestricted walking. **Walkability:** 4. **Opened:** 1966. **Architect:** Robert (Red) Lawrence. **Season:** Year-round. **High:** April-Sept. **Tee times:** Call golf shop. **Miscellaneous:** Reduced fees (weekdays, twilight, seniors, juniors), range (grass), credit cards (MC, V), BF, FF.
Notes: Ranked 4th in 2001 Best in State; 27th in 1996 America's Top 75 Affordable Courses.
Reader Comments: That mountain air does wonders with my distance! … Very challenging … The greens can be like putting on linoleum … A real test from the back tees … Very long and difficult … An alumni favorite.
Special Notes: Also has a 3-hole beginner course.

ZUNI MOUNTAIN GOLF COURSE
PU-1523 Horizon Ave., Milan, 87021, Cibola County, (505)287-8202, 80 miles from Albuquerque. **Facility Holes:** 9. **Yards:** 6,556/5,880. **Par:** 72/74. **Course Rating:** 69.8/71.2. **Slope:** 113/123. **Green Fee:** $9. **Cart Fee:** $14/Cart. **Walking Policy:** Unrestricted walking. **Opened:** 1957. **Season:** Year-round. **High:** June-Aug. **To obtain tee times:** Call golf shop. **Miscellaneous:** Metal spikes, range (grass).

★★★ ADIRONDACK GOLF & COUNTRY CLUB
PU-88 Golf Rd., Peru, 12972, Clinton County, (518)643-8403, (800)346-1761, 70 miles from Montreal, Quebec, Canada. **E-mail:** support@adirondackgolfclub.com. **Web:** www.adirondack-golfclub.com. **Facility Holes:** 18. **Yards:** 6,851/5,069. **Par:** 72/72. **Course Rating:** 71.9/67.9. **Slope:** 123/115. **Green Fee:** $19/$31. **Cart Fee:** $14/Person. **Walking Policy:** Unrestricted walking. **Walkability:** 2. **Opened:** 1990. **Architect:** Geoffrey Cornish/Brian Silva. **Season:** March-Dec. **High:** July-Aug. **To obtain tee times:** Call golf shop. **Miscellaneous:** Reduced fees (weekdays, twilight, seniors, juniors), range (grass), credit cards (MC, V, D).
Reader Comments: Challenging, good greens ... Great course, must play when in area ... Pretty course, tight & short ... Carolina-style layout.

★★ AFTON GOLF CLUB
PU-Afton Lake Rd., Afton, 13730, Chenango County, (607)639-2454, (800)238-6618, 23 miles from Binghamton. **Facility Holes:** 18. **Yards:** 6,268/4,835. **Par:** 72/72. **Course Rating:** 69.0/65.6. **Slope:** 113/110. **Green Fee:** $16/$20. **Cart Fee:** $18/Cart. **Walking Policy:** Unrestricted walking. **Walkability:** 3. **Architect:** Graden Decker. **Season:** April-Nov. **High:** May-Oct. **To obtain tee times:** Call up to 30 days in advance. **Miscellaneous:** Reduced fees (weekdays, seniors, juniors), metal spikes, BF, FF.

★★½ AIRWAY MEADOWS GOLF COURSE
PU-125 Brownville Rd., Gansevoort, 12831, Saratoga County, (518)792-4144, 10 miles from Saratoga Springs. **Web:** www.airwaymeadowsgolf.com. **Facility Holes:** 18. **Yards:** 6,427/4,823. **Par:** 72/71. **Course Rating:** 71.2/67.4. **Slope:** 125/114. **Green Fee:** $20/$24. **Cart Fee:** $11/Person. **Walking Policy:** Unrestricted walking. **Walkability:** 3. **Opened:** 1999. **Architect:** James Heber. **Season:** March-Dec. **High:** June-Sept. **To obtain tee times:** Call up to 5 days in advance. **Miscellaneous:** Reduced fees (weekdays), range (grass), credit cards (MC, V, D), BF, FF.

ALDER CREEK GOLF COURSE & COUNTRY INN
PU-Rt. 12, Alder Creek, 13301, Oneida County, (315)831-5222. **Facility Holes:** 9. **Yards:** 3,208/2,741. **Par:** 36/36. **Course Rating:** 35.1/34.4. **Green Fee:** $14/$18. **Cart Fee:** $22/Cart. **To obtain tee times:** Call golf shop. **Miscellaneous:** Lodging (8 rooms).

ALLEGHENY HILLS GOLF COURSE
PU-9622 Hardys Corner Rd., Rushford, 14777, Allegany County, (716)437-2163. **Facility Holes:** 18. **Yards:** 5,450/4,765. **Par:** 70/70. **Course Rating:** 65.7/66.3. **Slope:** 108/116. **Green Fee:** $14. **Cart Fee:** $18/Cart. **Walking Policy:** Unrestricted walking. **Opened:** 1960. **Architect:** Conrad Bruckert. **Season:** April-Nov. **High:** June-Sept. **To obtain tee times:** Call golf shop. **Miscellaneous:** Reduced fees (weekdays), credit cards (MC, V), FF.

★½ AMHERST AUDUBON GOLF COURSE
PU-500 Maple Rd., Williamsville, 14221, Erie County, (716)631-7139. **Facility Holes:** 18. **Yards:** 6,635/5,963. **Par:** 71/72. **Course Rating:** 69.5/74.2. **Slope:** 112/105. **Green Fee:** $16/$20. **Cart Fee:** $20/Cart. **Walking Policy:** Unrestricted walking. **Walkability:** 1. **Opened:** 1928. **Architect:** William Harries. **Season:** April-Nov. **High:** June-Aug. **To obtain tee times:** Call golf shop. **Miscellaneous:** Reduced fees (weekdays, twilight).

★½ APALACHIN GOLF COURSE
PU-607 S. Apalachin Rd., Apalachin, 13732, Tioga County, (607)625-2682, 20 miles from Binghamton. **Facility Holes:** 18. **Yards:** 5,727/5,727. **Par:** 71/72. **Green Fee:** $21/$25. **Cart Fee:** Included in green fee. **Walking Policy:** Unrestricted walking. **Walkability:** 2. **Opened:** 1964. **Architect:** John Martin, Tim Shearer. **Season:** April-Dec. **High:** May-Aug. **To obtain tee times:** Call golf shop. **Miscellaneous:** Reduced fees (weekdays, seniors, juniors), metal spikes.

★★★½ APPLE GREENS GOLF COURSE
PU-161 South St., Highland, 12528, Ulster County, (845)883-5500, 6 miles from Poughkeepsie. **E-mail:** applegreen@golflink.net. **Web:** www.applegreens.com. **Facility Holes:** 18. **Yards:** 6,576/4,959. **Par:** 71/71. **Course Rating:** 70.4/67.6. **Slope:** 124/122. **Green Fee:** $22/$35. **Cart Fee:** $26/Cart. **Walking Policy:** Walking at certain times. **Walkability:** 3. **Opened:** 1995. **Architect:** John Magaletta. **Season:** March-Dec. **To obtain tee times:** Call up to 7 days in advance. **Miscellaneous:** Reduced fees (twilight, seniors, juniors), range (grass/mats), credit cards (MC, V, AE, D), FF.
Reader Comments: Quality course for the money, conditions great ... Fun course, keep out of apple trees ... It is beautiful and sits right in an apple orchard ... Play in fall, slow but you can pick and eat apples all day.

NEW YORK

★★★ **BEAVER ISLAND STATE PARK GOLF COURSE**
PU-Beaver Island State Park, Grand Island, 14072, Erie County, (716)773-7143, 8 miles from Buffalo. **Facility Holes:** 18. **Yards:** 6,697/6,178. **Par:** 72/74. **Course Rating:** 69.8/73.0. **Slope:** 108/114. **Green Fee:** $17/$21. **Cart Fee:** $20/Cart. **Walking Policy:** Unrestricted walking. **Walkability:** 1. **Opened:** 1937. **Architect:** William Harries/A. Russell Tyron. **Season:** April-Nov. **To obtain tee times:** Call up to 4 days in advance. **Miscellaneous:** Reduced fees (weekdays, twilight, seniors, juniors), range (grass/mats), credit cards (MC, V), BF, FF.
Reader Comments: Nice course for the $$ ... Solid all around, great state course, wide open ... Far too slow a pace ... Great value, a challenge ... Crowded ... Nice state park course ... Good public course.

★★½ **BEEKMAN COUNTRY CLUB**
PU-11 Country Club Rd., Hopewell Junction, 12533, Dutchess County, (845)226-7700, 40 miles from White Plains. **Web:** www.beekmancc.com. **Facility Holes:** 27. **Green Fee:** $23/$50. **Cart Fee:** $10/Person. **Walking Policy:** Walking at certain times. **Walkability:** 3. **Opened:** 1963. **Architect:** Phil Shatz. **Season:** April-Nov. **To obtain tee times:** Call up to 7 days in advance. **Miscellaneous:** Reduced fees (weekdays, twilight, seniors, juniors), range (grass/mats), credit cards (MC, V, AE), BF, FF.
HIGHLAND/VALLEY (18 Combo)
Yards: 6,124/5,031. **Par:** 71/71. **Course Rating:** 70.3/71.2. **Slope:** 125/123.
TACONIC/HIGHLAND (18 Combo)
Yards: 6,267/5,275. **Par:** 72/72. **Course Rating:** 71.6/72.6. **Slope:** 128/128.
TACONIC/VALLEY (18 Combo)
Yards: 6,107/5,122. **Par:** 71/71. **Course Rating:** 70.4/70.8. **Slope:** 121/121.

BELDEN HILL GOLF CLUB
PU-1820 NYR #7, Belden, 13787, Broome County, (607)693-3257. **Facility Holes:** 18. **Yards:** 6,008/4,828. **Par:** 72/72. **Course Rating:** 68.0/69.1. **Slope:** 113/118. **Green Fee:** $12/$15. **Cart Fee:** $9/Cart. **To obtain tee times:** Call golf shop.

★★ **BERGEN POINT COUNTRY CLUB**
PU-69 Bergen Ave., West Babylon, 11704, Suffolk County, (516)661-8282, 30 miles from New York City. **Facility Holes:** 18. **Yards:** 6,637/5,707. **Par:** 71/71. **Course Rating:** 71.3/71.8. **Slope:** 124/123. **Green Fee:** $22/$35. **Cart Fee:** $27/Cart. **Walking Policy:** Unrestricted walking. **Walkability:** 3. **Opened:** 1972. **Architect:** William F. Mitchell. **Season:** March-Dec. **To obtain tee times:** Call up to 7 days in advance. **Miscellaneous:** Reduced fees (weekdays, twilight, seniors, juniors), range (mats), BF, FF.

BETHPAGE STATE PARK GOLF COURSES
PU-99 Quaker Meetinghouse Rd., Farmingdale, 11735, Nassau County, (516)249-4040, ? miles from Manhattan. **Web:** www.nysparks.state.ny.us. **Facility Holes:** 90. **Walking Policy:** ?restricted walking. **Architect:** A.W. Tillinghast. **To obtain tee times:** Call up to 7 days in ?ance. **Miscellaneous:** Reduced fees (weekdays, twilight, seniors), range (mats), credit ?s (MC, V, AE, D), BF, FF.
★★½ **BLACK COURSE** (18) *Value+, Condition+*
?: 7,295/6,281. **Par:** 71/71. **Course Rating:** 76.6/71.4. **Slope:** 148/134. **Green Fee:** ?39. **Walkability:** 5. **Opened:** 1936. **Season:** April-Nov. **High:** April-Nov.
? 10th in 2001 Best in State; 4th in 1996 America's Top 75 Affordable Courses.
? **Comments:** Can't wait for the US Open ... Awesome ... Toughest course ever played ... ?blic course going ... Best course ever played, extremely difficult ... Golf on steroids, huge ? great terrain ... This is a US Open course at the price of a pitch-and-putt course ... ?st masterpiece.
BLUE COURSE (18)
?684/6,213. **Par:** 72/72. **Course Rating:** 71.7/75.0. **Slope:** 124/129. **Green Fee:** $9/$29. ? $29/Cart. **Walkability:** 4. **Opened:** 1935. **Season:** Year-round. **High:** April-Nov.
?mments: Tough course ... Good course, needs a little work ... Hard to walk, very crowd-?ld trees ... Just might be the toughest front 9 on Long Island ... Hilly, front 9 demanding, ?vated greens ... Front 9 best.
GREEN COURSE (18) *Value*
?7/5,903. **Par:** 71/71. **Course Rating:** 69.5/73.0. **Slope:** 121/126. **Green Fee:** $9/$29. ?4. **Opened:** 1935. **Season:** April-Dec. **High:** April-Nov.
?ments: Scenic, challenging ... Good for run-up shots ... Great variety on hole designs, ?nstruct greens like this anymore ... Never should have allowed carts ... The Little
? COURSE (18) *Value+*
?6,198. **Par:** 70/70. **Course Rating:** 72.2/75.1. **Slope:** 127/130. **Green Fee:** $9/$29. ?Cart. **Walkability:** 3. **Opened:** 1935. **Season:** Year-round. **High:** May-Sept.
?ents: Great course for mid handicapper ... Championship course, long, hilly, beauti-?st hole in golf, 453 yards, up-hill, par 4 ... Could be better maintained ... Need a

★★★ ARROWHEAD GOLF COURSE
PU-7185 East Taft Rd., East Syracuse, 13057, Onondaga County, (315)656-7563. **Facility Holes:** 27. **Yards:** 6,700/5,156. **Par:** 72/73. **Course Rating:** 70.9/68.5. **Slope:** 113/109. **Green Fee:** $18. **Cart Fee:** $20/Cart. **Walking Policy:** Unrestricted walking. **Walkability:** 1. **Opened:** 1968. **Architect:** Dick Snyder. **Season:** April-Nov. **High:** May-Sept. **To obtain tee times:** Call golf shop. **Miscellaneous:** Reduced fees (seniors, juniors), BF, FF.
Reader Comments: Great condition year round, watered fairways, challenging course … Course always in good shape … Nice executive course, fun for the family … Can be very slow, good starter course.

ARTHUR CARTER AMSTERDAM MUNICIPAL GOLF COURSE
PU-Upper Van Dyke Ave., Amsterdam, 12010, Montgomery County, (518)842-6480. **Facility Holes:** 18. **Yards:** 6,702/5,333. **Par:** 71/74. **Course Rating:** 70.2/70.2. **Slope:** 110/110. **Green Fee:** $16/$22. **Cart Fee:** $11/Person. **To obtain tee times:** Call golf shop.

★★ AUBURN GOLF & COUNTRY CLUB
SP-East Lake Rd., Auburn, 13021, Cayuga County, (315)253-3152, 3 miles from Auburn. **Web:** www.auburngolf.com. **Facility Holes:** 18. **Yards:** 6,434/5,777. **Par:** 70/72. **Course Rating:** 70.4/73.1. **Slope:** 118/121. **Green Fee:** $14/$20. **Cart Fee:** $24/Cart. **Walking Policy:** Unrestricted walking. **Walkability:** 1. **Opened:** 1915. **Architect:** Tom Bendelow. **Season:** March-Nov. **High:** June-Aug. **To obtain tee times:** Call up to 3 days in advance. **Miscellaneous:** Reduced fees (weekdays), range (grass), credit cards (MC, V, AE), BF, FF.

★★★½ BALLSTON SPA COUNTRY CLUB
SP-Rte. 67, Ballston Spa, 12020, Saratoga County, (518)885-7935, 20 miles from Albany. **E-mail:** jchefti@aol.com. **Facility Holes:** 18. **Yards:** 6,215/5,757. **Par:** 71/74. **Course Rating:** 69.3/69.4. **Slope:** 124/122. **Green Fee:** $45/$55. **Cart Fee:** Included in green fee. **Walkability:** 4. **Opened:** 1926. **Architect:** Pete Craig. **Season:** April-Nov. **High:** June-Sept. **To obtain tee times:** Call golf shop. **Miscellaneous:** Range (grass/mats), credit cards (MC, V).
Reader Comments: Not a championship caliber course, but very nice, near Saratoga … Tough placements make up for distance … Overall good condition.

★★★ BARKER BROOK GOLF CLUB
PU-6080 Rogers Rd., Oriskany Falls, 13425, Oneida County, (315)821-6438, 13 miles Utica. **Facility Holes:** 18. **Yards:** 6,402/5,501. **Par:** 72/72. **Course Rating:** 70.6/71.8. **Slope:** 120/118. **Green Fee:** $15/$18. **Cart Fee:** $20/Cart. **Walking Policy:** Unrestricted walking. **Walkability:** 3. **Opened:** 1965. **Architect:** David Keshler/C. Miner. **Season:** April-Nov. **High:** June-Aug. **To obtain tee times:** Call golf shop. **Miscellaneous:** Reduced fees (weekday, light), metal spikes, range (grass/mats), credit cards (MC, V).
Reader Comments: Interesting … Very generous staff … Outstanding golf experience … the hills and bunkers that kill … No 2 holes are alike, use all your clubs … Great design … Very good value, nice course.

★★★ BATAVIA COUNTRY CLUB
SP-7909 Batavia-Byron Rd., Batavia, 14020, Genesee County, (716)343-76 (800)343-7660, 4 miles from Batavia. **Web:** www.bataviacc.com. **Facility Holes:** 6,533/5,372. **Par:** 72/72. **Course Rating:** 70.6/71.1. **Slope:** 119/117. **Green Fee:** $20/Cart. **Walking Policy:** Walking at certain times. **Walkability:** 3. O **Architect:** Tryon & Schwartz. **Season:** April-Oct. **High:** July-Aug. **To obtain** shop. **Miscellaneous:** Reduced fees (weekdays, twilight, seniors), metal credit cards (MC, V, D).
Reader Comments: Well-kept, friendly, semi-private course … Good pace … people … Course was rough … Hilly back 9, starts with back-to-back pa a championship course.

BATH COUNTRY CLUB
SP-330 May St., Bath, 14810, Steuben County, (607)776-5043, **Facility Holes:** 18. **Yards:** 6,407/5,272. **Par:** 72/72. **Course Rating: Green Fee:** $24. **Cart Fee:** $13/Person. **Walking Policy:** Walking 4. **Opened:** 1950. **Architect:** Robert Tallman. **Season:** April-N 7 days in advance. **Miscellaneous:** Range (grass), credit car

★★½ BATTLE ISLAND STATE PARK
PU-2150 Rte. 48, Battle Island State Park, Fulton, 13069 21 miles from Syracuse. **Facility Holes:** 18. **Yards:** 5,973 67.9/68.7. **Slope:** 109. **Green Fee:** $9/$17. **Cart Fee:** $2 walking. **Walkability:** 3. **Opened:** 1932. **Season:** April-N **times:** Call golf shop. **Misc:** Reduced fees (seniors, j

cannon … Good condition considering heavy play.

★★★½ YELLOW COURSE (18) *Value*
Yards: 6,339/5,966. **Par:** 71/71. **Course Rating:** 70.1/72.2. **Slope:** 121/123. **Green Fee:** $9/$29.
Cart Fee: $27/Cart. **Walkability:** 2. **Opened:** 1958. **Season:** Year-round. **High:** May-Sept.
Reader Comments: Often set up as a 9-hole course … Great bunkers … Fun course, confidence
builder … Easiest of Bethpage's courses .., Reservation system impossible … No way to get onto
the back … Good step up from a beginner course.

BLACKHEAD MOUNTAIN COUNTRY CLUB

PU-Crow's Nest Rd., Round Top, 12473, Greene County, (518)622-3157. **E-mail:** pmaas-
samann@aol.com. **Web:** www.blackheadmountaingolf.com. **Facility Holes:** 18. **Yards:**
6,076/4,993. **Par:** 72/72. **Course Rating:** 69.9/119.0. **Slope:** 133/70.2. **Green Fee:** $22. **Cart
Fee:** $22/Cart. **Walking Policy:** Walking at certain times. **Walkability:** 5. **Opened:** 1990.
Architect: Nicholas Psiahas. **Season:** April-Nov. **High:** July-Aug. **To obtain tee times:** Call up to
7 days in advance. **Miscellaneous:** Reduced fees (guests, twilight, juniors), range (grass),
lodging (24 rooms), credit cards (MC, V, AE), BF, FF.

★★★½ BLUE HILL GOLF CLUB
PU-285 Blue Hill Rd., Pearl River, 10965, Rockland County, (845)735-2094, 20 miles from
New York. **Facility Holes:** 27. **Green Fee:** $32/$37. **Cart Fee:** $30/Cart. **Walking Policy:**
Unrestricted walking. **Walkability:** 3. **Opened:** 1924. **Architect:** Stephen Kay. **Season:** March-
Dec. **High:** April-Oct. **To obtain tee times:** Call up to 2 days in advance. **Miscellaneous:**
Reduced fees (weekdays, twilight, seniors, juniors), BF, FF.
LAKE/PINES (18 Combo)
Par: 72/72. **Course Rating:** 70.0/70.6. **Slope:** 116/117.
PINES/WOODLAND (18 Combo)
Yards: 6,471/5,651. **Par:** 72/72. **Course Rating:** 70.6/69.8. **Slope:** 124/119.
WOODLAND/LAKE (18 Combo)
Par: 72/72. **Course Rating:** 70.0/70.6. **Slope:** 116/117.

★½ BLUE STONE GOLF CLUB
PU-44 Scott St., Oxford, 13830, Chenango County, (607)843-8352, 28 miles from
Binghamton. **E-mail:** blue-stone@citilink.net. **Facility Holes:** 18. **Yards:** 6,068/4,290. **Par:**
70/72. **Course Rating:** 66.1/65.2. **Slope:** 121/100. **Green Fee:** $12/$17. **Cart Fee:** $20/Cart.
Walking Policy: Unrestricted walking. **Walkability:** 3. **Opened:** 1930. **Architect:** Bradley/Race.
Season: March-Dec. **High:** June-Sept. **To obtain tee times:** Call golf shop. **Miscellaneous:**
Reduced fees (weekdays, juniors), BF, FF.

★★ BLUFF POINT GOLF & COUNTRY CLUB
SP-75 Bluff Point Dr., Plattsburgh, 12901, Clinton County, (518)563-3420, (800)438-0985,
60 miles from Montreal. **Web:** www.bluffpoint.com. **Facility Holes:** 18. **Yards:** 6,309/5,295. **Par:**
72/74. **Course Rating:** 70.6/71.0. **Slope:** 122/121. **Green Fee:** $23/$38. **Cart Fee:** $13/Person.
Walking Policy: Unrestricted walking. **Walkability:** 2. **Opened:** 1890. **Architect:** A.W. Tillinghast.
Season: April-Oct. **High:** July-Aug. **To obtain tee times:** Call up to 5 days in advance.
Miscellaneous: Reduced fees (weekdays, guests, twilight), range (grass), lodging (12 rooms),
credit cards (MC, V), BF, FF.

★★ BRAEMAR COUNTRY CLUB
SP-4704 Ridge Rd. West, Spencerport, 14559, Monroe County, (716)352-5360. **Facility
Holes:** 18. **Yards:** 6,767/5,428. **Par:** 72/72. **Course Rating:** 71.4/70.2. **Slope:** 121/113. **Green
Fee:** $16/$20. **Opened:** 1928. **Architect:** Morrison & Morrison. **To obtain tee times:** Call golf
shop. **Miscellaneous:** Metal spikes.

★★ BRANTINGHAM GOLF CLUB
PU-P.O. Box 151, Brantingham, 13312, Lewis County, (315)348-8861, 55 miles from Utica.
Facility Holes: 18. **Yards:** 5,268/4,886. **Par:** 71/74. **Course Rating:** 64.5. **Slope:** 97. **Green Fee:**
$16. **Cart Fee:** $18/Cart. **Walking Policy:** Unrestricted walking. **Walkability:** 1. **Architect:** Fred
Rhone. **Season:** April-Oct. **High:** July-Aug. **To obtain tee times:** Call golf shop. **Miscellaneous:**
Reduced fees (twilight), metal spikes, FF.

★★½ BRENTWOOD COUNTRY CLUB
PU-100 Pennsylvania Ave., Brentwood, 11717, Suffolk County, (631)436-6060, 45 miles from
New York City. **Facility Holes:** 18. **Yards:** 6,173/5,835. **Par:** 72/72. **Course Rating:** 69.3/68.4.
Slope: 121/111. **Green Fee:** $18/$28. **Cart Fee:** $26/Cart. **Walking Policy:** Unrestricted walk-
ing. **Walkability:** 1. **Opened:** 1920. **Architect:** Devereux Emmet. **Season:** March-Dec. **High:**
May-July. **Tee times:** Call golf shop. **Misc:** Reduced fees (weekdays, twilight, seniors, juniors).

★★ BRIAR CREEK GOLF COURSE
PU-2347 Pangburn Rd., Princetown, 12056-4013, Schenectady County, (518)355-6145, 10

miles from Albany. **Facility Holes:** 18. **Yards:** 5,667/5,187. **Par:** 70/71. **Green Fee:** $17/$22. **Cart Fee:** $22/Cart. **Walking Policy:** Unrestricted walking. **Walkability:** 2. **Opened:** 1963. **Architect:** Bob Smith. **Season:** April-Nov. **High:** May-Aug. **To obtain tee times:** Call golf shop. **Miscellaneous:** Reduced fees (weekdays, seniors).

★★ BRIGHTON PARK GOLF COURSE

PU-Brompton Rd., Town of Tonawanda, 14150, Erie County, (716)695-2580, 5 miles from Buffalo. **Facility Holes:** 18. **Yards:** 6,535/5,852. **Par:** 72/73. **Course Rating:** 70.7/73.5. **Slope:** 108/109. **Green Fee:** $16/$19. **Cart Fee:** $18/Cart. **Walking Policy:** Unrestricted walking. **Walkability:** 1. **Opened:** 1963. **Architect:** William Harries/A. Russell Tyron. **Season:** April-Nov. **High:** June-Aug. **To obtain tee times:** Call golf shop. **Miscellaneous:** Reduced fees (weekdays, twilight, seniors), range (grass).

★★★★ BRISTOL HARBOUR GOLF & RESORT

R-5410 Seneca Point Rd., Canandaigua, 14424, Ontario County, (716)396-2460, (800)288-8248, 30 miles from Rochester. **Facility Holes:** 18. **Yards:** 6,700/5,500. **Par:** 72/72. **Course Rating:** 72.6/73.0. **Slope:** 126/126. **Green Fee:** $30/$52. **Cart Fee:** Included in green fee. **Walking Policy:** Mandatory carts. **Walkability:** 4. **Opened:** 1972. **Architect:** Robert Trent Jones. **Season:** March-Nov. **High:** July-Sept. **To obtain tee times:** Call up to 7 days in advance. **Miscellaneous:** Reduced fees (weekdays, guests, twilight, seniors, juniors), range (grass/mats), lodging (75 rooms), credit cards (MC, V, AE), BF, FF.
Reader Comments: Panoramic views, tough course ... Nice track that needs to mature ... Play when leaves are changing-wow ... Beautiful course but pricey ... Great course, beautiful views ... Great shape, 156 traps ... Worth the drive.

★★★ BROCKPORT COUNTRY CLUB

SP-3739 County Line Rd., Brockport, 14420, Monroe County, (716)638-6486, 20 miles from Rochester. **E-mail:** burklew@ibm.net. **Web:** www.brockportcc.com. **Facility Holes:** 18. **Yards:** 6,600/5,000. **Par:** 72/72. **Course Rating:** 70.1/68.0. **Slope:** 130/112. **Green Fee:** $17/$25. **Cart Fee:** $13/Person. **Walking Policy:** Unrestricted walking. **Walkability:** 4. **Opened:** 1975. **Architect:** Joe Basso. **Season:** Year-round. **High:** April-Oct. **To obtain tee times:** Call golf shop. **Miscellaneous:** Reduced fees (twilight, seniors, juniors), range (grass/mats), credit cards (MC, V, AE, D), BF, FF.
Reader Comments: Course conditions very good, friendly people ... Good design, a few interesting holes ... Tricky greens, par 3s are difficult ... Good layout ... Can be slow.

BROOKHAVEN GOLF COURSE

SP-333 Alpine Meadows Rd., Porters Corners, 12859, Saratoga County, (518)893-7458, 8.5 miles from Saratoga. **Facility Holes:** 18. **Yards:** 6,587/4,806. **Par:** 71/70. **Course Rating:** 71.3/68.3. **Slope:** 125/113. **Green Fee:** $15/$20. **Cart Fee:** $22/Cart. **Walking Policy:** Unrestricted walking. **Walkability:** 2. **Opened:** 1963. **Season:** April-Nov. **High:** July-Sept. **Tee times:** Call up to 2 days in advance. **Miscellaneous:** Reduced fees (weekdays), FF.

BROOKLAWN GOLF COURSE

PU-Old Thompson Rd., Mattydale, 13211, Onondaga County, (315)463-1831, 2 miles from Syracuse. **Facility Holes:** 18. **Yards:** 5,014/4,465. **Par:** 64/66. **Green Fee:** $12/$14. **Cart Fee:** $18/Cart. **Walking Policy:** Unrestricted walking. **Walkability:** 1. **Opened:** 1920. **Season:** March-Nov. **High:** April-Sept. **To obtain tee times:** Call golf shop. **Miscellaneous:** Reduced fees (seniors, juniors), credit cards (MC, V, AE).

BURDEN LAKE COUNTRY CLUB

SP-104 Totem Lodge Rd., Averill Park, 12018, Rensselaer County, (518)674-1770. **Facility Holes:** 18. **Yards:** 6,205/4,880. **Par:** 71/71. **Course Rating:** 70.3/68.7. **Slope:** 122/114. **Green Fee:** $20/$25. **Cart Fee:** $26/Cart. **To obtain tee times:** Call golf shop.

★★★½ BYRNCLIFF GOLF CLUB

R-Rte. 20A, Varysburg, 14167, Wyoming County, (716)535-7300, 35 miles from Buffalo. **Web:** www.byrncliff.com. **Facility Holes:** 18. **Yards:** 6,783/5,545. **Par:** 72/73. **Course Rating:** 73.1/75.1. **Slope:** 115/119. **Green Fee:** $30/$34. **Cart Fee:** Included in green fee. **Walking Policy:** Unrestricted walking. **Walkability:** 3. **Opened:** 1965. **Architect:** Russ Tryon. **Season:** March-Nov. **High:** June-Aug. **To obtain tee times:** Call up to 7 days in advance. **Miscellaneous:** Reduced fees (weekdays, guests, twilight, seniors), range (grass/mats), credit cards (MC, V, AE, D), BF, FF.
Reader Comments: Great views, especially in autumn ... Mostly average, hilly ... Nice layout, but some blind shots ... Autumn is the best time to play ... Very scenic but overbooked ... Very hilly, good condition, very playable ... A good time.

★½ C-WAY GOLF CLUB

PU-37093 NYS Rte 12, Clayton, 13624, Jefferson County, (315)686-4562, 72 miles from

Syracuse. **E-mail:** cwny@gisco.net. **Web:** www.thousandislands.com/cway. **Facility Holes:** 18. **Yards:** 6,120/5,780. **Par:** 71/71. **Course Rating:** 66.0/67.0. **Slope:** 102/101. **Green Fee:** $17. **Cart Fee:** $20/Cart. **Walking Policy:** Unrestricted walking. **Walkability:** 2. **Opened:** 1964. **Season:** May-Nov. **To obtain tee times:** Call up to 3 days in advance. **Miscellaneous:** Range (grass/mats), lodging (50 rooms), credit cards (MC, V).

★★★ CAMILLUS COUNTRY CLUB

SP-5690 Bennetts Corners Rd., Camillus, 13031, Onondaga County, (315)672-3770, 20 miles from Syracuse. **Facility Holes:** 18. **Yards:** 6,368/5,573. **Par:** 73/73. **Course Rating:** 69.4/71.4. **Slope:** 124/115. **Green Fee:** $18/$20. **Cart Fee:** $22/Cart. **Walking Policy:** Unrestricted walking. **Walkability:** 5. **Opened:** 1962. **Season:** March-Nov. **High:** June-Sept. **To obtain tee times:** Call up to 7 days in advance. **Miscellaneous:** Reduced fees (weekdays, seniors, juniors), range (grass), credit cards (MC, V), BF, FF.
Reader Comments: Very hilly, 300-yard drive is likely … A very nice course, improves each year … Sidehill lies … Difficult par 3s all around … Simple course, rolling hills … Hilly, several doglegs.

★½ CANAJOHARIE COUNTRY CLUB

SP-Rte. 163, Canajoharie, 13317, Montgomery County, (518)673-8183, 37 miles from Utica. **Facility Holes:** 18. **Yards:** 5,854/5,144. **Par:** 71/72. **Course Rating:** 67.9/68.5. **Slope:** 115/115. **Green Fee:** $14/$18. **Walking Policy:** Unrestricted walking. **Walkability:** 3. **Opened:** 1940. **Architect:** Scott & John North. **Season:** April-Oct. **High:** June-Aug. **To obtain tee times:** Call golf shop. **Miscellaneous:** Reduced fees (juniors), range (grass), credit cards (MC, V).

★★★ CANASAWACTA COUNTRY CLUB

SP-Country Club Rd., Norwich, 13815, Chenango County, (607)336-2685, 37 miles from Binghamton. **Facility Holes:** 18. **Yards:** 6,271/5,166. **Par:** 70/71. **Course Rating:** 69.9/68.8. **Slope:** 120/114. **Green Fee:** $18/$22. **Cart Fee:** $22/Cart. **Walking Policy:** Unrestricted walking. **Walkability:** 3. **Opened:** 1920. **Architect:** Russell Bailey. **Season:** April-Oct. **High:** June-Aug. **To obtain tee times:** Call golf shop. **Miscellaneous:** Reduced fees (twilight, juniors), range (grass), credit cards (MC, V).
Reader Comments: Well maintained, slow play … Long course, No. 10 is 1/2 mile from clubhouse.

CARDINAL CREEK GOLF CLUB

SP-7061 Ridge Rd. W., Brockport, 14420, Monroe County, (716)637-4302. **Facility Holes:** 18. **Yards:** 5,618/4,856. **Par:** 70/72. **Course Rating:** 64.8. **Slope:** 98. **Green Fee:** $12. **Cart Fee:** $10/Person. **To obtain tee times:** Call golf shop.

★½ CARDINAL HILLS GOLF COURSE

PU-Rt. 241 Conewango Rd., Randolph, 14772, Cattaraugus County, (716)358-5409, 20 miles from Jamestown. **Facility Holes:** 18. **Yards:** 6,096/5,753. **Par:** 72/72. **Course Rating:** 69.5/70.5. **Slope:** 110/108. **Green Fee:** $18. **Cart Fee:** $22/Cart. **Walking Policy:** Unrestricted walking. **Walkability:** 3. **Season:** April-Nov. **High:** July-Aug. **To obtain tee times:** Call golf shop. **Miscellaneous:** Reduced fees (weekdays, twilight), credit cards (MC, V).

CARLOWDEN COUNTRY CLUB

SP-Carlowen Rd., P.O. Box 61, Denmark, 13631, Lewis County, (315)493-0624, 5 miles from Carthage. **Facility Holes:** 18. **Yards:** 6,100. **Par:** 72. **Course Rating:** 70.1. **Slope:** 120. **Green Fee:** $16/$20. **Cart Fee:** $22/Cart. **Walking Policy:** Unrestricted walking. **Walkability:** 3. **Opened:** 1925. **Architect:** P.H. Dolson. **Season:** April-Nov. **High:** March-Aug. **To obtain tee times:** Call up to 1 day in advance. **Miscellaneous:** Reduced fees (weekdays), range BF, FF.

★★★½ CARVEL COUNTRY CLUB

PU-Ferris Rd., Pine Plains, 12567, Dutchess County, (518)398-7101, 55 miles from Albany. **Facility Holes:** 18. **Yards:** 7,080/5,066. **Par:** 73/75. **Course Rating:** 73.2. **Slope:** 122. **Green Fee:** $25/$45. **Cart Fee:** Included in green fee. **Walking Policy:** Mandatory carts. **Walkability:** 4. **Opened:** 1968. **Architect:** William F. Mitchell. **Season:** April-Nov. **High:** June-Aug. **To obtain tee times:** Call up to 7 days in advance. **Miscellaneous:** Reduced fees (weekdays, twilight, seniors), range (mats), credit cards (MC, V, AE, D), BF, FF.
Reader Comments: Tough course in wind … Nice course, hilly … Never played it when it wasn't windy … Very long from tips … Back 9 too confined … Challenging course, prepare for big wind on back 9 … Fast greens, mandatory carts.

★½ CASOLWOOD GOLF COURSE

PU-New Boston Rd., Box 163, Canastota, 13032, Madison County, (315)697-9164, 15 miles from Syracuse. **E-mail:** rterquick2@aol.com. **Facility Holes:** 18. **Yards:** 6,100/5,700. **Par:** 71/71. **Green Fee:** $15. **Cart Fee:** $18/Cart. **Walking Policy:** Unrestricted walking. **Walkability:** 2. **Opened:** 1969. **Architect:** Richard L. Quick/Richard A. Quick. **Season:** March-Dec. **High:** June-Sept. **To obtain tee times:** Call golf shop. **Miscellaneous:** Reduced fees (weekdays, seniors), credit cards (MC, V), BF, FF.

★★★★ CASPERKILL COUNTRY CLUB
SP-2330 South Rd., Poughkeepsie, 12601, Dutchess County, (845)433-2222, 70 miles from New York City. **Web:** www.casperkill.com. **Facility Holes:** 18. **Yards:** 6,691/4,868. **Par:** 72/72. **Course Rating:** 72.5/67.6. **Slope:** 133/117. **Green Fee:** $33/$55. **Cart Fee:** $27/Cart. **Walking Policy:** Unrestricted walking. **Walkability:** 3. **Opened:** 1944. **Architect:** Robert Trent Jones. **Season:** April-Nov. **High:** May-Sept. **To obtain tee times:** Call up to 2 days in advance. **Miscellaneous:** Reduced fees (weekdays, twilight, juniors), range (mats), credit cards (MC, V, AE, D, DC), BF, FF.
Reader Comments: Interesting Trent Jones course ... Greens very difficult ... Very nice layout to look at & play ... Excellent layout and condition ... An outstanding old-fashioned course that plays over an assortment of up and downhill holes.

CEDAR VIEW GOLF COURSE
PU-Rte. 37C, Rooseveltown, 13683, St. Lawrence County, (315)764-9104, 70 miles from Syracuse. **Facility Holes:** 18. **Yards:** 6,027/5,175. **Par:** 72/72. **Course Rating:** 68.8/69.6. **Slope:** 119/121. **Green Fee:** $13/$16. **Cart Fee:** $18/Cart. **Walking Policy:** Unrestricted walking. **Walkability:** 1. **Opened:** 1986. **Season:** May-Oct. **High:** July-Aug. **To obtain tee times:** Call golf shop. **Miscellaneous:** Reduced fees (twilight, juniors), metal spikes, credit cards (MC, V).

CEDARS GOLF COURSE
PU-East Rd., Rt. 1, Lowville, 13367, Lewis County, (315)376-6267. **Facility Holes:** 18. **Yards:** 5,647/4,857. **Par:** 71/71. **Course Rating:** 66.8/68.2. **Slope:** 121/115. **Green Fee:** $18. **Cart Fee:** $20/Cart. **Opened:** 1979. **Architect:** Mena Uink. **Season:** March-Nov. **To obtain tee times:** Call golf shop. **Miscellaneous:** Reduced fees (twilight).

CEE-JAY GOLF COURSE
PU-203 Bateman Rd., Laurens, 13796, Otsego County, (607)263-5291. **Facility Holes:** 18. **Yards:** 5,092/4,129. **Par:** 69/69. **Course Rating:** 63.5/64.1. **Slope:** 100/102. **Green Fee:** $10/$12. **Cart Fee:** $16/Cart. **To obtain tee times:** Call golf shop.

★★★½ CENTENNIAL GOLF CLUB
PU-185 Simpson Rd., Carmel, 10512, Putnam County, (845)225-5700, 55 miles from New York City. **Web:** centennialgolf.com. **Facility Holes:** 27. **Green Fee:** $95/$125. **Cart Fee:** Included in green fee. **Walking Policy:** Walking at certain times. **Walkability:** 5. **Opened:** 1998. **Architect:** Larry Nelson. **Season:** April-Dec. **High:** May-Oct. **To obtain tee times:** Call up to 7 days in advance. **Miscellaneous:** Reduced fees (weekdays, twilight), range (grass/mats), credit cards (MC, V, AE), BF, FF.
LAKES/FAIRWAYS (18 Combo)
Yards: 7,133/5,208. **Par:** 72/72. **Course Rating:** 71.4/73.9. **Slope:** 134/138.
MEADOW/FAIRWAYS (18 Combo)
Yards: 7,050/5,208. **Par:** 72/72. **Course Rating:** 71.3/73.5. **Slope:** 129/136.
MEADOW/LAKES (18 Combo)
Yards: 7,115/5,208. **Par:** 72/72. **Course Rating:** 73.8/70.5. **Slope:** 135/126.
Reader Comments: Best in the area, expensive ... Great course, need all types of shots ... Beautiful views ... Should include free range balls at these prices ... Like a private club ... It's a little pricey.

★★★ CENTERPOINTE COUNTRY CLUB
SP-2231 Brickyard Rd., Canandaigua, 14424, Ontario County, (716)924-5346, 25 miles from Rochester. **Facility Holes:** 18. **Yards:** 6,787/5,171. **Par:** 71/71. **Course Rating:** 72.2/69.3. **Slope:** 119/112. **Green Fee:** $15/$35. **Cart Fee:** $20/Person. **Walking Policy:** Walking at certain times. **Walkability:** 2. **Opened:** 1963. **Architect:** John Thornton/Elmer Michaels. **Season:** April-Nov. **High:** July-Sept. **To obtain tee times:** Call up to 3 days in advance. **Miscellaneous:** Reduced fees (weekdays, twilight, seniors, juniors), metal spikes, range (grass), credit cards (MC, V), BF, FF.
Reader Comments: Hard to obtain tee times, many tournaments ... A pleasure to play ... Greens rolled true, fairways in good condition, fairly open ... Fairways are in very good condition ... Great course, fairly easy but enjoyable.

★★½ CENTRAL VALLEY GOLF CLUB
PU-206 Smith Clove Rd., Central Valley, 10917, Orange County, (845)928-6924, 50 miles from New York City. **Facility Holes:** 18. **Yards:** 5,644/5,317. **Par:** 70/73. **Course Rating:** 67.8/70.9. **Slope:** 122/123. **Green Fee:** $25/$35. **Cart Fee:** $26/Cart. **Walking Policy:** Unrestricted walking. **Walkability:** 5. **Opened:** 1922. **Architect:** Hal Purdy. **Season:** April-Dec. **High:** May-Sept. **To obtain tee times:** Call up to 7 days in advance. **Miscellaneous:** Reduced fees (weekdays, seniors), metal spikes, credit cards (MC, V, AE), BF, FF.

CHAUTAUQUA GOLF CLUB
R-Rte. 394, Chautauqua, 14722, Chautauqua County, (716)357-6211, 70 miles from Buffalo. **Facility Holes:** 36. **Green Fee:** $19/$34. **Cart Fee:** $11/Person. **Walking Policy:** Unrestricted walking. **Season:** April-Nov. **High:** June-Aug. **To obtain tee times:** Call golf shop. **Miscellaneous:** Reduced fees (weekdays, twilight), metal spikes, range (grass/mats), credit cards (MC, V).
★★★★ **HILLS COURSE** (18)
Yards: 6,412/5,076. **Par:** 72/72. **Course Rating:** 72.1/72.7. **Slope:** 118/110. **Walkability:** 5. **Opened:** 1994. **Architect:** X.G. Hassenplug.
Reader Comments: Well maintained, beautiful fall & spring … Great staff, very heavy play in July & August … Nicest people anywhere, great hill views … One of the most beautiful sites in upstate NY.
★★★★ **LAKE COURSE** (18)
Yards: 6,462/5,423. **Par:** 72/74. **Course Rating:** 71.1/71.7. **Slope:** 115/108. **Walkability:** 2. **Opened:** 1913. **Architect:** Donald Ross.
Reader Comments: Rangers really work, but very nice about it … Basically a back and forth layout … Great people, play both courses before supper … One of the most beautiful sites in upstate NY.

★★★ CHENANGO VALLEY STATE PARK
PU-153 State Park Rd., Chenango Forks, 13746, Broome County, (607)648-9804, 10 miles from Binghamton. **Facility Holes:** 18. **Yards:** 6,271/5,246. **Par:** 72/72. **Course Rating:** 70.6/69.5. **Slope:** 124/116. **Green Fee:** $17/$21. **Cart Fee:** $20/Cart. **Walking Policy:** Unrestricted walking. **Walkability:** 5. **Opened:** 1932. **Architect:** Hal Purdy. **Season:** April-Nov. **High:** July-Aug. **To obtain tee times:** Call up to 6 days in advance. **Miscellaneous:** Reduced fees (weekdays, seniors, juniors), credit cards (MC, V, AE, D), FF.
Reader Comments: Avoid the crowds and slow play, play before the July 4th or after Labor Day … This course is great all around … Fun state park course … Deer are everywhere, natural setting, great golf … State park course.

★★★★ CHERRY CREEK GOLF LINKS
PU-Reeves Ave., Riverhead, 11901, Suffolk County, (631)369-6500, 3 miles from Riverhead. **E-mail:** jakstkcak@aol.com. **Web:** www.cherrycreeklinks.com. **Facility Holes:** 18. **Yards:** 7,187/5,676. **Par:** 73/73. **Course Rating:** 73.7/72.5. **Slope:** 128/125. **Walking Policy:** Walking at certain times. **Walkability:** 2. **Opened:** 1996. **Architect:** Young/Young. **Season:** Year-round. **High:** May-Nov. **To obtain tee times:** Call up to 7 days in advance. **Miscellaneous:** Reduced fees (weekdays, twilight, juniors), range (grass), credit cards (MC, V, AE, D), BF, FF.
Reader Comments: Exceptionally nice clubhouse … Well-maintained, par-6 18th … Good putting practice greens, good range, challenging … Great chance for eagle on No. 18.

★★★ CHESTNUT HILL COUNTRY CLUB
PU-1330 Broadway, Darien Center, 14040, Genesee County, (716)547-9699, 30 miles from Buffalo. **Web:** www.chestnuthillcc.com. **Facility Holes:** 18. **Yards:** 6,653/5,466. **Par:** 72/72. **Course Rating:** 72.0/70.6. **Slope:** 119/115. **Green Fee:** $20/$35. **Cart Fee:** Included in green fee. **Walking Policy:** Mandatory carts. **Walkability:** 4. **Season:** April-Nov. **To obtain tee times:** Call up to 7 days in advance. **Miscellaneous:** Reduced fees (weekdays, seniors), metal spikes, range (grass), credit cards (MC, V, D), BF, FF.
Reader Comments: Good spring and fall, place very busy in summer … Course well maintained, service very good … Difficult to get starting times … Too many tournaments.

★★ CHILI COUNTRY CLUB
SP-760 Scottsville - Chili Rd., Scottsville, 14546, Monroe County, (716)889-9325, 10 miles from Rochester. **Web:** www.chiligolf.com. **Facility Holes:** 18. **Yards:** 6,618/5,488. **Par:** 72/72. **Course Rating:** 71.3/72.4. **Slope:** 124/117. **Green Fee:** $10/$18. **Cart Fee:** $20/Cart. **Walking Policy:** Unrestricted walking. **Walkability:** 2. **Opened:** 1959. **Architect:** Joe DeMino. **Season:** March-Nov. **High:** June-Aug. **To obtain tee times:** Call golf shop. **Miscellaneous:** Reduced fees (weekdays, twilight, seniors, juniors), range (grass), credit cards (MC, V, D), BF, FF.

CHRISTMAN'S WINDHAM HOUSE
R-5742 Rte. 23, Windham, 12496, Greene County, (518)734-3824, (888)294-4053, 23 miles from Catskill. **E-mail:** christ@mhcable.com. **Web:** www.windhamhouse.com. **Facility Holes:** 18. **Yards:** 5,680/4,279. **Par:** 70/70. **Course Rating:** 72.0/69.0. **Slope:** 129/105. **Green Fee:** $18/$22. **Cart Fee:** $32/Cart. **Walking Policy:** Unrestricted walking. **Walkability:** 3. **Opened:** 1965. **Architect:** Brian Christman. **Season:** April-Nov. **High:** May-Oct. **To obtain tee times:** Call up to 30 days in advance. **Miscellaneous:** Reduced fees (weekdays, guests, twilight), range (grass/mats), lodging (50 rooms), credit cards (MC, V, AE), BF, FF.

CHURCHVILLE GOLF CLUB
PU-629 Kendall Rd., Churchville, 14428, Monroe County, (716)293-0680. **Facility Holes:** 27. **Green Fee:** $12/$13. **Cart Fee:** $13/Person. **To obtain tee times:** Call golf shop.

EIGHTEEN HOLE COURSE (18)
Yards: 6,671/6,092. **Par:** 72/72. **Course Rating:** 69.8/72.0. **Slope:** 105/111.
NINE HOLE COURSE (9)
Yards: 6,390/5,812. **Par:** 72/72. **Course Rating:** 68.6. **Slope:** 105.

★★★ **CITY OF AMSTERDAM MUNICIPAL GOLF COURSE**
PU-158 Van Dyke Ave., Amsterdam, 12010, Montgomery County, (518)842-4265, 15 miles
from Schenectady. **E-mail:** bcoates@superior.com. **Facility Holes:** 18. **Yards:** 6,370/5,352. **Par:**
71/74. **Course Rating:** 70.2/70.2. **Slope:** 120/110. **Green Fee:** $19/$21. **Cart Fee:** $20/Cart.
Walking Policy: Unrestricted walking. **Walkability:** 5. **Opened:** 1938. **Architect:** Robert Trent
Jones. **Season:** April-Oct. **High:** May-July. **To obtain tee times:** Call golf shop. **Miscellaneous:**
Reduced fees (weekdays, twilight, seniors, juniors), range (grass/mats), BF, FF.
Reader Comments: Top-notch course design, needs better grooming and drainage, very hilly ...
Hidden jewel ... Lots of elevation changes ... Fairways and greens excellent ... A Trent Jones
design.

★★ **CLEARVIEW GOLF CLUB**
PU-202-12 Willets Point Blvd., Bayside, 11360, Queens County, (718)229-2570, 8 miles from
New York City. **Facility Holes:** 18. **Yards:** 6,473/5,721. **Par:** 70/70. **Course Rating:** 70.1/70.4.
Slope: 119/115. **Green Fee:** $19/$33. **Cart Fee:** $27/Cart. **Walking Policy:** Unrestricted walk-
ing. **Walkability:** 2. **Opened:** 1929. **Architect:** William H. Tucker. **Season:** Year-round. **High:**
April-Oct. **To obtain tee times:** Call up to 2 days in advance. **Miscellaneous:** Reduced fees
(twilight, seniors, juniors), credit cards (MC, V, AE, D), BF, FF.

COBLESKILL GOLF COURSE
SP-Rte. 7, Cobleskill, 12043, Schoharie County, (518)234-4045, 35 miles from Albany. **Web:**
www.nocrowds.com/enjoygolf. **Facility Holes:** 18. **Yards:** 6,133/5,212. **Par:** 70/73. **Course
Rating:** 69.2/70.1. **Slope:** 116/118. **Green Fee:** $20/$24. **Cart Fee:** $25/Cart. **Walking Policy:**
Unrestricted walking. **Opened:** 1929. **To obtain tee times:** Call up to 2 days in advance.
Miscellaneous: Credit cards (MC, V), BF, FF.

★★★★½ **COLGATE UNIVERSITY SEVEN OAKS GOLF CLUB** *Value, Pace*
SP-East Lake and Payne Sts., Hamilton, 13346, Madison County, (315)824-1432, 41 miles
from Syracuse. **Facility Holes:** 18. **Yards:** 6,915/5,315. **Par:** 72/72. **Course Rating:** 72.3/71.0.
Slope: 127/128. **Green Fee:** $25/$52. **Cart Fee:** $23/Cart. **Walking Policy:** Unrestricted walk-
ing. **Walkability:** 1. **Opened:** 1956. **Architect:** Robert Trent Jones. **Season:** April-Oct. **High:**
June-Aug. **To obtain tee times:** Call golf shop. **Miscellaneous:** Reduced fees (guests, juniors),
metal spikes, range (grass), caddies, credit cards (MC, V).
Reader Comments: Great layout, golf course was in great shape from tee to green ... Greens are
quick, smooth and true, the best in central New York ... Long, difficult, interesting and well conditioned course ... Good solid RTJ course ... You need to play this course ... A classic.

★★★★ **COLONIAL SPRINGS GOLF COURSE**
PU-1 Long Island Ave., East Farmingdale, 11735, Suffolk County, (516)643-1056,
(800)643-0051, 33 miles from New York City. **Facility Holes:** 27. **Green Fee:** $59/$95. **Cart
Fee:** Included in green fee. **Walking Policy:** Mandatory carts. **Walkability:** 3. **Opened:** 1995.
Architect: Arthur Hills. **Season:** March-Dec. **High:** April-Nov. **To obtain tee times:** Call golf
shop. **Miscellaneous:** Reduced fees (weekdays, twilight), range (grass/mats), credit cards
(MC, V, AE), BF, FF.
LAKES/PINES (18 Combo)
Yards: 6,793/5,467. **Par:** 72/72. **Course Rating:** 72.6/71.4. **Slope:** 129/123.
PINES/VALLEY (18 Combo)
Yards: 6,811/5,485. **Par:** 72/72. **Course Rating:** 71.8/70.5. **Slope:** 126/119.
VALLEY/LAKES (18 Combo)
Yards: 6,746/5,448. **Par:** 72/72. **Course Rating:** 72.6/71.4. **Slope:** 129/123.
Reader Comments: Great driving range and putting green ... Excellent condition, rolling course ...
Since maturing, this course has come into its own ... Three different 9s ... Private club feeling ...
Quality course, not too difficult, pricey.

CONCORD RESORT HOTEL
R-Chalet Rd., Kiamesha Lake, 12751, Sullivan County, (914)794-4000, (888)448-9686,
90 miles from New York. **Web:** www.concordresort.com. **Facility Holes:** 36. **Cart Fee:** Included
in green fee. **Season:** April-Nov. **High:** May-Oct. **To obtain tee times:** Call up to 30 days in
advance. **Miscellaneous:** Reduced fees (weekdays, guests, twilight), lodging (42 rooms),
credit cards (MC, V, AE, D, DC), BF, FF.
★★★ **INTERNATIONAL COURSE** (18)
Yards: 6,619/5,564. **Par:** 71/71. **Course Rating:** 72.2/73.6. **Slope:** 127/125. **Green Fee:**
$45/$55. **Walking Policy:** Unrestricted walking. **Walkability:** 5. **Opened:** 1950. **Architect:** Alfred
H. Tull. **Miscellaneous:** Range (grass/mats).

Reader Comments: Interesting holes ... Picturesque in fall ... Memorable ... Fair and not crowded ... Beautiful, expensive and tough ... Worth a trip from NYC ... Good course for beginner ... Yardage poorly marked.

★★★★ **MONSTER COURSE** (18)
Yards: 7,966/5,201. **Par:** 72/72. **Course Rating:** 76.4/70.6. **Slope:** 142/121. **Green Fee:** $45/$95. **Walking Policy:** Mandatory carts. **Walkability:** 3. **Opened:** 1963. **Architect:** Joseph Finger. **Miscellaneous:** Range (grass).
Notes: 72nd in 1996 America's Top 75 Upscale Courses.
Reader Comments: More than just long, very nice course & setting ... One hell of a course ... Not what it used to be anymore ... Always fun to play once a year ... Great layout.

★★★★½ **CONKLIN PLAYERS CLUB** *Value, Condition+, Pace*
PU-1520 Conklin Rd., Conklin, 13748, Broome County, (607)775-3042, 70 miles from Syracuse. **E-mail:** sales@conklinplayers.com. **Web:** www.conklinplayers.com. **Facility Holes:** 18. **Yards:** 6,772/4,699. **Par:** 72/72. **Course Rating:** 72.5/67.8. **Slope:** 127/116. **Green Fee:** $28/$38. **Cart Fee:** $10/Person. **Walking Policy:** Walking at certain times. **Walkability:** 5. **Opened:** 1991. **Architect:** R. Rickard/R. Brown/M. Brown. **Season:** April-Nov. **High:** June-Sept. **To obtain tee times:** Call golf shop. **Miscellaneous:** Reduced fees (weekdays, seniors), range (grass), credit cards (MC, V, AE, D), FF.
Reader Comments: Always in outstanding condition ... Very professional, well taken care of ... Beautiful, hilly setting great course ... Best course in area, very pretty course ... Gets heavy play ... Above average public course, dramatic elevation changes, very scenic ... Great strategic course, very scenic.

★★★ **COPAKE COUNTRY CLUB**
PU-44 Golf Course Rd., Craryville, 12521, Columbia County, (518)325-4338, 15 miles from Hudson. **Facility Holes:** 18. **Yards:** 6,129/5,329. **Par:** 72/72. **Course Rating:** 68.8/69.6. **Slope:** 113/113. **Green Fee:** $15/$30. **Cart Fee:** $12/Person. **Walking Policy:** Unrestricted walking. **Walkability:** 3. **Season:** Year-round. **High:** April-Nov. **To obtain tee times:** Call golf shop. **Miscellaneous:** Reduced fees (weekdays, seniors, juniors), credit cards (MC, V), FF.
Reader Comments: Layout is very nice ... If they'd put a little time and effort into the course, it would be great ... Hilly, open, some short holes ... Tough ... Great mountain views, quite challenging ... Great views.

★★½ **COUNTRY CLUB AT LAKE MACGREGOR**
SP-187 Hill St., Mahopac, 10541, Putnam County, (914)628-4200, 50 miles from New York City. **Web:** www.lakemacgregor.com. **Facility Holes:** 18. **Yards:** 6,575/5,807. **Par:** 71/73. **Course Rating:** 73.0/76.9. **Slope:** 129/135. **Green Fee:** $30/$55. **Cart Fee:** $15/Person. **Walking Policy:** Walking at certain times. **Walkability:** 3. **Opened:** 1955. **Architect:** William F. Mitchell. **Season:** March-Dec. **High:** June-Sept. **To obtain tee times:** Call up to 4 days in advance. **Miscellaneous:** Reduced fees (weekdays, twilight, seniors, juniors), range (grass), credit cards (MC, V, AE), BF, FF.

★★½ **CRAB MEADOW GOLF CLUB**
PU-220 Waterside Rd., Northport, 11768, Suffolk County, (631)757-8800, 28 miles from New York City. **Facility Holes:** 18. **Yards:** 6,774/5,799. **Par:** 72/72. **Course Rating:** 70.2/72.6. **Slope:** 116/116. **Green Fee:** $35. **Cart Fee:** $27/Cart. **Walking Policy:** Unrestricted walking. **Walkability:** 3. **Opened:** 1960. **Architect:** William F. Mitchell. **Season:** March-Dec. **High:** April-Sept. **To obtain tee times:** Call golf shop. **Miscellaneous:** Reduced fees (twilight, seniors, juniors), range (mats).

★½ **CRAGIE BRAE GOLF CLUB**
PU-4391 Union St., Scottsville, 14546, Monroe County, (716)889-1440, 10 miles from Rochester. **Facility Holes:** 18. **Yards:** 6,400/5,900. **Par:** 72/72. **Course Rating:** 68.5/68.5. **Slope:** 115/115. **Green Fee:** $13/$15. **Cart Fee:** $20/Cart. **Walking Policy:** Walking at certain times. **Walkability:** 3. **Opened:** 1963. **Architect:** James G. Harrison. **Season:** April-Nov. **High:** May-July. **To obtain tee times:** Call golf shop. **Miscellaneous:** Reduced fees (seniors, juniors), metal spikes, range (grass).

★★½ **CRAIG WOOD GOLF COURSE**
PU-Cascade Rd. Rte. 73, Lake Placid, 12946, Essex County, (518)523-9811, (877)999-9473, 135 miles from Albany. **E-mail:** info@neparkdistrict.com. **Web:** www.neparkdistrict.com. **Facility Holes:** 18. **Yards:** 6,554/5,500. **Par:** 72/72. **Course Rating:** 70.6/70.2. **Slope:** 114/118. **Green Fee:** $15/$25. **Cart Fee:** $14/Person. **Walking Policy:** Unrestricted walking. **Walkability:** 3. **Opened:** 1920. **Architect:** Seymour Dunn. **Season:** May-Oct. **High:** July-Sept. **To obtain tee times:** Call golf shop. **Miscellaneous:** Reduced fees (guests, twilight), range (grass/mats), credit cards (MC, V, AE, D), BF, FF.

CRESTWOOD GOLF CLUB
PU-Rte. 291, Marcy, 13403, Oneida County, (315)736-0478, 8 miles from Utica. **Facility Holes:** 18. **Yards:** 6,959/5,913. **Par:** 72/72. **Course Rating:** 70.7. **Slope:** 121. **Green Fee:** $12/$17. **Cart Fee:** $20/Cart. **Walking Policy:** Unrestricted walking. **Opened:** 1958. **Season:** April-Nov. **High:** June-Aug. **To obtain tee times:** Call golf shop. **Miscellaneous:** Reduced fees (weekdays, twilight), credit cards (MC, V), BF, FF.

★★½ CRONINS GOLF RESORT
R-Golf Course Rd., Warrensburg, 12885, Warren County, (518)623-9336, 7 miles from Lake George. **Facility Holes:** 18. **Yards:** 6,121/5,757. **Par:** 70/71. **Course Rating:** 69.3/68.3. **Slope:** 119/117. **Green Fee:** $20/$22. **Cart Fee:** $24/Cart. **Walking Policy:** Unrestricted walking. **Walkability:** 2. **Opened:** 1930. **Architect:** Patrick Cronin. **Season:** April-Nov. **High:** June-Sept. **To obtain tee times:** Call up to 7 days in advance. **Miscellaneous:** Reduced fees (guests, twilight, seniors), range (grass), lodging (25 rooms), credit cards (MC, V, AE, D), BF, FF.

★★½ DANDE FARMS COUNTRY CLUB
SP-13278 Carney Road, Akron, 14001, Erie County, (716)542-2027, 20 miles from Buffalo. **Facility Holes:** 18. **Yards:** 6,622/6,017. **Par:** 71/72. **Course Rating:** 70.5/72.1. **Slope:** 113/110. **Green Fee:** $20/$23. **Cart Fee:** $24/Cart. **Walking Policy:** Unrestricted walking. **Walkability:** 2. **Season:** April-Oct. **High:** July-Aug. **To obtain tee times:** Call golf shop. **Miscellaneous:** Reduced fees (seniors), metal spikes, credit cards (MC, V, AE, D).

DAVIS COUNTRYSIDE MEADOWS
PU-11070 Perry Rd., Pavilion, 14525, Genesee County, (716)584-8390, 45 miles from Buffalo. **Web:** www.dcmeadows.com. **Facility Holes:** 18. **Yards:** 6,100/4,880. **Par:** 72/72. **Course Rating:** 67.3/66.1. **Slope:** 111/106. **Green Fee:** $14/$16. **Cart Fee:** $18/Cart. **Walking Policy:** Unrestricted walking. **Walkability:** 3. **Opened:** 1995. **Architect:** Dave Penders. **Season:** April-Nov. **To obtain tee times:** Call golf shop. **Miscellaneous:** Reduced fees (seniors), range (grass/mats), credit cards (MC, V, D), BF, FF.

★★★½ DEERFIELD COUNTRY CLUB
SP-100 Craig Hill Dr., Brockport, 14420, Monroe County, (716)392-8080, 20 miles from Rochester. **E-mail:** mprotos@deerfieldcc.com. **Web:** www.deerfieldcc.com. **Facility Holes:** 27. **Yards:** 7,083/5,623. **Par:** 72/72. **Course Rating:** 73.9/72.4. **Slope:** 138/123. **Green Fee:** $14/$29. **Cart Fee:** $8/Person. **Walking Policy:** Unrestricted walking. **Walkability:** 3. **Opened:** 1963. **Architect:** Peter Craig. **Season:** April-Oct. **To obtain tee times:** Call up to 7 days in advance. **Miscellaneous:** Reduced fees (weekdays, twilight, seniors), metal spikes, range (grass), credit cards (MC, V, AE, D), BF, FF.
Reader Comments: The poor man's Oak Hill ... Front and back 9s dramatically different ... Nice greens, nice layout, no frills ... LPGA course ... Long, tight and very challenging ... Great value ... Very long, difficult ... Challenging layout.
Special Notes: Also has a 9-hole course.

★★★ DEERWOOD GOLF COURSE
PU-1818 Sweeney St., North Tonawanda, 14120, Niagara County, (716)695-8525, 12 miles from Buffalo. **Facility Holes:** 27. **Green Fee:** $10/$20. **Cart Fee:** $20/Cart. **Walking Policy:** Unrestricted walking. **Walkability:** 1. **Opened:** 1975. **Architect:** Tryon & Schwartz. **Season:** April-Dec. **High:** May-Oct. **To obtain tee times:** Call golf shop. **Miscellaneous:** Credit cards (MC, V), BF, FF.
BUCK/DOE (18 Combo)
Yards: 6,931/6,055. **Par:** 72/72. **Course Rating:** 72.5/74.0. **Slope:** 118/120.
BUCK/FAWN (18 Combo)
Yards: 6,568/5,691. **Par:** 72/72. **Course Rating:** 70.7/71.8. **Slope:** 117/119.
DOE/FAWN (18 Combo)
Yards: 6,521/5,614. **Par:** 72/72. **Course Rating:** 70.6/72.1. **Slope:** 117/121.
Reader Comments: 27 holes, well run ... Well maintained and managed ... Great place to play if you like to wait ... Excellent for price ... A good value ... Amazing new 9 holes, short but tricky, all around nice.

DELAWARE PARK GOLF COURSE
PU-, Buffalo, 14216, Erie County, (716)835-2533, 1 mile from Buffalo. **Facility Holes:** 18. **Yards:** 5,359/5,359. **Par:** 68/68. **Green Fee:** $5/$13. **Walking Policy:** Unrestricted walking. **Walkability:** 1. **Season:** April-Oct. **To obtain tee times:** Call golf shop. **Miscellaneous:** Reduced fees (seniors, juniors), BF, FF.

DELHI COLLEGE GOLF COURSE
PU-85 Scotch Mountain Rd., Delhi, 13753, Delaware County, (607)746-4653. **E-mail:**

arehardb@delhi.edu. **Web:** www.delhi.edu. **Facility Holes:** 18. **Yards:** 6,401/4,869. **Par:** 72/72. **Course Rating:** 70.8/68.0. **Slope:** 122/114. **Green Fee:** $22/$28. **Cart Fee:** $11/Person. **Walking Policy:** Unrestricted walking. **Walkability:** 4. **Opened:** 1965. **Season:** April-Nov. **High:** June-Aug. **To obtain tee times:** Call up to 5 days in advance. **Miscellaneous:** Reduced fees (weekdays, twilight, seniors, juniors), range (grass), credit cards (MC, V), BF, FF.

DELPHI FALLS GOLF COURSE
PU-2127 Oran-Delphi Rd., Delphi Falls, 13051, Onondaga County, (315)662-3611, 15 miles from Syracuse. **Facility Holes:** 18. **Yards:** 4,627/4,169. **Par:** 69/70. **Green Fee:** $13/$16. **Cart Fee:** $20/Cart. **Walking Policy:** Unrestricted walking. **Opened:** 1967. **Season:** April-Nov. **To obtain tee times:** Call golf shop. **Misc:**Reduced fees (weekdays), BF, FF.

DIMMOCK HILL GOLF COURSE
PU-638 Dimmock Hill Rd., Binghamton, 13905, Broome County, (607)729-5511. **Facility Holes:** 18. **Yards:** 5,312/4,834. **Par:** 66/69. **Green Fee:** $12. **To obtain tee times:** Call golf shop.

★★½ DINSMORE GOLF COURSE
PU-Old Post Rd., Mills Norrie State Park, Staatsburg, 12580, Dutchess County, (845)889-4071. **Facility Holes:** 18. **Yards:** 5,719/4,567. **Par:** 70/70. **Course Rating:** 65.7/64.2. **Slope:** 106/103. **Green Fee:** $18/$22. **Cart Fee:** $24/Cart. **To obtain tee times:** Call golf shop.

★★ DOMENICO'S GOLF COURSE
PU-13 Church Rd., Whitesboro, 13492, Oneida County, (315)736-9812, 4 miles from Utica. **Facility Holes:** 18. **Yards:** 6,715/5,458. **Par:** 72/75. **Course Rating:** 70.5/71.5. **Slope:** 118/115. **Green Fee:** $16/$18. **Cart Fee:** $22/Cart. **Walking Policy:** Unrestricted walking. **Walkability:** 2. **Opened:** 1982. **Architect:** Joseph Spinella. **Season:** March-Nov. **High:** May-Oct. **To obtain tee times:** Call golf shop. **Miscellaneous:** Reduced fees (weekdays, twilight), FF.

★★★ DOUGLASTON GOLF CLUB
PU-63-20 Marathon Pkwy., Douglaston, 11363, Queens County, (718)224-6566, 15 miles from Manhattan. **Facility Holes:** 18. **Yards:** 5,585/4,602. **Par:** 67/67. **Course Rating:** 66.2/65.6. **Slope:** 111/107. **Green Fee:** $19/$30. **Cart Fee:** $27/Cart. **Walking Policy:** Unrestricted walking. **Walkability:** 4. **Opened:** 1927. **Architect:** William H. Tucker. **Season:** Year-round. **High:** April-Sept. **To obtain tee times:** Call golf shop. **Miscellaneous:** Reduced fees (twilight, seniors, juniors), metal spikes, credit cards (MC, V, AE, D), FF.
Reader Comments: City course, some ups and downs, too short ... Greens are slow but true ... Old course, different, many par 3s ... Back 9 like a different course ... Tough to master.

★★½ DRUMLINS WEST GOLF CLUB
PU-800 Nottingham Rd., Syracuse, 13224, Onondaga County, (315)446-5580, 5 miles from Syracuse. **Facility Holes:** 18. **Yards:** 6,030/4,790. **Par:** 70/70. **Course Rating:** 68.2/71.0. **Green Fee:** $5/$10. **Cart Fee:** $24/Cart. **Walking Policy:** Unrestricted walking. **Walkability:** 4. **Opened:** 1935. **Architect:** Leonard MacComber. **Season:** March-Dec. **High:** May-Aug. **To obtain tee times:** Call golf shop. **Miscellaneous:** Reduced fees (twilight, seniors, juniors), metal spikes, range (grass/mats), credit cards (MC, V, D), BF, FF.

★★½ DUNWOODIE GOLF CLUB
PU-Wasylenko Lane, Yonkers, 10701, Westchester County, (914)231-3490, 15 miles from New York City. **Facility Holes:** 18. **Yards:** 5,815/4,511. **Par:** 70/72. **Course Rating:** 68.3/67.8. **Slope:** 117/117. **Green Fee:** $37/$42. **Cart Fee:** $22/Cart. **Walking Policy:** Unrestricted walking. **Walkability:** 4. **Season:** Year-round. **High:** April-Nov. **To obtain tee times:** Call golf shop. **Miscellaneous:** Reduced fees (twilight, seniors, juniors), metal spikes, range (grass), credit cards (MC, V, AE).

★★★½ DURAND EASTMAN GOLF COURSE
PU-1200 Kings Highway N., Rochester, 14617, Monroe County, (716)342-9810, 5 miles from Rochester. **Facility Holes:** 18. **Yards:** 6,089/5,727. **Par:** 70/72. **Course Rating:** 68.8/71.7. **Slope:** 112/113. **Green Fee:** $12/$13. **Walking Policy:** Unrestricted walking. **Walkability:** 3. **Opened:** 1935. **Architect:** Robert Trent Jones. **Season:** April-Nov. **High:** June-Aug. **To obtain tee times:** Call golf shop. **Miscellaneous:** Reduced fees (weekdays, seniors, juniors), metal spikes, range (grass).
Reader Comments: Excellent design, but very slow play ... A Robert Trent Jones Sr. course. There are beutiful views, many hills ... Some views include Lake Ontario ... You better hit straight.

★★★ DUTCH HOLLOW COUNTRY CLUB
SP-Benson Rd., Owasco, 13130, Cayuga County, (315)784-5052, 19 miles from Syracuse. **Facility Holes:** 18. **Yards:** 6,460/5,045. **Par:** 71/72. **Course Rating:** 68.5/69.0. **Slope:** 116/117. **Green Fee:** $17/$20. **Cart Fee:** $11/Person. **Walking Policy:** Unrestricted walking. **Walkability:** 3. **Opened:** 1965. **Architect:** Willard S. Hall. **Season:** April-Nov. **High:** May-Sept. **To obtain tee times:** Call golf shop. **Miscellaneous:** Reduced fees (weekdays, twilight, seniors, juniors), metal spikes, range (grass), credit cards (MC, V).
Reader Comments: Very friendly, nice pro shop, good prices ... Good layout ... Beautiful course, excellent value ... Challenging, target golf ... Fair ... Scenic, good value, so-so layout.

★★ DYKER BEACH GOLF COURSE
PU-86th St. and 7th Ave., Brooklyn, 11228, Kings County, (718)836-9722, 8 miles from New York City. **Facility Holes:** 18. **Yards:** 6,548/5,696. **Par:** 71/72. **Course Rating:** 68.8. **Slope:** 113. **Green Fee:** $18/$22. **Cart Fee:** $25/Cart. **Walking Policy:** Unrestricted walking. **Walkability:** 2. **Opened:** 1928. **Architect:** John Van Kleek. **Season:** Year-round. **High:** May-Oct. **To obtain tee times:** Call golf shop. **Miscellaneous:** Reduced fees (weekdays, twilight, seniors, juniors), metal spikes, credit cards (MC, V, AE, D).

★★★ EAGLE CREST GOLF CLUB
PU-1004 Ballston Lake Rd., Rte. 146A, Clifton Park, 12065, Saratoga County, (518)877-7082, 12 miles from Saratoga. **Web:** www.eaglecrestgolf.com. **Facility Holes:** 18. **Yards:** 6,861/5,094. **Par:** 72/72. **Course Rating:** 72.8/68.5. **Slope:** 120/112. **Green Fee:** $22/$26. **Cart Fee:** $24/Person. **Walking Policy:** Unrestricted walking. **Walkability:** 2. **Opened:** 1962. **Season:** March-Dec. **High:** June-Sept. **To obtain tee times:** Call up to 3 days in advance. **Miscellaneous:** Reduced fees (weekdays, twilight, seniors, juniors), range (grass), credit cards (MC, V), BF, FF.
Reader Comments: Nice course to walk ... Just too crowded ... Good place to have a tournament ... Nice course, very organized & challenging course, the only problem was the pace of play ... Good test of golf ... Average, making improvements.

★★★ EAGLE VALE GOLF COURSE
PU-4344 Nine Mile Point Rd., Fairport, 14450, Monroe County, (716)377-5200, 15 miles from Rochester. **E-mail:** proshop@eaglevale.com. **Web:** www.eaglevale.com. **Facility Holes:** 18. **Yards:** 6,584/5,801. **Par:** 71/72. **Course Rating:** 71.0/73.0. **Slope:** 121/121. **Green Fee:** $25/$38. **Cart Fee:** Included in green fee. **Walking Policy:** Walking at certain times. **Walkability:** 2. **Opened:** 1987. **Architect:** Bill Brown/Neil Hirsch. **Season:** April-Nov. **High:** May-Sept. **To obtain tee times:** Call up to 7 days in advance. **Miscellaneous:** Reduced fees (weekdays, seniors, juniors), range (mats), credit cards (MC, V, AE, D), BF, FF.
Reader Comments: Good layout, superb greens ... Course manicured nicely ... Some hidden trouble ... Only a couple of challenging holes.

EDGEWOOD GOLF COURSE
SP-Crow Hill Rd., Laurens, 13796, Otsego County, (607)432-2713. **E-mail:** kcs2020@hotmail.com. **Facility Holes:** 18. **Yards:** 6,062/5,674. **Par:** 72/74. **Green Fee:** $8/$12. **Cart Fee:** $14/Cart. **Walking Policy:** Unrestricted walking. **Walkability:** 4. **Opened:** 1963. **Season:** April-Oct. **High:** June-Sept. **To obtain tee times:** Call golf shop. **Miscellaneous:** BF, FF.

EISENHOWER PARK GOLF
PU-Eisenhower Park, East Meadow, 11554, Nassau County, (516)572-0327, 20 miles from New York City. **Facility Holes:** 54. **Cart Fee:** $29/Cart. **Walking Policy:** Unrestricted walking. **Walkability:** 1. **Architect:** Robert Trent Jones. **Season:** Year-round. **High:** May-Oct. **To obtain tee times:** Call golf shop. **Miscellaneous:** Reduced fees (weekdays, seniors), range,BF, FF.
★★ **BLUE COURSE** (18)
Yards: 6,026/5,800. **Par:** 72/72. **Course Rating:** 68.7/74.1. **Slope:** 112/122. **Green Fee:** $12/$28. **Opened:** 1947.
★★★½ **RED COURSE** (18) *Value*
Yards: 6,756/5,449. **Par:** 72/72. **Course Rating:** 71.5/69.8. **Slope:** 119/115. **Green Fee:** $13/$30. **Opened:** 1914.
Reader Comments: A very nice muni ... Great public course ... The most improved course on LI ... Very crowded & slow play as a result ... Good walking course, best of 3 at Eisenhower ... Excellent course, looks like a county club-type course.
★★ **WHITE COURSE** (18)
Yards: 6,269/5,920. **Par:** 72/72. **Course Rating:** 69.5/71.4. **Slope:** 115/117. **Green Fee:** $12/$28. **Opened:** 1947.

ELKDALE COUNTRY CLUB
SP-Rte. 353, Salamanca, 14779, Cattaraugus County, (716)945-5553. **Facility Holes:** 18. **Yards:** 6,200. **Par:** 70. **To obtain tee times:** Call golf shop.

★★½ ELM TREE GOLF COURSE
PU-283 State Rte. No.13, Cortland, 13045, Cortland County, (607)753-1341, 30 miles from Syracuse. **Facility Holes:** 18. **Yards:** 6,251/5,520. **Par:** 70/74. **Course Rating:** 66.4/66.3. **Slope:** 100/99. **Green Fee:** $10/$16. **Cart Fee:** $22/Cart. **Walking Policy:** Unrestricted walking. **Walkability:** 3. **Opened:** 1966. **Architect:** Alder Jones. **Season:** March-Nov. **High:** March-Dec. **To obtain tee times:** Call golf shop. **Miscellaneous:** Reduced fees (weekdays, guests, twilight), range (grass/mats), credit cards (MC, V), BF, FF.

★★½ ELMA MEADOWS GOLF CLUB
PU-1711 Girdle Rd., Elma, 14059, Erie County, (716)655-3037, 10 miles from Buffalo. **Facility Holes:** 18. **Yards:** 6,316/6,000. **Par:** 70/75. **Course Rating:** 70.7/74.0. **Slope:** 118/106. **Green Fee:** $11/$13. **Cart Fee:** $20/Cart. **Walking Policy:** Unrestricted walking. **Walkability:** 3. **Opened:** 1959. **Architect:** William Harries/A. Russell Tyron. **Season:** April-Nov. **To obtain tee times:** Call golf shop. **Miscellaneous:** Reduced fees (weekdays, seniors, juniors), range (grass), BF, FF.

ELMS GOLF CLUB
PU-9613 Elms Rd. N., Sandy Creek, 13145, Oswego County, (315)387-5297. **Facility Holes:** 18. **Yards:** 6,039. **Par:** 70. **To obtain tee times:** Call golf shop.

★★ ELY PARK MUNICIPAL GOLF COURSE
PU-67 Ridge Rd., Binghamton, 13905, Broome County, (607)772-7231. **Facility Holes:** 18. **Yards:** 6,410/4,872. **Par:** 71/73. **Course Rating:** 69.4/71.0. **Slope:** 115/117. **Green Fee:** $12/$13. **Cart Fee:** $18/Cart. **Walking Policy:** Unrestricted walking. **Walkability:** 4. **Opened:** 1932. **Architect:** Ernest E. Smith. **Season:** April-Nov. **To obtain tee times:** Call up to 7 days in advance. **Miscellaneous:** Reduced fees (seniors, juniors), metal spikes, range (grass/mats), BF, FF.

EMERALD CREST GOLF CLUB
PU-3989 St. Rte. 3, Fulton, 13069, Oswego County, (315)593-1016, 18 miles from Syracuse. **Facility Holes:** 18. **Yards:** 5,445/4,365. **Par:** 68/68. **Course Rating:** 66.2/62.7. **Slope:** 112/96. **Green Fee:** $15. **Cart Fee:** $20/Cart. **Walking Policy:** Unrestricted walking. **Walkability:** 3. **Opened:** 1961. **Season:** April-Nov. **High:** June-Sept. **To obtain tee times:** Call golf shop. **Miscellaneous:** Reduced fees (weekdays), credit cards (MC, V), FF.

★★★★ EN-JOIE GOLF CLUB
PU-722 W. Main St., Endicott, 13760, Broome County, (607)785-1661, (888)436-5643, 9 miles from Binghamton. **E-mail:** golf@enjoiegolf.com. **Web:** www.enjoiegolf.com. **Facility Holes:** 18. **Yards:** 7,016/5,205. **Par:** 72/74. **Course Rating:** 73.0/69.8. **Slope:** 125/118. **Green Fee:** $28/$32. **Cart Fee:** $24/Person. **Walking Policy:** Walking at certain times. **Walkability:** 2. **Opened:** 1927. **Architect:** Dr. Michael Hurdzan. **Season:** April-Nov. **To obtain tee times:** Call golf shop. **Miscellaneous:** Reduced fees (weekdays, seniors, juniors), range (grass/mats), credit cards (MC, V), BF, FF.
Reader Comments: Home of BC Open … A real classic … Where else can you play a PGA Tour stop for under $50? … Very cheap for a tour course.

★★★½ ENDWELL GREENS GOLF CLUB
PU-3675 Sally Piper Rd., Endwell, 13760, Broome County, (607)785-4653, (877)281-6863, 5 miles from Binghamton. **E-mail:** pga4653@aol.com. **Facility Holes:** 18. **Yards:** 7,104/5,382. **Par:** 72/76. **Course Rating:** 73.5/69.0. **Slope:** 129/113. **Green Fee:** $20/$27. **Cart Fee:** $12/Person. **Walking Policy:** Walking at certain times. **Walkability:** 4. **Opened:** 1968. **Architect:** Geoffrey Cornish. **Season:** Year-round. **High:** June-Aug. **To obtain tee times:** Call golf shop. **Miscellaneous:** Reduced fees (weekdays, seniors, juniors), metal spikes, range (grass/mats), lodging (10 rooms), credit cards (MC, V, D).
Reader Comments: This is a fun course (needs a little work) … Fairly long, very large greens … Great course, long and a lot of doglegs … Good for all abilities … Very hilly, but many interesting holes … Tough test from the tips.

EVER GREEN COUNTRY CLUB
SP-92 Schuurman Rd., Castleton-On-Hudson, 12033, Rensselaer County, (518)477-6224, 7 miles from Albany. **Web:** www.evergreencountryclub.com. **Facility Holes:** 36. **Yards:** 7,244/5,594. **Par:** 72/75. **Course Rating:** 73.5/76.5. **Slope:** 131/141. **Green Fee:** $15/$22. **Walking Policy:** Unrestricted walking. **Walkability:** 3. **Opened:** 1961. **Architect:** Ed Van Kappen. **Season:** Year-round. **High:** April-Dec. **To obtain tee times:** Call up to 5 days in

advance. **Miscellaneous:** Reduced fees (weekdays, twilight, seniors, juniors), metal spikes, range (grass), credit cards (MC, V, D), BF, FF.
Special Notes: Also has a private 18-hole course.

★½ **FILLMORE GOLF CLUB**
SP-Tollgate Hill Rd., Locke, 13092, Cayuga County, (315)497-3145, 19 miles from Auburn.
E-mail: fillmore@baldcom.net. **Facility Holes:** 18. **Yards:** 5,523/4,374. **Par:** 71/71. **Course Rating:** 67.1/66.1. **Slope:** 115/115. **Green Fee:** $15/$17. **Cart Fee:** $22/Cart. **Walking Policy:** Unrestricted walking. **Walkability:** 3. **Opened:** 1965. **Architect:** Alder Jones. **Season:** April-Oct. **High:** June-Aug. **To obtain tee times:** Call golf shop. **Miscellaneous:** Reduced fees (weekdays, seniors, juniors), range (grass), credit cards (MC, V), BF, FF.

★½ **FORD HILL COUNTRY CLUB**
PU-Rte. 26, Ford Hill Rd., Whitney Point, 13862, Broome County, (607)692-8938, 19 miles from Binghamton. **Facility Holes:** 36. **Green Fee:** $16/$18. **Cart Fee:** $20/Cart. **Walking Policy:** Unrestricted walking. **Walkability:** 2. **Opened:** 1951. **Architect:** Richard L. Driscoll. **Season:** April-Nov. **High:** June-Sept. **To obtain tee times:** Call golf shop. **Miscellaneous:** Reduced fees (weekdays, juniors), metal spikes, credit cards (MC, V, AE, D), BF, FF.
BLUE/ORANGE (18 Combo)
Yards: 5,436/5,436. **Par:** 70/70. **Course Rating:** 68.0/68.0. **Slope:** 105/105.
RED/BLUE (18 Combo)
Yards: 5,254/5,254. **Par:** 69/69. **Course Rating:** 68.0/68.0. **Slope:** 105/105.
RED/ORANGE (18 Combo)
Yards: 5,218/5,218. **Par:** 69/69. **Course Rating:** 68.0/68.0. **Slope:** 105/105.
RED/WHITE (18 Combo)
Yards: 5,299/5,299. **Par:** 69/69. **Course Rating:** 68.0/68.0. **Slope:** 105/105.

★★★ **FOREST PARK GOLF COURSE**
PU-101 Forest Park Dr., Woodhaven, 11421, Queens County, (718)296-0999, 10 miles from Bronx. **Facility Holes:** 18. **Yards:** 6,037/5,431. **Par:** 70/72. **Course Rating:** 65.5/69.5. **Slope:** 111/108. **Green Fee:** $24/$26. **Cart Fee:** $23/Cart. **Walking Policy:** Unrestricted walking. **Walkability:** 3. **Opened:** 1901. **Architect:** Mr. Elliot. **Season:** Year-round. **High:** April-Sept. **To obtain tee times:** Call golf shop. **Miscellaneous:** Reduced fees (weekdays, twilight, seniors, juniors), metal spikes, credit cards (MC, V).
Reader Comments: Good place for value … Like most NYC munis, this track is rarely watered.

FORESTBURGH COUNTRY CLUB
SP-80 Tannery Rd., Rte. 42 S., Forestburgh, 12777, Sullivan County, (845)794-6542. **Web:** www.forestburgh.com. **Facility Holes:** 18. **Yards:** 6,700. **Par:** 72/72. **Course Rating:** 72.3. **Slope:** 140/140. **Green Fee:** $37/$52. **Cart Fee:** $11/Person. **Walkability:** 5. **Opened:** 1997. **Architect:** W. F. Mitchell. **Season:** March-Dec. **High:** May-Oct. **To obtain tee times:** Call golf shop. **Miscellaneous:** Reduced fees (twilight), range (mats).

★★ **FOX RUN GOLF CLUB**
PU-129 Alban Hills Dr., Johnstown, 12095, Fulton County, (518)762-3717, 40 miles from Albany. **Facility Holes:** 18. **Yards:** 6,005/5,094. **Par:** 70/70. **Course Rating:** 66.3/67.6. **Slope:** 103/105. **Green Fee:** $12/$18. **Cart Fee:** $20/Cart. **Walking Policy:** Walking at certain times. **Walkability:** 1. **Opened:** 1980. **Architect:** Attillio Albanese. **Season:** April-Nov. **High:** June-Aug. **To obtain tee times:** Call golf shop. **Miscellaneous:** Reduced fees (weekdays, twilight, seniors, juniors), metal spikes, credit cards (MC, V).

★★★ **FOXFIRE AT VILLAGE GREEN**
PU-One Village Blvd., Baldwinsville, 13027, Onondaga County, (315)638-2930, 9 miles from Syracuse. **E-mail:** foxfire@twcny.rr.com. **Facility Holes:** 18. **Yards:** 6,856/5,401. **Par:** 72/74. **Course Rating:** 72.8/71.5. **Slope:** 127/115. **Green Fee:** $22/$24. **Cart Fee:** $11/Person. **Walking Policy:** Walking at certain times. **Walkability:** 2. **Opened:** 1974. **Architect:** Hal Purdy. **Season:** March-Nov. **High:** May-Sept. **To obtain tee times:** Call golf shop. **Miscellaneous:** Reduced fees (weekdays, seniors, juniors), metal spikes, range (grass/mats), credit cards (MC, V), BF, FF.
Reader Comments: It's very tight … A few challenging holes, makes you think … Nice layout, some tough holes … Nice course … Too narrow for weekend golfers … Challenging par 5s.

FREAR PARK GOLF COURSE
PU-Lavin Court & Park Blvd., Troy, 12180, Rensselaer County, (518)270-4553, 12 miles from Albany. **Facility Holes:** 18. **Yards:** 6,234/6,234. **Par:** 71/71. **Green Fee:** $18/$20. **Cart Fee:** $20/Cart. **Season:** April-Nov. **To obtain tee times:** Call golf shop. **Miscellaneous:** Reduced fees (seniors), credit cards (MC, V).

★★★ GARRISON GOLF CLUB
PU-2015 Rte. 9, Garrison, 10524, Putnam County, (845)424-4747, 50 miles from New York City. **E-mail:** joespivak@garrisongolfclub.com. **Facility Holes:** 18. **Yards:** 6,470/5,041. **Par:** 72/70. **Course Rating:** 72.1/69.9. **Slope:** 134/124. **Green Fee:** $40/$80. **Cart Fee:** Included in green fee. **Walking Policy:** Walking at certain times. **Walkability:** 5. **Opened:** 1962. **Architect:** Dick Wilson. **Season:** April-Dec. **To obtain tee times:** Call up to 7 days in advance. **Miscellaneous:** Reduced fees (weekdays, twilight, seniors), range (grass/mats), credit cards (MC, V, AE), BF, FF.
Reader Comments: Great views overlooking the Hudson River, nice layout with some challenging holes … Played in a wind storm, still enjoyed course … Beautiful views of the Hudson, West Point … Not too forgiving … Beautiful first hole.

GENEGANTSLET GOLF CLUB
PU-686 State Hwy. 12, Greene, 13778, Chenango County, (607)656-8191, 15 miles from Binghamton. **E-mail:** genygolf@aol.com. **Facility Holes:** 18. **Yards:** 6,547/4,894. **Par:** 71/71. **Course Rating:** 70.0/68.0. **Slope:** 117/108. **Green Fee:** $17/$20. **Cart Fee:** $20/Cart. **Walking Policy:** Unrestricted walking. **Walkability:** 1. **Opened:** 1956. **Architect:** Larry Reistetter. **Season:** April-Nov. **High:** June-Sept. **To obtain tee times:** Call up to 7 days in advance. **Miscellaneous:** Reduced fees (weekdays, twilight, seniors, juniors), credit cards (MC, V, AE, D), BF, FF.

GENESEE VALLEY GOLF COURSE
PU-1000 E. River Rd., Rochester, 14623, Monroe County, (716)424-2920. **Facility Holes:** 36. **Green Fee:** $13/$14. **Cart Fee:** $18/Cart. **Walking Policy:** Unrestricted walking. **Architect:** Frances Baker. **Season:** May-Nov. **To obtain tee times:** Call golf shop. **Miscellaneous:** Reduced fees (twilight, seniors, juniors), range (grass/mats), BF, FF.
★½ **NORTH COURSE (18)**
Yards: 6,374/6,007. **Par:** 71/77. **Course Rating:** 69.3/73.2. **Slope:** 104/112. **Opened:** 1900.
★½ **SOUTH COURSE (18)**
Yards: 5,270/5,270. **Par:** 67/69. **Course Rating:** .0/67.4. **Slope:** 93/100. **Opened:** 1927.

GLEN COVE GOLF COURSE
SP-Lattingtown Rd., Glen Cove, 11542, Nassau County, (516)671-0033, 20 miles from Queens. **Facility Holes:** 18. **Yards:** 4,815/4,148. **Par:** 66/66. **Course Rating:** 63.4/65.6. **Slope:** 108/98. **Green Fee:** $13/$15. **Cart Fee:** $24/Cart. **Opened:** 1970. **Architect:** William Mitchell. **Season:** April-Nov. **To obtain tee times:** Call golf shop. **Miscellaneous:** Reduced fees (seniors), range (mats).

★★★½ GLEN OAK GOLF COURSE
PU-711 Smith Rd., East Amherst, 14051, Erie County, (716)688-5454, 25 miles from Buffalo. **Facility Holes:** 18. **Yards:** 6,821/5,561. **Par:** 72/72. **Course Rating:** 72.6/71.9. **Slope:** 130/118. **Green Fee:** $25/$47. **Cart Fee:** Included in green fee. **Walking Policy:** Mandatory carts. **Walkability:** 3. **Opened:** 1969. **Architect:** Robert Trent Jones. **Season:** March-Nov. **High:** June-April. **To obtain tee times:** Call golf shop. **Miscellaneous:** Reduced fees (weekdays, twilight, seniors), range (grass/mats), credit cards (MC, V), BF, FF.
Reader Comments: A challenging Robert Trent Jones Sr. layout … Good chipping green for warmup, but be prepared to use your sand wedge … The best public course in the Buffalo area … Should be able to walk, too many outings, a fine layout.

★★ GOLDEN OAK GOLF CLUB
PU-679 NY, Rte. 79 S., Windsor, 13865, Broome County, (607)655-3217, 12 miles from Binghamton. **Facility Holes:** 18. **Yards:** 5,500/4,500. **Par:** 69/69. **Course Rating:** 70.8/65.0. **Slope:** 117/112. **Green Fee:** $13/$16. **Cart Fee:** $20/Cart. **Walking Policy:** Unrestricted walking. **Walkability:** 3. **Opened:** 1972. **Architect:** Paul Kern. **Season:** March-Nov. **High:** May-Sept. **To obtain tee times:** Call up to 2 days in advance. **Miscellaneous:** Reduced fees (weekdays), credit cards (MC, V), BF, FF.

THE GOLF CLUB AT MANSION RIDGE
PU-1292 Orange Tpke., Monroe, 10950, Orange County, (845)782-7888, 35 miles from New York City. **Facility Holes:** 18. **Yards:** 6,889/4,785. **Par:** 72/72. **Course Rating:** 73.5/68.1. **Slope:** 138/127. **Green Fee:** $100/$125. **Cart Fee:** Included in green fee. **Walking Policy:** Mandatory cart. **Walkability:** 3. **Opened:** 1999. **Architect:** Jack Nicklaus. **Season:** April-Nov. **High:** June-Sept. **To obtain tee times:** Call golf shop. **Miscellaneous:** Reduced fees (twilight), range (grass/mats), credit cards (MC, V, AE, D).

GOLF CLUB OF NEWPORT
PU-Honey Hill Rd., Newport, 13416, Herkimer County, (315)843-8333, (888)770-0592, 12 miles from Utica. **Facility Holes:** 18. **Yards:** 7,067/5,042. **Par:** 72/72. **Course Rating:** 73.7/69.1.

Slope: 120/115. **Green Fee:** $15/$18. **Cart Fee:** $22/Cart. **Walking Policy:** Unrestricted walking. **Walkability:** 3. **Opened:** 1968. **Architect:** Geoffrey Cornish. **Season:** April-Nov. **High:** July-Sept. **To obtain tee times:** Call up to 7 days in advance. **Miscellaneous:** Reduced fees (weekdays, twilight, seniors), range (grass), FF.

GOLF COURSE OF TRUMANSBURG
PU-23 Halsey St., Trumansburg, 14886, Tompkins County, (607)387-8844, 75 miles from Syracuse. **Web:** www.trumansburggolf.com. **Facility Holes:** 18. **Yards:** 6,373/4,946. **Par:** 72/72. **Course Rating:** 70.6/68.2. **Slope:** 122/115. **Green Fee:** $17/$19. **Cart Fee:** $22/Cart. **Walking Policy:** Unrestricted walking. **Walkability:** 3. **Opened:** 1969. **Architect:** Wes White/ Bob Tallman. **Season:** April-Nov. **High:** June-Aug.**Tee times:** Call up to 30 days in advance. **Miscellaneous:** Reduced fees (weekdays, seniors), credit cards (MC, V, AE), BF, FF.

GRANDVIEW FARMS GOLF COURSE
PU-400 Hartwell Rd., E. Berkshire, 13736, Tioga County, (607)657-2619, 25 miles from Binghamton. **Facility Holes:** 18. **Yards:** 5,818/4,185. **Par:** 70/70. **Green Fee:** $9/$15. **Cart Fee:** $13/Person. **Walking Policy:** Unrestricted walking. **Walkability:** 4. **Opened:** 1991. **Architect:** Howard I. Coon. **Season:** April-Nov. **High:** May-Sept. **To obtain tee times:** Call golf shop. **Miscellaneous:** Reduced fees (weekdays), metal spikes, range (grass), credit cards (MC, V, D, Debit Card), FF.

GREAT ROCK GOLF CLUB
SP-141 Fairway Dr., Wading River, 11792, Suffolk County, (631)929-1200. **E-mail:** info@greatrockgolfclub.com. **Web:** www.greatrockgolfclub.com. **Facility Holes:** 18. **Yards:** 6,193/5,106. **Par:** 71/71. **Course Rating:** 70.0/69.6. **Slope:** 125/120. **Green Fee:** $40/$80. **Cart Fee:** Included in green fee. **Walking Policy:** Walking at certain times. **Walkability:** 5. **Season:** Year-round. **High:** April-Oct. **To obtain tee times:** Call up to 5 days in advance. **Miscellaneous:** Range (grass/mats), credit cards (MC, V, AE, D), FF.

★★★½ GREEN LAKES STATE PARK GOLF CLUB
PU-7900 Green Lakes Rd., Fayetteville, 13066, Onondaga County, (315)637-0258, 7 miles from Syracuse. **Facility Holes:** 18. **Yards:** 6,212/5,481. **Par:** 71/74. **Course Rating:** 68.4/70.6. **Slope:** 113/120. **Green Fee:** $20/$24. **Cart Fee:** $20/Person. **Walking Policy:** Unrestricted walking. **Walkability:** 4. **Opened:** 1936. **Architect:** Robert Trent Jones. **Season:** April-Nov. **High:** May-Sept. **To obtain tee times:** Call golf shop. **Miscellaneous:** Reduced fees (weekdays, seniors, juniors), metal spikes, credit cards (MC, V).
Reader Comments: Beautiful view, great layout … Very crowded, tough course to walk … Plush … Course is great but speed of play, wow … Good for state course, crowded, hard to get tee time … A fine course, well done … Great course.

GREEN RIDGE GOLF CLUB
PU-204 Gregory Rd., Johnson, 10933, Orange County, (845)335-1317, 15 miles from Port Jervis. **Facility Holes:** 18. **Yards:** 5,500/4,770. **Par:** 72/72. **Green Fee:** $14/$18. **Cart Fee:** $22/Cart. **Walking Policy:** Unrestricted walking. **Opened:** 1965. **Season:** April-Nov. **Tee times:** Call golf shop. **Miscellaneous:** Reduced fees (twilight, seniors), credit cards (MC, V, AE, D).

GREENVIEW COUNTRY CLUB
PU-1720 Whig Hill Rd., West Monroe, 13167, Oswego County, (315)668-2244, 15 miles from Syracuse. **Facility Holes:** 36. **Walking Policy:** Walking at certain times. **Walkability:** 2. **Season:** April-Nov. **High:** June-Aug. **To obtain tee times:** Call golf shop. **Misc:** Reduced fees (weekdays, twilight, seniors, juniors), metal spikes, range (grass/mats), credit cards (MC, V, AE).
GREEN VALLEY COURSE (18)
Yards: 5,877/5,265. **Par:** 73/73. **Green Fee:** $17/$18. **Cart Fee:** $16/Cart.
★★½ **GREENVIEW COURSE** (18)
Yards: 6,299/5,864. **Par:** 71/72. **Course Rating:** 69.5. **Slope:** 116. **Green Fee:** $14/$17. **Cart Fee:** $17/Cart. **Opened:** 1960. **Architect:** Glen Green.

★★★★½ GREYSTONE GOLF CLUB
PU-1400 Atlantic Ave., Walworth, 14568, Wayne County, (315)524-0022, (800)810-2325, 12 miles from Rochester. **Web:** www.234golf.com. **Facility Holes:** 18. **Yards:** 6,500/5,300. **Par:** 72/72. **Course Rating:** 70.2/70.7. **Slope:** 121/122. **Green Fee:** $28/$38. **Cart Fee:** $12/Person. **Walking Policy:** Walking at certain times. **Walkability:** 4. **Opened:** 1996. **Architect:** Craig Schreiner. **Season:** April-Oct. **High:** June-Aug. **To obtain tee times:** Call golf shop. **Miscellaneous:** Reduced fees (weekdays, twilight, seniors), range (grass), credit cards (MC, V, AE), BF, FF.
Reader Comments: Wonderful experience, every hole is distinctive … Pseudo Scottish course, I like the fairway mounding … I would tell anyone to try this beauty … Easily the best public course within 75 miles … An enchanting course with elevation changes … Links golf in NY.

GRIFFINS' GREENS GOLF COURSE
PU-229 St. Rte. 104A, Oswego, 13126, Oswego County, (315)343-2996, 5 miles from Oswego. **Facility Holes:** 18. **Yards:** 5,332/5,332. **Par:** 70/70. **Green Fee:** $9/$14. **Cart Fee:** $18/Cart. **Walking Policy:** Unrestricted walking. **Walkability:** 3. **Opened:** 1975. **Architect:** G. Cornish. **Season:** March-Nov. **High:** May-Sept. **To obtain tee times:** Call golf shop. **Miscellaneous:** Reduced fees (seniors), FF.

GROSSINGER COUNTRY CLUB
PU-127 Grossinger Rd., Liberty, 12754, Sullivan County, (914)292-9000, (888)448-9686, 98 miles from New York City. **E-mail:** tbarker@catskill.net. **Web:** www.grossingergolf.com. **Facility Holes:** 27. **Season:** April-Nov. **High:** May-Oct. **To obtain tee times:** Call up to 30 days in advance. **Miscellaneous:** Reduced fees (weekdays, twilight), range (grass), credit cards (MC, V, AE), BF, FF.
★★★★   **THE BIG G (18)**
Yards: 6,907/5,730. **Par:** 71/73. **Course Rating:** 72.9/73.2. **Slope:** 134/137. **Green Fee:** $45/$82. **Cart Fee:** Included in green fee. **Walking Policy:** Mandatory carts. **Walkability:** 3. **Opened:** 1968. **Architect:** Joe Finger.
Reader Comments: The best public course in New York State ... Old course, love to play it ... Best course in Catskills ... Loved it ... It's the Augusta of the Catskills ... Slow play.
★★★   **THE LITTLE G (9)**
Yards: 3,268/3,024. **Par:** 36/36. **Course Rating:** 35.9/36.6. **Slope:** 126/130. **Green Fee:** $20. **Cart Fee:** $15/Person. **Walking Policy:** Unrestricted walking. **Walkability:** 4. **Opened:** 1925. **Architect:** A.W. Tillinghast.
Reader Comments: Back 9 takes your breath away ... A must play although out of way ... One of the best, spectacular views! ... Great, tough course ... A fun, basic course in the country and a great value ... Best in area.

★½   GROVER CLEVELAND GOLF COURSE
PU-3781 Main St., Amherst, 14226, Erie County, (716)862-9470, 3 miles from Buffalo. **Facility Holes:** 18. **Yards:** 5,584/5,584. **Par:** 69/69. **Course Rating:** 65.5/65.5. **Slope:** 101/101. **Green Fee:** $9/$10. **Cart Fee:** $19/Cart. **Walking Policy:** Unrestricted walking. **Walkability:** 2. **Opened:** 1912. **Season:** April-Nov. **To obtain tee times:** Call golf shop. **Miscellaneous:** Reduced fees (weekdays, seniors, juniors), range (mats), credit cards (MC, V), FF.

GULL HAVEN GOLF COURSE
PU-Gull Haven Dr., Central Islip, 11722, Suffolk County, (631)436-6059, 50 miles from New York City. **Facility Holes:** 9. **Yards:** 2,585/2,374. **Par:** 35/35. **Course Rating:** 65.7/70.5. **Slope:** 111/120. **Green Fee:** $18. **Cart Fee:** $13/Person. **Architect:** Doug Jansen. **Season:** Year-round. **To obtain tee times:** Call golf shop. **Miscellaneous:** Reduced fees (weekdays), credit cards (MC, V), FF.

HALES MILLS COUNTRY CLUB
PU-146 Steele Rd., Johnstown, 12095, Fulton County, (518)736-4622, 25 miles from Schnectady. **Facility Holes:** 18. **Yards:** 5,995/4,983. **Par:** 71/71. **Green Fee:** $14. **Cart Fee:** $14/Cart. **Opened:** 1995. **Architect:** Larry Hollenbeck. **To obtain tee times:** Call golf shop. **Miscellaneous:** Range (grass), credit cards (MC, V, D).

★★★   HANAH COUNTRY INN & GOLF RESORT
PU-Rte. 30, Margaretville, 12455, Delaware County, (845)586-4849, (800)752-6494, 42 miles from Kingston. **Facility Holes:** 18. **Yards:** 7,033/5,294. **Par:** 72/72. **Course Rating:** 73.5/69.7. **Slope:** 133/123. **Green Fee:** $40/$55. **Cart Fee:** Included in green fee. **Walking Policy:** Mandatory carts. **Opened:** 1992. **Architect:** Koji Nagasaka. **Season:** April-Oct. **High:** June-July. **To obtain tee times:** Call golf shop. **Miscellaneous:** Reduced fees (weekdays, guests, twilight, seniors), range (grass/mats), credit cards (MC, V, AE, D), BF, FF.
Reader Comments: Layout is different and very challenging ... Great package deals ... Great resort course, fun, some tricky holes, well maintained.

★★★½   HARBOR LINKS GOLF COURSE
PU-1 Fairway Dr., Port Washington, 11050, Nassau County, (516)767-4816, (877)342-7267, 25 miles from New York City. **E-mail:** kmiller@palmergolf.com. **Web:** www.harborlinks.com. **Facility Holes:** 27. **Yards:** 6,927/5,465. **Par:** 72/72. **Course Rating:** 73.2/71.5. **Slope:** 128/119. **Green Fee:** $40/$90. **Cart Fee:** Included in green fee. **Walking Policy:** Walking at certain times. **Walkability:** 4. **Opened:** 1998. **Architect:** Michael Hurdzan/Dana Fry. **Season:** April-Nov. **High:** May-Oct. **To obtain tee times:** Call golf shop. **Miscellaneous:** Reduced fees (twilight, seniors, juniors), range (grass/mats), credit cards (MC, V, AE), BF, FF.
Reader Comments: Expensive public course, but good ... Ease of getting there, but needs clubhouse ... Nice course, expensive on weekend, old sand mine.
Special Notes: Also has a 9-hole executive course.

HARBOUR POINTE GOLF COURSE
PU-1380 Oak Orchard Rd., Waterport, 14571, Orleans County, (585)682-3922, 30 miles from Rochester. **Facility Holes:** 18. **Yards:** 5,610/5,197. **Par:** 70/72. **Course Rating:** 66.8/69.0. **Slope:** 97/95. **Green Fee:** $19. **Cart Fee:** $18/Cart. **Opened:** 1961. **Architect:** Joe Dimino. **Season:** May-Oct. **To obtain tee times:** Call golf shop. **Miscellaneous:** Reduced fees (seniors), range (grass).

HARLEM VALLEY GOLF CLUB
SP-Wheeler Rd., Wingdale, 12594, Dutchess County, (845)832-9957. **Facility Holes:** 9. **Yards:** 6,016/6,016. **Par:** 35/35. **Green Fee:** $17/$20. **Cart Fee:** $22/Cart. **Walking Policy:** Unrestricted walking. **Opened:** 1937. **Season:** April-Nov. **To obtain tee times:** Call golf shop. **Miscellaneous:** Reduced fees (seniors), FF.

★★★½ **HEATHERWOOD GOLF COURSE**
PU-303 Arrowhead Lane, Centereach, 11720, Suffolk County, (631)473-9000, 8 miles from Hauppauge. **Facility Holes:** 18. **Yards:** 4,109/3,395. **Par:** 60/60. **Course Rating:** 58.6/58.9. **Slope:** 95/91. **Green Fee:** $25/$28. **Cart Fee:** $24/Cart. **Opened:** 1960. **Season:** Year-round. **To obtain tee times:** Call golf shop. **Miscellaneous:** Reduced fees (twilight, seniors).
Reader Comments: No par 5 holes, good for irons … Executive course … Great condition, all year-round … Short course, great to work on your game .

HERITAGE COUNTRY CLUB
SP-4301 Watson Blvd., Johnson City, 13790, Broome County, (607)755-6313, 15 miles from Binghamton. **Web:** www.heritagecc.com. **Facility Holes:** 27. **Yards:** 6,266/5,420. **Par:** 70/73. **Course Rating:** 68.6/68.6. **Slope:** 117/115. **Green Fee:** $28/$33. **Cart Fee:** $12/Person. **Walkability:** 4. **Opened:** 1937. **Architect:** John Van Kleek. **Season:** March-Dec. **To obtain tee times:** Call golf shop. **Miscellaneous:** Credit cards (MC, V, AE, D).
Special Notes: Also has a 9-hole Homestead Course.

HICKORY HILLS GOLF COURSE
PU-156 Rte. 17A, Warwick, 10990, Orange County, (845)988-9501. **Facility Holes:** 18. **Yards:** 6,400/5,898. **Par:** 72/72. **Course Rating:** 72.8/74.2. **Slope:** 123/125. **Green Fee:** $12/$36. **Cart Fee:** $24/Cart. **Walking Policy:** Unrestricted walking. **Walkability:** 5. **Opened:** 1993. **Architect:** Hal Purdy. **Season:** March-Dec. **High:** May-Sept. **To obtain tee times:** Call golf shop. **Miscellaneous:** Reduced fees (weekdays, twilight), range (grass), BF, FF.

HICKORY RIDGE GOLF & COUNTRY CLUB
SP-15816 Lynch Rd., Holley, 14470, Orleans County, (585)638-4653, (888)346-5458, 20 miles from Rochester. **Web:** www.hickoryridgegolfandcountryclub.com. **Facility Holes:** 18. **Yards:** 6,333/5,038. **Par:** 72/72. **Course Rating:** 70.9/69.8. **Slope:** 125/124. **Green Fee:** $17/$20. **Cart Fee:** $18/Person. **Opened:** 1995. **Architect:** Peter Craig. **Season:** April-Nov. **To obtain tee times:** Call up to 4 days in advance. **Miscellaneous:** Reduced fees (seniors, juniors), range (grass), credit cards (MC, V, AE, D).

HIDDEN VALLEY GOLF CLUB
PU-189 Castle Rd., Whitesboro, 13492, Oneida County, (315)736-9953, 5 miles from Utica. **Facility Holes:** 18. **Yards:** 6,456/5,517. **Par:** 71/73. **Course Rating:** 70.0/69.0. **Slope:** 109/106. **Green Fee:** $16/$17. **Cart Fee:** $9/Person. **Opened:** 1960. **Season:** March-Nov. **To obtain tee times:** Call golf shop. **Miscellaneous:** Metal spikes, range (grass).

HIGHLAND MEADOWS
PU-24201 NYS Rte. 342, Watertown, 13601, Jefferson County, (315)785-0108, 5 miles from Watertown. **Facility Holes:** 18. **Yards:** 6,241/5,231. **Par:** 72/72. **Course Rating:** 69.6/69.6. **Slope:** 116/112. **Green Fee:** $18/$21. **Walking Policy:** Unrestricted walking. **Walkability:** 2. **Opened:** 1996. **Architect:** James Doolittle. **Season:** April-Nov. **High:** June-April. **To obtain tee times:** Call golf shop. **Miscellaneous:** Range (grass), credit cards (MC, V, D), FF.

HIGHLAND PARK GOLF COURSE
SP-Franklin SR, Auburn, 13021, Cayuga County, (315)253-3381, 25 miles from Syracuse. **Facility Holes:** 18. **Yards:** 6,401/5,285. **Par:** 71/71. **Course Rating:** 70.8/73.0. **Slope:** 120/122. **Green Fee:** $28. **Cart Fee:** $22/Person. **Opened:** 1925. **Season:** April-Oct. **To obtain tee times:** Call golf shop. **Miscellaneous:** Range (grass/mats), credit cards (MC, V).

★★★★½ **HILAND GOLF CLUB** *Pace*
SP-195 Haviland Rd., Queensbury, 12804, Warren County, (518)761-4653, 45 miles from Albany. **E-mail:** hiland@kempersports.com. **Facility Holes:** 18. **Yards:** 6,732/5,677. **Par:** 72/72. **Course Rating:** 72.8/72.5. **Slope:** 130/124. **Green Fee:** $38. **Cart Fee:** $13/Person. **Walking**

Policy: Walking at certain times. **Walkability:** 2. **Opened:** 1988. **Architect:** Steven Kay. **Season:** April-Dec. **To obtain tee times:** Call up to 7 days in advance. **Miscellaneous:** Reduced fees (weekdays, guests, twilight), range (grass/mats), cards (MC, V, AE), BF, FF.
Reader Comments: Expensive for this area, but the best public course in the Capital district … New owners will spend more on upkeep … Fabulous value midway between NYC & Montreal.

★★ HILLENDALE GOLF COURSE
SP-218 N. Applegate Rd., Ithaca, 14850, Tompkins County, (607)273-2363, 50 miles from Syracuse. **E-mail:** dargolfer@aol.com. **Web:** www.hillendale.com. **Facility Holes:** 18. **Yards:** 6,002/5,705. **Par:** 71/73. **Course Rating:** 68.8/69.3. **Slope:** 115/116. **Green Fee:** $16/$18. **Cart Fee:** $20/Cart. **Walking Policy:** Unrestricted walking. **Walkability:** 3. **Opened:** 1912. **Architect:** Novickas/Sommer. **Season:** April-Nov. **High:** June-Sept. **To obtain tee times:** Call golf shop. **Miscellaneous:** Reduced fees (weekdays, twilight, seniors, juniors), metal spikes, range (grass), credit cards (MC, V), BF, FF.

HILLVIEW GOLF COURSE
PU-4717 Berry Rd., Fredonia, 14063, Chautauqua County, (716)679-4571, 25 miles from Jamestown. **Facility Holes:** 18. **Yards:** 6,149/5,201. **Par:** 70/72. **Course Rating:** 68.3. **Slope:** 106. **Green Fee:** $15/$20. **Cart Fee:** $20/Cart. **Opened:** 1936. **Architect:** A. W. Porter. **Season:** April-Nov. **To obtain tee times:** Call golf shop. **Miscellaneous:** Reduced fees (twilight).

★★★ HOLBROOK COUNTRY CLUB
PU-Patchogue-Holbrook Rd., Holbrook, 11741, Suffolk County, (631)467-3417, 5 miles from Patchogue. **Facility Holes:** 18. **Yards:** 6,252/4,746. **Par:** 71. **Green Fee:** $23/$28. **Cart Fee:** $26/Cart. **Opened:** 1992. **Season:** March-Dec. **To obtain tee times:** Call golf shop. **Miscellaneous:** Reduced fees (twilight, seniors, juniors), range (mats), credit cards (MC, V), BF, FF.
Reader Comments: Moves slow when backed up, just long enough … Enjoyable to play … Tight course, hit straight or stay home … All shots needed … Too many holes alike … Good value.

★★★ HOLIDAY VALLEY RESORT
R-Rte. 219, Ellicottville, 14731, Cattaraugus County, (716)699-2346, 48 miles from Buffalo. **Facility Holes:** 18. **Yards:** 6,555/5,381. **Par:** 72/73. **Course Rating:** 71.3/74.0. **Slope:** 125/115. **Green Fee:** $15/$34. **Cart Fee:** $13/Person. **Walking Policy:** Walking at certain times. **Walkability:** 5. **Opened:** 1961. **Architect:** Russ Tryon. **Season:** April-Oct. **High:** June-Sept. **To obtain tee times:** Call golf shop. **Miscellaneous:** Reduced fees (weekdays, guests, twilight), metal spikes, range (grass/mats), lodging (500 rooms), credit cards (MC, V, AE, D), BF, FF.
Reader Comments: Beautiful scenery … Very expensive … Pretty scenic … One of best public courses in Westchester … Always a pleasure to golf there … Speed up play.

HOLLAND HILLS GOLF COURSE
SP-10438 Holland-Glenwood Rd., Glenwood, 14069, Erie County, (716)537-2345, 25 miles from Buffalo. **Facility Holes:** 18. **Yards:** 6,355/6,140. **Par:** 72/75. **Course Rating:** 71.3/72.0. **Slope:** 115/108. **Green Fee:** $17/$20. **Cart Fee:** $16/Cart. **Opened:** 1958. **Season:** May-Oct. **To obtain tee times:** Call golf shop. **Miscellaneous:** Range (mats).

HUDSON VALLEY RESORT & SPA
R-400 Granite Rd., Kerhonkson, 12446, Ulster County, (845)626-2972, (888)684-7264, 20 miles from Kingston. **E-mail:** golf@hudsonvalleyresort.com. **Web:** hudsonvalleyresort.com. **Facility Holes:** 18. **Yards:** 6,351/5,300. **Par:** 70/70. **Course Rating:** 69.6/69.3. **Slope:** 119/110. **Green Fee:** $17/$33. **Cart Fee:** Included in green fee. **Walking Policy:** Walking at certain times. **Walkability:** 3. **Opened:** 1998. **Architect:** Lee Chen. **Season:** April-Nov. **High:** June-Sept. **To obtain tee times:** Call up to 30 days in advance. **Miscellaneous:** Reduced fees (weekdays, guests, twilight, seniors, juniors), range (grass/mats), lodging (306 rooms), credit cards (MC, V, AE, D), BF, FF.

HYDE PARK GOLF COURSE
PU-4343 Porter Rd., Niagara Falls, 14305, Niagara County, (716)297-2067, 20 miles from Buffalo. **Facility Holes:** 36. **Green Fee:** $17/$20. **Cart Fee:** $20/Cart. **Walking Policy:** Unrestricted walking. **Opened:** 1920. **Season:** April-Oct. **High:** June-Aug. **To obtain tee times:** Call up to 4 days in advance. **Miscellaneous:** Reduced fees (seniors, juniors), metal spikes, range (grass/mats), FF.
★½ **NORTH COURSE** (18)
Yards: 6,400/5,700. **Par:** 70/70. **Course Rating:** 70.0/72.0. **Slope:** 110/110. **Walkability:** 1. **Architect:** William Harries.
★½ **RED/WHITE COURSE** (18)
Yards: 6,850/6,500. **Par:** 71/71. **Architect:** William Harries/David Gordon.

INDIAN HILLS GOLF COURSE
SP-150 Indian Hills Rd., Painted Post, 14870, Steuben County, (607)523-7315, 5 miles from Painted Post. **Facility Holes:** 18. **Yards:** 6,626/5,120. **Par:** 72/72. **Course Rating:** 71.4. **Slope:** 121. **Green Fee:** $21/$25. **Walking Policy:** Unrestricted walking. **Walkability:** 1. **Opened:** 1962. **Season:** March-Nov. **To obtain tee times:** Call up to 3 days in advance. **Miscellaneous:** Reduced fees (juniors), range (grass/mats), credit cards (MC, V, D), BF, FF.

★★½ INDIAN ISLAND COUNTRY CLUB
PU-Riverside Dr., Riverhead, 11901, Suffolk County, (516)727-7776, 70 miles from New York City. **Facility Holes:** 18. **Yards:** 6,374/5,545. **Par:** 72/72. **Course Rating:** 70.3/71.3. **Slope:** 122/122. **Green Fee:** $9/$20. **Cart Fee:** $27/Cart. **Walking Policy:** Unrestricted walking. **Walkability:** 1. **Opened:** 1972. **Architect:** William F. Mitchell. **Season:** March-Dec. **High:** May-Sept. **To obtain tee times:** Call golf shop. **Miscellaneous:** Reduced fees (twilight, seniors, juniors), range (mats).

★★★½ INLET GOLF CLUB *Value*
PU-Rte. 28, Inlet, 13360, Hamilton County, (315)357-3503, 10 miles from Old Forge. **Facility Holes:** 18. **Yards:** 6,154/5,450. **Par:** 70/73. **Course Rating:** 70.2/71.0. **Slope:** 119/118. **Green Fee:** $20/$30. **Cart Fee:** $10/Person. **Walking Policy:** Unrestricted walking. **Walkability:** 3. **Season:** May-Oct. **To obtain tee times:** Call golf shop. **Miscellaneous:** Reduced fees (weekdays, twilight), FF.
Reader Comments: Short front 9, longer & tougher back 9 ... An Adirondack course, which is very pretty and nice ... Condition is improving ... Backwoods gem ... Narrow, great value ... Good course, lots of wildlife ... Beautifully manicured.

ISLAND OAKS GOLF CLUB
SP-7470 Chase Rd., Lima, 14485, Lima County, (716)624-5490, 20 miles from Rochester. **Facility Holes:** 18. **Yards:** 6,059/5,228. **Par:** 71/71. **Slope:** 120/117. **Green Fee:** $17/$23. **Cart Fee:** $11/Person. **Walking Policy:** Walking at certain times. **Walkability:** 3. **Opened:** 1994. **Season:** March-Nov. **To obtain tee times:** Call golf shop. **Miscellaneous:** Reduced fees (weekdays, seniors), range (grass), credit cards (MC, V, AE), BF, FF.

★★★½ ISLAND'S END GOLF & COUNTRY CLUB
SP-Rte. 25, Greenport, 11944, Suffolk County, (631)477-0777, 2 miles from Greenport. **Facility Holes:** 18. **Yards:** 6,639/5,039. **Par:** 72/72. **Course Rating:** 71.4/6906.0. **Slope:** 123/117. **Green Fee:** $27/$45. **Cart Fee:** $15/Person. **Walking Policy:** Walking at certain times. **Walkability:** 2. **Opened:** 1961. **Architect:** Herbert Strong. **Season:** Year-round. **High:** May-Oct. **To obtain tee times:** Call up to 1 day in advance. **Miscellaneous:** Range (grass), credit cards (MC, V), BF, FF.
Reader Comments: A hidden gem for the general golfing public ... I only wish more than one hole overlooked the Long Island Sound ... Well maintained, playable ... Great condition, fast greens, beautiful views.

IVES HILL GOLF COURSE
SP-435 Flower Ave. W., Watertown, 13601, Jefferson County, (315)782-1771, 65 miles from Syracuse. **Facility Holes:** 18. **Yards:** 6,646/5,667. **Par:** 72/73. **Course Rating:** 71.4/71.6. **Slope:** 119/124. **Green Fee:** $20/$30. **Cart Fee:** $22/Cart. **Walkability:** 4. **Opened:** 1897. **Architect:** Maurice McCarthy. **Season:** April-Oct. **To obtain tee times:** Call golf shop. **Miscellaneous:** Range (grass), FF.

★★★ JAMES BAIRD STATE PARK GOLF CLUB
PU-122C Freedom Plains Rd., Pleasant Valley, 12569, Dutchess County, (845)473-6200, 5 miles from Poughkeepsie. **Web:** www.nysparks.com. **Facility Holes:** 18. **Yards:** 6,616/5,541. **Par:** 71/74. **Course Rating:** 71.3/70.9. **Slope:** 124/122. **Green Fee:** $14/$17. **Cart Fee:** $26/Cart. **Walking Policy:** Unrestricted walking. **Walkability:** 2. **Opened:** 1947. **Architect:** Robert Trent Jones. **Season:** April-Nov. **High:** May-Aug. **To obtain tee times:** Call golf shop. **Miscellaneous:** Reduced fees (weekdays, twilight, seniors, juniors), range (grass/mats), credit cards (MC, V, AE, D), BF, FF.
Reader Comments: Requires precision shots on many holes ... Enjoyable, but very slow to play ... Good value, course was in great shape ... Well-maintained state course ... Best value in area, could be conditioned better ... Plain.

KINGSWOOD GOLF CLUB
PU-111 County Rd. 41, Hudson Falls, 12839, Washington County, (518)747-8888, 12 miles from Lake George. **Facility Holes:** 18. **Yards:** 6,571/5,184. **Par:** 71/71. **Course Rating:** 71.9/69.8. **Slope:** 128/116. **Green Fee:** $26/$34. **Cart Fee:** $13/Person. **Opened:** 1991. **Architect:** Mike Woodbury. **Season:** April-Nov. **To obtain tee times:** Call golf shop. **Misc:** Reduced fees (weekdays, twilight, seniors), range (grass), credit cards (MC, V).

★★½ KISSENA PARK GOLF COURSE
PU-164-15 Booth Memorial Ave., Flushing, 11365, Queens County, (718)939-4594, 15 miles from New York City. **Facility Holes:** 18. **Yards:** 4,727/4,425. **Par:** 64/64. **Course Rating:** 61.8/65.6. **Slope:** 101/106. **Green Fee:** $16/$18. **Cart Fee:** $13/Person. **Walking Policy:** Unrestricted walking. **Walkability:** 5. **Opened:** 1937. **Architect:** John Van Kleek. **Season:** Year-round. **High:** June-Sept. **To obtain tee times:** Call golf shop. **Miscellaneous:** Reduced fees (weekdays, twilight, seniors, juniors), metal spikes, range (mats).

★★★ KUTSHER'S COUNTRY CLUB
R-Kutsher Rd., Monticello, 12701, Sullivan County, (845)794-6000, 80 miles from New York City. **E-mail:** kutshers@warwick.net. **Web:** www.kutshers.com. **Facility Holes:** 18. **Yards:** 7,001/5,676. **Par:** 71/71. **Course Rating:** 74.1/73.1. **Slope:** 129/128. **Green Fee:** $40/$60. **Cart Fee:** Included in green fee. **Walking Policy:** Mandatory carts. **Walkability:** 4. **Opened:** 1962. **Architect:** William F. Mitchell. **Season:** April-Nov. **High:** July-Aug. **To obtain tee times:** Call up to 7 days in advance. **Miscellaneous:** Reduced fees (weekdays, guests, twilight), range (grass/mats), BF, FF.
Reader Comments: Nice layout ... Very hilly front 9 ... Good resort course ... A good test ... Very narrow ... Great layout ... Good test of golf ... Has potential ... Solid course ... Good resort course ... Great layout, no weak holes.

★★½ LA TOURETTE GOLF CLUB
PU-1001 Richmond Hill Rd., Staten Island, 10306, Richmond County, (718)351-1889. **Facility Holes:** 18. **Yards:** 6,692/5,493. **Par:** 72/72. **Course Rating:** 70.7/70.9. **Slope:** 119/115. **Green Fee:** $20/$22. **Cart Fee:** $25/Cart. **Walking Policy:** Unrestricted walking. **Walkability:** 3. **Opened:** 1930. **Architect:** John Van Kleek. **Season:** Year-round. **High:** May-Sept. **To obtain tee times:** Call golf shop. **Miscellaneous:** Reduced fees (twilight, seniors, juniors), metal spikes, range (mats), credit cards (MC, V).

LAKE PLACID RESORT
R-1 Olympic Dr., Lake Placid, 12946, Essex County, (518)523-4460, (800)874-1980, 20 miles from Plattsburgh. **E-mail:** golf@lpresort.com. **Web:** www.lpresort.com. **Facility Holes:** 45. **Cart Fee:** Included in green fee. **Walking Policy:** Unrestricted walking. **Season:** April-Oct. **High:** July-Sept. **To obtain tee times:** Call golf shop. **Misc:** Reduced fees (weekdays, guests, twilight), range (grass), lodging (207 rooms), credit cards (MC, V, AE, D, DC, CB), BF, FF.
★★★★ LINKS COURSE (18) *Pace+*
Yards: 7,006/5,133. **Par:** 71/71. **Course Rating:** 74.9/72.1. **Slope:** 128/111. **Green Fee:** $46/$65. **Walkability:** 2. **Opened:** 1909. **Architect:** Seymour Dunn.
Reader Comments: A fun links course in the mountains ... Awesome mountain views ... Links-style excellent, difficult ... Scenery beautiful, lots of trouble, facilities above average ... Great scenery, stay out of the bunkers ... Challenging.
★★★½ MOUNTAIN COURSE (18)
Yards: 6,216/4,784. **Par:** 70/70. **Course Rating:** 70.8/72.0. **Slope:** 126/120. **Green Fee:** $39. **Walkability:** 4. **Opened:** 1910. **Architect:** Alex Findlay/Alister Mackenzie.
Reader Comments: Great layout, great condition, top service ... Too many hidden greens ... Fun, blind shots, short par 4s ... MacKenzie's redesign is a lot more fun second time around ... Great old course, could use some work ... Pricey.
Special Notes: Also has a 9-hole executive course.

★★★ LAKE SHORE COUNTRY CLUB
SP-1165 Greenleaf Rd., Rochester, 14612, Monroe County, (716)663-0300, 5 miles from Rochester. **Facility Holes:** 18. **Yards:** 6,343/5,561. **Par:** 70/73. **Course Rating:** 67.2/72.0. **Slope:** 116/117. **Green Fee:** $24. **Cart Fee:** $11/Person. **Walking Policy:** Unrestricted walking. **Walkability:** 2. **Opened:** 1932. **Architect:** Calvin Black. **Season:** April-Nov. **High:** June-Aug. **To obtain tee times:** Call golf shop. **Miscellaneous:** Range (grass/mats), credit cards (MC, V, D).
Reader Comments: Relatively short course, great conditioning ... Not difficult but have to keep it in bounds ... Nice test, pretty course ... Nice, too short, overpriced.

LAKESIDE COUNTRY CLUB
SP-200 E. Lake Rd., Penn Yan, 14527, Yates County, (315)536-7252, 45 miles from Rochester. **E-mail:** keok@aol.com. **Facility Holes:** 18. **Yards:** 6,609/5,395. **Par:** 72/73. **Course Rating:** 71.5/69.7. **Slope:** 128/114. **Green Fee:** $20/Cart. **Walking Policy:** Mandatory carts. **Walkability:** 4. **Opened:** 1935. **Season:** April-Oct. **High:** June-Sept. **To obtain tee times:** Call up to 2 days in advance. **Miscellaneous:** Range (grass), credit cards (MC, V, AE, D), BF, FF.

★½ LE ROY COUNTRY CLUB
SP-7759 E. Main Rd., Le Roy, 14482, Genesee County, (716)768-7330, 20 miles from Rochester. **Facility Holes:** 18. **Yards:** 6,422/5,589. **Par:** 71/74. **Course Rating:** 69.8/71.0.

Slope: 116/117. **Green Fee:** $15/$20. **Cart Fee:** $20/Cart. **Walking Policy:** Unrestricted walking. **Walkability:** 2. **Opened:** 1930. **Architect:** Don Woodward. **Season:** April-Nov. **High:** June-Aug. **To obtain tee times:** Call up to 7 days in advance. **Miscellaneous:** Reduced fees (weekdays, twilight, seniors, juniors), range (grass), caddies, credit cards (MC, V), BF, FF.

★★★★ LEATHERSTOCKING GOLF COURSE
R-60 Lake St., Cooperstown, 13326, Otsego County, (607)547-5275, 50 miles from Albany. **Facility Holes:** 18. **Yards:** 6,416/5,178. **Par:** 72/72. **Course Rating:** 70.8/69.2. **Slope:** 135/116. **Green Fee:** $80. **Cart Fee:** $17/Person. **Walking Policy:** Walking at certain times. **Walkability:** 4. **Opened:** 1909. **Architect:** Devereux Emmet. **Season:** April-Nov. **High:** June-Oct. **To obtain tee times:** Call up to 6 days in advance. **Miscellaneous:** Reduced fees (guests, twilight), range (grass), lodging (136 rooms), credit cards (MC, V, AE), BF, FF.
Reader Comments: Last 4 holes are long, hard and beautiful ... A great challenge ... Too expensive ... Excellent, many beautiful holes ... Very nice course in a great town ... The three best finishing holes anywhere ... Super course.

★★★½ LIDO GOLF CLUB
PU-255 Lido Blvd., Lido Beach, 11561, Nassau County, (516)889-8181, 10 miles from New York City. **E-mail:** jmmonte2000@aol.com. **Web:** www.doubleeaglegolf.com. **Facility Holes:** 18. **Yards:** 6,896/5,291. **Par:** 72/72. **Course Rating:** 73.5/71.4. **Slope:** 128/114. **Green Fee:** $25/$44. **Walking Policy:** Unrestricted walking. **Walkability:** 1. **Opened:** 1948. **Architect:** Robert Trent Jones. **Season:** Year-round. **High:** May-Sept. **To obtain tee times:** Call up to 8 days in advance. **Miscellaneous:** Reduced fees (twilight), range (mats), credit cards (MC, V, AE), BF, FF.
Reader Comments: This course is great ... During the summer, the course never plays the same twice (winds) ... Lots of forced carries over water ... Potentially nice course ruined by tedious round ... Great links design, much improved.

★★★ LIMA GOLF & COUNTRY CLUB
SP-2681 Plank Rd., Lima, 14485, Livingston County, (716)624-1490, 20 miles from Rochester. **Facility Holes:** 18. **Yards:** 6,768/5,624. **Par:** 72/74. **Course Rating:** 71.8/74.0. **Slope:** 115/117. **Green Fee:** $17/$22. **Cart Fee:** $10/Person. **Walking Policy:** Unrestricted walking. **Walkability:** 1. **Opened:** 1963. **Season:** March-Nov. **To obtain tee times:** Call golf shop. **Miscellaneous:** Reduced fees (weekdays, seniors), range (grass), credit cards (MC, V, AE), BF, FF.
Reader Comments: Has some very challenging holes ... Well maintained ... Very open layout with very good greens ... Nice layout, fast greens ... Nice layout, some easy holes ... Old course, always great shape.

★★★★½ LINKS AT HIAWATHA LANDING *Service, Value, Condition, Pace*
PU-2350 Marshland Rd., Apalachin, 13732, Tioga County, (607)687-6952, (800)304-6533, 10 miles from Binghamton. **E-mail:** info@hiawathalinks.com. **Web:** www.hiawathalinks.com. **Facility Holes:** 18. **Yards:** 7,104/5,101. **Par:** 72/72. **Course Rating:** 73.5/68.4. **Slope:** 131/113. **Green Fee:** $31/$49. **Cart Fee:** $11/Person. **Walking Policy:** Unrestricted walking. **Walkability:** 2. **Opened:** 1994. **Architect:** Brian Silva/Mark Mungeam. **Season:** March-Nov. **High:** June-Sept. **To obtain tee times:** Call up to 7 days in advance. **Miscellaneous:** Reduced fees (weekdays, twilight, juniors), range (grass), credit cards (MC, V, AE, D), BF, FF.
Reader Comments: A real pleasure ... Excellent links course, small clubhouse ... Best course in southern NY ... Target golf, Scottish style ... Upper-tier public course, excellent practice facilities ... Overrated ... Worth your time ... Great in fall when leaves change.

LINKS AT SHIRLEY
PU-333 William Floyd Pkwy., Shirley, 11967, Suffolk County, (631)395-7272, 40 miles from New York City. **E-mail:** golf@linksatshirley.com. **Web:** www.linksatshirley.com. **Facility Holes:** 36. **Yards:** 7,030/5,137. **Par:** 72/72. **Course Rating:** 74.0/70.2. **Slope:** 129/113. **Green Fee:** $65/$80. **Cart Fee:** $15/Cart. **Walking Policy:** Walking at certain times. **Opened:** 2000. **Architect:** Jeff Myers. **Season:** Year-round. **High:** May-Sept. **To obtain tee times:** Call up to 7 days in advance. **Miscellaneous:** Reduced fees (weekdays, twilight, seniors, juniors), range (grass/mats), credit cards (MC, V, AE, D), BF, FF.
Notes: Golf Digest school site.
Special Notes: Also has an 18-hole par-3 course.

THE LINKS AT UNION VALE
SP-153 N. Parliman Rd., Lagrangeville, 12540, Dutchess County, (845)223-1000, 14 miles from Poughkeepsie. **Web:** www.thelinksatunionvale.com. **Facility Holes:** 18. **Yards:** 6,839/5,198. **Par:** 72/72. **Course Rating:** 72.6/72.0. **Slope:** 128/126. **Green Fee:** $38/$52. **Cart Fee:** $13/Person. **Walking Policy:** Unrestricted walking. **Walkability:** 2. **Opened:** 2000. **Architect:** Stephen Kay. **Season:** March-Dec. **High:** June-Sept. **To obtain tee times:** Call golf

shop. **Miscellaneous:** Reduced fees (weekdays, twilight, seniors, juniors), range (grass/mats), credit cards (MC, V, AE), BF, FF.

★★★ LIVERPOOL GOLF & COUNTRY CLUB

PU-7209 Morgan Rd., Liverpool, 13090, Onondaga County, (315)457-7170, 5 miles from Syracuse. **E-mail:** 2pollgolf@aol.com. **Facility Holes:** 18. **Yards:** 6,473/5,487. **Par:** 71/73. **Course Rating:** 70.7/69.3. **Slope:** 120/115. **Green Fee:** $22/$24. **Cart Fee:** $24/Cart. **Walking Policy:** Unrestricted walking. **Walkability:** 1. **Opened:** 1949. **Architect:** Archie S. Ajemian and Sons. **Season:** Year-round. **High:** April-Nov. **To obtain tee times:** Call up to 7 days in advance. **Miscellaneous:** Reduced fees (weekdays, twilight, seniors, juniors), range (grass), credit cards (MC, V), BF, FF.
Reader Comments: Fast greens … Very good layout … US Open-style rough during parts of season … Good layout, maintenance could be better … Excellent condition, always open, flat … Good course for long hitters, long & straight.

LIVINGSTON GOLF COURSE

SP-Rte. 20A, Geneseo, 14454, Livingston County, (716)243-4430, 20 miles from Rochester. **Facility Holes:** 18. **Yards:** 6,442/5,241. **Par:** 72/72. **Course Rating:** 71.1/70.1. **Slope:** 129/118. **Green Fee:** $16/$18. **Walking Policy:** Walking at certain times. **Walkability:** 3. **Season:** March-Nov. **High:** May-Sept. **To obtain tee times:** Call up to 7 days in advance. **Miscellaneous:** Reduced fees (weekdays), range (grass), credit cards (MC, V).

★★★ LOCHMOR GOLF COURSE

PU-CR 104, Loch Sheldrake, 12759, Sullivan County, (914)434-1257, 8 miles from Monticello. **Facility Holes:** 18. **Yards:** 6,426/5,129. **Par:** 71/71. **Course Rating:** 69.6/69.4. **Slope:** 117/116. **Green Fee:** $19/$25. **Cart Fee:** $15/Person. **Walking Policy:** Walking at certain times. **Walkability:** 4. **Season:** April-Oct. **High:** June-Sept. **To obtain tee times:** Call up to 3 days in advance. **Miscellaneous:** Reduced fees (weekdays, guests, twilight, juniors), range (grass/mats), credit cards (MC, V), BF, FF.
Reader Comments: Good layout & grooming … Good municipal course, front 9 wide open … Up one side of the mountain down the other … Great town course … Average course, some holes the same … Work in progress, improving.

★★★★ LONG ISLAND NATIONAL GOLF CLUB

PU-1793 Northville Tpke., Riverhead, 11901, Suffolk County, (516)727-4653, 60 miles from Manhattan. **Web:** www.longislandnational.com. **Facility Holes:** 18. **Yards:** 6,838/5,006. **Par:** 71/71. **Course Rating:** 73.6/65.3. **Slope:** 131/114. **Green Fee:** $80/$100. **Cart Fee:** Included in green fee. **Walking Policy:** Mandatory carts. **Walkability:** 1. **Opened:** 1999. **Architect:** Robert Trent Jones Jr. **Season:** March-Nov. **To obtain tee times:** Call golf shop. **Miscellaneous:** Reduced fees (twilight), range (grass), credit cards (MC, V, AE).
Reader Comments: New course, give it a couple of years … Excellent condition, very interesting layout … One of the better new public courses around NY … Good value in expensive region … Wind always blows … Like Shinnecock.

LOON LAKE GOLF COURSE

PU-Hwy. 26, Rte. 99, Box 137, Loon Lake, 12951, Franklin County, (518)891-3249, 85 miles from Montreal. **Facility Holes:** 18. **Yards:** 5,200/4,700. **Par:** 70/70. **Course Rating:** 67.0/67.0. **Green Fee:** $10/$18. **Cart Fee:** $22/Person. **Walking Policy:** Unrestricted walking. **Walkability:** 5. **Opened:** 1895. **Architect:** Seymour Dunn. **Season:** May-Nov. **High:** July-Aug. **To obtain tee times:** Call up to 30 days in advance. **Miscellaneous:** Reduced fees (weekdays, seniors, juniors), BF, FF.

LYNDON GOLF CLUB

PU-7054 East Genesee, Rte. #5, Fayetteville, 13066, Onondaga County, (315)446-1885. **E-mail:** ncgolf99@aol.com. **Facility Holes:** 18. **Yards:** 4,900/4,900. **Par:** 65/69. **Green Fee:** $8/$14. **Cart Fee:** $20/Cart. **Walking Policy:** Unrestricted walking. **Walkability:** 1. **Season:** March-Dec. **High:** May-Sept. **To obtain tee times:** Call golf shop. **Miscellaneous:** Reduced fees (seniors), FF.

MALONE GOLF CLUB

SP-79 Golf Course Rd., Malone, 12953, Franklin County, (518)483-2926, 70 miles from Montreal. **E-mail:** mgc@westelcom.com. **Web:** www.malonegolfclub.com. **Facility Holes:** 36. **Green Fee:** $29/$38. **Cart Fee:** $14/Person. **Walking Policy:** Unrestricted walking. **Architect:** Robert T. Jones/W.Wilkinson/A. Murray. **Season:** April-Oct. **To obtain tee times:** Call up to 90 days in advance. **Miscellaneous:** Reduced fees (weekdays, twilight), credit cards (MC, V, AE), BF, FF.
★★★★ **EAST COURSE** (18)
Yards: 6,545/5,224. **Par:** 72/73. **Course Rating:** 71.5/69.9. **Slope:** 123/117. **Walkability:** 5. **Opened:** 1939.

Reader Comments: Both courses are a challenge, good condition … A good challenge, but fair for errant shots … Pretty hilly with undulating greens and some tight holes … Overall a good experience … Great test … Great par 3s.

★★★★ **WEST COURSE (18)**
Yards: 6,592/5,272. **Par:** 71/72. **Course Rating:** 71.4/70.1. **Slope:** 124/119. **Walkability:** 2. **Opened:** 1987.
Reader Comments: A much tougher course with water in play as well as being tighter on most holes … Not as forgiving as the East Course … You need to play a more mental game by keeping the ball in play … Short holes.

★★★★ **MANSION RIDGE GOLF CLUB**
SP-1292 Orange Tpke., Monroe, 10950, Orange County, (845)782-7888, 50 miles from New York City. **E-mail:** mansianridge@americangolf.com. **Web:** www.americangolf.com. **Facility Holes:** 18. **Yards:** 6,889/4,785. **Par:** 72/72. **Course Rating:** 73.5/67.9. **Slope:** 138/121. **Green Fee:** $40/$135. **Cart Fee:** Included in green fee. **Walking Policy:** Mandatory carts. **Walkability:** 4. **Opened:** 1999. **Architect:** Jack Nicklaus. **Season:** April-Nov. **High:** May-Sept. **To obtain tee times:** Call up to 7 days in advance. **Miscellaneous:** Reduced fees (weekdays, twilight), range (grass/mats), credit cards (MC, V, AE, D, DC, CB), BF, FF.
Reader Comments: Great Nicklaus design … Still growing … More than half the holes have forced carries … Good course, bring a short game … Worth the effort to find … Play it once or twice a year as a treat.

MAPLE HILL GOLF COURSE
PU-Conrad Rd., Marathon, 13803, Cortland County, (607)849-3285, 30 miles from Binghamton. **Facility Holes:** 18. **Yards:** 6,440/4,640. **Par:** 70/70. **Course Rating:** 70.8/66.5. **Slope:** 119/109. **Green Fee:** $15/$18. **Cart Fee:** $18/Cart. **Walking Policy:** Unrestricted walking. **Walkability:** 4. **Opened:** 1965. **Season:** April-Nov. **High:** June-Sept. **To obtain tee times:** Call golf shop. **Miscellaneous:** Reduced fees (weekdays, seniors, juniors), BF, FF.

★★ **MAPLE MOOR GOLF COURSE**
PU-1128 N. St., White Plains, 10605, Westchester County, (914)946-1830, 20 miles from New York City. **Facility Holes:** 18. **Yards:** 6,226/5,812. **Par:** 71/74. **Course Rating:** 68.8/71.9. **Slope:** 110/119. **Green Fee:** $17/$45. **Cart Fee:** $25/Cart. **Walking Policy:** Unrestricted walking. **Walkability:** 2. **Opened:** 1923. **Architect:** Archie Capper. **Season:** April-Dec. **High:** May-Aug. **To obtain tee times:** Call golf shop. **Miscellaneous:** Reduced fees (twilight, seniors, juniors), metal spikes, credit cards (MC, V).

MAPLEHURST COUNTRY CLUB
SP-1508 Big Tree Rd., Lakewood, 14750, Chautauqua County, (716)763-9058, 4 miles from Jamestown. **Facility Holes:** 18. **Yards:** 6,165/5,376. **Par:** 70/70. **Course Rating:** 66.0/68.0. **Slope:** 113/111. **Green Fee:** $19/$20. **Cart Fee:** $20/Cart. **Walking Policy:** Unrestricted walking. **Walkability:** 5. **Opened:** 1934. **Season:** April-Nov. **High:** June-Aug. **To obtain tee times:** Call up to 2 days in advance. **Miscellaneous:** Reduced fees (weekdays, twilight, seniors), range (grass), BF, FF.

★★ **MARINE PARK GOLF CLUB**
PU-2880 Flatbush Ave., Brooklyn, 11234, Kings County, (718)338-7113, 5 miles from New York City. **Facility Holes:** 18. **Yards:** 6,866/5,323. **Par:** 72/72. **Course Rating:** 70.5. **Slope:** 118. **Green Fee:** $24/$26. **Cart Fee:** $24/Cart. **Walking Policy:** Unrestricted walking. **Walkability:** 1. **Opened:** 1964. **Architect:** Robert Trent Jones. **Season:** Year-round. **High:** May-Aug. **To obtain tee times:** Call golf shop. **Miscellaneous:** Reduced fees (weekdays, twilight, seniors, juniors), metal spikes, credit cards (MC, V, AE, D).

★★★½ **MARK TWAIN GOLF CLUB**
PU-2275 Corning Rd., Elmira, 14903, Chemung County, (607)737-5770, 50 miles from Binghamton. **Facility Holes:** 18. **Yards:** 6,829/5,571. **Par:** 72/76. **Course Rating:** 73.6/72.3. **Slope:** 123/121. **Green Fee:** $20. **Cart Fee:** $22/Cart. **Walking Policy:** Unrestricted walking. **Walkability:** 4. **Opened:** 1939. **Architect:** Donald Ross. **Season:** April-Oct. **High:** June-Aug. **To obtain tee times:** Call golf shop. **Miscellaneous:** Reduced fees (weekdays, twilight, seniors, juniors), range (grass/mats), credit cards (MC, V, D), BF, FF.
Reader Comments: Well laid-out municipal course … With the exception of two holes, quiet and serene … Your work begins when you reach the greens … Best value for the money.

★★★★½ **MARK TWAIN STATE PARK**
PU-201 Middle Rd., Horseheads, 14845, Chemung County, (607)796-5059, 10 miles from Elmira. **Facility Holes:** 18. **Yards:** 6,625/4,930. **Par:** 72/72. **Course Rating:** 71.6/67.5. **Slope:** 117/108. **Green Fee:** $9/$21. **Cart Fee:** $22/Cart. **Walking Policy:** Unrestricted walking. **Walkability:** 3. **Opened:** 1940. **Architect:** Archibald Craig. **Season:** April-Nov. **High:** June-Sept. **To obtain tee times:** Call golf shop. **Miscellaneous:** Reduced fees (twilight, seniors, juniors),

metal spikes, range (grass), credit cards (MC, V, AE).
Reader Comments: Good golf overall … Nice vistas, good course for all levels … You must play this jewel of a course … Finest state course in New York, great layout, well maintained … One of the best public values in upstate NY.

MARVIN'S GOLF COURSE
SP-, Macedon, 14502, Wayne County, (315)986-4455, 20 miles from Rochester. **Facility Holes:** 18. **Yards:** 6,139/5,241. **Par:** 70/73. **Course Rating:** 68.4/69.2. **Slope:** 112/108. **Green Fee:** $18/$21. **Cart Fee:** $10/Person. **Walking Policy:** Unrestricted walking. **Walkability:** 2. **Opened:** 1973. **Season:** April-Nov. **To obtain tee times:** Call golf shop. **Miscellaneous:** Reduced fees (seniors), range (grass), credit cards (MC, V), BF, FF.

★★ MASSENA COUNTRY CLUB
PU-Rte. 131, Massena, 13662, St. Lawrence County, (315)769-2293, 160 miles from Syracuse. **Facility Holes:** 18. **Yards:** 6,602/5,361. **Par:** 71/75. **Course Rating:** 70.1/70.0. **Slope:** 114/109. **Green Fee:** $22/$24. **Cart Fee:** $24/Cart. **Walking Policy:** Unrestricted walking. **Walkability:** 2. **Opened:** 1926. **Architect:** Albert Murray. **High:** April-Nov. **To obtain tee times:** Call golf shop. **Miscellaneous:** Reduced fees (twilight), range (grass/mats), caddies, credit cards (MC, V), BF, FF.

★★★★ MCCANN MEMORIAL GOLF CLUB *Value*
PU-155 Wilbur Blvd., Poughkeepsie, 12603, Dutchess County, (845)471-3917, 65 miles from New York City. **Facility Holes:** 18. **Yards:** 6,524/5,354. **Par:** 72/72. **Course Rating:** 71.5/71.1. **Slope:** 122/114. **Green Fee:** $30/$35. **Cart Fee:** $24/Cart. **Walking Policy:** Unrestricted walking. **Walkability:** 2. **Opened:** 1972. **Architect:** William F. Mitchell. **Season:** April-Dec. **To obtain tee times:** Call golf shop. **Miscellaneous:** Reduced fees (seniors, juniors), range (grass), BF, FF.
Reader Comments: Good muni … Some interesting holes … Great layout but slow play … Huge greens, challenging tree-lined layout … Great muni course considering amount of play … Excellent city course … Great value.

★★★★ MCCONNELLSVILLE GOLF CLUB *Value, Pace*
SP-Blossvale Rd., McConnellsville, 13401, Oneida County, (315)245-1157, 30 miles from Syracuse. **Facility Holes:** 18. **Yards:** 6,317/5,539. **Par:** 70/72. **Course Rating:** 69.8/71.1. **Slope:** 119/106. **Green Fee:** $22. **Cart Fee:** $10/Person. **Walking Policy:** Unrestricted walking. **Opened:** 1941. **Season:** April-Nov. **To obtain tee times:** Call golf shop. **Miscellaneous:** Metal spikes, range (grass), FF.
Reader Comments: Short, tight fairways make it challenging … Nice course … Always nice, great layout … Short but not easy … Excellent course, facilities and restaurant … Old established course … Fast greens … Long par 4s.

★★★ MIDDLE ISLAND COUNTRY CLUB
PU-Yapank Rd., Middle Island, 11953, Suffolk County, (631)924-5100, 75 miles from New York City. **E-mail:** reholohan@middleislandcc.com. **Web:** www.middleislandcc.com. **Facility Holes:** 27. **Green Fee:** $32/$40. **Cart Fee:** $15/Person. **Walking Policy:** Walking at certain times. **Walkability:** 3. **Opened:** 1964. **Architect:** Baier Lustgarten. **Season:** Year-round. **To obtain tee times:** Call golf shop. **Miscellaneous:** Reduced fees (weekdays, twilight), metal spikes, range (mats).
DOGWOOD/OAKTREE (18 Combo)
Yards: 6,934/5,809. **Par:** 72/74. **Course Rating:** 73.2/73.2. **Slope:** 130/127.
DOGWOOD/SPRUCE (18 Combo)
Yards: 7,015/5,909. **Par:** 72/74. **Course Rating:** 73.2/73.2. **Slope:** 130/127.
OAKTREE/SPRUCE (18 Combo)
Yards: 7,027/5,906. **Par:** 72/72. **Course Rating:** 73.2/73.2. **Slope:** 130/127.
Reader Comments: Some tight fairways lined with trees … Three very good 9s … Conditioning could make this a great course … Nice layout, good value … 27 holes that are long & challenging.

MIDLAKES CLUB
PU-Rd. 3 Bockes Road, Skaneateles, 13152, Onondaga County, (315)673-4916. **Facility Holes:** 18. **Yards:** 5,863/5,052. **Par:** 70/70. **Green Fee:** $18/$20. **Cart Fee:** $10/Person. **Opened:** 1978. **Architect:** Chris Staples. **Season:** April-Dec. **To obtain tee times:** Call golf shop. **Miscellaneous:** Reduced fees (seniors), credit cards (MC, V).
Special Notes: Formerly Skaneateles Greens Country Club.

★★½ MILL POND GOLF COURSE
PU-300 Mill Rd., Medford, 11763, Suffolk County, (631)732-8249, 63 miles from New York City. **E-mail:** info@golfatmillpond.com. **Web:** www.golfatmillpond.com. **Facility Holes:** 18. **Green Fee:** $50/$65. **Cart Fee:** Included in green fee. **Walking Policy:** Walking at certain times.

Opened: 1999. **Architect:** Buddy Johnson. **Season:** Year-round. **High:** June-Aug. **To obtain tee times:** Call up to 7 days in advance. **Miscellaneous:** Reduced fees (weekdays, twilight, seniors, juniors), range (mats), credit cards (MC, V, AE, D), BF, FF.

MILL ROAD ACRES GOLF COURSE
PU-30 Mill Rd., Latham, 12110, Albany County, (518)785-4653, 10 miles from Albany. **Facility Holes:** 18. **Yards:** 3,025/2,395. **Par:** 58/59. **Green Fee:** $15/$18. **Cart Fee:** $15/Cart. **Walking Policy:** Unrestricted walking. **Opened:** 1973. **Season:** April-Oct. **To obtain tee times:** Call golf shop. **Miscellaneous:** Reduced fees (weekdays, seniors), range (grass), credit cards (MC, V, D), FF.

★★½ MOHANSIC GOLF CLUB
PU-Baldwin Rd., Yorktown Heights, 10598, Westchester County, (914)962-9400, 37 miles from New York City. **Facility Holes:** 18. **Yards:** 6,500/5,594. **Par:** 70/75. **Course Rating:** 69.9/75.2. **Slope:** 120/127. **Green Fee:** $17/$40. **Cart Fee:** $25/Cart. **Walking Policy:** Unrestricted walking. **Walkability:** 3. **Opened:** 1925. **Architect:** Tom Winton. **Season:** April-Dec. **High:** June-Aug. **To obtain tee times:** Call golf shop. **Miscellaneous:** Reduced fees (weekdays, twilight, seniors, juniors), metal spikes, range (mats).

MOHAWK RIVER COUNTRY CLUB & CHATEAU
SP-847 Riverview Rd., Rexford, 12148, Saratoga County, (518)399-1920, 15 miles from Albany. **Facility Holes:** 18. **Yards:** 7,140/5,815. **Par:** 73/74. **Course Rating:** 73.7/73.4. **Slope:** 128/124. **Green Fee:** $19/$22. **Cart Fee:** $22/Cart. **Walking Policy:** Unrestricted walking. **Opened:** 1964. **Season:** March-Nov. **To obtain tee times:** Call up to 2 days in advance. **Miscellaneous:** Reduced fees (weekdays), range (grass), credit cards (MC, V, AE).

MONROE COUNTRY CLUB
SP-63 Still & Stage Rds., Monroe, 10950, Orange County, (845)783-9045. **Facility Holes:** 18. **Yards:** 5,428. **Par:** 70. **Course Rating:** 66.4. **Slope:** 116. **Green Fee:** $24/$30. **Cart Fee:** $34/Cart. **To obtain tee times:** Call golf shop. **Miscellaneous:** Reduced fees (weekdays, seniors), credit cards (MC, V, AE).

★★★★ MONTAUK DOWNS STATE PARK GOLF COURSE *Value*
PU-S. Fairview Ave., Montauk, 11954, Suffolk County, (516)668-1100, 110 miles from New York City. **Facility Holes:** 18. **Yards:** 6,762/5,797. **Par:** 72/72. **Course Rating:** 73.3/75.9. **Slope:** 133/135. **Green Fee:** $30/$36. **Cart Fee:** $14/Person. **Walking Policy:** Unrestricted walking. **Walkability:** 3. **Opened:** 1968. **Architect:** Robert Trent Jones. **Season:** Year-round. **To obtain tee times:** Call golf shop. **Miscellaneous:** Reduced fees (twilight, seniors), range (mats), credit cards (MC, V, AE, D), BF, FF.
Notes: Ranked 18th in 1999 Best in State.
Reader Comments: Great layout, very challenging, very scenic … Remember it's a state course, great layout … Tricky when wind is up … Bring your sleeping bag … Fabulous Robert Trent Jones Sr. design.

★½ MOSHOLU GOLF COURSE
PU-3700 Jerome Ave., Bronx, 10467, Bronx County, (718)655-9164. **Facility Holes:** 9. **Yards:** 6,382/5,676. **Par:** 71/70. **Course Rating:** 70.6/76.2. **Slope:** 120/133. **Green Fee:** $10/$26. **Cart Fee:** $27/Cart. **Opened:** 1914. **Architect:** Stephen Kay. **To obtain tee times:** Call golf shop. **Miscellaneous:** Metal spikes, credit cards (MC, V).

★★★★ NEVELE GRAND RESORT & COUNTRY CLUB
R-Rte. 209 - Nevele Road, Ellenville, 12428, Ulster County, (845)647-6000, (800)647-6000, 90 miles from New York. **Web:** www.nevele.com. **Facility Holes:** 27. **Green Fee:** $35/$65. **Cart Fee:** Included in green fee. **Walking Policy:** Walking at certain times. **Walkability:** 2. **Opened:** 1955. **Architect:** Tom Fazio/Robert Trent Jones. **Season:** April-Nov. **High:** May-Sept. **To obtain tee times:** Call up to 30 days in advance. **Miscellaneous:** Reduced fees (weekdays, guests, twilight, juniors), range (grass/mats), lodging (700 rooms), credit cards (MC, V, AE, D, DC), BF, FF.
BLUE/RED (18 Combo)
Yards: 6,823/5,145. **Par:** 70/70. **Course Rating:** 72.7/72.8. **Slope:** 130/129.
RED/WHITE (18 Combo)
Yards: 6,532/4,600. **Par:** 70/70. **Course Rating:** 71.4/71.1. **Slope:** 128/126.
WHITE/BLUE (18 Combo)
Yards: 6,573/4,600. **Par:** 70/70. **Course Rating:** 71.8/71.1. **Slope:** 126/126.
Reader Comments: Very fair, can score … Great service, good hotel package … 3 unique nines, loved everything … Quiet, scenic, good variety of holes … Nice setting … Tied with Grossingers as best in Catskills.

★★½ THE NEW COURSE AT ALBANY
PU-65 O'Neil Rd., Albany, 12208, Albany County, (518)438-2208, 3 miles from Albany.
Facility Holes: 18. **Yards:** 6,300/4,990. **Par:** 71/71. **Course Rating:** 69.4/72.0. **Slope:** 117/113.
Green Fee: $22. **Cart Fee:** $11/Person. **Walking Policy:** Unrestricted walking. **Walkability:** 4.
Opened: 1991. **Architect:** Bob Smith/Ed Bosse. **Season:** April-Nov. **High:** June-Sept. **To obtain tee times:** Call up to 1 day in advance. **Miscellaneous:** Reduced fees (twilight), metal spikes, range (grass/mats), credit cards (MC, V), BF.

★★½ NEW YORK COUNTRY CLUB
SP-103 Brick Church Rd., New Hempstead, 10977, Rockland County, (914)362-5800, (888)740-6800, 22 miles from New York City. **E-mail:** nycountryclub@aol.com. **Web:** nycountryclub.com. **Facility Holes:** 18. **Yards:** 6,673/5,671. **Par:** 72/72. **Course Rating:** 72.3/72.5. **Slope:** 134/131. **Green Fee:** $80/$135. **Cart Fee:** Included in green fee. **Walking Policy:** Walking at certain times. **Walkability:** 5. **Opened:** 1998. **Architect:** Stephen Kay. **Season:** Year-round. **High:** April-Nov. **To obtain tee times:** Call golf shop. **Miscellaneous:** Reduced fees (weekdays, twilight), range (grass), credit cards (MC, V, AE, D), BF, FF.

NEWARK VALLEY GOLF CLUB
PU-10626 Rte. 38, Newark Valley, 13811, Tioga County, (607)642-3376, 20 miles from Binghamton. **Facility Holes:** 18. **Yards:** 5,400/4,262. **Par:** 68/70. **Course Rating:** 62.0/62.8. **Slope:** 95/98. **Green Fee:** $12/$16. **Cart Fee:** $18/Cart. **Walking Policy:** Unrestricted walking. **Walkability:** 2. **Opened:** 1959. **Architect:** Nelson Cleveland. **Season:** April-Nov. **High:** June-Aug. **To obtain tee times:** Call up to 14 days in advance. **Miscellaneous:** Reduced fees (weekdays, seniors, juniors), FF.

★½ NIAGARA COUNTY GOLF COURSE
PU-314 Davison Rd., Lockport, 14094, Niagara County, (716)439-7954. **Facility Holes:** 18. **Yards:** 6,464/5,182. **Par:** 72/73. **Course Rating:** 69.3/74.1. **Slope:** 108/102. **Green Fee:** $10/$18. **Cart Fee:** $20/Cart. **Walking Policy:** Unrestricted walking. **Walkability:** 1. **Opened:** 1964. **Season:** April-Nov. **To obtain tee times:** Call golf shop. **Miscellaneous:** Reduced fees (twilight, seniors, juniors), range (grass), BF, FF.

★★ NIAGARA ORLEANS COUNTRY CLUB
PU-Telegraph Rd, Middleport, 14105, Niagara County, (716)735-9000, 7 miles from Lockport. **Facility Holes:** 18. **Yards:** 6,018/5,109. **Par:** 71/71. **Course Rating:** 65.0/65.0. **Slope:** 106/106. **Green Fee:** $15/$18. **Cart Fee:** $22/Cart. **Walking Policy:** Unrestricted walking. **Walkability:** 3. **Opened:** 1931. **Season:** April-Nov. **High:** June-Aug. **To obtain tee times:** Call up to 7 days in advance. **Miscellaneous:** Reduced fees (weekdays, twilight, seniors, juniors), BF, FF.

NICK STONER MUNICIPAL GOLF COURSE
PU-1803 State Hwy. 10, Caroga Lake, 12032, Fulton County, (518)835-4220, 50 miles from Albany. **Facility Holes:** 18. **Yards:** 6,200/5,800. **Par:** 70/72. **Course Rating:** 69.5/68.0. **Slope:** 110/115. **Green Fee:** $14/$16. **Cart Fee:** $19/Cart. **Walking Policy:** Unrestricted walking. **Walkability:** 3. **Opened:** 1929. **Season:** March-Oct. **To obtain tee times:** Call golf shop. **Miscellaneous:** Reduced fees (twilight), metal spikes, FF.

NORTH COUNTRY GOLF CLUB
SP-862 Hayford Rd., Rouses Point, 12979, Clinton County, (518)297-5814, 45 miles from Montreal. **E-mail:** ncgc@primelink1.net. **Web:** www.members.spree.com/sip/ncgc. **Facility Holes:** 18. **Yards:** 6,483/5,325. **Par:** 72/72. **Course Rating:** 71.0/71.0. **Slope:** 126/113. **Green Fee:** $18/$20. **Cart Fee:** $21/Cart. **Walking Policy:** Unrestricted walking. **Walkability:** 2. **Opened:** 1936. **Season:** April-Oct. **High:** June-Aug. **To obtain tee times:** Call golf shop. **Miscellaneous:** Reduced fees (twilight), range (grass/mats), credit cards (MC, V, D), BF, FF.

★★ OAK RUN GOLF CLUB
SP-4185 Lake Ave., Lockport, 14094, Niagara County, (716)434-8851, 20 miles from Buffalo. **Facility Holes:** 18. **Yards:** 6,670/5,181. **Par:** 70/71. **Course Rating:** 70.8/68.0. **Slope:** 118/109. **Green Fee:** $17/$19. **Cart Fee:** $20/Cart. **Walking Policy:** Unrestricted walking. **Opened:** 1990. **Season:** March-Dec. **To obtain tee times:** Call golf shop. **Miscellaneous:** Reduced fees (twilight, seniors), credit cards (MC, V, AE, D), FF.

★★ OLD HICKORY GOLF CLUB
SP-6653 Big Tree Rd., Livonia, 14487, Livingston County, (716)346-2450, 20 miles from Rochester. **Facility Holes:** 18. **Yards:** 6,650/5,450. **Par:** 72/72. **Course Rating:** 70.2/70.7. **Slope:** 109/111. **Green Fee:** $15/$18. **Cart Fee:** $11/Person. **Walking Policy:** Unrestricted walking. **Walkability:** 3. **Opened:** 1990. **Architect:** Pete Craig. **Season:** April-Nov. **High:** June-Sept. **To obtain tee times:** Call golf shop. **Miscellaneous:** Reduced fees (seniors, juniors), range (grass), credit cards (MC, V), BF, FF.

ORCHARD CREEK GOLF CLUB
PU-6700 Dunnsville Rd., Altamont, 12009, Albany County, (518)861-5000, 12 miles from Albany. **E-mail:** golf@orchardcreek.com. **Web:** www.orchardcreek.com. **Facility Holes:** 18. **Yards:** 6,553/4,828. **Par:** 71/70. **Course Rating:** 72.2/68.4. **Slope:** 133/117. **Green Fee:** $25/$30. **Cart Fee:** $24/Cart. **Walking Policy:** Unrestricted walking. **Walkability:** 2. **Opened:** 2000. **Architect:** Paul Cowley. **Season:** April-Dec. **High:** June-Oct. **To obtain tee times:** Call up to 2 days in advance. **Miscellaneous:** Reduced fees (weekdays, seniors, juniors), range (grass), credit cards (MC, V), BF, FF.

ORCHARD VALLEY GOLF CLUB
PU-4693 Cherry Valley Tpke., LaFayette, 13084, Onondaga County, (315)677-5180, 12 miles from Syracuse. **Facility Holes:** 9. **Yards:** 5,884/5,238. **Par:** 70/70. **Course Rating:** 70.0/75.0. **Green Fee:** $12/$24. **Cart Fee:** $14/Cart. **Walking Policy:** Unrestricted walking. **Walkability:** 1. **Season:** April-Oct. **To obtain tee times:** Call golf shop. **Miscellaneous:** Reduced fees (twilight, seniors, juniors), metal spikes, range (grass/mats), credit cards (MC, V), FF.

★★★½ OYSTER BAY TOWN GOLF COURSE
PU-#1 Southwoods Rd., Woodbury, 11797, Nassau County, (516)677-5980, 35 miles from New York. **Facility Holes:** 18. **Yards:** 6,351/5,109. **Par:** 70/70. **Course Rating:** 71.5/70.4. **Slope:** 131/126. **Green Fee:** $42/$67. **Cart Fee:** $0/Cart. **Walking Policy:** Unrestricted walking. **Walkability:** 4. **Opened:** 1989. **Architect:** Tom Fazio. **Season:** Year-round. **To obtain tee times:** Call golf shop. **Miscellaneous:** Reduced fees (weekdays, twilight, seniors, juniors), range (mats), BF, FF.
Reader Comments: Carry a light bag over this hilly terrain ... Nice, but needs work ... Tight fairways ... Tough, tight course, good mix of hazards ... One of the best public setups ... Tight.

PARKVIEW FAIRWAYS
PU-7100 Boughton Rd., Victor, 14564, Ontario County, (716)657-7867. **Facility Holes:** 18. **Yards:** 6,900/5,300. **Par:** 72/72. **Green Fee:** $15/$22. **Walking Policy:** Unrestricted walking. **Walkability:** 3. **Opened:** 1994. **Architect:** Pete Craig. **Season:** Year-round. **High:** May-Sept. **To obtain tee times:** Call up to 7 days in advance. **Miscellaneous:** Reduced fees (weekdays, seniors, juniors), range (grass), credit cards (MC, V, D), BF, FF.

PARTRIDGE RUN GOLF COURSE
PU-70 Sullivan Dr., Canton, 13617, St. Lawrence County, (315)386-4444, 130 miles from Syracuse. **E-mail:** krmag@PGA.com. **Web:** www.village.canton.ny.us. **Facility Holes:** 18. **Yards:** 6,569/5,267. **Par:** 72/72. **Course Rating:** 71.7/70.1. **Slope:** 130/114. **Green Fee:** $18/$20. **Cart Fee:** $20/Cart. **Walking Policy:** Unrestricted walking. **Walkability:** 1. **Opened:** 1995. **Season:** April-Nov. **High:** June-Aug. **To obtain tee times:** Call golf shop. **Miscellaneous:** Reduced fees (weekdays, twilight), range (grass), credit cards (MC, V), BF, FF.

PEEK'N PEAK RESORT
R-1405 Olde Rd., Findley Lake, 14736, Chautauqua County, (716)355-4141, 20 miles from Erie, PA. **E-mail:** pk-n-pk@travelbase.com. **Web:** www.pknpk.com. **Facility Holes:** 36. **Season:** April-Nov. **High:** June-Sept. **To obtain tee times:** Call golf shop. **Miscellaneous:** Reduced fees (weekdays, guests, twilight, seniors), metal spikes, range (grass), lodging (200 rooms), credit cards (MC, V, AE, D), BF, FF.
★★★½ LOWER COURSE (18)
Yards: 6,260/5,328. **Par:** 72/72. **Course Rating:** 69.0/69.5. **Slope:** 115/112. **Green Fee:** $23/$39. **Cart Fee:** $11/Person. **Walking Policy:** Unrestricted walking. **Walkability:** 1. **Opened:** 1974. **Architect:** Fred Garbin.
Reader Comments: A real test ... Nice valley course ... Lower in name only ... Flat and friendly ... Nice resort course, a little slow .... Expensive, nice clubhouse ... Excellent condition, resort very nice.
★★★★½ UPPER COURSE (18) *Pace*
Yards: 6,888/4,835. **Par:** 72/72. **Course Rating:** 72.5/67.5. **Slope:** 131/116. **Green Fee:** $64/$83. **Cart Fee:** Included in green fee. **Walking Policy:** Mandatory carts. **Walkability:** 5. **Opened:** 1991. **Architect:** John Exley.
Reader Comments: Very pretty, very scenic, nicely spread out ... Hardly see anyone else on the course, way too expensive for the area ... Great in fall ... Excellent condition & views ... Nice course, look forward to playing again ... Beautiful golf course.

PELHAM-SPLIT ROCK GOLF COURSE
PU-870 Shore Rd., Bronx, 10464, Bronx County, (718)885-1258, 8 miles from New York City. **Facility Holes:** 36. **Green Fee:** $10/$28. **Cart Fee:** $19/Cart. **Walking Policy:** Unrestricted walking. **Season:** Year-round. **High:** May-Sept. **To obtain tee times:** Call golf shop. **Miscellaneous:** Reduced fees (weekdays, twilight, seniors, juniors), metal spikes, credit cards (MC, V, AE).

NEW YORK

★★ **PELHAM COURSE** (18)
Yards: 6,601/5,554. **Par:** 71/73. **Course Rating:** 70.9/70.4. **Slope:** 116/113. **Walkability:** 2. **Opened:** 1901. **Architect:** Lawrence Van Etten.
★★½ **SPLIT ROCK COURSE** (18)
Yards: 6,714/5,509. **Par:** 71/71. **Course Rating:** 72.0/71.7. **Slope:** 129/122. **Walkability:** 3. **Opened:** 1934. **Architect:** John Van Kleek.

★½ **PHEASANT HOLLOW COUNTRY CLUB**
PU-2670 Phillips Rd., Castleton, 12033, Rensselaer County, (518)479-4653, 6 miles from Albany. **Facility Holes:** 9. **Yards:** 3,361/3,053. **Par:** 37/35. **Course Rating:** 70.0/73.5. **Slope:** 119/123. **Green Fee:** $12/$15. **Cart Fee:** $20/Cart. **Walking Policy:** Unrestricted walking. **Walkability:** 2. **Opened:** 1962. **Architect:** William F. Mitchell. **Season:** April-Nov. **High:** May-Nov. **To obtain tee times:** Call up to 3 days in advance. **Miscellaneous:** Reduced fees (weekdays, twilight, seniors, juniors), metal spikes, range (grass), credit cards (MC, V, D), BF, FF. **Special Notes:** Formerly Evergreen Golf Course.

★★ **PHILIP J. ROTELLA GOLF COURSE**
PU-Thiells and Mt. Ivy Road, Thiells, 10984, Rockland County, (845)354-1616, 20 miles from New York City. **Facility Holes:** 18. **Yards:** 6,502/4,856. **Par:** 72/72. **Course Rating:** 71.4/68.1. **Slope:** 128/117. **Green Fee:** $12/$34. **Cart Fee:** $24/Cart. **Walking Policy:** Walking at certain times. **Walkability:** 4. **Opened:** 1985. **Architect:** Hal Purdy. **Season:** March-Dec. **High:** May-Aug. **To obtain tee times:** Call golf shop. **Miscellaneous:** Reduced fees (twilight, seniors, juniors), range (mats).

★½ **PINE GROVE COUNTRY CLUB**
SP-4050 Milton Ave, Camillus, 13031, Onondaga County, (315)672-9272, 4 miles from Syracuse. **Facility Holes:** 18. **Yards:** 5,311/4,626. **Par:** 69/69. **Green Fee:** $12/$15. **Cart Fee:** $20/Cart. **Walking Policy:** Unrestricted walking. **Walkability:** 1. **Opened:** 1960. **Architect:** Barry Jordan. **Season:** March-Nov. **High:** June-Sept. **To obtain tee times:** Call golf shop. **Miscellaneous:** Reduced fees (weekdays, twilight, seniors), metal spikes, credit cards (MC, V, AE, D), BF, FF.

★★★½ **PINE HILLS COUNTRY CLUB**
SP-1 Country Club Drive, Manorville, 11949, Suffolk County, (631)878-7103, 15 miles from The Hamptons. **Facility Holes:** 18. **Yards:** 7,200/5,300. **Par:** 73/73. **Course Rating:** 74.0/70.3. **Slope:** 129/119. **Green Fee:** $35/$40. **Cart Fee:** $30/Cart. **Walking Policy:** Walking at certain times. **Walkability:** 3. **Opened:** 1972. **Architect:** Roger Tooker. **Season:** Year-round. **High:** April-Oct. **To obtain tee times:** Call golf shop. **Miscellaneous:** Reduced fees (twilight, seniors), range (grass/mats), credit cards (MC, V).
Reader Comments: Play this one from the tips and you'll need oxygen ... Good playing conditions ... Always improving, greens much better, great practice area ... Great country club-type condition ... Very short course, excellent condition.

PINE HILLS GOLF COURSE
SP-247 Jones Rd., Frankfort, 13340, Herkimer County, (315)733-5030, 10 miles from Utica. **Facility Holes:** 18. **Yards:** 6,070/4,912. **Par:** 70/74. **Green Fee:** $12/$13. **Cart Fee:** $20/Cart. **Walkability:** 2. **Opened:** 1954. **Architect:** Carl Grygiel, Sr. **Season:** March-Nov. **To obtain tee times:** Call golf shop. **Miscellaneous:** Reduced fees (twilight), range (grass), FF.

PINES GOLF COURSE
SP-6919 SR 3, Pulaski, 13142, Oswego County, (315)298-8100. **Facility Holes:** 18. **Yards:** 6,060/5,380. **Par:** 71/71. **Course Rating:** 71.0/73.0. **Slope:** 110/114. **Green Fee:** $13/$18. **Cart Fee:** $20/Cart. **Opened:** 1960. **Architect:** Bob Bingham. **Season:** April-Oct. **To obtain tee times:** Call golf shop. **Miscellaneous:** Reduced fees (juniors), credit cards (MC, V).

PIONEER HILLS GOLF COURSE
PU-3230 Ballston-Galway Rd., Ballston Spa, 12020, Saratoga County, (518)885-7000, 20 miles from Albany. **Facility Holes:** 18. **Yards:** 5,422/4,533. **Par:** 70/70. **Green Fee:** $20/$25. **Cart Fee:** $12/Person. **Walking Policy:** Unrestricted walking. **Walkability:** 3. **Opened:** 1995. **Season:** April-Nov. **High:** June-Aug. **To obtain tee times:** Call up to 7 days in advance. **Miscellaneous:** Credit cards (MC, V).

PORT BAY GOLF CLUB
PU-7430 E. Port Bay Rd., Wolcott, 14590, Wayne County, (315)594-8295, 35 miles from Rochester. **Facility Holes:** 18. **Yards:** 6,000/4,500. **Par:** 72/72. **Green Fee:** $13/$17. **Cart Fee:** $10/Person. **Walking Policy:** Unrestricted walking. **Walkability:** 3. **Opened:** 1962. **Architect:** Robert Beardsley. **Season:** April-Nov. **High:** May-Sept. **To obtain tee times:** Call golf shop. **Miscellaneous:** Reduced fees (weekdays, twilight, seniors), credit cards (MC, V), BF, FF.

QUEENSBURY COUNTRY CLUB
SP-SR 149, Lake George, 12845, Warren County, (518)793-3711, 55 miles from Albany. **Web:** www.lakegeorgegolf.com/queensbury. **Facility Holes:** 18. **Yards:** 6,015/4,755. **Par:** 70/70. **Course Rating:** 67.4/66.5. **Slope:** 112/106. **Green Fee:** $15/$22. **Walking Policy:** Unrestricted walking. **Walkability:** 3. **Opened:** 1954. **Architect:** Mark Cassidy/Scot Smith. **Season:** April-Nov. **High:** June-Sept. **To obtain tee times:** Call up to 7 days in advance. **Miscellaneous:** Reduced fees (twilight), range (grass/mats), credit cards (MC, V), BF, FF.

★★★★½ RADISSON GREENS GOLF CLUB
SP-8055 Potter Rd., Baldwinsville, 13027, Onondaga County, (315)638-0092, 15 miles from Syracuse. **E-mail:** radgreens@aol.com. **Web:** www.radissongreens.com. **Facility Holes:** 18. **Yards:** 7,010/5,543. **Par:** 72/73. **Course Rating:** 73.3/70.0. **Slope:** 135/124. **Green Fee:** $27/$37. **Cart Fee:** $25/Person. **Walking Policy:** Walking at certain times. **Walkability:** 3. **Opened:** 1977. **Architect:** Robert Trent Jones. **Season:** March-Nov. **High:** May-Sept. **To obtain tee times:** Call golf shop. **Miscellaneous:** Reduced fees (weekdays, seniors), range (grass), credit cards (MC, V), BF, FF.
Reader Comments: Great layout and in great shape … My favorite, every shot is challenging … Great layout, good value, good test … Very challenging, if you are playing well, you will use every club in your bag … Lots of fun & challenging … Top notch … Sand trap heaven.

RAINBOW GOLF COURSE
SP-3822 Route 26, Greenville, 12083, Greene County, (518)966-5343. **E-mail:** golfrainbow@aol.com. **Web:** www.golfrainbow.com. **Facility Holes:** 18. **Yards:** 6,283/4,348. **Par:** 71/71. **Course Rating:** 71.5/68.0. **Slope:** 126/119. **Green Fee:** $20/$29. **Cart Fee:** $22/Cart. **Opened:** 1957. **Season:** April-Dec. **To obtain tee times:** Call golf shop. **Miscellaneous:** Range (grass/mats), lodging (7 rooms), credit cards (MC, V, AE, D).

RED HOOK GOLF CLUB
SP-650 Rte. 199, Red Hook, 12571, Dutchess County, (845)758-8652, 100 miles from New York City. **Facility Holes:** 18. **Yards:** 6,571/5,155. **Par:** 72/71. **Course Rating:** 70.2/68.5. **Slope:** 123/118. **Green Fee:** $32/$40. **Cart Fee:** $15/Person. **Walking Policy:** Unrestricted walking. **Opened:** 1931. **Architect:** Dave Horn. **Season:** April-Nov. **High:** June-Sept. **To obtain tee times:** Call up to 2 days in advance. **Miscellaneous:** Reduced fees (juniors), range (grass), credit cards (MC, V, D), BF, FF.

RICCI MEADOWS GOLF COURSE
PU-1939 Oak Orchard Rd. (Rte. 98), Albion, 14411, Orleans County, (716)682-3280, 30 miles from Rochester. **Facility Holes:** 18. **Yards:** 5,268/4,597. **Par:** 71/72. **Course Rating:** 63.0/63.4. **Slope:** 102/100. **Green Fee:** $12/$14. **Cart Fee:** $10/Person. **Walking Policy:** Unrestricted walking. **Walkability:** 1. **Opened:** 1957. **Season:** April-Nov. **High:** June-Aug. **To obtain tee times:** Call golf shop. **Miscellaneous:** Reduced fees (weekdays, seniors), metal spikes, range (grass/mats), BF, FF.

RIVERSIDE COUNTRY CLUB
PU-647 County Rte. 37, Central Square, 13036, Oswego County, (315)676-7714. **Facility Holes:** 18. **Yards:** 3,485/3,485. **Par:** 58/58. **Green Fee:** $10/$14. **Cart Fee:** $14/Cart. **Opened:** 1967. **Architect:** Larry Packard. **Season:** April-Nov. **To obtain tee times:** Call golf shop.

★★ RIVERVIEW COUNTRY CLUB
PU-847 Riverview Rd, Rexford, 12148, Saratoga County, (518)399-2345, 15 miles from Albany. **Facility Holes:** 18. **Yards:** 7,095/5,815. **Par:** 73/74. **Course Rating:** 73.7/73.4. **Slope:** 128/124. **Green Fee:** $19/$24. **Cart Fee:** $22/Cart. **Walking Policy:** Unrestricted walking. **Walkability:** 3. **Opened:** 1964. **Season:** April-Nov. **High:** June-Aug. **To obtain tee times:** Call golf shop. **Miscellaneous:** Reduced fees (weekdays, twilight, seniors, juniors), metal spikes, range (grass), credit cards (MC, V, AE).

ROBERT MOSES STATE PARK
PU-South and Robert Moses Causeway, Babylon, 11702, Suffolk County, (631)669-0449, 40 miles from New York City. **Facility Holes:** 18. **Yards:** 3,045. **Par:** 55. **Green Fee:** $9. **Walking Policy:** Unrestricted walking. **Opened:** 1967. **Season:** April-Dec. **High:** May-Aug. **To obtain tee times:** Call golf shop. **Miscellaneous:** Reduced fees (seniors).

★★★½ ROCK HILL COUNTRY CLUB
PU-105 Clancy Rd., Manorville, 11949, Suffolk County, (631)878-2250, 60 miles from New York City. **Facility Holes:** 18. **Yards:** 7,050/5,390. **Par:** 71/72. **Course Rating:** 73.6/70.7. **Slope:** 136/120. **Green Fee:** $15/$42. **Cart Fee:** $32/Cart. **Walking Policy:** Walking at certain times. **Walkability:** 4. **Opened:** 1965. **Architect:** Frank Duane. **Season:** Year-round. **To obtain tee times:** Call up to 7 days in advance. **Miscellaneous:** Reduced fees (weekdays, twilight,

seniors, juniors), range (grass/mats), BF, FF.
Reader Comments: Challenging, aptly-named course in improved shape … Improved tremendously in last several years, good test when wind blows … Challenging.

★★½ ROCKLAND LAKE STATE PARK GOLF CLUB
PU-100 Route 9 W, Congers, 10920, Rockland County, (845)268-8250, 20 miles from New York City. **Facility Holes:** 36. **Yards:** 6,864/5,663. **Par:** 72/72. **Course Rating:** 72.3/71.1. **Slope:** 126/122. **Green Fee:** $24/$29. **Cart Fee:** $26/Cart. **Walking Policy:** Unrestricted walking. **Walkability:** 3. **Opened:** 1969. **Season:** March-Dec. **High:** April-Oct. **To obtain tee times:** Call golf shop. **Miscellaneous:** Reduced fees (twilight, seniors, juniors), range (mats), credit cards (MC, V, AE, D), BF, FF.
Special Notes: Also has an 18-hole executive course.

ROGUE'S ROOST GOLF CLUB
PU-Rt. 31, Bridgeport, 13030, Madison County, (315)633-0945, 12 miles from Syracuse. **Facility Holes:** 36. **Green Fee:** $20/$24. **Cart Fee:** $22/Cart. **Walking Policy:** Walking at certain times. **Walkability:** 2. **Architect:** Bill Galloway. **Season:** April-Nov. **High:** May-Sept. **To obtain tee times:** Call up to 7 days in advance. **Miscellaneous:** Reduced fees (weekdays), range (grass), credit cards (MC, V, AE, D), BF, FF.
★★★½ EAST COURSE (18)
Yards: 6,700/5,670. **Par:** 71/74. **Course Rating:** 70.9/69.7. **Slope:** 118/113. **Opened:** 1996.
Reader Comments: Two courses have own flavor … Grade is rising, someone doing their homework … Fairways & greens impressive … Dull … Fairly new, challenging … Excellent fairways & greens … Varied types of holes, aging well.
WEST COURSE (18)
Yards: 6,400/5,480. **Par:** 71/74. **Course Rating:** 68.6/68.5. **Slope:** 114/108. **Opened:** 1966.

ROLLING ACRES GOLF COURSE
PU-7795 Dewitt Rd., Pike, 14130, Wyoming County, (716)567-8557. **Facility Holes:** 18. **Yards:** 5,500/4,757. **Par:** 70/71. **Green Fee:** $14/$16. **Cart Fee:** $16/Person. **Opened:** 1987. **Season:** April-Nov. **To obtain tee times:** Call golf shop. **Miscellaneous:** Credit cards (MC, V).

ROLLING OAKS GOLF COURSE
PU-181 Rte. 25A, Rocky Point, 11778, Suffolk County, (631)744-3200, 5 miles from Port Jefferson. **Facility Holes:** 18. **Yards:** 5,000. **Par:** 65. **Course Rating:** 63.0. **Slope:** 110. **Green Fee:** $23/$28. **Cart Fee:** $16/Person. **Walking Policy:** Unrestricted walking. **Walkability:** 3. **Season:** Year-round. **To obtain tee times:** Call up to 2 days in advance. **Miscellaneous:** Credit cards (MC, V, AE), BF, FF.

★★★★ ROME COUNTRY CLUB
SP-5342 Rte. 69, Rome, 13440, Oneida County, (315)336-6464, 25 miles from Syracuse. **E-mail:** romecc@email.msn.com. **Web:** www.romecountryclub.com. **Facility Holes:** 18. **Yards:** 6,775/5,505. **Par:** 72/75. **Course Rating:** 73.6/71.3. **Slope:** 128/118. **Green Fee:** $24/$27. **Cart Fee:** $22/Cart. **Walking Policy:** Unrestricted walking. **Walkability:** 3. **Opened:** 1929. **Season:** Year-round. **High:** May-Sept. **To obtain tee times:** Call golf shop. **Miscellaneous:** Reduced fees (weekdays, twilight), range (grass/mats), credit cards (MC, V, D), BF, FF.
Reader Comments: Difficult to play because of creeks crossing fairways … Good value, good layout, nice people … Excellent condition, nice people, challenging layout … Great public course … A great challenge near home … Challenging.

★★½ RONDOUT GOLF CLUB
PU-Box 194 Whitfield Rd, Accord, 12404, Ulster County, (914)626-2513, (888)894-9455, 15 miles from Kingston. **Facility Holes:** 18. **Yards:** 6,468/4,956. **Par:** 72/72. **Course Rating:** 72.7/68.4. **Slope:** 128/116. **Green Fee:** $21/$31. **Cart Fee:** $14/Person. **Walking Policy:** Walking at certain times. **Walkability:** 2. **Opened:** 1970. **Architect:** Hal Purdy. **Season:** March-Nov. **To obtain tee times:** Call up to 7 days in advance. **Miscellaneous:** Reduced fees (weekdays, twilight, juniors), range (grass/mats), credit cards (MC, V, D), BF, FF.

ROSE BROOK GOLF COURSE
SP-12486 Beebe Rd., Silver Creek, 14136, Chautauqua County, (716)934-2825. **E-mail:** rosebgolf@aol.com. **Web:** www.rosebrookgolf.com. **Facility Holes:** 18. **Yards:** 6,300/6,000. **Par:** 72/72. **Course Rating:** 69.0/70.4. **Slope:** 109/113. **Green Fee:** $10/$20. **Cart Fee:** $10/Person. **Walking Policy:** Unrestricted walking. **Walkability:** 3. **Opened:** 1970. **Architect:** Manguso/Emerson. **Season:** April-Nov. **High:** May-Sept. **To obtain tee times:** Call golf shop. **Miscellaneous:** Reduced fees (weekdays, guests, twilight, seniors, juniors), credit cards (MC, V, AE), BF, FF.

★★½ ROTHLAND GOLF COURSE
PU-12089 Clarence Center Rd., Akron, 14001, Erie County, (716)542-4325, 15 miles from Buffalo. **E-mail:** play@rothland.com. **Web:** www.rothlandgolf.com. **Facility Holes:** 27. **Green Fee:** $20/$26. **Cart Fee:** $21/Cart. **Walking Policy:** Unrestricted walking. **Walkability:** 2. **Opened:** 1976. **Architect:** Bill Roth. **Season:** April-Nov. **High:** June-Sept. **To obtain tee times:** Call up to 7 days in advance. **Miscellaneous:** Reduced fees (weekdays, twilight, seniors), range (grass), credit cards (MC, V, AE, D), BF, FF.
GOLD/WHITE (18 Combo)
Yards: 6,176/5,519. **Par:** 72/72. **Course Rating:** 68.1/68.0. **Slope:** 112/112.
RED/GOLD (18 Combo)
Yards: 6,486/5,843. **Par:** 72/72. **Course Rating:** 70.2/71.3. **Slope:** 113/112.
RED/WHITE (18 Combo)
Yards: 6,348/5,878. **Par:** 72/72. **Course Rating:** 68.7/69.5. **Slope:** 110/110.

★★★★ THE SAGAMORE GOLF CLUB
R-110 Sagamore Rd., Bolton Landing, 12814, Warren County, (518)644-9400, 60 miles from Albany. **Facility Holes:** 18. **Yards:** 6,890/5,261. **Par:** 70/71. **Course Rating:** 72.9/73.0. **Slope:** 130/122. **Green Fee:** $70/$115. **Cart Fee:** Included in green fee. **Walking Policy:** Mandatory carts. **Walkability:** 5. **Opened:** 1928. **Architect:** Donald Ross. **Season:** April-Oct. **High:** May-Sept. **To obtain tee times:** Call golf shop. **Miscellaneous:** Reduced fees (twilight, juniors), range (grass), credit cards (MC, V, AE, D), BF, FF.
Notes: Ranked 15th in 2001 Best in State.
Reader Comments: Beautiful course, tight & wooded ... Great condition, layout excellent.

★★ SALMON CREEK COUNTRY CLUB
SP-355 Washington St., Spencerport, 14559, Monroe County, (716)352-4300, 6 miles from Rochester. **Facility Holes:** 18. **Yards:** 6,400/5,525. **Par:** 72/73. **Course Rating:** 69.5/71.4. **Slope:** 121/114. **Green Fee:** $19/$23. **Cart Fee:** $22/Person. **Walking Policy:** Unrestricted walking. **Walkability:** 3. **Opened:** 1963. **Architect:** Pete Craig. **Season:** March-Dec. **To obtain tee times:** Call up to 7 days in advance. **Miscellaneous:** Reduced fees (seniors), range (grass/mats), credit cards (MC, V), BF, FF.

★ SANCTUARY COUNTRY CLUB
PU-Rte. 118, Yorktown Heights, 10598, Westchester County, (914)962-8050, 2 miles from Yorktown Heights. **Facility Holes:** 18. **Yards:** 5,810/5,124. **Par:** 71/73. **Course Rating:** 68.6/68.6. **Slope:** 116/116. **Green Fee:** $25/$37. **Cart Fee:** $24/Cart. **Walking Policy:** Walking at certain times. **Walkability:** 3. **Opened:** 1955. **Architect:** Nat Squire. **Season:** March-Nov. **High:** May-Aug. **To obtain tee times:** Call golf shop. **Miscellaneous:** Reduced fees (weekdays, twilight, seniors, juniors), credit cards (MC, V, AE, D), FF.

SARANAC INN GOLF & COUNTRY CLUB *Pace*
PU-HCI Box 16, Saranac Lake, 12983, Franklin County, (518)891-1402, 120 miles from Montreal. **E-mail:** golf@saranacinn.com. **Web:** www.saranacinn.com. **Facility Holes:** 18. **Yards:** 6,631/5,263. **Par:** 72/72. **Course Rating:** 71.5/73.6. **Slope:** 124/128. **Green Fee:** $45/$55. **Cart Fee:** Included in green fee. **Walking Policy:** Walking at certain times. **Walkability:** 3. **Opened:** 1901. **Architect:** Seymour Dunn. **Season:** May-Oct. **High:** July-Sept. **To obtain tee times:** Call up to 30 days in advance. **Miscellaneous:** Reduced fees (twilight), range (grass), lodging (10 rooms), credit cards (MC, V, AE), BF, FF.

SARATOGA NATIONAL GOLF CLUB
PU-458 Union Ave., Saratoga Springs, 12866, Saratoga County, (518)583-4653, 25 miles from Albany. **Web:** www.golfsaratoga.com. **Facility Holes:** 18. **Yards:** 7,237/5,762. **Par:** 72/72. **Course Rating:** 74.5/74.2. **Slope:** 143/140. **Green Fee:** $110/$125. **Cart Fee:** Included in green fee. **Walking Policy:** Unrestricted walking. **Opened:** 2000. **Architect:** Roger Rulewich. **To obtain tee times:** Call golf shop. **Miscellaneous:** Range (grass).
Notes: Ranked 5th in 2001 Best New Upscale Courses.

★★★★ SARATOGA SPA GOLF COURSE *Value*
PU-Saratoga Spa State Park, 60 Roosevelt Dr, Saratoga Springs, 12866, Saratoga County, (518)584-2006, 24 miles from Albany. **Facility Holes:** 27. **Yards:** 7,149/5,649. **Par:** 72/72. **Course Rating:** 73.7/72.5. **Slope:** 130/122. **Green Fee:** $22/$25. **Cart Fee:** $26/Cart. **Walking Policy:** Unrestricted walking. **Walkability:** 2. **Opened:** 1962. **Architect:** William F. Mitchell. **Season:** April-Dec. **To obtain tee times:** Call up to 7 days in advance. **Miscellaneous:** Reduced fees (seniors, juniors), range (grass), credit cards (MC, V, AE, D), BF, FF.
Reader Comments: A terrific course, value you can't beat ... Outstanding value, good test ... One of the few good courses near Saratoga ... Nice walk in the woods ... Tough greens ... Championship layout.
Special Notes: Also has a 9-hole executive course.

★★ SAXON WOODS GOLF COURSE
PU-315 Old Mamaroneck Rd., Scarsdale, 10583, Westchester County, (914)725-4688, 5 miles from White Plains. **Facility Holes:** 18. **Yards:** 6,240/5,617. **Par:** 71/73. **Course Rating:** 70.4/71.9. **Slope:** 124/124. **Green Fee:** $10/$45. **Walking Policy:** Unrestricted walking. **Walkability:** 2. **Opened:** 1931. **Architect:** Tom Winton. **Season:** April-Dec. **High:** June-Sept. **To obtain tee times:** Call up to 7 days in advance. **Miscellaneous:** Reduced fees (weekdays, twilight, seniors, juniors), range (mats), BF, FF.

★★★ SCHENECTADY GOLF COURSE
PU-400 Oregon Ave., Schenectady, 12309, Schenectady County, (518)382-5155, 18 miles from Albany. **Facility Holes:** 18. **Yards:** 6,570/5,275. **Par:** 72/72. **Course Rating:** 71.1/68.1. **Slope:** 123/115. **Green Fee:** $19/$21. **Cart Fee:** $21/Cart. **Walking Policy:** Unrestricted walking. **Walkability:** 2. **Opened:** 1935. **Architect:** Jim Thomson. **Season:** April-Dec. **To obtain tee times:** Call golf shop. **Miscellaneous:** Reduced fees (weekdays, seniors, juniors), range (grass), BF, FF.
Reader Comments: This course is improving, the city is putting a lot of money into it … With some upkeep this course could be great … Muni course, no reservations … Well groomed, pleasure to play here … Good layout, bargain.

SENECA GOLF CLUB
PU-7346 State Fair Blvd., Baldwinsville, 13027, Onondaga County, (315)635-5695, 6 miles from Syracuse. **Facility Holes:** 9. **Yards:** 5,758/5,030. **Par:** 70/70. **Course Rating:** 68.2/67.0. **Slope:** 109/109. **Green Fee:** $12/$15. **Cart Fee:** $20/Cart. **Walking Policy:** Unrestricted walking. **Walkability:** 2. **Opened:** 1928. **Season:** April-Nov. **High:** May-Sept. **To obtain tee times:** Call golf shop. **Miscellaneous:** Reduced fees (seniors, juniors), range (grass), credit cards (MC, V), BF, FF.

★★★★½ SENECA LAKE COUNTRY CLUB *Service+, Value+, Pace+*
SP-Rt. 14S, Geneva, 14456, Ontario County, (315)789-4681. **Facility Holes:** 18. **Yards:** 6,259/5,341. **Par:** 72/72. **Course Rating:** 71.1/71.0. **Slope:** 113/114. **Green Fee:** $15. **Opened:** 1932. **To obtain tee times:** Call golf shop.
Reader Comments: Friendly atmosphere and golf like no other … One of the nicest courses I have played … The staff is extremely polite and you just get a real sense that they care about the place, I would recommend it to anyone … Has a great view of lake and surrounding area … Great elevation changes.

★★★ SHADOW LAKE GOLF & RACQUET CLUB
PU-1850 Five Mile Line Rd., Penfield, 14526, Monroe County, (716)385-2010, 10 miles from Rochester. **Facility Holes:** 27. **Yards:** 6,164/5,498. **Par:** 71/72. **Course Rating:** 68.5/70.5. **Slope:** 111/112. **Green Fee:** $10/$22. **Walking Policy:** Walking at certain times. **Opened:** 1977. **Architect:** Pete Craig. **Season:** March-Dec. **High:** June-Aug. **To obtain tee times:** Call golf shop. **Miscellaneous:** Reduced fees (weekdays, twilight, seniors), metal spikes, credit cards (MC, V, AE).
Reader Comments: Crowded but well managed … Nice course, gets a lot of rounds … Can be slow at times … People are very friendly … Challenging, good 19th hole … Still a challenge, friendly staff … Short course.
Special Notes: Also has a 9-hole executive course.

★★★½ SHADOW PINES GOLF CLUB
PU-600 Whalen Rd., Penfield, 14526, Monroe County, (716)385-8550, 10 miles from Rochester. **Web:** www.234golf.com. **Facility Holes:** 18. **Yards:** 6,763/5,292. **Par:** 72/72. **Course Rating:** 72.4/70.4. **Slope:** 124/123. **Green Fee:** $16/$23. **Cart Fee:** $12/Person. **Walking Policy:** Mandatory carts. **Walkability:** 4. **Opened:** 1985. **Architect:** Pete Craig/Gardner Odenbach. **Season:** March-Nov. **High:** June-Sept. **To obtain tee times:** Call up to 7 days in advance. **Miscellaneous:** Reduced fees (weekdays, twilight, seniors), range (grass/mats), credit cards (MC, V, AE), BF, FF.
Reader Comments: Challenging, could be crowded; good greens …Tight layout, nice course … Narrow, requires straight play … Tough, keep it on the short stuff …Lots of rounds, but pace is OK.

SHAMROCK GOLF & COUNTRY CLUB
SP-Airport Rd., Oriskany, 13424, Oneida County, (315)336-9858. **Facility Holes:** 18. **Yards:** 6,323/5,047. **Par:** 70/72. **Green Fee:** $15/$16. **Cart Fee:** $18/Cart. **Opened:** 1960. **Architect:** A.F. Reed. **Season:** April-Nov. **To obtain tee times:** Call golf shop. **Miscellaneous:** Reduced fees (twilight), range (grass/mats), credit cards (MC, V).

★★★★½ SHENANDOAH GOLF CLUB *Condition+*
R-5218 Patrick Rd., Verona, 13478, Oneida County, (315)361-8518, 30 miles from Syracuse. **Web:** www.turning-stone.com. **Facility Holes:** 27. **Yards:** 7,129/5,185. **Par:** 72/72. **Course**

Rating: 74.1/71.6. **Slope:** 142/120. **Green Fee:** $80/$105. **Cart Fee:** Included in green fee. **Walking Policy:** Unrestricted walking. **Walkability:** 3. **Opened:** 2000. **Architect:** Rick Smith. **Season:** April-Nov. **High:** May-Oct. **To obtain tee times:** Call up to 2 days in advance. **Miscellaneous:** Reduced fees (guests, twilight), range (grass), lodging (350 rooms), credit cards (MC, V, AE, D), BF, FF. **Notes:** Ranked 9th in 2001 Best New Upscale Courses.
Reader Comments: Great course in upstate New York, worth drive even from NYC ... Casino next door makes it worth a full day ... Some short, boring holes ... Wide open off the tee ... Back 9 better than front ... When done, stop by and play the par-3 course. **Special Notes:** Also has a 9-hole course.

★★★ SHERIDAN PARK GOLF CLUB
PU-Center Park Dr., Tonawanda, 14150, Erie County, (716)875-1811, 3 miles from Buffalo. **Facility Holes:** 18. **Yards:** 6,534/5,656. **Par:** 71/74. **Course Rating:** 71.3/74.0. **Slope:** 116/116. **Green Fee:** $16/$19. **Cart Fee:** $18/Cart. **Walking Policy:** Unrestricted walking. **Walkability:** 2. **Opened:** 1933. **Architect:** William Harries. **Season:** April-Nov. **High:** June-Aug. **To obtain tee times:** Call golf shop. **Miscellaneous:** Reduced fees (weekdays, twilight), range (mats).
Reader Comments: Great course, needs some work ... September and October best time to play ... Basic town course too much play, needs better conditioning ... Good price, nice layout.

★★★½ SILO RIDGE COUNTRY CLUB
PU-P.O. Box 86, Amenia, 12501, Dutchess County, (845)373-9200, (866)745-6743, 25 miles from Poughkeepsie. **Web:** www.siloridge.com. **Facility Holes:** 18. **Yards:** 6,617/5,601. **Par:** 72/72. **Course Rating:** 71.8/72.1. **Slope:** 135/131. **Green Fee:** $22/$44. **Cart Fee:** $26/Cart. **Walking Policy:** Walking at certain times. **Walkability:** 3. **Opened:** 1992. **Architect:** Al Zikorus. **Season:** April-Nov. **High:** June-Aug. **To obtain tee times:** Call up to 6 days in advance. **Misc:** Reduced fees (weekdays, seniors, juniors), range (mats), credit cards (MC, V, AE, D).
Reader Comments: Greens finally improved ... Great par 3s on back 9 ... Enjoyable, great back 9 greens ... Don't hit it in rough ... A blend of flat and hilly holes ... North boring, South better. **Special Notes:** Formerly Island Green Country Club.

SILVER CREEK GOLF CLUB
PU-1790 East River Rd., Waterloo, 13165, Seneca County, (315)539-8076, 40 miles from Rochester. **E-mail:** silvercreek@flare.net. **Facility Holes:** 18. **Yards:** 5,942/5,435. **Par:** 70/70. **Course Rating:** 68.3/71.0. **Slope:** 115/116. **Green Fee:** $13/$17. **Cart Fee:** $10/Cart. **Walking Policy:** Unrestricted walking. **Walkability:** 2. **Opened:** 1964. **Season:** April-Nov. **To obtain tee times:** Call up to 10 days in advance. **Miscellaneous:** Reduced fees (weekdays, seniors, juniors), range (grass), credit cards (MC, V, D), BF, FF.

★★½ SILVER LAKE GOLF COURSE
PU-915 Victory Blvd., Staten Island, 10301, Richmond County, (718)447-5686. **Facility Holes:** 18. **Yards:** 6,138/5,202. **Par:** 69/69. **Course Rating:** 68.8/71.2. **Slope:** 119/119. **Green Fee:** $19/$22. **Cart Fee:** $25/Cart. **Walking Policy:** Unrestricted walking. **Walkability:** 5. **Opened:** 1929. **Architect:** John Van Kleek. **Season:** Year-round. **High:** March-Oct. **To obtain tee times:** Call up to 11 days in advance. **Miscellaneous:** Reduced fees (weekdays, twilight, seniors, juniors), metal spikes, credit cards (MC, V, AE), BF, FF.

SIX-S GOLF COURSE
PU-5920 Co. Rt. 16, Belfast, 14711, Allegany County, (716)365-2201, 65 miles from Buffalo. **Facility Holes:** 36. **Green Fee:** $11/$12. **Cart Fee:** $10/Person. **Walking Policy:** Unrestricted walking. **Walkability:** 2. **Architect:** William F. Short. **Season:** March-Nov. **To obtain tee times:** Call golf shop. **Miscellaneous:** Reduced fees (weekdays, twilight, seniors, juniors), metal spikes, range (grass), credit cards (MC, V, D), FF.
EAST COURSE (18)
Yards: 5,927/5,927. **Par:** 72/72. **Course Rating:** 70.4/67.4. **Slope:** 124/116.
★★ **WEST COURSE** (18)
Yards: 6,210/4,826. **Par:** 72/72. **Course Rating:** 69.5/69.7. **Slope:** 120/115. **Opened:** 1965.

SKENE VALLEY GOLF COURSE
PU-129 County Route 9A, Whitehall, 12887, Washington County, (518)499-1685, 25 miles from Glens Fall. **Facility Holes:** 18. **Yards:** 6,838/5,688. **Par:** 72/73. **Course Rating:** 71.8/71.8. **Slope:** 121/117. **Green Fee:** $17/$20. **Cart Fee:** $21/Cart. **Walking Policy:** Unrestricted walking. **Walkability:** 2. **Opened:** 1967. **Architect:** Mark Cassidy. **Season:** April-Oct. **High:** July-Sept. **To obtain tee times:** Call golf shop. **Miscellaneous:** Metal spikes, range (grass), FF.

SKYLINE GOLF COURSE
PU-9113 Brewerton Rd., Brewerton, 13029, Onondaga County, (315)699-5338. **Facility Holes:** 18. **Yards:** 6,235/5,555. **Par:** 71/73. **Course Rating:** 69.6. **Slope:** 112. **Fee:** $14/$16. **Cart Fee:** $18/Cart. **Opened:** 1965. **Season:** March-Oct. **To obtain tee times:** Call golf shop.

SLEEPY HOLLOW GOLF COURSE
PU-8600 Country Club Dr., Rome, 13440, Oneida County, (315)336-4110. **Facility Holes:** 18.
Yards: 4,720/4,172. **Par:** 68/68. **Green Fee:** $10/$12. **Opened:** 1957. **Architect:** Ed Waller.
Season: April-Nov. **To obtain tee times:** Call golf shop.

★★½ **SMITHTOWN LANDING GOLF CLUB**
PU-495 Landing Ave., Smithtown, 11787, Suffolk County, (631)979-6534, 35 miles from New
York. **Facility Holes:** 18. **Yards:** 6,114/5,263. **Par:** 72/72. **Course Rating:** 70.9/69.8. **Slope:**
125/122. **Green Fee:** $21/$29. **Cart Fee:** $25/Cart. **Walking Policy:** Unrestricted walking.
Walkability: 3. **Architect:** Stephen Kay. **Season:** Year-round. **High:** May-Sept. **To obtain tee
times:** Call golf shop. **Miscellaneous:** Reduced fees (weekdays), metal spikes, range (mats).

SOARING EAGLES GOLF COURSE
PU-201 Middle Rd., Horseheads, 14845, Chemung County, (607)739-0551, 15 miles from
Elmira. **Web:** www.nysparks.com. **Facility Holes:** 18. **Yards:** 6,625/4,930. **Par:** 72/72. **Course
Rating:** 71.6/67.5. **Slope:** 117/108. **Green Fee:** $9/$21. **Cart Fee:** $22/Cart. **Walking Policy:**
Unrestricted walking. **Walkability:** 3. **Opened:** 1963. **Architect:** Archibald Craig. **Season:** April-
Nov. **High:** June-Aug. **To obtain tee times:** Call up to 4 days in advance. **Miscellaneous:**
Reduced fees (weekdays, seniors, juniors), range (grass/mats), credit cards (MC, V, D),
BF, FF.

SODUS BAY HEIGHTS GOLF COURSE
SP-7030 Bayview Dr., Sodus Point, 14555, Wayne County, (315)483-6777, 26 miles from
Rochester. **Facility Holes:** 18. **Yards:** 6,729/5,543. **Par:** 72/72. **Course Rating:** 72.1/71.5.
Slope: 127/123. **Green Fee:** $45/$50. **Cart Fee:** Included in green fee. **Walking Policy:**
Mandatory carts. **Walkability:** 3. **Opened:** 1924. **Season:** April-Oct. **High:** June-Aug. **To obtain
tee times:** Call up to 7 days in advance. **Miscellaneous:** Credit cards (MC, V), FF.

SOUTH HILLS COUNTRY CLUB
SP-3108 Busti-Stillwater Rd., Jamestown, 14701, Chautauqua County, (716)664-4653.
Facility Holes: 18. **Yards:** 6,105/4,681. **Par:** 72/72. **Course Rating:** 67.5/66.0. **Slope:** 116/105.
Green Fee: $17/$19. **Cart Fee:** $18/Cart. **Opened:** 1964. **Season:** April-Jan. **To obtain tee
times:** Call golf shop. **Miscellaneous:** Reduced fees (seniors).

★★ **SOUTH SHORE COUNTRY CLUB**
SP-5076 Southwestern Blvd., Hamburg, 14075, Erie County, (716)649-6674. **Facility Holes:**
18. **Yards:** 6,873/5,728. **Par:** 72/72. **Green Fee:** $20/$25. **Cart Fee:** $10/Person. **Opened:** 1920.
Architect: W. Stiles/J. Van Kleek. **Season:** April-Nov. **To obtain tee times:** Call golf shop.
Miscellaneous: Reduced fees (twilight, seniors), range (grass/mats), cards (MC, V).

★★ **SOUTH SHORE GOLF COURSE**
PU-200 Huguenot Ave., Staten Island, 10312, Richmond County, (718)984-0101, 18 miles
from Manhattan. **Facility Holes:** 18. **Yards:** 6,366/5,435. **Par:** 72/72. **Course Rating:** 69.9/69.8.
Slope: 113/114. **Green Fee:** $16/$18. **Cart Fee:** $24/Cart. **Walking Policy:** Unrestricted walk-
ing. **Walkability:** 1. **Opened:** 1927. **Architect:** Devereux Emmet/Alfred H. Tull. **Season:** Year-
round. **High:** May-Sept. **To obtain tee times:** Call golf shop. **Miscellaneous:** Reduced fees (twilight, seniors, juniors), metal spikes, credit cards (MC, V).

★★★½ **SPOOK ROCK GOLF COURSE**
PU-233 Spook Rock Rd., Suffern, 10901, Rockland County, (845)357-3085, 30 miles from
New York City. **Facility Holes:** 18. **Yards:** 6,894/4,953. **Par:** 72/72. **Course Rating:** 73.1/68.1.
Slope: 127/120. **Green Fee:** $50. **Cart Fee:** $30/Cart. **Walking Policy:** Unrestricted walking.
Walkability: 2. **Opened:** 1970. **Architect:** Frank Duane. **Season:** April-Dec. **High:** May-Sept. **To
obtain tee times:** Call golf shop. **Misc:** Reduced fees (twilight, seniors), range (mats), BF, FF.
Reader Comments: Like this very much ... Excellent facility ... Interesting holes, a little slow ...
Requires some iron tee shots ... Nice course, well maintained.

★★ **SPRAIN LAKE GOLF CLUB**
PU-290 Grassy Sprain Rd., Yonkers, 10710, Westchester County, (914)779-9827, 10 miles
from New York City. **Facility Holes:** 18. **Yards:** 6,010/5,500. **Par:** 70/71. **Course Rating:**
68.0/70.2. **Slope:** 113/115. **Green Fee:** $35/$45. **Cart Fee:** $24/Cart. **Walking Policy:**
Unrestricted walking. **Walkability:** 3. **Opened:** 1940. **Architect:** Tom Winton. **Season:** April-Dec.
High: April-Sept. **To obtain tee times:** Call up to 7 days in advance. **Miscellaneous:** Reduced
fees (weekdays, twilight, seniors, juniors), BF, FF.

★★★½ **SPRING LAKE GOLF CLUB**
PU-30 East Bartlett Rd., Middle Island, 11953, Suffolk County, (631)924-5115, 45 miles from
New York City. **Web:** www.usegolf.com. **Facility Holes:** 27. **Yards:** 7,048/5,732. **Par:** 72/72.

Course Rating: 73.2/70.0. Slope: 128/120. Green Fee: $25/$40. Cart Fee: $30/Cart. Walking Policy: Walking at certain times. Walkability: 3. Opened: 1967. Architect: Jurgens & Company. Season: Year-round. High: April-Oct. To obtain tee times: Call up to 10 days in advance. Miscellaneous: Reduced fees (weekdays, twilight), metal spikes, range (grass/mats), credit cards (MC, V, AE), BF, FF.

Reader Comments: Country club feel … Long hard course … Greens usually perfect … Big dog gets a workout here … Best in Long Island, kept like a private club … Another excellent course to be played … My favorite golf course.

Special Notes: Also has a 9-hole Sandpiper Course.

SPRINGBROOK GOLF COURSE
PU-827 Old State Rd., Sterling, 13156, Oswego County, (315)947-6115. Facility Holes: 18. Yards: 2,628/2,276. Par: 35/35. Green Fee: $15/$16. Cart Fee: $17/Cart. Opened: 1995. Architect: Alan Tomlinson. Season: April-Nov. High: July-Aug. To obtain tee times: Call golf shop. Miscellaneous: Reduced fees (seniors), range (mats), BF, FF.

★★★ ST. LAWRENCE UNIVERSITY GOLF & COUNTRY CLUB
PU-90 E. Main St., Canton, 13617, St. Lawrence County, (315)386-4600, 68 miles from Ottawa, Canada. Facility Holes: 18. Yards: 6,694/5,430. Par: 72/73. Course Rating: 72.1/73.1. Slope: 122/120. Green Fee: $20/$24. Cart Fee: $24/Cart. Walking Policy: Unrestricted walking. Walkability: 2. Opened: 1936. Architect: Devereux Emmet. Season: April-Nov. High: May-Aug. To obtain tee times: Call up to 8 days in advance. Miscellaneous: Reduced fees (guests), range (grass/mats), lodging (96 rooms), credit cards (MC, V), BF, FF.

Reader Comments: Some tight driving holes … A real gem, great value … A north country must … Great layout through old white pine growth … Course due for upgrade … Great condition, enjoyable to play … Twice-a-year type course.

★★★½ STADIUM GOLF CLUB
PU-333 Jackson Ave., Schenectady, 12304, Schenectady County, (518)374-9104, 15 miles from Albany. Facility Holes: 18. Yards: 5,959/5,423. Par: 71/71. Course Rating: 69.5/68.5. Slope: 113/106. Green Fee: $22/$26. Cart Fee: $24/Cart. Walking Policy: Unrestricted walking. Walkability: 2. Opened: 1966. Architect: Douglas Hennel. Season: April-Nov. High: May-Sept. To obtain tee times: Call up to 2 days in advance. Miscellaneous: Reduced fees (juniors), range (grass), credit cards (MC, V), BF, FF.

Reader Comments: Great course maintenance … Wide open, only need one ball … Good drainage for early season play … Well kept … Best of the lot … Don't miss this one … Great value.

STAMFORD GOLF COURSE
SP-Taylor Rd., Stamford, 12167, Delaware County, (607)652-7398, 55 miles from Albany. Facility Holes: 18. Yards: 6,501/5,700. Par: 70/73. Course Rating: 69.9. Slope: 111. Green Fee: $22/$30. Cart Fee: $30/Cart. Walking Policy: Unrestricted walking. Opened: 1894. Architect: John Farmer. Season: April-Oct. High: June-Aug. To obtain tee times: Call golf shop. Miscellaneous: Reduced fees (weekdays), range (grass), credit cards (MC, V), BF, FF.

STONE DOCK GOLF COURSE
PU-Berme Rd., High Falls, 12440, Ulster County, (845)687-7107, 15 miles from Kingston. Facility Holes: 9. Yards: 6,500/5,025. Par: 36/36. Course Rating: 70.0/68.0. Slope: 118/111. Green Fee: $18/$22. Cart Fee: $20/Cart. Walking Policy: Unrestricted walking. Walkability: 2. Opened: 1969. Architect: Tom Davenport. Season: April-Nov. High: June-Aug. To obtain tee times: Call golf shop. Miscellaneous: Reduced fees (juniors), credit cards (MC, V, D), FF.

STONEBRIDGE GOLF & COUNTRY CLUB
PU-Graffenburg Rd., New Hardford, 13413, Oneida County, (315)733-5663. Facility Holes: 18. Yards: 6,835/5,775. Par: 72/72. Course Rating: 70.3/72.9. Slope: 120/121. Green Fee: $14/$16. Cart Fee: $20/Cart. Opened: 1955. Season: April-Nov. To obtain tee times: Call golf shop. Miscellaneous: Reduced fees (twilight), range (grass/mats).

★★½ STONEBRIDGE GOLF LINKS & COUNTRY CLUB
SP-Veterans Memorial Hwy., Hauppauge, 11788, Suffolk County, (631)724-7500, 30 miles from New York City. E-mail: stonebridgeglcc@aol.com. Facility Holes: 18. Yards: 6,245/4,780. Par: 70/70. Course Rating: 70.0/67.8. Slope: 124/114. Green Fee: $47/$75. Cart Fee: Included in green fee. Walking Policy: Mandatory carts. Walkability: 3. Opened: 2000. Architect: Gil Hanse/George Bahto. Season: Year-round. High: May-Sept. To obtain tee times: Call up to 7 days in advance. Miscellaneous: Reduced fees (weekdays, twilight), range (mats), credit cards (MC, V, AE), BF, FF.

STONEHEDGES GOLF COURSE
PU-Lick & Stevens Rds., Groton, 13073, Tompkins County, (607)898-3754. Facility Holes: 18. Yards: 6,396/5,048. Par: 72/73. Course Rating: 71.7/68.9. Slope: 122/114. Green Fee:

$15/$17. **Cart Fee:** $20/Cart. **Season:** April-Nov. **To obtain tee times:** Call golf shop. **Miscellaneous:** Reduced fees (weekdays).

★★★ STONY FORD GOLF COURSE

PU-211 Rte. 416, Montgomery, 12549, Orange County, (914)457-1532, 60 miles from New York City. **Facility Holes:** 18. **Yards:** 6,551/5,856. **Par:** 72/73. **Course Rating:** 72.4/74.0. **Slope:** 129/129. **Green Fee:** $14/$36. **Cart Fee:** $11/Person. **Walking Policy:** Unrestricted walking. **Walkability:** 3. **Opened:** 1968. **Architect:** Hal Purdy. **Season:** March-Dec. **High:** May-Oct. **To obtain tee times:** Call golf shop. **Miscellaneous:** Reduced fees (weekdays, twilight, seniors, juniors), range (grass), BF, FF.
Reader Comments: A great municipal track, residents pay no more than $18 on weekends … Great views … Pro is a great guy … Walking allowed, but heavily played … Some great holes.

SULLIVAN COUNTY COUNTRY CLUB

SP-Route 52, Liberty, 12754, Sullivan County, (845)292-9584, 60 miles from Newburgh. **Facility Holes:** 18. **Yards:** 6,651/5,822. **Par:** 72/78. **Course Rating:** 69.5. **Slope:** 120. **Green Fee:** $15/$20. **Cart Fee:** $22/Cart. **Walking Policy:** Unrestricted walking. **Walkability:** 3. **Opened:** 1925. **Season:** May-Nov. **To obtain tee times:** Call golf shop. **Miscellaneous:** FF.

★★½ SUNKEN MEADOW STATE PARK GOLF CLUB

PU-Sunken Meadow State Park, Rte. 25A, Kings Park, 11754, Suffolk County, (631)544-0036, 40 miles from New York City. **Facility Holes:** 27. **Green Fee:** $22/$27. **Cart Fee:** $13/Person. **Walking Policy:** Unrestricted walking. **Opened:** 1964. **Architect:** Alfred H. Tull. **Season:** Year-round. **To obtain tee times:** Call up to 3 days in advance. **Miscellaneous:** Reduced fees (seniors), range (mats), credit cards (MC, V, AE, D), BF, FF.
BLUE/GREEN (18 Combo)
Yards: 6,185/5,638. **Par:** 71/71. **Course Rating:** 68.7/70.4. **Slope:** 111/112. **Walkability:** 2.
BLUE/RED (18 Combo)
Yards: 6,100/5,627. **Par:** 71/71. **Course Rating:** 68.2/70.0. **Slope:** 112/112. **Walkability:** 3.
RED/GREEN (18 Combo)
Yards: 6,165/5,567. **Par:** 72/72. **Course Rating:** 68.5/70.3. **Slope:** 112/113. **Walkability:** 3.

SUNSET VALLEY GOLF COURSE

PU-724 Hunt Rd., Lakewood, 14750, Chautauqua County, (716)664-7508. **Facility Holes:** 18. **Yards:** 2,807/2,582. **Par:** 54/54. **Green Fee:** $11/$12. **Cart Fee:** $20/Person. **Opened:** 1960. **Season:** Year-round. **To obtain tee times:** Call golf shop. **Misc:** Reduced fees (seniors).

SWAN LAKE COUNTRY CLUB

SP-Mt. Hope Rd., Swan Lake, 12783, Sullivan County, (845)292-0323, (888)254-5818. **E-mail:** central@nymetro.net. **Web:** www.swanlakegolf&countryclub.com. **Facility Holes:** 18. **Yards:** 6,820/5,339. **Par:** 72/72. **Course Rating:** 71.8/70.2. **Slope:** 132/118. **Green Fee:** $40/$55. **Cart Fee:** $15/Person. **Opened:** 1950. **Season:** April-Nov. **To obtain tee times:** Call golf shop. **Miscellaneous:** Reduced fees (seniors), range (mats), lodging (225 rooms), credit cards (MC, V, AE, D).

★★★★ SWAN LAKE GOLF CLUB

PU-373 River Rd., Manorville, 11949, Suffolk County, (516)369-1818, 10 miles from Riverhead. **Facility Holes:** 18. **Yards:** 7,011/5,245. **Par:** 72/72. **Course Rating:** 72.5/69.0. **Slope:** 121/112. **Green Fee:** $33/$37. **Cart Fee:** $30/Person. **Walking Policy:** Walking at certain times. **Walkability:** 1. **Opened:** 1979. **Architect:** Don Jurgens. **Season:** Year-round. **To obtain tee times:** Call golf shop. **Misc:** Reduced fees (twilight), credit cards (MC, V, AE), FF.
Reader Comments: Relatively good course conditions year round … Course was very beautiful … Great course for high handicapper … Great place for outings … Keep it in the short grass, a few hard water holes.

SYCAMORE COUNTRY CLUB

PU-Route 143 Tompkins Rd., Ravena, 12143, Albany County, (518)756-6635. **Facility Holes:** 18. **Yards:** 6,528/5,607. **Par:** 71/71. **Course Rating:** 70.1/70.7. **Slope:** 115/114. **Green Fee:** $18/$21. **Cart Fee:** $22/Cart. **Opened:** 1971. **Architect:** Frank Duane. **Season:** March-Nov. **To obtain tee times:** Call golf shop. **Miscellaneous:** Reduced fees (seniors), range (grass).

TALLGRASS GOLF CLUB

PU-24 Cooper St., Shoreham, 11786, Suffolk County, (631)209-9359, 65 miles from New York City. **E-mail:** tobrien@eaglgolf.com. **Web:** www.eaglgolf.com. **Facility Holes:** 18. **Yards:** 6,587/5,044. **Par:** 71/71. **Course Rating:** 71.8/68.6. **Slope:** 127/116. **Fee:** $30/$67. **Cart Fee:** $15/Person. **Walking Policy:** Walking at certain times. **Walkability:** 2. **Opened:** 2000. **Architect:** Gil Hanse. **Season:** Year-round. **High:** April-Sept. **To obtain tee times:** Call up to 7 days in advance. **Misc:** Reduced fees (weekdays, twilight, seniors, juniors), range (grass/mats), cards (MC, V, AE), BF, FF.

TANNER VALLEY GOLF COURSE
SP-4040 Tanner Rd., Syracuse, 13215, Onondaga County, (315)492-8113, 5 miles from Syracuse. **Facility Holes:** 18. **Yards:** 6,081. **Par:** 71. **Course Rating:** 68.4. **Slope:** 116. **Green Fee:** $12/$20. **Cart Fee:** $20/Person. **Walking Policy:** Unrestricted walking. **Walkability:** 2. **Opened:** 1966. **Architect:** Burt Brothers. **Season:** April-Nov. **High:** May-Sept. **To obtain tee times:** Call up to 7 days in advance. **Miscellaneous:** Reduced fees (weekdays, seniors, juniors), range (grass), BF, FF.

★★★½ TARRY BRAE GOLF CLUB
PU-Pleasant Valley Rd., South Fallsburg, 12779, Sullivan County, (914)434-2620, 10 miles from Montecello. **Web:** www.tarrybrae.com. **Facility Holes:** 18. **Yards:** 6,965/5,825. **Par:** 72/76. **Course Rating:** 73.4/72.2. **Slope:** 129/126. **Green Fee:** $20/$30. **Cart Fee:** $15/Person. **Walking Policy:** Walking at certain times. **Walkability:** 4. **Opened:** 1962. **Architect:** William F. Mitchell. **Season:** April-Nov. **High:** July-Sept. **To obtain tee times:** Call up to 3 days in advance. **Miscellaneous:** Reduced fees (weekdays, twilight, juniors), range (grass/mats), credit cards (MC, V), BF, FF.
Reader Comments: Great local course ... Very nice ... The layout is good, but the course needs a lot of work, especially the greens ... Nice course ... Tough greens, narrow fairways, great fun.

★★★½ TENNANAH LAKE GOLF & TENNIS CLUB
SP-100 Belle Rd., Suite 2, Roscoe, 12776, Sullivan County, (607)498-5502, (888)561-3935, 60 miles from Middletown. **E-mail:** tlgtgolf@aol.com. **Web:** www.tennanah.com. **Facility Holes:** 18. **Yards:** 6,546/5,164. **Par:** 72/72. **Course Rating:** 72.1/70.1. **Slope:** 128/120. **Green Fee:** $32/$36. **Cart Fee:** $15/Cart. **Walking Policy:** Walking at certain times. **Walkability:** 4. **Opened:** 1911. **Architect:** Alfred H. Tull. **Season:** April-Oct. **To obtain tee times:** Call golf shop. **Miscellaneous:** Reduced fees (weekdays, guests, twilight, seniors, juniors), range (grass/mats), lodging (24 rooms), credit cards (MC, V, AE), BF, FF.
Reader Comments: Nice mountain course ... Good value with the stay-and-play package ... A challenging layout, hilly, narrow fairways ... Located in the western end of the Catskills ... Best trout fishing east of Mississippi ... Tight.

★★★★ TERRY HILLS GOLF COURSE
PU-5122 Clinton St. Rd., Batavia, 14020, Genesee County, (716)343-0860, (800)825-8633, 30 miles from Buffalo. **E-mail:** terryhills@aol.com. **Web:** www.terryhills.com. **Facility Holes:** 27. **Green Fee:** $18/$26. **Cart Fee:** $12/Person. **Walking Policy:** Walking at certain times. **Walkability:** 4. **Opened:** 1930. **Architect:** Parker Terry/Mark Mungeam/Ed Ault. **Season:** March-Nov. **High:** May-Sept. **To obtain tee times:** Call up to 7 days in advance. **Miscellaneous:** Reduced fees (twilight, seniors, juniors), credit cards (MC, V, AE, D), BF, FF.
EAST/SOUTH (18 Combo)
Yards: 6,140/5,169. **Par:** 72/72. **Course Rating:** 68.3/68.3. **Slope:** 118/111.
NORTH/EAST (18 Combo)
Yards: 6,280/5,240. **Par:** 72/72. **Course Rating:** 68.8/68.3. **Slope:** 118/111.
SOUTH/NORTH (18 Combo)
Yards: 6,358/5,177. **Par:** 72/72. **Course Rating:** 69.4/67.4. **Slope:** 115/107.
Reader Comments: They squeezed in a new 9 with rolling fairways and small greens ... One of the nicest public courses around ... Everything's good about it ... Great course for seniors, great value ... Short course with small greens.

★★★★½ THENDARA GOLF CLUB *Value*
SP-Fifth Street, Thendara, 13472, Herkimer County, (315)369-3136, 55 miles from Utica. **Facility Holes:** 18. **Yards:** 6,435/5,757. **Par:** 72/73. **Course Rating:** 70.2/72.8. **Slope:** 124/121. **Green Fee:** $30. **Cart Fee:** $20/Cart. **Walking Policy:** Walking at certain times. **Walkability:** 3. **Opened:** 1921. **Architect:** Donald Ross. **Season:** May-Oct. **High:** July-Sept. **To obtain tee times:** Call golf shop. **Miscellaneous:** Reduced fees (twilight), range (grass/mats), credit cards (MC, V), BF, FF.
Reader Comments: Two distinctly different 9s ... A Donald Ross jewel in the Adirondacks ... Very nice course, great condition ... An old cours, immaculate ... Front 9 open, back 9 tight ... One of the nicest courses in the Adirondacks ... Pro course ... Beautiful mountain setting.

★★½ THOMAS CARVEL COUNTRY CLUB
PU-Ferris Rd., Pine Plains, 12567, Dutchess County, (518)398-7101, 30 miles from Poughkeepsie. **Facility Holes:** 18. **Yards:** 7,080/5,066. **Par:** 73/75. **Course Rating:** 73.5/69.0. **Slope:** 127/115. **Green Fee:** $20/$45. **Cart Fee:** Included in green fee. **Walking Policy:** Mandatory carts. **Walkability:** 5. **Opened:** 1968. **Architect:** William F. Mitchell. **Season:** April-Nov. **High:** June-Sept. **To obtain tee times:** Call up to 7 days in advance. **Miscellaneous:** Reduced fees (weekdays, twilight, seniors), range (mats), credit cards (MC, V, AE), BF, FF.

THOUSAND ISLANDS GOLF CLUB
PU-County Rd. 100, Wellesley Island E., Wellesley Island, 13640, Jefferson County, (315)482-9454, 35 miles from Watertown. **E-mail:** tigolf@thousandislands.com. **Web:** thousandislands.com/tigolfclub. **Facility Holes:** 36. **Walking Policy:** Walking at certain times. **Season:** April-Oct. **High:** June-Sept. **To obtain tee times:** Call golf shop. **Miscellaneous:** Reduced fees (weekdays, guests, twilight, juniors), range (grass), lodging (20 rooms), credit cards (MC, V, AE, D).
LAKE COURSE (18)
Yards: 5,005/4,425. **Par:** 70/70. **Green Fee:** $18/$23. **Cart Fee:** Included in green fee. **Walkability:** 4. **Opened:** 1990.
★★½ OLD COURSE (18)
Yards: 6,402/5,240. **Par:** 72/74. **Course Rating:** 69.2/68.5. **Slope:** 118/114. **Green Fee:** $28/$33. **Cart Fee:** $14/Person. **Walkability:** 3. **Opened:** 1894. **Architect:** Seth Raynor.

TICONDEROGA GOLF COURSE
PU-9N South, Hague Rd., Ticonderoga, 12883, Essex County, (518)585-2801. **Facility Holes:** 18. **Yards:** 6,273/5,015. **Par:** 71/72. **Course Rating:** 69.7/69.4. **Slope:** 120/115. **Green Fee:** $27. **Cart Fee:** $12/Person. **Opened:** 1929. **Architect:** Seymour Dunn. **Season:** April-Oct. **To obtain tee times:** Call golf shop. **Miscellaneous:** Reduced fees (twilight),cards (MC, V, AE, D).

★★ TIMBER POINT GOLF COURSE
PU-Great River Rd., Great River, 11739, Suffolk County, (631)581-2401, 50 miles from New York City. **E-mail:** acgolfinc@aol.com. **Facility Holes:** 27. **Green Fee:** $9/$35. **Cart Fee:** $27/Cart. **Walking Policy:** Unrestricted walking. **Walkability:** 1. **Opened:** 1927. **Architect:** H.S. Colt and C.H. Alison/William Mitche. **Season:** Year-round. **High:** June-Aug. **To obtain tee times:** Call golf shop. **Miscellaneous:** Reduced fees (weekdays, twilight, seniors, juniors), range (mats).
RED/BLUE (18 Combo)
Yards: 6,642/5,455. **Par:** 72/72. **Course Rating:** 72.3/71.7. **Slope:** 123/119.
RED/WHITE (18 Combo)
Yards: 6,441/5,358. **Par:** 72/72. **Course Rating:** 70.8/70.5. **Slope:** 119/117.
WHITE/BLUE (18 Combo)
Yards: 6,525/5,367. **Par:** 72/72. **Course Rating:** 71.7/71.2. **Slope:** 122/119.

★★★ TIOGA COUNTRY CLUB
SP-151 Ro-Ki Blvd, Nichols, 13812, Tioga County, (607)699-3881, 25 miles from Binghamton. **E-mail:** tiogacc@clarityconnect.com. **Facility Holes:** 18. **Yards:** 6,080/5,193. **Par:** 71/72. **Course Rating:** 69.4/70.2. **Slope:** 123/119. **Green Fee:** $26/$33. **Cart Fee:** Included in green fee. **Walking Policy:** Unrestricted walking. **Walkability:** 5. **Opened:** 1967. **Architect:** Hal Purdy. **Season:** April-Nov. **High:** May-Sept. **To obtain tee times:** Call up to 4 days in advance. **Miscellaneous:** Reduced fees (twilight), metal spikes, credit cards (MC, V), BF, FF.
Reader Comments: Unique layout, 5 par 5s, 6 par 3s ... Interesting layout, well kept ... Moderately priced, good variety.

★★½ TOMASSO'S CHEMUNG GOLF COURSE
PU-5799 Country Rd. #60, Waverly, 14892, Chemung County, (607)565-2323, 12 miles from Elmira. **Facility Holes:** 18. **Yards:** 6,000/5,525. **Par:** 69/69. **Course Rating:** 66.3/66.0. **Green Fee:** $13/$15. **Walking Policy:** Unrestricted walking. **Walkability:** 1. **Opened:** 1962. **Architect:** Lou Tomasso. **Season:** Year-round. **To obtain tee times:** Call golf shop. **Miscellaneous:** Reduced fees (weekdays, twilight, seniors), metal spikes, credit cards (MC, V, AE), FF.

★★★★ TOWN OF COLONIE GOLF COURSE *Value*
PU-418 Consaul Rd., Schenectady, 12304, Schenectady County, (518)374-4181. **Facility Holes:** 27. **Green Fee:** $20/$24. **Cart Fee:** $20/Cart. **Opened:** 1969. **Architect:** Willard Byrd/Robert Trent Jones. **Season:** April-Oct. **To obtain tee times:** Call golf shop. **Miscellaneous:** Reduced fees (seniors), range (grass).
BLUE/RED COURSE (18 Combo)
Yards: 6,709/5,648. **Par:** 72/72. **Course Rating:** 71.8/71.4. **Slope:** 120/120.
RED/WHITE COURSE (18 Combo)
Yards: 6,704/5,628. **Par:** 72/72. **Course Rating:** 71.7/71.3. **Slope:** 120/120.
WHITE/BLUE COURSE (18 Combo)
Yards: 6,845/5,810. **Par:** 72/72. **Course Rating:** 72.5/72.3. **Slope:** 120/120.
Reader Comments: Course gets a lot of play ... Play with a retiree who knows everyone ... Best town-owned public course in area ... Good public course ... Will play again.

★★★ TOWN OF WALLKILL GOLF CLUB
PU-40 Sands Rd., Middletown, 10940, Orange County, (845)361-1022, 55 miles from New York City. **E-mail:** golf760@aol.com. **Facility Holes:** 18. **Yards:** 6,437/5,171. **Par:** 72/72.

Course Rating: 70.6/69.7. **Slope:** 128/122. **Green Fee:** $12/$40. **Cart Fee:** $26/Cart. **Walking Policy:** Unrestricted walking. **Walkability:** 4. **Opened:** 1991. **Architect:** Steve Esposito. **Season:** March-Dec. **To obtain tee times:** Call up to 7 days in advance. **Miscellaneous:** Reduced fees (weekdays, twilight, seniors, juniors), range ,BF, FF.
Reader Comments: Nice layout … Keep driver in bag … Greens difficult to hold … Very good public course … Bring a snack, you will be out on there awhile … Enjoyable, scenic.

TOWNE ISLE GOLF COURSE
PU-6113 Town Island Rd., Kirkville, 13082, Onondaga County, (315)656-3522, 12 miles from Syracuse. **E-mail:** djw863@aol.com. **Facility Holes:** 18. **Yards:** 6,955/5,755. **Par:** 70/73. **Course Rating:** 72.0. **Slope:** 111. **Green Fee:** $13/$15. **Cart Fee:** $20/Cart. **Walking Policy:** Unrestricted walking. **Walkability:** 1. **Opened:** 1958. **Architect:** Bill Grygiel Sr. **Season:** March-Nov. **High:** May-Aug. **To obtain tee times:** Call up to 7 days in advance. **Miscellaneous:** Reduced fees (weekdays), range (grass), FF.

★★★½ TRI COUNTY COUNTRY CLUB
SP-Rte. 39, Forestville, 14062, Chautauqua County, (716)965-9723, 50 miles from Buffalo. **Facility Holes:** 18. **Yards:** 6,639/5,574. **Par:** 71/72. **Course Rating:** 70.9/71.0. **Slope:** 118/113. **Green Fee:** $24/$27. **Cart Fee:** $11/Person. **Walking Policy:** Unrestricted walking. **Walkability:** 4. **Opened:** 1924. **Architect:** Al Shart. **Season:** April-Oct. **High:** July-Aug. **To obtain tee times:** Call golf shop. **Miscellaneous:** Reduced fees (weekdays), range, credit cards (MC, V).
Reader Comments: Long from the blue, great pace to play. Nice grillroom … Fun course! … Not your average flat course … A gem, tough greens … Pretty course, kept in good shape, best time to play in fall … Good layout.

TRIPLE CREEK GOLF COURSE
SP-8793 SR 408, Nunda, 14517, Livingston County, (716)468-2116, 45 miles from Rochester. **E-mail:** smarsh6465@aol.com. **Facility Holes:** 18. **Yards:** 6,100/4,800. **Par:** 70/70. **Course Rating:** 67.7/70.5. **Slope:** 117/110. **Green Fee:** $20/Cart. **Walking Policy:** Unrestricted walking. **Walkability:** 3. **Opened:** 1966. **Architect:** Freeman Barber/Scott Marsh. **Season:** April-Nov. **High:** May-Sept. **To obtain tee times:** Call up to 7 days in advance. **Miscellaneous:** Reduced fees (weekdays, seniors, juniors), range (grass/mats), credit cards (MC, V), BF, FF.

TRUMANSBURG GOLF COURSE
PU-23 Halsey St., Trumansburg, 14886, Tompkins County, (607)387-8844, 12 miles from Ithaca. **Web:** www.trumansburggolf.com. **Facility Holes:** 18. **Yards:** 6,373/4,963. **Par:** 72/72. **Course Rating:** 70.6/68.2. **Slope:** 122/115. **Green Fee:** $17/$19. **Cart Fee:** $22/Cart. **Walking Policy:** Unrestricted walking. **Walkability:** 3. **Opened:** 1969. **Season:** April-Nov. **High:** June-Aug. **To obtain tee times:** Call golf shop. **Miscellaneous:** Reduced fees (weekdays, seniors), credit cards (MC, V, AE), BF, FF.

TUPPER LAKE COUNTRY CLUB
PU-Country Club Rd., Tupper Lake, 12986, Franklin County, (518)359-3701, 120 miles from Albany. **Facility Holes:** 18. **Yards:** 6,254/5,389. **Par:** 71/71. **Green Fee:** $24. **Cart Fee:** $24/Cart. **Walking Policy:** Unrestricted walking. **Walkability:** 3. **Opened:** 1932. **Architect:** Donald Ross. **Season:** April-Oct. **High:** July-Aug. **To obtain tee times:** Call up to 4 days in advance. **Miscellaneous:** Range (mats), credit cards (MC, V), BF, FF.

TURIN HIGHLANDS GOLF COURSE
PU-East Rd., Turin, 13473, Lewis County, (315)348-9912. **Facility Holes:** 18. **Yards:** 6,552/5,639. **Par:** 72/72. **Course Rating:** 72.0/72.0. **Slope:** 114. **Green Fee:** $17. **Cart Fee:** $20/Cart. **Opened:** 1969. **Architect:** William Harries. **Season:** May-Oct. **To obtain tee times:** Call golf shop. **Miscellaneous:** Range (grass), credit cards (MC, V).

TWIN BROOKS GOLF COURSE
PU-Franklin Rd., Waddington, 13694, St. Lawrence County, (315)388-4480. **Facility Holes:** 18. **Yards:** 6,353/5,247. **Par:** 71/71. **Green Fee:** $12/$15. **Cart Fee:** $16/Cart. **Opened:** 1964. **Architect:** Red Thomas. **Season:** April-Nov. **To obtain tee times:** Call golf shop.

TWIN HICKORY GOLF COURSE
SP-1799 turnpike Rd., Hornell, 14843, Steuben County, (607)324-1441. **Facility Holes:** 18. **Yards:** 6,287/4,910. **Par:** 72/72. **Course Rating:** 70.5/69.5. **Slope:** 114/112. **Green Fee:** $13/$15. **Cart Fee:** $10/Person. **Opened:** 1965. **Architect:** John Sherburne. **Season:** April-Dec. **To obtain tee times:** Call golf shop.

★★★½ TWIN HILLS GOLF COURSE
PU-5719 Ridge Rd. W., Spencerport, 14559, Monroe County, (716)352-4800, 15 miles from

Rochester. **Facility Holes:** 18. **Yards:** 6,360/4,670. **Par:** 71/71. **Course Rating:** 69.1/66.8. **Slope:** 110/114. **Green Fee:** $20/$25. **Cart Fee:** $22/Cart. **Walking Policy:** Unrestricted walking. **Walkability:** 3. **Opened:** 1970. **Architect:** Pete Craig. **Season:** April-Nov. **To obtain tee times:** Call up to 5 days in advance. **Miscellaneous:** Reduced fees (weekdays, seniors), range (grass), credit cards (MC, V, D), FF.

Reader Comments: Some blind tee shots … Long holes & good sized greens … Very well-kept public course … Short, but challenging … A bit overpriced, nice fairways … Excellent greens, a great public course.

TWIN PONDS GOLF & COUNTRY CLUB
PU-169 Main St., New York Mills, 13417, Oneida County, (315)736-0550. **Facility Holes:** 18. **Yards:** 6,205/5,765. **Par:** 70/73. **Course Rating:** 67.4/70.7. **Slope:** 106/112. **Green Fee:** $15/$19. **Cart Fee:** $11/Person. **Walking Policy:** Unrestricted walking. **Season:** March-Oct. **High:** June-Aug. **To obtain tee times:** Call up to 3 days in advance. **Miscellaneous:** Credit cards (MC, V, AE, D), FF.

★★ VALLEY VIEW GOLF CLUB
PU-620 Memorial Pkwy., Utica, 13501, Oneida County, (315)732-8755. **Facility Holes:** 18. **Yards:** 6,583/5,942. **Par:** 71/73. **Course Rating:** 69.2/72.6. **Slope:** 118/116. **Green Fee:** $12/$15. **Cart Fee:** $11/Person. **Walking Policy:** Unrestricted walking. **Walkability:** 4. **Opened:** 1936. **Architect:** Robert Trent Jones. **Season:** April-Nov. **High:** April-Aug. **To obtain tee times:** Call golf shop. **Miscellaneous:** Reduced fees (twilight), range (grass).

★★ VAN CORTLANDT PARK GOLF CLUB
PU-Van Cortlandt Park S. and Bailey Ave., Bronx, 10471, Bronx County, (718)543-4595, 5 miles from New York. **Web:** www.americangolf.com. **Facility Holes:** 18. **Yards:** 6,122/5,421. **Par:** 70/70. **Course Rating:** 68.9/73.0. **Slope:** 112/120. **Green Fee:** $19/$30. **Cart Fee:** $27/Cart. **Walking Policy:** Unrestricted walking. **Walkability:** 4. **Opened:** 1895. **Architect:** Tom Bendelow. **Season:** Year-round. **High:** April-Oct. **To obtain tee times:** Call up to 10 days in advance. **Miscellaneous:** Reduced fees (weekdays, twilight, seniors, juniors), metal spikes, credit cards (MC, V, AE, D), BF, FF.

★★½ VAN PATTEN GOLF COURSE
PU-Main St., Clifton Park, 12065, Saratoga County, (518)877-5400, 18 miles from Albany. **Facility Holes:** 27. **Green Fee:** $19/$23. **Cart Fee:** $11/Person. **Season:** April-Nov. **To obtain tee times:** Call golf shop.
RED/BLUE COURSE (18 Combo)
Yards: 6,195/5,260. **Par:** 70/70. **Course Rating:** 71.5/70.7. **Slope:** 120/115.
WHITE/BLUE COURSE (18 Combo)
Yards: 6,185/5,105. **Par:** 71/71. **Course Rating:** 70.8/69.3. **Slope:** 116/112.
WHITE/RED COURSE (18 Combo)
Yards: 6,630/5,515. **Par:** 72/72. **Course Rating:** 71.1/70.1. **Slope:** 121/113.

VICTOR HILLS GOLF CLUB
PU-1460 Brace Rd., Victor, 14564, Ontario County, (716)924-3480, 18 miles from Rochester. **Facility Holes:** 45. **Green Fee:** $21. **Cart Fee:** $20/Cart. **Walking Policy:** Unrestricted walking. **Opened:** 1973. **Architect:** Pete Craig. **High:** May-Sept. **To obtain tee times:** Call golf shop. **Miscellaneous:** Reduced fees (twilight), metal spikes, credit cards (MC, V).
★★★½ **NORTH COURSE** (18)
Yards: 6,440/6,454. **Par:** 72/72. **Course Rating:** 71.3/72.6. **Slope:** 119/117. **Walkability:** 3.
Reader Comments: Major drawback is heavy play, otherwise great, challenging … Great staff … Two great courses for the price … A bit too slow … Huge, slow greens … Hilly course.
★★★ **SOUTH COURSE** (18)
Yards: 6,663/5,670. **Par:** 72/72. **Course Rating:** 71.5/72.9. **Slope:** 121/119. **Walkability:** 2.
Reader Comments: Beautifully maintained, very professional staff … Major drawback is too crowded … A new 18 should speed up play … Two great courses for the price … Good greens, but play can be very slow, still a great value.
Special Notes: Also has a 9-hole executive course.

★★★½ VILLA ROMA COUNTRY CLUB
R-Villa Roma Rd., Callicoon, 12723, Sullivan County, (914)887-5097, (800)727-8455, 100 miles from New York City. **Facility Holes:** 18. **Yards:** 6,499/5,329. **Par:** 72/72. **Course Rating:** 70.9/70.3. **Slope:** 124/119. **Green Fee:** $50/$65. **Cart Fee:** Included in green fee. **Walking Policy:** Mandatory carts. **Walkability:** 3. **Opened:** 1987. **Architect:** David Postlethwaite. **Season:** April-Nov. **High:** June-Sept. **To obtain tee times:** Call golf shop. **Miscellaneous:** Reduced fees (weekdays, guests, twilight, seniors, juniors), range (grass), credit cards (MC, V, AE, D), BF, FF.
Reader Comments: Beautiful layout, tough greens … Awesome … Sidehills everywhere … Scenic course … Excellent course, tricky greens.

WA-NOA GOLF CLUB
SP-6920 Minoa-Bridgeport Rd., East Syracuse, 13057, Onondaga County, (315)656-8213.
Facility Holes: 18. **Yards:** 6,180/5,645. **Par:** 70/75. **Course Rating:** 68.5/71.0. **Slope:** 112/110.
Green Fee: $19. **Cart Fee:** $18/Cart. **Opened:** 1971. **Season:** March-Dec. **To obtain tee times:**
Call golf shop. **Miscellaneous:** Reduced fees (seniors, juniors), range (grass).

WALDEN OAKS GOLF COURSE
SP-3369 Walden Oaks Blvd., Cortland, 13045, Cortland County, (607)753-9452. **Facility
Holes:** 18. **Yards:** 6,229/5,662. **Par:** 71/72. **Green Fee:** $14/$17. **Cart Fee:** $10/Person.
Opened: 1993. **Season:** April-Dec. **To obtain tee times:** Call golf shop. **Miscellaneous:**
Reduced fees (seniors), range (grass), credit cards (MC, V).

★★½ **WATERTOWN GOLF CLUB**
SP-P.O. Box 927, Watertown, 13601, Jefferson County, (315)782-4040, 70 miles from
Syracuse. **Facility Holes:** 18. **Yards:** 6,309/5,492. **Par:** 72/73. **Course Rating:** 69.4/67.9. **Slope:**
113/114. **Green Fee:** $20. **Cart Fee:** $9/Cart. **Walking Policy:** Unrestricted walking. **Walkability:**
1. **Opened:** 1926. **Architect:** Geoffrey S. Cornish/James Huber. **Season:** April-Oct. **High:** June-
Aug. **To obtain tee times:** Call golf shop. **Miscellaneous:** Reduced fees (twilight), metal spikes,
range (grass), credit cards (MC, V, AE).

★★★★ **WAYNE HILLS COUNTRY CLUB**
SP-2250 Gannett Rd., Lyons, 14489, Wayne County, (315)946-6944, 30 miles from
Rochester. **Facility Holes:** 18. **Yards:** 6,854/5,556. **Par:** 72/73. **Course Rating:** 72.8/72.0.
Slope: 125/116. **Green Fee:** $33/$45. **Cart Fee:** Included in green fee. **Walking Policy:**
Mandatory carts. **Walkability:** 3. **Opened:** 1959. **Architect:** Lawrence Packard. **Season:** April-
Nov. **To obtain tee times:** Call up to 3 days in advance. **Miscellaneous:** Reduced fees (week-
days, twilight, juniors), range (grass), credit cards (MC, V), BF, FF.
Reader Comments: Pace of play was spectacular … Great golf course, some nice holes …
Excellent condition, great par 3s … Pretty course, challenging course … Great course, best-kept
secret in upstate NY.

WEBSTER GOLF CLUB
SP-440 Salt Rd., Webster, 14580, Monroe County, (716)265-1920, 10 miles from Rochester.
Web: www.webstergolf.com. **Facility Holes:** 36. **Season:** April-Nov. **High:** June-Aug. **To obtain
tee times:** Call golf shop. **Miscellaneous:** Metal spikes, range (grass), credit cards (MC, V),
BF, FF.
★★★½ **EAST COURSE** (18)
Yards: 7,089/5,710. **Par:** 71/73. **Course Rating:** 73.2/73.0. **Slope:** 128/121. **Green Fee:**
$21/$24. **Cart Fee:** $22/Person. **Walking Policy:** Walking at certain times. **Walkability:** 2.
Opened: 1957. **Architect:** James G. Harrison. **Miscellaneous:** Reduced fees (weekdays).
Reader Comments: Solid, good length, trouble for someone who hooks or slices … Excellent
greens and course conditions … Very flat, needs more bunkers … Very flat … Long holes, small
greens … Slow play on weekends.
★★½ **WEST COURSE** (18)
Yards: 6,003/5,400. **Par:** 70/70. **Course Rating:** 66.6/68.5. **Slope:** 106/108. **Green Fee:**
$15/$18. **Cart Fee:** $15/Person. **Walking Policy:** Unrestricted walking. **Walkability:** 1. **Opened:**
1974. **Architect:** Tom Murphy/Eddie Rieflin. **Miscellaneous:** Reduced fees (weekdays,
seniors, juniors).

★★★½ **WELLSVILLE COUNTRY CLUB**
SP-Riverside Dr, Wellsville, 14895, Allegany County, (716)593-6337, 30 miles from Orlean.
Web: www.wellsvillecountryclub.com. **Facility Holes:** 18. **Yards:** 6,253/5,527. **Par:** 71/72.
Course Rating: 71.5/70.4. **Slope:** 121/120. **Green Fee:** $30. **Cart Fee:** $12/Person. **Walking
Policy:** Unrestricted walking. **Walkability:** 1. **Opened:** 1911. **Season:** April-Nov. **To obtain tee
times:** Call up to 7 days in advance. **Miscellaneous:** Reduced fees (weekdays), range (grass),
credit cards (MC, V, AE), BF, FF.
Reader Comments: Excellent challenge … Fun on the right day … Excellent course with fast &
small greens … Short and simple, nice finisher, small greens and flat … Tough, tight course …
Good variety of holes … Best course in area.

★★½ **WEST POINT GOLF COURSE**
M-Route 218, Building 1230, West Point, 10996, Orange County, (845)938-2435, 45 miles
from New York City. **Facility Holes:** 18. **Yards:** 6,036/4,647. **Par:** 70/71. **Course Rating:**
70.0/67.5. **Slope:** 127/117. **Green Fee:** $32/$45. **Cart Fee:** $11/Person. **Walking Policy:**
Unrestricted walking. **Walkability:** 5. **Opened:** 1948. **Architect:** Robert Trent Jones. **Season:**
April-Nov. **High:** May-Aug. **To obtain tee times:** Call up to 3 days in advance. **Miscellaneous:**
Reduced fees (twilight, juniors), credit cards (MC, V), BF, FF.

★★★ WEST SAYVILLE GOLF CLUB
PU-Montauk Hwy., West Sayville, 11796, Suffolk County, (516)567-1704, 45 miles from New York City. **Facility Holes:** 18. **Yards:** 6,715/5,387. **Par:** 72/72. **Course Rating:** 72.5/71.2. **Slope:** 124/119. **Green Fee:** $22/$35. **Cart Fee:** $14/Person. **Walking Policy:** Unrestricted walking. **Walkability:** 1. **Opened:** 1968. **Architect:** William F. Mitchell. **Season:** March-Jan. **To obtain tee times:** Call up to 7 days in advance. **Miscellaneous:** Reduced fees (weekdays, twilight, seniors, juniors), range (grass/mats), credit cards (MC, V, D), BF, FF.
Reader Comments: Links-type, muni course by the water … County course … One of the better layouts on Long Island … Old-style course … Could use improvements … Another county course near ocean.

WESTERN TURNPIKE GOLF COURSE
SP-Western Ave., Guilderland, 12084, Albany County, (518)456-0786. **Web:** www.western-turnpike.com. **Facility Holes:** 27. **Green Fee:** $22/$25. **Cart Fee:** $24/Cart. **Architect:** James Thomson. **Season:** April-Dec. **To obtain tee times:** Call golf shop. **Miscellaneous:** Range (grass).
BLUE/RED COURSE (18 Combo)
Yards: 6,366/5,137. **Par:** 72/72. **Course Rating:** 70.6/69.0. **Slope:** 127/117.
BLUE/WHITE COURSE (18 Combo)
Yards: 5,978/4,981. **Par:** 72/72. **Course Rating:** 68.9/68.1. **Slope:** 123/118.
RED/WHITE COURSE (18 Combo)
Yards: 6,404/5,100. **Par:** 72/72. **Course Rating:** 71.3/68.7. **Slope:** 126/118.

★★½ WESTPORT COUNTRY CLUB
PU-Liberty St., Westport, 12993, Essex County, (518)962-4470, (800)600-6655, 90 miles from Montreal. **Facility Holes:** 18. **Yards:** 6,544/5,256. **Par:** 72/72. **Course Rating:** 71.5/70.5. **Slope:** 120/112. **Green Fee:** $25/$40. **Cart Fee:** $10/Person. **Walking Policy:** Walking at certain times. **Walkability:** 3. **Opened:** 1898. **Architect:** Tom Winton. **Season:** April-Oct. **High:** June-Aug. **To obtain tee times:** Call golf shop. **Miscellaneous:** Reduced fees (weekdays, guests, twilight, juniors), metal spikes, range (grass/mats), credit cards (MC, V, D), BF, FF.

WESTVALE GOLF CLUB
SP-100 Golf View Dr., Camillus, 13031, Onondaga County, (315)487-0131. **Facility Holes:** 18. **Yards:** 5,647/5,169. **Par:** 67/67. **Course Rating:** 66.2/67.5. **Slope:** 100/101. **Green Fee:** $13/$16. **Cart Fee:** $18/Cart. **Opened:** 1928. **Season:** March-Dec. **To obtain tee times:** Call golf shop. **Miscellaneous:** Reduced fees (weekdays, seniors).

WHISPERING HILLS GOLF COURSE
SP-1 Pine Alley, Conesus, 14435, Livingston County, (716)346-2100. **Facility Holes:** 18. **Yards:** 6,471/5,156. **Par:** 71/71. **Course Rating:** 70.9/68.9. **Slope:** 116/111. **Green Fee:** $17/$18. **Cart Fee:** $24/Cart. **Opened:** 1973. **Architect:** Joe Checho. **Season:** March-Nov. **To obtain tee times:** Call golf shop. **Miscellaneous:** Reduced fees (seniors, juniors), range (grass), credit cards (MC, V, AE, D).

★★★½ WHITEFACE CLUB ON LAKE PLACID
R-P.O. Box 231, Lake Placid, 12946, Essex County, (518)523-2551, (800)422-6757, 150 miles from Albany. **Web:** www.whitefaceclub.com. **Facility Holes:** 18. **Yards:** 6,490/5,635. **Par:** 72/74. **Course Rating:** 70.6/73.9. **Slope:** 123/125. **Green Fee:** $25/$36. **Cart Fee:** $30/Cart. **Walking Policy:** Unrestricted walking. **Walkability:** 3. **Opened:** 1898. **Architect:** John Van Kleek. **Season:** May-Oct. **High:** July-Sept. **To obtain tee times:** Call golf shop. **Miscellaneous:** Reduced fees (weekdays, guests, twilight, juniors), range (grass), credit cards (MC, V, AE, D), BF, FF.
Reader Comments: Short course, narrow, distance control a must here … Beautiful setting, well groomed, solid … Excellent mountain views … Plenty of dogleg lefts … Greens need more attention.

★★★ WILD WOOD COUNTRY CLUB
SP-1201 W. Rush Rd., Rush, 14543, Monroe County, (716)334-5860, 15 miles from Rochester. **Facility Holes:** 18. **Yards:** 6,431/5,368. **Par:** 71/72. **Course Rating:** 71.0/75.9. **Slope:** 127/129. **Green Fee:** $22/$24. **Cart Fee:** $11/Person. **Walking Policy:** Unrestricted walking. **Walkability:** 4. **Opened:** 1968. **Architect:** Pete Craig. **Season:** April-Nov. **To obtain tee times:** Call up to 7 days in advance. **Miscellaneous:** Reduced fees (seniors), range (grass), credit cards (MC, V), FF.
Reader Comments: Good course but pricey … Great short course, but tight and tricky … Could be challenging, good value … Crazy greens very hard to read … Played during wet spring, otherwise higher score.

★★★½ **WILLOWBROOK COUNTRY CLUB**
SP-4200 Lake Ave., Lockport, 14094, Niagara County, (716)434-0111, 15 miles from Buffalo.
Facility Holes: 27. **Green Fee:** $15/$25. **Cart Fee:** $12/Person. **Walking Policy:** Walking at certain times. **Walkability:** 3. **Opened:** 1956. **Architect:** George Graff/Jim Charbonneau. **Season:** March-Nov. **High:** May-Sept. **To obtain tee times:** Call up to 7 days in advance.
Miscellaneous: Reduced fees (weekdays, twilight, seniors, juniors), metal spikes, range (grass), credit cards (MC, V), FF.
NORTH/SOUTH (18 Combo)
Yards: 6,329/4,979. **Par:** 72/72. **Course Rating:** 70.0/67.8. **Slope:** 114/118.
NORTH/WEST (18 Combo)
Yards: 6,399/5,006. **Par:** 71/71. **Course Rating:** 70.3/68.3. **Slope:** 115/116.
SOUTH/WEST (18 Combo)
Yards: 6,100/4,713. **Par:** 71/71. **Course Rating:** 68.9/66.3. **Slope:** 112/112.
Reader Comments: Cost for seniors makes a great value, crowded … Very nice all-around experience, 27 holes gives them ability to accommodate large groups and still keep tee times … Good, they put money back into course for upgrade.

WILLOWBROOK GOLF CLUB
PU-25075 NYS Rte. 37, Watertown, 13601, Jefferson County, (315)782-8192, 2 miles from Watertown. **Facility Holes:** 27. **Green Fee:** $18. **Cart Fee:** $18/Cart. **Walking Policy:** Unrestricted walking. **Walkability:** 1. **Opened:** 1957. **Season:** April-Oct. **High:** June-Aug. **To obtain tee times:** Call up to 7 days in advance. **Miscellaneous:** Range (grass), credit cards (MC, V), BF, FF.
RED/YELLOW COURSE (18 Combo)
Yards: 6,450/5,447. **Par:** 72/74. **Course Rating:** 69.0/70.9. **Slope:** 104/111.
WHITE/RED COURSE (18 Combo)
Yards: 6,356/5,336. **Par:** 72/74. **Course Rating:** 68.4/70.2. **Slope:** 104/110.
YELLOW/WHITE COURSE (18 Combo)
Yards: 6,316/5,380. **Par:** 72/74. **Course Rating:** 68.8/69.9. **Slope:** 104/110.

WILLOWBROOK GOLF COURSE
PU-3267 NYS Rte. 215, Cortland, 13045, Cortland County, (607)756-7382. **Facility Holes:** 18. **Yards:** 6,020/5,080. **Par:** 70/70. **Course Rating:** 66.0/67.0. **Slope:** 110/108. **Green Fee:** $12/$15. **Cart Fee:** $22/Cart. **Opened:** 1928. **Season:** April-Nov. **To obtain tee times:** Call golf shop. **Miscellaneous:** Credit cards (MC, V).

WILLOWCREEK GOLF CLUB
SP-3069 SR 352, Big Flats, 14814, Chemung County, (607)562-8898, 5 miles from Corning. **E-mail:** willowcreekgolfclub@info.com. **Web:** www.willowcreekgolfclub.com. **Facility Holes:** 27. **Yards:** 6,820/5,400. **Par:** 72/72. **Course Rating:** 72.2/70.0. **Slope:** 126/121. **Green Fee:** $19. **Cart Fee:** $22/Cart. **Walking Policy:** Unrestricted walking. **Walkability:** 3. **Opened:** 1974. **Architect:** Robert Tallman. **Season:** March-Dec. **High:** May-Sept. **To obtain tee times:** Call up to 7 days in advance. **Miscellaneous:** Reduced fees (juniors), range (grass), credit cards (MC, V), BF, FF.

★★★½ **WINDHAM COUNTRY CLUB**
PU-36 South St., Windham, 12496, Greene County, (518)734-9910, 45 miles from Albany. **E-mail:** www.drarich299@aol.com. **Web:** www.windhamcountryclub.com. **Facility Holes:** 18. **Yards:** 6,088/4,876. **Par:** 71/72. **Course Rating:** 69.9/68.4. **Slope:** 127/114. **Green Fee:** $34/$43. **Cart Fee:** Included in green fee. **Walking Policy:** Walking at certain times. **Walkability:** 4. **Opened:** 1927. **Architect:** Seth Raynor. **Season:** April-Nov. **High:** June-Sept. **To obtain tee times:** Call golf shop. **Miscellaneous:** Reduced fees (weekdays, guests, twilight, seniors, juniors), credit cards (MC, V, AE), FF.
Reader Comments: Skied the mountain in February and played the course in June … Short mountain course, fun to play … Beautiful course, pace of play slow … Very nice … A little pricey.

WINDING BROOK COUNTRY CLUB
SP-2839 Rte. 203, Valatie, 12184, Columbia County, (518)758-9117. **Facility Holes:** 18. **Yards:** 6,614/5,855. **Par:** 72/72. **Course Rating:** 68.9/72.4. **Slope:** 110/121. **Green Fee:** $18/$20. **Cart Fee:** $20/Cart. **Opened:** 1962. **Architect:** Paul Roth. **Season:** Year-round. **To obtain tee times:** Call golf shop. **Miscellaneous:** Credit cards (MC, V).

WINDING HILLS GOLF COURSE
PU-1847 SR 17K, Montgomery, 12549, Orange County, (845)457-5908, 60 miles from New York City. **Facility Holes:** 18. **Yards:** 2,595/2,160. **Par:** 57/57. **Green Fee:** $15/$18. **Cart Fee:** $12/Cart. **Walking Policy:** Unrestricted walking. **Walkability:** 3. **Opened:** 1997. **Architect:** Steve Espisito. **Season:** March-Nov. **High:** June-Aug. **To obtain tee times:** Call golf shop. **Miscellaneous:** Reduced fees (weekdays), credit cards (MC, V, AE, D, DC), BF, FF.

WINDY HILLS GOLF COURSE
PU-219 Windy Hill Rd., Greenwich, 12834, Washington County, (518)692-4902, 13 miles from Saratoga. **Facility Holes:** 18. **Yards:** 6,062/5,470. **Par:** 71/71. **Course Rating:** 69.5/70.7. **Slope:** 117/114. **Green Fee:** $15. **Cart Fee:** $9/Person. **Walking Policy:** Unrestricted walking. **Walkability:** 3. **Opened:** 1995. **Architect:** Joseph Kehn. **Season:** April-Nov. **High:** May-Sept. **To obtain tee times:** Call up to 4 days in advance. **Miscellaneous:** Reduced fees (weekdays), credit cards (MC, V, D), BF, FF.

★★½ **WINGED PHEASANT GOLF LINKS**
SP-1475 Sand Hill Rd., Shortsville, 14548, Ontario County, (716)289-8846, 20 miles from Rochester. **Facility Holes:** 18. **Yards:** 6,400/5,835. **Par:** 70/72. **Course Rating:** 69.0/72.0. **Slope:** 118/119. **Green Fee:** $21/$23. **Cart Fee:** $24/Cart. **Walking Policy:** Walking at certain times. **Walkability:** 3. **Opened:** 1963. **Architect:** Pete Craig. **Season:** March-Nov. **High:** June-Aug. **To obtain tee times:** Call golf shop. **Miscellaneous:** Reduced fees (weekdays, twilight, seniors, juniors), range (grass/mats), credit cards (MC, V, AE, D).

WOODCREST GOLF CLUB
PU-Cheese Factory Rd., Chittenango, 13037, Madison County, (315)687-9401. **Facility Holes:** 18. **Yards:** 6,182/5,162. **Par:** 71/71. **Course Rating:** 68.5/69.0. **Slope:** 114/116. **Green Fee:** $16. **Cart Fee:** $18/Cart. **Opened:** 1991. **Season:** April-Oct. **To obtain tee times:** Call golf shop. **Miscellaneous:** Credit cards (MC, V).

WOODGATE PINES GOLF CLUB
PU-2965 Hayes Rd. W, Boonville, 13309, Oneida County, (315)942-5442, 35 miles from Utica. **Facility Holes:** 18. **Yards:** 5,731/4,550. **Par:** 70/70. **Green Fee:** $20/$22. **Cart Fee:** $22/Cart. **Opened:** 1928. **Season:** April-Nov. **High:** July-Aug. **To obtain tee times:** Call golf shop. **Miscellaneous:** Credit cards (MC, V, D), BF, FF.

WOODHAVEN GOLF COURSE
PU-169 Forest Ln., Oneonta, 13820, Otsego County, (607)433-2301, 50 miles from Binghamton. **Facility Holes:** 9. **Yards:** 4,988/4,332. **Par:** 68/68. **Course Rating:** 64.0. **Slope:** 106. **Green Fee:** $10/$15. **Cart Fee:** $12/Cart. **Season:** April-Nov. **To obtain tee times:** Call golf shop. **Miscellaneous:** Reduced fees (seniors), range (grass).

ANGEL'S TRACE GOLF LINKS
PU-1215 Angel's Club Dr. S.W., Sunset Beach, 28468, Brunswick County, (910)579-2277, (800)718-5733, 18 miles from N. Myrtle Beach. **E-mail:** angeltrace@2khiway.net. **Web:** www.golfangelstrace.com. **Facility Holes:** 36. **Green Fee:** $10/$55. **Walking Policy:** Mandatory carts. **Walkability:** 3. **Opened:** 1995. **Architect:** Clyde Johnston. **Season:** Year-round. **Miscellaneous:** Reduced fees (juniors), range (grass), credit cards (MC, V, AE), BF, FF.

★★★★ **NORTH COURSE** (18)
Yards: 6,640/4,524. **Par:** 72/72. **Course Rating:** 73.6/68.2. **Slope:** 139/118. **Cart Fee:** $20/Person. **High:** Feb.-April.
Reader Comments: Two excellent layouts ... Beautiful facility ... Well maintained ... Fun to play and bent-grass greens a plus ... Very good course, friendly folks, great price but slow play ... Fairway bunkers placed well, hit 3-wood all day.

★★★½ **SOUTH COURSE** (18)
Yards: 6,866/4,811. **Par:** 72/72. **Course Rating:** 74.1/67.7. **Slope:** 139/121. **Cart Fee:** $18/Person. **To obtain tee times:** Call golf shop.
Reader Comments: Good condition, considering the amount of rain in the area ... Nice layout, variety of holes, including elevation changes, water, woods ... Nice clubhouse and pro shop, would play this course again ... Tough, love it.

★★★½ **BALD HEAD ISLAND CLUB** *Pace*
R-P.O. Box 3070, Bald Head Island, 28461, Brunswick County, (910)457-7310, (800)234-1666, 30 miles from Wilmington. **Web:** baldheadisland.com. **Facility Holes:** 18. **Yards:** 6,855/4,810. **Par:** 72/72. **Course Rating:** 74.3/70.1. **Slope:** 139/117. **Green Fee:** $53/$85. **Cart Fee:** $17/Person. **Walking Policy:** Walking at certain times. **Walkability:** 2. **Opened:** 1975. **Architect:** George Cobb. **Season:** Year-round. **High:** May-Sept. **To obtain tee times:** Call up to 7 days in advance. **Miscellaneous:** Reduced fees (guests, juniors), range (grass), credit cards (MC, V, AE, D), BF, FF.
Reader Comments: A lot of movement, picturesque ... Always in great condition, 3-hour rounds ... Off the beaten track ... Worth the ferry ride ... Great test.

★★★½ **BAYONET AT PUPPY CREEK**
PU-349 S. Parker Church Rd., Raeford, 28736, Hoke County, (910)904-1500, (888)229-6638, 8 miles from Fayetteville. **E-mail:** bayonetpc@aol.com. **Web:** www.bayonetgolf.com. **Facility Holes:** 18. **Yards:** 7,036/4,453. **Par:** 72/72. **Course Rating:** 74.0/67.5. **Slope:** 134/115. **Green Fee:** $22/$34. **Cart Fee:** $12/Person. **Walking Policy:** Walking at certain times. **Walkability:** 3. **Opened:** 1995. **Architect:** Willard Byrd. **Season:** Year-round. **High:** April-May. **To obtain tee times:** Call golf shop. **Miscellaneous:** Reduced fees (weekdays, guests, twilight, seniors, juniors), range (grass), credit cards (MC, V, AE), BF, FF.
Reader Comments: Fun layout ... Poor clubhouse, course is a gem ... Diamond in the rough ... Course was good, snack bar lacking ... Nice layout, new course ... Excellent layout, good test of golf ... Greens could have used some TLC.

★★★ **BEACON RIDGE GOLF & COUNTRY CLUB**
R-6000 Longleaf Dr., West End, 27376, Moore County, (910)673-2950, (800)416-5204, 10 miles from Pinehurst. **Facility Holes:** 18. **Yards:** 6,414/4,730. **Par:** 72/72. **Course Rating:** 70.7/67.1. **Slope:** 125/115. **Green Fee:** $20/$36. **Cart Fee:** $16/Person. **Walking Policy:** Mandatory carts. **Walkability:** 3. **Opened:** 1988. **Architect:** Gene Hamm. **Season:** Year-round. **High:** March-May. **To obtain tee times:** Call golf shop. **Miscellaneous:** Reduced fees (weekdays, guests, twilight, seniors, juniors), range (grass), credit cards (MC, V, D), BF, FF.
Reader Comments: Lots of hills, very fast greens, a bargain compared to Pinehurst ... Great service, great course ... If I lived in North Carolina, this would be my home ... Too much elevation change ... Difficult ... Very good condition.

★★½ **BEAU RIVAGE RESORT & GOLF CLUB**
R-649 Rivage Promenade, Wilmington, 28412, New Hanover County, (910)392-9022, (800)628-7080, 7 miles from Wilmington. **Facility Holes:** 18. **Yards:** 6,709/4,612. **Par:** 72/72. **Course Rating:** 72.5/67.1. **Slope:** 136/114. **Green Fee:** $20/$40. **Cart Fee:** Included in green fee. **Walkability:** 5. **Opened:** 1988. **Architect:** Joe Gestner/Eddie Lewis. **Season:** Year-round. **High:** March-Sept. **To obtain tee times:** Call golf shop. **Miscellaneous:** Reduced fees (weekdays, guests, twilight), range (grass), lodging (30 rooms), credit cards (MC, V, AE, D).

★½ **BEL AIRE GOLF CLUB**
PU-1518 Pleasant Ridge Rd., Greensboro, 27409, Guilford County, (336)668-2413. **Facility Holes:** 18. **Yards:** 6,152/5,212. **Par:** 72/73. **Course Rating:** 70.5/69.9. **Slope:** 111/107. **Green Fee:** $25/$35. **Cart Fee:** Included in green fee. **Walking Policy:** Mandatory carts. **Walkability:** 2. **Opened:** 1969. **Architect:** Lee Evans/Red Brame. **Season:** Year-round. **High:** April-Sept. **To obtain tee times:** Call up to 3 days in advance. **Miscellaneous:** Reduced fees (twilight, seniors), credit cards (MC, V, AE, D).

NORTH CAROLINA

★★½ **BELVEDERE COUNTRY CLUB**
SP-2368 Country Club Dr., Hampstead, 28443, Pender County, (910)270-2703, 15 miles from Wilmington. **Facility Holes:** 18. **Yards:** 6,275/4,583. **Par:** 71/72. **Course Rating:** 71.7/68.3. **Slope:** 129/114. **Green Fee:** $20/$45. **Cart Fee:** Included in green fee. **Walking Policy:** Mandatory carts. **Walkability:** 2. **Opened:** 1970. **Architect:** Russell T. Burney. **Season:** Year-round. **To obtain tee times:** Call golf shop. **Miscellaneous:** Reduced fees (guests, twilight, seniors, juniors), range (mats), credit cards (MC, V), BF, FF.

★★★½ **BIRKDALE GOLF CLUB**
PU-16500 Birkdale Commons Pkwy., Huntersville, 28078, Mecklenburg County, (704)895-8038, 15 miles from Charlotte. **Web:** www.birkdale.com. **Facility Holes:** 18. **Yards:** 7,013/5,175. **Par:** 72/72. **Course Rating:** 74.1/69.7. **Slope:** 138/123. **Green Fee:** $39/$65. **Cart Fee:** Included in green fee. **Walking Policy:** Walking at certain times. **Walkability:** 3. **Opened:** 1997. **Architect:** Arnold Palmer/Ed Seay. **Season:** Year-round. **High:** April-Nov. **To obtain tee times:** Call up to 8 days in advance. **Miscellaneous:** Reduced fees (weekdays, twilight, juniors), range (grass/mats), credit cards (MC, V, AE, D, DC), BF, FF.
Reader Comments: Large greens, but get on right tier … Room to roam off the tee … Good variety in length of holes … Good conditions, overpriced … Very pricey, good mix of holes … Some Sunday holes, but overall good.

★★★ **BLACK MOUNTAIN GOLF COURSE**
PU-106 Montreat Rd., Black Mountain, 28711, Buncombe County, (828)669-2710, 15 miles from Asheville. **Facility Holes:** 18. **Yards:** 6,181/4,959. **Par:** 71/71. **Course Rating:** 69.5/69.0. **Slope:** 129/113. **Green Fee:** $20/$28. **Cart Fee:** $12/Person. **Walking Policy:** Walking at certain times. **Walkability:** 5. **Opened:** 1928. **Architect:** Ross Taylor. **Season:** Year-round. **High:** May-Oct. **To obtain tee times:** Call up to 6 days in advance. **Miscellaneous:** Reduced fees (weekdays), credit cards (MC, V), BF, FF.
Reader Comments: Some good holes, No. 17 is a good challenge … No. 17 is awesome … The longest hole (par 6) is fun to play … Long wait at par 6.

★½ **BLAIR PARK GOLF CLUB**
PU-1901 S. Main St., High Point, 27260, Guilford County, (336)883-3497, 18 miles from Greensboro. **Facility Holes:** 18. **Yards:** 6,449/5,171. **Par:** 72/72. **Course Rating:** 70.8/69.5. **Slope:** 122/113. **Green Fee:** $11/$13. **Cart Fee:** $11/Person. **Walking Policy:** Walking at certain times. **Walkability:** 3. **Opened:** 1936. **Architect:** Rick Briley. **Season:** Year-round. **High:** June-Aug. **To obtain tee times:** Call golf shop. **Miscellaneous:** Reduced fees (twilight, seniors, juniors), metal spikes.

★★★½ **BLUE RIDGE COUNTRY CLUB**
R-Hwy. 221, Marion, 28752, McDowell County, (828)756-4013, (800)845-8430, 35 miles from Asheville. **E-mail:** inn@wnc.link. **Web:** www.blueridgecc.com. **Facility Holes:** 18. **Yards:** 6,862/5,203. **Par:** 72/72. **Course Rating:** 72.9/70.4. **Slope:** 136/124. **Green Fee:** $25/$48. **Cart Fee:** Included in green fee. **Walking Policy:** Unrestricted walking. **Walkability:** 3. **Opened:** 1995. **Architect:** Clifton/Ezell/Clifton. **Season:** Year-round. **High:** May-Nov. **To obtain tee times:** Call golf shop. **Miscellaneous:** Reduced fees (weekdays, guests, twilight, seniors, juniors), range (grass), lodging (13 rooms), credit cards (MC, V, AE, D), BF, FF.
Reader Comments: Fun mountain course, joy to play … What a pleasant surprise … This course was a real challenge … True mountain course … The front was more forgiving, good for the start of a round … The river makes for great holes.

★★½ **BOGUE BANKS COUNTRY CLUB**
SP-152 Oak Leaf Dr., Pine Knoll Shores, 28512, Carteret County, (252)726-1034, 20 miles from New Bern. **E-mail:** bbcc@clis.com. **Web:** www.boguebankscc.com. **Facility Holes:** 18. **Yards:** 6,015/5,002. **Par:** 72/72. **Course Rating:** 69.5/69.3. **Slope:** 123/115. **Green Fee:** $17/$33. **Cart Fee:** $12/Person. **Walking Policy:** Walking at certain times. **Walkability:** 1. **Opened:** 1971. **Architect:** Maurice Brackett. **Season:** Year-round. **High:** March-Sept. **To obtain tee times:** Call golf shop. **Miscellaneous:** Reduced fees (twilight), credit cards (MC, V), BF, FF.

★★★½ **BOONE GOLF CLUB**
PU-433 Fairway Dr., Boone, 28607, Watauga County, (828)264-8760, 90 miles from Charlotte. **E-mail:** info@boonegolfclub.com. **Web:** www.boonegolfclub.com. **Facility Holes:** 18. **Yards:** 6,401/5,199. **Par:** 71/71. **Course Rating:** 70.1/69.1. **Slope:** 120/113. **Green Fee:** $30/$40. **Cart Fee:** $12/Person. **Walking Policy:** Unrestricted walking. **Walkability:** 2. **Opened:** 1959. **Architect:** Ellis Maples. **Season:** April-Nov. **High:** June-Sept. **To obtain tee times:** Call up to 7 days in advance. **Miscellaneous:** Reduced fees (weekdays, twilight), credit cards (MC, V), BF, FF.
Reader Comments: Fun to play, fast greens … Excellent Ellis Maples design … Great course that is in great condition … Surrounding scenery is unbeatable … The best public course in mountains.

★★★ BRANDYWINE BAY GOLF & COUNTRY CLUB
PU-224 Brandywine Blvd., Morehead City, 28557, Carteret County, (252)247-2541, 40 miles from New Bern. **Facility Holes:** 18. **Yards:** 6,609/5,191. **Par:** 71/71. **Course Rating:** 72.0/68.6. **Slope:** 121/113. **Green Fee:** $27/$40. **Cart Fee:** Included in green fee. **Walking Policy:** Walking at certain times. **Walkability:** 1. **Opened:** 1980. **Architect:** Bruce Devlin. **Season:** Year-round. **High:** April-Oct. **To obtain tee times:** Call golf shop. **Miscellaneous:** Reduced fees (twilight), credit cards (MC, V).
Reader Comments: Nice course, muddy cart paths … Although not the best course I've played, I do feel it is the best in the Crystal Coast area … Fun layout, in good condition … Costly during summer months … Did not like layout.

★½ BRIARCREEK GOLF CLUB
SP-Cherry St., High Shoals, 28077, Gaston County, (704)922-4208, 15 miles from Charlotte. **Facility Holes:** 18. **Yards:** 6,533/4,415. **Par:** 72/72. **Course Rating:** .0/64.9. **Slope:** 119/109. **Green Fee:** $17/$23. **Opened:** 1969. **To obtain tee times:** Call golf shop. **Miscellaneous:** Metal spikes, range (/).

★★★½ BRICK LANDING PLANTATION GOLF & COUNTRY CLUB
R-1900 Goose Creek Rd., Ocean Isle Beach, 28469, Brunswick County, (910)754-5545, (800)438-3006, 15 miles from N. Myrtle Beach. **E-mail:** golf@bricklanding.com. **Web:** www.bricklanding.com. **Facility Holes:** 18. **Yards:** 6,752/4,707. **Par:** 72/71. **Course Rating:** 72.1/67.0. **Slope:** 141/116. **Green Fee:** $31/$61. **Cart Fee:** $21/Person. **Walking Policy:** Mandatory carts. **Walkability:** 2. **Opened:** 1988. **Architect:** H.M. Brazeal. **Season:** Year-round. **To obtain tee times:** Call golf shop. **Miscellaneous:** Reduced fees (twilight, juniors), range (grass), lodging (38 rooms), credit cards (MC, V, AE), BF, FF.
Reader Comments: Toughest 6,400 yards at the beach … Impossible when windy … Always a treat & challenge … Take your straight game … Very nice, lots of water … Long and narrow … Water everywhere … Pretty course … Maybe quirky.

★★½ BRIERWOOD GOLF CLUB
SP-Hwy. 179, Shallotte, 28459, Brunswick County, (910)754-4660, (888)274-3796, 35 miles from Wilmington. **E-mail:** brierwoodlemindspring.com. **Web:** golfbrierwood.com. **Facility Holes:** 18. **Yards:** 6,607/4,863. **Par:** 72/72. **Course Rating:** 72.8/68.3. **Slope:** 127/117. **Green Fee:** $25/$55. **Cart Fee:** Included in green fee. **Walking Policy:** Mandatory carts. **Walkability:** 2. **Opened:** 1966. **Architect:** Ben Ward. **Season:** Year-round. **High:** Feb.-May. **To obtain tee times:** Call up to 120 days in advance. **Miscellaneous:** Reduced fees (weekdays, twilight, juniors), credit cards (MC, V), BF, FF.

★★½ BROADMOOR GOLF LINKS
PU-101 French Broad Lane, Fletcher, 28732, Henderson County, (828)687-1500, 7 miles from Asheville. **E-mail:** par@brinet.com. **Web:** broadmoorgolflinks.com. **Facility Holes:** 18. **Yards:** 7,115/5,082. **Par:** 72/72. **Course Rating:** 73.3/69.7. **Slope:** 132/117. **Green Fee:** $27/$39. **Cart Fee:** Included in green fee. **Walking Policy:** Mandatory carts. **Walkability:** 1. **Opened:** 1992. **Architect:** Karl Litten. **Season:** Year-round. **High:** April-Oct. **To obtain tee times:** Call up to 14 days in advance. **Miscellaneous:** Reduced fees (weekdays, seniors), range (grass), credit cards (MC, V), BF, FF.
Special Notes: Formerly French Broad Golf Center.

★★★½ BRUNSWICK PLANTATION GOLF RESORT
R-Hwy. 17 N., Calabash, 28467, Brunswick County, (910)287-7888, (800)848-0290, 25 miles from Myrtle Beach. **Web:** www.brunswickplantation.com. **Facility Holes:** 27. **Green Fee:** $35/$80. **Walking Policy:** Mandatory carts. **Walkability:** 1. **Opened:** 1992. **Architect:** Willard Byrd/Clyde Johnston. **Season:** Year-round. **To obtain tee times:** Call up to 365 days in advance. **Miscellaneous:** Reduced fees (weekdays, guests, twilight, juniors), range (grass), lodging (150 rooms), credit cards (MC, V, AE), BF, FF.
AZALEA/MAGNOLIA (18)
Yards: 6,717/5,140. **Par:** 72/72. **Course Rating:** 72.8/70.4. **Slope:** 132/126.
DOGWOOD/AZALEA (18)
Yards: 6,772/5,087. **Par:** 72/72. **Course Rating:** 72.8/70.4. **Slope:** 132/126.
MAGNOLIA/DOGWOOD (18)
Yards: 6,779/5,210. **Par:** 72/72. **Course Rating:** 72.7/70.4. **Slope:** 131/115.
Reader Comments: Very good place to plan golf vacation … New holes are disappointing … Tough greens with breaks that are hard to read … Just opened, nice … 3 nines, excellent restaurant.

BRUSHY MOUNTAIN GOLF CLUB
SP-300 Golf Course Lane, Taylorsville, 28681, Alexander County, (828)632-4804, 55 miles from Charlotte. **Facility Holes:** 18. **Yards:** 6,700/5,210. **Par:** 72/75. **Course Rating:** 71.2/69.0. **Slope:** 124/116. **Green Fee:** $30/$35. **Cart Fee:** Included in green fee. **Walking Policy:** Walking

at certain times. **Walkability:** 3. **Opened:** 1963. **Season:** Year-round. **High:** May-Aug. **To obtain tee times:** Call up to 3 days in advance. **Miscellaneous:** Reduced fees (weekdays, seniors), range (grass), credit cards (MC, V), BF, FF.

BRYAN PARK & GOLF CLUB
PU-6275 Bryan Park Rd., Brown Summit, 27214, Guilford County, (336)375-2200, 10 miles from Greensboro. **Web:** www.bryanpark.com. **Facility Holes:** 36. **Cart Fee:** $13/Person. **Season:** Year-round. **High:** March-Oct. **To obtain tee times:** Call up to 7 days in advance. **Miscellaneous:** Reduced fees (weekdays, twilight, seniors, juniors), range (grass), credit cards (MC, V, AE), BF, FF.

★★★★ **CHAMPIONS COURSE** (18)
Yards: 7,135/5,395. **Par:** 72/72. **Course Rating:** 74.4/71.0. **Slope:** 130/122. **Green Fee:** $23/$36. **Walking Policy:** Mandatory carts. **Walkability:** 4. **Opened:** 1990. **Architect:** Rees Jones.
Notes: Ranked 16th in 2001 Best in State; 12th in 1996 America's Top 75 Affordable Courses.
Reader Comments: Great course creative holes … Good length … Brand new greens and clubhouse … Must use cart, too long to walk … Beautiful course … Good layout, good condition … Enjoyable.

★★★★ **PLAYERS COURSE** (18)
Yards: 7,076/5,260. **Par:** 72/72. **Course Rating:** 73.0/70.5. **Slope:** 128/120. **Green Fee:** $17/$33. **Walking Policy:** Unrestricted walking. **Walkability:** 3. **Opened:** 1974. **Architect:** George Cobb/Rees Jones.
Reader Comments: Not too demanding, but still enjoyable … Nice layout, varied terrain … Not as tough as Champions … Killer 1st hole … Solid track with nice variety … Good layout… Long, easy layout … Excellent … Beautiful.

★★ **BUNCOMBE COUNTY MUNICIPAL GOLF CLUB**
PU-226 Fairway Dr., Asheville, 28805, Buncombe County, (828)298-1867. **Facility Holes:** 18. **Yards:** 6,814/4,744. **Par:** 72/72. **Course Rating:** 71.1/67.2. **Slope:** 122/115. **Green Fee:** $15/$20. **Cart Fee:** $12/Person. **Walking Policy:** Unrestricted walking. **Walkability:** 2. **Opened:** 1927. **Architect:** Donald Ross. **Season:** Year-round. **High:** April-Oct. **To obtain tee times:** Call golf shop. **Miscellaneous:** Reduced fees (weekdays, twilight, juniors), credit cards (MC, V), BF, FF.

★★★ **CALABASH GOLF LINKS**
R-820 Thomasboro Rd., Calabash, 28467, Brunswick County, (910)575-5000, (800)841-5971, 10 miles from Myrtle Beach. **E-mail:** info@calabashgolf.com. **Web:** www.calabashgolf.com. **Facility Holes:** 18. **Yards:** 6,641/4,907. **Par:** 72/72. **Course Rating:** 72.0/68.4. **Slope:** 128/108. **Green Fee:** $50/$90. **Cart Fee:** Included in green fee. **Walking Policy:** Mandatory carts. **Walkability:** 1. **Opened:** 1997. **Architect:** Willard Byrd. **Season:** Year-round. **High:** March-Nov. **To obtain tee times:** Call up to 180 days in advance. **Miscellaneous:** Reduced fees (guests, twilight, juniors), range (grass), credit cards (MC, V, AE, D), FF.
Reader Comments: Very friendly course … Still needs to mature … Good course, not expensive … Course is in good condition … Great course with mom and pop atmosphere … Very short and small greens … Beautiful course, nice people.

★★★ **CAPE GOLF & RACQUET CLUB**
SP-535 The Cape Blvd., Wilmington, 28412, New Hanover County, (910)799-3110, (800)291-9847, 55 miles from Myrtle Beach. **Web:** teetimes.com. **Facility Holes:** 18. **Yards:** 6,805/4,948. **Par:** 72/72. **Course Rating:** 73.1/69.3. **Slope:** 133/118. **Green Fee:** $25/$45. **Cart Fee:** Included in green fee. **Walking Policy:** Mandatory carts. **Walkability:** 3. **Opened:** 1985. **Architect:** Gene Hamn. **Season:** Year-round. **High:** April-Sept. **To obtain tee times:** Call golf shop. **Miscellaneous:** Reduced fees (weekdays, guests, twilight, seniors), range (grass), credit cards (MC, V), BF, FF.
Reader Comments: Layout not memorable, however some holes were fun to play … Great springy fairways, really spin the ball … Nice fairways … Not in very good condition … Isolated location.

★★½ **CAROLINA LAKES GOLF CLUB**
PU-53 Carolina Lakes Rd., Sanford, 27330, Harnett County, (919)499-5421, (800)942-8633, 18 miles from Sanford. **E-mail:** clakes@alltel.net. **Web:** www.fayettevillenc.com/carolina-lakes. **Facility Holes:** 18. **Yards:** 6,400/5,010. **Par:** 70/70. **Course Rating:** 70.7/67.0. **Slope:** 117/110. **Green Fee:** $10/$18. **Cart Fee:** $12/Person. **Walking Policy:** Walking at certain times. **Walkability:** 3. **Opened:** 1981. **Architect:** Roger Rulewich/Jim Hickey. **Season:** Year-round. **High:** March-May. **To obtain tee times:** Call golf shop. **Miscellaneous:** Reduced fees (weekdays, guests, twilight, seniors, juniors), range (grass/mats), credit cards (MC, V).

★★★ **CAROLINA NATIONAL GOLF CLUB**
SP-1643 Goley Hewett Rd., S.E., Bolivia, 28422, Brunswick County, (910)755-5200,

(888)200-6455, 35 miles from Myrtle Beach. **E-mail:** cngccxaranda.net. **Web:** www.caroli-nanatl.com. **Facility Holes:** 27. **Green Fee:** $55/$95. **Cart Fee:** Included in green fee. **Walking Policy:** Mandatory carts. **Walkability:** 2. **Opened:** 1998. **Architect:** Fred Couples/Gene Bates. **Season:** Year-round. **High:** Feb.-June. **To obtain tee times:** Call golf shop. **Miscellaneous:** Reduced fees (weekdays, juniors), range (grass), credit cards (MC, V, AE, D), BF, FF.
EGRET/HERON (18)
Yards: 7,017/4,759. **Par:** 72/72. **Course Rating:** 73.4/63.5. **Slope:** 136/116.
EGRET/IBIS (18)
Yards: 6,944/4,631. **Par:** 72/72. **Course Rating:** 74.0/67.1. **Slope:** 147/111.
HERON/IBIS (18)
Yards: 6,961/4,548. **Par:** 72/72. **Course Rating:** 74.2/66.6. **Slope:** 145/114.
Reader Comments: Several truly memorable holes, good condition; a little pricey ... Need course layout book to know where to hit ... Beautiful low country gem, you must play it ... Nice layout, lots of water ... Great layout, forced carries.

★★½ **CAROLINA PINES GOLF & COUNTRY CLUB**
SP-390 Carolina Pines Blvd., New Bern, 28560, Craven County, (919)444-1000, 15 miles from New Bern. **Facility Holes:** 18. **Yards:** 6,280/4,766. **Par:** 72/72. **Course Rating:** 70.1/67.8. **Slope:** 124/116. **Green Fee:** $18. **Cart Fee:** $11/Person. **Walking Policy:** Walking at certain times. **Walkability:** 2. **Opened:** 1968. **Architect:** Ron Borsset. **Season:** Year-round. **To obtain tee times:** Call up to 5 days in advance. **Miscellaneous:** Reduced fees (twilight), range (grass), credit cards (MC, V).

★★½ **CAROLINA SHORES GOLF & COUNTRY CLUB**
PU-99 Carolina Shores Dr., Calabash, 28467, Brunswick County, (910)579-2181, (800)579-8292, 7 miles from Myrtle Beach. **E-mail:** csgc@mindspring.com. **Web:** www.caroli-nashoresgolf.com. **Facility Holes:** 18. **Yards:** 6,783/5,385. **Par:** 72/72. **Course Rating:** 72.6/72.0. **Slope:** 128/122. **Green Fee:** $16/$44. **Cart Fee:** $20/Person. **Walking Policy:** Mandatory carts. **Walkability:** 2. **Opened:** 1974. **Architect:** Tom Jackson. **Season:** Year-round. **High:** Feb.-April. **To obtain tee times:** Call up to 365 days in advance. **Miscellaneous:** Reduced fees (weekdays, twilight, juniors), range (grass), credit cards (MC, V, AE), BF, FF.

★★★½ **THE CAROLINA**
PU-277 Avenue of the Carolina, Whispering Pines, 28327, Moore County, (910)949-2811, (888)725-6372, 45 miles from Raleigh. **Facility Holes:** 18. **Yards:** 6,928/4,828. **Par:** 72/72. **Course Rating:** 73.2/68.6. **Slope:** 142/117. **Green Fee:** $49/$85. **Cart Fee:** Included in green fee. **Walking Policy:** Walking at certain times. **Walkability:** 4. **Opened:** 1997. **Architect:** Arnold Palmer/Ed Seay. **Season:** Year-round. **High:** March-June. **To obtain tee times:** Call up to 90 days in advance. **Miscellaneous:** Reduced fees (weekdays, twilight, juniors), range (grass), credit cards (MC, V, AE, D), BF, FF.
Reader Comments: A good test of golf ... Brutal from the back tees ... A well-designed course with significant elevation changes ... The clubhouse is less than impressive ... Fairly new course, has some difficult holes ... Nice greens.

★★½ **CHARLOTTE GOLF LINKS**
PU-11500 Providence Rd., Charlotte, 28277, Mecklenburg County, (704)846-7990. **Web:** www.carolinatrail.com. **Facility Holes:** 18. **Yards:** 6,700/5,279. **Par:** 71/72. **Course Rating:** 71.8/70.0. **Slope:** 120/112. **Green Fee:** $21/$36. **Cart Fee:** $14/Person. **Walking Policy:** Walking at certain times. **Walkability:** 2. **Opened:** 1993. **Architect:** Tom Doak. **Season:** Year-round. **High:** Feb.-Nov. **To obtain tee times:** Call up to 7 days in advance. **Miscellaneous:** Reduced fees (weekdays, twilight, seniors, juniors), range (grass), credit cards (MC, V, AE, D), BF, FF.

★★ **CHARLOTTE NATIONAL GOLF CLUB**
SP-6920 Howey Bottoms Rd., Indian Trail, 28079, Union County, (704)882-8282, 15 miles from Charlotte. **Facility Holes:** 18. **Yards:** 7,227/5,423. **Par:** 72/72. **Course Rating:** 74.9/71.3. **Slope:** 129/127. **Green Fee:** $22/$45. **Cart Fee:** Included in green fee. **Walking Policy:** Walking at certain times. **Walkability:** 3. **Opened:** 1996. **Architect:** Russell Breeden. **Season:** Year-round. **High:** March-Oct. **To obtain tee times:** Call golf shop. **Miscellaneous:** Reduced fees (weekdays, seniors), range (grass/mats), credit cards (MC, V, AE).

★★★ **CHATUGE SHORES GOLF COURSE**
PU-260 Golf Course Rd., Hayesville, 28904, Clay County, (828)389-8940, 110 miles from Asheville. **Facility Holes:** 18. **Yards:** 6,687/4,950. **Par:** 72/72. **Course Rating:** 71.8/68.8. **Slope:** 126/118. **Green Fee:** $18/$22. **Cart Fee:** $11/Person. **Walking Policy:** Unrestricted walking. **Walkability:** 3. **Opened:** 1971. **Architect:** John V. Townsend. **Season:** Year-round. **To obtain tee times:** Call up to 3 days in advance. **Miscellaneous:** Reduced fees (weekdays), range (grass/mats), credit cards (MC, V), BF, FF.

Reader Comments: Well laid out, mountain course, greens always good ... Good course but weird layout ... Simply a good test of golf ... Beautiful setting ... Several blind shots because of hills.

★½ CHEROKEE HILLS GOLF & COUNTRY CLUB
SP-Harshaw Rd., Murphy, 28906, Cherokee County, (828)837-5853, (800)334-3905, 90 miles from Altanta. **Facility Holes:** 18. **Yards:** 6,724/5,172. **Par:** 72/72. **Course Rating:** 70.0/68.0. **Slope:** 113/117. **Green Fee:** $15. **Cart Fee:** $11/Person. **Walking Policy:** Walking at certain times. **Walkability:** 4. **Opened:** 1969. **Architect:** Wells and West Inc. **Season:** Year-round. **To obtain tee times:** Call up to 7 days in advance. **Miscellaneous:** Reduced fees (twilight, juniors), metal spikes, range (grass), lodging (12 rooms), credit cards (MC, V, AE), FF.

★★½ CHEVIOT HILLS GOLF CLUB
PU-7301 Capital Blvd., Raleigh, 27616, Wake County, (919)876-9920. **Facility Holes:** 18. **Yards:** 6,505/4,965. **Par:** 71/71. **Course Rating:** 71.0/68.8. **Slope:** 130/123. **Green Fee:** $16/$25. **Cart Fee:** $11/Person. **Walking Policy:** Walking at certain times. **Walkability:** 3. **Opened:** 1930. **Architect:** Gene Hamm. **Season:** Year-round. **High:** March-Oct. **To obtain tee times:** Call up to 5 days in advance. **Miscellaneous:** Reduced fees (twilight), metal spikes, range (mats), credit cards (MC, V), FF.

★★½ CLEGHORN PLANTATION GOLF & COUNTRY CLUB
SP-183 Golf Circle, Rutherfordton, 28139, Rutherford County, (828)286-9117, 70 miles from Charlotte. **E-mail:** cleghorngolf@blueridge.net. **Web:** cleghorngolfclub.com. **Facility Holes:** 18. **Yards:** 6,903/4,751. **Par:** 72/73. **Course Rating:** 74.6/68.1. **Slope:** 134/111. **Green Fee:** $7/$20. **Walking Policy:** Mandatory carts. **Walkability:** 3. **Opened:** 1969. **Architect:** George Cobb. **Season:** Year-round. **To obtain tee times:** Call up to 14 days in advance. **Miscellaneous:** Reduced fees (weekdays, seniors), range (grass), credit cards (MC, V, D), BF, FF.

CLIFFWOOD GOLF CLUB
PU-3811 Martin Luther King Dr., Lumberton, 28358, Robeson County, (910)738-9400. **Facility Holes:** 18. **Yards:** 6,206/5,094. **Par:** 72/72. **Course Rating:** 69.7/69.1. **Slope:** 125/116. **Green Fee:** $10/$12. **Cart Fee:** $11/Person. **Walking Policy:** Walking at certain times. **Walkability:** 2. **Opened:** 1991. **Season:** Year-round. **To obtain tee times:** Call golf shop. **Miscellaneous:** Reduced fees (weekdays), metal spikes, range (grass), credit cards (MC, V), FF.

★★★ THE CLUB AT LONGLEAF
SP-2001 Midland Rd., Southern Pines, 28387, Moore County, (910)692-6100, (800)889-5323, 60 miles from Raleigh. **E-mail:** longleaf@pinehurst.net. **Web:** www.dan-maples.com/longleaf. **Facility Holes:** 18. **Yards:** 6,600/4,719. **Par:** 71/71. **Course Rating:** 71.0/65.8. **Slope:** 123/114. **Green Fee:** $54/$84. **Cart Fee:** Included in green fee. **Walking Policy:** Mandatory carts. **Walkability:** 3. **Opened:** 1988. **Architect:** Dan Maples. **Season:** Year-round. **To obtain tee times:** Call golf shop. **Miscellaneous:** Reduced fees (weekdays, guests, twilight, juniors), range (grass), credit cards (MC, V), FF.
Reader Comments: Front 9 open, back 9 wooded ... Bizarre par 5, wide open front 9 ... Very flat ... Front 9 easier, fun ... Nice playable course located in Pinehurst ... Outstanding value, good course for higher handicappers.

COUNTRY CLUB OF WHISPERING PINES
SP-2 Clubhouse Blvd., Whispering Pines, 28327, Moore County, (910)949-3000, 55 miles from Raleigh. **E-mail:** gpccwp@pinehurst.net. **Web:** www.whisperingpinesnc.com. **Facility Holes:** 36. **Green Fee:** $55/$89. **Cart Fee:** Included in green fee. **Walking Policy:** Mandatory carts. **Walkability:** 2. **Opened:** 1959. **Architect:** Ellis Maples. **Season:** Year-round. **High:** March-Oct. **To obtain tee times:** Call golf shop. **Miscellaneous:** Reduced fees (guests, juniors), range (grass), lodging (40 rooms), credit cards (MC, V), BF, FF.
★★½ PINES COURSE (18)
Yards: 7,138/5,542. **Par:** 72/72. **Course Rating:** 73.9/72.0. **Slope:** 125/123.
★★★ RIVER COURSE (18)
Yards: 6,521/5,140. **Par:** 71/71. **Course Rating:** 70.3/69.8. **Slope:** 128/121.
Reader Comments: Fun ... 9 holes hilly; 9 holes level; greens mixed size ... Lots of water for the Pinehurst area ... Short, but a great course ... Beautiful, older course with a very friendly and accommodating staff.

★★½ CRESCENT GOLF CLUB
PU-220 Laurel Valley Way, Salisbury, 28144, Rowan County, (704)647-0025, 35 miles from Charlotte. **E-mail:** rdesmond@salisbury.net. **Web:** www.crescentgolfclub.com. **Facility Holes:** 18. **Yards:** 6,822/5,163. **Par:** 72/72. **Course Rating:** 73.1/65.4. **Slope:** 130/112. **Walking Policy:** Walking at certain times. **Walkability:** 3. **Opened:** 1998. **Architect:** John LaFoy. **Season:** Year-round. **High:** April-Oct. **To obtain tee times:** Call up to 7 days in advance. **Miscellaneous:**

NORTH CAROLINA

Reduced fees (weekdays, twilight, seniors, juniors), range (grass), credit cards (MC, V), BF, FF.

★★ CROOKED CREEK GOLF CLUB
PU-764 Crooked Creek Rd., Hendersonville, 28739, Henderson County, (828)692-2011, 20 miles from Asheville. **Facility Holes:** 18. **Yards:** 6,652/5,546. **Par:** 72/72. **Course Rating:** 71.3/65.1. **Slope:** 128/108. **Green Fee:** $15. **Cart Fee:** $10/Person. **Walking Policy:** Walking at certain times. **Walkability:** 1. **Opened:** 1968. **Architect:** Alex Guin & Stewart Goodin. **Season:** Year-round. **High:** April-Sept. **To obtain tee times:** Call up to 2 days in advance.

★★★½ CROOKED CREEK GOLF CLUB
SP-4621 Shady Greens Dr., Fuquay-Varina, 27526, Wake County, (919)557-7529, 12 miles from Raleigh. **E-mail:** jhillccgc@aol.com. **Web:** www.playcrookedcreek.com. **Facility Holes:** 18. **Yards:** 6,271/4,635. **Par:** 71/71. **Course Rating:** 70.6/68.0. **Slope:** 137/116. **Green Fee:** $23/$40. **Cart Fee:** $15/Person. **Walking Policy:** Walking at certain times. **Walkability:** 4. **Opened:** 1994. **Architect:** Chuck Smith. **Season:** Year-round. **High:** April-Oct. **To obtain tee times:** Call up to 7 days in advance. **Miscellaneous:** Reduced fees (weekdays, twilight, seniors, juniors), range (grass), credit cards (MC, V), BF, FF.
Reader Comments: Back 9 interesting course, assimilates a mountain course ... Like this course, a challenge, 12th hole tough par 5 ... Funky but fun layout, good, cheap golf ... Two different courses, front & back, very nice.

★★★½ THE CROSSINGS GOLF CLUB
SP-4023 Wake Forest Rd., Durham, 27703, Durham County, (919)598-8686, 5 miles from Durham. **E-mail:** mikecrossings@aol.com. **Web:** thecrossings.citysearch.com. **Facility Holes:** 18. **Yards:** 6,700/5,008. **Par:** 72/72. **Course Rating:** 72.1/69.1. **Slope:** 138/120. **Green Fee:** $20/$36. **Cart Fee:** $13/Person. **Walking Policy:** Walking at certain times. **Opened:** 1997. **Architect:** Ron Garl. **Season:** Year-round. **High:** April-Nov. **To obtain tee times:** Call up to 7 days in advance. **Miscellaneous:** Reduced fees (weekdays, twilight, seniors, juniors), credit cards (MC, V, AE), BF, FF.
Reader Comments: Interesting holes, but layout does not encourage fast play ... Increased popularity has slowed play ... Lots of water back 9, 9th par 5 crosses same lake twice.
Special Notes: Formerly The Crossings at Grove Park.

★★★½ CROW CREEK GOLF CLUB
PU-240 Hickman Rd. N.W., Calabash, 28467, Brunswick County, (910)287-3081, (877)287-3081. **E-mail:** crowcreek@mindspring.com. **Web:** www.crowcreek.com. **Facility Holes:** 18. **Yards:** 7,101/5,097. **Par:** 72/72. **Course Rating:** 74.3/69.3. **Slope:** 131/116. **Green Fee:** $30/$100. **Cart Fee:** Included in green fee. **Walking Policy:** Walking at certain times. **Opened:** 1999. **Architect:** Rick Robbins. **Season:** Year-round. **To obtain tee times:** Call golf shop. **Miscellaneous:** Reduced fees (juniors), range (grass), credit cards (MC, V), FF.
Reader Comments: Front 9 was in good condition ... Great undulating greens ... Quality warmup for your Myrtle Beach trip ... Forgiving fairways ... Do you like fast greens? ... Great for a new course ... 18 unique holes.

★½ CRYSTAL SPRINGS GOLF CLUB
PU-Highway 51 & Miller Rd., Pineville, 28134, Mecklenburg County, (704)588-2640, 10 miles from Charlotte. **Facility Holes:** 18. **Yards:** 6,387/4,496. **Par:** 71/71. **Course Rating:** 69.4/64.5. **Slope:** 114/102. **Walkability:** 3. **Opened:** 1972. **Architect:** John J. Criscione/Gene Thomas. **To obtain tee times:** Call golf shop. **Miscellaneous:** Reduced fees (weekdays), metal spikes.

★★★★½ THE CURRITUCK CLUB
SP-1 Clubhouse Dr. Hwy. 12, Corolla, 27927, Currituck County, (252)453-9400, (888)453-9400, 60 miles from Virginia Beach. **E-mail:** danny.agapion@ourclub. **Web:** thecurrituckgolfclub.com. **Facility Holes:** 18. **Yards:** 6,885/4,766. **Par:** 72/72. **Course Rating:** 74.0/68.5. **Slope:** 136/120. **Green Fee:** $45/$135. **Cart Fee:** Included in green fee. **Walking Policy:** Unrestricted walking. **Walkability:** 2. **Opened:** 1996. **Architect:** Rees Jones. **Season:** Year-round. **To obtain tee times:** Call up to 7 days in advance. **Miscellaneous:** Reduced fees (guests, twilight, juniors), range (grass/mats), credit cards (MC, V, AE), BF, FF.
Notes: Ranked 24th in 1999 Best in State.
Reader Comments: By far the best on or near the Outer Banks ... Beautiful, resort price ... Good pace of play ... Orville and Wilbur would have loved the wind here ... Good course ... Challenging but a little pricey in the summer months.

★★★½ CYPRESS LAKES GOLF COURSE
PU-2126 Cypress Lakes Rd., Hope Mills, 28348, Cumberland County, (910)483-0359, (800)789-0793, 10 miles from Fayetteville. **E-mail:** lenesline@aol.com. **Web:** cypresstock.com. **Facility Holes:** 18. **Yards:** 6,943/5,272. **Par:** 72/74. **Course Rating:** 73.2/69.7. **Slope:** 133/118.

NORTH CAROLINA

Green Fee: $16/$25. **Cart Fee:** $14/Person. **Walking Policy:** Walking at certain times. **Walkability:** 2. **Opened:** 1968. **Architect:** L.B. Floyd. **Season:** Year-round. **To obtain tee times:** Call up to 30 days in advance. **Miscellaneous:** Reduced fees (weekdays, seniors, juniors), metal spikes, range (grass), credit cards (MC, V), BF, FF.
Reader Comments: Solid course … Limited trouble … Great greens … Fast undulating greens … Every hole different … Super people … Par 3s tough … Excellent greens … Great service and course in good shape … Nice layout.

★★★★ CYPRESS LANDING GOLF CLUB
SP-600 Clubhouse Dr., Chocowinity, 27817, Beaufort County, (252)946-7788, 19 miles from Greenville. **Facility Holes:** 18. **Yards:** 6,850/4,989. **Par:** 72/72. **Course Rating:** 72.8/68.8. **Slope:** 130/118. **Green Fee:** $30/$36. **Cart Fee:** Included in green fee. **Walking Policy:** Mandatory cart. **Walkability:** 3. **Opened:** 1996. **Architect:** Bill Love. **Season:** Year-round. **To obtain tee times:** Call golf shop. **Miscellaneous:** Reduced fees (weekdays), range (grass), credit cards (MC, V).
Reader Comments: Good course, not too crowded :.. Great sleeper, out of the way … Tough 18th hole … I want to play this course again .·. A little pricey, good course … One of the best in eastern NC … Very nice view of Pamlico Sound.

DEER BROOK GOLF CLUB
SP-201 Deer Brook Dr., Shelby, 28150, Cleveland County, (704)482-4653. **E-mail:** dbrook@shelby.net. **Facility Holes:** 18. **Yards:** 6,911/5,034. **Par:** 72/72. **Course Rating:** 734.0/69.4. **Slope:** 133/122. **Green Fee:** $29/$46. **Cart Fee:** Included in green fee. **Walking Policy:** Walking at certain times. **Walkability:** 3. **Opened:** 1999. **Architect:** Rick Robbins/Brain Lussier. **Season:** Year-round. **High:** April-Nov. **To obtain tee times:** Call golf shop. **Miscellaneous:** Reduced fees (twilight, seniors, juniors), range (grass), credit cards (MC, V, AE, D), BF, FF.

★★★ DEERCROFT GOLF CLUB
SP-30000 Deercroft Dr., Wagram, 28396, Scotland County, (910)369-3107, (800)787-7323, 12 miles from Pinehurst. **E-mail:** golfatdeercroft.com. **Facility Holes:** 18. **Yards:** 6,745/5,443. **Par:** 72/72. **Course Rating:** 72.6/67.0. **Slope:** 125/113. **Green Fee:** $15/$40. **Cart Fee:** $17/Person. **Walking Policy:** Walking at certain times. **Walkability:** 3. **Opened:** 1984. **Architect:** Gardner Gildey. **Season:** Year-round. **To obtain tee times:** Call up to 14 days in advance. **Miscellaneous:** Reduced fees (weekdays, twilight, seniors, juniors), range (grass), credit cards (MC, V, AE), BF, FF.
Reader Comments: This is one of my favorite courses to play at Pinehurst, very enjoyable … Nice layout, needs drainage work … Course in good condition … Fairways too narrow, otherwise great … Average course … Tough course.

★★★★ DEVIL'S RIDGE GOLF CLUB
SP-5107 Linksland Dr., Holly Springs, 27540, Wake County, (919)557-6100, 10 miles from Raleigh. **E-mail:** klay.barrow@ourclub.com. **Web:** devilsridgecc.com. **Facility Holes:** 18. **Yards:** 7,002/5,244. **Par:** 72/72. **Course Rating:** 73.7/69.8. **Slope:** 138/121. **Green Fee:** $29/$46. **Cart Fee:** $16/Person. **Walking Policy:** Walking at certain times. **Walkability:** 3. **Opened:** 1991. **Architect:** John LaFoy. **Season:** Year-round. **To obtain tee times:** Call up to 5 days in advance. **Miscellaneous:** Reduced fees (weekdays, twilight, seniors, juniors), range (grass), credit cards (MC, V, AE), BF, FF.
Reader Comments: The area is overflowing with golf atmosphere. I cannot say enough about the condition of the course, especially for the price … Scenic design, houses line fairways … Service superior, good as a home course.

★★★ THE DIVIDE
PU-6803 Stevens Mill Rd., Matthews, 28105, Mecklenburg County, (704)882-8088, 20 miles from Charlotte. **Web:** www.charlottegolf.com. **Facility Holes:** 18. **Yards:** 6,973/5,213. **Par:** 72/73. **Course Rating:** 74.4/70.3. **Slope:** 137. **Green Fee:** $32/$44. **Cart Fee:** Included in green fee. **Walkability:** 5. **Opened:** 1995. **Architect:** John Cassell. **Season:** Year-round. **To obtain tee times:** Call golf shop. **Miscellaneous:** Reduced fees (seniors, juniors), range (grass), credit cards (MC, V, AE).
Reader Comments: Good layout, suffers from lots of play … Very friendly … Home construction distracting … Basic golf, no frills … Good, tough layout, fair price … Very friendly staff.

★½ DUCK HAVEN GOLF CLUB
PU-1202 Eastwood Rd., Wilmington, 28403, New Hanover County, (910)791-7983. **Facility Holes:** 18. **Yards:** 6,453/5,361. **Par:** 71/72. **Course Rating:** 71.6/71.8. **Slope:** 125/121. **Green Fee:** $15/$20. **Cart Fee:** Included in green fee. **Walking Policy:** Unrestricted walking. **Walkability:** 1. **Opened:** 1961. **Architect:** Raiford Trask Sr. **Season:** Year-round. **High:** March-Oct. **To obtain tee times:** Call golf shop. **Miscellaneous:** Reduced fees (weekdays, twilight, seniors, juniors), metal spikes.

★★★ DUCK WOODS COUNTRY CLUB

SP-50 S. Dogwood Trail, Kitty Hawk, 27949, Dare County, (252)261-2609, 70 miles from Norfolk, VA. **E-mail:** dwgolf@ecinet2000.com. **Facility Holes:** 18. **Yards:** 6,589/5,182. **Par:** 72/72. **Course Rating:** 72.3/70.8. **Slope:** 128/120. **Green Fee:** $45/$90. **Cart Fee:** Included in green fee. **Walking Policy:** Mandatory carts. **Walkability:** 1. **Opened:** 1969. **Architect:** Ellis Maples. **Season:** Year-round. **To obtain tee times:** Call up to 5 days in advance. **Miscellaneous:** Reduced fees (juniors), range (grass), credit cards (MC, V), BF, FF.
Reader Comments: Lots of water holes … A North Carolina challenge … Check wind speed before the round … More water than golf course … Pleasant course. Friendly staff … A lot of water, very good course, however.

★★★★ DUKE UNIVERSITY GOLF CLUB

PU-Rte. 751 and Science Dr., Durham, 27708, Durham County, (919)681-2288. **Facility Holes:** 18. **Yards:** 7,045/5,505. **Par:** 72/73. **Course Rating:** 73.9/71.2. **Slope:** 137/124. **Green Fee:** $38/$53. **Cart Fee:** $17/Cart. **Walking Policy:** Unrestricted walking. **Opened:** 1957. **Architect:** Robert Trent Jones/Rees Jones. **Season:** Year-round. **High:** March-Sept. **To obtain tee times:** Call golf shop. **Miscellaneous:** Reduced fees (weekdays, twilight, seniors, juniors), range (grass), credit cards (MC, V), BF, FF.
Notes: Ranked 15th in 2001 Best in State; 17th in 1996 America's Top 75 Affordable Courses.
Reader Comments: A personal top 5, love the variation in holes … A bit overpriced … Great design makes you think more about course management …Expensive, not very good mix of holes … Bring your "A" game … Almost perfect.

★★★ EAGLE CHASE GOLF CLUB

PU-3215 Brantley Rd., Marshville, 28103, Union County, (704)385-9000, 30 miles from Charlotte. **E-mail:** ecgc3215@aol.com. **Facility Holes:** 18. **Yards:** 6,723/5,139. **Par:** 72/72. **Course Rating:** 72.6/69.6. **Slope:** 128/121. **Green Fee:** $15/$26. **Cart Fee:** $13/Person. **Walking Policy:** Unrestricted walking. **Walkability:** 4. **Opened:** 1994. **Architect:** Tom Jackson. **Season:** Year-round. **To obtain tee times:** Call up to 5 days in advance. **Miscellaneous:** Reduced fees (twilight, seniors, juniors), range (grass), credit cards (MC, V, AE).
Reader Comments: Good track … Very challenging … A hilly course, but always in good shape … Awesome tee shot on No. 2 … Great staff … Fun to play … Great par 3s … Great holes, tough greens, hard to score … Average course.

★★ EAGLE CREST GOLF COURSE

PU-4400 Auburn Church Rd., Garner, 27529, Wake County, (919)772-6104, 5 miles from Raleigh. **E-mail:** eaglecrest@mindspring.com. **Facility Holes:** 18. **Yards:** 6,514/4,875. **Par:** 71/71. **Course Rating:** 70.5/67.3. **Slope:** 118/113. **Green Fee:** $15/$23. **Cart Fee:** $11/Person. **Walking Policy:** Unrestricted walking. **Walkability:** 2. **Opened:** 1968. **Architect:** Baucom & Assoc. **Season:** Year-round. **High:** April-Sept. **To obtain tee times:** Call golf shop. **Miscellaneous:** Reduced fees (weekdays, twilight, seniors, juniors), metal spikes, range (grass), credit cards (MC, V, AE).

★★★ ECHO FARMS GOLF & COUNTRY CLUB

SP-4114 Echo Farms Blvd., Wilmington, 28412, New Hanover County, (910)791-9318. **Facility Holes:** 18. **Yards:** 7,004/5,232. **Par:** 72/72. **Course Rating:** 74.6/72.3. **Slope:** 129/122. **Green Fee:** $25/$50. **Cart Fee:** Included in green fee. **Walking Policy:** Mandatory carts. **Walkability:** 2. **Opened:** 1974. **Architect:** Gene Hamm. **Season:** Year-round. **To obtain tee times:** Call up to 7 days in advance. **Miscellaneous:** Reduced fees (weekdays, guests, twilight, seniors, juniors), range (grass), credit cards (MC, V, AE, D), BF, FF.
Reader Comments: Getting better … Fun course, good condition, good staff, great value … The place to play in that area … Recent redesign very successful.

★★★½ THE EMERALD GOLF CLUB

SP-5000 Clubhouse Dr., New Bern, 28562, Craven County, (252)633-4440. **E-mail:** jbriele@emeraldgc.com. **Web:** www.emeraldgc.com. **Facility Holes:** 18. **Yards:** 6,924/5,287. **Par:** 72/72. **Course Rating:** 73.8/68.2. **Slope:** 129/114. **Green Fee:** $39/$45. **Cart Fee:** Included in green fee. **Walking Policy:** Mandatory carts. **Walkability:** 2. **Opened:** 1988. **Architect:** Rees Jones. **Season:** Year-round. **High:** April-Oct. **To obtain tee times:** Call up to 7 days in advance. **Miscellaneous:** Reduced fees (twilight, juniors), range (grass), credit cards (MC, V), BF, FF.
Reader Comments: Tight layout for the high handicapper, bring plenty of balls, you will plunk them in many of the water-oriented holes … One of the toughest finishing holes in NC … Fun course to play, good condition … New course.

★★★½ ETOWAH VALLEY COUNTRY CLUB

R-450 Brickyard Rd., Etowah, 28729, Henderson County, (828)891-7141, (800)451-8174, 18 miles from Asheville. **Facility Holes:** 27. **Green Fee:** $31. **Cart Fee:** $15/Person. **Walking**

NORTH CAROLINA

Policy: Walking at certain times. **Opened:** 1967. **Architect:** Edmund Ault. **Season:** Year-round. **High:** April-Oct. **To obtain tee times:** Call golf shop. **Miscellaneous:** Metal spikes, range (grass/mats), credit cards (MC, V, AE, D).
SOUTH/NORTH (18 Combo)
Yards: 6,911/5,391. **Par:** 73/73. **Course Rating:** 72.4/69.9. **Slope:** 125/117. **Walkability:** 3.
SOUTH/WEST (18 Combo)
Yards: 7,108/5,524. **Par:** 72/72. **Course Rating:** 73.3/71.3. **Slope:** 125/119. **Walkability:** 1.
WEST/NORTH (18 Combo)
Yards: 7,005/5,363. **Par:** 73/73. **Course Rating:** 73.1/70.2. **Slope:** 125/117. **Walkability:** 2.
Reader Comments: Very good course if you're in the area ... Good layout ... Challenging but playable ... Pace was slow ... Ducks on the greens, good speed on greens ... Very good course, challenging 3 nines.

FAIRFIELD HARBOUR GOLF CLUB
R-1105 Barkentine Dr., New Bern, 28560, Craven County, (252)638-5338, 12 miles from New Bern. **E-mail:** fhgcgolf@hotmail.com. **Web:** www.fairfieldharbourgolf.com. **Facility Holes:** 36. **Cart Fee:** Included in green fee. **Walkability:** 3. **Season:** Year-round. **To obtain tee times:** Call up to 30 days in advance. **Miscellaneous:** Reduced fees (weekdays, guests, twilight, seniors, juniors), range (grass), credit cards (MC, V), BF, FF.
★★½   **HARBOUR POINTE COURSE** (18)
Yards: 6,650/5,100. **Par:** 72/72. **Course Rating:** 71.8/68.6. **Slope:** 125/111. **Green Fee:** $15/$32. **Walking Policy:** Mandatory carts. **Opened:** 1989. **Architect:** Rees Jones.
★★★   **SHORELINE COURSE** (18)
Yards: 6,802/5,200. **Par:** 72/72. **Course Rating:** 72.1/70.0. **Slope:** 128/118. **Green Fee:** $20/$32. **Walking Policy:** Walking at certain times. **Opened:** 1972. **Architect:** Dominic Palumbo.

FERGUSON FARMS GOLF
SP-5428 White Chapel Rd., Staley, 27350, Randolph County, (336)622-1802, 25 miles from Greensboro. **Facility Holes:** 18. **Yards:** 3,411/2,449. **Par:** 36/35. **Green Fee:** $18/$24. **Cart Fee:** Included in green fee. **Walking Policy:** Unrestricted walking. **Walkability:** 4. **Opened:** 1980. **Season:** Year-round. **High:** May-July. **To obtain tee times:** Call golf shop. **Miscellaneous:** Reduced fees (twilight, seniors, juniors), credit cards (MC, V, AE, D).

★★½   **FIRETHORNE COUNTRY CLUB**
SP-1108 Firethorne Club Dr., Waxhaw, 28173, Union County, (704)843-3111, 5 miles from Charlotte. **E-mail:** firthrnecc@aol.com. **Web:** firethornecountryclub.com. **Facility Holes:** 18. **Yards:** 6,904/4,626. **Par:** 72/72. **Course Rating:** 74.5/68.4. **Slope:** 145/120. **Green Fee:** $50/$65. **Cart Fee:** Included in green fee. **Walking Policy:** Mandatory carts. **Walkability:** 3. **Opened:** 1998. **Architect:** Tom Jackson. **Season:** Year-round. **High:** April-Nov. **To obtain tee times:** Call up to 2 days in advance. **Miscellaneous:** Range (grass/mats), credit cards (MC, V), BF, FF.

★★   **FOX SQUIRREL COUNTRY CLUB**
SP-591 S. Shore Dr., Boiling Spring Lakes, 28461, Brunswick County, (910)845-2625, 25 miles from Wilmington. **Facility Holes:** 18. **Yards:** 6,762/5,349. **Par:** 72/72. **Course Rating:** 72.5/70.7. **Slope:** 125/117. **Green Fee:** $15/$20. **Cart Fee:** $12/Person. **Walking Policy:** Unrestricted walking. **Walkability:** 1. **Opened:** 1962. **Architect:** Ed Ricobboni. **Season:** Year-round. **High:** June-Sept. **To obtain tee times:** Call golf shop. **Miscellaneous:** Metal spikes, credit cards (MC, V).

FOXFIRE RESORT & COUNTRY CLUB
R-9 Foxfire Blvd., Jackson Springs, 27281, Moore County, (910)295-5555, 60 miles from Raleigh. **Web:** www.foxfiregolfcc.com. **Facility Holes:** 36. **Green Fee:** $31/$81. **Cart Fee:** $18/Person. **Walking Policy:** Mandatory carts. **Opened:** 1968. **Architect:** Gene Hamm. **Season:** Year-round. **To obtain tee times:** Call golf shop. **Miscellaneous:** Reduced fees (guests, juniors), range (grass/mats), credit cards (MC, V, AE), BF, FF.
★★★½   **GREY COURSE** (18)
Yards: 6,851/5,256. **Par:** 72/72. **Course Rating:** 73.5/70.5. **Slope:** 131/119. **Walkability:** 2.
Reader Comments: Course upgrade makes this a terrific Pinehurst value ... Both of those courses are in excellent shape & are very playable for all handicaps ... Good challenge, greens & fairways excellent ... Tougher than the scorecard looks.
★★★   **RED COURSE** (18)
Yards: 6,742/5,273. **Par:** 72/72. **Course Rating:** 72.4/70.3. **Slope:** 129/115. **Walkability:** 3.
Reader Comments: Survive the first six holes for a terrific round ... Great hole variety, 18th a bear ... Great track now that renovations have matured ... New management, new clubhouse, and new treatment. Wonderful experience.

★½ GASTONIA MUNICIPAL GOLF CLUB

PU-530 Niblick Dr., Gastonia, 28052, Gaston County, (704)866-6945, 20 miles from Charlotte. **Facility Holes:** 9. **Yards:** 6,474/4,341. **Par:** 71/71. **Course Rating:** 71.3/66.1. **Slope:** 128/110. **Green Fee:** $9/$14. **Cart Fee:** $9/Person. **Walking Policy:** Unrestricted walking. **Walkability:** 3. **Opened:** 1931. **Architect:** J. Porter Gibson. **Season:** Year-round. **High:** April-Sept. **To obtain tee times:** Call golf shop. **Miscellaneous:** Reduced fees (twilight), metal spikes, credit cards (MC, V).

★★★ GATES FOUR COUNTRY CLUB

SP-6775 Irongate Dr., Fayetteville, 28306, Cumberland County, (910)425-2176. **Web:** www.gatesfour.com. **Facility Holes:** 18. **Yards:** 6,865/5,368. **Par:** 72/72. **Course Rating:** 73.9/72.2. **Slope:** 137/127. **Green Fee:** $16/$36. **Cart Fee:** $14/Person. **Walking Policy:** Walking at certain times. **Walkability:** 2. **Opened:** 1971. **Architect:** Willard Byrd. **Season:** Year-round. **To obtain tee times:** Call golf shop. **Miscellaneous:** Reduced fees (weekdays, guests, twilight, seniors, juniors), range (grass), credit cards (MC, V), BF, FF.
Reader Comments: Hard, hard and hard … Fun course but still a challenge … Good design … Tee times hard to come by on weekend … Tight fairways … Well designed and maintained.

★★★½ GLEN CANNON COUNTRY CLUB

SP-Wilson Rd., Brevard, 28712, Transylvania County, (828)884-9160, 25 miles from Asheville. **Facility Holes:** 18. **Yards:** 6,548/5,172. **Par:** 72/72. **Course Rating:** 71.7/69.1. **Slope:** 124/117. **Green Fee:** $25/$50. **Cart Fee:** Included in green fee. **Walkability:** 2. **Opened:** 1967. **Architect:** Willie B. Lewis. **Season:** Year-round. **High:** April-Oct. **To obtain tee times:** Call golf shop. **Miscellaneous:** Reduced fees (twilight), metal spikes, range (grass), credit cards (MC, V).
Reader Comments: Great mountain course … Water on 15 holes! … Playable, pretty course … Lots of ladies play … Waterfall hole outstanding … Play this one if you have the time … Take a camera for the second hole.

★½ GOLF CLUB AT PAW CREEK

PU-7942 Pawtuckett Rd., Charlotte, 28214, Mecklenburg County, (704)394-5909, 12 miles from Charlotte. **Facility Holes:** 18. **Yards:** 6,530/5,125. **Par:** 71/73. **Course Rating:** 71.6/65.5. **Slope:** 134/111. **Green Fee:** $22/$35. **Cart Fee:** Included in green fee. **Walking Policy:** Walking at certain times. **Walkability:** 2. **Opened:** 1959. **Architect:** Russell Breeden. **Season:** Year-round. **High:** April-Oct. **To obtain tee times:** Call up to 7 days in advance. **Miscellaneous:** Reduced fees (weekdays, twilight, seniors, juniors), range (grass/mats), credit cards (MC, V, AE, D, DC, CB), BF, FF.
Special Notes: Formerly Pawtucket Golf Club.

GRANDOVER RESORT & CONFERENCE CENTER

R-1000 Club Rd., Greensboro, 27407, Guilford County, (336)323-3838, (800)472-6301. **E-mail:** d.frace@grandover.com. **Web:** www.grandover.com. **Facility Holes:** 36. **Green Fee:** $75. **Cart Fee:** Included in green fee. **Walking Policy:** Walking at certain times. **Walkability:** 4. **Architect:** David Graham/Gary Panks. **Season:** Year-round. **To obtain tee times:** Call golf shop. **Miscellaneous:** Range (grass), lodging (247 rooms), credit cards (MC, V, AE, D, DC), BF, FF.
★★★★½ **EAST COURSE** (18) *Condition*
Yards: 7,100/5,500. **Par:** 72/72. **Course Rating:** 74.3/71.7. **Slope:** 140/121. **Opened:** 1996.
Reader Comments: Always in great shape and consistently tough … Great shape but not a particularly memorable layout … Love it, very well thought out … Very nice course, a bit pricey in relation to other courses in the area … Worth your time.
★★★½ **WEST COURSE** (18)
Yards: 6,800/5,050. **Par:** 72/72. **Course Rating:** 72.5/69.2. **Slope:** 136/116. **Opened:** 1997.
Notes: Ranked 23rd in 1999 Best in State.
Reader Comments: Perfect condition but overpriced for the layout … Expensive (very) … Excellent complex.

★½ GREAT SMOKIES RESORT GOLF CLUB

R-One Holiday Inn Dr., Asheville, 28806, Buncombe County, (828)253-5874, (800)733-3211. **Facility Holes:** 18. **Yards:** 5,900/4,600. **Par:** 70/70. **Course Rating:** 69.5/67.0. **Slope:** 118/113. **Green Fee:** $25/$30. **Cart Fee:** $15/Person. **Walking Policy:** Unrestricted walking. **Walkability:** 3. **Opened:** 1974. **Architect:** William B. Lewis. **Season:** Year-round. **To obtain tee times:** Call up to 30 days in advance. **Miscellaneous:** Reduced fees (weekdays, guests, twilight), metal spikes, lodging (275 rooms), credit cards (MC, V, AE, D, DC), BF, FF.

★★★★ GREENSBORO NATIONAL GOLF CLUB

PU-330 Niblick Dr., Summerfield, 27358, Rockingham County, (336)342-1113, 8 miles from Greensboro. **Facility Holes:** 18. **Yards:** 7,072/4,911. **Par:** 72/72. **Course Rating:** 73.8/69.1.

Slope: 142/110. **Green Fee:** $35/$40. **Cart Fee:** Included in green fee. **Walking Policy:** Walking at certain times. **Walkability:** 4. **Opened:** 1995. **Architect:** Don and Mark Charles. **Season:** Year-round. **High:** Feb.-Dec. **To obtain tee times:** Call up to 7 days in advance. **Miscellaneous:** Reduced fees (seniors, juniors), range (grass/mats), credit cards (MC, V, AE, D), BF, FF.
Reader Comments: In addition to having a great course, this facility is also equipped with tremendous teaching facilities and professional instruction … Facilities very good, keep course in shape … Nice course … Very smooth greens.

★★★ THE GROVE PARK INN RESORT
R-290 Macon Ave., Asheville, 28804, Buncombe County, (828)252-2711, (800)438-5800.
Facility Holes: 18. **Yards:** 6,501/4,644. **Par:** 70/70. **Course Rating:** 71.7/68.6. **Slope:** 126/111.
Green Fee: $50/$80. **Cart Fee:** Included in green fee. **Walking Policy:** Walking at certain times.
Walkability: 3. **Opened:** 1894. **Architect:** Willie Park/Donald Ross. **Season:** Year-round. **High:** April-Nov. **To obtain tee times:** Call golf shop. **Miscellaneous:** Lodging (550 rooms), credit cards (MC, V, AE, D, Diners Club).
Reader Comments: Great setting … A nice course, great hotel and restaurant, too. Love it … Excellent resort course with rich history … Take a step back in time.

★★★ HAWKSNEST GOLF & SKI RESORT
PU-2058 Skyland Dr., Banner Elk, 28607, Watauga County, (828)963-6561, (800)822-4295, 70 miles from Winston-Salem. **E-mail:** hawksnets@boone.net. **Web:** hawksnest-resort.com.
Facility Holes: 18. **Yards:** 6,244/4,799. **Par:** 72/72. **Course Rating:** 68.6/69.4. **Slope:** 113/110.
Green Fee: $22/$42. **Cart Fee:** Included in green fee. **Walking Policy:** Mandatory carts.
Walkability: 5. **Opened:** 1969. **Architect:** Property owners. **Season:** April-Nov. **High:** June-Oct.
To obtain tee times: Call golf shop. **Miscellaneous:** Reduced fees (weekdays, twilight), metal spikes, credit cards (MC, V, AE, D), BF, FF.
Reader Comments: One of my favorites … Wonderful mountain views! Unique course. Can be a bit cold up there even in the middle of the summer … The weather changes by the minute … Nice layout but in bad shape.

★★ HEDINGHAM GOLF CLUB
SP-4801 Harbour Towne Dr., Raleigh, 27604, Wake County, (919)250-3030. **Facility Holes:** 18. **Yards:** 6,604/4,828. **Par:** 72/72. **Course Rating:** 72.1/66.8. **Slope:** 124/107. **Green Fee:** $20/$31. **Cart Fee:** $14/Person. **Walking Policy:** Walking at certain times. **Walkability:** 4. **Opened:** 1992. **Architect:** David Postlethwait. **Season:** Year-round. **To obtain tee times:** Call golf shop. **Miscellaneous:** Reduced fees (weekdays, twilight, seniors, juniors), range (grass/mats), credit cards (MC, V, AE, D).

★★★ HIGH HAMPTON INN & COUNTRY CLUB
R-Hwy. 107 S., Box 338, Cashiers, 28717, Jackson County, (828)743-2450, (800)334-2551, 65 miles from Asheville. **Facility Holes:** 18. **Yards:** 6,012/3,748. **Par:** 71/71. **Course Rating:** 68.5. **Slope:** 120. **Green Fee:** $20/$41. **Cart Fee:** $14/Person. **Walking Policy:** Unrestricted walking. **Walkability:** 3. **Opened:** 1923. **Architect:** George Cobb. **Season:** April-Nov. **High:** June-Aug. **To obtain tee times:** Call golf shop. **Miscellaneous:** Reduced fees (guests, twilight), range (grass), credit cards (MC, V, AE, D).
Reader Comments: Best value for golfer … Staff was very courteous and helpful … Great scenery, good fairways, greens excellent … Late in year, well maintained.

★★★ HIGHLAND CREEK GOLF CLUB
PU-7001 Highland Creek Pkwy., Charlotte, 28269, Mecklenburg County, (704)875-9000, 10 miles from Charlotte. **E-mail:** johbes@aol.com. **Web:** www.highland-creekgolf.com. **Facility Holes:** 18. **Yards:** 7,008/5,005. **Par:** 72/72. **Course Rating:** 73.3/70.1. **Slope:** 133/128. **Green Fee:** $45/$60. **Cart Fee:** Included in green fee. **Walking Policy:** Mandatory carts. **Walkability:** 5. **Opened:** 1993. **Architect:** Clifton/Ezell/Clifton. **Season:** Year-round. **High:** March-Oct. **To obtain tee times:** Call up to 7 days in advance. **Miscellaneous:** Reduced fees (weekdays, twilight, seniors, juniors), range (grass), credit cards (MC, V, AE, D, DC), BF, FF.
Reader Comments: The creek comes into play to penalize good tee shots … Love the global positioning devices on carts … Slow … Good layout spoiled by unsightly power lines … Good value overplayed … Good layout.

★½ HILLCREST GOLF CLUB
PU-2450 S. Stratford Rd., Winston-Salem, 27103, Forsyth County, (336)765-5269. **Facility Holes:** 27. **Green Fee:** $14/$18. **Cart Fee:** $12/Person. **Walking Policy:** Unrestricted walking. **Walkability:** 1. **Opened:** 1931. **Architect:** J. T. Jones. **Season:** Year-round. **To obtain tee times:** Call up to 3 days in advance. **Miscellaneous:** Reduced fees (weekdays, twilight, seniors, juniors), metal spikes, credit cards (MC, V, D), BF, FF.
CEDARSIDE/HILLSIDE (18 Combo)
Yards: 5,839/5,531. **Par:** 72/74. **Course Rating:** 66.5/68.5. **Slope:** 104/107.
CEDARSIDE/LAKESIDE (18 Combo)

Yards: 5,848/5,484. Par: 72/73. Course Rating: 66.5/70.0. Slope: 104/111.
HILLSIDE/LAKESIDE (18 Combo)
Yards: 5,869/5,485. Par: 72/73. Course Rating: 66.5/70.0. Slope: 104/111.

HOPE MILLS GOLF COURSE
PU-3625 Golfview Rd., Hope Mills, 28348, Cumberland County, (910)425-7125, 6 miles from Fayetteville. **Facility Holes:** 18. **Yards:** 6,200/4,600. **Par:** 70/70. **Course Rating:** 69.5/67.3. **Slope:** 127/112. **Green Fee:** $13/$27. **Cart Fee:** Included in green fee. **Walking Policy:** Walking at certain times. **Walkability:** 4. **Season:** Year-round. **High:** March-Nov. **To obtain tee times:** Call golf shop. **Miscellaneous:** Reduced fees (seniors), range (grass), credit cards (MC, V, AE, D).

★★★½ HOUND EARS CLUB
SP-P.O. Box 188, Blowing Rock, 28604, Watauga County, (828)963-4321, 90 miles from Asheville. **Facility Holes:** 18. **Yards:** 6,395/4,959. **Par:** 72/73. **Course Rating:** 70.1/68.5. **Slope:** 127/119. **Green Fee:** $45/$100. **Cart Fee:** $15/Person. **Walking Policy:** Walking at certain times. **Walkability:** 3. **Opened:** 1963. **Architect:** George Cobb. **Season:** April-Oct. **To obtain tee times:** Call golf shop. **Miscellaneous:** Reduced fees (juniors), range (grass), credit cards (MC, V, AE), BF, FF.
Reader Comments: Great course. Good food ... A fun golf course ... Greens make it a test ... Beautiful and challenging mountain course ... Food super ... A lot of blind shots ... It started snowing, but still a delight.

★★★½ HYLAND HILLS GOLF CLUB
R-115 Fairway Ave., Southern Pines, 28387, Moore County, (910)692-3752, (888)315-2296, 5 miles from Pinehurst. **Facility Holes:** 18. **Yards:** 6,726/4,677. **Par:** 72/72. **Course Rating:** 70.4/66.8. **Slope:** 124/109. **Green Fee:** $20/$55. **Cart Fee:** $19/Person. **Walking Policy:** Walking at certain times. **Walkability:** 3. **Opened:** 1974. **Architect:** Tom Jackson. **Season:** Year-round. **To obtain tee times:** Call up to 365 days in advance. **Miscellaneous:** Reduced fees (twilight, juniors), range (grass), lodging (52 rooms), credit cards (MC, V), FF.
Reader Comments: Fun & relatively easy ... Overall the best ... Improved condition ... The best public course in Pinehurst ... Very nice ... Just average ... Slow play, hard hat course in places ... Rough greens, nice fairways and scenic.

★★ INDIAN VALLEY GOLF COURSE
PU-1005 Indian Valley Dr., Burlington, 27217, Alamance County, (336)584-7871, 20 miles from Greensboro. **Facility Holes:** 18. **Yards:** 6,610/5,606. **Par:** 70/70. **Course Rating:** 71.3/68.4. **Slope:** 115/113. **Green Fee:** $9/$14. **Cart Fee:** $9/Person. **Walking Policy:** Unrestricted walking. **Opened:** 1967. **Architect:** Ellis Maples. **Season:** Year-round. **High:** April-Oct. **To obtain tee times:** Call golf shop. **Miscellaneous:** Reduced fees (weekdays, guests, twilight, seniors, juniors), metal spikes, range (grass), credit cards (MC, V).

★★★★ JAMESTOWN PARK GOLF CLUB
PU-7014 E. Fork Rd., Jamestown, 27282, Guilford County, (336)454-4912, 3 miles from Greensboro. **Facility Holes:** 18. **Yards:** 6,665/5,298. **Par:** 72/72. **Course Rating:** 72.6/70.7. **Slope:** 126/118. **Green Fee:** $16/$19. **Cart Fee:** $10/Person. **Walking Policy:** Walking at certain times. **Walkability:** 3. **Opened:** 1972. **Architect:** John Townsend. **Season:** Year-round. **To obtain tee times:** Call golf shop. **Miscellaneous:** Reduced fees (seniors, juniors), range (grass), credit cards (MC, V, D), BF, FF.
Reader Comments: Hole variety will make you use all 14 clubs ... Great value ... You can walk for under $20 ... Nice course at a great value ... Beautiful grounds, well kept.

★★★★½ JEFFERSON LANDING CLUB
R-Highway 16 - 88, Jefferson, 28640, Ashe County, (336)982-7767, (800)292-6274, 80 miles from Winston-Salem. **E-mail:** www.bullvannoy@yahoo.com. **Web:** www.jeffersonlanding.com. **Facility Holes:** 18. **Yards:** 7,111/4,960. **Par:** 72/72. **Slope:** 121/103. **Green Fee:** $35/$59. **Cart Fee:** $15/Person. **Walking Policy:** Mandatory carts. **Walkability:** 3. **Opened:** 1991. **Architect:** Larry Nelson/Dennis Lehmann. **Season:** April-Nov. **High:** May-Oct. **To obtain tee times:** Call golf shop. **Miscellaneous:** Reduced fees (weekdays, guests, twilight, seniors, juniors), range (grass/mats), lodging (50 rooms), credit cards (MC, V, AE, D), BF, FF.
Reader Comments: An excellent course and value for a resort ... I recommend it highly ... Mountain gem ... Fun to play, tricky; lots of elevation change ... Most enjoyable mountain course I ever played ... Great accommodations and staff.

★★★★ KEITH HILLS COUNTRY CLUB *Value*
SP-Country Club Dr., Buies Creek, 27506, Harnett County, (910)893-5051, (800)334-4111, 30 miles from Raleigh. **E-mail:** khcc@mailcenter.com. **Web:** www.campbell.edu/keith hills. **Facility Holes:** 18. **Yards:** 6,703/5,225. **Par:** 72/72. **Course Rating:** 71.6/69.6. **Slope:** 129/120. **Green Fee:** $18/$36. **Cart Fee:** $14/Person. **Walking Policy:** Walking at certain times.

Walkability: 4. **Opened:** 1975. **Architect:** Ellis Maples. **Season:** Year-round. **To obtain tee times:** Call golf shop. **Miscellaneous:** Reduced fees (twilight, seniors, juniors), range (grass), credit cards (MC, V), BF, FF.
Reader Comments: During school year can get crowded with students from university ... Course is in good condition with very good greens ... Well worth some travel to play it ... The drive is worth it ... Great round ... Wonderful variation.

LAKE LURE GOLF & BEACH RESORT
R-309 Winesap Rd., Lake Lure, 28746, Rutherford County, (828)625-2888, (800)260-1040, 9 miles from Lake Lure. **E-mail:** eparks@lakeluregolf.com. **Web:** www.lakeluregolf.com. **Facility Holes:** 36. **Cart Fee:** Included in green fee. **Season:** Year-round. **High:** March-Oct. **To obtain tee times:** Call up to 14 days in advance. **Miscellaneous:** Reduced fees (guests, twilight, juniors), range (grass), lodging (50 rooms), credit cards (MC, V, AE, D), BF, FF.
★★★★ **APPLE VALLEY GOLF CLUB** (18)
Yards: 6,756/4,661. **Par:** 72/72. **Course Rating:** 72.8/66.3. **Slope:** 139/114. **Green Fee:** $33/$50. **Walking Policy:** Mandatory carts. **Walkability:** 3. **Opened:** 1986. **Architect:** Dan Maples.
Reader Comments: This is the better of the two ... Got lost between holes, nice fairways ... Another pretty place to play ... Too many short par 4s ... Nice views, always in great shape ... Great variety, some really outstanding holes.
★★★ **BALD MOUNTAIN GOLF CLUB** (18)
Yards: 6,575/4,808. **Par:** 72/72. **Course Rating:** 72.8/67.9. **Slope:** 137/118. **Green Fee:** $41/$50. **Walking Policy:** Walking at certain times. **Walkability:** 4. **Opened:** 1968. **Architect:** W.B. Lewis.
Reader Comments: Hard to get to, pretty setting ... The greens were gone, green fee too high ... Not as nice as Apple Valley but still fun to play ... Nice mountain course, wonderful view.

★★★½ **LANE TREE GOLF CLUB**
SP-2317 Salem Church Rd., Goldsboro, 27530, Wayne County, (919)734-1245, 43 miles from Raleigh. **E-mail:** lanetree@esn.net. **Web:** www.lanetree.com. **Facility Holes:** 18. **Yards:** 7,016/5,217. **Par:** 72/73. **Course Rating:** 72.4/68.9. **Slope:** 131/120. **Green Fee:** $10/$25. **Cart Fee:** $14/Person. **Walking Policy:** Walking at certain times. **Walkability:** 3. **Opened:** 1992. **Architect:** John Lafoy. **Season:** Year-round. **High:** April-Oct. **To obtain tee times:** Call up to 5 days in advance. **Miscellaneous:** Reduced fees (weekdays, twilight, seniors), range (grass), credit cards (MC, V), FF.
Reader Comments: A nice scenic course ... Beautiful setting, good greens, 18th hole very hard ... Still fairly new & developing.

★★★★½ **LEGACY GOLF LINKS** *Service, Value, Pace*
PU-12615 U.S. Hwy. 15-501 S., Aberdeen, 28315, Moore County, (910)944-8825, (800)344-8825, 70 miles from Raleigh. **E-mail:** mriddle@legacygolfmgmt.com. **Web:** www.legacypinehurst.com. **Facility Holes:** 18. **Yards:** 7,014/4,948. **Par:** 72/72. **Course Rating:** 73.2/68.3. **Slope:** 132/120. **Green Fee:** $39/$99. **Cart Fee:** Included in green fee. **Walking Policy:** Mandatory carts. **Walkability:** 3. **Opened:** 1991. **Architect:** Jack Nicklaus. **Season:** Year-round. **To obtain tee times:** Call golf shop. **Miscellaneous:** Reduced fees (weekdays, guests, twilight, juniors), range (grass), credit cards (MC, V, AE), BF, FF.
Reader Comments: One of the most beautiful and fun places to play in the Pinehurst area ... Beautiful, good challenge ... Jack Jr. did good, a pleasure to play.

★★ **LINCOLN COUNTRY CLUB**
SP-2108 Country Club Rd., Lincolnton, 28092, Lincoln County, (704)735-1382, 20 miles from Charlotte. **Facility Holes:** 18. **Yards:** 6,467/5,011. **Par:** 72/72. **Course Rating:** 70.4/69.0. **Slope:** 125/118. **Green Fee:** $22/$28. **Cart Fee:** Included in green fee. **Walking Policy:** Unrestricted walking. **Opened:** 1991. **Architect:** Peter Tufts. **Season:** Year-round. **High:** April-Oct. **To obtain tee times:** Call golf shop. **Miscellaneous:** Reduced fees (weekdays, seniors, juniors), metal spikes, range (grass), credit cards (MC, V).

★★ **THE LINKS AT MAGNOLIA**
SP-171 Magnolia Country Club Lane, Magnolia, 28453, Duplin County, (910)289-2126, 40 miles from Wilmington. **E-mail:** gsmither@golfsat.net. **Facility Holes:** 18. **Yards:** 6,400/4,600. **Par:** 71/71. **Course Rating:** 69.8/68.3. **Slope:** 120/109. **Green Fee:** $19. **Cart Fee:** $11/Person. **Walking Policy:** Unrestricted walking. **Walkability:** 2. **Opened:** 1974. **Architect:** J.P. Smith/Doug Smith. **Season:** Year-round. **High:** March-Nov. **To obtain tee times:** Call up to 7 days in advance. **Miscellaneous:** Reduced fees (weekdays, guests, twilight, seniors, juniors), credit cards (MC, V, D), BF, FF.
Special Notes: Formerly Magnolia Country Club.

★★★½ **LINVILLE GOLF COURSE**
R-Linville Ave., Linville, 28646, Avery County, (828)733-4363, 60 miles from Asheville. **Facility**

Holes: 18. **Yards:** 6,780/5,086. **Par:** 72/72. **Course Rating:** 72.5/69.3. **Slope:** 134/121. **Green Fee:** $80. **Cart Fee:** Included in green fee. **Walking Policy:** Mandatory carts. **Walkability:** 3. **Opened:** 1924. **Architect:** Donald Ross. **Season:** May-Oct. **To obtain tee times:** Call up to 4 days in advance. **Miscellaneous:** Range (grass), BF, FF.
Notes: Ranked 24th in 2001 Best in State; 19th in 1996 America's Top 75 Affordable Courses.
Reader Comments: Like putting on glass … Trout in streams … Classic short course … Worth it … A special time … Old Donald Ross, great experience … The best in the state … Best mountain course around … Doesn't get any better.

★★★½ LITTLE RIVER FARM GOLF LINKS
PU-500 Little River Farm Rd., Carthage, 28327, Moore County, (910)949-4600, (888)766-6536, 5 miles from Pinehurst. **E-mail:** golf@littleriver.com. **Web:** www.littleriver.com. **Facility Holes:** 18. **Yards:** 6,909/5,092. **Par:** 72/72. **Course Rating:** 73.6/69.4. **Slope:** 132/118. **Green Fee:** $40/$70. **Cart Fee:** $18/Person. **Walking Policy:** Mandatory carts. **Walkability:** 5. **Opened:** 1996. **Architect:** Dan Maples. **Season:** Year-round. **To obtain tee times:** Call golf shop. **Miscellaneous:** Range (grass), credit cards (MC, V), BF, FF.
Reader Comments: Very difficult … Typical Maples, had best round ever there … Great layout, toughest par 5s, nice place … A few too many tricky holes …Fun course.

★★★ LOCHMERE GOLF CLUB
SP-2511 Kildare Farm Rd., Cary, 27511, Wake County, (919)851-0611, 5 miles from Raleigh. **E-mail:** tim.reeser@ourclub.com. **Web:** lochmere.com. **Facility Holes:** 18. **Yards:** 6,627/4,767. **Par:** 71/71. **Course Rating:** 71.7/68.4. **Slope:** 132/120. **Green Fee:** $24/$34. **Cart Fee:** $16/Person. **Walking Policy:** Walking at certain times. **Walkability:** 1. **Opened:** 1986. **Architect:** Gene Hamm. **Season:** Year-round. **To obtain tee times:** Call up to 5 days in advance. **Miscellaneous:** Reduced fees (twilight, seniors, juniors), range (grass), credit cards (MC, V), BF, FF.
Reader Comments: Good course except after a heavy rain … Scenic design, housing lines fairways … Wet at times & very crowded … Keeps getting better … Great service and course layout.

★★★★ LOCKWOOD FOLLY COUNTRY CLUB *Value, Pace*
SP-19 Clubhouse Dr. S.W., Holden Beach, 28462, Brunswick County, (910)842-5666, (877)562-9663, 40 miles from Myrtle Beach. **E-mail:** lockwoodfolly@mindspring.com. **Web:** www.lockwoodfolly.com. **Facility Holes:** 18. **Yards:** 6,836/5,524. **Par:** 72/72. **Course Rating:** 73.8/70.9. **Slope:** 139/122. **Green Fee:** $46/$73. **Cart Fee:** Included in green fee. **Walking Policy:** Mandatory carts. **Walkability:** 2. **Opened:** 1988. **Architect:** Willard Byrd. **Season:** Year-round. **To obtain tee times:** Call up to 30 days in advance. **Miscellaneous:** Reduced fees (weekdays, guests, twilight, juniors), range (grass), credit cards (MC, V), BF, FF.
Reader Comments: Different from most Myrtle Beach area courses … Fairways are tight and you use all clubs in your bag … Fair for ladies, still a challenge … Beautiful setting in low country, mature … Difficult course.

THE LODGE GOLF COURSE
PU-19400 Andrew Jackson Hwy., Laurinburg, 28352, Scotland County, (910)277-0311, 25 miles from Pinehurst. **Facility Holes:** 18. **Yards:** 6,570/4,830. **Par:** 72/72. **Course Rating:** 69.4/65.5. **Slope:** 112/102. **Green Fee:** $15/$26. **Cart Fee:** $12/Person. **Walking Policy:** Unrestricted walking. **Walkability:** 1. **Opened:** 1984. **Architect:** Tom Jackson. **Season:** Year-round. **To obtain tee times:** Call golf shop. **Miscellaneous:** Reduced fees (twilight, seniors), range (grass).

★★★ MAGGIE VALLEY RESORT & COUNTRY CLUB
R-1819 Country Club Rd., Maggie Valley, 28751, Haywood County, (828)926-6013, (800)438-3861, 40 miles from Asheville. **E-mail:** golf@maggievalleyresort.com. **Web:** www.maggievalleyresort.com. **Facility Holes:** 18. **Yards:** 6,377/4,579. **Par:** 72/72. **Course Rating:** 70.2/65.9. **Slope:** 120/113. **Green Fee:** $15/$42. **Cart Fee:** $15/Person. **Walking Policy:** Walking at certain times. **Walkability:** 3. **Opened:** 1963. **Architect:** Bill Prevost. **Season:** Year-round. **High:** April-Oct. **To obtain tee times:** Call golf shop. **Miscellaneous:** Reduced fees (weekdays, twilight, juniors), range (grass/mats), lodging (75 rooms), credit cards (MC, V, AE, D), BF, FF.
Reader Comments: Excellent layout … Very pleasant mountain course … Undulating greens … For golfing couples … Nicely landscaped … A tad neglected but nice … Scenery outstanding … Very scenic … Lovely, fair layout.

★★★★½ MAGNOLIA GREENS GOLF PLANTATION *Condition*
PU-1800 Linkwood Circle, Leland, 28451, Brunswick County, (910)383-0999, (800)677-7534, 5 miles from Wilmington. **E-mail:** magnoliagolf@navi-gator.com. **Web:** www.magnolia-greens.com. **Facility Holes:** 27. **Green Fee:** $29/$54. **Cart Fee:** $20/Person. **Walking Policy:** Mandatory carts. **Walkability:** 2. **Opened:** 1998. **Architect:** Tom Jackson. **Season:** Year-round.

High: March-May. **To obtain tee times:** Call up to 180 days in advance. **Miscellaneous:** Reduced fees (weekdays, guests, twilight, seniors, juniors), range (grass), lodging (48 rooms), credit cards (MC, V, AE, D), BF, FF.
CAMELLIA/AZALEA (18)
Yards: 7,103/5,186. **Par:** 72/72. **Course Rating:** 75.3/70.0. **Slope:** 139/122.
MAGNOLIA/AZALEA (18)
Yards: 6,987/5,066. **Par:** 72/72. **Course Rating:** 74.4/69.1. **Slope:** 134/120.
MAGNOLIA/CAMELLIA (18)
Yards: 7,182/5,312. **Par:** 72/72. **Course Rating:** 75.3/70.3. **Slope:** 138/120.
Reader Comments: Worth the stop ... Excellent condition and fun to play ... Great conditioning, new 9 is interesting; a real up & comer ... Best public course in Wilmington area ... Great greens, nice fairways ... Fabulous greens.

★★ **MALLARD HEAD COUNTRY CLUB**
SP-185 Mallard Way, Mooresville, 28117, Iredell County, (704)664-7031, 25 miles from Charlotte. **Facility Holes:** 18. **Yards:** 6,904/5,469. **Par:** 72/72. **Course Rating:** 72.8/70.5. **Slope:** 121/121. **Green Fee:** $16/$23. **Cart Fee:** $10/Person. **Walking Policy:** Walking at certain times. **Walkability:** 3. **Opened:** 1979. **Architect:** George Cobb. **Season:** Year-round. **To obtain tee times:** Call golf shop. **Miscellaneous:** Reduced fees (weekdays, seniors), range (grass), credit cards (MC, V).

★★★★ **MARSH HARBOUR GOLF LINKS**
PU-Hwy. 179, Calabash, 28467, Brunswick County, (910)579-3161, (800)377-2315, 15 miles from Myrtle Beach. **Facility Holes:** 18. **Yards:** 6,690/4,795. **Par:** 71/71. **Course Rating:** 72.4/67.7. **Slope:** 134/115. **Green Fee:** $19/$80. **Cart Fee:** $20/Person. **Walkability:** 3. **Opened:** 1980. **Architect:** Dan Maples. **Season:** Year-round. **To obtain tee times:** Call golf shop. **Miscellaneous:** Reduced fees (guests), range (grass), credit cards (MC, V, AE).
Reader Comments: Beautiful & challenging course ... Narrow course ... Played here years ago but never forgotten ... Will always be one of my all-time favorites.

★★★½ **MEADOWLANDS GOLF CLUB**
R-P.O. Box 4159 - Calabash Rd. NW, Calabash, 28467, Brunswick County, (910)287-7529, (888)287-7529, 50 miles from Wilmington. **E-mail:** meadowlands@nccoast.net. **Web:** www.meadowlandsgolf.com. **Facility Holes:** 18. **Yards:** 7,054/5,041. **Par:** 72/72. **Course Rating:** 74.8/70.2. **Slope:** 136/119. **Green Fee:** $20/$69. **Cart Fee:** $21/Person. **Walking Policy:** Walking at certain times. **Walkability:** 2. **Opened:** 1997. **Architect:** Willard Byrd. **Season:** Year-round. **High:** Feb.-May. **To obtain tee times:** Call golf shop. **Miscellaneous:** Reduced fees (weekdays, guests, twilight, seniors, juniors), range (grass), credit cards (MC, V), BF, FF.
Reader Comments: Toughest Willard Byrd course around ... Long course even if you keep in the fairways ... Nice change to beach courses ... Courteous and organized staff ... Thought I was in Scotland near Calabash.

★★★½ **MEADOWLANDS GOLF COURSE** *Pace*
PU-582 Motsinger Rd., Winston-Salem, 27107, Davidson County, (336)769-1011, 6 miles from Winston-Salem. **Facility Holes:** 18. **Yards:** 6,706/4,745. **Par:** 72/72. **Course Rating:** 72.7/67.4. **Slope:** 135/117. **Green Fee:** $38/$44. **Cart Fee:** Included in green fee. **Walking Policy:** Walking at certain times. **Walkability:** 5. **Opened:** 1995. **Architect:** Hale Irwin/Stan Gentry. **Season:** Year-round. **High:** April-Oct. **To obtain tee times:** Call golf shop. **Miscellaneous:** Reduced fees (weekdays, seniors, juniors), metal spikes, range (grass), credit cards (MC, V, AE).
Reader Comments: Best overall course in the area ... No development on the course, you feel as if you are away from everything ... Layout overall not memorable.

★★★★½ **MID PINES INN & GOLF CLUB** *Service, Pace*
R-1010 Midland Rd., Southern Pines, 28387, Moore County, (910)692-9362, (800)323-2114, 70 miles from Raleigh. **E-mail:** info@rossresorts.com. **Web:** www.pineneedles-midpines.com. **Facility Holes:** 18. **Yards:** 6,515/4,907. **Par:** 72/72. **Course Rating:** 71.4/68.2. **Slope:** 127/120. **Green Fee:** $59/$135. **Cart Fee:** Included in green fee. **Walking Policy:** Unrestricted walking. **Walkability:** 2. **Opened:** 1921. **Architect:** Donald Ross. **Season:** Year-round. **To obtain tee times:** Call golf shop. **Miscellaneous:** Reduced fees (weekdays, guests, twilight, juniors), range (grass), caddies, lodging (112 rooms), credit cards (MC, V, AE), BF, FF.
Reader Comments: Great Donald Ross layout, almost all greens are elevated and require an extra club approach. First-class service ... Never waited on tee box ... Good layout, not always in top condition ... Superb, excellent course. Perfect ... Challenging old-time course ... Short, tight, undulating greens.

★★★★ **MILL CREEK GOLF CLUB**
SP-1700 St. Andrews Dr., Mebane, 27302, Alamance County, (919)563-4653, 20 miles from Durham. **E-mail:** ronpdmzgolf4some@aol.com. **Web:** millcreekgc.com. **Facility Holes:** 18.

Yards: 7,004/4,884. **Par:** 72/72. **Course Rating:** 73.7/67.5. **Slope:** 141/113. **Green Fee:** $38/$55. **Cart Fee:** Included in green fee. **Walking Policy:** Walking at certain times. **Walkability:** 4. **Opened:** 1995. **Architect:** Rick Robbins/Gary Koch. **Season:** Year-round. **To obtain tee times:** Call up to 7 days in advance. **Miscellaneous:** Reduced fees (weekdays, twilight, seniors, juniors), range (grass), credit cards (MC, V, AE, D, DC), BF, FF. **Notes:** Ranked 6th in 1996 Best New Affordable Courses.

Reader Comments: Challenging layout … Very difficult course … Best in the area … Worth going out of your way … Great course in middle of nowhere, gnarly rough … Nice course, nice people … A lot of effort has been made to improve.

★★ MONROE COUNTRY CLUB
PU-Hwy. 601-S., Monroe, 28112, Union County, (704)282-4661, 20 miles from Charlotte. **Facility Holes:** 18. **Yards:** 6,759/4,964. **Par:** 72/73. **Course Rating:** 71.8/68.6. **Slope:** 118/117. **Green Fee:** $14/$19. **Cart Fee:** $11/Person. **Walking Policy:** Walking at certain times. **Walkability:** 3. **Opened:** 1936. **Architect:** Donald Ross/Tom Jackson. **Season:** Year-round. **To obtain tee times:** Call up to 5 days in advance. **Miscellaneous:** Reduced fees (weekdays, seniors, juniors), range (grass/mats), credit cards (MC, V), BF, FF.

★★½ MOREHEAD CITY COUNTRY CLUB
SP-Country Club Rd., Morehead City, 28557, Carteret County, (252)726-4917, 20 miles from New Bern. **Facility Holes:** 18. **Yards:** 6,255/4,801. **Par:** 72/72. **Course Rating:** 71.4/68.9. **Slope:** 119/115. **Green Fee:** $45. **Cart Fee:** Included in green fee. **Walking Policy:** Mandatory cart. **Walkability:** 1. **Opened:** 1950. **Architect:** C.C. McCuiston/Philip Ball. **Season:** Year-round. **To obtain tee times:** Call golf shop. **Miscellaneous:** Range (grass), credit cards (MC, V, AE).

★★★★½ MOUNT MITCHELL GOLF CLUB *Value, Condition*
PU-7590 Hwy. 80 S., Burnsville, 28714, Yancey County, (828)675-5454, 20 miles from Asheville. **E-mail:** mmgc@burnsville.com. **Web:** www.burnsville.come/mmgc. **Facility Holes:** 18. **Yards:** 6,495/5,455. **Par:** 72/72. **Course Rating:** 71.3/70.9. **Slope:** 141/131. **Green Fee:** $35/$69. **Cart Fee:** Included in green fee. **Walking Policy:** Walking at certain times. **Walkability:** 2. **Opened:** 1975. **Architect:** Fred Hawtree. **Season:** April-Nov. **High:** May-Oct. **To obtain tee times:** Call up to 14 days in advance. **Miscellaneous:** Reduced fees (weekdays, guests), lodging (40 rooms), credit cards (MC, V, AE), FF.

Reader Comments: Manicured to perfection … Panoramic views, very well kept, greens excellent … Awesome views, tight course … Super mountain, valley course, cart paths only, tough on seniors … My favorite … Perfect golf package … Well planned … Slow play.

★★★ MOUNTAIN AIRE GOLF CLUB
PU-1104 Golf Course Rd., West Jefferson, 28694, Ashe County, (336)877-4716, 80 miles from Winston-Salem. **E-mail:** mountainaire@skybest.com. **Web:** www.mountainaire.com. **Facility Holes:** 18. **Yards:** 6,404/4,265. **Par:** 72/72. **Course Rating:** 69.8/63.9. **Slope:** 122/108. **Green Fee:** $14/$25. **Cart Fee:** $12/Person. **Walking Policy:** Unrestricted walking. **Walkability:** 5. **Opened:** 1950. **Season:** March-Nov. **High:** July-Sept. **To obtain tee times:** Call golf shop. **Miscellaneous:** Reduced fees (weekdays, twilight, juniors), range (grass), credit cards (MC, V), BF, FF.

Reader Comments: Excellent venue for golf … Very friendly people, never crowded and very reasonably priced … Absolutely beautiful, great place … Chilly even in summer.

★★★★ MOUNTAIN GLEN GOLF CLUB
SP-Box 326, Newland, 28657, Avery County, (828)733-5804, 50 miles from Asheville. **Facility Holes:** 18. **Yards:** 6,723/5,506. **Par:** 72/72. **Course Rating:** 70.0/68.0. **Slope:** 129/113. **Green Fee:** $40/$48. **Cart Fee:** $0/Person. **Walking Policy:** Walking at certain times. **Walkability:** 1. **Opened:** 1964. **Architect:** George W. Cobb. **Season:** April-Nov. **High:** June-Oct. **To obtain tee times:** Call golf shop. **Miscellaneous:** Metal spikes, range (grass), BF, FF.

Reader Comments: The best value in the mountains … Excellent playing condition, really enjoyed playing here … Very nice people, fastest greens ever, hard to find but worth it, nice scenery, played in winter … Nice course.

★★★★ NAGS HEAD GOLF LINKS
SP-5615 S. Seachase Dr., Nags Head, 27959, Dare County, (252)441-8073, (800)851-9404, 75 miles from Virginia Beach. **Facility Holes:** 18. **Yards:** 6,126/4,415. **Par:** 71/71. **Course Rating:** 68.8/64.7. **Slope:** 130/117. **Green Fee:** $40/$100. **Cart Fee:** Included in green fee. **Walking Policy:** Walking at certain times. **Walkability:** 1. **Opened:** 1987. **Architect:** Bob Moore. **Season:** Year-round. **To obtain tee times:** Call up to 365 days in advance. **Miscellaneous:** Reduced fees (guests, twilight, juniors), range (grass/mats), credit cards (MC, V, AE), BF, FF.

Reader Comments: Advertised as a links layout but homes line almost every hole … Cart path only … Although not long, tight fairways. Wind is a killer.

★★★★½ **NATIONAL GOLF CLUB** *Pace*
SP-1 Royal Troon Dr., Pinehurst, 28374, Moore County, (910)295-5340, (800)471-4339. **E-mail:** proshop@nationalgolfclub.com. **Web:** www.nationalgolfclub.com. **Facility Holes:** 18.
Yards: 7,122/5,378. **Par:** 72/72. **Course Rating:** 75.3/72.1. **Slope:** 137/125. **Green Fee:** $95/$210. **Cart Fee:** Included in green fee. **Walking Policy:** Walking at certain times.
Walkability: 2. **Opened:** 1988. **Architect:** Jack Nicklaus. **Season:** Year-round. **High:** March-Nov.
To obtain tee times: Call golf shop. **Miscellaneous:** Reduced fees (weekdays), range (grass), lodging (20 rooms), credit cards (MC, V, AE), BF, FF.
Reader Comments: Better have a high fade in your bag ... Very tough layout, challenge ... Very difficult course ... Too difficult for average players ... Nicklaus at his best, great condition ... Very good.

★★★★½ **THE NEUSE GOLF CLUB** *Service, Value, Condition, Pace*
SP-918 Birkdale Dr., Clayton, 27520, Johnston County, (919)550-0550, 15 miles from
Raleigh. **Web:** neusegolf.com. **Facility Holes:** 18. **Yards:** 7,010/5,478. **Par:** 72/72. **Course Rating:** 73.5/72.2. **Slope:** 136/126. **Green Fee:** $23/$36. **Cart Fee:** $16/Person. **Walking Policy:** Walking at certain times. **Walkability:** 4. **Opened:** 1993. **Architect:** John LaFoy. **Season:** Year-round. **High:** April-Oct. **To obtain tee times:** Call up to 5 days in advance. **Miscellaneous:** Reduced fees (weekdays, twilight, seniors, juniors), range (grass), credit cards (MC, V, AE), BF, FF.
Notes: Ranked 32nd in 1996 America's Top 75 Affordable Courses.
Reader Comments: The par 3s are well designed ... Beautiful layout along Neuse River ... Excellent conditioning ... Nicest I have played ... All-around great experience ... Very good condition, some unique holes I like it ... Interesting.

★★½ **NORTH CAROLINA NATIONAL GOLF CLUB**
SP-1000 Broken Arrow Dr., Statesville, 28677, Iredell County, (704)873-4653, 10 miles from
Charlotte. **Web:** ncnationalgolfclub.com. **Facility Holes:** 18. **Yards:** 7,086/4,548. **Par:** 72/72.
Course Rating: 73.8/66.6. **Slope:** 133/113. **Green Fee:** $28/$38. **Cart Fee:** Included in green fee. **Walking Policy:** Walking at certain times. **Walkability:** 5. **Opened:** 1998. **Season:** Year-round. **High:** May-Aug. **To obtain tee times:** Call golf shop. **Miscellaneous:** Reduced fees (weekdays, twilight, seniors), range (grass), credit cards (MC, V), BF, FF.
Special Notes: Formerly Broken Arrow Golf Links.

★★★★ **NORTH SHORE COUNTRY CLUB** *Service, Value, Pace*
SP-101 N. Shore Dr., Sneads Ferry, 28460, Onslow County, (910)327-2410, (800)828-5035, 25 miles from Wilmington. **Web:** www.northshorecountryclub.com. **Facility Holes:** 18. **Yards:** 6,866/5,039. **Par:** 72/72. **Course Rating:** 72.8/68.7. **Slope:** 134/122. **Green Fee:** $30/$50. **Cart Fee:** Included in green fee. **Walking Policy:** Mandatory carts. **Walkability:** 3. **Opened:** 1988.
Architect: Bob Moore. **Season:** Year-round. **To obtain tee times:** Call golf shop.
Miscellaneous: Reduced fees (weekdays, twilight, juniors), range (grass), credit cards (MC, V).
Reader Comments: Extremely well maintained, challenging course ... Good variety of yardages to suit high and low handicappers ... An inexpensive, quality alternative to the Myrtle Beach courses ... Costly during summer ... Great place.

★★★ **OAK HOLLOW GOLF COURSE**
PU-3400 N. Centennial St., High Point, 27265, Guilford County, (336)883-3260, 8 miles from
Greensboro. **Facility Holes:** 18. **Yards:** 6,483/4,796. **Par:** 72/72. **Course Rating:** 71.6/67.4.
Slope: 124/114. **Green Fee:** $15/$18. **Cart Fee:** $12/Person. **Walking Policy:** Walking at certain times. **Walkability:** 3. **Opened:** 1972. **Architect:** Pete Dye. **Season:** Year-round. **To obtain tee times:** Call up to 2 days in advance. **Miscellaneous:** Reduced fees (seniors, juniors), range (grass/mats), BF, FF.
Reader Comments: This city-owned course is as good as most private clubs in area ... A bit pricey ... Well-maintained course ... Very crowded, grounds not well kept ... Great muni.

★★ **OAK ISLAND GOLF & COUNTRY CLUB**
PU-928 Caswell Beach Rd., Oak Island, 28465, Brunswick County, (910)278-5275, 23 miles from Wilmington. **Facility Holes:** 18. **Yards:** 6,608/5,437. **Par:** 72/72. **Slope:** 128/121. **Green Fee:** $35/$52. **Cart Fee:** Included in green fee. **Walking Policy:** Mandatory carts. **Opened:** 1969. **Architect:** George Cobb. **Season:** Year-round. **To obtain tee times:** Call golf shop. **Miscellaneous:** Reduced fees (weekdays), metal spikes, range (grass), credit cards (MC, V), FF.

★★★★ **OAK VALLEY GOLF CLUB**
SP-261 Oak Valley Blvd., Advance, 27006, Davie County, (336)940-2000, 10 miles from
Winston-Salem. **Facility Holes:** 18. **Yards:** 7,058/5,197. **Par:** 72/72. **Course Rating:** 74.0/68.0.
Slope: 144/125. **Green Fee:** $28/$47. **Cart Fee:** $14/Person. **Walking Policy:** Walking at certain times. **Walkability:** 3. **Opened:** 1995. **Architect:** Arnold Palmer/Ed Seay. **Season:** Year-round.

To obtain tee times: Call golf shop. **Miscellaneous:** Reduced fees (weekdays, twilight, seniors, juniors), range (grass), credit cards (MC, V, AE).
Reader Comments: This Arnold Palmer course is excellent and playable for all golfers … Great routing, excellent value … Has become the best golf in the area … Nice place to play.

★★★ OCEAN HARBOUR GOLF LINKS
PU-9686 Scenic Drive, Calabash, 28467, Brunswick County, (910)579-3588, (877)592-4653, 2 miles from Calabash. **Web:** www.oceanharbour.com. **Facility Holes:** 18. **Yards:** 6,859/5,056. **Par:** 72/72. **Course Rating:** 75.6/72.4. **Slope:** 142/126. **Green Fee:** $20/$61. **Cart Fee:** $20/Person. **Walking Policy:** Walking at certain times. **Walkability:** 3. **Opened:** 1989. **Architect:** Clyde Johnston. **Season:** Year-round. **To obtain tee times:** Call golf shop. **Miscellaneous:** Reduced fees (guests, juniors), range (grass), credit cards (MC, V, AE).
Reader Comments: Tough finishing holes, good mix of holes … A real beauty, great trees, seldom busy … Great layout, poor condition.

★★ OCEAN ISLE BEACH GOLF COURSE
SP-6000 Pro Shop Dr., S.W., Ocean Isle Beach, 28470, Brunswick County, (910)579-2610, 30 miles from Myrtle Beach. **Facility Holes:** 18. **Yards:** 6,626/5,075. **Par:** 72/72. **Course Rating:** 71.8/69.5. **Slope:** 132/111. **Green Fee:** $10/$30. **Cart Fee:** $18/Person. **Walking Policy:** Walking at certain times. **Walkability:** 2. **Opened:** 1977. **Architect:** Russell Breeden/Dan Breeden. **Season:** Year-round. **To obtain tee times:** Call golf shop. **Miscellaneous:** Reduced fees (weekdays, twilight, juniors), metal spikes, range (grass), credit cards (MC, V, AE, D).

OCEAN RIDGE PLANTATION
PU-351 Ocean Ridge Pkwy., Sunset Beach, 28469, Brunswick County, (910)287-1717, (800)233-1801, 9 miles from North Myrtle Beach. **E-mail:** teetimes@lionspaw.com. **Web:** www.lionspaw.com. **Facility Holes:** 54. **Season:** Year-round. **To obtain tee times:** Call up to 365 days in advance. **Miscellaneous:** Reduced fees (weekdays, guests, twilight, juniors), range (grass), credit cards (MC, V, AE, D), BF, FF.

★★½ **LION'S PAW GOLF LINKS** (18)
Yards: 7,003/5,363. **Par:** 72/72. **Course Rating:** 75.0/70.3. **Slope:** 137/129. **Green Fee:** $20/$50. **Cart Fee:** $20/Person. **Walking Policy:** Mandatory carts. **Walkability:** 3. **Opened:** 1991. **Architect:** Willard Byrd.
Reader Comments: Difficult layout, overpriced … Great course, wide open … Overbooked, slow … Nice layout, great service, great greens.

★★★½ **PANTHER'S RUN GOLF CLUB** (18)
Yards: 7,089/5,023. **Par:** 72/72. **Course Rating:** 72.4/68.3. **Slope:** 142/118. **Green Fee:** $20/$50. **Cart Fee:** $20/Person. **Walking Policy:** Mandatory carts. **Walkability:** 3. **Opened:** 1995. **Architect:** Tim Cate.
Reader Comments: Fun, beautiful, and challenging with great conditioning … Layout is different, good service, great shape every time … Difficult layout … Overpriced … Great course.

★★★★½ **TIGER'S EYE GOLF LINKS** (18)
Yards: 7,014/5,136. **Par:** 72/72. **Course Rating:** 73.5/70.1. **Slope:** 144/128. **Green Fee:** $45/$90. **Cart Fee:** $21/Cart. **Walking Policy:** Unrestricted walking. **Walkability:** 4. **Opened:** 2000. **Architect:** Tim Cate. **High:** March-May.
Notes: Ranked 11th in 2001 Best in State.
Reader Comments: Another perfect course … Greens are wonderfully tough, course is a real gem … Spent lots of dollars to create a lovely course … Very nice course. Worth your time … Overbooked at times … Can be slow.

★★★★ OLDE BEAU GOLF CLUB AT ROARING GAP
SP-Hwy. 21, Roaring Gap, 28668, Alleghany County, (910)363-3044, (800)752-1634, 60 miles from Winston-Salem. **Facility Holes:** 18. **Yards:** 6,705/4,912. **Par:** 72/75. **Course Rating:** 71.2/67.5. **Slope:** 131/118. **Green Fee:** $50/$65. **Cart Fee:** $13/Person. **Walking Policy:** Mandatory carts. **Walkability:** 5. **Opened:** 1991. **Architect:** Billy Satterfield. **Season:** March-Dec. **To obtain tee times:** Call golf shop. **Miscellaneous:** Range (grass), credit cards (MC, V, AE), BF, FF.
Reader Comments: Fantastic mountain course … Great course conditions & views … Target golf at its best … A true mountain course, beautiful … Wow … The front 9 great, the back is too steep … Pretty views.

OLDE FORT GOLF COURSE
PU-3189 River Rd. SE, Winnabow, 28479, Brunswick County, (910)371-9940, 12 miles from Wilmington. **Facility Holes:** 18. **Yards:** 6,311/4,580. **Par:** 72/72. **Course Rating:** 68.4/64.6. **Slope:** 108/99. **Green Fee:** $16/$21. **Cart Fee:** Included in green fee. **Walking Policy:** Unrestricted walking. **Walkability:** 4. **Opened:** 1990. **Season:** Year-round. **High:** March-Nov. **To obtain tee times:** Call golf shop. **Miscellaneous:** Reduced fees (weekdays, seniors, juniors), metal spikes.

★★★ OLDE POINT COUNTRY CLUB
SP-Country Club Dr. & Hwy. 17, N., Hampstead, 28443, Pender County, (910)270-2403, 18 miles from Wilmington. **Web:** oldepoint@aol.com. **Facility Holes:** 18. **Yards:** 6,913/5,133. **Par:** 72/72. **Course Rating:** 72.5/69.0. **Slope:** 136/115. **Green Fee:** $25/$45. **Cart Fee:** $16/Person. **Walking Policy:** Mandatory carts. **Walkability:** 4. **Opened:** 1974. **Architect:** Jerry Turner. **Season:** Year-round. **High:** March-April. **To obtain tee times:** Call golf shop. **Miscellaneous:** Reduced fees (weekdays), range (grass), credit cards (MC, V, AE), BF, FF.
Reader Comments: Fun to play … Some great holes … Course does not drain … Wet … Play it just for No. 11… Back 9 scenic and challenging … Best hot dogs in the country … Slow bent-grass greens … One of best in coastal region.

★★★★½ OYSTER BAY GOLF LINKS
PU-Hwy. 179, Sunset Beach, 28468, Brunswick County, (800)697-8372, (800)377-2315, 18 miles from Myrtle Beach, SC. **Facility Holes:** 18. **Yards:** 6,785/4,825. **Par:** 71/71. **Course Rating:** 74.1/67.7. **Slope:** 137/117. **Green Fee:** $30/$105. **Cart Fee:** $18/Person. **Walkability:** 2. **Opened:** 1983. **Architect:** Dan Maples. **Season:** Year-round. **To obtain tee times:** Call golf shop. **Miscellaneous:** Reduced fees (guests), metal spikes, range (grass), credit cards (MC, V, AE).
Reader Comments: Best course I've played all over the US … Great condition and design … Somewhat tricked up … Great holes, great views, great course … Good layout, great vistas … Played both these courses years ago but never forgotten … Loved all the oyster shells.

PEARL GOLF LINKS
PU-1300 Pearl Blvd. S.W., Sunset Beach, 28468, Brunswick County, (910)579-8132, (888)947-3275, 30 miles from Myrtle Beach. **E-mail:** info@thepearl.com. **Web:** www.thepearl-golf.com. **Facility Holes:** 36. **Cart Fee:** Included in green fee. **Walking Policy:** Mandatory carts. **Walkability:** 3. **Opened:** 1987. **Architect:** Dan Maples. **Season:** Year-round. **High:** March-May. **To obtain tee times:** Call golf shop. **Miscellaneous:** Reduced fees (twilight, juniors), range (grass), credit cards (MC, V, AE, D), BF, FF.
★★★★ EAST COURSE (18) *Pace*
Yards: 6,749/5,125. **Par:** 72/72. **Course Rating:** 73.1/73.9. **Slope:** 135/129. **Green Fee:** $35/$69.
Reader Comments: Good blend of golf and nature … Food was good and fast … I'll be back … Nos. 16 and 17 have spectacular views … Enjoyable … Good course in good shape … Very good facilities, not very long.
★★★★½ WEST COURSE (18) *Pace+*
Yards: 7,000/5,188. **Par:** 72/72. **Course Rating:** 73.2/73.4. **Slope:** 132/127. **Green Fee:** $31/$69.
Reader Comments: Very good test of golf … Great course layout … Winter has taken its toll on these greens … Enjoyable … Great course, tight … Always enjoy this one.

★½ PINE GROVE GOLF CLUB
PU-1108 Costner Rd., Shelby, 28150, Cleveland County, (704)487-0455, 45 miles from Charlotte. **Facility Holes:** 18. **Yards:** 6,238/4,774. **Par:** 70/70. **Course Rating:** 67.1/65.1. **Slope:** 106/103. **Green Fee:** $9/$15. **Cart Fee:** $12/Person. **Walking Policy:** Walking at certain times. **Walkability:** 4. **Opened:** 1960. **Architect:** Namon Hamrick. **Season:** Year-round. **To obtain tee times:** Call up to 3 days in advance. **Miscellaneous:** Reduced fees (weekdays, seniors), BF, FF.

★★ PINE KNOLLS GOLF CLUB
PU-1100 Quail Hollow Rd., Kernersville, 27284, Forsyth County, (336)993-8300, 9 miles from Winston-Salem. **E-mail:** jrs1948go@aol. **Web:** pkgc. **Facility Holes:** 18. **Yards:** 6,311/4,480. **Par:** 71/72. **Course Rating:** 70.4/64.8. **Slope:** 123/109. **Green Fee:** $15/$20. **Cart Fee:** $13/Person. **Walking Policy:** Walking at certain times. **Walkability:** 3. **Opened:** 1969. **Architect:** Clyde Holder. **Season:** Year-round. **To obtain tee times:** Call up to 7 days in advance. **Miscellaneous:** Reduced fees (weekdays, twilight, seniors, juniors), metal spikes, range (grass/mats), credit cards (MC, V, AE), BF, FF.

★★★★½ PINE NEEDLES LODGE & GOLF CLUB *Service+, Value, Pace*
R-1005 Midland Rd, Southern Pines, 28387, Moore County, (910)692-8611, (800)747-7272, 70 miles from Raleigh. **E-mail:** info@rossresorts.com. **Web:** www.rossresorts.com. **Facility Holes:** 18. **Yards:** 6,708/5,039. **Par:** 71/71. **Course Rating:** 72.2/68.4. **Slope:** 131/118. **Green Fee:** $75/$175. **Cart Fee:** Included in green fee. **Walking Policy:** Unrestricted walking. **Walkability:** 2. **Opened:** 1927. **Architect:** Donald Ross. **Season:** Year-round. **To obtain tee times:** Call golf shop. **Miscellaneous:** Reduced fees (guests, juniors), range (grass), caddies, lodging (81 rooms), credit cards (MC, V, AE), BF, FF.
Notes: Ranked 14th in 2001 Best in State.
Reader Comments: Made me fall in love with Donald Ross. "Thinking golf" … Great course, great environment, great treatment … Expected more … Traditional, timeless layout.

★½ PINE TREE GOLF CLUB
PU-1680 Pine Tree Lane, Kernersville, 27284, Forsyth County, (910)993-5598, 10 miles from Greensboro. **E-mail:** twpga@aol.com. **Facility Holes:** 18. **Yards:** 6,682/4,954. **Par:** 71/72. **Course Rating:** 71.0/67.0. **Slope:** 120/112. **Green Fee:** $15/$19. **Cart Fee:** $11/Person. **Walking Policy:** Walking at certain times. **Walkability:** 3. **Opened:** 1970. **Architect:** Gene Hamm. **Season:** Year-round. **High:** April-Nov. **To obtain tee times:** Call up to 10 days in advance. **Miscellaneous:** Reduced fees (seniors), range (grass), credit cards (MC, V), FF.

PINEHURST RESORT & COUNTRY CLUB
R-Carolina Vista Dr., Pinehurst, 28374, Moore County, (910)235-8141, (800)795-4653, 70 miles from Raleigh. **Facility Holes:** 144. **Season:** Year-round. **To obtain tee times:** Call golf shop. **Misc:** Reduced fees (twilight), range (grass), caddies, lodging (250 rooms), credit cards (MC, V, AE, D, DC, CB).

★★★★ PINEHURST NO. 1 (18)
Yards: 6,128/5,307. **Par:** 70/73. **Course Rating:** 69.4/70.5. **Slope:** 116/117. **Green Fee:** $70/$150. **Cart Fee:** Included in green fee. **Walking Policy:** Unrestricted walking. **Walkability:** 2. **Opened:** 1898. **Architect:** Donald Ross.
Reader Comments: Easy, danger is in front of you. Needs to be in better shape for three-figure green fee … Basic golf.

★★★★★ PINEHURST NO. 2 (18) *Condition+, Pace*
Yards: 7,189/5,035. **Par:** 72/74. **Course Rating:** 75.3/69.6. **Slope:** 135/124. **Fee:** $245/$325. **Walking Policy:** Unrestricted walking. **Walkability:** 2. **Opened:** 1907. **Architect:** Donald Ross. **Notes:** Ranked 9th in 2001-2002 America's 100 Greatest; 1st in 2001 Best in State.
Reader Comments: Absolute must for any serious golfer to experience, turtle-back greens of Ross at his finest is an unforgetable experience … Thinking of Payne Stewart while playing … Walking up No. 18 is like a pilgrimage … Best course in the world … Fun off the tee, genius around the greens.

★★★ PINEHURST NO. 3 (18)
Yards: 5,682/5,232. **Par:** 70/71. **Course Rating:** 67.2/69.9. **Slope:** 115/117. **Fee:** $70/$150. **Walking Policy:** Unrestricted walking. **Walkability:** 2. **Opened:** 1910. **Architect:** Donald Ross.
Reader Comments: Tough greens, tight … Small greens … No. 3 is a great warmup for No. 2 … Crowned greens will get you … How do you describe a masterpiece? … Overpriced … Good intro to Donald Ross greens … Short.

★★★★ PINEHURST NO. 4 (18)
Yards: 7,117/5,217. **Par:** 72/72. **Course Rating:** 74.5/70.6. **Slope:** 136/123. **Fee:** $155/$225. **Walking Policy:** Unrestricted walking. **Walkability:** 3. **Opened:** 1999. **Architect:** Tom Fazio. **Notes:** Ranked 5th in 2001 Best in State; 3rd in 2000 Best New Upscale Courses.
Reader Comments: Should be in top 100 in US … Best service ever … A golfer's dream … Fazio meets Ross … A great experience … Second best at Pinehurst, could host a PGA stop … Lots of bunkers … Great tribute course to Pinehurst.

★★★ PINEHURST NO. 5 (18)
Yards: 6,848/5,248. **Par:** 72/72. **Course Rating:** 73.4/70.1. **Slope:** 137/119. **Green Fee:** $85/$150. **Cart Fee:** Included in green fee. **Walking Policy:** Unrestricted walking. **Walkability:** 2. **Opened:** 1961. **Architect:** Ellis Maples.
Reader Comments: Classic course … Course in great shape … Good, fair course … Only three par 3s … Really tough with water in front … Shot under par … Good course.

★★★★ PINEHURST NO. 6 (18)
R-U.S. Hwy. 15-501, Pinehurst, 28374, Moore County, (910)235-8145, (800)795-4653. **Yards:** 7,157/5,436. **Par:** 72/72. **Course Rating:** 75.6/71.2. **Slope:** 139/125. **Green Fee:** $85/$150. **Walking Policy:** Mandatory carts. **Walkability:** 3. **Opened:** 1979. **Architect:** Tom Fazio/George Fazio.
Reader Comments: Beautiful parkland track, but overpriced due to Pinehurst name … Very expensive but excellent course … The most underrated of the resort courses.

★★★★ PINEHURST NO. 7 (18)
R-U.S. Hwy. 15-501, Pinehurst, 28374, Moore County, (910)235-8140, (800)795-4653. **Yards:** 7,125/4,996. **Par:** 72/72. **Course Rating:** 74.4/69.7. **Slope:** 140/122. **Fee:** $145/$215. **Walking Policy:** Unrestricted walking. **Walkability:** 5. **Opened:** 1986. **Architect:** Rees Jones. **Notes:** Ranked 18th in 2001 Best in State.
Reader Comments: My favorite Pinehurst course after No. 2 … Pricey resort but golf at its best … Great course, too slow … Good but not great … A pleasure to play, always in good condition.

★★★★½ PINEHURST NO. 8 (18) *Condition+, Pace+*
R-Murdocksville Rd., Pinehurst, 28374, Moore County, (910)235-8760, (800)795-4653. **Yards:** 7,092/5,177. **Par:** 72/72. **Course Rating:** 74.0/69.8. **Slope:** 135/122. **Fee:** $155/$225. **Walking Policy:** Unrestricted walking. **Walkability:** 5. **Opened:** 1995. **Architect:** Tom Fazio. **Notes:** Ranked 8th in 2001 Best in State; 3rd in 1996 Best New Upscale Courses.
Reader Comments: Expensive, but worth playing nonetheless … Beautiful design and great shot values … Good variety of holes, great condition and caddies … Great Fazio layout … Good course, a little overrated … Crown greens like No. 2 … It ought to be the next US Open course … Great place to golf.

PINEWILD COUNTRY CLUB OF PINEHURST

SP-Hwy. 211, Pinehurst, 28374, Moore County, (910)295-5145, (800)523-1499, 4 miles from Pinehurst. **E-mail:** golf@pinewildcc.com. **Web:** www.pinewildcc.com. **Facility Holes:** 36. **Cart Fee:** $18/Person. **Walking Policy:** Walking at certain times. **Season:** Year-round. **High:** March-June. **To obtain tee times:** Call golf shop. **Miscellaneous:** Reduced fees (guests, juniors), range (grass), credit cards (MC, V), BF, FF.

★★★★   HOLLY COURSE (18)
Yards: 7,024/5,475. **Par:** 72/72. **Course Rating:** 73.4/71.4. **Slope:** 131/126. **Green Fee:** $40/$80. **Walkability:** 3. **Opened:** 1996. **Architect:** Gary Player.
Reader Comments: Fine greens & no OB stakes … Best player-friendly course I've played … Challenging, fair, fast greens … Too many blind tee shots, large greens.

MAGNOLIA COURSE (18)
Yards: 7,276/5,362. **Par:** 72/72. **Course Rating:** 75.0/71.1. **Slope:** 135/121. **Green Fee:** $40/$90. **Walkability:** 2. **Opened:** 1988. **Architect:** Gene Hamm.

★★★★   THE PIT GOLF LINKS

PU-Highway 5 (between Pinehurst & Aberdeen), Pinehurst, 28374, Moore County, (910)944-1600, (800)574-4653, 35 miles from Fayetteville. **E-mail:** pit@pinehurst.net. **Web:** www.pitgolf.com. **Facility Holes:** 18. **Yards:** 6,600/4,759. **Par:** 71/72. **Course Rating:** 72.3/68.4. **Slope:** 139/121. **Green Fee:** $54/$89. **Cart Fee:** Included in green fee. **Walking Policy:** Unrestricted walking. **Walkability:** 3. **Opened:** 1985. **Architect:** Dan Maples. **Season:** Year-round. **High:** March-Nov. **To obtain tee times:** Call up to 365 days in advance. **Miscellaneous:** Reduced fees (twilight, juniors), metal spikes, range (grass), credit cards (MC, V), BF, FF.
Reader Comments: Not as tough as its reputation … Great condition and fast greens … A true test of your game … Good mix of holes, kept it in the fairways … Love the island par 3 …Frustrating … My favorite in the Sandhills.

★★★★   THE PLANTATION GOLF CLUB   *Pace*

SP-Midland Rd., Pinehurst, 28374, Moore County, (910)695-3193, (800)633-2685, 50 miles from Raleigh. **E-mail:** pro4u@mindspring.com. **Facility Holes:** 18. **Yards:** 7,123/4,845. **Par:** 72/73. **Course Rating:** 74.0/68.9. **Slope:** 140/123. **Green Fee:** $60/$115. **Cart Fee:** $0/Person. **Walking Policy:** Mandatory carts. **Walkability:** 4. **Opened:** 1993. **Architect:** Arnold Palmer/Ed Seay. **Season:** Year-round. **To obtain tee times:** Call golf shop. **Miscellaneous:** Reduced fees (guests), range (grass), credit cards (MC, V), BF, FF.
Notes: Ranked 20th in 1999 Best in State.
Reader Comments: Great Palmer course … Another great layout, worth it … Good condition … Bring your "A" game … Rounding into shape … 18 different holes, well designed … Great course with temporary clubhouse.

★★★½   PORTERS NECK PLANTATION & COUNTRY CLUB

SP-8403 Vintage Club Dr., Wilmington, 28411, New Hanover County, (910)686-1177, (800)947-8177, 3 miles from Wilmington. **Web:** porters-neck.com. **Facility Holes:** 18. **Yards:** 7,209/5,268. **Par:** 72/72. **Course Rating:** 75.6/71.2. **Slope:** 140/124. **Green Fee:** $50/$95. **Cart Fee:** Included in green fee. **Walking Policy:** Mandatory carts. **Walkability:** 3. **Opened:** 1991. **Architect:** Tom Fazio. **Season:** Year-round. **To obtain tee times:** Call up to 60 days in advance. **Miscellaneous:** Reduced fees (weekdays), range (grass), credit cards (MC, V), BF, FF.
Notes: Ranked 19th in 2001 Best in State.
Reader Comments: Nice layout, keeps you thinking … Great golf & service … Good test … Wonderful … Big bent-grass greens … Pretty tight, some greens in poor shape.

★★   QUAIL RIDGE GOLF COURSE

SP-5634 Quail Ridge Dr., Sanford, 27330, Lee County, (919)776-6623, (800)344-6276, 30 miles from Raleigh. **E-mail:** quailridge@cybernet2k.com. **Web:** www.golfersresource.com. **Facility Holes:** 18. **Yards:** 6,875/5,280. **Par:** 72/73. **Course Rating:** 73.2/70.8. **Slope:** 125/117. **Green Fee:** $25/$35. **Walking Policy:** Walking at certain times. **Walkability:** 3. **Opened:** 1965. **Architect:** Gene Hamm/Ellis Maples. **Season:** Year-round. **High:** March-June. **To obtain tee times:** Call up to 5 days in advance. **Miscellaneous:** Reduced fees (weekdays, guests, twilight, seniors, juniors), range (grass/mats), credit cards (MC, V), BF, FF.

★½   QUAKER MEADOWS GOLF CLUB

PU-826 N. Green St., Morganton, 28655, Burke County, (828)437-2677, 45 miles from Asheville. **Web:** gmgolf.com. **Facility Holes:** 18. **Yards:** 6,410/5,002. **Par:** 71/71. **Course Rating:** 70.0/68.2. **Slope:** 117/110. **Green Fee:** $10/$14. **Cart Fee:** $10/Person. **Walking Policy:** Walking at certain times. **Opened:** 1968. **Architect:** Russell Breeden. **Season:** Year-round. **High:** March-Dec. **To obtain tee times:** Call up to 4 days in advance. **Miscellaneous:** Range (grass), credit cards (MC, V, AE, D), BF, FF.

★★½ QUAKER NECK COUNTRY CLUB
SP-299 Country Club Rd., Trenton, 28585, Jones County, (252)224-5736, (800)657-5156, 10 miles from New Bern. **E-mail:** quakerneck@cconnect.net. **Web:** www.quakerneck.com. **Facility Holes:** 18. **Yards:** 6,575/4,953. **Par:** 72/72. **Course Rating:** 71.7/68.5. **Slope:** 126/115. **Green Fee:** $15/$19. **Cart Fee:** $12/Person. **Walking Policy:** Unrestricted walking. **Walkability:** 3. **Opened:** 1966. **Architect:** Russell T. Burney. **Season:** Year-round. **To obtain tee times:** Call up to 4 days in advance. **Miscellaneous:** Reduced fees (weekdays, twilight), range (grass), credit cards (MC, V, AE, D), BF, FF.

★★½ QUARRY HILLS COUNTRY CLUB
SP-George Bason Rd., Graham, 27253, Alamance County, (336)578-2602, 20 miles from Chapel Hill. **Web:** www.quarryhillscc.com. **Facility Holes:** 18. **Yards:** 6,617/4,905. **Par:** 70/70. **Course Rating:** 71.9/68.0. **Slope:** 130/116. **Green Fee:** $25/$44. **Cart Fee:** Included in green fee. **Walking Policy:** Unrestricted walking. **Walkability:** 4. **Opened:** 1970. **Architect:** Ellis Maples/Ed Seay. **Season:** Year-round. **High:** March-Nov. **To obtain tee times:** Call golf shop. **Miscellaneous:** Reduced fees (weekdays), range (grass/mats), credit cards (MC, V, AE, D).

★★★ REEDY CREEK GOLF COURSE
PU-585 Reedy Creek Rd., Four Oaks, 27524, Johnston County, (919)934-7502, (800)331-2572, 20 miles from Raleigh. **E-mail:** reedycrk@sprynet.com. **Facility Holes:** 18. **Yards:** 6,426/4,632. **Par:** 72/72. **Course Rating:** 70.2/67.5. **Slope:** 126/116. **Green Fee:** $11/$25. **Cart Fee:** $10/Person. **Walking Policy:** Walking at certain times. **Walkability:** 3. **Opened:** 1988. **Architect:** Gene Hamm. **Season:** Year-round. **To obtain tee times:** Call golf shop. **Miscellaneous:** Reduced fees (weekdays, guests, twilight, seniors, juniors), range (grass), credit cards (MC, V, D), FF.
Reader Comments: Not bad for the price … Nicely kept course and a good golf value … Challenging course, great service … Very well maintained, Bermuda greens nice contrast …

★★★★ REEMS CREEK GOLF CLUB
SP-Pink Fox Cove Rd., Weaverville, 28787, Buncombe County, (828)645-4393, (800)762-8379, 12 miles from Asheville. **Web:** www.reemscreekgolf.com. **Facility Holes:** 18. **Yards:** 6,492/4,605. **Par:** 72/72. **Course Rating:** 70.5/66.9. **Slope:** 130/114. **Green Fee:** $44/$50. **Cart Fee:** Included in green fee. **Walking Policy:** Mandatory carts. **Walkability:** 3. **Opened:** 1989. **Architect:** Martin Hawtree/Fred Hawtree. **Season:** Year-round. **High:** March-Nov. **To obtain tee times:** Call up to 30 days in advance. **Miscellaneous:** Reduced fees (weekdays, guests, juniors), range (grass), credit cards (MC, V, AE), BF, FF.
Reader Comments: A little too hilly … One of the best kept courses in the state … Beautiful sand traps and greens … Great views, fairways are slick.

★★★ REYNOLDS PARK GOLF CLUB
PU-2391 Reynolds Park Rd., Winston-Salem, 27107, Forsyth County, (336)650-7660. **E-mail:** reynoldspark@americangolf.com. **Web:** americangolf.com. **Facility Holes:** 18. **Yards:** 6,534/5,446. **Par:** 71/73. **Course Rating:** 70.8/65.1. **Slope:** 121/109. **Green Fee:** $15/$21. **Cart Fee:** $12/Person. **Walking Policy:** Walking at certain times. **Walkability:** 3. **Opened:** 1939. **Architect:** Ellis Maples. **Season:** Year-round. **High:** March-May. **To obtain tee times:** Call up to 7 days in advance. **Miscellaneous:** Reduced fees (weekdays, twilight, seniors, juniors), range (grass/mats), credit cards (MC, V, AE, D, DC), BF, FF.
Reader Comments: The pace of play is very dependent upon the time of day, as many leagues make the course overcrowded in the evenings … One of the best buys for the price.

★★ RICHMOND PINES COUNTRY CLUB
SP-145 Richmond Pines Dr., Rockingham, 28379, Richmond County, (910)895-3279, 50 miles from Charlotte. **E-mail:** rrrpro@aol.com. **Facility Holes:** 18. **Yards:** 6,267/5,051. **Par:** 72/72. **Course Rating:** 69.9/65.0. **Slope:** 127/113. **Green Fee:** $11/$17. **Cart Fee:** $12/Person. **Walking Policy:** Unrestricted walking. **Walkability:** 3. **Opened:** 1926. **Architect:** Donald Ross. **Season:** Year-round. **To obtain tee times:** Call golf shop. **Miscellaneous:** Reduced fees (seniors), range (grass), credit cards (MC, V), BF, FF.

★★★ RIVER BEND GOLF CLUB
PU-3005 Longwood Dr., Shelby, 28150, Cleveland County, (704)482-4286, 45 miles from Charlotte. **E-mail:** rbapro@carolina.rr.com. **Facility Holes:** 18. **Yards:** 6,770/5,225. **Par:** 72/72. **Course Rating:** 72.4/69.5. **Slope:** 134/119. **Green Fee:** $21/$39. **Cart Fee:** Included in green fee. **Walking Policy:** Walking at certain times. **Walkability:** 3. **Opened:** 1965. **Architect:** Russell Breeden. **Season:** Year-round. **High:** April-Oct. **To obtain tee times:** Call up to 7 days in advance. **Miscellaneous:** Reduced fees (weekdays, seniors, juniors), range (grass), credit cards (MC, V, D), BF, FF.
Reader Comments: Always in perfect condition … Easy course to walk, country club feel … Grass was outstanding, greens, fairways … Not a lot of fun … Good course.

★★ RIVER LANDING AT SANDY RIDGE
PU-2025 Sandy Ridge Rd., Colfax, 27235, Guilford County, (336)668-1171, 5 miles from Greensboro. **Facility Holes:** 9. **Yards:** 3,067/2,666. **Par:** 72/72. **Cart Fee:** Included in green fee. **Walking Policy:** Unrestricted walking. **Walkability:** 3. **Season:** Year-round. **High:** June-Sept. **To obtain tee times:** Call up to 7 days in advance. **Miscellaneous:** Reduced fees (seniors), metal spikes.
Special Notes: Formerly Sandy Ridge Golf Course.

★★★★½ RIVER RIDGE GOLF CLUB
SP-3224 Auburn-Knightdale Rd., Raleigh, 27610, Wake County, (919)661-8374. **Facility Holes:** 18. **Yards:** 6,651/5,769. **Par:** 72/71. **Course Rating:** 72.3/70.3. **Slope:** 135/125. **Green Fee:** $22/$53. **Cart Fee:** Included in green fee. **Walking Policy:** Walking at certain times. **Walkability:** 3. **Opened:** 1997. **Architect:** Chuck Smith. **Season:** Year-round. **To obtain tee times:** Call up to 7 days in advance. **Miscellaneous:** Reduced fees (weekdays, twilight, seniors, juniors), range (grass), credit cards (MC, V).
Reader Comments: Course is challenging yet fair … A great place … The staff is friendly and courteous and really makes one feel at home …The course is always in great shape. Even when crowded, the pace of play isn't all that bad .

★★★★½ RIVERS EDGE GOLF CLUB *Service, Pace*
PU-2000 Arnold Palmer Dr., Shallotte, 28470, Brunswick County, (910)755-3434, (877)748-3718, 30 miles from Myrtle Beach. **Web:** www.river 18.com. **Facility Holes:** 18. **Yards:** 6,909. **Par:** 72. **Course Rating:** 74.7. **Slope:** 149. **Green Fee:** $60/$100. **Walking Policy:** Mandatory carts. **Opened:** 1999. **Architect:** Arnold Palmer/Ed Seay/Erik Larsen. **To obtain tee times:** Call up to 365 days in advance. **Miscellaneous:** Range (grass), included in fee), credit cards (MC, V, AE), BF, FF.
Notes: Ranked 12th in 2001 Best in State; 7th in 2000 Best New Upscale Courses.
Reader Comments: I was treated absolutely fantastic by the staff from the very first minute on site … The scenery is spectacular and the golf course is challenging, well laid out and in great shape … The clubhouse sits atop a bluff overlooking the 9th & 18th holes … Awesome course … I was treated great.

RIVERWOOD GOLF CLUB
PU-400 Riverwood Dr., Clayton, 27520, Johnston County, (919)550-1919, 20 miles from Raleigh. **E-mail:** sunbeltgolfgroup.com. **Facility Holes:** 18. **Yards:** 7,012/4,970. **Par:** 72/72. **Course Rating:** 73.8/68.8. **Slope:** 130/115. **Green Fee:** $20/$31. **Cart Fee:** $13/Person. **Walking Policy:** Walking at certain times. **Walkability:** 4. **Opened:** 1997. **Architect:** David Postlethwait. **Season:** Year-round. **High:** April-Sept. **To obtain tee times:** Call golf shop. **Miscellaneous:** Reduced fees (weekdays, twilight, seniors, juniors), range (grass/mats), credit cards (MC, V, AE, D).

ROCK BARN GOLF & COUNTRY CLUB
SP-3791 Golf Dr., Conover, 28613, Catawba County, (828)459-9279, (888)725-2276, 60 miles from Charlotte. **Facility Holes:** 36. **Yards:** 6,553/6,040. **Par:** 72/72. **Course Rating:** 71.2/69.5. **Slope:** 130/126. **Green Fee:** $31/$38. **Cart Fee:** $12/Person. **Walking Policy:** Walking at certain times. **Walkability:** 3. **Opened:** 1969. **Architect:** Russell Breeden/Tom Jackson. **Season:** Year-round. **High:** March-Oct. **To obtain tee times:** Call golf shop. **Miscellaneous:** Reduced fees (weekdays, seniors), range (grass), credit cards (MC, V, AE, D), BF, FF.

★★★½ ROCKY RIVER GOLF CLUB AT CONCORD
PU-6900 Speedway Blvd., Concord, 28027, Cabarrus County, (704)455-1200, 9 miles from Charlotte. **E-mail:** RRgolf@ctc.net. **Web:** www.rockyrivergolf.com. **Facility Holes:** 18. **Yards:** 6,970/4,754. **Par:** 72/72. **Course Rating:** 73.5/68.4. **Slope:** 137/119. **Green Fee:** $24/$46. **Cart Fee:** $12/Person. **Walking Policy:** Walking at certain times. **Walkability:** 3. **Opened:** 1997. **Architect:** Dan Maples. **Season:** Year-round. **High:** April-Oct. **To obtain tee times:** Call up to 6 days in advance. **Miscellaneous:** Reduced fees (weekdays, twilight, seniors, juniors), range (grass), credit cards (MC, V, AE), BF, FF.
Reader Comments: Great little course … A little short … Stays is good shape all year long … Easier to play than the course rating, slope might suggest … Pretty venue … Challenging, but slow play … Interesting course … Penalty.

★★★½ SALEM GLEN COUNTRY CLUB
SP-1000 Glen Day Dr., Clemmons, 27012, Forsyth County, (336)712-1010, 15 miles from Winston-Salem. **E-mail:** brad@salemglen.com. **Web:** www.salemglen.com. **Facility Holes:** 18. **Yards:** 7,012/5,054. **Par:** 71/71. **Course Rating:** 72.4/67.7. **Slope:** 132/116. **Green Fee:** $23/$33. **Cart Fee:** $12/Person. **Walking Policy:** Walking at certain times. **Walkability:** 4. **Opened:** 1997. **Architect:** Bruce Borland/Glen Day. **Season:** Year-round. **High:** March-Sept. **To**

obtain tee times: Call golf shop. **Miscellaneous:** Reduced fees (weekdays, twilight, seniors, juniors), range (grass), credit cards (MC, V, AE, D), BF, FF.

Reader Comments: Favorite course in Winston area … Beautiful clubhouse, contrasting 9s; nice greens … Will improve with another year … Excellent layout … Must play, will eventually become private … Nice fairways and practice facilities.

★½ SAND HILLS GOLF CLUB

PU-U.S. Highway #1 S., Pinebluff, 28373, Moore County, (910)281-3169, (888)281-3169, 12 miles from Pinehurst. **E-mail:** flatt1loe@aol.com. **Web:** sandhillsgolfclub.com. **Facility Holes:** 18. **Yards:** 7,094/5,180. **Par:** 72/72. **Course Rating:** 72.9/67.8. **Slope:** 134/113. **Green Fee:** $25/$40. **Cart Fee:** Included in green fee. **Walking Policy:** Unrestricted walking. **Walkability:** 2. **Opened:** 1972. **Architect:** Frank Hicks. **Season:** Year-round. **High:** April-June. **To obtain tee times:** Call up to 60 days in advance. **Miscellaneous:** Reduced fees (weekdays, guests, twilight, seniors, juniors), metal spikes, range (grass), lodging (40 rooms), credit cards (MC, V), BF, FF.

Special Notes: Formerly Pinebluff Golf Club.

★★★★ SANDPIPER BAY GOLF & COUNTRY CLUB

PU-800 Sandpiper Bay Dr., Sunset Beach, 28468, Brunswick County, (910)579-9120, (800)356-5827, 25 miles from Myrtle Beach. **E-mail:** ssbpiper@insoave.net. **Web:** www.sand-piperbaygolf.com. **Facility Holes:** 27. **Yards:** 6,910/4,869. **Par:** 72/71. **Course Rating:** 72.6/68.3. **Slope:** 125/113. **Green Fee:** $20/$67. **Cart Fee:** $21/Person. **Walking Policy:** Mandatory carts. **Walkability:** 2. **Opened:** 1987. **Architect:** Dan Maples. **Season:** Year-round. **To obtain tee times:** Call golf shop. **Miscellaneous:** Reduced fees (weekdays), range (grass), credit cards (MC, D), BF, FF.

Reader Comments: Great use of water and sand instead of tight trees to make it tough … Good course for everyone with selection of tee boxes … Staff one of the best … Play often … Beautiful course and helpful staff … Wet.

SANDY RIDGE COUNTRY CLUB

PU-211 Clubhouse Dr., Dunn, 28334, Sampson County, (910)892-6424, 50 miles from Raleigh. **Facility Holes:** 18. **Yards:** 6,419/4,424. **Par:** 72/72. **Course Rating:** 68.5/65.2. **Slope:** 120/103. **Green Fee:** $15/$25. **Cart Fee:** Included in green fee. **Walking Policy:** Walking at certain times. **Walkability:** 1. **Opened:** 1989. **Architect:** L. B. Wilson. **Season:** Year-round. **High:** March-Nov. **To obtain tee times:** Call golf shop. **Miscellaneous:** FF.

★★★ SAPPHIRE MOUNTAIN GOLF CLUB

R-50 Slicer's Ave., Sapphire, 28774, Jackson County, (828)743-1174, 60 miles from Asheville. **E-mail:** smggp@aol.com. **Facility Holes:** 18. **Yards:** 6,185/4,547. **Par:** 70/70. **Course Rating:** 69.3/65.9. **Slope:** 127/114. **Green Fee:** $45/$75. **Cart Fee:** Included in green fee. **Walking Policy:** Mandatory carts. **Walkability:** 5. **Opened:** 1981. **Architect:** Ron Garl. **Season:** Year-round. **To obtain tee times:** Call up to 30 days in advance. **Miscellaneous:** Reduced fees (guests, twilight, juniors), metal spikes, credit cards (MC, V, AE), BF, FF.

Reader Comments: After round, pro shop staff offered to call another course to see if a tee time was available, made the time and gave us driving directions-wow.

★★ SCOTHURST GOLF COURSE

SP-Hwy. 20 E. P.O. Box 88, Lumber Bridge, 28357, Robeson County, (910)843-5357, 20 miles from Fayetteville. **Web:** marvinrea54@hotmail.com. **Facility Holes:** 18. **Yards:** 7,000/5,150. **Par:** 72/72. **Course Rating:** 72.9/70.0. **Slope:** 118/111. **Green Fee:** $22/$30. **Cart Fee:** Included in green fee. **Walking Policy:** Walking at certain times. **Opened:** 1965. **Architect:** Averett Nash. **Season:** Year-round. **To obtain tee times:** Call up to 7 days in advance. **Miscellaneous:** Reduced fees (weekdays), range (grass), credit cards (V), BF, FF.

★★★ SEA SCAPE GOLF LINKS

R-300 Eckner St., Kitty Hawk, 27949, Dare County, (252)261-2158, 70 miles from Norfolk. **E-mail:** info@seascapegolf.com. **Web:** www.seascapegolf.com. **Facility Holes:** 18. **Yards:** 6,409/5,536. **Par:** 72/73. **Course Rating:** 70.4/70.9. **Slope:** 123/117. **Green Fee:** $45/$85. **Cart Fee:** Included in green fee. **Walking Policy:** Walking at certain times. **Walkability:** 2. **Opened:** 1968. **Architect:** Art Wall. **Season:** Year-round. **High:** June-Sept. **To obtain tee times:** Call up to 180 days in advance. **Miscellaneous:** Reduced fees (guests, twilight, juniors), range (grass), credit cards (MC, V, D), BF, FF.

Reader Comments: Excellent elevation changes for seaside course … Too much sand … Fun but tough! … Front 9 windy. Back in forest … Enjoyable … Bring lots of balls … Scenic area … Long, hilly large, hard greens.

SEA TRAIL PLANTATION

R-211 Clubhouse Rd., Sunset Beach, 28468, Brunswick County, (910)287-1125, (800)546-5748, 2 miles from Sunset Beach. **E-mail:** seatrail@infoave.net. **Web:** www.sea-

trail.com. **Facility Holes:** 54. **Cart Fee:** $20/Person. **Walking Policy:** Mandatory carts.
Walkability: 1. **Season:** Year-round. **High:** March-May. **To obtain tee times:** Call up to 365 days in advance. **Miscellaneous:** Reduced fees (guests, twilight, juniors), range (grass), lodging (300 rooms), credit cards (MC, V, AE, D, DC), BF, FF.

★★★ **DAN MAPLES COURSE** (18)
Yards: 6,751/5,090. **Par:** 72/72. **Course Rating:** 72.4/69.0. **Slope:** 129/115. **Green Fee:** $25/$65. **Opened:** 1985. **Architect:** Dan Maples.
Reader Comments: Sea Trails was a delight, 3 courses, all with their own character ... Great discount packages and great golf ... Nice course ... Great test of golf ... Staff very friendly.

★★★½ **REES JONES COURSE** (18)
Yards: 6,761/4,912. **Par:** 72/72. **Course Rating:** 72.4/68.5. **Slope:** 132/115. **Green Fee:** $29/$72. **Opened:** 1989. **Architect:** Rees Jones.
Reader Comments: Great discount packages and great golf ... Nice course ... Good layout, needs grooming ... Well kept ... Staff very friendly.

★★★★ **WILLARD BYRD COURSE** (18)
Yards: 6,750/4,697. **Par:** 72/72. **Course Rating:** 72.1/67.9. **Slope:** 128/111. **Green Fee:** $19/$62. **Opened:** 1990. **Architect:** Willard Byrd.

★★★★ **SEVEN LAKES COUNTRY CLUB**
SP-P.O. Box 686, West End, 27376, Moore County, (910)673-1092, (888)475-2537, 10 miles from Pinehurst. **E-mail:** donfenissan.net. **Web:** www.sevenlakes.com. **Facility Holes:** 18. **Yards:** 6,927/5,018. **Par:** 72/72. **Course Rating:** 74.1/69.7. **Slope:** 142/128. **Green Fee:** $30/$55. **Cart Fee:** $18/Person. **Walking Policy:** Mandatory carts. **Walkability:** 3. **Opened:** 1976. **Architect:** Peter Tufts. **Season:** Year-round. **High:** April-June. **To obtain tee times:** Call golf shop.
Miscellaneous: Reduced fees (juniors), range (grass), credit cards (MC, V), BF, FF.
Reader Comments: I could not say enough great things about the course or staff... Each hole is distinct, superb layout ... Great holes & layout for middle handicapper... Superior design ... Fair test of golf.

★½ **SHAMROCK GOLF CLUB**
PU-1722 Shamrock Dr., Burlington, 27215, Alamance County, (336)227-8566, 35 miles from Raleigh. **Facility Holes:** 18. **Yards:** 6,416/5,017. **Par:** 72/72. **Course Rating:** 70.5/68.5. **Slope:** 125/114. **Green Fee:** $11/$16. **Walking Policy:** Walking at certain times. **Walkability:** 3. **Opened:** 1952. **Architect:** Calvin Walker. **Season:** Year-round. **To obtain tee times:** Call golf shop. **Miscellaneous:** Reduced fees (weekdays, twilight, seniors, juniors), metal spikes, range (grass), credit cards (MC, V), BF, FF.

SILO RUN GOLF CLUB
PU-4032 Rockford Rd., Boonville, 27011, Yadkin County, (336)367-3133, 20 miles from Winston Salem. **Facility Holes:** 18. **Yards:** 6,900/5,001. **Par:** 71/71. **Course Rating:** 72.9/6.7. **Slope:** 132/115. **Green Fee:** $3/$19. **Cart Fee:** $12/Person. **Walking Policy:** Walking at certain times. **Walkability:** 4. **Opened:** 1994. **Architect:** Thomas Peagram. **Season:** Year-round. **High:** May-June. **To obtain tee times:** Call golf shop. **Miscellaneous:** Reduced fees (weekdays, seniors, juniors), range (grass), credit cards (MC, V), BF, FF.

★★★ **SILVER CREEK GOLF CLUB**
PU-601 Pelletier Loop Rd., Swansboro, 28584, Carteret County, (252)393-8058, (800)393-6605, 3 miles from Emerald Isle Bridge. **E-mail:** scgc@tcp1.com. **Web:** www.emeraldislegolf.com. **Facility Holes:** 18. **Yards:** 7,005/5,412. **Par:** 72/72. **Course Rating:** 74.3/69.2. **Slope:** 139/123. **Green Fee:** $30/$48. **Cart Fee:** Included in green fee. **Walking Policy:** Walking at certain times. **Walkability:** 3. **Opened:** 1986. **Architect:** Gene Hamm. **Season:** Year-round. **High:** June-Sept. **To obtain tee times:** Call up to 30 days in advance. **Miscellaneous:** Reduced fees (twilight, seniors, juniors), range (grass/mats), caddies, credit cards (MC, V), BF, FF.
Reader Comments: Some outstanding holes ... Nice layout, poor maintenance ... Great greens ... Great course ... Gusts make this course a nightmare ... Too high a price, will be nice.

SKYBROOK GOLF CLUB
SP-14720 Northgreen Dr., Huntersville, 28078, Mecklenburg County, (704)948-6611, 15 miles from Charlotte. **Facility Holes:** 18. **Yards:** 7,028/5,355. **Par:** 72/72. **Course Rating:** 73.4/71.0. **Slope:** 132/122. **Green Fee:** $44/$65. **Cart Fee:** Included in green fee. **Walking Policy:** Mandatory carts. **Opened:** 2000. **Architect:** John Lafoy. **Season:** Year-round. **To obtain tee times:** Call golf shop. **Miscellaneous:** Reduced fees (weekdays), range (grass), credit cards (MC, V, AE).

★★★★½ **THE SOUND GOLF LINKS AT ALBEMARLE PLANTATION**
SP-371 Albemarle Blvd., Hertford, 27944, Perquimans County, (252)426-5555, (800)535-0704, 80 miles from Norfolk. **E-mail:** soundlinks@inteliport. **Web:** albemarle.net. **Facility Holes:** 18. **Yards:** 6,500/4,665. **Par:** 72/72. **Course Rating:** 70.1/66.3. **Slope:** 125/113.

Green Fee: $29/$48. **Cart Fee:** Included in green fee. **Walking Policy:** Mandatory carts. **Walkability:** 1. **Opened:** 1990. **Architect:** Dan Maples. **Season:** Year-round. **High:** April-Sept. **To obtain tee times:** Call golf shop. **Miscellaneous:** Reduced fees (juniors), range (grass), lodging (10 rooms), credit cards (MC, V), BF, FF.
Reader Comments: This is an exceptional bargain, it appeares to be lightly played ... All of the staff is very cordial ... This course is built in a marsh and eats golf balls ... Spectacular hidden gem ... Scenic, excellent layout.

★★½ SOURWOOD FOREST GOLF COURSE
PU-8055 Pleasanthill Church Rd., Snow Camp, 27349, Alamance County, (336)376-8166, 15 miles from Burlington. **Facility Holes:** 18. **Yards:** 6,862/5,012. **Par:** 72/72. **Course Rating:** 73.4/70.1. **Slope:** 133/119. **Green Fee:** $11/$18. **Cart Fee:** $10/Person. **Walking Policy:** Walking at certain times. **Walkability:** 3. **Opened:** 1990. **Architect:** Elmo Cobb. **Season:** Year-round. **To obtain tee times:** Call up to 7 days in advance. **Miscellaneous:** Reduced fees (weekdays, twilight, seniors, juniors), range (grass), credit cards (MC, V), FF.

★★★½ SPRINGDALE COUNTRY CLUB
R-200 Golfwatch Rd., Canton, 28716, Haywood County, (828)235-8451, (800)553-3027, 15 miles from Asheville. **E-mail:** steven@springdalegolf.com. **Web:** www.springdalegolf.com. **Facility Holes:** 18. **Yards:** 6,812/5,421. **Par:** 72/72. **Course Rating:** 72.5/72.4. **Slope:** 130/121. **Green Fee:** $40/$55. **Cart Fee:** Included in green fee. **Walking Policy:** Walking at certain times. **Walkability:** 4. **Opened:** 1968. **Architect:** Joseph Holmes. **Season:** Year-round. **High:** April-Oct. **To obtain tee times:** Call golf shop. **Miscellaneous:** Range (grass), lodging (55 rooms), credit cards (MC, V, AE), BF, FF.
Reader Comments: Nice setting, very good challenge to play ... The most beautiful scenery I've ever seen ... Greens were challenging, excellent experience ... Great mountain view ... A variety of holes and friendly staff ... Nice lodge.

ST. JAMES PLANTATION
SP-Hwy. 211., Southport, 28461, Brunswick County, (910)253-3008, (800)247-4806, 28 miles from Wilmington. **Facility Holes:** 54. **Season:** Year-round. **Miscellaneous:** Reduced fees (weekdays, twilight, seniors, juniors), range (grass), credit cards (MC, V).
★★★ GAUNTLET (18)
Yards: 7,050/5,048. **Par:** 72/72. **Course Rating:** 75.0/69.7. **Slope:** 142/119. **Green Fee:** $11/$74. **Cart Fee:** $19/Person. **Walking Policy:** Mandatory cart. **Walkability:** 2. **Opened:** 1990. **Architect:** P.B. Dye. **High:** March-May. **To obtain tee times:** Call golf shop.
Reader Comments: What a gem ... Last 4 holes are outstanding ... Add this one to a Myrtle Beach trip ... Lots of water ... Great layout, excellent service ... Ocean make course tough, wind can be tough ... Long carries over marshlands.
★★★★½ MEMBERS CLUB (18)
Yards: 6,887/5,113. **Par:** 72/72. **Course Rating:** 73.9/71.0. **Slope:** 135/123. **Green Fee:** $43/$98. **Cart Fee:** Included in green fee. **Walking Policy:** Mandatory carts. **Walkability:** 3. **Opened:** 1996. **Architect:** Hale Irwin. **Miscellaneous:** BF, FF.
Reader Comments: Challenging but very nice ... Good value ... Very forgiving, not very long, a wide fairway course ... Nice setting, good track ... Very interesting, nice course & people ... No. 15 interesting when wind blows.
★★★★½ PLAYERS CLUB (18)
Yards: 7,062/4,470. **Par:** 72/70. **Course Rating:** 75.1/66.6. **Slope:** 149/113. **Green Fee:** $48/$98. **Cart Fee:** Included in green fee. **Walking Policy:** Mandatory carts. **Walkability:** 2. **Opened:** 1997. **Architect:** Tim Cate. **Miscellaneous:** FF.
Reader Comments: Must keep in play, good track ... Great people, very nice & well kept course ... Tight fairways, very difficult ... Could be played at times by local seniors for $25-30 per round including cart ... Good value.

★★★½ STAR HILL GOLF & COUNTRY CLUB
SP-202 Clubhouse Dr., Cape Carteret, 28584, Carteret County, (252)393-8111, (800)845-8214, 1 mile from Cape Carteret. **E-mail:** starhill@mail.clis.com. **Facility Holes:** 27. **Green Fee:** $40/$55. **Cart Fee:** Included in green fee. **Walking Policy:** Unrestricted walking. **Walkability:** 1. **Opened:** 1967. **Architect:** Russell T. Burney. **Season:** Year-round. **To obtain tee times:** Call golf shop. **Miscellaneous:** Reduced fees (guests, twilight, juniors), range (grass), credit cards (MC, V), BF, FF.
PINES/LAKES (18 Combo)
Yards: 6,610/4,871. **Par:** 72/72. **Course Rating:** 71.0/67.5. **Slope:** 122/108. **High:** April-Oct.
SANDS/LAKES (18 Combo)
Yards: 6,575/4,740. **Par:** 72/72. **Course Rating:** 70.9/73.2. **Slope:** 121/109. **High:** May-Oct.
SANDS/PINES (18 Combo)
Yards: 6,421/4,649. **Par:** 72/72. **Course Rating:** 70.5/73.6. **Slope:** 118/107. **High:** May-Oct.
Reader Comments: Wife and I love this little gem ... Excellent, better every year ... Fun layout, great for everyone ... Nice course, feels too high ... Great layout, immaculate condition ... OK ... 3 nines, very nice, but crowded.

STONEBRIDGE GOLF CLUB

SP-2721 Swilcan Burn, Monroe, 28112, Union County, (704)283-8998, (888)337-2582, 10 miles from Charlotte. **E-mail:** tim_mervosh@msn.com. **Web:** www.stonebridgegolfclub.com. **Facility Holes:** 18. **Yards:** 6,923/5,145. **Par:** 72/72. **Course Rating:** 73.6/69.6. **Slope:** 132/120. **Green Fee:** $21/$35. **Cart Fee:** $14/Person. **Walking Policy:** Walking at certain times. **Walkability:** 1. **Opened:** 1997. **Architect:** Richard B. Osborne. **Season:** Year-round. **High:** April-Oct. **To obtain tee times:** Call up to 7 days in advance. **Miscellaneous:** Reduced fees (weekdays, twilight, seniors, juniors), range (grass), credit cards (MC, V, AE), BF, FF.

★★★½ STONEY CREEK GOLF CLUB

PU-911 Golf House Rd. E., Stoney Creek, 27377, Guilford County, (336)449-5688, 12 miles from Greensboro. **E-mail:** dereece@triadrr.com. **Web:** www.stoneycreekgolf.com. **Facility Holes:** 18. **Yards:** 7,101/4,737. **Par:** 72/72. **Course Rating:** 74.5/69.8. **Slope:** 144/123. **Green Fee:** $25/$35. **Cart Fee:** $15/Person. **Walking Policy:** Walking at certain times. **Walkability:** 4. **Opened:** 1992. **Architect:** Tom Jackson. **Season:** Year-round. **To obtain tee times:** Call up to 7 days in advance. **Miscellaneous:** Reduced fees (weekdays, twilight, seniors, juniors), range (grass), credit cards (MC, V, AE), BF, FF.
Reader Comments: What golfing should be like … Course always is in good shape, service has always been very good … Challenging … Excellent facilities, driver not needed on many holes … A nice course, difficult greens … Overpriced.

★★★★ TALAMORE RESORT

PU-48 Talamore Dr., Southern Pines, 28387, Moore County, (910)692-5884, 2 miles from Pinehurst. **Web:** travel@talamore.com. **Facility Holes:** 18. **Yards:** 7,020/4,945. **Par:** 71/72. **Course Rating:** 72.9/69.0. **Slope:** 142/125. **Green Fee:** $39/$95. **Cart Fee:** Included in green fee. **Walking Policy:** Walking at certain times. **Walkability:** 4. **Opened:** 1992. **Architect:** Rees Jones. **Season:** Year-round. **To obtain tee times:** Call golf shop. **Miscellaneous:** Reduced fees (guests, twilight, juniors), range (grass), credit cards (MC, V), BF, FF.
Notes: Ranked 18th in 1997 Best in State.
Reader Comments: Good challenge, resort cottages a great place to stay … Good facility … One of Pinehurst's better tracks … Nice layout, a bit pricey, great greens … Expensive, but worth the price.

TANGLEWOOD PARK

PU-4061 Clemmons Rd., Clemmons, 27012, Forsyth County, (336)778-6320, 8 miles from Winston-Salem. **Web:** www.tanglewoodpark.org.com. **Facility Holes:** 36. **Cart Fee:** $14/Person. **Walking Policy:** Walking at certain times. **Architect:** Robert Trent Jones. **Season:** Year-round. **Miscellaneous:** Reduced fees (weekdays, guests, twilight, seniors, juniors), range (grass), credit cards (MC, V).
★★★★ CHAMPIONSHIP COURSE (18)
Yards: 7,018/5,119. **Par:** 70/74. **Course Rating:** 74.5/70.9. **Slope:** 140/130. **Green Fee:** $20/$43. **Walkability:** 3. **Opened:** 1957.
Notes: Ranked 9th in 2001 Best in State.
Reader Comments: Too many sand traps … Top notch … Can see why this is a Sr. Tour mainstay … Great golf course facilities and well stocked … Challenging, slow, fair greens … Great course, fun to play … Championship course.
★★★ REYNOLDS COURSE (18)
Yards: 6,537/5,308. **Par:** 72/72. **Course Rating:** 71.8/71.5. **Slope:** 135/122. **Green Fee:** $13/$19. **Walkability:** 4. **Opened:** 1959. **To obtain tee times:** Call golf shop.
Reader Comments: Average course … Great layout, tight fairways, great staff.

THISTLE GOLF CLUB

PU-8840 Old Georgetown Rd., Sunset Beach, 28470, Brunswick County, (910)575-8700, (800)571-6710, 25 miles from Myrtle Beach. **Web:** www.thistlegolf.com. **Facility Holes:** 27. **Green Fee:** $39/$90. **Cart Fee:** $20/Person. **Walking Policy:** Walking at certain times. **Walkability:** 2. **Opened:** 1999. **Architect:** Tim Cate. **Season:** Year-round. **High:** Sept.-May. **To obtain tee times:** Call up to 365 days in advance. **Miscellaneous:** Reduced fees (juniors), range (grass), credit cards (MC, V, AE), BF, FF.
★★★★ NORTH/WEST (18) *Value, Pace*
Yards: 6,997/4,612. **Par:** 72/72. **Course Rating:** 74.9/67.2. **Slope:** 136/112.
Reader Comments: Cool layout, links style, bunkers that went down into lakes … Fun day … Awesome layout … Wonderful layout … Hell when the wind blows hard.
SOUTH/NORTH (18)
Yards: 6,801/4,468. **Par:** 71/72. **Course Rating:** 73.4/65.8. **Slope:** 137/109.
WEST/SOUTH (18)
Yards: 6,898/4,566. **Par:** 71/71. **Course Rating:** 74.3/66.2. **Slope:** 137/113.

THE TILLERY TRADITION COUNTRY CLUB
SP-214 Tradition Dr., Mt. Gilead, 27306, Montgomery County, (910)439-5578, (877)472-7211, 40 miles from Charlotte. **Web:** www.tillerytradition.com. **Facility Holes:** 18. **Yards:** 6,930/4,668. **Par:** 72/71. **Course Rating:** 73.6/66.4. **Slope:** 132/114. **Green Fee:** $34/$46. **Cart Fee:** $14/Person. **Walking Policy:** Walking at certain times. **Walkability:** 4. **Opened:** 2000. **Architect:** J. T. Russell & Sons. **Season:** Year-round. **High:** May-Oct. **To obtain tee times:** Call up to 14 days in advance. **Miscellaneous:** Reduced fees (weekdays, twilight, seniors, juniors), range (grass), credit cards (MC, V), BF, FF.

★★★★½ **TOBACCO ROAD GOLF CLUB** *Condition*
PU-442 Tobacco Rd., Sanford, 27330, Lee County, (919)775-1940, (877)284-3762, 20 miles from Pinehurst. **Web:** www.tobaccoroadgolf.com. **Facility Holes:** 18. **Yards:** 6,554/5,094. **Par:** 71/71. **Course Rating:** 73.2/70.4. **Slope:** 150/128. **Green Fee:** $48/$95. **Cart Fee:** Included in green fee. **Walking Policy:** Unrestricted walking. **Walkability:** 4. **Opened:** 1999. **Architect:** Mike Strantz. **Season:** June-Dec. **High:** March-May. **To obtain tee times:** Call up to 180 days in advance. **Miscellaneous:** Reduced fees (weekdays, juniors), range (grass), credit cards (MC, V, AE), FF.
Notes: Ranked 22nd in 2001 Best in State; tied for 10th in 1999 Best New Upscale Public.
Reader Comments: Visually intimidating, take plenty of balls … A unique golf experience in excellent shape and service … Most different course in NC, tough … You'll either love it or hate it.

TOT HILL FARM GOLF CLUB
SP-3183 Tot Hill Farm Rd., Asheboro, 27205, Randolph County, (336)857-4450, (800)868-4455. **E-mail:** thfgolfclub@rtmc.net. **Web:** www.tothillfarm.com. **Facility Holes:** 18. **Yards:** 6,614/4,853. **Par:** 72/72. **Course Rating:** 72.2/69.1. **Slope:** 135/122. **Green Fee:** $34/$60. **Cart Fee:** Included in green fee. **Walking Policy:** Unrestricted walking. **Walkability:** 4. **Opened:** 2000. **Architect:** Mike Strantz. **Season:** Year-round. **High:** March-June. **To obtain tee times:** Call up to 180 days in advance. **Miscellaneous:** Reduced fees (twilight), range (grass/mats), credit cards (MC, V, AE), BF, FF.

★½ **TOWN OF MOORESVILLE GOLF COURSE**
PU-800 Golf Course Dr. @ Wilson Ave., Mooresville, 28115, Iredell County, (704)663-2539, 25 miles from Charlotte. **E-mail:** croberts@ci.mooresville.nc.us. **Web:** http://golfmooresville.com. **Facility Holes:** 18. **Yards:** 6,603/4,917. **Par:** 72/72. **Course Rating:** 72.4/68.5. **Slope:** 126/113. **Green Fee:** $13/$18. **Cart Fee:** $12/Person. **Walking Policy:** Unrestricted walking. **Walkability:** 3. **Opened:** 1940. **Architect:** Donald Ross/J. Porter Gibson. **Season:** Year-round. **High:** April-Oct. **To obtain tee times:** Call up to 7 days in advance. **Miscellaneous:** Reduced fees (seniors, juniors), range (grass), credit cards (MC, V), BF, FF.

THE TRADITION
PU-3800 Prosperity Church Rd., Charlotte, 28269, Mecklenberg County, (704)549-9400. **Web:** www.charlottegolf.com. **Facility Holes:** 18. **Yards:** 6,978/5,422. **Par:** 72/72. **Course Rating:** 72.9/69.4. **Slope:** 140/126. **Green Fee:** $21/$36. **Cart Fee:** $14/Person. **Walking Policy:** Walking at certain times. **Walkability:** 3. **Opened:** 1996. **Architect:** John Cassell. **Season:** Year-round. **High:** March-Sept. **To obtain tee times:** Call golf shop. **Miscellaneous:** Reduced fees (weekdays, twilight, seniors, juniors), range (grass), credit cards (MC, V, AE), BF, FF.

★★★★½ **TRILLIUM LINKS & LAKE CLUB** *Condition, Pace*
SP-245 Links Dr., Cashiers, 28717, Jackson County, (828)743-4251, (888)909-7171, 70 miles from Asheville. **E-mail:** links@dnet.net. **Web:** www.trilliumnc.com. **Facility Holes:** 18. **Yards:** 6,505/4,340. **Par:** 71/71. **Course Rating:** 72.4/66.0. **Slope:** 134/120. **Green Fee:** $95/$125. **Cart Fee:** Included in green fee. **Walking Policy:** Mandatory carts. **Walkability:** 5. **Opened:** 1998. **Architect:** Morris Hatalsky. **Season:** April-Oct. **High:** July-Oct. **To obtain tee times:** Call golf shop. **Miscellaneous:** Reduced fees (weekdays, twilight), range (grass/mats), credit cards (MC, V, AE), BF, FF.
Reader Comments: If you're looking for mountain golf in NC, this is it … Very difficult golf, penalizing, wrist-breaking rough, not for beginners … Spectacular staff and conditioning … Breath-taking scenery … Only one totally absurd hole … Exciting layout … Fantastic course & view.

★½ **TWIN OAKS GOLF COURSE**
PU-320 Twin Oaks Rd., Statesville, 28625, Iredell County, (704)872-3979, 50 miles from Charlotte. **Facility Holes:** 18. **Yards:** 6,094/4,729. **Par:** 72/72. **Course Rating:** 68.0/65.9. **Slope:** 111/104. **Green Fee:** $12/$22. **Cart Fee:** Included in green fee. **Walking Policy:** Walking at certain times. **Walkability:** 1. **Opened:** 1960. **Season:** Year-round. **High:** April-Aug. **Tee times:** Call shop. **Misc:** Reduced fees (weekdays, seniors), range (grass), credit cards (MC, V, AE).

★★★★ **UNC FINLEY GOLF CLUB**
PU-Finley Golf Course Rd., Chapel Hill, 27515, Orange County, (919)962-2349. **E-mail:** mhw-golf@uncaa.unc.edu. **Facility Holes:** 18. **Yards:** 7,119/4,954. **Par:** 72/72. **Green Fee:** $45/$60.

Cart Fee: $16/Person. **Walking Policy:** Unrestricted walking. **Walkability:** 3. **Opened:** 1999. **Architect:** Tom Fazio. **Season:** Year-round. **To obtain tee times:** Call up to 7 days in advance. **Miscellaneous:** Reduced fees (weekdays, twilight), range (grass), credit cards (MC, V), FF. **Reader Comments:** As good as Duke ... Great renovation by Fazio ... Too difficult for mid to high handicappers ... Excellent remake, good ... Great Fazio renovation ... Front 9, nice but not very memorable ... What a terrific change.

★★★ WAKE FOREST GOLF CLUB

SP-13239 Capital Blvd., Wake Forest, 27587, Wake County, (919)556-3416, 12 miles from Raleigh. **E-mail:** dallgeyer@golfmatrix.com. **Facility Holes:** 18. **Yards:** 6,952/5,124. **Par:** 72/72. **Course Rating:** 74.4/70.0. **Slope:** 135/122. **Green Fee:** $25/$55. **Cart Fee:** Included in green fee. **Walking Policy:** Walking at certain times. **Walkability:** 3. **Opened:** 1967. **Architect:** Gene Hamm. **Season:** Year-round. **To obtain tee times:** Call up to 7 days in advance. **Miscellaneous:** Reduced fees (twilight, seniors, juniors), range (grass), credit cards (MC, V, AE), BF, FF. **Reader Comments:** Don't think you are playing a course associated with the university ... Starting hole is the longest par 5 in the country, 680 yards ... Great old-time country club.

★★ WALNUT WOOD GOLF COURSE

PU-3172 Alamance Church Rd., Julian, 27283, Guilford County, (910)697-8140, 15 miles from Greensboro. **Facility Holes:** 18. **Yards:** 6,409/4,962. **Par:** 73/73. **Course Rating:** 70.1/68.1. **Slope:** 126/114. **Green Fee:** $18/$23. **Walking Policy:** Walking at certain times. **Walkability:** 3. **Opened:** 1978. **Architect:** Ralph Clendenin. **Season:** Year-round. **To obtain tee times:** Call golf shop. **Miscellaneous:** Reduced fees (twilight, seniors), range (grass/mats), credit cards (MC, V), BF, FF.

★★★★ WARRIOR GOLF CLUB AT LAKE WRIGHT

SP-890 Lake Wright Rd., China Grove, 28023, Rowan County, (704)856-0871, 25 miles from Charlotte. **E-mail:** warrior@warriorgolf.com. **Web:** www.warriorgolf.com. **Facility Holes:** 18. **Yards:** 6,609/4,423. **Par:** 71/71. **Course Rating:** 71.5/64.1. **Slope:** 127/110. **Green Fee:** $35/$45. **Cart Fee:** Included in green fee. **Walking Policy:** Mandatory carts. **Walkability:** 3. **Opened:** 1999. **Architect:** Hale Irwin & Stan Gentry. **Season:** Year-round. **High:** May-Sept. **To obtain tee times:** Call up to 6 days in advance. **Miscellaneous:** Reduced fees (weekdays, twilight, seniors, juniors), range (grass), credit cards (MC, V). **Reader Comments:** Great challenge with the layout, greens fast ... The golf course and staff made my foursome's day enjoyable ... Good new course.

★★★½ WAYNESVILLE COUNTRY CLUB INN

R-Ninevah Rd., Waynesville, 28786, Haywood County, (704)452-4617, 25 miles from Asheville. **Web:** www.wccinn.com. **Facility Holes:** 27. **Green Fee:** $13/$28. **Cart Fee:** $15/Person. **Walking Policy:** Walking at certain times. **Walkability:** 4. **Opened:** 1926. **Architect:** Tom Jackson. **Season:** Year-round. **To obtain tee times:** Call golf shop. **Miscellaneous:** Reduced fees (guests, twilight, juniors), credit cards (MC, V), BF, FF.
CAROLINA/BLUE RIDGE (18 Combo)
Yards: 5,943/5,002. **Par:** 70/70. **Course Rating:** 66.8/67.0. **Slope:** 104/104.
CAROLINA/DOGWOOD (18 Combo)
Yards: 5,798/4,927. **Par:** 70/70. **Course Rating:** 66.4/66.6. **Slope:** 103/103.
DOGWOOD/BLUE RIDGE (18 Combo)
Yards: 5,803/4,565. **Par:** 70/70. **Course Rating:** 66.4/65.0. **Slope:** 105/100.
Reader Comments: Good course to play ... Though nothing spectacular, each set of 9 holes offers a pleasant mountain outing that should not be passed up ... Delight, 27 holes ... Too short, crowded, nice pro shop & staff.

★★ WENDELL COUNTRY CLUB

SP-180 Jake May Dr., Wendell, 27591, Wake County, (919)365-7337, 15 miles from Raleigh. **Facility Holes:** 18. **Yards:** 6,358/4,891. **Par:** 71/71. **Course Rating:** 69.5/68.0. **Slope:** 116/113. **Green Fee:** $13/$23. **Cart Fee:** $12/Person. **Walking Policy:** Walking at certain times. **Walkability:** 2. **Architect:** Ken Dye. **Season:** Year-round. **To obtain tee times:** Call golf shop. **Miscellaneous:** Reduced fees (seniors), credit cards (MC, V), BF, FF.

★½ WESTPORT GOLF COURSE

SP-7494 Golf Course Dr. S., Denver, 28037, Lincoln County, (704)483-5604, 25 miles from Charlotte. **Facility Holes:** 18. **Yards:** 6,805/5,600. **Par:** 72/72. **Course Rating:** 72.3/69.5. **Slope:** 123/118. **Green Fee:** $20/$28. **Cart Fee:** $12/Person. **Walking Policy:** Walking at certain times. **Walkability:** 3. **Opened:** 1968. **Architect:** Porter Gibson. **Season:** Year-round. **To obtain tee times:** Call up to 3 days in advance. **Miscellaneous:** Reduced fees (weekdays, twilight, seniors, juniors), range (grass), credit cards (MC, V, D), BF, FF.

★★ **WHISPERING WOODS GOLF CLUB**
SP-26 Sandpiper Dr., Whispering Pines, 28327, Moore County, (910)949-4653, (800)224-5061, 6 miles from Pinehurst. **E-mail:** thewoods@psinet.com. **Facility Holes:** 18. **Yards:** 6,334/4,924. **Par:** 70/71. **Course Rating:** 70.5/68.7. **Slope:** 122/122. **Green Fee:** $25/$50. **Walking Policy:** Unrestricted walking. **Walkability:** 4. **Opened:** 1974. **Architect:** Ellis Maples. **Season:** Year-round. **To obtain tee times:** Call golf shop. **Miscellaneous:** Reduced fees (twilight, juniors), credit cards (MC, V), BF, FF.

★★★½ **WOODBRIDGE GOLF LINKS**
PU-1007 New Camp Creek Church Rd., Kings Mountain, 28086, Cleveland County, (704)482-0353, 30 miles from Charlotte. **Facility Holes:** 18. **Yards:** 6,743/5,151. **Par:** 72/73. **Course Rating:** 72.3/70.4. **Slope:** 131/127. **Green Fee:** $28/$38. **Cart Fee:** Included in green fee. **Walking Policy:** Walking at certain times. **Walkability:** 4. **Opened:** 1976. **Architect:** Bob Toski/Porter Gibson. **Season:** Year-round. **High:** April-Oct. **To obtain tee times:** Call golf shop. **Miscellaneous:** Reduced fees (twilight), range (grass), credit cards (MC, V).
Reader Comments: Diamond in the rough, great layout ... Good older course ... No. 12 is a journey ... The back 9 is great ... Rangers actually do their job! ... Very nice, somewhat challenging, nice greens ... Outstanding.

WOODLAKE COUNTRY CLUB
R-400 Woodlake Blvd., Vass, 28394, Moore County, (910)245-7137, (888)843-5253, 12 miles from Pinehurst. **E-mail:** woodlakecc@hotmail.com. **Web:** www.woodlakecc.com. **Facility Holes:** 36. **Cart Fee:** Included in green fee. **Walking Policy:** Mandatory carts. **Season:** Year-round. **High:** March-May. **To obtain tee times:** Call up to 60 days in advance. **Miscellaneous:** Reduced fees (weekdays, guests, twilight, juniors), range (grass), lodging (70 rooms), credit cards (MC, V, AE), BF, FF.
★★★★ **MAPLES** (18)
Yards: 7,043/5,303. **Par:** 72/72. **Course Rating:** 73.2/71.6. **Slope:** 134/130. **Green Fee:** $70. **Walkability:** 4. **Opened:** 1974. **Architect:** Ellis Maples.
Reader Comments: Great design by Ellis Maples, good condition ... 77 not too bad for the 1st time ... Low holes, soggy after rain ... Lake views on 5 holes ... Nice course, lots of water ... Good, solid golf course ... Worth a look.
★★★ **PALMER** (18)
Yards: 6,962/5,223. **Par:** 72/72. **Course Rating:** 73.5/69.6. **Slope:** 133/118. **Green Fee:** $29/$70. **Walkability:** 3. **Opened:** 1996. **Architect:** Arnold Palmer.
Reader Comments: Concentrate on keeping ball dry ... Love the course ... Excellent strategy and fair course ... Great Sandhills course ... Boring layout ... Beautiful course, plenty of water ... OK place to visit ... Great ... Windy.

NORTH DAKOTA

BEULAH MUNICIPAL GOLF COURSE

PU-Hwy. 49, Beulah, 58523, Mercer County, (701)873-2929, 80 miles from Bismarck. **Facility Holes:** 9. **Yards:** 3,121/2,613. **Par:** 35/36. **Course Rating:** .0/67.9. **Slope:** 0/109. **Green Fee:** $13/$15. **Cart Fee:** $15/Cart. **Walking Policy:** Unrestricted walking. **Walkability:** 3. **To obtain tee times:** Call golf shop. **Miscellaneous:** Range (grass).

★★ BOIS DE SIOUX GOLF CLUB

PU-N. 4th St. and 13th Ave., Wahpeton, 58075, Richland County, (701)642-3673, 45 miles from Fargo. **Facility Holes:** 18. **Yards:** 6,648/5,500. **Par:** 72/72. **Course Rating:** 71.7/71.3. **Slope:** 122/115. **Green Fee:** $20/$22. **Cart Fee:** $22/Cart. **Walking Policy:** Unrestricted walking. **Walkability:** 1. **Opened:** 1924. **Architect:** Robert Bruce Harris. **Season:** April-Nov. **High:** May-Aug. **To obtain tee times:** Call up to 7 days in advance. **Miscellaneous:** Reduced fees (weekdays, juniors), range (grass/mats), credit cards (MC, V), BF, FF.

CARRINGTON GOLF CLUB

SP-P.O. Box 176, Carrington, 58421, Foster County, (701)652-2601. **Facility Holes:** 9. **Yards:** 2,890/2,600. **Par:** 36/36. **Course Rating:** 65.8/69.5. **Slope:** 106/111. **Green Fee:** $14. **Cart Fee:** $14/Cart. **Walking Policy:** Unrestricted walking. **Walkability:** 1. **Season:** April-Nov. **To obtain tee times:** Call golf shop. **Miscellaneous:** Reduced fees (juniors), range (grass), BF, FF.

EDGEWATER MUNICIPAL GOLF COURSE

PU-Hwy. 23, New Town, 58763, Mountrail County, (701)627-9407. **Facility Holes:** 9. **Yards:** 3,278/2,758. **Par:** 36/36. **Course Rating:** 70.4/71.4. **Slope:** 113/111. **Green Fee:** $16/$18. **Cart Fee:** $13/Cart. **Walking Policy:** Unrestricted walking. **Walkability:** 3. **Opened:** 1979. **Season:** April-Oct. **To obtain tee times:** Call golf shop. **Miscellaneous:** Range (grass), credit cards (MC, V), FF.

★★★½ EDGEWOOD GOLF COURSE

PU-19 Golf Ave., Fargo, 58102, Cass County, (701)232-2824. **E-mail:** gregm@pga.com. **Web:** www.fargogolfers.com. **Facility Holes:** 18. **Yards:** 6,369/5,176. **Par:** 71/71. **Course Rating:** 68.4/68.9. **Slope:** 122/115. **Green Fee:** $21/Cart. **Walking Policy:** Unrestricted walking. **Walkability:** 2. **Opened:** 1951. **Architect:** Robert Bruce Harris. **Season:** April-Nov. **High:** April-Nov. **To obtain tee times:** Call up to 3 days in advance. **Miscellaneous:** Reduced fees (twilight, seniors, juniors), range (grass/mats), credit cards (MC, V), BF, FF. **Notes:** Ranked 5th in 1999 Best in State.

Reader Comments: Great municipal course. Lots of mature trees so you better hit it straight … Challenging, excellent muni course … The outlook of the whole course is nice … Short, lots of trees, play it … Cut out of the trees, great value when in shape … Spring flooding causes problems.

★★★★½ HAWKTREE GOLF CLUB *Service, Value+, Condition+, Pace+*

PU-Burnt Creek Loop, Bismark, 58501, Burleigh County, (701)355-0995, (888)465-4295, 8 miles from Bismark. **E-mail:** hawktree@btigate.com. **Web:** www.hawktree.com. **Facility Holes:** 18. **Yards:** 7,085/4,868. **Par:** 72/72. **Course Rating:** 74.6/63.9. **Slope:** 135/107. **Green Fee:** $42/$45. **Walking Policy:** Unrestricted walking. **Walkability:** 3. **Opened:** 2000. **Architect:** Jim Engh. **Season:** April-Nov. **High:** May-Sept. **To obtain tee times:** Call up to 3 days in advance. **Miscellaneous:** Reduced fees (twilight), range (grass), credit cards (MC, V, AE, D, DC), BF, FF. **Notes:** Ranked 1st in 2001 Best in State; 2nd in 2000 Best New Affordable Courses.

Reader Comments: Makes great use of the natural landscape and views … At $40 a round an absolute steal … Black sand in bunkers … Very playable for women … Layout is top-notch, Best course in ND, if not the Midwest … If you get to North Dakota, don't miss the opportunity … The view itself is worth the trip.

★★★ HEART RIVER MUNICIPAL GOLF COURSE

PU-8th St. S.W., Dickinson, 58601, Stark County, (701)225-9412, 2 miles from Dickinson. **Facility Holes:** 18. **Yards:** 6,734/4,738. **Par:** 72/72. **Course Rating:** 71.5/67.2. **Slope:** 116/109. **Green Fee:** $16. **Cart Fee:** $16/Cart. **Walking Policy:** Unrestricted walking. **Walkability:** 3. **Opened:** 1983. **Architect:** Abe Epinosa/Dick Phelps/ Brad Benz. **Season:** March-Oct. **High:** June-Aug. **To obtain tee times:** Call up to 3 days in advance. **Miscellaneous:** Reduced fees (juniors), range (grass), credit cards (MC, V, D), BF, FF.

Reader Comments: Two distinct nines built in different eras … The old nine meanders back through a low level woodsy environment. Friendly courteous people who can play in about 3:45 … More fun on back … Good shape.

★★★ JAMESTOWN COUNTRY CLUB

SP-RR1 SE of City, Jamestown, 58401, Stutsman County, (701)252-5522, 3 miles from Jamestown. **Facility Holes:** 18. **Yards:** 6,567/5,252. **Par:** 72/72. **Course Rating:** 70.9/69.7. **Slope:** 122/114. **Green Fee:** $25/$30. **Cart Fee:** $24/Cart. **Walking Policy:** Unrestricted walk-

ing. **Walkability:** 1. **Opened:** 1963. **Season:** April-Oct. **High:** June-Aug. **To obtain tee times:** Call golf shop. **Miscellaneous:** Reduced fees (juniors), range (grass), credit cards (MC, V).
Reader Comments: Beautiful James River Valley ... Course is in good shape ... Traditional layout with good shot values ... Low play, wide open.

LANSFORD COUNTRY CLUB
SP-Box 66, Lansford, 58750, Bottineau County, (701)784-5585. **Facility Holes:** 9. **Yards:** 2,748/2,229. **Par:** 35/35. **Slope:** 89/94. **Opened:** 1960. **Season:** April-Oct. **To obtain tee times:** Call golf shop. **Miscellaneous:** Metal spikes, credit cards (MC, V).

★★½ LINCOLN PARK GOLF COURSE
PU-P.O. Box 12429, Grand Forks, 58208, Grand Forks County, (701)746-2788. **Facility Holes:** 18. **Yards:** 6,006/5,382. **Par:** 71/71. **Course Rating:** 67.0/69.7. **Slope:** 108/112. **Green Fee:** $13/$15. **Cart Fee:** $15/Cart. **Walking Policy:** Unrestricted walking. **Walkability:** 2. **Opened:** 1929. **Season:** April-Oct. **High:** May-July. **To obtain tee times:** Call golf shop. **Miscellaneous:** Reduced fees (twilight), credit cards (MC, V).

★★★★½ THE LINKS OF NORTH DAKOTA AT RED MIKE RESORT *Value, Pace*
PU-Hwy. 1804, Ray, 58849, Williams County, (701)568-2600, 27 miles from Williston. **Facility Holes:** 18. **Yards:** 7,092/5,249. **Par:** 72/72. **Course Rating:** 73.5/69.5. **Slope:** 126/114. **Green Fee:** $30/$35. **Cart Fee:** $18/Cart. **Walking Policy:** Unrestricted walking. **Walkability:** 3. **Opened:** 1995. **Architect:** Stephen Kay. **Season:** April-Oct. **High:** June-Sept. **To obtain tee times:** Call up to 7 days in advance. **Miscellaneous:** Reduced fees (twilight), range (grass), credit cards (MC, V), BF, FF.
Notes: Ranked 2nd in 2001 Best in State; 2nd in 1996 Best New Affordable Courses.
Reader Comments: Great course, worth the drive ... Can be wild in the wind ... Par 3s are great ... Excellent shape, great value, good camping ... Planned a 4000-mile trip around this gem.

★★½ MAPLE RIVER GOLF CLUB
PU-I-94 Exit 338, Mapleton, 58059, Cass County, (701)282-5415, 12 miles from Fargo. **Facility Holes:** 18. **Yards:** 6,643/5,550. **Par:** 72/74. **Course Rating:** 73.0/72.7. **Slope:** 124/121. **Green Fee:** $17/$19. **Cart Fee:** $20/Cart. **Walking Policy:** Unrestricted walking. **Walkability:** 2. **Opened:** 1966. **Season:** April-Oct. **High:** June-Aug. **To obtain tee times:** Call golf shop. **Miscellaneous:** Reduced fees (weekdays, seniors, juniors), range (grass), credit cards (MC, V), BF, FF.

★★★½ MINOT COUNTRY CLUB
SP-Country Rd. 15 W., Minot, 58701, Ward County, (701)839-6169, 4 miles from Minot. **E-mail:** mccshop@ndal.net. **Facility Holes:** 18. **Yards:** 6,565/5,270. **Par:** 72/72. **Course Rating:** 72.1/70.8. **Slope:** 131/123. **Green Fee:** $37. **Cart Fee:** $21/Person. **Walking Policy:** Unrestricted walking. **Walkability:** 2. **Opened:** 1929. **Architect:** Tom Vardon/Robert Bruce Harris. **Season:** April-Oct. **High:** June-Aug. **To obtain tee times:** Call up to 4 days in advance. **Miscellaneous:** Reduced fees (juniors), range (grass), credit cards (MC, V, AE), BF, FF.
Notes: Ranked 5th in 2001 Best in State.
Reader Comments: Always a pleasure to play ... Some weird holes ... Beautiful shape, good course, fairly long, great greens ... Trees, water, sand and hills.

MOTT COUNTRY CLUB
PU-P.O. Box 216, Mott, 58646, Hettinger County, (701)824-2825, 1 mile from Mott. **Facility Holes:** 9. **Yards:** 3,011/2,811. **Par:** 36/38. **Course Rating:** 69.3/66.6. **Slope:** 109/105. **Green Fee:** $12. **Cart Fee:** $14/Cart. **Walking Policy:** Unrestricted walking. **Walkability:** 3. **Season:** April-Nov. **To obtain tee times:** Call golf shop. **Miscellaneous:** Range (grass), BF, FF.

OAKES GOLF CLUB
PU-Rte. 1, Oakes, 58474, Dickey County, (701)742-2405, 57 miles from Valley City. **Facility Holes:** 9. **Yards:** 5,996/5,130. **Par:** 72/72. **Course Rating:** 68.3. **Green Fee:** $12/$15. **Cart Fee:** $16/Cart. **Walking Policy:** Unrestricted walking. **Walkability:** 5. **Opened:** 1952. **Season:** May-Oct. **To obtain tee times:** Call golf shop. **Miscellaneous:** Reduced fees (guests), FF.

PAINTED WOODS GOLF COURSE
PU-Hwy. 83 S., Washburn, 58577, McClean County, (701)462-8480, 35 miles from Bismarck. **Facility Holes:** 9. **Yards:** 2,819/2,619. **Par:** 36/37. **Course Rating:** 67.0/67.9. **Slope:** 106/112. **Green Fee:** $14. **Cart Fee:** $16/Cart. **Walking Policy:** Unrestricted walking. **Walkability:** 2. **Opened:** 1979. **Season:** May-Oct. **To obtain tee times:** Call golf shop. **Miscellaneous:** Reduced fees (juniors), range (grass), BF, FF.

NORTH DAKOTA

★★ **PLAINSVIEW GOLF COURSE AT GRAND FORKS AFB**
M-641 Alert Ave. Bldg.811, Grand Forks AFB, Grand Forks, 58205, Grand Forks County, (701)747-4279, 15 miles from Grand Forks. **E-mail:** malcolm.rodacker@grandforks.af.mil.com. **Facility Holes:** 18. **Yards:** 6,685/5,360. **Par:** 72/72. **Course Rating:** 69.9/65.9. **Slope:** 102/100. **Green Fee:** $8/$12. **Cart Fee:** $14/Cart. **Walking Policy:** Unrestricted walking. **Walkability:** 1. **Opened:** 1971. **Season:** April-Nov. **High:** June-July. **To obtain tee times:** Call golf shop. **Miscellaneous:** Reduced fees (juniors), range (grass/mats), credit cards (MC, V).

★★★ **PRAIRIE WEST GOLF COURSE**
PU-2709 Long Spur Trail, Mandan, 58554, Morton County, (701)667-3222, 2 miles from Bismarck. **E-mail:** olsonpwgolf@excite.com. **Facility Holes:** 18. **Yards:** 6,681/5,452. **Par:** 72/72. **Course Rating:** 71.6/70.1. **Slope:** 127/118. **Green Fee:** $18. **Cart Fee:** $18/Cart. **Walking Policy:** Unrestricted walking. **Walkability:** 2. **Opened:** 1992. **Architect:** Don Herfort. **Season:** March-Nov. **High:** May-Sept. **To obtain tee times:** Call up to 3 days in advance. **Miscellaneous:** Reduced fees (seniors, juniors), range (grass), credit cards (MC, V), BF, FF. **Reader Comments:** Nice solid course ... Some tight holes ... Little room for hooks or slices ... Great value ... Interesting, decent fairways.

RIVERS EDGE GOLF COURSE
PU-1664 26th Ave. NE, Manvel, 58256, Grand Forks County, (701)696-8268, 10 miles from Grand Forks. **Facility Holes:** 18. **Yards:** . **Par:** 72/72. **Course Rating:** 69.6/70.4. **Slope:** 122/123. **Green Fee:** $14/$16. **Cart Fee:** $18/Cart. **Walking Policy:** Unrestricted walking. **Walkability:** 3. **Opened:** 1995. **Architect:** Joel Goldstrand. **Season:** March-Nov. **To obtain tee times:** Call golf shop. **Miscellaneous:** Reduced fees (weekdays, seniors, juniors), range (grass), credit cards (MC, V), BF, FF.

★★★ **RIVERWOOD GOLF CLUB**
PU-725 Riverwood Dr., Bismarck, 58504, Burleigh County, (701)222-6462. **E-mail:** sraulsty@btigate.com. **Facility Holes:** 18. **Yards:** 6,941/5,196. **Par:** 72/72. **Course Rating:** 70.0/68.6. **Slope:** 130/112. **Green Fee:** $18. **Cart Fee:** $18/Cart. **Walking Policy:** Unrestricted walking. **Walkability:** 1. **Opened:** 1969. **Season:** April-Oct. **High:** June-Sept. **To obtain tee times:** Call golf shop. **Miscellaneous:** Reduced fees (seniors, juniors), range (grass), credit cards (MC, V, AE, D). **Reader Comments:** A delightful course, not far from the Missouri River. Many of the holes give a sense that you are the only golfers on the course. Many trees, but fairways wide enough that only the wildest shots get you in trouble ... Trees pose challenge ... Course through trees, very interesting, great to play.

★★½ **ROSE CREEK GOLF COURSE**
PU-1500 Rose Creek Pkwy. E., Fargo, 58104, Cass County, (701)235-5100. **Facility Holes:** 18. **Yards:** 6,625/5,584. **Par:** 71/71. **Course Rating:** 71.7/67.5. **Slope:** 124/112. **Green Fee:** $17/$21. **Cart Fee:** $20/Cart. **Walking Policy:** Unrestricted walking. **Walkability:** 1. **Opened:** 1993. **Architect:** Dick Phelps. **Season:** April-Oct. **High:** June-July. **To obtain tee times:** Call golf shop. **Miscellaneous:** Reduced fees (twilight, seniors, juniors), range (grass), credit cards (MC, V), BF, FF.

RUGBY GOLF CLUB
PU-P.O. Box 292, Rugby, 58368, Pierce County, (701)776-6917. **Facility Holes:** 9. **Yards:** 6,264/5,254. **Par:** 36/36. **Course Rating:** 69.4/70.0. **Slope:** 114/113. **Green Fee:** $15/$18. **Cart Fee:** $17/Cart. **Walking Policy:** Unrestricted walking. **Walkability:** 2. **Opened:** 1975. **Season:** April-Oct. **High:** June-Aug. **To obtain tee times:** Call golf shop. **Miscellaneous:** Reduced fees (weekdays), range (grass).

★★★ **SOURIS VALLEY GOLF CLUB**
PU-2400 14th Ave. S.W., Minot, 58701, Ward County, (701)838-4112. **Facility Holes:** 18. **Yards:** 6,815/5,474. **Par:** 72/72. **Course Rating:** 72.0/70.6. **Slope:** 119/120. **Green Fee:** $17. **Cart Fee:** $17/Cart. **Walking Policy:** Unrestricted walking. **Walkability:** 2. **Opened:** 1967. **Architect:** William James Spear. **Season:** April-Oct. **High:** June-Aug. **To obtain tee times:** Call golf shop. **Miscellaneous:** Reduced fees (twilight, seniors, juniors), credit cards (MC, V), BF, FF. **Reader Comments:** Very difficult course ... Heavy play ... Good, tough muni ... Great public course, great shape, interesting layout.

★★½ **TOM O'LEARY GOLF COURSE**
PU-1200 N. Washington St., Bismarck, 58501, Burleigh County, (701)222-6531. **Facility Holes:** 18. **Yards:** 5,369/4,109. **Par:** 68/68. **Course Rating:** 65.9/61.4. **Slope:** 111/100. **Green Fee:** $18. **Cart Fee:** $18/Person. **Walking Policy:** Unrestricted walking. **Walkability:** 4. **Opened:** 1987. **Architect:** David Gill/Garrett Gill. **Season:** April-Oct. **High:** April-Oct. **To obtain tee times:**

Call up to 1 day in advance. **Miscellaneous:** Reduced fees (seniors, juniors), range (grass), credit cards (MC, V, AE, D), BF, FF.

WESTRIDGE GOLF COURSE
PU-Hwy. 14 West/P.O. Box 336, Underwood, 58576, McLean County, (701)442-5555, 50 miles from Bismarck. **Facility Holes:** 9. **Yards:** 6,390/5,616. **Par:** 72/72. **Course Rating:** 69.3/70.7. **Slope:** 116/112. **Green Fee:** $13. **Cart Fee:** $17/Cart. **Walking Policy:** Unrestricted walking. **Walkability:** 3. **Opened:** 1989. **Season:** April-Oct. **High:** May-Sept. **To obtain tee times:** Call golf shop. **Miscellaneous:** Range (grass), FF.

WILLISTON MUNICIPAL GOLF COURSE
PU-, Williston, 58801, Williams County, (701)774-1321, 3 miles from Williston. **Facility Holes:** 9. **Yards:** 3,107/2,532. **Par:** 36/36. **Course Rating:** 66.8/67.4. **Slope:** 104/105. **Green Fee:** $13/$15. **Cart Fee:** $13/Cart. **Walking Policy:** Unrestricted walking. **Walkability:** 4. **Season:** April-Sept. **High:** June-Aug. **To obtain tee times:** Call golf shop. **Miscellaneous:** Reduced fees (seniors, juniors), range (grass), credit cards (MC, V, AE, D).

★★ **AIRPORT GOLF COURSE**
PU-900 N. Hamilton Rd., Columbus, 43219, Franklin County, (614)645-3127. **Facility Holes:** 18. **Yards:** 6,383/5,504. **Par:** 70/72. **Course Rating:** 68.1/68.8. **Slope:** 107/110. **Green Fee:** $14/$18. **Cart Fee:** $22/Cart. **Walking Policy:** Unrestricted walking. **Walkability:** 2. **Opened:** 1965. **Architect:** Jack Kidwell. **Season:** Year-round. **To obtain tee times:** Call up to 7 days in advance. **Misc:** Reduced fees (twilight, seniors, juniors), credit cards (MC, V), BF, FF.

AIRPORT GREENS GOLF COURSE
PU-28980 White Rd., Willoughby Hills, 44092, Lake County, (440)944-6164, 15 miles from Cleveland. **Facility Holes:** 18. **Yards:** 6,000/4,785. **Par:** 70/70. **Course Rating:** 67.0/65.9. **Slope:** 105/103. **Green Fee:** $21/$22. **Cart Fee:** $12/Person. **Walking Policy:** Unrestricted walking. **Walkability:** 3. **Opened:** 1991. **Season:** Year-round. **High:** June-Aug. **To obtain tee times:** Call up to 7 days in advance. **Miscellaneous:** Reduced fees (weekdays, seniors, juniors), range (grass), credit cards (MC, V), BF, FF.

★★★½ **APPLE VALLEY GOLF CLUB**
PU-433 Clubhouse Dr., Howard, 43028, Knox County, (740)397-7664, (800)359-7664, 6 miles from Mt. Vernon. **Web:** www.applevalleygolfcourse.com. **Facility Holes:** 18. **Yards:** 6,946/6,116. **Par:** 72/75. **Course Rating:** 72.4/72.9. **Slope:** 116/113. **Green Fee:** $19/$26. **Cart Fee:** $12/Person. **Walking Policy:** Walking at certain times. **Walkability:** 3. **Opened:** 1972. **Architect:** William Newcomb. **Season:** March-Nov. **To obtain tee times:** Call up to 90 days in advance. **Miscellaneous:** Reduced fees (weekdays, twilight, seniors, juniors), range (grass), credit cards (MC, V, AE, D), FF.
Reader Comments: Tough to play … It's just a beautiful track! … Everything excellent … Good test of golf, long par 4s on back … Good greens … Lots of variety … Tougher than it looks … Really liked the elevated tees … Lacks mature trees alongside fairways … Hidden gem.

ARROWHEAD PARK GOLF CLUB
SP-2211 Dirksen Rd., Minster, 45865, Shelby County, (419)628-3111, 65 miles from Dayton. **Facility Holes:** 18. **Yards:** 6,248/5,070. **Par:** 72/72. **Course Rating:** 69.3/68.6. **Slope:** 118/117. **Green Fee:** $20/$24. **Cart Fee:** $12/Person. **Walking Policy:** Unrestricted walking. **Walkability:** 3. **Opened:** 1967. **Season:** March-Dec. **To obtain tee times:** Call up to 7 days in advance. **Miscellaneous:** Range (grass/mats), credit cards (MC, V), BF, FF.

★★ **ASTORHURST COUNTRY CLUB**
PU-7000 Dunham Rd., Walton Hills, 44146, Cuyahoga County, (216)439-3636, 10 miles from Cleveland. **E-mail:** golfprods@aol.com. **Facility Holes:** 18. **Yards:** 6,083/5,299. **Par:** 71/73. **Course Rating:** 70.3/74.2. **Slope:** 120/124. **Green Fee:** $23/$27. **Cart Fee:** $22/Cart. **Walking Policy:** Walking at certain times. **Walkability:** 3. **Opened:** 1969. **Architect:** Harold Paddock. **Season:** Year-round. **High:** May-Sept. **To obtain tee times:** Call golf shop. **Miscellaneous:** Reduced fees (twilight, seniors, juniors), credit cards (MC, V, AE, D), BF, FF.

★★½ **ATWOOD RESORT GOLF COURSE**
R-2650 Lodge Rd., Dellroy, 44620, Carroll County, (330)735-2211, (800)362-6406, 25 miles from Canton. **Facility Holes:** 27. **Yards:** 6,152/4,188. **Par:** 70/70. **Course Rating:** 65.7/62.0. **Slope:** 102/91. **Green Fee:** $10/$23. **Cart Fee:** $11/Person. **Walking Policy:** Unrestricted walking. **Opened:** 1951. **Architect:** Oiler. **Season:** Year-round. **To obtain tee times:** Call up to 365 days in advance. **Miscellaneous:** Reduced fees (weekdays, guests, seniors, juniors), credit cards (MC, V, AE, D), BF, FF.
Special Notes: Also has a 9-hole par-3 course.

AUBURN SPRINGS COUNTRY CLUB
SP-10001 Stafford Rd., Chagrin Falls, 44023, Geauga County, (440)543-4448. **Facility Holes:** 18. **Yards:** 6,835/5,588. **Par:** 72/72. **Course Rating:** 71.5/71.5. **Slope:** 117/113. **Green Fee:** $16/$24. **Cart Fee:** $11/Cart. **Season:** Year-round. **To obtain tee times:** Call golf shop. **Miscellaneous:** Reduced fees (weekdays, seniors).

AUGLAIZE COUNTRY CLUB
SP-19062 Road 212, State Rte. 111, Defiance, 43512, Paulding County, (419)393-2211, 8 miles from Defiance. **Facility Holes:** 18. **Yards:** 6,500/5,600. **Par:** 72/72. **Course Rating:** 70.0. **Slope:** 117. **Green Fee:** $18/$23. **Cart Fee:** $13/Person. **Walking Policy:** Unrestricted walking. **Walkability:** 1. **Opened:** 1955. **Season:** Year-round. **High:** May-Oct. **To obtain tee times:** Call up to 10 days in advance. **Miscellaneous:** Reduced fees (weekdays, twilight, seniors, juniors), range (grass), credit cards (MC, V, D), BF, FF.

★★★★ AVALON LAKES GOLF COURSE
SP-One American Way, Warren, 44484, Trumbull County, (330)856-8898, 40 miles from Cleveland. **Facility Holes:** 18. **Yards:** 7,551/4,904. **Par:** 72/72. **Course Rating:** 76.9/68.5. **Slope:** 143/119. **Green Fee:** $50/$135. **Cart Fee:** $15/Person. **Walking Policy:** Unrestricted walking. **Walkability:** 2. **Opened:** 1968. **Architect:** Pete Dye. **Season:** April-Nov. **High:** June-Oct. **To obtain tee times:** Call golf shop. **Miscellaneous:** Reduced fees (weekdays, twilight), range (grass/mats), lodging (140 rooms), credit cards (MC, V, AE, D), FF.
Reader Comments: LPGA tour stop and worth playing ... A championship course for the public ... What a wonderful surprise ... A fantastic redesign by Pete Dye. A must play ... A little expensive ... Great greens.

★★½ AVALON SOUTH GOLF COURSE
PU-9794 E. Market St., Warren, 44484, Trumbull County, (330)856-4329, (800)828-2566X471, 60 miles from Cleveland. **E-mail:** dejackgolf@aol.com. **Facility Holes:** 18. **Yards:** 6,224/5,038. **Par:** 71/71. **Course Rating:** 68.6/68.1. **Slope:** 112/108. **Green Fee:** $15/$20. **Cart Fee:** $10/Person. **Walking Policy:** Unrestricted walking. **Walkability:** 2. **Opened:** 1930. **Season:** March-Nov. **To obtain tee times:** Call golf shop. **Miscellaneous:** Reduced fees (weekdays, seniors, juniors), range (grass), lodging (144 rooms), credit cards (MC, V, AE, D), BF, FF.

★★ AVON FIELD GOLF COURSE
PU-4081 Reading Rd., Cincinnati, 45229, Hamilton County, (513)281-0322, 5 miles from Cincinnati. **E-mail:** tedozzieksm@aol.com. **Web:** www.cincygolf.com. **Facility Holes:** 18. **Yards:** 4,963/4,234. **Par:** 66/66. **Course Rating:** 63.3/63.5. **Slope:** 103/103. **Green Fee:** $19/$20. **Cart Fee:** $11/Person. **Walking Policy:** Unrestricted walking. **Walkability:** 4. **Opened:** 1914. **Architect:** William B. Langford/Don Ross. **Season:** Year-round. **High:** May-Sept. **To obtain tee times:** Call up to 7 days in advance. **Miscellaneous:** Reduced fees (twilight, seniors, juniors), range (grass/mats), credit cards (MC, V), BF, FF.

AVONDALE GOLF CLUB
PU-38490 Detroit Rd., Avon, 44011, Lorain County, (440)934-4398. **Facility Holes:** 18. **Yards:** 6,258/5,400. **Par:** 71/73. **Course Rating:** 69.9/70.7. **Slope:** 118/114. **Green Fee:** $17/$20. **Cart Fee:** $11/Person. **Season:** Year-round. **To obtain tee times:** Call golf shop. **Miscellaneous:** Reduced fees (weekdays, seniors).

★★½ BARBERTON BROOKSIDE COUNTRY CLUB
PU-3727 Golf Course Dr., Norton, 44203, Summit County, (330)825-4539, 5 miles from Akron. **E-mail:** redt2golf@aol.com. **Facility Holes:** 18. **Yards:** 6,448/5,098. **Par:** 72/72. **Course Rating:** 72.0/71.8. **Slope:** 114/105. **Green Fee:** $15/$29. **Cart Fee:** $22/Cart. **Walking Policy:** Walking at certain times. **Walkability:** 3. **Opened:** 1921. **Season:** Year-round. **High:** April-Sept. **To obtain tee times:** Call golf shop. **Miscellaneous:** Reduced fees (weekdays, seniors, juniors), credit cards (MC, V), BF, FF.

★★★½ BEAVER CREEK MEADOWS GOLF COURSE
PU-12774 SR 7, Lisbon, 44432, Columbiana County, (330)385-3020, 30 miles from Youngstown. **Facility Holes:** 18. **Yards:** 6,500/5,500. **Par:** 71/72. **Course Rating:** 68.7/65.5. **Slope:** 116/113. **Green Fee:** $13/$17. **Cart Fee:** $18/Cart. **Walking Policy:** Unrestricted walking. **Walkability:** 3. **Opened:** 1984. **Architect:** Bruce Weber. **Season:** March-Dec. **Tee times:** Call golf shop. **Miscellaneous:** Reduced fees (weekdays), metal spikes, range (grass), BF, FF.
Reader Comments: Holes 10-15 are a nice stretch ... Enjoyable to play ... Excellent course for seniors and women. No. 12 is an exciting par 3 ... Fine golf course that gets lots of play ... Hard to walk.

★½ BEDFORD TRAILS GOLF COURSE
PU-713 Bedford Rd., Coitsville, 44436-9504, Mahoning County, (330)536-2234, 1 mile from Youngstown. **Facility Holes:** 18. **Yards:** 6,160/5,170. **Par:** 70/70. **Green Fee:** $12/$19. **Cart Fee:** $11/Person. **Walking Policy:** Unrestricted walking. **Walkability:** 1. **Opened:** 1962. **Architect:** Tom Grischow. **Season:** Year-round. **High:** May-Sept. **To obtain tee times:** Call golf shop. **Miscellaneous:** Reduced fees (weekdays, seniors, juniors), range (grass/mats), credit cards (MC, V), BF, FF.

★★★½ BENT TREE GOLF CLUB
PU-350 Bent Tree Rd., Sunbury, 43074, Delaware County, (740)965-5140, 10 miles from Columbus. **Facility Holes:** 18. **Yards:** 6,805/5,280. **Par:** 72/72. **Course Rating:** 72.1/69.2. **Slope:** 122/113. **Green Fee:** $47/$58. **Cart Fee:** Included in green fee. **Walking Policy:** Walking at certain times. **Walkability:** 3. **Opened:** 1988. **Architect:** Denis Griffiths & Assoc. **Season:** Year-round. **High:** May-Oct. **To obtain tee times:** Call golf shop. **Miscellaneous:** Reduced fees (weekdays, twilight, seniors, juniors), range (grass), credit cards (MC, V, AE, D).

OHIO

★★½ BERKSHIRE HILLS GOLF COURSE
PU-9758 Mayfield Rd., Chesterland, 44026, Geauga County, (440)729-9516, 3 miles from Chesterland. **Facility Holes:** 18. **Yards:** 6,607/5,512. **Par:** 72/73. **Course Rating:** 72.1/71.8. **Slope:** 129/122. **Green Fee:** $23/$29. **Cart Fee:** $11/Person. **Walking Policy:** Walking at certain times. **Walkability:** 4. **Season:** Year-round. **To obtain tee times:** Call up to 1 day in advance. **Miscellaneous:** Reduced fees (weekdays, seniors), range (grass), credit cards (MC, V), FF.

★½ BIG BEAVER CREEK GOLF COURSE
PU-1762 Zahn's Corner Rd., Piketon, 45661, Pike County, (740)289-3643, (800)554-6534, 59 miles from Columbus. **Facility Holes:** 18. **Yards:** 7,073/5,716. **Par:** 72/72. **Course Rating:** 73.5/72.3. **Slope:** 126/121. **Green Fee:** $14/$16. **Cart Fee:** $10/Person. **Walking Policy:** Unrestricted walking. **Walkability:** 4. **Opened:** 1996. **Architect:** D.W. Bloomfield. **Season:** Year-round. **High:** June-Sept. **To obtain tee times:** Call golf shop. **Miscellaneous:** Reduced fees (weekdays), range (grass), credit cards (MC, V), FF.

★★★ BIG MET GOLF CLUB
PU-4811 Valley Pkwy., Fairview Park, 44126, Cuyahoga County, (440)331-1070, 2 miles from Cleveland. **Facility Holes:** 18. **Yards:** 6,125/5,870. **Par:** 72/74. **Course Rating:** 68.0/72.0. **Slope:** 108/113. **Green Fee:** $13/$20. **Cart Fee:** $10/Person. **Walking Policy:** Unrestricted walking. **Walkability:** 3. **Opened:** 1926. **Architect:** Stanley Thompson. **Season:** March-Dec. **Tee times:** Call up to 5 days ahead. **Misc:** Reduced fees (seniors, juniors), credit cards (MC, V), BF, FF.

BLACK BROOK COUNTRY CLUB
SP-8900 Lakeshore Blvd., Mentor, 44060, Lake County, (440)951-0010, 35 miles from Cleveland. **Facility Holes:** 18. **Yards:** 6,211/5,398. **Par:** 70/73. **Course Rating:** 69.1/70.5. **Slope:** 118/117. **Green Fee:** $20/$23. **Cart Fee:** $11/Person. **Walking Policy:** Unrestricted walking. **Walkability:** 2. **Season:** Year-round. **To obtain tee times:** Call golf shop. **Miscellaneous:** Reduced fees (weekdays, seniors), range (grass), credit cards (MC, V), BF, FF.

BLACK DIAMOND GOLF COURSE
PU-7500 Township Rd. 103, Millersburg, 44654, Holmes County, (330)674-6110, 70 miles from Cleveland. **Web:** www.blackdiamondgolfcourse.com. **Facility Holes:** 18. **Yards:** 6,462/4,689. **Par:** 72/72. **Course Rating:** 71.3/66.8. **Slope:** 130/117. **Green Fee:** $32/$36. **Cart Fee:** Included in green fee. **Walking Policy:** Unrestricted walking. **Walkability:** 4. **Opened:** 2001. **Architect:** Barry Serafin. **Season:** March-Nov. **To obtain tee times:** Call golf shop. **Miscellaneous:** Reduced fees (weekdays), range (grass), credit cards (MC, V).

★★★ BLACKHAWK GOLF CLUB
PU-8830 Dustin Rd., Galena, 43021, Delaware County, (740)965-1042, 20 miles from Columbus. **E-mail:** blackhawkgc@compuserve.com. **Facility Holes:** 18. **Yards:** 6,550/4,726. **Par:** 71/71. **Course Rating:** 70.6/66.0. **Slope:** 115/106. **Green Fee:** $26. **Cart Fee:** $12/Person. **Walking Policy:** Unrestricted walking. **Walkability:** 3. **Opened:** 1964. **Architect:** Jack Kidwell. **Season:** March-Dec. **To obtain tee times:** Call golf shop. **Miscellaneous:** Reduced fees (twilight, seniors, juniors), metal spikes, range (grass), credit cards (MC, V, D), BF, FF.

★★★½ BLACKLICK WOODS GOLF COURSE
PU-7309 E. Livingston Ave., Reynoldsburg, 43068, Franklin County, (614)861-3193, 12 miles from Columbus. **Facility Holes:** 36. **Yards:** 6,819/5,018. **Par:** 72/75. **Course Rating:** 71.9/68.0. **Slope:** 124/116. **Green Fee:** $18. **Cart Fee:** $12/Person. **Walking Policy:** Unrestricted walking. **Walkability:** 3. **Opened:** 1965. **Architect:** Jack Kidwell/Jodie Kinney. **Season:** Year-round. **To obtain tee times:** Call golf shop. **Miscellaneous:** Reduced fees (twilight), range (grass/mats), credit cards (MC, V, AE, D), BF, FF.
Special Notes: Also has an 18-hole executive Green Course.

★★★ BLACKMOOR GOLF CLUB
SP-1220 Kragel Rd., Richmond, 43944, Jefferson County, (740)765-5502, 50 miles from Pittsburgh. **Facility Holes:** 18. **Yards:** 6,500/4,963. **Par:** 72/72. **Course Rating:** 71.2/72.0. **Slope:** 136/124. **Green Fee:** $25/$35. **Cart Fee:** Included in green fee. **Walking Policy:** Walking at certain times. **Walkability:** 4. **Opened:** 1995. **Architect:** John Robinson. **Season:** Year-round. **High:** May-Sept. **Tee times:** Call up to 15 days in advance. **Miscellaneous:** Reduced fees

OHIO

(weekdays, seniors), range (grass), credit cards (MC, V, AE, D), FF.
Reader Comments: Great par 3s … Hilly track with some interesting holes … Variety of lies worth the trip … Somewhat unfair … A thrill to play.

★★★½ BLUE ASH GOLF COURSE
PU-4040 Cooper Rd., Cincinnati, 45241, Hamilton County, (513)745-8577, 15 miles from Cincinnati. **Facility Holes:** 18. **Yards:** 6,643/5,125. **Par:** 72/72. **Course Rating:** 72.7/70.4. **Slope:** 135/125. **Green Fee:** $27. **Cart Fee:** $13/Person. **Walking Policy:** Unrestricted walking. **Walkability:** 3. **Opened:** 1979. **Architect:** Kidwell/Hurdzan. **Season:** Year-round. **High:** May-Oct. **To obtain tee times:** Call golf shop. **Miscellaneous:** Reduced fees (seniors, juniors), credit cards (MC, V), BF, FF.
Notes: Ranked 67th in 1996 America's Top 75 Affordable Courses.
Reader Comments: Great course … Used every club … Always a pleasant experience … Tight course with fast greens … New improvements are great! … Opening 3 holes will make or break your day.

★½ BLUFFTON GOLF CLUB
PU-8575 N. Dixie Hwy., Bluffton, 45817, Allen County, (419)358-6230, 15 miles from Lima. **Facility Holes:** 18. **Yards:** 6,633/5,822. **Par:** 72/72. **Course Rating:** 69.2/69.8. **Slope:** 103/95. **Green Fee:** $12. **Cart Fee:** $9/Person. **Walking Policy:** Unrestricted walking. **Opened:** 1941. **Architect:** Ken Mast. **Season:** March-Nov. **High:** June-Aug. **To obtain tee times:** Call golf shop. **Miscellaneous:** Reduced fees (weekdays, seniors, juniors), metal spikes, range (grass/mats).

★★★ BOB-O-LINK GOLF COURSE
PU-4141 Center Rd., Avon, 44011, Lorain County, (440)934-6217, 20 miles from Cleveland. **Facility Holes:** 27. **Green Fee:** $12/$14. **Cart Fee:** $20/Person. **Walking Policy:** Unrestricted walking. **Walkability:** 2. **Opened:** 1969. **Season:** Year-round. **High:** May-Sept. **To obtain tee times:** Call golf shop. **Miscellaneous:** Reduced fees (weekdays, seniors, juniors), metal spikes, range (grass), credit cards (MC, V).
RED/BLUE (18 Combo)
Yards: 6,052/4,808. **Par:** 71/71. **Course Rating:** 66.6/62.6. **Slope:** 115/112.
RED/WHITE (18 Combo)
Yards: 6,263/5,050. **Par:** 71/71. **Course Rating:** 66.6/62.6. **Slope:** 108/107.
WHITE/BLUE (18 Combo)
Yards: 6,383/5,103. **Par:** 72/72. **Course Rating:** 68.4/64.8. **Slope:** 115/115.
Reader Comments: Need to improve course condition … Average all-around course.

★★½ BOLTON FIELD GOLF COURSE
PU-6005 Alkire Rd., Columbus, 43119, Franklin County, (614)645-3050. **E-mail:** guyballz@aol.com. **Facility Holes:** 18. **Yards:** 7,034/5,204. **Par:** 72/72. **Course Rating:** 71.9/68.6. **Slope:** 118/113. **Green Fee:** $14/$19. **Cart Fee:** $22/Cart. **Walking Policy:** Unrestricted walking. **Walkability:** 2. **Opened:** 1971. **Architect:** Jack Kidwell. **Season:** Year-round. **To obtain tee times:** Call up to 7 days in advance. **Miscellaneous:** Reduced fees (weekdays, twilight, seniors, juniors), range (grass), credit cards (MC, V), BF, FF.

★★ BOSTON HILLS COUNTRY CLUB
PU-105/124 E. Hines Hill Rd., Boston Heights, 44236, Summit County, (330)656-2438, 30 miles from Cleveland. **E-mail:** bhcc@mainet.net. **Facility Holes:** 18. **Yards:** 6,117/4,987. **Par:** 71/71. **Course Rating:** 69.0/68.2. **Slope:** 114/108. **Green Fee:** $16/$27. **Cart Fee:** $22/Cart. **Walking Policy:** Unrestricted walking. **Walkability:** 2. **Opened:** 1923. **Architect:** Wink Chadwick. **Season:** Year-round. **High:** April-Sept. **To obtain tee times:** Call up to 7 days in advance. **Miscellaneous:** Reduced fees (weekdays, twilight, seniors, juniors), range (grass/mats), credit cards (MC, V, D), BF, FF.

★★½ BRANDYWINE COUNTRY CLUB
PU-5555 Akron Peninsula Rd., Peninsula, 44264, Summit County, (330)657-2525, 10 miles from Akron. **Facility Holes:** 27. **Yards:** 6,481/5,625. **Par:** 72/75. **Course Rating:** 70.2/70.5. **Slope:** 113/113. **Green Fee:** $22/$28. **Cart Fee:** $24/Cart. **Walking Policy:** Unrestricted walking. **Walkability:** 3. **Opened:** 1962. **Architect:** Earl Yesberger. **Season:** Year-round. **To obtain tee times:** Call up to 14 days in advance. **Miscellaneous:** Reduced fees (weekdays, twilight, seniors), BF, FF.
Special Notes: Also has a 9-hole par-3 course.

BRENTWOOD GOLF CLUB
PU-12415 Rte. 57, Grafton, 44044, Lorain County, (216)322-9254. **Facility Holes:** 18. **Yards:** 5,148/4,323. **Par:** 70/70. **Green Fee:** $15/$17. **Cart Fee:** $12/Person. **Season:** March-Dec. **To obtain tee times:** Call golf shop. **Miscellaneous:** Reduced fees (weekdays, seniors).

BRIAR HILL COUNTRY CLUB
PU-14451 Deshler Rd., North Baltimore, 45872, Wood County, (419)257-3641, 13 miles from Findlay. **E-mail:** briarhil@wcnet.org. **Web:** www.golfatbriarhill@wcnet.org. **Facility Holes:** 18. **Yards:** 6,014/4,707. **Par:** 70/70. **Course Rating:** 69.0/66.1. **Slope:** 115/107. **Green Fee:** $17/$18. **Cart Fee:** $20/Cart. **Walking Policy:** Unrestricted walking. **Walkability:** 3. **Opened:** 1965. **Season:** March-Nov. **High:** June-Sept. **To obtain tee times:** Call up to 14 days in advance. **Miscellaneous:** Reduced fees (weekdays, seniors, juniors), BF, FF.

★½ BRIARDALE GREENS GOLF COURSE
PU-24131 Briardale Ave., Euclid, 44123, Cuyahoga County, (216)289-8574, 8 miles from Cleveland. **Facility Holes:** 18. **Yards:** 6,127/4,977. **Par:** 70/70. **Course Rating:** 69.1/70.5. **Slope:** 116/118. **Green Fee:** $18/$22. **Cart Fee:** $10/Person. **Walking Policy:** Unrestricted walking. **Walkability:** 1. **Opened:** 1977. **Architect:** Dick LaConte. **Season:** Year-round. **To obtain tee times:** Call up to 7 days in advance. **Miscellaneous:** Reduced fees (seniors, juniors), range (mats), credit cards (MC, V), BF, FF.

★★½ BRIARWOOD GOLF COURSE
PU-2737 Edgerton Rd., Broadview Heights, 44147, Cuyahoga County, (440)237-5271, 22 miles from Cleveland. **E-mail:** briarwood27@aol.com. **Web:** www.briarwoodgolfcourse.com. **Facility Holes:** 27. **Green Fee:** $22/$30. **Cart Fee:** $12/Person. **Walking Policy:** Unrestricted walking. **Opened:** 1965. **Architect:** Ted McAnlis. **Season:** Year-round. **High:** April-Oct. **To obtain tee times:** Call up to 7 days in advance. **Miscellaneous:** Reduced fees (weekdays, twilight, seniors, juniors), range (grass), credit cards (MC, V), BF, FF.
RED/WHITE (18 Combo)
Yards: 7,098/5,368. **Par:** 72/72. **Course Rating:** 72.8/69.7. **Slope:** 125/113. **Walkability:** 3.
WHITE/BLUE (18 Combo)
Yards: 6,622/4,955. **Par:** 71/71. **Course Rating:** 70.8/67.0. **Slope:** 117/109. **Walkability:** 3.

BRONZWOOD GOLF CLUB
SP-9645 Kinsman Pymatuning Rd., Kinsman, 44428, Trumbull County, (330)876-5300. **Facility Holes:** 18. **Yards:** 6,029/4,773. **Par:** 70/70. **Course Rating:** 69.0/65.0. **Slope:** 108. **Green Fee:** $14/$17. **Cart Fee:** $18/Cart. **Season:** Year-round. **To obtain tee times:** Call golf shop. **Miscellaneous:** Reduced fees (weekdays, seniors).

BROOKLEDGE GOLF CLUB
PU-1621 E. Bailey Rd., Cuyahoga Falls, 44221, Cuyahoga County, (330)971-8430, 10 miles from Cleveland. **Facility Holes:** 18. **Yards:** 6,278/4,728. **Par:** 70/70. **Course Rating:** 68.9/66.2. **Slope:** 107/102. **Green Fee:** $26. **Cart Fee:** $20/Cart. **Walking Policy:** Unrestricted walking. **Walkability:** 3. **Opened:** 1992. **Architect:** Arthur Hills. **Season:** March-Nov. **High:** May-Sept. **To obtain tee times:** Call up to 14 days in advance. **Miscellaneous:** Reduced fees (seniors, juniors), metal spikes, range (grass/mats), credit cards (MC, V, D), BF, FF.

BROOKSIDE GOLF COURSE
PU-1399 Sandusky St., Ashland, 44805, Ashland County, (419)289-7933, 60 miles from Cleveland. **Facility Holes:** 18. **Yards:** 6,457/5,028. **Par:** 71/71. **Course Rating:** 69.8/68.3. **Slope:** 113/109. **Green Fee:** $16/$17. **Cart Fee:** $11/Person. **Walking Policy:** Mandatory carts. **Walkability:** 3. **Opened:** 1971. **Architect:** Kidwell & Hurdzan Inc. **Season:** Year-round. **High:** May-Sept. **To obtain tee times:** Call golf shop. **Miscellaneous:** Reduced fees (twilight, seniors, juniors), range (grass), credit cards (MC, V, D), BF, FF.

BRUNSWICK HILLS GOLF COURSE
PU-4900 Center Rd. (Rte. 303), Brunswick, 44212, Medina County, (330)225-7370, 15 miles from Cleveland. **Facility Holes:** 18. **Yards:** 6,590/4,958. **Par:** 72/72. **Course Rating:** 70.8/69.1. **Slope:** 119/110. **Green Fee:** $20/$24. **Cart Fee:** $11/Person. **Walking Policy:** Unrestricted walking. **Walkability:** 3. **Opened:** 1965. **Season:** March-Nov. **To obtain tee times:** Call golf shop. **Miscellaneous:** Reduced fees (weekdays, seniors, juniors), credit cards (MC, V, D), BF, FF.

★★ BUCKEYE HILLS COUNTRY CLUB
SP-13226 Miami Trace Rd., Greenfield, 45123, Highland County, (937)981-4136, 6 miles from Greenfield. **E-mail:** wet@bright.net. **Facility Holes:** 18. **Yards:** 6,393/4,907. **Par:** 71/72. **Course Rating:** 70.4/67.4. **Slope:** 121/113. **Green Fee:** $15/$20. **Cart Fee:** $11/Person. **Walking Policy:** Unrestricted walking. **Walkability:** 4. **Opened:** 1970. **Architect:** X. G. Hassenplug. **Season:** Year-round. **High:** March-Dec. **To obtain tee times:** Call up to 7 days in advance. **Miscellaneous:** Reduced fees (seniors), credit cards (MC, V), BF, FF.

BUCYRUS COUNTRY CLUB
SP-1330 E. Mansfield St., Bucyrus, 44820, Crawford County, (419)562-0381. **Facility Holes:** 18. **Yards:** 6,350/4,781. **Par:** 72/72. **Course Rating:** 70.2/66.9. **Slope:** 116/111. **Green Fee:** $13/$18. **Cart Fee:** $12/Person. **Season:** March-Nov. **To obtain tee times:** Call golf shop. **Miscellaneous:** Reduced fees (weekdays).

★★★½ BUNKER HILL GOLF COURSE
PU-3060 Pearl Rd., Medina, 44256, Medina County, (330)722-4174, (888)749-5827, 20 miles from Cleveland. **E-mail:** golfstud@apk.net. **Web:** www.bunkerhillgolf.com. **Facility Holes:** 18. **Yards:** 6,643/5,074. **Par:** 72/72. **Course Rating:** 70.9/68.2. **Slope:** 117/110. **Green Fee:** $24/$30. **Cart Fee:** $22/Cart. **Walking Policy:** Walking at certain times. **Walkability:** 3. **Opened:** 1927. **Architect:** Mateo and Sons. **Season:** Year-round. **To obtain tee times:** Call up to 30 days in advance. **Misc:** Reduced fees (weekdays, seniors, juniors), credit cards (MC, V), BF, FF.
Reader Comments: Short sporty course ... An improved and expanded challenge ... Finishing holes on each 9 are the most difficult I've ever played ... Redesign took a so-so course to the next level.

BURNING TREE GOLF COURSE
PU-4600 Ridgely Tract Rd. SE, Newark, 43056, Licking County, (740)522-3464, (800)830-4877, 30 miles from Columbus. **E-mail:** btgcol@aol.com. **Facility Holes:** 18. **Yards:** 6,328/5,804. **Par:** 71/71. **Course Rating:** 69.9/67.0. **Slope:** 119/114. **Green Fee:** $14/$17. **Cart Fee:** $20/Cart. **Walking Policy:** Unrestricted walking. **Walkability:** 1. **Opened:** 1975. **Architect:** Sherm Byers. **Season:** March-Nov. **High:** July-Sept. **To obtain tee times:** Call golf shop. **Miscellaneous:** Reduced fees (weekdays, seniors), range (grass), credit cards (MC, V, AE, D), FF.

★★½ CALIFORNIA GOLF COURSE
PU-5920 Kellogg Ave., Cincinnati, 45228, Hamilton County, (513)231-6513. **E-mail:** lkingksm@aol.com. **Facility Holes:** 18. **Yards:** 6,216/5,626. **Par:** 70/71. **Course Rating:** 70.0/71.4. **Slope:** 116/113. **Green Fee:** $16/$20. **Cart Fee:** $19/Cart. **Walking Policy:** Unrestricted walking. **Opened:** 1936. **Architect:** William H. Diddel. **Season:** Year-round. **To obtain tee times:** Call up to 7 days in advance. **Miscellaneous:** Reduced fees (seniors, juniors), credit cards (MC, V), BF, FF.

★★★★ CANDYWOOD GOLF CLUB
PU-765 Scoville N. Rd., Vienna, 44473, Trumbull County, (216)399-4217, 50 miles from Cleveland. **Facility Holes:** 18. **Yards:** 6,698/5,239. **Par:** 72/73. **Course Rating:** 71.4/69.0. **Slope:** 116/107. **Green Fee:** $19/$22. **Cart Fee:** $9/Person. **Walking Policy:** Unrestricted walking. **Walkability:** 2. **Opened:** 1967. **Season:** March-Dec. **To obtain tee times:** Call golf shop. **Miscellaneous:** Reduced fees (seniors, juniors), credit cards (MC, V), BF, FF.
Reader Comments: Maybe the best public greens in the area ... Good course, but too busy ... Huge greens are fast and true.

CARLISLE GOLF CLUB
SP-39709 Slife Rd., Grafton, 44044, Lorain County, (440)458-8011. **Facility Holes:** 18. **Yards:** 5,860/5,540. **Par:** 71/71. **Green Fee:** $14/$16. **Cart Fee:** $17/Cart. **Season:** Year-round. **To obtain tee times:** Call golf shop. **Miscellaneous:** Reduced fees (weekdays, seniors, juniors).

★★★½ CARROLL MEADOWS GOLF COURSE
PU-1130 Meadowbrook, Carrollton, 44615, Carroll County, (330)627-2663, (888)519-0576, 1 mile from Carrolton. **Facility Holes:** 18. **Yards:** 6,366/4,899. **Par:** 71/71. **Course Rating:** 69.4/67.4. **Slope:** 114/109. **Green Fee:** $14/$18. **Cart Fee:** $10/Person. **Walking Policy:** Unrestricted walking. **Walkability:** 3. **Opened:** 1989. **Architect:** John F. Robinson. **Season:** Year-round. **To obtain tee times:** Call golf shop. **Miscellaneous:** Reduced fees (weekdays, twilight, seniors, juniors), range (grass), credit cards (MC, V, AE), BF, FF.
Reader Comments: A hidden gem ... Tell your friends. It's a must play ... Interesting routing. Everything is well-defined ... I would play often if it were closer.

★★★★ CASSEL HILLS GOLF COURSE *Value*
PU-201 Clubhouse Way, Vandalia, 45377, Montgomery County, (937)890-1300, 5 miles from Dayton. **Facility Holes:** 18. **Yards:** 6,617/5,600. **Par:** 71/71. **Course Rating:** 72.6/69.6. **Slope:** 131/127. **Green Fee:** $18/$26. **Cart Fee:** $22/Cart. **Walking Policy:** Unrestricted walking. **Walkability:** 5. **Opened:** 1974. **Architect:** Bruce von Roxburg/Craig Schreiner. **Season:** Feb.-Dec. **High:** June-Aug. **To obtain tee times:** Call golf shop. **Miscellaneous:** Reduced fees (weekdays, twilight), credit cards (MC, V, D), BF, FF.
Reader Comments: Hilly back 9 is fun ... No driving range ... The 11th to 17th holes wind through the woods ... Excellent course ... Great signature hole in No. 11 ... Beautiful surroundings ... Great greens ... Lots of character ... Good value for your dollar ... A course you just like to play.

OHIO

★★★½ CASTLE SHANNON GOLF COURSE
PU-105 Castle Shannon Blvd., Hopedale, 43976, Jefferson County, (740)937-2373, (888)937-3311, 58 miles from Pittsburgh, PA. **Web:** www.pittsburghgolf.com. **Facility Holes:** 18. **Yards:** 6,896/4,752. **Par:** 71/71. **Course Rating:** 73.0/65.4. **Slope:** 132/110. **Green Fee:** $22/$35. **Cart Fee:** Included in green fee. **Walking Policy:** Walking at certain times. **Walkability:** 4. **Opened:** 1996. **Architect:** Gary Grandstaff. **Season:** Year-round. **To obtain tee times:** Call up to 365 days in advance. **Miscellaneous:** Reduced fees (weekdays, seniors), range (grass), credit cards (MC, V, AE, D).
Reader Comments: A young course, but in good shape … No. 2 is a tough par 3 … Mandatory carts on weekends … Beautiful course.

★★ CATAWBA WILLOWS GOLF & COUNTRY CLUB
PU-2590 E. Sand Rd., Port Clinton, 43452, Ottawa County, (419)734-2524. **Facility Holes:** 18. **Yards:** 5,572/4,557. **Par:** 71/71. **Course Rating:** 66.7/66.4. **Slope:** 113/107. **Green Fee:** $16/$19. **Cart Fee:** $19/Cart. **Season:** Year-round. **To obtain tee times:** Call golf shop. **Miscellaneous:** Reduced fees (weekdays), metal spikes.

★★½ CHAMPIONS GOLF COURSE
PU-3900 Westerville Rd., Columbus, 43224, Franklin County, (614)645-7111, 10 miles from Columbus. **E-mail:** oneiron@hotmail.com. **Facility Holes:** 18. **Yards:** 6,555/5,427. **Par:** 70/72. **Course Rating:** 71.2/71.2. **Slope:** 127/127. **Green Fee:** $29/$34. **Cart Fee:** $22/Cart. **Walking Policy:** Walking at certain times. **Walkability:** 3. **Opened:** 1948. **Architect:** Robert Trent Jones. **Season:** Year-round. **High:** April-Nov. **To obtain tee times:** Call golf shop. **Miscellaneous:** Reduced fees (weekdays, twilight, seniors, juniors), metal spikes, range (grass/mats), credit cards (MC, V), BF, FF.

★★★½ CHAPEL HILL GOLF COURSE
PU-7516 Johnstown Rd., Mount Vernon, 43050, Knox County, (740)393-3999, (800)393-3499, 28 miles from Columbus. **E-mail:** chapelhill@myaxiom.net. **Web:** www.chapelhillgolf-course.com. **Facility Holes:** 18. **Yards:** 6,900/4,600. **Par:** 72/72. **Course Rating:** 72.2/69.4. **Slope:** 128/119. **Green Fee:** $19/$25. **Cart Fee:** $11/Person. **Walking Policy:** Unrestricted walking. **Walkability:** 4. **Opened:** 1996. **Architect:** Barry Serafin. **Season:** Year-round. **High:** April-Oct. **To obtain tee times:** Call golf shop. **Miscellaneous:** Reduced fees (weekdays, twilight), range (grass), credit cards (MC, V), BF, FF.
Reader Comments: Lot of blind shots make it challenging and fun … GPS system speeds up play … A pleasure to play … Several backbreaking holes, including Nos. 9 and 18 … Too hard to walk … Staff is excellent.

★★ CHAPEL HILLS GOLF COURSE
PU-3381 Austinburg Rd., Ashtabula, 44004, Ashtabula County, (440)997-3791, (800)354-9608, 45 miles from Cleveland. **E-mail:** chgolf@knownet.net. **Web:** www.chapelhillsgolf.com. **Facility Holes:** 18. **Yards:** 5,971/4,507. **Par:** 72/72. **Course Rating:** 68.6/65.7. **Slope:** 112/104. **Green Fee:** $15/$20. **Cart Fee:** $10/Person. **Walking Policy:** Unrestricted walking. **Walkability:** 2. **Opened:** 1957. **Architect:** Bill Franklin. **Season:** March-Nov. **High:** June-Sept. **To obtain tee times:** Call golf shop. **Miscellaneous:** Reduced fees (weekdays, seniors, juniors), range (grass), credit cards (MC, V, AE), BF, FF.

★★★½ CHARDON LAKES GOLF COURSE
PU-470 South St., Chardon, 44024, Geauga County, (440)285-4653, 35 miles from Cleveland. **E-mail:** miketirpak@aol.com. **Facility Holes:** 18. **Yards:** 6,789/5,077. **Par:** 71/73. **Course Rating:** 73.1/66.6. **Slope:** 135/111. **Green Fee:** $23/$34. **Cart Fee:** $11/Person. **Walking Policy:** Unrestricted walking. **Walkability:** 3. **Opened:** 1931. **Architect:** Birdie Way/Don Tincher. **Season:** Year-round. **To obtain tee times:** Call golf shop. **Miscellaneous:** Reduced fees (weekdays, twilight, seniors, juniors), range (grass), credit cards (MC, V, AE, D), BF, FF.
Reader Comments: Old-style architecture … Tough from back tees … Good length and nice elevation changes … Good bang for your buck … Glass greens make it three-putt city.

★★★ CHEROKEE HILLS GOLF CLUB
PU-5740 Center Rd., Valley City, 44280, Medina County, (330)225-6122, 31 miles from Akron. **Web:** www.cherokeehillsgolf.com. **Facility Holes:** 18. **Yards:** 6,210/5,880. **Par:** 70/70. **Course Rating:** 68.3/70.3. **Slope:** 109/116. **Green Fee:** $17/$25. **Cart Fee:** $30/Cart. **Walking Policy:** Unrestricted walking. **Walkability:** 4. **Opened:** 1981. **Architect:** Brian Huntley. **Season:** Year-round. **High:** April-Oct. **To obtain tee times:** Call up to 365 days in advance. **Misc:** Reduced fees (weekdays, twilight, seniors, juniors), credit cards (MC, V), BF, FF.
Reader Comments: Narrow driving areas … Real good course for the average golfer as it's open and short … Hilly.

★★★ CHEROKEE HILLS GOLF COURSE
SP-4622 County Rd. 49 N., Bellefontaine, 43311, Logan County, (937)599-3221, 45 miles from Columbus. **Facility Holes:** 18. **Yards:** 6,448/5,327. **Par:** 71/74. **Course Rating:** 70.8/70.3. **Slope:** 115/108. **Green Fee:** $17/$21. **Cart Fee:** $11/Person. **Walking Policy:** Unrestricted walking. **Walkability:** 4. **Opened:** 1970. **Architect:** Chester Kurtz. **Season:** Year-round. **High:** April-Oct. **To obtain tee times:** Call golf shop. **Miscellaneous:** Reduced fees (weekdays, juniors), credit cards (MC, V, D), BF, FF.
Reader Comments: Nice course … Large price increase … Some water, some trees and a lot of good golf.

★★★ CHIPPEWA GOLF CLUB
PU-12147 Shank Rd., Doylestown, 44230, Wayne County, (330)658-6126, (800)321-1701, 5 miles from Akron. **E-mail:** cgc@concentric.net.com. **Web:** www.chipgolf.com. **Facility Holes:** 18. **Yards:** 6,273/4,877. **Par:** 71/72. **Course Rating:** 69.1/67.0. **Slope:** 109/103. **Green Fee:** $11/$18. **Cart Fee:** $19/Person. **Walking Policy:** Unrestricted walking. **Walkability:** 2. **Opened:** 1962. **Architect:** Harrison/Garbin. **Season:** Year-round. **High:** April-Oct. **To obtain tee times:** Call golf shop. **Miscellaneous:** Reduced fees (weekdays, seniors, juniors), range (grass/mats), credit cards (MC, V, AE, D), BF, FF.
Reader Comments: Demanding 3-hole stretch on back 9 … Tough greens … Course improvements are excellent … Layout and condition get better every year … Electrical poles need to go.

CHIPPEWA GOLF CLUB
SP-23550 W. Williston Rd., Curtice, 43412, Ottawa County, (419)836-8111, 6 miles from Toledo. **Facility Holes:** 18. **Yards:** 6,203/5,415. **Par:** 71/72. **Course Rating:** 68.3/69.6. **Slope:** 113/114. **Green Fee:** $14/$19. **Walking Policy:** Unrestricted walking. **Opened:** 1929. **Season:** March-Nov. **To obtain tee times:** Call golf shop.

CLEARVIEW GOLF CLUB
PU-8410 Lincoln St. SE, East Canton, 44730, Stark County, (330)488-0404, 6 miles from Canton. **Facility Holes:** 18. **Yards:** 5,890/5,198. **Par:** 69/73. **Course Rating:** 67.2/68.5. **Slope:** 105/107. **Green Fee:** $12/$22. **Cart Fee:** $20/Cart. **Walking Policy:** Unrestricted walking. **Walkability:** 3. **Opened:** 1948. **Architect:** William Powell. **Season:** March-Dec. **High:** May-Aug. **To obtain tee times:** Call golf shop. **Miscellaneous:** Reduced fees (weekdays, seniors, juniors), credit cards (MC, V), BF, FF.

★½ CLIFFSIDE GOLF COURSE
PU-100 Cliffside Dr., Gallipolis, 45631, Gallia County, (740)446-4653, 30 miles from Huntington. **Facility Holes:** 18. **Yards:** 6,598/5,268. **Par:** 72/72. **Course Rating:** 70.5/66.8. **Slope:** 115/109. **Green Fee:** $15/$16. **Cart Fee:** $10/Person. **Walking Policy:** Unrestricted walking. **Walkability:** 4. **Opened:** 1988. **Architect:** Jack Kidwell. **Season:** Year-round. **High:** April-Oct. **To obtain tee times:** Call golf shop. **Miscellaneous:** Reduced fees (weekdays), credit cards (MC, V).

CLIFFSIDE GOLF COURSE
PU-6510 S. State Rte. 202, Tipp City, 45371, Miami County, (937)667-6686, 10 miles from Dayton. **Facility Holes:** 27. **Green Fee:** $15/$18. **Cart Fee:** $20/Cart. **Walking Policy:** Unrestricted walking. **Opened:** 1972. **Season:** March-Nov. **High:** June-Aug. **To obtain tee times:** Call up to 2 days in advance. **Miscellaneous:** Reduced fees (weekdays), metal spikes, credit cards (MC, V, AE, D), FF.
LOWER COURSE (18)
Yards: 5,549/4,615. **Par:** 70/72. **Course Rating:** 67.3/67.4. **Slope:** 112/110. **Walkability:** 4.
TOP COURSE (9)
Yards: 2,922/2,812. **Par:** 36/36. **Walkability:** 2.

CLINTON HEIGHTS GOLF COURSE
PU-2760 E. Township Rd. 122, Tiffin, 44883, Seneca County, (419)447-8863, 25 miles from Findlay. **Facility Holes:** 18. **Yards:** 5,643/4,915. **Par:** 70/70. **Course Rating:** 65.7/67.5. **Slope:** 104/102. **Green Fee:** $15/$17. **Cart Fee:** $19/Cart. **Walking Policy:** Unrestricted walking. **Walkability:** 2. **Opened:** 1957. **Season:** March-Nov. **High:** April-Sept. **Tee times:** Call up to 1 day in advance. **Miscellaneous:** Reduced fees (twilight), credit cards (MC, V, AE, D), BF, FF.

★★★½ COLONIAL GOLFERS CLUB
PU-10985 Harding Hwy., Harrod, 45850, Allen County, (419)649-3350, (800)234-7468, 10 miles from Lima. **E-mail:** colonialgc@aol.com. **Facility Holes:** 18. **Yards:** 7,000/5,000. **Par:** 72/74. **Course Rating:** 72.2/68.7. **Slope:** 139/111. **Green Fee:** $17/$21. **Cart Fee:** $10/Person. **Walking Policy:** Unrestricted walking. **Walkability:** 4. **Opened:** 1973. **Architect:** Bob Holtsberry/Tom Holtsberry. **Season:** March-Nov. **High:** June-Aug. **To obtain tee times:** Call up to 14 days in advance. **Miscellaneous:** Reduced fees (weekdays, twilight, seniors, juniors),

range (grass), credit cards (MC, V, AE, D), BF, FF.
Reader Comments: Nice landscaping on the course … Not real hard … Pretty straightforward course with only a few challenging holes … Greens are not fast but in good shape … First-class people.

COMMUNITY GOLF COURSE
PU-2917 Berkley St., Dayton, 45409, Montgomery County, (937)293-2341. **Facility Holes:** 36. **Green Fee:** $20/$22. **Cart Fee:** $22/Cart. **Walking Policy:** Unrestricted walking. **Opened:** 1919. **Season:** Year-round. **To obtain tee times:** Call golf shop. **Miscellaneous:** Reduced fees (weekdays, seniors, juniors), range (grass), credit cards (MC, V), BF, FF.
★★ DALES COURSE (18)
Yards: 5,302/4,932. **Par:** 71/71. **Course Rating:** 67.3/65.9. **Slope:** 107/102. **Walkability:** 3.
★★ HILLS COURSE (18)
Yards: 6,304/5,187. **Par:** 71/71. **Course Rating:** 69.4/68.0. **Slope:** 126/123. **Walkability:** 5.

★★★★ COOKS CREEK GOLF CLUB
PU-16405 U.S. Hwy. 23 S., Ashville, 43103, Pickaway County, (740)983-3636, (800)430-4653, 15 miles from Columbus. **E-mail:** cookscrk@bright.net.com. **Web:** www.cookscreekgolf-club.com. **Facility Holes:** 18. **Yards:** 7,071/4,995. **Par:** 72/72. **Course Rating:** 73.7/68.2. **Slope:** 131/120. **Green Fee:** $38/$60. **Cart Fee:** Included in green fee. **Walking Policy:** Unrestricted walking. **Walkability:** 4. **Opened:** 1993. **Architect:** Michael Hurdzan/John Cook. **Season:** Year-round. **High:** May-Oct. **To obtain tee times:** Call up to 7 days in advance. **Miscellaneous:** Reduced fees (weekdays, twilight), range (grass/mats), credit cards (MC, V, AE), BF, FF.
Notes: Ranked 21st in 2001 Best in State; 9th in 1995 Best New Public Courses.
Reader Comments: Luxurious environment, but pricey … Breathtaking … Scenic course … Excellent design, lots of water … Can drive No. 2—a par 4! … Nice layout on rolling terrain near the river.

★★★ COPELAND HILLS GOLF CLUB
PU-41703 Metz Rd., Columbiana, 44408, Columbiana County, (330)482-3221, 20 miles from Youngstown. **E-mail:** lisabecka@aol.com. **Facility Holes:** 18. **Yards:** 6,859/5,763. **Par:** 72/74. **Course Rating:** 72.7/72.7. **Slope:** 121/120. **Green Fee:** $28/$32. **Cart Fee:** Included in green fee. **Walking Policy:** Unrestricted walking. **Walkability:** 2. **Opened:** 1960. **Architect:** R. Albert Anderson. **Season:** April-Nov. **High:** June-Aug. **To obtain tee times:** Call golf shop. **Misc:** Reduced fees (weekdays, seniors, juniors), metal spikes, range (grass), BF, FF.
Reader Comments: Elevated greens make it very tough … Lots of opportunity for trouble.

COSHOCTON PARK DISTRICT
PU-23253 SR 83, Coshocton, 43812, Coshocton County, (740)622-8083, 64 miles from Columbus. **Web:** www.hilltopgolf.com. **Facility Holes:** 18. **Yards:** 6,335/4,906. **Par:** 72/72. **Course Rating:** 68.4/66.3. **Slope:** 106/102. **Green Fee:** $14/$18. **Cart Fee:** $10/Person. **Walking Policy:** Unrestricted walking. **Walkability:** 4. **Opened:** 1938. **Season:** Year-round. **High:** May-Sept. **To obtain tee times:** Call golf shop. **Miscellaneous:** Reduced fees (weekdays, seniors, juniors), credit cards (MC, V), BF, FF.

★★★ COUNTRY ACRES GOLF CLUB
PU-17374 St. Rte. 694, Ottawa, 45875, Putnam County, (419)532-3434, 20 miles from Lima. **Facility Holes:** 18. **Yards:** 6,464/4,961. **Par:** 72/72. **Course Rating:** 69.9/67.9. **Slope:** 126/113. **Green Fee:** $17/$20. **Cart Fee:** $11/Person. **Walking Policy:** Unrestricted walking. **Walkability:** 2. **Opened:** 1978. **Architect:** John Simmons. **Season:** March-Dec. **High:** June-Sept. **To obtain tee times:** Call golf shop. **Miscellaneous:** Reduced fees (seniors, juniors), range (grass), credit cards (MC, V).
Reader Comments: Good course with fast greens … Wide open … Always very windy … Greens are hard and fast … No. 18-what a finisher.

★★ COUNTRYSIDE GOLF COURSE
PU-1421 Struthers Coit Rd., Lowellville, 44436, Mahoning County, (330)755-0016, 5 miles from Youngstown. **Facility Holes:** 18. **Yards:** 6,461/5,399. **Par:** 71/71. **Course Rating:** 70.5/70.1. **Green Fee:** $17/$19. **Cart Fee:** $16/Cart. **Walking Policy:** Unrestricted walking. **Walkability:** 2. **Opened:** 1967. **Season:** March-Nov. **To obtain tee times:** Call golf shop. **Miscellaneous:** Reduced fees (weekdays, seniors, juniors), credit cards (MC, V), BF, FF.

★★ CRANBERRY HILLS GOLF COURSE
PU-4891 Clovercrest Dr. N.W., Warren, 44483, Trumbull County, (330)847-2884, 1 mile from Champion. **Facility Holes:** 9. **Yards:** 2,745/2,418. **Par:** 35/35. **Green Fee:** $8/$13. **Cart Fee:** $14/Cart. **Walking Policy:** Unrestricted walking. **Walkability:** 2. **Opened:** 1930. **Season:** Year-round. **To obtain tee times:** Call golf shop. **Miscellaneous:** Reduced fees (weekdays, seniors, juniors), metal spikes, FF.

CREEKWOOD GOLF CLUB
PU-9691 N. Reed Rd., Columbia Station, 44028, Lorain County, (440)748-3188, 20 miles from Cleveland. **Facility Holes:** 18. **Yards:** 6,117/4,775. **Par:** 72/72. **Course Rating:** 68.8/69.1. **Slope:** 116/112. **Green Fee:** $20/$24. **Cart Fee:** $10/Person. **Walking Policy:** Unrestricted walking. **Walkability:** 2. **Opened:** 1960. **Architect:** David Sandvick. **Season:** Year-round. **High:** June-Sept. **To obtain tee times:** Call up to 7 days in advance. **Miscellaneous:** Reduced fees (weekdays, seniors, juniors), range (grass), credit cards (MC, V, D), BF, FF.

★★★ CROOKED TREE GOLF CLUB
PU-5171 Sentinel Oak Dr., Mason, 45040, Warren County, (513)398-3933, 30 miles from Cincinnati. **Facility Holes:** 18. **Yards:** 6,415/5,295. **Par:** 70/70. **Course Rating:** 71.3/69.7. **Slope:** 129/118. **Green Fee:** $27/$42. **Cart Fee:** Included in green fee. **Walking Policy:** Walking at certain times. **Walkability:** 3. **Opened:** 1989. **Architect:** Denny Acomb. **Season:** Year-round. **To obtain tee times:** Call up to 14 days in advance. **Miscellaneous:** Reduced fees (weekdays, twilight, seniors, juniors), credit cards (MC, V, AE), BF, FF.
Reader Comments: 6 par 3s ... A few Mickey Mouse holes ... Good greens ... Target golf ... Trouble everywhere.

CRYSTAL SPRINGS GOLF CLUB
PU-745 N. Hopewell Rd., Hopewell, 43746, Muskingum County, (740)787-1114, (800)787-1705, 45 miles from Columbus. **E-mail:** crystal@crystalspringsgolfclub.com. **Web:** www.crystalspringsgolfclub.com. **Facility Holes:** 18. **Yards:** 6,412/4,634. **Par:** 71/71. **Course Rating:** 70.1/66.2. **Slope:** 125/114. **Green Fee:** $16/$23. **Cart Fee:** $9/Person. **Walking Policy:** Unrestricted walking. **Walkability:** 4. **Opened:** 1998. **Architect:** Ronald Cutlip. **Season:** Year-round. **High:** May-Oct. **To obtain tee times:** Call golf shop. **Miscellaneous:** Reduced fees (twilight, seniors, juniors), credit cards (MC, V).

★★★½ CUMBERLAND TRAIL GOLF CLUB
PU-8244 Columbia Rd. S. W., Pataskala, 43062, Licking County, (740)964-9336, 18 miles from Columbus. **E-mail:** lmcgowan@cumberlandtrail.com. **Web:** www.cumberlandtrail.com. **Facility Holes:** 18. **Yards:** 7,205/5,469. **Par:** 72/72. **Course Rating:** 73.9/70.4. **Slope:** 130/119. **Green Fee:** $35/$55. **Cart Fee:** Included in green fee. **Walking Policy:** Unrestricted walking. **Walkability:** 1. **Opened:** 1999. **Architect:** Michael Hurdzan/David Whelchel. **Season:** Year-round. **High:** May-Sept. **To obtain tee times:** Call up to 7 days in advance. **Misc:** Reduced fees (weekdays, seniors), range (grass), included in fee), credit cards (MC, V, AE, D), BF, FF.
Reader Comments: Best public greens I've ever played on ... Front 9 mediocre, back 9 good ... Good new course with very good personnel.

★★★★ DARBY CREEK GOLF COURSE
PU-19300 Orchard Rd., Marysville, 43040, Union County, (937)349-7491, (800)343-2729, 18 miles from Dublin. **Web:** www.darbycreekgolf.com. **Facility Holes:** 18. **Yards:** 7,087/5,197. **Par:** 72/72. **Course Rating:** 73.7/69.3. **Slope:** 129/118. **Green Fee:** $30/$45. **Cart Fee:** Included in green fee. **Walking Policy:** Mandatory carts. **Walkability:** 3. **Opened:** 1993. **Architect:** Geoffrey S. Cornish/Brian Silva. **Season:** March-Nov. **High:** May-Oct. **To obtain tee times:** Call up to 7 days in advance. **Miscellaneous:** Reduced fees (weekdays, twilight, seniors, juniors), range (grass), credit cards (MC, V, AE, D), BF, FF.
Reader Comments: A very enjoyable round of golf ... A little hard to find ... Front 9 is links-style, back 9 is long and heavily wooded ... Service is wonderful ... Real challenge when windy ... A little something for everyone ... Price includes cart and range balls only on weekends.

DEER CREEK GOLF COURSE
PU-7691 E. Liberty St., Hubbard, 44425, Trumbull County, (330)534-1395. **Facility Holes:** 18. **Yards:** 6,136/4,979. **Par:** 71/71. **Green Fee:** $28/$30. **Cart Fee:** Included in green fee. **Season:** March-Dec. **Tee times:** Call golf shop. **Misc:** Reduced fees (weekdays, seniors).

★★★ DEER CREEK STATE PARK GOLF COURSE
R-20635 Waterloo Rd., Mount Sterling, 43143, Pickaway County, (740)869-3088, 45 miles from Columbus. **Web:** www.ohiostateparks.org. **Facility Holes:** 18. **Yards:** 7,116/5,611. **Par:** 72/72. **Course Rating:** 73.7/71.7. **Slope:** 113/113. **Green Fee:** $17/$22. **Cart Fee:** $12/Person. **Walking Policy:** Unrestricted walking. **Walkability:** 3. **Opened:** 1982. **Architect:** Jack Kidwell/Michael Hurdzan. **Season:** Year-round. **High:** June-Oct. **Tee times:** Call golf shop. **Miscellaneous:** Reduced fees (weekdays, guests, twilight, seniors, juniors), range (grass), credit cards (MC, V, AE, D), FF.
Reader Comments: Like playing golf in a state park ... Great layout that's underused ... Wide open ... Long par 4s, nice fairways .

★½ DEER LAKE GOLF CLUB
PU-6300 Lake Rd. W., Geneva, 44041, Ashtabula County, (440)466-8450, (800)468-8450, 6 miles from Geneva. **Facility Holes:** 18. **Yards:** 6,104/5,839. **Par:** 72/74. **Course Rating:** 67.3/70.5. **Slope:** 110/110. **Green Fee:** $15/$17. **Cart Fee:** $12/Person. **Walking Policy:** Unrestricted walking. **Walkability:** 1. **Opened:** 1967. **Architect:** Mr. Leoffler. **Season:** April-Nov. **High:** May-Sept. **To obtain tee times:** Call up to 10 days in advance. **Miscellaneous:** Reduced fees (weekdays, seniors, juniors), metal spikes, credit cards (MC, V, AE), BF, FF.

★★★★ DEER RIDGE GOLF CLUB
PU-900 Comfort Plaza Dr., Bellville, 44813, Richland County, (419)886-7090, 45 miles from Columbus. **Web:** www.bestcoursestoplay.com. **Facility Holes:** 18. **Yards:** 6,584/4,791. **Par:** 72/72. **Course Rating:** 71.8/67.6. **Slope:** 129/115. **Green Fee:** $25/$43. **Cart Fee:** Included in green fee. **Walking Policy:** Mandatory carts. **Walkability:** 5. **Opened:** 1999. **Architect:** Brian Huntley. **Season:** March-Dec. **High:** May-Oct. **To obtain tee times:** Call up to 14 days in advance. **Miscellaneous:** Reduced fees (twilight, seniors, juniors), range (grass/mats), credit cards (MC, V, AE, D), FF.
Reader Comments: Beautiful views and terrain … Great freeway access … Will use all your clubs … Tough par 3s … Going to be outstanding … New course will be a great one! Real tough but beautiful … Some greens are impossible to putt.

★★½ DEER TRACK GOLF CLUB
PU-9488 Leavitt Rd., Elyria, 44035, Lorain County, (440)986-5881, 30 miles from Cleveland. **E-mail:** deertrack@centuryinter.net.com. **Web:** www.deertrack.webjump.com. **Facility Holes:** 18. **Yards:** 6,410/5,191. **Par:** 71/71. **Course Rating:** 70.3/68.7. **Slope:** 124/115. **Green Fee:** $18/$21. **Cart Fee:** $22/Cart. **Walking Policy:** Unrestricted walking. **Walkability:** 1. **Opened:** 1989. **Architect:** Tony Dulio. **Season:** Year-round. **To obtain tee times:** Call golf shop. **Misc:** Reduced fees (seniors, juniors), range (grass/mats), credit cards (MC, V), BF, FF.

★★½ DEER TRACK GOLF COURSE
PU-6160 SR 727, Goshen, 45122, Clermont County, (513)625-2500, 24 miles from Cincinnati. **E-mail:** 4golf@cinti.net. **Web:** www.deertrackgolfcourse.com. **Facility Holes:** 18. **Yards:** 6,352/5,425. **Par:** 71/72. **Course Rating:** 70.7/70.5. **Slope:** 127/123. **Green Fee:** $22/$25. **Cart Fee:** $10/Person. **Walking Policy:** Unrestricted walking. **Walkability:** 1. **Opened:** 1996. **Architect:** Phillip Buress. **Season:** March-Nov. **To obtain tee times:** Call up to 7 days in advance. **Miscellaneous:** Reduced fees (seniors, juniors), range (grass), credit cards (MC, V), BF, FF.

★★½ DETWILER GOLF COURSE
PU-4001 N. Summit St., Toledo, 43611, Lucas County, (419)726-9353, 3 miles from Toledo. **Facility Holes:** 18. **Yards:** 6,497/5,137. **Par:** 71/71. **Course Rating:** 70.2/68.6. **Slope:** 114/108. **Green Fee:** $7/$26. **Cart Fee:** $12/Person. **Walking Policy:** Unrestricted walking. **Walkability:** 2. **Opened:** 1971. **Architect:** Arthur Hills. **Season:** Year-round. **To obtain tee times:** Call golf shop. **Miscellaneous:** Reduced fees (twilight, seniors, juniors), range (grass/mats), credit cards (MC, V, AE), BF, FF.

DOGWOOD GOLF COURSE
PU-2977 Newton Falls Rd., Diamond, 44412, Portage County, (330)538-2305. **Facility Holes:** 18. **Yards:** 5,715/5,715. **Par:** 71/71. **Green Fee:** $16. **Cart Fee:** $10/Person. **Season:** April-Nov. **To obtain tee times:** Call golf shop. **Miscellaneous:** Reduced fees (seniors, juniors).

DOGWOOD HILLS GOLF COURSE
PU-1193 Debord Rd., Chillicothe, 45601, Ross County, (740)663-2700, 12 miles from Chillicothe. **Facility Holes:** 18. **Yards:** 6,212/5,453. **Par:** 71/71. **Course Rating:** 69.8/71.2. **Slope:** 116/118. **Green Fee:** $14. **Cart Fee:** $11/Person. **Walking Policy:** Unrestricted walking. **Walkability:** 4. **Opened:** 1991. **Architect:** Don Gullion. **Season:** Year-round. **High:** April-Oct. **To obtain tee times:** Call golf shop. **Miscellaneous:** Range (grass), credit cards (MC, V), BF, FF.

★★½ DORLON GOLF CLUB
PU-18000 Station Rd., Columbia Station, 44028, Lorain County, (440)236-8234, 7 miles from Strongsville. **E-mail:** dorlon@compuserve.com. **Web:** www.dorlon.com. **Facility Holes:** 18. **Yards:** 7,154/5,691. **Par:** 72/74. **Course Rating:** 74.0/67.4. **Slope:** 131/118. **Green Fee:** $12/$25. **Cart Fee:** $16/Person. **Walking Policy:** Unrestricted walking. **Walkability:** 1. **Opened:** 1970. **Architect:** Dick LaConte. **Season:** Year-round. **High:** May-Sept. **To obtain tee times:** Call up to 14 days in advance. **Miscellaneous:** Reduced fees (weekdays, seniors, juniors), range (grass), credit cards (MC, V, Debit), BF, FF.

DOUGHTON GOLF COURSE
PU-2600 Lewis Seifert Rd., Hubbard, 44425, Trumbull County, (330)568-7005, (800)321-7005, 5 miles from Youngstown. **Facility Holes:** 18. **Yards:** 6,070/5,001. **Par:** 70/72. **Course Rating:** 69.2/67.9. **Slope:** 113/107. **Green Fee:** $18/$22. **Cart Fee:** $10/Person. **Walking Policy:** Unrestricted walking. **Walkability:** 2. **Opened:** 1927. **Architect:** H.D. Brown. **Season:** March-Dec. **To obtain tee times:** Call golf shop. **Miscellaneous:** Reduced fees (weekdays, seniors, juniors), credit cards (MC, V), BF, FF.

★★★★ EAGLE CREEK GOLF CLUB
PU-2406 New State Rd., Norwalk, 44857, Huron County, (419)668-8535, 1 mile from Norwalk. **E-mail:** eaglecreek@accnorwalk.com. **Web:** www.eaglecreekgolf.com. **Facility Holes:** 18. **Yards:** 6,557/4,908. **Par:** 71/71. **Course Rating:** 70.7/68.6. **Slope:** 126/116. **Green Fee:** $20/$32. **Cart Fee:** $12/Person. **Walking Policy:** Unrestricted walking. **Walkability:** 2. **Opened:** 1996. **Architect:** Brian Huntley. **Season:** March-Dec. **High:** May-Oct. **To obtain tee times:** Call golf shop. **Miscellaneous:** Reduced fees (weekdays, seniors, juniors), range (grass), credit cards (MC, V, AE, D), BF, FF.
Reader Comments: Great variety of holes ... Very good practice area ... Never tire of playing this course ... A hidden gem ... Great par 3s ... Some ordinary holes, but still fun to play.

★★½ EAGLES NEST GOLF COURSE
PU-1540 State Rte. No.28, Loveland, 45140, Clermont County, (513)722-1241, 15 miles from Cincinnati. **Facility Holes:** 18. **Yards:** 6,145/4,868. **Par:** 71/71. **Course Rating:** 69.7/66.9. **Slope:** 120/108. **Green Fee:** $17/$21. **Cart Fee:** $11/Person. **Walking Policy:** Unrestricted walking. **Walkability:** 1. **Opened:** 1960. **Architect:** Taylor Boyd. **Season:** Year-round. **To obtain tee times:** Call up to 7 days in advance. **Miscellaneous:** Reduced fees (seniors, juniors), metal spikes, range (grass/mats), credit cards (MC, V, D), BF, FF.

★★★★ EAGLESTICKS GOLF CLUB *Condition*
PU-2655 Maysville Pike, Zanesville, 43701, Muskingum County, (740)454-4900, (800)782-4493, 60 miles from Columbus. **Web:** www.eaglesticksgolf.com. **Facility Holes:** 18. **Yards:** 6,508/4,137. **Par:** 70/70. **Course Rating:** 70.1/63.7. **Slope:** 120/96. **Green Fee:** $26/$31. **Cart Fee:** $10/Person. **Walking Policy:** Unrestricted walking. **Walkability:** 4. **Opened:** 1990. **Architect:** Michael Hurdzan. **Season:** Year-round. **High:** May-Sept. **To obtain tee times:** Call up to 365 days in advance. **Miscellaneous:** Reduced fees (weekdays, twilight, seniors, juniors), range (grass), credit cards (MC, V, AE, D), BF, FF.
Notes: Ranked 19th in 2001 Best in State; 14th America's Top 75 Affordable Courses.
Reader Comments: Use lots of irons off the tee ... Great course, a must play ... Green are undulating ... Demands accurate shot placement ... Very good service from clubhouse to course ... Classy experience ... Great target golf ... Good layout, super greens ... Great par 3s ... Excellent facilities ... Great place for a 36-hole golf marathon.

ECHO VALLEY GOLF CLUB
PU-21056 Quarry Rd., Wellington, 44090, Lorain County, (440)647-2065. **Facility Holes:** 18. **Yards:** 6,110/5,278. **Par:** 71/71. **Green Fee:** $15/$17. **Cart Fee:** $17/Cart. **Season:** April-Nov. **To obtain tee times:** Call golf shop. **Miscellaneous:** Reduced fees (weekdays, seniors).

EDGEWATER GOLF CLUB
PU-2401 Fox Ave. NE, Minerva, 44657, Carroll County, (330)862-2630, (800)368-2548, 15 miles from Canton. **Facility Holes:** 18. **Yards:** 6,328/5,800. **Par:** 72/72. **Green Fee:** $10/$20. **Cart Fee:** $10/Person. **Walking Policy:** Unrestricted walking. **Walkability:** 1. **Opened:** 1926. **Season:** Year-round. **To obtain tee times:** Call up to 30 days in advance. **Miscellaneous:** Reduced fees (weekdays), range (grass), BF, FF.

EDGEWOOD GOLF CLUB
SP-6900 Market Ave. N., North Canton, 44721, Stark County, (330)499-2353, 4 miles from Canton. **E-mail:** jkerchner@aol.com. **Facility Holes:** 18. **Yards:** 6,102/5,378. **Par:** 70/72. **Course Rating:** 67.6/68.8. **Slope:** 104/110. **Green Fee:** $16/$25. **Cart Fee:** $12/Person. **Walking Policy:** Unrestricted walking. **Walkability:** 3. **Opened:** 1922. **Season:** Year-round. **High:** April-Nov. **To obtain tee times:** Call golf shop. **Miscellaneous:** Reduced fees (weekdays), range (grass), credit cards (MC, V, AE, D), BF, FF.

ELKS 797 GOLF CLUB
PU-2593 U.S. Rte. 22 E., Wilmington, 45177, Clinton County, (513)382-2666, (800)670-3557, 45 miles from Cincinnati. **Facility Holes:** 18. **Yards:** 6,047/4,728. **Par:** 71/72. **Course Rating:** 68.7/67.1. **Slope:** 121/114. **Green Fee:** $16/$18. **Cart Fee:** $12/Person. **Walking Policy:** Unrestricted walking. **Walkability:** 1. **Opened:** 1995. **Architect:** Barry Serafin. **Season:** Year-round. **High:** April-Sept. **To obtain tee times:** Call up to 7 days in advance. **Miscellaneous:** Reduced fees (seniors, juniors), range (mats), credit cards (MC, V), BF, FF.

ELKS COUNTRY CLUB
SP-19787A State Rte. 73, McDermott, 45652, Scioto County, (740)259-6241, 40 miles from Chillicothe. **Facility Holes:** 18. **Yards:** 6,677/5,660. **Par:** 72/74. **Course Rating:** 70.7/70.4. **Slope:** 116/115. **Green Fee:** $24/$29. **Cart Fee:** $13/Person. **Walking Policy:** Unrestricted walking. **Walkability:** 3. **Opened:** 1924. **Architect:** Donald Ross. **Season:** March-Dec. **High:** April-Sept. **To obtain tee times:** Call up to 5 days in advance. **Miscellaneous:** Reduced fees (weekdays), range (grass), credit cards (MC, V), FF.

★★★★ ELKS RUN GOLF CLUB *Condition, Pace*
PU-2000 Elklick Rd., Batavia, 45103, Clermont County, (513)735-6600, 18 miles from Cincinnati. **Facility Holes:** 18. **Yards:** 6,833/5,334. **Par:** 71/71. **Course Rating:** 72.5/70.5. **Slope:** 136/121. **Green Fee:** $85. **Cart Fee:** Included in green fee. **Walking Policy:** Unrestricted walking. **Walkability:** 3. **Opened:** 1999. **Architect:** Greg Norman. **Season:** March-Nov. **Tee times:** Call up to 30 days in advance. **Miscellaneous:** Range (grass), credit cards (MC, V, AE, D), FF.
Reader Comments: Fabulous course ... Dramatic elevation changes, beautiful greens and hardly anyone on the course ... Overpriced for this area ... More variety on back 9 ... amphitheater greens make it look like they will be seeking a tournament ... Punishing if you miss the fairway ... Built for the low handicapper.

THE ELMS COUNTRY CLUB
PU-1608 Manchester Rd. S.W., North Lawrence, 44666, Stark County, (330)833-2668, (800)600-3567, 45 miles from Cleveland. **E-mail:** theelmscc@aol.com. **Facility Holes:** 27. **Green Fee:** $21/$26. **Cart Fee:** $20/Cart. **Walking Policy:** Unrestricted walking. **Walkability:** 2. **Architect:** Ed Rottman. **Season:** March-Dec. **High:** May-Sept. **To obtain tee times:** Call up to 30 days in advance. **Miscellaneous:** Reduced fees (weekdays, twilight, seniors, juniors), range (grass/mats), credit cards (MC, V), BF, FF.
BACK 19-27 (9)
Yards: 3,071/2,438. **Par:** 36/36. **Course Rating:** 70.3/68.1. **Slope:** 111/103. **Opened:** 1965.
FRONT 18 (18)
Yards: 6,631/5,034. **Par:** 72/74. **Course Rating:** 70.3/67.2. **Slope:** 115/101. **Opened:** 1924.

EMERALD WOODS GOLF COURSE
PU-12501 N. Boone Rd., Columbia Station, 44028, Lorain County, (440)236-8940, 14 miles from Cleveland. **Facility Holes:** 45. **Cart Fee:** $22/Cart. **Walking Policy:** Unrestricted walking. **Walkability:** 3. **Opened:** 1967. **Architect:** Raymond McClain. **Season:** March-Nov. **High:** May-Sept. **Tee times:** Call up to 7 ahead. **Misc:** Reduced fees (weekdays, seniors), BF, FF.
★★ **AUDREY'S/HEATHER STONE COURSE** (18)
Yards: 6,673/5,295. **Par:** 70/71. **Course Rating:** 71.1/68.2. **Green Fee:** $21/$24.
Special Notes: Also has a 9-hole course.
★½ **SAINT ANDREWS/PINE VALLEY COURSE** (18)
Yards: 6,629/5,080. **Par:** 72/73. **Course Rating:** 72.1/66.4. **Green Fee:** $23/$24.
Special Notes: Also has a 9-hole course.

★★½ ERIE SHORES GOLF COURSE
PU-7298 Lake Rd. E., North Madison, 44057, Lake County, (440)428-3164, (800)225-3742, 40 miles from Cleveland. **Facility Holes:** 18. **Yards:** 6,000/4,750. **Par:** 70/70. **Course Rating:** 68.2/67.0. **Slope:** 116/108. **Green Fee:** $12/$16. **Cart Fee:** $11/Cart. **Walking Policy:** Unrestricted walking. **Walkability:** 1. **Opened:** 1957. **Architect:** Ben W. Zink. **Season:** Year-round. **High:** May-Sept. **To obtain tee times:** Call golf shop. **Miscellaneous:** Reduced fees (weekdays, seniors, juniors), metal spikes, range (grass/mats), credit cards (MC, V, D).

★½ ESTATE GOLF CLUB
PU-3871 Tschopp Rd., Lancaster, 43130, Fairfield County, (740)654-4444, (800)833-8463, 4 miles from Lancaster. **Facility Holes:** 18. **Yards:** 6,405/5,680. **Par:** 71/72. **Course Rating:** 69.9. **Slope:** 113. **Green Fee:** $15/$18. **Cart Fee:** $22/Cart. **Walking Policy:** Unrestricted walking. **Walkability:** 2. **Opened:** 1967. **Architect:** Donald Arledge. **Season:** Year-round. **To obtain tee times:** Call golf shop. **Miscellaneous:** Reduced fees (weekdays, twilight, seniors, juniors), range (grass), credit cards (MC, V), BF, FF.

★★★½ FAIRFIELD GOLF CLUB
PU-2200 John Gray Rd., Fairfield, 45014, Butler County, (513)867-5385, 2 miles from Cincinnati. **Facility Holes:** 18. **Yards:** 6,250/4,900. **Par:** 70/70. **Course Rating:** 69.5/68.8. **Slope:** 123/113. **Green Fee:** $23/$25. **Cart Fee:** $12/Person. **Walking Policy:** Unrestricted walking. **Walkability:** 3. **Opened:** 1968. **Architect:** Jack Kidwell/Michael Hurdzan. **Season:** March-Dec. **High:** June-Aug. **To obtain tee times:** Call up to 9 days in advance. **Miscellaneous:** Reduced fees (seniors, juniors), credit cards (MC, V), BF, FF.
Reader Comments: Several good water holes ... Well-maintained course, challenging, good value ... Best-kept secret in Cincinnati area ... So-so layout ... A good value.

★★ FAIRWAY PINES GOLF COURSE
PU-1777 Blase-Nemeth Rd., Painesville, 44077, Lake County, (440)357-7800, 26 miles from Cleveland. **Facility Holes:** 18. **Yards:** 6,663/5,081. **Par:** 71/71. **Course Rating:** 70.9/68.1. **Slope:** 112/106. **Green Fee:** $16/$19. **Opened:** 1989. **Architect:** X.G. Hassenplug. **To obtain tee times:** Call golf shop. **Miscellaneous:** Metal spikes.

★½ FALLEN TIMBERS FAIRWAYS
SP-7711 Timbers Blvd., Waterville, 43566, Lucas County, (419)878-4653, 12 miles from Toledo. **Facility Holes:** 18. **Yards:** 6,054/4,969. **Par:** 70/70. **Course Rating:** 67.7/65.8. **Slope:** 109/105. **Green Fee:** $16/$25. **Cart Fee:** $12/Person. **Walking Policy:** Unrestricted walking. **Walkability:** 1. **Opened:** 1992. **Season:** Year-round. **High:** June-Aug. **To obtain tee times:** Call golf shop. **Miscellaneous:** Reduced fees (weekdays, twilight, seniors, juniors), metal spikes, range (grass/mats), credit cards (MC, V, AE).

★★ FINDLAY HILLCREST GOLF CLUB
SP-800 W. Bigelow, Findlay, 45840, Hancock County, (419)423-7211, 40 miles from Toledo. **Facility Holes:** 18. **Yards:** 6,981/5,146. **Par:** 72/72. **Course Rating:** 71.7/67.8. **Slope:** 112/107. **Green Fee:** $20/$23. **Cart Fee:** $13/Person. **Architect:** Ed Rettig/Gene Cleary. **To obtain tee times:** Call golf shop. **Miscellaneous:** Credit cards (MC, V).

★★½ FIRE RIDGE GOLF COURSE
PU-1001 E. Jackson St., Millersburg, 46654, Holmes County, (330)674-3921, 40 miles from Canton. **E-mail:** frgc@bright.net. **Web:** www.fireridgegolf.com. **Facility Holes:** 18. **Yards:** 6,296/3,984. **Par:** 72/72. **Course Rating:** 70.4/66.5. **Slope:** 124/115. **Green Fee:** $10/$20. **Cart Fee:** $12/Person. **Walking Policy:** Walking at certain times. **Walkability:** 5. **Opened:** 1999. **Architect:** Ronald Cutlip. **Season:** March-Dec. **High:** June-Sept. **Tee times:** Call golf shop. **Miscellaneous:** Reduced fees (weekdays, twilight, seniors), credit cards (MC, V), BF, FF.

★★★ FLAGSTONE GOLF CLUB
PU-13683 St. Rte. 38, Marysville, 43040, Union County, (937)642-1816, (800)742-0899, 15 miles from Columbus. **Facility Holes:** 18. **Yards:** 6,323/5,111. **Par:** 72/72. **Course Rating:** 69.6/68.9. **Slope:** 115/113. **Green Fee:** $14/$19. **Walking Policy:** Unrestricted walking. **Opened:** 1925. **Season:** Year-round. **High:** May-Sept. **Tee times:** Call golf shop. **Miscellaneous:** Reduced fees (weekdays, twilight, seniors), metal spikes, credit cards (MC, V).
Reader Comments: Average ... Sporty course ... Accuracy counts ... Tricky greens ... Good mix of water, trees and hills.

★★★ FLYING 'B' GOLF COURSE
PU-13223 Middletown Rd. W., Salem, 44460, Columbiana County, (330)337-8138, 20 miles from Youngstown. **Facility Holes:** 18. **Yards:** 6,288/4,766. **Par:** 71/71. **Course Rating:** 69.5/66.6. **Slope:** 110/104. **Green Fee:** $19/$20. **Cart Fee:** $10/Person. **Walking Policy:** Unrestricted walking. **Walkability:** 3. **Opened:** 1959. **Season:** March-Dec. **High:** July-Sept. **To obtain tee times:** Call up to 365 days in advance. **Miscellaneous:** Reduced fees (weekdays, seniors), BF, FF.
Reader Comments: Above average ... You can't go wrong here—just don't tell anyone! ... Good layout if you have some time ... No. 10 could cost you strokes ... A little cramped ... Small greens ... Good course for beginners.

★★ FOREST HILLS GOLF COURSE
PU-41971 Oberlin Rd., Elyria, 44035, Lorain County, (440)323-2632, 30 miles from Cleveland. **Facility Holes:** 18. **Yards:** 6,161/5,125. **Par:** 70/71. **Course Rating:** 69.7/67.6. **Slope:** 117/105. **Green Fee:** $9/$17. **Cart Fee:** $11/Person. **Walking Policy:** Unrestricted walking. **Walkability:** 2. **Architect:** Charlie Smith. **Season:** March-Dec. **High:** March-Dec. **To obtain tee times:** Call up to 7 days in advance. **Miscellaneous:** Reduced fees (weekdays, seniors, juniors), range (grass/mats), credit cards (MC, V), BF, FF.

★½ FOREST OAKS GOLF COURSE
PU-U.S. Rte. No.422 and St. Rte. No.305, Southington, 44470, Trumbull County, (330)898-2852, 40 miles from Cleveland. **Facility Holes:** 27. **Yards:** 6,122/5,867. **Par:** 72/72. **Green Fee:** $17/$18. **Cart Fee:** $16/Cart. **Walking Policy:** Unrestricted walking. **Walkability:** 1. **Opened:** 1958. **Architect:** Myron Beechy. **Season:** March-Nov. **High:** May-Aug. **To obtain tee times:** Call golf shop. **Miscellaneous:** Reduced fees (weekdays, seniors, juniors), metal spikes, range (grass/mats), credit cards (MC, V, D). **Special Notes:** Also has a 9-hole course.

OHIO

FORREST CREASON GOLF COURSE

PU-1616 E. Poe Rd., Bowling Green, 43402, Wood County, (419)372-2674. **Facility Holes:** 18. **Yards:** 6,497/5,231. **Par:** 72/73. **Course Rating:** 70.7/70.1. **Slope:** 116/113. **Green Fee:** $17/$21. **Cart Fee:** $22/Cart. **Season:** March-Dec. **To obtain tee times:** Call golf shop. **Miscellaneous:** Reduced fees (weekdays, twilight, seniors, juniors).

★★★★ FOWLER'S MILL GOLF COURSE

PU-13095 Rockhaven Rd., Chesterland, 44026, Geauga County, (440)729-7569, 30 miles from Cleveland. **Web:** www.americangolf.com. **Facility Holes:** 27. **Green Fee:** $29/$67. **Cart Fee:** $3/Person. **Walking Policy:** Unrestricted walking. **Opened:** 1972. **Architect:** Pete Dye. **Season:** March-Dec. **To obtain tee times:** Call up to 14 days in advance. **Misc:** Reduced fees (weekdays, twilight, seniors, juniors), range (grass), credit cards (MC, V, AE), FF.
LAKE/RIVER (18 Combo)
Yards: 7,002/5,950. **Par:** 72/72. **Course Rating:** 74.7/73.9. **Slope:** 136/122. **Walkability:** 3.
Notes: Ranked 20th in 1999 Best in State; 55th in 1996 America's Top 75 Affordable Courses.
MAPLE/LAKE (18 Combo)
Yards: 6,595/5,913. **Par:** 72/72. **Course Rating:** 72.1/73.6. **Slope:** 128/123. **Walkability:** 3.
RIVER/MAPLE (18 Combo)
Yards: 6,385/5,797. **Par:** 72/72. **Course Rating:** 70.7/73.0. **Slope:** 125/123. **Walkability:** 2.
Reader Comments: Outstanding golf course ... An early Pete Dye that's playable for all ... Split fairways and railroad ties ... Par 3s tough from back tees ... The River and Lake 9s are best ... Very slow pace of play, plan to spend the day ... 4th hole on Lake Course the best ... Getting pricey.

★★★ FOX DEN GOLF CLUB

PU-2770 Call Rd., Stow, 44224, Summit County, (330)673-3443, (888)231-4693, 8 miles from Akron. **E-mail:** foxdengc@gateway.com. **Facility Holes:** 18. **Yards:** 6,406/5,223. **Par:** 72/72. **Course Rating:** 70.6/71.0. **Slope:** 125/114. **Green Fee:** $18/$30. **Cart Fee:** $11/Person. **Walking Policy:** Unrestricted walking. **Walkability:** 3. **Opened:** 1966. **Architect:** Frank Schmiedel. **Season:** March-Dec. **To obtain tee times:** Call up to 90 days in advance. **Miscellaneous:** Reduced fees (weekdays, seniors, juniors), range (grass), credit cards (MC, V, D), BF, FF.
Reader Comments: Not long, beautifully manicured, each hole uniquely designed ... Not long, but fun ... Good greens.

THE FOX'S DEN GOLF COURSE

PU-1221 Irmscher St., Celina, 45822, Mercer County, (419)586-3102. **Facility Holes:** 18. **Yards:** 6,874/5,436. **Par:** 72/72. **Course Rating:** 72.4/70.4. **Slope:** 125/117. **Green Fee:** $22/$25. **Cart Fee:** $10/Person. **Walking Policy:** Unrestricted walking. **Walkability:** 3. **Opened:** 1996. **Architect:** Jim Fazio. **Season:** Year-round. **To obtain tee times:** Call up to 8 days in advance. **Miscellaneous:** Reduced fees (weekdays, twilight, seniors), range (grass), credit cards (MC, V, D), BF, FF.

FOXFIRE GOLF CLUB

PU-10799 St. Rte. 104, Lockbourne, 43137, Pickaway County, (614)224-3694, 15 miles from Columbus. **E-mail:** bbarnett@netset.com. **Web:** www.foxfiregolfclub.com. **Facility Holes:** 36. **Walking Policy:** Unrestricted walking. **Walkability:** 3. **Season:** Year-round. **Tee times:** Call up to 14 days in advance. **Miscellaneous:** Range (grass/mats), credit cards (MC, V, AE), BF, FF.
★★★½ FOXFIRE COURSE (18)
Yards: 6,891/5,175. **Par:** 72/72. **Course Rating:** 72.7/69.1. **Slope:** 122/112. **Green Fee:** $18/$21. **Cart Fee:** $22/Cart. **Opened:** 1974. **Architect:** Jack Kidwell. **High:** June-Sept. **Miscellaneous:** Reduced fees (twilight, seniors, juniors).
Reader Comments: Fun place for an outing ... Large water hazards ... Back 9 harder than front.
★★★★½ PLAYERS CLUB (18)
Yards: 7,077/5,255. **Par:** 72/72. **Course Rating:** 74.2/70.3. **Slope:** 132/121. **Green Fee:** $25/$36. **Cart Fee:** $11/Person. **Opened:** 1993. **Architect:** Jack Kidwell/Barry Serafin. **High:** May-Sept. **Miscellaneous:** Reduced fees (twilight).
Reader Comments: Tough course, bring it all ... Good condition, nice layout ... Nice combo of open & wooded holes ... Water and treelined holes make this a solid test ... Nos. 14,15 and 16 are the Amen Corner of Columbus ... Out-standing employees and a nice course.

FRANKLIN VALLEY GOLF COURSE

SP-6954 Franklin Valley Rd., Jackson, 45640, Jackson County, (740)286-4903, 75 miles from Columbus. **Facility Holes:** 18. **Yards:** 6,371/4,927. **Par:** 71/73. **Course Rating:** 69.2/68.8. **Slope:** 108/108. **Green Fee:** $17. **Cart Fee:** $11/Person. **Walking Policy:** Unrestricted walking. **Walkability:** 4. **Opened:** 1962. **Season:** Year-round. **High:** April-Sept. **To obtain tee times:** Call up to 3 days in advance. **Miscellaneous:** Range (grass/mats), credit cards (MC, V), BF, FF.

FULLER'S FAIRWAYS

PU-4370 Clay Pike, Zanesville, 43701, Muskingum County, (740)452-9830, 5 miles from Zanesville. **Facility Holes:** 18. **Yards:** 5,600/4,100. **Par:** 70/70. **Course Rating:** 65.5/63.3. **Slope:** 103/96. **Green Fee:** $14. **Cart Fee:** $10/Person. **Walking Policy:** Unrestricted walking. **Walkability:** 3. **Opened:** 1972. **Architect:** Bob Fuller, Sr. **Season:** March-Nov. **To obtain tee times:** Call golf shop. **Miscellaneous:** Reduced fees (weekdays, seniors, juniors), range (grass), credit cards (MC, V, D), FF.

★★ GENEVA ON THE LAKE GOLF CLUB

PU-Almraz Dr., Geneva On The Lake, 44041, Ashtabula County, (440)466-8797, 45 miles from Cleveland. **Facility Holes:** 18. **Yards:** 6,569/5,292. **Par:** 73/73. **Course Rating:** 70.4/68.5. **Slope:** 118/112. **Green Fee:** $17/$18. **Opened:** 1927. **Architect:** Stanley Thompson. **To obtain tee times:** Call golf shop.

★★★★ GLENEAGLES GOLF CLUB

PU-2615 Glenwood Dr., Twinsburg, 44087, Summit County, (216)425-3334, 20 miles from Cleveland. **E-mail:** MJB4GLF@hotmail.com. **Facility Holes:** 18. **Yards:** 6,545/5,147. **Par:** 72/72. **Course Rating:** 72.2/69.4. **Slope:** 121/115. **Green Fee:** $23/$27. **Cart Fee:** $12/Person. **Walking Policy:** Unrestricted walking. **Walkability:** 2. **Opened:** 1990. **Architect:** Ted McAnlis. **Season:** April-Dec. **High:** May-Oct. **Tee times:** Call golf shop. **Miscellaneous:** Reduced fees (weekdays, twilight, seniors, juniors), range (grass), credit cards (MC, V), BF, FF.
Reader Comments: Great staff with a great pro shop with unbelievable prices ... Good course for walking ... Challenging greens ... Top course that is relatively inexpensive ... Needs a bigger clubhouse.

GLENVIEW MUNICIPAL GOLF COURSE

PU-10965 Springfield Pike, Cincinnati, 45246, Hamilton County, (513)771-1747, 15 miles from Cincinnati. **Web:** www.cincyrec.org. **Facility Holes:** 27. **Green Fee:** $20/$26. **Cart Fee:** $12/Person. **Walking Policy:** Unrestricted walking. **Walkability:** 3. **Opened:** 1970. **Architect:** Arthur Hills/Michael Hurdzan. **Season:** Year-round. **High:** April-Sept. **To obtain tee times:** Call golf shop. **Miscellaneous:** Reduced fees (weekdays, twilight, seniors, juniors), metal spikes, range (grass/mats), credit cards (MC, V), BF, FF.
EAST (9)
Yards: 3,359/2,634. **Par:** 36/36.
★★★ **WEST/SOUTH** (18)
Yards: 7,036/5,142. **Par:** 72/72. **Course Rating:** 74.2/69.9. **Slope:** 137/121.
Reader Comments: Always crowded ... Good facilities and service.

THE GOLF CENTER AT KINGS ISLAND

PU-6042 Fairway Dr., Mason, 45040, Warren County, (513)398-7700, 25 miles from Cincinnati. **Web:** www.thegolfcenter.com. **Facility Holes:** 45. **Cart Fee:** $12/Person. **Walkability:** 3. **Opened:** 1971. **Season:** Year-round. **To obtain tee times:** Call golf shop. **Miscellaneous:** Metal spikes, range (grass/mats), credit cards (MC, V, AE, D, CB), BF, FF.
★★★★ **BRUIN COURSE** (18)
Yards: 3,394/3,394. **Par:** 60/60. **Green Fee:** $13/$14. **Walking Policy:** Unrestricted walking. **Architect:** Jack Nicklaus/D.Muirhead. **Misc:** Reduced fees (weekdays, seniors, juniors).
Reader Comments: Pleasant place to play ... Overall great experience ... Excellent iron practice at a great price.
★★★½ **GRIZZLY COURSE (NORTH/SOUTH)** (27)
Green Fee: $28/$48. **Walking Policy:** Walking at certain times. **Architect:** J. Nicklaus/D. Muirhead/J. Morrish. **Miscellaneous:** Reduced fees (weekdays, twilight, seniors).
(NORTH/SOUTH) (18 Combo)
Yards: 6,784/5,156. **Par:** 72/72. **Course Rating:** 72.5/69.4. **Slope:** 136/122.
(NORTH/WEST) (18 Combo)
Yards: 6,795/5,210. **Par:** 72/72. **Course Rating:** 72.8/69.6. **Slope:** 136/125.
(SOUTH/WEST) (18 Combo)
Yards: 6,719/5,118. **Par:** 72/72. **Course Rating:** 72.4/69.6. **Slope:** 136/118.
Reader Comments: A fun course with fast greens ... Afternoon rates are a great value ... First-class operation in all respects.

★★★★½ THE GOLF CLUB AT YANKEE TRACE

PU-10000 Yankee St., Centerville, 45458, Montgomery County, (937)438-4653, 15 miles from Dayton. **E-mail:** yankeetrace@yankeetrace.org. **Web:** www.yankeetrace.org. **Facility Holes:** 21. **Yards:** 7,139/5,204. **Par:** 72/72. **Course Rating:** 75.5/70.5. **Slope:** 140/124. **Green Fee:** $33/$47. **Cart Fee:** $13/Person. **Walking Policy:** Unrestricted walking. **Walkability:** 2. **Opened:** 1995. **Architect:** Gene Bates. **Season:** March-Dec. **High:** March-Dec. **To obtain tee times:** Call up to 7 days in advance. **Miscellaneous:** Reduced fees (twilight, juniors), range (grass), credit cards (MC, V, AE, D), BF, FF.

OHIO

Reader Comments: Great clubhouse … A championship course, a pleasure to play … Last 4 holes are some of the toughest you'll find … Too pricey to play often … Very good public track, nice variety … Beautiful design and tough greens worth the money.
Special Notes: Also has 3 practice holes.

★★★ THE GOLF COURSES OF WINTON WOODS

PU-1515 W. Sharon Rd., Cincinnati, 45240, Hamilton County, (513)825-3770, 14 miles from Cincinnati. **E-mail:** glong@greatparks.org. **Web:** www.greatparks.org. **Facility Holes:** 27. **Yards:** 6,376/4,554. **Par:** 71/72. **Course Rating:** 70.0/65.8. **Slope:** 120/106. **Green Fee:** $20. **Cart Fee:** $12/Person. **Walking Policy:** Unrestricted walking. **Walkability:** 3. **Opened:** 1993. **Architect:** Michael Hurdzan. **Season:** March-Dec. **Tee times:** Call golf shop. **Miscellaneous:** Reduced fees (seniors, juniors), metal spikes, range (grass/mats), credit cards (MC, V), BF, FF.
Reader Comments: Some nice par 3s … Heavy play, staff is great … Good condition considering amount of play … Great city course.
Special Notes: Also has a 9-hole Meadow Links Course.

★★½ GRANDVIEW GOLF CLUB

PU-13404 Old State Rd., Middlefield, 44062, Geauga County, (440)834-1824, 8 miles from Chardon. **E-mail:** grandviewgolf@hotmail.com. **Facility Holes:** 18. **Yards:** 6,200/5,451. **Par:** 70/72. **Course Rating:** 70.4/70.2. **Slope:** 113/114. **Green Fee:** $11/$23. **Cart Fee:** $10/Person. **Walking Policy:** Unrestricted walking. **Walkability:** 4. **Opened:** 1929. **Architect:** Richard W. LaConte/Ted McAnlis. **Season:** March-Nov. **High:** May-Sept. **To obtain tee times:** Call golf shop. **Miscellaneous:** Reduced fees (seniors, juniors), credit cards (MC, V, AE), BF, FF.

★★★★ GRANVILLE GOLF COURSE

PU-555 Newark Rd., Granville, 43023, Licking County, (740)587-4653, 30 miles from Columbus. **Facility Holes:** 18. **Yards:** 6,559/5,197. **Par:** 71/71. **Course Rating:** 71.3/69.6. **Slope:** 128/123. **Green Fee:** $25/$39. **Cart Fee:** $12/Person. **Walking Policy:** Unrestricted walking. **Walkability:** 3. **Opened:** 1925. **Architect:** Donald Ross/Jack Kidwell. **Season:** Year-round. **High:** March-Oct. **Tee times:** Call up to 365 days in advance. **Miscellaneous:** Reduced fees (weekdays, twilight, seniors), range (grass/mats), credit cards (MC, V, AE), BF, FF.
Reader Comments: Outstanding holes and moderate cost … An older course with beautiful views … Prettiest 18th hole I've seen … Slick greens … Rustic feel … Donald Ross layout … Tough to get early tee time.

GREAT TRAIL GOLF COURSE

PU-10154 Great Trail Dr., Minerva, 44657, Carroll County, (330)868-6770, 15 miles from Canton. **Facility Holes:** 27. **Green Fee:** $14/$17. **Cart Fee:** $17/Cart. **Walking Policy:** Unrestricted walking. **Walkability:** 4. **Opened:** 1970. **Architect:** Romain Fry. **Season:** April-Nov. **High:** May-Sept. **To obtain tee times:** Call up to 14 days in advance. **Miscellaneous:** Reduced fees (weekdays, guests), range (grass), lodging (9 rooms), credit cards (MC, V, D), FF.
1-9/10-18 (18)
Yards: 5,791/4,548. **Par:** 71/72. **Course Rating:** 67.1/64.9. **Slope:** 112/101.
1-9/19-27 (18)
Yards: 5,888/4,660. **Par:** 71/72. **Course Rating:** 67.5/66.1. **Slope:** 110/102.
10-18/19-27 (18)
Yards: 6,087/4,512. **Par:** 72/72. **Course Rating:** 67.9/64.3. **Slope:** 111/97.

★★ GREEN CREST GOLF CLUB

PU-7813 Bethany Rd., Middletown, 45044, Butler County, (513)777-2090, 30 miles from Cincinnati. **Facility Holes:** 18. **Yards:** 6,230/4,884. **Par:** 70/72. **Course Rating:** 69.9/69.3. **Slope:** 125/115. **Green Fee:** $21/$23. **Cart Fee:** $11/Person. **Walking Policy:** Unrestricted walking. **Walkability:** 3. **Opened:** 1973. **Architect:** Harter. **Season:** Year-round. **To obtain tee times:** Call up to 7 days in advance. **Miscellaneous:** Reduced fees (seniors, juniors), metal spikes, credit cards (MC, V, AE, D), BF, FF.

★★★ GREEN HILLS GOLF CLUB

PU-1959 South Main St., Clyde, 43410, Sandusky County, (419)547-7947, (800)234-4766, 50 miles from Toledo. **Web:** www.greenhillsgolf.com. **Facility Holes:** 18. **Yards:** 6,239/5,437. **Par:** 71/74. **Course Rating:** 68.5/69.7. **Slope:** 102/100. **Green Fee:** $9/$22. **Cart Fee:** $20/Cart. **Walking Policy:** Walking at certain times. **Walkability:** 3. **Opened:** 1958. **Architect:** T. Crockett/B. Crockett/M. Fritz. **Season:** Feb.-Dec. **High:** May-Aug. **To obtain tee times:** Call up to 7 days in advance. **Miscellaneous:** Reduced fees (weekdays), range (grass), credit cards (MC, V, D), BF, FF.
Reader Comments: Nice, short course … Solid muni that's very busy.

OHIO

★★ GREEN VALLEY GOLF CLUB
SP-2673 Pleasant Valley Rd., N.E., New Philadelphia, 44663, Tuscarawas County, (330)364-2812, 20 miles from Canton. **Facility Holes:** 18. **Yards:** 6,500/5,200. **Par:** 72/73. **Course Rating:** 71.7/67.8. **Slope:** 119/115. **Green Fee:** $14/$15. **Cart Fee:** $17/Cart. **Walking Policy:** Unrestricted walking. **Walkability:** 4. **Opened:** 1961. **Season:** Year-round. **High:** May-Aug. **To obtain tee times:** Call golf shop. **Miscellaneous:** Reduced fees (weekdays, twilight, juniors), range (grass/mats), credit cards (MC, V, AE, D, Bank Debit Cards).

GREENTREE GOLF CLUB
PU-5505 Greentree Road, Lebanon, 45036, Warren County, (513)727-1009, 25 miles from Cincinnati. **Facility Holes:** 9. **Yards:** 3,368/2,499. **Par:** 36/36. **Green Fee:** $17/$18. **Cart Fee:** $20/Cart. **Walking Policy:** Unrestricted walking. **Walkability:** 3. **Opened:** 1999. **Architect:** Jody Kinney. **Season:** March-Dec. **High:** May-Sept. **To obtain tee times:** Call golf shop. **Miscellaneous:** Reduced fees (weekdays, seniors, juniors), metal spikes, FF.

★½ GROVEBROOK GOLF CLUB
SP-5525 Hoover Rd., Grove City, 43123, Franklin County, (614)875-2497, 6 miles from Columbus. **Facility Holes:** 18. **Yards:** 6,058/5,104. **Par:** 71/71. **Course Rating:** 67.7/67.8. **Slope:** 113/111. **Green Fee:** $15/$18. **Cart Fee:** $11/Person. **Walking Policy:** Unrestricted walking. **Walkability:** 2. **Opened:** 1961. **Architect:** Rotolo/Steele. **Season:** Year-round. **High:** April-Oct. **To obtain tee times:** Call up to 7 days in advance. **Miscellaneous:** Reduced fees (weekdays), credit cards (MC, V), BF, FF.

★★★★½ HAWKS NEST GOLF CLUB
PU-2800 E. Pleasant Home Rd., Creston, 44691, Wayne County, (330)435-4611, 6 miles from Wooster. **E-mail:** hawksnestgc@bright.net. **Web:** www.hawksnestgc.com. **Facility Holes:** 18. **Yards:** 6,670/4,767. **Par:** 72/72. **Course Rating:** 71.5/67.9. **Slope:** 124/110. **Green Fee:** $24/$31. **Cart Fee:** $11/Person. **Walking Policy:** Unrestricted walking. **Walkability:** 2. **Opened:** 1993. **Architect:** Steve Burns. **Season:** April-Dec. **High:** June-Sept. **To obtain tee times:** Call golf shop. **Miscellaneous:** Reduced fees (weekdays, seniors, juniors), range (grass), credit cards (MC, V, D), BF, FF.
Reader Comments: Great meatloaf sandwiches ... Awesome track ... Pace of play is a minus ... Beautiful setting in farm, pond on 16th hole... Awesome! Worth the drive ... Very challenging par 5s ... Always windy ... No two holes the same ... One of the best values in the state! ... Awesome layout in Amish country.

★★★½ HAWTHORNE HILLS GOLF CLUB
SP-1000 Fetter Rd., Lima, 45801, Allen County, (419)221-1891, 74 miles from Dayton. **Facility Holes:** 27. **Yards:** 6,710/5,695. **Par:** 72/72. **Course Rating:** 71.6/71.9. **Slope:** 119/118. **Green Fee:** $20/$23. **Cart Fee:** $11/Person. **Walking Policy:** Unrestricted walking. **Walkability:** 3. **Opened:** 1963. **Architect:** Harold Paddock. **Season:** March-Dec. **High:** May-Oct. **To obtain tee times:** Call up to 10 days in advance. **Miscellaneous:** Reduced fees (weekdays, twilight), range (grass), credit cards (MC, V), BF, FF.
Reader Comments: One of my favorites ... Great course ... A superior public course. Well maintained ... Always in great shape.
Special Notes: Also has a 9-hole executive course.

★★★★ HEATHERWOODE GOLF CLUB
PU-88 Heatherwoode Blvd., Springboro, 45066, Warren County, (513)748-3222, 15 miles from Dayton. **Facility Holes:** 18. **Yards:** 6,730/5,069. **Par:** 71/71. **Course Rating:** 72.9/69.8. **Slope:** 138/127. **Green Fee:** $46/$57. **Cart Fee:** Included in green fee. **Walking Policy:** Unrestricted walking. **Walkability:** 4. **Opened:** 1991. **Architect:** Denis Griffiths. **Season:** Year-round. **High:** April-Oct. **To obtain tee times:** Call up to 7 days in advance. **Miscellaneous:** Reduced fees (weekdays, twilight, seniors, juniors), range (grass/mats), credit cards (MC, V, AE), BF, FF.
Reader Comments: Tough when windy ... Fast greens are a challenge ... Holes are a little close to each other ... Nice atmosphere for an outing ... Former Nike Tour stop ... Nothing easy about this course. You'll love it.

★★★½ HEMLOCK SPRINGS GOLF CLUB
PU-4654 Cold Springs Rd., Geneva, 44041, Ashtabula County, (216)466-4044, (800)436-5625, 40 miles from Cleveland. **Facility Holes:** 18. **Yards:** 6,812/5,453. **Par:** 72/72. **Course Rating:** 72.8/73.8. **Slope:** 129/116. **Green Fee:** $12/$26. **Cart Fee:** $10/Person. **Walking Policy:** Unrestricted walking. **Walkability:** 3. **Opened:** 1961. **Architect:** Ben W. Zink. **Season:** April-Nov. **Tee times:** Call up to 365 days in advance. **Miscellaneous:** Reduced fees (weekdays, twilight, seniors, juniors), range (grass), credit cards (MC, V, AE, D), BF, FF.
Reader Comments: Fun course to play—can post a low number ... Very affordable course in the middle of nowhere ... Scenic and challenging ... Worth returning.

★★½ HIAWATHA GOLF COURSE
PU-901 Beech St., Mount Vernon, 43050, Knox County, (740)393-2886, 40 miles from Columbus. **Facility Holes:** 18. **Yards:** 6,721/5,100. **Par:** 72/74. **Course Rating:** 71.5/68.5. **Slope:** 121/116. **Green Fee:** $12/$15. **Cart Fee:** $11/Person. **Walking Policy:** Unrestricted walking. **Walkability:** 2. **Opened:** 1962. **Architect:** Jack Kidwell. **Season:** Year-round. **High:** April-Oct. **To obtain tee times:** Call golf shop. **Miscellaneous:** Reduced fees (weekdays, twilight, seniors, juniors), credit cards (MC, V, D), BF, FF.

★★½ HICKORY FLAT GREENS
PU-54188 Township Rd. 155, West Lafayette, 43845, Coshocton County, (740)545-7796, 2 miles from West Lafayette. **Facility Holes:** 18. **Yards:** 6,600/5,124. **Par:** 72/72. **Course Rating:** 70.4/68.3. **Slope:** 109/105. **Green Fee:** $17. **Cart Fee:** $12/Person. **Walking Policy:** Unrestricted walking. **Walkability:** 2. **Opened:** 1970. **Architect:** Jack Kidwell. **Season:** Year-round. **To obtain tee times:** Call golf shop. **Miscellaneous:** Reduced fees (weekdays, twilight, seniors, juniors), range (grass), credit cards (MC, V), BF, FF.

★★½ HICKORY GROVE GOLF CLUB
PU-6302 State Rte. 94, Harpster, 43323, Wyandot County, (614)496-2631, (800)833-6619, 15 miles from Marion. **Facility Holes:** 18. **Yards:** 6,874/5,376. **Par:** 72/76. **Course Rating:** 71.0/69.1. **Slope:** 108/105. **Green Fee:** $15. **Cart Fee:** $20/Person. **Walking Policy:** Unrestricted walking. **Walkability:** 3. **Opened:** 1963. **Architect:** J. Craig Bowman. **Season:** April-Oct. **To obtain tee times:** Call golf shop. **Miscellaneous:** Reduced fees (weekdays, twilight), range (grass), credit cards (MC, V, D), BF, FF.

★½ HICKORY GROVE GOLF COURSE
SP-1490 Fairway Dr., Jefferson, 44047, Ashtabula County, (440)576-3776, 55 miles from Cleveland. **E-mail:** par72hg@suite224. **Facility Holes:** 18. **Yards:** 6,500/5,593. **Par:** 72/73. **Course Rating:** 70.9/71.5. **Green Fee:** $10/$17. **Cart Fee:** $18/Cart. **Walking Policy:** Unrestricted walking. **Walkability:** 2. **Opened:** 1962. **Season:** April-Oct. **To obtain tee times:** Call golf shop. **Miscellaneous:** Range (grass), credit cards (MC, V), BF, FF.

★½ HICKORY NUT GOLF CLUB
PU-23601 Royalton Rd., Columbia Station, 44028, Lorain County, (440)236-8008, 1 mile from Strongsville. **Facility Holes:** 18. **Yards:** 6,194/5,771. **Par:** 71/73. **Course Rating:** 70.5. **Slope:** 112. **Green Fee:** $15/$30. **Cart Fee:** Included in green fee. **Walking Policy:** Unrestricted walking. **Walkability:** 1. **Opened:** 1968. **Season:** March-Nov. **High:** June-Sept. **To obtain tee times:** Call up to 7 days in advance. **Miscellaneous:** Reduced fees (weekdays, seniors, juniors), range (grass/mats), credit cards (MC, V, AE, D), BF, FF.

★★★ HICKORY WOODS GOLF COURSE
PU-1240 Hickory Woods Dr., Loveland, 45140, Clermont County, (513)575-3900, 15 miles from Cincinnati. **Web:** www.hickorywoods.com. **Facility Holes:** 18. **Yards:** 6,105/5,115. **Par:** 70/71. **Course Rating:** 70.1/69.4. **Slope:** 122/113. **Green Fee:** $18/$25. **Cart Fee:** $12/Person. **Walking Policy:** Unrestricted walking. **Walkability:** 3. **Opened:** 1983. **Architect:** Dennis Acomb. **Season:** Year-round. **To obtain tee times:** Call up to 7 days in advance. **Miscellaneous:** Reduced fees (seniors, juniors), credit cards (MC, V, AE), BF, FF.
Reader Comments: Tight back 9 ... Lots of hills and trees ... Clubhouse needs to be upgraded ... Don't stray left ... Old course, good variety of holes ... Hidden hazards for 1st timers.

★½ HIDDEN HILLS GOLF CLUB
PU-4886 Co. Rd. #16, Woodville, 43469, Sandusky County, (419)849-3693, (877)849-4653, 20 miles from Toledo. **Facility Holes:** 18. **Yards:** 5,687/4,747. **Par:** 72/72. **Course Rating:** 67.3/66.9. **Slope:** 111/103. **Green Fee:** $10/$17. **Cart Fee:** $18/Cart. **Walking Policy:** Unrestricted walking. **Walkability:** 2. **Opened:** 1968. **Architect:** Elizabeth Pierce. **Season:** April-Nov. **To obtain tee times:** Call golf shop. **Miscellaneous:** Reduced fees (weekdays, twilight, seniors, juniors), credit cards (MC, V, AE, D), BF, FF.

★½ HIDDEN LAKE GOLF COURSE
PU-5370 E. State Rd. 571, Tipp City, 45371, Miami County, (937)667-8880, 12 miles from Dayton. **Facility Holes:** 18. **Yards:** 6,562/5,357. **Par:** 72/72. **Course Rating:** 70.5/69.3. **Slope:** 114/111. **Green Fee:** $9/$18. **Walking Policy:** Unrestricted walking. **Opened:** 1988. **Architect:** Don Dick. **Season:** Year-round. **High:** March-Nov. **To obtain tee times:** Call golf shop. **Miscellaneous:** Reduced fees (seniors, juniors), metal spikes, range, credit cards (MC, V, AE, D).

HIGHLAND PARK GOLF COURSE
PU-3550 Green Rd., Highland Hills, 44122, Cuyahoga County, (216)348-7273. **Facility Holes:** 36. **Green Fee:** $15/$16. **Architect:** Sandy Alves. **To obtain tee times:** Call golf shop. **Miscellaneous:** Metal spikes.
★★　**BLUE COURSE** (18)
Yards: 6,740/5,589. **Par:** 71/71. **Course Rating:** 71.7/75.7. **Slope:** 119/125. **Opened:** 1929.
RED COURSE (18)
Yards: 6,322/5,416. **Par:** 71/71. **Course Rating:** 69.7/73.1. **Slope:** 113/119. **Opened:** 1927.

★★½　HILLIARD LAKES GOLF CLUB
PU-31665 Hilliard Rd., Westlake, 44145, Cuyahoga County, (440)871-9578, 15 miles from Cleveland. **E-mail:** hilliard18@aol.com. **Web:** www.hilliardlakesgolfcourse.com. **Facility Holes:** 18. **Yards:** 6,785/5,636. **Par:** 72/75. **Course Rating:** 70.0/74.0. **Slope:** 124/118. **Green Fee:** $18. **Cart Fee:** $24/Cart. **Walking Policy:** Unrestricted walking. **Walkability:** 1. **Opened:** 1968. **Architect:** Mr. Zaleski. **Season:** April-Nov. **To obtain tee times:** Call golf shop. **Miscellaneous:** Reduced fees (weekdays, seniors, juniors), range (grass/mats), credit cards (MC, V), BF, FF.

HILLVIEW GOLF COURSE
PU-6954 Wesselman Rd., Cleves, 45002, Hamilton County, (513)574-6670. **Facility Holes:** 18. **Yards:** 5,435/4,681. **Par:** 71/71. **Course Rating:** 65.2/63.2. **Slope:** 108/102. **Green Fee:** $23/$25. **Cart Fee:** Included in green fee. **Season:** Year-round. **To obtain tee times:** Call golf shop. **Miscellaneous:** Reduced fees (weekdays).

★★★　HINCKLEY HILLS GOLF COURSE
PU-300 State Rd., Hinckley, 44233, Medina County, (330)278-4861, 17 miles from Cleveland. **Facility Holes:** 18. **Yards:** 6,846/5,478. **Par:** 73/72. **Course Rating:** 71.6/70.9. **Slope:** 125/118. **Green Fee:** $28. **Cart Fee:** $24/Cart. **Walking Policy:** Walking at certain times. **Walkability:** 4. **Opened:** 1964. **Architect:** Harold Paddock Sr. **Season:** April-Nov. **To obtain tee times:** Call golf shop. **Miscellaneous:** Reduced fees (weekdays), credit cards (MC, V, AE), FF.
Reader Comments: Tough course, well maintained … Very hilly, I would love to know what the pros would shoot.

★½　HOLLY HILLS GOLF CLUB
PU-4966 St. Rte. 42 S., Waynesville, 45068, Warren County, (513)897-4921, 20 miles from Dayton. **E-mail:** hhgc1871@aol.com. **Web:** www.hollyhillsgolfclub.com. **Facility Holes:** 18. **Yards:** 6,785/5,358. **Par:** 71/71. **Course Rating:** 71.6/70.3. **Slope:** 126/117. **Green Fee:** $19/$23. **Cart Fee:** $12/Person. **Walking Policy:** Unrestricted walking. **Walkability:** 3. **Opened:** 1962. **Architect:** William H. Diddel. **Season:** Year-round. **High:** March-Sept. **To obtain tee times:** Call up to 7 days in advance. **Miscellaneous:** Reduced fees (weekdays, seniors, juniors), range (grass), credit cards (MC, V, AE, D), BF, FF.

★★½　HOMESTEAD GOLF COURSE
PU-5327 Worley Rd., Tipp City, 45371, Miami County, (937)698-4876, 15 miles from Dayton. **E-mail:** davek@erinet.com. **Facility Holes:** 18. **Yards:** 6,308/5,335. **Par:** 71/73. **Course Rating:** 70.3/70.7. **Slope:** 123/121. **Green Fee:** $18/$21. **Cart Fee:** $20/Cart. **Walking Policy:** Unrestricted walking. **Walkability:** 1. **Opened:** 1965. **Architect:** Bill Amick. **Season:** March-Dec. **To obtain tee times:** Call up to 7 days in advance. **Miscellaneous:** Credit cards (MC, V), BF, FF.

★½　HOMESTEAD SPRINGS GOLF COURSE
PU-5888 London Lancaster Rd., Groveport, 43125, Franklin County, (614)836-5872, 15 miles from Columbus. **Facility Holes:** 18. **Yards:** 6,463/4,907. **Par:** 72/72. **Course Rating:** 69.7. **Slope:** 111. **Green Fee:** $16/$20. **Cart Fee:** $10/Person. **Walking Policy:** Unrestricted walking. **Walkability:** 2. **Opened:** 1972. **Architect:** Harlan (Bud) Rainier. **Season:** Year-round. **To obtain tee times:** Call golf shop. **Miscellaneous:** Credit cards (MC, V, D).

★★★★　HUESTON WOODS STATE PARK
R-6962 Brown Rd., Oxford, 45056, Butler County, (513)523-8081, 25 miles from Cincinnati. **Facility Holes:** 18. **Yards:** 7,005/5,258. **Par:** 72/72. **Course Rating:** 73.1/69.1. **Slope:** 132/120. **Green Fee:** $18/$26. **Cart Fee:** $11/Person. **Walking Policy:** Unrestricted walking. **Walkability:** 3. **Opened:** 1969. **Architect:** Jack Kidwell. **Season:** Year-round. **High:** April-Oct. **To obtain tee times:** Call golf shop. **Miscellaneous:** Reduced fees (weekdays, guests, twilight, seniors, juniors), range (grass/mats), lodging (97 rooms), credit cards (MC, V, AE, D), BF, FF.
Reader Comments: The people are great and so is price … A real gem! … Beautiful … Traditional layout, no gimmicks, grip it and rip it … Long, tough and very tight … Pretty course, tough … More doglegs than a kennel.

INDIAN HOLLOW LAKE GOLF COURSE
PU-16525 Indian Hollow Rd., Grafton, 44044, Lorain County, (440)355-5344. **Facility Holes:** 18. **Yards:** 6,910/4,810. **Par:** 72/70. **Green Fee:** $15/$18. **Cart Fee:** $18/Cart. **Season:** April-Nov. **To obtain tee times:** Call golf shop. **Miscellaneous:** Reduced fees (weekdays, twilight, seniors, juniors).

★★★★ **INDIAN RIDGE GOLF CLUB**
PU-2600 Oxford-Millville Rd., Oxford, 45056, Butler County, (513)524-4653, (877)426-8365, 15 miles from Cincinnati. **E-mail:** golfclubtheridge@aol.com. **Web:** www.theindianridgegolf-club.com. **Facility Holes:** 18. **Yards:** 7,001/5,063. **Par:** 72/72. **Course Rating:** 73.7/69.6. **Slope:** 134/117. **Green Fee:** $16/$27. **Cart Fee:** $10/Person. **Walking Policy:** Walking at certain times. **Walkability:** 4. **Opened:** 1999. **Architect:** Brian Huntley. **Season:** March-Nov. **High:** May-Sept. **Tee times:** Call up to 10 days in advance. **Miscellaneous:** Reduced fees (weekdays, twilight, seniors, juniors), range (grass/mats), credit cards (MC, V, AE, D), BF, FF.
Reader Comments: New course has great potential ...Some very challenging holes ... Univ. of Miami practice course ... Best new course in the area ... Only two years old, it will only get better.

★★★★ **INDIAN SPRINGS GOLF CLUB**
PU-11111 State Rte. 161, Mechanicsburg, 43044, Champaign County, (937)834-2111, (800)752-7846, 23 miles from Dublin. **E-mail:** indiansprinsgc@yahoo.com. **Web:** www.geoci-ties.com/indianspringsgc. **Facility Holes:** 27. **Green Fee:** $24/$35. **Cart Fee:** $11/Person. **Walking Policy:** Unrestricted walking. **Walkability:** 4. **Opened:** 1990. **Architect:** Jack Kidwell. **Season:** March-Nov. **High:** June-Aug. **To obtain tee times:** Call up to 7 days in advance. **Miscellaneous:** Reduced fees (weekdays, seniors, juniors), range (grass), credit cards (MC, V), BF, FF.
LAKES/WOODS (18 Combo)
Yards: 6,949/5,176. **Par:** 72/72. **Course Rating:** 71.6/71.1. **Slope:** 132/125.
RESERVE/LAKES (18 Combo)
Yards: 7,008/5,463. **Par:** 72/72. **Course Rating:** 73.4/72.0. **Slope:** 132/124.
RESERVE/WOODS (18 Combo)
Yards: 7,123/5,733. **Par:** 72/72. **Course Rating:** 72.9/73.5. **Slope:** 137/131.
Notes: Ranked 36th in 1996 America's Top 75 Affordable Courses.
Reader Comments: Public golf at a good fee ... Plenty of woods ... Tough test from the tips ... Beautiful course ... New 9 not grown in yet, greens less severe than 3 years ago ... A little unfair ... Old 18 much better than new 9 ... Ownership change good for the course.

INDIAN VALLEY GOLF COURSE
PU-3950 Newtown Rd., Cincinnati, 45244, Hamilton County, (513)561-9491. **Facility Holes:** 18. **Yards:** 6,007/4,494. **Par:** 70/70. **Course Rating:** 68.3/70.4. **Slope:** 113/109. **Green Fee:** $18. **Cart Fee:** $21/Cart. **Season:** Year-round. **To obtain tee times:** Call golf shop. **Miscellaneous:** Reduced fees (seniors, juniors).

IRISH HILLS GOLF COURSE
PU-7020 Newark Rd., Mount Vernon, 43050, Knox County, (740)397-6252, 25 miles from Columbus. **Facility Holes:** 18. **Yards:** 6,503/5,890. **Par:** 71/75. **Course Rating:** 69.9/72.9. **Slope:** 115/120. **Green Fee:** $10/$13. **Cart Fee:** $9/Person. **Walking Policy:** Unrestricted walking. **Walkability:** 3. **Opened:** 1928. **Season:** March-Dec. **High:** May-Sept. **To obtain tee times:** Call golf shop. **Miscellaneous:** Credit cards (MC, V, AE), BF, FF.

★★★ **IRONWOOD GOLF CLUB**
SP-1015 W. Leggett, Wauseon, 43567, Fulton County, (419)335-0587, 30 miles from Toledo. **Facility Holes:** 18. **Yards:** 6,965/5,306. **Par:** 72/74. **Course Rating:** 72.7/69.8. **Slope:** 118/111. **Green Fee:** $14/$22. **Cart Fee:** $11/Person. **Walking Policy:** Unrestricted walking. **Walkability:** 1. **Opened:** 1971. **Architect:** Ben Hadden. **Season:** March-Nov. **High:** May-Sept. **Tee times:** Call up to 7 days in advance. **Misc:** Reduced fees (weekdays), range (grass), BF, FF.
Reader Comments: Back 9 very scenic with water ... Some weird holes ... Challenging course, good value.

★★★ **IRONWOOD GOLF COURSE**
PU-445 State Rd., Hinckley, 44233, Medina County, (330)278-7171, 6 miles from Hinckley. **Facility Holes:** 18. **Yards:** 6,360/5,785. **Par:** 71/74. **Course Rating:** 69.7/72.8. **Slope:** 118/124. **Green Fee:** $25/$27. **Cart Fee:** $22/Cart. **Walking Policy:** Unrestricted walking. **Walkability:** 3. **Opened:** 1967. **Architect:** Harold Paddock. **Season:** April-Nov. **To obtain tee times:** Call golf shop. **Miscellaneous:** Reduced fees (seniors), credit cards (MC, V), BF, FF.
Reader Comments: Course wanders through hills, valleys and river ... Difficult to walk but a very good test ... A course this beautiful and in such good shape should be played.

★★★★ J.E. GOOD PARK GOLF CLUB

PU-530 Nome Ave., Akron, 44320, Summit County, (330)864-0020, 35 miles from Cleveland. **Facility Holes:** 18. **Yards:** 6,663/4,926. **Par:** 71/71. **Course Rating:** 72.0/69.1. **Slope:** 123/115. **Green Fee:** $20/$25. **Cart Fee:** $10/Person. **Walking Policy:** Unrestricted walking. **Walkability:** 1. **Opened:** 1926. **Architect:** Bertie Way. **Season:** March-Dec. **High:** May-Sept. **To obtain tee times:** Call golf shop. **Miscellaneous:** Reduced fees (seniors, juniors), BF, FF.
Reader Comments: An excellent city-owned course … Many challenging holes … Nice tree-lined course, you're either straight or in trouble … Always in prime shape … Tight, dogleg holes, tough to score on.

★★½ JAMAICA RUN GOLF CLUB

PU-8781 Jamaica Rd., Germantown, 45327, Montgomery County, (937)866-4333, 15 miles from Dayton. **Facility Holes:** 18. **Yards:** 6,587/5,092. **Par:** 72/72. **Course Rating:** 70.8/68.6. **Slope:** 128/123. **Green Fee:** $17/$22. **Cart Fee:** $11/Person. **Walking Policy:** Unrestricted walking. **Walkability:** 2. **Opened:** 1989. **Architect:** Denny/Mays/Bowman. **Season:** Year-round. **High:** April-Dec. **To obtain tee times:** Call up to 7 days in advance. **Miscellaneous:** Reduced fees (weekdays, seniors, juniors), range (grass/mats), credit cards (MC, V), BF, FF.

JAYCEE GOLF COURSE

PU-12100 Pleasant Valley Rd., Chillicothe, 45601, Ross County, (740)775-7659, 60 miles from Columbus. **Facility Holes:** 18. **Yards:** 6,893/5,181. **Par:** 72/74. **Course Rating:** 72.0/69.8. **Slope:** 124/117. **Green Fee:** $10/$12. **Cart Fee:** $10/Person. **Walking Policy:** Unrestricted walking. **Opened:** 1957. **Architect:** Ted Cox/Jack Kidwell. **Season:** March-Dec. **High:** June-July. **To obtain tee times:** Call golf shop. **Miscellaneous:** Reduced fees (weekdays, seniors, juniors), metal spikes, range (grass), credit cards (MC, V).

★★★ JAYCEE PUBLIC GOLF COURSE

PU-2710 Jackson Rd., Zanesville, 43701, Muskingum County, (740)452-1860. **Facility Holes:** 18. **Yards:** 6,660/6,200. **Par:** 71/76. **Course Rating:** 67.8/72.3. **Slope:** 101/96. **Green Fee:** $15/$17. **Cart Fee:** $10/Person. **Walking Policy:** Unrestricted walking. **Walkability:** 3. **Opened:** 1949. **Architect:** Zanesville Jaycees. **Season:** Year-round. **Tee times:** Call golf shop. **Misc:** Reduced fees (twilight, seniors, juniors), range (grass), credit cards (MC, V), BF, FF.
Reader Comments: Many improvements over the last 5 years … Wide open … Long but so enjoyable, tough for women.

KENT STATE UNIVERSITY GOLF CLUB

PU-2346 State Rte. 59, Kent, 44240, Portage County, (330)672-2500. **Facility Holes:** 18. **Yards:** 5,642/4,367. **Par:** 70/69. **Course Rating:** 65.7. **Slope:** 118. **Green Fee:** $14/$24. **Cart Fee:** $10/Person. **Season:** March-Dec. **To obtain tee times:** Call golf shop. **Miscellaneous:** Reduced fees (weekdays, seniors, juniors).

★★ KINGS MILL GOLF COURSE

SP-2500 Berringer Rd., Waldo, 43356, Marion County, (740)726-2626, (877)218-8488, 35 miles from Columbus. **E-mail:** kingsmillohio@earthlink.net. **Web:** www.kingsmillgolf.com. **Facility Holes:** 18. **Yards:** 6,099/5,318. **Par:** 70/74. **Course Rating:** 68.1/68.8. **Slope:** 106/109. **Green Fee:** $19/$22. **Cart Fee:** $20/Cart. **Walking Policy:** Unrestricted walking. **Walkability:** 3. **Opened:** 1966. **Architect:** Jack Kidwell. **Season:** March-Dec. **High:** May-Sept. **To obtain tee times:** Call up to 7 days in advance. **Miscellaneous:** Reduced fees (weekdays, twilight, juniors), metal spikes, credit cards (MC, V), FF.

★½ KINGSWOOD GOLF COURSE

PU-4188 Irwin Simpson Rd., Mason, 45040, Warren County, (513)398-5252, 14 miles from Cincinnati. **Facility Holes:** 18. **Yards:** 6,305/5,462. **Par:** 71/74. **Course Rating:** 69.8/66.3. **Slope:** 116/113. **Green Fee:** $18/$33. **Cart Fee:** $22/Person. **Walking Policy:** Walking at certain times. **Walkability:** 3. **Opened:** 1970. **Season:** Year-round. **High:** June-Sept. **To obtain tee times:** Call up to 7 days in advance. **Miscellaneous:** Reduced fees (weekdays, seniors, juniors), metal spikes, BF, FF.

KITTY HAWK GOLF CLUB

PU-3383 Chuck Wagner Lane, Dayton, 45414, Montgomery County, (937)237-5424. **Facility Holes:** 54. **Green Fee:** $18/$20. **Cart Fee:** $22/Cart. **Walking Policy:** Unrestricted walking. **Walkability:** 1. **Opened:** 1962. **Architect:** Robert Bruce Harris. **Season:** Year-round. **High:** April-Oct. **To obtain tee times:** Call golf shop. **Miscellaneous:** Reduced fees (seniors, juniors), range (grass), credit cards (MC, V).
★★ **EAGLE COURSE** (18)
Yards: 7,115/5,887. **Par:** 72/75. **Course Rating:** 72.8/74.3. **Slope:** 120/123.
Special Notes: Also has an 18-hole par-3 course.

★½ **HAWK COURSE** (18)
Yards: 6,766/5,638. **Par:** 72/73. **Course Rating:** 71.1/73.3. **Slope:** 118/121.
Special Notes: Also has an 18-hole par-3 course.

LAKELAND GOLF COURSE

PU-3770 Country Rd. 23, Fostoria, 44830, Seneca County, (419)894-6440. **Facility Holes:** 18.
Yards: 5,485/4,741. **Par:** 70/72. **Course Rating:** 66.1/66.1. **Slope:** 103/106. **Green Fee:**
$12/$15. **Cart Fee:** $10/Person. **Season:** March-Nov. **To obtain tee times:** Call golf shop.
Miscellaneous: Reduced fees (weekdays).

★★½ **LAKESIDE GOLF COURSE**

PU-PO Box 680, St Rt 60, Beverly, 45715, Washington County, (740)984-4265, 18 miles from
Marietta. **Facility Holes:** 18. **Yards:** 6,318/4,384. **Par:** 70/70. **Course Rating:** 71.4/67.0. **Slope:**
109/103. **Green Fee:** $27/$30. **Cart Fee:** Included in green fee. **Walking Policy:** Unrestricted
walking. **Walkability:** 3. **Opened:** 1959. **Season:** Year-round. **To obtain tee times:** Call up to 7
days in advance. **Miscellaneous:** Reduced fees (weekdays, twilight), range (grass), lodging
(40 rooms), credit cards (MC, V, AE, D), FF.

★½ **LAKESIDE GOLF COURSE**

PU-2404 S.E. River Rd., Lake Milton, 44429, Mahoning County, (330)547-2797. **Facility
Holes:** 18. **Yards:** 6,330/5,940. **Par:** 72/72. **Green Fee:** $16. **Cart Fee:** $18/Cart. **Architect:**
Edmund B. Ault. **Season:** March-Dec. **To obtain tee times:** Call golf shop. **Miscellaneous:**
Reduced fees (twilight, seniors, juniors), metal spikes.

★★ **LARCH TREE GOLF COURSE**

PU-2765 N. Snyder Rd., Trotwood, 45426, Montgomery County, (937)854-1951, 6 miles from
Dayton. **E-mail:** larchtree@erinet.com. **Web:** www.larchtree.com. **Facility Holes:** 18. **Yards:**
6,982/5,912. **Par:** 72/74. **Course Rating:** 71.5/72.7. **Slope:** 107/107. **Green Fee:** $15/$24. **Cart
Fee:** $12/Person. **Walking Policy:** Unrestricted walking. **Walkability:** 1. **Opened:** 1971.
Architect: Jack Kidwell. **Season:** March-Dec. **High:** April-Sept. **To obtain tee times:** Call up to
7 days in advance. **Miscellaneous:** Reduced fees (seniors, juniors), range (grass), credit
cards (MC, V, AE, D), BF, FF.

★★★½ **LEGENDARY RUN GOLF COURSE**

PU-915 Legendary Run Dr., Cincinnati, 45245, Clermont County, (513)753-1919, 15 miles
from Cincinnati. **E-mail:** michaelmccaw@yahoo.com. **Web:** www.legendaryrun.com. **Facility
Holes:** 19. **Yards:** 6,558/5,033. **Par:** 72/72. **Course Rating:** 72.2/69.7. **Slope:** 128/117. **Green
Fee:** $25/$34. **Cart Fee:** $13/Person. **Walking Policy:** Unrestricted walking. **Walkability:** 3.
Opened: 1999. **Architect:** Arthur Hills. **Season:** Year-round. **High:** April-Oct. **To obtain tee
times:** Call up to 14 days in advance. **Miscellaneous:** Reduced fees (weekdays, twilight,
seniors, juniors), range (grass), credit cards (MC, V, AE).
Reader Comments: Lots of tee options … Natural layout with wide variety of holes … Friendly service … Disappointing back 9 is too long to walk … Large greens with mild contours … Demanding
course with strong par 4s.

★★★★ **THE LEGENDS OF MASSILLON**

PU-2700 Augusta Dr., Massillon, 44646, Stark County, (330)830-4653, (888)830-7277, 60
miles from Cleveland. **Web:** www.thelegends.com. **Facility Holes:** 18. **Yards:** 7,002/4,696. **Par:**
72/72. **Course Rating:** 73.7/67.0. **Slope:** 121/108. **Green Fee:** $22/$34. **Cart Fee:** $10/Person.
Walking Policy: Unrestricted walking. **Walkability:** 2. **Opened:** 1995. **Architect:** John Robinson.
Season: April-Oct. **High:** June-Sept. **To obtain tee times:** Call golf shop. **Miscellaneous:**
Reduced fees (weekdays, twilight, seniors, juniors), range (grass), credit cards (MC, V).
Reader Comments: Everything excellent, except my score … A great course … The staff is always
ready to help … Rate this course one to play when in town … Highly recommend it … Good course
but overrated … Better than most public fee courses … If you're not smart you'll suffer … Even the
food is better than everywhere else.

★★★ **LIBERTY HILLS GOLF CLUB**

PU-665 Rd. 190 W., Bellefontaine, 43311, Logan County, (937)592-4653, (800)816-2255, 50
miles from Columbus. **E-mail:** rclark@bright.net. **Web:** www.libertyhillsgolfclub.com. **Facility
Holes:** 18. **Yards:** 6,005/4,400. **Par:** 70/70. **Course Rating:** 68.0/64.0. **Slope:** 124/104. **Green
Fee:** $18/$21. **Cart Fee:** $11/Person. **Walking Policy:** Unrestricted walking. **Walkability:** 3.
Opened: 1920. **Architect:** Barry Serafin. **Season:** Feb.-Dec. **High:** May-Oct. **To obtain tee
times:** Call golf shop. **Miscellaneous:** Reduced fees (weekdays, seniors, juniors), range
(grass/mats), credit cards (MC, V), BF, FF.
Reader Comments: Enjoyable course, nice atmosphere … Fun layout to play at a good value.

★★ LICKING SPRINGS TROUT & GOLF CLUB
PU-2250 Horns Hill Rd., Newark, 43055, Licking County, (740)366-2770, (800)204-3638, 35 miles from Columbus. **Web:** www.lickingspringsgolf.com. **Facility Holes:** 18. **Yards:** 6,400/5,035. **Par:** 71/71. **Course Rating:** 70.0/68.7. **Slope:** 119/107. **Green Fee:** $13/$18. **Cart Fee:** $11/Person. **Walking Policy:** Unrestricted walking. **Walkability:** 4. **Opened:** 1960. **Architect:** Jack Kidwell. **Season:** Year-round. **To obtain tee times:** Call golf shop. **Misc:** Reduced fees (weekdays, twilight, seniors, juniors), credit cards (MC, V, AE), BF, FF.

★★★★ THE LINKS AT ECHO SPRINGS
PU-5940 Loudon St., Johnstown, 43031, Licking County, (740)587-1890, (800)597-3240, 30 miles from Columbus. **E-mail:** rpotes@alink.com. **Web:** www.echosprings1.com. **Facility Holes:** 18. **Yards:** 6,900/4,465. **Par:** 72/72. **Course Rating:** 72.4/65.0. **Slope:** 127/108. **Green Fee:** $22/$26. **Cart Fee:** $12/Person. **Walking Policy:** Walking at certain times. **Walkability:** 3. **Opened:** 1996. **Architect:** Barry Serafin. **Season:** March-Dec. **High:** May-Oct. **To obtain tee times:** Call up to 7 days in advance. **Miscellaneous:** Reduced fees (weekdays), range (grass), credit cards (MC, V, AE), BF, FF.
Reader Comments: Friendly staff ... A short course but you'll use most of your clubs ... Quick greens, windy, hilly ... Needs middle set of tees ... Slow play, but good value ... A beautiful mix of links and traditional golf ... Only negative is that you cannot walk it on the weekends.

THE LINKS AT THE RENAISSANCE
PU-26111 John Rd., Olmsted Township, 44138, Cuyahoga County, (440)235-0501, 8 miles from Cleveland. **Facility Holes:** 18. **Yards:** 4,745/3,501. **Par:** 65/65. **Course Rating:** 63.6/60.1. **Slope:** 107/96. **Green Fee:** $15/$18. **Cart Fee:** $10/Person. **Walking Policy:** Unrestricted walking. **Walkability:** 2. **Opened:** 1985. **Architect:** Michael Hurdzan/Jack Kidwell. **Season:** Year-round. **High:** April-Oct. **To obtain tee times:** Call up to 1 day in advance. **Miscellaneous:** Reduced fees (weekdays, seniors, juniors), range (grass), credit cards (MC, V), BF, FF.

LITTLE MOUNTAIN COUNTRY CLUB
SP-7667 Hermitage Rd., Concord, 44077, Lake County, (440)358-7888, 25 miles from Cleveland. **Facility Holes:** 18. **Yards:** 6,616/5,375. **Par:** 70/72. **Course Rating:** 72.7. **Slope:** 131. **Green Fee:** $36/$48. **Cart Fee:** $16/Person. **Walking Policy:** Unrestricted walking. **Walkability:** 5. **Opened:** 2000. **Architect:** Hurdzan/Fry. **Season:** March-Dec. **High:** June-Sept. **To obtain tee times:** Call up to 14 days in advance. **Miscellaneous:** Credit cards (MC, V, AE, D), BF, FF.

LOCUST HILLS GOLF CLUB
PU-5575 N. River Rd., Springfield, 45502, Clark County, (937)265-5152, (800)872-4918, 6 miles from Springfield. **Facility Holes:** 36. **Green Fee:** $13/$18. **Cart Fee:** $10/Person. **Walking Policy:** Unrestricted walking. **Walkability:** 3. **Opened:** 1966. **Architect:** The Kitchens. **Season:** Year-round. **To obtain tee times:** Call golf shop. **Miscellaneous:** Reduced fees (juniors), range (grass), credit cards (MC, V).
GOLD COURSE (18)
Yards: 6,708/4,616. **Par:** 72/72. **Course Rating:** 70.9/65.7. **Slope:** 118/103.
★★ **RED COURSE** (18)
Yards: 6,576/4,641. **Par:** 72/72. **Course Rating:** 68.3/63.7. **Slope:** 109/100.

★★★★½ LONGABERGER GOLF CLUB *Service, Condition+, Pace+*
PU-One Long Dr., Nashport, 43830, Licking County, (740)763-1100, 50 miles from Columbus. **E-mail:** mkaido@longaberger.com. **Facility Holes:** 18. **Yards:** 7,243/4,985. **Par:** 72/72. **Course Rating:** 75.2/68.9. **Slope:** 138/122. **Green Fee:** $115. **Cart Fee:** Included in green fee. **Walking Policy:** Unrestricted walking. **Walkability:** 3. **Opened:** 1999. **Architect:** Arthur Hills/Brian Yoder. **Season:** April-Nov. **High:** June-Sept. **Tee times:** Call golf shop. **Miscellaneous:** Reduced fees (juniors), range (grass), credit cards (MC, V, AE, D), BF, FF. **Notes:** Ranked 12th in 2001 Best in State; 1st in 2000 Best New Upscale Courses.
Reader Comments: How much better can "big time" public golf get? ... No. 4 alone is worth the money ... Just about perfect, although expensive ... Great layout, no parallel fairways ... Every hole a new adventure ... If you're looking to shoot a low score, go elsewhere. Arthur Hills should be proud of what he didn't do to this wonderful piece of land ... A public course with a private club feel.

★½ LOST NATION GOLF COURSE
PU-38890 Hodgson Rd., Willoughby, 44094, Lake County, (440)953-4280, 25 miles from Cleveland. **Facility Holes:** 18. **Yards:** 6,400/5,700. **Par:** 72/73. **Course Rating:** 69.4/70.9. **Slope:** 113/112. **Green Fee:** $13/$19. **Cart Fee:** $12/Person. **Walking Policy:** Unrestricted walking. **Walkability:** 2. **Opened:** 1928. **Architect:** H.S. Colt/C.H. Allison. **Season:** Year-round. **High:** April-Oct. **Tee times:** Call up to 7 days in advance. **Miscellaneous:** Reduced fees (weekdays, seniors, juniors), metal spikes, range (grass/mats), credit cards (MC, V, D), BF, FF.

OHIO

LOUDON MEADOWS GOLF CLUB
SP-11072 W. SR 18, Fostoria, 44830, Seneca County, (419)435-8500, (800)686-4653, 30 miles from Toledo. **Facility Holes:** 18. **Yards:** 6,183/4,900. **Par:** 71/72. **Course Rating:** 68.1/67.5. **Slope:** 112/109. **Green Fee:** $15/$17. **Cart Fee:** $12/Person. **Walking Policy:** Unrestricted walking. **Walkability:** 1. **Season:** March-Nov. **High:** May-Sept. **To obtain tee times:** Call golf shop. **Miscellaneous:** Reduced fees (weekdays, twilight, seniors), range (grass), credit cards (MC, V), BF, FF.

LOYAL OAK GOLF COURSE
PU-2909 S. Cleve-Mass Rd., Norton, 44203, Summit County, (330)825-2904, 10 miles from Akron. **Facility Holes:** 27. **Walking Policy:** Unrestricted walking. **Opened:** 1928. **Season:** March-Nov. **High:** May-Sept. **To obtain tee times:** Call golf shop. **Miscellaneous:** Reduced fees (seniors, juniors), metal spikes.
★½ **FIRST/SECOND (18)**
Yards: 6,245/5,602. **Par:** 70/70. **Course Rating:** 69.1/70.9. **Slope:** 111/109. **Green Fee:** $13/$17.
★½ **THIRD COURSE (9)**
Yards: 2,845/2,845. **Par:** 35/35. **Green Fee:** $9.

★½ LYONS DEN GOLF
PU-Rte. 93 at 21, Canal Fulton, 44614, Stark County, (330)854-9910, (800)801-6007, 14 miles from Akron. **E-mail:** lyonsgolf@aol.com. **Facility Holes:** 18. **Yards:** 5,520/4,519. **Par:** 69/69. **Course Rating:** 65.0/65.0. **Slope:** 97/102. **Green Fee:** $12/$20. **Cart Fee:** $18/Cart. **Walking Policy:** Unrestricted walking. **Walkability:** 3. **Opened:** 1962. **Architect:** Bill Lyons. **Season:** Year-round. **High:** May-Sept. **To obtain tee times:** Call golf shop. **Miscellaneous:** Reduced fees (weekdays, seniors, juniors), metal spikes, range (grass/mats), credit cards (MC, V).

MADDEN GOLF COURSE
PU-2100 Nicholas Rd., Dayton, 45418, Montgomery County, (937)268-0111. **Facility Holes:** 18. **Yards:** 6,326/5,056. **Par:** 72/71. **Course Rating:** 68.6/68.7. **Slope:** 113/120. **Green Fee:** $20/$22. **Cart Fee:** $22/Cart. **Season:** Year-round. **To obtain tee times:** Call golf shop. **Miscellaneous:** Reduced fees (weekdays, seniors, juniors).

★½ MAHONING GOLF COURSE
PU-710 East Liberty St., Girard, 44420, Trumbull County, (330)545-2519, 45 miles from Cleveland. **E-mail:** mahoningcc@prod.net. **Facility Holes:** 18. **Yards:** 6,276/5,810. **Par:** 70/73. **Green Fee:** $13/$18. **Cart Fee:** $16/Cart. **Walking Policy:** Unrestricted walking. **Walkability:** 1. **Opened:** 1919. **Season:** Year-round. **High:** May-Nov. **To obtain tee times:** Call up to 7 days in advance. **Miscellaneous:** Reduced fees (weekdays, seniors, juniors), metal spikes, credit cards (MC, V, AE, D), FF.

MAJESTIC SPRINGS GOLF COURSE
PU-1631 Todd's Fork Rd., Wilmington, 45177, Clinton County, (937)383-1474, 45 miles from Cincinnati. **Facility Holes:** 18. **Yards:** 6,464/4,487. **Par:** 71/71. **Course Rating:** 70.9/66.0. **Slope:** 129/111. **Green Fee:** $24/$30. **Cart Fee:** $10/Person. **Walking Policy:** Unrestricted walking. **Opened:** 2000. **Architect:** Barry Serafin. **Season:** Year-round. **To obtain tee times:** Call golf shop. **Miscellaneous:** Reduced fees (weekdays).

★★★ MALLARD CREEK GOLF COURSE
PU-34500 E. Royalton Rd., Columbia Station, 44028, Lorain County, (440)236-8231. **Facility Holes:** 27. **Yards:** 6,630/5,777. **Par:** 72/74. **Course Rating:** 71.1/73.1. **Slope:** 116/118. **Green Fee:** $31/$36. **Cart Fee:** Included in green fee. **Season:** Year-round. **To obtain tee times:** Call golf shop. **Miscellaneous:** Reduced fees (weekdays, twilight, seniors).
Reader Comments: Tee off early or play slow ... Wide open and very forgiving ... No bunkers, flat, you would think it should play faster.
Special Notes: Also has a 9-hole course.

★★★½ MANAKIKI GOLF CLUB
PU-35501 Eddy Rd., Willoughby, 44094, Lake County, (440)942-2500, 18 miles from Cleveland. **Facility Holes:** 18. **Yards:** 6,625/5,390. **Par:** 72/72. **Course Rating:** 71.4/72.8. **Slope:** 128/121. **Green Fee:** $16/$26. **Cart Fee:** $11/Person. **Walking Policy:** Unrestricted walking. **Walkability:** 4. **Opened:** 1929. **Architect:** Donald Ross. **Season:** March-Dec. **High:** June-Sept. **To obtain tee times:** Call up to 5 days in advance. **Miscellaneous:** Reduced fees (seniors, juniors), metal spikes, credit cards (MC, V), BF, FF.
Reader Comments: Nice elevation changes ... 'Manakiki' means "many maples" which describes this course to a tee! ... Good value.

★★½ MAPLE RIDGE GOLF COURSE
PU-Rte. 45, P.O. Box 17, Austinburg, 44010, Ashtabula County, (440)969-1368, (800)922-1368, 50 miles from Cleveland. **Facility Holes:** 18. **Yards:** 6,001/5,400. **Par:** 70/70. **Course Rating:** 68.5/69.0. **Slope:** 113/115. **Green Fee:** $16/$18. **Cart Fee:** $22/Cart. **Walking Policy:** Unrestricted walking. **Walkability:** 3. **Opened:** 1960. **Architect:** Lawrence Porter. **Season:** Year-round. **High:** May-Sept. **To obtain tee times:** Call golf shop. **Miscellaneous:** Reduced fees (seniors, juniors), metal spikes, credit cards (MC, V), FF.

★★★★ MAPLECREST GOLF COURSE
PU-219 Tallmadge Rd., Kent, 44240, Portage County, (330)673-2722, 5 miles from Akron. **Facility Holes:** 18. **Yards:** 6,412/5,285. **Par:** 71/72. **Course Rating:** 69.2/67.8. **Slope:** 108/113. **Green Fee:** $14/$28. **Cart Fee:** $20/Cart. **Walking Policy:** Unrestricted walking. **Walkability:** 3. **Opened:** 1926. **Architect:** Edward Ashton. **Season:** March-Dec. **High:** May-Sept. **To obtain tee times:** Call golf shop. **Miscellaneous:** Reduced fees (weekdays, seniors), range (mats), credit cards (MC, V), FF.
Reader Comments: Beautiful landscaping ... Never saw so many flowers on a golf course ... Best par 3s in the county.

MAR-O-DEL GOLF COURSE
PU-604 Somerlot Hoffman Rd. E., Marion, 43302, Marion County, (614)389-4119, (800)627-6335, 35 miles from Columbus. **Facility Holes:** 18. **Yards:** 6,844/5,296. **Par:** 72/72. **Course Rating:** 73.5. **Green Fee:** $16/$17. **Cart Fee:** $20/Cart. **Walking Policy:** Unrestricted walking. **Walkability:** 1. **Opened:** 1965. **Season:** April-Dec. **High:** May-Sept. **To obtain tee times:** Call golf shop. **Miscellaneous:** Reduced fees (seniors, juniors), credit cards (MC, V), FF.

★★★½ MAUMEE BAY RESORT GOLF COURSE
R-1750 Park Rd. No.2, Oregon, 43618, Lucas County, (419)836-9009, 12 miles from Toledo. **E-mail:** mbryda@amfacpnr.com. **Web:** maumeebayresort.com. **Facility Holes:** 18. **Yards:** 6,941/5,221. **Par:** 72/72. **Course Rating:** 73.3/70.5. **Slope:** 129/118. **Green Fee:** $11/$28. **Cart Fee:** $15/Person. **Walking Policy:** Walking at certain times. **Walkability:** 2. **Opened:** 1991. **Architect:** Arthur Hills. **Season:** April-Nov. **High:** June-Sept. **To obtain tee times:** Call up to 7 days in advance. **Miscellaneous:** Reduced fees (weekdays, twilight, seniors, juniors), range (grass/mats), lodging (120 rooms), credit cards (MC, V, AE, D, DC), BF, FF.
Reader Comments: Everyone should play at least once ... Wind provides good challenge ... Bring a lot of balls ... Slightly expensive, great amenities, a lot of fun ... A British Isles course in Toledo, Ohio.

MAYFAIR COUNTRY CLUB
PU-2229 Raber Rd., Uniontown, 44685, Summit County, (330)699-2209, 40 miles from Cleveland. **Facility Holes:** 36. **Architect:** Edmund B. Ault. **To obtain tee times:** Call golf shop.
★★ EAST COURSE (18)
Yards: 5,288/4,769. **Par:** 64/65.8. **Course Rating:** 99.0/100.0. **Slope:** 68/68. **Green Fee:** $21/$23.
★★★ WEST COURSE (18)
Yards: 6,048/5,435. **Par:** 70/70. **Course Rating:** 68.5/69.6. **Slope:** 116/109. **Green Fee:** $27/$30.
Reader Comments: All par 5s are automatic pars ... Very nice golf course.

MERCER COUNTY ELKS GOLF CLUB
SP-3242 US Rte. 127, Celina, 45822, Mercer County, (419)925-4215, 8 miles from Celina. **Facility Holes:** 18. **Yards:** 6,331/4,962. **Par:** 72/72. **Course Rating:** 69.9/70.1. **Slope:** 119/117. **Green Fee:** $22/$27. **Cart Fee:** $11/Person. **Walking Policy:** Unrestricted walking. **Walkability:** 3. **Opened:** 1960. **Season:** Year-round. **High:** May-Oct. **To obtain tee times:** Call golf shop. **Miscellaneous:** Range (grass), credit cards (MC, V, D), BF, FF.

★★ MIAMI SHORES GOLF COURSE
PU-Rutherford Dr., Troy, 45373, Miami County, (937)335-4457, 15 miles from Dayton. **E-mail:** mitchellpga@erinet.com. **Web:** www.troy-ohio-usa.com. **Facility Holes:** 18. **Yards:** 6,212/5,192. **Par:** 72/72. **Course Rating:** 67.6/68.5. **Slope:** 97/101. **Green Fee:** $20. **Cart Fee:** $11/Person. **Walking Policy:** Unrestricted walking. **Walkability:** 1. **Opened:** 1949. **Architect:** Donald Ross. **Season:** March-Dec. **High:** May-Nov. **To obtain tee times:** Call golf shop. **Miscellaneous:** Reduced fees (twilight), credit cards (MC, V), BF, FF.

★★★½ MIAMI WHITEWATER FOREST GOLF COURSE
PU-8801 Mount Hope Rd., Harrison, 45030, Hamilton County, (513)367-4627, 18 miles from Cincinnati. **Facility Holes:** 18. **Yards:** 6,780/5,093. **Par:** 72/72. **Course Rating:** 72.1/69.3. **Slope:** 125/110. **Green Fee:** $17/$20. **Cart Fee:** $12/Person. **Walking Policy:** Unrestricted walking.

Walkability: 2. **Opened:** 1959. **Architect:** Hamilton County Park District. **Season:** March-Dec. **To obtain tee times:** Call golf shop. **Miscellaneous:** Reduced fees (seniors, juniors), metal spikes, range (mats), credit cards (MC, V), BF, FF.
Reader Comments: Great course, great people … Played here 30 years and never tire of it … Nice course than plays harder then it looks … Much improved … Tough 9th hole partly over water … Best public facility in Cincinnati.

★★★ MILL CREEK GOLF CLUB

SP-7259 Penn Rd., Ostrander, 43061, Delaware County, (740)666-7711, (800)695-5175,˙10 miles from Dublin. **E-mail:** millcreekgolf@cs.com. **Web:** millcreekgolfclub.com. **Facility Holes:** 18. **Yards:** 6,300/5,100. **Par:** 72/72. **Course Rating:** 69.0/70.0. **Slope:** 116/113. **Green Fee:** $18/$25. **Cart Fee:** $10/Person. **Walking Policy:** Unrestricted walking. **Walkability:** 1. **Opened:** 1973. **Architect:** Bill Black. **Season:** Feb.-Dec. **High:** May-Sept. **To obtain tee times:** Call up to 14 days in advance. **Miscellaneous:** Reduced fees (weekdays, seniors, juniors), range (grass), credit cards (MC, V, AE, D), FF.
Reader Comments: Easy to walk … A track that is not too hard, not too easy … The people treat you like family … Fun, wooded, pleasant … Good golf course.

MILL CREEK PARK GOLF COURSE

PU-W. Golf Dr., Boardman, 44512, Mahoning County, (330)740-7112, 7 miles from Youngstown. **Facility Holes:** 54. **Green Fee:** $17/$21. **Cart Fee:** $19/Cart. **Walking Policy:** Unrestricted walking. **Walkability:** 1. **Architect:** Donald Ross. **Season:** April-Nov. **High:** June-Sept. **To obtain tee times:** Call golf shop. **Miscellaneous:** Reduced fees (twilight, seniors, juniors), metal spikes, credit cards (MC, V).
★★★½ **NORTH COURSE** (18)
Yards: 6,412/5,889. **Par:** 70/74. **Course Rating:** 71.9/74.4. **Slope:** 124/117. **Opened:** 1928.
Reader Comments: Best public course for the price in the area … Not as difficult as the South Course … Overused … Very enjoyable … Very reasonably priced.
Special Notes: Also have an 18-hole par-3 course.
★★★½ **SOUTH COURSE** (18) *Value*
Yards: 6,511/6,102. **Par:** 70/75. **Course Rating:** 71.8/74.9. **Slope:** 129/118. **Opened:** 1937.
Reader Comments: Neat old Ross course … Very nice tree-lined track … Better 18 of the 36.
Special Notes: Also have an 18-hole par-3 course.

MILLSTONE HILLS GOLF COURSE

PU-2235 Euclid Rd., New London, 44851, Huron County, (419)929-6477. **Facility Holes:** 18. **Yards:** 6,451/4,866. **Par:** 72/72. **Green Fee:** $11/$13. **Cart Fee:** $15/Cart. **Season:** March-Oct. **To obtain tee times:** Call golf shop. **Miscellaneous:** Reduced fees (seniors, juniors).

★½ MINERVA LAKE GOLF CLUB

PU-2955 Minerva Lake Rd., Columbus, 43231, Franklin County, (614)882-9988, 10 miles from Columbus. **Web:** www.minervalakegolf.com. **Facility Holes:** 18. **Yards:** 5,638. **Par:** 69. **Course Rating:** 67.8. **Slope:** 103. **Green Fee:** $13/$18. **Cart Fee:** $20/Cart. **Walking Policy:** Unrestricted walking. **Walkability:** 2. **Opened:** 1931. **Architect:** Woody Waugh. **Season:** March-Jan. **High:** April-Sept. **To obtain tee times:** Call up to 7 days in advance. **Miscellaneous:** Reduced fees (weekdays, twilight, seniors, juniors), credit cards (MC, V, D), BF, FF.

★★★★ MOHICAN HILLS GOLF CLUB *Service, Value*

PU-25 Ashland County Rd. 1950, Jeromesville, 44840, Ashland County, (419)368-3303, 10 miles from Wooster. **Facility Holes:** 18. **Yards:** 6,536/4,976. **Par:** 72/72. **Course Rating:** 71.1/67.9. **Slope:** 122/112. **Green Fee:** $19/$24. **Cart Fee:** $12/Person. **Walking Policy:** Unrestricted walking. **Walkability:** 3. **Architect:** Jack Kidwell. **Season:** March-Dec. **To obtain tee times:** Call up to 14 days in advance. **Miscellaneous:** Reduced fees (weekdays), range (grass), credit cards (MC, V), BF, FF.
Reader Comments: Always in great shape! … Best value in golf … A real gem … Always worth going back … Good shape & scenic.

★★★½ MOSS CREEK GOLF CLUB

PU-1 Club Dr., Clayton, 45315, Montgomery County, (937)837-4653, (800)889-4653, 6 miles from Dayton. **Facility Holes:** 18. **Yards:** 7,223/5,046. **Par:** 72/72. **Course Rating:** 74.1/68.8. **Slope:** 132/121. **Green Fee:** $19/$37. **Cart Fee:** $12/Person. **Walking Policy:** Walking at certain times. **Walkability:** 3. **Opened:** 1999. **Architect:** Denis Griffiths/Chi Chi Rodriguez. **Season:** Year-round. **High:** April-Oct. **To obtain tee times:** Call up to 7 days in advance. **Miscellaneous:** Reduced fees (weekdays, twilight), range (grass), credit cards (MC, V), BF, FF.
Reader Comments: Course is great, but food service … Water and out-of-bounds place a premium on shotmaking … Demanding bunkers, excellent greens … Some of longest holes you'll play.

NATURE TRAILS GOLF COURSE
PU-6730 Liberty Township Rd. 69, Kansas, 44841, Seneca County, (419)986-5229. **Facility Holes:** 18. **Yards:** 5,555/4,619. **Par:** 73/76. **Course Rating:** 65.3/64.3. **Slope:** 98/98. **Green Fee:** $14/$16. **Cart Fee:** $18/Cart. **Walking Policy:** Unrestricted walking. **Season:** March-Nov. **To obtain tee times:** Call golf shop. **Miscellaneous:** Reduced fees (weekdays, seniors), credit cards (MC, V), BF, FF.

★★ NEUMANN GOLF COURSE
PU-7215 Bridgetown Rd., Cincinnati, 45248, Hamilton County, (513)574-1320, 10 miles from Cincinnati. **E-mail:** bterasksm@aol.com. **Facility Holes:** 27. **Green Fee:** $19. **Cart Fee:** $11/Person. **Walking Policy:** Unrestricted walking. **Walkability:** 4. **Opened:** 1965. **Architect:** William H. Diddel. **Season:** Year-round. **To obtain tee times:** Call up to 14 days in advance. **Miscellaneous:** Reduced fees (weekdays, twilight, seniors, juniors), metal spikes, range (mats), credit cards (MC, V), BF, FF.
RED/BLUE (18 Combo)
Yards: 6,069/4,288. **Par:** 70/72. **Course Rating:** 67.7/60.3. **Slope:** 105/90.
RED/WHITE (18 Combo)
Yards: 5,957/4,349. **Par:** 71/72. **Course Rating:** 67.7/60.9. **Slope:** 108/91.
WHITE/BLUE (18 Combo)
Yards: 6,200/4,279. **Par:** 71/72. **Course Rating:** 68.9/60.9. **Slope:** 111/90.

NEW ALBANY LINKS GOLF CLUB
SP-7001 New Albany Links Dr., New Albany, 43054, Franklin County, (614)855-8532, 7 miles from Columbus. **Facility Holes:** 18. **Yards:** 7,004/5,551. **Par:** 72/72. **Course Rating:** 73.6/71.7. **Slope:** 133/123. **Green Fee:** $34/$41. **Cart Fee:** $14/Person. **Walking Policy:** Unrestricted walking. **Opened:** 2000. **Architect:** Barry Serafin. **Season:** Year-round. **Tee times:** Call golf shop. **Notes:** Ranked 9th in 2001 Best New Affordable Courses.

★★ NORTHMOOR GOLF CLUB
SP-8330 State Rte. 703 E., Celina, 45822, Mercer County, (419)394-4896, 30 miles from Lima. **E-mail:** bobp@bright.net. **Facility Holes:** 18. **Yards:** 5,802/5,086. **Par:** 70/70. **Course Rating:** 66.8/68.0. **Slope:** 102/102. **Green Fee:** $13/$18. **Cart Fee:** $8/Person. **Walking Policy:** Unrestricted walking. **Walkability:** 1. **Opened:** 1923. **Architect:** Alex (Nipper) Campbell. **Season:** Year-round. **High:** April-Nov. **Tee times:** Call up to 21 days in advance. **Misc:** Reduced fees (weekdays), range (grass/mats), credit cards (MC, V, AE, D), FF.

★★ OAK GROVE GOLF COURSE
PU-14901 German Church Rd., Atwater, 44201, Portage County, (330)823-8823, 4 miles from Alliance. **Web:** ohio.oakgrovegolfcourse.com. **Facility Holes:** 18. **Yards:** 6,570/5,550. **Par:** 71/75. **Course Rating:** 69.4/70.5. **Green Fee:** $15/$17. **Cart Fee:** $11/Person. **Walking Policy:** Unrestricted walking. **Walkability:** 2. **Opened:** 1928. **Season:** Year-round. **High:** May-Sept. **To obtain tee times:** Call golf shop. **Miscellaneous:** Reduced fees (weekdays, seniors), range (grass), credit cards (MC, V), BF, FF.

OAK HARBOR GOLF CLUB
PU-10433 Country Rd. 17, Oak Harbor, 43449, Ottawa County, (419)898-1493, (800)252-1729, 20 miles from Toledo. **E-mail:** oakharborgolfclub.com. **Web:** oakharborgolfclub.com. **Facility Holes:** 18. **Yards:** 6,541/5,232. **Par:** 72/72. **Course Rating:** 70.2/69.9. **Slope:** 114/107. **Green Fee:** $18/$20. **Cart Fee:** $10/Person. **Walking Policy:** Unrestricted walking. **Walkability:** 1. **Opened:** 1964. **Architect:** Mel Hoover. **Season:** April-Nov. **High:** May-Sept. **To obtain tee times:** Call golf shop. **Miscellaneous:** Reduced fees (twilight, seniors, juniors), range (grass/mats), credit cards (MC, V, AE, D), BF, FF.

OAK KNOLLS GOLF CLUB
PU-6700 SR 43, Kent, 44240, Portage County, (330)673-6713, 10 miles from Akron. **Facility Holes:** 36. **Green Fee:** $21/$29. **Cart Fee:** $20/Cart. **Walking Policy:** Unrestricted walking. **Walkability:** 3. **To obtain tee times:** Call golf shop. **Miscellaneous:** Reduced fees (weekdays, twilight, seniors, juniors), metal spikes, range (grass/mats), credit cards (MC, V, D), BF, FF.
★★½ **EAST COURSE** (18)
Yards: 6,882/5,508. **Par:** 72/73. **Course Rating:** 71.8/70.1. **Slope:** 118/111. **Opened:** 1963. **Architect:** Howard Morrette. **Season:** Year-round. **High:** April-Nov.
★★ **WEST COURSE** (18)
Yards: 6,373/5,681. **Par:** 72/72. **Course Rating:** 69.0/71.3. **Slope:** 112/112. **Opened:** 1970. **Architect:** Jon Wegenek. **Season:** April-Oct. **High:** May-Oct.

★★★½ OAK SHADOWS GOLF CLUB
PU-1063 Oak Shadows Dr., New Philadelphia, 44663, Tuscarawas County, (330)343-2426, (888)802-7289, 30 miles from Canton. **Facility Holes:** 18. **Yards:** 7,015/5,207. **Par:** 72/72. **Course Rating:** 73.0/73.6. **Slope:** 132/127. **Green Fee:** $15/$30. **Cart Fee:** $10/Person. **Walking Policy:** Walking at certain times. **Walkability:** 4. **Opened:** 1996. **Architect:** John Robinson. **Season:** Year-round. **High:** April-Oct. **To obtain tee times:** Call golf shop. **Miscellaneous:** Reduced fees (weekdays, twilight, seniors, juniors), range (grass/mats), credit cards (MC, V, AE, D), BF, FF.
Reader Comments: Lots of hills, ponds and streams … Unique layout, great greens … Very challenging with few level lies … Bring your "A" game … Beautiful, scenic views give an open feel … Some quirky holes but a good challenge … Could use a bigger clubhouse.

OAK'S GOLF CLUB
PU-2425 Kemp Rd., Lima, 45806, Allen County, (419)999-2586, 3 miles from Lima. **E-mail:** oaksgolfclub@aol.com. **Facility Holes:** 18. **Yards:** 6,500/5,020. **Par:** 72/72. **Slope:** 124/121. **Green Fee:** $18/$23. **Cart Fee:** $12/Person. **Walking Policy:** Unrestricted walking. **Walkability:** 1. **Opened:** 1957. **Season:** Year-round. **High:** May-Aug. **Tee times:** Call golf shop. **Misc:** Reduced fees (weekdays, twilight, juniors), credit cards (MC, V, AE, D), BF, FF.

OAKHAVEN GOLF CLUB
PU-2871 US 23 N, Delaware, 43015, Delaware County, (740)363-9900, (888)504-6281, 20 miles from Columbus. **E-mail:** oakhaven@compusteve.com. **Web:** www.oakhaven.com. **Facility Holes:** 18. **Yards:** 6,638/4,704. **Par:** 72/72. **Course Rating:** 70.9/65.8. **Slope:** 122/108. **Green Fee:** $25/$30. **Cart Fee:** $10/Person. **Walking Policy:** Walking at certain times. **Walkability:** 3. **Opened:** 1997. **Architect:** David Savic. **Season:** Year-round. **High:** May-Sept. **To obtain tee times:** Call up to 7 days in advance. **Miscellaneous:** Reduced fees (weekdays, twilight, seniors), range (grass/mats), credit cards (MC, V, AE), BF, FF.

OLDE DUTCH MILL GOLF COURSE
PU-2745 Grandview Rd., Lake Milton, 44429, Mahoning County, (330)654-4100, 15 miles from Youngstown. **E-mail:** olddutchgc@aol.com. **Web:** www.oldedutchmill.com. **Facility Holes:** 18. **Yards:** 6,537/5,062. **Par:** 72/72. **Course Rating:** 71.5/69.7. **Slope:** 126/115. **Green Fee:** $14/$20. **Cart Fee:** $10/Person. **Walking Policy:** Unrestricted walking. **Walkability:** 3. **Opened:** 1954. **Season:** Year-round. **High:** May-Sept. **To obtain tee times:** Call up to 365 days in advance. **Miscellaneous:** Reduced fees (weekdays, seniors, juniors), credit cards (MC, V, AE, D), BF, FF.
Special Notes: Formerly Spring Lakes Golf Course.

★★★½ ORCHARD HILLS GOLF & COUNTRY CLUB
SP-11414 Caves Rd., Chesterland, 44026, Geauga County, (440)729-1963, 20 miles from Cleveland. **E-mail:** tpatter625@aol.com. **Facility Holes:** 18. **Yards:** 6,409/5,651. **Par:** 72/72. **Course Rating:** 71.1/72.6. **Slope:** 126/122. **Green Fee:** $21/$32. **Cart Fee:** $13/Person. **Walking Policy:** Unrestricted walking. **Walkability:** 3. **Opened:** 1962. **Architect:** Gordon Alves. **Season:** April-Nov. **High:** May-Sept. **To obtain tee times:** Call golf shop. **Miscellaneous:** Reduced fees (weekdays, seniors, juniors), credit cards (MC, V), BF, FF.
Reader Comments: Play in the fall during apple season … Tight, narrow fairways and small greens … Good luck 2-putting the 18th green! … Good course to practice irons … I expected more—overrated … Very well kept and not expensive.

★★½ OTTAWA PARK GOLF COURSE
PU-13120 Anne Road, Toledo, 43606, Lucas County, (419)472-2059. **Facility Holes:** 18. **Yards:** 5,079/4,715. **Par:** 71/71. **Course Rating:** 64.2/67.2. **Slope:** 110/111. **Green Fee:** $13. **Cart Fee:** $20/Cart. **Walking Policy:** Unrestricted walking. **Walkability:** 4. **Opened:** 1899. **Architect:** Sylvanus Pierson Jermain/Arthur Hill. **High:** June-Aug. **To obtain tee times:** Call golf shop. **Miscellaneous:** Reduced fees (twilight, seniors, juniors), metal spikes, credit cards (MC, V, AE, D).

★★★ OXBOW GOLF & COUNTRY CLUB
PU-County Rd. 85, Belpre, 45714, Washington County, (740)423-6771, (800)423-0443, 120 miles from Columbus. **Facility Holes:** 18. **Yards:** 6,558/4,858. **Par:** 71/72. **Course Rating:** 70.9/68.8. **Slope:** 117/109. **Green Fee:** $15/$20. **Cart Fee:** $12/Person. **Walking Policy:** Unrestricted walking. **Walkability:** 2. **Opened:** 1974. **Architect:** Jack Kidwell. **Season:** Year-round. **To obtain tee times:** Call golf shop. **Miscellaneous:** Reduced fees (seniors, juniors), range (grass/mats), credit cards (MC, V, AE, D), BF, FF.
Reader Comments: Rolling terrain, fast greens … A good test of golf … Nice layout.

PAINESVILLE COUNTRY CLUB
PU-84 Golf Dr., Painesville, 44077, Lake County, (440)354-3469, (800)400-6233, 30 miles from Cleveland. **E-mail:** pvcc@ameritech.net. **Facility Holes:** 18. **Yards:** 5,956/5,435. **Par:** 71/71. **Course Rating:** 69.0/71.3. **Slope:** 120/120. **Green Fee:** $19/$23. **Cart Fee:** $12/Person. **Walking Policy:** Unrestricted walking. **Opened:** 1928. **Architect:** Lamoran. **Season:** Year-round. **To obtain tee times:** Call golf shop. **Miscellaneous:** Reduced fees (weekdays, seniors), range (grass), credit cards (MC, V, D), BF, FF.

PARADISE LAKE GOLF & BANQUET CENTER
PU-1900 Randolph Rd., Mogadore, 44260, Portage County, (330)628-1313, 10 miles from Kent. **Facility Holes:** 18. **Yards:** 5,613/5,135. **Par:** 71/70. **Course Rating:** 66.7/71.2. **Slope:** 102/102. **Green Fee:** $29/$37. **Cart Fee:** Included in green fee. **Walking Policy:** Unrestricted walking. **Opened:** 1974. **Architect:** Mike Rainieri. **Season:** Year-round. **High:** April-Sept. **To obtain tee times:** Call up to 30 days in advance. **Miscellaneous:** Reduced fees (weekdays, twilight), range (grass), credit cards (MC, V), BF, FF.

★★★½ **PEBBLE CREEK GOLF CLUB**
PU-4300 Algire Rd., Lexington, 44904, Richland County, (419)884-3434, 4 miles from Mansfield. **Facility Holes:** 18. **Yards:** 6,554/5,195. **Par:** 72/72. **Course Rating:** 70.8/69.1. **Slope:** 117/113. **Green Fee:** $18/$22. **Cart Fee:** $11/Person. **Walking Policy:** Unrestricted walking. **Walkability:** 3. **Opened:** 1971. **Architect:** Richard W. LaConte/Jack Kidwell. **Season:** March-Nov. **To obtain tee times:** Call golf shop. **Miscellaneous:** Reduced fees (weekdays, seniors, juniors), range (grass), credit cards (MC, V, AE, D), BF, FF.
Reader Comments: Hard to find but well worth the trouble … When greens are good, course is tough … Too many blind shots … Need all the shots.

PEBBLE CREEK GOLF COURSE
PU-9799 Prechtel Rd., Cincinnati, 45252, Hamilton County, (513)385-4442. **E-mail:** mikejf@fuse.net. **Web:** www.pebblecreek-sugarridge.com. **Facility Holes:** 18. **Yards:** 6,144/4,612. **Par:** 71/70. **Course Rating:** 69.1/65.7. **Slope:** 130/120. **Green Fee:** $29/$40. **Cart Fee:** Included in green fee. **Walking Policy:** Mandatory carts. **Walkability:** 3. **Opened:** 1991. **Architect:** Mike Macke. **Season:** Year-round. **To obtain tee times:** Call up to 7 days in advance. **Miscellaneous:** Reduced fees (weekdays, twilight, seniors, juniors), credit cards (MC, V, AE, D), BF, FF.

PENN TERRA GOLF COURSE
PU-7500 Salem Rd., Lewisburg, 45338, Preble County, (937)962-4515. **Facility Holes:** 18. **Yards:** 6,121/5,328. **Par:** 70/72. **Course Rating:** 68.0/67.9. **Slope:** 115/114. **Green Fee:** $20/$31. **Cart Fee:** Included in green fee. **Season:** Feb.-Dec. **To obtain tee times:** Call golf shop. **Miscellaneous:** Reduced fees (weekdays, twilight).

★½ **PHEASANT RUN GOLF COURSE**
PU-711 Pheasant Run Dr., La Grange, 44050, Lorain County, (440)355-5035, 35 miles from Cleveland. **Facility Holes:** 18. **Yards:** 6,345/5,006. **Par:** 72/72. **Course Rating:** 69.3/67.5. **Slope:** 111/108. **Green Fee:** $12/$15. **Cart Fee:** $17/Person. **Walking Policy:** Unrestricted walking. **Walkability:** 1. **Opened:** 1964. **Season:** Year-round. **High:** March-Nov. **To obtain tee times:** Call golf shop. **Miscellaneous:** Reduced fees (seniors, juniors), credit cards (MC, V).

PIKE RUN GOLF CLUB
PU-10807 Rd. H, Ottawa, 45875, Putnam County, (419)523-4669, 25 miles from Lima. **Facility Holes:** 18. **Yards:** 6,299/4,634. **Par:** 71/71. **Course Rating:** 69.0/65.7. **Slope:** 115/105. **Green Fee:** $16/$18. **Cart Fee:** $11/Person. **Walking Policy:** Unrestricted walking. **Walkability:** 1. **Opened:** 1995. **Season:** Year-round. **High:** May-Sept. **To obtain tee times:** Call up to 7 days in advance. **Miscellaneous:** Reduced fees (weekdays, seniors, juniors), range (grass), credit cards (MC, V, AE, D), BF, FF.

★★ **PINE BROOK GOLF COURSE**
PU-11043 N. Durkee Rd., Grafton, 44044, Lorain County, (440)748-2939, 22 miles from Cleveland. **Facility Holes:** 18. **Yards:** 6,262/5,225. **Par:** 70/70. **Course Rating:** 66.8/68.9. **Slope:** 113/109. **Green Fee:** $19/$23. **Cart Fee:** $20/Cart. **Walking Policy:** Unrestricted walking. **Walkability:** 2. **Opened:** 1959. **Architect:** Pete Dye. **Season:** Year-round. **High:** April-Nov. **To obtain tee times:** Call golf shop. **Miscellaneous:** Reduced fees (weekdays, seniors, juniors), range (grass/mats), credit cards (MC, V), FF.

★★½ **PINE HILL GOLF COURSE**
SP-4382 Kauffman Rd., Carroll, 43112, Fairfield County, (614)837-3911, 18 miles from Columbus. **Facility Holes:** 18. **Yards:** 6,673/4,927. **Par:** 72/72. **Course Rating:** 69.9/66.6. **Slope:** 119/109. **Green Fee:** $17/$20. **Cart Fee:** $10/Person. **Walking Policy:** Unrestricted

walking. **Walkability:** 3. **Opened:** 1965. **Architect:** Jack Kidwell. **Season:** Year-round. **High:** May-Oct. **To obtain tee times:** Call golf shop. **Miscellaneous:** Credit cards (MC, V, D), FF.

★★★★½ PINE HILLS GOLF CLUB

PU-433 W. 130th St., Hinckley, 44233, Medina County, (330)225-4477, 20 miles from Cleveland. **Facility Holes:** 18. **Yards:** 6,482/5,685. **Par:** 72/73. **Course Rating:** 71.2/74.3. **Slope:** 124/126. **Green Fee:** $34. **Cart Fee:** $10/Person. **Walking Policy:** Unrestricted walking. **Walkability:** 5. **Opened:** 1957. **Architect:** Harold Paddock. **Season:** April-Dec. **To obtain tee times:** Call golf shop. **Miscellaneous:** Reduced fees (seniors), credit cards (MC, V), BF, FF. **Reader Comments:** A beautiful course that's great for entertaining clients … Country club quality at public price … Great layout and nice people … Hilly, tight … Excellent finishing hole … Best public course in Cleveland area … Lots of flowers.

★★½ PINE LAKES GOLF CLUB

R-6233 W. Liberty St., Hubbard, 44425, Trumbull County, (330)534-9026, 5 miles from Youngstown. **E-mail:** jvterrara@aol.com. **Web:** www.golfpinelakes.com. **Facility Holes:** 18. **Yards:** 6,463/4,884. **Par:** 72/73. **Course Rating:** 70.3/67.4. **Slope:** 121/114. **Green Fee:** $16. **Walking Policy:** Walking at certain times. **Opened:** 1999. **Architect:** Brian Huntley. **Season:** Year-round. **High:** May-Oct. **To obtain tee times:** Call golf shop. **Miscellaneous:** Reduced fees (weekdays, guests, twilight, seniors, juniors), metal spikes, range (grass/mats), lodging (6 rooms), credit cards (MC, V, D), BF, FF.

PINE LAKES GOLF COURSE

PU-901 E. High St., Mount Gilead, 43338, Morrow County, (419)946-1856. **Facility Holes:** 18. **Yards:** 6,285/4,957. **Par:** 71/72. **Course Rating:** 68.2/67.4. **Slope:** 109/106. **Green Fee:** $23/$27. **Cart Fee:** Included in green fee. **Season:** March-Nov. **To obtain tee times:** Call golf shop. **Miscellaneous:** Reduced fees (weekdays, seniors).

★½ PINE RIDGE COUNTRY CLUB

PU-30601 Ridge Rd., Wickliffe, 44092, Lake County, (440)943-0293, (800)254-7275, 15 miles from Cleveland. **Facility Holes:** 18. **Yards:** 6,137/5,672. **Par:** 71/75. **Course Rating:** 69.6/73.0. **Slope:** 118/122. **Green Fee:** $20/$22. **Cart Fee:** $13/Person. **Opened:** 1924. **Architect:** Harold Paddock. **Season:** Year-round. **High:** April-Oct. **To obtain tee times:** Call golf shop. **Miscellaneous:** Reduced fees (weekdays, twilight, seniors), caddies, credit cards (MC, V).

★★ PINE VALLEY GOLF CLUB

PU-469 Reimer Rd., Wadsworth, 44281, Medina County, (330)335-3375, 1 mile from Wadsworth. **Facility Holes:** 18. **Yards:** 6,097/5,268. **Par:** 72/74. **Course Rating:** 68.5/67.9. **Slope:** 109/107. **Green Fee:** $17/$22. **Cart Fee:** $20/Person. **Walking Policy:** Unrestricted walking. **Walkability:** 2. **Opened:** 1962. **Architect:** Cliff Deming. **Season:** March-Nov. **High:** May-Oct. **To obtain tee times:** Call up to 5 days in advance. **Miscellaneous:** Reduced fees (weekdays, seniors), range (grass), credit cards (MC, V), FF.

THE PINES GOLF CLUB

PU-1319 N. Millborne Rd., Orrville, 44667, Wayne County, (330)684-1414, (888)684-1020, 25 miles from Akron. **Facility Holes:** 18. **Yards:** 6,525/5,181. **Par:** 71/72. **Course Rating:** 70.8/69.7. **Slope:** 119/114. **Green Fee:** $12/$18. **Cart Fee:** $8/Person. **Walking Policy:** Unrestricted walking. **Walkability:** 3. **Opened:** 1963. **High:** May-Sept. **To obtain tee times:** Call golf shop. **Miscellaneous:** Reduced fees (weekdays, seniors, juniors), range (grass/mats), credit cards (MC, V).

★★★★ PIPESTONE GOLF CLUB

PU-4344 Benner Rd., Miamisburg, 45342, Montgomery County, (937)866-4653, 8 miles from Dayton. **E-mail:** pipestn@aol.com. **Web:** kempersports.com. **Facility Holes:** 18. **Yards:** 6,939/5,207. **Par:** 72/72. **Course Rating:** 72.1/69.2. **Slope:** 137/121. **Green Fee:** $27/$37. **Cart Fee:** $12/Person. **Walking Policy:** Unrestricted walking. **Walkability:** 4. **Opened:** 1992. **Architect:** Arthur Hills. **Season:** March-Dec. **High:** May-Sept. **To obtain tee times:** Call up to 7 days in advance. **Miscellaneous:** Reduced fees (twilight, seniors, juniors), range (grass), credit cards (MC, V), BF, FF. **Reader Comments:** Fast, tiered greens … Some neat holes, tight fairways … Great staff & clubhouse … Green fees are well worth what you get in return … Walkable … Undulating greens … Best public course in the Dayton area … This is a must. Some holes need to be redone … Soft greens and plush fairways, great service.

★★★ PLEASANT HILL GOLF CLUB

PU-6487 Hankins Rd., Middletown, 45044, Butler County, (513)539-7220, 15 miles from Cincinnati. **Facility Holes:** 18. **Yards:** 6,586/4,723. **Par:** 71/71. **Course Rating:** 70.9/66.9. **Slope:** 117/107. **Green Fee:** $17/$23. **Cart Fee:** $11/Person. **Walking Policy:** Unrestricted walking. **Walkability:** 2. **Opened:** 1969. **Architect:** Jack Kidwell. **Season:** Year-round. **High:** April-Oct.

To obtain tee times: Call golf shop. **Miscellaneous:** Reduced fees (seniors, juniors), range (grass), credit cards (MC, V), BF, FF.

Reader Comments: Open course makes it easy to find balls ... Family run and well done ... Nos. 8 and 17 very good holes.

★★½ PLEASANT HILL GOLF COURSE

PU-13461 Aquilla Rd., Chardon, 44024, Geauga County, (440)285-2428, 30 miles from Cleveland. **Facility Holes:** 27. **Green Fee:** $10/$20. **Cart Fee:** $20/Cart. **Walking Policy:** Unrestricted walking. **Walkability:** 2. **Opened:** 1965. **Architect:** Dalton Pfouts. **Season:** March-Nov. **High:** June-July. **To obtain tee times:** Call golf shop. **Miscellaneous:** Reduced fees (weekdays, seniors), metal spikes, credit cards (MC, V).

FRONT/BACK (18 Combo)
Yards: 6,212/5,446. **Par:** 71/71. **Course Rating:** 67.5. **Slope:** 113.
FRONT/MIDDLE (18 Combo)
Yards: 6,308/5,174. **Par:** 70/70. **Course Rating:** 67.5. **Slope:** 113.
MIDDLE/BACK (18 Combo)
Yards: 6,351/5,276. **Par:** 71/71. **Course Rating:** 67.5. **Slope:** 113.

★★★ PLEASANT VALLEY COUNTRY CLUB

PU-3830 Hamilton Rd., Medina, 44256, Medina County, (330)725-5770, 25 miles from Cleveland. **Facility Holes:** 18. **Yards:** 6,912/4,984. **Par:** 72/72. **Course Rating:** 73.4/68.9. **Slope:** 123/113. **Green Fee:** $25/$29. **Cart Fee:** $22/Cart. **Walking Policy:** Unrestricted walking. **Walkability:** 2. **Opened:** 1970. **Architect:** Jack Kidwell. **Season:** April-Nov. **High:** June-Aug. **To obtain tee times:** Call golf shop. **Miscellaneous:** Reduced fees (weekdays, juniors), FF.

Reader Comments: Humble little course at a very good price ... Greens could use improvement, otherwise nice.

★★★ PLEASANT VIEW GOLF CLUB

PU-14605 Louisville St. NE, Paris, 44669, Stark County, (330)862-2034, 12 miles from Canton. **E-mail:** p.u.g.c.@camnet.com. **Web:** www.pleasantviewgolf.com. **Facility Holes:** 18. **Yards:** 6,240/4,990. **Par:** 71/72. **Course Rating:** 67.2/68.7. **Slope:** 104/108. **Green Fee:** $16/$22. **Cart Fee:** $10/Person. **Walking Policy:** Unrestricted walking. **Walkability:** 3. **Opened:** 1965. **Architect:** Fred Garbin. **Season:** Feb.-Dec. **High:** June-Sept. **Tee times:** Call golf shop. **Miscellaneous:** Reduced fees (weekdays, seniors, juniors), credit cards (MC, V), BF, FF.

Reader Comments: The 17th hole is a great par 3 over water ... Nice pro shop ... Good test for intermediate to low handicap players ... Great mix of holes and beautiful views ... Very challenging, very hilly and tops out at 6,800 yards.

★★½ POWDERHORN GOLF COURSE

PU-3991 Bates Rd., Madison, 44057, Lake County, (216)428-5951, (800)863-3742, 40 miles from Cleveland. **Web:** www.ohio-golf.com. **Facility Holes:** 18. **Yards:** 6,004/4,881. **Par:** 70/70. **Course Rating:** 68.5/67.6. **Slope:** 117/113. **Green Fee:** $19/$21. **Cart Fee:** $12/Person. **Walking Policy:** Unrestricted walking. **Walkability:** 4. **Opened:** 1981. **Architect:** Anderson/Lesniak. **Season:** Year-round. **High:** April-Oct. **To obtain tee times:** Call golf shop. **Miscellaneous:** Reduced fees (weekdays, seniors, juniors), credit cards (MC, V, D), BF, FF.

PRAIRIE VIEW GOLF CLUB

PU-SR 67 26820, Waynesfield, 45896, Auglaize County, (419)568-7888, 12 miles from Wapakoneta. **E-mail:** p.v.golf@brightnet.com. **Facility Holes:** 18. **Yards:** 6,348/5,575. **Par:** 72/72. **Slope:** 115/113. **Green Fee:** $12/$16. **Cart Fee:** $10/Person. **Walking Policy:** Unrestricted walking. **Walkability:** 2. **Opened:** 1991. **Architect:** Charles Buffenbarger. **Season:** March-Nov. **High:** May-Sept. **To obtain tee times:** Call golf shop. **Miscellaneous:** Reduced fees (weekdays, seniors, juniors), range (grass/mats), credit cards (MC, V), BF, FF.

★★★ PUNDERSON STATE PARK GOLF COURSE

PU-11755 Kinsman Rd., Newbury, 44065, Geauga County, (440)564-5465, 25 miles from Cleveland. **Facility Holes:** 18. **Yards:** 6,815/5,769. **Par:** 72/72. **Course Rating:** 72.9/72.3. **Slope:** 125/122. **Green Fee:** $24/$30. **Cart Fee:** $12/Person. **Walking Policy:** Walking at certain times. **Walkability:** 3. **Opened:** 1969. **Architect:** Jack Kidwell. **Season:** March-Nov. **High:** June-Aug. **To obtain tee times:** Call golf shop. **Miscellaneous:** Reduced fees (weekdays, twilight, seniors), lodging (57 rooms), credit cards (MC, V, AE, D, DC), BF, FF.

Reader Comments: Long and tough, hard to believe it's a state park ... Pricey for what it is ... Very nice layout through the woods ... Big and fast greens ... Mostly average holes ... Nice golf facility and layout.

QUAIL HOLLOW RESORT & COUNTRY CLUB
SP-11080 Concord-Hambden Rd., Painesville, 44077, Lake County, (440)350-3500, (800)792-0258, 30 miles from Cleveland. **E-mail:** steveranney@ourclub.com. **Facility Holes:** 36. **Cart Fee:** $19/Person. **Walking Policy:** Unrestricted walking. **Walkability:** 4. **Season:** April-Nov. **High:** May-Sept. **To obtain tee times:** Call golf shop. **Miscellaneous:** Reduced fees (weekdays, twilight, juniors), range (grass/mats), lodging (150 rooms), BF, FF.
★★★★½ **DEVLIN-VON HAGGE COURSE** (18) *Condition, Pace*
Yards: 6,712/4,389. **Par:** 72/72. **Course Rating:** 72.2/65.7. **Slope:** 130/107. **Green Fee:** $65/$90. **Opened:** 1972. **Architect:** B. Devlin/R. von Hagge. **Misc:** Credit cards (MC, V, AE, D).
Reader Comments: Wonderful course ... Expensive ... Fast, fast greens ... 9th hole is murder ... A fun course which is not easy ... Beautiful, great shape, great service ... I play four rounds here each year and always enjoy it thoroughly.
★★★★½ **WEISKOPF-MORRISH COURSE** (18) *Condition, Pace*
Yards: 6,872/5,166. **Par:** 71/71. **Course Rating:** 73.9/70.0. **Slope:** 130/117. **Fee:** $50/$75. **Opened:** 1996. **Architect:** Tom Weiskopf/Jay Morrish. **Misc:** Credit cards (MC, V, AE, DC).
Notes: Ranked 15th in 1999 Best in State; 9th in 1996 Best New Upscale Courses.
Reader Comments: Unique variety of holes challenge players of varying skills ... Greens are icy fast and in great shape ... A must-play if given the chance ... No.16 should be a par 4 instead of 5 ... Outstanding! Marvelous condition ... Great condition, well staffed.

★★★½ **RACCOON HILL GOLF CLUB**
PU-485 Judson Rd., Kent, 44240, Portage County, (330)673-2111, 10 miles from Akron. **Facility Holes:** 18. **Yards:** 6,068/4,650. **Par:** 71/71. **Course Rating:** 69.2/67.0. **Slope:** 115/106. **Green Fee:** $15/$26. **Cart Fee:** $9/Person. **Walking Policy:** Unrestricted walking. **Opened:** 1989. **Architect:** Bill Snetsinger. **Season:** March-Nov. **High:** May-Sept. **To obtain tee times:** Call golf shop. **Miscellaneous:** Reduced fees (weekdays, twilight, seniors, juniors), metal spikes.
Reader Comments: Good walking course ... Interesting layout ... Pace of play good ... Kinda short, but well run and kept ... Some holes are unnaturally squeezed into available space.

★★★ **RACCOON INTERNATIONAL GOLF CLUB**
PU-3275 Worthington Rd. S.W., Granville, 43023, Licking County, (740)587-0921, (888)692-7898, 15 miles from Columbus, Oh. **Facility Holes:** 18. **Yards:** 6,700/6,194. **Par:** 72/72. **Course Rating:** 70.3/68.6. **Slope:** 116/107. **Green Fee:** $15/$20. **Cart Fee:** $10/Person. **Walking Policy:** Walking at certain times. **Walkability:** 3. **Opened:** 1973. **Architect:** Marian Packard. **Season:** Year-round. **Tee times:** Call up to 14 days in advance. **Miscellaneous:** Reduced fees (weekdays, guests, twilight), range (grass/mats), credit cards (MC, V), BF, FF.
Reader Comments: Priced right ... Lies would improve if the raccoons left ... Some interesting holes ... Good vacation spot.

★★★½ **RAINTREE COUNTRY CLUB**
PU-4350 Mayfair Rd., Uniontown, 44685, Summit County, (330)699-3232, (800)371-0017, 5 miles from Akron. **Facility Holes:** 18. **Yards:** 6,936/5,030. **Par:** 72/72. **Course Rating:** 73.0/68.5. **Slope:** 127/114. **Green Fee:** $15/$32. **Cart Fee:** $10/Person. **Walking Policy:** Walking at certain times. **Walkability:** 3. **Opened:** 1992. **Architect:** Brian Huntley. **Season:** March-Dec. **High:** May-Sept. **Tee times:** Call golf shop. **Miscellaneous:** Reduced fees (weekdays, guests, twilight, seniors, juniors), range (grass/mats), credit cards (MC, V), BF, FF.
Reader Comments: Fine course ... Some blind shots ... Staff is always eager to help ... Decent course, but not worth the price ... Excellent layout, worth playing anytime, great facilities.

★★½ **RAYMOND MEMORIAL GOLF CLUB**
PU-3860 Trabue Rd., Columbus, 43228, Franklin County, (614)645-8454, 5 miles from Columbus. **Facility Holes:** 18. **Yards:** 7,000/5,800. **Par:** 72/72. **Course Rating:** 69.9/67.9. **Slope:** 113/113. **Green Fee:** $14/$18. **Cart Fee:** $21/Cart. **Walking Policy:** Unrestricted walking. **Walkability:** 3. **Opened:** 1953. **Architect:** Robert Trent Jones. **Season:** Year-round. **High:** April-Sept. **To obtain tee times:** Call golf shop. **Miscellaneous:** Reduced fees (weekdays, twilight, seniors, juniors), metal spikes, credit cards (MC, V).

★★★★½ **RED HAWK RUN GOLF CLUB** *Value*
PU-18441 U. S. Hwy. 224 E., Findlay, 45840, Hancock County, (419)894-4653, (877)484-3429, 5 miles from Findlay. **E-mail:** Hawk@redhawkrun.com. **Web:** www.redhawkrun.com. **Facility Holes:** 18. **Yards:** 7,155/4,997. **Par:** 72/72. **Course Rating:** 74.4/68.8. **Slope:** 132/117. **Green Fee:** $26/$37. **Walking Policy:** Unrestricted walking. **Walkability:** 1. **Opened:** 1999. **Architect:** Arthur Hills/Steve Forrest. **Season:** April-Nov. **High:** May-Aug. **To obtain tee times:** Call up to 7 days in advance. **Miscellaneous:** Reduced fees (weekdays, seniors), range (grass), credit cards (MC, V, AE), BF, FF.
Notes: Ranked 6th in 2000 Best New Affordable Courses.
Reader Comments: Nice practice area ... Will be great course when it matures ... Excellent layout ... Good test, water on 11 holes ... Delightful challenge on flat terrain ... Don't jump on the wrong tees—it will eat you alive ... Fun to play.

★½ REEVES GOLF COURSE
PU-4747 Playfield Lane, Cincinnati, 45226, Hamilton County, (513)321-1433. **Facility Holes:** 27. **Yards:** 6,200/5,630. **Par:** 70/74. **Course Rating:** 68.4/70.2. **Slope:** 109/102. **Green Fee:** $17. **Cart Fee:** $11/Person. **Walking Policy:** Unrestricted walking. **Walkability:** 1. **Opened:** 1965. **Architect:** William H. Diddel. **Season:** Year-round. **High:** May-Sept. **To obtain tee times:** Call golf shop. **Miscellaneous:** Reduced fees (seniors, juniors), metal spikes, range (grass/mats). **Special Notes:** Also has a 9-hole par-3 course.

REID MEMORIAL PARK GOLF COURSE
PU-1325 Bird Rd., Springfield, 45505, Clark County, (937)324-7725, 43 miles from Columbus. **E-mail:** breid@ci.springfield.oh.us. **Facility Holes:** 36. **Green Fee:** $18/$20. **Cart Fee:** $22/Person. **Walking Policy:** Unrestricted walking. **Opened:** 1967. **Architect:** Jack Kidwell. **Season:** Year-round. **High:** April-Oct. **To obtain tee times:** Call up to 8 days in advance. **Miscellaneous:** Range (grass), credit cards (MC, V), BF, FF.
★★★ NORTH COURSE (18)
Yards: 6,760/5,035. **Par:** 72/72. **Course Rating:** 72.5/69.2. **Slope:** 131/118. **Walkability:** 4.
Reader Comments: Rolling hills, some water and sand ... Very scenic ... A couple of rigged up holes.
★★½ SOUTH COURSE (18)
Yards: 6,500/4,895. **Par:** 72/72. **Course Rating:** 69.0/66.5. **Slope:** 110/102. **Walkability:** 1.

★★★★ THE RESERVE AT THUNDER HILL
PU-7050 Griswold Rd., Madison, 44057, Geauga County, (440)298-3474, 35 miles from Cleveland. **Facility Holes:** 18. **Yards:** 7,223/5,524. **Par:** 72/72. **Course Rating:** 78.0. **Slope:** 151/127. **Green Fee:** $25/$30. **Cart Fee:** Included in green fee. **Opened:** 1976. **Architect:** Fred Slagle. **Season:** April-Dec. **High:** May-Sept. **To obtain tee times:** Call golf shop. **Miscellaneous:** Reduced fees (seniors, juniors), metal spikes, credit cards (MC, V).
Reader Comments: Various tee box options to challenge even the longest hitters ... Tight and tree lined ... Many forced carrires ... Better each year ... Impossible for the average golfer ... Bring a lot of ammo, trouble everywhere! ... Greens are so big they should have area codes.

★★★½ RESERVE RUN GOLF CLUB
PU-625 E. Western Reserve Rd., Poland, 44514, Mahoning County, (330)758-1017, 12 miles from Youngstown. **E-mail:** ebattery9. **Facility Holes:** 18. **Yards:** 6,162/5,381. **Par:** 70/70. **Course Rating:** 68.9/67.5. **Slope:** 119/113. **Green Fee:** $25/$30. **Cart Fee:** Included in green fee. **Walking Policy:** Unrestricted walking. **Walkability:** 3. **Opened:** 1999. **Architect:** Barry Serafin. **Season:** March-Dec. **High:** April-Oct. **To obtain tee times:** Call up to 365 days in advance. **Miscellaneous:** Reduced fees (seniors, juniors), credit cards (MC, V), BF, FF.
Reader Comments: Scenic, fair and playable ... New course with a wise layout ... Will be a great course in a couple of years ... Bring driver for par-3 8th ... Affordable and fun ... Short par 3s give shot at hole-in-one.

RICELAND GOLF COURSE
PU-11977 E. Lincoln Way, Orrville, 44667, Wayne County, (330)683-1876, (800)555-3044, 20 miles from Canton. **Facility Holes:** 18. **Yards:** 6,284/5,015. **Par:** 71/73. **Course Rating:** 67.5/65.5. **Slope:** 105/97. **Green Fee:** $15/$20. **Cart Fee:** $10/Person. **Walking Policy:** Unrestricted walking. **Walkability:** 3. **Season:** April-Oct. **High:** June-Aug. **To obtain tee times:** Call golf shop. **Miscellaneous:** Reduced fees (weekdays, seniors), range (grass), BF, FF.

★★ RICKENBACKER GOLF CLUB
SP-5600 Airbase Rd., Groveport, 43125, Pickaway County, (614)491-5000, 15 miles from Columbus. **Facility Holes:** 18. **Yards:** 7,003/5,476. **Par:** 72/72. **Course Rating:** 72.6/71.2. **Slope:** 117/117. **Green Fee:** $21/$24. **Walking Policy:** Walking at certain times. **Walkability:** 1. **Opened:** 1959. **Architect:** Col. Frank Hager. **Season:** Year-round. **High:** May-Sept. **To obtain tee times:** Call golf shop. **Miscellaneous:** Reduced fees (weekdays), range (grass), credit cards (MC, V, D), BF, FF.

★★★ RIDGE TOP GOLF COURSE
PU-7441 Tower Rd., Medina, 44256, Medina County, (330)725-5500, (800)679-9839, 20 miles from Cleveland. **Facility Holes:** 18. **Yards:** 6,211/4,968. **Par:** 71/71. **Course Rating:** 70.0/67.9. **Slope:** 114/107. **Green Fee:** $20/$27. **Cart Fee:** $20/Cart. **Walking Policy:** Unrestricted walking. **Walkability:** 3. **Opened:** 1970. **Architect:** Robert Pennington. **Season:** March-Dec. **High:** May-Sept. **To obtain tee times:** Call golf shop. **Miscellaneous:** Reduced fees (weekdays, seniors, juniors), credit cards (MC, V, D).
Reader Comments: Tough greens are very fast but fair ... Nice layout, challenging ... Some interesting holes ... Not overly long ... Well taken care of, friendly management.

OHIO

RIDGEWOOD GOLF COURSE
PU-6505 Ridge Rd., Parma, 44129, Cuyahoga County, (440)888-1057, 10 miles from Cleveland. **Facility Holes:** 18. **Yards:** 6,074/4,688. **Par:** 70/74. **Slope:** 114/107. **Green Fee:** $17/$20. **Cart Fee:** $11/Person. **Walking Policy:** Unrestricted walking. **Walkability:** 3. **Opened:** 1925. **Season:** March-Nov. **High:** May-Sept. **To obtain tee times:** Call golf shop. **Miscellaneous:** Reduced fees (seniors, juniors), range (grass), credit cards (MC, V), BF, FF.

★½ RIVER BEND GOLF COURSE
PU-5567 Upper River Rd., Miamisburg, 45342, Montgomery County, (937)859-8121, 5 miles from Dayton. **Facility Holes:** 18. **Yards:** 7,000/5,980. **Par:** 72/75. **Course Rating:** 70.8/71.4. **Slope:** 112/121. **Green Fee:** $13/$20. **Cart Fee:** $11/Person. **Walking Policy:** Unrestricted walking. **Walkability:** 1. **Opened:** 1963. **Architect:** Robert Bruce Harris. **Season:** Year-round. **High:** April-Oct. **To obtain tee times:** Call up to 7 days in advance. **Miscellaneous:** Reduced fees (seniors, juniors), range (grass/mats), credit cards (MC, V, D), BF, FF.

★★★★½ RIVER GREENS GOLF COURSE
SP-22749 State Rte. 751, West Lafayette, 43845, Coshocton County, (740)545-7817, (888)584-4495, 25 miles from New Philadelphia. **E-mail:** rggolf@clover.net. **Web:** www.river-greens.com. **Facility Holes:** 27. **Green Fee:** $18/$21. **Cart Fee:** $11/Person. **Walking Policy:** Unrestricted walking. **Walkability:** 1. **Opened:** 1967. **Architect:** Jack Kidwell. **Season:** March-Dec. **High:** March-Sept. **To obtain tee times:** Call golf shop. **Miscellaneous:** Reduced fees (seniors, juniors), range (grass/mats), credit cards (MC, V).
GREENS/PINES (18 Combo)
Yards: 6,668/5,324. **Par:** 72/72. **Course Rating:** 71.0/69.2. **Slope:** 112/109.
PINES/RIVER (18 Combo)
Yards: 6,534/5,130. **Par:** 72/72. **Course Rating:** 70.6/68.3. **Slope:** 117/109.
RIVER/GREENS (18 Combo)
Yards: 6,561/5,248. **Par:** 72/73. **Course Rating:** 71.1/70.2. **Slope:** 120/115.
Reader Comments: Rule#1: stay out of the pines ... My favorite—just a great course for the average golfer ... Greens are always nice.

★★★½ RIVERBY HILLS GOLF CLUB
SP-16571 W. River Rd., Bowling Green, 43402, Wood County, (419)878-5941, 9 miles from Bowling Green. **Facility Holes:** 18. **Yards:** 6,856/5,316. **Par:** 72/72. **Course Rating:** 72.1/69.4. **Slope:** 125/113. **Green Fee:** $22/$26. **Cart Fee:** $12/Person. **Walking Policy:** Unrestricted walking. **Walkability:** 4. **Opened:** 1926. **Architect:** Harold Paddock. **Season:** March-Nov. **High:** June-Aug. **To obtain tee times:** Call golf shop. **Miscellaneous:** Reduced fees (seniors, juniors), range (grass), credit cards (MC, V), BF, FF.
Reader Comments: Sneaky long last 4 holes will bring you to your knees ... Always in good condition ... A bit high on cost but they get it.

RIVERSIDE GOLF CLUB
PU-10005 Columbia Rd., Olmsted Falls, 44138, Cuyahoga County, (216)235-8006. **Facility Holes:** 18. **Yards:** 5,498/5,162. **Par:** 69/69. **Course Rating:** 66.1/68.8. **Slope:** 106/111. **Green Fee:** $18. **Cart Fee:** $10/Person. **Season:** Year-round. **To obtain tee times:** Call golf shop. **Miscellaneous:** Reduced fees (weekdays).

RIVERSIDE GOLF COURSE
PU-37895 State Rte. 7, Sardis, 43946, Monroe County, (740)483-1536. **Facility Holes:** 27. **Yards:** 6,710/4,768. **Par:** 72/73. **Course Rating:** 70.7/66.1. **Slope:** 111/103. **Green Fee:** $18. **Cart Fee:** $9/Person. **Season:** Year-round. **To obtain tee times:** Call golf shop. **Miscellaneous:** Reduced fees (weekdays).

RIVERSIDE GREENS
PU-20010 County Rd. F, Stryker, 43557, Williams County, (419)682-2053. **Facility Holes:** 18. **Yards:** 5,432/4,660. **Par:** 70/72. **Course Rating:** 65.6/67.0. **Slope:** 104/104. **Green Fee:** $16/$18. **Cart Fee:** $18/Cart. **Season:** March-Nov. **To obtain tee times:** Call golf shop. **Miscellaneous:** Reduced fees (weekdays, seniors).

★★★½ RIVERVIEW GOLF COURSE
PU-3903 SR 82 SW, Newton Falls, 44444, Trumbull County, (330)898-5674, 6 miles from Warren. **E-mail:** gwilthew@aol.com. **Facility Holes:** 18. **Yards:** 6,585/5,206. **Par:** 72/72. **Course Rating:** 71.6/70.5. **Slope:** 116/112. **Green Fee:** $20/$23. **Cart Fee:** $10/Person. **Walking Policy:** Unrestricted walking. **Walkability:** 1. **Opened:** 1962. **Season:** March-Dec. **To obtain tee times:** Call golf shop. **Miscellaneous:** Reduced fees (seniors, juniors), metal spikes, range (grass), credit cards (MC, V), BF, FF.
Reader Comments: From start to finish, a very nice place ... Another public course with character ... More golf balls than fish in the Mahoning River ... Treat you very well.

ROBINS' RIDGE GOLF COURSE
PU-57770 Fairway Dr., Senecaville, 43780, Guernsey County, (614)685-6029. **Facility Holes:** 18. **Yards:** 6,461/5,322. **Par:** 72/72. **Green Fee:** $11/$12. **Cart Fee:** $9/Person. **Season:** April-Nov. **To obtain tee times:** Call golf shop. **Miscellaneous:** Reduced fees (seniors).

ROCKY FORK GOLF & TENNIS CENTER
PU-9965 State Rte. 124, Hillsboro, 45133, Highland County, (937)393-9004. **Facility Holes:** 18. **Yards:** 6,577/4,897. **Par:** 71/71. **Course Rating:** 71.0/70.0. **Slope:** 126/104. **Green Fee:** $28. **Opened:** 1977. **To obtain tee times:** Call golf shop. **Miscellaneous:** Metal spikes.

★½ ROLLING ACRES GOLF COURSE
PU-63 State Route 511, Nova, 44859, Ashland County, (419)652-3160, 12 miles from Ashland. **Facility Holes:** 18. **Yards:** 6,590/5,022. **Par:** 71/71. **Course Rating:** 70.2/68.6. **Slope:** 117/109. **Green Fee:** $10/$19. **Cart Fee:** $19/Cart. **Walking Policy:** Unrestricted walking. **Walkability:** 3. **Opened:** 1963. **Season:** March-Nov. **High:** June-Aug. **To obtain tee times:** Call golf shop. **Miscellaneous:** Reduced fees (weekdays, seniors, juniors), metal spikes, credit cards (MC, V, AE).

★★ ROLLING GREEN GOLF CLUB
PU-15900 Mayfield Rd., Huntsburg, 44046, Geauga County, (440)636-5171, (888)833-7442, 50 miles from Cleveland. **Facility Holes:** 18. **Yards:** 6,641/5,643. **Par:** 71/71. **Course Rating:** 70.1/71.9. **Slope:** 120/114. **Green Fee:** $14/$22. **Cart Fee:** $20/Cart. **Walking Policy:** Unrestricted walking. **Walkability:** 2. **Opened:** 1970. **Season:** April-Nov. **High:** June-Aug. **To obtain tee times:** Call golf shop. **Miscellaneous:** Reduced fees (weekdays, seniors, juniors), range (grass), credit cards (MC, V), FF.

★½ ROLLING GREEN GOLF COURSE
PU-7656 Lutz Ave. NW, Massillon, 44646, Stark County, (330)854-3800. **Facility Holes:** 18. **Yards:** 5,007/4,813. **Par:** 69/70. **Green Fee:** $8/$15. **Cart Fee:** $7/Person. **Walking Policy:** Unrestricted walking. **Walkability:** 1. **Opened:** 1969. **Architect:** Ray Stefanik. **Season:** Year-round. **To obtain tee times:** Call golf shop. **Miscellaneous:** Reduced fees (weekdays, seniors), range (mats), credit cards (MC, V), BF, FF.

★★ ROLLING MEADOWS GOLF CLUB
PU-11233 Industrial Pkwy., Marysville, 43040, Union County, (614)873-4567, 15 miles from Columbus. **Facility Holes:** 18. **Yards:** 6,750/5,832. **Par:** 71/71. **Course Rating:** 71.1/72.0. **Slope:** 119/119. **Green Fee:** $19/$26. **Cart Fee:** $10/Person. **Walking Policy:** Unrestricted walking. **Walkability:** 3. **Opened:** 1996. **Architect:** David Savic. **Season:** Feb.-Dec. **To obtain tee times:** Call up to 7 days in advance. **Miscellaneous:** Reduced fees (weekdays, seniors), credit cards (MC, V, AE, D), BF, FF.

★★★½ ROSES RUN COUNTRY CLUB
PU-2636 N. River Rd., Stow, 44224, Summit County, (330)688-4653, 30 miles from Cleveland. **E-mail:** jilllockhart@neo.rr.com. **Web:** www.rosesrun.com. **Facility Holes:** 18. **Yards:** 6,859/4,964. **Par:** 72/72. **Course Rating:** 73.3/69.3. **Slope:** 128/116. **Green Fee:** $22/$44. **Cart Fee:** Included in green fee. **Walking Policy:** Mandatory carts. **Walkability:** 5. **Opened:** 1999. **Architect:** Brian Huntley. **Season:** April-Nov. **High:** June-Aug. **To obtain tee times:** Call golf shop. **Miscellaneous:** Reduced fees (weekdays, seniors), range (grass/mats), credit cards (MC, V, AE).
Reader Comments: Gorgeous views … Great layout … Back 9 is extremely difficult to score … Two par 5s have little landing area for 2nd shots … Average golf course … The back 9 seems squeezed together … Fast greens, nice layout.

★★★½ ROYAL AMERICAN LINKS GOLF CLUB
PU-3300 Miller Paul Rd., Galena, 43021, Delaware County, (614)965-1215, 17 miles from Columbus. **E-mail:** ralagc@aolcom. **Web:** americangolf.com. **Facility Holes:** 18. **Yards:** 6,859/5,172. **Par:** 72/72. **Course Rating:** 72.5/69.2. **Slope:** 127/117. **Green Fee:** $26/$45. **Cart Fee:** $10/Person. **Walking Policy:** Unrestricted walking. **Walkability:** 1. **Opened:** 1992. **Architect:** Michael Hurdzan. **Season:** Year-round. **To obtain tee times:** Call up to 14 days in advance. **Miscellaneous:** Reduced fees (weekdays, twilight, seniors), range (grass), credit cards (MC, V, AE, D).
Reader Comments: Lots of water … Big greens … Too expensive … Conditions were great, and the service was excellent … A good job of spacing groups out for a good pace of play … Treat you like a member … Great experience, but a little expensive.

ROYAL CREST GOLF CLUB
PU-23310 Royalton Rd., Columbia Station, 44028, Lorain County, (216)236-5644, 20 miles from Cleveland. **E-mail:** etkadam@juno.com. **Facility Holes:** 18. **Yards:** 6,746/5,903. **Par:** 71/73. **Course Rating:** 70.5/72.0. **Slope:** 108/112. **Green Fee:** $21/$22. **Cart Fee:** $22/Cart. **Walking Policy:** Unrestricted walking. **Walkability:** 2. **Opened:** 1966. **Architect:** William Burdick. **Season:** April-Dec. **High:** May-Sept. **To obtain tee times:** Call golf shop. **Miscellaneous:** Reduced fees (weekdays, seniors, juniors), range (grass), FF.

★½ RUNNING FOX GOLF COURSE
PU-310 Sunset, Chillicothe, 45601, Ross County, (740)775-9955, 42 miles from Columbus. **Facility Holes:** 27. **Green Fee:** $10/$12. **Cart Fee:** $19/Person. **Walking Policy:** Unrestricted walking. **Walkability:** 2. **Opened:** 1974. **Architect:** Ted Cox. **Season:** Year-round. **High:** June-July. **To obtain tee times:** Call golf shop. **Miscellaneous:** Reduced fees (weekdays, seniors, juniors), metal spikes, range (grass/mats), credit cards (MC, V, AE, D).
RED/BLUE (18 Combo)
Yards: 6,549/5,645. **Par:** 72/72. **Course Rating:** 70.5/68.5. **Slope:** 113/108.
RED/WHITE (18 Combo)
Yards: 6,538/5,685. **Par:** 72/72. **Course Rating:** 70.5/68.5. **Slope:** 113/108.
WHITE/BLUE (18 Combo)
Yards: 6,568/6,220. **Par:** 72/72. **Course Rating:** 70.5/68.5. **Slope:** 113/108.

★★ SAFARI GOLF CLUB AT THE COLUMBUS ZOO
PU-10245 Riverside Dr., Powell, 43065, Delaware County, (614)645-3444, 15 miles from Columbus. **E-mail:** bstaten471@aol.com. **Facility Holes:** 18. **Yards:** 6,507/4,827. **Par:** 72/72. **Course Rating:** 70.2/68.0. **Slope:** 11/110. **Green Fee:** $19/$23. **Cart Fee:** $11/Person. **Walking Policy:** Unrestricted walking. **Walkability:** 1. **Opened:** 1952. **Architect:** Jimmy Duros. **Season:** Year-round. **High:** May-Oct. **To obtain tee times:** Call golf shop. **Miscellaneous:** Reduced fees (twilight, seniors, juniors), metal spikes, range (grass), credit cards (MC, V, D), BF, FF.

★★★★ SAINT DENIS GOLF COURSE
PU-10660 Chardon Rd., Chardon, 44024, Geauga County, (440)285-2183, (800)843-5676, 25 miles from Cleveland. **Facility Holes:** 18. **Yards:** 6,600/5,900. **Par:** 72/72. **Course Rating:** 72.5/72.0. **Slope:** 115/117. **Green Fee:** $22/$26. **Cart Fee:** $10/Person. **Walking Policy:** Unrestricted walking. **Walkability:** 3. **Opened:** 1967. **To obtain tee times:** Call golf shop. **Miscellaneous:** Reduced fees (weekdays, seniors), metal spikes, credit cards (MC, V). **Reader Comments:** Fast play ... Creativity in shot making is a must ... A great place to play.

★★½ SALEM HILLS GOLF & COUNTRY CLUB
SP-12688 Salem-Warren Rd., Salem, 44460, Mahoning County, (330)337-8033, 15 miles from Youngstown. **Facility Holes:** 18. **Yards:** 7,146/5,597. **Par:** 72/72. **Course Rating:** 74.3/69.7. **Slope:** 126/114. **Green Fee:** $25. **Cart Fee:** $10/Person. **Walking Policy:** Unrestricted walking. **Walkability:** 2. **Opened:** 1966. **Season:** April-Nov. **High:** June-Aug. **To obtain tee times:** Call golf shop. **Miscellaneous:** Reduced fees (weekdays, seniors, juniors), range (grass/mats), credit cards (MC, V).

★★★ SALT FORK STATE PARK GOLF COURSE
R-14755 Cadiz Rd., Lore City, 43755, Guernsey County, (614)432-7185, (800)282-7275, 6 miles from Cambridge. **Facility Holes:** 18. **Yards:** 6,056/5,241. **Par:** 71/71. **Course Rating:** 68.3/69.7. **Slope:** 126/123. **Green Fee:** $14/$18. **Cart Fee:** $12/Person. **Walking Policy:** Unrestricted walking. **Walkability:** 5. **Opened:** 1972. **Architect:** Jack Kidwell. **Season:** Year-round. **High:** May-Oct. **To obtain tee times:** Call up to 365 days in advance. **Miscellaneous:** Reduced fees (weekdays, guests, seniors, juniors), metal spikes, range (grass/mats), lodging (148 rooms), credit cards (MC, V, AE, D), BF, FF. **Reader Comments:** Fabulous course ... 14 clubs may not be enough ... Lots of sidehill lies ... Take your pack mule ... Huge changes in elevation, plays longer than yardage.

THE SANCTUARY
PU-2400 Applegrove St., NW, North Canton, 44720, Stark County, (330)499-7710, (800)203-0331, 6 miles from Canton. **E-mail:** cbennell@aol.com. **Facility Holes:** 18. **Yards:** 6,750/4,850. **Par:** 71/71. **Green Fee:** $26/$40. **Cart Fee:** $10/Person. **Walking Policy:** Walking at certain times. **Walkability:** 3. **Opened:** 2002. **Architect:** Brian Huntley. **Season:** March-Dec. **High:** May-Sept. **To obtain tee times:** Call golf shop. **Miscellaneous:** Reduced fees (weekdays, twilight, seniors, juniors), credit cards (MC, V), BF, FF.

★★★½ SAWMILL CREEK GOLF & RACQUET CLUB
R-300 Sawmill, Huron, 44839, Erie County, (419)433-3789, (800)729-6455, 60 miles from Cleveland. **Web:** sawmillcreek.com. **Facility Holes:** 18. **Yards:** 6,702/5,124. **Par:** 71/71. **Course Rating:** 72.3/69.4. **Slope:** 128/115. **Green Fee:** $25/$63. **Cart Fee:** $15/Person. **Walking Policy:**

Walking at certain times. **Walkability:** 1. **Opened:** 1974. **Architect:** George Fazio/Tom Fazio. **Season:** March-Nov. **High:** June-Dec. **To obtain tee times:** Call up to 7 days in advance. **Misc:** Reduced fees (weekdays), lodging (245 rooms), credit cards (MC, V, AE, D), BF, FF. **Reader Comments:** Wish more holes had views of the lake ... Will definitely play again when in the area ... No flat putts, greens are tough ... Great service.

SEBASTIAN HILLS GOLF CLUB

PU-1100 Knollhaven Dr., Xenia, 45385, Greene County, (937)372-2468, 15 miles from Dayton. **Facility Holes:** 18. **Yards:** 6,646/4,668. **Par:** 72/72. **Course Rating:** 72.5/68.5. **Slope:** 132/114. **Green Fee:** $22/$27. **Cart Fee:** $12/Person. **Walking Policy:** Unrestricted walking. **Opened:** 2999. **Architect:** Steve Burns. **Season:** Year-round. **To obtain tee times:** Call golf shop. **Miscellaneous:** Reduced fees (twilight), credit cards (MC, V).

SENECA GOLF COURSE

PU-975 Metro Valley Pkwy., Broadview Heights, 44147, Cuyahoga County, (216)348-7274. **Facility Holes:** 36. **Green Fee:** $15/$16. **Cart Fee:** $18/Cart. **Season:** April-Nov. **To obtain tee times:** Call golf shop. **Miscellaneous:** Reduced fees (weekdays, seniors, juniors).
A COURSE (18)
Yards: 6,559/6,387. **Par:** 71/72. **Course Rating:** 71.2/74.6. **Slope:** 118/118.
B COURSE (18)
Yards: 6,639/5,473. **Par:** 72/73. **Course Rating:** 71.6/75.1. **Slope:** 121/121.

SENECA HILLS GOLF COURSE

PU-4044 W. Township Rd. 98, Tiffin, 44883, Seneca County, (419)447-9446, 50 miles from Toledo. **Facility Holes:** 18. **Yards:** 6,121/4,991. **Par:** 70/71. **Course Rating:** 68.3/67.6. **Slope:** 113/109. **Green Fee:** $14/$16. **Cart Fee:** $20/Cart. **Walking Policy:** Unrestricted walking. **Walkability:** 2. **Opened:** 1965. **Season:** Year-round. **To obtain tee times:** Call up to 7 days in advance. **Miscellaneous:** Reduced fees (weekdays, twilight, seniors, juniors), range (grass), credit cards (MC, V, D), BF, FF.

★★½ SEVEN HILLS COUNTRY CLUB

PU-11700 Willliam Penn Ave. NE, Hartville, 44632, Stark County, (330)877-9303, 12 miles from Canton. **E-mail:** www.prodigy.net. **Facility Holes:** 18. **Yards:** 6,939/5,592. **Par:** 72/72. **Course Rating:** 73.0/72.4. **Slope:** 131/126. **Green Fee:** $19/$31. **Cart Fee:** $22/Person. **Walking Policy:** Walking at certain times. **Walkability:** 4. **Opened:** 1969. **Architect:** William Newcomb. **Season:** March-Nov. **High:** May-Sept. **To obtain tee times:** Call up to 90 days in advance. **Miscellaneous:** Reduced fees (weekdays), range (grass), BF, FF. **Reader Comments:** Favorite holes on this course are all of them ... Country club atmosphere ... Rolling terrain, tough course to score on ... Always in good condition ... Fairways are perfect ... Narrow fairways and ponds make straight tee shots very important ... Back tees are quality golf.

★★★★½ SHAKER RUN GOLF CLUB

PU-4361 Greentree Rd., Lebanon, 45036, Warren County, (513)727-0007, 8 miles from Lebanon. **Web:** www.shakerrungolfclub.com. **Facility Holes:** 27. **Green Fee:** $40/$76. **Cart Fee:** Included in green fee. **Walking Policy:** Walking at certain times. **Walkability:** 4. **Opened:** 1979. **Architect:** Arthur Hills/Michael Hurdzan. **Season:** Year-round. **High:** April-Oct. **To obtain tee times:** Call up to 14 days in advance. **Miscellaneous:** Reduced fees (weekdays, twilight, seniors, juniors), range (grass), credit cards (MC, V, AE), BF, FF.
LAKESIDE/MEADOWS (18)
Yards: 6,991/5,046. **Par:** 72/72. **Course Rating:** 73.7/68.4. **Slope:** 136/118.
MEADOWS/WOODLANDS (18)
Yards: 7,092/5,161. **Par:** 72/72. **Course Rating:** 74.1/69.6. **Slope:** 134/119.
WOODLANDS/LAKESIDE (18)
Yards: 6,963/5,075. **Par:** 72/72. **Course Rating:** 74.0/68.8. **Slope:** 138/121.
Notes: Ranked 22nd in 2001 Best in State.
Reader Comments: Must play all 27 holes ... Played in the worst weather possible and still had a great day ... Great design ... A little pricey for the area ... New 9 is wide open ... Original 18 great, new 9 is OK ... Excellent, memorable holes ... Tough course.

★★ SHAMROCK GOLF CLUB

PU-4436 Powell Rd., Powell, 43065, Delaware County, (614)792-6630, 12 miles from Columbus. **Web:** www.shamrockgolfclub.com. **Facility Holes:** 18. **Yards:** 6,300/5,400. **Par:** 71/71. **Course Rating:** 67.5/68.0. **Slope:** 115/110. **Green Fee:** $21/$26. **Cart Fee:** $12/Person. **Walking Policy:** Walking at certain times. **Walkability:** 2. **Opened:** 1988. **Architect:** Jack Kidwell and Michael Hurdzan. **Season:** Year-round. **High:** April-Sept. **To obtain tee times:** Call up to 7 days in advance. **Miscellaneous:** Reduced fees (seniors, juniors), range (grass/mats), credit cards (MC, V, AE, D), BF, FF.

OHIO

★★★½ SHARON WOODS GOLF COURSE
PU-11355 Swing Road, Cincinnati, 45241, Hamilton County, (513)769-4325, 15 miles from Cincinnati. Web: greatparks.org. **Facility Holes:** 18. **Yards:** 6,652/5,288. **Par:** 70/70. **Course Rating:** 72.0/68.3. **Slope:** 131/116. **Green Fee:** $21. **Cart Fee:** $12/Person. **Walking Policy:** Unrestricted walking. **Walkability:** 4. **Opened:** 1938. **Architect:** William H. Diddel. **Season:** March-Dec. **High:** May-Sept. **To obtain tee times:** Call golf shop. **Miscellaneous:** Reduced fees (seniors, juniors), metal spikes, credit cards (MC, V), BF, FF.
Reader Comments: Won't find a better course in this area for the price … No. 3 eats all who play it … Old course with huge trees.

★★★ SHAWNEE HILLS GOLF COURSE
PU-18753 Egbert Rd., Bedford, 44146, Cuyahoga County, (440)232-7184, 10 miles from Cleveland. **Facility Holes:** 27. **Yards:** 6,366/5,884. **Par:** 71/73. **Course Rating:** 69.9/72.5. **Slope:** 114/116. **Green Fee:** $13/$20. **Cart Fee:** $10/Person. **Walking Policy:** Unrestricted walking. **Walkability:** 3. **Opened:** 1957. **Architect:** Ben W. Zink. **Season:** March-Dec. **High:** May-Sept. **To obtain tee times:** Call up to 5 days in advance. **Miscellaneous:** Reduced fees (weekdays, seniors, juniors), metal spikes, range (mats), credit cards (MC, V), BF, FF.
Reader Comments: Good layout, but a bit short … Nice condition for Metro park course … Some very unique holes.
Special Notes: Also has a 9-hole par-3 course.

★½ SHAWNEE LOOKOUT GOLF CLUB
PU-2030 Lawrenceburg, North Bend, 45052, Hamilton County, (513)941-0120, 15 miles from Cincinnati. **Facility Holes:** 18. **Yards:** 6,016/4,912. **Par:** 70/70. **Green Fee:** $8/$16. **Cart Fee:** $12/Person. **Walking Policy:** Unrestricted walking. **Walkability:** 5. **Opened:** 1979. **Architect:** Jack Kidwell/Michael Hurdzan. **Season:** March-Nov. **High:** May-Aug. **To obtain tee times:** Call golf shop. **Miscellaneous:** Reduced fees (seniors, juniors), credit cards (MC, V), BF, FF.

★★★ SHAWNEE STATE PARK GOLF COURSE
R-U.S. Route 52, Friendship, 45630, Scioto County, (740)858-6681. **Facility Holes:** 18. **Yards:** 6,837/5,748. **Par:** 72/72. **Course Rating:** 71.6/71.7. **Slope:** 117/117. **Green Fee:** $18. **Cart Fee:** $13/Person. **Walking Policy:** Unrestricted walking. **Walkability:** 1. **Opened:** 1982. **Architect:** Jack Kidwell/Michael Hurdzan. **Season:** March-Nov. **High:** May-Aug. **To obtain tee times:** Call golf shop. **Miscellaneous:** Reduced fees (seniors), range (grass), credit cards (MC, V), FF.
Reader Comments: Beautiful course with great pro shop … Pleasant surprise for a state owned course.

★★½ SHELBY OAKS GOLF CLUB
SP-9900 Sidney Freyburg Rd., Sidney, 45365, Shelby County, (937)492-2883, 3 miles from Sidney. **E-mail:** fridley@bright.net. **Facility Holes:** 27. **Green Fee:** $20/$23. **Cart Fee:** $12/Person. **Walking Policy:** Unrestricted walking. **Walkability:** 3. **Opened:** 1964. **Architect:** Ken Killian/Dick Nugent. **Season:** March-Nov. **High:** May-Sept. **To obtain tee times:** Call up to 10 days in advance. **Miscellaneous:** Reduced fees (weekdays, twilight), credit cards (MC, V), BF, FF.
SOUTH/NORTH (18 Combo)
Yards: 6,561/5,465. **Par:** 72/72. **Course Rating:** 70.5/70.5. **Slope:** 115/111.
SOUTH/WEST (18 Combo)
Yards: 6,100/5,700. **Par:** 72/72. **Course Rating:** 70.5/70.5. **Slope:** 113/111.
WEST/NORTH (18 Combo)
Yards: 6,650/5,205. **Par:** 72/72. **Course Rating:** 70.9/70.9. **Slope:** 115/111.

★★ SKYLAND GOLF COURSE
PU-2085 Center Rd., Hinckley, 44233, Medina County, (330)225-5698, 20 miles from Cleveland. **Facility Holes:** 18. **Yards:** 6,239/5,491. **Par:** 72/74. **Course Rating:** 68.9/70.7. **Slope:** 113/112. **Green Fee:** $18/$24. **Cart Fee:** $20/Cart. **Walking Policy:** Unrestricted walking. **Walkability:** 3. **Opened:** 1932. **Architect:** James O. Rhodes. **Season:** April-Oct. **High:** June-Sept. **To obtain tee times:** Call golf shop. **Miscellaneous:** Reduced fees (weekdays, seniors, juniors), range (grass), credit cards (MC, V, AE), BF, FF.

★★★ SKYLAND PINES GOLF CLUB
PU-3550 Columbus Rd. NE, Canton, 44705, Stark County, (330)454-5131, 5 miles from Canton. **Facility Holes:** 18. **Yards:** 6,467/5,279. **Par:** 72/72. **Course Rating:** 69.6/69.6. **Slope:** 113/113. **Green Fee:** $17/$28. **Cart Fee:** $10/Person. **Walking Policy:** Unrestricted walking. **Walkability:** 2. **Season:** Year-round. **High:** April-Dec. **To obtain tee times:** Call golf shop. **Miscellaneous:** Reduced fees (weekdays), range (grass/mats), credit cards (MC, V, AE, D), BF, FF.
Reader Comments: Always enjoyable … Best greens … What a bargain! … Plays a lot tougher than it looks.

SLEEPY HOLLOW COUNTRY CLUB
SP-374 Homeworth Rd., Alliance, 44601, Columbiana County, (330)821-8865, (800)834-9913, 50 miles from Cleveland. **Facility Holes:** 18. **Yards:** 6,294/5,268. **Par:** 71/71. **Course Rating:** 68.9/72.9. **Slope:** 118/113. **Green Fee:** $17/$23. **Cart Fee:** $9/Person. **Walking Policy:** Walking at certain times. **Walkability:** 3. **Opened:** 1927. **Season:** Year-round. **High:** May-Oct. **To obtain tee times:** Call golf shop. **Miscellaneous:** Reduced fees (weekdays), credit cards (MC, V), BF, FF.

★★★★ SLEEPY HOLLOW GOLF COURSE
PU-9445 Brecksville Rd., Brecksville, 44141, Cuyahoga County, (440)526-4285, 15 miles from Cleveland. **E-mail:** jsf@clevelandmetroparks.com. **Web:** www.clevelandmetroparks.com. **Facility Holes:** 18. **Yards:** 6,630/5,715. **Par:** 71/73. **Course Rating:** 72.7/71.6. **Slope:** 132/120. **Green Fee:** $23/$26. **Cart Fee:** $11/Person. **Walking Policy:** Unrestricted walking. **Walkability:** 4. **Opened:** 1924. **Architect:** Stanley Thompson. **Season:** March-Dec. **High:** May-Sept. **To obtain tee times:** Call golf shop. **Miscellaneous:** Reduced fees (seniors, juniors), metal spikes, range (mats), credit cards (MC, V), BF, FF.
Reader Comments: Old course making comeback ... Classic course, greens severe ... Beautiful view from No. 1 tee ... Slick greens ... Great long par 3s.

SLEEPY HOLLOW GOLF COURSE
PU-6029 E. State Rte. 101, Clyde, 43410, Sandusky County, (419)547-0770, 50 miles from Toledo. **Facility Holes:** 18. **Yards:** 6,371/5,204. **Par:** 71/72. **Course Rating:** 69.3/68.4. **Slope:** 113/110. **Green Fee:** $11/$19. **Cart Fee:** $20/Person. **Walking Policy:** Unrestricted walking. **Walkability:** 2. **Opened:** 1961. **Architect:** Mike Fritz/Howard Wiedle/Kit Hetrick. **Season:** April-Nov. **High:** June-Sept. **To obtain tee times:** Call golf shop. **Miscellaneous:** Reduced fees (weekdays, seniors, juniors), metal spikes, range (grass), credit cards (MC, V, D).

SNYDER PARK GOLF COURSE
PU-Snyder Park Rd., Springfield, 45504, Clark County, (937)324-7383, 20 miles from Dayton. **Facility Holes:** 18. **Yards:** 6,381/5,347. **Par:** 72/72. **Course Rating:** 69.9/70.2. **Slope:** 118/116. **Green Fee:** $18/$20. **Cart Fee:** $11/Person. **Walking Policy:** Unrestricted walking. **Walkability:** 2. **Opened:** 1920. **Season:** Year-round. **High:** May-Sept. **To obtain tee times:** Call up to 8 days in advance. **Miscellaneous:** Reduced fees (twilight, seniors, juniors), credit cards (MC, V).

★★★ SOUTH TOLEDO GOLF CLUB
SP-3915 Heatherdowns Blvd, Toledo, 43614, Lucas County, (419)385-4678. **E-mail:** naszy43614@aol. **Facility Holes:** 18. **Yards:** 6,508/5,315. **Par:** 71/71. **Course Rating:** 70.8/70.0. **Slope:** 124/116. **Green Fee:** $20/$25. **Cart Fee:** $28/Cart. **Walking Policy:** Unrestricted walking. **Walkability:** 1. **Opened:** 1925. **Season:** March-Dec. **High:** June-Aug. **To obtain tee times:** Call up to 30 days in advance. **Miscellaneous:** Reduced fees (weekdays, twilight, seniors, juniors), range (mats), credit cards (MC, V, AE), BF, FF.
Reader Comments: Comfortable course with good amenities ... Greens are small and well trapped ... Green fees out of balance with similar courses ... Lots of trees and fun to play.

SPLIT ROCK GOLF COURSE
PU-10210 Scioto Darby Rd., Orient, 43146, Pickaway County, (614)877-9755, 10 miles from Columbus. **Facility Holes:** 18. **Yards:** 6,809/5,046. **Par:** 72/72. **Course Rating:** 72.0/68.1. **Slope:** 125/116. **Green Fee:** $15/$19. **Cart Fee:** $11/Person. **Walking Policy:** Unrestricted walking. **Walkability:** 3. **Opened:** 1998. **Architect:** Michael Hurdzan/Dana Fry. **Season:** March-Dec. **High:** June-Aug. **To obtain tee times:** Call golf shop. **Miscellaneous:** Reduced fees (weekdays), range (grass), credit cards (MC, V), BF, FF.

★★ SPRING HILLS GOLF CLUB
PU-SR 43, Box 128, East Springfield, 43925, Jefferson County, (740)543-3270, 13 miles from Steubenville. **Facility Holes:** 18. **Yards:** 6,558/5,560. **Par:** 71/71. **Course Rating:** 70.9/67.0. **Slope:** 119/119. **Green Fee:** $14/$16. **Cart Fee:** $14/Person. **Walking Policy:** Unrestricted walking. **Walkability:** 2. **Opened:** 1970. **Season:** Year-round. **To obtain tee times:** Call golf shop. **Misc:** Reduced fees (weekdays, seniors, juniors), range (grass), credit cards (MC, V), BF, FF.

SPRING HILLS GOLF CLUB
PU-6571 Cleveland Massillon Rd., Clinton, 44216, Summit County, (330)825-2439, 8 miles from Akron. **Facility Holes:** 18. **Yards:** 6,233/5,121. **Par:** 70/70. **Course Rating:** 68.4/67.5. **Slope:** 110/108. **Green Fee:** $14/$22. **Cart Fee:** $10/Person. **Walking Policy:** Unrestricted walking. **Walkability:** 3. **Opened:** 1963. **Season:** March-Nov. **To obtain tee times:** Call golf shop. **Miscellaneous:** Metal spikes, credit cards (MC, V, D).

SPRINGBROOK GOLF CLUB
PU-4200 Ottawa Rd., Lima, 45801, Allen County, (419)225-8037, 65 miles from Dayton.
Facility Holes: 18. **Yards:** 6,045/5,102. **Par:** 71/71. **Course Rating:** 67.7/69.1. **Slope:** 108/110.
Green Fee: $17/$19. **Cart Fee:** $11/Person. **Opened:** 1931. **Season:** Year-round. **To obtain tee times:** Call golf shop. **Miscellaneous:** Reduced fees (twilight, seniors, juniors).

SPRINGVALE GOLF CLUB
PU-5871 Canterbury Rd., North Olmsted, 44070, Cuyahoga County, (440)777-0678. **Facility Holes:** 18. **Yards:** 6,303/5,100. **Par:** 70/70. **Course Rating:** 69.0/67.7. **Slope:** 112/110. **Green Fee:** $16/$30. **Cart Fee:** Included in green fee. **Walking Policy:** Walking at certain times. **Walkability:** 2. **Opened:** 1927. **Season:** Year-round. **High:** April-Oct. **To obtain tee times:** Call golf shop. **Miscellaneous:** Reduced fees (weekdays, seniors, juniors), range (grass/mats), credit cards (MC, V, AE), BF, FF.

SPUYTEN DUYVAL GOLF CLUB
PU-9501 W. Central Ave., Sylvania, 43560, Lucas County, (419)829-2891, 6 miles from Toledo. **Facility Holes:** 18. **Yards:** 6,246/4,872. **Par:** 71/71. **Course Rating:** 68.3/66.1. **Slope:** 111/106. **Green Fee:** $13/$24. **Cart Fee:** $20/Cart. **Walking Policy:** Unrestricted walking. **Walkability:** 1. **Opened:** 1928. **Architect:** Cal Wilson. **Season:** Feb.-Dec. **High:** May-Sept. **Tee times:** Call up to 1 day ahead. **Misc:** Reduced fees (weekdays, twilight, seniors, juniors), range (grass/mats), credit cards (MC, V), BF, FF.

★★½ ST. ALBANS GOLF CLUB
PU-3833 Northridge Rd. NW, Alexandria, 43001, Licking County, (740)924-8885, 25 miles from Columbus. **Facility Holes:** 18. **Yards:** 6,732/5,513. **Par:** 71/71. **Course Rating:** 71.6/71.1. **Slope:** 112/112. **Green Fee:** $28. **Cart Fee:** Included in green fee. **Walking Policy:** Unrestricted walking. **Walkability:** 3. **Opened:** 1988. **Architect:** Tony Price. **Season:** March-Dec. **To obtain tee times:** Call up to 14 days in advance. **Miscellaneous:** Reduced fees (seniors), credit cards (MC, V, AE, D), FF.

★★½ STONE RIDGE GOLF CLUB
PU-1553 Muirfield Ln., Bowling Green, 43402, Wood County, (419)353-2582, (877)504-2582, 2 miles from Bowling Green. **E-mail:** monty@glasscity.net. **Web:** stoneridgegolfclub.com. **Facility Holes:** 18. **Yards:** 6,920/5,080. **Par:** 72/72. **Course Rating:** 72.7/68.6. **Slope:** 129/119. **Green Fee:** $24/$45. **Cart Fee:** Included in green fee. **Walking Policy:** Unrestricted walking. **Walkability:** 2. **Opened:** 1999. **Architect:** Arthur Hills/Steve Forrest. **Season:** Year-round. **High:** April-Aug. **To obtain tee times:** Call up to 7 days in advance. **Miscellaneous:** Reduced fees (weekdays, twilight, seniors, juniors), range (grass/mats), credit cards (MC, V, AE, D), BF, FF.

★★★★½ STONEWATER GOLF CLUB *Condition*
SP-1 Club Dr., Highland Heights, 44143, Cuyahoga County, (440)461-4653, 16 miles from Cleveland. **E-mail:** jon@stonewatergolf.com. **Web:** www.stonewatergolf.com. **Facility Holes:** 18. **Yards:** 7,002/5,500. **Par:** 71/71. **Course Rating:** 74.8/72.6. **Slope:** 138/132. **Green Fee:** $50/$90. **Cart Fee:** Included in green fee. **Walking Policy:** Walking at certain times. **Walkability:** 3. **Opened:** 1996. **Architect:** Hurdzan/Fry Golf Design. **Season:** Feb.-Dec. **High:** May-Sept. **To obtain tee times:** Call up to 14 days in advance. **Miscellaneous:** Reduced fees (weekdays, twilight), range (grass), caddies, credit cards (MC, V, AE), BF, FF.
Notes: Ranked 14th in 2001 Best in State.
Reader Comments: Deep bunkers ... Weaves in and out of a wildlife perserve ... Greens in excellent shape ... Expensive ... Wide fairways ... Reminds you of being in North Carolina ... Manicured like a tour course ... Great practice range.

SUBURBAN GOLF CLUB
PU-State Rte. 15 N, Bryan, 43506, Williams County, (419)636-9988. **Facility Holes:** 18. **Yards:** 6,100/4,779. **Par:** 72/72. **Course Rating:** 67.1/65.2. **Slope:** 106/100. **Green Fee:** $12/$15. **Cart Fee:** $16/Cart. **Season:** April-Oct. **To obtain tee times:** Call golf shop.

★★★½ SUGAR BUSH GOLF CLUB
PU-11186 North State Rte. 88, Garrettsville, 44231, Portage County, (330)527-4202, 33 miles from Cleveland. **Facility Holes:** 18. **Yards:** 6,571/4,727. **Par:** 72/72. **Course Rating:** 72.4/66.4. **Slope:** 121/106. **Walkability:** 4. **Opened:** 1965. **Architect:** Harold Paddock. **Season:** March-Nov. **To obtain tee times:** Call golf shop. **Miscellaneous:** Reduced fees (weekdays, twilight, seniors, juniors), metal spikes, credit cards (MC, V), BF, FF.
Reader Comments: Psst—everyone in Cleveland loves this course ... Small, sloping fast greens ... Very good course ... Nice challenge ... Great old course, good greens ... An enjoyable course with fast greens.

★★½ SUGAR CREEK GOLF COURSE
SP-950 Elmore E. Rd., Elmore, 43416, Ottawa County, (419)862-2551, 20 miles from Toledo.
E-mail: srodawalt@aol.com. **Facility Holes:** 18. **Yards:** 6,331/5,092. **Par:** 71/71. **Course Rating:**
66.5/64.4. **Slope:** 102/98. **Green Fee:** $12/$18. **Cart Fee:** $22/Cart. **Walking Policy:** Walking at
certain times. **Walkability:** 3. **Opened:** 1963. **Architect:** Stan Neeb/Leon Neeb. **Season:** March-
Dec. **High:** June-Sept. **To obtain tee times:** Call golf shop. **Miscellaneous:** Reduced fees
(weekdays, twilight, seniors, juniors), range (grass/mats), credit cards (MC, V), FF.

★★ SUGAR ISLE GOLF COUNTRY
PU-2469 Dayton Lakeview Rd., New Carlisle, 45344, Clark County, (937)845-8699, 15 miles
from Dayton. **Facility Holes:** 18. **Yards:** 6,754/5,636. **Par:** 72/72. **Course Rating:** 70.2/71.1.
Slope: 107/110. **Green Fee:** $16/$20. **Cart Fee:** $11/Person. **Walking Policy:** Unrestricted walk-
ing. **Walkability:** 2. **Opened:** 1974. **Architect:** Jack Kidwell/Michael Hurdzan. **Season:** Year-
round. **High:** June-Sept. **To obtain tee times:** Call golf shop. **Miscellaneous:** Reduced fees
(weekdays, seniors), range (grass), credit cards (MC, V).

★★ SUNNYHILL GOLF COURSE
PU-3734 Sunnybrook Rd., Kent, 44240, Portage County, (330)673-1785, 5 miles from Akron.
E-mail: 27sunny@gateway.net. **Facility Holes:** 27. **Yards:** 6,289/5,083. **Par:** 71/72. **Course
Rating:** 69.4/69.1. **Slope:** 119/113. **Green Fee:** $23/$26. **Cart Fee:** $10/Person. **Walking Policy:**
Unrestricted walking. **Walkability:** 3. **Opened:** 1921. **Architect:** Ferdinand Garbin. **Season:**
April-Dec. **To obtain tee times:** Call golf shop. **Miscellaneous:** Reduced fees (weekdays,
seniors, juniors), range (mats), credit cards (MC, V, D).
Special Notes: Also has a 9-hole Middle Course.

★★★ SWEETBRIAR GOLF & PRO SHOP
PU-750 Jaycox Rd., Avon Lake, 44012, Lorain County, (440)933-9001, 20 miles from
Cleveland. **Facility Holes:** 27. **Green Fee:** $17/$22. **Cart Fee:** $21/Cart. **Walking Policy:**
Unrestricted walking. **Opened:** 1966. **Architect:** Ron Palmer. **Season:** Year-round. **High:** May-
Oct. **To obtain tee times:** Call golf shop. **Miscellaneous:** Reduced fees (twilight, seniors,
juniors), metal spikes, range (mats), credit cards (MC, V).
FIRST/SECOND (18 Combo)
Yards: 6,491/5,521. **Par:** 72/74. **Course Rating:** 68.7/68.9. **Slope:** 106/105.
FIRST/THIRD (18 Combo)
Yards: 6,075/5,414. **Par:** 70/73. **Course Rating:** 66.3/68.0. **Slope:** 100/105. **Walkability:** 1.
SECOND/THIRD (18 Combo)
Yards: 6,292/5,411. **Par:** 72/73. **Course Rating:** 67.5/68.3. **Slope:** 104/104. **Walkability:** 1.
Reader Comments: Much improved older course … Good staff and pro shop … A fair test.

SYCAMORE HILLS GOLF CLUB
SP-3728 W. Hayes Ave. (U.S. Route 6), Fremont, 43420, Sandusky County, (419)332-5716,
(800)336-5716, 3 miles from Fremont. **E-mail:** sycamorehills@ezworks.net. **Web:**
www.sycamorehillsgolf.com. **Facility Holes:** 27. **Green Fee:** $18/$21. **Cart Fee:** $22/Cart.
Walking Policy: Unrestricted walking. **Walkability:** 2. **Opened:** 1995. **Architect:** Bryan Huntley.
Season: March-Dec. **To obtain tee times:** Call golf shop. **Miscellaneous:** Reduced fees (week-
days, seniors, juniors), range (grass), credit cards (MC, V, D), BF, FF.
BLUE/WHITE (18)
Yards: 6,393/5,134. **Par:** 70/72. **Course Rating:** 69.6/68.2. **Slope:** 117/112.
RED/BLUE (18)
Yards: 6,221/5,076. **Par:** 70/72. **Course Rating:** 67.3/66.3. **Slope:** 110/107.
WHITE/RED (18)
Yards: 6,126/4,910. **Par:** 70/72. **Course Rating:** 68.1/67.8. **Slope:** 117/107.

SYCAMORE SPRINGS GOLF COURSE
SP-Eagle Township Country Rd. 25, Arlington, 45814, Hancock County, (419)365-5109, 5
miles from Findlay. **Facility Holes:** 18. **Yards:** 6,612/5,190. **Par:** 72/72. **Course Rating:**
70.9/68.9. **Slope:** 119/113. **Green Fee:** $20/$24. **Cart Fee:** $11/Person. **Walking Policy:**
Unrestricted walking. **Walkability:** 1. **Opened:** 1958. **Season:** March-Dec. **High:** May-Oct. **Tee
times:** Call golf shop. **Misc:** Reduced fees (seniors, juniors), range, cards (MC, V, D), BF, FF.

★★½ TABLE ROCK GOLF CLUB
PU-3005 Wilson Rd., Centerburg, 43011, Knox County, (740)625-6859, (800)688-6859, 20
miles from Columbus. **E-mail:** info@tablerock.com. **Web:** www.tablerock.com. **Facility Holes:**
18. **Yards:** 6,729/5,303. **Par:** 72/72. **Course Rating:** 71.4/69.2. **Slope:** 119/115. **Green Fee:**
$15/$23. **Cart Fee:** $13/Person. **Walking Policy:** Unrestricted walking. **Walkability:** 1. **Opened:**
1973. **Architect:** Jack Kidwell. **Season:** Year-round. **Tee times:** Call up to 14 days ahead. **Misc:**
Reduced fees (weekdays, twilight, seniors, juniors), range, cards (MC, V, AE, D), BF, FF.

OHIO

TAM O'SHANTER GOLF COURSE
PU-5055 Hills and Dales Rd. NW, Canton, 44708, Stark County, (330)477-5111, (800)462-9964, 50 miles from Cleveland. **E-mail:** tamogolf@aol.com. **Web:** www.tamoshantergolf.com. **Facility Holes:** 36. **Green Fee:** $15/$30. **Cart Fee:** $10/Person. **Walking Policy:** Unrestricted walking. **Walkability:** 3. **Season:** March-Dec. **High:** May-Sept. **Tee times:** Call golf shop. **Misc:** Reduced fees (weekdays, seniors, juniors), range (grass), credit cards (MC, V), BF, FF.
★★★ **DALES COURSE** (18)
Yards: 6,538/5,012. **Par:** 70/72. **Course Rating:** 70.4/67.5. **Slope:** 117/108. **Opened:** 1928. **Architect:** Leonard Macomber.
Reader Comments: Always enjoyable … Best greens … Nice course.
★★½ **HILLS COURSE** (18)
Yards: 6,362/5,076. **Par:** 70/72. **Course Rating:** 69.4/68.0. **Slope:** 115/108. **Opened:** 1930. **Architect:** Merle Paul.

★★ TAMARAC GOLF CLUB
PU-500 Stevick Rd., Lima, 45807, Allen County, (419)331-2951, 4 miles from Lima. **Facility Holes:** 27. **Yards:** 6,109/5,029. **Par:** 72/72. **Course Rating:** 69.8/67.9. **Slope:** 112/108. **Green Fee:** $15/$20. **Cart Fee:** $18/Person. **Walking Policy:** Unrestricted walking. **Walkability:** 2. **Opened:** 1950. **Architect:** Bob Holopeter. **Season:** March-Dec. **High:** April-Sept. **To obtain tee times:** Call golf shop. **Miscellaneous:** Reduced fees (weekdays, twilight, seniors), range (grass), credit cards (MC, V, D), BF, FF.
Special Notes: Also has 9-hole par-3 course.

TAMARON COUNTRY CLUB
SP-2162 W. Alexis Rd., Toledo, 43613, Lucas County, (419)474-0501. **Web:** www.tamaroncc.com. **Facility Holes:** 18. **Yards:** 6,067/5,157. **Par:** 70/73. **Course Rating:** 69.0/68.9. **Slope:** 118/115. **Green Fee:** $13/$27. **Cart Fee:** $12/Person. **Walking Policy:** Walking at certain times. **Walkability:** 4. **Opened:** 1926. **Season:** Year-round. **Tee times:** Call golf shop. **Miscellaneous:** Reduced fees (seniors, juniors), credit cards (MC, V), BF, FF.

★★½ TAMER WIN GOLF & COUNTRY CLUB
PU-2940 Niles Cortland Rd. NE, Cortland, 44410, Trumbull County, (330)637-2881, 20 miles from Youngstown. **E-mail:** twgolf2881@aol.com. **Facility Holes:** 18. **Yards:** 6,275/5,623. **Par:** 71/74. **Course Rating:** 70.0/71.6. **Slope:** 114/116. **Green Fee:** $19/$21. **Cart Fee:** $10/Person. **Walking Policy:** Unrestricted walking. **Walkability:** 3. **Opened:** 1961. **Architect:** Charles E. Winch. **Season:** April-Nov. **High:** June-Aug. **To obtain tee times:** Call up to 365 days in advance. **Miscellaneous:** Reduced fees (seniors, juniors), credit cards (MC, V, AE, D), BF, FF.

★★ TANGLEWOOD GOLF CLUB
PU-1086 Cheshire Rd., Delaware, 43015, Delaware County, (740)548-6715, 10 miles from Columbus. **E-mail:** jscott@midohio.net. **Web:** www.midohio.net/tanglewood. **Facility Holes:** 18. **Yards:** 6,950/6,300. **Par:** 72/72. **Course Rating:** 69.0/69.0. **Slope:** 113/113. **Green Fee:** $22/$25. **Cart Fee:** $10/Person. **Walking Policy:** Walking at certain times. **Walkability:** 1. **Opened:** 1967. **Architect:** Jack Kidwell. **Season:** March-Dec. **To obtain tee times:** Call up to 7 days in advance. **Miscellaneous:** Reduced fees (weekdays), metal spikes, range (grass), credit cards (MC, V), FF.

TANGLEWOOD GOLF COURSE
SP-9802 Dowling Rd., Perrysburg, 43551, Wood County, (419)833-1725, 12 miles from Toledo. **Facility Holes:** 18. **Yards:** 5,822/4,599. **Par:** 72/72. **Course Rating:** 65.7/64.0. **Slope:** 99/95. **Green Fee:** $13/$15. **Cart Fee:** $18/Cart. **Walking Policy:** Unrestricted walking. **Walkability:** 1. **Opened:** 1950. **Architect:** Richard Wyckoff. **Season:** April-Nov. **High:** May-Sept. **To obtain tee times:** Call golf shop. **Miscellaneous:** Reduced fees (seniors).

★★★½ TANNENHAUF GOLF CLUB
PU-11411 McCallum Ave., Alliance, 44601, Stark County, (330)823-4402, (800)533-5140, 10 miles from Canton. **E-mail:** tanenhauf@bright.net. **Web:** www.tannenhaufgolf.com. **Facility Holes:** 18. **Yards:** 6,694/4,763. **Par:** 72/72. **Course Rating:** 71.3/66.1. **Slope:** 121/109. **Green Fee:** $18/$28. **Cart Fee:** $10/Person. **Walking Policy:** Unrestricted walking. **Walkability:** 2. **Opened:** 1959. **Architect:** James G. Harrison/Fred Garvin. **Season:** Year-round. **High:** May-Oct. **To obtain tee times:** Call golf shop. **Miscellaneous:** Reduced fees (weekdays, twilight, seniors, juniors), range (grass), credit cards (MC, V, AE, D), BF, FF.
Reader Comments: More challenging than it appears … Must use short woods or long irons off most tees … Well maintained … A hidden gem.

★★ THORN APPLE COUNTRY CLUB
SP-1051 Alton Darby Creek Rd., Galloway, 43119, Franklin County, (614)878-7703, 10 miles from Columbus. **Facility Holes:** 18. **Yards:** 7,037/5,901. **Par:** 72/74. **Course Rating:** 72.6/71.7. **Slope:** 116/115. **Green Fee:** $17/$20. **Cart Fee:** $20/Cart. **Walking Policy:** Unrestricted walking. **Walkability:** 2. **Opened:** 1966. **Architect:** Jack Kidwell. **Season:** Year-round. **High:** April-Oct. **To obtain tee times:** Call up to 7 days in advance. **Miscellaneous:** Reduced fees (twilight), metal spikes, credit cards (MC, V).

THUNDERBIRD HILLS GOLF CLUB
PU-1316 Mudbrook Rd., SR 13, Huron, 44839, Erie County, (419)433-4552, 40 miles from Cleveland. **E-mail:** golfinc@aolcom. **Web:** thunderbirdhills.com. **Facility Holes:** 36. **Cart Fee:** $12/Person. **Walkability:** 3. **Architect:** Bruce Palmer. **To obtain tee times:** Call golf shop. **Miscellaneous:** Reduced fees (weekdays, twilight, seniors, juniors), metal spikes, range (mats), credit cards (MC, V, D), BF, FF.

★★★★ NORTH COURSE (18)
Yards: 6,464/5,993. **Par:** 72/74. **Course Rating:** 70.3/74.0. **Slope:** 109/121. **Green Fee:** $19/$21. **Walking Policy:** Unrestricted walking. **Opened:** 1960. **Season:** Year-round.
Reader Comments: Lots of water, blind shots, a course to talk about … The old course is great fun to play, scenic, nicely maintained and a good value … Too many golfers … Great pro shop … A bit short by today's standards … I like the South better but both are good value … All different type holes … Well maintained, challenging and fair priced.

★★★ SOUTH COURSE (18)
Yards: 6,235/4,660. **Par:** 72/72. **Course Rating:** 68.9/65.6. **Slope:** 114/103. **Green Fee:** $20/$23. **Walking Policy:** Walking at certain times. **Opened:** 1995. **Season:** April-Oct.
Reader Comments: Short course, but nice … Trees need to fill in … Wind can be problematic.

TIMBERVIEW GOLF CLUB
PU-1107 London Ave., Marysville, 43040, Union County, (937)644-4653, (800)833-4887, 30 miles from Columbus. **Facility Holes:** 18. **Yards:** 6,202/5,073. **Par:** 71/71. **Course Rating:** 69.1/67.9. **Slope:** 111/109. **Green Fee:** $15/$20. **Cart Fee:** $8/Person. **Walking Policy:** Unrestricted walking. **Walkability:** 1. **Opened:** 1989. **Architect:** Bob Lewis. **Season:** Year-round. **To obtain tee times:** Call up to 7 days in advance. **Miscellaneous:** Reduced fees (weekdays, twilight, seniors), range (grass), credit cards (MC, V), BF, FF.

★★★ TREE LINKS GOLF COURSE
PU-3482 C.R. 10, Bellefontaine, 43311, Logan County, (937)592-7888, (800)215-7888, 35 miles from Columbus. **Web:** www.treelinks.com. **Facility Holes:** 18. **Yards:** 6,421/4,727. **Par:** 73/73. **Course Rating:** 70.1/66.6. **Slope:** 121/115. **Green Fee:** $16/$23. **Cart Fee:** Included in green fee. **Walking Policy:** Unrestricted walking. **Walkability:** 5. **Opened:** 1992. **Season:** Year-round. **To obtain tee times:** Call up to 7 days in advance. **Miscellaneous:** Reduced fees (weekdays, seniors), range (grass), credit cards (MC, V), BF, FF.
Reader Comments: Short and scenic … Hit lots of irons … Improves each year … Many blind holes, interesting, elevation changes … Challenging design, needs cart paths paved … No clubhouse.

★★★½ TURKEYFOOT LAKE GOLF LINKS
PU-294 W. Turkeyfoot Lake Rd., Akron, 44319, Summit County, (330)644-5971, (800)281-4484, 5 miles from Akron. **E-mail:** tykgolf@aol. **Facility Holes:** 27. **Green Fee:** $16/$28. **Cart Fee:** $22/Cart. **Walking Policy:** Unrestricted walking. **Walkability:** 3. **Opened:** 1925. **Architect:** Harry Smith. **Season:** March-Dec. **To obtain tee times:** Call golf shop. **Miscellaneous:** Reduced fees (weekdays, seniors, juniors), BF, FF.

FIRST/SECOND (18 Combo)
Yards: 6,168/5,190. **Par:** 71/72. **Course Rating:** 70.0/68.4. **Slope:** 116/111.

FIRST/THIRD (18 Combo)
Yards: 5,452/4,678. **Par:** 71/72. **Course Rating:** 66.8/61.3. **Slope:** 116/111.

SECOND/THIRD (18 Combo)
Yards: 5,122/4,322. **Par:** 70/70. **Course Rating:** 65.0/65.1. **Slope:** 116/111.
Reader Comments: Very sandy … Need local knowledge … Lots of distractions on lake 9—including boats and bikinis … Nice course … Fastest greens in the area.

★★★ TURNBERRY GOLF COURSE
PU-1145 Clubhouse Rd., Pickerington, 43147, Fairfield County, (614)645-2582, 12 miles from Columbus. **Facility Holes:** 18. **Yards:** 6,757/5,440. **Par:** 72/73. **Course Rating:** 71.1/68.8. **Slope:** 114/110. **Green Fee:** $22/$27. **Cart Fee:** $11/Person. **Walking Policy:** Walking at certain times. **Walkability:** 3. **Opened:** 1991. **Architect:** Arthur Hills. **Season:** Year-round. **High:** May-Sept. **To obtain tee times:** Call golf shop. **Miscellaneous:** Reduced fees (weekdays, twilight, seniors, juniors), range (grass), credit cards (MC, V), BF, FF.
Reader Comments: Usually in good shape … Long if the wind blows … Links course, nice finishing holes … Service is solid if not spectacular … Too tricked up.

OHIO

★★ **TWIN LAKES GOLF COURSE**
SP-2220 Marion Ave. Rd., Mansfield, 44903-9411, Richland County, (419)529-3777, 2 miles from Mansfield. **Facility Holes:** 18. **Yards:** 6,343/5,843. **Par:** 71/75. **Course Rating:** 70.0/69.8. **Green Fee:** $15/$18. **Cart Fee:** $11/Person. **Walking Policy:** Unrestricted walking. **Walkability:** 3. **Opened:** 1960. **Architect:** Jack Kidwell. **Season:** March-Nov. **High:** May-Sept. **To obtain tee times:** Call golf shop. **Miscellaneous:** Reduced fees (weekdays, twilight, seniors, juniors), credit cards (MC, V), BF, FF.

★★ **TWIN RUN GOLF COURSE**
PU-2505 Eaton Rd., Hamilton, 45013, Butler County, (513)868-5833, 15 miles from Cincinnati. **E-mail:** jdsmall726@aolcom. **Facility Holes:** 18. **Yards:** 6,561/5,391. **Par:** 72/74. **Course Rating:** 71.3/69.9. **Slope:** 123/112. **Green Fee:** $18. **Cart Fee:** $11/Person. **Walking Policy:** Unrestricted walking. **Walkability:** 3. **Opened:** 1963. **Architect:** William H. Diddel. **Season:** March-Dec. **High:** March-Oct. **To obtain tee times:** Call golf shop. **Miscellaneous:** Reduced fees (seniors, juniors), range (grass), credit cards (MC, V), BF, FF.

UPPER LANSDOWNE GOLF LINKS
PU-17565 Winchester Rd., Ashville, 43103, Pickaway County, (740)983-2989, (800)858-2989, 25 miles from Columbus. **Facility Holes:** 18. **Yards:** 6,691/4,979. **Par:** 72/72. **Course Rating:** 70.8. **Slope:** 114. **Green Fee:** $14/$17. **Cart Fee:** $10/Person. **Walking Policy:** Unrestricted walking. **Walkability:** 3. **Opened:** 1964. **Architect:** Jack Kidwell. **Season:** March-Nov. **High:** April-Oct. **To obtain tee times:** Call up to 7 days in advance. **Miscellaneous:** Range (grass), credit cards (MC, V).

VALLEAIRE GOLF CLUB
SP-6969 Boston Rd., Hinckley, 44233, Medina County, (440)237-9191, 20 miles from Cleveland. **Facility Holes:** 18. **Yards:** 6,442/5,552. **Par:** 72/72. **Course Rating:** 70.2/70.9. **Slope:** 117/116. **Green Fee:** $13/$25. **Cart Fee:** $11/Person. **Walking Policy:** Walking at certain times. **Walkability:** 2. **Season:** April-Dec. **High:** June-Sept. **To obtain tee times:** Call golf shop. **Miscellaneous:** Reduced fees (seniors, juniors), credit cards (MC, V), FF.

★★★½ **VALLEY VIEW GOLF CLUB**
PU-1212 Cuyahoga St., Akron, 44313, Summit County, (330)928-9034. **Facility Holes:** 27. **Green Fee:** $22/$24. **Cart Fee:** $18/Cart. **Walking Policy:** Unrestricted walking. **Walkability:** 2. **Opened:** 1958. **Architect:** Carl Springer. **Season:** March-Dec. **High:** May-Oct. **To obtain tee times:** Call up to 7 days in advance. **Miscellaneous:** Reduced fees (weekdays, seniors), FF.
RIVER/LAKES (18 Combo)
Yards: 6,183/5,277. **Par:** 72/72. **Course Rating:** 68.2/68.7. **Slope:** 111/115.
VALLEY/LAKES (18 Combo)
Yards: 6,168/5,464. **Par:** 72/72. **Course Rating:** 68.2/69.3. **Slope:** 109/112.
VALLEY/RIVER (18 Combo)
Yards: 6,293/5,327. **Par:** 72/72. **Course Rating:** 68.7/69.2. **Slope:** 111/114.
Reader Comments: Unbelievable views ... Good variety of holes ... An easy course ...Well-kept secret ... Lakes & River 9s better than the Valley 9.

VALLEY VIEW GOLF CLUB
PU-2106 State Rte. 598, Galion, 44833, Crawford County, (419)468-1226. **Facility Holes:** 18. **Yards:** 6,514/4,819. **Par:** 72/72. **Slope:** 113. **Green Fee:** $12/$13. **Cart Fee:** $20/Cart. **Opened:** 1964. **Architect:** Lee Stuckman. **Season:** March-Nov. **To obtain tee times:** Call golf shop. **Miscellaneous:** Reduced fees (seniors, juniors), range (grass/mats), credit cards (MC, V).

★★½ **VALLEY VIEW GOLF COURSE**
PU-1401 George Rd., Lancaster, 43130, Fairfield County, (740)687-1112, (800)281-7305, 20 miles from Columbus. **Facility Holes:** 18. **Yards:** 6,400/5,706. **Par:** 71/74. **Course Rating:** 68.9. **Slope:** 117/114. **Green Fee:** $17/$19. **Cart Fee:** $22/Cart. **Walking Policy:** Unrestricted walking. **Walkability:** 3. **Opened:** 1956. **Architect:** Bill George. **Season:** Year-round. **High:** April-Oct. **To obtain tee times:** Call golf shop. **Miscellaneous:** Reduced fees (weekdays, twilight, seniors, juniors), credit cards (MC, V), BF, FF.

★★★½ **VALLEYWOOD GOLF CLUB**
SP-13502 Airport Hwy., Swanton, 43558, Lucas County, (419)826-3991, 15 miles from Toledo. **Facility Holes:** 18. **Yards:** 6,364/5,588. **Par:** 71/73. **Course Rating:** 69.6/71.6. **Slope:** 115/121. **Green Fee:** $20/$24. **Cart Fee:** $11/Person. **Walking Policy:** Unrestricted walking. **Walkability:** 3. **Opened:** 1929. **Season:** Feb.-Dec. **High:** April-Nov. **To obtain tee times:** Call golf shop. **Miscellaneous:** Reduced fees (seniors), range (grass), credit cards (MC, V, D), BF, FF.
Reader Comments: Nothing to get excited about, but a decent course ... Plays tougher than rating ... Greens are small and fast.

OHIO

VETERANS MEMORIAL PARK GOLF COURSE
PU-15906 SR 309 E., Kenton, 43326, Hardin County, (419)674-4573, 60 miles from Columbus. **Facility Holes:** 18. **Yards:** 6,315/4,712. **Par:** 72/72. **Course Rating:** 69.7/66.2. **Slope:** 116/107. **Green Fee:** $16. **Cart Fee:** $12/Person. **Walking Policy:** Unrestricted walking. **Walkability:** 3. **Season:** March-Nov. **High:** June-Sept. **To obtain tee times:** Call up to 3 days in advance. **Miscellaneous:** Reduced fees (juniors), credit cards (MC, V), BF, FF.

VILLAGE GREEN GOLF COURSE
PU-Lake Rd. & Rte. 193, North Kingsville, 44068, Ashtabula County, (440)224-0931, 50 miles from Erie. **Facility Holes:** 18. **Yards:** 6,600/5,645. **Par:** 71/71. **Course Rating:** 71.0. **Slope:** 112. **Green Fee:** $13/$17. **Cart Fee:** $25/Person. **Walking Policy:** Unrestricted walking. **Walkability:** 3. **Season:** April-Nov. **Tee times:** Call golf shop. **Misc:** Reduced fees (twilight, seniors).

VILLAGE VIEW GOLF COURSE
PU-210 S. Main St., Croton, 43013, Licking County, (740)893-4653, 25 miles from Columbus. **Facility Holes:** 18. **Yards:** 6,544/5,427. **Par:** 73/73. **Green Fee:** $18/$24. **Cart Fee:** Included in green fee. **Walking Policy:** Unrestricted walking. **Walkability:** 2. **Opened:** 1993. **Architect:** Harold Compton. **Season:** Year-round. **To obtain tee times:** Call golf shop. **Miscellaneous:** Reduced fees (seniors), range (grass), credit cards (MC, V, AE).

★★★★ THE VINEYARD GOLF COURSE
PU-600 Nordyke Rd., Cincinnati, 45255, Hamilton County, (513)474-3007, 10 miles from Cincinnati. **E-mail:** sdanker@greatparks.org. **Web:** greatparks.org. **Facility Holes:** 18. **Yards:** 6,789/4,747. **Par:** 71/71. **Course Rating:** 72.8/65.7. **Slope:** 132/113. **Green Fee:** $23/$28. **Cart Fee:** $13/Person. **Walking Policy:** Unrestricted walking. **Walkability:** 3. **Opened:** 1987. **Architect:** Jack Kidwell/Michael Hurdzan. **Season:** March-Nov. **High:** May-Oct. **Tee times:** Call up to 10 days in advance. **Misc:** Reduced fees (seniors, juniors), credit cards (MC, V), BF, FF. **Notes:** Ranked 74th in 1996 America's Top 75 Affordable Courses.
Reader Comments: Multi-level greens place a premium on accuracy ... Hills, trees, rustic setting with a very service-oriented approach ... Every hole has something ... Greens are too tricked up ... Always in good condition, let carts off path ... Always a good day here ... Pace of play is excellent.

VISTA VIEW GOLF COURSE
SP-2300 Vista View Dr., Nashport, 43830, Licking County, (740)453-4758, 4 miles from Zanesville. **Facility Holes:** 18. **Yards:** 6,701/5,079. **Par:** 71/71. **Course Rating:** 72.4/70.3. **Slope:** 113/107. **Green Fee:** $10/$15. **Cart Fee:** $10/Person. **Walking Policy:** Unrestricted walking. **Walkability:** 1. **Opened:** 1974. **Architect:** Jack Kidwell. **Season:** Year-round. **High:** April-Sept. **To obtain tee times:** Call up to 14 days in advance. **Miscellaneous:** Reduced fees (weekdays, twilight, seniors, juniors), range (grass), BF, FF.

WAVERLY GOLF CLUB
SP-973 Golf Course Rd., Waverly, 45690, Pike County, (740)947-7422, 5 miles from Waverly. **Facility Holes:** 18. **Yards:** 6,100/5,159. **Par:** 71/71. **Course Rating:** 68.8/71.4. **Slope:** 114/116. **Green Fee:** $11. **Cart Fee:** $20/Cart. **Walking Policy:** Unrestricted walking. **Walkability:** 2. **Opened:** 1952. **Season:** Feb.-Nov. **High:** July-Aug. **To obtain tee times:** Call golf shop. **Miscellaneous:** Reduced fees (twilight), metal spikes, BF, FF.

WEATHERWAX GOLF COURSE
PU-5401 Mosiman Rd., Middletown, 45042, Butler County, (513)425-7886, 45 miles from Cincinnati. **Facility Holes:** 36. **Green Fee:** $25. **Cart Fee:** $12/Person. **Walking Policy:** Unrestricted walking. **Walkability:** 2. **Opened:** 1972. **Architect:** Arthur Hills. **Season:** Year-round. **High:** May-Oct. **To obtain tee times:** Call up to 7 days in advance. **Miscellaneous:** Reduced fees (seniors, juniors), range (grass), credit cards (MC, V), BF, FF.
★★★★ **VALLEYVIEW/HIGHLANDS COURSE** (18)
Yards: 6,799/5,253. **Par:** 72/72. **Course Rating:** 72.4/68.8. **Slope:** 125/113.
Reader Comments: Wide fairways, big greens ... Fun test ... Can play long, great value ... Very good facilities ... Excellent service.
★★★★ **WOODSIDE/MEADOWS COURSE** (18) *Value*
Yards: 7,189/5,547. **Par:** 72/72. **Course Rating:** 73.8/71.3. **Slope:** 123/114.
Reader Comments: 36 holes of pure golf ... Good for the money ... Great variety of holes and course styles ... Greens very fast, course very challenging ... Everything was wonderful.

WEST'S MOGADORE COUNTRY CLUB
PU-197 N. Cleveland Ave., Mogadore, 44260, Portage County, (330)628-2611, 10 miles from Akron. **Facility Holes:** 18. **Yards:** 5,750/4,705. **Par:** 70/70. **Course Rating:** 65.8/65.3. **Slope:** 108/105. **Green Fee:** $14/$20. **Cart Fee:** $10/Person. **Walking Policy:** Unrestricted walking. **Walkability:** 3. **Opened:** 1950. **Season:** Year-round. **High:** May-Sept. **To obtain tee times:** Call golf shop. **Miscellaneous:** Reduced fees (seniors).

OHIO

★★★★ WESTCHESTER GOLF COURSE
PU-6300 Bent Grass Blvd., Canal Winchester, 43110, Franklin County, (614)834-4653, 12 miles from Columbus. **Facility Holes:** 18. **Yards:** 6,800/5,482. **Par:** 72/72. **Course Rating:** 71.5/70.4. **Slope:** 127/121. **Green Fee:** $25/$41. **Cart Fee:** $9/Person. **Walking Policy:** Walking at certain times. **Walkability:** 3. **Opened:** 1998. **Architect:** Michael Hurdzan/Dana Fry/Bill Kerman. **Season:** Feb.-Dec. **To obtain tee times:** Call up to 7 days in advance. **Miscellaneous:** Reduced fees (twilight, seniors, juniors), range (grass), credit cards (MC, V), BF, FF.
Reader Comments: Nice greens ... Pretty piece of land ... You have to play here ... Lots of trees ... Slightly overpriced ... Need proper clubhouse.

★½ WESTERN ROW GOLF COURSE
PU-7392 Mason-Montgomery Rd., Mason, 45040, Warren County, (513)398-8886, 19 miles from Cincinnati. **Facility Holes:** 18. **Yards:** 6,746/5,701. **Par:** 72/72. **Course Rating:** 71.4/71.2. **Slope:** 121/120. **Green Fee:** $21. **Cart Fee:** $22/Cart. **Walking Policy:** Unrestricted walking. **Walkability:** 1. **Opened:** 1963. **Architect:** William H. Diddel. **Season:** Year-round. **To obtain tee times:** Call golf shop. **Miscellaneous:** Reduced fees (seniors), credit cards (MC, V, D), BF, FF.

WGC GOLF COURSE
SP-944 Country Club Dr., Xenia, 45385, Greene County, (937)372-1202, 10 miles from Dayton. **E-mail:** golfwgc@aol.com. **Web:** daytongolf.com/wgc. **Facility Holes:** 18. **Yards:** 6,565/4,671. **Par:** 71/71. **Course Rating:** 70.3/68.1. **Slope:** 117/112. **Green Fee:** $21/$25. **Cart Fee:** $12/Person. **Walking Policy:** Unrestricted walking. **Walkability:** 3. **Opened:** 1925. **Architect:** MIC. **Season:** Year-round. **High:** May-Oct. **To obtain tee times:** Call up to 7 days in advance. **Miscellaneous:** Reduced fees (weekdays, twilight, seniors, juniors), range (grass/mats), credit cards (MC, V, AE), BF, FF.

★★½ WHETSTONE GOLF CLUB
PU-5211 Marion Mt. Gilead Rd., Caledonia, 43314, Marion County, (740)389-4343, (800)272-3215, 6 miles from Marion. **Web:** whetstonegolf.com. **Facility Holes:** 18. **Yards:** 6,674/5,023. **Par:** 72/72. **Course Rating:** 71.7/73.6. **Slope:** 120/111. **Green Fee:** $17/$20. **Cart Fee:** $11/Person. **Walking Policy:** Unrestricted walking. **Walkability:** 2. **Opened:** 1971. **Architect:** Dick LaConte. **Season:** Year-round. **To obtain tee times:** Call up to 7 days in advance. **Miscellaneous:** Reduced fees (weekdays, twilight, seniors), range (grass), credit cards (MC, V), FF.

WILDFIRE GOLF CLUB
PU-4230 Friendship Dr., New Concord, 43762, Muskingum County, (740)826-7606, 7 miles from Zanesville. **Facility Holes:** 18. **Yards:** 6,000/4,286. **Par:** 71/73. **Course Rating:** 69.0/67.0. **Slope:** 117/108. **Green Fee:** $8/$11. **Cart Fee:** $8/Cart. **Walking Policy:** Unrestricted walking. **Walkability:** 4. **Opened:** 1968. **Season:** Year-round. **High:** May-Aug. **To obtain tee times:** Call golf shop. **Miscellaneous:** Reduced fees (twilight, seniors, juniors).

★★★½ WILKSHIRE GOLF COURSE
PU-10566 Wilkshire Blvd. NE, Bolivar, 44612, Tuscarawas County, (330)874-2525, (800)555-5973, 12 miles from Canton. **Facility Holes:** 18. **Yards:** 6,545/5,042. **Par:** 72/72. **Course Rating:** 70.4/69.5. **Slope:** 114/111. **Green Fee:** $18/$26. **Cart Fee:** $10/Person. **Walking Policy:** Walking at certain times. **Walkability:** 2. **Opened:** 1970. **Architect:** Burkhart/Easterday. **Season:** Year-round. **High:** May-Sept. **Tee times:** Call golf shop. **Misc:** Reduced fees (weekdays), range (grass/mats), credit cards (MC, V, AE, D), BF, FF.
Reader Comments: Better every year ... Narrow fairways ... Very good public course ... Woman friendly layout, well stocked clubhouse ... Sneaky long ... Nice layout along river's edge ... Would play every chance I get.

★½ WILLANDALE GOLF CLUB
PU-2870 Winklepleck Rd., Sugarcreek, 44681, Tuscarawas County, (330)852-4395, 8 miles from New Philadelphia. **Facility Holes:** 18. **Yards:** 6,200/6,006. **Par:** 72/72. **Course Rating:** 67.4/66.4. **Slope:** 107/100. **Green Fee:** $13. **Cart Fee:** $10/Person. **Walking Policy:** Walking at certain times. **Walkability:** 2. **Opened:** 1929. **Season:** Year-round. **High:** June-Sept. **To obtain tee times:** Call up to 2 days in advance. **Miscellaneous:** Reduced fees (weekdays, seniors), range (grass/mats), credit cards (MC, V, Debit card.), BF, FF.

WILLOW CREEK GOLF CLUB
PU-15905 Darrow Rd., Vermilion, 44089, Erie County, (440)967-4101, 40 miles from Cleveland. **Facility Holes:** 18. **Yards:** 6,356/5,419. **Par:** 72/76. **Course Rating:** 68.0/68.0. **Slope:** 108/111. **Green Fee:** $16/$19. **Cart Fee:** $10/Person. **Walking Policy:** Unrestricted walking. **Walkability:** 1. **Opened:** 1948. **Architect:** Dick Palmer. **Season:** March-Dec. **High:** May-Oct. **To obtain tee times:** Call up to 7 days in advance. **Miscellaneous:** Reduced fees (weekdays, seniors), range (grass), credit cards (MC, V), BF, FF.

★★ WILLOW RUN GOLF COURSE
SP-State Rtes. 310 and 161, Alexandria, 43001, Licking County, (740)927-1932. **Facility Holes:** 18. **Yards:** 6,253/5,094. **Par:** 71/73. **Course Rating:** 68.9/69.9. **Slope:** 113/113. **Green Fee:** $14/$18. **Cart Fee:** $10/Person. **Walking Policy:** Unrestricted walking. **Walkability:** 2. **Opened:** 1964. **Architect:** Jack Kidwell. **Season:** Year-round. **High:** April-Oct. **To obtain tee times:** Call up to 7 days in advance. **Miscellaneous:** Reduced fees (weekdays), credit cards (MC, V, AE, D), BF, FF.

★★★★ WINDMILL LAKES GOLF CLUB
PU-6544 SR 14, Ravenna, 44266, Portage County, (330)297-0440, 30 miles from Cleveland. **E-mail:** hpage@windmill-lakes-golf.com. **Facility Holes:** 18. **Yards:** 6,936/5,368. **Par:** 70/70. **Course Rating:** 73.8/70.4. **Slope:** 128/115. **Green Fee:** $23/$49. **Cart Fee:** $10/Person. **Walking Policy:** Walking at certain times. **Walkability:** 1. **Opened:** 1971. **Architect:** Edward Ault Sr. **High:** May-Sept. **To obtain tee times:** Call golf shop. **Miscellaneous:** Reduced fees (twilight, seniors, juniors), range (grass/mats), credit cards (MC, V, D), BF, FF.
Reader Comments: Very long, better bring the ERC II ... Always in great shape, beautiful greens ... Super nice layout ... Pace of play doesn't warrant price ... Better than most private courses ... Incredible pro shop ... No. 1 green looks like a mogul run on a ski slope ... Golf as golf should be ... Five sets of tees ... Excellent test ... Course is always in superb shape.

WINDY HILL GOLF COURSE
PU-6231 Weaver Rd., Conneaut, 44030, Ashtabula County, (440)594-5251, 30 miles from Erie, PA. **E-mail:** windy@suite224.net. **Web:** www.windyhillgolf.com. **Facility Holes:** 18. **Yards:** 6,902/5,399. **Par:** 72/72. **Course Rating:** 72.3/69.6. **Slope:** 119/112. **Green Fee:** $14/$20. **Cart Fee:** $10/Person. **Walking Policy:** Walking at certain times. **Walkability:** 2. **Opened:** 1968. **Season:** Year-round. **High:** May-Oct. **To obtain tee times:** Call golf shop. **Miscellaneous:** Reduced fees (weekdays, seniors, juniors), metal spikes, BF, FF.

★★★ WOODLAND GOLF CLUB
PU-4900 Swisher Rd., Cable, 43009, Champaign County, (937)653-8875, (888)395-2001, 36 miles from Columbus. **Facility Holes:** 18. **Yards:** 6,473/4,886. **Par:** 71/71. **Course Rating:** 70.3/67.7. **Slope:** 123/119. **Green Fee:** $19/$22. **Cart Fee:** $11/Person. **Walking Policy:** Unrestricted walking. **Walkability:** 5. **Opened:** 1972. **Architect:** Jack Kidwell. **Season:** Year-round. **High:** April-Oct. **To obtain tee times:** Call golf shop. **Miscellaneous:** Reduced fees (seniors, juniors), range (grass), credit cards (MC, V, D).
Reader Comments: Hilly, scenic and challenging ... Presents a good variety of shots ... Lots of woods and very nice.

★★½ THE WOODS GOLF CLUB
PU-12083 U.S. 127 S., Van Wert, 45891, Van Wert County, (419)238-0441, 40 miles from Ft. Wayne. **Facility Holes:** 18. **Yards:** 6,775/5,025. **Par:** 72/72. **Course Rating:** 70.4/70.4. **Slope:** 118/116. **Green Fee:** $16/$20. **Cart Fee:** $9/Person. **Walking Policy:** Unrestricted walking. **Walkability:** 1. **Opened:** 1962. **Architect:** William James Spear. **Season:** March-Dec. **To obtain tee times:** Call golf shop. **Miscellaneous:** Reduced fees (seniors), range (grass/mats), credit cards (MC, V), BF, FF.

WOODY RIDGE GOLF COURSE
SP-6362 Rte. 598, Shelby, 44875, Crawford County, (419)347-1588, 75 miles from Columbus. **Facility Holes:** 18. **Yards:** 6,180/5,010. **Par:** 72/72. **Green Fee:** $12/$15. **Cart Fee:** $20/Cart. **Walking Policy:** Unrestricted walking. **Walkability:** 1. **Opened:** 1968. **Season:** March-Nov. **High:** March-Nov. **To obtain tee times:** Call golf shop. **Miscellaneous:** Reduced fees (seniors), range (grass), credit cards (MC, V).

★★ WOOLDRIDGE WOODS GOLF AND SWIM CLUB
SP-1313 S. Main St., Mansfield, 44907, Richland County, (419)756-1026, 60 miles from Columbus. **Facility Holes:** 18. **Yards:** 5,963/5,089. **Par:** 71/71. **Course Rating:** 67.2/68.4. **Slope:** 105/105. **Green Fee:** $14/$17. **Cart Fee:** $10/Person. **Walking Policy:** Unrestricted walking. **Walkability:** 3. **Opened:** 1924. **Season:** Year-round. **High:** June-Aug. **To obtain tee times:** Call golf shop. **Miscellaneous:** Reduced fees (weekdays, twilight, seniors, juniors), metal spikes, range (grass/mats), credit cards (MC, V).

WOUSSICKETT GOLF COURSE
PU-6311 Mason Rd., Sandusky, 44870, Erie County, (419)359-1141, (800)950-4766, 60 miles from Cleveland. **Web:** www.greenhillsgolf.com. **Facility Holes:** 18. **Yards:** 5,992/4,916. **Par:** 70/71. **Course Rating:** 66.6/67.6. **Slope:** 98/101. **Green Fee:** $9/$22. **Cart Fee:** $20/Cart. **Walking Policy:** Walking at certain times. **Walkability:** 3. **Opened:** 1984. **Architect:** T.Crockett/B.Crockett. **Season:** March-Dec. **High:** June-Aug. **Tee times:** Call up to 7 days in advance. **Misc:** Reduced fees (weekdays), range (grass), credit cards (MC, V, D), BF, FF.

OHIO

★½ WYANDOT GOLF COURSE
SP-3032 Columbus Rd., Centerburg, 43011, Knox County, (740)625-5370, (800)986-4653, 25 miles from Columbus. **Facility Holes:** 18. **Yards:** 6,422/5,486. **Par:** 72/72. **Course Rating:** 68.4/70.3. **Slope:** 113/115. **Green Fee:** $14/$19. **Cart Fee:** $11/Person. **Walking Policy:** Unrestricted walking. **Walkability:** 1. **Opened:** 1978. **Architect:** Noah Salyers. **Season:** Year-round. **High:** April-Oct. **To obtain tee times:** Call golf shop. **Miscellaneous:** Reduced fees (weekdays, seniors), metal spikes, credit cards (MC, V, AE, D).

★★★★½ YANKEE RUN GOLF COURSE *Service*
PU-7610 Warren Sharon Rd., Brookfield, 44403, Trumbull County, (330)448-8096, (800)446-5346, 60 miles from Pittsburgh, PA. **E-mail:** kmcmul3492.com. **Web:** www.yankeerun.com. **Facility Holes:** 18. **Yards:** 6,501/5,140. **Par:** 70/73. **Course Rating:** 70.7/69.0. **Slope:** 119/109. **Green Fee:** $25/$30. **Cart Fee:** $10/Person. **Walking Policy:** Unrestricted walking. **Walkability:** 4. **Opened:** 1931. **Architect:** Bill Jones/Jerry Mathews. **Season:** March-Dec. **High:** May-Oct. **To obtain tee times:** Call golf shop. **Miscellaneous:** Reduced fees (weekdays, seniors, juniors), credit cards (MC, V, AE, D), FF.
Reader Comments: Need every club in your bag ... Best surprise this year, a thoroughly enjoyable day ... Stay below the hole ... Short but tough! ... Fast paced course up and down tees to greens ... Great practice facility.

★★★½ ZOAR VILLAGE GOLF CLUB
PU-P.O. Box 647, Zoar, 44697, Tuscarawas County, (330)874-4653, (888)874-4654, 1 mile from Zoar. **Facility Holes:** 18. **Yards:** 6,585/5,235. **Par:** 72/72. **Course Rating:** 70.7/69.7. **Slope:** 117/115. **Green Fee:** $22/$26. **Cart Fee:** $10/Cart. **Walking Policy:** Walking at certain times. **Walkability:** 2. **Opened:** 1975. **Architect:** Geoffrey Cornish. **Season:** Year-round. **High:** May-Sept. **To obtain tee times:** Call golf shop. **Miscellaneous:** Reduced fees (weekdays, seniors), range (grass), credit cards (MC, V), BF, FF.
Reader Comments: Must visit Zoar Tavern 1/4 mile up the road after your round ... Good greens, subtle breaks, wide open ... The Pro Football Hall of Fame is only 20 minutes away ... Very nice ... This one you gotta play, large greens, very nice.

★★ ADAMS MUNICIPAL GOLF COURSE
PU-5801 E. Tuxedo Blvd., Bartlesville, 74006, Washington County, 9183313900, 45 miles from Tulsa. **Facility Holes:** 18. **Yards:** 6,819/5,655. **Par:** 72/74. **Course Rating:** 72.0/71.8. **Slope:** 119/117. **Green Fee:** $16/$17. **Cart Fee:** $16/Cart. **Walking Policy:** Unrestricted walking. **Opened:** 1963. **Architect:** Floyd Farley. **Season:** Year-round. **High:** March-Oct. **To obtain tee times:** Call golf shop. **Miscellaneous:** Reduced fees (weekdays, twilight, seniors, juniors), range (grass), BF, FF.

ALVA GOLF & COUNTRY CLUB
SP-P.O. Box 42, Alva, 73717, Woods County, (580)327-2296, 85 miles from Ponca City. **Facility Holes:** 18. **Yards:** 7,036/5,734. **Par:** 72/72. **Course Rating:** 68.0/71.0. **Slope:** 118/118. **Green Fee:** $11/$21. **Cart Fee:** $15/Cart. **Walking Policy:** Unrestricted walking. **Walkability:** 3. **Opened:** 1957. **Architect:** Floyd Farley. **Season:** Year-round. **High:** April-July. **To obtain tee times:** Call golf shop. **Miscellaneous:** Reduced fees (weekdays), range (grass), BF, FF.

★★★ ARROWHEAD GOLF COURSE
PU-HC-67, Box 6, Canadian, 74425, Pittsburg County, (918)339-2769, (866)602-4653, 20 miles from McAlester. **Facility Holes:** 18. **Yards:** 6,741/5,342. **Par:** 72/75. **Course Rating:** 71.4/70.7. **Slope:** 119/126. **Green Fee:** $9/$15. **Cart Fee:** $18/Person. **Walking Policy:** Unrestricted walking. **Walkability:** 2. **Opened:** 1965. **Architect:** Floyd Farley. **Season:** Year-round. **High:** March-Oct. **To obtain tee times:** Call up to 7 days in advance. **Miscellaneous:** Reduced fees (weekdays, twilight, seniors, juniors), range (grass), credit cards (MC, V, AE, D), BF, FF.
Reader Comments: Great course in the trees with wonderful views of the lake ... Lots of doglegs ... One weird par 5 ... Good greens, nice fairways ... Worth a round.

ATOKA TRAILS GOLF CLUB
PU-220 City Lake Rd., Atoka, 74525, Atoka County, (580)889-7171, 2 miles from Atoka. **E-mail:** dcochran@oio.net. **Facility Holes:** 9. **Yards:** 6,233/2,479. **Par:** 72/72. **Course Rating:** 68.5/68.5. **Slope:** 109/109. **Green Fee:** $7/$14. **Cart Fee:** $16/Cart. **Walking Policy:** Unrestricted walking. **Walkability:** 3. **Opened:** 1971. **Architect:** Floyd Farley. **Season:** Year-round. **High:** March-Sept. **To obtain tee times:** Call golf shop. **Miscellaneous:** Reduced fees (twilight), BF, FF.

★★★½ BAILEY RANCH GOLF CLUB
PU-10105 Larkin Bailey Blvd., Owasso, 74055, Tulsa County, (918)274-4653, 8 miles from Tulsa. **Facility Holes:** 18. **Yards:** 6,753/4,898. **Par:** 72/72. **Course Rating:** 73.1/68.4. **Slope:** 132/115. **Green Fee:** $15/$23. **Cart Fee:** $10/Person. **Walking Policy:** Walking at certain times. **Walkability:** 3. **Opened:** 1993. **Architect:** Bland Pittman. **Season:** Year-round. **High:** April-Oct. **To obtain tee times:** Call golf shop. **Miscellaneous:** Reduced fees (weekdays, twilight, seniors, juniors), range (grass), credit cards (MC, V, AE, D).
Reader Comments: Good value and seldom crowded ... The most fun golf in Oklahoma, especially finishing holes along the water ... Best value around ... Long walks from green to next tee ... Good links-style course.

★★★ BATTLE CREEK GOLF CLUB
PU-3200 N. Battle Creek Dr., Broken Arrow, 74012, Tulsa County, (918)259-8633, 5 miles from Tulsa. **Facility Holes:** 18. **Yards:** 7,273/5,580. **Par:** 72/72. **Course Rating:** 76.4/69.8. **Slope:** 130/118. **Green Fee:** $17/$46. **Cart Fee:** $11/Person. **Walking Policy:** Walking at certain times. **Walkability:** 5. **Opened:** 1997. **Architect:** Bland Pittman. **Season:** Year-round. **High:** April-Oct. **To obtain tee times:** Call golf shop. **Miscellaneous:** Reduced fees (weekdays, guests, twilight, seniors, juniors), range (grass), credit cards (MC, V, AE, D).
Reader Comments: Must keep the ball in play here ... Course is easy to walk and fun to ride ... Skyline views of Tulsa from clubhouse and course ... Needs some maturity.

BLACKWELL GOLF COURSE
PU-333 Country Club Lane, Blackwell, 74631, Kay County, (580)363-1228, 17 miles from Ponca City. **Facility Holes:** 9. **Yards:** 6,273/5,297. **Par:** 71/71. **Course Rating:** 69.8/68.1. **Slope:** 106/99. **Green Fee:** $8/$12. **Cart Fee:** $16/Cart. **Walking Policy:** Unrestricted walking. **Walkability:** 2. **Opened:** 1939. **Architect:** Perry Maxwell. **Season:** Year-round. **High:** June-Oct. **To obtain tee times:** Call golf shop. **Miscellaneous:** Reduced fees (twilight, juniors), range (grass), credit cards (MC, V, AE, D), BF, FF.

★★★½ BOILING SPRINGS GOLF CLUB
PU-R.R. 2 Box 204-1A, Woodward, 73801, Woodward County, (580)256-1206, 130 miles from Oklahoma City. **Facility Holes:** 18. **Yards:** 6,511/4,944. **Par:** 71/75. **Course Rating:** 71.3/68.6. **Slope:** 120/117. **Green Fee:** $12/$25. **Cart Fee:** $15/Person. **Walking Policy:** Unrestricted walking. **Walkability:** 4. **Opened:** 1979. **Architect:** Don Sechrest. **Season:** Year-

round. **High:** April-Oct. **To obtain tee times:** Call golf shop. **Miscellaneous:** Reduced fees (weekdays, seniors, juniors), range (grass), credit cards (MC, V, AE, D).

Reader Comments: Elevation changes in Oklahoma, go figure … Tight … Wonderful layout, challenging short course … Bring your irons … Good golf at a small price.

BRENT BRUEHL MEMORIAL GOLF COURSE
PU-1400 Chandler Rd., Purcell, 73080, McClain County, (405)527-5114, 30 miles from Oklahoma City. **E-mail:** pgca@telepath.com. **Facility Holes:** 18. **Yards:** 6,318/5,234. **Par:** 71/71. **Course Rating:** 70.1/69.8. **Slope:** 119/114. **Green Fee:** $16. **Cart Fee:** $20/Cart. **Walking Policy:** Walking at certain times. **Walkability:** 3. **Opened:** 1995. **Architect:** Mike Gowens. **Season:** Year-round. **To obtain tee times:** Call golf shop. **Miscellaneous:** Reduced fees (twilight, seniors, juniors), range (grass), credit cards (MC, V), BF, FF.

BRISTOW COUNTRY CLUB
SP-Country Club Dr., Bristow, 74010, Creek County, (918)367-5156, 30 miles from Tulsa. **Facility Holes:** 9. **Yards:** 6,247/5,343. **Par:** 72/73. **Course Rating:** 68.6/70.8. **Slope:** 111/122. **Green Fee:** $10/$14. **Cart Fee:** $18/Cart. **Walking Policy:** Unrestricted walking. **Walkability:** 3. **Season:** Year-round. **High:** May-Sept. **To obtain tee times:** Call golf shop. **Miscellaneous:** Reduced fees (weekdays, twilight), range (grass), credit cards (MC, V, D).

BROADMOORE GOLF COURSE
PU-500 Willow Pine Dr., Oklahoma City, 73160, Oklahoma County, (405)794-1529. **Facility Holes:** 18. **Yards:** 6,514/5,623. **Par:** 71/73. **Green Fee:** $14/$16. **Cart Fee:** $18/Cart. **Walking Policy:** Unrestricted walking. **Walkability:** 2. **Opened:** 1960. **Architect:** Duffy Martin. **Season:** Year-round. **To obtain tee times:** Call golf shop. **Miscellaneous:** Metal spikes, credit cards (MC, V).

BROOKSIDE GOLF COURSE
PU-9016 S. Shields, Oklahoma City, 73160, Oklahoma County, (405)632-9666. **Facility Holes:** 9. **Yards:** 3,005. **Par:** 35/38. **Green Fee:** $10/$11. **Cart Fee:** $17/Cart. **Walking Policy:** Unrestricted walking. **Walkability:** 1. **Opened:** 1954. **Architect:** Duffy Martin. **Season:** Year-round. **High:** April-Nov. **To obtain tee times:** Call golf shop. **Miscellaneous:** Reduced fees (weekdays, twilight, seniors), range (grass), credit cards (MC, V).

★★★★½ CEDAR CREEK GOLF COURSE
R-P.O. Box 10, Broken Bow, 74728, McCurtain County, (580)494-6456, 60 miles from Paris, TX. **Facility Holes:** 18. **Yards:** 6,724/5,762. **Par:** 72/72. **Course Rating:** 72.1. **Slope:** 132. **Green Fee:** $15/$20. **Cart Fee:** $9/Person. **Walking Policy:** Unrestricted walking. **Walkability:** 5. **Opened:** 1975. **Architect:** Floyd Farley/Art Proctor. **Season:** Year-round. **High:** June-Sept. **To obtain tee times:** Call up to 60 days in advance. **Miscellaneous:** Reduced fees (weekdays, guests, twilight, seniors, juniors), range (grass), credit cards (MC, V, AE, D), BF, FF.

Reader Comments: Scenic, hidden secret … Stay below the hole on sharply sloping greens … View across lake on No. 16 is memorable.

CEDAR LAKES GOLF COURSE
M-4746 Monrovia St., Fort Sill, 73503, Comanche County, (580)442-3875, 15 miles from Lawton. **Facility Holes:** 18. **Yards:** 6,725/5,477. **Par:** 72/72. **Course Rating:** 71.8/71.1. **Slope:** 123/123. **Green Fee:** $12/$18. **Walkability:** 4. **Opened:** 1954. **To obtain tee times:** Call golf shop. **Miscellaneous:** Reduced fees (weekdays).
Special Notes: Military personnel only.

CEDAR VALLEY GOLF CLUB
PU-210 Par Ave., Guthrie, 73044, Logan County, (405)282-4800, 25 miles from Oklahoma City. **Facility Holes:** 36. **Green Fee:** $15/$16. **Cart Fee:** $20/Person. **Walking Policy:** Unrestricted walking. **Opened:** 1975. **Architect:** Duffy Martin/Floyd Farley. **Season:** Year-round. **High:** April-Oct. **To obtain tee times:** Call up to 1 day in advance. **Miscellaneous:** Reduced fees (weekdays, twilight, seniors, juniors), range (grass), BF, FF.
★★★½ AUGUSTA COURSE (18)
Yards: 6,602/5,170. **Par:** 70/72. **Course Rating:** 70.3/69.1. **Slope:** 108/114. **Walkability:** 4. **Miscellaneous:** Credit cards (MC, V, AE, D).
Reader Comments: Friendly pro shop … Many excellent golf holes … Friendly- fast play … Fairways in need of work.
★★½ INTERNATIONAL COURSE (18)
Yards: 6,520/4,955. **Par:** 70/72. **Course Rating:** 71.1/68.4. **Slope:** 112/115. **Walkability:** 3. **Miscellaneous:** Credit cards (MC, V, AE, D, DC).

CHANDLER GOLF COURSE
PU-Rte. 2, Box 1845, Chandler, 74834, Lincoln County, (405)258-3068, 35 miles from Oklahoma City. **Facility Holes:** 9. **Yards:** 6,364/5,026. **Par:** 72/76. **Course Rating:** 69.7/69.7.

Slope: 111/111. Green Fee: $10/$12. Cart Fee: $20/Cart. Walking Policy: Unrestricted walking. Walkability: 5. Opened: 1972. Season: Year-round. High: May-Aug. To obtain tee times: Call golf shop. Miscellaneous: Reduced fees (weekdays, twilight, juniors), range (grass), BF, FF.

CHEROKEE GROVE GOLF CLUB

PU-519 Quail Run Rd., Grove, 74344, Delaware County, (918)786-9852, 45 miles from Joplin. Facility Holes: 9. Yards: 3,240/2,657. Par: 36/36. Course Rating: 70.7/69.2. Slope: 128/109. Green Fee: $18. Cart Fee: $20/Cart. Walking Policy: Unrestricted walking. Walkability: 4. Opened: 1979. Architect: Vince Bizik. Season: Year-round. High: May-Oct. To obtain tee times: Call golf shop. Miscellaneous: Range (grass), credit cards (MC, V), BF, FF.

CHEROKEE TRAILS GOLF COURSE

PU-S. Hwy. 62, Tahlequah, 74465, Cherokee County, (918)458-4294, 60 miles from Tulsa. Facility Holes: 9. Yards: 6,460/5,300. Par: 72/72. Course Rating: 71.2/69.8. Slope: 121/117. Green Fee: $5/$10. Cart Fee: $15/Cart. Walking Policy: Unrestricted walking. Walkability: 1. Opened: 1954. Architect: Amon Baker. Season: Year-round. High: June-Sept. To obtain tee times: Call golf shop. Miscellaneous: Reduced fees (twilight, seniors, juniors), range (grass), credit cards (MC, V).

CHERRY SPRINGS GOLF COURSE

SP-700 E. Balentine Rd., Tahlequah, 74464, Cherokee County, (918)456-5100, 55 miles from Tulsa. E-mail: hcberry@swbell.net. Web: cherry springs.com. Facility Holes: 18. Yards: 6,814/4,950. Par: 72/72. Course Rating: 72.8/63.9. Slope: 127/99. Green Fee: $14/$16. Cart Fee: $20/Cart. Walking Policy: Unrestricted walking. Walkability: 4. Opened: 1989. Architect: Burl Berry. Season: Year-round. High: March-Oct. To obtain tee times: Call golf shop. Miscellaneous: Reduced fees (weekdays, twilight, seniors), range (grass), credit cards (MC, V, AE, D), FF.

★★★★½ CHICKASAW POINT G. CSE. *Service, Value, Condition+, Pace*

PU-P. O. 279, Kingston, 73439, Marshall County, (580)564-2581, (877)242-8040, 4 miles from Kingston. Facility Holes: 18. Yards: 7,085/5,285. Par: 72/72. Course Rating: 74.5/72.2. Slope: 125/126. Green Fee: $35/$60. Cart Fee: Included in green fee. Walking Policy: Unrestricted walking. Walkability: 4. Opened: 1999. Architect: Randy Heckenkemper. Season: Year-round. High: March-Nov. To obtain tee times: Call up to 30 days in advance. Miscellaneous: Reduced fees (weekdays, guests, twilight, seniors, juniors), range (grass), lodging (178 rooms), credit cards (MC, V, AE, D, DC), BF, FF.
Notes: Ranked 4th in 2001 Best in State.
Reader Comments: The state of Oklahoma finally did something right ... Great course, one of top two public courses in Oklahoma ... Great value ... Pretty lakeside location ... A real pleasure to play.

CHOCTAW CREEK GOLF COURSE

PU-2200 N. Hiwassee Rd., Choctaw, 73020, Oklahoma County, (405)769-7166, 8 miles from Oklahoma City. E-mail: grinacres@aol.com. Facility Holes: 18. Yards: 6,625/5,200. Par: 71/74. Course Rating: 70.6/71.1. Slope: 122/123. Green Fee: $9/$15. Cart Fee: $18/Person. Walking Policy: Unrestricted walking. Walkability: 3. Opened: 1989. Architect: Tom Billings. Season: Year-round. High: March-Oct. To obtain tee times: Call up to 7 days in advance. Miscellaneous: Reduced fees (weekdays, twilight, seniors, juniors), range (grass), credit cards (MC, V, D), BF, FF.

CIMARRON NATIONAL GOLF CLUB

PU-500 Duffy's Way, Guthrie, 73044, Logan County, (405)282-7888, 20 miles from Oklahoma City. Facility Holes: 36. Green Fee: $16/$18. Cart Fee: $18/Cart. Architect: Floyd Farley. Season: Year-round. To obtain tee times: Call golf shop. Miscellaneous: Reduced fees (weekdays), range (grass), credit cards (MC, V, AE, D), BF, FF.
★★★ AQUA CANYON COURSE (18)
Yards: 6,415/5,339. Par: 70/71. Course Rating: 69.6/68.2. Slope: 114/110. Walking Policy: Unrestricted walking. Walkability: 4. Opened: 1994.
Reader Comments: Rolling hills on several holes ... One of my favorite places to play ... Medium length with lots of water ... Open course, quite playable ... No bunkers.
★★★ CIMARRON COURSE (18)
Yards: 6,653/5,559. Par: 70/70. Course Rating: 68.1/72.8. Slope: 120/132. Walking Policy: Walking at certain times. Walkability: 5. Opened: 1992.
Reader Comments: Tough, but one of my favorite places to play ... Lots of water and trees ... Beautiful layout, tight fairways ... Lots of fun and a great facility ... Several unfair holes.

CLARY FIELDS GOLF CLUB

PU-9999 S. 49th West Ave, Sapulpa, 74066, Creek County, (918)248-4080, 5 miles from

Tulsa. **Facility Holes:** 18. **Yards:** 6,705/5,064. **Par:** 71/71. **Course Rating:** 72.4/69.2. **Slope:** 118/114. **Green Fee:** $32/$45. **Cart Fee:** Included in green fee. **Walking Policy:** Walking at certain times. **Walkability:** 2. **Opened:** 2000. **Architect:** Tripp Davis. **Season:** Year-round. **High:** April-Nov. **To obtain tee times:** Call up to 7 days in advance. **Miscellaneous:** Reduced fees (twilight, seniors, juniors), range (grass), credit cards (MC, V, AE, D), BF, FF.

★★★½ COFFEE CREEK GOLF COURSE
PU-4000 N. Kelly, Edmond, 73003, Oklahoma County, (405)340-4653, 8 miles from Oklahoma City. **E-mail:** ssmelser@mmcable.com. **Web:** coffeecreekgc.com. **Facility Holes:** 18. **Yards:** 6,700/5,200. **Par:** 70/70. **Course Rating:** 71.5/70.5. **Slope:** 129/122. **Green Fee:** $20/$25. **Cart Fee:** $13/Person. **Walking Policy:** Unrestricted walking. **Walkability:** 3. **Opened:** 1991. **Season:** Year-round. **High:** April-Oct. **To obtain tee times:** Call up to 5 days in advance. **Miscellaneous:** Reduced fees (weekdays, twilight, seniors, juniors), range (grass), credit cards (MC, V, AE, D), BF, FF.
Reader Comments: Excellent course with fast paced play … Add more bunkers … You've got to be an early bird for tee times … Staff was very nice … Back 9 is outstanding … Fairways range from wide open to extremely tight.

COMANCHE GOLF COURSE
PU-HC 64, Comanche, 73529, Stephens County, (580)439-8879, 12 miles from Duncan. **Facility Holes:** 9. **Yards:** 3,056/2,856. **Par:** 36/36. **Walking Policy:** Unrestricted walking. **Walkability:** 3. **Opened:** 1968. **Season:** Year-round. **High:** May-June. **To obtain tee times:** Call golf shop. **Miscellaneous:** Reduced fees (twilight, seniors, juniors).

CRIMSON CREEK GOLF CLUB
PU-800 Babcock Dr., El Reno, 73036, Canadian County, (405)422-4653, 25 miles from Oklahoma City. **E-mail:** dormie1@aol.com. **Web:** www.crimsoncreek.com. **Facility Holes:** 18. **Yards:** 6,992/5,491. **Par:** 72/72. **Course Rating:** 74.2/73.5. **Slope:** 128/132. **Green Fee:** $16/$19. **Cart Fee:** $9/Person. **Walking Policy:** Unrestricted walking. **Walkability:** 4. **Opened:** 1998. **Architect:** P.B. Dye. **Season:** Year-round. **High:** May-Sept. **To obtain tee times:** Call up to 7 days in advance. **Miscellaneous:** Reduced fees (weekdays, twilight, seniors, juniors), range (grass), credit cards (MC, V, AE, D), BF, FF.

CUSHING COUNTRY CLUB
SP-Route 2, SE, Cushing, 74023, Payne County, (918)225-6734, 18 miles from Stillwater. **Facility Holes:** 18. **Yards:** 6,292/5,260. **Par:** 70/70. **Course Rating:** 69.5/68.9. **Slope:** 115/99. **Green Fee:** $21/$35. **Walkability:** 3. **Opened:** 1921. **Architect:** Perry Maxwell. **To obtain tee times:** Call golf shop. **Miscellaneous:** Reduced fees (weekdays).

DIETRICH MEMORIAL GOLF & COUNTRY CLUB
SP-S. Country Club Rd., Anadarko, 73005, Caddo County, (405)247-5075, 60 miles from Oklahoma City. **Facility Holes:** 9. **Yards:** 6,076/5,373. **Par:** 71/71. **Course Rating:** 66.8/69.9. **Slope:** 102/119. **Green Fee:** $7/$13. **Cart Fee:** $10/Cart. **Walking Policy:** Unrestricted walking. **Walkability:** 3. **Opened:** 1947. **Season:** Year-round. **High:** April-July. **To obtain tee times:** Call golf shop. **Miscellaneous:** Reduced fees (weekdays, twilight), range (grass).

DOBY SPRINGS GOLF COURSE
PU-70 Doby Springs Rd., Buffalo, 73834, Harper County, (580)735-2654, 30 miles from Woodward. **Facility Holes:** 9. **Yards:** 3,068/2,465. **Par:** 36/37. **Slope:** 112/108. **Green Fee:** $6. **Walkability:** 2. **Opened:** 1980. **To obtain tee times:** Call golf shop.

DRUMRIGHT GOLF COURSE
PU-Hwy. 33, Drumright, 74030, Payne County, (918)352-9424, 45 miles from Tulsa. **Facility Holes:** 18. **Yards:** 6,545/5,248. **Par:** 72/72. **Course Rating:** 71.5. **Slope:** 123. **Green Fee:** $10/$12. **Cart Fee:** $20/Cart. **Walking Policy:** Unrestricted walking. **Walkability:** 3. **Opened:** 20. **Architect:** Unknown. **Season:** Year-round. **High:** April-Nov. **To obtain tee times:** Call golf shop. **Miscellaneous:** Reduced fees (weekdays, twilight), credit cards (MC, V), BF, FF.

DUNCAN GOLF & COUNTRY CLUB
SP-1800 N. Country Club Rd., Duncan, 73533, Stephens County, (580)255-7706, 70 miles from Oklahoma City. **Facility Holes:** 18. **Yards:** 6,450/5,397. **Par:** 71/71. **Course Rating:** 71.6/71.8. **Slope:** 124/125. **Green Fee:** $20. **Opened:** 1919. **Architect:** Perry Maxwell. **To obtain tee times:** Call golf shop.

EAGLE CREST GOLF COURSE
PU-40th & Border, Muskogee, 74401, Muskogee County, (918)682-0866. **Facility Holes:** 27. **Yards:** 6,506/4,517. **Par:** 72/72. **Course Rating:** 69.7/66.8. **Slope:** 119/112. **Green Fee:** $15/$18. **Cart Fee:** $20/Cart. **Walking Policy:** Unrestricted walking. **Walkability:** 3. **Opened:**

OKLAHOMA

1987. **Season:** Year-round. **High:** April-Nov. **To obtain tee times:** Call golf shop.
Miscellaneous: Reduced fees (weekdays, twilight, seniors, juniors), range (grass), credit cards (MC, V, AE, D).
Special Notes: Also has a 9-hole Village Course.

EARLYWINE PARK GOLF COURSE
PU-11500 S. Portland Ave., Oklahoma City, 73170, Oklahoma County, (405)691-1727.
Facility Holes: 36. **Green Fee:** $16. **Cart Fee:** $19/Person. **Walking Policy:** Unrestricted walking. **Season:** Year-round. **To obtain tee times:** Call golf shop. **Miscellaneous:** Reduced fees (weekdays, twilight, seniors, juniors), range (grass), credit cards (MC, V), BF, FF.
★★★½ **NORTH COURSE** (18)
Yards: 6,721/4,843. **Par:** 72/72. **Course Rating:** 71.9/70.4. **Slope:** 126/122. **Walkability:** 4.
Opened: 1977. **Architect:** Randy Heckenkemper.
Reader Comments: Tight course ... Hole #12 is beautiful ... Better hit it straight, lots of native grass here.
★★½ **SOUTH COURSE** (18)
Yards: 6,505/5,020. **Par:** 70/70. **Course Rating:** 72.5/71.6. **Slope:** 114/117. **Walkability:** 2.
Opened: 1976. **Architect:** Floyd Farley.

★★½ ELK CITY GOLF & COUNTRY CLUB
SP-108 Lakeridge Rd., Elk City, 73644, Beckham County, (405)225-3556, 100 miles from Oklahoma City. **Facility Holes:** 18. **Yards:** 6,090/4,678. **Par:** 71/71. **Course Rating:** 69.4/67.7. **Slope:** 109/114. **Green Fee:** $10/$18. **Cart Fee:** $18/Cart. **Walking Policy:** Unrestricted walking. **Walkability:** 2. **Opened:** 1954. **Architect:** Bob Dunning/Don Sechrest. **Season:** Year-round. **To obtain tee times:** Call golf shop. **Miscellaneous:** Reduced fees (weekdays, twilight), range (grass), credit cards (MC, V, D), BF, FF.

FAIRVIEW LAKESIDE COUNTRY CLUB
SP-Longdale St., Longdale, 73755, Blaine County, (580)227-3225, 55 miles from Oklahoma City. **Facility Holes:** 9. **Yards:** 3,126/2,623. **Par:** 35/35. **Course Rating:** 67.0/67.7. **Green Fee:** $10. **Opened:** 1964. **To obtain tee times:** Call golf shop.

FALCONHEAD RESORT & COUNTRY CLUB
SP-605 Falconhead Dr., Burneyville, 73430, Love County, (580)276-9284, 25 miles from Ardmore. **E-mail:** fpoa@brightok.net. **Web:** www.redriver.net/falconhead. **Facility Holes:** 18. **Yards:** 6,404/5,280. **Par:** 72/71. **Course Rating:** 70.2/70.3. **Slope:** 125/120. **Green Fee:** $26/$35. **Cart Fee:** Included in green fee. **Walking Policy:** Mandatory carts. **Walkability:** 3. **Opened:** 1960. **Architect:** Waco Turner. **Season:** Year-round. **To obtain tee times:** Call golf shop. **Miscellaneous:** Reduced fees (guests, juniors), range (grass), lodging (16 rooms), credit cards (MC, V, AE, D), FF.

★★★ FIRE LAKE GOLF COURSE
PU-1901 S. Gordon Cooper, Shawnee, 74801, Pottawatomie County, (405)275-4471, 30 miles from Oklahoma City. **E-mail:** mwood@potawatomi.org. **Web:** support.potawatomi.org. **Facility Holes:** 18. **Yards:** 6,335/4,992. **Par:** 70/71. **Course Rating:** 69.6. **Slope:** 121. **Green Fee:** $10/$15. **Cart Fee:** $18/Person. **Walking Policy:** Unrestricted walking. **Walkability:** 2. **Opened:** 1982. **Architect:** Don Sechrest. **Season:** Year-round. **High:** March-Nov. **To obtain tee times:** Call up to 7 days in advance. **Miscellaneous:** Reduced fees (twilight, seniors, juniors), range (grass), credit cards (MC, V, D), BF, FF.
Reader Comments: Good value for a very nice course ... Makes you place your shot ... Lots of water.

★★★★½ FOREST RIDGE GOLF CLUB *Condition, Pace*
SP-7501 E. Kenosha, Broken Arrow, 74014, Wagoner County, (918)357-2282, 12 miles from Tulsa. **E-mail:** marketing@forestridge.com. **Web:** www.forestridge.com. **Facility Holes:** 18. **Yards:** 7,069/5,341. **Par:** 71/72. **Course Rating:** 74.8/73.3. **Slope:** 137/132. **Green Fee:** $30/$75. **Cart Fee:** Included in green fee. **Walking Policy:** Unrestricted walking. **Walkability:** 3. **Opened:** 1989. **Architect:** Randy Heckenkemper. **Season:** Year-round. **To obtain tee times:** Call golf shop. **Miscellaneous:** Reduced fees (weekdays, twilight), range (grass), credit cards (MC, V, AE, D), BF, FF.
Notes: Ranked 5th in 2001 Best in State.
Reader Comments: Magnificent course ... Staff is knowledgeable and helpful ... First rate experience ... Best public course in Oklahoma ... Public course that feels like a posh club ... Tight, bring lots of balls ... Must play.

★★★ FORT COBB STATE PARK GOLF COURSE
R-P.O. Box 497, Fort Cobb, 73038, Caddo County, (405)643-2398, 6 miles from Fort Cobb.
Facility Holes: 18. **Yards:** 6,620/5,485. **Par:** 70/71. **Course Rating:** 69.8/74.4. **Slope:** 117/129. **Green Fee:** $14/$16. **Cart Fee:** $9/Person. **Walking Policy:** Unrestricted walking. **Walkability:** 2.

Opened: 1960. **Architect:** Floyd Farley/Don Sechrest. **Season:** Year-round. **High:** May-Sept. **To obtain tee times:** Call golf shop. **Miscellaneous:** Reduced fees (weekdays, twilight, seniors, juniors), range (grass), credit cards (MC, V, AE, D).
Reader Comments: Front 9 is open but back side is tight ... Very scenic course to someone visting the area ... Water holes on back 9.

FORT SILL GOLF CLUB
M-Bldg 1275 Quinette Rd., Fort Sill, 73501, Comanche County, (580)353-0411, 50 miles from Oklahoma City. **Facility Holes:** 18. **Yards:** 6,505/5,197. **Par:** 72/72. **Course Rating:** 71.8/70.6. **Slope:** 128/124. **Green Fee:** $9/$12. **Opened:** 1947. **Architect:** Ralph (Lefty) Mace. **To obtain tee times:** Call golf shop.

★★ FOUNTAINHEAD STATE GOLF COURSE
R-Hwy. 69 W., Checotah, 74426, McIntosh County, (918)689-3209, 60 miles from Tulsa. **E-mail:** fountpro@aol.com. **Facility Holes:** 18. **Yards:** 6,919/4,864. **Par:** 72/72. **Course Rating:** 71.3/67.3. **Slope:** 116/98. **Green Fee:** $7/$15. **Cart Fee:** $9/Cart. **Walking Policy:** Unrestricted walking. **Walkability:** 3. **Opened:** 1964. **Architect:** Floyd Farley. **Season:** Year-round. **High:** March-Oct. **To obtain tee times:** Call golf shop. **Miscellaneous:** Reduced fees (weekdays, twilight, seniors, juniors), range (grass), credit cards (MC, V, AE, D), BF, FF.

GIL MORGAN MUNICIPAL GOLF COURSE
PU-800 E. 7th, Wewoka, 74884, Seminole County, (405)257-3292, 75 miles from Oklahoma City. **Facility Holes:** 9. **Yards:** 6,555/5,400. **Par:** 72/72. **Course Rating:** 69.7/69.5. **Slope:** 112/110. **Green Fee:** $10/$13. **Cart Fee:** $16/Cart. **Walking Policy:** Unrestricted walking. **Walkability:** 5. **Opened:** 1950. **Architect:** Floyd Farley. **Season:** Year-round. **High:** April-Sept. **To obtain tee times:** Call golf shop. **Miscellaneous:** Range (grass), BF, FF.

★½ GLEN EAGLES GOLF COURSE
PU-20239 E. 41st St., Broken Arrow, 74014, Wagoner County, (918)355-4422, 30 miles from Tulsa. **Facility Holes:** 18. **Yards:** 6,909/5,257. **Par:** 72/72. **Course Rating:** 72.2/73.0. **Slope:** 115/116. **Green Fee:** $14/$16. **Cart Fee:** $18/Person. **Walking Policy:** Unrestricted walking. **Walkability:** 2. **Opened:** 1994. **Season:** Year-round. **High:** May-Sept. **To obtain tee times:** Call golf shop. **Miscellaneous:** Reduced fees (seniors, juniors), range (grass/mats), credit cards (MC, V, D).

★★★ THE GOLF CLUB AT CIMARRON TRAILS
PU-1400 Lovers Lane, Perkins, 74059, Payne County, (405)547-5701, 10 miles from Stillwater. **E-mail:** spool@cimarrontrails.com. **Web:** cimarrontrails.com. **Facility Holes:** 18. **Yards:** 6,859/5,128. **Par:** 72/72. **Course Rating:** 74.0/70.0. **Slope:** 125/113. **Green Fee:** $10/$20. **Cart Fee:** $11/Person. **Walking Policy:** Unrestricted walking. **Walkability:** 3. **Opened:** 1994. **Architect:** Kevin Benedict. **Season:** Year-round. **High:** April-Oct. **To obtain tee times:** Call up to 7 days in advance. **Miscellaneous:** Reduced fees (weekdays, twilight, seniors, juniors), range (grass), credit cards (MC, V, AE, D), BF, FF.
Reader Comments: Wonderful, in great shape ... Ego booster with some good holes ... A well-kept secret ... Greens in good shape during hot weather.

GREENS GOLF COURSE
PU-Hwy 44, Burns Flat, 73624, Washita County, (580)562-4354, 90 miles from Oklahoma City. **Facility Holes:** 9. **Yards:** 6,574/5,756. **Par:** 72/74. **Green Fee:** $8/$10. **Cart Fee:** $16/Cart. **Walking Policy:** Unrestricted walking. **Walkability:** 2. **Opened:** 1963. **Season:** Year-round. **High:** March-Oct. **To obtain tee times:** Call golf shop. **Miscellaneous:** Reduced fees (weekdays, seniors, juniors), range (grass), credit cards (MC, V).

HENRIETTA COUNTRY CLUB
SP-Country Club Rd., Henrietta, 74437, Okmulgee County, (918)652-8664, 45 miles from Tulsa. **E-mail:** soonerlan@aol.com. **Facility Holes:** 18. **Yards:** 6,006/5,250. **Par:** 72/73. **Course Rating:** 68.8. **Slope:** 123. **Green Fee:** $11/$14. **Cart Fee:** $18/Cart. **Walking Policy:** Unrestricted walking. **Walkability:** 5. **Opened:** 1921. **Season:** Year-round. **To obtain tee times:** Call golf shop. **Miscellaneous:** Reduced fees (weekdays), range (grass), credit cards (MC, V), BF, FF.

★★★½ HERITAGE HILLS GOLF COURSE
PU-3140 Tee Dr., Claremore, 74017, Rogers County, (918)341-0055, 30 miles from Tulsa. **E-mail:** snaphk@aol.com. **Facility Holes:** 18. **Yards:** 6,760/5,324. **Par:** 71/72. **Course Rating:** 72.7/70.0. **Slope:** 129/117. **Green Fee:** $18. **Cart Fee:** $20/Cart. **Walking Policy:** Unrestricted walking. **Walkability:** 3. **Opened:** 1977. **Architect:** Don Sechrest. **Season:** Year-round. **High:** April-Aug. **To obtain tee times:** Call up to 3 days in advance. **Miscellaneous:** Reduced fees (weekdays, twilight, seniors, juniors), range (grass), credit cards (MC, V, AE), BF, FF.
Reader Comments: Best par 5s in Oklahoma ... Greens run firm and fast ... Hidden gem ... Great

bang for the buck … Enjoyable from white tees and tough from the blues … Very helpful staff … Great course no one knows about … Lots of trees … Worth playing.

IDABEL COUNTRY CLUB
PU-Lincoln Rd., Idabel, 74745, McCurtain County, (580)286-6836, 200 miles from Tulsa. **Facility Holes:** 18. **Yards:** 2,860/2,092. **Par:** 35/35. **Course Rating:** 34.1/33.4. **Slope:** 116/109. **Green Fee:** $15/$20. **Walkability:** 1. **Opened:** 1974. **Season:** Year-round. **To obtain tee times:** Call golf shop.

★½ INDIAN HILLS GOLF COURSE
SP-1890 Country Club Dr., Catoosa, 74015, Rogers County, (918)266-2207, 3 miles from Tulsa. **Facility Holes:** 18. **Yards:** 6,639/5,748. **Par:** 72/73. **Course Rating:** 71.5/72.9. **Slope:** 124/127. **Green Fee:** $14/$16. **Cart Fee:** $9/Person. **Walking Policy:** Unrestricted walking. **Opened:** 1921. **Architect:** Perry Maxwell. **Season:** Year-round. **High:** March-Oct. **To obtain tee times:** Call golf shop. **Miscellaneous:** Reduced fees (weekdays, twilight, seniors, juniors), metal spikes, credit cards (MC, V).
Special Notes: Formerly Spunky Creek Country Club.

★★★½ JIMMIE AUSTIN UNIVERSITY OF OKLAHOMA GOLF COURSE
PU-1 Par Dr., Norman, 73069, Cleveland County, (405)325-6716, 15 miles from Oklahoma City. **Facility Holes:** 18. **Yards:** 7,197/5,310. **Par:** 72/72. **Course Rating:** 74.9/71.6. **Slope:** 134/119. **Green Fee:** $33/$40. **Cart Fee:** $22/Cart. **Walking Policy:** Unrestricted walking. **Walkability:** 4. **Opened:** 1951. **Architect:** Bob Cupp. **Season:** Year-round. **High:** May-Oct. **To obtain tee times:** Call up to 3 days in advance. **Miscellaneous:** Reduced fees (weekdays, twilight, seniors, juniors), range (grass), credit cards (MC, V, AE), BF, FF.
Notes: Ranked 10th in 1999 Best in State.
Reader Comments: Used to be top notch, still nice … Bring your 'A' Game … Good course, but pricey for non-students.

★★★ JOHN CONRAD REGIONAL GOLF COURSE
PU-711 S. Douglas Blvd., Midwest City, 73130, Oklahoma County, (405)732-2209, 1 mile from Oklahoma City. **Facility Holes:** 18. **Yards:** 6,854/5,511. **Par:** 72/74. **Course Rating:** 72.0/70.8. **Slope:** 124/119. **Green Fee:** $15. **Cart Fee:** $19/Cart. **Walking Policy:** Unrestricted walking. **Walkability:** 2. **Opened:** 1971. **Architect:** Floyd Farley. **Season:** Year-round. **To obtain tee times:** Call up to 7 days in advance. **Miscellaneous:** Reduced fees (twilight, seniors, juniors), range (grass/mats), credit cards (MC, V), BF, FF.
Reader Comments: Great challenge … Good public course … The facilities are OK … Beautiful scenery and layout.

KAH-WAH-C GOLF COURSE
PU-Rte. 2, Fairfax, 74637, Osage County, (918)642-5351, 32 miles from Ponca City. **Facility Holes:** 9. **Yards:** 3,100/2,740. **Par:** 36/37. **Course Rating:** 69.5/69.8. **Slope:** 118/119. **Green Fee:** $8/$10. **Cart Fee:** $7/Person. **Walking Policy:** Unrestricted walking. **Walkability:** 2. **Opened:** 1922. **Season:** Year-round. **High:** April-Nov. **To obtain tee times:** Call golf shop. **Miscellaneous:** Reduced fees (juniors), BF, FF.

★★★★½ KARSTEN CREEK *Service, Condition+, Pace+*
SP-1800 S. Memorial Dr., Stillwater, 74074, Payne County, (405)743-1658, 5 miles from Stillwater. **E-mail:** osupistol@aol.com. **Facility Holes:** 18. **Yards:** 7,095/4,906. **Par:** 72/72. **Course Rating:** 74.8/70.1. **Slope:** 142/127. **Green Fee:** $225. **Cart Fee:** Included in green fee. **Walking Policy:** Unrestricted walking. **Walkability:** 4. **Opened:** 1994. **Architect:** Tom Fazio. **Season:** Year-round. **High:** April-Oct. **To obtain tee times:** Call golf shop. **Miscellaneous:** Range (grass), caddies, credit cards (MC, V, AE), FF.
Notes: Ranked 2nd in 2001 Best in State; 16th in 1996 America's Top 75 Upscale Courses.
Reader Comments: Could play it every day … Too expensive but great … On most of the holes, you don't see anything but the hole you are playing … One of the best in the country … A real treat, a must! … Beautiful, huge greens … No houses and no crowds … Excellent course but expensive.

KEYSTONE GOLF COURSE
SP-South Airport Rd., P.O. Box 289, Cleveland, 74020, Pawnee County, (918)358-2277, 1 mile from Cleveland. **Facility Holes:** 9. **Yards:** 3,078/2,968. **Par:** 36/37. **Course Rating:** 69.8/70.8. **Slope:** 109/108. **Green Fee:** $9/$12. **Cart Fee:** $15/Cart. **Walking Policy:** Unrestricted walking. **Walkability:** 2. **Opened:** 1971. **Season:** Year-round. **To obtain tee times:** Call golf shop. **Miscellaneous:** Reduced fees (weekdays, juniors), credit cards (MC, V, D), BF, FF.

★★★ KICKING BIRD GOLF COURSE
PU-1600 E. Danforth Rd., Edmond, 73034, Oklahoma County, (405)341-5350, 10 miles from Oklahoma City. **Web:** www.ci.edmond.ok.us. **Facility Holes:** 18. **Yards:** 6,722/5,051. **Par:** 70/70.

Course Rating: 71.8/69.3. **Slope:** 123/112. **Green Fee:** $17/$22. **Cart Fee:** $10/Person. **Walking Policy:** Unrestricted walking. **Walkability:** 3. **Opened:** 1971. **Architect:** Floyd Farley/Mark Hayes. **Season:** Year-round. **To obtain tee times:** Call up to 7 days in advance. **Miscellaneous:** Reduced fees (weekdays, twilight, seniors, juniors), range (grass/mats), credit cards (MC, V, AE, D), BF, FF.
Reader Comments: Save your strength for No.18, it's all uphill ... Kid-friendly course ... Well-maintained muni.

★★½ LAFORTUNE PARK GOLF COURSE
PU-5501 S. Yale Ave., Tulsa, 74135, Tulsa County, (918)596-8627. **Facility Holes:** 36. **Yards:** 6,970/5,780. **Par:** 72/73. **Course Rating:** 72.8/72.9. **Slope:** 123/122. **Green Fee:** $10/$17. **Cart Fee:** $10/Person. **Walking Policy:** Unrestricted walking. **Walkability:** 2. **Opened:** 1960. **Architect:** Floyd Farley. **Season:** Year-round. **High:** April-Sept. **To obtain tee times:** Call up to 7 days in advance. **Miscellaneous:** Reduced fees (twilight, seniors, juniors), range (grass/mats), credit cards (MC, V), BF, FF.
Special Notes: Also has an 18-hole par-3 course.

LAKE HEFNER GOLF CLUB
PU-4491 S. Lake Hefner Dr., Oklahoma City, 73116, Oklahoma County, (405)843-1565. **Facility Holes:** 39. **Green Fee:** $11/$16. **Cart Fee:** $19/Cart. **Walking Policy:** Unrestricted walking. **Walkability:** 3. **Season:** Year-round. **To obtain tee times:** Call golf shop. **Miscellaneous:** Reduced fees (twilight, seniors, juniors), range (grass), credit cards (MC, V), BF, FF.
★★★½ NORTH COURSE (18)
Yards: 6,970/5,169. **Par:** 72/72. **Course Rating:** 74.2/69.6. **Slope:** 128/117. **Opened:** 1995. **Architect:** Randy Heckenkemper.
Reader Comments: View of lake on most holes ... Recently redone, worth playing ... One of few courses overseeded in winter ... Great facilities ... Lots of water ... Pleasant surprise.
★★★ SOUTH COURSE (18)
Yards: 6,305/5,393. **Par:** 70/73. **Course Rating:** 68.9/71.2. **Slope:** 111/115. **Opened:** 1963. **Architect:** Floyd Farley.
Reader Comments: Back 9 better than front 9 ... Needs more trees and less water.
Special Notes: Also has a 3-hole Academy Course.

★★½ LAKE MURRAY RESORT GOLF
R-3310 S. Lake Murray Dr., Ardmore, 73401, Carter County, (405)223-6613, (866)602-4653, 90 miles from Dallas. **Web:** otrd.state.ok.us. **Facility Holes:** 18. **Yards:** 6,250/4,800. **Par:** 70/71. **Course Rating:** 69.2/70.8. **Slope:** 122/122. **Green Fee:** $14/$18. **Cart Fee:** $18/Person. **Walking Policy:** Unrestricted walking. **Walkability:** 2. **Opened:** 1960. **Architect:** Floyd Farley/Art Proctor. **Season:** Year-round. **To obtain tee times:** Call up to 7 days in advance. **Miscellaneous:** Reduced fees (weekdays, twilight, seniors, juniors), range (grass), lodging (100 rooms), credit cards (MC, V, AE, D), BF, FF.

★★½ LAKE TEXOMA GOLF RESORT
R-P.O. Box 279, Kingston, 73439, Marshall County, (580)564-3333, 65 miles from Dallas. **Facility Holes:** 18. **Yards:** 6,523/5,747. **Par:** 71/74. **Course Rating:** 71.4/68.7. **Slope:** 126/111. **Green Fee:** $14/$18. **Cart Fee:** $18/Cart. **Walking Policy:** Unrestricted walking. **Walkability:** 3. **Opened:** 1958. **Architect:** Floyd Farley. **Season:** Year-round. **High:** March-Oct. **To obtain tee times:** Call up to 7 days in advance. **Miscellaneous:** Reduced fees (weekdays, twilight, seniors, juniors), range (grass), lodging (100 rooms), credit cards (MC, V, AE, D), BF, FF.

LAKESIDE GOLF COURSE
PU-129 E. Colorado, Walters, 73572, Cotton County, (580)875-3829, 25 miles from Lawton. **Facility Holes:** 18. **Yards:** 5,146/4,093. **Par:** 70/68. **Course Rating:** 63.9/63.9. **Slope:** 103/103. **Green Fee:** $7. **Cart Fee:** $16/Cart. **Walking Policy:** Unrestricted walking. **Walkability:** 2. **Opened:** 1947. **Architect:** R. L. Pearson. **Season:** Year-round. **High:** May-Oct. **To obtain tee times:** Call golf shop. **Miscellaneous:** FF.

★★ LAKESIDE MEMORIAL GOLF CLUB
PU-5201 N. Washington, Stillwater, 74075, Payne County, (405)372-3399, 60 miles from Oklahoma City. **E-mail:** golfpro@stillwater.org. **Facility Holes:** 18. **Yards:** 6,698/5,124. **Par:** 70/71. **Course Rating:** 73.0/71.5. **Slope:** 128/122. **Green Fee:** $14/$19. **Cart Fee:** $10/Person. **Walking Policy:** Unrestricted walking. **Walkability:** 3. **Opened:** 1946. **Architect:** Labron Harris Sr. **Season:** Year-round. **To obtain tee times:** Call up to 5 days in advance. **Miscellaneous:** Reduced fees (twilight, seniors, juniors), range (grass), credit cards (MC, V), BF, FF.

★★½ LAKEVIEW GOLF COURSE
PU-3905 N. Commerce, Ardmore, 73401, Carter County, (405)223-4260, 88 miles from Oklahoma City. **Facility Holes:** 18. **Yards:** 6,881/5,032. **Par:** 71/72. **Course Rating:** 71.2/67.5. **Slope:** 114/113. **Green Fee:** $12/$15. **Cart Fee:** $18/Cart. **Walking Policy:** Unrestricted walk-

ing. **Walkability:** 2. **Opened:** 1971. **Architect:** Fillmore Vaughn. **Season:** Year-round. **High:** April-Sept. **To obtain tee times:** Call golf shop. **Miscellaneous:** Reduced fees (weekdays, twilight, seniors, juniors), range (grass), credit cards (MC, V, AE, D), BF, FF.

LAKEWOOD GOLF COURSE
PU-3101 Lakewood Dr., Ada, 74820, Pontotoc County, (580)332-5151, 80 miles from Oklahoma City. **Facility Holes:** 9. **Yards:** 5,990/5,390. **Par:** 71/71. **Course Rating:** 67.8. **Slope:** 112. **Green Fee:** $8/$10. **Cart Fee:** $18/Cart. **Walking Policy:** Unrestricted walking. **Walkability:** 5. **Opened:** 1968. **Season:** Year-round. **To obtain tee times:** Call golf shop. **Miscellaneous:** Reduced fees (weekdays, twilight), FF.

LAWTON MUNICIPAL GOLF COURSE
PU-Airport Rd., Lawton, 73502, Comanche County, (580)353-4493, 50 miles from Wichita Falls. **Facility Holes:** 18. **Yards:** 6,800/5,325. **Par:** 72/74. **Course Rating:** 72.9. **Slope:** 102/100. **Green Fee:** $10/$12. **Cart Fee:** $18/Cart. **Walking Policy:** Unrestricted walking. **Walkability:** 1. **Architect:** Jack Greer. **Season:** Year-round. **High:** April-June. **To obtain tee times:** Call golf shop. **Miscellaneous:** Reduced fees (juniors).

★★★ LEW WENTZ MEMORIAL GOLF COURSE
PU-2928 L.A. Cann Dr., Ponca City, 74604, Kay County, (405)767-0433, 80 miles from Tulsa. **Facility Holes:** 18. **Yards:** 6,400/5,450. **Par:** 71/70. **Course Rating:** 70.0/71.8. **Slope:** 125/123. **Green Fee:** $39. **Cart Fee:** Included in green fee. **Walking Policy:** Unrestricted walking. **Walkability:** 3. **Opened:** 1940. **Architect:** Floyd Farley. **Season:** Year-round. **To obtain tee times:** Call golf shop. **Miscellaneous:** Reduced fees (weekdays, seniors, juniors), credit cards (MC, V).
Reader Comments: Great layout along a lake ... Beautiful layout-back 9 along lake.

LINCOLN PARK GOLF COURSE
PU-4001 NE Grand Blvd., Oklahoma City, 73111, Oklahoma County, (405)424-1421. **Facility Holes:** 36. **Green Fee:** $11/$16. **Cart Fee:** $19/Cart. **Walking Policy:** Unrestricted walking. **Walkability:** 4. **Opened:** 1925. **Architect:** Arthur Jackson. **Season:** Year-round. **To obtain tee times:** Call up to 7 days in advance. **Miscellaneous:** Reduced fees (twilight, seniors, juniors), range (grass), credit cards (MC, V), BF, FF.
★★★ **EAST COURSE** (18)
Yards: 6,535/5,276. **Par:** 70/71. **Course Rating:** 70.0/70.8. **Slope:** 120/117.
Reader Comments: Lots of trees on several holes ... Very busy course.
★★★★ **WEST COURSE** (18)
Yards: 6,576/5,343. **Par:** 71/72. **Course Rating:** 70.1/72.4. **Slope:** 122/125.
Reader Comments: Hard to get on this course ... Booked solid ... Some great holes, good value ... Very good city park.

LINDSAY MUNICIPAL GOLF COURSE
PU-Hwy. 76, Lindsay, 73052, McClain County, (405)756-3611, 35 miles from Norman. **Web:** www.teedoffattelepath.com. **Facility Holes:** 9. **Yards:** 3,285/2,989. **Par:** 36/75. **Course Rating:** 70.0/73.4. **Slope:** 118/125. **Green Fee:** $7/$9. **Cart Fee:** $15/Cart. **Walking Policy:** Unrestricted walking. **Walkability:** 2. **Opened:** 1962. **Season:** Year-round. **To obtain tee times:** Call golf shop. **Miscellaneous:** Range (grass), FF.

MEADOWLAKE MUNICIPAL GOLF COURSE
PU-2000 W. Rupe, Enid, 73703, Garfield County, (580)234-3080, 12 miles from Oklahoma City. **Facility Holes:** 18. **Yards:** 6,416/5,801. **Par:** 71/73. **Course Rating:** 71.3/74.2. **Slope:** 117/125. **Green Fee:** $10/$17. **Cart Fee:** $9/Cart. **Walking Policy:** Unrestricted walking. **Walkability:** 2. **Opened:** 1950. **Architect:** Tripp Davis. **Season:** Year-round. **High:** April-Sept. **To obtain tee times:** Call up to 4 days in advance. **Miscellaneous:** Reduced fees (twilight, seniors, juniors), range (grass), credit cards (MC, V), BF, FF.

MOHAWK PARK GOLF CLUB
PU-5223 E. 41st St. N., Tulsa, 74115, Tulsa County, (918)425-6871. **E-mail:** harrington@pga.com. **Web:** tulsagolf.org. **Facility Holes:** 36. **Green Fee:** $10/$19. **Cart Fee:** $22/Cart. **Walking Policy:** Unrestricted walking. **Walkability:** 2. **Season:** Year-round. **High:** April-Oct. **To obtain tee times:** Call up to 7 days in advance. **Miscellaneous:** Reduced fees (twilight, seniors, juniors), range (grass), credit cards (MC, V, AE, D), BF, FF.
★★ **PECAN VALLEY COURSE** (18)
Yards: 6,499/5,130. **Par:** 70/70. **Course Rating:** 71.6/69.6. **Slope:** 124/119. **Opened:** 1957. **Architect:** Floyd Farley/Jerry Slack.
★★ **WOODBINE COURSE** (18)
Yards: 6,898/6,202. **Par:** 72/76. **Course Rating:** 71.0/73.9. **Slope:** 115/127. **Opened:** 1934. **Architect:** William H. Diddel.

OKEENE MUNICIPAL GOLF COURSE
PU-401 S. Phillips, Okeene, 73763, Blaine County, (580)822-3435, 24 miles from Enid. **Facility Holes:** 9. **Yards:** 2,932/2,752. **Par:** 35/35. **Course Rating:** 69.0/69.0. **Green Fee:** $10/$13. **Cart Fee:** $13/Cart. **Walking Policy:** Unrestricted walking. **Walkability:** 1. **Opened:** 1950. **Season:** Year-round. **High:** March-Sept. **To obtain tee times:** Call golf shop. **Miscellaneous:** Reduced fees (weekdays, twilight, juniors), range (grass).

OSAGE CREEK GOLF COURSE
PU-Hwy. 28 - Will Rogers Tpke., Adair, 74330, Mayes County, (918)785-4166, 32 miles from Tulsa. **Facility Holes:** 18. **Yards:** 7,024/5,540. **Par:** 72/72. **Course Rating:** 73.8/74.8. **Slope:** 111/111. **Green Fee:** $10/$12. **Cart Fee:** $16/Cart. **Walking Policy:** Unrestricted walking. **Walkability:** 1. **Opened:** 1986. **Architect:** Charles Bland. **Season:** Year-round. **To obtain tee times:** Call golf shop. **Miscellaneous:** Reduced fees (weekdays, seniors), credit cards (MC, V).

PAGE BELCHER GOLF COURSE
PU-6666 S. Union Ave., Tulsa, 74132, Tulsa County, (918)446-1529. **E-mail:** pagebgc@aol.com. **Facility Holes:** 36. **Green Fee:** $16/$19. **Cart Fee:** $21/Cart. **Walking Policy:** Unrestricted walking. **Walkability:** 3. **Season:** Year-round. **High:** April-Oct. **To obtain tee times:** Call up to 7 days in advance. **Miscellaneous:** Reduced fees (weekdays, twilight, seniors, juniors), range (grass), credit cards (MC, V, AE, D), BF, FF.
★★½ **OLD PAGE COURSE** (18)
Yards: 6,826/5,532. **Par:** 71/71. **Course Rating:** 72.0/71.5. **Slope:** 123/118. **Opened:** 1977. **Architect:** Leon Howard.
★★★ **STONE CREEK COURSE** (18)
Yards: 6,539/5,144. **Par:** 71/71. **Course Rating:** 72.3/69.9. **Slope:** 132/127. **Opened:** 1987. **Architect:** Don Sechrest.
Notes: Ranked 7th in 1999 Best in State; 41st in 1996 America's Top 75 Affordable Courses. **Reader Comments:** Lots of bunkers and water ... Fair tee boxes for women ... Pleasure to hit off Zoysia fairways ... Excellent layout for under $20 ... TLC needed for this one.

PATRICIA ISLAND GOLF CLUB
PU-4980 Club House Rd., Grove, 74344, Delaware County, (918)786-3338. **Facility Holes:** 18. **Yards:** 6,815/5,222. **Par:** 72/72. **Course Rating:** 72.2. **Slope:** 122. **Green Fee:** $33/$40. **Cart Fee:** Included in green fee. **Walking Policy:** Walking at certain times. **Walkability:** 2. **Opened:** 1999. **Architect:** Tripp Davis. **Season:** Year-round. **High:** April-Sept. **To obtain tee times:** Call golf shop. **Miscellaneous:** Reduced fees (twilight), credit cards (MC, V, AE, D).

PAULS VALLEY MUNICIPAL GOLF COURSE
PU-South Airport Rd., Pauls Valley, 73075, Garvin County, (405)238-7462, 50 miles from Oklahoma City. **Facility Holes:** 9. **Yards:** 3,403/2,602. **Par:** 72/72. **Course Rating:** 70.2/70.1. **Slope:** 108/125. **Green Fee:** $9/$11. **Cart Fee:** $17/Cart. **Walking Policy:** Walking at certain times. **Walkability:** 1. **Opened:** 1992. **Season:** Year-round. **High:** March-Oct. **To obtain tee times:** Call golf shop. **Miscellaneous:** Range (grass).

PEORIA RIDGE GOLF COURSE
PU-10301 S. 600 Rd., Miami, 74354, Ottawa County, (918)542-7676, 25 miles from Joplin, MO. **E-mail:** peoriaridge.com. **Web:** peoriaridge.com. **Facility Holes:** 18. **Yards:** 6,960/4,946. **Par:** 72. **Course Rating:** 74.1. **Slope:** 127. **Green Fee:** $30/$40. **Cart Fee:** Included in green fee. **Walking Policy:** Unrestricted walking. **Walkability:** 3. **Opened:** 2000. **Architect:** Bland Pittman. **Season:** Year-round. **High:** April-Sept. **To obtain tee times:** Call up to 7 days in advance. **Miscellaneous:** Reduced fees (seniors, juniors), range (grass), credit cards (MC, V, AE), BF, FF.

PRAIRIE WEST GOLF CLUB
SP-Rader Park, Weatherford, 73096, Custer County, (580)772-3832, 60 miles from Oklahoma City. **Facility Holes:** 18. **Yards:** 6,543/4,979. **Par:** 71/73. **Course Rating:** 71.2/62.4. **Slope:** 125/93. **Green Fee:** $13/$18. **Cart Fee:** $18/Cart. **Walking Policy:** Unrestricted walking. **Walkability:** 3. **Architect:** Labron Harris. **Season:** Year-round. **To obtain tee times:** Call golf shop. **Miscellaneous:** Reduced fees (twilight, seniors, juniors), range (grass), credit cards (MC, V), BF, FF.
Special Notes: Formerly Weatherford Golf Course.

PRYOR MUNICIPAL GOLF COURSE
PU-East Highway 69A, Pryor, 74361, Mayes County, (918)825-3056, 28 miles from Tulsa. **Facility Holes:** 18. **Yards:** 6,549/5,649. **Par:** 72/72. **Course Rating:** 71.2/68.1. **Slope:** 124/109. **Green Fee:** $9/$14. **Cart Fee:** $18/Cart. **Walking Policy:** Unrestricted walking. **Walkability:** 2.

OKLAHOMA

Season: Year-round. **High:** April-Oct. **To obtain tee times:** Call golf shop. **Miscellaneous:** Reduced fees (twilight, seniors, juniors).

★★ QUARTZ MOUNTAIN GOLF COURSE
R-Rte. 1, Box 35, Lone Wolf, 73655, Kiowa County, (580)563-2520, 17 miles from Altus. **Facility Holes:** 18. **Yards:** 6,595/5,706. **Par:** 71/71. **Course Rating:** 70.8/73.4. **Slope:** 119/123. **Green Fee:** $11/$16. **Cart Fee:** $9/Person. **Walking Policy:** Unrestricted walking. **Walkability:** 2. **Opened:** 1958. **Architect:** Floyd Farley/Art Proctor. **Season:** Year-round. **High:** May-Aug. **To obtain tee times:** Call golf shop. **Miscellaneous:** Reduced fees (weekdays, twilight, seniors, juniors), range (grass), credit cards (MC, V, AE, D).

RIVERSIDE MUNICIPAL GOLF COURSE
PU-Rte. 1, Box 3625, Clinton, 73601, Custer County, (580)323-5958, 120 miles from Oklahoma City. **Facility Holes:** 18. **Yards:** 6,880/4,921. **Par:** 70/70. **Course Rating:** 68.8/70.2. **Slope:** 113/119. **Green Fee:** $7/$18. **Cart Fee:** $18/Cart. **Walking Policy:** Unrestricted walking. **Walkability:** 1. **Opened:** 1925. **Season:** Year-round. **To obtain tee times:** Call golf shop. **Miscellaneous:** Reduced fees (weekdays, twilight, seniors, juniors), range (grass), credit cards (MC, V), BF, FF.

ROCK CREEK GOLF COURSE
PU-Hwy. 69, Hugo, 74743, Choctaw County, (580)326-6130, 100 miles from Dallas. **Facility Holes:** 9. **Yards:** 5,995. **Par:** 72. **Course Rating:** 69.0. **Slope:** 106. **Green Fee:** $8/$10. **Cart Fee:** $16/Cart. **Walking Policy:** Unrestricted walking. **Walkability:** 2. **Opened:** 1972. **Season:** Year-round. **High:** May-Aug. **To obtain tee times:** Call golf shop. **Miscellaneous:** Reduced fees (weekdays, juniors), metal spikes, range (grass).

ROMAN NOSE GOLF COURSE
PU-St. Hwy. 8A, Watonga, 73772, Blaine County, (580)623-7989, 60 miles from Oklahoma City. **Facility Holes:** 18. **Yards:** 6,139/4,599. **Par:** 70/70. **Course Rating:** 70.5. **Slope:** 123. **Green Fee:** $10/$15. **Cart Fee:** $18/Cart. **Walking Policy:** Unrestricted walking. **Walkability:** 5. **Opened:** 1957. **Architect:** Floyd Farley/Tripp Davis. **Season:** Year-round. **High:** May-Sept. **To obtain tee times:** Call up to 7 days in advance. **Miscellaneous:** Reduced fees (weekdays, twilight, seniors, juniors), lodging (57 rooms), credit cards (MC, V, AE, D), BF, FF.

★★★ SAND SPRINGS MUNICIPAL GOLF COURSE
PU-1801 N. McKinley, Sand Springs, 74063, Tulsa County, (918)246-2606, 8 miles from Tulsa. **Facility Holes:** 18. **Yards:** 6,113/4,692. **Par:** 71/70. **Course Rating:** 69.5/68.4. **Slope:** 125/118. **Green Fee:** $8/$18. **Cart Fee:** $19/Cart. **Walking Policy:** Unrestricted walking. **Walkability:** 4. **Opened:** 1956. **Architect:** Floyd Farley. **Season:** Year-round. **To obtain tee times:** Call golf shop. **Miscellaneous:** Reduced fees (weekdays, twilight, seniors, juniors), range (grass), credit cards (MC, V), BF, FF.
Reader Comments: Huge elevation changes ... Lots of variety with sand, water, tight, open, flat, hilly ... Very friendly ... Underrated muni course with super greens ... Awesome layout.

★½ SAPULPA MUNICIPAL GOLF COURSE
PU-Hwy. 66, Sapulpa, 74067, Creek County, (918)224-0237, 15 miles from Tulsa. **Facility Holes:** 18. **Yards:** 6,675/5,087. **Par:** 71/70. **Course Rating:** 72.4/69.2. **Slope:** 128/112. **Green Fee:** $14/$16. **Cart Fee:** $19/Cart. **Walking Policy:** Unrestricted walking. **Walkability:** 2. **Opened:** 1995. **Architect:** Jerry Slack/Mark Hayes. **Season:** Year-round. **High:** June-Aug. **To obtain tee times:** Call golf shop. **Miscellaneous:** Reduced fees (weekdays, twilight, seniors, juniors), credit cards (MC, V, D).

SAYRE GOLF COURSE
PU-, Sayre, 73662, Beckham County, (580)928-9046, 25 miles from Weatherford. **Facility Holes:** 9. **Yards:** 3,098/2,486. **Par:** 36/36. **Green Fee:** $10/$12. **Opened:** 1973. **Season:** Year-round. **To obtain tee times:** Call golf shop.

★★ SEQUOYAH STATE PARK GOLF CLUB
R-Hwy. 51, Hulbert, 74441, Cherokee County, (918)772-2297, 45 miles from Tulsa. **Facility Holes:** 18. **Yards:** 5,860/5,555. **Par:** 70/73. **Course Rating:** 66.7/69.9. **Slope:** 109/113. **Green Fee:** $15/$22. **Cart Fee:** $18/Person. **Walking Policy:** Unrestricted walking. **Walkability:** 4. **Opened:** 1954. **Architect:** Floyd Farley. **Season:** Year-round. **High:** May-Sept. **To obtain tee times:** Call up to 7 days in advance. **Miscellaneous:** Reduced fees (weekdays, twilight, seniors, juniors), range (grass), lodging (204 rooms), credit cards (MC, V, AE, D), BF, FF.

SHANGRI-LA GOLF RESORT
R-R.R. No.3, Afton, 74331, Delaware County, (918)257-4204, (800)331-4060, 90 miles from Tulsa. **Facility Holes:** 36. **Cart Fee:** Included in green fee. **Walking Policy:** Walking at certain

times. **Architect:** Don Sechrest. **Season:** Year-round. **To obtain tee times:** Call golf shop. **Miscellaneous:** Reduced fees (guests, juniors), range (grass), credit cards (MC, V, AE, D), BF, FF.

★★★★½   **BLUE COURSE** (18)
Yards: 7,012/5,892. **Par:** 72/73. **Course Rating:** 73.7/74.8. **Slope:** 131/126. **Green Fee:** $90/$95. **Walkability:** 3. **Opened:** 1970.
Reader Comments: Nice view of the lake … Very challenging … Excellent … Outstanding service.

★★★★½   **GOLD COURSE** (18)
Yards: 5,802/4,586. **Par:** 70/71. **Course Rating:** 67.9/66.8. **Slope:** 124/112. **Green Fee:** $85/$90. **Walkability:** 4. **Opened:** 1980.
Reader Comments: Perfect short resort course … Enjoyable par 3s … Little easier than Blue Course but same challenges … Fun to play.

SHATTUCK GOLF & COUNTRY CLUB
SP-1 1/2 South Shattuck Hwy. 283, Shattuck, 73858, Ellis County, (580)938-2445, 25 miles from Woodward. **Facility Holes:** 9. **Yards:** 3,156/2,870. **Par:** 36/36. **Green Fee:** $8/$12. **Cart Fee:** $14/Cart. **Walking Policy:** Unrestricted walking. **Walkability:** 3. **Architect:** Ned Stuart. **Season:** Year-round. **High:** June-Sept. **To obtain tee times:** Call golf shop. **Miscellaneous:** Reduced fees (weekdays, twilight).

★★★★   **SILVERHORN GOLF CLUB**
PU-11411 N. Kelley Ave., Oklahoma City, 73131, Oklahoma County, (405)752-1181, 10 miles from Oklahoma City. **Facility Holes:** 18. **Yards:** 6,800/4,943. **Par:** 71/71. **Course Rating:** 73.4/71.0. **Slope:** 128/113. **Green Fee:** $22/$31. **Cart Fee:** $9/Person. **Walking Policy:** Unrestricted walking. **Walkability:** 3. **Opened:** 1991. **Architect:** Randy Heckenkemper. **Season:** Year-round. **To obtain tee times:** Call golf shop. **Miscellaneous:** Reduced fees (weekdays, twilight, seniors, juniors), metal spikes, range (grass), credit cards (MC, V, AE, D), BF, FF.
Reader Comments: Keeping the ball out of the rough is at a premium … Relatively short, scenic layout … Quality course.

★★½   **SOUTH LAKES GOLF COURSE**
PU-9253 S. Elwood, Jenks, 74037, Tulsa County, (918)746-3760, 10 miles from Tulsa. **Facility Holes:** 18. **Yards:** 6,340/5,242. **Par:** 71/71. **Course Rating:** 68.6/70.4. **Slope:** 113/116. **Green Fee:** $18. **Cart Fee:** $20/Cart. **Walking Policy:** Unrestricted walking. **Walkability:** 2. **Opened:** 1989. **Architect:** Randy Heckenkemper. **Season:** Year-round. **High:** April-Oct. **To obtain tee times:** Call golf shop. **Miscellaneous:** Reduced fees (twilight, seniors, juniors), range (grass/mats), credit cards (MC, V), BF, FF.

STROUD MUNICIPAL GOLF COURSE
PU-Hwy 99 North, Stroud, 74079, Lincoln County, (918)968-2105, 45 miles from Tulsa. **Facility Holes:** 9. **Yards:** 6,300/5,426. **Par:** 70/70. **Course Rating:** 70.2/68.4. **Slope:** 118/113. **Green Fee:** $8/$10. **Cart Fee:** $8/Person. **Walking Policy:** Unrestricted walking. **Walkability:** 2. **Opened:** 1972. **Season:** Year-round. **High:** May-Nov. **To obtain tee times:** Call golf shop. **Miscellaneous:** Reduced fees (weekdays, twilight, seniors, juniors), range (grass), credit cards (MC, V).

SUGAR CREEK CANYON GOLF CLUB
PU-200 W. Sugar Creek Rd., Hinton, 73047, Caddo County, (405)542-3974, 20 miles from Weatherford. **E-mail:** mrpars@hintonet.net. **Facility Holes:** 18. **Yards:** 6,837/5,145. **Par:** 71/71. **Course Rating:** 73.1/70.5. **Slope:** 125/121. **Green Fee:** $12/$19. **Cart Fee:** $18/Person. **Walking Policy:** Unrestricted walking. **Walkability:** 3. **Opened:** 1999. **Architect:** Mark Hayes. **Season:** Year-round. **High:** April-Oct. **To obtain tee times:** Call up to 7 days in advance. **Miscellaneous:** Reduced fees (weekdays, twilight, seniors, juniors), range (grass), credit cards (MC, V, AE), BF, FF.

SULPHUR HILLS GOLF COURSE
PU-Country Club Dr., Sulphur, 73086, Murray County, (580)622-5057, 1 mile from Sulphur. **Facility Holes:** 9. **Yards:** 6,450/5,760. **Par:** 72/78. **Course Rating:** 69.5/72.0. **Slope:** 107/107. **Green Fee:** $7/$10. **Cart Fee:** $16/Cart. **Walking Policy:** Unrestricted walking. **Walkability:** 2. **Opened:** 1965. **Season:** Year-round. **High:** May-Sept. **To obtain tee times:** Call golf shop. **Miscellaneous:** Reduced fees (twilight, juniors).

SUNSET HILLS GOLF COURSE
PU-Sunset Lane, Guymon, 73942, Texas County, (580)338-7404, 120 miles from Amarillo. **Facility Holes:** 18. **Yards:** 6,732/5,780. **Par:** 71/74. **Course Rating:** 70.3/68.0. **Slope:** 108/112. **Green Fee:** $10/$13. **Cart Fee:** $18/Cart. **Walking Policy:** Unrestricted walking. **Walkability:** 4. **Opened:** 1932. **Architect:** Bob Dunning. **Season:** Year-round. **To obtain tee times:** Call golf shop. **Miscellaneous:** Reduced fees (twilight), range (grass), BF, FF.

SYCAMORE SPRINGS GOLF COURSE
SP-Rte 2, 2555 Golf Course Rd., Wilburton, 74578, Latimer County, (918)465-3161, 75 miles from Fort Smith, Arkansas. **Facility Holes:** 9. **Yards:** 5,895/5,355. **Par:** 70/70. **Green Fee:** $9/$11. **Cart Fee:** $14/Cart. **Walking Policy:** Unrestricted walking. **Walkability:** 2. **Opened:** 1972. **Season:** Year-round. **High:** June-Oct. **To obtain tee times:** Call golf shop. **Miscellaneous:** Reduced fees (weekdays, twilight, juniors), range (grass).
Special Notes: Formerly Latimer County Golf Club.

TENKILLER GOLF CLUB
PU-Rte. 1, Box 189, Vian, 74962, Sequoyah County, (918)773-8436, 80 miles from Tulsa. **E-mail:** proshop@tenkillergolf.com. **Web:** tenkillergolf.com. **Facility Holes:** 18. **Yards:** 6,455/5,538. **Par:** 72/74. **Course Rating:** 69.8/74.0. **Slope:** 117/120. **Green Fee:** $12/$18. **Walking Policy:** Unrestricted walking. **Walkability:** 3. **Opened:** 1970. **Season:** Year-round. **To obtain tee times:** Call golf shop. **Miscellaneous:** Reduced fees (weekdays, seniors, juniors), range (grass), lodging (12 rooms), credit cards (MC, V), BF, FF.
Special Notes: Formerly East Lake Hills Resort Golf Course.

★★½ THUNDERCREEK GOLF COURSE
PU-2300 W. Hwy. 270, Mc Alester, 74502, Pittsburg County, (918)423-5799, 90 miles from Tulsa. **Facility Holes:** 18. **Yards:** 6,835/5,033. **Par:** 72/72. **Course Rating:** 69.5/72.0. **Slope:** 135/110. **Green Fee:** $12/$18. **Cart Fee:** $20/Person. **Walking Policy:** Unrestricted walking. **Walkability:** 3. **Opened:** 1994. **Season:** Year-round. **High:** March-June. **To obtain tee times:** Call golf shop. **Miscellaneous:** Reduced fees (twilight), range (grass), credit cards (MC, V, AE, D).

TISHOMINGO GOLF AND RECREATION
PU-St. Hwy. 99, Tishomingo, 73460, Johnston County, (580)371-2604, 35 miles from Ardmore. **Facility Holes:** 9. **Yards:** 3,187/2,480. **Par:** 36/36. **Green Fee:** $10/$12. **Cart Fee:** $14/Cart. **Walking Policy:** Walking at certain times. **Walkability:** 2. **Opened:** 1940. **Season:** Year-round. **High:** June-Aug. **To obtain tee times:** Call golf shop. **Miscellaneous:** Range (grass).

TRADITION GOLF CLUB
PU-15200 Traditions Blvd., Edmond, 73013, Oklahoma County, (405)844-4488, 4 miles from Oklahoma City. **Facility Holes:** 18. **Yards:** 6,470/5,075. **Par:** 70/70. **Course Rating:** 71.3. **Slope:** 119. **Green Fee:** $23/$40. **Cart Fee:** $13/Person. **Walking Policy:** Walking at certain times. **Walkability:** 3. **Opened:** 2001. **Architect:** R. Wigington/D. Wigington/T. Givens. **Season:** Year-round. **High:** March-Nov. **To obtain tee times:** Call up to 5 days in advance. **Miscellaneous:** Reduced fees (weekdays, twilight, seniors, juniors), range (grass/mats), credit cards (MC, V, AE, D), BF, FF.

★★½ TROSPER PARK GOLF COURSE
PU-2301 SE 29th, Oklahoma City, 73129, Oklahoma County, (405)677-8874. **Facility Holes:** 18. **Yards:** 6,631/5,067. **Par:** 71/71. **Course Rating:** 71.5/74.1. **Slope:** 125/114. **Green Fee:** $10/$16. **Cart Fee:** $19/Cart. **Walking Policy:** Unrestricted walking. **Walkability:** 3. **Opened:** 1960. **Architect:** Arthur Jackson. **Season:** Year-round. **High:** May-Oct. **To obtain tee times:** Call golf shop. **Miscellaneous:** Reduced fees (twilight, seniors, juniors), range (grass), credit cards (MC, V), BF, FF.

TURKEY CREEK GOLF CLUB
SP-Hwy 51 W., Hennessey, 73742, Kingfisher County, (405)853-2100, 50 miles from Oklahoma City. **Facility Holes:** 18. **Yards:** 6,300/4,895. **Par:** 70/70. **Course Rating:** 68.0/69.6. **Slope:** 114/118. **Green Fee:** $10/$20. **Cart Fee:** Included in green fee. **Walking Policy:** Unrestricted walking. **Walkability:** 1. **Opened:** 1969. **Architect:** Mark Hayes/Jerry Slack. **Season:** Year-round. **High:** April-Nov. **To obtain tee times:** Call golf shop. **Miscellaneous:** Credit cards (MC, V, D).
Special Notes: Formerly Hennessey Country Club.

TWIN OAKS GOLF COURSE
PU-Rte. 2, Duncan, 73533, Stephens County, (580)252-4714, 60 miles from Oklahoma City. **Facility Holes:** 18. **Yards:** 6,312/4,323. **Par:** 71/71. **Green Fee:** $7/$9. **Walkability:** 3. **Opened:** 1968. **Architect:** Riley Parr. **To obtain tee times:** Call golf shop.
Special Notes: Formerly Cowboy Creek Golf Course.

VINITA GOLF AND TENNIS CLUB
PU-South Fairgounds Rd., Vinita, 74301, Craig County, (918)256-8100, 40 miles from Tulsa. **Facility Holes:** 9. **Yards:** 6,200/5,048. **Par:** 70/70. **Course Rating:** 69.6/65.6. **Slope:** 112/102. **Green Fee:** $18/$22. **Cart Fee:** Included in green fee. **Walking Policy:** Unrestricted walking.

Walkability: 3. **Opened:** 1922. **Season:** Year-round. **To obtain tee times:** Call golf shop.
Miscellaneous: Range (grass), credit cards (MC, V), BF, FF.

WESTBURY COUNTRY CLUB
SP-2101 Westbury Dr., Yukon, 73099, Canadian County, (405)324-0707, 10 miles from
Oklahoma City. **Facility Holes:** 18. **Yards:** 6,874/6,276. **Par:** 72/74. **Course Rating:** 72.3/71.6.
Slope: 122/130. **Green Fee:** $15/$17. **Cart Fee:** $19/Cart. **Walking Policy:** Unrestricted walk-
ing. **Walkability:** 1. **Opened:** 1975. **Season:** Year-round. **High:** April-Sept. **To obtain tee times:**
Call golf shop. **Miscellaneous:** Reduced fees (weekdays, twilight), range (grass/mats), credit
cards (MC, V, AE, D).

★★ WESTWOOD PARK GOLF COURSE
PU-2400 Westport Dr., Norman, 73069, Cleveland County, (405)292-9700, 17 miles from
Oklahoma City. **E-mail:** westwoodgolf@aol.com. **Facility Holes:** 18. **Yards:** 6,015/5,525. **Par:**
70/74. **Course Rating:** 67.7/71.0. **Slope:** 108/120. **Green Fee:** $8/$16. **Cart Fee:** $20/Cart.
Walking Policy: Unrestricted walking. **Walkability:** 1. **Opened:** 1967. **Architect:** Floyd Farley.
Season: Year-round. **High:** March-Oct. **To obtain tee times:** Call up to 7 days in advance.
Miscellaneous: Reduced fees (weekdays, twilight, seniors, juniors), range (grass), credit
cards (MC, V), BF, FF.

★★★½ WHITE HAWK GOLF CLUB
SP-14515 S. Yale Ave., Bixby, 74008, Tulsa County, (918)366-4653, 10 miles from Tulsa.
Facility Holes: 18. **Yards:** 6,982/5,148. **Par:** 72/72. **Course Rating:** 74.1. **Slope:** 134. **Green
Fee:** $12/$37. **Cart Fee:** $8/Person. **Walking Policy:** Unrestricted walking. **Walkability:** 3.
Opened: 1994. **Architect:** Randy Heckenkemper. **Season:** Year-round. **High:** March-Oct. **To
obtain tee times:** Call up to 7 days in advance. **Miscellaneous:** Reduced fees (weekdays, twi-
light, seniors, juniors), range (grass), credit cards (MC, V, AE, D, DC), BF, FF.
Reader Comments: Wide open front 9, tight back ... Well maintained and kept ... Wind blows on
most days ... Overall a very pleasant play.

WILDHORSE GOLF COURSE
PU-128 Wildhorse Dr., Velma, 73491, Stephens County, (580)444-3338, 16 miles from
Duncan. **E-mail:** peav/rw@texaco.com. **Facility Holes:** 9. **Yards:** 6,074/4,762. **Par:** 70/70.
Course Rating: 62.4. **Green Fee:** $7/$10. **Cart Fee:** $16/Cart. **Walking Policy:** Unrestricted
walking. **Walkability:** 3. **Opened:** 1968. **Season:** Year-round. **To obtain tee times:** Call golf
shop. **Miscellaneous:** Reduced fees (weekdays, juniors), FF.

WOODWARD MUNICIPAL GOLF COURSE
PU-Crystal Beach Park, Woodward, 73802, Woodward County, (580)256-9028, 150 miles
from Oklahoma City. **Facility Holes:** 9. **Yards:** 3,163/2,983. **Par:** 35/38. **Course Rating:**
68.5/72.5. **Slope:** 95/110. **Green Fee:** $10/$12. **Cart Fee:** $16/Cart. **Walking Policy:**
Unrestricted walking. **Walkability:** 1. **Season:** Year-round. **High:** April-Sept. **To obtain tee
times:** Call golf shop. **Miscellaneous:** Reduced fees (twilight), range (grass).

ASPEN LAKES GOLF COURSE
PU-16900 Aspen Lakes Dr., Sisters, 97759, Deschutes County, (541)549-4653, 20 miles from Bend. **E-mail:** pam@aspenlakes.com. **Web:** www.aspenlakes.com. **Facility Holes:** 18. **Yards:** 7,302/5,594. **Par:** 72/72. **Course Rating:** 75.4/71.7. **Slope:** 135/125. **Green Fee:** $40/$50. **Cart Fee:** $28/Cart. **Walking Policy:** Unrestricted walking. **Walkability:** 3. **Opened:** 1997. **Architect:** William Overdorf. **Season:** March-Dec. **High:** June-Oct. **To obtain tee times:** Call up to 30 days in advance. **Miscellaneous:** Reduced fees (twilight, juniors), range (grass/mats), credit cards (MC, V, AE, D), BF, FF.
Notes: Ranked 8th in 2001 Best New Affordable Courses.

BAKER CITY GOLF CLUB
PU-2801 Indiana Ave., Baker City, 97814, Baker County, (541)523-2358, 130 miles from Boise Idaho. **Facility Holes:** 18. **Yards:** 6,340/5,750. **Par:** 70/72. **Course Rating:** 67.7/71.0. **Slope:** 118/120. **Green Fee:** $20. **Cart Fee:** $20/Cart. **Walking Policy:** Unrestricted walking. **Walkability:** 3. **Opened:** 1934. **Season:** March-Oct. **High:** June-Aug. **To obtain tee times:** Call golf shop. **Miscellaneous:** Reduced fees (juniors), credit cards (MC, V).

BANDON DUNES GOLF RESORT
R-57744 Round Lake Dr., Bandon, 97411, Coos County, (541)347-4380, (888)345-6008, 16 miles from Coos Bay. **E-mail:** thval@bandondunesgolf.com. **Web:** www.bandondunesgolf.com. **Facility Holes:** 36. **Green Fee:** $50/$150. **Walking Policy:** Unrestricted walking. **Walkability:** 2. **Season:** Year-round. **To obtain tee times:** Call up to 365 days in advance. **Miscellaneous:** Reduced fees (weekdays, guests), range (grass), caddies, lodging (69 rooms), credit cards (MC, V, AE, D), BF, FF.
★★★★½ **BANDON DUNES COURSE** (18) *Value, Condition+, Pace+*
Yards: 6,844/5,178. **Par:** 72/72. **Course Rating:** 74.2/72.1. **Slope:** 138/127. **Opened:** 1999. **Architect:** David McLay Kidd/James Kidd. **High:** May-Dec.
Notes: Ranked 1st in 2001 Best in State; 1st in 1999 Best New Upscale Public.
Reader Comments: Great course, great scenery, love walking-only policy. Buy yardage book or spend the $35 bucks for a caddie ... Awesome! I drove 5 hours to get there—was worth every bit ... My favorite golf course ever! Golf as it was meant to be ... Nothing can compare to this experience. Utopia ... My #1 pick.
PACIFIC DUNES COURSE (18)
Yards: 6,557/5,107. **Par:** 71/71. **Course Rating:** 72.9/71.1. **Slope:** 133/131. **Opened:** 2001. **Architect:** Tom Doak. **High:** May-Oct.
Notes: Ranked 1st in 2001 Best New Upscale Public.

BATTLE CREEK GOLF CLUB
PU-6161 Commercial St. SE, Salem, 97306, Marion County, (503)585-1402. **Facility Holes:** 18. **Yards:** 6,015/4,945. **Par:** 72/72. **Course Rating:** 117.0/113.0. **Slope:** 68.8/68.5. **Green Fee:** $25/$26. **Cart Fee:** $22/Cart. **Walking Policy:** Unrestricted walking. **Walkability:** 2. **Opened:** 1959. **Architect:** Bill Stevely. **Season:** Year-round. **To obtain tee times:** Call golf shop. **Miscellaneous:** Reduced fees (weekdays, seniors, juniors), metal spikes, range (grass), credit cards (MC, V), BF, FF.

BLACK BUTTE RANCH
R-Hwy. 20, Black Butte Ranch, 97759, Deschutes County, (541)595-1500, (800)399-2322, 29 miles from Bend. **E-mail:** ghanway@blackbutteranch.com. **Web:** www.blackbutteranch.com. **Facility Holes:** 36. **Green Fee:** $32/$65. **Cart Fee:** $30/Cart. **Walking Policy:** Unrestricted walking. **Season:** March-Oct. **High:** June-Sept. **Miscellaneous:** Reduced fees (weekdays, twilight, juniors), range (grass), credit cards (MC, V, AE, D), BF, FF.
★★★★ **BIG MEADOW COURSE** (18)
Yards: 6,850/5,678. **Par:** 72/72. **Course Rating:** 71.3/70.4. **Slope:** 125/124. **Walkability:** 2. **Opened:** 1971. **Architect:** Robert Muir Graves. **To obtain tee times:** Call up to 7 days in advance.
Reader Comments: Every hole has a view of the lake ... Mountain views were outstanding ... Nice grass in fairways and greens ... Pretty setting, wide and hilly ... Great, straightforward golf... Excellent vistas, pines, aspens.
★★★½ **GLAZE MEADOW COURSE** (18)
Yards: 6,574/5,616. **Par:** 72/72. **Course Rating:** 71.5/72.1. **Slope:** 128/120. **Walkability:** 3. **Opened:** 1982. **Architect:** Gene (Bunny) Mason. **To obtain tee times:** Call golf shop.
Notes: Ranked 12th in 1997 Best in State.
Reader Comments: Good balance of precision & power ... Overpriced ... Great, a couple quirky holes ... Resort play at a reasonable price ... Beautiful ponderosas, vistas ... Outstanding service ... Excellent traditional-style course.

★★ BROADMOOR GOLF COURSE
PU-3509 NE Columbia Blvd., Portland, 97211, Multnomah County, (503)281-1337, 4 miles from Portland. **Facility Holes:** 18. **Yards:** 6,467/5,388. **Par:** 72/74. **Course Rating:** 70.2/69.5.

Slope: 122/111. **Green Fee:** $22/$26. **Cart Fee:** $24/Cart. **Walking Policy:** Unrestricted walking. **Walkability:** 3. **Opened:** 1931. **Architect:** George Junor. **Season:** Year-round. **High:** May-Sept. **To obtain tee times:** Call golf shop. **Miscellaneous:** Reduced fees (weekdays, juniors), metal spikes, credit cards (MC, V).

★★½ **CEDAR LINKS GOLF CLUB**
PU-3155 Cedar Links Dr., Medford, 97504, Jackson County, (541)773-4373, (800)853-2754.
Facility Holes: 18. **Yards:** 6,215/5,145. **Par:** 70/71. **Course Rating:** 68.9/68.7. **Slope:** 114/112.
Green Fee: $22/$24. **Cart Fee:** $9/Person. **Walking Policy:** Unrestricted walking. **Walkability:** 2.
Opened: 1972. **Architect:** Coverstone/Graves. **Season:** Year-round. **High:** April-Sept. **To obtain tee times:** Call golf shop. **Miscellaneous:** Reduced fees (seniors, juniors), metal spikes, range (mats), credit cards (MC, V, D).

★★ **COLWOOD NATIONAL GOLF CLUB**
PU-7313 NE Columbia Blvd., Portland, 97218, Multnomah County, (503)254-5515. **Facility Holes:** 18. **Yards:** 6,200/5,800. **Par:** 70/74. **Course Rating:** 69.1/71.0. **Slope:** 115/111. **Green Fee:** $26/$39. **Cart Fee:** $22/Cart. **Walking Policy:** Unrestricted walking. **Walkability:** 1. **Opened:** 1930. **Architect:** A. Vernon Macan. **Season:** Year-round. **High:** April-Oct. **Tee times:** Call golf shop. **Miscellaneous:** Reduced fees (juniors), metal spikes, credit cards (MC, V).

CROOKED RIVER RANCH GOLF COURSE
SP-5195 Club House Rd., Crooked River Ranch, 97760, Deschutes County, (541)923-6343.
Facility Holes: 18. **Yards:** 6,156/5,000. **Par:** 71/72. **Course Rating:** 69.2/67.4. **Slope:** 119/111.
Green Fee: $25/$30. **Cart Fee:** $25/Cart. **To obtain tee times:** Call golf shop.

EAGLE CREST RESORT
R-1522 Cline Falls Rd., Redmond, 97756, Deschutes County, (541)923-4653, (877)818-0286, 5 miles from Redmond. **E-mail:** bobh@ecresort.eagle-crest.com. **Facility Holes:** 54.
Cart Fee: $25/Cart. **Walking Policy:** Unrestricted walking. **High:** June-Oct. **Misc:** Reduced fees (juniors), range (grass), lodging (100 rooms), credit cards (MC, V, AE, D), BF, FF.
MID IRON COURSE (18)
Yards: 4,160/2,982. **Par:** 63/63. **Course Rating:** 60.3/56.5. **Slope:** 100/91. **Green Fee:** $35.
Walkability: 3. **Season:** March-Nov. **To obtain tee times:** Call up to 14 days in advance.
★★★½ **RESORT COURSE** (18)
Yards: 6,673/5,395. **Par:** 72/72. **Course Rating:** 71.5/69.8. **Slope:** 128/120. **Green Fee:** $55.
Walkability: 3. **Opened:** 1986. **Architect:** Gene (Bunny) Mason. **Tee times:** Call golf shop.
Reader Comments: Accommodations nice, long course, fun ... Almost impossible to walk, only 1 memorable hole ... Great course ... Wide open ... Resort course, well designed ... Good value ... Beautiful courses.
★★★★ **RIDGE COURSE** (18)
Yards: 6,927/4,792. **Par:** 72/72. **Course Rating:** 73.0/66.1. **Slope:** 131/115. **Green Fee:** $65.
Walkability: 2. **Opened:** 1993. **Architect:** John Thronson. **Season:** Year-round. **To obtain tee times:** Call up to 14 days in advance.
Reader Comments: Good resort course, suitable for almost anyone ... Super practice area ... Hilly but good test ... Excellent and fun layout ... Better than its sister.

★★★★ **EAGLE POINT GOLF COURSE** *Value*
PU-100 Eagle Point Dr., Eagle Point, 97524, Jackson County, (541)826-8225, 9 miles from Medford. **E-mail:** epgolf@moriah.com. **Web:** http://www.moriah.com/epgolf/. **Facility Holes:** 18.
Yards: 7,099/5,071. **Par:** 72/72. **Course Rating:** 74.3/68.9. **Slope:** 135/114. **Green Fee:** $50/$58. **Cart Fee:** $10/Person. **Walking Policy:** Unrestricted walking. **Walkability:** 2. **Opened:** 1996. **Architect:** Robert Trent Jones Jr. **Season:** Year-round. **High:** March-Oct. **To obtain tee times:** Call up to 30 days in advance. **Miscellaneous:** Reduced fees (weekdays, twilight, seniors, juniors), range (grass), credit cards (MC, V, AE), BF, FF.
Notes: Ranked 8th in 2001 Best in State.
Reader Comments: Excellent young course, great drainage when the winter rains come ... A super value ... Immaculate condition, uncrowded ... Great greens, impossible rough ... Great track! Well-maintained, nice new clubhouse.

★★★ **EASTMORELAND GOLF COURSE**
PU-2425 SE Bybee Blvd., Portland, 97202, Multnomah County, (503)775-2900. **E-mail:** east-crc@aol.com. **Facility Holes:** 18. **Yards:** 6,529/5,646. **Par:** 72/74. **Course Rating:** 71.7/71.4.
Slope: 123/117. **Green Fee:** $21/$23. **Cart Fee:** $26/Cart. **Walking Policy:** Unrestricted walking. **Walkability:** 2. **Opened:** 1918. **Architect:** H. Chandler Egan. **Season:** Year-round. **To obtain tee times:** Call up to 6 days in advance. **Miscellaneous:** Reduced fees (seniors, juniors), range (mats), credit cards (MC, V), BF, FF.
Notes: Ranked 15th in 2001 Best in State; 37th in 1996 America's Top 75 Affordable.
Reader Comments: Best value around ... Excellent course, narrow fairways, lots of trees, some water ... Great value, minutes from downtown ... Challenging ... Tight & lots of trouble.

★★★★ **ELKHORN VALLEY GOLF COURSE** *Value, Pace*
PU-32295 N. Fork Rd., Lyons, 97358, Marion County, (503)897-3368, 36 miles from Salem.
Web: www.elkhorngolf.com. **Facility Holes:** 18. **Yards:** 6,242/3,774. **Par:** 71/71. **Course Rating:**
70.6/61.9. **Slope:** 126/98. **Green Fee:** $34/$38. **Cart Fee:** $22/Cart. **Walking Policy:**
Unrestricted walking. **Walkability:** 1. **Opened:** 1976. **Architect:** Don Cutler. **Season:** March-
Nov. **High:** June-Sept. **To obtain tee times:** Call golf shop. **Miscellaneous:** Reduced fees
(juniors), metal spikes, credit cards (MC, V, AE, D), BF, FF.
Reader Comments: Great design, amazing fast greens … Beautiful location, 2nd 9 not quite ready
… Beautiful mountain valley course … This is a must-play course, both scenic and challenging …
Spectacular setting … Severe hazards.

★★★ **EMERALD VALLEY GOLF CLUB**
SP-83301 Dale Kuni Rd., Creswell, 97426, Lane County, (541)895-2174, 10 miles from
Eugene. **Facility Holes:** 18. **Yards:** 6,873/5,371. **Par:** 72/73. **Course Rating:** 73.0/70.8. **Slope:**
126/122. **Green Fee:** $28/$31. **Cart Fee:** $22/Cart. **Walking Policy:** Unrestricted walking.
Walkability: 2. **Opened:** 1964. **Architect:** Bob Baldock. **Season:** Year-round. **High:** June-Sept.
To obtain tee times: Call golf shop. **Miscellaneous:** Reduced fees (weekdays, twilight, seniors,
juniors), range (grass/mats), credit cards (MC, V, AE).
Reader Comments: Good course all the way around … Difficult greens, great value … Long &
treelined … Greens fees too high, especially for the condition it is in … Nice, fairly easy layout.

★★½ **FOREST HILLS GOLF COURSE**
SP-36260 SW Tongue Lane, Cornelius, 97113, Washington County, (503)357-3347, 25 miles
from Portland. **Facility Holes:** 18. **Yards:** 6,173/5,673. **Par:** 72/74. **Course Rating:** 69.7/72.1.
Slope: 126/123. **Green Fee:** $34. **Cart Fee:** $24/Cart. **Walking Policy:** Unrestricted walking.
Walkability: 2. **Opened:** 1927. **Architect:** Don Bell. **Season:** Year-round. **High:** April-Oct. **To
obtain tee times:** Call up to 7 days in advance. **Miscellaneous:** Reduced fees (juniors), range
(grass/mats), credit cards (MC, V, AE), BF, FF.

★★★ **GEARHART GOLF LINKS**
PU-N. Marion St., Gearhart, 97138, Clatsop County, (503)738-3538, 90 miles from Portland.
Facility Holes: 18. **Yards:** 6,218/5,353. **Par:** 72/74. **Course Rating:** 71.0/73.1. **Slope:** 133/137.
Green Fee: $35/$45. **Cart Fee:** $25/Cart. **Walking Policy:** Unrestricted walking. **Walkability:** 2.
Opened: 1892. **Season:** Year-round. **High:** April-Nov. **To obtain tee times:** Call golf shop.
Miscellaneous: Reduced fees (twilight, juniors), range (grass), lodging (100 rooms), credit
cards (MC, V), BF, FF.
Reader Comments: Fun course to play… Totally redone, a real challenge, a must play … Rain and
wind made it challenging … Seaside links style, recently remodeled both clubhouse and course,
Scottish bunkering … Old back and forth links style, narrow fairways.

GLENDOVEER GOLF COURSE
PU-14015 NE Glisan, Portland, 97230, Multnomah County, (503)253-7507. **Facility Holes:** 36.
Green Fee: $21/$24. **Cart Fee:** $25/Cart. **Walking Policy:** Unrestricted walking. **Opened:** 1926.
Season: Year-round. **To obtain tee times:** Call golf shop. **Miscellaneous:** Reduced fees
(seniors, juniors), metal spikes, range (mats), BF, FF.
★★½ **EAST COURSE** (18)
Yards: 6,510/5,100. **Par:** 73/73. **Course Rating:** 70.4/71.4. **Slope:** 124/117. **Walkability:** 4.
Architect: John Junor.
★★★ **WEST COURSE** (18)
Yards: 6,129/5,018. **Par:** 71/72. **Course Rating:** 67.5/70.8. **Slope:** 111/110. **Walkability:** 2.
Architect: Frank Stenzel.
Reader Comments: For as much play as these two courses get, they are in great condition …
Great public course … Revamped 4 holes, making play longer and harder.

★★½ **THE GOLF CLUB OF OREGON**
PU-905 NW Spring Hill Dr., Albany, 97321, Benton County, (541)928-8338, 20 miles from
Salem. **Facility Holes:** 18. **Yards:** 5,836/5,089. **Par:** 70/71. **Course Rating:** 67.8/68.9. **Slope:**
111/117. **Green Fee:** $25. **Cart Fee:** $20/Cart. **Walking Policy:** Unrestricted walking.
Walkability: 2. **Opened:** 1930. **Season:** Year-round. **To obtain tee times:** Call up to 7 days in
advance. **Miscellaneous:** Reduced fees (seniors, juniors), metal spikes, range (mats), BF, FF.

★★★ **GRANTS PASS GOLF CLUB**
SP-230 Espey Rd., Grants Pass, 97527, Josephine County, (541)476-0849. **Facility Holes:**
18. **Yards:** 6,425/5,300. **Par:** 72/73. **Course Rating:** 71.5/71.4. **Slope:** 131/121. **Green Fee:** $30.
Cart Fee: $20/Cart. **Walking Policy:** Unrestricted walking. **Walkability:** 3. **Opened:** 1947.
Architect: Bob Baldock/Robert L. Baldock. **Season:** Year-round. **High:** March-Oct. **To obtain
tee times:** Call golf shop. **Miscellaneous:** Reduced fees (juniors), range,cards (MC, V).
Reader Comments: Good course … Odd layout.

OREGON

★★½ HARBOR LINKS GOLF COURSE
PU-601 Harbor Isles Blvd., Klamath Falls, 97601, Klamath County, (541)882-0609. **E-mail:** harbor@cvc.net. **Facility Holes:** 18. **Yards:** 6,272/5,709. **Par:** 72/72. **Course Rating:** 69.3/71.2. **Slope:** 117/119. **Green Fee:** $25/$38. **Cart Fee:** $22/Cart. **Walking Policy:** Unrestricted walking. **Walkability:** 1. **Opened:** 1986. **Architect:** Ken Black. **Season:** Year-round. **To obtain tee times:** Call up to 7 days in advance. **Miscellaneous:** Reduced fees (weekdays, twilight, seniors, juniors), range (mats), credit cards (MC, V, AE), BF, FF.

HERON LAKES GOLF COURSE
PU-3500 N. Victory Blvd., Portland, 97217, Multnomah County, (503)289-1818. **Facility Holes:** 36. **Cart Fee:** $26/Cart. **Walking Policy:** Unrestricted walking. **Walkability:** 1. **Season:** Year-round. **High:** March-Oct. **To obtain tee times:** Call golf shop. **Miscellaneous:** Metal spikes, range (grass/mats), credit cards (MC, V, AE, D).
★★★ GREAT BLUE COURSE (18)
Yards: 6,916/5,285. **Par:** 72/72. **Course Rating:** 73.6/69.8. **Slope:** 132/120. **Green Fee:** $31. **Opened:** 1971. **Architect:** Robert Trent Jones/Robert T. Jones Jr. **Miscellaneous:** Reduced fees (weekdays, seniors, juniors).
Reader Comments: Good course, crowded on weekends due to low price ... Excellent design ... Great test of golf ... If you don't like water, stay away ... Good value, tough course ... Excellent for a busy course ... A good challenge.
★★★ GREENBACK COURSE (18)
Yards: 6,608/5,240. **Par:** 72/72. **Course Rating:** 71.6/69.4. **Slope:** 123/113. **Green Fee:** $19/$21. **Opened:** 1970. **Architect:** Robert Trent Jones Jr. **Miscellaneous:** Reduced fees (seniors, juniors).
Reader Comments: Tough, long course ... Great layout but not maintained well ... Good average little muni, a little short. Good for casual game ... Great course, good use of water ... Open links-style course, lots of trouble.

HIDDEN VALLEY GOLF COURSE
PU-775 N. River Rd., Cottage Grove, 97424, Lane County, (541)942-3046, 20 miles from Eugene. **Facility Holes:** 9. **Yards:** 2,771/2,355. **Par:** 35/35. **Course Rating:** 66.6/68.4. **Slope:** 108/114. **Green Fee:** $11/$16. **Cart Fee:** $16/Cart. **Walking Policy:** Unrestricted walking. **Walkability:** 2. **Opened:** 1929. **Architect:** Ray Vincent. **Season:** Year-round. **High:** May-Sept. **To obtain tee times:** Call golf shop. **Miscellaneous:** Reduced fees (weekdays, seniors, juniors).

★★★½ INDIAN CREEK GOLF COURSE
PU-3605 Brookside Dr., Hood River, 97031, Hood River County, (541)386-7770, (866)386-7770, 60 miles from Portland. **E-mail:** icgolf@gorge.net. **Web:** indiancreekgolf.com. **Facility Holes:** 18. **Yards:** 6,150/4,547. **Par:** 72/72. **Course Rating:** 70.2/67.7. **Slope:** 124/116. **Green Fee:** $28/$38. **Cart Fee:** $25/Cart. **Walking Policy:** Unrestricted walking. **Walkability:** 4. **Opened:** 1990. **Season:** Year-round. **High:** March-Oct. **To obtain tee times:** Call up to 7 days in advance. **Miscellaneous:** Reduced fees (weekdays, twilight, seniors, juniors), range (grass/mats), credit cards (MC, V), BF, FF.
Reader Comments: Beautiful view Mt. Hood ... Easy if no wind, but wind makes it impossible ... Clean, well-maintained, up & down, great view ... Very tough course, take a dozen golf balls ... Scenic layout, fun to play.

★★★ JUNIPER GOLF CLUB
SP-139 SE Sisters Ave., Redmond, 97756, Deschutes County, (541)548-3121, (800)600-3121. **E-mail:** pga1@bendnet.com. **Facility Holes:** 18. **Yards:** 6,525/5,598. **Par:** 72/72. **Course Rating:** 70.8/70.9. **Slope:** 127/119. **Green Fee:** $20/$35. **Cart Fee:** $25/Cart. **Walking Policy:** Unrestricted walking. **Walkability:** 2. **Opened:** 1952. **Architect:** Tim Berg. **Season:** Year-round. **High:** May-Oct. **To obtain tee times:** Call up to 30 days in advance. **Miscellaneous:** Reduced fees (juniors), range (grass/mats), credit cards (MC, V, AE), BF, FF.
Reader Comments: Enjoyed it ... Great old course ... Not too exciting ... Great value for late afternoon play.

★★★ KAH-NEE-TA HIGH DESERT RESORT & CASINO
R-6823 Hwy. 8, Warm Springs, 97761, Wasco County, (541)553-4971, (800)831-0100, 115 miles from Portland. **E-mail:** kah-nee-taresort.com. **Facility Holes:** 18. **Yards:** 6,352/5,195. **Par:** 72/73. **Course Rating:** 70.1/70.0. **Slope:** 124/119. **Green Fee:** $30/$38. **Cart Fee:** $25/Cart. **Walking Policy:** Unrestricted walking. **Walkability:** 1. **Opened:** 1972. **Architect:** William P. Bell/Bunny Mason. **Season:** Year-round. **High:** May-Dec. **To obtain tee times:** Call up to 30 days in advance. **Miscellaneous:** Reduced fees (weekdays, guests, seniors, juniors), metal spikes, range (grass/mats), lodging (169 rooms), credit cards (MC, V, AE, D, DC), BF, FF.
Reader Comments: Great complex with casino ... Slow play ... Resort course, good value, need cart ... A great links golf experience, wind is a major factor ... Great condition ... Pretty good little course, a little out of the way.

★½ KENTUCK GOLF COURSE

PU-675 Golf Course Lane, North Bend, 97459, Coos County, (541)756-4464, 4 miles from North Bend. **Facility Holes:** 18. **Yards:** 5,393/4,469. **Par:** 70/70. **Course Rating:** 65.5/69.8. **Slope:** 99/107. **Green Fee:** $16/$18. **Cart Fee:** $20/Cart. **Walking Policy:** Unrestricted walking. **Walkability:** 2. **Opened:** 1962. **Season:** Year-round. **High:** May-Sept. **To obtain tee times:** Call golf shop. **Miscellaneous:** Range (grass), credit cards (MC, V, D).

LAKERIDGE GOLF COURSE

PU-Klamath Hwy. 140, Lakeview, 97630, Lake County, (541)947-3855, 3 miles from Lakeview. **E-mail:** lakeridge@transport.com. **Facility Holes:** 9. **Yards:** 3,323/2,965. **Par:** 36/37. **Course Rating:** 70.0/71.6. **Slope:** 119/121. **Green Fee:** $18. **Cart Fee:** $15/Cart. **Walking Policy:** Unrestricted walking. **Walkability:** 1. **Season:** Year-round. **High:** June-Aug. **To obtain tee times:** Call golf shop. **Miscellaneous:** Reduced fees (seniors, juniors), metal spikes, range (grass), credit cards (MC, V).

★½ LAKESIDE GOLF & FITNESS CLUB

SP-3245 NE 50th St., Lincoln City, 97367, Lincoln County, (541)994-8442, 50 miles from Salem. **E-mail:** proshop@lakeside-golf.com. **Web:** lakeside-golf.com. **Facility Holes:** 18. **Yards:** 5,007/4,318. **Par:** 65/69. **Course Rating:** 62.3/62.4. **Slope:** 102/98. **Green Fee:** $27/$40. **Cart Fee:** $25/Cart. **Walking Policy:** Unrestricted walking. **Walkability:** 4. **Opened:** 1925. **Architect:** Peter Jacobsen. **Season:** Year-round. **High:** March-Oct. **To obtain tee times:** Call up to 30 days in advance. **Miscellaneous:** Reduced fees (weekdays, twilight, seniors, juniors), metal spikes, range (mats), credit cards (MC, V, AE, D), BF, FF.

★★★½ LANGDON FARMS GOLF CLUB

PU-24377 NE Airport Rd., Aurora, 97002, Marion County, (503)678-4653, 15 miles from Portland. **E-mail:** bthompson@heritagegolfgroup.com. **Web:** www.langdonfarms.com. **Facility Holes:** 18. **Yards:** 6,950/5,249. **Par:** 71/71. **Course Rating:** 73.3/69.4. **Slope:** 125/114. **Green Fee:** $49/$84. **Cart Fee:** Included in green fee. **Walking Policy:** Unrestricted walking. **Walkability:** 3. **Opened:** 1995. **Architect:** John Fought/Robert Cupp. **Season:** Year-round. **High:** May-Oct. **To obtain tee times:** Call golf shop. **Miscellaneous:** Reduced fees (weekdays, twilight, juniors), range (grass/mats), credit cards (MC, V, AE, D), BF, FF.
Reader Comments: Excellent layout, challenging, greens in fantastic shape ... Great condition ... Nice facilities, fun ... Contrived links, big bunkers, overpriced ... Wide open ... Too many knolls in fairways ... Try 9-hole putting course.

★★★★ LOST TRACKS GOLF CLUB *Service, Pace*

PU-60205 Sunset View Dr., Bend, 97702, Deschutes County, (541)385-1818. **Facility Holes:** 18. **Yards:** 7,003/5,287. **Par:** 72/73. **Course Rating:** 72.7/71.1. **Slope:** 131/128. **Green Fee:** $29/$48. **Cart Fee:** $25/Person. **Walking Policy:** Unrestricted walking. **Walkability:** 2. **Opened:** 1996. **Architect:** Brian Whitcomb. **Season:** Year-round. **High:** June-Sept. **To obtain tee times:** Call golf shop. **Miscellaneous:** Reduced fees (guests, twilight, seniors, juniors), range (grass), credit cards (MC, V).
Reader Comments: Lots of fun ... Good course ... Mountains, lava, trees & lakes ... One of the warmest welcomes ever: I stayed an extra day for more fine golf ... One of my favorites ... Too bad there are so many houses ... Tough greens.

MALLARD CREEK GOLF COURSE

SP-31966 Bellinger Scale Rd., Lebanon, 97355, Linn County, (541)259-4653, 50 miles from Eugene. **E-mail:** john@mallardcreekgc.com. **Web:** www.mallardcreekgc.com. **Facility Holes:** 18. **Yards:** 6,938/5,399. **Par:** 72/71. **Course Rating:** 73.3/71.5. **Slope:** 138/139. **Green Fee:** $35/$40. **Cart Fee:** $24/Cart. **Walking Policy:** Unrestricted walking. **Walkability:** 3. **Opened:** 2000. **Architect:** Mike Stark. **Season:** Year-round. **High:** May-Oct. **To obtain tee times:** Call up to 7 days in advance. **Miscellaneous:** Reduced fees (juniors), range (grass/mats), credit cards (MC, V), BF, FF.

★★★½ MCNARY GOLF CLUB

SP-155 McNary Estates Dr. N., Keizer, 97303, Marion County, (503)393-4653, 45 miles from Portland. **E-mail:** ghatmcnary@aol.com. **Facility Holes:** 18. **Yards:** 6,215/5,325. **Par:** 71/71. **Course Rating:** 69.2/70.4. **Slope:** 121/117. **Green Fee:** $30/$40. **Cart Fee:** $24/Cart. **Walking Policy:** Unrestricted walking. **Walkability:** 2. **Opened:** 1962. **Season:** Year-round. **High:** April-Oct. **To obtain tee times:** Call golf shop. **Miscellaneous:** Reduced fees (weekdays, twilight, juniors), credit cards (MC, V).
Reader Comments: Lots of houses, keep it to the fairway ... Excellent condition, wonderful course ... Great course.

★★★★ MEADOW LAKES GOLF COURSE
PU-300 Meadow Lakes Dr., Prineville, 97754, Crook County, (541)447-7113, (800)577-2797, 38 miles from Bend. **Facility Holes:** 18. **Yards:** 6,731/5,155. **Par:** 72/72. **Course Rating:** 71.7/69.0. **Slope:** 125/121. **Green Fee:** $20/$32. **Cart Fee:** $12/Person. **Walking Policy:** Unrestricted walking. **Walkability:** 2. **Opened:** 1993. **Architect:** William Robinson. **Season:** Year-round. **High:** May-Oct. **To obtain tee times:** Call golf shop. **Miscellaneous:** Range (grass/mats), credit cards (MC, V, D), BF, FF.
Notes: 1996 Golf Digest's Environmental Leaders in Golf Award.
Reader Comments: Not an exciting layout, but water on every hole makes it interesting … Good course … Take great care to stay out of water … Excellent value and nice people … Excellent layout, great value … Great.

MERIWETHER NATIONAL GOLF CLUB
PU-5200 SW Rood Bridge Rd., Hillsboro, 97123, Washington County, (503)648-4143, 25 miles from Portland. **Facility Holes:** 27. **Green Fee:** $24/$30. **Cart Fee:** $20/Cart. **Walking Policy:** Walking at certain times. **Walkability:** 2. **Architect:** Fred Federsfield. **Season:** Year-round. **High:** April-Oct. **To obtain tee times:** Call golf shop. **Miscellaneous:** Reduced fees (juniors), metal spikes, range (grass), credit cards (MC, V).
NORTH/SOUTH (18)
Yards: 6,779/5,727. **Par:** 72/72. **Course Rating:** 71.2. **Slope:** 117/114. **Opened:** 1993.
SOUTH/WEST (18)
Yards: 6,752/5,665. **Par:** 72/72. **Course Rating:** 71.3/72.3. **Slope:** 115/114. **Opened:** 1993.
WEST/NORTH (18)
Yards: 6,719/5,766. **Par:** 72/73. **Course Rating:** 71.3/67.2. **Slope:** 121/112. **Opened:** 1960.
Special Notes: Also has a 9-hole executive course.

★★½ MOUNTAIN HIGH GOLF COURSE
PU-60650 China Hat Rd., Bend, 97702, Deschutes County, (541)382-1111. **Facility Holes:** 18. **Yards:** 6,656/5,268. **Par:** 72/72. **Course Rating:** 72.0/69.2. **Slope:** 131/120. **Green Fee:** $40/$48. **Cart Fee:** Included in green fee. **Walking Policy:** Unrestricted walking. **Walkability:** 2. **Opened:** 1986. **Season:** April-Nov. **High:** May-Oct. **To obtain tee times:** Call golf shop. **Miscellaneous:** Metal spikes, range (mats), credit cards (MC, V).

★★ MOUNTAIN VIEW GOLF CLUB
PU-27195 SE Kelso Rd., Boring, 97009, Clackamas County, (503)663-4869, 15 miles from Portland. **Facility Holes:** 18. **Yards:** 6,056/5,294. **Par:** 71/73. **Course Rating:** 69.2/69.2. **Slope:** 122/111. **Green Fee:** $23/$28. **Cart Fee:** $25/Cart. **Walking Policy:** Unrestricted walking. **Walkability:** 3. **Opened:** 1963. **Architect:** Jack Waltmeyer. **Season:** Year-round. **High:** March-Oct. **To obtain tee times:** Call up to 7 days in advance. **Miscellaneous:** Reduced fees (weekdays, seniors, juniors), metal spikes, range (mats), credit cards (MC, V, D), BF, FF.

★★★½ MYRTLE CREEK GOLF COURSE
PU-1316 Fairway Dr., Myrtle Creek, 97457, Douglas County, (541)863-4653, (888)869-7853, 220 miles from Portland. **E-mail:** mcgc@rosenet.net. **Web:** www.cybergolf.com/myrtlecreekgolf.com. **Facility Holes:** 18. **Yards:** 6,710/4,868. **Par:** 72/72. **Course Rating:** 72.3/69.4. **Slope:** 139/124. **Green Fee:** $23/$33. **Cart Fee:** $20/Cart. **Walking Policy:** Unrestricted walking. **Walkability:** 4. **Opened:** 1997. **Architect:** Graham Cooke. **Season:** Year-round. **High:** April-Oct. **To obtain tee times:** Call up to 14 days in advance. **Miscellaneous:** Reduced fees (weekdays, guests, twilight, seniors, juniors), metal spikes, range (grass), credit cards (MC, V), BF, FF.
Reader Comments: Just a pleasure … Hilly, very challenging, take a cart … Challenging, fun, back 9 hilly … Hilly, good shape … I liked this course, round was quick, condition was good … Target course … Fun course, caring staff.

NINE PEAKS GOLF COURSE
PU-1152 NW Golf Course Dr., Madras, 97741, Jefferson County, (541)475-3511. **Facility Holes:** 18. **Yards:** 6,582/5,745. **Par:** 72/72. **Course Rating:** 68.4/67.3. **Slope:** 107/107. **Green Fee:** $16. **Opened:** 1962. **To obtain tee times:** Call golf shop. **Miscellaneous:** Metal spikes.

OAK HILLS GOLF CLUB
PU-1919 Recreation Lane, Sutherlin, 97479, Douglas County, (541)459-4422, 12 miles from Roseburg. **Web:** www.golfoakhills.com. **Facility Holes:** 18. **Yards:** 6,811/5,388. **Par:** 72/72. **Course Rating:** 71.6/71.9. **Slope:** 129/122. **Green Fee:** $22/$25. **Cart Fee:** $20/Cart. **Walkability:** 3. **Opened:** 1971. **Season:** Year-round. **High:** May-Oct. **To obtain tee times:** Call golf shop. **Miscellaneous:** Reduced fees (weekdays, twilight, juniors), range (grass/mats), credit cards (MC, V).

OREGON

★★½ OAK KNOLL GOLF COURSE
PU-6335 Hwy. 22, Independence, 97351, Polk County, (503)378-0344, 6 miles from Salem. **Facility Holes:** 18. **Yards:** 6,208/5,239. **Par:** 72/72. **Course Rating:** 68.6/69.2. **Slope:** 113/113. **Green Fee:** $15/$27. **Cart Fee:** $14/Person. **Walking Policy:** Unrestricted walking. **Walkability:** 1. **Opened:** 1926. **Architect:** Bill Ashby. **Season:** Year-round. **High:** June-Sept. **To obtain tee times:** Call golf shop. **Miscellaneous:** Reduced fees (weekdays, twilight, seniors, juniors), metal spikes, range (grass/mats), credit cards (MC, V), BF, FF.

★★½ OCEAN DUNES GOLF LINKS
PU-3345 Munsel Lake Rd., Florence, 97439, Lane County, (541)997-3232, (800)468-4833, 60 miles from Eugene. **Facility Holes:** 18. **Yards:** 6,018/5,044. **Par:** 71/73. **Course Rating:** 70.0/73.8. **Slope:** 124/129. **Green Fee:** $28/$35. **Cart Fee:** $24/Cart. **Walking Policy:** Unrestricted walking. **Walkability:** 3. **Opened:** 1963. **Architect:** William Robinson. **Season:** Year-round. **High:** June-Nov. **To obtain tee times:** Call golf shop. **Miscellaneous:** Reduced fees (twilight, seniors, juniors), metal spikes, range (grass), credit cards (MC, V, D), BF, FF.

OLALLA VALLEY GOLF COURSE
PU-1022 Olalla Rd., Toledo, 97391, Lincoln County, (541)336-2121, 7 miles from Newport. **Facility Holes:** 18. **Yards:** 6,027/5,507. **Par:** 72/74. **Course Rating:** 69.2/72.7. **Slope:** 127/124. **Green Fee:** $22. **Cart Fee:** $18/Cart. **Walking Policy:** Unrestricted walking. **Walkability:** 4. **Season:** Year-round. **High:** June-Oct. **To obtain tee times:** Call golf shop. **Miscellaneous:** Reduced fees (juniors), range (grass), credit cards (MC, V).

★★½ OREGON CITY GOLF CLUB
PU-20124 S. Beavercreek Rd., Oregon City, 97045, Clackamas County, (503)518-2846, 6 miles from Portland. **Facility Holes:** 18. **Yards:** 5,964/5,259. **Par:** 71/75. **Course Rating:** 67.9/69.4. **Slope:** 116/113. **Green Fee:** $18/$32. **Cart Fee:** $25/Cart. **Walking Policy:** Unrestricted walking. **Walkability:** 2. **Opened:** 1922. **Architect:** H. Beals/R. Seon/J. Herberger. **Season:** Year-round. **To obtain tee times:** Call up to 14 days in advance. **Miscellaneous:** Reduced fees (weekdays, seniors, juniors), range (mats), credit cards (MC, V, D), BF, FF.

★★★★½ OREGON GOLF ASSOCIATION MEMBERS COURSE AT TUKWILA
PU-2850 Hazelnut Dr., Woodburn, 97071, Marion County, (503)981-6105. **Facility Holes:** 18. **Yards:** 6,650/5,498. **Par:** 72/72. **Course Rating:** 71.7/71.8. **Slope:** 131/129. **Green Fee:** $51. **Cart Fee:** $22/Cart. **Walking Policy:** Unrestricted walking. **Walkability:** 2. **Opened:** 1996. **Architect:** William Robinson. **Season:** Year-round. **To obtain tee times:** Call up to 5 days in advance. **Miscellaneous:** Reduced fees (twilight, juniors), range (grass/mats), credit cards (MC, V, D), BF, FF.
Notes: Ranked tied for 8th in 1996 Best New Affordable Courses.
Reader Comments: Short, playable course, back-to-back par 5s ... Great condition ... Great, a challenge ... Challenges entire game ... I'll return ... Front 9 through hazelnut trees is special ... Great course, great greens, nice facility.

★★★★ PERSIMMON COUNTRY CLUB *Service, Pace*
SP-500 SE Butler Rd., Gresham, 97080, Multnomah County, (503)661-1800, 25 miles from Portland. **E-mail:** www.persimmongolf.com. **Facility Holes:** 18. **Yards:** 6,678/4,852. **Par:** 72/72. **Course Rating:** 71.2/66.1. **Slope:** 125/112. **Green Fee:** $45/$75. **Cart Fee:** Included in green fee. **Walking Policy:** Unrestricted walking. **Walkability:** 4. **Opened:** 1993. **Architect:** Gene "Bunny" Mason. **Season:** Year-round. **High:** May-Sept. **To obtain tee times:** Call golf shop. **Miscellaneous:** Reduced fees (twilight), metal spikes, range (grass/mats), credit cards (MC, V, AE, D).
Reader Comments: Best course I've ever played ... Views of 4 mountains ... Very challenging, mountain views ... Tough, gorgeous ... Great golf! Facilities super ... Good course, too expensive ... Very hilly, long walk, must be accurate.

★★★★½ PUMPKIN RIDGE GOLF CLUB
PU-12930 Old Pumpkin Ridge Rd., North Plains, 97133, Washington County, (503)647-9977, (888)594-4653, 20 miles from Portland. **E-mail:** benh@pumpkinridge.com. **Web:** www.pumpkinridge.com. **Facility Holes:** 18. **Yards:** 6,839/5,206. **Par:** 71/71. **Course Rating:** 73.8/70.4. **Slope:** 139/125. **Green Fee:** $120. **Cart Fee:** $15/Person. **Walking Policy:** Unrestricted walking. **Walkability:** 2. **Opened:** 1992. **Architect:** Bob Cupp. **Season:** Year-round. **High:** May-Oct. **To obtain tee times:** Call golf shop. **Miscellaneous:** Reduced fees (weekdays, twilight, juniors), range (grass/mats), caddies, credit cards (MC, V, AE, D, DC), BF, FF.
Notes: Ranked 81st in 1997-98 America's 100 Greatest; 7th in 2001 Best in State.
Reader Comments: Among top public golf courses in the U.S., Outstanding ... Good course, challenging ... Great service, great condition, beautiful setting, customer service gave me a gift bag at the practice tee ... Solid, overpriced, very good but not best area ... Traditional layout ... Completely enjoyable.

★★★★ QUAIL RUN GOLF COURSE
PU-16725 Northridge Dr., La Pine, 97739, Deschutes County, (541)536-1303, (800)895-4653, 10 miles from Sunriver. **Facility Holes:** 9. **Yards:** 7,024/5,414. **Par:** 72/72. **Course Rating:** 73.4/71.0. **Slope:** 135/128. **Green Fee:** $35/$38. **Cart Fee:** $12/Person. **Walking Policy:** Unrestricted walking. **Walkability:** 2. **Opened:** 1991. **Architect:** Jim Ramey. **High:** March-Nov. **To obtain tee times:** Call up to 180 days in advance. **Miscellaneous:** Reduced fees (twilight, juniors), range (grass), credit cards (MC, V), BF, FF.
Reader Comments: The best 9 holer you will ever play … Most impressive 9-hole course … Very clean course, kept up well … Fun course … Very good 9-hole course … Really nice 9 holes.

★★★ QUAIL VALLEY GOLF COURSE
PU-12565 NW Aerts Rd., Banks, 97106, Washington County, (503)324-4444, 20 miles from Portland. **E-mail:** qvgc@teleport.com. **Web:** quailvalleygolf.com. **Facility Holes:** 18. **Yards:** 6,603/5,519. **Par:** 72/72. **Course Rating:** 71.1/71.1. **Slope:** 119/115. **Green Fee:** $26/$39. **Cart Fee:** $24/Person. **Walking Policy:** Unrestricted walking. **Walkability:** 1. **Opened:** 1994. **Architect:** John Zoller Jr. **Season:** Year-round. **To obtain tee times:** Call up to 7 days in advance. **Miscellaneous:** Reduced fees (weekdays, juniors), range (grass/mats), credit cards (MC, V, AE, D), BF, FF.
Reader Comments: Gets windy. Slightly overpriced … Good drainage, challenging & fun … Another good course … Out of the way, but nice.

★★½ RED TAIL GOLF COURSE
PU-8200 SW Scholls Ferry Rd., Beaverton, 97008, Washington County, (503)646-5166, 4 miles from Portland. **E-mail:** chris@redtail.com. **Web:** www.golfredtail.com. **Facility Holes:** 18. **Yards:** 7,107/5,601. **Par:** 72/72. **Course Rating:** 74.4/73.0. **Slope:** 135/131. **Green Fee:** $25/$35. **Cart Fee:** $25/Cart. **Walking Policy:** Unrestricted walking. **Walkability:** 2. **Opened:** 1966. **Architect:** John Zoller. **Season:** Year-round. **High:** June-Sept. **To obtain tee times:** Call up to 7 days in advance. **Miscellaneous:** Reduced fees (seniors, juniors), range (mats), credit cards (MC, V, AE, D), BF, FF.
Special Notes: Formerly Progress Downs Golf Course.

THE RESERVE VINEYARDS & GOLF CLUB
SP-4805 SW 229th Ave., Aloha, 97007, Washington County, (503)649-8191, 20 miles from Portland. **Web:** www.reservegolf.com. **Facility Holes:** 36. **Green Fee:** $45/$79. **Cart Fee:** $20/Cart. **Walking Policy:** Unrestricted walking. **Walkability:** 1. **Season:** Year-round. **To obtain tee times:** Call up to 14 days in advance. **Miscellaneous:** Reduced fees (weekdays, twilight, juniors), range (grass), credit cards (MC, V, AE, D), BF, FF.
★★★★½ CUPP COURSE (18) *Condition*
Yards: 6,852/5,198. **Par:** 72/72. **Course Rating:** 72.6/69.6. **Slope:** 132/115. **Opened:** 1998. **Architect:** Bob Cupp.
Reader Comments: Top quality, top value … A must-play, fairways in good shape, plenty of hazards for wayward irons, greens fast, challenging … Clay soil impedes run-up shots … Nice links layout … Course immaculate, service great.
★★★★½ FOUGHT COURSE (18) *Condition*
Yards: 7,172/5,189. **Par:** 72/72. **Course Rating:** 74.3/70.1. **Slope:** 134/121. **Opened:** 1997. **Architect:** John Fought.
Notes: Ranked 12th in 1999 Best in State.
Reader Comments: Nice track, good test … Best of the best … Didn't realize how much I liked it until after the round. Solid course nicely follows the natural landscape … Lots of sand, must control drives, good walking course … Great layout and shape … Gets too much play … Technical and tactical challenge.

★★★½ RESORT AT THE MOUNTAIN
R-68010 E. Fairway Ave., Welches, 97067, Clackamas County, (503)622-3151, (800)669-4653, 45 miles from Portland. **Facility Holes:** 27. **Green Fee:** $24/$48. **Cart Fee:** $28/Cart. **Walking Policy:** Unrestricted walking. **Walkability:** 2. **Opened:** 1928. **Season:** Year-round. **High:** May-Oct. **To obtain tee times:** Call golf shop. **Miscellaneous:** Reduced fees (weekdays, guests, twilight, juniors), lodging (170 rooms), credit cards (MC, V, AE, D, DC, CB), BF, FF.
FOXGLOVE/PINECONE (18 Combo)
Yards: 6,405/4,979. **Par:** 72/72. **Course Rating:** 70.7/68.5. **Slope:** 120/119.
FOXGLOVE/THISTLE (18 Combo)
Yards: 6,302/4,742. **Par:** 70/70. **Course Rating:** 68.3/67.1. **Slope:** 122/114.
PINECONE/THISTLE (18 Combo)
Yards: 6,225/4,617. **Par:** 70/70. **Course Rating:** 69.4/66.0. **Slope:** 122/109.
Reader Comments: Hills … A little overpriced, three 9s only one really good layout … Terrific scenery, good layout … Nice weekend trip … Tight fairways, beautiful scenery … 27 holes of fun in the mountains.

OREGON

★★★½ RIVER'S EDGE GOLF RESORT
R-400 NW Pro Shop Dr., Bend, 97701, Deschutes County, (541)389-2828. **Facility Holes:** 18. **Yards:** 6,683/5,381. **Par:** 72/73. **Course Rating:** 72.0/71.2. **Slope:** 134/136. **Green Fee:** $24/$48. **Cart Fee:** $13/Person. **Walking Policy:** Unrestricted walking. **Opened:** 1988. **Architect:** Robert Muir Graves. **Season:** Year-round. **High:** May-Sept. **To obtain tee times:** Call golf shop. **Miscellaneous:** Reduced fees (weekdays, guests, twilight, juniors), range (grass/mats), credit cards (MC, V), BF, FF.
Reader Comments: Very tricky short course ... Changes in elevations make for challenge ... Bring your A-game ... Challenge, great staff, overpriced ... Exceptional value ... Some tricky holes.

★★ RIVERIDGE GOLF COURSE
PU-3800 N. Delta Hwy., Eugene, 97408, Lane County, (541)345-9160. **Facility Holes:** 18. **Yards:** 6,256/5,146. **Par:** 71/71. **Course Rating:** 68.6/67.7. **Slope:** 116/112. **Green Fee:** $24/$30. **Cart Fee:** $20/Cart. **Walking Policy:** Unrestricted walking. **Walkability:** 3. **Opened:** 1990. **Architect:** Ric Jeffries. **Season:** Year-round. **High:** May-Sept. **To obtain tee times:** Call golf shop. **Miscellaneous:** Reduced fees (weekdays, seniors, juniors), metal spikes, range (grass/mats), credit cards (MC, V).

★★½ ROSE CITY MUNICIPAL GOLF CLUB
PU-2200 NE 71st, Portland, 97213, Multnomah County, (503)253-4744. **Facility Holes:** 18. **Yards:** 6,455/5,619. **Par:** 72/72. **Course Rating:** 70.9/71.6. **Slope:** 118/117. **Green Fee:** $11/$22. **Cart Fee:** $26/Cart. **Walking Policy:** Unrestricted walking. **Walkability:** 2. **Opened:** 1923. **Architect:** George Otten. **Season:** Year-round. **High:** May-Oct. **To obtain tee times:** Call golf shop. **Miscellaneous:** Reduced fees (weekdays), credit cards (MC, V, D), BF, FF.

★★★★½ RUNNING Y RANCH RESORT *Value, Condition, Pace+*
R-5790 Coopers Hawk Rd., Klamath Falls, 97601, Klamath County, (541)850-5580, (888)850-0261, 10 miles from Klamath Falls. **E-mail:** runningy.com. **Web:** www.runningy.com. **Facility Holes:** 18. **Yards:** 7,133/4,842. **Par:** 72/72. **Course Rating:** 73.0/66.3. **Slope:** 125/120. **Green Fee:** $37/$55. **Cart Fee:** $26/Cart. **Walking Policy:** Unrestricted walking. **Walkability:** 2. **Opened:** 1997. **Architect:** Arnold Palmer/Ed Seay/Erik Larsen. **Season:** Year-round. **High:** May-Nov. **To obtain tee times:** Call up to 14 days in advance. **Miscellaneous:** Reduced fees (guests, juniors), range (grass), lodging (83 rooms), credit cards (MC, V, AE, D), BF, FF. **Notes:** Ranked 6th in 2001 Best in State.
Reader Comments: Beautiful course, player friendly, staff is friendly & helpful ... Loved it ... Great course, best layout ... Outstanding, 9th hole bad ... Perfect fairways, lighting-fast greens that hold, scenery ... Affordable, fair for all skill levels ... Great golf experience, tough greens ... Great staff.

★★★★ SALEM GOLF CLUB
SP-2025 Golf Course Rd., Salem, 97302, Marion County, (503)363-6652. **Facility Holes:** 18. **Yards:** 6,200/5,163. **Par:** 72/72. **Course Rating:** 69.6/70.0. **Slope:** 114/113. **Green Fee:** $35/$40. **Cart Fee:** $24/Cart. **Walking Policy:** Unrestricted walking. **Walkability:** 1. **Opened:** 1928. **Architect:** Ercel Kay. **Season:** Year-round. **High:** July-Sept. **To obtain tee times:** Call golf shop. **Miscellaneous:** Reduced fees (twilight, juniors), metal spikes, range (grass/mats), caddies, credit cards (MC, V).
Reader Comments: Very nice old-style course, big trees, small greens ... Old course, old growth, very fun to play ... Heavily treed, small greens.

★★★ SALMON RUN GOLF COURSE
PU-99040 S. Bank Chetcho River Rd., Brookings, 97415, Curry County, (541)469-4888. **E-mail:** claveran@harborside.com. **Web:** www.salmonrun.net. **Facility Holes:** 18. **Opened:** 2000. **Architect:** Mike Stark/Troy Claveran. **To obtain tee times:** Call golf shop.
Reader Comments: Pretty views, very narrow, fun ... Overpriced, overall course condition poor ... Pretty land, has dogleg par 3 ... Beautiful surroundings ... New course ... Overpriced ... Beautiful new course ... Unique course.

★½ SANDELIE GOLF COURSE
PU-28333 SW Mountain Rd., West Linn, 97068, Clackamas County, (503)655-1461. **Facility Holes:** 18. **Yards:** 5,894/5,406. **Par:** 70/70. **Slope:** 99/109. **Green Fee:** $16/$18. **Opened:** 1970. **Architect:** Harvey Junor. **To obtain tee times:** Call golf shop. **Miscellaneous:** Metal spikes.

★★★★ SANDPINES GOLF LINKS
PU-1201 35th St., Florence, 97439, Lane County, (541)997-1940, (800)917-4653, 60 miles from Eugene. **E-mail:** info@sandpines.com. **Web:** www.sandpines.com. **Facility Holes:** 18. **Yards:** 6,954/5,346. **Par:** 72/72. **Course Rating:** 74.9/72.7. **Slope:** 130/129. **Green Fee:** $35/$50. **Cart Fee:** $26/Cart. **Walking Policy:** Unrestricted walking. **Walkability:** 2. **Opened:** 1993. **Architect:** Rees Jones. **Season:** Year-round. **To obtain tee times:** Call golf shop. **Miscellaneous:** Reduced fees (twilight, juniors), metal spikes, range (grass/mats), credit cards

(MC, V, AE), BF, FF.
Notes: Ranked 12th in 2001 Best in State; 1st in 1996 America's Top 75 Affordable Courses.
Reader Comments: Incredible value, outstanding ... What every course should be ... A little pricey ... Scenic, good service, good pace ... Poor man's Spyglass ... Links, plays hard in wind ... Wonderful place, sand dunes.

SANTIAM GOLF CLUB
PU-8724 Golf Club Rd. SE, Aumsville, 97325, Marion County, (503)769-3485, 15 miles from Salem. **Facility Holes:** 18. **Yards:** 6,392/5,469. **Par:** 72/72. **Course Rating:** 69.9/70.7. **Slope:** 123/119. **Green Fee:** $26/$29. **Cart Fee:** $20/Cart. **Walking Policy:** Unrestricted walking. **Walkability:** 2. **Opened:** 1958. **Architect:** Fred Federspiel. **Season:** Year-round. **To obtain tee times:** Call golf shop. **Miscellaneous:** Reduced fees (weekdays, seniors, juniors), range (grass), credit cards (MC, V), BF, FF.

SHADOW BUTTE GOLF CLUB
PU-1345 Golf Course Rd., Ontario, 97914, Malheur County, (541)889-9022, (888)303-4653, 60 miles from Boise. **Facility Holes:** 18. **Yards:** 6,795/5,742. **Par:** 72/74. **Course Rating:** 70.4/73.3. **Slope:** 116/120. **Green Fee:** $10/$12. **Cart Fee:** $16/Cart. **Walking Policy:** Unrestricted walking. **Walkability:** 2. **Opened:** 1968. **Season:** Feb.-Nov. **High:** March-June. **To obtain tee times:** Call golf shop. **Miscellaneous:** Reduced fees (juniors), metal spikes, range (grass), credit cards (MC, V).

★★½ SHIELD CREST GOLF COURSE
SP-3151 Shield Crest Dr., Klamath Falls, 97603, Klamath County, (541)884-5305, 70 miles from Medford. **E-mail:** byrdie@internetcds.com. **Facility Holes:** 18. **Yards:** 7,005/5,464. **Par:** 72/74. **Course Rating:** 71.8/68.2. **Slope:** 117/116. **Green Fee:** $21/$25. **Cart Fee:** $11/Person. **Walking Policy:** Unrestricted walking. **Walkability:** 2. **Opened:** 1989. **Season:** March-Nov. **High:** July-Sept. **To obtain tee times:** Call golf shop. **Miscellaneous:** Reduced fees (weekdays, seniors, juniors), range (grass), credit cards (MC, V).

★★★½ STONERIDGE GOLF CLUB
PU-500 E. Antelope Rd., Eagle Point, 97524, Jackson County, (541)830-4653, 8 miles from Medford. **Facility Holes:** 18. **Yards:** 6,738/4,986. **Par:** 72/72. **Course Rating:** 72.3/69.0. **Slope:** 134/123. **Green Fee:** $25/$30. **Cart Fee:** $10/Person. **Walking Policy:** Unrestricted walking. **Walkability:** 4. **Opened:** 1995. **Architect:** James Cochran. **Season:** Year-round. **High:** May-Oct. **To obtain tee times:** Call up to 7 days in advance. **Miscellaneous:** Reduced fees (twilight), metal spikes, range (grass/mats), credit cards (MC, V), BF, FF.
Reader Comments: Very interesting. Good value ... Favorite course, beautiful, moderately difficult ... Great scenery. Good variety of holes ... Fun course ... Excellent layout, good pace of play ... Good value, will use all your clubs.

SUNRIVER LODGE & RESORT
R-Sunriver, Deschutes County, (541)593-3750, (800)547-3922, 12 miles from Bend. **E-mail:** sunriver-resort.com. **Facility Holes:** 54. **Cart Fee:** Included in green fee. **Walking Policy:** Unrestricted walking. **High:** June-Aug. **To obtain tee times:** Call golf shop. **Miscellaneous:** Range (grass), credit cards (MC, V, AE, D, DC), BF, FF.
★★★★½ **CROSSWATER CLUB** (18) *Condition*
P.O. Box 4818, Sunriver, 97707, Deschutes County, (541)593-6196, (800)547-3922
Yards: 7,683/5,359. **Par:** 72/72. **Course Rating:** 76.9/69.8. **Slope:** 153/125. **Green Fee:** $95/$175. **Walkability:** 2. **Opened:** 1995. **Architect:** Bob Cupp/John Fought. **Season:** April-Oct. **Miscellaneous:** Reduced fees (guests, twilight, juniors), lodging (200 rooms).
Notes: Ranked 96th in 2001-2002 America's 100 Greatest; 3rd in 2001 Best in State; 1st in 1995 Best New Resort Courses.
Reader Comments: If you have a secret weakness, this course will find it ... Incredible place ... Very tough & fun ... Not for hackers ... Not from tips! ... Too demanding for any but low-handicappers ... A little expensive, but great ... Doesn't get any better ... Tough & stunning, what a treat.
★★★★ **NORTH WOODLANDS COURSE** (18)
R-P. O. Box 3609, Sunriver, 97707, Deschutes County, (541)593-3703, (800)547-3922
Yards: 6,880/5,446. **Par:** 72/72. **Course Rating:** 73.0/70.3. **Slope:** 131/118. **Green Fee:** $55/$125. **Walkability:** 2. **Opened:** 1981. **Architect:** Robert Trent Jones Jr. **Season:** May-Nov. **Miscellaneous:** Reduced fees (weekdays, guests, twilight, juniors).
Notes: Ranked 11th in 2001 Best in State.
Reader Comments: Excellent resort course ... A must-play, user friendly ... Sporty layout ... spectacular views ... Fun & scenic ... OK but not as good as expected ... Nice, slow ... Wonderful course, fabulous setting.
★★★★ **SOUTH MEADOWS COURSE** (18)
R-P. O. Box 3609, Sunriver, 97707, Deschutes County, (541)593-3750, (800)547-3922
Yards: 7,012/5,304. **Par:** 71/71. **Course Rating:** 72.8/69.8. **Slope:** 128/127. **Green Fee:** $55/$125. **Walkability:** 1. **Opened:** 1999. **Architect:** John Fought. **Season:** April-Nov.

OREGON

Miscellaneous: Reduced fees (weekdays, guests, twilight, juniors).
Reader Comments: Traps, water, good test ... Nice, overpriced, slow play... Excellent course ... Great views, challenging ... A great spot! Much better ... New remodel is great ... Remodeled course a winner.

★★★★ TOKATEE GOLF CLUB *Value*
PU-54947 McKenzie Hwy., Blue River, 97413, Lane County, (541)822-3220, (800)452-6376, 47 miles from Eugene. **E-mail:** tokatee@pond.net. **Web:** www.tokatee.com. **Facility Holes:** 18. **Yards:** 6,806/5,018. **Par:** 72/72. **Course Rating:** 72.4/67.8. **Slope:** 127/109. **Green Fee:** $37. **Cart Fee:** $28/Cart. **Walking Policy:** Unrestricted walking. **Walkability:** 2. **Opened:** 1966. **Architect:** Ted Robinson. **Season:** Feb.-Nov. **High:** July-Sept. **To obtain tee times:** Call golf shop. **Miscellaneous:** Reduced fees (juniors), metal spikes, range (grass), credit cards (MC, V), BF, FF.
Notes: Ranked 13th in 2001 Best in State.
Reader Comments: Breathtaking, can't remember a single shot! ... Outstanding views, great condition, terrific value ... Great track, beautiful mountain setting ... Best value in Oregon ... Starts easy, becomes challenging, great setting.

★½ TOP O SCOTT GOLF COURSE
PU-12000 S.E. Stevens Rd., Portland, 97266, Clackamas County, (503)654-5050, 6 miles from Portland. **Facility Holes:** 18. **Yards:** 4,826/3,670. **Par:** 67/67. **Course Rating:** 64.5/65.4. **Slope:** 100/101. **Green Fee:** $17/$19. **Cart Fee:** $22/Cart. **Walking Policy:** Unrestricted walking. **Walkability:** 3. **Opened:** 1926. **Season:** Year-round. **High:** May-Oct. **To obtain tee times:** Call golf shop. **Miscellaneous:** Reduced fees (seniors, juniors), metal spikes, range (mats), credit cards (MC, V).

★★★ TRYSTING TREE GOLF CLUB
PU-34028 Electric Rd., Corvallis, 97333, Benton County, (541)752-3332, 34 miles from Salem. **E-mail:** thetree@peak.org. **Facility Holes:** 18. **Yards:** 7,014/5,516. **Par:** 72/72. **Course Rating:** 73.9/71.3. **Slope:** 129/118. **Green Fee:** $28. **Cart Fee:** $22/Cart. **Walking Policy:** Unrestricted walking. **Walkability:** 1. **Opened:** 1988. **Architect:** Ted Robinson. **Season:** Year-round. **High:** May-Oct. **To obtain tee times:** Call golf shop. **Miscellaneous:** Reduced fees (juniors), metal spikes, range (grass/mats), credit cards (MC, V, D).
Reader Comments: Back 9 more challenging, but fun all the way ... Very different front & back 9s ... Prices were high but pace is great ... Great university course.

UMATILLA GOLF COURSE
PU-705 Willamette, Umatilla, 97882, Umatilla County, (541)922-3006, 54 miles from Walla Walla. **Facility Holes:** 18. **Yards:** 6,000/5,700. **Par:** 70/72. **Course Rating:** 68.9/74.0. **Slope:** 119/113. **Green Fee:** $10/$16. **Walking Policy:** Unrestricted walking. **Opened:** 1968. **Season:** Year-round. **High:** March-Oct. **To obtain tee times:** Call golf shop. **Miscellaneous:** Reduced fees (juniors), metal spikes, range (grass), credit cards (MC, V, D).

VERNONIA GOLF CLUB
PU-15961 Timber Rd. E, Vernonia, 97064, Columbia County, (503)429-6811, (800)644-6535, 35 miles from Portland. **Facility Holes:** 18. **Yards:** 5,750/5,116. **Par:** 70/73. **Course Rating:** 68.5/69.8. **Slope:** 111/114. **Green Fee:** $18/$25. **Cart Fee:** $24/Cart. **Walking Policy:** Unrestricted walking. **Walkability:** 3. **Opened:** 1928. **Architect:** Fred R. Fulmer III. **Season:** Year-round. **To obtain tee times:** Call golf shop. **Miscellaneous:** Reduced fees (weekdays, seniors, juniors), metal spikes, range (grass), credit cards (MC, V), BF, FF.

★★★½ WESTIN SALISHAN LODGE & GOLF RESORT
R-Hwy. 101, Gleneden Beach, 97388, Lincoln County, (541)764-3632, (800)890-0387, 58 miles from Salem. **E-mail:** mswiftsalishan.com. **Web:** www.salishan.com. **Facility Holes:** 18. **Yards:** 6,453/5,389. **Par:** 72/72. **Course Rating:** 72.3/72.3. **Slope:** 132/128. **Green Fee:** $35/$65. **Cart Fee:** $30/Cart. **Walking Policy:** Unrestricted walking. **Walkability:** 3. **Opened:** 1965. **Architect:** Fred Federspiel. **Season:** Year-round. **High:** June-Oct. **To obtain tee times:** Call golf shop. **Miscellaneous:** Reduced fees (guests, juniors), range (mats), lodging (205 rooms), credit cards (MC, V, AE, D, DC), BF, FF.
Notes: Ranked 14th in 1997 Best in State; 68th in 1996 America's Top 75 Affordable Courses.
Reader Comments: Difficult, tight, hilly ... Very challenging ... Nice layout, tough with wind ... Great resort course ... Challenging, very nice getaway ... Made improvements in last 5 years.

★★★★ WIDGI CREEK GOLF CLUB *Pace*
SP-18707 SW Century Dr., Bend, 97702, Deschutes County, (541)382-4449, 160 miles from Portland. **E-mail:** www.widgi.com. **Web:** www.widgi.com. **Facility Holes:** 18. **Yards:** 6,903/5,070. **Par:** 72/72. **Course Rating:** 71.9/67.4. **Slope:** 134/119. **Green Fee:** $29/$80. **Cart Fee:** $28/Person. **Walking Policy:** Unrestricted walking. **Walkability:** 2. **Opened:** 1991.

OREGON

Architect: Robert Muir Graves. **Season:** March-Nov. **High:** June-Sept. **To obtain tee times:** Call up to 30 days in advance. **Miscellaneous:** Reduced fees (weekdays, guests, twilight, juniors), range (grass), lodging (6 rooms), credit cards (MC, V, D), BF, FF.
Reader Comments: Great design ... Tough, narrow greens ... Narrow, tough greens, may not need to hit driver often, need good iron play ... Beautiful course ... Fun as always ... Very friendly crew.

WILDHORSE RESORT GOLF COURSE

PU-72787 Hwy. 331, Pendleton, 97801, Umatilla County, (541)276-5588, (800)654-9453, 5 miles from Pendleton. **E-mail:** wildgolf@uc.net.com. **Web:** www.wildhorseresort.com. **Facility Holes:** 18. **Yards:** 7,112/5,718. **Par:** 72/72. **Course Rating:** 73.8/72.1. **Slope:** 125/122. **Green Fee:** $25/$30. **Cart Fee:** $26/Cart. **Walking Policy:** Unrestricted walking. **Walkability:** 2. **Opened:** 1998. **Architect:** John Steidel. **Season:** Year-round. **High:** April-Sept. **To obtain tee times:** Call golf shop. **Miscellaneous:** Reduced fees (weekdays, guests, twilight, juniors), range (grass), lodging (200 rooms), credit cards (MC, V, AE, D), BF, FF.

★★½ ALLENTOWN MUNICIPAL GOLF COURSE
PU-3400 Tilghman St., Allentown, 18104, Lehigh County, (610)395-9926, 65 miles from Philadelphia. **Facility Holes:** 18. **Yards:** 6,763/4,917. **Par:** 72/72. **Course Rating:** 71.9/67.0. **Slope:** 125/113. **Green Fee:** $16/$24. **Cart Fee:** $22/Person. **Walking Policy:** Unrestricted walking. **Walkability:** 3. **Opened:** 1952. **Architect:** Ault/Clark. **Season:** Year-round. **High:** May-Sept. **To obtain tee times:** Call up to 7 days in advance. **Miscellaneous:** Reduced fees (twilight, seniors, juniors), range (grass), credit cards (MC, V), BF, FF.

★★★ AMERICAN LEGION COUNTRY CLUB
SP-Country Club Rd., Mount Union, 17066, Huntingdon County, (814)542-4343. **Facility Holes:** 18. **Yards:** 6,521/5,791. **Par:** 74/74. **Course Rating:** 70.9/72.3. **Slope:** 118/120. **Green Fee:** $15/$18. **Cart Fee:** $24/Cart. **Opened:** 1920. **Season:** Year-round. **To obtain tee times:** Call golf shop.
Reader Comments: Only course I've played with a par-6 hole ... Unique layout ... Friendly staff ... Long course in nice country ... Very good test, excellent greens.

★★ APPLEWOOD GOLF COURSE
PU-Mt. Zion Rd., Harding, 18643, Luzerne County, (570)388-2500, 15 miles from Wilkes-Barre. **E-mail:** applewd@epix.net. **Facility Holes:** 9. **Yards:** 2,812/2,145. **Par:** 35/35. **Course Rating:** 33.2/32.0. **Slope:** 110/106. **Green Fee:** $13/$19. **Cart Fee:** $13/Person. **Walking Policy:** Unrestricted walking. **Walkability:** 3. **Opened:** 1995. **Architect:** Jim Blaukovitch & Associates. **Season:** April-Nov. **High:** May-Sept. **To obtain tee times:** Call golf shop. **Miscellaneous:** Reduced fees (weekdays, twilight), metal spikes, range (mats), credit cards (MC, V).

★★★½ ARMITAGE GOLF COURSE *Value*
PU-800 Orrs Bridge Rd., Mechanicsburg, 17050, Cumberland County, (717)737-5344, 5 miles from Harrisburg. **Facility Holes:** 18. **Yards:** 6,000/5,200. **Par:** 70/70. **Course Rating:** 67.2/67.6. **Slope:** 116/111. **Green Fee:** $17/$25. **Cart Fee:** $10/Person. **Walking Policy:** Unrestricted walking. **Walkability:** 3. **Opened:** 1962. **Architect:** Ed Ault. **Season:** March-Nov. **High:** May-Sept. **To obtain tee times:** Call up to 7 days in advance. **Miscellaneous:** Reduced fees (twilight, seniors, juniors), range (grass/mats), credit cards (MC, V), BF, FF.
Reader Comments: Best bargain in the area ... Driver not always best selection ... Narrow fairways, hilly, excellent greens ... Very good attention to small things ... Course is short ... Staff makes you feel like a country-club member ... Flower beds reminiscent of Augusta.

★★ ARNOLD'S GOLF CLUB
SP-Route 339 South, Nescopeck, 18635, Luzerne County, (570)752-7022. **E-mail:** jbcris@sunlink.net. **Facility Holes:** 18. **Yards:** 5,134/4,143. **Par:** 70/70. **Course Rating:** 68.5/69.5. **Slope:** 115/116. **Green Fee:** $16/$19. **Cart Fee:** $11/Person. **Walking Policy:** Mandatory carts. **Walkability:** 4. **Opened:** 1981. **Architect:** Arnold Crisman. **High:** April-Oct. **To obtain tee times:** Call golf shop. **Miscellaneous:** Credit cards (MC, V), FF.

★★½ ARROWHEAD GOLF COURSE
PU-1539 Weavertown Rd., Douglassville, 19518, Berks County, (610)582-4258, 9 miles from Reading. **Facility Holes:** 27. **Yards:** 6,002/6,002. **Par:** 71/71. **Course Rating:** 68.9/73.4. **Slope:** 116/124. **Green Fee:** $16/$25. **Cart Fee:** $20/Cart. **Walking Policy:** Unrestricted walking. **Opened:** 1954. **Architect:** John McLean. **To obtain tee times:** Call golf shop. **Miscellaneous:** Reduced fees (weekdays, twilight), metal spikes, range (grass/mats). **Special Notes:** Also has a 9-hole Blue Course.

★★½ ASHBOURNE COUNTRY CLUB
SP-Ashbourne & Oak Lane Rds, Cheltenham, 19012, Montgomery County, (215)635-3090, 5 miles from Philadelphia. **Web:** www.ashbourne.com. **Facility Holes:** 18. **Yards:** 6,037/5,263. **Par:** 70/72. **Course Rating:** 69.2/71.5. **Slope:** 121/125. **Green Fee:** $39/$75. **Cart Fee:** Included in green fee. **Walking Policy:** Walking at certain times. **Walkability:** 3. **Opened:** 1924. **Architect:** J. Franklyn Meehan. **High:** May-Oct. **To obtain tee times:** Call golf shop. **Miscellaneous:** Reduced fees (weekdays, twilight, juniors), credit cards (MC, V, AE, D).

★★★ AUBREYS GOLF CLUB
SP-Mercer Rd., Butler, 16001, Butler County, (724)287-4832. **Facility Holes:** 18. **Yards:** 6,350/5,545. **Par:** 71/71. **Course Rating:** 68.0. **Slope:** 114. **Green Fee:** $14/$18. **Opened:** 1964. **Architect:** John Aubrey. **To obtain tee times:** Call golf shop. **Miscellaneous:** Metal spikes.
Reader Comments: Difficult course, nice staff ... Front 9 a cakewalk, back rates among the most difficult in western PA. ... Not for everyone, you'll love it or hate it ... The back, what a challenge.

★★★½ BAVARIAN HILLS GOLF COURSE
PU-1 Mulligan Rd., St. Mary's, 15857, Elk County, (814)834-3602, 135 miles from Pittsburgh. **Facility Holes:** 18. **Yards:** 5,986/4,693. **Par:** 71/73. **Course Rating:** 68.8/67.2. **Slope:** 126/115.

Green Fee: $22/$29. **Cart Fee:** $10/Person. **Walking Policy:** Unrestricted walking. **Walkability:** 5. **Opened:** 1990. **Architect:** Bill Love/Brian Ault. **Season:** April-Nov. **High:** June-Sept. **To obtain tee times:** Call up to 7 days in advance. **Miscellaneous:** Reduced fees (weekdays), range (mats), credit cards (MC, V), BF, FF.
Reader Comments: Variety of shots, lots of fun ... A gem in the mountains of northwestern Pennsylvania ... A must to play and worth the trip ... Need to think! ... Yard markers good ... Majestic mountain scenery.

★★★ BEDFORD SPRINGS GOLF COURSE

PU-2138 Business 220 South, Bedford, 15522, Bedford County, (814)623-8700, 80 miles from Pittsburgh. **Facility Holes:** 18. **Yards:** 7,000/5,535. **Par:** 74/74. **Course Rating:** 73.0/72.5. **Slope:** 130/125. **Green Fee:** $10/$25. **Cart Fee:** $13/Person. **Walking Policy:** Mandatory carts. **Walkability:** 3. **Opened:** 1923. **Architect:** Donald Ross. **Season:** Year-round. **To obtain tee times:** Call up to 7 days in advance. **Miscellaneous:** Reduced fees (weekdays, twilight, seniors, juniors), range (grass), credit cards (MC, V), BF, FF.
Reader Comments: Classic old course ... Good for all handicaps ... Great for longball hitters ... Scenic ... Fast greens, long par 5s, well bunkered.

BELLES SPRING GOLF COURSE

PU-P.O. Box 149, Mackeyville, 17750, Clinton County, (570)726-4222. **Web:** www.bellessprings.com. **Facility Holes:** 18. **Yards:** 6,937/5,547. **Par:** 72/74. **Course Rating:** 73.2/71.6. **Slope:** 124/119. **Green Fee:** $18/$21. **Cart Fee:** $12/Person. **Walking Policy:** Unrestricted walking. **Walkability:** 4. **Opened:** 1969. **Architect:** Edmund B. Ault. **Season:** March-Dec. **To obtain tee times:** Call golf shop. **Miscellaneous:** Range (grass), credit cards (MC, V, D), BF, FF.

★★ BENSALEM COUNTRY CLUB

PU-2000 Brown Ave., Bensalem, 19020, Bucks County, (215)639-5556, 20 miles from Philadelpia. **Facility Holes:** 18. **Yards:** 6,131/5,554. **Par:** 70/70. **Course Rating:** 68.2/65.6. **Slope:** 119/111. **Green Fee:** $40/$50. **Cart Fee:** Included in green fee. **Walking Policy:** Walking at certain times. **Season:** Year-round. **To obtain tee times:** Call up to 7 days in advance. **Miscellaneous:** Reduced fees (weekdays, twilight, seniors, juniors), range (mats), credit cards (MC, V, AE), BF, FF.

★★★★ BETHLEHEM MUNICIPAL GOLF CLUB *Value*

PU-400 Illicks Mills Rd., Bethlehem, 18017, Northampton County, (610)691-9393, 8 miles from Allentown. **Facility Holes:** 27. **Yards:** 7,017/5,119. **Par:** 71/71. **Course Rating:** 73.6/70.6. **Slope:** 127/113. **Green Fee:** $12/$25. **Cart Fee:** $12/Person. **Walking Policy:** Unrestricted walking. **Walkability:** 3. **Opened:** 1956. **Architect:** William Gordon/David Gordon. **Season:** Year-round. **High:** May-Oct. **To obtain tee times:** Call golf shop. **Miscellaneous:** Reduced fees (weekdays, twilight, seniors, juniors), range (grass/mats), credit cards (MC, V), BF, FF.
Reader Comments: Good condition, roomy ... Pro shop guys are the most pleasant I've met ... Quick greens, bargain greens fees ... A very pleasant way to spend 3 hrs and 45 minutes ... Municipal course in excellent shape.
Special Notes: Also has a 9-hole executive course.

BLACK HAWK GOLF COURSE

PU-644 Blackhawk Rd., Beaver Falls, 15010, Beaver County, (724)843-2542, 35 miles from Pittsburgh. **E-mail:** blckhawk@tristate.pgh.net. **Facility Holes:** 36. **Green Fee:** $14/$23. **Cart Fee:** $11/Person. **Walking Policy:** Unrestricted walking. **Walkability:** 2. **Opened:** 1927. **Architect:** Paul Frable. **Season:** Year-round. **High:** May-Sept. **To obtain tee times:** Call up to 7 days in advance. **Miscellaneous:** Reduced fees (weekdays, seniors), range (grass/mats), credit cards (MC, V, AE, D), BF, FF.
★★★½ FIRST COURSE (18)
Yards: 6,114/5,365. **Par:** 72/72. **Course Rating:** 67.7/68.6. **Slope:** 113/113. **Miscellaneous:** Metal spikes.
Reader Comments: Economical and convenient ... Great fast greens, good public course ... Up and down challenges ... Old-style, small greens; short on hazards ... Plenty of play.
★★★ SECOND COURSE (18)
Yards: 6,285/5,552. **Par:** 72/72. **Course Rating:** 67.7/68.6. **Slope:** 112/113.
Reader Comments: Wide fairways, big greens, friendly pro ... Hilly, gets a lot of play ... Long, challenging ... Need to be Tiger to reach in two.

★★½ BLACKWOOD GOLF COURSE

PU-510 Red Corner Rd., Douglassville, 19518, Berks County, (610)385-6200, 12 miles from Reading. **E-mail:** msnairn@aol.com. **Web:** www.blackwoodgolf.com. **Facility Holes:** 18. **Yards:** 6,403/4,826. **Par:** 70/70. **Course Rating:** 68.6/62.0. **Slope:** 115/95. **Green Fee:** $17/$28. **Cart Fee:** $22/Cart. **Walking Policy:** Unrestricted walking. **Walkability:** 2. **Opened:** 1970. **Architect:** William Gordon. **Season:** Year-round. **To obtain tee times:** Call golf shop. **Miscellaneous:** Reduced fees (weekdays, twilight, seniors), metal spikes, range (grass/mats), FF.

PENNSYLVANIA

★★ BLUE MOUNTAIN VIEW GOLF COURSE
PU-Blue Mt. Dr., RD 1, Box 106, Fredericksburg, 17026, Lebanon County, (717)865-4401, 23 miles from Harrisburg. **Facility Holes:** 18. **Yards:** 6,010/4,520. **Par:** 71/73. **Course Rating:** 68.2/64.9. **Slope:** 110/101. **Green Fee:** $13/$21. **Cart Fee:** $9/Person. **Walking Policy:** Unrestricted walking. **Walkability:** 2. **Opened:** 1963. **Architect:** William and David Gordon. **Season:** Year-round. **High:** May-Sept. **To obtain tee times:** Call up to 14 days in advance. **Miscellaneous:** Reduced fees (weekdays, seniors, juniors), range (grass), credit cards (MC, V), BF, FF.

BLUEBERRY HILL GOLF CLUB
PU-Warren & Onoville Rd., Russell, 16345, Warren County, (814)757-8620. **Facility Holes:** 18. **Yards:** 6,716/5,813. **Par:** 72/72. **Course Rating:** 71.5/72.6. **Slope:** 122/119. **Green Fee:** $18. **Cart Fee:** $20/Cart. **Opened:** 1961. **Architect:** James Harrison & Ferdinand. **Season:** April-Nov. **To obtain tee times:** Call golf shop. **Miscellaneous:** Reduced fees (twilight), metal spikes, credit cards (MC, V).

★½ BON-AIR GOLF CLUB
PU-505 McCormick Rd., Coraopolis, 15108, Allegheny County, (412)262-2992, 10 miles from Pittsburgh. **Facility Holes:** 18. **Yards:** 5,821/4,809. **Par:** 71/73. **Course Rating:** 68.5/69.5. **Slope:** 117/120. **Green Fee:** $12/$18. **Cart Fee:** $12/Person. **Walking Policy:** Unrestricted walking. **Walkability:** 4. **Opened:** 1932. **Season:** Year-round. **High:** April-Sept. **To obtain tee times:** Call golf shop. **Miscellaneous:** Reduced fees (weekdays, seniors), metal spikes, credit cards (MC, V, AE).

BRIARWOOD GOLF CLUB
PU-4775 W. Market St., York, 17404, York County, (717)792-9776, (800)432-1555, 40 miles from Baltimore, MD. **E-mail:** briarwood@blazenet.net. **Facility Holes:** 36. **Green Fee:** $23/$31. **Cart Fee:** $13/Person. **Walking Policy:** Unrestricted walking. **Walkability:** 3. **Season:** Year-round. **High:** April-Nov. **Tee times:** Call up to 180 days in advance. **Miscellaneous:** Reduced fees (weekdays, guests, twilight, seniors, juniors), credit cards (MC, V, MAC/Cirrus), BF, FF.
★★★½ **EAST COURSE** (18)
Yards: 6,608/5,193. **Par:** 72/72. **Course Rating:** 71.2/69.2. **Slope:** 122/114. **Opened:** 1955. **Architect:** Charles Klingensmith. **Miscellaneous:** Range (grass/mats).
Reader Comments: Shorter course … Use every club … Challenging course, some great holes … Nice layout … Good old public course … Value.
★★½ **WEST COURSE** (18)
Yards: 6,400/4,820. **Par:** 70/70. **Course Rating:** 70.6/67.5. **Slope:** 120/112. **Opened:** 1990. **Architect:** Ault/Clark & Assoc.

★★★★ THE BRIDGES GOLF CLUB
PU-6729 York Rd, Abbottstown, 17301, Adams County, (717)624-9551, (800)942-2444, 17 miles from York. **Facility Holes:** 18. **Yards:** 6,713/5,104. **Par:** 72/72. **Course Rating:** 71.7/69.6. **Slope:** 132/113. **Green Fee:** $36/$60. **Cart Fee:** Included in green fee. **Walking Policy:** Walking at certain times. **Walkability:** 3. **Opened:** 1995. **Architect:** Altland Brothers. **Season:** Year-round. **High:** May-Sept. **To obtain tee times:** Call up to 7 days in advance. **Miscellaneous:** Reduced fees (weekdays, guests, twilight, seniors, juniors), range (grass/mats), lodging (13 rooms), credit cards (MC, V, AE), BF, FF.
Reader Comments: Great par 5s … Would play there all the time if closer … Immaculate, pristine, divine … Funky holes … Level of service rivals far more expensive clubs … Nice clubhouse … Nice accommodations on-site … Outstanding!!! … Great golf, good pro shop, food okay.

★★★½ BUCK HILL GOLF CLUB
SP-Golf Dr., Buck Hill Falls, 18323, Monroe County, (570)595-7730, 50 miles from Allentown. **E-mail:** podunko@ptd.net. **Web:** www.buckhillfalls.com. **Facility Holes:** 27. **Green Fee:** $40/$75. **Cart Fee:** Included in green fee. **Walking Policy:** Mandatory carts. **Opened:** 1901. **Architect:** Donald Ross. **Season:** April-Oct. **High:** May-Aug. **To obtain tee times:** Call up to 7 days in advance. **Miscellaneous:** Reduced fees (weekdays, twilight), range (grass), credit cards (MC, V), BF, FF.
RED/BLUE (18 Combo)
Yards: 6,150/5,870. **Par:** 70/72. **Course Rating:** 69.8/69.8. **Slope:** 118/120. **Walkability:** 4.
RED/WHITE (18 Combo)
Yards: 6,300/5,620. **Par:** 70/72. **Course Rating:** 69.4/71.0. **Slope:** 121/124. **Walkability:** 4.
WHITE/BLUE (18 Combo)
Yards: 6,450/5,550. **Par:** 72/72. **Course Rating:** 70.4/72.8. **Slope:** 124/126. **Walkability:** 3.
Reader Comments: A spectacular course to play in the fall … Much better with new water system … Best course in the Poconos … Great views … Great condition, excellent layout, needs better practice areas.

PENNSYLVANIA

★★★½ BUCKNELL GOLF CLUB
SP-P.O. Box 297, Lewisburg, 17837, Union County, (570)523-8193, 60 miles from Harrisburg. **E-mail:** bpkelly@bucknell.edu. **Facility Holes:** 18. **Yards:** 6,253/4,851. **Par:** 70/71. **Course Rating:** 70.0/67.8. **Slope:** 132/122. **Green Fee:** $36/$40. **Cart Fee:** $16/Person. **Walking Policy:** Unrestricted walking. **Walkability:** 3. **Opened:** 1930. **Architect:** Edmund B. Ault. **Season:** Year-round. **High:** May-Sept. **To obtain tee times:** Call up to 7 days in advance. **Miscellaneous:** Reduced fees (weekdays), range (grass), credit cards (MC, V), BF, FF.
Reader Comments: Short, tight ... Not too long, but tricky ... Very mature! ... Nice layout ... Excellent maintenance ... Great greens ... Probably best in central Pennsylvania.

★★★ BUFFALO GOLF COURSE
PU-201 Monroe Rd., Sarver, 16055, Butler County, (724)353-2440, 25 miles from Pittsburgh. **Facility Holes:** 18. **Yards:** 6,324/5,247. **Par:** 71/73. **Course Rating:** 69.7/71.0. **Slope:** 117/105. **Green Fee:** $14/$21. **Cart Fee:** $10/Person. **Walking Policy:** Unrestricted walking. **Walkability:** 1. **Opened:** 1967. **Season:** March-Dec. **High:** June-Aug. **To obtain tee times:** Call up to 7 days in advance. **Miscellaneous:** Reduced fees (seniors, juniors), metal spikes, credit cards (MC, V, D), BF, FF.
Reader Comments: Nice course for the money ... Easy course to walk ... Friendly ... Very good greens and challenging ... Need a course ranger.

BUTLER'S GOLF COURSE
PU-800 Rock Run Rd., Elizabeth, 15037, Allegheny County, (412)751-9121, (800)932-1001, 15 miles from Pittsburgh. **E-mail:** info@butlersgolf.com. **Web:** www.butlersgolf.com. **Facility Holes:** 36. **Green Fee:** $24/$33. **Cart Fee:** $13/Person. **Walking Policy:** Unrestricted walking. **Walkability:** 3. **Season:** Year-round. **High:** March-Nov. **To obtain tee times:** Call up to 8 days in advance. **Miscellaneous:** Reduced fees (weekdays, twilight, seniors, juniors), metal spikes, range (grass), lodging (4 rooms), credit cards (MC, V, AE, D, DC), BF, FF.
LAKESIDE (18)
Yards: 6,689/5,491. **Par:** 72/72. **Course Rating:** 71.3/71.1. **Slope:** 130/123.
★★½ **WOODSIDE** (18)
Yards: 6,606/5,560. **Par:** 72/72. **Course Rating:** 68.9/70.8. **Slope:** 117/119. **Opened:** 1928. **Architect:** John Butler.

★★★ BUTTER VALLEY GOLF PORT
PU-S. 7th St., Bally, 19503, Berks County, (610)845-2491. **E-mail:** bvgp@buttervalley.com. **Web:** www.buttervalley.com. **Facility Holes:** 18. **Yards:** 6,211/4,950. **Par:** 71/71. **Course Rating:** 67.7/65.7. **Slope:** 115/107. **Green Fee:** $18/$27. **Cart Fee:** $22/Cart. **Opened:** 1969. **Season:** Year-round. **To obtain tee times:** Call up to 1 day in advance. **Miscellaneous:** Reduced fees (twilight), credit cards (MC, V), BF, FF.
Reader Comments: Improving every year ... GPS is a plus ... Help in pro shop extremely courteous ... Course is also an airport, planes land on course ... Scenery is very good.

★★½ CABLE HOLLOW GOLF CLUB
PU-RD #2, Norberg Rd, Russell, 16345, Warren County, (814)757-4765, 150 miles from Pittsburgh. **Facility Holes:** 18. **Yards:** 6,300/5,200. **Par:** 72/73. **Course Rating:** 68.7/69.0. **Slope:** 108/109. **Green Fee:** $9/$17. **Cart Fee:** $18/Cart. **Walking Policy:** Unrestricted walking. **Walkability:** 2. **Opened:** 1968. **Season:** March-Nov. **High:** May-Sept. **To obtain tee times:** Call golf shop. **Miscellaneous:** Reduced fees (weekdays, twilight, seniors), metal spikes, credit cards (MC, V, AE, D).

CALEDONIA GOLF CLUB
PU-9515 Golf Course Rd., Fayetteville, 17222, Franklin County, (717)352-7271. **Facility Holes:** 18. **Yards:** 5,154/4,907. **Par:** 68/70. **Course Rating:** 67.1/68.9. **Slope:** 118/118. **Green Fee:** $14/$16. **Cart Fee:** $12/Person. **Opened:** 1924. **Season:** April-Nov. **To obtain tee times:** Call golf shop. **Miscellaneous:** Reduced fees (twilight, seniors), metal spikes, credit cards (MC, V).

CARMICHAELS GOLF CLUB
PU-RR1, Carmichaels, 15320, Greene County, (724)966-7500. **Facility Holes:** 18. **Yards:** 5,338/4,704. **Par:** 70/70. **Course Rating:** 63.1/63.2. **Slope:** 112/113. **Green Fee:** $10/$15. **Cart Fee:** $10/Cart. **Season:** Year-round. **To obtain tee times:** Call golf shop. **Miscellaneous:** Metal spikes.

CARRADAM GOLF CLUB
PU-2151 Wendel-Hahntown Rd., North Huntingdon, 15642, Westmoreland County, (412)863-6860, 28 miles from Pittsburgh. **E-mail:** colleen@carradam.com. **Web:** www.carradam.com. **Facility Holes:** 18. **Yards:** 5,904/5,460. **Par:** 71/76. **Course Rating:** 68.4/71.9. **Slope:** 113/120. **Green Fee:** $21/$23. **Cart Fee:** $11/Person. **Walkability:** 4. **Opened:** 1964. **Architect:**

James G. Harrison. **Season:** Year-round. **High:** April-Oct. **To obtain tee times:** Call up to 5 days in advance. **Miscellaneous:** Reduced fees (weekdays, seniors, juniors), range (grass/mats), credit cards (MC, V, AE, D, DC, CB), BF, FF.

CARROLL VALLEY GOLF RESORT
R-121 Sanders Rd., Fairfield, 17320, Adams County, (717)642-8252, (800)548-8504, 10 miles from Gettysburg. **Facility Holes:** 36. **Architect:** Edmund B. Ault. **High:** April-Oct. **Tee times:** Call golf shop. **Miscellaneous:** Reduced fees (weekdays, guests, twilight, seniors).
★★★★½ **CARROLL VALLEY COURSE** (18)
Yards: 6,633/5,005. **Par:** 71/72. **Course Rating:** 71.2/67.6. **Slope:** 120/114. **Green Fee:** $22/$29. **Cart Fee:** $12/Person. **Walking Policy:** Walking at certain times. **Walkability:** 3. **Opened:** 1965. **Season:** Year-round. **Miscellaneous:** Metal spikes, credit cards (MC, V, D).
Reader Comments: Nice resort with good food ... Great layout ... Long but not terribly difficult ... An enjoyable course with nice views.
★★★★ **MOUNTAIN VIEW COURSE** (18)
Yards: 6,343/5,024. **Par:** 71/70. **Course Rating:** 70.2/68.2. **Slope:** 122/113. **Green Fee:** $24/$30. **Cart Fee:** $13/Person. **Walking Policy:** Unrestricted walking. **Walkability:** 2. **Opened:** 1979. **Season:** March-Nov. **Miscellaneous:** Range (grass/mats), credit cards (MC, V, AE, D).
Reader Comments: Front 9 is links, back 9 woody, good mix ... Some great holes, some plain holes ... Very scenic course ... Good value.

★★★½ **CASTLE HILLS GOLF COURSE**
PU-110 W. Oakwood Way, New Castle, 16105, Lawrence County, (724)652-8122, 40 miles from Pittsburgh. **Facility Holes:** 18. **Yards:** 6,501/5,530. **Par:** 72/73. **Course Rating:** 69.7/73.3. **Slope:** 118/114. **Green Fee:** $16/$20. **Cart Fee:** $10/Person. **Walking Policy:** Unrestricted walking. **Walkability:** 2. **Opened:** 1930. **Season:** March-Dec. **High:** May-Sept. **To obtain tee times:** Call golf shop. **Miscellaneous:** Reduced fees (weekdays, seniors, juniors), range (grass), credit cards (MC, V, D).
Reader Comments: Tight fairways, great par 3s ... Fun course, great chili dogs ... Course in very good condition.

★★ **CEDAR RIDGE GOLF COURSE**
PU-1225 Barlow Two Taverns Rd., Gettysburg, 17325, Adams County, (717)359-4480, 5 miles from Gettysburg. **Facility Holes:** 18. **Yards:** 6,132/5,546. **Par:** 72/72. **Course Rating:** 69.5/69.3. **Slope:** 114/114. **Green Fee:** $15/$20. **Cart Fee:** $11/Person. **Walking Policy:** Unrestricted walking. **Walkability:** 2. **Opened:** 1987. **Architect:** Roger Weaver. **Season:** Year-round. **To obtain tee times:** Call up to 2 days in advance. **Miscellaneous:** Reduced fees (weekdays, twilight, seniors), metal spikes, credit cards (V, AE, D), BF, FF.

CEDARBROOK GOLF COURSE
PU-215 Route 981, Belle Vernon, 15012, Westmoreland County, (724)929-8300, 25 miles from Pittsburgh. **E-mail:** palonder@cedarbrookgolf.com. **Web:** www.cedarbrookgolf.com. **Facility Holes:** 36. **Green Fee:** $22/$32. **Cart Fee:** $12/Person. **Walking Policy:** Unrestricted walking. **Walkability:** 3. **Opened:** 1986. **Architect:** Michael Hurdzan. **Season:** Year-round. **High:** May-Sept. **To obtain tee times:** Call up to 7 days in advance. **Miscellaneous:** Reduced fees (weekdays, twilight, seniors, juniors), range (grass), credit cards (MC, V, AE, D), BF, FF.
★★★½ **GOLD COURSE** (18)
Yards: 6,710/5,138. **Par:** 72/72. **Course Rating:** 72.4/70.2. **Slope:** 135/121.
Reader Comments: Nice layout, fairly new ... Very nice challenge! Recommend ... Good public course, heavily played ... Good reputation ... Always in good shape, accommodating staff.
★★★½ **RED COURSE** (18)
Yards: 6,154/4,577. **Par:** 71/71. **Course Rating:** 68.3/65.3. **Slope:** 120/111.

★★★ **CENTER SQUARE GOLF CLUB**
PU-Rte. 73 and Whitehall Rd., Center Square, 19422, Montgomery County, (610)584-5700, 25 miles from Philadelphia. **Facility Holes:** 18. **Yards:** 6,296/5,598. **Par:** 71/73. **Course Rating:** 69.3/70.6. **Slope:** 119/114. **Green Fee:** $17/$26. **Cart Fee:** $36/Cart. **Walking Policy:** Walking at certain times. **Walkability:** 4. **Opened:** 1963. **Architect:** Edward Ault. **Season:** Year-round. **High:** April-Oct. **To obtain tee times:** Call golf shop. **Miscellaneous:** Reduced fees (twilight, seniors), range (grass), credit cards (MC, V, AE).
Reader Comments: First-class layout ... Wide fairways ... Fun, diverse terrain ... Very easy layout ... Old course with small greens ... Friendly staff.

★★★★ **CENTER VALLEY CLUB**
PU-3300 Center Valley Pky., Center Valley, 18034, Lehigh County, (610)791-5580, 3 miles from Allentown/Bethlehem. **E-mail:** chweiner@centervalleyclubgolf.com. **Web:** www.centervalleyclubgolf.com. **Facility Holes:** 18. **Yards:** 6,916/4,925. **Par:** 72/72. **Course Rating:** 74.1/70.6. **Slope:** 135/123. **Green Fee:** $25/$70. **Cart Fee:** Included in green fee. **Walking Policy:** Unrestricted walking. **Walkability:** 2. **Opened:** 1992. **Architect:** Geoffrey S. Cornish. **Season:**

PENNSYLVANIA

April-Dec. **High:** May-Sept. **To obtain tee times:** Call up to 7 days in advance. **Miscellaneous:** Reduced fees (twilight), range (grass/mats), credit cards (MC, V, AE, D, Debit), BF, FF. **Reader Comments:** Fantastic in every way … The staff from greeters, to starter, to rangers and snack servers are very service-oriented and friendly … Linksy front, traditional back … Each year gets better.

★★★★ CHAMPION LAKES GOLF COURSE
PU-RD 1 Box 285, Bolivar, 15923, Westmoreland County, (724)238-5440, 50 miles from Pittsburgh. **Web:** www.pagolf.com. **Facility Holes:** 18. **Yards:** 6,608/5,556. **Par:** 71/74. **Course Rating:** 69.0/72.1. **Slope:** 128/127. **Green Fee:** $25/$30. **Cart Fee:** $10/Person. **Walking Policy:** Unrestricted walking. **Walkability:** 3. **Opened:** 1968. **Season:** Year-round. **High:** May-Oct. **To obtain tee times:** Call golf shop. **Miscellaneous:** Reduced fees (weekdays), metal spikes, range (grass/mats), lodging (15 rooms), credit cards (MC, V, AE).
Reader Comments: Beautiful course and scenery … Long and always breezy… Excellent, friendly service, and the price is right … The rough is tough.

★★½ CHAPEL HILL GOLF COURSE
PU-2023 Old Lancaster Pike, Reading, 19608, Berks County, (610)775-8815, 4 miles from Reading. **Facility Holes:** 18. **Yards:** 6,089/4,352. **Par:** 70/70. **Course Rating:** 69.4/63.6. **Slope:** 122/105. **Green Fee:** $19/$23. **Walking Policy:** Unrestricted walking. **Walkability:** 2. **Opened:** 1992. **Architect:** William D. Holloway. **Season:** Year-round. **High:** May-Sept. **To obtain tee times:** Call up to 4 days in advance. **Miscellaneous:** Reduced fees (weekdays, twilight, seniors), credit cards (MC, V), FF.

★½ CHEROKEE GOLF COURSE
PU-217 Elysburg Rd., Danville, 17821, Northumberland County, (570)275-2005, (888)843-1633, 3 miles from Danville on Rt. 54. **Facility Holes:** 18. **Yards:** 6,037/4,524. **Par:** 72/72. **Course Rating:** 68.4/65.1. **Slope:** 114/102. **Green Fee:** $15/$19. **Cart Fee:** $10/Person. **Walking Policy:** Unrestricted walking. **Walkability:** 1. **Opened:** 1973. **Architect:** Brouse Family. **Season:** Year-round. **High:** May-Aug. **To obtain tee times:** Call golf shop. **Miscellaneous:** Reduced fees (weekdays), metal spikes, credit cards (MC, V, AE, D).

CHERRY VALLEY GOLF COURSE
PU-Cherry Valley Rd., Stroudsburg, 18360, Monroe County, (570)421-1350. **Facility Holes:** 18. **Yards:** 6,063/5,275. **Par:** 71/71. **Course Rating:** 69.3/70.4. **Slope:** 123/119. **Green Fee:** $27/$40. **Cart Fee:** Included in green fee. **Season:** Year-round. **To obtain tee times:** Call golf shop. **Miscellaneous:** Reduced fees (twilight, seniors).

CHERRY WOOD GOLF COURSE
PU-204 Truxall Rd., Apollo, 15613, Westmoreland County, (724)727-2546, 35 miles from Pittsburgh. **Facility Holes:** 9. **Yards:** 6,230/3,970. **Par:** 70/70. **Course Rating:** 69.7/60.9. **Slope:** 117/99. **Green Fee:** $16/$18. **Cart Fee:** $20/Cart. **Walking Policy:** Unrestricted walking. **Walkability:** 3. **Opened:** 1997. **Architect:** John S. Chernega. **Season:** April-Nov. **High:** June-Aug. **To obtain tee times:** Call up to 7 days in advance. **Miscellaneous:** Reduced fees (weekdays, seniors), metal spikes, range (grass), credit cards (MC, V), BF, FF.

CHESTNUT RIDGE GOLF CLUB
PU-1762 Old William Penn Hwy., Blairsville, 15717, Indiana County, (724)459-7188, (800)770-0000, 35 miles from Pittsburgh. **Facility Holes:** 36. **Cart Fee:** $10/Person. **Walking Policy:** Unrestricted walking. **Season:** March-Dec. **High:** June-Oct. **To obtain tee times:** Call up to 7 days in advance. **Miscellaneous:** Reduced fees (weekdays, twilight), metal spikes, range (grass), credit cards (MC, V, AE), BF, FF.
★★★★½ CHESTNUT RIDGE COURSE (18)
Yards: 6,321/5,130. **Par:** 72/72. **Course Rating:** 70.7/70.2. **Slope:** 129/119. **Green Fee:** $25/$30. **Walkability:** 2. **Opened:** 1964. **Architect:** Harrison/Garbin.
Reader Comments: Best kept secret in western PA … Expensive, but oh what a play! … Hard to beat … Target golf, tough narrow fairways … good value.
★★★★½ TOM'S RUN COURSE (18) *Condition, Pace*
Yards: 6,812/5,363. **Par:** 72/72. **Course Rating:** 73.0/71.0. **Slope:** 135/126. **Green Fee:** $45/$50. **Walkability:** 3. **Opened:** 1993. **Architect:** Bill Love/Brian Ault/Tom Clark.
Reader Comments: Course condition excellent … Great, great course … Pricey, worth it … Beautiful mountain views … Great restaurant … Unbelievable walk through nature … Country club atmosphere.

★★★ CHIPPEWA GOLF CLUB
PU-128 Chippewa Rd., Bentleyville, 15314, Washington County, (724)239-4841. **Facility Holes:** 18. **Yards:** 6,051/5,104. **Par:** 70/70. **Course Rating:** 67.9/69.0. **Slope:** 108/108. **Green Fee:** $15/$19. **Cart Fee:** $11/Person. **Walking Policy:** Unrestricted walking. **Walkability:** 3. **To obtain tee times:** Call up to 7 days in advance. **Miscellaneous:** Reduced fees (twilight,

seniors, juniors), credit cards (MC, V), FF.

Reader Comments: Course is a great value, well maintained, friendly atmosphere, staff helpful and considerate ... Solid value, diverse, fair test.

★★½ CLARION OAKS GOLF COURSE

PU-I-80 Exit 9N Pa. Rte. 68, Clarion, 16214, Clarion County, (814)226-8888, 90 miles from Pittsburgh. **Facility Holes:** 18. **Yards:** 6,990/5,439. **Par:** 72/72. **Course Rating:** 73.0/71.0. **Slope:** 117/118. **Green Fee:** $15/$22. **Cart Fee:** $10/Person. **Walking Policy:** Walking at certain times. **Opened:** 1974. **Architect:** X.G. Hassenplug. **Season:** April-Oct. **High:** June-Aug. **Tee times:** Call golf shop. **Miscellaneous:** Reduced fees (weekdays), metal spikes, range (grass). **Special Notes:** Formerly Mayfield Golf Club.

CLOVERLEAF GOLF CLUB

PU-Cloverleaf Dr. Box 55, Delmont, 15626, Westmoreland County, (724)468-4173, 25 miles from Pittsburgh. **Facility Holes:** 27. **Green Fee:** $18/$21. **Cart Fee:** $10/Person. **Walking Policy:** Unrestricted walking. **Walkability:** 3. **Opened:** 1954. **Architect:** Wynn Tredway. **Season:** Year-round. **High:** May-Sept. **To obtain tee times:** Call golf shop. **Miscellaneous:** Reduced fees (seniors, juniors), metal spikes, FF.
FIRST 9/SECOND 9 COURSE (18)
Yards: 6,215/6,015. **Par:** 72/76.
FIRST 9/THIRD 9 COURSE (18)
Yards: 6,135/5,838. **Par:** 72/76.
SECOND 9/THIRD 9 COURSE (18)
Yards: 6,016/5,839. **Par:** 72/76.

COBB'S CREEK GOLF CLUB

PU-72 Lansdowne Ave., Philadelphia, 19151, Philadelphia County, (215)877-8707. **Facility Holes:** 36. **Cart Fee:** $15/Person. **Walking Policy:** Unrestricted walking. **Walkability:** 4. **Season:** Year-round. **Tee times:** Call up to 7 days in advance. **Miscellaneous:** Reduced fees (weekdays, twilight, seniors, juniors), metal spikes, range (grass/mats), credit cards (MC, V), BF, FF.
KARA KUNG COURSE (18)
Yards: 5,762/5,421. **Par:** 71/72. **Course Rating:** 66.7/70.3. **Slope:** 115/119.
Green Fee: $11/$26.
★★½ OLDE COURSE (18)
Yards: 6,202/5,433. **Par:** 71/71. **Course Rating:** 68.6/69.8. **Slope:** 117/118.
Green Fee: $14/$35. **Opened:** 1916. **Architect:** Hugh Wilson.

★★½ CONLEY'S RESORT INN

R-740 Pittsburgh Rd. - Rt. 8, Butler, 16002, Butler County, (724)586-7711, (800)344-7303, 20 miles from Pittsburgh. **Facility Holes:** 18. **Yards:** 6,200/5,625. **Par:** 72/72. **Course Rating:** 69.0/69.0. **Slope:** 110/110. **Green Fee:** $26/$36. **Cart Fee:** $13/Person. **Walking Policy:** Walking at certain times. **Walkability:** 3. **Opened:** 1963. **Architect:** Nicholas Iannotti. **Season:** Year-round. **High:** April-Oct. **To obtain tee times:** Call up to 2 days in advance. **Miscellaneous:** Reduced fees (weekdays, guests, twilight, seniors), lodging (56 rooms), credit cards (MC, V, AE, D, DC, Check Card).

CONOCODELL GOLF CLUB

PU-112 Coldspring Rd., Fayetteville, 17222, Franklin County, (717)352-3222, 19 miles from Gettysburg. **Facility Holes:** 9. **Yards:** 6,090/4,990. **Par:** 70/72. **Slope:** 114/110. **Green Fee:** $14. **Cart Fee:** $9/Person. **Walking Policy:** Unrestricted walking. **Walkability:** 1. **Opened:** 1962. **Season:** March-Dec. **High:** April-Nov. **To obtain tee times:** Call golf shop. **Miscellaneous:** Reduced fees (twilight, seniors), BF, FF.

★★★ COOL CREEK COUNTRY CLUB

PU-Cool Creek Rd., Wrightsville, 17368, York County, (717)252-3691, (800)942-2444, 10 miles from Lancaster. **E-mail:** skeeney@coolcreekgolf.com. **Web:** www.coolcreekgolf.com. **Facility Holes:** 18. **Yards:** 6,521/5,703. **Par:** 71/70. **Course Rating:** 71.1/72.6. **Slope:** 118/118. **Green Fee:** $25/$34. **Cart Fee:** $14/Person. **Walking Policy:** Unrestricted walking. **Walkability:** 3. **Opened:** 1948. **Architect:** Chester Ruby. **Season:** Year-round. **To obtain tee times:** Call golf shop. **Miscellaneous:** Reduced fees (weekdays, guests, twilight, seniors, juniors), range (mats), credit cards (MC, V, AE), BF, FF.

Reader Comments: A nice easy-walking course ... Starts slow but back 9 very competitive ... Really like Cool Creek ... Small greens ... Nice layout, hilly, wooded ... Great people, well manicured.

★★ COREY CREEK GOLF CLUB

SP-U.S. Rte. No.6 E., Mansfield, 16933, Tioga County, (570)662-3520, 35 miles from Elmira, NY. **E-mail:** goleepix.net. **Web:** www.coreycreekgolf.com. **Facility Holes:** 18. **Yards:** 6,571/4,920. **Par:** 72/72. **Course Rating:** 71.1/66.0. **Slope:** 120/110. **Green Fee:** $12/$27. **Cart**

Fee: $12/Person. **Walking Policy:** Walking at certain times. **Walkability:** 4. **Opened:** 1927. **Architect:** Herb Peterson/Jack Marsh. **Season:** April-Nov. **High:** May-Oct. **Tee times:** Call up to 365 days ahead. **Misc:** Reduced fees (weekdays, twilight), range, cards (MC, V), BF, FF.

COUDERSPORT GOLF CLUB

PU-Rte. 44 S., Coudersport, 16915, Potter County, (814)274-9122. **Facility Holes:** 18. **Yards:** 5,819/4,748. **Par:** 72/72. **Course Rating:** 67.7/67.1. **Slope:** 115/109. **Green Fee:** $18/$25. **Cart Fee:** $12/Person. **Walking Policy:** Unrestricted walking. **Walkability:** 4. **Opened:** 1935. **Season:** April-Nov. **High:** June-Aug. **To obtain tee times:** Call golf shop. **Miscellaneous:** Reduced fees (twilight, seniors), range (grass), credit cards (MC, V), BF, FF.

★★★★½ COUNTRY CLUB AT WOODLOCH SPRINGS

SP-Woodloch Dr., Hawley, 18428, Wayne County, (717)685-8102, 7 miles from Scranton. **E-mail:** woodgolf@woodloch.com. **Web:** www.woodloch.com. **Facility Holes:** 18. **Yards:** 6,579/4,973. **Par:** 72/72. **Course Rating:** 72.3/71.6. **Slope:** 143/130. **Green Fee:** $60/$75. **Cart Fee:** Included in green fee. **Walking Policy:** Walking at certain times. **Walkability:** 5. **Opened:** 1992. **Architect:** Rocky Roquemore. **Season:** April-Nov. **High:** May-Oct. **To obtain tee times:** Call up to 10 days in advance. **Miscellaneous:** Reduced fees (weekdays), range (grass/mats), credit cards (MC, V, AE, D), BF, FF.

Reader Comments: A course as it should be, great … In the mountains … Service and clubhouse worth it … Incredible elevation changes … Breathtaking … Challenging layout, very fast greens.

COUNTRY CLUB OF HERSHEY

R-1000 E. Derry Rd., Hershey, 17033, Dauphin County, (717)533-2464, (800)900-4653, 12 miles from Harrisburg. **Facility Holes:** 54. **Miscellaneous:** Reduced fees (weekdays, twilight, seniors, juniors), range (grass), lodging (18 rooms), credit cards (MC, V, AE), BF, FF.

★★★★ EAST COURSE (18)

Yards: 7,061/5,645. **Par:** 71/71. **Course Rating:** 73.6/71.6. **Slope:** 128/127. **Green Fee:** $93. **Cart Fee:** Included in green fee. **Walking Policy:** Mandatory carts. **Walkability:** 3. **Opened:** 1970. **Architect:** George Fazio. **Season:** Year-round. **High:** May-Oct. **Tee times:** Call golf shop.

Reader Comments: Excellent track, very challenging, great course … Bring your long irons … Long, tough, thick rough … Hardest Hershey course … Most greens elevated … Good course, great service … Excellent, challenging resort course.

★★★½ SOUTH COURSE (18)

Yards: 6,332/4,979. **Par:** 71/72. **Course Rating:** 69.9/69.6. **Slope:** 121/107. **Green Fee:** $65. **Cart Fee:** $8/Person. **Walking Policy:** Walking at certain times. **Walkability:** 4. **Opened:** 1927. **Architect:** Maurice McCarthy. **Season:** Year-round. **High:** May-Sept.

Reader Comments: Local knowledge is very handy … Always been the 'other' course in Hershey … Beautiful old-style layout … Short but challenging … Smells like chocolate … Great everything! Best public course in state.

★★★★½ WEST COURSE (18) *Pace*

Yards: 6,860/5,908. **Par:** 73/76. **Course Rating:** 73.1/74.7. **Slope:** 131/127. **Green Fee:** $115/$135. **Cart Fee:** Included in green fee. **Walking Policy:** Mandatory carts. **Walkability:** 4. **Opened:** 1930. **Architect:** Maurice McCarthy. **Season:** March-Dec. **High:** May-Oct. **To obtain tee times:** Call golf shop.

Reader Comments: Short, tight, tough … Course is loaded with history from all the greats that have played there … Still my favorite in all PA … Great old course with the character of Merion … Outstanding course and service … Excellent, challenging resort course.

CRICKET HILL GOLF CLUB

SP-Rte. 6, Between Hawley & Honesdale, Hawley, 18428, Wayne County, (570)226-4366. **Facility Holes:** 18. **Yards:** 5,800/4,932. **Par:** 70/70. **Course Rating:** 67.3/68.8. **Slope:** 104/106. **Green Fee:** $22/$24. **Cart Fee:** $20/Cart. **Season:** April-Nov. **To obtain tee times:** Call golf shop. **Miscellaneous:** Reduced fees (twilight, seniors), credit cards (MC, V).

CROSS CREEK RESORT

PU-Rd. 3 Box 152, Titusville, 16354, Venango County, (814)827-9611, (800)461-3173, 4 miles from Erie. **E-mail:** ccresor@csonline.net. **Web:** www.crosscreekresort.com. **Facility Holes:** 27. **Green Fee:** $36/$40. **Cart Fee:** $14/Person. **Walking Policy:** Walking at certain times. **Walkability:** 3. **Opened:** 1959. **Season:** April-Oct. **High:** June-Aug. **To obtain tee times:** Call up to 7 days in advance. **Miscellaneous:** Metal spikes, range (grass/mats), lodging (94 rooms), credit cards (MC, V, AE, D), BF, FF.

★★★ NORTH COURSE (18)

Yards: 6,467/5,226. **Par:** 70/72. **Rating:** 68.6/68.4. **Slope:** 112/108. **Architect:** Wynn Tredway.

SOUTH COURSE (9)

Yards: 3,137/2,417. **Par:** 36/36. **Rating:** 34.0/33.1. **Slope:** 0/108. **Architect:** Ferdinand Garbin.

Reader Comments: Well maintained and manicured … Some of the hardest par 3s, plus good distance holes … Excellent food … Interesting holes, especially par-3 third … Tiny greens …Weekend package, good value.

CROSSGATES GOLF COURSE
PU-One Crossland Pass, Millersville, 17551, Lancaster County, (717)872-4500, 3 miles from Lancaster. **Web:** www.crossgatesgolf.com. **Facility Holes:** 18. **Yards:** 6,100/4,738. **Par:** 72/72. **Course Rating:** 69.9/67.4. **Slope:** 122/113. **Green Fee:** $24/$29. **Cart Fee:** $13/Person. **Walking Policy:** Walking at certain times. **Walkability:** 3. **Opened:** 1994. **Architect:** Fred Garbin. **Season:** Year-round. **High:** May-Sept. **To obtain tee times:** Call up to 10 days in advance. **Miscellaneous:** Reduced fees (weekdays, twilight, seniors, juniors), range (grass), credit cards (MC, V, D), BF, FF.

★★★ CULBERTSON HILLS GOLF RESORT
R-Rte. 6N W., Edinboro, 16412, Erie County, (814)734-3114, (800)734-8191, 15 miles from Erie. **E-mail:** chpro@surferie.net. **Web:** www.culbertsonhills.com. **Facility Holes:** 18. **Yards:** 6,813/5,514. **Par:** 72/72. **Course Rating:** 72.4/71.4. **Slope:** 128/124. **Green Fee:** $18/$27. **Cart Fee:** $13/Person. **Walking Policy:** Walking at certain times. **Walkability:** 3. **Opened:** 1931. **Architect:** Tom Bendelow. **Season:** March-Nov. **High:** June-Sept. **To obtain tee times:** Call golf shop. **Miscellaneous:** Reduced fees (weekdays, twilight, seniors, juniors), metal spikes, lodging (105 rooms), credit cards (MC, V), BF, FF.
Reader Comments: Fun out and back course … Good old-style course with mature trees. L-o-n-g, bring your driver. No sand traps … My favorite course; I'd rather break par here than at St Andrews! … Drive it straight to score, but greens pretty open.

★★ CUMBERLAND GOLF CLUB
SP-2395 Ritner Hwy., Carlisle, 17013, Cumberland County, (717)249-5538, 5 miles from Carlisle. **Facility Holes:** 18. **Yards:** 6,900. **Par:** 72. **Course Rating:** 70.4. **Slope:** 121. **Green Fee:** $13/$18. **Cart Fee:** $18/Cart. **Opened:** 1962. **Architect:** James Gilmore Harrison/Ferdinand Garbin. **Season:** March-Dec. **High:** April-Sept. **To obtain tee times:** Call golf shop. **Miscellaneous:** Metal spikes, range (grass/mats), credit cards (MC, V, AE, D).

★★★★ DAUPHIN HIGHLANDS GOLF COURSE
PU-650 S. Harrisburg St., Harrisburg, 17113, Dauphin County, (717)986-1984, 5 miles from Harrisburg. **Web:** www.pateetimes.com. **Facility Holes:** 18. **Yards:** 7,035/5,327. **Par:** 72/72. **Course Rating:** 73.4/70.1. **Slope:** 125/114. **Green Fee:** $23/$32. **Cart Fee:** $13/Person. **Walking Policy:** Unrestricted walking. **Walkability:** 5. **Opened:** 1995. **Architect:** Bill Love. **Season:** March-Dec. **High:** May-Sept. **To obtain tee times:** Call up to 6 days in advance. **Miscellaneous:** Reduced fees (weekdays, twilight, seniors, juniors), range (grass/mats), credit cards (MC, V), BF, FF.
Reader Comments: A "must-play" course … Great layout, maturing nicely … Demanding par 4s … Always enjoy playing it … Greens could be cut shorter… Great public course.

★★ DEEP VALLEY GOLF COURSE
PU-169 Hartmann Rd., Harmony, 16037, Butler County, (724)452-8021, 25 miles from Pittsburgh. **Facility Holes:** 18. **Yards:** 6,310/6,310. **Par:** 72/72. **Green Fee:** $12/$19. **Cart Fee:** $22/Cart. **Walking Policy:** Unrestricted walking. **Walkability:** 2. **Opened:** 1958. **Season:** March-Dec. **To obtain tee times:** Call golf shop. **Miscellaneous:** Reduced fees (seniors), metal spikes, FF.

★★★½ DEER RUN GOLF CLUB
SP-287 Monier Road, Gibsonia, 15044, Allegheny County, (724)265-4800, 3 miles from Pittsburgh. **Facility Holes:** 18. **Yards:** 7,018/5,238. **Par:** 72/73. **Course Rating:** 74.2/71.2. **Slope:** 134/128. **Green Fee:** $28/$36. **Cart Fee:** $14/Person. **Walking Policy:** Walking at certain times. **Walkability:** 3. **Opened:** 1994. **Architect:** Ron Forse. **Season:** Year-round. **High:** May-Aug. **To obtain tee times:** Call golf shop. **Miscellaneous:** Metal spikes, range (grass), credit cards (MC, V), BF, FF.
Reader Comments: A great place for a match, price is right … Nice clubhouse … Keeps improving … Short course but challenging … Great layout … Elevation changes … Good, testing course, uses all 14 clubs.

DEL-MAR GOLF COURSE
SP-Smiley Stop Rd., Wampum, 16157, Lawrence County, (724)758-9499, 38 miles from Pittsburgh. **Facility Holes:** 18. **Yards:** 6,415/5,143. **Par:** 72/73. **Course Rating:** 70.6/71.0. **Slope:** 123/120. **Green Fee:** $15/$17. **Cart Fee:** $20/Cart. **Season:** Year-round. **Tee times:** Call golf shop. **Miscellaneous:** Reduced fees (twilight, seniors), metal spikes, credit cards (D).

★★★ DONEGAL HIGHLANDS GOLF CLUB
PU-Route 31 and Clay Pike, Donegal, 15628, Westmoreland County, (724)423-7888, 35 miles from Pittsburgh. **E-mail:** blackdog@donegalhighlandsgolf.com. **Web:** www.donegalhighlandsgolf.com. **Facility Holes:** 18. **Yards:** 6,350/4,545. **Par:** 72/72. **Course Rating:** 70.1/65.7.

Slope: 123/113. **Green Fee:** $18/$28. **Cart Fee:** $13/Person. **Walking Policy:** Unrestricted walking. **Walkability:** 2. **Opened:** 1991. **Architect:** James Gayton/Ron Forse. **Season:** March-Nov. **High:** May-Sept. **To obtain tee times:** Call up to 7 days in advance. **Miscellaneous:** Reduced fees (weekdays, seniors, juniors), range (grass), credit cards (MC, V, AE, D), BF, FF.
Reader Comments: Nice golf for your $ … Short course, not difficult but good people running the show … Very nice greens and fairways … Links course … Two different 9s—one open, the other woodsy.

★★★ DOWN RIVER GOLF CLUB
PU-134 Rivers Bend Drive, Everett, 15537, Bedford County, (814)652-5193, 40 miles from Altoona. **Facility Holes:** 18. **Yards:** 6,900/5,513. **Par:** 72/73. **Course Rating:** 72.0/70.7. **Slope:** 128/118. **Green Fee:** $18/$20. **Cart Fee:** $12/Person. **Walking Policy:** Unrestricted walking. **Walkability:** 2. **Opened:** 1967. **Architect:** X.G. Hassenplug. **Season:** Year-round. **High:** April-Oct. **To obtain tee times:** Call up to 10 days in advance. **Miscellaneous:** Reduced fees (weekdays, twilight, juniors), range (grass), credit cards (MC, V, AE, D), BF, FF.
Reader Comments: Easy course to play … Nice, very playable course … Good condition, some real nice golf holes, sitting along Juniata River… Beautiful scenery … Course in great shape … One of the best public courses I've played … Long but wide open.

★★★ DOWNING GOLF COURSE
PU-Troupe Rd., Harborcreek, 16421, Erie County, (814)899-5827, 6 miles from Erie. **Facility Holes:** 18. **Yards:** 7,175/6,259. **Par:** 72/74. **Course Rating:** 73.0/74.4. **Slope:** 114/115. **Green Fee:** $15/$19. **Cart Fee:** $20/Cart. **Walking Policy:** Unrestricted walking. **Walkability:** 1. **Opened:** 1962. **Architect:** Harrison. **Season:** Year-round. **High:** March-Nov. **To obtain times:** Call up to 3 days in advance. **Misc:** Reduced fees (twilight), range (grass), BF, FF.
Reader Comments: Great value, good course, slow pace … Condition overall was great for a public links … Long and flat, fun day … Has returned to great course … Two completely different 9s … Superb value, great condition.

★★★½ DOWNINGTOWN COUNTRY CLUB
PU-85 Country Club Drive, Downingtown, 19335, Chester County, (610)269-2000, 25 miles from Philadelphia. **E-mail:** proshop@golfdowningtown. **Web:** www.golfdowningtown.com. **Facility Holes:** 18. **Yards:** 6,619/5,092. **Par:** 72/72. **Course Rating:** 72.9/69.4. **Slope:** 132/119. **Green Fee:** $53/$63. **Cart Fee:** $20/Person. **Walking Policy:** Unrestricted walking. **Walkability:** 2. **Opened:** 1967. **Architect:** George Fazio. **Season:** Year-round. **High:** May-Sept. **To obtain tee times:** Call up to 7 days in advance. **Miscellaneous:** Reduced fees (weekdays, twilight, seniors, juniors), credit cards (MC, V, AE), BF, FF.
Reader Comments: Great clubhouse and food … Terrific course, great challenge … Tough course and rough, last seven holes are terrific … Great redo of old course … Great course to walk.

★★½ DUCK HOLLOW GOLF CLUB
PU-347 Duck Hollow Rd., Uniontown, 15401, Fayette County, (724)439-3150, 40 miles from Pittsburgh. **Facility Holes:** 18. **Yards:** 6,538/6,112. **Par:** 72/74. **Course Rating:** 69.5/68.9. **Slope:** 120/115. **Green Fee:** $15/$25. **Cart Fee:** $13/Person. **Walking Policy:** Walking at certain times. **Walkability:** 3. **Opened:** 1975. **Season:** Year-round. **High:** April-Oct. **To obtain tee times:** Call golf shop. **Miscellaneous:** Reduced fees (weekdays, seniors, juniors), metal spikes, range (grass), credit cards (MC, V, D), BF, FF.

★★★ EAGLE ROCK RESORT
PU-1031 Valley of Lakes, Hazelton, 18201, Luzerne County, (570)384-6616, (888)384-6660, 48 miles from Allentown. **E-mail:** rcheler@eglrock.com. **Web:** www.eglrock.com. **Facility Holes:** 18. **Yards:** 7,140/5,325. **Par:** 72/72. **Course Rating:** 73.2/69.7. **Slope:** 126/116. **Green Fee:** $30/$45. **Cart Fee:** $14/Person. **Walking Policy:** Walking at certain times. **Walkability:** 3. **Opened:** 2000. **Architect:** Palmer Course DesignCo./Randy Gracie. **Season:** March-Nov. **To obtain tee times:** Call up to 14 days in advance. **Miscellaneous:** Reduced fees (twilight), range (grass/mats), lodging (80 rooms), credit cards (MC, V, AE), BF, FF.
Reader Comments: This is a virtually unknown course that is absolutely stunning … One of the most scenic mountain areas you will find in northeast PA … Beautiful views, excellent condition, a challenge … Great new course, fun to play.

★★★½ EDGEWOOD IN THE PINES GOLF COURSE
PU-R.R.1, Box 1601-A, Drums, 18222, Luzerne County, (570)788-1101, 5 miles from Hazleton. **Facility Holes:** 18. **Yards:** 6,721/5,184. **Par:** 72/72. **Course Rating:** 71.9/69.9. **Slope:** 132/118. **Green Fee:** $13/$28. **Cart Fee:** $12/Person. **Walking Policy:** Walking at certain times. **Walkability:** 3. **Opened:** 1980. **Architect:** David Gordon. **Season:** Year-round. **High:** May-Aug. **To obtain tee times:** Call golf shop. **Miscellaneous:** Reduced fees (weekdays, twilight), metal spikes, credit cards (MC, V, AE).
Reader Comments: Good layout, always nice to play … Confidence builder … Very nice public course … Terrific, beautiful scenery.

PENNSYLVANIA

ELK VALLEY GOLF & RECREATION
PU-7085 Van Camp Rd., Girard, 16417, Erie County, (814)474-2356, (888)398-0584, 8 miles from Erie. **Web:** www.elkvalleygolfcourse.com. **Facility Holes:** 18. **Yards:** 6,500/4,881. **Par:** 72/72. **Course Rating:** 69.4/68.6. **Slope:** 109/108. **Green Fee:** $17/$20. **Cart Fee:** $12/Person. **Walking Policy:** Walking at certain times. **Walkability:** 2. **Opened:** 1972. **Architect:** Bob Herbstritt. **Season:** Year-round. **High:** May-Oct. **Tee times:** Call up to 7 days in advance. **Misc:** Reduced fees (weekdays), range (grass/mats), credit cards (MC, V, AE), BF, FF.

★★★ EMPORIUM COUNTRY CLUB
SP-Cameron Rd., Star Rte., Emporium, 15834, Cameron County, (814)486-2241, 50 miles from Bradford. **Facility Holes:** 18. **Yards:** 6,032/5,233. **Par:** 72/72. **Course Rating:** 68.5/69.0. **Slope:** 118/115. **Green Fee:** $14/$27. **Cart Fee:** $11/Person. **Walking Policy:** Mandatory carts. **Walkability:** 5. **Opened:** 1954. **Architect:** Members. **Season:** March-Nov. **To obtain tee times:** Call golf shop. **Miscellaneous:** Reduced fees (weekdays, juniors), metal spikes, range (grass/mats), credit cards (MC, V), BF, FF.
Reader Comments: Neat course in the mountains … Back 9 narrow and challenging with many trees …Worth the trip … Nice course, hidden in the hills … Like a private club … Scenic back 9 is great.

★½ ERIE GOLF CLUB
PU-6050 Old Zuck Rd., Erie, 16506, Erie County, (814)866-0641. **Facility Holes:** 18. **Yards:** 5,682/4,977. **Par:** 69/72. **Course Rating:** 67.2/68.2. **Slope:** 111/109. **Green Fee:** $11/$14. **Cart Fee:** $15/Person. **Walking Policy:** Unrestricted walking. **Opened:** 1964. **Architect:** James Gilmore Harrison. **Season:** March-Nov. **High:** April-Oct. **To obtain tee times:** Call golf shop. **Miscellaneous:** Reduced fees (twilight, seniors, juniors), metal spikes.

★½ EXETER GOLF CLUB
PU-811 Shelbourne Rd., Reading, 19606, Berks County, (610)779-1211. **Facility Holes:** 9. **Yards:** 5,550/4,450. **Par:** 70/70. **Green Fee:** $14/$18. **Cart Fee:** $20/Cart. **Walking Policy:** Unrestricted walking. **Walkability:** 3. **Opened:** 1957. **Architect:** Enrico Filippini. **Season:** Year-round. **High:** April-Nov. **To obtain tee times:** Call golf shop. **Miscellaneous:** Reduced fees (weekdays, twilight), metal spikes, credit cards (MC, V).

★★★½ FAIRVIEW GOLF COURSE
PU-2399 Quentin Road, Lebanon, 17042, Lebanon County, (717)273-3411, (800)621-6557, 5 miles from Lebanon. **E-mail:** jonesview@aol.com. **Web:** www.distinctgolf.com. **Facility Holes:** 18. **Yards:** 6,227/5,221. **Par:** 71/73. **Course Rating:** 69.2/72.9. **Slope:** 106/115. **Green Fee:** $12/$28. **Cart Fee:** $12/Person. **Walking Policy:** Unrestricted walking. **Walkability:** 2. **Opened:** 1959. **Architect:** Frank Murray/Russell Roberts. **Season:** Year-round. **To obtain tee times:** Call up to 14 days in advance. **Miscellaneous:** Reduced fees (weekdays, twilight, seniors, juniors), range (mats), credit cards (MC, V), BF, FF.
Reader Comments: Interesting to play … Good value for the money … Short course … Tough par 3s … Very professional staff … Always well maintained … Good variety of holes.

FAIRWAYS GOLF COURSE
PU-750 Country Club Ln., Warrington, 18976, Bucks County, (215)343-9979, 34 miles from Philadelphia. **Facility Holes:** 18. **Yards:** 4,503/3,923. **Par:** 65/65. **Slope:** 104/103. **Green Fee:** $22/$27. **Cart Fee:** $16/Person. **Season:** Year-round. **To obtain tee times:** Call golf shop. **Misc:** Reduced fees (twilight, seniors, juniors), metal spikes, credit cards (MC, V, AE).

★½ FERNWOOD RESORT & COUNTRY CLUB
PU-Rte. 209, Bushkill, 18324, Monroe County, (570)588-9500, (800)233-8103, 12 miles from Stroudsburg. **Facility Holes:** 18. **Yards:** 6,100/4,800. **Par:** 71/71. **Course Rating:** 68.8/63.3. **Slope:** 125/115. **Green Fee:** $38/$46. **Cart Fee:** Included in green fee. **Walking Policy:** Mandatory carts. **Walkability:** 3. **Opened:** 1968. **Architect:** Nicholas Psiahas. **Season:** April-Nov. **To obtain tee times:** Call up to 7 days in advance. **Misc:** Reduced fees (guests, twilight), metal spikes, range (grass/mats), lodging (900 rooms), credit cards (MC, V, AE), BF, FF.

★★★ FIVE PONDS GOLF CLUB
PU-1225 West Street Road, Warminster, 18974, Bucks County, (215)956-9727, 14 miles from Philadelphia. **E-mail:** 5ponds@warminstertownship.org. **Web:** www.warminstertownship.org. **Facility Holes:** 18. **Yards:** 6,681/5,365. **Par:** 71/71. **Course Rating:** 71.5/70.1. **Slope:** 123/117. **Green Fee:** $26/$30. **Cart Fee:** $12/Person. **Walking Policy:** Walking at certain times. **Walkability:** 2. **Opened:** 1988. **Architect:** X.G. Hassenplug. **Season:** Year-round. **High:** March-Nov. **To obtain tee times:** Call up to 7 days in advance. **Miscellaneous:** Reduced fees (weekdays, twilight, seniors, juniors), range (grass), credit cards (MC, V, MAC), BF, FF.
Reader Comments: Outstanding service, condition and value … Tight fairways … Challenging doglegs … Good front, tough back … Tough course, excellent conditions.

★★ FLATBUSH GOLF COURSE

PU-940 Littlestown Rd., Littletown, 17340, Adams County, (717)359-7125, (800)942-2444, 40 miles from Harrisburg. **Facility Holes:** 18. **Yards:** 6,671/5,247. **Par:** 71/71. **Course Rating:** 71.6/69.6. **Slope:** 121/119. **Green Fee:** $19/$23. **Cart Fee:** $10/Person. **Walking Policy:** Unrestricted walking. **Walkability:** 3. **Opened:** 1989. **Architect:** Ault/Clark & Assoc. **Season:** Year-round. **High:** April-Oct. **To obtain tee times:** Call golf shop. **Miscellaneous:** Reduced fees (twilight, seniors), metal spikes, range (grass), credit cards (MC, V), BF, FF.

★★½ FLYING HILLS GOLF COURSE

PU-10 Village Center Dr., Reading, 19607, Berks County, (610)775-4063, 5 miles from Reading. **Facility Holes:** 18. **Yards:** 6,023/5,176. **Par:** 70/70. **Course Rating:** 68.2/68.8. **Slope:** 118/118. **Green Fee:** $19/$22. **Cart Fee:** $21/Person. **Walking Policy:** Unrestricted walking. **Walkability:** 4. **Opened:** 1971. **Architect:** Mr. Rahenkamp. **Season:** Year-round. **To obtain tee times:** Call golf shop. **Miscellaneous:** Reduced fees (weekdays), BF, FF.

FORT CHERRY GOLF CLUB

PU-Ft. Cherry Rd., McDonald, 15057, Washington County, (724)926-4182, 20 miles from Pittsburgh. **Facility Holes:** 18. **Yards:** 6,205/5,441. **Par:** 70/71. **Course Rating:** 68.5/71.9. **Slope:** 117/119. **Green Fee:** $21/$27. **Cart Fee:** $8/Person. **Walking Policy:** Walking at certain times. **Walkability:** 4. **Season:** Year-round. **To obtain tee times:** Call up to 40 days in advance. **Miscellaneous:** Reduced fees (weekdays, seniors), range (mats), lodging (30 rooms), credit cards (MC, V), BF, FF.

★★½ FOUR SEASONS GOLF CLUB

PU-750 Slocum Ave., Exeter, 18643-1030, Luzerne County, (570)655-8869, 6 miles from Wilkes-Barre. **E-mail:** fsggp@aol.com. **Web:** www.gothamgolf.com. **Facility Holes:** 18. **Yards:** 5,524/4,136. **Par:** 70/70. **Course Rating:** 64.5/62.0. **Slope:** 102/91. **Green Fee:** $13/$20. **Cart Fee:** $11/Person. **Walking Policy:** Walking at certain times. **Walkability:** 1. **Opened:** 1960. **Season:** Year-round. **High:** April-Sept. **To obtain tee times:** Call up to 7 days in advance. **Misc:** Reduced fees (weekdays, twilight), metal spikes, credit cards (MC, V, AE, D), BF, FF.

FOUR SEASONS GOLF COURSE

PU-949 Church St., Landisville, 17538, Lancaster County, (717)898-0104, 65 miles from Philadelphia. **Facility Holes:** 18. **Yards:** 6,320/5,007. **Par:** 70/72. **Course Rating:** 69.6/67.9. **Slope:** 120/111. **Green Fee:** $16/$25. **Cart Fee:** $13/Person. **Walking Policy:** Unrestricted walking. **Opened:** 1961. **Architect:** Richard Funk. **Season:** Year-round. **To obtain tee times:** Call up to 7 days in advance. **Miscellaneous:** Reduced fees (weekdays, twilight, seniors, juniors), credit cards (MC, V), BF, FF.

★★★ FOX HOLLOW GOLF CLUB

PU-2020 Trumbauersville Rd., Quakertown, 18951, Bucks County, (215)538-1920. **E-mail:** fxggp@aol.com. **Facility Holes:** 18. **Yards:** 6,613/4,984. **Par:** 71/71. **Course Rating:** 70.2/67.1. **Slope:** 123/120. **Green Fee:** $18/$45. **Cart Fee:** $10/Person. **Walking Policy:** Walking at certain times. **Walkability:** 1. **Opened:** 1957. **Architect:** Dave Gordon. **Season:** Year-round. **To obtain tee times:** Call up to 10 days in advance. **Miscellaneous:** Reduced fees (weekdays, twilight, seniors, juniors), range (grass), credit cards (MC, V, AE), BF, FF.
Reader Comments: Fun course ... Nice views ... Good value and service ... Good course from back tees ... Still has crazy par-5 15th ... Not bad for the price ... They are working on improving the course.

★★½ FOX RUN GOLF COURSE

PU-4240 River Road, Beaver Falls, 15010, Beaver County, (724)847-3568, 30 miles from Pittsburgh. **Facility Holes:** 18. **Yards:** 6,510/5,337. **Par:** 72/72. **Course Rating:** 69.6/72.2. **Slope:** 113/117. **Green Fee:** $14/$22. **Cart Fee:** $10/Person. **Walking Policy:** Unrestricted walking. **Walkability:** 2. **Opened:** 1962. **Architect:** Max Mesing. **Season:** Year-round. **High:** May-Sept. **To obtain tee times:** Call golf shop. **Miscellaneous:** Reduced fees (seniors, juniors), range (grass/mats), credit cards (MC, V), BF, FF.

★★★½ FOXCHASE GOLF CLUB

PU-300 Stevens Rd., Stevens, 17578, Lancaster County, (717)336-3673, 50 miles from Philadelphia. **E-mail:** foxchasegc@desupernet.net. **Web:** www.foxchasegolf.com. **Facility Holes:** 18. **Yards:** 6,796/4,690. **Par:** 72/72. **Course Rating:** 72.7/66.9. **Slope:** 124/116. **Green Fee:** $20/$43. **Cart Fee:** Included in green fee. **Walking Policy:** Walking at certain times. **Walkability:** 3. **Opened:** 1991. **Architect:** John Thompson. **Season:** Year-round. **High:** April-Oct. **To obtain tee times:** Call golf shop. **Miscellaneous:** Reduced fees (weekdays, twilight, seniors, juniors), range (grass/mats), credit cards (MC, V, D).
Reader Comments: Greens are consistent and immaculate ... Tough par 3s ... Wide open, good service, enjoyable ... Very friendly ... Improves each year ... Solid but not spectacular.

PENNSYLVANIA

★ **FRANKLIN D. ROOSEVELT GOLF CLUB**
PU-20th & Pattison Ave., Philadelphia, 19145, Philadelphia County, (215)462-8997. **Facility Holes:** 18. **Yards:** 5,894/5,413. **Par:** 69/69. **Course Rating:** 68.7. **Slope:** 113. **Green Fee:** $21/$29. **Cart Fee:** $25/Cart. **Walking Policy:** Unrestricted walking. **Walkability:** 1. **Opened:** 1933. **Season:** Year-round. **High:** April-Sept. **To obtain tee times:** Call golf shop. **Miscellaneous:** Reduced fees (weekdays, twilight, seniors, juniors), metal spikes, range (grass), credit cards (MC, V).

★★★ **GALEN HALL COUNTRY CLUB**
PU-Galen Hall Rd. P.O. Box 129, Wernersville, 19565, Berks County, (610)678-9535, 10 miles from Reading. **Web:** www.galenhallcountryclub.com. **Facility Holes:** 18. **Yards:** 6,271/5,117. **Par:** 72/73. **Course Rating:** 70.2/68.8. **Slope:** 121/113. **Green Fee:** $10/$25. **Cart Fee:** $13/Person. **Walking Policy:** Walking at certain times. **Walkability:** 4. **Opened:** 1911. **Architect:** Alex Findlay/A.W.Tillinghast. **Season:** Year-round. **High:** May-Oct. **To obtain tee times:** Call golf shop. **Miscellaneous:** Reduced fees (weekdays, twilight, seniors, juniors), metal spikes, range (grass), lodging (9 rooms), credit cards (MC, V, AE, D), BF, FF. **Reader Comments:** A true hidden gem, from the hand that shaped Winged Foot ... Elevation changes, many interesting holes ... Previous knowledge is especially helpful... Tough course ... Good value ... No. 15 has an island green ... Beautiful setting.

★★½ **GENERAL WASHINGTON COUNTRY CLUB**
PU-2750 Egypt Rd., Audubon, 19403, Montgomery County, (610)666-7600, 20 miles from Philadelphia. **Facility Holes:** 18. **Yards:** 6,400/5,300. **Par:** 71/72. **Course Rating:** 70.3/70.5. **Slope:** 119/119. **Green Fee:** $14/$29. **Cart Fee:** $11/Person. **Walking Policy:** Walking at certain times. **Walkability:** 3. **Opened:** 1945. **Architect:** William F. Mitchell. **Season:** Year-round. **High:** April-Oct. **To obtain tee times:** Call up to 7 days in advance. **Miscellaneous:** Reduced fees (twilight, seniors, juniors), range (mats), credit cards (MC, V, AE, D), BF, FF.

★★½ **GILBERTSVILLE GOLF CLUB**
PU-2944 Lutheran Rd., Gilbertsville, 19525, Montgomery County, (610)323-3222. **Facility Holes:** 18. **To obtain tee times:** Call golf shop.

★★½ **GLEN BROOK GOLF CLUB**
PU-Glenbrook Rd., Stroudsburg, 18360, Monroe County, (570)421-3680, 75 miles from New York City. **Web:** www.glenbrookgolfclub.com. **Facility Holes:** 18. **Yards:** 6,536/5,234. **Par:** 72/72. **Course Rating:** 70.9/69.2. **Slope:** 125/123. **Green Fee:** $38/$45. **Cart Fee:** Included in green fee. **Walking Policy:** Walking at certain times. **Walkability:** 3. **Opened:** 1924. **Architect:** Robert White. **Season:** April-Dec. **To obtain tee times:** Call up to 14 days in advance. **Miscellaneous:** Reduced fees (weekdays, guests, twilight, seniors), metal spikes, lodging (12 rooms), credit cards (MC, V), FF.

★★★★ **GOLDEN OAKS COUNTRY CLUB**
SP-10 Stonehedge Rd., Fleetwood, 19522, Berks County, (610)944-8633, 18 miles from Reading. **E-mail:** Corporateservices@americangolf.com. **Web:** www.americangolf.com. **Facility Holes:** 18. **Yards:** 7,106/5,120. **Par:** 72/72. **Course Rating:** 74.4/68.5. **Slope:** 128/108. **Green Fee:** $49/$70. **Cart Fee:** Included in green fee. **Opened:** 1994. **Architect:** Jim Blaukovitch. **Season:** Year-round. **To obtain tee times:** Call golf shop. **Miscellaneous:** Credit cards (MC, V, AE). **Reader Comments:** An excellent public facility ... Great course with a few superb holes ... Great facility ... Good variation, slick greens ... A real hidden gem!! ... Nicest public golf course in SE Pennsylvania ... Fantastic course, great clubhouse.

★★ **THE GOLF CLUB AT SHEPHERD HILLS**
PU-1160 S. Krocks Rd., Wescosville, 18106, Lehigh County, (610)391-0644. **Facility Holes:** 18. **Yards:** 6,500/5,842. **Par:** 70/73. **Course Rating:** 69.5/70.8. **Slope:** 116/115. **Green Fee:** $20/$30. **Cart Fee:** $12/Person. **Walking Policy:** Unrestricted walking. **Walkability:** 1. **Opened:** 1964. **Architect:** Leo Frazer. **Season:** Year-round. **High:** May-Sept. **To obtain tee times:** Call golf shop. **Miscellaneous:** Reduced fees (weekdays), credit cards (MC, V).

THE GOLF COURSE AT GLEN MILLS
PU-221 Glen Mills Rd., Glen Mills, 19342, Delaware County, (610)558-2142, 15 miles from Philadelphia. **Facility Holes:** 18. **Yards:** 6,636/4,703. **Par:** 71/71. **Course Rating:** 71.0/62.0. **Slope:** 131/114. **Green Fee:** $40/$85. **Cart Fee:** Included in green fee. **Walking Policy:** Unrestricted walking. **Walkability:** 3. **Opened:** 2001. **Architect:** Bobby Weed. **Season:** Year-round. **High:** April-Nov. **To obtain tee times:** Call up to 7 days in advance. **Miscellaneous:** Reduced fees (weekdays, twilight, seniors, juniors), range (grass/mats), credit cards (MC, V, AE, D), BF, FF. **Notes:** Ranked 7th in 2001 Best New Upscale Courses.

GOSPEL HILL GOLF & COUNTRY CLUB
SP-4415 Steimer Rd., Erie, 16510, Erie County, (814)899-5700. **Facility Holes:** 18. **Yards:** 5,527/5,299. **Par:** 70/70. **Course Rating:** 65.3/69.3. **Slope:** 109/113. **Green Fee:** $13/$16. **Cart Fee:** $18/Cart. **Opened:** 1959. **Architect:** Ed Kerner. **Season:** March-Dec. **To obtain tee times:** Call golf shop. **Miscellaneous:** Reduced fees (twilight).

★★½ GRAND VIEW GOLF CLUB
PU-1000 Clubhouse Dr., North Braddock, 15104, Allegheny County, (412)351-5390, 8 miles from Pittsburgh. **E-mail:** gvga@pgh.net. **Web:** pittsburghgolf.com. **Facility Holes:** 18. **Yards:** 6,151/4,817. **Par:** 71/71. **Course Rating:** 71.9/69.4. **Slope:** 132/122. **Green Fee:** $35/$45. **Cart Fee:** Included in green fee. **Walking Policy:** Walking at certain times. **Walkability:** 5. **Opened:** 1996. **Architect:** Garbin. **Season:** Year-round. **High:** April-Oct. **To obtain tee times:** Call up to 7 days in advance. **Miscellaneous:** Reduced fees (twilight, seniors, juniors), range (grass/mats), credit cards (MC, V, AE, D), BF, FF.

★★★ GRANDVIEW GOLF CLUB
PU-2779 Carlisle Rd., York, 17404, York County, (717)764-2674, 4 miles from York. **E-mail:** grandviewinc@netzero.net. **Web:** www.golfgrandview.com. **Facility Holes:** 18. **Yards:** 6,639/5,578. **Par:** 72/73. **Course Rating:** 71.0/71.0. **Slope:** 122/119. **Green Fee:** $16/$27. **Cart Fee:** $12/Person. **Walking Policy:** Unrestricted walking. **Walkability:** 3. **Opened:** 1924. **Season:** Year-round. **To obtain tee times:** Call golf shop. **Miscellaneous:** Reduced fees (weekdays, guests, twilight, seniors, juniors), credit cards (MC, V, D), BF, FF.
Reader Comments: Long course … A neat old course … All of the par 5s are reachable … Comfortable and enjoyable … Super greens … Just love this course.

GRANDVIEW GOLF CLUB
PU-RD2 Box196, Curwensville, 16833, Clearfield County, (814)236-3369. **Facility Holes:** 18. **Yards:** 6,334/5,214. **Par:** 71/73. **Course Rating:** 70.2/70.6. **Slope:** 117/114. **Green Fee:** $14/$18. **Cart Fee:** $12/Person. **Walking Policy:** Unrestricted walking. **Walkability:** 4. **Opened:** 1978. **Architect:** John G. Harrison. **Season:** April-Oct. **High:** June-Aug. **To obtain tee times:** Call up to 7 days in advance. **Misc:** Range (grass), credit cards (MC, V, AE, D), BF, FF.

GREAT COVE GOLF RECREATION
SP-Hist County Road 80, McConnelsburg, 17233, Fulton County, (717)485-9924. **Facility Holes:** 18. **Yards:** 6,780/5,580. **Par:** 71/72. **Course Rating:** 70.9/65.5. **Slope:** 118/110. **Green Fee:** $20/$25. **Cart Fee:** Included in green fee. **Opened:** 1963. **Season:** April-Dec. **To obtain tee times:** Call golf shop. **Misc:** Reduced fees (twilight, seniors), credit cards (MC, V).

★★★ GREEN ACRES GOLF
PU-RR1, Bernville, 19506, Berks County, (610)488-6698, 15 miles from Reading. **Facility Holes:** 18. **Yards:** 6,070/5,490. **Par:** 70/70. **Green Fee:** $14/$19. **Cart Fee:** $10/Person. **Opened:** 1965. **Architect:** Leon Stacherski. **Season:** March-Dec. **To obtain tee times:** Call golf shop. **Miscellaneous:** Reduced fees (twilight, seniors, juniors), metal spikes.
Reader Comments: Ego-building course … Flat, wide open, great for beginners, fun for all, great value … Congenial management … Great scenery … Front more fun than back.

★★½ GREEN ACRES GOLF CLUB
PU-RD No.4, Rte. 408, Titusville, 16354, Crawford County, (814)827-3589, 2 miles from Hydentown. **Facility Holes:** 9. **Yards:** 5,660/5,660. **Par:** 72/72. **Green Fee:** $10/$12. **Cart Fee:** $14/Cart. **Walking Policy:** Unrestricted walking. **Walkability:** 2. **Opened:** 1974. **Architect:** A. Kalkbrenner/D. Kalkbrenner/R. Howe. **Season:** April-Oct. **High:** June-Sept. **To obtain tee times:** Call golf shop. **Miscellaneous:** Reduced fees (seniors), metal spikes, range (grass), BF, FF.

★★ GREEN MEADOWS GOLF COURSE
PU-2451 N Brickyard Rd., North East, 16428, Erie County, (814)725-5009, (877)453-1974, 15 miles from Erie. **E-mail:** threebs2@aol.com. **Facility Holes:** 18. **Yards:** 5,988/5,144. **Par:** 72/71. **Course Rating:** 67.1/68.0. **Slope:** 102/102. **Green Fee:** $12/$18. **Cart Fee:** $10/Person. **Walking Policy:** Unrestricted walking. **Walkability:** 1. **Opened:** 1975. **Architect:** Bob Boyd. **Season:** April-Oct. **High:** June-Aug. **To obtain tee times:** Call golf shop. **Miscellaneous:** Reduced fees (weekdays, seniors), range (grass/mats), credit cards (MC, V, D), BF, FF.

★★★½ GREEN MEADOWS GOLF COURSE
PU-R.D. 2, Box 224 Rte. 19, Volant, 16156, Lawrence County, (724)530-7330, 45 miles from Pittsburgh. **Facility Holes:** 18. **Yards:** 6,543/5,220. **Par:** 72/72. **Course Rating:** 68.4/71.0. **Slope:** 108/107. **Green Fee:** $15/$18. **Cart Fee:** $9/Person. **Walking Policy:** Unrestricted walking. **Walkability:** 4. **Opened:** 1964. **Season:** March-Dec. **High:** April-Sept. **Tee times:** Call golf shop. **Miscellaneous:** Reduced fees (weekdays, seniors, juniors), range (grass/mats), credit

cards (MC, V, D).
Reader Comments: One of the nicest courses in PA ... Like playing this course ... Very long course, especially for seniors ... Good condition and good management ...Too many blind shots ... Long par 5s ... Worth the drive from Pittsburgh.

★★★ GREEN POND COUNTRY CLUB
PU-3604 Farmersville Rd., Bethlehem, 18020, Northampton County, (610)691-9453. **Facility Holes:** 18. **Yards:** 6,521/5,541. **Par:** 71/74. **Course Rating:** 69.4/69.7. **Slope:** 126/112. **Green Fee:** $22/$45. **Cart Fee:** $13/Person. **Walking Policy:** Walking at certain times. **Walkability:** 2. **Opened:** 1931. **Architect:** Alex Findlay. **Season:** Year-round. **High:** April-Nov. **To obtain tee times:** Call up to 7 days in advance. **Miscellaneous:** Reduced fees (seniors, juniors), range (grass), credit cards (MC, V, AE, D), BF, FF.
Reader Comments: Easy to walk, tries to stay open all winter ... Short, tight, excellent greens ... These greens are fast ... Needs fairway work.

★★★½ GREENCASTLE GREENS GOLF CLUB
PU-2000 Castlegreen Dr., Greencastle, 17225, Franklin County, (717)597-1188, (717)593-9192, 75 miles from Baltimore. **Facility Holes:** 18. **Yards:** 6,908/5,315. **Par:** 72/74. **Course Rating:** 72.6/70.3. **Slope:** 129/124. **Green Fee:** $17/$28. **Cart Fee:** $12/Person. **Walking Policy:** Walking at certain times. **Walkability:** 5. **Opened:** 1991. **Architect:** Bob Elder. **Season:** Year-round. **To obtain tee times:** Call up to 7 days in advance. **Misc:** Reduced fees (weekdays, twilight, seniors, juniors), range (grass/mats), credit cards (MC, V, AE), BF, FF.
Reader Comments: Nice course and value ... Okay! Potential but inconsistent ... Best small course you can play in central PA ... Great par 3s ... Play it twice, club selection imperative ... Nice mountain views ... Very long when the wind blows.

★★½ GROFF'S FARM GOLF CLUB
PU-650 Pinkerton Rd., Mount Joy, 17552, Lancaster County, (717)653-2048, 60 miles from Philadelphia. **E-mail:** cgroff5510@aol.com. **Web:** www.groffsfarmgolfclub.com. **Facility Holes:** 18. **Yards:** 6,403/4,863. **Par:** 71/71. **Course Rating:** 70.6/67.3. **Slope:** 121/107. **Green Fee:** $22/$28. **Cart Fee:** $13/Person. **Walking Policy:** Unrestricted walking. **Walkability:** 3. **Opened:** 1998. **Architect:** Ed Beidel. **Season:** Year-round. **To obtain tee times:** Call golf shop. **Miscellaneous:** Reduced fees (weekdays, twilight, seniors, juniors), range (grass/mats), lodging (2 rooms), credit cards (MC, V, D), BF, FF.

★★★½ HARRISBURG NORTH GOLF RESORT
R-1724 Rte. 25, Millersburg, 17061, Dauphin County, (717)692-3664, (800)442-4652, 24 miles from Harrisburg. **Facility Holes:** 18. **Yards:** 6,960/6,600. **Par:** 71/71. **Course Rating:** 68.8/69.2. **Slope:** 115/117. **Green Fee:** $10/$18. **Cart Fee:** $27/Person. **Walking Policy:** Unrestricted walking. **Walkability:** 3. **Opened:** 1963. **Architect:** Harlin Wills. **Season:** Year-round. **High:** May-Sept. **To obtain tee times:** Call golf shop. **Miscellaneous:** Range (grass), lodging (14 rooms), credit cards (MC, V), BF, FF.
Reader Comments: Good variety, good service, great view ... Nice greens, No. 10 very difficult par-3 ... Brand new clubhouse ... Good greens.

★★★★ HARTEFELD NATIONAL GOLF COURSE
PU-1 Hartefeld Dr., Avondale, 19311, Chester County, (610)268-8800, (800)240-7373, 35 miles from Philadelphia. **E-mail:** macuff@hartefeld.com. **Web:** www.hartefeld.com. **Facility Holes:** 18. **Yards:** 6,969/5,065. **Par:** 71/71. **Course Rating:** 73.2/69.8. **Slope:** 131/123. **Green Fee:** $55/$110. **Cart Fee:** Included in green fee. **Walking Policy:** Unrestricted walking. **Walkability:** 3. **Opened:** 1995. **Architect:** Tom Fazio. **Season:** Year-round. **High:** April-Nov. **To obtain tee times:** Call up to 14 days in advance. **Miscellaneous:** Reduced fees (twilight), range (grass/mats), credit cards (MC, V, AE, D), BF, FF.
Notes: Ranked 20th in 2001 Best in State; 6th in 1996 Best New Upscale Courses.
Reader Comments: I love everything about this place ... Locker room facilities, services are outstanding ... Best public course in the East ... Food is awesome ... A superb layout ... Wonderful junior program ... A bit pricey but the best facility in this area for golf, food, locker room and practice.

HAWK LAKE GOLF CLUB
PU-1605 Loucks Rd., York, 17404, York County, (717)764-2224. **E-mail:** ytggp@aol.com. **Web:** www.gothamgolf.com. **Facility Holes:** 18. **Yards:** 6,516/5,116. **Par:** 72/72. **Green Fee:** $39/$55. **Cart Fee:** Included in green fee. **Walking Policy:** Walking at certain times. **Walkability:** 3. **Opened:** 2001. **Architect:** James Ganley. **Season:** Year-round. **High:** May-Sept. **To obtain tee times:** Call up to 7 days in advance. **Miscellaneous:** Reduced fees (twilight, seniors), range (grass/mats), credit cards (MC, V, AE), FF.
Special Notes: Formerly Yorktown Golf Course.

PENNSYLVANIA

★★★½ **HAWK VALLEY GOLF CLUB**
PU-1309 Crestview Dr., Denver, 17517, Lancaster County, (717)445-5445, (800)522-4295, 5 miles from Denver. **E-mail:** hawkvalley@desupernet.net. **Web:** www.golfthehawk.com. **Facility Holes:** 18. **Yards:** 6,628/5,661. **Par:** 72/72. **Course Rating:** 70.3/70.2. **Slope:** 132/119. **Green Fee:** $22/$30. **Cart Fee:** $12/Person. **Walking Policy:** Walking at certain times. **Walkability:** 3. **Opened:** 1971. **Architect:** William Gordon. **Season:** Year-round. **High:** March-Nov. **To obtain tee times:** Call golf shop. **Miscellaneous:** Reduced fees (juniors), metal spikes, credit cards (MC, V, AE, D), BF, FF.
Reader Comments: Hidden gem, good shape, great greens ... Short course, small greens ... Some of the fastest, toughest greens, nice layout ... Good layout ... Good public course ... Country club conditions.

★★★½ **HERITAGE HILLS GOLF RESORT & CONFERENCE CENTER**
R-2700 Mt. Rose Ave., York, 17402, York County, (717)755-4653, (800)942-2444. **E-mail:** don@hhgr.com. **Web:** www.hhgr.com. **Facility Holes:** 18. **Yards:** 6,628/5,147. **Par:** 71/72. **Course Rating:** 70.8/69.9. **Slope:** 122/111. **Green Fee:** $32/$40. **Cart Fee:** $16/Person. **Walking Policy:** Walking at certain times. **Walkability:** 3. **Opened:** 1989. **Architect:** Russell Roberts. **Season:** Year-round. **High:** April-Oct. **To obtain tee times:** Call up to 14 days in advance. **Miscellaneous:** Reduced fees (weekdays, guests, twilight, seniors), range (mats), lodging (104 rooms), credit cards (MC, V, AE, D), BF, FF.
Reader Comments: Busy but always in great condition ... Toughest finishing hole in area ... Nice large bunkers ... Unusual holes ... Great restaurant.

HI-LEVEL GOLF COURSE
PU-Fern Rd., Kossuth, 16331, Clarion County, (814)797-1813, 100 miles from Pittsburgh. **E-mail:** hilevel@penn.com. **Facility Holes:** 23. **Yards:** 5,692/4,677. **Par:** 72/72. **Green Fee:** $14/$17. **Cart Fee:** $17/Cart. **Opened:** 1968. **Architect:** Ed Hess. **Season:** April-Nov. **To obtain tee times:** Call golf shop. **Miscellaneous:** Credit cards (MC, V, D).
Special Notes: Also has a 5-hole executive course.

★★★ **HICKORY HEIGHTS GOLF CLUB**
PU-116 Hickory Heights Dr., Bridgeville, 15017, Allegheny County, (412)257-0300, 12 miles from Pittsburgh. **Facility Holes:** 18. **Yards:** 6,531/5,002. **Par:** 72/72. **Course Rating:** 71.6/69.6. **Slope:** 131/125. **Green Fee:** $29/$49. **Cart Fee:** Included in green fee. **Walking Policy:** Walking at certain times. **Walkability:** 4. **Opened:** 1992. **Architect:** Michael Hurdzan. **Season:** Year-round. **To obtain tee times:** Call up to 7 days in advance. **Misc:** Reduced fees (weekdays, twilight, seniors, juniors), metal spikes, range (grass), credit cards (MC, V, AE), BF, FF.
Reader Comments: A hilly, tight course, narrow fairways, weaves around homes ... A bit pricey but a tough, well-manicured track ... Don't like having back-to-back par 3s on front side ... Design a little funky, but fun.

HICKORY HEIGHTS GOLF CLUB
PU-Rd. 1 & Lehman Rd., Spring Grove, 17362, York County, (717)225-4247. **E-mail:** lks2256724@aol.com. **Facility Holes:** 18. **Yards:** 5,980/4,640. **Par:** 71/71. **Course Rating:** 67.2/67.4. **Slope:** 122/118. **Green Fee:** $18/$23. **Cart Fee:** $10/Person. **Walkability:** 4. **Season:** March-Dec. **High:** May-Oct. **To obtain tee times:** Call up to 7 days in advance. **Miscellaneous:** Reduced fees (weekdays, seniors), range (grass/mats), credit cards (MC, V), BF, FF.

HICKORY VALLEY GOLF CLUB
PU-1921 Ludwig Rd., Gilbertsville, 19525, Montgomery County, (610)754-9862, 25 miles from Philadelphia. **E-mail:** hkryvlypro@aol.com. **Web:** www.hickoryvalley.com. **Facility Holes:** 36. **Cart Fee:** $12/Person. **Walking Policy:** Walking at certain times. **Opened:** 1968. **Architect:** Ron Pritchard. **Season:** Year-round. **High:** April-Oct. **To obtain tee times:** Call up to 7 days in advance. **Miscellaneous:** Reduced fees (twilight, seniors, juniors), range (mats), credit cards (MC, V, D), BF, FF.
★★★½ **AMBASSADOR COURSE** (18)
Yards: 6,442/5,058. **Par:** 72/72. **Course Rating:** 70.3/69.0. **Slope:** 116/116. **Green Fee:** $19/$38. **Walkability:** 2.
Reader Comments: Fun course to play ... Par-5 finishing hole is a true 3-shot par 5 ... Go for 36 holes in one day ... Fast greens ... Tight, control important ... Owners put a lot back into course.
★★★½ **PRESIDENTIAL COURSE** (18)
Yards: 6,676/5,271. **Par:** 72/72. **Course Rating:** 72.8/71.2. **Slope:** 133/128. **Green Fee:** $28/$55. **Walkability:** 1.
Reader Comments: Nice course ... Good test of golf ... Best value daily-fee course in the Philadelphia area ... Back 9 is far superior to the front ... Perfect mix of holes ... Best of everything in PA.

PENNSYLVANIA

HICKORY VFW GOLF COURSE
PU-4586 E. State St., Hermitage, 16148, Mercer County, (724)346-6903. **Facility Holes:** 18. **Yards:** 6,405/5,228. **Par:** 71/72. **Green Fee:** $14/$19. **Cart Fee:** $10/Person. **Walking Policy:** Unrestricted walking. **Walkability:** 2. **Opened:** 1930. **Architect:** George Lee. **Season:** Year-round. **To obtain tee times:** Call up to 14 days in advance. **Miscellaneous:** Reduced fees (weekdays, twilight, seniors, juniors), credit cards (MC, V), BF, FF.

★★★ HIDDEN VALLEY FOUR SEASONS RESORT
R-One Craighead Dr., Hidden Valley, 15502, Somerset County, (814)443-8444, (800)458-0175, 60 miles from Pittsburgh. **E-mail:** hvr@shol.com. **Web:** www.hiddenvalleyresort.com. **Facility Holes:** 18. **Yards:** 6,589/5,027. **Par:** 72/72. **Course Rating:** 73.5/69.2. **Slope:** 142/129. **Green Fee:** $35/$50. **Cart Fee:** Included in green fee. **Walking Policy:** Mandatory carts. **Walkability:** 5. **Opened:** 1987. **Architect:** Russell Roberts. **Season:** April-Oct. **To obtain tee times:** Call golf shop. **Miscellaneous:** Reduced fees (weekdays, guests, twilight), metal spikes, range (grass/mats), credit cards (MC, V, AE, D, DC), BF, FF.
Reader Comments: Great starting hole—picturesque ... Very serene ... Short but a lot of trouble.

★★★½ HIDDEN VALLEY GOLF COURSE
PU-1753 Panther Valley Rd., Pine Grove, 17963, Schuylkill County, (570)739-4455, (800)428-4631, 45 miles from Harrisburg. **E-mail:** hvgolf@sunlink.net. **Web:** www.distinctgolf.com. **Facility Holes:** 18. **Yards:** 6,361/5,212. **Par:** 72/72. **Course Rating:** 71.7/71.8. **Slope:** 125/121. **Green Fee:** $29. **Cart Fee:** $12/Person. **Walking Policy:** Unrestricted walking. **Walkability:** 3. **Opened:** 1958. **Season:** Year-round. **To obtain tee times:** Call up to 14 days in advance. **Miscellaneous:** Reduced fees (twilight, seniors), range (grass/mats), credit cards (MC, V), BF, FF.
Reader Comments: Nice layout ... Beautiful mountain course, secluded ... One of the consistently best public courses I play on ... Very playable ... Tight fairways ... Very nice golf for money.

★★★★½ HIDEAWAY HILLS GOLF CLUB
PU-Carney Road, Kresgville, 18333, Monroe County, (610)681-6000, 30 miles from Allentown. **Web:** www.hideawaygolf.com. **Facility Holes:** 18. **Yards:** 6,933/5,047. **Par:** 72/72. **Course Rating:** 72.7/68.4. **Slope:** 127/116. **Green Fee:** $29/$42. **Cart Fee:** $15/Person. **Walking Policy:** Mandatory carts. **Walkability:** 5. **Opened:** 1994. **Architect:** Joseph Farda. **Season:** March-Dec. **To obtain tee times:** Call up to 7 days in advance. **Miscellaneous:** Reduced fees (guests, twilight), range (grass), lodging (36 rooms), credit cards (MC, V, AE, D), FF.
Reader Comments: Great mountain course ... Unique holes with elevation changes ... You'll love the par 5s ... A hidden gem maybe! ... Play this course every fall ... The scenery is excellent.

HIGHLANDER GOLF COURSE
PU-Rte. 6N. & I-79, Edinboro, 16412, Erie County, (814)734-4135. **Facility Holes:** 18. **Yards:** 5,116/3,961. **Par:** 67/67. **Green Fee:** $16/$19. **Cart Fee:** $8/Person. **Walking Policy:** Unrestricted walking. **Walkability:** 3. **Opened:** 1965. **Season:** March-Nov. **To obtain tee times:** Call golf shop. **Misc:** Reduced fees (weekdays, twilight, seniors), metal spikes, range (grass).

★★★★ HONEY RUN GOLF & COUNTRY CLUB
SP-3131 S. Salem Church Rd., York, 17404, York County, (717)792-9771, (800)475-4657, 3 miles from York. **Facility Holes:** 18. **Yards:** 6,797/5,948. **Par:** 72/72. **Course Rating:** 72.4/74.0. **Slope:** 123/125. **Green Fee:** $20/$32. **Cart Fee:** $13/Person. **Walking Policy:** Walking at certain times. **Walkability:** 4. **Opened:** 1971. **Architect:** Edmund B. Ault. **Season:** Year-round. **High:** May-Aug. **To obtain tee times:** Call golf shop. **Miscellaneous:** Reduced fees (weekdays, guests, twilight, seniors, juniors), metal spikes, range (grass), credit cards (MC, V).
Reader Comments: Great opening hole ... Nice layout ... Large, wonderful greens ... Best New Course Nominee.

HONEYBROOK GOLF CLUB
SP-1422 Cambridge Rd., Honey Brook, 19344, Chester County, (610)273-0207, 40 miles from Philadelphia. **E-mail:** michael@honeybrookgolf.com. **Web:** www.honeybrookgolf.com. **Facility Holes:** 18. **Yards:** 6,341/4,961. **Par:** 70/70. **Course Rating:** 70.4/68.8. **Slope:** 128/115. **Green Fee:** $22/$59. **Cart Fee:** $13/Person. **Walking Policy:** Unrestricted walking. **Walkability:** 3. **Opened:** 2000. **Architect:** Jim Blaukovitch. **Season:** Year-round. **High:** May-Oct. **To obtain tee times:** Call up to 14 days in advance. **Miscellaneous:** Reduced fees (weekdays, twilight, seniors, juniors), range (grass/mats), credit cards (MC, V, AE, D), BF, FF.

★★½ HORSHAM VALLEY GOLF CLUB
PU-500 Babylon Rd., Ambler, 19002, Montgomery County, (215)646-4707, 15 miles from Philadelphia. **Web:** www.horshamvalleygolf.com. **Facility Holes:** 18. **Yards:** 5,115/4,430. **Par:** 66/66. **Course Rating:** 62.4/60.8. **Slope:** 102/96. **Green Fee:** $18/$30. **Cart Fee:** $24/Cart.

Walking Policy: Unrestricted walking. **Walkability:** 1. **Opened:** 1957. **Architect:** Jack Melville/Doug Melville. **Season:** Year-round. **To obtain tee times:** Call up to 7 days in advance. **Miscellaneous:** Reduced fees (weekdays, twilight, seniors, juniors), range (grass), credit cards (MC, V, AE, D), BF, FF.

INDIAN LAKE RESORT
PU-700 S. Shore Trail, Indian Lake, 15926, Somerset County, (814)754-4653, 15 miles from Johnstown. **Facility Holes:** 18. **Yards:** 6,199/5,244. **Par:** 72/72. **Course Rating:** 70.2/70.0. **Slope:** 128/124. **Green Fee:** $18/$20. **Cart Fee:** $12/Person. **Walking Policy:** Unrestricted walking. **Walkability:** 2. **Architect:** Musser Engineering Inc. **Season:** March-Nov. **High:** June-Aug. **To obtain tee times:** Call golf shop. **Miscellaneous:** Reduced fees (weekdays, guests, twilight), metal spikes, range (grass/mats), credit cards (MC, V, AE, D), BF, FF.

INDIAN RUN GOLF CLUB
PU-1975 Avella Road, Avella, 15312, Washington County, (724)587-0330, 50 miles from Pittsburgh. **Facility Holes:** 18. **Yards:** 6,256/4,886. **Par:** 72/72. **Course Rating:** 70.7/69.3. **Slope:** 129/123. **Green Fee:** $25/$35. **Cart Fee:** Included in green fee. **Walking Policy:** Walking at certain times. **Walkability:** 4. **Opened:** 1998. **Architect:** David Black. **Season:** Year-round. **To obtain tee times:** Call golf shop. **Miscellaneous:** Reduced fees (weekdays, seniors), credit cards (MC, V, AE, D), FF.

★½ INDIAN RUN GOLF COURSE
PU-RD No. 2, Mc Clure, 17841, Snyder County, (570)658-2080. **Facility Holes:** 18. **Yards:** 5,456/5,056. **Par:** 71/71. **Green Fee:** $13/$17. **Cart Fee:** $18/Cart. **Opened:** 1970. **Architect:** Bill Riden. **Season:** April-Oct. **To obtain tee times:** Call golf shop. **Miscellaneous:** Metal spikes.

★★ INGLESIDE GOLF CLUB
PU-104 Horseshoe Drive, Thorndale, 19372, Chester County, (610)384-9128, 30 miles from Philadelphia. **E-mail:** gm@golfingleside.com. **Web:** www.golfingleside.com. **Facility Holes:** 18. **Yards:** 5,106/4,800. **Par:** 68/68. **Course Rating:** 64.2/62.9. **Slope:** 112/109. **Green Fee:** $19/$30. **Cart Fee:** $14/Person. **Walking Policy:** Unrestricted walking. **Walkability:** 3. **Opened:** 1964. **Architect:** Unknown. **Season:** Year-round. **To obtain tee times:** Call golf shop. **Miscellaneous:** Reduced fees (twilight, seniors, juniors), range (grass/mats), credit cards (MC, V), BF, FF.

★★★½ IRON MASTERS COUNTRY CLUB
SP-Country Club Road, Roaring Spring, 16673, Bedford County, (814)224-2915, 15 miles from Altoona. **Facility Holes:** 18. **Yards:** 6,644/5,683. **Par:** 72/75. **Course Rating:** 72.2/73.6. **Slope:** 130/119. **Green Fee:** $30/$35. **Cart Fee:** Included in green fee. **Walking Policy:** Unrestricted walking. **Opened:** 1962. **Architect:** Edmund B. Ault. **Season:** April-Dec. **High:** June-Aug. **To obtain tee times:** Call golf shop. **Miscellaneous:** Reduced fees (weekdays, juniors), credit cards (MC, V).
Reader Comments: Narrow fairways ... Nice course ... Good test, a pleasure to play ... Very scenic ... Very tight ... Mature ... Excellent condition.

IRON VALLEY GOLF CLUB
PU-246 Rexmont Rd., Cornwall, 17016, Lebanon County, (717)279-7409, 3 miles from Lebanon. **Web:** www.ironvalley.com. **Facility Holes:** 18. **Yards:** 7,026/4,905. **Par:** 72/72. **Course Rating:** 74.9/69.2. **Slope:** 138/123. **Green Fee:** $65. **Cart Fee:** Included in green fee. **Walking Policy:** Mandatory carts. **Walkability:** 5. **Opened:** 2001. **Architect:** P.B. Dye. **Season:** Year-round. **To obtain tee times:** Call golf shop. **Miscellaneous:** Reduced fees (twilight), range (grass/mats), credit cards (MC, V, AE, D).

IRWIN COUNTRY CLUB
PU-594 Simpson Rd., Irwin, 15642, Westmoreland County, (742)863-6016, 35 miles from Pittsburgh. **Web:** www.irwincountryclub.com. **Facility Holes:** 18. **Yards:** 5,577/4,741. **Par:** 70/70. **Course Rating:** 66.8/67.5. **Slope:** 119/115. **Green Fee:** $16/$18. **Cart Fee:** $11/Person. **Walking Policy:** Unrestricted walking. **Walkability:** 3. **Opened:** 1958. **Architect:** James Harrison. **Season:** Year-round. **High:** April-Sept. **To obtain tee times:** Call up to 2 days in advance. **Miscellaneous:** Reduced fees (weekdays, seniors, juniors), metal spikes, BF, FF.

JACKSON VALLEY GOLF COURSE
PU-1947 Jackson Run Road, Warren, 16365, Warren County, (814)489-7803, 50 miles from Erie. **Web:** www.jacksonvalley.com. **Facility Holes:** 18. **Yards:** 6,442/5,642. **Par:** 71/73. **Course Rating:** 69.3/71.4. **Slope:** 117/116. **Green Fee:** $18/$20. **Cart Fee:** $11/Person. **Walking Policy:** Walking at certain times. **Walkability:** 4. **Opened:** 1961. **Season:** March-Dec. **High:** May-Sept. **To obtain tee times:** Call golf shop. **Miscellaneous:** Reduced fees (weekdays, guests), lodging (12 rooms), credit cards (MC, V, D).

★★½ **JEFFERSONVILLE GOLF CLUB**
PU-2400 W. Main St., Jeffersonville, 19403, Montgomery County, (610)539-0422, 22 miles from Philadelphia. **Facility Holes:** 18. **Yards:** 6,450/5,880. **Par:** 70/72. **Course Rating:** 69.7/71.4. **Slope:** 128/131. **Green Fee:** $21/$28. **Cart Fee:** $12/Person. **Walking Policy:** Unrestricted walking. **Walkability:** 3. **Opened:** 1931. **Architect:** Donald Ross. **Season:** Year-round. **High:** May-Sept. **To obtain tee times:** Call up to 7 days in advance. **Miscellaneous:** Reduced fees (twilight, seniors, juniors), range (grass), credit cards (MC, V), BF, FF.

★½ **JOHN F. BYRNE GOLF COURSE**
PU-9500 Leon St., Philadelphia, 19114, Philadelphia County, (215)632-8666. **Facility Holes:** 18. **Yards:** 5,200/4,662. **Par:** 67/67. **Course Rating:** 65.0/61.4. **Slope:** 107/98. **Green Fee:** $16/$20. **Cart Fee:** $26/Cart. **Walking Policy:** Unrestricted walking. **Walkability:** 4. **Season:** Year-round. **High:** May-Oct. **To obtain tee times:** Call golf shop. **Miscellaneous:** Reduced fees (weekdays, twilight, seniors, juniors), metal spikes, credit cards (MC, V, AE, D).

★★½ **KIMBERTON GOLF CLUB**
PU-Rte. 23, Kimberton, 19442, Chester County, (610)933-8836, 30 miles from Philadelphia. **E-mail:** kimbertongolf@aol.com. **Facility Holes:** 18. **Yards:** 6,304/5,010. **Par:** 70/71. **Course Rating:** 69.4/67.4. **Slope:** 123/112. **Green Fee:** $15/$33. **Cart Fee:** $22/Cart. **Walking Policy:** Unrestricted walking. **Walkability:** 1. **Opened:** 1962. **Architect:** George Fazio. **Season:** Year-round. **To obtain tee times:** Call up to 7 days in advance. **Miscellaneous:** Reduced fees (weekdays, twilight, seniors, juniors), credit cards (MC, V), BF, FF.

★★★ **KRENDALE GOLF COURSE**
PU-131 N. Eberhart Rd., Butler, 16001, Butler County, (724)482-4065, 30 miles from Pittsburgh. **Facility Holes:** 27. **Green Fee:** $16/$19. **Cart Fee:** $18/Cart. **Walking Policy:** Unrestricted walking. **Opened:** 1949. **Season:** April-Dec. **High:** June-Aug. **Tee times:** Call up to 7 days in advance. **Misc:** Reduced fees (weekdays, twilight, seniors), metal spikes, FF.
NORTH/SOUTH COURSE (18)
Yards: 6,674/5,885. **Par:** 71/71. **Walkability:** 4.
SOUTH/WEST COURSE (18)
Yards: 6,843/5,874. **Par:** 71/71. **Walkability:** 4.
WEST/NORTH COURSE (18)
Yards: 6,453/5,579. **Par:** 71/71. **Walkability:** 3.
Reader Comments: 27 holes to choose from … Some blind holes … Nice course overall … Tight fairways, lots of fun, nice challenge … 175-yard island par-3.

★★★ **LAKE ARTHUR COUNTRY CLUB**
PU-255 Isle Rd., Butler, 16001, Butler County, (724)865-2765. **Facility Holes:** 18. **Yards:** 6,629/6,629. **Par:** 72/72. **Course Rating:** 72.7/69.4. **Slope:** 116/111. **Green Fee:** $14/$21. **Cart Fee:** $28/Cart. **Opened:** 1957. **Architect:** Wynn Tredway. **Season:** Year-round. **To obtain tee times:** Call golf shop. **Miscellaneous:** Metal spikes.
Reader Comments: Nice layout … Good improvements over the last few years … Management is doing great job of fixing up and improving each year … Multiple tees are great.

LAKE VUE NORTH GOLF COURSE
PU-591 Pittsburgh Rd., Butler, 16002, Butler County, (724)586-7097, 40 miles from Pittsburgh. **E-mail:** tpbigblue@aol.com. **Facility Holes:** 18. **Yards:** 6,055/5,140. **Par:** 72/73. **Green Fee:** $13/$28. **Cart Fee:** Included in green fee. **Walking Policy:** Unrestricted walking. **Opened:** 1972. **Season:** Year-round. **To obtain tee times:** Call up to 7 days in advance. **Miscellaneous:** Reduced fees (seniors), FF.

★★½ **LANCASTER HOST GOLF & RESORT**
R-2300 Lincoln Hwy. E., Lancaster, 17602, Lancaster County, (717)299-5500, 45 miles from Harrisburg. **Web:** www.lancasterhost.com. **Facility Holes:** 18. **Yards:** 6,849/5,411. **Par:** 71/71. **Course Rating:** 70.8/70.1. **Slope:** 124/122. **Green Fee:** $18/$51. **Walking Policy:** Unrestricted walking. **Walkability:** 3. **Opened:** 1967. **Architect:** Gordon & Gordon. **Season:** March-Dec. **High:** May-Nov. **To obtain tee times:** Call golf shop. **Miscellaneous:** Reduced fees (twilight), range (grass), lodging (325 rooms), credit cards (MC, V, AE), BF, FF.

★★★ **LEBANON VALLEY GOLF COURSE**
PU-240 Golf Rd., Myerstown, 17067, Lebanon County, (717)866-4481, **Facility Holes:** 18. **Yards:** 6,211/5,796. **Par:** 71/71. **Course Rating:** 67.8/67.8. **Slope:** 129/127. **Green Fee:** $23/$30. **Cart Fee:** Included in green fee. **Season:** Year-round. **To obtain tee times:** Call golf shop. **Miscellaneous:** Reduced fees (seniors), credit cards (MC, V, D).
Reader Comments: Great old course … Greens are always excellent … Can't wait to play it again … New clubhouse… Best deal in central PA … Good course for seniors … Short course … New owners, working hard.

★★★ LENAPE HEIGHTS GOLF COURSE
PU-950 Golf Course Rd., Ford City, 16226, Armstrong County, (724)763-2201, 40 miles from Pittsburgh. **Facility Holes:** 18. **Yards:** 6,145/4,869. **Par:** 71/71. **Course Rating:** 69.0/67.6. **Slope:** 119/114. **Green Fee:** $15/$20. **Cart Fee:** $10/Person. **Walking Policy:** Unrestricted walking. **Walkability:** 3. **Opened:** 1967. **Architect:** Ferdinand Garbin. **Season:** Year-round. **Tee times:** Call golf shop. **Misc:** Reduced fees (weekdays), credit cards (MC, V, AE, D), FF.
Reader Comments: Gets better every year ... New 12,000 square foot clubhouse ... A super place to play golf! ... Pack a lunch, weekend rounds can be long.

★★½ LIMEKILN GOLF CLUB
PU-1176 Limekiln Pike, Ambler, 19002, Montgomery County, (215)643-0643, 10 miles from Philadelphia. **E-mail:** rob@limegolf.net. **Web:** www.limegolf.com. **Facility Holes:** 27. **Green Fee:** $26/$35. **Cart Fee:** $12/Person. **Walking Policy:** Walking at certain times. **Walkability:** 2. **Opened:** 1966. **Architect:** Wrenn/Janis. **Season:** Year-round. **To obtain tee times:** Call golf shop. **Miscellaneous:** Reduced fees (twilight, seniors), range (grass/mats), credit cards (MC, V), BF, FF.
BLUE/RED (18 Combo)
Yards: 6,200/5,282. **Par:** 70/72. **Course Rating:** 67.5/67.5. **Slope:** 114/114.
RED/WHITE (18 Combo)
Yards: 6,240/5,227. **Par:** 70/71. **Course Rating:** 67.8/67.8. **Slope:** 114/114.
WHITE/BLUE (18 Combo)
Yards: 6,415/5,848. **Par:** 70/71. **Course Rating:** 68.7/68.7. **Slope:** 114/114.

★½ LIMERICK GOLF CLUB
PU-765 N. Lewis Rd., Linfield, 19468, Montgomery County, (610)495-6945. **E-mail:** Info@limerickgolfclub.com. **Web:** limerickgolfclub.com. **Facility Holes:** 18. **Yards:** 6,098/4,801. **Par:** 71/71. **Course Rating:** 67.9/66.2. **Slope:** 113/107. **Green Fee:** $22/$32. **Cart Fee:** $22/Cart. **Season:** Year-round. **To obtain tee times:** Call golf shop. **Miscellaneous:** Reduced fees (weekdays, twilight, seniors).

★★★½ LINDEN HALL GOLF CLUB
R-R.D. No. 1, Dawson, 15428, Fayette County, (724)529-2366, (800)944-3238, 37 miles from Pittsburgh. **Web:** www.lindenhallpa.com. **Facility Holes:** 18. **Yards:** 6,675/5,900. **Par:** 72/77. **Course Rating:** 71.2/73.6. **Slope:** 122/123. **Green Fee:** $20/$29. **Cart Fee:** $24/Cart. **Walking Policy:** Unrestricted walking. **Walkability:** 2. **Opened:** 1950. **Architect:** Pete Snead. **Season:** Year-round. **High:** May-Sept. **To obtain tee times:** Call up to 7 days in advance. **Miscellaneous:** Reduced fees (weekdays, guests, seniors, juniors), range (grass), lodging (75 rooms), credit cards (MC, V, AE, D), BF, FF.
Reader Comments: Good layout ... No. 18 a thrill ... Good length, walkable, No. 6 a great par 4 ... Some picturesque holes, front 9 better than back ... No. 13 a beautiful par 5 ... From the back tees it will test you and your bag ... Beautiful mountain layout.

LINDENWOOD GOLF CLUB
PU-360 Galley Rd., Canonsburg, 15317, Washington County, (724)745-9889, 14 miles from Pittsburgh. **Facility Holes:** 36. **Green Fee:** $26/$32. **Cart Fee:** $24/Cart. **Walking Policy:** Walking at certain times. **Walkability:** 2. **Opened:** 1963. **Season:** March-Nov. **High:** May-Aug. **To obtain tee times:** Call golf shop. **Miscellaneous:** Metal spikes, range (grass), credit cards (MC, V, AE, D, Diners' Club).
GOLD/BLUE (18 Combo)
Yards: 6,434/5,018. **Par:** 71/71. **Course Rating:** 68.2/68.2. **Slope:** 118/118.
RED/BLUE (18 Combo)
Yards: 6,665/5,137. **Par:** 71/71. **Course Rating:** 71.0/68.2. **Slope:** 128/119.
RED/GOLD (18 Combo)
Yards: 6,700/5,217. **Par:** 72/72. **Course Rating:** 70.0/70.0. **Slope:** 131/131.
Special Notes: Also has a 9-hole executive course.

★★★★ THE LINKS AT GETTYSBURG
PU-601 Mason-Dixon Rd., Gettysburg, 17325, Adams County, (717)359-8000, 40 miles from Baltimore. **Web:** www.thelinksatgettysburg.com. **Facility Holes:** 18. **Yards:** 7,031/4,861. **Par:** 72/72. **Course Rating:** 73.9/68.8. **Slope:** 128/116. **Green Fee:** $50/$75. **Cart Fee:** Included in green fee. **Walking Policy:** Unrestricted walking. **Walkability:** 4. **Opened:** 1999. **Architect:** Lindsay Ervin/Steve Klein. **Season:** Year-round. **High:** May-Oct. **To obtain tee times:** Call up to 14 days in advance. **Miscellaneous:** Reduced fees (twilight), range (grass/mats), credit cards (MC, V, AE), BF, FF.
Reader Comments: A memorable experience ... Great layout and plenty of challenge ... Some interesting holes with unique local stone outcroppings ... Pampered from the time you drop your bags off ... Bring your camera ... Should host a PGA Tour event, awesome.

THE LINKS AT SPRING CHURCH
PU-3257 Balsiger Rd., Apollo, 15613, Armstrong County, (724)478-5478, (877)725-4657, 22 miles from Pittsburgh. **E-mail:** dss@pga.com. **Web:** www.springchurch.com. **Facility Holes:** 18. **Yards:** 6,785/4,920. **Par:** 72/72. **Course Rating:** 72.6/68.2. **Slope:** 130/116. **Green Fee:** $45/$55. **Cart Fee:** Included in green fee. **Walking Policy:** Unrestricted walking. **Walkability:** 2. **Opened:** 2000. **Architect:** Dominic Palombo. **Season:** March-Nov. **To obtain tee times:** Call up to 14 days in advance. **Miscellaneous:** Reduced fees (juniors), range (mats), credit cards (MC, V, AE, D), BF, FF.

★★½ LOCH NAIRN GOLF CLUB
PU-514 McCue Rd., Avondale, 19311, Chester County, (610)268-2234, 40 miles from Philadelphia. **Facility Holes:** 18. **Yards:** 6,315/5,341. **Par:** 70/70. **Course Rating:** 69.8/68.7. **Slope:** 120/117. **Green Fee:** $18/$36. **Cart Fee:** $12/Person. **Walking Policy:** Unrestricted walking. **Walkability:** 3. **Opened:** 1970. **Architect:** H. C. Smedley. **Season:** Year-round. **High:** April-Oct. **To obtain tee times:** Call up to 6 days in advance. **Miscellaneous:** Reduced fees (weekdays, twilight, seniors, juniors), credit cards (MC, V, AE, D), BF, FF.

★★★ LOCUST VALLEY GOLF CLUB
PU-5525 Locust Valley Rd., Coopersburg, 18036, Lehigh County, (610)282-4711, 45 miles from Philadelphia. **E-mail:** kdslvgc@aol.com. **Facility Holes:** 18. **Yards:** 6,503/5,310. **Par:** 72/72. **Course Rating:** 71.0/71.3. **Slope:** 132/121. **Green Fee:** $23/$33. **Cart Fee:** $13/Person. **Walking Policy:** Unrestricted walking. **Walkability:** 2. **Opened:** 1954. **Architect:** William Gordon & Sons. **Season:** March-Dec. **High:** April-Oct. **To obtain tee times:** Call up to 7 days in advance. **Miscellaneous:** Reduced fees (weekdays, twilight, seniors), metal spikes, credit cards (MC, V), BF, FF.
Reader Comments: Tight, hilly, unforgiving … Good service and conditions … Real nice course, play it a lot … Slow pace on weekends.

★★½ LOST CREEK GOLF CLUB
SP-Rte. No. 35, Oakland Mills, 17076, Juniata County, (717)463-2450, 30 miles from Harrisburg. **Facility Holes:** 18. **Yards:** 6,579/5,318. **Par:** 71/71. **Course Rating:** 70.6/68.9. **Slope:** 116/113. **Green Fee:** $16/$24. **Cart Fee:** $14/Person. **Walking Policy:** Unrestricted walking. **Walkability:** 3. **Opened:** 1965. **Season:** Year-round. **High:** March-Oct. **To obtain tee times:** Call golf shop. **Miscellaneous:** Reduced fees (weekdays, seniors), range (mats), BF, FF.

★★½ MACOBY RUN GOLF COURSE
PU-5275 McLeans Station Rd., Green Lane, 18054, Montgomery County, (215)541-0161, 20 miles from Allentown. **Web:** www.macobyrun.com. **Facility Holes:** 18. **Yards:** 6,238/4,938. **Par:** 72/72. **Course Rating:** 69.7/67.9. **Slope:** 116/110. **Green Fee:** $15/$27. **Cart Fee:** $18/Cart. **Walking Policy:** Unrestricted walking. **Walkability:** 4. **Opened:** 1991. **Architect:** David Horn, Architerra P.C. **Season:** Year-round. **High:** June-Sept. **To obtain tee times:** Call up to 7 days in advance. **Miscellaneous:** Reduced fees (weekdays, twilight, seniors, juniors), metal spikes, range (grass/mats), credit cards (MC, V, D), BF, FF.

MAHONING VALLEY GOLF COURSE
PU-Golf Road off Rt 443, Tamaqua, 18252, Schuylkill County, (570)386-4515, 30 miles from Allentown. **E-mail:** mvgl@ptd.net. **Web:** www.mahoningvalleygolf.com. **Facility Holes:** 18. **Yards:** 5,795/5,000. **Par:** 70/70. **Course Rating:** 68.0/67.0. **Slope:** 113/113. **Green Fee:** $12/$15. **Cart Fee:** $22/Person. **Walking Policy:** Unrestricted walking. **Walkability:** 4. **Opened:** 1958. **Season:** Year-round. **To obtain tee times:** Call up to 7 days in advance. **Miscellaneous:** Reduced fees (weekdays, twilight, seniors), metal spikes, range (grass), BF, FF.

★★★½ MAINLAND GOLF COURSE
PU-Rittenhouse Rd. and Clemens Rd., Mainland, 19451, Montgomery County, (215)256-9548, 15 miles from Philadelphia. **E-mail:** mainlandgolf@erols.com. **Web:** www.mainlandgolf.com. **Facility Holes:** 18. **Yards:** 6,146/4,849. **Par:** 70/70. **Course Rating:** 68.5/65.3. **Slope:** 118/111. **Green Fee:** $32/$42. **Cart Fee:** Included in green fee. **Walking Policy:** Unrestricted walking. **Walkability:** 3. **Opened:** 1963. **Season:** Year-round. **High:** May-Sept. **To obtain tee times:** Call up to 365 days in advance. **Miscellaneous:** Reduced fees (twilight, seniors, juniors), range (mats), credit cards (MC, V, AE, D), BF, FF.
Reader Comments: Short, but fun design … Course in good shape, close to home … The course has been upgraded to make it harder … Improving each year … Fair course … Good for beginners.

★★★ MAJESTIC RIDGE GOLF CLUB
PU-2437 Adin Lane, Chambersburg, 17201, Franklin County, (717)267-3444, (888)743-4346, 50 miles from Harrisburg. **E-mail:** mrgcpga@innernet.net. **Facility Holes:** 18. **Yards:** 6,481/4,349. **Par:** 72/70. **Course Rating:** 72.3/64.4. **Slope:** 132/112. **Green Fee:** $11/$26. **Cart Fee:** $14/Person. **Walking Policy:** Unrestricted walking. **Walkability:** 5. **Opened:** 1992. **Season:**

Year-round. **To obtain tee times:** Call golf shop. **Miscellaneous:** Reduced fees (weekdays, twi-light, seniors), range (grass/mats), credit cards (MC, V, AE, D), BF, FF.
Reader Comments: Hilly, target golf … Lots of blind tee shots … Placement of tee shot a must … Fast greens which I love … Nicely maintained course.

★★½ MANADA GOLF CLUB
PU-609 Golf Lane, Grantville, 17028, Dauphin County, (717)469-2400, (800)942-2444, 15 miles from Harrisburg. **Facility Holes:** 18. **Yards:** 6,705/5,276. **Par:** 72/72. **Course Rating:** 70.7/68.8. **Slope:** 117/111. **Green Fee:** $20/$27. **Cart Fee:** $13/Person. **Walking Policy:** Unrestricted walking. **Walkability:** 2. **Opened:** 1963. **Architect:** William Gordon. **Season:** Year-round. **To obtain tee times:** Call up to 365 days in advance. **Miscellaneous:** Reduced fees (weekdays, twilight, seniors, juniors), credit cards (MC, V), BF, FF.

MANNITTO GOLF CLUB
PU-Rd. 1, Box 258, New Alexandria, 15670, Westmoreland County, (724)668-8150. **E-mail:** mannittogolfclub.com. **Facility Holes:** 18. **Yards:** 7,000/5,037. **Par:** 71/71. **Course Rating:** 71.5/74.2. **Slope:** 125/118. **Green Fee:** $18/$19. **Cart Fee:** $19/Cart. **Opened:** 1960. **Architect:** George Beljan. **Season:** Year-round. **To obtain tee times:** Call golf shop. **Miscellaneous:** Reduced fees (seniors), metal spikes.

★★½ MANOR GOLF CLUB
PU-R.D. 8, Bran Rd., Sinking Spring, 19608, Berks County, (610)678-9597, 75 miles from Philadelphia. **Facility Holes:** 18. **Yards:** 5,425/4,660. **Par:** 70/70. **Course Rating:** 65.7/62.2. **Slope:** 108/101. **Green Fee:** $15/$22. **Cart Fee:** $10/Person. **Walking Policy:** Unrestricted walk-ing. **Walkability:** 4. **Opened:** 1923. **Architect:** Alex Findlay. **Season:** Year-round. **High:** April-Oct. **To obtain tee times:** Call golf shop. **Miscellaneous:** Reduced fees (weekdays, twilight, juniors), metal spikes, range (grass), BF, FF.

★½ MANOR VALLEY COUNTRY CLUB
PU-2095 Denmark Manor Rd., Export, 15632, Westmoreland County, (724)744-4242, 28 miles from Pittsburgh. **Facility Holes:** 18. **Yards:** 6,327/6,327. **Par:** 72/79. **Green Fee:** $17/$18. **Cart Fee:** $10/Person. **Walking Policy:** Unrestricted walking. **Walkability:** 2. **Opened:** 1963. **Architect:** Frye Brothers. **Season:** March-Dec. **High:** April-Oct. **To obtain tee times:** Call golf shop. **Miscellaneous:** Reduced fees (seniors).

★★½ MAYAPPLE GOLF LINKS
PU-1 Mayapple Dr., Carlisle, 17013, Cumberland County, (717)258-4088, 1 mile from Carlisle. **Facility Holes:** 18. **Yards:** 6,541/5,595. **Par:** 71/72. **Course Rating:** 71.3/69.6. **Slope:** 116/114. **Green Fee:** $12/$19. **Cart Fee:** $11/Person. **Walking Policy:** Walking at certain times. **Walkability:** 1. **Opened:** 1990. **Architect:** Ron Garl. **Season:** Year-round. **To obtain tee times:** Call up to 14 days in advance. **Miscellaneous:** Reduced fees (weekdays, guests, twilight, seniors, juniors), range (grass), credit cards (MC, V, AE), BF, FF.

MEADOW LANE GOLF COURSE
PU-510 Hamil Rd., Indiana, 15701, Indiana County, (724)465-5604, 60 miles from Pittsburgh. **Facility Holes:** 18. **Yards:** 6,060/4,836. **Par:** 70/71. **Course Rating:** 65.3/66.8. **Slope:** 107/112. **Green Fee:** $17/$20. **Cart Fee:** $12/Person. **Walking Policy:** Unrestricted walking. **Walkability:** 3. **Opened:** 1965. **Architect:** Cecil Spadafora. **Season:** March-Dec. **To obtain tee times:** Call golf shop. **Miscellaneous:** Reduced fees (weekdays, twilight), range (grass), credit cards (MC, V), BF, FF.

★★★ MEADOWINK GOLF CLUB
PU-4076 Bulltown Rd., Murrysville, 15668, Westmoreland County, (724)327-8243, 20 miles from Pittsburgh. **Facility Holes:** 18. **Yards:** 6,139/5,103. **Par:** 72/72. **Course Rating:** 68.2/66.9. **Slope:** 125/118. **Green Fee:** $20/$26. **Cart Fee:** $12/Person. **Walking Policy:** Unrestricted walk-ing. **Walkability:** 3. **Opened:** 1970. **Architect:** Ferdinand Garbin. **Season:** Year-round. **High:** April-Nov. **To obtain tee times:** Call up to 7 days in advance. **Miscellaneous:** Reduced fees (weekdays, seniors), credit cards (MC, V), BF, FF.
Reader Comments: Short course … Excellent condition … Very affordable, nicely run golf course … Very good public course … Easy short course … Solid not spectacular.

★★ MERCER PUBLIC GOLF COURSE
PU-281 Golf Rd., Mercer, 16137, Mercer County, (724)662-9951, 60 miles from Pittsburgh. **Facility Holes:** 18. **Yards:** 6,194/5,366. **Par:** 72/72. **Course Rating:** 70.4/69.4. **Slope:** 111/111. **Green Fee:** $13/$16. **Cart Fee:** $10/Person. **Walking Policy:** Walking at certain times. **Walkability:** 2. **Opened:** 1959. **Architect:** Mike Maneini. **Season:** Year-round. **High:** May-Sept. **To obtain tee times:** Call golf shop. **Miscellaneous:** Reduced fees (seniors), metal spikes, range (grass), BF, FF.

★★½ **MIDDLETOWN COUNTRY CLUB**
PU-420 N. Bellevue Ave., Langhorne, 19047, Bucks County, (215)757-6953, 14 miles from Philadelphia. **Facility Holes:** 18. **Yards:** 6,081/5,230. **Par:** 69/73. **Course Rating:** 67.7/69.4. **Slope:** 112/113. **Green Fee:** $23/$28. **Cart Fee:** $26/Cart. **Walking Policy:** Unrestricted walking. **Opened:** 1918. **Season:** Year-round. **High:** May-Oct. **To obtain tee times:** Call golf shop. **Miscellaneous:** Reduced fees (weekdays, twilight, seniors, juniors), metal spikes, credit cards (MC, V, AE, D).

★★★½ **MILL RACE GOLF COURSE**
R-RR No. 2, Box 81-B, Benton, 17814, Columbia County, (570)925-2040, 35 miles from Wilke-Barre. **Facility Holes:** 18. **Yards:** 6,096/4,791. **Par:** 70/71. **Course Rating:** 68.6/68.3. **Slope:** 126/122. **Green Fee:** $14/$18. **Cart Fee:** $10/Person. **Walking Policy:** Walking at certain times. **Walkability:** 1. **Opened:** 1970. **Architect:** Geoffrey Cornish. **Season:** March-Nov. **High:** May-Aug. **To obtain tee times:** Call golf shop. **Miscellaneous:** Reduced fees (weekdays, seniors, juniors), range (grass), credit cards (MC, V).
Reader Comments: A challenging but fair course that tests more than driving distance ... Always a challenge, a favorite of mine ... Some back holes remind you of Myrtle Beach layouts ... Always in nice shape.

★★★ **MOCCASIN RUN GOLF COURSE**
PU-Box 402, Schoff Rd., Atglen, 19310, Chester County, (610)593-7322, 40 miles from Philadelphia. **E-mail:** mlk@epix.net. **Web:** www.moccasinrun.com. **Facility Holes:** 18. **Yards:** 6,400/5,275. **Par:** 72/72. **Course Rating:** 70.6/70.4. **Slope:** 119/120. **Green Fee:** $23/$35. **Cart Fee:** $12/Person. **Walking Policy:** Unrestricted walking. **Walkability:** 3. **Opened:** 1988. **Architect:** John Thompson. **Season:** Year-round. **High:** April-Oct. **To obtain tee times:** Call golf shop. **Miscellaneous:** Reduced fees (weekdays, twilight, seniors, juniors), range (grass/mats), credit cards (MC, V, All Debit Cards), BF, FF.
Reader Comments: Great track ... First few holes are a little tight but after that it is a fun course to play ... Good scoring opportunity if you are willing to take some risks ... Nice mom and pop course.

★★½ **MOHAWK TRAILS GOLF COURSE**
PU-RD No. 7, Box 243, New Castle, 16102, Lawrence County, (724)667-8570, 50 miles from Pittsburgh. **Facility Holes:** 18. **Yards:** 6,324. **Par:** 72. **Course Rating:** 70.3. **Slope:** 108. **Green Fee:** $16/$18. **Cart Fee:** $20/Cart. **Walking Policy:** Unrestricted walking. **Walkability:** 3. **Opened:** 1965. **Architect:** Eichenlaub family. **Season:** March-Dec. **High:** May-Sept. **To obtain tee times:** Call up to 365 days in advance. **Miscellaneous:** Reduced fees (weekdays, seniors, juniors), range (grass), FF.

★★½ **MONROE VALLEY GOLF CLUB**
PU-23 Ironwood Lane, Jonestown, 17038, Lebanon County, (717)865-2375, 20 miles from Harrisburg. **Facility Holes:** 18. **Yards:** 6,884/5,254. **Par:** 72/72. **Course Rating:** 71.9/65.0. **Slope:** 115/108. **Green Fee:** $15/$25. **Cart Fee:** $11/Person. **Walking Policy:** Unrestricted walking. **Walkability:** 2. **Opened:** 1968. **Architect:** Edmund B. Ault. **Season:** Year-round. **High:** May-Sept. **To obtain tee times:** Call golf shop. **Miscellaneous:** Reduced fees (weekdays, twilight, seniors, juniors), range (grass/mats), credit cards (MC, V).

★★★★ **MOUNT AIRY LODGE GOLF COURSE**
R-42 Woodland Rd., Mount Pocono, 18344, Monroe County, (570)839-8811, (800)441-4410, 30 miles from Scranton. **Facility Holes:** 18. **Yards:** 7,123/5,771. **Par:** 72/73. **Course Rating:** 74.3/73.3. **Slope:** 138/122. **Green Fee:** $40/$50. **Cart Fee:** $16/Cart. **Walking Policy:** Mandatory cart. **Walkability:** 5. **Opened:** 1980. **Architect:** Hal Purdy. **Season:** April-Nov. **High:** May-Sept. **To obtain tee times:** Call golf shop. **Miscellaneous:** Reduced fees (weekdays, guests, twilight), range (/), credit cards (MC, V, AE, D).
Reader Comments: An excellent variety of challenging holes ... Great layout but the course needs TLC ... 18 holes of the best in the world ... Breathtaking views ... Nice mountain course.

MOUNT ODIN PARK GOLF CLUB
PU-Mt. Odin Park Dr., Greensburg, 15601, Westmoreland County, (724)834-2640, 30 miles from Pittsburgh. **E-mail:** bernpga@sgi.net. **Facility Holes:** 18. **Yards:** 5,395/4,733. **Par:** 70/72. **Course Rating:** 65.0/68.0. **Slope:** 108/104. **Green Fee:** $15/$16. **Cart Fee:** $9/Person. **Walking Policy:** Unrestricted walking. **Walkability:** 4. **Opened:** 1935. **Architect:** X.G. Hassenplug. **Season:** March-Dec. **High:** April-Sept. **To obtain tee times:** Call golf shop. **Miscellaneous:** Metal spikes, range (grass/mats).

★★½ **MOUNTAIN LAUREL RESORT**
R-Rte. 534, White Haven, 18661, Luzerne County, (570)443-7424, 1-800-458-5921, 38 miles from Scranton. **E-mail:** info@mountainlaurelresort.com. **Web:** www.mountainlaurelresort.com. **Facility Holes:** 18. **Yards:** 6,868/5,631. **Par:** 72/72. **Course Rating:** 72.3/71.9. **Green Fee:**

$33/$44. **Cart Fee:** Included in green fee. **Opened:** 1970. **Season:** March-Dec. **To obtain tee times:** Call golf shop. **Miscellaneous:** Reduced fees (twilight, seniors), metal spikes, credit cards (MC, V, AE, D).

MOUNTAIN MANOR INN & GOLF CLUB
SP-Creek Rd. Box 1067, Marshall's Creek, 18335, Monroe County, (717)223-1290, 100 miles from Philadelphia. **Facility Holes:** 36. **Green Fee:** $22/$32. **Cart Fee:** $36/Cart. **Walking Policy:** Unrestricted walking. **Architect:** Russell Scott. **Season:** March-Nov. **High:** April-Oct. **To obtain tee times:** Call golf shop. **Miscellaneous:** Reduced fees (weekdays, guests, twilight), metal spikes, lodging (100 rooms), FF.
★★　**BLUE/YELLOW COURSE** (18)
Yards: 6,233/5,079. **Par:** 71/71. **Course Rating:** 68.5/68.5. **Slope:** 115/115. **Walkability:** 2. **Opened:** 1945. **Miscellaneous:** Range (mats).
★★★　**ORANGE/SILVER COURSE** (18)
Yards: 6,426/5,146. **Par:** 73/73. **Course Rating:** 71.0/71.5. **Slope:** 132/124. **Walkability:** 5. **Opened:** 1956.
Reader Comments: Great place to play when western NJ courses are full (weekends) … Too many blind shots … Slightly more challenging than beautiful … Quirky, goofy, 678-yard par 6.

★★★½　MOUNTAIN VALLEY GOLF COURSE
PU-1021 Brockton Mountain Dr., Barnesville, 18214, Schuylkill County, (570)467-2242, 10 miles from Hazleton. **E-mail:** mtvalley@csrlink.net. **Web:** www.mtvalleygolf.com. **Facility Holes:** 27. **Green Fee:** $12/$22. **Cart Fee:** $10/Person. **Walking Policy:** Walking at certain times. **Walkability:** 4. **Opened:** 1969. **Architect:** Ault/Clark & Assoc. **Season:** Year-round. **High:** April-Oct. **To obtain tee times:** Call up to 7 days in advance. **Miscellaneous:** Reduced fees (twilight, seniors, juniors), range (grass/mats), credit cards (MC, V), BF, FF.
MAPLE/PINE (18)
Yards: 6,472/4,885. **Par:** 72/72. **Course Rating:** 70.5/70.5. **Slope:** 131/119.
OAK/MAPLE (18)
Yards: 6,591/5,003. **Par:** 72/72. **Course Rating:** 71.1/71.2. **Slope:** 130/121.
PINE/OAK (18)
Yards: 6,449/4,766. **Par:** 72/72. **Course Rating:** 70.6/69.5. **Slope:** 130/116.
Reader Comments: Nice course, with 27 holes … Beautiful view of the western Poconos … Lots of work been done to this gem to be 27 holes … The view is worth the play, bring clubs and camera … Newly refurbished will be great when mature … Tight course, very challenging, nice staff.

★★　MURRYSVILLE GOLF CLUB
PU-3804 Sardis Rd., Murrysville, 15668, Westmoreland County, (724)327-0726, 20 miles from Pittsburgh. **Facility Holes:** 18. **Yards:** 5,575/5,250. **Par:** 70/74. **Course Rating:** 64.4/67.2. **Slope:** 99/107. **Green Fee:** $18/$20. **Cart Fee:** $10/Person. **Walking Policy:** Unrestricted walking. **Walkability:** 2. **Opened:** 1930. **Architect:** James Noble, Sr. **Season:** April-Dec. **High:** June-Sept. **To obtain tee times:** Call golf shop. **Miscellaneous:** Reduced fees (seniors, juniors), metal spikes, credit cards (MC, V), BF, FF.

NEMACOLIN WOODLANDS RESORT & SPA
R-Rte. 40 E., Farmington, 15437, Fayette County, (724)329-6111, (800)422-2736, 65 miles from Pittsburgh. **Web:** www.nemacolin.com. **Facility Holes:** 36. **Cart Fee:** Included in green fee. **Walking Policy:** Mandatory carts. **Walkability:** 2. **To obtain tee times:** Call up to 30 days in advance. **Miscellaneous:** Reduced fees (guests, twilight), range (grass/mats), credit cards (MC, V, AE, D, DC), BF, FF.
★★★★½　**MYSTIC ROCK COURSE** (18)
Yards: 6,832/4,800. **Par:** 72/72. **Course Rating:** 75.0/68.8. **Slope:** 146/125. **Green Fee:** $130/$150. **Opened:** 1995. **Architect:** Pete Dye/Mike O'Conner. **Season:** April-Oct. **High:** June-Aug.
Notes: Ranked 4th in 1995 Best New Resort Courses.
Reader Comments: Great experience, serious golf, wonderful accommodations, good food, excellent service … What a track … Wonderful golf experience … Just outstanding … Simply the best in southwest Pennsylvania.
★★★½　**WOODLANDS LINKS COURSE** (18)
Yards: 6,814/4,825. **Par:** 71/71. **Course Rating:** 73.0/67.3. **Slope:** 131/115. **Green Fee:** $84. **Opened:** 1976. **Architect:** Joe Hardy/Willard Rockwell. **Season:** Year-round. **High:** May-Aug.
Reader Comments: Expensive, worth it … Fair test of golf skills. Beautiful facility … Lots of sand … Mature course, great views, playable … Primo greens … Nice scenery…. Very scenic particularly the back 9 …. Spectacular design.

NESHAMINY VALLEY GOLF CLUB
PU-Almshouse Rd., Jamison, 18929, Bucks County, (215)343-6930, 33 miles from Philadelphia. **Facility Holes:** 18. **Yards:** 5,961/5,534. **Par:** 70/70. **Course Rating:** 68.7/66.6. **Slope:** 118/114. **Green Fee:** $23/$29. **Cart Fee:** $11/Cart. **Walking Policy:** Unrestricted

walking. **Opened:** 1969. **Architect:** The Schneider Family. **Season:** Year-round. **To obtain tee times:** Call golf shop. **Miscellaneous:** Reduced fees (weekdays, twilight, seniors), metal spikes, credit cards (MC, V, AE).

★★ NORTH FORK COUNTRY CLUB

SP-120 Court Dr., Johnstown, 15905, Somerset County, (814)288-2822, 65 miles from Pittsburgh. **Facility Holes:** 18. **Yards:** 6,470/5,762. **Par:** 72/72. **Course Rating:** 71.2/72.0. **Slope:** 130/114. **Green Fee:** $20/$22. **Cart Fee:** $12/Person. **Walking Policy:** Unrestricted walking. **Walkability:** 4. **Opened:** 1934. **Architect:** Fred Garbin. **Season:** April-Nov. **High:** June-Sept. **To obtain tee times:** Call up to 7 days in advance. **Miscellaneous:** Reduced fees (juniors), credit cards (MC, V, AE, D), BF, FF.

★★★½ NORTH HILLS GOLF COURSE

PU-1450 N. Center St., Corry, 16407, Erie County, (814)664-4477, 1 mile from Corry. **Facility Holes:** 18. **Yards:** 6,800/5,146. **Par:** 71/72. **Course Rating:** 71.0/71.4. **Slope:** 115/119. **Green Fee:** $11/$28. **Cart Fee:** $20/Person. **Walking Policy:** Unrestricted walking. **Walkability:** 3. **Opened:** 1967. **Architect:** Edmond Ault. **Season:** April-Oct. **High:** July-Aug. **To obtain tee times:** Call golf shop. **Miscellaneous:** Reduced fees (weekdays, twilight), metal spikes, range (grass), credit cards (MC, V).

Reader Comments: Great public course … Incredible course for the money … Excellent course, good shape, tough greens … Traditional, mature course, long … Best public course in this area.

★★½ NORTH PARK GOLF COURSE

PU-Kummer Rd., Allison Park, 15101, Allegheny County, (724)935-1967, 10 miles from Pittsburgh. **Facility Holes:** 18. **Yards:** 6,805/5,352. **Par:** 72/72. **Course Rating:** 71.0/69.9. **Slope:** 117/115. **Green Fee:** $15/$18. **Cart Fee:** $18/Cart. **Walking Policy:** Unrestricted walking. **Walkability:** 4. **Opened:** 1934. **Architect:** X.G. Hassenplug. **Season:** Year-round. **High:** April-Oct. **To obtain tee times:** Call golf shop. **Miscellaneous:** Reduced fees (seniors, juniors), metal spikes, range (mats), credit cards (MC, V), FF.

★★ NORTHAMPTON VALLEY COUNTRY CLUB

SP-P.O. Box 703, Richboro, 18954, Bucks County, (215)355-2234, 15 miles from Philadelphia. **E-mail:** golf@nvgc.com. **Web:** www.nvgc.com. **Facility Holes:** 18. **Yards:** 6,377/5,586. **Par:** 70/70. **Course Rating:** 69.2/70.0. **Slope:** 123/118. **Green Fee:** $28/$36. **Cart Fee:** $15/Person. **Walking Policy:** Walking at certain times. **Walkability:** 2. **Opened:** 1964. **Architect:** Ed Ault. **Season:** Year-round. **High:** April-Nov. **To obtain tee times:** Call up to 8 days in advance. **Miscellaneous:** Reduced fees (weekdays, twilight, seniors, juniors), range (mats), credit cards (MC, V, AE, D), BF, FF.

NORVELT GOLF CLUB

SP-Off of Rte. 981, Mount Pleasant, 15666, Westmoreland County, (724)423-5400. **Web:** www.norveltgolfclub.com. **Facility Holes:** 27. **Yards:** 6,417/5,061. **Par:** 72/72. **Course Rating:** 68.3/68.7. **Slope:** 120/112. **Green Fee:** $17/$21. **Cart Fee:** $12/Person. **Walking Policy:** Unrestricted walking. **Walkability:** 3. **Opened:** 1968. **Architect:** Larry S. Liprando. **Season:** Year-round. **To obtain tee times:** Call up to 7 days in advance. **Miscellaneous:** Reduced fees (weekdays, seniors, juniors), metal spikes, credit cards (MC, V), BF, FF.
Special Notes: Also has a 9-hole executive course.

OAK LAKE GOLF COURSE

PU-1208 Oaklake Rd., New Kensington, 15068, Westmoreland County, (724)727-2400. **Facility Holes:** 18. **Yards:** 5,706/5,465. **Par:** 72/72. **Course Rating:** 67.1/68.2. **Slope:** 125/126. **Green Fee:** $18/$22. **Cart Fee:** $12/Person. **Opened:** 1950. **Season:** April-Nov. **Tee times:** Call golf shop. **Misc:** Reduced fees (weekdays, seniors), metal spikes, credit cards (MC, V).

★★ OAKBROOK GOLF COURSE

PU-251 Golf Course Rd., Stoystown, 15563, Somerset County, (814)629-5892, 3 miles from Jennerstown. **Facility Holes:** 18. **Yards:** 5,935/5,400. **Par:** 71/73. **Course Rating:** 66.6/69.4. **Slope:** 107/110. **Green Fee:** $20/$22. **Cart Fee:** $12/Person. **Walking Policy:** Unrestricted walking. **Walkability:** 2. **Opened:** 1965. **Architect:** H.J. Hillegas. **Season:** April-Nov. **High:** May-Aug. **To obtain tee times:** Call up to 7 days in advance. **Miscellaneous:** Reduced fees (seniors), range (grass/mats), credit cards (MC, V), BF, FF.

OAKLAND BEACH GOLF CLUB

PU-11866 Oakland Beach Dr., Conneaut Lake, 16316, Crawford County, (814)382-5665, 30 miles from Erie. **E-mail:** obgc@toolcity.net. **Web:** www.oaklandbeach.com. **Facility Holes:** 18. **Yards:** 6,783/5,133. **Par:** 71/72. **Course Rating:** 70.9/69.6. **Slope:** 117/112. **Green Fee:** $11/$15. **Cart Fee:** $15/Person. **Walking Policy:** Walking at certain times. **Walkability:** 3. **Opened:** 1927. **Architect:** Paul McGuire. **Season:** April-Nov. **High:** May-Sept. **Tee times:** Call golf shop. **Misc:** Reduced fees (weekdays, seniors), range, cards (MC, V, AE, D), BF, FF.

OAKMONT EAST GOLF COURSE
PU-Rte. 909 Hulton Rd., Oakmont, 15139, Allegheny County, (412)828-5335, 16 miles from Pittsburgh. **Facility Holes:** 18. **Yards:** 5,750/5,750. **Par:** 72/72. **Course Rating:** 65.5/65.5. **Slope:** 113/113. **Green Fee:** $18/$21. **Cart Fee:** $12/Person. **Walking Policy:** Unrestricted walking. **Opened:** 1938. **Architect:** Emil Loeffler & John McGlynn. **Season:** Year-round. **To obtain tee times:** Call golf shop. **Miscellaneous:** Reduced fees (seniors, juniors), metal spikes, credit cards (MC, V).

★★★★ OLDE HOMESTEAD GOLF CLUB
PU-6598 Rte. 309, New Tripoli, 18066, Lehigh County, (610)298-4653, 15 miles from Allentown. **Facility Holes:** 18. **Yards:** 6,900/5,013. **Par:** 72/72. **Course Rating:** 73.8/68.5. **Slope:** 132/115. **Green Fee:** $28/$55. **Cart Fee:** Included in green fee. **Walking Policy:** Walking at certain times. **Walkability:** 4. **Opened:** 1995. **Architect:** Jim Blaukovitch. **Season:** Year-round. **To obtain tee times:** Call up to 7 days in advance. **Miscellaneous:** Reduced fees (weekdays, twilight, seniors, juniors), range (grass/mats), credit cards (MC, V, AE), BF, FF.
Reader Comments: Excellent design out in the country ... Windswept and worth every cent ... New course in great condition ... Great layout with great view ... Fun to play.

★★★★ OLDE STONEWALL GOLF CLUB
PU-1495 Mercer Rd., Ellwood City, 16117, Beaver County, (724)752-4653, 30 miles from Pittsburgh. **E-mail:** golfpro@infoline.net. **Web:** www.oldestonewall.com. **Facility Holes:** 18. **Yards:** 6,944/5,051. **Par:** 70/70. **Course Rating:** 73.2/69.7. **Slope:** 140/123. **Green Fee:** $80/$135. **Cart Fee:** Included in green fee. **Walking Policy:** Unrestricted walking. **Walkability:** 3. **Opened:** 1999. **Architect:** Michael Hurdzan/Dana Fry. **Season:** April-Nov. **High:** May-Oct. **To obtain tee times:** Call up to 14 days in advance. **Miscellaneous:** Range (grass), credit cards (MC, V, AE, DC), BF, FF.
Notes: Ranked 16th in 2001 Best in State.
Reader Comments: Great Hurdzan design ... Incredible scenery... Some awesome tees ... A must play in the fall... Great clubhouse ... Better than many country club courses ... Worth the buck and a half.

OVER LAKE GOLF COURSE
PU-10601 Ridge Rd., Girard, 16417, Erie County, (814)774-3361. **Facility Holes:** 18. **Yards:** 5,933/5,159. **Par:** 70/70. **Course Rating:** 68.3. **Slope:** 106. **Green Fee:** $21/$22. **Cart Fee:** $20/Cart. **Opened:** 1973. **Season:** April-Nov. **To obtain tee times:** Call golf shop. **Miscellaneous:** Reduced fees (seniors), metal spikes.

★★½ OVERLOOK GOLF COURSE
PU-2040 Lititz Pike, Lancaster, 17601, Lancaster County, (717)569-9551, 60 miles from Philadelphia. **E-mail:** bkreider@manheimtownship.org. **Web:** www.manheimtownship.org. **Facility Holes:** 18. **Yards:** 6,100/4,962. **Par:** 70/71. **Course Rating:** 69.2/68.4. **Slope:** 110/113. **Green Fee:** $14/$26. **Cart Fee:** $12/Person. **Walking Policy:** Unrestricted walking. **Walkability:** 3. **Opened:** 1928. **Architect:** Abe Domback. **Season:** Year-round. **High:** April-Oct. **To obtain tee times:** Call up to 14 days in advance. **Miscellaneous:** Reduced fees (weekdays, seniors, juniors), range (grass/mats), credit cards (MC, V), BF, FF.

★★½ PANORAMA GOLF COURSE
PU-Rte. 1, Forest City, 18421, Susquehanna County, (570)222-3525, 2 miles from Forest City. **Facility Holes:** 18. **Yards:** 7,256/5,345. **Par:** 72/74. **Course Rating:** 73.0. **Slope:** 122/112. **Walkability:** 2. **Opened:** 1964. **Season:** April-Nov. **High:** July-Aug. **To obtain tee times:** Call golf shop. **Miscellaneous:** Reduced fees (weekdays, seniors), range (grass), credit cards (MC, V).

★½ PARK GOLF COURSE
PU-13115 State Highway 618, Conneaut Lake, 16316, Crawford County, (814)382-9974, 10 miles from Meadville. **E-mail:** parkgolf@toolcity.net. **Facility Holes:** 18. **Yards:** 6,000/4,778. **Par:** 71/71. **Course Rating:** 68.0/66.7. **Slope:** 113/109. **Green Fee:** $15/$20. **Cart Fee:** $10/Person. **Walking Policy:** Unrestricted walking. **Walkability:** 1. **Opened:** 1945. **Season:** April-Oct. **High:** May-Sept. **To obtain tee times:** Call golf shop. **Miscellaneous:** Reduced fees (seniors), metal spikes.

★★½ PARK HILLS COUNTRY CLUB
SP-Highland Ave., Altoona, 16602, Blair County, (814)944-2631. **E-mail:** djapga@charter.net. **Facility Holes:** 18. **Yards:** 6,032/4,877. **Par:** 71/70. **Course Rating:** 69.4/68.3. **Slope:** 126/121. **Green Fee:** $30/$46. **Cart Fee:** Included in green fee. **Walking Policy:** Walking at certain times. **Walkability:** 4. **Opened:** 1966. **Architect:** James Gilmore Harrison. **Season:** March-Nov. **High:** May-Sept. **To obtain tee times:** Call up to 3 days in advance. **Miscellaneous:** Credit cards (MC, V), BF, FF.

PENNSYLVANIA

★★ PARLINE GOLF COURSE
PU-4545 E. Harrisburg Pike, Elizabethtown, 17022, Lancaster County, (717)367-7794. **Facility Holes:** 18. **Yards:** 6,505/4,843. **Par:** 72/72. **Course Rating:** 70.5/66.7. **Slope:** 119/108. **Green Fee:** $15/$20. **Cart Fee:** $8/Person. **Opened:** 1991. **Architect:** Roy Sauder. **Season:** Year-round. **To obtain tee times:** Call golf shop. **Miscellaneous:** Reduced fees (twilight, seniors), metal spikes.

★★★ PAXON HOLLOW COUNTRY CLUB
PU-850 Paxon Hollow Rd., Media, 19063, Delaware County, (610)353-0220, 10 miles from Philadelphia. **E-mail:** paxongolf@aol.com. **Web:** www.marple.net/paxongolf/. **Facility Holes:** 18. **Yards:** 5,655/4,952. **Par:** 71/72. **Course Rating:** 67.6/69.8. **Slope:** 122/118. **Green Fee:** $18/$35. **Cart Fee:** $15/Person. **Opened:** 1927. **Architect:** James Blaukovitch. **Season:** Year-round. **High:** May-Sept. **To obtain tee times:** Call up to 7 days in advance. **Miscellaneous:** Reduced fees (weekdays, twilight, seniors), range (grass), credit cards (MC, V, AE, D, DC), BF, FF.
Reader Comments: My home course; great 18th! ... Excellent course, but could speed up play ... Good food, good on-course water and a good banquet hall ... Good course, close to Philly ... Hilly course, tough greens, great conditions, beautiful facilities.

PENN NATIONAL GOLF CLUB & INN
PU-3720 Clubhouse Dr., Fayetteville, 17222, Franklin County, (717)352-3000, (800)221-7366, 39 miles from Harrisburg. **E-mail:** dbeegs@supernet.com. **Web:** www.penngolf.com. **Facility Holes:** 36. **Green Fee:** $19/$40. **Cart Fee:** $15/Person. **Walking Policy:** Unrestricted walking. **Walkability:** 3. **Season:** Year-round. **High:** April-Oct. **To obtain tee times:** Call up to 30 days in advance. **Miscellaneous:** Reduced fees (weekdays, twilight, seniors, juniors), range (grass), lodging (36 rooms), credit cards (MC, V, AE, D), BF, FF.
★★★★½ **FOUNDERS COURSE** (18) *Pace*
Yards: 6,958/5,367. **Par:** 72/72. **Course Rating:** 73.2/71.4. **Slope:** 129/123. **Opened:** 1968. **Architect:** Edmund B. Ault.
Reader Comments: Mature course perfect for resort clientele ... Traditional beautiful golf course ... Old course still rules ... Excellent course to stay and play ... Many trees force accuracy ... Friendly staff ... Great traditional layout with no weak holes and a set of great finishing holes.
★★★★½ **IRON FORGE COURSE** (18) *Condition, Pace*
Yards: 7,009/5,246. **Par:** 72/72. **Course Rating:** 73.8/70.3. **Slope:** 133/120. **Opened:** 1996. **Architect:** Bill Love.
Reader Comments: The only links-style course I've played that I liked ... Great course, package price, lodging and staff ... Great complex! ... Beautiful links-style golf course, rolling hills, great views, well kept, a pleasure to play ... With wind a real challenge, don't try it from the black tees.

PENNSYLVANIA STATE UNIVERSITY GOLF COURSE
PU-1523 W. College Ave., State College, 16801, Centre County, (814)865-4653, 5 miles from State College. **E-mail:** dtw3@psu.edu. **Web:** www.psu.edu/dept\golfcourses. **Facility Holes:** 36. **Cart Fee:** $15/Person. **High:** May-Oct. **To obtain tee times:** Call up to 8 days in advance. **Miscellaneous:** Range (mats), credit cards (MC, V, AE, D), BF, FF.
★★★½ **BLUE COURSE** (18)
Yards: 6,525/5,128. **Par:** 72/72. **Course Rating:** 72.0/69.8. **Slope:** 128/118. **Green Fee:** $30. **Walking Policy:** Unrestricted walking. **Walkability:** 2. **Opened:** 1970. **Architect:** Harrison and Garbin/Tom Clark. **Season:** April-Nov. **Miscellaneous:** Reduced fees (twilight, juniors).
Reader Comments: Returned as an alumnae, loved it ... Excellent course with a variety of holes ... Well maintained ... Penn State Blue is one of my favorite layouts ... Established greens, small greens, wide open, well cared for.
★★★ **WHITE COURSE** (18)
Yards: 6,008/5,212. **Par:** 70/70. **Course Rating:** 68.2/69.4. **Slope:** 115/116. **Green Fee:** $23. **Walking Policy:** Walking at certain times. **Walkability:** 3. **Opened:** 1994. **Architect:** Harrison and Garbin/Tom Clark. **Season:** March-Nov. **Miscellaneous:** Reduced fees (twilight).
Reader Comments: Great family course ... Fun to play ... Slow play as all the good golfers are on the Blue course ... Lots of sand ... Wide open, good greens, great views.

★½ PERRY GOLF COURSE
PU-220 Zion's Church Rd., Shoemakersville, 19555, Berks County, (610)562-3510, 12 miles from Reading. **E-mail:** perrygolf1@aol.com. **Facility Holes:** 18. **Yards:** 6,000/4,686. **Par:** 70/70. **Course Rating:** 68.1/68.5. **Slope:** 112/116. **Green Fee:** $11/$17. **Cart Fee:** $10/Person. **Walking Policy:** Unrestricted walking. **Walkability:** 1. **Opened:** 1964. **Season:** Year-round. **To obtain tee times:** Call golf shop. **Miscellaneous:** Reduced fees (twilight, seniors), metal spikes, FF.

★★ PICKERING VALLEY GOLF CLUB
PU-450 S. White Horse Rd., Phoenixville, 19460, Chester County, (610)933-2223, 20 miles from Philadelphia. **Facility Holes:** 18. **Yards:** 6,572/5,135. **Par:** 72/72. **Course Rating:**

71.0/65.5. **Slope:** 127/117. **Green Fee:** $24/$33. **Cart Fee:** $24/Cart. **Walking Policy:** Walking at certain times. **Walkability:** 3. **Opened:** 1985. **Architect:** John Thompson. **Season:** Year-round. **To obtain tee times:** Call up to 7 days in advance. **Miscellaneous:** Reduced fees (weekdays, twilight, seniors), range (grass), credit cards (MC, V).

★★★½ PILGRIM'S OAK GOLF COURSE
PU-1107 Pilgrim's Pathway, Peach Bottom, 17563, Lancaster County, (717)548-3011, 24 miles from Lancaster. **E-mail:** pilgrim@epix.net. **Web:** www.pilgrimsoak.com. **Facility Holes:** 18. **Yards:** 6,766/5,064. **Par:** 72/71. **Course Rating:** 73.4/70.7. **Slope:** 138/129. **Green Fee:** $20/$36. **Cart Fee:** $12/Person. **Walking Policy:** Unrestricted walking. **Walkability:** 5. **Opened:** 1996. **Architect:** Michael Hurdzan. **Season:** Year-round. **To obtain tee times:** Call golf shop. **Miscellaneous:** Reduced fees (weekdays, twilight, seniors), range (grass), credit cards (MC, V, AE, D, Debit Card), BF, FF.
Reader Comments: Interesting layout ... A new high-end course with nice scenery and thoughtful risk/reward design ... Great hidden gem, has tour feel on some holes ... Beautifully landscaped ... Courteous personnel, fair fees, good condition ... Little bit remote but worth the drive.

★★★ PINE ACRES COUNTRY CLUB
SP-1401 W. Warren Rd., Bradford, 16701, McKean County, (814)362-2005, 8 miles from Bradford. **Facility Holes:** 18. **Yards:** 6,700/5,600. **Par:** 72/72. **Course Rating:** 70.3/72.3. **Slope:** 120/120. **Green Fee:** $24. **Cart Fee:** $22/Cart. **Walking Policy:** Unrestricted walking. **Walkability:** 2. **Opened:** 1965. **Architect:** James G. Harrison. **Season:** April-Nov. **High:** June-Aug. **To obtain tee times:** Call up to 30 days in advance. **Miscellaneous:** Reduced fees (weekdays), range (grass), credit cards (MC, V), BF, FF.
Reader Comments: Always in great shape even late in August ... The pro staff treats you like you are someone special ... Most fun course in town ... A treat in the trees ... Short course but enjoyable enough ... Greens slope back to front.

★★★ PINE CREST COUNTRY CLUB
PU-101 Country Club Dr., Lansdale, 19446, Montgomery County, (215)855-6112, 25 miles from Philadelphia. **Web:** www.pincrestcountryclub.com. **Facility Holes:** 18. **Yards:** 6,331/5,284. **Par:** 70/70. **Course Rating:** 69.3/68.1. **Slope:** 122/118. **Green Fee:** $21/$50. **Cart Fee:** $14/Person. **Walking Policy:** Walking at certain times. **Walkability:** 2. **Opened:** 1990. **Architect:** Ron Prichard. **Season:** Year-round. **High:** May-Sept. **To obtain tee times:** Call up to 10 days in advance. **Miscellaneous:** Reduced fees (weekdays, twilight, seniors, juniors), credit cards (MC, V, AE, D), BF, FF.
Reader Comments: Well maintained; well defined fairways ... Outstanding greens ... Interesting mix of holes ... Short, tight course. Great clubhouse.

★★★½ PINE GROVE GOLF COURSE
PU-38 Fairway Dr., Grove City, 16127, Mercer County, (724)458-8394, 60 miles from Pittsburgh. **E-mail:** chutzgolf@pathway.net. **Facility Holes:** 18. **Yards:** 5,833/5,051. **Par:** 72/72. **Course Rating:** 66.8/68.7. **Slope:** 119/112. **Green Fee:** $18/$20. **Cart Fee:** $10/Person. **Walking Policy:** Unrestricted walking. **Walkability:** 2. **Opened:** 1957. **Architect:** John Deitrick. **Season:** April-Oct. **High:** May-Aug. **To obtain tee times:** Call golf shop. **Miscellaneous:** Reduced fees (weekdays), metal spikes, credit cards (MC, V, D), FF.
Reader Comments: Just like a country club, great public course ... User-friendly course ... Good bang for your buck ... Pleasant play and easy walking.

★½ PINE HILL GOLF COURSE
PU-263 Leech Rd., Greenville, 16125, Mercer County, (724)588-8053, 60 miles from Pittsburgh. **E-mail:** lorenos@pathway.net. **Web:** www.pinehillgc.com. **Facility Holes:** 18. **Yards:** 6,013/5,430. **Par:** 72/72. **Course Rating:** 67.1/66.9. **Slope:** 98/103. **Green Fee:** $12/$16. **Cart Fee:** $18/Cart. **Walking Policy:** Unrestricted walking. **Walkability:** 1. **Opened:** 1967. **Architect:** Charles Loreno. **Season:** April-Nov. **High:** May-Aug. **To obtain tee times:** Call golf shop. **Miscellaneous:** Reduced fees (weekdays, seniors, juniors), range (grass/mats), BF, FF.

★½ PINE HILLS GOLF COURSE
PU-140 S Keyser Ave., Taylor, 18517, Lackawanna County, (570)562-0138, 3 miles from Scranton. **E-mail:** gkozar@attglobal.net. **Facility Holes:** 27. **Yards:** 6,011/5,304. **Par:** 71/71. **Green Fee:** $9/$13. **Cart Fee:** $20/Cart. **Walking Policy:** Unrestricted walking. **Walkability:** 3. **Opened:** 1967. **Architect:** Andrew Evanish. **Season:** Year-round. **High:** June-Sept. **To obtain tee times:** Call golf shop. **Misc:** Reduced fees (weekdays, twilight, seniors), metal spikes, FF.
Special Notes: Also has a 9-hole pitch & putt course.

★★★½ PINECREST COUNTRY CLUB
SP-100 Franklin Ave., Brookville, 15825, Jefferson County, (814)849-4666. **Facility Holes:** 18. **Yards:** 5,741/5,213. **Par:** 70/72. **Course Rating:** 68.3/68.7. **Slope:** 116/115. **Green Fee:** $25/$29. **Cart Fee:** $24/Cart. **Opened:** 1927. **Season:** March-Nov. **To obtain tee times:** Call golf

shop. **Miscellaneous:** Metal spikes.
Reader Comments: Usually in good condition, a little short, enjoyable … Great clubhouse and restaurant, pretty course.

PITTSBURGH NORTH GOLF CLUB
PU-3800 Bakerstown Rd., Bakerstown, 15007, Allegheny County, (724)443-3800, 16 miles from Pittsburgh. **Facility Holes:** 27. **Green Fee:** $16/$23. **Cart Fee:** $20/Person. **Walking Policy:** Walking at certain times. **Walkability:** 3. **Architect:** O.J. Price. **Season:** Year-round. **To obtain tee times:** Call golf shop. **Miscellaneous:** Reduced fees (seniors, juniors), range (grass/mats), credit cards (MC, V, D), BF, FF.
★★½ **18-HOLE COURSE** (18)
Yards: 7,021/5,075. **Par:** 72/73. **Course Rating:** 73.3/68.4. **Slope:** 134/114. **Opened:** 1950.
FOX COURSE (9)
Yards: 2,796/2,051. **Par:** 35/35. **Course Rating:** 68.0/65.0. **Slope:** 121/111. **Opened:** 1994.

★★ PLEASANT VALLEY GOLF CLUB
PU-8467 Pleasant Valley Rd., Stewartstown, 17363, York County, (717)993-2184, 5 miles from Baltimore, MD. **Facility Holes:** 18. **Yards:** 6,497/5,462. **Par:** 72/74. **Course Rating:** 69.7/70.5. **Slope:** 116/117. **Green Fee:** $18/$23. **Cart Fee:** $12/Person. **Walking Policy:** Unrestricted walking. **Walkability:** 3. **Opened:** 1964. **Season:** Year-round. **High:** April-Nov. **To obtain tee times:** Call golf shop. **Miscellaneous:** Reduced fees (weekdays, twilight, seniors, juniors), metal spikes, range (grass/mats), credit cards (MC, V, AE, D), BF, FF.

★½ PLEASANT VALLEY GOLF COURSE
PU-R.R. No. 1, Box 58, Vintondale, 15961, Indiana County, (814)446-6244, 10 miles from Johnstown. **Facility Holes:** 18. **Yards:** 6,498/5,361. **Par:** 71/72. **Course Rating:** 69.8/70.3. **Slope:** 124/115. **Green Fee:** $13/$15. **Cart Fee:** $11/Person. **Walking Policy:** Walking at certain times. **Opened:** 1966. **Architect:** Telford M. Dixon. **Season:** March-Dec. **High:** May-Oct. **To obtain tee times:** Call golf shop. **Miscellaneous:** Reduced fees (weekdays, juniors), metal spikes, range (grass), credit cards (MC, V, D).

POCONO MANOR INN & GOLF CLUB
R-P.O. Box 7, Pocono Manor, 18349, Monroe County, (570)839-7111, (800)233-8150, 20 miles from Scranton. **Facility Holes:** 36. **Green Fee:** $23/$38. **Cart Fee:** $20/Person. **Walking Policy:** Mandatory carts. **Season:** April-Nov. **To obtain tee times:** Call up to 7 days in advance. **Miscellaneous:** Reduced fees (weekdays, guests, twilight), range (grass), lodging (250 rooms), credit cards (MC, V, AE), BF, FF.
★★★ **EAST COURSE** (18)
Yards: 6,565/5,977. **Par:** 72/75. **Course Rating:** 69.0/74.0. **Slope:** 118/117. **Walkability:** 4. **Opened:** 1919. **Architect:** Donald Ross.
Reader Comments: Play often, small greens a real challenge … Long, challenging … Use every club in your bag … Great staff … Vacation course—very pleasant experience.
★★ **WEST COURSE** (18)
Yards: 7,013/5,236. **Par:** 72/72. **Course Rating:** 72.3/72.0. **Slope:** 117/114. **Walkability:** 2. **Opened:** 1960. **Architect:** George Fazio.

PONDEROSA GOLF COURSE
PU-2728 Route 168, Hookstown, 15050, Beaver County, (724)947-4745, 25 miles from Pittsburgh. **Facility Holes:** 18. **Yards:** 6,625/5,525. **Par:** 71/73. **Course Rating:** 70.1/68.7. **Slope:** 120/113. **Green Fee:** $17/$22. **Cart Fee:** $24/Cart. **Walking Policy:** Unrestricted walking. **Walkability:** 4. **Opened:** 1964. **Architect:** Ed Ault. **Season:** Year-round. **To obtain tee times:** Call up to 14 days in advance. **Miscellaneous:** Credit cards (MC, V, AE, D), BF, FF.

★★★½ QUAIL VALLEY GOLF CLUB
SP-901 Teeter Rd., Littletown, 17340, Adams County, (717)359-8453, 45 miles from Baltimore. **Facility Holes:** 18. **Yards:** 7,042/5,218. **Par:** 72/72. **Course Rating:** 72.9/69.5. **Slope:** 123/113. **Green Fee:** $20/$30. **Cart Fee:** $12/Person. **Walking Policy:** Unrestricted walking. **Walkability:** 2. **Opened:** 1993. **Architect:** Paul Hicks. **Season:** Year-round. **To obtain tee times:** Call golf shop. **Miscellaneous:** Reduced fees (weekdays, twilight, seniors, juniors), range (grass), credit cards (MC, V), BF, FF.
Reader Comments: Nice, out of the way, tough, great value … Has an interesting island hole … Unusual layout … With some work, could be really good course … Great finishing hole … Beautiful tough course, some tight fairways.

★★★★ QUICKSILVER GOLF CLUB
PU-2000 Quicksilver Rd., Midway, 15060, Washington County, (724)796-1811, 18 miles from Pittsburgh. **Facility Holes:** 18. **Yards:** 7,120/5,067. **Par:** 72/74. **Course Rating:** 75.7/68.6. **Slope:** 145/115. **Green Fee:** $40/$65. **Cart Fee:** Included in green fee. **Walking Policy:** Walking at certain times. **Walkability:** 2. **Opened:** 1990. **Architect:** Don Nagode/Arnold Palmer. **Season:**

PENNSYLVANIA

March-Dec. **High:** April-Oct. **To obtain tee times:** Call up to 6 days in advance. **Miscellaneous:** Reduced fees (twilight, seniors, juniors), metal spikes, range (grass), credit cards (MC, V, AE, D, DC), BF, FF.

Reader Comments: Used to be a senior tour stop ... One of the best public facilities in the Pittsburgh area ... Fast greens, difficult layout ... Best greens in western Penn. ... Best to play after 3 p.m. ...Tough par 3s ... Solid test of golf.

★★½ RANGE END GOLF CLUB

PU-303 Golf Club Ave., Dillsburg, 17019, York County, (717)432-4114, 20 miles from Harrisburg. **E-mail:** scott.rangeend@paonline.com. **Web:** www.rangeendgolfclub.com. **Facility Holes:** 18. **Yards:** 6,300/4,926. **Par:** 71/71. **Course Rating:** 70.3/71.6. **Slope:** 126/120. **Green Fee:** $20/$31. **Cart Fee:** $14/Person. **Walking Policy:** Unrestricted walking. **Walkability:** 2. **Opened:** 1954. **Season:** Year-round. **High:** April-Oct. **To obtain tee times:** Call up to 14 days in advance. **Miscellaneous:** Reduced fees (weekdays), range (grass/mats), credit cards (MC, V, D), BF, FF.

★★★ RICH MAIDEN GOLF COURSE

PU-234 Rich Maiden Rd., Fleetwood, 19522, Berks County, (610)926-1606, (800)905-9555, 10 miles from Reading. **Facility Holes:** 18. **Yards:** 5,635/5,145. **Par:** 69/70. **Course Rating:** 63.6/64.9. **Slope:** 97/99. **Green Fee:** $18/$23. **Cart Fee:** $20/Cart. **Walking Policy:** Unrestricted walking. **Walkability:** 3. **Opened:** 1932. **Architect:** Jake Merkel. **Season:** Year-round. **High:** April-Aug. **To obtain tee times:** Call golf shop. **Miscellaneous:** Reduced fees (weekdays, twilight, seniors, juniors), FF.

Reader Comments: Good short course ... Most enjoyable course ... Great fun for the price ... Short course, good for the ego ... Friendly atmosphere.

RITTSWOOD GOLF CLUB

PU-239 Sheldon Rd., Valencia, 16059, Butler County, (724)586-2721, 40 miles from Pittsburgh. **Facility Holes:** 18. **Yards:** 6,531/5,235. **Par:** 72/72. **Green Fee:** $15/$20. **Cart Fee:** $12/Person. **Walking Policy:** Unrestricted walking. **Walkability:** 3. **Opened:** 1966. **Architect:** Garbin/Harrison. **Season:** March-Dec. **High:** April-Nov. **To obtain tee times:** Call golf shop. **Miscellaneous:** Reduced fees (seniors), range (grass), FF.

★½ RIVER VALLEY COUNTRY CLUB

SP-RD 4, Box 582, Westfield, 16950, Tioga County, (814)367-2202, 30 miles from Corning. **Facility Holes:** 18. **Yards:** 6,258/5,625. **Par:** 72/72. **Course Rating:** 70.2/67.1. **Slope:** 116/111. **Green Fee:** $15/$18. **Cart Fee:** $24/Person. **Walking Policy:** Unrestricted walking. **Walkability:** 5. **Opened:** 1964. **Architect:** Geoffrey Cornish. **Season:** April-Nov. **High:** June-Aug. **To obtain tee times:** Call golf shop. **Misc:** Reduced fees (weekdays), credit cards (MC, V, AE, D).

★★★½ RIVERSIDE GOLF CLUB

PU-24527 Hwy. 19, Cambridge Springs, 16403, Crawford County, (814)398-4537, (877)228-5322, 18 miles from Erie. **Facility Holes:** 18. **Yards:** 6,334/5,287. **Par:** 71/72. **Course Rating:** 69.7/69.5. **Slope:** 125/120. **Green Fee:** $17/$28. **Cart Fee:** $13/Person. **Walking Policy:** Walking at certain times. **Walkability:** 1. **Opened:** 1915. **Architect:** Unknown. **Season:** April-Nov. **High:** June-Aug. **To obtain tee times:** Call up to 30 days in advance. **Miscellaneous:** Reduced fees (weekdays, twilight, seniors, juniors), range (grass), lodging (75 rooms), credit cards (MC, V, AE, D), BF, FF.

Reader Comments: Challenging, good greens, good pace, needs better drainage ... Flat course with lots of sand and five tough par 3s ... One of my favorites, a good buy ... A true test ... No. 13 green will humble a professional.

★★½ RIVERVIEW GOLF COURSE

PU-97 Golf Course Dr., Bunola, 15037, Allegheny County, (412)384-7596, 3 miles from Elizabeth. **E-mail:** sford301@home.com. **Web:** www.riverviewpa.com. **Facility Holes:** 18. **Yards:** 6,382/4,871. **Par:** 71/71. **Course Rating:** 70.1/67.3. **Slope:** 120/114. **Green Fee:** $18/$31. **Cart Fee:** $24/Cart. **Walking Policy:** Walking at certain times. **Walkability:** 2. **Opened:** 1962. **Season:** Year-round. **High:** May-Sept. **To obtain tee times:** Call up to 8 days in advance. **Miscellaneous:** Reduced fees (weekdays, seniors, juniors), metal spikes, range (grass/mats), credit cards (MC, V, AE, D), BF, FF.

ROHANNA'S GOLF COURSE

PU-Rte. 2, Waynesburg, 15370, Greene County, (724)627-6423. **Facility Holes:** 18. **Yards:** 6,017/5,392. **Par:** 70/70. **Course Rating:** 66.0/62.0. **Slope:** 105/95. **Green Fee:** $13/$18. **Cart Fee:** $20/Cart. **Season:** Year-round. **To obtain tee times:** Call golf shop. **Miscellaneous:** Reduced fees (weekdays, seniors), credit cards (MC, V).

ROLLING ACRES GOLF COURSE

PU-350 Achortown Rd., Beaver Falls, 15010, Beaver County, (724)843-6736, 35 miles from Pittsburgh. **Web:** www.rollingacresgolf.com. **Facility Holes:** 27. **Green Fee:** $17/$22. **Cart Fee:** $11/Person. **Walking Policy:** Unrestricted walking. **Opened:** 1965. **Architect:** James Harrison. **Season:** March-Nov. **High:** May-Sept. **To obtain tee times:** Call golf shop. **Miscellaneous:** Reduced fees (seniors), credit cards (MC, V), FF.

NORTH/SOUTH COURSE (18)
Yards: 6,576/5,606. **Par:** 73/73. **Course Rating:** 70.1/71.1. **Slope:** 115/116.
SOUTH/WEST COURSE (18)
Yards: 6,207/5,226. **Par:** 72/72. **Course Rating:** 67.4/68.9. **Slope:** 110/112.
WEST/NORTH COURSE (18)
Yards: 6,047/5,086. **Par:** 71/71. **Course Rating:** 66.9/67.8. **Slope:** 112/109.

★½ ROLLING FIELDS GOLF COURSE

PU-Hankey Church Rd., Murraysville, 15668, Westmoreland County, (724)335-7522, 15 miles from Pittsburgh. **Facility Holes:** 18. **Yards:** 6,085/5,025. **Par:** 70/72. **Course Rating:** 68.9. **Slope:** 105/110. **Green Fee:** $13/$18. **Cart Fee:** $20/Cart. **Walking Policy:** Unrestricted walking. **Walkability:** 4. **Opened:** 1955. **Architect:** John Chernega. **Season:** Year-round. **To obtain tee times:** Call up to 7 days in advance. **Miscellaneous:** Reduced fees (weekdays, seniors, juniors), metal spikes, credit cards (MC, V), FF.

★★½ ROLLING GREEN GOLF CLUB

PU-Rt. 136, Eighty-four, 15301, Washington County, (724)222-9671, 20 miles from Pittsburgh. **Facility Holes:** 18. **Yards:** 6,000/4,500. **Par:** 71/71. **Green Fee:** $18/$20. **Cart Fee:** $20/Cart. **Walking Policy:** Walking at certain times. **Walkability:** 3. **Opened:** 1957. **Season:** March-Oct. **High:** May-July. **To obtain tee times:** Call golf shop. **Miscellaneous:** Reduced fees (weekdays, seniors, juniors), metal spikes, credit cards (MC, V).

★★ ROLLING HILLS GOLF COURSE

PU-RD No. 1, Rte. 208, Pulaski, 16143, Lawrence County, (724)964-8201, 10 miles from Youngstown. **Facility Holes:** 18. **Yards:** 6,000/5,552. **Par:** 71/76. **Course Rating:** 66.4/66.2. **Slope:** 105/107. **Green Fee:** $11/$18. **Cart Fee:** $11/Person. **Walking Policy:** Unrestricted walking. **Walkability:** 3. **Opened:** 1967. **Architect:** Frank Kwolsek. **Season:** Year-round. **High:** May-Sept. **To obtain tee times:** Call golf shop. **Miscellaneous:** Reduced fees (weekdays, seniors, juniors), credit cards (MC, V), FF.

★½ ROLLING MEADOWS GOLF CLUB

PU-23 Rolling Meadows Rd., Ashland, 17921, Schuylkill County, (570)875-1204, 12 miles from Pottsville. **Web:** www.rollingmeadowsgolf.com. **Facility Holes:** 18. **Yards:** 5,200/5,200. **Par:** 68/69. **Course Rating:** 70.0/72.0. **Green Fee:** $14/$16. **Cart Fee:** $14/Cart. **Walking Policy:** Unrestricted walking. **Walkability:** 3. **Opened:** 1964. **Season:** Year-round. **High:** June-Aug. **To obtain tee times:** Call golf shop. **Miscellaneous:** Reduced fees (weekdays, twilight, seniors).

ROSE RIDGE GOLF COURSE

PU-4769 Route 910, Allison Park, 15101, Allegheny County, (724)443-5020, 15 miles from Pittsburgh. **E-mail:** info@roseridgegolfcourse.com. **Web:** www.roseridgegolfcourse.com. **Facility Holes:** 18. **Yards:** 6,520/5,555. **Par:** 72/72. **Course Rating:** 68.9/68.9. **Slope:** 121/121. **Green Fee:** $12/$16. **Cart Fee:** $10/Cart. **Walkability:** 2. **Opened:** 1967. **Season:** Year-round. **To obtain tee times:** Call golf shop. **Miscellaneous:** Metal spikes.

★★★½ ROYAL OAKS GOLF CLUB

PU-3350 W. Oak St., Lebanon, 17042, Lebanon County, (717)274-2212, 15 miles from Hershey. **E-mail:** rogcggp@aol.com. **Facility Holes:** 18. **Yards:** 6,486/4,695. **Par:** 71/71. **Course Rating:** 71.4/66.9. **Slope:** 121/109. **Green Fee:** $18/$49. **Cart Fee:** Included in green fee. **Walking Policy:** Walking at certain times. **Walkability:** 2. **Opened:** 1992. **Architect:** Ron Forse. **Season:** Year-round. **Tee times:** Call up to 7 days in advance. **Miscellaneous:** Reduced fees (weekdays, twilight, seniors, juniors), range (grass), credit cards (MC, V, AE), BF, FF.
Reader Comments: One of the best public layouts in central Penn. ... Tight fairways, good greens ... Long and hard ... The bent-grass turf is great ... Anyone visiting the Lebanon area won't be disappointed with this one ... Great layout, could play it every day.

★★½ SAXON GOLF COURSE

PU-839 Ekastown Rd., Sarver, 16055, Butler County, (724)353-2130. **Facility Holes:** 27. **Yards:** 6,603/5,131. **Par:** 72/72. **Green Fee:** $17/$21. **Cart Fee:** $19/Cart. **Walking Policy:** Unrestricted walking. **Walkability:** 1. **Opened:** 1960. **Architect:** Frank E. Ekas. **Season:** April-Nov. **High:** July-Aug. **To obtain tee times:** Call golf shop. **Miscellaneous:** Range (grass). **Special Notes:** Also has a 9-hole course.

PENNSYLVANIA

★★★ SCRANTON MUNICIPAL GOLF COURSE
PU-1099 Golf Club Road, Lake Ariel, 18436, Lackawanna County, (570)689-2686, 10 miles from Scranton. **Facility Holes:** 18. **Yards:** 6,638/5,763. **Par:** 72/73. **Course Rating:** 69.9/70.6. **Slope:** 113/112. **Green Fee:** $15/$24. **Cart Fee:** $20/Cart. **Walking Policy:** Unrestricted walking. **Walkability:** 4. **Opened:** 1960. **Season:** April-Dec. **High:** June-Aug. **To obtain tee times:** Call golf shop. **Miscellaneous:** Range (grass/mats), BF, FF.
Reader Comments: For a muni, it is the best … Tough … Needs work … Forgiving, wide open.

★★½ SEVEN SPRINGS COUNTRY CLUB
PU-357 Pineview Dr., Elizabeth, 15037, Allegheny County, (412)384-7730, 3 miles from Elizabeth. **E-mail:** mkuehner@home.com. **Web:** www.7springsgc.com. **Facility Holes:** 18. **Yards:** 6,139/4,941. **Par:** 71/71. **Course Rating:** 68.0/66.4. **Slope:** 115/102. **Green Fee:** $16/$25. **Cart Fee:** $22/Cart. **Walking Policy:** Walking at certain times. **Walkability:** 3. **Opened:** 1954. **Architect:** Edward J. Rack. **Season:** Year-round. **High:** May-Oct. **To obtain tee times:** Call up to 7 days in advance. **Miscellaneous:** Reduced fees (weekdays, twilight, seniors, juniors), metal spikes, range (grass), credit cards (MC, V, D), FF.

★★★½ SEVEN SPRINGS MOUNTAIN RESORT GOLF COURSE
R-777 Waterwheel Dr., Champion, 15622, Westmoreland County, (814)352-7777, (800)452-2223, 60 miles from Pittsburgh. **E-mail:** mtrimbur@7springs.com. **Web:** www.7springs.com. **Facility Holes:** 18. **Yards:** 6,360/5,384. **Par:** 71/72. **Course Rating:** 71.7/68.3. **Slope:** 132/111. **Green Fee:** $55/$65. **Cart Fee:** Included in green fee. **Walking Policy:** Walking at certain times. **Walkability:** 3. **Opened:** 1969. **Architect:** X.G.Hassenplug. **Season:** April-Nov. **High:** June-Sept. **To obtain tee times:** Call golf shop. **Miscellaneous:** Reduced fees (weekdays, guests, twilight), range (grass), lodging (500 rooms), credit cards (MC, V, D), BF, FF.
Reader Comments: Beautiful mountain views, excellent condition, great seafood buffet … Scenic, great elevation changes … Beautiful surroundings, slow pace … Good mountain resort course.

SHADE MOUNTAIN GOLF CLUB
PU-Rte. 104, Middleburg, 17842, Snyder County, (570)837-2155. **Facility Holes:** 18. **Yards:** 6,698/5,522. **Par:** 72/72. **Course Rating:** 71.1/68.8. **Slope:** 126/117. **Green Fee:** $16/$22. **Cart Fee:** $12/Cart. **Opened:** 1969. **Architect:** Edmund B. Ault. **Season:** April-Nov. **Tee times:** Call golf shop. **Miscellaneous:** Metal spikes.

★★½ SHADOW BROOK GOLF COURSE
PU-615 5R 6E, Tunkhannock, 18657, Wyoming County, (570)836-5417, (800)955-0295. **E-mail:** shadowb@epix.net. **Web:** www.shadowbrookresort.com. **Facility Holes:** 18. **Yards:** 5,907/4,700. **Par:** 71/71. **Course Rating:** 68.1/66.3. **Slope:** 115/110. **Green Fee:** $16/$22. **Cart Fee:** $10/Person. **Walking Policy:** Unrestricted walking. **Walkability:** 3. **Opened:** 1958. **Architect:** Karl Schmidt/Geoffrey S. Cornish. **Season:** April-Jan. **High:** April-Oct. **Tee times:** Call golf shop. **Miscellaneous:** Reduced fees (guests, twilight, seniors), range (grass), lodging (73 rooms), credit cards (MC, V, AE, D, DC).

★★★ SHAWNEE INN GOLF RESORT
R-River Rd., Shawnee-on-Delaware, 18356, Monroe County, (570)424-4050, (800)742-9633, 90 miles from New York City. **E-mail:** golf@shawneeinn.com. **Web:** www.shawneeinn.com. **Facility Holes:** 27. **Green Fee:** $40/$80. **Cart Fee:** Included in green fee. **Walking Policy:** Mandatory carts. **Opened:** 1906. **Architect:** A.W. Tillinghast/W.H. Diddel. **Season:** April-Dec. **High:** May-Oct. **To obtain tee times:** Call golf shop. **Miscellaneous:** Reduced fees (weekdays, guests, twilight, seniors), range (grass/mats), credit cards (MC, V, AE, D, DC), BF, FF.
RED/BLUE (18 Combo)
Yards: 6,800/5,650. **Par:** 72/74. **Course Rating:** 72.2/71.4. **Slope:** 132/121. **Walkability:** 1.
RED/WHITE (18 Combo)
Yards: 6,589/5,424. **Par:** 72/74. **Course Rating:** 72.4/71.1. **Slope:** 131/121. **Walkability:** 2.
WHITE/BLUE (18 Combo)
Yards: 6,665/5,398. **Par:** 72/74. **Course Rating:** 72.8/72.5. **Slope:** 129/123. **Walkability:** 1.
Reader Comments: Old course, fun to play … Best service I've ever received … Challenging 27-hole layout, many great holes … Most of the course is located on an island in the Delaware River.

★★ SILVER SPRINGS GOLF CLUB
PU-136 Sample Bridge Rd., Mechanicsburg, 17050, Cumberland County, (717)766-0462, (877)766-0462, 10 miles from Harrisburg. **E-mail:** fun@silverspringgolfcourse.com. **Web:** www.silverspringgolfcourse.com. **Facility Holes:** 18. **Yards:** 6,000/5,500. **Par:** 70/70. **Course Rating:** 68.0/66.0. **Slope:** 114/109. **Green Fee:** $17/$23. **Cart Fee:** $20/Cart. **Walking Policy:** Walking at certain times. **Walkability:** 3. **Opened:** 1970. **Architect:** George Fazio. **Season:** Year-round. **High:** April-Oct. **To obtain tee times:** Call up to 14 days in advance. **Miscellaneous:** Reduced fees (weekdays, twilight, seniors, juniors), range (grass/mats), credit cards (MC, V), FF.

★★½ SINKING VALLEY COUNTRY CLUB
SP-Route 3, Altoona, 16601, Blair County, (814)684-0662. **Facility Holes:** 18. **Yards:** 6,735/5,760. **Par:** 72/75. **Course Rating:** 72.0/70.0. **Slope:** 123/120. **Green Fee:** $30. **Walkability:** 5. **Opened:** 1967. **Architect:** Edmund B. Ault. **To obtain tee times:** Call golf shop. **Miscellaneous:** Metal spikes.

★★½ SKIPPACK GOLF COURSE
PU-Stump Hall & Cedars Rd., Skippack, 19474, Montgomery County, (610)584-4226, 25 miles from Philadelphia. **E-mail:** scooter1973@msn.com. **Web:** www.americangolf.com. **Facility Holes:** 18. **Yards:** 6,007/5,734. **Par:** 70/70. **Course Rating:** 69.0/68.0. **Slope:** 120/115. **Green Fee:** $16. **Walking Policy:** Walking at certain times. **Walkability:** 4. **Season:** Year-round. **High:** April-Oct. **To obtain tee times:** Call up to 7 days in advance. **Miscellaneous:** Reduced fees (weekdays, twilight, seniors, juniors), range (mats), credit cards (MC, V, AE, D), BF, FF.

★½ SKYLINE GOLF COURSE
PU-118 Petrilak Road, Greenfield Twp., 18407, Lackawanna County, (570)282-5993, 15 miles from Scranton. **E-mail:** skylnegolf@aol.com. **Web:** www.members.aol.com/skylnegolf. **Facility Holes:** 18. **Yards:** 4,719/3,866. **Par:** 66/66. **Green Fee:** $9/$11. **Cart Fee:** $10/Person. **Walking Policy:** Unrestricted walking. **Walkability:** 2. **Opened:** 1959. **Architect:** Carl Weinschenk/Andrew Petrilak. **Season:** April-Dec. **High:** June-Aug. **To obtain tee times:** Call golf shop. **Miscellaneous:** Reduced fees (seniors), FF.

★★★★½ SKYTOP LODGE *Service+, Condition*
R-#1 Skytop, Route 390, Skytop, 18357, Monroe County, (570)595-8910, (800)345-7759, 35 miles from Scranton. **Web:** www.skytop.com. **Facility Holes:** 18. **Yards:** 6,505/5,864. **Par:** 72/73. **Course Rating:** 71.5/73.5. **Slope:** 125/130. **Green Fee:** $25/$50. **Cart Fee:** $20/Person. **Walking Policy:** Walking at certain times. **Walkability:** 1. **Opened:** 1928. **Architect:** Robert White. **Season:** April-Dec. **High:** June-Sept. **To obtain tee times:** Call golf shop. **Miscellaneous:** Range (grass), lodging (200 rooms), credit cards (MC, V, AE), BF, FF.
Reader Comments: Good Pocono course ... New holes are great ... Good facilities ... Good condition, nice pro shop and pro ... Superb resort.

★★★½ SOUTH HILLS GOLF CLUB
PU-925 Westminster Ave., Hanover, 17331, York County, (717)637-7500, 35 miles from Baltimore. **E-mail:** southhills@blazenet.net. **Facility Holes:** 27. **Green Fee:** $20/$26. **Cart Fee:** $12/Person. **Walking Policy:** Walking at certain times. **Walkability:** 3. **Opened:** 1959. **Architect:** Ault/Clark. **Season:** Year-round. **High:** April-Sept. **To obtain tee times:** Call up to 7 days in advance. **Miscellaneous:** Reduced fees (weekdays, seniors, juniors), range (grass), BF, FF.
NORTH/SOUTH (18 Combo)
Yards: 6,575/5,704. **Par:** 71/71. **Course Rating:** 70.5/71.9. **Slope:** 121/119.
NORTH/WEST (18 Combo)
Yards: 6,709/5,196. **Par:** 72/72. **Course Rating:** 71.8/69.8. **Slope:** 131/118.
SOUTH/WEST (18 Combo)
Yards: 6,478/5,076. **Par:** 71/71. **Course Rating:** 70.4/68.5. **Slope:** 124/114.
Reader Comments: Elevation changes make course tougher ... Fun to play ... Old course, mature trees, nice setting, great course ... Good greens ... Lots of water ... Good value for your money.

SOUTH PARK GOLF COURSE
PU-E. Park Dr., Library, 15129, Allegheny County, (412)835-3545, 8 miles from Pittsburgh. **Facility Holes:** 27. **Green Fee:** $15/$18. **Cart Fee:** $18/Cart. **Walking Policy:** Unrestricted walking. **Season:** Year-round. **High:** April-Oct. **To obtain tee times:** Call golf shop. **Miscellaneous:** Reduced fees (seniors, juniors), metal spikes, BF, FF.
★½ 18-HOLE COURSE (18)
Yards: 6,584/5,580. **Par:** 72/73. **Course Rating:** 70.9/70.6. **Slope:** 123/114. **Walkability:** 4. **Opened:** 1928.
9-HOLE COURSE (9)
Yards: 2,652/2,652. **Par:** 34/34. **Course Rating:** 32.8/32.8. **Slope:** 107/107. **Walkability:** 3. **Opened:** 1932.

★★★½ SOUTHMOORE GOLF COURSE
PU-235 Moorestown Dr., Bath, 18014, Northampton County, (610)837-7200, 15 miles from Allentown. **E-mail:** emuschlitz@aol.com. **Web:** www.southmooregolf.com. **Facility Holes:** 18. **Yards:** 6,183/4,955. **Par:** 71/71. **Course Rating:** 71.2/65.0. **Slope:** 126/112. **Green Fee:** $25/$55. **Cart Fee:** $13/Person. **Walking Policy:** Walking at certain times. **Walkability:** 3. **Opened:** 1994. **Architect:** Jim Blaukovich. **Season:** Year-round. **To obtain tee times:** Call up to 5 days in advance. **Miscellaneous:** Reduced fees (weekdays, guests, twilight, seniors, juniors), metal spikes, range (grass), credit cards (MC, V, AE), BF, FF.

PENNSYLVANIA

Reader Comments: Good value, fair course, nice greens ... Accommodating head pro ... Great fairways ... Greens are challenging ... Always in nice condition.

★★ SPORTSMANS GOLF CLUB
SP-3800 Linglestown Rd., Harrisburg, 17110, Dauphin County, (717)545-0023. **Facility Holes:** 18. **Yards:** 6,541/5,334. **Par:** 71/73. **Course Rating:** 73.0/70.8. **Slope:** 130/125. **Green Fee:** $23. **Cart Fee:** $12/Person. **Walking Policy:** Unrestricted walking. **Walkability:** 2. **Opened:** 1965. **Architect:** James Gilmore Harrison/Ferdinand Garbin. **Season:** Year-round. **High:** April-Oct. **To obtain tee times:** Call golf shop. **Miscellaneous:** Reduced fees (weekdays, twilight, seniors), range (grass/mats), credit cards (MC, V).

★★½ SPRING HOLLOW GOLF COURSE
PU-3350 Schuylkill Rd., Spring City, 19475, Chester County, (610)948-5566, 20 miles from Reading. **Web:** www.spring-hollow.com. **Facility Holes:** 18. **Yards:** 6,218/5,075. **Par:** 70/70. **Course Rating:** 69.1/67.7. **Slope:** 113/113. **Green Fee:** $15/$26. **Cart Fee:** $13/Person. **Walking Policy:** Walking at certain times. **Walkability:** 4. **Opened:** 1994. **Architect:** John Thompson. **Season:** Year-round. **High:** April-Oct. **To obtain tee times:** Call golf shop. **Miscellaneous:** Reduced fees (weekdays, twilight, seniors, juniors), credit cards (MC, V).

★½ SPRINGDALE GOLF CLUB
PU-65 Springdale Drive, Uniontown, 15401, Fayette County, (724)439-4400, 50 miles from Pittsburgh. **Facility Holes:** 18. **Yards:** 5,850/4,951. **Par:** 70/71. **Course Rating:** 67.5/68.5. **Slope:** 115/115. **Green Fee:** $12/$15. **Cart Fee:** $20/Person. **Walking Policy:** Unrestricted walking. **Walkability:** 2. **Season:** March-Nov. **High:** June-Aug. **To obtain tee times:** Call golf shop. **Miscellaneous:** Reduced fees (weekdays, seniors), metal spikes.

★★½ SPRINGFIELD GOLF & COUNTRY CLUB
PU-400 W. Sproul Rd., Springfield, 19064, Delaware County, (610)543-9860, 10 miles from Philadelphia. **E-mail:** caspgapro@aol.com. **Facility Holes:** 18. **Yards:** 5,985/5,019. **Par:** 70/71. **Course Rating:** 69.0/69.2. **Slope:** 127/122. **Green Fee:** $32/$41. **Cart Fee:** $15/Person. **Walking Policy:** Unrestricted walking. **Walkability:** 4. **Opened:** 1935. **Season:** March-Dec. **High:** April-Oct. **To obtain tee times:** Call up to 3 days in advance. **Miscellaneous:** Reduced fees (twilight, seniors), credit cards (MC, V, D), BF, FF.

★★★★ SPRINGWOOD GOLF CLUB
PU-601 Chestnut Hill Rd., York, 17402, York County, (717)747-9663. **E-mail:** swoodgolf@aol.com. **Facility Holes:** 18. **Yards:** 6,826/5,075. **Par:** 72/72. **Course Rating:** 73.4/69.7. **Slope:** 131/113. **Green Fee:** $25/$60. **Cart Fee:** Included in green fee. **Walking Policy:** Mandatory cart. **Walkability:** 4. **Opened:** 1998. **Architect:** Tom Clark/Dan Schlegel. **Season:** Year-round. **High:** April-Oct. **Tee times:** Call golf shop. **Miscellaneous:** Reduced fees (guests, twilight), range (grass/mats), credit cards (MC, V, AE, D, DC).
Reader Comments: For a relatively new course in southeastern Penn., this course has a manicured layout and wonderful service ... Target golf ... Great 19th hole ... Great variety of holes ... Awesome clubhouse.

★★ STANDING STONE GOLF CLUB
PU-Rte. 26 N., Huntingdon, 16652, Huntingdon County, (814)643-4800, 30 miles from State College. **Facility Holes:** 18. **Yards:** 6,593/5,278. **Par:** 70/71. **Course Rating:** 71.4/71.1. **Slope:** 120/120. **Green Fee:** $20/$25. **Cart Fee:** $11/Person. **Walking Policy:** Unrestricted walking. **Walkability:** 3. **Opened:** 1973. **Architect:** Geoffrey Cornish. **Season:** March-Nov. **To obtain tee times:** Call golf shop. **Miscellaneous:** Reduced fees (twilight), metal spikes, range (grass), credit cards (MC, V), FF.

STATE COLLEGE ELKS COUNTRY CLUB
SP-Rte. 322 Box 8, Boalsburg, 16827, Centre County, (814)466-6451, 5 miles from State College. **Facility Holes:** 18. **Yards:** 6,369/5,097. **Par:** 71/72. **Course Rating:** 70.9/70.2. **Slope:** 123/119. **Green Fee:** $40. **Cart Fee:** $16/Person. **Walking Policy:** Unrestricted walking. **Walkability:** 3. **Opened:** 1964. **Architect:** Erdman. **Season:** March-Dec. **High:** June-Sept. **To obtain tee times:** Call up to 3 days in advance. **Miscellaneous:** Range (grass), credit cards (MC, V, AE), BF, FF.

★★★★ STONE HEDGE COUNTRY CLUB
PU-R.D. No. 4, Tunkhannock, 18657, Wyoming County, (570)836-5108, (800)452-2582, 22 miles from Scranton. **E-mail:** stonehedge@epix.net. **Facility Holes:** 18. **Yards:** 6,644/5,046. **Par:** 71/71. **Course Rating:** 71.9/69.7. **Slope:** 124/122. **Green Fee:** $25/$43. **Cart Fee:** Included in green fee. **Walking Policy:** Mandatory cart. **Walkability:** 4. **Opened:** 1991. **Architect:** Jim Blaukovitch. **Season:** April-Dec. **High:** May-Sept. **To obtain tee times:** Call golf shop. **Misc:** Reduced fees (weekdays, twilight, seniors), range (grass), credit cards (MC, V).

PENNSYLVANIA

Reader Comments: In the middle of nowhere, but worth a trip ... Best layout ... Improvements being done ... Would be worthy of one's ashes! ... Diamond in the midst of Pennsylvania's Appalachian Mountain ... Has great potential... Bring your A game ... What a challenge.

★★★★½ STOUGHTON ACRES GOLF CLUB *Value+*
PU-904 Sunset Dr., Butler, 16001, Butler County, (724)285-3633, 40 miles from Pittsburgh.
Facility Holes: 18. **Yards:** 6,100/5,012. **Par:** 71/72. **Course Rating:** 67.3/68.5. **Slope:** 114/116.
Walking Policy: Unrestricted walking. **Walkability:** 3. **Opened:** 1964. **Architect:** Van Smith.
Season: April-Dec. **High:** June-Aug. **Tee times:** Call golf shop. **Misc:** Metal spikes, FF.
Reader Comments: Best golf for the money ... Open, relatively easy course, with a couple of spectacular holes ... If you don't enjoy yourself here, then quit golfing! ... Nice course and nice owners ... Best kept secret in the area ... Shhhh! Don't let this one get out.

★★★★ SUGARLOAF GOLF CLUB *Value*
PU-RR 2, Box 508, Sugarloaf, 18249, Luzerne County, (570)384-4097, (888)342-5784, 6
miles from Hazleton. **E-mail:** sgc@sugarloafgolfclub.com. **Web:** www.sugarloafgolfclub.com.
Facility Holes: 18. **Yards:** 6,845/5,620. **Par:** 72/72. **Course Rating:** 73.0/72.8. **Slope:** 122/120.
Green Fee: $17/$25. **Cart Fee:** $28/Cart. **Walking Policy:** Walking at certain times. **Walkability:**
3. **Opened:** 1967. **Architect:** Geoffrey Cornish. **Season:** March-Nov. **High:** June-Aug. **To obtain
tee times:** Call up to 7 days in advance. **Miscellaneous:** Reduced fees (weekdays, twilight,
seniors), range (grass), credit cards (MC, V, AE, D, MAC), FF.
Reader Comments: Well-kept course ... Great layout ... Friendly staff ... Cheap lunch $5 for sandwich, fries, and soda ... Get the early tee times.

SUMMIT COUNTRY CLUB
SP-Country Club Rd., Cresson, 16630, Cambria County, (814)886-9985, 12 miles from
Altoona. **Facility Holes:** 18. **Yards:** 6,748/5,451. **Par:** 72/76. **Course Rating:** 72.8/71.4. **Slope:**
133/126. **Green Fee:** $20/$27. **Cart Fee:** $17/Person. **Walking Policy:** Unrestricted walking.
Walkability: 4. **Opened:** 1923. **Architect:** Ault & Associates. **Season:** April-Nov. **High:** June-Oct.
To obtain tee times: Call up to 7 days in advance. **Miscellaneous:** Reduced fees (twilight),
range (grass), credit cards (MC, V, AE), BF, FF.

SUMMIT HILLS GOLF CLUB
PU-1235 Country Club Rd., Clarks Summit, 18411, Lackawanna County, (570)586-4427.
Facility Holes: 18. **Yards:** 6,004/5,609. **Par:** 72/72. **Course Rating:** 68.7/67.0. **Slope:** 117/110.
Green Fee: $13/$15. **Cart Fee:** $20/Cart. **Season:** Year-round. **To obtain tee times:** Call golf
shop. **Miscellaneous:** Metal spikes.

★★★ SUNCREST GOLF COURSE
PU-137 Brownsdale Rd., Butler, 16001, Butler County, (724)586-5508. **Facility Holes:** 18.
Yards: 6,243/5,513. **Par:** 72/72. **Course Rating:** 69.3/70.7. **Slope:** 112/112. **Green Fee:**
$11/$17. **Cart Fee:** $11/Person. **Opened:** 1938. **Season:** April-Nov. **To obtain tee times:** Call
golf shop. **Miscellaneous:** Reduced fees (seniors), metal spikes.
Reader Comments: Short course .·. Excellent value, nice greens ... Treated very well by everybody who helped us ... Lots of hills, scenic ... Always in good condition ... Great finishing hole.

★★★ SUNSET GOLF COURSE
PU-Geyer's Church Rd. & Sunset Dr., Middletown, 17057, Dauphin County, (717)944-5415,
12 miles from Harrisburg. **Facility Holes:** 18. **Yards:** 6,328/5,255. **Par:** 70/71. **Course Rating:**
69.1/69.9. **Slope:** 113/113. **Green Fee:** $10/$20. **Cart Fee:** $11/Cart. **Walking Policy:**
Unrestricted walking. **Walkability:** 3. **Opened:** Air Force. **Season:** Year-round. **High:** May-Sept.
To obtain tee times: Call golf shop. **Miscellaneous:** Reduced fees (seniors, juniors), metal
spikes, range (mats), credit cards (MC, V).
Reader Comments: Fun watching airplanes landing at HIA ... Good course, great views, a mustplay for locals ... Not the best, but good value ... A good value.

★½ SYLVAN HEIGHTS GOLF COURSE
PU-Rte. 65, Ellwood-New Castle Rd., New Castle, 16101, Lawrence County, (724)658-8021,
50 miles from Pittsburgh. **Facility Holes:** 18. **Yards:** 6,081/6,781. **Par:** 71/71. **Course Rating:**
69.8/70.0. **Slope:** 128/118. **Green Fee:** $9/$13. **Cart Fee:** $15/Person. **Walking Policy:**
Unrestricted walking. **Walkability:** 2. **Season:** April-Nov. **High:** May-Aug. **To obtain tee times:**
Call golf shop. **Miscellaneous:** Reduced fees (seniors), FF.

★★★★ TAM O'SHANTER GOLF CLUB
PU-2961 S. Hermitage Rd., Hermitage, 16148, Mercer County, (724)981-3552, 12 miles from
Youngstown. **Facility Holes:** 18. **Yards:** 6,537/5,385. **Par:** 72/76. **Course Rating:** 69.4/70.2.
Slope: 121/113. **Green Fee:** $21/$25. **Cart Fee:** $10/Person. **Walking Policy:** Walking at certain
times. **Walkability:** 3. **Opened:** 1931. **Architect:** Emil Loeffler. **Season:** March-Dec. **High:** May-
Sept. **Tee times:** Call up to 365 days in advance. **Misc:** Reduced fees (weekdays, guests, twi-

light, seniors, juniors), range (grass/mats), credit cards (MC, V, D), BF, FF.
Reader Comments: One of the best courses I have ever played … Well-stocked pro shop … Mature layout, challenging yet playable … Super fast greens … Always in excellent condition … Service and price are great.

★★★ TAMIMENT RESORT & CONFERENCE CENTER GOLF CLUB

R-Bushkill Falls Rd., Tamiment, 18371, Pike County, (570)588-6652, (800)233-8105, 75 miles from New York. **Facility Holes:** 18. **Yards:** 6,858/5,598. **Par:** 72/72. **Course Rating:** 72.7/71.9. **Slope:** 130/124. **Green Fee:** $15/$45. **Cart Fee:** $15/Person. **Walkability:** 3. **Opened:** 1951. **Architect:** Robert Trent Jones. **Season:** April-Nov. **High:** May-Sept. **To obtain tee times:** Call golf shop. **Miscellaneous:** Reduced fees (weekdays, guests, twilight, seniors, juniors), range (mats), credit cards (MC, V, AE, D).
Reader Comments: Beautiful mountain course in excellent shape … Long par 3s … Good course design … Always enjoyable … Play smart … Improvements noticeable.

★★★½ TANGLEWOOD GOLF COURSE

PU-Rd. 1 & Tanglewood Rd., Pulaski, 16143, Lawrence County, (724)964-8702, (800)465-3610, 50 miles from Pittsburgh. **Facility Holes:** 18. **Yards:** 6,053/5,598. **Par:** 72/76. **Course Rating:** 68.2/70.2. **Slope:** 119/116. **Green Fee:** $13/$19. **Cart Fee:** $20/Cart. **Walking Policy:** Unrestricted walking. **Walkability:** 3. **Opened:** 1963. **Architect:** Joseph B. Clingan. **Season:** March-Nov. **High:** May-Sept. **To obtain tee times:** Call golf shop. **Miscellaneous:** Reduced fees (weekdays, seniors, juniors), metal spikes, range (grass), credit cards (MC, V, AE), BF, FF.
Reader Comments: Hilly, tight course, need straight shots … Nice course … Great use of terrain.

★★★ TANGLEWOOD MANOR GOLF CLUB & LEARNING CENTER

PU-Scotland Rd., Quarryville, 17566, Lancaster County, (717)786-2500, 10 miles from Lancaster. **Web:** www.twgolf.com. **Facility Holes:** 18. **Yards:** 6,457/5,321. **Par:** 72/74. **Course Rating:** 70.7/70.0. **Slope:** 118/118. **Green Fee:** $18/$28. **Cart Fee:** $13/Person. **Walking Policy:** Walking at certain times. **Walkability:** 3. **Opened:** 1969. **Architect:** Chester Ruby. **Season:** March-Dec. **High:** May-Oct. **To obtain tee times:** Call up to 14 days in advance. **Miscellaneous:** Reduced fees (weekdays, twilight, seniors, juniors), range (grass/mats), credit cards (MC, V, D), BF, FF.
Reader Comments: Beautiful layout … Interesting holes … Risk/reward worth the gamble … Kept in great condition … Recently redesigned and irrigation added … Much improved course conditions and facility, fair fees.

TATTERSALL GOLF CLUB

PU-1520 Tattersall Way, West Chester, 19380, Chester County, (610)738-4410, 20 miles from Philadelphia. **Web:** www.tattersallgolfclub.com. **Facility Holes:** 18. **Yards:** 6,826/5,286. **Par:** 72/72. **Course Rating:** 72.0/65.8. **Slope:** 132/111. **Green Fee:** $55/$108. **Walking Policy:** Unrestricted walking. **Walkability:** 5. **Opened:** 2000. **Architect:** Rees Jones. **Season:** Year-round. **High:** April-Oct. **To obtain tee times:** Call up to 14 days in advance. **Miscellaneous:** Reduced fees (twilight), range (grass), credit cards (MC, V, AE), BF, FF.

THREE PONDS GOLF CLUB

PU-RR2, Box 262, Elysburg, 17824, Northumberland County, (570)672-9064. **Web:** www.3ponds.homepage.com. **Facility Holes:** 18. **Yards:** 6,137/5,094. **Par:** 71/71. **Course Rating:** 69.1/69.8. **Slope:** 127/121. **Green Fee:** $15/$20. **Cart Fee:** $22/Cart. **Walking Policy:** Walking at certain times. **Walkability:** 3. **Opened:** 1960. **Season:** Year-round. **To obtain tee times:** Call up to 14 days in advance. **Miscellaneous:** Credit cards (MC, V), FF.

★½ TIMBER RIDGE GOLF CLUB

PU-RR 6, Box 2057, Mount Pleasant, 15666, Westmoreland County, (724)547-1909, 17 miles from Pittsburgh. **Facility Holes:** 18. **Yards:** 6,340/5,277. **Par:** 72/72. **Course Rating:** 69.6/74.4. **Slope:** 126/124. **Green Fee:** $16/$18. **Cart Fee:** $12/Person. **Walking Policy:** Unrestricted walking. **Walkability:** 3. **Opened:** 1983. **Architect:** Fred Garbin. **Season:** Year-round. **High:** June-Oct. **To obtain tee times:** Call golf shop. **Miscellaneous:** Reduced fees (weekdays, seniors, juniors), metal spikes, credit cards (MC, V, AE, D), FF.

★★★★ TOFTREES RESORT

R-1 Country Club Lane, State College, 16803, Centre County, (814)238-7600, (800)252-3551, 90 miles from Harrisburg. **Web:** wwwtoftrees.com. **Facility Holes:** 18. **Yards:** 7,018/5,555. **Par:** 72/72. **Course Rating:** 74.3/72.2. **Slope:** 138/125. **Green Fee:** $40/$64. **Cart Fee:** $15/Person. **Walking Policy:** Walking at certain times. **Walkability:** 3. **Opened:** 1968. **Architect:** Ed Ault. **Season:** Year-round. **High:** May-Oct. **To obtain tee times:** Call up to 14 days in advance. **Miscellaneous:** Reduced fees (weekdays, guests, twilight, seniors, juniors), range (grass), lodging (105 rooms), credit cards (MC, V, AE, D, DC), BF, FF.

PENNSYLVANIA

Reader Comments: Hit it straight or take a chainsaw ... Tight greens ... Wind is a constant challenge ... Demanding layout from tips ... A hidden jewel! ... Remote but worth the trip ... Beautiful resort course ... Awesome layout ... Beautiful Poa annua fairways ... Excellent course and service.

★★★ TOWANDA COUNTRY CLUB
SP-RR 06, Box 6180, Towanda, 18848, Bradford County, (570)265-6939, 1 mile from Towanda. **E-mail:** tcc@sosbbs. **Facility Holes:** 18. **Yards:** 5,958/5,127. **Par:** 71/76. **Course Rating:** 68.0/69.0. **Slope:** 112/102. **Green Fee:** $39/$43. **Cart Fee:** Included in green fee. **Walking Policy:** Mandatory carts. **Walkability:** 4. **Opened:** 1927. **Architect:** Bill Glenn/Warner Burger. **Season:** March-Dec. **High:** June-Sept. **To obtain tee times:** Call golf shop. **Miscellaneous:** Credit cards (MC, V), BF, FF.
Reader Comments: I wish it was closer ... Short course ... Demands accuracy ... Good condition ... Course is a bit hilly ... Difficult to walk.

TREASURE LAKE GOLF CLUB
SP-13 Treasure Lake, Dubois, 15801, Clearfield County, (814)375-1807, 110 miles from Pittsburgh. **Facility Holes:** 36. **Green Fee:** $16/$21. **Cart Fee:** $13/Person. **Walking Policy:** Unrestricted walking. **Architect:** Dominic Palombo. **Season:** April-Dec. **High:** May-Sept. **To obtain tee times:** Call up to 14 days in advance. **Miscellaneous:** Reduced fees (twilight, juniors), range (grass), credit cards (MC, V, AE, D), BF, FF.
★★★★ GOLD COURSE (18)
Yards: 6,284/5,198. **Par:** 72/74. **Course Rating:** 71.4/71.4. **Slope:** 135/129. **Walkability:** 5. **Opened:** 1972.
Reader Comments: The nicest course I've played in Pennsylvania ... Tight ... Tree-lined, difficult ... Beautiful course through wooded area, narrow ... Humbling course, must place shots to score well ... Good greens, scenic, good layout.
SILVER COURSE (18)
Yards: 6,641/5,682. **Par:** 72/75. **Course Rating:** 72.1/73.0. **Slope:** 120/123. **Walkability:** 2. **Opened:** 1982.

★★ TURBOT HILLS GOLF COURSE
PU-Route 405 North, Milton, 17847, Northumberland County, (570)742-7455, 1 mile from Milton. **Facility Holes:** 18. **Yards:** 6,557/5,242. **Par:** 71/74. **Course Rating:** 71.5/69.2. **Slope:** 120/116. **Green Fee:** $15/$19. **Cart Fee:** $11/Person. **Walking Policy:** Unrestricted walking. **Walkability:** 3. **Opened:** 1927. **Season:** Year-round. **High:** June-Sept. **To obtain tee times:** Call golf shop. **Miscellaneous:** Range (grass/mats), credit cards (MC, V, AE).

★★★½ TURTLE CREEK GOLF COURSE
PU-303 W. Ridge Pike, Limerick, 19468, Montgomery County, (610)489-5133, 15 miles from King of Prussia. **Web:** www.turtlecreekgolf.com. **Facility Holes:** 18. **Yards:** 6,702/5,131. **Par:** 72/72. **Course Rating:** 72.1/68.6. **Slope:** 127/115. **Green Fee:** $25/$50. **Cart Fee:** Included in green fee. **Walking Policy:** Unrestricted walking. **Walkability:** 3. **Opened:** 1997. **Architect:** Ed Beidel. **Season:** March-Jan. **To obtain tee times:** Call up to 10 days in advance. **Misc:** Reduced fees (twilight, seniors), range (grass/mats), credit cards (MC, V), BF, FF.
Reader Comments: As good as it gets for a newer course ... Great par-5 finishing hole over water ... Great value ... Friendly staff ... Nice links-style course ... Tough par 3s ... Use all your clubs ... Good value ... Good greens ... Should monitor pace of play better sometimes.

TWIN LAKES COUNTRY CLUB
PU-3625 Shankweiler Rd., Allentown, 18104, Lehigh County, (610)395-3369, 50 miles from Philadelphia. **Facility Holes:** 18. **Yards:** 6,600/5,800. **Par:** 71/71. **Green Fee:** $30/$42. **Cart Fee:** $13/Person. **Walking Policy:** Mandatory carts. **Opened:** 1956. **Architect:** Joe F. Peter. **Season:** March-Dec. **High:** April-Sept. **To obtain tee times:** Call golf shop. **Miscellaneous:** Reduced fees (twilight, seniors, juniors), credit cards (MC, V, AE), BF, FF.

★★★ TWIN PONDS GOLF COURSE
PU-700 Gilbertsville Rd., Gilbertsville, 19525, Montgomery County, (610)369-1901. **Facility Holes:** 18. **Yards:** 5,588/4,747. **Par:** 70/70. **Course Rating:** 65.5/67.7. **Slope:** 111/119. **Green Fee:** $20/$28. **Cart Fee:** $10/Person. **Walking Policy:** Walking at certain times. **Walkability:** 2. **Opened:** 1963. **Season:** Year-round. **High:** April-Sept. **To obtain tee times:** Call golf shop. **Miscellaneous:** Reduced fees (weekdays, twilight, seniors), metal spikes, range (grass).
Reader Comments: Short course ... Excellent greens ... Great for seniors ... Good value ... Old course with small greens ... OK.

★½ TWINING VALLEY GOLF & FITNESS CLUB
PU-1400 Twining Rd., Dresher, 19025, Montgomery County, (215)659-9917, 5 miles from Philadelphia. **E-mail:** w-faffy@hotmail.com. **Web:** www.twiningvalley.com. **Facility Holes:** 18. **Yards:** 6,513/5,300. **Par:** 71/72. **Course Rating:** 65.9. **Slope:** 114. **Green Fee:** $22/$28. **Cart Fee:** $14/Person. **Walking Policy:** Unrestricted walking. **Walkability:** 4. **Opened:** 1931.

Architect: Jock Mellville/Hugh Reilly. **Season:** Year-round. **To obtain tee times:** Call up to 7 days in advance. **Miscellaneous:** Reduced fees (twilight, seniors), metal spikes, range (grass/mats), credit cards (MC, V, AE, D), BF, FF.

★★★½ TYOGA COUNTRY CLUB

SP-RR 6, Pine Creek Rd., Wellsboro, 16901, Tioga County, (570)724-1653, 50 miles from Corning, NY. **Web:** www.tyogacc.com. **Facility Holes:** 18. **Yards:** 6,335/5,227. **Par:** 71/73. **Course Rating:** 71.3/70.8. **Slope:** 135/128. **Green Fee:** $45/$49. **Cart Fee:** Included in green fee. **Walking Policy:** Mandatory carts. **Walkability:** 5. **Opened:** 1923. **Architect:** Edmund B. Ault. **Season:** April-Nov. **High:** June-Sept. **To obtain tee times:** Call golf shop. **Miscellaneous:** Range (grass), credit cards (MC, V), BF, FF.
Reader Comments: Course is a joy to play regardless of how you score … Very hilly, nice setting, challenging … Worth the visit … Very good condition long and hilly … Excellent mountain layout … Avoid dry spells … Beautiful layout.

★★★ UPPER PERK GOLF COURSE

PU-2324 Ott Road, Pennsburg, 18073, Montgomery County, (215)679-5594, 50 miles from Philadelphia. **Facility Holes:** 18. **Yards:** 6,381/5,249. **Par:** 71/71. **Course Rating:** 70.0/69.6. **Slope:** 117/113. **Green Fee:** $18/$30. **Cart Fee:** $20/Cart. **Walking Policy:** Walking at certain times. **Walkability:** 2. **Opened:** 1977. **Architect:** Bob Hendricks. **Season:** March-Dec. **To obtain tee times:** Call up to 10 days in advance. **Miscellaneous:** Reduced fees (weekdays, twilight, seniors, juniors), credit cards (MC, V), BF, FF.
Reader Comments: A favorite … Excellent course … Always in good condition … Pace of play excellent, great value … Gets a lot of play.

★½ VALLEY FORGE GOLF CLUB

PU-401 N. Gulf Rd., King Of Prussia, 19406, Montgomery County, (610)337-1776, 25 miles from Philadelphia. **E-mail:** valleyforgegolf@aol.com. **Web:** www.valleyforgegolf.com. **Facility Holes:** 18. **Yards:** 6,200/5,668. **Par:** 71/73. **Course Rating:** 68.1/70.0. **Slope:** 107/113. **Green Fee:** $12/$27. **Cart Fee:** $13/Cart. **Walking Policy:** Unrestricted walking. **Walkability:** 3. **Opened:** 1929. **Architect:** Alex Findlay. **Season:** Year-round. **To obtain tee times:** Call golf shop. **Miscellaneous:** Reduced fees (weekdays, twilight, seniors, juniors), metal spikes, range (mats), credit cards (MC, V), BF, FF.

★★ VALLEY GREEN GOLF & COUNTRY CLUB

PU-RD No. 2, Box 449F, Greensburg, 15601, Westmoreland County, (724)837-6366, 40 miles from Pittsburgh. **Facility Holes:** 18. **Yards:** 6,345/5,450. **Par:** 72/72. **Course Rating:** 67.5/67.5. **Slope:** 104/104. **Green Fee:** $17/$21. **Cart Fee:** $20/Cart. **Walking Policy:** Unrestricted walking. **Walkability:** 1. **Opened:** 1965. **Architect:** X.G. Hassenplug. **Season:** Year-round. **High:** April-Oct. **To obtain tee times:** Call golf shop. **Miscellaneous:** Reduced fees (seniors), metal spikes, range (grass), credit cards (MC, V, AE), FF.

★★ VALLEY GREEN GOLF COURSE

PU-1227 Valley Green Rd., Etters, 17319, York County, (717)938-4200, 15 miles from Harrisburg. **Facility Holes:** 18. **Yards:** 6,000/5,500. **Par:** 71/71. **Course Rating:** 67.0/67.0. **Slope:** 110/109. **Green Fee:** $16/$25. **Cart Fee:** $13/Person. **Walking Policy:** Unrestricted walking. **Walkability:** 3. **Opened:** 1964. **Architect:** Short/Leggett. **Season:** Year-round. **To obtain tee times:** Call up to 14 days in advance. **Miscellaneous:** Reduced fees (weekdays, twilight, seniors, juniors), metal spikes, credit cards (MC, V), BF, FF.

★½ VENANGO TRAIL GOLF COURSE

SP-1305 Freeport Rd., Mars, 16046, Butler County, (724)776-4400, 18 miles from Pittsburgh. **E-mail:** super@venangogolf.com. **Web:** www.venangogolf.com. **Facility Holes:** 18. **Yards:** 6,200/5,518. **Par:** 72/72. **Course Rating:** 69.9/74.0. **Slope:** 120/117. **Green Fee:** $11/$22. **Cart Fee:** $10/Person. **Walking Policy:** Walking at certain times. **Walkability:** 3. **Opened:** 1954. **Architect:** James Gilmore Harrison. **Season:** Year-round. **High:** May-Sept. **To obtain tee times:** Call golf shop. **Miscellaneous:** Reduced fees (weekdays, seniors, juniors), credit cards (MC, V, AE, D), BF, FF.

★★ VENANGO VALLEY INN & GOLF CLUB

PU-Rte. 19, Venango, 16440, Crawford County, (814)398-4330, 30 miles from Erie. **E-mail:** loreno@stargate.net. **Facility Holes:** 18. **Yards:** 6,202/4,751. **Par:** 71/71. **Course Rating:** 68.7/66.2. **Slope:** 112/105. **Green Fee:** $13/$18. **Cart Fee:** $10/Person. **Walking Policy:** Unrestricted walking. **Walkability:** 2. **Opened:** 1972. **Architect:** Paul E. Erath. **Season:** Year-round. **High:** April-Nov. **To obtain tee times:** Call up to 14 days in advance. **Miscellaneous:** Reduced fees (weekdays, seniors, juniors), credit cards (MC, V, D), FF.

VFW COUNTRY CLUB
SP-824 Indian Springs Rd., Indiana, 15701, Indiana County, (724)465-5131. **Facility Holes:** 18. **Yards:** 5,895/4,841. **Par:** 71/71. **Course Rating:** 68.9/68.0. **Slope:** 114/106. **Green Fee:** $16/$20. **Cart Fee:** $20/Cart. **Walking Policy:** Unrestricted walking. **Walkability:** 3. **Season:** Year-round. **To obtain tee times:** Call golf shop. **Miscellaneous:** Credit cards (MC, V).

VILLAGE GREEN
PU-4050 Henderson Rd., Hickory, 15340, Washington County, (724)356-4653. **E-mail:** scameron@pulsenet.com. **Facility Holes:** 18. **Yards:** 6,398/5,085. **Par:** 71/71. **Course Rating:** 69.9/63.9. **Slope:** 124/117. **Green Fee:** $18/$19. **Cart Fee:** $11/Person. **Walking Policy:** Unrestricted walking. **To obtain tee times:** Call up to 7 days in advance. **Miscellaneous:** Reduced fees (weekdays, seniors), credit cards (MC, V, D), FF.
Special Notes: Formerly Godwin's Village Green.

★★★ WATER GAP COUNTRY CLUB
SP-Mountain Rd., Delaware Water Gap, 18327, Monroe County, (570)476-0300, 70 miles from New York City. **E-mail:** wgcc1.@noln. **Web:** www.watergapcountryclub.com. **Facility Holes:** 18. **Yards:** 6,237/5,199. **Par:** 72/74. **Course Rating:** 69.0/69.0. **Slope:** 124/120. **Green Fee:** Included in green fee. **Walking Policy:** Walking at certain times. **Walkability:** 5. **Opened:** 1921. **Architect:** Robert White. **Season:** March-Nov. **High:** June-Sept. **To obtain tee times:** Call golf shop. **Miscellaneous:** Reduced fees (weekdays, twilight), metal spikes, lodging (23 rooms), credit cards (MC, V, AE, D), FF.
Reader Comments: Typical Pocono course—tight, small greens … Need some luck, need to know the course … Short course, mostly iron shots, uphill sidehill, downhill … Very nice old course.

WAYNESBORO MUNICIPAL
PU-165 Cemetary Ave., Waynesboro, 17268, Franklin County, (717)762-3734, 70 miles from Baltimore. **Facility Holes:** 18. **Yards:** 5,488/5,488. **Par:** 72/72. **Course Rating:** 70.4/68.4. **Slope:** 98/94. **Green Fee:** $11/$13. **Cart Fee:** $14/Person. **Walking Policy:** Unrestricted walking. **Walkability:** 3. **Opened:** 1958. **Season:** Year-round. **To obtain tee times:** Call golf shop. **Miscellaneous:** Reduced fees (seniors, juniors), metal spikes, credit cards (MC, V, D), FF.

★★½ WEDGEWOOD GOLF CLUB
PU-4875 Limeport Pike, Coopersburg, 18036, Lehigh County, (610)797-4551, 4 miles from Allentown. **E-mail:** wedgewood@netcarrier.com. **Web:** www.distinctgolf.com. **Facility Holes:** 27. **Green Fee:** $19/$39. **Cart Fee:** $22/Cart. **Walking Policy:** Walking at certain times. **Walkability:** 2. **Opened:** 1963. **Architect:** William Gordon/David Gordon. **Season:** Year-round. **To obtain tee times:** Call up to 14 days in advance. **Miscellaneous:** Reduced fees (weekdays, twilight, seniors), metal spikes, range (grass), credit cards (MC, V).
MAPLE/OAK (18 Combo)
Yards: 6,278/5,391. **Par:** 70/71. **Course Rating:** 69.3/67.0. **Slope:** 122/110.
PINE/MAPLE (18 Combo)
Yards: 6,159/5,622. **Par:** 71/72. **Course Rating:** 68.9/65.9. **Slope:** 122/108.
PINE/OAK (18 Combo)
Yards: 6,031/5,141. **Par:** 71/71. **Course Rating:** 68.5/66.4. **Slope:** 120/108.

WESTOVER GOLF CLUB
SP-401 S. Schuylkill Ave., Norristown, 19403, Montgomery County, (610)539-4502, 25 miles from Philadelphia. **Facility Holes:** 18. **Yards:** 6,300/4,950. **Par:** 70/70. **Course Rating:** 69.8/68.5. **Slope:** 122/117. **Green Fee:** $12/$37. **Cart Fee:** $13/Person. **Walking Policy:** Walking at certain times. **Walkability:** 3. **Opened:** 1967. **Architect:** George Fazio. **Season:** Year-round. **High:** April-Oct. **To obtain tee times:** Call up to 5 days in advance. **Miscellaneous:** Reduced fees (twilight, seniors, juniors), range (grass), credit cards (MC, V, AE, D), BF, FF.

WHISPERING PINES GOLF COURSE
PU-15630 Middle Rd., Meadville, 16335, Crawford County, (814)333-2817. **Facility Holes:** 18. **Yards:** 6,226/4,910. **Par:** 71/71. **Course Rating:** 69.0/66.7. **Slope:** 116/118. **Green Fee:** $8/$11. **Cart Fee:** $11/Person. **Walking Policy:** Unrestricted walking. **Opened:** 1965. **Season:** April-Nov. **Tee times:** Call golf shop. **Misc:** Reduced fees (twilight, seniors), credit cards (MC, V, AE).

WHITE BIRCH GOLF COURSE
PU-660 Tuscarora Park Rd., Barnesville, 18214, Schuylkill County, (570)467-2525, 45 miles from Allentown. **E-mail:** linda@whitebirch.com. **Web:** www.whitebirchgolfcourse.com. **Facility Holes:** 27. **Yards:** 5,040/4,580. **Par:** 69/69. **Green Fee:** $7/$15. **Cart Fee:** $10/Person. **Walking Policy:** Walking at certain times. **Walkability:** 4. **Opened:** 1963. **Season:** April-Nov. **High:** May-Sept. **To obtain tee times:** Call up to 7 days in advance. **Miscellaneous:** Reduced fees (weekdays, twilight, seniors), metal spikes, range (mats), BF, FF.
Special Notes: Also has a 9-hole executive course.

WHITE DEER PARK & GOLF COURSE

PU-352 Allenwood Camp Ln., Montgomery, 17752, Lycoming County, (570)547-2186, 8 miles from Williamsport. **Facility Holes:** 36. **Green Fee:** $14/$26. **Cart Fee:** $13/Person. **Walking Policy:** Unrestricted walking. **Season:** Year-round. **Miscellaneous:** Reduced fees (weekdays, twilight, seniors, juniors), metal spikes, range (grass), credit cards (MC, V, D), BF, FF.

★★★½ **CHALLENGE** (18)
Yards: 6,605/4,742. **Par:** 72/72. **Course Rating:** 71.6/68.4. **Slope:** 133/125. **Walkability:** 4. **Opened:** 1989. **Architect:** Lindsay Ervin. **To obtain tee times:** Call up to 28 days in advance.
Reader Comments: Excellent layout, very scenic … I played my best round all year … Requires good iron play, fast greens … Difficult layout … Still making improvements.

★★ **VINTAGE** (18)
Yards: 6,405/4,843. **Par:** 72/72. **Course Rating:** 69.7/68.5. **Slope:** 122/120. **Walkability:** 3. **Opened:** 1965. **Architect:** Kenneth J. Polakowski. **To obtain tee times:** Call golf shop.

★★★½ WHITETAIL GOLF CLUB

PU-2679 Klein Rd., Bath, 18014, Northampton County, (610)837-9626, 7 miles from Allentown. **Web:** www.whitetailgolfclub.com. **Facility Holes:** 18. **Yards:** 6,432/5,152. **Par:** 72/72. **Course Rating:** 70.6/65.3. **Slope:** 128/113. **Green Fee:** $23/$50. **Cart Fee:** Included in green fee. **Walking Policy:** Walking at certain times. **Walkability:** 3. **Opened:** 1993. **Architect:** Jim Blaukovitch. **Season:** Year-round. **To obtain tee times:** Call up to 7 days in advance. **Miscellaneous:** Reduced fees (weekdays, twilight, seniors, juniors), range (grass), credit cards (MC, V, AE), BF, FF.
Reader Comments: Good design, hilly … Good test of golf, excellent conditions, good value, great greens … Good food … Run like a course should be … Will be better course when it matures … Great experience.

WHITETAIL GOLF RESORT

R-11573 Blairs Valley Rd., Mercersburg, 17236, Franklin County, (717)328-4169, (888)493-4169, 90 miles from Baltimore. **E-mail:** jalsip@whitetailgolfresort.com. **Web:** whitetailgolfresort.com. **Facility Holes:** 18. **Yards:** 6,950/5,234. **Par:** 72/72. **Course Rating:** 73.5/70.5. **Slope:** 138/123. **Green Fee:** $43/$56. **Cart Fee:** Included in green fee. **Walking Policy:** Mandatory carts. **Walkability:** 5. **Opened:** 2001. **Architect:** Rick Robbins. **Season:** March-Nov. **High:** April-July. **To obtain tee times:** Call up to 30 days in advance. **Miscellaneous:** Reduced fees (weekdays, twilight, seniors), range (grass), credit cards (MC, V, AE, D), BF, FF.

★★★★ WILKES-BARRE GOLF CLUB

PU-1001 Fairway Dr., Wilkes-Barre, 18702, Luzerne County, (570)472-3590, 10 miles from Wilkes-Barre. **Web:** www.wilkes-barregolfclub.com. **Facility Holes:** 18. **Yards:** 7,020/5,425. **Par:** 72/73. **Course Rating:** 72.8/72.6. **Slope:** 125/121. **Green Fee:** $20/$24. **Cart Fee:** $14/Person. **Walking Policy:** Walking at certain times. **Walkability:** 3. **Opened:** 1968. **Architect:** Geoffrey Cornish. **Season:** March-Nov. **High:** April-Sept. **To obtain tee times:** Call up to 7 days in advance. **Miscellaneous:** Reduced fees (weekdays, twilight, seniors, juniors), range (grass/mats), credit cards (MC, V, AE), BF, FF.
Reader Comments: Always in good condition … Exactly what a muni should be … Great practice facility … Well maintained, nice clubhouse, county owned, busy.

★★★ WILLOW HOLLOW GOLF COURSE

PU-619 Prison Road, Leesport, 19533, Berks County, (610)373-1505, 6 miles from Reading. **E-mail:** willowhollowgolf@netscape.net. **Web:** www.distinctgolf.com. **Facility Holes:** 18. **Yards:** 5,810/4,435. **Par:** 70/70. **Course Rating:** 67.1/64.1. **Slope:** 105/99. **Green Fee:** $12/$24. **Cart Fee:** $11/Person. **Walking Policy:** Walking at certain times. **Walkability:** 3. **Opened:** 1959. **Architect:** Harvey Haupt. **Season:** Year-round. **High:** April-Oct. **To obtain tee times:** Call up to 14 days in advance. **Miscellaneous:** Reduced fees (weekdays, twilight, seniors), credit cards (MC, V), FF.
Reader Comments: Short course … Good for women and seniors … Usually in good shape … Nice price, good place to practice … Don't let length fool you, small sleek greens.

WILLOW RUN INN & GOLF COURSE

PU-RR 2, Box 2990, Berwick, 18603, Columbia County, (570)752-1000. **Facility Holes:** 18. **Yards:** 5,427/4,630. **Par:** 72/72. **Course Rating:** 72.0/65.5. **Slope:** 65.5/108. **Green Fee:** $12/$16. **Cart Fee:** $26/Cart. **Walking Policy:** Unrestricted walking. **Season:** Year-round. **To obtain tee times:** Call golf shop. **Miscellaneous:** Metal spikes, credit cards (MC, V, AE, D).

★★ WOODLAND HILLS COUNTRY CLUB

SP-4166 Lower Saucon Road, Hellertown, 18055, Northampton County, (610)838-7192, 5 miles from Hellertown. **Web:** www.woodlandhillscountryclub.com. **Facility Holes:** 18. **Yards:** 6,761/4,863. **Par:** 72/72. **Course Rating:** 70.3/66.7. **Slope:** 121/104. **Green Fee:** $27/$32. **Cart Fee:** $13/Person. **Walking Policy:** Walking at certain times. **Walkability:** 3. **Opened:** 1968.

PENNSYLVANIA

Architect: Henry Bartholemew. **Season:** Year-round. **To obtain tee times:** Call up to 10 days in advance. **Miscellaneous:** Reduced fees (weekdays, seniors, juniors), metal spikes, range (grass), credit cards (MC, V), BF, FF.

WOODLOCH SPRINGS COUNTRY CLUB

SP-RD #1, Hawley, 18428, Wayne County, (570)685-2100, (800)572-6658, 35 miles from Scranton. **Facility Holes:** 18. **Yards:** 6,127/4,973. **Par:** 72/72. **Course Rating:** 70.4/71.6. **Slope:** 133/130. **Green Fee:** $60/$75. **Cart Fee:** Included in green fee. **Walking Policy:** Walking at certain times. **Walkability:** 5. **Opened:** 1992. **Architect:** Rocky Rogermore. **Season:** April-Nov. **High:** June-Oct. **To obtain tee times:** Call golf shop. **Miscellaneous:** Range (mats), credit cards (MC, V, AE, D).

★★★½ WYNCOTE GOLF CLUB

PU-50 Wyncote Dr., Oxford, 19363, Chester County, (610)932-8900, 50 miles from Philadelphia. **E-mail:** jimp@wyncote.com. **Web:** www.wyncote.com. **Facility Holes:** 18. **Yards:** 7,012/5,454. **Par:** 72/72. **Course Rating:** 74.0/71.6. **Slope:** 130/126. **Green Fee:** $30/$65. **Cart Fee:** $20/Person. **Walking Policy:** Unrestricted walking. **Walkability:** 2. **Opened:** 1993. **Architect:** Brian Ault/Ault Clark & Associates. **Season:** Year-round. **To obtain tee times:** Call up to 14 days in advance. **Miscellaneous:** Reduced fees (weekdays, twilight, seniors, juniors), range (grass/mats), caddies, credit cards (MC, V, AE, D), BF, FF.
Notes: Ranked 25th in 1999 Best in State.
Reader Comments: Good links-style layout ... Best greens in Pennsylvania ... Course requires solid approach shots ... Outstanding customer service ... Good marshals ... Terrific condition ... Scotland in the Northeast! ... Fairways like carpet.

RHODE ISLAND

BRISTOL GOLF CLUB
PU-95 Tupelo St., Bristol, 02809, Bristol County, (401)253-9844. **Facility Holes:** 9. **Yards:** 2,097/2,097. **Par:** 32/32. **Green Fee:** $10/$12. **Cart Fee:** $15/Cart. **To obtain tee times:** Call golf shop.

★★½ **COUNTRY VIEW GOLF CLUB**
PU-49 Club Lane, Harrisville, 02830, Providence County, (401)568-7157, 15 miles from Providence. **E-mail:** rickcvgc@aol.com. **Facility Holes:** 18. **Yards:** 6,067/4,755. **Par:** 70/70. **Course Rating:** 69.2/67.0. **Slope:** 119/105. **Green Fee:** $16/$30. **Cart Fee:** $24/Cart. **Walking Policy:** Unrestricted walking. **Walkability:** 3. **Opened:** 1965. **Architect:** Carl Dexter. **Season:** Year-round. **High:** April-Oct. **To obtain tee times:** Call up to 6 days in advance. **Miscellaneous:** Reduced fees (weekdays, twilight, seniors, juniors), credit cards (MC, V, D), BF, FF.

★★½ **CRANSTON COUNTRY CLUB**
PU-69 Burlingame Rd., Cranston, 02921, Providence County, (401)826-1683, 7 miles from Providence. **E-mail:** ejgolfpro@aol.com. **Facility Holes:** 18. **Yards:** 6,750/5,499. **Par:** 71/72. **Course Rating:** 71.4/71.9. **Slope:** 126/120. **Green Fee:** $28/$37. **Cart Fee:** $14/Person. **Walking Policy:** Unrestricted walking. **Walkability:** 3. **Opened:** 1970. **Architect:** Geoffrey Cornish. **Season:** Year-round. **High:** May-Oct. **To obtain tee times:** Call up to 2 days in advance. **Miscellaneous:** Reduced fees (weekdays, twilight, seniors), range (grass/mats), credit cards (MC, V, D).

★★★½ **EXETER COUNTRY CLUB**
SP-320 Ten Rod Rd., Exeter, 02822, Washington County, (401)295-8212, 15 miles from Warwick. **Facility Holes:** 18. **Yards:** 6,923/5,733. **Par:** 72/72. **Course Rating:** 72.3/72.0. **Slope:** 125/115. **Green Fee:** $25/$35. **Cart Fee:** $22/Cart. **Walking Policy:** Unrestricted walking. **Walkability:** 3. **Opened:** 1969. **Architect:** Geoffrey S. Cornish. **Season:** April-Nov. **High:** May-Sept. **To obtain tee times:** Call up to 2 days in advance. **Miscellaneous:** Reduced fees (twilight), range (grass), credit cards (MC, V), BF, FF.
Reader Comments: Very crowded on weekends … Nice course, long, great greens … Nice Cornish layout with front nine encircling the back nine.

★★½ **FOSTER COUNTRY CLUB**
SP-67 Johnson Rd., Foster, 02825, Providence County, (401)397-7750, 32 miles from Providence. **Facility Holes:** 18. **Yards:** 6,200/5,500. **Par:** 72/74. **Course Rating:** 71.5/70.0. **Slope:** 117/112. **Green Fee:** $25/$32. **Cart Fee:** $24/Cart. **Walking Policy:** Unrestricted walking. **Walkability:** 3. **Opened:** 1964. **Season:** March-Jan. **High:** May-Sept. **To obtain tee times:** Call up to 7 days in advance. **Miscellaneous:** Reduced fees (weekdays, twilight, juniors), credit cards (MC, V, AE), BF, FF.

★★½ **FOXWOODS GOLF & COUNTRY CLUB**
SP-87 Kingstown Rd., Richmond, 02898, Washington County, (401)539-4653. **E-mail:** rajohnson@mptn.org. **Facility Holes:** 18. **Yards:** 6,004/4,881. **Par:** 70/70. **Course Rating:** 69.1/67.7. **Slope:** 131/126. **Green Fee:** $37/$53. **Cart Fee:** Included in green fee. **Walking Policy:** Mandatory carts. **Walkability:** 5. **Opened:** 1995. **Architect:** Tripp Davis III. **Season:** April-Dec. **High:** June-Oct. **To obtain tee times:** Call up to 7 days in advance. **Miscellaneous:** Reduced fees (seniors), range (grass/mats), credit cards (MC, V, AE), BF, FF.

★★★ **GREEN VALLEY COUNTRY CLUB**
SP-371 Union St., Portsmouth, 02871, Newport County, (401)849-2162, 5 miles from Newport. **E-mail:** gucc@tiac.net. **Facility Holes:** 18. **Yards:** 6,830/5,459. **Par:** 71/71. **Course Rating:** 72.0/69.5. **Slope:** 126/120. **Green Fee:** $40/$43. **Cart Fee:** $24/Cart. **Walking Policy:** Walking at certain times. **Walkability:** 3. **Opened:** 1957. **Architect:** Manuel Raposa. **Season:** April-Dec. **High:** June-Nov. **To obtain tee times:** Call up to 3 days in advance. **Miscellaneous:** Reduced fees (weekdays, twilight), metal spikes, range (grass/mats), credit cards (MC, V, AE, D), BF, FF.
Reader Comments: Tough for nonmembers to get on … Can be very windy … Nice course … Play it if possible, long but fair … Scenic ocean views.

★★½ **LAUREL LANE GOLF CLUB**
PU-309 Laurel Lane, West Kingston, 02892, Washington County, (401)783-3844, 25 miles from Providence. **Facility Holes:** 18. **Yards:** 6,031/5,381. **Par:** 71/70. **Course Rating:** 68.1/70.8. **Slope:** 120/120. **Green Fee:** $25/$30. **Cart Fee:** $22/Cart. **Walking Policy:** Unrestricted walking. **Walkability:** 3. **Opened:** 1961. **Architect:** Richard Holly Sr./John Thoren/John Bota. **Season:** Year-round. **To obtain tee times:** Call golf shop. **Miscellaneous:** Reduced fees (weekdays, twilight, juniors), range (grass/mats), credit cards (MC, V), BF, FF.

★½ MEADOW BROOK GOLF CLUB

PU-163 Kingstown Rd., Wyoming, 02898, Washington County, (401)539-8491, 32 miles from Providence. **Facility Holes:** 18. **Yards:** 6,075/5,605. **Par:** 71/73. **Green Fee:** $12/$15. **Cart Fee:** $15/Cart. **Walking Policy:** Unrestricted walking. **Walkability:** 2. **Opened:** 1929. **Architect:** Rob Roy Rawlings. **Season:** April-Feb. **High:** July-Aug. **To obtain tee times:** Call golf shop. **Miscellaneous:** Reduced fees (weekdays, twilight), metal spikes, range (grass).

★½ MELODY HILL GOLF COURSE

PU-Off Saw Mill Rd., Harmony, 02829, Providence County, (401)949-9851, 15 miles from Providence. **Facility Holes:** 18. **Yards:** 6,185. **Par:** 71. **Course Rating:** 69.0. **Slope:** 113. **Green Fee:** $20/$23. **Cart Fee:** $24/Cart. **Walking Policy:** Unrestricted walking. **Walkability:** 3. **Opened:** 1967. **Architect:** Samuel Mitchell. **Season:** April-Nov. **High:** May-Sept. **To obtain tee times:** Call golf shop. **Miscellaneous:** Reduced fees (twilight, seniors), BF, FF.

★★★½ MONTAUP COUNTRY CLUB

SP-500 Anthony Rd., Portsmouth, 02871, Newport County, (401)683-0955, 15 miles from Newport. **Facility Holes:** 18. **Yards:** 6,446/5,432. **Par:** 71/73. **Course Rating:** 71.7/71.5. **Slope:** 126/120. **Green Fee:** $37/$42. **Cart Fee:** $28/Person. **Walking Policy:** Unrestricted walking. **Walkability:** 1. **Opened:** 1923. **Architect:** Geoffrey S. Cornish. **Season:** Year-round. **High:** May-Sept. **To obtain tee times:** Call up to 1 day in advance. **Miscellaneous:** Credit cards (MC, V), BF, FF.

Reader Comments: Awesome veiws, great greens, great holes ... Nice layout ... Best public course in RI.

★★★ NORTH KINGSTOWN MUNICIPAL GOLF COURSE

PU-615 Callahan Road, North Kingstown, 02852, Washington County, (401)294-0684, 15 miles from Providence. **Facility Holes:** 18. **Yards:** 6,161/5,227. **Par:** 70/70. **Course Rating:** 69.3/69.5. **Slope:** 123/115. **Green Fee:** $28/$35. **Cart Fee:** $24/Cart. **Walking Policy:** Unrestricted walking. **Walkability:** 2. **Opened:** 1943. **Architect:** Unknown. **Season:** March-Dec. **High:** June-Sept. **To obtain tee times:** Call up to 2 days in advance. **Miscellaneous:** Reduced fees (weekdays, twilight, seniors, juniors), range (grass), BF, FF.

Reader Comments: Great course, fun to golf there ... Nice muni course ... Try to find this golf course ... Best value in the state ... Recent improvements to clubhouse.

★★★★ RICHMOND COUNTRY CLUB

PU-74 Sandy Pond Rd., Richmond, 02832, Washington County, (401)364-9200, 30 miles from Providence. **Facility Holes:** 18. **Yards:** 6,826/4,974. **Par:** 71/71. **Course Rating:** 72.1/70.4. **Slope:** 121/113. **Green Fee:** $30/$35. **Cart Fee:** $22/Cart. **Walking Policy:** Unrestricted walking. **Walkability:** 1. **Opened:** 1993. **Architect:** Geoffrey S. Cornish/Brian Silva. **Season:** April-Nov. **High:** June-Sept. **To obtain tee times:** Call golf shop. **Miscellaneous:** Reduced fees (weekdays, twilight), credit cards (MC, V).

Reader Comments: Narrow and long, tough—worth the drive ... Like a piece of NC in RI ... Odd layout, very penal in nature ... A personal favorite ... A bargain for New England golf ... Some claim too easy, just right for us.

★★★½ TRIGGS MEMORIAL GOLF COURSE

PU-1533 Chalkstone Ave., Providence, 02909, Providence County, (401)521-8460. **Facility Holes:** 18. **Yards:** 6,596/5,598. **Par:** 72/73. **Course Rating:** 71.9. **Slope:** 126. **Green Fee:** $29/$32. **Cart Fee:** $25/Cart. **Walking Policy:** Unrestricted walking. **Walkability:** 2. **Opened:** 1933. **Architect:** Donald Ross. **Season:** Year-round. **High:** June-Aug. **To obtain tee times:** Call golf shop. **Miscellaneous:** Reduced fees (seniors), metal spikes, credit cards (MC, V).

Reader Comments: Long course ... Challenging Ross course ... Tough greens, great layout ... Nothing fancy, just a great Donald Ross golf course ... Links-style course, high handicapper will struggle ... Lots of history ... Ken Venturi won here 50 years ago.

★★★ WINNAPAUG COUNTRY CLUB

SP-184 Shore Rd., Westerly, 02891, Washington County, (401)596-1237, (800)538-9948, 30 miles from Providence. **Facility Holes:** 18. **Yards:** 6,345/5,113. **Par:** 72/72. **Course Rating:** 70.6/69.1. **Slope:** 124/110. **Green Fee:** $30/$35. **Cart Fee:** $24/Cart. **Walking Policy:** Unrestricted walking. **Walkability:** 3. **Opened:** 1922. **Architect:** Donald Ross. **Season:** Year-round. **To obtain tee times:** Call up to 7 days in advance. **Miscellaneous:** Reduced fees (weekdays, guests, twilight, seniors, juniors), metal spikes, range (grass), lodging (60 rooms), credit cards (MC, V, AE), BF, FF.

Reader Comments: Out of bounds 16 of 18 holes—tough ... layout is hilly & curvy ... Open all year ... Undulating greens are fast and fun.

★★★½ ABERDEEN COUNTRY CLUB *Pace*
PU-701 Bucks Trail, Longs, 29568, Horry County, (843)399-2660, (800)344-5590, 6 miles from Myrtle Beach. **E-mail:** shopp@sccoast.net. **Web:** www.mbn.com. **Facility Holes:** 27. **Green Fee:** $31/$78. **Cart Fee:** $21/Person. **Walking Policy:** Unrestricted walking. **Walkability:** 3. **Opened:** 1990. **Architect:** Tom Jackson. **Season:** Year-round. **High:** Feb.-May. **To obtain tee times:** Call up to 365 days in advance. **Miscellaneous:** Reduced fees (twilight, juniors), range (grass), credit cards (MC, V, AE, D, DC, CB), BF, FF.
HIGHLANDS/MEADOWS (18 Combo)
Yards: 6,729/4,972. **Par:** 72/72. **Course Rating:** 72.2/67.7. **Slope:** 134/113.
MEADOWS/WOODLANDS (18 Combo)
Yards: 6,751/4,972. **Par:** 72/72. **Course Rating:** 72.3/68.3. **Slope:** 136/117.
WOODLANDS/HIGHLANDS (18 Combo)
Yards: 6,850/4,956. **Par:** 72/72. **Course Rating:** 72.9/68.5. **Slope:** 138/116.
Reader Comments: Better than ever … Some fun holes, and usually a great value. Good course to play as a warm-up in a golf package … Tight course. Lots of water. Great greens … Long course, excellent fairways, many traps.

★½ AIKEN GOLF CLUB
SP-555 Highland Park Dr., Aiken, 29801, Aiken County, (803)649-6029, 20 miles from Augusta. **Web:** www.aikengolfclub.com. **Facility Holes:** 18. **Yards:** 6,200/5,400. **Par:** 70/70. **Course Rating:** 68.0. **Slope:** 115. **Green Fee:** $15/$25. **Cart Fee:** $11/Person. **Walking Policy:** Unrestricted walking. **Walkability:** 3. **Opened:** 1912. **Architect:** J.R. Inglis. **Season:** Year-round. **To obtain tee times:** Call golf shop. **Miscellaneous:** Reduced fees (twilight), metal spikes, credit cards (MC, V, AE), FF.

★★★ ARCADIAN SHORES GOLF CLUB
PU-701 Hilton Rd., Myrtle Beach, 29577, Horry County, (843)449-5217, 120 miles from Charleston. **E-mail:** wmbr@sccoast.net. **Facility Holes:** 18. **Yards:** 6,938/5,229. **Par:** 72/72. **Course Rating:** 73.2/69.9. **Slope:** 136/117. **Green Fee:** $39/$88. **Cart Fee:** Included in green fee. **Walking Policy:** Mandatory carts. **Walkability:** 3. **Opened:** 1974. **Architect:** Rees Jones. **Season:** Year-round. **High:** March-May. **To obtain tee times:** Call up to 365 days in advance. **Miscellaneous:** Reduced fees (guests, juniors), range (grass), lodging (385 rooms), credit cards (MC, V, AE, D), BF, FF.
Reader Comments: Five holes on front 9 are some of Jones' best … Hole designs were good … Good all-around course, loved it … Would play it again.

★★★★ ARROWHEAD COUNTRY CLUB
PU-1201 Burcal Rd., Myrtle Beach, 29579, Horry County, (843)236-3243, (800)236-3243, 3 miles from Myrtle Beach. **E-mail:** arrow@sccoast.net. **Web:** www.arrowheadcc.com. **Facility Holes:** 27. **Yards:** 6,666/4,812. **Par:** 72/72. **Course Rating:** 71.1/71.2. **Slope:** 130/116. **Green Fee:** $41/$90. **Cart Fee:** Included in green fee. **Walking Policy:** Mandatory carts. **Walkability:** 3. **Opened:** 1994. **Architect:** Tom Jackson/Ray Floyd. **Season:** Year-round. **To obtain tee times:** Call golf shop. **Miscellaneous:** Reduced fees (juniors), range (grass), credit cards (MC, V, AE), BF, FF.
Reader Comments: Classical design, great waterway holes … Good course, always good condition, good price … Good course to begin or end a golf vacation … Imaginative layout, lots of different clubs needed.
Special Notes: Also has a 9-hole course.

★★★ AZALEA SANDS GOLF CLUB
PU-2100 Hwy. 17 S., North Myrtle Beach, 29582, Horry County, (843)272-6191, (800)252-2312, 10 miles from Myrtle Beach. **Facility Holes:** 18. **Yards:** 6,902/5,172. **Par:** 72/72. **Course Rating:** 72.5/70.2. **Slope:** 123/119. **Green Fee:** $26/$60. **Cart Fee:** Included in green fee. **Walking Policy:** Walking at certain times. **Walkability:** 1. **Opened:** 1972. **Architect:** Gene Hamm. **Season:** Year-round. **To obtain tee times:** Call golf shop. **Miscellaneous:** Reduced fees (guests, twilight, juniors), credit cards (MC, V, AE, D), FF.
Reader Comments: True greens … Player friendly … Fun to play, well maintained … Very courteous staff … Good, solid beach course, great greens … For price and course condition, best value in Myrtle Beach.

BAREFOOT RESORT & GOLF
PU-4980 46th Ave. S. Ext., North Myrtle Beach, 29582, Horry County, (843)399-7238, (877)237-3767. **Web:** www.barefootgolf.com. **Facility Holes:** 72. **Cart Fee:** Included in green fee. **Walking Policy:** Unrestricted walking. **Opened:** 2000. **Season:** Year-round. **To obtain tee times:** Call golf shop. **Miscellaneous:** Credit cards (MC, V, AE).
DYE COURSE (18)
Yards: 7,343/5,021. **Par:** 72/72. **Course Rating:** 75.3/69.1. **Slope:** 149/119. **Green Fee:** $85/$150. **Architect:** Pete Dye.
Notes: Golf Digest School site.

★★★★½ **FAZIO COURSE** (18) *Pace*
Yards: 6,834/4,820. **Par:** 71/71. **Course Rating:** 73.2/68.4. **Slope:** 149/122. **Green Fee:** $70/$130. **Architect:** Tom Fazio.
Notes: Golf Digest School site.
Reader Comments: This ranks among the top tier courses already at the Beach ... Highly playable for middle and high handicap players. Service was outstanding ... 2nd toughest at Barefoot. Avoid the traps ... Visual feast ... Long par 4s. Excellent greens ... All holes are different ... Kind of expensive for Myrtle Beach, but great course to play.

★★★★½ **LOVE COURSE** (18) *Pace*
Yards: 7,047/5,346. **Par:** 72/72. **Course Rating:** 73.7/71.8. **Slope:** 137/124. **Green Fee:** $70/$130. **Architect:** Davis Love III.
Notes: Golf Digest School site. Ranked 14th in 2001 Best in State; 6th in 2000 Best New Upscale Courses.
Reader Comments: Unique holes accompanied with great green complexes ... Diverse design, gracious staff, a must play ...Interesting driving course ... Wide fairways. Interesting ruins holes ... Instantly in my top five in Myrtle Beach ... Fast greens! Fringes shaved down like Pinehurst No. 2.

NORMAN COURSE (18)
Yards: 7,035/4,953. **Par:** 72/72. **Course Rating:** 73.5/68.2. **Slope:** 137/117. **Green Fee:** $70/$130. **Architect:** Greg Norman.
Notes: Golf Digest School site.

BAY TREE GOLF PLANTATION
PU-P.O. Box 240, North Myrtle Beach, 29597, Horry County, (843)399-6166, (800)845-6191, 8 miles from Myrtle Beach. **E-mail:** btgolf@sccoast.net. **Web:** www.baytreegolfplantation.com. **Facility Holes:** 54. **Green Fee:** $19/$42. **Cart Fee:** $20/Person. **Walking Policy:** Walking at certain times. **Walkability:** 2. **Opened:** 1972. **Architect:** George Fazio/Russell Breedon. **Season:** Year-round. **High:** Feb.-May. **To obtain tee times:** Call golf shop. **Miscellaneous:** Reduced fees (juniors), range (grass), lodging (350 rooms), credit cards (MC, V), BF, FF.

★★★½ **GOLD COURSE** (18)
Yards: 6,942/5,264. **Par:** 72/72. **Course Rating:** 72.0/69.7. **Slope:** 135/117.
Reader Comments: Staff was very nice ... Beautiful course ... A great layout that requires all the shots. The best value in Myrtle Beach ... Warm up and be ready ... Large trees, nice landscape.

★★★ **GREEN COURSE** (18)
Yards: 7,044/5,362. **Par:** 72/72. **Course Rating:** 72.5/69.0. **Slope:** 135/118.
Reader Comments: Outstanding service and course conditions ... Very scenic, tight ... Recent renovations really paying off ... Stay away if you don't like water.

★★★½ **SILVER COURSE** (18)
Yards: 6,871/5,417. **Par:** 72/72. **Course Rating:** 70.5/69.0. **Slope:** 131/116.
Reader Comments: A fun, forgiving course to play. Course conditions superb ... Tight, overall good ... Best kept secret in Myrtle Beach area.

★★★ BEACHWOOD GOLF CLUB
R-1520 Hwy. 17 South, North Myrtle Beach, 29582, Horry County, (803)272-6168, (800)526-4889, 12 miles from Myrtle Beach. **E-mail:** info@beachwood.com. **Web:** www.beachwoodgolf.com. **Facility Holes:** 18. **Yards:** 6,844/4,947. **Par:** 72/72. **Course Rating:** 71.4/67.6. **Slope:** 120/111. **Green Fee:** $18/$46. **Cart Fee:** $20/Person. **Walking Policy:** Mandatory carts. **Walkability:** 1. **Opened:** 1968. **Architect:** Gene Hamm. **Season:** Year-round. **High:** March-Nov. **To obtain tee times:** Call golf shop. **Miscellaneous:** Reduced fees (twilight, seniors, juniors), range (grass), credit cards (MC, V, AE), FF.
Reader Comments: Good condition ... Good tourist course ... Bermuda greens ... Old but good.

BEECH CREEK GOLF CLUB
PU-1800 Sam Gillespie Blvd., Sumter, 29154, Sumter County, (803)499-4653, 28 miles from Columbia. **E-mail:** beechcreekgolfclub@yahoo.com. **Web:** www.golfbeechcreek.com. **Facility Holes:** 18. **Yards:** 6,805/5,245. **Par:** 72/72. **Course Rating:** 72.5/69.7. **Slope:** 128/119. **Green Fee:** $20/$33. **Cart Fee:** Included in green fee. **Walking Policy:** Walking at certain times. **Walkability:** 4. **Opened:** 1990. **Architect:** Ron Goodson. **Season:** Year-round. **To obtain tee times:** Call up to 7 days in advance. **Miscellaneous:** Range (grass/mats), credit cards (MC, V, AE), BF, FF.

BELLE TERRE GOLF COURSE
R-4073 U.S. Hwy. 501, Myrtle Beach, 29579, Horry County, (843)236-8888, (800)340-0072, 3 miles from Myrtle Beach. **E-mail:** bellterr@sccoast.net. **Web:** www.belleterre.com. **Facility Holes:** 27. **Opened:** 1995. **Architect:** Rees Jones. **Season:** Year-round. **To obtain tee times:** Call golf shop. **Miscellaneous:** Reduced fees (guests, juniors), range (grass), credit cards (MC, V, AE, D), FF.

★★★½ **CHAMPIONSHIP COURSE** (18)
Yards: 7,013/5,049. **Par:** 72/72. **Course Rating:** 74.0/69.6. **Slope:** 134/126. **Green Fee:** $20/$70. **Cart Fee:** $18/Person. **Walking Policy:** Mandatory carts. **Walkability:** 2.

★★★ SKINS COURSE (9)
Yards: 1,597/1,384. **Par:** 29/29. **Green Fee:** $15/$30. **Cart Fee:** $15/Person. **Walking Policy:** Unrestricted walking. **Walkability:** 1.
Reader Comments: Just good golf, excellent track, you can play as easy or difficult as you want ... Fun but too much water ... Back 9 is a good challenge ... Hard course but fun to play ... Hard for hackers ... Best service I've ever seen. Awesome ... Need to choose the right set of tees to play ... Close to awesome! ... Enjoyable ... Best exec course ever played ... Service was outstanding ... A trip to reality for hackers.

★★ BERKELEY COUNTRY CLUB
SP-Old Hwy. 52, Moncks Corner, 29461, Berkeley County, (843)761-4880, 20 miles from Charleston. **Facility Holes:** 18. **Yards:** 6,711/5,100. **Par:** 72/72. **Course Rating:** 71.2/67.9. **Slope:** 114/106. **Green Fee:** $17/$23. **Cart Fee:** $12/Person. **Walking Policy:** Walking at certain times. **Walkability:** 1. **Opened:** 1959. **Architect:** George Cobb. **Season:** Year-round. **To obtain tee times:** Call up to 2 days in advance. **Miscellaneous:** Reduced fees (weekdays, seniors, juniors), range (grass), credit cards (MC, V), BF, FF.

★★★½ BLACK BEAR GOLF CLUB
PU-Hwy. 9 W., North Myrtle Beach, 29582, Horry County, (843)756-0550, (800)842-8390, 11 miles from North Myrtle Beach. **Web:** www.golfblackbear.com. **Facility Holes:** 18. **Yards:** 6,787/4,859. **Par:** 72/72. **Course Rating:** 72.7/67.9. **Slope:** 132/113. **Green Fee:** $33/$70. **Cart Fee:** Included in green fee. **Walking Policy:** Mandatory carts. **Walkability:** 2. **Opened:** 1989. **Architect:** Tom Jackson. **Season:** Year-round. **To obtain tee times:** Call golf shop. **Miscellaneous:** Reduced fees (weekdays, guests, twilight, seniors, juniors), range (grass), credit cards (MC, V), BF, FF.
Reader Comments: Lot of challenging holes around and over water, like par-4 8th and par-5 18th ... Well conditioned, well designed golf course ... Good low score opportunities.

★★★½ BLACKMOOR GOLF CLUB
R-6100 Longwood Rd., Hwy. 707, Murrells Inlet, 29576, Horry County, (843)650-5555, (888)650-5556, 12 miles from Myrtle Beach. **E-mail:** blkmoor@sccoast.net. **Web:** www.black-moor.com. **Facility Holes:** 18. **Yards:** 6,614/4,807. **Par:** 72/72. **Course Rating:** 71.1/67.9. **Slope:** 126/115. **Green Fee:** $32/$73. **Cart Fee:** $20/Person. **Walking Policy:** Mandatory carts. **Walkability:** 3. **Opened:** 1990. **Architect:** Gary Player. **Season:** Year-round. **High:** Feb.-May. **To obtain tee times:** Call up to 180 days in advance. **Miscellaneous:** Reduced fees (guests, juniors), metal spikes, range (grass), credit cards (MC, V), BF, FF.
Reader Comments: Was in excellent conditions ... Alligators keep things interesting. Great staff ... Definitely a replay ... Beautiful course, challenging ... Very enjoyable for all skill levels.

★★★ BONNIE BRAE GOLF CLUB
SP-1116 Ashmore Bridge Rd., Greenville, 29605, Greenville County, (864)277-9838, 3 miles from Mauldin. **Facility Holes:** 18. **Yards:** 6,484/5,316. **Par:** 72/74. **Course Rating:** 70.7/69.6. **Slope:** 127/116. **Green Fee:** $16/$25. **Cart Fee:** $10/Person. **Walking Policy:** Walking at certain times. **Walkability:** 2. **Opened:** 1961. **Architect:** Charles Willimon. **Season:** Year-round. **To obtain tee times:** Call up to 7 days in advance. **Miscellaneous:** Reduced fees (twilight), range (grass), credit cards (MC, V, D), BF, FF.
Reader Comments: Some interesting holes ... Good job improving course conditions, 5th green impossible ... Wide fairways, large firm greens ... Only course in my area that allows my 4-year-old to play.

★★ BOSCOBEL GOLF CLUB
SP-Hwy. 76, Pendleton, 29670, Anderson County, (864)646-3991, 28 miles from Greenville. **Facility Holes:** 18. **Yards:** 6,400/5,023. **Par:** 71/72. **Course Rating:** 69.8/67.8. **Slope:** 115/114. **Green Fee:** $13/$19. **Cart Fee:** $18/Cart. **Walking Policy:** Unrestricted walking. **Walkability:** 3. **Opened:** 1932. **Architect:** Fred Bolton. **Season:** Year-round. **High:** April-June. **To obtain tee times:** Call golf shop. **Miscellaneous:** Reduced fees (twilight), credit cards (MC, V), BF, FF.

BURNING RIDGE GOLF CLUB
R-Hwy. 501 W., Conway, 29577, Horry County, (843)347-0538, (800)833-6337, 5 miles from Myrtle Beach. **Web:** www.linksgroup.com. **Facility Holes:** 36. **Green Fee:** $29/$74. **Cart Fee:** Included in green fee. **Walking Policy:** Mandatory carts. **Walkability:** 3. **Architect:** Gene Hamm. **Season:** Year-round. **High:** March-June. **To obtain tee times:** Call golf shop. **Miscellaneous:** Reduced fees (weekdays, twilight, juniors), range (grass), credit cards (MC, V, AE, D), FF.
★★★ EAST COURSE (18)
Yards: 6,780/4,524. **Par:** 72/72. **Course Rating:** 73.1/65.4. **Slope:** 132/111. **Opened:** 1985.
Reader Comments: Best deal in area, play from tips ... Good facilities, staff very good and helpful ... Some fairways narrow, lots of water ... Tough course, bring your 'A' game.

SOUTH CAROLINA

★★★ **WEST COURSE** (18)
Yards: 6,714/4,831. **Par:** 72/72. **Course Rating:** 73.0/66.5. **Slope:** 128/118. **Opened:** 1980.
Reader Comments: Challenging course with lots of trees … Small greens on par 3s, good fairways … Older course, good value.

★★★★½ **CALEDONIA GOLF & FISH CLUB** *Service, Condition, Pace*
PU-369 Caledonia Dr., Pawleys Island, 29585, Georgetown County, (843)237-3675, (800)483-6800, 1 mile from Pawleys Island. **Web:** www.fishclub.com. **Facility Holes:** 18. **Yards:** 6,526/4,957. **Par:** 70/70. **Course Rating:** 70.9/68.2. **Slope:** 132/113. **Green Fee:** $85/$150. **Cart Fee:** Included in green fee. **Walking Policy:** Unrestricted walking. **Walkability:** 3. **Opened:** 1994. **Architect:** Mike Strantz. **Season:** Year-round. **To obtain tee times:** Call golf shop. **Miscellaneous:** Reduced fees (juniors), credit cards (MC, V, AE, D), FF.
Notes: Ranked 23rd in 2001 Best in State; 31st in 1996 America's Top 75 Upscale Courses.
Reader Comments: Fair, but testing course … One you can play over and over … A 'must play.' Great use of a very small site … Looks like Augusta when you drive in. Play it from the back … Make sure to sit on the porch at 18 and watch golfers try to hit over the water.

★★½ **CALHOUN COUNTRY CLUB**
SP-Rte. 3 Country Club Rd., St. Matthews, 29135, Calhoun County, (803)823-2465, 3 miles from St. Matthews. **Facility Holes:** 18. **Yards:** 6,339/4,812. **Par:** 71/71. **Course Rating:** 70.9/66.4. **Slope:** 119/110. **Green Fee:** $22/$26. **Cart Fee:** Included in green fee. **Walking Policy:** Walking at certain times. **Walkability:** 4. **Opened:** 1957. **Architect:** Ellis Maples. **Season:** Year-round. **High:** Jan.-May. **To obtain tee times:** Call golf shop. **Miscellaneous:** Reduced fees (weekdays, twilight, seniors, juniors), metal spikes, range (grass), credit cards (MC, V), BF, FF.

★½ **CAROLINA DOWNS COUNTRY CLUB**
PU-294 Shiloh Rd., York, 29745, York County, (803)684-5878, 18 miles from Charlotte. **Facility Holes:** 18. **Yards:** 6,335/4,624. **Par:** 72/72. **Course Rating:** 69.5/67.4. **Slope:** 141/123. **Green Fee:** $23/$28. **Cart Fee:** Included in green fee. **Walking Policy:** Walking at certain times. **Walkability:** 2. **Opened:** 1984. **Architect:** Boony Harper. **Season:** Year-round. **High:** May-Oct. **To obtain tee times:** Call golf shop. **Miscellaneous:** Reduced fees (weekdays, seniors, juniors), range (grass), credit cards (MC, V, AE, D).

★★½ **CAROLINA SPRINGS GOLF CLUB**
SP-1680 Scuffletown Rd., Fountain Inn, 29644, Greenville County, (864)862-3551, 8 miles from Greenville. **Facility Holes:** 27. **Green Fee:** $30/$42. **Cart Fee:** Included in green fee. **Walking Policy:** Walking at certain times. **Walkability:** 2. **Opened:** 1968. **Architect:** Russel Breeden. **Season:** Year-round. **High:** April-Sept. **To obtain tee times:** Call golf shop. **Miscellaneous:** Reduced fees (weekdays, twilight, seniors, juniors), range (grass/mats), credit cards (MC, V, AE, D).
PINES/CEDAR (18 Combo)
Yards: 6,676/5,084. **Par:** 72/72. **Course Rating:** 72.6/68.9. **Slope:** 132/116.
WILLOWS/CEDAR (18 Combo)
Yards: 6,643/5,135. **Par:** 72/72. **Course Rating:** 72.0/68.5. **Slope:** 126/113.
WILLOWS/PINES (18 Combo)
Yards: 6,815/5,223. **Par:** 72/72. **Course Rating:** 72.8/69.3. **Slope:** 130/119.

★★★½ **CEDAR CREEK GOLF CLUB**
SP-2475 Club Dr., Aiken, 29803, Aiken County, (803)648-4206, 5 miles from Aiken. **E-mail:** cedarcr005@aol.com. **Facility Holes:** 18. **Yards:** 7,206/5,182. **Par:** 72/72. **Course Rating:** 74.1/68.6. **Slope:** 142/113. **Green Fee:** $36. **Cart Fee:** Included in green fee. **Walking Policy:** Walking at certain times. **Walkability:** 4. **Opened:** 1991. **Architect:** Arthur Hills. **Season:** Year-round. **To obtain tee times:** Call golf shop. **Miscellaneous:** Reduced fees (weekdays, twilight, seniors, juniors), metal spikes, range (grass), credit cards (MC, V, AE), BF, FF.
Reader Comments: Course management a must … Really fun to play … Wooded fairways, challenging layout … Could be outstanding … Nice course with great finishing trio of holes.

★★ **CHARLESTON MUNICIPAL GOLF COURSE**
PU-2110 Maybank Hwy., Charleston, 29412, Charleston County, (843)795-6517. **E-mail:** whetsellh@ci.charleston.sc.us. **Facility Holes:** 18. **Yards:** 6,411/5,202. **Par:** 72/72. **Course Rating:** 70.2/69.2. **Slope:** 112/114. **Green Fee:** $9/$15. **Cart Fee:** $10/Person. **Walking Policy:** Unrestricted walking. **Walkability:** 1. **Opened:** 1927. **Architect:** John E. Adams. **Season:** Year-round. **To obtain tee times:** Call up to 7 days in advance. **Miscellaneous:** Reduced fees (twilight, seniors, juniors), metal spikes, range (grass/mats), credit cards (MC, V), BF, FF.

★★★½ **CHARLESTON NATIONAL COUNTRY CLUB**
SP-1360 National Dr., Mount Pleasant, 29466, Charleston County, (843)884-7799, 10 miles from Charleston. **E-mail:** bartwolfe@aol.com. **Web:** www.charlestonnationalgolf.com. **Facility**

Holes: 18. **Yards:** 6,975/5,103. **Par:** 72/72. **Course Rating:** 74.0/70.8. **Slope:** 140/126. **Green Fee:** $32/$75. **Cart Fee:** Included in green fee. **Walking Policy:** Mandatory carts. **Walkability:** 3. **Opened:** 1989. **Architect:** Rees Jones. **Season:** Year-round. **High:** March-May. **To obtain tee times:** Call up to 180 days in advance. **Miscellaneous:** Reduced fees (weekdays, guests, twilight, seniors, juniors), range (grass/mats), credit cards (MC, V, AE, D), BF, FF.
Reader Comments: Excellent links-style course. Well maintained and challenging greens. Not for the timid or errant shotmaker … Lots of forced carries over hazards … Great 3s, only 1 bad hole … Interesting doglegs/lay ups … 17th hole is very odd … Great value.

★★★★ CHERAW STATE PARK GOLF COURSE *Value+, Pace*
PU-100 State Park Rd., Cheraw, 29520, Chesterfield County, (843)537-2215, (800)868-9630, 40 miles from Florence. **Facility Holes:** 18. **Yards:** 6,900/5,408. **Par:** 72/72. **Course Rating:** 73.4/70.8. **Slope:** 130/120. **Green Fee:** $13/$18. **Cart Fee:** $12/Person. **Walking Policy:** Walking at certain times. **Walkability:** 3. **Opened:** 1992. **Architect:** Tom Jackson. **Season:** Year-round. **To obtain tee times:** Call up to 14 days in advance. **Miscellaneous:** Reduced fees (weekdays), range (grass/mats), lodging (8 rooms), credit cards (MC, V), BF, FF.
Reader Comments: First-class challenge … Beautiful course some very demanding holes … A great state park to play … Interesting layout, not crowded, no houses, just forest … Well kept. Nice greens … Thank God nobody knows about it.

★★½ CHEROKEE VALLEY GOLF CLUB
SP-253 Chinquapin Rd., Tigerville, 29688, Greenville County, (864)895-6758, (800)531-3634, 15 miles from Greenville. **Facility Holes:** 18. **Yards:** 6,713/4,545. **Par:** 72/72. **Course Rating:** 72.1/69.7. **Slope:** 135/119. **Green Fee:** $25/$39. **Cart Fee:** Included in green fee. **Walking Policy:** Mandatory carts. **Walkability:** 5. **Opened:** 1993. **Architect:** P.B. Dye. **Season:** Year-round. **To obtain tee times:** Call up to 7 days in advance. **Miscellaneous:** Reduced fees (weekdays, twilight, seniors, juniors), range (grass), credit cards (MC, V, AE), BF, FF.

★★★ CHESTER GOLF CLUB
SP-770 Old Richburg Rd., Chester, 29706, Chester County, (803)581-5733, 45 miles from Charlotte. **Web:** www.leroysprings.com. **Facility Holes:** 18. **Yards:** 6,811/5,347. **Par:** 72/72. **Course Rating:** 72.0/70.1. **Slope:** 124/116. **Green Fee:** $20/$25. **Cart Fee:** $14/Person. **Walking Policy:** Walking at certain times. **Walkability:** 2. **Opened:** 1971. **Architect:** Russell Breeden. **Season:** Year-round. **To obtain tee times:** Call up to 7 days in advance. **Miscellaneous:** Reduced fees (weekdays, seniors), range (grass), credit cards (MC, V), BF, FF.
Reader Comments: This course is one of the greatest values for the money I have played. The greens are great and fairways are always well groomed … Fun par-3 hole.

★★ CHICKASAW POINT COUNTRY CLUB
SP-503 So. Hogan Dr., Westminster, 29693, Oconee County, (864)972-9623. **Facility Holes:** 18. **Yards:** 6,135/4,495. **Par:** 72/72. **Course Rating:** 70.0/66.0. **Slope:** 117/114. **Green Fee:** $22/$26. **Opened:** 1979. **Architect:** Russell Breeden. **To obtain tee times:** Call golf shop. **Miscellaneous:** Metal spikes.

THE CLUB AT SEABROOK ISLAND
R-1002 Landfall Way, Seabrook Island, 29455, Charleston County, (843)768-1000, (800)845-2475, 20 miles from Charleston. **E-mail:** sigolf@carol.net. **Web:** www.seabrookresort.com. **Facility Holes:** 36. **Green Fee:** $65/$135. **Cart Fee:** Included in green fee. **Walking Policy:** Unrestricted walking. **Walkability:** 2. **Season:** Year-round. **High:** March-June. **To obtain tee times:** Call up to 7 days in advance. **Miscellaneous:** Reduced fees (juniors), range (grass), lodging (225 rooms), credit cards (MC, V, AE, D, DC), BF, FF.
★★★★ CROOKED OAKS COURSE (18)
Yards: 6,754/5,137. **Par:** 72/72. **Course Rating:** 72.7/71.8. **Slope:** 136/123. **Opened:** 1979. **Architect:** Robert T. Jones.
Reader Comments: One of Jones' best in the South, and I'm not one of his fans … Far and away the best putting surfaces in the state … Long and tough.
★★★★ OCEAN WINDS COURSE (18)
Yards: 6,761/5,572. **Par:** 72/72. **Course Rating:** 73.0/73.3. **Slope:** 139/127. **Opened:** 1976. **Architect:** Willard Byrd.
Reader Comments: I could play this course everyday! … Very difficult layout, very good condition … Great links holes … Winds make it a great challenge.

★★★ COBB'S GLEN COUNTRY CLUB
SP-2201 Cobb's Way, Anderson, 29621, Anderson County, (864)226-7688, (800)624-7688, 3 miles from Anderson. **E-mail:** cobbsglen@carol.net. **Web:** www.cobbsglen.com. **Facility Holes:** 18. **Yards:** 7,002/5,312. **Par:** 72/72. **Course Rating:** 72.3/72.0. **Slope:** 129/121. **Green Fee:** $20/$29. **Cart Fee:** $13/Person. **Walking Policy:** Walking at certain times. **Walkability:** 3. **Opened:** 1975. **Architect:** George Cobb. **Season:** Year-round. **High:** April-May. **To obtain tee**

times: Call golf shop. **Miscellaneous:** Reduced fees (weekdays, seniors, juniors), metal spikes, range (grass), credit cards (MC, V, AE), BF, FF.
Reader Comments: Staff are uniformly courteous and attentive. Fairways are mostly generous, but this course is long ... Course condition fair ... Long but now narrow ... 18th is tough par 4.

COLDSTREAM COUNTRY CLUB

SP-2121 Lake Murray Blvd., Columbia, 29063, Lexington County, (803)781-0114, 10 miles from Columbia. **E-mail:** golf@the isp.net. **Web:** www.coldstream.com. **Facility Holes:** 18. **Yards:** 6,155/5,047. **Par:** 71/71. **Course Rating:** 70.0/68.6. **Slope:** 133/125. **Green Fee:** $33/$39. **Cart Fee:** Included in green fee. **Walking Policy:** Walking at certain times. **Walkability:** 3. **Opened:** 1974. **Season:** Year-round. **To obtain tee times:** Call up to 30 days in advance. **Miscellaneous:** Reduced fees (weekdays, guests, twilight, seniors, juniors), credit cards (MC, V, AE), BF, FF.

★★★ COLONIAL CHARTERS GOLF CLUB

PU-301 Charter Dr., Longs, 29301, Horry County, (843)399-4653, (800)833-6337, 20 miles from Myrtle Beach. **Facility Holes:** 18. **Yards:** 6,769/5,079. **Par:** 72/72. **Course Rating:** 73.0/70.2. **Slope:** 131/120. **Green Fee:** $29/$65. **Cart Fee:** Included in green fee. **Walkability:** 3. **Opened:** 1988. **Architect:** John Simpson. **Season:** Year-round. **To obtain tee times:** Call golf shop. **Miscellaneous:** Reduced fees (twilight, juniors), range (grass), credit cards (MC, V, D).
Reader Comments: Old course, forgiving, playable ... Very good staff ... OK course for an average golfer ... Good golf course, some areas need work ... Out a little but worth the ride ... Very user friendly.

★★★ COOPER'S CREEK GOLF CLUB

SP-700 Wagener Hwy. No. 113, Pelion, 29123, Lexington County, (803)894-3666, (800)828-8463, 25 miles from Columbia. **Facility Holes:** 18. **Yards:** 6,582/4,565. **Par:** 72/73. **Course Rating:** 70.6/63.6. **Slope:** 131/99. **Green Fee:** $8/$15. **Cart Fee:** $15/Person. **Walking Policy:** Unrestricted walking. **Walkability:** 3. **Opened:** 1973. **Architect:** Red Chase. **Season:** Year-round. **High:** April-Oct. **To obtain tee times:** Call golf shop. **Miscellaneous:** Range (grass), credit cards (MC, V, AE).
Reader Comments: Worth playing ... A diamond in the rough. Very enjoyable ... Very well kept course ... Wide open fairways, good greens ... Good value.

★★★½ COOSAW CREEK COUNTRY CLUB

SP-4210 Club Course Dr., North Charleston, 29420, Dorchester County, (843)767-9000, 10 miles from Charleston. **Web:** www.coosawcreek.com. **Facility Holes:** 18. **Yards:** 6,593/5,064. **Par:** 71/71. **Course Rating:** 71.3/69.1. **Slope:** 129/117. **Green Fee:** $22/$46. **Cart Fee:** $17/Person. **Walking Policy:** Walking at certain times. **Walkability:** 3. **Opened:** 1993. **Architect:** Arthur Hills. **Season:** Year-round. **To obtain tee times:** Call up to 7 days in advance. **Miscellaneous:** Reduced fees (weekdays, juniors), range (grass), credit cards (MC, V, AE), BF, FF.
Reader Comments: Good condition ... Very well maintained fairways and greens. A few blind greens ... Short tight and a challenge for all levels ... Use all your sticks ... Good value course that is in pretty good shape.

★★★ COUNTRY CLUB OF BEAUFORT

SP-8 Barnwell Dr., Beaufort, 29902, Beaufort County, (843)522-1605, (800)869-1617, 38 miles from Hilton Head. **Facility Holes:** 18. **Yards:** 6,506/4,764. **Par:** 72/72. **Course Rating:** 71.5/67.8. **Slope:** 130/120. **Green Fee:** $29/$45. **Cart Fee:** Included in green fee. **Walking Policy:** Walking at certain times. **Walkability:** 2. **Opened:** 1973. **Architect:** Russell Breeden. **Season:** Year-round. **To obtain tee times:** Call up to 4 days in advance. **Miscellaneous:** Reduced fees (twilight, juniors), range (grass), credit cards (MC, V, AE, D), BF, FF.
Reader Comments: Good golf, Nos. 17 & 18 great closers ... Fun course, good value ... Great pace of play and very low cost.

★★★★ COUNTRY CLUB OF HILTON HEAD

SP-70 Skull Creek Dr., Hilton Head Island, 29926, Beaufort County, (843)681-4653, 35 miles from Savannah. **Facility Holes:** 18. **Yards:** 6,919/5,373. **Par:** 72/72. **Course Rating:** 73.6/71.3. **Slope:** 132/123. **Green Fee:** $52/$85. **Cart Fee:** Included in green fee. **Walking Policy:** Walking at certain times. **Walkability:** 2. **Opened:** 1987. **Architect:** Rees Jones. **Season:** Year-round. **To obtain tee times:** Call up to 120 days in advance. **Miscellaneous:** Reduced fees (twilight, juniors), range (grass/mats), credit cards (MC, V, AE, DC), BF, FF.
Reader Comments: Top-notch condition, great challenge for low/high handicapper ... Long for women ... Interesting layout, challenge to play, enjoyed my round.

★½ COUNTRY CLUB OF SUMMERVILLE

SP-400 Country Club Blvd., Summerville, 29483, Dorchester County, (843)873-2210, 20 miles from Charleston. **E-mail:** ccsville@dycon.com. **Facility Holes:** 18. **Yards:** 6,001/5,400.

Par: 71/71. **Course Rating:** 68.8/68.9. **Slope:** 114/110. **Green Fee:** $17/$33. **Cart Fee:** $13/Person. **Walking Policy:** Walking at certain times. **Walkability:** 1. **Opened:** 1925. **Architect:** Ricciboni/Kemp. **Season:** Year-round. **High:** March-July. **To obtain tee times:** Call up to 10 days in advance. **Miscellaneous:** Reduced fees (weekdays, twilight, juniors), credit cards (MC, V, AE, D), BF, FF.

CRESCENT POINTE GOLF CLUB

PU-1 Crescent Pointe, Bluffton, 29910, Beaufort County, (843)341-2500, (888)292-7778, 9 miles from Hilton Head Island. **Facility Holes:** 18. **Yards:** 6,773/5,219. **Par:** 71/71. **Course Rating:** 72.9/70.2. **Slope:** 137/124. **Green Fee:** $39/$125. **Cart Fee:** Included in green fee. **Walking Policy:** Walking at certain times. **Walkability:** 2. **Opened:** 2000. **Architect:** Arnold Palmer. **Season:** Year-round. **To obtain tee times:** Call up to 365 days in advance. **Miscellaneous:** Reduced fees (twilight, juniors), range (grass), credit cards (MC, V, AE, D), BF, FF.

★★★★ CROWFIELD GOLF & COUNTRY CLUB *Value*

SP-300 Hamlet Circle, Goose Creek, 29445, Berkeley County, (843)764-4618, 20 miles from Charleston. **E-mail:** crowgolf@aol.com. **Web:** www.chrlstngolf.com. **Facility Holes:** 18. **Yards:** 7,003/5,682. **Par:** 72/72. **Course Rating:** 73.7/67.3. **Slope:** 134/121. **Green Fee:** $30/$69. **Cart Fee:** Included in green fee. **Walking Policy:** Walking at certain times. **Walkability:** 4. **Opened:** 1990. **Architect:** Bob Spence. **Season:** Year-round. **To obtain tee times:** Call golf shop. **Miscellaneous:** Reduced fees (weekdays, twilight), range (grass), credit cards (MC, V, AE, D). **Reader Comments:** Long and hard slope, great greens, a challenge for everyone … Back 9 layout is good … Great, challenging course run by an outstanding, friendly staff … Challenging par 5s, small greens … Tight course, demands shotmaking, not just bombing the tee shot … Tough from back tees.

★★½ CYPRESS BAY GOLF CLUB

R-Hwy. 17, North Myrtle Beach, 29566, Horry County, (843)249-1017, (800)833-5638, 7 miles from Myrtle Beach. **Facility Holes:** 18. **Yards:** 6,502/4,920. **Par:** 72/72. **Course Rating:** 71.2/69.0. **Slope:** 122/113. **Green Fee:** $28/$59. **Cart Fee:** $19/Person. **Walking Policy:** Walking at certain times. **Walkability:** 1. **Opened:** 1972. **Architect:** Russell Breeden. **Season:** Year-round. **To obtain tee times:** Call golf shop. **Miscellaneous:** Reduced fees (twilight), metal spikes.

DAUFUSKIE ISLAND CLUB & RESORT

R-P.O. Box 23285, Hilton Head Island, 29925, Beaufort County, (843)341-4810, (800)648-6778. **Web:** www.daufuskieresort.com. **Facility Holes:** 36. **Green Fee:** $80/$145. **Cart Fee:** Included in green fee. **Walking Policy:** Unrestricted walking. **Walkability:** 1. **Season:** Year-round. **To obtain tee times:** Call up to 45 days in advance. **Miscellaneous:** Reduced fees (guests, twilight), range (grass), lodging (86 rooms), credit cards (MC, V, AE, D, DC), BF, FF.
★★★★ **BLOODY POINT (18)**
Yards: 6,900/5,220. **Par:** 72/72. **Course Rating:** 73.2/69.7. **Slope:** 135/126. **Opened:** 1991. **Architect:** Tom Weiskopf/Jay Morrish.
Reader Comments: Park-like setting on unique island … When the wind blows, this is brutal … Enjoy the boat ride and great golf.
★★★★½ **MELROSE COURSE (18)** *Value, Condition+, Pace+*
Yards: 7,081/5,575. **Par:** 72/72. **Course Rating:** 74.2/72.3. **Slope:** 138/126. **Opened:** 1987. **Architect:** Jack Nicklaus.
Reader Comments: Great finishing holes, beautiful views … Best in Hilton Head … Beautiful, impeccable condition, a must play … Must use all 14 clubs … Loved that each hole is physically separate … Felt like I had my own private course.

DEER TRACK GOLF RESORT

R-1705 Platt Blvd., Surfside Beach, 29575, Horry County, (843)650-2146, (800)548-9186, 2 miles from Myrtle Beach. **Facility Holes:** 36. **Green Fee:** $8/$42. **Cart Fee:** $20/Cart. **Walking Policy:** Walking at certain times. **Walkability:** 1. **Opened:** 1974. **Architect:** Bob Toski/Porter Gibson. **Season:** Year-round. **To obtain tee times:** Call golf shop. **Miscellaneous:** Reduced fees (weekdays, guests, twilight, juniors), range (grass/mats), credit cards (MC, V, AE), BF, FF.
★★½ **SOUTH COURSE (18)**
Yards: 6,916/5,226. **Par:** 71/71. **Course Rating:** 72.9/70.6. **Slope:** 119/120.
★★ **TOSKI LINKS (18)**
Yards: 7,203/5,353. **Par:** 72/72. **Course Rating:** 73.5/69.6. **Slope:** 121/119.

★★★½ DIAMOND BACK GOLF CLUB

PU-615 Log Cabin Rd., Loris, 29569, Horry County, (843)756-3264, (877)600-3264, 20 miles from North Myrtle Beach. **E-mail:** rattle@sccoast.net. **Web:** www.diamondbackgolf.com. **Facility Holes:** 18. **Yards:** 6,928/4,945. **Par:** 72/72. **Course Rating:** 74.0/68.5. **Slope:** 139/121.

Green Fee: $5/$88. **Cart Fee:** $21/Person. **Walking Policy:** Mandatory carts. **Walkability:** 3. **Opened:** 1999. **Architect:** Russell Breeden. **Season:** Year-round. **High:** Feb.-May. **To obtain tee times:** Call golf shop. **Miscellaneous:** Reduced fees (juniors), range (grass), credit cards (MC, V, AE), BF, FF.
Reader Comments: I'd play this course over and over again … A difficult, demanding, driving course … Challenging greens, beautiful scenery, great condition, an incredible bargain … Short and tight … Greens are well taken care of and very fast but true …Some marvelous par 3s … A hidden luxury.

★★★★ **THE DUNES GOLF & BEACH CLUB** *Pace*
SP-9000 N. Ocean Blvd., Myrtle Beach, 29572, Horry County, (843)449-5914. **E-mail:** clifmannpga@aol.com. **Web:** www.dunesgolfandbeachclub.com. **Facility Holes:** 18. **Yards:** 7,165/5,390. **Par:** 72/72. **Course Rating:** 72.1/72.3. **Slope:** 141/132. **Green Fee:** $80/$133. **Cart Fee:** Included in green fee. **Walking Policy:** Unrestricted walking. **Walkability:** 2. **Opened:** 1948. **Architect:** Robert Trent Jones. **Season:** Year-round. **To obtain tee times:** Call golf shop. **Miscellaneous:** Range (grass), credit cards (MC, V, AE), BF, FF.
Notes: Ranked 5th in 2001 Best in State.
Reader Comments: Great layout, worth the price … Historic layout, beautiful greens, No. 13 is neat … A rare pleasure … Variety of shaped holes. Lot of sand and undulated greens. Some tight holes and some driver holes … A great course, very enjoyable even for a 20-handicapper … Doesn't get much better.

★★★½ **THE DUNES WEST GOLF CLUB**
SP-3535 Wando Plantation Way, Mount Pleasant, 29466, Charleston County, (843)856-9000, 10 miles from Charleston. **Web:** www.golfduneswest.com. **Facility Holes:** 18. **Yards:** 6,871/5,278. **Par:** 72/72. **Course Rating:** 73.5/69.2. **Slope:** 138/118. **Green Fee:** $39/$85. **Cart Fee:** Included in green fee. **Walking Policy:** Mandatory carts. **Walkability:** 2. **Opened:** 1991. **Architect:** Arthur Hills. **Season:** Year-round. **To obtain tee times:** Call up to 30 days in advance. **Miscellaneous:** Reduced fees (weekdays, guests, twilight, juniors), metal spikes, range (grass), credit cards (MC, V, AE), BF, FF.
Reader Comments: Forgiving layout, tough back 9 … Very good overall … Pretty clubhouse, nice course … Exceptional value, must have all the shots … Smooth roll on greens.

DUSTY HILLS COUNTRY CLUB
SP-225 Country Club Rd., Marion, 29571, Marion County, (843)423-2721, 20 miles from Florence. **Facility Holes:** 18. **Yards:** 6,120/4,995. **Par:** 72/74. **Course Rating:** 69.0/68.0. **Slope:** 114/101. **Green Fee:** $12/$26. **Cart Fee:** $12/Person. **Walking Policy:** Unrestricted walking. **Walkability:** 2. **Opened:** 1928. **Season:** Year-round. **To obtain tee times:** Call golf shop. **Miscellaneous:** Reduced fees (guests, seniors), range (grass), BF.

★★★ **EAGLE NEST GOLF CLUB**
PU-Hwy. 17 N., North Myrtle Beach, 29597, Horry County, (843)249-1449, (800)543-3113, 1 mile from North Myrtle Beach. **E-mail:** eaglenestgolf@worldnet.att.net. **Web:** www.golg-eagle.com. **Facility Holes:** 18. **Yards:** 6,901/5,105. **Par:** 72/72. **Course Rating:** 73.0/69.8. **Slope:** 128/117. **Green Fee:** $52. **Cart Fee:** Included in green fee. **Walking Policy:** Walking at certain times. **Walkability:** 3. **Opened:** 1972. **Architect:** Gene Hamm. **Season:** Year-round. **To obtain tee times:** Call golf shop. **Miscellaneous:** Reduced fees (twilight), metal spikes, range (grass/mats), credit cards (MC, V).
Reader Comments: Enjoyed playing the course … Great back 9, must work shots.

★★★½ **EAGLE'S POINTE GOLF CLUB**
PU-1 Eagle's Pointe Dr., Bluffton, 29910, Beaufort County, (843)686-4457, (888)325-1833, 7 miles from Hilton Head. **Web:** www.eaglespointe.com. **Facility Holes:** 18. **Yards:** 6,738/5,210. **Par:** 71/71. **Course Rating:** 72.5/69.8. **Slope:** 130/119. **Green Fee:** $50/$86. **Cart Fee:** Included in green fee. **Walking Policy:** Walking at certain times. **Walkability:** 1. **Opened:** 1998. **Architect:** Davis Love III. **Season:** Year-round. **To obtain tee times:** Call golf shop. **Miscellaneous:** Reduced fees (weekdays, twilight, juniors), range (grass), credit cards (MC, V, AE, D), BF, FF.
Reader Comments: This will be an outstanding course. Deceiving doglegs and par 3s … Great fairways … Great diversity of holes … Enjoyable.

★★½ **EASTPORT GOLF CLUB**
PU-Hwy. 17, North Myrtle Beach, 29597, Horry County, (843)249-3997, (800)334-9035, 2 miles from North Myrtle Beach. **Facility Holes:** 18. **Yards:** 6,202/4,698. **Par:** 70/70. **Course Rating:** 69.1/65.7. **Slope:** 116/114. **Green Fee:** $6/$33. **Cart Fee:** $20/Cart. **Walking Policy:** Mandatory carts. **Walkability:** 3. **Opened:** 1988. **Architect:** Denis Griffiths & Assoc. **Season:** Year-round. **High:** Feb.-May. **To obtain tee times:** Call up to 1 day in advance. **Miscellaneous:** Reduced fees (weekdays, guests, juniors), credit cards (MC, V), FF.

★★½ EDISTO BEACH GOLF CLUB
R-24 Fairway Dr., Edisto Island, 29438, Colleton County, (843)869-1111, 45 miles from Charleston. **Facility Holes:** 18. **Yards:** 6,212/5,306. **Par:** 71/72. **Course Rating:** 69.9/70.3. **Slope:** 127/120. **Green Fee:** $41/$48. **Cart Fee:** Included in green fee. **Walking Policy:** Walking at certain times. **Walkability:** 1. **Opened:** 1973. **Architect:** Tom Jackson. **Season:** Year-round. **To obtain tee times:** Call up to 30 days in advance. **Miscellaneous:** Reduced fees (weekdays, juniors), credit cards (MC, V, D), FF.

★★ FALCON'S LAIR GOLF COURSE
SP-1308 Falcon's Dr., Walhalla, 29691, Oconee County, (864)638-0000, 40 miles from Greenville. **Facility Holes:** 18. **Yards:** 6,955/5,238. **Par:** 72/74. **Course Rating:** 73.2/70.6. **Slope:** 134/123. **Green Fee:** $18/$30. **Cart Fee:** $12/Person. **Walking Policy:** Walking at certain times. **Walkability:** 5. **Opened:** 1991. **Architect:** Harry Bowers. **Season:** Year-round. **High:** April-Oct. **To obtain tee times:** Call golf shop. **Miscellaneous:** Reduced fees (weekdays, twilight, seniors, juniors), range (grass/mats), credit cards (MC, V, AE), FF.

★★★ FORT MILL GOLF CLUB
SP-101 Country Club Dr., P.O. Box 336, Fort Mill, 29716, York County, (803)547-2044, 15 miles from Charlotte. **Facility Holes:** 18. **Yards:** 6,826/5,427. **Par:** 72/72. **Course Rating:** 72.7/71.6. **Slope:** 123/125. **Green Fee:** $19/$30. **Cart Fee:** $14/Person. **Walking Policy:** Walking at certain times. **Walkability:** 2. **Opened:** 1948. **Architect:** Donald Ross/George Cobb. **Season:** Year-round. **High:** April-Oct. **To obtain tee times:** Call up to 3 days in advance. **Miscellaneous:** Reduced fees (weekdays, seniors), range (grass), credit cards (MC, V, D), BF, FF.
Reader Comments: Donald Ross design on front 9, love it … Good course to walk, well kept.

★★½ FOX CREEK GOLF CLUB
SP-Hwy. 15 S., Lydia, 29079, Darlington County, (843)332-0613, 20 miles from Florence. **Facility Holes:** 18. **Yards:** 6,903/5,271. **Par:** 72/72. **Course Rating:** 72.7/67.9. **Slope:** 128/106. **Green Fee:** $20/$25. **Cart Fee:** Included in green fee. **Walking Policy:** Walking at certain times. **Walkability:** 1. **Opened:** 1988. **Architect:** James Goodson/Woody Morgan. **Season:** Year-round. **To obtain tee times:** Call golf shop. **Miscellaneous:** Reduced fees (weekdays, guests, seniors, juniors), range (grass), credit cards (MC, V, D).

★★★ FOXBORO GOLF CLUB
SP-1438 Wash Davis Rd., Summerton, 29148, Clarendon County, (803)478-7000, (800)468-7061, 75 miles from Charleston. **Facility Holes:** 18. **Yards:** 6,889/5,386. **Par:** 72/72. **Course Rating:** 71.9/68.4. **Slope:** 121/114. **Green Fee:** $15/$29. **Cart Fee:** Included in green fee. **Walking Policy:** Mandatory carts. **Walkability:** 1. **Opened:** 1988. **Architect:** Porter Gibson. **Season:** Year-round. **High:** Feb.-May. **To obtain tee times:** Call up to 30 days in advance. **Miscellaneous:** Reduced fees (juniors), range (grass), credit cards (MC, V, AE, D).
Reader Comments: Have done a lot of work on drainage … Open links-style course … Flat course, great greens.

FRIPP ISLAND RESORT
R-88 Ocean Creek Blvd., Fripp Island, 29920, Beaufort County, (843)838-1576, (800)845-4100, 19 miles from Beaufort. **Web:** www.frippislandresort.com. **Facility Holes:** 36. **Cart Fee:** Included in green fee. **Walking Policy:** Unrestricted walking. **Season:** Year-round. **Miscellaneous:** Range (grass), lodging (300 rooms), BF, FF.
★★★★½ **OCEAN CREEK (18)** *Value, Pace*
Yards: 6,643/4,884. **Par:** 71/71. **Course Rating:** 72.0/69.5. **Slope:** 132/121. **Green Fee:** $44/$84. **Walkability:** 3. **Opened:** 1995. **Architect:** Davis Love III. **High:** March-Oct. **To obtain tee times:** Call golf shop. **Miscellaneous:** Reduced fees (guests, twilight, juniors), credit cards (Resort charge card only).
Reader Comments: Very interesting course, challenging … Outstanding scenery, greens excellent.
★★★★ **OCEAN POINT GOLF LINKS (18)** *Pace*
Yards: 6,556/4,908. **Par:** 72/72. **Course Rating:** 72.2/69.5. **Slope:** 132/113. **Green Fee:** $55/$84. **Walkability:** 2. **Opened:** 1962. **Architect:** George W. Cobb. **High:** April-Nov. **To obtain tee times:** Call up to 30 days in advance. **Miscellaneous:** Reduced fees (weekdays, guests, twilight, juniors), metal spikes, credit cards (MC, V, AE, D).
Reader Comments: Beachy and forest settings on same course … Great course. Would like to play again … Wind blows always, beautiful views … Back 9 is the best, ocean scenic.

★★★★ GLEN DORNOCH WATERWAY GOLF LINKS *Service*
R-4840 Glen Dornoch Way, Little River, 29566, Horry County, (843)249-2541, (800)717-8784, 15 miles from Myrtle Beach. **E-mail:** glen@sccoast.net. **Web:** www.glendornoch.com. **Facility Holes:** 18. **Yards:** 6,850/5,002. **Par:** 72/72. **Course Rating:** 73.2/69.8. **Slope:** 141/129. **Green Fee:** $48/$103. **Cart Fee:** $20/Person. **Walking Policy:** Mandatory carts. **Walkability:** 3.

Opened: 1996. **Architect:** Clyde Johnston. **Season:** Year-round. **To obtain tee times:** Call golf shop. **Miscellaneous:** Range (grass), credit cards (MC, V, AE).
Notes: Ranked 22nd in 1999 Best in State.
Reader Comments: Awesome course. Very difficult from the tips. Better than advertised … Great all-around golf experience. Beautiful clubhouse overlooks scenic waterway, as do several holes. Very friendly staff … No. 16 will test you … Very tight course … Strategic shot placement … Wide variety of holes.

★★★½ GOLDEN BEAR GOLF CLUB

SP-72 Golden Bear Way, Hilton Head, 29926, Beaufort County, (843)689-2200, 42 miles from Savannah. **Web:** www.goldenbeargolfclub.com. **Facility Holes:** 18. **Yards:** 7,014/4,974. **Par:** 72/72. **Course Rating:** 73.7/69.3. **Slope:** 132/120. **Green Fee:** $49/$74. **Cart Fee:** $21/Person. **Walking Policy:** Walking at certain times. **Walkability:** 2. **Opened:** 1992. **Architect:** Bruce Burland. **Season:** Year-round. **To obtain tee times:** Call golf shop. **Miscellaneous:** Reduced fees (guests, twilight, juniors), metal spikes, range (grass), credit cards (MC, V, AE).
Reader Comments: Places a premium on accuracy off the tee … Links style, different course … Loved the rocking chairs overlooking the putting green. Great practice facility … Nice variety of holes, no two alike. Conditions excellent. One of the best values on Hilton Head.

★★ GOLDEN HILLS GOLF & COUNTRY CLUB

SP-100 Scotland Dr., Lexington, 29072, Lexington County, (803)957-3355, 15 miles from Columbia. **Facility Holes:** 18. **Yards:** 6,561/4,951. **Par:** 71/71. **Course Rating:** 71.2/68.0. **Slope:** 134/113. **Green Fee:** $19/$40. **Cart Fee:** $10/Person. **Walking Policy:** Unrestricted walking. **Walkability:** 2. **Opened:** 1988. **Architect:** Ron Garl. **Season:** Year-round. **To obtain tee times:** Call golf shop. **Miscellaneous:** Reduced fees (weekdays), metal spikes, credit cards (MC, V), BF, FF.

GOLF CLUB AT WESCOTT PLANTATION

PU-5000 Wescott Club Dr., North Charleston, 29485, Dorchester County, (843)871-2135, (866)214-4653, 7 miles from North Charleston. **E-mail:** trobertson@bellsouth.net. **Facility Holes:** 27. **Green Fee:** $37/$47. **Cart Fee:** Included in green fee. **Walking Policy:** Unrestricted walking. **Walkability:** 2. **Opened:** 2000. **Architect:** Dr. Michael Hurdzan. **Season:** Year-round. **High:** March-May. **To obtain tee times:** Call up to 14 days in advance. **Miscellaneous:** Reduced fees (twilight, seniors, juniors), range (grass), credit cards (MC, V, AE), BF, FF.
BURN KILL/BLACK ROBIN (18 Combo)
Yards: 7,197/5,088. **Par:** 72/72.
OAK FOREST/BLACK ROBIN (18 Combo)
Yards: 7,197/5,088. **Par:** 72/72.
OAK FOREST/BURN KILL (18 Combo)
Yards: 7,197/5,088. **Par:** 72/72. **Course Rating:** 74.1/70.2. **Slope:** 135/114.

★★★½ THE GOLF CLUB OF SOUTH CAROLINA AT CRICKENTREE

SP-1084 Langford Rd., Blythewood, 29016, Richland County, (803)754-8600, 12 miles from Columbia. **Web:** www.simgrp.com. **Facility Holes:** 18. **Yards:** 7,002/4,791. **Par:** 72/72. **Course Rating:** 74.2/71.3. **Slope:** 140/130. **Green Fee:** $39/$49. **Cart Fee:** Included in green fee. **Walking Policy:** Mandatory carts. **Walkability:** 4. **Opened:** 1987. **Architect:** Ken Killian. **Season:** Year-round. **High:** Feb.-April. **To obtain tee times:** Call golf shop. **Miscellaneous:** Reduced fees (weekdays, twilight, seniors, juniors), range (grass), credit cards (MC, V), BF, FF.
Reader Comments: Toughest course I have ever played … Challenging layout … The more you play it, the better you'll play it … Attractive … Bring your 'A' game … Could play this course 1,000 times and not get bored.

GRANDE DUNES GOLF CLUB

PU-8700 Golf Village Lane, Myrtle Beach, 29579, Horry County, (843)449-7070. **Web:** www.grandedunes.com. **Facility Holes:** 18. **Yards:** 7,618/5,353. **Par:** 72/72. **Course Rating:** 77.3/71.2. **Slope:** 142/123. **Green Fee:** $79/$160. **Cart Fee:** Included in green fee. **Opened:** 2001. **Architect:** Roger Rulewich. **Season:** Year-round. **To obtain tee times:** Call golf shop.

★★★★ HARBOUR TOWN GOLF LINKS *Service*

R-11 Lighthouse Lane, Hilton Head Island, 29928, Beaufort County, (843)363-4485, (800)955-8337, 45 miles from Savannah. **Web:** www.seapines.com. **Facility Holes:** 18. **Yards:** 6,916/5,019. **Par:** 71/71. **Course Rating:** 74.0/69.0. **Slope:** 136/117. **Green Fee:** $165/$215. **Cart Fee:** Included in green fee. **Walking Policy:** Unrestricted walking. **Walkability:** 1. **Opened:** 1969. **Architect:** Pete Dye. **Season:** Year-round. **To obtain tee times:** Call golf shop. **Miscellaneous:** Reduced fees (guests, juniors), range (grass), credit cards (MC, V, AE, D).
Notes: Ranked 66th in 2001-2002 America's 100 Greatest; 1st in 2001 Best in State; 8th in 1996 America's Top 75 Upscale Courses.
Reader Comments: The renovation is outstanding … A bit long for this amateur even from the forward tees. No. 18 is just as beautiful as it looks on television … A great walk.

HARBOUR VIEW GOLF COMPLEX
PU-901 Hwy. 17, Little River, 29566, Horry County, (843)249-9117. **Facility Holes:** 9. **Yards:** 2,138/2,138. **Par:** 27/27. **Green Fee:** $15. **Walking Policy:** Unrestricted walking. **Walkability:** 1. **Season:** Year-round. **High:** June-Aug. **To obtain tee times:** Call golf shop. **Miscellaneous:** Range (grass/mats), credit cards (MC, V), BF, FF.

★★★★½ HEATHER GLEN GOLF LINKS *Pace*
PU-Hwy. 17 N., Little River, 29566, Horry County, (843)249-9000, (800)868-4536, 12 miles from Myrtle Beach. **E-mail:** glen@sccoast.net. **Web:** www.heatherglen.com. **Facility Holes:** 27. **Green Fee:** $30/$81. **Cart Fee:** $20/Person. **Walking Policy:** Mandatory carts. **Walkability:** 2. **Opened:** 1987. **Architect:** Willard Byrd/Clyde Johnston. **Season:** Year-round. **To obtain tee times:** Call golf shop. **Miscellaneous:** Reduced fees (juniors), range (grass), credit cards (MC, V, AE).
RED/BLUE (18 Combo)
Yards: 6,771/5,053. **Par:** 72/72. **Course Rating:** 72.4/69.3. **Slope:** 127/117.
RED/WHITE (18 Combo)
Yards: 6,783/5,101. **Par:** 72/72. **Course Rating:** 72.4/69.3. **Slope:** 130/117.
WHITE/BLUE (18 Combo)
Yards: 6,822/5,127. **Par:** 72/72. **Course Rating:** 72.4/69.3. **Slope:** 130/117.
Reader Comments: Great layout that is aging well. On a busy day, still got around in four hours … Above average for the area … Very tight and tough … Should get more notice than it does, but I'm happy if the crowds stay away … Best customer service … Classic golf holes you remember, a challenge.

★★★½ HERITAGE CLUB
PU-Hwy. 17 S., Pawleys Island, 29585, Georgetown County, (843)237-3424, (800)377-2315, 20 miles from Myrtle Beach. **Facility Holes:** 18. **Yards:** 7,100/5,325. **Par:** 71/71. **Course Rating:** 74.2/71.0. **Slope:** 137/125. **Green Fee:** $43/$105. **Cart Fee:** $21/Person. **Walking Policy:** Mandatory carts. **Opened:** 1986. **Architect:** Dan Maples. **Season:** Year-round. **High:** March-May. **To obtain tee times:** Call up to 365 days in advance. **Miscellaneous:** Reduced fees (guests), metal spikes, range (grass/mats), credit cards (MC, V, AE).
Notes: Ranked 21st in 1999 Best in State.
Reader Comments: Great layout. Great clubhouse … Lots of water … Great back 9 … Felt guilty to leave a divot … Think you are a good putter? … Not overdone architecture like much of Myrtle Beach. Wonderful live oaks. Solid sequence of par 5s. Wonderful entrance is like Augusta.

★★★½ HERON POINT GOLF CLUB
R-6980 Blue Heron Blvd., Myrtle Beach, 29588, Horry County, (803)650-6664, (800)786-1671. **E-mail:** golfinsc@msn.com. **Web:** heronpointgolfclub.com. **Facility Holes:** 18. **Yards:** 6,477/4,734. **Par:** 72/72. **Course Rating:** 71.0/69.2. **Slope:** 120/121. **Green Fee:** $12/$38. **Cart Fee:** Included in green fee. **Walking Policy:** Unrestricted walking. **Walkability:** 2. **Opened:** 1989. **Architect:** Willard Byrd. **Season:** Year-round. **High:** Feb.-May. **To obtain tee times:** Call golf shop. **Miscellaneous:** Reduced fees (weekdays, guests, twilight, seniors, juniors), range (grass), credit cards (MC, V, D), BF, FF.
Reader Comments: Nice course but tight, good service … Have to place shots … A good playable course.

★★★½ HICKORY KNOB GOLF CLUB
R-Rte. 4, Box 199-B, McCormick, 29835, McCormick County, (864)391-2450, (800)491-1764, 8 miles from McCormick. **E-mail:** hickory-knobsp@prt.state.sc.us. **Facility Holes:** 18. **Yards:** 6,560/4,905. **Par:** 72/72. **Course Rating:** 71.9/70.3. **Slope:** 132/124. **Green Fee:** $13/$18. **Cart Fee:** $12/Person. **Walking Policy:** Unrestricted walking. **Walkability:** 3. **Architect:** Tom Jackson. **Season:** Year-round. **High:** March-May. **To obtain tee times:** Call golf shop. **Miscellaneous:** Reduced fees (weekdays, twilight, seniors, juniors), range (grass), lodging (77 rooms), credit cards (MC, V), BF, FF.
Reader Comments: Even though this course is operated by the state parks department, it stays in great shape throughout the year. You'd swear it's a resort by the way it looks and plays … Tough … Outstanding value.

HIDDEN CYPRESS GOLF CLUB
PU-672 Col. Thomas Heyward Rd., Bluffton, 29910, Beaufort County, (843)705-4999, (866)705-4999. **E-mail:** edlinm@delwebb.com. **Facility Holes:** 18. **Yards:** 6,946/4,984. **Par:** 72/72. **Course Rating:** 73.2/68.3. **Slope:** 133/114. **Green Fee:** $50/$80. **Cart Fee:** $15/Person. **Walking Policy:** Walking at certain times. **Walkability:** 2. **Opened:** 2000. **Architect:** Mark McCumber/Jeff Lucovsky. **Season:** Year-round. **To obtain tee times:** Call up to 60 days in advance. **Miscellaneous:** Reduced fees (guests, juniors), range (grass), credit cards (MC, V, AE, D), BF, FF.

★ HILLANDALE GOLF COURSE

PU-105 S. Parker Rd., Greenville, 29609, Greenville County, (864)250-1700, 8 miles from Greenville. **Facility Holes:** 18. **Yards:** 5,545/5,545. **Par:** 72/72. **Green Fee:** $15/$20. **Cart Fee:** Included in green fee. **Walking Policy:** Unrestricted walking. **Walkability:** 2. **Opened:** 1930. **Season:** Year-round. **High:** June-Nov. **To obtain tee times:** Call golf shop. **Miscellaneous:** Reduced fees (weekdays, seniors).

★★½ HILLCREST GOLF CLUB

PU-1099 Old St. Matthews Rd., Orangeburg, 29116, Orangeburg County, (803)533-6030, 2 miles from Orangeburg. **Facility Holes:** 18. **Yards:** 6,722/5,208. **Par:** 72/72. **Course Rating:** 72.0/69.1. **Slope:** 128/117. **Green Fee:** $13/$15. **Cart Fee:** $10/Person. **Walking Policy:** Unrestricted walking. **Walkability:** 1. **Opened:** 1972. **Architect:** Russell Breeden. **Season:** Year-round. **To obtain tee times:** Call golf shop. **Miscellaneous:** Reduced fees (juniors), metal spikes, range (grass/mats), credit cards (MC, V, AE, D), BF, FF.

★★★½ HILTON HEAD NATIONAL GOLF CLUB

PU-60 Hilton Head National Dr., Bluffton, 29910, Beaufort County, (843)842-5900, (888)955-1234, 1 mile from Hilton Head Island. **E-mail:** hhngc@hargray.com. **Web:** www.scratch-golf.com. **Facility Holes:** 27. **Green Fee:** $40/$105. **Cart Fee:** Included in green fee. **Walking Policy:** Mandatory carts. **Walkability:** 1. **Opened:** 1989. **Architect:** Gary Player/Bobby Weed. **Season:** Year-round. **To obtain tee times:** Call golf shop. **Miscellaneous:** Reduced fees (weekdays, guests, twilight, juniors), metal spikes, range (grass), credit cards (MC, V, AE), BF, FF.
NATIONAL/PLAYER (18 Combo)
Yards: 6,659/4,563. **Par:** 72/72. **Course Rating:** 72.0/66.2. **Slope:** 128/106.
PLAYER/WEED (18 Combo)
Yards: 6,718/4,682. **Par:** 72/72. **Course Rating:** 71.7/66.0. **Slope:** 132/111.
WEED/NATIONAL (18 Combo)
Yards: 6,655/4,631. **Par:** 72/72. **Course Rating:** 71.5/66.0. **Slope:** 125/108.
Reader Comments: Always in excellent shape … Hourglass double green on 9, 18 kind of funky … Very challenging, especially, the Player 9. The greens were like putting on carpet. Very picturesque and the staff was great … Some beautiful, but challenging holes … Requires accuracy, not length.

★★★½ HUNTER'S CREEK GOLF & COUNTRY CLUB

SP-702 Hunter's Creek Blvd., Greenwood, 29649, Greenwood County, (864)223-9286, (888)763-6741, 47 miles from Greenville. **E-mail:** steph@emeraldis.com. **Web:** hunter-screekcc.com. **Facility Holes:** 27. **Green Fee:** $28/$50. **Cart Fee:** Included in green fee. **Walking Policy:** Walking at certain times. **Walkability:** 4. **Opened:** 1994. **Architect:** Tom Jackson. **Season:** Year-round. **To obtain tee times:** Call golf shop. **Miscellaneous:** Reduced fees (weekdays, juniors), range (grass), credit cards (MC, V), FF.
MAPLE/WILLOW (18 Combo)
Yards: 6,999/4,977. **Par:** 72/72. **Course Rating:** 73.6/67.5. **Slope:** 133/119.
OAK/MAPLE (18 Combo)
Yards: 6,920/5,000. **Par:** 72/72. **Course Rating:** 73.6/67.8. **Slope:** 133/122.
WILLOW/OAK (18 Combo)
Yards: 6,837/4,931. **Par:** 72/72. **Course Rating:** 73.6/67.8. **Slope:** 133/122.
Reader Comments: Very enjoyable, good layout … 27 of the toughest.

★★★ INDIAN RIVER GOLF CLUB

SP-200 Congaree Hunt Dr., West Columbia, 29170, Lexington County, (803)955-0080, 15 miles from Columbia. **Facility Holes:** 18. **Yards:** 6,507/4,643. **Par:** 71/71. **Course Rating:** 71.7/66.9. **Slope:** 133/113. **Green Fee:** $17/$23. **Cart Fee:** Included in green fee. **Walking Policy:** Walking at certain times. **Walkability:** 4. **Opened:** 1992. **Architect:** Lyndell Young. **Season:** Year-round. **High:** March-May. **To obtain tee times:** Call golf shop. **Miscellaneous:** Reduced fees (weekdays, guests, twilight, seniors, juniors), metal spikes, range (grass), credit cards (MC, V, AE).
Reader Comments: Good layout, with spacious fairways … In middle of nowhere, good deal for price.

★★★ INDIAN WELLS GOLF CLUB

PU-100 Woodlake Dr., Garden City, 29576, Horry County, (843)651-1505, (800)833-6337, 10 miles from Myrtle Beach. **Facility Holes:** 18. **Yards:** 6,624/4,872. **Par:** 72/72. **Course Rating:** 71.9/68.2. **Slope:** 125/118. **Green Fee:** $5/$40. **Cart Fee:** $18/Person. **Walking Policy:** Walking at certain times. **Walkability:** 2. **Opened:** 1984. **Architect:** Gene Hamm. **Season:** Year-round. **To obtain tee times:** Call golf shop. **Miscellaneous:** Reduced fees (guests, twilight, juniors), range (grass), credit cards (MC, V, D).
Reader Comments: Open and flat course … Water on 15 of 18 holes … Good greens.

SOUTH CAROLINA

★★ INDIGO CREEK GOLF PLANTATION
PU-P.O. Box 15437, Surfside Beach, 29587, Horry County, (843)650-0381, (800)833-6337, 10 miles from Myrtle Beach. **Facility Holes:** 18. **Yards:** 6,750/4,921. **Par:** 72/72. **Course Rating:** 72.4/69.7. **Slope:** 134/126. **Green Fee:** $26/$60. **Cart Fee:** Included in green fee. **Opened:** 1990. **Architect:** Willard Byrd. **Season:** Year-round. **To obtain tee times:** Call golf shop. **Miscellaneous:** Reduced fees (twilight), metal spikes, range (grass), credit cards (MC, V, D).

THE INTERNATIONAL CLUB
PU-1560 Tournament Blvd., Murrells Inlet, 29576, Georgetown County, (843)651-9995. **Facility Holes:** 18. **Yards:** 6,857/5,639. **Par:** 72/72. **Course Rating:** 72.8/71.0. **Slope:** 131/120. **Green Fee:** $40/$80. **Cart Fee:** Included in green fee. **Opened:** 2000. **Architect:** Willard Byrd. **Season:** Year-round. **To obtain tee times:** Call golf shop.

★★★★ INTERNATIONAL WORLD TOUR GOLF LINKS
PU-2000 World Tour Blvd., Myrtle Beach, 29579, Horry County, (843)236-2000, (877)377-7773. **E-mail:** info@worldtourmb.com. **Web:** www.worldtourmb.com. **Facility Holes:** 27. **Green Fee:** $105/$160. **Cart Fee:** Included in green fee. **Walking Policy:** Unrestricted walking. **Walkability:** 1. **Opened:** 1999. **Architect:** Mel Graham. **Season:** Year-round. **To obtain tee times:** Call up to 365 days in advance. **Miscellaneous:** Reduced fees (weekdays), range (grass), included in fee), credit cards (MC, V, AE), BF, FF.
CHAMPIONSHIP/INTERNATIONAL (18)
Yards: 6,688/5,129. **Par:** 72/72. **Course Rating:** 72.9/70.2. **Slope:** 133/117.
INTERNATIONAL/WORLD TOUR (18)
Yards: 6,633/4,955. **Par:** 72/72. **Course Rating:** 72.3/69.0. **Slope:** 135/115.
OPEN/CHAMPIONSHIP (18)
Yards: 6,525/5,344. **Par:** 72/72. **Course Rating:** 72.2/71.4. **Slope:** 130/120.
Reader Comments: Meet some great and famous holes … Holes similar in style to the real hole, all in all, they did a nice job … They make you feel as if they actually enjoy their job and care that you have a great experience … Nice creation, fun to play, price high … Easy course, despite championship holes.

★★½ ISLAND GREEN GOLF CLUB
PU-455 Sunehanna Dr., Unit STE-1, Myrtle Beach, 29575, Horry County, (843)650-2186. **Facility Holes:** 27. **Green Fee:** $25/$71. **Cart Fee:** $21/Cart. **Walking Policy:** Walking at certain times. **Walkability:** 3. **Opened:** 1979. **Architect:** William Mooney. **Season:** Year-round. **To obtain tee times:** Call golf shop. **Miscellaneous:** Reduced fees (twilight, juniors), credit cards (MC, V).
DOGWOOD/HOLLY (18 Combo)
Yards: 6,200/4,610. **Par:** 72/72. **Course Rating:** 66.4/66.8. **Slope:** 115/116.
DOGWOOD/TALL OAKS (18 Combo)
Yards: 6,012/4,596. **Par:** 72/72. **Course Rating:** 69.0/66.8. **Slope:** 118/115.
HOLLY/TALL OAKS (18 Combo)
Yards: 6,243/4,704. **Par:** 72/72. **Course Rating:** 67.0/67.0. **Slope:** 115/115.

★★★ ISLAND WEST GOLF CLUB
R-U.S. Hwy. 278, Bluffton, 29910, Beaufort County, (843)689-6660, 25 miles from Savannah. **Facility Holes:** 18. **Yards:** 6,803/4,938. **Par:** 72/72. **Course Rating:** 72.1/66.5. **Slope:** 129/116. **Green Fee:** $39/$79. **Cart Fee:** Included in green fee. **Walking Policy:** Mandatory carts. **Walkability:** 1. **Opened:** 1991. **Architect:** Fuzzy Zoeller/Clyde Johnston. **Season:** Year-round. **To obtain tee times:** Call golf shop. **Miscellaneous:** Reduced fees (guests, twilight, juniors), range (grass), credit cards (MC, V, AE, D), BF, FF.
Reader Comments: Good course, no houses lining the fairways … Very playable for all skill levels, very attractive.

KIAWAH ISLAND RESORT
R-12 Kiawah Beach Dr., Kiawah Island, 29455, Charleston County, (843)768-2121, (888)854-2924, 21 miles from Charleston. **E-mail:** mike_vegis@kiawahresort.com. **Web:** www.kiawahgolf.com. **Facility Holes:** 90. **Walking Policy:** Unrestricted walking. **Walkability:** 2. **Season:** Year-round. **High:** March-Nov. **To obtain tee times:** Call golf shop. **Miscellaneous:** Reduced fees (guests, twilight, juniors), range (grass), lodging (800 rooms), credit cards (MC, V, AE, D, DC), BF, FF.
★★★★½ COUGAR POINT (18) *Pace*
Yards: 6,875/4,776. **Par:** 72/72. **Course Rating:** 73.0/67.6. **Slope:** 134/118. **Green Fee:** $89/$149. **Cart Fee:** Included in green fee. **Opened:** 1996. **Architect:** Gary Player.
Reader Comments: Not as well known but every bit as good as the resort's other courses … Since redone by Player, absolutely great … Great variety of holes … The holes are challenging and demand some rigorous thinking before each shot is struck.

★★★½ **OAK POINT GOLF COURSE** (18) *Pace*
Yards: 6,759/4,956. **Par:** 72/72. **Course Rating:** 73.8/69.8. **Slope:** 140/121. **Green Fee:** $55/$90. **Cart Fee:** Included in green fee. **Opened:** 1989. **Architect:** Clyde Johnston.
Reader Comments: Inexpensive, quiet and beautiful! ... Wonderful layout, very underrated ... Mostly good holes.

★★★★★ **THE OCEAN COURSE** (18) *Condition*
Yards: 7,296/5,327. **Par:** 72/72. **Course Rating:** 78.0/72.9. **Slope:** 152/133. **Green Fee:** $160/$245. **Cart Fee:** Included in green fee. **Opened:** 1991. **Architect:** Pete Dye.
Notes: Ranked 67th in 2001-2002 America's 100 Greatest; 2nd in 2001 Best in State; 7th in 1996 America's Top 75 Upscale Courses.
Reader Comments: Now that the course has been renovated it's a lot easier ... Has to one of prettiest and toughest golf courses anywhere ... Great course in an awesome setting. Not for the faint of heart. Pete Dye at his best ... Wind is greatest challenge ... Mentally exhausting, great par 3s.

★★★★½ **OSPREY POINT** (18) *Pace*
Yards: 6,871/5,023. **Par:** 72/72. **Course Rating:** 72.9/70.0. **Slope:** 137/121. **Green Fee:** $90/$179. **Cart Fee:** Included in green fee. **Opened:** 1988. **Architect:** Tom Fazio.
Reader Comments: Beautiful course, beautiful clubhouse, excellent service, polite staff, but watch out for the alligators in the drop areas! ... Manicured to the 'nth' degree with plenty of challenging risk/reward holes ... Expensive but outstanding golf.

★★★★ **TURTLE POINT** (18) *Pace*
Yards: 7,054/5,210. **Par:** 72/72. **Course Rating:** 74.2/71.5. **Slope:** 141/126. **Green Fee:** $85/$145. **Opened:** 1981. **Architect:** Jack Nicklaus. **High:** March-Nov.
Reader Comments: New greens. The oceanside holes are great, and all in all a great experience ... Some out of bounds area near the fairway edges ... Nicklaus' renovations make it one of the top courses in South Carolina, rivaling The Ocean Course.

LADY'S ISLAND COUNTRY CLUB
SP-139 Frances Marion Circle, Beaufort, 29902, Beaufort County, (843)524-3635, 7 miles from Beaufort. **Web:** www.liccgolf.com. **Facility Holes:** 36. **Green Fee:** $35/$39. **Cart Fee:** Included in green fee. **Walking Policy:** Walking at certain times. **Walkability:** 1. **Opened:** 1971. **Season:** Year-round. **To obtain tee times:** Call golf shop. **Miscellaneous:** Range (grass), credit cards (MC, V, AE, D).
MARSH COURSE (18)
Yards: 6,000/5,192. **Par:** 72/72. **Course Rating:** 67.4/68.4. **Slope:** 104/107.
★½ **PINES COURSE** (18)
Yards: 7,003/5,357. **Par:** 72/72. **Course Rating:** 73.4/71.0. **Slope:** 124/126.

★★★½ **LAKE MARION GOLF CLUB**
R-P.O. Box 160, Santee, 29142, Orangeburg County, (803)854-2554, (800)344-6534, 50 miles from Columbia. **E-mail:** santeegolf@aol. **Web:** santeegolf@aol. **Facility Holes:** 18. **Yards:** 6,670/5,254. **Par:** 72/72. **Course Rating:** 72.1/69.8. **Slope:** 121/112. **Green Fee:** $25/$48. **Cart Fee:** Included in green fee. **Walking Policy:** Mandatory carts. **Walkability:** 3. **Opened:** 1979. **Architect:** Eddie Riccoboni. **Season:** Year-round. **High:** Feb.-June. **To obtain tee times:** Call golf shop. **Miscellaneous:** Reduced fees (juniors), metal spikes, range (grass/mats), credit cards (MC, V, AE), FF.
Reader Comments: Good for price ... Old course, tight, fun to play ... Somewhat long ... Super deal ... Interesting and fun to play ... Tough par 4s, uphill approaches, nice greens.

★★★½ **LAKEWOOD LINKS GOLF CLUB**
SP-3600 Greenview Pkwy., Sumter, 29150, Sumter County, (803)481-5700, 40 miles from Columbia. **E-mail:** slinkinc@ftc-i.net. **Web:** http://www.geocities.com/augusta/fairway/7462. **Facility Holes:** 18. **Yards:** 6,857/5,042. **Par:** 72/72. **Course Rating:** 71.7/68.2. **Slope:** 123/116. **Green Fee:** $20/$35. **Cart Fee:** Included in green fee. **Walking Policy:** Mandatory carts. **Walkability:** 2. **Opened:** 1989. **Architect:** J. Porter Gibson. **Season:** Year-round. **To obtain tee times:** Call up to 365 days in advance. **Miscellaneous:** Reduced fees (weekdays, guests, twilight, seniors, juniors), range (grass), credit cards (MC, V), BF, FF.
Reader Comments: Very nice course to play, excellent condition ... Staff great ... Water, water everywhere.

★★★ **LEGEND OAK'S PLANTATION GOLF CLUB**
SP-118 Legend Oaks Way, Summerville, 29485, Dorchester County, (843)821-4077, (888)821-4077, 19 miles from Charleston. **Facility Holes:** 18. **Yards:** 6,974/4,945. **Par:** 72/72. **Course Rating:** 72.3/69.4. **Slope:** 124/116. **Green Fee:** $30/$48. **Walking Policy:** Walking at certain times. **Walkability:** 2. **Opened:** 1994. **Architect:** Scott Pool. **Season:** Year-round. **To obtain tee times:** Call golf shop. **Miscellaneous:** Reduced fees (twilight, seniors, juniors), range (grass), credit cards (MC, V, AE), BF, FF.
Reader Comments: Need to play ... Epitome of Low Country landscape ... Excellent layout, good par 4s ... You'll use every club in your bag.

SOUTH CAROLINA

THE LEGENDS AT PARRIS ISLAND
PU-Marine Corps. Recruit Depot, Parris Island, 299005, Beaufort County, (843)228-2240, 30 miles from Hilton Head. **E-mail:** lainsmith@signature-is.com. **Facility Holes:** 18. **Yards:** 6,872/4,972. **Par:** 72/72. **Course Rating:** 74.0/69.0. **Slope:** 129/114. **Green Fee:** $23. **Cart Fee:** $12/Person. **Walking Policy:** Unrestricted walking. **Walkability:** 2. **Opened:** 2000. **Architect:** Clyde Johnston. **Season:** Year-round. **High:** Oct.-May. **To obtain tee times:** Call up to 5 days in advance. **Miscellaneous:** Reduced fees (twilight, juniors), range (grass), credit cards (MC, V, AE, D), BF, FF.

THE LEGENDS
R-Hwy. 501, Myrtle Beach, 29577, Horry County, (843)236-5181, (800)377-2315, 5 miles from Myrtle Beach. **Facility Holes:** 54. **Green Fee:** $30/$80. **Cart Fee:** $21/Person. **Walking Policy:** Mandatory carts. **Season:** Year-round. **To obtain tee times:** Call golf shop. **Miscellaneous:** Reduced fees (guests), range (grass/mats), credit cards (MC, V, AE), BF, FF.
★★★★ **HEATHLAND COURSE** (18)
Yards: 6,785/5,115. **Par:** 71/71. **Course Rating:** 72.3/71.0. **Slope:** 127/121. **Walkability:** 3. **Opened:** 1990. **Architect:** Tom Doak.
Reader Comments: Wide open and lengthy but fairly easy to score on … They take care of you … Great Scottish layout, bunkers are severe … Spectacular, hard in the wind! … Target golf, not for squeamish! … Good package, course … A great place to play and stay … Cheap trip to Scotland.
★★★½ **MOORLAND COURSE** (18)
Yards: 6,799/4,905. **Par:** 72/72. **Course Rating:** 72.8/72.8. **Slope:** 135/118. **Walkability:** 4. **Opened:** 1990. **Architect:** P.B. Dye.
Reader Comments: Great unique course. Worth every penny. Enjoy the course but don't go out thinking your going to shoot low … A strategic challenge … Very unusual course, mounding, always in good condition, bring your 'A' game.
★★★★ **PARKLAND COURSE** (18)
Yards: 7,170/5,543. **Par:** 72/72. **Course Rating:** 74.9/71.0. **Slope:** 137/125. **Walkability:** 2. **Opened:** 1992. **Architect:** Legends Group Design.
Reader Comments: Great course through the woods … Quiet, beautiful … Nice variety of short and long, straight and dogleg holes … Extremely difficult for short hitters … Deceptive landing areas … Great course, great complex.

THE LINKS AT CYPRESS BAY
PU-P.O. Box 680, Little River, 29566, Horry County, (843)249-1025, (800)833-6337, 25 miles from Myrtle Beach. **Facility Holes:** 18. **Yards:** 6,502/5,004. **Par:** 72/72. **Course Rating:** 70.0/69.0. **Slope:** 118/113. **Green Fee:** $31/$54. **Walking Policy:** Walking at certain times. **Opened:** 1970. **Architect:** Russell Breeden. **Season:** Year-round. **To obtain tee times:** Call golf shop. **Miscellaneous:** Reduced fees (guests, twilight, juniors), metal spikes, credit cards (MC, V, D).

★★★ THE LINKS AT STONO FERRY
PU-5365 Forest Oaks Dr., Hollywood, 29449, Charleston County, (843)763-1817, 12 miles from Charleston. **Facility Holes:** 18. **Yards:** 6,606/4,928. **Par:** 72/72. **Course Rating:** 71.9/69.2. **Slope:** 136/119. **Green Fee:** $25/$50. **Cart Fee:** $30/Person. **Walking Policy:** Unrestricted walking. **Walkability:** 2. **Opened:** 1989. **Architect:** Ron Garl. **Season:** Year-round. **To obtain tee times:** Call golf shop. **Miscellaneous:** Reduced fees (weekdays, twilight, seniors, juniors), range (grass), credit cards (MC, V, AE, D, DC), BF, FF.
Reader Comments: Good family outing type course … Great weekday rates. Challenging par 5s … Best value around Charleston … Great course for the money. Nice back 9 along the ICW.

★★★ LINKS O'TRYON
SP-11250 Newcut Rd., Campobello, 29322, Spartanburg County, (864)468-4995, (888)525-4657, 20 miles from Greenville. **Facility Holes:** 18. **Yards:** 6,951/4,938. **Par:** 72/72. **Course Rating:** 73.6/67.4. **Slope:** 137/114. **Green Fee:** $35/$45. **Cart Fee:** Included in green fee. **Walking Policy:** Walking at certain times. **Walkability:** 4. **Opened:** 1987. **Architect:** Tom Jackson. **Season:** Year-round. **High:** March-Nov. **To obtain tee times:** Call golf shop. **Miscellaneous:** Reduced fees (weekdays, twilight), range (grass), credit cards (MC, V, AE, D).
Reader Comments: All you can handle … Interesting layout … Nice foothills course, slick greens … Small greens … A sleeper! … Good greens … Nice views, wind … Hard par 3s.

★★½ LINRICK GOLF COURSE
PU-356 Campground Rd., Columbia, 29203, Richland County, (803)754-6331, 7 miles from Columbia. **Facility Holes:** 18. **Yards:** 6,919/5,243. **Par:** 73/73. **Course Rating:** 72.8/69.4. **Slope:** 125. **Green Fee:** $10/$12. **Walking Policy:** Unrestricted walking. **Opened:** 1972. **Architect:** Russell Breeden. **Season:** Year-round. **High:** March-Sept. **To obtain tee times:** Call golf shop. **Miscellaneous:** Reduced fees (seniors, juniors), metal spikes, range (grass).

LITCHFIELD BEACH & GOLF RESORT

R-Hwy 17S, Pawleys Island, 29585, Georgetown County, (843)237-3411, (800)844-5590, 20 miles from Myrtle Beach. **E-mail:** info@mbn.com. **Web:** www.mbn.com. **Facility Holes:** 54. **Green Fee:** $40/$82. **Cart Fee:** $20/Person. **Walking Policy:** Unrestricted walking. **Walkability:** 2. **Season:** Year-round. **To obtain tee times:** Call golf shop. **Miscellaneous:** Reduced fees (guests, twilight, juniors), range (grass/mats), caddies, credit cards (MC, V, AE, D, DC).

★★★ **LITCHFIELD COUNTRY CLUB** (18)
Yards: 6,752/5,264. **Par:** 72/72. **Course Rating:** 72.6/69.9. **Slope:** 130/119. **Opened:** 1966. **Architect:** Willard Byrd.
Reader Comments: A tradition at the beach ... Excellent mature course ... Should shoot a low number here ... Tough greens. Very good service. Keep straight or hit a house ... Classic design, Southern hospitality.

★★★★½ **THE RIVER CLUB** (18)
Yards: 6,677/5,084. **Par:** 72/72. **Course Rating:** 72.2/66.5. **Slope:** 125/110. **Opened:** 1986. **Architect:** Tom Jackson.
Reader Comments: Best greens ... Accuracy is most important. Lots of water, No. 18 a real treat ... New A1 bent greens, unknown gem ... True test for golfing skills.

★★★★ **WILLBROOK PLANTATION GOLF CLUB** (18)
Yards: 6,704/4,963. **Par:** 72/72. **Course Rating:** 71.8/67.7. **Slope:** 125/118. **Opened:** 1988. **Architect:** Dan Maples.
Reader Comments: Very forgiving course. Wonderful staff. Tough greens ... Natural beauty ... Beautiful scenery, lots of bunkers ... Rangers and starters friendly ... Playable all levels. Women love it ... 4 great par 5s, each unique.

★★★★½ **THE LONG BAY CLUB** *Service*

R-350 Foxtail Dr., Longs, 29568, Horry County, (843)399-2222, (800)344-5590, 15 miles from North Myrtle Beach. **E-mail:** info@mbn.com. **Web:** www.mbn.com. **Facility Holes:** 18. **Yards:** 7,021/5,598. **Par:** 72/72. **Course Rating:** 74.3/72.1. **Slope:** 137/127. **Green Fee:** $46/$94. **Cart Fee:** $20/Person. **Walking Policy:** Unrestricted walking. **Walkability:** 5. **Opened:** 1988. **Architect:** Jack Nicklaus. **Season:** Year-round. **High:** Feb.-May. **To obtain tee times:** Call golf shop. **Miscellaneous:** Reduced fees (guests, twilight, juniors), range (grass/mats), credit cards (MC, V, AE, D, DC), BF, FF.
Reader Comments: Will definitely test you from the tips ... Not a level stance all day ... Challenging greens, memorable ... Great test of golf ... Long carries over marsh ... Very fair test of Nicklaus golf.

★★★½ **MAN O' WAR GOLF**

R-5601 Leeshire Blvd., Myrtle Beach, 29579, Horry County, (843)236-8000, 3 miles from Myrtle Beach. **Web:** www.mysticalgolf.com. **Facility Holes:** 18. **Yards:** 6,967/5,033. **Par:** 72/72. **Course Rating:** 72.4/71.2. **Slope:** 130/114. **Green Fee:** $44/$93. **Cart Fee:** Included in green fee. **Walking Policy:** Mandatory carts. **Walkability:** 1. **Opened:** 1996. **Architect:** Dan Maples. **Season:** Year-round. **High:** March-April. **To obtain tee times:** Call up to 365 days in advance. **Miscellaneous:** Reduced fees (juniors), range (grass), credit cards (MC, V), FF.
Reader Comments: Lots of water, tough for a high handicapper. Interesting course to play, definitely a thinking man's golf course ... A good challenge, all around the course ... Great price for a very good course ... Very friendly staff, great greens.

★★★½ **MIDLAND VALLEY COUNTRY CLUB**

SP-151 Midland Dr., Aiken, 29829, Aiken County, (803)663-7332, (800)486-0240, 10 miles from Augusta, GA. **E-mail:** mvccqprodigy.net. **Facility Holes:** 18. **Yards:** 6,849/5,542. **Par:** 71/74. **Course Rating:** 72.1/71.8. **Slope:** 127/125. **Green Fee:** $21/$40. **Cart Fee:** Included in green fee. **Walking Policy:** Mandatory carts. **Walkability:** 3. **Opened:** 1961. **Architect:** Ellis Maples. **Season:** Year-round. **High:** March-May. **To obtain tee times:** Call golf shop. **Miscellaneous:** Reduced fees (seniors), range (grass), credit cards (MC, V, AE, D), BF, FF.
Reader Comments: Good course all around ... Shotmaker's course ... Well kept course ... Home course, great layout and challenge.

MONTICELLO GOLF COURSE

SP-500 Hwy. 61, McCormick, 29835, McCormick County, (864)391-4175, 40 miles from Augusta. **E-mail:** slvgolf@wctel.net. **Web:** savannahlakesvillage.net. **Facility Holes:** 18. **Yards:** 7,032/5,037. **Par:** 72/72. **Course Rating:** 73.7/69.7. **Slope:** 138/123. **Green Fee:** $45. **Cart Fee:** $15/Person. **Walking Policy:** Unrestricted walking. **Walkability:** 3. **Opened:** 1999. **Architect:** Tom Clark. **Season:** Year-round. **To obtain tee times:** Call golf shop. **Miscellaneous:** Range (grass), lodging (40 rooms), credit cards (MC, V, D), BF, FF.
Notes: Ranked 8th in 2000 Best New Affordable Courses.

SOUTH CAROLINA

MYRTLE BEACH NATIONAL GOLF CLUB
R-4900 National Dr., Myrtle Beach, 29579, Horry County, (843)448-2308, (800)344-5590, 8 miles from Myrtle Beach. **E-mail:** info@mbn.com. **Web:** www.mbn.com. **Facility Holes:** 54. **Cart Fee:** $20/Person. **Walking Policy:** Unrestricted walking. **Architect:** Arnold Palmer/Francis Duane. **Season:** Year-round. **High:** Feb.-May. **To obtain tee times:** Call up to 365 days in advance. **Miscellaneous:** Reduced fees (guests, twilight, juniors), range (grass/mats), credit cards (MC, V, AE, D, DC), BF, FF.
★★★★ **KINGS NORTH** (18)
Yards: 7,017/4,816. **Par:** 72/72. **Course Rating:** 72.6/67.0. **Slope:** 136/122. **Green Fee:** $100/$122. **Walkability:** 2. **Opened:** 1973.
Notes: Ranked 22nd in 2001 Best in State.
Reader Comments: Great course, definitely worth experiencing … King at his best … A few really challenging holes, great clubhouse … The most interesting (fun) layout I have ever played, although a little gimmicky at times. Worth playing once just to experience 'The Gambler' … Good for all levels.
★★★ **SOUTHCREEK** (18)
Yards: 6,416/4,723. **Par:** 72/72. **Course Rating:** 70.5/66.5. **Slope:** 123/109. **Green Fee:** $27/$62. **Walkability:** 2. **Opened:** 1975.
Reader Comments: Nice layout, good greens, expect to shoot a good score … Short, tight, tricky.
★★★★ **WEST COURSE** (18) *Pace+*
Yards: 6,866/5,307. **Par:** 72/72. **Course Rating:** 73.0/69.0. **Slope:** 119/109. **Green Fee:** $27/$62. **Walkability:** 1. **Opened:** 1973.
Reader Comments: Great test from back tees … Excellent, makes you think about shots … It wasn't just a round of golf, it was a memorable moment … Park-like setting.

MYRTLEWOOD GOLF CLUB
SP-Hwy. 17 at 48th Ave. N., Myrtle Beach, 29577, Horry County, (843)449-5134, (800)283-3633. **Web:** www.myrtlebeachtrips.com. **Facility Holes:** 36. **Green Fee:** $27/$64. **Cart Fee:** $20/Person. **Walking Policy:** Mandatory carts. **Walkability:** 1. **Season:** Year-round. **To obtain tee times:** Call golf shop. **Miscellaneous:** Range (grass), credit cards (MC, V, AE, D), BF, FF.
★★★½ **PALMETTO COURSE** (18)
Yards: 6,953/5,176. **Par:** 72/72. **Course Rating:** 73.7/70.1. **Slope:** 135/117. **Opened:** 1973. **Architect:** Edmund Ault.
Reader Comments: Enjoyed the courses but not as challenging as I had hoped … Friendly course … I like it and I'll be back … Easy to get to.
★★★ **PINEHILLS COURSE** (18)
Yards: 6,640/4,906. **Par:** 72/72. **Course Rating:** 72.0/67.4. **Slope:** 125/113. **Opened:** 1993. **Architect:** Arthur Hills.
Reader Comments: Great layout. Terrific staff … A player friendly course, reasonable rates … Driving landing areas small, leave driver home.

★★★½ NORTHWOODS GOLF CLUB
PU-201 Powell Rd., Columbia, 29203, Richland County, (803)786-9242, 4 miles from Columbia. **Facility Holes:** 18. **Yards:** 6,800/5,000. **Par:** 72/72. **Course Rating:** 71.9/67.8. **Slope:** 122/116. **Green Fee:** $19/$28. **Cart Fee:** $11/Person. **Walking Policy:** Walking at certain times. **Walkability:** 3. **Opened:** 1990. **Architect:** P.B. Dye. **Season:** Year-round. **To obtain tee times:** Call golf shop. **Miscellaneous:** Reduced fees (weekdays, twilight, seniors, juniors), range (grass/mats), credit cards (MC, V, AE).
Reader Comments: Just what a course should be. A tough but fair test of golf … Best grill in Columbia … A good afternoon round … Very friendly atmosphere … Unusual challenges of deep fairway bunkers, bunkers hiding greens. Greens have some severe slopes … A sleeper.

★★★ OAK HILLS GOLF & COUNTRY CLUB
PU-7629 Fairfield Rd., Columbia, 29203, Richland County, (803)735-9830, (800)263-5218, 1 mile from Columbia. **E-mail:** golf3@mindspring.com. **Web:** oakhillsgolf.com. **Facility Holes:** 18. **Yards:** 6,894/4,574. **Par:** 72/72. **Course Rating:** 72.4/65.8. **Slope:** 122/110. **Green Fee:** $39/$49. **Cart Fee:** Included in green fee. **Walking Policy:** Walking at certain times. **Walkability:** 5. **Opened:** 1990. **Architect:** Steve Melnyk. **Season:** Year-round. **To obtain tee times:** Call golf shop. **Miscellaneous:** Reduced fees (weekdays, twilight, seniors, juniors), range (grass/mats), credit cards (MC, V, AE, D).
Reader Comments: Worth playing … Hilly and tricky.

★★ OAKDALE COUNTRY CLUB
SP-3700 W. Lake Dr., Florence, 29501, Florence County, (843)662-0368, 5 miles from Florence. **Facility Holes:** 18. **Yards:** 6,300/5,000. **Par:** 72/73. **Course Rating:** 70.3/68.8. **Slope:** 123/114. **Green Fee:** $15/$20. **Cart Fee:** $10/Person. **Walking Policy:** Unrestricted walking. **Walkability:** 1. **Opened:** 1964. **Architect:** Roland (Robby) Robertson. **Season:** Year-round. **To obtain tee times:** Call golf shop. **Miscellaneous:** Metal spikes, range (grass/mats), BF, FF.

SOUTH CAROLINA

OCEAN CREEK GOLF COURSE
R-90B Ocean Creek Blvd., Fripp Island, 29920, Beaufort County, (813)838-1576, (800)933-0050, 30 miles from Hilton Head. **E-mail:** frippislandresort.com. **Facility Holes:** 18. **Yards:** 6,629/4,824. **Par:** 71/71. **Course Rating:** 72.0/69.5. **Slope:** 132/121. **Green Fee:** $49/$84. **Cart Fee:** Included in green fee. **Walking Policy:** Unrestricted walking. **Walkability:** 2. **Opened:** 1995. **Architect:** Davis Love III/Bob Spence. **Season:** Year-round. **High:** April-Sept. **To obtain tee times:** Call up to 30 days in advance. **Miscellaneous:** Reduced fees (guests, twilight, juniors), range (grass), lodging (370 rooms), BF, FF.

OCEAN POINT GOLF LINKS
R-250 Ocean Point Dr., Fripp Island, 29920, Beaufort County, (803)838-1521, (800)845-4100, 20 miles from Beaufort. **Facility Holes:** 18. **Yards:** 6,590/4,951. **Par:** 72/72. **Course Rating:** 72.2/69.5. **Slope:** 129/113. **Green Fee:** $44/$69. **Cart Fee:** Included in green fee. **Walking Policy:** Walking at certain times. **Walkability:** 1. **Opened:** 1964. **Architect:** George Cobb. **Season:** Year-round. **To obtain tee times:** Call golf shop. **Miscellaneous:** Reduced fees (weekdays, guests, twilight, juniors), range (grass/mats), credit cards (MC, V, AE, D).

★★★ OLD CAROLINA GOLF CLUB
PU-89 Old Carolina Dr., Bluffton, 29910, Beaufort County, (843)785-6363, (888)785-7274, 5 miles from Hilton Head Island. **Web:** www.oldcarolinagolf.com. **Facility Holes:** 18. **Yards:** 6,805/4,725. **Par:** 72/71. **Course Rating:** 73.1/67.0. **Slope:** 142/121. **Green Fee:** $49/$89. **Cart Fee:** Included in green fee. **Walking Policy:** Walking at certain times. **Walkability:** 3. **Opened:** 1996. **Architect:** Clyde Johnston. **Season:** Year-round. **High:** March-Oct. **To obtain tee times:** Call up to 90 days in advance. **Miscellaneous:** Reduced fees (guests, twilight, juniors), range (grass), credit cards (MC, V, AE, D), BF, FF.
Reader Comments: Great target golf course ... Challenging, great variety of holes, water on 14 holes, great greens condition and speed. Play the right tees, deserves every point of slope and course ratings ... For layout near HHI, great value.

★★★½ OLD SOUTH GOLF LINKS
PU-50 Buckingham Plantation Dr., Bluffton, 29910, Beaufort County, (843)785-5353, (800)257-8997, 1 mile from Hilton Head Island. **E-mail:** oldsouthgolf@digitel.net. **Web:** oldsouthgolf.com. **Facility Holes:** 18. **Yards:** 6,772/4,776. **Par:** 72/71. **Course Rating:** 72.4/69.6. **Slope:** 129/123. **Green Fee:** $36/$60. **Cart Fee:** $29/Person. **Walking Policy:** Unrestricted walking. **Walkability:** 2. **Opened:** 1991. **Architect:** Clyde Johnston. **Season:** Year-round. **High:** March-April. **To obtain tee times:** Call up to 120 days in advance. **Miscellaneous:** Reduced fees (guests, twilight, juniors), metal spikes, range (grass), credit cards (MC, V, AE, D), BF, FF.
Reader Comments: The best kept secret around Hilton Head Island ... Really enjoy the par 4s on the marsh ... Magnificent vistas of water ... Good test for all golfers, great shape, good value ... Really great test, scenic, short 17th hole is a monster.

★★★½ OYSTER REEF GOLF CLUB
SP-155 High Bluff Rd., Hilton Head Island, 29925, Beaufort County, (843)681-7717, (800)728-6662, 35 miles from Savannah. **E-mail:** orgc99@aol.com. **Facility Holes:** 18. **Yards:** 7,027/5,288. **Par:** 72/72. **Course Rating:** 73.7/69.8. **Slope:** 131/118. **Green Fee:** $48/$89. **Cart Fee:** Included in green fee. **Walkability:** 2. **Opened:** 1982. **Architect:** Rees Jones. **Season:** Year-round. **To obtain tee times:** Call golf shop. **Miscellaneous:** Reduced fees (guests, juniors), range (grass), credit cards (MC, V, AE, D).
Reader Comments: Beautiful low country course ... Again, always in good condition ... Par-3 No. 6 stunning ...Georgeous scenery challenge to one's accuracy, focus.

PALMETTO DUNES RESORT
R-2 Leamington Lane, Hilton Head Island, 29928, Beaufort County, (843)785-1140, (800)827-3006, 50 miles from Savannah. **E-mail:** csinclair@greenwooddevelopment.com. **Web:** palmettodunesresort.com. **Facility Holes:** 54. **Cart Fee:** Included in green fee. **Walking Policy:** Unrestricted walking. **Season:** Year-round. **High:** March-Oct. **To obtain tee times:** Call up to 90 days in advance. **Miscellaneous:** Reduced fees (weekdays, guests, juniors), credit cards (MC, V, AE), BF, FF.
★★★★½ **ARTHUR HILLS COURSE** (18) *Condition, Pace*
Yards: 6,651/4,999. **Par:** 72/72. **Course Rating:** 71.4/68.5. **Slope:** 127/118. **Green Fee:** $92/$148. **Walkability:** 2. **Opened:** 1986. **Architect:** Arthur Hills. **Miscellaneous:** Range (grass).
Reader Comments: A truly beautiful golf course. Excellent layout. Some very difficult golf holes over water or marsh. Great condition ... Excellent course, was treated like a king ... Well maintained, well designed, well treated, fun ... Greens in great condition in winter ... Last 3 finishing holes unbelievable.

SOUTH CAROLINA

★★★★ **GEORGE FAZIO COURSE** (18) *Pace*
Yards: 6,875/5,273. **Par:** 70/70. **Course Rating:** 74.2/70.8. **Slope:** 132/127. **Green Fee:** $74/$95. **Walkability:** 1. **Opened:** 1974. **Architect:** George Fazio.
Reader Comments: Always enjoy this course, lots of sand & water … Nothing fancy, but good test of golf … Very nice course, hard but fair … Love to play, excellent condition & challenge.

★★★ **ROBERT TRENT JONES COURSE** (18)
Yards: 6,710/5,425. **Par:** 72/72. **Course Rating:** 72.2/70.3. **Slope:** 123/123. **Green Fee:** $74/$95. **Walkability:** 1. **Opened:** 1969. **Architect:** Robert Trent Jones. **Miscellaneous:** Range (grass/mats).
Reader Comments: Lots of wind, enjoyable … Good resort course … Great value in golf package, but very long for women … No. 10 tough with ocean wind … A sentimental favorite of mine.

PALMETTO HALL PLANTATION
R-108 Fort Howell Dr., Hilton Head Island, 29926, Beaufort County, (843)689-4100, (800)827-3006, 30 miles from Savannah. **E-mail:** bfaulkner@greenwooddevelopment.com.
Facility Holes: 36. **Green Fee:** $55/$95. **Cart Fee:** Included in green fee. **Walkability:** 2. **Season:** Year-round. **High:** March-Nov. **To obtain tee times:** Call up to 60 days in advance. **Misc:** Reduced fees (guests, juniors), range (grass), credit cards (MC, V, AE), BF, FF.

★★★★ **ARTHUR HILLS COURSE** (18) *Pace*
Yards: 6,918/4,956. **Par:** 72/72. **Course Rating:** 74.0/68.6. **Slope:** 140/119. **Walking Policy:** Mandatory carts. **Opened:** 1991. **Architect:** Arthur Hills.
Reader Comments: Play at least once if you can … A tough layout … Challenging, good variety of holes with no repetition … Fun from the white tees, tough from the blue tees … Lulls you into a false sense of security just when you think it's easy, no way.

★★★★ **ROBERT CUPP COURSE** (18)
Yards: 7,079/5,220. **Par:** 72/72. **Course Rating:** 75.2/71.1. **Slope:** 144/126. **Walking Policy:** Unrestricted walking. **Opened:** 1993. **Architect:** Bob Cupp.
Reader Comments: Sister course not as pretty, but beautiful clubhouse … A difficult course but I don't care for the trapezoidal designs … Some don't like the angular shapes. Great! Stay away. Better than some say.

★★½ **PATRIOTS POINT LINKS ON CHARLESTON HARBOR**
PU-1 Patriots Point Rd., Mount Pleasant, 29464, Charleston County, (843)881-0042, (800)221-2424, 2 miles from Charleston. **E-mail:** chad@patriotspointlinks.com. **Web:** patriotspointlinks.com. **Facility Holes:** 18. **Yards:** 6,838/5,562. **Par:** 72/72. **Course Rating:** 72.1/71.0. **Slope:** 118/115. **Green Fee:** $45/$80. **Cart Fee:** Included in green fee. **Walking Policy:** Walking at certain times. **Walkability:** 1. **Opened:** 1981. **Architect:** Willard Byrd. **Season:** Year-round. **High:** March-May. **To obtain tee times:** Call up to 90 days in advance. **Miscellaneous:** Reduced fees (weekdays, guests, twilight, juniors), range (grass), lodging (150 rooms), credit cards (MC, V, AE, D), BF, FF.

★★★★ **PAWLEYS PLANTATION GOLF & COUNTRY CLUB**
R-Hwy. 17 S., Pawleys Island, 29585, Georgetown County, (843)237-6200, (800)367-9959, 30 miles from Myrtle Beach. **E-mail:** info@pawleysplantation.com. **Web:** www.pawleysplantation.com. **Facility Holes:** 18. **Yards:** 7,026/4,979. **Par:** 72/72. **Course Rating:** 75.3/70.5. **Slope:** 146/124. **Green Fee:** $55/$100. **Cart Fee:** $21/Person. **Walking Policy:** Mandatory carts. **Walkability:** 1. **Opened:** 1988. **Architect:** Jack Nicklaus. **Season:** Year-round. **High:** March-April. **To obtain tee times:** Call golf shop. **Miscellaneous:** Reduced fees (guests, juniors), range (grass), lodging (175 rooms), credit cards (MC, V, AE, D), BF, FF.
Notes: Ranked 23rd in 1999 Best in State.
Reader Comments: Breathtaking design, very challenging, #13 and #17 were worth the drive from Atlanta by themselves … Very challenging holes along the marsh—especially with strong winds. Very enjoyable … Very interesting layout, excellent staff … A must play, great place.

★★ **PAWPAW COUNTRY CLUB**
SP-600 George St., Bamberg, 29003, Bamberg County, (803)245-4171, 50 miles from Columbia. **Facility Holes:** 18. **Yards:** 6,733/5,010. **Par:** 72/72. **Course Rating:** 72.3/67.5. **Slope:** 133/114. **Green Fee:** $12/$17. **Cart Fee:** $9/Person. **Walking Policy:** Unrestricted walking. **Walkability:** 1. **Architect:** Russell Breeden. **To obtain tee times:** Call golf shop. **Miscellaneous:** Reduced fees (weekdays, juniors), range (grass), credit cards (MC, V).

★★★½ **PERSIMMON HILL GOLF CLUB**
PU-126 Golf Club Rd., Saluda, 29138, Saluda County, (803)275-3522, 35 miles from Augusta. **E-mail:** mo@pga.com. **Facility Holes:** 18. **Yards:** 6,925/5,449. **Par:** 72/73. **Course Rating:** 72.3/71.1. **Slope:** 122/121. **Green Fee:** $25/$35. **Cart Fee:** Included in green fee. **Walking Policy:** Walking at certain times. **Walkability:** 2. **Opened:** 1962. **Architect:** Russell Breeden. **Season:** Year-round. **High:** March-May. **To obtain tee times:** Call golf shop. **Miscellaneous:** Reduced fees (weekdays, twilight), range (grass/mats), credit cards (MC, V, AE), BF, FF.

Reader Comments: My secret place! One of my favorite 'fun' courses … Another diamond in the rough. Challenging, … Long with small greens … Challenging, fun course in an out-of-the-way location. Friendly staff. Great value … Quality for money … Gem in state, great layout, condition.

★★★★ **PINE FOREST COUNTRY CLUB**
SP-1000 Congressional Blvd., Summerville, 29483, Dorchester County, (803)851-1193, 3 miles from Summerville. **E-mail:** pineforest@kempersports.com. **Web:** pineforestcountryclub.com. **Facility Holes:** 18. **Yards:** 6,905/5,007. **Par:** 72/72. **Course Rating:** 73.6/67.7. **Slope:** 140/120. **Green Fee:** $27/$65. **Cart Fee:** Included in green fee. **Walking Policy:** Walking at certain times. **Walkability:** 3. **Opened:** 1992. **Architect:** Bob Spence. **Season:** Year-round. **High:** Feb.-May. **To obtain tee times:** Call up to 7 days in advance. **Miscellaneous:** Reduced fees (weekdays, twilight, seniors, juniors), range (grass), credit cards (MC, V, AE, D), BF, FF.
Reader Comments: A truly outstanding championship course. The most challenging course in the Charleston area … Good test of golf, good value … Trees everywhere, loved it … Nice course, challenging with nice facilities.

★★★★ **PINE LAKES INTERNATIONAL COUNTRY CLUB** *Service*
SP-5603 Woodside Ave., Myrtle Beach, 29577, Horry County, (843)449-6459, (800)446-6817. **Web:** www.pinelakes.com. **Facility Holes:** 18. **Yards:** 6,700/5,162. **Par:** 71/71. **Course Rating:** 72.0/70.5. **Slope:** 130/121. **Green Fee:** $45/$110. **Cart Fee:** Included in green fee. **Walking Policy:** Mandatory carts. **Walkability:** 1. **Opened:** 1927. **Architect:** Robert White. **Season:** Year-round. **High:** Sept.-May. **To obtain tee times:** Call golf shop. **Miscellaneous:** Reduced fees (guests, twilight), range (grass/mats), credit cards (MC, V, AE), BF, FF.
Reader Comments: Service was excellent! … A real walk into memory lane, another great place to play … Real Scottish atmosphere … Spend the extra money for the Rolls carts! … Great chowder.

★★ **PINETUCK GOLF CLUB**
SP-2578 Tuckaway Rd., Rock Hill, 29730, York County, (803)327-1141, 20 miles from Charlotte. **E-mail:** pinetuck@rhtc.com. **Web:** pinetuck.com. **Facility Holes:** 18. **Yards:** 6,567/4,870. **Par:** 71/71. **Course Rating:** 71.7/68.2. **Slope:** 127/116. **Green Fee:** $18/$24. **Cart Fee:** $14/Person. **Walking Policy:** Walking at certain times. **Walkability:** 2. **Opened:** 1971. **Architect:** George Dunlap. **Season:** Year-round. **High:** April-Oct. **To obtain tee times:** Call golf shop. **Miscellaneous:** Reduced fees (weekdays, twilight, seniors, juniors), range (grass), credit cards (MC, V), BF, FF.

THE PLAYERS COURSE
SP-300 Players Course Dr., Manning, 29102, Clarendon County, (803)478-2500. **Facility Holes:** 18. **Yards:** 7,007/5,375. **Par:** 72/72. **Course Rating:** 72.0/68.3. **Slope:** 120/111. **Green Fee:** $25/$30. **Cart Fee:** Included in green fee. **Season:** Year-round. **To obtain tee times:** Call golf shop. **Miscellaneous:** Reduced fees (seniors), metal spikes, credit cards (MC, V).

POCALLA SPRINGS COUNTRY CLUB
SP-1700 Hwy. 15 S., Sumter, 29150, Sumter County, (803)481-8322. **Facility Holes:** 18. **Yards:** 6,350/5,500. **Par:** 71/71. **Course Rating:** 68.0/65.0. **Slope:** 115/111. **Green Fee:** $11/$13. **Walking Policy:** Walking at certain times. **Walkability:** 2. **Opened:** 1920. **Season:** Year-round. **High:** March-Aug. **To obtain tee times:** Call golf shop. **Miscellaneous:** Reduced fees (weekdays, guests, twilight, seniors, juniors), metal spikes, range (grass), credit cards (MC, V), BF, FF.

PORT ROYAL GOLF CLUB
R-10A Grasslawn Ave., Hilton Head, 29928, Beaufort County, (843)681-1760, (800)234-6318, 40 miles from Savannah. **E-mail:** amergolf@hargray.com. **Web:** www.hiltonheadgolf.net. **Facility Holes:** 54. **Cart Fee:** Included in green fee. **Walking Policy:** Mandatory carts. **Season:** Year-round. **High:** March-May. **To obtain tee times:** Call up to 90 days in advance. **Miscellaneous:** Reduced fees (guests, twilight, juniors), range (grass/mats), credit cards (MC, V, AE, D), BF, FF.
★★★½ **BARONY COURSE** (18)
Yards: 6,530/5,253. **Par:** 72/72. **Course Rating:** 71.6/70.1. **Slope:** 129/115. **Green Fee:** $60/$93. **Walkability:** 1. **Opened:** 1968. **Architect:** George Cobb.
Reader Comments: I never go to Hilton Head without playing Port Royal facilities.
★★½ **PLANTER'S ROW COURSE** (18)
Yards: 6,520/5,126. **Par:** 72/72. **Course Rating:** 71.7/68.9. **Slope:** 133/116. **Green Fee:** $60/$93. **Walkability:** 2. **Opened:** 1983. **Architect:** Willard Byrd.
★★★ **ROBBER'S ROW COURSE** (18)
Yards: 6,642/5,000. **Par:** 72/72. **Course Rating:** 72.6/70.4. **Slope:** 134/115. **Green Fee:** $65/$98. **Walkability:** 2. **Opened:** 1968. **Architect:** Pete Dye.
Reader Comments: Most forgiving for women … Good condition, bring your best sand wedge … Nice clubhouse … Fantastic greens … Good design, some holes are on sites of the Civil War.

★★★½ POSSUM TROT GOLF CLUB
R-Possum Trot Rd., North Myrtle Beach, 29582, Horry County, (843)272-5341,
(800)626-8768. **Facility Holes:** 18. **Yards:** 6,966/5,160. **Par:** 72/72. **Course Rating:** 73.0/69.6.
Slope: 127/111. **Green Fee:** $32/$72. **Cart Fee:** Included in green fee. **Walking Policy:** Walking
at certain times. **Walkability:** 3. **Opened:** 1968. **Architect:** Russell Breeden. **Season:** Year-
round. **To obtain tee times:** Call golf shop. **Miscellaneous:** Reduced fees (twilight, juniors),
range (grass/mats), credit cards (MC, V, AE, D), BF, FF.
Reader Comments: Old course, playable … Fun course to play … Best value on the beach.

PRESTWICK COUNTRY CLUB
PU-1001 Links Rd., Myrtle Beach, 29575, Horry County, (843)293-4100, (888)250-1767, 5
miles from Myrtle Beach. **E-mail:** prescc@sccoast.net. **Web:** prestwickcountryclub.com.
Facility Holes: 18. **Yards:** 7,086/5,210. **Par:** 72/72. **Course Rating:** 74.5/71.9. **Slope:** 140/121.
Green Fee: $35/$90. **Cart Fee:** $20/Person. **Walking Policy:** Walking at certain times.
Walkability: 2. **Opened:** 1989. **Architect:** Pete Dye/P.B. Dye. **Season:** Year-round. **High:** Feb.-
June. **To obtain tee times:** Call up to 365 days in advance. **Miscellaneous:** Reduced fees
(juniors), range (grass), credit cards (MC, V), BF, FF.

★★★ QUAIL CREEK GOLF CLUB
PU-Hwy. 501 W., Myrtle Beach, 29578, Horry County, (843)347-0549, (800)833-6337. **Facility
Holes:** 18. **Yards:** 6,812/5,287. **Par:** 72/72. **Course Rating:** 72.8/70.2. **Slope:** 119/112. **Green
Fee:** $41. **Cart Fee:** $19/Person. **Walking Policy:** Walking at certain times. **Walkability:** 3.
Opened: 1966. **Architect:** Gene Hamm. **Season:** Year-round. **High:** Feb.-May. **To obtain tee
times:** Call up to 7 days in advance. **Miscellaneous:** Reduced fees (twilight, juniors), range
(grass), credit cards (MC, V, AE, D), BF, FF.
Reader Comments: Easiest of Links Group; wide fairways … Excellent course for the money. An
interesting mix of holes. Will not beat you up but offers a fair challenge … Player friendly.

★★½ RACCOON RUN GOLF CLUB
PU-8950 Hwy. 707, Myrtle Beach, 29588, Horry County, (843)650-2644, 10 miles from Myrtle
Beach. **Facility Holes:** 18. **Yards:** 7,349/5,535. **Par:** 73/73. **Course Rating:** 74.0/69.5. **Slope:**
120/109. **Green Fee:** $18/$35. **Cart Fee:** $18/Person. **Walking Policy:** Mandatory carts.
Walkability: 1. **Opened:** 1977. **Architect:** Gene Hamm. **Season:** June-Dec. **To obtain tee times:**
Call up to 180 days in advance. **Miscellaneous:** Reduced fees (juniors), credit cards (MC, V).

★★★½ REGENT PARK GOLF CLUB
PU-5055 Regent Pkwy., Fort Mill, 29715, York County, (803)547-1300, (800)671-5550, 16
miles from Charlotte. **E-mail:** tlregentpark@comporium.net. **Web:** www.regentparkgc.com.
Facility Holes: 18. **Yards:** 6,729/5,245. **Par:** 71/71. **Course Rating:** 72.7/69.5. **Slope:** 135/123.
Green Fee: $44/$64. **Cart Fee:** Included in green fee. **Walking Policy:** Mandatory carts.
Walkability: 4. **Opened:** 1994. **Architect:** Ron Garl. **Season:** Year-round. **To obtain tee times:**
Call up to 5 days in advance. **Miscellaneous:** Reduced fees (guests, twilight, seniors, juniors),
range (grass/mats), credit cards (MC, V, AE, D), BF, FF.
Reader Comments: Charlotte area's best public course … A test, pretty course, nice facilities …
Great course, lots of fun, need to be long off tee … Good mix of holes, elevation changes … Take
time to play, great holes.

★★½ RIVER CLUB ON THE ASHLEY
SP-222 Fairington Dr., Summerville, 29485, Dorchester County, (843)873-7110, (800)230-
1639, 19 miles from Charleston. **Facility Holes:** 18. **Yards:** 6,712/5,025. **Par:** 72/72. **Course
Rating:** 71.2/68.1. **Slope:** 117/114. **Green Fee:** $15/$30. **Cart Fee:** $15/Cart. **Walking Policy:**
Walking at certain times. **Walkability:** 1. **Opened:** 1971. **Architect:** Russell Breeden. **Season:**
Year-round. **To obtain tee times:** Call up to 30 days in advance. **Miscellaneous:** Reduced fees
(weekdays, twilight, juniors), range (grass), credit cards (MC, V), BF, FF.

★★★ RIVER FALLS PLANTATION
SP-100 Player Blvd., Duncan, 29334, Spartanburg County, (864)433-9192, 10 miles from
Greenville. **E-mail:** proshop345@aol.com. **Web:** www.riverfallsgolf.com. **Facility Holes:** 18.
Yards: 6,734/4,928. **Par:** 72/72. **Course Rating:** 72.1/68.2. **Slope:** 127/125. **Green Fee:**
$24/$34. **Cart Fee:** $15/Person. **Walking Policy:** Walking at certain times. **Walkability:** 5.
Opened: 1990. **Architect:** Gary Player. **Season:** Year-round. **High:** March-June. **To obtain tee
times:** Call golf shop. **Miscellaneous:** Reduced fees (guests, seniors, juniors), range (grass),
credit cards (MC, V, AE, D), BF, FF.
Reader Comments: Excellent track has one or two quirky holes, a Player trademark … Well kept …
Stay in the fairway on this one … Fairways very, very, tight, small greens.

SOUTH CAROLINA

THE RIVER GOLF CLUB
PU-307 Riverside Blvd., North Augusta, 29841, Aiken County, (803)202-0110, 1 mile from Augusta. **E-mail:** riverclub@gabn.net. **Web:** www.rivergolfclub.com. **Facility Holes:** 18. **Yards:** 6,847/5,081. **Par:** 71/71. **Course Rating:** 72.2/68.4. **Slope:** 130/114. **Green Fee:** $15/$30. **Cart Fee:** $13/Person. **Walking Policy:** Mandatory carts. **Walkability:** 1. **Opened:** 1998. **Architect:** Jim Fazio. **Season:** Year-round. **High:** March-June. **To obtain tee times:** Call golf shop. **Miscellaneous:** Reduced fees (weekdays, twilight, seniors, juniors), range (grass), credit cards (MC, V, AE), BF, FF.
Notes: Ranked 8th in 2001 Best in State; 5th in 1999 Best New Affordable Public.

★★★½ **RIVER HILLS GOLF & COUNTRY CLUB**
PU-3670 Ceder Creek Run, Little River, 29566, Horry County, (803)399-2100, (800)264-3810, 10 miles from Myrtle Beach. **Web:** www.riverhillsgolf.com. **Facility Holes:** 18. **Yards:** 7,006/4,932. **Par:** 72/72. **Course Rating:** 73.3/67.7. **Slope:** 136/120. **Green Fee:** $15/$55. **Cart Fee:** $20/Person. **Walking Policy:** Mandatory carts. **Walkability:** 3. **Opened:** 1989. **Architect:** Tom Jackson. **Season:** Year-round. **To obtain tee times:** Call golf shop. **Miscellaneous:** Reduced fees (twilight, juniors), range (grass), credit cards (MC, V), BF, FF.
Reader Comments: Excellent course. Many challenging golf holes. Not for the high handicapper ... Great greens, fun course ... This course used to be a 'secret' good course, now more play it ... Helpful staff ... Must play target golf.

★★★ **RIVER OAKS GOLF PLANTATION**
R-831 River Oaks Dr., Myrtle Beach, 29577, Horry County, (843)236-2222. **Facility Holes:** 27. **Green Fee:** $25/$60. **Cart Fee:** Included in green fee. **Walking Policy:** Mandatory cart. **Opened:** 1987. **Architect:** Gene Hamm. **Season:** Year-round. **To obtain tee times:** Call golf shop. **Miscellaneous:** Reduced fees (guests, twilight, juniors), metal spikes, range (grass), credit cards (MC, V, AE).
BEAR/FOX (18 Combo)
Yards: 6,778/5,133. **Par:** 72/72. **Course Rating:** 72.0/69.7. **Slope:** 126/116.
OTTER/BEAR (18 Combo)
Yards: 6,877/5,188. **Par:** 72/72. **Course Rating:** 72.5/69.7. **Slope:** 125/118.
OTTER/FOX (18 Combo)
Yards: 6,791/5,043. **Par:** 72/72. **Course Rating:** 71.7/69.7. **Slope:** 125/118.
Reader Comments: Good value ... Good blend of holes and hazards ... Beautiful oak trees ... Tight, hard to work ball with water on each side of the fairway.

★★★ **ROBBERS ROOST GOLF COURSE**
PU-1400 Hwy. 17 N., North Myrtle Beach, 29582, Horry County, (843)249-1471, (800)352-2384. **Web:** www.robbersroost.com. **Facility Holes:** 18. **Yards:** 7,148/5,387. **Par:** 70/72. **Course Rating:** 74.4/70.2. **Slope:** 137/116. **Green Fee:** $29/$56. **Cart Fee:** Included in green fee. **Walking Policy:** Mandatory carts. **Walkability:** 1. **Opened:** 1968. **Architect:** Russell Breeden. **Season:** Year-round. **To obtain tee times:** Call golf shop. **Miscellaneous:** Reduced fees (twilight, juniors), range (grass), credit cards (MC, V, AE, D), BF, FF.
Reader Comments: Typical beach course ... Easy to keep it in play; nice par 5s ... OK for average golfer ... Variety of shots ... Long par 4s, water, trees, super par 5s.

★★ **ROLLING HILLS GOLF CLUB**
PU-1790 Hwy. 501, Galavants Ferry, 29544, Horry County, (803)358-4653, (800)633-2380, 20 miles from Conway. **Facility Holes:** 18. **Yards:** 6,749/5,141. **Par:** 72/72. **Course Rating:** 72.6/68.3. **Slope:** 133/109. **Green Fee:** $13/$18. **Cart Fee:** $20/Person. **Walking Policy:** Walking at certain times. **Walkability:** 3. **Opened:** 1988. **Architect:** Gene Hamm. **Season:** Year-round. **To obtain tee times:** Call up to 7 days in advance. **Miscellaneous:** Reduced fees (weekdays, guests, twilight, seniors, juniors), metal spikes, range (grass), credit cards (MC, V, AE), BF, FF.

★★ **ROSE HILL COUNTRY CLUB**
SP-1 Rosehill Dr., Bluffton, 29910, Beaufort County, (843)757-2160. **Facility Holes:** 27. **Green Fee:** $49. **Opened:** 1982. **Architect:** Gene Hamm. **To obtain tee times:** Call golf shop. **Miscellaneous:** Metal spikes.
EAST/SOUTH (18 Combo)
Yards: 6,464/5,082. **Par:** 72/72. **Course Rating:** 71.4/69.1. **Slope:** 117/115.
EAST/WEST (18 Combo)
Yards: 6,808/5,276. **Par:** 72/72. **Course Rating:** 73.1/69.4. **Slope:** 123/118.
SOUTH/WEST (18 Combo)
Yards: 6,822/5,218. **Par:** 72/72. **Course Rating:** 72.9/69.7. **Slope:** 121/117.

★★½ SALUDA VALLEY COUNTRY CLUB

SP-598 Beaver Dam Rd., Williamston, 29697, Anderson County, (864)847-7102, 20 miles from Greenville. **Facility Holes:** 18. **Yards:** 6,430/5,126. **Par:** 72/72. **Course Rating:** 70.8/69.4. **Slope:** 119/114. **Green Fee:** $15/$21. **Cart Fee:** $10/Person. **Walking Policy:** Unrestricted walking. **Walkability:** 2. **Opened:** 1964. **Architect:** William B. Lewis. **Season:** Year-round. **High:** April-Oct. **To obtain tee times:** Call golf shop. **Miscellaneous:** Reduced fees (weekdays), metal spikes, range (grass/mats), credit cards (MC, V), FF.

SANDY POINT GOLF CLUB

SP-3451 Middendorf Rd., Hartsville, 29550, Darlington County, (843)335-8950. **E-mail:** sandypointgolf@yahoo.com. **Facility Holes:** 18. **Yards:** 6,840/6,045. **Par:** 72/72. **Course Rating:** 73.0/69.3. **Slope:** 127/121. **Green Fee:** $20/$27. **Cart Fee:** Included in green fee. **Walking Policy:** Walking at certain times. **Walkability:** 4. **Opened:** 1981. **Architect:** J. B. Ammons. **Season:** Year-round. **High:** April-Aug. **To obtain tee times:** Call golf shop. **Miscellaneous:** Reduced fees (seniors), credit cards (MC, V, D), BF, FF.

★★★ SANTEE NATIONAL GOLF CLUB

R-Hwy. 6 W., Santee, 29142, Orangeburg County, (803)854-3531, (800)448-0152, 60 miles from Charleston. **E-mail:** headpro@gte.com. **Web:** www.santeenational.com. **Facility Holes:** 18. **Yards:** 6,858/4,748. **Par:** 72/72. **Course Rating:** 72.1/68.2. **Slope:** 120/116. **Green Fee:** $25/$47. **Cart Fee:** Included in green fee. **Walking Policy:** Mandatory carts. **Walkability:** 2. **Opened:** 1989. **Architect:** Porter Gibson. **Season:** Year-round. **High:** Feb.-May. **To obtain tee times:** Call golf shop. **Miscellaneous:** Reduced fees (guests, twilight), metal spikes, range (grass), lodging (8 rooms), credit cards (MC, V, AE, D), BF, FF.
Reader Comments: Interesting layout … Worth the trip … Great service, great staff. Can't beat it.

★★½ SEA GULL GOLF CLUB

PU-7829 Ocean Hwy., Pawleys Island, 29585, Georgetown County, (843)237-4285, (800)833-6337, 20 miles from Myrtle Beach. **E-mail:** topgull@aol.com. **Web:** www.linksgroup.com. **Facility Holes:** 18. **Yards:** 6,910/5,250. **Par:** 72/72. **Course Rating:** 74.0/69.6. **Slope:** 134/120. **Green Fee:** $34/$70. **Cart Fee:** Included in green fee. **Walking Policy:** Walking at certain times. **Walkability:** 3. **Opened:** 1967. **Architect:** Gene Hamm. **Season:** Year-round. **High:** Feb.-May. **To obtain tee times:** Call golf shop. **Miscellaneous:** Reduced fees (juniors), lodging (100 rooms), credit cards (MC, V, AE, D), BF, FF.

SEA PINES PLANTATION CLUB

R-100 N. Sea Pines Dr., Hilton Head Island, 29928, Beaufort County, (843)842-8484, (800)732-7463, 30 miles from Savannah. **E-mail:** ocsm@seapines. **Web:** www.seapines.com. **Facility Holes:** 36. **Cart Fee:** Included in green fee. **Walking Policy:** Unrestricted walking. **Walkability:** 2. **Season:** Year-round. **High:** Feb.-May. **To obtain tee times:** Call up to 90 days in advance. **Miscellaneous:** Reduced fees (guests, twilight, juniors), range (grass), credit cards (MC, V, AE, D), BF, FF.
★★★ OCEAN COURSE (18)
Yards: 6,906/5,325. **Par:** 72/72. **Course Rating:** 72.8/71.1. **Slope:** 133/124. **Green Fee:** $85/$105. **Opened:** 1960. **Architect:** George Cobb, Mark McCumber.
Reader Comments: Has some great holes … Even saw deer grazing on the course.
★★★ SEA MARSH COURSE (18)
Yards: 6,515/5,054. **Par:** 72/72. **Course Rating:** 70.0/69.8. **Slope:** 120/123. **Green Fee:** $74/$95. **Opened:** 1964. **Architect:** George Cobb/Clyde Johnson.
Reader Comments: Good basic course.

★★½ SHADOWMOSS PLANTATION GOLF CLUB

SP-20 Dunvegan Dr., Charleston, 29414, Charleston County, (843)556-8251, (800)338-4971. **Facility Holes:** 18. **Yards:** 6,700/5,200. **Par:** 72/72. **Course Rating:** 72.5/71.0. **Slope:** 133/123. **Green Fee:** $22/$55. **Cart Fee:** Included in green fee. **Walking Policy:** Unrestricted walking. **Walkability:** 1. **Opened:** 1971. **Architect:** Russell Breeden. **Season:** Year-round. **High:** March-May. **Tee times:** Call up to 365 days in advance. **Miscellaneous:** Reduced fees (weekdays, guests, twilight, juniors), metal spikes, range (grass), credit cards (MC, V, AE, D), BF, FF.

★★★ SHIPYARD GOLF CLUB

R-P.O. Drawer 7229, Hilton Head Island, 29938, Beaufort County, (843)686-8802. **Facility Holes:** 27. **Green Fee:** $59/$88. **Cart Fee:** Included in green fee. **Walking Policy:** Mandatory carts. **Walkability:** 2. **Architect:** George W. Cobb. **To obtain tee times:** Call golf shop. **Miscellaneous:** Reduced fees (twilight), range (grass/mats), credit cards (MC, V, AE).
BRIGANTINE/CLIPPER (18 Combo)
Yards: 6,858/5,202. **Par:** 72/72. **Rating:** 73.0/70.5. **Slope:** 128/116. **Season:** Year-round. **High:** Feb.-May.

CLIPPER/GALLEON (18 Combo)
Yards: 6,878/5,391. **Par:** 72/72. **Rating:** 73.0/70.5. **Slope:** 129/119. **Season:** Year-round.
GALLEON/BRIGANTINE (18 Combo)
Yards: 6,738/5,127. **Par:** 72/72. **Rating:** 72.6/68.8. **Slope:** 128/114.
Reader Comments: Good layout, wife's favorite … Nice practice area, too much hidden … Another place to have fun … Very pedestrian … Most fun course for high handicaps.

★★★ **SOUTH CAROLINA NATIONAL GOLF CLUB**
SP-8 Waveland Ave., Cat Island, 29902, Beaufort County, (843)524-0300, 1 mile from Beaufort. **E-mail:** www.scnational.com. **Web:** www.scnational.com. **Facility Holes:** 18. **Yards:** 6,625/4,970. **Par:** 71/71. **Course Rating:** 72.0/67.4. **Slope:** 126/116. **Green Fee:** $35/$69. **Cart Fee:** Included in green fee. **Walking Policy:** Unrestricted walking. **Walkability:** 2. **Opened:** 1986. **Architect:** George W. Cobb. **Season:** Year-round. **High:** March-April. **To obtain tee times:** Call up to 30 days in advance. **Miscellaneous:** Reduced fees (weekdays, guests, twilight, juniors), range (grass), credit cards (MC, V, AE, D), BF, FF.
Reader Comments: Back-to-back par 3s across the marsh are the best I've seen … Short with lots of strategy.

★★★ **SPRING LAKE COUNTRY CLUB**
SP-1375 Spring Lake Rd., York, 29745, York County, (803)684-4898, 20 miles from Charlotte. **Facility Holes:** 18. **Yards:** 6,748/4,975. **Par:** 72/72. **Course Rating:** 72.8/67.3. **Slope:** 126/108. **Green Fee:** $17/$26. **Cart Fee:** $14/Person. **Walking Policy:** Walking at certain times. **Walkability:** 3. **Opened:** 1960. **Architect:** Fred Bolton/Bob Renaud. **Season:** Year-round. **High:** April-Oct. **To obtain tee times:** Call golf shop. **Miscellaneous:** Reduced fees (juniors), metal spikes, range (grass), credit cards (MC, V), BF, FF.
Reader Comments: Great greens … Great layout, tough Bermuda greens.

SPRINGFIELD GOLF CLUB
PU-990 Springfield Pkwy, Fort Mill, 29715, York County, (803)548-3318, (866)304-4653, 15 miles from Charlotte. **E-mail:** jcafarellaz@aol.com. **Web:** www.leroysprings.com. **Facility Holes:** 18. **Yards:** 6,923/4,854. **Par:** 72/72. **Course Rating:** 73.4/68.8. **Slope:** 139/129. **Green Fee:** $29/$50. **Cart Fee:** Included in green fee. **Walking Policy:** Walking at certain times. **Walkability:** 4. **Opened:** 2001. **Architect:** Clyde Johnston. **Season:** Year-round. **High:** April-Oct. **To obtain tee times:** Call up to 7 days in advance. **Miscellaneous:** Reduced fees (weekdays, twilight, seniors, juniors), credit cards (MC, V, AE, D), BF, FF.

★★★★ **STONEY POINT GOLF CLUB** *Pace*
SP-709 Swing About Dr., Greenwood, 29648, Greenwood County, (864)942-0900, 35 miles from Greenville. **E-mail:** proshop@stoneypointgolfclub.com. **Web:** www.stoneypointgolfclub.com. **Facility Holes:** 18. **Yards:** 6,760/5,060. **Par:** 72/72. **Course Rating:** 72.1/70.3. **Slope:** 125/120. **Green Fee:** $15/$22. **Cart Fee:** $15/Person. **Walking Policy:** Walking at certain times. **Walkability:** 3. **Opened:** 1990. **Architect:** Tom Jackson. **Season:** Year-round. **To obtain tee times:** Call up to 14 days in advance. **Miscellaneous:** Reduced fees (twilight, seniors, juniors), range (grass), credit cards (MC, V, D), BF, FF.
Reader Comments: Outstanding value if you walk … Really liked the way holes set up off the tee … Best kept secret in upstate SC … Good layout … Beautiful lake course, no rough.

★★ **SUMMERSETT GOLF CLUB**
SP-111 Pilot Rd., Greenville, 29609, Greenville County, (864)834-4781, 5 miles from Greenville. **Facility Holes:** 18. **Yards:** 6,025/4,910. **Par:** 72/72. **Course Rating:** 68.3/67.6. **Slope:** 114/119. **Green Fee:** $12/$19. **Cart Fee:** $11/Person. **Walking Policy:** Walking at certain times. **Walkability:** 3. **Opened:** 1938. **Architect:** Tom Jackson. **Season:** Year-round. **High:** April-Aug. **To obtain tee times:** Call golf shop. **Miscellaneous:** Reduced fees (seniors), metal spikes, credit cards (MC, V).

SUMTER NATIONAL GOLF CLUB
SP-7305 Myrtle Beach Hwy., Gable, 29051, Sumter County, (803)495-3550, 20 miles from Florence. **E-mail:** slinkinc@ftc.i.net. **Facility Holes:** 18. **Yards:** 7,000/5,344. **Par:** 72/72. **Course Rating:** 73.0/70.2. **Slope:** 127/119. **Green Fee:** $20/$38. **Cart Fee:** Included in green fee. **Walking Policy:** Mandatory carts. **Walkability:** 1. **Opened:** 1971. **Architect:** Russell Breeden. **Season:** Year-round. **High:** March-April. **To obtain tee times:** Call up to 365 days in advance. **Miscellaneous:** Reduced fees (weekdays, guests, twilight, seniors, juniors), range (grass), credit cards (MC, V), BF, FF.
Special Notes: Formerly Pineview Golf Club.

★★★★ **SURF GOLF & BEACH CLUB**
SP-1701 Springland Lane, North Myrtle Beach, 29597, Horry County, (843)249-1524, (800)765-7873, 60 miles from Wilmington. **Facility Holes:** 18. **Yards:** 6,842/5,178. **Par:** 72/72. **Course Rating:** 73.1/68.2. **Slope:** 131/109. **Green Fee:** $38/$75. **Cart Fee:** $18/Person.

Walking Policy: Mandatory carts. **Walkability:** 1. **Opened:** 1960. **Architect:** George Cobb. **Season:** Year-round. **To obtain tee times:** Call golf shop. **Miscellaneous:** Range (grass/mats), credit cards (MC, V), BF, FF.

Reader Comments: Best conditioned course in all of Myrtle Beach! … Kicked my butt … Best G-2 bent greens on the Strand … Good old course, good shape, offers variety … Super run facility. Worked us in for a replay even though they were booked.

★★★★½ TIDEWATER GOLF CLUB & PLANTATION

PU-1400 Tidewater Dr., North Myrtle Beach, 29582, Horry County, (843)249-3829, (800)446-5363, 10 miles from Myrtle Beach. **Web:** www.tide-water.com. **Facility Holes:** 18. **Yards:** 7,078/4,615. **Par:** 72/72. **Course Rating:** 74.8/67.1. **Slope:** 144/115. **Green Fee:** $90/$135. **Cart Fee:** Included in green fee. **Walking Policy:** Unrestricted walking. **Walkability:** 3. **Opened:** 1990. **Architect:** Ken Tomlinson. **Season:** Year-round. **To obtain tee times:** Call up to 365 days in advance. **Miscellaneous:** Reduced fees (weekdays, juniors), range (grass), lodging (100 rooms), credit cards (MC, V, AE), BF, FF.
Notes: Ranked 20th in 2001 Best in State; 29th in 1996 America's Top 75 Upscale Courses.
Reader Comments: Classic layout in a beautiful setting, great par 3s and great waterfront holes … Challenging to all skill levels … I don't see how it was left off the top 100 list … The par-3 3rd and 12th are probably two of the best anywhere … Holes 12 and 13 along the waterway are awesome.

★★½ TIMBERLAKE PLANTATION GOLF CLUB

SP-284 Club Dr., Chapin, 29036, Lexington County, (803)345-9909, 30 miles from Columbia. **Facility Holes:** 18. **Yards:** 6,703/5,111. **Par:** 72/72. **Course Rating:** 73.2/69.8. **Slope:** 132/118. **Green Fee:** $16/$22. **Cart Fee:** $13/Person. **Walking Policy:** Unrestricted walking. **Walkability:** 2. **Opened:** 1986. **Architect:** Willard Byrd. **Season:** Year-round. **To obtain tee times:** Call golf shop. **Miscellaneous:** Reduced fees (weekdays, guests, seniors, juniors), metal spikes, range (grass), credit cards (MC, V, AE).

★★★½ TOURNAMENT PLAYER'S CLUB OF MYRTLE BEACH

PU-1199 TPC Blvd., Murrell's Inlet, 29576, Horry County, (843)357-3399, (888)742-8721, 90 miles from Charleston. **E-mail:** tpcmbbox@mail.pgatour.com. **Web:** www.tpc-mb.com. **Facility Holes:** 18. **Yards:** 6,950/5,118. **Par:** 72/72. **Course Rating:** 74.0/70.3. **Slope:** 145/125. **Green Fee:** $54/$153. **Cart Fee:** $22/Person. **Walking Policy:** Walking at certain times. **Walkability:** 2. **Opened:** 1999. **Architect:** Tom Fazio/Lanny Wadkins. **Season:** Year-round. **High:** March-June. **To obtain tee times:** Call golf shop. **Miscellaneous:** Reduced fees (twilight, juniors), range (grass), credit cards (MC, V, AE), BF, FF.
Notes: Ranked 25th in 2001 Best in State; 9th in 1999 Best New Upscale Public.
Reader Comments: Long par 4s … Friendly layout … As with all TPCs, they make you feel like a pro. Clubhouse, grill room and locker room are all top notch. Tough course … Great TPC course, beautifully conditioned … Challenging but overpriced.

★★★★ TRADITION GOLF CLUB

PU-1027 Willbrook Blvd., Pawleys Island, 29585, Georgetown County, (843)237-5041, 20 miles from Myrtle Beach. **Web:** www.tradition.com. **Facility Holes:** 18. **Yards:** 6,919/5,111. **Par:** 72/72. **Course Rating:** 73.0/68.4. **Slope:** 130/113. **Green Fee:** $42/$89. **Cart Fee:** Included in green fee. **Walking Policy:** Walking at certain times. **Walkability:** 4. **Opened:** 1995. **Architect:** Ron Garl. **Season:** Year-round. **High:** March-April. **To obtain tee times:** Call golf shop. **Miscellaneous:** Reduced fees (twilight), range (grass), credit cards (MC, V, AE), BF, FF.
Reader Comments: A good course for people of all handicaps. Lots of sand and water… Fun layout, fun greens … Stately Southern property and course. Challenging, yet fair and fun … Great practice range and green.

★★★★½ TRUE BLUE GOLF CLUB

PU-900 Blue Stem Dr., Pawleys Island, 29585, Georgetown County, (803)235-0900, (888)483-6800, 20 miles from Myrtle Beach. **E-mail:** trueblue@s.c.coast.net. **Web:** www.true-bluegolfl.com. **Facility Holes:** 18. **Yards:** 7,062/4,995. **Par:** 72/72. **Course Rating:** 74.3/71.4. **Slope:** 145/123. **Green Fee:** $80/$130. **Cart Fee:** Included in green fee. **Walking Policy:** Unrestricted walking. **Walkability:** 2. **Opened:** 1998. **Architect:** Mike Strantz. **Season:** Year-round. **To obtain tee times:** Call golf shop. **Miscellaneous:** Range (grass/mats), credit cards (MC, V, AE, D), BF, FF.
Notes: Ranked 13th in 2001 Best in State.
Reader Comments: Nothing like it in Myrtle Beach. Another wild ride from Mike Strantz. Great job with Pine Valley-like waste bunkering. Great 3 opening holes … Waste bunkers and mounding add great character to nearly every hole … 10th hole is a 'killer.'.

★★★★ VERDAE GREENS GOLF CLUB

R-650 Verdae Blvd., Greenville, 29607, Greenville County, (864)676-1500, (800)849-7529, 90 miles from Charlotte. **Facility Holes:** 18. **Yards:** 7,041/5,012. **Par:** 72/72. **Course Rating:** 74.2/68.1. **Slope:** 140/116. **Green Fee:** $38/$52. **Cart Fee:** Included in green fee. **Walking**

Policy: Walking at certain times. **Walkability:** 4. **Opened:** 1989. **Architect:** Willard Byrd.
Season: Year-round. **High:** March-Oct. **To obtain tee times:** Call up to 7 days in advance.
Miscellaneous: Reduced fees (weekdays, guests, twilight, seniors, juniors), range (grass),
lodging (275 rooms), credit cards (MC, V, AE, D), BF, FF.
Reader Comments: Great location … Neat course adjacent to Embassy Suites … Tough greens …
USGA rough, fast greens … Great course … Championship course, very challenging, well main-
tained, courteous personnel.

★★½ VILLAGE GREEN GOLF CLUB
SP-Hwy. 176, Gramling, 29348, Spartanburg County, (864)472-2411, 14 miles from
Spartanburg. **Facility Holes:** 18. **Yards:** 6,372/5,280. **Par:** 72/74. **Course Rating:** 71.0/70.0.
Slope: 122/123. **Green Fee:** $15/$20. **Cart Fee:** $11/Person. **Walking Policy:** Unrestricted walk-
ing. **Walkability:** 3. **Opened:** 1969. **Architect:** Russell Breeden/Dan Breeden. **Season:** Year-
round. **To obtain tee times:** Call golf shop. **Miscellaneous:** Reduced fees (seniors), range
(grass), credit cards (MC, V), BF, FF.

★★★★ WACHESAW PLANTATION EAST
SP-911 Riverwood Dr., Murrells Inlet, 29576, Georgetown County, (843)357-2090,
(888)922-0027, 90 miles from Charleston. **E-mail:** info@wachesaweast.com. **Web:** www.wach-
esaweast.com. **Facility Holes:** 18. **Yards:** 6,993/4,995. **Par:** 72/72. **Course Rating:** 73.6/68.8.
Slope: 135/117. **Green Fee:** $55/$107. **Walking Policy:** Walking at certain times. **Walkability:** 1.
Opened: 1996. **Architect:** Clyde Johnston. **Season:** Year-round. **Tee times:** Call golf shop.
Misc: Reduced fees (guests, juniors), range (grass/mats), credit cards (MC, V, AE), BF, FF.
Reader Comments: Course where LPGA played … Staff could not have been more helpful .. A
jewel, not as expensive as other 'surcharge' courses, but a much better value than nearly all the oth-
ers … Not crowded in summer … A tough high quality course.

★★★½ THE WALKER COURSE AT CLEMSON UNIVERSITY
SP-110 Madren Center Dr., Clemson, 29634, Pickens County, (864)656-0236, 40 miles from
Greenville. **Web:** www.clemson.edu. **Facility Holes:** 18. **Yards:** 6,911/4,667. **Par:** 72/72. **Course
Rating:** 72.8/65.7. **Slope:** 137/107. **Green Fee:** $18/$36. **Walking Policy:** Unrestricted walking.
Walkability: 4. **Opened:** 1995. **Architect:** D.J. DeVictor. **Season:** Year-round. **To obtain tee
times:** Call up to 7 days in advance. **Misc:** Reduced fees (weekdays, twilight, seniors, juniors),
range (grass/mats), lodging (89 rooms), credit cards (MC, V, AE, D), BF, FF.
Reader Comments: Several holes are well crafted, multiple ways to play … This course is very
hilly, walkable for those in good physical condition … Beautiful course, a real challenge.

WATERFORD GOLF CLUB
SP-1900 Clubhouse Rd., Rock Hill, 29730, York County, (803)324-0300, (888)203-9222, 15
miles from Charlotte. **E-mail:** waterfordgc@aol.com. **Web:** charlottegolf.com. **Facility Holes:**
18. **Yards:** 6,913/5,196. **Par:** 72/72. **Course Rating:** 72.2/68.2. **Slope:** 132/112. **Green Fee:**
$35/$50. **Cart Fee:** Included in green fee. **Walking Policy:** Walking at certain times.
Walkability: 3. **Opened:** 1997. **Architect:** Hale Irwin/Stan Gentry. **Season:** Year-round. **To
obtain tee times:** Call up to 7 days in advance. **Miscellaneous:** Reduced fees (weekdays,
twilight, seniors, juniors), range (grass), credit cards (MC, V, AE, D), BF, FF.

★★★ WATERWAY HILLS GOLF CLUB
R-9731 Hwy. 17 N., Restaurant Row, Myrtle Beach, 29578, Horry County, (843)449-6488,
(800)344-5590. **E-mail:** info@mbn.com. **Web:** www.mbn.com. **Facility Holes:** 27. **Green Fee:**
$27/$69. **Cart Fee:** $21/Person. **Walking Policy:** Walking at certain times. **Walkability:** 2.
Opened: 1975. **Architect:** Robert Trent Jones/Rees Jones. **Season:** Year-round. **To obtain tee
times:** Call golf shop. **Miscellaneous:** Reduced fees (guests, twilight, juniors), range (grass),
credit cards (MC, V, AE, D, DC, CB), BF, FF.
LAKES/RAVINES (18 Combo)
Yards: 6,339/4,825. **Par:** 72/72. **Course Rating:** 70.6/67.3. **Slope:** 123/110.
OAKS/LAKES (18 Combo)
Yards: 6,461/5,069. **Par:** 72/72. **Course Rating:** 71.0/68.7. **Slope:** 119/113.
RAVINES/OAKS (18 Combo)
Yards: 6,420/4,914. **Par:** 72/72. **Course Rating:** 70.8/67.6. **Slope:** 121/113.
Reader Comments: A classic … Ride over inland waterway is the best part … Confidence booster
… Great course for the money.

★★★ WEDGEFIELD PLANTATION GOLF CLUB
SP-Hwy 701 N., Georgetown, 29440, Georgetown County, (843)546-8587, 5 miles from
Georgetown. **E-mail:** info@wedgefield.com. **Web:** wedgefield.com. **Facility Holes:** 18. **Yards:**
6,299/5,254. **Par:** 72/73. **Course Rating:** 70.2/69.9. **Slope:** 124/119. **Green Fee:** $35/$55. **Cart
Fee:** Included in green fee. **Walking Policy:** Mandatory carts. **Walkability:** 1. **Opened:** 1974.
Architect: Porter Gibson. **Season:** Year-round. **High:** March-May. **To obtain tee times:** Call golf
shop. **Miscellaneous:** Reduced fees (twilight), metal spikes, range (grass), credit cards

(MC, V), BF, FF.
Reader Comments: Nice par 3s and finishing holes… Challenging, choose your shots carefully … Out of the way, but a must play.

★★★ THE WELLMAN CLUB
PU-Hwy. 41-51 S., 328 Clubhouse Dr.., Johnsonville, 29555, Florence County, (843)386-2521, 42 miles from Myrtle Beach. **E-mail:** wellmanclub@wellmanclub.com. **Web:** www.wellmanclub.com. **Facility Holes:** 18. **Yards:** 7,018/5,281. **Par:** 72/72. **Course Rating:** 73.9/69.5. **Slope:** 129/105. **Green Fee:** $16/$35. **Cart Fee:** $15/Person. **Walking Policy:** Walking at certain times. **Walkability:** 3. **Opened:** 1966. **Architect:** Ellis Maples/Ed Seay. **Season:** Year-round. **To obtain tee times:** Call golf shop. **Miscellaneous:** Reduced fees (weekdays, guests, twilight, seniors, juniors), range (grass), credit cards (MC, V), BF, FF.
Reader Comments: Excellent shape, challenging … Course is generally in good shape.

★½ WHITE PINES GOLF CLUB
PU-614 Mary Lane, Camden, 29020, Kershaw County, (803)432-7442, 5 miles from Camden. **Facility Holes:** 18. **Yards:** 6,373/4,806. **Par:** 72/72. **Course Rating:** 69.4/66.9. **Slope:** 115/112. **Green Fee:** $17/$25. **Cart Fee:** Included in green fee. **Walking Policy:** Mandatory carts. **Walkability:** 1. **Opened:** 1969. **Architect:** Griffen Fletcher. **Season:** Year-round. **Tee times:** Call golf shop. **Misc:** Reduced fees (weekdays, guests, seniors), range (grass).

★★★ WICKED STICK GOLF LINKS
R-1051 Coventry Rd., Myrtle Beach, 29575, Horry County, (843)215-2500, (800)797-8425, 5 miles from Myrtle Beach. **E-mail:** wkdstk@sccoast.net. **Web:** www.wickedstick.com. **Facility Holes:** 18. **Yards:** 7,001/4,911. **Par:** 72/72. **Course Rating:** 72.2/70.1. **Slope:** 129/123. **Green Fee:** $35/$57. **Cart Fee:** $20/Person. **Walking Policy:** Walking at certain times. **Walkability:** 1. **Opened:** 1995. **Architect:** Clyde Johnston/John Daly. **Season:** Year-round. **To obtain tee times:** Call golf shop. **Miscellaneous:** Reduced fees (guests, twilight, juniors), range (grass/mats), credit cards (MC, V, AE), BF, FF.
Reader Comments: Nice course, Scottish feel … Always in good shape … A slugfest, wide open and long … Multiple tee boxes allowed course to be enjoyed by whole family. Just enough rough, water, sand (pot bunkers) to really test you.

WILD DUNES RESORT
R-5881 Palmetto Dr., Isle of Palms, 29451, Charleston County, (843)886-2301, (800)845-8880, 12 miles from Charleston. **Facility Holes:** 36. **Cart Fee:** Included in green fee. **Architect:** Tom Fazio. **Season:** Year-round. **To obtain tee times:** Call golf shop.
★★★★ HARBOR COURSE (18) *Pace*
Yards: 6,446/4,774. **Par:** 70/70. **Course Rating:** 70.9/68.1. **Slope:** 124/117. **Green Fee:** $60/$119. **Walking Policy:** Mandatory carts. **Walkability:** 3. **Opened:** 1986. **Miscellaneous:** Reduced fees (weekdays, guests, twilight, juniors), credit cards (MC, V, AE, D), BF, FF.
Reader Comments: Another great course at Wild Dunes … Tough, lots of water, and a bit narrow … Stronger course than its reputation … Nos. 2, 4, 17, 18 make the course … Great experience.
★★★★½ LINKS COURSE (18)
Yards: 6,722/4,849. **Par:** 72/72. **Course Rating:** 72.7/69.1. **Slope:** 131/121. **Green Fee:** $50/$145. **Walking Policy:** Unrestricted walking. **Walkability:** 2. **Opened:** 1980. **Miscellaneous:** Reduced fees (guests, juniors), metal spikes, range (grass/mats), caddies, credit cards (MC, V, AE, D, Diners Club).
Notes: Ranked 7th in 2001 Best in State; 26th in 1996 America's Top 75 Upscale Course.
Reader Comments: Great golf course … Very tough finishing hole … Watch out for the last two holes, tough when its windy … Could play this layout everyday … Ocean holes are beautiful … Bagger Vance would feel at home … Two reachable par 5s … Back 9 best stretch anywhere.

WILD WING PLANTATION
R-1000 Wild Wing Blvd., Conway, 29526, Horry County, (843)347-9464, (800)736-9464, 7 miles from Myrtle Beach. **E-mail:** wildwing@sccoast.net. **Web:** www.wildwing.com. **Facility Holes:** 72. **Cart Fee:** $20/Person. **Walking Policy:** Mandatory carts. **Season:** Year-round. **High:** March-April. **Tee times:** Call golf shop. **Miscellaneous:** Reduced fees (weekdays, guests, twilight), range (grass), lodging (144 rooms), credit cards (MC, V, AE, D), BF, FF.
★★★★ AVOCET COURSE (18) *Condition*
Yards: 7,127/5,298. **Par:** 72/72. **Course Rating:** 74.4/70.4. **Slope:** 129/118. **Green Fee:** $30/$108. **Walkability:** 2. **Opened:** 1993. **Architect:** Larry Nelson/Jeff Brauer.
Reader Comments: Love layout, nice greens, fun … One of the best in Myrtle Beach … Always a pleasure to play nice facility … Fun course with 4 risk reward par 5s … Price good, picturesque, interesting, good condition, wide landing areas … Excellent pub.
★★★★ FALCON COURSE (18)
Yards: 7,082/5,190. **Par:** 72/72. **Course Rating:** 74.4/70.4. **Slope:** 134/118. **Green Fee:** $30/$90. **Walkability:** 3. **Opened:** 1994. **Architect:** Rees Jones.
Reader Comments: Probably one of the top courses in Myrtle Beach … Tough but fair with the

best greens, almost too fast ... Challenge for most handicappers, good course ... Nice facility, busy ... May be best year-round greens at the beach.

★★★★½ **HUMMINGBIRD COURSE** (18) *Value, Condition*
Yards: 6,853/5,168. **Par:** 72/72. **Course Rating:** 73.6/69.5. **Slope:** 135/123. **Green Fee:** $26/$77. **Walkability:** 2. **Opened:** 1992. **Architect:** Willard Byrd.

Reader Comments: Doesn't get the reviews of some of the other Wild Wing courses, but every bit as impressive ... Tough track ... Great conditioned golf course ... Must play the right tees. Whites are short (layups at 180 to 200 on some holes) ... Pure golf, layout exceptional, excellent condition.

★★★★½ **WOOD STORK COURSE** (18) *Condition*
Yards: 7,044/5,409. **Par:** 72/72. **Course Rating:** 74.1/70.7. **Slope:** 130/121. **Green Fee:** $25/$84. **Walkability:** 1. **Opened:** 1991. **Architect:** Willard Byrd.

Reader Comments: A must play ... Fair, challenging ... Great bent grass greens. After a ho-hum first 6 holes this course winds beautifully through the trees and is the best of the four ... Consistently good conditions ... Prices that can't be beat ... Courses are pretty and hard.

WINYAH BAY GOLF CLUB
PU-South Island Rd., Georgetown, 29440, Georgetown County, (843)527-7765, (877)527-7765. **Facility Holes:** 18. **Yards:** 6,100/4,700. **Par:** 70/70. **Course Rating:** 66.9/65.1. **Slope:** 116/111. **Green Fee:** $25/$60. **Cart Fee:** $20/Cart. **Walking Policy:** Walking at certain times. **Walkability:** 2. **Opened:** 1998. **Architect:** Matt Sapochak. **Season:** Year-round. **To obtain tee times:** Call golf shop. **Miscellaneous:** Reduced fees (juniors), range (grass), credit cards (MC, V), BF, FF.

★★★★½ **THE WITCH**
R-1900 Hwy. 544, Conway, 29526, Horry County, (843)347-2706, 8 miles from Myrtle Beach. **Web:** www.mysticalgolf.com. **Facility Holes:** 18. **Yards:** 6,702/4,812. **Par:** 71/71. **Course Rating:** 71.2/69.0. **Slope:** 133/109. **Green Fee:** $44/$93. **Cart Fee:** Included in green fee. **Walking Policy:** Mandatory carts. **Walkability:** 2. **Opened:** 1989. **Architect:** Dan Maples. **Season:** Year-round. **High:** March-April. **To obtain tee times:** Call up to 365 days in advance. **Miscellaneous:** Reduced fees (juniors), range (grass), credit cards (MC, V), FF.

Reader Comments: Beautiful course with no housing to distract from setting. Some very, very challenging holes ... Good holes through woods, watch out for alligators ... Nice beach course without gimmicks ... Bridges and water everywhere ... Lots of trouble to carry in front of greens.

★★★★ **THE WIZARD GOLF COURSE**
R-4601 Leeshore Blvd., Myrtle Beach, 29579, Horry County, (843)236-9393, 8 miles from Myrtle Beach. **Web:** www.mysticalgolf.com. **Facility Holes:** 18. **Yards:** 6,721/4,972. **Par:** 71/71. **Course Rating:** 70.4/71.2. **Slope:** 119/121. **Green Fee:** $44/$90. **Cart Fee:** Included in green fee. **Walking Policy:** Mandatory carts. **Walkability:** 2. **Opened:** 1996. **Architect:** Dan Maples. **Season:** Year-round. **High:** March-April. **To obtain tee times:** Call up to 365 days in advance. **Miscellaneous:** Reduced fees (juniors), range (grass), credit cards (MC, V), FF.

Reader Comments: Great course. Tough but playable ... Great condition of the greens and fairways will improve your game. Good mix of water and sand hazards. Clubhouse built like a castle ... This is a fun course that rewards shot selection. A long drive is not necessary to do well ... Water everywhere, good greens.

WOODFIN RIDGE GOLF CLUB
SP-215 So. Woodfin Ridge Dr., Inman, 29349, Spartanburg County, (864)578-0023, 9 miles from Spartanburg. **Web:** www.woodfinridge.com. **Facility Holes:** 18. **Yards:** 7,107/5,105. **Par:** 72/72. **Course Rating:** 73.6/69.9. **Slope:** 134/121. **Green Fee:** $25/$39. **Cart Fee:** Included in green fee. **Walking Policy:** Unrestricted walking. **Walkability:** 3. **Opened:** 2000. **Architect:** Bill Bergin. **Season:** Year-round. **High:** March-Sept. **To obtain tee times:** Call up to 7 days in advance. **Miscellaneous:** Reduced fees (weekdays, twilight, seniors, juniors), range (grass), credit cards (MC, V, AE), BF, FF.

SOUTH DAKOTA

ABERDEEN LINKS GOLF COURSE
SP-1500 NW 8th Ave., Aberdeen, 57401, Brown County, (605)225-8135. **E-mail:** ablinks@nvc.net. **Facility Holes:** 9. **Yards:** 2,574/2,171. **Par:** 34/34. **Course Rating:** 63.4/63.4. **Slope:** 100/100. **Green Fee:** $6/$12. **Cart Fee:** $8/Person. **Walking Policy:** Unrestricted walking. **Season:** April-Nov. **To obtain tee times:** Call golf shop. **Miscellaneous:** Reduced fees (weekdays), range (grass), credit cards (MC, V, D).

BELLE FOURCHE COUNTRY CLUB
PU-S. Hwy. 85, Belle Fourche, 57717, Butte County, (605)892-3472. **Facility Holes:** 9. **Yards:** 3,012/2,554. **Par:** 36/36. **Course Rating:** 68.9/68.0. **Slope:** 122/117. **Green Fee:** $22/$24. **Cart Fee:** $20/Cart. **Walking Policy:** Unrestricted walking. **Walkability:** 3. **Opened:** 1927. **Season:** April-Nov. **To obtain tee times:** Call golf shop. **Miscellaneous:** Reduced fees (weekdays), range (grass), credit cards (MC, V, AE, D), BF, FF.

★★★★ THE BLUFFS *Value, Pace*
PU-2021 E. Main St., Vermillion, 57069, Clay County, (605)677-7058, 60 miles from Sioux Falls. **E-mail:** covbluff@usd.edu. **Web:** www.bluffsliving.com. **Facility Holes:** 18. **Yards:** 6,684/4,926. **Par:** 72/72. **Course Rating:** 72.4/63.9. **Slope:** 123/100. **Green Fee:** $16/$20. **Cart Fee:** $21/Cart. **Walking Policy:** Unrestricted walking. **Walkability:** 3. **Opened:** 1996. **Architect:** Pat Wyss. **Season:** March-Nov. **High:** June-Aug. **To obtain tee times:** Call up to 7 days in advance. **Miscellaneous:** Range (grass), credit cards (MC, V), BF, FF.
Reader Comments: Fun and challenging course. Friendly staff and superb clubhouse ... Very interesting bluff holes. Local knowledge is critical ... Interesting, well-conditioned course on a wetland along the Nebraska Bluffs of the Missouri River.

BRANDON GOLF COURSE
PU-2100 E. Aspen Blvd., Brandon, 57005, Minnehaha County, (605)582-7100, 1 mile from Brandon. **E-mail:** bgc@splitrocktel.net. **Facility Holes:** 18. **Yards:** 6,243/5,073. **Par:** 71/71. **Course Rating:** 70.1/69.7. **Slope:** 110/109. **Green Fee:** $17/$19. **Cart Fee:** $11/Person. **Walking Policy:** Unrestricted walking. **Walkability:** 2. **Opened:** 1980. **Architect:** Wyss Associates. **Season:** April-Nov. **To obtain tee times:** Call up to 7 days in advance. **Miscellaneous:** Range (grass), credit cards (MC, V, D), BF, FF.

BROADLAND CREEK NATIONAL GOLF CLUB
PU-N. Hwy. 37, Huron, 57350, Beadle County, (605)353-8525. **Facility Holes:** 18. **Yards:** 3,152/2,721. **Par:** 36/36. **Course Rating:** 69.8/75.4. **Slope:** 110/122. **Green Fee:** $16. **Cart Fee:** $17/Cart. **Architect:** Garrett Gill. **To obtain tee times:** Call golf shop.

★★ CENTRAL VALLEY GOLF CLUB
SP-Hwy. 38, Hartford, 57033, Minnehaha County, (605)528-6122, 8 miles from Sioux Falls. **Facility Holes:** 18. **Yards:** 6,326/5,115. **Par:** 72/72. **Course Rating:** 70.1/68.6. **Slope:** 121/110. **Green Fee:** $16/$20. **Cart Fee:** $24/Cart. **Walking Policy:** Unrestricted walking. **Walkability:** 3. **Opened:** 1969. **Architect:** Mike Smith. **Season:** March-Oct. **High:** May-Aug. **To obtain tee times:** Call up to 7 days in advance. **Miscellaneous:** Reduced fees (weekdays, seniors, juniors), range (grass/mats), credit cards (MC, V, AE), BF, FF.

★★½ EDGEBROOK GOLF COURSE
PU-Rte. #1 Box 1A, Brookings, 57006, Brookings County, (605)692-6995, 1 mile from Brookings. **Facility Holes:** 18. **Yards:** 6,078/5,041. **Par:** 70/70. **Course Rating:** 68.1/68.0. **Slope:** 113/111. **Green Fee:** $12/$17. **Cart Fee:** $16/Cart. **Walkability:** 2. **Opened:** 1974. **Architect:** Pat Wyss. **Season:** April-Oct. **High:** May-July. **To obtain tee times:** Call golf shop. **Miscellaneous:** Metal spikes, range (grass).

★★★ ELMWOOD GOLF COURSE
PU-2604 W. Russell, Sioux Falls, 57104, Minnehaha County, (605)367-7092, (888)709-6095. **E-mail:** elmwood@dakotagolf.com. **Web:** www.dakotagolf.com. **Facility Holes:** 27. **Yards:** 6,850/5,750. **Par:** 72/72. **Course Rating:** 72.1/72.0. **Slope:** 129/125. **Green Fee:** $16/$18. **Cart Fee:** $11/Person. **Walking Policy:** Unrestricted walking. **Walkability:** 1. **Opened:** 1923. **Architect:** Lawrence Packard. **Season:** April-Nov. **High:** May-Sept. **To obtain tee times:** Call up to 7 days in advance. **Miscellaneous:** Reduced fees (twilight), range (grass/mats), credit cards (MC, V, D), BF, FF.
Reader Comments: A fast pace for the value & easy course ... Old course, well taken care of ... Nice old-style muni. A lot of trees, fun, inexpensive, but not overly remarkable.
Special Notes: Also has a 9-hole course.

★★½ FOX RUN GOLF COURSE
PU-600 W. 27th St., Yankton, 57078, Yankton County, (605)668-5205, 75 miles from Sioux Falls. **Facility Holes:** 18. **Yards:** 6,792/5,209. **Par:** 72/72. **Course Rating:** 70.8/68.6. **Slope:**

122/115. **Green Fee:** $16/$19. **Cart Fee:** $18/Cart. **Walking Policy:** Unrestricted walking. **Walkability:** 2. **Opened:** 1993. **Architect:** Pat Wyss. **Season:** March-Nov. **To obtain tee times:** Call up to 7 days in advance. **Miscellaneous:** Reduced fees (weekdays), range (grass/mats), credit cards (MC, V), BF, FF.

★★★½ HART RANCH GOLF COURSE

PU-Spring Creek Rd., Rapid City, 57702, Pennington County, (605)341-5703, 8 miles from Rapid City. **E-mail:** golf@hartranch.com. **Web:** www.hartranch.com. **Facility Holes:** 18. **Yards:** 6,841/4,999. **Par:** 72/72. **Course Rating:** 72.5/70.1. **Slope:** 127/124. **Green Fee:** $30/$32. **Cart Fee:** $22/Cart. **Walking Policy:** Unrestricted walking. **Walkability:** 3. **Opened:** 1985. **Architect:** Pat Wyss. **Season:** March-Nov. **High:** June-Aug. **To obtain tee times:** Call up to 7 days in advance. **Miscellaneous:** Range (grass), credit cards (MC, V, AE, D), BF, FF.
Reader Comments: Great views of the Black Hills ... Extremely challenging, great holes ... Green fees are high for the area, greens are inconsistent.

★★★★½ HILLCREST GOLF & COUNTRY CLUB

SP-2206 Mulberry, Yankton, 57078, Yankton County, (605)665-4621, 50 miles from Sioux Falls. **Facility Holes:** 18. **Yards:** 6,874/5,726. **Par:** 72/72. **Course Rating:** 72.2/72.2. **Slope:** 130/126. **Green Fee:** $35/$40. **Cart Fee:** $24/Cart. **Walking Policy:** Unrestricted walking. **Walkability:** 2. **Opened:** 1953. **Architect:** Chic Adams. **Season:** March-Dec. **High:** April-Nov. **To obtain tee times:** Call up to 7 days in advance. **Miscellaneous:** Reduced fees (weekdays), range (grass), credit cards (MC, V), BF, FF.
Reader Comments: #17 outstanding—excellent greens ... Length is not a problem, the greens are the killer ... Excellent, long, old course in great condition.

★★ HILLSVIEW GOLF CLUB

PU-4201 SD Hwy. 34, Pierre, 57501, Hughes County, (605)224-6191, 180 miles from Rapid City. **Facility Holes:** 18. **Yards:** 6,828/5,470. **Par:** 72/73. **Course Rating:** 71.4/73.9. **Slope:** 122/119. **Green Fee:** $16. **Cart Fee:** $18/Cart. **Walking Policy:** Unrestricted walking. **Walkability:** 1. **Opened:** 1965. **Architect:** Charles Maddox. **Season:** April-Oct. **High:** June-Aug. **To obtain tee times:** Call golf shop. **Miscellaneous:** Reduced fees (juniors), metal spikes, range (grass/mats), credit cards (MC, V).

LAKEVIEW GOLF COURSE

PU-3300 N. Ohlman St., Mitchell, 57301, Davison County, (605)995-8460, 1 mile from Mitchell. **E-mail:** turfexp@aol.com. **Facility Holes:** 18. **Yards:** 6,670/5,808. **Par:** 72/73. **Course Rating:** 71.3/72.6. **Slope:** 124/125. **Green Fee:** $20. **Cart Fee:** $10/Person. **Walking Policy:** Unrestricted walking. **Walkability:** 2. **Opened:** 1978. **Architect:** Richard Watson. **Season:** March-Nov. **To obtain tee times:** Call golf shop. **Miscellaneous:** Range (grass), credit cards (MC, V), BF, FF.

★★ LEE PARK GOLF COURSE

PU-2 Elk Dr., Aberdeen, 57401, Brown County, (605)626-7092, 200 miles from Sioux Falls. **Facility Holes:** 18. **Yards:** 6,346/5,138. **Par:** 72/72. **Course Rating:** 69.6/68.3. **Slope:** 128/122. **Green Fee:** $16/$18. **Cart Fee:** $18/Cart. **Walking Policy:** Unrestricted walking. **Walkability:** 1. **Opened:** 1933. **Season:** April-Oct. **To obtain tee times:** Call up to 3 days in advance. **Miscellaneous:** Reduced fees (weekdays, twilight), range (grass/mats), credit cards (MC, V, D), BF, FF.

★★★★ MEADOWBROOK GOLF COURSE

PU-3625 Jackson Blvd., Rapid City, 57702, Pennington County, (605)394-4191. **Facility Holes:** 18. **Yards:** 7,054/5,603. **Par:** 72/72. **Course Rating:** 73.0/71.1. **Slope:** 138/130. **Green Fee:** $19/$26. **Cart Fee:** $18/Cart. **Walking Policy:** Unrestricted walking. **Walkability:** 2. **Opened:** 1976. **Architect:** David Gill. **Season:** Year-round. **High:** April-Oct. **To obtain tee times:** Call golf shop. **Miscellaneous:** Reduced fees (weekdays, seniors, juniors), range (grass/mats).
Notes: Ranked 2nd in 2001 Best in State; 56th in 1996 America's Top 75 Affordable Courses.
Reader Comments: You use every club in the bag ... Nice layout, lots of slow days ... Challenging, well manicured home course.

★★★★ PRAIRIE GREEN GOLF COURSE

PU-600 E. 69th St., Sioux Falls, 57108, Minnehaha County, (605)367-6076, (800)585-6076. **E-mail:** prairiegreen@dakotagolf.com. **Web:** www.dakotagolf.com. **Facility Holes:** 18. **Yards:** 7,179/5,250. **Par:** 72/72. **Course Rating:** 74.2/70.2. **Slope:** 134/122. **Green Fee:** $23/$27. **Cart Fee:** $11/Person. **Walking Policy:** Unrestricted walking. **Walkability:** 3. **Opened:** 1995. **Architect:** Dick Nugent. **Season:** March-Nov. **To obtain tee times:** Call up to 7 days in advance. **Miscellaneous:** Reduced fees (weekdays, twilight, seniors, juniors), range (grass), credit cards (MC, V, AE, D), BF, FF.

SOUTH DAKOTA

Notes: Ranked 4th in 2001 Best in State; 5th in 1996 Best New Affordable Courses.
Reader Comments: Excellent links-type course in the South Dakota wind tunnel … Long, hard course—set up for big hitter … No trees & windy … Tough, flat, good value … Nice layout, very playable … Good prairie-style target golf.

RAPID CITY ELKS GOLF COURSE
SP-3333 E. 39th St., Rapid City, 57703, Pennington County, (605)393-0522, 3 miles from Rapid City. **Facility Holes:** 18. **Yards:** 6,126/4,932. **Par:** 72/72. **Course Rating:** 70.9/69.9. **Slope:** 131/131. **Green Fee:** $17/$21. **Cart Fee:** $20/Cart. **Walking Policy:** Unrestricted walking. **Walkability:** 3. **Opened:** 1960. **Architect:** Pat Wyss. **Season:** April-Nov. **High:** June-Sept. **To obtain tee times:** Call golf shop. **Miscellaneous:** Range (grass), credit cards (MC, V, D).

★★★★ SOUTHERN HILLS GOLF COURSE
PU-W. Hwy. 18, Hot Springs, 57747, Fall River County, (605)745-6400, 45 miles from Rapid City. **Facility Holes:** 9. **Yards:** 2,969/2,435. **Par:** 35/35. **Course Rating:** 35.1/34.7. **Slope:** 130/121. **Green Fee:** $22. **Cart Fee:** $22/Cart. **Walking Policy:** Unrestricted walking. **Walkability:** 5. **Opened:** 1979. **Architect:** Dick Phelps/Brad Benz. **Season:** March-Nov. **High:** June-Sept. **To obtain tee times:** Call golf shop. **Miscellaneous:** Range (grass), credit cards (MC, V, D), BF, FF.
Reader Comments: Fun track, lots of interesting holes, I always want to play this 9-holer more than once. One problem, need a shuttle for the range … Excellent course—needs to expand to 18 holes … Great scenery.

SPEARFISH CANYON COUNTRY CLUB
SP-120 Spearfish Canyon Dr., Spearfish, 57783, Lawrence County, (605)642-7156. **E-mail:** sccc@vcn.com. **Facility Holes:** 18. **Yards:** 6,616/5,399. **Par:** 71/72. **Course Rating:** 71.0/70.3. **Slope:** 121/118. **Green Fee:** $25/$43. **Cart Fee:** $12/Person. **Walking Policy:** Unrestricted walking. **Walkability:** 5. **Opened:** 1922. **Season:** Year-round. **High:** May-Sept. **To obtain tee times:** Call up to 7 days in advance. **Miscellaneous:** Reduced fees (weekdays, juniors), range (grass), credit cards (MC, V), BF, FF.

★★½ TWO RIVERS GOLF CLUB
PU-150 S. Oak Tree Lane, Dakota Dunes, 57049, Union County, (605)232-3241, 1 mile from Sioux City. **Facility Holes:** 18. **Yards:** 5,820/5,246. **Par:** 70/73. **Course Rating:** 69.0/71.0. **Slope:** 120/112. **Green Fee:** $19. **Cart Fee:** $11/Person. **Walking Policy:** Unrestricted walking. **Walkability:** 1. **Opened:** 1921. **Season:** April-Nov. **To obtain tee times:** Call up to 7 days in advance. **Miscellaneous:** Reduced fees (weekdays), range (grass), credit cards (MC, V, AE, D), BF, FF.

★★½ WATERTOWN MUNICIPAL GOLF COURSE
PU-351 S. Lake Dr., Watertown, 57201, Codington County, (605)882-6262. **Facility Holes:** 27. **Green Fee:** $17/$20. **Cart Fee:** $18/Cart. **Walking Policy:** Unrestricted walking. **Walkability:** 1. **Architect:** Phil Wigton. **Season:** April-Oct. **To obtain tee times:** Call golf shop. **Miscellaneous:** Range (grass), credit cards (MC, V).
RED/BLUE (18 Combo)
Yards: 5,220/5,858. **Par:** 72/78. **Course Rating:** 67.4/71.3. **Slope:** 106/114.
RED/YELLOW (18 Combo)
Yards: 6,231/5,615. **Par:** 72/75. **Course Rating:** 69.4/71.7. **Slope:** 109/113.
YELLOW/BLUE (18 Combo)
Yards: 6,001/5,470. **Par:** 72/75. **Course Rating:** 68.4/70.9. **Slope:** 108/111.

★★★½ WILLOW RUN GOLF COURSE
PU-E. Hwy. 38/42, Sioux Falls, 57103, Minnehaha County, (605)335-5900. **Facility Holes:** 18. **Yards:** 6,505/4,855. **Par:** 71/71. **Course Rating:** 71.1/68.7. **Slope:** 127/119. **Green Fee:** $14/$17. **Walking Policy:** Unrestricted walking. **Opened:** 1988. **Architect:** Joel Goldstrand. **Season:** March-Nov. **High:** May-Oct. **To obtain tee times:** Call golf shop. **Miscellaneous:** Reduced fees (weekdays, twilight, seniors, juniors), metal spikes, range (grass), credit cards (MC, V).
Reader Comments: Very tight course, lots of fun, fair green fees … Great hilly target-style design, but lacking in conditioning … Enjoyable course with a lot of variety, good value … Nice elevation changes … Watch out for the wind.

ANDREW JOHNSON GOLF CLUB
PU-615 Lick Hollow Rd., Greeneville, 37744, Greene County, (423)636-1476, (800)421-2149, 1 mile from Greenville. **Facility Holes:** 18. **Yards:** 6,103/4,776. **Par:** 70/70. **Course Rating:** 68.1/66.6. **Slope:** 114/113. **Green Fee:** $14/$16. **Cart Fee:** $12/Person. **Walking Policy:** Walking at certain times. **Walkability:** 2. **Opened:** 1989. **Architect:** Robert Walker. **Season:** Year-round. **High:** April-Aug. **To obtain tee times:** Call golf shop. **Miscellaneous:** Reduced fees (weekdays), range (grass), credit cards (MC, V).

★½ AUDUBON PARK GOLF COURSE
PU-4160 Park Ave., Memphis, 38117, Shelby County, (901)683-6941. **E-mail:** audubon-golf@msn.com. **Facility Holes:** 18. **Yards:** 6,347/5,615. **Par:** 70/71. **Course Rating:** 68.3. **Slope:** 104. **Cart Fee:** $24/Cart. **Walking Policy:** Unrestricted walking. **Walkability:** 2. **Opened:** 1952. **Season:** Year-round. **To obtain tee times:** Call up to 7 days in advance. **Miscellaneous:** Reduced fees (weekdays, seniors, juniors), range (grass), BF, FF.

★★★ BANEBERRY GOLF & RESORT
R-704 Harrison Ferry Rd., Baneberry, 37890, Jefferson County, (865)674-2500, (800)951-4653, 35 miles from Knoxville. **E-mail:** golfrest@baneberrygolf.com. **Web:** www.baneberrygolf.com. **Facility Holes:** 18. **Yards:** 6,694/4,829. **Par:** 71/72. **Course Rating:** 72.6/68.5. **Slope:** 125/117. **Green Fee:** $14/$17. **Cart Fee:** $13/Person. **Walking Policy:** Unrestricted walking. **Walkability:** 2. **Opened:** 1972. **Architect:** Bob Thompson. **Season:** Year-round. **High:** April-Oct. **To obtain tee times:** Call golf shop. **Miscellaneous:** Reduced fees (weekdays, juniors), range (grass), lodging (36 rooms), credit cards (MC, V, AE, D), BF, FF.
Reader Comments: Interesting course, modest fee ... Nice owners, friendly, beautiful setting, very reasonable rates ... Great pro ... Very nice course & management ... Great staff.

★★★★ BEAR TRACE AT CHICKASAW
PU-9555 State Rte. 100, Henderson, 38340, Chester County, (731)989-4700, (888)944-2327, 20 miles from Jackson. **E-mail:** griffpga@msn.com. **Web:** www.beartrace.com. **Facility Holes:** 18. **Yards:** 7,118/5,375. **Par:** 72/72. **Course Rating:** 73.4/71.9. **Slope:** 134/123. **Green Fee:** $14/$40. **Cart Fee:** $15/Cart. **Walking Policy:** Walking at certain times. **Walkability:** 3. **Opened:** 2000. **Architect:** Jack Nicklaus. **Season:** Year-round. **High:** April-Sept. **To obtain tee times:** Call up to 365 days in advance. **Miscellaneous:** Reduced fees (twilight, seniors, juniors), range (grass), credit cards (MC, V, AE, D), BF, FF.
Reader Comments: A great layout. Fun to play. Snake habitats an interesting twist ... Nice course ... Beautiful course in a somewhat isolated location ... Playable for average golfers, a bargain for serious golfer... New, much potential.

★★★½ BEAR TRACE AT CUMBERLAND MOUNTAIN
PU-407 Wild Plum Lane, Crossville, 38555, Cumberland County, (931)707-1640, (888)800-2327, 5 miles from Crossville. **Web:** www.beartrace.com. **Facility Holes:** 18. **Yards:** 6,900/5,066. **Par:** 72/72. **Course Rating:** 72.0/70.0. **Slope:** 130/120. **Green Fee:** $15/$35. **Cart Fee:** $15/Person. **Walking Policy:** Walking at certain times. **Walkability:** 4. **Opened:** 1998. **Architect:** Jack Nicklaus. **Season:** Year-round. **High:** March-June. **To obtain tee times:** Call up to 90 days in advance. **Miscellaneous:** Reduced fees (weekdays, twilight, seniors, juniors), range (grass), credit cards (MC, V, AE, D), BF, FF.
Notes: Ranked 9th in 2001 Best in State.
Reader Comments: A wonderful choice, can't go wrong ... Scenic back 9, average front 9 ... Front & back different ... New, good layout ... Good tee options ... Great layout, condition good, play slow.

★★★★ BEAR TRACE AT HARRISON BAY
PU-8919 Harrison Bay Rd., Harrison, 37341, Hamilton County, (423)326-0885, (877)611-2327, 20 miles from Chattanooga. **E-mail:** beartrace@mindspring.com. **Web:** www.beartrace.com. **Facility Holes:** 18. **Yards:** 7,140/5,290. **Par:** 72/72. **Green Fee:** $45/$55. **Cart Fee:** Included in green fee. **Walking Policy:** Walking at certain times. **Walkability:** 3. **Opened:** 1999. **Architect:** Jack Nicklaus/Jim Lipe. **Season:** Year-round. **High:** April-Oct. **To obtain tee times:** Call up to 30 days in advance. **Miscellaneous:** Reduced fees (twilight, seniors, juniors), range (grass), credit cards (MC, V, AE, D), BF, FF.
Reader Comments: Lots of wildlife, lovely scenery ... Great design, nice clubhouse ... Beautiful, long, tough track ... Tour potential ... Great test of golf. Very scenic ... Great value. Best layout of the Trace but really out of the way.

★★★★ BEAR TRACE AT TIMS FORD STATE PARK
PU-891 Wiseman Bend Rd., Winchester, 37398, Franklin County, (931)968-0995, (888)558-2327, 90 miles from Nashville. **E-mail:** mdaniels@pga.com. **Web:** www.beartrace.com. **Facility Holes:** 18. **Yards:** 6,800/4,900. **Par:** 71/71. **Slope:** 130. **Green Fee:** $25/$35. **Cart Fee:** $15/Person. **Walking Policy:** Walking at certain times. **Walkability:** 4. **Opened:** 1999. **Architect:** Jack Nicklaus. **Season:** Year-round. **To obtain tee times:** Call up to

14 days in advance. **Miscellaneous:** Reduced fees (weekdays, twilight, seniors), range (grass), credit cards (MC, V, AE, D), BF, FF.

Reader Comments: A gem, a challenging layout ... Great driving range and course design ... New, will be great ... Tough but fair course, lots of sand in strategic places, beautiful ... Pretty course, a lot of variety.

★★ BENT TREE GOLF COURSE
PU-2993 Paul Coffman Dr., Jackson, 38301, Madison County, (901)425-8620, 83 miles from Memphis. **Facility Holes:** 18. **Yards:** 6,845/4,722. **Par:** 72/72. **Green Fee:** $21. **Cart Fee:** Included in green fee. **Walking Policy:** Unrestricted walking. **Opened:** 1997. **Season:** Year-round. **To obtain tee times:** Call golf shop. **Miscellaneous:** Range (grass), credit cards (MC, V, D), BF, FF.

★★½ BRAINERD GOLF COURSE
PU-5203 Old Mission Rd., Chattanooga, 37411, Hamilton County, (423)855-2692. **Web:** www.chattanooga.gov/cpr/golf. **Facility Holes:** 18. **Yards:** 6,468/5,403. **Par:** 72/72. **Course Rating:** 69.8/69.9. **Slope:** 119/118. **Green Fee:** $10/$20. **Cart Fee:** $10/Person. **Walking Policy:** Walking at certain times. **Walkability:** 2. **Opened:** 1926. **Architect:** Donald Ross. **Season:** Year-round. **High:** April-Sept. **To obtain tee times:** Call golf shop. **Miscellaneous:** Reduced fees (weekdays, seniors, juniors), credit cards (MC, V).

★★★ BROWN ACRES GOLF COURSE
PU-406 Brown Rd., Chattanooga, 37421, Hamilton County, (423)855-2680, 5 miles from Chattanooga. **Facility Holes:** 18. **Yards:** 6,774/4,923. **Par:** 71/71. **Course Rating:** 72.5/66.1. **Slope:** 122/110. **Green Fee:** $15/$20. **Cart Fee:** $10/Person. **Walking Policy:** Walking at certain times. **Walkability:** 3. **Opened:** 1975. **Architect:** Grant Wencel. **Season:** Year-round. **High:** April-Oct. **To obtain tee times:** Call golf shop. **Miscellaneous:** Reduced fees (seniors, juniors), range (grass/mats), credit cards (MC, V).

Reader Comments: Excellent condition ... One of my favorites, but crowded at times ... Good course, flat ... Flat course, good greens, wide fairways ... Next to Interstate ... Much better than it used to be ... Excellent course.

★★ BUFFALO VALLEY GOLF COURSE
PU-190 Country Club Dr., Unicoi, 37692, Unicoi County, (423)928-1022, 3 miles from Johnson City. **Facility Holes:** 18. **Yards:** 6,665/4,775. **Par:** 71/72. **Course Rating:** 71.7/69.6. **Slope:** 119/111. **Green Fee:** $16/$20. **Cart Fee:** $12/Person. **Walking Policy:** Unrestricted walking. **Walkability:** 3. **Season:** Year-round. **Tee times:** Call up to 7 days in advance. **Misc:** Reduced fees (weekdays, seniors, juniors), metal spikes, range, credit cards (MC, V), BF, FF.

CAMELOT COUNTRY CLUB
PU-908 Pressman's Home Rd., Rogersville, 37857, Hawkins County, (423)272-7570, 10 miles from Rogersville. **Facility Holes:** 18. **Yards:** 6,844/5,035. **Par:** 73/73. **Course Rating:** 72.3/68.2. **Slope:** 119/110. **Green Fee:** $24/$32. **Cart Fee:** Included in green fee. **Walking Policy:** Unrestricted walking. **Walkability:** 4. **Opened:** 1987. **Architect:** Robert Thomason. **Season:** Feb.-Dec. **High:** May-Sept. **Tee times:** Call golf shop. **Miscellaneous:** Reduced fees (seniors, juniors), range (grass), lodging (100 rooms), credit cards (MC, V, AE, D), BF, FF.

CARROLL LAKE GOLF CLUB
SP-1305 Carroll Lake Rd., McKenzie, 38201, Carroll County, (731)352-2998, (800)871-2128, 45 miles from Jackson. **Facility Holes:** 18. **Yards:** 6,020/4,868. **Par:** 71/71. **Course Rating:** 68.0/68.0. **Slope:** 123/120. **Green Fee:** $9/$17. **Cart Fee:** $20/Cart. **Walking Policy:** Unrestricted walking. **Walkability:** 3. **Opened:** 1961. **Architect:** R. Albert Anderson. **Season:** Year-round. **High:** May-Sept. **To obtain tee times:** Call up to 1 day in advance. **Miscellaneous:** Reduced fees (weekdays, seniors, juniors), credit cards (MC, V, D), BF, FF.

★★ CATTAILS AT MEADOW VIEW
PU-1901 Meadowview Pkwy., Kingsport, 37660, Sullivan County, (423)578-6622. **Facility Holes:** 18. **Yards:** 6,704/4,452. **Par:** 71/71. **Course Rating:** 72.5/65.9. **Slope:** 130/116. **Green Fee:** $33. **Cart Fee:** $10/Person. **Walking Policy:** Unrestricted walking. **Walkability:** 3. **Opened:** 1998. **Architect:** Denis Griffiths. **Season:** Year-round. **High:** May-Oct. **To obtain tee times:** Call up to 7 days in advance. **Miscellaneous:** Reduced fees (seniors, juniors), metal spikes, range (grass), lodging (195 rooms), credit cards (MC, V, AE, D), BF, FF.

★★½ CLINCHVIEW GOLF & COUNTRY CLUB
PU-970 Hwy. 11 W., Bean Station, 37708, Grainger County, (865)993-2892, 50 miles from Knoxville. **Facility Holes:** 18. **Yards:** 6,901/4,724. **Par:** 72/72. **Course Rating:** 72.3/66.3. **Slope:** 121/110. **Green Fee:** $15/$18. **Cart Fee:** $11/Person. **Walking Policy:** Unrestricted walking. **Walkability:** 1. **Opened:** 1969. **Season:** Year-round. **To obtain tee times:** Call up to 7 days in advance. **Miscellaneous:** Reduced fees (twilight), range (grass), credit cards (MC, V, AE), FF.

★★½ THE CLUB AT BIG CREEK
SP-6195 Woodstock-Cuba Rd., Millington, 38053, Shelby County, (901)353-1654, 2 miles from Memphis. **E-mail:** mm2ncreek@aol.com. **Facility Holes:** 18. **Yards:** 7,052/5,086. **Par:** 72/72. **Course Rating:** 72.8/69.6. **Slope:** 121/111. **Green Fee:** $18/$32. **Cart Fee:** $11/Person. **Walking Policy:** Walking at certain times. **Walkability:** 2. **Opened:** 1977. **Architect:** G.S. Mitchell. **Season:** Year-round. **To obtain tee times:** Call up to 7 days in advance. **Miscellaneous:** Reduced fees (weekdays, guests, twilight, seniors, juniors), range (grass), credit cards (MC, V, AE), BF, FF.

★★½ COUNTRY HILLS GOLF COURSE
PU-1501 Saundersville Rd., Hendersonville, 37075, Sumner County, (615)824-1100, 10 miles from Nashville. **Facility Holes:** 18. **Yards:** 6,100/4,800. **Par:** 70/70. **Course Rating:** 71.2/67.8. **Slope:** 119/114. **Green Fee:** $14/$27. **Cart Fee:** $10/Person. **Walking Policy:** Unrestricted walking. **Walkability:** 4. **Opened:** 1990. **Architect:** Leon Howard. **Season:** Year-round. **To obtain tee times:** Call up to 7 days in advance. **Miscellaneous:** Reduced fees (weekdays, twilight, seniors, juniors), range (grass), credit cards (MC, V, AE), BF, FF.

THE CROSSINGS GOLF CLUB
SP-2585 Hwy. 81 N., Jonesboro, 37659, Washington County, (423)348-8844, 75 miles from Knoxville. **Facility Holes:** 18. **Yards:** 6,366/5,072. **Par:** 72/72. **Course Rating:** 70.1/68.2. **Slope:** 118/112. **Green Fee:** $25. **Cart Fee:** $10/Person. **Walking Policy:** Unrestricted walking. **Walkability:** 2. **Opened:** 1994. **Architect:** Gary Roger Baird. **Season:** Year-round. **High:** March-Oct. **To obtain tee times:** Call golf shop. **Miscellaneous:** Metal spikes, range (grass), credit cards (MC, V, AE, D).

★★★ CUMBERLAND GARDENS RESORT
PU-Hwy. 70 E., Crab Orchard, 37723, Cumberland County, (931)484-5285, 45 miles from Knoxville. **E-mail:** cgardens@usit.net. **Web:** www.midtenn.net. **Facility Holes:** 18. **Yards:** 6,689/5,021. **Par:** 72/72. **Course Rating:** 74.2/70.9. **Slope:** 132/123. **Green Fee:** $25/$36. **Cart Fee:** Included in green fee. **Walkability:** 5. **Opened:** 1988. **Architect:** Robert Renaud. **Season:** Year-round. **High:** April-Oct. **To obtain tee times:** Call golf shop. **Miscellaneous:** Reduced fees (weekdays, guests), metal spikes, range (grass), lodging (32 rooms), credit cards (MC, V, AE, D). **Reader Comments:** Great views … Scenic, tough holes … Beautiful mountain-top course, especially hole No. 5, must see … Beautiful views … Spectacular views, hidden … Layout difficult, beautiful course.

★½ DAVY CROCKETT GOLF COURSE
PU-4380 Range Line Rd., Memphis, 38127, Shelby County, (901)358-3375. **E-mail:** budy@davycrockettgolf.com. **Web:** www.davycrockettgolf.com. **Facility Holes:** 18. **Yards:** 6,200/5,900. **Par:** 72/72. **Course Rating:** 68.5/67.2. **Slope:** 118/114. **Green Fee:** $12/$13. **Cart Fee:** $20/Cart. **Walking Policy:** Unrestricted walking. **Walkability:** 4. **Opened:** 1961. **Architect:** Harry Isabelle. **Season:** Year-round. **To obtain tee times:** Call golf shop. **Miscellaneous:** Reduced fees (weekdays, seniors, juniors), credit cards (MC, V, D), BF, FF.

★★ DEAD HORSE LAKE GOLF COURSE
PU-9891 Sherrill Blvd., Knoxville, 37932, Knox County, (865)693-5270, 10 miles from Knoxville. **E-mail:** kyle@deadhorselake.com. **Web:** www.deadhorselake.com. **Facility Holes:** 18. **Yards:** 6,225/5,132. **Par:** 71/73. **Course Rating:** 69.1. **Slope:** 116. **Green Fee:** $16/$23. **Cart Fee:** $12/Person. **Walking Policy:** Unrestricted walking. **Walkability:** 2. **Opened:** 1973. **Architect:** Joe Parker/Pete Parker. **Season:** Year-round. **High:** May-Aug. **To obtain tee times:** Call up to 7 days in advance. **Miscellaneous:** Reduced fees (seniors), metal spikes, range (grass/mats), credit cards (MC, V), BF, FF.

★★★½ DEER CREEK GOLF CLUB
SP-445 Deer Creek Dr., Crossville, 38558, Cumberland County, (931)456-0178, 60 miles from Knoxville. **Facility Holes:** 18. **Yards:** 6,251/4,917. **Par:** 72/72. **Course Rating:** 69.6/67.2. **Slope:** 122/114. **Green Fee:** $15/$23. **Cart Fee:** $13/Person. **Walking Policy:** Walking at certain times. **Walkability:** 3. **Opened:** 1989. **Architect:** Robert Renaud. **Season:** Year-round. **High:** March-Oct. **To obtain tee times:** Call golf shop. **Miscellaneous:** Range (grass/mats), credit cards (MC, V, D), FF. **Reader Comments:** Nice course, a little short, at times busy. Fun … Good management … Great tight course … Short, but worth the play and price … Always in good shape … Nice course, beautiful area & setting … Excellent service.

DEER CREEK GOLF CLUB
R-135 Golf Dr., Saulsbury, 38067, Hardeman County, (731)376-8050, (800)844-7685, 60 miles from Memphis. **E-mail:** deercreek01@msn.com. **Facility Holes:** 18. **Yards:** 7,000/5,142.

Par: 72/73. Course Rating: 73.5/68.9. Slope: 128/116. Green Fee: $14/$18. Cart Fee: $14/Person. Walking Policy: Walking at certain times. Walkability: 3. Opened: 1999. Architect: Mike Brady. Season: Year-round. High: April-Dec. To obtain tee times: Call up to 7 days in advance. Miscellaneous: Reduced fees (weekdays), range (grass), credit cards (MC, V, AE, D, DC), BF, FF.

★★★ DEERFIELD RESORT
R-161 The Clubhouse Dr., LaFollette, 37766, Campbell County, (423)566-0040, (800)325-2788, 45 miles from Knoxville. E-mail: jfields@ccdi.net. Web: www.greensatdeerfield.com. Facility Holes: 18. Yards: 6,716/4,776. Par: 71/71. Course Rating: 72.8/69.8. Slope: 131/125. Green Fee: $30/$35. Cart Fee: Included in green fee. Walking Policy: Mandatory carts. Walkability: 4. Opened: 1995. Architect: Bobby Clampett. Season: Year-round. High: April-Oct. To obtain tee times: Call up to 7 days in advance. Miscellaneous: Reduced fees (weekdays), range (grass), lodging (200 rooms), credit cards (MC, V, D), BF, FF.
Reader Comments: Hard day's work ... You haven't seen hills till you've been here ... Great greens, beautiful scenery ... Hilly, difficult ... Tough course. Good condition, very tight ... Very quiet setting, great holes.

★★½ DYERSBURG MUNICIPAL GOLF COURSE
PU-1358 Golf Course Rd., Dyersburg, 38024, Dyer County, (901)286-7620. Facility Holes: 18. Yards: 6,592/5,746. Par: 71/71. Course Rating: 69.7/71.0. Slope: 118/116. Green Fee: $8. Cart Fee: $14/Cart. Walking Policy: Unrestricted walking. Walkability: 3. Architect: Scott Nall. Season: Year-round. High: May-Sept. To obtain tee times: Call golf shop. Miscellaneous: Metal spikes.

★★★½ EAGLE'S LANDING GOLF CLUB
PU-1556 Old Knox Hwy., Sevierville, 37876, Sevier County, (865)429-4223, 20 miles from Knoxville. Facility Holes: 18. Yards: 6,919/4,591. Par: 72/72. Course Rating: 73.5/68.8. Slope: 134/120. Green Fee: $30/$50. Cart Fee: Included in green fee. Walking Policy: Mandatory carts. Walkability: 3. Opened: 1994. Architect: D.J. DeVictor. Season: Year-round. To obtain tee times: Call up to 30 days in advance. Miscellaneous: Reduced fees (weekdays, twilight, juniors), metal spikes, range (grass), credit cards (MC, V), BF, FF.
Reader Comments: I'll play anytime ... Real winner, beautiful. ... Fairly plain, not worth price ... Little slow ... Magnificent, challenging, price a little high ... Key is accuracy, great service.

★★★½ EASTLAND GREEN GOLF COURSE
PU-550 Club House Lane, Clarksville, 37043, Montgomery County, (931)358-9051, 35 miles from Nashville. Facility Holes: 27. Yards: 6,437/4,790. Par: 72/72. Course Rating: 71.5/68.4. Slope: 123/116. Green Fee: $18/$23. Cart Fee: $18/Cart. Walking Policy: Unrestricted walking. Walkability: 3. Opened: 1990. Architect: East Green Development Corp. Season: Year-round. To obtain tee times: Call up to 7 days in advance. Miscellaneous: Reduced fees (twilight, seniors, juniors), metal spikes, range (grass), credit cards (MC, V, AE, D), BF, FF.
Reader Comments: Good shape year-round, good rates, a favorite ... Front and back different, fun ... Awesome greens, fun ... Old-style country course ... Spectacular setting ... Excellent greens, fun course ... Nice, gets lots of play.
Special Notes: Also has a 9-hole course.

★★★★ EGWANI FARMS GOLF COURSE
PU-3920 Singleton Station Rd., Rockford, 37853, Blount County, (865)970-7132, 8 miles from Knoxville. Facility Holes: 18. Yards: 6,708/4,680. Par: 72/72. Course Rating: 71.9/66.1. Slope: 126/113. Green Fee: $45/$50. Cart Fee: Included in green fee. Walking Policy: Unrestricted walking. Opened: 1991. Architect: D.J. DeVictor. Season: Year-round. To obtain tee times: Call golf shop. Miscellaneous: Range (grass), credit cards (MC, V).
Reader Comments: Very friendly, great staff ... Staff is great, open course with options for scoring ... Owners appreciate your business ... Tight, good greens ... One of the better golf courses in the area ... Expensive, good condition.

★★ ELIZABETHTON MUNICIPAL GOLF CLUB
PU-185 Buck Van Hess Dr., Elizabethton, 37643, Carter County, (423)542-8051, 9 miles from Johnson City. Facility Holes: 18. Yards: 6,339/4,335. Par: 72/72. Course Rating: 71.2/67.7. Slope: 129/118. Green Fee: $14/$21. Cart Fee: Included in green fee. Walking Policy: Unrestricted walking. Walkability: 3. Opened: 1934. Architect: D.J. DeVictor. Season: Year-round. High: April-Sept. To obtain tee times: Call golf shop. Miscellaneous: Range (grass), credit cards (MC, V).

★★★ FALCON RIDGE GOLF CLUB
SP-400 Summit Chase, Cedar Grove, 38321, Carroll County, (731)968-1212, 19 miles from Jackson. E-mail: dgremmels@msn.com. Web: www.falconridgegc.com. Facility Holes: 18. Yards: 6,917/5,211. Par: 72/72. Course Rating: 71.8/70.2. Slope: 119/116. Green Fee:

$36/$39. **Cart Fee:** Included in green fee. **Walking Policy:** Mandatory carts. **Walkability:** 4.
Opened: 2000. **Architect:** David Gremmels. **Season:** Year-round. **High:** May-Sept. **To obtain tee times:** Call up to 30 days in advance. **Miscellaneous:** Reduced fees (weekdays, twilight, seniors, juniors), range (grass), credit cards (MC, V, AE), BF, FF.
Reader Comments: New course, excellent layout, imagination … Good course, great value, fun for all golfers … Still a new course and rough around the edges. Will be great once it matures … Beautiful course, good people.

★★★½ FALL CREEK FALLS STATE PARK GOLF COURSE
PU-Rte. 3, Pikeville, 37367, Bledsoe County, (423)881-5706, (800)250-8610, 20 miles from Pikeville. **E-mail:** bmaxwell@mail.state.tn.us. **Web:** www.state.tn.us/environment/index.html.
Facility Holes: 18. **Yards:** 6,669/4,417. **Par:** 72/72. **Course Rating:** 71.6/68.2. **Slope:** 127/114. **Green Fee:** $21/$24. **Cart Fee:** $11/Person. **Walking Policy:** Unrestricted walking. **Walkability:** 2. **Opened:** 1972. **Architect:** Joe Lee. **Season:** Year-round. **High:** May-Oct. **To obtain tee times:** Call up to 90 days in advance. **Miscellaneous:** Reduced fees (seniors, juniors), range (grass), credit cards (MC, V, AE, D), FF.
Reader Comments: Tight course, lots of sand … Setting is great, accuracy required … Best for your money in TN … One of the best ever … Great layout, reasonable … Scenic, narrow … Good open, mildly hilly … Great value, fun.

FOREST HILL GOLF COURSE
PU-200 Kubo Rd., Drummonds, 38023-0157, Tipton County, (901)835-2152, 20 miles from Memphis. **Facility Holes:** 18. **Yards:** 6,609/5,220. **Par:** 72/72. **Course Rating:** 71.5/69.8. **Slope:** 122/118. **Green Fee:** $15/$25. **Cart Fee:** $10/Person. **Walking Policy:** Walking at certain times. **Walkability:** 3. **Opened:** 1993. **Architect:** Hiroshi Kubo. **Season:** Year-round. **High:** March-Oct. **To obtain tee times:** Call golf shop. **Miscellaneous:** Reduced fees (weekdays, twilight, seniors), range (grass), credit cards (MC, V).

★★½ FORREST CROSSING GOLF COURSE
PU-750 Riverview Dr., Franklin, 37064, Williamson County, (615)794-9400, 15 miles from Nashville. **Facility Holes:** 18. **Yards:** 6,968/5,011. **Par:** 72/72. **Course Rating:** 73.6/69.1. **Slope:** 125/114. **Green Fee:** $22/$39. **Cart Fee:** $10/Person. **Walking Policy:** Walking at certain times. **Walkability:** 1. **Opened:** 1988. **Architect:** Gary Roger Baird. **Season:** Year-round. **High:** March-Oct. **To obtain tee times:** Call up to 7 days in advance. **Miscellaneous:** Reduced fees (weekdays, twilight, seniors, juniors), metal spikes, range (grass/mats), credit cards (MC, V, AE, D, DC), BF, FF.

★★ FOX MEADOWS GOLF COURSE
PU-3064 Clarke Rd., Memphis, 38115, Shelby County, (901)362-0232. **Facility Holes:** 18. **Yards:** 6,545/5,095. **Par:** 71/72. **Course Rating:** 69.9/66.7. **Slope:** 108/102. **Green Fee:** $13/$15. **Cart Fee:** $20/Cart. **Walking Policy:** Unrestricted walking. **Walkability:** 1. **Opened:** 1960. **Architect:** Chic Adams. **Season:** Year-round. **High:** May-Sept. **To obtain tee times:** Call golf shop. **Miscellaneous:** Reduced fees (seniors, juniors), metal spikes.

★½ GALLOWAY GOLF COURSE
PU-3815 Walnut Grove Rd., Memphis, 38111, Shelby County, (901)685-7805. **Facility Holes:** 18. **Yards:** 5,844/5,472. **Par:** 71/73. **Course Rating:** 67.4/71.3. **Slope:** 109/117. **Green Fee:** $13/$15. **Cart Fee:** $19/Cart. **Walking Policy:** Unrestricted walking. **Opened:** 1926. **Season:** Year-round. **High:** April-Oct. **To obtain tee times:** Call golf shop. **Miscellaneous:** Reduced fees (juniors), metal spikes.

★★★ GATLINBURG GOLF COURSE
PU-520 Dollywood Lane, Pigeon Forge, 37868, Sevier County, (865)453-3912, (800)231-4128, 5 miles from Pigeon Forge. **Facility Holes:** 18. **Yards:** 6,281/4,718. **Par:** 71/72. **Course Rating:** 72.3/68.9. **Slope:** 132/117. **Green Fee:** $25/$35. **Cart Fee:** $16/Person. **Walking Policy:** Walking at certain times. **Walkability:** 5. **Opened:** 1955. **Architect:** William B. Langford/Bob Cupp. **Season:** Year-round. **High:** May-Oct. **To obtain tee times:** Call golf shop. **Miscellaneous:** Reduced fees (twilight, juniors), metal spikes, credit cards (MC, V).
Reader Comments: Hilliest course I've ever played, scenic par 3s … Good course, great greens. good value … Very nice, simple course … Good up & down fairways … Scenic course, good conditions, tough, good service … Short but tricky.

★★★★½ GRAYSBURG HILLS GOLF COURSE *Condition*
PU-910 Graysburg Hills Rd., Chuckey, 37641, Greene County, (423)234-8061, 12 miles from Greenville. **Web:** www.graysburghillsgolf.com. **Facility Holes:** 27. **Green Fee:** $20/$26. **Cart Fee:** $12/Person. **Walking Policy:** Walking at certain times. **Walkability:** 3. **Opened:** 1978. **Architect:** Rees Jones/Larry Packard. **Season:** Year-round. **High:** April-Oct. **To obtain tee times:** Call up to 365 days in advance. **Miscellaneous:** Reduced fees (twilight), range (grass), credit cards (MC, V, AE, D), BF, FF.

FODDERSTACK/CHIMNEYTOP (18 Combo)
Yards: 6,875/5,362. **Par:** 72/72. **Course Rating:** 73.0/70.5. **Slope:** 134/123.
KNOBS/CHIMNEYTOP (18 Combo)
Yards: 6,743/5,474. **Par:** 72/72. **Course Rating:** 72.2/71.3. **Slope:** 133/125.
KNOBS/FODDERSTACK (18 Combo)
Yards: 6,834/5,562. **Par:** 72/72. **Course Rating:** 72.8/71.2. **Slope:** 128/122.
Reader Comments: Layout exceptional, don't miss playing this gem ... Great course, great value ... Great service, crowded ... As peaceful a place as you'd ever want to play, and for a great price. A truly rewarding golf experience.

★★★½ GREYSTONE GOLF CLUB
PU-2555 Hwy. 70 E., Dickson, 37056, Dickson County, (615)446-0044, 25 miles from Nashville. **E-mail:** greystonegc@yahoo.com. **Web:** www.greystonegc.com. **Facility Holes:** 18. **Yards:** 6,858/4,919. **Par:** 72/72. **Course Rating:** 73.1/69.0. **Slope:** 131/123. **Green Fee:** $30/$55. **Cart Fee:** Included in green fee. **Walking Policy:** Mandatory carts. **Walkability:** 4. **Opened:** 1998. **Architect:** Mark McCumber. **Season:** Year-round. **High:** April-Aug. **To obtain tee times:** Call up to 7 days in advance. **Miscellaneous:** Reduced fees (weekdays, twilight, juniors), range (grass), credit cards (MC, V, AE), BF, FF.
Reader Comments: Nice layout, friendly ... Excellent ... Challenging, drives must be straight ... Fun ... Must play, great layout, service awesome ... Wonderful design, great facilities ... Heather off fairways slows pace. Nice layout.

★★½ HARPETH HILLS GOLF COURSE
PU-2424 Old Hickory Blvd., Nashville, 37221, Davidson County, (615)862-8493. **Facility Holes:** 18. **Yards:** 6,900/5,200. **Par:** 72/72. **Course Rating:** 73.1/71.2. **Slope:** 126/124. **Green Fee:** $14. **Walking Policy:** Unrestricted walking. **Opened:** 1968. **Season:** Year-round. **High:** May-Sept. **To obtain tee times:** Call golf shop. **Miscellaneous:** Metal spikes, range (grass).

★★★★ HEATHERHURST GOLF CLUB
R-Stonehenge Dr., Fairfield Glade, 38557, Cumberland County, (931)484-3799, 6 miles from Crossfield. **Facility Holes:** 27. **Green Fee:** $16/$38. **Walking Policy:** Walking at certain times. **Opened:** 1988. **Architect:** Gary Roger Baird. **Season:** Year-round. **High:** April-Oct. **To obtain tee times:** Call golf shop. **Miscellaneous:** Metal spikes, range (grass), credit cards (MC, V, AE, D).
CREEK/MOUNTAIN (18 Combo)
Yards: 6,800/4,789. **Par:** 72/72. **Course Rating:** 70.2/66.9. **Slope:** 123/112.
PINE/CREEK (18 Combo)
Yards: 6,700/4,630. **Par:** 72/72. **Course Rating:** 69.2/66.8. **Slope:** 119/111.
PINE/MOUNTAIN (18 Combo)
Yards: 6,650/4,637. **Par:** 72/72. **Course Rating:** 69.4/66.1. **Slope:** 120/110.
Reader Comments: Great track ... Always in tip top shape ... Clubhouse, grounds are well-kept. Course layout is great with hills, ponds and flats ... Good resort course.

★★★½ HENRY HORTON STATE PARK GOLF COURSE
PU-4358 Nashville Hwy., Chapel Hill, 37034, Marshall County, (931)364-2319, 30 miles from Nashville. **Facility Holes:** 18. **Yards:** 7,060/5,625. **Par:** 72/73. **Course Rating:** 74.3/72.1. **Slope:** 128/117. **Green Fee:** $19/$21. **Cart Fee:** $11/Person. **Walking Policy:** Unrestricted walking. **Walkability:** 3. **Opened:** 1963. **Season:** Year-round. **High:** May-July. **To obtain tee times:** Call golf shop. **Miscellaneous:** Reduced fees (seniors, juniors), range (grass), lodging (72 rooms), credit cards (MC, V, AE).
Reader Comments: Long, excellent upkeep ... Huge greens, tree-lined fairways ... Longest holes, fun, friendly ... One of my favorite state park courses ... Good greens, great wildlife.

HERMITAGE GOLF COURSE
PU-3939 Old Hickory Blvd., Old Hickory, 37138, Davidson County, (615)847-4001, 10 miles from Nashville. **E-mail:** proshop@hermitagegolf.com. **Web:** www.hermitagegolf.com. **Facility Holes:** 36. **Walking Policy:** Unrestricted walking. **Walkability:** 2. **Season:** Year-round. **To obtain tee times:** Call up to 5 days in advance. **Miscellaneous:** Reduced fees (weekdays, twilight, juniors), range (grass/mats), credit cards (MC, V, AE, D), BF, FF.
★★★★ GENERAL'S RETREAT (18)
Yards: 6,773/5,437. **Par:** 72/72. **Course Rating:** 72.3/70.8. **Slope:** 129/120. **Green Fee:** $31/$39. **Cart Fee:** $16/Person. **Opened:** 1986. **Architect:** Gary Baird. **High:** April-Oct.
Reader Comments: Pricey but a good occasional course ... Awesome ... Beautiful holes on river ... Slow, no marshals, good condition ... Good, playable ... One of best in area ... Great value, beautifully manicured course.
PRESIDENT'S RESERVE (18)
Yards: 7,157/5,138. **Par:** 72/72. **Course Rating:** 74.2/69.0. **Slope:** 129/115. **Green Fee:** $56/$64. **Cart Fee:** Included in green fee. **Opened:** 2000. **Architect:** Denis Griffiths. **High:** March-Oct.

HIDDEN VALLEY GOLF CLUB
SP-307 Henderson Rd., Jackson, 38305, Madison County, (731)424-3146. **Facility Holes:** 18. **Yards:** 6,801/5,146. **Par:** 72/72. **Course Rating:** 72.7/72.4. **Slope:** 126/117. **Green Fee:** $17/$20. **Opened:** 1970. **Architect:** George Curtis. **To obtain tee times:** Call golf shop.

★★ HIGHLAND RIM GOLF COURSE
PU-1725 New Hope Rd., Joelton, 37080, Cheatham County, (615)746-0400, 25 miles from Nashville. **Facility Holes:** 18. **Yards:** 6,200/4,417. **Par:** 71/71. **Course Rating:** 70.2/65.5. **Slope:** 123/110. **Green Fee:** $31/$39. **Walking Policy:** Mandatory carts. **Walkability:** 4. **Opened:** 1999. **Architect:** Jim Kirkley/Mary Mills. **Season:** Year-round. **High:** April-Oct. **To obtain tee times:** Call up to 7 days in advance. **Miscellaneous:** Reduced fees (twilight, seniors, juniors), range (grass/mats), credit cards (MC, V), BF, FF.

★½ HUNTERS POINT GOLF CLUB
PU-Highway 231 N., Lebanon, 37087, Wilson County, (615)444-7521, 25 miles from Nashville. **Facility Holes:** 18. **Yards:** 6,573/5,600. **Par:** 72/73. **Course Rating:** 69.6/71.5. **Slope:** 108/111. **Green Fee:** $11/$18. **Cart Fee:** $11/Person. **Walking Policy:** Unrestricted walking. **Walkability:** 1. **Opened:** 1966. **Architect:** Robert Renaud. **Season:** Year-round. **To obtain tee times:** Call up to 7 days in advance. **Miscellaneous:** Reduced fees (weekdays, seniors, juniors), range (grass), credit cards (MC, V, AE, D), FF.

★★½ INDIAN HILLS GOLF CLUB
PU-405 Calumet Trace, Murfreesboro, 37127, Rutherford County, (615)895-3642, 25 miles from Nashville. **E-mail:** dave@indianhillsgc.com. **Web:** www.indianhillsgc.com. **Facility Holes:** 18. **Yards:** 6,716/5,237. **Par:** 72/72. **Course Rating:** 72.9/70.3. **Slope:** 126/118. **Green Fee:** $10/$25. **Cart Fee:** $10/Person. **Walking Policy:** Walking at certain times. **Walkability:** 2. **Opened:** 1988. **Season:** Year-round. **High:** April-Oct. **To obtain tee times:** Call up to 7 days in advance. **Miscellaneous:** Reduced fees (weekdays, twilight, seniors, juniors), range (grass), credit cards (MC, V, AE), BF, FF.

★★ IRONWOOD GOLF COURSE
PU-3801 Ironwood Rd., Cookeville, 38501, Putnam County, (931)528-2331, 80 miles from Nashville. **Facility Holes:** 18. **Yards:** 6,321/5,033. **Par:** 72/72. **Course Rating:** 69.8/68.5. **Slope:** 122/112. **Green Fee:** $12. **Cart Fee:** $12/Person. **Walking Policy:** Unrestricted walking. **Walkability:** 3. **Opened:** 1971. **Architect:** Bobby Nichols. **Season:** Year-round. **High:** May-Sept. **To obtain tee times:** Call golf shop. **Miscellaneous:** Reduced fees (weekdays, seniors, juniors), range (grass/mats), credit cards (MC, V, D), BF, FF.

★★½ KNOXVILLE GOLF COURSE
PU-3925 Schaad Rd., Knoxville, 37912, Knox County, (865)691-7143. **Facility Holes:** 18. **Yards:** 6,528/5,325. **Par:** 72/72. **Course Rating:** 71.5/69.7. **Slope:** 119/110. **Green Fee:** $10/$14. **Walking Policy:** Unrestricted walking. **Opened:** 1984. **Architect:** D.J. DeVictor. **Season:** Year-round. **High:** April-Nov. **To obtain tee times:** Call golf shop. **Miscellaneous:** Reduced fees (weekdays, twilight, seniors, juniors), metal spikes, credit cards (MC, V).

★★½ LAMBERT ACRES GOLF CLUB
SP-3402 Tuckaleechee Park, Maryville, 37803, Blount County, (865)982-9838, 4 miles from Maryville. **Facility Holes:** 27. **Green Fee:** $17. **Cart Fee:** $8/Person. **Walking Policy:** Unrestricted walking. **Walkability:** 3. **Opened:** 1965. **Architect:** Don Charles. **Season:** Year-round. **High:** May-Oct. **To obtain tee times:** Call golf shop. **Miscellaneous:** Metal spikes.
RED/ORANGE (18 Combo)
Yards: 6,282/4,753. **Par:** 72/72. **Course Rating:** 70.1/68.3. **Slope:** 121/105.
RED/WHITE (18 Combo)
Yards: 6,480/4,511. **Par:** 72/72. **Course Rating:** 70.8/66.2. **Slope:** 118/102.
WHITE/ORANGE (18 Combo)
Yards: 6,292/4,704. **Par:** 72/72. **Course Rating:** 69.6/66.4. **Slope:** 119/105.

★★★★ LANDMARK GOLF CLUB AT AVALON
SP-1299 Oak Chase Blvd., Lenoir City, 37772, Loudon County, (865)986-4653, (877)471-4653, 12 miles from Knoxville. **Web:** www.avalongolf.com. **Facility Holes:** 18. **Yards:** 6,764/5,261. **Par:** 72/72. **Course Rating:** 72.2/70.0. **Slope:** 131/113. **Green Fee:** $34/$52. **Cart Fee:** Included in green fee. **Walking Policy:** Walking at certain times. **Walkability:** 5. **Opened:** 1997. **Architect:** Joe Lee/Rocky Roquemore. **Season:** Year-round. **High:** April-Nov. **To obtain tee times:** Call up to 30 days in advance. **Miscellaneous:** Reduced fees (weekdays, twilight), range (grass), credit cards (MC, V, AE, D), BF, FF.
Reader Comments: Great greens, great service, great experience ... Should be used for mini-tour ... Great course layout, exceptional service ... Too many short par 4s.
Special Notes: Formerly The Medalist at Avalon Golf Club.

TENNESSEE

LAUREL VALLEY COUNTRY CLUB
PU-702 Country Club Dr., Townsend, 37882, Blount County, (865)448-6690. **Web:** www.laurelvalleygolf.com. **Facility Holes:** 18. **Yards:** 6,070/4,555. **Par:** 70/70. **Course Rating:** 69.7/68.0. **Slope:** 123/114. **Green Fee:** $16/$26. **Cart Fee:** $14/Person. **To obtain tee times:** Call golf shop.

★★½ THE LEGACY GOLF COURSE
PU-100 Ray Floyd Dr., Springfield, 37172, Robertson County, (615)384-4653, 25 miles from Nashville. **E-mail:** info@golfthelegacy.com. **Web:** www.golfthelegacy.com. **Facility Holes:** 18. **Yards:** 6,755/4,860. **Par:** 72/72. **Course Rating:** 73.3/68.2. **Slope:** 131/118. **Green Fee:** $15/$27. **Cart Fee:** $12/Person. **Walking Policy:** Unrestricted walking. **Walkability:** 3. **Opened:** 1996. **Architect:** Ray Floyd/Augusta Golf, Inc. **Season:** Year-round. **High:** March-Oct. **To obtain tee times:** Call up to 5 days in advance. **Miscellaneous:** Reduced fees (twilight, seniors, juniors), range (grass), credit cards (MC, V, AE), BF, FF.

★★★★ LEGENDS CLUB OF TENNESSEE (ROPER'S KNOB)
SP-1500 Legends Club Lane, Franklin, 37069, Williamson County, (615)791-8100, 15 miles from Nashville. **E-mail:** pjackson@legendsclub.com. **Web:** www.legendsclub.com. **Facility Holes:** 36. **Yards:** 7,113/5,290. **Par:** 71/71. **Course Rating:** 74.7/71.4. **Slope:** 129/121. **Green Fee:** $77/$88. **Cart Fee:** Included in green fee. **Walking Policy:** Mandatory carts. **Walkability:** 2. **Opened:** 1992. **Architect:** Tom Kite/Bob Cupp. **Season:** Year-round. **High:** April-Oct. **To obtain tee times:** Call golf shop. **Miscellaneous:** Reduced fees (weekdays, twilight, juniors), range (grass), credit cards (MC, V, AE, D), BF, FF.
Reader Comments: Excellent fairway grass! Never a bad lie … Awesome … Beautiful 36 holes … Tough, wind always blows … Very good test for good shots … Absolutely beautiful.
Special Notes: Also has an 18-hole private course.

★★ LONG HOLLOW GOLF COURSE
PU-1080 Long Hollow Pike, Gallatin, 37066, Sumner County, (615)451-3120, 25 miles from Nashville. **Facility Holes:** 18. **Yards:** 6,000/4,952. **Par:** 70/70. **Course Rating:** 66.7/66.6. **Slope:** 109/101. **Green Fee:** $18/$20. **Cart Fee:** $20/Person. **Walking Policy:** Unrestricted walking. **Walkability:** 1. **Opened:** 1983. **Architect:** Kevin Tucker. **Season:** Year-round. **High:** May-Sept. **To obtain tee times:** Call golf shop. **Miscellaneous:** Reduced fees (weekdays), range (grass/mats), credit cards (MC, V).

★★ MCCABE FIELD GOLF COURSE
PU-46th Ave. & Murphy Rd., Nashville, 37209, Davidson County, (615)862-8491. **Facility Holes:** 27. **Green Fee:** $18. **Cart Fee:** $18/Cart. **Walking Policy:** Unrestricted walking. **Walkability:** 1. **Opened:** 1939. **Season:** Year-round. **High:** April-Sept. **To obtain tee times:** Call golf shop. **Miscellaneous:** Reduced fees (seniors, juniors), metal spikes, credit cards (MC, V).
MIDDLE/NORTH (18 Combo)
Yards: 6,481/5,876. **Par:** 71/71. **Course Rating:** 69.6/69.6. **Slope:** 112/112.
MIDDLE/SOUTH (18 Combo)
Yards: 6,023/5,590. **Par:** 70/70. **Course Rating:** 68.6/68.6. **Slope:** 110/110.
NORTH/SOUTH (18 Combo)
Yards: 6,522/5,866. **Par:** 71/71. **Course Rating:** 69.7/69.7. **Slope:** 111/111.

★★ MOCCASIN BEND GOLF CLUB
PU-381 Moccasin Bend Rd., Chattanooga, 37405, Hamilton County, (423)267-3585, 3 miles from Chattanooga. **E-mail:** wggolff@aol.com. **Facility Holes:** 18. **Yards:** 6,469/5,290. **Par:** 72/72. **Course Rating:** 69.6/69.0. **Slope:** 111/109. **Green Fee:** $14/$19. **Cart Fee:** $10/Person. **Walking Policy:** Unrestricted walking. **Walkability:** 2. **Opened:** 1966. **Architect:** Alex McKay. **Season:** Year-round. **To obtain tee times:** Call golf shop. **Miscellaneous:** Reduced fees (twilight, seniors, juniors), range (grass), credit cards (MC, V).

★★★ MONTGOMERY BELL STATE PARK GOLF COURSE
PU-800 Hotel Ave., Burns, 37029, Dickson County, (615)797-2578, (800)250-8613, 35 miles from Nashville. **Facility Holes:** 18. **Yards:** 6,196/4,961. **Par:** 71/72. **Course Rating:** 69.3/68.8. **Slope:** 121/116. **Green Fee:** $20/$22. **Cart Fee:** $22/Person. **Walking Policy:** Unrestricted walking. **Walkability:** 3. **Opened:** 1970. **Architect:** Gary Roger Baird. **Season:** Year-round. **High:** May-Oct. **To obtain tee times:** Call up to 6 days in advance. **Miscellaneous:** Reduced fees (seniors, juniors), range (grass), lodging (115 rooms), credit cards (MC, V, AE, D), BF, FF.
Reader Comments: Tight and secluded, very peaceful … State park course, beautifully maintained, offers a challenge to all players … Nice, many hills … Average course but you will enjoy. Leave your troubles in the city.

MOUNTAIN VIEW GOLF COURSE
PU-1925 Allardt-Tinshtown, Allardt, 38504, Fentress County, (931)879-6473. **Facility Holes:** 18. **Yards:** 6,697/5,296. **Par:** 70/70. **Green Fee:** $12/$24. **Cart Fee:** $11/Person. **Architect:** C.D. Hendren. **To obtain tee times:** Call golf shop.

★★★★ MT. AIRY GOLF & ATHLETIC CLUB
SP-100 Madison Dr., Dunlap, 37327, Sequatchie County, (423)949-7274, 40 miles from Dunlap. **E-mail:** www.mtairygolf@bledsoe.net. **Web:** www.mtairygolf.com. **Facility Holes:** 18. **Yards:** 6,850/4,855. **Par:** 72/72. **Course Rating:** 72.3. **Slope:** 132. **Green Fee:** $15/$20. **Cart Fee:** $12/Person. **Walking Policy:** Unrestricted walking. **Walkability:** 5. **Opened:** 1995. **Architect:** Dennis Mills. **Season:** Year-round. **High:** April-Oct. **To obtain tee times:** Call golf shop. **Miscellaneous:** Reduced fees (weekdays, twilight, seniors), range (grass), credit cards (MC, V, D).
Reader Comments: Very mountainous course, challenging course ... Super course and layout ... Fairways are great! Some exceptional par 5s ... Liked the course, too far to drive often.

★★½ NASHBORO GOLF CLUB
PU-1101 Nashboro Blvd., Nashville, 37217, Davidson County, (615)367-2311. **Facility Holes:** 18. **Yards:** 6,887/5,485. **Par:** 72/75. **Course Rating:** 73.5/72.3. **Slope:** 134/121. **Green Fee:** $35/$48. **Cart Fee:** Included in green fee. **Walking Policy:** Walking at certain times. **Walkability:** 4. **Opened:** 1975. **Architect:** B.J. Wyre. **Season:** Year-round. **To obtain tee times:** Call up to 10 days in advance. **Miscellaneous:** Reduced fees (weekdays, twilight, seniors), range (grass/mats), credit cards (MC, V, AE, D), FF.

★★★½ OLD FORT GOLF CLUB
PU-1028 Golf Lane, Murfreesboro, 37129, Rutherford County, (615)896-2448, 25 miles from Nashville. **E-mail:** twkpga@aol.com. **Facility Holes:** 18. **Yards:** 6,859/4,971. **Par:** 72/72. **Course Rating:** 73.1/69.4. **Slope:** 127/114. **Green Fee:** $21/$25. **Cart Fee:** $9/Person. **Walking Policy:** Unrestricted walking. **Walkability:** 2. **Opened:** 1985. **Architect:** Leon Howard. **Season:** Year-round. **High:** April-Sept. **To obtain tee times:** Call up to 5 days in advance. **Miscellaneous:** Reduced fees (seniors, juniors), range (grass), credit cards (MC, V), BF, FF.
Reader Comments: Good variety, no blind tee shots ... Great layout ... Excellent course ... Good staff. Greens in good shape ... Staff & course great ... Great course, reasonably priced, great shape, not real hard but by no means easy.

OLD ISLAND GOLF & RESIDENTIAL COMMUNITY
PU-148 Braemere Rd., Kingsport, 37664, Sullivan County, (423)279-1700. **E-mail:** info@old-island.com. **Web:** www.oldisland.com. **Facility Holes:** 18. **Yards:** 6,466/5,199. **Par:** 72/72. **Course Rating:** 70.9/69.0. **Slope:** 125/115. **Green Fee:** $18/$34. **Cart Fee:** $12/Person. **Opened:** 1999. **Architect:** Tom Clark. **To obtain tee times:** Call golf shop.

★★★ ORGILL PARK GOLF COURSE
PU-9080 Bethuel Rd., Millington, 38053, Shelby County, (901)872-3610, 5 miles from Memphis. **E-mail:** jesse@orgillpark.com. **Web:** www.orgillpark.com. **Facility Holes:** 18. **Yards:** 6,408/4,676. **Par:** 70/71. **Course Rating:** 69.5/68.3. **Slope:** 114/108. **Green Fee:** $14/$15. **Cart Fee:** $14/Person. **Walking Policy:** Unrestricted walking. **Walkability:** 3. **Opened:** 1972. **Architect:** Press Maxwell. **Season:** Year-round. **High:** April-Oct. **To obtain tee times:** Call golf shop. **Miscellaneous:** Reduced fees (weekdays, seniors, juniors), metal spikes, range (grass), credit cards (MC, V, AE, D), BF, FF.
Reader Comments: No bunkers (sand), hardy slow greens ... Fairly easy, open, no traps, good walk ... Not bad for an out-of-the-way public ... Worth the money ... Best county-run park course in area.

★★★½ PARIS LANDING GOLF COURSE
PU-16055 Hwy.79 N., Buchanan, 38222, Henry County, (731)641-4459, 40 miles from Clarksville. **Facility Holes:** 18. **Yards:** 6,612/6,408. **Par:** 72/72. **Course Rating:** 72.9/72.9. **Slope:** 126/124. **Green Fee:** $19/$20. **Cart Fee:** $22/Person. **Walking Policy:** Unrestricted walking. **Walkability:** 5. **Opened:** 1971. **Architect:** Benjamin Wihry. **Season:** Year-round. **To obtain tee times:** Call golf shop. **Miscellaneous:** Range (grass), lodging (130 rooms), credit cards (MC, V, AE, D).
Reader Comments: Nothing too special, but impressive for a state-run course. Beautiful views of river ... Very scenic course, not in best shape, nice resort area ... Well-run state park course, in good shape, great golf for the money.

★★★½ PATRIOT HILLS GOLF CLUB
SP-735 Constitution Dr., Jefferson City, 37760, Jefferson County, (865)475-4466, 30 miles from Knoxville. **Web:** www.dandridgegolf.com. **Facility Holes:** 18. **Yards:** 6,710/4,974. **Par:** 72/72. **Course Rating:** 72.4/67.1. **Slope:** 126/115. **Green Fee:** $16/$21. **Cart Fee:** $11/Person.

Walking Policy: Unrestricted walking. **Walkability:** 4. **Opened:** 1997. **Architect:** Jerry Hodge/Randall Hodge& Greg Hodge. **Season:** Year-round. **High:** March-Oct. **To obtain tee times:** Call up to 7 days in advance. **Miscellaneous:** Reduced fees (weekdays, twilight), range (grass), credit cards (MC, V, D), BF, FF.
Reader Comments: Wonderful experience, warm staff, interesting course ... Scenic, good service, nice stop ... Could play every day ... Too many blind shots ... Super ... Beautiful setting, good greens & friendly.

★★★½ PICKWICK LANDING STATE PARK GOLF COURSE
PU-Hwy. No. 57 & 128, Pickwick Dam, 38365, Hardin County, (731)689-3149, 120 miles from Memphis. **Facility Holes:** 18. **Yards:** 6,478/5,229. **Par:** 72/72. **Course Rating:** 70.2/68.7. **Slope:** 118/115. **Green Fee:** $19/$22. **Cart Fee:** $22/Person. **Walking Policy:** Unrestricted walking. **Walkability:** 5. **Opened:** 1973. **Architect:** Benjamin Wihry. **Season:** Year-round. **High:** March-Oct. **To obtain tee times:** Call up to 14 days in advance. **Miscellaneous:** Reduced fees (weekdays, twilight, seniors, juniors), range (grass), lodging (100 rooms), credit cards (MC, V, AE, D, DC), BF, FF.
Reader Comments: Good course, rustic ... A heck of a golf course ... Well-maintained, typical Tennessee state-park golf course, challenging layout ... Very good ... Course is a gem, no gimmie holes ... Better than average.

★★ PINE HILL GOLF COURSE
PU-1005 Alice Ave., Memphis, 38106, Shelby County, (901)775-9434. **Facility Holes:** 18. **Yards:** 5,908/5,014. **Par:** 72/73. **Course Rating:** 65.9/66.7. **Slope:** 114/116. **Green Fee:** $9/$11. **Walking Policy:** Unrestricted walking. **Season:** Year-round. **High:** May-Sept. **To obtain tee times:** Call golf shop. **Miscellaneous:** Reduced fees (seniors, juniors), metal spikes, range (grass), credit cards (MC, V, AE).

PINE OAKS GOLF CLUB
PU-1709 Buffalo Rd., Johnson City, 37604, Washington County, (423)434-6250. **Facility Holes:** 18. **Yards:** 6,271/4,905. **Par:** 71/73. **Course Rating:** 68.4/69.1. **Slope:** 109/114. **Green Fee:** $15/$19. **Cart Fee:** $12/Person. **Walking Policy:** Unrestricted walking. **Walkability:** 3. **Opened:** 1962. **Architect:** Alex McKay. **Season:** Year-round. **To obtain tee times:** Call up to 7 days in advance. **Miscellaneous:** Reduced fees (weekdays, twilight, juniors), metal spikes, credit cards (MC, V), BF, FF.

★★★ QUAIL RIDGE GOLF COURSE
PU-4055 Altruria Rd., Bartlett, 38135, Shelby County, (901)386-6951, 5 miles from Memphis. **Facility Holes:** 18. **Yards:** 6,632/5,238. **Par:** 71/70. **Course Rating:** 71.8/70.8. **Slope:** 128/117. **Green Fee:** $20/$32. **Cart Fee:** $11/Person. **Walking Policy:** Unrestricted walking. **Walkability:** 3. **Opened:** 1994. **Architect:** David Pfaff. **Season:** Year-round. **High:** April-Sept. **To obtain tee times:** Call up to 5 days in advance. **Miscellaneous:** Reduced fees (twilight, seniors, juniors), range (grass/mats), credit cards (MC, V, AE, D), BF, FF.
Reader Comments: Very friendly staff ... Tough to walk, prices a little high ... Average layout, needs work, good value ... Always in great shape, greens are bent & sweet, back 9 tough ... Good condition, good service, some tough holes.

★★ THE QUARRY GOLF CLUB
PU-1001 Reads Lake Rd., Chattanooga, 37415, Hamilton County, (423)875-8888, 6 miles from Chattanooga. **Facility Holes:** 9. **Yards:** 2,890. **Par:** 34. **Green Fee:** $15/$18. **Cart Fee:** $10/Person. **Walking Policy:** Unrestricted walking. **Walkability:** 2. **Opened:** 1972. **Architect:** Joe Lee. **Season:** Year-round. **Tee times:** Call up to 3 days in advance. **Miscellaneous:** Reduced fees (weekdays, seniors, juniors), range (grass), credit cards (MC, V, AE, D), BF, FF.

RIDGEWOOD GOLF COURSE
PU-387 County Rd., Athens, 37303, Mc Minn County, (423)263-5672. **Facility Holes:** 18. **Yards:** 6,444/5,401. **Par:** 72/72. **Course Rating:** 71.1/67.6. **Slope:** 119/114. **Green Fee:** $10/$12. **Opened:** 1960. **To obtain tee times:** Call golf shop.

★★★★ RIVER ISLANDS GOLF CLUB
PU-9610 Kodak Rd., Kodak, 37764, Knox County, (865)933-0100, 15 miles from Knoxville. **Web:** www.riverislandsgolf.com. **Facility Holes:** 18. **Yards:** 7,001/4,973. **Par:** 72/72. **Course Rating:** 75.4/69.4. **Slope:** 133/118. **Green Fee:** $29/$49. **Cart Fee:** Included in green fee. **Walking Policy:** Mandatory carts. **Walkability:** 2. **Opened:** 1990. **Architect:** Arthur Hills. **Season:** Year-round. **High:** April-Nov. **Tee times:** Call up to 30 days in advance. **Misc:** Reduced fees (weekdays, twilight), range (grass), credit cards (MC, V, AE, D), FF.
Notes: Ranked 7th in 2001 Best in State.
Reader Comments: Take camera and plenty of balls, course has great natural landscape and a lot of water ... When was last time you played in the middle of a river? ... Tremendous course, unique setting, beautiful ... Overall favorite.

TENNESSEE

★★★ RIVER RUN GOLF CLUB
PU-1701 Tennessee Ave., Crossville, 38555, Cumberland County, (931)456-4060, (800)465-3069, 60 miles from Knoxville. **E-mail:** riverruntn@multipro.com. **Web:** www.cumberlandgolf.com. **Facility Holes:** 18. **Yards:** 6,550/4,844. **Par:** 72/72. **Course Rating:** 71.9/70.0. **Slope:** 124/121. **Green Fee:** $24/$29. **Cart Fee:** Included in green fee. **Walking Policy:** Walking at certain times. **Walkability:** 5. **Opened:** 1983. **Architect:** Ron Garl/Bob Renau. **Season:** Year-round. **To obtain tee times:** Call golf shop. **Miscellaneous:** Reduced fees (guests, twilight, seniors), range (grass), lodging (45 rooms), credit cards (MC, V, AE, D), BF, FF.
Reader Comments: Course improving under new ownership. The trickiest little par-3 island green you'll find … Course continues to make improvements … Has changed for the better.

★★★½ ROAN VALLEY GOLF ESTATES
SP-Hwy. 421 S., Mountain City, 37683, Johnson County, (423)727-7931, 20 miles from Boone, NC. **E-mail:** sjadams@boone.net. **Facility Holes:** 18. **Yards:** 6,736/4,370. **Par:** 72/72. **Course Rating:** 71.8/68.9. **Slope:** 120/107. **Green Fee:** $33/$42. **Cart Fee:** Included in green fee. **Walking Policy:** Walking at certain times. **Walkability:** 5. **Opened:** 1982. **Architect:** Dan Maples. **Season:** April-Dec. **High:** May-Oct. **To obtain tee times:** Call golf shop. **Miscellaneous:** Reduced fees (weekdays, juniors), metal spikes, credit cards (MC, V), BF, FF.
Reader Comments: Super, wide open, real challenging … Best course in east Tennessee … Beautiful back 9, greens too small, good value … Beautiful mountain views … One of the best layouts I have played … A fun course.

★★★½ SADDLE CREEK GOLF CLUB
PU-1480 Fayetteville Hwy., Lewisburg, 37091, Marshall County, (931)270-7280, 50 miles from Nashville. **E-mail:** saddlecreekgc@hotmail.com. **Web:** www.saddlecreekgolfclub.com. **Facility Holes:** 18. **Yards:** 6,700/4,999. **Par:** 72/72. **Course Rating:** 71.9/67.9. **Slope:** 127/120. **Green Fee:** $19/$26. **Cart Fee:** $10/Person. **Walking Policy:** Unrestricted walking. **Walkability:** 3. **Opened:** 1995. **Architect:** Gene Bates. **Season:** Year-round. **High:** May-Sept. **To obtain tee times:** Call up to 7 days in advance. **Miscellaneous:** Reduced fees (weekdays, twilight, seniors, juniors), range (grass), credit cards (MC, V, AE), BF, FF.
Reader Comments: Front 9 wooded, back 9 open. Great greens and fairways. Staff friendly. Nice range … Worth the drive, fun to play … Par 5s are risk-reward gems … Beautiful, challenging layout, excellently maintained … Play it.

★★★½ SHILOH FALLS GOLF CLUB
SP-205 Clubhouse Lane, Counce, 38326, Hardin County, (731)689-5050, 100 miles from Memphis. **E-mail:** shilohfalls@centurytel.net. **Web:** www.shilohfallsgolf.com. **Facility Holes:** 18. **Yards:** 6,724/5,156. **Par:** 72/72. **Course Rating:** 73.6/71.2. **Slope:** 131/122. **Green Fee:** $28/$49. **Cart Fee:** Included in green fee. **Walking Policy:** Walking at certain times. **Walkability:** 5. **Opened:** 1993. **Architect:** Jerry Pate. **Season:** Year-round. **High:** April-Oct. **Tee times:** Call up to 14 days in advance. **Miscellaneous:** Reduced fees (weekdays, twilight, seniors, juniors), range (grass), lodging (52 rooms), credit cards (MC, V, AE, D, DC), BF, FF.
Reader Comments: Good Bermuda, nice small-town layout … Fun and fair course. A walk in the woods … Solid course, good experience … Interesting holes … worth playing time & again.

SMYRNA MUNICIPAL GOLF COURSE
PU-101 Sam Ridley Pkwy., Smyrna, 37167, Rutherford County, (615)459-2666. **Facility Holes:** 27. **Yards:** 6,414/5,264. **Par:** 72/72. **Course Rating:** 70.4/71.1. **Slope:** 120/118. **Green Fee:** $19. **Cart Fee:** $10/Person. **Walking Policy:** Unrestricted walking. **Walkability:** 3. **Opened:** 1976. **Architect:** Ed Connor. **Season:** Year-round. **Tee times:** Call up to 3 days in advance. **Miscellaneous:** Reduced fees (seniors, juniors), range (grass), credit cards (MC, V), BF, FF. **Special Notes:** Also has a 9-hole executive course.

★½ SOUTHWEST POINT GOLF COURSE
PU-2000 Decatur Hwy., Kingston, 37763, Roane County, (865)376-5282, 40 miles from Knoxville. **Facility Holes:** 18. **Yards:** 6,723/6,086. **Par:** 72/74. **Course Rating:** 70.3/70.2. **Slope:** 113. **Green Fee:** $23/$26. **Cart Fee:** Included in green fee. **Walking Policy:** Unrestricted walking. **Walkability:** 2. **Opened:** 1964. **Architect:** Alex McKay. **Season:** Year-round. **High:** May-Oct. **To obtain tee times:** Call up to 14 days in advance. **Miscellaneous:** Reduced fees (weekdays, seniors), credit cards (MC, V, AE, D), BF, FF.

SPARTA GOLF & COUNTRY CLUB
SP-128 Lester Flat Rd, Sparta, 38583, White County, (931)738-5836, 100 miles from Nashville. **Facility Holes:** 9. **Yards:** 2,759/2,133. **Par:** 35/36. **Course Rating:** 66.5/69.7. **Slope:** 112/110. **Green Fee:** $7. **Opened:** 1960. **To obtain tee times:** Call golf shop.

TENNESSEE

★★★½ SPRINGHOUSE GOLF CLUB
R-18 Springhouse Lane, Nashville, 37214, Davidson County, (615)871-7759. **Web:** www.opry-landhotels.com. **Facility Holes:** 18. **Yards:** 7,007/5,126. **Par:** 72/72. **Course Rating:** 74.0/70.2. **Slope:** 133/118. **Green Fee:** $60/$75. **Cart Fee:** Included in green fee. **Walking Policy:** Mandatory carts. **Walkability:** 3. **Opened:** 1990. **Architect:** Larry Nelson/Jeff Brauer. **Season:** Year-round. **High:** April-Oct. **To obtain tee times:** Call up to 7 days in advance. **Miscellaneous:** Reduced fees (weekdays, twilight, seniors, juniors), range (grass), lodging (2900 rooms), credit cards (MC, V, AE, D, DC), BF, FF.
Reader Comments: Greens are fast and true. Great condition … Loved this links-style course … A bit expensive, worth the money … Too pricey … Classy, slow play, able to score … Short, fun, easy … Solid golf, greens great.

★★★ STONEBRIDGE GOLF CLUB
PU-3049 Davies Plantation Rd., Lakeland, 38002, Shelby County, (901)382-1886, 5 miles from Memphis. **E-mail:** jdbank@PGA.com. **Web:** www.stonebridgegolf.com. **Facility Holes:** 18. **Yards:** 6,753/4,978. **Par:** 71/71. **Course Rating:** 73.3/68.7. **Slope:** 133/117. **Green Fee:** $25/$54. **Cart Fee:** Included in green fee. **Walking Policy:** Walking at certain times. **Walkability:** 3. **Opened:** 1972. **Architect:** George W. Cobb. **Season:** Year-round. **High:** April-Sept. **To obtain tee times:** Call up to 5 days in advance. **Miscellaneous:** Reduced fees (weekdays, twilight), range (grass/mats), credit cards (MC, V, AE, D), BF, FF.
Reader Comments: One of the most accessible in Memphis area … Excellent course, tough to walk … A little pricey … Great shape, narrow.

★★★★ STONEHENGE GOLF CLUB
PU-222 Fairfield Blvd., Fairfield Glade, 38558, Cumberland County, (931)484-3731, 60 miles from Knoxville. **Web:** www.stonehengegolf.com. **Facility Holes:** 18. **Yards:** 6,549/5,043. **Par:** 72/72. **Course Rating:** 71.8/69.6. **Slope:** 135/124. **Green Fee:** $59/$79. **Cart Fee:** Included in green fee. **Walking Policy:** Mandatory carts. **Walkability:** 4. **Opened:** 1984. **Architect:** Joe Lee/Rocky Roquemore. **Season:** March-Nov. **High:** Sept.-Oct. **To obtain tee times:** Call golf shop. **Miscellaneous:** Reduced fees (guests, twilight, juniors), range (grass), credit cards (MC, V, AE, D), BF, FF.
Notes: Ranked 4th in 2001 Best in State; 40th in 1996 America's Top 75 Affordable Courses.
Reader Comments: Fairways wet, atmosphere is unbeatable. Death Drop par-3 is tough … Tough course, spectacular layout, what views! Pricey but worth it … Great mountain golf … Every shot has value.

★★★ SUNTERRA BENT CREEK GOLF VILLAGE
R-3919 E. Pkwy., Gatlinburg, 37738, Sevier County, (865)436-3947, (800)251-9336, 12 miles from Gatlinburg. **E-mail:** bentcreek@earthlink.net. **Web:** www.bentcreekgolfcourse.com. **Facility Holes:** 18. **Yards:** 6,182/5,111. **Par:** 72/73. **Course Rating:** 70.3/69.2. **Slope:** 127/117. **Green Fee:** $20/$35. **Cart Fee:** $16/Person. **Walking Policy:** Walking at certain times. **Walkability:** 3. **Opened:** 1972. **Architect:** Gary Player. **Season:** Year-round. **High:** April-Nov. **To obtain tee times:** Call golf shop. **Miscellaneous:** Reduced fees (weekdays, guests, twilight, seniors, juniors), lodging (86 rooms), credit cards (MC, V, AE, D), BF, FF.
Reader Comments: Expensive for what you get in area … Back 9 in bad shape, front 9 is wonderful … Great setting, fun course.

★★½ SWAN LAKE GOLF COURSE
PU-581 Dunbar Cave Rd., Clarksville, 37043, Montgomery County, (931)648-0479, 40 miles from Nashville. **E-mail:** jvaughn@cityofclarksville.com. **Facility Holes:** 18. **Yards:** 6,419/5,155. **Par:** 71/72. **Course Rating:** 70.5/69.0. **Slope:** 116/112. **Green Fee:** $16/$18. **Cart Fee:** $18/Cart. **Walking Policy:** Unrestricted walking. **Walkability:** 3. **Architect:** Benjamin Wihry. **Season:** Year-round. **To obtain tee times:** Call up to 6 days in advance. **Miscellaneous:** Reduced fees (seniors), credit cards (MC, V), BF, FF.

★½ T.O. FULLER GOLF COURSE
PU-1400 Pavillion Dr., Memphis, 38109, Shelby County, (901)543-7771. **Facility Holes:** 18. **Yards:** 6,000/5,656. **Par:** 72/73. **Course Rating:** 71.0/72.0. **Slope:** 117/110. **Green Fee:** $16/$18. **Cart Fee:** $11/Person. **Walking Policy:** Unrestricted walking. **Walkability:** 4. **Opened:** 1956. **Architect:** City of Memphis. **Season:** Year-round. **High:** May-Dec. **To obtain tee times:** Call golf shop. **Miscellaneous:** Reduced fees (weekdays, seniors, juniors), metal spikes, credit cards (MC, V, AE, D).

★★★ TED RHODES GOLF COURSE
PU-1901 Ed Temple Blvd., Nashville, 37208, Davidson County, (615)862-8463. **Facility Holes:** 18. **Yards:** 6,660/5,732. **Par:** 72/72. **Course Rating:** 71.8/68.3. **Slope:** 120/115. **Green Fee:** $8/$16. **Cart Fee:** $14/Cart. **Walking Policy:** Unrestricted walking. **Opened:** 1994. **Architect:** Gary Roger Baird. **Season:** Year-round. **High:** May-Sept. **To obtain tee times:** Call

golf shop. **Miscellaneous:** Reduced fees (seniors, juniors), metal spikes, range (grass).
Reader Comments: Challenging layout, need some knowledge of course, trouble is subtle … Best muni in state … Staff tops anywhere … Well-designed for muni, not the best maintained.

★★★★ THE TENNESSEAN GOLF CLUB

PU-900 Olde Tennessee Trail, Paris, 38242, Henry County, (731)642-7271, (866)710-4653, 100 miles from Nashville. **E-mail:** info@tennesseangolfclub.com. **Web:** www.tennesseangolf-club.com. **Facility Holes:** 18. **Yards:** 7,182/4,777. **Par:** 72/72. **Course Rating:** 74.4/67.8. **Slope:** 134/118. **Green Fee:** $27/$37. **Cart Fee:** $12/Person. **Walking Policy:** Unrestricted walking. **Walkability:** 4. **Opened:** 1999. **Architect:** Keith Foster. **Season:** March-Dec. **High:** April-Oct. **To obtain tee times:** Call up to 180 days in advance. **Miscellaneous:** Reduced fees (twilight, juniors), range (grass), credit cards (MC, V, AE, D), BF, FF.
Notes: Ranked 6th in 2001 Best in State; 7th in 2000 Best New Affordable Courses.
Reader Comments: Excellent layout … Great, hard … Overrated but nice … Greens severely undulating … Beautiful, must play, great value … Best in Tennessee, bar none … Best I've played, it will humble you.

★★★★ THREE RIDGES GOLF COURSE

PU-6101 Wise Springs Rd., Knoxville, 37918, Knox County, (865)687-4797. **E-mail:** sboyle@forestergolfinc.com. **Web:** www.threeridges.com. **Facility Holes:** 18. **Yards:** 7,035/5,225. **Par:** 72/72. **Course Rating:** 73.2/70.7. **Slope:** 128/121. **Green Fee:** $10/$27. **Cart Fee:** $13/Person. **Walking Policy:** Unrestricted walking. **Walkability:** 5. **Opened:** 1991. **Architect:** Ault/Clark & Assoc. **Season:** Year-round. **High:** April-Oct. **To obtain tee times:** Call golf shop. **Miscellaneous:** Reduced fees (weekdays, twilight, seniors, juniors), range (grass), credit cards (MC, V, AE, D), BF, FF.
Reader Comments: One of the best-kept secrets … Very nice course … Outstanding! Outstanding! Outstanding! … You would never know it's a muni … An excellent course, good greens & fairways.

★★★ TWELVE STONES CROSSING GOLF CLUB

SP-1201 Twelve Stones Crossing, Goodlettsville, 37072, Sumner County, (615)855-1201, 9 miles from Nashville. **E-mail:** pgathomas@mindspring.com. **Web:** www.twelvestonesgolfclub.com. **Facility Holes:** 18. **Yards:** 6,922/5,081. **Par:** 72/72. **Course Rating:** 73.9/70.3. **Slope:** 132/121. **Green Fee:** $34/$49. **Cart Fee:** Included in green fee. **Walking Policy:** Unrestricted walking. **Walkability:** 4. **Opened:** 1999. **Architect:** Bill Bergin. **Season:** Year-round. **High:** April-Oct. **To obtain tee times:** Call up to 7 days in advance. **Miscellaneous:** Reduced fees (twilight, seniors, juniors), range (grass), credit cards (MC, V, AE, D, DC), BF, FF.
Reader Comments: Lots of shots, didn't know a course could have so many hills … Good all-around course … Great course, challenging … Many houses, good conditions … Up & coming course, very hilly … Beautiful new course, love it.

★★½ TWO RIVERS GOLF COURSE

PU-3140 McGavock Pike, Nashville, 37214, Davidson County, (615)889-2675, 10 miles from Nashville. **Facility Holes:** 18. **Yards:** 6,595/5,336. **Par:** 72/72. **Course Rating:** 71.5/70.4. **Slope:** 120/116. **Green Fee:** $19. **Cart Fee:** $10/Cart. **Walking Policy:** Unrestricted walking. **Walkability:** 2. **Opened:** 1973. **Architect:** Dave Bennett/Leon Howard. **Season:** Year-round. **High:** March-Sept. **To obtain tee times:** Call up to 7 days in advance. **Miscellaneous:** Reduced fees (weekdays), credit cards (MC, V), BF, FF.

★★½ WARRIOR'S PATH STATE PARK

PU-1687 Fall Creek Rd., Kingsport, 37663, Sullivan County, (423)323-4990, 90 miles from Knoxville. **E-mail:** markpath@aol.com. **Web:** www.tnstateparks.com. **Facility Holes:** 18. **Yards:** 6,601/5,328. **Par:** 72/72. **Course Rating:** 71.5/72.4. **Slope:** 123/117. **Green Fee:** $17/$20. **Cart Fee:** $11/Person. **Walking Policy:** Unrestricted walking. **Walkability:** 4. **Opened:** 1972. **Architect:** George Cobb. **Season:** Year-round. **To obtain tee times:** Call up to 7 days in advance. **Miscellaneous:** Reduced fees (weekdays, seniors, juniors), range (grass/mats), credit cards (MC, V, AE, D), BF, FF.

WHITE OAKS GOLF COURSE

PU-705 CR 105, Athens, 37303, McMinn County, (423)745-3349, 40 miles from Chattanooga. **Facility Holes:** 18. **Yards:** 6,760/4,809. **Par:** 72/72. **Course Rating:** 72.1/69.3. **Slope:** 124/118. **Green Fee:** $12/$15. **Cart Fee:** $12/Person. **Walking Policy:** Walking at certain times. **Walkability:** 3. **Opened:** 1992. **Architect:** Don Wyatt/Richard Davis. **Season:** Year-round. **High:** May-Sept. **To obtain tee times:** Call golf shop. **Miscellaneous:** Reduced fees (seniors), range (grass/mats), credit cards (MC, V, AE, D), BF, FF.

★★ WHITTLE SPRINGS GOLF COURSE

PU-3113 Valley View Dr., Knoxville, 37917, Knox County, (865)525-1022, (800)527-1022.
Facility Holes: 18. **Yards:** 6,000/4,884. **Par:** 70/70. **Course Rating:** 68.3/67.4. **Slope:** 106/111.
Green Fee: $14. **Cart Fee:** $11/Person. **Walking Policy:** Unrestricted walking. **Walkability:** 1.
Season: Year-round. **To obtain tee times:** Call up to 7 days in advance. **Miscellaneous:**
Reduced fees (weekdays, seniors, juniors), metal spikes, range (grass), FF.

★★★½ WILLOW CREEK GOLF CLUB

SP-12003 Kingston Pike, Knoxville, 37922, Knox County, (865)675-0100, 12 miles from
Knoxville. **E-mail:** tinwhistl1@aol.com. **Web:** www.willowcreekgolf.com. **Facility Holes:** 18.
Yards: 6,986/5,557. **Par:** 72/74. **Course Rating:** 73.5/71.9. **Slope:** 130/119. **Green Fee:**
$30/$40. **Cart Fee:** $15/Person. **Walking Policy:** Walking at certain times. **Walkability:** 2.
Opened: 1988. **Architect:** Bill Oliphant. **Season:** Year-round. **High:** May-Oct. **To obtain tee
times:** Call golf shop. **Miscellaneous:** Range (grass), credit cards (MC, V, AE), BF, FF.
Reader Comments: Worth the drive, friendly course, fun to play … It's so plush my dad wanted to
play barefoot … Very nice, costs a little more … Awesome golf course … Sometimes too slow …
Beautiful course.

WILLOWBROOK GOLF CLUB

PU-6751 McMinnville Hwy., Manchester, 37355, Coffee County, (931)728-8989,
(931)728-8989, 5 miles from Manchester. **Facility Holes:** 18. **Yards:** 6,689/5,304. **Par:** 72/72.
Course Rating: 72.7/71.4. **Slope:** 128/122. **Green Fee:** $18/$30. **Cart Fee:** $9/Person. **Walking
Policy:** Walking at certain times. **Walkability:** 2. **Opened:** 1995. **Architect:** Jerry Lemons.
Season: Year-round. **High:** April-Oct. **Tee times:** Call golf shop. **Miscellaneous:** Reduced fees
(weekdays, guests, twilight, seniors, juniors), range (grass), credit cards (MC, V, AE).

★★★½ WINDTREE GOLF CLUB

PU-810 Nonaville Rd., Mount Juliet, 37122, Wilson County, (615)754-4653, 15 miles from
Nashville. **Web:** www.windtreegolf.com. **Facility Holes:** 18. **Yards:** 6,557/5,126. **Par:** 72/72.
Course Rating: 71.1/69.6. **Slope:** 124/117. **Green Fee:** $25/$46. **Cart Fee:** $11/Cart. **Walking
Policy:** Walking at certain times. **Walkability:** 3. **Opened:** 1991. **Architect:** John LaFoy. **Season:**
Year-round. **High:** March-Oct. **To obtain tee times:** Call up to 5 days in advance.
Miscellaneous: Reduced fees (twilight, seniors, juniors), range (grass), credit cards (MC, V,
AE, D, Debit card), BF, FF.
Reader Comments: Great course, great shape, staff made sure we had whatever we needed, price
was reasonable … Great layout … A little pricey … Always in good shape … I always score well
here, go figure … Nicely playable.

★★★★ WOODLAKE GOLF CLUB *Service*

PU-330 Woodlake Blvd., Tazewell, 37879, Claiborne County, (423)626-6060, (877)423-4653,
45 miles from Knoxville. **E-mail:** woodlake@centuryinter.net. **Web:** www.woodlakegolf.com.
Facility Holes: 18. **Yards:** 6,771/4,985. **Par:** 72/72. **Course Rating:** 72.1/69.3. **Slope:** 127/118.
Green Fee: $30/$40. **Cart Fee:** Included in green fee. **Walking Policy:** Walking at certain times.
Walkability: 3. **Opened:** 1999. **Architect:** Chip Powell. **Season:** Year-round. **To obtain tee
times:** Call golf shop. **Miscellaneous:** Reduced fees (seniors, juniors), range (grass/mats),
credit cards (MC, V, D), BF, FF.
Reader Comments: Very nice course, reasonable price … Nice piece of land … A gem in every
way … Best experience this year … Very impressed … New course, great … Fun to play, short,
easy … Beautiful course, hidden gem.

★½ ALICE MUNICIPAL GOLF COURSE
PU-Texas Blvd., Alice, 78332, Jim Wells County, (361)664-7033, 40 miles from Corpus Christi. **Facility Holes:** 18. **Yards:** 6,099/5,066. **Par:** 71/72. **Course Rating:** 67.8/65.6. **Slope:** 108/100. **Green Fee:** $6/$7. **Cart Fee:** $15/Cart. **Walking Policy:** Unrestricted walking. **Walkability:** 1. **Architect:** Ralph Plummer. **Season:** Year-round. **High:** April-Aug. **To obtain tee times:** Call golf shop. **Miscellaneous:** Reduced fees (seniors), credit cards (MC, V).

★½ ALPINE GOLF COURSE
PU-2385 Smelley Rd., Longview, 75605, Gregg County, (903)753-4515, 45 miles from Shreveport. **E-mail:** alpgc@aol.com. **Facility Holes:** 18. **Yards:** 5,996/4,795. **Par:** 70/70. **Course Rating:** 67.4/67.4. **Slope:** 108/108. **Green Fee:** $19. **Cart Fee:** $8/Person. **Walking Policy:** Unrestricted walking. **Walkability:** 2. **Opened:** 1955. **Architect:** W.L. Benningfield. **Season:** Year-round. **To obtain tee times:** Call Golf Shop. **Miscellaneous:** Credit cards (MC, V, AE, D), FF.

★★★½ ALSATIAN GOLF COURSE
PU-1339 Country Road, Castroville, 78009, Medina County, (830)931-3100. **Facility Holes:** 18. **Yards:** 6,882/4,920. **Par:** 72/72. **Course Rating:** 72.3/68.7. **Slope:** 127/110. **Green Fee:** $26/$35. **Cart Fee:** Included in green fee. **Opened:** 1995. **Architect:** Steve Mrak. **Season:** Year-round. **To obtain tee times:** Call golf shop. **Miscellaneous:** Reduced fees (twilight, seniors), credit cards (MC, V, AE).
Reader Comments: Good people, course layout and condition … Great alternative to expensive San Antonio courses … Best course in this area for your money … Fun course, good pace, liked GPS on carts … New management, improving.

★★★ ANDREWS COUNTY GOLF COURSE
PU-920 Golf Course Rd., Andrews, 79714, Andrews County, (915)524-1462, 36 miles from Odessa. **Facility Holes:** 18. **Yards:** 6,300/5,331. **Par:** 70/72. **Course Rating:** 68.9/69.7. **Slope:** 116/110. **Green Fee:** $18/$25. **Cart Fee:** $19/Cart. **Walking Policy:** Unrestricted walking. **Walkability:** 1. **Opened:** 1950. **Architect:** Warren Cantrell. **Season:** Year-round. **To obtain tee times:** Call golf shop. **Miscellaneous:** Range (grass/mats), credit cards (MC, V, AE, D), BF, FF.
Reader Comments: Neat course—great value … Fast greens … Great value, good condition, walkable, fair … Good layout.

ARROWHEAD GOLF COURSE AT COMANCHE TRAIL
PU-4200 S. Grand, Amarillo, 79103, Potter County, (806)378-4281. **E-mail:** geoprio@aol.com. **Facility Holes:** 36. **Cart Fee:** $20/Cart. **Season:** Year-round. **To obtain tee times:** Call golf shop. **Miscellaneous:** Reduced fees (seniors, juniors).
ARROWHEAD COURSE (18)
Yards: 6,940/6,018. **Par:** 72/72. **Course Rating:** 71.9/67.4. **Slope:** 121/112. **Green Fee:** $16/$17. **Opened:** 1999. **Architect:** Bob Cupp.
TOMAHAWK COURSE (18)
Yards: 7,180/5,524. **Par:** 72/72. **Course Rating:** 72.9/68.7. **Slope:** 117/108. **Green Fee:** $12/$14. **Opened:** 1991. **Architect:** Charles Howard.

★½ ASCARATE PARK GOLF COURSE
PU-6900 Delta Dr., El Paso, 79905, El Paso County, (915)772-7381. **Facility Holes:** 27. **Yards:** 6,505/5,650. **Par:** 71/72. **Course Rating:** 69.4/66.2. **Slope:** 114/107. **Green Fee:** $5/$10. **Cart Fee:** $16/Cart. **Walking Policy:** Unrestricted walking. **Opened:** 1958. **Architect:** George Hoffman. **Season:** Year-round. **High:** Year-round. **To obtain tee times:** Call golf shop. **Miscellaneous:** Reduced fees (weekdays, twilight, seniors, juniors), metal spikes, range **Special Notes:** Also has a 9-hole course.

AUGUSTA PINES GOLF CLUB
SP-18 Augusta Pines Dr., Spring, 77389, Harris County, (832)381-1010. **Facility Holes:** 18. **Yards:** 7,041/5,606. **Par:** 72/72. **Course Rating:** 73.6/72.8. **Slope:** 125/121. **Green Fee:** $45/$79. **Cart Fee:** Included in green fee. **Opened:** 2000. **Season:** Year-round. **To obtain tee times:** Call up to 5 days in advance. **Miscellaneous:** Reduced fees (weekdays, twilight, juniors).

★★★★ THE BANDIT GOLF CLUB
PU-6019 FM 725, New Braunfels, 78130, Guadalupe County, (830)609-4665, (888)923-7846, 5 miles from New Braunfels. **Facility Holes:** 18. **Yards:** 6,928/5,253. **Par:** 71/71. **Course Rating:** 73.6/70.3. **Slope:** 133/126. **Green Fee:** $33/$43. **Cart Fee:** Included in green fee. **Walking Policy:** Unrestricted walking. **Walkability:** 4. **Opened:** 1997. **Architect:** Keith Foster. **Season:** Year-round. **To obtain tee times:** Call up to 7 days in advance. **Miscellaneous:** Reduced fees (seniors, juniors), range (grass), credit cards (MC, V, AE, D), BF, FF.
Reader Comments: A unique design with cleverly hidden hazards and severe doglegs … Great

condition, challenging but fair ... Good greens ... No. 18 tests your shot making ability ... Elevations uncommon for old ranch site.

BARTON CREEK RESORT & COUNTRY CLUB

R-8212 Barton Club Dr., Austin, 78735, Travis County, (512)301-7096, (800)336-6158, 12 miles from Austin. **E-mail:** chip.gist@ourclub.com. **Web:** www.clubcorp.com. **Facility Holes:** 72. **Cart Fee:** Included in green fee. **Walking Policy:** Unrestricted walking. **Season:** Year-round. **To obtain tee times:** Call golf shop. **Miscellaneous:** Range, metal spikes, credit cards (MC, V, AE).

★★★★ **CANYONS COURSE** (18)
Yards: 7,161/5,078. **Par:** 72/72. **Course Rating:** 74.0. **Slope:** 135. **Green Fee:** $160.
Walkability: 4. **Opened:** 2000. **Architect:** Tom Fazio. **Miscellaneous:** Reduced fees (twilight).
Notes: Ranked 12th in 2001 Best in State; 10th in 2000 Best New Upscale Courses.
Reader Comments: Beautiful setting ... No homes on course yet, so you are out in the woods by yourself ... Every hole is breathtaking! ... Fabulous practice facility ... Great course, great design ... Maybe best of the four courses ... New course, serious ups and downs, swirling winds.

★★★★ **CRENSHAW-COORE COURSE** (18)
Yards: 6,678/4,843. **Par:** 71/71. **Course Rating:** 71.0/67.2. **Slope:** 124/110. **Green Fee:** $95.
Walkability: 3. **Opened:** 1991. **Architect:** Ben Crenshaw/Bill Coore.
Notes: Ranked 24th in 1999 Best in State.
Reader Comments: Plush, excellent facility ... Great course ... Great design ... Huge greens, more links-type holes than the other courses ... First-class treatment by staff ... Visual treat ... Hilly terrain adds challenge.

★★★★½ **FAZIO COURSE** (18) *Condition*
Yards: 6,956/5,207. **Par:** 72/72. **Course Rating:** 74.0/69.4. **Slope:** 135/120. **Green Fee:** $135.
Walkability: 4. **Opened:** 1986. **Architect:** Tom Fazio.
Notes: Ranked 7th in 2001 Best in State; 21st in 1996 America's Top 75 Upscale Courses.
Reader Comments: Challenging and fun ... Super condition, service and facilities ... As good as it gets in Texas! ... The original Barton Creek Course is still the standard by which resort courses in this area should be measured ... Little expensive, but quality.

★★★★ **PALMER-LAKESIDE COURSE** (18) *Pace+*
Yards: 6,657/5,067. **Par:** 71/71. **Course Rating:** 71.0/71.0. **Slope:** 124/124. **Green Fee:** $95.
Walkability: 4. **Opened:** 1986. **Architect:** Arnold Palmer/Ed Seay.
Reader Comments: Beautiful setting, great staff ... Nice course, great service, good bunkers ... My personal favorite of Barton Creek courses ... Signature par-3 hole is as beautiful as any hole in golf.

★★ BATTLE LAKE GOLF COURSE

PU-4443 Battle Lake Road, Mart, 76664, McLennan County, (254)876-2837, 15 miles from Waco. **E-mail:** chig63@aol.com. **Web:** www.battlelakegolf.com. **Facility Holes:** 18. **Yards:** 6,608/5,254. **Par:** 72/74. **Course Rating:** 70.7/69.3. **Slope:** 116/112. **Cart Fee:** $11/Person. **Walking Policy:** Unrestricted walking. **Walkability:** 3. **Season:** Year-round. **To obtain tee times:** Call up to 14 days in advance. **Miscellaneous:** Reduced fees (weekdays, twilight, seniors, juniors), metal spikes, range (grass/mats), credit cards (MC, V, AE, D), BF, FF.

★★★ THE BATTLEGROUND AT DEER PARK GOLF COURSE

PU-1600 Georgia Ave., Deer Park, 77536, Harris County, (281)478-4653, 20 miles from Houston. **E-mail:** lgantz@deerparktx.org. **Facility Holes:** 18. **Yards:** 6,942/5,526. **Par:** 72/72. **Course Rating:** 73.6/73.1. **Slope:** 130/134. **Green Fee:** $24/$32. **Cart Fee:** $11/Person. **Walking Policy:** Unrestricted walking. **Walkability:** 2. **Opened:** 1996. **Architect:** Tom Knickerbocker/Charlie Epps. **Season:** Year-round. **To obtain tee times:** Call up to 7 days in advance. **Miscellaneous:** Reduced fees (weekdays, twilight, seniors, juniors), metal spikes, range (grass/mats), credit cards (MC, V, AE), BF, FF.
Reader Comments: Driving range and 3-hole practice layout good for a warm-up ... One of the top five courses in the greater Houston area for value ... Solid but not special ... Tough course when wind blows ... Fast greens.

★★★½ BAY FOREST GOLF COURSE *Value*

PU-201 Bay Forest Dr., LaPorte, 77571, Harris County, (281)471-4653, 20 miles from Houston. **Facility Holes:** 18. **Yards:** 6,756/5,094. **Par:** 72/72. **Course Rating:** 72.4/69.0. **Slope:** 126/113. **Green Fee:** $13/$22. **Cart Fee:** $20/Cart. **Walking Policy:** Unrestricted walking. **Walkability:** 1. **Opened:** 1988. **Architect:** Riviere/Marr. **Season:** Year-round. **High:** March-Dec. **To obtain tee times:** Call golf shop. **Miscellaneous:** Reduced fees (twilight, seniors), metal spikes, range (grass), credit cards (MC, V, AE, D), BF, FF.
Reader Comments: For a daily-fee course, hard to beat ... Nice design ... Generally in excellent shape ... Some of the best greens in the area ... Stern test, but fair ... Well worth a visit.

★★★ BAYOU DIN GOLF CLUB

PU-8537 LaBelle Rd., Beaumont, 77705, Jefferson County, (409)796-1327, 85 miles from

Houston. **Web:** www.aquilagolf.com. **Facility Holes:** 27. **Green Fee:** $13/$19. **Cart Fee:** $9/Person. **Walking Policy:** Unrestricted walking. **Walkability:** 2. **Opened:** 1961. **Architect:** Jimmy Witcher/Warren Howard. **Season:** Year-round. **To obtain tee times:** Call up to 7 days in advance. **Miscellaneous:** Reduced fees (weekdays, twilight, seniors, juniors), range (grass), credit cards (MC, V, AE, D), BF, FF.

BAYOU BACK/LINKS 9 (18 Combo)
Yards: 6,495/5,233. **Par:** 71/71. **Course Rating:** 70.6/64.7. **Slope:** 118/105.
BAYOU FRONT/BAYOU BACK (18 Combo)
Yards: 6,285/5,339. **Par:** 71/71. **Course Rating:** 68.5/64.4. **Slope:** 108/98.
BAYOU FRONT/LINKS 9 (18 Combo)
Yards: 7,020/5,672. **Par:** 72/72. **Course Rating:** 72.1/66.1. **Slope:** 116/103.
Reader Comments: Links 9 is a must-play, but very busy … 27 holes, play the new 9 twice … Narrow fairways … Played the old 18, new 9 hard to get on.

★★ BAYOU GOLF CLUB
PU-2800 Ted Dudley Dr., Texas City, 77590, Galveston County, (409)643-5850, 30 miles from Houston. **E-mail:** sstaffa@texas-city-tx.org. **Facility Holes:** 18. **Yards:** 6,665/5,448. **Par:** 72/73. **Course Rating:** 71.0/73.0. **Slope:** 114/118. **Green Fee:** $10/$14. **Cart Fee:** $16/Cart. **Walking Policy:** Unrestricted walking. **Walkability:** 1. **Opened:** 1974. **Architect:** Joe Finger. **Season:** Year-round. **To obtain tee times:** Call up to 3 days in advance. **Miscellaneous:** Reduced fees (weekdays, twilight, seniors, juniors), range (grass), credit cards (MC, V), BF, FF.

BEAR CREEK GOLF CLUB
PU-3500 Bear Creek Court, DFW Airport, 75261, Dallas County, (972)456-3200. **E-mail:** andy.gaudet@ourclub.com. **Web:** clubcorpgolf.com. **Facility Holes:** 36. **Green Fee:** $48/$88. **Cart Fee:** Included in green fee. **Walking Policy:** Walking at certain times. **Walkability:** 3. **Opened:** 1981. **Architect:** Ted Robinson. **Season:** Year-round. **High:** March-Oct. **To obtain tee times:** Call up to 7 days in advance. **Miscellaneous:** Reduced fees (weekdays, twilight, seniors, juniors), range (grass), credit cards (MC, V, AE, D), BF, FF.

★★★ **EAST COURSE** (18)
Yards: 6,670/5,620. **Par:** 72/72. **Course Rating:** 72.5/72.4. **Slope:** 127/124.
Reader Comments: Beautiful layout, very nice facilities … If it weren't for the jets flying overhead (DFW), you'd think you were out in the country … Roller coaster golf course … Challenging and beautiful … Good course, could be better maintained.

★★★½ **WEST COURSE** (18)
Yards: 6,675/5,570. **Par:** 72/72. **Course Rating:** 72.7/72.5. **Slope:** 130/122.
Reader Comments: Play both courses for a really good value … Tee ball in play a must … Gets lots of play …: Cost is a little high … Great course.

BEAR CREEK GOLF WORLD
PU-16001 Clay Rd., Houston, 77084, Harris County, (281)855-4720. **Facility Holes:** 54. **Cart Fee:** $13/Person. **Walking Policy:** Walking at certain times. **Walkability:** 1. **Season:** Year-round. **To obtain tee times:** Call up to 3 days in advance. **Miscellaneous:** Reduced fees (weekdays, twilight, seniors, juniors), range (grass), credit cards (MC, V, AE, D), BF, FF.

★★★ **CHALLENGER COURSE** (18)
Yards: 5,295/4,432. **Par:** 66/66. **Course Rating:** 64.2/64.7. **Slope:** 103/103. **Green Fee:** $12/$24. **Opened:** 1968. **Architect:** Bruce Littell.
Reader Comments: Excellent course, good diversity … Challenging executive course … Good practice course … Stay in the fairway, there are lots of trees.

★★½ **MASTERS COURSE** (18)
Yards: 7,131/5,544. **Par:** 72/72. **Course Rating:** 74.1/72.1. **Slope:** 133/125. **Green Fee:** $33/$59. **Opened:** 1972. **Architect:** Jay Riviere.
Notes: Ranked 20th in 1999 Best in State.

★★½ **PRESIDENTS COURSE** (18)
Yards: 6,562/5,728. **Par:** 72/72. **Course Rating:** 69.1/70.6. **Slope:** 110/111. **Green Fee:** $19/$40. **Opened:** 1968. **Architect:** Jay Riviere.

★½ BERGSTROM GOLF COURSE
PU-10330 Golf Course Rd., Austin, 78719, Travis County, (512)530-4653, 10 miles from Austin. **Facility Holes:** 18. **Yards:** 6,576/5,300. **Par:** 71/72. **Course Rating:** 69.5/70.5. **Slope:** 115/116. **Green Fee:** $10/$15. **Cart Fee:** $10/Person. **Walking Policy:** Unrestricted walking. **Walkability:** 3. **Opened:** 1954. **Architect:** Curly Tice/George Williams. **Season:** Year-round. **To obtain tee times:** Call golf shop. **Miscellaneous:** Reduced fees (weekdays, twilight, seniors, juniors), range (grass), credit cards (MC, V, D), BF, FF.
Special Notes: Formerly The Cedars on Bergstrom.

★★★ BLACKHAWK GOLF CLUB
PU-2714 Kelly Lane, Pflugerville, 78660, Travis County, (512)251-9000, 15 miles from Austin. **E-mail:** bhgc@swbell.net. **Web:** www.ccsi.com. **Facility Holes:** 18. **Yards:** 7,103/5,538.

Par: 72/72. **Course Rating:** 73.5/71.1. **Slope:** 123/121. **Green Fee:** $37/$48. **Cart Fee:** $11/Person. **Walking Policy:** Walking at certain times. **Walkability:** 2. **Opened:** 1991. **Architect:** Hollis Stacy/Charles Howard. **Season:** Year-round. **To obtain tee times:** Call up to 7 days in advance. **Miscellaneous:** Reduced fees (weekdays, twilight, seniors, juniors), metal spikes, range (grass/mats), credit cards (MC, V, AE), BF, FF.
Reader Comments: Good greens ... Good layout but not exceptional ... A lot of golf course for money, terrific shape ... Links golf is the only golf ... Wind, water or sand on every approach.

BLACKHORSE GOLF CLUB
PU-12205 Fry Rd., Cypress, 77433, Harris County, (281)304-1747, 20 miles from Houston. **E-mail:** klouvar@blackhorsegolfclub.com. **Web:** www.blackhorsegolfclub.com. **Facility Holes:** 36. **Green Fee:** $59/$69. **Cart Fee:** Included in green fee. **Walking Policy:** Unrestricted walking. **Walkability:** 3. **Opened:** 2000. **Architect:** Peter Jacobsen/Jim Hardy. **Season:** Year-round. **To obtain tee times:** Call up to 30 days in advance. **Miscellaneous:** Reduced fees (weekdays, twilight, seniors, juniors), metal spikes, range (grass), credit cards (MC, V, AE, D, DC), BF, FF.
NORTH COURSE (18)
Yards: 7,301/5,065. **Par:** 72/72. **Course Rating:** 75.0/69.1. **Slope:** 130/115.
SOUTH COURSE (18)
Yards: 7,171/4,843. **Par:** 72/68.5. **Course Rating:** 74.7/123.0. **Slope:** 138.

★★★ BLUEBONNET COUNTRY GOLF COURSE
SP-Rte. 2, Box 3471, Navasota, 77868, Grimes County, (936)894-2207. **Facility Holes:** 18. **Yards:** 6,495/5,159. **Par:** 72/72. **Course Rating:** 71.0/70.4. **Slope:** 129/129. **Green Fee:** $6/$18. **Cart Fee:** $18/Cart. **Walking Policy:** Walking at certain times. **Walkability:** 4. **Opened:** 1972. **Architect:** Jay Riviere. **Season:** Year-round. **To obtain tee times:** Call golf shop. **Miscellaneous:** Reduced fees (weekdays, twilight, seniors, juniors), metal spikes, credit cards (MC, V, AE, D).
Reader Comments: Good layout ... Nice people ... Natural layout ... Could be great with higher budget ... Big greens.

★★½ BLUEBONNET HILL GOLF CLUB
PU-9100 Decker Lane, Austin, 78724, Travis County, (512)272-4228. **E-mail:** bbhillpro@aol.com. **Facility Holes:** 18. **Yards:** 6,503/5,241. **Par:** 72/72. **Course Rating:** 70.0/69.4. **Slope:** 113/115. **Green Fee:** $13/$27. **Cart Fee:** $20/Cart. **Walking Policy:** Unrestricted walking. **Walkability:** 3. **Opened:** 1991. **Architect:** Jeff Brauer. **Season:** Year-round. **High:** March-June. **To obtain tee times:** Call up to 5 days in advance. **Miscellaneous:** Reduced fees (weekdays, twilight, seniors, juniors), metal spikes, range (grass), credit cards (MC, V), BF, FF.

★★★ BRACKENRIDGE PARK MUNICIPAL GOLF COURSE
PU-2315 Ave. B, San Antonio, 78215, Bexar County, (210)226-5612, 2 miles from San Antonio. **Facility Holes:** 18. **Yards:** 6,185/5,216. **Par:** 72/72. **Course Rating:** 70.1/69.2. **Slope:** 122/112. **Green Fee:** $12/$19. **Cart Fee:** $18/Cart. **Walking Policy:** Unrestricted walking. **Walkability:** 1. **Opened:** 1916. **Architect:** A.W. Tillinghast. **Season:** Year-round. **To obtain tee times:** Call up to 7 days in advance. **Miscellaneous:** Reduced fees (weekdays, twilight, seniors, juniors), metal spikes, credit cards (MC, V), BF, FF.
Reader Comments: Great food ... Good history ... Nice course ... Texas golf was invented here ... Good old course, clubhouse ... A grand old lady ... Improving all the time ... Crowded, slow play.

★★ BRIARWOOD GOLF CLUB
SP-4511 Briarwood Dr., Tyler, 75709, Smith County, (903)593-7741, 3 miles from Tyler. **E-mail:** briarwoodgolf@juno.com. **Web:** www.briarwoodgc.com. **Facility Holes:** 18. **Yards:** 6,487/4,735. **Par:** 71/71. **Course Rating:** 71.1/66.1. **Slope:** 125/115. **Green Fee:** $13/$33. **Cart Fee:** $12/Person. **Walking Policy:** Unrestricted walking. **Walkability:** 4. **Opened:** 1955. **Architect:** Lee Singletary. **Season:** Year-round. **High:** March-Oct. **To obtain tee times:** Call up to 3 days in advance. **Miscellaneous:** Reduced fees (weekdays, twilight, seniors, juniors), metal spikes, range (grass), credit cards (MC, V), BF, FF.

★★★½ BRIDLEWOOD GOLF CLUB
PU-4000 West Windsor Dr., Flower Mound, 75028, Denton County, (972)355-4800, 20 miles from Dallas. **Web:** www.bridlewoodgolf.com. **Facility Holes:** 18. **Yards:** 7,036/5,278. **Par:** 72/72. **Course Rating:** 73.6/70.7. **Slope:** 130/120. **Green Fee:** $70/$88. **Cart Fee:** Included in green fee. **Walking Policy:** Unrestricted walking. **Walkability:** 3. **Opened:** 1997. **Architect:** D.A. Weibring/Maury Miller. **Season:** Year-round. **To obtain tee times:** Call up to 6 days in advance. **Miscellaneous:** Reduced fees (weekdays, twilight, seniors, juniors), range (grass), credit cards (MC, V, AE, D), BF, FF.
Reader Comments: Good place to play, wide open ... Staff is excellent ... Nice layout well, maintained ... Love clubhouse ... Great weather ... Large practice facility.

★★ BROCK PARK GOLF COURSE
PU-8201 John Ralston Rd., Houston, 77044, Harris County, (281)458-1350. **Facility Holes:** 18. **Yards:** 6,487/5,650. **Par:** 72/74. **Course Rating:** 70.7. **Slope:** 114. **Green Fee:** $4/$12. **Cart Fee:** $17/Cart. **Walking Policy:** Unrestricted walking. **Walkability:** 5. **Opened:** 1952. **Architect:** A.C. Ray. **To obtain tee times:** Call golf shop. **Miscellaneous:** Reduced fees (weekdays, twilight), metal spikes, range (grass).

★★ BROWNSVILLE GOLF CENTER
PU-1800 W. San Marcelo, Brownsville, 78526, Cameron County, (956)541-2582. **Facility Holes:** 18. **Yards:** 6,066/5,104. **Par:** 70/70. **Course Rating:** 69.5/69.5. **Slope:** 113/113. **Green Fee:** $10/$15. **Cart Fee:** $10/Person. **Walking Policy:** Unrestricted walking. **Walkability:** 1. **Opened:** 1972. **Architect:** Don Sechrest. **Season:** Year-round. **High:** Jan.-April. **To obtain tee times:** Call up to 7 days in advance. **Miscellaneous:** Reduced fees (twilight, juniors), credit cards (MC, V, AE, D), BF, FF.

★½ BRYAN GOLF COURSE
PU-206 W. Villa Maria, Bryan, 77801, Brazos County, (979)823-0126, 84 miles from Houston. **Facility Holes:** 18. **Yards:** 6,243/5,857. **Par:** 70/70. **Course Rating:** 69.6/67.3. **Slope:** 110/106. **Green Fee:** $9/$16. **Cart Fee:** $9/Person. **Walking Policy:** Unrestricted walking. **Walkability:** 2. **Opened:** 1925. **Architect:** Fred Marburry. **Season:** Year-round. **To obtain tee times:** Call up to 7 days in advance. **Miscellaneous:** Reduced fees (weekdays, twilight, seniors, juniors), credit cards (MC, V, AE, D), BF, FF.

★★★ THE BUCKHORN GOLF COURSE
PU-36 FM 473, Comfort, 78013, Kendal County, (830)995-5351, 48 miles from San Antonio. **Web:** www.buckhorngolfcourse.com. **Facility Holes:** 18. **Yards:** 6,637/4,616. **Par:** 71/71. **Course Rating:** 71.4/66.0. **Slope:** 117/109. **Green Fee:** $27/$34. **Cart Fee:** Included in green fee. **Walking Policy:** Walking at certain times. **Walkability:** 3. **Opened:** 2000. **Architect:** Art Schuapeter. **Season:** Year-round. **High:** Jan.-June. **To obtain tee times:** Call up to 7 days in advance. **Miscellaneous:** Reduced fees (weekdays, twilight, seniors, juniors), metal spikes, range (grass), credit cards (MC, V, AE, D), BF, FF.
Reader Comments: Friendly folks ... Great seniors layout ... Good overall experience ... A steal for Hill Country experience, great product ... Good elevation changes, course still needs work.

★★★★ BUFFALO CREEK GOLF CLUB
SP-624 Country Club Dr., Rockwall, 75087, Rockwall County, (972)771-4003, 15 miles from Dallas. **Facility Holes:** 18. **Yards:** 7,012/5,209. **Par:** 71/71. **Course Rating:** 73.8/67.0. **Slope:** 135/113. **Green Fee:** $40/$91. **Cart Fee:** Included in green fee. **Walking Policy:** Unrestricted walking. **Walkability:** 3. **Opened:** 1992. **Architect:** Tom Weiskopf/Jay Morrish. **Season:** Year-round. **To obtain tee times:** Call golf shop. **Miscellaneous:** Reduced fees (weekdays, twilight, seniors, juniors), range (grass), credit cards (MC, V, AE, DC), BF, FF.
Reader Comments: Nos. 6 and 18 are 2 of the best par 4s in the state ... Good fair test of golf ... A favorite ... Great service, beautiful course ... Very well maintained high-end course ... Great course, good facilities ... Great design, tees make great course ... Somewhat pricey but awesome course.

★★½ CANYON LAKE GOLF CLUB
SP-405 Watts Lane, Canyon Lake, 78133, Comal County, (830)899-3372, 25 miles from San Antonio. **Facility Holes:** 18. **Yards:** 6,528/4,726. **Par:** 72/72. **Course Rating:** 70.1/67.9. **Slope:** 126/114. **Green Fee:** $20/$30. **Cart Fee:** Included in green fee. **Walking Policy:** Unrestricted walking. **Walkability:** 4. **Opened:** 1980. **Season:** Year-round. **High:** Nov.-May. **To obtain tee times:** Call golf shop. **Miscellaneous:** Reduced fees (weekdays, guests, twilight, seniors, juniors), range (grass), credit cards (MC, V, AE, D).

★★★★½ CANYON SPRINGS GOLF CLUB
PU-24400 Canyon Golf Rd., San Antonio, 78258, Bexar County, (210)497-1770, (888)800-1511, 3 miles from San Antonio. **E-mail:** duane.devalle@ourclub.com. **Web:** www.canyonspringscc.com. **Facility Holes:** 18. **Yards:** 7,077/5,234. **Par:** 72/72. **Course Rating:** 72.8/70.0. **Slope:** 130/115. **Green Fee:** $60/$99. **Cart Fee:** Included in green fee. **Walking Policy:** Mandatory carts. **Walkability:** 4. **Opened:** 1998. **Architect:** Tom Walker. **Season:** Year-round. **To obtain tee times:** Call up to 7 days in advance. **Miscellaneous:** Reduced fees (weekdays, twilight, seniors, juniors), range (grass), credit cards (MC, V, AE, D), BF, FF.
Notes: Ranked 16th in 2001 Best in State.
Reader Comments: Maybe the best in San Antonio ... Great daily-fee course ... Awesome greens, elevations, food ... Wonderful views of Hill Country ... Need to play at least twice.

★★★ CAPE ROYALE GOLF COURSE
SP-Lake Livingstone, Coldspring, 77331, San Jacinto County, (936)-653-5323,

(800)707-7022, 40 miles from Conroe. **E-mail:** phendrix@lcc.net. **Facility Holes:** 18. **Yards:** 6,088/4,941. **Par:** 70/70. **Course Rating:** 66.1/64.7. **Slope:** 113/103. **Green Fee:** $11/$28. **Cart Fee:** $10/Person. **Walking Policy:** Walking at certain times. **Walkability:** 5. **Opened:** 1972. **Architect:** Bruce Littell. **Season:** Year-round. **To obtain tee times:** Call golf shop. **Miscellaneous:** Reduced fees (weekdays, twilight, seniors, juniors), range (grass), credit cards (MC, V, AE, D), BF, FF.
Reader Comments: Interesting layout … Challenging holes … Short course—fun to play … 2 completely different 9s … Short, tight and tricky greens.

★½ **CASA BLANCA GOLF COURSE**
PU-3900 Casa Blanca, Laredo, 78041, Webb County, (956)791-7262. **Facility Holes:** 18. **Yards:** 6,390/5,631. **Par:** 72/72. **Course Rating:** 71.0/68.9. **Slope:** 115/115. **Green Fee:** $8/$10. **Cart Fee:** $14/Cart. **Walking Policy:** Unrestricted walking. **Opened:** 1922. **Architect:** Carter Morrish/Roy Becthol. **Season:** Year-round. **High:** Feb.-Oct. **To obtain tee times:** Call golf shop. **Miscellaneous:** Reduced fees (weekdays, seniors, juniors), metal spikes, range (grass), credit cards (MC, V, AE, D).

★★★½ **CEDAR CREEK GOLF COURSE**
PU-8250 Vista Colina, San Antonio, 78255, Bexar County, (210)695-5050, 20 miles from San Antonio. **Facility Holes:** 18. **Yards:** 7,103/5,535. **Par:** 72/72. **Course Rating:** 73.4/70.8. **Slope:** 132/113. **Green Fee:** $30/$44. **Cart Fee:** Included in green fee. **Walking Policy:** Unrestricted walking. **Walkability:** 4. **Opened:** 1989. **Architect:** Finger/Dye/Spann. **Season:** Year-round. **High:** March-Oct. **To obtain tee times:** Call up to 365 days in advance. **Miscellaneous:** Reduced fees (weekdays, twilight, seniors, juniors), metal spikes, range (grass/mats), credit cards (MC, V, AE, D), BF, FF.
Reader Comments: Best muni you could ever play outside of Bethpage Black and Red … Great layout, my favorite in San Antonio … Beautiful hills, a tough walk … New owners building on great progress of former owners … Interesting, quiet, challenging, long, pretty with great wildlife.

★★½ **CEDAR CREST GOLF COURSE**
PU-1800 Southerland, Dallas, 75223, Dallas County, (214)670-7615. **Facility Holes:** 18. **Yards:** 6,550/5,594. **Par:** 71/75. **Course Rating:** 71.0/76.0. **Slope:** 121/116. **Green Fee:** $11/$14. **Cart Fee:** $18/Cart. **Walking Policy:** Unrestricted walking. **Opened:** 1923. **Architect:** A.W. Tillinghast. **Season:** Year-round. **High:** April-Sept. **To obtain tee times:** Call golf shop. **Miscellaneous:** Reduced fees (twilight, seniors, juniors), metal spikes, range (grass), caddies, credit cards (MC, V, AE, D).

★★ **CHAMBERS COUNTY GOLF COURSE**
PU-1 Pinchback Dr., Anahuac, 77514, Chambers County, (409)267-8235, 43 miles from Houston. **Facility Holes:** 18. **Yards:** 6,909/5,014. **Par:** 72/73. **Course Rating:** 71.5/67.5. **Slope:** 116/106. **Green Fee:** $10/$15. **Cart Fee:** $17/Person. **Walking Policy:** Unrestricted walking. **Walkability:** 1. **Opened:** 1975. **Architect:** Leon Howard/R.T. Pinchback. **Season:** Year-round. **To obtain tee times:** Call golf shop. **Miscellaneous:** Reduced fees (weekdays, twilight), range (grass/mats), credit cards (MC, V, AE, D), BF, FF.

CHASE OAKS GOLF CLUB
PU-7201 Chase Oaks Blvd., Plano, 75025, Collin County, (972)517-7777, 14 miles from Dallas. **E-mail:** mailbox@chaseoaks.com. **Web:** www.chaseoaks.com. **Facility Holes:** 27. **Cart Fee:** $12/Person. **Walking Policy:** Walking at certain times. **Walkability:** 4. **Architect:** Robert von Hagge/Bruce Devlin. **Season:** Year-round. **High:** April-Nov. **To obtain tee times:** Call golf shop. **Miscellaneous:** Reduced fees (weekdays, twilight, seniors, juniors), range (grass/mats), credit cards (MC, V, AE, D, DC), BF, FF.
★★★ **BLACK JACK COURSE (18)**
Yards: 6,762/5,105. **Par:** 72/72. **Course Rating:** 74.4/70.0. **Slope:** 139/128. **Green Fee:** $37/$57. **Opened:** 1986.
Reader Comments: One of the best overall routings in Dallas and worth fighting the traffic … Hilly, good test of golf skills.
SAWTOOTH COURSE (9)
Yards: 3,250/2,746. **Par:** 36/36. **Course Rating:** 70.1/72.0. **Slope:** 130/124. **Green Fee:** $29. **Opened:** 1981.

★½ **CHEROKEE COUNTRY CLUB**
SP-Henderson Highway, Jacksonville, 75766, Cherokee County, (903)586-2141. **Facility Holes:** 18. **Yards:** 6,208/5,145. **Par:** 71/73. **Course Rating:** 69.1/69.8. **Slope:** 119/125. **Green Fee:** $15/$20. **Cart Fee:** $20/Cart. **Walking Policy:** Walking at certain times. **Walkability:** 3. **Opened:** 1936. **Season:** Year-round. **High:** April-Aug. **To obtain tee times:** Call golf shop. **Miscellaneous:** Metal spikes, range (grass/mats), credit cards (MC, V, D).

★★½ CHESTER W. DITTO GOLF CLUB
PU-801 Brown Blvd., Arlington, 76011, Tarrant County, (817)275-5941, 20 miles from Dallas. **Facility Holes:** 18. **Yards:** 6,727/5,555. **Par:** 72/72. **Course Rating:** 70.8/71.2. **Slope:** 117/116. **Green Fee:** $17/$20. **Cart Fee:** $10/Person. **Walking Policy:** Unrestricted walking. **Walkability:** 4. **Opened:** 1982. **Architect:** Killian/Nugent. **Season:** Year-round. **To obtain tee times:** Call golf shop. **Miscellaneous:** Reduced fees (weekdays, twilight, seniors, juniors), metal spikes, range (grass/mats), credit cards (MC, V, D), BF, FF.

★★★ CIELO VISTA GOLF COURSE
PU-1510 Hawkins, El Paso, 79925, El Paso County, (915)591-4927. **E-mail:** cieloep@aol.com. **Facility Holes:** 18. **Yards:** 6,411/5,421. **Par:** 71/71. **Course Rating:** 69.4/69.4. **Slope:** 122/113. **Green Fee:** $18/$22. **Cart Fee:** $18/Cart. **Walking Policy:** Unrestricted walking. **Walkability:** 1. **Opened:** 1977. **Architect:** Marvin Ferguson. **Season:** Year-round. **To obtain tee times:** Call golf shop. **Miscellaneous:** Reduced fees (weekdays, twilight), range (grass), credit cards (MC, V, D), BF, FF.
Reader Comments: Good course … Reasonable rates and good service … Nice small course, challenging.

★★★½ CIRCLE C RANCH GOLF CLUB
PU-7401 Hwy. 45, Austin, 78739, Travis County, (512)288-4297. **E-mail:** bogengolfing@aol.com. **Facility Holes:** 18. **Yards:** 6,859/5,236. **Par:** 72/72. **Course Rating:** 72.7/69.9. **Slope:** 122/120. **Green Fee:** $36/$51. **Cart Fee:** $14/Cart. **Walking Policy:** Walking at certain times. **Walkability:** 4. **Opened:** 1992. **Architect:** Jay Morrish. **Season:** Year-round. **To obtain tee times:** Call up to 7 days in advance. **Miscellaneous:** Reduced fees (weekdays, twilight, juniors), range (grass), credit cards (MC, V, AE), BF, FF.
Reader Comments: Great layout … Plenty of tests … Few easy holes, but not unplayable … Fast greens and good pace of play … Keep it in the fairway … Great Hill Country course … Beautiful setting and excellent course, in good condition despite drought conditions … A great value.

★★½ CLEAR LAKE GOLF CLUB
PU-1202 Reseda Dr., Houston, 77062, Harris County, (281)488-0250, 15 miles from Downtown Houston. **Web:** www.clearlakegolf.com. **Facility Holes:** 18. **Yards:** 6,757/5,924. **Par:** 72/72. **Course Rating:** 71.7/71.1. **Slope:** 113/111. **Green Fee:** $19/$36. **Cart Fee:** Included in green fee. **Walking Policy:** Walking at certain times. **Walkability:** 3. **Opened:** 1964. **Architect:** Jay Riviere. **Season:** Year-round. **To obtain tee times:** Call up to 7 days in advance. **Miscellaneous:** Reduced fees (twilight, seniors, juniors), range (grass), credit cards (MC, V, AE, D), BF, FF.

★★ CLEBURNE MUNICIPAL GOLF COURSE
PU-2500 Country Club Rd., Cleburne, 76031, Johnson County, (817)645-9078. **Facility Holes:** 18. **Yards:** 6,326/5,084. **Par:** 71/71. **Green Fee:** $9/$11. **Opened:** 1930. **Season:** Year-round. **To obtain tee times:** Call golf shop. **Miscellaneous:** Reduced fees (twilight), metal spikes.

★★★★½ THE CLIFFS RESORT
R-160 Cliffs Dr., Graford, 76449, Palo Pinto County, (940)779-4040, (888)843-2543, 75 miles from Fort Worth. **Web:** www.thecliffsresort.com. **Facility Holes:** 18. **Yards:** 6,808/4,876. **Par:** 71/71. **Course Rating:** 73.9/68.4. **Slope:** 143/124. **Green Fee:** $40/$80. **Cart Fee:** Included in green fee. **Walking Policy:** Mandatory carts. **Walkability:** 5. **Opened:** 1988. **Architect:** Bruce Devlin/Robert von Hagge. **Season:** Year-round. **High:** April-Oct. **To obtain tee times:** Call up to 7 days in advance. **Miscellaneous:** Reduced fees (weekdays, guests, twilight, juniors), range (grass), lodging (90 rooms), credit cards (MC, V, AE, D), BF, FF.
Reader Comments: Best views in Texas … Helpful … Tricky course, too many blind shots … Beautiful and challenging layout … Bring some balls, this one can get tough … Doesn't feel like Texas.

★★ THE CLUB AT RUNAWAY BAY
SP-400 Half Moon Way, Runaway Bay, 76426, Wise County, (940)575-2225, 45 miles from Fort Worth. **E-mail:** probob@ntws.net. **Web:** www.runawaybaytexas.com. **Facility Holes:** 18. **Yards:** 7,032/5,446. **Par:** 72/72. **Course Rating:** 73.1/68.2. **Slope:** 124/108. **Green Fee:** $30/$50. **Cart Fee:** $10/Person. **Walking Policy:** Walking at certain times. **Walkability:** 3. **Opened:** 1968. **Architect:** Leon Howard. **Season:** Year-round. **To obtain tee times:** Call golf shop. **Miscellaneous:** Reduced fees (guests, twilight, juniors), range (grass), credit cards (MC, V, AE, D), BF, FF.

★★★½ COLUMBIA LAKES
R-188 Freeman Blvd., West Columbia, 77486, Brazoria County, (979)345-5151, (800)231-1030, 50 miles from Houston. **Facility Holes:** 18. **Yards:** 6,967/5,280. **Par:** 72/72.

Course Rating: 73.2/71.7. **Slope:** 133/122. **Green Fee:** $50/$65. **Cart Fee:** Included in green fee. **Walking Policy:** Unrestricted walking. **Walkability:** 2. **Opened:** 1972. **Architect:** Jack Miller/Tom Fazio. **Season:** Year-round. **To obtain tee times:** Call up to 7 days in advance. **Miscellaneous:** Reduced fees (weekdays, guests), range (grass/mats), lodging (160 rooms), credit cards (MC, V, AE, D, DC), BF, FF.

Reader Comments: Good resort setting ... Some challenging holes, good condition ... Dramatic old oaks, pecans, wildlife ... Very long, good greens ... Good quick greens ... New pro/pro shop good value.

COMANCHE TRAIL GOLF CLUB
PU-4200 S. Grand, Amarillo, 79103, Randall County, (806)378-4281. **E-mail:** gpriolo@arn.net. **Facility Holes:** 36. **Cart Fee:** $20/Cart. **Walking Policy:** Unrestricted walking. **Walkability:** 2. **Season:** Year-round. **High:** April-Sept. **To obtain tee times:** Call golf shop. **Miscellaneous:** Reduced fees (twilight, seniors, juniors), range (grass), credit cards (MC, V, D), BF, FF.
ARROWHEAD COURSE (18)
Yards: 6,940/5,279. **Par:** 72/72. **Course Rating:** 71.9/70.2. **Slope:** 121/118. **Green Fee:** $13/$17. **Opened:** 1999. **Architect:** Bob Cupp.
★★½ **TOMAHAWK COURSE** (18)
Yards: 7,180/5,524. **Par:** 72/72. **Course Rating:** 72.9/70.0. **Slope:** 117/108. **Green Fee:** $9/$13. **Opened:** 1990. **Architect:** Charles Howard.

★★ COMANCHE TRAIL GOLF COURSE
PU-800 Comanche Park Rd., Big Spring, 79720, Howard County, (915)264-2366, 37 miles from Midland. **E-mail:** jbird@nwol.net. **Facility Holes:** 18. **Yards:** 6,975/5,950. **Par:** 71/72. **Course Rating:** 68.9/66.1. **Slope:** 113/98. **Green Fee:** $10/$15. **Cart Fee:** $18/Cart. **Walking Policy:** Unrestricted walking. **Walkability:** 3. **Opened:** 1934. **Architect:** William Cantrell. **Season:** Year-round. **High:** April-Oct. **To obtain tee times:** Call golf shop. **Miscellaneous:** Reduced fees (seniors, juniors), credit cards (MC, V, AE, D), BF, FF.

★★ CONNALLY GOLF COURSE
PU-7900 Concord Rd., Waco, 76705, McLennan County, (254)799-6561, 5 miles from Waco. **E-mail:** jickybarg@aol.com. **Facility Holes:** 18. **Yards:** 6,975/5,950. **Par:** 72/73. **Course Rating:** 72.5/72.6. **Slope:** 116/120. **Green Fee:** $12/$16. **Cart Fee:** $10/Person. **Walking Policy:** Unrestricted walking. **Walkability:** 2. **Opened:** 1959. **Architect:** Ralph Plummer. **Season:** Year-round. **To obtain tee times:** Call up to 7 days in advance. **Miscellaneous:** Reduced fees (twilight, seniors, juniors), metal spikes, range (grass/mats), credit cards (MC, V), BF, FF.

★★★ COTTONWOOD CREEK GOLF COURSE
PU-5200 Bagby Dr., Waco, 76711, McLennan County, (254)752-2474. **E-mail:** davidst@ci.waco.tx.us. **Web:** www.waco-texas.com. **Facility Holes:** 18. **Yards:** 7,140/5,716. **Par:** 72/72. **Course Rating:** 73.5/71.9. **Slope:** 129. **Green Fee:** $14/$17. **Cart Fee:** $12/Person. **Walking Policy:** Unrestricted walking. **Walkability:** 3. **Opened:** 1985. **Architect:** Joe Finger. **Season:** Year-round. **High:** March-Oct. **To obtain tee times:** Call up to 5 days in advance. **Miscellaneous:** Reduced fees (weekdays, twilight, seniors, juniors), range (grass), credit cards (MC, V), BF, FF.

Reader Comments: Good design ... Always accommodating ... Good bang for buck ... Excellent public course, best in state!! ... Always crowded (muni) ... Long, windy ... Excellent course for all levels ... Best muni I have played.

★★½ COUNTRY VIEW GOLF CLUB
PU-240 W. Beltline Rd., Lancaster, 75146, Dallas County, (972)227-0995, 13 miles from Dallas. **Facility Holes:** 18. **Yards:** 6,609/5,048. **Par:** 71/71. **Course Rating:** 71.0/68.2. **Slope:** 120/114. **Green Fee:** $12/$17. **Cart Fee:** $20/Cart. **Walking Policy:** Unrestricted walking. **Opened:** 1989. **Architect:** Ron Garl. **Season:** Year-round. **High:** April-Oct. **To obtain tee times:** Call golf shop. **Miscellaneous:** Reduced fees (twilight, seniors, juniors), metal spikes, range (grass), credit cards (MC, V, D).

★★ COYOTE RIDGE GOLF CLUB
PU-1680 Bandera Dr., Carrollton, 75010, Denton County, (972)939-0666, 18 miles from Dallas. **Web:** www.coyoteridgegolf.com. **Facility Holes:** 18. **Yards:** 6,795/4,995. **Par:** 71/71. **Course Rating:** 72.8/70.0. **Slope:** 130/118. **Green Fee:** $30/$62. **Cart Fee:** $12/Person. **Walking Policy:** Walking at certain times. **Walkability:** 2. **Opened:** 1999. **Architect:** Williams, Gill & Associates. **Season:** Year-round. **High:** April-June. **To obtain tee times:** Call up to 7 days in advance. **Miscellaneous:** Reduced fees (twilight, seniors, juniors), range (grass), credit cards (MC, V, AE, D), BF, FF.

THE CREEKS AT BEECHWOOD
R-15801 Championship Pkwy., Fort Worth, 76177, Tarrant County, (817)497-2582, 20 miles from Fort Worth. **E-mail:** josborne@troongolf.com. **Web:** www.troongolf.com. **Facility Holes:**

18. **Yards:** 7,154/4,949. **Par:** 72/72. **Course Rating:** 75.6/64.5. **Slope:** 143/110. **Green Fee:** $45/$85. **Cart Fee:** Included in green fee. **Walking Policy:** Unrestricted walking. **Walkability:** 3. **Opened:** 2000. **Architect:** Greg Norman. **Season:** Year-round. **High:** April-June. **To obtain tee times:** Call up to 30 days in advance. **Miscellaneous:** Reduced fees (weekdays, twilight, seniors, juniors), metal spikes, range (grass), lodging (286 rooms), credit cards (MC, V, AE), BF, FF.

★★★½ CREEKVIEW GOLF CLUB
PU-1602 E. Hwy. 175, Crandall, 75114, Kaufman County, (972)427-3811, 20 miles from Dallas. **Facility Holes:** 18. **Yards:** 7,238/5,459. **Par:** 72/72. **Course Rating:** 74.1/71.2. **Slope:** 119/115. **Green Fee:** $31/$43. **Cart Fee:** Included in green fee. **Walking Policy:** Mandatory carts. **Walkability:** 2. **Opened:** 1995. **Architect:** Dick Phelps. **Season:** Year-round. **High:** March-June. **To obtain tee times:** Call up to 7 days in advance. **Miscellaneous:** Reduced fees (weekdays, twilight, seniors, juniors), range (grass/mats), credit cards (MC, V, AE, D), BF, FF.
Reader Comments: One of the best courses for the money in the Dallas area ... The course is always in great shape and usually easy to get on ... Slow play on weekends ... Windy conditions make it tough ... Best bent greens and lush fairways.

★★★½ CROSS TIMBERS GOLF COURSE *Pace*
PU-1181 S. Stewart, Azle, 76020, Parker County, (817)444-4940, 14 miles from Fort Worth. **Facility Holes:** 18. **Yards:** 6,734/5,051. **Par:** 72/72. **Course Rating:** 71.5/68.2. **Slope:** 128/113. **Green Fee:** $18/$22. **Cart Fee:** $10/Person. **Walking Policy:** Unrestricted walking. **Walkability:** 5. **Opened:** 1995. **Architect:** Jeff Brauer. **Season:** Year-round. **High:** March-Oct. **To obtain tee times:** Call golf shop. **Miscellaneous:** Reduced fees (weekdays, twilight, seniors, juniors), metal spikes, range (grass), credit cards (MC, V, AE).
Reader Comments: 1st hole amazing ... A nice course away from the bustle of Dallas/Ft. Worth ... Nice staff and good scenery to go with a good course ... Extreme topography for north Texas ... Beware the Cross Timbers bounce ... Great layout ... Great setting! ... Very hilly, but fun to play.

★★½ CRYSTAL FALLS GOLF COURSE
PU-3400 Crystal Falls Pkwy., Leander, 78641, Travis County, (512)259-5855, 14 miles from Austin. **Facility Holes:** 18. **Yards:** 6,654/5,194. **Par:** 72/72. **Course Rating:** 72.3/70.0. **Slope:** 126/123. **Green Fee:** $18/$27. **Cart Fee:** $13/Person. **Walking Policy:** Unrestricted walking. **Walkability:** 5. **Opened:** 1990. **Architect:** Charles Howard/Jack Miller. **Season:** Year-round. **To obtain tee times:** Call up to 3 days in advance. **Miscellaneous:** Reduced fees (weekdays, twilight, seniors, juniors), range (grass), credit cards (MC, V), BF, FF.

★★½ CYPRESS LAKES GOLF CLUB
PU-18700 Cypresswood Dr., Cypress, 77429, Harris County, (281)304-8515, 15 miles from Houston. **Web:** www.cypresslakesgolf.net. **Facility Holes:** 18. **Yards:** 7,023/5,351. **Par:** 72/72. **Course Rating:** 72.6/70.6. **Slope:** 126/120. **Green Fee:** $42/$70. **Cart Fee:** Included in green fee. **Walking Policy:** Unrestricted walking. **Walkability:** 2. **Opened:** 1999. **Architect:** Jim Fazio. **Season:** Year-round. **High:** March-Oct. **To obtain tee times:** Call up to 7 days in advance. **Miscellaneous:** Reduced fees (weekdays, twilight, seniors, juniors), range (grass), credit cards (MC, V, AE), BF, FF.

CYPRESSWOOD GOLF CLUB
PU-21602 Cypresswood Dr., Spring, 77373, Harris County, (281)821-6300, 16 miles from Houston. **E-mail:** cmartinez@cypresswood.com. **Web:** www.cypresswood.com. **Facility Holes:** 54. **Cart Fee:** Included in green fee. **Walking Policy:** Unrestricted walking. **Season:** Year-round. **High:** March-May. **To obtain tee times:** Call up to 8 days in advance. **Miscellaneous:** Reduced fees (weekdays, twilight, seniors, juniors), metal spikes, range (grass/mats), credit cards (MC, V, AE, D), BF, FF.
★★★ CREEK COURSE (18)
Yards: 6,937/5,549. **Par:** 72/72. **Course Rating:** 72.0/69.1. **Slope:** 124/113. **Green Fee:** $36/$58. **Walkability:** 3. **Opened:** 1988. **Architect:** Rick Forester.
Reader Comments: Good course ... The price was right ... Always great greens, tough but fair ... This course is 1 of 3 Cypresswood Courses which are all great courses and good values ... Needs work around hazards.
★★★ CYPRESS COURSE (18)
Yards: 6,906/5,599. **Par:** 72/72. **Course Rating:** 71.8/67.6. **Slope:** 123/111. **Green Fee:** $36/$58. **Walkability:** 3. **Opened:** 1987. **Architect:** Rick Forester.
Reader Comments: Good course ... Starter was helpful ... Great holes ... Great greens, fun, short par 4s ... Good variety ... Best 54 holes of golf in Houston, great value.
★★★★ TRADITION COURSE (18)
Yards: 7,220/5,255. **Par:** 72/72. **Course Rating:** 74.4/68.9. **Slope:** 134/122. **Green Fee:** $75. **Walkability:** 4. **Opened:** 1998. **Architect:** Keith Foster.
Notes: Ranked 15th in 2001 Best in State.
Reader Comments: Great new track ... My favorite golf course in Houston ... A championship

course, great holes, feels like you are on tour … Excellent staff … Each hole is carved through woods! … Bring your A game or the course will eat you up … Long with fairly open landing areas … Hardly any water hazards. Loved it.

★★½ DEL LAGO GOLF RESORT
R-600 Del Lago Blvd., Montgomery, 77356-5349, Montgomery County, (936)582-7570, (800)335-5246, 50 miles from Houston. **E-mail:** 104746.570@compuserve.com. **Web:** www.dellago.com. **Facility Holes:** 18. **Yards:** 6,794/5,180. **Par:** 72/72. **Course Rating:** 72.6/71.7. **Slope:** 131/122. **Green Fee:** $50/$65. **Cart Fee:** Included in green fee. **Walking Policy:** Walking at certain times. **Walkability:** 2. **Opened:** 1985. **Architect:** Dave Marr/Jay Riviere. **Season:** Year-round. **High:** May-Oct. **To obtain tee times:** Call golf shop. **Miscellaneous:** Reduced fees (weekdays, guests, twilight, seniors, juniors), range (grass/mats), credit cards (MC, V, AE, D), FF.

★★★ DELAWARE SPRINGS GOLF COURSE
PU-Hwy. 281 South, Burnet, 78611, Burnet County, (512)756-8951, 50 miles from Austin. **Facility Holes:** 18. **Yards:** 6,819/5,770. **Par:** 72/71. **Course Rating:** 72.0/66.5. **Slope:** 121/107. **Green Fee:** $16/$26. **Cart Fee:** $9/Person. **Walking Policy:** Walking at certain times. **Walkability:** 3. **Opened:** 1992. **Architect:** Dave Axland/Don Proctor. **Season:** Year-round. **To obtain tee times:** Call up to 14 days in advance. **Miscellaneous:** Reduced fees (twilight, seniors, juniors), metal spikes, range (grass), credit cards (MC, V, AE, D), BF, FF.
Reader Comments: Beautiful scenery! Watch out for snakes! … Fine small-town course … Check out turkeys and deer… Reasonable price … Hill Country views … Best muni in TX … Senior value.

★★ DEVINE GOLF COURSE
PU-116 Malone Dr., Devine, 78016, Medina County, (830)665-9943, 30 miles from San Antonio. **Facility Holes:** 18. **Yards:** 6,600/5,100. **Par:** 72/72. **Course Rating:** 70.4/67.5. **Slope:** 121/105. **Green Fee:** $12/$18. **Cart Fee:** $16/Cart. **Walking Policy:** Unrestricted walking. **Walkability:** 3. **Opened:** 1968. **Architect:** Built by members, Steve Mrak. **Season:** Year-round. **High:** May-July. **To obtain tee times:** Call golf shop. **Miscellaneous:** Reduced fees (twilight, seniors, juniors), credit cards (MC, V, AE, D).

★★★★ DIAMONDBACK GOLF CLUB *Pace*
PU-1510 E. Industrial Blvd., Abilene, 79602, Taylor County, (915)690-9190, (888)545-6262, 170 miles from Fort Worth. **E-mail:** bhelm23@hotmail.com. **Facility Holes:** 18. **Yards:** 6,977/5,006. **Par:** 71/71. **Course Rating:** 73.7/71.8. **Slope:** 134/124. **Green Fee:** $27/$36. **Cart Fee:** Included in green fee. **Walking Policy:** Unrestricted walking. **Walkability:** 3. **Opened:** 1999. **Architect:** George Williams/Charles Coody. **Season:** Year-round. **To obtain tee times:** Call up to 4 days in advance. **Miscellaneous:** Reduced fees (weekdays, twilight, seniors, juniors), range (grass), credit cards (MC, V, AE, D), BF, FF.
Reader Comments: Beautiful course that looks like something out of an Arizona golf brochure, in west Texas! For a new course, very exciting and challenging … Great practice facility as well.

★★★★ EAGLE POINT GOLF CLUB
PU-2211 135E North, Denton, 76205, Denton County, (940)387-5180, 35 miles from Dallas/Fort Worth. **Facility Holes:** 18. **Yards:** 6,647/5,056. **Par:** 72/72. **Course Rating:** 71.2/64.1. **Slope:** 119/102. **Green Fee:** $11/$25. **Cart Fee:** $20/Cart. **Walking Policy:** Unrestricted walking. **Walkability:** 3. **Season:** Year-round. **High:** March-Nov. **To obtain tee times:** Call golf shop. **Miscellaneous:** Reduced fees (guests, twilight, seniors, juniors), range (grass), lodging (150 rooms), credit cards (MC, V, AE, D, DC).
Reader Comments: Worth the drive out to this one! … Great new course for the Houston area … Elevation changes uncommon to Houston … Good practice range … Great value, tough course; No. 16 is a killer … Still maturing … Some surprises.

EAGLE'S BLUFF COUNTRY CLUB
SP-99 Eagle's Bluff Blvd., Bullard, 75757, Cherokee County, (903)825-2999, (877)972-4653, 90 miles from Dallas. **E-mail:** mcotepga@hotmail.com. **Web:** www.eaglesbluff.com. **Facility Holes:** 18. **Yards:** 6,421/4,967. **Par:** 71/71. **Course Rating:** 71.1/69.5. **Slope:** 133/123. **Green Fee:** $49/$62. **Cart Fee:** Included in green fee. **Walking Policy:** Mandatory carts. **Walkability:** 3. **Opened:** 1999. **Architect:** Carlton Gipson. **Season:** Year-round. **To obtain tee times:** Call up to 5 days in advance. **Miscellaneous:** Reduced fees (weekdays, twilight, seniors), range (grass), credit cards (MC, V, AE, D), BF, FF.

★★ ECHO CREEK COUNTRY CLUB
SP-FM 317, Athens, 75778, Henderson County, (903)852-7094, 20 miles from Tyler. **Facility Holes:** 18. **Yards:** 6,200/5,000. **Par:** 71/73. **Course Rating:** 69.2/69.2. **Slope:** 120/118. **Green Fee:** $12/$18. **Cart Fee:** $18/Cart. **Walking Policy:** Unrestricted walking. **Walkability:** 3. **Opened:** 1989. **Architect:** Rusty Lambert. **Season:** Year-round. **To obtain tee times:** Call golf shop. **Miscellaneous:** Reduced fees (guests, seniors), range (grass).

★½ ELM GROVE GOLF COURSE
PU-3202 Milwaukee, Lubbock, 79407, Lubbock County, (806)799-7801. **E-mail:** elmgrovegolfclub@aol.com. **Web:** www.elmgrovegolfclub.com. **Facility Holes:** 18. **Yards:** 6,401/5,480. **Par:** 71/72. **Course Rating:** 69.8. **Slope:** 110. **Green Fee:** $8/$16. **Cart Fee:** $9/Person. **Walking Policy:** Unrestricted walking. **Walkability:** 2. **Opened:** 1953. **Architect:** Warren Cantrell/W.G. McMillan. **Season:** Year-round. **High:** March-Oct. **To obtain tee times:** Call up to 6 days in advance. **Miscellaneous:** Reduced fees (twilight, seniors, juniors), range (grass/mats), credit cards (MC, V, AE, D, Debit), BF, FF.

ENNIS COUNTRY CLUB
SP-2905 Country Club Rd., Ennis, 75119, Ellis County, (972)875-3641, 35 miles from Dallas. **Web:** www.enniscc.com. **Facility Holes:** 18. **Yards:** 6,278/4,890. **Par:** 71/71. **Course Rating:** 69.9/69.7. **Slope:** 128/115. **Green Fee:** $20/$28. **Cart Fee:** $9/Person. **Walking Policy:** Walking at certain times. **Walkability:** 2. **Opened:** 1999. **Architect:** John Ponko. **Season:** Year-round. **To obtain tee times:** Call up to 4 days in advance. **Miscellaneous:** Reduced fees (twilight), credit cards (MC, V, AE), BF, FF.

★★★★ EVERGREEN POINT GOLF CLUB
PU-1530 Evergreen Point Rd., Baytown, 77520, Harris County, (281)837-9000, 20 miles from Houston. **Facility Holes:** 18. **Yards:** 7,000/5,298. **Par:** 72/72. **Course Rating:** 73.0/72.2. **Slope:** 129/130. **Green Fee:** $22/$33. **Cart Fee:** $20/Cart. **Walking Policy:** Unrestricted walking. **Walkability:** 3. **Opened:** 1996. **Architect:** Jay Riviere/Dave Marr. **Season:** Year-round. **To obtain tee times:** Call up to 7 days in advance. **Miscellaneous:** Reduced fees (twilight, seniors, juniors), range (grass), credit cards (MC, V, AE, D, DC), BF, FF.
Reader Comments: Great course any day! ... Another bargain ... For only 40 bucks, you get the best course in the bay area ... Tight fairways with moderate hills (yes, hills in the Houston area!) ... Much better than your typical Houston-area track ... Excellent value for good test of golf.

★★★★½ THE FALLS GOLF CLUB & RESORT *Value, Pace*
SP-1750 N. Falls Dr., New Ulm, 78950, Colorado County, (979)992-3123, (800)992-3930, 60 miles from Houston. **E-mail:** thefalls@thefallsresort.com. **Web:** www.the fallsresort.com. **Facility Holes:** 18. **Yards:** 6,757/5,326. **Par:** 72/73. **Course Rating:** 72.3/70.0. **Slope:** 135/125. **Green Fee:** $50/$65. **Cart Fee:** Included in green fee. **Walking Policy:** Walking at certain times. **Walkability:** 3. **Opened:** 1985. **Architect:** Jay Riviere/Dave Marr. **Season:** Year-round. **High:** March-June. **To obtain tee times:** Call up to 4 days in advance. **Miscellaneous:** Reduced fees (weekdays, guests), metal spikes, range (grass/mats), lodging (19 rooms), credit cards (MC, V, AE, D), BF, FF.
Reader Comments: Best course in Houston area ... Brutally tough but outstanding ... Challenging course but very playable ... Great course in the middle of nowhere... A Hidden Jewel ... Too remote for routine play.

FIREWHEEL GOLF PARK
PU-600 W. Blackburn Rd., Garland, 75044, Dallas County, (972)205-2795, 10 miles from Dallas. **Facility Holes:** 36. **Green Fee:** $18/$26. **Cart Fee:** $20/Cart. **Walkability:** 3. **Walking Policy:** Unrestricted walking. **Architect:** Dick Phelps. **Season:** Year-round. **High:** April-Sept. **To obtain tee times:** Call golf shop. **Miscellaneous:** Reduced fees (twilight, seniors), metal spikes, range (grass/mats), credit cards (MC, V, AE).
★★★ LAKES COURSE (18)
Yards: 6,625/5,215. **Par:** 71/71. **Course Rating:** 72.0/69.1. **Slope:** 126/110. **Opened:** 1987.
Reader Comments: Great public course ... You must play both courses ... A must-play when in town ... Old course not bad either ... Beautiful scenery and conditions.
★★★ OLD COURSE (18)
Yards: 7,054/5,692. **Par:** 72/72. **Course Rating:** 74.1/71.7. **Slope:** 129/117. **Walkability:** 2. **Opened:** 1983.
Reader Comments: Great value, tough layout ... Good course but rough around the edges ... Good bargain ... Fairways could use work in the heat of summer.

FISH CREEK GOLF CLUB
PU-6201 Mulligan Dr., Montgomery, 77316, Montgomery County, (936)588-8800, 30 miles from Houston. **Web:** fishcreekgolf.com. **Facility Holes:** 18. **Yards:** 6,834/5,293. **Par:** 72/72. **Course Rating:** 73.4/72.8. **Slope:** 130/127. **Green Fee:** $30/$79. **Cart Fee:** Included in green fee. **Walking Policy:** Unrestricted walking. **Walkability:** 3. **Opened:** 2001. **Architect:** Steve Elkington. **Season:** Year-round. **To obtain tee times:** Call up to 7 days in advance. **Miscellaneous:** Reduced fees (twilight, seniors, juniors), metal spikes, range (grass), credit cards (MC, V, AE), BF, FF.
Special Notes: Additional 9 holes to be added in 2002.

TEXAS

★★★ FLYING L RANCH GOLF COURSE
R-P.O. Box 1959, Bandera, 78003, Bandera County, (830)796-8466, (800)646-5407, 40 miles from San Antonio. **Web:** www.flyingl.com. **Facility Holes:** 18. **Yards:** 6,646/5,442. **Par:** 72/72. **Course Rating:** 71.0/69.9. **Slope:** 123/109. **Green Fee:** $17/$20. **Cart Fee:** $10/Person. **Walking Policy:** Unrestricted walking. **Walkability:** 2. **Opened:** 1975. **Season:** Year-round. **To obtain tee times:** Call up to 7 days in advance. **Miscellaneous:** Reduced fees (weekdays, guests, seniors, juniors), metal spikes, range (grass), credit cards (MC, V, AE, D), BF, FF.
Reader Comments: Friendly people, good track and great service ... Good bargain ... Well-kept, back 9 could be more of a challenge ... A jewel in the Hill Country ... Challenging layout for all levels ... Established resort—they try hard.

★★★½ FOREST CREEK GOLF CLUB
PU-99 Twin Ridge Pkwy., Round Rock, 78664, Williamson County, (512)388-2874, 10 miles from Austin. **E-mail:** troy.dickson@ourclub.com. **Web:** www.forestcreek.com. **Facility Holes:** 18. **Yards:** 7,147/5,394. **Par:** 72/72. **Course Rating:** 73.8/71.9. **Slope:** 136/124. **Green Fee:** $47/$60. **Cart Fee:** Included in green fee. **Walking Policy:** Walking at certain times. **Walkability:** 4. **Opened:** 1989. **Architect:** Dick Phelps. **Season:** Year-round. **High:** March-Oct. **To obtain tee times:** Call up to 7 days in advance. **Miscellaneous:** Reduced fees (weekdays, twilight, seniors, juniors), range (grass/mats), credit cards (MC, V, AE, D, DC), BF, FF.
Reader Comments: Interesting layout ... Pace of play can be a problem ... Fun course, great buy ... Challenging course. Good practice facilities ... Big oak trees everywhere, nice greens.

★★ FORT BROWN MEMORIAL GOLF COURSE
PU-300 River Levee Rd., Brownsville, 78520, Cameron County, (956)541-0394, (956)685-7202. **Facility Holes:** 18. **Yards:** 6,172/4,803. **Par:** 72/72. **Course Rating:** 67.0/67.0. **Slope:** 108/108. **Green Fee:** $7/$8. **Cart Fee:** $8/Person. **Walking Policy:** Unrestricted walking. **Walkability:** 1. **Opened:** 1958. **Season:** Year-round. **High:** Jan.-March. **To obtain tee times:** Call golf shop. **Miscellaneous:** Reduced fees (twilight, juniors), range (grass), credit cards (MC, V, AE).

FOUR SEASONS RESORT & CLUB
R-4150 N. MacArthur Blvd, Irving, 75038, Dallas County, (972)717-2530, (800)332-3442, 10 miles from Dallas. **Facility Holes:** 36. **Green Fee:** $150/$170. **Cart Fee:** $25/Person. **Walking Policy:** Unrestricted walking. **Walkability:** 3. **Opened:** 1986. **Architect:** Jay Morrish/Byron Nelson/Ben Crenshaw. **Season:** Year-round. **To obtain tee times:** Call golf shop. **Miscellaneous:** Reduced fees (guests, twilight), range (grass), credit cards (MC, V, AE, DC), BF, FF.
★★★★ TPC COURSE (18)
Yards: 6,899/5,340. **Par:** 70/70. **Course Rating:** 73.5/70.6. **Slope:** 135/116.
Reader Comments: Great shape as always ... Great facility, but pricey ... New trees have added beauty ... Wonderful hotel, service, course is hard but fun ... Too pretty to play.
Special Notes: Also has an 18-hole private Cottonwood Valley Course.

★½ FOX CREEK GOLF COURSE
PU-Rte. 3, Hempstead, 77445, Waller County, (409)826-2131, (877)290-3997, 40 miles from Houston. **E-mail:** foxcreek31@aol.com. **Web:** www.foxcreekgolf.com. **Facility Holes:** 18. **Yards:** 6,180/4,680. **Par:** 71/71. **Course Rating:** 69.4. **Slope:** 114. **Green Fee:** $10/$16. **Cart Fee:** $9/Person. **Walking Policy:** Unrestricted walking. **Walkability:** 2. **Season:** Year-round. **To obtain tee times:** Call up to 7 days in advance. **Miscellaneous:** Reduced fees (weekdays, seniors, juniors), range (mats), credit cards (MC, V), BF, FF.

FREEPORT GOLF COURSE
PU-830 Slaughter Rd., Freeport, 77541, Brazoria County, (979)233-8311. **E-mail:** pinkey@beamans.com. **Facility Holes:** 18. **Yards:** 6,169/5,787. **Par:** 71/71. **Course Rating:** 69.0/71.2. **Slope:** 113/112. **Green Fee:** $10/$13. **Cart Fee:** $17/Cart. **Walking Policy:** Unrestricted walking. **Walkability:** 2. **Opened:** 1975. **Season:** Year-round. **To obtain tee times:** Call golf shop. **Miscellaneous:** Range (grass), BF, FF.

★★½ GABE LOZANO SR. GOLF CENTER
PU-4401 Old Brownsville Rd., Corpus Christi, 78405, Nueces County, (361)883-3696, 3 miles from Corpus Christi. **Facility Holes:** 27. **Yards:** 6,953/5,149. **Par:** 72/72. **Course Rating:** 72.6/68.8. **Slope:** 128/112. **Green Fee:** $12/$15. **Cart Fee:** $8/Person. **Walking Policy:** Unrestricted walking. **Walkability:** 2. **Opened:** 1962. **Architect:** Leon Howard. **Season:** Year-round. **High:** Feb.-April. **To obtain tee times:** Call up to 2 days in advance. **Miscellaneous:** Reduced fees (weekdays, twilight, seniors, juniors), metal spikes, range (grass), credit cards (MC, V), BF, FF.
Special Notes: Also has a 9-hole executive course.

TEXAS

★½ GAINESVILLE MUNICIPAL GOLF CLUB
PU-200 S. Rusk, Gainesville, 76240, Cooke County, (940)668-4560. **Facility Holes:** 18. **Yards:** 6,546/5,012. **Par:** 71/74. **Course Rating:** 71.3. **Slope:** 123. **Green Fee:** $12/$15. **Opened:** 1955. **Architect:** Ralph Plummer. **To obtain tee times:** Call golf shop. **Miscellaneous:** Metal spikes.

★★½ GALVESTON ISLAND MUNICIPAL GOLF COURSE
PU-1700 Sydnor Lane, Galveston, 77554, Galveston County, (409)741-4626, 50 miles from Houston. **Facility Holes:** 18. **Yards:** 6,969/5,407. **Par:** 72/73. **Course Rating:** 73.0/71.4. **Slope:** 131/121. **Green Fee:** $13/$25. **Cart Fee:** $10/Person. **Walking Policy:** Unrestricted walking. **Opened:** 1989. **Architect:** Carlton Gipson. **Season:** Year-round. **High:** April-Oct. **To obtain tee times:** Call golf shop. **Miscellaneous:** Reduced fees (weekdays, guests, twilight, seniors, juniors), metal spikes, range (grass/mats), credit cards (MC, V, AE, D).

GARDEN VALLEY GOLF RESORT
R-22049 FM 1995, Lindale, 75771, Smith County, (903)882-6107, (800)443-8577, 80 miles from Dallas. **Facility Holes:** 36. **Season:** Year-round. **High:** March-Oct. **To obtain tee times:** Call golf shop. **Miscellaneous:** Reduced fees (weekdays, guests, twilight, seniors, juniors), range (grass), lodging (13 rooms), credit cards (MC, V, AE), FF.
★★★★ DOGWOOD COURSE (18)
Yards: 6,754/5,532. **Par:** 72/72. **Course Rating:** 72.4/72.5. **Slope:** 132/130. **Green Fee:** $45/$64. **Cart Fee:** Included in green fee. **Walking Policy:** Mandatory carts. **Walkability:** 5. **Opened:** 1992. **Architect:** John Sanford.
Reader Comments: A must play ... Beautiful layout ... Back 9 better ... You get lots of shot choices and it is in a beautiful spot ... Garden of Eden ... My favorite! Augusta of Texas.
★★ HUMMINGBIRD COURSE (18)
Yards: 6,446/5,131. **Par:** 71/71. **Course Rating:** 71.0/69.0. **Slope:** 128/125. **Green Fee:** $8/$21. **Cart Fee:** $12/Person. **Walking Policy:** Unrestricted walking. **Walkability:** 4. **Architect:** Leon Howard.

★★★½ GLEANNLOCH FARMS GOLF CLUB
PU-19393 Champions Forest Dr., Spring, 77379, Harris County, (281)225-1200, 10 miles from Houston. **E-mail:** mstroman@entouch.net. **Web:** www.golfgleannloch.com. **Facility Holes:** 27. **Green Fee:** $50/$65. **Cart Fee:** Included in green fee. **Walking Policy:** Unrestricted walking. **Walkability:** 2. **Opened:** 1999. **Architect:** Jay Riviere. **Season:** Year-round. **To obtain tee times:** Call up to 5 days in advance. **Miscellaneous:** Reduced fees (twilight, seniors, juniors), range (grass), credit cards (MC, V, AE), BF, FF.
GLEANN/LOCH (18 Combo)
Yards: 6,959/5,003. **Par:** 71/71. **Course Rating:** 72.9/69.5. **Slope:** 129/114.
LOCH/PADDOCK (18 Combo)
Yards: 7,301/5,332. **Par:** 72/72. **Course Rating:** 74.7/71.3. **Slope:** 131/117.
PADDOCK/GLEANN (18 Combo)
Yards: 7,052/5,103. **Par:** 71/71. **Course Rating:** 73.4/69.9. **Slope:** 131/117.
Reader Comments: Good test, but needs to mature ... Great links course, best on north side Houston ... Outstanding layout! Great shot variety ... Solid, difficult in the wind ... Good if mowed, a little pricey ... Will only improve with age.

★★½ GLENBROOK GOLF COURSE
PU-8205 N. Bayou Dr., Houston, 77017, Harris County, (713)649-8089, 15 miles from Houston. **Facility Holes:** 18. **Yards:** 6,427/5,258. **Par:** 71/71. **Course Rating:** 70.7/70.7. **Slope:** 120/117. **Green Fee:** $13/$17. **Cart Fee:** $8/Person. **Walking Policy:** Unrestricted walking. **Walkability:** 3. **Opened:** 1924. **Architect:** Robert McKinney. **Season:** Year-round. **To obtain tee times:** Call golf shop. **Miscellaneous:** Reduced fees (weekdays, twilight, seniors, juniors), metal spikes, credit cards (MC, V, AE, D), BF, FF.

★★★★ THE GOLF CLUB AT CASTLE HILLS
PU-699 Lady of the Lake Blvd., Lewisville, 75056, Denton County, (972)899-7400. **E-mail:** gm.castle@palmergolf.com. **Web:** www.thegolfclubch@msn.com. **Facility Holes:** 18. **Yards:** 7,152/5,481. **Par:** 72/72. **Course Rating:** 74.3/71.4. **Slope:** 139/119. **Green Fee:** $80/$100. **Cart Fee:** Included in green fee. **Walking Policy:** Walking at certain times. **Walkability:** 4. **Opened:** 1999. **Architect:** Jay Morrish/Carter Morrish. **Season:** Year-round. **High:** April-Oct. **To obtain tee times:** Call up to 7 days in advance. **Miscellaneous:** Reduced fees (weekdays, twilight, seniors, juniors), range (grass), credit cards (MC, V, AE), BF, FF.
Reader Comments: Awesome course ... Great layout and clubhouse ... Great golf course, no houses on course ... Brutal from back tees, best bent-grass greens in north Texas ... Great design ... Tough in the wind.

★★★ THE GOLF CLUB AT CINCO RANCH
PU-23030 Cinco Ranch Blvd., Katy, 77450, Fort Bend County, (281)395-4653, 20 miles from

Houston. **Facility Holes:** 18. **Yards:** 7,044/5,263. **Par:** 72/72. **Course Rating:** 73.7/70.3. **Slope:** 132/118. **Green Fee:** $40/$50. **Cart Fee:** Included in green fee. **Walkability:** 2. **Opened:** 1994. **Architect:** Carlton Gipson. **Season:** Year-round. **High:** April-June. **To obtain tee times:** Call golf shop. **Miscellaneous:** Reduced fees (weekdays, twilight, seniors, juniors), metal spikes, range (grass), credit cards (MC, V, AE, D).
Reader Comments: Strategic delight ... Great practice range. Wind always blows ... Very enjoyable day. ... Fairly new course with small trees—will only get better as it ages.

★★★½ THE GOLF CLUB AT FOSSIL CREEK
PU-3401 Clubgate Dr., Fort Worth, 76137, Tarrant County, (817)498-5538, 10 miles from Fort Worth. **Web:** www.fossil-creek.com. **Facility Holes:** 18. **Yards:** 6,865/5,066. **Par:** 72/72. **Course Rating:** 73.6/68.5. **Slope:** 131/111. **Green Fee:** $25/$75. **Cart Fee:** Included in green fee. **Walking Policy:** Mandatory carts. **Walkability:** 5. **Opened:** 1987. **Architect:** Arnold Palmer/Ed Seay. **Season:** Year-round. **High:** April-Oct. **To obtain tee times:** Call up to 5 days in advance. **Miscellaneous:** Reduced fees (weekdays, twilight, seniors, juniors), range (grass), credit cards (MC, V, AE, D, DC), BF, FF.
Reader Comments: Excellent course with several breathtaking holes ... Good service in pro shop ... Conditions much improved ... Best course in Forth Worth ... Good greens ... Very expensive.

THE GOLF CLUB AT STAR RANCH
PU-2500 FM 685, Hutto, 78634, Williamson County, (512)252-4653, 10 miles from Austin. **E-mail:** lbowman@palmergolf.com. **Web:** www.starranchgolf.com. **Facility Holes:** 18. **Yards:** 7,017/4,990. **Par:** 71/71. **Course Rating:** 73.8/64.2. **Slope:** 131/110. **Green Fee:** $55/$65. **Cart Fee:** Included in green fee. **Walking Policy:** Walking at certain times. **Walkability:** 4. **Opened:** 2001. **Architect:** R. Bechtol, R. Russell, C. Morrish. **Season:** Year-round. **High:** March-Oct. **To obtain tee times:** Call up to 7 days in advance. **Miscellaneous:** Reduced fees (weekdays, twilight, seniors, juniors), credit cards (MC, V, AE), BF, FF.

★★★½ THE GOLF CLUB OF TEXAS *Service*
PU-13600 Briggs Ranch, San Antonio, 78245, Bexar County, (210)677-0027, (877)465-3839. **E-mail:** golfclubtx@aol.com. **Web:** www.golfcluboftexas.com. **Facility Holes:** 18. **Yards:** 7,022/4,823. **Par:** 72/72. **Course Rating:** 73.1/67.9. **Slope:** 135/109. **Green Fee:** $60/$95. **Cart Fee:** Included in green fee. **Walking Policy:** Unrestricted walking. **Walkability:** 3. **Opened:** 1999. **Architect:** R. Bechtol/R. Russell/L.Trevino. **Season:** Year-round. **To obtain tee times:** Call up to 30 days in advance. **Miscellaneous:** Reduced fees (weekdays, twilight, seniors, juniors), range (grass), credit cards (MC, V, AE, D, DC, CB), BF, FF.
Reader Comments: Awesome greens ... Very long, good food, good grass ... Great traditional layout ... New course, fun, very hospitable ... Too wide open, few shade trees ... Good clubhouse food ... Great breakfast tacos.

★★★ GRAPEVINE GOLF COURSE
PU-3800 Fairway Dr., Grapevine, 76051, Tarrant County, (817)410-3377, 15 miles from Dallas. **E-mail:** misbell@ci.grapevine.tx.us. **Web:** www.ci.grapevine.tx.us. **Facility Holes:** 18. **Yards:** 6,901/4,954. **Par:** 72/72. **Course Rating:** 73.3/71.7. **Slope:** 132/114. **Green Fee:** $23/$27. **Cart Fee:** $13/Person. **Walking Policy:** Unrestricted walking. **Walkability:** 3. **Opened:** 1979. **Architect:** Joe Finger/Byron Nelson. **Season:** Year-round. **To obtain tee times:** Call up to 3 days in advance. **Miscellaneous:** Reduced fees (weekdays, twilight, seniors, juniors), range (grass/mats), credit cards (MC, V, AE, DC), BF, FF.
Reader Comments: A beautiful and mature course, even in the brown of Texas winter... A demanding course, but fun to play for low and high handicappers ... New 9 very good ... Much improved ... Lots of character ... Excellent value.

★½ GRAYSON COUNTY COLLEGE GOLF COURSE
PU-56 Golf Drive, Denison, 75020, Grayson County, (903)786-9719, 70 miles from Dallas. **E-mail:** golfcourseii@texoma.net. **Facility Holes:** 18. **Yards:** 6,633/4,876. **Par:** 72/72. **Course Rating:** 70.0/67.7. **Slope:** 114/108. **Green Fee:** $10/$14. **Cart Fee:** $18/Cart. **Walking Policy:** Unrestricted walking. **Walkability:** 3. **Opened:** 1961. **Architect:** Joe Finger. **Season:** Year-round. **To obtain tee times:** Call up to 6 days in advance. **Miscellaneous:** Reduced fees (weekdays, twilight, juniors), metal spikes, range (grass), credit cards (MC, V), BF, FF.

★★★½ GREATWOOD GOLF CLUB
PU-6767 Greatwood Pkwy., Sugar Land, 77479, Fort Bend County, (281)343-9999, (888)343-4001, 4 miles from Sugar Land. **Web:** www.greatwoodgolfclub.com. **Facility Holes:** 18. **Yards:** 6,836/5,220. **Par:** 72/72. **Course Rating:** 72.3/70.0. **Slope:** 138/125. **Green Fee:** $48/$70. **Cart Fee:** Included in green fee. **Walking Policy:** Mandatory carts. **Walkability:** 3. **Opened:** 1990. **Architect:** Carlton Gipson. **Season:** Year-round. **To obtain tee times:** Call up to 7 days in advance. **Miscellaneous:** Reduced fees (twilight, seniors, juniors), metal spikes, range (grass/mats), credit cards (MC, V, AE, D, DC), BF, FF.
Reader Comments: Well-maintained course with a personality ... Good layout, challenging holes,

TEXAS

fast greens … A lot of sand … Difficult pin positions … Best 3 finishing holes in Houston … Fairways need mowing.

★★ GREEN MEADOWS GOLF CLUB
PU-6138 Franz Rd., Katy, 77493, Harris County, (281)391-3670, 8 miles from Houston.
Facility Holes: 18. **Yards:** 5,440/4,949. **Par:** 70/70. **Course Rating:** 66.3/70.5. **Slope:** 104/110.
Green Fee: $10/$21. **Cart Fee:** $10/Person. **Walking Policy:** Unrestricted walking. **Walkability:**
1. **Opened:** 1965. **Architect:** Jay Riviere. **Season:** Year-round. **High:** Jan.-Aug. **To obtain tee times:** Call golf shop. **Miscellaneous:** Reduced fees (twilight, seniors), metal spikes, credit cards (MC, V, AE, D).

★½ GUS WORTHAM PARK GOLF COURSE
PU-7000 Capitol, Houston, 77011, Harris County, (713)921-3227. **Facility Holes:** 18. **Yards:**
6,400/6,000. **Par:** 72/74. **Course Rating:** 69.5/74.2. **Slope:** 113/118. **Green Fee:** $10/$14. **Cart Fee:** $18/Cart. **Walking Policy:** Unrestricted walking. **Season:** Year-round. **High:** April-May.
To obtain tee times: Call golf shop. **Miscellaneous:** Reduced fees (weekdays, twilight, seniors, juniors), metal spikes, range (grass), credit cards (MC, V, AE).

★½ HAWKS CREEK GOLF CLUB
PU-6520 White Settlement, Fort Worth, 76114, Tarrant County, (817)738-8402. **Facility Holes:**
18. **Green Fee:** $25/$50. **Walkability:** 3. **Opened:** 1954. **Architect:** John Colligan. **Season:** Year-round. **To obtain tee times:** Call golf shop. **Miscellaneous:** Reduced fees (weekdays, twilight, seniors, juniors), range (grass), credit cards (MC, V, AE, D).

★½ HEATHER RUN GOLF & FISH CLUB
SP-1600 Western Oaks Dr., Waco, 76712, McLennan County, (254)772-8100. **E-mail:**
gregg@juster.com. **Web:** www.heathernrungolf.com. **Facility Holes:** 18. **Yards:** 6,400/5,040.
Par: 70/70. **Course Rating:** 70.7/68.7. **Slope:** 127/120. **Green Fee:** $10/$15. **Cart Fee:**
$12/Person. **Walking Policy:** Unrestricted walking. **Walkability:** 3. **Opened:** 1969. **Architect:**
Greg Juster. **Season:** Year-round. **High:** March-June. **To obtain tee times:** Call up to 14 days in advance. **Miscellaneous:** Reduced fees (weekdays, guests, twilight, seniors, juniors), metal spikes, range (grass), credit cards (MC, V, AE, D).

★★ HENRY HOMBERG MUNICIPAL GOLF COURSE
PU-5940 Babe Zaharias Dr., Beaumont, 77705, Jefferson County, (409)842-3220, 75 miles from Houston. **Facility Holes:** 18. **Yards:** 6,786/5,660. **Par:** 72/73. **Course Rating:** 71.2/70.0.
Slope: 116/116. **Green Fee:** $8/$9. **Cart Fee:** $15/Cart. **Walking Policy:** Unrestricted walking. **Walkability:** 1. **Opened:** 1930. **Architect:** Ralph Plummer. **Season:** Year-round. **High:** March-June. **To obtain tee times:** Call golf shop. **Miscellaneous:** Reduced fees (weekdays, twilight, seniors, juniors), metal spikes, range (grass/mats), credit cards (MC, V, AE).

★★★½ HERMANN PARK GOLF COURSE
PU-2215 N. MacGregor, Houston, 77030, Harris County, (713)526-0077. **E-mail:**
pstark@bslgolf.com. **Web:** www.houston.sidewalk.msn.com/bslgolf. **Facility Holes:** 18. **Yards:**
6,014/4,724. **Par:** 70/70. **Course Rating:** 67.9/63.7. **Slope:** 117/99. **Green Fee:** $19/$29. **Cart Fee:** $13/Person. **Walking Policy:** Walking at certain times. **Walkability:** 2. **Opened:** 1922.
Architect: John Bredemus/Carlton Gipson. **Season:** Year-round. **High:** April-Oct. **To obtain tee times:** Call up to 3 days in advance. **Miscellaneous:** Reduced fees (twilight, seniors, juniors), range (grass/mats), credit cards (MC, V, AE), BF, FF.
Reader Comments: Old, short, inner-city course—refurbished … Too slow on weekend … Great redo of an urban golf gem … Better than it used to be … Short fun course … Surprisingly good for heavily played public course … Nice old course.

★★★½ HIDDEN CREEK GOLF CLUB
PU-700 S. Burleson Ave., Burleson, 76028, Tarrant County, (817)447-4444, 14 miles from Fort Worth. **E-mail:** blaing@hiddencreekgolfcourse.com. **Web:**
www.hiddencreekgolfcourse.com. **Facility Holes:** 18. **Yards:** 6,753/4,968. **Par:** 71/71. **Course Rating:** 73.8. **Slope:** 139. **Green Fee:** $27/$50. **Cart Fee:** Included in green fee. **Walking Policy:** Unrestricted walking. **Walkability:** 4. **Opened:** 1997. **Architect:** Steve Plumer. **Season:** Year-round. **To obtain tee times:** Call up to 7 days in advance. **Miscellaneous:** Reduced fees (weekdays, twilight, seniors, juniors), range (grass), credit cards (MC, V, AE, D), BF, FF.
Reader Comments: Excellent course, courteous staff, great pricing, wow! … A great layout, one of my personal favorites … Watch for the creeks … Holes 16-18 are extremely difficult … Best bang for the buck anywhere.

HIDDEN HILLS PUBLIC GOLF COURSE
PU-N. Hwy. 70, Pampa, 79066, Gray County, (806)669-5866, 56 miles from Amarillo. **Facility Holes:** 18. **Yards:** 6,463/5,196. **Par:** 71/71. **Course Rating:** 69.4/68.0. **Slope:** 122/116. **Green Fee:** $7/$12. **Cart Fee:** $17/Cart. **Walking Policy:** Unrestricted walking. **Walkability:** 5. **Opened:**

1990. **Architect:** Ray Hardy. **Season:** Year-round. **High:** May-Sept. **To obtain tee times:** Call golf shop. **Miscellaneous:** Reduced fees (weekdays, twilight, seniors, juniors), range (grass), credit cards (MC, V).

★★★½ HIGH MEADOW RANCH GOLF CLUB

PU-37300 Golf Club Trail, Magnolia, 77355, Montgomery County, (281)356-7700, 40 miles from Houston. **E-mail:** highmeadowranch@aol.com. **Web:** www.highmeadowranchgolf.com. **Facility Holes:** 18. **Yards:** 7,370/4,954. **Par:** 72/72. **Course Rating:** 75.7/69.7. **Slope:** 133/136. **Green Fee:** $30/$67. **Cart Fee:** $12/Person. **Walking Policy:** Unrestricted walking. **Walkability:** 4. **Opened:** 1999. **Architect:** Tim Nugent/David Ogrin. **Season:** Year-round. **To obtain tee times:** Call up to 7 days in advance. **Miscellaneous:** Reduced fees (weekdays, twilight, seniors, juniors), range (grass), credit cards (MC, V, AE, D), BF, FF.
Notes: Ranked 23rd in 2001 Best in State.
Reader Comments: Prettiest course ... 3 loops of 6 holes ... Fantastic design ... A breath of fresh air ... houses lining the course ... Golf the way it was meant to be.

★★★★ HILL COUNTRY GOLF CLUB

R-9800 Hyatt Resort Dr., San Antonio, 78251, Bexar County, (210)520-4040, (888)901-4653, 15 miles from San Antonio. **Web:** www. sanantonio. hyatt. com. **Facility Holes:** 18. **Yards:** 6,913/4,781. **Par:** 72/72. **Course Rating:** 73.9/67.8. **Slope:** 136/114. **Green Fee:** $60/$120. **Cart Fee:** Included in green fee. **Walking Policy:** Unrestricted walking. **Walkability:** 3. **Opened:** 1993. **Architect:** Arthur Hills. **Season:** Year-round. **High:** March-Nov. **To obtain tee times:** Call golf shop. **Miscellaneous:** Reduced fees (weekdays, twilight, juniors), metal spikes, range (grass/mats), credit cards (MC, V, AE, D, DC), BF, FF.
Reader Comments: Superb service... Expensive ... Nothing could get better ... Too expensive, amenities are great ... Best course in San Antonio ... Great par 5s ... Good course ... Hotel is a must ... Pampered.

HOGAN PARK GOLF COURSE

PU-3600 N. Fairground Rd., Midland, 79705, Midland County, (915)685-7360. **Facility Holes:** 27. **Walking Policy:** Unrestricted walking. **Walkability:** 2. **Season:** Year-round. **High:** May-Oct. **To obtain tee times:** Call golf shop. **Miscellaneous:** Reduced fees (weekdays, twilight, seniors, juniors), metal spikes, range (grass), credit cards (MC, V).
★★★½ EIGHTEEN HOLE COURSE (18)
Yards: 6,615/5,775. **Par:** 70/70. **Course Rating:** 68.5/69.0. **Slope:** 111/103. **Green Fee:** $12/$17. **Cart Fee:** $17/Cart. **Opened:** 1959. **Architect:** Charles Campbell/Jimmy Gamewell.
Reader Comments: A very good course to spend Sunday afternoon ... Harder than its slope rating ... Can reach all par 5s in 2 ... Wide open fairways ... Learn to play in strong west Texas wind.
★★★ NINE HOLE COURSE (9)
Yards: 3,410/2,710. **Par:** 36/36. **Course Rating:** 68.9/69.5. **Slope:** 111/103. **Green Fee:** $12. **Opened:** 1983.
Reader Comments: This course has been expanded to 36 holes and the new front 9 is the best at the complex ... Par-4 3rd hole is particularly treacherous with water all along the left side and sand and scrub mesquite guarding the right.

HORSESHOE BAY RESORT

R-Bay W. Blvd., Horseshoe Bay, 78657, Burnet County, (830)598-6561, 45 miles from Austin. **Web:** www.horseshoe-bay-resort.com. **Facility Holes:** 54. **Green Fee:** $70/$121. **Cart Fee:** Included in green fee. **Architect:** Robert Trent Jones. **Season:** Year-round. **High:** March-Nov. **To obtain tee times:** Call golf shop. **Miscellaneous:** Reduced fees (weekdays, guests, juniors), metal spikes, range (grass), credit cards (MC, V, AE, D).
★★★★ APPLEROCK COURSE (18) *Condition, Pace*
Yards: 6,999/5,509. **Par:** 72/72. **Course Rating:** 73.9/71.6. **Slope:** 134/117. **Walkability:** 4. **Opened:** 1986.
Reader Comments: Impressed, beautiful, fair, loved it ... Great layout ... What to say? Go to Horseshoe Bay! Terrific view ... Great golf... New greens good, good shotmakers value, scenic.
★★★½ RAM ROCK COURSE (18)
Yards: 6,946/5,306. **Par:** 71/71. **Course Rating:** 73.9/71.4. **Slope:** 137/121. **Walking Policy:** Mandatory cart. **Walkability:** 5. **Opened:** 1981.
Notes: Ranked 10th in 2001 Best in State.
Reader Comments: Tough layout ... Plush, excellent facility, very hard, pros would be tested ... Great layout ... Many deer on the course ... Bring your 2-iron, this course is long.
★★★★ SLICK ROCK (18) *Condition*
Yards: 6,834/5,832. **Par:** 72/72. **Course Rating:** 72.6/70.2. **Slope:** 125/115. **Walking Policy:** Mandatory cart. **Walkability:** 2. **Opened:** 1972.
Reader Comments: Easiest of 3 ... Pretty course and very playable ... Great golf course ... Well maintained and managed ... Super facilities.

HOUSTON NATIONAL GOLF CLUB

SP-16500 Houston National Blvd., Houston, 77095, Harris County, (281)304-1400, 15 miles from Houston. **Facility Holes:** 18. **Yards:** 7,337/5,558. **Par:** 72/72. **Course Rating:** 75.8/73.2. **Slope:** 133/126. **Green Fee:** $45/$65. **Cart Fee:** Included in green fee. **Walking Policy:** Mandatory carts. **Walkability:** 2. **Opened:** 2000. **Architect:** Von Hagge/Smelek/Baril. **Season:** Year-round. **To obtain tee times:** Call up to 5 days in advance. **Miscellaneous:** Reduced fees (weekdays, twilight, seniors, juniors), range (grass), credit cards (MC, V, AE, D), BF, FF.

HOUSTON OAKS GOLF & COUNTRY CLUB

SP-22602 Hegar Rd., Hockley, 77447, Waller County, (936)931-2917, (800)865-4657, 30 miles from Houston. **Web:** www.houstonoaksgolfclub.com. **Facility Holes:** 36. **Green Fee:** $18/$57. **Cart Fee:** Included in green fee. **Walking Policy:** Unrestricted walking. **Walkability:** 1. **Season:** Year-round. **To obtain tee times:** Call up to 5 days in advance. **Miscellaneous:** Reduced fees (weekdays, twilight, seniors, juniors), range (grass), credit cards (MC, V, AE, D), BF, FF.

★★½ **LINKS COURSE (18)**
Yards: 6,397/5,011. **Par:** 72/73. **Course Rating:** 70.8/68.3. **Slope:** 120/109. **Opened:** 1956. **Architect:** Tom Fazio.
OAKS COURSE (18)
Yards: 6,420/5,396. **Par:** 71/72. **Course Rating:** 70.3/70.9. **Slope:** 120/118. **Opened:** 1960. **Architect:** Ralph Plummer.

★★★★ THE HOUSTONIAN GOLF CLUB *Service+*

R-12610 FM 1464, Richmond, 77469, Fort Bend County, (281)494-4244, 10 miles from Houston. **E-mail:** mhoffman@houstoniangolf.com. **Web:** www.houstoniangolf.com. **Facility Holes:** 18. **Yards:** 7,110/5,375. **Par:** 72/72. **Course Rating:** 74.1/71.0. **Slope:** 132/121. **Green Fee:** $75/$105. **Cart Fee:** $10/Person. **Walking Policy:** Unrestricted walking. **Walkability:** 2. **Opened:** 1999. **Architect:** Rees Jones. **Season:** Year-round. **High:** March-Nov. **To obtain tee times:** Call golf shop. **Miscellaneous:** Reduced fees (weekdays, twilight, juniors), range (grass), caddies, credit cards (MC, V, AE, D, DC), BF, FF.
Reader Comments: 1st-class in every way ... Very attentive staff ... Water everywhere—on 12 of 18 holes ... Nice resort course ... Conditioning was perfect! ... Very windy and lots of water.

INDIAN CREEK GOLF CLUB

PU-1650 W. Frankford, Carrollton, 75007, Denton County, (972)492-3620, (800)369-4137, 10 miles from Dallas. **Facility Holes:** 36. **Green Fee:** $22/$28. **Cart Fee:** $10/Person. **Walking Policy:** Unrestricted walking. **Walkability:** 1. **Architect:** Dick Phelps. **Season:** Year-round. **High:** March-Oct. **To obtain tee times:** Call golf shop. **Miscellaneous:** Reduced fees (weekdays, twilight, seniors, juniors), range (grass/mats), credit cards (MC, V).

★★★ **CREEKS COURSE (18)**
Yards: 7,218/4,967. **Par:** 72/72. **Course Rating:** 74.7/68.2. **Slope:** 136/114. **Opened:** 1984.
Reader Comments: Nice, lush course ... Trees, water, traps, tough.
★★★ **LAKES COURSE (18)**
Yards: 7,060/5,367. **Par:** 72/72. **Course Rating:** 72.9/69.9. **Slope:** 135/114. **Opened:** 1987.
Reader Comments: Lots of water but still open ... Lakes has bent greens, Creeks has Bermuda ... Fairways could be better... Flat, lots of traps and water ... The price is right, course in good shape ... Winds through condos, expensive.

★★★½ IRON HORSE GOLF COURSE

PU-6200 Skylark Circle, North Richland Hill, 76180, Tarrant County, (817)485-6666, (888)522-9921, 10 miles from Fort Worth. **Web:** www.ironhorsetx.com. **Facility Holes:** 18. **Yards:** 6,580/5,083. **Par:** 70/70. **Course Rating:** 71.8/69.6. **Slope:** 130/119. **Green Fee:** $30/$40. **Cart Fee:** $12/Person. **Walking Policy:** Unrestricted walking. **Walkability:** 4. **Opened:** 1990. **Architect:** Dick Phelps. **Season:** Year-round. **To obtain tee times:** Call up to 3 days in advance. **Miscellaneous:** Reduced fees (weekdays, twilight, seniors, juniors), range (grass), credit cards (MC, V, AE, DC), BF, FF.
Reader Comments: Target golf ... Hit it straight off the tee ... Boxes and fairways in great shape ... Fun course with helpful staff ... Consistently good ... One of, if not the best, public courses in the Ft. Worth area ... Slow play ... Tricky valleys and streams, along with hills and tough greens.

★★½ J.F. SAMMONS PARK GOLF COURSE

PU-2727 W. Adams Ave., Temple, 76504, Bell County, (254)771-2030, 50 miles from Austin. **Facility Holes:** 18. **Yards:** 6,100/4,450. **Par:** 70/70. **Course Rating:** 69.8/65.8. **Slope:** 129/110. **Green Fee:** $6/$13. **Cart Fee:** $10/Person. **Walking Policy:** Unrestricted walking. **Walkability:** 2. **Opened:** 1987. **Season:** Year-round. **To obtain tee times:** Call golf shop. **Miscellaneous:** Reduced fees (weekdays, twilight, seniors, juniors), range (grass), credit cards (MC, V, AE), BF, FF.

★★★ JERSEY MEADOW GOLF COURSE
PU-8502 Rio Grande, Jersey Village, 77040, Harris County, (713)896-0900. **Facility Holes:** 18. **Yards:** 6,610/5,151. **Par:** 71/72. **Course Rating:** 70.5/70.2. **Slope:** 118/120. **Green Fee:** $26/$40. **Walking Policy:** Walking at certain times. **Walkability:** 1. **Opened:** 1956. **Architect:** Carlton Gipson. **Season:** Year-round. **To obtain tee times:** Call up to 7 days in advance. **Miscellaneous:** Reduced fees (weekdays, twilight, seniors, juniors), range (grass), credit cards (MC, V, AE), BF, FF.
Reader Comments: Nice greens ... Best greens in area.

★★★ JIMMY CLAY GOLF COURSE
PU-5400 Jimmy Clay Dr., Austin, 78744, Travis County, (512)444-0999. **Facility Holes:** 18. **Yards:** 6,857/5,036. **Par:** 72/72. **Course Rating:** 72.4/68.5. **Slope:** 124/110. **Green Fee:** $14/$16. **Cart Fee:** $10/Cart. **Walking Policy:** Unrestricted walking. **Opened:** 1974. **Architect:** Joseph Finger. **Season:** Year-round. **To obtain tee times:** Call golf shop. **Miscellaneous:** Reduced fees (weekdays, twilight, seniors, juniors), metal spikes, range (grass), BF, FF.
Reader Comments: Nice muni ... Great practice facility ... Lighted driving range and three pitching greens with plenty of room to bring out the shag bag ... Good old course.

★★ JOHN PITMAN MUNICIPAL GOLF COURSE
PU-S. Main St., Hereford, 79045, Deaf Smith County, (806)363-7139. **Facility Holes:** 18. **Yards:** 6,545/4,870. **Par:** 71/71. **Course Rating:** 69.6/66.2. **Slope:** 113/113. **Green Fee:** $9/$12. **Cart Fee:** $18/Cart. **Walking Policy:** Unrestricted walking. **Walkability:** 4. **Opened:** 1972. **Season:** Year-round. **High:** March-Sept. **To obtain tee times:** Call golf shop. **Miscellaneous:** Reduced fees (weekdays, seniors, juniors), range (grass), credit cards (MC, V).

★★★ KEETON PARK GOLF COURSE
PU-2323 Jim Miller Rd., Dallas, 75227, Dallas County, (214)670-8784. **E-mail:** mrpause@msn.com. **Web:** www.keetonpark.com. **Facility Holes:** 18. **Yards:** 6,511/5,054. **Par:** 72/72. **Course Rating:** 70.6/68.1. **Slope:** 120/113. **Green Fee:** $11/$17. **Cart Fee:** $20/Cart. **Walking Policy:** Unrestricted walking. **Walkability:** 2. **Opened:** 1978. **Architect:** Dave Bennett. **Season:** Year-round. **High:** April-July. **To obtain tee times:** Call up to 4 days in advance. **Miscellaneous:** Reduced fees (weekdays, twilight, seniors, juniors), metal spikes, range (grass), caddies, credit cards (MC, V, AE), BF, FF.
Reader Comments: Best-kept secret in Dallas ... Very narrow ... 1st 5 holes the toughest ... Good place to play a quick round ... Nice track, but gets a lot of play.

★★½ KILLEEN MUNICIPAL GOLF COURSE
PU-406 Roy Reynolds Dr., Killeen, 76543, Bell County, (254)699-6034, 50 miles from Austin. **Facility Holes:** 18. **Yards:** 6,700/5,109. **Par:** 72/72. **Course Rating:** 69.5/68.3. **Slope:** 107/109. **Green Fee:** $9/$13. **Cart Fee:** $16/Cart. **Walking Policy:** Unrestricted walking. **Walkability:** 3. **Opened:** 1969. **Architect:** Jay Riviere. **Season:** Year-round. **To obtain tee times:** Call golf shop. **Miscellaneous:** Reduced fees (twilight, seniors, juniors), range (grass), credit cards (MC, V).

★★½ KINGWOOD COVE GOLF CLUB
PU-805 Hamblen Rd., Kingwood, 77339, Harris County, (281)358-1155, 20 miles from Houston. **Facility Holes:** 18. **Yards:** 6,722/5,601. **Par:** 71/71. **Course Rating:** 71.9/73.2. **Slope:** 118/114. **Green Fee:** $25/$33. **Cart Fee:** Included in green fee. **Walking Policy:** Unrestricted walking. **Walkability:** 3. **Opened:** 1967. **Season:** Year-round. **To obtain tee times:** Call golf shop. **Miscellaneous:** Reduced fees (weekdays, twilight, seniors, juniors), range (grass/mats), credit cards (MC, V, AE, D), BF, FF.

★★½ L.B. HOUSTON PARK GOLF COURSE
PU-11223 Luna Rd., Dallas, 75229, Dallas County, (214)670-6322. **Facility Holes:** 18. **Yards:** 6,705/5,596. **Par:** 72/73. **Course Rating:** 70.8/72.8. **Slope:** 126/113. **Green Fee:** $7/$17. **Cart Fee:** $18/Cart. **Walking Policy:** Unrestricted walking. **Walkability:** 1. **Opened:** 1967. **Architect:** Dave Bennett/Leon Howard. **To obtain tee times:** Call golf shop. **Miscellaneous:** Reduced fees (weekdays, twilight, seniors, juniors), metal spikes, range (grass), credit cards (MC, V, AE, D).

★½ L.E. RAMEY GOLF COURSE
PU-FM 3320, Kingsville, 78363, Kleberg County, (361)592-1101, 30 miles from Corpus Christi. **Facility Holes:** 18. **Yards:** 6,995/5,540. **Par:** 72/72. **Course Rating:** 72.5/71.3. **Slope:** 128/107. **Green Fee:** $8/$10. **Cart Fee:** $15/Cart. **Walking Policy:** Unrestricted walking. **Walkability:** 1. **Opened:** 1974. **Season:** Year-round. **High:** March-June. **To obtain tee times:** Call golf shop. **Miscellaneous:** Reduced fees (weekdays, twilight), metal spikes, range (grass), credit cards (MC, V, AE, D).

TEXAS

LA CANTERA GOLF CLUB
R-17865 Babcock Rd., San Antonio, 78255, Bexar County, (210)558-2365. **E-mail:** ryan.wilson@westin.com. **Web:** www.lacanteragolfclub.com. **Facility Holes:** 36. **Green Fee:** $60/$130. **Cart Fee:** Included in green fee. **Walking Policy:** Unrestricted walking. **Walkability:** 4. **Season:** Year-round. **High:** March-April. **To obtain tee times:** Call up to 30 days in advance.
Miscellaneous: Reduced fees (weekdays, twilight, juniors), metal spikes, range (grass), lodging (508 rooms), credit cards (MC, V, AE, D, DC, CB), BF, FF.
THE PALMER COURSE (18)
Yards: 6,926/5,066. **Par:** 71/71. **Course Rating:** 74.2/65.3. **Slope:** 142/116. **Opened:** 2001.
Architect: Arnold Palmer.
★★★★½ **THE RESORT COURSE** (18) *Condition*
Yards: 7,001/4,953. **Par:** 72/72. **Course Rating:** 72.5/67.1. **Slope:** 134/108. **Opened:** 1994.
Architect: Tom Weiskopf/Jay Morrish.
Notes: Ranked 21st in 2001 Best in State; 1st in 1995 Best New Public Courses.
Reader Comments: Beautiful resort ... Great service ... Great, strategic layout... Beautiful Texas Hill Country scenery ... World-class PGA championship course and home to the Texas Open ... Best greens I've ever played ... Scenic golf course but a walker's nightmare ... Brutal par-5 1st hole ... Golf at its finest.

★★★½ LADY BIRD JOHNSON MUNICIPAL GOLF COURSE
PU-341 Golfers Loop, Fredericksburg, 78624, Gillespie County, (830)997-4010, (800)950-8147, 70 miles from San Antonio. **Facility Holes:** 18. **Yards:** 6,448/5,094. **Par:** 72/72. **Course Rating:** 70.6/69.0. **Slope:** 126/117. **Green Fee:** $17/$24. **Cart Fee:** $9/Person. **Walking Policy:** Unrestricted walking. **Walkability:** 3. **Opened:** 1969. **Architect:** Jeffrey Brauer. **Season:** Year-round. **High:** April-July. **To obtain tee times:** Call up to 7 days in advance. **Miscellaneous:** Reduced fees (weekdays), range (grass/mats), credit cards (MC, V, AE, D), BF, FF.
Reader Comments: This may be a muni, but it will give you everything that you want in a course and more ... 1st-class new clubhouse ... Well maintained ... Great shopping attractions for wife while you play ... Neat town, great German food ... Great value, play the tips.

★★½ LAKE ARLINGTON GOLF COURSE
PU-1516 Green Oaks Blvd. W., Arlington, 76013, Tarrant County, (817)451-6101, 25 miles from Dallas. **Facility Holes:** 18. **Yards:** 6,637/5,485. **Par:** 71/71. **Course Rating:** 70.7/71.0. **Slope:** 117/114. **Green Fee:** $10/$12. **Cart Fee:** $8/Person. **Walking Policy:** Unrestricted walking. **Opened:** 1963. **Architect:** Ralph Plummer. **Season:** Year-round. **High:** April-Aug. **To obtain tee times:** Call golf shop. **Miscellaneous:** Reduced fees (twilight, seniors, juniors), metal spikes, range (grass), credit cards (MC, V, D).

★★½ LAKE PARK GOLF COURSE
PU-6 Lake Park Rd., Lewisville, 75067, Denton County, (972)219-5661, 15 miles from Dallas. **E-mail:** mruhga@eaglgolf.com. **Facility Holes:** 18. **Yards:** 6,135/4,960. **Par:** 70/70. **Course Rating:** 68.3. **Slope:** 108. **Green Fee:** $12/$30. **Cart Fee:** $12/Person. **Walking Policy:** Unrestricted walking. **Walkability:** 1. **Opened:** 1996. **Architect:** Richard Watson/Jeffrey Brauer. **Season:** Year-round. **To obtain tee times:** Call up to 3 days in advance. **Miscellaneous:** Reduced fees (weekdays, twilight, seniors, juniors), metal spikes, range (grass), credit cards (MC, V, AE, DC), BF, FF.

★★ LAKE WHITNEY COUNTRY CLUB
SP-155 Country Club Rd., Whitney, 76692, Hill County, (254)694-2313, 55 miles from Fort Worth. **E-mail:** lwcc@whitneytx.net. **Facility Holes:** 18. **Yards:** 6,296/5,020. **Par:** 70/71. **Course Rating:** 67.6/69.8. **Slope:** 113/113. **Green Fee:** $11/$15. **Cart Fee:** $11/Person. **Walking Policy:** Unrestricted walking. **Walkability:** 3. **Opened:** 1968. **Architect:** Leon Howard. **Season:** Year-round. **To obtain tee times:** Call golf shop. **Miscellaneous:** Reduced fees (weekdays, guests, twilight, seniors, juniors), range (grass/mats), FF.

LAKEWAY RESORT
R-510 Lakeway Dr., Austin, 78734, Travis County, (512)261-7173, 12 miles from Austin. **E-mail:** Contactus@clubcorp.com. **Facility Holes:** 36. **Green Fee:** $40/$50. **Cart Fee:** $13/Person. **Walking Policy:** Unrestricted walking. **Architect:** Leon Howard. **Season:** Year-round. **To obtain tee times:** Call golf shop. **Miscellaneous:** Reduced fees (weekdays, juniors), metal spikes, range (grass/mats), credit cards (MC, V, AE).
★★★ **LIVE OAK COURSE** (18)
Yards: 6,652/5,403. **Par:** 72/72. **Course Rating:** 71.6. **Slope:** 121. **Walkability:** 1. **Opened:** 1966.
Reader Comments: Fairly short, but very tight Hill Country course ... Beautiful layout ... Lots of deer, fun golf.
★★★ **YAUPON COURSE** (18)
Yards: 6,590/5,032. **Par:** 72/72. **Course Rating:** 71.5/69.4. **Slope:** 123/119. **Walkability:** 5. **Opened:** 1971.

Reader Comments: Take along someone that knows the course or plan to play it twice … Slick greens can be a test … Fun course once you're familiar with the holes … A nice little course.

★★ LANDA PARK MUNICIPAL GOLF COURSE
PU-310 Golf Course Dr., New Braunfels, 78130, Comal County, (830)608-2174, 30 miles from San Antonio. **Facility Holes:** 18. **Yards:** 6,103/4,919. **Par:** 72/72. **Course Rating:** 68.9/67.4. **Slope:** 112/106. **Green Fee:** $15. **Cart Fee:** $18/Person. **Walking Policy:** Unrestricted walking. **Walkability:** 2. **Opened:** 1932. **Architect:** Dave Bennett/Leon Howard. **Season:** Year-round. **High:** Jan.-Aug. **To obtain tee times:** Call golf shop.

LEGACY HILLS GOLF CLUB
PU-301 Del Webb Blvd., Georgetown, 78628, Williamson County, (512)864-1222, (800)909-1969, 25 miles from Austin. **E-mail:** corys@delwebb.com. **Web:** www.golftexasbest.com. **Facility Holes:** 18. **Yards:** 7,088/6,536. **Par:** 72/72. **Course Rating:** 73.4/71.5. **Slope:** 127/118. **Green Fee:** $34/$71. **Cart Fee:** Included in green fee. **Walking Policy:** Walking at certain times. **Walkability:** 4. **Opened:** 1996. **Architect:** Billy Casper/Greg Nash. **Season:** Year-round. **High:** Feb.-June. **To obtain tee times:** Call up to 3 days in advance. **Miscellaneous:** Reduced fees (guests, twilight), range (grass), credit cards (MC, V, AE, D), BF, FF.

★½ LEON VALLEY GOLF COURSE
PU-709 E. 24th Ave., Belton, 76513, Bell County, (254)939-5271. **E-mail:** beltongolf@aol.com. **Web:** www.leonvalley.com. **Facility Holes:** 18. **Yards:** 6,652/5,370. **Par:** 72/73. **Course Rating:** 70.1/69.7. **Slope:** 117/114. **Green Fee:** $11/$14. **Cart Fee:** $9/Person. **Walking Policy:** Unrestricted walking. **Walkability:** 1. **Opened:** 1959. **Architect:** Dick Normand. **Season:** Year-round. **High:** April-Sept. **To obtain tee times:** Call golf shop. **Miscellaneous:** Reduced fees (twilight, seniors, juniors), range (grass/mats), credit cards (MC, V, D).

THE LINKS AT WATERCHASE
PU-8951 Creek Run Rd., Fort Worth, 76120, Tarrant County, (817)861-4653. **Web:** www.waterchasegolf.com. **Facility Holes:** 18. **Yards:** 7,304/4,941. **Par:** 72/72. **Course Rating:** 75.4/70.9. **Slope:** 145/123. **Green Fee:** $30/$75. **Cart Fee:** Included in green fee. **Opened:** 2000. **Season:** Year-round. **To obtain tee times:** Call up to 7 days in advance. **Miscellaneous:** Reduced fees (weekdays, twilight, seniors).

★★½ LIONS MUNICIPAL GOLF COURSE
PU-2901 Enfield Rd., Austin, 78703, Travis County, (512)477-6963. **Facility Holes:** 18. **Yards:** 6,001/4,931. **Par:** 71/71. **Course Rating:** 68.9/67.6. **Slope:** 118/115. **Green Fee:** $12/$14. **Opened:** 1934. **Architect:** Leon Howard. **Season:** Year-round. **High:** June-Aug. **To obtain tee times:** Call golf shop. **Miscellaneous:** Reduced fees (twilight), metal spikes.

★★★½ LONGWOOD GOLF CLUB
SP-13300 Longwood Trace, Cypress, 77429, Harris County, (281)373-4100, 10 miles from Houston. **Facility Holes:** 27. **Green Fee:** $55/$65. **Cart Fee:** Included in green fee. **Walking Policy:** Walking at certain times. **Walkability:** 3. **Opened:** 1995. **Architect:** Keith Fergus/Harry Yewens. **Season:** Year-round. **To obtain tee times:** Call up to 7 days in advance. **Miscellaneous:** Reduced fees (weekdays, twilight, seniors, juniors), range (grass), credit cards (MC, V, AE, D, DC), BF, FF.
PALMETTO/POST OAK (18 Combo)
Yards: 6,647/4,872. **Par:** 72/72. **Course Rating:** 72.2/72.2. **Slope:** 133/133.
PINE/PALMETTO (18 Combo)
Yards: 6,758/4,860. **Par:** 72/72. **Course Rating:** 72.8/68.9. **Slope:** 136/123.
POST OAK/PINE (18 Combo)
Yards: 6,925/5,094. **Par:** 72/70. **Course Rating:** 73.6/69.9. **Slope:** 139/124.
Reader Comments: Slightly high green fee, but a beautiful course with championship layout … I recommend this course to all … Beautiful 27 holes. 3 9s have different obstacles … Nice facility, excellent golf course … Always in good condition … Awesome value.

LOS LAGOS GOLF CLUB
PU-1720 S. Paul Longoria, Edinburg, 78539, Hidalgo County, (956)316-0444, 5 miles from McAllen. **E-mail:** britglfpro@pga.com. **Facility Holes:** 18. **Yards:** 7,200/6,200. **Par:** 72/72. **Course Rating:** 74.7/67.0. **Slope:** 132/115. **Green Fee:** $19/$45. **Cart Fee:** Included in green fee. **Walking Policy:** Walking at certain times. **Walkability:** 5. **Architect:** Robert Von Hagge. **Season:** Year-round. **To obtain tee times:** Call up to 3 days in advance. **Miscellaneous:** Reduced fees (weekdays, twilight, juniors), credit cards (MC, V, AE), BF, FF.

LOST VALLEY RESORT GOLF COURSE
R-Highway 16, Bandera, 78003, Bandera County, (830)460-7958, (800)378-8681, 30 miles from San Antonio. **Facility Holes:** 18. **Yards:** 6,210/5,905. **Par:** 72/72. **Course**

Rating: 69.2. Slope: 116. Green Fee: $10/$15. Cart Fee: $10/Person. Walking Policy: Walking at certain times. Walkability: 3. Opened: 1955. Season: Year-round. High: April-Aug. To obtain tee times: Call golf shop. Miscellaneous: Reduced fees (guests, twilight, seniors, juniors), metal spikes, credit cards (MC, V, AE).

MAGNOLIA CREEK GOLF LINKS
PU-1501 West Bay Area Blvd., League City, 77573, Galveston County, (281)557-0555, 10 miles from Houston. Facility Holes: 27. Green Fee: $50/$68. Cart Fee: Included in green fee. Walking Policy: Unrestricted walking. Walkability: 3 Opened: 2000. Architect: Thomas Clark. Season: Feb.-Dec. High: March-May. To obtain tee times: Call golf shop. Miscellaneous: Reduced fees (weekdays, twilight, seniors, juniors), range (grass), credit cards (MC, V, AE), BF, FF.
(IRELAND/ENGLAND) (18 Combo)
Yards: 7,344/5,370. Par: 72/72. Course Rating: 74.9/66.1. Slope: 137/113.
(SCOTLAND/ENGLAND) (18 Combo)
Yards: 7,333/5,500. Par: 72/72. Course Rating: 75.1/66.1. Slope: 133/115.
(SCOTLAND/IRELAND) (18 Combo)
Yards: 7,349/5,380. Par: 72/72. Course Rating: 75.2/66.6. Slope: 137/114. .

★½ MAXWELL GOLF CLUB
PU-1002 S. 32nd St., Abilene, 79602, Taylor County, (915)692-2737, 160 miles from Dallas. Facility Holes: 18. Yards: 6,125/5,031. Par: 71/71. Course Rating: 68.1/66.5. Slope: 111/105. Green Fee: $12/$17. Cart Fee: $17/Cart. Walking Policy: Unrestricted walking. Walkability: 3. Opened: 1930. Architect: George Williams. Season: Year-round. High: July-Aug. To obtain tee times: Call golf shop. Miscellaneous: Reduced fees (twilight, seniors, juniors), metal spikes, range (grass), credit cards (MC, V, AE), BF, FF.

★★★★ MEADOWBROOK FARMS GOLF CLUB *Service*
PU-9595 S. Fry Rd., Katy, 77494, Harris County, (281)693-4653, 5 miles from Houston. E-mail: mbrkfarms@aol.com. Web: www.meadowbrookfarms.com. Facility Holes: 18. Yards: 7,100/5,000. Par: 72/72. Course Rating: 74.2/64.1. Slope: 137/108. Green Fee: $60/$85. Cart Fee: Included in green fee. Walking Policy: Unrestricted walking. Walkability: 1. Opened: 1999. Architect: Greg Norman. Season: Year-round. High: March-July. To obtain tee times: Call up to 30 days in advance. Miscellaneous: Reduced fees (weekdays, twilight, seniors, juniors), range (grass), credit cards (MC, V, AE), BF, FF.
Notes: Ranked 17th in 2001 Best in State.
Reader Comments: A true country club for day. The Greg Norman course is public but it makes you feel as if you are playing in your own privated club ... Best of the newer courses in Houston ... Great layout, good greens ... A treat to play, beautiful greens ... Great greens! Great staff.

★★½ MEADOWBROOK GOLF COURSE
PU-1815 Jenson Rd., Fort Worth, 76112, Tarrant County, (817)457-4616, 5 miles from Ft. Worth. Facility Holes: 18. Yards: 6,363/5,000. Par: 71/71. Course Rating: 70.2/68.4. Slope: 126/116. Green Fee: $6/$20. Cart Fee: $18/Cart. Walking Policy: Unrestricted walking. Walkability: 3. Opened: 1924. Season: Year-round. High: March-Oct. To obtain tee times: Call golf shop. Miscellaneous: Reduced fees (twilight, seniors, juniors), credit cards (MC, V, AE, D), BF, FF.

MEADOWBROOK MUNICIPAL GOLF COMPLEX
PU-601 Municipal Dr., Lubbock, 79403, Lubbock County, (806)765-6679. Facility Holes: 36. Green Fee: $15/$19. Cart Fee: $9/Person. Walking Policy: Unrestricted walking. Opened: 1934. Season: Year-round. To obtain tee times: Call golf shop. Miscellaneous: Reduced fees (weekdays, twilight, seniors, juniors), range (grass/mats), credit cards (MC, V, D).
★★★ CANYON (18)
Yards: 6,450/5,511. Par: 72/72. Course Rating: 71.6/74.3. Slope: 120/117. Walkability: 3. Architect: Warren Cantrell/Baxter Spann. High: April-Sept.
Reader Comments: Exceptional value for seniors ... Good course layout ... Best course layout I've seen ... Canyon—rugged course.
★★ CREEK (18)
Yards: 6,276/5,011. Par: 70/70. Course Rating: 69.0/70.5. Slope: 117/113. Walkability: 2. Architect: Warren Cantrell. High: June-Oct.

★★★½ MEMORIAL PARK GOLF COURSE
PU-1001 E. Memorial Loop Park Dr., Houston, 77007, Harris County, (713)862-4033. E-mail: glennchilders@msn.com. Facility Holes: 18. Yards: 7,164/5,459. Par: 72/72. Course Rating: 73.0/67.7. Slope: 122/114. Green Fee: $23/$32. Cart Fee: $10/Person. Walking Policy: Unrestricted walking. Walkability: 1. Opened: 1936. Architect: John Bredemus/Baxter Spann. Season: Year-round. To obtain tee times: Call up to 3 days in advance. Miscellaneous: Reduced fees (weekdays, twilight), range (grass/mats), credit cards (MC, V, AE, D), BF, FF.

Reader Comments: One of the best in Houston ... A great muni ... Old course, redone in 1993, lots of play ... Houston gold equals Memorial Park ... Best city-owned course anywhere ... Majestic, traditional, awesome ... One of the best public courses around.

★½ MESQUITE GOLF COURSE

PU-825 N. Highway 67, Mesquite, 75150, Dallas County, (972)270-7457, 15 miles from Dallas. **Facility Holes:** 18. **Yards:** 6,280/5,028. **Par:** 71/72. **Course Rating:** 69.1/70.2. **Slope:** 116/113. **Green Fee:** $9/$27. **Cart Fee:** $9/Person. **Walking Policy:** Unrestricted walking. **Walkability:** 3. **Opened:** 1963. **Architect:** Marvin Ferguson. **Season:** Year-round. **High:** April-Oct. **To obtain tee times:** Call up to 7 days in advance. **Miscellaneous:** Reduced fees (weekdays, twilight, seniors, juniors), metal spikes, range (grass/mats), credit cards (MC, V, AE, D, DC), BF, FF.

★★★½ MILL CREEK GOLF RESORT

R-1610 Club Circle, Salado, 76571, Bell County, (254)947-5698, (800)736-3441, 50 miles from Austin. **Web:** www.millcreekgolfresort.com. **Facility Holes:** 27. **Green Fee:** $52/$62. **Cart Fee:** Included in green fee. **Walking Policy:** Mandatory carts. **Walkability:** 3. **Opened:** 1981. **Architect:** Robert Trent Jones Jr. **Season:** Year-round. **To obtain tee times:** Call up to 2 days in advance. **Miscellaneous:** Reduced fees (weekdays, guests), range (grass/mats), lodging (23 rooms), credit cards (MC, V), BF, FF.

CREEK 1/CREEK 2 (18 Combo)
Yards: 6,486/5,250. **Par:** 71. **Course Rating:** 70.0. **Slope:** 128.
CREEK 1/CREEK 3 (18 Combo)
Yards: 6,582/5,239. **Par:** 70. **Course Rating:** 69.7. **Slope:** 125.
CREEK 2/CREEK 3 (18 Combo)
Yards: 6,420/5,017. **Par:** 69. **Course Rating:** 68.9. **Slope:** 124.

Reader Comments: Great layout, great service ... Great design, lots of trouble ... Played in January - great deal ... An enjoyable relaxing round, the creek is everywhere ... Great true greens.

★★★½ MISSION DEL LAGO GOLF COURSE

PU-1250 Mission Grande, San Antonio, 78221, Bexar County, (210)627-2522, 2 miles from San Antonio. **Facility Holes:** 18. **Yards:** 7,200/5,601. **Par:** 72/72. **Course Rating:** 73.6/70.2. **Slope:** 130/121. **Green Fee:** $26/$34. **Cart Fee:** Included in green fee. **Walking Policy:** Unrestricted walking. **Walkability:** 5. **Opened:** 1989. **Architect:** Denis Griffiths. **Season:** Year-round. **High:** April-July. **To obtain tee times:** Call up to 7 days in advance. **Miscellaneous:** Reduced fees (weekdays, guests, twilight, seniors, juniors), metal spikes, range (grass), credit cards (MC, V, AE, D), BF, FF.

★★½ MORRIS WILLIAMS GOLF COURSE

PU-4305 Manor Rd., Austin, 78723, Travis County, (512)926-1298. **Facility Holes:** 18. **Yards:** 6,636/4,943. **Par:** 72/72. **Course Rating:** 71.5/69.3. **Slope:** 121/117. **Green Fee:** $15/$16. **Cart Fee:** $20/Cart. **Walking Policy:** Unrestricted walking. **Walkability:** 3. **Opened:** 1964. **Architect:** Leon Howard. **Season:** Year-round. **High:** March-Oct. **To obtain tee times:** Call up to 1 day in advance. **Miscellaneous:** Reduced fees (weekdays, twilight, seniors, juniors), metal spikes, range (grass), credit cards (MC, V, D), BF, FF.

★★ NOCONA HILLS COUNTRY CLUB

SP-179 Country Club Dr., Nocona, 76255, Montague County, (940)825-3444, 58 miles from Wichita Falls. **Facility Holes:** 18. **Yards:** 6,155/4,971. **Par:** 72/72. **Course Rating:** 70.2/64.1. **Slope:** 111/103. **Green Fee:** $8/$18. **Cart Fee:** $17/Cart. **Walking Policy:** Walking at certain times. **Walkability:** 5. **Opened:** 1973. **Architect:** Leon Howard/Charles Howard. **Season:** Year-round. **High:** April-Aug. **To obtain tee times:** Call golf shop. **Miscellaneous:** Reduced fees (seniors, juniors), range (grass), lodging (28 rooms), credit cards (MC, V, D), BF, FF.

NUEVA VISTA GOLF CLUB

PU-6101 W. Wadley, Midland, 79707, Midland County, (915)520-0500. **Facility Holes:** 18. **Yards:** 6,900/5,270. **Par:** 72/72. **Course Rating:** 71.7/67.5. **Slope:** 114/112. **Green Fee:** $30/$35. **Cart Fee:** Included in green fee. **Walking Policy:** Unrestricted walking. **Walkability:** 2. **Opened:** 1999. **Architect:** George Williams. **Season:** Year-round. **High:** April-Oct. **To obtain tee times:** Call up to 5 days in advance. **Miscellaneous:** Reduced fees (weekdays, twilight, seniors, juniors), range (grass), credit cards (MC, V, AE, D), BF, FF.

OAK HOLLOW GOLF CLUB

PU-2005 N. McDonald Hwy. 5, McKinney, 75069, Collin County, (972)562-0670. **Facility Holes:** 18. **Yards:** 6,679/5,080. **Par:** 70/70. **Course Rating:** 72.3/68.8. **Slope:** 121/115. **Green Fee:** $10/$28. **Cart Fee:** $10/Person. **Walking Policy:** Unrestricted walking. **Opened:** 1999. **Architect:** Maury Miller. **Season:** Year-round. **To obtain tee times:** Call golf shop. **Miscellaneous:** Reduced fees (weekdays, twilight, seniors, juniors), range (grass), credit cards (MC, V), BF, FF.

★★★½ OLD ORCHARD GOLF CLUB
PU-13134 FM 1464, Richmond, 77469, Fort Bend County, (281)277-3300, 15 miles from Houston. **Facility Holes:** 27. **Green Fee:** $35/$65. **Cart Fee:** Included in green fee. **Walking Policy:** Unrestricted walking. **Walkability:** 2. **Opened:** 1990. **Architect:** C. Gibson/H. Yewens/ K. Forgus. **Season:** Year-round. **To obtain tee times:** Call golf shop. **Miscellaneous:** Reduced fees (twilight, seniors, juniors), metal spikes, range (grass/mats), credit cards (MC, V, AE).
BARN/RANGE (18 Combo)
Yards: 6,927/5,166. **Par:** 72/72. **Course Rating:** 73.6/69.4. **Slope:** 127/114.
STABLES/BARN (18 Combo)
Yards: 6,888/5,035. **Par:** 72/72. **Course Rating:** 73.5/69.0. **Slope:** 130/113.
STABLES/RANGE (18 Combo)
Yards: 6,687/5,010. **Par:** 72/72. **Course Rating:** 71.7/68.1. **Slope:** 124/111.
Reader Comments: The best in Texas, great design ... A really good test 3 9s ... Huge old pecan trees ... Tight and fairly tough, first-class without too high green fees ... One of my favorite places to play, course always improving, service always excellent ... Old horse farm, no homes, plush.

★★½ OLMOS BASIN GOLF CLUB
PU-7022 N. McCullough Ave., San Antonio, 78216, Bexar County, (210)826-4041. **Facility Holes:** 18. **Yards:** 6,896/5,748. **Par:** 72/72. **Course Rating:** 71.0/71.0. **Slope:** 123/120. **Green Fee:** $14/$16. **Opened:** 1963. **Architect:** George Hoffman. **To obtain tee times:** Call golf shop.

OLYMPIA HILLS GOLF & CONFERENCE CENTER
PU-12900 Mount Olympus, Universal City, 78148, Bexar County, (210)945-4653, (888)945-6463, 15 miles from San Antonio. **Web:** www.olympiahills-golf.com. **Facility Holes:** 18. **Yards:** 6,923/5,534. **Par:** 72/72. **Course Rating:** 73.4/72.3. **Slope:** 132/128. **Green Fee:** $40/$50. **Cart Fee:** Included in green fee. **Walking Policy:** Unrestricted walking. **Walkability:** 3. **Opened:** 2000. **Architect:** Finger/Dye/Spann. **Season:** Year-round. **To obtain tee times:** Call up to 7 days in advance. **Miscellaneous:** Reduced fees (weekdays, twilight, seniors, juniors), range (grass), credit cards (MC, V, AE, D), BF, FF.
Notes: Ranked 4th in 2001 Best New Affordable Courses.

★★½ OSO BEACH MUNICIPAL GOLF COURSE
PU-5601 S. Alameda, Corpus Christi, 78412, Nueces County, (361)991-5351. **Facility Holes:** 18. **Yards:** 6,223/4,994. **Par:** 70/70. **Course Rating:** 69.9/68.8. **Slope:** 119/118. **Green Fee:** $12/$15. **Cart Fee:** $16/Cart. **Walking Policy:** Walking at certain times. **Walkability:** 1. **Opened:** 1938. **Architect:** John Bredemus. **Season:** Year-round. **To obtain tee times:** Call golf shop. **Miscellaneous:** Reduced fees (twilight, seniors, juniors), credit cards (MC, V), BF, FF.

P.A.R. COUNTRY CLUB
SP-Farm Road, Comanche, 76442, Comanche County, (254)879-2296. **Facility Holes:** 18. **Yards:** 6,068/4,548. **Par:** 72/72. **Course Rating:** 67.9/67.4. **Slope:** 108/110. **Green Fee:** $13/$16. **Cart Fee:** $8/Person. **Opened:** 1963. **Season:** Year-round. **To obtain tee times:** Call golf shop. **Miscellaneous:** Credit cards (MC, V).

★★★★½ PAINTED DUNES DESERT GOLF COURSE *Value+, Condition*
PU-12000 McCombs, El Paso, 79934, El Paso County, (915)821-2122. **E-mail:** pdgolf@gte.net. **Facility Holes:** 27. **Green Fee:** $19/$24. **Cart Fee:** $11/Person. **Walking Policy:** Unrestricted walking. **Walkability:** 3. **Opened:** 1991. **Architect:** Ken Dye. **Season:** Year-round. **High:** July-Oct. **To obtain tee times:** Call up to 7 days in advance. **Miscellaneous:** Reduced fees (weekdays, twilight, seniors, juniors), range (grass/mats), credit cards (MC, V, AE), BF, FF.
EAST/WEST (18 Combo)
Yards: 6,925/5,701. **Par:** 72/72. **Course Rating:** 72.7/67.6. **Slope:** 134/122.
Notes: Ranked 14th in 2001 Best in State.
NORTH/EAST (18 Combo)
Yards: 6,904/5,615. **Par:** 72/72. **Course Rating:** 72.3/66.6. **Slope:** 128/116.
WEST/NORTH (18 Combo)
Yards: 6,941/5,662. **Par:** 72/72. **Course Rating:** 72.6/66.8. **Slope:** 131/120.
Reader Comments: A must-play if you are in El Paso ... Take plenty of balls ... What an absolute gem in the middle of nowhere ... Great, great, great ... Great desert layout, great value, watch out for winds ... Nice new public course.

★½ PALACIO REAL COUNTRY CLUB
PU-Monte Cristo Rd., Edinburg, 78539, Hidalgo County, (956)381-0964. **Facility Holes:** 18. **Yards:** 6,204/4,550. **Par:** 71/70. **Course Rating:** 70.4/68.6. **Slope:** 115/113. **Green Fee:** $12/$14. **Cart Fee:** $14/Cart. **Walking Policy:** Walking at certain times. **Walkability:** 1. **Opened:** 1974. **Season:** Year-round. **To obtain tee times:** Call golf shop. **Miscellaneous:** Reduced fees (weekdays, twilight), range (grass), lodging (6 rooms), credit cards (MC, V, AE, D).

★★½ PALO DURO CREEK GOLF CLUB

SP-50 Country Club Dr., Canyon, 79015, Randall County, (806)655-1106, 12 miles from Amarillo. **Facility Holes:** 18. **Yards:** 6,865/5,120. **Par:** 72/74. **Course Rating:** 72.1/66.9. **Slope:** 117/105. **Green Fee:** $10/$15. **Cart Fee:** $16/Cart. **Walking Policy:** Unrestricted walking. **Walkability:** 2. **Architect:** Henry Hughes. **Season:** Year-round. **High:** April-Sept. **To obtain tee times:** Call golf shop. **Miscellaneous:** Reduced fees (twilight, seniors, juniors), range (grass), credit cards (MC, V).

★★ PASADENA MUNICIPAL GOLF COURSE

PU-1000 Duffer, Houston, 77034, Harris County, (281)481-0834. **Facility Holes:** 18. **Yards:** 6,750/4,910. **Par:** 72/72. **Course Rating:** 72.2/67.9. **Slope:** 118/108. **Green Fee:** $9/$13. **Cart Fee:** $19/Cart. **Walking Policy:** Unrestricted walking. **Walkability:** 4. **Opened:** 1978. **Architect:** Jay Riviere. **Season:** Year-round. **High:** March-Aug. **To obtain tee times:** Call golf shop. **Miscellaneous:** Reduced fees (weekdays, twilight, seniors, juniors), metal spikes, range (grass), credit cards (MC, V, AE, D, Diners Club).

PEACH TREE GOLF CLUB

SP-6212 CR 152 W., Bullard, 75757, Smith County, (903)894-7079, 9 miles from Tyler. **E-mail:** golfpro@easttexasgolf.com. **Web:** www.easttexasgolf.com. **Facility Holes:** 36. **Cart Fee:** $12/Person. **Walking Policy:** Unrestricted walking. **Season:** Year-round. **Miscellaneous:** Metal spikes, range (grass), credit cards (MC, V, AE, D), BF, FF.

★★★ OAKHURST COURSE (18)

Yards: 6,813/5,086. **Par:** 72/72. **Course Rating:** 72.3/69.0. **Slope:** 126/118. **Green Fee:** $18/$33. **Walkability:** 3. **Opened:** 1993. **Architect:** Carlton Gipson. **To obtain tee times:** Call up to 6 days in advance. **Miscellaneous:** Reduced fees (twilight, seniors).
Reader Comments: Course has matured in the past years ... Three tough finishing holes, always into the wind ... Tough in the summer ... Nice design and layout-lots of trees-fun to play tee to green ... Best in area ... Good course for average golfer ... Nice greens.

★½ PEACH TREE COURSE (18)

Yards: 5,556/4,467. **Par:** 70/71. **Course Rating:** 65.7/65.5. **Slope:** 109/111. **Green Fee:** $13/$19. **Walkability:** 1. **Opened:** 1986. **Architect:** Dan Hurst. **To obtain tee times:** Call golf shop. **Miscellaneous:** Reduced fees (weekdays, twilight, seniors, juniors).

★★ PECAN HOLLOW GOLF COURSE

PU-4501 E. 14th St., Plano, 75074, Collin County, (972)941-7600. **Facility Holes:** 18. **Yards:** 6,848/5,301. **Par:** 72/72. **Course Rating:** 71.9/71.3. **Slope:** 122/118. **Green Fee:** $13/$16. **Walkability:** 1. **Opened:** 1960. **Architect:** Don January/Billy Martindale. **To obtain tee times:** Call golf shop. **Miscellaneous:** Metal spikes.
Special Notes: Formerly Plano Municipal Golf Course.

★★★★ PECAN VALLEY GOLF CLUB

PU-4700 Pecan Valley Dr., San Antonio, 78223, Bexar County, (210)333-9018, 6 miles from San Antonio. **E-mail:** pvgc@texas.net. **Web:** thetexasgolftrail.com. **Facility Holes:** 18. **Yards:** 7,010/5,335. **Par:** 71/71. **Course Rating:** 73.9/65.7. **Slope:** 131/118. **Green Fee:** $75/$85. **Cart Fee:** Included in green fee. **Walking Policy:** Unrestricted walking. **Walkability:** 2. **Opened:** 1963. **Architect:** J. Press Maxwell. **Season:** Year-round. **High:** Feb.-May. **To obtain tee times:** Call up to 7 days in advance. **Miscellaneous:** Reduced fees (weekdays, twilight, seniors, juniors), range (grass), credit cards (MC, V, AE, D, DC), FF.
Reader Comments: Wonderful renovation of a classic Texas course ... Very playable, with many tee options ... Historic course built before golf carts so it is easy to walk ... Classic course in great condition ... Stay out of trees ... Tricky greens with many undulations ... Huge oaks and tree-lined (tight) fairways!

PECAN VALLEY GOLF COURSE

PU-6400 Pecan Dr., Fort Worth, 76126, Tarrant County, (817)249-1845, 2 miles from Dallas. **Facility Holes:** 36. **Cart Fee:** $20/Cart. **Walking Policy:** Unrestricted walking. **Architect:** Ralph Plummer/Bland Pittman. **Season:** Year-round. **High:** April-Nov. **To obtain tee times:** Call golf shop. **Miscellaneous:** Reduced fees (weekdays, twilight, seniors, juniors), metal spikes, range (grass), credit cards (MC, V, AE, D).

★★ HILLS COURSE (18)

Yards: 6,577/5,275. **Par:** 72/72. **Course Rating:** 71.4/69.7. **Slope:** 128/115. **Green Fee:** $12/$16. **Walkability:** 2. **Opened:** 1981.

★★½ RIVER COURSE (18)

Yards: 6,562/5,419. **Par:** 71/72. **Course Rating:** 71.3/69.6. **Slope:** 124/109. **Green Fee:** $15/$20. **Walkability:** 1. **Opened:** 1963.

PERRYTON MUNICIPAL GOLF COURSE

SP-402 SE 24th. St., Perryton, 79070, Ochiltree County, (806)435-5381. **Facility Holes:** 18.

Yards: 6,431/5,257. **Par:** 72/72. **Course Rating:** 69.2/67.0. **Slope:** 116/111. **Green Fee:** $8/$11. **Cart Fee:** $16/Cart. **Opened:** 1976. **Season:** Year-round. **To obtain tee times:** Call golf shop. **Miscellaneous:** Reduced fees (seniors, juniors).

PHEASANT TRAILS GOLF COURSE
PU-11352 Schuman Rd., Dumas, 79029, Moore County, (806)935-7375, 45 miles from Amarillo. **E-mail:** cnelson@xit.net. **Facility Holes:** 18. **Yards:** 6,481/5,292. **Par:** 71/71. **Course Rating:** 69.5/70.5. **Slope:** 111/117. **Green Fee:** $10/$13. **Cart Fee:** $18/Cart. **Walking Policy:** Unrestricted walking. **Walkability:** 3. **Opened:** 1945. **Season:** Year-round. **High:** March-Nov. **To obtain tee times:** Call golf shop. **Miscellaneous:** Reduced fees (twilight, seniors, juniors), range (grass), credit cards (MC, V), BF, FF.

★★½ PHILLIPS COUNTRY CLUB
SP-1609 N. Sterling Rd., Borger, 79007, Hutchinson County, (806)274-6812. **Facility Holes:** 18. **Yards:** 6,200/5,212. **Par:** 72/72. **Course Rating:** 69.1/68.1. **Slope:** 105/105. **Green Fee:** $10/$15. **Walking Policy:** Unrestricted walking. **Opened:** 1941. **Architect:** Phillips Petroleum Employees. **To obtain tee times:** Call golf shop. **Miscellaneous:** Reduced fees (weekdays, twilight), range (grass), credit cards (MC, V, AE, D).

★★★★ PINE FOREST GOLF CLUB
SP-2509 Riverside Dr., Bastrop, 78602, Bastrop County, (512)321-1181, 30 miles from Austin. **E-mail:** golfer@bluebon.net. **Web:** www.pineforestgolfclub.com. **Facility Holes:** 18. **Yards:** 6,600/4,946. **Par:** 72/72. **Course Rating:** 71.5/69.0. **Slope:** 126/114. **Green Fee:** $25/$35. **Cart Fee:** Included in green fee. **Walking Policy:** Mandatory carts. **Walkability:** 5. **Opened:** 1979. **Architect:** Don January/Billy Martindale. **Season:** Year-round. **To obtain tee times:** Call up to 7 days in advance. **Miscellaneous:** Reduced fees (twilight, seniors), range (grass), credit cards (MC, V, AE, D), BF, FF.
Reader Comments: Good, tight layout … You don't get many breathers … If you haven't played this course, you will be in for a surprise … Greens and fairways are in great condition … Beautiful on Colorado River… 'Sleeper' … Great Layout … Excellent greens and a good challenge with steep sloped greens … Nice clubhouse and good food.

PINE RIDGE GOLF COURSE
PU-5615 Pine Mill Road, Paris, 75462, Lamar County, (903)785-8076, 2 miles from Paris. **Facility Holes:** 18. **Yards:** 5,855/4,462. **Par:** 72/72. **Course Rating:** 67.1. **Slope:** 106. **Green Fee:** $10/$12. **Cart Fee:** $18/Cart. **Walking Policy:** Unrestricted walking. **Walkability:** 2. **Opened:** 1987. **Architect:** Raney/Exum. **Season:** Year-round. **High:** March-Nov. **To obtain tee times:** Call up to 7 days in advance. **Miscellaneous:** Reduced fees (weekdays), range (grass), credit cards (MC, V, D), BF, FF.

★★★ PINNACLE COUNTRY CLUB
SP-200 Pinnacle Club Dr., Mabank, 75147, Henderson County, (903)451-9797, 60 miles from Dallas. **Facility Holes:** 18. **Yards:** 6,641/5,222. **Par:** 71/71. **Course Rating:** 72.9/70.8. **Slope:** 135/129. **Green Fee:** $16/$35. **Cart Fee:** $10/Person. **Walking Policy:** Walking at certain times. **Walkability:** 4. **Opened:** 1988. **Architect:** Don January. **Season:** Year-round. **High:** March-July. **To obtain tee times:** Call up to 3 days in advance. **Miscellaneous:** Reduced fees (weekdays, twilight, seniors), range (grass/mats), credit cards (MC, V, AE), BF, FF.
Reader Comments: Tight shotmakers course … Hidden away. Hard to find, but worthwhile experience … Beautiful trip through the woods, have to hit the fairway …Greens and fairways are outstanding … Favors a fade.

★★½ PLANTATION GOLF CLUB
PU-4701 Plantation Lane, Frisco, 75035, Collin County, (972)335-4653, 20 miles from Dallas. **E-mail:** perry.arthur@clubcorp.com. **Facility Holes:** 18. **Yards:** 6,382/5,945. **Par:** 72/72. **Course Rating:** 70.9/70.4. **Slope:** 122/113. **Green Fee:** $39/$58. **Cart Fee:** Included in green fee. **Walking Policy:** Mandatory cart. **Walkability:** 1. **Opened:** 1988. **Architect:** Richard Ellis. **To obtain tee times:** Call golf shop. **Miscellaneous:** Reduced fees (weekdays, twilight, seniors, juniors), range (grass), credit cards (MC, V, AE, D).

★★½ PRAIRIE LAKES GOLF COURSE
PU-3202 S.E. 14th St., Grand Prairie, 75052, Dallas County, (972)263-0661, 5 miles from Dallas. **E-mail:** bwpga@flash.net. **Web:** www.prairielakesgolf.com. **Facility Holes:** 27. **Green Fee:** $16/$18. **Cart Fee:** $21/Cart. **Walking Policy:** Unrestricted walking. **Walkability:** 1. **Opened:** 1964. **Architect:** Ralph Plummer. **Season:** Year-round. **High:** May-Sept. **To obtain tee times:** Call up to 3 days in advance. **Miscellaneous:** Reduced fees (twilight, seniors, juniors), range (grass), credit cards (MC, V, AE, D), BF, FF.
RED/BLUE (18 Combo)
Yards: 6,500/5,465. **Par:** 72/72. **Course Rating:** 71.0/65.3. **Slope:** 118/102.

RED/WHITE (18 Combo)
Yards: 6,219/5,176. **Par:** 71/71. **Course Rating:** 69.5/64.2. **Slope:** 94/98.
WHITE/BLUE (18 Combo)
Yards: 6,309/5,275. **Par:** 71/71. **Course Rating:** 69.5/64.3. **Slope:** 112/98.

★★ **QUAIL CREEK COUNTRY CLUB**
SP-Highway 21, San Marcos, 78666, Hays County, (512)353-1665. **Facility Holes:** 18. **Yards:** 6,424/4,993. **Par:** 72/72. **Course Rating:** 70.3/68.9. **Slope:** 116/112. **Green Fee:** $18/$25. **Opened:** 1968. **To obtain tee times:** Call golf shop. **Miscellaneous:** Metal spikes.

★★★★ **THE QUARRY GOLF CLUB**
PU-444 E. Basse Rd., San Antonio, 78209, Bexar County, (210)824-4500, (800)347-7759. **E-mail:** proshop@quarrygolf.com. **Web:** www.quarrygolf.com. **Facility Holes:** 18. **Yards:** 6,740/4,897. **Par:** 71/71. **Course Rating:** 72.4/67.4. **Slope:** 128/115. **Green Fee:** $59/$110. **Cart Fee:** Included in green fee. **Walking Policy:** Unrestricted walking. **Walkability:** 3. **Opened:** 1993. **Architect:** Keith Foster. **Season:** Year-round. **High:** Oct.-June. **To obtain tee times:** Call up to 30 days in advance. **Miscellaneous:** Reduced fees (twilight, juniors), metal spikes, range (grass), credit cards (MC, V, AE, D, DC), FF.
Notes: Ranked 13th in 2001 Best in State; 28th in 1996 America's Top 75 Upscale Courses.
Reader Comments: Amazing setting on back 9 ... Great holes, innovative concept ... Target course ... Very dramatic, good greens and food ... Reload is one of the truly great holes ... Immaculate condition, even in dry, summer ... Nos. 13 and 17 worth the trip.

★★★★ **QUICKSAND GOLF COURSE**
PU-2305 Pulliam St., San Angelo, 76905, Tom Green County, (915)482-8337, (877)520-4653. **E-mail:** quicksandgc.com. **Web:** www.quicksandgc.com. **Facility Holes:** 18. **Yards:** 7,171/5,023. **Par:** 72/72. **Course Rating:** 75.0/69.5. **Slope:** 140/121. **Green Fee:** $17/$32. **Cart Fee:** $9/Person. **Walking Policy:** Walking at certain times. **Walkability:** 2. **Opened:** 1997. **Architect:** Michael Hurdzan/Dana Fry. **Season:** Year-round. **High:** March-Oct. **To obtain tee times:** Call golf shop. **Miscellaneous:** Reduced fees (twilight, juniors), metal spikes, range (grass), credit cards (MC, V, AE, D).
Reader Comments: Bring a sand wedge! ... New and improving, tough in the wind, good food ... Last three holes are exceptional ... A favorite, great value, very challenging ... Great greens, good layout ... Excellent course in excellent condition.

★½ **RABBIT RUN AT BROOKS ROAD**
PU-Brooks Rd., Beaumont, 77720, Jefferson County, (409)866-7545. **Facility Holes:** 18. **Yards:** 6,258/4,773. **Par:** 70/70. **Green Fee:** $8/$10. **Cart Fee:** $15/Cart. **Opened:** 1995. **Architect:** Johnnie Barlow. **Season:** Feb.-Dec. **To obtain tee times:** Call golf shop. **Miscellaneous:** Metal spikes.

RANCHO VIEJO RESORT & COUNTRY CLUB
SP-No.1 Rancho Viejo Dr., Rancho Viejo, 78575, Cameron County, (956)350-4000, (800)531-7400, 10 miles from Brownsville. **Web:** www.playrancho.com. **Facility Holes:** 36. **Green Fee:** $35/$40. **Cart Fee:** $12/Person. **Walking Policy:** Walking at certain times. **Walkability:** 1. **Opened:** 1971. **Architect:** Dennis W. Arp. **Season:** Year-round. **High:** Oct.-April. **To obtain tee times:** Call golf shop. **Miscellaneous:** Reduced fees (guests, juniors), range (grass), lodging (63 rooms), credit cards (MC, V, AE), BF, FF.
★★½ **EL ANGEL COURSE (18)**
Yards: 6,318/5,087. **Par:** 71/72. **Course Rating:** 71.5/67.6. **Slope:** 120/113.
★★½ **EL DIABLO COURSE (18)**
Yards: 6,847/5,556. **Par:** 70/73. **Course Rating:** 73.7/70.7. **Slope:** 129/122.

★★ **RATLIFF RANCH GOLF LINKS**
PU-7500 N. Grandview, Odessa, 79768, Ector County, (915)550-8181, 3 miles from Odessa. **Facility Holes:** 18. **Yards:** 6,800/4,900. **Par:** 72/72. **Course Rating:** 73.0/68.9. **Slope:** 122/110. **Green Fee:** $12/$17. **Cart Fee:** $10/Person. **Walking Policy:** Unrestricted walking. **Walkability:** 2. **Opened:** 1988. **Architect:** Jeff Brauer. **Season:** Year-round. **High:** April-Sept. **To obtain tee times:** Call up to 3 days in advance. **Miscellaneous:** Reduced fees (weekdays, twilight, seniors, juniors), range (grass), credit cards (MC, V, AE, D), BF, FF.

★★★½ **RAYBURN COUNTRY CLUB & RESORT**
R-1000 Wingate Blvd., Sam Rayburn, 75951, Jasper County, (409)698-2271, (800)882-1442, 80 miles from Houston. **Facility Holes:** 27. **Green Fee:** $28/$35. **Cart Fee:** $20/Cart. **Walking Policy:** Walking at certain times. **Walkability:** 5. **Opened:** 1967. **Architect:** Riviere/von Hagge/Devlin/R.T. Jones. **Season:** Year-round. **To obtain tee times:** Call golf shop. **Miscellaneous:** Reduced fees (twilight, juniors), range (grass/mats), credit cards (MC, V, AE, D), BF, FF.

BLUE/GOLD (18 Combo)
Yards: 6,731/5,824. **Par:** 72/72. **Course Rating:** 71.3/72.2. **Slope:** 116/126.
BLUE/GREEN (18 Combo)
Yards: 6,719/5,237. **Par:** 72/72. **Course Rating:** 72.5/71.0. **Slope:** 129/123.
GOLD/GREEN (18 Combo)
Yards: 6,728/5,301. **Par:** 72/72. **Course Rating:** 72.2/71.0. **Slope:** 124/118.
Reader Comments: I love the course ... A good golf value ... Hilly and interesting ... Beautiful scenery ... Very challenging—3 different 9's—3 different looks ... Excellent lakeside layout, ample fairways.

★★½ **RED WOLF RUN GOLF CLUB**
PU-27350 Afton Way, Huffman, 77336, Harris County, (281)324-1841, 20 miles from Houston. **Facility Holes:** 18. **Yards:** 6,940/5,553. **Par:** 72/72. **Course Rating:** 74.2/73.3. **Slope:** 131/130. **Green Fee:** $23/$36. **Cart Fee:** Included in green fee. **Walking Policy:** Walking at certain times. **Walkability:** 4. **Opened:** 1971. **Architect:** Jay Riviere. **Season:** Year-round. **High:** Sept.-April. **To obtain tee times:** Call up to 7 days in advance. **Miscellaneous:** Reduced fees (weekdays, guests, twilight, seniors, juniors), range (grass), credit cards (MC, V, AE), BF, FF. **Special Notes:** Formerly Lake Houston Golf Club.

REEVES COUNTY GOLF COURSE
PU-88 Starley Dr., Pecos, 79772, Reeves County, (915)447-2858. **Facility Holes:** 18. **Yards:** 6,405/4,933. **Par:** 71/71. **Course Rating:** 68.8/68.5. **Slope:** 104/93. **Green Fee:** $18/$25. **Cart Fee:** $10/Person. **Walking Policy:** Unrestricted walking. **Walkability:** 1. **Opened:** 1942. **Season:** Year-round. **To obtain tee times:** Call golf shop. **Miscellaneous:** Reduced fees (seniors, juniors), range (grass), FF.

★★★★ **RIDGEVIEW RANCH GOLF CLUB**
PU-2501 Ridgeview Dr., Plano, 75025, Collin County, (972)390-1039. **Facility Holes:** 18. **Yards:** 7,025/5,335. **Par:** 72/72. **Course Rating:** 74.1/70.4. **Slope:** 130/117. **Green Fee:** $30/$53. **Cart Fee:** $13/Person. **Walking Policy:** Walking at certain times. **Walkability:** 3. **Opened:** 1995. **Architect:** Jeff Braurer. **Season:** Year-round. **To obtain tee times:** Call golf shop. **Miscellaneous:** Reduced fees (twilight, seniors, juniors), range (grass/mats), credit cards (MC, V, AE), BF, FF.
Reader Comments: One of my favorite places to play ... Oh wow, what a nice golf course ... Great course ... Many interesting, challenging holes ... Best $ value in Dallas area ... Too hard for the average player ... Nice 1st hole .

★★★½ **RIO COLORADO GOLF COURSE**
PU-FM 2668 and Riverside Park, Bay City, 77414, Matagorda County, (979)244-2955, 80 miles from Houston. **Facility Holes:** 18. **Yards:** 6,824/5,020. **Par:** 72/72. **Course Rating:** 73.1/69.1. **Slope:** 127/116. **Green Fee:** $13/$20. **Cart Fee:** $11/Person. **Walking Policy:** Unrestricted walking. **Walkability:** 2. **Opened:** 1993. **Architect:** Gary Player Design Company. **Season:** Year-round. **High:** April-Oct. **To obtain tee times:** Call golf shop. **Miscellaneous:** Reduced fees (twilight, seniors, juniors), metal spikes, range, credit cards (MC, V, AE).
Reader Comments: Open front, tight back ... Flat course, long par 5s, plenty of bunkers, nice ... Good course for the area ... Would be worth double closer to Houston ... Fun course to play.

★★★ **RIVER BEND RESORT**
R-Rte. 8, Box 649, Brownsville, 78520, Cameron County, (956)548-0192, 3 miles from Brownsville. **Facility Holes:** 18. **Yards:** 6,828/5,126. **Par:** 72/72. **Course Rating:** 72.6/71.7. **Slope:** 119/119. **Green Fee:** $14/$19. **Cart Fee:** $9/Person. **Walking Policy:** Unrestricted walking. **Walkability:** 1. **Opened:** 1985. **Architect:** Mike Ingram. **Season:** Year-round. **High:** Oct.-April. **To obtain tee times:** Call up to 3 days in advance. **Miscellaneous:** Reduced fees (weekdays, twilight), range (grass), credit cards (MC, V), BF, FF.
Reader Comments: Beautiful fairways, ball sat up nicely ... Nice course, good condition, a little expensive ... Needs better upkeep ... Farthest course south in U.S.

★★ **RIVER CREEK PARK GOLF COURSE**
PU-1177 Farmarket Rd., Burkburnett, 76354, Wichita County, (940)855-3361, 10 miles from Wichita Falls. **Facility Holes:** 18. **Yards:** 6,800/5,100. **Par:** 71/73. **Course Rating:** 69.0/69.1. **Slope:** 104/104. **Green Fee:** $7/$8. **Cart Fee:** $10/Person. **Walking Policy:** Unrestricted walking. **Architect:** Buddy Pierson/Richard Boyd. **Season:** Year-round. **High:** May-July. **To obtain tee times:** Call golf shop. **Miscellaneous:** Reduced fees (twilight, seniors, juniors), metal spikes, range (grass), credit cards (MC, V).

★★★★ **RIVER RIDGE GOLF CLUB** *Pace*
PU-3133 Brazos Oak Lane, Sealy, 77474, Austin County, (979)885-3333, (800)553-7517, 35 miles from Houston. **E-mail:** headpro@riverridgegolfclub.com. **Web:** www.riverridgegolf-club.com. **Facility Holes:** 27. **Green Fee:** $55/$72. **Cart Fee:** Included in green fee. **Walking**

Policy: Unrestricted walking. **Walkability:** 3. **Opened:** 1998. **Architect:** Jay Riviere. **Season:** Year-round. **To obtain tee times:** Call up to 7 days in advance. **Miscellaneous:** Reduced fees (weekdays, twilight, seniors, juniors), range (grass), credit cards (MC, V, AE), BF, FF.
PARKLAND/RIDGE (18 Combo)
Yards: 7,201/5,486. **Par:** 72/72. **Course Rating:** 73.6/71.3. **Slope:** 133/122.
RIVER/PARKLAND (18 Combo)
Yards: 6,946/5,344. **Par:** 71/71. **Course Rating:** 71.5/70.8. **Slope:** 129/121.
RIVER/RIDGE (18 Combo)
Yards: 6,925/5,228. **Par:** 71/71. **Course Rating:** 72.1/70.1. **Slope:** 125/119.
Reader Comments: Very good 27 holes of golf … Easy layout with good greens, lets you play conservative or difficult shots … Challenging and beautiful setting … A good addition to the Houston area … Best public course in Houston, classic style … Awesome golf… Quiet and country-like.

RIVER TERRACE
SP-16777 Wallisville Road, Houston, 77049, Harris County, (281)452-2183, 13 miles from Houston. **Facility Holes:** 18. **Yards:** 6,690/5,740. **Par:** 72/72. **Course Rating:** 70.7/66.4. **Slope:** 118/106. **Green Fee:** $15/$16. **Cart Fee:** $16/Cart. **Walking Policy:** Unrestricted walking. **Walkability:** 1. **Opened:** 1998. **Architect:** Darrell Witt. **Season:** Year-round. **To obtain tee times:** Call golf shop. **Miscellaneous:** Reduced fees (twilight, seniors, juniors), range (grass), credit cards (MC, V, AE), FF.

★★½ RIVERCHASE GOLF CLUB
PU-700 Riverchase Dr., Coppell, 75019, Dallas County, (972)462-8281, 5 miles from Dallas. **Facility Holes:** 18. **Yards:** 6,593/6,041. **Par:** 71/71. **Course Rating:** 72.0/70.5. **Slope:** 124/119. **Green Fee:** $25/$65. **Cart Fee:** Included in green fee. **Walking Policy:** Walking at certain times. **Walkability:** 2. **Opened:** 1988. **Architect:** George Fazio. **Season:** Year-round. **To obtain tee times:** Call golf shop. **Miscellaneous:** Reduced fees (weekdays, twilight, seniors, juniors), range (grass/mats), credit cards (MC, V, AE), BF, FF.

★★★ RIVERSIDE GOLF CLUB
PU-3000 Riverside Pkwy., Grand Prairie, 75050, Dallas County, (817)640-7800, 15 miles from Dallas. **E-mail:** riverside_gc@hotmail.com. **Web:** www.americangolf.com. **Facility Holes:** 18. **Yards:** 7,025/5,175. **Par:** 72/72. **Course Rating:** 74.4/69.5. **Slope:** 132/113. **Green Fee:** $45/$55. **Cart Fee:** Included in green fee. **Walking Policy:** Unrestricted walking. **Walkability:** 3. **Opened:** 1984. **Architect:** Roger Packard. **Season:** Year-round. **High:** April-Oct. **To obtain tee times:** Call up to 7 days in advance. **Miscellaneous:** Reduced fees (weekdays, twilight, seniors, juniors), range (grass), credit cards (MC, V, AE, D, DC), BF, FF.
Reader Comments: Great layout … Most enjoyable, great fairways, greens … No. 18 will challenge you! … Course has too many water hazards and becomes more of a target course … Lots of water, fun to play with tough holes.

★½ RIVERSIDE GOLF CLUB
PU-3301 Riverside Club Road, San Angelo, 76903, Tom Green County, (915)653-6130. **E-mail:** jfagolf@wcc.net. **Facility Holes:** 18. **Yards:** 6,499/5,397. **Par:** 72/72. **Course Rating:** 70.5/69.8. **Slope:** 113/105. **Green Fee:** $11/$16. **Cart Fee:** $8/Person. **Walking Policy:** Unrestricted walking. **Walkability:** 1. **Opened:** 1965. **Architect:** John Dublin. **To obtain tee times:** Call golf shop. **Miscellaneous:** Reduced fees (juniors), metal spikes, range (grass/mats), credit cards (MC, V, D).

★★½ RIVERSIDE GOLF COURSE
PU-302 McWright Rd., Victoria, 77901, Victoria County, (512)573-4521, 94 miles from San Antonio. **Facility Holes:** 27. **Green Fee:** $10/$12. **Cart Fee:** $12/Cart. **Walking Policy:** Unrestricted walking. **Walkability:** 1. **Architect:** Ralph Plummer/Jay Riviere. **Season:** Year-round. **High:** May-Sept. **To obtain tee times:** Call golf shop. **Miscellaneous:** Reduced fees (weekdays, juniors), metal spikes.
RED/BLUE (18 Combo)
Yards: 6,488/5,121. **Par:** 72/72. **Course Rating:** 71.4/70.4. **Slope:** 122/117.
RED/WHITE (18 Combo)
Yards: 6,606/5,497. **Par:** 72/72. **Course Rating:** 71.4/70.4. **Slope:** 122/117. **Opened:** 1953.
WHITE/BLUE (18 Combo)
Yards: 6,430/5,150. **Par:** 72/72. **Course Rating:** 70.8/70.4. **Slope:** 121/117. **Opened:** 1953.

★★½ RIVERSIDE GOLF COURSE
PU-1020 Grove Blvd., Austin, 78741, Travis County, (512)386-7077, 2 miles from Austin. **E-mail:** riversidegc@hotmail.com. **Facility Holes:** 18. **Yards:** 6,562/5,334. **Par:** 71/71. **Course Rating:** 70.3/69.6. **Slope:** 122/112. **Green Fee:** $12/$25. **Cart Fee:** $10/Person. **Walking Policy:** Unrestricted walking. **Walkability:** 3. **Opened:** 1948. **Architect:** Perry Maxwell. **Season:** Year-round. **To obtain tee times:** Call up to 7 days in advance. **Miscellaneous:** Reduced fees (weekdays, twilight, seniors, juniors), credit cards (MC, V, AE, D, DC), BF, FF.

★★★ RIVERSIDE MUNICIPAL GOLF COURSE

PU-203 McDonald, San Antonio, 78210, Bexar County, (210)533-8371. **Facility Holes:** 27.
Yards: 6,729/5,730. **Par:** 72/72. **Course Rating:** 72.0/72.0. **Slope:** 128/121. **Green Fee:** $6/$16.
Cart Fee: $15/Cart. **Walking Policy:** Unrestricted walking. **Opened:** 1929. **Architect:** Vern
Schmidt. **Season:** Year-round. **High:** April-Sept. **To obtain tee times:** Call golf shop.
Miscellaneous: Reduced fees (weekdays, guests, twilight, seniors, juniors), metal spikes,
credit cards (MC, V, AE, D).
Reader Comments: Good par 3s ... Tough par 5s ... Flat river layout but challenging ... Good muni
... Friendly golfers ... Most improved San Antonio muni ... Wonderful contrast between front and
back 9s ... Very good course city owned.
Special Notes: Also has a 9-hole par-3 course.

RIVERWOOD GOLF COURSE

PU-Eagle St., Vidor, 77662, Orange County, (409)768-1710. **Facility Holes:** 18. **Yards:**
6,771/5,114. **Par:** 71/71. **Green Fee:** $6/$8. **Opened:** 1977. **Architect:** Johnny Barlow. **To obtain
tee times:** Call golf shop. **Miscellaneous:** Metal spikes.

ROCKWOOD GOLF COURSE

PU-1851 Jacksboro Hwy., Fort Worth, 76114, Tarrant County, (817)624-1771, 2 miles from
Fort Worth. **Facility Holes:** 27. **Green Fee:** $13/$18. **Cart Fee:** $19/Cart. **Walking Policy:**
Unrestricted walking. **Opened:** 1940. **Architect:** John Bredemus. **Season:** Year-round.
To obtain tee times: Call up to 7 days in advance. **Miscellaneous:** Reduced fees (weekdays,
twilight, seniors, juniors), range (grass), credit cards (MC, V, AE, D), BF, FF.
★½ **THE ROCK (18)**
Yards: 6,350/6,070. **Par:** 70/73. **Course Rating:** 69.5/65.6. **Slope:** 111/103. **Walkability:** 2.
★½ **TRINITY (9)**
Yards: 3,652/2,958. **Par:** 36/38. **Course Rating:** 37.9/33.4. **Slope:** 129/108. **Walkability:** 3.

ROSS ROGERS GOLF CLUB

PU-722 N.W. 24th St., Amarillo, 79107, Potter County, (806)378-3086. **Facility Holes:** 36.
Green Fee: $10/$14. **Cart Fee:** $20/Cart. **Walking Policy:** Unrestricted walking. **Architect:**
James Rettenberry. **Season:** Year-round. **To obtain tee times:** Call golf shop. **Miscellaneous:**
Reduced fees (weekdays, seniors, juniors), range (grass/mats), credit cards (MC, V, D).
★★ **EAST COURSE (18)**
Yards: 6,858/5,575. **Par:** 72/72. **Course Rating:** 70.8/69.5. **Slope:** 112/111. **Walkability:** 2.
Opened: 1977.
★★ **WEST COURSE (18)**
Yards: 6,602/5,392. **Par:** 72/72. **Course Rating:** 69.2/68.2. **Slope:** 110/108. **Walkability:** 1.
Opened: 1940.

★★★★ ROY KIZER GOLF COURSE

PU-5400 Jimmy Clay Dr., Austin, 78744, Travis County, (512)444-0999. **Facility Holes:** 18.
Yards: 6,749/5,018. **Par:** 71/71. **Course Rating:** 71.6. **Slope:** 125. **Green Fee:** $18/$28. **Cart
Fee:** $10/Person. **Walking Policy:** Unrestricted walking. **Walkability:** 2. **Opened:** 1994.
Architect: Randolph Russell. **Season:** Year-round. **High:** April-Nov. **To obtain tee times:** Call
up to 3 days in advance. **Miscellaneous:** Reduced fees (weekdays, twilight, seniors, juniors),
metal spikes, range (grass), credit cards (MC, V, D), BF, FF.
Reader Comments: Best muni ever, fun and fair, great design ...Links-style course in great shape
... Bird estuary on site brings beautiful wildlife right into the city ... Great practice facility ... The
most for your money in Austin ... Best public links course I've played.

★★★ SAN SABA MUNICIPAL GOLF COURSE

PU-Golf Course Rd., County Rd. 102, San Saba, 76877, San Saba County, (915)372-3212,
90 miles from Austin. **E-mail:** mcn@centex.net. **Facility Holes:** 18. **Yards:** 6,904/5,246. **Par:**
72/72. **Course Rating:** 71.5/69.0. **Slope:** 119/109. **Green Fee:** $12/$18. **Cart Fee:** $9/Person.
Walking Policy: Unrestricted walking. **Walkability:** 1. **Opened:** 1972. **Architect:** Sorrell Smith.
Season: Year-round. **To obtain tee times:** Call golf shop. **Miscellaneous:** Metal spikes, range
(grass), credit cards (MC, V, AE), BF, FF.
Reader Comments: Tee placements make the course challenging for pros and beginners ... Great
back 9, front 9 a drag ... Interesting layout ... Good muni ... Gets dry in summer ... Poor layout ...
... Lots of pecan trees.

★★½ SCOTT SCHREINER KERRVILLE MUNICIPAL GOLF COURSE

PU-1 Country Club Dr., Kerrville, 78028, Kerr County, (830)257-4982, 60 miles from
San Antonio. **E-mail:** pga@kerrville.org. **Web:** www.kerrville.org. **Facility Holes:** 18. **Yards:**
6,453/4,826. **Par:** 70/70. **Course Rating:** 71.6/67.8. **Slope:** 126/104. **Green Fee:** $12/$18. **Cart
Fee:** $18/Cart. **Walking Policy:** Unrestricted walking. **Walkability:** 2. **Opened:** 1921. **Architect:**
John Bredemus/R.D. Kaiser/Joe Finger. **Season:** Year-round. **To obtain tee times:** Call up to 7

days in advance. **Miscellaneous:** Reduced fees (twilight, juniors), range (grass), credit cards (MC, V), BF, FF.

★★ SEVEN OAKS RESORT & COUNTRY CLUB

SP-1300 Circle Dr., Mission, 78572, Hidalgo County, (956)581-6267, 7 miles from McAllen.
E-mail: seven_oaks_resort@yahoo.com. **Web:** www.7oaksresort.com. **Facility Holes:** 18.
Yards: 6,089/4,867. **Par:** 70/70. **Course Rating:** 69.3/69.0. **Slope:** 113/111. **Green Fee:** $17.
Cart Fee: $17/Cart. **Walking Policy:** Unrestricted walking. **Walkability:** 1. **Opened:** 1983.
Season: Year-round. **To obtain tee times:** Call golf shop. **Miscellaneous:** Reduced fees
(juniors), range (grass/mats), credit cards (MC, V, AE, D), BF, FF.

★★½ SHADOW HILLS GOLF COURSE

PU-6002 3rd St., Lubbock, 79499, Lubbock County, (806)793-9700. **E-mail:** shgc@door.net.
Facility Holes: 18. **Yards:** 6,777/5,594. **Par:** 72/72. **Course Rating:** 71.2/71.2. **Slope:** 118/118.
Green Fee: $10/$19. **Cart Fee:** $9/Person. **Walking Policy:** Unrestricted walking. **Walkability:** 3.
Opened: 1982. **Season:** Year-round. **High:** June-Aug. **To obtain tee times:** Call golf shop.
Miscellaneous: Reduced fees (weekdays, twilight, seniors, juniors), metal spikes, range
(grass), credit cards (MC, V, D).

★½ SHARPSTOWN MUNICIPAL GOLF COURSE

PU-6600 Harbor Town Dr., Houston, 77036, Harris County, (713)988-2099. **Facility Holes:** 18.
Yards: 6,660/5,883. **Par:** 70/72. **Course Rating:** 69.7/72.0. **Slope:** 113/113. **Green Fee:** $7/$17.
Cart Fee: $17/Cart. **Walking Policy:** Unrestricted walking. **Walkability:** 1. **Opened:** 1957.
Architect: Ralph Plummer/Jay Riviere. **Season:** Year-round. **High:** April-Oct. **To obtain tee
times:** Call up to 3 days in advance. **Miscellaneous:** Reduced fees (weekdays, twilight,
seniors, juniors), range (mats), credit cards (MC, V), FF.

SHARY MUNICIPAL GOLF COURSE

PU-2201 Mayberry, Mission, 78572, Hidalgo County, (956)580-8770, 6 miles from McAllen.
Facility Holes: 27. **Green Fee:** $12. **Cart Fee:** $17/Cart. **Walking Policy:** Unrestricted walking.
Walkability: 1. **Season:** Year-round. **High:** Jan.-March. **To obtain tee times:** Call golf shop.
Miscellaneous: Reduced fees (juniors), range (grass), credit cards (MC, V, AE, D, Diner's
Club).
★★ **18-HOLE COURSE** (18)
Yards: 6,025/4,893. **Par:** 71/71. **Course Rating:** 68.9/68.8. **Slope:** 105/105. **Opened:** 1929.
Architect: George Williams.
9-HOLE COURSE (9)
Yards: 3,143/2,754. **Par:** 36/36. **Course Rating:** 72.4/70.2. **Slope:** 122/107. **Opened:** 1994.

SHERRILL PARK GOLF COURSE

PU-2001 E. Lookout Dr., Richardson, 75082, Collin County, (972)234-1416, 10 miles from
Dallas. **Facility Holes:** 36. **Cart Fee:** $10/Person. **Walking Policy:** Unrestricted walking.
Walkability: 3. **Season:** Year-round. **To obtain tee times:** Call up to 7 days in advance.
Miscellaneous: Reduced fees (weekdays, twilight, seniors, juniors), range (grass), credit
cards (MC, V), BF, FF.
★★★ **COURSE NO. 1** (18)
Yards: 6,900/5,182. **Par:** 72/72. **Course Rating:** 72.4/70.0. **Slope:** 124/120. **Green Fee:**
$22/$30. **Opened:** 1973. **Architect:** D.A. Weibring and Golf Resources.
Reader Comments: Much improved after redesign ... Good muni ... Don't need a driver ...
Enjoyable place to play and not overpriced ... Drive on 18 is pure and testy ... Lovely treelined golf
course ... Hot, dry summer! But fun ... Good muni if you can get on.
★★ **COURSE NO. 2** (18)
Yards: 6,083/5,476. **Par:** 70/70. **Course Rating:** 66.0/66.0. **Slope:** 113/109. **Green Fee:**
$14/$17. **Opened:** 1976. **Architect:** D.A. Weibring.

★★★ SIENNA PLANTATION GOLF CLUB

PU-1 Waters Lake Blvd., Missouri City, 77459, Fort Bend County, (281)778-4653, 30 miles
from Houston. **E-mail:** brookssimmons@entouch.net. **Web:** www.siennagolf.com. **Facility
Holes:** 18. **Yards:** 7,151/5,239. **Par:** 72/72. **Course Rating:** 73.9/71.7. **Slope:** 129/124. **Green
Fee:** $31/$51. **Cart Fee:** $14/Person. **Walking Policy:** Walking at certain times. **Walkability:** 2.
Opened: 2000. **Architect:** Arthur Hills/Mike Dasher. **Season:** Year-round. **High:** April-May.
To obtain tee times: Call up to 7 days in advance. **Miscellaneous:** Reduced fees (weekdays,
twilight, seniors, juniors), credit cards (MC, V, AE, D), BF, FF.
Reader Comments: A great course ... long and tight ... What a layout! Hills masterpiece ... Great
new place to play, you can lay up or go for it, good people ... Needs 2 or 3 years of growth ... One
of the better new courses in the Houston area.

★★★½ SILVERHORN GOLF CLUB OF TEXAS

PU-1100 W. Bitters Rd., San Antonio, 78216, Bexar County, (210)545-5300, 12 miles from

San Antonio. **Facility Holes:** 18. **Yards:** 6,922/5,271. **Par:** 72/72. **Course Rating:** 73.1/66.4. **Slope:** 129/109. **Green Fee:** $75/$80. **Cart Fee:** Included in green fee. **Walking Policy:** Unrestricted walking. **Walkability:** 2. **Opened:** 1995. **Architect:** Randy Heckenkemper. **Season:** Year-round. **To obtain tee times:** Call golf shop. **Miscellaneous:** Reduced fees (twilight, seniors, juniors), metal spikes, range (grass), credit cards (MC, V, AE, D).
Reader Comments: Nice upscale course … Long but very challenging … Great site for value … Great facilities, very tough … Tree-lined fairways are a killer … An exciting well-run operation … Wonderful course-pricey … A number of fun thinking par 5s … Good layout.

★★ SINTON MUNICIPAL GOLF COURSE
PU-Robert Welder Park Hwy. No. 181, Sinton, 78387, San Patricio County, (361)364-9013, 30 miles from Corpus Christi. **Facility Holes:** 18. **Yards:** 6,572/5,412. **Par:** 72/72. **Course Rating:** 71.1/71.0. **Slope:** 116/118. **Green Fee:** $9/$10. **Cart Fee:** $18/Cart. **Walking Policy:** Unrestricted walking. **Walkability:** 1. **Opened:** 1956. **Season:** Year-round. **High:** Dec.-Aug. **To obtain tee times:** Call golf shop. **Miscellaneous:** Reduced fees (juniors), range (grass), FF.

★★★★ SKY CREEK RANCH GOLF CLUB
PU-600 Promontory Dr., Keller, 76248, Tarrant County, (817)498-1414, 10 miles from Fort Worth. **Facility Holes:** 18. **Yards:** 6,953/5,390. **Par:** 72/72. **Course Rating:** 73.4/72.8. **Slope:** 136/132. **Green Fee:** $45/$85. **Walking Policy:** Walking at certain times. **Opened:** 1999. **Architect:** Robert Trent Jones Jr./Gary Linn. **Season:** Year-round. **High:** March-Oct. **To obtain tee times:** Call up to 7 days in advance. **Miscellaneous:** Reduced fees (weekdays, twilight, seniors, juniors), range (grass), credit cards (MC, V, AE, D, DC), BF, FF.
Reader Comments: Excellent layout … Nice course … Tough track … Beautiful new course, could be outstanding … Top notch greens … A great new course! Super layout … Tremendous course—too steep $.

★★½ SLEEPY HOLLOW GOLF & COUNTRY CLUB
SP-4747 S. Loop 12, Dallas, 75216, Dallas County, (214)371-3433, 7 miles from Dallas. **Facility Holes:** 36. **Yards:** 7,031/5,878. **Par:** 71/71. **Course Rating:** 73.4/74.1. **Slope:** 125/123. **Green Fee:** $20/$30. **Cart Fee:** $12/Person. **Walking Policy:** Unrestricted walking. **Walkability:** 2. **Opened:** 1961. **Architect:** Press Maxwell. **Season:** Year-round. **High:** March-Nov. **To obtain tee times:** Call golf shop. **Miscellaneous:** Reduced fees (twilight), metal spikes, range (grass), credit cards (MC, V, AE, D), FF.
Special Notes: Also has an 18-hole private course.

★★★★ SOUTH PADRE ISLAND GOLF CLUB
R-1 Golf House Dr., Laguna Vista, 78578, Cameron County, (956)943-5678, 7 miles from South Padre Island. **E-mail:** spigc@ies.net. **Web:** www.spigolf.com. **Facility Holes:** 18. **Yards:** 6,931/5,406. **Par:** 72/72. **Course Rating:** 73.1/68.0. **Slope:** 130/116. **Green Fee:** $29/$60. **Cart Fee:** Included in green fee. **Walking Policy:** Unrestricted walking. **Walkability:** 3. **Opened:** 1997. **Architect:** Chris Cole/Steve Caplinger. **Season:** Year-round. **High:** May-Aug. **To obtain tee times:** Call golf shop. **Miscellaneous:** Reduced fees (weekdays, guests, twilight, seniors, juniors), metal spikes, range (grass), credit cards (MC, V, AE, D), FF.
Reader Comments: Good facility, great layout, watch for snakes … Too windy!! … A very nice championship course … Will get better as course matures … Bring your low punch shot … By far the best course in the Rio Grande Valley of Texas.

★★★★ SOUTHERN OAKS GOLF CLUB
PU-13765 Southern Oaks Dr., Burleson, 76028, Tarrant County, (817)426-2400. **Web:** www.southernoaksgolf.com. **Facility Holes:** 18. **Yards:** 7,302/5,369. **Par:** 71/71. **Course Rating:** 75.0/71.6. **Slope:** 132/120. **Green Fee:** $50/$65. **Cart Fee:** Included in green fee. **Walking Policy:** Unrestricted walking. **Walkability:** 3. **Opened:** 1999. **Architect:** Mark Brooks. **Season:** Year-round. **High:** March-Nov. **To obtain tee times:** Call golf shop. **Miscellaneous:** Reduced fees (weekdays, twilight, seniors, juniors), range (grass), credit cards (MC, V, AE, D).
Notes: Ranked 24th in 2001 Best in State.
Reader Comments: Championship golf course at muni prices … Mark Brooks staff is super … Great layout, long par 4s, excellent value … Enjoyable course, but bring your sand game … Deep bunkers and treelined with generous fairways … Very demanding but fair.

★★★ SOUTHWYCK GOLF CLUB
PU-2901 Clubhouse Dr., Pearland, 77584, Brazoria County, (713)436-9999, 10 miles from Houston. **Facility Holes:** 18. **Yards:** 7,015/5,211. **Par:** 72/72. **Course Rating:** 72.9/68.9. **Slope:** 123/112. **Green Fee:** $35/$48. **Cart Fee:** $12/Person. **Walking Policy:** Walking at certain times. **Walkability:** 3. **Opened:** 1988. **Architect:** Ken Kavanaugh. **Season:** Year-round. **High:** March-Oct. **To obtain tee times:** Call up to 7 days in advance. **Miscellaneous:** Reduced fees (weekdays, twilight, seniors, juniors), range (grass), credit cards (MC, V, AE, D), BF, FF.
Reader Comments: Links layout, rough severe, windy … Good potential … No trees! … Nice layout, fun course … Wind, wind, go away … Lots of sand … Good greens.

TEXAS

★★★★½ **SQUAW VALLEY GOLF COURSE** *Value+, Condition, Pace*
PU-HCR 51-45B Hwy. 67, Glen Rose, 76043, Somervell County, (254)897-7956, (800)831-8259, 60 miles from Fort Worth. **Facility Holes:** 18. **Yards:** 7,062/5,014. **Par:** 72/72. **Course Rating:** 73.6/70.0. **Slope:** 130/117. **Green Fee:** $22/$30. **Cart Fee:** $10/Person. **Walking Policy:** Walking at certain times. **Walkability:** 4. **Opened:** 1992. **Architect:** Jeff Brauer. **Season:** Year-round. **High:** April-Oct. **To obtain tee times:** Call golf shop. **Miscellaneous:** Reduced fees (weekdays, twilight, seniors), metal spikes, range (grass/mats), credit cards (MC, V, D).
Reader Comments: Best condition and staff for the money without question ... This is one that everyone should play! ... Wide fairways and big greens ... Fun to play.

★★½ **STEPHEN F. AUSTIN GOLF COURSE**
SP-Park Rd. 38, San Felipe, 77473, Austin County, (979)885-2811, 40 miles from Houston. **E-mail:** rkbco@evi.net. **Web:** www.sfaustingc.com. **Facility Holes:** 18. **Yards:** 5,813/5,137. **Par:** 70/70. **Course Rating:** 67.3/69.7. **Slope:** 120/111. **Green Fee:** $19/$27. **Cart Fee:** $10/Person. **Walking Policy:** Walking at certain times. **Walkability:** 3. **Opened:** 1953. **Architect:** Members. **Season:** Year-round. **To obtain tee times:** Call golf shop. **Miscellaneous:** Reduced fees (seniors), range (grass), credit cards (MC, V, AE, D), BF, FF.

★★★½ **STEVENS PARK GOLF COURSE**
PU-1005 N. Montclair, Dallas, 75208, Dallas County, (214)670-7506. **Facility Holes:** 18. **Yards:** 6,005/5,000. **Par:** 71/71. **Course Rating:** 69.2/68.0. **Slope:** 120/118. **Green Fee:** $14/$17. **Cart Fee:** $18/Cart. **Walking Policy:** Unrestricted walking. **Walkability:** 4. **Opened:** 1922. **Architect:** Arthur Davis. **Season:** Year-round. **To obtain tee times:** Call up to 4 days in advance. **Miscellaneous:** Reduced fees (weekdays, twilight, seniors, juniors), credit cards (MC, V, D), BF, FF.
Reader Comments: One of my favorite 'old style' courses ... Good course although crowded and slow on weekends ... Nice views of trees, exclusive neighborhoods and the Dallas skyline.

★★★★ **SUGARTREE GOLF CLUB** *Value, Pace*
SP-Hwy. 1189, P.O. Box 98, Dennis, 76439, Parker County, (817)596-4991, 35 miles from Fort Worth. **Web:** www.sugartreegolf.com. **Facility Holes:** 18. **Yards:** 6,775/5,254. **Par:** 71/71. **Course Rating:** 72.8/71.0. **Slope:** 138/126. **Green Fee:** $27/$36. **Cart Fee:** $10/Person. **Walking Policy:** Unrestricted walking. **Walkability:** 3. **Opened:** 1987. **Architect:** Phil Lumsden. **Season:** Year-round. **High:** April-Oct. **To obtain tee times:** Call up to 7 days in advance. **Miscellaneous:** Reduced fees (weekdays, twilight, seniors, juniors), range (grass), credit cards (MC, V, AE, D), BF, FF.
Reader Comments: Don't pass this one by, you'll regret it ... Beautiful layout ... Tough, tight track from tips ... Never crowded ... Lot of course for the money ... Worth the drive from DFW ... Shotmaker's course ... Lots of doglegs and lots of character.

★★★½ **SWEETWATER COUNTRY CLUB**
SP-1900 Country Club Lane, Sweetwater, 79556, Nolan County, (915)235-8093, 45 miles from Abilene. **Facility Holes:** 18. **Yards:** 6,362/5,316. **Par:** 71/72. **Course Rating:** 70.0. **Slope:** 118. **Green Fee:** $15/$25. **Cart Fee:** $16/Cart. **Walking Policy:** Unrestricted walking. **Walkability:** 2. **Opened:** 1957. **Architect:** M.C. Alston. **Season:** Year-round. **To obtain tee times:** Call golf shop. **Miscellaneous:** Reduced fees (twilight), range (grass/mats), BF, FF.
Reader Comments: Fair course ... Best little course in Texas ... A small town haven for golfers ... Best sports facility in Houston ... Great gym, good food ... Both courses are long, but not too narrow.

★★★½ **TANGLERIDGE GOLF CLUB**
PU-818 TangleRidge Dr., Grand Prairie, 75052, Dallas County, (972)299-6837, 30 miles from Dallas. **Facility Holes:** 18. **Yards:** 6,835/5,187. **Par:** 72/72. **Course Rating:** 72.2/70.2. **Slope:** 129/117. **Green Fee:** $28/$49. **Cart Fee:** $12/Person. **Walking Policy:** Unrestricted walking. **Walkability:** 4. **Opened:** 1995. **Architect:** Jeff Brauer. **Season:** Year-round. **To obtain tee times:** Call up to 7 days in advance. **Miscellaneous:** Reduced fees (twilight, seniors, juniors), range (grass), credit cards (MC, V, AE, D), BF, FF.
Notes: Ranked 12th in 1999 Best in State.
Reader Comments: Great layout ... Nice design ... Average condition ... Have to hit every shot in your bag ... Nice course and nice people.

★★★½ **TANGLEWOOD RESORT**
R-290 Tanglewood Circle, Pottsboro, 75076, Grayson County, (903)786-4140, (800)833-6569, 68 miles from Dallas. **E-mail:** twgolf@texoma.net. **Web:** www.tanglewoodresort.com. **Facility Holes:** 18. **Yards:** 6,993/4,925. **Par:** 72/72. **Course Rating:** 73.7/67.5. **Slope:** 128/104. **Green Fee:** $38/$48. **Cart Fee:** $14/Person. **Walking Policy:** Walking at certain times. **Walkability:** 3. **Opened:** 1971. **Architect:** Ralph Plummer/Arnold Palmer. **Season:** Year-round. **High:** Sept.-

Nov. **To obtain tee times:** Call up to 7 days in advance. **Miscellaneous:** Reduced fees (twilight, juniors), range (grass), credit cards (MC, V, AE, D), BF, FF.
Reader Comments: A good challenge from back tees ... Well-maintained course ... Excellent! Best course in northern Texas ... Good value for the money-nice course ... Good resort ... Lovely area, especially the wildlife.

★★★★ TAPATIO SPRINGS RESORT & CONFERENCE CENTER
SP-W. Johns Rd., Boerne, 78006, Kendall County, (830)537-4197, (800)999-3299, 25 miles from San Antonio. **E-mail:** jess@tapatio.com. **Web:** www.tapatio.com. **Facility Holes:** 27. **Green Fee:** $80/$95. **Cart Fee:** Included in green fee. **Walking Policy:** Mandatory carts. **Walkability:** 4. **Opened:** 1980. **Architect:** Bill Johnston. **Season:** Year-round. **To obtain tee times:** Call up to 7 days in advance. **Miscellaneous:** Reduced fees (weekdays, guests, twilight, juniors), range (grass/mats), lodging (123 rooms), credit cards (MC, V, AE, D), BF, FF.
LAKES/VALLEY (18 Combo)
Yards: 6,504/5,185. **Par:** 72/72. **Course Rating:** 71.4/70.4. **Slope:** 133/127.
RIDGE/LAKES (18 Combo)
Yards: 6,265/4,757. **Par:** 70/70. **Course Rating:** 70.5/67.9. **Slope:** 130/118.
VALLEY/RIDGE (18 Combo)
Yards: 6,513/5,122. **Par:** 72/72. **Course Rating:** 71.7/70.2. **Slope:** 133/126.
Reader Comments: Very nice Hill Country course ... Most beautiful land in Texas ... Great condition always ... Nice resort course ... Greens can be hard ... Hard to get to, but rewarding, great food and service ... Gift from God ... Fascinating design with a nice clubhouse.

TENISON PARK GOLF COURSE
PU-3501 Samuell, Dallas, 75223, Dallas County, (214)670-1402, 3 miles from Dallas. **E-mail:** dmasanda@tenisonpark.com. **Web:** www.tenisonpark.com. **Facility Holes:** 36. **Green Fee:** $14/$17. **Walking Policy:** Unrestricted walking. **Season:** Year-round. **High:** March-June.
To obtain tee times: Call up to 4 days in advance. **Miscellaneous:** Reduced fees (weekdays, twilight, seniors, juniors), range (mats), credit cards (MC, V, AE), BF, FF.
★★★ **TENISON GLEN** (18)
Yards: 6,605/5,107. **Par:** 72/72. **Course Rating:** 71.2/70.8. **Slope:** 122/115. **Cart Fee:** $20/Cart.
Walkability: 2. **Opened:** 1927. **Architect:** Ralph Plummer.
Reader Comments: Lot of history, nice new facelift ... Challenging, tight muni course ... Course always in OK shape.
★★★ **TENISON HIGHLANDS** (18)
Yards: 7,078/4,883. **Par:** 72/75. **Course Rating:** 72.0/72.2. **Slope:** 121/118. **Cart Fee:** $17/Cart.
Walkability: 4. **Opened:** 2000. **Architect:** D.A. Weibring/Steve Wolford.
Reader Comments: Excellent big city course ... A hilly site for the middle of Dallas ... Renovation opened in fall, needs a bit of maturity ... Very well laid out in the heart of east Dallas ... Lee Trevino played here.

★½ TEXAS A&M UNIVERSITY GOLF COURSE
PU-3152 TAMU, College Station, 77843, Brazos County, (409)845-1723, 100 miles from Houston. **E-mail:** rkahlich@rec.tamu.edu. **Web:** www.recsports.tamu.edu.com. **Facility Holes:** 18. **Yards:** 6,479/4,871. **Par:** 71/71. **Course Rating:** 70.2/71.4. **Slope:** 122/111. **Green Fee:** $20/$25. **Cart Fee:** $20/Cart. **Walking Policy:** Unrestricted walking. **Walkability:** 3. **Opened:** 1951. **Architect:** Ralph Plummer/Jackie Burke Jr. **Season:** Year-round. **To obtain tee times:** Call up to 7 days in advance. **Miscellaneous:** Reduced fees (weekdays, twilight, seniors, juniors), metal spikes, range (grass), credit cards (MC, V, AE, D), BF, FF.

★★★★ TEXAS STAR GOLF COURSE
PU-1400 Texas Star Pkwy., Euless, 76040, Tarrant County, (817)685-7888, (888)839-7827, 6 miles from Dallas. **Web:** www.texasstargolf.com. **Facility Holes:** 18. **Yards:** 6,936/4,962. **Par:** 71/71. **Course Rating:** 73.6/69.7. **Slope:** 135/124. **Green Fee:** $57/$77. **Cart Fee:** Included in green fee. **Walking Policy:** Unrestricted walking. **Walkability:** 4. **Opened:** 1997. **Architect:** Keith Foster. **Season:** Year-round. **To obtain tee times:** Call up to 5 days in advance. **Miscellaneous:** Reduced fees (twilight, seniors, juniors), range (grass/mats), credit cards (MC, V, AE, D, DC), BF, FF.
Reader Comments: Great layout with the toughest greens in north Texas ... Excellent staff ... Good value ... Best city-run course ... Excellent shape ... First class for a public course ... Some really neat holes! ... Audubon areas are beautiful... Blind shots all over ... The best public greens I have played ... Bring lots-o-balls.

★★★★ TIERRA SANTA GOLF CLUB *Condition*
PU-1901 Club de Amistad, Weslaco, 78596, Hidalgo County, (956)973-1811, (800)838-5769, 3.5 miles from Weslaco. **Web:** www.tierrasantacc.com. **Facility Holes:** 18. **Yards:** 7,101/5,283. **Par:** 72/72. **Course Rating:** 74.5/72.5. **Slope:** 140/125. **Green Fee:** $26/$39. **Cart Fee:** $12/Person. **Walking Policy:** Unrestricted walking. **Walkability:** 3. **Opened:** 1997. **Architect:** Jeff Brauer. **Season:** Year-round. **To obtain tee times:** Call up to 2 days in advance.

Miscellaneous: Reduced fees (weekdays, guests, twilight, seniors, juniors), range (grass), credit cards (MC, V, AE, D, DC).

Reader Comments: Great course for this part of the state … Definitely worth the trip … Great practice area, no pull carts … Oh and the greens, talk about a true roll … The best course in south TX.

★★★★ TIERRA VERDE GOLF CLUB

PU-7005 Golf Club Dr., Arlington, 76001, Tarrant County, (817)478-8500. **Facility Holes:** 18. **Yards:** 6,995/5,111. **Par:** 72/72. **Course Rating:** 73.3/70.5. **Slope:** 129/119. **Green Fee:** $51/$60. **Cart Fee:** Included in green fee. **Opened:** 2000. **Architect:** David Graham/Gary Panks. **Season:** Jan.-Nov. **To obtain tee times:** Call golf shop. **Miscellaneous:** Reduced fees (weekdays, seniors), metal spikes, credit cards (MC, V, D).

Reader Comments: My favorite course … Fun to play … Excellent value … City course with a country feel … Best city course for your $$, excellent condition … Great setting … Fun course.

★★★ TIMARRON GOLF & COUNTRY CLUB

PU-14000 Byron Nelson Pkwy., Southlake, 76092, Tarrant County, (817)481-7529, 20 miles from Ft. Worth. **Facility Holes:** 18. **Yards:** 7,100/5,330. **Par:** 72/72. **Course Rating:** 74.2/71.3. **Slope:** 137/120. **Green Fee:** $45/$60. **Cart Fee:** Included in green fee. **Walking Policy:** Mandatory carts. **Opened:** 1994. **Architect:** Byron Nelson /Baxter Spann. **Season:** Year-round. **High:** March-April. **To obtain tee times:** Call golf shop. **Miscellaneous:** Reduced fees (weekdays), metal spikes, range (grass), credit cards (MC, V, AE).

Notes: Ranked 9th in 1999 Best in State; 7th in 1995 Best New Public Courses.

Reader Comments: Interesting finishing hole … Beautiful design, fun to play … Modern layout with some great holes and blind shots … Carts tell exact yardage to pin and/or water … Great par-5 18th with island green … Best course in Dallas area, beautiful clubhouse.

★ TIMBER-VIEW GOLF COURSE

PU-4508 E. Enon, Fort Worth, 76140, Tarrant County, (817)478-3601, 10 miles from Fort Worth. **Facility Holes:** 18. **Yards:** 6,491/5,406. **Par:** 72/72. **Green Fee:** $9/$18. **Cart Fee:** $16/Cart. **Walking Policy:** Unrestricted walking. **Walkability:** 1. **Opened:** 1963. **Architect:** Thomas Fouts. **Season:** Year-round. **High:** March-Sept. **To obtain tee times:** Call golf shop. **Miscellaneous:** Reduced fees (weekdays, seniors).

TONY BUTLER GOLF COURSE

PU-2640 S. M St., Harlingen, 78550, Cameron County, (956)430-6685, 120 miles from Corpus Christi. **Facility Holes:** 27. **Cart Fee:** $9/Person. **Walking Policy:** Unrestricted walking. **Season:** Year-round. **High:** Oct.-March. **To obtain tee times:** Call golf shop. **Miscellaneous:** Reduced fees (juniors), metal spikes, range (grass), credit cards (MC, V).

★★ 18-HOLE COURSE (18)
Yards: 6,320/5,680. **Par:** 71/71. **Course Rating:** 69.1/69.1. **Slope:** 113/112. **Green Fee:** $10. **Opened:** 1927. **Architect:** Dennis W. Arp.

9-HOLE COURSE (9)
Yards: 2,881/2,467. **Par:** 35/35. **Opened:** 1929.

★★★★ TOUR 18

PU-3102 FM 1960 E., Humble, 77338, Harris County, (281)540-1818, (800)856-8687, 22 miles from Houston. **Web:** www.tour18.com. **Facility Holes:** 18. **Yards:** 6,782/5,380. **Par:** 72/72. **Course Rating:** 72.2/66.6. **Slope:** 126/113. **Green Fee:** $65/$95. **Cart Fee:** Included in green fee. **Walking Policy:** Mandatory carts. **Walkability:** 3. **Opened:** 1992. **Architect:** Dennis Wilkerson. **Season:** Year-round. **To obtain tee times:** Call up to 30 days in advance. **Miscellaneous:** Reduced fees (twilight, juniors), range (grass/mats), credit cards (MC, V, AE), BF, FF.

Reader Comments: Not gimmicky, just a solid, fun track … A great course with good service … Like the concept … Great to play the replica holes … Good course, must play at least one time … You don't pay Rolex prices for a fake … This fun course is a must.

★★★★ TOUR 18 GOLF CLUB

PU-8718 Amen Corner, Flower Mound, 75022, Tarrant County, (817)430-2000, (800)946-5310, 10 miles from Dallas. **E-mail:** sbrady@palmergolf.com. **Web:** www.tour18golf.com. **Facility Holes:** 18. **Yards:** 7,033/5,493. **Par:** 72/72. **Course Rating:** 74.3/66.3. **Slope:** 138/119. **Green Fee:** $59/$95. **Cart Fee:** Included in green fee. **Walking Policy:** Mandatory carts. **Walkability:** 4. **Opened:** 1995. **Architect:** Dave Edsall. **Season:** Year-round. **To obtain tee times:** Call up to 30 days in advance. **Miscellaneous:** Reduced fees (twilight), range (grass/mats), credit cards (MC, V, AE), BF, FF.

Reader Comments: Great fun playing fantasy golf on course that replicated great holes … 19th hole seems to be a Dallas Cowboys hangout … Makes one appreciate great design … Expensive! … Lightning fast greens.

THE TRAILS OF FRISCO GOLF CLUB
SP-10411 Teel Pkwy., Frisco, 75034, Collin County, (972)668-4653. **Facility Holes:** 18. **Yards:** 6,959/5,104. **Par:** 71/71. **Course Rating:** 74.0/65.0. **Slope:** 138/111. **Green Fee:** $55/$75. **Cart Fee:** Included in green fee. **Opened:** 2000. **Season:** Year-round. **To obtain tee times:** Call up to 7 days in advance. **Miscellaneous:** Reduced fees (weekdays, twilight, seniors, juniors).

★½ TREELINE GOLF CLUB
SP-17505 N. Eldridge Pkwy., Tomball, 77375, Harris County, (281)376-1542, (888)800-5199, 12 miles from Houston. **E-mail:** rampy@treelinegolf.com. **Web:** www.treelinegolf.com. **Facility Holes:** 18. **Yards:** 6,010/4,752. **Par:** 70/70. **Course Rating:** 68.4/62.3. **Slope:** 117/99. **Green Fee:** $13/$33. **Cart Fee:** $10/Person. **Walking Policy:** Unrestricted walking. **Walkability:** 2. **Opened:** 1953. **Architect:** Jay Riviere. **Season:** Year-round. **To obtain tee times:** Call up to 6 days in advance. **Miscellaneous:** Reduced fees (weekdays, twilight, seniors, juniors), range (grass), credit cards (MC, V, AE, D), BF, FF.

THE TRIBUTE GOLF CLUB
R-1000 Boyd Rd, The Colony, 75056, Denton County, (972)370-5465, 20 miles from Dallas. **Web:** www.thetexasgolftrail.com. **Facility Holes:** 18. **Yards:** 7,002/5,302. **Par:** 72/72. **Course Rating:** 73.2/65.6. **Slope:** 128/111. **Green Fee:** $50/$105. **Cart Fee:** Included in green fee. **Walking Policy:** Walking at certain times. **Walkability:** 1. **Opened:** 2000. **Architect:** Tripp Davis. **Season:** Year-round. **To obtain tee times:** Call up to 7 days in advance. **Miscellaneous:** Reduced fees (weekdays, guests, twilight, seniors, juniors), range (grass), lodging (7 rooms), credit cards (MC, V, AE, D, DC), FF.

★★★ TURTLE HILL GOLF COURSE
PU-Rte. 373 N., P.O. Box 660, Muenster, 76252, Cooke County, (940)759-4896, (877)759-4896, 18 miles from Gainesville. **E-mail:** theturtle@nortexinfo.net. **Web:** www.theturtle.com. **Facility Holes:** 18. **Yards:** 6,510/4,821. **Par:** 72/73. **Course Rating:** 72.2/69.5. **Slope:** 123/116. **Green Fee:** $22/$34. **Cart Fee:** Included in green fee. **Walking Policy:** Unrestricted walking. **Walkability:** 5. **Opened:** 1993. **Architect:** Dick Murphy. **Season:** Year-round. **High:** April-Sept. **To obtain tee times:** Call golf shop. **Miscellaneous:** Reduced fees (weekdays, twilight, seniors, juniors), metal spikes, range (grass/mats), credit cards (MC, V, D).
Reader Comments: Nice scenic fairways … Should get better with improvements initiated by new owner … Scenic course … North Texas secret … Best greens in Texas for $ … Remote location, hilly … Great greens … Several interesting holes.

★★★ TWIN CREEKS GOLF CLUB
PU-501 Twin Creeks Dr., Allen, 75013, Collin County, (972)390-8888, 20 miles from Dallas. **E-mail:** tcarter@twincreeks.co. **Web:** www.twincreeks.com. **Facility Holes:** 18. **Yards:** 6,924/4,790. **Par:** 72/72. **Course Rating:** 73.2/66.5. **Slope:** 131/107. **Green Fee:** $40/$60. **Cart Fee:** $15/Person. **Walking Policy:** Unrestricted walking. **Walkability:** 2. **Opened:** 1995. **Architect:** Palmer Course Design Co. **Season:** Year-round. **To obtain tee times:** Call up to 5 days in advance. **Miscellaneous:** Reduced fees (weekdays, twilight, seniors, juniors), range (grass/mats), credit cards (MC, V, AE, D, DC), BF, FF.
Reader Comments: Well-maintained, enjoyable layout … This could be a wonderful facility with better maintenance … Nice track … Too expensive for what you get … Short but tough.

★★½ TWIN WELLS GOLF COURSE
PU-2000 E. Shady Grove Rd., Irving, 75060, Dallas County, (972)438-4340, 2 miles from Texas Stadium. **Facility Holes:** 18. **Yards:** 6,636/6,239. **Par:** 72/72. **Course Rating:** 70.9/69.3. **Slope:** 117/113. **Green Fee:** $18/$28. **Cart Fee:** $22/Cart. **Walking Policy:** Unrestricted walking. **Walkability:** 2. **Opened:** 1988. **Architect:** Brian Ault/Bill Love. **Season:** Year-round. **High:** March-Dec. **To obtain tee times:** Call golf shop. **Miscellaneous:** Reduced fees (weekdays, twilight, seniors, juniors), range (grass/mats), credit cards (MC, V, AE).

★ TYLER FAMILY GOLF CENTER
PU-800 Bellwood Golf Rd., Tyler, 75709, Smith County, (903)597-2100. **Facility Holes:** 18. **Cart Fee:** $0/Cart. **Walking Policy:** Unrestricted walking. **Season:** Year-round. **To obtain tee times:** Call golf shop. **Miscellaneous:** Range (grass), BF.
Special Notes: Formerly Cross Creek Golf Club.

UNDERWOOD GOLF COMPLEX
M-3200 Coe Ave., El Paso, 79904, El Paso County, (915)562-2066. **E-mail:** kaerwerb@bliss.army.mil. **Facility Holes:** 36. **Green Fee:** $6/$18. **Cart Fee:** $16/Cart. **Walking Policy:** Unrestricted walking. **Season:** Year-round. **To obtain tee times:** Call golf shop. **Miscellaneous:** Reduced fees (weekdays, twilight, juniors), range (grass), credit cards (MC, V, D), BF, FF.

SUNRISE COURSE (18)
Yards: 6,942/5,498. **Par:** 72/72. **Course Rating:** 73.1/71.1. **Slope:** 126/124. **Walkability:** 3.
Opened: 1993. **Architect:** Finger-Dye-Spann.
★★★ **SUNSET COURSE** (18)
Yards: 6,629/5,531. **Par:** 72/72. **Course Rating:** 70.4/70.4. **Slope:** 120/109. **Walkability:** 1.
Opened: 1945.
Reader Comments: Grass on greens kept very well ... Flat ... Narrow fairways with lots of rough ...
This is an army course, well kept.

★★ **VALLEY INN & COUNTRY CLUB**
SP-FM Rd. 802 and Central Blvd., Brownsville, 78520, Cameron County, (956)548-9199.
Facility Holes: 18. **Yards:** 6,538/4,924. **Par:** 70/71. **Course Rating:** 72.3/69.7. **Slope:** 125/116.
Green Fee: $15/$17. **Cart Fee:** $18/Cart. **Walking Policy:** Walking at certain times. **Walkability:**
2. **Opened:** 1917. **Season:** Year-round. **High:** Jan.-March. **To obtain tee times:** Call up to 7
days in advance. **Miscellaneous:** Reduced fees (twilight), credit cards (MC, V, AE, D), BF, FF.

WATERVIEW GOLF CLUB
PU-9509 Waterview Pkwy., Rowlett, 75089, Dallas County, (972)463-8900. **Facility Holes:** 18.
Yards: 7,191/5,472. **Par:** 72/72. **Course Rating:** 74.1/65.6. **Slope:** 128/106. **Green Fee:**
$20/$54. **Cart Fee:** Included in green fee. **Opened:** 2000. **Season:** Year-round. **To obtain tee
times:** Call up to 7 days in advance. **Miscellaneous:** Reduced fees (weekdays, twilight,
seniors, juniors).

★★★½ **WATERWOOD NATIONAL RESORT & COUNTRY CLUB** *Pace*
R-One Waterwood, Huntsville, 77320, San Jacinto County, (936)891-5050, (877)441-5211,
75 miles from Houston. **E-mail:** headpro@txucom.net. **Web:** www.waterwoodnational.com.
Facility Holes: 18. **Yards:** 6,906/5,029. **Par:** 71/73. **Course Rating:** 73.7/68.0. **Slope:** 142/117.
Green Fee: $45/$65. **Cart Fee:** Included in green fee. **Walking Policy:** Unrestricted walking.
Walkability: 3. **Opened:** 1975. **Architect:** Pete Dye. **Season:** Year-round. **To obtain tee times:**
Call up to 7 days in advance. **Miscellaneous:** Reduced fees (twilight, seniors, juniors), range
(grass), credit cards (MC, V, AE, D), BF, FF.
Notes: Ranked 8th in 2001 Best in State.
Reader Comments: Course that will test the best ... Undergoing lots of upgrades ... Unbelievably
terraced greens ... Best thing is beer and hamburger ... New management bringing back great
course ... Great challenge—could use a little work though.

★★★ **WEDGEWOOD GOLF CLUB**
PU-5454 Hwy. 105 W., Conroe, 77304, Montgomery County, (409)441-4653, 50 miles from
Houston. **E-mail:** wdgewood@lcc.net. **Web:** http://houstonsidewalk.com/bslgolf. **Facility Holes:**
18. **Yards:** 6,817/5,071. **Par:** 72/72. **Course Rating:** 73.7/69.6. **Slope:** 134/128. **Green Fee:**
$20/$40. **Cart Fee:** $10/Person. **Walking Policy:** Unrestricted walking. **Walkability:** 4. **Opened:**
1988. **Architect:** Ron Prichard. **Season:** Year-round. **To obtain tee times:** Call up to 7 days in
advance. **Miscellaneous:** Reduced fees (weekdays, twilight, seniors, juniors), range
(grass/mats), credit cards (MC, V, AE), BF, FF.
Reader Comments: Very tight, what a challenge ... Tough course ... Excellent course and value!
... Best topography in area ... A great course and good price ... Almost unplayable for first timers,
too many blind shots ... Gorgeous, plush, hilly, tight, challenging.

★½ **WEEKS PARK MUNICIPAL GOLF COURSE**
PU-4400 Lake Park Dr., Wichita Falls, 76302, Wichita County, (940)767-6107. **Facility Holes:**
18. **Yards:** 6,470/4,915. **Par:** 72/73. **Course Rating:** 70.0/67.8. **Slope:** 117/109. **Green Fee:**
$12/$15. **Cart Fee:** $10/Person. **Walking Policy:** Unrestricted walking. **Walkability:** 1. **Architect:**
Jeff Brauer. **Season:** Year-round. **High:** March-Oct. **To obtain tee times:** Call up to 7 days in
advance. **Miscellaneous:** Reduced fees (weekdays, twilight, seniors, juniors), credit cards
(MC, V), FF.

WESTIN STONEBRIAR RESORT
R-1549 Legacy Dr., Frisco, 75007, Collin County, (972)668-8748, 25 miles from Dallas.
E-mail: graig.pullen@ourclub.com. **Web:** www.stonebriar.com. **Facility Holes:** 18. **Yards:**
7,021/5,208. **Par:** 72/72. **Course Rating:** 73.8/71.0. **Slope:** 133/121. **Green Fee:** $115. **Cart
Fee:** Included in green fee. **Walking Policy:** Mandatory carts. **Walkability:** 3. **Opened:** 2000.
Architect: Tom Fazio. **Season:** Year-round. **To obtain tee times:** Call up to 30 days in advance.
Miscellaneous: Range (grass/mats), lodging (301 rooms), credit cards (MC, V), BF, FF.

WHITE BLUFF RESORT
R-22 Misty Valley Circle, Whitney, 76692, Hill County, (254)694-4000, (888)944-8325, 40
miles from Waco. **E-mail:** mhicks@whitebluffresort.com. **Web:** www.whitebluffresort.com.
Facility Holes: 36. **Green Fee:** $50/$75. **Cart Fee:** Included in green fee. **Walking Policy:**
Unrestricted walking. **Walkability:** 3. **Architect:** Bruce Lietzke/Lee Singletary. **Season:** Year-

round. **To obtain tee times:** Call up to 7 days in advance. **Miscellaneous:** Reduced fees (guests, twilight, juniors), range (grass), credit cards (MC, V, AE, D), BF, FF.
NEW COURSE (18)
Yards: 6,965/5,589. **Par:** 72/72. **Course Rating:** 73.9/73.3. **Slope:** 139/128. **Opened:** 1998.
★★★★ **OLD COURSE** (18)
Yards: 6,866/5,292. **Par:** 72/72. **Course Rating:** 73.3/72.4. **Slope:** 132/128. **Opened:** 1993.
Reader Comments: Good, old design … Good condition and superb greens … Never crowded … Good value… Outstanding course, great facilities, let's go! … Some really good golf holes.

WHITE WING GOLF CLUB
PU-151 Dove Hollow Trail, Georgetown, 78626, Williamson County, (512)864-1244, (800)909-1969, 25 miles from Austin. **E-mail:** corys@delwebb.com. **Web:** www. golftexasbest.com. **Facility Holes:** 18. **Yards:** 6,700/5,159. **Par:** 72/72. **Course Rating:** 71.6/70.1. **Slope:** 126/118. **Green Fee:** $34/$71. **Cart Fee:** Included in green fee. **Walking Policy:** Walking at certain times. **Walkability:** 4. **Opened:** 2000. **Architect:** Billy Casper/ Greg Nash. **Season:** Year-round. **High:** Feb.-June. **To obtain tee times:** Call up to 3 days in advance. **Miscellaneous:** Reduced fees (guests, twilight), range (grass), credit cards (MC, V, AE, D), BF, FF.

★★★★ **WHITESTONE GOLF CLUB**
PU-10650 Hwy. 377 S., Benbrook, 76126, Tarrant County, (817)249-9996, 15 miles from Fort Worth. **Facility Holes:** 18. **Yards:** 7,117/5,201. **Par:** 72/72. **Course Rating:** 74.4/71.2. **Slope:** 135/125. **Green Fee:** $25/$52. **Cart Fee:** Included in green fee. **Walking Policy:** Mandatory carts. **Walkability:** 4. **Opened:** 2000. **Architect:** Jeff Brauer/Jay Morrish. **Season:** Year-round. **To obtain tee times:** Call up to 7 days in advance. **Miscellaneous:** Reduced fees (weekdays, twilight, seniors, juniors), range (grass/mats), credit cards (MC, V, AE), BF, FF.
Reader Comments: New course, has potential, good layout, good greens … Great service friendly … Keep it straight … A lot of sand, fairly new needs to mature… Nice and new … Very fast greens, great course … The par-4 9th can be reached with wind at your back.

★★★ **WILLOW SPRINGS GOLF CLUB**
PU-202 Coliseum Rd., San Antonio, 78219, Bexar County, (210)226-6721, 2 miles from San Antonio. **Facility Holes:** 18. **Yards:** 7,221/5,631. **Par:** 72/72. **Course Rating:** 73.9/72.5. **Slope:** 134/120. **Green Fee:** $16/$19. **Cart Fee:** $19/Cart. **Walking Policy:** Unrestricted walking. **Walkability:** 2. **Opened:** 1923. **Architect:** Emil Loeffler/John McGlynn. **Season:** Year-round. **To obtain tee times:** Call up to 7 days in advance. **Miscellaneous:** Reduced fees (weekdays, twilight, seniors, juniors), credit cards (MC, V, AE, D), BF, FF.
Reader Comments: Great course to walk, friendly folks … Beautiful layout, well groomed … Excellent service, good value … Not fancy but good price … Best muni I've played … Flat and wide open, but great for the price.

★★★½ **WINDROSE GOLF COURSE**
PU-6235 Pinelakes Blvd., Spring, 77379, Harris County, (281)370-8900, 20 miles from Houston. **Web:** www.windrosegolfclub.com. **Facility Holes:** 18. **Yards:** 7,203/5,355. **Par:** 72/72. **Course Rating:** 73.0/69.3. **Slope:** 128/117. **Green Fee:** $50/$68. **Cart Fee:** Included in green fee. **Walking Policy:** Mandatory carts. **Walkability:** 2. **Opened:** 1998. **Architect:** Rick Forester. **Season:** Year-round. **High:** March-June. **To obtain tee times:** Call up to 7 days in advance. **Miscellaneous:** Reduced fees (weekdays, twilight, seniors, juniors), range (grass), credit cards (MC, V, AE), BF, FF.
Reader Comments: Wonderful greens… Best greens in state greens… Nice local addition … Plenty of room to rip it.

★★★★ **WOODBRIDGE GOLF CLUB**
PU-7400 Country Club Dr., Wylie, 75098, Collin County, (972)429-5100, 20 miles from Dallas. **E-mail:** wbgolf@gte.net. **Facility Holes:** 18. **Yards:** 7,016/4,939. **Par:** 72/72. **Course Rating:** 74.1/67.0. **Slope:** 141/109. **Green Fee:** $41/$67. **Cart Fee:** Included in green fee. **Walking Policy:** Walking at certain times. **Walkability:** 2. **Opened:** 1999. **Architect:** Lee Singletary. **Season:** Year-round. **High:** April-July. **To obtain tee times:** Call up to 4 days in advance. **Miscellaneous:** Reduced fees (weekdays, twilight, seniors, juniors), range (grass), credit cards (MC, V, AE), BF, FF.
Reader Comments: What a great layout … A PGA event should be held here … Narrow landing areas … Good course … Will be great when it matures … Tough greens … Very difficult … Solid layout, tough test.

★★★ **WOODLAKE GOLF CLUB**
SP-6500 Woodlake Pkwy., San Antonio, 78244, Bexar County, (210)661-6124. **Facility Holes:** 18. **Yards:** 6,691/5,305. **Par:** 72/72. **Course Rating:** 71.6/70.8. **Slope:** 129/121. **Green Fee:** $22/$28. **Walking Policy:** Unrestricted walking. **Opened:** 1972. **Architect:** Desmond Muirhead. **Season:** Year-round. **To obtain tee times:** Call up to 7 days in advance. **Miscellaneous:**

Reduced fees (weekdays, twilight, seniors), metal spikes, range (grass), credit cards (MC, V, AE, D), BF, FF.

Reader Comments: A championship course … Needs work, good history … Course was excellent, service good, nice place to play … Hard, small greens! … Doing great things, very nice … Needs some TLC … On the way to being restored to past condition.

★★ WOODLAND HILLS GOLF COURSE
PU-319 Woodland Hills Dr., Nacogdoches, 75961, Nacogdoches County, (936)564-2762, 120 miles from Houston. **E-mail:** woodlandhills@cox-internet.com. **Facility Holes:** 18. **Yards:** 6,620/5,069. **Par:** 72/73. **Course Rating:** 72.6/72.9. **Slope:** 133/123. **Green Fee:** $10/$22. **Cart Fee:** $10/Person. **Walking Policy:** Unrestricted walking. **Walkability:** 5. **Opened:** 1972. **Architect:** Don January/Bill Martindale. **Season:** Year-round. **To obtain tee times:** Call up to 15 days in advance. **Miscellaneous:** Reduced fees (weekdays, twilight, seniors, juniors), range (grass), credit cards (MC, V, AE), BF, FF.

THE WOODLANDS RESORT & COUNTRY CLUB
R-2301 N. Millbend Dr., The Woodlands, 77380, Montgomery County, (281)367-1100, (800)433-2624, 22 miles from Houston. **E-mail:** chris.farnsworth@the-woodlands.net. **Web:** www.woodlandsresort.com. **Facility Holes:** 36. **Walking Policy:** Unrestricted walking. **Season:** Year-round. **High:** Sept.-Nov. **Miscellaneous:** Reduced fees (weekdays, twilight, juniors), range (grass/mats), lodging (400 rooms), credit cards (MC, V, AE, D, DC), BF, FF.

★★★★ PINES COURSE (18)
Yards: 6,881/5,245. **Par:** 72/72. **Course Rating:** 72.2/72.1. **Slope:** 126/120. **Green Fee:** $49/$69. **Cart Fee:** $14/Person. **Walkability:** 3. **Opened:** 1976. **Architect:** Joe Lee. **To obtain tee times:** Call up to 7 days in advance.

Reader Comments: Great place to play, you have to hit all the shots … Excellent course conditions, well managed.

★★★★ TPC AT THE WOODLANDS (18)
Yards: 7,018/5,326. **Par:** 72/72. **Course Rating:** 73.7/72.1. **Slope:** 136/128. **Green Fee:** $90/$130. **Cart Fee:** Included in green fee. **Walkability:** 2. **Opened:** 1985. **Architect:** Robert von Hagge/Devlin. **To obtain tee times:** Call up to 30 days in advance.

Notes: Ranked 22nd in 2001 Best in State.

Reader Comments: Great test … Nice to play where pros play … Great course, many of best holes in Texas … Gracious hospitality … Beautiful and peaceful layout … Use power cart … Pricey.

★★½ WORLD HOUSTON GOLF CLUB
PU-4000 Greens Rd., Houston, 77032, Harris County, (281)449-8384. **E-mail:** golf@worldhoustongolf.com. **Web:** www.worldhoustongolf.com. **Facility Holes:** 18. **Yards:** 6,642/5,204. **Par:** 72/72. **Course Rating:** 71.2/71.4. **Slope:** 119/123. **Green Fee:** $26/$36. **Cart Fee:** Included in green fee. **Walking Policy:** Unrestricted walking. **Walkability:** 1. **Architect:** Garrett Gill/George B. Williams. **Season:** Year-round. **To obtain tee times:** Call up to 7 days in advance. **Miscellaneous:** Reduced fees (twilight, seniors, juniors), metal spikes, credit cards (MC, V, AE, D), BF, FF.

★★ Z BOAZ GOLF COURSE
PU-3240 Lackland Rd., Fort Worth, 76116, Tarrant County, (817)738-6287. **Facility Holes:** 18. **Yards:** 6,033/4,782. **Par:** 70/70. **Course Rating:** 69.6/68.0. **Slope:** 124/107. **Green Fee:** $11/$13. **Cart Fee:** $19/Cart. **Walking Policy:** Unrestricted walking. **Walkability:** 3. **Opened:** 1937. **Architect:** Ralph Plummer. **Season:** Year-round. **High:** April-Aug. **To obtain tee times:** Call golf shop. **Miscellaneous:** Reduced fees (weekdays, twilight, seniors, juniors), credit cards (MC, V, D).

UTAH

★½ **BEN LOMOND GOLF COURSE**
PU-1800 N. Hwy. #89, Ogden, 84404, Weber County, (801)782-7754, 5 miles from Ogden.
Facility Holes: 18. **Yards:** 6,176/5,445. **Par:** 72/72. **Course Rating:** 67.9/69.2. **Slope:** 112/112.
Green Fee: $16/$20. **Cart Fee:** $20/Cart. **Walking Policy:** Unrestricted walking. **Walkability:** 1.
Opened: 1956. **Season:** Feb.-Dec. **High:** May-Aug. **To obtain tee times:** Call golf shop.
Miscellaneous: Reduced fees (seniors, juniors), credit cards (MC, V), BF, FF.

★★★★½ **BIRCH CREEK GOLF CLUB**
PU-550 East 100 North, Smithfield, 84335, Cache County, (435)563-6825, 7 miles from
Logan. **Facility Holes:** 18. **Yards:** 6,770/5,734. **Par:** 72/72. **Course Rating:** 72.2/70.7. **Slope:**
124/117. **Green Fee:** $18/$20. **Cart Fee:** $20/Cart. **Walking Policy:** Unrestricted walking.
Walkability: 4. **Opened:** 1953. **Architect:** Dale Schvaneveldt/Joseph B. Williams. **Season:**
March-Nov. **High:** May-Sept. **To obtain tee times:** Call golf shop. **Miscellaneous:** Reduced fees
(weekdays, seniors, juniors), range (grass/mats), credit cards (MC, V, D), BF, FF.
Reader Comments: Changes in elevation ... Walkable ... Always treated with courtesy and respect
... Great course ... Greatly improved.

★★★½ **BONNEVILLE GOLF COURSE**
PU-954 Connor St., Salt Lake City, 84108, Salt Lake County, (801)583-9513, 4 miles from
Salt Lake. **Facility Holes:** 18. **Yards:** 6,824/5,860. **Par:** 72/74. **Course Rating:** 71.0/71.6. **Slope:**
120/119. **Green Fee:** $20. **Cart Fee:** $20/Cart. **Walking Policy:** Unrestricted walking.
Walkability: 4. **Opened:** 1929. **Architect:** William F. Bell. **Season:** March-Nov. **High:** April-Sept.
To obtain tee times: Call golf shop. **Miscellaneous:** Reduced fees (seniors, juniors), range
(grass/mats), credit cards (MC, V).
Reader Comments: Great course located overlooking Salt Lake City ... Challenging layout, good
greens ... Elevation changes, mature, walkable ... Great views ... Long and mean, No. 18 is a killer.

★★★★ **BOUNTIFUL RIDGE GOLF COURSE**
PU-2430 S. Bountiful Blvd., Bountiful, 84010, Davis County, (801)298-6040, 5 miles from
Salt Lake City. **Facility Holes:** 18. **Yards:** 6,523/5,098. **Par:** 71/72. **Course Rating:** 70.2/67.6.
Slope: 122/116. **Green Fee:** $19/$21. **Cart Fee:** $10/Person. **Walking Policy:** Unrestricted walk-
ing. **Walkability:** 4. **Opened:** 1975. **Architect:** William H. Neff. **Season:** March-Nov. **High:** May-
Aug. **To obtain tee times:** Call golf shop. **Miscellaneous:** Reduced fees (seniors, juniors),
credit cards (MC, V), BF, FF.
Reader Comments: One of the finest public courses I've ever played ... The only reason it isn't
perfect is that they don't have room for a driving range ... Beautiful challenging layout ...
Outstanding vistas ... Huge greens.

★★½ **CEDAR RIDGE GOLF COURSE**
PU-200 East 900 North, Cedar City, 84720, Iron County, (435)586-2970, 170 miles from
Las Vegas. **Facility Holes:** 18. **Yards:** 6,635/5,076. **Par:** 71/71. **Course Rating:** 69.7/68.5.
Slope: 118/113. **Green Fee:** $20. **Cart Fee:** $9/Person. **Walking Policy:** Unrestricted walking.
Walkability: 2. **Opened:** 1962. **Architect:** John Evans. **Season:** Feb.-Dec. **High:** April-Oct.
To obtain tee times: Call golf shop. **Miscellaneous:** Reduced fees (seniors), range
(grass/mats), credit cards (MC, V), BF, FF.

CORAL CANYON GOLF COURSE
PU-1925 N. Canyon Greens Dr., Washington, 84780, Washington County, (435)688-1700,
7 miles from St. George. **Web:** www.coralcanyongolf.com. **Facility Holes:** 18. **Yards:**
7,029/5,026. **Par:** 72/72. **Course Rating:** 73.0/69.1. **Slope:** 137/122. **Green Fee:** $83. **Cart Fee:**
Included in green fee. **Opened:** 2000. **Architect:** Keith Foster. **Season:** Year-round. **High:** Oct.-
May. **To obtain tee times:** Call golf shop. **Miscellaneous:** Reduced fees (twilight).

★★★ **DAVIS PARK GOLF COURSE**
PU-1074 E. Nicholls Rd., Fruit Heights, 84037, Davis County, (801)546-4154, 17 miles from
Salt Lake City. **Facility Holes:** 18. **Yards:** 6,555/5,317. **Par:** 71/71. **Course Rating:** 70.9/68.8.
Slope: 123/119. **Green Fee:** $20/$22. **Cart Fee:** $10/Person. **Walking Policy:** Unrestricted
walking. **Walkability:** 2. **Opened:** 1964. **Architect:** Pierre Hualde/Ernie Schnieter. **Season:**
Feb.-Dec. **High:** May-Sept. **Tee times:** Call up to 7 days in advance. **Miscellaneous:** Reduced
fees (weekdays, seniors, juniors), range (grass/mats), credit cards (MC, V, AE), BF, FF.
Reader Comments: Very long and challenging ... Good course in need of new clubhouse ... Pace
of play is good, except on Saturdays ... Outstanding beauty, fun to play ... Good fairways ... Greens
could use some work.

DINALAND GOLF COURSE
PU-675 S. 2000 East, Vernal, 84078, Uintah County, (435)781-1428, 180 miles from
Salt Lake City. **E-mail:** kmccurdy@easilink.com. **Facility Holes:** 18. **Yards:** 6,773/5,094. **Par:**
72/72. **Course Rating:** 71.5/67.7. **Slope:** 129/116. **Green Fee:** $16/$18. **Cart Fee:** $17/Cart.

Walking Policy: Unrestricted walking. Walkability: 3. Opened: 1994. Architect: Jim McPhiliomy. Season: Feb.-Dec. High: April-Sept. Tee times: Call up to 7 days in advance. Miscellaneous: Reduced fees (seniors, juniors), range (grass), credit cards (MC, V), BF, FF.

★★★ DIXIE RED HILLS GOLF CLUB

PU-645 West 1250 North, St. George, 84770, Washington County, (435)634-5852, 100 miles from Las Vegas. Facility Holes: 9. Yards: 2,564. Par: 34. Course Rating: 65.9. Slope: 119. Green Fee: $25. Cart Fee: $22/Cart. Walking Policy: Unrestricted walking. Walkability: 1. Opened: 1965. Season: Year-round. To obtain tee times: Call up to 14 days in advance. Miscellaneous: Range (grass/mats), credit cards (MC, V, AE), BF, FF.
Reader Comments: Very accommodating! ... Nice little 9-hole ... The holes through the red rocks are great ... Fun course to walk.

★★½ EAGLE MOUNTAIN GOLF COURSE

PU-960 E. 700 S., Brigham City, 84302, Box Elder County, (435)723-3212, 45 miles from Salt Lake City. Facility Holes: 18. Yards: 6,769/4,767. Par: 71/71. Course Rating: 71.4/65.4. Slope: 119/101. Green Fee: $17/$18. Cart Fee: $9/Person. Walking Policy: Unrestricted walking. Walkability: 4. Opened: 1989. Architect: William H. Neff. Season: March-Nov. High: April-Sept. To obtain tee times: Call golf shop. Miscellaneous: Range, credit cards (MC, V), BF, FF.

★★★½ EAGLEWOOD GOLF COURSE

PU-1110 E. Eaglewood Dr., North Salt Lake City, 84054, Davis County, (801)299-0088, 10 miles from Salt Lake City. Facility Holes: 18. Yards: 6,800/5,200. Par: 71/71. Course Rating: 71.1/68.8. Slope: 121/112. Green Fee: $20. Cart Fee: $10/Person. Walking Policy: Unrestricted walking. Walkability: 4. Opened: 1994. Architect: Keith Foster. Season: March-Nov. High: June-Aug. To obtain tee times: Call golf shop. Miscellaneous: Reduced fees (weekdays, juniors), metal spikes, range (grass), credit cards (MC, V).
Reader Comments: Beautiful scenery up against the mountains with incredible sunsets overlooking the Great Salt Lake ... Great layout, well maintained ... Good design, tough, slow, tight.

★★★★ ENTRADA AT SNOW CANYON

SP-2511 W. Entrada Trail, St. George, 84770, Washington County, (435)674-7500, 325 miles from Salt Lake City. E-mail: stevesharpgolfentrada.com. Web: www.golfentrada.com. Facility Holes: 18. Yards: 7,262/5,454. Par: 72/72. Course Rating: 75.1/70.8. Slope: 132/121. Green Fee: $30/$85. Cart Fee: Included in green fee. Walking Policy: Mandatory carts. Walkability: 3. Opened: 1996. Architect: Johnny Miller/Fred Bliss. Season: Year-round. To obtain tee times: Call up to 30 days in advance. Miscellaneous: Reduced fees (twilight), range (grass), credit cards (MC, V, AE, D), BF, FF.
Notes: Ranked 2nd in 2001 Best in State.
Reader Comments: Great layout ... Most fun golf course in Utah ... Love last 4 holes! ... The back nine is beautiful, so short, and so tough ... Desert, lava, water, tough ... Awesome views.

★★★ GLADSTAN GOLF CLUB

PU-One Gladstan Dr., Payson, 84651, Utah County, (801)465-2549, (800)634-3009, 20 miles from Provo. Facility Holes: 18. Yards: 6,509/4,782. Par: 71/71. Course Rating: 70.7/67.4. Slope: 121/111. Green Fee: $20/$22. Cart Fee: $10/Person. Walking Policy: Unrestricted walking. Walkability: 5. Opened: 1988. Architect: William H. Neff. Season: March-Nov. High: May-Sept. To obtain tee times: Call golf shop. Miscellaneous: Reduced fees (seniors, juniors), range (grass/mats), credit cards (MC, V, AE, D), BF, FF.
Reader Comments: Beautiful surroundings, peaceful place to play a round ... Always feel welcome ... Beautiful course ... Watch the back 9.

★★★ GLEN EAGLE AT SYRACUSE GOLF CLUB

PU-3176 W. 1700 S., Syracuse, 84075, Davis County, (801)773-4653, 20 miles from Salt Lake City. E-mail: Fernau@USwest.com. Web: golfgleneagle.com. Facility Holes: 18. Yards: 7,065/4,805. Par: 72/72. Course Rating: 72.8/66.2. Slope: 130/113. Green Fee: $20. Cart Fee: $10/Person. Walking Policy: Unrestricted walking. Walkability: 3. Opened: 1999. Architect: William H. Neff. Season: Year-round. High: May-Sept. To obtain tee times: Call up to 2 days in advance. Miscellaneous: Range (grass), credit cards (MC, V, AE, D), BF, FF.
Reader Comments: Links course ... Tight, good greens.

★★ GLENDALE GOLF COURSE

PU-1630 W. 2100 S., Salt Lake City, 84119, Salt Lake County, (801)974-2403. Facility Holes: 18. Yards: 6,908/5,815. Par: 72/73. Course Rating: 70.9/72.5. Slope: 117/120. Green Fee: $20. Cart Fee: $22/Cart. Walking Policy: Unrestricted walking. Walkability: 1. Opened: 1973. Architect: William F. Bell. Season: Feb.-Nov. High: April-July. To obtain tee times: Call golf shop. Miscellaneous: Reduced fees (weekdays, seniors, juniors), range (grass), credit cards (MC, V, D), BF, FF.

UTAH

★★★ GLENMOOR GOLF & COUNTRY CLUB
PU-9800 S. 4800 W., South Jordon, 84095, Salt Lake County, (801)280-1742, 12 miles from Salt Lake City. **Facility Holes:** 18. **Yards:** 6,900/5,800. **Par:** 72/72. **Course Rating:** 71.3/71.5. **Slope:** 121/121. **Green Fee:** $22. **Cart Fee:** $20/Cart. **Walking Policy:** Unrestricted walking. **Walkability:** 3. **Opened:** 1965. **Architect:** William H. Neff. **Season:** Year-round. **High:** April-Oct. **To obtain tee times:** Call up to 7 days in advance. **Miscellaneous:** Reduced fees (seniors), range (grass), credit cards (MC, V), BF, FF.
Reader Comments: Target golf ... Best greens in state ... Variety of shots needed ... Great views ... Nice course ... Easy walking.

★★★★½ THE GOLF CLUB AT THANKSGIVING POINT *Service*
PU-2095 N. Thanksgiving Way, Lehi, 84043, Utah County, (801)768-7401, 20 miles from Salt Lake City. **Web:** www.thanskgivingpointgolfshop.com. **Facility Holes:** 18. **Yards:** 7,728/5,838. **Par:** 72/72. **Course Rating:** 76.2/72.8. **Slope:** 140/135. **Green Fee:** $35/$75. **Cart Fee:** Included in green fee. **Walking Policy:** Mandatory carts. **Walkability:** 3. **Opened:** 1997. **Architect:** Johnny Miller/Fred Bliss. **Season:** April-Nov. **High:** May-Oct. **To obtain tee times:** Call up to 14 days in advance. **Miscellaneous:** Reduced fees (twilight, seniors), range (grass), credit cards (MC, V, AE, D, DC), BF, FF.
Notes: Ranked 3rd in 2001 Best in State.
Reader Comments: Great challenge for the average golfer ... Beautiful, built around Jordan River ... Spectacular gem in the middle of an unlikely setting ... Fantastic layout, severe greens ... Difficult, new course.

★★★★ GREEN SPRING GOLF COURSE
PU-588 N. Green Spring Dr., Washington, 84780, Washington County, (435)673-7888, 2 miles from St. George. **Web:** greenspringgolfcourse.com. **Facility Holes:** 18. **Yards:** 6,629/4,952. **Par:** 71/71. **Course Rating:** 71.9/68.9. **Slope:** 130/118. **Green Fee:** $21/$36. **Cart Fee:** $11/Person. **Walking Policy:** Unrestricted walking. **Walkability:** 4. **Opened:** 1989. **Architect:** Gene Bates. **Season:** Year-round. **Tee times:** Call up to 60 days in advance. **Miscellaneous:** Reduced fees (twilight, juniors), range (grass), credit cards (MC, V, D), BF, FF.
Notes: Ranked 9th in 1999 Best in State.
Reader Comments: Great greens! ... Your heart will really get pumping on holes over the canyon ... Price is great, condition of course is fantastic and pace is as fast as you can play ... Interesting river shots.

★★★★ HOBBLE CREEK GOLF CLUB
PU-E. Hobble Creek Canyon Rd., Springville, 84663, Utah County, (801)489-6297, 15 miles from Provo. **Facility Holes:** 18. **Yards:** 6,315/5,435. **Par:** 71/73. **Course Rating:** 69.4/69.5. **Slope:** 120/117. **Green Fee:** $9/$18. **Cart Fee:** $22/Person. **Walking Policy:** Unrestricted walking. **Walkability:** 3. **Opened:** 1966. **Architect:** William F. Bell. **Season:** March-Nov. **High:** April-Sept. **To obtain tee times:** Call up to 7 days in advance. **Miscellaneous:** Reduced fees (seniors, juniors), range (grass), credit cards (MC, V), BF, FF.
Reader Comments: Canyon course, beautiful in fall, walkable ... Keep ball in fairway ... Nice old style mountain/valley golf course ... Narrow fairways, great food, good price ... Beautiful mountain setting, not a long course but has its challenges.

★★★½ HOMESTEAD GOLF CLUB
R-700 N. Homestead Dr., Midway, 84049, Wasatch County, (435)654-5588, (800)327-7220. **E-mail:** homesteadresort.com. **Web:** www.homesteadresort.com. **Facility Holes:** 18. **Yards:** 7,017/5,091. **Par:** 72/72. **Course Rating:** 73.0/68.8. **Slope:** 135/118. **Green Fee:** $25/$45. **Cart Fee:** $10/Person. **Walking Policy:** Unrestricted walking. **Walkability:** 3. **Opened:** 1990. **Architect:** Bruce Summerhays. **Season:** April-Nov. **High:** June-Sept. **To obtain tee times:** Call golf shop. **Miscellaneous:** Reduced fees (weekdays, guests, twilight, seniors), range (grass), lodging (155 rooms), credit cards (MC, V, AE, D, DC), BF, FF.
Reader Comments: Best resort course in Utah ... Lovely course and setting, great employees ... Relatively new and trees are not fully developed ... Pretty course, great for the vacationing family.

★★½ LAKESIDE GOLF COURSE
PU-1201 N. 1100 W., West Bountiful, 84087, Davis County, (801)295-1019, 10 miles from Salt Lake City. **E-mail:** mikebic@msn.com. **Facility Holes:** 18. **Yards:** 6,030/4,895. **Par:** 71/71. **Course Rating:** 67.2/66.5. **Slope:** 113/115. **Green Fee:** $15/$20. **Cart Fee:** $10/Person. **Walking Policy:** Unrestricted walking. **Walkability:** 1. **Opened:** 1966. **Architect:** William H. Neff. **Season:** March-Nov. **High:** June-Aug. **Tee times:** Call up to 4 days in advance. **Miscellaneous:** Reduced fees (seniors, juniors), range (grass/mats), credit cards (MC, V, D), BF, FF.

UTAH

★★★½ LOGAN RIVER GOLF COURSE
PU-550 W. 1000 S., Logan, 84321, Cache County, (435)750-0123, (888)750-0123, 80 miles from Salt Lake City. **Facility Holes:** 18. **Yards:** 6,502/5,048. **Par:** 71/71. **Course Rating:** 70.5/78.9. **Slope:** 124/117. **Green Fee:** $17. **Walking Policy:** Unrestricted walking. **Walkability:** 2. **Opened:** 1993. **Architect:** Robert Muir Graves. **Season:** March-Oct. **High:** June-Sept. **Tee times:** Call golf shop. **Misc:** Reduced fees (seniors, juniors), range , credit cards (MC, V).
Reader Comments: Tightest course I've ever played ... Good food also! ... Short and tight ... Bring a lot of balls ... Leave the driver in the bag.

★½ MEADOW BROOK GOLF COURSE
PU-4197 S. 1300 W., Taylorsville, 84123, Salt Lake County, (801)266-0971, 4 miles from Salt Lake City. **Facility Holes:** 18. **Yards:** 6,800/5,605. **Par:** 72/72. **Course Rating:** 70.0/67.9. **Slope:** 110/104. **Green Fee:** $17/$18. **Walking Policy:** Unrestricted walking. **Walkability:** 1. **Opened:** 1953. **Architect:** Mick Riley. **Season:** March-Dec. **High:** May-Oct. **To obtain tee times:** Call golf shop. **Miscellaneous:** Reduced fees (weekdays, seniors, juniors), metal spikes, range (grass), caddies.

★★★★ MOAB GOLF CLUB *Value, Pace*
PU-2705 S.E. Bench Rd., Moab, 84532, Grand County, (435)259-6488, 220 miles from Salt Lake City. **E-mail:** moabgolf@citlink.net. **Facility Holes:** 18. **Yards:** 6,819/4,725. **Par:** 72/72. **Course Rating:** 72.2/69.6. **Slope:** 125/110. **Green Fee:** $25. **Cart Fee:** $12/Person. **Walking Policy:** Unrestricted walking. **Walkability:** 3. **Opened:** 1960. **Season:** Year-round. **High:** March-Nov. **To obtain tee times:** Call golf shop. **Miscellaneous:** Reduced fees (juniors), range (grass), credit cards (MC, V), BF, FF.
Reader Comments: Gorgeous red cliffs/green fairways ... Most fun course, most fun town ... Mix of old and new, good value ... Not as fancy as Sedona but just as pretty ... Great value ... Unbelievable scenery.

★★★ MOUNT OGDEN GOLF COURSE
PU-1787 Constitution Way, Ogden, 84403, Weber County, (801)629-0699. **Facility Holes:** 18. **Yards:** 6,400/5,020. **Par:** 71/72. **Course Rating:** 70.5/69.5. **Slope:** 132/118. **Green Fee:** $18. **Cart Fee:** $10/Person. **Walking Policy:** Unrestricted walking. **Walkability:** 5. **Opened:** 1985. **Architect:** William H. Neff. **Season:** March-Nov. **High:** May-Sept. **To obtain tee times:** Call up to 4 days in advance. **Miscellaneous:** Reduced fees (seniors, juniors), range (grass), credit cards (MC, V), BF, FF.
Reader Comments: Spectacular views and challenging course ... Very steep ... Tight, tight, tight ... Good service, great course ... Need extra balls ... Not at all forgiving.

MOUNTAIN DELL GOLF CLUB
PU-Parleys Canyon, Salt Lake City, 84109, Salt Lake County, (801)582-3812, 6 miles from Salt Lake City. **Facility Holes:** 36. **Green Fee:** $22/$26. **Cart Fee:** $22/Cart. **Walking Policy:** Unrestricted walking. **Walkability:** 5. **Architect:** William H. Neff. **Season:** March-Nov. **To obtain tee times:** Call up to 7 days in advance. **Miscellaneous:** Reduced fees (weekdays, twilight, seniors, juniors), range (grass), credit cards (MC, V, AE, D), BF, FF.
★★★½ CANYON COURSE (18)
Yards: 6,787/5,447. **Par:** 72/73. **Course Rating:** 71.3/71.1. **Slope:** 126/112. **Opened:** 1962.
Reader Comments: Fun, refreshing course ... Very good public course ... If you can't play the Lake, the Canyon is a challenge.
★★★½ LAKE COURSE (18)
Yards: 6,709/5,066. **Par:** 71/71. **Course Rating:** 72.2/67.6. **Slope:** 129/109. **Opened:** 1991.
Reader Comments: Lots of wildlife—moose, deer, elk, fox, rabbits ... Mountain course, beautiful in spring, fall ... Good layout ... Demanding ... Narrow.

★★ MOUNTAIN VIEW GOLF CLUB
PU-2400 W. 8660 S., West Jordan, 84084, Salt Lake County, (801)255-9211, 10 miles from Salt Lake City. **Facility Holes:** 18. **Yards:** 6,764/5,827. **Par:** 72/72. **Course Rating:** 70.2/69.9. **Slope:** 112/118. **Green Fee:** $10/$20. **Cart Fee:** $20/Cart. **Walking Policy:** Unrestricted walking. **Walkability:** 1. **Opened:** 1968. **Architect:** William H. Neff. **Season:** Feb.-Dec. **High:** May-Sept. **To obtain tee times:** Call golf shop. **Miscellaneous:** Reduced fees (seniors, juniors), range (grass), credit cards (MC, V), BF, FF.

★★ MURRAY PARKWAY GOLF CLUB
PU-6345 S. Murray Pkwy. Ave., Murray, 84123, Salt Lake County, (801)262-4653, 8 miles from Salt Lake City. **Facility Holes:** 18. **Yards:** 6,800/5,800. **Par:** 72/72. **Course Rating:** 71.3/71.0. **Slope:** 120/118. **Green Fee:** $21. **Cart Fee:** $10/Person. **Walking Policy:** Unrestricted walking. **Walkability:** 1. **Opened:** 1986. **Architect:** Robert Muir Graves. **Season:** Feb.-Dec. **High:** April-Oct. **To obtain tee times:** Call up to 7 days in advance. **Miscellaneous:** Reduced fees (seniors, juniors), range (grass/mats), credit cards (MC, V, D), BF, FF.

★★★ OLD MILL GOLF CLUB

PU-6080 S. Wasatch Blvd., Salt Lake City, 84121, Salt Lake County, (801)424-1302, 10 miles from Salt Lake City. **Facility Holes:** 18. **Yards:** 6,769/5,618. **Par:** 71/71. **Course Rating:** 69.9/68.3. **Slope:** 125/115. **Green Fee:** $26. **Cart Fee:** $12/Person. **Walking Policy:** Unrestricted walking. **Walkability:** 4. **Opened:** 1998. **Architect:** Gene Bates. **Season:** Year-round. **To obtain tee times:** Call up to 7 days in advance. **Miscellaneous:** Reduced fees (seniors, juniors), range (grass/mats), credit cards (MC, V, AE, D), BF, FF.
Reader Comments: Beautiful layout of two completely different 9s … Always on time and pace, keeps moving … Love this course … Great views, demanding.

★★★ PARK CITY GOLF CLUB

PU-Lower Park Ave., Park City, 84060, Summit County, (435)615-5800, 25 miles from Salt Lake City. **E-mail:** csanchez@parkcity2002.com. **Web:** parkcitygolfclub.com. **Facility Holes:** 18. **Yards:** 6,562/5,527. **Par:** 72/72. **Course Rating:** 71.2/71.3. **Slope:** 124/122. **Green Fee:** $22/$37. **Cart Fee:** $12/Person. **Walking Policy:** Unrestricted walking. **Walkability:** 3. **Opened:** 1963. **Architect:** William H. Neff. **Season:** April-Nov. **High:** June-Sept. **To obtain tee times:** Call golf shop. **Miscellaneous:** Range (mats), credit cards (MC, V, AE, D), BF, FF.
Reader Comments: Look out for moose … Park City's best course; scenery great … Played golf and skied the same day … Ball goes long way … Tricky breaks on greens … Well kept course.

★★½ THE RESERVE AT EAST BAY

PU-1860 S. E. Bay Blvd., Provo, 84601, Utah County, (801)373-6262, 49 miles from Salt Lake City. **Facility Holes:** 27. **Yards:** 6,932/5,125. **Par:** 72/72. **Course Rating:** 72.1/66.6. **Slope:** 123/106. **Green Fee:** $20/$22. **Cart Fee:** $20/Cart. **Walking Policy:** Unrestricted walking. **Walkability:** 2. **Opened:** 1986. **Architect:** William H. Neff. **Season:** March-Nov. **High:** May-Aug. **To obtain tee times:** Call up to 1 day in advance. **Miscellaneous:** Reduced fees (twilight), range (grass), credit cards (MC, V, AE, D), BF, FF.
Special Notes: Also has a 9-hole junior course.

★★½ RIVER OAKS GOLF CLUB

PU-9300 S. Riverside Dr., Sandy, 84070, Salt Lake County, (801)561-4000, 10 miles from Salt Lake City. **E-mail:** desantis@mail.mstar.net. **Facility Holes:** 18. **Yards:** 6,350/4,316. **Par:** 70/70. **Course Rating:** 70.5/66.0. **Slope:** 131/115. **Green Fee:** $24/$27. **Cart Fee:** $10/Person. **Walking Policy:** Unrestricted walking. **Walkability:** 3. **Opened:** 1999. **Architect:** William H. Neff. **Season:** March-Nov. **High:** April-Oct. **To obtain tee times:** Call up to 7 days in advance. **Miscellaneous:** Reduced fees (weekdays, seniors, juniors), range (grass), credit cards (MC, V, AE, D), BF, FF.

★★★½ RIVERBEND GOLF COURSE

PU-12800 S. 1040 W., Riverton, 84065, Salt Lake County, (801)253-3673, 15 miles from Salt Lake City. **Facility Holes:** 18. **Yards:** 6,876/5,081. **Par:** 72/72. **Course Rating:** 69.9/68.7. **Slope:** 118/111. **Green Fee:** $13/$24. **Cart Fee:** $11/Person. **Walking Policy:** Unrestricted walking. **Walkability:** 5. **Opened:** 1994. **Architect:** Gene Bates. **Season:** Year-round. **To obtain tee times:** Call up to 7 days in advance. **Miscellaneous:** Reduced fees (seniors, juniors), range (grass), credit cards (MC, V, AE, D), BF, FF.
Notes: Ranked 7th in 1997 Best in State.
Reader Comments: Wind can really make this course interesting … Demanding, great vistas … Great view from elevated 10th tee … Fun course but always slow play … Awesome!!!

ROOSEVELT GOLF COURSE

PU-1155 Clubhouse Dr., Roosevelt, 84066, Duchesne County, (435)722-9644, 142 miles from Salt Lake City. **Facility Holes:** 18. **Yards:** 7,049/5,021. **Par:** 72/72. **Course Rating:** 72.1/69.2. **Slope:** 121/114. **Green Fee:** $17. **Cart Fee:** $9/Person. **Walking Policy:** Unrestricted walking. **Season:** Feb.-Nov. **To obtain tee times:** Call golf shop. **Miscellaneous:** Reduced fees (juniors), range (grass), credit cards (MC, V, AE, D), BF, FF.

★★ ROSE PARK GOLF CLUB

PU-1386 N. Redwood Rd., Salt Lake City, 84116, Salt Lake County, (801)596-5030, 2 miles from Salt Lake City. **E-mail:** steve.elliott@ci.slc.ut.us. **Facility Holes:** 18. **Yards:** 6,696/5,816. **Par:** 72/75. **Course Rating:** 69.6/70.8. **Slope:** 109/112. **Green Fee:** $20. **Cart Fee:** $11/Person. **Walking Policy:** Unrestricted walking. **Walkability:** 2. **Opened:** 1960. **Architect:** Mick Riley/William F. Bell. **Season:** Feb.-Dec. **High:** April-Sept. **To obtain tee times:** Call up to 7 days in advance. **Miscellaneous:** Reduced fees (seniors, juniors), range (grass), credit cards (MC, V, AE), BF, FF.

★★½ ROUND VALLEY COUNTRY CLUB
PU-1875 E. Round Valley Rd., Morgan, 84050, Morgan County, (801)829-3796, 3 miles from Morgan. **E-mail:** rdvlygolf@aol.com. **Facility Holes:** 18. **Yards:** 6,732/5,153. **Par:** 72/72. **Course Rating:** 71.5/69.0. **Slope:** 122/114. **Green Fee:** $18. **Walking Policy:** Unrestricted walking. **Walkability:** 3. **Season:** Year-round. **High:** June-Oct. **To obtain tee times:** Call golf shop. **Miscellaneous:** Reduced fees (weekdays, seniors, juniors), range (grass), credit cards (MC, V, AE, D).

★★★ SCHNEITER'S BLUFF AT WEST POINT
PU-300 N. 3500 W., West Point, 84015, Davis County, (801)773-0731, 20 miles from Salt Lake City. **E-mail:** golfer@PMBS.net. **Web:** schneitersgolf.com. **Facility Holes:** 18. **Yards:** 6,833/5,419. **Par:** 72/72. **Course Rating:** 70.2/67.3. **Slope:** 115/113. **Green Fee:** $20. **Cart Fee:** $10/Cart. **Walking Policy:** Unrestricted walking. **Walkability:** 2. **Opened:** 1995. **Architect:** E. Schneiter/B. Schneiter/J. Schneiter. **Season:** Year-round. **Tee times:** Call golf shop. **Misc:** Reduced fees (seniors, juniors), range (grass), credit cards (MC, V, AE, D), BF, FF.
Reader Comments: New course in very good shape ... Flat, often windy ... New course, will be great in a few years ... Can't lose your ball, easy on, easy score.

SCHNEITER'S PEBBLE BROOK GOLF LINKS
PU-8968 South 1300 E., Sandy, 84094, Salt Lake County, (801)566-2181, 7 miles from Salt Lake City. **Facility Holes:** 18. **Yards:** 4,469/4,121. **Par:** 68/68. **Course Rating:** 63.6/66.8. **Slope:** 100/106. **Green Fee:** $20. **Cart Fee:** $22/Cart. **Walking Policy:** Unrestricted walking. **Walkability:** 4. **Opened:** 1973. **Architect:** Ernie Schneiter. **Season:** Year-round. **High:** April-Oct. **To obtain tee times:** Call golf shop. **Miscellaneous:** Reduced fees (seniors, juniors), range (grass/mats), credit cards (MC, V, AE, D), BF, FF.

★★★ SCHNEITER'S RIVERSIDE GOLF COURSE
PU-5460 S. Weber Dr., Ogden, 84405, Weber County, (801)399-4636, 30 miles from Salt Lake City. **Facility Holes:** 18. **Yards:** 6,177/5,217. **Par:** 71/71. **Course Rating:** 68.4/68.5. **Slope:** 114/113. **Green Fee:** $18. **Cart Fee:** $18/Cart. **Walking Policy:** Walking at certain times. **Walkability:** 2. **Opened:** 1961. **Architect:** Ernie Schneiter. **Season:** March-Nov. **High:** May-Sept. **To obtain tee times:** Call golf shop. **Miscellaneous:** Reduced fees (seniors, juniors), range (grass/mats), credit cards (MC, V, AE, D), BF, FF.
Reader Comments: Excellent, mature public course ... Course is always in excellent shape ... Fun place to play, but crowded ... Making great improvements ... Short; tight; treelined; friendly staff ... Very slow play.

★★ SHERWOOD HILLS RESORT GOLF COURSE
R-Highway 89-91, Wellsville, 84339, Cache County, (435)245-6055, 6 miles from Logan. **Facility Holes:** 9. **Yards:** 3,315/2,830. **Par:** 36/37. **Course Rating:** 69.8/70.5. **Slope:** 109/111. **Green Fee:** $19/$20. **Cart Fee:** $20/Cart. **Walking Policy:** Unrestricted walking. **Walkability:** 3. **Opened:** 1973. **Architect:** Mark Dixon Ballif. **Season:** March-Nov. **High:** June-Oct. **To obtain tee times:** Call up to 10 days in advance. **Miscellaneous:** Reduced fees (weekdays, guests, seniors), range (grass), lodging (85 rooms), credit cards (MC, V), BF, FF.

★★★★ SKY MOUNTAIN GOLF COURSE *Value*
PU-1030 N. 2600 W., Hurricane, 84737, Washington County, (435)635-7888. **Facility Holes:** 18. **Yards:** 6,312/5,044. **Par:** 72/72. **Course Rating:** 69.9/66.4. **Slope:** 115/107. **Green Fee:** $16/$30. **Cart Fee:** $10/Person. **Walking Policy:** Unrestricted walking. **Walkability:** 4. **Opened:** 1994. **Architect:** Jeff Hardin. **Season:** Year-round. **High:** Oct.-May. **To obtain tee times:** Call golf shop. **Miscellaneous:** Metal spikes, range (grass), credit cards (MC, V, AE, D), BF, FF.
Reader Comments: Friendly staff ... Views outstanding ... Good layout ... Nice layout ... Wonderful public facility, I play it every year ... Short course, some challenging holes ... A lost ball can go a mile ... One of my favorites ... Beautiful service.

★★★½ SOUTH MOUNTAIN GOLF CLUB
PU-1247 E. Rambling Rd., Draper, 84020, Salt Lake County, (801)495-0500. **E-mail:** southmountaingolf@juno.com. **Web:** www.southmountaingolf.com. **Facility Holes:** 18. **Yards:** 7,080/5,165. **Par:** 72/72. **Course Rating:** 73.4/69.8. **Slope:** 130/118. **Green Fee:** $30/$49. **Cart Fee:** Included in green fee. **Walking Policy:** Mandatory carts. **Opened:** 1998. **Architect:** David Graham/Gary Panks. **Season:** Year-round. **To obtain tee times:** Call up to 7 days in advance. **Miscellaneous:** Reduced fees (weekdays, twilight, seniors, juniors), range (grass), credit cards (MC, V, AE, D), BF, FF.
Notes: Ranked 8th in 2001 Best in State.
Reader Comments: Nice course ... Tough course, links type, but good ... Length is premium ... Excellent new championship course! ... Could be great with conditioning.

UTAH

★★½ SOUTHGATE GOLF CLUB
PU-1975 S. Tonaquint Dr., St. George, 84770, Washington County, (435)628-0000, 120 miles from Las Vegas. **E-mail:** southgate@mindspring.com. **Web:** www.cityofstgeorge.com/golf. **Facility Holes:** 18. **Yards:** 6,138/5,504. **Par:** 70/70. **Course Rating:** 69.1/64.4. **Slope:** 118/101. **Green Fee:** $28. **Cart Fee:** $22/Cart. **Walking Policy:** Unrestricted walking. **Walkability:** 3. **Opened:** 1984. **Architect:** William H. Neff. **Season:** Year-round. **Tee times:** Call up to 14 days ahead. **Misc:** Reduced fees (twilight, juniors), range, credit cards (MC, V, AE), BF, FF.

★★ SPANISH OAKS GOLF CLUB
PU-2300 E. Powerhouse Rd., Spanish Fork, 84660, Utah County, (801)798-9816, 7 miles from Provo. **E-mail:** rchristensen@spanishfork.org. **Facility Holes:** 18. **Yards:** 6,358/5,319. **Par:** 72/73. **Course Rating:** 69.5/70.2. **Slope:** 127/119. **Green Fee:** $20/$22. **Cart Fee:** $20/Cart. **Walking Policy:** Unrestricted walking. **Opened:** 1983. **Architect:** Billy Casper/Gary Darling. **Season:** Year-round. **To obtain tee times:** Call golf shop. **Miscellaneous:** Reduced fees (twilight, seniors, juniors), range (grass/mats), credit cards (MC, V, AE), BF, FF.

★★½ ST. GEORGE GOLF CLUB
PU-2190 S. 1400 E., St. George, 84790, Washington County, (435)634-5854, 110 miles from Las Vegas. **Facility Holes:** 18. **Yards:** 7,213/5,197. **Par:** 73/73. **Course Rating:** 71.7/68.9. **Slope:** 123/114. **Green Fee:** $18/$27. **Cart Fee:** $11/Person. **Walking Policy:** Unrestricted walking. **Walkability:** 3. **Opened:** 1976. **Architect:** David Bingaman. **Season:** Year-round. **To obtain tee times:** Call up to 14 days in advance. **Miscellaneous:** Credit cards (MC, V, AE), BF, FF.

★★ STANSBURY PARK GOLF CLUB
PU-#1 Country Club Dr., Tooele, 84074, Tooele County, (801)328-1483, 25 miles from Salt Lake City. **Facility Holes:** 18. **Yards:** 6,831/5,722. **Par:** 72/72. **Course Rating:** 71.6/71.5. **Slope:** 125/121. **Green Fee:** $16/$18. **Cart Fee:** $8/Person. **Walking Policy:** Unrestricted walking. **Opened:** 1972. **Architect:** William H. Neff. **Season:** Feb.-Dec. **High:** May-July. **To obtain tee times:** Call up to 7 days in advance. **Miscellaneous:** Reduced fees (weekdays, juniors), range (grass), credit cards (MC, V), BF, FF.

STONEBRIDGE GOLF CLUB AT LAKE PARK
PU-4415 Links Dr., West Valley City, 84120, Salt Lake County, (801)908-7888, 5 miles from Salt Lake City. **E-mail:** pjphillis@pga.com. **Web:** www.golfstonebridgeutah.com. **Facility Holes:** 27. **Green Fee:** $18/$30. **Cart Fee:** $10/Person. **Walking Policy:** Unrestricted walking. **Walkability:** 2. **Opened:** 1999. **Architect:** Johnny Miller. **Season:** Year-round. **High:** April-Sept. **To obtain tee times:** Call up to 7 days in advance. **Miscellaneous:** Reduced fees (weekdays, twilight, seniors, juniors), range (grass), credit cards (MC, V, AE, D), BF, FF.
CREEKSIDE/SAGEBRUSH (18 Combo)
Yards: 7,164/5,221. **Par:** 71/71. **Course Rating:** 74.2/70.4. **Slope:** 139/138.
★★½ **CREEKSIDE/SUNRISE** (18 Combo)
Yards: 7,127/5,141. **Par:** 71/71. **Course Rating:** 73.4/70.4. **Slope:** 135/125.
SUNRISE/SAGEBRUSH (18 Combo)
Yards: 7,095/5,290. **Par:** 72/72. **Course Rating:** 73.4/70.5. **Slope:** 138/127.

★★★★ SUNBROOK GOLF CLUB
PU-2366 W. Sunbrook Drive, St. George, 84770, Washington County, (435)634-5866, 120 miles from Las Vegas. **Facility Holes:** 27. **Green Fee:** $22/$38. **Cart Fee:** $10/Person. **Walking Policy:** Unrestricted walking. **Walkability:** 3. **Opened:** 1990. **Architect:** Ted G. Robinson/John Harbottle. **Season:** Year-round. **High:** Oct.-May. **To obtain tee times:** Call golf shop. **Miscellaneous:** Range (grass/mats), credit cards (MC, V).
POINTE/BLACKROCK (18 Combo)
Yards: 6,758/5,155. **Par:** 72/72. **Course Rating:** 73.8/71.4. **Slope:** 133/125.
POINTE/WOODBRIDGE (18 Combo)
Yards: 6,818/5,286. **Par:** 72/72. **Course Rating:** 73.0/71.1. **Slope:** 129/121.
WOODBRIDGE/BLACKROCK (18 Combo)
Yards: 6,828/5,233. **Par:** 72/72. **Course Rating:** 74.0/74.1. **Slope:** 134/126.
Notes: Ranked 5th in 1999 Best in State.
Reader Comments: Wide fairways, hilly ... Island green fun ... Worth the drive up from Vegas ... Good variety ... Great resort course ... Unique lava formations.

★★½ TRI-CITY GOLF COURSE
PU-1400 N. 200 E., American Fork, 84003, Utah County, (801)756-3594, 30 miles from Salt Lake City. **Facility Holes:** 18. **Yards:** 7,077/6,304. **Par:** 72/73. **Course Rating:** 73.0/73.0. **Slope:** 125/124. **Green Fee:** $18. **Cart Fee:** $9/Person. **Walking Policy:** Unrestricted walking. **Walkability:** 2. **Opened:** 1972. **Architect:** Joe Williams. **Season:** March-Nov. **High:** May-Sept. **Tee times:** Call 10 days ahead. **Miscellaneous:** Reduced fees (seniors, juniors), range, credit cards (MC, V), BF, FF.

★★★★ VALLEY VIEW GOLF COURSE *Value*
PU-2501 E. Gentile, Layton, 84040, Davis County, (801)546-1630, 15 miles from Salt Lake City. **E-mail:** valley@co.davis.ut.us. **Facility Holes:** 18. **Yards:** 6,652/5,755. **Par:** 72/74. **Course Rating:** 71.0/73.2. **Slope:** 123/125. **Green Fee:** $20/$22. **Cart Fee:** $22/Cart. **Walking Policy:** Unrestricted walking. **Walkability:** 5. **Opened:** 1974. **Architect:** William Hull. **Season:** March-Nov. **High:** May-Sept. **To obtain tee times:** Call golf shop. **Miscellaneous:** Reduced fees (seniors, juniors), range (grass), credit cards (MC, V, AE, D), BF, FF.
Notes: Ranked 7th in 2001 Best in State.
Reader Comments: Beautiful mature course ... Wide variety of terrain, some change in elevation, and secluded mountain setting ... Worth the trip ... Excellent track ... Always improving the course ... One of the best in the state.

WASATCH STATE PARK GOLF CLUB
PU-P.O. Box 10, Midway, 84049, Wasatch County, (435)654-0532, 35 miles from Salt Lake City. **Facility Holes:** 36. **Architect:** William H. Neff. **Season:** March-Nov. **To obtain tee times:** Call golf shop. **Miscellaneous:** Reduced fees (seniors, juniors), range (grass/mats), credit cards (MC, V), BF, FF.
★★★★½ LAKE (18) *Value+*
Yards: 6,942/5,573. **Par:** 72/72. **Course Rating:** 72.0/71.5. **Slope:** 128/123. **Green Fee:** $18/$20. **Cart Fee:** $20/Cart. **Walking Policy:** Unrestricted walking. **Walkability:** 2. **Opened:** 1962.
Reader Comments: Secluded, delightful ... 36 great holes of golf located in the mountains overlooking Heber Valley ... One of the most beautiful locations for a golf course ... Huge greens, always a challenge.
★★★★ MOUNTAIN (18) *Value+*
Yards: 6,459/5,009. **Par:** 71/71. **Course Rating:** 70.4/67.4. **Slope:** 125/119. **Green Fee:** $20/$22. **Cart Fee:** $11/Person. **Walking Policy:** Walking at certain times. **Walkability:** 3. **Opened:** 1998.
Reader Comments: Good muni ... Just added new 9 on mountain... Spectacular views ... Crown jewel of Utah golf ... Great color in fall... Must have cart, superb vistas hard to improve.

★★½ WEST RIDGE GOLF COURSE
PU-5055 S. W. Ridge Blvd., West Valley City, 84118, Salt Lake County, (801)966-4653, 10 miles from Salt Lake City. **Facility Holes:** 18. **Yards:** 6,734/5,027. **Par:** 71/71. **Course Rating:** 72.2/68.1. **Slope:** 125/118. **Green Fee:** $16/$18. **Cart Fee:** $9/Person. **Walking Policy:** Unrestricted walking. **Walkability:** 4. **Opened:** 1991. **Architect:** William H. Neff. **Season:** March-Nov. **High:** April-Aug. **To obtain tee times:** Call golf shop. **Miscellaneous:** Reduced fees (weekdays, seniors, juniors), range (grass), credit cards (MC, V, AE, D).

★★★★ WINGPOINTE GOLF COURSE *Value*
PU-3602 W. 100 N., Salt Lake City, 84122, Salt Lake County, (801)575-2345. **Facility Holes:** 18. **Yards:** 7,101/5,228. **Par:** 72/72. **Course Rating:** 73.3/72.0. **Slope:** 131/125. **Green Fee:** $22. **Cart Fee:** $22/Cart. **Walking Policy:** Unrestricted walking. **Walkability:** 3. **Opened:** 1990. **Architect:** Arthur Hills. **Season:** Year-round. **High:** May-Oct. **To obtain tee times:** Call golf shop. **Miscellaneous:** Reduced fees (weekdays, seniors, juniors), range (grass), credit cards (MC, V, AE, D), FF.
Notes: Ranked 10th in 2001 Best in State.
Reader Comments: Great links course located next to the Salt Lake City airport ... Great links course, very challenging ... Next door to the airport and very windy, but an enjoyable track ... Always in great shape, staff is excellent ... Noisy course because of air traffic.

★★★½ WOLF CREEK GOLF RESORT
SP-3900 N. Wolf Creek Dr., Eden, 84310, Weber County, (801)745-3365, (877)492-1051, 10 miles from Ogden. **E-mail:** chris@homesteadresort.com. **Facility Holes:** 18. **Yards:** 6,845/5,332. **Par:** 72/72. **Course Rating:** 73.4/71.0. **Slope:** 134/127. **Green Fee:** $20/$25. **Cart Fee:** $10/Person. **Walking Policy:** Unrestricted walking. **Walkability:** 3. **Opened:** 1965. **Architect:** Mark Dixon Ballif. **Season:** April-Oct. **High:** June-Sept. **To obtain tee times:** Call up to 7 days in advance. **Miscellaneous:** Reduced fees (weekdays, guests, twilight, seniors, juniors), range (grass/mats), credit cards (MC, V, AE).
Reader Comments: Fine mountain course with great scenery ... Of the seven days of golf in Utah, this was the best golf outing ... Great views, long from back tees ... Really neat mountain course.

★★ ALBURG COUNTRY CLUB
SP-230 Rte.129, South Alburg, 05440, Grand Isle County, (802)796-3586, 40 miles from Burlington. **E-mail:** golf@alburg.com. **Web:** www.alburg.com. **Facility Holes:** 18. **Yards:** 6,434/5,536. **Par:** 72/75. **Course Rating:** 70.2/71.2. **Slope:** 119/120. **Green Fee:** $12/$25. **Cart Fee:** $20/Cart. **Walking Policy:** Unrestricted walking. **Walkability:** 3. **Opened:** 1967. **Architect:** Dick Ellison. **Season:** May-Oct. **High:** July-Aug. **To obtain tee times:** Call golf shop. **Miscellaneous:** Reduced fees (weekdays, twilight, juniors), metal spikes, range (grass/mats).

BARTON GOLF CLUB
PU-548 Telfer Hill, Barton, 05822, Orleans County, (802)525-1126, 25 miles from St. Johnsbury. **E-mail:** barbill@together.net. **Facility Holes:** 18. **Yards:** 5,800/5,200. **Par:** 70/72. **Course Rating:** 68.0/68.0. **Slope:** 115/115. **Green Fee:** $15. **Cart Fee:** $10/Person. **Walking Policy:** Unrestricted walking. **Walkability:** 2. **Opened:** 1990. **Architect:** Brian King. **Season:** May-Nov. **To obtain tee times:** Call golf shop. **Miscellaneous:** Reduced fees (twilight), credit cards (MC, V), FF.

★★★½ BASIN HARBOR CLUB
R-Basin Harbor Rd., Vergennes, 05491, Addison County, (802)475-2309, 30 miles from Burlington. **E-mail:** pennie@basinharbor.com. **Web:** www.basinharbor.com. **Facility Holes:** 18. **Yards:** 6,511/5,700. **Par:** 72/72. **Course Rating:** 70.7/67.1. **Slope:** 120/113. **Green Fee:** $37/$47. **Cart Fee:** $30/Cart. **Walking Policy:** Unrestricted walking. **Walkability:** 2. **Opened:** 1927. **Architect:** A. Campbell/W. Mitchell/G. Cornish. **Season:** May-Oct. **High:** July-Aug. **To obtain tee times:** Call up to 2 days in advance. **Miscellaneous:** Reduced fees (guests, twilight, juniors), range (grass), lodging (136 rooms), credit cards (MC, V), BF, FF.
Reader Comments: Beautiful setting ... Charming ... Can be windy on the lake holes ... Scenic views of Lake Champlain ... Fast greens, great vacation spot ... Very fair ... A very pleasant experience ... Excellent greens, impressive mosquitoes ... Try to play once a year, worth it ... Not a typical VT course.

BRATTLEBORO COUNTRY CLUB
SP-Upper Dummerston Rd., Brattleboro, 05301, Windham County, (802)257-7380, 5 miles from Brattleboro. **Web:** www.brattleborogolf.com. **Facility Holes:** 18. **Yards:** 6,508/5,059. **Par:** 71/71. **Course Rating:** 71.0/70.0. **Slope:** 123/116. **Green Fee:** $40/$50. **Cart Fee:** $18/Person. **Walking Policy:** Unrestricted walking. **Walkability:** 4. **Opened:** 1914. **Architect:** Tom MacNamara/Steve Durkee. **High:** June-Aug. **To obtain tee times:** Call golf shop. **Miscellaneous:** Reduced fees (juniors), range (grass), credit cards (MC, V).

CEDAR KNOLL COUNTRY CLUB
PU-Highway VT #116, Hinesburg, 05461, Chittenden County, (802)482-3186, 15 miles from Burlington. **Facility Holes:** 27. **Green Fee:** $22. **Cart Fee:** $23/Cart. **Walking Policy:** Unrestricted walking. **Walkability:** 3. **Opened:** 1994. **Architect:** Raymond Ayer. **Season:** April-Oct. **High:** July-Aug. **To obtain tee times:** Call golf shop. **Miscellaneous:** Reduced fees (twilight, seniors), range (grass/mats), credit cards (MC, V, AE, D).
NORTH/SOUTH (18 Combo)
Yards: 5,863/4,646. **Par:** 71/70. **Course Rating:** 68.5/68.0. **Slope:** 119/108.
NORTH/WEST (18 Combo)
Yards: 6,541/5,360. **Par:** 72/72. **Course Rating:** 70.8/69.5. **Slope:** 124/112.
SOUTH/WEST (18 Combo)
Yards: 6,072/4,924. **Par:** 71/70. **Course Rating:** 67.7/67.1. **Slope:** 117/109.

★★ CHAMPLAIN COUNTRY CLUB
SP-Rte. 7 North, Swanton, 05488, Franklin County, (802)527-1187, 3 miles from St. Albans. **Web:** www.champlaincountryclub.com. **Facility Holes:** 18. **Yards:** 6,237/5,266. **Par:** 70/70. **Course Rating:** 69.9/70.4. **Slope:** 123/117. **Green Fee:** $25/$28. **Cart Fee:** $26/Cart. **Walking Policy:** Unrestricted walking. **Walkability:** 1. **Opened:** 1915. **Architect:** Duer Irving Sewall/Graham Cook. **Season:** April-Nov. **High:** July-Sept. **To obtain tee times:** Call golf shop. **Miscellaneous:** Reduced fees (weekdays, twilight), range , credit cards (MC, V, D), BF, FF.

★★★ COUNTRY CLUB OF BARRE
SP-Plainfield Rd., Barre, 05641, Washington County, (802)476-7658, 4 miles from Barre. **Facility Holes:** 18. **Yards:** 6,218/5,407. **Par:** 71/71. **Course Rating:** 70.2/71.7. **Slope:** 123/124. **Green Fee:** $35. **Cart Fee:** $15/Person. **Walking Policy:** Unrestricted walking. **Walkability:** 4. **Opened:** 1924. **Architect:** Wayne Stiles. **Season:** May-Nov. **High:** June-Sept. **To obtain tee times:** Call up to 7 days in advance. **Miscellaneous:** Range (grass/mats), credit cards (MC, V), BF, FF.
Reader Comments: Several blind holes, tough but nice ... Very scenic ... Demanding layout ... Tight and fairly long ... Hilly ... Most underrated course in Vermont ... Give it a try, you will not be disappointed ... Looks are deceiving, many holes with potential to score well.

★★★ CROWN POINT COUNTRY CLUB
SP-Weathersfield Center Rd., Springfield, 05156, Windsor County, (802)885-1010, 100 miles from Hartford. **Facility Holes:** 18. **Yards:** 6,602/5,542. **Par:** 72/72. **Course Rating:** 71.2/71.3. **Slope:** 123/117. **Green Fee:** $40/$50. **Cart Fee:** $30/Cart. **Walking Policy:** Unrestricted walking. **Walkability:** 3. **Opened:** 1953. **Architect:** William F. Mitchell. **Season:** April-Nov. **High:** June-Aug. **To obtain tee times:** Call up to 3 days in advance. **Miscellaneous:** Reduced fees (weekdays, twilight, seniors, juniors), range (grass/mats), credit cards (MC, V), BF, FF.
Reader Comments: Good value especially compared to other area courses ... Sloping fairways make it tough to position drives ... Good clubhouse and food. Great views ... Fast greens, beautiful scenery, great par 3s ... A real test of skill. Key as usual is keeping ball in the fairway.

ENOSBURG FALLS COUNTRY CLUB
PU-11 Elm St., Enosburg Falls, 05450, Franklin County, (802)933-2296, 15 miles from Saint Albans. **Facility Holes:** 18. **Yards:** 5,897/4,869. **Par:** 72/72. **Course Rating:** 67.4/67.1. **Slope:** 116/110. **Green Fee:** $20/$23. **Cart Fee:** $20/Cart. **Walking Policy:** Unrestricted walking. **Walkability:** 3. **Opened:** 1962. **Season:** May-Oct. **High:** June-Aug. **To obtain tee times:** Call golf shop. **Miscellaneous:** Credit cards (MC, V).

★½ ESSEX COUNTRY CLUB
PU-332 Old Stage Rd., Essex Junction, 05452, Chittenden County, (802)879-3232, 10 miles from Burlington. **Facility Holes:** 18. **Yards:** 6,500/5,700. **Par:** 72/72. **Course Rating:** 70.4/69.0. **Slope:** 117/112. **Green Fee:** $23/$25. **Cart Fee:** $24/Cart. **Walking Policy:** Unrestricted walking. **Walkability:** 2. **Opened:** 1988. **Architect:** Graham Cooke. **Season:** May-Nov. **High:** June-Oct. **To obtain tee times:** Call up to 7 days in advance. **Miscellaneous:** Reduced fees (twilight), range (grass/mats), credit cards (MC, V, AE), BF, FF.

★★★★ GLENEAGLES GOLF COURSE AT THE EQUINOX *Service*
R-Historic Rte. 7-A., Manchester Village, 05254, Bennington County, (802)362-3223, 70 miles from Albany. **Facility Holes:** 18. **Yards:** 6,423/5,082. **Par:** 71/71. **Course Rating:** 71.3/65.2. **Slope:** 129/117. **Green Fee:** $85/$95. **Cart Fee:** $18/Person. **Walking Policy:** Walking at certain times. **Walkability:** 3. **Opened:** 1926. **Architect:** Rees Jones/Walter Travis. **Season:** May-Nov. **High:** May-Sept. **To obtain tee times:** Call golf shop. **Miscellaneous:** Reduced fees (guests, twilight), lodging (183 rooms), credit cards (MC, V, AE, D).
Notes: Ranked 4th in 2001 Best in State.
Reader Comments: Lovely course. If you stay at Equinox you must have a few at the Marsh Tavern ... Go back in time to 1769 when it was established ... Beautiful views, nice greens & pace ... Classic Vermont location & ambience ... Very good service.

★★★★ GREEN MOUNTAIN NATIONAL GOLF COURSE
PU-Rte. 100 - Barrows-Towne Rd., Killington, 05751, Rutland County, (802)422-4653, 15 miles from Rutland. **E-mail:** gmngc@vermontel.net. **Web:** www.gmngc.com. **Facility Holes:** 18. **Yards:** 6,589/4,740. **Par:** 71/71. **Course Rating:** 72.6/68.0. **Slope:** 138/118. **Green Fee:** $44/$57. **Cart Fee:** $18/Person. **Walking Policy:** Walking at certain times. **Walkability:** 3. **Opened:** 1996. **Architect:** Gene Bates. **Season:** May-Nov. **High:** July-Sept. **To obtain tee times:** Call up to 7 days in advance. **Miscellaneous:** Reduced fees (weekdays, twilight, juniors), range (grass/mats), credit cards (MC, V, AE, D), BF, FF.
Notes: Ranked 5th in 2001 Best in State; 5th in 1997 Best New Upscale Public Courses.
Reader Comments: Played early morning round & completed in less than 4 hours ... Beautiful mountain course ... Feel like your the only ones on the course ... Felt pushed by the clocks on the course ... If you're off the fairway the ball is gone ... Huge elevation changes ... Bring lots of balls.

★★½ HAYSTACK GOLF CLUB
PU-70 Spyglass Dr., Wilmington, 05363, Windham County, (802)464-8301, 3 miles from Wilmington. **E-mail:** golfinfo@haystackgolf.com. **Web:** www.haystackgolf.com. **Facility Holes:** 18. **Yards:** 6,549/5,396. **Par:** 72/74. **Course Rating:** 71.5/71.4. **Slope:** 128/122. **Green Fee:** $40/$49. **Cart Fee:** $16/Person. **Walking Policy:** Walking at certain times. **Walkability:** 3. **Opened:** 1972. **Architect:** Desmond Muirhead. **Season:** May-Oct. **High:** July-Sept. **To obtain tee times:** Call golf shop. **Miscellaneous:** Reduced fees (weekdays, guests, twilight, juniors), range (grass), credit cards (MC, V, AE, D), BF, FF.

JOHN P. LARKIN COUNTRY CLUB
SP-N. Main St., Windsor, 05089, Windsor County, (802)674-6491, 7 miles from Windsor. **Facility Holes:** 9. **Yards:** 5,382/4,924. **Par:** 68/72. **Course Rating:** 65.1/68.2. **Slope:** 105/109. **Green Fee:** $20/$25. **Cart Fee:** $22/Cart. **Walking Policy:** Unrestricted walking. **Walkability:** 5. **Opened:** 1923. **Architect:** MIT Students. **Season:** April-Oct. **High:** June-Aug. **To obtain tee times:** Call golf shop. **Miscellaneous:** Credit cards (MC, V).

VERMONT

★★★½ KILLINGTON GOLF RESORT
R-4763 Killington Rd., Killington, 05751, Rutland County, (802)422-6700, 16 miles from Rutland. **E-mail:** dpfannenstein@killington.com. **Web:** www.killingtongolf.com. **Facility Holes:** 18. **Yards:** 6,326/5,108. **Par:** 72/72. **Course Rating:** 70.6/71.2. **Slope:** 126/123. **Green Fee:** $51. **Cart Fee:** $16/Person. **Walking Policy:** Unrestricted walking. **Walkability:** 4. **Opened:** 1984. **Architect:** Geoffrey Cornish. **Season:** May-Oct. **High:** June-Oct. **To obtain tee times:** Call up to 14 days in advance. **Miscellaneous:** Reduced fees (twilight, juniors), metal spikes, range (mats), lodging (750 rooms), credit cards (MC, V, AE, D), BF, FF.
Reader Comments: Only a few people there in early June ... Nice mountain layout, good work out to walk ... Scenic, hilly, reservations a must ... Worth the price a least once ... Up hills, down dales, over rivers and everything else you can imagine ... You will talk about it for many years to come.

★★★ KWINIASKA GOLF CLUB
SP-5531 Spear St., Shelburne, 05482, Chittenden County, (802)985-3672, 7 miles from Burlington. **E-mail:** mdbailey@kwiniaska.com. **Web:** www.kwiniaska.com. **Facility Holes:** 18. **Yards:** 7,048/5,627. **Par:** 72/72. **Course Rating:** 72.5/72.6. **Slope:** 128/119. **Green Fee:** $30. **Cart Fee:** $24/Cart. **Walking Policy:** Unrestricted walking. **Walkability:** 3. **Opened:** 1964. **Architect:** Bradford Caldwell. **Season:** April-Nov. **High:** May-Sept. **To obtain tee times:** Call up to 1 day in advance. **Miscellaneous:** Reduced fees (twilight), range (grass), credit cards (MC, V), BF, FF.
Reader Comments: Nice fun course for an afternoon off ... Long course, a little wet, course was crowded ... Interesting varied holes ... Surprisingly good ... Deceptive, flat front 9, hilly back 9 ... Unreal layout, lots of potential, too slow on weekends ... Nice folks.

★★½ LAKE MOREY COUNTRY CLUB
R-179 Club House Rd., Fairlee, 05045, Orange County, (802)333-4800, (800)423-1227, 50 miles from Springfield. **E-mail:** lkmorey@sover.net. **Web:** www.lakemoreycc.com. **Facility Holes:** 18. **Yards:** 6,024/4,942. **Par:** 70/70. **Course Rating:** 68.4/68.0. **Slope:** 118/116. **Green Fee:** $30/$37. **Cart Fee:** $29/Cart. **Walking Policy:** Walking at certain times. **Walkability:** 3. **Opened:** 1910. **Architect:** Geoffrey Cornish. **Season:** April-Nov. **High:** May-Sept. **To obtain tee times:** Call up to 4 days in advance. **Miscellaneous:** Reduced fees (guests, twilight, seniors), range (grass/mats), lodging (140 rooms), credit cards (MC, V, D), BF, FF.

★★ LAKE ST. CATHERINE COUNTRY CLUB
SP-Rte. 30 Lake Rd., Poultney, 05764, Rutland County, (802)287-9341, 15 miles from Rutland. **Facility Holes:** 18. **Yards:** 6,293/4,940. **Par:** 72/72. **Course Rating:** 70.9/68.2. **Slope:** 127/116. **Green Fee:** $20/$27. **Cart Fee:** $27/Cart. **Walking Policy:** Unrestricted walking. **Walkability:** 5. **Opened:** 1996. **Season:** April-Oct. **High:** June-Aug. **To obtain tee times:** Call golf shop. **Miscellaneous:** Range (grass/mats), credit cards (MC, V), FF.

★★ MONTAGUE GOLF CLUB
SP-2 Golf Lane, Randolph, 05060, Orange County, (802)728-3806, 20 miles from Montpilier. **Facility Holes:** 18. **Yards:** 5,910/5,064. **Par:** 70/71. **Course Rating:** 68.6/68.7. **Slope:** 115/117. **Green Fee:** $25/$30. **Cart Fee:** $25/Cart. **Walking Policy:** Unrestricted walking. **Walkability:** 1. **Opened:** 1925. **Season:** April-Oct. **High:** June-Aug. **To obtain tee times:** Call golf shop. **Miscellaneous:** Reduced fees (weekdays, twilight), range, credit cards (MC, V), BF, FF.

★★★ MOUNT SNOW GOLF CLUB
R-Country Club Rd., West Dover, 05356, Windham County, (802)464-5642, (800)451-4211, 26 miles from Brattleboro. **E-mail:** jmorelli@mountsnow.com. **Web:** www.thegolfschool.com. **Facility Holes:** 18. **Yards:** 6,894/5,436. **Par:** 72/72. **Course Rating:** 73.3/72.8. **Slope:** 130/121. **Green Fee:** $54. **Cart Fee:** $32/Cart. **Walking Policy:** Unrestricted walking. **Walkability:** 5. **Opened:** 1964. **Architect:** Geoffrey Cornish. **Season:** May-Nov. **High:** July-Sept. **To obtain tee times:** Call up to 7 days in advance. **Miscellaneous:** Reduced fees (weekdays, guests, twilight, juniors), metal spikes, range (grass/mats), lodging (365 rooms), credit cards (MC, V, AE, D), BF, FF.
Reader Comments: Some great views & good challenges ... Mountain course lots of elevation changes ... Nice layout ... Very slow ... A lot of blind shots ... Very scenic, difficult.

★★ MT. ANTHONY COUNTRY CLUB
PU-180 Country Club Dr., Bennington, 05201, Bennington County, (802)447-7079, 30 miles from Albany. **Facility Holes:** 18. **Yards:** 6,146/4,942. **Par:** 71/71. **Course Rating:** 70.5/67.7. **Slope:** 125/106. **Green Fee:** $30/$35. **Cart Fee:** $12/Person. **Walking Policy:** Unrestricted walking. **Walkability:** 4. **Opened:** 1897. **Architect:** Jay Jerome. **Season:** April-Nov. **To obtain tee times:** Call up to 7 days in advance. **Miscellaneous:** Reduced fees (weekdays), metal spikes, range (grass), credit cards (MC, V, AE, D), BF, FF.

VERMONT

★★★½ NESHOBE GOLF CLUB
SP-Town Farm Rd., Brandon, 05733, Rutland County, (802)247-3611, 15 miles from Rutland. **E-mail:** neshgolf@together.net. **Web:** www.neshobe.com. **Facility Holes:** 18. **Yards:** 6,362/5,042. **Par:** 72/71. **Course Rating:** 71.6/64.9. **Slope:** 125/115. **Green Fee:** $34/$36. **Cart Fee:** $28/Cart. **Walking Policy:** Unrestricted walking. **Walkability:** 3. **Opened:** 1959. **Architect:** Steve Durkee. **Season:** April-Oct. **High:** June-Aug. **To obtain tee times:** Call up to 3 days in advance. **Miscellaneous:** Reduced fees (twilight, juniors), range (grass), credit cards (MC, V), BF, FF.
Reader Comments: New back 9 is wonderful … A hidden Vermont gem … Greens are great to putt … Unlike any other, but too many tournaments during the season brings it down two notches … Surrounded by cow pastures, but course is gem! … The State's best test of golf from back tees.

★★½ NEWPORT COUNTRY CLUB
SP-Pine Hill Rd., Newport, 05855, Orleans County, (802)334-2391, 80 miles from Burlington. **Facility Holes:** 18. **Yards:** 6,453/5,312. **Par:** 72/72. **Course Rating:** 69.4/69.5. **Slope:** 109/110. **Green Fee:** $25. **Cart Fee:** $23/Cart. **Walking Policy:** Unrestricted walking. **Walkability:** 2. **Opened:** 1922. **Architect:** Ralph Barton. **Season:** April-Oct. **High:** June-July. **To obtain tee times:** Call up to 1 day in advance. **Miscellaneous:** Reduced fees (twilight), range (grass), credit cards (MC, V), BF, FF.

OKEMO VALLEY GOLF CLUB
R-89 Fox Lane, Ludlow, 05149, Windsor County, (802)228-1396, 45 miles from Brattleboro. **Web:** www.okemo.com. **Facility Holes:** 18. **Yards:** 6,400/5,105. **Par:** 70/70. **Course Rating:** 71.1/70.1. **Slope:** 130/125. **Green Fee:** $80. **Cart Fee:** Included in green fee. **Opened:** 2000. **Architect:** Steve Durkee. **To obtain tee times:** Call golf shop.

★★★ ORLEANS COUNTRY CLUB
SP-Rte. 58, P.O. Box 217, Orleans, 05860, Orleans County, (802)754-2333, 70 miles from Burlington. **Facility Holes:** 18. **Yards:** 6,200/5,595. **Par:** 72/72. **Course Rating:** 69.3/71.8. **Slope:** 121/124. **Green Fee:** $24. **Cart Fee:** $22/Cart. **Walking Policy:** Unrestricted walking. **Walkability:** 1. **Opened:** 1929. **Architect:** Alex Reid. **Season:** April-Oct. **High:** June-Sept. **To obtain tee times:** Call golf shop. **Miscellaneous:** Metal spikes, range (grass), credit cards (MC, V).
Reader Comments: Food very good … Friendly atmosphere … Ethan Allen's steam whistle is disruptive … Feels like VT … Play with locals … Flat. Very walkable. Great food … Fun little course.

★★½ PROCTOR-PITTSFORD COUNTRY CLUB
PU-Corn Hill Rd., Pittsford, 05763, Rutland County, (802)483-9379, 3 miles from Rutland. **Facility Holes:** 18. **Yards:** 6,052/5,446. **Par:** 70/72. **Course Rating:** 69.4/66.1. **Slope:** 121/115. **Green Fee:** $32. **Cart Fee:** $13/Cart. **Walking Policy:** Unrestricted walking. **Walkability:** 3. **Opened:** 1927. **Architect:** Henry Collin/Ray Keyser. **Season:** April-Oct. **High:** June-Aug. **To obtain tee times:** Call up to 2 days in advance. **Miscellaneous:** Reduced fees (twilight), range (grass), credit cards (MC, V), BF, FF.

★★½ RALPH MYHRE GOLF COURSE OF MIDDLEBURY COLLEGE
PU-Rte. 30, Middlebury, 05753, Addison County, (802)443-5125, 1 mile from Middlebury. **E-mail:** jdayton@middlebury.edu. **Web:** www.middlebury.edu. **Facility Holes:** 18. **Yards:** 6,379/5,337. **Par:** 71/71. **Course Rating:** 71.3/66.9. **Slope:** 129/120. **Green Fee:** $35. **Cart Fee:** $15/Person. **Walking Policy:** Unrestricted walking. **Walkability:** 3. **Opened:** 1927. **Architect:** Ralph Myhre. **Season:** April-Oct. **High:** July-Aug. **To obtain tee times:** Call golf shop. **Miscellaneous:** Reduced fees (twilight, juniors), range (grass/mats), credit cards (MC, V), BF, FF.

★★ ROCKY RIDGE GOLF CLUB
SP-7470 Rt. 116, St. George, 05495, Chittenden County, (802)482-2191, 12 miles from Burlington. **E-mail:** biggolf@aol.com. **Web:** www.rockyridge.com. **Facility Holes:** 18. **Yards:** 6,000/5,230. **Par:** 72/72. **Course Rating:** 69.1/68.7. **Slope:** 124/110. **Green Fee:** $22. **Cart Fee:** $22/Cart. **Walking Policy:** Unrestricted walking. **Walkability:** 3. **Opened:** 1963. **Architect:** Ernest Farrington. **Season:** April-Nov. **High:** June-Aug. **To obtain tee times:** Call golf shop. **Miscellaneous:** Reduced fees (twilight), range (mats), credit cards (MC, V, AE, D), BF, FF.

★★★★½ RUTLAND COUNTRY CLUB
SP-N. Grove St., Rutland, 05701, Rutland County, (802)773-3254. **E-mail:** pgaprogn@aol.com. **Facility Holes:** 18. **Yards:** 6,134/5,368. **Par:** 70/71. **Course Rating:** 69.7/71.6. **Slope:** 125/125. **Green Fee:** $84. **Cart Fee:** Included in green fee. **Walking Policy:** Mandatory carts. **Walkability:** 3. **Opened:** 1902. **Architect:** Wayne E. Stiles/John Van Kleek. **Season:** May-Oct. **High:** June-Sept. **To obtain tee times:** Call up to 2 days in advance. **Miscellaneous:** Credit cards (MC, V, D), BF, FF.

Notes: Ranked 4th in 1997 Best in State.
Reader Comments: A real challenge ... Very fast greens and someone with local knowledge a real plus ... # 13 is one of the toughest and longest par 5s you will ever play ... This is a great course with great history ... A gem, one of the best in VT.

★★★½ ST. JOHNSBURY COUNTRY CLUB

SP-Rte. 5 Memorial Dr., St. Johnsbury, 05819, Caledonia County, (802)748-9894, (800)748-8899, 175 miles from Boston. **Facility Holes:** 18. **Yards:** 6,323/4,685. **Par:** 70/70. **Course Rating:** 70.4/65.8. **Slope:** 129/104. **Green Fee:** $33/$38. **Cart Fee:** $13/Person. **Walking Policy:** Unrestricted walking. **Walkability:** 4. **Opened:** 1923. **Architect:** Willie Park/Mungo Park-Cornish/J.Havers. **Season:** April-Oct. **High:** July-Aug. **To obtain tee times:** Call golf shop. **Miscellaneous:** Reduced fees (guests, twilight), metal spikes, range (grass/mats), credit cards (MC, V).
Reader Comments: Back 9 especially good ... Well worth the price ... Too hilly ... Challenging, beautiful vistas, well designed ... Very nice layout, great service.

★★★½ STOWE COUNTRY CLUB

R-Cape Cod Rd., Stowe, 05672, Lamoille County, (802)253-4893, (800)253-4754, 37 miles from Burlington. **E-mail:** jnicholls@stowe.com. **Web:** www.stowe.com. **Facility Holes:** 18. **Yards:** 6,206/5,346. **Par:** 72/74. **Course Rating:** 70.4/66.5. **Slope:** 122/115. **Green Fee:** $42/$69. **Cart Fee:** $16/Person. **Walking Policy:** Unrestricted walking. **Walkability:** 3. **Opened:** 1950. **Architect:** Walter Barcomb. **Season:** May-Oct. **High:** June-Sept. **To obtain tee times:** Call up to 30 days in advance. **Miscellaneous:** Reduced fees (weekdays, guests, twilight), range (grass), credit cards (MC, V, AE, D, DC, CB), BF, FF.
Reader Comments: Great course in the mountains ... Gorgeous views, quaint village ... Waited on every hole ... Fun layout.

★★★ STRATTON MOUNTAIN COUNTRY CLUB

R-R.R. 1 Box 145, Stratton Mountain, 05155, Windham County, (802)297-4114, (800)787-2886, 40 miles from Rutland. **Web:** www.stratton.com. **Facility Holes:** 27. **Green Fee:** $69/$99. **Cart Fee:** $17/Person. **Walking Policy:** Walking at certain times. **Opened:** 1965. **Architect:** Geoffrey Cornish. **Season:** May-Oct. **High:** July-Aug. **To obtain tee times:** Call golf shop. **Miscellaneous:** Reduced fees (weekdays, guests, twilight, juniors), range (grass/mats), lodging (400 rooms), credit cards (MC, V, AE, D), BF, FF.
LAKE/FOREST (18 Combo)
Yards: 6,526/5,153. **Par:** 72/74. **Course Rating:** 71.2/69.8. **Slope:** 125/123. **Walkability:** 4.
LAKE/MOUNTAIN (18 Combo)
Yards: 6,602/5,410. **Par:** 72/74. **Course Rating:** 72.0/71.1. **Slope:** 125/124. **Walkability:** 3.
MOUNTAIN/FOREST (18 Combo)
Yards: 6,478/5,163. **Par:** 72/74. **Course Rating:** 71.2/69.9. **Slope:** 126/123. **Walkability:** 4.

★★★ SUGARBUSH GOLF COURSE

R-Golf Course Rd., Warren, 05674, Washington County, (802)583-6725, (800)537-8427, 45 miles from Burlington. **E-mail:** gloniewski@sugarbush.com. **Web:** www.sugarbush.com. **Facility Holes:** 18. **Yards:** 6,524/5,187. **Par:** 72/72. **Course Rating:** 71.7/70.4. **Slope:** 128/119. **Green Fee:** $35/$52. **Cart Fee:** $18/Person. **Walking Policy:** Walking at certain times. **Walkability:** 5. **Opened:** 1962. **Architect:** Robert Trent Jones. **Season:** May-Oct. **High:** July-Aug. **To obtain tee times:** Call golf shop. **Miscellaneous:** Reduced fees (guests, twilight, juniors), metal spikes, range (grass), lodging (150 rooms), credit cards (MC, V, AE, D), BF, FF.
Reader Comments: Hilly, challenging, tough lies ... Nice view ... Pace of play before 9:30 under 4 hours ... More mountain golf.

★★★★ VERMONT NATIONAL COUNTRY CLUB *Service, Condition*

PU-1227 Dorset St., South Burlington, 05403, Chittenden County, (802)864-7770. **E-mail:** jimg@vnccgolf.com. **Web:** www.vnccgolf.com. **Facility Holes:** 18. **Yards:** 7,035/4,966. **Par:** 72/72. **Course Rating:** 74.2/69.2. **Slope:** 133/116. **Green Fee:** $85/$100. **Cart Fee:** Included in green fee. **Walking Policy:** Unrestricted walking. **Walkability:** 3. **Opened:** 1999. **Architect:** Jack Nicklaus/Jack Nicklaus Jr. **Season:** April-Nov. **High:** June-Oct. **To obtain tee times:** Call up to 3 days in advance. **Miscellaneous:** Reduced fees (twilight), range (grass), credit cards (MC, V, AE, D, DC), BF, FF.
Reader Comments: This course adds a touch of class to the Vermont golf scene ... Interesting course set among marshes against the back drop of mountains ... Many forced carries ... Definitely worth a visit.

★★½ WEST BOLTON GOLF CLUB

PU-5161 Stage Rd., Jericho, 05465, Chittenden County, (802)434-4321, 20 miles from Burlington. **E-mail:** wbgc4golf@aol.com. **Web:** www.westboltongolfclub.com. **Facility Holes:** 18. **Yards:** 5,880/5,094. **Par:** 72/72. **Course Rating:** 66.3/65.7. **Slope:** 109/103. **Green Fee:**

$18/$23. **Cart Fee:** $25/Cart. **Walking Policy:** Unrestricted walking. **Walkability:** 3. **Opened:** 1983. **Architect:** Xen Wheeler. **Season:** May-Oct. **High:** May-Aug. **To obtain tee times:** Call up to 7 days in advance. **Miscellaneous:** Reduced fees (twilight, seniors, juniors), credit cards (MC, V, D), BF, FF.

★★★ WILLISTON GOLF CLUB

PU-424 Golf Course Rd., Williston, 05495, Chittenden County, (802)878-3747, 7 miles from Burlington. **Facility Holes:** 18. **Yards:** 5,725/4,753. **Par:** 69/72. **Course Rating:** 68.0/64.1. **Slope:** 118/106. **Green Fee:** $23. **Cart Fee:** $25/Cart. **Walking Policy:** Unrestricted walking. **Walkability:** 2. **Opened:** 1926. **Architect:** Ben Murray. **Season:** May-Nov. **To obtain tee times:** Call up to 4 days in advance. **Miscellaneous:** Reduced fees (twilight), credit cards (MC, V), BF, FF.

Reader Comments: Very tight course, in good shape … Condition excellent for a public golf course … Course not long but lots of hazards … Very busy golf course with 4-5 hour rounds … A pleasure to play … Play long irons on most tees … Leave the driver in the trunk.

★★★½ WINDHAM GOLF CLUB

SP-6802 Popple Dungeon Rd., N. Windham, 05143, Windsor County, (802)875-2517, 15 miles from Manchester. **E-mail:** windhamgolf.com. **Web:** www.windhamgolf.com. **Facility Holes:** 18. **Yards:** 6,801/4,979. **Par:** 72/72. **Course Rating:** 72.3/64.7. **Slope:** 129/113. **Green Fee:** $55/$72. **Cart Fee:** Included in green fee. **Walking Policy:** Unrestricted walking. **Walkability:** 3. **Opened:** 1964. **Architect:** Don Warner. **Season:** May-Oct. **High:** July-Sept. **To obtain tee times:** Call golf shop. **Miscellaneous:** Reduced fees (weekdays, twilight, juniors), range (grass), credit cards (MC, V, AE), BF, FF.

Reader Comments: Long walk between holes, fun layout … Keep this course a secret … Jekyll & Hyde 9s … A gem hidden in Vermont's interior … Old and new 9s make a beautiful mix … Very enjoyable.

Special Notes: Formerly Tater Hill Country Club.

★★★★ WOODSTOCK COUNTRY CLUB

R-Fourteen The Green, Woodstock, 05091, Windsor County, (802)457-6674, 30 miles from Rutland. **E-mail:** jfgpro@aol.com. **Facility Holes:** 18. **Yards:** 6,053/4,924. **Par:** 70/71. **Course Rating:** 69.7/69.0. **Slope:** 123/113. **Green Fee:** $62/$82. **Cart Fee:** $18/Person. **Walking Policy:** Unrestricted walking. **Walkability:** 1. **Opened:** 1895. **Architect:** Robert Trent Jones. **Season:** May-Nov. **High:** June-Sept. **To obtain tee times:** Call golf shop. **Miscellaneous:** Reduced fees (weekdays, guests, twilight), range (grass), lodging (144 rooms), credit cards (MC, V, AE), BF, FF.

Reader Comments: Wonderful short layout with trout streams throughout … Lots of water comes into play … Course a little too narrow … A must in autumn … Unique Vermont experience … Challenging … Difficult but engaging.

VIRGINIA

★★½ ALGONKIAN REGIONAL PARK GOLF COURSE
PU-47001 Fairway Dr., Sterling, 20165, Loudoun County, (703)450-4655, 20 miles from
Washington, DC. **Facility Holes:** 18. **Yards:** 7,015/5,795. **Par:** 72/72. **Course Rating:** 73.5/74.0.
Slope: 125/113. **Green Fee:** $23/$34. **Cart Fee:** $26/Cart. **Walking Policy:** Unrestricted walk-
ing. **Walkability:** 3. **Opened:** 1972. **Architect:** Ed Ault. **Season:** Year-round. **To obtain tee times:**
Call up to 7 days in advance. **Miscellaneous:** Reduced fees (weekdays, guests, seniors,
juniors), range (mats), credit cards (MC, V, ATM Debit), BF, FF.

ALLEGHANY COUNTRY CLUB
SP-111A E. Country Club Lane., Covington, 24426, Alleghany County, (540)862-5789.
Facility Holes: 9. **Yards:** 6,280/5,410. **Par:** 71/73. **Course Rating:** 67.6/70.1. **Slope:** 109/113.
Green Fee: $10. **Cart Fee:** $5/Person. **To obtain tee times:** Call golf shop.

ASHLEY PLANTATION COUNTRY CLUB
SP-919 Greenfield St., Daleville, 24083, Botetourt County, (540)992-4653, 12 miles from
Roanoke. **Facility Holes:** 18. **Yards:** 6,915/4,690. **Par:** 73/73. **Course Rating:** 72.3/66.3. **Slope:**
121/111. **Green Fee:** $15/$28. **Cart Fee:** $13/Person. **Walking Policy:** Walking at certain times.
Walkability: 4. **Opened:** 1999. **Architect:** Russell Breeden. **Season:** Year-round. **High:** May-
Oct. **To obtain tee times:** Call up to 5 days in advance. **Miscellaneous:** Range (grass/mats),
credit cards (MC, V), BF, FF.

AUBURN HILLS GOLF CLUB
PU-1581 Turnberry Ln., Riner, 24149, Montgomery County, (540)381-4995, 30 miles from
Roanoke. **Web:** www.auburnhillsgolf.com. **Facility Holes:** 18. **Yards:** 6,534/4,807. **Par:** 72/72.
Course Rating: 71.9/67.2. **Slope:** 127/113. **Green Fee:** $16/$25. **Cart Fee:** $12/Person.
Walking Policy: Walking at certain times. **Walkability:** 3. **Opened:** 1999. **Architect:** Algie Pulley.
Season: Year-round. **To obtain tee times:** Call golf shop. **Miscellaneous:** Reduced fees (week-
days, seniors), range (grass), credit cards (MC, V, AE, D), BF, FF.

★★★★ AUGUSTINE GOLF CLUB
SP-76 Monument Dr., Stafford, 22554, Stafford County, (540)720-7374, 30 miles from
Washington, DC. **E-mail:** www.info@augustinegolf.com. **Web:** www.augustinegolf.com.
Facility Holes: 18. **Yards:** 6,850/4,838. **Par:** 71/71. **Course Rating:** 74.3/68.2. **Slope:** 142/119.
Green Fee: $44/$79. **Cart Fee:** Included in green fee. **Walking Policy:** Unrestricted walking.
Walkability: 3. **Opened:** 1995. **Architect:** Rick Jacobson. **Season:** Year-round. **High:** April-Nov.
To obtain tee times: Call up to 7 days in advance. **Miscellaneous:** Reduced fees (weekdays,
twilight, seniors, juniors), range (grass/mats), credit cards (MC, V, AE, D), BF, FF.
Notes: Ranked 10th in 1999 Best in State; 5th in 1996 Best New Upscale Courses.
Reader Comments: The holes are awe-inspiring, tough, but not impossble with rolling fairways and
undulating greens … Challenging … Public course with a private course layout and conditioning …
Great warm-up on our way to Myrtle … Super starting hole … Fast & true greens.

★★★ BELMONT GOLF COURSE
PU-1600 Hilliard Rd., Richmond, 23228, Henrico County, (804)501-4653, 5 miles from
Richmond. **Web:** www.co.henrico.va.us.com. **Facility Holes:** 18. **Yards:** 6,350/5,418. **Par:**
71/73. **Course Rating:** 70.6/72.6. **Slope:** 126/130. **Green Fee:** $18/$21. **Cart Fee:** $11/Person.
Walking Policy: Unrestricted walking. **Walkability:** 2. **Opened:** 1903. **Architect:** A.W. Tillinghast.
Season: Year-round. **High:** April-Sept. **To obtain tee times:** Call up to 7 days in advance.
Miscellaneous: Reduced fees (weekdays, seniors, juniors), credit cards (MC, V), BF, FF.
Reader Comments: Very reasonable price for the quality of the course … Very walker-friendly
course … I enjoyed it even though I am a high handicapper. The first hole is a real killer … Lots of
trees that were in play … Best value in Richmond.

★★★★ BIDE-A-WEE GOLF CLUB
PU-1 Bide-A-Wee Drive, Portsmouth, 23701, Portsmouth City County, (757)393-8600,
5 miles from Portsmouth. **Facility Holes:** 18. **Yards:** 7,069/5,518. **Par:** 72/74. **Course Rating:**
72.2/66.4. **Slope:** 121/113. **Green Fee:** $25/$35. **Cart Fee:** $10/Person. **Walking Policy:**
Walking at certain times. **Walkability:** 2. **Opened:** 1999. **Architect:** Curtis Strange/Tom Clark.
Season: Year-round. **To obtain tee times:** Call up to 7 days in advance. **Miscellaneous:**
Reduced fees (weekdays, twilight, seniors, juniors), range (grass/mats), credit cards (MC, V,
D), BF, FF.
Reader Comments: The new, improved course is wonderful … Curtis Strange redesigned what
was a dog track and turned it into a real jewel. Greens are magnificent and layout a challenge from
all tees … Fun to play.

★★★½ BIRDWOOD GOLF COURSE
R-410 Golf Course Drive, Charlottesville, 22903, Albemarle County, (804)293-4653, 1 mile
from Charlottesville. **E-mail:** birdwood@bearsheadinn.com. **Web:** www.bearsheadinn.com.

Facility Holes: 18. **Yards:** 6,820/5,041. **Par:** 72/72. **Course Rating:** 72.8/65.2. **Slope:** 132/116. **Green Fee:** $17/$60. **Cart Fee:** $15/Person. **Walking Policy:** Walking at certain times. **Walkability:** 3. **Opened:** 1984. **Architect:** Lindsay Ervin. **Season:** Year-round. **High:** April-Oct. **To obtain tee times:** Call up to 7 days in advance. **Miscellaneous:** Reduced fees (weekdays, guests, twilight, juniors), range (grass/mats), credit cards (MC, V, AE), BF, FF.
Reader Comments: A wonderful course for college kids to enjoy a quality round for under $20 … A true challenge to walk (very hilly) and a true challenge to play … Island green great hole.

★★½ **BIRKDALE GOLF CLUB**
SP-8511 Royal Birkdale Dr., Chesterfield, 23832, Chesterfield County, (804)739-8800, 15 miles from Richmond. **Facility Holes:** 18. **Yards:** 6,566/5,390. **Par:** 71/71. **Course Rating:** 71.3/71.2. **Slope:** 126/122. **Green Fee:** $56. **Cart Fee:** Included in green fee. **Walking Policy:** Mandatory carts. **Walkability:** 3. **Opened:** 1990. **Architect:** Dan Maples. **Season:** Year-round. **To obtain tee times:** Call golf shop. **Miscellaneous:** Reduced fees (weekdays, guests, twilight, seniors, juniors), range (grass/mats), credit cards (MC, V, AE), BF, FF.

★½ **BOW CREEK GOLF COURSE**
PU-3425 Clubhouse Rd., Virginia Beach, 23452, Virginia Beach City County, (757)431-3763, 10 miles from Norfolk. **Facility Holes:** 18. **Yards:** 5,917/5,181. **Par:** 70/70. **Course Rating:** 70.4/68.4. **Slope:** 114/104. **Green Fee:** $25. **Cart Fee:** $10/Person. **Walking Policy:** Unrestricted walking. **Walkability:** 1. **Opened:** 1960. **Architect:** John Aragona/Fred Sappenfield. **Season:** Year-round. **High:** April-Sept. **To obtain tee times:** Call golf shop. **Miscellaneous:** Reduced fees (twilight, seniors, juniors), range (grass), credit cards (MC, V).

BOWLING GREEN COUNTRY CLUB
SP-838 Bowling Green Rd., Front Royal, 22630, Warren County, (540)635-2024, (800)659-0163, 45 miles from Washington, DC. **E-mail:** bgccva@yahoo. **Facility Holes:** 36. **Green Fee:** $10/$26. **Cart Fee:** $10/Person. **Walking Policy:** Walking at certain times. **Architect:** Lynwood Morrison. **Season:** Year-round. **High:** April-Oct. **To obtain tee times:** Call up to 7 days in advance. **Miscellaneous:** Reduced fees (weekdays, twilight), range (grass), credit cards (MC, V, D), BF, FF.
NORTH COURSE (18)
Yards: 6,464/5,010. **Par:** 71/71. **Course Rating:** 70.2/65.2. **Slope:** 123/113. **Walkability:** 3. **Opened:** 1983.
SOUTH COURSE (18)
Yards: 5,929/4,853. **Par:** 70/72. **Course Rating:** 68.4/63.7. **Slope:** 117/104. **Walkability:** 4. **Opened:** 1992.

★★½ **BRAMBLETON REGIONAL PARK GOLF COURSE**
PU-42180 Ryan Rd., Ashburn, 20147, Loudoun County, (703)327-3403. **Facility Holes:** 18. **Yards:** 6,764/5,684. **Par:** 72/72. **Course Rating:** 71.2/72.0. **Slope:** 121/121. **Green Fee:** $29/$36. **Cart Fee:** $27/Cart. **To obtain tee times:** Call golf shop.

★★★ **BRISTOW MANOR GOLF CLUB**
PU-11507 Valley View Dr., Bristow, 20136, Prince William County, (703)368-3558, 25 miles from Washington, DC. **Web:** americangolf.com. **Facility Holes:** 18. **Yards:** 7,102/5,527. **Par:** 72/74. **Course Rating:** 72.9/73.4. **Slope:** 129/128. **Green Fee:** $25/$69. **Cart Fee:** Included in green fee. **Walking Policy:** Walking at certain times. **Walkability:** 2. **Opened:** 1993. **Architect:** Ken Killian. **Season:** Year-round. **High:** April-Oct. **To obtain tee times:** Call up to 7 days in advance. **Miscellaneous:** Reduced fees (weekdays, twilight, seniors, juniors), range (grass), credit cards (MC, V, AE, D), BF, FF.
Reader Comments: Good links design in the middle of rolling VA countryside … Two dramatically different nines … Somewhat difficult … Loved the zoysia grass … Watch for No. 7.

BROAD RUN GOLF & PRACTICE FACILITY
PU-10201 Golf Academy Dr., Bristow, 20136, Prince William County, (703)365-2443, 20 miles from Washington, DC. **E-mail:** rzarlengo@golfmatrix.com. **Web:** broadrungolfpractice.com. **Facility Holes:** 9. **Yards:** 3,070/2,221. **Par:** 35/35. **Course Rating:** 70.4/62.9. **Slope:** 135/115. **Green Fee:** $16/$28. **Cart Fee:** $15/Person. **Walking Policy:** Unrestricted walking. **Walkability:** 2. **Opened:** 1998. **Architect:** Rick Jacobson. **Season:** Year-round. **High:** April-Sept. **To obtain tee times:** Call up to 7 days in advance. **Miscellaneous:** Reduced fees (weekdays, twilight, seniors, juniors), range (grass/mats), credit cards (MC, V, D), BF, FF.

★★ **THE BROOKWOODS GOLF CLUB**
PU-7325 Club Dr., Quinton, 23141, New Kent County, (804)932-3737, 15 miles from Richmond. **E-mail:** brookwoodsgolf@aol.com. **Facility Holes:** 18. **Yards:** 6,485/5,057. **Par:** 72/72. **Course Rating:** 71.2/69.5. **Slope:** 123/119. **Green Fee:** $16/$23. **Cart Fee:** $11/Person. **Walking Policy:** Walking at certain times. **Walkability:** 3. **Opened:** 1974. **Architect:** Algie Pulley.

Season: Year-round. **High:** April-Oct. **To obtain tee times:** Call up to 7 days in advance. **Miscellaneous:** Reduced fees (twilight, seniors, juniors), range (grass), credit cards (MC, V, D, DC), FF.

★★½ BRYCE RESORT GOLF COURSE

R-P.O. Box 3, Basye, 22810, Shenandoah County, (540)856-2124, (800)821-1444, 100 miles from Washington, DC. **E-mail:** golfinfo@bryceresort.com. **Web:** www.bryceresort.com. **Facility Holes:** 18. **Yards:** 6,261/5,240. **Par:** 71/71. **Course Rating:** 68.8/70.1. **Slope:** 122/120. **Green Fee:** $28/$50. **Cart Fee:** Included in green fee. **Walking Policy:** Mandatory carts. **Walkability:** 2. **Opened:** 1968. **Architect:** Ed Ault. **Season:** March-Dec. **To obtain tee times:** Call up to 4 days in advance. **Miscellaneous:** Reduced fees (weekdays, twilight), range (grass), credit cards (MC, V, AE, D), BF, FF.

★★★★ BULL RUN COUNTRY CLUB

PU-3520 James Madison Hwy., Haymarket, 20169, Prince William County, (703)753-7777, (877)753-7770, 12 miles from Manassas. **E-mail:** bullruncc@aol.com. **Web:** www.bullruncc.com. **Facility Holes:** 18. **Yards:** 6,961/5,069. **Par:** 72/72. **Course Rating:** 73.1/68.3. **Slope:** 134/110. **Green Fee:** $45/$85. **Cart Fee:** Included in green fee. **Walking Policy:** Walking at certain times. **Walkability:** 3. **Opened:** 1999. **Architect:** Rick Jacobson. **Season:** Year-round. **High:** April-Oct. **To obtain tee times:** Call up to 8 days in advance. **Miscellaneous:** Reduced fees (weekdays, twilight, seniors, juniors), range (grass/mats), credit cards (MC, V, AE, D, DC), BF, FF.
Reader Comments: Tough, interesting layout … Enjoyable layout with a mix of long & short holes - great fairways. Time to grow will make it great … Looks easier than it is.

CAHOON PLANTATION

PU-1501 Cedar Rd., Chesapeake, 23322, City of Chesapeake County, (757)436-2775. **Web:** www.cahoonplantation.com. **Facility Holes:** 27. **Green Fee:** $29/$69. **Cart Fee:** Included in green fee. **Opened:** 1999. **Architect:** Tom Clark. **To obtain tee times:** Call golf shop.
SALTIRE/TRICOLOUR COURSE (18 Combo)
Yards: 6,618/5,226. **Par:** 72/72. **Course Rating:** 71.1/69.0. **Slope:** 112/113.
UNION JACK/SALTIRE COURSE (18 Combo)
Yards: 6,676/5,193. **Par:** 72/72. **Course Rating:** 71.2/68.7. **Slope:** 118/112.
UNION JACK/TRICOLOUR COURSE (18 Combo)
Yards: 6,672/5,257. **Par:** 72/72. **Course Rating:** 70.8/68.9. **Slope:** 117/112.

★★ CARPER'S VALLEY GOLF CLUB

PU-1400 Millwood Pike, Winchester, 22602, Frederick County, (540)662-4319, 65 miles from Washington, DC. **Facility Holes:** 18. **Yards:** 6,125/4,930. **Par:** 70/71. **Course Rating:** 69.5/67.5. **Slope:** 118/107. **Green Fee:** $10/$25. **Cart Fee:** $15/Person. **Walking Policy:** Walking at certain times. **Walkability:** 2. **Opened:** 1962. **Architect:** Ed Ault. **Season:** Year-round. **High:** April-Nov. **To obtain tee times:** Call up to 5 days in advance. **Miscellaneous:** Reduced fees (weekdays, twilight, juniors), metal spikes, range (grass/mats), credit cards (MC, V), BF, FF.

★★½ CAVERNS COUNTRY CLUB RESORT

R-910 T.C. Northcott Bv., Luray, 22835, Page County, (540)743-7111, 80 miles from Washington, DC. **E-mail:** luraycaverns@rica.net. **Web:** www.luraycaverns.com. **Facility Holes:** 18. **Yards:** 6,499/5,499. **Par:** 72/72. **Course Rating:** 71.2/72.4. **Slope:** 117/120. **Green Fee:** $24/$33. **Cart Fee:** $13/Person. **Walking Policy:** Unrestricted walking. **Walkability:** 3. **Opened:** 1976. **Architect:** Mal Purdy. **Season:** Year-round. **High:** April-June. **To obtain tee times:** Call up to 7 days in advance. **Miscellaneous:** Reduced fees (weekdays), metal spikes, lodging (63 rooms), credit cards (MC, V, AE, D).

CEDAR HILLS COUNTRY CLUB

SP-RR No. 1 Box 598, Jonesville, 24263, Lee County, (540)346-1535, 85 miles from Knoxville. **Facility Holes:** 18. **Yards:** 6,466/5,057. **Par:** 71/71. **Course Rating:** 69.3/65.2. **Slope:** 111/101. **Green Fee:** $10/$15. **Cart Fee:** $10/Person. **Walking Policy:** Unrestricted walking. **Walkability:** 2. **Opened:** 1967. **Architect:** Horace Smith. **Season:** Year-round. **High:** April-Oct. **To obtain tee times:** Call golf shop. **Miscellaneous:** Reduced fees (weekdays, juniors), metal spikes, range (grass/mats), credit cards (MC, V).

CHESAPEAKE GOLF CLUB

PU-1201 Club House Dr., Chesapeake, 23322, City of Chesapeake County, (757)547-1122, 7 miles from Norfolk. **Facility Holes:** 18. **Yards:** 6,241/5,044. **Par:** 70/70. **Course Rating:** 69.4/68.0. **Slope:** 115/115. **Green Fee:** $15/$33. **Cart Fee:** Included in green fee. **Walking Policy:** Walking at certain times. **Opened:** 1986. **Season:** Year-round. **High:** March-Nov. **To obtain tee times:** Call up to 7 days in advance. **Miscellaneous:** Reduced fees (weekdays, twilight, seniors, juniors), range (mats), credit cards (MC, V, AE), BF, FF.
Special Notes: Formerly Seven Springs Golf Club.

VIRGINIA

CLEAR CREEK GOLF CLUB
PU-732 Harleywood Rd., Bristol, 24202, Washington County, (540)466-4833, 100 miles from Knoxville. **Facility Holes:** 18. **Yards:** 6,516/4,665. **Par:** 71/71. **Course Rating:** 71.9. **Slope:** 133. **Green Fee:** $18/$23. **Cart Fee:** $11/Person. **Walking Policy:** Walking at certain times. **Walkability:** 3. **Opened:** 1997. **Architect:** Jack Sykes/Chris Chrisman. **Season:** Year-round. **To obtain tee times:** Call up to 30 days in advance. **Miscellaneous:** Reduced fees (weekdays, seniors, juniors), metal spikes, range (grass), credit cards (MC, V, AE), BF, FF.

★★★★ THE COLONIAL GOLF COURSE *Pace*
PU-8285 Diascund Rd ., Williamsburg, 23089, James City County, (757)566-1600, (800)566-6660, 12 miles from Williamsburg. **E-mail:** jb@golfcolonial.com. **Web:** golfcolonial.com. **Facility Holes:** 18. **Yards:** 6,885/4,568. **Par:** 72/72. **Course Rating:** 73.2/66.3. **Slope:** 133/109. **Green Fee:** $40/$85. **Cart Fee:** Included in green fee. **Walking Policy:** Unrestricted walking. **Walkability:** 3. **Opened:** 1995. **Architect:** Lester George. **Season:** Year-round. **High:** March-Nov. **To obtain tee times:** Call golf shop. **Miscellaneous:** Reduced fees (twilight, seniors, juniors), range (grass/mats), credit cards (MC, V, AE, D), BF, FF.
Reader Comments: This is the surprise of the state—a fine course, plenty tough and away from the crowds ... Good prize for a good mind ... Quiet, secluded course with nice facilities—6th hole is worth the experience ... Challenging greens, long par 4s.

★★★½ COUNTRYSIDE GOLF CLUB
PU-One Countryside Rd. NW, Roanoke, 24017, Roanoke County, (540)563-0391. **Facility Holes:** 18. **Yards:** 6,815/5,185. **Par:** 70/70. **Course Rating:** 71.3/69.8. **Slope:** 121/114. **Green Fee:** $28/$33. **Cart Fee:** Included in green fee. **To obtain tee times:** Call golf shop.
Reader Comments: A scorer's heaven, great par 3s ... Tough from back tee ... Great value for nice course ... Friendly staff, good discount for group, good winter conditions.

★★★ THE CROSSINGS GOLF CLUB
PU-800 Virginia Center Pkwy., Glen Allen, 23060, Henrico County, (804)261-0000, 9 miles from Richmond. **Web:** www.thecrossingsgolf.com. **Facility Holes:** 18. **Yards:** 6,619/5,625. **Par:** 72/72. **Course Rating:** 70.7/73.2. **Slope:** 126/128. **Green Fee:** $24/$57. **Cart Fee:** $12/Person. **Walking Policy:** Walking at certain times. **Walkability:** 3. **Opened:** 1979. **Architect:** Joe Lee. **Season:** Year-round. **To obtain tee times:** Call up to 14 days in advance. **Miscellaneous:** Reduced fees (weekdays, twilight, juniors), range (grass/mats), credit cards (MC, V, AE, D), BF, FF.
Reader Comments: Great layout. Great service. Solid golf course ... A few challenging holes ... GPS new on carts ... Very clean and nice to play ... Great greens.

★★★★ CYPRESS CREEK GOLFERS' CLUB
SP-600 Cypress Creek Pkwy., Smithfield, 23430, Isle of White County, (757)365-4774, 14 miles from Newport News. **Web:** www.golfsouth.com. **Facility Holes:** 18. **Yards:** 7,159/5,136. **Par:** 72/72. **Course Rating:** 74.1/68.8. **Slope:** 130/113. **Green Fee:** $35/$55. **Cart Fee:** Included in green fee. **Walking Policy:** Unrestricted walking. **Walkability:** 3. **Opened:** 1998. **Architect:** Tom Clark/Curtis Strange. **Season:** Year-round. **High:** April-Oct. **To obtain tee times:** Call golf shop. **Miscellaneous:** Reduced fees (weekdays, twilight, juniors), range (grass/mats), credit cards (MC, V, AE).
Reader Comments: Striking layout with attention to preserving and incorporating natural features ... Many tricky holes. Glad we played with regulars the 1st time ... Worth long drive from civilization.

★★★ CYPRESS POINT COUNTRY CLUB
SP-5340 Club Head Rd., Virginia Beach, 23455, Virginia Beach City County, (757)490-8822. **Facility Holes:** 18. **Yards:** 6,680/5,440. **Par:** 72/72. **Course Rating:** 71.5/70.8. **Slope:** 124/114. **Green Fee:** $33/$39. **Cart Fee:** Included in green fee. **Walking Policy:** Walking at certain times. **Walkability:** 2. **Opened:** 1987. **Architect:** Tom Clark/Brian Ault. **Season:** Year-round. **High:** April-Oct. **To obtain tee times:** Call golf shop. **Miscellaneous:** Range (grass), credit cards (MC, V, AE), BF, FF.
Reader Comments: Excellent course ... Well maintained, not overly challenging.

★★★★½ DRAPER VALLEY GOLF CLUB
PU-2800 Big Valley Drive, Draper, 24324, Pulaski County, (540)980-4653, (866)980-4653, 60 miles from Roanoke. **E-mail:** drapergolf@psknet.com. **Web:** drapervalleygolf.com. **Facility Holes:** 18. **Yards:** 7,072/4,793. **Par:** 72/72. **Course Rating:** 73.3/65.6. **Slope:** 125/113. **Green Fee:** $16/$28. **Cart Fee:** $12/Person. **Walking Policy:** Walking at certain times. **Walkability:** 3. **Opened:** 1992. **Architect:** Harold Louthen. **Season:** Year-round. **To obtain tee times:** Call up to 7 days in advance. **Miscellaneous:** Reduced fees (weekdays, twilight, seniors, juniors), range (grass), credit cards (MC, V, D), BF, FF.
Reader Comments: Dollar for dollar, tough to beat ... A long hitter's paradise, wide fairways ... Outstanding condition. Very long course.

VIRGINIA

★★½ **FAIRFAX NATIONAL GOLF CLUB**
SP-16850 Sudley Rd., Centreville, 20120, Fairfax County, (703)631-9226, 15 miles from Washington, DC. **Facility Holes:** 27. **Green Fee:** $42/$59. **Walking Policy:** Walking at certain times. **Walkability:** 2. **Season:** Year-round. **High:** March-Nov. **To obtain tee times:** Call up to 7 days in advance. **Miscellaneous:** Reduced fees (weekdays, twilight, seniors, juniors), range (grass/mats), credit cards (MC, V), BF, FF.
BULL RUN/CEDARS COURSE (18 Combo)
Yards: 7,048/5,983. **Par:** 73/73. **Course Rating:** 72.4. **Slope:** 121.
CEDARS/SUDLEY COURSE (18 Combo)
Yards: 6,883/5,955. **Par:** 72/72. **Course Rating:** 72.1. **Slope:** 119.
SUDLEY/BULL RUN COURSE (18 Combo)
Yards: 6,958/5,972. **Par:** 73/73. **Course Rating:** 72.5. **Slope:** 122.

FORD'S COLONY COUNTRY CLUB
R-240 Ford's Colony Dr., Williamsburg, 23188, James City County, (757)258-4130, (800)334-6033, 5 miles from Williamsburg. **Web:** www.fordscolony.com. **Facility Holes:** 54. **Green Fee:** $40/$90. **Cart Fee:** Included in green fee. **Walking Policy:** Mandatory carts. **Walkability:** 3. **Architect:** Dan Maples. **Season:** Year-round. **High:** April-Oct. **To obtain tee times:** Call up to 7 days in advance. **Miscellaneous:** Reduced fees (weekdays, guests, twilight, juniors), range (grass/mats), credit cards (MC, V, AE), BF, FF.
★★★★ **BLACKHEATH COURSE** (18)
Yards: 6,621/5,390. **Par:** 71/71. **Course Rating:** 71.8/70.5. **Slope:** 133/119. **Opened:** 1999.
Reader Comments: Wonderful variety, challenging but playable … Fairly long which requires shotmaking … Great course, fast greens, challenging layout … Beautiful course with lots of water in play.
★★★★½ **BLUE HERON COURSE** (18) *Pace*
Yards: 6,769/5,424. **Par:** 71/71. **Course Rating:** 72.3. **Slope:** 124/109. **Opened:** 1987.
Reader Comments: Excellent challenge, scenic … The only thing better than this golf course is its wine list—you must stay for dinner … Beautiful clubhouse … Great course, fast greens, challenging layout.
★★★★½ **MARSH HAWK COURSE** (18) *Condition*
Yards: 6,738/5,579. **Par:** 72/72. **Course Rating:** 72.3/72.3. **Slope:** 124/124. **Opened:** 1985.
Reader Comments: Good value during fall & winter … Perfect greens. No trick holes … Challenging design. Tough for short hitters … Excellent variety, some cavernous bunkers…. Good test. Watch the water.

★★★ **FOREST GREENS GOLF CLUB**
PU-4500 Poa Annua Lane, Triangle, 22172, Prince William County, (703)221-0123, 32 miles from Washington, DC. **Facility Holes:** 18. **Yards:** 6,839/5,007. **Par:** 72/72. **Course Rating:** 71.8/68.7. **Slope:** 129/119. **Green Fee:** $20/$38. **Cart Fee:** $11/Person. **Walking Policy:** Walking at certain times. **Walkability:** 4. **Opened:** 1996. **Architect:** Clyde Johnston. **Season:** Year-round. **High:** April-Sept. **To obtain tee times:** Call golf shop. **Miscellaneous:** Reduced fees (weekdays, twilight, seniors, juniors), range (grass), credit cards (MC, V), BF, FF.
Reader Comments: Good combination of hard and playable holes … Good course, very forgiving … Hilly, excellent make-up of challenging holes.

★★★★ **THE GAUNTLET GOLF CLUB AT CURTIS PARK**
SP-18 Fairway Dr., Fredericksburg, 22406, Stafford County, (540)752-0963, (888)755-7888, 10 miles from Fredericksburg. **Facility Holes:** 18. **Yards:** 6,857/4,955. **Par:** 72/72. **Course Rating:** 72.8/69.8. **Slope:** 137/126. **Green Fee:** $42/$65. **Cart Fee:** Included in green fee. **Walking Policy:** Walking at certain times. **Walkability:** 3. **Opened:** 1995. **Architect:** P.B. Dye. **Season:** Year-round. **High:** March-Nov. **To obtain tee times:** Call up to 7 days in advance. **Miscellaneous:** Reduced fees (weekdays, twilight, seniors), range (grass), credit cards (MC, V), BF, FF.
Notes: Ranked 10th in 1996 Best New Affordable Courses.
Reader Comments: An absolutely beautiful and deceptively difficult course. Bring plenty of balls … This course kicks my butt every time … Lots of water … Plenty of risk, but rewarding … Scenic, very tough if windy … Looks harder than it is … Great shape.

★★★ **GENERAL'S RIDGE GOLF COURSE**
PU-9701 Manassas Dr., Manassas Park, 20111, Prince William County, (703)335-0777, 20 miles from Washington, DC. **Facility Holes:** 18. **Yards:** 6,651/4,747. **Par:** 72/72. **Course Rating:** 72.5/68.1. **Slope:** 133/118. **Green Fee:** $15/$30. **Cart Fee:** $12/Person. **Walking Policy:** Walking at certain times. **Walkability:** 5. **Opened:** 1996. **Architect:** Jerry Slack. **Season:** Year-round. **High:** April-Oct. **To obtain tee times:** Call golf shop. **Miscellaneous:** Reduced fees (weekdays, twilight, seniors, juniors), metal spikes, range (grass), credit cards (MC, V), BF, FF.
Reader Comments: Fun course, very hilly! … Most challenging, most enjoyable … True links, huge greens … Tight, rolling terrain. Need a yardage book to judge carries.

★★ GLENWOOD GOLF CLUB
PU-3100 Creighton Rd., Richmond, 23223, Henrico County, (804)226-1793, 3 miles from Richmond. **Facility Holes:** 18. **Yards:** 6,464/5,197. **Par:** 71/75. **Course Rating:** 70.0/72.1. **Slope:** 114/120. **Green Fee:** $12/$23. **Cart Fee:** $12/Person. **Walking Policy:** Walking at certain times. **Walkability:** 2. **Opened:** 1927. **Architect:** Fred Findlay. **Season:** Year-round. **High:** May-Oct. **To obtain tee times:** Call up to 7 days in advance. **Miscellaneous:** Reduced fees (weekdays, twilight, seniors, juniors), credit cards (MC, V), FF.

GOLDEN HORSESHOE GOLF CLUB
R-401 S. England St., Williamsburg, 23185, City of Williamsburg County, (757)220-7696, (800)447-8679, 45 miles from Richmond. **Facility Holes:** 36. **Cart Fee:** Included in green fee. **Walking Policy:** Unrestricted walking. **Walkability:** 3. **Season:** Year-round. **To obtain tee times:** Call up to 30 days in advance. **Miscellaneous:** Reduced fees (guests, twilight, juniors), metal spikes, range (grass/mats), credit cards (MC, V, AE, D, DC), BF, FF.

★★★★½ **GOLD COURSE** (18) *Condition, Pace*
Yards: 6,817/5,168. **Par:** 71/71. **Course Rating:** 73.8/69.8. **Slope:** 144/126. **Green Fee:** $40/$130. **Opened:** 1963. **Architect:** Robert Trent Jones.
Notes: Golf Digest School site. Ranked 7th in 2001 Best in State.
Reader Comments: Great course, great par 3s ... The four par 3s are as beautiful as any I've ever played ... If Spyglass gets 5 stars, then this RTJ gets 7 ... Not too unreasonable for 'vacation budget' ... Fantastic elvation changes from the tee boxes ... Very tight course ... The service was outstanding.
Special Notes: Also has a 9-hole executive course.

★★★★½ **GREEN COURSE** (18) *Pace*
Yards: 7,120/5,348. **Par:** 72/72. **Course Rating:** 75.1/70.5. **Slope:** 138/120. **Green Fee:** $30/$95. **Opened:** 1991. **Architect:** Rees Jones.
Notes: Golf Digest School site. Ranked 8th in 1997 Best in State.
Reader Comments: Great course in great shape; wide, sculpted fairways ... Rolling terrain ... More forgiving than sister course ... Back 9 is better than front ... Tough course. Good finishing hole.
Special Notes: Also has a 9-hole executive course.

★★ GOOSE CREEK GOLF CLUB
PU-43001 Golf Club Rd., Leesburg, 20175, Loudoun County, (703)729-2500, 35 miles from Washington, DC. **E-mail:** info@goosecreekgolf.com. **Web:** www.goosecreekgolf.com. **Facility Holes:** 18. **Yards:** 6,400/5,235. **Par:** 72/72. **Course Rating:** 70.3/71.3. **Slope:** 121/120. **Green Fee:** $25/$49. **Cart Fee:** Included in green fee. **Walking Policy:** Walking at certain times. **Walkability:** 2. **Opened:** 1952. **Architect:** William Gordon. **Season:** Year-round. **High:** April-Oct. **To obtain tee times:** Call up to 14 days in advance. **Miscellaneous:** Reduced fees (weekdays, twilight, seniors, juniors), credit cards (MC, V, AE), BF, FF.

GORDON TRENT GOLF COURSE, INC.
PU-2160 Golf Course Rd., Stuart, 24171, Patrick County, (540)694-3805. **Facility Holes:** 18. **Yards:** 5,503/4,343. **Par:** 70/70. **Course Rating:** 64.8/62.8. **Slope:** 110/108. **Green Fee:** $10/$12. **Cart Fee:** $7/Person. **Architect:** Al Jamison/Claude Bingham. **To obtain tee times:** Call golf shop. **Miscellaneous:** Metal spikes.

GREEN'S FOLLY GOLF COURSE
PU-1085 Green's Folly Rd., South Boston, 24592, Halifax County, (804)572-4998, 60 miles from Raleigh. **E-mail:** www.greensfolly.com. **Web:** www.greensfolly.com. **Facility Holes:** 18. **Yards:** 6,800/5,600. **Par:** 71/75. **Course Rating:** 72.0/68.0. **Slope:** 121/120. **Green Fee:** $10/$15. **Cart Fee:** $9/Person. **Walking Policy:** Unrestricted walking. **Walkability:** 3. **Architect:** Fred Findlay. **Season:** Year-round. **To obtain tee times:** Call golf shop. **Miscellaneous:** Reduced fees (weekdays, twilight, seniors, juniors), range (grass/mats), BF, FF.

GREENDALE GOLF COURSE
PU-6700 Telegraph Rd., Alexandria, 22310, Fairfax County, (703)971-3788. **Facility Holes:** 18. **Yards:** 6,353/5,454. **Par:** 70/70. **Course Rating:** 70.9/70.4. **Slope:** 128/115. **Green Fee:** $25/$29. **Cart Fee:** $23/Cart. **To obtain tee times:** Call golf shop.

★★½ THE HAMPTONS GOLF COURSE
PU-320 Butler Farm Rd., Hampton, 23666, Hampton City County, (757)766-9148. **E-mail:** mlmiller@city.hampton.va.us. **Web:** www.hampton.gov/thehamptons. **Facility Holes:** 27. **Green Fee:** $17/$19. **Cart Fee:** $10/Person. **Walking Policy:** Walking at certain times. **Walkability:** 1. **Opened:** 1989. **Architect:** Michael Hurdzan. **Season:** Year-round. **To obtain tee times:** Call up to 5 days in advance. **Miscellaneous:** Reduced fees (seniors, juniors), range (grass), credit cards (MC, V, AE), BF, FF.
LAKES/LINKS (18 Combo)
Yards: 6,283/4,965. **Par:** 71/71. **Course Rating:** 69.4/67.2. **Slope:** 110/103.

WOODS/LAKES (18 Combo)
Yards: 6,401/5,398. **Par:** 71/71. **Course Rating:** 70.9/65.7. **Slope:** 118/107.
WOODS/LINKS (18 Combo)
Yards: 5,940/4,857. **Par:** 70/70. **Course Rating:** 66.8/60.4. **Slope:** 106/88.

★★★½ HANGING ROCK GOLF CLUB
PU-1500 Red Lane, Salem, 24135, Salem City County, (540)389-7275, (800)277-7497,
9 miles from Roanoke. **E-mail:** hangingrockgolf@aol.com. **Web:** hangingrockgolf.com. **Facility
Holes:** 18. **Yards:** 6,828/4,463. **Par:** 73/72. **Course Rating:** 72.3/62.6. **Slope:** 125/106. **Green
Fee:** $23/$33. **Cart Fee:** $13/Person. **Walking Policy:** Walking at certain times. **Walkability:** 3.
Opened: 1991. **Architect:** Russell Breeden. **Season:** Year-round. **High:** April-Oct. **To obtain tee
times:** Call up to 3 days in advance. **Miscellaneous:** Reduced fees (weekdays, guests,
twilight, seniors, juniors), metal spikes, range (grass/mats), credit cards (MC, V), BF, FF.
Reader Comments: Some of the most undulating and fastest greens I ever tried to putt on ...
Allowed my wife to ride free ... Very nice course, hidden find ... Good course, great views, good
value ... Good course & buy.

★★★★ HELL'S POINT GOLF CLUB
PU-2700 Atwoodtown Rd., Virginia Beach, 23456, Virginia Beach City County,
(757)721-3400, (888)821-3401, 15 miles from Norfolk. **E-mail:** rdodson@cmfa.com.
Web: www.hellspoint.com. **Facility Holes:** 18. **Yards:** 6,966/5,003. **Par:** 72/72. **Course Rating:**
73.3/71.2. **Slope:** 130/116. **Green Fee:** $34/$65. **Cart Fee:** Included in green fee. **Walking
Policy:** Unrestricted walking. **Walkability:** 1. **Opened:** 1982. **Architect:** Rees Jones. **Season:**
Year-round. **High:** March-Nov. **To obtain tee times:** Call golf shop. **Miscellaneous:** Reduced
fees (weekdays, guests, twilight, seniors, juniors), range (grass/mats), credit cards (MC, V,
AE, D), BF, FF.
Reader Comments: Classic layout ... Shotmaker's course. Friendly staff ... Beautiful location, lots
of wildlife, longest 6000-yard course you'll ever play ... Greens in great condition, true, fast, fair ...
Holes that aren't particularly long, just strategic ... Wooded, water, big greens, hard course.

★★★ HERNDON CENTENNIAL GOLF CLUB
PU-909 Ferndale Ave., Herndon, 20170, Fairfax County, (703)471-5769, 30 miles from
Washington, DC. **E-mail:** gene.fleming@town.herndon.va.us. **Web:** www.town.herndon.va.us.
Facility Holes: 18. **Yards:** 6,445/5,025. **Par:** 71/71. **Course Rating:** 68.7/68.4. **Slope:** 116/114.
Green Fee: $27/$34. **Cart Fee:** $13/Person. **Walking Policy:** Unrestricted walking. **Walkability:**
2. **Opened:** 1979. **Architect:** Edmond Ault. **Season:** Year-round. **High:** April-Oct. **To obtain tee
times:** Call up to 7 days in advance. **Miscellaneous:** Reduced fees (weekdays, twilight,
seniors, juniors), range (grass), credit cards (MC, V, D), BF, FF.
Reader Comments: Nice, friendly muni, always congenial players ... Short course.

★★★ HERON RIDGE GOLF CLUB
PU-2973 Heron Ridge Drive, Virginia Beach, 23456, Virginia Beach City County,
(757)426-3800. **E-mail:** golfpro@heronridge. **Web:** www.heronridge.com. **Facility Holes:** 18.
Yards: 7,017/5,011. **Par:** 72/72. **Course Rating:** 73.9/68.5. **Slope:** 131/111. **Green Fee:**
$34/$59. **Cart Fee:** Included in green fee. **Walking Policy:** Mandatory carts. **Walkability:** 2.
Opened: 1999. **Architect:** Fred Couples/Gene Bates. **Season:** Year-round. **High:** March-Nov.
To obtain tee times: Call golf shop. **Miscellaneous:** Reduced fees (weekdays, twilight, seniors,
juniors), range (grass), credit cards (MC, V, AE), BF, FF.
Reader Comments: Difficult in the wind ... Some super holes ... Challenging, fun, great.

HIGHLAND SPRINGS GOLF COURSE
PU-300 Lee Ave,, Highland Springs, 23075, Henrico County, (804)737-4716. **Facility Holes:**
18. **Yards:** 6,368/4,640. **Par:** 70/69. **Course Rating:** 71.9/66.4. **Slope:** 126/113. **Green Fee:**
$12/$18. **Cart Fee:** $15/Person. **To obtain tee times:** Call golf shop.

★★★½ HIGHLANDS GOLFERS' CLUB
PU-8136 Highland Glen Dr., Chesterfield, 23838, Chesterfield County, (804)796-4800,
15 miles from Richmond. **E-mail:** wwoolwine@golfmatrix.com. **Web:** golfmatrix.com. **Facility
Holes:** 18. **Yards:** 6,711/5,019. **Par:** 72/72. **Course Rating:** 72.1/68.7. **Slope:** 133/120. **Green
Fee:** $36/$56. **Cart Fee:** Included in green fee. **Walking Policy:** Mandatory carts. **Walkability:**
4. **Opened:** 1995. **Architect:** Barton Tuck. **Season:** Year-round. **High:** May-Sept. **To obtain tee
times:** Call up to 7 days in advance. **Miscellaneous:** Reduced fees (twilight, seniors, juniors),
range (grass), credit cards (MC, V, AE), BF, FF.
Reader Comments: Beautiful landscaping & challenging ... Good layout, good player can go
low ...A must play ... A shotmaker's course. Tough but fun ... Challenging course, interesting variety
of holes.

★★ HOLLOWS GOLF COURSE
SP-14501 Greenwood Church Rd., Montpelier, 23192, Hanover County, (804)798-2949,

VIRGINIA

10 miles from Richmond. **E-mail:** hollows@erols.com. **Facility Holes:** 27. **Green Fee:** $19/$25. **Cart Fee:** $11/Person. **Walking Policy:** Unrestricted walking. **Walkability:** 3. **Opened:** 1984. **Architect:** Brian Ault/Tom Clark. **Season:** Year-round. **High:** April-Nov. **To obtain tee times:** Call golf shop. **Miscellaneous:** Reduced fees (weekdays, twilight, seniors, juniors), metal spikes, credit cards (MC, V), BF, FF.
COTTAGE/ROAD (18 Combo)
Yards: 5,969/4,642. **Par:** 70/70. **Course Rating:** 67.9/63.3. **Slope:** 112/103.
LAKE/COTTAGE (18 Combo)
Yards: 5,829/4,662. **Par:** 70/70. **Course Rating:** 67.7/63.6. **Slope:** 115/106.
LAKE/ROAD (18 Combo)
Yards: 5,966/4,750. **Par:** 70/70. **Course Rating:** 68.0/67.1. **Slope:** 112/109.

HOLSTON HILLS COUNTRY CLUB
SP-1000 Country Club Rd., Marion, 24354, Smyth County, (540)783-7484, 40 miles from Bristol. **E-mail:** rwlincoln.hhcc@smyth.net. **Facility Holes:** 18. **Yards:** 6,536/5,171. **Par:** 72/75. **Course Rating:** 70.8/70.6. **Slope:** 126/119. **Green Fee:** $22/$28. **Cart Fee:** $10/Person. **Walking Policy:** Unrestricted walking. **Walkability:** 4. **Opened:** 1946. **Architect:** Edmund B. Ault. **Season:** Year-round. **High:** May-Aug. **To obtain tee times:** Call golf shop. **Miscellaneous:** Reduced fees (weekdays), credit cards (MC, V), BF, FF.

THE HOMESTEAD RESORT
R-P.O. Box 2000, Hot Springs, 24445, Bath County, (540)839-7994, (800)838-1766, 65 miles from Roanoke. **Web:** www.thehomestead.com. **Facility Holes:** 54. **Cart Fee:** Included in green fee. **Walking Policy:** Unrestricted walking. **Season:** March-Nov. **High:** April-Oct. **To obtain tee times:** Call golf shop. **Miscellaneous:** Reduced fees (guests, twilight, juniors), metal spikes, range (grass/mats), caddies, lodging (500 rooms), credit cards (MC, V, AE, D, DC), BF, FF.
★★★★½ **CASCADES COURSE** (18)
Yards: 6,679/4,967. **Par:** 70/70. **Course Rating:** 73.0/70.3. **Slope:** 137/124. **Green Fee:** $100/$165. **Walkability:** 3. **Opened:** 1923. **Architect:** William Flynn.
Notes: Ranked 48th in 2001-2002 America's 100 Greatest; 1st in 2001 Best in State.
Reader Comments: Gorgeous vistas, lightning fast greens Paradise! ... Quite simply the best mountain course in the country, bar none. The history is evident from the moment you step in the clubhouse. Course plays long ... Beautifully sited, hole after hole ... Great setting, good service ... Top notch, tough.
★★★★ **LOWER CASCADES COURSE** (18)
Yards: 6,619/4,726. **Par:** 72/70. **Course Rating:** 72.2/65.5. **Slope:** 127/116. **Green Fee:** $45/$103. **Walkability:** 3. **Opened:** 1962. **Architect:** Robert Trent Jones.
Reader Comments: A nice variety of holes ... Streams meander throughout course, par 3s are the toughest ... Very enjoyable, challenging, fair.
★★★½ **THE OLD COURSE** (18)
Yards: 6,211/4,952. **Par:** 72/72. **Course Rating:** 69.0/67.7. **Slope:** 129/116. **Green Fee:** $45/$103. **Walkability:** 5. **Opened:** 1892. **Architect:** Donald Ross.
Reader Comments: Less severe lies, fun to play ... Beautiful views ... High rating ... Excellent practice area ... Good old course. Great shape ... Friendly, helpful staff ... A wonderful surprise. Excellent course ... Small fast greens.

★★★ **HONEY BEE GOLF CLUB**
PU-2500 S. Independence Blvd, Virginia Beach, 23456, Virginia Beach City County, (757)471-2768. **Facility Holes:** 18. **Yards:** 6,075/4,929. **Par:** 70/70. **Course Rating:** 69.6/67.0. **Slope:** 123/104. **Green Fee:** $27/$44. **Cart Fee:** Included in green fee. **Walking Policy:** Walking at certain times. **Walkability:** 1. **Opened:** 1988. **Architect:** Rees Jones. **Season:** Year-round. **To obtain tee times:** Call up to 7 days in advance. **Miscellaneous:** Reduced fees (weekdays, twilight, seniors, juniors), range (grass), credit cards (MC, V, AE), BF, FF.
Reader Comments: Short, tough ... Nice executive-type course ... Good variety of holes ... Like to play, good ladies program ... A flat course ... Good course.

HUNTING HAWK GOLF CLUB
PU-15201 Ashland Rd., Glen Allen, 23059, Hanover County, (804)749-1900, 12 miles from Richmond. **Facility Holes:** 18. **Yards:** 6,832/5,164. **Par:** 71/72. **Course Rating:** 73.3/69.7. **Slope:** 137/120. **Green Fee:** $15/$45. **Cart Fee:** $14/Person. **Walking Policy:** Unrestricted walking. **Walkability:** 3. **Opened:** 2000. **Architect:** W. R. Love. **Season:** Year-round. **To obtain tee times:** Call up to 7 days in advance. **Miscellaneous:** Reduced fees (twilight, juniors), range (grass), credit cards (MC, V, AE), BF, FF.

★★★ **IVY HILL GOLF CLUB**
SP-1327 Ivy Hill Dr., Forrest, 24551, Bedford County, (804)525-2680. **Web:** www.ivyhillgolf.com. **Facility Holes:** 18. **Yards:** 7,047/4,893. **Par:** 72/72. **Course Rating:** 74.2/67.8. **Slope:** 130/110. **Green Fee:** $19/$24. **Cart Fee:** $13/Person. **Walking Policy:** Walking at certain times. **Walkability:** 5. **Opened:** 1972. **Architect:** J. Porter Gibson.

Season: Year-round. **High:** April-Oct. **To obtain tee times:** Call golf shop. **Miscellaneous:** Reduced fees (weekdays, seniors), range (grass/mats), credit cards (MC, V), BF, FF.
Reader Comments: Great tee boxes, improvement to course ... Hilly, a lot of elevation changes ... New owner made good changes ... Greens are great, pro is excellent.

★½ **JORDAN POINT GOLF CLUB**
SP-Jordan Point Rd., Hopewell, 23860, Prince George County, (804)458-0141, 80 miles from Richmond. **Facility Holes:** 18. **Yards:** 6,585/4,944. **Par:** 72/72. **Course Rating:** 70.7/68.6. **Slope:** 129/113. **Green Fee:** $19/$24. **Cart Fee:** $11/Person. **Walking Policy:** Walking at certain times. **Walkability:** 3. **Opened:** 1955. **Architect:** Russell Breeden. **Season:** Year-round. **High:** April-Oct. **To obtain tee times:** Call golf shop. **Miscellaneous:** Reduced fees (seniors), credit cards (MC, V, AE, D).

KASTLE GREENS GOLF CLUB
PU-11446 Rogues Rd., Midland, 22728, Fauquier County, (540)788-4410, (877)283-4653, 18 miles from Manassas. **E-mail:** kggolf@erols.com. **Web:** www.kastlegreens.com. **Facility Holes:** 18. **Yards:** 6,732/5,331. **Par:** 72/72. **Course Rating:** 73.8/70.5. **Slope:** 132/122. **Green Fee:** $20/$32. **Cart Fee:** $13/Person. **Walking Policy:** Walking at certain times. **Walkability:** 1. **Opened:** 1998. **Architect:** Gary Cordova. **Season:** Year-round. **High:** April-Sept. **To obtain tee times:** Call up to 7 days in advance. **Miscellaneous:** Reduced fees (weekdays, twilight, seniors), range (grass/mats), credit cards (MC, V), BF, FF.

★½ **KEMPSVILLE GREENS GOLF CLUB**
PU-4840 Princess Anne Rd., Virginia Beach, 23462, Virginia Beach City County, (757)474-8441. **Facility Holes:** 18. **Yards:** 5,849/4,538. **Par:** 70/70. **Course Rating:** 67.8/63.8. **Slope:** 114/94. **Green Fee:** $12/$20. **Cart Fee:** $9/Person. **Walking Policy:** Unrestricted walking. **Walkability:** 1. **Opened:** 1954. **Architect:** Ellis Maples. **Season:** Year-round. **High:** June-Aug. **To obtain tee times:** Call golf shop. **Miscellaneous:** Reduced fees (weekdays, twilight, seniors, juniors), metal spikes, range (grass/mats), credit cards (MC, V).

★★★ **KILN CREEK GOLF & COUNTRY CLUB**
SP-1003 Brick Kiln Blvd., Newport News, 23602, Newport News City County, (757)988-3220, 30 miles from Norfolk. **Facility Holes:** 18. **Yards:** 6,889/5,313. **Par:** 72/72. **Course Rating:** 73.4/69.5. **Slope:** 130/119. **Green Fee:** $35/$60. **Cart Fee:** Included in green fee. **Walking Policy:** Mandatory carts. **Walkability:** 3. **Opened:** 1989. **Architect:** Tom Clark. **Season:** Year-round. **High:** April-Oct. **To obtain tee times:** Call golf shop. **Miscellaneous:** Reduced fees (weekdays), range (grass/mats), credit cards (MC, V, AE), BF, FF.
Reader Comments: Back tees are monsters. Very tough par 3s. 460-yard,par-4 finish ... Better course for walking than riding.

KINDERTON COUNTRY CLUB
SP-7900 Kinderton Dr., Clarksville, 23927, Mecklenburg County, (804)374-8822. **Facility Holes:** 18. **Yards:** 6,414/4,984. **Par:** 71/72. **Course Rating:** 71.5/68.5. **Slope:** 128/115. **Green Fee:** $20/$30. **Cart Fee:** $10/Person. **To obtain tee times:** Call golf shop.

KINGSMILL RESORT & CLUB
R-1010 Kingsmill Rd., Williamsburg, 23185, James City County, (757)253-3906, (800)832-5665, 50 miles from Richmond. **Web:** www.kingsmill.com. **Facility Holes:** 63. **Cart Fee:** Included in green fee. **Walking Policy:** Mandatory carts. **Season:** Year-round. **High:** March-Nov. **To obtain tee times:** Call up to 30 days in advance. **Miscellaneous:** Reduced fees (guests, twilight), metal spikes, range (grass/mats), lodging (400 rooms), credit cards (MC, V, AE, D), BF, FF.
★★★★ **PLANTATION COURSE** (18) *Pace*
Yards: 6,543/4,880. **Par:** 72/72. **Course Rating:** 71.3/67.9. **Slope:** 119/116. **Green Fee:** $55/$105. **Walkability:** 3. **Opened:** 1986. **Architect:** Arnold Palmer/Ed Seay.
Reader Comments: Beautiful layout ... Outstanding staff ... Awesome. I might like this course better than the River course, where they play Michelob ... Difficult rough ... Excellent facility for golf.
★★★★½ **RIVER COURSE** (18)
Yards: 6,837/4,646. **Par:** 71/71. **Course Rating:** 73.3/65.3. **Slope:** 137/116. **Green Fee:** $65/$145. **Walkability:** 4. **Opened:** 1975. **Architect:** Pete Dye.
Notes: Ranked 12th in 1997 Best in State.
Reader Comments: Only thing bad: my putting that day ... Love to play it again ... Beautiful holes on the river, great course ... Harder than Chinese trigonometry ... Must keep in play ... Outstanding staff ... Wonderful greens, tough course ... It intimidates you on your first time.
Special Notes: Also has a 9-hole par-3 course.
★★★★½ **WOODS COURSE** (18) *Value, Condition*
Yards: 6,784/5,140. **Par:** 72/72. **Course Rating:** 72.7/68.7. **Slope:** 131/120. **Green Fee:** $60/$105. **Walkability:** 3. **Opened:** 1995. **Architect:** Tom Clark/Curtis Strange.
Notes: Ranked 13th in 1997 Best in State.

VIRGINIA

Reader Comments: The best … Outstanding staff … Scenic, difficult, fun … Impeccable grounds keeping, very natural … Everything is good.
Special Notes: Also has a 9-hole par-3 course.

★★★★ KISKIACK GOLF CLUB
R-8104 Club Dr., Williamsburg, 23188, James City County, (757)566-2200, (800)989-4728, 45 miles from Richmond. **E-mail:** kiskiackgolf@hotmail.com. **Facility Holes:** 18. **Yards:** 6,775/4,902. **Par:** 72/71. **Course Rating:** 72.5/67.8. **Slope:** 134/112. **Green Fee:** $25/$70. **Cart Fee:** Included in green fee. **Walking Policy:** Mandatory carts. **Walkability:** 3. **Opened:** 1997. **Architect:** John LaFoy/Vinny Giles. **Season:** Year-round. **To obtain tee times:** Call up to 30 days in advance. **Miscellaneous:** Reduced fees (twilight, juniors), range (grass/mats), credit cards (MC, V, AE, D), BF, FF.
Reader Comments: Good challenge. Tough rough … Gem hidden in the shadows of Kingsmill, Ford's Colony … A good layout which keeps your interest … Lots of variety. Good risk-reward choices … If you are traveling I-64, it is worth the stop … Speedy greens.

★★ LAKE CHESDIN GOLF CLUB
SP-21801 Lake Chesdin Pkwy., Chesterfield, 23838, Chesterfield County, (804)590-0031, 20 miles from Richmond. **Web:** www.chesdin.com. **Facility Holes:** 18. **Yards:** 6,767/5,054. **Par:** 72/72. **Course Rating:** 72.5/69.6. **Slope:** 133/116. **Green Fee:** $50/$60. **Cart Fee:** Included in green fee. **Walking Policy:** Mandatory carts. **Walkability:** 3. **Opened:** 1999. **Architect:** Barton Tuck. **Season:** Year-round. **To obtain tee times:** Call up to 7 days in advance. **Miscellaneous:** Reduced fees (twilight), range (grass/mats), credit cards (MC, V, AE), BF, FF.

★★ LAKE WRIGHT GOLF COURSE
PU-6282 N. Hampton Blvd., Norfolk, 23502, Norfolk City County, (757)459-2255. **Facility Holes:** 18. **Yards:** 6,174/5,297. **Par:** 70/70. **Course Rating:** 68.8/68.2. **Slope:** 116/105. **Green Fee:** $18/$21. **Cart Fee:** $20/Person. **Walking Policy:** Walking at certain times. **Walkability:** 2. **Opened:** 1969. **Architect:** Al Jamison. **Season:** Year-round. **High:** April-Nov. **To obtain tee times:** Call golf shop. **Miscellaneous:** Reduced fees (weekdays, seniors, juniors), range (grass/mats), BF, FF.

★★★ LAKEVIEW GOLF COURSE
SP-4101 Shen Lake Dr., Harrisonburg, 22801, Rockingham County, (540)434-8937, 2 miles from Harrisonburg. **E-mail:** DaveGoodenGolf@Yahoo. **Web:** LakeviewGolf.net. **Facility Holes:** 27. **Green Fee:** $22/$25. **Cart Fee:** $26/Cart. **Walking Policy:** Unrestricted walking. **Walkability:** 3. **Opened:** 1962. **Architect:** Ed Ault. **Season:** Year-round. **High:** April-Oct. **To obtain tee times:** Call up to 7 days in advance. **Miscellaneous:** Reduced fees (twilight), range (mats), credit cards (MC, V), BF, FF.
LAKE/PEAK (18 Combo)
Yards: 6,517/5,637. **Par:** 72/72. **Course Rating:** 70.3/71.8. **Slope:** 122/113.
LAKE/SPRING (18 Combo)
Yards: 6,589/5,383. **Par:** 72/72. **Course Rating:** 70.0/70.1. **Slope:** 122/115.
PEAK/SPRING (18 Combo)
Yards: 6,726/5,410. **Par:** 72/72. **Course Rating:** 70.6/70.1. **Slope:** 121/116.
Reader Comments: Challenging … Hills, valleys, water and woods … Enjoyable for all handicaps … Lake 9th hole requires a long blind drive and a long iron to a green guarded in front by a pond …Nice, walkable.

★★★★ LANSDOWNE GOLF CLUB *Condition*
R-44050 Woodridge Pkwy., Lansdowne, 20176, Loudoun County, (703)729-4071, (800)541-4801, 35 miles from Washington, DC. **Facility Holes:** 18. **Yards:** 7,057/5,213. **Par:** 72/72. **Course Rating:** 74.6/70.6. **Slope:** 139/124. **Green Fee:** $85/$95. **Cart Fee:** Included in green fee. **Walking Policy:** Mandatory cart. **Walkability:** 5. **Opened:** 1991. **Architect:** Robert Trent Jones Jr. **Season:** Year-round. **High:** April-Nov. **To obtain tee times:** Call golf shop. **Miscellaneous:** Reduced fees (guests, twilight), range (grass/mats), credit cards (MC, V, AE).
Reader Comments: Super layout and fine facilities … Nice upscale facility … Great course to play, plenty of risk-reward shots … Perfect fairways … Last 3 holes uphill … Some short quirky par 4s … Must play at least once a year.

★½ LEE PARK GOLF COURSE
PU-3108 Homestead Dr., Petersburg, 23805, Petersburg City County, (804)733-5667, 25 miles from Richmond. **Facility Holes:** 18. **Yards:** 6,037/4,946. **Par:** 70/70. **Course Rating:** 68.0/62.2. **Slope:** 108/96. **Green Fee:** $17/$20. **Cart Fee:** $10/Person. **Walking Policy:** Unrestricted walking. **Walkability:** 1. **Opened:** 1945. **Architect:** Fred Findley. **Season:** Year-round. **High:** June-Aug. **To obtain tee times:** Call golf shop. **Miscellaneous:** Reduced fees (weekdays, twilight, seniors, juniors), range (grass/mats), credit cards (MC, V).

VIRGINIA

★★★ LEE'S HILL GOLFERS' CLUB
SP-10200 Old Dominion Pkwy., Fredericksburg, 22408, Spotsylvania County, (540)891-0111, (800)930-3636, 50 miles from Washington, DC. **E-mail:** amullins@golfmatrix.com. **Web:** www.leeshillgc.com. **Facility Holes:** 18. **Yards:** 6,805/5,064. **Par:** 72/72. **Course Rating:** 72.4/69.2. **Slope:** 128/115. **Green Fee:** $36/$52. **Cart Fee:** Included in green fee. **Walking Policy:** Mandatory carts. **Walkability:** 1. **Opened:** 1993. **Architect:** Bill Love. **Season:** Year-round. **High:** April-Oct. **To obtain tee times:** Call up to 7 days in advance. **Miscellaneous:** Reduced fees (weekdays, guests, twilight), range (grass/mats), caddies, credit cards (MC, V, AE).
Reader Comments: Good track, still improving, playable ... Some nice holes ... Enjoyed history aspect of course (Civil War).

★★★★½ THE LEGENDS AT STONEHOUSE *Service*
SP-9550 Old Stage Rd., Toano, 23168, James City County, (757)566-1138, (888)825-3436, 10 miles from Williamsburg. **E-mail:** jburton@legendsgolf.com. **Web:** www.legendsgolf.com. **Facility Holes:** 18. **Yards:** 6,963/5,085. **Par:** 71/71. **Course Rating:** 75.0/69.1. **Slope:** 140/121. **Green Fee:** $59/$79. **Cart Fee:** $20/Person. **Walking Policy:** Unrestricted walking. **Walkability:** 4. **Opened:** 1996. **Architect:** Mike Strantz. **Season:** Year-round. **High:** March-Oct. **To obtain tee times:** Call golf shop. **Miscellaneous:** Reduced fees (weekdays, twilight), range (grass), credit cards (MC, V, AE), BF, FF.
Notes: Ranked 6th in 2001 Best in State; 1st in 1996 Best New Upscale Courses.
Reader Comments: Forgiving from the tee, but accurate approach shots a must ... Front 9 great, great finish ... Very good clubhouse, long & tough, stunning course worth every penny ... Awesome, Strantz at his best, powerful par 3s, back 9 is tough ... A player's course, not for high-handicapper.

★★ MARINERS LANDING GOLF & COUNTRY CLUB
SP-2052 Lake Retreat Rd., Huddleston, 24104, Bedford County, (540)297-7888, 35 miles from Roanoke. **E-mail:** mcgcc@hotmail.com. **Web:** www.marinerslanding.com. **Facility Holes:** 18. **Yards:** 7,155/5,170. **Par:** 72/72. **Course Rating:** 74.5/68.1. **Slope:** 130/113. **Green Fee:** $27/$39. **Cart Fee:** Included in green fee. **Walking Policy:** Mandatory carts. **Walkability:** 4. **Opened:** 1994. **Architect:** Robert Trent Jones. **Season:** Year-round. **To obtain tee times:** Call up to 7 days in advance. **Miscellaneous:** Reduced fees (weekdays, twilight, juniors), range (grass), lodging (30 rooms), credit cards (MC, V, D), BF, FF.

★★★ MASSANUTTEN RESORT GOLF COURSE
R-P.O. Box 1227, Harrisonburg, 22801, Rockingham County, (540)289-4941, 100 miles from Washington, DC. **Web:** www.massresort.com. **Facility Holes:** 27. **Yards:** 6,408/5,117. **Par:** 72/73. **Course Rating:** 70.5/69.8. **Slope:** 123/128. **Green Fee:** $40/$50. **Cart Fee:** Included in green fee. **Walking Policy:** Unrestricted walking. **Walkability:** 5. **Opened:** 1975. **Architect:** Frank Duane/Richard Watson. **Season:** Year-round. **High:** May-Oct. **To obtain tee times:** Call up to 14 days in advance. **Miscellaneous:** Reduced fees (guests, juniors), range (mats), credit cards (MC, V, AE, D), BF, FF.
Reader Comments: Tough mountain course, challenging ... Great setting, but needs work ... Great views, good vacation spot.
Special Notes: Also has a 9-hole course.

★★★ MEADOWS FARMS GOLF COURSE
PU-4300 Flat Run Rd., Locust Grove, 22508, Orange County, (540)854-9890, 16 miles from Fredericksburg. **E-mail:** blewis@nsgemlink.com. **Web:** www.meadowsfarms.com. **Facility Holes:** 27. **Green Fee:** $19/$39. **Cart Fee:** Included in green fee. **Walking Policy:** Walking at certain times. **Opened:** 1993. **Architect:** Bill Ward. **Season:** Year-round. **High:** April-Nov. **To obtain tee times:** Call golf shop. **Miscellaneous:** Reduced fees (weekdays, twilight, seniors, juniors), credit cards (MC, V), BF, FF.
ISLAND GREEN/LONGEST HOLE (18 Combo)
Yards: 7,005/4,541. **Par:** 72/72. **Course Rating:** 73.2/65.3. **Slope:** 129/109. **Walkability:** 3. **Miscellaneous:** Range (grass), lodging (3 rooms).
ISLAND GREEN/WATERFALL (18 Combo)
Yards: 6,058/4,075. **Par:** 70/70. **Course Rating:** 68.9/62.8. **Slope:** 123/100. **Walkability:** 3. **Miscellaneous:** Range (grass/mats).
LONGEST HOLE/WATERFALL (18 Combo)
Yards: 6,871/4,424. **Par:** 72/72. **Course Rating:** 72.7/65.1. **Slope:** 123/105. **Walkability:** 4. **Miscellaneous:** Range (grass/mats), lodging (3 rooms).
Reader Comments: An excellent new course, with some innovative gimmicks—including the longest hole in the 48 States ... Senior rates for in-season play ... Really fun course ... Good value ... Unique layout. Longest hole a bear.

★★½ MILL QUARTER PLANTATION GOLF COURSE
SP-1525 Mill Quarter Dr., Powhatan, 23139, Powhatan County, (804)598-4221, (804)598-4221, 22 miles from Richmond. **E-mail:** ddaniels@millquarter.com. **Web:**

www.millquarter.com. **Facility Holes:** 18. **Yards:** 6,943/4,936. **Par:** 72/72. **Course Rating:** 72.2/73.6. **Slope:** 118/123. **Green Fee:** $16/$28. **Cart Fee:** $28/Cart. **Walking Policy:** Walking at certain times. **Walkability:** 1. **Opened:** 1973. **Architect:** Ed Ault. **Season:** Year-round. **To obtain tee times:** Call golf shop. **Miscellaneous:** Reduced fees (weekdays, guests, twilight, seniors), range (grass), credit cards (MC, V, AE), FF.

NEWPORT NEWS GOLF CLUB AT DEER RUN
PU-901 Clubhouse Way, Newport News, 23608, Newport News City County, (757)886-7925, 10 miles from Williamsburg. **Facility Holes:** 36. **Walkability:** 2. **Opened:** 1966. **Architect:** Edmund B. Ault. **Season:** Year-round. **High:** April-Nov. **To obtain tee times:** Call golf shop. **Miscellaneous:** Range (grass/mats), credit cards (MC, V).
★★★½ **CARDINAL COURSE** (18)
Yards: 6,624/4,789. **Par:** 72/72. **Course Rating:** 70.9/62.8. **Slope:** 118/102. **Green Fee:** $27. **Cart Fee:** $18/Cart. **Walking Policy:** Unrestricted walking.
Reader Comments: Nice course, back 9 a real challenge … Nice challenge, especially No. 17 … Good golf, fine greenkeepers.
★★★½ **DEER RUN COURSE** (18)
Yards: 7,209/5,295. **Par:** 72/72. **Course Rating:** 73.7/70.0. **Slope:** 133/113. **Green Fee:** $36. **Cart Fee:** Included in green fee. **Walking Policy:** Mandatory cart.
Reader Comments: Demanding course, good food in clubhouse … Many deer … Rough kept high, great value … Best bargain.

★½ OCEAN VIEW GOLF COURSE
PU-9610 Norfolk Ave., Norfolk, 23503, Norfolk City County, (757)480-2094. **Facility Holes:** 18. **Yards:** 6,200/5,642. **Par:** 70/70. **Course Rating:** 69.5/69.0. **Slope:** 117/116. **Green Fee:** $15. **Cart Fee:** Included in green fee. **Walking Policy:** Walking at certain times. **Opened:** 1929. **Season:** Year-round. **High:** April-Oct. **To obtain tee times:** Call golf shop. **Miscellaneous:** Reduced fees (weekdays, twilight, seniors, juniors), metal spikes, credit cards (MC, V).

★½ OLD MONTEREY GOLF CLUB
SP-1112 Tinker Creek Lane NE, Roanoke, 24019, Roanoke City County, (540)563-0400. **Facility Holes:** 18. **Yards:** 6,760/5,540. **Par:** 71/71. **Course Rating:** 70.6/69.6. **Slope:** 113/115. **Green Fee:** $18/$20. **Cart Fee:** $30/Person. **Architect:** Fred Findlay. **Season:** Year-round. **High:** April-Oct. **To obtain tee times:** Call golf shop. **Miscellaneous:** Reduced fees (weekdays), metal spikes.

★★★★½ OLDE MILL GOLF RESORT
R-2258 Stone Mountain Rd., Laurel Fork, 24352, Carroll County, (540)398-2211, (800)753-5005, 55 miles from Winston-Salem. **E-mail:** oldemill@tcia.net. **Web:** www.oldemill.net. **Facility Holes:** 18. **Yards:** 6,833/4,876. **Par:** 72/72. **Course Rating:** 72.7/70.4. **Slope:** 127/134. **Green Fee:** $32/$56. **Cart Fee:** Included in green fee. **Walking Policy:** Walking at certain times. **Walkability:** 4. **Opened:** 1973. **Architect:** Ellis Maples. **Season:** Year-round. **To obtain tee times:** Call up to 30 days in advance. **Miscellaneous:** Reduced fees (weekdays, guests, twilight), range (grass), credit cards (MC, V, AE, D), FF.
Reader Comments: A perfect mountain golf course. Beautiful views, challenging course. Spectacular fall colors … Beautiful hard course … Water on 10 holes … View from 10th tee great … Tough. Bring lots of balls.

OSPREYS AT BELMONT BAY
PU-13401 Potomac Path Dr., Woodbridge, 22191, Prince William County, (703)497-1384, 20 miles from Washington, DC. **Facility Holes:** 18. **Yards:** 5,567/4,285. **Par:** 70/70. **Course Rating:** 68.2/65.3. **Slope:** 127/108. **Green Fee:** $28/$45. **Cart Fee:** Included in green fee. **Walking Policy:** Mandatory carts. **Season:** Year-round. **To obtain tee times:** Call up to 5 days in advance. **Miscellaneous:** Reduced fees (weekdays, guests, twilight, seniors, juniors), credit cards (MC, V, AE, D), BF, FF.

★★ OWL'S CREEK GOLF CENTER
PU-411 S. Birdneck Rd., Virginia Beach, 23451, Virginia Beach City County, (757)428-2800, 15 miles from Norfolk. **Facility Holes:** 18. **Yards:** 3,779/2,575. **Par:** 62/62. **Course Rating:** 59.2/59.9. **Slope:** 77/86. **Green Fee:** $11/$13. **Cart Fee:** $9/Person. **Walking Policy:** Walking at certain times. **Walkability:** 1. **Opened:** 1988. **Architect:** Brooks Parker. **Season:** Year-round. **To obtain tee times:** Call up to 5 days in advance. **Miscellaneous:** Reduced fees (twilight, seniors, juniors), range (grass/mats), credit cards (MC, V, AE, D), BF, FF.

★★½ PEN PARK
PU-1400 Pen Park Rd., Charlottesville, 22901, Albemarle County, (804)977-0615. **Facility Holes:** 18. **Yards:** 6,051/4,568. **Par:** 70/70. **Course Rating:** 68.5/62.0. **Slope:** 118/105. **Green Fee:** $21/$23. **Cart Fee:** $14/Person. **Walking Policy:** Unrestricted walking. **Walkability:** 3. **Opened:** 1973. **Architect:** Buddy Loving/Bill Love. **Season:** Year-round. **To obtain tee times:**

VIRGINIA

Call up to 2 days in advance. **Miscellaneous:** Reduced fees (weekdays, twilight, seniors, juniors), range (grass/mats), credit cards (MC, V), BF, FF.

★★½ PENDERBROOK GOLF CLUB
SP-3700 Golf Trail Lane, Fairfax, 22033, Fairfax County, (703)385-3700, 14 miles from Washington, DC. **Facility Holes:** 18. **Yards:** 6,152/5,042. **Par:** 71/72. **Course Rating:** 71.2/69.1. **Slope:** 130/121. **Green Fee:** $27/$35. **Cart Fee:** $13/Person. **Walking Policy:** Unrestricted walking. **Opened:** 1979. **Architect:** Edmund B. Ault. **Season:** Year-round. **High:** March-Oct. **To obtain tee times:** Call golf shop. **Miscellaneous:** Reduced fees (weekdays, seniors, juniors), metal spikes, credit cards (MC, V).

★★★ PIANKATANK RIVER GOLF CLUB
SP-P.O. Box 424, Rte. 708, Hartfield, 23071, Middlesex County, (804)776-6516, (800)303-3384, 60 miles from Richmond. **Facility Holes:** 18. **Yards:** 6,751/4,894. **Par:** 72/72. **Course Rating:** 73.6/70.0. **Slope:** 130/113. **Green Fee:** Included in green fee. **Walking Policy:** Walking at certain times. **Walkability:** 4. **Opened:** 1996. **Architect:** Algie Pulley. **Season:** Year-round. **High:** April-Nov. **To obtain tee times:** Call golf shop. **Miscellaneous:** Reduced fees (weekdays, guests, twilight, seniors, juniors), range (grass), credit cards (MC, V).
Reader Comments: A bargain ... Nice variety of holes and the views of the river are nice ... Excellent, great scenic layout ... This course is always in great shape. The front 9 is hilly, but the back 9 is more open.

PINE HILLS GOLF CLUB
PU-65 Jackson Chase Dr., Middletown, 22645, Warren County, (540)635-7814, 3 miles from Front Royal. **E-mail:** teetime@shentel.net. **Web:** www.jacksonchase.com. **Facility Holes:** 18. **Yards:** 6,575/4,006. **Par:** 72/72. **Course Rating:** 70.8/67.3. **Slope:** 125/111. **Green Fee:** $20/$35. **Cart Fee:** Included in green fee. **Walking Policy:** Walking at certain times. **Opened:** 1998. **Architect:** Shapemasters. **Season:** Year-round. **To obtain tee times:** Call up to 7 days in advance. **Miscellaneous:** Reduced fees (twilight, seniors, juniors), range (grass), credit cards (MC, V, AE), BF, FF.

★★★ PLEASANT VALLEY GOLFERS' CLUB
SP-4715 Pleasant Valley Rd., Chantilly, 20151, Fairfax County, (703)631-7902, 20 miles from Washington, DC. **Web:** www.golfmid.com. **Facility Holes:** 18. **Yards:** 6,915/5,106. **Par:** 72/72. **Course Rating:** 135.0/118.0. **Slope:** 72.9/68.9. **Green Fee:** $49/$79. **Cart Fee:** Included in green fee. **Walking Policy:** Mandatory carts. **Walkability:** 2. **Opened:** 1998. **Architect:** Tom Clark. **Season:** Year-round. **High:** April-Oct. **To obtain tee times:** Call golf shop. **Miscellaneous:** Reduced fees (twilight), range (grass/mats), caddies, credit cards (MC, V, AE), BF, FF.
Reader Comments: Open terrain. Tough in the wind. Nice combination of long and short holes ... Memorable holes ... Nice greens ... Growing into an excellent course.

★★★ POHICK BAY REGIONAL GOLF COURSE
PU-10301 Gunston Rd., Lorton, 22079, Fairfax County, (703)339-8585, 15 miles from Washington, DC. **Facility Holes:** 18. **Yards:** 6,405/4,948. **Par:** 72/72. **Course Rating:** 71.7/68.9. **Slope:** 131/121. **Green Fee:** $19/$37. **Cart Fee:** $27/Cart. **Walking Policy:** Unrestricted walking. **Walkability:** 5. **Opened:** 1982. **Architect:** George W. Cobb/John LaFoy. **Season:** Year-round. **High:** April-Oct. **To obtain tee times:** Call up to 7 days in advance. **Miscellaneous:** Reduced fees (weekdays, twilight, seniors, juniors), range (mats), credit cards (MC, V), BF, FF.
Reader Comments: Some very interesting holes. Good set of par 3s ... Challenging track. Usually in pretty ood condition. Very slow on weekends ... Short, tight, hilly, challenging.

★★ PRINCE WILLIAM GOLF COURSE
PU-14631 Vint Hill Rd, Nokesville, 20181, Prince William County, (703)754-7111, (800)218-8463, 8 miles from Manassas. **Facility Holes:** 18. **Yards:** 6,606/5,455. **Par:** 70/72. **Course Rating:** 70.1/71.6. **Slope:** 119/119. **Green Fee:** $23/$38. **Walking Policy:** Walking at certain times. **Walkability:** 2. **Season:** Year-round. **High:** April-Oct. **To obtain tee times:** Call golf shop. **Miscellaneous:** Reduced fees (twilight, seniors), metal spikes, range (mats), credit cards (MC, V, AE).

★★★★ RASPBERRY FALLS GOLF & HUNT CLUB
PU-41601 Raspberry Dr., Leesburg, 20176, Loudoun County, (703)779-2555, 3 miles from Washington, DC. **E-mail:** steve@raspberryfalls.com. **Web:** www.raspberryfalls.com. **Facility Holes:** 18. **Yards:** 7,191/4,854. **Par:** 72/72. **Course Rating:** 75.6/67.8. **Slope:** 140/113. **Green Fee:** $65/$93. **Walking Policy:** Unrestricted walking. **Walkability:** 4. **Opened:** 1996. **Architect:** Gary Player. **Season:** Year-round. **High:** April-Nov. **To obtain tee times:** Call golf shop. **Miscellaneous:** Reduced fees (weekdays, twilight), range (grass), credit cards (MC, V, AE, D),

BF, FF.
Notes: Ranked 7th in 1999 Best in State.
Reader Comments: Couldn't find a fault … Great layout, beautiful holes, deer crossing … Player knows how to play and design. Are they bunkers, hazards or mining pits? … Great course, too expensive … Great design, tough bunkers … The course is so beautiful naturally, it's worth the cash. It's a must.

★★½ RED WING LAKE GOLF COURSE
PU-1080 Prosperity Rd., Virginia Beach, 23451, Virginia Beach City County, (757)437-4845.
E-mail: tebbetts@pga.com. **Web:** teetimes.com. **Facility Holes:** 18. **Yards:** 7,080/5,285.
Par: 72/72. **Course Rating:** 73.7/68.1. **Slope:** 125/102. **Green Fee:** $11/$31. **Cart Fee:** $12/Person. **Walking Policy:** Walking at certain times. **Walkability:** 1. **Opened:** 1971. **Architect:** George Cobb. **Season:** Year-round. **High:** April-Oct. **To obtain tee times:** Call up to 7 days in advance. **Miscellaneous:** Reduced fees (weekdays, guests, twilight, seniors, juniors), range (grass), credit cards (MC, V, AE, D), BF, FF.

★★½ RESTON NATIONAL GOLF COURSE
PU-11875 Sunrise Valley Dr., Reston, 22091, Fairfax County, (703)620-9333, 25 miles from Washington, DC. **Facility Holes:** 18. **Yards:** 6,871/5,936. **Par:** 71/72. **Course Rating:** 72.9/74.3. **Slope:** 126/132. **Green Fee:** $59/$85. **Cart Fee:** Included in green fee. **Walking Policy:** Unrestricted walking. **Walkability:** 2. **Opened:** 1967. **Architect:** Edmund Ault. **Season:** Year-round. **To obtain tee times:** Call up to 7 days in advance. **Miscellaneous:** Reduced fees (weekdays, twilight, seniors, juniors), metal spikes, credit cards (MC, V, AE, D, DC), BF, FF.

★½ RINGGOLD GOLF CLUB
PU-1493 Ringgold Rd., Ringgold, 24586, Pittsylvania County, (804)822-8728, 5 miles from Danville. **Facility Holes:** 18. **Yards:** 6,588/4,816. **Par:** 72/72. **Course Rating:** 72.3/64.2. **Slope:** 124/107. **Green Fee:** $10/$15. **Cart Fee:** $10/Person. **Walking Policy:** Unrestricted walking. **Walkability:** 3. **Opened:** 1962. **Architect:** Gene Hamm. **Season:** Year-round. **To obtain tee times:** Call golf shop. **Miscellaneous:** Reduced fees (weekdays, seniors), range (mats), credit cards (MC, V), FF.

★★★ THE RIVER COURSE
PU-8400 River Course Dr., Radford, 24141, City of Radford County, (540)633-6732. **E-mail:** therivercourse@aol.com. **Web:** rivercourse.net. **Facility Holes:** 18. **Yards:** 7,182/5,109. **Par:** 72/72. **Course Rating:** 73.4/69.3. **Slope:** 124/122. **Green Fee:** $35/$50. **Cart Fee:** Included in green fee. **Walking Policy:** Walking at certain times. **Opened:** 2000. **Architect:** Dan Schlegel. **Season:** Year-round. **To obtain tee times:** Call up to 7 days in advance. **Miscellaneous:** Reduced fees (weekdays, twilight, seniors, juniors), range (grass/mats), credit cards (MC, V, AE), BF, FF.
Reader Comments: Still maturing … Lots of exciting holes … Definitely a great new golf course … Good future.

★★★½ RIVER'S BEND GOLF CLUB
PU-11700 Hogans Alley, Chester, 23836, Chesterfield County, (804)530-1000, (800)354-2363, 10 miles from Richmond. **E-mail:** riversbend@aol.com. **Web:** www.riversbend-golf.com. **Facility Holes:** 18. **Yards:** 6,671/4,932. **Par:** 71/71. **Course Rating:** 71.9/67.8. **Slope:** 132/117. **Green Fee:** $19/$39. **Cart Fee:** $15/Person. **Walking Policy:** Unrestricted walking. **Walkability:** 4. **Opened:** 1990. **Architect:** Steve Smyers. **Season:** Year-round. **High:** April-Oct. **To obtain tee times:** Call up to 7 days in advance. **Miscellaneous:** Reduced fees (weekdays, twilight, seniors, juniors), range (grass), credit cards (MC, V, AE, D), BF, FF.
Reader Comments: Fun to play. Worth the drive … A great course on the way to Myrtle Beach … Enjoyable course, don't go left … Great layout, great views … Great personnel, challenging course, fast greens.

★★★★½ RIVERFRONT GOLF CLUB *Value, Condition+*
SP-5200 River Club Dr., Suffolk, 23435, Suffolk City County, (757)484-2200, 10 miles from Norfolk. **E-mail:** chrisbrems@linkcorp.com. **Web:** www.riverfrontgolf.com. **Facility Holes:** 18. **Yards:** 6,735/5,259. **Par:** 72/72. **Course Rating:** 72.5/69.7. **Slope:** 129/117. **Green Fee:** $39/$69. **Cart Fee:** Included in green fee. **Walking Policy:** Walking at certain times. **Walkability:** 1. **Opened:** 1999. **Architect:** Tom Doak. **Season:** Year-round. **High:** April-Sept. **To obtain tee times:** Call up to 7 days in advance. **Miscellaneous:** Reduced fees (weekdays, twilight, seniors, juniors), range (grass), credit cards (MC, V, AE, D), BF, FF.
Reader Comments: Fantastic views, No. 3 the hardest in southeast Va. … Long par 4s challenging … Scenic, challenging … Spectacular views. A must-play in Tidal Marshes … Great conditions and views … One of the best courses I've played … Scenic, excellent, challenging, good mix.

★★★★½ ROYAL NEW KENT GOLF CLUB *Condition*
PU-5300 Bailey Road, Providence Forge, 23160, New Kent County, (804)966-7023,

(888)253-4363, 20 miles from Williamsburg. **Web:** www.legendsgolf.com. **Facility Holes:** 18. **Yards:** 7,291/5,231. **Par:** 72/72. **Course Rating:** 76.5/72.0. **Slope:** 147/130. **Green Fee:** $40/$85. **Cart Fee:** $20/Person. **Walking Policy:** Unrestricted walking. **Walkability:** 4. **Opened:** 1996. **Architect:** Mike Strantz. **Season:** Year-round. **High:** March-Nov. **To obtain tee times:** Call golf shop. **Miscellaneous:** Range (grass), credit cards (MC, V, AE).
Notes: Ranked 84th in 1999-2000 America's 100 Greatest; 3rd in 2001 Best in State; 1st in 1997 Best New Upscale Courses.
Reader Comments: Top notch course, fun and challenging. A great experience every time ... Fantastic links course, love the sheep ... Terrific layout, you have to work at every shot ... Play with someone who's been there before—some blind shots ... Don't expect to set the course record—just enjoy ... Wish I had a camera ... Only for good players, period, the ultimate test.

★★★ ROYAL VIRGINIA GOLF CLUB
PU-3181 Dukes Rd., Hadensville, 23067, Goochland County, (804)457-2041, 31 miles from Charlottesville. **Facility Holes:** 18. **Yards:** 7,106. **Par:** 72. **Course Rating:** 73.4. **Slope:** 131. **Green Fee:** $15/$24. **Walking Policy:** Walking at certain times. **Opened:** 1993. **Architect:** Algie Pulley. **Season:** Year-round. **High:** Dec.-Feb. **To obtain tee times:** Call golf shop. **Miscellaneous:** Reduced fees (weekdays, twilight, seniors), metal spikes, credit cards (MC, V).
Reader Comments: Long from whites ... Tough but fair ... Long and elevation changes ... Not crowded ... Up and coming, recently hosted state open ... Condition of the course isn't equal to the good layout, but great specials available ... Nice people ... Great layout.

★★½ SHENANDOAH CROSSING RESORT & COUNTRY CLUB
PU-1944 Shenandoah Crossing Dr., Gordonsville, 22942, Louisa County, (540)832-9543, 30 miles from Charlottesville. **Facility Holes:** 18. **Yards:** 6,192/4,713. **Par:** 72/72. **Course Rating:** 69.8/66.5. **Slope:** 119/111. **Green Fee:** $30/$35. **Cart Fee:** Included in green fee. **Walking Policy:** Mandatory carts. **Walkability:** 4. **Opened:** 1991. **Architect:** Buddy Loving. **Season:** Year-round. **High:** March-Nov. **To obtain tee times:** Call up to 7 days in advance. **Miscellaneous:** Reduced fees (weekdays, twilight, seniors, juniors), range (grass), lodging (12 rooms), credit cards (MC, V), FF.

★★★½ SHENANDOAH VALLEY GOLF CLUB *Value*
SP-134 Golf Club Circle, Front Royal, 22630, Warren County, (540)636-4653, 15 miles from Winchester. **E-mail:** golf@sugcgolf.com. **Web:** www.sugcgolf.com. **Facility Holes:** 27. **Green Fee:** $12/$35. **Cart Fee:** $15/Person. **Walking Policy:** Walking at certain times. **Walkability:** 3. **Opened:** 1966. **Architect:** Buddy Loving. **Season:** Year-round. **High:** March-Nov. **To obtain tee times:** Call up to 7 days in advance. **Miscellaneous:** Reduced fees (weekdays, twilight, juniors), range (grass/mats), credit cards (MC, V, AE, D), BF, FF.
BLUE/RED (18 Combo)
Yards: 6,399/5,000. **Par:** 72/73. **Course Rating:** 71.1/67.8. **Slope:** 126/116.
RED/WHITE (18 Combo)
Yards: 6,121/4,700. **Par:** 71/71. **Course Rating:** 69.6/66.3. **Slope:** 122/114.
WHITE/BLUE (18 Combo)
Yards: 6,330/4,900. **Par:** 71/71. **Course Rating:** 70.7/66.2. **Slope:** 122/113.
Reader Comments: Not hard, good value ... Maintained well, exceptional value for this area ... Good shotmaking course ... All-day rate ... Always a nice day ... Old reliable ... Beautiful valley views.

★★★½ SHENVALEE GOLF CLUB
R-P.O. Box 930, New Market, 22844, Shenandoah County, (540)740-9930, 95 miles from Washington, DC. **Facility Holes:** 27. **Green Fee:** $26/$29. **Cart Fee:** $15/Person. **Walking Policy:** Walking at certain times. **Walkability:** 3. **Opened:** 1924. **Architect:** Edmund B. Ault. **Season:** Year-round. **High:** March-Nov. **To obtain tee times:** Call up to 7 days in advance. **Miscellaneous:** Reduced fees (weekdays, guests, twilight), range (grass/mats), lodging (42 rooms), credit cards (MC, V, AE, D), BF, FF.
CREEK/MILLER (18 Combo)
Yards: 6,595/4,757. **Par:** 71/71. **Course Rating:** 71.1/65.0. **Slope:** 120/102.
OLDE/CREEK (18 Combo)
Yards: 6,358/4,821. **Par:** 71/72. **Course Rating:** 70.1/65.2. **Slope:** 117/103.
OLDE/MILLER (18 Combo)
Yards: 6,297/4,738. **Par:** 71/71. **Course Rating:** 70.1/65.1. **Slope:** 119/104.
Reader Comments: A great 27-hole resort course with super service ... Just off the interstate, good value ... Three 9s interesting, great food, lodging ... The view from No. 3 on the Creek of the mountains and Shenandoah valley is second to none.

★★ SKYLAND LAKES GOLF COURSE
PU-Mile Post 202.2 Blue Ridge Pkwy., Fancy Gap, 24328, Carroll County, (540)728-4923, 50 miles from Winston-Salem. **Facility Holes:** 18. **Yards:** 6,500/5,955. **Par:** 71/71. **Course**

VIRGINIA

Rating: 70.0/69.0. **Slope:** 119/118. **Green Fee:** $18/$27. **Cart Fee:** Included in green fee. **Walking Policy:** Mandatory carts. **Walkability:** 3. **Opened:** 1990. **Architect:** Welch DeBoard. **Season:** Year-round. **To obtain tee times:** Call golf shop. **Miscellaneous:** Reduced fees (weekdays, twilight, seniors, juniors), credit cards (MC, V, D), FF.

★★★ SLEEPY HOLE GOLF COURSE
PU-4700 Sleepy Hole Rd., Suffolk, 23435, Suffolk City County, (757)538-4100, 12 miles from Norfolk. **E-mail:** sgolfcours@aol.com. **Facility Holes:** 18. **Yards:** 6,813/5,121. **Par:** 72/72. **Course Rating:** 72.6/64.8. **Slope:** 124/108. **Green Fee:** $24/$36. **Cart Fee:** Included in green fee. **Walking Policy:** Unrestricted walking. **Walkability:** 2. **Opened:** 1972. **Architect:** Russell Breeden. **Season:** Year-round. **To obtain tee times:** Call golf shop. **Miscellaneous:** Reduced fees (weekdays, twilight, seniors, juniors), range (grass/mats), credit cards (MC, V, AE), BF, FF.
Reader Comments: They don't make 'em like this anymore … Favorite, tight, requires imagination to score well … Hidden away course, good bargain … Plays longer than yardage.

SOMERSET GOLF CLUB
SP-35448 Somerset Ridge Rd., Locust Grove, 22508, Orange County, (540)423-1500, 16 miles from Fredericksburg. **E-mail:** somersetgac@hotmail.com. **Facility Holes:** 18. **Yards:** 6,832/5,195. **Par:** 72/72. **Course Rating:** 73.6/65.5. **Slope:** 136/114. **Green Fee:** $35/$45. **Cart Fee:** $14/Person. **Walking Policy:** Unrestricted walking. **Walkability:** 4. **Opened:** 1997. **Architect:** Jerry Slack. **Season:** Year-round. **High:** March-Oct. **To obtain tee times:** Call golf shop. **Miscellaneous:** Reduced fees (weekdays, twilight, seniors, juniors), range (grass/mats), credit cards (MC, V, AE, D).

★★★ SOUTH RIDING GOLFERS' CLUB
SP-43237 Golf View Dr., South Riding, 20152, Loudoun County, (703)327-3673, 25 miles from Washington, DC. **Web:** www.golfmatrix.com. **Facility Holes:** 18. **Yards:** 7,147/5,004. **Par:** 72/72. **Course Rating:** 74.5/69.4. **Slope:** 133/116. **Green Fee:** $40/$75. **Cart Fee:** Included in green fee. **Walking Policy:** Mandatory carts. **Walkability:** 2. **Opened:** 1997. **Architect:** Dan Maples. **Season:** Year-round. **To obtain tee times:** Call golf shop. **Miscellaneous:** Reduced fees (weekdays, twilight), range (grass/mats), credit cards (MC, V, AE), BF.
Reader Comments: Good combination of holes. A must play in Northern Virginia … Good layout in good shape … Challenging for us mid-handicaps … Good hole variety … Bring your putting game, fun and challenging.

★★ SOUTH WALES GOLF COURSE
SP-18363 Golf Lane, Jeffersonton, 22724, Culpeper County, (540)937-3250, 50 miles from Washington, DC. **Facility Holes:** 18. **Yards:** 7,077/5,020. **Par:** 71/73. **Course Rating:** 73.2/68.5. **Slope:** 123/104. **Green Fee:** $12/$31. **Cart Fee:** $22/Cart. **Walking Policy:** Unrestricted walking. **Walkability:** 3. **Opened:** 1960. **Architect:** Edmund B. Ault. **Season:** Year-round. **High:** April-Oct. **To obtain tee times:** Call golf shop. **Miscellaneous:** Reduced fees (weekdays, twilight, seniors, juniors), metal spikes, range (mats), credit cards (MC, V, D).

★★★½ STONELEIGH GOLF CLUB
SP-35271 Prestwick Court, Round Hill, 20141, Loudoun County, (703)589-1402, 40 miles from Washington, DC. **E-mail:** stoneleigh@erols.com. **Web:** www.stoneleighgolf.com. **Facility Holes:** 18. **Yards:** 6,709/4,837. **Par:** 72/72. **Course Rating:** 73.1/69.1. **Slope:** 141/121. **Green Fee:** $48/$58. **Cart Fee:** Included in green fee. **Walking Policy:** Walking at certain times. **Walkability:** 4. **Opened:** 1992. **Architect:** Lisa Maki. **Season:** Year-round. **High:** March-Nov. **To obtain tee times:** Call golf shop. **Miscellaneous:** Range (grass/mats), caddies, credit cards (MC, V).
Reader Comments: Historic golf … Nice scenery … Blind shots rolling hills … Fast greens, some unfair holes … Great view on No. 2 … Holes 2 and 3 are killers.

★★ STUMPY LAKE GOLF CLUB
PU-4797 E. Indian River Rd., Virginia Beach, 23456, Virginia Beach City County, (757)467-6119. **Facility Holes:** 18. **Yards:** 6,800/5,200. **Par:** 72/72. **Course Rating:** 71.8/67.1. **Slope:** 121/97. **Green Fee:** $19/$23. **Cart Fee:** $11/Person. **Walking Policy:** Walking at certain times. **Opened:** 1944. **Architect:** Robert Trent Jones. **Season:** Year-round. **High:** April-Oct. **To obtain tee times:** Call up to 7 days in advance. **Miscellaneous:** Reduced fees (weekdays, twilight, seniors, juniors), range (grass/mats), credit cards (MC, V, AE), BF, FF.

★★★ SUFFOLK GOLF COURSE
PU-1227 Holland Rd., Suffolk, 23434, Suffolk City County, (757)539-6298, 2 miles from Suffolk. **Facility Holes:** 18. **Yards:** 6,340/5,561. **Par:** 72/72. **Course Rating:** 70.3/71.1. **Slope:** 121/112. **Green Fee:** $12/$17. **Cart Fee:** $9/Person. **Walking Policy:** Walking at certain times. **Walkability:** 2. **Opened:** 1950. **Architect:** Dick Wilson. **Season:** Year-round. **To obtain tee times:** Call golf shop. **Miscellaneous:** Reduced fees (weekdays, seniors, juniors), range

(mats), credit cards (V, AE, D), BF, FF.
Reader Comments: Scenic, good layout, reasonable prices ... Cheap, well-run city course ... Fun little course, sneaky hard on some holes ... Great doglegs on back 9 ... Might not use a driver from Nos. 11-17, good closing par 5.

SWANNANOA COUNTRY CLUB
PU-RR 1, Afton, 22920, Nelson County, (540)943-8864. **Facility Holes:** 18. **Yards:** 7,020/6,600. **Par:** 70/70. **Course Rating:** 68.0/64.0. **Slope:** 112/107. **Green Fee:** $12/$16. **Cart Fee:** $10/Person. **To obtain tee times:** Call golf shop.

★★★ SYCAMORE CREEK GOLF COURSE
PU-1991 Manakin Rd., Manakin Sabot, 23103, Goochland County, (804)784-3544, 15 miles from Richmond. **Facility Holes:** 18. **Yards:** 6,256/4,431. **Par:** 70/70. **Course Rating:** 70.6/64.6. **Slope:** 126/111. **Green Fee:** $33/$45. **Cart Fee:** Included in green fee. **Walking Policy:** Walking at certain times. **Walkability:** 4. **Opened:** 1992. **Architect:** Michael Hurzdan. **Season:** Year-round. **To obtain tee times:** Call up to 7 days in advance. **Miscellaneous:** Reduced fees (weekdays, twilight, seniors, juniors), range (grass), credit cards (MC, V, AE, D), BF, FF.
Reader Comments: Several very nice, interesting holes ... One of the best kept secrets in VA. Not a long course, but I promise you will have fun and remember it when you leave. Par 4, No 16 a true test and one of the best par 4s in the state ... Can score low. Good value ... Play slow at times.

★★★ TARTAN GOLF COURSE
R-633 St. Andrews Lane, Weens, 22576, Lancaster County, (804)438-6200, (800)248-4337, 65 miles from Richmond. **E-mail:** tartangolf@kaballero.com. **Facility Holes:** 18. **Yards:** 6,586/5,121. **Par:** 72/72. **Course Rating:** 71.5/69.2. **Slope:** 124/116. **Green Fee:** $25/$53. **Cart Fee:** $12/Person. **Walking Policy:** Unrestricted walking. **Walkability:** 2. **Opened:** 1959. **Architect:** Sir Guy Campbell/George Cobb. **Season:** Year-round. **To obtain tee times:** Call golf shop. **Miscellaneous:** Reduced fees (weekdays, guests, twilight), range (grass), credit cards (MC, V, AE), BF, FF.
Reader Comments: Nice track, very pretty in spring with all the flowers in bloom ... Fun to play, difficult but fair ... An old-style course ... Very enjoyable and easy to walk.

★★★½ THE TIDES INN
R-Golden Eagle Dr., Irvington, 22480, Lancaster County, (804)438-5501, (800)843-3746, 70 miles from Richmond. **Facility Holes:** 18. **Yards:** 6,963/5,384. **Par:** 72/72. **Course Rating:** 74.3/70.9. **Slope:** 134/126. **Green Fee:** $40/$70. **Cart Fee:** $15/Person. **Walking Policy:** Walking at certain times. **Walkability:** 3. **Opened:** 1976. **Architect:** George Cobb. **Season:** March-Dec. **High:** April-Oct. **To obtain tee times:** Call golf shop. **Miscellaneous:** Reduced fees (weekdays, guests), metal spikes, range (grass/mats), credit cards (MC, V, AE).
Notes: Ranked 14th in 1997 Best in State.
Reader Comments: A beautiful course with great service ... Classic, some real challenges ... Nos. 9 and 18 feature major water, can be intimidating ... Great scenery, well maintained.

★★★½ TPC OF VIRGINIA BEACH
PU-2500 Tournament Dr., Virginia Beach, 23456, Virginia Beach City County, (757)563-9440, (877)484-3872, 15 miles from Norfolk. **Web:** www.playatpc.com. **Facility Holes:** 18. **Yards:** 7,432/5,314. **Par:** 72/72. **Course Rating:** 75.8/70.1. **Slope:** 142/114. **Green Fee:** $75/$115. **Cart Fee:** Included in green fee. **Walking Policy:** Mandatory carts. **Opened:** 1999. **Architect:** Pete Dye/Curtis Strange. **Season:** Year-round. **To obtain tee times:** Call golf shop. **Miscellaneous:** Reduced fees (guests), range (grass), credit cards (MC, V, AE), BF, FF.
Reader Comments: Expensive, but best in VA beach ... Excellent test, pros are challenged ... Good condition, lots of bunkers ... Pricey but worth it.

★★★★½ TRADITION AT STONEHOUSE *Service, Condition+*
PU-9550 Old Stage Rd., Toano, 23168, James City County, (757)566-1138. **E-mail:** jburton@traditionalclubs.com. **Web:** www.traditionalclubs.com. **Facility Holes:** 18. **Yards:** 6,963/5,085. **Par:** 71/71. **Course Rating:** 75.0/69.1. **Slope:** 140/121. **Green Fee:** $59/$69. **Cart Fee:** Included in green fee. **Walking Policy:** Walking at certain times. **Walkability:** 4. **Opened:** 1996. **Architect:** Mike Strantz. **Season:** Year-round. **To obtain tee times:** Call up to 7 days in advance. **Miscellaneous:** Reduced fees (weekdays, juniors), range (grass), credit cards (MC, V, AE, D), BF, FF.
Notes: Ranked 4th in 1999 Best in State.
Reader Comments: Must keep in play ... Best par 3s I've ever played ... Several signature quality holes ... Huge fast greens.

TWIN LAKES GOLF COURSE
PU-6201 Union Mill Rd., Clifton, 20124, Fairfax County, (703)631-9099, 20 miles from Washington, DC. **Facility Holes:** 36. **Cart Fee:** $25/Cart. **Walking Policy:** Unrestricted walking. **Walkability:** 3. **Season:** Year-round. **High:** April-Oct. **To obtain tee times:** Call golf shop.

Miscellaneous: Reduced fees (weekdays, seniors, juniors), range (grass/mats), credit cards (MC, V), BF, FF.

★★★ **LAKES COURSE** (18)
Yards: 6,788/5,627. **Par:** 73/73. **Course Rating:** 72.0/70.7. **Slope:** 132/119. **Green Fee:** $27/$31. **Opened:** 1967. **Architect:** Charles Schalestock.
Reader Comments: A good, challenging course that makes a serious effort to speed up play … Beautiful course in fall … Hilly but walkable … Solid muni.

★★★ **OAKS COURSE** (18)
Yards: 6,710/4,686. **Par:** 71/71. **Course Rating:** 73.0/65.7. **Slope:** 139/109. **Green Fee:** $31/$37. **Opened:** 1998. **Architect:** Denis Griffiths.
Reader Comments: Good golf investment … A good, solid, challenging golf course for a muni … Tougher layout.

★★★½ **VIRGINIA NATIONAL GOLF CLUB**
PU-1400 Parker Lane, Bluemont, 20135, Loudoun County, (888)283-4653, (888)283-4653, 20 miles from Leesburg. **E-mail:** cliff@virginianational.com. **Web:** www.virginianational.com. **Facility Holes:** 18. **Yards:** 6,950/5,193. **Par:** 72/72. **Course Rating:** 73.0/68.3. **Slope:** 136/116. **Green Fee:** $40/$70. **Walking Policy:** Unrestricted walking. **Opened:** 1999. **Architect:** Jerry Matthews. **Season:** March-Nov. **High:** May-Sept. **To obtain tee times:** Call up to 7 days in advance. **Miscellaneous:** Reduced fees (weekdays, twilight, seniors), range (grass), credit cards (MC, V, AE), BF, FF.
Reader Comments: Sneaky good course … Great rates for locals, tough, long course … Great scenery … New course, has some beautiful mountain views along the Shenandoah River … Relatively unknown, very good … Tough test, don't spray the ball … Great greens.

★★★ **VIRGINIA OAKS GOLF CLUB**
SP-7950 Virginia Oaks Dr., Gainesville, 20155, Prince William County, (703)754-4200, 1 mile from Gainesville. **Facility Holes:** 18. **Yards:** 6,928/4,852. **Par:** 72/71. **Course Rating:** 73.5/72.0. **Slope:** 133/115. **Green Fee:** $39/$85. **Cart Fee:** Included in green fee. **Walking Policy:** Walking at certain times. **Walkability:** 2. **Opened:** 1995. **Architect:** P.B. Dye. **Season:** Year-round. **High:** April-Oct. **To obtain tee times:** Call golf shop. **Miscellaneous:** Reduced fees (weekdays, twilight, juniors), range (grass/mats), credit cards (MC, V, AE, D), BF, FF.
Reader Comments: Beautiful design … Good greens … Playable layout for a change. Great variety of holes … New home construction too close to playing grounds … Tough course. Always in very good condition.

VIRGINIA TECH GOLF COURSE
PU-1 Duckpond Dr., Blacksburg, 24061, Montgomery County, (540)231-6435. **Facility Holes:** 18. **Yards:** 6,448/5,364. **Par:** 70/72. **Course Rating:** 69.7/69.5. **Slope:** 108/106. **Green Fee:** $16/$20. **Cart Fee:** $12/Person. **To obtain tee times:** Call golf shop.

★★★★ **WESTFIELDS GOLF CLUB**
PU-13940 Balmoral Greens Ave., Clifton, 20124, Fairfax County, (703)631-3300, 20 miles from Washington, DC. **E-mail:** westfield3@mindspring.com. **Web:** westfieldgolf.com. **Facility Holes:** 18. **Yards:** 6,897/4,597. **Par:** 71/71. **Course Rating:** 73.1/65.9. **Slope:** 136/114. **Green Fee:** $50/$94. **Cart Fee:** Included in green fee. **Walking Policy:** Unrestricted walking. **Walkability:** 3. **Opened:** 1998. **Architect:** Fred Couples/Gene Bates. **Season:** Year-round. **To obtain tee times:** Call up to 7 days in advance. **Miscellaneous:** Reduced fees (weekdays, twilight), range (grass/mats), lodging (400 rooms), credit cards (MC, V, AE, D, DC), BF, FF.
Reader Comments: Nice layout wide winding areas but approach shots have less room for error … Very good layout, true greens … A fun play, but can't afford it but once a year … Correct tee selection makes it enjoyable. Missing a green is punishing … Service is top notch … Just a terrific course and facility.

★★½ **WESTLAKE GOLF & COUNTRY CLUB**
SP-360 Chestnut Creek Dr., Hardy, 24101, Franklin County, (540)721-4214, (800)296-7277, 20 miles from Roanoke. **Facility Holes:** 18. **Yards:** 6,540/4,582. **Par:** 72/72. **Course Rating:** 71.7/65.6. **Slope:** 128/114. **Green Fee:** $19/$24. **Cart Fee:** $11/Person. **Walking Policy:** Walking at certain times. **Opened:** 1989. **Architect:** Russell Breeden. **Season:** Year-round. **High:** May-Sept. **To obtain tee times:** Call golf shop. **Miscellaneous:** Reduced fees (twilight, juniors), metal spikes, range (grass), credit cards (MC, V).

★★½ **WESTPARK GOLF CLUB**
SP-59 Clubhouse Dr. S.W., Leesburg, 20175, Loudoun County, (703)777-7023, 20 miles from Fairfax. **E-mail:** eliaspga@aol.com. **Facility Holes:** 18. **Yards:** 6,521/5,027. **Par:** 71/71. **Course Rating:** 71.1/69.0. **Slope:** 121/111. **Green Fee:** $22/$30. **Cart Fee:** $15/Person. **Walking Policy:** Walking at certain times. **Walkability:** 3. **Opened:** 1968. **Architect:** Edward Ault. **High:** April-Oct. **To obtain tee times:** Call golf shop. **Miscellaneous:** Reduced fees (weekdays, twilight, seniors), metal spikes, range (mats), credit cards (MC, V, AE, Diners CLub).

★★★½ WILLIAMSBURG NATIONAL GOLF CLUB
PU-3700 Centerville Rd., Williamsburg, 23188, James City County, (757)258-9642, (800)826-5732, 40 miles from Richmond. **E-mail:** wngc@widomaker.com. **Web:** www.wngc.com. **Facility Holes:** 18. **Yards:** 6,950/5,200. **Par:** 72/72. **Course Rating:** 72.9/69.7. **Slope:** 130/127. **Green Fee:** $33/$53. **Cart Fee:** $16/Person. **Walking Policy:** Walking at certain times. **Walkability:** 3. **Opened:** 1995. **Architect:** Jim Lipe. **Season:** Year-round. **High:** April-Oct. **To obtain tee times:** Call golf shop. **Miscellaneous:** Reduced fees (weekdays, guests), range (grass), credit cards (MC, V, AE), BF, FF.
Reader Comments: Very fun to play…Trouble visible off tee, making it tough but fair … Excellent course, scenic, fast greens … Difficult for short hitters … Fine practice facilities, always busy … Great for the average player … Good overall test, good par 3s.

WINTERGREEN RESORT
R-P.O. Box 706, Wintergreen, 22958, Nelson County, (804)325-8250, (800)266-2444, 43 miles from Charlottesville. **Web:** www.wintergreenresort.com. **Facility Holes:** 45. **Green Fee:** $70/$80. **Cart Fee:** $19/Person. **Walking Policy:** Unrestricted walking. **To obtain tee times:** Call up to 14 days in advance. **Miscellaneous:** Lodging (350 rooms), BF, FF.
★★★★ DEVIL'S KNOB GOLF CLUB (18)
Yards: 6,576/5,101. **Par:** 70/70. **Course Rating:** 72.8/68.6. **Slope:** 133/118. **Walkability:** 5. **Opened:** 1976. **Architect:** Ellis Maples. **Season:** April-Oct. **High:** July-Sept. **Miscellaneous:** Reduced fees (weekdays, guests, twilight), range (grass/mats), credit cards (MC, V, AE, D).
Reader Comments: Challenge if you fade or slice. Greens are like glass … Well maintained, good staff, nice upscale facility … Great mountain golf but leave the big club home; off the fairway means off the mountain. Requires you to think your way around … Not long but tricky.
★★★★ STONEY CREEK
Walkability: 3. **Opened:** 1988. **Architect:** Rees Jones. **Season:** Year-round. **High:** April-Nov. **Miscellaneous:** Reduced fees (weekdays, guests), range (grass), credit cards (MC, V, AE). **Notes:** Ranked 6th in 1997 Best in State.
STONEY CREEK - MONOCAN/SHAMOKIN (18 Combo)
Yards: 7,005/5,500. **Par:** 72/72. **Course Rating:** 74.0/71.8. **Slope:** 132/127.
STONEY CREEK - MONOCAN/TUCKAHOE (18 Combo)
Yards: 6,951/5,462. **Par:** 72/72. **Course Rating:** 74.0/71.6. **Slope:** 130/129.
STONEY CREEK - SHAMOKIN/TUCKAHOE (18 Combo)
Yards: 6,998/5,594. **Par:** 72/72. **Course Rating:** 73.8/72.4. **Slope:** 130/128.
Reader Comments: Greens are anything but flat, Crenshaw's touch required. Incredible views … Always a challenge … Three different nines: one tight, one open, one long, all with great views and interesting layouts to challenge both skills & course management.

WINTON COUNTRY CLUB
SP-Hwy. 151, Clifford, 24533, Amherst County, (434)946-7336, 20 miles from Lynchburg. **E-mail:** wintonpro@aol. **Facility Holes:** 18. **Yards:** 6,833/5,341. **Par:** 71/73. **Course Rating:** 71.2/70.8. **Slope:** 123/118. **Green Fee:** $35/$50. **Cart Fee:** Included in green fee. **Walking Policy:** Walking at certain times. **Opened:** 1971. **Season:** Year-round. **To obtain tee times:** Call up to 14 days in advance. **Miscellaneous:** Reduced fees (weekdays), range (grass), credit cards (MC, V), BF, FF.

★★ WOLF CREEK GOLF & COUNTRY CLUB
SP-Rte. 1 Box 421, Bastian, 24314, Bland County, (540)688-4610, 20 miles from Wytheville. **Facility Holes:** 18. **Yards:** 6,380/4,788. **Par:** 71/71. **Course Rating:** 71.3/71.0. **Slope:** 122/128. **Green Fee:** $15/$20. **Cart Fee:** $10/Person. **Walkability:** 4. **Opened:** 1982. **Architect:** Maurice Brackett. **Season:** Year-round. **High:** April-Oct. **To obtain tee times:** Call golf shop. **Miscellaneous:** Reduced fees (weekdays, seniors, juniors), range (grass), credit cards (MC, V, AE), FF.

★★½ WOODLANDS GOLF COURSE
PU-9 Woodland Rd., Hampton, 23663, Hampton City County, (757)727-1195. **Facility Holes:** 18. **Yards:** 5,391/4,154. **Par:** 69/69. **Course Rating:** 65.6/62.9. **Slope:** 113/106. **Green Fee:** $12/$16. **Cart Fee:** $16/Cart. **Walking Policy:** Unrestricted walking. **Walkability:** 1. **Opened:** 1927. **Architect:** Donald Ross. **Season:** Year-round. **High:** April-Sept. **To obtain tee times:** Call golf shop. **Miscellaneous:** Reduced fees (weekdays, seniors, juniors), credit cards (MC, V).

WASHINGTON

★★★½ ALDERBROOK GOLF & YACHT CLUB
R-300 Country Club Drive, Union, 98592, Mason County, (360)898-2560, (888)898-2560, 35 miles from Olympia. **E-mail:** mfields@greatputt.com. **Web:** www.alderbrookgolf.com. **Facility Holes:** 18. **Yards:** 6,326/5,500. **Par:** 72/73. **Course Rating:** 70.3/71.5. **Slope:** 118/116. **Green Fee:** $32/$35. **Cart Fee:** $24/Cart. **Walking Policy:** Unrestricted walking. **Walkability:** 2. **Opened:** 1966. **Architect:** Ray Coleman. **Season:** Year-round. **High:** June-Sept. **To obtain tee times:** Call up to 7 days in advance. **Miscellaneous:** Reduced fees (weekdays, guests, twilight, seniors, juniors), range (grass), lodging (88 rooms), credit cards (MC, V), BF, FF.
Reader Comments: Top notch, first-class operation ... Keep it straight, OB both sides of rough ... A jewel off the beaten path ... Beautiful mountain views.

★★★★ APPLE TREE GOLF COURSE
PU-8804 Occidental Ave., Yakima, 98908, Yakima County, (509)966-5877, 170 miles from Seattle. **Web:** www.appletreegolf.com. **Facility Holes:** 18. **Yards:** 6,892/5,428. **Par:** 72/72. **Course Rating:** 73.3/72.0. **Slope:** 129/124. **Green Fee:** $27/$53. **Cart Fee:** $25/Cart. **Walking Policy:** Unrestricted walking. **Walkability:** 3. **Opened:** 1992. **Architect:** John Steidel/Apple Tree Partnership. **Season:** Year-round. **High:** March-Oct. **To obtain tee times:** Call up to 30 days in advance. **Miscellaneous:** Reduced fees (weekdays, twilight, seniors, juniors), range (grass), credit cards (MC, V), BF, FF.
Notes: Ranked 9th in 1999 Best in State.
Reader Comments: The apple-shaped par 3 and a walk through the apple orchards makes this course a must in Washington State ... The best course in central Washington. Very unique like playing four different courses in one ... This course also has a unique apple sandtrap on the 18th which is made of fine volcanic rock ... Sweet course and amazing restaurant.

★★★ AUBURN GOLF COURSE
PU-29630 Green River Rd., Auburn, 98002, King County, (253)833-2350. **Facility Holes:** 18. **Yards:** 6,350/6,004. **Par:** 71/71. **Course Rating:** 69.5/68.4. **Slope:** 116/109. **Green Fee:** $19/$21. **Cart Fee:** $10/Cart. **Walking Policy:** Unrestricted walking. **Walkability:** 3. **Opened:** 1969. **Architect:** Milton Bauman/Glenn Proctor. **Season:** Year-round. **High:** June-Sept. **To obtain tee times:** Call golf shop. **Miscellaneous:** Metal spikes.
Reader Comments: Great improvements last few years ... Hidden value ... Comely little course, 'cliff hole' is fun ... Lots of improvements made.

★★★ AVALON GOLF LINKS
PU-19345 Kelleher Rd., Burlington, 98233, Skagit County, (360)757-1900, (800)624-0202, 55 miles from Seattle. **E-mail:** bkruhlak@avalonlinks.com. **Web:** www.avalonlinks.com. **Facility Holes:** 27. **Green Fee:** $22/$42. **Cart Fee:** $25/Cart. **Walking Policy:** Unrestricted walking. **Walkability:** 1. **Opened:** 1991. **Architect:** Robert Muir Graves. **Season:** Year-round. **High:** May-Sept. **To obtain tee times:** Call up to 7 days in advance. **Miscellaneous:** Reduced fees (weekdays, twilight, seniors, juniors), range (grass), caddies, credit cards (MC, V), BF, FF.
NORTH/SOUTH (18 Combo)
Yards: 6,803/5,534. **Par:** 72/72. **Course Rating:** 73.3/72.7. **Slope:** 132/127.
NORTH/WEST (18 Combo)
Yards: 6,629/5,236. **Par:** 72/72. **Course Rating:** 72.3/71.6. **Slope:** 125/122.
WEST/SOUTH (18 Combo)
Yards: 6,576/5,318. **Par:** 72/72. **Course Rating:** 71.3/72.2. **Slope:** 129/122.
Reader Comments: Beautiful landscape, good facilities ... 27 holes carved out of the forest ... Great variety ... A great challenge. Many bunkers, both sand and grass. Fairways and greens are kept in good shape ... Play North/South ... Great, friendly service.

★★★ BATTLE CREEK GOLF COURSE
PU-6006 Meridian Ave. N., Marysville, 98271, Snohomish County, (360)659-7931, (800)655-7931, 30 miles from Seattle. **Facility Holes:** 18. **Yards:** 6,575/5,391. **Par:** 73/73. **Course Rating:** 71.2/70.5. **Slope:** 121/121. **Green Fee:** $23/$30. **Cart Fee:** $22/Cart. **Walking Policy:** Unrestricted walking. **Walkability:** 3. **Opened:** 1990. **Architect:** Fred Jacobson. **Season:** Year-round. **To obtain tee times:** Call up to 7 days in advance. **Miscellaneous:** Reduced fees (weekdays, twilight, seniors, juniors), range (grass), credit cards (MC, V), BF, FF.
Reader Comments: The fairways are good and the greens are fair. Worth the price to play ... A little out of the way, but worth the trip. The course is pretty technical and demands that you plan shots carefully ... Fun course.

★★ BELLEVUE MUNICIPAL GOLF COURSE
PU-5500 140th N.E., Bellevue, 98005, King County, (425)452-7250. **Facility Holes:** 18. **Yards:** 5,800/5,100. **Par:** 71/71. **Course Rating:** 66.5/68.6. **Slope:** 110/111. **Green Fee:** $20. **Cart Fee:** $23/Cart. **Walking Policy:** Unrestricted walking. **Walkability:** 1. **Opened:** 1969. **Season:** Year-round. **High:** May-Aug. **To obtain tee times:** Call golf shop. **Miscellaneous:** Reduced fees (twilight, seniors, juniors), metal spikes, range (mats).

WASHINGTON

★★★ BROOKDALE GOLF COURSE
PU-1802 Brookdale Rd. E., Tacoma, 98445, Pierce County, (253)537-4400, (800)281-2428.
Facility Holes: 18. **Yards:** 6,435/5,835. **Par:** 71/74. **Course Rating:** 70.3/73.1. **Slope:** 119/120.
Green Fee: $10/$23. **Cart Fee:** $20/Cart. **Walking Policy:** Unrestricted walking. **Walkability:** 2.
Opened: 1931. **Architect:** Al Smith. **Season:** Year-round. **To obtain tee times:** Call golf shop.
Miscellaneous: Reduced fees (weekdays, twilight, seniors, juniors), metal spikes, credit cards
(MC, V), FF.
Reader Comments: Good course to play year-round ... Old course, easy test ... Good course in
rain ... Wide open, nice greens, inexpensive ... My kids play Brookdale at every opportunity ...
Great prices for seniors ... Excellent management ... Condition, condition, condition.

★★★ CAMALOCH GOLF COURSE
PU-326 N. E. Camano Dr., Camano Island, 98282, Island County, (360)387-3084,
(800)628-0469, 45 miles from Seattle. **Facility Holes:** 18. **Yards:** 6,200/5,232. **Par:** 72/72.
Course Rating: 70.0/70.0. **Slope:** 118/114. **Green Fee:** $19/$29. **Cart Fee:** $23/Cart. **Walking
Policy:** Unrestricted walking. **Walkability:** 2. **Opened:** 1990. **Architect:** Bill Overdorf. **Season:**
Year-round. **High:** May-Sept. **To obtain tee times:** Call up to 7 days in advance.
Miscellaneous: Reduced fees (weekdays, twilight, seniors, juniors), metal spikes, range
(grass), credit cards (MC, V, D), BF, FF.
Reader Comments: Nice course, a short drive from northern Seattle and easy to get on during the
season. The greens and fairways are excellent ... Fun course, very nice people ... This is a good
course to work on iron play. The fairways are tight in places with plenty of meandering creeks and
ponds. Worth the price.

CAMAS MEADOW GOLF CLUB
PU-4105 NW Camas Meadows Dr., Camas, 98607, Clark County, (360)833-2000,
(800)750-6511, 5 miles from Vancouver. **E-mail:** email@camasmeadow.com. **Web:**
www.camasmeadows.com. **Facility Holes:** 18. **Yards:** 6,518/4,859. **Par:** 72/71. **Course
Rating:** 71.3/67.9. **Slope:** 130/122. **Green Fee:** $35/$70. **Cart Fee:** Included in green fee.
Walking Policy: Unrestricted walking. **Walkability:** 2. **Opened:** 2000. **Architect:** Andy Raugust.
Season: Year-round. **To obtain tee times:** Call up to 30 days in advance. **Miscellaneous:**
Reduced fees (weekdays, twilight, juniors), credit cards (MC, V, AE, D), BF, FF.

★★★★ CANYON LAKES GOLF COURSE *Value*
PU-3700 Canyon Lakes Dr., Kennewick, 99337, Benton County, (509)582-3736. **E-mail:**
info@canyonlakesgolfcourse.com. **Web:** www.canyonlakesgolfcourse.com. **Facility Holes:** 18.
Yards: 7,026/5,533. **Par:** 72/72. **Course Rating:** 73.4/72.0. **Slope:** 127/124. **Green Fee:**
$24/$34. **Cart Fee:** $13/Person. **Walking Policy:** Unrestricted walking. **Walkability:** 3. **Opened:**
1981. **Architect:** John Steidel. **Season:** Year-round. **To obtain tee times:** Call up to 7 days in
advance. **Miscellaneous:** Reduced fees (weekdays, guests, twilight, juniors), range (grass),
lodging (87 rooms), credit cards (MC, V, AE), BF, FF.
Reader Comments: Fun course; super greens ... Requires solid long iron play and a delicate touch
on the greens ... This was the best course I have played in years!! ... As the name would imply,
very hilly and quite the challenge.

★★★ CAPITOL CITY GOLF CLUB
PU-5225 Yelm Hwy. S.E., Olympia, 98513, Thurston County, (360)491-5111, (800)994-2582.
Facility Holes: 18. **Yards:** 6,536/5,510. **Par:** 72/72. **Course Rating:** 70.9/71.7. **Slope:** 123/122.
Green Fee: $17/$22. **Cart Fee:** $13/Person. **Walking Policy:** Unrestricted walking. **Opened:**
1961. **Architect:** Norman Woods. **Season:** Year-round. **High:** June-Aug. **To obtain tee times:**
Call golf shop. **Miscellaneous:** Reduced fees (weekdays, twilight, seniors, juniors), metal
spikes, range (grass), credit cards (MC, V).
Reader Comments: This is one of the best all-year courses ... A GREAT course ... Outstanding
public course for your money, dry year round.

★½ CARNATION GOLF COURSE
PU-1810 W Snoqualmie River Rd. N.E., Carnation, 98014, King County, (425)333-4151, 10
miles from Redmond. **E-mail:** cgc@accessone.com. **Web:** www.carnationgolf.com. **Facility
Holes:** 18. **Yards:** 6,011/4,599. **Par:** 72/72. **Course Rating:** 67.7/65.0. **Slope:** 111/102. **Green
Fee:** $22/$29. **Cart Fee:** $24/Cart. **Walking Policy:** Unrestricted walking. **Walkability:** 1.
Opened: 1967. **Architect:** Bob Tachell. **Season:** Year-round. **High:** May-Oct. **To obtain tee
times:** Call up to 14 days in advance. **Miscellaneous:** Reduced fees (weekdays, twilight,
seniors, juniors), metal spikes, range (grass/mats), credit cards (MC, V).

★★★ CEDARCREST GOLF CLUB
PU-6810 84th St. N.E., Marysville, 98270, Snohomish County, (360)659-3566, 35 miles from
Seattle. **Facility Holes:** 18. **Yards:** 5,811/4,846. **Par:** 70/70. **Course Rating:** 67.0/66.6. **Slope:**
114/112. **Green Fee:** $24. **Cart Fee:** $20/Cart. **Walking Policy:** Unrestricted walking.

Walkability: 3. **Opened:** 1927. **Architect:** John Steidel. **Season:** Year-round. **High:** May-Oct. **To obtain tee times:** Call up to 7 days in advance. **Miscellaneous:** Reduced fees (weekdays, twilight, seniors, juniors), metal spikes, credit cards (MC, V), BF, FF.

Reader Comments: A newly renovated course, lots of water … The pro was always very helpful … It could use a little bit better drainage, but other than that it is a very fun course to play … Not a bad course overall, a little on the short side though.

★★½ CEDARS GOLF CLUB

PU-15001 N.E. 181st St., Brush Prairie, 98606, Clark County, (360)687-4233, 20 miles from Portland. **Facility Holes:** 18. **Yards:** 6,423/5,216. **Par:** 72/73. **Course Rating:** 71.6/71.2. **Slope:** 135/126. **Green Fee:** $24/$26. **Cart Fee:** $22/Cart. **Walking Policy:** Walking at certain times. **Walkability:** 3. **Opened:** 1975. **Architect:** Jerry James. **Season:** Year-round. **High:** April-Oct. **To obtain tee times:** Call up to 7 days in advance. **Miscellaneous:** Reduced fees (juniors), range (grass), credit cards (MC, V), BF, FF.

CHEVY CHASE GOLF CLUB

PU-7401 Cape George Rd., Port Townsend, 98368, Jefferson County, (360)385-0704. **Facility Holes:** 18. **Yards:** 6,745/5,407. **Par:** 72/73. **Course Rating:** 77.5/70.3. **Slope:** 122/114. **Green Fee:** $20/$26. **Cart Fee:** $26/Cart. **To obtain tee times:** Call golf shop.

★★★ CHEWELAH GOLF & COUNTRY CLUB

SP-2537 Sand Canyon Rd., Chewelah, 99109, Stevens County, (509)935-6807, 40 miles from Spokane. **Facility Holes:** 27. **Yards:** 6,645/5,393. **Par:** 72/72. **Course Rating:** 72.2/66.1. **Slope:** 126/114. **Green Fee:** $10/$20. **Cart Fee:** $24/Cart. **Walking Policy:** Walking at certain times. **Walkability:** 4. **Opened:** 1976. **Architect:** Keith Hellstrom/Jim Kraus. **Season:** April-Nov. **High:** June-Sept. **To obtain tee times:** Call up to 21 days in advance. **Miscellaneous:** Reduced fees (seniors, juniors), range (mats), credit cards (MC, V), BF, FF.

Reader Comments: Great value … Beautiful course, now adding an executive 9 … Many trees, soon to be 27 holes … Short course but plenty challenging. Great greens.
Special Notes: Also has a 9-hole course.

★★★½ CLASSIC COUNTRY CLUB

PU-4908 208th St. E., Spanaway, 98387, Pierce County, (253)847-4440, (800)924-9557, 60 miles from Seattle. **Facility Holes:** 18. **Yards:** 6,793/5,580. **Par:** 72/72. **Course Rating:** 73.6/73.3. **Slope:** 133/128. **Green Fee:** $20/$45. **Cart Fee:** $23/Cart. **Walking Policy:** Unrestricted walking. **Opened:** 1991. **Architect:** Bill Overdorf. **Season:** Year-round. **High:** May-Oct. **To obtain tee times:** Call golf shop. **Miscellaneous:** Reduced fees (weekdays, twilight, seniors, juniors), metal spikes, range (grass/mats), credit cards (MC, V, AE, JCB).

Reader Comments: Very nicely conditioned course. People are wonderful to deal with … Great, challenging course … Twilight rates good. Nice course … Make the long drive, it's worth it … Good shotmaker's layout … One of public's best layouts and year-round conditions.

★★★½ COLUMBIA POINT GOLF COURSE

PU-225 Columbia Point Dr., Richland, 99352, Benton County, (509)946-0710. **Web:** www.cybergolf.com/columbiapoint. **Facility Holes:** 18. **Yards:** 6,571/4,692. **Par:** 72/72. **Course Rating:** 70.0/65.9. **Slope:** 121/107. **Green Fee:** $16/$32. **Cart Fee:** $12/Person. **Walking Policy:** Unrestricted walking. **Walkability:** 3. **Opened:** 1997. **Architect:** Jim Engh. **Season:** Year-round. **High:** March-Oct. **Tee times:** Call up to 10 days ahead. **Miscellaneous:** Reduced fees (weekdays, twilight, seniors, juniors), range, credit cards (MC, V, AE), BF, FF.

Reader Comments: Mmany interesting holes, lots of fun … Great course … Fair to all golfers, best service … Back 9 has a Scottish flavor … Great golf for the $ … Easy to walk.

★★★½ THE CREEK AT QUALCHAN GOLF COURSE

PU-301 E. Meadowlane Rd., Spokane, 99224, Spokane County, (509)448-9317, 5 miles from Spokane. **Facility Holes:** 18. **Yards:** 6,599/5,389. **Par:** 72/72. **Course Rating:** 71.6/72.3. **Slope:** 127/126. **Green Fee:** $17/$23. **Cart Fee:** $25/Cart. **Walking Policy:** Unrestricted walking. **Walkability:** 3. **Opened:** 1993. **Architect:** William Robinson. **Season:** March-Nov. **High:** June-Sept. **To obtain tee times:** Call golf shop. **Miscellaneous:** Reduced fees (juniors), metal spikes, range (grass), credit cards (MC, V), BF, FF.

Reader Comments: Great value … Very fair test for a great price … My favorite! Very tough, great back 9, nice bunkers … Enjoyable … Excellent, excellent, excellent … Best new course in eastern WA … Challenging course, many tough tee shots.

★★½ DESERT AIRE GOLF COURSE

SP-505 Club House Way W., Desert Aire, 99349, Grant County, (509)932-4439, 60 miles from Yakima. **Facility Holes:** 18. **Yards:** 6,501/5,786. **Par:** 72/73. **Course Rating:** 70.5/72.6. **Slope:** 115/120. **Green Fee:** $16/$24. **Cart Fee:** $24/Person. **Walking Policy:** Unrestricted walking. **Walkability:** 1. **Opened:** 1975. **Architect:** Jim Krause. **Season:** Year-round. **Tee times:** Call up to 7 days in advance. **Miscellaneous:** Range (grass), credit cards (MC, V), BF, FF.

★★★★½ DESERT CANYON GOLF RESORT *Condition*
R-1201 Desert Canyon Blvd., Orondo, 98843, Douglas County, (509)784-1111, (800)258-4173, 25 miles from Wenatchee. **E-mail:** desertcanyon@desertcanyon.com. **Web:** www.desertcanyon.com. **Facility Holes:** 18. **Yards:** 7,293/4,899. **Par:** 72/72. **Course Rating:** 74.0/67.5. **Slope:** 127/104. **Green Fee:** $48/$85. **Cart Fee:** Included in green fee. **Walking Policy:** Mandatory carts. **Walkability:** 5. **Opened:** 1993. **Architect:** Jack Frei. **Season:** March-Nov. **High:** June-Oct. **To obtain tee times:** Call golf shop. **Miscellaneous:** Reduced fees (weekdays, twilight, seniors, juniors), range (grass), lodging (10 rooms), credit cards (MC, V, AE), BF, FF.
Notes: Ranked 5th in 2001 Best in State; 35th in 1996 America's Top 75 Upscale Courses.
Reader Comments: On a high bluff above the Columbia River, this course is very scenic. Lots of changes in elevation. Hole #6 on the Desert 9 is as good as it gets, a GREAT par 5 and a thrill to play ... Because of its location, very few people know of its existence, too bad. Maybe the best course for your money in the Pacific Northwest.

★★★½ DOWNRIVER GOLF CLUB
PU-3225 N. Columbia Circle, Spokane, 99205, Spokane County, (509)327-5269. **Facility Holes:** 18. **Yards:** 6,130/5,592. **Par:** 71/73. **Course Rating:** 68.8/70.9. **Slope:** 115/114. **Green Fee:** $19. **Cart Fee:** $25/Cart. **Walking Policy:** Unrestricted walking. **Walkability:** 2. **Opened:** 1916. **Architect:** Local Citizens Committee. **Season:** March-Nov. **High:** May-Aug. **To obtain tee times:** Call golf shop. **Miscellaneous:** Range (mats), credit cards (MC, V).
Reader Comments: Beautiful course ... Old mature, wooded course. Great setting ... Short course, tree lined... Best shorter layout for the money ... Beautiful old pines, gorgeous on a summer morning ... Old and still good.

★★★½ DRUIDS GLEN GOLF CLUB/ACCESS GOLF LLC
PU-29925 207th Ave. S.E., Kent, 98042, King County, (253)638-1200, 25 miles from Seattle. **E-mail:** taddavis@seanet.com. **Web:** druidsglengolf.com. **Facility Holes:** 18. **Yards:** 7,146/5,354. **Par:** 72/72. **Course Rating:** 74.9/65.8. **Slope:** 134/119. **Green Fee:** $24/$55. **Cart Fee:** $14/Person. **Walking Policy:** Unrestricted walking. **Walkability:** 3. **Opened:** 1997. **Architect:** Keith Foster. **Season:** Year-round. **High:** April-Sept. **To obtain tee times:** Call up to 7 days in advance. **Miscellaneous:** Reduced fees (weekdays, twilight, seniors, juniors), metal spikes, range (grass/mats), credit cards (MC, V, AE), BF, FF.
Reader Comments: Excellent course condition. The fairways are short but not hard and the greens are comparable to Pumpkin Ridge, very fast. Good course to play and worth the price ... It must be one of the best kept secrets in the Puget Sound because I never have a problem getting on in the morning and, with a cart, can finish this course in under 3 hours.

★★★★ DUNGENESS GOLF & COUNTRY CLUB
SP-1965 Woodcock Rd., Sequim, 98382, Clallam County, (360)683-6344, (800)447-6826, 91 miles from Seattle. **E-mail:** skip@dungenessgolf.com. **Web:** www.dungenessgolf.com. **Facility Holes:** 18. **Yards:** 6,456/5,347. **Par:** 72/72. **Course Rating:** 70.1/70.3. **Slope:** 126/119. **Green Fee:** $27/$30. **Cart Fee:** $23/Cart. **Walking Policy:** Unrestricted walking. **Walkability:** 2. **Opened:** 1970. **Architect:** Ray Coleman. **Season:** Year-round. **High:** March-Oct. **To obtain tee times:** Call up to 60 days in advance. **Miscellaneous:** Reduced fees (weekdays, twilight, juniors), metal spikes, range (grass), lodging (7 rooms), credit cards (MC, V, AE), BF, FF.
Reader Comments: Talk about freedom. Excellent and courteous staff ... Dry, staff great ... The best course in the state of Washington. It's a must play if you're ever in the Pacific Northwest. I can't say enough good things about the place ... Great course all year long.

★★★½ EAGLEMONT GOLF CLUB
SP-4127 Eaglemont Dr., Mount Vernon, 98274, Skagit County, (360)424-0800, (800)368-8876, 23 miles from Bellingham. **Facility Holes:** 18. **Yards:** 7,006/5,307. **Par:** 72/72. **Course Rating:** 74.6/70.7. **Slope:** 140/121. **Green Fee:** $39/$63. **Cart Fee:** Included in green fee. **Walking Policy:** Mandatory carts. **Walkability:** 5. **Opened:** 1994. **Architect:** John Steidel. **Season:** Year-round. **High:** May-Sept. **To obtain tee times:** Call up to 7 days in advance. **Miscellaneous:** Reduced fees (weekdays, twilight, juniors), metal spikes, range (grass), credit cards (MC, V, AE), BF, FF.
Reader Comments: This challenging course makes you hit a lot of long irons off the tee to target areas. The greens rolled true ... Great layout ... Great elevation change & variety ... This course is very tough, but worth the price ...One of my favorites in western Washington.

★★★½ ECHO FALLS COUNTRY CLUB
PU-20414 121 First Ave. S.E., Snohomish, 98296, Snohomish County, (360)668-3030, 10 miles from Bellevue. **Facility Holes:** 18. **Yards:** 6,123/4,357. **Par:** 70/71. **Course Rating:** 69.4/64.6. **Slope:** 132/115. **Green Fee:** $27/$47. **Cart Fee:** $13/Person. **Walking Policy:** Unrestricted walking. **Walkability:** 3. **Opened:** 1992. **Architect:** Jack Frei. **Season:** Year-round. **High:** April-Sept. **To obtain tee times:** Call golf shop. **Miscellaneous:** Reduced fees (weekdays, guests, twilight, seniors, juniors), metal spikes, range (mats), credit cards (MC, V, AE).

WASHINGTON

★★★ ELK RUN GOLF CLUB
PU-22500 S.E. 275th Place, Maple Valley, 98038, King County, (425)432-8800, (800)244-8631, 35 miles from Seattle. **Facility Holes:** 18. **Yards:** 5,847/5,400. **Par:** 71/71. **Course Rating:** 68.7/70.4. **Slope:** 117/115. **Green Fee:** $27/$35. **Cart Fee:** $24/Cart. **Walking Policy:** Unrestricted walking. **Walkability:** 3. **Opened:** 1989. **Architect:** Pete Peterson. **Season:** Year-round. **To obtain tee times:** Call up to 5 days in advance. **Miscellaneous:** Reduced fees (weekdays, seniors, juniors), metal spikes, range (mats), credit cards (MC, V).
Reader Comments: For the money, it's the best course I've played. A lot of variation from hole-to-hole makes for a fun round. Plays remarkably well in wet weather, as well ... Great variety of holes. Use all clubs ... Great pro, player friendly ... Front 9 treed and tight. Not much play, great people, nice clubhouse.

★★ ENUMCLAW GOLF CLUB
PU-45220 288 Ave. S.E., Enumclaw, 98022, King County, (360)825-2827, 40 miles from Seattle. **Facility Holes:** 18. **Yards:** 5,561/5,211. **Par:** 70/71. **Course Rating:** 66.0/68.8. **Slope:** 106/110. **Green Fee:** $19. **Cart Fee:** $22/Cart. **Walking Policy:** Unrestricted walking. **Walkability:** 3. **Season:** Year-round. **High:** July-Aug. **To obtain tee times:** Call golf shop. **Miscellaneous:** Reduced fees (seniors, juniors), metal spikes, credit cards (MC, V).

★★★ ESMERALDA GOLF COURSE
PU-3933 E. Courtland, Spokane, 99217, Spokane County, (509)487-6291. **Facility Holes:** 18. **Yards:** 6,249/5,594. **Par:** 70/72. **Course Rating:** 68.7/72.5. **Slope:** 108/116. **Green Fee:** $19. **Cart Fee:** $29/Cart. **Walking Policy:** Unrestricted walking. **Walkability:** 2. **Opened:** 1956. **Architect:** Francis James. **Season:** March-Nov. **High:** April-Sept. **To obtain tee times:** Call golf shop. **Miscellaneous:** Reduced fees (twilight, seniors, juniors), metal spikes, range (grass/mats), credit cards (MC, V), BF, FF.
Reader Comments: Very friendly people. Very good mix of fairways and holes ... Very good for the price ... What you see is what you get ... Greens look slow, putt fast ... Old, short course, reasonable rates ... Best course to start the season on ... Always green in summer ... Friendly pro shop.

★★ THE FAIRWAYS AT WEST TERRACE
PU-9810 W. Melville Rd, Cheney, 99004, Spokane County, (509)747-8418, 8 miles from Spokane. **Facility Holes:** 18. **Yards:** 6,459/5,152. **Par:** 72/72. **Course Rating:** 69.0/68.9. **Slope:** 117/120. **Green Fee:** $14/$20. **Cart Fee:** $24/Cart. **Walking Policy:** Unrestricted walking. **Walkability:** 1. **Opened:** 1987. **Season:** Year-round. **High:** May-Oct. **To obtain tee times:** Call golf shop. **Miscellaneous:** Reduced fees (weekdays, twilight, seniors, juniors), range (grass), credit cards (MC, V, D), BF, FF.

★★½ FOSTER GOLF LINKS
PU-13500 Interuban Ave. S., Tukwila, 98168, King County, (206)242-4221, 6 miles from Seattle. **Facility Holes:** 18. **Yards:** 4,804/4,544. **Par:** 68/70. **Course Rating:** 61.9/64.8. **Slope:** 98/103. **Green Fee:** $21/$23. **Cart Fee:** $22/Cart. **Walking Policy:** Unrestricted walking. **Walkability:** 1. **Opened:** 1925. **Architect:** George Eddie. **Season:** Year-round. **High:** May-Oct. **To obtain tee times:** Call up to 7 days in advance. **Miscellaneous:** Reduced fees (weekdays, twilight, seniors, juniors), metal spikes, credit cards (MC, V), FF.

★★ GALLERY GOLF COURSE
M-3065 N. Cowpens Rd., Whidbey Island, Oak Harbor, 98278, Island County, (360)257-2178, 60 miles from Seattle. **E-mail:** ggc@mwrwhidbey.com. **Facility Holes:** 18. **Yards:** 6,351/5,454. **Par:** 72/74. **Course Rating:** 70.0/69.7. **Slope:** 117/110. **Green Fee:** $14/$23. **Cart Fee:** $16/Cart. **Walking Policy:** Unrestricted walking. **Walkability:** 3. **Opened:** 1948. **Architect:** U.S. Navy. **Season:** Year-round. **To obtain tee times:** Call golf shop. **Miscellaneous:** Reduced fees (twilight, juniors), metal spikes, range (grass), credit cards (MC, V, AE, D), BF, FF.

★★★ GLENEAGLES GOLF COURSE
PU-7619 Country Club Dr., Arlington, 98223, Snohomish County, (360)435-6713, (888)232-4653, 42 miles from Seattle. **Facility Holes:** 18. **Yards:** 5,901/4,507. **Par:** 70/70. **Course Rating:** 69.8/66.4. **Slope:** 136/120. **Green Fee:** $21/$26. **Cart Fee:** $10/Person. **Walking Policy:** Unrestricted walking. **Walkability:** 3. **Opened:** 1995. **Architect:** William Teufel. **Season:** Year-round. **To obtain tee times:** Call up to 7 days in advance. **Miscellaneous:** Reduced fees (weekdays, twilight, seniors, juniors), metal spikes, range (grass), credit cards (MC, V, AE, D, DC), BF, FF.
Reader Comments: Awesome value, great summer rates, lots of trees ... Has great senior rates ... Very challenging tee shots, water and tight ... Multiple tees for all levels.

WASHINGTON

GOLD MOUNTAIN GOLF COMPLEX
PU-7263 W. Belfair Valley Rd., Bremerton, 98312, Kitsap County, (360)415-5432, 5 miles from Bremerton. **Facility Holes:** 36. **Cart Fee:** $24/Cart. **Walking Policy:** Unrestricted walking. **Walkability:** 3. **Season:** Year-round. **Miscellaneous:** Reduced fees (weekdays, twilight, seniors, juniors), range (grass), credit cards (MC, V), BF, FF.

★★★★ **CASCADE COURSE** (18) *Value*
Yards: 6,707/5,306. **Par:** 71/74. **Course Rating:** 71.3/69.9. **Slope:** 120/116. **Green Fee:** $23/$29. **Opened:** 1970. **Architect:** Jack Reimer. **To obtain tee times:** Call up to 30 days in advance.
Reader Comments: Aims to please ... Fun to play ... Both good values ... The best courses in WA ... Great greens. Very good, very quiet course ... Great older course ... A perfect 36-hole day ... Great course, one of best winter courses.

★★★★½ **OLYMPIC COURSE** (18) *Value*
Yards: 7,003/5,220. **Par:** 72/72. **Course Rating:** 73.5/70.0. **Slope:** 131/116. **Green Fee:** $33/$40. **Opened:** 1996. **Architect:** John Harbottle. **To obtain tee times:** Call golf shop.
Notes: Ranked 10th in 2001 Best in State.
Reader Comments: Best public course in Washington State. 36 holes with no houses on or in sight of the golf complex. Fairways are the best anywhere and the greens are very fast and smooth ... Fantastic! Great course at any price, and it happens to be $36! Great and varied holes, wonderful conditioning, beautiful scenery. This course is a treat ... Absolutely the best.

THE GOLF CLUB AT HAWK'S PRAIRIE
PU-8383 Vicwood Lane, Lacey, 98516, Thurston County, (360)455-8383, (800)558-3348, 10 miles from Olympia. **E-mail:** zepper68@yahoo.com. **Facility Holes:** 36. **Walkability:** 4. **Season:** Year-round. **High:** April-Sept. **Miscellaneous:** Reduced fees (weekdays, twilight, seniors, juniors), range (grass), credit cards (MC, V, AE), BF, FF.

★★★★½ **THE LINKS** (18)
Yards: 6,887/5,202. **Par:** 72/72. **Course Rating:** 72.8/64.9. **Slope:** 123/105. **Green Fee:** $23/$38. **Cart Fee:** $12/Person. **Walking Policy:** Unrestricted walking. **Opened:** 1999. **Architect:** Peter L. H. Thompson. **To obtain tee times:** Call golf shop.
Notes: Ranked 10th in 1999 Best New Affordable Public.
Reader Comments: Very walkable and some great holes ... Super design, uncrowded ... A fun challenging course ... Good links course for NW ... Beautifully manicured, even the cart paths were being cleaned ... Beautiful course and layout ... My favorite course, links style ... Open links course where you can hit the big drive.
Special Notes: Formerly Vicwood Golf Links.

★★★ **THE WOODLANDS** (18)
Yards: 7,170/5,600. **Par:** 72/72. **Course Rating:** 75.1/73.0. **Slope:** 135/127. **Green Fee:** $30/$53. **Cart Fee:** Included in green fee. **Walking Policy:** Walking at certain times. **Opened:** 1995. **Architect:** Bill Overdorf. **To obtain tee times:** Call up to 7 days in advance.
Notes: Ranked 64th in 1996 America's Top 75 Affordable Courses.
Reader Comments: Great value ... Tough course, you earn a good score here ... Fair, no tricks ... Great course, good yardage markers ... A scenic ride through the fir forest.
Special Notes: Formerly Meriwood Golf Course.

THE GOLF CLUB AT NEWCASTLE
PU-15500 Six Penny Lane, Newcastle, 98059, King County, (425)793-4653, 20 miles from Seattle. **Web:** www.newcastlegolf.com. **Facility Holes:** 36. **Cart Fee:** Included in green fee. **Walking Policy:** Unrestricted walking. **Architect:** Bob Cupp/Fred Couples. **Season:** Year-round. **High:** April-Oct. **To obtain tee times:** Call up to 7 days in advance. **Miscellaneous:** Reduced fees (twilight, juniors), range (grass/mats), caddies, credit cards (MC, V, AE, D, DC, Check Card/Debit), BF, FF.

CHINA CREEK COURSE (18)
Yards: 6,416/4,566. **Par:** 70/70. **Course Rating:** 71.4/66.1. **Slope:** 126/112. **Green Fee:** $45/$90. **Walkability:** 4. **Opened:** 2001.

★★★ **COAL CREEK COURSE** (18)
Yards: 7,024/5,153. **Par:** 72/72. **Course Rating:** 73.7/69.4. **Slope:** 133/119. **Green Fee:** $100/$150. **Walkability:** 5. **Opened:** 1999.
Reader Comments: Incredible views on every hole ... Very fun, but tough to score on first time visit. Amazing clubhouse. Unparalleled views! Seattle and Bellevue skylines are breathtaking ... Perfect service and the course is maintained magnificently.

★½ **GRANDVIEW GOLF COURSE**
PU-7738 Portal Way, Custer, 98240, Whatcom County, (360)366-3947, (877)644-4653. **Facility Holes:** 18. **Yards:** 6,425/5,422. **Par:** 72/72. **Course Rating:** 69.9/70.2. **Slope:** 117/116. **Green Fee:** $18/$25. **Cart Fee:** $21/Cart. **Walking Policy:** Unrestricted walking. **Walkability:** 1. **Season:** Year-round. **Tee times:** Call up to 7 days in advance. **Miscellaneous:** Reduced fees (weekdays, twilight, seniors, juniors), metal spikes, credit cards (MC, V, AE, D), BF, FF.

GREEN MOUNTAIN GOLF COURSE

PU-2817 NE Ingle Rd., Vancouver, 98682, Clark County, (360)833-8463, (800)443-6612, 5 miles from Vancouver. **E-mail:** greenmountainrejor2j@earthlink.net. **Facility Holes:** 18. **Yards:** 6,170/5,187. **Par:** 72/72. **Course Rating:** 69.8/70.8. **Slope:** 122/115. **Green Fee:** $20/$39. **Cart Fee:** $24/Cart. **Walking Policy:** Unrestricted walking. **Walkability:** 3. **Opened:** 1999. **Architect:** Gene Mason. **Season:** Year-round. **High:** June-Sept. **To obtain tee times:** Call up to 10 days in advance. **Miscellaneous:** Reduced fees (weekdays, twilight, seniors, juniors), range (grass/mats), credit cards (MC, V), FF.

★★★½ HANGMAN VALLEY GOLF COURSE *Value*

PU-E. 2210 Hangman Valley Rd., Spokane, 99223, Spokane County, (509)448-1212. **E-mail:** hvgc@att.net. **Facility Holes:** 18. **Yards:** 6,906/5,699. **Par:** 72/71. **Course Rating:** 71.9/71.6. **Slope:** 126/118. **Green Fee:** $16/$22. **Cart Fee:** $24/Cart. **Walking Policy:** Unrestricted walking. **Walkability:** 3. **Opened:** 1969. **Architect:** Bob Baldock. **Season:** April-Oct. **High:** June-Oct. **To obtain tee times:** Call golf shop. **Miscellaneous:** Reduced fees (seniors, juniors), metal spikes, range (mats), credit cards (MC, V, D), BF.

Reader Comments: 2 great 600+ yarders here ... Nice course, great rates ... Very challenging par 5s ... Best value, great course.

★★★½ HARBOUR POINTE GOLF CLUB

PU-11817 Harbour Pointe Blvd., Mukilteo, 98275, Snohomish County, (425)355-6060, (800)233-3128, 15 miles from Seattle. **E-mail:** harbourpointe@msn.com. **Web:** www.harbourpt.com. **Facility Holes:** 18. **Yards:** 6,862/4,842. **Par:** 72/72. **Course Rating:** 72.8/68.8. **Slope:** 135/117. **Green Fee:** $28/$65. **Cart Fee:** $15/Person. **Walking Policy:** Unrestricted walking. **Walkability:** 3. **Opened:** 1990. **Architect:** Arthur Hills. **Season:** Year-round. **To obtain tee times:** Call up to 7 days in advance. **Miscellaneous:** Reduced fees (weekdays, twilight, seniors, juniors), metal spikes, range (grass/mats), credit cards (MC, V, AE), BF, FF. **Notes:** Ranked 58th in 1996 America's Top 75 Affordable Courses.

Reader Comments: Great course gets better all the time ... The greens are excellent and very fast and smooth. The greens hold approach shots, and the fairways are like walking on padded carpet ... If visiting the Seattle area, a must play ... View of Puget Sound incredible ... Great service and views, fun, challenging.

★★★ HIGH CEDARS GOLF CLUB

PU-14604 149th St. Court E., Orting, 98360, Pierce County, (360)893-3171, 14 miles from Tacoma. **Facility Holes:** 27. **Yards:** 6,303/5,409. **Par:** 71/71. **Course Rating:** 69.7/70.7. **Slope:** 114/115. **Green Fee:** $22/$30. **Cart Fee:** $22/Cart. **Walking Policy:** Unrestricted walking. **Walkability:** 1. **Opened:** 1971. **Season:** Year-round. **High:** April-Nov. **To obtain tee times:** Call golf shop. **Miscellaneous:** Reduced fees (weekdays, twilight, seniors, juniors), metal spikes, range (mats), credit cards (MC, V).

Reader Comments: Play can be slow to start a round, 2 of the first 4 holes are par 3s, but challenging shots and beautiful views make it worth the wait ... Nice local course ... Working to make it a beauty ... Wide fairways, very flat.

Special Notes: Also has a 9-hole executive course.

★★★★ HOMESTEAD FARMS GOLF RESORT

R-115 E. Homestead Blvd., Lynden, 98264, Whatcom County, (360)354-1196, (800)354-1196, 15 miles from Bellingham. **Web:** www.homesteadfarmsgolf.com. **Facility Holes:** 18. **Yards:** 6,927/5,570. **Par:** 72/72. **Course Rating:** 73.6/72.5. **Slope:** 130/130. **Green Fee:** $25/$50. **Cart Fee:** $12/Person. **Walking Policy:** Unrestricted walking. **Walkability:** 2. **Opened:** 1995. **Architect:** Bill Overdorf. **Season:** Year-round. **To obtain tee times:** Call up to 7 days in advance. **Miscellaneous:** Reduced fees (weekdays, guests, twilight, seniors, juniors), range (grass), lodging (20 rooms), credit cards (MC, V, AE, D), BF, FF.

Reader Comments: Beautiful course with plenty of water and sand to keep you thinking. The new clubhouse facilities are outstanding ... In great shape all seasons, a little spendy ... Excellent staff, course, facilities ... No. 1 course I've played this year.

★★★ HORSESHOE LAKE GOLF CLUB

PU-1250 S.W. Clubhouse Ct., Port Orchard, 98367, Kitsap County, (253)857-3326, 10 miles from Tacoma. **Web:** www.hlgolf.com. **Facility Holes:** 18. **Yards:** 6,105/5,115. **Par:** 71/71. **Course Rating:** 68.0/68.0. **Slope:** 116/112. **Green Fee:** $20/$35. **Walking Policy:** Mandatory carts. **Walkability:** 3. **Opened:** 1992. **Architect:** Jim Richardson. **Season:** Year-round. **To obtain tee times:** Call up to 7 days in advance. **Miscellaneous:** Reduced fees (weekdays, twilight, seniors, juniors), metal spikes, range (mats), credit cards (MC, V, AE, D), BF, FF.

Reader Comments: This course is one of the nice hidden secrets of Gig Harbor Peninsula. The front 9 is well kept and walkable ... Fun course to play ... Great price, challenging course ... Sweet back nine ... Tight fairways and beautiful canyon on back 9 ... Unusual and fun course.

HOT SPRINGS GOLF COURSE
PU-One St. Martin Rd., Carson, 98610, Skamania County, (509)427-5150, (800)607-3678, 45 miles from Portland. **E-mail:** geofflee@skamania.net. **Facility Holes:** 18. **Yards:** 6,407/5,244. **Par:** 72/72. **Course Rating:** 69.8/69.1. **Slope:** 113/110. **Green Fee:** $20/$25. **Cart Fee:** $10/Cart. **Walking Policy:** Unrestricted walking. **Walkability:** 1. **Opened:** 1991. **Season:** Feb.-Dec. **High:** June-Oct. **To obtain tee times:** Call up to 7 days in advance. **Miscellaneous:** Reduced fees (seniors, juniors), metal spikes, range (grass), lodging (22 rooms), credit cards (MC, V), FF.

★★★★ INDIAN CANYON GOLF COURSE *Value*
PU-W. 4304 West Dr., Spokane, 99224, Spokane County, (509)747-5353. **Facility Holes:** 18. **Yards:** 6,255/5,943. **Par:** 72/72. **Course Rating:** 69.8/70.2. **Slope:** 121/125. **Green Fee:** $23. **Cart Fee:** $23/Cart. **Walking Policy:** Unrestricted walking. **Walkability:** 4. **Opened:** 1935. **Architect:** H. Chandler Egan. **Season:** April-Oct. **Tee times:** Call golf shop. **Miscellaneous:** Reduced fees (twilight, juniors), metal spikes, range (grass/mats), credit cards (MC, V). **Notes:** Ranked 6th in 2001 Best in State; 6th in 1996 America's Top 75 Affordable Courses. **Reader Comments:** A bad day at the Canyon is better than a great day at many other courses I've played over the years ... An awesome course, the best value for your money in Spokane, awesome layout, some great holes, they keep it in great shape and most of all very user-friendly on the wallet ... A classic course, must play in Spokane.

★★½ JACKSON PARK GOLF COURSE
PU-1000 NE 135th St., Seattle, 98125, King County, (206)363-4747. **Facility Holes:** 27. **Yards:** 6,186/5,540. **Par:** 71/74. **Course Rating:** 68.2/70.2. **Slope:** 115/117. **Green Fee:** $18/$22. **Cart Fee:** $20/Cart. **Walking Policy:** Unrestricted walking. **Walkability:** 3. **Opened:** 1928. **Architect:** Henry Tucker, Frank James. **Season:** Year-round. **High:** March-Sept. **To obtain tee times:** Call golf shop. **Miscellaneous:** Reduced fees (twilight, seniors, juniors), metal spikes, range (mats), credit cards (MC, V). **Special Notes:** Also has a 9-hole par-3 course.

★★½ JEFFERSON PARK GOLF COURSE
PU-4101 Beacon Ave. S., Seattle, 98108, King County, (206)762-4513. **Facility Holes:** 27. **Yards:** 6,182/5,449. **Par:** 70/72. **Course Rating:** 68.3/70.2. **Slope:** 112/116. **Green Fee:** $25/$28. **Cart Fee:** $22/Cart. **Walking Policy:** Unrestricted walking. **Walkability:** 3. **Opened:** 1917. **Architect:** Robert Johnstone. **Season:** Year-round. **To obtain tee times:** Call up to 7 days in advance. **Miscellaneous:** Reduced fees (weekdays, twilight, seniors, juniors), metal spikes, range (mats), credit cards (MC, V), BF, FF. **Special Notes:** Also has 9-hole Par-3 course.

★★★½ KAYAK POINT GOLF COURSE
PU-15711 Marine Dr., Stanwood, 98292, Snohomish County, (360)652-9676, (800)562-3094, 45 miles from Seattle. **Web:** www.kayakgolf.com. **Facility Holes:** 18. **Yards:** 6,719/5,332. **Par:** 72/72. **Course Rating:** 72.9/71.1. **Slope:** 138/125. **Green Fee:** $20/$33. **Cart Fee:** $27/Cart. **Walking Policy:** Unrestricted walking. **Walkability:** 4. **Opened:** 1977. **Architect:** Ron Fream. **Season:** Year-round. **High:** May-Sept. **To obtain tee times:** Call golf shop. **Miscellaneous:** Reduced fees (weekdays, twilight, seniors, juniors), metal spikes, range (grass/mats), credit cards (MC, V, AE), BF, FF. **Notes:** Ranked 39th in 1996 America's Top 75 Affordable Courses. **Reader Comments:** Best course I've played for the price ... Absolutely beautiful course, great value ... A tree-lined challenge, drive straight not long ... Very nice course with some long and narrow holes. They offer some great discount deals ... Difficult, imposing course but fair, truly beautiful. Great clubhouse and food service.

★½ KENWANDA GOLF COURSE
PU-14030 Kenwanda Dr., Snohomish, 98296, Snohomish County, (360)668-1166, (866)300-1166, 10 miles from Everett. **E-mail:** fiddlersbluff@earthlink.net. **Facility Holes:** 18. **Yards:** 5,336/5,336. **Par:** 69/72. **Course Rating:** 64.1/68.7. **Slope:** 101/110. **Green Fee:** $20. **Cart Fee:** $20/Cart. **Walking Policy:** Unrestricted walking. **Walkability:** 3. **Opened:** 1962. **Architect:** Dr. Roy Goss/Ken Harris. **Season:** Year-round. **High:** April-Sept. **To obtain tee times:** Call up to 7 days in advance. **Miscellaneous:** Metal spikes, credit cards (MC, V), FF.

★★★½ LAKE CHELAN GOLF COURSE
PU-1501 Golf Course Dr., Chelan, 98816, Chelan County, (509)682-8026, (800)246-5361, 45 miles from Wenatchee. **Facility Holes:** 18. **Yards:** 6,440/5,501. **Par:** 72/72. **Course Rating:** 70.3/70.9. **Slope:** 119/113. **Green Fee:** $23/$30. **Cart Fee:** $23/Cart. **Walking Policy:** Unrestricted walking. **Walkability:** 3. **Opened:** 1971. **Architect:** Ron Sloan. **Season:** March-Nov. **High:** June-Aug. **To obtain tee times:** Call golf shop. **Miscellaneous:** Reduced fees (twilight, seniors, juniors), metal spikes, range (grass), credit cards (MC, V), BF, FF.

WASHINGTON

★★★★ LAKE PADDEN GOLF COURSE *Value+*

PU-4882 Samish Way, Bellingham, 98226, Whatcom County, (360)738-7400, 80 miles from Seattle. **Facility Holes:** 18. **Yards:** 6,675/5,496. **Par:** 72/72. **Course Rating:** 72.0/71.9. **Slope:** 124/122. **Green Fee:** $18/$24. **Cart Fee:** $24/Cart. **Walking Policy:** Unrestricted walking. **Walkability:** 2. **Opened:** 1970. **Architect:** Proctor & Goss. **Season:** Year-round. **High:** May-Sept. **Tee times:** Call golf shop. **Misc:** Reduced fees (seniors, juniors), range (grass/mats), credit cards (MC, V, AE), BF, FF.

Reader Comments: A tremendous value. You get to play a treed, interesting golf course in good condition for less than $20! ... Should be rated in top affordable courses in the country. Great course for all levels of play. Super service, all-around good muni ... Make the trip, this course is fun!

★★★ LAKE SPANAWAY GOLF COURSE

PU-15602 Pacific Ave., Tacoma, 98444, Pierce County, (253)531-3660, 30 miles from Seattle. **Facility Holes:** 18. **Yards:** 6,938/5,459. **Par:** 71/74. **Course Rating:** 73.0/71.3. **Slope:** 125/118. **Green Fee:** $16/$22. **Cart Fee:** $22/Cart. **Walking Policy:** Unrestricted walking. **Walkability:** 2. **Opened:** 1967. **Architect:** A. Vernon Macan. **Season:** Year-round. **High:** March-Oct. **To obtain tee times:** Call up to 7 days in advance. **Miscellaneous:** Reduced fees (weekdays, seniors, juniors), metal spikes, range (grass/mats), credit cards (MC, V, AE, D), BF, FF.

Reader Comments: Great public course ... Long, fair and tough ... Big trees ... Quality public course at great price ... Good muni course ... Best golf value in Tacoma area.

★★★ LAKE WILDERNESS GOLF COURSE

PU-25400 Witte Rd. S.E., Maple Valley, 98038, King County, (425)432-9405, 30 miles from Seattle. **Facility Holes:** 18. **Yards:** 5,218/4,544. **Par:** 70/70. **Course Rating:** 66.1/66.6. **Slope:** 118/117. **Green Fee:** $12/$22. **Cart Fee:** $20/Cart. **Walking Policy:** Unrestricted walking. **Walkability:** 3. **Architect:** Ray Coleman. **Season:** Year-round. **High:** May-Sept. **To obtain tee times:** Call up to 7 days in advance. **Miscellaneous:** Reduced fees (weekdays, twilight, seniors, juniors), metal spikes, credit cards (MC, V, AE, D), BF, FF.

Reader Comments: Fun to play ... Good course ... Little slow on weekend, fun holes ... Reasonable price, well maintained.

★★½ LAKELAND VILLAGE GOLF COURSE

SP-Old Ranch Rd., Allyn, 98524, Mason County, (360)275-6100, 40 miles from Olympia. **Web:** www.lakelandliving.com. **Facility Holes:** 27. **Green Fee:** $20/$33. **Cart Fee:** $24/Cart. **Walking Policy:** Unrestricted walking. **Walkability:** 3. **Opened:** 1972. **Architect:** Bunny Mason. **Season:** Year-round. **High:** May-Oct. **To obtain tee times:** Call up to 7 days in advance. **Miscellaneous:** Reduced fees (weekdays, twilight, seniors, juniors), metal spikes, range (grass), credit cards (MC, V), BF, FF.

GENERATION 1/GENERATION 2 (18 Combo)
Yards: 5,724/4,925. **Par:** 71/72. **Course Rating:** 68.8/69.2. **Slope:** 117/119.
GENERATION 2/GENERATION 3 (18 Combo)
Yards: 6,471/5,334. **Par:** 72/72. **Course Rating:** 71.5/71.0. **Slope:** 122/121.
GENERATION 3/GENERATION 1 (18 Combo)
Yards: 5,915/5,081. **Par:** 72/72. **Course Rating:** 68.5/69.6. **Slope:** 114/117.

★★★★ LEAVENWORTH GOLF CLUB

SP-9101 Icicle Rd., Leavenworth, 98826, Chelan County, (509)548-7267, 110 miles from Seattle. **E-mail:** lgc@crcwnet.com. **Web:** www.leavenworthgolf.com. **Facility Holes:** 18. **Yards:** 5,711/5,343. **Par:** 71/71. **Course Rating:** 66.7/67.3. **Slope:** 111/113. **Green Fee:** $26/$29. **Cart Fee:** $24/Cart. **Walking Policy:** Unrestricted walking. **Walkability:** 2. **Opened:** 1927. **Season:** April-Oct. **Tee times:** Call golf shop. **Misc:** Credit cards (MC, V, AE, D), BF, FF.

Reader Comments: Great course next to mountains ... Beautiful setting, short but fun ... Fun little course. Beautiful! ... This place has the best customer service I have ever seen ... Wooded, narrow fairways. Pretty course.

★★★ LEGION MEMORIAL GOLF COURSE

PU-144 W Marine View Dr., Everett, 98201, Snohomish County, (425)259-4653. **Facility Holes:** 18. **Yards:** 6,900/4,805. **Par:** 72/72. **Course Rating:** 71.2/65.9. **Slope:** 116/100. **Green Fee:** $22/$30. **Cart Fee:** $21/Cart. **Walking Policy:** Unrestricted walking. **Walkability:** 2. **Opened:** 1934. **Architect:** Steve Burns. **Season:** Year-round. **High:** May-Sept. **To obtain tee times:** Call golf shop. **Miscellaneous:** Reduced fees (seniors, juniors), credit cards (MC, V).

Reader Comments: This course holds up extremely well during the winter (rainy) season. One of the better courses in the area, but a little on the pricey side ... Great winter course: Fairly forgiving and wide open, hard to get into trouble. Nice greens and fairways ... This is a good easy course to play. The fairways are wide and in excellent shape.

★★★½ LEWIS RIVER GOLF COURSE
PU-3209 Lewis River Rd., Woodland, 98674, Cowlitz County, (360)225-8254, (800)341-9426, 30 miles from Portland. **Facility Holes:** 18. **Yards:** 6,352/5,260. **Par:** 72/73. **Course Rating:** 69.5/68.9. **Slope:** 124/118. **Green Fee:** $25/$31. **Cart Fee:** $24/Cart. **Walking Policy:** Unrestricted walking. **Walkability:** 2. **Opened:** 1968. **Season:** Year-round. **High:** June-Sept. **To obtain tee times:** Call golf shop. **Miscellaneous:** Reduced fees (twilight, seniors, juniors), metal spikes, range (grass), credit cards (MC, V).
Reader Comments: Beautiful mountain valley course ... Always lush and playable ... Excellent ... Constantly improving ... Beautiful course ... Lots of water. Great shape ... Great back 9.

★★★½ LIBERTY LAKE GOLF CLUB
PU-E. 24403 Sprague, Liberty Lake, 99019, Spokane County, (509)255-6233, 20 miles from Spokane. **Facility Holes:** 18. **Yards:** 6,373/5,801. **Par:** 70/74. **Course Rating:** 69.8/75.7. **Slope:** 121/134. **Green Fee:** $16/$22. **Cart Fee:** $25/Cart. **Walking Policy:** Unrestricted walking. **Walkability:** 3. **Opened:** 1959. **Architect:** Curly Houston. **Season:** Year-round. **To obtain tee times:** Call golf shop. **Miscellaneous:** Reduced fees (twilight, seniors, juniors), metal spikes, range (grass/mats), credit cards (MC, V, D), BF, FF.
Reader Comments: Excellent mix of fairways and greens. Very friendly people ... Longer than you think ... Changes continue to improve course ... Best $ value in Spokane.

★★½ LIPOMA FIRS GOLF COURSE
PU-18615 110th Ave. E., Puyallup, 98374, Pierce County, (253)841-4396, (800)649-4396, 10 miles from Tacoma. **Facility Holes:** 27. **Green Fee:** $17/$22. **Cart Fee:** $20/Cart. **Walking Policy:** Unrestricted walking. **Opened:** 1989. **Architect:** Bill Stowe. **Season:** Year-round. **High:** April-Oct. **To obtain tee times:** Call golf shop. **Miscellaneous:** Reduced fees (weekdays, twilight, seniors, juniors), metal spikes, range (grass/mats).
GOLD/BLUE (18 Combo)
Yards: 6,805/5,517. **Par:** 72/72. **Course Rating:** 72.2/70.8. **Slope:** 122/116.
GREEN/BLUE (18 Combo)
Yards: 6,687/5,473. **Par:** 72/72. **Course Rating:** 70.0/70.6. **Slope:** 122/117.
GREEN/GOLD (18 Combo)
Yards: 6,722/5,476. **Par:** 72/72. **Course Rating:** 72.1/70.4. **Slope:** 122/117.

★★½ MADRONA LINKS GOLF COURSE
PU-3604 22nd Ave. N.W., Gig Harbor, 98335, Pierce County, (253)851-5193, 2 miles from Tacoma. **Facility Holes:** 18. **Yards:** 5,602/4,737. **Par:** 71/73. **Course Rating:** 65.5/65.6. **Slope:** 110/110. **Green Fee:** $20/$22. **Cart Fee:** $20/Cart. **Walking Policy:** Unrestricted walking. **Opened:** 1978. **Architect:** Ken Tyson. **Season:** Year-round. **High:** March-Oct. **To obtain tee times:** Call golf shop. **Miscellaneous:** Reduced fees (twilight, seniors, juniors), metal spikes, range (grass/mats), credit cards (MC, V).

★★★½ MAPLEWOOD GOLF COURSE
PU-4050 Maple Valley Hwy., Renton, 98058, King County, (425)430-6800, 2 miles from Renton. **Facility Holes:** 18. **Yards:** 6,005/5,400. **Par:** 72/72. **Course Rating:** 68.8/69.1. **Slope:** 115/115. **Green Fee:** $17/$28. **Cart Fee:** $22/Cart. **Walking Policy:** Unrestricted walking. **Walkability:** 2. **Opened:** 1927. **Architect:** Al Smith. **Season:** Year-round. **To obtain tee times:** Call golf shop. **Miscellaneous:** Reduced fees (seniors, juniors), metal spikes, range (mats), credit cards (MC, V), BF, FF.
Reader Comments: Surprise course ... Nice! Good price and challenging ... This course is well worth the price and they have the best bar and restaurant. The greens are receptive and in good condition. The fairways are good and tight in places.

★★★★½ MCCORMICK WOODS GOLF COURSE
PU-5155 McCormick Woods Dr. S.W., Port Orchard, 98367, Kitsap County, (360)895-0130, (800)373-0130, 2 miles from Port Orchard. **Web:** www.mccormickwoodsgolf.com. **Facility Holes:** 18. **Yards:** 7,040/5,758. **Par:** 72/72. **Course Rating:** 74.6/73.6. **Slope:** 136/131. **Green Fee:** $25/$55. **Cart Fee:** $13/Person. **Walking Policy:** Unrestricted walking. **Walkability:** 3. **Opened:** 1988. **Architect:** Jack Frei. **Season:** Year-round. **High:** July-Sept. **To obtain tee times:** Call up to 30 days in advance. **Miscellaneous:** Reduced fees (weekdays, twilight, seniors), metal spikes, range (grass/mats), credit cards (MC, V, AE, D, DC, CB), BF, FF.
Notes: Ranked 7th in 1999 Best in State.
Reader Comments: Peaceful, scenic, great track ... A great course. Impeccably kept with some challenging holes. This is one of the gems of Gig Harbor Peninsula golf ... Wow! What a fantastic course. Excellent pro shop and staff ... Favorite Washington course, beautiful setting ... Good course, nice people, and fun time.

★★½ MEADOW PARK GOLF COURSE
PU-7108 Lakewood Dr. W., Tacoma, 98467, Pierce County, (253)473-3033, 27 miles from Seattle. **Facility Holes:** 27. **Yards:** 6,093/5,262. **Par:** 71/73. **Course Rating:** 68.9/70.2. **Slope:** 116/115. **Green Fee:** $22/$25. **Cart Fee:** $22/Cart. **Walking Policy:** Unrestricted walking. **Walkability:** 3. **Opened:** 1917. **Architect:** John Steidel. **Season:** Year-round. **To obtain tee times:** Call up to 7 days in advance. **Miscellaneous:** Reduced fees (weekdays, twilight, seniors, juniors), metal spikes, range (mats), credit cards (MC, V), BF, FF. **Special Notes:** Also has a 9-hole executive course.

★★★★ MEADOWWOOD GOLF COURSE *Value*
PU-E. 24501 Valley Way, Liberty Lake, 99019, Spokane County, (509)255-9539, 12 miles from Spokane. **Facility Holes:** 18. **Yards:** 6,846/5,880. **Par:** 72/72. **Course Rating:** 72.1/73.5. **Slope:** 126/131. **Green Fee:** $12/$22. **Cart Fee:** $23/Cart. **Walking Policy:** Walking at certain times. **Walkability:** 3. **Opened:** 1988. **Architect:** Robert Muir Graves. **Season:** March-Nov. **High:** May-Aug. **To obtain tee times:** Call golf shop. **Miscellaneous:** Reduced fees (twilight, seniors, juniors), metal spikes, range (mats), credit cards (MC, V, D), BF, FF. **Reader Comments:** An awesome course for the price, would easily cost 70-80 dollars in California, only 18 dollars in Spokane, a supreme value … One of the best public golf courses that you can play … Wind, wind, super course … Nice golf course, grip it & rip it!!

★★★ MINT VALLEY GOLF CLUB
PU-4002 Pennsylvania St., Longview, 98632, Cowlitz County, (360)577-3395, (800)928-8929, 38 miles from Portland. **Facility Holes:** 18. **Yards:** 6,379/5,231. **Par:** 71/71. **Course Rating:** 70.4/69.0. **Slope:** 119/109. **Green Fee:** $15/$24. **Cart Fee:** $24/Cart. **Walking Policy:** Unrestricted walking. **Walkability:** 1. **Opened:** 1976. **Architect:** Ron Fream. **Season:** Year-round. **High:** June-Sept. **To obtain tee times:** Call up to 7 days in advance. **Misc:** Reduced fees (weekdays, twilight, seniors, juniors), range (grass/mats), credit cards (MC, V), BF, FF. **Reader Comments:** Very nice for the money. Very nice people in the clubhouse … Fine public course … Small, interesting, coupon values, worth the money … Sporty course at reasonable rates.

MOSES POINTE GOLF RESORT
SP-4524 Westshore Dr., Moses Lake, 98837, Grant County, (509)764-2275. **Web:** www.mosespointe.com. **Facility Holes:** 18. **Yards:** 7,428/5,807. **Par:** 72/72. **Course Rating:** 75.6/73.8. **Slope:** 134/132. **Green Fee:** $22/$45. **Cart Fee:** $12/Person. **Walking Policy:** Unrestricted walking. **Walkability:** 2. **Opened:** 1999. **Architect:** Mike Moore/David Soushek. **Season:** Year-round. **High:** March-Oct. **To obtain tee times:** Call up to 14 days in advance. **Miscellaneous:** Reduced fees (twilight, seniors, juniors), credit cards (MC, V, AE), FF.

★★ MOUNT ADAMS COUNTRY CLUB
SP-1250 Rockyford Rd., Toppenish, 98948, Yakima County, (509)865-4440, 2 miles from Toppenish. **Facility Holes:** 18. **Yards:** 6,261/5,707. **Par:** 72/73. **Course Rating:** 70.1/72.8. **Slope:** 123/127. **Green Fee:** $23. **Cart Fee:** $23/Cart. **Walking Policy:** Unrestricted walking. **Walkability:** 1. **Architect:** Designed by members. **Season:** Year-round. **Tee times:** Call golf shop. **Misc:** Reduced fees (weekdays, juniors), range, credit cards (MC, V), BF, FF.

★★★ MOUNT SI GOLF COURSE
PU-9010 Boalch Ave. S.E., Snoqualmie, 98065, King County, (425)888-1541, 27 miles from Seattle. **E-mail:** matt@mtsigolf.com. **Web:** www.mtsigolf.com. **Facility Holes:** 18. **Yards:** 6,304/5,439. **Par:** 72/72. **Course Rating:** 68.5/68.8. **Slope:** 116/108. **Green Fee:** $24/$35. **Cart Fee:** $24/Cart. **Walking Policy:** Unrestricted walking. **Walkability:** 2. **Opened:** 1927. **Architect:** Gary Barter/John Sanford. **Season:** Year-round. **To obtain tee times:** Call up to 365 days in advance. **Miscellaneous:** Reduced fees (weekdays, twilight, seniors, juniors), metal spikes, range (mats), credit cards (MC, V), BF, FF. **Reader Comments:** Nice course. Fairly forgiving and wide open … Plenty of open space to work on your mistakes without being overly penalized … Very friendly staff, great food, fun course to walk due to views, great putting surface.

NEWAUKUM VALLEY GOLF COURSE
PU-153 Newaukum Golf Dr., Chehalis, 98532, Lewis County, (360)748-0461, 85 miles from Seattle. **Facility Holes:** 27. **Green Fee:** $12/$23. **Cart Fee:** $20/Cart. **Walking Policy:** Unrestricted walking. **Walkability:** 3. **Opened:** 1979. **Architect:** H.M. Date/J.H. Date. **Season:** Year-round. **Tee times:** Call golf shop. **Misc:** Reduced fees (weekdays, twilight, seniors, juniors), credit cards (MC, V), BF, FF.
EAST/WEST (18 Combo)
Yards: 6,213/5,287. **Par:** 72/72. **Course Rating:** 68.7/69.6. **Slope:** 112/115.
SOUTH/EAST (18 Combo)
Yards: 6,168/5,102. **Par:** 72/72. **Course Rating:** 68.8/68.3. **Slope:** 112/112.

WASHINGTON

SOUTH/WEST (18 Combo)
Yards: 6,491/5,519. **Par:** 72/72. **Course Rating:** 69.9/70.6. **Slope:** 113/112.

★½ **NILE GOLF CLUB**
SP-6601 244th S.W., Mountlake Terrace, 98043, Snohomish County, (425)776-5154, 5 miles from Seattle. **Facility Holes:** 18. **Yards:** 5,000/4,578. **Par:** 67/67. **Course Rating:** 64.0/65.4. **Slope:** 104/105. **Green Fee:** $28. **Cart Fee:** $22/Cart. **Walking Policy:** Unrestricted walking. **Walkability:** 3. **Opened:** 1969. **Architect:** Norman Woods. **Season:** Year-round. **High:** March-Oct. **To obtain tee times:** Call up to 3 days in advance. **Miscellaneous:** Reduced fees (seniors, juniors), metal spikes, credit cards (MC, V), BF, FF.

★½ **NISQUALLY VALLEY GOLF CLUB**
PU-15425 Mosman St. S.W., Yelm, 98597, Thurston County, (360)458-3332, (800)352-2645, 15 miles from Olympia. **Facility Holes:** 18. **Yards:** 6,007/5,751. **Par:** 72/72. **Course Rating:** 68.2/71.6. **Slope:** 116/123. **Green Fee:** $17. **Cart Fee:** $15/Cart. **Walking Policy:** Unrestricted walking. **Walkability:** 1. **Opened:** 1960. **Season:** Year-round. **High:** April-Oct. **To obtain tee times:** Call up to 7 days in advance. **Miscellaneous:** Reduced fees (twilight, seniors, juniors), metal spikes, credit cards (MC, V), FF.

★★★ **NORTH BELLINGHAM GOLF COURSE**
PU-205 W. Smith Rd., Bellingham, 98226, Whatcom County, (360)398-8300, (888)322-6242. **E-mail:** nbgc@caitacusa.com. **Web:** nbellinghamgc.com. **Facility Holes:** 18. **Yards:** 6,816/5,160. **Par:** 72/72. **Course Rating:** 72.5/68.9. **Slope:** 125/112. **Green Fee:** $19/$39. **Cart Fee:** $12/Person. **Walking Policy:** Unrestricted walking. **Walkability:** 2. **Opened:** 1995. **Architect:** Ted Locke. **Season:** Year-round. **To obtain tee times:** Call up to 7 days in advance. **Miscellaneous:** Reduced fees (weekdays, twilight, seniors, juniors), range (grass/mats), credit cards (MC, V, AE, D, DC, CB), FF.
Reader Comments: Wonderful practice facilities ... Open course, target golf ... Good greens, links style, windy ... Challenging course, amazingly dry in winter ... Good links-type course ... Good views of mountains ... Very windy, all of the time ... Close to being No. 1 ... A well-kept secret.

★★★½ **NORTH SHORE GOLF & COUNTRY CLUB**
PU-4101 N. Shore Blvd. N.E., Tacoma, 98422, Pierce County, (253)927-1375, (800)447-1375. **E-mail:** ngolfcours@aol.com. **Web:** northshoregc.com. **Facility Holes:** 18. **Yards:** 6,305/5,442. **Par:** 71/73. **Course Rating:** 69.9/70.7. **Slope:** 120/119. **Green Fee:** $20/$30. **Cart Fee:** $34/Cart. **Walking Policy:** Unrestricted walking. **Walkability:** 2. **Opened:** 1961. **Architect:** Glen Proctor/RoyGoss. **Season:** Year-round. **High:** May-Sept. **To obtain tee times:** Call up to 7 days in advance. **Miscellaneous:** Reduced fees (weekdays, twilight, juniors), metal spikes, range (grass/mats), credit cards (MC, V, AE, D), BF, FF.
Reader Comments: A wide variety of holes and many elevation changes ... Some great holes. Tougher than it looks ... A great neighborhood course. Provides plenty of challenge with a different look on every hole. Greens and fairways are always in great shape ... Beautiful layout.

★★ **OAKSRIDGE GOLF COURSE**
PU-1052 Monte-Elma Rd., Elma, 98541, Grays Harbor County, (360)482-3511, 80 miles from Seattle. **E-mail:** royaloak@techline.com. **Facility Holes:** 18. **Yards:** 5,643/5,423. **Par:** 70/72. **Course Rating:** 65.3/68.9. **Slope:** 100/108. **Green Fee:** $13/$17. **Cart Fee:** $17/Cart. **Walking Policy:** Unrestricted walking. **Walkability:** 1. **Opened:** 1935. **Season:** Year-round. **To obtain tee times:** Call golf shop. **Miscellaneous:** Reduced fees (seniors, juniors), metal spikes, range (mats), credit cards (MC, V, AE, D), BF, FF.

★★ **OCEAN SHORES GOLF COURSE**
R-500 Canal Dr. N.E., Ocean Shores, 98569, Grays Harbor County, (360)289-3357, 130 miles from Seattle. **E-mail:** lespedal@techline.com. **Facility Holes:** 18. **Yards:** 6,252/5,173. **Par:** 71/72. **Course Rating:** 70.2/69.6. **Slope:** 115/115. **Green Fee:** $14/$27. **Cart Fee:** $24/Cart. **Walking Policy:** Unrestricted walking. **Walkability:** 2. **Opened:** 1965. **Architect:** Ray Coleman. **Season:** Year-round. **To obtain tee times:** Call golf shop. **Miscellaneous:** Reduced fees (seniors, juniors), metal spikes, credit cards (MC, V), BF, FF.

OTHELLO GOLF CLUB
PU-P.O. Box 185, Bench Rd., Othello, 99344, Adams County, (509)488-2376, 45 miles from Pasco. **Facility Holes:** 18. **Yards:** 6,200. **Par:** 70. **Course Rating:** 68.6. **Slope:** 115. **Green Fee:** $18/$20. **Cart Fee:** $21/Cart. **Walking Policy:** Unrestricted walking. **Walkability:** 1. **Opened:** 1965. **Architect:** John Reimer. **Season:** Year-round. **To obtain tee times:** Call golf shop. **Miscellaneous:** Reduced fees (juniors), range (grass), credit cards (MC, V), BF, FF.

★★★★ PORT LUDLOW GOLF COURSE

R-751 Highland Dr., Port Ludlow, 98365, Jefferson County, (360)437-0272, (800)732-1239, 40 miles from Seattle. **E-mail:** golfteetimes@orminc.com. **Web:** visitportludlow.com.
Facility Holes: 27. **Green Fee:** $29/$55. **Cart Fee:** $14/Person. **Walking Policy:** Unrestricted walking. **Walkability:** 3. **Opened:** 1975. **Architect:** Robert Muir Graves. **Season:** Year-round. **High:** May-Sept. **To obtain tee times:** Call golf shop. **Miscellaneous:** Reduced fees (weekdays, guests, twilight), lodging (225 rooms), range (grass/mats), credit cards (MC, V, AE), BF, FF.
TIDE/TIMBER (18 Combo) *Pace+*
Yards: 6,787/5,598. **Par:** 72/72. **Course Rating:** 72.7/72.9. **Slope:** 131/126.
TIMBER/TRAIL (18 Combo)
Yards: 6,746/5,112. **Par:** 72/72. **Course Rating:** 73.6/70.8. **Slope:** 138/124.
TRAIL/TIDE (18 Combo)
Yards: 6,683/5,192. **Par:** 72/72. **Course Rating:** 73.1/71.3. **Slope:** 138/124.
Reader Comments: A beautiful golf course. Some vistas are so breathtaking you want to just stay and enjoy rather than hit your next shot … 27 holes—Trail 9 is toughest I've ever played … Nice walking course … Awesome challenge of skills … Watch for specials.

★★★ QUAIL RIDGE GOLF COURSE

PU-3600 Swallows Nest Dr., Clarkston, 99403, Asotin County, (509)758-8501, 100 miles from Spokane. **Facility Holes:** 18. **Yards:** 5,861/4,675. **Par:** 71/71. **Course Rating:** 68.1/66.2. **Slope:** 114/107. **Green Fee:** $17/$19. **Cart Fee:** $21/Cart. **Walking Policy:** Unrestricted walking.
Walkability: 4. **Opened:** 1966. **Architect:** Mark Poe. **Season:** Year-round. **High:** April-Sept.
To obtain tee times: Call golf shop. **Miscellaneous:** Reduced fees (seniors, juniors), range (mats), credit cards (MC, V).
Reader Comments: Beautiful, green, lush, well maintained and run. My 2nd most favorite … Hilly, but interesting … Very nice since the addition of the new 9 … Great layout, accuracy and length needed to score … Rolling terrain, busy but fun course … Nice pro shop and clubhouse … Great service staff … Best drainage in area … Short, but fair.

★★★ RIVERBEND GOLF COMPLEX

PU-2019 W. Meeker St., Kent, 98032, King County, (253)854-3673, 18 miles from Seattle.
Facility Holes: 27. **Yards:** 6,633/5,538. **Par:** 72/72. **Course Rating:** 70.1/70.1. **Slope:** 119/114.
Green Fee: $19/$23. **Cart Fee:** $20/Cart. **Walking Policy:** Unrestricted walking. **Walkability:** 2.
Opened: 1989. **Architect:** John Steidel. **Season:** Year-round. **High:** April-Sept. **To obtain tee times:** Call golf shop. **Miscellaneous:** Reduced fees (weekdays, twilight, seniors, juniors), metal spikes, range (mats), caddies, credit cards (MC, V).
Reader Comments: Great course. Busy, but a fairly good pace of play. Well maintained. Not real hilly, but still a challenge … Good condition, easy to walk, challenging … Great junior golf program … Very picturesque, good challenge … A great value.
Special Notes: Also has a 9-hole par 3.

★★½ RIVERSIDE COUNTRY CLUB

PU-1451 N.W. Airport Rd., Chehalis, 98532, Lewis County, (360)748-8182, (800)242-9486, 27 miles from Olympia. **E-mail:** riversidecc@localaccess.com. **Facility Holes:** 18. **Yards:** 6,155/5,456. **Par:** 71/72. **Course Rating:** 69.3/71.2. **Slope:** 118/116. **Green Fee:** $14/$25. **Cart Fee:** $22/Cart. **Walking Policy:** Unrestricted walking. **Walkability:** 2. **Opened:** 1927. **Architect:** Roy Goss/Glenn Proctor. **Season:** Year-round. **High:** March-Oct. **To obtain tee times:** Call golf shop. **Miscellaneous:** Reduced fees (weekdays, twilight, seniors, juniors), metal spikes, range (grass/mats), credit cards (MC, V), BF, FF.

★★ ROLLING HILLS GOLF COURSE

PU-2485 N.E. McWilliams Rd., Bremerton, 98311, Kitsap County, (360)479-1212. **Facility Holes:** 18. **Yards:** 5,936/5,486. **Par:** 70/71. **Course Rating:** 68.7/71.0. **Slope:** 120/120. **Green Fee:** $24/$26. **Cart Fee:** $24/Cart. **Walking Policy:** Unrestricted walking. **Walkability:** 3.
Opened: 1972. **Architect:** Don Hogan. **Season:** Year-round. **High:** April-Oct. **To obtain tee times:** Call up to 7 days in advance. **Miscellaneous:** Reduced fees (seniors, juniors), metal spikes, range (mats), credit cards (MC, V, AE, D), BF, FF.

★★ SAGE HILLS GOLF CLUB

PU-10400 Sagehill Rd. SE, Warden, 98857, Grant County, (509)349-2603, 2 miles from Warden. **Facility Holes:** 18. **Yards:** 6,591/5,128. **Par:** 71/73. **Course Rating:** 71.4/69.0. **Slope:** 122/114. **Green Fee:** $17/$22. **Cart Fee:** $11/Person. **Walking Policy:** Unrestricted walking.
Walkability: 3. **Opened:** 1967. **Season:** March-Nov. **High:** May-Aug. **To obtain tee times:** Call golf shop. **Miscellaneous:** Reduced fees (weekdays, guests, seniors, juniors), range (mats), credit cards (MC, V).
Special Notes: Formerly Warden Golf Course.

SEMIAHMOO GOLF & COUNTRY CLUB

SP-8720 Semiahmoo Pkwy., Blaine, 98230, Whatcom County, (360)371-7005, (800)231-4425, 40 miles from Vancouver. **Web:** www.semiahmoo.com. **Facility Holes:** 54. **Cart Fee:** $17/Person. **Walking Policy:** Unrestricted walking. **Season:** Year-round. **High:** May-Sept. **Miscellaneous:** Reduced fees (weekdays, guests, twilight, juniors), range (grass/mats), lodging (200 rooms), credit cards (MC, V, AE), BF, FF.

LOOMIS TRAIL COURSE (18) *Pace*

Yards: 7,137/5,399. **Par:** 72/72. **Course Rating:** 75.1/71.9. **Slope:** 145/125. **Green Fee:** $75. **Walkability:** 1. **Opened:** 1992. **Architect:** Graham Cooke. **To obtain tee times:** Call up to 30 days in advance.

Notes: Ranked 7th in 2001 Best in State.

★★★★ SEMIAHMOO COURSE (18) *Pace*

Yards: 7,005/5,288. **Par:** 72/72. **Course Rating:** 74.5/71.6. **Slope:** 130/126. **Green Fee:** $39/$65. **Walkability:** 2. **Opened:** 1986. **Architect:** Arnold Palmer/Ed Seay. **To obtain tee times:** Call up to 7 days in advance.

Notes: Ranked 8th in 2001 Best in State; 69th in 1996 America's Top 75 Upscale Courses.
Reader Comments: This was the best course I have ever played … Nice Palmer layout, user friendly … This course always is a treat to play. The fairways are well maintained and the club atmosphere is very positive … Good year-round resort course … Good duo with Loomis Trail.
Special Notes: Also has an 18-hole private course.

★★★★ SHUKSAN GOLF CLUB

PU-1500 E. Axton Rd., Bellingham, 98226, Whatcom County, (360)398-8888, (800)801-8897, 5 miles from Bellingham. **E-mail:** shuksangolf@home.com. **Web:** shuksangolf.com. **Facility Holes:** 18. **Yards:** 6,742/5,253. **Par:** 72/72. **Course Rating:** 72.2/68.5. **Slope:** 135/118. **Green Fee:** $22/$41. **Cart Fee:** $12/Person. **Walking Policy:** Unrestricted walking. **Walkability:** 4. **Opened:** 1994. **Architect:** Rick Dvorak. **Season:** Year-round. **High:** May-Sept. **To obtain tee times:** Call up to 7 days in advance. **Miscellaneous:** Reduced fees (weekdays, twilight, seniors, juniors), range (grass/mats), credit cards (MC, V, D), BF, FF.
Reader Comments: Beautiful views, tough but fair, a gem … One of the best courses for the price in the Pacific Northwest … What a deal! Fun, fun course with spectacular views, another almost target golf but fun.

★½ SIMILK BEACH GOLF COURSE

PU-12518 Christiansen Rd., Anacortes, 98221, Skagit County, (360)293-3444, 5 miles from Anacortes. **Facility Holes:** 18. **Yards:** 6,177/5,788. **Par:** 72/74. **Course Rating:** 68.4/72.3. **Slope:** 110/112. **Green Fee:** $20/$23. **Cart Fee:** $22/Cart. **Walking Policy:** Unrestricted walking. **Walkability:** 3. **Opened:** 1955. **Architect:** Jim Turner. **Season:** Year-round. **To obtain tee times:** Call up to 14 days in advance. **Miscellaneous:** Reduced fees (weekdays, juniors), metal spikes, range (mats), credit cards (MC, V), BF, FF.

★★★½ SKAMANIA LODGE GOLF COURSE

R-1131 Skamania Lodge Way, Stevenson, 98671, Skamania County, (509)427-2541, (800)293-0418, 45 miles from Portland. **E-mail:** guyp@skamania.com. **Facility Holes:** 18. **Yards:** 5,776/4,362. **Par:** 70/70. **Course Rating:** 68.9/65.2. **Slope:** 127/115. **Green Fee:** $25/$49. **Cart Fee:** $26/Cart. **Walking Policy:** Unrestricted walking. **Walkability:** 3. **Opened:** 1993. **Architect:** Bunny Mason. **Season:** Year-round. **High:** May-Oct. **To obtain tee times:** Call golf shop. **Miscellaneous:** Reduced fees (guests, twilight, juniors), metal spikes, range (grass/mats), lodging (195 rooms), credit cards (MC, V, AE, D, DC), BF, FF.
Reader Comments: Very narrow course with great views. Can find deals in Portland newspaper that help. Very nice people working there. Can't beat the 19th hole … Difficult but scenic … Short and sporty, country club atmosphere … Scenery is spectacular, little margin for errant shots.

★★★ SNOHOMISH GOLF COURSE

PU-7805 147th Ave. S.E., Snohomish, 98290, Snohomish County, (360)568-2676, (800)560-2676, 20 miles from Seattle. **E-mail:** links399@aol.com. **Web:** snohomishgolf.com. **Facility Holes:** 18. **Yards:** 6,858/5,980. **Par:** 72/74. **Course Rating:** 72.7/74.1. **Slope:** 126/129. **Green Fee:** $23/$30. **Cart Fee:** $22/Cart. **Walking Policy:** Unrestricted walking. **Walkability:** 3. **Opened:** 1967. **Architect:** Roy Goss. **Season:** Year-round. **To obtain tee times:** Call up to 7 days in advance. **Miscellaneous:** Reduced fees (weekdays, twilight, seniors, juniors), metal spikes, range (grass/mats), credit cards (MC, V, D), BF, FF.
Reader Comments: Love this course!!! … Very busy course. Well maintained, plays long and fairly tough … Good course … Long, good course at good price.

★★★½ SNOQUALMIE FALLS GOLF COURSE

PU-35109 Fish Hatchery Rd. SE, Fall City, 98024, King County, (425)222-5244, 25 miles from Seattle. **Facility Holes:** 18. **Yards:** 5,452/5,224. **Par:** 71/71. **Course Rating:** 64.9/69.6. **Slope:** 102/114. **Green Fee:** $21/$28. **Cart Fee:** $22/Cart. **Walking Policy:** Unrestricted walking. **Walkability:** 1. **Opened:** 1963. **Architect:** Emmett Jackson. **Season:** Year-round.

High: April-Nov. **To obtain tee times:** Call up to 6 days in advance. **Miscellaneous:** Reduced fees (weekdays, seniors, juniors), metal spikes, range (grass), credit cards (MC, V), FF.
Reader Comments: Fun, simple course ... Nice (busy) executive course. Good for the beginner, but challenging enough for anyone ... A pleasant little course that borders the Snoqualmie River. It's flat and very walkable ... Prettiest scenery on earth! ... Price is right.

★★★½ SUDDEN VALLEY GOLF & COUNTRY CLUB
SP-2145 Lake Whatcom Blvd., Bellingham, 98226, Whatcom County, (360)734-6435, 8 miles from Bellingham. **E-mail:** gregp@suddenvalley.com. **Web:** www.suddenvalleygolf.com. **Facility Holes:** 18. **Yards:** 6,553/5,627. **Par:** 72/72. **Course Rating:** 71.8/72.8. **Slope:** 126/124. **Green Fee:** $25/$45. **Cart Fee:** $24/Cart. **Walking Policy:** Unrestricted walking. **Walkability:** 3. **Opened:** 1970. **Architect:** Ted Robinson. **Season:** Year-round. **High:** July-Sept. **To obtain tee times:** Call up to 7 days in advance. **Miscellaneous:** Reduced fees (weekdays, twilight, juniors), range (grass/mats), credit cards (MC, V, AE), BF, FF.
Reader Comments: Very creative, great golf course ... Views, lake, can walk ... Very nicely managed, beautiful course ... Distinct 9s.

★★½ SUMNER MEADOWS GOLF LINKS
PU-14802 8th St. E., Sumner, 98390, Pierce County, (253)863-8198, (888)258-3348, 5 miles from Sumner. **Web:** www.cybergolf.com. **Facility Holes:** 18. **Yards:** 6,801/5,295. **Par:** 72/72. **Course Rating:** 72.3/69.8. **Slope:** 124/115. **Green Fee:** $13/$33. **Cart Fee:** $13/Person. **Walking Policy:** Unrestricted walking. **Walkability:** 1. **Opened:** 1995. **Architect:** Lynn William Horn. **Season:** Year-round. **To obtain tee times:** Call up to 14 days in advance. **Miscellaneous:** Reduced fees (weekdays, twilight, seniors, juniors), metal spikes, range (grass/mats), credit cards (MC, V, AE), BF, FF.

★★ SUN DANCE GOLF COURSE
PU-9725 N. Nine Mile Rd., Nine Mile Falls, 99026, Spokane County, (509)466-4040, 9 miles from Spokane. **E-mail:** forcedcarry@hotmail.com. **Web:** www.sundancegc.com. **Facility Holes:** 18. **Yards:** 6,268/5,452. **Par:** 70/72. **Course Rating:** 69.4/70.8. **Slope:** 111/114. **Green Fee:** $14/$18. **Cart Fee:** $24/Cart. **Walking Policy:** Unrestricted walking. **Walkability:** 1. **Opened:** 1964. **Architect:** Dale Knott. **Season:** March-Oct. **High:** May-Sept. **To obtain tee times:** Call up to 7 days in advance. **Miscellaneous:** Reduced fees (twilight, seniors, juniors), range (mats), credit cards (MC, V, D), BF, FF.

★★½ SUN WILLOWS GOLF CLUB
PU-2035 N. 20th St., Pasco, 99301, Franklin County, (509)545-3440, 110 miles from Spokane. **Web:** www.sunwillows.xtcom.com. **Facility Holes:** 18. **Yards:** 6,800/5,600. **Par:** 72/72. **Course Rating:** 70.1/68.2. **Slope:** 119/119. **Green Fee:** $18/$24. **Cart Fee:** $12/Person. **Walking Policy:** Unrestricted walking. **Walkability:** 2. **Opened:** 1959. **Architect:** Robert Muir Graves. **Season:** Year-round. **To obtain tee times:** Call up to 10 days in advance. **Miscellaneous:** Reduced fees (twilight, seniors, juniors), range (grass), credit cards (MC, V, AE), BF, FF.

★★★ SUNLAND GOLF & COUNTRY CLUB
SP-109 Hilltop Dr., Sequim, 98382, Clallam County, (360)683-6800, 100 miles from Seattle. **Facility Holes:** 18. **Yards:** 6,319/5,557. **Par:** 72/73. **Course Rating:** 70.4/71.5. **Slope:** 120/120. **Green Fee:** $28/$33. **Cart Fee:** $22/Cart. **Walking Policy:** Unrestricted walking. **Opened:** 1971. **Architect:** A. Vernon Macan. **Season:** Year-round. **High:** April-Sept. **To obtain tee times:** Call golf shop. **Miscellaneous:** Reduced fees (juniors), metal spikes, range (grass), credit cards (MC, V).
Reader Comments: Very good, but narrow fairways ... Plays well in winter ... Narrow fairways, fast greens, pleasant ... Tight holes ... Best value in NW, wish I lived there.

★★ SUNTIDES GOLF COURSE
PU-231 Pence Rd., Yakima, 98908, Yakima County, (509)966-9065, 2 miles from Yakima. **E-mail:** pacobleigh@aol.com. **Web:** www.suntidesgolf.com. **Facility Holes:** 18. **Yards:** 6,178/5,509. **Par:** 70/70. **Course Rating:** 68.4/68.3. **Slope:** 113/109. **Green Fee:** $22. **Cart Fee:** $22/Cart. **Walking Policy:** Unrestricted walking. **Walkability:** 1. **Opened:** 1963. **Architect:** Joe Grier. **Season:** Feb.-Dec. **To obtain tee times:** Call golf shop. **Miscellaneous:** Reduced fees (juniors), range (mats), credit cards (MC, V), FF.

★½ TALL CHIEF GOLF COURSE
PU-1313 Snoqualmie River Rd. S.E., Fall City, 98024, King County, (425)222-5911, 21 miles from Seattle. **Facility Holes:** 18. **Yards:** 5,422/4,867. **Par:** 70/71. **Course Rating:** 66.0/66.5. **Slope:** 119/117. **Green Fee:** $20/$24. **Cart Fee:** $22/Cart. **Walking Policy:** Unrestricted walking. **Walkability:** 3. **Opened:** 1965. **Architect:** Frank Avant. **Season:** Year-round. **High:** June-Sept. **To obtain tee times:** Call golf shop. **Miscellaneous:** Reduced fees (weekdays, twilight, seniors, juniors), metal spikes, credit cards (MC, V).

THREE LAKES GOLF COURSE

SP-2695 Golf Dr., Malaga, 98828, Chelan County, (509)663-5448. **Facility Holes:** 18.
Yards: 5,327/5,201. **Par:** 69/69. **Course Rating:** 65.2/70.1. **Slope:** 104/121. **Green Fee:** $20.
Opened: 1953. **To obtain tee times:** Call golf shop. **Miscellaneous:** Metal spikes.

★★★ THREE RIVERS GOLF COURSE

PU-2222 S. River Rd., Kelso, 98626, Cowlitz County, (360)423-4653, (800)286-7765,
40 miles from Portland. **E-mail:** knightgolf@pga.com. **Facility Holes:** 18. **Yards:** 6,666/5,393.
Par: 72/72. **Course Rating:** 71.2/69.9. **Slope:** 119/113. **Green Fee:** $13/$23. **Cart Fee:**
$24/Cart. **Walking Policy:** Unrestricted walking. **Walkability:** 3. **Opened:** 1982. **Architect:**
Robert Muir Graves. **Season:** Year-round. **To obtain tee times:** Call up to 7 days in advance.
Miscellaneous: Reduced fees (twilight, seniors, juniors), metal spikes, range (grass/mats),
credit cards (MC, V), BF, FF.
Reader Comments: One of the best conditioned in any weather ... Driest course in NW ... Dry
course on Mount St. Helens' ash dredging ... Best winter course around ... Great value here, really
hard to get a tee time on weekends ... Good winter course.

★★★ TRI-CITY COUNTRY CLUB

SP-314 N. Underwood, Kennewick, 99336, Benton County, (509)783-6014, 120 miles from
Spokane. **E-mail:** isaacchrs@aol.com. **Web:** tccountryclub.com. **Facility Holes:** 18. **Yards:**
4,855/4,300. **Par:** 65/65. **Course Rating:** 62.2/65.2. **Slope:** 108/115. **Green Fee:** $22/$30. **Cart
Fee:** $25/Cart. **Walking Policy:** Unrestricted walking. **Walkability:** 3. **Opened:** 1938. **Architect:**
Bert Lesley. **Season:** Year-round. **High:** April-Oct. **To obtain tee times:** Call up to 2 days in
advance. **Miscellaneous:** Reduced fees (juniors), BF, FF.
Reader Comments: Short semi-private course, great condition, great pro, demands good wedge
play, fast greens ... Great short course ... Deceptively tight ... Good for short game ... Old golf
course but well kept ... Accuracy a must ... Made to feel welcome.

★★★ TRI-MOUNTAIN GOLF COURSE

PU-1701 N.W. 299th St., Ridgefield, 98642, Clark County, (360)887-3004, (888)874-6686,
15 miles from Portland. **E-mail:** tri-chuck@juno.com. **Web:** www.cybergolf.com. **Facility Holes:**
18. **Yards:** 6,580/5,284. **Par:** 72/72. **Course Rating:** 71.1/69.8. **Slope:** 120/117. **Green Fee:**
$18/$34. **Cart Fee:** $24/Cart. **Walking Policy:** Unrestricted walking. **Walkability:** 2. **Opened:**
1994. **Architect:** William Robinson. **Season:** Year-round. **To obtain tee times:** Call up to 7 days
in advance. **Miscellaneous:** Reduced fees (weekdays, twilight, seniors, juniors), range (mats),
credit cards (MC, V), BF, FF.
Reader Comments: A lot of bang for the buck. Top notch chipping area. The greens are always
great ... Give it a try! ... Greens were excellent ... Windy, good layout, tricky ... Good layout.

★★★★ TROPHY LAKE GOLF & CASTING CLUB *Service*

PU-3900 S. W. Lake Flora Rd., Port Orchard, 98366, Kitsap County, (360)874-3777, 15 miles
from Seattle. **E-mail:** rwhitney@heritagegolfgroup.com. **Web:** www.trophylakegolf.com.
Facility Holes: 18. **Yards:** 7,216/5,123. **Par:** 72/72. **Course Rating:** 74.3/70.3. **Slope:** 137/125.
Green Fee: $34/$79. **Cart Fee:** Included in green fee. **Walking Policy:** Unrestricted walking.
Walkability: 3. **Opened:** 1999. **Architect:** John Fought. **Season:** Year-round. **High:** April-Oct.
To obtain tee times: Call up to 30 days in advance. **Miscellaneous:** Reduced fees (weekdays,
twilight, juniors), range (grass), credit cards (MC, V, AE, D), BF, FF.
Reader Comments: Outstanding service, incredible views ... Perfect in every way! ... Good new
course, can also fly fish ... Recommend very highly ... A really nice clubhouse and well stocked
pro shop. This would be a great facility for a company tournament ... Great course, amazing
practice facility.

★★★ TUMWATER VALLEY MUNICIPAL GOLF COURSE

PU-4611 Tumwater Valley Dr., Tumwater, 98501, Thurston County, (360)943-9500,
(888)943-9500, 60 miles from Seattle. **Facility Holes:** 18. **Yards:** 7,154/5,428. **Par:** 72/72.
Course Rating: 73.4/71.0. **Slope:** 118/115. **Green Fee:** $16/$22. **Cart Fee:** $10/Person.
Walking Policy: Unrestricted walking. **Walkability:** 2. **Opened:** 1970. **Architect:** John Graham.
Season: Year-round. **High:** March-Oct. **To obtain tee times:** Call up to 7 days in advance.
Miscellaneous: Reduced fees (weekdays, twilight, juniors), metal spikes, range (grass), credit
cards (MC, V), BF, FF.
Reader Comments: Wide open, but long ... Fun open course ... Good public course. Some long
holes, affordable ... Good summer course ... Good muni.

★½ TYEE VALLEY GOLF COURSE

PU-2401 S. 192nd St., Seattle, 98188, King County, (206)878-3540. **Facility Holes:** 18.
Yards: 5,926/5,257. **Par:** 71/73. **Course Rating:** 68.8/69.9. **Slope:** 119/123. **Green Fee:**
$18/$19. **Opened:** 1968. **Architect:** Roy Moore. **To obtain tee times:** Call golf shop.
Miscellaneous: Metal spikes.

WASHINGTON

★★½ **VETERANS MEMORIAL GOLF COURSE**
PU-201 E. Rees, Walla Walla, 99362, Walla Walla County, (509)527-4507. **E-mail:** weman@wwics.com. **Facility Holes:** 18. **Yards:** 6,646/5,732. **Par:** 72/72. **Slope:** 114/121. **Green Fee:** $20. **Cart Fee:** $24/Cart. **Walking Policy:** Unrestricted walking. **Walkability:** 2. **Architect:** Frank James. **Season:** Year-round. **To obtain tee times:** Call golf shop. **Miscellaneous:** Reduced fees (seniors, juniors), metal spikes, range (grass/mats), credit cards (MC, V), BF, FF.

★★½ **WALTER E. HALL MEMORIAL GOLF COURSE**
PU-1226 W. Casino Rd., Everett, 98204, Snohomish County, (425)353-4653, 25 miles from Seattle. **E-mail:** thwalterhall@juno.com. **Web:** www.walterhallgolf.com. **Facility Holes:** 18. **Yards:** 6,450/5,657. **Par:** 72/73. **Course Rating:** 69.6/71.6. **Slope:** 117/118. **Green Fee:** $17/$27. **Cart Fee:** $22/Cart. **Walking Policy:** Unrestricted walking. **Walkability:** 1. **Opened:** 1972. **Architect:** John Steidel. **Season:** Year-round. **High:** April-Sept. **To obtain tee times:** Call golf shop. **Miscellaneous:** Reduced fees (weekdays, seniors, juniors), metal spikes, credit cards (MC, V), BF, FF.

★★ **WANDERMERE GOLF COURSE**
PU-N. 13700 Wandermere Road, Spokane, 99208, Spokane County, (509)466-8023, 10 miles from Spokane. **E-mail:** wandgolf@aol.com. **Web:** www.wandermere.com. **Facility Holes:** 18. **Yards:** 6,050/5,205. **Par:** 70/71. **Course Rating:** 68.4/69.4. **Slope:** 108/107. **Green Fee:** $18/$20. **Cart Fee:** $25/Cart. **Walking Policy:** Unrestricted walking. **Walkability:** 3. **Opened:** 1929. **Architect:** Lee Wayne Ross. **Season:** March-Dec. **High:** April-Nov. **To obtain tee times:** Call golf shop. **Miscellaneous:** Reduced fees (seniors, juniors), range (grass/mats), credit cards (MC, V), BF, FF.

WASHINGTON NATIONAL GOLF CLUB
PU-14330 SE Husky Way, Auburn, 98092, King County, (253)333-5000, 30 miles from Seattle. **E-mail:** rwhitney@heritagegolfgroup.com. **Web:** www.washingtonnationalgolfclub.com. **Facility Holes:** 18. **Yards:** 7,304/5,117. **Par:** 72/72. **Course Rating:** 75.6/70.3. **Slope:** 141/118. **Green Fee:** $39/$104. **Cart Fee:** Included in green fee. **Walking Policy:** Unrestricted walking. **Walkability:** 2. **Opened:** 2000. **Architect:** John Fought. **Season:** Year-round. **To obtain tee times:** Call up to 30 days in advance. **Miscellaneous:** Reduced fees (weekdays, twilight, juniors), range (grass/mats), credit cards (MC, V, AE), BF, FF.

★½ **WEST RICHLAND MUNICIPAL GOLF COURSE**
PU-4000 Fallon Dr., West Richland, 99352, Benton County, (509)967-2165, 200 miles from Seattle. **Facility Holes:** 18. **Yards:** 6,103/5,516. **Par:** 70/70. **Course Rating:** 67.7/70.3. **Slope:** 114/114. **Green Fee:** $13. **Cart Fee:** $20/Cart. **Walking Policy:** Unrestricted walking. **Walkability:** 1. **Opened:** 1950. **Season:** Year-round. **High:** March-Oct. **To obtain tee times:** Call golf shop. **Miscellaneous:** Metal spikes, range (grass).

★★★ **WEST SEATTLE GOLF COURSE**
PU-4470 35th Ave. S.W., Seattle, 98126, King County, (206)935-5187, 5 miles from Seattle. **Facility Holes:** 18. **Yards:** 6,600/5,700. **Par:** 72/72. **Course Rating:** 70.9/72.6. **Slope:** 119/123. **Green Fee:** $18/$22. **Cart Fee:** $20/Cart. **Walking Policy:** Unrestricted walking. **Walkability:** 3. **Opened:** 1939. **Architect:** H. C. Egan. **Season:** Year-round. **High:** May-Sept. **To obtain tee times:** Call golf shop. **Miscellaneous:** Reduced fees (twilight, seniors, juniors), metal spikes, credit cards (MC, V).
Reader Comments: Improved course. Staff is excellent … Good municipal layout, easy to keep pace … This is the best course within Seattle. Very challenging and good views of downtown on a couple of holes. The fairways are tight and sloped in places requiring well placed tee shots. The greens are in good shape.

WILLOWS RUN GOLF CLUB
PU-10402 Willows Rd. N.E., Redmond, 98052, King County, (425)883-1200, 10 miles from Seattle. **Web:** www.willowsrun.com. **Facility Holes:** 45. **Green Fee:** $24/$55. **Cart Fee:** $27/Cart. **Walking Policy:** Unrestricted walking. **Walkability:** 1. **Opened:** 1999. **Architect:** Ted Locke. **Season:** Year-round. **High:** March-Nov. **To obtain tee times:** Call up to 7 days in advance. **Miscellaneous:** Reduced fees (weekdays, twilight, seniors, juniors), metal spikes, range (grass/mats), caddies, credit cards (MC, V, AE), BF, FF.
COYOTE CREEK COURSE (18)
Yards: 6,375/5,326. **Par:** 72/72. **Course Rating:** 69.5/69.3. **Slope:** 118/113.
Special Notes: Also has a 9-hole executive course.
★★½ **EAGLE'S TALON COURSE** (18)
Yards: 6,915/5,751. **Par:** 72/72. **Course Rating:** 72.4/72.3. **Slope:** 122/119.
Special Notes: Also has a 9-hole executive course.

WEST VIRGINIA

ALPINE LAKE RESORT
R-700 West Alpine Drive, Terra Alta, 26764, Preston County, (304)789-2481, (800)752-7179, 30 miles from Morgantown. **Web:** www.alpinelake.com. **Facility Holes:** 18. **Yards:** 6,069/4,902. **Par:** 72/73. **Course Rating:** 69.1/68.8. **Slope:** 122/111. **Green Fee:** $15/$27. **Cart Fee:** $12/Person. **Walking Policy:** Walking at certain times. **Walkability:** 4. **Opened:** 1968. **Architect:** Brian Farse. **Season:** April-Oct. **High:** May-Sept. **To obtain tee times:** Call golf shop. **Miscellaneous:** Reduced fees (twilight, seniors), range (grass/mats), lodging (35 rooms), credit cards (MC, V, AE, D).

BARBOUR COUNTRY CLUB
SP-US Rte. 119 S., Philippi, 26416, Barbour County, (304)457-2156, 15 miles from Clarksburg. **Facility Holes:** 9. **Yards:** 5,596/4,770. **Par:** 70/71. **Course Rating:** 66.6/67.3. **Slope:** 112/104. **Green Fee:** $12/$16. **Cart Fee:** $20/Cart. **Architect:** John Walsh. **To obtain tee times:** Call golf shop.

BEAVER CREEK GOLF CLUB
SP-800 Country Club Dr., Beaver, 25813, Raleigh County, (304)763-9116, (800)842-5604, 6 miles from Beckley. **Facility Holes:** 18. **Yards:** 5,040/3,865. **Par:** 70/70. **Course Rating:** 71.2/68.5. **Slope:** 133/129. **Green Fee:** $11/$13. **Cart Fee:** $11/Person. **Walking Policy:** Unrestricted walking. **Walkability:** 3. **Opened:** 1986. **Season:** Year-round. **High:** April-Sept. **To obtain tee times:** Call up to 5 days in advance. **Miscellaneous:** Reduced fees (weekdays, seniors), metal spikes, range (grass), credit cards (MC, V, AE, D), FF.

★★½ BEL MEADOW COUNTRY CLUB
SP-Rte. 1 Box 450, Mount Clare, 26408, Harrison County, (304)623-3701, 5 miles from Clarksburg. **Web:** www.belmeadow.com. **Facility Holes:** 18. **Yards:** 6,938/5,517. **Par:** 72/72. **Course Rating:** 73.0/71.5. **Slope:** 126/122. **Green Fee:** $17/$20. **Cart Fee:** $12/Person. **Walking Policy:** Walking at certain times. **Walkability:** 1. **Opened:** 1965. **Architect:** Robert Trent Jones. **Season:** Year-round. **High:** May-Sept. **To obtain tee times:** Call up to 7 days in advance. **Miscellaneous:** Reduced fees (weekdays, twilight, seniors, juniors), metal spikes, range (grass/mats), credit cards (MC, V, AE, D), BF, FF.

★½ BIG BEND GOLF CLUB
PU-P.O. Box 329, Riverview Dr., Tornado, 25202, Kanawha County, (304)722-0400, 15 miles from Charleston. **Facility Holes:** 18. **Yards:** 6,327/5,762. **Par:** 71/72. **Course Rating:** 69.6. **Slope:** 116. **Green Fee:** $14/$17. **Cart Fee:** $10/Person. **Walking Policy:** Unrestricted walking. **Walkability:** 1. **Opened:** 1964. **Architect:** Kanawha County Parks. **Season:** Year-round. **To obtain tee times:** Call golf shop. **Miscellaneous:** Reduced fees (twilight), range (grass), credit cards (MC, V), BF, FF.

★★★★ CACAPON RESORT
R-Rt. 1, Box 230, Berkeley Springs, 25411, Morgan County, (304)258-1022, (800)225-5982, 25 miles from Hagerstown. **Facility Holes:** 18. **Yards:** 6,827/5,647. **Par:** 72/72. **Course Rating:** 72.3/70.6. **Slope:** 126/118. **Green Fee:** $23/$28. **Cart Fee:** $22/Cart. **Walking Policy:** Unrestricted walking. **Walkability:** 2. **Opened:** 1974. **Architect:** Robert Trent Jones. **Season:** Year-round. **High:** April-Oct. **To obtain tee times:** Call up to 7 days in advance. **Miscellaneous:** Reduced fees (seniors), range (grass), lodging (48 rooms), credit cards (MC, V, AE, D, Diner's Club), BF, FF.
Reader Comments: A must play for serious golfers ... Great scenery ... Fall colors are awesome ... Lots of trees ... Great design.

★★★½ CANAAN VALLEY RESORT GOLF COURSE
R-HC70, Box 330, Davis, 26260, Tucker County, (304)866-4121x2632, (800)622-4121, 185 miles from Washington. **Facility Holes:** 18. **Yards:** 6,984/5,820. **Par:** 72/72. **Course Rating:** 73.3/73.8. **Slope:** 130/127. **Green Fee:** $24/$33. **Cart Fee:** $28/Cart. **Walking Policy:** Unrestricted walking. **Walkability:** 2. **Opened:** 1968. **Architect:** Geoffrey Cornish. **Season:** April-Nov. **High:** May-Oct. **To obtain tee times:** Call up to 60 days in advance. **Miscellaneous:** Reduced fees (weekdays, guests, twilight, seniors), metal spikes, range (grass/mats), lodging (250 rooms), credit cards (MC, V, AE, D, Diners Club), BF, FF.
Reader Comments: The fairways are soft and the service is excellent ... Flat, wide, large greens ... A great test to shotmaking ... Great fairways ... Large landing areas ... Deer everywhere.

CLEAR FORK VALLEY COUNTRY CLUB
SP-Rte. 971, Oceana, 24870, Wyoming County, (304)682-6209, 50 miles from Charleston. **Facility Holes:** 18. **Yards:** 5,743/4,932. **Par:** 70/70. **Course Rating:** 65.3/67.0. **Slope:** 96/109. **Green Fee:** $14/$17. **Opened:** 1959. **To obtain tee times:** Call golf shop.

DEERFIELD COUNTRY CLUB
SP-New Jackson Mill Rd., Weston, 26452, Lewis County, (304)269-1139, 20 miles from Clarksburg. **Facility Holes:** 9. **Yards:** 3,405/2,827. **Par:** 36/36. **Course Rating:** 72.3/70.4. **Slope:** 120/114. **Green Fee:** $24/$29. **Cart Fee:** Included in green fee. **To obtain tee times:** Call golf shop.

★★½ ESQUIRE GOLF COURSE
PU-Esquire Dr., Barboursville, 25504, Cabell County, (304)736-1476, 10 miles from Huntington. **Facility Holes:** 18. **Yards:** 6,905/5,250. **Par:** 72/72. **Course Rating:** 72.2/69.2. **Slope:** 116/104. **Green Fee:** $28/$30. **Cart Fee:** Included in green fee. **Walking Policy:** Walking at certain times. **Walkability:** 2. **Opened:** 1975. **Architect:** X.G. Hassenplug. **Season:** Year-round. **High:** April-Oct. **To obtain tee times:** Call golf shop. **Miscellaneous:** Range (grass), credit cards (MC, V, AE).

★★★★½ GLADE SPRINGS RESORT
R-200 Lake Dr., Daniels, 25832, Raleigh County, (304)763-2050, (800)634-5233, 8 miles from Beckley. **Web:** www.gladesprings.com. **Facility Holes:** 18. **Yards:** 6,941/4,884. **Par:** 72/72. **Course Rating:** 73.5/67.6. **Slope:** 135/118. **Green Fee:** $80. **Cart Fee:** Included in green fee. **Walking Policy:** Unrestricted walking. **Walkability:** 3. **Opened:** 1973. **Architect:** George Cobb. **Season:** Year-round. **High:** June-Sept. **To obtain tee times:** Call golf shop. **Miscellaneous:** Reduced fees (guests, twilight, juniors), range (grass), lodging (88 rooms), credit cards (MC, V, AE, D), BF, FF.
Notes: Ranked 5th in 1997 Best in State.
Reader Comments: Great course to play in the fall … Toughest set of par-3 holes in West Virginia … Huge greens, great fairways … Great stop on way to Myrtle Beach … I got treated like a king … Challenging, but fair … Saw a lot of deer … Great service.

GLENVILLE GOLF CLUB
PU-Sycamore Road, Glenville, 26351, Gilmer County, (304)462-5907, 55 miles from Clarksburg. **Facility Holes:** 9. **Yards:** 2,840/2,312. **Par:** 35/37. **Course Rating:** 65.4. **Slope:** 111. **Green Fee:** $14. **Cart Fee:** $16/Cart. **Walking Policy:** Unrestricted walking. **Walkability:** 3. **Opened:** 1948. **Season:** March-Oct. **High:** May-Aug. **To obtain tee times:** Call golf shop. **Miscellaneous:** Credit cards (MC, V).

★★½ GOLF CLUB OF WEST VIRGINIA
PU-Box 199, Rte. 1, Waverly, 26184, Wood County, (304)464-4420, 10 miles from Parkersburg. **Web:** www.kempersports.com. **Facility Holes:** 18. **Yards:** 6,018/5,011. **Par:** 70/71. **Course Rating:** 68.9/67.9. **Slope:** 116/109. **Green Fee:** $22/$32. **Cart Fee:** Included in green fee. **Walking Policy:** Unrestricted walking. **Walkability:** 4. **Opened:** 1950. **Architect:** Lauren Parish. **Season:** Year-round. **To obtain tee times:** Call golf shop. **Miscellaneous:** Reduced fees (weekdays, twilight, seniors, juniors), credit cards (MC, V, D), BF, FF.

★★★ GRANDVIEW COUNTRY CLUB
PU-1500 Scottridge Dr., Beaver, 25813, Raleigh County, (304)763-2520, 8 miles from Beckley. **Facility Holes:** 18. **Yards:** 6,834/4,910. **Par:** 72/72. **Course Rating:** 70.2/67.3. **Slope:** 112/107. **Green Fee:** $14/$18. **Cart Fee:** $18/Cart. **Walking Policy:** Walking at certain times. **Walkability:** 3. **Opened:** 1973. **Architect:** Randy Scott/Glenn Scott. **Season:** May-Nov. **High:** June-Aug. **To obtain tee times:** Call golf shop. **Miscellaneous:** Metal spikes, range (grass).
Reader Comments: Short with small greens, very hilly … Wide fairways, tiny greens … Lots of people … Family owned & operated, a real hidden treat.

THE GREENBRIER
R-300 W. Main St., White Sulphur Springs, 24986, Greenbrier County, (304)536-7862, (800)624-6070, 250 miles from Washington. **E-mail:** joanna_honaker@greenbrier.com. **Web:** www.greenbrier.com. **Facility Holes:** 54. **Green Fee:** $90/$300. **Cart Fee:** Included in green fee. **Walking Policy:** Walking at certain times. **Season:** Year-round. **High:** April-Oct. **To obtain tee times:** Call golf shop. **Miscellaneous:** Reduced fees (guests, juniors), range (grass/mats), caddies, lodging (750 rooms), credit cards (MC, V, AE, D, DC), BF, FF.
★★★★½ **GREENBRIER COURSE** (18) *Condition+*
Yards: 6,675/5,095. **Par:** 72/72. **Course Rating:** 73.1/69.8. **Slope:** 135/118. **Walkability:** 2. **Opened:** 1924. **Architect:** Seth Raynor/Jack Nicklaus.
Notes: Ranked 2nd in 2001 Best in State.
Reader Comments: Best Greenbrier course by far … Championship level … You can't beat their service anywhere … Expensive, but super … Worth the fee.
★★★★½ **MEADOWS COURSE** (18)
Yards: 6,807/5,001. **Par:** 71/71. **Course Rating:** 72.4/68.5. **Slope:** 132/115. **Walkability:** 2. **Opened:** 1999. **Architect:** Bob Cupp.
Reader Comments: Not as famous as the Old White or Greenbrier but every bit as good … Good

mix of mountain and valley holes ... Streams meander through the course ... Par-3s are excellent ... New holes greatly improved the course ... The most scenic of the courses.

★★★★½ OLD WHITE COURSE (18) *Condition*
Yards: 6,652/5,179. **Par:** 70/70. **Course Rating:** 72.2/69.7. **Slope:** 131/119. **Walkability:** 3.
Opened: 1913. **Architect:** C.B. Macdonald/S.J. Raynor.
Notes: Ranked 3rd in 2001 Best in State.
Reader Comments: Great course ... Classy, traditional layout ... One of my favorite old layouts ... Watched Snead on the range and was in awe!

★★★ GREENHILLS COUNTRY CLUB
SP-Rte. 56, Ravenswood, 26164, Jackson County, (304)273-3396, 38 miles from Charleston.
Facility Holes: 18. **Yards:** 6,252/5,192. **Par:** 72/74. **Course Rating:** 69.3/69.0. **Slope:** 119/108.
Green Fee: $19/$24. **Cart Fee:** $13/Person. **Walking Policy:** Unrestricted walking. **Walkability:** 3. **Opened:** 1959. **Architect:** Paul Lemon. **Season:** Year-round. **Tee times:** Call golf shop. **Misc:** Reduced fees (weekdays, guests), range (grass/mats), credit cards (MC, V, AE, D), BF, FF.
Reader Comments: Very hilly ... Interesting ... Great course, great service ... Fast greens ... Short course ... Several blind shots ... Super greens.

★★½ HIGHLAND SPRINGS GOLF COURSE
PU-1600 Washington Pike, Wellsburg, 26070, Brooke County, (304)737-2201, 35 miles from Pittsburgh. **Facility Holes:** 18. **Yards:** 6,853/5,739. **Par:** 72/75. **Course Rating:** 72.4/72.1. **Slope:** 118/113. **Green Fee:** $7/$18. **Walking Policy:** Unrestricted walking. **Walkability:** 4. **Opened:** 1963. **Architect:** James Gilmore Harrison. **Season:** March-Dec. **High:** June-Aug. **To obtain tee times:** Call golf shop. **Miscellaneous:** Reduced fees (weekdays, seniors, juniors), metal spikes, credit cards (MC, V).

LAKEVIEW GOLF RESORT & SPA
R-1 Lakeview Drive, Morgantown, 26505, Monongalia County, (304)594-2011, (800)624-8300, 10 miles from Morgantown. **Web:** www.lakeviewresort.com.
Facility Holes: 36. **Cart Fee:** Included in green fee. **Walking Policy:** Mandatory carts. **High:** April-Oct. **To obtain tee times:** Call golf shop. **Miscellaneous:** Reduced fees (weekdays, guests, twilight, juniors), lodging (187 rooms), credit cards (MC, V, AE, D, Diners Club), BF, FF.
★★★½ LAKEVIEW COURSE (18)
Yards: 6,800/5,432. **Par:** 72/72. **Course Rating:** 72.8/71.8. **Slope:** 130/118. **Green Fee:** $39/$69. **Walkability:** 3. **Opened:** 1954. **Architect:** Jim Harrison. **Season:** March-Dec.
Notes: Ranked 5th in 1999 Best in State.
Reader Comments: Great packages for the price ... Tight tree-lined holes, great views, accommodations and food ... Breathtaking ... Super place.
★★★ MOUNTAINVIEW COURSE (18)
Yards: 6,447/5,242. **Par:** 72/72. **Course Rating:** 71.9/70.2. **Slope:** 126/124. **Green Fee:** $29/$49. **Walkability:** 4. **Opened:** 1984. **Architect:** Brian Ault. **Season:** April-Nov.
Reader Comments: Very nice views ... Not as scenic as Lakeview Course, too short doglegs ... Vast elevation changes ... Does not get the reputation or play that its sister course gets but it has its own set of challenges ... It's golf in the hills.

★★½ LAVELETTE GOLF CLUB
PU-Lynn Oak Dr., Lavalette, 25535, Wayne County, (304)525-7405, 5 miles from Huntington.
Facility Holes: 18. **Yards:** 6,262/5,257. **Par:** 71/71. **Course Rating:** 69.5/72.6. **Slope:** 118/120. **Green Fee:** $15/$17. **Cart Fee:** $11/Person. **Walking Policy:** Unrestricted walking. **Opened:** 1991. **Architect:** Bill Ward. **Season:** Year-round. **High:** May-Sept. **Tee times:** Call golf shop. **Misc:** Reduced fees (weekdays), range (grass/mats), credit cards (MC, V, AE, D).

★★ LEWISBURG ELKS COUNTRY CLUB
SP-Rte. 219 N., Lewisburg, 24901, Greenbrier County, (304)645-3660, 2 miles from Lewisburg. **Facility Holes:** 18. **Yards:** 5,609/4,314. **Par:** 70/70. **Course Rating:** 66.8/64.5. **Slope:** 111/114. **Green Fee:** $17/$20. **Cart Fee:** $11/Person. **Walking Policy:** Unrestricted walking. **Walkability:** 3. **Opened:** 1940. **Architect:** Ray Vaughan. **Season:** Year-round. **High:** May-Oct. **To obtain tee times:** Call golf shop. **Miscellaneous:** Credit cards (MC, V), FF.

★★★★ LOCUST HILL GOLF COURSE
SP-1 St. Andrews Dr., Charles Town, 25414, Jefferson County, (304)728-7300, 55 miles from Washington. **Facility Holes:** 18. **Yards:** 7,005/5,112. **Par:** 72/72. **Course Rating:** 73.5/72.0. **Slope:** 128/120. **Green Fee:** $22/$46. **Cart Fee:** Included in green fee. **Walking Policy:** Walking at certain times. **Walkability:** 3. **Opened:** 1991. **Architect:** Edward Ault/Guy Rando. **Season:** Year-round. **To obtain tee times:** Call up to 14 days in advance. **Miscellaneous:** Reduced fees (weekdays, guests, twilight, seniors), credit cards (MC, V), BF, FF.
Reader Comments: Great course, nice layout ... Tough course ... Last 3 holes have lots of water to avoid ... Challenging course.

MEADOW PONDS GOLF COURSE

PU-Rte. 7 W., Cassville, 26527, Monongalia County, (304)328-5570, 60 miles from Pittsburgh. **Facility Holes:** 18. **Yards:** 5,328/5,026. **Par:** 69/69. **Course Rating:** 64.9/63.9. **Slope:** 102/100. **Green Fee:** $10/$12. **Walking Policy:** Unrestricted walking. **Opened:** 1963. **Architect:** Bob Holt. **To obtain tee times:** Call golf shop. **Miscellaneous:** Reduced fees (weekdays), metal spikes, range (grass), credit cards (MC, V, AE, D).

MILL CREEK GOLF COURSE

SP-Rte 1, Keyser, 26726, Mineral County, (304)289-3160, 55 miles from Martinsburg. **Facility Holes:** 9. **Yards:** 6,200/5,800. **Par:** 70/72. **Course Rating:** 66.6/66.6. **Slope:** 106/106. **Green Fee:** $15/$17. **Cart Fee:** $15/Cart. **To obtain tee times:** Call golf shop.

MOUNTAINEER GOLF & COUNTRY CLUB

SP-Rte. 19, Pursglove, 26546, Monongalia County, (304)328-5520. **E-mail:** www.mtrgolfer@aol.com. **Web:** www.mountaineergolf.com. **Facility Holes:** 18. **Yards:** 6,131/4,817. **Par:** 72/72. **Course Rating:** 68.5/63.7. **Slope:** 113/100. **Green Fee:** $12/$14. **Cart Fee:** $11/Person. **Walking Policy:** Unrestricted walking. **Walkability:** 3. **Season:** Year-round. **High:** April-Sept. **To obtain tee times:** Call golf shop. **Miscellaneous:** Reduced fees (weekdays), range (grass/mats), credit cards (MC, V), BF, FF.

MOUNTAINEERS WOODVIEW GOLF COURSE

PU-Ballentine Rd., New Cumberland, 26047, Hancock County, (304)564-5765, 30 miles from Wheeling. **Facility Holes:** 18. **Yards:** 6,077/5,295. **Par:** 71/72. **Course Rating:** 65.9/71.0. **Slope:** 118/109. **Green Fee:** $15/$19. **Cart Fee:** $10/Person. **Walking Policy:** Walking at certain times. **Walkability:** 4. **Opened:** 1958. **Architect:** Robert Hillis. **Season:** March-Nov. **High:** April-Nov. **To obtain tee times:** Call golf shop. **Miscellaneous:** Reduced fees (seniors, juniors), range (grass), credit cards (MC, V).

OAKHURST LINKS

PU-1 Montague Dr., P.O. Box 639, White Sulpher Springs, 24986, Greenbrier County, (304)536-1884, 3 miles from White Sulphur Springs. **E-mail:** oakhurst@metone.net. **Web:** www.oakhurstlinks.com. **Facility Holes:** 9. **Yards:** 2,235. **Par:** 34. **Green Fee:** $80. **Walking Policy:** Unrestricted walking. **Walkability:** 4. **Opened:** 1884. **Architect:** Russel Montague/Bob Cupp. **Season:** May-Nov. **To obtain tee times:** Call up to 30 days in advance. **Miscellaneous:** Credit cards (MC, V, AE).

OGLEBAY RESORT & CONFERENCE CENTER

PU-Oglebay Park, Rte. 88N., Wheeling, 26003, Ohio County, (304)243-4050, (800)752-9436, 55 miles from Pittsburgh. **E-mail:** speidel@hgo.net. **Web:** www.oglebay-resort.com. **Facility Holes:** 54. **To obtain tee times:** Call up to 60 days in advance. **Miscellaneous:** Credit cards (MC, V, AE, D), BF, FF.

★★★★½ **ARNOLD PALMER COURSE** (18)
Yards: 6,717/5,125. **Par:** 71/72. **Course Rating:** 71.9/69.6. **Slope:** 135/117. **Green Fee:** $65. **Cart Fee:** Included in green fee. **Walking Policy:** Mandatory carts. **Walkability:** 3. **Opened:** 2000. **Architect:** Arnold Palmer. **Season:** April-Nov. **High:** May-Sept. **Miscellaneous:** Reduced fees (twilight), range (grass), lodging (202 rooms).
Reader Comments: Links-style course, fast greens, holds well ... Huge, rock hard greens, good driving course ... A great layout, hilly terrain, scenic views ... New course needs to mature.

★★★ **CRISPIN COURSE** (18)
Yards: 5,627/5,100. **Par:** 71/71. **Course Rating:** 66.6/68.4. **Slope:** 109/103. **Green Fee:** $18. **Cart Fee:** $12/Person. **Walking Policy:** Unrestricted walking. **Walkability:** 4. **Opened:** 1933. **Architect:** Robert Biery. **Season:** Year-round. **Miscellaneous:** Metal spikes, range (mats), caddies.
Reader Comments: Great greens ... Hilly ... A lot of slope on the fairways ... Nice mountain views ... Good for the high-handicapper.

★★★★ **SPEIDEL CLUB** (18)
Yards: 7,000/5,241. **Par:** 71/71. **Course Rating:** 73.5/69.7. **Slope:** 137/120. **Green Fee:** $55. **Cart Fee:** Included in green fee. **Walking Policy:** Unrestricted walking. **Walkability:** 3. **Opened:** 1971. **Architect:** Robert Trent Jones. **Season:** April-Nov. **Miscellaneous:** Reduced fees (twilight), metal spikes, range (grass), caddies, lodging (202 rooms).
Notes: Ranked 5th in 2001 Best in State; 69th in 1996 America's Top 75 Affordable Courses.
Reader Comments: More tree-lined holes, not as open as Palmer course ... Par-5 5th hole over water is great ... Use all your shots ... Will test your skills ... Great scenic views ... Lots of up and down hills ... Very picturesque especially in the fall ... The Mercedes of resorts in WV ... Lighted driving range.

WEST VIRGINIA

★★★½ **PIPESTEM GOLF CLUB**
PU-Pipestem State Park, Pipestem, 25979, Summers County, (304)466-1800, (800)225-5982, 25 miles from Beckley. **Facility Holes:** 18. **Yards:** 6,884/5,600. **Par:** 72/72. **Course Rating:** 72.5/72.2. **Slope:** 125/119. **Green Fee:** $17/$28. **Cart Fee:** $20/Cart. **Walking Policy:** Unrestricted walking. **Walkability:** 3. **Opened:** 1970. **Architect:** Geoffrey Cornish. **Season:** Year-round. **High:** May-Sept. **To obtain tee times:** Call golf shop. **Miscellaneous:** Reduced fees (weekdays, seniors), metal spikes, range (grass), lodging (142 rooms), credit cards (MC, V, AE, D, DC), BF, FF.
Reader Comments: One of the most scenic courses you would ever want to play, it truly is almost like heaven … Breathtaking views on holes 16 & 17 … Tough course … Plays long … Perfect greens, an abundance of wildlife … Outstanding layout, cannot see other holes while playing.

POLISH PINES
PU-Rte. 220 S., Keyser, 26726, Mineral County, (301)786-4131. **Facility Holes:** 9. **Yards:** 5,178/2,109. **Par:** 68/34. **Green Fee:** $18/$20. **Cart Fee:** $7/Person. **To obtain tee times:** Call golf shop.

PRESTON COUNTRY CLUB
SP-Rte. 7, Kingwood, 26537, Preston County, (304)329-2100, 20 miles from Morgantown. **Facility Holes:** 18. **Yards:** 7,001/5,398. **Par:** 72/72. **Course Rating:** 73.2/70.2. **Slope:** 130/115. **Green Fee:** $20/$26. **Cart Fee:** $15/Person. **Walking Policy:** Walking at certain times. **Walkability:** 1. **Opened:** 1925. **Season:** April-Nov. **To obtain tee times:** Call up to 7 days in advance. **Miscellaneous:** Range (grass), credit cards (MC, V), BF, FF.

★★ **RIVERSIDE GOLF CLUB**
PU-Rte. 1, Mason, 25260, Mason County, (304)773-5354, (800)261-3031, 60 miles from Charleston. **Facility Holes:** 18. **Yards:** 6,198/4,842. **Par:** 70/72. **Course Rating:** 69.2/72.0. **Slope:** 118/117. **Green Fee:** $15/$18. **Cart Fee:** $10/Person. **Walking Policy:** Unrestricted walking. **Walkability:** 1. **Opened:** 1975. **Architect:** Kidwell/Hurdzan. **Season:** March-Dec. **High:** May-Sept. **To obtain tee times:** Call golf shop. **Miscellaneous:** Reduced fees (weekdays), credit cards (MC, V), BF, FF.

RIVERVIEW COUNTRY CLUB
SP-Rte. 17, Madison, 25130, Boone County, (304)369-9835, 25 miles from Charleston. **Facility Holes:** 18. **Yards:** 6,069/5,069. **Par:** 70/70. **Course Rating:** 67.8/69.3. **Slope:** 114/116. **Green Fee:** $15/$20. **Cart Fee:** $10/Person. **Walking Policy:** Unrestricted walking. **Walkability:** 4. **Opened:** 1964. **Season:** Year-round. **High:** April-Oct. **To obtain tee times:** Call golf shop. **Miscellaneous:** Reduced fees (weekdays), range (grass), credit cards (MC, V, AE, D).

RIVIERA GOLF COURSE
SP-Rte. 2, Lesage, 25537, Cabell County, (304)736-7778, 5 miles from Huntington. **Facility Holes:** 18. **Yards:** 6,200/5,400. **Par:** 70/69. **Course Rating:** 66.9/66.6. **Slope:** 108/104. **Green Fee:** $17/$19. **Cart Fee:** $10/Person. **Walking Policy:** Unrestricted walking. **Walkability:** 1. **Opened:** 1957. **Architect:** Patsy Jefferson. **Season:** Year-round. **To obtain tee times:** Call up to 7 days in advance. **Miscellaneous:** Credit cards (MC, V, AE), FF.

ROANE COUNTY COUNTRY CLUB
SP-Tucker's Run Rd., Spencer, 25276, Roane County, (304)927-2899, 40 miles from Charleston. **Facility Holes:** 9. **Yards:** 6,304/4,396. **Par:** 72/72. **Green Fee:** $12/$22. **Cart Fee:** Included in green fee. **To obtain tee times:** Call golf shop.

★½ **SANDY BRAE GOLF COURSE**
PU-19 Osborne Mills Rd., Clendenin, 25045, Kanawha County, (304)965-6800, 25 miles from Charleston. **Facility Holes:** 18. **Yards:** 5,648/5,312. **Par:** 69/74. **Course Rating:** 66.7. **Slope:** 101/98. **Green Fee:** $11/$14. **Cart Fee:** $8/Person. **Walking Policy:** Unrestricted walking. **Opened:** 1965. **Architect:** Edmund B. Ault. **Season:** Year-round. **High:** April-Oct. **To obtain tee times:** Call golf shop. **Miscellaneous:** Reduced fees (weekdays, twilight, seniors), metal spikes, credit cards (MC, V).

★★½ **SCARLET OAKS COUNTRY CLUB**
SP-2 Dairy Rd., Poca, 25159, Putnam County, (304)755-8079, 15 miles from Charleston. **Facility Holes:** 18. **Yards:** 6,700/5,036. **Par:** 72/72. **Course Rating:** 72.3/69.3. **Slope:** 129/109. **Green Fee:** $27/$30. **Walking Policy:** Mandatory carts. **Walkability:** 4. **Opened:** 1980. **Architect:** McDavid Family. **Season:** Year-round. **To obtain tee times:** Call golf shop. **Miscellaneous:** Range (grass), credit cards (MC, V, AE, D, DC), BF, FF.

WEST VIRGINIA

SHAWNEE GOLF COURSE
PU-Rte. 25, Institute, 25112, Kanawha County, (304)341-8030, 4 miles from Charleston.
Facility Holes: 9. **Yards:** 2,978. **Par:** 36. **Course Rating:** 67.3. **Slope:** 106. **Green Fee:** $9/$12.
Cart Fee: $10/Person. **Walking Policy:** Unrestricted walking. **Walkability:** 1. **Architect:**
Gary Player. **Season:** Year-round. **High:** April-Oct. **To obtain tee times:** Call golf shop.
Miscellaneous: Reduced fees (seniors), credit cards (MC, V).

★½ SLEEPY HOLLOW GOLF & COUNTRY CLUB
SP-Golf Course Rd., Charles Town, 25414, Jefferson County, (304)725-5210, 25 miles
from Hagerstown. **Web:** www.teetimegolfpass.sleepyhollow.com. **Facility Holes:** 18. **Yards:**
6,600/5,766. **Par:** 72/72. **Course Rating:** 70.6/72.3. **Slope:** 115/104. **Green Fee:** $10/$23.
Cart Fee: $13/Person. **Walking Policy:** Unrestricted walking. **Walkability:** 3. **Opened:** 1962.
Architect: M. Glenn, W. Glenn. **Season:** Year-round. **Tee times:** Call golf shop. **Miscellaneous:**
Reduced fees (weekdays, twilight, seniors), metal spikes, range (grass), BF, FF.

★★★★½ SNOWSHOE MOUNTAIN RESORT *Service, Condition+*
R-10 Snowshoe Dr., Snowshoe, 26209, Pocahantas County, (304)572-6500, (877)441-4386,
30 miles from Elkins. **E-mail:** www.gwilliams@snowshoemtn.com. **Web:**
www.snowshoemtn.com. **Facility Holes:** 18. **Yards:** 7,045/4,363. **Par:** 72/72. **Course Rating:**
75.5/65.3. **Slope:** 142/120. **Green Fee:** $59/$90. **Cart Fee:** Included in green fee. **Walking
Policy:** Unrestricted walking. **Walkability:** 5. **Opened:** 1993. **Architect:** Gary Player. **Season:**
April-Oct. **High:** May-Sept. **To obtain tee times:** Call up to 14 days in advance. **Miscellaneous:**
Reduced fees (weekdays, guests, twilight), metal spikes, range (grass), lodging (900 rooms),
credit cards (MC, V, AE), BF, FF.
Notes: Ranked 4th in 2001 Best in State.
Reader Comments: Best golf in WV ... Beautiful layout and scenery ... Best mountain course I've
ever played ... Very good range & practice area ... Beautiful views, fun to play ... Can't say enough,
every hole is more beautiful than last ... You can play bad & still enjoy the view.

★½ SOUTH HILLS GOLF CLUB
PU-1253 Gihon Rd., Parkersburg, 26101, Wood County, (304)422-8381, 70 miles from
Charleston. **Facility Holes:** 18. **Yards:** 6,467/4,842. **Par:** 71/71. **Course Rating:** 71.2/70.3.
Slope: 129/115. **Green Fee:** $13/$18. **Cart Fee:** $12/Person. **Walking Policy:** Unrestricted walk-
ing. **Walkability:** 3. **Opened:** 1953. **Architect:** Gary Grandstaff. **Season:** Year-round.
To obtain tee times: Call golf shop. **Miscellaneous:** Reduced fees (seniors, juniors), range
(grass/mats), credit cards (MC, V, AE).

★★ STONEBRIDGE GOLF CLUB
SP-1959 Golf Course Rd., Martinsburg, 25401, Berkeley County, (304)263-4653, 1 mile from
Martinsburg. **E-mail:** www.golfstoneridge@aol.com. **Facility Holes:** 18. **Yards:** 6,253/5,056.
Par: 72/72. **Course Rating:** 69.7/67.9. **Slope:** 119/108. **Green Fee:** $20/$30. **Cart Fee:**
$16/Person. **Walking Policy:** Walking at certain times. **Walkability:** 3. **Opened:** 1922. **Architect:**
Bob Elder. **Season:** Year-round. **High:** April-Oct. **To obtain tee times:** Call golf shop.
Miscellaneous: Reduced fees (weekdays, guests, twilight), range (grass/mats), credit cards
(MC, V, AE, D), BF, FF.

★★ SUGARWOOD GOLF CLUB
PU-Sugarwood Rd., Lavalette, 25535, Wayne County, (304)523-6500, 6 miles from
Huntington. **E-mail:** sugarwoodgc@aol. **Facility Holes:** 18. **Yards:** 6,522/5,478. **Par:** 72/73.
Course Rating: 71.8/72.5. **Slope:** 129/118. **Green Fee:** $16/$20. **Cart Fee:** $11/Person.
Walking Policy: Walking at certain times. **Walkability:** 1. **Opened:** 1965. **Architect:**
Dave Whechel. **Season:** Year-round. **To obtain tee times:** Call golf shop. **Miscellaneous:** Metal
spikes, credit cards (MC, V), BF, FF.

★★★ TWIN FALLS STATE PARK GOLF COURSE
R-P.O. Box 1023, Mullens, 25882, Wyoming County, (304)294-4044, (800)225-5982,
23 miles from Beckley. **Facility Holes:** 18. **Yards:** 6,382/5,202. **Par:** 71/74. **Course Rating:**
71.3/70.3. **Slope:** 132/124. **Green Fee:** $20/$23. **Cart Fee:** $20/Cart. **Walking Policy:**
Unrestricted walking. **Walkability:** 3. **Opened:** 1968. **Architect:** Geoffrey Cornish/
George Cobb. **Season:** Year-round. **High:** May-Sept. **To obtain tee times:** Call golf shop.
Miscellaneous: Reduced fees (weekdays, seniors), metal spikes, lodging (20 rooms), credit
cards (MC, V, AE, D, DC), BF, FF.
Reader Comments: Built in the old links style between mountains ... Different course depending on
pin positions.

★★½ **TYGART LAKE GOLF COURSE**
PU-Rte.1 Box 449-B, Grafton, 26354, Taylor County, (304)265-3100, 4 miles from Grafton.
E-mail: www.bjwestfall@access.mountain.net. **Web:** www.tygartlakegolfcourse@access.
mountain.net. **Facility Holes:** 18. **Yards:** 6,257/5,420. **Par:** 72/75. **Course Rating:** 70.0/71.0.
Slope: 115/113. **Green Fee:** $23/$32. **Cart Fee:** Included in green fee. **Walking Policy:** Walking
at certain times. **Walkability:** 2. **Opened:** 1969. **Architect:** James Gilmore Harrison/
Ferdinand Garbin. **Season:** Year-round. **High:** May-Oct. **To obtain tee times:** Call up to 7 days
in advance. **Miscellaneous:** Reduced fees (twilight), range (grass/mats), credit cards
(MC, V), BF, FF.

VALLEY VIEW GOLF COURSE
PU-Rte. #220 South, Moorefield, 26836, Hardy County, (304)538-6564, 145 miles from
Washington. **Facility Holes:** 18. **Yards:** 6,129/4,928. **Par:** 71/72. **Course Rating:** 68.0/65.4.
Slope: 108/110. **Green Fee:** $16/$19. **Cart Fee:** $15/Cart. **Walking Policy:** Unrestricted
walking. **Walkability:** 3. **Opened:** 1969. **Architect:** Russell Roberts. **Season:** Year-round.
High: May-Aug. **To obtain tee times:** Call golf shop. **Miscellaneous:** Reduced fees (twilight),
metal spikes, range (grass).

WHITE OAK COUNTRY CLUB
SP-Summerly Rd., Oak Hill, 25901, Fayette County, (304)465-5639, 15 miles from Beckley.
E-mail: www.rpenartay@hotmail.com. **Facility Holes:** 18. **Yards:** 5,680/4,762. **Par:** 70/72.
Course Rating: 66.6/68.1. **Slope:** 117/112. **Green Fee:** $25/$30. **Cart Fee:** Included in green
fee. **Walking Policy:** Walking at certain times. **Walkability:** 5. **Opened:** 1922. **Season:**
Feb.-Dec. **High:** May-Oct. **To obtain tee times:** Call golf shop. **Miscellaneous:** Range (grass),
credit cards (MC, V), BF, FF.

WOODBRIER
PU-250 Top Flite Dr., Martinsburg, 25401, Berkeley County, (304)274-9818, 4 miles from
Martinsburg. **Facility Holes:** 9. **Yards:** 2,809/2,533. **Par:** 36/36. **Course Rating:** 68.2/68.2.
Slope: 114/110. **Green Fee:** $11/$13. **Cart Fee:** $9/Person. **Walking Policy:** Unrestricted walk-
ing. **Walkability:** 3. **Opened:** 1966. **Season:** Year-round. **High:** April-Oct. **To obtain tee times:**
Call golf shop. **Miscellaneous:** Metal spikes, credit cards (None), FF.

★★★ **WOODRIDGE PLANTATION GOLF CLUB**
R-301 Woodridge Dr., Mineral Wells, 26150, Wood County, (304)489-1800, (800)869-1001,
7 miles from Parkersburg. **Facility Holes:** 18. **Yards:** 6,830/5,031. **Par:** 71/71. **Course Rating:**
72.7/70.5. **Slope:** 128/116. **Green Fee:** $20/$38. **Cart Fee:** Included in green fee. **Walking
Policy:** Mandatory carts. **Walkability:** 2. **Opened:** 1993. **Architect:** John Salyers. **Season:** Year-
round. **To obtain tee times:** Call golf shop. **Miscellaneous:** Reduced fees (weekdays, twilight,
seniors, juniors), range (grass), credit cards (MC, V, AE, D).
Reader Comments: Had two eagles at this course, great place ... An eye appealing course ... Nice
layout, but course condition must improve ... Interesting layout ... Flat for the most part.

THE WOODS RESORT
R-Mountain Lake Rd., Hedgesville, 25427, Berkeley County, (304)754-7222, (800)248-2222,
90 miles from Washington. **Facility Holes:** 36. **Walkability:** 3. **Architect:** Ray Johnston.
Season: Year-round. **Miscellaneous:** Reduced fees (weekdays, twilight, seniors, juniors),
range (grass/mats), BF, FF.
★★★½ **MOUNTAIN VIEW COURSE** (18)
Yards: 6,608/4,900. **Par:** 72/71. **Course Rating:** 70.9/68.0. **Slope:** 121/110. **Green Fee:**
$24/$35. **Cart Fee:** $13/Person. **Walking Policy:** Walking at certain times. **Opened:** 1989. **High:**
April-Sept. **To obtain tee times:** Call golf shop. **Miscellaneous:** Credit cards (MC, V, AE).
Reader Comments: A bit short, play the tips ... Challenging & playable ... Some very scenic holes
... Great course, friendly staff ... Trees everywhere, nice layout ... Uneven lies guaranteed.
★★★½ **STONY LICK COURSE** (18)
Yards: 3,685/3,045. **Par:** 62/62. **Green Fee:** $20/$28. **Cart Fee:** $11/Person. **Walking Policy:**
Unrestricted walking. **Opened:** 2002. **High:** March-Nov. **To obtain tee times:** Call up to 5 days
in advance. **Miscellaneous:** Lodging (100 rooms), credit cards (MC, V, AE, D).
Reader Comments: Awesome front 9 ... Enjoyable ... Pretty scenery ... Good variety ... A
mountain course ... My favorite ... Excellent food, great par 3s.

WORTHINGTON GOLF CLUB
PU-3414 Roseland Ave, Parkersburg, 26104, Wood County, (304)428-4297, 70 miles from Charleston. **E-mail:** www.worthingtongolf@juno.com. **Facility Holes:** 18. **Yards:** 6,106/4,967. **Par:** 71/71. **Course Rating:** 68.0/67.1. **Slope:** 108/107. **Green Fee:** $15/$17. **Cart Fee:** $12/Person. **Walking Policy:** Unrestricted walking. **Walkability:** 1. **Opened:** 1941. **Architect:** A.P. Taylor. **Season:** April-Oct. **Tee times:** Call golf shop. **Misc:** Reduced fees (seniors), credit cards (MC, V, D), FF.

★★★★ ABBEY SPRINGS GOLF COURSE
R-Country Club Dr., Fontana on Geneva Lake, 53125, Walworth County, (414)275-6111,
50 miles from Milwaukee. **E-mail:** golfpro@elknet.net. **Web:** www.abbeysprings.com. **Facility
Holes:** 18. **Yards:** 6,466/5,439. **Par:** 72/72. **Course Rating:** 71.4/72.4. **Slope:** 133/129. **Green
Fee:** $70/$80. **Cart Fee:** Included in green fee. **Walking Policy:** Walking at certain times.
Walkability: 5. **Opened:** 1971. **Architect:** Ken Killian/Dick Nugent. **Season:** April-Nov. **High:**
June-Oct. **To obtain tee times:** Call up to 30 days in advance. **Miscellaneous:** Reduced fees
(weekdays, juniors), range (grass), credit cards (MC, V, AE, D), BF, FF.
Reader Comments: Beautiful course. Front and back 9s are very different from each other ...
Challenging and scenic ... Pack plenty of ammo ... Lots of woods makes challenging ... Great
greens ... Very nice facility ... Hilly, scenic setting.

★★½ ALPINE RESORT GOLF COURSE
R-P.O. Box 200, Egg Harbor, 54209, Door County, (920)868-3232, 60 miles from Green Bay.
E-mail: alpine@mail.wiscnet.net. **Web:** www.alpineresort.com. **Facility Holes:** 27. **Green Fee:**
$22/$26. **Cart Fee:** $24/Cart. **Walking Policy:** Unrestricted walking. **Walkability:** 4. **Opened:**
1926. **Architect:** Francis H. Schaller. **Season:** May-Oct. **High:** July-Aug. **To obtain tee times:**
Call golf shop. **Miscellaneous:** Reduced fees (weekdays, guests, twilight), metal spikes,
lodging (40 rooms), credit cards (MC, V, AE).
RED/BLUE (18 Combo)
Yards: 5,858/5,440. **Par:** 71/70. **Course Rating:** 67.6/70.5. **Slope:** 114/117.
RED/WHITE (18 Combo)
Yards: 6,047/5,879. **Par:** 70/73. **Course Rating:** 67.9/72.4. **Slope:** 109/118.
WHITE/BLUE (18 Combo)
Yards: 6,207/5,837. **Par:** 71/73. **Course Rating:** 69.4/72.8. **Slope:** 117/122.

★★★★ ANTIGO BASS LAKE COUNTRY CLUB
SP-W. 10650 Bass Lake Road, Deerbrook, 54424, Langlade County, (715)623-6196,
50 miles from Green Bay. **Facility Holes:** 18. **Yards:** 6,308/4,769. **Par:** 71/71. **Course Rating:**
70.1/67.4. **Slope:** 125/115. **Green Fee:** $35. **Cart Fee:** $12/Person. **Walking Policy:**
Unrestricted walking. **Walkability:** 3. **Opened:** 1961. **Architect:** Edward Lawrence Packard.
Season: April-Nov. **High:** June-Sept. **To obtain tee times:** Call up to 7 days in advance.
Miscellaneous: Reduced fees (juniors), range (grass), credit cards (MC, V, AE, D), BF, FF.
Reader Comments: Friendly staff, scenic, good facilities ... Nice layout, challenging and fun ...
Course maintained great ... Relaxing course ... Short course, but fun to play.

★★½ BARABOO COUNTRY CLUB
SP-1010 Lake St., Hwy.123 S., Baraboo, 53913, Sauk County, (608)356-8195,
(800)657-4981, 35 miles from Madison. **E-mail:** info@baraboocountryclub.com.
Web: www.baraboocountryclub.com. **Facility Holes:** 18. **Yards:** 6,570/5,681. **Par:** 72/72.
Course Rating: 71.3/72.5. **Slope:** 124/122. **Green Fee:** $32/$39. **Cart Fee:** $15/Person.
Walking Policy: Unrestricted walking. **Walkability:** 4. **Opened:** 1962. **Architect:** Edward
Lawrence Packard. **Season:** April-Nov. **To obtain tee times:** Call up to 7 days in advance.
Miscellaneous: Reduced fees (weekdays, twilight), range (grass), credit cards (MC, V),
BF, FF.

★★ BEAVER DAM COUNTRY CLUB
PU-Hwy. 33 NW and W8884 Sunset Dr., Beaver Dam, 53916, Dodge County, (920)885-6614,
2 miles from Beaver Dam. **Facility Holes:** 18. **Yards:** 6,011/5,190. **Par:** 72/70. **Course Rating:**
68.3/69.4. **Slope:** 116/114. **Green Fee:** $22/$26. **Cart Fee:** $24/Cart. **Walking Policy:** Walking
at certain times. **Walkability:** 3. **Opened:** 1969. **Season:** May-Oct. **To obtain tee times:** Call golf
shop. **Miscellaneous:** Reduced fees (twilight), credit cards (MC, V, AE, D), BF, FF.

BIG OAKS GOLF COURSE
PU-6117 123rd Place, Pleasant Prairie, 53158, Kenosha County, (262)694-4200, 30 miles
from Milwaukee. **Facility Holes:** 27. **Green Fee:** $17/$23. **Cart Fee:** $23/Cart. **Walking Policy:**
Unrestricted walking. **Walkability:** 3. **Season:** Year-round. **To obtain tee times:** Call up to 7
days in advance. **Miscellaneous:** Reduced fees (twilight), range (grass/mats), credit cards
(MC, V), FF.
★½ BIG OAKS COURSE (18)
Yards: 6,071/5,809. **Par:** 72/72. **Opened:** 2001.
NORTH COURSE (9)
Yards: 2,963/2,834. **Par:** 36/36. **Opened:** 1987.

BLACKWOLF RUN GOLF CLUB
R-1111 W. Riverside Dr., Kohler, 53044, Sheboygan County, (920)457-4446, (800)618-5535,
55 miles from Milwaukee. **E-mail:** david.albrecht@kohler.com. **Web:** www.blackwolfrun.com.
Facility Holes: 36. **Cart Fee:** Included in green fee. **Walking Policy:** Unrestricted walking.

Walkability: 4. **Opened:** 1988. **Architect:** Pete Dye. **Season:** April-Nov. **High:** June-Sept. **To obtain tee times:** Call golf shop. **Miscellaneous:** Reduced fees (twilight), range (grass), lodging (357 rooms), credit cards (MC, V, AE, D), BF, FF.

★★★★½ **MEADOW VALLEYS COURSE** (18) *Condition+, Pace*
Yards: 7,142/5,065. **Par:** 72/72. **Course Rating:** 74.7/69.5. **Slope:** 143/125. **Green Fee:** $169. **Notes:** Ranked 8th in 2001 Best in State.
Reader Comments: Heaven! … Tremendous service, course condition … A great day no matter what you shot … Beautiful, tough … A lot of $, worth every penny … Every hole is different and a challenge … No. 1 in Midwest … Tough, fair. Lots of waste area & long grass.

★★★★★ **RIVER COURSE** (18) *Condition+, Pace*
Yards: 6,991/5,115. **Par:** 72/72. **Course Rating:** 74.9/70.7. **Slope:** 151/128. **Green Fee:** $179. **Notes:** Ranked 70th in 2001-2002 America's 100 Greatest; 3rd in 2001 Best in State; 12th in 1996 America's Top 75 Upscale Courses.
Reader Comments: Nice but very expensive … Beautiful course, pace was too slow, golfer's paradise … Awesome, too hard for average players … Terrific routing through the woods … Is unparalleled anywhere in Wisconsin … 1st class in everything … A real golf experience, A-1.

★★★★ **THE BOG**
PU-3121 County Hwy. I, Saukville, 53080, Ozaukee County, (414)284-7075, (800)484-3264, 28 miles from Milwaukee. **Web:** www.golfthebog.com. **Facility Holes:** 18. **Yards:** 7,110/5,110. **Par:** 72/72. **Course Rating:** 74.9/70.3. **Slope:** 142/124. **Green Fee:** $75/$125. **Cart Fee:** Included in green fee. **Walking Policy:** Unrestricted walking. **Walkability:** 2. **Opened:** 1995. **Architect:** Arnold Palmer/Ed Seay. **Season:** April-Nov. **To obtain tee times:** Call up to 45 days in advance. **Miscellaneous:** Reduced fees (weekdays, twilight), range (grass), credit cards (MC, V, AE, D), BF, FF.
Reader Comments: Gorgeous wetland area … Overpriced, plays fair, greens fast, should play once … Great layout & practice facilities.

★★★½ **THE BRIDGES GOLF COURSE**
PU-2702 Shopko Drive, Madison, 53704, Dane County, (608)244-1822. **E-mail:** bridge-spro@pga.com. **Web:** www.golfthebridges.com. **Facility Holes:** 18. **Yards:** 6,888/5,322. **Par:** 72/72. **Course Rating:** 73.0/70.4. **Slope:** 124/119. **Green Fee:** $28/$31. **Cart Fee:** $13/Person. **Walking Policy:** Unrestricted walking. **Walkability:** 2. **Opened:** 2000. **Architect:** Feick Design Group. **Season:** March-Dec. **High:** June-Aug. **To obtain tee times:** Call up to 7 days in advance. **Miscellaneous:** Reduced fees (weekdays, twilight, seniors, juniors), range (grass/mats), credit cards (MC, V, AE, D), BF, FF.
Reader Comments: New course, great layout … Very good course layout … New course, friendly staff, easy to walk … Target golf … Lots of water … 1st year, not bad… Great new course & helpful pro & staff.

★½ **BRIDGEWOOD GOLF COURSE**
PU-1040 Bridgewood Dr., Neenah, 54956, Winnebago County, (920)722-9819. **Facility Holes:** 18. **Yards:** 6,030/5,907. **Par:** 71/71. **Course Rating:** 65.1. **Green Fee:** $16/$17. **Cart Fee:** $15/Cart. **Walking Policy:** Unrestricted walking. **Walkability:** 2. **Opened:** 1949. **Architect:** Jack Taylor. **Season:** April-Nov. **High:** May-Aug. **To obtain tee times:** Call golf shop. **Miscellaneous:** Reduced fees (weekdays, seniors, juniors), metal spikes.

BRIGHTON DALE GOLF CLUB
PU-830-248th Ave., Kansasville, 53139, Kenosha County, (262)878-1440, 21 miles from Kenosha. **Facility Holes:** 45. **Green Fee:** $15/$28. **Cart Fee:** $24/Cart. **Walking Policy:** Unrestricted walking. **Walkability:** 3. **Season:** March-Nov. **To obtain tee times:** Call up to 12 days in advance. **Miscellaneous:** Reduced fees (weekdays), range (mats), credit cards (MC, V), BF, FF.

★★★½ **BLUE SPRUCE COURSE** (18) *Value*
Yards: 6,687/5,988. **Par:** 72/72. **Course Rating:** 72.0/72.1. **Slope:** 129/125. **Opened:** 1992. **Architect:** David Gill.
Reader Comments: A great every-Saturday course, challenging with great variety … Fair tracks, can't beat the price … Good layout, big practice green, small practice range … Nice layout, 45 holes and well kept … Narrow—water & woods.

RED PINE COURSE (9)
Yards: 3,512/2,851. **Par:** 36/36. **Course Rating:** 72.9/71.8. **Slope:** 132/126. **Opened:** 1972. **Architect:** Edmund B. Ault.

★★★ **WHITE BIRCH COURSE** (18)
Yards: 6,977/6,206. **Par:** 72/72. **Course Rating:** 73.3/73.2. **Slope:** 130/126. **Opened:** 1992. **Architect:** David Gill.
Reader Comments: Pace of play is slow, but good condition … Inexpensive. A bit of the prairie and northwoods combined … Par 3s are difficult, long, greens are good … Great price & service … Long, narrow, lots of pine trees.

★★★★½ BRISTLECONE PINES GOLF CLUB *Condition*

SP-1500 E. Arlene Dr., Hartland, 53029, Waukesha County, (262)367-7880, 20 miles from Milwaukee. **Facility Holes:** 18. **Yards:** 7,005/5,033. **Par:** 71/71. **Course Rating:** 74.1/69.4. **Slope:** 138/120. **Green Fee:** $70/$80. **Cart Fee:** Included in green fee. **Walking Policy:** Unrestricted walking. **Walkability:** 3. **Opened:** 1996. **Architect:** Scott Miller. **Season:** April-Nov. **High:** June-Sept. **To obtain tee times:** Call up to 2 days in advance. **Miscellaneous:** Reduced fees (weekdays, twilight), range (grass), caddies, credit cards (MC, V, AE), BF, FF.
Reader Comments: Beautiful course with wide fairways … Treatment and service of a private club … Wide fairways but difficult approaches and challenging, subtle greens. Tall fescue grasses if you miss the fairways.

★★★ BRISTOL OAKS COUNTRY CLUB

SP-16801 - 75th St., Bristol, 53104, Kenosha County, (262)857-2302, 25 miles from Milwaukee. **E-mail:** info@bristoloaks.com. **Web:** www.bristoloaks.com. **Facility Holes:** 18. **Yards:** 6,319/5,437. **Par:** 72/72. **Course Rating:** 70.1/70.9. **Slope:** 120/116. **Green Fee:** $18/$24. **Cart Fee:** $25/Cart. **Walking Policy:** Walking at certain times. **Walkability:** 2. **Opened:** 1964. **Architect:** Edward Lockie. **Season:** Year-round. **High:** May-Oct. **To obtain tee times:** Call golf shop. **Miscellaneous:** Reduced fees (weekdays, twilight, seniors), range (grass/mats), credit cards (MC, V, AE).
Reader Comments: Confidence builder. Not very difficult, the staff is friendly … Slow play … Basic golf … Steady improvement in many areas.

★★★★ THE BROADLANDS GOLF CLUB *Pace*

PU-18 Augusta Way, North Prairie, 53153, Waukesha County, (262)392-6320, 35 miles from Milwaukee. **E-mail:** broadlands@milwpc.com. **Web:** www.broadlandsgolfclub.com. **Facility Holes:** 18. **Yards:** 6,846/4,952. **Par:** 72/72. **Course Rating:** 72.0/63.3. **Slope:** 122/107. **Green Fee:** $31/$37. **Cart Fee:** $13/Person. **Walking Policy:** Unrestricted walking. **Walkability:** 3. **Opened:** 2000. **Architect:** Jacobson Golf Course Design, Inc. **Season:** April-Nov. **High:** June-Sept. **To obtain tee times:** Call up to 21 days in advance. **Miscellaneous:** Reduced fees (twilight, seniors, juniors), range (grass), credit cards (MC, V), BF, FF.
Reader Comments: Great new course, the 16th is one of the finest holes I have every played … Greens are difficult to hold, great layout, facilities … Gorgeous course, polite staff … Links-style, keep it straight.

★★★★ BROWN COUNTY GOLF COURSE *Value+*

PU-897 Riverdale Dr., Oneida, 54155, Brown County, (920)497-1731, 7 miles from Green Bay. **Facility Holes:** 18. **Yards:** 6,729/5,801. **Par:** 72/73. **Course Rating:** 72.1/72.7. **Slope:** 133/127. **Green Fee:** $22/$43. **Cart Fee:** $28/Cart. **Walking Policy:** Unrestricted walking. **Walkability:** 3. **Opened:** 1957. **Architect:** Edward Lawrence Packard. **Season:** April-Nov. **High:** May-Oct. **To obtain tee times:** Call up to 7 days in advance. **Miscellaneous:** Reduced fees (seniors, juniors), range (grass/mats), credit cards (MC, V), BF, FF.
Reader Comments: Long hitter's dream, fair course, greens OK … Old course well maintained … Tough, fair, good value … Fast greens. Love the layout … Absolutely remarkable for the price (or any price).

★★★★ BROWN DEER PARK GOLF COURSE

PU-7835 N. Green Bay Rd., Milwaukee, 53209, Milwaukee County, (414)352-8080, 10 miles from Milwaukee. **Facility Holes:** 18. **Yards:** 6,759/5,927. **Par:** 71/71. **Course Rating:** 72.9/68.7. **Slope:** 133/125. **Green Fee:** $29/$75. **Cart Fee:** $25/Cart. **Walking Policy:** Unrestricted walking. **Walkability:** 3. **Opened:** 1929. **Architect:** George Hansen/Roger Packard/Andy North. **Season:** April-Nov. **High:** June-Sept. **To obtain tee times:** Call up to 5 days in advance. **Miscellaneous:** Reduced fees (weekdays, seniors, juniors), range (grass), credit cards (MC, V), BF, FF.
Notes: Ranked 9th in 2001 Best in State.
Reader Comments: A challenging, tight layout, thick rough … Constantly being improved and provides a good test of golf … Cheap and very tough, if rough is up so are your scores … Great old course … Old classic layout.

★★ BROWNS LAKE GOLF COURSE

PU-3110 S. Browns Lake Dr., Burlington, 53105, Racine County, (262)878-3714, 25 miles from Milwaukee. **Facility Holes:** 18. **Yards:** 6,449/5,706. **Par:** 72/73. **Course Rating:** 70.2/70.4. **Slope:** 122/121. **Green Fee:** $20. **Cart Fee:** $24/Cart. **Walking Policy:** Unrestricted walking. **Walkability:** 3. **Opened:** 1923. **Architect:** David Gill. **Season:** April-Oct. **High:** June-Sept. **To obtain tee times:** Call golf shop. **Miscellaneous:** Reduced fees (seniors, juniors), metal spikes, range (grass).

WISCONSIN

★★★½ BUTTERNUT HILLS GOLF COURSE
PU-Golf Road and Country Road B, Sarona, 54870, Washburn County, (715)635-4396.
Facility Holes: 18. **Yards:** 5,561/4,894. **Par:** 70/70. **Course Rating:** 66.5/67.7. **Slope:** 112/111.
Green Fee: $16/$18. **Opened:** 1978. **Architect:** Carl Marshall. **To obtain tee times:** Call golf
shop. **Miscellaneous:** Reduced fees (juniors), metal spikes.
Reader Comments: Challenging course, with a variety of obstacles, small greens, real fun, a
great value ... Fun, short, sometimes slow ... Pricey, worth it ... Short course, easy to score,
good ambiance.

★½ CASTLE ROCK GOLF COURSE
PU-W. 6285 Welch Prairie Rd., Mauston, 53948, Juneau County, (608)847-4658,
(800)851-4653, 2 miles from Mauston. **E-mail:** crgc@mwt.net. **Web:**
www.castlerockgolfcourse.com. **Facility Holes:** 18. **Yards:** 6,182/5,318. **Par:** 72/71.
Course Rating: 70.1/70.6. **Slope:** 126/122. **Green Fee:** $25/$28. **Cart Fee:** $27/Cart.
Walking Policy: Unrestricted walking. **Walkability:** 3. **Opened:** 1991. **Architect:** Art
Johnson/Jim Van Pee/Gary Van Pee. **Season:** March-Oct. **High:** May-Sept. **To obtain tee
times:** Call golf shop. **Miscellaneous:** Reduced fees (weekdays, twilight, seniors, juniors),
range (grass), credit cards (MC, V), BF, FF.

CATHEDRAL PINES GOLF COURSE
PU-501 Golf Course Rd., Suring, 54174, Oconto County, (920)842-2803, 40 miles from
Green Bay. **Facility Holes:** 18. **Yards:** 6,131/4,719. **Par:** 71/71. **Course Rating:** 74.6/68.0.
Slope: 141/119. **Green Fee:** $18/$22. **Cart Fee:** $12/Person. **Walking Policy:** Unrestricted
walking. **Walkability:** 3. **Opened:** 1999. **Architect:** Marty Gharrity/Bob Lohmann. **Season:**
April-Nov. **High:** May-Oct. **Tee times:** Call up to 14 days in advance. **Miscellaneous:** Reduced
fees (weekdays, twilight, seniors, juniors), range (grass), credit cards (MC, V, AE, D), BF, FF.

★★★ CHASKA GOLF COURSE
PU-Wisconsin Ave. Exit 138 W., Appleton, 54912, Outagamie County, (920)757-5757,
90 miles from Milwaukee. **E-mail:** chaskagolf@aol.com. **Web:** www.chaskagolf.com. **Facility
Holes:** 18. **Yards:** 6,912/5,864. **Par:** 72/72. **Course Rating:** 72.8/73.2. **Slope:** 129/126. **Green
Fee:** $23/$29. **Cart Fee:** $32/Cart. **Walking Policy:** Unrestricted walking. **Walkability:** 2.
Opened: 1975. **Architect:** Lawrence Packard. **Season:** April-Nov. **High:** June-Sept. **To obtain
tee times:** Call golf shop. **Miscellaneous:** Reduced fees (twilight, seniors, juniors), range
(grass), credit cards (MC, V), BF, FF.
Reader Comments: Plush fairways and greens. Sand, sand and more sand ... Trees need to
mature, large greens, wide open ... Lots of sand, nice shape ... Stays wet after rain.

CHEQUAMEGON BAY GOLF CLUB
PU-3000 Golf Course Rd., Ashland, 54806, Ashland County, (715)682-8004. **E-mail:**
chad@pga.com. **Web:** golfashland.com. **Facility Holes:** 18. **Yards:** 6,566/5,134. **Par:** 72/72.
Course Rating: 71.8/69.6. **Slope:** 128/119. **Green Fee:** $27/$30. **Cart Fee:** $12/Person.
Walking Policy: Unrestricted walking. **Walkability:** 3. **Opened:** 1998. **Architect:** S. Campbell/G.
Gill. **Season:** April-Nov. **High:** June-Sept. **To obtain tee times:** Call up to 30 days in advance.
Miscellaneous: Reduced fees (weekdays), range (grass), credit cards (MC, V, AE), BF, FF.

★★★ CHERRY HILLS LODGE & GOLF COURSE *Pace*
R-5905 Dunn Rd., Sturgeon Bay, 54235, Door County, (920)743-3240, (800)545-2307,
40 miles from Green Bay. **E-mail:** cherryhl@itol.com. **Web:** www.golfdoorcounty.com. **Facility
Holes:** 18. **Yards:** 6,163/5,432. **Par:** 72/72. **Course Rating:** 69.2/71.0. **Slope:** 121/122. **Green
Fee:** $21/$30. **Cart Fee:** $14/Person. **Walking Policy:** Unrestricted walking. **Walkability:** 4.
Opened: 1977. **Season:** April-Nov. **High:** June-Sept. **To obtain tee times:** Call golf shop.
Miscellaneous: Reduced fees (weekdays, twilight, seniors, juniors), range (grass), lodging
(31 rooms), credit cards (MC, V, AE, D), BF, FF.
Reader Comments: Fun layout, many unique holes ... Some hills & cliff holes, great views ...
Difficult, very hilly but fairways in not so good condition ... Short, wide open front, doglegs on back.

★★★ CHRISTMAS MOUNTAIN VILLAGE GOLF CLUB
R-S. 944 Christmas Mountain Rd., Wisconsin Dells, 53965, Sauk County, (608)254-3971, 40
miles from Madison. **E-mail:** mvkrause@dellsnet.com. **Web:** www.dells.com. **Facility Holes:**
27. **Yards:** 6,786/5,095. **Par:** 72/72. **Course Rating:** 72.9/69.7. **Slope:** 133/120. **Green Fee:**
$32/$65. **Cart Fee:** Included in green fee. **Walking Policy:** Walking at certain times.
Walkability: 3. **Opened:** 1970. **Architect:** Art Johnson/D.J. DeVictor. **Season:** April-Nov. **High:**
June-Sept. **To obtain tee times:** Call golf shop. **Miscellaneous:** Reduced fees (twilight, seniors,
juniors), range (grass), credit cards (MC, V, AE, D), BF, FF.
Reader Comments: A resort-type course ... New 9 outstanding ... Resort course, hilly ... Back 9 is
unbelievable ... Great service & people ... Fast greens, challenge from the tips.
Special Notes: Also has new 9-hole course.

★★★★½ CLIFTON HIGHLANDS GOLF COURSE *Value*
PU-Cty. Rds. MM & F, Prescott, 54021, Pierce County, (715)262-5141, (800)657-6845, 30 miles from St. Paul, MN. **E-mail:** info@cliftonhighlands.com. **Web:** www.cliftonhighlands.com. **Facility Holes:** 27. **Yards:** 6,632/5,235. **Par:** 72/72. **Course Rating:** 71.8/69.8. **Slope:** 127/119. **Green Fee:** $20/$32. **Cart Fee:** $26/Cart. **Walking Policy:** Unrestricted walking. **Walkability:** 3. **Opened:** 1974. **Architect:** Dr. Gordon Emerson. **Season:** March-Nov. **High:** May-Sept. **To obtain tee times:** Call up to 7 days in advance. **Miscellaneous:** Reduced fees (weekdays, twilight, seniors, juniors), range (grass/mats), credit cards (MC, V), BF, FF.
Reader Comments: Holes vary, well groomed, great $ value ... Always in excellent condition ... A country sleeper ... Good course. Good people ... Very playable. Nice layout. Challenging.
Special Notes: Also has a 9-hole par-3 course.

★★★½ CLIFTON HOLLOW GOLF CLUB
PU-12166 W. 820th. Ave., River Falls, 54022, Pierce County, (715)425-9781, (800)487-8879, 30 miles from St. Paul. **E-mail:** don@cliftonhollow.com. **Web:** www.cliftonhollow.com. **Facility Holes:** 27. **Yards:** 6,429/5,038. **Par:** 71/72. **Course Rating:** 70.6/69.5. **Slope:** 121/115. **Green Fee:** $25/$30. **Cart Fee:** $13/Person. **Walking Policy:** Unrestricted walking. **Walkability:** 3. **Opened:** 1973. **Architect:** Gordon Emerson. **Season:** March-Nov. **High:** June-Sept. **To obtain tee times:** Call up to 7 days in advance. **Miscellaneous:** Reduced fees (weekdays, twilight, seniors, juniors), range (grass), credit cards (MC, V, D), BF, FF.
Reader Comments: Excellent for all players ... Pace quick, price low ... Rolling, challenging, well conditioned, old clubhouse ... A great place to play ... Kind of quirky layout, but very playable.
Special Notes: Also has a 9-hole par-3 course.

★★★ THE COACHMAN'S GOLF RESORT
R-984 County Hwy. A, Edgerton, 53534, Rock County, (608)884-8484, 15 miles from Madison. **Facility Holes:** 27. **Green Fee:** $23/$26. **Cart Fee:** $25/Cart. **Opened:** 1990. **Architect:** R. C. Greaves. **Season:** April-Oct. **To obtain tee times:** Call golf shop. **Miscellaneous:** Metal spikes.
RED/BLUE (18 Combo)
Yards: 6,190/4,830. **Par:** 71/71. **Course Rating:** 69.2/68.7. **Slope:** 115/112.
RED/WHITE (18 Combo)
Yards: 6,180/5,021. **Par:** 71/71. **Course Rating:** 68.0. **Slope:** 111.
WHITE/BLUE (18 Combo)
Yards: 6,420/5,000. **Par:** 72/72. **Course Rating:** 69.5. **Slope:** 114.
Reader Comments: Very heavy weekend play, excellent food ... Nice for stay & play usage ... Great for couples stay & play ... Short but nice. Good course for couples ... Great course.
Special Notes: Formerly Coachman's Inn.

★★★★ COUNTRY CLUB OF WISCONSIN
PU-2241 Highway. W., Grafton, 53024, Ozaukee County, (262)375-2444, 20 miles from Milwaukee. **Web:** www.ccwgolf.com. **Facility Holes:** 18. **Yards:** 7,049/5,499. **Par:** 72/72. **Course Rating:** 74.5/67.3. **Slope:** 136/119. **Green Fee:** $30/$59. **Cart Fee:** $13/Person. **Walking Policy:** Walking at certain times. **Walkability:** 4. **Opened:** 1994. **Architect:** Mattingly/Kuehn. **Season:** April-Nov. **High:** May-Sept. **To obtain tee times:** Call up to 7 days in advance. **Miscellaneous:** Reduced fees (weekdays, twilight, juniors), range (grass), credit cards (MC, V, AE), BF, FF.
Reader Comments: Tight, interesting ... Beautiful greens, challenging layout ... Maturing well, greens a little fast for average golfer... Really nice course, enjoyable ... Can score here if you play smart ... Great condition, too expensive.

★½ COUNTRYSIDE GOLF CLUB
PU-W. 726 Weiler Rd., Kaukauna, 54130, Outagamie County, (920)766-2219, 2 miles from Kaukauna. **Facility Holes:** 18. **Yards:** 6,183/5,187. **Par:** 71/71. **Course Rating:** 69.1/69.0. **Slope:** 115/111. **Green Fee:** $18/$22. **Cart Fee:** $25/Cart. **Walking Policy:** Unrestricted walking. **Walkability:** 2. **Opened:** 1964. **Season:** April-Oct. **High:** June-Aug. **To obtain tee times:** Call golf shop. **Miscellaneous:** Reduced fees (weekdays, seniors, juniors), range (grass).

★★★½ CRYSTAL SPRINGS GOLF CLUB
PU-N. 8055 French Rd., Seymour, 54165, Outagamie County, (920)833-6348, (800)686-2984, 17 miles from Green Bay. **E-mail:** tim@crystalspringsgolf.com. **Web:** www.crystalspringsgolf.com. **Facility Holes:** 21. **Yards:** 6,596/5,497. **Par:** 72/73. **Course Rating:** 70.7/70.5. **Slope:** 120/116. **Green Fee:** $17/$24. **Cart Fee:** $25/Cart. **Walking Policy:** Unrestricted walking. **Walkability:** 1. **Opened:** 1967. **Architect:** Edward Lockie. **Season:** April-Oct. **High:** May-Aug. **To obtain tee times:** Call up to 7 days in advance. **Miscellaneous:** Reduced fees (twilight, seniors, juniors), range (grass/mats), credit cards (MC, V), BF, FF.
Reader Comments: Nice course, 9 & 18 are tough ... A great challenge, excellent finishing holes ... Great course ... Short back 9, good layout ... Pace of play too slow on weekends ... Has some of the best greens.
Special Notes: Also has 3-hole kids' course—First Tee facility.

WISCONSIN

★★½ CUMBERLAND GOLF CLUB
PU-2400 5th St., Cumberland, 54829, Barron County, (715)822-4333, 2 miles from Cumberland. **Facility Holes:** 18. **Yards:** 6,272/5,004. **Par:** 72/71. **Course Rating:** 70.7/70.1. **Slope:** 129/116. **Green Fee:** $23/$26. **Cart Fee:** $24/Cart. **Walking Policy:** Unrestricted walking. **Walkability:** 4. **Opened:** 1991. **Architect:** Don Herfort. **Season:** April-Oct. **High:** June-Aug. **To obtain tee times:** Call golf shop. **Miscellaneous:** Reduced fees (weekdays), range (grass), credit cards (MC, V).

★★ CURRIE PARK GOLF COURSE
PU-3535 N. Mayfair Rd., Milwaukee, 53222, Milwaukee County, (414)453-7030, 11 miles from Milwaukee. **Web:** www.countryparks.com. **Facility Holes:** 18. **Yards:** 6,420/5,811. **Par:** 71/72. **Course Rating:** 68.6/72.4. **Slope:** 115/120. **Green Fee:** $11/$22. **Cart Fee:** $24/Cart. **Walking Policy:** Unrestricted walking. **Walkability:** 3. **Architect:** George Hansen. **Season:** April-Nov. **High:** June-Aug. **To obtain tee times:** Call golf shop. **Miscellaneous:** Reduced fees (twilight, seniors, juniors), credit cards (MC, V).

★★★ DEERTRAK GOLF COURSE
PU-W. 930 Hwy. O, Oconomowoc, 53066, Dodge County, (920)474-4444, 25 miles from Milwaukee. **Facility Holes:** 18. **Yards:** 6,313/5,114. **Par:** 72/72. **Course Rating:** 70.2/69.2. **Slope:** 120/116. **Green Fee:** $26/$31. **Walking Policy:** Unrestricted walking. **Walkability:** 4. **Opened:** 1986. **Architect:** Don Chapman. **To obtain tee times:** Call golf shop. **Miscellaneous:** Reduced fees (seniors), credit cards (MC, V).
Reader Comments: For the price it's too easy … Unique hole designs, great course, good value … Good shape … Outstanding course, neat layout, a beautiful place to play … Very good value … Fast play … Beautiful course.

★★½ DELBROOK GOLF COURSE
PU-700 S. 2nd St., Delavan, 53115, Walworth County, (262)728-3966, 45 miles from Milwaukee. **Facility Holes:** 18. **Yards:** 6,519/5,599. **Par:** 72/72. **Course Rating:** 70.8/71.3. **Slope:** 123/121. **Green Fee:** $11/$24. **Cart Fee:** $10/Person. **Walking Policy:** Unrestricted walking. **Walkability:** 2. **Opened:** 1928. **Architect:** James Foulis. **Season:** March-Nov. **High:** June-Aug. **To obtain tee times:** Call golf shop. **Miscellaneous:** Reduced fees (weekdays, twilight), range (grass), credit cards (MC, V, AE, D).

★★½ DEVIL'S HEAD RESORT & CONVENTION CENTER
R-S. 6330 Bluff Rd., Merrimac, 53561, Sauk County, (608)493-2251, (800)472-6670, 35 miles from Madison. **E-mail:** info@www.devils-head.com. **Web:** www.devils-head.com. **Facility Holes:** 18. **Yards:** 6,861/5,141. **Par:** 73/73. **Course Rating:** 72.4/64.4. **Slope:** 129/113. **Green Fee:** $26/$59. **Cart Fee:** Included in green fee. **Walking Policy:** Walking at certain times. **Walkability:** 5. **Opened:** 1973. **Architect:** Art Johnson. **Season:** April-Oct. **High:** June-Aug. **To obtain tee times:** Call golf shop. **Miscellaneous:** Reduced fees (weekdays, twilight), credit cards (MC, V, AE, D).

★★★½ DOOR CREEK GOLF COURSE
PU-4321 Vilas, Cottage Grove, 53527, Dane County, (608)839-5656, 3 miles from Madison. **Facility Holes:** 27. **Yards:** 6,475/5,189. **Par:** 71/71. **Course Rating:** 70.5/69.7. **Slope:** 119/111. **Green Fee:** $24/$26. **Cart Fee:** $12/Person. **Walking Policy:** Unrestricted walking. **Walkability:** 3. **Opened:** 1990. **Architect:** Bradt Family. **Season:** Year-round. **High:** April-Oct. **To obtain tee times:** Call up to 7 days in advance. **Miscellaneous:** Reduced fees (weekdays, seniors, juniors), range (grass/mats), credit cards (MC, V, D), BF, FF.
Reader Comments: Great fairways & greens, good value … Course, gets better each year … Great staff, always smiling, owners take pride in the quality of the course … Sunday get-together course … Wide open, fair, fast greens.
Special Notes: Also has a 9-hole executive course.

★★★ DRETZKA PARK GOLF COURSE
PU-12020 W. Bradley Rd., Milwaukee, 53224, Milwaukee County, (414)354-7300. **Facility Holes:** 18. **Yards:** 6,832/5,680. **Par:** 72/72. **Course Rating:** 70.8/74.6. **Slope:** 124/123. **Green Fee:** $23/$27. **Cart Fee:** $24/Cart. **Walking Policy:** Unrestricted walking. **Walkability:** 5. **Opened:** 1967. **Architect:** Evert Kincaid. **Season:** March-Nov. **High:** May-Sept. **To obtain tee times:** Call golf shop. **Miscellaneous:** Reduced fees (twilight, seniors, juniors), range (grass/mats), credit cards (MC, V), BF, FF.
Reader Comments: Top-notch public course, long, and annual changes … Great course, long and challenging … Excellent muni, huge greens … Affordable but difficult to get tee time … Great variety of holes.

★★★½ DRUGAN'S CASTLE MOUND
PU-W. 7665 Sylvester Rd., Holmen, 54636, La Crosse County, (608)526-3225, 12 miles from LaCrosse. **E-mail:** drugansgolfdine@centurytel.net. **Web:** www.drugans.com. **Facility Holes:** 18. **Yards:** 6,583/4,852. **Par:** 72/72. **Course Rating:** 70.7/67.5. **Slope:** 120/110. **Green Fee:** $24/$27. **Cart Fee:** $12/Person. **Walking Policy:** Unrestricted walking. **Walkability:** 3. **Opened:** 1970. **Season:** April-Dec. **High:** May-Sept. **To obtain tee times:** Call up to 365 days in advance. **Miscellaneous:** Reduced fees (twilight, seniors, juniors), credit cards (MC, V, AE, D), BF, FF.
Reader Comments: Challenging, not easy to walk … Nice variety of holes … Some great holes … Always improving. Greens fine … Great views.

EAGLE BLUFF GOLF COURSE
PU-Route 1 County Trunk D, Hurley, 54534, Iron County, (715)561-3552, 3 miles from Hurley. **Web:** www.hurley.ci.wi.com/golf. **Facility Holes:** 18. **Yards:** 5,870/5,327. **Par:** 70/68. **Course Rating:** 67.9/73.1. **Slope:** 122/126. **Green Fee:** $20. **Cart Fee:** $18/Cart. **Walking Policy:** Unrestricted walking. **Walkability:** 3. **Opened:** 1967. **Architect:** Homer Fieldhouse. **Season:** April-Nov. **High:** May-Oct. **To obtain tee times:** Call golf shop. **Miscellaneous:** Credit cards (MC, V, AE), BF, FF.

★★★★ EAGLE RIVER GOLF COURSE
PU-527 McKinley Blvd., Eagle River, 54521, Vilas County, (715)479-8111, (800)280-1477, 70 miles from Wausau. **E-mail:** eagleriverlongball@yahoo.com. **Web:** www.eaglerivergolf-course.com. **Facility Holes:** 18. **Yards:** 6,112/5,105. **Par:** 71/71. **Course Rating:** 69.4/67.8. **Slope:** 121/119. **Green Fee:** $25/$32. **Cart Fee:** $14/Person. **Walking Policy:** Unrestricted walking. **Walkability:** 3. **Opened:** 1923. **Architect:** Don Herfort. **Season:** April-Nov. **High:** June-Sept. **To obtain tee times:** Call up to 30 days in advance. **Miscellaneous:** Reduced fees (guests, twilight, juniors), range (grass), credit cards (MC, V, D), BF, FF.
Reader Comments: Well-kept secret … Couldn't believe they could get away with calling themselves the Augusta of the North, until I played it, and believed it … Tight fairways, small greens, fun … Fast and tight fairways.

EDGEWOOD GOLF COURSE
PU-W240, S10050 Castle Rd., Big Bend, 53103, Waukesha County, (262)662-3110, 20 miles from Milwaukee. **E-mail:** frreeman@aol.com. **Facility Holes:** 36. **Cart Fee:** $13/Person. **Walkability:** 3. **Opened:** 1969. **Architect:** Fred Millies. **Season:** March-Dec. **To obtain tee times:** Call up to 7 days in advance. **Miscellaneous:** Reduced fees (weekdays, twilight, seniors, juniors), range (grass), credit cards (MC, V, AE, D, DC), BF, FF.
★★½ OAKS (18)
Yards: 6,783/5,411. **Par:** 72/72. **Course Rating:** 72.3/70.8. **Slope:** 134/126. **Green Fee:** $35/$45. **Walking Policy:** Mandatory carts.
★★ PINES (18)
Yards: 6,551/5,386. **Par:** 72/72. **Course Rating:** 70.7/69.9. **Slope:** 122/117. **Green Fee:** $23/$33. **Walking Policy:** Unrestricted walking.
Reader Comments: Tougher course than you'd think … Good value … Front 9 is fun, back 9 more difficult … Good balance of challenging holes … Variety, great value … A little pricey.

★★★ EVANSVILLE COUNTRY CLUB
PU-8501 Cemetery Rd., Evansville, 53536, Rock County, (608)882-6524, 25 miles from Madison. **Facility Holes:** 18. **Yards:** 6,559/5,366. **Par:** 72/72. **Course Rating:** 71.2/70.7. **Slope:** 126/119. **Green Fee:** $23/$26. **Cart Fee:** $24/Cart. **Walking Policy:** Unrestricted walking. **Walkability:** 3. **Opened:** 1964. **Architect:** Built by members. **Season:** April-Nov. **High:** June-Sept. **To obtain tee times:** Call up to 14 days in advance. **Miscellaneous:** Reduced fees (weekdays, seniors, juniors), range (grass), credit cards (MC, V, D), BF, FF.
Reader Comments: Nice mature course … Always in great shape … Very good greens, mature trees make missing fairways costly … Course was in great shape, good food, nice people.

★★★½ EVERGREEN GOLF CLUB
PU-N. 6246 U.S. Hwy. 12, Elkhorn, 53121, Walworth County, (262)723-5722, 3 miles from Elkhorn. **E-mail:** evergreen@elknct.net. **Web:** www.evergreengolf.com. **Facility Holes:** 27. **Green Fee:** $27/$34. **Cart Fee:** $15/Person. **Walking Policy:** Walking at certain times. **Walkability:** 3. **Opened:** 1973. **Architect:** Dick Nugent/Gary Welsh. **Season:** March-Dec. **High:** May-Sept. **To obtain tee times:** Call up to 21 days in advance. **Miscellaneous:** Reduced fees (weekdays, twilight, seniors, juniors), range (mats), credit cards (MC, V, AE, D), BF, FF.
EAST/SOUTH (18 Combo)
Yards: 6,537/5,284. **Par:** 72/72. **Course Rating:** 71.9/70.6. **Slope:** 127/120.
NORTH/EAST (18 Combo)
Yards: 6,306/5,343. **Par:** 72/72. **Course Rating:** 70.9/71.3. **Slope:** 125/121.
NORTH/SOUTH (18 Combo)
Yards: 6,541/5,435. **Par:** 72/72. **Course Rating:** 71.8/71.5. **Slope:** 128/123.

WISCONSIN

Reader Comments: Great value, interesting holes ... Well-maintained course, very busy in summer ... Can play tough from the back tees ... Short, great holes, nice doglegs, very good condition ... Good bargain, well kept ... A surprise, interesting shots.

★½ FAR VU GOLF COURSE

PU-4985 State Rd. 175, Oshkosh, 54901, Winnebago County, (920)231-2631, 6 miles from Fond Du Lac. **E-mail:** jpfeiffer48@hotmail.com. **Web:** www.farvugc.com. **Facility Holes:** 18. **Yards:** 6,192/5,381. **Par:** 72/74. **Course Rating:** 69.3/71.1. **Green Fee:** $20/$22. **Cart Fee:** $24/Cart. **Walking Policy:** Unrestricted walking. **Walkability:** 2. **Opened:** 1964. **Architect:** Norman Pfeiffer. **Season:** March-Nov. **To obtain tee times:** Call up to 7 days in advance. **Miscellaneous:** Reduced fees (seniors, juniors), credit cards (MC, V), BF, FF.

★★★ FOREST HILLS PUBLIC GOLF COURSE

PU-600 Losey Blvd. N., La Crosse, 54601, La Crosse County, (608)784-0567. **E-mail:** holtzer@execac.com. **Web:** www.forest-hills.net. **Facility Holes:** 18. **Yards:** 6,063/5,275. **Par:** 71/72. **Course Rating:** 69.5/70.4. **Slope:** 123/119. **Green Fee:** $22/$24. **Cart Fee:** $22/Cart. **Walking Policy:** Unrestricted walking. **Walkability:** 3. **Opened:** 1901. **Season:** April-Nov. **High:** June-Aug. **To obtain tee times:** Call up to 14 days in advance. **Miscellaneous:** Range (grass), credit cards (MC, V, D, DC), BF, FF.
Reader Comments: Very hilly, train holds up play ... The course is very nice. The green fees are a little too much for the course ... Good layout. Slow play.

FOX HILLS RESORT

R-250 W. Church St., Mishicot, 54228, Manitowoc County, (920)755-2376, (800)950-7615, 30 miles from Green Bay. **E-mail:** foxhills@dct.com. **Web:** www.fox-hills.com. **Facility Holes:** 45. **Cart Fee:** $27/Cart. **Walking Policy:** Unrestricted walking. **Walkability:** 2. **Season:** April-Nov. **High:** July-Aug. **To obtain tee times:** Call up to 14 days in advance. **Miscellaneous:** Range (grass), lodging (335 rooms), credit cards (MC, V, AE, D), BF, FF.

★★½ BLUE/WHITE COURSE (18)
Yards: 6,044/5,390. **Par:** 71/71. **Course Rating:** 69.1/70.9. **Slope:** 123/120. **Green Fee:** $20/$24. **Opened:** 1964. **Architect:** Edward Lockie. **Miscellaneous:** Reduced fees (weekdays, twilight, seniors).

★★★½ NATIONAL COURSE (18)
Yards: 7,010/5,366. **Par:** 72/72. **Course Rating:** 73.8/71.0. **Slope:** 136/124. **Green Fee:** $40/$45. **Opened:** 1988. **Architect:** Bob Lohmann. **Miscellaneous:** Reduced fees (weekdays, guests, twilight, seniors, juniors).
Reader Comments: Nice links layout. Lots of buried elephants ... Windy, long par 4s ... Very windy & long ... Good links style for resort course ... Tests all your shots and skill ... Difficult. Good use of land and hole placement.

RED/BLUE COURSE (18)
Yards: 6,220/5,598. **Par:** 71/71. **Course Rating:** 70.0/72.0. **Slope:** 122/120. **Green Fee:** $20/$24. **Opened:** 1964. **Architect:** Edward Lockie. **Miscellaneous:** Reduced fees (weekdays, twilight, seniors).

WHITE/RED COURSE (18)
Yards: 6,406/5,692. **Par:** 72/72. **Course Rating:** 70.5/72.3. **Slope:** 123/121. **Green Fee:** $20/$24. **Opened:** 1964. **Architect:** Edward Lockie. **Miscellaneous:** Reduced fees (weekdays, twilight, seniors).

★★★★ FOXFIRE GOLF CLUB

PU-Hwy. 54 & Hwy. 10, Waupaca, 54981, Waupaca County, (715)256-1700, 60 miles from Green Bay. **E-mail:** foxfire1@execpc.com. **Web:** www.foxfiregc.com. **Facility Holes:** 18. **Yards:** 6,528/5,022. **Par:** 70/70. **Course Rating:** 70.9/69.4. **Slope:** 124/115. **Green Fee:** $23/$34. **Cart Fee:** $14/Person. **Walking Policy:** Unrestricted walking. **Walkability:** 1. **Opened:** 1996. **Architect:** David Truttman & Assoc. **Season:** March-Nov. **High:** June-Aug. **To obtain tee times:** Call golf shop. **Miscellaneous:** Reduced fees (weekdays, twilight, seniors, juniors), range (grass), lodging (80 rooms), credit cards (MC, V, AE, D), BF, FF.
Reader Comments: Water, sand, tall grass—hit it straight ... Totally different front/back ... Fairways close together ... Nice layout, good deal ... Short, very challenging, service great ... Plush links layout, both friendly and challenging.

GENEVA NATIONAL GOLF CLUB

R-1221 Geneva National Ave. S., Lake Geneva, 53147, Walworth County, (262)245-7000, 45 miles from Milwaukee. **E-mail:** palomagolf@aol.com. **Web:** www.genevanationalresort.com. **Facility Holes:** 54. **Cart Fee:** Included in green fee. **Walking Policy:** Mandatory carts. **Walkability:** 4. **Season:** March-Oct. **High:** May-Sept. **To obtain tee times:** Call golf shop. **Miscellaneous:** Reduced fees (weekdays, guests, twilight), range (grass), credit cards (MC, V, AE, D), BF, FF.

★★★★ GARY PLAYER COURSE (18)
Yards: 7,018/4,823. **Par:** 72/72. **Course Rating:** 74.4/68.4. **Slope:** 138/125. **Green Fee:**

$50/$125. **Opened:** 2000. **Architect:** Gary Player.
Reader Comments: Another beauty in Wisconsin ... Thoughtful & attractive layout ... Beautiful views ... Friendly, best of the 3 courses there ... Expensive, but a fabulous course ... Some outstanding holes, some average.
★★★★½ **PALMER COURSE** (18)
Yards: 7,177/4,892. **Par:** 72/72. **Course Rating:** 74.7/68.5. **Slope:** 140/122. **Green Fee:** $45/$110. **Opened:** 1991. **Architect:** Arnold Palmer/Ed Seay.
Notes: Ranked 10th in 1997 Best in State.
Reader Comments: Great shape, nice layout, fairways like greens ... Pricey, but you feel like a member ... Great layout, woodsy ... Great service, beautiful scenery ... Great condition.
★★★★½ **TREVINO COURSE** (18) *Condition, Pace*
Yards: 7,116/5,261. **Par:** 72/72. **Course Rating:** 74.2/70.2. **Slope:** 135/124. **Green Fee:** $45/$110. **Opened:** 1991. **Architect:** Lee Trevino/William Graves Design Co.
Reader Comments: Very nice course, 1 goofy hole ... Nice layout, top-notch practice range ... Nice greens ... Great value.

★½ **GEORGE WILLIAMS GOLF COURSE**
PU-100 N. Lake Shore, Williams Bay, 53191, Walworth County, (262)245-9507, 40 miles from Milwaukee. **Web:** www.augeowms.org. **Facility Holes:** 18. **Yards:** 5,066/4,721. **Par:** 67/68.
Course Rating: 63.4/65.5. **Slope:** 102/106. **Green Fee:** $18/$22. **Cart Fee:** $21/Cart. **Walking Policy:** Unrestricted walking. **Walkability:** 2. **Opened:** 1902. **Architect:** James Naismith.
Season: April-Nov. **High:** June-Aug. **To obtain tee times:** Call up to 7 days in advance.
Miscellaneous: Reduced fees (weekdays, twilight, seniors, juniors), lodging (80 rooms), credit cards (MC, V), BF, FF.

★★★ **GLACIER WOOD GOLF CLUB**
PU-604 Water St., Iola, 54945, Waupaca County, (715)445-3831, 15 miles from Waupaca.
Facility Holes: 18. **Yards:** 6,520/5,113. **Par:** 71/71. **Course Rating:** 71.6/65.2. **Slope:** 130/116.
Green Fee: $23/$29. **Cart Fee:** $13/Person. **Walking Policy:** Unrestricted walking. **Walkability:** 3. **Opened:** 1999. **Architect:** Art Johnson. **Season:** April-Nov. **High:** June-Aug. **To obtain tee times:** Call up to 7 days in advance. **Miscellaneous:** Reduced fees (weekdays), credit cards (MC, V), BF, FF.
Reader Comments: A hidden gem ... Picturesque, very friendly ... Not too difficult, very playable ... Some holes play short ... New 9 needs a little time ... Excellent course ... Neat layout combining old 9 and new 9.

★★ **GOLDEN SANDS GOLF COMMUNITY**
SP-300 Naber Rd., Cecil, 54111, Shawano County, (715)745-2189, 25 miles from Green Bay.
Facility Holes: 18. **Yards:** 6,122/4,888. **Par:** 71/72. **Course Rating:** 69.2/68.5. **Slope:** 117/113.
Green Fee: $20/$24. **Cart Fee:** $24/Cart. **Walking Policy:** Unrestricted walking. **Walkability:** 3.
Opened: 1970. **Season:** April-Nov. **High:** June-Aug. **To obtain tee times:** Call golf shop.
Miscellaneous: Reduced fees (twilight), range (grass), credit cards (MC, V, AE, D), BF, FF.

★★ **THE GOLF CLUB AT CAMELOT**
PU-W192 Highway 67, Lomira, 53048, Dodge County, (920)269-4949, (800)510-4949, 30 miles from Milwaukee. **Facility Holes:** 18. **Yards:** 6,121/5,338. **Par:** 70/72. **Course Rating:** 68.8/70.2. **Slope:** 124/123. **Green Fee:** $18/$29. **Cart Fee:** $26/Cart. **Walking Policy:** Unrestricted walking. **Walkability:** 4. **Opened:** 1966. **Architect:** Homer Fieldhouse. **Season:** Jan.-Oct. **High:** May-Sept. **To obtain tee times:** Call up to 7 days in advance. **Miscellaneous:** Reduced fees (weekdays, guests, twilight, seniors, juniors), range (grass/mats), credit cards (MC, V), BF, FF.

THE GOLF COURSES OF LAWSONIA
PU-W2615 S. Valley View Dr., Green Lake, 54941, Green Lake County, (920)294-3320, (800)529-4453, 35 miles from Oshkosh. **Web:** www.lawsonia.com. **Facility Holes:** 36.
Green Fee: $48/$58. **Cart Fee:** $17/Person. **Walking Policy:** Walking at certain times. **Season:** April-Nov. **High:** June-Sept. **To obtain tee times:** Call golf shop. **Miscellaneous:** Reduced fees (weekdays, guests, twilight), range (grass/mats), lodging (150 rooms), BF, FF.
★★★★½ **LINKS COURSE** (18)
Yards: 6,764/5,078. **Par:** 72/71. **Course Rating:** 72.8/68.9. **Slope:** 130/114. **Walkability:** 5.
Opened: 1930. **Architect:** William B. Langford. **Miscellaneous:** Credit cards (MC, V, AE, D).
Notes: Ranked 10th in 2001 Best in State; 60th in 1996 America's Top 75 Affordable Courses.
Reader Comments: Great value, wonderful old-style course ... Nice links design, has stood the test of time ... Tough elevated greens ... Lots of fun ... None like it in Midwest ... Large elevated greens & wide open but tough to score.
★★★★½ **WOODLANDS COURSE** (18) *Pace*
Yards: 6,618/5,106. **Par:** 72/72. **Course Rating:** 71.5/69.1. **Slope:** 129/120. **Walkability:** 3.
Opened: 1982. **Architect:** Rocky Roquemore. **Miscellaneous:** Credit cards (V, AE, D).

WISCONSIN

Notes: Ranked 10th in 1999 Best in State.
Reader Comments: One word says it all: WOW! You get more than you pay for here ... Beautiful layout & scenery, a little expensive ... Fabulous ... Great course, lots of fun ... Great value, great variety ... This place is fun.

GRAND GENEVA RESORT & SPA
R-7036 Grand Geneva Way, Lake Geneva, 53147, Walworth County, (262)248-2556, (800)558-3417, 40 miles from Milwaukee. **E-mail:** golf@grandgeneva.com. **Web:** www.grand-geneva.com. **Facility Holes:** 36. **Cart Fee:** Included in green fee. **Walking Policy:** Mandatory carts. **Walkability:** 5. **Opened:** 1969. **Season:** Year-round. **High:** May-Oct. **To obtain tee times:** Call up to 14 days in advance. **Miscellaneous:** Range (grass/mats), lodging (355 rooms), credit cards (MC, V, AE, D, DC), BF, FF.
★★★★½ **BRUTE COURSE** (18) *Pace*
Yards: 6,997/5,244. **Par:** 72/72. **Course Rating:** 73.8/70.0. **Slope:** 136/129. **Green Fee:** $65/$130. **Architect:** Robert Bruce Harris. **Miscellaneous:** Reduced fees (weekdays, guests, twilight).
Reader Comments: A magnificent course, aptly named ... Tough, great condition ... Everything was great ... Pricey, but a great treat ... Fantastic layout & condition ... First-class ... Lots of sand, very long ... Great service and pace.
★★★★ **HIGHLANDS COURSE** (18)
Yards: 6,633/5,038. **Par:** 71/71. **Course Rating:** 71.5/68.3. **Slope:** 125/115. **Green Fee:** $65/$115. **Architect:** Pete Dye/Jack Nicklaus/Bob Cupp. **Miscellaneous:** Reduced fees (weekdays, twilight).
Reader Comments: Very fair ... Big greens ... My favorite resort, too expensive ... Course layout improved ... A good resort course, the staff was attentive ... Not very difficult but picturesque.

★★ GRANT PARK GOLF COURSE
PU-100 E. Hawthorne Ave., South Milwaukee, 53172, Milwaukee County, (414)762-4646, 12 miles from Milwaukee. **Facility Holes:** 18. **Yards:** 5,174/5,147. **Par:** 67/71. **Course Rating:** 64.1/68.4. **Slope:** 110/103. **Green Fee:** $11/$24. **Cart Fee:** $15/Person. **Walking Policy:** Unrestricted walking. **Walkability:** 2. **Opened:** 1920. **Architect:** George Hansen. **Season:** Year-round. **To obtain tee times:** Call golf shop. **Miscellaneous:** Reduced fees (weekdays, twilight, seniors, juniors), range (grass), credit cards (MC, V), BF, FF.

★★ GREENFIELD PARK GOLF COURSE
PU-2028 W. Greenfield, West Allis, 53226, Milwaukee County, (414)453-1750, 10 miles from Milwaukee. **Web:** www.countyparks.com. **Facility Holes:** 18. **Yards:** 6,026/5,572. **Par:** 69/71. **Course Rating:** 66.7/68.4. **Slope:** 113/120. **Green Fee:** $11/$22. **Cart Fee:** $24/Cart. **Walking Policy:** Unrestricted walking. **Walkability:** 3. **Architect:** George Hansen. **Season:** April-Nov. **High:** June-Aug. **To obtain tee times:** Call golf shop. **Miscellaneous:** Reduced fees (twilight, seniors, juniors), credit cards (MC, V).

★½ HALLIE GOLF CLUB
PU-2196 110th Street, Chippewa Falls, 54729, Chippewa County, (715)723-8524, (800)830-3007, 1 mile from Eau Claire. **E-mail:** edsgolf@discovernet.net. **Web:** www.halliegolf.com. **Facility Holes:** 18. **Yards:** 5,787/4,822. **Par:** 70/70. **Course Rating:** 67.5/63.1. **Slope:** 120/112. **Green Fee:** $20/$25. **Cart Fee:** $13/Person. **Walking Policy:** Unrestricted walking. **Walkability:** 2. **Opened:** 1928. **Architect:** Art Tungen. **Season:** April-Oct. **High:** June-July. **To obtain tee times:** Call golf shop. **Miscellaneous:** Reduced fees (weekdays, seniors, juniors), range (grass/mats), credit cards (MC, V, AE).

HANSEN PARK GOLF COURSE
PU-9800 W. Underwood Creek Pkwy., Wauwatosa, 53226, Milwaukee County, (414)453-4454, 8 miles from Milwaukee. **Web:** www.countyparks.com. **Facility Holes:** 18. **Yards:** 2,217/2,217. **Par:** 55/55. **Green Fee:** $6/$10. **Cart Fee:** $15/Cart. **Walking Policy:** Unrestricted walking. **Walkability:** 2. **Season:** April-Nov. **High:** June-Aug. **To obtain tee times:** Call golf shop. **Miscellaneous:** Reduced fees (seniors, juniors).

★★ HARTFORD GOLF CLUB
SP-7072 Lee Rd., Hartford, 53027, Washington County, (262)673-2710, 30 miles from Milwaukee. **Facility Holes:** 18. **Yards:** 6,520/5,622. **Par:** 72/74. **Course Rating:** 70.7/75.2. **Slope:** 121/121. **Green Fee:** $24/$29. **Cart Fee:** $24/Person. **Walking Policy:** Unrestricted walking. **Walkability:** 3. **Opened:** 1933. **Architect:** Killian/Nugent. **Season:** April-Nov. **High:** May-Oct. **To obtain tee times:** Call golf shop. **Miscellaneous:** Reduced fees (twilight), range (grass), caddies, credit cards (MC, V), BF, FF.

★★★½ **HAWTHORNE HILLS GOLF CLUB** *Value*
PU-4720 County Hwy. I, Saukville, 53080, Ozaukee County, (262)692-2151, 25 miles from Milwaukee. **Facility Holes:** 18. **Yards:** 6,657/5,352. **Par:** 72/72. **Course Rating:** 70.8/69.4. **Slope:** 119/114. **Green Fee:** $13/$26. **Cart Fee:** $24/Cart. **Walking Policy:** Unrestricted walking. **Walkability:** 3. **Opened:** 1965. **Architect:** Bob Lohmann. **Season:** April-Nov. **High:** June-Sept. **To obtain tee times:** Call up to 10 days in advance. **Miscellaneous:** Reduced fees (weekdays, seniors, juniors), credit cards (MC, V, D), FF.
Reader Comments: One of the best bargains in the area ... Very good value, fun ... Walk-on and enjoy a fair game ... Very good municipal course ... Very good management and course condition ... Easy but fun.

★★★½ **HAYWARD GOLF & TENNIS CLUB**
PU-16005 Wittwer St., Hayward, 54843, Sawyer County, (715)634-2760. **Web:** www.haywardgolf.com. **Facility Holes:** 18. **Yards:** 6,685/5,200. **Par:** 72/72. **Course Rating:** 71.8/70.0. **Slope:** 125/119. **Green Fee:** $30. **Cart Fee:** $26/Cart. **Walking Policy:** Unrestricted walking. **Walkability:** 2. **Opened:** 1924. **Architect:** Ken Killian. **Season:** April-Nov. **High:** June-Oct. **To obtain tee times:** Call up to 30 days in advance. **Miscellaneous:** Reduced fees (twilight, juniors), range (grass), credit cards (MC, V), BF, FF.
Reader Comments: Nice layout, good blend of trees and water ... Excellent condition, easy to walk ... Excellent course condition despite heavy play ... Great greens ... Well managed, well designed, nice clubhouse ... Challenging, easy walk.

HIAWATHA GOLF CLUB
PU-10229 Ellsworth Rd., Tomah, 54660, Monroe County, (608)372-5589, 40 miles from La Crosse. **Facility Holes:** 18. **Yards:** 6,520/5,263. **Par:** 72/72. **Course Rating:** 70.5/69.4. **Slope:** 122/117. **Green Fee:** $21/$27. **Cart Fee:** $13/Person. **Walking Policy:** Unrestricted walking. **Walkability:** 3. **Opened:** 1959. **Architect:** Gilmore Graves. **Season:** March-Nov. **High:** June-Aug. **To obtain tee times:** Call up to 14 days in advance. **Miscellaneous:** Reduced fees (weekdays), range (grass), credit cards (MC, V, AE, D), BF, FF.

★★½ **HICKORY HILLS COUNTRY CLUB**
PU-W 3095 Hickory Hills Rd., Chilton, 53014, Calumet County, (920)849-2912, (888)849-2912, 25 miles from Appleton. **Facility Holes:** 18. **Yards:** 6,130/5,916. **Par:** 71/72. **Slope:** 121/117. **Green Fee:** $14/$15. **Walking Policy:** Unrestricted walking. **Walkability:** 2. **Season:** April-Nov. **To obtain tee times:** Call golf shop. **Miscellaneous:** Reduced fees (weekdays), range (mats), credit cards (MC), FF.

★★½ **HIGH CLIFF GOLF COURSE**
PU-W. 5055 Golf Course Rd., Sherwood, 54169, Calumet County, (920)734-1162, 2 miles from Sherwood. **Facility Holes:** 18. **Yards:** 6,106/4,932. **Par:** 71/71. **Course Rating:** 67.1/62.7. **Slope:** 113/104. **Green Fee:** $16/$22. **Cart Fee:** $22/Cart. **Walking Policy:** Unrestricted walking. **Walkability:** 3. **Opened:** 1968. **Architect:** Homer Fieldhouse. **To obtain tee times:** Call golf shop. **Miscellaneous:** Reduced fees (seniors, juniors), range (grass), credit cards (MC, V, D).

★★★ **HILLMOOR GOLF CLUB**
SP-333 E.Main Street, Lake Geneva, 53147, Walworth County, (262)248-4570, (877)944-2462, 70 miles from Chicago. **Web:** www.hillmoor.com. **Facility Holes:** 18. **Yards:** 6,350/5,360. **Par:** 72/72. **Course Rating:** 71.0/65.3. **Slope:** 125/113. **Green Fee:** $24/$38. **Cart Fee:** $15/Person. **Walking Policy:** Walking at certain times. **Walkability:** 3. **Opened:** 1924. **Architect:** James Foulis. **Season:** March-Dec. **High:** May-Nov. **To obtain tee times:** Call up to 14 days in advance. **Miscellaneous:** Reduced fees (weekdays, twilight, seniors, juniors), range (grass/mats), credit cards (MC, V, D), BF, FF.
Reader Comments: Very hilly, greens in great condition ... Some great holes, but several boring ones ... One of best conditioned courses in state ... Back 9 especially beautiful ... Several very good holes, up-and-down terrain.

★★ **HON-E-KOR COUNTRY CLUB**
PU-1141 Riverview Dr., Box 439, Kewaskum, 53040, Washington County, (262)626-2520, 5 miles from West Bend. **Facility Holes:** 27. **Green Fee:** $20/$25. **Cart Fee:** $25/Cart. **Walking Policy:** Unrestricted walking. **Walkability:** 4. **Opened:** 1962. **Architect:** Jim Korth. **Season:** April-Oct. **High:** June-Aug. **To obtain tee times:** Call up to 7 days in advance. **Miscellaneous:** Reduced fees (weekdays), credit cards (MC, V), BF, FF.
RED/BLUE (18 Combo)
Yards: 6,011/5,164. **Par:** 70/71. **Course Rating:** 68.7/70.3. **Slope:** 118/122.
RED/WHITE (18 Combo)
Yards: 5,959/5,145. **Par:** 70/71. **Course Rating:** 66.0/70.3. **Slope:** 116/122.
WHITE/BLUE (18 Combo)
Yards: 6,033/5,161. **Par:** 70/70. **Course Rating:** 67.6/70.3. **Slope:** 120/122.

WISCONSIN

HORSESHOE BAY GOLF CLUB
SP-5335 Horseshoe Bay Rd., Egg Harbor, 54209, Door County, (920)868-3741, (877)599-4653, 60 miles from Green Bay. **E-mail:** tbauman@itol.com. **Web:** www.hsbfarms.com. **Facility Holes:** 18. **Yards:** 7,101/5,386. **Par:** 72/72. **Course Rating:** 74.0/71.0. **Slope:** 134/122. **Green Fee:** $95/$110. **Cart Fee:** Included in green fee. **Walking Policy:** Unrestricted walking. **Walkability:** 2. **Opened:** 2000. **Architect:** Rick Robbins/ Brian Lussier. **Season:** April-Nov. **High:** July-Aug. **Tee times:** Call up to 6 days in advance. **Misc:** Reduced fees (twilight), range (grass/mats), credit cards (MC, V, AE, D), BF, FF.

THE HOUSE ON THE ROCK RESORT
R-400 Springs Dr., Spring Green, 53588, Iowa County, (608)588-7000, (800)822-7774, 35 miles from Madison. **E-mail:** daven@thehouseontherock.com. **Web:** www.thehouseontherock.com. **Facility Holes:** 27. **Green Fee:** $45/$65. **Cart Fee:** Included in green fee. **Walking Policy:** Walking at certain times. **Opened:** 1969. **Season:** April-Oct. **High:** May-Sept. **To obtain tee times:** Call golf shop. **Misc:** Reduced fees (weekdays, guests, twilight), range (grass), lodging (80 rooms), credit cards (MC, V, AE, D), BF, FF.
★★★★½ **NORTH NINE** (9) *Condition, Pace*
Yards: 3,262/2,659. **Par:** 36/36. **Course Rating:** 71.8/68.3. **Slope:** 132/122. **Walkability:** 5. **Architect:** Roger Packard/Andy North.
Reader Comments: One of my favorites ... Great value & conditions ... In perfect condition, pace of play was great ... Very plush, beautiful course ... Nice location & course ... Beautiful but pricey.
THE SPRINGS COURSE (18)
Yards: 6,562/5,334. **Par:** 72/72. **Course Rating:** 71.5/70.3. **Slope:** 132/123. **Walkability:** 3. **Architect:** Robert Trent Jones.
Special Notes: Formerly The Springs Golf Club Resort.

★★★½ HUDSON COUNTRY CLUB
SP-201 Carmichael Rd., Hudson, 54016, St. Croix County, (715)386-6515, 55 miles from Eau Claire. **Facility Holes:** 18. **Yards:** 6,435/5,074. **Par:** 71/71. **Course Rating:** 71.0/69.1. **Slope:** 129/127. **Green Fee:** $28/$33. **Cart Fee:** $26/Cart. **Walking Policy:** Unrestricted walking. **Opened:** 1955. **Season:** April-Nov. **To obtain tee times:** Call golf shop. **Miscellaneous:** Credit cards (MC, V, D), FF.
Reader Comments: Very hilly, study distances, short, packed ... Redone in fine style, hard to walk ... Back 9 is very picturesque ... Pricey, need to speed up play, great shape, fastest greens around.

★★★½ IDLEWILD GOLF COURSE
PU-4146 Golf Valley Dr., Sturgeon Bay, 54235, Door County, (920)743-3334, 40 miles from Green Bay. **E-mail:** info@idlewildgolf.com. **Web:** www.idlewildgolf.com. **Facility Holes:** 18. **Yards:** 6,889/5,886. **Par:** 72/72. **Course Rating:** 72.7/73.4. **Slope:** 130/128. **Green Fee:** $20/$26. **Cart Fee:** $13/Person. **Walking Policy:** Unrestricted walking. **Walkability:** 2. **Opened:** 1978. **Season:** April-Oct. **High:** June-Aug. **To obtain tee times:** Call up to 365 days in advance. **Miscellaneous:** Reduced fees (weekdays, guests, twilight, seniors, juniors), range (grass), credit cards (MC, V), BF, FF.
Reader Comments: Very well groomed, with interesting mix of holes ... Nice, playable layout. Must stay on fairways ... Nice course.

★½ INSHALLA COUNTRY CLUB
R-N11060 Clear Lake Rd., Tomahawk, 54487, Lincoln County, (715)453-3130, 3 miles from Tomahawk. **Facility Holes:** 18. **Yards:** 5,659/5,269. **Par:** 70/70. **Course Rating:** 66.6/65.5. **Slope:** 109/104. **Green Fee:** $20/$27. **Cart Fee:** $14/Person. **Walking Policy:** Unrestricted walking. **Walkability:** 2. **Opened:** 1964. **Architect:** John Hein/John F. Hein. **Season:** April-Nov. **High:** June-Aug. **To obtain tee times:** Call up to 7 days in advance. **Miscellaneous:** Reduced fees (twilight, juniors), range (grass), lodging (2 rooms), credit cards (MC, V, AE, D), BF, FF.

★★★ IVES GROVE GOLF LINKS
PU-14101 Washington Ave., Sturtevant, 53177, Racine County, (262)878-3714, 6 miles from Racine. **Facility Holes:** 27. **Green Fee:** $18/$24. **Cart Fee:** $27/Cart. **Walking Policy:** Unrestricted walking. **Walkability:** 2. **Opened:** 1971. **Architect:** David Gill. **Season:** April-Nov. **High:** May-Sept. **To obtain tee times:** Call up to 7 days in advance. **Miscellaneous:** Reduced fees (seniors, juniors), range (grass/mats), credit cards (MC, V), BF, FF.
BLUE/RED (18 Combo)
Yards: 7,000/5,370. **Par:** 72/72. **Course Rating:** 73.0. **Slope:** 131.
RED/WHITE (18 Combo)
Yards: 6,965/5,440. **Par:** 72/72. **Course Rating:** 72.8. **Slope:** 130.
WHITE/BLUE (18 Combo)
Yards: 6,985/5,380. **Par:** 72/72. **Course Rating:** 73.0. **Slope:** 131.
Reader Comments: A long ball hitter's dream! ... Great shape, flat, lots of bunkers ... Friendly staff, good value ... Tough in the wind ... Offers variety.

WISCONSIN

★★★ JOHNSON PARK GOLF COURSE
PU-6200 Northwestern Ave., Racine, 53406, Racine County, (262)637-2840, 20 miles from Milwaukee. **E-mail:** info@racinegolfonline.com. **Web:** www.racinegolfonline.com. **Facility Holes:** 18. **Yards:** 6,657/5,948. **Par:** 72/74. **Course Rating:** 71.5/73.6. **Slope:** 124/125. **Green Fee:** $18/$24. **Cart Fee:** $26/Cart. **Walking Policy:** Unrestricted walking. **Walkability:** 4. **Opened:** 1931. **Architect:** Todd Sloan. **Season:** March-Dec. **High:** May-Sept. **To obtain tee times:** Call up to 7 days in advance. **Miscellaneous:** Reduced fees (weekdays, seniors, juniors), metal spikes, range (grass/mats), credit cards (MC, V, D), BF, FF.
Reader Comments: Great for tournaments … Have pace of play program everyone should use … Great public course … Some very interesting holes, doglegs hilly … Always busy, good pace, good value … Good price but they race you around.

KETTLE HILLS GOLF COURSE
PU-3375 State Hwy. 167 W., Richfield, 53076, Washington County, (262)255-2200, 20 miles from Milwaukee. **Web:** www.kettlehills.com. **Facility Holes:** 36. **Green Fee:** $22/$29. **Architect:** Don Zimmermann. **Season:** March-Dec. **High:** June-Sept. **To obtain tee times:** Call up to 9 days in advance. **Miscellaneous:** Reduced fees (weekdays, twilight, seniors, juniors), range (grass/mats). credit cards (MC, V), BF, FF.
★★★ PONDS/WOODS COURSE (18)
Yards: 6,787/5,171. **Par:** 72/72. **Course Rating:** 72.5/69.6. **Slope:** 128/123. **Cart Fee:** $11/Person. **Walking Policy:** Unrestricted walking. **Walkability:** 4. **Opened:** 1987.
Reader Comments: Challenging holes, good course … Beautiful course, tough holes, great condition, challenged every part of my game … Tough greens, great layout, fun, scenic.
★★½ VALLEY COURSE (18)
Yards: 6,455/5,088. **Par:** 72/72. **Course Rating:** 70.9/69.2. **Slope:** 122/116. **Cart Fee:** $9/Person. **Walking Policy:** Walking at certain times. **Walkability:** 3. **Opened:** 1990.

★★★★ KETTLE MORAINE GOLF CLUB *Pace*
PU-4299 Highway 67, Dousman, 53118, Waukesha County, (262)965-6200, 4 miles from Dousman. **Facility Holes:** 18. **Yards:** 6,406/5,203. **Par:** 72/72. **Course Rating:** 70.3/69.5. **Slope:** 118/116. **Green Fee:** $27/$32. **Cart Fee:** $14/Person. **Walking Policy:** Unrestricted walking. **Walkability:** 3. **Opened:** 1969. **Architect:** Dwayne Dewey Laak. **Season:** April-Nov. **High:** May-Sept. **To obtain tee times:** Call up to 14 days in advance. **Miscellaneous:** Reduced fees (twilight), range (grass), credit cards (MC, V), BF, FF.
Reader Comments: Wonderful golf … Out of the way, but challenging, fast greens … Excellent value, course and personnel … Very playable, nice layout … Variety of holes … Nice course, great Bloody Marys.

★★★ KILKARNEY HILLS GOLF CLUB *Value*
PU-163 Radio Rd, River Falls, 54022, St. Croix County, (715)425-8501, (800)466-7999, 23 miles from St. Paul. **E-mail:** pat@kilkarney.com. **Web:** www.kilkarneyhills.com. **Facility Holes:** 18. **Yards:** 6,434/5,055. **Par:** 72/73. **Course Rating:** 70.8/64.4. **Slope:** 120/107. **Green Fee:** $16/$28. **Cart Fee:** $13/Person. **Walking Policy:** Unrestricted walking. **Walkability:** 3. **Opened:** 1994. **Architect:** Gordon Emerson. **Season:** April-Nov. **High:** May-Sept. **To obtain tee times:** Call up to 7 days in advance. **Miscellaneous:** Reduced fees (weekdays, twilight, seniors, juniors), range (grass), credit cards (MC, V), BF, FF.
Reader Comments: Reasonable cost, great course … The 11th hole is a monster… If not for slow play would be great … Open and growing … Great value.

★★★ KOSHKONONG MOUNDS COUNTRY CLUB
SP-W7670 Koshkonong Mounds Rd., Fort Atkinson, 53538, Jefferson County, (920)563-2823, 40 miles from Madison. **Facility Holes:** 18. **Yards:** 6,432/5,813. **Par:** 71/72. **Course Rating:** 70.0/72.1. **Slope:** 121/121. **Green Fee:** $20/$23. **Cart Fee:** $22/Person. **Walking Policy:** Walking at certain times. **Opened:** 1944. **Architect:** Art Johnson. **Season:** April-Oct. **High:** May-Aug. **To obtain tee times:** Call golf shop. **Miscellaneous:** Credit cards (MC, V).
Reader Comments: Nice course, friendly … Super condition … Pretty, not very long but challenging, some fairways are too close together … Nice variety … Tough and tricky in midsummer.

★★ KRUEGER-HASKELL GOLF COURSE
PU-1611 Hackett St., Beloit, 53511, Rock County, (608)362-6503, 90 miles from Chicago. **Facility Holes:** 18. **Yards:** 6,103/5,550. **Par:** 70/71. **Course Rating:** 69.0/71.5. **Slope:** 121. **Green Fee:** $18/$25. **Cart Fee:** $24/Cart. **Walking Policy:** Unrestricted walking. **Walkability:** 3. **Opened:** 1917. **Architect:** Stanley Pelchar. **Season:** March-Dec. **High:** June-Oct. **To obtain tee times:** Call golf shop. **Miscellaneous:** Reduced fees (twilight, seniors, juniors), BF, FF.

LAKE ARROWHEAD GOLF COURSE

PU-1195 Apache Lane, Nekoosa, 54457, Adams County, (715)325-2929, 13 miles from Wisconsin Rapids. **E-mail:** lakearro@wctc.net. **Web:** www.lakearrowheadgolf.com. **Facility Holes:** 36. **Green Fee:** $32/$49. **Cart Fee:** $13/Person. **Walkability:** 2. **Season:** April-Oct. **High:** April-Oct. **To obtain tee times:** Call golf shop. **Miscellaneous:** Range (grass), credit cards (MC, V, D), BF, FF.

★★★★½ **LAKES COURSE** (18)

Yards: 7,105/5,272. **Par:** 72/72. **Course Rating:** 74.8/71.0. **Slope:** 140/124. **Walking Policy:** Walking at certain times. **Opened:** 1998. **Architect:** Ken Killian. **Miscellaneous:** Reduced fees (twilight, juniors).

Reader Comments: Very good course layout, great value ... Expensive, beautiful ... Great getaway to a course rich in beauty and the sweet smell of pine trees. Prettiest place I've ever played ... New course, beautiful setting, challenging and fun.

★★★★½ **PINES COURSE** (18) *Value, Pace*

Yards: 6,624/5,213. **Par:** 72/72. **Course Rating:** 72.3/70.2. **Slope:** 135/125. **Walking Policy:** Unrestricted walking. **Opened:** 1983. **Architect:** Killian/Nugent. **Miscellaneous:** Reduced fees (twilight).

Reader Comments: Great woodlands layout. Superb conditions. One of the best in the state. Sand, sand and more sand! ... The sounds of silence! Beautiful course ... Challenging course with narrow fairways, good value ... Beautiful older course, well maintained. Excellent staff ... Beautiful, tight.

★½ LAKE BEULAH COUNTRY CLUB

SP-N9430 E. Shore Drive, Mukwonago, 53149, Walworth County, (262)363-8147, 20 miles from Milwaukee. **Facility Holes:** 27. **Yards:** 5,715/4,891. **Par:** 68/69. **Course Rating:** 66.7/69.8. **Slope:** 108/113. **Green Fee:** $19/$24. **Cart Fee:** $24/Cart. **Walking Policy:** Unrestricted walking. **Walkability:** 2. **Architect:** RoyJacobs/James Jacobs. **Season:** April-Nov. **High:** June-Aug. **To obtain tee times:** Call up to 10 days in advance. **Miscellaneous:** Reduced fees (seniors), credit cards (MC, V), FF.

Special Notes: Also has a 9-hole regulation course.

★★½ LAKE BREEZE GOLF CLUB

PU-6333 Highway 110, Winneconne, 54986, Winnebago County, (920)582-7585, (800)330-9189, 10 miles from Oshkosh. **E-mail:** PGAPro14@aol.com. **Facility Holes:** 18. **Yards:** 6,896/5,748. **Par:** 72/72. **Course Rating:** 72.2/71.9. **Slope:** 121/118. **Green Fee:** $18/$22. **Cart Fee:** $12/Person. **Walking Policy:** Unrestricted walking. **Walkability:** 2. **Opened:** 1991. **Architect:** Homer Fieldhouse. **Season:** April-Oct. **To obtain tee times:** Call up to 7 days in advance. **Miscellaneous:** Reduced fees (twilight, seniors, juniors), range (grass), credit cards (MC, V), BF, FF.

★★★ LAKE LAWN RESORT GOLF COURSE

R-2400 E. Geneva St., Hwy. 50 E., Delavan, 53115, Walworth County, (262)728-7950, (800)338-5253, 45 miles from Milwaukee. **E-mail:** golfshop@lakelawnresort.com. **Web:** www.lakelawnresort.com. **Facility Holes:** 18. **Yards:** 6,201/5,054. **Par:** 70/70. **Course Rating:** 70.0/69.4. **Slope:** 124/116. **Green Fee:** $18/$69. **Cart Fee:** Included in green fee. **Walking Policy:** Walking at certain times. **Walkability:** 3. **Opened:** 1921. **Architect:** Dick Nugent. **Season:** March-Nov. **High:** May-Sept. **To obtain tee times:** Call up to 14 days in advance. **Miscellaneous:** Reduced fees (weekdays, guests, twilight), range (grass), lodging (284 rooms), credit cards (MC, V, AE, D, DC, CB), BF, FF.

Reader Comments: Great resort course, greens in nice shape ... Average resort course ... Narrow fairways, good resort ... Very nice resort & course, excellent family getaway; price right, no problems ... Short but very challenging approaches.

★½ LAKE PARK GOLF COURSE

PU-N. 112 W. 17300 Mequon Rd., Germantown, 53022, Washington County, (262)255-4200, 15 miles from Milwaukee. **Facility Holes:** 27. **Green Fee:** $10/$29. **Cart Fee:** $12/Person. **Walking Policy:** Unrestricted walking. **Walkability:** 2. **Opened:** 1974. **Architect:** Lloyd B. Robinson. **Season:** April-Nov. **High:** June-Aug. **To obtain tee times:** Call golf shop. **Misc:** Reduced fees (weekdays, twilight, seniors), metal spikes, credit cards (MC, V), FF.

RED/BLUE (18 Combo)
Yards: 6,642/5,875. **Par:** 72/73. **Course Rating:** 71.9/76.0. **Slope:** 126/129.
RED/WHITE (18 Combo)
Yards: 7,010/6,069. **Par:** 72/75. **Course Rating:** 73.6/77.2. **Slope:** 131/134.
WHITE/BLUE (18 Combo)
Yards: 6,812/6,068. **Par:** 72/76. **Course Rating:** 72.9/77.0. **Slope:** 126/131.

★½ LAKE SHORE GOLF COURSE

PU-2175 Punhoqua St., Oshkosh, 54901, Winnebago County, (920)235-6200, 85 miles from Milwaukee. **Facility Holes:** 18. **Yards:** 6,030/5,162. **Par:** 70/71. **Course Rating:** 68.2/69.4. **Slope:** 120/119. **Green Fee:** $17/$18. **Cart Fee:** $19/Cart. **Walking Policy:** Unrestricted walking. **Walkability:** 1. **Opened:** 1920. **Architect:** Williams/Gill. **Season:** April-Oct. **To obtain tee times:** Call golf shop. **Miscellaneous:** Reduced fees (weekdays, twilight, seniors, juniors), range (grass/mats), credit cards (MC, V), BF, FF.

★★½ LAKE WINDSOR GOLF CLUB
SP-4628 Golf Rd., Windsor, 53598, Dane County, (608)255-6100, 5 miles from Madison. **Facility Holes:** 27. **Green Fee:** $10/$20. **Cart Fee:** $9/Person. **Walking Policy:** Unrestricted walking. **Walkability:** 3. **Opened:** 1963. **Season:** April-Dec. **High:** June-Aug. **To obtain tee times:** Call up to 7 days in advance. **Miscellaneous:** Reduced fees (weekdays, juniors), credit cards (MC, V), BF, FF.
RED/BLUE (18 Combo)
Yards: 5,983/5,143. **Par:** 71/71. **Course Rating:** 68.0/72.0. **Slope:** 115/122.
RED/WHITE (18 Combo)
Yards: 6,228/5,348. **Par:** 72/72. **Course Rating:** 69.2/73.0. **Slope:** 118/127.
WHITE/BLUE (18 Combo)
Yards: 6,157/5,215. **Par:** 71/71. **Course Rating:** 68.5/73.0. **Slope:** 118/127.

★★½ LAKE WISCONSIN COUNTRY CLUB
SP-N1076 Golf Rd., Prairie Du Sac, 53578, Columbia County, (608)643-2405, 2 miles from Prairie Du Sac. **E-mail:** jebud@merr.com. **Facility Holes:** 18. **Yards:** 5,860/5,147. **Par:** 70/71. **Course Rating:** 68.2/69.3. **Slope:** 116/115. **Green Fee:** $33/$38. **Cart Fee:** $27/Cart. **Walking Policy:** Unrestricted walking. **Walkability:** 2. **Opened:** 1925. **Season:** March-Nov. **High:** June-Aug. **To obtain tee times:** Call up to 7 days in advance. **Miscellaneous:** Range (grass), credit cards (MC, V, AE), BF, FF.

★★★ LAKEWOODS FOREST RIDGES GOLF COURSE
R-H.C. 73, Cable, 54821, Bayfield County, (715)794-2698, (800)255-5937, 80 miles from Duluth. **E-mail:** info@lakewoodsresort.com. **Web:** www.lakewoodsresort.com. **Facility Holes:** 18. **Yards:** 6,270/4,442. **Par:** 71/71. **Course Rating:** 70.9/66.9. **Slope:** 137/123. **Green Fee:** $45/$55. **Cart Fee:** Included in green fee. **Walking Policy:** Mandatory carts. **Walkability:** 4. **Opened:** 1995. **Architect:** Joel Goldstrand. **Season:** April-Oct. **Tee times:** Call golf shop. **Misc:** Reduced fees (guests, twilight), range (grass/mats), credit cards (MC, V, D), BF, FF.
Reader Comments: Course is outstanding, peaceful and serene. It's a great place to play ... Narrow & difficult, unfair landing areas ... Very challenging course, excellent condition, unique holes ... Cut through the woods. Some neat holes.

LINCOLN PARK GOLF COURSE
PU-1000 West Hampton Avenue, Milwaukee, 53209, Milwaukee County, (414)962-2400, 5 miles from Milwaukee. **Web:** www.countyparks.com. **Facility Holes:** 9. **Yards:** 2,538/2,538. **Par:** 33/33. **Green Fee:** $11/$22. **Cart Fee:** $25/Cart. **Walking Policy:** Unrestricted walking. **Walkability:** 2. **Opened:** 1928. **Season:** Year-round. **To obtain tee times:** Call golf shop. **Miscellaneous:** Reduced fees (twilight, seniors, juniors), credit cards (MC, V), FF.

LITTLE RIVER COUNTRY CLUB
SP-N2235 Shore Dr., Marinette, 54143, Marinette County, (715)732-2221, 2 miles from Marinette. **Web:** www.geocities.com/lr.cc. **Facility Holes:** 18. **Yards:** 5,749/5,083. **Par:** 70/71. **Course Rating:** 65.7/68.0. **Slope:** 108/111. **Green Fee:** $21/$24. **Cart Fee:** $23/Cart. **Walking Policy:** Unrestricted walking. **Walkability:** 1. **Opened:** 1927. **Season:** April-Nov. **To obtain tee times:** Call up to 7 days in advance. **Miscellaneous:** Reduced fees (weekdays, juniors), range (grass), credit cards (MC, V), BF, FF.

★★½ LUCK GOLF COURSE
PU-1520 S. Shore Dr., Luck, 54853, Polk County, (715)472-2939, (866)465-3582, 65 miles from St. Paul. **Facility Holes:** 18. **Yards:** 6,122/5,198. **Par:** 71/72. **Course Rating:** 70.0/70.4. **Slope:** 122/119. **Green Fee:** $21/$29. **Cart Fee:** $13/Person. **Walking Policy:** Unrestricted walking. **Walkability:** 3. **Opened:** 1938. **Architect:** Gordon Emerson. **Season:** April-Oct. **High:** June-Aug. **To obtain tee times:** Call up to 10 days in advance. **Miscellaneous:** Reduced fees (weekdays, juniors), range (grass), credit cards (MC, V), BF, FF.

★★★ MADELINE ISLAND GOLF CLUB
SP-P.O. Box 83, La Pointe, 54850, Ashland County, (715)747-3212, 25 miles from Ashland. **Facility Holes:** 18. **Yards:** 6,366/5,506. **Par:** 71/72. **Course Rating:** 71.0/71.7. **Slope:** 131/127. **Green Fee:** $36/$47. **Cart Fee:** $26/Cart. **Walking Policy:** Unrestricted walking. **Walkability:** 3. **Opened:** 1966. **Architect:** Robert Trent Jones. **Season:** May-Oct. **High:** June-Sept. **Tee times:** Call golf shop. **Misc:** Reduced fees (twilight, juniors), range (grass), credit cards (MC, V).

WISCONSIN

★★ MAPLE GROVE COUNTRY CLUB
PU-W. 4142 County B, West Salem, 54669, La Crosse County, (608)786-0340, 10 miles from La Crosse. **E-mail:** tacmgcc@fflax.net. **Facility Holes:** 18. **Yards:** 6,485/5,578. **Par:** 71/71. **Course Rating:** 70.1/70.9. **Slope:** 122/121. **Green Fee:** $22/$24. **Cart Fee:** $26/Cart. **Walking Policy:** Unrestricted walking. **Walkability:** 3. **Opened:** 1929. **Architect:** Leland Thompson. **Season:** April-Nov. **High:** June-Aug. **To obtain tee times:** Call up to 6 days in advance. **Miscellaneous:** Reduced fees (weekdays, twilight, seniors), metal spikes, range (grass), credit cards (MC, V), BF, FF.

★★½ MAPLECREST COUNTRY CLUB
PU-9401 18th St., Kenosha, 53144, Kenosha County, (262)859-2887, 25 miles from Milwaukee. **Facility Holes:** 18. **Yards:** 6,396/5,056. **Par:** 71/71. **Course Rating:** 70.9/71.0. **Slope:** 121/124. **Green Fee:** $19/$26. **Cart Fee:** $25/Cart. **Walking Policy:** Unrestricted walking. **Walkability:** 2. **Opened:** 1929. **Architect:** Leonard Macomber. **Season:** March-Nov. **High:** May-Oct. **To obtain tee times:** Call up to 7 days in advance. **Miscellaneous:** Reduced fees (twilight, seniors), range (grass), credit cards (MC, V), FF.

★½ MARSHFIELD COUNTRY CLUB
PU-11426 Wren Rd., Marshfield, 54449, Wood County, (715)384-4409, (800)690-4409, 1 mile from Marshfield. **Facility Holes:** 18. **Yards:** 6,004/5,376. **Par:** 70/70. **Slope:** 115/111. **Green Fee:** $17/$18. **Cart Fee:** $20/Cart. **Walking Policy:** Unrestricted walking. **Season:** April-Nov. **High:** May-Sept. **Tee times:** Call golf shop. **Miscellaneous:** Reduced fees (weekdays, twilight, seniors, juniors), metal spikes, range (grass/mats), credit cards (MC, V, AE, D).

★★★★ MASCOUTIN GOLF CLUB
PU-W1635 County Trunk A, Berlin, 54923, Green Lake County, (920)361-2360, 20 miles from Oshkosh. **E-mail:** mcc@dotnet.com. **Web:** www.mascoutingolf.com. **Facility Holes:** 27. **Green Fee:** $27/$45. **Cart Fee:** $14/Person. **Walking Policy:** Walking at certain times. **Walkability:** 3. **Opened:** 1975. **Architect:** Larry Packard/Rick Jacobson. **Season:** April-Nov. **High:** June-Sept. **To obtain tee times:** Call golf shop. **Miscellaneous:** Reduced fees (weekdays, twilight, juniors), range (grass), credit cards (MC, V), FF.
BLUE/RED (18 Combo)
Yards: 6,883/5,118. **Par:** 72/69. **Course Rating:** 72.9/69.4. **Slope:** 130/120.
RED/WHITE (18) Combo
Yards: 6,821/5,133. **Par:** 72/73. **Course Rating:** 72.8/69.9. **Slope:** 130/122.
WHITE/BLUE (18 Combo)
Yards: 6,860/5,009. **Par:** 72/72. **Course Rating:** 72.9/68.9. **Slope:** 130/119.
Reader Comments: Great layout, doglegs, sand, water, has it all ... Little surprises, beautiful shape ... Busy place, even in October ... Great variety ... Great contrasting 9s ... Tough greens. A great layout ... Excellent course.

★½ MAXWELTON BRAES GOLF RESORT
PU-7670 Hwy. 57, Baileys Harbor, 54202, Door County, (920)839-2321, 18 miles from Sturgeon Bay. **E-mail:** information@maxwelton-braes.com. **Web:** www.maxwelton-braes.com. **Facility Holes:** 18. **Yards:** 6,041/5,857. **Par:** 70/74. **Course Rating:** 68.7/74.0. **Slope:** 114/122. **Green Fee:** $22/$27. **Cart Fee:** $12/Person. **Walking Policy:** Unrestricted walking. **Walkability:** 3. **Opened:** 1929. **Architect:** George O'Neil/Joseph A. Roseman. **Season:** April-Nov. **High:** June-Sept. **To obtain tee times:** Call golf shop. **Miscellaneous:** Reduced fees (twilight, juniors), lodging (24 rooms), credit cards (MC, V, AE, D), BF, FF.

★★ MAYVILLE GOLF CLUB
PU-325 S. German St., Mayville, 53050, Dodge County, (920)387-2999, 25 miles from Fond du Lac. **Facility Holes:** 18. **Yards:** 6,173/5,235. **Par:** 71/72. **Course Rating:** 69.5/70.0. **Slope:** 119/115. **Green Fee:** $24/$29. **Cart Fee:** $14/Person. **Walking Policy:** Unrestricted walking. **Walkability:** 4. **Opened:** 1931. **Architect:** Bob Lohmann. **Season:** April-Nov. **High:** June-Aug. **To obtain tee times:** Call up to 7 days in advance. **Miscellaneous:** Reduced fees (weekdays, twilight, seniors, juniors), credit cards (MC, V), BF, FF.

★★★ MCGAUSLIN BROOK GOLF & COUNTRY CLUB
SP-17067 Clubhouse Lane, Lakewood, 54138, Oconto County, (715)276-7623, 75 miles from Green Bay. **Facility Holes:** 18. **Yards:** 5,926/4,886. **Par:** 70/70. **Course Rating:** 67.1/62.5. **Slope:** 115/105. **Green Fee:** $22/$27. **Cart Fee:** $22/Cart. **Walking Policy:** Unrestricted walking. **Walkability:** 2. **Opened:** 1965. **Season:** April-Oct. **High:** July-Aug. **Tee times:** Call up to 3 days in advance. **Miscellaneous:** Reduced fees (weekdays), credit cards (MC, V, AE, D). **Reader Comments:** Front 9 offers roomy fairways, open rough areas, back 9 has more character and beauty, mature trees, fairways are not as wide or open ... Nice resort course, fun layout. ·

★★ MEADOW LINKS GOLF COURSE

PU-1540 Johnston Dr., Manitowoc, 54220, Manitowoc County, (920)682-6842, 35 miles from Green Bay. **Facility Holes:** 18. **Yards:** 5,934/5,254. **Par:** 72/72. **Course Rating:** 67.8/69.2. **Slope:** 114/114. **Green Fee:** $13/$20. **Cart Fee:** $20/Cart. **Walking Policy:** Unrestricted walking. **Walkability:** 3. **Opened:** 1929. **Season:** April-Oct. **High:** June-Aug. **To obtain tee times:** Call golf shop. **Miscellaneous:** Reduced fees (seniors, juniors), credit cards (MC, V).

★★★ MEEK-KWON PARK GOLF COURSE

PU-6333 W. Bonniwell Rd, 136N., Mequon, 53097, Ozaukee County, (262)242-1310, 25 miles from Milwaukee. **Facility Holes:** 18. **Yards:** 6,486/5,249. **Par:** 70/70. **Course Rating:** 70.6/69.5. **Slope:** 122/117. **Green Fee:** $13/$26. **Cart Fee:** $24/Cart. **Walking Policy:** Unrestricted walking. **Walkability:** 4. **Opened:** 1974. **Season:** April-Nov. **High:** June-Sept. **To obtain tee times:** Call up to 10 days in advance. **Miscellaneous:** Reduced fees (weekdays, seniors, juniors), credit cards (MC, V, D), FF.
Reader Comments: Fast and not too many people play it ... More challenging than I thought it would be ... Slow play ... Excellent value. Great improvements in fairways, greens and tee boxes, excellent ... Great views, good county course.

★★½ MERRILL GOLF CLUB

PU-1604 O'Day St., Merrill, 54452, Lincoln County, (715)536-2529, 20 miles from Wausaw. **Facility Holes:** 18. **Yards:** 6,456/5,432. **Par:** 72/72. **Course Rating:** 70.2/70.0. **Slope:** 120/111. **Green Fee:** $12/$21. **Cart Fee:** $21/Cart. **Walking Policy:** Unrestricted walking. **Walkability:** 3. **Opened:** 1932. **Architect:** Tom Vardon. **Season:** April-Oct. **High:** June-Aug. **To obtain tee times:** Call golf shop. **Miscellaneous:** Reduced fees (weekdays, twilight, seniors, juniors), range (mats), credit cards (MC, V, AE, D).

★★★ MID-VALLEE GOLF COURSE

PU-3134 Apple Creek Rd., De Pere, 54115, Brown County, (920)532-6674, 10 miles from Green Bay. **Facility Holes:** 27. **Green Fee:** $18/$24. **Cart Fee:** $22/Cart. **Walking Policy:** Unrestricted walking. **Walkability:** 3. **Opened:** 1963. **Architect:** Edward Lockie. **Season:** April-Oct. **High:** June-Aug. **To obtain tee times:** Call golf shop. **Miscellaneous:** Reduced fees (weekdays, twilight, seniors, juniors), range (grass/mats), credit cards (MC, V).
BLUE/WHITE (18 Combo)
Yards: 6,134/5,025. **Par:** 70/70. **Course Rating:** 69.1. **Slope:** 122/119.
RED/BLUE (18 Combo)
Yards: 6,024/4,952. **Par:** 70/70. **Course Rating:** 69.1. **Slope:** 122/120.
RED/WHITE (18 Combo)
Yards: 6,078/5,193. **Par:** 70/70. **Course Rating:** 69.1/68.3. **Slope:** 122/118.
Reader Comments: Bent-grass fairways are improving, great value ... In good shape, good value ... Short course, but fair ... Good condition, OK design ... Perfect stop on your way to Packer's game ... Slow play at times, a friendly staff.

MILL RUN GOLF CLUB

PU-3905 Kane Rd., Eau Claire, 54703, Eau Claire County, (715)858-7960, (800)241-1766, 65 miles from Minneapolis-St. Paul. **Web:** www.millrungolf.com. **Facility Holes:** 36. **Cart Fee:** $13/Person. **Walking Policy:** Unrestricted walking. **Season:** March-Nov. **High:** April-Oct. **To obtain tee times:** Call golf shop. **Misc:** Range (grass), credit cards (MC, V), BF, FF.
★★★½ HIDDEN CREEK AT MILL RUN (18)
Yards: 6,078/4,744. **Par:** 70/71. **Course Rating:** 68.7/66.6. **Slope:** 116/109. **Green Fee:** $23/$26. **Walkability:** 2. **Opened:** 1981. **Architect:** Gordon Emerson. **Miscellaneous:** Reduced fees (weekdays, seniors, juniors).
Reader Comments: Lots of trees ... Good value, nice layout ... Course is the best ever, everyone should play it ... Short, but well kept.
WILD RIDGE AT MILL RUN (18)
Yards: 7,034/5,252. **Par:** 72/72. **Course Rating:** 73.5/70.3. **Slope:** 133/120. **Green Fee:** $38/$40. **Walkability:** 4. **Opened:** 1999. **Architect:** Greg Martin. **Misc:** Reduced fees (twilight).

★★½ MUSKEGO LAKES COUNTRY CLUB

SP-S. 100 W. 14020 Loomis Rd., Muskego, 53150, Waukesha County, (414)425-6500, 13 miles from Milwaukee. **E-mail:** mlcc@muskegolakes.com. **Web:** www.muskegolakes.com. **Facility Holes:** 18. **Yards:** 6,498/5,493. **Par:** 71/72. **Course Rating:** 71.5/71.7. **Slope:** 126/123. **Green Fee:** $22/$34. **Cart Fee:** $14/Person. **Walking Policy:** Unrestricted walking. **Walkability:** 2. **Opened:** 1969. **Architect:** Larry Packard. **Season:** March-Nov. **High:** May-Sept. **To obtain tee times:** Call up to 7 days in advance. **Miscellaneous:** Reduced fees (weekdays, twilight, seniors, juniors), range (grass/mats), credit cards (MC, V, AE, D), BF, FF.

WISCONSIN

★★½ MYSTERY HILLS GOLF CLUB
PU-3149 Dickinson Rd., De Pere, 54115, Brown County, (920)336-6077, 2 miles from Green Bay. **Facility Holes:** 27. **Yards:** 6,254/5,569. **Par:** 72/72. **Course Rating:** 70.1/72.2. **Slope:** 120/120. **Green Fee:** $21/$23. **Cart Fee:** $26/Cart. **Walking Policy:** Unrestricted walking. **Walkability:** 4. **Opened:** 1963. **Season:** March-Nov. **High:** May-Sept. **To obtain tee times:** Call up to 30 days in advance. **Miscellaneous:** Reduced fees (weekdays, seniors, juniors), range (grass/mats), credit cards (MC, V, D), BF, FF.
Special Notes: Also has a 9-hole executive course.

★★★★ NAGA-WAUKEE GOLF COURSE   *Value*
PU-1897 Maple Ave., Pewaukee, 53072, Waukesha County, (262)367-2153, 20 miles from Milwaukee. **Facility Holes:** 18. **Yards:** 6,780/5,796. **Par:** 72/72. **Course Rating:** 71.8/72.6. **Slope:** 125/125. **Green Fee:** $20/$35. **Cart Fee:** $13/Person. **Walking Policy:** Unrestricted walking. **Walkability:** 3. **Opened:** 1966. **Architect:** Lawrence Packard. **Season:** April-Dec. **High:** May-Sept. **To obtain tee times:** Call golf shop. **Miscellaneous:** Reduced fees (weekdays, twilight, seniors, juniors), metal spikes, range (grass/mats), credit cards (MC, V).
Reader Comments: Best muni in Wisconsin ... Great layout, difficult to get tee time ... Good course, hills, hills & more hills ... Must play, great course, beautiful ... Excellent layout, great price ... Great course & value.

NEMADJI GOLF COURSE
PU-5 N. 58th St. E., Superior, 54880, Douglas County, (715)394-0266, 1 mile from Superior. **E-mail:** suppro@aol.com. **Web:** www.nemadjigolf.com. **Facility Holes:** 36. **Green Fee:** $12/$25. **Cart Fee:** $20/Cart. **Walking Policy:** Unrestricted walking. **Season:** April-Nov. **High:** June-Sept. **To obtain tee times:** Call up to 14 days in advance. **Miscellaneous:** Reduced fees (twilight, juniors), range (grass/mats), caddies, credit cards (MC, V, AE, D), BF, FF.
★★★★ EAST/WEST COURSE (18)
Yards: 6,701/5,252. **Par:** 72/72. **Course Rating:** 72.7/70.7. **Slope:** 133/124. **Walkability:** 3. **Opened:** 1981. **Architect:** D.W. Herfort.
Reader Comments: Beautiful course, deer all over, great shape, played in under 4 hours ... Great golf, great value ... Too many playing, play was slow ... Course condition and value are great.
★★★ NORTH/SOUTH COURSE (18)
Yards: 6,362/4,983. **Par:** 71/71. **Course Rating:** 69.7/67.8. **Slope:** 120/114. **Walkability:** 1. **Opened:** 1932. **Architect:** Stanley Pelchar.
Reader Comments: Good, not as tough as other courses ... Basic golf, great value ... Good scoring course, wide & flat fairways ... Course condition and value are great. Excellent value.

★★★ NEW BERLIN HILLS GOLF COURSE
PU-13175 W. Graham St., New Berlin, 53151, Waukesha County, (262)780-5200, 9 miles from Milwaukee. **E-mail:** newberlin@crowngolf.com. **Facility Holes:** 18. **Yards:** 6,517/5,346. **Par:** 71/71. **Course Rating:** 71.7/70.8. **Slope:** 127/123. **Green Fee:** $18/$31. **Cart Fee:** $13/Person. **Walking Policy:** Unrestricted walking. **Walkability:** 3. **Opened:** 1908. **Season:** April-Nov. **High:** May-Sept. **To obtain tee times:** Call golf shop. **Miscellaneous:** Reduced fees (seniors, juniors), credit cards (MC, V).
Reader Comments: A lot of improvement last few years ... Nice urban course, tends to flood ... Very hard fast greens, nice layout, creek comes into play often, nice new clubhouse.

★★★★ NEW RICHMOND GOLF CLUB
SP-1226 180th Ave., New Richmond, 54017, St. Croix County, (715)246-6724, 30 miles from St. Paul. **Facility Holes:** 27. **Yards:** 6,716/5,547. **Par:** 72/73. **Course Rating:** 72.5/71.7. **Slope:** 136/129. **Green Fee:** $28/$33. **Cart Fee:** $12/Person. **Walking Policy:** Unrestricted walking. **Walkability:** 3. **Opened:** 1923. **Architect:** Willie Kidd/Don Herfort. **Season:** April-Oct. **To obtain tee times:** Call up to 5 days in advance. **Miscellaneous:** Reduced fees (seniors, juniors), range (grass), credit cards (MC, V), BF, FF.
Reader Comments: Excellent course ... Well-kept secret, not sure I want your readers to know about it ... Old course, in great condition ... Good challenging layout, good variety ... Nice course, busy, long rounds ... Lovely unsung gem.
Special Notes: Also has a 9-hole Links Course.

★★ NICOLET COUNTRY CLUB
PU-Hwy. 8, 5245 Fairway Ct., Laona, 54541, Forest County, (715)674-4780, 1 mile from Laona. **E-mail:** nccgolf@newnorth.net. **Web:** www.nicoletcountryclub.com. **Facility Holes:** 18. **Yards:** 4,713/4,093. **Par:** 67/67. **Course Rating:** 62.2/62.3. **Slope:** 104/100. **Green Fee:** $19/$23. **Cart Fee:** $22/Cart. **Walking Policy:** Unrestricted walking. **Walkability:** 2. **Opened:** 1960. **Season:** April-Nov. **High:** June-Oct. **To obtain tee times:** Call up to 7 days in advance. **Miscellaneous:** Reduced fees (juniors), range (grass), credit cards (MC, V), BF, FF.

★★★ NIPPERSINK GOLF CLUB & RESORT

PU-N. 1055 Tombeau Rd., Genoa City, 53128, Walworth County, (262)279-6311, (888)744-6944, 50 miles from Chicago. **E-mail:** nippergolf@aol.com. **Web:** www.nip-persinkgolf.com. **Facility Holes:** 18. **Yards:** 6,600/5,827. **Par:** 71/71. **Course Rating:** 72.3/67.1. **Slope:** 126/113. **Green Fee:** $22/$32. **Cart Fee:** $26/Cart. **Walking Policy:** Walking at certain times. **Walkability:** 3. **Opened:** 1922. **Architect:** James Foulis, Jr. **Season:** March-Nov. **High:** May-Oct. **To obtain tee times:** Call golf shop. **Miscellaneous:** Reduced fees (weekdays, guests, twilight, seniors, juniors), lodging (44 rooms), credit cards (MC, V, D), BF, FF.
Reader Comments: Great deal ... Wonderful old course, better conditions in the last 2 years ... Very pleasant staff ... Fun to play.

★★★★ NORTHBROOK COUNTRY CLUB *Value*

SP-407 NorthBrook Dr., Luxemburg, 54217, Kewaunee County, (920)845-2383, 15 miles from Green Bay. **E-mail:** jnadeau601@aol.com. **Facility Holes:** 18. **Yards:** 6,223/5,495. **Par:** 71/72. **Course Rating:** 69.2/70.9. **Slope:** 121/116. **Green Fee:** $16/$25. **Cart Fee:** $12/Person. **Walking Policy:** Unrestricted walking. **Walkability:** 2. **Opened:** 1971. **Architect:** Ed Langert. **Season:** March-Nov. **High:** June-Aug. **To obtain tee times:** Call up to 7 days in advance. **Miscellaneous:** Reduced fees (weekdays, seniors, juniors), range (grass), caddies, credit cards (MC, V), BF, FF.
Reader Comments: Always fun to play, front very straight, back more of a challenge ... Very good! Hole 10 is awesome! ... One of the best in area ... Short, nice greens, good value ... Always immaculate, a few tough holes.

★★★★½ NORTHWOOD GOLF COURSE *Value*

PU-3131 Golf Course Rd., Rhinelander, 54501, Oneida County, (715)282-6565, 2 miles from Rhinelander. **Facility Holes:** 18. **Yards:** 6,724/5,338. **Par:** 72/72. **Course Rating:** 73.1/71.3. **Slope:** 140/129. **Green Fee:** $31. **Cart Fee:** $30/Cart. **Walking Policy:** Unrestricted walking. **Walkability:** 4. **Opened:** 1989. **Architect:** Don Herfort. **Season:** April-Oct. **High:** June-Aug. **To obtain tee times:** Call up to 14 days in advance. **Miscellaneous:** Reduced fees (twilight, juniors), range (grass), credit cards (MC, V), BF, FF.
Reader Comments: Tight, great greens, good value ... Straight hits a must, very wooded ... Great course, people were great, food excellent ... Treacherous, frustrating, outstanding ... First-rate, you'll hit every club, best greens, fast.

OAK RIDGE GOLF COURSE

SP-1238 Bowers Lake Rd., Milton, 53563, Rock County, (608)868-4353, 4 miles from Janesville. **Facility Holes:** 27. **Yards:** 5,949/5,519. **Par:** 71/72. **Course Rating:** 69.9/69.5. **Slope:** 117/111. **Green Fee:** $20/$23. **Cart Fee:** $20/Cart. **Walking Policy:** Unrestricted walking. **Walkability:** 2. **Opened:** 1975. **Season:** March-Oct. **High:** June-Aug. **To obtain tee times:** Call up to 7 days in advance. **Miscellaneous:** Reduced fees (seniors, juniors), range (grass), credit cards (MC, V, D), BF, FF.
Special Notes: Also has a 9-hole course.

★★★ OAKWOOD PARK GOLF COURSE

PU-3600 W. Oakwood Rd., Franklin, 53132, Milwaukee County, (414)281-6700, 8 miles from Milwaukee. **E-mail:** progolf@execpc.com. **Web:** www.mkegolf.com. **Facility Holes:** 18. **Yards:** 7,008/6,179. **Par:** 72/72. **Course Rating:** 72.5/74.4. **Slope:** 121/123. **Green Fee:** $13/$29. **Cart Fee:** $25/Cart. **Walking Policy:** Unrestricted walking. **Walkability:** 2. **Opened:** 1971. **Architect:** Edward Lawrence Packard. **Season:** April-Dec. **High:** June-Sept. **To obtain tee times:** Call up to 5 days in advance. **Miscellaneous:** Reduced fees (weekdays, seniors, juniors), range (grass/mats), credit cards (MC, V), BF, FF.
Reader Comments: Good layout, OK facilities, a good challenge ... Great practice areas ... Long, fairly wide open, but you'll need every club in the bag ... Long, open, great muni for serious golfer ... Nice course, very open fairways.

★★★★½ OLD HICKORY COUNTRY CLUB *Pace*

SP-Hwy. 33 E., W7596, Beaver Dam, 53916, Dodge County, (920)887-7577, 30 miles from Madison. **E-mail:** stevek@internetwis.com. **Web:** www.oldhickorycc.com. **Facility Holes:** 18. **Yards:** 6,721/5,372. **Par:** 72/73. **Course Rating:** 72.5/72.8. **Slope:** 129/127. **Green Fee:** $40/$50. **Cart Fee:** $14/Person. **Walking Policy:** Unrestricted walking. **Walkability:** 4. **Opened:** 1920. **Architect:** Tom Bendelow. **Season:** April-Oct. **High:** June-Aug. **To obtain tee times:** Call up to 7 days in advance. **Miscellaneous:** Range (grass/mats), credit cards (MC, V), FF.
Reader Comments: Old course, lots of trees ... Great value ... A classic course, tree-lined fairways ... Just a classy place ... Some blind holes, but still a joy ... Tough course, fast greens ... Beautiful course, fees are high.

WISCONSIN

★★½ **OLYMPIA SPORTS CENTER**
PU-965 Cannongate Rd., Oconomowoc, 53066, Waukesha County, (262)567-6048, 30 miles from Milwaukee. **E-mail:** oldeighlander@hotmail.com. **Web:** www.olympiasportscenter.com. **Facility Holes:** 18. **Yards:** 6,458/5,688. **Par:** 72/71. **Course Rating:** 70.5/72.4. **Slope:** 118/119. **Green Fee:** $24/$28. **Cart Fee:** $12/Person. **Walking Policy:** Walking at certain times. **Walkability:** 2. **Opened:** 1971. **Architect:** Randy Warobick. **Season:** March-Dec. **To obtain tee times:** Call up to 7 days in advance. **Miscellaneous:** Reduced fees (weekdays, twilight, seniors, juniors), range (grass), lodging (300 rooms), credit cards (MC, V, AE, D), BF, FF.

THE ORCHARDS AT EGG HARBOR GOLF CLUB
PU-8125 Elm Rd., Egg Harbor, 54209-0176, Door County, (920)868-2483, (888)463-4653, 45 miles from Green Bay. **E-mail:** thorchards@itol.com. **Web:** www.orchardsateggharbor.com. **Facility Holes:** 18. **Yards:** 7,005/5,400. **Par:** 72/72. **Course Rating:** 74.4. **Slope:** 130/121. **Green Fee:** $39/$47. **Cart Fee:** $12/Person. **Walking Policy:** Walking at certain times. **Opened:** 2000. **Architect:** William Newcomb. **Season:** April-Nov. **To obtain tee times:** Call golf shop. **Miscellaneous:** Reduced fees (twilight), range (grass), FF.

★½ **PAGANICA GOLF COURSE**
PU-3850 Silverlake St., Oconomowoc, 53066, Waukesha County, (262)567-0171, 29 miles from Milwaukee. **Facility Holes:** 18. **Yards:** 6,576/5,663. **Par:** 72/74. **Course Rating:** 70.7/71.5. **Slope:** 116/116. **Green Fee:** $26/$28. **Cart Fee:** $13/Person. **Walking Policy:** Unrestricted walking. **Walkability:** 2. **Opened:** 1965. **Architect:** Luke Frye. **Season:** April-Nov. **High:** June-Aug. **To obtain tee times:** Call up to 7 days in advance. **Miscellaneous:** Reduced fees (seniors), range (grass), BF, FF.

★★ **PECKS WILDWOOD GOLF COURSE**
PU-10080 Highway 70 W., Minocqua, 54548, Oneida County, (715)356-3477, 70 miles from Wausau. **Facility Holes:** 18. **Yards:** 5,869/5,483. **Par:** 71/71. **Course Rating:** 68.6/71.0. **Slope:** 115/118. **Green Fee:** $25. **Cart Fee:** $20/Cart. **Walking Policy:** Unrestricted walking. **Opened:** 1983. **To obtain tee times:** Call golf shop. **Miscellaneous:** Range (mats), credit cards (MC, V).

★★★½ **PENINSULA STATE PARK GOLF COURSE**
PU-Hwy. 42, Ephraim, 54211, Door County, (920)854-5791, 70 miles from Green Bay. **Facility Holes:** 18. **Yards:** 6,304/5,428. **Par:** 71/72. **Course Rating:** 69.8/70.6. **Slope:** 123/121. **Green Fee:** $24/$28. **Cart Fee:** $24/Cart. **Walking Policy:** Unrestricted walking. **Walkability:** 4. **Opened:** 1921. **Architect:** Edward Lawrence Packard. **Season:** May-Nov. **High:** June-Sept. **To obtain tee times:** Call up to 14 days in advance. **Miscellaneous:** Reduced fees (twilight, juniors), range (grass), credit cards (MC, V), BF, FF.
Reader Comments: Hilly scenic views. Slow play! ... Perfect layout for a relaxing round in a beautiful location ... Great layout cut through a state park ... Good front 9, fantastic back 9.

★★½ **PETRIFYING SPRINGS GOLF COURSE**
PU-4909 7th St., Kenosha, 53144, Kenosha County, (262)552-9052, 1 mile from Kenosha. **Facility Holes:** 18. **Yards:** 5,979/5,588. **Par:** 71/72. **Course Rating:** 67.8/70.9. **Slope:** 119/122. **Green Fee:** $22/$28. **Cart Fee:** $24/Cart. **Walking Policy:** Unrestricted walking. **Walkability:** 3. **Opened:** 1936. **Architect:** Joseph A. Roseman. **Season:** March-Nov. **High:** June-Aug. **To obtain tee times:** Call golf shop. **Miscellaneous:** Credit cards (MC, V), BF, FF.

★½ **PINEWOOD COUNTRY CLUB**
PU-4660 Lakewood Rd., Harshaw, 54529, Oneida County, (715)282-5500, (888)674-6396, 15 miles from Minocqua. **E-mail:** cbgolf1@newnorth.net. **Web:** www.pinewoodcc.com. **Facility Holes:** 18. **Yards:** 6,245/4,854. **Par:** 70/70. **Course Rating:** 69.8/67.7. **Slope:** 123/115. **Green Fee:** $20/$27. **Cart Fee:** $13/Person. **Walking Policy:** Unrestricted walking. **Walkability:** 5. **Opened:** 1962. **Architect:** Al Broman Jr. **Season:** April-Oct. **High:** July-Aug. **To obtain tee times:** Call up to 30 days in advance. **Miscellaneous:** Reduced fees (twilight, juniors), range (grass/mats), lodging (8 rooms), credit cards (MC, V, D), BF, FF.

★★½ **PLEASANT VIEW GOLF CLUB**
PU-1322 Pleasant View Dr., Middleton, 53562, Dane County, (608)831-6666, 1 mile from Madison. **Facility Holes:** 18. **Yards:** 6,436/5,514. **Par:** 72/72. **Course Rating:** 70.0/67.5. **Slope:** 122/116. **Green Fee:** $25/$29. **Cart Fee:** $28/Cart. **Walking Policy:** Unrestricted walking. **Walkability:** 5. **Opened:** 1957. **Architect:** Art Johnson. **Season:** April-Oct. **High:** June-Aug. **To obtain tee times:** Call golf shop. **Miscellaneous:** Reduced fees (weekdays, twilight, seniors, juniors), range (grass/mats), credit cards (MC, V).
Special Notes: Also has a par-3 course.

★★★½ PORTAGE COUNTRY CLUB
SP-E. Hwy. No. 33, Portage, 53901, Columbia County, (608)742-5121, 6 miles from Portage.
Facility Holes: 18. **Yards:** 6,356/4,946. **Par:** 72/74. **Course Rating:** 70.4/68.0. **Slope:** 127/119.
Green Fee: $30/$36. **Cart Fee:** $15/Person. **Walking Policy:** Unrestricted walking. **Walkability:**
3. **Architect:** Art Johnson. **Season:** April-Oct. **High:** June-Aug. **To obtain tee times:** Call up to 7
days in advance. **Misc:** Reduced fees (weekdays), range (grass), credit cards (MC, V), BF, FF.
Reader Comments: Long carries over marsh, tough for short hitters … Very scenic … Tight fairways, undulating greens … Great setups.

★★★ QUIT-QUI-OC GOLF CLUB
PU-500 Quit-Qui-Oc Lane, Elkhart Lake, 53020, Sheboygan County, (920)876-2833, 50 miles
from Milwaukee. **E-mail:** qqqgolf@aol.com. **Facility Holes:** 27. **Yards:** 6,178/5,134. **Par:** 70/71.
Course Rating: 69.6/64.9. **Slope:** 119/109. **Green Fee:** $23/$26. **Cart Fee:** $13/Person.
Walking Policy: Unrestricted walking. **Walkability:** 4. **Opened:** 1925. **Architect:**
Bendelow/Wiese. **Season:** April-Nov. **High:** June-Sept. **To obtain tee times:** Call up to 4 days
in advance. **Miscellaneous:** Reduced fees (weekdays, guests, twilight, seniors, juniors), range
(grass/mats), credit cards (MC, V, D), BF, FF.
Reader Comments: Nice people, a sporty little course … It appears short and gentle, but it's a real
challenge …Better know how to play sidehill 'lies … Plenty of changes in elevation … A gem of a
course, variety of holes.
Special Notes: Also has a 9-hole course.

★★★ RAINBOW SPRINGS GOLF CLUB
PU-S103 W33599 Hwy. 99, Mukwonago, 53149, Waukesha County, (262)363-4550,
(800)465-3631, 30 miles from Milwaukee. **Facility Holes:** 36. **Yards:** 6,914/5,135. **Par:** 72/72.
Course Rating: 73.4/69.8. **Slope:** 132/120. **Green Fee:** $22/$26. **Cart Fee:** $13/Person.
Walking Policy: Walking at certain times. **Opened:** 1964. **Architect:** Francis Schroedel.
Season: April-Nov. **High:** June-Sept. **To obtain tee times:** Call golf shop. **Misc:** Reduced fees
(weekdays, twilight, seniors, juniors), metal spikes, range (grass), credit cards (MC, V).
Reader Comments: Long course & scenic … Extremely challenging … Lots of H2O. Bring extra
balls … Water everywhere, odd layout … Looks easy, plays hard, water water everywhere.
Special Notes: Also has an 18-hole executive course.

★★★★ REEDSBURG COUNTRY CLUB
SP-Hwy. 33, Reedsburg, 53959, Sauk County, (608)524-6000, 14 miles from Wisconsin Dells.
Facility Holes: 18. **Yards:** 6,300/5,324. **Par:** 72/73. **Course Rating:** 70.5/70.3. **Slope:** 129/124.
Green Fee: $38. **Cart Fee:** $14/Person. **Walking Policy:** Walking at certain times. **Walkability:**
4. **Opened:** 1924. **Architect:** Ken Killian/Dick Nugent. **Season:** March-Nov. **High:** June-Aug.
To obtain tee times: Call golf shop. **Miscellaneous:** Reduced fees (weekdays, twilight), range
(grass), credit cards (MC, V).
Reader Comments: Great town course, mature trees, good variety … Always a pleasure to play,
short, some tight holes … Excellent shape … Interesting & challenging … Just beautiful … Well-
kept course … Fantastic greens.

★★★ REID GOLF COURSE
PU-1100 E. Fremont, Appleton, 54915, Outagamie County, (920)832-5926. **Facility Holes:** 18.
Yards: 5,968/5,296. **Par:** 71/72. **Course Rating:** 67.6/69.1. **Slope:** 114/115. **Green Fee:**
$16/$19. **Cart Fee:** $19/Cart. **Walking Policy:** Unrestricted walking. **Walkability:** 3. **Opened:**
1941. **Architect:** Miller Cohenen. **Season:** April-Oct. **High:** June-Aug. **To obtain tee times:** Call
golf shop. **Miscellaneous:** Reduced fees (twilight, seniors, juniors), metal spikes, range.
Reader Comments: A good muni, great greens … Average course … The best municipal that I
have played.

★★★ THE RIDGES GOLF COURSE
SP-2311 Griffith Ave., Wisconsin Rapids, 54494, Wood County, (715)424-3204, 90 miles from
Madison. **E-mail:** ridges@wctc.net. **Web:** www.ridgesgolfcourse.com. **Facility Holes:** 18. **Yards:**
6,289/5,018. **Par:** 72/72. **Course Rating:** 71.3/69.9. **Slope:** 131/124. **Green Fee:** $32/$42. **Cart
Fee:** $26/Person. **Walking Policy:** Unrestricted walking. **Walkability:** 3. **Opened:** 1963.
Architect: Dave Murgatroyd. **Season:** April-Oct. **To obtain tee times:** Call golf shop.
Miscellaneous: Range (grass/mats), credit cards (MC, V, AE, D), BF, FF.
Reader Comments: Back 9 gets a little tight with overgrown foliage, a lot of water on the back, a
great shotmaker's course … Narrow shorter fairway course, workable, pleasant course.

★★★ RIVER FALLS GOLF CLUB
SP-1011 E. Division St., River Falls, 54022, Pierce County, (715)425-0032, (800)688-1511,
3 miles from River Falls. **E-mail:** rfgc2@pressenter.com. **Facility Holes:** 18. **Yards:**
6,596/5,142. **Par:** 72/72. **Course Rating:** 72.0/69.9. **Slope:** 126/118. **Green Fee:** $21/$29. **Cart
Fee:** $24/Cart. **Walking Policy:** Unrestricted walking. **Walkability:** 3. **Opened:** 1929. **Season:**

April-Oct. **High:** May-Sept. **To obtain tee times:** Call golf shop. **Miscellaneous:** Reduced fees (seniors, juniors), range (grass), credit cards (MC, V, AE).

Reader Comments: Price was right! Very unique … Nice layout … Has some blind holes. Bring someone who has played it before … Must ride, steep between tees.

★★ RIVERDALE COUNTRY CLUB

PU-5008 South 12th St., Sheboygan, 53081, Sheboygan County, (920)458-2561, 50 miles from Milwaukee. **Facility Holes:** 18. **Yards:** 5,875/5,651. **Par:** 70/72. **Course Rating:** 67.4/71.3. **Slope:** 109/116. **Green Fee:** $19/$24. **Cart Fee:** $22/Cart. **Walking Policy:** Unrestricted walking. **Walkability:** 2. **Opened:** 1929. **Season:** April-Nov. **High:** June-Sept. **To obtain tee times:** Call up to 7 days in advance. **Miscellaneous:** Reduced fees (weekdays), range (grass), credit cards (MC, V), BF, FF.

★★★ RIVERMOOR COUNTRY CLUB

SP-30802 Waterford Dr., Waterford, 53185, Racine County, (262)534-2500, 20 miles from Milwaukee. **E-mail:** info@rivermoor.com. **Web:** www.rivermoor.com. **Facility Holes:** 18. **Yards:** 6,256/5,728. **Par:** 70/75. **Course Rating:** 70.2/73.1. **Slope:** 124/126. **Green Fee:** $25/$32. **Cart Fee:** $13/Person. **Walking Policy:** Unrestricted walking. **Walkability:** 2. **Opened:** 1929. **Architect:** Billy Sixty Jr. **Season:** March-Nov. **High:** May-Oct. **To obtain tee times:** Call up to 7 days in advance. **Miscellaneous:** Reduced fees (twilight, seniors), range (grass), credit cards (MC, V, D), BF, FF.

Reader Comments: Old course, fun to play … Pricey but nice … Sporty, mature, short course … Fast greens, narrow fairways … Tight little course! Get ready to play out of the woods.

★★★½ RIVERSIDE GOLF COURSE

PU-2100 Golf Course Rd., Janesville, 53545, Rock County, (608)757-3080, 35 miles from Madison. **E-mail:** julgolf@aol.com. **Facility Holes:** 18. **Yards:** 6,508/5,147. **Par:** 72/72. **Course Rating:** 70.7/68.9. **Slope:** 123/116. **Green Fee:** $22/$25. **Cart Fee:** $12/Person. **Walking Policy:** Unrestricted walking. **Walkability:** 3. **Opened:** 1924. **Architect:** Robert Bruce Harris. **Season:** April-Nov. **High:** May-Sept. **To obtain tee times:** Call golf shop. **Miscellaneous:** Reduced fees (weekdays, seniors, juniors), range (grass), credit cards (MC, V), BF, FF.

Reader Comments: Excellent value, nice course … Never gets boring, great food … Fun to play … Fairways needed to be thicker (more grass) … Shotmaker's advantage … Great course.

★★★½ ROCK RIVER HILLS GOLF COURSE

SP-Main St. Rd., Horicon, 53032, Dodge County, (920)485-4990, 45 miles from Milwaukee. **Facility Holes:** 18. **Yards:** 6,300/5,160. **Par:** 70/70. **Course Rating:** 70.5/70.0. **Slope:** 127/121. **Green Fee:** $22/$30. **Cart Fee:** $24/Cart. **Walking Policy:** Unrestricted walking. **Walkability:** 2. **Opened:** 1969. **Architect:** Homer Fieldhouse/Bob Lohmann. **Season:** March-Nov. **High:** May-Sept. **To obtain tee times:** Call golf shop. **Miscellaneous:** Reduced fees (twilight, seniors, juniors), range (grass), credit cards (MC, V), BF, FF.

Reader Comments: A very nice course, neat layout, an overall value … A good bargain … A hidden treasure … Excellent value, must play … Delightful course, fun, challenging, scenic … Fun course, short but tight.

★★★½ ROLLING MEADOWS GOLF COURSE   *Value*

PU-560 W. Rolling Meadows Dr., Fond Du Lac, 54937, Fond Du Lac County, (920)929-3735, 55 miles from Milwaukee. **E-mail:** fd/cnty@dotnet.com. **Facility Holes:** 27. **Green Fee:** $27/$28. **Cart Fee:** $25/Cart. **Walking Policy:** Unrestricted walking. **Walkability:** 2. **Architect:** Nugent & Associates. **Season:** April-Nov. **High:** May-Sept. **To obtain tee times:** Call up to 5 days in advance. **Miscellaneous:** Reduced fees (weekdays, seniors, juniors), range (grass/mats), lodging (300 rooms), credit cards (MC, V), BF, FF.

BLUE/RED (18 Combo)
Yards: 6,988/5,406. **Par:** 72/72. **Course Rating:** 73.5/71.0. **Slope:** 129/121. **Opened:** 1996.
RED/WHITE (18 Combo)
Yards: 7,000/5,100. **Par:** 72/72. **Course Rating:** 73.5/69.5. **Slope:** 131/121. **Opened:** 1973.
WHITE/BLUE (18 Combo)
Yards: 6,962/5,177. **Par:** 72/72. **Course Rating:** 73.4/69.7. **Slope:** 128/118. **Opened:** 1996.

Reader Comments: Excellent mix of holes for a muni … What a deal, awesome … Tough course, fun … Great variety … 27 strong, challenging holes … Long course.

★★½ ROYAL SCOT GOLF COURSE & SUPPER CLUB

PU-4831 Church Rd., New Franken, 54229, Brown County, (920)866-2356, 5 miles from Green Bay. **Facility Holes:** 18. **Yards:** 6,572/5,474. **Par:** 72/72. **Course Rating:** 70.7/70.7. **Slope:** 122/118. **Green Fee:** $20/$23. **Cart Fee:** $26/Cart. **Walking Policy:** Unrestricted walking. **Walkability:** 2. **Opened:** 1971. **Architect:** Don Herfort. **Season:** March-Nov. **High:** May-Sept. **To obtain tee times:** Call up to 5 days in advance. **Miscellaneous:** Reduced fees (seniors, juniors), range (grass), credit cards (MC, V, D), BF, FF.

WISCONSIN

★★★★ SAINT CROIX NATIONAL GOLF CLUB
PU-1603 County Rd. V, Somerset, 54025, St. Croix County, (715)247-4200, (866)525-4624, 4 miles from Somerset. **E-mail:** golf@saintcroixnational.com. **Web:** www. saintcroixnational.com. **Facility Holes:** 18. **Yards:** 6,909/5,251. **Par:** 72/72. **Course Rating:** 73.9/66.3. **Slope:** 138/119. **Green Fee:** $26/$46. **Cart Fee:** $13/Person. **Walking Policy:** Unrestricted walking. **Walkability:** 5. **Opened:** 1996. **Architect:** Joel Goldstrand. **Season:** March-Nov. **To obtain tee times:** Call up to 7 days in advance. **Miscellaneous:** Reduced fees (weekdays, twilight, seniors, juniors), range (grass), credit cards (MC, V, AE, D), BF, FF.
Reader Comments: Scenic and challenging ... Just beautiful ... Rolling forest ... Very hilly ... Lots of elevated tee boxes ... Beautiful, trees everywhere, animals all over ... Can't carry enough balls.

★★★ SCENIC VIEW COUNTRY CLUB
PU-4415 Club Dr., Slinger, 53086, Washington County, (262)644-5661, (800)472-6411, 20 miles from Milwaukee. **Web:** www.svgolf.com. **Facility Holes:** 18. **Yards:** 6,296/5,358. **Par:** 72/71. **Course Rating:** 68.6/70.1. **Slope:** 115/115. **Green Fee:** $20/$26. **Cart Fee:** $26/Person. **Walking Policy:** Unrestricted walking. **Walkability:** 4. **Opened:** 1961. **Architect:** Robert Raasch. **Season:** March-Nov. **High:** June-Aug. **To obtain tee times:** Call golf shop. **Miscellaneous:** Reduced fees (weekdays, seniors), range (grass), credit cards (MC, V, AE).
Reader Comments: The price is right ... Very pleasing to the eye ... Making improvements.

★★★★ SENTRYWORLD GOLF COURSE
PU-601 N. Michigan Ave., Stevens Point, 54481, Portage County, (715)345-1600, 90 miles from Madison. **E-mail:** sentryworld@g2a.net. **Web:** www.sentryworld.com. **Facility Holes:** 18. **Yards:** 6,951/5,108. **Par:** 72/72. **Course Rating:** 74.4/71.0. **Slope:** 142/126. **Green Fee:** $47/$74. **Cart Fee:** Included in green fee. **Walking Policy:** Unrestricted walking. **Walkability:** 3. **Opened:** 1982. **Architect:** Robert Trent Jones Jr. **Season:** April-Oct. **High:** June-Aug. **To obtain tee times:** Call up to 365 days in advance. **Miscellaneous:** Reduced fees (weekdays, twilight), range (grass), credit cards (MC, V, AE), BF, FF.
Notes: Ranked 4th in 2001 Best in State; 18th in 1996 America's Top 75 Upscale Courses.
Reader Comments: Sand, trees, water, trouble. Must be straight and long ... Great test. Fun to play ... Superb conditions ... Nice course, a little tricked up ... Beautiful, a joy to be on, price is steep.

★★ SHAWANO LAKE GOLF CLUB
PU-W5714 Lake Drive, Shawano, 54166, Shawano County, (715)524-4890, 25 miles from Green Bay. **E-mail:** golftc@mail.wisc.net. **Facility Holes:** 18. **Yards:** 6,231/5,496. **Par:** 71/71. **Course Rating:** 72.9/70.4. **Slope:** 124/124. **Green Fee:** $18/$25. **Cart Fee:** $11/Person. **Walking Policy:** Unrestricted walking. **Walkability:** 4. **Opened:** 1922. **Architect:** Marty Garrity. **Season:** March-Jan. **High:** May-Sept. **To obtain tee times:** Call up to 14 days in advance. **Miscellaneous:** Reduced fees (weekdays, guests, twilight, seniors, juniors), range (grass), credit cards (MC, V), BF, FF.

★★ SHEBOYGAN TOWN & COUNTRY CLUB
PU-W1945 County J, Sheboygan, 53083, Sheboygan County, (920)467-2509, 5 miles from Sheboygan. **E-mail:** golftc@dotnet.com. **Web:** www.townandcountrygolf.com. **Facility Holes:** 27. **Green Fee:** $22/$26. **Cart Fee:** $22/Cart. **Walking Policy:** Unrestricted walking. **Walkability:** 3. **Opened:** 1962. **Architect:** Homer Fieldhouse. **Season:** April-Nov. **High:** May-Sept. **To obtain tee times:** Call up to 5 days in advance. **Miscellaneous:** Reduced fees (weekdays, twilight, seniors, juniors), range (grass), credit cards (MC, V, D), BF, FF.
BERMS/PIGEON RUN (18 Combo)
Yards: 5,990/4,974. **Par:** 71/71. **Course Rating:** 68.1/67.9. **Slope:** 117/112.
BERMS/RIVERWOODS (18 Combo)
Yards: 5,827/5,593. **Par:** 71/71. **Course Rating:** 68.0/64.7. **Slope:** 115/108.
PIGEON RUN/RIVERWOODS (18 Combo)
Yards: 6,223/5,882. **Par:** 72/72. **Course Rating:** 69.4/65.9. **Slope:** 119/112.

SILVER SPRING GOLF COURSE
PU-N56 W21318 Silver Spring Dr., Menomonee Falls, 53051, Waukesha County, (262)252-4666, 7 miles from Menomonee Falls. **Facility Holes:** 36. **Cart Fee:** $14/Person. **Walking Policy:** Walking at certain times. **Season:** March-Nov. **High:** June-Sept. **To obtain tee times:** Call up to 7 days in advance. **Miscellaneous:** Reduced fees (weekdays, twilight), range (grass/mats), credit cards (MC, V, AE), BF, FF.
★★★½ FALLS COURSE (18)
Yards: 5,564/5,160. **Par:** 70/72. **Course Rating:** 71.8/70.5. **Slope:** 123/120. **Green Fee:** $28/$32. **Walkability:** 2. **Opened:** 1994. **Architect:** Ron Kuhlman/Tom Kramer.
★★★ ISLAND COURSE (18)
Yards: 6,744/5,616. **Par:** 72/70. **Course Rating:** 72.4/67.9. **Slope:** 134/124. **Green Fee:** $35/$39. **Walkability:** 3. **Opened:** 1986. **Architect:** Ron Kuhlman.
Reader Comments: Always a great deal ... Island green is a challenge, a lot of outings on this course, pace of play suffers ... Nice practice area, good specials ... What a challenge.

★★★½ SKYLINE GOLF CLUB
SP-11th and Golf Rd., Black River Falls, 54615, Jackson County, (715)284-2613, 125 miles from Madison. **E-mail:** skyline@cuttingedge.net. **Facility Holes:** 18. **Yards:** 6,371/5,122. **Par:** 72/72. **Course Rating:** 70.6/69.4. **Slope:** 123/112. **Green Fee:** $25/$27. **Cart Fee:** $28/Cart. **Walking Policy:** Unrestricted walking. **Walkability:** 5. **Opened:** 1957. **Architect:** Edward L. Packard/Brent Wadsworth. **Season:** April-Nov. **High:** May-Sept. **Tee times:** Call golf shop. **Miscellaneous:** Reduced fees (guests, twilight), range (grass), credit cards (MC, V, D), BF, FF.
Reader Comments: Great shape ... Difficult greens to putt ... Wouldn't miss it ... Pretty course. Hard work. Elevation changes.

★★½ SONGBIRD HILLS GOLF CLUB
PU-W259 N8700 Hwy. J, Hartland, 53029, Waukesha County, (262)246-7050, 15 miles from Milwaukee. **Facility Holes:** 18. **Yards:** 5,556/5,074. **Par:** 70/70. **Course Rating:** 66.2/64.0. **Slope:** 110/105. **Green Fee:** $20/$24. **Cart Fee:** $22/Cart. **Walking Policy:** Unrestricted walking. **Walkability:** 4. **Opened:** 1992. **Architect:** Harold E. Hoffman. **Season:** April-Nov. **High:** June-Aug. **To obtain tee times:** Call golf shop. **Miscellaneous:** Reduced fees (weekdays, twilight, seniors, juniors), metal spikes, range (grass), credit cards (MC, V).

★★½ SOUTH HILLS COUNTRY CLUB
PU-3047 Hwy. 41, Franksville, 53126, Racine County, (262)835-4441, (800)736-4766, 15 miles from Milwaukee. **Facility Holes:** 18. **Yards:** 6,403/6,107. **Par:** 72/76. **Course Rating:** 69.4/75.0. **Slope:** 118/125. **Green Fee:** $18/$22. **Cart Fee:** $24/Cart. **Walking Policy:** Unrestricted walking. **Walkability:** 2. **Opened:** 1927. **High:** May-Oct. **To obtain tee times:** Call golf shop. **Miscellaneous:** Reduced fees (weekdays), metal spikes, range (grass/mats), credit cards (MC, V, AE).

★★★ SPARTA MUNICIPAL GOLF COURSE
PU-1210 E. Montgomery St., Sparta, 54656, Monroe County, (608)269-3022, 25 miles from La Crosse. **Facility Holes:** 18. **Yards:** 6,544/5,648. **Par:** 72/72. **Course Rating:** 70.8/71.6. **Slope:** 127/125. **Green Fee:** $20/$23. **Cart Fee:** $23/Cart. **Walking Policy:** Unrestricted walking. **Walkability:** 1. **Opened:** 1984. **Architect:** Art Johnson. **Season:** April-Nov. **High:** June-Aug. **To obtain tee times:** Call golf shop. **Miscellaneous:** Reduced fees (seniors, juniors), range (grass), credit cards (MC, V), BF, FF.
Reader Comments: Great for seniors, gets a lot of play ... Nice course, fun, lots of play, affordable ... A great muni.

★★★★ SPOONER GOLF CLUB
SP-County Trunk H N., Spooner, 54801, Washburn County, (715)635-3580, 85 miles from Eau Claire. **Facility Holes:** 18. **Yards:** 6,417/5,084. **Par:** 71/72. **Course Rating:** 70.9/68.8. **Slope:** 128/117. **Green Fee:** $27/$31. **Cart Fee:** $26/Cart. **Walking Policy:** Unrestricted walking. **Walkability:** 3. **Opened:** 1930. **Architect:** Tom Vardon/Gordon Emerson. **Season:** April-Oct. **High:** July-Aug. **To obtain tee times:** Call up to 21 days in advance. **Miscellaneous:** Reduced fees (weekdays, twilight), range (grass), credit cards (MC, V), BF, FF.
Reader Comments: Beautiful old course, great to play ... Fast greens, excellent condition, hard to walk ... Well maintained, fast greens, excellent fairway conditions ... Nice layout, very playable ... Tough final 2 holes.

★★ SPRING VALLEY COUNTRY CLUB
PU-23913 Wilmot Rd., Salem, 53168, Kenosha County, (262)862-2626, 8 miles from Kenosha. **Facility Holes:** 18. **Yards:** 6,354/5,968. **Par:** 70/70. **Course Rating:** 70.1/68.9. **Slope:** 119/113. **Green Fee:** $21. **Cart Fee:** $13/Person. **Walking Policy:** Unrestricted walking. **Walkability:** 3. **Opened:** 1924. **Architect:** William B. Langford/Theodore J. Moreau. **Season:** Year-round. **High:** March-Nov. **To obtain tee times:** Call golf shop. **Miscellaneous:** Reduced fees (weekdays, twilight, seniors), range (grass), credit cards (MC, V), FF.

★★½ SPRING VALLEY GOLF COURSE
PU-400 Van Buren Rd., Spring Valley, 54767, Pierce County, (715)778-5513, (800)236-0009, 40 miles from St. Paul. **Facility Holes:** 18. **Yards:** 6,114/4,735. **Par:** 71/72. **Course Rating:** 70.0/68.0. **Slope:** 124/116. **Green Fee:** $16/$19. **Cart Fee:** $10/Person. **Walking Policy:** Unrestricted walking. **Walkability:** 5. **Opened:** 1974. **Architect:** Gordon Emerson. **Season:** April-Oct. **High:** May-Sept. **To obtain tee times:** Call golf shop. **Miscellaneous:** Reduced fees (weekdays, twilight, seniors, juniors), credit cards (MC, V, AE, D).

★★★ SQUIRES COUNTRY CLUB
PU-4970 Country Club Rd., Port Washington, 53074, Ozaukee County, (262)285-3402, 30 miles from Milwaukee. **E-mail:** squirescc@nconnect.net. **Web:** www.squirescc.com. **Facility Holes:** 18. **Yards:** 5,823/5,014. **Par:** 70/69. **Course Rating:** 68.0/68.6. **Slope:** 119/117. **Green Fee:** $26. **Cart Fee:** $13/Person. **Walking Policy:** Unrestricted walking. **Walkability:** 3.

WISCONSIN

Opened: 1927. Architect: Clarence St. Peter. Season: April-Nov. High: May-Sept. To obtain tee times: Call up to 10 days in advance. Miscellaneous: Reduced fees (weekdays, twilight, seniors, juniors), range (grass), credit cards (MC, V, D), FF.

Reader Comments: Nice mix of links and Northwoods holes … Short holes, hilly, great views … Lake Michigan views make you forget the course.

★★★★ ST. GERMAIN MUNICIPAL GOLF CLUB
PU-9041 Hwy. 70 W., P.O. 385, St. Germain, 54558, Vilas County, (715)542-2614, 3 miles from St. Germain. Web: www.stgermain-golfclub.com. Facility Holes: 18. Yards: 6,651/5,233. Par: 72/72. Course Rating: 72.2/70.3. Slope: 130/121. Green Fee: $25/$38. Cart Fee: $12/Person. Walking Policy: Unrestricted walking. Walkability: 3. Opened: 1993. Architect: Don Stepanik, Jr. Season: April-Oct. High: July-Sept. To obtain tee times: Call up to 14 days in advance. Miscellaneous: Reduced fees (twilight), range (grass), credit cards (MC, V, AE, D), BF, FF.

Reader Comments: Nice, tight course, greens rough … Best in area … Excellent course, beautiful location … Wonderful course, enjoyable, wooded … Many trees, facilities beautiful, people great … Old 9 holes good, new 9 holes great.

★★ SUN PRAIRIE GOLF COURSE
PU-Happy Valley Rd., Sun Prairie, 53590, Dane County, (608)837-6211, 2 miles from Sun Prairie. Facility Holes: 18. Yards: 6,658/5,289. Par: 72/73. Course Rating: 71.3/65.0. Slope: 117/102. Green Fee: $22/$24. Cart Fee: $22/Cart. Walking Policy: Unrestricted walking. Walkability: 3. Opened: 1961. Season: April-Nov. High: June-Aug. To obtain tee times: Call golf shop. Miscellaneous: Range (grass), credit cards (MC, V).

TEAL WING GOLF CLUB
R-12425 N. Ross Road, Hayward, 54843, Sawyer County, (715)462-9051, 20 miles from Hayward. E-mail: rossteal@cheqnet.net. Web: www.tealwing.com. Facility Holes: 18. Yards: 6,379/5,218. Par: 72/72. Course Rating: 72.1/71.2. Slope: 139/127. Green Fee: $30/$53. Cart Fee: $12/Person. Walking Policy: Unrestricted walking. Walkability: 3. Opened: 1995. Architect: Ross Associates. Season: May-Oct. High: July-Aug. To obtain tee times: Call golf shop. Miscellaneous: Reduced fees (weekdays, guests, twilight, juniors), metal spikes, range (grass), lodging (25 rooms), credit cards (MC, V), BF, FF.

★★★ TELEMARK GOLF COURSE
R-41885 Valhalla Townhouse Rd., Cable, 54821, Bayfield County, (715)798-3104, 100 miles from Eau Claire. E-mail: slgr@cheqnet.net. Web: www.cable4fun.com/golf27.htm. Facility Holes: 18. Yards: 6,403/5,691. Par: 72/72. Course Rating: 70.6/67.0. Slope: 128/119. Green Fee: $28. Cart Fee: $12/Person. Walking Policy: Walking at certain times. Walkability: 4. Opened: 1970. Architect: Art Johnson. Season: May-Oct. High: June-Sept. To obtain tee times: Call up to 30 days in advance. Miscellaneous: Reduced fees (twilight), range (grass), lodging (8 rooms), credit cards (MC, V), BF, FF.

Reader Comments: Don't miss this one! Hard to walk … Never crowded … Nice wooded course, not very crowded & inexpensive … Beautiful scenery in the trees, some water, greens need TLC … Lots of woods, tight in hollows.

★½ THAL ACRES LINKS & LANES
PU-N6109 CTHM, Westfield, 53964, Marquette County, (608)296-2850, 50 miles from Madison. Facility Holes: 18. Yards: 5,672/5,211. Par: 70/72. Course Rating: 66.5/69.3. Slope: 114/118. Green Fee: $20/$26. Cart Fee: $24/Cart. Walking Policy: Unrestricted walking. Walkability: 2. Opened: 1963. Season: April-Nov. Tee times: Call up to 60 days in advance. Misc: Reduced fees (weekdays, seniors), range (grass), credit cards (MC, V).

TIMBER RIDGE GOLF CLUB
PU-10030 Timber Ridge Rd., Minocqua, 54548, Oneida County, (715)356-9502, (888)457-4343, 50 miles from Wausau. E-mail: info@timberridgegolfclub.com. Web: www.timberridgegolfclub.com. Facility Holes: 18. Yards: 6,627/5,488. Par: 72/72. Course Rating: 71.8/71.7. Slope: 127/123. Green Fee: $42/$68. Cart Fee: Included in green fee. Walking Policy: Walking at certain times. Walkability: 3. Opened: 1977. Architect: Roger Packard. Season: April-Oct. High: June-Sept. To obtain tee times: Call golf shop. Miscellaneous: Reduced fees (guests, juniors), credit cards (MC, V, AE, D), BF, FF.

★★ TRAPP RIVER GOLF CLUB
PU-Hwy. WW, Wausau, 54403, Marathon County, (715)675-3044, 8 miles from Wausau. E-mail: welsgof@aol.com. Facility Holes: 18. Yards: 6,335/4,935. Par: 72/72. Course Rating: 69.3/67.3. Slope: 116/109. Green Fee: $16/$22. Cart Fee: $13/Person. Walking Policy: Unrestricted walking. Walkability: 2. Opened: 1963. Architect: Farmer Sloan. Season: April-Nov. High: June-Aug. To obtain tee times: Call up to 7 days in advance. Misc: Reduced fees (twilight, seniors, juniors), range (grass/mats), credit cards (MC, V, AE, D), BF, FF.

WISCONSIN

★★★★ **TRAPPERS TURN GOLF CLUB**
PU-652 Trappers Turn Dr., Wisconsin Dells, 53965, Sauk County, (608)253-7000, (800)221-8876, 50 miles from Madison. **E-mail:** trappers@midplains.net. **Web:** www.trappersturn.com. **Facility Holes:** 27. **Green Fee:** $48/$75. **Cart Fee:** Included in green fee. **Walking Policy:** Walking at certain times. **Walkability:** 5. **Opened:** 1991. **Architect:** Andy North/Roger Packard. **Season:** April-Nov. **High:** May-Sept. **To obtain tee times:** Call up to 30 days in advance. **Miscellaneous:** Reduced fees (weekdays, guests, twilight, seniors), range (grass), credit cards (MC, V, AE, D), BF, FF.
ARBOR/LAKE (18 Combo)
Yards: 6,831/5,017. **Par:** 72/72. **Course Rating:** 73.3/69.7. **Slope:** 133/123.
CANYON/ARBOR (18 Combo)
Yards: 6,738/5,000. **Par:** 72/72. **Course Rating:** 73.3/69.7. **Slope:** 133/123.
LAKE/CANYON (18 Combo)
Yards: 6,759/5,017. **Par:** 72/72. **Course Rating:** 72.8/69.4. **Slope:** 133/122.
Reader Comments: Combo of links holes and woods ... Nice course, you'll enjoy ... Super course ... Some gorgeous holes ... Pricey but worth it, beautiful, great service ... Shouldn't be missed. Excellent.

★★★ **TREE ACRES GOLF COURSE**
PU-5254 Pleasant Dr., Plover, 54467, Portage County, (715)341-4530, 10 miles from Stevens Point. **E-mail:** jackdavis@voyager.net. **Facility Holes:** 27. **Green Fee:** $21/$25. **Cart Fee:** $12/Person. **Walking Policy:** Unrestricted walking. **Walkability:** 1. **Opened:** 1991. **Architect:** Don Stepanik. **Season:** April-Oct. **High:** May-Aug. **To obtain tee times:** Call up to 7 days in advance. **Miscellaneous:** Reduced fees (weekdays, seniors, juniors), range (grass), credit cards (MC, V), BF, FF.
BIRCH/ARBOR (18 Combo)
Yards: 6,409/4,747. **Par:** 72/72. **Course Rating:** 70.1/71.0. **Slope:** 122/120.
PINE/ARBOR (18 Combo)
Yards: 6,828/5,326. **Par:** 72/72. **Course Rating:** 72.2/72.4. **Slope:** 123/121.
PINE/BIRCH (18 Combo)
Yards: 6,701/5,079. **Par:** 72/72. **Course Rating:** 71.5/68.7. **Slope:** 121/119.
Reader Comments: Wide variety of holes ... New 9 great ... New layout of 27 holes is major improvement ... New additions good.

★★★½ **TROUT LAKE GOLF & COUNTRY CLUB**
PU-3800 Hwy. 51 N., Arbor Vitae, 54568, Vilas County, (715)385-2189, 80 miles from Wausau. **Web:** www.troutlakegolf.com. **Facility Holes:** 18. **Yards:** 6,175/5,263. **Par:** 72/71. **Course Rating:** 69.9/70.3. **Slope:** 124/122. **Green Fee:** $24/$35. **Cart Fee:** $13/Person. **Walking Policy:** Unrestricted walking. **Walkability:** 2. **Opened:** 1926. **Architect:** Charles Maddox/Frank P. MacDonald. **Season:** April-Oct. **High:** June-Aug. **To obtain tee times:** Call up to 14 days in advance. **Miscellaneous:** Reduced fees (twilight), credit cards (MC, V), BF, FF.
Reader Comments: The greens are the best in Midwest ... Tough and challenging ... Great Northwoods course ... Old course, needs improvements ... Significant improvement ... Fun to play.

★★★★½ **TROY BURNE GOLF CLUB**
PU-295 Lindsay Rd., Hudson, 54016, St. Croix County, (715)381-9800, (877)888-8633, 20 miles from St. Paul. **E-mail:** Ceakins@pga.com. **Web:** www.troyburne.com. **Facility Holes:** 18. **Yards:** 7,003/4,932. **Par:** 71/71. **Course Rating:** 74.8/69.6. **Slope:** 140/122. **Green Fee:** $79. **Cart Fee:** $13/Person. **Walking Policy:** Unrestricted walking. **Walkability:** 3. **Opened:** 1999. **Architect:** Michael Hurdzan/Dana Fry/Tom Lehman. **Season:** April-Oct. **To obtain tee times:** Call up to 20 days in advance. **Miscellaneous:** Reduced fees (twilight), range (grass), credit cards (MC, V, AE, D), BF, FF.
Reader Comments: Traditional Scottish links-style course; rate this highest I have ever played for condition ... Very challenging ... Fun ... Front 9 bunkers too penal ... Awesome course tee to green. One of the best in the nation ... Good driving course, a lot of fun gambling opportunities.

★★★★ **TURTLEBACK GOLF & CONFERENCE CENTER**
PU-W. Allen Rd., Rice Lake, 54868, Barron County, (715)234-7641, (888)300-9443, 1 mile from Rice Lake. **E-mail:** turtlebk@chibardun.net. **Web:** www.turtlebackgolf.com. **Facility Holes:** 18. **Yards:** 6,604/5,291. **Par:** 71/71. **Course Rating:** 72.0/73.6. **Slope:** 130/126. **Green Fee:** $23/$32. **Cart Fee:** $24/Cart. **Walking Policy:** Unrestricted walking. **Walkability:** 3. **Opened:** 1982. **Architect:** Todd Severud. **Season:** April-Oct. **High:** May-Sept. **To obtain tee times:** Call up to 21 days in advance. **Miscellaneous:** Reduced fees (weekdays, seniors, juniors), range (grass), credit cards (MC, V), BF, FF.
Reader Comments: Very playable, imaginative holes ... Challenging well-conditioned course. Challenging greens ... Hilly, challenging, very fast greens ... Good track, fun to play, long ... Best value in Wisconsin ... Outstanding course.

WISCONSIN

★★★ **TUSCUMBIA GOLF CLUB**
SP-637 Illinois Ave., Green Lake, 54941, Green Lake County, (920)294-3240, (800)294-3381, 65 miles from Milwaukee. **E-mail:** tusky@dotnet.com. **Web:** www.tuscumbiacc.com. **Facility Holes:** 18. **Yards:** 6,301/5,619. **Par:** 71/71. **Course Rating:** 70.1/73.2. **Slope:** 122/123. **Green Fee:** $30/$41. **Cart Fee:** $12/Person. **Walking Policy:** Unrestricted walking. **Walkability:** 2. **Opened:** 1896. **Architect:** Tom Bendelow. **Season:** March-Nov. **To obtain tee times:** Call up to 20 days in advance. **Miscellaneous:** Reduced fees (twilight, seniors, juniors), metal spikes, range (grass/mats), credit cards (MC, V, D).
Reader Comments: Wisconsin's oldest course ... Always feel like I'm getting a bargain on a great golf course ... Narrow fairways, lots of trees, gets little play because of the difficulty.

★½ **TWIN LAKES COUNTRY CLUB**
SP-1230 Legion Dr., Twin Lakes, 53181, Kenosha County, (262)877-2500, 50 miles from Milwaukee. **E-mail:** auc@genevaonline.com. **Web:** www.twin-lakes-countryclub.com. **Facility Holes:** 18. **Yards:** 6,023/5,060. **Par:** 70/71. **Course Rating:** 68.4/68.4. **Slope:** 120/117. **Green Fee:** $19/$25. **Cart Fee:** $13/Person. **Walking Policy:** Unrestricted walking. **Walkability:** 3. **Opened:** 1912. **Architect:** Leonard Macomber. **Season:** March-Nov. **High:** May-Oct. **To obtain tee times:** Call up to 7 days in advance. **Miscellaneous:** Reduced fees (weekdays, twilight, seniors), range (grass/mats), credit cards (MC, V), BF, FF.

★★ **TWIN OAKS GOLF COURSE**
PU-4871 County Hwy. R, Denmark, 54208, Brown County, (920)863-2716, 5 miles from Green Bay. **Facility Holes:** 18. **Yards:** 6,468/5,214. **Par:** 72/72. **Course Rating:** 69.6/68.3. **Slope:** 116/103. **Green Fee:** $16/$20. **Cart Fee:** $11/Person. **Walking Policy:** Unrestricted walking. **Walkability:** 2. **Opened:** 1968. **Season:** March-Nov. **High:** June-Aug. **To obtain tee times:** Call golf shop. **Miscellaneous:** Reduced fees (weekdays, seniors, juniors), metal spikes, range (grass), credit cards (MC, V, D).

★★★ **TWO OAKS NORTH GOLF CLUB**
PU-Cty. Hwy. F, Wautoma, 54982, Waushara County, (920)787-7132, (800)236-6257, 35 miles from Oshkosh. **E-mail:** twooaks@network20l0.net. **Web:** www.twooaksgolf.com. **Facility Holes:** 18. **Yards:** 6,552/5,034. **Par:** 72/72. **Course Rating:** 70.7/68.3. **Slope:** 120/111. **Green Fee:** $14/$32. **Cart Fee:** $26/Cart. **Walking Policy:** Unrestricted walking. **Walkability:** 3. **Opened:** 1995. **Architect:** Bob Lohmann/John Houdek. **Season:** April-Nov. **High:** June-Aug. **Tee times:** Call up to 10 days in advance. **Miscellaneous:** Reduced fees (weekdays, guests, twilight, seniors, juniors), range (grass/mats), credit cards (MC, V, AE, D), BF, FF.
Reader Comments: Front 9 short, not much trouble. Back 9 challenging. Nice, a little overpriced.

★★★★½ **UNIVERSITY RIDGE GOLF COURSE** *Condition*
PU-7120 County Trunk PD, Verona, 53593, Dane County, (608)845-7700, (800)897-4343, 8 miles from Madison. **E-mail:** gm.university@palmergolf.com. **Web:** www.uwbadgers.com. **Facility Holes:** 18. **Yards:** 6,888/5,005. **Par:** 72/72. **Course Rating:** 73.2/68.9. **Slope:** 142/121. **Green Fee:** $34/$54. **Cart Fee:** $15/Person. **Walking Policy:** Unrestricted walking. **Walkability:** 3. **Opened:** 1991. **Architect:** Robert Trent Jones Jr. **Season:** April-Oct. **High:** May-Sept. **To obtain tee times:** Call up to 14 days in advance. **Miscellaneous:** Reduced fees (twilight, juniors), range (grass/mats), credit cards (MC, V, AE), BF, FF.
Notes: Ranked 5th in 2001 Best in State.
Reader Comments: Excellent design, a test ... Great design and value ... Class, class, class ... Simply the best for your buck ... Great condition, nice pace for a weekend, beautiful ... Perfect fairways, perfect layout.

★★ **UTICA GOLF COURSE**
PU-2330 Knott Rd., Oshkosh, 54904, Winnebago County, (920)233-4446, 5 miles from Oshkosh. **Facility Holes:** 18. **Yards:** 6,185/5,368. **Par:** 72/72. **Course Rating:** 68.8/69.9. **Slope:** 117/117. **Green Fee:** $20/$22. **Cart Fee:** $24/Cart. **Walking Policy:** Unrestricted walking. **Walkability:** 2. **Opened:** 1974. **Architect:** Robert Petzel. **Season:** April-Nov. **High:** May-Sept. **To obtain tee times:** Call up to 10 days in advance. **Miscellaneous:** Reduced fees (weekdays, seniors, juniors), range (grass), credit cards (MC, V), BF, FF.

★★★ **VOYAGER VILLAGE COUNTRY CLUB**
SP-28851 Kilkare Rd., Danbury, 54830, Burnett County, (715)259-3911, (800)782-0329, 15 miles from Webster. **E-mail:** voyagervillage@centurytel.net. **Web:** www.voyagervillage.com. **Facility Holes:** 27. **Yards:** 6,638/5,711. **Par:** 72/72. **Course Rating:** 71.6/72.4. **Slope:** 123/122. **Green Fee:** $29/$33. **Cart Fee:** $27/Cart. **Walking Policy:** Unrestricted walking. **Walkability:** 3. **Opened:** 1970. **Architect:** William James Spear. **Season:** April-Nov. **High:** June-Sept. **To obtain tee times:** Call up to 5 days in advance. **Miscellaneous:** Reduced fees (weekdays, twilight), range (grass), credit cards (MC, V), BF, FF.

WISCONSIN

Reader Comments: Above average, speedy for the area ... Priced right, few people, natural setting ... Beautiful setting ... Very scenic course ... Small greens.
Special Notes: Also has a 9-hole par-3 course.

★★½ **WANAKI GOLF COURSE**
PU-20830 W. Libson Rd., Menomonee Falls, 53051, Waukesha County, (262)252-3480.
Facility Holes: 18. **Yards:** 6,569/5,012. **Par:** 71/70. **Course Rating:** 71.4/69.2. **Slope:** 127/117.
Green Fee: $25/$35. **Cart Fee:** $27/Cart. **Walking Policy:** Unrestricted walking. **Walkability:** 1.
Opened: 1970. **Architect:** Billy Sixty Jr. **Season:** March-Nov. **High:** May-Oct. **To obtain tee times:** Call up to 6 days in advance. **Miscellaneous:** Reduced fees (weekdays, twilight, seniors, juniors), credit cards (MC, V), BF, FF.

★★★★½ **WASHINGTON COUNTY GOLF COURSE** *Value+, Condition, Pace*
PU-6439 Clover Rd., Hartford, 53027, Washington County, (262)670-6616, (888)383-4653.
E-mail: jjstatz@yahoo.com. **Web:** www.golfwcgc.com. **Facility Holes:** 18. **Yards:** 7,007/5,200.
Par: 72/72. **Course Rating:** 73.1/69.5. **Slope:** 130/118. **Green Fee:** $17/$53. **Cart Fee:**
$14/Person. **Walking Policy:** Unrestricted walking. **Walkability:** 3. **Opened:** 1997. **Architect:**
Arthur Hills/Brian Yoder. **Season:** April-Nov. **High:** June-Sept. **To obtain tee times:** Call golf
shop. **Miscellaneous:** Reduced fees (twilight, seniors, juniors), range (grass), credit cards
(MC, V, AE), BF, FF.
Reader Comments: Good variety, nice layout ... Good value, flat terrain but fairways and greens in great shape ... Just like Ireland ... Links-style makes it interesting ... Great layout. Outstanding condition. Laid back.

WENDELL PETTINGER - WILD RIDGE GOLF CLUB
PU-3905 Kane Rd., Eau Claire, 54703, Eau Claire County, (715)834-1766, (800)241-1766,
90 miles from Minneapolis. **E-mail:** millrungolf@ecol.net. **Web:** www.millrungolf.com.
Facility Holes: 36. **Cart Fee:** $13/Person. **Walking Policy:** Unrestricted walking. **Season:** April-Dec.**To obtain tee times:** Call golf shop. **Miscellaneous:** Reduced fees (weekdays, twilight), range (grass), credit cards (MC, V, AE), BF, FF.
MILL RUN COURSE (18)
Yards: 6,076/4,744. **Par:** 70/71. **Course Rating:** 68.7/66.9. **Slope:** 117/109. **Green Fee:**
$23/$26. **Walkability:** 1. **Opened:** 1980. **Architect:** Gordon Emerson. **High:** April-Oct.
★★★★ **WILD RIDGE GOLF COURSE** (18)
Yards: 7,034/5,252. **Par:** 72/72. **Course Rating:** 73.5/70.3. **Slope:** 133/126. **Green Fee:**
$38/$40. **Walkability:** 3. **Opened:** 1999. **Architect:** Greg Martin. **High:** June-Aug.
Reader Comments: Beautiful, challenging, lot of up & down terrain, lots of water, undulating greens, good test ... Many holes bordered by prairie grasses, contoured greens, scenic ... Love this course, difficult rough, bring extra balls.

★★½ **WESTERN LAKES GOLF CLUB**
SP-W287 N1963 Oakton Rd., Pewaukee, 53072, Waukesha County, (262)691-1181, 20 miles
from Milwaukee. **E-mail:** wlgc1@juno.com. **Facility Holes:** 18. **Yards:** 6,587/5,618. **Par:** 72/72.
Course Rating: 71.2/71.8. **Slope:** 124/123. **Green Fee:** $24/$34. **Cart Fee:** $26/Cart. **Walking Policy:** Unrestricted walking. **Walkability:** 3. **Opened:** 1963. **Architect:** Lawrence Packard.
Season: April-Nov. **High:** June-Sept. **To obtain tee times:** Call golf shop. **Miscellaneous:**
Reduced fees (weekdays, twilight), range (grass/mats), credit cards (MC, V, AE).

★½ **WESTHAVEN GOLF CLUB**
PU-1400 Westhaven St., Oshkosh, 54904, Winnebago County, (920)233-4640. **Facility Holes:**
18. **Yards:** 5,902/5,181. **Par:** 70/70. **Course Rating:** 67.6/71.6. **Slope:** 115/118. **Green Fee:**
$18/$24. **Cart Fee:** $24/Cart. **Walking Policy:** Unrestricted walking. **Walkability:** 2. **Opened:**
1969. **Architect:** Homer Fieldhouse. **Season:** April-Nov. **High:** April-Sept. **To obtain tee times:**
Call up to 180 days in advance. **Miscellaneous:** Reduced fees (twilight, seniors, juniors),
range (grass), credit cards (MC, V, AE, D), BF, FF.

★★★★ **WHISPERING SPRINGS GOLF CLUB** *Value, Pace*
PU-380 Whispering Springs Dr., Fond Du Lac, 54935, Fond Du Lac County, (920)921-8053,
4 miles from Fond du Lac. **Web:** www.whisperingspringsgolf.com. **Facility Holes:** 18. **Yards:**
6,961/5,207. **Par:** 72/72. **Course Rating:** 73.9/70.3. **Slope:** 134/122. **Green Fee:** $34/$41. **Cart
Fee:** $14/Person. **Walking Policy:** Unrestricted walking. **Walkability:** 1. **Opened:** 1997.
Architect: Bob Lohmann/Michael Benkusky. **Season:** March-Nov. **High:** May-Sept. **To obtain
tee times:** Call golf shop. **Miscellaneous:** Reduced fees (weekdays, twilight, seniors, juniors),
range (grass), credit cards (MC, V, D), BF, FF.
Reader Comments: Great value, nice new course ... Nicely laid out, very pretty ... A real find ... Tough, challenging, fun ... Excellent conditions, fair price ... Wind, fast greens, bent fairways ... Several great holes.

WISCONSIN

WHISTLING STRAITS GOLF CLUB
PU-N8501 Cty Rd. LS, Sheboygan, 53081, Sheboygan County, (920)565-6062, (800)618-5535, 5 miles from Sheboygan. **Web:** www.whistlingstraits.com. **Facility Holes:** 36. **Walkability:** 4. **Architect:** Pete Dye. **Season:** April-Oct. **High:** Jan.-Sept. **To obtain tee times:** Call golf shop. **Miscellaneous:** Reduced fees (twilight), range (grass), caddies (included in fee), lodging (357 rooms), credit cards (MC, V, AE, D), BF, FF.
IRISH COURSE (18)
Yards: 7,201/5,109. **Par:** 72/72. **Course Rating:** 75.6/70.0. **Slope:** 146/126. **Green Fee:** $196. **Cart Fee:** Included in green fee. **Walking Policy:** Unrestricted walking. **Opened:** 2000.
★★★★★ **STRAITS COURSE (18)** *Condition+*
Yards: 7,288/5,381. **Par:** 72/72. **Course Rating:** 76.7/72.2. **Slope:** 151/132. **Green Fee:** $248. **Cart Fee:** $21/Person. **Walking Policy:** Walking with Caddie. **Opened:** 1997.
Notes: Ranked 2nd in 2001 Best in State; 2nd in 1999 Best New Upscale Public.
Reader Comments: Awesome layout, great scenery, huge undulating greens ... Transported to Scotland ... Absolutely the best. Awesome! Golf as it should be ... No greater course this side of Pebble Beach ... Great but hard for average player ... Spectacular lakeside vistas and routing ... Nothing like it in Midwest.

WHITE EAGLE GOLF CLUB
PU-1293 County Rd. V, Hudson, 54016, St. Croix County, (715)549-4653, (888)465-3004, 20 miles from St. Paul. **Facility Holes:** 18. **Yards:** 7,178/4,995. **Par:** 72/72. **Course Rating:** 74.7/69.2. **Slope:** 140/118. **Green Fee:** $55/$70. **Walking Policy:** Mandatory carts. **Walkability:** 4. **Opened:** 2000. **Architect:** Garrett Gill. **Season:** April-Nov. **High:** June-Sept. **To obtain tee times:** Call up to 14 days in advance. **Miscellaneous:** Reduced fees (weekdays, twilight), range (grass), credit cards (MC, V, AE, D), BF, FF.

★★★ WHITNALL PARK GOLF CLUB
PU-5879 S. 92nd St., Hales Corners, 53130, Milwaukee County, (414)425-7931, 5 miles from Milwaukee. **Facility Holes:** 18. **Yards:** 6,335/5,879. **Par:** 71/74. **Course Rating:** 69.6/72.6. **Slope:** 118/120. **Green Fee:** $12/$27. **Cart Fee:** $24/Cart. **Walking Policy:** Unrestricted walking. **Walkability:** 4. **Opened:** 1932. **Architect:** George Hansen. **Season:** April-Nov. **High:** June-Sept. **To obtain tee times:** Call golf shop. **Miscellaneous:** Reduced fees (twilight, seniors, juniors), credit cards (MC, V).
Reader Comments: Nice old course, can be slow to play ... Above average county course ... Fun on occasion, drivable par 4s.

★★★★ WILDERNESS RESORT & GOLF COURSE
R-856 Canyon Dr., Wisconsin Dells, 53965, Sauk County, (608)253-4653, 35 miles from Madison. **Web:** www.golfwildernesswoods.com. **Facility Holes:** 29. **Yards:** 6,644/5,511. **Par:** 72/72. **Course Rating:** 73.1/67.7. **Slope:** 131/119. **Green Fee:** $65/$75. **Cart Fee:** ncluded in green fee. **Walking Policy:** Mandatory carts. **Walkability:** 4. **Opened:** 1997. **Architect:** Art Johnson. **Season:** April-Oct. **High:** May-Sept. **To obtain tee times:** Call up to 30 days in advance. **Miscellaneous:** Reduced fees (weekdays, guests, twilight), range (grass/mats), lodging (380 rooms), credit cards (MC, V, AE, D), BF, FF.
Reader Comments: A real surprise ... Very scenic, great variety of holes ... Challenging but fun ... Nice design, worth the money ... Fun, some very good layouts, elevated tees ... Spectacular scenery ... Great condition.
Special Notes: Also has a 6-hole Lakes Course and a 5-hole Canyon Course.

★★½ WILLOW RUN GOLF CLUB
SP-N8 W26506 Golf Rd., Pewaukee, 53072, Waukesha County, (262)544-8585, 15 miles from Milwaukee. **E-mail:** jdee@mggi.com. **Web:** www.willowrungolf.com. **Facility Holes:** 18. **Yards:** 6,384/5,183. **Par:** 71/71. **Course Rating:** 71.0/70.0. **Slope:** 119/114. **Green Fee:** $28/$32. **Cart Fee:** $26/Cart. **Walking Policy:** Walking at certain times. **Walkability:** 2. **Opened:** 1966. **Architect:** Dewey Slocum. **Season:** March-Dec. **High:** May-Aug. **To obtain tee times:** Call up to 7 days in advance. **Miscellaneous:** Reduced fees (weekdays, twilight, seniors, juniors), range (grass/mats), credit cards (MC, V), BF, FF.

★★½ WINAGAMIE GOLF COURSE
SP-3501 Winagamie Dr., Neenah, 54956, Winnebago County, (920)757-5453, 6 miles from Appleton. **Facility Holes:** 18. **Yards:** 6,355/5,422. **Par:** 73/73. **Course Rating:** 69.5/69.9. **Slope:** 115/115. **Green Fee:** $16/$18. **Cart Fee:** $20/Cart. **Walking Policy:** Unrestricted walking. **Walkability:** 2. **Opened:** 1963. **Architect:** Julius Jacobson. **Season:** April-Nov. **High:** May-Aug. **To obtain tee times:** Call golf shop. **Miscellaneous:** Reduced fees (weekdays, twilight, seniors, juniors), range (grass), credit cards (MC, V).

WISCONSIN

★★ **WISCONSIN RIVER GOLF CLUB**
PU-705 W. River Dr., Stevens Point, 54481, Portage County, (715)344-9152, 100 miles from Madison. **Facility Holes:** 18. **Yards:** 6,695/4,924. **Par:** 72/72. **Course Rating:** 71.9/68.5. **Slope:** 126/118. **Green Fee:** $21/$24. **Cart Fee:** $11/Person. **Walking Policy:** Unrestricted walking. **Walkability:** 2. **Opened:** 1961. **Architect:** Larry Roberts. **Season:** March-Nov. **High:** May-Sept. **To obtain tee times:** Call up to 7 days in advance. **Miscellaneous:** Reduced fees (seniors, juniors), range (grass), credit cards (MC, V, D), BF, FF.

★★ **WOODSIDE COUNTRY CLUB**
PU-530 Erie Rd., Green Bay, 54311, Brown County, (920)468-5729. **Facility Holes:** 18. **Yards:** 5,817/5,291. **Par:** 71/71. **Course Rating:** 67.6/69.8. **Slope:** 115/115. **Green Fee:** $17/$19. **Cart Fee:** $20/Cart. **Walking Policy:** Unrestricted walking. **Walkability:** 3. **Season:** April-Oct. **High:** June-Aug. **To obtain tee times:** Call golf shop. **Miscellaneous:** Reduced fees (weekdays, seniors, juniors), metal spikes, credit cards (MC, V).

YAHARA HILLS GOLF COURSE
PU-6701 E. Broadway, Madison, 53718, Dane County, (608)838-3126. **Facility Holes:** 36. **Green Fee:** $18/$22. **Cart Fee:** $24/Cart. **Walking Policy:** Unrestricted walking. **Walkability:** 3. **Opened:** 1967. **Architect:** Art Johnson. **Season:** April-Oct. **High:** May-Aug. **To obtain tee times:** Call up to 7 days in advance. **Miscellaneous:** Reduced fees (seniors, juniors), metal spikes, range (grass), credit cards (MC, V, D), BF, FF.
★★★ **EAST COURSE** (18)
Yards: 7,200/6,115. **Par:** 72/72. **Course Rating:** 71.9/73.4. **Slope:** 116/118.
Reader Comments: Wide open, free from most trouble … Good value … Diverse holes make a decent challenge.
★★★ **WEST COURSE** (18)
Yards: 7,000/5,705. **Par:** 72/73. **Course Rating:** 71.6/71.4. **Slope:** 118/116.
Reader Comments: Good course for novice golfers, very good condition … Good condition but both courses have too many similar holes … Inexpensive course, huge greens tilted back to front … Greens were rough … Appreciate customers.

WYOMING

★★ AIRPORT GOLF CLUB
PU-4801 Central, Cheyenne, 82009, Laramie County, (307)637-6418, 100 miles from Denver. **E-mail:** mikelepore@msn.com. **Facility Holes:** 18. **Yards:** 6,121/5,661. **Par:** 70/74. **Course Rating:** 67.8/68.4. **Slope:** 109/106. **Green Fee:** $14. **Cart Fee:** $20/Cart. **Walking Policy:** Unrestricted walking. **Walkability:** 2. **Opened:** 1927. **Season:** Year-round. **High:** April-Oct. **To obtain tee times:** Call up to 2 days in advance. **Miscellaneous:** Reduced fees (twilight), range (grass), credit cards (MC, V, AE, D), BF, FF.

★★★ BELL NOB GOLF CLUB
PU-4600 Overdale Dr., Gillette, 82718, Campbell County, (307)686-7069, 140 miles from Rapid City. **Facility Holes:** 18. **Yards:** 7,024/5,555. **Par:** 72/72. **Course Rating:** 70.8/70.6. **Slope:** 119/116. **Green Fee:** $21. **Cart Fee:** $11/Person. **Walking Policy:** Unrestricted walking. **Walkability:** 4. **Opened:** 1981. **Architect:** Frank Hummel. **Season:** April-Oct. **High:** June-Sept. **To obtain tee times:** Call up to 7 days in advance. **Miscellaneous:** Range (grass), credit cards (MC, V), BF, FF.
Reader Comments: Excellent shape and fun to play ... Watch out for antelope.

★★★½ BUFFALO GOLF CLUB
PU-P.O. Box 759, Buffalo, 82834, Johnson County, (307)684-5266, 110 miles from Casper. **Facility Holes:** 18. **Yards:** 6,556/5,512. **Par:** 71/72. **Course Rating:** 69.5/69.7. **Slope:** 114/115. **Green Fee:** $22. **Cart Fee:** $20/Cart. **Walking Policy:** Unrestricted walking. **Walkability:** 4. **Opened:** 1928. **Architect:** Bill Poirot. **Season:** April-Oct. **High:** May-Oct. **Tee times:** Call up to 30 days in advance. **Miscellaneous:** Range (grass/mats), credit cards (MC, V), BF, FF.
Reader Comments: Beautiful, hilly, old mountain course ... Almost as many deer as trees.

★★½ CASPER MUNICIPAL GOLF COURSE
PU-2120 Allendale, Casper, 82601, Natrona County, (307)234-2405, 120 miles from Cheyenne. **E-mail:** progolfgm@aol.com. **Facility Holes:** 27. **Green Fee:** $15. **Cart Fee:** $8/Person. **Walking Policy:** Unrestricted walking. **Walkability:** 3. **Opened:** 1929. **Architect:** Robert Muir Graves/Keith Foster. **Season:** March-Nov. **High:** May-Sept. **To obtain tee times:** Call up to 1 day in advance. **Miscellaneous:** Range (grass/mats), credit cards (MC, V), BF, FF.
HIGHLANDS/LINKS (18 Combo)
Yards: 6,562/5,500. **Par:** 71/73. **Course Rating:** 69.7/69.7. **Slope:** 113/118.
HIGHLANDS/PARK (18 Combo)
Yards: 6,253/5,492. **Par:** 70/72. **Course Rating:** 68.1/69.3. **Slope:** 108/113.
PARK/LINKS (18 Combo)
Yards: 6,317/5,384. **Par:** 71/71. **Course Rating:** 68.4/68.8. **Slope:** 108/112.

CHEYENNE COUNTRY CLUB
SP-800 Stinner Rd., Cheyenne, 82001, Laramie County, (307)637-2230, 120 miles from Denver. **Facility Holes:** 18. **Yards:** 6,619/5,320. **Par:** 72/73. **Course Rating:** 69.2/70.2. **Slope:** 114/113. **Green Fee:** $24/$50. **Cart Fee:** $19/Cart. **Walking Policy:** Unrestricted walking. **Walkability:** 2. **Opened:** 1912. **Architect:** Dick Phelps. **Season:** March-Dec. **High:** June-Aug. **To obtain tee times:** Call golf shop. **Miscellaneous:** Range (grass/mats), credit cards (MC, V).

COTTONWOOD COUNTRY CLUB
PU-West 15th St., Torrington, 82240, Goshen County, (307)532-3868, 60 miles from Cheyenne. **Facility Holes:** 18. **Yards:** 6,298/5,344. **Par:** 72/73. **Course Rating:** 69.9/70.5. **Slope:** 126/127. **Green Fee:** $15/$16. **Cart Fee:** $14/Cart. **Walking Policy:** Unrestricted walking. **Walkability:** 1. **Season:** Year-round. **High:** May-Aug. **To obtain tee times:** Call golf shop. **Miscellaneous:** Range (grass), credit cards (MC, V), BF, FF.

★★½ DOUGLAS COMMUNITY CLUB
PU-64 Golf Course Rd., Douglas, 82633, Converse County, (307)358-5099, 50 miles from Casper. **E-mail:** douglasgc@vcn.com. **Facility Holes:** 18. **Yards:** 6,253/5,323. **Par:** 71/72. **Course Rating:** 68.4/68.5. **Slope:** 107/103. **Green Fee:** $18. **Cart Fee:** $9/Person. **Walking Policy:** Unrestricted walking. **Walkability:** 3. **Opened:** 1974. **Architect:** Vern Knisley. **Season:** April-Oct. **High:** April-Oct. **To obtain tee times:** Call up to 7 days in advance. **Miscellaneous:** Range (grass), credit cards (MC, V), BF, FF.

FRANCIS E. WARREN AFB GOLF COURSE
PU-7103 Randall Ave., F.E. Warren AFB, 82005, Laramie County, (307)773-3556, 1 mile from Cheyenne. **Facility Holes:** 18. **Yards:** 6,652/5,036. **Par:** 72/73. **Course Rating:** 69.6/67.0. **Slope:** 112/111. **Green Fee:** $9/$16. **Cart Fee:** $16/Cart. **Walking Policy:** Unrestricted walking. **Walkability:** 1. **Opened:** 1949. **Architect:** U.S. Government. **Season:** Year-round. **High:** April-Oct. **To obtain tee times:** Call golf shop. **Miscellaneous:** Reduced fees (twilight), range (grass), credit cards (MC, V).

GREEN HILLS MUNICIPAL GOLF COURSE
PU-1455 Airport Rd., Worland, 82401, Washakie County, (307)347-8972, 180 miles from Billings, MT. **Facility Holes:** 18. **Yards:** 6,444/5,104. **Par:** 72/72. **Course Rating:** 69.3/68.0. **Slope:** 113/113. **Green Fee:** $16/$18. **Cart Fee:** $16/Cart. **Walking Policy:** Unrestricted walking. **Walkability:** 3. **Opened:** 1954. **Architect:** Dennis Smith/Dennis Bower. **Season:** April-Oct. **High:** June-Aug. **Tee times:** Call golf shop. **Misc:** Reduced fees (juniors), range (grass).

★★★★ JACKSON HOLE GOLF & TENNIS CLUB
R-5000 Spring Gulch Rd., Jackson, 83001, Teton County, (307)733-3111, 8 miles from Jackson. **Facility Holes:** 18. **Yards:** 7,168/6,036. **Par:** 72/73. **Course Rating:** 72.3/73.2. **Slope:** 133/125. **Green Fee:** $85/$125. **Cart Fee:** Included in green fee. **Walking Policy:** Walking at certain times. **Walkability:** 1. **Opened:** 1963. **Architect:** Robert Trent Jones Jr. **Season:** April-Oct. **High:** June-Aug. **To obtain tee times:** Call golf shop. **Miscellaneous:** Reduced fees (twilight), range (grass), credit cards (MC, V, AE).
Notes: Ranked 1st in 2001 Best in State; 40th in 1996 America's Top 75 Upscale Courses.
Reader Comments: Can't beat the view … The scenery is absolutely magnificient! Great course with plenty of challenges to test your golf … Teton Mountains are breathtaking.

★★ JACOBY GOLF COURSE
PU-University of Wyoming, Laramie, 82071, Albany County, (307)745-3111, 140 miles from Denver. **Web:** www.uwyo.edu/jacobygc. **Facility Holes:** 18. **Yards:** 6,590/5,480. **Par:** 70/72. **Course Rating:** 69.3/69.3. **Slope:** 114/121. **Green Fee:** $14/$21. **Cart Fee:** $18/Cart. **Walking Policy:** Unrestricted walking. **Walkability:** 2. **Opened:** 1932. **Season:** March-Oct. **High:** June-Aug. **To obtain tee times:** Call golf shop. **Miscellaneous:** Reduced fees (juniors), range (grass), credit cards (MC, V).

★★ KENDRICK GOLF COURSE
PU-Big Goose Rd., Sheridan, 82801, Sheridan County, (307)674-8148, 125 miles from Billings. **Facility Holes:** 18. **Yards:** 6,800/5,549. **Par:** 72/73. **Course Rating:** 71.3/70.8. **Slope:** 116/113. **Green Fee:** $19. **Cart Fee:** $19/Cart. **Walking Policy:** Unrestricted walking. **Walkability:** 3. **Opened:** 1940. **Architect:** Edward A. Hunnicutt/Frank Hummel. **Season:** April-Oct. **High:** May-July. **To obtain tee times:** Call golf shop. **Miscellaneous:** Reduced fees (juniors), range (grass), credit cards (MC, V).

LANDER GOLF & COUNTRY CLUB
PU-1 Golf Course Dr., Lander, 82520, Fremont County, (307)332-4653. **Facility Holes:** 18. **Yards:** 6,574/4,770. **Par:** 71/71. **Course Rating:** 70.8. **Slope:** 113. **Green Fee:** $20. **Opened:** 1933. **To obtain tee times:** Call golf shop.

NEW CASTLE COUNTRY CLUB
SP-2302 W. Main St., Newcastle, 82701, Weston County, (307)746-2639. **Facility Holes:** 9. **Yards:** 3,241/2,783. **Par:** 36/38. **Course Rating:** 69.4/71.1. **Slope:** 113/113. **Green Fee:** $9. **Opened:** 1966. **To obtain tee times:** Call golf shop.

★★★ OLIVE GLENN GOLF & COUNTRY CLUB
SP-802 Meadow Lane, Cody, 82414, Park County, (307)587-5551, 102 miles from Billings. **E-mail:** oliveglenn@tritel.net. **Facility Holes:** 18. **Yards:** 6,880/5,654. **Par:** 72/72. **Course Rating:** 71.6/71.2. **Slope:** 124/120. **Green Fee:** $21/$35. **Cart Fee:** $10/Person. **Walking Policy:** Unrestricted walking. **Walkability:** 2. **Opened:** 1970. **Architect:** Bob Baldock. **Season:** April-Oct. **High:** June-Aug. **To obtain tee times:** Call up to 7 days in advance. **Miscellaneous:** Reduced fees (juniors), range (grass/mats), credit cards (MC, V), BF, FF.
Notes: Ranked 5th in 2001 Best in State.
Reader Comments: Friendly, unpretentious, challenging … Beautiful … Delightful restaurant.

POWDER HORN GOLF CLUB
SP-14 Clubhouse Rd., Sheridan, 82801, Sheridan County, (307)672-5323, 120 miles from Billings. **E-mail:** proshop@fiberpipe.net. **Web:** www.thepowderhorn.com. **Facility Holes:** 18. **Yards:** 6,934/4,596. **Par:** 72/72. **Course Rating:** 72.3/64.5. **Slope:** 128/110. **Green Fee:** $41/$69. **Cart Fee:** Included in green fee. **Walking Policy:** Unrestricted walking. **Walkability:** 3. **Opened:** 1997. **Architect:** Dick Bailey. **Season:** April-Oct. **High:** May-Sept. **To obtain tee times:** Call up to 7 days in advance. **Miscellaneous:** Reduced fees (weekdays, guests, juniors), range (grass), lodging (10 rooms), credit cards (MC, V, AE, D, DC, CB), BF, FF.

★★½ POWELL COUNTRY CLUB
PU-600 Hwy. 114, Powell, 82435, Park County, (307)754-7259, 7 miles from Powell. **E-mail:** powellgolf@tritel.net. **Facility Holes:** 18. **Yards:** 6,498/5,067. **Par:** 72/72. **Course Rating:** 69.6/67.3. **Slope:** 117/113. **Green Fee:** $18/$22. **Cart Fee:** $22/Cart. **Walking Policy:** Unrestricted walking. **Walkability:** 3. **Opened:** 1949. **Architect:** Local Grounds

WYOMING

Committee. **Season:** March-Nov. **High:** May-Aug. **To obtain tee times:** Call up to 7 days in advance. **Miscellaneous:** Reduced fees (weekdays, juniors), range (grass), credit cards (MC, V), BF, FF.

PURPLE SAGE MUNICIPAL GOLF COURSE
PU-19th and Country Club Dr., Evanston, 82930, Uinta County, (307)789-2383, 75 miles from Salt Lake City. **E-mail:** psgc@allwest.net. **Facility Holes:** 9. **Yards:** 2,960/2,684. **Par:** 36/36. **Course Rating:** 67.5/68.9. **Slope:** 110/119. **Green Fee:** $18. **Cart Fee:** $18/Cart. **Walking Policy:** Unrestricted walking. **Walkability:** 3. **Opened:** 1956. **Season:** May-Oct. **High:** April-Oct. **To obtain tee times:** Call up to 3 days in advance. **Miscellaneous:** Reduced fees (seniors, juniors), range (grass/mats), credit cards (MC, V), BF, FF.

★★ RENDEZVOUS MEADOWS GOLF CLUB
PU-55 Clubhouse Rd., Pinedale, 82941, Sublette County, (307)367-4252, 1 mile from Pinedale. **E-mail:** mlauger@wyoming.com. **Facility Holes:** 9. **Yards:** 3,255/2,760. **Par:** 36/36. **Course Rating:** 69.8/70.3. **Slope:** 118/118. **Green Fee:** $15/$20. **Cart Fee:** $10/Person. **Walking Policy:** Unrestricted walking. **Walkability:** 2. **Opened:** 1985. **Architect:** William Hull. **Season:** April-Oct. **High:** July-Aug. **To obtain tee times:** Call golf shop. **Miscellaneous:** Reduced fees (weekdays), range (grass/mats), credit cards (MC, V), BF, FF.

★★★½ RIVERTON COUNTRY CLUB
SP-4275 Country Club Dr., Riverton, 82501, Fremont County, (307)856-4779, 117 miles from Casper. **E-mail:** recgolf@wyoming.com. **Facility Holes:** 18. **Yards:** 7,064/5,549. **Par:** 72/72. **Course Rating:** 72.2/71.0. **Slope:** 128/119. **Green Fee:** $20/$38. **Cart Fee:** $15/Person. **Walking Policy:** Unrestricted walking. **Walkability:** 2. **Opened:** 1953. **Architect:** Richard Watson. **Season:** March-Nov. **High:** May-Oct. **To obtain tee times:** Call up to 7 days in advance. **Miscellaneous:** Reduced fees (twilight), range (grass), credit cards (MC, V), BF, FF.
Reader Comments: Great value ... Lots of water ... Rough is very rough.

★★ SARATOGA INN RESORT
R-P.O. Box 869 - 601 East Pic Pike Road, Saratoga, 82331, Carbon County, (307)326-5261, (800)594-0178, 80 miles from Laramie. **Facility Holes:** 9. **Yards:** 3,425/2,943. **Par:** 36/36. **Course Rating:** 69.7/71.4. **Slope:** 112/113. **Green Fee:** $35. **Cart Fee:** $20/Cart. **Walking Policy:** Unrestricted walking. **Walkability:** 1. **Opened:** 1950. **Season:** May-Oct. **To obtain tee times:** Call golf shop. **Miscellaneous:** Reduced fees (juniors), lodging (50 rooms), credit cards (MC, V, AE, D), BF, FF.

SHERIDAN COUNTRY CLUB
SP-1992 West 5th St., Sheridan, 82801, Sheridan County, (307)674-8135, 150 miles from Billings. **Facility Holes:** 9. **Yards:** 6,225/5,921. **Par:** 72/72. **Course Rating:** 68.2/73.0. **Slope:** 118/117. **Green Fee:** $20. **Cart Fee:** $20/Cart. **Walking Policy:** Unrestricted walking. **Walkability:** 2. **Opened:** 1920. **Season:** April-Nov. **High:** June-Aug. **To obtain tee times:** Call golf shop. **Miscellaneous:** Credit cards (MC, V, AE), BF, FF.

SINCLAIR GOLF CLUB
SP-Golf Course Rd., Sinclair, 82334, Carson County, (307)324-7767, 8 miles from Rawlins. **E-mail:** sinclairgolfclub@excite.com. **Facility Holes:** 9. **Yards:** 5,865/5,405. **Par:** 71/72. **Course Rating:** 67.1/68.3. **Slope:** 107/113. **Green Fee:** $16/$18. **Cart Fee:** $18/Cart. **Walking Policy:** Unrestricted walking. **Walkability:** 1. **Opened:** 1947. **Season:** April-Oct. **High:** June-Aug. **To obtain tee times:** Call up to 14 days in advance. **Miscellaneous:** Reduced fees (weekdays), range (mats), credit cards (MC, V), BF, FF.

STAR VALLEY RANCH COUNTRY CLUB
SP-1800 Cedar Creek Dr., Thayne, 83127, Lincoln County, (307)883-2899, 50 miles from Jackson. **E-mail:** ebuchler@juno.com. **Web:** www.starvalleywy.com. **Facility Holes:** 27. **Green Fee:** $16/$37. **Cart Fee:** $17/Cart. **Walking Policy:** Unrestricted walking. **Walkability:** 3. **Architect:** Harold Stewart. **Season:** April-Oct. **High:** June-Aug. **To obtain tee times:** Call golf shop. **Miscellaneous:** Reduced fees (weekdays, twilight), range (grass), credit cards (MC, V).
ASPEN HILLS (9)
Yards: 6,260/5,430. **Par:** 72/72. **Course Rating:** 68.3/69.7. **Slope:** 119/123. **Opened:** 1972.
★★★ CEDAR CREEK (18)
Yards: 6,446/5,950. **Par:** 73/73. **Course Rating:** 69.3/71.0. **Slope:** 116/121. **Opened:** 1970.

★★★½ TETON PINES RESORT & COUNTRY CLUB
R-3450 Clubhouse Dr., Jackson, 83001, Teton County, (307)733-1733, (800)238-2223, 5 miles from Jackson. **E-mail:** info@tetonpines.com. **Web:** www.tetonpines.com. **Facility Holes:** 18. **Yards:** 7,412/5,486. **Par:** 72/72. **Course Rating:** 74.8/70.1. **Slope:** 137/124. **Green Fee:** $60/$180. **Cart Fee:** Included in green fee. **Walking Policy:** Walking with Caddie. **Walkability:** 2. **Opened:** 1987. **Architect:** Arnold Palmer/Ed Seay. **Season:** May-Oct. **High:** July-

WYOMING

Sept. **Tee times:** Call up to 365 days in advance. **Misc:** Reduced fees (guests, juniors), range (grass/mats), caddies, lodging (18 rooms), credit cards (MC, V, AE, DC), BF, FF. **Notes:** Ranked 3rd in 2001 Best in State.

Reader Comments: Beautiful views ... Very beautiful and expensive ... Can't afford to play it very often ... A must play course ... Pretty scenery.

TORRINGTON MUNICIPAL GOLF COURSE
PU-W. 15th. St., Torrington, 82240, Goshen County, (307)532-3868. **Facility Holes:** 18. **Yards:** 6,298/5,344. **Par:** 72/73. **Course Rating:** 69.9/70.5. **Slope:** 126/127. **Green Fee:** $15/$16. **Cart Fee:** $14/Cart. **Walking Policy:** Unrestricted walking. **Walkability:** 2. **Season:** Year-round. **High:** June-Aug. **To obtain tee times:** Call golf shop. **Miscellaneous:** Reduced fees (weekdays), range (grass), credit cards (MC, V).

WHEATLAND GOLF CLUB
PU-1253 E. Cole Rd., Wheatland, 82201, Platte County, (307)322-3675. **Facility Holes:** 9. **Yards:** 6,226/5,204. **Par:** 72/72. **Course Rating:** 67.9/68.5. **Slope:** 113/108. **Green Fee:** $15/$18. **Walking Policy:** Unrestricted walking. **Walkability:** 3. **Opened:** 1960. **Season:** April-Oct. **To obtain tee times:** Call golf shop. **Miscellaneous:** Range (grass), credit cards (MC, V, AE, D), BF, FF.

★★★ WHITE MOUNTAIN GOLF COURSE
PU-1501 Clubhouse Dr., Rock Springs, 82901, Sweetwater County, (307)352-1415. **Facility Holes:** 18. **Yards:** 7,000/5,666. **Par:** 72/73. **Course Rating:** 72.4/73.1. **Slope:** 122/115. **Green Fee:** $15. **Cart Fee:** $15/Person. **Walking Policy:** Unrestricted walking. **Opened:** 1979. **Architect:** Dick Phelps/Donald G. Brauer. **Season:** April-Oct. **High:** June-Sept. **To obtain tee times:** Call golf shop. **Miscellaneous:** Reduced fees (juniors), range (grass/mats).

Reader Comments: Long course but playable for all but very high handicappers ... In great shape ... Friendly atmosphere.

Part II

Canada

CANADA

ALBERTA

ATHABASCA GOLF & COUNTRY CLUB
SP-P.O. Box 2225, Athabasca, T9S 2B7, (780)675-4599, (888)475-4599, 1 mile from Athabasca. **E-mail:** proshop@athagolf.com. **Web:** www.athagolf.com. **Facility Holes:** 18. **Yards:** 6,800/5,400. **Par:** 72/72. **Course Rating:** 73.3/73.7. **Slope:** 133/125. **Green Fee:** $28/$30. **Cart Fee:** $25/Cart. **Walking Policy:** Unrestricted walking. **Walkability:** 4. **Opened:** 1960. **Architect:** Sid Puddicombe. **Season:** April-Oct. **High:** July-Aug. **To obtain tee times:** Call up to 5 days in advance. **Miscellaneous:** Range (grass), credit cards (MC, V), BF, FF.

BANFF SPRINGS GOLF COURSE
R-One Golf Course Rd., Banff, T0L 0C0, (403)762-6833, 70 miles from Calgary. **E-mail:** jason.getty@fairmont.com. **Web:** www.banffsprings.com. **Facility Holes:** 27. **Walking Policy:** Unrestricted walking. **Walkability:** 3. **Season:** May-Oct. **High:** July-Sept. **To obtain tee times:** Call up to 160 days in advance. **Miscellaneous:** Range (mats), lodging (780 rooms), credit cards (MC, V, AE, D, DC), BF, FF.
★★★★½   **STANLEY THOMPSON 18 (18)**   *Value+*
Yards: 7,072/5,607. **Par:** 71/71. **Course Rating:** 74.4/72.5. **Slope:** 142/139. **Green Fee:** $75/$165. **Cart Fee:** Included in green fee. **Opened:** 1928. **Architect:** Stanley Thompson. **Miscellaneous:** Reduced fees (guests).
Reader Comments: Classic design, spectacular views ... Wonderful service ... You pay a lot however it has been the most memorable golf experience of my life.
★★★½   **TUNNEL 9 (9)**
Yards: 3,325/2,806. **Par:** 36/36. **Course Rating:** 73.8/67.0. **Slope:** 134/121. **Cart Fee:** $20/Person. **Opened:** 1989. **Architect:** William Robinson. **Miscellaneous:** Reduced fees ().
Reader Comments: Looks easy for 9 holes, but is challenging ... High end course with good value.

★★★½   **BARRHEAD GOLF CLUB**
PU-P.O. Box 4090, Barrhead, T7N 1A1, (780)674-3053, (888)674-3053, 60 miles from Edmonton. **E-mail:** bargolf@telusplanet.net. **Facility Holes:** 18. **Yards:** 6,593/5,341. **Par:** 72/72. **Course Rating:** 72.0/71.0. **Slope:** 127/120. **Green Fee:** $18/$32. **Cart Fee:** $25/Cart. **Walking Policy:** Unrestricted walking. **Walkability:** 3. **Opened:** 1991. **Architect:** Les Furber. **Season:** May-Oct. **High:** June-Aug. **To obtain tee times:** Call up to 4 days in advance. **Miscellaneous:** Reduced fees (twilight), range (grass/mats), credit cards (MC, V, AE), BF, FF.
Reader Comments: Excellent value and a very challenging course ... Nice scenery, good layout ... Holes 14-17 tough.

★★   **BROADMOOR PUBLIC GOLF COURSE**
PU-2100 Oak St., Sherwood Park, T8A 0V9, (780)467-7373, 10 miles from Edmonton. **Facility Holes:** 18. **Yards:** 6,550/5,750. **Par:** 71/71. **Course Rating:** 69.5/70.4. **Slope:** 122/120. **Green Fee:** $28/$34. **Cart Fee:** $27/Cart. **Walking Policy:** Unrestricted walking. **Walkability:** 3. **Opened:** 1960. **Architect:** Norman H. Woods. **Season:** March-Oct. **To obtain tee times:** Call up to 3 days in advance. **Miscellaneous:** Reduced fees (weekdays, twilight, seniors, juniors), range (grass/mats), credit cards (MC, V, AE), BF, FF.

★★★½   **CANMORE GOLF & CURLING CLUB**
SP-2000 8th Ave., Canmore, TIW 142, (403)678-4785, 55 miles from Calgary. **E-mail:** canpro@telusplanet.net. **Facility Holes:** 18. **Yards:** 6,309/5,258. **Par:** 71/72. **Course Rating:** 69.1/68.7. **Slope:** 122/119. **Green Fee:** $48. **Cart Fee:** $17/Cart. **Walking Policy:** Unrestricted walking. **Walkability:** 3. **Opened:** 1926. **Architect:** Bill Newis. **Season:** April-Oct. **High:** June-Sept. **To obtain tee times:** Call golf shop. **Miscellaneous:** Reduced fees (guests, juniors), range (mats), credit cards (MC, V, AE, Debit Card), BF, FF.
Reader Comments: Underrated mountain course ... Old cabin for a pro shop has real charm ... Nice mountain course ... Enjoyable day—good value ... A nice country course ... Great small-town course in mountain setting ... Very scenic and reasonably priced ... Couldn't ask for more.

★★★★½   **COLONIALE GOLF & COUNTRY CLUB**
SP-10 Country Club Dr., Beaumont, T4X 1M1, (780)929-4653, 2 miles from Edmonton. **E-mail:** cgcc@telusplanet.net. **Facility Holes:** 18. **Yards:** 7,020/5,666. **Par:** 72/72. **Course Rating:** 73.8/72.1. **Slope:** 145/126. **Green Fee:** $30/$55. **Cart Fee:** Included in green fee. **Walking Policy:** Mandatory carts. **Walkability:** 3. **Opened:** 1993. **Architect:** Bill Newis. **Season:** April-Oct. **High:** May-Sept. **To obtain tee times:** Call golf shop. **Miscellaneous:** Reduced fees (weekdays, twilight, seniors, juniors), range (grass/mats), credit cards (MC, V), BF, FF.
Reader Comments: Good value and very challenging ... Links-style course ... Forces you to think on every hole ... Spectacular layout ... Do not like mandatory power carts.

CANADA

★★★ **CONNAUGHT GOLF CLUB**
SP-2802 13th Ave. S.E., Medicine Hat, T1A 3P9, (403)526-0737, 185 miles from Calgary. **E-mail:** knotpros@telusplanet.net. **Facility Holes:** 18. **Yards:** 6,993/5,800. **Par:** 72/73. **Course Rating:** 74.0/73.5. **Slope:** 128/126. **Green Fee:** $32/$36. **Cart Fee:** $30/Cart. **Walking Policy:** Unrestricted walking. **Walkability:** 2. **Architect:** A.L. (Ron) Ehlert. **Season:** April-Oct. **To obtain tee times:** Call up to 2 days in advance. **Miscellaneous:** Reduced fees (juniors), range (mats), credit cards (MC, V, AE).
Reader Comments: A treat to play ... The pro shop and clubhouse service is second to none ... The greens have vastly improved over the past few years ... Very challenging course ... Not too difficult but enough to keep you interested.

COUNTRYSIDE GOLF COURSE
PU-51466 Range Rd. 232, Sherwood Park, T8B 1L1, (780)467-9254, 6 miles from Edmonton. **E-mail:** golf@apexmail.com. **Facility Holes:** 27. **Green Fee:** $25/$30. **Cart Fee:** $24/Cart. **Walking Policy:** Unrestricted walking. **Season:** April-Oct. **To obtain tee times:** Call up to 5 days in advance. **Miscellaneous:** Reduced fees (seniors, juniors), range (grass/mats), credit cards (MC, V, AE), BF, FF.
PRAIRIES (18)
Yards: 6,980/5,874. **Par:** 72/73. **Walkability:** 2. **Opened:** 1986. **Architect:** J. Solomon.
WOODLANDS (9)
Yards: 2,844/2,487. **Par:** 36/36. **Walkability:** 3. **Opened:** 1985. **Architect:** Harry Seutter.

★★★½ **D'ARCY RANCH GOLF CLUB**
PU-Hwy. 2A and Milligan Dr., Okotoks, T0L 1T0, (403)938-4455, (800)803-8810, 14 miles from Calgary. **E-mail:** darcy@darcyranchgolf.com. **Web:** www.darcyranchgolf.com. **Facility Holes:** 18. **Yards:** 6,919/5,567. **Par:** 72/73. **Course Rating:** 72.7/70.4. **Slope:** 130/117. **Green Fee:** $55. **Cart Fee:** $13/Person. **Walking Policy:** Unrestricted walking. **Walkability:** 4. **Opened:** 1991. **Architect:** Finger/Dye/Spann. **Season:** April-Oct. **High:** May-Sept. **To obtain tee times:** Call up to 2 days in advance. **Miscellaneous:** Reduced fees (twilight, juniors), range (grass/mats), credit cards (MC, V, AE), BF, FF.
Reader Comments: Nice staff ... One of my favorite local clubs ... An excellent setup ... Challenging public course ... Good value ... Good dining room ... If it's windy, stay in control ... One of my favorite courses.

★★½ **DINOSAUR TRAIL GOLF & COUNTRY CLUB**
PU-P.O. Box 1511, Drumheller, T0J 0Y0, (403)823-5622, (866)833-3466, 110 miles from Calgary. **E-mail:** dinogolf@telusplanet.net. **Web:** www.dinosaurtrailgolf.com. **Facility Holes:** 18. **Yards:** 6,401/5,093. **Par:** 72/73. **Course Rating:** 71.2/68.4. **Slope:** 135/110. **Green Fee:** $36. **Cart Fee:** $30/Cart. **Walking Policy:** Walking at certain times. **Walkability:** 5. **Opened:** 1995. **Architect:** Sid Puddicombe. **Season:** May-Oct. **High:** June-Sept. **To obtain tee times:** Call up to 14 days in advance. **Miscellaneous:** Reduced fees (seniors, juniors), range (grass/mats), BF, FF, credit cards (MC, V), BF, FF.

DOUBLE DAM GOLF COURSE
PU-General Delivery, Rosalind, T0B 3YO, (780)375-2154, 23 miles from Camrose. **Facility Holes:** 18. **Yards:** 5,227/5,227. **Par:** 67/67. **Green Fee:** $16. **Cart Fee:** $17/Cart. **Walking Policy:** Unrestricted walking. **Walkability:** 2. **Opened:** 1989. **Season:** May-Oct. **High:** July-Sept. **Tee times:** Call golf shop. **Miscellaneous:** Range (grass/mats), credit cards (MC), BF, FF.

★★½ **THE DUNES GOLF & WINTER CLUB**
PU-RR #1, Site 4, Box 1, Grande Prairie, T8V 5N3, (780)538-4333, (888)224-2252. **E-mail:** dunes@telusplanet.net. **Facility Holes:** 18. **Yards:** 6,436/5,274. **Par:** 71/72. **Course Rating:** 69.3/70.1. **Slope:** 124/120. **Green Fee:** $25/$36. **Cart Fee:** $26/Cart. **Walking Policy:** Unrestricted walking. **Walkability:** 3. **Opened:** 1992. **Architect:** Mel Watchhorn. **Season:** May-Oct. **High:** May-June. **To obtain tee times:** Call golf shop. **Miscellaneous:** Reduced fees (seniors), range (grass/mats), credit cards (MC, V, AE), BF, FF.

★½ **EAGLE ROCK GOLF COURSE**
PU-TWP 510, RR 234, South Edmonton, T6H 4N6, (780)464-4653, 5 miles from Edmonton. **Facility Holes:** 18. **Yards:** 6,660/5,644. **Par:** 71/71. **Course Rating:** 72.0/71.4. **Slope:** 123/121. **Green Fee:** $21/$35. **Cart Fee:** $25/Cart. **Walking Policy:** Unrestricted walking. **Walkability:** 3. **Opened:** 1990. **Architect:** Sid Puddicome. **Season:** April-Oct. **High:** June-Aug. **To obtain tee times:** Call up to 7 days in advance. **Miscellaneous:** Reduced fees (weekdays, twilight, seniors, juniors), range (grass), credit cards (MC, V), BF, FF.

FAIRWAYS WEST GOLF COURSE
PU-Hiwy. 22, Alder Flats, T0C 0A0, (780)388-3060. **Facility Holes:** 18. **Yards:** 6,890/5,500. **Par:** 72/72. **Green Fee:** $17/$19. **Cart Fee:** $22/Cart. **To obtain tee times:** Call golf shop.

★★★½ GOOSE HUMMOCK GOLF RESORT
PU-2 Miles N. of Gibbons, Hwy. 28, Gibbons, T0A 1N0, (780)921-2444, 10 miles from Edmonton. **E-mail:** goosehum@telusplanet.net. **Web:** www.golfthegoose.com. **Facility Holes:** 18. **Yards:** 6,604/5,408. **Par:** 71/71. **Course Rating:** 72.5/71.5. **Slope:** 135/121. **Green Fee:** $28/$35. **Cart Fee:** $26/Cart. **Walking Policy:** Unrestricted walking. **Walkability:** 2. **Opened:** 1989. **Architect:** William Robinson. **Season:** April-Oct. **High:** June-Sept. **To obtain tee times:** Call up to 7 days in advance. **Miscellaneous:** Reduced fees (twilight, seniors, juniors), range (grass/mats), credit cards (MC, V, AE, Debit Card), BF, FF.
Reader Comments: Very challenging … Beautiful in September! … Most difficult course in area. Interesting holes … Course management a must.

★★ HENDERSON LAKE GOLF CLUB
PU-2727 S. Parkside Dr., Lethbridge, T1K 0C6, (403)329-6767, 120 miles from Calgary. **E-mail:** hlgc@home.com. **Facility Holes:** 18. **Yards:** 6,512/5,976. **Par:** 70/75. **Course Rating:** 70.5/73.1. **Slope:** 120/123. **Green Fee:** $30. **Cart Fee:** $25/Cart. **Walking Policy:** Unrestricted walking. **Walkability:** 1. **Opened:** 1917. **Architect:** Norman H. Woods. **Season:** April-Oct. **To obtain tee times:** Call up to 2 days in advance. **Miscellaneous:** Reduced fees (twilight, juniors), metal spikes, credit cards (MC, V), BF, FF.

★★★½ HERITAGE POINTE GOLF & COUNTRY CLUB
R-R.R. No.1, Heritage Pointe Dr., De Winton, T0L 0X0, (403)256-2002, 6 miles from Calgary. **E-mail:** inform@heritagepointe.com. **Web:** www.heritagepointe.com. **Facility Holes:** 27. **Green Fee:** $90. **Cart Fee:** Included in green fee. **Walking Policy:** Unrestricted walking. **Walkability:** 5. **Opened:** 1992. **Architect:** Ron Garl. **Season:** April-Oct. **High:** April-Oct. **To obtain tee times:** Call up to 7 days in advance. **Miscellaneous:** Reduced fees (twilight, seniors, juniors), range (grass), credit cards (MC, V, AE, DC), BF, FF.
DESERT/HERITAGE (18 Combo)
Yards: 7,044/4,967. **Par:** 72/73. **Course Rating:** 74.0/68.0. **Slope:** 128/129.
POINTE/DESERT (18 Combo)
Yards: 6,936/4,944. **Par:** 72/72. **Course Rating:** 73.0/67.0. **Slope:** 131/125.
POINTE/HERITAGE (18 Combo)
Yards: 6,904/4,773. **Par:** 72/73. **Course Rating:** 73.0/66.0. **Slope:** 137/128.
Reader Comments: Difficult course, lots of water … Good facilities … Challenging, well maintained … Beautiful clubhouse … Some great holes … Stay within your game.

HINTON GOLF CLUB
PU-Hwy. 16 W., Hinton, T7V 1Y2, (780)865-2905, 175 miles from Edmonton. **Facility Holes:** 18. **Yards:** 6,729/5,700. **Par:** 72/72. **Course Rating:** 72.0/70.0. **Slope:** 125/120. **Green Fee:** $32/$35. **Cart Fee:** $27/Cart. **Walking Policy:** Unrestricted walking. **Walkability:** 3. **Opened:** 1964. **Architect:** N/A. **High:** May-Sept. **To obtain tee times:** Call golf shop. **Miscellaneous:** Reduced fees (twilight, juniors), range (grass/mats), credit cards (MC, V, AE), BF, FF.

★★½ INDIAN LAKES GOLF CLUB
PU-Hwy 60 South of Hwy 16, Enoch, T7X 3Y3, (780)470-4653, 6 miles from Edmonton. **Web:** www.indianlakes.ab.ca.com. **Facility Holes:** 18. **Yards:** 6,650/5,600. **Par:** 71/71. **Course Rating:** 69.5/67.0. **Slope:** 128/128. **Green Fee:** $23/$26. **Cart Fee:** $24/Cart. **Walking Policy:** Unrestricted walking. **Walkability:** 2. **Opened:** 1989. **Architect:** William Robinson. **Season:** April-Oct. **High:** June-Aug. **To obtain tee times:** Call golf shop. **Miscellaneous:** Reduced fees (seniors, juniors), range (grass).

★★★ IRONHEAD GOLF & COUNTRY CLUB
PU-P.O. Box 69, Wabamun, T0E 2K0, (780)892-4653, 30 miles from Edmonton. **E-mail:** johnb@ironheadgolfcourse.com. **Web:** www.ironheadgolfcourse.com. **Facility Holes:** 18. **Yards:** 6,805/5,442. **Par:** 72/72. **Course Rating:** 72.0/70.4. **Slope:** 132/124. **Green Fee:** $22/$27. **Cart Fee:** $23/Cart. **Walking Policy:** Unrestricted walking. **Walkability:** 4. **Opened:** 1987. **Architect:** Les Furber. **Season:** April-Oct. **High:** July-Aug. **To obtain tee times:** Call up to 5 days in advance. **Miscellaneous:** Reduced fees (weekdays, juniors), metal spikes, range (grass/mats), credit cards (MC, V, AE), BF, FF.
Reader Comments: Great layout, condition of course improving … Beautiful course … Tee boxes are so good, they could be the greens on some courses! Fantastic.

★★★★½ JASPER PARK LODGE GOLF COURSE *Service, Value, Pace*
R-Box 40, Jasper, T0E 1E0, (780)852-6089, 210 miles from Edmonton. **E-mail:** jplgolf@fairmont.com. **Web:** www.fairmont.com. **Facility Holes:** 18. **Yards:** 6,663/5,935. **Par:** 71/75. **Course**

Rating: 71.1/73.1. **Slope:** 124/130. **Green Fee:** $59/$119. **Cart Fee:** $16/Person. **Walking Policy:** Unrestricted walking. **Walkability:** 3. **Opened:** 1925. **Architect:** Stanley Thompson. **Season:** April-Oct. **High:** June-Sept. **To obtain tee times:** Call golf shop. **Miscellaneous:** Reduced fees (guests, twilight, juniors), range (grass/mats), lodging (450 rooms), credit cards (MC, V, AE, D, DC), BF, FF.
Reader Comments: Outstanding resort course and not overly punishing … You chase deer from the fairway while a bear is watching … Beautiful course … Stay alert for bears, elk and deer … World-class setting … Breathtaking.

KANANASKIS COUNTRY GOLF CLUB
R-P.O. Box 1710, Kananaskis Village, T0L 2H0, (403)591-7070, (877)591-2525, 50 miles from Calgary. **E-mail:** proshop@kananaskisgolf.com. **Web:** www.kananaskisgolf.com. **Facility Holes:** 36. **Green Fee:** $50/$65. **Cart Fee:** $14/Person. **Walking Policy:** Unrestricted walking. **Opened:** 1983. **Architect:** Robert Trent Jones. **Season:** May-Oct. **High:** May-Oct. **To obtain tee times:** Call golf shop. **Miscellaneous:** Reduced fees (twilight, seniors, juniors), metal spikes, range (grass/mats), credit cards (MC, V, AE), BF, FF.
★★★★½ **MT. KIDD COURSE** (18) *Value+*
Yards: 7,083/5,539. **Par:** 72/72. **Course Rating:** 72.8/71.5. **Slope:** 134/127. **Walkability:** 3.
Reader Comments: Fantastic course, very challenging, superior layout and scenery … A true RTJ Sr. masterpiece set in the Canadian Rockies … A must play for all golfers … Played the course once while it was snowing—what a remarkable experience … If timing is right, can play both courses in one day.
★★★★½ **MT. LORETTE COURSE** (18) *Value+, Condition, Pace*
Yards: 7,102/5,429. **Par:** 72/72. **Course Rating:** 74.1/69.8. **Slope:** 137/123. **Walkability:** 2.
Reader Comments: Very challenging water hazards … I enjoy the course, however, I prefer Mt. Kidd … A setting to die for … You are treated like a king … For the money, this is the best course I've ever played … Free valet parking … Big difference between blue & white tees.

★★½ LAKESIDE GREENS GOLF & COUNTRY CLUB
SP-555 Lakeside Greens Dr., Chestermere, T1X 1O5, (403)569-9111, 4 miles from Calgary. **E-mail:** bull-trout@hotmail.com. **Facility Holes:** 18. **Yards:** 6,804/5,063. **Par:** 71/71. **Course Rating:** 72.5/68.8. **Slope:** 134/118. **Green Fee:** $25/$55. **Cart Fee:** $28/Cart. **Walking Policy:** Unrestricted walking. **Walkability:** 1. **Opened:** 1992. **Architect:** Bill Newis. **Season:** April-Oct. **To obtain tee times:** Call golf shop. **Miscellaneous:** Reduced fees (weekdays, twilight), range (mats), credit cards (MC, V, AE, Debit Card), BF, FF.

★★½ LAND-O-LAKES GOLF CLUB
SP-102 Fairway Dr., Coaldale, T1M 1H1, (403)345-2582, 6 miles from Lethbridge. **Facility Holes:** 18. **Yards:** 6,459/5,634. **Par:** 71/72. **Course Rating:** 72.0/73.0. **Slope:** 119/126. **Green Fee:** $24/$28. **Cart Fee:** $26/Cart. **Walking Policy:** Unrestricted walking. **Walkability:** 3. **Opened:** 1987. **Architect:** Les Furber. **Season:** April-Oct. **High:** June-Aug. **To obtain tee times:** Call up to 2 days in advance. **Miscellaneous:** Reduced fees (weekdays, juniors), range (grass/mats), credit cards (MC, V, Interac), BF, FF.

LAST HILL GOLF & RV PARK
PU-Box 406, Eckville, TOM OKO, (430)746-3179, 25 miles from Red Deer. **Facility Holes:** 18. **Yards:** 6,553/5,546. **Par:** 72/72. **Course Rating:** 71.9/71.6. **Slope:** 126/126. **Green Fee:** $22/$28. **Cart Fee:** $24/Cart. **Walking Policy:** Unrestricted walking. **Walkability:** 3. **Opened:** 1983. **Architect:** Les Furber/Puddicombe Assoc. **Season:** April-Oct. **High:** June-Aug. **To obtain tee times:** Call up to 4 days in advance. **Miscellaneous:** Reduced fees (weekdays, juniors), range (grass/mats), credit cards (MC, V, Interac), BF, FF.

★★★ THE LINKS AT SPRUCE GROVE
PU-Calahoo Rd., Spruce Grove, T7X 3B4, (780)962-4653, 10 miles from Edmonton. **Facility Holes:** 18. **Yards:** 6,767/5,748. **Par:** 72/72. **Course Rating:** 71.0/72.0. **Slope:** 125/126. **Green Fee:** $33/$39. **Cart Fee:** $28/Cart. **Walking Policy:** Unrestricted walking. **Walkability:** 3. **Opened:** 1983. **Architect:** William Robinson. **Season:** April-Oct. **To obtain tee times:** Call up to 2 days in advance. **Miscellaneous:** Reduced fees (weekdays, twilight, seniors, juniors), metal spikes, range (grass), credit cards (MC, V, AE), BF, FF.
Reader Comments: Good value … Good layout and reasonable challenge for all skill levels … It was tougher than I thought … Need fence on holes No. 1 and No. 8 beside driving range … The clubhouse is first class … Narrow & tough.

THE LINKS OF GLENEAGLES
PU-100 GlenEagles Dr., Cochrane, T4C 1P5, (403)932-1100, 9 miles from Calgary. **E-mail:** jeff-gleneagles@home.com. **Web:** www.gleneaglesgolf.com. **Facility Holes:** 18. **Yards:** 7,019/5,222. **Par:** 72/72. **Course Rating:** 74.0/70.5. **Slope:** 139/124. **Green Fee:** $45/$68. **Cart Fee:** $28/Cart. **Walking Policy:** Unrestricted walking. **Walkability:** 4. **Opened:** 1998. **Architect:** Les Furber. **Season:** April-Oct. **High:** June-Sept. **To obtain tee times:** Call up to 60 days in

advance. **Miscellaneous:** Reduced fees (twilight, juniors), range (grass), credit cards (MC, V, AE, Debit), BF, FF.
Notes: Ranked 3rd in 1999 Best New Canadian.

★★½ **MAPLE RIDGE GOLF COURSE**
PU-1240 Mapleglade Dr. S.E., Calgary, T2P 2M5, (403)974-1825. **Facility Holes:** 18. **Yards:** 6,576/5,832. **Par:** 72/72. **Course Rating:** 70.2/72.5. **Slope:** 117/129. **Green Fee:** $23/$25. **Opened:** 1985. **To obtain tee times:** Call golf shop. **Miscellaneous:** Metal spikes, range (/).

★★ **MCCALL LAKE GOLF COURSE**
PU-1600 32nd Ave. N.E., Calgary, T2P 2M5, (403)291-3596. **Facility Holes:** 27. **Yards:** 6,788/5,568. **Par:** 71/71. **Course Rating:** 71.3/71.7. **Slope:** 121/127. **Green Fee:** $26. **Cart Fee:** $25/Cart. **Walking Policy:** Unrestricted walking. **Walkability:** 2. **Opened:** 1982. **Architect:** Bill Newis. **High:** April-Sept. **To obtain tee times:** Call golf shop. **Miscellaneous:** Reduced fees (twilight), metal spikes, range (mats), credit cards (MC, V, Debit).
Special Notes: Also has 9-hole par-3 course.

MCKENZIE MEADOWS GOLF CLUB
PU-17215 McKenzie Meadows Dr. SE, Calgary, T2H 0J9, (403)257-2255. **E-mail:** admin.mckenzie@home.com. **Web:** www.mckenziemeadows.com. **Facility Holes:** 18. **Yards:** 6,508/5,132. **Par:** 72/72. **Course Rating:** 70.5/67.8. **Slope:** 124/116. **Green Fee:** $42/$45. **Cart Fee:** $25/Cart. **Walking Policy:** Unrestricted walking. **Walkability:** 3. **Opened:** 1996. **Architect:** Gary Browning & Associates. **Season:** April-Oct. **High:** May-Sept. **To obtain tee times:** Call up to 3 days in advance. **Miscellaneous:** Reduced fees (weekdays, twilight), range (grass), credit cards (MC, V, AE), BF, FF.

★★½ **MEDICINE HAT GOLF & COUNTRY CLUB**
SP-#1 Parkview Dr. NE, Medicine Hat, T1A 7E9, (403)527-8086, 180 miles from Calgary. **Facility Holes:** 18. **Yards:** 6,612/5,606. **Par:** 72/72. **Course Rating:** 72.5/72.5. **Slope:** 131/123. **Green Fee:** $37/$40. **Cart Fee:** $33/Cart. **Walking Policy:** Unrestricted walking. **Walkability:** 2. **Opened:** 1933. **Architect:** Tom Bendelow. **Season:** April-Oct. **High:** June-Aug. **To obtain tee times:** Call up to 2 days in advance. **Miscellaneous:** Reduced fees (twilight), range (mats), credit cards (MC, V), BF, FF.

★★ **OLDS GOLF CLUB**
PU-R.R. #1, Site 2, Box 13, Olds, T4H 1P2, (403)556-8008, (800)310-9297, 45 miles from Calgary. **E-mail:** oldsgolf@telusplanet.net. **Facility Holes:** 18. **Yards:** 6,662/5,886. **Par:** 72/73. **Course Rating:** 70.4/72.5. **Slope:** 121/121. **Green Fee:** $26/$28. **Cart Fee:** $25/Cart. **Walking Policy:** Unrestricted walking. **Walkability:** 3. **Opened:** 1982. **Season:** April-Oct. **High:** April-Oct. **To obtain tee times:** Call golf shop. **Miscellaneous:** Reduced fees (weekdays, juniors), range (grass), credit cards (MC, V, Debit Cards), BF, FF.

★★★½ **PARADISE CANYON GOLF & RESORT**
R-185 Canyon Blvd., Lethbridge, T1K 6V1, (403)381-7500, (877)707-GOLF, 120 miles from Calgary. **Facility Holes:** 18. **Yards:** 6,810/5,282. **Par:** 71/71. **Course Rating:** 73.1/70.6. **Slope:** 132/127. **Green Fee:** $25/$45. **Cart Fee:** $30/Cart. **Walking Policy:** Unrestricted walking. **Walkability:** 4. **Opened:** 1992. **Architect:** Bill Newis. **Season:** March-Nov. **High:** June-Sept. **To obtain tee times:** Call golf shop. **Miscellaneous:** Reduced fees (weekdays, twilight), range (grass/mats), lodging (50 rooms), credit cards (MC, V, AE).
Reader Comments: Lots of elevation changes ... Good solid golf course ... Large mounding between holes so you feel like you have the whole course to yourself ... The rough was very thick ... Desert golf gone north ... Tight and demanding ... Plays tough from the tips.
Special Notes: Formerly Paradise Canyon Golf & Country Club.

★★★ **PHEASANTBACK GOLF & COUNTRY CLUB**
PU-P.O. Box 1625, Stettler, T0C 2L0, (403)742-4653, 5 miles from Stettler. **Facility Holes:** 18. **Yards:** 6,186/4,631. **Par:** 71/71. **Course Rating:** 70.0/67.5. **Slope:** 127/113. **Green Fee:** $27/$32. **Cart Fee:** $25/Cart. **Walking Policy:** Unrestricted walking. **Walkability:** 5. **Opened:** 1995. **Architect:** William Robinson. **Season:** April-Oct. **High:** June-Sept. **To obtain tee times:** Call golf shop. **Miscellaneous:** Reduced fees (guests, twilight, juniors), range (grass), credit cards (MC, V), BF, FF.
Reader Comments: Tough for a high handicapper ... Water! Water! Water! ... Hidden gem ... Will only get better with time ... Lots of water, keep it straight ... Enjoyable.

★★½ **PICTURE BUTTE GOLF CLUB**
SP-P.O. Box 359, Picture Butte, T0K 1V0, (403)732-4157, 20 miles from Lethbridge. **E-mail:** pbpro@telusplanet.net. **Facility Holes:** 18. **Yards:** 6,390/5,127. **Par:** 72/73. **Course Rating:** 70.5/71.5. **Slope:** 116/122. **Green Fee:** $14/$28. **Cart Fee:** $28/Cart. **Walking Policy:** Unrestricted walking. **Walkability:** 2. **Opened:** 1963. **Architect:** Les Furber/Jim Eremko.

Season: March-Oct. **High:** May-Aug. **To obtain tee times:** Call up to 6 days in advance. **Miscellaneous:** Reduced fees (weekdays, twilight, seniors, juniors), range (grass), credit cards (MC, V, Interac), BF, FF.

PIPESTONE PUTTERS GOLF CLUB

PU-Pipestone Club Dr., Wembley, T0H 3S0, (780)766-2720. **Facility Holes:** 18. **Yards:** 5,851/5,110. **Par:** 71/70. **Course Rating:** 69.0. **Slope:** 106. **Green Fee:** $18/$20. **Cart Fee:** $20/Cart. **To obtain tee times:** Call golf shop.

★★★ PONOKA COMMUNITY GOLF COURSE

PU-P.O. Box 4145, Ponoka, T4J 1R5, (403)783-4626, 60 miles from Edmonton. **Web:** www.ponokagolf.com. **Facility Holes:** 18. **Yards:** 6,500/5,800. **Par:** 72/72. **Course Rating:** 69.9/72.4. **Slope:** 121/131. **Green Fee:** $23/$27. **Cart Fee:** $25/Cart. **Walking Policy:** Unrestricted walking. **Walkability:** 3. **Opened:** 1987. **Architect:** William Robinson. **Season:** April-Oct. **Tee times:** Call golf shop. **Misc:** Range (grass), credit cards (MC, V, AE, DC).
Reader Comments: Great golf, back 9 fantastic … Hard course, have to have a good short game … Liked this course, return at least once a year … A very nice natural course with changes in elevation … Worth a stop … Off main roads, good course.

★★★½ THE RANCH GOLF & COUNTRY CLUB

SP-52516 Range Rd. 262, Spruce Grove, T7Y 1A5, (780)470-4700, 3 miles from Edmonton. **Facility Holes:** 18. **Yards:** 6,526/5,082. **Par:** 71/71. **Course Rating:** 70.4/70.7. **Slope:** 129/124. **Green Fee:** $16/$49. **Cart Fee:** Included in green fee. **Walking Policy:** Unrestricted walking. **Walkability:** 3. **Opened:** 1989. **Architect:** Western Golf. **Season:** April-Oct. **High:** June-Aug. **To obtain tee times:** Call up to 3 days in advance. **Miscellaneous:** Reduced fees (weekdays, twilight, juniors), range (mats), credit cards (MC, V, AE), BF, FF.
Reader Comments: Links-style course with multiple tee boxes to provide a wide variety of options for all golfers … Excellent for the high handicapper as well as the intermediate skilled golfer.

★★★ REDWOOD MEADOWS GOLF & COUNTRY CLUB

SP-100-2 Tsuu T'ina Dr., Redwood Meadows, T3Z 3G6, (403)949-3663, 15 miles from Calgary. **E-mail:** deanwalk@cadvision.com. **Web:** www.redwoodmeadows.com. **Facility Holes:** 18. **Yards:** 7,058/6,023. **Par:** 72/73. **Course Rating:** 72.7/74.0. **Slope:** 129/134. **Green Fee:** $60/$75. **Cart Fee:** $30/Cart. **Walking Policy:** Unrestricted walking. **Walkability:** 2. **Opened:** 1976. **Architect:** Stan Leonard. **Season:** May-Oct. **To obtain tee times:** Call up to 120 days in advance. **Miscellaneous:** Reduced fees (twilight, juniors), range (grass), credit cards (MC, V, AE, Debit), BF, FF.
Reader Comments: Rustic country setting—hard course … Great natural beauty … My favorite course in the Calgary area; long from the tips with lots of woods … Very imaginative design … Beautiful foothills course.

★★★ RIVER BEND GOLF & RECREATION AREA

PU-P.O. Box 157, Red Deer, T4N 5E8, (403)343-8311, 4 miles from Red Deer. **E-mail:** riverbend@reddeer.net. **Web:** www.riverbend.reddeer.net. **Facility Holes:** 18. **Yards:** 6,700/5,514. **Par:** 72/72. **Course Rating:** 71.9/70.4. **Slope:** 129/119. **Green Fee:** $29/$33. **Cart Fee:** $26/Cart. **Walking Policy:** Unrestricted walking. **Walkability:** 1. **Opened:** 1986. **Architect:** William Robinson. **Season:** April-Oct. **To obtain tee times:** Call up to 6 days in advance. **Misc:** Reduced fees (juniors), range (grass/mats), credit cards (MC, V, AE, Debit), BF, FF.
Reader Comments: An excellent course, good greens … Good variety of golf holes … Wide fairways, large greens, several water holes … A challenging, interesting course in a pretty setting … Wicked rough really slowed pace of play.

★★½ RIVERSIDE GOLF COURSE

PU-8630 Rowland Rd., Edmonton, T6A 3X1, (780)496-8702. **Facility Holes:** 18. **Yards:** 6,306/5,984. **Par:** 71/75. **Course Rating:** 71.0/74.0. **Slope:** 114. **Green Fee:** $24/$27. **Cart Fee:** $20/Cart. **Walking Policy:** Unrestricted walking. **Walkability:** 3. **Opened:** 1951. **Season:** April-Oct. **To obtain tee times:** Call up to 2 days in advance. **Miscellaneous:** Metal spikes, credit cards (MC, V), BF, FF.

★★ SHAGANAPPI POINT GOLF COURSE

PU-1200-26 St. S.W., Calgary, T2P 2M5, (403)974-1810, 2 miles from Downtown Calgary. **Facility Holes:** 27. **Yards:** 5,195/4,707. **Par:** 68/70. **Course Rating:** 66.1. **Slope:** 112. **Green Fee:** $20/$29. **Cart Fee:** $26/Cart. **Walking Policy:** Unrestricted walking. **Walkability:** 3. **Opened:** 1917. **Season:** April-Oct. **High:** June-Aug. **To obtain tee times:** Call up to 4 days in advance. **Miscellaneous:** Reduced fees (twilight, seniors, juniors), range (mats), credit cards (MC, V, Debit Card), BF, FF.
Special Notes: Also has a 9-hole executive course.

★★½ SHAW-NEE SLOPES GOLF COURSE
SP-820 James McKevitt Rd. S.W., Calgary, T2Y2E7, (403)256-1444. **Facility Holes:** 18.
Yards: 6,478/5,691. **Par:** 72/72. **Course Rating:** 70.5/71.0. **Slope:** 122/123. **Green Fee:**
$35/$38. **Cart Fee:** $26/Cart. **Walking Policy:** Unrestricted walking. **Walkability:** 3. **Opened:**
1965. **Architect:** R.F. Moote & Assoc. Ltd. **Season:** April-Nov. **High:** June-Aug. **To obtain tee**
times: Call golf shop. **Miscellaneous:** Reduced fees (weekdays, twilight, seniors), range
(mats), credit cards (MC, V).

★½ SHERWOOD PARK GOLF COURSE
PU-52321 Range Rd. 233, Sherwood Park, T8B 1C8, (780)467-5060, 1 mile from Sherwood
Park. **Facility Holes:** 18. **Yards:** 6,045/5,859. **Par:** 70/72. **Course Rating:** 67.3/73.3. **Slope:**
112/129. **Green Fee:** $23/$25. **Cart Fee:** $24/Cart. **Walking Policy:** Unrestricted walking.
Walkability: 3. **Opened:** 1960. **Architect:** William Brinkworth. **Season:** April-Oct. **High:** May-
Sept. **To obtain tee times:** Call golf shop. **Miscellaneous:** Reduced fees (weekdays, twilight),
range (grass/mats), credit cards (MC, V).

★★★★½ SILVERTIP GOLF COURSE *Condition+*
R-1000 SilverTip Trail, Canmore, T1W 2V1, (403)678-1600, (877)877-5444, 45 miles from
Calgary. **E-mail:** gandrew@silvertipresort.com. **Web:** www.silvertipresort.com. **Facility Holes:**
18. **Yards:** 7,200/5,131. **Par:** 72/72. **Course Rating:** 74.1/69.0. **Slope:** 153/131. **Green Fee:**
$85/$129. **Cart Fee:** Included in green fee. **Walking Policy:** Mandatory carts. **Walkability:** 5.
Opened: 1998. **Architect:** Les Furber. **Season:** May-Oct. **High:** May-Oct. **Tee times:** Call golf
shop. **Misc:** Reduced fees (twilight), range (grass/mats), credit cards (MC, V, AE), BF, FF.
Notes: Ranked 2nd in 1999 Best New Canadian.
Reader Comments: New course & very challenging ... Extreme mountainside golf with great views
... One of North America's most beautiful.

SPRUCE MEADOWS GOLF & COUNTRY CLUB
PU-P.O. Box 548, Sexsmith, TOH 3C0, (780)568-4653, 12 miles from Grande Prairie. **E-mail:**
smeadows@telusplanet.net. **Web:** www.smeadow@telusplanet.net. **Facility Holes:** 18. **Yards:**
6,527/5,909. **Par:** 71/72. **Course Rating:** 73.0/73.0. **Slope:** 117. **Green Fee:** $25. **Cart Fee:**
$20/Cart. **Walking Policy:** Unrestricted walking. **Walkability:** 2. **Opened:** 1982. **Architect:** Ed
Sodergren. **Season:** April-Oct. **High:** May-July. **To obtain tee times:** Call up to 7 days in
advance. **Miscellaneous:** Reduced fees (weekdays, guests, seniors, juniors), range
(grass/mats), credit cards (MC, V), BF, FF.

STEWART CREEK GOLF CLUB
PU-Box 8570, Canmore, T1W 2V3, (877)993-4653. **Facility Holes:** 18. **Yards:** 6,023/5,156.
Par: 72/72. **Green Fee:** $65/$125. **Cart Fee:** Included in green fee. **Architect:** Gary Browning.
To obtain tee times: Call golf shop.
Notes: Ranked 2nd in 2001 Best New Canadian Courses.

★★ VICTORIA GOLF COURSE
PU-12130 River Rd., Edmonton, T5N 0E0, (780)496-4710. **E-mail:**
barbara.ursuliak@gov.edmonton.ab.ca. **Facility Holes:** 18. **Yards:** 6,081/6,081. **Par:** 71/73.
Course Rating: 66.8/72.1. **Slope:** 99/112. **Green Fee:** $27/$30. **Cart Fee:** $20/Cart. **Walking**
Policy: Unrestricted walking. **Walkability:** 2. **Opened:** 1907. **Architect:** City of Edmonton.
Season: April-Oct. **High:** June-Aug. **To obtain tee times:** Call up to 2 days in advance.
Miscellaneous: Reduced fees (weekdays, seniors, juniors), range (mats), credit cards
(MC, V), BF, FF.

WESTLOCK GOLF CLUB
PU-Hwy. 18, Westlock, T7P 2P6, (780)349-2478. **Facility Holes:** 18. **Yards:** 6,537/5,457. **Par:**
71/71. **Course Rating:** 70.5/71.0. **Slope:** 124/115. **Green Fee:** $14/$24. **Cart Fee:** $24/Cart. **To**
obtain tee times: Call golf shop.

★★½ WINTERGREEN GOLF & COUNTRY CLUB
SP-P.O. Bag No.2, Bragg Creek, TOL 0K0, (403)949-3333, 20 miles from Calgary. **E-mail:**
bmacdonald@skiwintergreen.com. **Web:** www.skiwintergreen.com. **Facility Holes:** 18. **Yards:**
6,692/5,061. **Par:** 72/72. **Course Rating:** 72.5/69.9. **Slope:** 134/128. **Green Fee:** $45/$55. **Cart**
Fee: $28/Cart. **Walking Policy:** Unrestricted walking. **Walkability:** 4. **Opened:** 1991. **Architect:**
Bill Newis. **Season:** May-Oct. **High:** June-Sept. **To obtain tee times:** Call up to 4 days in
advance. **Miscellaneous:** Reduced fees (weekdays, twilight, seniors, juniors), range
(grass/mats), credit cards (MC, V, AE, Debit Card), BF, FF.

★★★★½ **WOLF CREEK GOLF RESORT**
R-R.R. No.3 Site 10, Ponoka, T4J 1R3, (403)783-6050, 70 miles from Edmonton. **E-mail:** wlfcreek@telusplanet.net. **Web:** www.wolfcreekgolf.com. **Facility Holes:** 27. **Green Fee:** $50/$56. **Cart Fee:** $28/Cart. **Walking Policy:** Unrestricted walking. **Walkability:** 3. **Opened:** 1984. **Architect:** Rod Whitman. **Season:** April-Oct. **High:** May-Sept. **To obtain tee times:** Call golf shop. **Miscellaneous:** Reduced fees (weekdays, twilight, seniors, juniors), range (grass), credit cards (MC, V, AE, DC), BF, FF.
EAST/SOUTH (18 Combo)*Pace*
Yards: 6,818/5,144. **Par:** 70/70. **Course Rating:** 74.2/69.0. **Slope:** 135/117.
SOUTH/WEST (18 Combo)
Yards: 6,730/4,990. **Par:** 70/70. **Course Rating:** 74.5/69.0. **Slope:** 135/117.
WEST/EAST (18 Combo)
Yards: 6,516/4,880. **Par:** 70/70. **Course Rating:** 72.3/69.0. **Slope:** 138/117.
Reader Comments: A test for all, must be straight … Great course, very narrow in spots … Great links course … Excellent, challenging, different … Not for a beginner … A wind-swept masterpiece … Firm fast greens … When the wind is blowing it is a very difficult course … A welcome challenge.

BRITISH COLUMBIA

★★ **ARBUTUS RIDGE GOLF & COUNTRY CLUB**
SP-3515 Telegraph Rd., Cobble Hill, V0R 1L0, (250)743-5000, (800)446-5322, 18 miles from Victoria. **E-mail:** info_arbutus@golfbc.com. **Web:** www.arbutusridgegolf.com. **Facility Holes:** 18. **Yards:** 6,168/5,113. **Par:** 70/71. **Course Rating:** 69.9/64.8. **Slope:** 123/109. **Green Fee:** $55/$70. **Cart Fee:** Included in green fee. **Walking Policy:** Unrestricted walking. **Walkability:** 3. **Opened:** 1988. **Architect:** William/Robinson. **Season:** Year-round. **To obtain tee times:** Call golf shop. **Miscellaneous:** Reduced fees (weekdays, twilight, juniors), range (grass/mats), credit cards (MC, V, AE), BF, FF.

★★ **BELMONT GOLF COURSE**
PU-22555 Telegraph Trail, Langley, V1M 354, (604)888-9898, 10 miles from Langley. **E-mail:** tpeverley@goodgolfbc.com. **Web:** www.goodgolfbc.com. **Facility Holes:** 18. **Yards:** 6,416/4,951. **Par:** 70/70. **Course Rating:** 70.5/68.1. **Slope:** 122/114. **Green Fee:** $40/$48. **Cart Fee:** $30/Cart. **Walking Policy:** Unrestricted walking. **Walkability:** 3. **Opened:** 1993. **Architect:** Les Furber. **Season:** Year-round. **High:** May-Oct. **Tee times:** Call up to 5 days in advance. **Misc:** Reduced fees (weekdays, twilight, juniors), credit cards (MC, V, AE), BF, FF.

★★★★½ **BIG SKY GOLF & COUNTRY CLUB**
R-1690 Airport Rd., Pemberton, V0N 2L0, (604)894-6106, (800)668-7900, 85 miles from Vancouver. **E-mail:** bigsky@bigskygolf.com. **Web:** www.bigskygolf.com. **Facility Holes:** 18. **Yards:** 7,001/5,208. **Par:** 72/72. **Course Rating:** 73.5/70.0. **Slope:** 133/114. **Green Fee:** $60/$150. **Cart Fee:** $32/Cart. **Walking Policy:** Unrestricted walking. **Walkability:** 1. **Opened:** 1994. **Architect:** Bob Cupp. **Season:** April-Oct. **High:** July-Aug. **To obtain tee times:** Call golf shop. **Miscellaneous:** Reduced fees (weekdays, twilight, juniors), range (grass/mats), caddies, credit cards (MC, V, AE, JTB), BF, FF.
Reader Comments: Course very playable … Beautiful course surrounded by mountains, great practice facilities, friendly staff, a 'must-play' if you're in the Whistler area … Challenging course that rewards good shots … Friendly from minute one … Setting of golf course is spectacular.

★★ **BURNABY MOUNTAIN GOLF COURSE**
PU-7600 Halifax St., Burnaby, V5A 4M8, (604)280-7355, 10 miles from Vancouver. **Facility Holes:** 18. **Yards:** 6,301/5,830. **Par:** 71/72. **Green Fee:** $31. **Cart Fee:** $26/Cart. **Walking Policy:** Unrestricted walking. **Walkability:** 3. **Opened:** 1969. **Season:** Year-round. **High:** April-Sept. **To obtain tee times:** Call golf shop. **Miscellaneous:** Reduced fees (twilight, seniors, juniors), metal spikes, range (mats), credit cards (MC, V).

★★★½ **CASTLEGAR GOLF CLUB**
PU-P.O. Box 3430, Castlegar, V1N 3N8, (250)365-5006, (800)660-0324, 180 miles from Spokane, WA. **E-mail:** cgargolf@look.ca. **Web:** www.golfcastlegar.com. **Facility Holes:** 18. **Yards:** 6,677/6,178. **Par:** 72/76. **Course Rating:** 72.6/75.9. **Slope:** 127/133. **Green Fee:** $23/$38. **Cart Fee:** $27/Cart. **Walking Policy:** Unrestricted walking. **Walkability:** 3. **Opened:** 1958. **Architect:** Designed by members. **Season:** April-Oct. **High:** April-Oct. **Tee times:** Call golf shop. **Misc:** Reduced fees (weekdays, twilight), range, credit cards (MC, V), BF, FF.
Reader Comments: Casual atmosphere … Excellent greens … Natural beauty and variety … Saw a bear! … Peaceful with deer and bear sightings, nice layout … Friendly local atmosphere, welcome tourists, rolling well-treed terrain, tricky sloping greens … Forces you to concentrate.

★★★★½ **CHATEAU WHISTLER GOLF CLUB** *Service*
R-4612 Blackcomb Way, Whistler, V0N 1B4, (604)938-2095, (877)938-2092, 75 miles from Vancouver. **E-mail:** dave.hodgson@fairmont.com. **Web:** www.chateauwhistlerresort.com. **Facility Holes:** 18. **Yards:** 6,635/5,157. **Par:** 72/72. **Course Rating:** 73.0/70.0. **Slope:** 145/124. **Green Fee:** $110/$175. **Cart Fee:** Included in green fee. **Walking Policy:** Mandatory carts. **Walkability:** 4. **Opened:** 1993. **Architect:** Robert Trent Jones Jr. **Season:** May-Oct. **High:** July-Aug. **To obtain tee times:** Call golf shop. **Miscellaneous:** Reduced fees (guests, twilight, juniors), lodging (558 rooms), credit cards (MC, V, AE, D, DC), BF, FF.
Reader Comments: Unbelievable scenery ... Front 9 is mainly uphill and different, back 9 is downhill and fun ... Makes you play for position ... Mountainside location, watch for bears ... Too, too hard ... One of Canada's best courses ... Take a camera ... Every hole is different ... Lots of blind shots.

★★★ **CHRISTINA LAKE GOLF CLUB**
SP-339 2nd Ave., Christina Lake, V0H 1E0, (250)447-9313, 12 miles from Grand Forks. **E-mail:** kevsgolf@sunshinecable.com. **Web:** www.christinalakegolfclub.com. **Facility Holes:** 18. **Yards:** 6,615/5,725. **Par:** 72/73. **Course Rating:** 71.5/71.3. **Slope:** 125/123. **Green Fee:** $25/$40. **Cart Fee:** $28/Cart. **Walking Policy:** Unrestricted walking. **Walkability:** 2. **Opened:** 1963. **Architect:** Les Furber. **Season:** April-Oct. **High:** July-Aug. **To obtain tee times:** Call up to 3 days in advance. **Miscellaneous:** Reduced fees (twilight, juniors), range (grass), credit cards (MC, V, Direct Debit), BF, FF.
Reader Comments: Good rural course ... Good service, friendly pro shop staff ... Great integration of new modern 9 with older traditional 9 ... Very scenic.

★★★★ **CORDOVA BAY GOLF COURSE**
PU-5333 Cordova Bay Rd., Victoria, V8Y 2L3, (250)658-4075, 15 miles from Downtown Victoria. **E-mail:** jim.goddard@cordovabaygolf.com. **Web:** www.cordovabaygolf.com. **Facility Holes:** 18. **Yards:** 6,642/5,269. **Par:** 72/72. **Course Rating:** 72.0/72.0. **Slope:** 122/119. **Green Fee:** $49/$52. **Cart Fee:** $34/Cart. **Walking Policy:** Unrestricted walking. **Walkability:** 1. **Opened:** 1991. **Architect:** William Robinson. **Season:** Year-round. **High:** May-Sept. **To obtain tee times:** Call golf shop. **Miscellaneous:** Reduced fees (weekdays, twilight, juniors), range (mats), credit cards (MC, V, AE), BF, FF.
Reader Comments: One of the few courses in Canada that is playable all year ... Always in great shape ... A few blind shots to the green ... Some challenging long par 4s ... A spectacular layout with ocean views and mountain vistas ... Beautiful landscaping.

★★★★ **CROWN ISLE RESORT & GOLF COMMUNITY**
R-399 Clubhouse Dr., Courtenay, V9N 9G3, (250)703-5050, (888)338-8439, 100 miles from Victoria, BC. **E-mail:** info@crownisle.com. **Web:** www.crownisle.com. **Facility Holes:** 18. **Yards:** 7,024/5,169. **Par:** 72/72. **Course Rating:** 74.2/68.5. **Slope:** 133/114. **Green Fee:** $35/$65. **Cart Fee:** $30/Cart. **Walking Policy:** Unrestricted walking. **Walkability:** 2. **Opened:** 1993. **Architect:** Graham Cooke & Assoc. **Season:** Year-round. **To obtain tee times:** Call golf shop. **Miscellaneous:** Reduced fees (weekdays, twilight, juniors), range (grass/mats), lodging (40 rooms), credit cards (MC, V, AE, Interact), BF, FF.
Reader Comments: Great practice areas ... Both tall trees and open holes, spectacular clubhouse, great place or a getaway ... Beautiful view of Comax Glacier ... Excellent service and extravagant clubhouse ... Can't wait to visit again.

★★ **DUNCAN MEADOWS GOLF COURSE**
SP-Highway 18 & North Rd., Duncan, V9L 6K9, (250)746-8993, 35 miles from Victoria. **Facility Holes:** 18. **Yards:** 6,616/5,356. **Par:** 72/72. **Course Rating:** 71.8/67.0. **Slope:** 129/119. **Green Fee:** $20/$40. **Cart Fee:** $28/Cart. **Walking Policy:** Unrestricted walking. **Walkability:** 3. **Opened:** 1993. **Architect:** Claude Muret. **Season:** Year-round. **High:** May-Oct. **To obtain tee times:** Call up to 7 days in advance. **Miscellaneous:** Reduced fees (twilight, seniors, juniors), range (grass/mats), credit cards (MC, V), BF, FF.

★★★★ **DUNES AT KAMLOOPS**
SP-652 Dunes Dr., Kamloops, V2B 8M8, (250)579-3300, (888)881-4653, 7 miles from Downtown Kamloops. **E-mail:** info@golfthedunes.com. **Web:** www.golfthedunes.com. **Facility Holes:** 18. **Yards:** 7,120/5,405. **Par:** 72/72. **Course Rating:** 73.8/72.0. **Slope:** 126/122. **Green Fee:** $56. **Cart Fee:** $32/Cart. **Walking Policy:** Unrestricted walking. **Walkability:** 2. **Opened:** 1996. **Architect:** Graham Cooke. **Season:** March-Nov. **High:** April-Sept. **To obtain tee times:** Call golf shop. **Miscellaneous:** Reduced fees (twilight), metal spikes, range (grass), credit cards (MC, V, AE, DC), BF, FF.
Reader Comments: Be prepared to come to this course with your 'A' game in mind ... Semi-links, well conditioned course in a scenic riverside canyon setting ... Limited but good grill ... Excellent driving range and putting greens ... Really fast greens.

★★★ EAGLE POINT GOLF & COUNTRY CLUB
R-8888 Barnhartvale Rd., Kamloops, V2C 6W1, (250)573-2453, (888)863-2453, 225 miles from Vancouver. **E-mail:** eaglepoint@telus.net. **Web:** www.golfeaglepoint.com. **Facility Holes:** 18. **Yards:** 6,762/5,315. **Par:** 72/72. **Course Rating:** 71.8/70.6. **Slope:** 128/126. **Green Fee:** $49/$55. **Cart Fee:** $28/Cart. **Walking Policy:** Unrestricted walking. **Walkability:** 4. **Opened:** 1991. **Architect:** Robert Heaslip. **Season:** March-Nov. **High:** April-Oct. **To obtain tee times:** Call golf shop. **Miscellaneous:** Reduced fees (weekdays, guests, twilight, juniors), range (grass/mats), credit cards (MC, V, AE), BF, FF.
Reader Comments: Challenging ... Playable for the mid-handicapper ... One of my favorite BC courses ... Mountain slopes setting with some tricky holes.

★★★★ EAGLE RANCH GOLF COURSE
SP-Athalmer Rd., Invermere, V0A 1K3, (250)342-0820, (877)877-3889, 180 miles from Calgary. **E-mail:** info@eagleranchresort.com. **Web:** www.eagleranchresort.com. **Facility Holes:** 18. **Yards:** 6,637/5,086. **Par:** 72/72. **Course Rating:** 71.9/68.8. **Slope:** 138/125. **Green Fee:** $55/$89. **Cart Fee:** Included in green fee. **Walking Policy:** Walking at certain times. **Walkability:** 4. **Opened:** 2000. **Architect:** William Robinson. **Season:** April-Oct. **High:** April-Sept. **To obtain tee times:** Call golf shop. **Miscellaneous:** Reduced fees (weekdays, twilight), range (grass), credit cards (MC, V, AE), BF, FF.
Reader Comments: 16th hole par-3 is across a "large" canyon to a postage stamp green. Lovely to look at—tough to play ... What a great experience ... The course is incredible and I have never been treated better ... Price is a bit high ... Would play it everyday if I could afford it ... Too tough for most.

★★ EAGLECREST GOLF CLUB
SP-2035 Island Hwy. W., Qualicum Beach, V9K 1G1, (250)752-6311, (800)567-1320, 25 miles from Nanaimo. **Facility Holes:** 18. **Yards:** 6,013/5,430. **Par:** 71/71. **Course Rating:** 70.6/71.0. **Slope:** 126/123. **Green Fee:** $25/$40. **Cart Fee:** $27/Cart. **Walking Policy:** Unrestricted walking. **Walkability:** 3. **Opened:** 1971. **Architect:** Warren Radomski. **Season:** Year-round. **High:** May-Oct. **To obtain tee times:** Call golf shop. **Miscellaneous:** Reduced fees (weekdays, guests, twilight, juniors), metal spikes, range (mats), credit cards (MC, V, AE).

★★★ FAIRMONT HOT SPRINGS RESORT
R-P.O. Box 10, Fairmont Hot Springs, V0B 1L0, (250)345-6514, (800)663-4979, 180 miles from Calgary. **E-mail:** info@fairmonthotsprings.com. **Web:** www.fairmonthotsprings.com. **Facility Holes:** 18. **Yards:** 6,522/5,488. **Par:** 72/72. **Course Rating:** 70.9/71.4. **Slope:** 121/125. **Green Fee:** $40/$55. **Cart Fee:** $26/Cart. **Walking Policy:** Unrestricted walking. **Walkability:** 3. **Opened:** 1963. **Architect:** Lloyd Wilder. **Season:** April-Oct. **High:** May-Sept. **To obtain tee times:** Call golf shop. **Miscellaneous:** Reduced fees (weekdays, guests, twilight, juniors), credit cards (MC, V, AE, D), BF, FF.
Reader Comments: Great value ... A challenging course for both novice and experienced golfer, along with some breathtaking views ... Lovely scenery ... Tricky greens.

★★★★ FAIRVIEW MOUNTAIN GOLF CLUB *Value*
SP-Old Golf Course Rd., Oliver, V0H 1T0, (250)498-3521, (888)955-4657, 70 miles from Kelowna. **E-mail:** fvgolf@otvcablelan.net. **Web:** www.fairviewmountain.com. **Facility Holes:** 18. **Yards:** 6,557/5,382. **Par:** 72/73. **Course Rating:** 71.5/73.5. **Slope:** 129/127. **Green Fee:** $45/$48. **Cart Fee:** $30/Person. **Walking Policy:** Unrestricted walking. **Walkability:** 4. **Opened:** 1991. **Architect:** Les Furber. **Season:** March-Nov. **High:** June-Sept. **Tee times:** Call. **Misc:** Reduced fees (twilight, juniors), range (mats), credit cards (MC, V, AE), BF, FF.
Reader Comments: One of our favorites, a gem, hard to find ... Don't go looking for your ball—rattlers! ... Very challenging ... Great course, cart is a must ... Each hole is unique, great views, difficult to walk.

★★★ FAIRWINDS GOLF & COUNTRY CLUB
R-3730 Fairwinds Dr., Nanoose Bay, V9P 9J6, (250)468-7666, (888)781-2777, 6 miles from Nanaimo. **E-mail:** wstouffer@fairwinds.bc.ca. **Web:** www.fairwinds.bc.ca. **Facility Holes:** 18. **Yards:** 6,151/5,173. **Par:** 71/71. **Course Rating:** 70.2/69.8. **Slope:** 126/121. **Green Fee:** $35/$55. **Cart Fee:** $29/Cart. **Walking Policy:** Unrestricted walking. **Walkability:** 4. **Opened:** 1988. **Architect:** Les Furber/Jim Eremko. **Season:** Year-round. **High:** May-Oct. **To obtain tee times:** Call up to 5 days in advance. **Miscellaneous:** Reduced fees (twilight, juniors), metal spikes, range (grass/mats), lodging (29 rooms), credit cards (MC, V, AE), BF, FF.
Reader Comments: Short but challenging and very natural ... Good golf ... Lovely setting, nice clubhouse.

★★★½ THE FALLS GOLF & COUNTRY CLUB
SP-8341 Nixon Rd., Rosedale, V0X 1X0, (604)794-3300, (800)862-3168, 60 miles from Vancouver. **E-mail:** thefalls@telus.net. **Web:** www.thefalls.bc.ca. **Facility Holes:** 18. **Yards:**

6,426/4,892. **Par:** 71/71. **Course Rating:** 70.6/63.7. **Slope:** 130/112. **Green Fee:** $35/$80. **Cart Fee:** Included in green fee. **Walking Policy:** Mandatory carts. **Walkability:** 5. **Opened:** 1996. **Architect:** Ted Locke/Rick Wellsby. **Season:** Feb.-Nov. **High:** June-Sept. **To obtain tee times:** Call golf shop. **Miscellaneous:** Reduced fees (weekdays, guests, twilight, seniors, juniors), range (grass), credit cards (MC, V), FF.

Reader Comments: Outstanding golf course ... Tough, scenic and well groomed ... You'll want to play this one again and again ... All putts go towards the valley—even uphill putts ... One hole overlooks Frazier Valley, awesome.

★½ FORT LANGLEY GOLF COURSE

SP-9782 McKinnon Crescent, Fort Langley, V1M 2R5, (604)888-5911, 10 miles from Vancouver. **Facility Holes:** 18. **Yards:** 6,428/5,681. **Par:** 70/75. **Course Rating:** 70.0/71.5. **Slope:** 115/126. **Green Fee:** $30/$35. **Cart Fee:** $26/Cart. **Walking Policy:** Unrestricted walking. **Walkability:** 3. **Opened:** 1968. **Architect:** James Bryce/Tony Turney. **Season:** Year-round. **High:** May-Sept. **To obtain tee times:** Call golf shop. **Miscellaneous:** Reduced fees (weekdays, twilight, seniors, juniors), metal spikes, range (grass), credit cards (MC, V, AE, Diners Club).

★★ FRASERVIEW GOLF COURSE

PU-7800 Vivian St., Vancouver, V5S 2V8, (604)257-6923. **Facility Holes:** 18. **Yards:** 6,700/5,890. **Par:** 72/72. **Course Rating:** 71.4/72.6. **Slope:** 121/116. **Green Fee:** $40/$45. **Cart Fee:** $27/Cart. **Walking Policy:** Unrestricted walking. **Walkability:** 3. **Opened:** 1934. **Architect:** Thomas McBroom. **Season:** Year-round. **High:** April-Nov. **To obtain tee times:** Call up to 5 days in advance. **Miscellaneous:** Reduced fees (twilight, seniors, juniors), credit cards (MC, V, AE), BF, FF.

★★★½ FURRY CREEK GOLF & COUNTRY CLUB

PU-150 Country Club Rd., Lions Bay, VON 2E0, (604)896-2216, (888)922-9461, 12 miles from Lions Bay. **E-mail:** info_furry@golfbc.com. **Web:** www.furrycreekgolf.ca. **Facility Holes:** 18. **Yards:** 6,017/4,730. **Par:** 72/71. **Course Rating:** 69.1/68.8. **Slope:** 122/119. **Green Fee:** $70/$100. **Cart Fee:** Included in green fee. **Walking Policy:** Mandatory carts. **Walkability:** 5. **Opened:** 1993. **Architect:** Robert Muir Graves. **Season:** March-Oct. **High:** June-Sept. **Tee times:** Call up to 10 days in advance. **Miscellaneous:** Reduced fees (weekdays, twilight, seniors, juniors), metal spikes, range (grass), credit cards (MC, V, AE), FF.

Reader Comments: Beautiful views—playing golf on the side of a mountain ... Hilly course, too many blind shots ... A bit too target golf for me, but what views ... Put the driver away and play position ... Novelty design, exciting ... Takes you from top of the mountains to the ocean.

★★★★ GALLAGHER'S CANYON GOLF & COUNTRY CLUB

SP-4320 Gallagher's Dr. W., Kelowna, V1W 3Z9, (250)861-4240, (800)446-5322, 2 miles from Kelowna. **E-mail:** phopley-gallaghers@golfbc.com. **Web:** www.golfbc.com. **Facility Holes:** 27. **Yards:** 6,792/5,574. **Par:** 72/73. **Course Rating:** 72.2/72.9. **Slope:** 123/129. **Green Fee:** $35/$90. **Cart Fee:** $32/Person. **Walking Policy:** Unrestricted walking. **Walkability:** 3. **Opened:** 1980. **Architect:** William Robinson/Les Furber. **Season:** April-Oct. **High:** May-Sept. **To obtain tee times:** Call golf shop. **Miscellaneous:** Reduced fees (twilight, juniors), metal spikes, range (grass), credit cards (MC, V, AE), BF, FF.

Reader Comments: Excellent vacation course ... Mix of old and new holes, hilly ... Beautiful fairways winding through a pine forest ... Awesome course.

Special Notes: Also has a 9-hole course.

★★★★ GOLDEN GOLF & COUNTRY CLUB *Value*

SP-576 Dogtooth Rd., Golden, V0A 1H0, (250)344-2700, (866)727-7222, 150 miles from Calgary. **E-mail:** golfgolden@redshift.bc.ca. **Web:** www.golfgolden.com. **Facility Holes:** 18. **Yards:** 6,818/5,380. **Par:** 72/72. **Course Rating:** 72.7/70.0. **Slope:** 137/121. **Green Fee:** $39/$50. **Cart Fee:** $25/Cart. **Walking Policy:** Unrestricted walking. **Walkability:** 4. **Opened:** 1985. **Architect:** Les Furber. **High:** May-Sept. **Tee times:** Call golf shop. **Miscellaneous:** Reduced fees (twilight, juniors), range (grass), credit cards (MC, V, AE), BF, FF.

Reader Comments: Must play ... Great river holes, wildlife, no houses ... Out of the way course, but worth the trip ... Scenery.

★★½ GORGE VALE GOLF CLUB

SP-1005 Craigflower Rd., Victoria, V9A 2X9, (250)386-3401, 2 miles from Victoria. **E-mail:** office@gorgevalegolf.com. **Web:** www.gorgevalegolf.com. **Facility Holes:** 18. **Yards:** 6,452/5,729. **Par:** 72/74. **Course Rating:** 70.4/74.4. **Slope:** 121/137. **Green Fee:** $50/$65. **Cart Fee:** $32/Cart. **Walking Policy:** Unrestricted walking. **Walkability:** 4. **Opened:** 1930. **Architect:** A. Vernon Macan. **Season:** Year-round. **High:** April-Sept. **To obtain tee times:** Call golf shop. **Miscellaneous:** Reduced fees (juniors), metal spikes, range (grass/mats), credit cards (MC, V), BF, FF.

CANADA

★★★★ GREYWOLF GOLF COURSE
R-1860 Greywolf Dr., Panorama, V0A 1T0, (250)342-6941, (800)663-2929, 80 miles from Calgary. **E-mail:** pfsmith@intrawest.com. **Web:** www.panoramaresort.com. **Facility Holes:** 18. **Yards:** 7,140/5,400. **Par:** 72/72. **Course Rating:** 73.5/69.6. **Slope:** 137/122. **Green Fee:** $65/$105. **Cart Fee:** Included in green fee. **Walking Policy:** Mandatory carts. **Walkability:** 5. **Opened:** 1999. **Architect:** Doug Carrick. **Season:** May-Oct. **To obtain tee times:** Call pro shop. **Miscellaneous:** Reduced fees (twilight), lodging (500 rooms), credit cards (MC, V, AE), FF. **Notes:** Ranked 1st in 1999 Best New Canadian.
Reader Comments: This is a MUST for every serious golfer … Best scenery in the world, makes a bad round seem a lot better … Slow play because of trouble you can get into … Outstanding design … Lots of sloping fairways … Unpredictable weather, extreme golf … Takes every shot you know.

★★★★ HARVEST GOLF CLUB
R-2725 Klo Rd., Kelowna, V1W 4S8, (250)862-3103, (800)257-8577, 200 miles from Vancouver. **E-mail:** proshop@harvestgolf.com. **Web:** www.harvestgolf.com. **Facility Holes:** 18. **Yards:** 7,109/5,454. **Par:** 72/72. **Course Rating:** 73.3/70.9. **Slope:** 128/120. **Green Fee:** $44/$85. **Cart Fee:** $32/Cart. **Walking Policy:** Unrestricted walking. **Walkability:** 3. **Opened:** 1994. **Architect:** Graham Cooke. **Season:** March-Oct. **High:** May-Sept. **To obtain tee times:** Call up to 365 days in advance. **Miscellaneous:** Reduced fees (twilight, juniors), range (grass/mats), credit cards (MC, V, AE), BF, FF.
Reader Comments: In superb condition … Must play while in Kelowna … Scenic course through Okanagan Orchard … Wide fairways with sloping greens and a view of Okanagan Lake and Kelowna … Service excellent … Too many holes the same.

★★½ KELOWNA SPRINGS GOLF CLUB
SP-480 Penno Rd., Kelowna, V1X 6S3, (250)765-4653. **E-mail:** golf@kelownasprings.com. **Web:** www.kelownasprings.com. **Facility Holes:** 18. **Yards:** 6,156/5,225. **Par:** 71/71. **Course Rating:** 69.6/70.0. **Slope:** 117/118. **Green Fee:** $30/$45. **Cart Fee:** $27/Cart. **Walking Policy:** Unrestricted walking. **Walkability:** 1. **Opened:** 1990. **Architect:** Les Furber. **Season:** March-Nov. **High:** May-Sept. **To obtain tee times:** Call up to 90 days in advance. **Miscellaneous:** Reduced fees (twilight, juniors), credit cards (MC, V, AE, Debit), BF, FF.

★★★★ KOKANEE SPRINGS GOLF RESORT
R-Box 96, Crawford Bay, V0B 1E0, (250)227-9362, (800)979-7999, 120 miles from Spokane, WA. **Facility Holes:** 18. **Yards:** 6,537/5,747. **Par:** 71/74. **Course Rating:** 72.0/68.4. **Slope:** 135/128. **Green Fee:** $41/$46. **Cart Fee:** $12/Person. **Walking Policy:** Unrestricted walking. **Walkability:** 5. **Opened:** 1967. **Architect:** Norman Woods. **Season:** April-Oct. **High:** July-Sept. **To obtain tee times:** Call golf shop. **Miscellaneous:** Reduced fees (guests, twilight, juniors), metal spikes, range (grass/mats), lodging (26 rooms), credit cards (MC, V, AE).
Reader Comments: A great mountain course … View of glacier on 4th hole … Need to improve clubhouse area … Seclusion, variety, great greens & bunkers … What a venue … They came and picked me up from the local campground and dropped me off when I was done … Beautiful course in quiet secluded town.

THE LONE WOLF GOLF CLUB
PU-P.O. Box 300, Taylor, V0C 2K0, (250)789-3711, 12 miles from Fort St. John. **Facility Holes:** 18. **Yards:** 6,817/5,968. **Par:** 72/73. **Course Rating:** 72.5/68.5. **Slope:** 128/118. **Green Fee:** $22/$28. **Cart Fee:** $25/Cart. **Walking Policy:** Unrestricted walking. **Walkability:** 2. **Opened:** 1995. **Architect:** Albers Bros. **Season:** April-Oct. **High:** June-Aug. **Tee times:** Call. **Misc:** Reduced fees (weekdays, seniors, juniors), range, credit cards (MC, V, AE), BF, FF.

★★★ MAYFAIR LAKES GOLF & COUNTRY CLUB
SP-5460 #7 Rd., Richmond, V6V 1R7, (604)276-0505, (800)446-5322, 7 miles from Vancouver. **Web:** www.mayfairlakes.com. **Facility Holes:** 18. **Yards:** 6,641/5,277. **Par:** 71/72. **Course Rating:** 71.3/71.3. **Slope:** 123/126. **Green Fee:** $45/$85. **Cart Fee:** $30/Cart. **Walking Policy:** Unrestricted walking. **Walkability:** 1. **Opened:** 1989. **Architect:** Les Furber. **Season:** Year-round. **To obtain tee times:** Call golf shop. **Miscellaneous:** Reduced fees (weekdays, twilight, seniors, juniors), metal spikes, range (grass/mats), credit cards (MC, V, AE), BF, FF.
Reader Comments: Nice facility, well maintained, good food … Bring your ball retriever (10 holes with water)… Greens are like putting on glass … Grooming is immaculate … Very flat, not easy to score … Newly renovated clubhouse adds to value.

★★½ MCCLEERY GOLF COURSE
PU-7188 MacDonald St., Vancouver, V6N 1G2, (604)257-8191. **Facility Holes:** 18. **Yards:** 6,265/5,010. **Par:** 71/71. **Course Rating:** 69.6/67.1. **Slope:** 126/110. **Green Fee:** $34/$37. **Cart Fee:** $26/Cart. **Walking Policy:** Unrestricted walking. **Walkability:** 2. **Opened:** 1959. **Architect:** Ted Baker & Associates. **Season:** Year-round. **High:** April-Oct. **Tee times:** Call golf shop. **Miscellaneous:** Reduced fees (twilight, seniors, juniors), range (mats), credit cards (MC, V).

★★★½ MEADOW GARDENS GOLF COURSE
SP-19675 Meadow Gardens Way, Pitt Meadows, V3Y 1Z2, (604)465-5474, (800)667-6758, 12 miles from Vancouver. **E-mail:** sharonkyle@home.com. **Facility Holes:** 18. **Yards:** 7,041/5,519. **Par:** 72/72. **Course Rating:** 73.1/71.3. **Slope:** 126/116. **Green Fee:** $37/$55. **Cart Fee:** $28/Cart. **Walking Policy:** Unrestricted walking. **Walkability:** 2. **Opened:** 1994. **Architect:** Les Furber/Jim Eremko. **Season:** Year-round. **High:** April-Sept. **To obtain tee times:** Call up to 7 days in advance. **Miscellaneous:** Reduced fees (weekdays, twilight, seniors, juniors), range (grass/mats), caddies, credit cards (MC, V, AE, DC), BF, FF.
Reader Comments: Top value for the money … Very walkable … Good use of the natural waterways on some of the holes … Excellent finishing hole … Plenty of water.

★★★½ MORGAN CREEK GOLF COURSE
SP-3500 Morgan Creek Way, Surrey, V3S 0J7, (604)531-4653, (800)513-6555, 35 miles from Vancouver. **E-mail:** admin@morgancreekgolf.com. **Web:** www.morgancreekgolf.com. **Facility Holes:** 18. **Yards:** 6,954/5,221. **Par:** 72/73. **Course Rating:** 73.2/69.4. **Slope:** 133/120. **Green Fee:** $55/$90. **Cart Fee:** $32/Cart. **Walking Policy:** Unrestricted walking. **Walkability:** 2. **Opened:** 1995. **Architect:** Thomas McBroom. **Season:** Year-round. **High:** June-Sept. **To obtain tee times:** Call golf shop. **Miscellaneous:** Reduced fees (weekdays, twilight, seniors, juniors), range (grass), credit cards (MC, V, AE, DC), BF, FF.
Reader Comments: Many environmentally sensitive areas, beautiful clubhouse … Good challenging course layout … Par-3 8th hole is outstanding … Not a bad lie on the fairways … Easily one of the most challenging and best maintained courses open to public play on the mainland.

★★★½ MORNINGSTAR GOLF CLUB
PU-525 Lowry's Rd., Parksville, V9P 2R8, (250)248-8161, 30 miles from Nanaimo. **Facility Holes:** 18. **Yards:** 7,018/5,313. **Par:** 72/72. **Course Rating:** 74.5/71.2. **Slope:** 139/135. **Green Fee:** $25/$55. **Cart Fee:** $30/Cart. **Walking Policy:** Unrestricted walking. **Walkability:** 1. **Opened:** 1990. **Architect:** Les Furber. **Season:** Year-round. **To obtain tee times:** Call up to 7 days in advance. **Miscellaneous:** Reduced fees (weekdays, guests, twilight, juniors), metal spikes, range (grass), credit cards (MC, V, AE), BF, FF.
Reader Comments: Excellent layout, very good service … Maybe a little overpriced … Challenging, greens quite fast … Terrific par-3s.

★★★ NANAIMO GOLF CLUB
SP-2800 Highland Blvd., Nanaimo, V9S 3N8, (250)758-6332, 70 miles from Victoria. **E-mail:** admin@nangolf.nisa.com. **Web:** www.nangolf.nisa.com. **Facility Holes:** 18. **Yards:** 6,667/5,648. **Par:** 72/72. **Course Rating:** 71.9/67.3. **Slope:** 129/118. **Green Fee:** $36/$55. **Cart Fee:** $29/Cart. **Walking Policy:** Unrestricted walking. **Walkability:** 2. **Opened:** 1962. **Architect:** A. Vernon Macan. **Season:** Year-round. **To obtain tee times:** Call golf shop. **Miscellaneous:** Reduced fees (twilight, juniors), metal spikes, range (mats), credit cards (MC, V), BF, FF.
Reader Comments: Nice course right in city, good views … Course well laid out … Not many hills, quite walkable.

★★★★ NICKLAUS NORTH GOLF COURSE
SP-8080 Nicklaus North Blvd., Whistler, V0N 1B0, (604)938-9898, (800)386-9898, 75 miles from Vancouver. **E-mail:** info_nicklaus@golfbc.com. **Web:** www.nicklausnorth.com. **Facility Holes:** 18. **Yards:** 6,908/4,730. **Par:** 71/71. **Course Rating:** 72.2/66.3. **Slope:** 133/113. **Green Fee:** $125/$205. **Cart Fee:** Included in green fee. **Walking Policy:** Unrestricted walking. **Walkability:** 1. **Opened:** 1995. **Architect:** Jack Nicklaus. **Season:** May-Oct. **High:** July-Sept. **To obtain tee times:** Call golf shop. **Miscellaneous:** Reduced fees (twilight, juniors), range (grass), lodging (24 rooms), credit cards (MC, V, AE, DC), BF, FF.
Reader Comments: Fantastic course, but expensive … Excellent scenery … Wonderful lake & mountain setting … Narrow fairways, bears, slow play.

NORTHLANDS GOLF COURSE
PU-3400 Anne MacDonald Way, North Vancouver, V7G 2S7, (604)924-2950. **E-mail:** craddocl@dnv.org. **Web:** www.golfnorthlands.com. **Facility Holes:** 18. **Yards:** 6,504/5,135. **Par:** 71/71. **Course Rating:** 71.6/70.1. **Slope:** 135/123. **Green Fee:** $35/$50. **Cart Fee:** $28/Cart. **Walking Policy:** Unrestricted walking. **Walkability:** 4. **Opened:** 1997. **Architect:** Les Furber. **Season:** Year-round. **High:** May-Sept. **To obtain tee times:** Call up to 3 days in advance. **Miscellaneous:** Reduced fees (weekdays, twilight, seniors, juniors), metal spikes, credit cards (MC, V, AE), BF, FF.

NORTHVIEW GOLF & COUNTRY CLUB
PU-6857 168th St., Surrey, V3S 8E7, (604)576-4653, (888)574-2211, 18 miles from Vancouver. **E-mail:** golf@northviewgolf.com. **Web:** www.northviewgolf.com. **Facility Holes:** 36. **Cart Fee:** $30/Cart. **Walking Policy:** Unrestricted walking. **Architect:** Arnold Palmer. **Season:** Year-round. **To obtain tee times:** Call golf shop. **Miscellaneous:** Reduced fees (weekdays, twi-

light, seniors, juniors), range (grass/mats), credit cards (MC, V, AE, DC), BF, FF.

★★★½ **CANAL COURSE** (18)
Yards: 7,101/5,314. **Par:** 72/72. **Course Rating:** 74.4/70.1. **Slope:** 137/108. **Green Fee:** $40/$70. **Walkability:** 1. **Opened:** 1995.
Reader Comments: Fairly flat ... Good golf course that makes you want play it over and over because you know someday you will beat it ... Long hittter's paradise ... Fairways are wide open and forgiving ... Misplaced approach shots punished ... Fantastic closing 3 holes.

★★★½ **RIDGE COURSE** (18)
Yards: 6,900/5,231. **Par:** 72/72. **Course Rating:** 72.8/70.1. **Slope:** 131/123. **Green Fee:** $50/$95. **Walkability:** 3. **Opened:** 1994.
Reader Comments: Best course in the area ... Just 2 hours north of Seattle ... PGA Tour stop ... Offers risk-reward shots ... Rough around tournament time is thick so bring a few extra balls ... One of Canada's best ... Excellent variety of holes.

THE OKANAGAN GOLF CLUB
PU-3200 via Centrale, Kelowna, V1V 2A4, (250)765-5955, (800)446-5322. **Web:** www.okana-gangolfclub.com. **Facility Holes:** 36. **Cart Fee:** $32/Cart. **Walking Policy:** Unrestricted walking. **Season:** April-Oct. **Miscellaneous:** Reduced fees (twilight), credit cards (MC, V, AE), BF, FF.
BEAR COURSE (18)
Yards: 6,468/5,100. **Par:** 72/72. **Course Rating:** 69.8/68.4. **Slope:** 122/108. **Green Fee:** $70/$85. **Walkability:** 4. **Opened:** 1999. **Architect:** Bill O'Leary. **To obtain tee times:** Call golf shop. **Miscellaneous:** Range (grass/mats).
QUAIL COURSE (18)
Yards: 6,765/4,713. **Par:** 72/72. **Course Rating:** 72.8/73.3. **Slope:** 133/132. **Green Fee:** $48/$95. **Walkability:** 3. **Opened:** 1993. **Architect:** Les Furber. **To obtain tee times:** Call up to 60 days in advance. **Miscellaneous:** Metal spikes, range (grass), lodging (27 rooms).

★★½ OLYMPIC VIEW GOLF CLUB
PU-643 Latoria Rd., Victoria, V9C 3A3, (250)474-3671, (800)446-5322, 20 miles from Victoria. **E-mail:** jsmith_olympic@golfbc.com. **Web:** www.olympicviewgolf.com. **Facility Holes:** 18. **Yards:** 6,530/5,308. **Par:** 72/73. **Course Rating:** 71.8/70.7. **Slope:** 127/125. **Green Fee:** $35/$65. **Cart Fee:** $35/Cart. **Walking Policy:** Unrestricted walking. **Walkability:** 3. **Opened:** 1990. **Architect:** William Robinson. **Season:** Year-round. **To obtain tee times:** Call golf shop. **Miscellaneous:** Reduced fees (weekdays, twilight, juniors), metal spikes, range (grass), credit cards (MC, V, AE, D, DC), BF, FF.

★★½ OSOYOOS GOLF & COUNTRY CLUB
SP-12300 Golf Course Drive, Osoyoos, V0H 1V0, (250)495-7003, 81 miles from Kelowna. **E-mail:** mail@golfosoyoos.com. **Web:** www.golfosoyoos.com. **Facility Holes:** 27. **Green Fee:** $30/$43. **Cart Fee:** $30/Cart. **Walking Policy:** Unrestricted walking. **Walkability:** 3. **Opened:** 1971. **Architect:** Boyd Barr. **Season:** March-Nov. **High:** June-Sept. **To obtain tee times:** Call golf shop. **Miscellaneous:** Reduced fees (twilight, juniors), range (grass/mats), credit cards (MC, V, AE), BF, FF.
DESERT/MEADOWS (18 Combo)
Yards: 6,318/5,303. **Par:** 72/72. **Course Rating:** 69.8/71.8. **Slope:** 118/123.
PARK/DESERT (18 Combo)
Yards: 6,223/5,109. **Par:** 72/72. **Course Rating:** 69.8/71.8. **Slope:** 118/123.
PARK/MEADOWS (18 Combo)
Yards: 6,323/5,214. **Par:** 72/72. **Course Rating:** 69.7/71.7. **Slope:** 116/121. **Miscellaneous:** Metal spikes.

★★★ PEACE PORTAL GOLF COURSE
SP-16900 4th Ave., South Surrey, V4P 2Y9, (604)538-4818, (800)354-7544, 30 miles from Vancouver. **E-mail:** info@peaceportalgolf.com. **Web:** www.peaceportalgolf.com. **Facility Holes:** 18. **Yards:** 6,363/5,621. **Par:** 72/73. **Course Rating:** 70.9/73.0. **Slope:** 126/133. **Green Fee:** $46/$50. **Cart Fee:** $27/Cart. **Walking Policy:** Unrestricted walking. **Walkability:** 4. **Opened:** 1928. **Architect:** Francis L. James. **Season:** Year-round. **High:** May-Sept. **To obtain tee times:** Call up to 7 days in advance. **Miscellaneous:** Reduced fees (twilight, juniors), metal spikes, range (grass/mats), credit cards (MC, V, AE, DC), BF, FF.
Reader Comments: Best conditions to be found in South Surrey ... Very well maintained ... Picturesque older course carved through hills and gullies and framed by Douglas fir and hemlocks ... Not very long, but sea air makes it play at least 400 yards longer ... Elevated greens ... Wow, what big trees.

CANADA

★★ PENTICTON GOLF & COUNTRY CLUB
SP-600 Comox St., Penticton, V2A 6K3, (250)492-8727, 40 miles from Kelowna.
E-mail: pentictongolf@img.net. **Facility Holes:** 18. **Yards:** 6,131/5,609. **Par:** 70/72. **Course Rating:** 70.0/73.0. **Slope:** 127/130. **Green Fee:** $40. **Cart Fee:** $23/Cart. **Walking Policy:** Unrestricted walking. **Walkability:** 1. **Opened:** 1920. **Architect:** Les Furber. **Season:** Feb.-Dec. **Tee times:** Call golf shop. **Misc:** Reduced fees (guests, twilight, juniors), credit cards (MC, V), BF, FF.

★★½ PITT MEADOWS GOLF CLUB
SP-13615 Harris Rd., Pitt Meadows, V3Y 2R8, (604)465-4711, 20 miles from Vancouver. **E-mail:** dlooyen@pittmeadowsgolf.com. **Web:** www.pittmeadowsgolf.com. **Facility Holes:** 18. **Yards:** 6,516/5,927. **Par:** 72/74. **Course Rating:** 71.8/73.3. **Slope:** 125/123. **Green Fee:** $40/$60. **Cart Fee:** $28/Cart. **Walking Policy:** Unrestricted walking. **Walkability:** 1. **Opened:** 1963. **Architect:** Built by members. **Season:** Year-round. **High:** March-Oct. **To obtain tee times:** Call up to 1 day in advance. **Miscellaneous:** Reduced fees (juniors), metal spikes, range (grass/mats), credit cards (MC, V), BF, FF.

PREDATOR RIDGE GOLF RESORT
R-301 Village Center Place, Vernon, V1H 1T2, (250)542-3436, (888)578-6688, 36 miles from Kelowna. **E-mail:** resmgr@predatorridge.com. **Web:** www.predatorridge.com. **Facility Holes:** 27. **Green Fee:** $72/$95. **Cart Fee:** $40/Cart. **Walking Policy:** Unrestricted walking. **Walkability:** 4. **Opened:** 1991. **Architect:** Les Furber. **Season:** April-Oct. **High:** May-Sept. **To obtain tee times:** Call golf shop. **Miscellaneous:** Reduced fees (guests, twilight, juniors), metal spikes, range (grass), credit cards (MC, V, AE), BF, FF.
★★★★½ **OSPREY/PEREGRINE** (18)
Yards: 7,087/5,514. **Par:** 71/71. **Course Rating:** 76.0/72.9. **Slope:** 131/131.
Reader Comments: Several holes will stick in your memory for a long time ... Service was outstanding ... Good variety of holes ... Beautiful setting ... Fun from white tees, impossible from back ... Very large, fast greens ... Play the right tee's and you can have a great time.
RED TAIL/OSPREY (18)
Yards: 7,099/5,373. **Par:** 71/71. **Course Rating:** 76.0/72.9. **Slope:** 131/131.
RED TAIL/PEREGRINE (18)
Yards: 7,144/5,513. **Par:** 72/72. **Course Rating:** 76.0/72.9. **Slope:** 131/131.

PRINCE RUPERT CENTENNIAL GOLF
SP-523 9th Ave. W., Prince Rupert, V8J 2S9, (250)624-2000. **E-mail:** moe_the_pro@hotmail.com. **Facility Holes:** 18. **Yards:** 5,808/5,526. **Par:** 70/71. **Course Rating:** 68.9/73.4. **Slope:** 119/132. **Green Fee:** $18/$30. **Cart Fee:** $27/Cart. **Walking Policy:** Unrestricted walking. **Walkability:** 3. **Opened:** 1969. **Season:** March-Nov. **High:** May-Sept. **To obtain tee times:** Call up to 2 days in advance. **Miscellaneous:** Reduced fees (twilight, seniors, juniors), metal spikes, credit cards (MC, V, AE), BF, FF.

★★★★ RADIUM RESORT
R-Stanley St. and Columbia Ave., Radium Hot Springs, V0A 1M0, (250)347-6200, (800)667-6444, 90 miles from Banff. **E-mail:** headpro@radiumresort.com. **Web:** www.radiumresort.com. **Facility Holes:** 36. **Yards:** 6,767/5,163. **Par:** 72/72. **Course Rating:** 72.3/70.3. **Slope:** 129/126. **Green Fee:** $40/$60. **Cart Fee:** $25/Cart. **Walking Policy:** Unrestricted walking. **Walkability:** 2. **Opened:** 1988. **Architect:** Les Furber. **Season:** March-Oct. **High:** May-Sept. **To obtain tee times:** Call up to 180 days in advance. **Miscellaneous:** Reduced fees (weekdays, guests, twilight, juniors), range (grass), credit cards (MC, V, AE), BF, FF.
Reader Comments: Great par 3s ... Used to be my favorite, 'til Greywolf opened ... Excellent course layout with a wide variety of holes ... Challenge for all golfers ... Hard to beat, solid course ... High calibre course at a good bargain ... Overlooking Columbia River, scenic course.

RADIUM RESORT
PU-Box 310, 8100 Golf Course Rd., Radium Hot Springs, V0A 1M0, (250)347-6266, (800)667-6444. **E-mail:** headpro@radiumresort.com. **Web:** www.radiumresort.com. **Facility Holes:** 36. **Yards:** 5,306/4,972. **Par:** 69/69. **Course Rating:** 64.9/69.2. **Slope:** 106/122. **Green Fee:** $27/$40. **Cart Fee:** $25/Cart. **Walking Policy:** Unrestricted walking. **Walkability:** 3. **Opened:** 1957. **Season:** April-Oct. **High:** May-Sept. **To obtain tee times:** Call up to 180 days in advance. **Miscellaneous:** Reduced fees (weekdays, guests, twilight, juniors), lodging (100 rooms), credit cards (MC, V, AE, DC), BF, FF.

CANADA

★★★ THE REDWOODS
PU-22011 88th Ave., Langley, V1M 2M3, (604)882-5132, (877)882-5130, 25 miles from Vancouver. **E-mail:** info@redwoods-golf.com. **Web:** www.redwoods-golf.com. **Facility Holes:** 18. **Yards:** 6,516/5,452. **Par:** 71/71. **Course Rating:** 72.3/71.3. **Slope:** 131/123. **Green Fee:** $15/$65. **Cart Fee:** $28/Cart. **Walking Policy:** Unrestricted walking. **Walkability:** 3. **Opened:** 1994. **Architect:** Ted Locke. **Season:** Year-round. **High:** June-Sept. **To obtain tee times:** Call up to 30 days in advance. **Miscellaneous:** Reduced fees (weekdays, twilight, seniors, juniors), metal spikes, range (mats), credit cards (MC, V, AE), BF, FF.
Reader Comments: Walkable ... Some nice changes in elevation ... Very memorable ... Tight course that winds through a forest ... Every time I've played I've been impressed ... Use your first round to "see" the course ... Would love to play it twice in one day ... A tough walk, great value.

REVELSTOKE GOLF CLUB
PU-170 Columbia Park Drive, Revelstoke, V0E 2S0, (250)837-2440, 110 miles from Kamloops. **Facility Holes:** 18. **Yards:** 6,521/5,847. **Par:** 72/74. **Course Rating:** 70.9/74.3. **Slope:** 122/130. **Green Fee:** $43. **Walking Policy:** Unrestricted walking. **Walkability:** 2. **Opened:** 1925. **Architect:** Norman Woods. **Season:** April-Nov. **High:** June-Sept. **To obtain tee times:** Call golf shop. **Miscellaneous:** Reduced fees (twilight), range (grass), credit cards (MC, V), BF, FF.

★★★ RIVERSHORE GOLF LINKS
SP-330 Rivershore Drive, Kamloops, V2H 1S1, (250)573-4622, (866)886-4653, 10 miles from Kamloops. **E-mail:** rivershore_golf@telus.net. **Web:** www.rivershoregolflinks.com. **Facility Holes:** 18. **Yards:** 7,007/5,445. **Par:** 72/72. **Course Rating:** 74.8/71.3. **Slope:** 135/122. **Green Fee:** $46/$60. **Cart Fee:** $28/Cart. **Walking Policy:** Unrestricted walking. **Walkability:** 1. **Opened:** 1982. **Architect:** Robert Trent Jones. **Season:** March-Nov. **High:** April-Sept. **To obtain tee times:** Call up to 30 days in advance. **Miscellaneous:** Reduced fees (weekdays, guests, twilight, juniors), range (grass/mats), credit cards (MC, V, AE), BF, FF.
Reader Comments: Excellent RTJ Sr. semi-links course along the Thompson River ... Attentive staff ... Fun & challenging especially in wind ... Flat, easy walk.

★★½ RIVERSIDE GOLF RESORT
SP-5097 Riverview Dr., Fairmont Hot Springs, V0B 1L0, (250)345-6346, (800)665-2112, 180 miles from Calgary. **E-mail:** info@golfriverside.com. **Web:** www.golfriverside.com. **Facility Holes:** 18. **Yards:** 6,507/5,370. **Par:** 71/71. **Course Rating:** 71.0/70.3. **Slope:** 128/119. **Green Fee:** $39/$65. **Cart Fee:** $25/Cart. **Walking Policy:** Unrestricted walking. **Walkability:** 1. **Opened:** 1988. **Architect:** Bill Newis. **Season:** April-Nov. **High:** April-Nov. **To obtain tee times:** Call up to 3 days in advance. **Miscellaneous:** Reduced fees (weekdays, guests, twilight, juniors), range (grass/mats), credit cards (MC, V), BF, FF.

★★★ RIVERWAY PUBLIC GOLF COURSE
PU-9001 Riverway Place, Burnaby, V5J 5J3, (604)280-4653, 2 miles from Vancouver. **Facility Holes:** 18. **Yards:** 7,004/5,437. **Par:** 72/72. **Course Rating:** 73.4/72.0. **Slope:** 132/125. **Green Fee:** $42. **Cart Fee:** $26/Cart. **Walking Policy:** Unrestricted walking. **Walkability:** 2. **Opened:** 1995. **Architect:** Les Furber. **Season:** Year-round. **High:** May-Oct. **To obtain tee times:** Call up to 2 days in advance. **Miscellaneous:** Reduced fees (twilight, seniors, juniors), metal spikes, range (mats), credit cards (MC, V), BF, FF.
Reader Comments: A municipal course, fairly flat, some difficult holes ... As close to links as possible in a public course ... Almost treeless ... Very good hole & shot variety for muni ... Good eating facility though very small ... Great links layout.

★★ ROSSLAND TRAIL COUNTRY CLUB
SP-P.O. Box 250, Trail, V1R 4L5, (250)693-2255, 10 miles from Trail. **E-mail:** golfrtee@wkpowerlink.com. **Web:** www.golfcanada.com. **Facility Holes:** 27. **Yards:** 6,489/5,786. **Par:** 72/72. **Course Rating:** 70.1/73.1. **Slope:** 121/129. **Green Fee:** $40. **Cart Fee:** $28/Cart. **Walking Policy:** Unrestricted walking. **Walkability:** 2. **Opened:** 1963. **Architect:** Reg Stone/Roy Stone. **Season:** March-Nov. **To obtain tee times:** Call golf shop. **Miscellaneous:** Reduced fees (twilight, juniors), range (grass), credit cards (MC, V), BF, FF.
Special Notes: Also has a 9-hole Rossland Course.

★★ SHADOW RIDGE GOLF CLUB
SP-3770 Bulman, Kelowna, V1Y 7P7, (250)765-7777. **E-mail:** shadow_ridge@the sun.net. **Web:** www.golfokanagan.com. **Facility Holes:** 18. **Yards:** 6,475/5,777. **Par:** 71/72. **Course Rating:** 70.3/74.0. **Slope:** 121/130. **Green Fee:** $30/$40. **Cart Fee:** $26/Cart. **Walking Policy:** Unrestricted walking. **Walkability:** 1. **Opened:** 1988. **High:** April-Oct. **To obtain tee times:** Call golf shop. **Miscellaneous:** Reduced fees (weekdays, guests, twilight, juniors), metal spikes, range (mats), credit cards (MC, V, AE), BF, FF.

CANADA

★★ SHANNON LAKE GOLF COURSE
PU-2649 Shannon Lake Rd., Westbank, V4T 1V6, (250)768-4577, 5 miles from Kelowna. E-mail: shannonlk@home.com. **Web:** www.golfokanagan.com. **Facility Holes:** 18. **Yards:** 6,316/5,494. **Par:** 71/72. **Course Rating:** 70.9/70.9. **Slope:** 125/116. **Green Fee:** $33/$42. **Cart Fee:** $26/Cart. **Walking Policy:** Unrestricted walking. **Walkability:** 3. **Opened:** 1985. **Architect:** Bob Kains. **Season:** March-Oct. **High:** June-Aug. **To obtain tee times:** Call golf shop. **Misc:** Reduced fees (weekdays, guests, twilight, juniors), metal spikes, credit cards (MC, V), BF, FF.

★★½ SPALLUMCHEEN GOLF & COUNTRY CLUB
PU-P.O. Box 218, 9701 - Hwy. 97 N., Vernon, V1T 6M2, (250)545-5824, 8 miles from Vernon. **E-mail:** spallumcheen_estates@telus.net. **Web:** www.spallumcheengolf.com. **Facility Holes:** 27. **Yards:** 6,423/5,294. **Par:** 71/71. **Course Rating:** 70.2/74.6. **Slope:** 118/129. **Green Fee:** $39/$48. **Cart Fee:** $30/Cart. **Walking Policy:** Unrestricted walking. **Walkability:** 2. **Opened:** 1972. **Architect:** Bill Simms/Cyril Foster. **Season:** March-Nov. **High:** June-Sept. **To obtain tee times:** Call golf shop. **Miscellaneous:** Reduced fees (twilight), metal spikes, range (grass/mats), credit cards (MC, V, AE), BF, FF.
Special Notes: Also has a 9-hole executive course.

★★★ SQUAMISH VALLEY GOLF & COUNTRY CLUB
SP-2458 Mamquam Rd., Squamish, V0N 3G0, (604)898-9691, (888)349-3688, 50 miles from Vancouver. **E-mail:** svgcc@mountain-inter.net. **Web:** www.squamishvalleygolf.com. **Facility Holes:** 18. **Yards:** 6,495/5,148. **Par:** 72/72. **Course Rating:** 71.8/69.9. **Slope:** 125/113. **Green Fee:** $35/$55. **Cart Fee:** $30/Cart. **Walking Policy:** Unrestricted walking. **Walkability:** 1. **Opened:** 1970. **Architect:** Gordon McKay/Robert Muir Graves. **Season:** Year-round. **High:** May-Sept. **To obtain tee times:** Call up to 7 days in advance. **Miscellaneous:** Reduced fees (twilight, seniors, juniors), range (grass/mats), credit cards (MC, V), BF, FF.
Reader Comments: Underrated, the best value of any course in the Whistler corridor ... Nice mountain views and good combination of hazards.

ST. EUGENE MISSION GOLF RESORT
R-7725 Mission Rd., Cranbrook, V1C 7E5, (250)417-3417, (877)417-3133, 4 miles from Cranbrook. **E-mail:** links@golfsteugene. **Web:** golfsteugene.com. **Facility Holes:** 18. **Yards:** 7,007/5,398. **Par:** 72/72. **Course Rating:** 72.8/65.6. **Slope:** 130/110. **Green Fee:** $49/$69. **Cart Fee:** $13/Person. **Walking Policy:** Unrestricted walking. **Walkability:** 2. **Opened:** 2000. **Architect:** Les Furber. **Season:** April-Oct. **High:** July-Sept. **To obtain tee times:** Call golf shop. **Miscellaneous:** Reduced fees (twilight, juniors), range (grass), credit cards (MC, V, AE), FF.
Notes: Ranked 3rd in 2001 Best New Canadian Courses.

★★★★ STOREY CREEK GOLF CLUB
SP-McGimpsey Rd., Campbell River, V9W 6J3, (250)923-3673, 7 miles from Campbell River. **E-mail:** storeycreek@connected.bc.ca. **Web:** www.storeycreek.bc.ca. **Facility Holes:** 18. **Yards:** 6,697/5,434. **Par:** 72/72. **Course Rating:** 72.5/72.0. **Slope:** 133/129. **Green Fee:** $34/$48. **Cart Fee:** $30/Cart. **Walking Policy:** Unrestricted walking. **Walkability:** 2. **Opened:** 1989. **Architect:** Les Furber. **Season:** Year-round. **High:** April-Sept. **To obtain tee times:** Call up to 2 days in advance. **Miscellaneous:** Reduced fees (guests, twilight, juniors), range (grass/mats), credit cards (MC, V), BF, FF.
Reader Comments: Best course on Vancouver Island by far ... Out in nature ... Better hit it straight ... Helpful starter ... Carved out of forest, many bunkers & water hazards ... Have to play it again to try & get even—course beat me up last round ... Excellent layout, challenging course.

★★ SUMMERLAND GOLF & COUNTRY CLUB
SP-2405 Mountain Ave., Summerland, V0H 1Z0, (250)494-9554, (877)955-7955, 3 miles from Summerland. **Web:** www.summerlandgolf.com. **Facility Holes:** 18. **Yards:** 6,535/5,655. **Par:** 72/72. **Course Rating:** 70.7/73.4. **Slope:** 121/128. **Green Fee:** $35/$45. **Cart Fee:** $28/Cart. **Walking Policy:** Unrestricted walking. **Walkability:** 2. **Opened:** 1980. **Architect:** Jim McIntyre. **Season:** March-Nov. **To obtain tee times:** Call golf shop. **Miscellaneous:** Reduced fees (guests, twilight, juniors), credit cards (MC, V), BF, FF.

★★★ SUNSET RANCH GOLF & COUNTRY CLUB
SP-4001 Anderson Rd., Kelowna, V1X 7V8, (250)765-7700, (877)606-7700. **E-mail:** sunset@silk.net. **Web:** www.sunsetranchbc.com. **Facility Holes:** 18. **Yards:** 6,558/5,752. **Par:** 72/72. **Course Rating:** 71.2/76.3. **Slope:** 133/131. **Green Fee:** $29/$49. **Cart Fee:** $25/Cart. **Walking Policy:** Unrestricted walking. **Walkability:** 3. **Opened:** 1991. **Architect:** J. Bruce Carr. **Season:** April-Oct. **To obtain tee times:** Call golf shop. **Miscellaneous:** Reduced fees (twilight, juniors), metal spikes, range (grass), credit cards (MC, V, AE), FF.
Reader Comments: Great setting, cut into the side of a mountain, quite challenging, but fun at the same time ... Interesting, scenic valley-side layout requires accuracy off the tee ... Greens with subtle breaks toward the valley floor demand attention for consistent scoring.

CANADA

★★★ SWAN-E-SET BAY RESORT & COUNTRY CLUB
SP-16651 Rannie Rd., Pitt Meadows, V3Y 1Z1, (604)465-3888, (800)235-8188, 27 miles from Vancouver. **E-mail:** swaneset@axionet.com. **Web:** www.swaneset.com. **Facility Holes:** 36. **Yards:** 7,000/5,632. **Par:** 72/72. **Course Rating:** 73.8/71.5. **Slope:** 130/120. **Green Fee:** $40/$85. **Cart Fee:** $25/Cart. **Walking Policy:** Unrestricted walking. **Walkability:** 2. **Opened:** 1993. **Architect:** Lee Trevino. **Season:** Year-round. **High:** April-Oct. **To obtain tee times:** Call up to 7 days in advance. **Miscellaneous:** Reduced fees (weekdays, twilight, juniors), range (grass/mats), credit cards (MC, V, AE, DC), BF, FF.
Reader Comments: Views fantastic and the clubhouse was amazing ... Lacked any excitement ... Hit the fairways or be prepared to score high ... Great mountain views ... Lots of wildlife, lots of fescue along the fairways ... Well bunkered ... A solid golfer's design, no tricked up holes ... Beautiful clubhouse.
Special Notes: Also has an 18-hole private Links Course.

★★★★ TRICKLE CREEK GOLF RESORT *Condition*
R-500 Gerry Sorensen Way, Kimberley, V1A 2H8, (250)427-3389, (888)874-2553, 150 miles from Calgary. **E-mail:** trickle@rockies.net. **Web:** www.tricklecreek.com. **Facility Holes:** 18. **Yards:** 6,896/5,082. **Par:** 72/72. **Course Rating:** 72.5/64.1. **Slope:** 130/110. **Green Fee:** $54/$89. **Cart Fee:** Included in green fee. **Walking Policy:** Unrestricted walking. **Walkability:** 5. **Opened:** 1993. **Architect:** Les Furber. **Season:** May-Oct. **High:** July-Sept. **To obtain tee times:** Call golf shop. **Miscellaneous:** Reduced fees (twilight), range (grass), lodging (80 rooms), credit cards (MC, V, AE), BF, FF.
Reader Comments: Great mountain course! ... Cart a must ... Green fees a bit pricey ... One of Canada's best ... Not exactly cheap, but a very nice golf course ... One of many great golf courses in the area ... Tough—but fair ... Nice course, treated well but overrated ... 18 great holes.

★★★½ UNIVERSITY GOLF CLUB
PU-5185 University Blvd., Vancouver, V6T 1X5, (604)224-1818. **E-mail:** mmather@university-golf.com. **Web:** www.universitygolf.com. **Facility Holes:** 18. **Yards:** 6,584/5,653. **Par:** 72/72. **Course Rating:** 71.0/70.9. **Slope:** 122/114. **Green Fee:** $35/$60. **Cart Fee:** $32/Cart. **Walking Policy:** Unrestricted walking. **Walkability:** 3. **Opened:** 1929. **Architect:** Davey Black. **Season:** Year-round. **High:** March-Oct. **To obtain tee times:** Call up to 7 days in advance. **Misc:** Reduced fees (twilight), metal spikes, range (mats), credit cards (MC, V, AE), BF, FF.
Reader Comments: My winter playground ... This is an old golf course in great shape but they need to replace the sand in the traps ... A beautiful track ... Heavily wooded, generous landing areas ... A bit sloppy in wet weather ... Good course with long par-5 holes ... Lots of trees.

★★★ VERNON GOLF & COUNTRY CLUB
SP-800 Kalamalka Lake Rd., Vernon, V1T 6V2, (250)542-9126, 2 miles from Vernon. **E-mail:** pro@vernongolf.com. **Web:** www.vernongolf.com. **Facility Holes:** 18. **Yards:** 6,597/5,666. **Par:** 72/74. **Course Rating:** 71.1/71.4. **Slope:** 123/118. **Green Fee:** $30/$65. **Cart Fee:** $28/Cart. **Walking Policy:** Unrestricted walking. **Walkability:** 3. **Opened:** 1913. **Architect:** Ernie Brown/Graham Cooke. **Season:** March-Nov. **High:** April-Sept. **To obtain tee times:** Call golf shop. **Misc:** Reduced fees (twilight, juniors), range (mats), credit cards (MC, V, AE), BF, FF.
Reader Comments: Good retirement course; no one in a hurry ... Harder than it looks. Great friendly staff ... Good course, always enjoyable playing ... Excellent greens ... Hilly ... A traditonal, mature course always in excellent condition ... Good facilities, helpful staff ... Neat little course, some nice holes.

★★★★½ WESTWOOD PLATEAU GOLF & COUNTRY CLUB *Service+, Pace*
PU-3251 Plateau Blvd., Coquitlam, V3E 3B8, (604)552-0777, (800)580-0785, 12 miles from Vancouver. **E-mail:** dboudraa@westwood/plateau.bc.ca. **Web:** www.westwoodplateaugolf.bc.ca. **Facility Holes:** 27. **Yards:** 6,770/5,014. **Par:** 72/72. **Course Rating:** 71.9/68.2. **Slope:** 136/123. **Green Fee:** $99/$149. **Cart Fee:** Included in green fee. **Walking Policy:** Mandatory carts. **Walkability:** 4. **Opened:** 1995. **Architect:** Michael Hurdzan. **Season:** April-Oct. **To obtain tee times:** Call up to 7 days in advance. **Miscellaneous:** Reduced fees (weekdays, juniors), range (grass/mats), credit cards (MC, V, AE, DC), BF, FF.
Reader Comments: A perfect round of mountain golf ... You must play it if in Vancouver area ... Great views if the sun should shine ... Excellent links course that winds through a hillside housing development ... Target golf ... A very memorable golfing experience ... Great variety of holes.
Special Notes: Also has a 9-hole course.

★★★★ WHISTLER GOLF CLUB
R-4001 Whistler Way, Whistler, V0N 1B4, (604)932-3280, (800)376-1777, 80 miles from Vancouver. **E-mail:** akrisma@tourismwhistler.com. **Web:** www.whistlergolf.com. **Facility Holes:** 18. **Yards:** 6,676/5,434. **Par:** 72/72. **Course Rating:** 71.3/70.5. **Slope:** 132/120. **Green Fee:** $69/$149. **Cart Fee:** $35/Cart. **Walking Policy:** Unrestricted walking. **Walkability:** 1. **Opened:** 1982. **Architect:** Arnold Palmer. **Season:** May-Oct. **High:** July-Aug. **To obtain tee times:** Call up to 365 days in advance. **Miscellaneous:** Reduced fees (twilight, juniors), range (grass/mats),

credit cards (MC, V, AE), BF, FF.
Reader Comments: Beautiful surroundings, very playable course … Don't miss this one. Not too long, but tricky, target golf … Nice views, tight course … Soak up the views … Another hilly adventure … Unbelievable views, ran into a bear on the course … Long wide fairways, trees.

MANITOBA

★★★★ CLEAR LAKE GOLF COURSE
PU-Box 328, Onanole, R0J 1N0, (204)848-4653, 150 miles from Winnipeg. **Facility Holes:** 18. **Yards:** 6,070/6,070. **Par:** 72/72. **Course Rating:** 69.3/72.7. **Slope:** 120/130. **Green Fee:** $24/$28. **Cart Fee:** $13/Person. **Walking Policy:** Unrestricted walking. **Walkability:** 4. **Opened:** 1933. **Architect:** Stanley Thompson. **Season:** May-Oct. **High:** June-Aug. **To obtain tee times:** Call golf shop. **Miscellaneous:** Reduced fees (twilight, juniors), metal spikes, credit cards (MC, V).
Reader Comments: Absolutely beautiful early in the morning … Great course, slow pace, price a bit high … Great resort course, good value.

★★★★ FALCON LAKE GOLF COURSE
PU-South Shore Rd. & Green, Falcon Lake, R0E 0N0, (204)349-2554, 85 miles from Winnipeg. **Facility Holes:** 18. **Yards:** 6,937/5,978. **Par:** 72/73. **Course Rating:** 72.6/72.0. **Slope:** 121/115. **Green Fee:** $26/$30. **Cart Fee:** $23/Cart. **Walking Policy:** Unrestricted walking. **Walkability:** 2. **Opened:** 1958. **Architect:** Norman Woods. **Season:** April-Oct. **High:** July-Aug. **To obtain tee times:** Call golf shop. **Miscellaneous:** Reduced fees (weekdays, twilight, seniors, juniors), metal spikes, range (grass/mats), credit cards (MC, V, AE).
Reader Comments: Just a grand old course carved out of the wilderness … Wonderful classic design, mature forest and great greens … Generous fairways but lots of traps and trees to keep you honest … Plays long at times … Very enjoyable.

★★★★ HECLA GOLF COURSE AT GULL HARBOR RESORT *Value*
R-P.O. Box 1000, Riverton, R0C 2R0, (204)279-2072, (800)267-6700, 110 miles from Winnipeg. **Web:** gullharbourresort.com. **Facility Holes:** 18. **Yards:** 6,696/5,496. **Par:** 72/72. **Course Rating:** 71.7/70.7. **Slope:** 122/118. **Green Fee:** $23/$30. **Cart Fee:** $27/Cart. **Walking Policy:** Unrestricted walking. **Walkability:** 2. **Opened:** 1975. **Architect:** Jack Thompson. **Season:** May-Oct. **High:** May-Sept. **To obtain tee times:** Call golf shop. **Miscellaneous:** Reduced fees (twilight, seniors, juniors), range (grass), lodging (92 rooms), credit cards (MC, V, AE, DC), BF, FF.
Reader Comments: Challenging and fun … One of the four best in the province … Great service, great price, great pace of play and the course is awesome … Very scenic … Challenge for all golfers.

JOHN BLUMBERG GOLF COURSE
PU-4540 Portage Ave., Headingley, R4H IC8, (204)986-3490, 1 mile from Winnipeg. **E-mail:** benjamin@autobahn.mb.ca. **Facility Holes:** 27. **Green Fee:** $18/$22. **Cart Fee:** $23/Cart. **Walking Policy:** Unrestricted walking. **Walkability:** 5. **Opened:** 1969. **Architect:** Robbie Robinson. **Season:** April-Oct. **High:** May-Sept. **To obtain tee times:** Call up to 7 days in advance. **Miscellaneous:** Reduced fees (twilight, seniors, juniors), range (grass/mats), credit cards (MC, V, AE), BF, FF.
★★ **EMERALD COURSE** (18)
Yards: 6,343/5,844. **Par:** 71/71. **Course Rating:** 70.2/68.0. **Slope:** 116/111.
GOLD COURSE (9)
Yards: 2,739/2,560. **Par:** 34/34. **Course Rating:** 65.5/63.0. **Slope:** 111/111.

★★★ LARTERS AT ST. ANDREWS GOLF & COUNTRY CLUB
SP-30 River Rd., St. Andrews, R1A 2V1, (204)334-2107, 5 miles from Winnipeg. **E-mail:** geoffk@larters.com. **Web:** www.larters.com. **Facility Holes:** 18. **Yards:** 6,226/5,274. **Par:** 70/70. **Course Rating:** 70.0/69.7. **Slope:** 120/113. **Green Fee:** $27/$32. **Cart Fee:** $30/Cart. **Walking Policy:** Unrestricted walking. **Walkability:** 1. **Opened:** 1990. **Architect:** David Wagner. **Season:** April-Oct. **High:** June-Aug. **To obtain tee times:** Call up to 7 days in advance. **Miscellaneous:** Reduced fees (twilight, juniors), range (grass/mats), credit cards (MC, V, AE, DC), BF, FF.
Reader Comments: Stays in good shape … Opening 4 holes are among the toughest, so be prepared to play from the outset … The greens can be exceptional, especially in mid-summer … One of my favorite courses in Manitoba … Water in play on several holes.

THE LINKS AT QUARRY OAKS
PU-Box 3629, Hwy. 311 E., Steinbach, R0A 2A0, (204)326-4653, 35 miles from Winnipeg. **E-mail:** robin@golfquarry.com. **Web:** www.golfquarry.com. **Facility Holes:** 27. **Green Fee:** $25/$35. **Cart Fee:** Included in green fee. **Walking Policy:** Unrestricted walking. **Walkability:** 3. **Opened:** 1992. **Architect:** Les Furber. **Season:** April-Oct. **High:** June-Sept. **To obtain tee times:** Call up to 14 days in advance. **Miscellaneous:** Reduced fees (weekdays, twilight), range (grass), credit cards (MC, V, AE), BF, FF.

★★★½ **DESERT/OAK** (18)
Yards: 6,808/5,136. **Par:** 72/72. **Course Rating:** 72.1/65.5. **Slope:** 136/110.
Reader Comments: Great service, variety, pace ... Bring your "A" game ... Wow! Variety, challenge, everything ... Accuracy very important ... Links-style course ... Overrated.

OAK/QUARRY (18)
Yards: 7,000/5,407. **Par:** 72/72. **Course Rating:** 73.7/66.9. **Slope:** 140/119.

QUARRY/DESERT (18)
Yards: 7,100/5,405. **Par:** 72/72. **Course Rating:** 74.2/67.2. **Slope:** 139/118.

SCOTSWOOD LINKS
PU-Hwy. 2, Elm Creek, R0G 0N0, (204)436-2600. **Facility Holes:** 18. **Yards:** 6,180/5,363. **Par:** 70/70. **Green Fee:** $15/$18. **Cart Fee:** $22/Cart. **To obtain tee times:** Call golf shop.

★★½ SELKIRK GOLF & COUNTRY CLUB
SP-100 Sutherland Ave., Selkirk, R1A 2B1, (204)482-2050, 20 miles from Winnipeg. **Web:** ww.selkirkgolfcourse.com. **Facility Holes:** 18. **Yards:** 6,433/5,862. **Par:** 71/72. **Course Rating:** 69.4/72.2. **Slope:** 117/117. **Green Fee:** $15/$28. **Cart Fee:** $27/Cart. **Walking Policy:** Unrestricted walking. **Walkability:** 1. **Opened:** 1931. **Architect:** Jack Thompson. **Season:** April-Oct. **To obtain tee times:** Call up to 3 days in advance. **Miscellaneous:** Reduced fees (twilight), range (mats), credit cards (MC, V, AE, Debit Card), BF, FF.

★★★½ STEINBACH FLY-IN GOLF COURSE
SP-P.O. Box 3716, Steinbach, R0A 2A0, (204)326-6813. **Facility Holes:** 18. **Yards:** 6,544/5,445. **Par:** 72/73. **Course Rating:** 72.3/70.2. **Slope:** 125/115. **Green Fee:** $14/$26. **Cart Fee:** $26/Cart. **Walking Policy:** Unrestricted walking. **Walkability:** 1. **Opened:** 1970. **Architect:** Robbie Robinson. **Season:** April-Oct. **High:** May-Sept. **To obtain tee times:** Call golf shop. **Miscellaneous:** Reduced fees (weekdays, twilight, seniors, juniors), range (grass), credit cards (MC, V).
Reader Comments: A very fair course with great variety in holes ... Lots of water due to creek meandering through most holes ... Plays easy, except when there is wind (which is almost always) ... I loved it, challenging, good for the hacker.

★★★½ TEULON GOLF & COUNTRY CLUB
SP-Hwy. 7 N., Teulon, R0C 3B0, (204)886-4653, 30 miles from Winnipeg. **E-mail:** teulongc.mb.sympatico.com. **Facility Holes:** 18. **Yards:** 6,426/5,256. **Par:** 72/71. **Course Rating:** 71.0/69.0. **Slope:** 115/111. **Green Fee:** $15/$27. **Cart Fee:** $24/Cart. **Walking Policy:** Unrestricted walking. **Walkability:** 2. **Opened:** 1961. **Architect:** Robert Heaslip. **Season:** April-Oct. **High:** June-Sept. **To obtain tee times:** Call up to 5 days in advance. **Miscellaneous:** Reduced fees (weekdays, twilight, seniors, juniors), range (grass/mats), credit cards (MC, V, AE), BF, FF.
Reader Comments: They have the best greens in Manitoba—quick and in excellent shape ... Most fairways are open on the tee shot ... Not many trees however they cut the fairway fairly narrow which makes it challenging even for the expert ... Well laid out ... Small-town service & food.

WINKLER GOLF CLUB
PU-15th St. W., Winkler, R6W 4B1, (204)325-7582. **Facility Holes:** 18. **Yards:** 6,451/5,185. **Par:** 71/74. **Course Rating:** 69.5/68.6. **Slope:** 108/114. **Green Fee:** $18/$20. **Cart Fee:** $20/Cart. **To obtain tee times:** Call golf shop.

NEW BRUNSWICK

★★★½ ALGONQUIN GOLF COURSE & ACADEMY
R-465 Brandy Cove Rd., St. Andrews-by the Sea, E5B 2L6, (506)529-7142, 60 miles from Saint John. **E-mail:** lindon.garron@fairmont.com. **Facility Holes:** 27. **Yards:** 6,908/5,027. **Par:** 71/71. **Course Rating:** 73.7/68.7. **Slope:** 134/112. **Green Fee:** $70/$125. **Cart Fee:** Included in green fee. **Walking Policy:** Unrestricted walking. **Walkability:** 4. **Opened:** 2000. **Architect:** Thomas McBroom. **Season:** April-Nov. **High:** June-Sept. **To obtain tee times:** Call golf shop. **Miscellaneous:** Reduced fees (guests, twilight, juniors), range (grass), lodging (238 rooms),

credit cards (MC, V, AE, D, DC, En R.), BF, FF.
Reader Comments: Enjoy the layout, nice views … Very scenic … Completely redone, destination resort course … It's new, but so was great wine at one time … Beautiful course, great views.
Special Notes: Also has a 9-hole executive course.

★★★ AROOSTOOK VALLEY COUNTRY CLUB
SP-, Four Falls, E71 5K3, (207)476-8083, (800)980-8747, 3 miles from Fort Fairfield, ME. **E-mail:** llansen@nb.net. **Facility Holes:** 18. **Yards:** 6,304/5,397. **Par:** 72/72. **Course Rating:** 69.4/69.4. **Slope:** 122/122. **Green Fee:** $25. **Cart Fee:** $22/Cart. **Walking Policy:** Unrestricted walking. **Walkability:** 4. **Opened:** 1927. **Architect:** Howard Watson. **Season:** May-Nov. **High:** July-Aug. **To obtain tee times:** Call golf shop. **Miscellaneous:** Reduced fees (juniors), range (grass), credit cards (MC, V, Interac), BF, FF.
Reader Comments: Tough walk, various lakes … Different … Dramatic par 5s, fast greens, great variety … Very friendly and helpful staff.

★½ COUNTRY MEADOWS GOLF CLUB
SP-149 Catamount Rd., Indian Mountain, E1G 3A7, (506)858-8909, 8 miles from Moncton. **E-mail:** golfing@countrymeadows.nb.ca. **Web:** www.countrymeadows.nb.ca. **Facility Holes:** 18. **Yards:** 6,314/5,363. **Par:** 72/72. **Course Rating:** 69.1/71.1. **Slope:** 116/119. **Green Fee:** $23/$25. **Cart Fee:** $25/Cart. **Walking Policy:** Unrestricted walking. **Walkability:** 2. **Opened:** 1973. **Architect:** Doug Sullivan. **Season:** May-Oct. **To obtain tee times:** Call up to 2 days in advance. **Miscellaneous:** Reduced fees (weekdays), metal spikes, range (grass), credit cards (MC, V, AE), BF, FF.

★★★ COVERED BRIDGE GOLF & COUNTRY CLUB
PU-190 Golf Club Rd., Hartland, E7P3K4, (506)375-1112, (888)346-5777, 65 miles from Fredericton. **Web:** www.coveredbridgegolf.nb.ca. **Facility Holes:** 18. **Yards:** 6,609/5,412. **Par:** 72/72. **Course Rating:** 71.3/71.6. **Slope:** 132/122. **Green Fee:** $35. **Cart Fee:** $28/Cart. **Walking Policy:** Unrestricted walking. **Walkability:** 3. **Opened:** 1992. **Architect:** John Robinson. **Season:** April-Oct. **High:** June-Sept. **To obtain tee times:** Call golf shop. **Miscellaneous:** Reduced fees (guests), range (grass), lodging (12 rooms), credit cards (MC, V, AE, DC), BF, FF.
Reader Comments: Great target course, not crowded, challenging … Fun, wind can be a factor … A good test of golf … Course draped over and around huge hill… Every hole is interesting and challenging … Some fabulous tee shots … Absolutely my favorite NB course … Maturing well.

★★★★ EDMUNDSTON GOLF CLUB
SP-570 Victoria St., C.P. 263, Edmundston, E3V 3K9, (506)735-3086, 200 miles from Quebec City. **Facility Holes:** 18. **Yards:** 6,694/5,342. **Par:** 73/73. **Course Rating:** 71.6/69.5. **Slope:** 124/119. **Green Fee:** $30/$45. **Cart Fee:** $30/Cart. **Walking Policy:** Unrestricted walking. **Walkability:** 3. **Opened:** 1926. **Architect:** Albert Murray. **Season:** May-Nov. **High:** June-Aug. **To obtain tee times:** Call up to 2 days in advance. **Miscellaneous:** Reduced fees (guests, twilight), range (mats), credit cards (MC, V, AE), BF, FF.
Reader Comments: Lots of tight fairways … Bring all your clubs … Majestic trees … Exceptional, golf at it's best … Difficult, fun at every turn … Interesting and challenging golf … Superb—strong par 3s.

★★ FREDERICTON GOLF & CURLING CLUB
SP-331 Golf Club Rd., Fredericton, E3B 4Z9, (506)443-7710. **E-mail:** hgcogolf@nbnet.nb.ca. **Web:** www.hgcogolf.hypermart.net. **Facility Holes:** 18. **Yards:** 6,285/5,450. **Par:** 70/72. **Course Rating:** 67.7/72.0. **Slope:** 120/122. **Green Fee:** $35/$45. **Cart Fee:** $30/Cart. **Walking Policy:** Unrestricted walking. **Walkability:** 3. **Opened:** 1917. **Architect:** C. Robinson/G. Cornish/W. Robinson. **Season:** May-Nov. **High:** July-Sept. **To obtain tee times:** Call up to 1 day in advance. **Miscellaneous:** Range (grass), credit cards (MC, V, AE), BF, FF.

GAGE GOLF & CURLING ASSOCIATION
PU-55 Fraser Ave., CFB Gagetown, E2V 2R6, (506)357-3002. **Facility Holes:** 18. **Yards:** 5,831/5,397. **Par:** 70/71. **Course Rating:** 69.7. **Slope:** 118. **Green Fee:** $30. **Cart Fee:** $25/Cart. **Season:** April-Oct. **To obtain tee times:** Call golf shop.

GOLF BOUCTOUCHE
PU-Case Postale 568, Bouctouche, E0A 1G0, (506)743-5251, 30 miles from Moncton. **Facility Holes:** 18. **Yards:** 6,182/5,301. **Par:** 72/72. **Course Rating:** 68.0/69.0. **Slope:** 114/113. **Green Fee:** $22/$25. **Cart Fee:** $26/Cart. **Walking Policy:** Unrestricted walking. **Walkability:** 1. **Opened:** 1982. **Season:** May-Oct. **High:** July-Aug. **To obtain tee times:** Call golf shop. **Miscellaneous:** Reduced fees (weekdays), range (grass), caddies, credit cards (MC, V).

GOWAN BRAE GOLF & COUNTRY CLUB
SP-150 Youghall Dr., Bathurst, E2A 3Z1, (506)546-2707. **E-mail:** golfing@gowanbraegolf.nb.ca. **Web:** www.gowanbraegolf.nb.ca. **Facility Holes:** 18. **Yards:**

6,577/5,979. **Par:** 72/74. **Course Rating:** 72.3/73.0. **Slope:** 131/125. **Green Fee:** $45. **Cart Fee:** $32/Cart. **Walking Policy:** Unrestricted walking. **Walkability:** 2. **Opened:** 1958. **Architect:** Robbie Robinson. **Season:** May-Oct. **High:** July-Sept. **To obtain tee times:** Call up to 2 days in advance. **Miscellaneous:** Reduced fees (twilight), range (grass/mats), credit cards (MC, V, Inter-Act), BF, FF.

GRAND FALLS GOLF CLUB
SP-803 Main St., Grand-Sault, E3Y 1A7, (506)475-6008, 120 miles from Fredericton. **E-mail:** drmroy@nbnet.nb.ca. **Web:** www.sn2000.nb.ca. **Facility Holes:** 18. **Yards:** 6,632/5,122. **Par:** 72/72. **Course Rating:** 70.6/68.6. **Slope:** 122/111. **Green Fee:** $25/$35. **Cart Fee:** $30/Cart. **Walking Policy:** Unrestricted walking. **Walkability:** 4. **Opened:** 1990. **Architect:** Bob Moote. **Season:** May-Oct. **To obtain tee times:** Call golf shop. **Miscellaneous:** Reduced fees (juniors), range (grass), credit cards (MC, V), BF, FF.

★★★ HAMPTON COUNTRY CLUB
PU-William Bell Dr., Rte. 100, Hampton, E0G 1Z0, (506)832-3411, 18 miles from Saint John. **Facility Holes:** 18. **Yards:** 6,291/5,430. **Par:** 72/73. **Course Rating:** 69.9/72.0. **Slope:** 118/132. **Green Fee:** $32/$35. **Cart Fee:** $25/Cart. **Walking Policy:** Unrestricted walking. **Walkability:** 3. **Opened:** 1972. **Architect:** Cecil Manuge. **Season:** May-Oct. **High:** June-Aug. **To obtain tee times:** Call golf shop. **Miscellaneous:** Reduced fees (twilight), range (grass), credit cards (MC, V).
Reader Comments: 660-yard par 6 ... Wow! Top-notch, fun to play ... Service very good ... Hilly in spots ... Par-6 hole is fun ... Local knowledge essential to score ... Excellent value for the money ... The course plays tougher than the slope indicates ... Good layout.

LAKESIDE GOLF CLUB
SP-1896 Rte. 134, Lakeville, E1H 1A7, (506)861-9441, 3 miles from Moncton. **E-mail:** lksgolf@nbnet.nb.ca. **Web:** www.lakesidegolf.nb.ca. **Facility Holes:** 18. **Yards:** 5,880/5,612. **Par:** 70/71. **Course Rating:** 67.3/68.3. **Slope:** 110/117. **Green Fee:** $28. **Cart Fee:** $28/Cart. **Walking Policy:** Unrestricted walking. **Walkability:** 1. **Opened:** 1926. **Season:** May-Oct. **High:** June-Aug. **To obtain tee times:** Call up to 2 days in advance. **Miscellaneous:** Range (grass/mats), credit cards (MC, V, AE), BF, FF.

LE CLUB DE GOLF DE ST. IGNACE
SP-20 Berube Rd., St. Ignace, E4X 2H1, (506)876-3737, 55 miles from Moncton. **Facility Holes:** 18. **Yards:** 6,325/5,694. **Par:** 72/72. **Course Rating:** 70.2/73.0. **Slope:** 125/131. **Green Fee:** $25/$30. **Cart Fee:** $25/Cart. **Walking Policy:** Unrestricted walking. **Walkability:** 4. **Opened:** 1984. **Architect:** Geoffrey Cornish. **Season:** April-Oct. **High:** July-Sept. **To obtain tee times:** Call up to 2 days in advance. **Miscellaneous:** Reduced fees (weekdays), range (grass/mats), credit cards (MC, V, AE), BF, FF.

★★★½ MACTAQUAC PROVINCIAL PARK GOLF CLUB
PU-1256 Route 105, Mactaquac, E6L 1B5, (506)363-4925, 15 miles from Fredericton. **Facility Holes:** 18. **Yards:** 7,030/5,756. **Par:** 72/72. **Course Rating:** 74.0/71.0. **Slope:** 131/117. **Green Fee:** $40. **Cart Fee:** $30/Cart. **Walking Policy:** Unrestricted walking. **Walkability:** 2. **Opened:** 1970. **Architect:** William F. Mitchell. **Season:** May-Oct. **To obtain tee times:** Call golf shop. **Miscellaneous:** Reduced fees (twilight), range (grass), credit cards (MC, V, AE), BF, FF.
Reader Comments: Interesting holes ... "Jumbo golf" with long holes, huge bunkers, big greens ... Pars are tough but bogeys are easy ... Huge greens, wide fairways.

★★½ MAGNETIC HILL GOLF & COUNTRY CLUB
PU-1 Tee Time Dr., Moncton, E1G 3T7, (506)858-1611. **E-mail:** maghill@auracom.com. **Web:** www.maghillgolf.com. **Facility Holes:** 18. **Yards:** 5,692/5,292. **Par:** 70/70. **Course Rating:** 66.4/69.2. **Slope:** 112/115. **Green Fee:** $29. **Cart Fee:** $27/Cart. **Walking Policy:** Unrestricted walking. **Walkability:** 3. **Opened:** 1967. **Season:** May-Oct. **High:** June-Aug. **To obtain tee times:** Call golf shop. **Miscellaneous:** Range (grass/mats), credit cards (MC, V).

MAPLEWOOD GOLF & COUNTRY CLUB
PU-2572 Route 115, Irishtown, E1H 2L8, (506)858-7840, 6 miles from Moncton. **Facility Holes:** 18. **Yards:** 6,301/5,081. **Par:** 71/71. **Course Rating:** 69.3/67.2. **Slope:** 118/111. **Green Fee:** $26. **Cart Fee:** $26/Cart. **Walking Policy:** Unrestricted walking. **Walkability:** 2. **Opened:** 1983. **Architect:** Dale Rasmussen. **Season:** May-Oct. **High:** July-Aug. **To obtain tee times:** Call golf shop. **Miscellaneous:** Credit cards (MC, V, AE), BF, FF.

MIRAMICHI GOLF & COUNTRY CLUB
SP-930 Water St., Miramichi, E1N 4C3, (506)622-2068. **Web:** http://www.compuwer.nb.ca.mgcc.com. **Facility Holes:** 18. **Yards:** 6,358/5,466. **Par:** 72/72. **Course Rating:** 70.9/66.3. **Slope:** 125/116. **Green Fee:** $35. **Cart Fee:** $30/Cart. **Walking Policy:** Unrestricted walking. **Walkability:** 1. **Opened:** 1925. **Architect:** John Robinson. **Season:**

May-Oct. **High:** May-Sept. **To obtain tee times:** Call up to 2 days in advance. **Miscellaneous:** Range (grass), credit cards (MC, V), BF, FF.

★★★ MONCTON GOLF AND COUNTRY CLUB

SP-212 Coverdale Rd., Riverview, E1B 4T9, (506)387-3855, 1 mile from Moncton. **Facility Holes:** 18. **Yards:** 6,263/5,654. **Par:** 70/72. **Course Rating:** 69.0/71.4. **Slope:** 123/119. **Green Fee:** $40. **Cart Fee:** $30/Cart. **Walking Policy:** Unrestricted walking. **Walkability:** 1. **Opened:** 1929. **Architect:** Stanley Thompson. **Season:** May-Oct. **High:** June-Sept. **To obtain tee times:** Call golf shop. **Miscellaneous:** Reduced fees (twilight), range (grass), credit cards (MC, V, AE), BF, FF.
Reader Comments: Wonderful short course. Par 3s will keep your score above par … Well wooded, challenging, good test … Long par 3s … Accuracy required—ball positioning a must … Nice layout … Great new holes but pesky insects detract from course.

★★½ PETITCODIAC VALLEY GOLF & COUNTRY CLUB

SP-Golf Course Rd., Petitcodiac, E0A 2H0, (506)756-8129, 25 miles from Moncton. **Facility Holes:** 18. **Yards:** 5,932/5,581. **Par:** 71/71. **Course Rating:** 66.7/71.1. **Slope:** 114/119. **Green Fee:** $24. **Cart Fee:** $20/Cart. **Walking Policy:** Unrestricted walking. **Walkability:** 3. **Opened:** 1960. **Season:** April-Oct. **High:** July-Sept. **To obtain tee times:** Call golf shop. **Miscellaneous:** Reduced fees (guests, seniors, juniors), range (grass), credit cards (MC, V).

PINE NEEDLES GOLF & COUNTRY CLUB

SP-54 Glaude Rd., Haute Aboujagane, E4P 5N6, (506)532-4634, 20 miles from Moncton. **E-mail:** pineneed@fundy.net. **Web:** www.pineneedlesgolf.nb.ca. **Facility Holes:** 36. **Green Fee:** $27. **Cart Fee:** $27/Cart. **Walking Policy:** Unrestricted walking. **Walkability:** 2. **Season:** May-Oct. **High:** July-Aug. **To obtain tee times:** Call up to 2 days in advance. **Miscellaneous:** Reduced fees (twilight), credit cards (MC, V), BF, FF.
★★★½ **PINE COURSE** (18)
Yards: 5,919/5,280. **Par:** 71/72. **Course Rating:** 66.2/69.4. **Slope:** 106/119. **Opened:** 1973.
★★★½ **RIVER COURSE** (18)
Yards: 6,424/5,404. **Par:** 72/73. **Course Rating:** 72.0/70.4. **Slope:** 127/125. **Opened:** 1990.
Reader Comments: Long and interesting, staff is friendly as are the members.

RESTIGOUCHE GOLF & COUNTRY CLUB

PU-Box 8 Site 11 R.R. 2, Campbellton, E3N 3E8, (506)789-7628. **Facility Holes:** 18. **Yards:** 5,652/4,989. **Par:** 70/73. **Course Rating:** 69.1/69.0. **Slope:** 126/119. **Green Fee:** $20/$27. **Cart Fee:** $22/Cart. **Walking Policy:** Unrestricted walking. **Walkability:** 5. **Opened:** 1923. **Season:** May-Oct. **High:** July-Aug. **To obtain tee times:** Call golf shop. **Miscellaneous:** Metal spikes, credit cards (MC, V).

★★ RIVERBEND GOLF & FISHING CLUB

PU-541 Rte. 628 Durham Bridge, Fredericton, E6C 1J9, (506)452-7277, 15 miles from Fredericton. **E-mail:** golfing@riverbendgolf.nb.ca. **Web:** www.riverbendgolf.nb.ca. **Facility Holes:** 18. **Yards:** 6,406/5,425. **Par:** 71/71. **Course Rating:** 71.0/66.1. **Slope:** 126/114. **Green Fee:** $23/$29. **Cart Fee:** $28/Cart. **Walking Policy:** Unrestricted walking. **Walkability:** 1. **Opened:** 1992. **Architect:** Graham Cooke and Associates. **Season:** April-Oct. **High:** May-Sept. **To obtain tee times:** Call up to 2 days in advance. **Miscellaneous:** Reduced fees (weekdays), range (grass), credit cards (MC, V), BF, FF.

★★★ ROCKWOOD PARK GOLF COURSE

PU-1255 Sandy Point Road, Saint John, E2L 4B3, (506)634-0090. **Facility Holes:** 18. **Yards:** 6,017/5,023. **Par:** 70/69. **Course Rating:** 68.0/69.0. **Slope:** 117/113. **Green Fee:** $22/$30. **Cart Fee:** $26/Cart. **Walking Policy:** Unrestricted walking. **Walkability:** 4. **Opened:** 1973. **Season:** April-Oct. **High:** June-Sept. **To obtain tee times:** Call golf shop. **Miscellaneous:** Reduced fees (twilight, seniors, juniors), range (mats), credit cards (MC, V, AE), BF, FF.
Reader Comments: Huge tough greens … Hidden gem, accuracy essential, No. 17 worth the trip … Big greens … Challenging and exceptionally picturesque … One of the best municipal courses … Fun course to play.

ROYAL OAKS ESTATES & GOLF COURSE

PU-1746 Elmwood Dr., Moncton, E1H 2H6, (506)384-3330, (866)769-6257, 6 miles from Moncton. **E-mail:** golf@nbnet.nb.ca. **Web:** www.royaloaks.nb.ca. **Facility Holes:** 18. **Yards:** 7,103/5,325. **Par:** 72/72. **Course Rating:** 76.2/70.7. **Slope:** 143/118. **Green Fee:** $65/$90. **Cart Fee:** $20/Person. **Walking Policy:** Unrestricted walking. **Walkability:** 3. **Opened:** 2000. **Architect:** Rees Jones. **Season:** May-Oct. **High:** June-Sept. **To obtain tee times:** Call up to 7 days in advance. **Miscellaneous:** Reduced fees (twilight), range (grass), caddies, lodging (3 rooms), credit cards (MC, V, AE), BF, FF.

CANADA

ST. STEPHEN GOLF CLUB
PU-Old Bay Rd., P.O. Box 272, St. Stephen, E3L 2X2, (506)466-5336, 60 miles from Saint John. **Facility Holes:** 18. **Yards:** 6,075/6,075. **Par:** 71/71. **Course Rating:** 69.1/74.0. **Slope:** 122/124. **Green Fee:** $25. **Cart Fee:** $23/Cart. **Walking Policy:** Unrestricted walking. **Walkability:** 2. **Opened:** 1982. **Architect:** Clayton Van Tassel. **Season:** May-Oct. **High:** July-Sept. **To obtain tee times:** Call golf shop. **Miscellaneous:** Reduced fees (twilight), range (grass/mats), credit cards (V, AE), BF, FF.

★★½ SUSSEX GOLF & CURLING CLUB
SP-148 Picadilly Rd., Picadilly, E4E 5H8, (506)433-9040, 40 miles from Saint John. **E-mail:** proshop@sussexgolf.com. **Web:** www.sussexgolf.com. **Facility Holes:** 18. **Yards:** 6,518/5,625. **Par:** 72/73. **Course Rating:** 69.7/72.0. **Slope:** 117/119. **Green Fee:** $30/$35. **Cart Fee:** $25/Cart. **Walking Policy:** Unrestricted walking. **Walkability:** 4. **Opened:** 1973. **Season:** May-Oct. **High:** June-Aug. **To obtain tee times:** Call up to 1 day in advance. **Miscellaneous:** Range (grass), credit cards (MC, V, AE), BF, FF.

★★ WESTFIELD GOLF & COUNTRY CLUB
SP-8 Golf Club Rd., Grand Bay - Westfield, E5K 3C8, (506)757-2907, 20 miles from Saint John. **E-mail:** westgc@nbnet.nb.ca. **Web:** www.westfieldgolf.net. **Facility Holes:** 18. **Yards:** 5,804/5,605. **Par:** 69/72. **Course Rating:** 68.8/71.7. **Slope:** 113/115. **Green Fee:** $40/$45. **Cart Fee:** $25/Cart. **Walking Policy:** Unrestricted walking. **Walkability:** 4. **Opened:** 1919. **Season:** May-Oct. **High:** June-Sept. **To obtain tee times:** Call golf shop. **Miscellaneous:** Credit cards (V), BF, FF.

NEWFOUNDLAND

BLOMIDON GOLF & COUNTRY CLUB
SP-Wess Valley Rd., Corner Brook, A2H 6J3, (709)634-5550. **Facility Holes:** 18. **Yards:** 5,500/5,400. **Par:** 69/72. **Course Rating:** 67.0/70.0. **Slope:** 116/121. **Green Fee:** $30/$35. **Cart Fee:** $25/Cart. **Walking Policy:** Unrestricted walking. **Walkability:** 5. **Opened:** 1952. **Architect:** Alfred H. Tull. **Season:** May-Oct. **High:** June-Aug. **To obtain tee times:** Call golf shop. **Miscellaneous:** Metal spikes, range (grass), credit cards (MC, V, Debit).

★★★★½ TERRA NOVA GOLF RESORT
R-P.O. Box 160, Port Blandford, A0C 2G0, (709)543-2525, 140 miles from Saint John. **Facility Holes:** 27. **Yards:** 6,546/5,423. **Par:** 71/71. **Course Rating:** 71.9/72.5. **Slope:** 128/129. **Green Fee:** $35/$67. **Cart Fee:** $31/Cart. **Walking Policy:** Walking at certain times. **Walkability:** 3. **Opened:** 1984. **Architect:** Robbie Robinson/Doug Carrick. **Season:** May-Oct. **To obtain tee times:** Call golf shop. **Miscellaneous:** Reduced fees (weekdays, guests, twilight, seniors, juniors), range (grass/mats), caddies, credit cards (MC, V, AE, D, En Route), BF, FF.
Reader Comments: A hidden treasure! … Watch out for the moose … Fall colors are amazing … Beautiful scenery … Fairways cut a little long … Much like a links-type course … Good opportunity to see bald eagles and maybe the occasional fox, moose, lynx or black bear during play … Truly a delight to play.
Special Notes: Also has a 9-hole course.

NOVA SCOTIA

★★★ ABERCROMBIE GOLF CLUB
SP-Abercrombie RR #3, Station Main, New Glasgow, B2H 5E7, (902)755-4653, 90 miles from Halifax. **Web:** www.3.ns.sympatico.ca/nsga. **Facility Holes:** 18. **Yards:** 6,100. **Par:** 71. **Course Rating:** 71.0. **Slope:** 125. **Green Fee:** $42. **Cart Fee:** $18/Person. **Walking Policy:** Unrestricted walking. **Walkability:** 3. **Opened:** 1918. **Architect:** Clinton E. Robinson. **Season:** May-Oct. **To obtain tee times:** Call golf shop. **Miscellaneous:** Reduced fees (twilight), range (grass/mats), credit cards (V), FF.
Reader Comments: A good value … Good, fair test of golf … Excellent fairways, greens, clubhouse.

★★★ AMHERST GOLF CLUB
SP-P.O. Box 26, Amherst, B4H 3Z6, (902)667-8730, 2 miles from Amherst. **Facility Holes:** 18. **Yards:** 6,367/5,439. **Par:** 71/71. **Course Rating:** 71.0/71.0. **Slope:** 122/115. **Green Fee:** $28/$38. **Cart Fee:** $27/Cart. **Walking Policy:** Unrestricted walking. **Walkability:** 3. **Opened:**

1906. **Architect:** Clinton E. Robinson. **Season:** May-Oct. **To obtain tee times:** Call golf shop. **Miscellaneous:** Reduced fees (weekdays, twilight), range (grass), credit cards (V), BF, FF. Reader Comments: Solid golf course, scenic … Old course with character … Slick greens … Delightful to play … Great finishing hole … Easy access from main highway, limited pro shop and practice area … Well worth a return visit … A good challenge when the winds are up.

★★ ANTIGONISH GOLF & COUNTRY CLUB

SP-P.O. Box 1341, Antigonish, B2G 2L7, (902)863-4797. **E-mail:** ed.ryan@ns.sympatico.ca. **Web:** www.antigonishgolfclub.ca. **Facility Holes:** 18. **Yards:** 6,605/5,109. **Par:** 72/72. **Course Rating:** 73.0/69.0. **Slope:** 130/118. **Green Fee:** $25/$40. **Cart Fee:** $27/Cart. **Walking Policy:** Unrestricted walking. **Walkability:** 3. **Opened:** 1926. **Architect:** Bob Moote. **Season:** May-Oct. **High:** July-Aug. **To obtain tee times:** Call golf shop. **Miscellaneous:** Reduced fees (twilight), range (grass), credit cards (MC, V, AE), BF, FF.

★★★★½ BELL BAY GOLF CLUB *Condition*

PU-761 Hwy 205, Baddeck, B0E 1B0, (902)295-1333, (800)565-3077, 60 miles from Sydney. **E-mail:** bellbay@auracom.com. **Web:** www.bellbaygolfclub.com. **Facility Holes:** 18. **Yards:** 7,037/5,185. **Par:** 72/72. **Course Rating:** 74.7/70.0. **Slope:** 137/120. **Green Fee:** $69. **Cart Fee:** $30/Cart. **Walking Policy:** Unrestricted walking. **Walkability:** 3. **Opened:** 1997. **Architect:** Thomas McBroom. **Season:** May-Oct. **High:** July-Sept. **To obtain tee times:** Call up to 150 days in advance. **Miscellaneous:** Reduced fees (juniors), range (grass), credit cards (MC, V, AE, DC, Debit Card), BF, FF.
Reader Comments: Wow … Beautiful … Last 4 holes are awesome … Impressive view from 18th tee … Local player has a distinct advantage … Best finishing holes I've ever played … Slow play, but course layout excellent … I felt like a jewel thief—a gem at a steal … A great view of Baddeck Bay.

★★½ BRIGHTWOOD GOLF & COUNTRY CLUB

SP-227 School St., Dartmouth, B3A 2Y5, (902)469-7879, 1 mile from Halifax. **Web:** www.brightwood.ns.ca. **Facility Holes:** 18. **Yards:** 5,247/4,759. **Par:** 68/70. **Course Rating:** 66.6/67.5. **Slope:** 112/116. **Green Fee:** $70. **Cart Fee:** $15/Person. **Walking Policy:** Unrestricted walking. **Walkability:** 5. **Opened:** 1914. **Architect:** Donald Ross. **Season:** May-Nov. **To obtain tee times:** Call up to 1 day in advance. **Miscellaneous:** Credit cards (MC, V, AE), BF, FF.

★★★ DUNDEE RESORT GOLF CLUB

R-R.R. 2, West Bay, B0E 3K0, (902)345-0420, (800)565-1774, 17 miles from Port Hawkesbury. **E-mail:** dundee@capebretonresorts.com. **Web:** www.capebretonresorts.com. **Facility Holes:** 18. **Yards:** 6,475/5,236. **Par:** 72/72. **Course Rating:** 71.9/71.7. **Slope:** 135/131. **Green Fee:** $35/$50. **Cart Fee:** $31/Cart. **Walking Policy:** Unrestricted walking. **Walkability:** 4. **Opened:** 1977. **Architect:** Bob Moote. **Season:** May-Oct. **High:** June-Sept. **To obtain tee times:** Call golf shop. **Miscellaneous:** Reduced fees (weekdays, guests, twilight, juniors), lodging (99 rooms), credit cards (MC, V, AE, D, DC, Enroute), BF, FF.
Reader Comments: Great scenery, hilly … Difficult when wind blows … Breathtaking views and interesting holes … Even if your golf is bad, you are in for a treat … Outstanding, highly recommend … Be warned, all putts break towards the lake.

FOX HARB'R RESORT

PU-1337 Fox Harb'r Rd., Wallace, B0K 1Y0, (902)257-1801, 35 miles from Truro. **E-mail:** mail@foxharbr.ns.ca. **Web:** www.foxharbr.com. **Facility Holes:** 27. **Yards:** 7,205/5,336. **Par:** 72/72. **Course Rating:** 75.4/66.4. **Slope:** 141/119. **Green Fee:** $150/$200. **Cart Fee:** Included in green fee. **Walking Policy:** Unrestricted walking. **Walkability:** 2. **Opened:** 2000. **Architect:** Graham Cooke. **Season:** June-Oct. **To obtain tee times:** Call up to 1 day in advance. **Miscellaneous:** Range (grass), lodging (72 rooms), credit cards (MC, V, AE, DC), FF. **Special Notes:** Also has a 9-hole par-3 course.

★★★★½ GLEN ARBOUR GOLF CLUB *Service+, Condition+*

PU-40 Clubhouse Ln., Hammonds Plains, B4B 1T4, (902)832-4944, (877)835-4653, 15 miles from Halifax. **E-mail:** golf@glenarbour.com. **Web:** www.glenarbour.com. **Facility Holes:** 27. **Yards:** 6,800/4,736. **Par:** 72/72. **Course Rating:** 73.6/67.6. **Slope:** 138/120. **Green Fee:** $90/$115. **Walking Policy:** Unrestricted walking. **Walkability:** 3. **Opened:** 1999. **Architect:** Graham Cooke. **Season:** May-Oct. **High:** July-Aug. **To obtain tee times:** Call up to 60 days in advance. **Miscellaneous:** Reduced fees (twilight), range (grass/mats), credit cards (MC, V, AE, DC), BF, FF.
Notes: Ranked 2nd in 2000 Best New Canadian Courses.
Reader Comments: Great layout, fast greens, fine test … Absolutely beautiful … A grand golf course … Large undulating greens, many at hilltops … Fantastic course at a steep price.
Special Notes: Also has a 9-hole par-3 course.

GRANDVIEW GOLF & COUNTRY CLUB
SP-431 Crane Hill Road, Westphal, B2Z 1J5, (902)435-3278, 6 miles from Dartmouth. **E-mail:** grandview@accesswave.ca. **Facility Holes:** 18. **Yards:** 6,475/5,571. **Par:** 72/73. **Course Rating:** 71.5/71.4. **Slope:** 128/127. **Green Fee:** $48/$50. **Cart Fee:** $27/Cart. **Walking Policy:** Unrestricted walking. **Walkability:** 1. **Opened:** 1988. **Architect:** Cornish/Robinson. **Season:** May-Nov. **High:** June-Sept. **To obtain tee times:** Call up to 3 days in advance. **Miscellaneous:** Reduced fees (twilight), range (grass), credit cards (MC, V, AE, DC, CB), BF, FF.

★★★★½ HIGHLANDS LINKS GOLF COURSE *Value, Pace*
PU-Cape Breton Highlands Nt'l Pk., Ingonish Beach, B0C 1L0, (902)285-2600, (800)441-1118, 70 miles from Sydney. **E-mail:** highlandslinks@pch.gc.ca. **Web:** www.highlandslinks-golf.com. **Facility Holes:** 18. **Yards:** 6,596/5,243. **Par:** 72/72. **Course Rating:** 73.9/73.3. **Slope:** 141/131. **Green Fee:** $17/$38. **Cart Fee:** $33/Cart. **Walking Policy:** Unrestricted walking. **Walkability:** 4. **Opened:** 1941. **Architect:** Stanley Thompson/Graham Cooke. **Season:** May-Oct. **High:** July-Sept. **To obtain tee times:** Call golf shop. **Miscellaneous:** Reduced fees (twilight, juniors), caddies, credit cards (MC, V, AE), BF, FF.
Reader Comments: Breathtaking views, and an inventive, time-tested layout ... Very scenic, excellent layout, offers a variety of golf challenges, well worth repeat visits ... The scenery will compensate for poor scoring ... Views exceptional ... A must play ... You look back as much as you look forward.

★★★ KEN-WO COUNTRY CLUB
SP-9514 Commercial St., New Minas, B4N 3E9, (902)681-5388, 60 miles from Halifax. **E-mail:** gsingleton@ken-wo.com. **Web:** www.ken-wo.com. **Facility Holes:** 18. **Yards:** 6,284/5,531. **Par:** 70/71. **Course Rating:** 69.7/72.5. **Slope:** 122/127. **Green Fee:** $35/$45. **Cart Fee:** $26/Cart. **Walking Policy:** Unrestricted walking. **Walkability:** 3. **Opened:** 1921. **Season:** April-Oct. **High:** June-Sept. **To obtain tee times:** Call up to 3 days in advance. **Miscellaneous:** Reduced fees (twilight), range (grass), credit cards (MC, V, AE), BF, FF.
Reader Comments: Good test of golf ... Nice course, solid back 9 ... Mix of farmland & woods ... A friendly enjoyable course ... Fun golf course, needs a better practice facility ... Very friendly course ... Nice clubhouse.

LINGAN GOLF & COUNTRY CLUB
SP-1225 Grand Lake Rd., Hwy. 4, Sydney, B1P 6J9, (902)562-1112, 260 miles from Halifax. **Web:** www.nsga.ns.ca. **Facility Holes:** 18. **Yards:** 6,620/5,834. **Par:** 72/74. **Course Rating:** 71.4/73.5. **Slope:** 125/127. **Green Fee:** $44. **Cart Fee:** $29/Cart. **Walking Policy:** Unrestricted walking. **Walkability:** 2. **Opened:** 1913. **Architect:** Stanley Thompson/C.E. (Robbie) Robinson. **Season:** May-Oct. **To obtain tee times:** Call golf shop. **Miscellaneous:** Range (grass), credit cards (MC, V, AE), FF.

★★★★½ NORTHUMBERLAND LINKS *Value*
PU-1776 Gulf Shore Rd., Pugwash, BOK 1LO, (902)243-2808, (800)882-9661, 60 miles from Moncton. **E-mail:** norlinks@istar.ca. **Web:** www.norlinks.pugwash.ns.ca. **Facility Holes:** 18. **Yards:** 6,515/5,588. **Par:** 71/72. **Course Rating:** 72.8/74.3. **Slope:** 131/129. **Green Fee:** $25/$40. **Cart Fee:** $26/Cart. **Walking Policy:** Unrestricted walking. **Walkability:** 2. **Opened:** 1935. **Architect:** Cornish/Robinson. **Season:** May-Nov. **High:** June-Sept. **To obtain tee times:** Call up to 365 days in advance. **Miscellaneous:** Reduced fees (weekdays, twilight), range (grass), credit cards (MC, V, AE, D), BF, FF.
Reader Comments: Friendly and helpful staff ... A return visit is a must ... Excellent scenery, ocean views ... Enjoyable but open to wind, off water ... A course you want to play over and over... Great views of PEI and the Confederation Bridge ... Classic & modern, it's all here ... Fastest greens ever.

OSPREY RIDGE GOLF CLUB
SP-270 Harold Whynot Road, Bridgewater, B4V 2W6, (902)543-6666, 60 miles from Halifax. **E-mail:** info@ospreyridge.ns.ca. **Web:** www.ospreyridge.ns.ca. **Facility Holes:** 18. **Yards:** 6,575/5,098. **Par:** 72/72. **Course Rating:** 72.3/70.9. **Slope:** 137/126. **Green Fee:** $39/$49. **Cart Fee:** $28/Cart. **Walking Policy:** Unrestricted walking. **Walkability:** 4. **Opened:** 1998. **Architect:** Graham Cooke. **Season:** April-Oct. **High:** June-Sept. **To obtain tee times:** Call up to 3 days in advance. **Misc:** Reduced fees (twilight), range (grass), credit cards (MC, V, AE, DC), BF, FF.

★★½ PARAGON GOLF & COUNTRY CLUB
SP-368 Brookside Dr., Kingston, B0P 1R0, (902)765-2554, (877)414-2554, 100 miles from Halifax. **E-mail:** paragon.golf@nv.sympatico.ca. **Facility Holes:** 18. **Yards:** 6,245/5,580. **Par:** 72/72. **Course Rating:** 69.6/72.7. **Slope:** 120/124. **Green Fee:** $35. **Cart Fee:** $29/Cart. **Walking Policy:** Unrestricted walking. **Walkability:** 3. **Opened:** 1964. **Architect:** Gordie Shaw. **Season:** April-Oct. **High:** April-Oct. **To obtain tee times:** Call up to 2 days in advance. **Miscellaneous:** Reduced fees (twilight), credit cards (V), BF, FF.

★★★★ **THE PINES RESORT HOTEL GOLF COURSE**
R-103 Shore Rd., Digby, B0V 1A0, (902)245-7709, (800)667-4637, 160 miles from Halifax. **Web:** www.signatureresorts.com. **Facility Holes:** 18. **Yards:** 6,222/5,865. **Par:** 71/75. **Course Rating:** 70.0/73.0. **Slope:** 121/131. **Green Fee:** $55. **Cart Fee:** $33/Cart. **Walking Policy:** Unrestricted walking. **Walkability:** 2. **Opened:** 1931. **Architect:** Stanley Thompson. **Season:** April-Oct. **High:** July-Sept. **To obtain tee times:** Call up to 90 days in advance. **Miscellaneous:** Lodging (145 rooms), credit cards (MC, V, AE, D, DC, Debit), FF.
Reader Comments: Course is fair to all skill levels ... Superb inn ... Very interesting holes ... Easy to play ... Nice traditional course, lots of trees ... Great hotel.

★★½ **THE TRURO GOLF CLUB**
SP-86 Golf St., Truro, B2N 5C7, (902)893-4650, 50 miles from Halifax. **E-mail:** gordie@truro-golfclub.ns.ca. **Facility Holes:** 18. **Yards:** 6,342/5,636. **Par:** 71/72. **Course Rating:** 70.9/72.4. **Slope:** 121/125. **Green Fee:** $46. **Cart Fee:** $26/Cart. **Walking Policy:** Unrestricted walking. **Walkability:** 1. **Opened:** 1903. **Architect:** Robbie Robinson/Stanley Thompson. **Season:** May-Oct. **To obtain tee times:** Call golf shop. **Miscellaneous:** Reduced fees (twilight), range (grass), credit cards (MC, V, AE), FF.

ONTARIO

AGUASABON GOLF COURSE
PU-Beach Rd., Terrace Bay, P0T 2W0, (807)825-3844, 130 miles from Thunder Bay. **E-mail:** saadams@schreiber.lakeheadu.ca. **Facility Holes:** 9. **Yards:** 3,200/2,900. **Par:** 36/37. **Course Rating:** 69.2/70.8. **Slope:** 113/118. **Green Fee:** $18/$25. **Cart Fee:** $20/Cart. **Walking Policy:** Unrestricted walking. **Walkability:** 3. **Opened:** 1964. **Season:** May-Oct. **To obtain tee times:** Call golf shop. **Miscellaneous:** Reduced fees (seniors, juniors), range (grass), credit cards (MC, V), BF, FF.

★★★★½ **ANGUS GLEN GOLF CLUB** *Condition*
PU-10080 Kennedy Rd., Markham, L6C 1N9, (905)887-5157, 25 miles from Toronto. **Web:** www.angusglen.com. **Facility Holes:** 18. **Yards:** 7,400/5,721. **Par:** 72/72. **Course Rating:** 76.0/73.3. **Slope:** 143/129. **Green Fee:** $85/$110. **Cart Fee:** Included in green fee. **Walkability:** 3. **Opened:** 1994. **Architect:** Doug Carrick. **Season:** April-Nov. **High:** May-Oct. **To obtain tee times:** Call golf shop. **Miscellaneous:** Range (grass/mats), credit cards (MC, V, AE, Diners Club).
Reader Comments: A real shotmaker's course ... A great experience ... Beautifully sculpted and maintained ... Well kept course but always booked, 9 minutes or less apart, plays great ... Fast greens, tight fairways ... Outstanding, not to be missed.

BALLANTRAE GOLF & COUNTRY CLUB
PU-1 Masters S., Stouffville, L4A 7Z5, (905)640-6333, 30 miles from Toronto. **E-mail:** ballantrae@psinet.com. **Web:** www.ballantraegolfclub.com. **Facility Holes:** 18. **Yards:** 6,808/5,041. **Par:** 72/72. **Course Rating:** 72.4. **Slope:** 130/106. **Green Fee:** $65/$80. **Cart Fee:** $28/Cart. **Walking Policy:** Unrestricted walking. **Walkability:** 2. **Opened:** 2000. **Architect:** Doug Carrick/Ian Andrew. **Season:** May-Nov. **To obtain tee times:** Call up to 21 days in advance. **Miscellaneous:** Reduced fees (weekdays, twilight), range (grass/mats), credit cards (MC, V, Debit), BF, FF.

★★★ **BAY OF QUINTE COUNTRY CLUB**
SP-1830 Old Highway #2, Belleville, K8N 4Z9, (613)968-7063, 115 miles from Toronto. **E-mail:** bofqgolf@sympatico.ca. **Web:** www.bayofquintegolf.com. **Facility Holes:** 18. **Yards:** 6,840/5,701. **Par:** 72/73. **Course Rating:** 72.4/72.7. **Slope:** 125/122. **Green Fee:** $29/$40. **Cart Fee:** $30/Cart. **Walking Policy:** Unrestricted walking. **Walkability:** 2. **Opened:** 1921. **Architect:** Howard Watson. **Season:** April-Nov. **To obtain tee times:** Call up to 5 days in advance. **Misc:** Reduced fees (twilight, juniors), range (grass/mats), credit cards (MC, V), BF, FF.
Reader Comments: Good value, nice short, tight course with good greens, very playable for all levels ... RR tracks go right through course ... A course that rewards accuracy, then length ... Test of power game.

★★★ **BEECHWOOD GOLF & COUNTRY CLUB**
SP-4680 Thorold Townline Rd., Niagara Falls, L2E 6S4, (905)680-4653. **E-mail:** beechwood@beechwoodgolf.com. **Web:** www.beechwoodgolf.com. **Facility Holes:** 18. **Yards:** 6,700/5,400. **Par:** 72/72. **Course Rating:** 73.0/69.8. **Slope:** 127/116. **Green Fee:** $44/$50. **Cart Fee:** $32/Cart. **Walking Policy:** Unrestricted walking. **Walkability:** 3. **Opened:** 1960. **Architect:** R.F. Moote and Associates/B. Antonsen. **Season:** April-Nov. **High:** May-Sept. **To obtain tee**

times: Call golf shop. **Miscellaneous:** Reduced fees (weekdays, twilight), credit cards (MC, V, AE), BF, FF.
Reader Comments: Need many shots ... No warm-up area during off season ... Some of the fastest greens around ... Good play ... Too many power lines in the way, lush fairways.

★★★ BROCKVILLE COUNTRY CLUB
SP-P.O. Box 42, Brockville, K6V 5T7, (613)342-3023, 1 mile from Brockville. **Facility Holes:** 18. **Yards:** 6,343/5,288. **Par:** 72/72. **Course Rating:** 70.4/72.2. **Slope:** 126/129. **Green Fee:** $48. **Walking Policy:** Unrestricted walking. **Walkability:** 5. **Opened:** 1914. **Architect:** Stanley Thompson/C.E. (Robbie) Robinson. **Season:** May-Oct. **High:** July-Aug. **To obtain tee times:** Call golf shop. **Miscellaneous:** Reduced fees (twilight, juniors), range (grass/mats), credit cards (MC, V).
Reader Comments: Challenging ... Interesting par 3s, many elevation changes ... Excellent layout.

★★★ BROOKLEA GOLF & COUNTRY CLUB
SP-Highway 93, Midland, L4R 4K6, (705)526-7532, (800)257-0428, 90 miles from Toronto. **E-mail:** clubhouse@brookleagolf.com. **Web:** www.brookleagolf.com. **Facility Holes:** 27. **Yards:** 6,645/5,585. **Par:** 72/72. **Course Rating:** 71.2/71.4. **Slope:** 126/126. **Green Fee:** $40/$48. **Cart Fee:** $32/Cart. **Walking Policy:** Unrestricted walking. **Walkability:** 3. **Opened:** 1959. **Architect:** Rene Muylaert. **Season:** April-Nov. **High:** June-Sept. **To obtain tee times:** Call up to 30 days in advance. **Miscellaneous:** Reduced fees (weekdays, guests, twilight), range (grass), credit cards (MC, V, AE, DC), BF, FF.
Reader Comments: Part links, part park, nice experience ... Great course, good value, friendly staff, fair to all golfers ... Well groomed, easy access ... Excellent 19th hole ... Front 9 very good ... Price is right.
Special Notes: Also has a 9-hole executive course.

★½ CALABOGIE HIGHLANDS RESORT & GOLF CLUB
PU-981 Barryvale Rd., Calabogie, K0J 1H0, (613)752-2171, (877)224-4653, 55 miles from Ottawa. **E-mail:** info@calabogiehighlandsgolf.com. **Web:** www.calabogiehighlandsgolf.com. **Facility Holes:** 27. **Yards:** 6,735/5,632. **Par:** 72/72. **Course Rating:** 71.4/72.0. **Slope:** 126/129. **Green Fee:** $26/$29. **Cart Fee:** $26/Cart. **Walking Policy:** Unrestricted walking. **Walkability:** 4. **Opened:** 1983. **Architect:** Dolgos & Assoc. **Season:** April-Nov. **High:** June-Sept. **To obtain tee times:** Call up to 7 days in advance. **Miscellaneous:** Reduced fees (weekdays, guests, twilight, juniors), range (grass/mats), lodging (16 rooms), credit cards (MC, V, AE), BF, FF.
Special Notes: Also has 9-hole course.

★★½ CALEDON COUNTRY CLUB
PU-2121 Old Baseline Rd., R.R. No.1, Inglewood, L0N 1K0, (905)838-0121, 10 miles from Toronto. **E-mail:** info@golfcaledon.com. **Web:** www.golfcaledon.com. **Facility Holes:** 18. **Yards:** 6,140/5,414. **Par:** 71/73. **Course Rating:** 71.5/70.5. **Slope:** 132/121. **Green Fee:** $35/$68. **Cart Fee:** $34/Cart. **Walking Policy:** Unrestricted walking. **Walkability:** 5. **Opened:** 1961. **Architect:** Rene Muylaert. **Season:** April-Nov. **To obtain tee times:** Call up to 7 days in advance. **Miscellaneous:** Reduced fees (twilight, seniors, juniors), metal spikes, range (grass/mats), credit cards (MC, V, AE, DC), BF, FF.

CARDINAL GOLF CLUB
PU-2740 Hwy. 9, R.R. No.1, Kettleby, L0G 1J0, (905)841-7378, 20 miles from Toronto. **Web:** www.cardinalgolfclub.com. **Facility Holes:** 54. **Green Fee:** $35/$55. **Cart Fee:** $16/Person. **Walking Policy:** Unrestricted walking. **Walkability:** 3. **Opened:** 1989. **Architect:** Dan Lavis. **Season:** April-Dec. **High:** May-Sept. **To obtain tee times:** Call up to 14 days in advance. **Miscellaneous:** Reduced fees (weekdays, twilight, seniors, juniors), range (grass/mats), credit cards (MC, V, AE, DC, Direct), BF, FF.
★★½ EAST COURSE (18)
Yards: 6,450/5,362. **Par:** 72/72. **Course Rating:** 69.9/71.7. **Slope:** 114/116.
Special Notes: Also has a Kettle Creek executive course.
WEST COURSE (18)
Yards: 6,315/5,305. **Par:** 71/71. **Course Rating:** 69.1/67.6. **Slope:** 113/115.
Special Notes: Also has a Kettle Creek executive course.

CARLISLE GOLF & COUNTRY CLUB
PU-523 Carlisle Rd., Carlisle, L0R 1H0, (905)689-8820, (800)661-4343, 10 miles from Burlington. **Facility Holes:** 27. **Green Fee:** $40/$60. **Cart Fee:** $32/Cart. **Walking Policy:** Unrestricted walking. **Walkability:** 3. **Opened:** 1991. **Architect:** Ted Baker. **Season:** April-Oct. **To obtain tee times:** Call up to 7 days in advance. **Miscellaneous:** Reduced fees (weekdays, twilight, seniors), range (grass/mats), credit cards (MC, V, AE), BF, FF.
★★★ NORTH/EAST (18)
Yards: 6,650/5,455. **Par:** 72/72. **Course Rating:** 70.6/72.9. **Slope:** 119/105.

Reader Comments: They always treat us great ... The course is nice, but not extremely hard ... Sometimes a little slow ... Short but sweet, fairways gorgeous ... Very tight ... Three different 9s give you interesting combinations.

NORTH/SOUTH (18)
Yards: 6,800/5,330. **Par:** 72/72.
SOUTH/EAST (18)
Yards: 6,350/5,445. **Par:** 72/72.

CENTENNIAL GOLF COURSE
PU-R.R. 11 320 Thompson Rd., Thunder Bay, (807)767-4600. **Facility Holes:** 9. **Yards:** 3,316/2,962. **Par:** 36/36. **Course Rating:** 35.8/35.8. **Slope:** 123/107. **Green Fee:** $20. **Cart Fee:** $22/Cart. **Walking Policy:** Unrestricted walking. **Walkability:** 1. **Opened:** 1985. **Season:** May-Sept. **High:** June-July. **To obtain tee times:** Call golf shop. **Miscellaneous:** Reduced fees (twilight), metal spikes, range (grass), credit cards (MC, V, AE).

CHAPPLES GOLF COURSE
PU-530 Chapples Dr., Thunder Bay, (807)625-2582. **Facility Holes:** 18. **Yards:** 6,184/5,555. **Par:** 71/71. **Course Rating:** 69.5/70.6. **Slope:** 108/111. **Green Fee:** $21. **Cart Fee:** $22/Cart. **Walking Policy:** Unrestricted walking. **Walkability:** 1. **Season:** April-Oct. **High:** June-Aug. **To obtain tee times:** Call golf shop. **Miscellaneous:** Reduced fees (juniors), metal spikes, range (grass), credit cards (MC, V).

★★ CHIPPEWA GOLF & COUNTRY CLUB
SP-400 Rankin St. Highway 21 North, Southampton, N0H 2L0, (519)797-3684, 20 miles from Owen Sound. **E-mail:** chippewag@bmts.com. **Web:** www.brucecountygolf.com. **Facility Holes:** 18. **Yards:** 6,420/5,392. **Par:** 72/72. **Course Rating:** 69.5/70.0. **Slope:** 116/109. **Green Fee:** $22/$35. **Cart Fee:** $26/Cart. **Walking Policy:** Unrestricted walking. **Walkability:** 2. **Opened:** 1964. **Architect:** S. Thompson. **Season:** April-Oct. **High:** July-Aug. **To obtain tee times:** Call up to 7 days in advance. **Miscellaneous:** Reduced fees (twilight, seniors), range (grass), credit cards (MC, V, AE), BF, FF.

★★½ DEER RUN GOLF CLUB
PU-Bloomfield Rd. No.1, Blenheim, N0P 1A0, (519)676-1566, 11 miles from Chotham. **Facility Holes:** 27. **Yards:** 6,548/5,567. **Par:** 72/72. **Course Rating:** 72.9/71.9. **Slope:** 136/122. **Green Fee:** $16/$27. **Cart Fee:** $14/Person. **Walking Policy:** Unrestricted walking. **Walkability:** 3. **Opened:** 1993. **Architect:** Bill Dickie Assoc. **Season:** March-Dec. **High:** June-Sept. **To obtain tee times:** Call golf shop. **Miscellaneous:** Reduced fees (weekdays, twilight), credit cards (MC, V, AE), FF.
Special Notes: Additional 9-hole course opening spring of 2002.

DEERHURST RESORT
R-1235 Deerhurst Dr., Huntsville, P1H 2E8, (705)789-2381, (800)461-4393, 120 miles from Toronto. **E-mail:** rwood@deerhurst.newcastlehotels.com. **Web:** www.deerhurst.on.ca. **Facility Holes:** 36. **Cart Fee:** Included in green fee. **To obtain tee times:** Call golf shop. **Miscellaneous:** Range (grass/mats), lodging (460 rooms), credit cards (MC, V, AE, D, DC), BF, FF.
★★★★½ DEERHURST HIGHLANDS (18)
Yards: 7,011/5,393. **Par:** 72/73. **Course Rating:** 74.5/71.2. **Slope:** 140/125. **Green Fee:** $85/$145. **Walking Policy:** Mandatory carts. **Walkability:** 5. **Opened:** 1990. **Architect:** Bob Cupp/T. McBroom. **Season:** May-Oct. **High:** June-Sept. **Miscellaneous:** Reduced fees (weekdays, guests, twilight, juniors).
Reader Comments: Good golf ... Very scenic ... Great value for a first-rate course ... Terrific par-3s, best resort course in Canada, slow play at times, worth every penny ... Beautiful setting ... A pleasure ... What a test of golf ... Great mix of long and short holes.
★★½ DEERHURST LAKESIDE (18)
Yards: 4,700/3,800. **Par:** 65/65. **Course Rating:** 62.4/63.0. **Slope:** 101/104. **Green Fee:** $35/$60. **Walking Policy:** Walking at certain times. **Walkability:** 3. **Opened:** 1972. **Architect:** C.E. Robinson/T.McBroom. **Season:** April-Oct. **High:** May-Sept. **Miscellaneous:** Reduced fees (guests, twilight, juniors).

DELHI GOLF & COUNTRY CLUB
SP-905 James St., Delhi, N4B 2E2, (519)582-1621, 40 miles from London. **E-mail:** delhigolf@on.a1bn.com. **Facility Holes:** 18. **Yards:** 6,400/5,200. **Par:** 71/72. **Course Rating:** 71.3/69.4. **Slope:** 114/121. **Green Fee:** $20/$29. **Cart Fee:** $29/Cart. **Walking Policy:** Unrestricted walking. **Walkability:** 3. **Opened:** 1960. **Architect:** George Coreno. **Season:** March-Dec. **High:** May-Sept. **To obtain tee times:** Call up to 7 days in advance. **Miscellaneous:** Reduced fees (weekdays, twilight, seniors, juniors), range (grass), credit cards (MC, V, AE, Debit), BF, FF.

CANADA

★★½ **DELTA PINESTONE RESORT**
SP-P.O. Box 809, Haliburton, K0M 1S0, (705)457-3444, (800)461-0357, 120 miles from Toronto. **E-mail:** rvillamere@deltahotels.com. **Web:** www.deltahotels.com. **Facility Holes:** 18. **Yards:** 6,024/5,448. **Par:** 71/73. **Course Rating:** 70.4/72.6. **Slope:** 141/137. **Green Fee:** $49/$65. **Cart Fee:** $32/Cart. **Walking Policy:** Unrestricted walking. **Walkability:** 4. **Opened:** 1976. **Architect:** J. Elstone/J. Davidson. **Season:** May-Oct. **To obtain tee times:** Call golf shop. **Miscellaneous:** Reduced fees (weekdays, guests), lodging (103 rooms), credit cards (MC, V, AE, DC), FF.
Special Notes: Formerly Pinestone Golf & Conference Center.

★★½ **DON VALLEY GOLF COURSE**
PU-4200 Yonge St., Toronto, M2P 1N9, (416)392-2465. **Facility Holes:** 18. **Yards:** 6,109/5,048. **Par:** 71/73. **Course Rating:** 70.0/69.0. **Slope:** 124/120. **Green Fee:** $45/$49. **Cart Fee:** $35/Cart. **Walking Policy:** Unrestricted walking. **Walkability:** 3. **Opened:** 1956. **Architect:** Howard Watson/David Moote. **Season:** April-Dec. **High:** May-Sept. **To obtain tee times:** Call up to 5 days in advance. **Miscellaneous:** Reduced fees (twilight, seniors, juniors), caddies, credit cards (MC, V, AE), BF, FF.

★★★ **DOON VALLEY GOLF CLUB**
PU-500 Doon Valley Dr., Kitchener, N2P 1B4, (519)741-2939, 60 miles from Toronto. **Facility Holes:** 18. **Yards:** 6,193/5,507. **Par:** 72/73. **Course Rating:** 68.1. **Slope:** 115/106. **Green Fee:** $28/$35. **Cart Fee:** $25/Cart. **Walking Policy:** Unrestricted walking. **Walkability:** 2. **Opened:** 1955. **Architect:** Clinton E. Robinson. **Season:** April-Nov. **High:** May-Oct. **To obtain tee times:** Call up to 7 days in advance. **Miscellaneous:** Reduced fees (weekdays, twilight, juniors), range (grass), credit cards (MC, V, AE), BF, FF.
Reader Comments: A bargain … Very enjoyable, good facilities … Very nice layout. Nice course. Moves well … Busy, always in good condition, have to be able to hit draws… Nice & open for average players … Easy access.

DUNDEE COUNTRY CLUB
PU-RR #4, New Dundee, NOB 2E1, (519)696-2650. **Web:** www.golfnorth.ca. **Facility Holes:** 18. **Yards:** 6,357/5,412. **Par:** 72/72. **Course Rating:** 71.6/71.0. **Slope:** 129/110. **Green Fee:** $20/$50. **Cart Fee:** $30/Cart. **Season:** April-Nov. **To obtain tee times:** Call up to 7 days in advance. **Miscellaneous:** Reduced fees (twilight), range (grass), credit cards (MC, V, AE).

★★★★½ **EAGLE CREEK GOLF COURSE** *Condition*
PU-109 Royal Troon Lane, Ottawa, K0A 1T0, (613)832-0728, 18 miles from Ottawa. **Web:** eaglecreekgolf.ca. **Facility Holes:** 18. **Yards:** 7,093/5,413. **Par:** 72/72. **Course Rating:** 74.3/71.5. **Slope:** 134/125. **Green Fee:** $60/$70. **Cart Fee:** $30/Cart. **Walking Policy:** Unrestricted walking. **Walkability:** 3. **Opened:** 1991. **Architect:** Ken Venturi/Ken Skodacek. **Season:** April-Oct. **To obtain tee times:** Call golf shop. **Miscellaneous:** Metal spikes, range (grass), credit cards (MC, V, AE, DC), BF, FF.
Reader Comments: Ken Venturi design—tight and a bit gimmicky, but a blast to play … Fun, love all the par 5s … Great design, excellent greens … It's one of my favorites … No hole the same, charming and challenging … Under wet conditions, it became one of the toughest courses I have ever played.

EMBRUN GOLF CLUB
PU-1483 Notre Dame St., Embrun, K0A 1W0, (613)443-4653. **Facility Holes:** 9. **Yards:** 1,115/1,115. **Par:** 28/28. **Green Fee:** $13. **To obtain tee times:** Call golf shop.

EMERALD GREENS GOLF COURSE
PU-R.R. 12 2370 Dawson Rd., Thunder Bay, P7B 5E3, (807)767-4511, 4 miles from Thunder Bay. **Facility Holes:** 9. **Yards:** 2,600/2,400. **Par:** 34/34. **Course Rating:** 66.0/65.8. **Slope:** 102/102. **Green Fee:** $22. **Cart Fee:** $20/Cart. **Walking Policy:** Unrestricted walking. **Walkability:** 3. **Opened:** 1977. **Season:** May-Nov. **High:** June-Sept. **To obtain tee times:** Call up to 2 days in advance. **Miscellaneous:** Reduced fees (weekdays, juniors), metal spikes, range (grass/mats), BF, FF.

★★ **FANSHAWE GOLF CLUB**
SP-2835 Sunningdale Rd. East, London, N5X 3Y7, (519)661-4435. **Facility Holes:** 36. **Yards:** 6,233/6,425. **Par:** 70/70. **Course Rating:** 69.0/71.2. **Slope:** 108/121. **Green Fee:** $24. **Cart Fee:** $26/Cart. **Walking Policy:** Unrestricted walking. **Walkability:** 3. **Opened:** 1958. **Architect:** John Moffatt Sr. **Season:** April-Nov. **High:** May-Sept. **To obtain tee times:** Call golf shop. **Miscellaneous:** Reduced fees (twilight), metal spikes, range (grass), credit cards (MC, V).
Special Notes: Also has an 18-hole course.

FIRE FIGHTERS ROLLING HILLS GOLF CLUB

PU-Warden Ave., Gromley, L0H 1G0, (905)888-1955, 12 miles from Toronto. **Facility Holes:** 54. **Cart Fee:** $25/Cart. **Walking Policy:** Unrestricted walking. **Season:** April-Nov. **High:** June-Sept. **To obtain tee times:** Call golf shop. **Miscellaneous:** Reduced fees (weekdays, twilight, seniors), metal spikes, credit cards (MC, V, AE).

★½ **BLUE** (18)
Yards: 6,340/5,664. **Par:** 72/75. **Course Rating:** 68.5. **Slope:** 112. **Green Fee:** $32/$38. **Walkability:** 3. **Opened:** 1979.
GOLD (18)
Yards: 4,010/3,681. **Par:** 62/62. **Green Fee:** $24/$30. **Walkability:** 2. **Opened:** 1994. **Architect:** Rene Muylaert/Charles Muylaert.
★★ **RED** (18)
Yards: 4,894/4,894. **Par:** 70/70. **Course Rating:** 61.3. **Slope:** 95. **Green Fee:** $28/$34. **Walkability:** 1. **Opened:** 1979.

★★ FLAMBOROUGH HILLS GOLF CLUB

SP-P.O. Box 9, Copetown, L0R 1J0, (905)627-1743, 15 miles from Hamilton. **E-mail:** flamhill@skyline.net. **Web:** www.flamborohills-golf.com. **Facility Holes:** 27. **Green Fee:** $30/$45. **Cart Fee:** $32/Cart. **Walking Policy:** Unrestricted walking. **Walkability:** 3. **Opened:** 1960. **Season:** April-Nov. **High:** June-Sept. **To obtain tee times:** Call up to 7 days in advance. **Miscellaneous:** Reduced fees (weekdays, seniors), range (mats), credit cards (MC, V), FF.

HILLS/LAKES (18 Combo)
Yards: 6,580/5,280. **Par:** 73/73. **Course Rating:** 69.5/69.2. **Slope:** 114/118.
HILLS/WOODS (18 Combo)
Yards: 6,331/5,458. **Par:** 73/73. **Course Rating:** 68.5/70.9. **Slope:** 116/121.
WOODS/LAKES (18 Combo)
Yards: 6,259/5,292. **Par:** 72/72. **Course Rating:** 69.0/70.0. **Slope:** 114/117.

★★★★½ FOREST CITY NATIONAL GOLF CLUB *Service, Value+, Pace*

PU-16540 Robin's Hill Rd., London, N6A 4C1, (519)451-0994. **E-mail:** brentholmes@hotmail.com. **Web:** fcngolf.com. **Facility Holes:** 18. **Yards:** 6,850/5,119. **Par:** 72/74. **Course Rating:** 73.6/69.4. **Slope:** 141/116. **Green Fee:** $58/$65. **Cart Fee:** Included in green fee. **Walking Policy:** Unrestricted walking. **Walkability:** 3. **Opened:** 1993. **Architect:** Craig Schreiner. **Season:** April-Nov. **High:** June-Aug. **To obtain tee times:** Call golf shop. **Miscellaneous:** Reduced fees (weekdays), twilight, range (grass), credit cards (MC, V, Debit Card), BF, FF. **Reader Comments:** Great practice facility … Course is spread out with each hole on its own … Drop your bag off, get your clubs cleaned while you park the car—great service … A tremendous challenge & power carts keep play going 4 hours or less for 18 holes … A gem, memorable … Great test of all the clubs.

FORT WILLIAM COUNTRY CLUB

SP-R.R. 4, 1350 Mountain Rd., Thunder Bay, P7J 1C2, (807)475-4721. **E-mail:** fwcc@air.on.ca. **Web:** www.fortwilliamcc.on.ca. **Facility Holes:** 18. **Yards:** 6,670/5,304. **Par:** 72/74. **Course Rating:** 72.6/71.7. **Slope:** 134/118. **Green Fee:** $50/$60. **Cart Fee:** $30/Cart. **Walking Policy:** Unrestricted walking. **Walkability:** 3. **Opened:** 1923. **Architect:** Stanley Thompson. **Season:** May-Oct. **High:** June-Aug. **To obtain tee times:** Call up to 2 days in advance. **Miscellaneous:** Reduced fees (juniors), credit cards (MC, V, Debit), BF, FF.

★★★★½ GLEN ABBEY GOLF CLUB

PU-1333 Dorval Dr., Oakville, L6J 4Z3, (905)844-1800, 20 miles from Toronto. **E-mail:** cneale@clublink.ca. **Web:** www.clublink.ca. **Facility Holes:** 18. **Yards:** 7,112/5,520. **Par:** 73/74. **Course Rating:** 75.5/71.4. **Slope:** 140/117. **Green Fee:** $125/$230. **Cart Fee:** Included in green fee. **Walking Policy:** Mandatory carts. **Walkability:** 3. **Opened:** 1977. **Architect:** Jack Nicklaus. **Season:** April-Nov. **High:** June-Sept. **To obtain tee times:** Call golf shop. **Miscellaneous:** Range (grass), credit cards (MC, V, AE, DC), BF, FF. **Reader Comments:** Canadian Open site … Treated like royalty, magnificent … Best public course in Ontario, incredible shape but too expensive … Slow play … Out of average man's price range … Holes in the valley are outstanding … Strong 3s.

GLEN EAGLE GOLF CLUB

PU-15731 Hwy. 50, Bolton, L7E 5R8, (905)880-0131, (800)665-3915, 12 miles from Toronto. **E-mail:** info@gleneaglegolf.com. **Web:** gleneaglegolf.com. **Facility Holes:** 27. **Green Fee:** $58/$65. **Cart Fee:** $14/Person. **Walking Policy:** Unrestricted walking. **Walkability:** 5. **Opened:** 1962. **Architect:** Rene Muylaert. **Season:** March-Nov. **High:** May-Sept. **To obtain tee times:** Call up to 7 days in advance. **Miscellaneous:** Reduced fees (twilight), range (grass/mats), credit cards (MC, V, AE), BF, FF.

★★★ **BLUE/RED** (18)
Yards: 7,004/5,520. **Par:** 72/74. **Course Rating:** 73.8/70.7. **Slope:** 128/120.

CANADA

Reader Comments: 27 solid holes, busy, slow play, quite hilly, big greens but very playable ... Great opening hole with both the tee & green well elevated above the middle of the fairway ... The course offers a good challenge with well placed tee shots essential ... Red & Blue the best ... Very hilly, cart a must.
BLUE/YELLOW (18)
Yards: 6,686/5,448. **Par:** 72/73. **Course Rating:** 72.0/70.7. **Slope:** 128/120.
YELLOW/RED (18)
Yards: 6,770/5,526. **Par:** 72/75. **Course Rating:** 72.8/70.7. **Slope:** 133/120.

GODERICH SUNSET GOLF CLUB
SP-263 Picton St. W. RR 6, Goderich, N7A 3Y3, (519)524-8047. **Facility Holes:** 18. **Yards:** 5,850/5,505. **Par:** 70/70. **Course Rating:** 68.5/69.8. **Slope:** 126/114. **Green Fee:** $20/$24. **Cart Fee:** $24/Cart. **To obtain tee times:** Call golf shop.

GORMLEY GREEN GOLF CLUB
PU-P.O. Box 489 12657 Woodbine Ave., Gormley, L0H 1G0, (905)888-1219, (800)276-9542, 12 miles from Markham. **E-mail:** ajacque@clublink.ca. **Facility Holes:** 36. **Walking Policy:** Unrestricted walking. **Season:** March-Oct. **Tee times:** Call up to 30 days ahead. **Misc:** Reduced fees (weekdays, twilight), range (grass), credit cards (MC, V, AE, DC), BF, FF.
★★ **CIRCLE COURSE** (18)
Yards: 6,618/5,658. **Par:** 70/70. **Course Rating:** 72.0/71.9. **Slope:** 115/125. **Green Fee:** $15/$56. **Cart Fee:** $16/Person. **Walkability:** 2. **Opened:** 1978. **Architect:** Rene Muylaert/Charles Muylaert. **High:** May-July.
★★½ **CREEK COURSE** (18)
Yards: 6,948/5,958. **Par:** 72/72. **Course Rating:** 73.1/74.6. **Slope:** 128/139. **Green Fee:** $19/$62. **Cart Fee:** $16/Cart. **Walkability:** 4. **Architect:** Rene Muylaert.

GREENWOOD GOLF CLUB
SP-2212 London Line, Sarnia, N7T 7H2, (519)542-2770. **Facility Holes:** 18. **Yards:** 6,276/5,903. **Par:** 70/70. **Course Rating:** 70.4/69.2. **Slope:** 129/126. **Green Fee:** $20/$30. **Cart Fee:** $28/Cart. **Walking Policy:** Unrestricted walking. **Opened:** 1963. **Architect:** Stanley White. **Season:** March-Dec. **High:** May-Sept. **To obtain tee times:** Call up to 3 days in advance. **Miscellaneous:** Reduced fees (twilight), range (grass), credit cards (MC, V), BF, FF.

HAWK RIDGE GOLF CLUB
PU-P.O. Box 874, Orillia, L3V 6K8, (705)329-4653, (888)462-4295, 60 miles from Toronto. **E-mail:** hrgweb@hawkridgegolf.com. **Web:** www.hawkridgegolf.com. **Facility Holes:** 36. **Green Fee:** $35/$49. **Cart Fee:** $30/Cart. **Walking Policy:** Unrestricted walking. **Walkability:** 2. **Season:** Year-round. **High:** May-Oct. **To obtain tee times:** Call up to 7 days in advance. **Miscellaneous:** Reduced fees (guests, twilight, seniors, juniors), range (grass/mats), credit cards (MC, V, AE), BF, FF.
★★★½ **MEADOW'S NEST** (18)
Yards: 6,933/5,994. **Par:** 72/72. **Course Rating:** 72.0/72.0. **Slope:** 120/120. **Opened:** 1991.
Reader Comments: Very strong winds most of the time ... Usually easy to get tee times ... Very playable, huge difference in 9s ... Very slow but great value ... Fun course to play ... Length is too much from certain tees for average golfer.
TIMBER RIDGE (18)
Yards: 6,584/5,739. **Par:** 71/71. **Opened:** 1999.

HIDDEN LAKE GOLF CLUB
SP-1137 #1 Side Rd., Burlington, L7R 3X4, (905)336-3660, 35 miles from Toronto. **Web:** www.hiddenlakegolf.com. **Facility Holes:** 36. **Green Fee:** $25/$65. **Cart Fee:** $32/Cart. **Walking Policy:** Unrestricted walking. **Walkability:** 3. **Architect:** Dick Kirkpatrick. **Season:** April-Nov. **High:** May-Sept. **To obtain tee times:** Call up to 7 days in advance. **Miscellaneous:** Reduced fees (weekdays, twilight, seniors, juniors), range (grass), credit cards (MC, V, AE), BF, FF.
★★★½ **NEW COURSE** (18)
Yards: 6,645/5,017. **Par:** 72/71. **Course Rating:** 72.1/68.9. **Slope:** 124/117. **Opened:** 1984.
Reader Comments: Always enjoyable and a good test ... Good mix of holes and variety of shots ... Excellent facilities ... Good greens ... A golfer's golf course.
OLD COURSE (18)
Yards: 6,622/5,331. **Par:** 71/70. **Course Rating:** 71.1/69.7. **Slope:** 122/112. **Opened:** 1963.

★★★½ **HOCKLEY VALLEY RESORT**
R-R.R. No.1, Orangeville, L9W 2Y8, (519)942-0754, 30 miles from Toronto. **E-mail:** jsheppard@hockley.com. **Web:** www.hockley.com. **Facility Holes:** 18. **Yards:** 6,403/4,646. **Par:** 70/70. **Course Rating:** 71.0/71.0. **Slope:** 130/126. **Green Fee:** $50/$105. **Cart Fee:** Included in green fee. **Walking Policy:** Mandatory carts. **Walkability:** 5. **Opened:** 1989. **Architect:** Thomas McBroom. **Season:** April-Nov. **High:** May-Oct. **To obtain tee times:** Call up to 7 days in advance. **Miscellaneous:** Reduced fees (weekdays, guests, twilight), range (grass/mats),

lodging (104 rooms), credit cards (MC, V, AE, D, DC), BF, FF.
Reader Comments: Spectacular vistas … I enjoy it, love the elevated tee boxes, a lot of blind shots … Nice friendly place to play … Rolling hills, no sand traps but tough enough … Links style, beautiful scenery … Sure need a cart with good brakes, hilly.

HOMESTEAD RESORT
R-Homestead Dr., Durham, N0G 1R0, (519)369-3771. **Facility Holes:** 18. **Yards:** 5,244/4,894. **Par:** 68/68. **Course Rating:** 63.0/69.0. **Slope:** 105/109. **Green Fee:** $18/$24. **Cart Fee:** $25/Cart. **To obtain tee times:** Call golf shop.

★½ HORNBY GLEN GOLF COURSE
PU-8286 Hornby Rd., Hornby, L0P 1E0, (905)878-3421, 3 miles from Mississauga. **E-mail:** hornbygolf@on.aibn.com. **Web:** www.hornbyglen.com. **Facility Holes:** 18. **Yards:** 6,740/5,698. **Par:** 72/73. **Course Rating:** 70.5/69.5. **Slope:** 110/108. **Green Fee:** $38/$43. **Cart Fee:** $30/Cart. **Walking Policy:** Unrestricted walking. **Walkability:** 2. **Opened:** 1964. **Architect:** Robert Moote/David S. Moote. **Season:** April-Nov. **To obtain tee times:** Call up to 7 days in advance. **Miscellaneous:** Reduced fees (weekdays, twilight, seniors, juniors), range (grass), credit cards (MC, V, Debit), BF, FF.

HORSESHOE VALLEY RESORT
R-R.R. No.1 Horseshoe Valley Rd., Barrie, L4M 4Y8, (705)835-2790, (800)461-5627, 60 miles from Toronto. **E-mail:** golfhr@horseshoeresort.com. **Web:** www.horseshoeresort.com. **Facility Holes:** 27. **Architect:** Rene Muylaert. **Season:** April-Oct. **High:** June-Sept. **To obtain tee times:** Call golf shop. **Miscellaneous:** Reduced fees (weekdays, guests, twilight, juniors), lodging (102 rooms), credit cards (MC, V, AE, DC), BF, FF.
HIGHLANDS COURSE (9)
Yards: 6,750/5,900. **Par:** 36/36. **Course Rating:** 71.0/74.0. **Slope:** 124/129. **Green Fee:** $39/$49. **Cart Fee:** $32/Cart. **Walking Policy:** Unrestricted walking. **Walkability:** 3. **Opened:** 1990. **Miscellaneous:** Range (grass).
★★★ VALLEY COURSE (18)
Yards: 6,202/5,232. **Par:** 72/72. **Course Rating:** 69.7/70.9. **Slope:** 131/129. **Green Fee:** $49/$85. **Cart Fee:** Included in green fee. **Walking Policy:** Walking at certain times. **Walkability:** 4. **Opened:** 1974. **Miscellaneous:** Range (grass/mats).
Reader Comments: Great variety—some bad holes, many excellent … tight course … Have to use carts on weekends.

★★ HUMBER VALLEY GOLF COURSE
PU-40 Beattie Ave., Rexdale, M9W 2M3, (416)392-2488. **Facility Holes:** 18. **Yards:** 5,446/4,690. **Par:** 70/70. **Course Rating:** 65.8. **Slope:** 113. **Green Fee:** $25/$28. **Opened:** 1921. **Architect:** StanleyThompson. **To obtain tee times:** Call golf shop. **Miscellaneous:** Metal spikes.

HUNTSVILLE DOWNS GOLF LIMITED
PU-182 Golf Course Rd., Huntsville, P1H 1N7, (705)789-1000, 140 miles from Toronto. **E-mail:** hdgc@surenet.net. **Web:** www.golfcoursecanada.com/huntsvilledowns. **Facility Holes:** 18. **Yards:** 6,270/5,217. **Par:** 72/72. **Course Rating:** 70.4/65.6. **Slope:** 129/122. **Green Fee:** $45/$50. **Cart Fee:** $30/Cart. **Walking Policy:** Unrestricted walking. **Walkability:** 4. **Opened:** 1998. **Architect:** John Robinson. **Season:** April-Oct. **High:** July-Aug. **Tee times:** Call golf shop. **Misc:** Reduced fees (twilight, juniors), range (grass), credit cards (MC, V, AE), BF, FF.

INDIAN CREEK GOLF & COUNTRY CLUB
SP-120 Indian Creek Rd. W., Chatham, N7M 5L6, (519)354-7666. **Facility Holes:** 18. **Yards:** 6,200/5,471. **Par:** 71/73. **Course Rating:** 68.6/71.4. **Slope:** 113/119. **Cart Fee:** $22/Cart. **Walking Policy:** Unrestricted walking. **Walkability:** 2. **Opened:** 1956. **Architect:** Paul Sironen. **Season:** March-Dec. **High:** May-Oct. **To obtain tee times:** Call golf shop. **Miscellaneous:** Reduced fees (twilight, seniors, juniors), metal spikes, credit cards (MC, V).

KENOGAMISIS GOLF COURSE
SP-P.O. Box 729, Geraldton, P0T 1M0, (807)854-1029, 180 miles from Thunder Bay. **Facility Holes:** 9. **Yards:** 6,558/5,982. **Par:** 72/74. **Course Rating:** 69.4/72.6. **Slope:** 114/116. **Green Fee:** $24. **Cart Fee:** $25/Cart. **Walking Policy:** Unrestricted walking. **Walkability:** 3. **Opened:** 1937. **Architect:** Stanley Thompson. **Season:** May-Sept. **To obtain tee times:** Call golf shop. **Miscellaneous:** Reduced fees (weekdays, juniors), credit cards (V), BF, FF.

★★★½ KINGSVILLE GOLF & COUNTRY CLUB
SP-640 C. Rd. 20 West, Kingsville, N9Y 2E9, (519)733-6585, 35 miles from Windsor. **E-mail:** kinggolf@mnsi.net. **Web:** www.kingsvillegolf.com. **Facility Holes:** 27. **Green Fee:** $47. **Cart Fee:** $16/Person. **Walking Policy:** Unrestricted walking. **Opened:** 1925. **Architect:** R.F. Moote and Associates. **Season:** March-Nov. **High:** April-Oct. **To obtain tee times:** Call up to 2 days in advance. **Misc:** Reduced fees (twilight, juniors), range (grass), credit cards (MC, V), BF, FF.

RED/GOLD (18 Combo)
Yards: 6,622/5,545. **Par:** 27/73. **Course Rating:** 72.9/71.3. **Slope:** 134/120. **Walkability:** 4.
RED/WHITE (18 Combo)
Yards: 6,364/5,808. **Par:** 72/73. **Course Rating:** 70.9/72.7. **Slope:** 126/120. **Walkability:** 2.
WHITE/GOLD (18 Combo)
Yards: 6,394/5,288. **Par:** 72/72. **Course Rating:** 71.1/70.0. **Slope:** 132/119. **Walkability:** 4.
Reader Comments: Red/White the easiest of the three … Big trees, very flat … Good mix … Well kept despite being busy most of the time … A bit pricey for the area … Great par 3s … Trees, water, fast greens, lots of character … Gold 9 most hilly in the county.

LAKE JOSEPH CLUB

R-RR 2, Port Carling, P0B 1J0, (705)765-2020, (800)291-9899, 120 miles from Toronto.
Facility Holes: 27. **Yards:** 6,985/5,081. **Par:** 72/72. **Course Rating:** 71.9/69.8. **Slope:** 132/123.
Green Fee: $70/$160. **Cart Fee:** $18/Person. **Walking Policy:** Unrestricted walking. **Walkability:**
5. **Opened:** 1996. **Architect:** Thomas McBroom. **Season:** May-Oct. **High:** July-Aug. **To obtain tee times:** Call golf shop. **Miscellaneous:** Reduced fees (twilight, juniors), range (grass), lodging (42 rooms), credit cards (MC, V, AE, Diner's Club).
Special Notes: Also has a 9-hole course.

LEGENDS ON THE NIAGARA

PU-P.. Box 510, Niagara Falls, L2E 6T2, (905)356-1140. **Facility Holes:** 45. **Green Fee:**
$119/$129. **Cart Fee:** Included in green fee. **Walkability:** 2. **Season:** April-Nov. **To obtain tee times:** Call up to 365 days in advance. **Miscellaneous:** Reduced fees (twilight), credit cards (MC, V, AE, DC).
BATTLEFIELD COURSE (18)
Yards: 7,224/5,428. **Par:** 72/72. **Walking Policy:** Mandatory carts. **Architect:** Douglas Carrick.
CHIPPAWA COURSE (9)
Yards: 2,201. **Par:** 30. **Walking Policy:** Unrestricted walking. **Architect:**
Thomas McBroom/Douglas Carrick.
USHERS CREEK COURSE (18)
Yards: 7,308/5,506. **Par:** 72/72. **Walking Policy:** Mandatory carts. **Architect:**
Thomas McBroom.

★★½ THE LINKS OF NIAGARA AT WILLODELL

SP-10325 Willodell Rd., Niagara Falls, L0S 1K0, (905)295-8181, (800)790-0912, 6 miles from Niagara Falls. **E-mail:** info@willo-dell.com. **Web:** www.willo-dell.com. **Facility Holes:** 18. **Yards:**
6,689/5,752. **Par:** 72/73. **Course Rating:** 71.7/71.6. **Slope:** 125/124. **Green Fee:** $36/$48. **Cart Fee:** $32/Cart. **Walking Policy:** Unrestricted walking. **Walkability:** 3. **Opened:** 1964. **Architect:**
Nicol Thompson. **Season:** March-Nov. **To obtain tee times:** Call up to 7 days in advance.
Miscellaneous: Reduced fees (weekdays, twilight, juniors), range (grass), credit cards (MC, V), BF, FF.

★★ THE LINKS OF ROCKWAY GLEN

SP-3290 9th St. Louth, St. Catharines, L2R 6P7, (905)641-4536, 5 miles from St. Catharines.
E-mail: rockway@niagra.com. **Web:** www.rockwayglen.com. **Facility Holes:** 18. **Yards:**
6,914/5,033. **Par:** 72/72. **Course Rating:** 72.0/68.9. **Slope:** 124/118. **Green Fee:** $40/$50. **Cart Fee:** $20/Cart. **Walking Policy:** Unrestricted walking. **Walkability:** 2. **Opened:** 1991. **Architect:**
Robert Moote. **Season:** April-Nov. **High:** June-Sept. **To obtain tee times:** Call up to 5 days in ahead. **Miscellaneous:** Reduced fees (weekdays), range (grass), credit cards (MC, V), BF, FF.

LIONHEAD GOLF & COUNTRY CLUB

PU-8525 Mississauga Rd., Brampton, L6V 3N2, (905)455-4900, 10 miles from Brampton.
Web: www.golflionhead.com. **Facility Holes:** 36. **Walking Policy:** Mandatory carts. **Opened:**
1991. **Architect:** Ted Baker. **Season:** April-Dec. **To obtain tee times:** Call golf shop.
Miscellaneous: Reduced fees (twilight), range (grass/mats), credit cards (MC, V, AE, DC), BF, FF.
★★★★ **LEGENDS COURSE** (18) *Condition*
Yards: 7,230/5,473. **Par:** 72/72. **Course Rating:** 76.4/69.5. **Slope:** 153/138. **Green Fee:**
$60/$145. **Cart Fee:** $15/Person. **Walkability:** 5. **High:** Jan.-Oct.
Reader Comments: Tough track … Narrow with forced carries … One of the toughest courses in Ontario … Great par 4s, very tough course … Wow, challenging, beautiful, good shape, great staff and service … Toughest track in town … Good variety of holes … Very slow round of golf even with carts.
★★★½ **MASTERS COURSE** (18)
Yards: 7,035/5,553. **Par:** 72/72. **Course Rating:** 75.0/72.0. **Slope:** 146/131. **Green Fee:**
$60/$135. **Cart Fee:** Included in green fee. **Walkability:** 4.
Reader Comments: Fine golf course … Beautiful facilities … Small, fast greens—not for the faint of heart … Takes 5 hrs at any time.

★★★½ **LOCH MARCH GOLF & COUNTRY CLUB**
PU-1755 Old Carp Rd., Kanata, K2K 1X7, (613)839-5885, 28 miles from Ottawa. **E-mail:** greatday@lochmarch.com. **Web:** www.lochmarch.com. **Facility Holes:** 18. **Yards:** 6,750/5,174. **Par:** 72/72. **Course Rating:** 71.6/64.6. **Slope:** 129.3/113. **Green Fee:** $51. **Cart Fee:** $26/Cart. **Walking Policy:** Unrestricted walking. **Walkability:** 3. **Opened:** 1987. **Architect:** Mark Fuller. **Season:** May-Oct. **To obtain tee times:** Call up to 2 days in advance. **Miscellaneous:** Metal spikes, range (grass/mats), credit cards (MC, V, AE, Interac), FF.
Reader Comments: Unforgiving fairways, fast greens … Leave driver at home … Always enjoyable.

LOMBARD GLEN GOLF CLUB
SP-R.R. No.1, Lombardy, K0G 1L0, (613)283-5318, 5 miles from Smith Falls. **Facility Holes:** 18. **Yards:** 6,061/4,890. **Par:** 70/71. **Course Rating:** 68.1/67.0. **Slope:** 113/111. **Green Fee:** $26/$27. **Cart Fee:** $26/Cart. **Walking Policy:** Unrestricted walking. **Walkability:** 1. **Opened:** 1967. **Architect:** David Moote. **Season:** April-Nov. **High:** June-Sept. **Tee times:** Call golf shop. **Miscellaneous:** Reduced fees (twilight), metal spikes, range (grass), credit cards (MC, V, AE).

★½ **MANDERLEY ON THE GREEN**
SP-5920 Prince of Wales Dr., North Gower, K0A 2T0, (613)489-2066, (800)555-9623, 6 miles from Ottawa. **E-mail:** manderley@primus.ca. **Web:** www.ottawagolf.com. **Facility Holes:** 18. **Yards:** 6,414/5,668. **Par:** 71/71. **Course Rating:** 70.0/72.0. **Slope:** 123/126. **Green Fee:** $18/$34. **Cart Fee:** $14/Person. **Walking Policy:** Unrestricted walking. **Walkability:** 2. **Opened:** 1964. **Architect:** Howard Watson. **Season:** April-Nov. **High:** June-Sept. **To obtain tee times:** Call up to 6 days in advance. **Miscellaneous:** Reduced fees (weekdays, twilight), metal spikes, range (grass/mats), credit cards (MC, V, AE), BF, FF.

MANITOUWADGE GOLF COURSE
PU-P.O. Box 3097, Manitouwadge, P0T 2C0, (807)826-4265, 250 miles from Thunder Bay. **Facility Holes:** 9. **Yards:** 3,250. **Par:** 36. **Course Rating:** 72.2. **Slope:** 129. **Cart Fee:** $24/Cart. **Walking Policy:** Unrestricted walking. **Walkability:** 4. **Opened:** 1971. **Season:** May-Sept. **High:** July-Aug. **To obtain tee times:** Call golf shop. **Miscellaneous:** Reduced fees (twilight, seniors, juniors), credit cards (MC, V, AE).

★★ **MAPLES OF BALLANTRAE LODGE & GOLF CLUB**
R-P. O. Box 10, Stouffville, L4A 7X5, (905)640-6077, 30 miles from Toronto. **Facility Holes:** 27. **Yards:** 6,715/5,250. **Par:** 72/73. **Course Rating:** 70.0/69.5. **Slope:** 126/116. **Green Fee:** $24/$55. **Cart Fee:** $30/Cart. **Walking Policy:** Unrestricted walking. **Walkability:** 3. **Opened:** 1982. **Architect:** R.F. Moote & Assoc. **Season:** April-Nov. **High:** June-Sept. **To obtain tee times:** Call up to 3 days in advance. **Miscellaneous:** Reduced fees (weekdays, guests, twilight, seniors, juniors), range (grass), lodging (20 rooms), credit cards (MC, V, AE), BF, FF. **Special Notes:** Also has a 9-hole executive course.

★★★ **MARKHAM GREEN GOLF CLUB**
SP-120 Rouge Bank Dr., Markham, L3S 4B7, (905)294-6156, 15 miles from Toronto. **E-mail:** pmorrell@ca.ibm.com. **Web:** www.markhamgreengolfclub.ca. **Facility Holes:** 9. **Yards:** 3,004/2,326. **Par:** 35/35. **Course Rating:** 34.5/36.2. **Slope:** 127/121. **Green Fee:** $44/$45. **Cart Fee:** $27/Cart. **Walking Policy:** Unrestricted walking. **Walkability:** 3. **Opened:** 1954. **Architect:** Jim Johnson. **Season:** April-Nov. **High:** July-Aug. **To obtain tee times:** Call up to 5 days in advance. **Miscellaneous:** Reduced fees (twilight, juniors), range (grass), credit cards (MC, V, AE), BF, FF.
Reader Comments: If you like valley courses, you will like this … Best 9-hole course in Ontario … Very tricky with lots of water … Bring lots of balls or keep it in the fairway.

METCALFE GOLF CLUB
SP-8th Line Rd., Metcalfe, K0A 2P0, (613)821-2701. **Facility Holes:** 18. **Yards:** 6,120/5,614. **Par:** 71/71. **Course Rating:** 69.1/71.6. **Slope:** 118/121. **Green Fee:** $28/$32. **Cart Fee:** $28/Cart. **To obtain tee times:** Call golf shop.

★★ **MILL RUN GOLF & COUNTRY CLUB**
SP-269 Durham Rd. #8, Uxbridge, L9P 1R1, (905)852-6212, (800)465-8633, 7 miles from Toronto. **Facility Holes:** 18. **Yards:** 6,800/5,385. **Par:** 72/72. **Course Rating:** 72.8/70.5. **Slope:** 131/117. **Green Fee:** $24/$37. **Cart Fee:** $25/Cart. **Walking Policy:** Unrestricted walking. **Walkability:** 2. **Opened:** 1985. **Architect:** Rene Muylaert. **Season:** April-Oct. **High:** June-Aug. **To obtain tee times:** Call golf shop. **Miscellaneous:** Reduced fees (weekdays, twilight, seniors, juniors), metal spikes, range (grass), credit cards (MC, V, AE).

★★★½ **MONTERRA GOLF AT BLUE MOUNTAIN RESORTS**
R-R.R. No.3, Collingwood, L9Y 3Z2, (705)445-0231x6531, 75 miles from Toronto. **E-mail:** mail@bluemountain.ca. **Web:** www.bluemountain.ca. **Facility Holes:** 18. **Yards:** 6,581/5,139.

Par: 72/72. **Course Rating:** 71.8/69.5. **Slope:** 129/116. **Green Fee:** $19/$84. **Cart Fee:** $15/Person. **Walking Policy:** Unrestricted walking. **Walkability:** 4. **Opened:** 1989. **Architect:** Thomas McBroom. **Season:** May-Oct. **High:** June-Sept. **Tee times:** Call up to 10 days in advance. **Miscellaneous:** Reduced fees (guests, twilight), credit cards (MC, V, AE), BF, FF.
Reader Comments: Lots of ups and downs … 18 unique holes. New challenge on every tee. Love it! … Fair tee positions for women, a rarity … Fast greens … Read the yardage book to score well … A thinker's course … Good variety of holes … No. 9 does not return to clubhouse—halfway house at No. 1.

MUNICIPAL GOLF COURSE
PU-R.R. 2 Twin City Crossroads, Thunder Bay, R7E6, (807)939-1331. **Facility Holes:** 9. **Yards:** 2,862/2,832. **Par:** 36/36. **Course Rating:** 64.6/66.2. **Slope:** 95/101. **Green Fee:** $21. **Cart Fee:** $22/Cart. **Walking Policy:** Unrestricted walking. **Walkability:** 1. **Season:** April-Oct. **High:** June-Aug. **To obtain tee times:** Call golf shop. **Miscellaneous:** Reduced fees (juniors), metal spikes, credit cards (MC, V).

★★★★½ NATIONAL PINES GOLF CLUB *Condition, Pace*
SP-8165 10 Sidroad, Innisfil, L95 4T3, (705)431-7000, (800)663-1549, 40 miles from Toronto. **Web:** www.golfnationalpines.com. **Facility Holes:** 18. **Yards:** 7,013/4,980. **Par:** 72/72. **Course Rating:** 74.5/69.0. **Slope:** 144/125. **Green Fee:** $77/$97. **Cart Fee:** $16/Person. **Walking Policy:** Unrestricted walking. **Opened:** 1992. **Architect:** Thomas McBroom. **Season:** April-Nov. **High:** June-Sept. **To obtain tee times:** Call up to 7 days in advance. **Miscellaneous:** Range (grass), credit cards (MC, V, AE, DC).
Reader Comments: Great golf day … Interesting holes … One of the best in Ontario and less expensive than many others … Greens are really tough … Play it if you can … You feel like you are the only group on the course … Worth the 45 minute drive … Great to walk … For long ball hitters.

★★★★ NOBLETON LAKES GOLF CLUB
PU-125 Nobleton Lakes Dr., Nobleton, L0G 1N0, (905)859-4070, 20 miles from Toronto. **Web:** www.nobletonlakesgolf.com. **Facility Holes:** 18. **Yards:** 7,089/5,819. **Par:** 72/72. **Course Rating:** 75.3/72.8. **Slope:** 145. **Green Fee:** $74/$80. **Cart Fee:** Included in green fee. **Walkability:** 5. **Opened:** 1975. **Architect:** Rene Muylaert/Charles Muylaert. **Season:** April-Nov. **High:** May-Oct. **To obtain tee times:** Call golf shop. **Miscellaneous:** Reduced fees (twilight), range (grass), credit cards (MC, V, AE).
Reader Comments: Superb layout … Hidden gem, great fall golf … Fast tricky greens, wildlife … A terrific course … Lots of variety of terrain and hole layouts … A great blend of elevation changes & scenic beauty … Lots of bunkers … Too many blind shots cause penalties.

NORTH SHORE GOLF COURSE
PU-P.O. Box 95, Red Rock, P0T 2P0, (807)887-2006, 70 miles from Thunder Bay. **E-mail:** nsgcinc@camcom.net. **Facility Holes:** 9. **Yards:** 6,500/6,048. **Par:** 72. **Course Rating:** 71.8/69.9. **Slope:** 131/121. **Green Fee:** $17/$22. **Cart Fee:** $23/Cart. **Walking Policy:** Unrestricted walking. **Walkability:** 3. **Opened:** 1960. **Season:** April-Oct. **High:** June-Sept. **To obtain tee times:** Call golf shop. **Miscellaneous:** Reduced fees (juniors), range (grass), credit cards (MC, V, AE, Interac), BF, FF.

★½ NORTHRIDGE PUBLIC GOLF COURSE
PU-320 Balmoral Dr., Brantford, N3R 7S2, (519)753-6112, 15 miles from Hamilton. **E-mail:** cbeachey@city.brantford.on.ca. **Facility Holes:** 18. **Yards:** 6,300/5,830. **Par:** 72/74. **Course Rating:** 68.5/73.3. **Slope:** 110/120. **Green Fee:** $29. **Cart Fee:** $27/Cart. **Walking Policy:** Unrestricted walking. **Walkability:** 2. **Opened:** 1957. **Season:** April-Nov. **High:** June-Sept. **To obtain tee times:** Call up to 7 days in advance. **Miscellaneous:** Reduced fees (twilight), range (grass), credit cards (MC, V, AE), BF, FF.

★★★ THE OAKS OF ST. GEORGE GOLF CLUB
SP-269 German School Rd., R.R. No.1, Paris, N3L 3E1, (519)448-3673, 2 miles from Brantford. **E-mail:** oaksofstgeorge@on.aibn.com. **Web:** www.oaksofstgeorge.ca. **Facility Holes:** 18. **Yards:** 6,338/5,628. **Par:** 72/72. **Course Rating:** 71.1/69.8. **Slope:** 123/118. **Green Fee:** $36/$42. **Cart Fee:** $26/Cart. **Walking Policy:** Unrestricted walking. **Walkability:** 3. **Opened:** 1992. **Architect:** David Moote/Robert Moote. **Season:** April-Oct. **High:** June-Aug. **To obtain tee times:** Call up to 7 days in advance. **Miscellaneous:** Reduced fees (twilight, seniors, juniors), range (grass/mats), credit cards (MC, V), BF, FF.
Reader Comments: Real gem, short but excellent layout … Tight layout … Price is right … Challenging course … I like it! … Think your way around this one … Beware the foxes, they might steal your golf balls … Great variety from hole to hole … 10th hole is beautiful.

★★★½ OLIVER'S NEST GOLF & COUNTRY CLUB *Pace*

PU-P.O. Box 75, Lindsay, K9V 4R8, (705)953-2093, (888)953-6378, 3 miles from Lindsay. **E-mail:** golf@oliversnest.com. **Web:** www.oliversnest.com. **Facility Holes:** 18. **Yards:** 6,625/5,185. **Par:** 71/72. **Course Rating:** 72.2/65.2. **Slope:** 127/111. **Green Fee:** $32/$48. **Cart Fee:** $30/Cart. **Walking Policy:** Unrestricted walking. **Walkability:** 3. **Opened:** 1997. **Architect:** Graham Cooke. **Season:** April-Oct. **High:** June-Sept. **To obtain tee times:** Call golf shop. **Miscellaneous:** Reduced fees (weekdays, twilight, seniors, juniors), range (grass), credit cards (MC, V, Debit cards), BF, FF.

Reader Comments: Tough finish ... Good value ... Always delayed ... Greens putt very true ... Good variety of holes ... Use every club in the bag ... Doesn't have finishing touches, but some neat holes ... Each week we drive 1 1/2 hours to play this course ... Some of best fairways in area.

OSPREY VALLEY RESORTS

PU-R.R. No.2, 18821 Main St., Alton, L0N 1A0, (519)927-9034, (800)833-1561, 20 miles from Toronto. **Facility Holes:** 54. **Green Fee:** $70/$105. **Cart Fee:** $30/Cart. **Walking Policy:** Unrestricted walking. **Architect:** Douglas Carrick. **Season:** April-Dec. **High:** May-Oct. **To obtain tee times:** Call golf shop. **Miscellaneous:** Metal spikes, credit cards (MC, V, AE, Interac), FF.

★★★½ HEATHLANDS LINKS (18)

Yards: 6,810/5,248. **Par:** 71/71. **Course Rating:** 72.6/69.0. **Slope:** 128/118. **Walkability:** 2. **Opened:** 1993. **Miscellaneous:** Reduced fees (twilight).

Reader Comments: Best kept secret in town ... Hidden gem ... Crowned greens and deep pot bunkers put a real emphasis on the short game ... Punishing fescue, not a good place to play if you spray the ball ... Wonderful course ... One of the best links-style courses in Canada.

ROYAL HOOT (18)

Yards: 7,087/5,154. **Par:** 72/72. **Walkability:** 2. **Opened:** 2001. **Miscellaneous:** Reduced fees (twilight, seniors).

ROYAL TOOT (18)

Yards: 7,106/5,372. **Par:** 72/72. **Walkability:** 3. **Opened:** 2001. **Miscellaneous:** Reduced fees (twilight, seniors).

PAKENHAM HIGHLANDS GOLF CLUB

PU-Hwy. 29 at McWatty Rd., Pakenham, K0A 2X0, (613)624-5550, 25 miles from Ottawa. **E-mail:** pak@calabogiehighlandsgolf.com. **Web:** www.calabogiehighlandsgolf.com. **Facility Holes:** 27. **Green Fee:** $26/$32. **Cart Fee:** $26/Cart. **Walking Policy:** Unrestricted walking. **Walkability:** 3. **Opened:** 1994. **Architect:** Rick Fleming. **Season:** April-Nov. **High:** June-Sept. **To obtain tee times:** Call up to 7 days in advance. **Miscellaneous:** Reduced fees (weekdays, twilight), credit cards (MC, V, AE), BF, FF.

CANYON/ISLAND (18)

Yards: 6,606/5,223. **Par:** 72/72. **Course Rating:** 70.9/69.3. **Slope:** 116/114.

★★ LAKE/CANYON (18)

Yards: 6,470/5,268. **Par:** 72/72. **Course Rating:** 70.2/69.7. **Slope:** 120/114.

LAKE/ISLAND (18)

Yards: 6,480/5,331. **Par:** 72/72. **Course Rating:** 70.0/69.8. **Slope:** 116/113.

PARRY SOUND GOLF & COUNTRY CLUB

SP-50 Geo. Hunt Memorial Dr., Parry Sound, P2A 2X3, (705)342-5262, 5 miles from Parry Sound. **E-mail:** abetts@vianet.on.ca. **Facility Holes:** 18. **Yards:** 5,896/4,865. **Par:** 71/72. **Course Rating:** 68.4/70.0. **Slope:** 133/119. **Green Fee:** $45/$50. **Cart Fee:** $30/Cart. **Walking Policy:** Unrestricted walking. **Walkability:** 3. **Opened:** 1983. **Architect:** Thomas McBroom. **Season:** May-Oct. **High:** June-Sept. **To obtain tee times:** Call up to 7 days in advance. **Misc:** Reduced fees (twilight, juniors), range (grass), credit cards (MC, V, AE), BF, FF.

PENINSULA GOLF CLUB

PU-P.O. Bag TM Peninsula Rd., Marathon, P0T 2E0, (807)229-1392, 180 miles from Thunder Bay. **E-mail:** btocheri@marathon.lakehead.u.ca. **Facility Holes:** 9. **Yards:** 6,032/5,352. **Par:** 72/71. **Course Rating:** 68.0/69.0. **Slope:** 128/111. **Green Fee:** $13/$20. **Cart Fee:** $20/Cart. **Walking Policy:** Unrestricted walking. **Walkability:** 4. **Opened:** 1952. **Architect:** Stanley Thompson. **Season:** May-Oct. **High:** June-Sept. **To obtain tee times:** Call golf shop. **Misc:** Reduced fees (seniors, juniors), metal spikes, range (mats), credit cards (V), BF, FF.

PENINSULA LAKES GOLF CLUB

SP-569 Hwy. 20 W., Fenwick, L0S 1C0, (905)892-8844, 15 miles from Niagra Falls. **E-mail:** info@penlakes.com. **Web:** www.penlakes.com. **Facility Holes:** 27. **Green Fee:** $28/$55. **Cart Fee:** $30/Cart. **Walking Policy:** Unrestricted walking. **Walkability:** 3. **Opened:** 1980. **Architect:** Rene Muylaert. **Season:** April-Nov. **High:** June-Oct. **To obtain tee times:** Call golf shop. **Miscellaneous:** Range (grass/mats), credit cards (MC, V, Debit), BF, FF.

ORCHARD/HILLSIDE (18)

Yards: 6,480/5,455. **Par:** 71/73. **Course Rating:** 70.6/70.8. **Slope:** 122/121.

CANADA

★★★★ QUARRY/HILLSIDE (18)
Yards: 6,500/5,523. **Par:** 71/73. **Course Rating:** 72.5/71.3. **Slope:** 127/121.
Reader Comments: First class ... This course is a gem ... A nice enjoyable course, not too hard, not too easy ... Enjoyable track on hilly terrain ... Outstanding ... Front 9 great ... Lack of length hurts this course—many memorable holes ... Well groomed, good layout.
QUARRY/ORCHARD (18)
Yards: 6,425/5,315. **Par:** 70/72. **Course Rating:** 70.6/69.9. **Slope:** 122/118.

★★★ PHEASANT RUN GOLF CLUB
PU-18033 Warden Ave., Sharon, L0G 1V0, (905)898-3917, 35 miles from Toronto. **E-mail:** proshop@pheasantrungolf.com. **Web:** www.pheasantrungolf.com. **Facility Holes:** 27. **Green Fee:** $50/$70. **Walking Policy:** Unrestricted walking. **Opened:** 1980. **Architect:** Rene Muylaert/Charles Muylaert. **Season:** April-Nov. **High:** June-Sept. **To obtain tee times:** Call up to 210 days in advance. **Miscellaneous:** Reduced fees (weekdays, twilight, juniors), range (grass/mats), credit cards (MC, V, AE), BF, FF.
MIDLANDS/HIGHLANDS (18 Combo)
Yards: 6,541/5,255. **Par:** 73/73. **Course Rating:** 72.8/67.0. **Slope:** 136/127. **Cart Fee:** $16/Person. **Walkability:** 5.
SOUTHERN UPLAND/HIGHLANDS (18 Combo)
Yards: 6,335/5,091. **Par:** 72/72. **Course Rating:** 71.0/65.3. **Slope:** 135/124. **Cart Fee:** $16/Cart. **Walkability:** 3.
SOUTHERN UPLAND/MIDLANDS (18 Combo)
Yards: 6,058/4,880. **Par:** 71/71. **Course Rating:** 70.9/65.0. **Slope:** 133/120. **Cart Fee:** $16/Person. **Walkability:** 3.
Reader Comments: 3 unique 9s: 2 tough, 1 flat and shorter. All fun ... You will use every club in your bag ... A lot of fun to play ... Worth the drive.

★★ PINE KNOT GOLF & COUNTRY CLUB
SP-5421 Hamilton Rd., Dorchester, N0L 1G6, (519)268-3352, (800)414-3270, 7 miles from London. **E-mail:** bkeating@pineknotgolf.com. **Web:** pineknotgolf.com. **Facility Holes:** 18. **Yards:** 6,500/5,003. **Par:** 71/71. **Course Rating:** 71.7/69.0. **Slope:** 127/115. **Green Fee:** $32/$38. **Cart Fee:** $28/Cart. **Walking Policy:** Unrestricted walking. **Walkability:** 2. **Opened:** 1992. **Architect:** John Robinson. **Season:** April-Dec. **High:** May-Sept. **To obtain tee times:** Call up to 5 days in advance. **Miscellaneous:** Reduced fees (twilight), range (grass/mats), credit cards (MC, V, AE), BF, FF.

PINES OF GEORGINA GOLF CLUB
SP-P.O. Box 44, Hwy. 48, Pefferlaw, L0E 1N0, (705)437-1669, 40 miles from Toronto. **Facility Holes:** 18. **Yards:** 6,012/5,457. **Par:** 70/70. **Course Rating:** 67.8/65.7. **Slope:** 112/107. **Green Fee:** $25/$38. **Cart Fee:** $15/Person. **Walking Policy:** Unrestricted walking. **Walkability:** 4. **Opened:** 1992. **Architect:** R.F. Moote & Assoc. **High:** April-Nov. **To obtain tee times:** Call up to 14 days in advance. **Miscellaneous:** Reduced fees (weekdays, twilight, juniors), credit cards (MC, V), BF, FF.

★★★ RENFREW GOLF CLUB
SP-1108 Golf Course Rd., Renfrew, K7V 4A4, (613)432-7729, (888)805-3739, 40 miles from Kanata. **E-mail:** info@renfrew.golf.can. **Web:** www.renfrewgolf.com. **Facility Holes:** 18. **Yards:** 6,440/5,650. **Par:** 71/74. **Course Rating:** 71.0/72.7. **Slope:** 124/125. **Green Fee:** $31/$33. **Cart Fee:** $32/Cart. **Walking Policy:** Unrestricted walking. **Walkability:** 4. **Opened:** 1929. **Architect:** George Cumming/Steven Ward. **Season:** May-Oct. **High:** June-Aug. **To obtain tee times:** Call up to 5 days in advance. **Miscellaneous:** Reduced fees (twilight, juniors), range (grass), credit cards (MC, V, AE), BF, FF.
Reader Comments: Very scenic, hilly, and challenging ... A must play! ... Rolling terrain ... Challenging for all.

★★★ RICHMOND HILL GOLF CLUB
PU-8755 Bathurst St., Richmond Hill, L4C 0H4, (905)889-4653, 5 miles from Toronto. **E-mail:** winstonrhgolf.com. **Web:** www.rhgolf.com. **Facility Holes:** 18. **Yards:** 6,004/4,935. **Par:** 70/70. **Course Rating:** 67.8/64.0. **Slope:** 120. **Green Fee:** $30/$65. **Cart Fee:** $32/Cart. **Walking Policy:** Unrestricted walking. **Walkability:** 3. **Opened:** 1992. **Architect:** Rene Muyleart. **Season:** April-Nov. **High:** May-Sept. **To obtain tee times:** Call up to 4 days in advance. **Miscellaneous:** Reduced fees (weekdays, twilight, seniors, juniors), range (mats), credit cards (MC, V, AE, Cash/Interac), BF, FF.
Reader Comments: Excellent facilities, course conditions excellent ... Lots of elevation changes on the back 9 ... Good shot variety for a short course ... Nos. 11 & 12 two of the best par-4s in southern Ontario ... Target course.

★★½ RICHVIEW GOLF & COUNTRY CLUB
SP-2204 Bronty Rd., Oakville, L6L 6M9, (905)827-1211. **Facility Holes:** 18. **Yards:** 6,100/5,200. **Par:** 71/71. **Course Rating:** 69.3/65.0. **Slope:** 115/107. **Green Fee:** $43/$52. **Cart Fee:** $30/Cart. **Walking Policy:** Unrestricted walking. **Walkability:** 3. **Opened:** 1965. **Architect:** Clinton E. Robinson. **Season:** Year-round. **To obtain tee times:** Call up to 10 days in advance. **Miscellaneous:** Reduced fees (twilight, seniors, juniors), credit cards (MC, V, AE), BF, FF.

RIVENDELL GOLF CLUB
SP-R.R. No.1 7359 Hwy. 38, Verona, K0H 2W0, (613)374-3404, 18 miles from Kingston. **E-mail:** info@rivendellgolf.on.ca. **Web:** www.rivendellgolf.on.ca. **Facility Holes:** 18. **Yards:** 6,218/5,173. **Par:** 71/71. **Course Rating:** 68.5/68.9. **Slope:** 116/116. **Green Fee:** $27/$31. **Cart Fee:** $23/Cart. **Walking Policy:** Unrestricted walking. **Walkability:** 3. **Opened:** 1979. **Architect:** Robert Heaslip. **Season:** April-Nov. **High:** July-Aug. **To obtain tee times:** Call up to 7 days in advance. **Miscellaneous:** Reduced fees (guests, twilight), credit cards (MC, V, Interac), FF.

★★ RIVER ROAD GOLF COURSE
PU-2115 River Rd., London, N6A 4C3, (519)661-4450, 100 miles from Toronto. **Facility Holes:** 18. **Yards:** 6,480/5,386. **Par:** 72/72. **Course Rating:** 72.6/70.0. **Slope:** 130/126. **Green Fee:** $26/$27. **Cart Fee:** $27/Cart. **Walking Policy:** Unrestricted walking. **Walkability:** 3. **Opened:** 1992. **Architect:** Bill Fox Sr. **Season:** March-Nov. **High:** May-Sept. **Tee times:** Call up to 2 days in advance. **Miscellaneous:** Reduced fees (twilight), credit cards (MC, V), BF, FF.

★★★ ROSELAND GOLF & CURLING CLUB
PU-455 Kennedy Dr. W., Windsor, N9G 1S8, (519)969-3810, 5 miles from Detroit. **E-mail:** roseland@city.windsor.on.ca. **Facility Holes:** 18. **Yards:** 6,588/5,914. **Par:** 72/75. **Course Rating:** 71.6/73.1. **Slope:** 125/123. **Green Fee:** $33/$39. **Cart Fee:** $30/Cart. **Walking Policy:** Unrestricted walking. **Walkability:** 1. **Opened:** 1928. **Architect:** Donald Ross. **Season:** March-Nov. **High:** May-Oct. **To obtain tee times:** Call golf shop. **Miscellaneous:** Reduced fees (weekdays, twilight, seniors), credit cards (MC, V), BF, FF.
Reader Comments: Very good ... Classic layout. Conditioning improving yearly ... Lots of play, busy, challenging ... My favorite walk in the park ... Bring all your clubs ... New pro shop.

★★★½ ROYAL ASHBURN GOLF CLUB
PU-995 Myrtle Rd. W., Ashburn, L0B 1A0, (905)686-1121, 18 miles from Whitby. **E-mail:** rage@istar.ca. **Web:** www.royalashburngolfclub.com. **Facility Holes:** 18. **Yards:** 7,019/5,828. **Par:** 72/73. **Course Rating:** 74.0/72.6. **Slope:** 129/126. **Green Fee:** $55/$65. **Cart Fee:** $30/Cart. **Walking Policy:** Unrestricted walking. **Walkability:** 2. **Opened:** 1961. **Architect:** Wilson Paterson. **Season:** April-Nov. **To obtain tee times:** Call up to 7 days in advance. **Miscellaneous:** Reduced fees (weekdays, twilight), range (grass/mats), credit cards (MC, V, AE), BF, FF.
Reader Comments: Lots of golf to be had here ... Classic old course; gimmicky 3rd hole ... A solid straight-forward test ... New name Royal Ashburn, great course, play it as often as we can ... A good challenge from the back tees ... Very traditional layout ... Very difficult for high handicap.
Special Notes: Formerly Thunderbird Golf & Country Club.

★★★ ROYAL WOODBINE GOLF CLUB
SP-195 Galaxy Blvd., Toronto, M9W 6R7, (416)674-4653, 1 mile from Toronto. **Facility Holes:** 18. **Yards:** 6,446/5,102. **Par:** 71/71. **Course Rating:** 72.3/71.2. **Slope:** 139/120. **Green Fee:** $100/$145. **Cart Fee:** Included in green fee. **Walking Policy:** Walking at certain times. **Walkability:** 3. **Opened:** 1992. **Architect:** Michael Hurdzan. **Season:** April-Nov. **High:** May-Sept. **To obtain tee times:** Call golf shop. **Miscellaneous:** Reduced fees (twilight), range (grass/mats), credit cards (MC, V, AE, Enroute), FF.
Reader Comments: Unique ... Good clubhouse and practice facility ... Shortish but tough ... Very crowded ... Below airport glide path.

SAUGEEN GOLF CLUB
SP-R.R. No. 2, Port Elgin, N0H 2C6, (519)389-4031, 25 miles from Owen Sound. **E-mail:** golf@saugeengolf.com. **Web:** saugeengolf.com. **Facility Holes:** 27. **Cart Fee:** $28/Cart. **Walking Policy:** Unrestricted walking. **Walkability:** 3. **Opened:** 1925. **Architect:** Stanley Thompson/David Moote. **Season:** April-Nov. **To obtain tee times:** Call up to 3 days in advance. **Miscellaneous:** Reduced fees (weekdays, guests, twilight), range (grass), credit cards (MC, V), BF, FF.
LEGACY/SUNRISE (18)
Yards: 6,398/5,086. **Par:** 72/73. **Course Rating:** 69.6/70.8. **Slope:** 114/121. **Green Fee:** $38.
SUNRISE/SUNSET (18)
Yards: 6,453. **Par:** 72/72. **Course Rating:** 70.6/70.2. **Slope:** 121/123. **Green Fee:** $38.
SUNSET/LEGACY (18)
Yards: 6,455/5,286. **Par:** 72/73. **Course Rating:** 69.4/71.0. **Slope:** 117/118. **Green Fee:** $38.

SAWMILL CREEK GOLF & COUNTRY CLUB
PU-3790 Lakeshore Dr., Camlachie, N0N 1E0, (519)899-4653, (888)729-6455, 50 miles from Detroit. **Web:** www.sawmill-creek.com. **Facility Holes:** 18. **Yards:** 6,278/4,976. **Par:** 70/70. **Course Rating:** 70.7/69.4. **Slope:** 131/124. **Green Fee:** $25/$35. **Cart Fee:** $30/Cart. **Walking Policy:** Unrestricted walking. **Walkability:** 2. **Opened:** 1999. **Architect:** Rene Muylaert. **Season:** April-Nov. **High:** May-Sept. **Tee times:** Call up to 5 days in advance. **Miscellaneous:** Reduced fees (weekdays, twilight), range (grass), lodging (6 rooms), credit cards (MC, V), BF, FF.

★★★★ SILVER LAKES GOLF & COUNTRY CLUB *Value, Pace*
SP-21114 Yonge St., R.R. No.1, Newmarket, L3Y 4V8, (905)836-8070, 5 miles from Newmarket. **E-mail:** parsleyis@home.com. **Facility Holes:** 18. **Yards:** 7,029/5,092. **Par:** 72/72. **Course Rating:** 73.6/70.1. **Slope:** 133/123. **Green Fee:** $55/$65. **Cart Fee:** $30/Cart. **Walking Policy:** Unrestricted walking. **Walkability:** 1. **Opened:** 1994. **Architect:** David Moote. **Season:** April-Nov. **High:** June-Aug. **Tee times:** Call up to 5 days in advance. **Misc:** Reduced fees (weekdays, twilight, seniors, juniors), range (grass), credit cards (MC, V, AE, DC), BF, FF.
Reader Comments: One-third the price of other high-end courses; twice the fun … Very easy walk … Always in great shape … Aqua range is unique … Great for tournaments … Bring bug repellent in spring … If you love doglegs you will like this course … Tight with lots of water, target golf.

★★★★ ST. ANDREWS VALLEY GOLF CLUB
PU-368 St. John Sideroad E., Aurora, L4G 3G8, (905)727-7888, 20 miles from Toronto. **E-mail:** golf@standrewsvalley.com. **Web:** www.standrewsvalley.com. **Facility Holes:** 18. **Yards:** 7,304/5,536. **Par:** 72/72. **Course Rating:** 77.4/68.5. **Slope:** 143/123. **Green Fee:** $42/$84. **Cart Fee:** $16/Person. **Walking Policy:** Unrestricted walking. **Walkability:** 4. **Opened:** 1993. **Architect:** Rene Muylaert. **Season:** April-Nov. **High:** June-Aug. **To obtain tee times:** Call up to 14 days in advance. **Miscellaneous:** Reduced fees (weekdays, twilight), range (grass/mats), credit cards (MC, V, AE, DC), BF, FF.
Reader Comments: Friendly staff … Deceptively difficult … Multiple hazards, punishing rough, roller-coaster greens … Don't challenge the 9th hole … Excellent driving range … Absolutely outstanding … A good test for anybody, choose the right tees … True golfers will love this course … A real gem.

ST. CLAIR PARKWAY GOLF COURSE
PU-132 Moore Line, Mooretown, N0N 1M0, (519)867-2810, (877)362-3344, 12 miles from Sarnia. **E-mail:** info@stclairparkway.com. **Web:** www.stclairparkway.com. **Facility Holes:** 18. **Yards:** 6,720/5,731. **Par:** 71/72. **Course Rating:** 70.5/71.0. **Slope:** 118/122. **Green Fee:** $32/$35. **Cart Fee:** $29/Cart. **Walking Policy:** Unrestricted walking. **Walkability:** 2. **Opened:** 1971. **Architect:** William Aimers. **Season:** April-Oct. **High:** May-Sept. **To obtain tee times:** Call up to 7 days in advance. **Miscellaneous:** Reduced fees (weekdays, twilight), range (grass), credit cards (MC, V, AE), BF, FF.

STRATHCONA GOLF COURSE
PU-500 Hodder Ave., Thunder Bay, (807)683-8251. **Facility Holes:** 18. **Yards:** 6,507/5,852. **Par:** 72/73. **Course Rating:** 73.4/72.9. **Slope:** 130/115. **Green Fee:** $21. **Cart Fee:** $22/Cart. **Walking Policy:** Unrestricted walking. **Walkability:** 3. **Season:** April-Oct. **High:** July-Aug. **To obtain tee times:** Call golf shop. **Miscellaneous:** Reduced fees (juniors), metal spikes, credit cards (MC, V).

SUMMERHEIGHTS GOLF LINKS
PU-1160 S. Branch Rd., Cornwall, K6H 5R6, (613)938-8009, 70 miles from Ottawa. **E-mail:** kathy@summerheightsgolf.com. **Web:** www.summerheightsgolf.com. **Facility Holes:** 36. **Green Fee:** $27/$32. **Cart Fee:** $30/Cart. **Walking Policy:** Unrestricted walking. **Walkability:** 2. **Architect:** Robert Heaslip. **Season:** April-Oct. **Tee times:** Call up to 2 days in advance. **Miscellaneous:** Reduced fees (twilight), range (grass), credit cards (MC, V, AE), BF, FF.
SOUTH/NORTH (18)
Yards: 6,345/5,372. **Par:** 72/72. **Course Rating:** 69.8/71.1. **Slope:** 120/123. **Opened:** 1962.
WEST (18)
Yards: 6,236/5,301. **Par:** 72/72. **Course Rating:** 69.5/70.0. **Slope:** 118/113. **Opened:** 1966.

★★½ SUTTON CREEK GOLF & COUNTRY CLUB
SP-R.R. No.2, Walker and Guesto, Essex, N8M 2X6, (519)726-6179, 10 miles from Windsor. **Facility Holes:** 18. **Yards:** 6,856/5,286. **Par:** 72/73. **Course Rating:** 72.5/70.5. **Slope:** 132/118. **Green Fee:** $30/$40. **Cart Fee:** $15/Person. **Walking Policy:** Unrestricted walking. **Walkability:** 2. **Opened:** 1988. **Architect:** Robert Heaslip. **Season:** April-Nov. **High:** June-Sept. **To obtain tee times:** Call golf shop. **Miscellaneous:** Reduced fees (weekdays, seniors, juniors), range (grass), credit cards (MC, V).

CANADA

★★ TAM O'SHANTER GOLF COURSE
PU-2481 Birchmount Rd., Toronto, M1T 2M6, (416)392-2547. **Facility Holes:** 18. **Yards:** 6,098/4,958. **Par:** 72/70. **Course Rating:** 68.4/67.2. **Slope:** 120/109. **Green Fee:** $20/$43. **Cart Fee:** $32/Cart. **Walking Policy:** Unrestricted walking. **Walkability:** 2. **Season:** April-Dec. **High:** May-Oct. **To obtain tee times:** Call golf shop. **Miscellaneous:** Reduced fees (weekdays, twilight, seniors, juniors), credit cards (MC, V, AE), BF, FF.

★½ THAMES VALLEY GOLF COURSE
PU-850 Sunninghill Ave., London, N6H 3L9, (519)661-4440. **Facility Holes:** 27. **Yards:** 6,219/5,650. **Par:** 70/74. **Course Rating:** 70.1/72.9. **Slope:** 124/126. **Green Fee:** $27. **Cart Fee:** $27/Cart. **Walking Policy:** Unrestricted walking. **Walkability:** 2. **Opened:** 1924. **Architect:** John Innes. **Season:** April-Nov. **High:** May-Sept. **To obtain tee times:** Call up to 2 days in advance. **Miscellaneous:** Reduced fees (twilight), credit cards (MC, V), BF, FF.
Special Notes: Also has a 9-hole executive course.

THUNDER BAY COUNTRY CLUB
SP-R.R. 17 1055 Oliver Rd., Thunder Bay, P7B 6C2, (807)344-8141. **E-mail:** brian@thunderbaycc.ca. **Web:** thunderbaycc.ca. **Facility Holes:** 9. **Yards:** 5,981/5,203. **Par:** 72/72. **Course Rating:** 69.1/69.0. **Slope:** 126/120. **Green Fee:** $35/$45. **Cart Fee:** $25/Cart. **Walking Policy:** Unrestricted walking. **Walkability:** 5. **Opened:** 1912. **Architect:** Stanley Thompson. **Season:** April-Oct. **High:** July-Aug. **To obtain tee times:** Call up to 2 days in advance. **Miscellaneous:** Reduced fees (seniors, juniors), range (grass), credit cards (MC, V), BF, FF.

THUNDERBIRD GOLF & ATHLETIC CLUB
PU-1927 Richardson Side Rd., Kanata, K2K 1X4, (613)836-4150. **Facility Holes:** 9. **Yards:** 1,074/1,074. **Par:** 27/27. **Green Fee:** $19. **To obtain tee times:** Call golf shop.

★★★★½ TIMBERWOLF GOLF CLUB *Value+, Pace*
PU-Maley Dr., Sudbury, P3L 1M2, (705)524-9653, 250 miles from Toronto. **E-mail:** ja@timberwolfgolf.com. **Web:** www.timberwolfgolf.com. **Facility Holes:** 18. **Yards:** 7,156/5,123. **Par:** 72/72. **Course Rating:** 74.8/65.0. **Slope:** 140/120. **Green Fee:** $45/$65. **Cart Fee:** $16/Person. **Walking Policy:** Unrestricted walking. **Walkability:** 3. **Opened:** 1999. **Architect:** Thomas McBroom. **Season:** May-Oct. **High:** June-Aug. **To obtain tee times:** Call up to 30 days in advance. **Miscellaneous:** Reduced fees (twilight), range (grass), included in fee), credit cards (MC, V, AE), BF, FF.
Notes: Ranked 1st in 2000 Best New Canadian Courses.
Reader Comments: Outstanding on all fronts ... Very very tough ... Considering the course is only 2 years old it's very lush and manicured ... This is a 'must play' ... Unbelievable value—a course like this in the 'Big City' would be 3 times the price ... Worth every penny and then some.

★★★★ UPPER CANADA GOLF COURSE *Value*
PU-R.R. No.1, Morrisburg, K0C 1X0, (613)543-2003, (800)437-2233, 50 miles from Ottawa. **Facility Holes:** 18. **Yards:** 6,900/6,008. **Par:** 72/73. **Course Rating:** 71.8/74.2. **Slope:** 121/130. **Green Fee:** $34/$39. **Cart Fee:** $30/Cart. **Walking Policy:** Unrestricted walking. **Walkability:** 1. **Opened:** 1966. **Architect:** Robbie Robinson. **Season:** April-Nov. **High:** June-Aug. **To obtain tee times:** Call golf shop. **Miscellaneous:** Reduced fees (twilight, seniors, juniors), range (grass), credit cards (MC, V, AE).
Reader Comments: Flat parkland course, but well laid out with lots of trees and water in play ... Tough track from the back tees ... Classic design with outstanding variety of holes ... Par number 4 and smile for a week ... Great greens ... Bird sanctuary next to the course.

★★★★ WHIRLPOOL GOLF COURSE
PU-3351 Niagara Pkwy., Niagara Falls, L2E 6T2, (905)356-1140, 4 miles from Niagara Falls. **E-mail:** wpgc@niagaraparks.com. **Web:** www.niagarapark.com. **Facility Holes:** 18. **Yards:** 7,019/6,392. **Par:** 72/72. **Course Rating:** 71.8/75.9. **Slope:** 126/126. **Green Fee:** $64/$69. **Cart Fee:** $32/Cart. **Walking Policy:** Unrestricted walking. **Walkability:** 2. **Opened:** 1951. **Architect:** Stanley Thompson/David Moote. **Season:** March-Nov. **High:** June-Sept. **To obtain tee times:** Call up to 180 days ahead. **Misc:** Reduced fees (weekdays, twilight), credit cards (MC, V, AE), BF, FF.
Reader Comments: Long par 4s ... Great layout ... Helicopters are annoying ... Worth the trip ... Playable for all handicaps ... A good test for long hitters, with a lot of elevation changes ... Par 5s make it fun ... Country club quality at municipal prices ... Rivals any private course.

WHISKY RUN GOLF CLUB
SP-631 Lorraine Rd., Port Colborne, L3K 5V3, (905)835-6864, (877)835-6868. **E-mail:** lou@whiskyrun.com. **Web:** www.whiskyrun.com. **Facility Holes:** 27. **Green Fee:** $30. **Cart Fee:** $15/Person. **Walking Policy:** Unrestricted walking. **Walkability:** 1. **Opened:** 1989. **Season:** March-Dec. **High:** May-Sept. **To obtain tee times:** Call up to 7 days in advance. **Miscellaneous:** Range (mats), credit cards (MC, V, AE), BF, FF.

FOX/OWL (18)
Yards: 4,899/4,094. **Par:** 70/70. **Course Rating:** 685.0/64.2. **Slope:** 106/100.
FOX/SERPENT (18)
Yards: 5,706/4,555. **Par:** 72/72. **Course Rating:** 72.6/65.6. **Slope:** 123/106.
OWL/SERPENT (18)
Yards: 4,899/4,113. **Par:** 70/70. **Course Rating:** 68.4/64.2. **Slope:** 109/97.

★★★★ **WOODEN STICKS GOLF CLUB**
PU-P. O. Box 848, Uxbridge, L9T 1N2, (905)852-4379. **E-mail:** wsticks@home.com. **Web:** www.woodensticks.com. **Facility Holes:** 18. **Opened:** 1999. **Architect:** Ron Garl. **To obtain tee times:** Call golf shop.
Notes: Ranked 3rd in 2000 Best New Canadian Courses.
Reader Comments: As good as promised … Did great job on St. Andrews holes … Worth playing at least once for the novelty of the replica holes … It's like a mini-vacation … Tricky if wind blows—lots of copy-cat holes … The original holes are better than the replicas.

PRINCE EDWARD ISLAND

BEAVER VALLEY GOLF CLUB
PU-Rte. 321, Martinvale, C0A 1G0, (902)583-3481, 34 miles from Charlottetown. **E-mail:** beavervalley@pei.sympatico.ca. **Web:** www.peisland.com/beavervalley. **Facility Holes:** 18.
Yards: 5,655/5,133. **Par:** 70/70. **Course Rating:** 68.5. **Slope:** 132/132. **Green Fee:** $16/$26.
Cart Fee: $24/Cart. **Walking Policy:** Unrestricted walking. **Walkability:** 3. **Opened:** 1996.
Architect: Norman Myers. **Season:** May-Oct. **High:** July-April. **Tee times:** Call golf shop.
Miscellaneous: Reduced fees (twilight, seniors, juniors), credit cards (MC, V, AE), BF, FF.

★★½ **BELVEDERE GOLF CLUB**
SP-1 Greensview Dr., Charlottetown, C1A 7K4, (902)368-7104. **Facility Holes:** 18. **Yards:** 6,425/5,380. **Par:** 72/74. **Course Rating:** 69.8/73.2. **Slope:** 121/123. **Green Fee:** $50/$65. **Cart Fee:** $25/Cart. **Walking Policy:** Unrestricted walking. **Walkability:** 1. **Opened:** 1902. **Architect:** Graham Cooke. **Season:** May-Nov. **To obtain tee times:** Call up to 2 days in advance.
Miscellaneous: Range (grass/mats), credit cards (MC, V).

BRUDENELL RIVER RESORT
R-, Roseneath, C0A 1R0, (902)652-8965, (800)377-8336, 30 miles from Charlottetown.
Facility Holes: 36. **Cart Fee:** $30/Cart. **Walking Policy:** Unrestricted walking. **Season:** May-Oct.
High: June-Sept. **Miscellaneous:** Range (grass), credit cards (MC, V, AE), FF.
★★★★ **BRUDENELL RIVER GOLF COURSE** (18) *Value*
Yards: 6,591/5,064. **Par:** 72/72. **Course Rating:** 72.6/69.0. **Slope:** 137/116. **Green Fee:** $48/$60. **Walkability:** 2. **Opened:** 1969. **Architect:** Robbie Robinson. **To obtain tee times:** Call up to 90 days in advance. **Miscellaneous:** Reduced fees (seniors), caddies ().
Reader Comments: A well run, fairly priced resort … Good range, good food, very hospitable people … Unique layout … Super stay & play resort … A personal favorite.
★★★★½ **DUNDARAVE GOLF COURSE** (18) *Value*
Yards: 7,284/4,997. **Par:** 72/72. **Course Rating:** 76.2/64.9. **Slope:** 139/112. **Green Fee:** $64/$80. **Walkability:** 3. **Opened:** 1999. **Architect:** Michael Hurdzan/Dana Fry. **Tee times:** Call up to 60 days ahead. **Misc:** Reduced fees (guests, twilight, seniors), lodging (160 rooms), BF.
Reader Comments: Good design, fun, challenging … 5 sets of tees make course enjoyable for all … Very pretty, big greens with lots of undulation, lots of bunkers … Very long, very hard … The resort is 1st class … Too slow & long distance green to tee … Favors slice too much but very nice.

CLYDE RIVER GOLF CLUB
PU-RR2, Clyde River, C0A 1H0, (902)675-2585, 8 miles from Charlottetown. **E-mail:** clyderiver@pei.sympatico.pe.ca. **Facility Holes:** 18. **Yards:** 6,076/5,588. **Par:** 72/72. **Course Rating:** 69.6/67.3. **Slope:** 126/122. **Green Fee:** $20/$25. **Cart Fee:** $25/Cart. **Walking Policy:** Unrestricted walking. **Season:** April-Oct. **To obtain tee times:** Call up to 2 days in advance.
Miscellaneous: Reduced fees (weekdays, twilight), credit cards (MC, V), BF, FF.

FOX MEADOW GOLF & COUNTRY CLUB
PU-167 Kinlock Rd., Stratford, C1A 7J6, (902)569-4653, (877)569-8337, 2 miles from Charlottetown. **E-mail:** info@foxmeadow.pe.ca. **Web:** www.foxmeadow.pe.ca. **Facility Holes:** 18. **Yards:** 6,836/5,389. **Par:** 72/72. **Course Rating:** 73.5/73.2. **Slope:** 127/127. **Green Fee:** $40/$60. **Cart Fee:** $29/Person. **Walking Policy:** Unrestricted walking. **Walkability:** 2. **Opened:** 2000. **Architect:** Robert Heaslip. **Season:** May-Oct. **High:** June-Sept. **To obtain tee times:** Call up to 365 days in advance. **Miscellaneous:** Reduced fees (twilight), range (grass), credit cards (MC, V), BF, FF.

★½ GLEN AFTON GOLF CLUB
PU-Nine Mile Creek R.R. 2, Cornwall, C0A 1H0, (902)675-3000, (866)675-3001, 15 miles from Charlottetown. **E-mail:** glenaftongolf@isn.net. **Web:** glenaftongolf.com. **Facility Holes:** 18. **Yards:** 5,980/5,572. **Par:** 70/70. **Course Rating:** 69.0/70.8. **Slope:** 111/118. **Green Fee:** $24/$27. **Cart Fee:** $24/Cart. **Walking Policy:** Unrestricted walking. **Walkability:** 2. **Opened:** 1973. **Architect:** William Robinson. **Season:** May-Oct. **High:** June-Sept. **To obtain tee times:** Call golf shop. **Miscellaneous:** Metal spikes, credit cards (MC, V, Interact), BF, FF.

★★★ GREEN GABLES GOLF COURSE
PU-Rte. No.6, Cavendish, C0A 1N0, (902)963-2488, 25 miles from Charlottetown. **Facility Holes:** 18. **Yards:** 6,459/5,589. **Par:** 72/74. **Course Rating:** 71.5/72.0. **Slope:** 122/124. **Green Fee:** $18/$38. **Cart Fee:** $26/Cart. **Walking Policy:** Unrestricted walking. **Walkability:** 4. **Opened:** 1939. **Architect:** Stanley Thompson. **Season:** May-Oct. **High:** June-Sept. **Tee times:** Call golf shop. **Misc:** Reduced fees (weekdays, twilight), range (grass), credit cards (MC, V). **Reader Comments:** Good value ... Near tourist sites ... Slow greens, good test of golf ... Course is inside a National Park ... Easy but enjoyable ... Lovely views ... Too many geese.

★★★★½ THE LINKS AT CROWBUSH COVE *Value+, Condition+*
PU-P.O. Box 204, Morell, C0A 1S0, (902)961-7300, (800)377-8337, 25 miles from Charlottetown. **E-mail:** crowbush@gov.pe.ca. **Web:** www.gov.pe.ca/golf. **Facility Holes:** 18. **Yards:** 6,903/4,965. **Par:** 72/72. **Course Rating:** 75.2/67.3. **Slope:** 148/120. **Green Fee:** $64/$80. **Cart Fee:** $30/Cart. **Walking Policy:** Unrestricted walking. **Walkability:** 3. **Opened:** 1993. **Architect:** Thomas McBroom. **Season:** May-Oct. **High:** June-Sept. **To obtain tee times:** Call golf shop. **Miscellaneous:** Reduced fees (guests, twilight, seniors), range (grass), credit cards (MC, V, AE), BF, FF. **Notes:** 1994 Golf Digest's Best New Canadian Course. **Reader Comments:** Can't wait to return ... I will remember this day for the rest of my life ... Worth the effort to get there ... Best scenery on the island ... YIKES! Golf heaven ... Unforgiving in spots ... If you can score well at Crowbush, you can score well anywhere ... Thought I was in Scotland.

★★★★ MILL RIVER GOLF COURSE
R-O'Leary RR#3, O'Leary, C0B 1V0, (902)859-8873, (800)377-8339, 35 miles from Summerside. **E-mail:** denard99@hotmail.com. **Facility Holes:** 18. **Yards:** 6,827/5,983. **Par:** 72/72. **Course Rating:** 75.0/70.5. **Slope:** 132/127. **Green Fee:** $33/$41. **Cart Fee:** $30/Cart. **Walking Policy:** Unrestricted walking. **Walkability:** 3. **Opened:** 1971. **Architect:** C.E. (Robbie) Robinson. **Season:** May-Oct. **High:** June-Sept. **To obtain tee times:** Call up to 180 days in advance. **Miscellaneous:** Reduced fees (twilight, seniors), range (grass), lodging (90 rooms), credit cards (MC, V, AE), BF, FF. **Reader Comments:** Very good layout, eye pleasing with abundance of flowers ... Nice resort ... A good challenge.

★½ RUSTICO RESORT GOLF & COUNTRY CLUB
R-R.R. No.3, South Rustico, C0A 1N0, (902)963-2357, (800)465-3734, 12 miles from Charlottetown. **E-mail:** rustico@auracom.com. **Web:** www.rusticoresort.com. **Facility Holes:** 18. **Yards:** 6,675/5,550. **Par:** 73/73. **Course Rating:** .0/71.8. **Slope:** 0/118. **Green Fee:** $23/$29. **Cart Fee:** $27/Cart. **Walking Policy:** Unrestricted walking. **Walkability:** 1. **Opened:** 1980. **Architect:** John Langdale. **Season:** April-Oct. **High:** July-Aug. **To obtain tee times:** Call golf shop. **Miscellaneous:** Reduced fees (weekdays, guests, twilight, seniors, juniors), metal spikes, range (grass), lodging (35 rooms), credit cards (MC, V, Diners Club).

★★½ STANHOPE GOLF & COUNTRY CLUB
PU-York R.R. No.1, Stanhope, C0A 1P0, (902)672-2842, 15 miles from Charlottetown. **Facility Holes:** 18. **Yards:** 6,600/5,785. **Par:** 72/74. **Course Rating:** 73.3/72.8. **Slope:** 131/120. **Green Fee:** $30/$45. **Cart Fee:** $29/Cart. **Walking Policy:** Unrestricted walking. **Walkability:** 2. **Opened:** 1970. **Architect:** Robbie Robinson. **Season:** May-Oct. **High:** June-Sept. **To obtain tee times:** Call golf shop. **Miscellaneous:** Reduced fees (weekdays, guests), range (grass), caddies, credit cards (MC, V, AE), BF, FF.

★★★ SUMMERSIDE GOLF & COUNTRY CLUB
PU-Bayview Dr., Summerside, C1N 5M4, (902)436-2505, (877)505-2505, 30 miles from Charlottetown. **E-mail:** sgc@auracom.com. **Facility Holes:** 18. **Yards:** 6,428/5,773. **Par:** 72/72. **Slope:** 125/119. **Green Fee:** $31/$37. **Cart Fee:** $26/Cart. **Walking Policy:** Unrestricted walking. **Walkability:** 1. **Opened:** 1926. **Architect:** John Watson. **Season:** April-Oct. **High:** June-Sept. **To obtain tee times:** Call up to 360 days in advance. **Miscellaneous:** Reduced fees (twilight), range (grass/mats), credit cards (MC, V, AE), BF, FF. **Reader Comments:** It tests everyone ... Needs a practice facility ... The first hole doesn't fit with the rest of the course, the other 17 holes are fun and challenging ... Short but challenging.

QUEBEC

BAIE MISSISQUOI GOLF CLUB
PU-321 Ave. Venise W., Venise-en-Quebec, J0J 2K0, (450)244-5932, 40 miles from Montreal.
E-mail: golfbaiemissisquoi@hotmail.com. **Facility Holes:** 18. **Yards:** 6,357/5,664. **Par:** 72/73.
Course Rating: 69.0/69.9. **Slope:** 114/113. **Green Fee:** $18/$31. **Cart Fee:** $25/Cart. **Walking
Policy:** Unrestricted walking. **Walkability:** 3. **Opened:** 1962. **Architect:** Gerry Huot. **Season:**
April-Oct. **High:** June-Aug. **To obtain tee times:** Call up to 3 days in advance. **Miscellaneous:**
Reduced fees (weekdays, twilight, juniors), range (grass/mats), credit cards (MC, V), BF, FF.

CLUB DE GOLF LACHUTE
PU-355 Ch Bethanie, Lachute, J8H 3X5, (450)562-5228. **E-mail:** 36@golflachute.com. **Web:**
www.golflachute.com. **Facility Holes:** 36. **Green Fee:** $33/$39. **Cart Fee:** $26/Cart. **To obtain
tee times:** Call golf shop.
#1 COURSE (18)
Yards: 6,711/5,644. **Par:** 72/72. **Course Rating:** 72.5/73.0. **Slope:** 150/115.
#2 COURSE (18)
Yards: 7,069/5,634. **Par:** 72/72. **Course Rating:** 72.5/73.0. **Slope:** 126/120.

CLUB DE GOLF METROPOLITAIN ANJOU B.D.F.R
PU-9555 Blvd. du Golf, Anjou, H1J 2Y2, (514)356-2666, 10 miles from Montreal. **E-mail:**
joseph@gc.aira.com. **Web:** www.golfmetropolitainanjou.com. **Facility Holes:** 36. **Yards:**
7,005/5,830. **Par:** 72/72. **Course Rating:** 73.0/73.6. **Slope:** 130/131. **Green Fee:** $30/$50.
Cart Fee: $25/Cart. **Walking Policy:** Unrestricted walking. **Walkability:** 2. **Opened:** 1998.
Architect: Graham Cooke. **Season:** April-Nov. **High:** May-Oct. **To obtain tee times:** Call up to 3
days in advance. **Miscellaneous:** Reduced fees (weekdays), range (mats), credit cards
(MC, V, AE, DC), BF, FF.
Special Notes: Also has an 18-hole executive course.

GOLF DORVAL
PU-2000 Ave. Revechon, Dorval, H9P 2S7, (514)631-6624, 5 miles from Montreal. **Facility
Holes:** 36. **Green Fee:** $20/$35. **Cart Fee:** $30/Cart. **Walking Policy:** Unrestricted walking.
Walkability: 2. **Opened:** 1982. **Architect:** Graham Cooke. **Season:** April-Oct. **High:** June-Aug.
To obtain tee times: Call golf shop. **Miscellaneous:** Reduced fees (weekdays, twilight,
seniors), range (mats), credit cards (MC, V), BF, FF.
GENTILLY (18)
Yards: 6,256/5,232. **Par:** 70/70. **Course Rating:** 69.5/69.5. **Slope:** 116/110.
★★ **OAKVILLE** (18)
Yards: 6,743/5,629. **Par:** 72/72. **Course Rating:** 71.9/71.1. **Slope:** 123/115.

GRAY ROCKS GOLF CLUB
R-525 Rue Principale, Mont Tremblant, J0T 1Z0, (819)425-2772, (800)567-6744, 78 miles
from Montreal. **E-mail:** info@grayrocks.com. **Web:** www.grayrocks.com. **Facility Holes:** 36.
Season: May-Oct. **High:** July-Sept. **To obtain tee times:** Call golf shop. **Miscellaneous:**
Reduced fees (weekdays, guests, twilight), lodging (150 rooms), credit cards (MC, V, AE), FF.
LA BELLE COURSE (18)
Yards: 6,330/5,623. **Par:** 72/72. **Course Rating:** 70.0/72.0. **Slope:** 119/118. **Green Fee:**
$30/$50. **Cart Fee:** $32/Cart. **Walking Policy:** Unrestricted walking. **Walkability:** 3. **Opened:**
1928. **Miscellaneous:** Range (mats), BF.
★★★ **LA BETE COURSE** (18)
Yards: 6,825/5,150. **Par:** 72/72. **Course Rating:** 73.0/69.8. **Slope:** 131/119. **Green Fee:**
$50/$115. **Cart Fee:** Included in green fee. **Walking Policy:** Mandatory carts. **Walkability:** 4.
Opened: 1998. **Architect:** Graham Cooke and Associates.
Reader Comments: Best resort in Canada … Glorious views … Halfway house inconvenient …
Interesting topography … A good mix of long and short holes … Second hole borders on unfair …
Some impossible holes but great setting.

★★★½ **LE CHATEAU MONTEBELLO**
R-392 Rue Notre Dame, Montebello, J0V 1L0, (819)423-4653, 60 miles from Montreal. **E-
mail:** francois.blambert@fairmont.com. **Facility Holes:** 18. **Yards:** 6,235/4,998. **Par:** 70/72.
Course Rating: 70.0/72.0. **Slope:** 129/128. **Green Fee:** $46/$65. **Cart Fee:** Included in green
fee. **Walking Policy:** Walking at certain times. **Walkability:** 4. **Opened:** 1929. **Architect:** Stanley
Thompson. **Season:** April-Oct. **High:** June-Sept. **To obtain tee times:** Call up to 7 days in
advance. **Miscellaneous:** Reduced fees (weekdays, twilight, juniors), range (grass/mats),
lodging (211 rooms), credit cards (MC, V, AE, D, DC).

Reader Comments: Some fantastic driving holes … Simply a joy to play … A Stanley Thompson classic … Should return number 9 to Thompson's original design—now its a par 3 to an elevated green with NO safety area—like hitting into a volcano … Spectacular views, fall color, very tight.

★★★★ LE CLUB DE GOLF CARLING LAKE
R-Rte. 327 N., Pine Hill, J0V 1A0, (514)337-1212, 60 miles from Montreal. E-mail: info@golf-carlinglake.com. Web: www.golfcarlinglake.com. Facility Holes: 18. Yards: 6,691/5,421. Par: 72/73. Course Rating: 71.5/71.5. Slope: 126/123. Green Fee: $44/$46. Cart Fee: $14/Person. Walking Policy: Mandatory carts. Walkability: 5. Opened: 1961. Architect: Howard Watson. Season: May-Oct. To obtain tee times: Call golf shop. Miscellaneous: Reduced fees (weekdays, twilight), metal spikes, lodging (100 rooms), credit cards (MC, V, AE), FF.
Reader Comments: Play in the fall—colors are outstanding … Scenic layout … Great design … Hidden jewel, very seldom busy … Super views in the fall … Outstanding accommodations on-site … Tough undulating greens … Good golf course … Off the beaten path … Will go back.

★★½ LE GOLF CHANTECLER
PU-2520, chemin Du Club, Ste. Adele, J8B 3C3, (450)229-3742, 30 miles from Montreal. E-mail: chantecler@golflachute.com. Web: www.golflachute.com/chantecler. Facility Holes: 18. Yards: 6,120/5,315. Par: 70/72. Course Rating: 69.0/71.0. Green Fee: $44/$50. Cart Fee: $28/Cart. Walking Policy: Walking at certain times. Walkability: 4. Opened: 1957. Season: May-Nov. High: June-Sept. To obtain tee times: Call up to 7 days in advance. Miscellaneous: Reduced fees (weekdays, guests, twilight, seniors, juniors), lodging (180 rooms), credit cards (MC, V), BF, FF.

LE MANOIR RICHELIEU
R-19 Ran Terrebonne, P.O. Box 338, Point-au-Pic, G0T 1M0, (418)665-2526, (800)665-8082, 75 miles from Quebec City. Facility Holes: 18. Yards: 6,300/5,205. Par: 71/72. Course Rating: 70.0/72.0. Slope: 131/115. Green Fee: $56/$80. Cart Fee: Included in green fee. Walking Policy: Mandatory cart. Walkability: 5. Opened: 1921. Architect: Herbert Strong. Season: May-Oct. High: June-Sept. To obtain tee times: Call golf shop. Miscellaneous: Reduced fees (weekdays, guests), lodging (400 rooms), credit cards (MC, V, AE).

★★★ LE ROYAL BROMONT GOLF CLUB
SP-400 Chemin Compton, Bromont, J2L 1E9, 450)534-5582, (888)281-0017, 45 miles from Montreal. Web: www.royalbromont.com. Facility Holes: 18. Yards: 7,036/5,181. Par: 72/72. Course Rating: 74.0/70.3. Slope: 132/123. Green Fee: $37/$57. Cart Fee: $27/Cart. Walking Policy: Unrestricted walking. Walkability: 2. Opened: 1993. Architect: Graham Cooke. Season: April-Oct. High: June-Sept. To obtain tee times: Call up to 7 days in advance. Miscellaneous: Reduced fees (twilight), range (mats), credit cards (MC, V, AE, DC, Interact), FF.
Reader Comments: Greens were fast and true … Great clubhouse … Front 9 in a field, back 9 in woods, very nice … Groomed beautifully … Great package deals for overnight accommodations with hotel very close by.

MONT STE. MARIE GOLF COURSE
PU-RR #1 Chemin De la Montagne, Lac St. Marie, J0X-1Z0, (800)567-1256, (800)567-1256. E-mail: esouligny@intrawest.com. Web: www.montstemarie.com. Facility Holes: 18. Yards: 6,609/5,432. Par: 72/74. Course Rating: 71.6/71.1. Slope: 128/122. Green Fee: $23/$35. Cart Fee: $16/Person. Walking Policy: Walking at certain times. Walkability: 3. Opened: 1976. Season: May-Oct. High: June-Aug. Tee times: Call up to 5 days in advance. Miscellaneous: Reduced fees (weekdays, twilight), range (grass), credit cards (MC, V, AE), BF, FF.

MONTREAL MUNICIPAL GOLF, LE VILLAGE
PU-4235 Viau St., Montreal, H2A 1M1, (514)872-4653. Facility Holes: 9. Yards: 1,531/1,385. Opened: 1923. Architect: Albert Murray. Season: May-Oct. To obtain tee times: Call golf shop. Miscellaneous: Reduced fees (weekdays, seniors, juniors), range (grass).

★★★½ OWL'S HEAD
R-181 Chemin Owl's Head, Mansonville, J0E 1X0, (450)292-3666, (800)363-3342, 75 miles from Montreal. E-mail: info@owlshead.com. Web: www.owlshead.com. Facility Holes: 18. Yards: 6,671/5,210. Par: 72/72. Course Rating: 72.0/69.0. Slope: 126/119. Green Fee: $35/$42. Cart Fee: $28/Cart. Walking Policy: Unrestricted walking. Walkability: 2. Opened: 1992. Architect: Graham Cooke. Season: May-Oct. To obtain tee times: Call up to 5 days in advance. Miscellaneous: Reduced fees (weekdays, twilight), range (grass/mats), lodging (45 rooms), credit cards (MC, V, AE), BF, FF.
Reader Comments: Gorgeous, great views! … Holes up & down the mountain … Crossing wind on downhill holes is a score killer … Great buy with our exchange rate … Getaway packages outstanding … Remote location.

CANADA

TREMBLANT GOLF RESORT
R-3005 Chemin Principal, Mont Tremblant, J0T 1Z0, (819)681-4653, (888)736-2526, 90 miles from Montreal. **Facility Holes:** 36. **Green Fee:** $40/$100. **Cart Fee:** Included in green fee. **Walkability:** 4. **Opened:** 1998. **Architect:** Michael Hurdzan/Dana Fry. **Season:** May-Oct. **High:** June-Sept. **To obtain tee times:** Call golf shop. **Miscellaneous:** Reduced fees (weekdays, guests, twilight), range (grass), lodging (1400 rooms), credit cards (MC, V, AE).
★★★★½ **LE DIABLE (THE DEVIL)** (18) *Condition+*
Yards: 7,056/4,651. **Par:** 71/71. **Course Rating:** 73.0/69.0. **Slope:** 131/122. **Walking Policy:** Mandatory cart.
Reader Comments: Wonderful … Tough but beautiful … Drawback is slow pace of play … Busy … Excellent and tough.
★★★★½ **LE GEANT (THE GIANT)** (18) *Condition*
Yards: 6,826/5,115. **Par:** 72/72. **Course Rating:** 73.0/68.2. **Slope:** 131/113.
Reader Comments: We must have showed up on the perfect day! Never saw the group in front of us and we played in just under 4 hours … Great golf experience … A true mountain course … Best track in Quebec … Beautiful setting, great views, keep your mind on your game … Long distance between green & tees.

SASKATCHEWAN

★★½ **COOKE MUNICIPAL GOLF COURSE**
PU-900 22nd St. E., Prince Albert, S6V 1P1, (306)763-2502, 90 miles from Saskatoon. **Facility Holes:** 18. **Yards:** 6,809/5,738. **Par:** 71/72. **Course Rating:** 71.2/72.6. **Slope:** 122/123. **Green Fee:** $19/$28. **Cart Fee:** $26/Cart. **Walking Policy:** Unrestricted walking. **Walkability:** 3. **Opened:** 1935. **Architect:** Hubert Cooke/Danny Jutras. **Season:** April-Oct. **High:** May-Aug. **To obtain tee times:** Call up to 1 day in advance. **Miscellaneous:** Reduced fees (twilight, juniors), range (grass/mats), credit cards (MC, V, AE, Debit), BF, FF.

★★½ **ELMWOOD GOLF & COUNTRY CLUB**
SP-P.O. Box 373, Swift Current, S9H 3V8, (306)773-2722. **Facility Holes:** 18. **Yards:** 6,380/5,610. **Par:** 71/74. **Course Rating:** 70.2/72.0. **Slope:** 120/119. **Green Fee:** $13/$24. **Cart Fee:** $25/Person. **Walking Policy:** Unrestricted walking. **Walkability:** 3. **Opened:** 1924. **Architect:** William Brinkworth. **Season:** April-Oct. **High:** May-Sept. **To obtain tee times:** Call golf shop. **Miscellaneous:** Metal spikes, range (grass), credit cards (MC, V, Interac).

★★½ **ESTEVAN WOODLAWN GOLF CLUB**
PU-P.O. Box 203, Estevan, S4A 2A3, (306)634-2017, 2 miles from Estevan. **E-mail:** wood-lawngolfclub@sympatico.sk.ca. **Facility Holes:** 18. **Yards:** 6,349/5,409. **Par:** 71/72. **Course Rating:** 70.0/73.0. **Slope:** 123/118. **Green Fee:** $25. **Cart Fee:** $28/Cart. **Walking Policy:** Unrestricted walking. **Walkability:** 1. **Opened:** 1945. **Architect:** Les Furber. **Season:** April-Oct. **To obtain tee times:** Call up to 2 days in advance. **Miscellaneous:** Reduced fees (juniors), range (grass), credit cards (MC, V, AE, Interact), BF, FF.

LONG CREEK GOLF & COUNTRY CLUB
PU-Box 369, Avonlea, SOH OCO, (306)868-4432. **E-mail:** rod.day@longcreek.ca. **Web:** www.longcreek.ca. **Facility Holes:** 18. **Yards:** 6,528/5,162. **Par:** 72/72. **Course Rating:** 71.5/70.6. **Slope:** 128/132. **Green Fee:** $13/$30. **Cart Fee:** $28/Cart. **Walking Policy:** Unrestricted walking. **Walkability:** 3. **Opened:** 1987. **Season:** April-Oct. **High:** June-Aug. **To obtain tee times:** Call golf shop. **Miscellaneous:** Reduced fees (weekdays, twilight, juniors), range (grass), credit cards (MC, V), BF, FF.

★★½ **MAINPRIZE REGIONAL PARK & GOLF COURSE**
PU-Box 488, Midale, S0C 1S0, (306)458-2452, 18 miles from Weyburn. **E-mail:** mainprize.park@sympatico.ca. **Web:** www.mainprizepark.com. **Facility Holes:** 18. **Yards:** 7,022/5,672. **Par:** 72/72. **Course Rating:** 74.7/72.2. **Slope:** 128/118. **Green Fee:** $17/$22. **Cart Fee:** $24/Cart. **Walking Policy:** Unrestricted walking. **Walkability:** 5. **Opened:** 1994. **Architect:** John Robinson. **Season:** May-Oct. **High:** July-Aug. **To obtain tee times:** Call up to 7 days in advance. **Miscellaneous:** Reduced fees (weekdays, juniors), range (grass), lodging (13 rooms), credit cards (MC, V, Interact), BF, FF.

★★★½ **NORTH BATTLEFORD GOLF & COUNTRY CLUB**
PU-No. 1 Riverside Drive, North Battleford, S9A 2Y3, (306)937-5659, 60 miles from Saskatoon. **E-mail:** golf@battlefords.com. **Web:** www.battlefords.com/golf. **Facility Holes:** 18. **Yards:** 6,638/5,609. **Par:** 72/74. **Course Rating:** 71.6/66.4. **Slope:** 119/112. **Green Fee:** $18/$28. **Cart Fee:** $24/Cart. **Walking Policy:** Unrestricted walking. **Walkability:** 3. **Opened:**

1969. **Architect:** Ray Buffel. **Season:** April-Oct. **High:** June-April. **To obtain tee times:** Call up to 2 days in advance. **Miscellaneous:** Reduced fees (twilight, seniors, juniors), range (grass), credit cards (MC, V), BF, FF.
Reader Comments: The par 5s were the best ... Has good version of Amen Corner ... Very good course and facilities ... Set along the Saskatchewan River ... Expensive, beautiful course ... Quickest greens in the province ... Very well maintained, a good test.

★★★★ WASKESIU GOLF COURSE

PU-P.O. Box 234, Waskesiu Lake, S0J 2Y0, (306)663-5302, 50 miles from Prince Albert. **E-mail:** lobstickgolf@sk.sympatico.ca. **Web:** www.waskesiugolf.com. **Facility Holes:** 18. **Yards:** 6,301/5,481. **Par:** 70/71. **Course Rating:** 69.7/72.1. **Slope:** 126/130. **Green Fee:** $22/$29. **Cart Fee:** $27/Cart. **Walking Policy:** Unrestricted walking. **Walkability:** 4. **Opened:** 1936. **Architect:** Stanley Thompson. **Season:** May-Oct. **High:** June-Aug. **To obtain tee times:** Call golf shop. **Miscellaneous:** Reduced fees (twilight, juniors), metal spikes, range (mats), credit cards (MC, V, AE), BF, FF.
Reader Comments: A solid challenge ... A walker's delight ... It is pristine, mature —the type of course you want to play in your bare feet. Gorgeous ... Classic old design ... Tee shots must be exactly placed ... A northern wonderland ... Many blind holes ... Take your camera.

THE WILLOWS GOLF & COUNTRY CLUB

PU-382 Cartwright Street, Saskatoon, S7T 1B1, (306)956-4653. **E-mail:** wgcc@sk.sympatico.ca. **Web:** www.willowsgolf.com. **Facility Holes:** 36. **Green Fee:** $36/$40. **Cart Fee:** $12/Person. **Walking Policy:** Unrestricted walking. **Walkability:** 2. **Opened:** 1991. **Architect:** Bill Newis. **Season:** April-Oct. **High:** April-Oct. **To obtain tee times:** Call up to 7 days in advance. **Miscellaneous:** Reduced fees (weekdays, twilight, seniors, juniors), range (grass/mats), credit cards (MC, V, AE, DC), BF, FF.
★★½ **BRIDGES/XENA COURSE** (18)
Yards: 7,070/5,564. **Par:** 72/72. **Course Rating:** 73.1/71.8. **Slope:** 130/128.
★★ **LAKES/ISLAND COURSE** (18)
Yards: 6,839/5,137. **Par:** 71/71. **Course Rating:** 72.5/69.4. **Slope:** 125/121.

Part III

Mexico

MEXICO
BAJA NORTE

BAJA COUNTRY CLUB
SP-Canon San Carlos KM. 15.25 S/N, Ensenada, (011)-52-617-75523, 8 miles from
Ensenada. **Facility Holes:** 18. **Yards:** 6,859/5,203. **Par:** 72/72. **Course Rating:** 73.1/69.5.
Slope: 131/117. **Green Fee:** $35/$45. **Walking Policy:** Mandatory carts. **Walkability:** 1.
Opened: 1991. **Architect:** Enrique Valenzuela. **Season:** Year-round. **To obtain tee times:** Call
up to 7 days in advance. **Miscellaneous:** Reduced fees (weekdays, twilight), metal spikes,
range (grass/mats), credit cards (MC, V), FF.

BAJAMAR OCEAN FRONT GOLF RESORT
R-KM 77.5 Carrectora Esenada Tijuana, Ensenada, (011)-52-615-50161, (800)225-2418,
20 miles from Ensenada. **E-mail:** patrickshawPGA@home.com. **Web:** golfbajamar.com.
Facility Holes: 27. **Green Fee:** $65/$80. **Cart Fee:** Included in green fee. **Walking Policy:**
Mandatory carts. **Walkability:** 3. **Opened:** 1975. **Architect:** David Fleming/Robert von
Hagge/Percy Clifford. **Season:** Year-round. **High:** May-Sept. **To obtain tee times:** Call up to 21
days in advance. **Miscellaneous:** Reduced fees (weekdays, guests, twilight, seniors, juniors),
range (grass), lodging (82 rooms), credit cards (MC, V, AE), BF, FF.
★★★★ **LAGOS/VISTA** (18 Combo)
Yards: 6,968/4,696. **Par:** 71/71. **Course Rating:** 74.0/68.1. **Slope:** 137/113.
★★★½ **OCEANO/LAGOS** (18 Combo)
Yards: 6,923/5,103. **Par:** 71/71. **Course Rating:** 73.6/70.8. **Slope:** 135/116. ★★★★
VISTA/OCEANO (18 Combo)
Yards: 7,165/5,175. **Par:** 72/72. **Course Rating:** 74.7/71.1. **Slope:** 138/119.
Reader Comments: Ocean front golf … This is a must play … Not an easy course … Beautiful
views from Ocean 9 … Some of the best Baja golf … 4 ocean holes breathtaking … Awesome play-
ing golf on the edge of the earth … As pretty as Pebble Beach.

MEXICALI COUNTRY CLUB
SP-PMB-5, P.O. Box 872, Calexico, 92232, Imperial County, (011)52-6563-6170, 1 mile
from Mexicali. **Facility Holes:** 18. **Yards:** 6,744/6,516. **Par:** 72/72. **Course Rating:** 72.0/71.2.
Slope: 126/123. **Green Fee:** $25/$40. **Cart Fee:** $10/Person. **Walking Policy:** Unrestricted walk-
ing. **Architect:** Larry Hughes. **Season:** Year-round. **High:** Oct.-April. **To obtain tee times:** Call
golf shop. **Miscellaneous:** Reduced fees (weekdays), range (grass), credit cards
(MC, V), BF, FF.

★★★★ **REAL DEL MAR GOLF CLUB**
R-19 1/2 KM Ensenada, Toll Rd., Tijuana, (011)-52-663-13406, (800)803-6038, 16 miles from
San Diego. **Facility Holes:** 18. **Yards:** 6,403/5,033. **Par:** 72/72. **Course Rating:** 70.5/68.5.
Slope: 131/119. **Green Fee:** $59/$69. **Cart Fee:** Included in green fee. **Walkability:** 3. **Opened:**
1993. **Architect:** Pedro Guerreca. **Season:** Year-round. **High:** June-Sept. **To obtain tee times:**
Call golf shop. **Miscellaneous:** Reduced fees (weekdays, guests, twilight, seniors, juniors),
range (grass/mats), caddies, lodging (76 rooms), credit cards (MC, V).
Reader Comments: Baja's best! Beautiful, great amenities … Rooms are better than course …
Tough course, well manicured … Very difficult course … Viva Mexico … Awesome specials …
Unique layout.

★★½ **TIJUANA COUNTRY CLUB**
SP-Blvd. Agua Caliente No. 11311, Col. Avia, Tijuana, (011)-52-668-17855, 20 miles from
San Diego. **Facility Holes:** 18. **Yards:** 6,869/5,517. **Par:** 72/72. **Course Rating:** 73.0/72.0.
Slope: 129/127. **Green Fee:** $22/$27. **Cart Fee:** $20/Person. **Walking Policy:** Unrestricted walk-
ing. **Opened:** 1927. **Architect:** William P. Bell. **To obtain tee times:** Call golf shop.
Miscellaneous: Reduced fees (twilight, seniors, juniors), metal spikes, range (grass), caddies,
credit cards (MC, V).

BAJA SUR

CABO DEL SOL
R-10.3 Carretera Transpeninsular Hwy., Cabo San Lucas, 23410, (011)-52-114-58200,
(800)386-2465, 4 miles from Cabo San Lucas. **E-mail:** bwheatley@cabodelsol.com.mx.
Facility Holes: 36. **Green Fee:** $110/$295. **Cart Fee:** Included in green fee. **Walking Policy:**
Walking at certain times. **Walkability:** 4. **Season:** Year-round. **High:** Oct.-June. **To obtain tee
times:** Call golf shop. **Miscellaneous:** Reduced fees (weekdays, guests, twilight), metal
spikes, range (grass), lodging (750 rooms), credit cards (MC, V, AE), BF, FF.
THE DESERT COURSE (18)
Opened: 2001. **Architect:** Tom Weiskopf.

MEXICO

★★★★½ **THE OCEAN COURSE** (18) *Condition+, Pace*
Yards: 7,037/4,696. **Par:** 72/72. **Course Rating:** 74.1/67.1. **Slope:** 137/111. **Opened:** 1994.
Architect: Jack Nicklaus.
Reader Comments: An outstanding course, perfectly maintained and a challenge for any level …
Service with a sense of style … Ocean holes are totally fabulous … Waves crashing, so beautiful it's
hard to play … The seaside 16th, 17th, and 18th holes are the most spectacular I have ever played.

★★★★ **CABO REAL GOLF CLUB**
PU-KM 19.5 Carreterra, Transpeninsular, San Jose Del Cabo, 23410, (011)-52-114-40040,
(011)-866-889-7406, 5 miles from Cabo San Lucas. **Web:** www.caboreal.com. **Facility Holes:**
18. **Yards:** 6,988/5,068. **Par:** 72/72. **Course Rating:** 74.1/69.4. **Slope:** 140/119. **Green Fee:**
$172/$187. **Cart Fee:** Included in green fee. **Walking Policy:** Mandatory carts. **Opened:** 1996.
Architect: Robert Trent Jones Jr. **Season:** Year-round. **To obtain tee times:** Call up to 2 days
in advance. **Miscellaneous:** Reduced fees (guests, twilight), metal spikes, range (grass), lodging (1800 rooms), credit cards (MC, V, AE), BF, FF.
Reader Comments: Excellent course, in great condition …Very expensive to play … Service was
good … Outstanding front 9, beautiful views … Nice combination of desert & ocean setting, great
challenge … Can't say enough good things about it … Pricey, but a real gem.

★★★½ **CABO SAN LUCAS COUNTRY CLUB** *Pace*
SP-Carretera Transpeninsular KM 3.6, Cabo San Lucas, 23410, (011)-52-114-34653,
(888)328-8501. **E-mail:** erjoss@aol.com. **Web:** www.golfincabo.com. **Facility Holes:** 18. **Yards:**
7,220/5,302. **Par:** 72/72. **Course Rating:** 75.4/70.9. **Slope:** 137/122. **Green Fee:** $80/$160. **Cart
Fee:** Included in green fee. **Walking Policy:** Mandatory carts. **Walkability:** 2. **Opened:** 1994.
Architect: Roy Dye. **Season:** Year-round. **To obtain tee times:** Call up to 30 days in advance.
Miscellaneous: Reduced fees (guests, twilight, juniors), range (grass/mats), lodging (62
rooms), credit cards (MC, V, AE), BF, FF.
Reader Comments: Excellent course for average golfer … All the holes began to look the same …
Long from tips … Great views, fun play … Long way from NYC to play, but worth it … Nice course,
visit the timeshares for a great deal.

★★½ **CAMPO DE GOLF SAN JOSE**
PU-Paseo Finisterra #1, San Jose del Cabo, 23400, (011)-52-114-20905, 150 miles from
La Paz. **E-mail:** cgolf@bcsi.telmex.nen.mx. **Facility Holes:** 9. **Yards:** 3,111/2,443. **Par:** 35/35.
Course Rating: 68.0/70.0. **Green Fee:** $55. **Cart Fee:** $50/Person. **Walking Policy:** Walking at
certain times. **Walkability:** 3. **Opened:** 1988. **Architect:** Mario Schjtanan/Joe Finger. **Season:**
Year-round. **High:** Nov.-Feb. **To obtain tee times:** Call golf shop. **Miscellaneous:** Credit cards
(MC, V, AE).

★★★★½ **ELDORADO GOLF COURSE** *Condition*
R-KM 20 Carretera Trans-Peninsula, San Jose del Cabo, (011)-52-114-45451, 5 miles from
Cabo San Lucas. **E-mail:** caboreal@bcs1.telemex.net.mx. **Web:** www.caboreal.com. **Facility
Holes:** 18. **Yards:** 7,050/5,771. **Par:** 72/72. **Course Rating:** 74.7/70.3. **Slope:** 143/131. **Green
Fee:** $204/$213. **Cart Fee:** Included in green fee. **Walking Policy:** Mandatory carts. **Opened:**
2000. **Architect:** Jack Nicklaus. **Season:** Year-round. **To obtain tee times:** Call up to 2 days in
advance. **Miscellaneous:** Reduced fees (guests, twilight), range (grass), credit cards (MC, V,
AE), BF, FF.
Reader Comments: Very good service … You could tell it was a Nicklaus design … Rates are high,
unless you started after 2:00 … Excellent, excellent excellent … Brings the Sea of Cortez into play
… Outstanding views, a real challenge … I'm speechless.

★★★★ **PALMILLA GOLF CLUB**
SP-Carretera Transpeninsular KM 27, San Jose del Cabo, (011)-52-114-45250, (800)386-
2465, 27 miles from San Jose del Cabo. **Facility Holes:** 27. **Green Fee:** $75/$180. **Cart Fee:**
Included in green fee. **Walking Policy:** Mandatory cart. **Miscellaneous:** Range (grass).
Opened: 1992. **Architect:** Jack Nicklaus. **Season:** Year-round. **High:** Oct.-May. **To obtain tee
times:** Call golf shop. **Miscellaneous:** Reduced fees (weekdays, guests), metal spikes, credit
cards (MC, V, AE).
ARROYO/OCEAN (18 Combo) *Pace*
Yards: 6,849/5,029. **Par:** 72/72. **Course Rating:** 73.4/62.8. **Slope:** 136/106.
MOUNTAIN/ARROYO (18 Combo)
Yards: 6,939/5,858. **Par:** 72/72. **Course Rating:** 74.3/67.1. **Slope:** 144/109.
MOUNTAIN/OCEAN (18 Combo)
Yards: 7,114/5,219. **Par:** 72/72. **Course Rating:** 74.9/68.8. **Slope:** 139/109.
Reader Comments: Real target golf … Another great Baja course, big arroyos … Stay in bounds
… Desert golf the way it was meant to be … A little too pricey … Superb 27-hole course …
Some world-class holes here … New 9 not as good as original 18 … Had the course to ourselves.

COLIMA

ISLA NAVIDAD GOLF CLUB
R-Paseo Country Club S/N, Isla Navidad, (011)-52-335-56476, 16 miles from Manzanillo.
Web: www.islanavidad.com.mx. **Facility Holes:** 27. **Green Fee:** $140/$195. **Cart Fee:** Included
in green fee. **Walking Policy:** Mandatory carts. **Opened:** 1993. **Architect:** Robert Von Hagge.
Season: Year-round. **High:** Oct.-May. **To obtain tee times:** Call up to 2 days in advance.
Miscellaneous: Reduced fees (guests), range (grass), lodging (200 rooms).credit cards
(MC, V, AE), BF, FF.
LAGOON COURSE (9)
Yards: 3,501/2,580. **Par:** 36/36. **Course Rating:** 74.0/70.8. **Slope:** 133/122. **Walkability:** 2.
MOUNTAIN COURSE (9)
Yards: 3,584/2,585. **Par:** 36/36. **Course Rating:** 73.9/69.8. **Slope:** 126/119. **Walkability:** 3.
Architect: Robert Von Hagge. **Miscellaneous:** Lodging (200 rooms).
★★★★½ **OCEAN COURSE** (9)
Yards: 3,442/2,462. **Par:** 36/36. **Course Rating:** 73.9/69.8. **Slope:** 126/119.
Reader Comments: Spectacular … Exquisite course. Perfect condition … Play golf and then go
and watch the sunset … Oasis in the middle of nowhere! … Excellent course, service and facilities
are wonderful.

★★ **LAS HADAS GOLF RESORT & MARINA**
R-Peninsula deSantiago, Manzanillo, 28860, (011)-52-333-10120, 800-2274727. **E-mail:**
hadasgolf@brisas.com.mx. **Web:** www.brisas.com.mx. **Facility Holes:** 18. **Yards:** 6,435/4,773.
Par: 71/71. **Course Rating:** 71.3/67.9. **Slope:** 139/117. **Green Fee:** $74. **Cart Fee:** $40/Cart.
Walking Policy: Walking with Caddie. **Walkability:** 1. **Opened:** 1974. **Architect:** Roy Dye/
Pete Dye. **Season:** Year-round. **High:** Nov.-April. **To obtain tee times:** Call up to 60 days in
advance. **Miscellaneous:** Reduced fees (guests), range (grass), caddies, lodging (250
rooms), credit cards (MC, V, AE), BF, FF.

GUERRERO

★★½ **ACAPULCO PRINCESS CLUB DE GOLF**
R-A.P. 1351, Acapulco, 39300, (011)-52-746-91000, 7 miles from Acapulco.
Facility Holes: 18. **Yards:** 6,355/5,400. **Par:** 72/72. **Course Rating:** 69.4/69.6.
Slope: 117/115. **Green Fee:** $70/$100. **Cart Fee:** Included in green fee. **Walking Policy:**
Mandatory carts. **Walkability:** 1. **Opened:** 1971. **Architect:** Ted Robinson. **Season:**
Year-round. **High:** Nov.-March. **To obtain tee times:** Call golf shop. **Miscellaneous:**
Reduced fees (guests, twilight, juniors), metal spikes, range (grass), lodging (1021 rooms),
credit cards (MC, V, AE, DC), BF, FF.

★★★ **CAMPO DE GOLF IXTAPA GOLF COURSE**
PU-Blvd. Ixtapa S/N, Ixtapa, 40880, (011)-52-755-31062, 3 miles from Zihuantanejo.
Facility Holes: 18. **Yards:** 6,868/5,801. **Par:** 72/72. **Course Rating:** 70.0. **Green Fee:** $50.
Cart Fee: $25/Cart. **Walking Policy:** Walking with Caddie. **Walkability:** 2. **Opened:** 1975.
Architect: Robert Trent Jones Jr. **Season:** Year-round. **High:** Dec.-April. **To obtain tee times:**
Call golf shop. **Miscellaneous:** Reduced fees (guests, twilight), range (grass/mats), caddies,
credit cards (MC, V, AE), BF, FF.
Reader Comments: Old traditional course. 2 or 3 blind shots … Watch out for alligators! Great
greens … Picturesque holes … A fun course in a fun location! You can drive through a coconut
harvest, chip over a alligator-filled lake, and putt right next to the beach! … A beauty.

★★★ **MARINA IXTAPA CLUB DE GOLF**
R-Calle De La Darsena s/n Lote 8 Final de, Ixtapa, 40880, (011)-52-755-31410, 130 miles
from Acapulco. **E-mail:** golf-dmi@travel.com.mx. **Web:** www.sidek.com.mx. **Facility Holes:** 18.
Yards: 6,793/5,228. **Par:** 72/72. **Course Rating:** 74.1/71.4. **Slope:** 138/117. **Green Fee:**
$61/$75. **Cart Fee:** Included in green fee. **Walking Policy:** Walking with Caddie. **Walkability:** 3.
Opened: 1994. **Architect:** Robert von Hagge. **Season:** Year-round. **High:** Oct.-April.
To obtain tee times: Call golf shop. **Miscellaneous:** Reduced fees (weekdays, guests, twilight,
seniors, juniors), metal spikes, range (grass/mats), caddies, credit cards (MC, V, AE), BF, FF.
Reader Comments: The most difficult course I've ever played … Great setup, friendly, challenging
… Location idyllic … Water on 14 holes! … Beautiful… Moguls, crocodiles and monkeys.

★★★½ **PIERRE MARQUES GOLF CLUB**
R-Playa Revolcadero, Acapulco, 39300, (011)-52-746-61000, 7 miles from Acapulco.
Facility Holes: 18. **Yards:** 6,557/5,197. **Par:** 72/73. **Course Rating:** 71.5/69.8. **Slope:** 127/116.
Green Fee: $70/$100. **Cart Fee:** Included in green fee. **Walking Policy:** Mandatory carts.

Walkability: 1. **Opened:** 1960. **Architect:** Percy Clifford. **Season:** Year-round. **High:** Nov.-March. **Tee times:** Call golf shop. **Misc:** Reduced fees (guests, twilight, juniors), metal spikes, range (grass), lodging (320 rooms), credit cards (MC, V, AE, DC), BF, FF.
Reader Comments: Good value … Fun golf … It is my favorite course, long good greens, marvelous experience. I am going back … Enjoyable course and resort … World class … Lots of iguanas, humid.

JALISCO

FLAMINGOS GOLF CLUB
PU-Carretera Tepic - Puerto Vallarta KM 145, Bucerias, 63732, Nayarit County, (011)52-329-65006. **E-mail:** ventasflamingosgolf.com.mx. **Web:** www.flamingosgolf.com.mx. **Facility Holes:** 18. **Yards:** 6,452/4,828. **Par:** 72/72. **Course Rating:** 72.8/68.2. **Slope:** 123/114. **Green Fee:** $62/$95. **Cart Fee:** Included in green fee. **Walking Policy:** Mandatory carts. **Walkability:** 3. **Opened:** 1978. **Architect:** Percy Clifford. **Season:** Year-round. **To obtain tee times:** Call up to 1 day in advance. **Miscellaneous:** Reduced fees (twilight, juniors), caddies, credit cards (MC, V), BF, FF.

FOUR SEASONS RESORT
R-Bahia De Banderas, Punta De Mita-Nayarit, 63734, (011)-52-329-16035, (800)332-3442, 25 miles from Puerto Vallarta. **E-mail:** sam.logan@fourseasons.com. **Web:** www.fshr.com. **Facility Holes:** 18. **Yards:** 7,014/5,037. **Par:** 72/72. **Course Rating:** 72.9/68.4. **Slope:** 131/116. **Green Fee:** $160. **Cart Fee:** Included in green fee. **Walking Policy:** Mandatory carts. **Walkability:** 2. **Opened:** 1999. **Architect:** Jack Nicklaus. **Season:** Year-round. **To obtain tee times:** Call golf shop. **Miscellaneous:** Reduced fees (twilight), range (grass), lodging (140 rooms), credit cards (MC, V, AE, D), BF, FF.
Special Notes: Formerly Punta Mita.

★★★½ MARINA VALLARTA CLUB DE GOLF
SP-Paseo de la Marina S/N, Puerto Vallarta, 48354, (011)-52-322-10073, 5 miles from Puerto Vallarta. **E-mail:** foremexico@corclub.com. **Web:** www.foremexico.com. **Facility Holes:** 18. **Yards:** 6,701/5,279. **Par:** 71/72. **Course Rating:** 73.2/70.1. **Slope:** 136/117. **Green Fee:** $85/$130. **Cart Fee:** Included in green fee. **Walking Policy:** Mandatory carts. **Opened:** 1989. **Architect:** Joe Finger. **Season:** Year-round. **Tee times:** Call up to 30 days in advance. **Misc:** Reduced fees (twilight), range (grass), caddies, credit cards (MC, V, AE), BF, FF.
Reader Comments: Best resort in Puerto Vallarta … Great design, caddies are wonderful …. Nearby airport distracting … Ocean views great—course overpriced … Great practice facility … Alligators in the water hazards … Narrow, small greens very playable.

VISTA VALLARTA CLUB DE GOLF
PU-Cirevito Universidad #653 Col. San Nicolas, Puerto Vallarta, 48390, (011)52-329-00030, 7 miles from Puerto Vallarta. **E-mail:** foremexico@ourclub.com. **Web:** www.foremexico.com. **Facility Holes:** 18. **Yards:** 7,057/5,251. **Par:** 72/72. **Course Rating:** 73.4/69.4. **Slope:** 136/115. **Green Fee:** $105/$160. **Cart Fee:** Included in green fee. **Walking Policy:** Mandatory carts. **Opened:** 2001. **Architect:** Jack Nicklaus. **Season:** Year-round. **To obtain tee times:** Call up to 30 days in advance. **Miscellaneous:** Reduced fees (twilight, juniors), range (grass), credit cards (MC, V, AE), BF, FF.

MORELOS

COUNTRY CLUB COCOYOC
R-Circuito Del Hombre S/N, Cocoyoc, 62738, (011)-52-735-61188, 65 miles from Mexico City. **Facility Holes:** 18. **Yards:** 6,287/5,250. **Par:** 72/72. **Course Rating:** 69.7/68.1. **Slope:** 127/116. **Green Fee:** $65. **Cart Fee:** $15/Cart. **Walking Policy:** Unrestricted walking. **Walkability:** 3. **Opened:** 1977. **Architect:** Mario Schjetnan. **Season:** Year-round. **Tee times:** Call golf shop. **Misc:** Reduced fees (weekdays, guests), range, caddies, cards (MC, V, AE), FF.

OAXACA

TANGOLUNDA GOLF COURSE
PU-Domicilio Conocido Bahia de Tangolunda, Bahia de Huatulco, 70989, (011)-52-958-10037, 150 miles from Oaxaca. **E-mail:** tangolundagolfcourse@hotmail.com. **Facility Holes:** 18. **Yards:** 6,870/5,605. **Par:** 72/72. **Rating:** 74.6/73.8. **Slope:** 131/126. **Green Fee:** $48/$65. **Cart Fee:** $39/Cart. **Walkability:** 5. **Opened:** 1991. **Architect:** Mario Schjetnan. **Season:** Year-round. **Tee times:** Call. **Misc:** Reduced fees (juniors), metal spikes, range (grass), caddies, credit cards (MC, V, AE).

MEXICO

QUINTANO ROO

★★½ **POK-TA-POK CLUB DE GOLF CANCUN**
R-KM 7.5 Blvd. Kukulcan, Hotel Zone, Cancun, 77500, (011)-52-988-31277, (988)312-77.
E-mail: poktapok@sybcom.com. **Web:** cancungolfclub.com. **Facility Holes:** 18. **Yards:**
6,602/5,244. **Par:** 72/72. **Course Rating:** 71.9/71.0. **Slope:** 121/120. **Green Fee:** $75/$105. **Cart
Fee:** Included in green fee. **Walking Policy:** Walking at certain times. **Walkability:** 2. **Architect:**
Robert Trent Jones Jr. **Season:** Year-round. **Tee times:** Call golf shop. **Miscellaneous:**
Reduced fees (guests, twilight), range (grass), caddies, credit cards (MC, V, AE), BF, FF.

SINALOA

★★★ **EL CID GOLF & COUNTRY CLUB**
R-Av. Camaron Sabalo S/N, Mazatlan, 82110, (011)-52-691-35611, (888)521-6011. **E-mail:**
cclub@elcid.com.mx. **Web:** www.elcid.com.mx. **Facility Holes:** 27. **Green Fee:** $55/$70.
Cart Fee: $35/Cart. **Walking Policy:** Walking at certain times. **Walkability:** 1. **Opened:** 1973.
Architect: Lee Trevino. **Season:** Year-round. **High:** Nov.-May. **To obtain tee times:** Call golf
shop. **Miscellaneous:** Reduced fees (guests, seniors, juniors), range (grass), caddies, lodging
(1300 rooms), credit cards (MC, V, AE), BF, FF.
EL MORO/CASTILLA (18 Combo)
Yards: 6,623/5,417. **Par:** 72/72. **Course Rating:** 71.8/71.1. **Slope:** 131/127.
MARINA/CASTILLA (18 Combo)
Yards: 6,657/5,220. **Par:** 72/72. **Course Rating:** 71.4/68.8. **Slope:** 124/122.
MARINA/EL MORO (18 Combo)
Yards: 6,880/5,329. **Par:** 72/72. **Course Rating:** 72.7/70.7. **Slope:** 126/124.
Reader Comments: Great caddies … Fun place, will go often … Narrow fairways. Greens difficult
to read … Saw about 50 iguanas on the course … Many nice homes line the course. Only hit two of
them … Good test of golf, hard to find some tees.

ESTRELLA DEL MAR GOLF AND BEACH RESORT COMM.
R-Camino Isla De la piedra KM10, Mazatlan, 82280, (011)-52-698-23300, (888)587-0609.
Facility Holes: 18. **Yards:** 7,002/5,442. **Par:** 72/72. **Course Rating:** 73.4/68.9. **Slope:** 125/113.
Green Fee: $65/$105. **Cart Fee:** Included in green fee. **Walkability:** 3. **Opened:** 1996.
Architect: Robert Trent Jones Jr. **Season:** Year-round. **High:** Nov.-April. **To obtain tee times:**
Call up to 30 days in advance. **Miscellaneous:** Reduced fees (guests, twilight), range (grass),
lodging (60 rooms), credit cards (MC, V), BF, FF.

SONORA

★★★½ **CLUB DE GOLF SAN CARLOS**
SP-Int.Campo deGolf ent.LomaBonita ySolimar, San Carlos, 85506, (011)-52-622-61102,
12 miles from Guaymas, Sonora. **E-mail:** golfmsccsidek.com.mx. **Facility Holes:** 18. **Yards:**
6,542/5,072. **Par:** 72/72. **Course Rating:** 71.0/68.3. **Slope:** 118/114. **Green Fee:** $40/$50. **Cart
Fee:** Included in green fee. **Walking Policy:** Mandatory carts. **Walkability:** 1. **Opened:** 1977.
Architect: Roy Dye. **Season:** Year-round. **High:** Oct.-April. **To obtain tee times:** Call golf shop.
Miscellaneous: Reduced fees (twilight, juniors), range (grass), lodging (125 rooms), credit
cards (MC, V), BF, FF.
Reader Comments: Good layout … Beautiful ocean views … Very nice clubhouse. Course
exceeded expectations.
Special Notes: Formerly Marina San Carlos Campo de Golf.

Part IV

The Islands

ABACO

★★★ TREASURE CAY GOLF CLUB
R-P.O. Box AB 22183, Treasure Cay, (242)365-8045, (800)327-1584. **E-mail:** info@treasurecay.com. **Web:** www.treasurecay.com. **Facility Holes:** 18. **Yards:** 6,985/5,690. **Par:** 72/73. **Green Fee:** $50/$60. **Cart Fee:** $25/Person. **Walking Policy:** Walking at certain times. **Walkability:** 1. **Opened:** 1965. **Architect:** Dick Wilson. **Season:** Year-round. **High:** Dec.-April. **To obtain tee times:** Call golf shop. **Miscellaneous:** Reduced fees (guests), range (grass), lodging (96 rooms), credit cards (MC, V, AE), BF, FF.
Reader Comments: Play this for unhurried tranquility … Desert-type course, windy … Generally very tight … Very little play … Kind of steep but it's all there is.

ARUBA

★★★★ TIERRA DEL SOL COUNTRY CLUB *Pace*
R-Malmokweg z/n, (011)297867-800, 10 miles from Oranjestad. **E-mail:** annbrown_tds @hotmail.com. **Web:** tdsteetime@setarnet.aw. **Facility Holes:** 18. **Yards:** 6,811/5,002. **Par:** 71/71. **Course Rating:** 74.2/70.6. **Slope:** 132/121. **Green Fee:** $98/$133. **Cart Fee:** Included in green fee. **Walking Policy:** Mandatory carts. **Walkability:** 4. **Opened:** 1995. **Architect:** Robert Trent Jones Jr. **Season:** Year-round. **High:** Dec.-April. **To obtain tee times:** Call up to 365 days in advance. **Miscellaneous:** Reduced fees (guests, twilight, juniors), range (grass), lodging (100 rooms), credit cards (MC, V, AE, D), BF, FF.
Reader Comments: Lots of cactus and beautiful ocean views … You can see the ocean on virtually all holes … Island tradewinds wreaks havoc with your ball … You have to become creative with your shots … Bring your knockdown shot … Difficult to get tee times, plan ahead … Wonderful setting.

BARBADOS

★★★★½ ROYAL WESTMORELAND BARBADOS
SP-Westmoreland, St. James, (246)419-7242, 5 miles from Bridgeton. **E-mail:** greg.schofield@royal-westmoreland. **Facility Holes:** 18. **Yards:** 6,870/5,333. **Par:** 72/72. **Course Rating:** 74.4/72.5. **Slope:** 130/124. **Green Fee:** $110/$220. **Cart Fee:** Included in green fee. **Walking Policy:** Unrestricted walking. **Walkability:** 4. **Opened:** 1994. **Architect:** Robert Trent Jones Jr. **Season:** Year-round. **To obtain tee times:** Call golf shop. **Miscellaneous:** Reduced fees (guests), range (grass), caddies, credit cards (MC, V, AE), BF, FF.
Reader Comments: Incredible experience … Greens young … Great views … Putts break to ocean! … Great island golf.

★★ SANDY LANE GOLF CLUB
R-Sandy Lane, St. James, (246)432-1311. **Facility Holes:** 18. **Yards:** 6,553/5,520. **Par:** 72/72. **Course Rating:** 70.2/70.8. **Slope:** 122/120. **Green Fee:** $55/$85. **Walking Policy:** Unrestricted . **Opened:** 1961. **Architect:** Robertson Ward. **Season:** Year-round. **High:** Dec.-April. **Tee times:** Call golf shop. **Misc:** Reduced fees (guests, twilight), , range, caddies, cards (MC, V, AE).

BERMUDA

★★★ BELMONT GOLF & COUNTRY CLUB
R-P.O. Box WK 251, Warwick, WKBX, (441)236-6400, 5 miles from Hamilton. **E-mail:** alex.belmont@ibl.bm. **Facility Holes:** 18. **Yards:** 5,800/4,900. **Par:** 70/72. **Course Rating:** 68.6/67.7. **Slope:** 128/116. **Green Fee:** $68. **Cart Fee:** $22/Person. **Walking Policy:** Walking at certain times. **Walkability:** 2. **Opened:** 1928. **Architect:** Devereux Emmet. **Season:** Year-round. **High:** April-Oct. **To obtain tee times:** Call golf shop. **Miscellaneous:** Reduced fees (guests, twilight, juniors), range (mats), credit cards (MC, V, AE), BF, FF.
Reader Comments: What a place, can't wait to go back, hooked … Short course, wind makes holes difficult … Somewhat quirky … Easy to play, no frills … Great views, beautiful condition … Blind holes, elevated greens. Very challenging for the average duffer … Excellent hotel, funky course setup, nice views.

★★★★½ THE MID OCEAN CLUB
SP-1 Mid Ocean Club Dr., St. George's, GE02, (441)293-0330, 7 miles from Hamilton.
E-mail: prshop@ibl.bm. **Facility Holes:** 18. **Yards:** 6,512/5,042. **Par:** 71/71. **Course Rating:** 72.0/69.5. **Slope:** 138/121. **Green Fee:** $190. **Cart Fee:** $45/Cart. **Walking Policy:** Unrestricted walking. **Walkability:** 5. **Opened:** 1922. **Architect:** C.B. Macdonald. **Season:** Year-round. **High:** May-Sept. **To obtain tee times:** Call golf shop. **Miscellaneous:** Range (grass/mats), caddies, credit cards (MC, V, AE).
Reader Comments: Best course in the Atlantic! … Absolutely first rate golf course … The caddies made this golf course a very memorable experience … The scenery was exquisite … The wind she does blow … Great 3 last holes … The best in Bermuda … 4 or 5 amazing holes.

★★★★ OCEAN VIEW GOLF COURSE
PU-2 Barkers Hill Rd, Devonshire, DVBX, (441)295-9077, 3 miles from Hamilton.
Facility Holes: 18. **Yards:** 2,940/2,450. **Par:** 35/36. **Course Rating:** 67.3/67.3. **Slope:** 122/119. **Green Fee:** $48/$50. **Cart Fee:** $22/Person. **Walking Policy:** Walking at certain times. **Walkability:** 3. **Season:** Year-round. **Tee times:** Call up to 14 days in advance. **Miscellaneous:** Reduced fees (twilight, juniors), range (grass/mats), credit cards (MC, V, AE), BF, FF.
Reader Comments: Bring lots of balls … Scenic, tricky, nice people … Good challenge, nice views … Breathtaking ocean views.

★★★½ PORT ROYAL GOLF COURSE
PU-Middle Rd., Southampton, SNBX, (441)234-0972. **Facility Holes:** 18. **Yards:** 6,561/5,577. **Par:** 71/72. **Course Rating:** 72.0/72.5. **Slope:** 134/127. **Green Fee:** $72/$82. **Cart Fee:** $50/Person. **Walking Policy:** Walking at certain times. **Walkability:** 3. **Opened:** 1970. **Architect:** Robert Trent Jones. **Season:** Year-round. **High:** April-Dec. **To obtain tee times:** Call up to 7 days in advance. **Miscellaneous:** Reduced fees (twilight, seniors, juniors), range (grass/mats), credit cards (MC, V, AE), BF, FF.
Reader Comments: Beautiful scenery, blue water, pink sand and challenging holes … Best test golf on island … Windy … Bring a camera … Challenging but fair … 16th is a great par 3 … A must play with a world class par 3 that will scare you … Nice to walk … Adjust putting stroke for sandy greens.

★★★ RIDDELL'S BAY GOLF & COUNTRY CLUB
SP-26 Riddell's Bay Rd., Warwick, WK04, (441)238-1060. **E-mail:** rbgcc@northrock.bay. **Web:** bermudashorts.bm/riddellsbay/. **Facility Holes:** 18. **Yards:** 5,668/5,324. **Par:** 70/72. **Course Rating:** 66.6/69.7. **Slope:** 118/114. **Green Fee:** $135. **Cart Fee:** Included in green fee. **Walking Policy:** Mandatory carts. **Walkability:** 2. **Opened:** 1922. **Architect:** Devereux Emmett. **Season:** Year-round. **Tee times:** Call golf shop. **Miscellaneous:** Credit cards (MC, V, AE), BF, FF.
Reader Comments: Very scenic around the course, Nice people there … Beautiful course … Nice experience … Beautiful, relaxed pace of play (no rush).

★★★★ SOUTHAMPTON PRINCESS GOLF COURSE
R-101 South Shore Rd., Southampton, SN02, (441)239-6952. **Facility Holes:** 18. **Yards:** 2,737/2,229. **Par:** 54/54. **Course Rating:** 53.7/53.2. **Slope:** 81/77. **Green Fee:** $66. **Cart Fee:** Included in green fee. **Walking Policy:** Walking at certain times. **Walkability:** 4. **Opened:** 1971. **Architect:** Ted Robinson. **Season:** Year-round. **Tee times:** Call golf shop. **Miscellaneous:** Reduced fees (guests, twilight, juniors), credit cards (MC, V, AE), BF, FF.
Reader Comments: Great irons test … Great views … Best executive course in the world … Very pretty course, fun to play … Challenging, accuracy needed.

★★★ ST. GEORGE'S GOLF COURSE
PU-1 Park Rd., St. George's, GE03, (441)297-8067, 1 mile from St. George's.
E-mail: sggc@northrock.bm. **Facility Holes:** 18. **Yards:** 4,043/3,344. **Par:** 62/62. **Course Rating:** 62.8/62.8. **Slope:** 103/100. **Green Fee:** $50/$55. **Cart Fee:** $22/Person. **Walking Policy:** Walking at certain times. **Walkability:** 3. **Opened:** 1985. **Architect:** Robert Trent Jones. **Season:** Year-round. **High:** April-Oct. **To obtain tee times:** Call up to 7 days in advance. **Miscellaneous:** Reduced fees (twilight, juniors), credit cards (MC, V, AE), BF, FF.
Reader Comments: Outstanding ocean view on first … Some of the par 4s could be par 3s … Short fun course … Very tight layout … Hidden gem.

CAYMAN ISLANDS

★★★½ **THE LINKS AT SAFE HAVEN**
SP-, Grand Cayman, (345)949-5988. **E-mail:** proshop@safehavenlimited.com. **Web:** www.safehavenlimited.com. **Facility Holes:** 18. **Yards:** 6,606/4,765. **Par:** 71/71. **Course Rating:** 75.1/71.2. **Slope:** 139/128. **Green Fee:** $110/$120. **Cart Fee:** Included in green fee. **Walking Policy:** Walking at certain times. **Walkability:** 1. **Opened:** 1994. **Architect:** Roy Case. **Season:** Year-round. **High:** Dec.-May. **To obtain tee times:** Call up to 1 day in advance. **Miscellaneous:** Reduced fees (twilight), range (grass), credit cards (MC, V, AE), BF, FF.
Reader Comments: Great layout! ... Plenty of water, on the ocean, windy ... No greenside bunkers ... Warm and beautiful ... Practice range with floating balls! ... Expensive but location explains it ... Nice views of the ocean.

DOMINICAN REPUBLIC

BAVARO RESORT GOLF COURSE
R-Bavaro Punta Cana, Augueg, (809)686-5797. **Facility Holes:** 18. **Yards:** 6,710/5,608. **Par:** 72/72. **Course Rating:** 73.5/74.0. **Slope:** 145/137. **Green Fee:** $37/$63. **Walking Policy:** Walking at certain times. **Walkability:** 1. **Season:** Year-round. **High:** Nov.-April. **To obtain tee times:** Call golf shop. **Miscellaneous:** Range (grass), credit cards (MC, V).

★★★★½ **CAMPO DE GOLF PLAYA GRANDE** *Value, Condition, Pace+*
R-, Rio San Juan, (809)582-3302, 48 miles from Puerto Plata Airport. **Facility Holes:** 18. **Yards:** 6,295/4,483. **Par:** 72/72. **Course Rating:** 74.9/69.4. **Slope:** 126/111. **Green Fee:** $60/$90. **Cart Fee:** Included in green fee. **Walking Policy:** Unrestricted walking. **Walkability:** 4. **Opened:** 1997. **Architect:** Robert Trent Jones. **Season:** Year-round. **High:** Nov.-April. **To obtain tee times:** Call golf shop. **Miscellaneous:** Reduced fees (guests), caddies, lodging (300 rooms), credit cards (MC, V, AE), BF, FF.
Reader Comments: Pebble Beach of the Caribbean! ... Most scenic I've ever played ... Gold tees really tough ... Oh baby, why can't this be close to home ... Fantastic vistas ... Beautiful atmosphere and beach.
Special Notes: Formerly Caribbean Village Playa Grande Golf Course.

CASA DE CAMPO RESORT & COUNTRY CLUB
R-, La Romana, (809)523-8115, (888)212-5073, 45 miles from Santo Domingo. **Facility Holes:** 36. **Cart Fee:** Included in green fee. **Architect:** Pete Dye. **Season:** Year-round. **High:** Dec.-April. **To obtain tee times:** Call golf shop. **Miscellaneous:** Reduced fees (guests, twilight, juniors), metal spikes, range (grass), caddies, lodging (285 rooms), credit cards (MC, V, AE).
★★★★½ **LINKS COURSE** (18) *Value, Condition, Pace*
Yards: 6,602/4,410. **Par:** 71/71. **Course Rating:** 70.0/65.7. **Slope:** 124/113. **Green Fee:** $90/$100. **Walking Policy:** Mandatory cart. **Walkability:** 2. **Opened:** 1976.
Reader Comments: Great caddies make tricky greens easy ... Definitely the best, I'll go back anytime ... Great lodging and food ... We enjoyed an all inclusive package which exceeded all expectations ... Fabulous ... Use all clubs ... Great links course, very fair to play ... Good course, not one of my favorites.
★★★★★ **TEETH OF THE DOG** (18)
Yards: 6,989/4,779. **Par:** 72/72. **Course Rating:** 74.1/72.9. **Slope:** 140/130. **Green Fee:** $90/$150. **Walkability:** 3. **Opened:** 1970.
Reader Comments: Awesome course ... Paradise ... Great caddies, great views, great golf ... As nice and pretty as you can play ... Nelson was a great caddie ... Loved the views ... 7 spectacular ocean holes ... The ultimate experience for very rich people.

CAYACOA COUNTRY CLUB
PU-Autopista Duarte Kilometer 20, Santo Domingo, (809)372-7441. **Facility Holes:** 18. **Yards:** 6,726/5,307. **Par:** 72/72. **Course Rating:** 73.5/71.9. **Slope:** 139/130. **Green Fee:** $30/$55. **Cart Fee:** Included in green fee. **Walking Policy:** Walking at certain times. **Walkability:** 1. **Season:** Year-round. **High:** Nov.-April. **To obtain tee times:** Call golf shop. **Miscellaneous:** Reduced fees (twilight, juniors), range (grass), caddies, credit cards (MC, V, AE).

★★½ **THE CLUB ON THE GREEN**
PU-Playa Dorado Golf Course, Puerto Plata, (809)320-4262. **Web:** www.playadoradogolf.com. **Facility Holes:** 18. **Yards:** 6,730/5,361. **Par:** 72/72. **Course Rating:** 71.5/69.9. **Slope:** 130/126. **Walking Policy:** Unrestricted walking. **Walkability:** 1. **Opened:** 1972. **Architect:** Robert Trent Jones. **Season:** Year-round. **High:** Sept.-May. **To obtain tee times:** Call

up to 30 days in advance. **Miscellaneous:** Reduced fees (guests, juniors), range , caddies, credit cards (MC, V), BF, FF.
Special Notes: Formerly Radisson Puerto Plata Golf Resort.

COCOTAL GOLF & COUNTRY CLUB
R-Playas de Bavaro, Punta Cana, (809)687-4653. **E-mail:** cocotal@codetef.net.co. **Facility Holes:** 18. **Yards:** 7,285/5,712. **Par:** 72/72. **Course Rating:** 75.2/73.1. **Slope:** 131/128. **Green Fee:** $85/$95. **Cart Fee:** Included in green fee. **Walking Policy:** Mandatory carts. **Walkability:** 1. **Opened:** 2000. **Architect:** Jose (Pepe) Gancedo. **Season:** Year-round. **High:** Dec.-April. **To obtain tee times:** Call golf shop. **Miscellaneous:** Reduced fees (guests), range (grass), lodging (1500 rooms), credit cards (MC, V, AE), BF, FF.

METRO COUNTRY CLUB
R-Juan Dolio, San Pedro De Macoris, (809)526-3515, 30 miles from Santo Domingo. **E-mail:** mcountry@codetel.net.do. **Web:** www.atlanticametro.com. **Facility Holes:** 18. **Yards:** 6,398/5,262. **Par:** 72/72. **Course Rating:** 70.5/69.9. **Slope:** 123/115. **Green Fee:** $55. **Cart Fee:** $25/Cart. **Walking Policy:** Walking at certain times. **Walkability:** 2. **Opened:** 1995. **Architect:** Charles Ankrom. **Season:** Year-round. **High:** Jan.-May. **To obtain tee times:** Call golf shop. **Miscellaneous:** Reduced fees (twilight), range (grass), caddies, credit cards (MC, V, AE).

GRAND BAHAMA ISLAND

FORTUNE HILLS GOLF & COUNTRY CLUB
R-P.O. Box 5-42619, Freeport, (242)373-4500. **Facility Holes:** 9. **Yards:** 6,916/6,164. **Par:** 72/74. **Course Rating:** 71.5/75.6. **Slope:** 116/125. **Green Fee:** $43. **Cart Fee:** $44/Cart. **Walking Policy:** Mandatory carts. **Walkability:** 2. **Opened:** 1971. **Architect:** Joe Lee. **Season:** Year-round. **High:** Jan.-April. **To obtain tee times:** Call up to 1 day in advance. **Miscellaneous:** Range (mats), lodging (24 rooms), credit cards (MC, V, D).

★★★½ THE LUCAYAN RESORT
R-P.O. Box F42500, Freeport, (242)373-1066, (800)582-2926, 2 miles from Freeport. **Facility Holes:** 18. **Yards:** 6,780/5,978. **Par:** 72/72. **Course Rating:** 72.1/74.5. **Slope:** 128/129. **Green Fee:** $96. **Cart Fee:** Included in green fee. **Walking Policy:** Walking at certain times. **Walkability:** 2. **Opened:** 1962. **Architect:** Dick Wilson. **Season:** Year-round. **High:** Oct.-March. **To obtain tee times:** Call golf shop. **Miscellaneous:** Reduced fees (guests, juniors), range (grass), caddies, lodging (600 rooms), credit cards (MC, V, AE, D).
Reader Comments: Nice resort course, green on No. 17 is huge ... Best in Bahamas ... Tough but fair, friendly folks ... A beautiful surprise ... Best course on the island ... Each fairway well separated by trees ... Tight fairways, plenty of trees & sand.

RESORT AT BAHAMIA
R-P.O. Box F-40207, Freeport, (242)350-7000, 52 miles from Palm Beach. **E-mail:** tomalfano@hotmail.com. **Facility Holes:** 36. **Green Fee:** $65/$95. **Walking Policy:** Mandatory carts. **Walkability:** 1. **Opened:** 1964. **Architect:** Jim Fazio. **Season:** Year-round. **Tee times:** Call golf shop. **Misc:** Reduced fees (guests, juniors), range (grass), lodging (965 rooms), credit cards (MC, V, AE, D), BF, FF.
★★★ EMERALD COURSE (18)
Yards: 6,679/5,722. **Par:** 72/75. **Course Rating:** 72.3/73.1. **Slope:** 121/121.
Reader Comments: Tough rough. Makes you play in the middle ... Bring a lot of balls ... Expect more in the Bahamas ... Very courteous and accommodating staff ... Typical tourist course ... Long challenging course ... Defined by palm-tree lined fairways ... Great pace of play.
★★½ RUBY COURSE (18)
Yards: 6,750/5,622. **Par:** 72/74. **Course Rating:** 72.4/72.4. **Slope:** 122/120. **Cart Fee:** Included.

JAMAICA

CAYMANAS GOLF COURSE
SP-Spanish Town, St. Catherine, (876)922-3388, 10 miles from Kingston. **E-mail:** play@caymanasgolfclub.com. **Web:** www.caymanasgolfclub.com. **Facility Holes:** 18. **Yards:** 6,732/5,512. **Par:** 72/72. **Course Rating:** 73.8/73.1. **Slope:** 133/127. **Green Fee:** $35/$50. **Cart Fee:** $20/Cart. **Walking Policy:** Unrestricted walking. **Walkability:** 3. **Opened:** 1958. **Architect:** Howard Watson. **Season:** Year-round. **Tee times:** Call golf shop. **Misc:** Reduced fees (weekdays, guests, juniors), range (grass), caddies, credit cards (MC, V, AE), BF, FF.

THE ISLANDS

★★★½ HALF MOON GOLF, TENNIS & BEACH CLUB
R-Rose Hall, Montego Bay, (876)953-2560, (800)626-0592, 7 miles from Montego Bay.
Facility Holes: 18. **Yards:** 7,119/5,148. **Par:** 72/72. **Course Rating:** 73.7/68.9. **Slope:** 127/115.
Green Fee: $130. **Cart Fee:** $30/Person. **Walking Policy:** Walking with Caddie. **Walkability:** 1.
Opened: 1961. **Architect:** Robert Trent Jones. **Season:** Year-round. **High:** Dec.-April. **To obtain tee times:** Call golf shop. **Miscellaneous:** Reduced fees (guests), metal spikes, range (grass), caddies, lodging (425 rooms), credit cards (MC, V, AE).
Reader Comments: Great caddies ... No ocean holes but luxurious ... Food good, service everywhere ... You would swear they trimmed the greens and fairways with scissors ... Wind adds to difficulty ... Super, a pleasure to play ... Pricey, good walking course.

★★½ NEGRIL HILLS GOLF CLUB
PU-Negril P.O., Westmoreland, (876)957-4638. **Facility Holes:** 9. **Yards:** 6,333/5,036. **Par:** 72/72. **Green Fee:** $58. **Cart Fee:** $35/Cart. **Walking Policy:** Unrestricted walking. **Walkability:** 5. **Opened:** 1994. **Architect:** Bob Simmons. **Season:** Year-round. **High:** Dec.-April. **To obtain tee times:** Call golf shop. **Miscellaneous:** Reduced fees (guests), metal spikes, range (grass), caddies, credit cards (MC, V).

THE RITZ-CARLETON WHITE WITCH GOLF COURSE
PU-1 Ritz-Carlton Dr., Rose Hall, (876)518-0174, 10 miles from Montego Bay. **E-mail:** white-witchgolf@rcrosehall.com. **Web:** www.rosehall.org. **Facility Holes:** 18. **Yards:** 6,718/5,397. **Par:** 71/71. **Course Rating:** 74.0/73.2. **Slope:** 139/126. **Green Fee:** $125/$139. **Cart Fee:** Included in green fee. **Walking Policy:** Mandatory carts. **Walkability:** 5. **Opened:** 2000. **Architect:** Robert Von Hagge. **Season:** Year-round. **High:** Dec.-April. **To obtain tee times:** Call up to 7 days in advance. **Miscellaneous:** Reduced fees (guests, twilight, juniors), included in fee), credit cards (MC, V, AE, D, DC), BF, FF.

★★★★ SANDALS GOLF & COUNTRY CLUB
SP-Upton, Ocho Rios, (876)975-0119, 2 miles from Ocho Rios. **E-mail:** sgcgolf@cwjamaica.com. **Web:** www.sandals.com. **Facility Holes:** 18. **Yards:** 6,311/4,961. **Par:** 71/72. **Course Rating:** 128.0/120.0. **Slope:** 70.9/69.3. **Green Fee:** $100. **Walking Policy:** Walking with Caddie. **Walkability:** 3. **Opened:** 1954. **Architect:** P.K. Saunders. **Season:** Year-round. **High:** Jan.-March. **To obtain tee times:** Call golf shop. **Miscellaneous:** Reduced fees (guests), metal spikes, range (grass/mats), caddies, credit cards (MC, V, AE, D), BF, FF.
Reader Comments: Excellent caddies, beautiful setting ... Open, not a lot of trouble ... Good views, rolling terrain, wet in December ... Foliage outstanding ... Golfing in paradise ... Friendly locals ... Listen to your caddy.

★★★½ SUPER CLUBS GOLF CLUB AT RUNAWAY BAY
R-Runaway Bay P.O. Box 58, St. Ann, (876)973-7319, 15 miles from Ocho Rios. **Facility Holes:** 18. **Yards:** 6,871/5,389. **Par:** 72/72. **Course Rating:** 72.4/70.3. **Slope:** 124/117. **Green Fee:** $50/$80. **Cart Fee:** $35/Cart. **Walking Policy:** Unrestricted walking. **Walkability:** 2. **Opened:** 1960. **Architect:** James Harris. **Season:** Year-round. **High:** Oct.-April. **To obtain tee times:** Call golf shop. **Miscellaneous:** Reduced fees (guests, juniors), range (grass/mats), caddies, lodging (236 rooms), credit cards (MC, V, AE), BF, FF.
Reader Comments: Great par 4s ... The caddies are a lot of fun ... Wide open and long ... Wiry rough ... Greens are like a billards table ... Good if you like wind ... Let the caddie read the putt, long but forgiving ... 1st time I played with a caddie, interesting and good for my game.

★★½ SUPERCLUBS GOLF CLUB
R-P.O. Box 531, Montego Bay No.2 Halfmoon, St. James, (876)953-3681. **Facility Holes:** 18. **Yards:** 6,600/5,400. **Par:** 72/73. **Course Rating:** 72.0/73.0. **Green Fee:** $80. **Cart Fee:** $35/Cart. **Walking Policy:** Unrestricted walking. **Walkability:** 1. **Opened:** 1971. **Architect:** Robert Moote. **Season:** Year-round. **High:** Nov.-April. **Tee times:** Call golf shop. **Miscellaneous:** Reduced fees (guests, juniors), metal spikes, range (grass), caddies, credit cards (MC, V, AE), BF, FF.
Special Notes: Formerly Ironshore Golf & Country Club.

★★★½ THE TRYALL CLUB, RESORT & VILLAS
R-Sandy Bay Main Rd., Hanover, (876)956-5681, 15 miles from Montego Bay. **E-mail:** tryall-club@cwjamaica.com. **Web:** www.thetryallclub.co.uk. **Facility Holes:** 18. **Yards:** 6,772/5,669. **Par:** 71/73. **Course Rating:** 72.5/72.5. **Slope:** 133/122. **Green Fee:** $150. **Cart Fee:** $27/Cart. **Walking Policy:** Unrestricted walking. **Walkability:** 3. **Opened:** 1959. **Architect:** Ralph Plummer. **Season:** Year-round. **High:** Dec.-April. **To obtain tee times:** Call golf shop. **Miscellaneous:** Reduced fees (guests), metal spikes, range (grass), caddies, credit cards (MC, V, AE, DC), BF, FF.
Reader Comments: Still by far, 'the best in Jamaica, mon' ... Expensive, but play it once for the experience ... Fast greens ... Best vacation I ever had ... Beautiful scenery ... Outstanding course ... Wind can be interesting ... I expected more, service is very good ... The caddies are the best.

THE ISLANDS

★★★ WYNDHAM ROSE HALL RESORT & COUNTRY CLUB
R-Box 999, Montego Bay, (876)953-2650x89, 10 miles from Montego Bay. **E-mail:** twhite128@hotmail.com. **Web:** www.wyndham.com. **Facility Holes:** 18. **Yards:** 6,637/5,162. **Par:** 71/71. **Green Fee:** $115/$130. **Cart Fee:** Included in green fee. **Walking Policy:** Mandatory carts. **Walkability:** 5. **Opened:** 2001. **Architect:** von Hagge/Smelek/Baril. **Season:** Year-round. **High:** Nov.-April. **To obtain tee times:** Call golf shop. **Miscellaneous:** Reduced fees (guests, twilight), metal spikes, range (grass), caddies (included in fee), lodging (488 rooms), credit cards (MC, V, AE, DC, Key card), BF, FF.
Reader Comments: Play early, it gets too hot in afternoon ... Caddies were very helpful, course winds through mountains and nice scenery ... Front 9 OK, back in hills very good ... Beautiful views ... What a mix, very humbling.

NEVIS

★★★★½ FOUR SEASONS RESORT NEVIS
R-P.O. Box 565, Pinney's Beach, (869)469-1111. **Facility Holes:** 18. **Yards:** 6,766/5,153. **Par:** 71/71. **Course Rating:** 73.6/71.5. **Slope:** 132/128. **Green Fee:** $150/$175. **Cart Fee:** Included in green fee. **Walking Policy:** Mandatory carts. **Walkability:** 5. **Opened:** 1991. **Architect:** Robert Trent Jones Jr. **Season:** Year-round. **To obtain tee times:** Call golf shop. **Miscellaneous:** Range (grass), lodging (198 rooms), credit cards (MC, V, AE, D, DC), BF, FF.
Reader Comments: Tough mountain terrain ... 600-yard, par 5 down the mountain ... Enjoyed this track immensely ... Unbelievable setting ... 15th is a roller coaster ... Spectacular views and elevations ... Spectacular, watch out for the goats.

NEW PROVIDENCE

★★ CABLE BEACH GOLF CLUB
R-W. Bay St., Nassau, (242)327-6000, (800)432-0221. **Facility Holes:** 18. **Yards:** 7,040/6,114. **Par:** 72/72. **Course Rating:** 72.0/72.0. **Green Fee:** $50/$75. **Cart Fee:** $60/Cart. **Walking Policy:** Walking at certain times. **Walkability:** 1. **Opened:** 1929. **Architect:** Devereux Emmet. **Season:** Year-round. **High:** Dec.-April. **To obtain tee times:** Call golf shop. **Miscellaneous:** Reduced fees (guests, juniors), metal spikes, range (grass/mats), credit cards (MC, V, AE).

★★½ PARADISE ISLAND GOLF CLUB
R-P.O. Box N-4777, Nassau, (242)363-3925. **Facility Holes:** 18. **Yards:** 6,770/6,003. **Par:** 72/73. **Course Rating:** 71.6/71.4. **Slope:** 114/124. **Green Fee:** $60/$155. **Cart Fee:** Included in green fee. **Walking Policy:** Mandatory cart. **Walkability:** 2. **Opened:** 1961. **Architect:** Dick Wilson. **Season:** Year-round. **High:** Nov.-April. **To obtain tee times:** Call golf shop. **Miscellaneous:** Reduced fees (weekdays, guests, juniors), metal spikes, range (grass/mats), credit cards (MC, V, AE, D).

★½ SOUTH OCEAN GOLF & BEACH RESORT
R-S. Ocean Dr., Nassau, (242)362-4391x23, 11 miles from Nassau. **E-mail:** clarion@batelnet.bs. **Web:** www.clarionnassau.com. **Facility Holes:** 18. **Yards:** 6,707/5,908. **Par:** 72/72. **Course Rating:** 72.5/75.0. **Slope:** 128/130. **Green Fee:** $75/$85. **Cart Fee:** $70/Cart. **Walking Policy:** Mandatory carts. **Walkability:** 4. **Opened:** 1972. **Architect:** Joe Lee. **Season:** Year-round. **To obtain tee times:** Call up to 2 days in advance. **Miscellaneous:** Reduced fees (guests, juniors), metal spikes, range (grass), lodging (259 rooms), credit cards (MC, V, AE, D, DC), BF, FF.

PUERTO RICO

★★★ BAHIA BEACH PLANTATION
PU-Rte. 187 Km. 4.2, Rio Grande, 00745, (787)256-5600, 16 miles from San Juan. **Facility Holes:** 18. **Yards:** 6,695/5,648. **Par:** 72/72. **Course Rating:** 71.5/72.5. **Slope:** 124/124. **Green Fee:** $40/$85. **Cart Fee:** Included in green fee. **Walking Policy:** Mandatory carts. **Walkability:** 1. **Opened:** 1991. **Architect:** J.B. Gold. **Season:** Year-round. **High:** Nov.-June. **To obtain tee times:** Call golf shop. **Miscellaneous:** Reduced fees (weekdays, twilight, seniors, juniors), range (grass/mats), credit cards (MC, V, AE, DC), BF, FF.

THE ISLANDS

★★ BERWIND COUNTRY CLUB
SP-Rte. 187 KM 4.7, Rio Grande, 00745, (787)876-3056, 15 miles from San Juan. **Facility Holes:** 18. **Yards:** 7,011/5,772. **Par:** 72/72. **Course Rating:** 72.6/72.1. **Slope:** 127/123. **Green Fee:** $50/$65. **Cart Fee:** Included in green fee. **Walking Policy:** Mandatory carts. **Walkability:** 1. **Opened:** 1966. **Architect:** Frank Murray. **Season:** Year-round. **To obtain tee times:** Call golf shop. **Miscellaneous:** Reduced fees (juniors), range (grass/mats), credit cards (MC, V, AE).

CAGUAS REAL GOLF COURSE
SP-Las Americas Expressway (Hwy. P.R. 52), Caguas, 00752, (561)743-1897, 25 miles from San Juan. **E-mail:** mail@sanford-golf.com. **Web:** www.sanford-golf.com. **Facility Holes:** 18. **Yards:** 6,700/4,900. **Par:** 71/71. **Opened:** 2002. **Architect:** John Sanford ASGCA. **Season:** Year-round. **To obtain tee times:** Call golf shop. **Miscellaneous:** Lodging (125 rooms). **Special Notes:** Opening Fall of 2002.

★★★★ DORADO DEL MAR COUNTRY CLUB
R-200 Dorado del Mar, Dorado, 00646, (787)796-3065, 25 miles from San Juan. **Facility Holes:** 18. **Yards:** 6,937/5,283. **Par:** 72/72. **Course Rating:** 75.2/71.9. **Slope:** 138/125. **Green Fee:** $60/$95. **Cart Fee:** Included in green fee. **Walking Policy:** Mandatory carts. **Walkability:** 3. **Opened:** 1998. **Architect:** Chi Chi Rodriguez. **Season:** Year-round. **To obtain tee times:** Call up to 7 days in advance. **Miscellaneous:** Reduced fees (weekdays, twilight, seniors, juniors), range (grass), lodging (300 rooms), credit cards (MC, V, AE), BF, FF.

HYATT DORADO BEACH RESORT
R-Carr. 693, Dorado, 00646, (787)796-8961, 22 miles from San Juan. **E-mail:** mrolon@doradpo.hyatt.com. **Facility Holes:** 36. **Cart Fee:** $25/Person. **Walking Policy:** Mandatory carts. **Walkability:** 3. **Opened:** 1958. **Architect:** Robert Trent Jones. **Season:** Year-round. **High:** Dec.-April. **Tee times:** Call up to 30 days in advance. **Miscellaneous:** Range (grass), credit cards (MC, V, AE, D), BF, FF.
★★★★ EAST COURSE (18)
Yards: 6,985/5,883. **Par:** 72/72. **Course Rating:** 72.5/74.2. **Slope:** 132/126. **Green Fee:** $70/$125. **Miscellaneous:** Reduced fees (guests, twilight, juniors).
★★½ WEST COURSE (18)
Yards: 6,913/5,883. **Par:** 72/74. **Course Rating:** 74.5/75.2. **Slope:** 132/132. **Green Fee:** $80/$125. **Miscellaneous:** Reduced fees (weekdays, guests, twilight, juniors).

HYATT REGENCY CERROMAR BEACH
R-Rte. 693, Dorado, 00646, (787)796-8915 xt. 3213, 26 miles from San Juan. **Facility Holes:** 36. **Green Fee:** $30/$105. **Cart Fee:** $20/Person. **Walking Policy:** Mandatory cart. **Walkability:** 2. **Opened:** 1971. **Architect:** Robert Trent Jones. **Season:** Year-round. **High:** Dec.-March. **Tee times:** Call golf shop. **Misc:** Reduced fees (weekdays, guests, twilight, seniors, juniors), range (grass), lodging (506 rooms), credit cards (MC, V, AE, D, Diners Club).
★★★ NORTH COURSE (18)
Yards: 6,841/5,547. **Par:** 72/72. **Course Rating:** 72.2/71.1. **Slope:** 125/121.
★★★ SOUTH COURSE (18)
Yards: 7,047/5,486. **Par:** 72/72. **Course Rating:** 73.1/70.8. **Slope:** 127/120.

PALMAS DEL MAR COUNTRY CLUB
R-1 Country Club Dr., Humacao, 00792, (787)285-2255, 1 mile from Humacao. **Facility Holes:** 36. **Cart Fee:** Included in green fee. **Walking Policy:** Mandatory carts. **Walkability:** 4. **Season:** Year-round. **High:** Dec.-April. **To obtain tee times:** Call golf shop. **Miscellaneous:** Reduced fees (weekdays, guests, twilight, seniors, juniors), range (grass), lodging (250 rooms), credit cards (MC, V, AE, D, DC, CB). BF, FF.
★★★★ FLAMBOYAN COURSE (18)
Yards: 7,117/5,434. **Par:** 72/72. **Course Rating:** 75.2/71.3. **Slope:** 136/125. **Green Fee:** $90/$170. **Opened:** 1998. **Architect:** Rees Jones.

★★★½ **PALM COURSE** (18)
Yards: 6,675/5,215. **Par:** 71/72. **Course Rating:** 73.1/71.3. **Slope:** 131/125. **Green Fee:** $90/$150. **Opened:** 1974. **Architect:** Gary Player.
Reader Comments: Some stunning holes … 18 is a par 5, great finishing hole … Fun course. Too many short holes … Nice layout, windy … Front 9 and back 9 are two different golf courses … Wide open, hard to lose balls … Beautiful views.

★½ **PUNTA BORINQUEN GOLF CLUB**
PU-Golf St., Ramey, Aguadilla, 00604, (787)890-2987, 25 miles from Mayaguez.
Facility Holes: 18. **Yards:** 6,869/4,908. **Par:** 72/71. **Course Rating:** 71.5/71.0. **Slope:** 130/119.
Green Fee: $18/$20. **Cart Fee:** $26/Cart. **Walking Policy:** Walking at certain times. **Walkability:** 3. **Opened:** 1948. **Architect:** Ferdinand Garbin. **Season:** Year-round. **High:** Nov.-March. **To obtain tee times:** Call golf shop. **Miscellaneous:** Reduced fees (weekdays, twilight, juniors), range (grass), caddies, credit cards (MC, V, AE, Debit Cards), BF, FF.

RIO MAR COUNTRY CLUB
R-Call Box 2888, Palmer, 00721, (787)888-6000, 25 miles from San Juan. **Facility Holes:** 36.
Green Fee: $75/$125. **Cart Fee:** Included in green fee. **Walkability:** 3. **Opened:** 1975. **Season:** Year-round. **High:** Dec.-May. **To obtain tee times:** Call golf shop. **Miscellaneous:** Reduced fees (guests, twilight, juniors), metal spikes, range (grass), credit cards (MC, V, AE).
★★★½ **OCEAN COURSE** (18)
Yards: 6,845/5,510. **Par:** 72/72. **Course Rating:** 70.7/69.0. **Slope:** 126/124. **Architect:** George Fazio/Tom Fazio.
Reader Comments: Great course, views and facilities … Expensive … Not a bad course, but not overly exciting either … Wide open, no rough … Great Color GPS System in place, made club selection easy.
★★★★ **RIVER COURSE** (18)
Yards: 6,945/5,119. **Par:** 72/72. **Course Rating:** 74.5/69.8. **Slope:** 135/120. **Walking Policy:** Mandatory cart. **Architect:** Greg Norman.
Reader Comments: A treat! … Better than its twin … Greens large … Converted me to a Greg Norman design fan … Narrow fairways. Well bunkered … More challenging than Ocean course … Great fun.

★★★★ **WYNDHAM EL CONQUISTADOR RESORT AND COUNTRY CLUB**
R-Rd. 987, K.M. 3.4, Las Croabas, 00738, (787)863-6784, 31 miles from San Juan. **Facility Holes:** 18. **Yards:** 6,662/5,131. **Par:** 72/72. **Course Rating:** 72.5/70.9. **Slope:** 131/130. **Green Fee:** $80/$165. **Cart Fee:** Included in green fee. **Walkability:** 5. **Opened:** 1992. **Architect:** Arthur Hills. **Season:** Year-round. **High:** Dec.-May. **To obtain tee times:** Call golf shop. **Miscellaneous:** Reduced fees (twilight, juniors), metal spikes, range (grass), lodging (918 rooms), credit cards (MC, V, AE).
Reader Comments: Bring lots of golf balls … Rarely a level lie except off the tee box … Yardages don't mean a thing … Windy … Unique layout … Banked fairways speed play & lengthen drives … Absolutely stunning! Loved it … Great par 5s.

ST. CROIX

★★½ **BUCCANEER HOTEL GOLF COURSE**
R-P.O. Box 218, Christiansted, 00820, (340)773-2100, (800)255-3881, 3 miles from Christiansted. **E-mail:** jljtcj@viaccess.net. **Web:** www.the buccaneer.com. **Facility Holes:** 18. **Yards:** 5,736/4,505. **Par:** 70/70. **Course Rating:** 67.3/64.3. **Slope:** 116/108. **Green Fee:** $30/$65. **Cart Fee:** $15/Person. **Walking Policy:** Unrestricted walking. **Walkability:** 4. **Opened:** 1973. **Architect:** Robert Joyce. **Season:** June-Dec. **High:** Dec.-April. **To obtain tee times:** Call up to 1 day in advance. **Miscellaneous:** Reduced fees (guests, juniors), lodging (136 rooms), credit cards (MC, V, AE, DC), FF.

★★★½ **CARAMBOLA GOLF CLUB** *Pace*
R-72 Estate River, Kingshill, 00851, (340)778-5638. **E-mail:** cgcgolf@viaccess.net. **Web:** www.golfvi.com. **Facility Holes:** 18. **Yards:** 6,843/5,424. **Par:** 72/73. **Course Rating:** 72.7/71.0. **Slope:** 131/123. **Green Fee:** $36/$76. **Cart Fee:** $14/Person. **Walking Policy:** Walking at certain times. **Walkability:** 3. **Opened:** 1966. **Architect:** Robert Trent Jones. **Season:** Year-round. **High:** Dec.-April. **To obtain tee times:** Call golf shop. **Miscellaneous:** Reduced fees (guests, twilight), metal spikes, range (grass), credit cards (MC, V, AE).
Reader Comments: Friendly members gave pointers … On-course service was terrific … Good restaurant and bar … Hilly terrain, breezy … Scenery was very enjoyable … Pace of play excellent … I had a life experience here! One morning I literally had the course to myself.

ST. KITTS

★★ ROYAL ST. KITTS GOLF CLUB
PU-P.O. Box 315, Frigate Bay, (869)465-8339, 2 miles from Basseterre. **Facility Holes:** 18. **Yards:** 6,918/5,349. **Par:** 72/72. **Course Rating:** 73.0/69.0. **Slope:** 125. **Green Fee:** $31/$35. **Cart Fee:** $40/Cart. **Walking Policy:** Mandatory cart. **Opened:** 1976. **Architect:** Harris/Thompson/Wolveridge/Fream. **Season:** Year-round. **High:** Dec.-May. **To obtain tee times:** Call golf shop. **Miscellaneous:** Reduced fees (guests, seniors, juniors), metal spikes, range (grass), credit cards (MC, V, AE, D).

ST. MAARTEN

★★ MULLET BAY GOLF CLUB
-P.O. Box 309, Phillipsburg, (599)552-8011, 10 miles from Phillipsburg. **Facility Holes: 18. **Yards:** 6,300/5,700. **Par:** 70/71. **Course Rating:** 69.0/68.0. **Slope:** 115/111. **Green Fee:** $65/$125. **Cart Fee:** Included in green fee. **Opened:** 1971. **Architect:** Joe Lee. **Season:** Year-round. **High:** Nov.-May. **To obtain tee times:** Call golf shop. **Miscellaneous:** Reduced fees (guests), metal spikes, range (grass), credit cards (MC, V, AE).

ST. THOMAS

★★★ MAHOGANY RUN GOLF COURSE
PU-No.1 Mahogany Run Rd. N., 00801, (340)777-6006, (800)253-7103. **E-mail:** mahoganyrun@hotmail.com. **Web:** www.st_thomas.com/mahogany. **Facility Holes:** 18. **Yards:** 6,022/4,873. **Par:** 70/70. **Course Rating:** 70.1/72.6. **Slope:** 123/111. **Green Fee:** $70/$100. **Cart Fee:** $15/Person. **Walking Policy:** Mandatory carts. **Walkability:** 4. **Opened:** 1980. **Architect:** George Fazio/Tom Fazio. **Season:** Year-round. **High:** Jan.-May. **To obtain tee times:** Call up to 2 days in advance. **Miscellaneous:** Reduced fees (twilight), metal spikes, range (grass/mats), credit cards (MC, V, AE, D), BF, FF.
Reader Comments: Very tight and windy, club selection tough ... Challenge the triangle, bring extra balls ... Too many blind shots ... Lots of fun ... Watch out for ocean-cliff holes.

TOBAGO

MOUNT IRVINE BAY GOLF CLUB
R-Mt. Irvine P.O. Box 222, Scarborough, W.I., (868)639-8871. **E-mail:** mtirvine@tstt.net.tt. **Web:** www.mtirvine.com. **Facility Holes:** 18. **Yards:** 6,793/5,558. **Par:** 72/74. **Course Rating:** 72.1/71.6. **Green Fee:** $48. **Cart Fee:** $36/Cart. **Walking Policy:** Unrestricted walking. **Walkability:** 3. **Opened:** 1968. **Architect:** Commander John D. Harris. **Season:** Year-round. **To obtain tee times:** Call golf shop. **Miscellaneous:** Reduced fees (guests), range (grass), caddies, lodging (105 rooms), credit cards (MC, V, AE, DC).

TURKS & CAICOS

★★★★ **PROVO GOLF CLUB**
R-Grace Bay Rd., Providenciales, (649)946-5991. **E-mail:** provgolf@tciway.com.
Web: www.provogolfclub.com. **Facility Holes:** 18. **Yards:** 6,642/4,979. **Par:** 72/72. **Course Rating:** 74.0/70.9. **Slope:** 136/125. **Green Fee:** $95/$120. **Cart Fee:** Included in green fee.
Walking Policy: Mandatory carts. **Walkability:** 1. **Opened:** 1992. **Architect:** Karl Litten. **Season:** Year-round. **To obtain tee times:** Call up to 90 days in advance. **Miscellaneous:** Reduced fees (guests), range (grass/mats), credit cards (MC, V, AE), FF.
Reader Comments: Trade winds … Almost too beautiful to be real … Windy as hell but a lot of fun … Makes you feel great to be alive and golfing … Flamingos are native to the course … Bring lots of balls … Very good service, but very expensive … Each hole was unique … 18 holes in 3 hours, every time … Only course on Turks and Caicos, but a good one.

Geographical Directory
by Town/City

A

Abbottstown, PA, The Bridges G.C., *680*
Aberdeen, MD,
Beechtree G.C., *321*
Ruggles G.Cse., *331*
Aberdeen, NC, Legacy G.L., *581*
Aberdeen, SD,
Aberdeen Links G.Cse., *749*
Lee Park G.Cse., *750*
Abilene, KS, Chisholm Trail G.Cse., *287*
Abilene, TX,
Diamondback G.C., *775*
Maxwell G.C., *786*
Abita Springs, LA, Abita Springs Golf & C.C., *307*
Absecon, NJ, Marriott's Seaview Resort, *506*
Acapulco, GUERRERO,
Acapulco Princess Club De Golf, *948*
Pierre Marques G.C., *948*
Accokeek, MD, Atlantic Golf at Potomac Ridge, *320*
Accord, NY, Rondout G.C., *553*
Ackworth, IA, Shady Oaks G.Cse., *283*
Acme, MI, Grand Traverse Resort and Spa, *377*
Acushnet, MA, Acushnet River Valley G.Cse., *335*
Acworth, GA,
Bentwater G.C., *180*
Centennial G.C., *182*
Cobblestone G.Cse., *184*
Ada, MI, Quail Ridge G.C., *401*
Ada, OK, Lakewood G.Cse., *660*
Adair, OK, Osage Creek G.Cse., *661*
Adairsville, GA, Barnsley Gardens, *180*
Adams, MN, Cedar River C.C., *422*
Addison, IL, Oak Meadows G.C., *239*
Adel, IA, River Valley G.Cse., *282*
Adrian, MI,
Centerview G.Cse., *364*
Woodlawn G.C., *419*
Advance, NC, Oak Valley G.C., *585*
Afton, NY, Afton G.C., *522*
Afton, OK, Shangri-La Golf Resort, *662*
Afton, VA, Swannanoa C.C., *834*
Aguadilla, PUERTO RICO, Punta Borinquen G.C., *959*
Aiea, HI, Pearl C.C., *205*
Aiken, SC,
Aiken G.C., *721*
Cedar Creek G.C., *724*
Midland Valley C.C., *736*
Akron, NY,
Dande Farms C.C., *532*
Rothland G.Cse., *554*
Akron, OH,
J.E. Good Park G.C., *624*
Turkeyfoot Lake G.L., *646*
Valley View G.C., *647*
Alameda, CA, Chuck Corica Golf Complex, *49*

Alamogordo, NM, Desert Lakes G.Cse., *515*
Alamosa, CO, Cattails G.C., *100*
Albany, MN, Albany G.Cse., *420*
Albany, NY, The New Course at Albany, *549*
Albany, OR, The G.C. of Oregon, *668*
Albert Lea, MN, Green Lea G.Cse., *428*
Albion, MI, Tomac Woods G.Cse., *413*
Albion, NY, Ricci Meadows G.Cse., *552*
Albuquerque, NM,
Arroyo del Oso Municipal G.Cse., *515*
Isleta Eagle G.Cse., *516*
Ladera G.Cse., *516*
Los Altos G.Cse., *517*
Paradise Hills G.C., *518*
Tijeras Arroyo G.Cse., *520*
University of New Mexico G.Cse., *521*
Alder Creek, NY, Alder Creek G.Cse. & Country Inn, *522*
Alder Flats, ALBERTA, Fairways West G.Cse., *900*
Aledo, IL, Hawthorn Ridge G.C., *229*
Alexandria, KY, A.J. Jolly G.Cse., *294*
Alexandria, OH,
St. Albans G.Cse., *643*
Willow Run G.Cse., *650*
Alexandria, VA, Greendale G.Cse., *823*
Algonquin, IL, G.C. of Illinois, *227*
Alhambra, CA, Alhambra Municipal G.Cse., *42*
Alice, TX, Alice Municipal G.Cse., *766*
Aliso Viejo, CA, Aliso Viejo G.C., *42*
Allardt, TN, Mountain View G.Cse., *760*
Allegan, MI, Cheshire Hills G.Cse., *364*
Allen, TX, Twin Creeks G.C., *800*
Allendale, MI, The Meadows G.C., *392*
Allentown, PA,
Allentown Municipal G.Cse., *678*
Twin Lakes C.C., *714*
Alliance, NE, Skyview G.Cse., *477*
Alliance, OH,
Sleepy Hollow C.C., *642*
Tannenhauf G.C., *645*
Allison Park, PA,
North Park G.Cse., *702*
Rose Ridge G.Cse., *708*
Alloway, NJ, Holly Hills G.C., *505*
Allyn, WA, Lakeland Village G.Cse., *845*
Alma, AR, Eagle Crest G.Cse., *38*
Aloha, OR, The Reserve Vineyards & G.C., *673*
Alpena, MI, Alpena G.C., *356*
Alpharetta, GA,
Crooked Creek G.C., *184*
RiverPines G.C., *194*
The Trophy Club of Atlanta, *197*
White Columns G.C., *197*
Alpine, AL, Alpine Bay G. & C.C., *2*
Altamont, NY, Orchard Creek G.C., *550*
Alto, MI,
Saskatoon G.C., *405*
Tyler Creek Recreation Area, *414*
Alton, IL,
Cloverleaf G.Cse., *221*
Spencer T. Olin Community G.Cse., *248*
The Woodlands G.C., *254*

Sudden Valley G. & C.C., *851*
Bellville, OH, Deer Ridge G.C., *613*
Belmont, MI,
Boulder Creek G.C., *359*
Grand Island Golf Ranch, *376*
Beloit, WI, Krueger-Haskell G.Cse., *874*
Belpre, OH, Oxbow G. & C.C., *631*
Belton, MO,
Eagle's Landing G.Cse., *455*
Southview G.C., *463*
Belton, TX, Leon Valley G.Cse., *785*
Belvidere, NJ, Apple Mountain G.C., *498*
Bemidji, MN,
Bemidji Town & C.C., *420*
Castle Highlands G.Cse., *422*
Benbrook, TX, Whitestone G.C., *802*
Bend, OR,
Lost Tracks G.C., *670*
Mountain High G.Cse., *671*
River's Edge Golf Resort, *674*
Widgi Creek G.C., *676*
Bennington, VT, Mt. Anthony C.C., *814*
Bensalem, PA, Bensalem C.C., *679*
Bensenville, IL, White Pines G.C., *253*
Bentleyville, PA, Chippewa G.C., *683*
Benton Harbor, MI,
Blossom Trails G.Cse., *359*
Lake Michigan Hills G.C., *386*
Benton, AR, Longhills G.C., *39*
Benton, KY, Kerry Landing G.Cse., *299*
Benton, PA, Mill Race G.Cse., *700*
Benzonia, MI, Pinecroft Plantation, *399*
Berkeley Springs, WV, Cacapon Resort,
854
Berkeley, CA, Tilden Park G.Cse., *93*
Berlin, MD,
The Bay Club, *320*
The Beach Club G.L., *320*
Deer Run G.C., *323*
Eagle's Landing G.Cse., *323*
Ocean City Golf & Yacht Club, *329*
River Run G.C., *330*
Rum Pointe Seaside G.L., *331*
Berlin, WI, Mascoutin G.C., *877*
Bernalillo, NM,
Santa Ana G.C., *519*
Twin Warriors G.C., *521*
Bernardston, MA, Crumpin-Fox Club, *339*
Bernice, LA, Meadow Lake G. & C.C., *310*
Bernville, PA, Green Acres Golf, *691*
Berwick, PA, Willow Run Inn & G.Cse., *717*
Bessemer, AL,
Bent Brook G.Cse., *2*
Frank House Municipal G.C., *4*
Bethany, CT, Woodhaven C.C., *124*
Bethel Island, CA, Bethel Island G.Cse., *44*
Bethel, ME, The Bethel Inn & C.C., *313*
Bethlehem, NH,
Bethlehem C.C., *490*
Maplewood C.C., *493*
Bethlehem, PA,
Bethlehem Municipal G.C., *679*
Green Pond C.C., *692*
Bettendorf, IA,
Hidden Hills G.Cse., *279*
Palmer Hills Municipal G.Cse., *281*
Beulah, MI,
Champion Hill, *364*
Crystal Lake G.C., *367*
Beulah, ND, Beulah Municipal G.Cse., *599*
Beverly Hills, FL, Twisted Oaks G.C., *175*

Beverly, MA, Beverly Golf & Tennis Club,
336
Beverly, OH, Lakeside G.Cse., *625*
Big Bend, WI, Edgewood G.Cse., *868*
Big Flats, NY, Willowcreek G.C., *566*
Big Rapids, MI,
Falcon Head G.C., *371*
Ferris State University, *371*
Meceola C.C., *392*
Big Sky, MT, Big Sky G.C., *467*
Big Spring, TX, Comanche Trail G.Cse., *773*
Bigfork, MT, Eagle Bend G.C., *468*
Billerica, MA, C.C. of Billerica, *338*
Billings, MT,
The Briarwood, *467*
Lake Hills G.Cse., *468*
Peter Yegen Jr. G.C., *469*
Biloxi, MS,
Dogwood Hills G.C., *445*
Edgewater Bay G.Cse., *445*
President Broadwater G.Cse., *449*
Sunkist C.C., *450*
Binghamton, NY,
Dimmock Hill G.Cse., *533*
Ely Park Municipal G.Cse., *535*
Birmingham, AL,
Eagle Point G.C., *4*
Highland Park G.C., *5*
Robert Trent Jones Golf Trail at Oxmoor
Valley G.C., *11*
Bishop, GA, Lane Creek G.C., *190*
Bishopville, MD, The Links at Lighthouse
Sound G.C., *327*
Bismarck, AR, DeGray Lake Resort State
Park G.Cse., *38*
Bismarck, ND,
Riverwood G.C., *601*
Tom O'Leary G.Cse., *601*
Bismark, ND, Hawktree G.C., *599*
Biwabik, MN, Giants Ridge Golf & Ski
Resort, *426*
Bixby, OK, White Hawk G.C., *665*
Black Butte Ranch, OR, Black Butte Ranch,
666
Black Mountain, NC, Black Mountain
G.Cse., *569*
Black River Falls, WI, Skyline G.C., *885*
Blackfoot, ID, Blackfoot Municipal G.Cse.,
209
Blacksburg, VA, Virginia Tech G.Cse., *835*
Blackwell, OK, Blackwell G.Cse., *652*
Blackwood, NJ, Ron Jaworski's Valleybrook
G.C., *511*
Blaine, WA, Semiahmoo G. & C.C., *850*
Blairsden, CA, Plumas Pines C.C., *77*
Blairsville, PA, Chestnut Ridge G.C., *683*
Blanchard, ID, Stoneridge C.C., *213*
Blenheim, ONTARIO, Deer Run G.C., *926*
Bloomingdale, IL,
Bloomingdale G.C., *217*
Indian Lakes Resort, *231*
Bloomington, IL,
The Den at Fox Creek G.C., *223*
Highland Park G.Cse., *230*
Prairie Vista G.Cse., *243*
Bloomington, IN,
Eagle Pointe Golf & Tennis Resort, *259*
Indiana University G.C., *263*
Blowing Rock, NC, Hound Ears Club, *580*
Blue Island, IL, The Meadows G.C. of Blue
Island, *236*
Blue River, OR, Tokatee G.C., *676*

Nelson Park G.Cse., *237*
Scovill G.C., *246*
Decorah, IA, Oneota G. & C.C., *281*
Deer Park, TX, The Battleground at Deer
   Park G.Cse., *767*
Deerbrook, WI, Antigo Bass Lake C.C., *862*
Deerfield Beach, FL, Deer Creek G.C., *138*
Deerwood, MN,
Cuyuna C.C., *423*
Ruttger's Bay Lake Lodge, *438*
Defiance, OH, Auglaize County Club, *603*
Delavan, WI,
Delbrook G.Cse., *867*
Lake Lawn Resort G.Cse., *875*
Delaware Water Gap, PA, Water Gap C.C.,
   716
Delaware, OH,
Oakhaven G.C., *631*
Tanglewood G.C., *645*
Delhi, NY, Delhi College G.Cse., *532*
Delhi, ONTARIO, Delhi G. & C.C., *926*
Dellroy, OH, Atwood Resort G.Cse., *603*
Delmont, PA, Cloverleaf G.C., *684*
Delphi Falls, NY, Delphi Falls G.Cse., *533*
Delray Beach, FL,
Delray Beach G.C., *138*
Polo Trace G.Cse., *163*
Delton, MI, Mullenhurst G.Cse., *393*
Deming, NM, Rio Mimbres C.C., *519*
Denison, TX, Grayson County College
   G.Cse., *779*
Denmark, NY, Carlowden C.C., *527*
Denmark, WI, Twin Oaks G.Cse., *888*
Dennis, MA, Dennis Highlands G.Cse., *339*
Dennis, TX, Sugartree G.C., *797*
Denton, TX, Eagle Point G.C., *775*
Denver, CO,
City Park G.C., *100*
Foothills G.Cse., *104*
Overland Park G.Cse., *109*
Park Hill G.C., *110*
Wellshire G.Cse., *115*
Willis Case G.Cse., *115*
Denver, NC, Westport G.Cse., *597*
Denver, PA, Hawk Valley G.C., *693*
Derby, KS, Hidden Lakes G.Cse., *289*
Derwood, MD, Needwood G.Cse., *328*
Des Moines, IA,
A.H. Blank G.Cse., *275*
Grandview G.Cse., *279*
Waveland G.Cse., *284*
Woodland Hills G.Cse., *285*
Desert Aire, WA, Desert Aire G.Cse., *839*
Desert Hot Springs, CA,
Desert Dunes G.C., *52*
Mission Lakes C.C., *70*
Desoto, KS, Oak Country G.Cse., *290*
Destin, FL,
Emerald Bay G.Cse., *142*
Indian Bayou G. & C.C., *149*
Kelly Plantation G.C., *150*
Regatta Bay G. & C.C., *164*
Sandestin Resort, *167*
Seascape Resort, *169*
Detroit Lakes, MN,
Detroit C.C., *424*
Ironman G.Cse., *429*
Wildflower at Fair Hills, *442*
Detroit, MI,
Palmer Park G.Cse., *397*
Rogell G.Cse., *404*
Rouge Park G.C., *404*

Devine, TX, Devine G.Cse., *775*
Devonshire, BERMUDA, Ocean View
   G.Cse., *953*
Dewey, AZ, Prescott G. & C.C., *29*
Dexter, MI, Hudson Mills Metro Park G.Cse.,
   382
Dexter, MO, Hidden Trails C.C., *456*
Diamond Bar, CA, Diamond Bar G.C., *53*
Diamond City, AR, Diamond Hills C.C., *38*
Diamond, OH, Dogwood G.Cse., *613*
Diamondhead, MS, Diamondhead C.C., *445*
Dickinson, ND, Heart River Municipal
   G.Cse., *599*
Dickson, TN, GreyStone G.C., *757*
Digby, NOVA SCOTIA, The Pines Resort
   Hotel G.Cse., *924*
Dillsburg, PA, Range End G.C., *707*
Dixon, IL, Lost Nation G.C., *235*
Dixville Notch, NH, The Balsams Grand
   Resort Hotel, *490*
Dodge City, KS, Mariah Hills G.Cse., *289*
Donegal, PA, Donegal Highlands G.C., *686*
Dora, AL, Horse Creek G.C., *5*
Dorado, PUERTO RICO,
Dorado del Mar C.C., *958*
Hyatt Dorado Beach Resort, *958*
Hyatt Regency Cerromar Beach, *958*
Dorchester, ONTARIO, Pine Knot G. & C.C.,
   935
Dorval, QUEBEC, Golf Dorval, *941*
Dothan, AL,
Dothan National G.C. & Hotel, *4*
Robert Trent Jones Golf Trail at Highland
   Oaks, *10*
Douglas, GA, Hinson Hills G.Cse., *188*
Douglas, WY, Douglas Community Club,
   892
Douglassville, PA,
Arrowhead G.Cse., *678*
Blackwood G.Cse., *679*
Douglaston, NY, Douglaston G.C., *533*
Douglasville, GA, Bear Creek G. & C.C.,
   180
Dousman, WI, Kettle Moraine G.C., *874*
Dover, DE, Eagle Creek G.C., *125*
Dover-Foxcroft, ME, Foxcroft G.C., *315*
Dowagiac, MI, Hampshire C.C., *379*
Downers Grove, IL, Downers Grove Park
   District G.Cse., *223*
Downey, CA, Rio Hondo G.C., *81*
Downingtown, PA, Downingtown C.C., *687*
Doylestown, OH, Chippewa G.C., *610*
Draper, UT, South Mountain G.C., *809*
Draper, VA, Draper Valley G.C., *821*
Dresher, PA, Twining Valley Golf & Fitness
   Club, *714*
Drumheller, ALBERTA, Dinosaur Trail G. &
   C.C., *899*
Drummond Island, MI, The Rock at
   Drummond Island, *403*
Drummonds, TN, Forest Hill G.Cse., *756*
Drumright, OK, Drumright G.Cse., *655*
Drums, PA, Edgewood In The Pines G.Cse.,
   687
Dubois, PA, Treasure Lake G.C., *714*
Dubuque, IA,
Bunker Hill G.Cse., *276*
The Meadows G.C., *280*
Dudley, MA, Webster Dudley G.C., *354*
Duluth, GA, St. Marlo C.C., *196*
Duluth, MN,
Enger Park G.C., *426*

Forsyth, IL, Hickory Point G.Cse., *229*
Fort Atkinson, WI, Koshkonong Mounds
C.C., *874*
Fort Carson, CO, Fort Carson G.C.. *104*
Fort Cobb, OK, Fort Cobb State Park
G.Cse., *656*
Fort Collins, CO,
Collindale G.C., *101*
SouthRidge G.C., *113*
Fort Dodge, IA,
American Legion G. & C.C., *275*
Lakeside Municipal G.Cse., *280*
Fort Fairfield, ME, Aroostook Valley C.C.,
313
Fort Kent, ME, Fort Kent G.C., *315*
Fort Knox, KY, Fort Knox, *297*
Fort Langley, BRITISH COLUMBIA, Fort
Langley G.Cse., *908*
Fort Leonard Wood, MO, Piney Valley
G.Cse., *461*
Fort Lupton, CO, Coyote Creek G.Cse., *102*
Fort Madison, IA, Sheaffer Memorial Golf
Park, *283*
Fort Meade, MD, The Courses Fort Meade,
323
Fort Mill, SC,
Fort Mill G.C., *729*
Regent Park G.C., *741*
Springfield G.C., *744*
Fort Morgan, CO, Fort Morgan G.Cse., *104*
Fort Myers, FL,
Eastwood G.Cse., *141*
Fort Myers C.C., *143*
Gateway G. & C.C., *144*
Gulf Harbour G. & C.C., *147*
The Legends G. & C.C., *152*
Fort Pierce, FL,
Fairwinds G.Cse., *142*
Gator Trace G. & C.C., *144*
Fort Polk, LA, Warrior Hills G.Cse., *312*
Fort Richardson, AK, Moose Run G.Cse.,
14
Fort Riley, KS, Custer Hill G.C., *287*
Fort Sill, OK,
Cedar Lakes G.Cse., *653*
Fort Sill G.C., *657*
Fort Smith, AR, Ben Geren Regional Park
G.Cse., *37*
Fort Wainwright, AK, Chena Bend G.C., *14*
Fort Walton Beach, FL, Fort Walton Beach
G.C., *143*
Fort Wayne, IN,
Autumn Ridge G.C., *255*
Brookwood G.C., *257*
Cherry Hill G.C., *257*
Chestnut Hill G.C., *257*
Fairview G.Cse., *260*
Riverbend G.Cse., *268*
Fort Worth, TX,
The Creeks at Beechwood, *773*
The G.C. at Fossil Creek, *779*
Hawks Creek G.C., *780*
The Links at WaterChase, *785*
Meadowbrook G.Cse., *786*
Pecan Valley G.Cse., *789*
Rockwood G.Cse., *794*
Timber-View G.Cse., *799*
Z Boaz G.Cse., *803*
Foster, RI, Foster C.C., *719*
Fostoria, OH,
Lakeland G.Cse., *625*
Loudon Meadows G.C., *627*

Fountain Hills, AZ,
Desert Canyon G.C., *19*
The G.C. at Eagle Mountain, *22*
SunRidge Canyon G.C., *33*
Fountain Inn, SC, Carolina Springs G.C.,
724
Fountain Valley, CA, Mile Square G.Cse.,
70
Four Falls, NEW BRUNSWICK, Aroostook
Valley C.C., *918*
Four Oaks, NC, Reedy Creek G.Cse., *590*
Fox Lake, IL, Fox Lake C.C., *226*
Foxboro, MA, Foxborough C.C., *341*
Francestown, NH, Tory Pines G.C., *496*
Frankenmuth, MI, The Fortress, *372*
Frankfort, IL, Green Garden C.C., *228*
Frankfort, KY, Juniper Hills G.Cse., *299*
Frankfort, NY, Pine Hills G.Cse., *551*
Franklin Lakes, NJ, High Mountain G.C.,
504
Franklin, IN, The Legends of Indiana
G.Cse., *264*
Franklin, KY, Country Creek G.Cse., *296*
Franklin, TN,
Forrest Crossing G.Cse., *756*
Legends Club of Tennessee, *759*
Franklin, WI, Oakwood Park G.Cse., *880*
Franklinton, LA, Gemstone Plantation G. &
C.C., *308*
Franksville, WI, South Hills C.C., *885*
Frederick, MD,
Clustered Spires G.Cse., *323*
Frederick G.C., *324*
Fredericksburg, PA, Blue Mountain View
G.Cse., *680*
Fredericksburg, TX, Lady Bird Johnson
Municipal G.Cse., *784*
Fredericksburg, VA,
The Gauntlet G.C. at Curtis Park, *822*
Lee's Hill Golfers' Club, *828*
Fredericton, NEW BRUNSWICK,
Fredericton Golf & Curling Club, *918*
Riverbend Golf & Fishing Club, *920*
Fredonia, NY, Hillview G.Cse., *541*
Freeland, MI,
Beech Hollow G.Cse., *357*
The G.C. at Apple Mountain, *375*
Twin Oaks G.Cse., *414*
Freeport, GRAND BAHAMA ISL.,
Fortune Hills G. & C.C., *955*
The Lucayan Resort, *955*
Resort at Bahamia, *955*
Freeport, IL, Park Hills G.C., *241*
Freeport, TX, Freeport G.Cse., *777*
Fremont, MI, Northwood G.Cse., *394*
Fremont, NE, Valley View G.Cse., *478*
Fremont, OH, Sycamore Hills G.C., *644*
French Lick, IN, French Lick Springs
Resort, *261*
Fresno, CA,
Fig Garden G.C., *56*
Riverside G.Cse., *82*
Friendship, OH, Shawnee State Park
G.Cse., *641*
Frigate Bay, ST. KITTS, Royal St. Kitts G.C.,
960
Fripp Island, SC,
Fripp Island Resort, *729*
Ocean Creek G.Cse., *738*
Ocean Point G.L., *738*
Frisco, TX,
Plantation G.C., *790*

Glen Mills, PA, The G.Cse. at Glen Mills, *690*
Glen Rose, TX, Squaw Valley G.Cse., *797*
Glencoe, AL, Robert Trent Jones Golf Trail at Silver Lakes G.C., *11*
Glencoe, IL, Glencoe G.C., *227*
Glencoe, MN, Glencoe C.C., *427*
Glendale Heights, IL, Glendale Lakes G.Cse., *227*
Glendale, AZ,
The 500 Club, *16*
The Legend at Arrowhead G.C., *25*
Glendale, CA, Scholl Canyon G.Cse., *86*
Glendive, MT, Cottonwood C.C., *467*
Gleneden Beach, OR, Westin Salishan Lodge & Golf Resort, *676*
Glenn Dale, MD, Glenn Dale G.C., *325*
Glenview, IL, Glenview Park District G.C., *227*
Glenville, WV, Glenville G.C., *855*
Glenwood, AR, Glenwood C.C., *38*
Glenwood, IL, Glenwoodie G.Cse., *227*
Glenwood, MN,
Minnewaska G.C., *433*
Pezhekee G.C., *436*
Glenwood, NY, Holland Hills G.Cse., *541*
Gobles, MI, Shamrock Hills G.Cse., *406*
Goderich, ONTARIO, Goderich Sunset G.C., *929*
Godfrey, IL, Rolling Hills G.Cse., *245*
Goffstown, NH, Stonebridge C.C., *496*
Gold Canyon, AZ,
Gold Canyon Golf Resort, *21*
Mountain Brook G.C., *27*
Golden Valley, MN,
Brookview G.Cse., *421*
Theodore Wirth G.Cse., *440*
Golden, BRITISH COLUMBIA, Golden G. & C.C., *908*
Golden, CO, Applewood G.Cse., *98*
Goldsboro, NC, Lane Tree G.C., *581*
Goleta, CA, Glen Annie G.Cse., *57*
Goodlettsville, TN, Twelve Stones Crossing G.C., *764*
Goodrich, MI, Goodrich C.C., *376*
Goodyear, AZ,
Eagle's Nest C.C. at Pebble Creek, *20*
Estrella Mountain G.Cse., *20*
Estrella Mountain Ranch G.C., *21*
Palm Valley G.C., *28*
Goose Creek, SC, Crowfield G. & C.C., *727*
Gordon, NE, Gordon G. & C.C., *473*
Gordonsville, VA, Shenandoah Crossing Resort & C.C., *832*
Gorham, ME, Gorham C.C., *315*
Gorham, NH, Androscoggin Valley C.C., *490*
Gormley, ONTARIO, Gormley Green G.C., *929*
Goshen, IN, Black Squirrel G.C., *255*
Goshen, OH, Deer Track G.Cse., *613*
Gothenburg, NE, Wild Horse G.C., *478*
Gowen, MI, The Links at Bowen Lake, *388*
Graeagle, CA, Graeagle Meadows G.Cse., *58*
Graford, TX, The Cliffs Resort, *772*
Grafton, OH,
Brentwood G.C., *606*
Carlisle G.C., *608*
Indian Hollow Lake G.Cse., *623*
Pine Brook G.Cse., *632*
Grafton, WI, C.C. of Wisconsin, *866*
Grafton, WV, Tygart Lake G.Cse., *860*

Graham, NC, Quarry Hills C.C., *590*
Grain Valley, MO, Valley Hills G.C., *465*
Gramling, SC, Village Green G.C., *746*
Granada Hills, CA, Knollwood C.C., *63*
Granby, MA, Westover G.Cse., *354*
Grand Bay - Westfield, NEW BRUNSWICK, Westfield G. & C.C., *921*
Grand Blanc, MI,
Grand Blanc G. & C.C., *376*
Woodfield G. & C.C., *419*
Grand Cayman, CAYMAN ISLANDS, The Links at Safe Haven, *954*
Grand Forks, ND,
Lincoln Park G.Cse., *600*
Plainsview G.Cse. at Grand Forks AFB, *601*
Grand Haven, MI, Grand Haven G.C., *376*
Grand Island, NE,
Grand Island Municipal G.Cse., *473*
Indianhead G.C., *475*
Grand Island, NY, Beaver Island State Park G.Cse., *524*
Grand Junction, CO,
The G.C. at Redlands Mesa, *105*
Tiara Rado G.Cse., *114*
Grand Lake, CO, Grand Lake G.Cse., *105*
Grand Ledge, MI,
Grand Ledge C.C., *377*
Ledge Meadows G.Cse., *388*
Grand Prairie, TX,
Prairie Lakes G.Cse., *790*
Riverside G.C., *793*
TangleRidge G.C., *797*
Grand Rapids, MI,
English Hills G.Cse., *371*
The G.C. at Thornapple Pointe, *375*
Gracewil C.C., *376*
Grand Rapids G.C., *377*
Indian Trails G.Cse., *384*
Lincoln C.C., *388*
Thousand Oaks G.C., *412*
Grand Rapids, MN,
Pokegama G.C., *436*
Wendigo G.Cse., *442*
Grand-Sault, NEW BRUNSWICK, Grand Falls G.C., *919*
Grande Prairie, ALBERTA, The Dunes Golf & Winter Club, *899*
Grandview, MO, River Oaks G.C., *462*
Grandville, MI, Maple Hill G.Cse., *390*
Granger, IA, Jester Park G.Cse., *279*
Granger, IN, Juday Creek G.Cse., *263*
Granite City, IL, Legacy G.C., *234*
Grant Park, IL, Minne Monesse G.C., *237*
Grant, MI, Brigadoon G.C., *361*
Grant, MN, Sawmill G.C., *439*
Grantham, NH, Eastman G.L., *491*
Grants Pass, OR, Grants Pass G.C., *668*
Grants, NM, Coyote De Malpais, *515*
Grantville, PA, Manada G.C., *699*
Granville, OH,
Granville G.Cse., *619*
Raccoon International G.C., *635*
Grapevine, TX, Grapevine G.Cse., *779*
Grass Valley, CA, Alta Sierra C.C., *42*
Grayling, MI,
Fox Run C.C., *373*
Grayling C.C., *378*
Grayslake, IL,
Brae Loch G.C., *218*
Stonewall Orchard G.C., *249*
Graysville, AL, Mountain View G.C., *8*
Great Barrington, MA, Egremont C.C., *340*

982

The Hamptons G.Cse., *823*
Woodlands G.Cse., *836*
Hanceville, AL, Cullman G.Cse., *4*
Hanover, IL, Storybrook C.C., *249*
Hanover, JAMAICA, The Tryall Club, Resort & Villas, *956*
Hanover, NH, Hanover C.C., *492*
Hanover, PA, South Hills G.C., *710*

Harbor Springs, MI,
Boyne Highlands Resort, *360*
Chestnut Valley G.Cse., *365*
Harbor Point G.Cse., *379*
Little Traverse Bay G.C., *389*
Harborcreek, PA, Downing G.Cse., *687*
Harding, PA, Applewood G.Cse., *678*
Hardinsburg, KY, Breckenridge County Community Center, *294*
Hardy, VA, Westlake G. & C.C., *835*
Harlingen, TX, Tony Butler G.Cse., *799*
Harmon, ME, Hermon Meadow G.C., *315*
Harmony, PA, Deep Valley G.Cse., *686*
Harmony, RI, Melody Hill G.Cse., *720*
Harpersville, AL, The Meadows G.C., *7*
Harpster, OH, Hickory Grove G.C., *621*
Harrisburg, PA,
Dauphin Highlands G.Cse., *686*
Sportsmans G.C., *711*
Harrison, AR, Harrison C.C., *38*
Harrison, MI,
Snow Snake Ski & Golf, *407*
The Tamaracks G.Cse., *410*
Harrison, OH, Miami Whitewater Forest G.Cse., *628*
Harrison, TN, Bear Trace at Harrison Bay, *752*
Harrisonburg, VA,
Lakeview G.Cse., *827*
Massanutten Resort G.Cse., *828*
Harrisville, RI, Country View G.C., *719*
Harrod, OH, Colonial Golfers Club, *610*
Harrodsburg, KY, Bright Leaf Golf Resort, *295*
Harshaw, WI, Pinewood C.C., *881*
Hart, MI, The Colonial G.Cse., *365*
Hartfield, VA, Piankatank River G.C., *830*
Hartford City, IN, Ki-Ann G.Cse., *263*
Hartford, CT,
Goodwin Park G.Cse., *118*
Keney G.Cse., *119*
Hartford, SD, Central Valley G.C., *749*
Hartford, WI,
Hartford G.C., *871*
Washington County G.Cse., *889*
Hartland, MI,
Dunham Hills G. & C.C., *368*
Hartland Glen G. & C.C., *379*
The Majestic at Lake Walden, *389*
Hartland, NEW BRUNSWICK, Covered Bridge G. & C.C., *918*
Hartland, WI,
Bristlecone Pines G.C., *864*
Songbird Hills G.C., *885*
Hartsburg, MO, Eagle Knoll G.C., *455*
Hartsville, SC, Sandy Point G.C., *743*
Hartville, OH, Seven Hills C.C., *640*
Hartwell, GA, Cateechee G.C., *182*
Harvard, IL,
Oak Grove G.Cse., *239*
Plum Tree National G.C., *242*
Harvard, MA, Shaker Hills G.C., *351*
Harwich, MA, Cranberry Valley G.Cse., *338*

Harwinton, CT, Fairview Farm G.Cse., *118*
Haslett, MI, Meridian Sun G.Cse., *392*
Hastings, MI,
Hastings C.C., *380*
River Bend G.Cse., *403*
Hastings, MN,
Afton Alps G.Cse., *420*
Bellwood Oaks G.Cse., *420*
Hidden Greens G.C., *428*
Hastings, NE, Southern Hills G.Cse., *477*
Hattiesburg, MS,
Canebrake G.C., *443*
Timberton G.C., *450*
USM's Van Hook G.Cse., *450*
Haughton, LA, Olde Oaks G.C., *310*
Hauppauge, NY, Stonebridge G.L. & C.C., *558*
Haute Aboujagane, NEW BRUNSWICK, Pine Needles G. & C.C., *920*
Haverhill, MA, Crystal Springs G.C., *339*
Havre de Grace, MD, Bulle Rock, *322*
Hawkinsville, GA, Southern Hills G.C., *195*
Hawley, MN, Hawley G. & C.C., *428*
Hawley, PA,
C.C. at Woodloch Springs, *685*
Cricket Hill G.C., *685*
Woodloch Springs C.C., *718*
Hayden Lake, ID, Avondale G.C., *209*
Hayesville, NC, Chatuge Shores G.Cse., *572*
Hayfield, MN, Oaks C.C., *435*
Haymarket, VA, Bull Run C.C., *820*
Hayward, CA, Skywest G.Cse., *88*
Hayward, WI,
Hayward Golf & Tennis Club, *872*
Teal Wing G.C., *886*
Hazelton, PA, Eagle Rock Resort, *687*
Headingley, MANITOBA, John Blumberg G.Cse., *916*
Heber Springs, AR, The Red Apple Inn & C.C., *40*
Hebron, CT,
Blackledge C.C., *116*
Tallwood C.C., *122*
Hedgesville, WV, The Woods Resort, *860*
Helen, GA, Innsbruck Resort & G.C., *189*
Helena, MT, Bill Roberts Municipal G.Cse., *467*
Hellertown, PA, Woodland Hills C.C., *717*
Hemet, CA,
Diamond Valley G.C., *54*
Seven Hills G.C., *86*
Hempstead, TX, Fox Creek G.Cse., *777*
Henderson, NV,
Black Mountain G. & C.C., *480*
Lake Las Vegas Resort, *483*
The Legacy G.C., *484*
The Revere at Anthem, *486*
Rio Secco G.C., *486*
Wild Horse G.C., *488*
Henderson, TN, Bear Trace at Chickasaw, *752*
Hendersonville, NC, Crooked Creek G.C., *574*
Hendersonville, TN, Country Hills G.Cse., *754*
Hennessey, OK, Turkey Creek G.C., *664*
Henrietta, OK, Henrietta C.C., *657*
Hercules, CA, Franklin Canyon G.Cse., *57*
Hereford, TX, John Pitman Municipal G.Cse., *783*
Hermitage, PA,

The Course at Wente Vineyards, *50*
Las Positas G.Cse., *65*
Poppy Ridge G.Cse., *78*
Livermore, IA, Spring Valley G.Cse., *283*
Liverpool, NY, Liverpool G. & C.C., *545*

Livonia, MI,
Fox Creek G.Cse., *372*
Idle Wyld G.C., *383*
Whispering Willows G.Cse., *417*
Livonia, NY, Old Hickory G.C., *549*
Loch Sheldrake, NY, Lochmor G.Cse., *545*
Lockbourne, OH, Foxfire G.C., *617*
Locke, NY, Fillmore G.C., *536*
Lockport, IL,
Big Run G.C., *216*
Broken Arrow G.C., *218*
Old Oak C.C., *240*
Prairie Bluff G.C., *242*
Woodbine G.Cse., *254*
Lockport, NY,
Niagara County G.Cse., *549*
Oak Run G.C., *549*
Willowbrook C.C., *566*
Locust Grove, VA,
Meadows Farms G.Cse., *828*
Somerset G.C., *833*
Lodi, CA,
Lockeford Springs G.Cse., *66*
Micke Grove G.L., *70*
Logan, UT, Logan River G.Cse., *807*
Logansport, IN,
Dykeman Park G.Cse., *259*
Logansport G.C., *265*
Lombardy, ONTARIO, Lombard Glen G.C., *932*
Lomira, WI, The G.C. at Camelot, *870*
Lompoc, CA, La Purisima G.Cse., *64*
London, KY, Crooked Creek G.C., *296*
London, ONTARIO,
Fanshawe G.C., *927*
Forest City National G.C., *928*
River Road G.Cse., *936*
Thames Valley G.Cse., *938*
Lone Wolf, OK, Quartz Mountain G.Cse., *662*
Long Beach, CA,
El Dorado Park G.C., *55*
Recreation Park G.Cse., *80*
Skylinks G.Cse., *88*
Long Grove, IA, Glynns Creek G.Cse., *278*
Long Grove, IL, Kemper Lakes G.Cse., *232*
Long Neck, DE, Baywood Greens, *125*
Longboat Key, FL, Longboat Key Club, *153*
Longdale, OK, Fairview Lakeside C.C., *656*
Longmont, CO,
Twin Peaks G.Cse., *114*
Ute Creek G.Cse., *114*
Longs, SC,
Aberdeen C.C., *721*
Colonial Charters G.C., *726*
The Long Bay Club, *736*
Longview, TX, Alpine G.Cse., *766*
Longview, WA, Mint Valley G.C., *847*
Longville, MN, Ridgewood G.Cse., *438*
Longwood, FL,
Diamond Players Club, *139*
The Legacy Club at Alaqua Lakes, *151*
Sabal Point C.C., *167*
Loon Lake, NY, Loon Lake G.Cse., *545*
Lopatcong, NJ, The Architects Club, *498*

Lore City, OH, Salt Fork State Park G.Cse., *639*
Loris, SC, Diamond Back G.C., *727*
Lorton, VA, Pohick Bay Regional G.Cse., *830*
Los Alamitos, CA, Cypress G.C., *51*
Los Alamos, NM, Los Alamos G.C., *517*
Los Angeles, CA,
Chester Washington G.Cse., *48*
Griffith Park, *59*
Rancho Park G.Cse., *79*
Louisville, CO, Coal Creek G.Cse., *101*
Louisville, KY,
Indian Springs G.C., *298*
Iroquois G.Cse., *299*
Penn Run G.Cse., *302*
Quail Chase G.C., *303*
Seneca G.Cse., *303*
Shawnee G.Cse., *303*
Loveland, CO,
Mariana Butte G.Cse., *108*
The Olde Course at Loveland, *109*
Loveland, OH,
Eagles Nest G.Cse., *614*
Hickory Woods G.Cse., *621*
Lowell, MI, Deer Run G.C., *368*
Lowellville, OH, Countryside G.Cse., *611*
Lowville, NY, Cedars G.Cse., *528*
Lubbock, TX,
Elm Grove G.Cse., *776*
Meadowbrook Municipal Golf Complex, *786*
Shadow Hills G.Cse., *795*
Lucas, KY, Barren River State Park G.Cse., *294*
Lucedale, MS, Lucedale Golf & Recreation, *447*
Luck, WI, Luck G.Cse., *876*
Ludington, MI,
Lakeside Links, *387*
Lincoln Hills G.C., *388*
Ludlow, VT, Okemo Valley G.C., *815*
Luling, LA, Willowdale G.C., *312*
Lum, MI, Lum International G.C., *389*
Lumber Bridge, NC, Scothurst G.Cse., *592*
Lumberton, NC, Cliffwood G.C., *573*
Luray, VA, Caverns C.C. Resort, *820*
Lusby, MD, Chesapeake Hills G.C., *323*
Lutherville, MD, Pine Ridge G.Cse., *329*
Lutsen, MN, Superior National G.Cse., *440*
Lutz, FL, Tournament Players Club of Tampa Bay, *174*
Luxemburg, WI, NorthBrook C.C., *880*
Lydia, SC, Fox Creek G.C., *729*
Lynden, WA, Homestead Farms Golf Resort, *843*
Lynn, MA, Larry Gannon G.C., *345*
Lynnfield, MA,
Colonial G.C., *338*
Sagamore Spring G.C., *350*
Sheraton Colonial G.C., *351*
Lyons, NY, Wayne Hills C.C., *564*
Lyons, OR, Elkhorn Valley G.Cse., *668*

M

Mabank, TX, Pinnacle C.C., *790*
Macedon, NY, Marvin's G.Cse., *547*
Mackeyville, PA, Belles Spring G.Cse., *679*
Mackinac Island, MI,
Grand Hotel G.C., *376*
Wawashkamo G.C., *415*
Macomb, MI,

Bello Woods G.C., *357*
Cracklewood G.C., *366*
Hickory Hollow G.Cse., *381*
Sycamore Hills G.C., *410*
Wolverine G.C., *418*
Macon, GA,
Barrington Hall G.C., *180*
Bowden G.Cse., *181*
Oakview G. & C.C., *192*
Mactaquac, NEW BRUNSWICK, Mactaquac
    Provincial Park G.C., *919*
Madera, CA, Madera Municipal G.Cse., *67*
Madison, IL, Gateway National G.L., *226*
Madison, ME, Lakewood G.Cse., *316*
Madison, MS, Caroline G.C., *444*
Madison, OH,
Powderhorn G.Cse., *634*
The Reserve at Thunder Hill, *636*
Madison, WI,
The Bridges G.Cse., *863*
Yahara Hills G.Cse., *891*
Madison, WV, Riverview C.C., *858*
Madras, OR, Nine Peaks G.Cse., *671*
Maggie Valley, NC, Maggie Valley Resort &
    C.C., *582*
Magnolia, NC, The Links at Magnolia, *581*
Magnolia, TX, High Meadow Ranch G.C.,
    781
Mahomet, IL, Lake of the Woods G.C., *233*
Mahopac, NY, C.C. at Lake MacGregor, *531*
Mahwah, NJ, Darlington County G.Cse., *501*
Mainland, PA, Mainland G.Cse., *698*
Makanda, IL, Stone Creek G.C., *249*
Malaga, WA, Three Lakes G.Cse., *852*
Malibu, CA, Malibu C.C., *68*
Malone, NY, Malone G.C., *545*
Mammoth Lakes, CA, Sierra Star G.C., *87*
Manahawkin, NJ, Ocean Acres C.C., *508*
Manakin Sabot, VA, Sycamore Creek
    G.Cse., *834*
Manalapan, NJ, Knob Hill G.C., *505*
Manassas Park, VA, General's Ridge
    G.Cse., *822*
Mancelona, MI,
Deer Run at Lakes of the North, *367*
Deer Run G.Cse., *368*
Lakes of the North Deer Run, *386*
Manchester Village, VT, Gleneagles G.Cse.
    at The Equinox, *813*
Manchester, CT, Manchester C.C., *119*
Manchester, KY, Big Hickory G.Cse. & C.C.,
    294
Manchester, NH, Derryfield C.C., *491*
Manchester, TN, Willowbrook G.C., *765*
Mandan, ND, Prairie West G.Cse., *601*
Manhattan, KS,
Colbert Hills G.Cse., *287*
Stagg Hill G.C., *291*
Manistee, MI, Manistee National Golf &
    Resort, *390*
Manitouwadge, ONTARIO, Manitouwadge
    G.Cse., *932*
Manitowoc, WI, Meadow Links G.Cse., *878*
Manning, SC, The Players Course, *740*
Manorville, NY,
Pine Hills C.C., *551*
Rock Hill C.C., *552*
Swan Lake G.C., *559*
Mansfield, OH,
Twin Lakes G.Cse., *647*
Wooldridge Woods Golf and Swim Club, *650*
Mansfield, PA, Corey Creek G.C., *684*

Mansonville, QUEBEC, Owl's Head, *942*
Manteno, IL, Manteno G.C., *236*
Manton, MI, Emerald Vale G.C., *370*
Manvel, ND, Rivers Edge G.Cse., *601*
Manzanillo, COLIMA, Las Hadas Golf
    Resort & Marina, *948*

Maple Grove, MN,
Rush Creek G.C., *438*
Sundance G.C., *440*
Maple Plain, MN, Pioneer Creek G.Cse.,
    436
Maple Valley, WA,
Elk Run G.C., *841*
Lake Wilderness G.Cse., *845*
Mapleton, ND, Maple River G.C., *600*
Maplewood, MN, Goodrich G.Cse., *427*
Marana, AZ, Heritage Highlands G. & C.C.,
    23
Marathon, NY, Maple Hill G.Cse., *546*
Marathon, ONTARIO, Peninsula G.C., *934*
Marcy, NY, Crestwood G.C., *532*
Marengo, IL, Marengo Ridge G.C., *236*
Margaretville, NY, Hanah Country Inn &
    Golf Resort, *539*
Margate, FL,
Carolina Club, *133*
Oriole Golf & Tennis Club of Margate, *159*
Marietta, GA, City Club Marietta, *183*
Marinette, WI, Little River C.C., *876*
Marion, IA,
Don Gardner Memorial G.Cse., *277*
Gardner G.Cse., *278*
Hunter's Ridge G.C., *279*
Marion, IL, Kokopelli G.C., *233*
Marion, IN,
Arbor Trace G.C., *255*
Shady Hills G.Cse., *270*
Walnut Creek G.Cse., *273*
Marion, NC, Blue Ridge C.C., *569*
Marion, OH, Mar-O-Del G.Cse., *628*
Marion, SC, Dusty Hills C.C., *728*
Marion, VA, Holston Hills C.C., *825*
Markham, ONTARIO,
Angus Glen G.C., *924*
Markham Green G.C., *932*
Marksville, LA, Tamahka Trails G.C., *312*
Marlton, NJ, Indian Spring C.C., *505*
Marne, MI, Western Greens G.Cse., *416*
Marquette, MI,
Chocolay Downs G.Cse., *365*
Marquette G. & C.C., *391*
Marriottsville, MD, Waverly Woods G.C.,
    332
Mars, PA, Venango Trail G.Cse., *715*
Marseilles, IL, The Bourne G.C., *218*
Marshall's Creek, PA, Mountain Manor Inn
    & G.C., *701*
Marshall, MI, The Medalist G.C., *392*
Marshall, MN, Marshall G.C., *432*
Marshalltown, IA, American Legion
    Memorial G.Cse., *275*
Marshfield, MA, Green Harbor G.C., *342*
Marshfield, WI, Marshfield C.C., *877*
Marshville, NC, Eagle Chase G.C., *576*
Marstons Mills, MA, Olde Barnstable
    Fairgrounds G.Cse., *347*
Mart, TX, Battle Lake G.Cse., *767*
Martinsburg, WV,
Stonebridge G.C., *859*
Woodbrier, *860*
Martinvale, P.E.I., Beaver Valley G.C., *939*

Mt. Gilead, NC, The Tillery Tradition C.C., 596
Mt. Holly, NJ, Springfield G.Ctr., 512
Mt. Laurel, NJ, Ramblewood C.C., 510
Mt. Pleasant, MI,
Bucks Run G.C., 362
Pleasant Hills G.C., 400
PohlCat G.Cse., 400
Riverwood Resort, 403
Mt. Prospect, IL,
Mount Prospect G.C., 237
Old Orchard C.C., 240
Mt. Sterling, KY, Old Silo G.C., 302
Mt. Vernon, IL, Indian Hills G.Cse., 231
Muenster, TX, Turtle Hill G.Cse., 800
Mukilteo, WA, Harbour Pointe G.C., 843
Mukwonago, WI,
Lake Beulah C.C., 875
Rainbow Springs G.C., 882
Mullens, WV, Twin Falls State Park G.Cse., 859
Muncie, IN, Maplewood G.C., 265
Mundelein, IL,
Countryside G.Cse., 222
Four Winds G.C., 225
Indian Valley C.C., 231
Pine Meadow G.C., 241
Steeple Chase G.C., 249
Village Green C.C., 252
Murfreesboro, TN,
Indian Hills G.C., 758
Old Fort G.C., 760
Murphy, NC, Cherokee Hills G. & C.C., 573
Murray, KY, Frances E. Miller G.Cse., 297
Murray, UT, Murray Parkway G.C., 807
Murraysville, PA, Rolling Fields G.Cse., 708
Murrell's Inlet, SC, Tournament Player's Club of Myrtle Beach, 745
Murrells Inlet, SC,
Blackmoor G.C., 723
The International Club, 733
Wachesaw Plantation East, 746
Murrieta, CA, The SCGA Members' Club at Rancho California, 85
Murrysville, PA,
Meadowink G.C., 699
Murrysville G.C., 701
Muscatine, IA, Muscatine Municipal G.Cse., 281
Muscle Shoals, AL, Cypress Lakes G. & C.C., 4
Muskego, WI, Muskego Lakes C.C., 878
Muskegon, MI,
Chase Hammond G.Cse., 364
Fruitport C.C., 373
Lincoln G.C., 388
Oak Ridge G.C., 395
Muskogee, OK, Eagle Crest G.Cse., 655
Myerstown, PA, Lebanon Valley G.Cse., 696
Myrtle Beach, SC,
Arcadian Shores G.C., 721
Arrowhead C.C., 721
Belle Terre G.Cse., 722
The Dunes Golf & Beach Club, 728
Grande Dunes G.C., 730
Heron Point G.C., 731
International World Tour G.L., 733
Island Green G.C., 733
The Legends, 735
Man O' War Golf, 736
Myrtle Beach National G.C., 737
Myrtlewood G.C., 737

Pine Lakes International C.C., 740
Prestwick C.C., 741
Quail Creek G.C., 741
Raccoon Run G.C., 741
River Oaks Golf Plantation, 742
Waterway Hills G.C., 746
Wicked Stick G.L., 747
The Wizard G.Cse., 748
Myrtle Creek, OR, Myrtle Creek G.Cse., 671

N

Nacogdoches, TX, Woodland Hills G.Cse., 803
Nags Head, NC, Nags Head G.L., 584
Nampa, ID,
Centennial G.C., 210
Ridgecrest G.C., 212
Nanaimo, BRITISH COLUMBIA, Nanaimo G.C., 910
Nanoose Bay, BRITISH COLUMBIA, Fairwinds G. & C.C., 907
Nantucket, MA, Miacomet G.C., 345
Napa, CA,
The Chardonnay G.C., 48
Napa G.Cse. at Kennedy Park, 72
Silverado C.C. & Resort, 88
Naperville, IL,
Country Lakes G.C., 222
Springbrook G.Cse., 248
Tamarack G.C., 250
Naples, FL,
The G.C. at Marco, 145
Lely Resort G. & C.C., 152
Marco Shores C.C., 154
The Naples Beach Hotel & G.C., 157
Naples Grande G.C., 157
Naples Lakes C.C., 158
Quality Inn & Suites Golf Resort, 164
Tiburon G.C., 173
Valencia G.Cse. at Orangetree, 175
Nashport, OH,
Longaberger G.C., 626
Vista View G.Cse., 648
Nashville, IN, Salt Creek G.C., 269
Nashville, MI, Mulberry Fore G.Cse., 393
Nashville, TN,
Harpeth Hills G.Cse., 757
McCabe Field G.Cse., 759
Nashboro G.C., 760
Springhouse G.C., 763
Ted Rhodes G.Cse., 763
Two Rivers G.Cse., 764
Nassau, NEW PROVIDENCE,
Cable Beach G.C., 957
Paradise Island G.C., 957
South Ocean Golf & Beach Resort, 957
Natchez, MS,
Beau Pre C.C., 443
Duncan Park G.Cse., 445
Nauvoo, IL, Great River Road G.C., 228
Navarre, FL, The Club at Hidden Creek, 135
Navasota, TX, Bluebonnet Country G.Cse., 769
Nebraska City, NE, Wildwood G.Cse., 478
Needles, CA, Needles Municipal G.Cse., 72
Neenah, WI,
Bridgewood G.Cse., 863
Winagamie G.Cse., 890
Nekoosa, WI, Lake Arrowhead G.Cse., 875
Nellis AFB, NV, Sunrise Vista G.C., 488
Neptune, NJ, Shark River G.Cse., 512

Winghaven C.C., *465*
O'Leary, P.E.I., Mill River G.Cse., *940*
Oak Bluffs, MA, Farm Neck G.C., *340*
Oak Brook, IL,
Oak Brook G.C., *238*
Oak Brook Hills Hotel & Resort, *238*
Oak Forest, IL, George W. Dunne National
  G.Cse., *226*
Oak Grove, MO, Bent Oak G.C., *452*
Oak Harbor, OH, Oak Harbor G.C., *630*
Oak Harbor, WA, Gallery G.Cse., *841*
Oak Hill, WV, White Oak C.C., *860*
Oak Island, NC, Oak Island G. & C.C., *585*
Oakes, ND, Oakes G.C., *600*
Oakland Mills, PA, Lost Creek G.C., *698*
Oakland, CA, Lake Chabot G.Cse., *64*
Oakland, MD, Oakland G.C., *328*
Oakland, ME, Waterville C.C., *319*
Oakland, MI,
Beaver Creek Golf Links, *357*
Twin Lakes G.C., *414*
Oakland, NE, Oakland G.C., *476*
Oakmont, PA, Oakmont East G.Cse., *703*
Oakville, ONTARIO,
Glen Abbey G.C., *928*
Richview G. & C.C., *936*
Ocala, FL, Golden Ocala G. & C.C., *145*
Ocean Isle Beach, NC,
Brick Landing Plantation G. & C.C., *570*
Ocean Isle Beach G.Cse., *586*
Ocean Shores, WA, Ocean Shores G.Cse.,
  848
Ocean Springs, MS,
Gulf Hills G.C., *446*
St. Andrews G.C., *449*
Ocean View, DE, Bear Trap Dunes G.C.,
  125
Oceana, WV, Clear Fork Valley C.C., *854*
Oceanside, CA, Oceanside Municipal
  G.Cse., *73*
Ocho Rios, JAMAICA, Sandals G. & C.C.,
  956
Ocoee, FL, Forest Lake G.C. of Ocoee, *143*
Oconomowoc, WI,
Deertrak G.Cse., *867*
Olympia Sports Center, *881*
Paganica G.Cse., *881*
Odessa, FL, The Eagles G.C., *141*
Odessa, TX, Ratliff Ranch G.L., *791*
Ogden, UT,
Ben Lomond G.Cse., *804*
Mount Ogden G.Cse., *807*
Schneiter's Riverside G.Cse., *809*
Ojai, CA,
Ojai Valley Inn & Spa, *73*
Soule Park G.Cse., *89*
Okeene, OK, Okeene Municipal G.Cse., *661*
Oklahoma City, OK,
Broadmoore G.Cse., *653*
Brookside G.Cse., *653*
Earlywine Park G.Cse., *656*
Lake Hefner G.Cse., *659*
Lincoln Park G.Cse., *660*
Silverhorn G.C., *663*
Trosper Park G.Cse., *664*
Okoboji, IA, Brooks G.C., *276*
Okotoks, ALBERTA, D'Arcy Ranch G.C.,
  899
Olathe, KS,
Heritage Park G.Cse., *288*
Lakeside Hills G.Cse., *289*
Old Hickory, TN, Hermitage G.Cse., *757*

Old Orchard Beach, ME, Dunegrass G.C.,
  314
Olds, ALBERTA, Olds G.C., *902*
Olive Branch, MS,
Cherokee Valley G.C., *444*
Links of Whispering Woods, *446*
Plantation G.C., *448*
Wedgewood G.Cse., *450*
Oliver, BRITISH COLUMBIA, Fairview
  Mountain G.C., *907*
Olmsted Falls, OH, Riverside G.C., *637*
Olmsted Township, OH, The Links at the
  Renaissance, *626*
Olney, MD, Trotters Glen G.Cse., *331*
Olympia, WA, Capitol City G.C., *838*
Olympic Valley, CA, Resort at Squaw
  Creek, *80*
Omaha, NE,
Benson Park G.Cse., *472*
Elmwood Park G.Cse., *473*
Johnny Goodman G.Cse., *475*
The Knolls G.Cse., *475*
Miracle Hill Golf & Tennis Center, *476*
Player's Club at Deer Creek, *476*
Stone Creek G.Cse., *477*
Tiburon G.C., *477*
Onamia, MN, Izatys Golf & Yacht Club, *429*
Onanole, MANITOBA, Clear Lake G.Cse.,
  916
Onaway, MI, Black Lake G.C., *358*
Oneida, WI, Brown County G.Cse., *864*
Onekama, MI, The Heathlands, *381*
Oneonta, AL, Limestone Springs G.C., *7*
Oneonta, NY, Woodhaven G.Cse., *567*
Onset Beach, MA, Bay Pointe C.C., *335*
Ontario, CA, Whispering Lakes G.Cse., *95*
Ontario, OR, Shadow Butte G.C., *675*
Opelika, AL, Robert Trent Jones Golf Trail at
  Grand National G.C., *9*
Orange City, IA, Landsmeer G.C., *280*
Orange Park, FL,
Eagle Harbor G.C., *141*
The G.C. at Fleming Island Plantation, *145*
Orange, CT,
Grassy Hill C.C., *118*
Orange Hills C.C., *120*
Orangeburg, SC, Hillcrest G.C., *732*
Orangeville, ONTARIO, Hockley Valley
  Resort, *929*
Oregon City, OR, Oregon City G.C., *672*
Oregon, IL, Silver Ridge G.Cse., *247*
Oregon, OH, Maumee Bay Resort G.Cse.,
  628
Orient, OH, Split Rock G.Cse., *642*
Orilla, ONTARIO, Hawk Ridge G.C., *929*
Oriskany Falls, NY, Barker Brook G.C., *523*
Oriskany, NY, Shamrock G. & C.C., *555*
Orland Park, IL, Silver Lake C.C., *247*
Orlando, FL,
Arnold Palmer's Bay Hill Club & Lodge, *128*
Eastwood G.C., *141*
Grand Cypress G.C., *146*
Hunter's Creek G.C., *148*
International G.C., *149*
Lake Orlando G.C., *151*
MetroWest C.C., *156*
Orlando World Center - Marriott, *160*
Orleans, IN, Saddlebrook G.C., *269*
Orleans, VT, Orleans C.C., *815*
Ormond Beach, FL,
Halifax Plantation G.C., *147*
River Bend G.C., *165*

Schaumburg, IL, Schaumburg G.C., *246*
Schenectady, NY,
Schenectady G.Cse., *555*
Stadium G.C., *558*
Town of Colonie G.Cse., *561*
Schererville, IN, Scherwood G.Cse., *269*
Schofield Barracks, HI, Leilehua G.Cse., *203*
Schoolcraft, MI, Olde Mill G.C., *396*
Scituate, MA,
Scituate C.C., *350*
Widow's Walk G.Cse., *354*
Scotch Plains, NJ, Ash Brook G.Cse., *498*
Scotts, MI, Indian Run G.C., *384*
Scottsbluff, NE, Riverview G. & C.C., *477*
Scottsboro, AL, Goose Pond Colony G.Cse., *5*
Scottsdale, AZ,
Gainey Ranch G.C., *21*
Grayhawk G.C., *22*
Kierland G.C., *23*
Legend Trail G.C., *25*
Marriott's Camelback G.C., *26*
McCormick Ranch G.C., *26*
Mountain Shadows, *27*
Orange Tree Golf Resort, *27*
Pavilion Lakes G.C., *28*
The Phoenician, *28*
The Sanctuary G.Cse. at Westworld, *31*
Scottsdale Silverado G.C., *31*
Starfire G.C. at Scottsdale C.C., *32*
Talking Stick G.C., *33*
Tournament Players Club of Scottsdale, *34*
Troon North G.C., *34*
Scottsville, NY,
Chili C.C., *529*
Cragie Brae G.C., *531*
Seabrook Island, SC, The Club at Seabrook Island, *725*
Sealy, TX, River Ridge G.C., *792*
Seaside, CA, Bayonet/Black Horse Golf Courses, *44*
Seattle, WA,
Jackson Park G.Cse., *844*
Jefferson Park G.Cse., *844*
Tyee Valley G.Cse., *852*
West Seattle G.Cse., *853*
Sebastian, FL, Sebastian Municipal G.Cse., *169*
Sebring, FL,
C.C. of Sebring, *137*
Golf Hammock C.C., *146*
Harder Hall C.C., *147*
Spring Lake Golf & Tennis Resort, *171*
Secor, IL, Fairlakes G.Cse., *225*
Sedona, AZ,
Oakcreek C.C., *27*
Sedona Golf Resort, *31*
Seekonk, MA, Firefly G.Cse., *341*
Selkirk, MANITOBA, Selkirk G. & C.C., *917*
Sellersburg, IN,
Covered Bridge G.C., *258*
Hidden Creek G.C., *262*
Selma, CA, Selma Valley G.Cse., *86*
Semmes, AL, Robert Trent Jones Golf Trail at Magnolia Grove, *10*
Seneca, KS, Seneca G.C., *291*
Senecaville, OH, Robins' Ridge G.Cse., *638*
Sequim, WA,
Dungeness G. & C.C., *840*
Sunland G. & C.C., *851*
Sevierville, TN, Eagle's Landing G.C., *755*

Sewell, NJ,
Maple Ridge G.C., *506*
Pitman G.Cse., *509*
Sexsmith, ALBERTA, Spruce Meadows G. & C.C., *904*
Seymour, IN, Shadowood G.Cse., *270*
Seymour, WI, Crystal Springs G.C., *866*
Shakopee, MN,
Lone Pine C.C., *431*
Stonebrooke G.C., *439*
Shalimar, FL, Shalimar Pointe G. & C.C., *169*
Shallotte, NC,
Brierwood G.C., *570*
Rivers Edge G.C., *591*
Sharon, ONTARIO, Pheasant Run G.C., *935*
Shattuck, OK, Shattuck G. & C.C., *663*
Shawano, WI, Shawano Lake G.C., *884*
Shawnee, KS, Tomahawk Hills G.C., *292*
Shawnee, OK, Fire Lake G.Cse., *656*
Shawnee-on-Delaware, PA, Shawnee Inn Golf Resort, *709*
Sheboygan, WI,
Riverdale C.C., *883*
Sheboygan Town & C.C., *884*
Whistling Straits G.C., *890*
Shelburne, VT, Kwiniaska G.C., *814*
Shelby Township, MI,
Cherry Creek G.C., *364*
Stony Creek G.Cse., *409*
Shelby, MI, Oceana G.C., *395*
Shelby, MT, Marias Valley G. & C.C., *469*
Shelby, NC,
Deer Brook G.C., *575*
Pine Grove G.C., *587*
River Bend G.C., *590*
Shelby, OH, Woody Ridge G.Cse., *650*
Shelbyville, KY,
Shelbyville C.C., *304*
Weissinger Hills G.Cse., *305*
Shelbyville, MI, Orchard Hills G.Cse., *396*
Shenandoah, IA, American Legion C.C., *275*
Shepherd, MI, Winding Brook G.C., *418*
Shepherdsville, KY, Maplehurst G.Cse., *301*
Sheridan, WY,
Kendrick G.Cse., *893*
Powder Horn G.C., *893*
Sheridan C.C., *894*
Sherwood Park, ALBERTA,
Broadmoor Public G.Cse., *898*
Countryside G.Cse., *899*
Sherwood Park G.Cse., *904*
Sherwood, WI, High Cliff G.Cse., *872*
Shirley, NY, Links at Shirley, *544*
Shoemakersville, PA, Perry G.Cse., *704*
Shoreham, NY, Tallgrass G.C., *559*
Short Hills, NJ, East Orange G.Cse., *502*
Shortsville, NY, Winged Pheasant G.L., *567*
Show Low, AZ, Silver Creek G.C., *32*
Shreveport, LA,
Huntington Park G.Cse., *309*
Northwood G. & C.C., *310*
Querbes Park G.Cse., *311*
Siasconset, MA, Siasconset G.C., *351*
Sicklerville, NJ, Freeway G.Cse., *502*
Sidney, NE, Hillside G.Cse., *474*
Sidney, OH, Shelby Oaks G.C., *641*
Sierra Vista, AZ, Pueblo Del Sol C.C., *29*
Sikeston, MO,
BootHeel G.C., *452*

Sikeston C.C., *463*
Siloam Springs, AR, Dawn Hill Golf & Racquet Club, *38*
Silver City, NM, Silver City G.Cse. at Scott Park, *520*
Silver Creek, NY, Rose Brook G.Cse., *553*
Silver Spring, MD, Hampshire Greens G.C., *326*
Silverthorne, CO, The Raven G.C. at Three Peaks, *111*
Silvis, IL, Tournament Players Club at Deere Run, *251*
Simi Valley, CA,
Lost Canyons G.C., *67*
Simi Hills G.C., *88*
Sinclair, WY, Sinclair G.C., *894*
Sinking Spring, PA, Manor G.C., *699*
Sinton, TX, Sinton Municipal G.Cse., *796*
Sioux City, IA, Green Valley Municipal G.C., *279*
Sioux Falls, SD,
Elmwood G.Cse., *749*
Prairie Green G.Cse., *750*
Willow Run G.Cse., *751*
Sisters, OR, Aspen Lakes G.Cse., *666*
Skaneateles, NY, Midlakes Club, *547*
Skippack, PA, Skippack G.Cse., *710*
Sky Valley, GA, Sky Valley Golf & Ski Resort, *195*
Skytop, PA, Skytop Lodge, *710*
Slidell, LA,
Oak Harbor G.C., *310*
Pinewood C.C., *311*
Royal G.C., *311*
Slinger, WI, Scenic View C.C., *884*
Smithfield, UT, Birch Creek G.C., *804*
Smithfield, VA, Cypress Creek Golfers' Club, *821*
Smithtown, NY, Smithtown Landing G.C., *557*
Smithville, MO, Paradise Pointe Golf Complex, *460*
Smyrna, DE, Garrisons Lake C.C., *126*
Smyrna, GA, Fox Creek G.C., *186*
Smyrna, TN, Smyrna Municipal G.Cse., *762*
Sneads Ferry, NC, North Shore C.C., *585*
Snellville, GA, Trophy Club of Gwinnett, *197*
Snohomish, WA,
Echo Falls C.C., *840*
Kenwanda G.Cse., *844*
Snohomish G.Cse., *850*
Snoqualmie, WA, Mount Si G.Cse., *847*
Snow Camp, NC, Sourwood Forest G.Cse., *594*
Snow Hill, MD, Nassawango C.C., *328*
Snowmass Village, CO, Snowmass Club G.Cse., *113*
Snowshoe, WV, Snowshoe Mountain Resort, *859*
Socorro, NM, New Mexico Tech G.Cse., *518*
Soda Springs, ID, Oregon Trail C.C., *211*
Sodus Point, NY, Sodus Bay Heights G.Cse., *557*
Soldotna, AK, Birch Ridge G.Cse., *14*
Solvang, CA,
The Alisal Ranch G.Cse., *42*
River Course at The Alisal, *81*
Somers, CT, Cedar Knob G.C., *116*
Somerset, KY, Eagle's Nest C.C., *297*
Somerset, NJ,
Quail Brook G.Cse., *510*
Spooky Brook G.Cse., *512*

Somerset, WI, Saint Croix National G.C., *884*
Sonoma, CA, Sonoma Mission Inn G. & C.C., *89*
Sonora, CA, Mountain Springs G.C., *72*
South Alburg, VT, Alburg C.C., *812*
South Bend, IN,
Blackthorn G.C., *255*
Elbel Park G.Cse., *259*
Erskine Park G.Cse., *259*
South Boston, VA, Green's Folly G.Cse., *823*
South Burlington, VT, Vermont National C.C., *816*
South Easton, MA, Easton C.C., *340*
South Edmonton, ALBERTA, Eagle Rock G.Cse., *899*
South Fallsburg, NY, Tarry Brae G.C., *560*
South Haven, MI,
HawksHead G.L., *380*
South Haven C.C., *408*
South Jordon, UT, Glenmoor G. & C.C., *806*
South Lake Tahoe, CA, Lake Tahoe G.Cse., *64*
South Lyon, MI,
Cattails G.C., *363*
Pebble Creek G.Cse., *397*
Tanglewood G.C., *410*
South Milwaukee, WI, Grant Park G.Cse., *871*
South Portland, ME, Sable Oaks G.C., *318*
South Riding, VA, South Riding Golfers' Club, *833*
South Rockwood, MI, Wesburn G.Cse., *416*
South Rustico, P.E.I., Rustico Resort G. & C.C., *940*
South Sandwich, MA, Holly Ridge G.C., *343*
South Sioux City, NE, Covington Links G.Cse., *472*
South Surrey, BRITISH COLUMBIA, Peace Portal G.Cse., *911*
South Windsor, CT, Topstone G.C., *123*
South Yarmouth, MA,
Bass River G.Cse., *335*
Blue Rock G.Cse., *336*
Southampton, BERMUDA,
Port Royal G.Cse., *953*
Southampton Princess G.Cse., *953*
Southampton, MA, South Hampton C.C., *351*
Southampton, ONTARIO, Chippewa G. & C.C., *926*
Southaven, MS, The Club at North Creek, *444*
Southern Pines, NC,
The Club at Longleaf, *573*
Hyland Hills G.C., *580*
Mid Pines Inn & G.C., *583*
Pine Needles Lodge & G.C., *587*
Talamore Resort, *595*
Southington, CT,
Pattonbrook C.C., *120*
Pine Valley G.Cse., *120*
Southington C.C., *122*
Southington, OH, Forest Oaks G.Cse., *616*
Southlake, TX, Timarron G. & C.C., *799*
Southport, NC, St. James Plantation, *594*
Southwick, MA,
Edgewood G.Cse. of Southwick, *340*
The Ranch G.C., *349*

Summerland, BRITISH COLUMBIA,
Summerland G. & C.C., *914*
Summerside, P.E.I., Summerside G. & C.C.,
940
Summerton, SC, Foxboro G.C., *729*
Summerville, SC,
C.C. of Summerville, *726*
Legend Oak's Plantation G.C., *734*
Pine Forest C.C., *740*
River Club on the Ashley, *741*
Sumner, WA, Sumner Meadows G.L., *851*
Sumter, SC,
Beech Creek G.C., *722*
Lakewood Links G.C., *734*
Pocalla Springs C.C., *740*
Sun City West, AZ, Hillcrest G.C., *23*
Sun Prairie, WI, Sun Prairie G.Cse., *886*
Sun Valley, ID,
Elkhorn Resort & G.C., *210*
Sun Valley Resort G.Cse., *213*
Sunbury, OH, Bent Tree G.C., *604*
Sunfield, MI, Centennial Acres G.Cse., *363*
Sunnyvale, CA, Sunnyvale G.Cse., *91*
Sunol, CA, Sunol Valley G.Cse., *91*
Sunrise, FL, Sunrise C.C., *172*
Sunriver, OR,
Sunriver Lodge & Resort, *675*
Sunset Beach, NC,
Angel's Trace G.L., *568*
Ocean Ridge Plantation, *586*
Oyster Bay G.L., *587*
Pearl G.L., *587*
Sandpiper Bay G. & C.C., *592*
Sea Trail Plantation, *592*
Thistle G.C., *595*
Superior, WI, Nemadji G.Cse., *879*
Surfside Beach, SC,
Deer Track Golf Resort, *727*
Indigo Creek Golf Plantation, *733*
Suring, WI, Cathedral Pines G.Cse., *865*
Surprise, AZ,
Coyote Lakes G.C., *19*
Desert Springs G.Cse., *19*
Granite Falls G.C., *22*
Happy Trails Resort, *23*
Surrey, BRITISH COLUMBIA,
Morgan Creek G.Cse., *910*
Northview G. & C.C., *910*
Sutherlin, OR, Oak Hills G.C., *671*
Sutter, CA, Southridge G.C., *89*
Sutton, MA, Blackstone National G.C., *336*
Suwanee, GA,
Laurel Springs G.C., *190*
Olde Atlanta G.C., *192*
Swainton, NJ, Sand Barrens G.C., *511*
Swan Lake, NY, Swan Lake C.C., *559*
Swansboro, NC, Silver Creek G.C., *593*
Swansea, IL, Clinton Hill G.C., *221*
Swansea, MA,
Swansea C.C., *352*
Touisset C.C., *353*
Swanton, OH, Valleywood G.C., *647*
Swanton, VT, Champlain C.C., *812*
Swartz Creek, MI, Genesee Valley
Meadows, *374*
Swedesboro, NJ, Beckett G.C., *498*
Sweetwater, TX, Sweetwater C.C., *797*
Swift Current, SASKATCHEWAN, Elmwood
G. & C.C., *943*
Sycamore, IL, Sycamore G.C., *250*
Sydney, NOVA SCOTIA, Lingan G. & C.C.,
923

Sylmar, CA, The Cascades G.C., *47*
Sylvania, OH, Spuyten Duyval G.C., *643*
Syracuse, IN,
Maxwelton G.C., *265*
South Shore G.C., *270*
Syracuse, NY,
Drumlins West G.C., *533*
Tanner Valley G.Cse., *560*
Syracuse, UT, Glen Eagle at Syracuse G.C.,
805

T

Tacoma, WA,
Brookdale G.Cse., *838*
Lake Spanaway G.Cse., *845*
Meadow Park G.Cse., *847*
North Shore G. & C.C., *848*
Tahlequah, OK,
Cherokee Trails G.Cse., *654*
Cherry Springs G.Cse., *654*
Talladega, AL, Timber Ridge G.C., *12*
Tallahassee, FL,
Don Veller Seminole G.Cse., *139*
Hilaman Park Municipal G.Cse., *148*
Tamaqua, PA, Mahoning Valley G.Cse., *698*
Tamarac, FL, Colony West C.C., *136*
Tamaroa, IL, Red Hawk C.C., *244*
Tamiment, PA, Tamiment Resort &
Conference Center G.C., *713*
Tampa, FL,
Babe Zaharias G.Cse., *129*
Northdale Golf & Tennis Club, *158*
Rocky Point G.Cse., *166*
Rogers Park G.Cse., *166*
University of South Florida G.Cse., *175*
Westchase G.C., *177*
Tarpon Springs, FL, Tarpon Springs G.C.,
172
Tavares, FL, Deer Island Golf & Lake Club,
138
Tawas City, MI,
Singing Bridge Golf, *407*
Tawas Creek G.C., *411*
Taylor, BRITISH COLUMBIA, The Lone
Wolf G.C., *909*
Taylor, MI,
Lakes of Taylor G.C., *386*
Taylor Meadows G.C., *411*
Taylor, PA, Pine Hills G.Cse., *705*
Taylorsville, KY, Tanglewood G.Cse., *304*
Taylorsville, NC, Brushy Mountain G.C.,
570
Taylorsville, UT, Meadow Brook G.Cse.,
807
Taylorville, IL, Lake Shore G.Cse., *234*
Tazewell, TN, Woodlake G.C., *765*
Teaneck, NJ, Overpeck County G.Cse., *508*
Tecumseh, MI, Raisin Valley G.C., *401*
Tehachapi, CA, Horse Thief C.C., *61*
Temecula, CA,
CrossCreek G.C., *51*
Redhawk G.C., *80*
Temecula Creek Inn, *92*
Temeku Hills G. & C.C., *92*
Tempe, AZ,
The ASU Karsten G.Cse., *17*
Ken McDonald G.Cse., *23*
Temperance, MI, Giant Oak Golf Club, *374*
Temple, TX, J.F. Sammons Park G.Cse., *782*
Terra Alta, WV, Alpine Lake Resort, *854*

Alphabetical Directory
by Course

The Broadlands G.Cse., 99
Broadmoor C.C., 256
Broadmoor C.C., 361
The Broadmoor G.C., 99
Broadmoor G.Cse., 666
Broadmoor G.L., 570
Broadmoor Public G.Cse., 898
Broadmoore G.Cse., 653
Brock Park G.Cse., 770
Brockport C.C., 526
Brockville C.C., 925
Broken Arrow G.C., 218
Bronzwood G.C., 607
Brook Hill G.C., 256
Brookdale G.Cse., 838
Brookhaven G.Cse., 526
Brooklawn G.Cse., 526
Brooklea G. & C.C., 925
Brookledge G.C., 607
Brookline G.C., 337
Brookmeadow C.C., 337
Brooks G.C., 276
Brookshire G.C., 256
Brookside G.C., 337
Brookside G.C., 46
Brookside G.Cse., 607
Brookside G.Cse., 653
Brooktree Municipal G.Cse., 421
Brookview G.Cse., 421
Brookwood C.C., 443
Brookwood G.C., 257
Brookwood G.Cse., 362
The Brookwoods G.C., 819
Brown Acres G.Cse., 753
Brown County G.Cse., 864
Brown Deer G.C., 276
Brown Deer Park G.Cse., 864
Browns Lake G.Cse., 864
Browns Mill G.Cse., 181
Brownsville G.Ctr., 770
Brudenell River Resort, 939
Brunswick G.C., 314
Brunswick Hills G.Cse., 607
Brunswick Plantation Golf Resort, 570
Brushy Mountain G.C., 570
Bryan G.Cse., 770
Bryan Park & G.C., 571
Bryce Resort G.Cse., 820
Bryden Canyon Public G.Cse., 209
Buccaneer Hotel G.Cse., 959
Buck Hill G.C., 680
Buckeye Hills C.C., 607
The Buckhorn G.Cse., 770
Bucknell G.C., 681
Bucks Run G.C., 362
Bucyrus C.C., 608
Buena Vista C.C., 499
Buenaventura G.Cse., 46
Buffalo Creek G.C., 770
Buffalo Creek, 132
Buffalo Dunes G.Cse., 286
Buffalo G.C., 892
Buffalo G.Cse., 681
Buffalo Grove G.C., 218
Buffalo Hill G.C., 467
Buffalo Run G.Cse., 100
Buffalo Valley G.Cse., 753
The Bull at Boone's Trace G.C., 295
Bull Creek G.C., 181
Bull Run C.C., 820
Bulle Rock, 322
Buncombe County Municipal G.C., 571

Bunker Hill G.Cse., 276
Bunker Hill G.Cse., 499
Bunker Hill G.Cse., 608
Bunker Hills G.Cse., 422
Bunker Links Municipal G.Cse., 218
Bunn G.Cse., 218
Burden Lake C.C., 526
Burley G.Cse., 209
Burnaby Mountain G.Cse., 905
Burning Oak C.C., 362
Burning Ridge G.C., 723
Burning Tree G.Cse., 608
Burns Park G.Cse., 37
Burr Oak G.C., 362
Butler's G.Cse., 681
Butter Valley Golf Port, 681
Butternut Farm G.C., 337
Butternut Hills G.Cse., 865
Byrncliff G.C., 526
Byron Hills G.C., 362
Byron Hills G.Cse., 218
C-Way G.C., 526
Caberfae Peaks Ski & Golf Resort, 362
Cabin Brook G.C., 295
Cable Beach G.C., 957
Cable Hollow G.C., 681
Cabo del Sol, 946
Cabo Real G.C., 947
Cabo San Lucas C.C., 947
Cacapon Resort, 854
Caguas Real G.Cse., 958
Cahoon Plantation, 820
Calabash G.L., 571
Calabogie Highlands Resort & G.C., 925
Caledon C.C., 925
Caledonia Golf & Fish Club, 724
Caledonia G.C., 681
Calhoun C.C., 724
California Club, 132
California G.Cse., 608
Calimesa C.C., 46
Callaway Gardens Resort, 182
Calusa C.C., 132
Calusa Lakes G.Cse., 132
Calvert City G. & C.C., 295
Calvert Crossing G.C., 308
Camaloch G.Cse., 838
Camarillo Springs G.Cse., 46
Camas Meadow G.C., 838
Cambridge C.C., 322
Cambridge G.C., 257
Camelot C.C., 753
Camillus C.C., 527
Campbell's Scottish Highlands G.Cse., 491
Campo de Golf Ixtapa G.Cse., 948
Campo de Golf Playa Grande, 954
Campo de Golf San Jose, 947
Canaan Valley Resort G.Cse., 854
Canajoharie C.C., 527
Canasawacta C.C., 527
Candia Woods G.L., 491
Candlestone Inn Golf & Resort, 362
Candlewood Valley C.C., 116
Candywood G.C., 608
Canebrake G.C., 443
Canmore Golf & Curling Club, 898
Cannon G.C., 422
Canoa Hills G.Cse., 18
Canterberry G.Cse., 100
Cantigny Golf, 219
Canton Public G.Cse., 116
Canyon Lake G.C., 770

Chapel Hill G.Cse., 609
Chapel Hill G.Cse., 683
Chapel Hills G.Cse., 609
Chapel Ridge G.C., 453
Chapples G.Cse., 926
Chardon Lakes G.Cse., 609
The Chardonnay G.C., 48
Charleston Municipal G.Cse., 724
Charleston National C.C., 724
Charleston Springs G.Cse., 500
Charlevoix C.C., 364
Charlie Vettiner G.Cse., 295
Charlotte G.L., 572
Charlotte National G.C., 572
Chase Hammond G.Cse., 364
Chase Oaks G.C., 771
Chaska G.Cse., 865
Chaska Town Course, 422
Chateau Elan Resort, 182
Chateau Whistler G.C., 906
Chattahoochee G.C., 183
Chatuge Shores G.Cse., 572
Chautauqua G.C., 529
Cheboygan G. & C.C., 364
Chena Bend G.C., 14
Chenango Valley State Park, 529
Chennault Park G.Cse., 308
Chequamegon Bay G.C., 865
Chequessett Yacht & C.C., 338
Cheraw State Park G.Cse., 725
Cherokee C.C., 771
Cherokee G.Cse., 683
Cherokee Grove G.C., 654
Cherokee Hills G. & C.C., 573
Cherokee Hills G.C., 609
Cherokee Hills G.Cse., 610
Cherokee Run G.C., 183
Cherokee Trails G.Cse., 654
Cherokee Valley G.C., 444
Cherokee Valley G.C., 725
Cherokee Village G.C., 37
Cherry Creek G.C., 364
Cherry Creek G.L., 529
Cherry Hill G.C., 257
Cherry Hills G.C., 220
Cherry Hills G.C., 453
Cherry Hills Lodge & G.Cse., 865
Cherry Island G.Cse., 48
Cherry Springs G.Cse., 654
Cherry Valley G.Cse., 683
Cherry Wood G.Cse., 683
Chesapeake Bay G.C., 322
Chesapeake G.C., 820
Chesapeake Hills G.C., 323
Cheshire Hills G.Cse., 364
Chesley Oaks G.Cse., 3
Chestatee G.C., 183
Chester G.C., 725
Chester W. Ditto G.C., 772
Chester Washington G.Cse., 48
Chestnut Hill C.C., 529
Chestnut Hill G.C., 257
Chestnut Ridge G.C., 683
Chestnut Valley G.Cse., 365
Cheviot Hills G.C., 573
Chevy Chase G.C., 220
Chevy Chase G.C., 839
Chewelah G. & C.C., 838
Cheyenne C.C., 892
Chi Chi Rodriguez G.C., 134
Chick Evans G.Cse., 220
Chickasaw Point C.C., 725

Chicopee G.C., 338
Chicopee Woods G.Cse., 183
Chili C.C., 529
Chimney Rock Municipal G.Cse., 481
China Lake G.C., 48
Chippewa G. & C.C., 926
Chippewa G.C., 610
Chippewa G.C., 610
Chippewa G.C., 683
Chisago Lakes G.Cse., 423
Chisholm Hills C.C., 365
Chisholm Trail G.Cse., 287
Chocolay Downs G.Cse., 365
Choctaw Creek G.Cse., 654
Chomonix G.Cse., 423
Christina Lake G.C., 906
Christman's Windham House, 529
Christmas Lake G.Cse., 257
Christmas Mountain Village G.C., 865
Chuck Corica Golf Complex, 49
Chula Vista Municipal G.Cse., 49
Churchville G.C., 529
Cielo Vista G.Cse., 772
Cimarron Golf Resort, 49
Cimarron National G.C., 654
Cimarrone G. & C.C., 134
Cinder Ridge G.L., 220
Cinnabar Hills G.C., 49
Circle C Ranch G.C., 772
Citronelle Municipal G.Cse., 3
Citrus Hills G. & C.C., 134
Citrus Springs G. & C.C., 134
City Club Marietta, 183
City of Amsterdam Municipal G.Cse., 530
City Park G.C., 100
City Park G.Cse., 308
Clarion Oaks G.Cse., 684
Clark Lake G.C., 365
Clarkston Creek G.C., 365
Clary Fields G.C., 654
Classic C.C., 839
Claycrest G.C., 453
Clayton G.Cse., 515
Clear Creek G.C., 444
Clear Creek G.C., 821
Clear Fork Valley C.C., 854
Clear Lake C.C., 210
Clear Lake G.C., 772
Clear Lake G.Cse., 916
Clearbrook G.C., 365
Clearview G.C., 530
Clearview G.C., 610
Clearwater C.C., 134
Cleburne Municipal G.Cse., 772
Cleghorn Plantation G. & C.C., 573
Cleveland Heights G.Cse., 135
The Cliffs Resort, 772
Cliffside G.Cse., 610
Cliffside G.Cse., 610
Cliffwood G.C., 573
Clifton Highlands G.Cse., 866
Clifton Hollow G.C., 866
Clifton Park G.Cse., 323
Clinchview G. & C.C., 753
Clinton C.C., 453
Clinton Heights G.Cse., 610
Clinton Hill G.C., 221
Cloverleaf G.C., 684
Cloverleaf G.Cse., 221
The Club & Lodge at The Bluffs on
    Thompson Creek, 308
The Club at Big Creek, 754

Goderich Sunset G.C., 929
Gogebic C.C., 375
Gold Canyon Golf Resort, 21
Gold Creek Resort, 187
Gold Hills G.C., 58
Gold Mountain Golf Complex, 842
The Golden Bear Club at Keene's Pointe, 144
Golden Bear G.C. at Hammock Creek, 144
Golden Bear G.C., 730
Golden Belt C.C., 288
Golden G. & C.C., 908
Golden Hills G. & C.C., 730
Golden Horseshoe G.C., 823
Golden Oak G.C., 537
Golden Oaks C.C., 690
Golden Ocala G. & C.C., 145
Golden Pheasant G.C., 503
Golden Sands Golf Community, 870
Golf at The Legacy, 427
Golf Bouctouche, 918
The G.Ctr. at Kings Island, 618
The G.C. at Amelia Island, 145
The G.C. at Apple Mountain, 375
The G.C. at Bradshaw Farm, 187
The G.C. at Camelot, 870
The G.C. at Castle Hills, 778
The G.C. at Cimarron Trails, 657
The G.C. at Cinco Ranch, 778
The G.C. at Cuscowilla, 187
The G.C. at Cypress Head, 145
The G.C. at Eagle Mountain, 22
The G.C. at Fleming Island Plantation, 145
The G.C. at Fossil Creek, 779
The G.C. at Genoa Lakes, 483
The G.C. at Hawk's Prairie, 842
The G.C. at Mansion Ridge, 537
The G.C. at Marco, 145
The G.C. at Newcastle, 842
G.C. at Paw Creek, 578
The G.C. at Redlands Mesa, 105
The G.C. at Roddy Ranch, 58
The G.C. at Shepherd Hills, 690
The G.C. at Star Ranch, 779
The G.C. at StoneBridge, 308
The G.C. at Thanksgiving Point, 806
The G.C. at Thornapple Pointe, 375
The G.C. at Valley View, 38
The G.C. at Vistoso, 22
G.C. at Wescott Plantation, 730
The G.C. at Whitehawk Ranch, 58
The G.C. at Wisp, 325
The G.C. at Yankee Trace, 618
G.C. of Illinois, 227
G.C. of Indiana, 261
G.C. of Jacksonville, 145
The G.C. of Jupiter, 146
G.C. of Michigan, 376
The G.C. of New Orleans at Eastover, 308
G.C. of Newport, 537
The G.C. of Oregon, 668
The G.C. of South Carolina at Crickentree, 730
The G.C. of Texas, 779
G.C. of West Virginia, 855
The G.Cse. at Glen Mills, 690
G.Cse. of Trumansburg, 538
The G.Cse.s at Incline Village, 483
The G.Cse.s at Kenton County, 298
The G.Cse.s of Lawsonia, 870
The G.Cse.s of Winton Woods, 619
Golf Dorval, 941

Golf Hammock C.C., 146
Golf Resort at Indian Wells, 58
Golfmohr G.Cse., 228
Goodrich C.C., 376
Goodrich G.Cse., 427
Goodwin Park G.Cse., 118
Goose Creek G.C., 58
Goose Creek G.C., 823
Goose Hummock Golf Resort, 900
Goose Pond Colony G.Cse., 5
Gordon G. & C.C., 473
Gordon Trent G.Cse., Inc., 823
Gorge Vale G.C., 908
Gorham C.C., 315
Gormley Green G.C., 929
Goshen Plantation C.C., 187
Gospel Hill G. & C.C., 691
Gowan Brae G. & C.C., 918
Gracewil C.C., 376
Graeagle Meadows G.Cse., 58
Grand Bear G.Cse., 446
Grand Blanc G. & C.C., 376
Grand Cypress G.C., 146
Grand Falls G.C., 919
Grand Geneva Resort & Spa, 871
Grand Haven G.C., 146
Grand Haven G.C., 376
Grand Hotel G.C., 376
Grand Island Golf Ranch, 376
Grand Island Municipal G.Cse., 473
Grand Lake G.Cse., 105
Grand Ledge C.C., 377
Grand Marais G.Cse., 228
Grand National G.C., 427
Grand Oak G.C., 261
Grand Oaks Resort G.Cse., 446
Grand Palms G. & C.C. Resort, 146
Grand Prairie G.Cse., 377
Grand Rapids G.C., 377
Grand Traverse Resort and Spa, 377
Grand View G.C., 691
Grand View G.Cse., 377
Grand View Lodge Resort, 427
Grande Dunes G.C., 730
Grande Valle G.C., 22
Grandote Peaks G.C., 105
Grandover Resort & Conference Center, 578
Grandview C.C., 342
Grandview C.C., 855
Grandview Farms G.Cse., 538
Grandview G. & C.C., 923
Grandview G.C., 377
Grandview G.C., 619
Grandview G.C., 691
Grandview G.C., 691
Grandview G.Cse., 279
Grandview G.Cse., 842
Granite Falls G.C., 22
Grant Park G.Cse., 871
Grants Pass G.C., 668
Granville G.Cse., 619
Grapevine G.Cse., 779
Grassmere C.C., 118
Grassy Hill C.C., 118
Gray Plantation G.C., 309
Gray Rocks G.C., 941
Grayhawk G.C., 22
Grayling C.C., 378
Graysburg Hills G.Cse., 756
Grayson County College G.Cse., 779
Great Cove Golf Recreation, 691
Great Gorge C.C., 503

Hastings C.C., 380
Haven G.C., 23
Hawaii C.C., 204
Hawaii Kai G.Cse., 200
Hawaii Prince G.C., 200
Hawk Hollow G.Cse., 380
Hawk Lake G.C., 692
Hawk Meadows at Dama Farms, 380
Hawk Pointe G.C., 504
Hawk Ridge G.C., 929
Hawk Valley G.C., 693
Hawks Creek G.C., 780
Hawks Nest G.C., 620
HawksHead G.L., 380
Hawksnest Golf & Ski Resort, 579
Hawktree G.C., 599
Hawley G. & C.C., 428
Hawthorn Ridge G.C., 229
Hawthorn Suites at Midlane Golf Resort, 229
Hawthorne Hills G.C., 620
Hawthorne Hills G.C., 872
Haymaker G.Cse., 105
Haystack G.C., 813
Hayward Golf & Tennis Club, 872
Headwaters C.C., 428
Heart River Municipal G.Cse., 599
Heather Glen G.L., 731
Heather Highlands G.C., 380
Heather Hill C.C., 342
Heather Hills G.Cse., 380
Heather Run Golf & Fish Club, 780
Heatherhurst G.C., 757
Heatherwood G.Cse., 540
Heatherwoode G.C., 620
The Heathlands, 381
Hecla G.Cse. at Gull Harbor Resort, 916
Hedingham G.C., 579
Helfrich G.Cse., 262
Hell's Point G.C., 824
Hemlock Springs G.C., 620
Henderson G.C., 188
Henderson Lake G.C., 900
Hendricks Field G.Cse., 504
Henrietta C.C., 657
Henry County C.C., 298
Henry Homberg Municipal G.Cse., 780
Henry Horton State Park G.Cse., 757
Heritage Bluffs G.C., 229
Heritage Club, 731
Heritage C.C., 342
Heritage C.C., 540
Heritage Eagle Bend G.C., 106
Heritage Glen G.C., 381
The Heritage G.C., 188
The Heritage G.Cse. at Westmoor, 106
Heritage Highlands G. & C.C., 23
Heritage Hills G.Cse., 473
Heritage Hills G.Cse., 657
Heritage Hills Golf Resort & Conference
    Center, 693
Heritage Palms G.C., 60
Heritage Park G.Cse., 288
Heritage Pointe G. & C.C., 900
Hermann Park G.Cse., 780
Hermitage G.Cse., 757
Hermon Meadow G.C., 315
Herndon Centennial G.C., 824
Heron Creek G. & C.C., 148
Heron Lakes G.Cse., 669
Heron Point G.C., 731
Heron Ridge G.C., 824
Hesperia G. & C.C., 60

Hessel Ridge G.Cse., 381
Hesston Golf Park, 288
Hi-Level G.Cse., 693
Hiawatha G.C., 872
Hiawatha G.Cse., 428
Hiawatha G.Cse., 621
Hickam G.Cse., 200
Hickory Flat Greens, 621
Hickory Grove G.C., 621
Hickory Grove G.Cse., 621
Hickory Heights G.C., 693
Hickory Heights G.C., 693
Hickory Hills C.C., 229
Hickory Hills C.C., 872
Hickory Hills G.C., 342
Hickory Hills G.C., 381
Hickory Hills G.Cse., 540
Hickory Hollow G.Cse., 381
Hickory Knob G.C., 731
Hickory Knoll G.Cse., 381
Hickory Nut G.C., 621
Hickory Point G.Cse., 229
Hickory Ridge C.C., 343
Hickory Ridge G. & C.C., 540
Hickory Ridge G.Ctr., 230
Hickory Stick G.C., 262
Hickory Valley G.C., 693
Hickory VFW G.Cse., 694
Hickory Woods G.Cse., 621
Hidden Creek G.C., 262
Hidden Creek G.C., 780
Hidden Cypress G.C., 731
Hidden Greens G.C., 428
Hidden Haven G.C., 429
Hidden Hills G.C., 621
Hidden Hills G.Cse., 279
Hidden Hills Public G.Cse., 780
Hidden Lake G.C., 929
Hidden Lake G.Cse., 621
Hidden Lakes G.Cse., 289
Hidden Lakes Golf Resort, 211
Hidden Oaks G.Cse., 309
Hidden Oaks G.Cse., 381
Hidden River Golf & Casting Club, 382
Hidden Trails C.C., 456
Hidden Valley C.C., 516
Hidden Valley Four Seasons Resort, 694
Hidden Valley G.C., 540
Hidden Valley G.C., 61
Hidden Valley G.C., 758
Hidden Valley G.Cse., 298
Hidden Valley G.Cse., 456
Hidden Valley G.Cse., 473
Hidden Valley G.Cse., 669
Hidden Valley G.Cse., 694
Hidden Valley G.L., 456
Hidden Valley Lake G. & C.C., 61
Hiddenbrooke G.C., 61
Hideaway Hills G.C., 694
High Bridge Hills G.C., 504
High Cedars G.C., 843
High Cliff G.Cse., 872
High Hampton Inn & C.C., 579
High Meadow Ranch G.C., 781
High Mountain G.C., 504
High Point C.C., 504
High Point G.C., 298
High Pointe G.C., 382
Highland Creek G.C., 579
Highland G.C., 188
Highland G.C., 382
Highland G.Cse., 211

Idabel C.C., 658
Idle Wyld G.C., 383
Idlewild G.Cse., 873
Illinois State University G.Cse., 231
Imperial Lakewoods G.C., 149
Indian Bayou G. & C.C., 149
Indian Bluff G.Cse., 231
Indian Boundary G.Cse., 231
Indian Canyon G.Cse., 844
Indian Creek G. & C.C., 930
Indian Creek G.C., 782
Indian Creek G.Cse., 474
Indian Creek G.Cse., 669
Indian Hills G.C., 61
Indian Hills G.C., 758
Indian Hills G.Cse., 231
Indian Hills G.Cse., 542
Indian Hills G.Cse., 658
Indian Hollow Lake G.Cse., 623
Indian Island C.C., 542
Indian Lake Hills G.Cse., 383
Indian Lake Resort, 695
Indian Lakes G.C., 900
Indian Lakes Resort, 231
Indian Meadows G.Cse., 474
Indian Mound G.C., 492
Indian Palms C.C. & Resort, 62
Indian Peaks G.C., 107
Indian Pines G.C., 6
Indian Ridge G.C., 622
Indian River G.C., 384
Indian River G.C., 732
Indian Run G.C., 384
Indian Run G.C., 695
Indian Run G.Cse., 695
Indian Spring C.C., 505
Indian Springs C.C., 62
Indian Springs G.C., 298
Indian Springs G.C., 623
Indian Springs Metro Park G.Cse., 384
Indian Trails C.C., 474
Indian Trails G.Cse., 384
Indian Tree G.C., 107
Indian Valley C.C., 231
Indian Valley G.C., 62
Indian Valley G.Cse., 580
Indian Valley G.Cse., 623
Indian Wells G.C., 732
Indiana University G.C., 263
Indianhead G.C., 475
Indigo Creek Golf Plantation, 733
Indigo Lakes G.C., 149
Industry Hills Sheraton Resort & Conference
    Center, 62
Ingersoll G.Cse., 231
Ingleside G.C., 695
Inkster Valley G.Cse., 384
Inlet G.C., 542
Inn of the Mountain Gods G.Cse., 516
Innsbrook Resort & Conference Center, 457
Innsbruck Resort & G.C., 189
Inshalla C.C., 873
Interlochen G. & C.C., 384
International City Municipal G.Cse., 189
The International Club, 733
International G.C., 149
International Links of Miami at Melreese
    G.Cse., 149
International World Tour G.L., 733
Inver Wood G.C., 429
Inverness Hotel & G.C., 107
Inwood G.Cse., 232

Irish Hills G.Cse., 623
Iron Eagle Municipal G.Cse., 475
Iron Horse G.Cse., 782
Iron Masters C.C., 695
Iron Valley G.C., 695
Ironhead G. & C.C., 900
Ironhorse G.C., 289
Ironhorse G.Cse., 232
Ironman G.Cse., 429
Ironwood, 263
Ironwood G.C., 384
Ironwood G.C., 623
Ironwood G.Cse., 149
Ironwood G.Cse., 232
Ironwood G.Cse., 384
Ironwood G.Cse., 623
Ironwood G.Cse., 758
Iroquois G.Cse., 299
Irv Warren Memorial G.Cse., 279
Irwin C.C., 695
Isla Navidad G.C., 948
The Island C.C., 309
Island Green G.C., 733
Island Hills G.C., 385
Island Oaks G.C., 542
Island View G.Cse., 429
Island West G.C., 733
Island's End G. & C.C., 542
Isle Dauphine G.C., 6
Isleta Eagle G.Cse., 516
Ives Grove G.L., 873
Ives Hill G.Cse., 542
Ivy Hill G.C., 825
Izatys Golf & Yacht Club, 429
J.E. Good Park G.C., 624
J.F. Sammons Park G.Cse., 782
Jacaranda G.C., 150
Jack O'Lantern Resort, 492
Jack Tone Golf, 62
Jackpot G.C., 483
Jackson Hole Golf & Tennis Club, 893
Jackson Park G.C., 232
Jackson Park G.Cse., 844
Jackson Valley G.Cse., 695
Jacksonville Beach G.C., 150
Jacoby G.Cse., 893
Jamaica Run G.C., 624
James Baird State Park G.C., 542
Jamestown C.C., 599
Jamestown Park G.C., 580
Jasper Municipal G.Cse., 263
Jasper Park Lodge G.Cse., 900
Javier's Fresno West G. & C.C., 63
Jaycee G.Cse., 624
Jaycee Public G.Cse., 624
Jefferson Landing Club, 580
Jefferson Park G.Cse., 844
Jeffersonville G.C., 696
Jekyll Island Golf Resort, 189
Jerome C.C., 211
Jersey Meadow G.Cse., 783
Jester Park G.Cse., 279
Jimmie Austin University of Oklahoma
    G.Cse., 658
Jimmy Clay G.Cse., 783
Joe Bartholomew G.Cse., 309
Joe Louis G.C., 232
Joe Wheeler State Park G.Cse., 6
John Blumberg G.Cse., 916
John Conrad Regional G.Cse., 658
John F. Byrne G.Cse., 696
John F. Kennedy G.C., 107

Lake Breeze G.C., 875
Lake Carlsbad G.Cse., 516
Lake Chabot G.Cse., 64
Lake Chelan G.Cse., 844
Lake Chesdin G.C., 827
Lake Cora Hills G.Cse., 386
Lake Doster G.C., 386
Lake Forest G.C., 386
Lake Guntersville G.C., 7
Lake Hefner G.C., 659
Lake Hills G.C., 264
Lake Hills G.Cse., 468
Lake James G.C., 264
Lake Joseph Club, 931
Lake Jovita G. & C.C., 151
Lake Las Vegas Resort, 483
Lake Lawn Resort G.Cse., 875
Lake Lure Golf & Beach Resort, 581
Lake Maloney G.Cse., 475
Lake Marion G.C., 734
Lake Michigan Hills G.C., 386
Lake Morey C.C., 814
Lake Murray Resort Golf, 659
Lake of the Woods G.C., 233
Lake of the Woods G.Cse., 458
Lake Orlando G.C., 151
Lake Padden G.Cse., 845
Lake Panorama National G.Cse., 280
Lake Park G.Cse., 784
Lake Park G.Cse., 875
Lake Placid Resort, 543
Lake Powell National G.C., 24
Lake Ridge G.Cse., 483
Lake Shastina Golf Resort, 64
Lake Shore C.C., 543
Lake Shore G.Cse., 234
Lake Shore G.Cse., 875
Lake Spanaway G.Cse., 845
Lake St. Catherine C.C., 814
Lake Tahoe G.Cse., 64
Lake Texoma Golf Resort, 659
Lake Valley G. & C.C., 458
Lake View C.C., 234
Lake Vue North G.Cse., 696
Lake Whitney C.C., 784
Lake Wilderness G.Cse., 845
Lake Windsor G.C., 876
Lake Wisconsin C.C., 876
Lake Worth G.C., 151
Lake Wright G.Cse., 827
Lakeland G.Cse., 625
Lakeland Hills G.Cse., 386
Lakeland Village G.Cse., 845
Lakepoint Resort G.Cse., 7
Lakeridge G.Cse., 670
Lakes of Taylor G.C., 386
Lakes of the North Deer Run, 386
Lakeside C.C., 190
Lakeside C.C., 475
Lakeside C.C., 543
Lakeside Golf & Fitness Club, 670
Lakeside G.C., 300
Lakeside G.C., 430
Lakeside G.C., 919
Lakeside G.Cse., 625
Lakeside G.Cse., 625
Lakeside G.Cse., 659
Lakeside G.Cse., 806
Lakeside Greens G. & C.C., 901
Lakeside Hills G.Cse., 289
Lakeside Links, 387
Lakeside Memorial G.C., 659

Lakeside Municipal G.Cse., 280
Lakeview C.C., 280
Lakeview G.Cse., 659
Lakeview G.Cse., 750
Lakeview G.Cse., 827
Lakeview Golf of Orono, 430
Lakeview Golf Resort & Spa, 856
Lakeview Hills C.C. & Resort, 387
Lakeview National G.Cse., 430
Lakeville C.C., 344
Lakeway Resort, 784
Lakewood C.C., 506
Lakewood C.C., 65
Lakewood G.Cse., 316
Lakewood G.Cse., 660
Lakewood G.Cse., 7
Lakewood Links G.C., 734
Lakewood Shores Resort, 387
Lakewoods Forest Ridges G.Cse., 876
Lakin Municipal G.Cse., 289
Lambert Acres G.C., 758
Lancaster Host Golf & Resort, 696
Land-O-Lakes G.C., 901
Landa Park Municipal G.Cse., 785
Lander G. & C.C., 893
Landings G.C., 190
Landmark G.C. at Avalon, 758
Landmark G.C. at Oak Quarry, 65
Landmark G.C., 65
Landsmeer G.C., 280
Lane Creek G.C., 190
Lane Tree G.C., 581
Langdon Farms G.C., 670
Langston G.Cse., 127
Lansbrook G.Cse., 151
Lansdowne G.C., 827
Lansford C.C., 600
Lapeer C.C., 387
Larch Tree G.Cse., 625
Larchmont G.Cse., 468
Larry Gannon G.C., 345
Larters at St. Andrews G. & C.C., 916
Larue County C.C., 300
Las Cruces C.C., 517
Las Hadas Golf Resort & Marina, 948
Las Positas G.Cse., 65
Las Sendas G.C., 24
Las Vegas G.C., 484
Las Vegas National G.C., 484
Las Vegas Paiute Resort, 484
Lassing Pointe G.Cse., 300
Last Hill Golf & RV Park, 901
Laura Walker G.Cse., 190
Laurel Greens Public Golfers Club, 234
Laurel Lane G.C., 719
Laurel Springs G.C., 190
Laurel Valley C.C., 759
Laurel View G.Cse., 119
Lavelette G.C., 856
Lawrence County C.C., 234
Lawton Municipal G.Cse., 660
Laytonsville G.Cse., 326
Le Chateau Montebello, 941
Le Club de Golf Carling Lake, 942
Le Club de Golf de St. Ignace, 919
Le Golf Chantecler, 942
Le Manoir Richelieu, 942
Le Mars Municipal G.Cse., 280
Le Roy C.C., 543
Le Royal Bromont G.C., 942
Leatherstocking G.Cse., 544
Leavenworth G.C., 845

Lebanon C.C., 458
Lebanon Valley G.Cse., 696
Ledge Meadows G.Cse., 388
The Ledges G.C., 234
The Ledges G.C., 316
Lee Park G.Cse., 750
Lee Park G.Cse., 827
Lee's Hill Golfers' Club, 828
The Legacy Club at Alaqua Lakes, 151
The Legacy Courses at Cragun's, 430
The Legacy G.C., 388
The Legacy G.C., 484
The Legacy G.Cse. at Lakewood Ranch, 151
The Legacy G.Cse., 759
Legacy G.L., 581
The Legacy Golf Resort, 24
Legacy Hills G.C., 785
Legacy Ridge G.Cse., 108
The Legend at Arrowhead G.C., 25
Legend Oak's Plantation G.C., 734
Legend Trail G.C., 25
Legendary Run G.Cse., 625
The Legends at Parris Island, 735
The Legends at Stonehouse, 828
Legends Butte G.C., 475
The Legends G. & C.C., 152
The Legends of Indiana G.Cse., 264
The Legends of Massillon, 625
Legends On The Niagara, 931
The Legends, 735
Legion Memorial G.Cse., 845
Leicester C.C., 345
Leilehua G.Cse., 203
Lely Resort G. & C.C., 152
Lemoore G.Cse., 65
Lenape Heights G.Cse., 697
Leo Donovan G.Cse., 234
Leo J. Martin Memorial Municipal G.Cse., 345
Leon Valley G.Cse., 785
Les Bolstad Univ. of Minnesota G.C., 430
Les Vieux Chenes G.C., 309
Leslie Park G.Cse., 388
Lester Park G.C., 431
Lew Wentz Memorial G.Cse., 660
Lewis River G.Cse., 846
Lewisburg Elks C.C., 856
Liberty C.C., 264
Liberty Hills G.C., 625
Liberty Lake G.C., 846
Lick Creek G.C., 234
Licking Springs Trout & G.C., 626
Lido G.C., 544
Lilac G.C., 388
Lima G. & C.C., 544
Limberlost G.C., 264
Limekiln G.C., 697
Limerick G.C., 697
Lincoln C.C., 388
Lincoln C.C., 581
Lincoln G.C., 388
Lincoln Greens G.Cse., 235
Lincoln Homestead State Park, 300
Lincoln Oaks G.Cse., 235
Lincoln Park G.Cse., 600
Lincoln Park G.Cse., 65
Lincoln Park G.Cse., 660
Lincoln Park G.Cse., 876
Lincoln Trail C.C., 300
Lincoln Valley G.C., 280
Linden Hall G.C., 697

Lindenwood G.C., 697
Lindsay Municipal G.Cse., 660
Lingan G. & C.C., 923
The Links at Bowen Lake, 388
The Links at Boynton Beach, 152
The Links at Challedon, 326
The Links at Continental Ranch, 25
The Links at Crowbush Cove, 940
The Links at Cypress Bay, 735
The Links at Echo Springs, 625
The Links at Gettysburg, 697
The Links at Grand Victoria, 264
The Links at Heartland Crossing, 265
The Links at Lake Erie G.C., 389
The Links at Lighthouse Sound G.C., 327
Links at Lilly Creek Resort, 300
The Links at Lost Plantation, 190
The Links at Madison Green, 152
The Links at Magnolia, 581
The Links at Northfork, 431
The Links at Pinewood, 389
The Links at Pointe West, 152
The Links at Quarry Oaks, 917
The Links at Queen Creek, 25
The Links at RiverLakes Ranch, 66
The Links at Safe Haven, 954
Links at Shirley, 544
The Links at Sierra Blanca, 517
The Links at Spanish Bay, 66
The Links at Spring Church, 698
The Links at Spruce Grove, 901
The Links at Stono Ferry, 735
The Links at the Renaissance, 626
The Links at Union Vale, 544
The Links at Victoria, 66
The Links at WaterChase, 785
The Links G.C., 191
The Links G.C., 265
The Links G.Cse., 235
Links O'Tryon, 735
The Links of GlenEagles, 901
The Links of Lake Bernadette, 152
The Links of Niagara at Willodell, 931
The Links of North Dakota at Red Mike Resort, 600
The Links of Novi, 389
The Links of Rockway Glen, 931
Links of Whispering Woods, 446
The Linksman G.C., 7
LinRick G.Cse., 735
Linville G.Cse., 581
Lionhead G. & C.C., 931
Lions Municipal G.Cse., 785
Lipoma Firs G.Cse., 846
Litchfield Beach & Golf Resort, 736
Litchfield G.Cse., 431
Little Bennett G.Cse., 327
Little Crow C.C., 431
Little Falls C.C., 431
Little Fishing Creek G.C., 191
Little Harbor C.C., 345
Little Mountain C.C., 626
Little Mountain G.Cse., 191
Little River C.C., 876
Little River Farm G.L., 582
Little Traverse Bay G.C., 389
Liverpool G. & C.C., 545
Livingston G.Cse., 545
Loch March G. & C.C., 932
Loch Nairn G.C., 698
Lochmere G. & C.C., 493
Lochmere G.C., 582

Maplewood C.C., 493
Maplewood G. & C.C., 919
Maplewood G.C., 265
Maplewood G.Cse., 846
Mar-O-Del G.Cse., 628
Marco Shores C.C., 154
Marcus Pointe G.C., 155
Marengo Ridge G.C., 236
Mariah Hills G.Cse., 289
Mariana Butte G.Cse., 108
Marias Valley G. & C.C., 469
Marina Ixtapa Club de Golf, 948
Marina Vallarta Club de Golf, 949
Marine Park G.C., 546
Mariners Landing G. & C.C., 828
Marion Oaks G.C., 391
Mark Twain G.C., 546
Mark Twain State Park, 546
Markham Green G.C., 932
Marlborough Golf Club, 327
Marquette G. & C.C., 391
Marquette Trails C.C., 391
Marriott's Bay Point Resort, 155
Marriott's Camelback G.C., 26
Marriott's Desert Springs Resort & Spa, 68
Marriott's Griffin Gate G.C., 301
Marriott's Lakewood G.C., 7
Marriott's Lincolnshire Resort, 236
Marriott's Rancho Las Palmas Resort &
    C.C., 68
Marriott's Seaview Resort, 506
Marriott's Shadow Ridge Resort, 68
Marsh Harbour G.L., 583
Marsh Landing C.C., 155
Marsh Ridge Resort, 391
Marshall G.C., 432
Marshfield C.C., 877
Martin County G. & C.C., 155
Marty Sanchez Links de Santa Fe, 517
Marvin's G.Cse., 547
Marysville G.Cse., 391
Maryvale G.C., 26
Marywood G.C. & Banquet Center, 391
Mascoutin G.C., 877
Massanutten Resort G.Cse., 828
Massena C.C., 547
Mather G.Cse., 68
Mattawang G.C., 506
Maumee Bay Resort G.Cse., 628
Mauna Kea Beach G.Cse., 204
Mauna Lani Resort, 204
Maxwell G.C., 786
Maxwelton Braes Golf Resort, 877
Maxwelton G.C., 265
Mayapple G.L., 699
Mayfair C.C., 155
Mayfair C.C., 628
Mayfair Lakes G. & C.C., 909
Mays Landing C.C., 506
Mayville G.C., 877
Maywood G.C., 301
McCabe Field G.Cse., 759
McCall Lake G.Cse., 902
McCall Municipal G.Cse., 211
McCann Memorial G.C., 547
McCleery G.Cse., 909
McConnellsville G.C., 547
McCormick Ranch G.C., 26
McCormick Woods G.Cse., 846
McGauslin Brook G. & C.C., 877
McGuire's Resort, 391
McKenzie Meadows G.C., 902

McNary G.C., 670
Meadow Brook G.C., 720
Meadow Brook G.Cse., 807
Meadow Gardens G.Cse., 910
Meadow Hills G.Cse., 108
Meadow Lake C.C., 459
Meadow Lake G. & C.C., 310
Meadow Lake G.Cse., 69
Meadow Lake Golf Resort, 469
Meadow Lakes G.Cse., 671
Meadow Lane G.Cse., 699
Meadow Links G.Cse., 878
Meadow Park G.Cse., 847
Meadow Ponds G.Cse., 857
Meadowbrook Farms G.C., 786
Meadowbrook G.C., 155
Meadowbrook G.Cse., 432
Meadowbrook G.Cse., 750
Meadowbrook G.Cse., 786
Meadowbrook Municipal Golf Complex, 786
Meadowink G.C., 699
Meadowlake G.C., 310
Meadowlake Municipal G.Cse., 660
Meadowlands G.C., 583
Meadowlands G.Cse., 583
Meadowlark G.C., 69
Meadowlark G.Cse., 236
Meadowlark Hills G.Cse., 476
Meadowood G.C., 301
The Meadows at Middlesex, 507
The Meadows Del Mar G.C., 69
Meadows Farms G.Cse., 828
The Meadows G.C. of Blue Island, 236
The Meadows G.C., 108
The Meadows G.C., 280
The Meadows G.C., 392
The Meadows G.C., 7
Meadows G.C., 507
The Meadows G.Cse., 433
Meadowview G.Cse., 236
MeadowWood G.Cse., 847
Meceola C.C., 392
The Medalist G.C., 392
Medicine Hat G. & C.C., 902
Meek-Kwon Park G.Cse., 878
Melody Hill G.Cse., 720
Memorial Park G.Cse., 786
Menifee Lakes C.C., 69
Meramec Lakes G.C., 459
Merced Hills G.C., 69
Mercer County Elks G.C., 628
Mercer Oaks G.C., 507
Mercer Public G.Cse., 699
Meridian Sun G.Cse., 392
Meriwether National G.C., 671
Merrill G.C., 878
Merrimack C.C., 345
Mesa Del Sol G.Cse., 26
Mesaba C.C., 433
Mesquite G.C., 69
Mesquite G.Cse., 787
Metcalfe G.C., 932
Metro C.C., 955
Metropolitan G.C., 191
MetroWest C.C., 156
Mexicali C.C., 946
Miacomet G.C., 345
Miami National G.C., 156
Miami National G.C., 156
Miami Shores C.C., 156
Miami Shores G.Cse., 628
Miami Whitewater Forest G.Cse., 628

Mt. Anthony C.C., 814
Mulberry Fore G.Cse., 393
Mulberry Hills G.C., 393
Mullenhurst G.Cse., 393
Mullet Bay G.C., 960
Municipal G.Cse., 933
Murphy Creek G.Cse., 109
Murray Parkway G.C., 807
Murrysville G.C., 701
Muscatine Municipal G.Cse., 281
Muskego Lakes C.C., 878
My Old Kentucky Home State Park G.C., 301
Myakka Pines G.C., 157
Myrtle Beach National G.C., 737
Myrtle Creek G.Cse., 671
Myrtlewood G.C., 737
Mystery Hills G.C., 879
Mystery Valley G.Cse., 191
Mystic Creek G.C., 393
Mystic Hills G.C., 265
Naga-Waukee G.C., 879
Nags Head G.L., 584
Nanaimo G.C., 910
Napa G.Cse. at Kennedy Park, 72
Naperbrook G.Cse., 237
The Naples Beach Hotel & G.C., 157
Naples Grande G.C., 157
Naples Lakes C.C., 158
NAS Brunswick G.Cse., 316
NAS G.Cse., 310
Nashboro G.C., 760
Nassawango C.C., 328
Natanis G.Cse., 316
The Natchez Trace G.C., 447
National G.C., 585
National Pines G.C., 933
The Natural at Beaver Creek Resort, 393
Nature Trails G.Cse., 630
Navy Marine G.C., 205
Needles Municipal G.Cse., 72
Needwood G.Cse., 328
Negril Hills G.C., 956
Nelson Park G.Cse., 237
Nemacolin Woodlands Resort & Spa, 701
Nemadji G.Cse., 879
Neshaminy Valley G.C., 701
Neshobe G.C., 815
Nettle Creek C.C., 238
Neumann G.Cse., 629
The Neuse G.C., 585
Nevel Meade G.Cse., 301
Nevele Grand Resort & C.C., 548
New Albany Links G.C., 630
New Berlin Hills G.C., 879
New Castle C.C., 893
The New Course at Albany, 549
New England C.C., 346
New Ewa Beach G.C., 205
New Jersey National G.C., 507
New Melle Lakes G.C., 460
New Mexico Military Institute G.Cse., 517
New Mexico State University G.Cse., 518
New Mexico Tech G.Cse., 518
New Prague G.C., 434
New Richmond G.C., 879
New Seabury C.C., 346
New York C.C., 549
Newark Valley G.C., 549
Newaukum Valley G.Cse., 847
Newman G.Cse., 238
Newport C.C., 815

Newport News G.C. at Deer Run, 829
Newton Commonwealth G.Cse., 346
Newton Public G.Cse., 290
Niagara County G.Cse., 549
Niagara Orleans C.C., 549
Nick Stoner Municipal G.Cse., 549
Nicklaus G.C. at Birch River, 191
Nicklaus North G.Cse., 910
Nicolet C.C., 879
Nile G.C., 848
Nine Peaks G.Cse., 671
Nippersink G.C. & Resort, 880
Nisqually Valley G.C., 848
Nob North G.Cse., 191
Nobleton Lakes G.C., 933
Nocona Hills C.C., 787
Nordic Hills Resort, 238
Normandie G.C., 460
Normandy Shores G.Cse., 158
North Battleford G. & C.C., 943
North Bellingham G.Cse., 848
North Carolina National G.C., 585
North Conway C.C., 494
North Country G.C., 549
North Fork C.C., 702
North Fulton G.Cse., 191
North Hill C.C., 346
North Hills G.Cse., 702
North Kent G.Cse., 394
North Kingstown Municipal G.Cse., 720
North Links G.Cse., 434
North Palm Beach C.C., 158
North Park G.Cse., 702
North Shore C.C., 585
North Shore G. & C.C., 848
North Shore G.Cse., 394
North Shore G.Cse., 933
North Star G.Cse., 15
Northampton Valley C.C., 702
NorthBrook G.C., 880
Northbrook G.C., 394
Northdale Golf & Tennis Club, 158
Northeast Harbor G.C., 316
Northern Hills G.Cse., 434
Northern Pines G.C., 469
Northfield G.C., 434
Northgate G.Cse., 484
Northlands G.Cse., 910
Northmoor G.C., 630
Northridge Public G.Cse., 933
Northstar-at-Tahoe Resort G.Cse., 72
Northumberland Links, 923
Northview G. & C.C., 910
Northville Hills G.C., 394
Northwest Park G.Cse., 328
Northwood G. & C.C., 310
Northwood G.Cse., 394
Northwood G.Cse., 880
Northwoods G.C., 737
Norton C.C., 346
Norvelt G.C., 702
Norwich G.Cse., 120
Norwood C.C., 347
Nueva Vista, 787
Nutters Crossing G.C., 328
Oak Bridge Club at Sawgrass, 158
Oak Brook G.C., 238
Oak Brook G.Cse., 238
Oak Brook Hills Hotel & Resort, 238
The Oak Club of Genoa, 238
Oak Country G.Cse., 290
Oak Creek G.C., 73

Prestwick C.C., 741
Prestwick G.C. at Wedgewood, 437
Priest Lake G.Cse., 212
Primm Valley G.C., 485
Prince Rupert Centennial Golf, 912
Prince William G.Cse., 830
Princeton G.C., 437
Princeton G.C., 510
Princeville Resort, 205
Proctor-Pittsford C.C., 815
Prospect Hill G.Cse., 317
Province Lake Golf, 317
Provo G.C., 961
Pryor Municipal G.Cse., 661
Pueblo City Park G.Cse., 111
Pueblo De Cochiti G.Cse., 519
Pueblo Del Sol C.C., 29
Pueblo El Mirage Resort, 30
Pukalani C.C., 206
Pumpkin Ridge G.C., 672
Punderson State Park G.Cse., 634
Punta Borinquen G.C., 959
Purgatory G.C., 268
Purple Hawk C.C., 437
Purple Sage G.Cse., 212
Purple Sage Municipal G.Cse., 894
Quail Brook G.Cse., 510
Quail Chase G.C., 303
Quail Creek C.C., 791
Quail Creek G.C., 461
Quail Creek G.C., 741
Quail Creek G.Cse., 282
Quail Creek G.Cse., 9
Quail Crossing G.C., 268
Quail Hollow G.C., 212
Quail Hollow G.Cse., 449
Quail Hollow Resort & C.C., 635
Quail Meadows G.Cse., 243
Quail Ranch G.C., 78
Quail Ridge G.C., 401
Quail Ridge G.Cse., 290
Quail Ridge G.Cse., 589
Quail Ridge G.Cse., 761
Quail Ridge G.Cse., 849
Quail Run G.Cse., 476
Quail Run G.Cse., 673
Quail Valley G.C., 706
Quail Valley G.Cse., 673
Quaker Meadows G.Cse., 589
Quaker Neck C.C., 590
Quality Inn & Suites Golf Resort, 164
The Quarry G.C., 761
The Quarry G.C., 791
Quarry Hills C.C., 590
Quarry Oaks G.C., 477
Quarry Ridge G.Cse., 121
Quartz Mountain G.Cse., 662
Quashnet Valley C.C., 349
Queensbury C.C., 552
Queenstown Harbor G.L., 329
Querbes Park G.Cse., 311
The Quest G.C., 401
Quicksand G.Cse., 791
Quicksilver G.C., 706
Quit-Qui-Oc G.C., 882
R.O. Speck Municipal G.Cse., 470
Rabbit Run at Brooks Road, 791
Raber G.Cse., 268
Raccoon Creek G.Cse., 111
Raccoon Hill G.C., 635
Raccoon International G.C., 635
Raccoon Run G.C., 741

Raceway G.C., 121
Rackham G.C., 401
Radisson Greens G.C., 552
Radisson Ponce de Leon Golf & Conference
    Resort, 164
Radium Resort, 912
Radium Resort, 912
Ragged Mountain G.C., 495
The Rail G.C., 244
Railside G.C., 244
Railwood G.C., 461
Rainbow G.Cse., 552
Rainbow Springs G.C., 882
RainTree C.C., 461
Raintree C.C., 635
Raintree G.C., 193
Raintree Golf Resort, 164
Raisin River C.C., 401
Raisin Valley G.C., 401
Ralph Myhre G.Cse. of Middlebury College,
    815
Ramblewood C.C., 510
Rammler G.C., 402
Rams Hill C.C., 78
Ramsey G.C., 437
The Ranch G. & C.C., 903
The Ranch G.C., 349
Rancho Bernardo Inn Resort, 78
Rancho Canada G.C., 79
Rancho Del Ray G.C., 79
Rancho Manana G.C., 30
Rancho Maria G.C., 79
Rancho Park G.Cse., 79
Rancho San Joaquin G.C., 79
Rancho San Marcos G.C., 79
Rancho Solano G.Cse., 80
Rancho Viejo Resort & C.C., 791
Rancocas G.C., 510
Randall Oaks G.C., 244
Randolph Park G.Cse., 30
Range End G.C., 707
Rapid City Elks G.Cse., 751
Raspberry Falls Golf & Hunt Club, 830
Ratliff Ranch G.L., 791
Rattle Run G.Cse., 402
The Raven G.C. at Sabino Springs, 30
The Raven G.C. at South Mountain, 30
The Raven G.C. at Three Peaks, 111
Ravines G. & C.C., 164
The Ravines G.C., 402
Rayburn C.C. & Resort, 791
Raymond Memorial G.C., 635
Razorback Park G.Cse., 39
Real Del Mar G.C., 946
Rebsamen Park G.Cse., 40
Recreation Park G.Cse., 80
The Red Apple Inn & C.C., 40
Red Carpet G.C., 282
Red Fox Run G.Cse., 402
Red Hawk C.C., 244
Red Hawk G.C., 402
Red Hawk G.C., 485
Red Hawk Ridge G.C., 111
Red Hawk Run G.C., 635
Red Hook G.C., 552
Red Lodge Mountain Resort G.Cse., 470
Red Tail G.Cse., 673
Red Wing Lake G.Cse., 831
Red Wolf Run G.C., 792
Reddeman Farms G.C., 402
Redgate Municipal G.Cse., 330
Redhawk G.C., 80

The SCGA Members' Club at Rancho California, 85
Schalamar Creek G. & C.C., 169
Schaumburg G.C., 246
Schenectady G.Cse., 555
Scherwood G.Cse., 269
Schifferdecker G.Cse., 463
Schneiter's Bluff at West Point, 809
Schneiter's Pebble Brook G.L., 809
Schneiter's Riverside G.Cse., 809
Scholl Canyon G.Cse., 86
Scituate C.C., 350
Scotch Pines G.Cse., 213
Scothurst G.Cse., 592
Scotland Run G.C., 511
Scotswood Links, 917
Scott Lake C.C., 406
Scott Schreiner Kerrville Muni G.Cse., 794
Scottsdale Silverado G.C., 31
Scovill G.C., 246
Scranton Municipal G.Cse., 709
Sea Gull G.C., 743
Sea Island G.C., 194
Sea Oaks G.C., 512
Sea Palms Resort, 195
Sea Pines Plantation Club, 743
The Sea Ranch G.L., 86
Sea Scape G.L., 592
Sea Trail Plantation, 592
Seamountain G.Cse., 206
Seascape G.C., 86
Seascape Resort, 169
Sebastian Hills G.C., 640
Sebastian Municipal G.Cse., 169
Sedona Golf Resort, 31
Selkirk G. & C.C., 917
Selma Valley G.Cse., 86
Semiahmoo G. & C.C., 850
Seneca G.C., 291
Seneca G.C., 555
Seneca G.Cse., 303
Seneca G.Cse., 640
Seneca Hills G.Cse., 640
Seneca Lake C.C., 555
Senica Oak Ridge G.C., 246
SentryWorld G.Cse., 884
Sepulveda G.Cse., 86
Sequoyah State Park G.C., 662
Settler's Hill G.Cse., 246
Settlers Bay G.C., 15
Seven Bridges G.C., 246
Seven Hills C.C., 640
Seven Hills G.C., 86
Seven Hills Golfers Club, 169
Seven Lakes C.C., 593
Seven Oaks Resort & C.C., 795
Seven Springs C.C., 709
Seven Springs G. & C.C., 169
Seven Springs Mountain Resort G.Cse., 709
Shade Mountain G.C., 709
Shadow Brook G.Cse., 709
Shadow Butte G.C., 675
Shadow Creek G.C., 487
Shadow Hills G.Cse., 795
Shadow Lake Golf & Racquet Club, 555
Shadow Mountain G.C., 31
Shadow Pines G.C., 555
Shadow Ridge G.C., 406
Shadow Ridge G.C., 913
Shadow Valley G.C., 213
Shadowmoss Plantation G.C., 743
Shadowood G.Cse., 270

Shady Hills G.Cse., 270
Shady Hollow G.Cse., 406
Shady Oaks C.C., 247
Shady Oaks G.Cse., 283
Shaganappi Point G.Cse., 903
Shagbark G.C., 406
Shaker Farms C.C., 351
Shaker Hills G.C., 351
Shaker Run G.C., 640
Shalimar Pointe G. & C.C., 169
Shamrock G. & C.C., 555
Shamrock G.C., 593
Shamrock G.C., 640
Shamrock G.Cse., 439
Shamrock Hills G.Cse., 406
Shamrock Hills G.Cse., 463
Shandin Hills G.C., 87
Shangri-La Golf Resort, 662
Shannon Lake G.Cse., 914
Shanty Creek, 406
Shark River G.Cse., 512
Sharon Woods G.Cse., 641
Sharp Park G.Cse., 87
Sharpstown Municipal G.Cse., 795
Shary Municipal G.Cse., 795
Shattuck G. & C.C., 663
Shattuck G.Cse., 495
Shaw-Nee Slopes G.Cse., 904
Shawano Lake G.C., 884
Shawnee G.Cse., 303
Shawnee G.Cse., 859
Shawnee Hills G.Cse., 641
Shawnee Inn Golf Resort, 709
Shawnee Lookout G.C., 641
Shawnee State Park G.Cse., 641
Sheaffer Memorial Golf Park, 283
Sheboygan Town & C.C., 884
Shelby Oaks G.C., 641
Shelbyville C.C., 304
Shell Landing G.C., 449
Shenandoah Crossing Resort & C.C., 832
Shenandoah G. & C.C., 407
Shenandoah G.C., 555
Shenandoah Valley G.C., 832
Shennecossett Municipal G.Cse., 122
Shenvalee G.C., 832
Shepherd's Crook G.Cse., 247
Shepherd's Hollow G.C., 407
Sheraton Colonial G.C., 351
Sheraton El Conquistador C.C., 32
Sheraton San Marcos G.C., 32
Sheraton Steamboat Resort & G.C., 112
Sheraton Tamarron Resort, 113
Sheraton Twin Brooks G.Cse., 351
Sheridan C.C., 894
Sheridan Park G.C., 556
Sherman Hills G.C., 169
Sherrill Park G.Cse., 795
Sherwood Forest G.C., 87
Sherwood Hills Resort G.Cse., 809
Sherwood Park G.Cse., 904
Shield Crest G.Cse., 675
Shiloh Falls G.C., 762
Shiloh Ridge Golf & Racquet Club, 449
Shiloh Springs G.C., 463
Shining Mountain G.C., 113
Shipyard G.C., 743
Shirkey G.C., 463
Shoal River C.C., 169
Shorecliffs G.C., 87
Shoreland C.C., 439
Shoreline G.Cse., 283

Shoreline G.L. at Mountain View, 87
Shoshone Golf & Tennis Club, 213
Shuksan G.C., 850
Siasconset G.C., 351
Siena G.C., 487
Sienna Plantation G.C., 795
Sierra Lakes G.C., 87
Sierra Nevada Golf Ranch, 487
Sierra Sage G.Cse., 487
Sierra Star G.C., 87
Signal Hill G.Cse., 170
Sikeston C.C., 463
Silo Ridge C.C., 556
Silo Ridge G. & C.C., 463
Silo Run G.C., 593
The Silos G.C., 304
Silver City G.Cse. at Scott Park, 520
Silver Creek G.C., 32
Silver Creek G.C., 556
Silver Creek G.C., 593
Silver Lake C.C., 247
Silver Lake G.Cse., 556
Silver Lakes G. & C.C., 937
Silver Oak G.Cse., 487
Silver Oaks G. & C.C., 170
Silver Ridge G.Cse., 247
Silver Spring G.Cse., 884
Silver Springs G.C., 709
Silver Springs G.Cse., 439
Silverado C.C. & Resort, 88
Silverbell G.Cse., 32
SilverHorn G.C. of Texas, 795
Silverhorn G.C., 663
SilverStone G.C., 487
Silverthorn C.C., 170
SilverTip G.Cse., 904
Sim Park G.Cse., 286
Simi Hills G.C., 88
Similk Beach G.Cse., 850
Simsbury Farms G.C., 122
Sinclair G.C., 894
Singing Bridge Golf, 407
Singing Hills Resort at Sycuan, 88
Sinking Valley C.C., 710
Sinnissippi G.Cse., 247
Sinton Municipal G.Cse., 796
Six-S G.Cse., 556
Skamania Lodge G.Cse., 850
Skene Valley G.Cse., 556
Skippack G.Cse., 710
Skungamaug River G.C., 122
Sky Creek Ranch G.C., 796
Sky Mountain G.C., 809
Sky Valley Golf & Ski Resort, 195
Skybrook G.C., 593
Skyland G.Cse., 641
Skyland Lakes G.Cse., 832
Skyland Pines G.C., 641
Skyline C.C., 351
Skyline G.C., 885
Skyline G.Cse., 556
Skyline G.Cse., 710
Skylinks G.Cse., 88
Skytop Lodge, 710
Skyview G.Cse., 477
Skywest G.Cse., 88
Sleeping Bear G.C., 407
Sleepy Hole G.Cse., 833
Sleepy Hollow C.C., 642
Sleepy Hollow G. & C.C., 796
Sleepy Hollow G. & C.C., 859
Sleepy Hollow G.C., 15

Sleepy Hollow G.Cse., 557
Sleepy Hollow G.Cse., 642
Sleepy Hollow G.Cse., 642
Smithtown Landing G.C., 557
Smock G.Cse., 270
Smyrna Municipal G.Cse., 762
Snag Creek G.Cse., 247
Snohomish G.Cse., 850
Snoqualmie Falls G.Cse., 850
Snow Snake Ski & Golf, 407
Snowmass Club G.Cse., 113
Snowshoe Mountain Resort, 859
Snyder Park G.Cse., 642
Soaring Eagles G.Cse., 557
Soboba Springs Royal Vista G.Cse., 88
Sodus Bay Heights G.Cse., 557
Somerset G.C., 833
Songbird Hills G.C., 885
Sonnenalp G.C., 113
Sonny Guy Municipal G.Cse., 449
Sonoma Mission Inn G. & C.C., 89
Sonoma Ranch G.Cse., 520
Souhegan Woods G.C., 496
Soule Park G.Cse., 89
The Sound G.L. at Albemarle Plantation, 593
Souris Valley G.C., 601
Sourwood Forest G.Cse., 594
South Carolina National G.C., 744
South Grove G.Cse., 270
South Hampton C.C., 351
South Haven C.C., 408
South Haven G.C., 40
South Hills C.C., 557
South Hills C.C., 885
South Hills G.C., 710
South Hills G.C., 859
South Lakes G.Cse., 663
South Mountain G.C., 809
South Ocean Golf & Beach Resort, 957
South Padre Island G.C., 796
South Park G.Cse., 710
South Riding Golfers' Club, 833
South River G.L., 331
South Shore C.C., 351
South Shore C.C., 557
South Shore G.C., 270
South Shore G.Cse., 247
South Shore G.Cse., 557
South Suburban G.Cse., 113
South Toledo G.C., 642
South Wales G.Cse., 833
Southampton Princess G.Cse., 953
Southbridge G.C., 195
Southern Dunes G. & C.C., 170
Southern Hills G.C., 439
Southern Hills G.Cse., 477
Southern Hills G.Cse., 751
Southern Oaks G.C., 311
Southern Oaks G.C., 796
Southerness G.C., 195
Southgate G.C., 810
Southington C.C., 122
Southmoor C.C., 408
Southmoore G.Cse., 710
SouthRidge G.C., 113
Southridge G.C., 89
Southview G.C., 463
Southwest Point G.Cse., 762
Southwick C.C., 352
Southwind G.Cse., 304
Southwinds G.Cse., 170

The Warren G.Cse. at Notre Dame, 273
Warren Valley G.Cse., 415
Warrenbrook G.Cse., 513
Warrior G.C. at Lake Wright, 597
Warrior Hills G.Cse., 312
Warrior's Path State Park, 764
Wasatch State Park G.C., 811
Wasco Valley Rose G.Cse., 94
Washakie Golf & RV Resort, 415
Washington County G.Cse., 889
Washington National G.C., 853
Washoe County G.C., 488
Wasioto Winds G.Cse., 305
Waskesiu G.Cse., 944
Water Gap C.C., 716
Water's Edge G.C., 252
Waterford G.C., 177
Waterford G.C., 746
Waterlefe Golf & River Club, 177
Watertown G.C., 564
Watertown Municipal G.Cse., 751
Waterview G.C., 801
Waterville C.C., 319
Waterway Hills G.C., 746
Waterwood National Resort & C.C., 801
Waubeeka G.L., 354
Waukewan G.C., 496
Waumbek G.C., 496
Waveland G.Cse., 284
Waverly G.C., 648
Waverly G.Cse., 284
Waverly Oaks G.C., 354
Waverly Woods G.C., 332
Wawashkamo G.C., 415
Wawonowin C.C., 415
Wayne C.C., 478
Wayne Hills C.C., 564
Waynesboro Municipal, 716
Waynesville C.C. Inn, 597
Weatherwax G.Cse., 648
WeaverRidge G.C., 252
Webb Memorial G.Cse., 312
Webster Dudley G.C., 354
Webster G.C., 564
Wedgefield Plantation G.C., 746
Wedgewood C.C., 513
Wedgewood G. & C.C., 177
Wedgewood G.C., 716
Wedgewood G.C., 801
Wedgewood G.Cse., 252
Wedgewood G.Cse., 450
Weeks Park Municipal G.Cse., 801
Weissinger Hills G.Cse., 305
Welk Resort Center, 95
Wellington G.C., 292
The Wellman Club, 747
Wellshire G.Cse., 115
Wellsville C.C., 564
Wendell C.C., 597
Wendell Pettinger - Wild Ridge G.C., 889
Wendigo G.Cse., 442
Wentworth G.C., 496
Wesburn G.Cse., 416
West Bolton G.C., 816
West Branch C.C., 416
West Loch G.Cse., 208
West Ottawa G.C., 416
West Palm Beach Municipal C.C., 177
West Plains C.C., 465
West Point G.Cse., 564
West Richland Municipal G.Cse., 853
West Ridge G.Cse., 811

West Sayville G.C., 565
West Seattle G.Cse., 853
West Woods G.C., 115
West's Mogadore C.C., 648
Westbrook Village G.C., 35
Westbrook Village G.C., 35
Westbrooke G.Cse., 416
Westbury C.C., 665
WestChase G.C., 273
Westchase G.C., 177
Westchester G. & C.C., 178
Westchester G.Cse., 649
Western Greens G.Cse., 416
Western Hills G.C., 124
Western Hills G.C., 293
Western Hills G.Cse., 305
Western Lakes G.C., 889
Western Row G.Cse., 649
Western Skies G.C., 35
Western Turnpike G.Cse., 565
Westfield G. & C.C., 921
Westfields G.C., 835
Westhaven G.C., 889
The Westin Innisbrook Resort, 178
The Westin Mission Hills Resort, 95
Westin Salishan Lodge & Golf Resort, 676
Westin Stonebriar Resort, 801
Westlake G. & C.C., 835
Westlock G.C., 904
Westminster C.C., 354
Westover G.C., 716
Westover G.Cse., 354
Westpark C.C., 835
Westport G.C., 565
Westport G.Cse., 597
Westridge G.C., 95
Westridge G.Cse., 602
Westside G.C., 312
Westvale G.C., 565
Westview G.Cse., 252
Westwood G.C., 285
Westwood G.C., 513
Westwood Park G.Cse., 665
Westwood Plateau G. & C.C., 915
WGC G.Cse., 649
Whaling City G.Cse., 354
Wheatland G.C., 895
Whetstone G.C., 649
Whiffle Tree Hill G.Cse., 416
Whirlpool G.Cse., 938
Whirlwind G.C., 36
Whiskey Creek G.C., 333
Whisky Run G.C., 938
Whisper Creek G.C., 253
Whispering Hills G.Cse., 565
Whispering Lakes G.Cse., 95
Whispering Pines G.C., 416
Whispering Pines G.C., 450
Whispering Pines G.Cse., 716
Whispering Springs G.C., 889
Whispering Willows G.Cse., 417
Whispering Woods G.C., 598
Whistler G.C., 915
Whistling Straits G.C., 890
White Birch G.Cse., 716
White Birch Hills G.Cse., 417
White Bluff Resort, 801
White Columns G.C., 197
White Deer C.C., 417
White Deer Park & G.Cse., 717
White Deer Run G.C., 253
White Eagle G.C., 890

Metro Area Index

Eagle Chase G.C.
Marshville, NC, 576
Firethorne C.C.
Waxhaw, NC, 577
Fort Mill G.C.
Fort Mill, SC, 729
Gastonia Municipal G.C.
Gastonia, NC, 578
Highland Creek G.C.
Charlotte, NC, 579
Lincoln C.C.
Lincolnton, NC, 581
Mallard Head C.C.
Mooresville, NC, 583
Monroe C.C.
Monroe, NC, 584
Oak Valley G.C.
Advance, NC, 585
Pine Grove G.C.
Shelby, NC, 587
Pinetuck G.C.
Rock Hill, SC, 740
Regent Park G.C.
Fort Mill, SC, 741
River Bend G.C.
Shelby, NC, 590
Rocky River G.C. at Concord
Harrisburg, NC, 591
Spring Lake C.C.
York, SC, 744
Stonebridge G.C.
Monroe, NC, 595
Town of Mooresville G.Cse.
Mooresville, NC, 596
The Tradition
Charlotte, NC, 596
Twin Oaks G.Cse.
Statesville, NC, 596
Warrior G.C.
China Grove, NC, 597
Waterford G.C.
Rock Hill, SC, 746
Westport G.Cse.
Denver, NC, 597
Woodbridge G.L.
Kings Mountain, NC, 598

CHICAGO
Antioch G.C.
Antioch, IL, 215
The Arboretum Club
Buffalo Grove, IL, 215
Arrowhead G.C.
Wheaton, IL, 215
Balmoral Woods C.C.
Crete, IL, 216
Bartlett Hills G.Cse.
Bartlett, IL, 216
Big Oaks G.Cse.
Kenosha, WI, 862
Big Run G.C.
Lockport, IL, 216
Bittersweet G.C.
Gurnee, IL, 216
Blackberry Oaks G.Cse.
Bristol, IL, 217
Blackhawk G.C.
St. Charles, IL, 217
Bloomingdale G.C.
Bloomingdale, IL, 217
Bon Vivant C.C.
Bourbonnais, IL, 217

Bonnie Brook G.C.
Waukegan, IL, 217
Bonnie Dundee G.C.
Carpentersville, IL, 217
Boone Creek G.C.
McHenry, IL, 218
Brae Loch G.C.
Grayslake, IL, 218
Brassie G.C.
Chesterton, IN, 256
Briar Leaf G.C.
La Porte, IN, 256
Bristol Oaks C.C.
Bristol, WI, 864
Broadmoor C.C.
Merrillville, IN, 256
Broken Arrow G.C.
Lockport, IL, 218
Buffalo Grove G.C.
Buffalo Grove, IL, 218
Cantigny Golf
Wheaton, IL, 219
Cardinal Creek G.Cse.
Beecher, IL, 219
Carillon G.C.
Plainfield, IL, 219
Carriage Greens C.C.
Darien, IL, 219
Cary C.C.
Cary, IL, 220
Chalet Hills G.C.
Cary, IL, 220
Chapel Hill C.C.
McHenry, IL, 220
Cherry Hills G.C.
Flossmoor, IL, 220
Chevy Chase G.C.
Wheeling, IL, 220
Chick Evans G.Cse.
Morton Grove, IL, 220
Cinder Ridge G.L.
Wilmington, IL, 220
Cog Hill G.C.
Lemont, IL, 221
Country Lakes G.C.
Naperville, IL, 222
Countryside G.Cse.
Mundelein, IL, 222
The Course at Aberdeen
Valparaiso, IN, 258
Cressmoor C.C.
Hobart, IN, 258
Crystal Woods G.C.
Woodstock, IL, 222
Deer Creek G.C.
University Park, IL, 222
Deerpath Park G.Cse.
Lake Forest, IL, 222
Deerfield Park District G.C.
Riverwoods, IL, 222
Downers Grove Park District G.Cse.
Downers Grove, IL, 223
Edgebrook C.C.
Sandwich, IL, 224
Edgebrook G.C.
Chicago, IL, 224
Evergreen G. & C.C.
Evergreen Park, IL, 225
Foss Park G.C.
North Chicago, IL, 225
Four Winds G.C.
Mundelein, IL, 225

Raisin Valley G.C.
　　Tecumseh, MI, 401
Rammler G.C.
　　Sterling Heights, MI, 402
Rattle Run G.Cse.
　　St. Clair, MI, 402
Reddeman Farms G.C.
　　Chelsea, MI, 402
Richmond Forest G.C.
　　Lenox, MI, 402
Riverview Highlands G.C.
　　Riverview, MI, 403
Rochester Hills G. & C.C.
　　Rochester, MI, 403
Rogell G.Cse.
　　Detroit, MI, 404
Rolling Hills G.C.
　　Lapeer, MI, 404
Rolling Meadows G.Cse.
　　Whitmore Lake, MI, 404
Romeo Golf Course & C.C.
　　Washington, MI, 404
Rouge Park G.C.
　　Detroit, MI, 404
Rush Lake Hills G.C.
　　Pinckney, MI, 405
Salem Hills G.C.
　　Northville, MI, 405
Salt River C.C.
　　Chesterfield, MI, 405
Shady Hollow G.Cse.
　　Romulus, MI, 406
Shenandoah G. & C.C.
　　West Bloomfield, MI, 407
South Toledo G.C.
　　Toledo, OH, 642
Southmoor C.C.
　　Burton, MI, 408
Springfield Oaks G.Cse.
　　Davisburg, MI, 408
Spuyten Duyval G.C.
　　Sylvania, OH, 643
St. Clair Shores C.C.
　　St. Clair Shores, MI, 408
Stonebridge G.C.
　　Ann Arbor, MI, 409
Stony Creek G.Cse.
　　Shelby Township, MI, 409
Sugar Creek G.Cse.
　　Elmore, OH, 644
Sugarbush G.C.
　　Davison, MI, 409
Swartz Creek G.Cse.
　　Flint, MI, 410
Sycamore Hills G.C.
　　Macomb, MI, 410
Sylvan Glen G.Cse.
　　Troy, MI, 410
Tamaron C.C.
　　Toledo, OH, 645
Tanglewood G.C.
　　South Lyon, MI, 410
Taylor Meadows G.C.
　　Taylor, MI, 411
Thorne Hills G.Cse.
　　Carleton, MI, 411
Timber Trace G.C.
　　Pinckney, MI, 412
Twin Lakes G.C.
　　Oakland, MI, 414
Tyrone Hills G.Cse.
　　Fenton, MI, 414

Warren Valley G.Cse.
　　Dearborn Heights, MI, 415
Wesburn G.Cse.
　　South Rockwood, MI, 416
Whispering Pines G.C.
　　Pinckney, MI, 416
Whispering Willows G.Cse.
　　Livonia, MI, 417
White Lake Oaks G.Cse.
　　White Lake, MI, 417
Whiteford Valley G.C.
　　Ottawa Lake, MI, 417
Willow Brook Public G.C.
　　Byron, MI, 418
Wolverine G.C.
　　Macomb, MI, 418
Woodfield G. & C.C.
　　Grand Blanc, MI, 419
Woodlawn G.C.
　　Adrian, MI, 419
HOUSTON
The Battleground at Deer Park G.Cse.
　　Deer Park, TX, 767
Bay Forest G.Cse.
　　LaPorte, TX, 767
Bayou G.C.
　　Texas City, TX, 768
Bear Creek Golf World
　　Houston, TX, 768
Bluebonnet Country G.Cse.
　　Navasota, TX, 769
Brock Park G.Cse.
　　Houston, TX, 770
Cape Royale G.Cse.
　　Coldspring, TX, 770
Chambers County G.Cse.
　　Anahuac, TX, 771
Clear Lake G.C.
　　Houston, TX, 772
Columbia Lakes
　　West Columbia, TX, 772
Cypress Lakes G.C.
　　Cypress, TX, 774
Cypresswood G.C.
　　Spring, TX, 774
Del Lago Golf Resort
　　Montgomery, TX, 775
Evergreen Point G.C.
　　Baytown, TX, 776
Fox Creek G.Cse.
　　Hempstead, TX, 777
Freeport G.Cse.
　　Freeport, TX, 777
Galveston Island Municipal G.Cse.
　　Galveston, TX, 778
Gleannloch Farms G.C.
　　Spring, TX, 778
Glenbrook G.Cse.
　　Houston, TX, 778
The G.C. at Cinco Ranch
　　Katy, TX, 778
Greatwood G.C.
　　Sugar Land, TX, 779
Green Meadows G.C.
　　Katy, TX, 780
Gus Wortham Park G.Cse.
　　Houston, TX, 780
Hermann Park G.Cse.
　　Houston, TX, 780
High Meadow Ranch G.C.
　　Magnolia, TX, 781

The Houstonian G.C.
  Richmond, TX, 782
Jersey Meadow G.Cse.
  Houston, TX, 783
Kingwood Cove G.C.
  Kingwood, TX, 783
Longwood G.C.
  Cypress, TX, 785
Meadowbrook Farms G.C.
  Katy, TX, 786
Memorial Park G.Cse.
  Houston, TX, 786
Old Orchard G.C.
  Richmond, TX, 788
Pasadena Municipal G.Cse.
  Houston, TX, 789
River Ridge G.C.
  Sealy, TX, 792
River Terrace
  Channelview, TX, 793
Sharpstown Municipal G.Cse.
  Houston, TX, 795
Sienna Plantation G.C.
  Missouri City, TX, 795
Southwyck G.C.
  Pearland, TX, 796
Stephen F. Austin G.Cse.
  San Felipe, TX, 797
Tour 18
  Humble, TX, 799
Treeline G.C.
  Tomball, TX, 800
Wedgewood G.C.
  Conroe, TX, 801
Windrose G.Cse.
  Spring, TX, 802
World Houston G.C.
  Houston, TX, 803
LOS ANGELES
Alhambra Municipal G.Cse.
  Alhambra, CA, 42
Alondra Park G.Cse.
  Lawndale, CA, 42
Anaheim Hills G.Cse.
  Anaheim, CA, 42
Azusa Greens G.Cse.
  Azusa, CA, 43
Birch Hills G.Cse.
  Brea, CA, 45
Brookside G.C.
  Pasadena, CA, 46
Buenaventura G.Cse.
  Ventura, CA, 46
Camarillo Springs G.Cse.
  Camarillo, CA, 46
The Cascades G.C.
  Sylmar, CA, 47
Chester Washington G.Cse.
  Los Angeles, CA, 48
Colton G.C.
  Colton, CA, 49
Costa Mesa C.C.
  Costa Mesa, CA, 50
Coyote Hills G.Cse.
  Fullerton, CA, 51
Cypress G.C.
  Los Alamitos, CA, 51
Dad Miller G.Cse.
  Anaheim, CA, 52
DeBell G.C.
  Burbank, CA, 52

Diamond Bar G.C.
  Diamond Bar, CA, 53
Eagle Glen G.C.
  Corona, CA, 55
El Dorado Park G.C.
  Long Beach, CA, 55
El Prado G.Cse.
  Chino, CA, 55
El Rancho Verde Royal Vista G.Cse.
  Rialto, CA, 55
El Rivino C.C.
  Riverside, CA, 56
Elkins Ranch G.Cse.
  Fillmore, CA, 56
Empire Lakes G.Cse.
  Rancho Cucamonga, CA, 56
General Old G.Cse.
  Riverside, CA, 57
Goose Creek G.C.
  Mira Loma, CA, 58
Green Tree G.Cse.
  Victorville, CA, 59
Griffith Park
  Los Angeles, CA, 59
Hansen Dam G.Cse.
  Pacoima, CA, 60
Hesperia G. & C.C.
  Hesperia, CA, 60
Indian Hills G.C.
  Riverside, CA, 61
Industry Hills Sheraton Resort & Conference Center
  City of Industry, CA, 62
Jurupa Hills C.C.
  Riverside, CA, 63
Knollwood C.C.
  Granada Hills, CA, 63
La Mirada G.Cse.
  La Mirada, CA, 63
Lakewood C.C.
  Lakewood, CA, 65
The Links at Victoria G.C.
  Carson, CA, 66
Los Angeles Royal Vista G.Cse.
  Walnut, CA, 66
Los Robles G.Cse.
  Thousand Oaks, CA, 66
Los Serranos G. & C.C.
  Chino Hills, CA, 67
Los Verdes G.Cse.
  Rancho Palos Verdes, CA, 67
Malibu C.C.
  Malibu, CA, 68
Meadowlark G.C.
  Huntington Beach, CA, 69
Mile Square G.C.
  Fountain Valley, CA, 70
Monarch Beach G.L.
  Dana Point, CA, 70
Montebello C.C.
  Montebello, CA, 70
Mountain Meadows G.C.
  Pomona, CA, 71
Mountain View C.C.
  Corona, CA, 72
Oak Creek G.C.
  Irvine, CA, 73
Palos Verdes G.C.
  Palos Verdes Estates, CA, 75
Pelican Hill G.C.
  Newport Coast, CA, 76

Rancho Park G.Cse.
    Los Angeles, CA, 79
Rancho San Joaquin G.C.
    Irvine, CA, 79
Recreation Park G.Cse.
    Long Beach, CA, 80
Rio Hondo G.C.
    Downey, CA, 81
River Ridge G.C.
    Oxnard, CA, 82
River View G.Cse.
    Santa Ana, CA, 82
Riverside G.Cse.
    Riverside, CA, 82
Robinson Ranch G.C.
    Santa Clarita, CA, 82
San Bernardino G.C.
    San Bernardino, CA, 83
San Dimas Canyon G.C.
    San Dimas, CA, 83
San Juan Hills C.C.
    San Juan Capistrano, CA, 84
Santa Anita G.Cse.
    Arcadia, CA, 85
Scholl Canyon G.Cse.
    Glendale, CA, 86
Sepulveda G.Cse.
    Encino, CA, 86
Shandin Hills G.C.
    San Bernardino, CA, 87
Simi Hills G.C.
    Simi Valley, CA, 88
Skylinks G.Cse.
    Long Beach, CA, 88
Sterling Hills G.C.
    Camarillo, CA, 90
Strawberry Farms G.C.
    Irvine, CA, 90
Tierra Rejada G.C.
    Moorpark, CA, 92
Tijeras Creek G.C.
    Rancho Santa Margarita, CA, 93
Tustin Ranch G.C.
    Tustin, CA, 93
Upland Hills C.C.
    Upland, CA, 94
Van Buren G.Ctr.
    Riverside, CA, 94
Westridge G.C.
    La Habra, CA, 95
Whispering Lakes G.Cse.
    Ontario, CA, 95
Whittier Narrows G.Cse.
    Rosemead, CA, 95
Willowick G.C.
    Santa Ana, CA, 96
Woodley Lakes G.Cse.
    Van Nuys, CA, 96

NEW YORK
Apple Mountain G.C.
    Belvidere, NJ, 498
Ash Brook G.Cse.
    Scotch Plains, NJ, 498

Beaver Brook C.C.
    Clinton, NJ, 498
Bergen Point C.C.
    West Babylon, NY, 524
Bey Lea G.C.
    Toms River, NJ, 498
Black Bear G.C.
    Franklin, NJ, 501

Blue Hill G.C.
    Pearl River, NY, 525
Bowling Green G.C.
    Milton, NJ, 499
Brentwood C.C.
    Brentwood, NY, 525
Bunker Hill G.Cse.
    Princeton, NJ, 499
Cedar Creek G.C.
    Bayville, NJ, 500
Centennial G.C.
    Carmel, NY, 528
Central Valley G.C.
    Central Valley, NY, 528
Charleston Springs G.Cse.
    Millstone Township, NJ, 500
Clearview G.C.
    Bayside, NY, 530
Colonial Springs G.Cse.
    East Farmingdale, NY, 530
Crab Meadow G.C.
    Northport, NY, 531
Cranbury G.C.
    West Windsor, NJ, 500
Cream Ridge G.C.
    Cream Ridge, NJ, 500
Crystal Springs G.C.
    Hamburg, NJ, 501
D. Fairchild-Wheeler G.Cse.
    Fairfield, CT, 117
Darlington County G.Cse.
    Mahwah, NJ, 501
Douglaston G.C.
    Douglaston, NY, 533
Dunwoodie G.C.
    Yonkers, NY, 533
Dyker Beach G.Cse.
    Brooklyn, NY, 534
E. Gaynor Brennan Municipal G.Cse.
    Stamford, CT, 117
Eagle Ridge G.Cse.
    Lakewood, NJ, 501
East Orange G.Cse.
    Short Hills, NJ, 502
Eisenhower Park Golf
    East Meadow, NY, 534
Emerson G.C.
    Emerson, NJ, 502
Farmstead G. & C.C.
    Lafayette, NJ, 502
Flanders Valley G.Cse.
    Flanders, NJ, 502
Forest Park G.Cse.
    Woodhaven, NY, 536
Francis A. Byrne G.C.
    West Orange, NJ, 502
Galloping Hill G.Cse.
    Union, NJ, 503
Gambler Ridge G.C.
    Cream Ridge, NJ, 503
Garrison G.C.
    Garrison, NY, 537
Glen Cove G.Cse.
    Glen Cove, NY, 537
Great Gorge C.C.
    McAfee, NJ, 503
Green Knoll G.Cse.
    Bridgewater, NJ, 503
Green Ridge G.C.
    Johnson, NY, 538
Gull Haven G.Cse.
    Central Islip, NY, 539

Mainland G.Cse.
Mainland, PA, 698
Manor G.C.
Sinking Spring, PA, 699
Maple Ridge G.C.
Sewell, NJ, 506
Marriott's Seaview Resort
Absecon, NJ, 506
Mays Landing C.C.
Mays Landing, NJ, 506
Middletown C.C.
Langhorne, PA, 700
Moccasin Run G.Cse.
Atglen, PA, 700
Neshaminy Valley G.C.
Jamison, PA, 701
Northampton Valley C.C.
Richboro, PA, 702
Ocean Acres C.C.
Manahawkin, NJ, 508
Ocean County G.Cse. at Atlantis
Tuckerton, NJ, 508
Olde Homestead G.C.
New Tripoli, PA, 703
Paxon Hollow C.C.
Media, PA, 704
Pennsauken C.C.
Pennsauken, NJ, 508
Perry G.Cse.
Shoemakersville, PA, 704
Pickering Valley G.C.
Phoenixville, PA, 704
Pilgrim's Oak G.Cse.
Peach Bottom, PA, 705
Pinelands G.C.
Winslow, NJ, 509
Pitman G.Cse.
Sewell, NJ, 509
Ramblewood C.C.
Mt. Laurel, NJ, 510
Rancocas G.C.
Willingboro, NJ, 510
Rich Maiden G.Cse.
Fleetwood, PA, 707
Rock Manor G.Cse.
Wilmington, DE, 126
Scotland Run G.C.
Williamstown, NJ, 511
Skippack G.Cse.
Skippack, PA, 710
Southmoore G.Cse.
Bath, PA, 710
Spring Hollow G.Cse.
Spring City, PA, 711
Springfield G. & C.C.
Springfield, PA, 711
Springfield G.Ctr.
Mt. Holly, NJ, 512
**Tanglewood Manor G.C. &
Learning Center**
Quarryville, PA, 713
Three Little Bakers C.C.
Wilmington, DE, 126
Town and Country G.L.
Woodstown, NJ, 513
Turtle Creek G.Cse.
Limerick, PA, 714
Twin Lakes C.C.
Allentown, PA, 714
Twin Ponds G.Cse.
Gilbertsville, PA, 714

Upper Perk G.Cse.
Pennsburg, PA, 715
Valley Forge G.C.
King Of Prussia, PA, 715
Wedgewood C.C.
Turnersville, NJ, 513
Wedgewood G.C.
Coopersburg, PA, 716
Westover G.C.
Norristown, PA, 716
Westwood G.C.
Woodbury, NJ, 513
Whitetail G.C.
Bath, PA, 717
Wild Oaks G.C.
Salem, NJ, 513
Willow Brook C.C.
Moorestown, NJ, 514
Willow Hollow G.Cse.
Leesport, PA, 717
Woodland Hills C.C.
Hellertown, PA, 717
Wyncote G.C.
Oxford, PA, 718

PHOENIX
The 500 Club
Glendale, AZ, 16
Aguila G.Cse.
Laveen, AZ, 16
Apache Creek G.C.
Apache Junction, AZ, 16
Arizona Biltmore C.C.
Phoenix, AZ, 16
**The Arizona Golf Resort & Conference
Center**
Mesa, AZ, 17
The ASU Karsten G.Cse.
Tempe, AZ, 17
The Boulders Club
Carefree, AZ, 17
Casa Grande Municipal G.Cse.
Casa Grande, AZ, 18
Cave Creek G.C.
Phoenix, AZ, 18
Club West G.C.
Phoenix, AZ, 18
Coyote Lakes G.C.
Surprise, AZ, 19
Desert Canyon G.C.
Fountain Hills, AZ, 19
Dobson Ranch G.C.
Mesa, AZ, 19
Dove Valley Ranch G.C.
Cave Creek, AZ, 19
Eagle's Nest C.C. at Pebble Creek
Goodyear, AZ, 20
Encanto G.Cse.
Phoenix, AZ, 20
Estrella Mountain G.Cse.
Goodyear, AZ, 20
Estrella Mountain Ranch G.C.
Goodyear, AZ, 21
Francisco Grande Resort & G.C.
Casa Grande, AZ, 21
The Foothills G.C.
Phoenix, AZ, 21
Gainey Ranch G.C.
Scottsdale, AZ, 21
Gold Canyon Golf Resort
Gold Canyon, AZ, 21
The G.C. at Eagle Mountain
Fountain Hills, AZ, 22

Grayhawk G.C.
Scottsdale, AZ, 22
Happy Trails Resort
Surprise, AZ, 23
Hillcrest G.C.
Sun City West, AZ, 23
Ken McDonald G.Cse.
Tempe, AZ, 23
Kierland G.C.
Scottsdale, AZ, 23
Kokopelli Golf Resort
Gilbert, AZ, 24
Las Sendas G.C.
Mesa, AZ, 24
The Legacy Golf Resort
Phoenix, AZ, 24
The Legend at Arrowhead G.C.
Glendale, AZ, 25
Legend Trail G.C.
Scottsdale, AZ, 25
The Links at Queen Creek
Queen Creek, AZ, 25
Longbow G.C.
Mesa, AZ, 25
Los Caballeros G.C.
Wickenburg, AZ, 26
Marriott's Camelback G.C.
Scottsdale, AZ, 26
Maryvale G.C.
Phoenix, AZ, 26
McCormick Ranch G.C.
Scottsdale, AZ, 26
Mountain Brook G.C.
Gold Canyon, AZ, 27
Mountain Shadows
Scottsdale, AZ, 27
Ocotillo G.C.
Chandler, AZ, 27
Orange Tree Golf Resort
Scottsdale, AZ, 27
Painted Mountain G.C.
Mesa, AZ, 28
Palm Valley G.C.
Goodyear, AZ, 28
Papago G.Cse.
Phoenix, AZ, 28
Pavilion Lakes G.C.
Scottsdale, AZ, 28
The Phoenician G.C.
Scottsdale, AZ, 28
Pueblo El Mirage Resort
El Mirage, AZ, 30
Rancho Manana G.C.
Cave Creek, AZ, 30
The Raven G.C. at Sabino Springs
Tucson, AZ, 30
The Raven G.C. at South Mountain
Phoenix, AZ, 30
The Sanctuary G.Cse. at Westworld
Scottsdale, AZ, 31
Sheraton San Marcos G.C.
Chandler, AZ, 32
Stonecreek G.C.
Phoenix, AZ, 33
SunRidge Canyon G.C.
Fountain Hills, AZ, 33
Superstition Springs G.C.
Mesa, AZ, 33
Talking Stick G.C.
Scottsdale, AZ, 33
Tatum Ranch G.C.
Cave Creek, AZ, 33

Tonto Verde G.C.
Rio Verde, AZ, 33
Tournament Players Club of Scottsdale
Scottsdale, AZ, 34
Troon North G.C.
Scottsdale, AZ, 34
Western Skies G.C.
Gilbert, AZ, 35
Westbrook Village G.C.
Peoria, AZ, 35
The Wigwam G. & C.C.
Litchfield Park, AZ, 36
WildFire at Desert Ridge G.C.
Phoenix, AZ, 36
SAN DIEGO
Balboa Park G.C.
San Diego, CA, 43
Bonita G.C.
Bonita, CA, 45
Carlton Oaks C.C.
Santee, CA, 47
Carmel Mountain Ranch C.C.
San Diego, CA, 47
Castle Creek C.C.
Escondido, CA, 47
Chula Vista Municipal G.Cse.
Bonita, CA, 49
Coronado G.Cse.
Coronado, CA, 50
Cottonwood at Rancho San Diego G.C.
El Cajon, CA, 50
Doubletree Carmel Highland Resort
San Diego, CA, 54
Eagle Crest G.C.
Escondido, CA, 54
EastLake C.C.
Chula Vista, CA, 55
Encinitas Ranch G.C.
Encinitas, CA, 56
Fallbrook G.C.
Fallbrook, CA, 56
Four Seasons Resort Aviara
Carlsbad, CA, 57
La Costa Resort & Spa
Carlsbad, CA, 63
Maderas C.C.
Poway, CA, 67
Meadow Lake G.Cse.
Escondido, CA, 69
The Meadows Del Mar G.C.
San Diego, CA, 69
Morgan Run Resort & Club
Rancho Santa Fe, CA, 71
Mount Woodson G.C.
Ramona, CA, 71
Oceanside Municipal G.Cse.
Oceanside, CA, 73
Pala Mesa Resort
Fallbrook, CA, 74
Rancho Bernardo Inn
San Diego, CA, 78
Redhawk G.C.
Temecula, CA, 80
Riverwalk G.C.
San Diego, CA, 82
San Clemente Municipal G.C.
San Clemente, CA, 83
San Luis Rey Downs Golf Resort
Bonsall, CA, 84

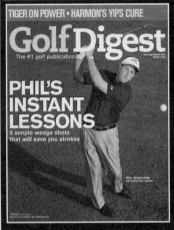